THE
ALL ENGLAND
LAW REPORTS

1987

Volume 1

Editor
PETER HUTCHESSON LL M
Barrister, New Zealand

Assistant Editor
BROOK WATSON
of Lincoln's Inn, Barrister
and of the New South Wales Bar

Consulting Editor
WENDY SHOCKETT
of Gray's Inn, Barrister

London
BUTTERWORTHS

UNITED KINGDOM Butterworth & Co (Publishers) Ltd,
                88 Kingsway, **London** WC2B 6AB and
                61A North Castle Street, **Edinburgh** EH2 3LJ

AUSTRALIA   Butterworths Pty Ltd, **Sydney, Melbourne,
                Brisbane, Adelaide, Perth, Canberra**
                and **Hobart**

CANADA   Butterworths. A division of Reed Inc, **Toronto** and **Vancouver**

NEW ZEALAND   Butterworths of New Zealand Ltd, **Wellington** and **Auckland**

SINGAPORE   Butterworth & Co (Asia) Pte Ltd, **Singapore**

SOUTH AFRICA   Butterworth Publishers (Pty) Ltd, **Durban** and **Pretoria**

USA   Butterworth Legal Publishers, **Seattle**, Washington,
                Boston, Massachusetts, **Austin**, Texas and
                St Paul, Minnesota
                D & S Publishers, **Clearwater**, Florida

Butterworth & Co (Publishers) Ltd

1987

ISBN 0 406 85161 1

Typeset by CCC, printed and bound in Great Britain by William Clowes Limited, Beccles and
London

House of Lords

The Lord High Chancellor: Lord Hailsham of St Marylebone

Lords of Appeal in Ordinary

Lord Keith of Kinkel
Lord Bridge of Harwich
Lord Brandon of Oakbrook
Lord Brightman
Lord Templeman

Lord Griffiths
Lord Mackay of Clashfern
Lord Ackner
Lord Oliver of Aylmerton
Lord Goff of Chieveley

Court of Appeal

The Lord High Chancellor

The Lord Chief Justice of England: Lord Lane
(President of the Criminal Division)

The Master of the Rolls: Sir John Francis Donaldson
(President of the Civil Division)

The President of the Family Division: Sir John Lewis Arnold

The Vice-Chancellor: Sir Nicolas Christopher Henry Browne-Wilkinson

Lords Justices of Appeal

Sir Tasker Watkins VC
Sir Patrick McCarthy O'Connor
Sir Michael John Fox
Sir Michael Robert Emanuel Kerr
Sir John Douglas May
Sir Christopher John Slade
Sir Francis Brooks Purchas
Sir George Brian Hugh Dillon
Sir Stephen Brown
Sir Roger Jocelyn Parker
Sir David Powell Croom-Johnson
Sir Anthony John Leslie Lloyd

Sir Brian Thomas Neill
Sir Michael John Mustill
Sir Martin Charles Nourse
Sir Iain Derek Laing Glidewell
Sir Alfred John Balcombe
Sir Ralph Brian Gibson
Sir John Dexter Stocker
Sir Harry Kenneth Woolf
Sir Donald James Nicholls
Sir Thomas Henry Bingham
Sir Thomas Patrick Russell
(appointed 12 January 1987)

Chancery Division

The Lord High Chancellor

The Vice-Chancellor

Sir John Norman Keates Whitford
Sir Raymond Henry Walton
Sir John Evelyn Vinelott
Sir Douglas William Falconer
Sir Jean-Pierre Frank Eugene Warner
Sir Peter Leslie Gibson

Sir David Herbert Mervyn Davies
Sir Jeremiah LeRoy Harman
Sir Richard Rashleigh Folliott Scott
Sir Leonard Hubert Hoffmann
Sir John Leonard Knox
Sir Peter Julian Millett

Queen's Bench Division

The Lord Chief Justice of England

Sir Bernard Caulfield
Sir William Lloyd Mars-Jones
Sir Leslie Kenneth Edward Boreham
Sir Alfred William Michael Davies
Sir Kenneth George Illtyd Jones
Sir Haydn Tudor Evans
Sir Peter Richard Pain
Sir Kenneth Graham Jupp
Sir Walter Derek Thornley Hodgson
Sir Frederick Maurice Drake
Sir Barry Cross Sheen
Sir David Bruce McNeill
Sir Christopher James Saunders French
Sir Thomas Patrick Russell
    (appointed Lord Justice of Appeal,
    12 January 1987)
Sir Peter Edlin Webster
Sir Peter Murray Taylor
Sir Murray Stuart-Smith
Sir Christopher Stephen Thomas Jonathan
    Thayer Staughton
Sir Donald Henry Farquharson
Sir Anthony James Denys McCowan
Sir Iain Charles Robert McCullough
Sir Hamilton John Leonard
Sir Alexander Roy Asplan Beldam
Sir David Cozens-Hardy Hirst
Sir John Stewart Hobhouse

Sir Michael Mann
Sir Andrew Peter Leggatt
Sir Michael Patrick Nolan
Sir Oliver Bury Popplewell
Sir William Alan Macpherson
Sir Philip Howard Otton
Sir Paul Joseph Morrow Kennedy
Sir Michael Hutchison
Sir Simon Denis Brown
Sir Anthony Howell Meurig Evans
Sir Mark Oliver Saville
Sir Johan Steyn
Sir Christopher Dudley Roger Rose
Sir Richard Howard Tucker
Sir Robert Alexander Gatehouse
Sir Patrick Neville Garland
Sir John Ormond Roch
Sir Michael John Turner
Sir Harry Henry Ognall
Sir John Downes Alliott
Sir Konrad Hermann Theodor Schiemann
Sir John Arthur Dalziel Owen
Sir Denis Robert Maurice Henry
Sir Francis Humphrey Potts
Sir Richard George Rougier
Sir Ian Alexander Kennedy
Sir Nicholas Addison Phillips
    (appointed 12 January 1987)

Family Division

The President of the Family Division

Sir John Brinsmead Latey
Sir Alfred Kenneth Hollings
Sir Charles Trevor Reeve
Dame Rose Heilbron
Sir Brian Drex Bush
Sir John Kember Wood
Sir Ronald Gough Waterhouse
Sir John Gervase Kensington Sheldon

Sir Thomas Michael Eastham
Dame Margaret Myfanwy Wood Booth
Sir Anthony Leslie Julian Lincoln
Dame Ann Elizabeth Oldfield Butler-Sloss
Sir Anthony Bruce Ewbank
Sir John Douglas Waite
Sir Anthony Barnard Hollis
Sir Swinton Barclay Thomas

CITATION

These reports are cited thus:

[1987] 1 All ER

REFERENCES

These reports contain references to the following major works of legal reference described in the manner indicated below.

Halsbury's Laws of England

The reference 26 Halsbury's Laws (4th edn) para 577 refers to paragraph 577 on page 296 of volume 26 of the fourth edition of Halsbury's Laws of England.

Halsbury's Statutes of England and Wales

The reference 27 Halsbury's Statutes (4th edn) 208 refers to page 208 of volume 27 of the fourth edition of Halsbury's Statutes of England and Wales, and the reference 39 Halsbury's Statutes (3rd edn) 895 refers to page 895 of volume 39 of the third edition of Halsbury's Statutes of England.

The Digest

References are to the green band reissue volumes of The Digest (formerly the English and Empire Digest).

The reference 36(2) Digest (Reissue) 764, *1398* refers to case number 1398 on page 764 of Digest Green Band Reissue Volume 36(2).

Halsbury's Statutory Instruments

The reference 1 Halsbury's Statutory Instruments (Grey Volume) 278 refers to page 278 of Grey Volume 1 of Halsbury's Statutory Instruments.

The reference 17 Halsbury's Statutory Instruments (4th reissue) 256 refers to page 256 of the fourth reissue of volume 17 of Halsbury's Statutory Instruments; references to other reissues are similar.

Cases reported in volume 1

Digest of cases reported in volume 1

House of Lords petitions

This list, which covers the period 10 December 1986 to 17 April 1987, sets out all cases which have formed the subject of a report in the All England Law Reports in which an Appeal Committee of the House of Lords has, subsequent to the publication of that report, dismissed a petition for leave to appeal either on a perusal of the papers or after an oral hearing. Where the result of a petition for leave to appeal was known prior to the publication of the relevant report a note of that result appears at the end of the report.

R v Nanayakkara [1987] 1 All ER 650, CA. Leave to appeal refused 8 April 1987 (Lord Bridge, Lord Templeman and Lord Oliver) (oral hearing).

R v Newham Juvenile Court, ex p F (a minor) [1986] 3 All ER 17, DC. Leave to appeal refused 10 December 1986 (Lord Bridge, Lord Brandon and Lord Oliver) (oral hearing)

CORRIGENDA

[1986] 3 All ER

p 146. **Johnston v Chief Constable of the Royal Ulster Constabulary.** Line *e* 4. For *'question 2'* read *'question 3'*.

p 767. **Netherlands Insurance Co Est 1845 Ltd v Karl Ljungberg & Co AB, The Mammoth Pine.** Line *h* 5 should read 'insistence did *not* of itself . . .'

p 860. **Spiliada Maritime Corp v Cansulex Ltd, The Spiliada.** Lines *c* 4 to *c* 6. Omit sentence 'Here a special . . . substantive matter'.

[1987] 1 All ER

p 405. **Re Basham (decd).** Line *d* 6 should read 'death. The *deceased* died intestate . . .'

p 565. **R v Panel on Take-overs and Mergers, ex p Datafin plc (Norton Opax plc intervening).** Line *d* 1 should read '. . . it is unlikely that the panel could be accused of'.

p 914. **R v Maginnis.** Line *e* 1 should read '. . . use of the word which should *not* be regarded . . .'

R v Hunt

HOUSE OF LORDS

LORD KEITH OF KINKEL, LORD TEMPLEMAN, LORD GRIFFITHS, LORD MACKAY OF CLASHFERN AND LORD ACKNER

20, 21, 22 OCTOBER, 4 DECEMBER 1986

Criminal law – Possession of controlled drugs – Exceptions to prohibition against possession – Burden of proof – Prosecution not adducing evidence that defendant did not fall within exception to prohibition against possession – Whether burden of proof lying on prosecution or defendant to establish that defendant falling within exception – Misuse of Drugs Regulations 1973, Sch 1, para 3.

The defendant was found to be in possession of a powder containing morphine mixed with two other substances which were not controlled drugs. He was charged with unlawfully possessing a controlled drug, namely morphine, contrary to s 5(2) of the Misuse of Drugs Act 1971. Under para 3[a] of Sch 1 to the Misuse of Drugs Regulations 1973 any preparation of morphine containing not more than 0·2% of morphine compounded with other ingredients was excepted from the prohibition on possession of controlled drugs contained in s 5 of the 1971 Act. At the trial the prosecution did not adduce evidence as to the proportion of morphine in the powder. The defendant submitted that there was no case to answer because the prosecution had failed to show that the powder was not within the exception contained in para 3, but following an adverse ruling by the judge he changed his plea to guilty and was sentenced to three months' imprisonment. The defendant appealed against his conviction to the Court of Appeal, contending that the burden lay on the prosecution to prove that he did not fall within the exception contained in para 3. The Court of Appeal dismissed the appeal, holding that the burden of proof was on the defendant to show that he did fall within the exception. The defendant appealed to the House of Lords, contending that if the defendant raised a statutory defence, then provided there was evidence to support the defence the burden was on the prosecution to negative the defence.

Held – There was no rule of law that the burden of proving a statutory defence lay on the defendant only where the statute specifically so provided, since a statute could place the burden of proof on the defendant by necessary implication and without doing so expressly. Each case turned on the construction of the particular legislation but the court should be very slow to infer from the statute that Parliament intended to impose an onerous duty on the defendant to prove his innocence in a criminal case. The occasions on which a statute would be construed as imposing a burden of proof on the defendant were generally limited to offences arising under enactments which prohibited the doing of an act save in specified circumstances or by persons of specified classes or within specified qualifications or with the licence or permission of specified authorities. On the true construction of para 3 of Sch 1 to the 1973 regulations the offence was possession of morphine in a prohibited form and therefore the burden lay on the prosecution to prove not only that the powder contained morphine but also that it was not morphine in the form permitted by para 3 of Sch 1. It followed that the Court of Appeal had been wrong to hold that the burden of proof in relation to para 3 lay on the defendant. The appeal would accordingly be allowed (see p 3 a, p 4 b c, p 10 e f, p 11 h j, p 12 b c, p 13 a b e to g, p 15 d e, p 18 g h and p 19 g, post).

---

a Paragraph 3 is set out at p 13 h j, post

Woolmington v DPP [1935] All ER Rep 1 and *R v Edwards* [1974] 2 All ER 1085 considered.

Decision of Court of Appeal [1986] 1 All ER 184 reversed.

Notes

For the burden of proof in criminal proceedings, see 11 Halsbury's Laws (4th edn) paras 354–357, and for cases on the subject, see 14(2) Digest (Reissue) 474–477, 3918–3948.

For the possession of controlled drugs, see 11 Halsbury's Laws (4th edn) para 1092 and 30 ibid para 750, and for cases on the subject, see 15 Digest (Reissue) 1068–1071, 9154–9169.

For the Misuse of Drugs Act 1971, s 5, see 41 Halsbury's Statutes (3rd edn) 884.

For the Misuse of Drugs Regulations 1973, Sch 1, para 3, see 13 Halsbury's Statutory Instruments (4th reissue) 313.

Cases referred to in opinions

Apothecaries' Co v Bentley (1824) 1 C & P 538, 171 ER 1307, NP.
Bird v Adams [1972] Crim LR 174, DC.
Davis v Scrace (1869) LR 4 CP 172.
Gatland v Metropolitan Police Comr [1968] 2 All ER 100, [1968] 2 QB 279, [1968] 2 WLR 1263, DC.
Jayasena v R [1970] 1 All ER 219, [1970] AC 618, [1970] 2 WLR 448, PC.
Jelfs v Ballard (1799) 1 Bos & P 468, 126 ER 1014.
John v Humphreys [1955] 1 All ER 793, [1955] 1 WLR 325, DC.
M'Naghten's Case (1843) 10 Cl & Fin 200, [1843–60] All ER Rep 229, 8 ER 718, HL.
Mancini v DPP [1941] 3 All ER 272, [1942] AC 1, HL.
Nimmo v Alexander Cowan & Sons Ltd [1967] 3 All ER 187, [1968] AC 107, [1967] 3 WLR 1169, HL.
R v Burke (1978) 67 Cr App R 220, CA.
R v Cousins [1982] 2 All ER 115, [1982] QB 526, [1982] 2 WLR 621, CA.
R v Davies (1913) 8 Cr App R 211, CCA.
R v Edwards [1974] 2 All ER 1085, [1975] QB 27, [1974] 3 WLR 285, CA.
R v Ewens [1966] 2 All ER 470, [1967] 1 QB 322, [1966] 2 WLR 1372, CCA.
R v Jarvis (1756) 1 East 643, 102 ER 249.
R v McPherson [1973] RTR 157, CA.
R v Oliver [1943] 2 All ER 800, [1944] KB 68, CCA.
R v Putland and Sorrell [1946] 1 All ER 85, CCA.
R v Schama, R v Abramovitch (1914) 84 LJKB 396, [1914–15] All ER Rep 204, CCA.
R v Scott (1921) 86 JP 69, CCC.
R v Turner (1816) 5 M & S 206, [1814–23] All ER Rep 713, 105 ER 1026.
Robertson v Bannister [1973] RTR 109, DC.
Spieres v Parker (1786) 1 Term Rep 141, 99 ER 1019.
Taylor v Humphries (1864) 17 CBNS 539, 144 ER 216.
Warner v Metropolitan Police Comr [1968] 2 All ER 356, [1969] AC 256, [1968] 2 WLR 1303, HL.
Woolmington v DPP [1935] AC 462, [1935] All ER Rep 1, HL.

Appeal

Richard Selwyn Russell Hunt appealed with leave of the Court of Appeal, Criminal Division, granted on 23 October 1985 against the decision of that court (Robert Goff LJ, Beldam and Hutchison JJ) ([1986] 1 All ER 184, [1986] QB 125) on 23 October 1985 whereby it dismissed his appeal against his conviction on 26 February 1985 in the Crown Court at Lewes before his Honour Judge Wingate QC on an indictment charging him with unlawfully possessing a controlled drug contrary to s 5(2) of the Misuse of Drugs Act 1971. The facts are set out in the opinion of Lord Griffiths.

Kenneth Zucker QC and *Geoffrey Greenwood* for the appellant.
Anthony Hacking QC and *Michael Warren* for the Crown.

Their Lordships took time for consideration.

4 December. The following opinions were delivered.

a

LORD KEITH OF KINKEL. My Lords, I have had the opportunity of considering in draft the speech prepared by my noble and learned friend Lord Griffiths. I agree with it, and for the reasons he gives would allow the appeal and quash the conviction.

LORD TEMPLEMAN. My Lords, by the Misuse of Drugs Act 1971, morphine was
b classified as a controlled drug. By s 5—

'(1) Subject to any regulations under section 7 of this Act for the time being in force, it shall not be lawful for a person to have a controlled drug in his possession.
(2) Subject to section 28 of this Act and subsection (4) below, it is an offence for a person to have a controlled drug in his possession in contravention of subsection (1)
c above...'

By s 5(4) if '... it is proved that the accused had a controlled drug in his possession, it shall be a defence for him to prove...' in certain defined circumstances that he intended to destroy the drug or to deliver the drug into lawful custody and that he took all reasonable steps to carry out his intention.

By s 7(1) the Secretary of State was given power by regulation to—
d

'(*a*) except from section ... 5(1) of this Act such controlled drugs as may be specified in the regulations; and (*b*) make such other provision he thinks fit for the purpose of making it lawful for persons to do things which ... it would otherwise be unlawful for them to do.'

By s 28(3)(*b*)(i), in proceeding for an offence under s 5(2), the accused shall be acquitted
e 'if he proves that he neither believed nor suspected nor had reason to suspect that the substance [involved in the alleged offence] was a controlled drug'.

By reg 4 of and Sch 1 to the Misuse of Drugs Regulations 1973, SI 1973/797, made pursuant to s 7 of the 1971 Act, the Secretary of State directed that s 5(1) 'shall not have effect in relation to' any preparation of morphine containing 'not more than 0·2 per cent.
f of morphine calculated as anhydrous morphine base' and compounded in such a way that the morphine cannot readily be recovered and does not constitute a risk to health.

Regulation 6 authorises certain persons to have a controlled drug in their possession, notwithstanding the provisions of s 5(1). The specified persons included a constable, a post office employee and a customs officer acting in the course of their respective occupations.

The onus of proving possession of a drug which by s 5(1) it is unlawful to possess lies
g on the prosecution. If that onus is discharged, it is for the accused to prove lawful authority under reg 6, or to establish the defence of lawful intention under s 5(4), or the defence of lack of knowledge under s 28. In my opinion the 1971 Act creates a statutory offence which must be proved by the prosecution and makes available statutory defences which must be proved by the accused.

The appellant was accused of 'possessing a controlled drug, contrary to section 5(2) of
h the Misuse of Drugs Act 1971'. The evidence established possession of a powder containing 'morphine mixed with caffeine and atropine'. If the powder contained not more than 0·2% of morphine, calculated and compounded in the manner specified in the regulations, then the accused did not possess a controlled drug 'contrary to section 5(2)'. The prosecution only tendered facts which might or might not amount to an
j offence.

In these circumstances, the decision of this House in *Woolmington v DPP* [1935] AC 462, [1935] All ER Rep 1 is not relevant. An accused may be convicted of a criminal offence if he commits an unlawful act with the requisite state of mind. *Woolmington v DPP* reaffirmed that in the absence of standing provisions to the contrary the prosecution must not only prove the act by direct or circumstantial evidence but must also prove the state of mind by evidence or by inference from fact. The 1971 Act is inconsistent with any duty on the prosecution save the duty of proving the unlawful act, namely possession

of a controlled drug contrary to s 5(2). A restricted defence is accorded to a particular
state of mind, but the onus of proving that defence, and other defences defined by the   *a*
1971 Act and the 1973 regulations, lies with the accused. Another statute may preserve
common law defences or create statutory defences and may doubtfully provide for the
onus of proof; the effect of *Woolmington v DPP* depends on the construction of the statute.

The present appeal is not concerned with defences. By s 5(2) it is an offence to be in
possession of a controlled drug in contravention of s 5(1). Possession of a powder
containing not more than 0·2% of morphine based and compounded in the manner   *b*
specified in reg 4 does not contravene s 5(1) and therefore does not contravene s 5(2).
Possession of a powder which contains morphine and does not comply with the conditions
specified by reg 4 contravenes s 5(1) and (2). The prosecution only proved possession of a
powder containing morphine. The appellant was therefore entitled to be acquitted.

LORD GRIFFITHS. My Lords, on 26 February 1985 in the Crown Court at Lewes the   *c*
appellant pleaded not guilty to an indictment charging him with possessing a controlled
drug contrary to s 5(2) of the Misuse of Drugs Act 1971, the particulars of the offence
being that he on 13 July 1984, at Eastbourne in the county of East Sussex, unlawfully
had in his possession a controlled drug, namely 154 mg of a powder containing morphine,
a Class A drug.

The prosecution called two police officers who gave evidence that on 13 July 1984 they   *d*
executed a search warrant at the appellant's home and there found, under an ashtray in
the bedroom, a paper fold containing a white powder. The appellant told the police that
he had bought the powder in Shaftesbury Avenue and that it was amphetamine sulphate.
The only other evidence for the prosecution was contained in the report of an analyst
which was by agreement read to the jury. The report showed that the powder was not
amphetamine sulphate and that it contained morphine. The report read: *e*

> 'On 19 July 1984 the following sealed item was received at the laboratory from
> Sussex Police, Eastbourne: RSE.1 Paper fold with powder. The paper fold, item
> RSE.1, contained 154 milligrams of off-white powder. This powder was found to
> contain morphine mixed with caffeine and atropine. Morphine is a controlled drug
> within the Misuse of Drugs Act 1971, Part I of Schedule 2 (Class A drugs). Caffeine   *f*
> and atropine are not controlled under the Misuse of Drugs Act 1971.'

At the close of the prosecution case counsel for the appellant submitted that there was
no case to answer. In order to understand the basis of that submission it is necessary to
set out the relevant statutory provisions which I take from the judgment of the Court of
Appeal ([1986] 1 All ER 184 at 186–187, [1986] QB 125 at 129–130):   *g*

> 'The defendant was charged with an offence under s 5(2) of the Misuse of Drugs
> Act 1971. Section 5(1) and (2) provides as follows: "(1) Subject to any regulations
> under section 7 of this Act for the time being in force, it shall not be lawful for a
> person to have a controlled drug in his possession. (2) Subject to section 28 of this
> Act and to subsection (4) below, it is an offence for a person to have a controlled   *h*
> drug in his possession in contravention of subsection (1) above." The expression
> "controlled drug" is defined in s 2(1)(a) of the Act, which provides that in the Act—
> "the expression 'controlled drug' means any substance or product for the time being
> specified in Part I, II or III of Schedule 2 to this Act . . ." Part I of Sch 2 is concerned
> with Class A drugs. Paragraph 1 of Pt I contains a list of "substances and products",
> including morphine. Paragraph 5 specifies "Any preparation or other product   *j*
> containing a substance or product for the time being specified in any of paragraphs
> 1 to 4 above." It follows that the powder of which the defendant was found to be in
> possession was a controlled drug by virtue of being a preparation or other product
> containing morphine. It is to be observed that s 5(1) of the Act is expressed to be
> "subject to any regulations under section 7 of this Act". Section 7(1) of the Act
> provides as follows: "The Secretary of State may by regulations—(a) except from
> section 3(1)(a) or (b), 4(1)(a) or (b) or 5(1) of this Act such controlled drugs as may be

a   specified in the regulations; and (b) make such other provisions as he thinks fit for
       the purpose of making it lawful for persons to do things which under any of the
       following provisions of this Act, that is to say sections 4(1), 5(1) and 6(1), it would
       otherwise be unlawful for them to do." In 1973 there came into force the Misuse of
       Drugs Regulations 1973, SI 1973/797, made in pursuance of various sections of the
       1971 Act, including s 7. Part II of the regulations is headed "Exemptions from
       Certain Provisions of the Misuse of Drugs Act 1971", and contains regs 4 to 13
b   inclusive. For present purposes, the regulation which is of immediate importance is
       reg 4(1) which provides as follows: "Sections 3(1) and 5(1) of the Act (which prohibit
       the importation, exportation and possession of controlled drugs) shall not have effect
       in relation to the controlled drugs specified in Schedule 1." The amended Sch 1 to
       the regulations, which was in force at the relevant time, is headed as follows:
       "Controlled Drugs Excepted from the Prohibition on Importation, Exportation and
c   Possession and Subject to the Requirements of Regulation 23". The schedule consists
       of nine paragraphs. Each paragraph specifies a particular controlled drug in the
       nature of a preparation or powder or mixture. The relevant paragraph for present
       purposes is para 3, which reads as follows: "Any preparation of medicinal opium or
       of morphine containing (in either case) not more than 0·2 per cent of morphine
       calculated as anhydrous morphine base, being a preparation compounded with one
d   or more other active or inert ingredients in such a way that the opium or, as the case
       may be, the morphine, cannot be recovered by readily applicable means or in a yield
       which would constitute a risk to health." It follows, therefore, that a controlled
       drug, being a preparation as described in para 3, is a controlled drug excepted from
       the prohibition on possession contained in s 5 of the Act. It was the submission of
       counsel for the defendant at the trial that there was no case to answer because the
e   prosecution had called no evidence as to the proportion of morphine contained in
       the powder found in the defendant's possession, or to the effect that the powder was
       not compound as specified in para 3 of Sch 1 to the regulations, and that it was not
       therefore open to the jury to hold, on the evidence, that the defendant was
       unlawfully in possession of a controlled drug contrary to s 5(2) of the Act.'

f   The judge ruled against the submission. The appellant changed his plea to guilty and
       after being formally convicted by the jury he was sentenced to three months'
       imprisonment suspended for two years.
           The judge did not give reasons for rejecting the submission of no case to answer but it
       is apparent from the discussion between the judge and counsel during the course of the
       submission that the judge rejected the submission because he was of opinion that Sch 1
g   only applied to possession by such persons as doctors, dentists, veterinary surgeons and
       pharmacists. For the reasons given by the Court of Appeal this was an erroneous view of
       the scope of the regulations and the prosecution do not seek to uphold the construction
       of the regulations adopted by the trial judge.
           The Court of Appeal, however, concluded that the ruling that there was a case to
       answer was correct, albeit it had been made for the wrong reason. The unchallenged
h   evidence of the prosecution established that the appellant had had morphine in his
       possession, and in these circumstances the Court of Appeal held that if the appellant
       wished to escape conviction the burden lay on him to prove on the balance of probability
       that the preparation of morphine fell within the relevant exception contained in the
       Misuse of Drugs Regulations 1973. As it was obvious that the appellant neither intended
       to nor could discharge this burden of proof, the Court of Appeal upheld the conviction.
j   The Court of Appeal gave leave to appeal to your Lordships' House and certified the
       following point of law of general public importance:

           'Whether in a prosecution for possession of a preparation or product containing
           morphine under Section 5 of the Misuse of Drugs Act 1971, where the morphine is
           of an unspecified amount and compounded with other ingredients, and where the
           Defence seeks to rely upon the exception to the said Section 5 set out in Regulation
           4(1) of and paragraph 3 of Schedule 1 to the Misuse of Drugs Regulations 1973 (as

amended) the burden falls upon the Defence to show that the said preparation or
product comes within the said exception.'   *a*

The appellant challenges the decision of the Court of Appeal by two entirely distinct
arguments. It is submitted that on the true construction of the 1971 Act and the 1973
regulations the Court of Appeal was wrong to hold that the burden was on the defendant
to prove that the powder fell within Sch 1 to the 1973 regulations, an argument
depending on a close consideration of this particular legislation. But the appellant also   *b*
raises an argument of far wider ranging significance based on the decision of this House
in *Woolmington v DPP* [1935] AC 462, [1935] All ER Rep 1 and involving the submission
that the leading case of *R v Edwards* [1974] 2 All ER 1085, [1975] QB 27 was wrongly
decided by the Court of Appeal.

I propose first to consider the argument based on *Woolmington v DPP*. The starting
point is the celebrated passage in the speech of Viscount Sankey LC ([1935] AC 462 at   *c*
481–482, [1935] All ER Rep 1 at 8):

> 'Throughout the web of the English Criminal Law one golden thread is always to
> be seen, that it is the duty of the prosecution to prove the prisoner's guilt subject to
> what I have already said as to the defence of insanity and subject also to any statutory
> exception. If, at the end of and on the whole of the case, there is a reasonable doubt,
> created by the evidence given by either the prosecution or the prisoner, as to   *d*
> whether the prisoner killed the deceased with a malicious intention, the prosecution
> has not made out the case and the prisoner is entitled to an acquittal. No matter
> what the charge or where the trial, the principle that the prosecution must prove
> the guilt of the prisoner is part of the common law of England and no attempt to
> whittle it down can be entertained.'
>   *e*

The appellant submits that in using the phrase 'any statutory exception' Viscount
Sankey was referring to statutory exceptions in which Parliament had by the use of
express words placed the burden of proof on the accused, in the same way as the judges
in *M'Naghten's Case* (1843) 10 Cl & Fin 200, 8 ER 718 had expressly placed the burden of
proving insanity on the accused. There are, of course, many examples of such statutory
drafting, of which a number are to be found in this Act: see s 5(4): 'In any proceedings   *f*
for an offence under subsection (2) above in which it is proved that the accused had a
controlled drug in his possession, it shall be a defence for him to prove . . .' (see also
s 28(2)(3)). Examples in other Acts are to be found conveniently collected in *Phipson on
Evidence* (13th edn, 1982) p 51, n 68.

The appellant also relies on a passage in the speech of Viscount Simon LC in *Mancini v
DPP* [1941] 3 All ER 272 at 279, [1942] AC 1 at 11, in which he said: *g*

> '*Woolmington's* case ([1935] AC 462, [1935] All ER Rep 1) is concerned with
> explaining and reinforcing the rule that the prosecution must prove the charge it
> makes beyond reasonable doubt, and consequently that, if, on the material before
> the jury, there is a reasonable doubt, the prisoner should have the benefit of it. The
> rule is of general application in all charges under the criminal law. (The only   *h*
> exceptions arise, as explained in *Woolmington's* case, in the defence of insanity and in
> offences where onus of proof is specially dealt with by statute.)'

It is submitted that the use of the word 'specially' indicates that Viscount Simon LC
considered that the reference in *Woolmington v DPP* was limited to express statutory
burdens of proof.

From this premise, it is argued that, as it is well settled that if a defendant raises any of   *j*
the common law defences such as accident, self-defence, provocation or duress and there
is evidence to support such a defence the judge must leave it to the jury with a direction
that the burden is on the prosecution to negative that defence, so it must follow that if a
defendant raises any statutory defence the same rule must apply, and provided there is
evidence to support such a defence the burden lies on the prosecution to negative it, the

only exceptions to this rule being those cases in which the statute has by express words
a placed the burden of proving the defence on the defendant.

However, in *Woolmington v DPP* the House was not concerned to consider the nature
of a statutory defence or on whom the burden of proving it might lie. The House was
considering a defence of accident to a charge of murder and were concerned to correct a
special rule which appeared to have emerged in charges of murder whereby once it was
proved that the defendant had killed the deceased a burden was held to lie on the
b defendant to excuse himself by proving that it was the result of an accident or that he
had been provoked to do so or had acted in self-defence. This in effect relieved the
prosecution of the burden of proving an essential element in the crime of murder,
namely the malicious intent and placed the burden on the accused to disprove it. It was
this aberration that was so trenchantly corrected by Viscount Sankey LC in the passage
already cited. In *Mancini v DPP* the House dealt with the duty of the judge to lay before
c the jury any line of defence which the facts might reasonably support and it also dealt
with the particular nature of the defence of provocation. In neither appeal was the House
concerned with a statutory defence and no argument was addressed on the nature or
scope of statutory exceptions.

Before the decision in *Woolmington v DPP* there had been a number of cases in which
in trials on indictment the courts had held that the burden of establishing a statutory
d defence fell on the defendant although the statute did not expressly so provide: see for
example *R v Turner* (1816) 5 M & S 206, [1814–23] All ER Rep 713, a decision under the
gaming Acts, and *Apothecaries' Co v Bentley* (1824) 1 C & P 538, 171 ER 1307 and *R v Scott*
(1921) 86 JP 69, decisions in which it was held that the defendant had the burden of
proving that he was licensed to perform an otherwise prohibited act.

I cannot accept that either Viscount Sankey LC or Viscount Simon LC intended to cast
e doubt on these long-standing decisions without having had the benefit of any argument
addressed to the House on the question of statutory exceptions. I am, therefore, unwilling
to read the reference to 'any statutory exception' (see *Woolmington v DPP* [1935] AC 462
at 481, [1935] All ER Rep 1 at 8) in the restricted sense in which the appellant invites us
to read it. It is also to be observed that Lord Devlin in *Jayesena v R* [1970] 1 All ER 219 at
221, [1970] AC 618 at 623, a decision of the Privy Council, commenting on *Woolmington*
f *v DPP* said:

> 'The House laid it down that, save in the case of insanity or of a statutory defence,
> there was no burden laid on the prisoner to prove his innocence and that it was
> sufficient for him to raise a doubt as to his guilt.'

g Lord Devlin does not appear to restrict a statutory defence to one in which the burden
of proof is expressly placed on the defendant.

In *R v Edwards* [1974] 2 All ER 1085, [1975] QB 27 the defendant had been convicted
in the Crown Court of selling intoxicating liquor without a justices' license contrary to
s 160(1)(*a*) of the Licensing Act 1964. Section 160(1)(*a*) provides:

> *h* 'Subject to the provisions of this Act, if any person—(*a*) sells or exposes for sale by
> retail any intoxicating liquor without holding a justices' licence or canteen licence
> authorising him to hold an excise licence for the sale of that liquor . . . he shall be
> guilty of an offence under this section.'

The prosecution had called no evidence that the defendant did not have a licence and
he appealed on the ground that the burden was on the prosecution to establish the lack
j of a licence. The Court of Appeal held that the burden was on the defendant to prove
that he held a licence and that as he had not done so he was rightly convicted.

After an extensive review of the authorities the Court of Appeal held that the same
rule applied to trials on indictment as was applied to summary trial by s 81 of the
Magistrates' Courts Act 1952, which provided:

> 'Where the defendant to an information or complaint relies for his defence on

any exception, exemption, proviso, excuse or qualification, whether or not it
accompanies the description of the offence or matter of complaint in the enactment a
creating the offence or on which the complaint is founded, the burden of proving
the exception, exemption, proviso, excuse or qualification shall be on him; and this
notwithstanding that the information or complaint contains an allegation negativing
the exception, exemption, proviso, excuse or qualification.'

(Section 81 of that Act has now been repealed and re-enacted in identical language in b
s 101 of the Magistrates' Courts Act 1980.)

A study of the old cases and practitioners' books led the court to conclude that when
Parliament established a new system of summary jurisdiction by the Summary
Jurisdiction Act 1848 (Jervis's Act) and enacted in s 14, which deals with proceedings on
the hearing of complaints and informations, the following proviso:

'Provided always, that if the Information or Complaint in any such Case shall c
negative any Exemption, Exception, Proviso, or Condition in the Statute on which
the same shall be framed, it shall not be necessary for the Prosecutor or Complainant
in that behalf to prove such Negative, but the Defendant may prove the Affirmative
thereof in his Defence, if he would have Advantage of the Same'

they were there stating the common law rules as to proof that the judges then applied to d
trials on indictment.

Counsel for the appellant in a most interesting argument has challenged that
conclusion and submitted that the common law rule at that time was that an exception
contained in the same clause of the Act which created the offence had to be negatived by
the prosecution but if the exception or proviso were in a subsequent clause of a statute
or, although in the same section, were not incorporated with the enabling clause by e
words of reference it was a matter of defence. From this general rule counsel submits
that there were but two exceptions, namely the burden on a defendant under the gaming
laws to show that he was qualified to keep guns, bows, dogs etc, and, secondly, that where
an Act was prohibited unless done pursuant to a stipulated licence or authority the
defendant had to prove that he possessed the necessary licence or authority.

The authorities certainly show that a rule of pleading had evolved by the beginning of f
the last century, and probably well before that, in the form of the general rule stated by
counsel for the appellant. One of the more celebrated statements of the rule is Lord
Mansfield CJ's dictum in *R v Jarvis* (1756) 1 East 643 at 644, 102 ER 249 at 251:

'For it is a known distinction that what comes by way of proviso in a statute must
be insisted on by way of defence by the party accused; but where exceptions are in
the enacting part of a law, it must appear in the charge that the defendant does not g
fall within any of them.'

However, as Mr Zukerman demonstrates in his learned article 'The Third Exception
to the Woolmington Rules' (1976) 92 LQR 402, the judges did not always regard the
rules of pleading and the rules as to the burden of proof as being the same. In *Spieres v
Parker* (1786) 1 Term Rep 141 at 144, 99 ER 1019 at 1020 Lord Mansfield CJ said that h
the prosecutor must 'negative the exceptions in the enacting clause, though he threw the
burden of proof upon the other side'. And in *Jelfs v Ballard* (1799) 1 Bos & P 468, 126 ER
1014 Buller J said: 'The Plaintiff must state in his Scire Facias every thing that entitles
him to recover; but it is a very different question what is to be proved by one party and
what by the other.'

Sometimes, however, the judges do appear to have applied the old pleading rules to j
determine the burden of proof. In *Taylor v Humphries* (1864) 17 CBNS 539, 144 ER 216
a publican was charged with opening his premises on a Sunday before 12.30 in the
afternoon otherwise than for the refreshment of travellers. The question for the court
was on whom the burden of proof lay to show that those found drinking in the premises
at 11.20 in the morning were 'travellers'. In the course of giving judgment Erle CJ said,
referring to the argument on behalf of the publican (17 CBNS 539 at 549, 144 ER 216 at
220):

'He further contended that, as the exception of refreshment to a traveller is
contained in the clause creating the prohibition, the burthen of proving that the
prohibition has been infringed, and that the case is not within the exception, is cast
on the informer . . . In this argument we think the appellant is well founded, and
that the statute ought to be construed on the principles that he has contended for.'

In *Davis v Scrace* (1869) LR 4 CP 172 a publican had been prosecuted under the
Metropolitan Police Act 1839 for selling liquor before one in the afternoon on a Sunday.
The Act provided, by s 42:

'. . . no Licensed Victualler or other Person shall open his House within the
Metropolitan Police District for the Sale of Wine, Spirits [etc] on *Sundays, Christmas
Day,* and *Good Friday* before the Hour of One in the Afternoon, except Refreshment
for Travellers.'

The court held that it was bound to follow *Taylor v Humphries.* Brett J said (at 176–177):

'It is quite impossible to distinguish this case from *Taylor v Humphries* . . . They
seem to have held that. though the word "except" is used in 11 and 12 Vict. c. 49
[sale of beer etc on Sunday (1848)], s. 1, it is not in truth an exception within the
meaning of the proviso in s. 14 of 11 and 12 Vict. c. 43 [the Summary Jurisdiction
Act 1848] and that therefore that proviso had no application to the case in hand. I
think we must adopt the same construction here.'

It seems likely that these cases played their part in leading Parliament to repeal s 14 of
the 1848 Act and to replace it by s 39(2) of the Summary Jurisdiction Act 1879, which
was in substantially the same language as the present s 101 of the 1980 Act. As Lord
Pearson pointed out in *Nimmo v Alexander Cowan & Sons Ltd* [1967] 3 All ER 187 at 202–
203, [1968] AC 107 at 135, Parliament was here emphasising that it was the substance
and effect as well as the form of the enactment that mattered when considering on whom
it was intended that the burden of proof should lie under any particular Act.

It seems to me that the probabilities are that Parliament when it enacted s 14 of the
1848 Act was intending to apply to summary trial that which it believed to be the rule
relating to burden of proof evolved by the judges on trials on indictment. It seems
unlikely that Parliament would have wished to introduce confusion by providing for
different burdens of proof in summary trials as opposed to trials on indictment. Looking
back over so many years, this must, to some extent, be speculation and I bear in mind
that whereas the defendant could give evidence on his own behalf in a summary trial it
was not until 1898 that he was allowed to do so in a trial on indictment, which might be
a reason for placing a heavier burden of proof on the prosecutions in trials on indictment.

However, my Lords, the common law adapts itself and evolves to meet the changing
patterns and needs of society; it is not static. By the time the 1879 Act was passed there
were already many offences that were triable both summarily and on indictment. This
list of offences has been growing steadily and the very crime with which we are concerned
in this appeal is such an example. It is conceded that in the case of exceptions within the
meaning of s 101 of the 1980 Act the burden of proving the exception has been
specifically placed on the defendant. The law would have developed on absurd lines if in
respect of the same offence the burden of proof today differed according to whether the
case was heard by the magistrates or on indictment. I observe that there would be no
possibility of presenting such a submission in respect of a crime triable in Scotland, for
the Criminal Procedure (Scotland) Act 1975, by ss 66 and 312(v), applies the same rule as
to the burden of proof in respect of exceptions to both trials on indictment and summary
trials. Although the language of ss 66 and 312(v) is slightly different from s 101 of the
1980 Act it is to the like effect.

There have been a number of cases considered by the Court of Appeal since *Woolmington
v DPP* [1935] AC 462, [1935] All ER Rep 1 concerning the burden of proof in licensing
cases both on indictment and on summary trial. There is no indication in any of these
cases that the court considered that there should be any difference of approach to the
burden of proof according to whether the case was tried summarily or on indictment:

see *R v Oliver* [1943] 2 All ER 800, [1944] KB 68, *R v Putland and Sorrell* [1946] 1 All ER 85, *John v Humphries* [1955] 1 All ER 793, [1955] 1 WLR 325 and *Robertson v Bannister* *a* [1973] RTR 109; see also *R v Ewens* [1966] 2 All ER 470, [1967] 1 QB 322, in which it was held that the Drugs (Prevention of Misuse) Act 1964 on its true construction placed an onus on the defendant to show that he was in possession of a prohibited drug by virtue of the issue of a prescription by a duly qualified medical practitioner.

Counsel for the appellant relied on three recent decisions of the Court of Appeal which he submitted support his submission that a statutory defence only places an evidentiary *b* burden on the defendant to raise the defence and that if this is done the burden remains on the prosecution to negative the defence. They are *R v Burke* (1978) 67 Cr App R 220, *R v McPherson* [1973] RTR 157 and *R v Cousins* [1982] 2 All ER 115, [1982] QB 526. In none of these cases was *R v Edwards* [1974] 2 All ER 1085, [1975] QB 27 either cited in argument or referred to in the judgment. In each case the Court of Appeal construed the relevant statutory provision as requiring the burden of proof to be discharged by the *c* prosecution. I do not regard these cases as intending to cast any doubt on the correctness of the decision in *R v Edwards* or as support for the proposition for which they were cited.

Whatever may have been its genesis I am satisfied that the modern rule was encapsulated by Lord Wilberforce in *Nimmo v Alexander Cowan & Sons Ltd* [1967] 3 All ER 187 at 199, [1968] AC 107 at 130, when speaking of the Scottish section which was *d* then the equivalent of the present s 101 of the Magistrates' Courts Act 1982:

'I would think, then, that the section merely states the orthodox principle (common to both the criminal and the civil law) that exceptions, etc., are to be set up by those who rely on them.'

I would summarise the position thus far by saying that *Woolmington v DPP* did not lay *e* down a rule that the burden of proving a statutory defence only lay on the defendant if the statute specifically so provided, that a statute can, on its true construction, place a burden of proof on the defendant although it does not so do so expressly and that if a burden of proof is placed on the defendant it is the same burden whether the case is tried summarily or on indictment, namely a burden that has to be discharged on the balance of probabilities. *f*

The real difficulty in these cases lies in determining on whom Parliament intended to place the burden of proof when the statute has not expressly so provided. It presents particularly difficult problems of construction when what might be regarded as a matter of defence appears in a clause creating the offence rather than in some subsequent proviso from which it may more readily be inferred that it was intended to provide for a separate *g* defence which a defendant must set up and prove if he wishes to avail himself of it. This difficulty was acutely demonstrated in *Nimmo v Alexander Cowan & Sons Ltd*. Section 29(1) of the Factories Act 1961 provides:

'There shall, so far as is reasonably practicable, be provided and maintained safe means of access to every place at which any person has at any time to work and every such place shall, so far as is reasonably practicable, be made and kept safe for *h* any person working there.'

The question before the House was whether the burden of proving that it was not reasonably practicable to make the working place safe lay on the defendant or the plaintiff in a civil action. However, as the section also created a summary offence, the same question would have arisen in a prosecution. In the event, the House divided 3 to 2 on *j* the construction of the section, Lord Reid and Lord Wilberforce holding that the section required the plaintiff or prosecution to prove that it was reasonably practicable to make the working place safe, the majority, Lord Guest, Lord Upjohn and Lord Pearson, holding that if the plaintiff or prosecution proved that the working place was not safe it was for the defendant to excuse himself by proving that it was not reasonably practicable to

make it safe. However, their Lordships were in agreement that if the linguistic
a construction of the statute did not clearly indicate on whom the burden should lie the
court should look to other considerations to determine the intention of Parliament, such
as the mischief at which the Act was aimed and practical considerations affecting the
burden of proof and, in particular, the ease or difficulty that the respective parties would
encounter in discharging the burden. I regard this last consideration as one of great
importance, for surely Parliament can never lightly be taken to have intended to impose
b an onerous duty on a defendant to prove his innocence in a criminal case, and a court
should be very slow to draw any such inference from the language of a statute.

When all the cases are analysed, those in which the courts have held that the burden
lies on the defendant are cases in which the burden can be easily discharged. This point
can be demonstrated by what, at first blush, appear to be two almost indistinguishable
cases that arose under wartime regulations. In *R v Oliver* [1943] 2 All ER 800, [1944] KB
c 68 the defendant was prosecuted for selling sugar without a licence. The material part of
the Sugar (Control) Order 1940, SR & O 1940/1069, by art 2 provided:

> 'Subject to any directions given or except under and in accordance with the terms
> of a licence permit or other authority granted by or on behalf of the Minister no . . .
> wholesaler shall by way of trade . . . supply . . . any sugar.'

d The Court of Criminal Appeal held that this placed the burden on the defendant to prove
that he had the necessary licence to sell sugar. In *R v Putland and Sorrell* [1946] 1 All ER
85, the defendant was charged with acquiring silk stockings without surrendering
clothing coupons. The material part of the Consumer Rationing (Consolidation) Order
1944, SR & O 1944/800, art 4 provided: 'A person shall not acquire rationed goods . . .
without surrendering . . . coupons.' The Court of Criminal Appeal there held that the
e burden was on the prosecution to prove that the clothing had been bought without the
surrender of coupons. The real distinction between these two cases lies in the comparative
difficulty which would face a defendant in discharging the burden of proof.

In *R v Oliver* it would have been a simple matter for the defendant to prove that he
had a licence if such was the case but in the case of purchase of casual articles of clothing
it might, as the court pointed out in *R v Putland and Sorrell*, be a matter of the utmost
f difficulty for a defendant to establish that he had given the appropriate number of
coupons for them. It appears to me that it was this consideration that led the court to
construe that particular regulation as imposing the burden of proving that coupons had
not been surrendered on the prosecution.

In *R v Edwards* [1974] 2 All ER 1085 at 1095, [1975] QB 27 at 39–40 the Court of
Appeal expressed its conclusion in the form of an exception to what it said was the
g fundamental rule of our criminal law that the prosecution must prove every element of
the charged. It said that the exception—

> 'is limited to offences arising under enactments which prohibit the doing of an
> act save in specified circumstances or by persons of specified classes or with specified
> qualifications or with the licence or permission of specified authorities.'

h
I have little doubt that the occasions on which a statute will be construed as imposing a
burden of proof on a defendant which do not fall within this formulation are likely to be
exceedingly rare. But I find it difficult to fit *Nimmo v Alexander Cowan & Sons Ltd* into
this formula, and I would prefer to adopt the formula as an excellent guide to construction
rather than as an exception to a rule. In the final analysis each case must turn on the
j construction of the particular legislation to determine whether the defence is an exception
within the meaning of s 101 of the 1980 Act, which the Court of Appeal rightly decided
reflects the rule for trials on indictment. With this one qualification I regard *R v Edwards*
as rightly decided.

My Lords, I am, of course, well aware of the body of distinguished academic opinion
that urges that wherever a burden of proof is placed on a defendant by statute the burden

should be an evidential burden and not a persuasive burden, and that it has the support of the distinguished signatories to the 11th Report of the Criminal Law Revision Committee, Evidence (General) (1972) (Cmnd 4991). My Lords, such a fundamental change is, in my view, a matter for Parliament and not a decision of your Lordships' House.

With these considerations in mind I turn now to the question of construction. The essence of the offence is having in one's possession a prohibited substance. In order to establish guilt the prosecution must therefore prove that the prohibited substance is in the possession of the defendant. As it is an offence to have morphine in one form but not an offence to have morphine in another form the prosecution must prove that the morphine is in the prohibited form for otherwise no offence is established. The Court of Appeal recognised the strength of this argument for it said ([1986] 1 All ER 184 at 190, [1986] QB 125 at 135):

> 'The offence, it will be remembered, is created by s 5(2) of the 1971 Act, under which it is an offence for a person to have a controlled drug in his possession in contravention of s 5(1). Section 5(1) provides that, subject to any regulations under s 7 of the Act for the time being in force, it shall not be lawful for a person to have a controlled drug in his possession. By virtue of para 4(1) of the regulations, s 5(1) of the Act shall not have effect in relation to the controlled drugs specified in Sch 1. If we restrict ourselves to the form and wording of these provisions, a strong argument can be advanced in favour of the proposition that this is simply a case where the possession of certain controlled drugs is prohibited, and the possession of others is not; that it must therefore be for the prosecution to prove that the controlled drug in the possession of the defendant is one the possession of which is prohibited; and that the prosecution must therefore negative the possibility that the drug in question is a controlled drug excluded from the prohibition in s 5(1) because it falls within Sch 1.'

The Court of Appeal rejected this construction primarily because it considered that all the regulations made pursuant to s 7 of the 1971 Act should be similarly construed as placing a burden on the defendant. But this approach does not, in my view, give sufficient weight to the difference between the two regulatory powers given to the Secretary of State by s 7(1). Under s 7(1)(a) a power is given to provide that it shall not be an offence to possess certain drugs; this is achieved by exempting them in reg 4. Under s 7(1)(b) a power is given to clothe certain persons with immunity for what would otherwise be unlawful acts and this is achieved by the remainder of the regulations in Pt II of the 1973 regulations. These latter regulations provide special defences to what would otherwise be unlawful acts and would, I accept, place a burden on defendants to bring themselves within the exceptions if it were necessary to do so. I say 'if it were necessary to do so' because of the extreme improbability that an exempted person would be charged with an offence.

However, I regard reg 4 as in a quite different category from the other regulations in Pt II. It deals not with exceptions to what would otherwise be unlawful but with the definition of the essential ingredients of an offence. This can be strikingly demonstrated by reference to reg 4(2), which provides:

> 'Sections 4(1) (which prohibits the production of and supply of controlled drugs) and 5(1) of the Act shall not have effect in relation to poppy-straw.'

Poppy-straw is shown in Pt I of Sch 2 to the 1971 Act as a Class A drug. But, Parliament having removed poppy-straw from the schedule by the regulation, where is there room for any burden to lie on a defendant if he is charged with possessing poppy-straw? The defendant's answer is simply that it is not an offence to possess poppy-straw. Clearly, one cannot approach the problem of poppy-straw by saying that the prosecution establishes a prima facie case by proving the possession of poppy-straw because it is a controlled drug within Pt I of Sch 2 to the 1971 Act when poppy-straw has been withdrawn from the

a schedule for the purposes of an offence under s 5(1). Both parts of reg 4 must be similarly construed and by parity of reasoning the prosecution cannot establish a prima facie case of possessing morphine by pointing to morphine in the schedule when the regulation has provided that it is not an offence to possess morphine in a particular form. The prosecution must prove as an essential element of the offence the possession of a prohibited substance and the burden therefore lies on the prosecution to prove not only

b that the powder contained morphine but also that it was not morphine in the form permitted by reg 4(1) and Sch 1 made thereunder.

I do not share the anxieties of the Court of Appeal that this may place an undue burden on the prosecution. It must be extremely rare for a prosecution to be brought under the 1971 Act without the substance in question having been analysed. If it has been analysed there will be no difficulty in producing evidence to show that it does not fall within Sch

c 1 to the 1973 regulations. I pause here to observe that the analyst was in court during this trial and could, no doubt, have given this evidence if called on to do so. In future the evidence can, of course, be included in the analyst's report. On the other hand if the burden of proof is placed on the defendant he may be faced with very real practical difficulties in discharging it. The suspected substance is usually seized by the police for the purpose of analysis and there is no statutory provision entitling the defendant to a

d proportion of it. Often there is very little of the substance and if it has already been analysed by the prosecution it may have been destroyed in the process. In those cases, which I would surmise are very rare, in which it is intended to prosecute without an analyst's report there will have to be evidence from which the inference can be drawn that the substance was a prohibited drug and such evidence may well permit of the inference that it was not one of the relatively harmless types of compounds containing

e little more than traces of the drugs which are contained in Sch 1 to the 1973 regulations.

Finally, my Lords, as this question of construction is obviously one of real difficulty I have regard to the fact that offences involving the misuse of hard drugs are among the most serious in the criminal calendar and, subject to certain special defences the burden whereof is specifically placed on the defendant, they are absolute. In these circumstances,

f it seems to me right to resolve any ambiguity in favour of the defendant and to place the burden of proving the nature of the substance involved in so serious an offence on the prosecution.

For these reasons, my Lords, I would answer the certified question in the negative. I would allow this appeal and quash the conviction.

g **LORD MACKAY OF CLASHFERN.** My Lords, I have had the advantage of reading in draft the speech prepared by my noble and learned friend Lord Griffiths, and I agree in the proposal he has made for disposal of this appeal and for answering the certified question for the reasons which he has given.

The analyst's certificate, as my noble and learned friend has narrated, stated that the powder analysed 'was found to contain morphine mixed with caffeine and atropine'. The

h relevant paragraph (para 3 of Sch 1 to the Misuse of Drugs Regulations 1973, SI 1973/ 797) refers to—

> 'Any preparation of medicinal opium or of morphine containing (in either case) not more than 0·2 per cent. of morphine calculated as anhydrous morphine base, being a preparation compounded with one or more other active or inert ingredients in such a way that the opium or, as the case may be, the morphine, cannot be
>
> j recovered by readily applicable means or in a yield which would constitute a risk to health.'

I should have thought it quite possible that what is described as 'morphine mixed with caffeine and atropine' could not be a preparation of morphine compounded with one or more other active or inert ingredients since I should have thought that in chemical usage a mixture is to be distinguished from a compound since in a mixture there would be no chemical bond between the constituents whereas in a compound there is such bond. However, the case has been argued on behalf of the Crown on the basis that the appellant could be guilty of a offence under s 5(2) of the Misuse of Drugs Act 1971 only if the percentage of morphine in the analysed powder was more than 0·2%. The Crown makes no distinction between the word 'mixture' and the word 'compound' in this context.

I consider that this case emphasises the need for absolute clarity in the terms of the analyst's certificate founded on by the prosecution in cases of this sort and, in my opinion, it would be wise where there is any possibility of one of the descriptions in the relevant schedule applying to the substance which is the subject of the certificate that the analyst should state expressly whether or not the substance falls within that description as well as stating whether or not it is a controlled drug within the meaning of the 1971 Act.

LORD ACKNER. My Lords, I gratefully adopt and therefore do not repeat the statement of the facts and the recital of the relevant legislation so succinctly set out in the speech of my noble and learned friend Lord Griffiths, which I have had the advantage of reading in draft. This appeal raises in essence three relatively short points of law, with which I will seek to deal seriatim.

1 *In order to place a burden of proof on the defendant, does Parliament have expressly so to provide or can it do so by necessary implication?*

It is the appellant's contention that the burden of proof in all cases of trials on indictment falls on the prosecution subject only to the defence of insanity and offences where the onus of proof is specially dealt with by statute. In support of this proposition counsel for the appellant relies principally on *Woolmington v DPP* [1935] AC 462, [1935] All ER Rep 1. That case was concerned with the constituent elements of the crime of murder. The facts were unusual. The appellant went to his mother-in-law's house where his wife, following a quarrel with him, had gone to stay. He went there to persuade her to return, but he killed her with a shot from a gun which he had fastened with a wire under his coat. He claimed that he had carried the gun with the view to threatening to commit suicide and that as he tried to use it for this purpose it went off and killed his wife. Swift J gave the following direction to the jury ([1935] AC 462 at 465, [1935] All ER Rep 1 at 3–4):

'Once it is shown . . . that somebody has died through the act of another, that is presumed to be murder, unless the person who has been guilty of the act which causes the death can satisfy a jury that what happened was something less, something which might be alleviated, something which might be reduced to a charge of manslaughter, or was something which was accidental, or was something which could be justified.'

In giving this direction Swift J relied on the following passage in *Foster's Crown Law* (1762) p 255:

'In every charge of murder, the fact of killing being first proved, all the circumstances of accident, necessity, or infirmity are to be satisfactorily proved by the prisoner, unless they arise out of the evidence produced against him; for the law presumeth the fact to have been founded in malice, unless the contrary appeareth.'

(See [1932] AC 462 at 475, [1935] All ER Rep 1 at 4.)

The House of Lords quashed the conviction on the ground of misdirection, approving *R v Davies* (1913) 8 Cr App R 211 and *R v Schama, R v Abramovitch* (1914) 84 LJKB 396, [1914–15] All ER Rep 204. Viscount Sankey LC made the classic statement ([1935] AC 462 at 481, [1935] All ER Rep 1 at 8):

'Throughout the web of the English Criminal Law one golden thread is always to be seen, that it is the duty of the prosecution to prove the prisoner's guilt subject to *a* what I have already said as to the defence of insanity and subject also to any statutory exception.'

It is, of course, axiomatic that a statute may impose on the accused the burden of proof of a particular defence to a statutory offence and may do so either expressly or by necessary implication. Whichever method Parliament uses it has created a 'statutory exception' and there is no difference in the quality or status of such an exception. As at
b the date of the decision in *Woolmington v DPP*, there were numerous examples of statutes in which the onus of proof of a particular defence had been placed on the accused, either expressly or, on a proper construction of the Act, by necessary implication. There is no warrant to be found either in the words used by Viscount Sankey LC quoted above or in their context for suggesting that 'statutory exception' is limited to *express* statutory exception. In *Mancini v DPP* [1941] 3 All ER 272 at 279, [1942] AC 1 at 11 Viscount
c Simon LC referred to Viscount Sankey LC's second exception as covering no more than 'offences where onus of proof is specially dealt with by statute'. I take the word 'specially' to mean no more than that the onus of proof is made the subject of a statutory provision, be this express or implied. Viscount Simon LC was not purporting to narrow the exception identified by Viscount Sankey LC, but merely to repeat it. If he had intended to narrow it to *express* statutory exceptions, this would have been so stated, but the
d resultant anomaly would then have required justification. Since, ex hypothesi, Parliament had by necessary implication from the words used in the statute made known its intention, by what authority could that intention be ignored? It is a constitutional platitude to state that where Parliament makes its intention known, either expressly or by necessary implication, the courts must give effect to what Parliament has provided. While the very nature of this appeal demonstrates the desirability of parliamentary
e draftsmen, whenever it is the intention of Parliament to place a burden of proof on the accused, so to provide in express terms, the proposition advanced by the appellant cannot be sustained.

2 *Where does the incidence of the burden of proof lie in the offence charged?*
Where Parliament has made no express provision as to the burden of proof, the court
f must construe the enactment under which the charge is laid. But the court is not confined to the language of the statute. It must look at the substance and the effect of the enactment. The first question which has to be decided is: what is the offence? Here there are the following alternatives: (a) the offence is being in possession of a controlled drug, viz morphine; or (b) the offence is being in possession of morphine other than a preparation of morphine as specified in para 3 of Sch 1 to the Misuse of Drugs Regulations
g 1973, SI 1973/797. Robert Goff LJ, giving the judgment of the Court of Appeal, Criminal Division, said ([1986] 1 All ER 184 at 190, [1986] QB 125 at 135):

> 'If we restrict ourselves to the form and wording of these provisions, a strong argument can be advanced in favour of the proposition that this is simply a case where the possession of certain controlled drugs is prohibited, and the possession of others is not; that it must therefore be for the prosecution to prove that the
h controlled drug in the possession of the defendant is one the possession of which is prohibited; and that the prosecution must therefore negative the possibility that the drug in question is a controlled drug excluded from the prohibition in s 5(1) because it falls within Sch 1.'

With respect, the Court of Appeal in my judgment would appear to have
j underestimated the strength of that argument. Counsel for the Crown rightly conceded that if Sch 1 to the 1973 regulations had removed entirely morphine from the list of controlled drugs the possession of which was prohibited, the case for the prosecution would have failed in limine once it was apparent, as it would be from the terms of the summons or information, that the controlled drug possession of which was charged by the prosecution was morphine. Indeed, this is what the Secretary of State so provided by

the regulations in relation to poppy-straw. This drug appears in Sch 2 to the 1971 Act as
a Class A drug. Regulation 4(2) provided in terms: *a*

> 'Sections 4(1) (which prohibits the production and supply of controlled drugs)
> and 5(1) of the Act shall not have effect in relation to poppy-straw.'

The Court of Appeal considered that if it restricted itself to the form and wording of
the provisions it would be adopting too narrow an approach. Robert Goff LJ said ([1986]
1 All ER 184 at 190–191, [1986] QB 125 at 135–136):   *b*

> 'In particular, we do not think that we can derive much assistance from the
> opening words of s 5(1), viz, "Subject to any regulations under section 7 of this Act
> for the time being in force . . .". We say this because the regulations do not only
> provide that s 5(1) shall not have effect in relation to the controlled drugs specified
> in Sch 1. They also provide, in para 6, for a general authority to possess conferred on
> certain persons when acting in certain capacities, for example, a constable when   *c*
> acting in the course of his duty as such, or a person engaged in the business of the
> Post Office when acting in the course of that business. In para 10, there is provision
> that certain persons may have in their possession any of the controlled drugs
> specified in Sch 2 and Sch 3; these persons are essentially professional persons such
> as practitioners, pharmacies, matrons, sisters, persons in charge of laboratories, and *d*
> others. We cannot think that it is incumbent on the prosecution, in a charge
> brought for an offence under s 5(2) of the Act, to negative the possibility that the
> defendant can take advantage of any of these provisions . . . Yet all these provisions,
> like para 4(1), form part of the "regulations under section 7 of this Act for the time
> being in force". Indeed, Pt II of the regulations is making provision for exceptions
> from certain provisions of the 1971 Act, and is therefore listing those circumstances *e*
> in which it is, for example, lawful to possess, or supply, or administer, or produce
> controlled drugs. Not surprisingly, many of these exceptions relate to the medical
> profession and other comparable professions; but, even where they do not, as in the
> case of para 4(1) and Sch 1, they relate to controlled drugs which anybody may
> innocently possess, and evidently include controlled drugs with medicinal properties.
> There is, we think, a strong argument that, in all the exceptions introduced by the   *f*
> 1973 regulations, the burden of proof should be consistent and for that reason
> should in each case rest on the defendant.'

Before us counsel for the appellant, in his able submissions, has emphasised the
significant difference between the two classes of regulations which the Secretary of State
is empowered to make under s 7 of the 1971 Act, a point which does not appear to have
been made before the Court of Appeal. Under powers given to him by virtue of s 7(1)(a)   *g*
the Secretary of State may by regulations 'except from section 3(1)(a) or (b), 4(1)(a) or (b)
or 5(1) of this Act such controlled drugs as may be specified in the regulations'.
Regulations made under that subsection are clearly directed at reducing the ambit of the
offences of importation and exportation of controlled drugs (s 3(1)(a) and (b)), of using or
supplying or offering to supply controlled drugs (s 4(1)(a) or (b)) and possession of *h*
controlled drugs (s 5(1)) by specifying controlled drugs which otherwise would have
been the subject matter of such offences. By contrast, s 7(1)(b) empowers the Secretary of
State by regulations to make such other provision as he thinks fit for the purpose of
making it lawful for persons to do things which under ss 4(1), 5(1) and 6(1) it would
otherwise be unlawful for them to do. Regulations made under this power, while leaving
the controlled drugs within the ambit of ss 4, 5 and 6, enable the Secretary of State to *j*
specify circumstances which will justify what otherwise would be unlawful activity.
Thus under reg 6 a general authority is conferred on certain persons when acting in
certain capacities to possess the controlled drug as exemplified by Robert Goff LJ in the
excerpt from the judgment of the Court of Appeal set out above. Counsel for the
appellant submits that the regulations made under s 7(1)(a), where made, affect the
definition of the offence, the ingredients of which *all* have to be proved by the

prosecution. He concedes, however, that regulations made under s 7(1)(b) provide
a exceptions or excuses, ie defences, and in relation to them the incidence of the burden of
proof is on the accused. While accepting these submissions I do not think they conclude
the question. The Court of Appeal, in construing the relevant statutory provisions in
order to ascertain where the burden of proof lay, rightly concluded, relying on the
decision of your Lordships' House in *Nimmo v Alexander Cowan & Sons Ltd* [1967] 3 All
ER 187, [1968] AC 107, that it was not restricted to the form or wording of the statutory
b provisions but was entitled to have regard to matters of policy. *Nimmo's* case concerned a
Scottish civil action brought by the pursuer against his employers for damages for breach
of their statutory duty under s 29(1) of the Factories Act 1961, which provided:

> 'There shall, so far as is reasonably practicable, be provided and maintained safe
> means of access to every place at which any person has at any time to work and
c > every such place shall, so far as is reasonably practicable, be made and kept safe for
> any person working there.'

The issue in that case was whether it was necessary for the pursuer to plead and to
prove that it was reasonably practicable for the defenders to make the place safe. Your
Lordships' House held, by a majority, that as a matter of construction the burden rested
on the defenders.
d Much was sought to be made by counsel for the appellants of the fact that this was a
civil action. This point is disposed of succinctly by Lord Pearson in his speech in these
terms ([1967] 3 All ER 187 at 202, [1968] AC 107 at 134):

> 'I should point out by way of introduction that the Factories Act, 1961, applies
> both to England and to Scotland (as did the earlier Acts relating to factories) and that
e > for a contravention of the Act the primary remedy—the only remedy expressly
> provided by the Act—is a prosecution under Part XII. The civil remedy arises only
> by implication, enabling a workman, for whose protection the provisions were
> enacted, to recover damages if the contravention of the Act—the breach of statutory
> duty—has caused him injury. The weight of the burden of proof is different in a
> civil action (needing, in England at any rate, proof on a balance of probabilities
f > instead of proof beyond reasonable doubt), but I think that the incidence of the
> burden of proof, determining what each party has to prove in order to succeed in
> the action, must be the same.'

Although Lord Reid dissented, his opinion on this point was identical (see [1967] 3 All
ER 187 at 189–190, [1968] AC 107 at 115).
g Lord Pearson, who, together with Lord Guest and Lord Upjohn, constituted the
majority, did not accept that they were confined, in construing the enactment, to the
arrangement of the sections and the forms of expression used in them (see [1967] 3 All
ER 187 at 200, [1968] AC 107 at 132). There were broader considerations to be taken
into account, in particular the practical consequences of holding that the burden of proof
rested on one party or the other.
h In my judgment, the Court of Appeal was entitled to have regard to the practical
consequences in this sense. If the result of holding that the burden of proof rested on the
prosecution to establish that the controlled drug had *not* been excepted by the Secretary
of State by regulations made under s 7(1)(a) of the 1971 Act would be to make the
prosecution of offences under the relevant sections particularly difficult or burdensome
with the consequence that the purpose of the legislation would be significantly frustrated,
j then this would be a relevant consideration to weigh against the grammatical form of
the legislation.
When dealing with the practical considerations, Robert Goff LJ stated ([1986] 1 All ER
184 at 191, [1986] QB 125 at 136):

> 'We are conscious of the fact that, in many cases, a prosecution launched under
> s 5(2) of the Act is not supported by an analyst's report, as for example where it is

based on an admission by the defendant (as to which see *Bird v Adams* [1972] Crim
LR 174); another example may arise where there is evidence of the supply to the *a*
defendant, or other evidence of his possession, but he has destroyed the drug in
question. Yet, if the burden rests on the prosecution to negative the possibility of
the drug falling within one of the exceptions in Sch 1 to the regulations, it would in
many cases be necessary for that purpose alone to produce evidence from an analyst.
On the other hand, it will be only in rare cases that a defendant will wish to invoke
any of the exceptions in the regulations. So far as the exceptions in Sch 1 are *b*
concerned, he is only likely to do so in specified circumstances, for example, where
he asserts that he has received a drug for medicinal purposes; and we can see no
great hardship in saying that, when he wishes to make such an assertion, the burden
should rest on the defendant to bring himself within the exception on which he
relies. It is not, we think, to be forgotten that we are here concerned with offences
relating to the possession of controlled drugs, offences which are regarded with such *c*
concern in modern society that Parliament has made them absolute: see *Warner v
Metropolitan Police Comr* [1968] 2 All ER 356, [1969] 2 AC 256.'

    With respect, I cannot share the concern which the Court of Appeal experienced at the
burden resting on the prosecution to negative the possibility of the drug falling within
one of the exceptions in Sch 1 to the 1973 regulations. If, as in this case, the prosecution *d*
obtains possession of the drug, then in order to discover the nature of the drug they
would in the ordinary course of events submit it to an analyst. There would have been
no difficulty in this case in the analyst's report containing an additional paragraph
negativing that it was a preparation within para 3 of Sch 1. The prosecution must always
establish, by admission or otherwise, that the accused had in his possession a controlled
drug. I see no practical difficulty in the case postulated by the Court of Appeal of an *e*
accused destroying the controlled drug. Such conduct would provide prima facie evidence
of the offence. In the instant case the accused, albeit wrongly, admitted that the drug was
amphetamine, a Class B drug. Had he destroyed it, and thereby prevented the prosecution
from analysing it, there would have been prima facie evidence that he was in possession
of a controlled drug which did not fall within one of the exceptions in Sch 1 to the 1973
regulations. The Court of Appeal envisaged that an accused was only likely to invoke the *f*
regulations in specified circumstances, providing as an example where he asserts that he
has received a drug for medicinal purposes. Such a situation comes under reg 6, made
pursuant to the powers of the Secretary of State under s 7(1)(*b*), and in such a situation it
is rightly conceded that the incidence of the burden of proof is on the accused.
    While I accept that the Court of Appeal was entitled to have regard to the practical
consequences of holding that the burden of proof rested on one party or the other and *g*
was not restricted to the formal wording of the relevant statutory provisions, those
practical considerations pointed in my judgment to the burden of negativing the
possibility of the drug being within one of the exceptions in Sch 1 to the 1973 regulations
resting on the prosecution.

h

3 *What is the weight of the burden of proof when it rests on an accused?*
    Where the burden of proof rests on the prosecution to negative the possibility of the
drug falling within one of the exceptions, it is, of course, common ground that the
prosecution must prove its case beyond reasonable doubt. It was, however, strongly
urged on your Lordships that if the burden had been on the defence, as indeed it is
conceded to be if reliance is being placed on reg 6, that burden is only an evidential one, *j*
that is to say an obligation to establish through evidence from the prosecution and/or
evidence from the defence that there is material which raises such a defence, so that it
becomes a live issue in the case.
    Although, in the light of my decision on the first two points, this question does not
arise, I have no hesitation in rejecting the submission of counsel for the appellant for the

following reasons. (i) It is accepted that, when Parliament by express words provides that
a the proof of the excuse shall lie on the accused, the legal burden of proof, that is to say
the ultimate burden of proof, is placed on the defendant, and that is discharged 'on the
balance of probabilities'. It cannot logically follow that if, ex hypothesi, Parliament has
by necessary implication placed the burden on the accused the weight of that burden
should be quite different. (ii) The hypothesis is that by necessary implication Parliament
has provided in a statute that *proof* of a particular exculpatory matter shall lie on the
b accused. However, the discharge of an evidential burden *proves* nothing: it merely raises
an issue. Accordingly, the mere raising of an issue by the defence would not satisfy the
obligation which Parliament has imposed. (iii) Section 101 of the Magistrates' Courts Act
1980 provides:

'Where the defendant to an information or complaint relies for his defence on
c   any exception, exemption, proviso, excuse or qualification, whether or not it
accompanies the description of the offence or matter of complaint in the enactment
creating the offence or on which the complaint is founded, the burden of proving
the exception, exemption, proviso, excuse or qualification shall be on him; and this
notwithstanding that the information or complaint contains an allegation negativing
the exception, exemption, proviso, excuse or qualification.'

d It is accepted that the words 'the burden of proving the exception . . . shall be on him'
impose the legal burden and that the decision of the Divisional Court in *Gatland v
Metropolitan Police Comr* [1968] 2 All ER 100, [1968] 2 QB 279 was correct. Counsel for
the appellant frankly concedes that, if his submission is right, the weight of the burden
would vary according to whether an accused is tried summarily or on indictment. This
anomaly becomes even more remarkable when one bears in mind the extent of hybrid
e offences, that is offences that can be tried either summarily or on indictment. If counsel
for the appellant is correct in his submissions it would follow that a Crown Court judge,
sitting with justices and hearing an appeal from conviction in a magistrate's court where
an exception etc was relied on by the appellant (defendant), would have to advise them
that the legal burden of establishing that offence was on the defendant. In the next case
which might be a trial on indictment for the selfsame offence, he would have to give to
f the jury an entirely different direction with regard to the weight of the burden of proof,
it being only the evidential burden. Such a remarkable situation cannot, in my judgment,
be attributed to the presumed intention of Parliament.

My Lords, in giving my reasons for allowing this appeal, answering the certified
question in the negative and quashing the conviction which are substantially the same as
those of my noble and learned friend Lord Griffiths, I have made no mention of *R v
g Edwards* [1974] 2 All ER 1085, [1975] QB 27. I have not done so firstly because I agree
with the Court of Appeal that this case does not fall within the principle stated in that
case ([1974] 2 All ER 1085 at 1095, [1975] QB 27 at 40) and secondly because it is clear
that the statement of principle is not intended to be exclusive in its effect. Lawton LJ in
giving the judgment of the Court of Appeal stated in terms: 'Whenever the prosecution
h seeks to rely on this exception, the court must construe the enactment under which the
charge is laid.'

R v Edwards provides, to my mind, a most helpful approach; but it still leaves to be
answered in every case where Parliament has made no express provision as to the
incidence of the burden of proof, the question: what is the proper construction of the
enactment?

j
Appeal allowed.

Solicitors: *Sylvester Small & Co* (for the appellant): *Director of Public Prosecutions.*

Mary Rose Plummer   Barrister.

D (a minor) v Berkshire County Council and others

FAMILY DIVISION

HOLLINGS AND WAITE JJ

4 FEBRUARY 1986

COURT OF APPEAL, CIVIL DIVISION

DILLON, STEPHEN BROWN AND WOOLF LJJ

19 MARCH 1986

HOUSE OF LORDS

LORD KEITH OF KINKEL, LORD BRANDON OF OAKBROOK, LORD GRIFFITHS, LORD MACKAY OF CLASHFERN AND LORD GOFF OF CHIEVELEY

8 OCTOBER, 4 DECEMBER 1986

Children and young persons – Care proceedings in juvenile court – Conditions to be satisfied before making order – Neglect or ill-treatment of child – Proper development of child 'is being' avoidably prevented or neglected etc – Is being – Child born with drug withdrawal symptoms because of mother's drug-taking during pregnancy – Whether child's proper development 'is being' avoidably prevented because of mother's actions during pregnancy – Whether juvenile court entitled to take into account mother's actions during pregnancy when making care order – Children and Young Persons Act 1969, s 1(2)(a).

On 12 March 1985 the mother, who was a registered drug addict and had taken drugs throughout her pregnancy, gave birth to a child which at the time of birth was suffering from drug withdrawal symptoms. The mother was aware that her drug-taking during pregnancy could harm the child. Because of its condition the child was placed in intensive care for several weeks following the birth. On 23 April the local authority obtained a place of safety order and on 1 August a juvenile court made a care order under s 1(2)(a)[a] of the Children and Young Persons Act 1969 committing the child to the care and control of the local authority on the ground, inter alia, that because of the mother's abuse of her own bodily health during pregnancy the child's proper development was being avoidably prevented or neglected or its health was being avoidably impaired or neglected or it was being ill-treated. The child, by its guardian ad litem, supported by the parents, appealed to the Divisional Court of the Family Division against the order. At the hearing of the appeal the issue arose whether, in determining whether a child's proper development 'is being' avoidably prevented etc, the juvenile court was restricted to considering the situation of the child at the date of the hearing or whether it was entitled to have regard to past treatment of the child including when the child was en ventre sa mère. The Divisional Court discharged the care order on the grounds that even if it were permissible to have regard to past events the whole of the mother's conduct in question had occurred before the child was born and would not be repeated and there was no evidence of the child's development being avoidably prevented etc since birth. On appeal by the local authority the Court of Appeal reinstated the care order. The child, supported by the parents, appealed to the House of Lords.

Held – Since the three alternative concepts referred to in s 1(2)(a) of the 1969 Act, namely the concepts of development, health and treatment, were themselves continuing concepts it followed that the term 'is being' in s 1(2)(a) denoted a continuing, rather than an instant, situation when applied to the impairment or neglect etc of a child's development, health or treatment. Accordingly, in deciding whether to make a care

---

a   Section 1(2), so far as material, is set out at p 33 *h j*, post

order under s 1 of the 1969 Act a juvenile court was required to consider whether, at the
point of time immediately before the process of protecting the child was put in motion,
a there was a continuing situation of impairment, neglect or ill-treatment etc. In doing so,
the court had to look at the present and also the past, and in respect of past events it was
permissible, when considering whether a child's proper development 'is being' avoidably
impaired, for the juvenile court to have regard to events before the child was born which
were having an adverse effect on the child's development or health. Furthermore, the
b court could have regard to the situation as it might be in the future if the situation was
likely to continue. Since the juvenile court had been entitled to take into account the
mother's drug-taking during pregnancy appeal would be dismissed (see p 33 *b*, p 40 *h j*,
p 41 *e* to *h*, p 42 *e f h j* to p 43 *a e f*, p 44 *e* to *h* and p 45 *c* to *e*, post).

    F v Suffolk CC (1981) 2 FLR 208 and *M v Westminster City Council* [1985] FLR 325
approved.
c   *Essex CC v TLR and KBR* (1978) 143 JP 309 considered.

    Per Lord Griffiths, Lord Mackay and Lord Goff. A juvenile court is not entitled to
conclude that a child's development 'is being' avoidably prevented or its health 'is being'
avoidably impaired by the mere fact of a past avoidable prevention of development or
impairment of health even if there are symptoms or effects which persist or manifest
themselves later, since it cannot be said in such circumstances that at the relevant time
d the child's health 'is being' avoidably impaired; all that can be said is that its health has
been avoidably impaired in the past (see p 43 *d* to *f j* to p 44 *d*, post).

Notes

For the grounds for a care order, see 24 Halsbury's Laws (4th edn) para 732.
    For the Children and Young Persons Act 1969, s 1, see 6 Halsbury's Statutes (4th edn)
e 229.

Cases referred to in judgments and opinions

A v Liverpool City Council [1981] 2 All ER 385, [1982] AC 363, [1981] 2 WLR 948, HL.
Caller v Caller [1966] 2 All ER 754, [1968] P 39, [1966] 3 WLR 437, DC.
Elliot v Joicey [1935] AC 209, [1935] All ER Rep 578, HL.
f *Essex CC v TLR and KBR* (1978) 143 JP 309, DC.
F v Suffolk CC (1981) 2 FLR 208.
M v Westminster City Council [1985] FLR 325, DC.
Paton v Trustees of BPAS [1978] 2 All ER 987, [1979] QB 276, [1978] 3 WLR 687.
Salaman, Re, De Pass v Sonnenthal [1908] 1 Ch 4, CA.
Villar v Gilbey [1907] AC 139, [1904–7] All ER Rep 779, HL.
g *W v Hertfordshire CC* [1985] 1 All ER 1001, CA; *affd* [1985] 2 All ER 301, [1985] AC 791,
    [1985] 2 WLR 892, HL.

Appeal

D, a child, by her guardian ad litem, appealed by way of case stated dated 1 August 1985
h by the justices for the county of Berkshire acting in and for the petty sessional division of
Reading whereby on the application of the Berkshire County Council (the local authority)
they made a care order in respect of the child pursuant to s 1 of the Children and Young
Persons Act 1969. By an order dated 22 January 1986 his Honour Judge Monier-Williams,
sitting as a judge of the High Court, ordered that the parents of the child be joined as
respondents to the appeal. The facts are set out in the judgment of Hollings J.

j

   Christopher Critchlow for the child.
   Barbara Slomnicka for the local authority.
   Paul Reid for the parents.

HOLLINGS J. This is an appeal by way of case stated from the decision of the juvenile
court sitting at the Civic Centre in Reading on 1 August 1985 whereby, pursuant to the

provisions of s 1(2)(a) of the Children and Young Persons Act 1969, on the application of
the Berkshire County Council (the local authority) for a care order under that section *a*
they decided that a baby girl (the child) should be made the subject of a care order,
because the condition laid down in para (a) of s 1(2) of that Act had, on the evidence and
on their findings, been satisfied. The child is represented by her guardian ad litem and is
the appellant.

Under that section it is provided that if the court before which a child is brought under
this section is of the opinion that any of the following conditions are satisfied with respect *b*
to that child, that is to say—

'(a) [which is the relevant condition] his proper development is being avoidably
prevented or neglected or his health is being avoidably impaired or neglected or he
is being ill-treated [there follow a number of other conditions in respect of which I
need only refer to the fact that paras (b) and (bb) refer to something which may *c*
happen in the future as compared with the phrase 'is being' in para (a)] and also that
[the child] is in need of care or control which [the child] is unlikely to receive unless
the court makes an order under that section in respect of [the child]',

then if those conditions, which have been referred to as the primary and secondary
conditions, are satisfied the court may, if it thinks fit, make such an order as is set out in
sub-s (3) of that section. Those orders include a supervision order and a care order as well *d*
as other orders.

In the proceedings before the juvenile court the guardian ad litem, acting on behalf of
the child, in response to the application for a care order by the local authority, asked the
juvenile court to make a supervision order, with a view to the child being restored at
some stage to the care of the mother or the mother and the father. In this appeal the
guardian ad litem seeks the discharge of the care order, submitting that in the *e*
circumstances the only proper and available course is the institution of wardship
proceedings.

The parents, who were not parties in the juvenile court proceedings but who were
given leave to intervene and call evidence, have been given leave to appear in this appeal
by this court, and they also appear by counsel. Their counsel supports the appeal of the *f*
guardian ad litem. The local authority appears by counsel to resist the appeal and to
support the decision of the justices.

In stating the case the justices found certain facts, and it is I think useful if I recite the
facts now which they found. They heard the case on 23, 24, 25 July and 1 August 1985.
They found the following facts. The child was born to her mother, who was then aged
29, on 12 March 1985 at the Royal Berkshire Hospital in Reading. At the time of her
birth the child was suffering from symptoms caused by withdrawal from narcotics. The *g*
mother had been a registered drug addict since 1982 and had been taking drugs for
approximately ten years. The mother continued to take drugs, both by oral means and
by injection, from the time that she knew that she was pregnant to the time when the
child was born. During the pregnancy the mother took drugs in excess of those which
were prescribed for her by her registered medical practitioner. The mother knew that by *h*
taking drugs while pregnant she could be causing damage to her child. The child was
kept in intensive care in hospital for several weeks immediately following the birth,
indeed until 19 May. A place of safety order was obtained by the Berkshire social services
on 23 April and successive interim care orders were in force from 13 May 1985 to the
date of the hearing. This meant that the child was never in the care or control of the
mother or of her father since her birth. They found that the medical condition in which *j*
the child was born was a direct result of deliberate and excessive taking of drugs by the
mother during pregnancy. They also found that the mother, and the father too,
continued to be addicted to drugs and remained so on the final day of the hearing of the
case.

The case stated by the justices then sets out the respective contentions of the guardian
ad litem, the local authority and the parents. Having set out those contentions and

having referred to the cases to which they were referred in the juvenile court proceedings,
a the justices said as follows: 'The Berkshire County Council decided to initiate these proceedings in the juvenile court and we had jurisdiction to hear the matter.' They then refer to the question of whether the wardship jurisdiction should have been allowed to take the place of the justices' jurisdiction. I will refer to that later in this judgment. They considered *A v Liverpool City Council* [1981] 2 All ER 385, [1982] AC 363 and on the basis of that decision they considered that their powers were sufficient to ensure that the best
b interests of the child were met. They accepted that the particular circumstances on which what I have called the primary condition was based would not recur since the child had now been born, but, as they say in their case, they took the view that a child's development is a continuing process which encompasses the past and the present 'and we considered that events in the past life of this child, even during the time when it was a fetus in the womb, were relevant'. For this reason they considered that they were entitled to have
c regard to the mother's abuse of her own bodily health during the pregnancy when deciding whether the condition in s 1(2)(a) of the 1969 Act was proved in respect of the child born of that pregnancy. They expressed themselves satisfied that this child's proper development was being avoidably prevented or neglected, or her health was being avoidably impaired or neglected, or she was being ill-treated. I should interpose to say that it is accepted that they were entitled to make a finding in that compendious form,
d referring to the various alternatives which are set out in that primary condition. And they accepted that in so deciding they should not look at the future development of the child. They further concluded that the child was in need of care or control which she was unlikely to receive unless an order was made, and they made a care order in respect of the child.

In respect of that latter decision, that is that the child was in need of care or control,
e which is the secondary condition, the guardian ad litem makes no complaint, and there is no appeal in respect of that condition, it being conceded that the child was at the time of the hearing before the justices, and indeed no doubt now, in need of care or control. The sole question for this court is whether the primary condition has been satisfied.

The justices then set out four questions on which they asked for the opinion of this
f court. I will refer to those questions towards the end of this judgment.

The construction of s 1(2)(a) of the 1969 Act has been the subject matter of consideration in two cases in particular to which this court has been referred. The first is *F v Suffolk CC* (1981) 2 FLR 208, a decision of McNeill J hearing the Crown Office list, and the second is *M v Westminster City Council* [1985] FLR 325, a decision by Bush and Butler-Sloss JJ in this court, the Family Divisional Court. Both *F v Suffolk CC* and *M v*
g *Westminster City Council* concerned children, or a child, who had during his or her lifetime been in the care of his or her mother. That is a distinction which has to be borne in mind when applying, so far as they are relevant, those decisions to the facts of this case.

In *F v Suffolk CC* 2 FLR 208 at 213 (which was referred to by Butler-Sloss J in *M v Westminster City Council*) McNeill J, having referred to *Essex CC v TLR and KBR* (1978) 143 JP 309, which I do not need to refer to myself, said:

h   'What the court has to consider, as I see it, is this: is there present avoidable neglect or prevention? That is the present tense application to these words. Is that something which is happening now, or it may be has happened, with the result that the proper development of the child is affected in those ways? The proper development of the child is a continuing process, past, present, and future and what the court has to look at, in my view, is the present conduct and its effect on the development of the
j   child in the past, at the present time and at any rate in the foreseeable future. Development being a continuing matter, I do not think this section is intended to rule out of consideration either mental development or development in its broadest and continuing sense.'

Having referred to that passage, with agreement and approval, but with some possible qualification as to how far it would apply in the foreseeable future, Butler-Sloss J

considered the case before her and Bush J in M v *Westminster City Council*. In that case the
mother had what were described as drink problems, which she had suffered from when *a*
having the care of the relevant children. However, by the time the application for a care
order came before the justices the particular drink problem was no longer present, and
the justices decided that the court must look at the situation when the proceedings were
started in the light of the subsequent relevant factors but the fact that the mother had
cared for the children well from 20 January until the hearing on 17 February did not
prevent them from holding that the primary condition under sub-para (*a*) was made out, *b*
and they expressed the view that although the children were to be left with the mother a
supervision order would not provide sufficient motivation for the mother and that a care
order was appropriate. It was from that decision that the appeal was made to the
Divisional Court. Butler-Sloss J said ([1985] FLR 325 at 335–336):

> 'If [counsel], for the appellant, is right [that is that one must look at the situation *c*
> as at the moment of the application], then there will be virtually no cases under
> s. 1(2)(*c*) where the children have been removed from home in which it would be
> possible to find the primary condition in the subsection proved. One has only got to
> take the example of the very young child who has been battered and who is then
> put in a foster home [but] who has recovered from the injuries by the time the case
> is heard, there having been perhaps a number of adjournments in order, as [counsel *d*
> for the local authority] in her submissions to us points out, to wait for the criminal
> proceedings that may arise; such a child by the time he is in foster care and has
> recovered from his injuries, as, fortunately, very young children often do, would
> not be, on the analogy of [counsel] for the appellant, conceivably within the ambit
> of "is being avoidably prevented". Or, indeed, one could have a situation, again with
> a very young child who, even 2 or 3 months before, had been taken away after a *e*
> long course of fairly minor injuries and was placed with foster parents and it would
> be impossible to say of such a child that the development is being avoidably
> prevented as at the date of the hearing, because there may be great difficulty in
> saying, with a very young child, how far that could possibly arise . . . For my part, I
> find it impossible to find that for the primary condition to be established the child's
> proper development can only be considered as being avoidably prevented at the *f*
> time of the hearing. A child's development is a continuing process. The present
> must be relevant in the context of what has happened in the past and it becomes a
> matter of degree as to how far in the past you go. It must be as, indeed, counsel for
> the children has urged upon us, in the interests of the children themselves that one
> should look at the past and, since we are considering the development of the
> children, we must look to see what it is that we must look at. I take the view that *g*
> this very restrictive approach, put forward with great enthusiasm by counsel for the
> appellant, is quite inappropriate to the way in which one should look at the proper
> development of a child. Therefore, the magistrates' approach to this case, whereby
> they said that you look at the position when the proceedings were started and are
> entitled to interpret it in the light of anything relevant which has happened since,
> was an entirely proper way for them to consider this matter, and it leaves out any *h*
> problems there may be as to the future because it is clear from their case that they
> did not consider the future in respect of the primary condition.'

Likewise Bush J on this aspect said this (at 340–341):

> 'The development of a child is a continuing matter and encompasses the past, *j*
> present and, to a certain extent, the future. The magistrates, in determining the
> primary condition, must have regard to the past treatment of the child as well as to
> the present. They must ask themselves on the day of the hearing: "Are we satisfied
> that his proper development is being avoidably prevented or neglected, or his health

a

is being avoidably impaired or neglected?" They are not bound to answer the question in the negative if, for example, there has been a temporary respite in the condition or treatment of the child. In my view "is being" is not temporal in the sense that it means "now", "this minute"; it is descriptive of the child, that is the child must fall into the category mentioned in the section. If the words used had been different then different considerations would apply. "Has been" would indicate some time in the past; "will be" would indicate some time in the future; "is being"

b

would indicate a situation over a period, not now at this precise moment but over a period of time sufficiently proximate to the date of the inquiry to indicate that it is the present, not history and not the days to come. It is the description of a continuing set of circumstances which may not obtain on the particular day on which the matter is being considered but represents a category which the description of the child fits. Whether the evidence available satisfies this criterion is a question of fact

c

and degree.'

Counsel for the local authority relies on the decision and the effect of the judgments in M v Westminster City Council, and for that purpose she makes a further submission, and that is that the justices are not only entitled to look at how the mother behaved towards her unborn child, but are also entitled to treat that unborn child as a child for the

d

purposes of the Act so that the damage which was caused to that unborn child was damage which did or might come within the purview of s 1(2)(a) as that sub-paragraph had been interpreted and construed in M v Westminster City Council. For that purpose counsel for the local authority has referred this court to not only the definition section in the 1969 Act and in the Child Care Act 1980, but also to a number of authorities and to a number of statutes in order to seek to establish what she contends for.

e

By s 70 of the 1969 Act, which is the definition section, it is provided that a child means a person under the age of 14. By s 87 of the Child Care Act 1980 'child' means a person under the age of 18. For the purposes of her submission counsel for the local authority has referred us to cases which have to do with wills and intestacy, with the maintenance of children, and with the rights of unborn children. She has referred us to *Caller v Caller* [1966] 2 All ER 754, [1968] P 39, which was a case where whether a father

f

had accepted an unborn child as a child of the family was under consideration. It was there held by the Divisional Court that the child even before birth could be accepted by the father for the purpose of his acceptance within the meaning of the Act then in force, so that he could be liable for the maintenance of that child when born, even though he had left the mother before birth. In the course of their judgments Karminski and Latey JJ made certain observations which were obiter and on which counsel for the authority

g

relies. I am satisfied that those observations were obiter and I do not find the facts of that case, or the decision in that case, of relevance or assistance to solve the present problem.

We were also referred to *Paton v Trustees of BPAS* [1978] 2 All ER 987, [1979] QB 276, a decision of Sir George Baker P, which, however, only decided that an unborn child or fetus cannot have any right of its own, at least until that fetus is born and becomes a child. Again I find that of little assistance in solving the present problem.

h

Counsel then referred us to a number of cases concerning wills and intestacy, in particular *Elliot v Joicey* [1935] AC 209, [1935] All ER Rep 578, which reviewed the earlier cases of *Villar v Gilbey* [1907] AC 139, [1904–7] All ER Rep 779 and *Re Salaman, De Pass v Sonnenthal* [1908] 1 Ch 4, and from that it is plain that in the case of wills a particularly favourable construction to a child en ventre sa mère would be given if that would secure for the child a benefit which that child would have got if the child had been born at the

j

relevant date. It is in my judgment a construction of its own particular kind to meet a particular case. Again I do not find it of assistance in deciding the present case.

Counsel has referred us to a number of statutes where it has been provided that the statute in question applies to a child en ventre sa mère, namely the Infant Life Preservation Act 1929, the Congenital Disabilities Act 1976, the Inheritance Act 1975 and the Law of

Property Act 1922. Those are all, I find, statutes passed to govern the particular matters with which those statutes were concerned, and once more I do not find the fact that those *a* statutes have referred specifically to them applying to a child en ventre sa mère of assistance in this case, and indeed one might say they point more the other way, in as much as it was deemed necessary to refer specifically to the statute applying to a child en ventre sa mère.

Added to that is the fact that care proceedings both under this Act and any other Act, it is common ground, can only be taken in respect of a living, born, child. In those *b* circumstances, having regard to that particular reason and the definition of a child as a 'person', and to the natural meaning of the word 'child', I am satisfied that this Act and this section applies only to a child from the moment of that child's birth. That does not mean, however, that what happened to that child while unborn was not to be looked at or considered by the justices, and how the mother had regard for or cared for her child during the pregnancy, it might be said, and the effect that her behaviour had on the *c* health of that child when born, together with the fact that the mother continues to abuse drugs, may be considered perhaps relevant evidence for the purpose of considering whether the child's proper development is being avoidably prevented or neglected or her health is being avoidably impaired. The difficulty which, however, I have found is this: that unlike M v Westminster City Council [1985] FLR 325 and F v Suffolk CC (1981) 2 FLR 208 the whole of the conduct, if I may so describe it, of the mother vis-á-vis the child *d* relates to the period before birth. The mother's present conduct vis-á-vis the child has never been tested, and of its very nature her previous conduct vis-á-vis this child can never be repeated. It is that circumstance which to my mind distinguishes this case from that of M v Westminster City Council, and indeed from F v Suffolk CC.

The only evidence before the justices as to the situation after the birth of the child was that this mother and father (of course we are chiefly concerned with the mother) *e* continue, or continued at least until the hearing before the justices, to take class A drugs. There was no evidence before the justices as to the effect that had or might have on her caring for the child. There was no evidence to suggest that her use or abuse of drugs would affect the child or that the parents would administer drugs to the child. Indeed no one has suggested that the mother would seek to do so, I hasten to add. As counsel for the local authority submitted in M v Westminster City Council, in the case of a battered *f* child who is now in the care of the local authority one cannot say that this condition does not apply, because the child is now in care. That is because the child was battered when in the care of the mother and alive, and it is only because of the intervention of the social services and the care application that the child is no longer with the mother. What the justices have realistically to be concerned with is not the situation technically as it is before them at the time but the situation in the continuum, as it has been described by *g* Butler-Sloss and Bush JJ. They had to look at the ability of the mother and the risk to the child in the light of the past, with some thought to the future, though not so far into the future. In the present case there is a notable absence of any such state of affairs.

That this child is in need of care and control is, as I said at the outset, conceded. However, in my judgment the justices, confined as they were to the provisions of that *h* section of the 1969 Act, as interpreted by the two cases to which I have referred, even though they were entitled to look at what happened during the pregnancy, ought not, in my judgment to have come to the conclusion that this condition has been satisfied in any of its respects, for the reasons I have already stated.

It remains therefore for me now to consider the four questions which have been posed to this court in the case stated. By the first question the justices ask: *j*

'Is it wrong in law for the Juvenile Court to find that the condition under Section 1(2)(a) of the Children and Young Persons Act 1969 is satisfied in circumstances where the child has never been in the care of either parent or out of the care of responsible agencies?'

My answer to that is that there may be cases in the future where it might be right to find a that condition proved, even though the child was never in the care of either parent, but it was wrong in this case. I do not propose to answer that question in the generality in which it is posed.

The second question is as follows:

b 'Is the condition in Section 1(2)(a) of the Children and Young Persons Act 1969 satisfied in respect of a child when the evidence [here I would add 'and when the *only* evidence'] of the child's proper development being avoidably prevented or neglected or its health being avoidably impaired or neglected or its being ill-treated relates to when the child was "en ventre sa mere"?'

I would answer that question, as amended, No.

The third question is:

c 'On the facts found could the Juvenile Court properly find that the proper development of the child is being avoidably prevented or neglected or her health is being avoidably impaired or neglected or she is being ill-treated?'

I have already answered that question No.

The fourth question is:

d 'In considering Section 1(2)(a) of the Children and Young Persons Act 1969 should the Juvenile Court have considered the availability of Wardship proceedings and/or proceedings under the Child Care Act 1980 and/or any other powers and procedures available to the local authority?'

Again I would answer that question No. The justices had only to consider the provisions of that section, bearing in mind the enjoinder in s 44 of the Children and Young Persons e Act 1933 that they must have regard to the welfare of the child. The availability or otherwise of wardship proceedings in my judgment is not a relevant consideration for the justices. It was for them to consider whether the conditions laid down in s 1(2)(a) had been satisfied or not. By the decision in, especially, *M v Westminster City Council* the meaning of the words 'is being' has been expanded somewhat, but not enough to cover the facts and circumstances of this case. As I say the answer is No, but of course wardship f proceedings are a relevant consideration here and now for the purposes of the welfare of the child, and I have no doubt that an application will be made in respect of that at the conclusion of this appeal.

For those reasons I would allow the appeal and discharge the care order.

g **WAITE J.** I agree that the appeal should be allowed for the reasons given by Hollings J, and I concur in the answers which he has given to the questions raised in the case stated.

Appeal allowed. Care order discharged. Leave to appeal to the Court of Appeal granted.

h *Solicitors: Rowberry Morris & Co*, Reading (for the child); *D C H Williams*, Reading (for the local authority); *Blandy & Blandy*, Reading (for the parents).

Bebe Chua   Barrister.

Appeal
The local authority appealed.

j *Nicholas Medawar QC* and *Barbara Slomnicka* for the local authority.
James Townend QC and *Christopher Critchlow* for the child.
Paul Reid for the parents.

STEPHEN BROWN LJ (giving the first judgment at the invitation of Dillon LJ). This is an appeal from a decision of the Divisional Court of the Family Division on 4 February

1986. On that occasion the Divisional Court allowed an appeal by way of case stated from
a decision of the justices at Reading on 1 August 1985 whereby they made a care order *a*
in respect of a little girl (the child) in favour of the Berkshire County Council (the local
authority).

The facts giving rise to these proceedings are sad but may be shortly stated. They
concern a little girl, who was born prematurely on 12 March 1985. She was born to a
mother who was addicted to heroin or a substitute and, as a result, she was born in a
condition where she herself was addicted to that drug and was suffering serious *b*
withdrawal symptoms. She was taken to a special care baby unit at the Royal Berkshire
Hospital, her health having deteriorated after her birth. She spent some six weeks in
hospital and, in the interim, the local authority placed the child on the abuse register. It
called a case conference to consider the circumstances of this little baby and it decided to
seek a care order from the juvenile court under the provisions of the Children and Young
Persons Act 1969. *c*

Those proceedings were commenced on 25 April and subsequently successive interim
care orders were made. It was arranged that the child should be separately represented
by a guardian ad litem, who was appointed from a panel kept by the juvenile court. On
19 May 1985 the child was discharged from intensive care at the hospital to foster parents.

It is part of the chronology of events that the mother, who was unmarried at the time
of the birth, married the father on 21 June 1985. The juvenile court commenced the *d*
hearing of the application by the local authority for a care order on 23 July and that
hearing continued until it was completed on 1 August when the juvenile court made a
care order in favour of the local authority.

The child, by her guardian ad litem, appealed by way of case stated from the decision
of the justices to the Divisional Court of the Family Division. The Divisional Court, as I
have indicated, allowed that appeal and the local authority, the first respondent in the *e*
proceedings before the Divisional Court, is the appellant before this court.

The facts found by the justices and stated in their case were as follows. [His Lordship
then set out the facts, set out in the judgment of Hollings J (at p 22 *g* to *j*, ante), and
continued:]

The justices accepted that the particular circumstances which gave rise to the physical
condition of the baby could not recur after the child had been born, but in para 7(b) of *f*
the case they stated:

'... However, we took the view that a child's development is a continuing process
which encompasses the past and the present and we considered that events in the
past life of this child, even during the time when it was a foetus in the womb, were
relevant. For this reason we considered we were entitled to have regard to the *g*
mother's abuse of her own bodily health during pregnancy when deciding whether
the condition in Section 1(2)(a) Children and Young Persons Act 1969 was proved
in respect of the child born of that pregnancy. We were satisfied that this child's
proper development was being avoidably prevented or neglected or her health was
being avoidably impaired or neglected or she was being ill-treated. In so deciding *h*
we accepted that we should not look at the future development of the child. We
further concluded that this child was in need of care or control which she was
unlikely to receive unless an order was made and we made a Care Order to the
[authority] in respect of the child.'

The appeal to the Divisional Court raised the question of the construction and *j*
application of s 1(2) of the 1969 Act. Section 1 provides:

'(1) Any local authority, constable or authorised person who reasonably believes
that there are grounds for making an order under this section in respect of a child
or young person may, subject to section 2(3) and (8) of this Act, bring him before a
juvenile court.

a   (2) If the court before which a child or young person is brought under this section is of opinion that any of the following conditions is satisfied with respect to him, that is to say—(a) his proper development is being avoidably prevented or neglected or his health is being avoidably impaired or neglected or he is being ill-treated . . . and also that he is in need of care or control which he is unlikely to receive unless the court makes an order under this section in respect of him, then, subject to the following provisions of this section and sections 2 and 3 of this Act,

b   the court may if it thinks fit make such an order . . .'

The submissions made to the Divisional Court, which it accepted and upheld, concerned the application and construction of s 1(2)(a). The submission which received approval was that, in this particular case, the only evidence before the justices as to the cause of the condition of the child related to events which had taken place before its

c birth; that there had been no opportunity for the mother to care for the child since the birth and accordingly no conduct on her part which could be said to have avoidably impaired the health or prevented the proper development of the child. Accordingly, applying the strict wording of s 1(2)(a) in its present tense, the condition was not satisfied which is the primary condition which enables a court to proceed to make a care order.

It is not in dispute, nor was it in dispute before the Divisional Court, that the child is

d in need of care or control. Submissions were made to the effect that this was a case in which the court should consider wardship proceedings as being the appropriate procedure. The Divisional Court came to the conclusion that the submissions made on behalf of the child and the mother, who was given leave to intervene before the Divisional Court, were made out and, accordingly, allowed the appeal.

Before this court counsel for the local authority submits that the Divisional Court fell

e into error. In his submission it looked too narrowly at the application of s 1(2)(a) and in effect overlooked the complete findings of the justices, including the continuing addiction of the parents. Counsel submitted that, in this case, the facts found by the justices supported their conclusion that the proper development of the child *was* being prevented and her health *was* being impaired and that this was avoidable. He submitted that this was attributable to conduct which was the deliberate conduct of the mother and, looking

f at the situation as a continuing state of affairs, it was appropriate to take into consideration the matters which had in fact taken place while the child was still in her mother's womb. He submits that the decision of the Divisional Court has in effect divided the process of the child's development artificially. It is artificial to disregard the period before birth and to have regard only to events which have occurred since the actual birth of the child.

Counsel for the local authority has invited the court's attention to M v *Westminster City*

g *Council* [1985] FLR 325 and, in particular, to a passage in the judgment of Butler-Sloss J (at 336):

    'For my part, I find it impossible to find that for the primary condition to be established the child's proper development can only be considered as being avoidably prevented at the time of the hearing. A child's development is a continuing process.

h   The present must be relevant in the context of what has happened in the past and it becomes a matter of degree as to how far in the past you go. It must be as, indeed, counsel for the children has urged upon us, in the interests of the children themselves that one should look at the past and, since we are considering the development of the children, we must look to see what it is that we must look at. I take the view that this very restrictive approach, put forward with great enthusiasm

j   by counsel for the appellant, is quite inappropriate to the way in which one should look at the proper development of a child. Therefore, the magistrates' approach to this case, whereby they said that you look at the position when the proceedings were started and are entitled to interpret it in the light of anything relevant which has happened since, was an entirely proper way for them to consider this matter, and it leaves out any problems there may be as to the future because it is clear from their case that they did not consider the future in respect of the primary condition.'

The facts of that case were different from the particular facts of the present case, but it is significant that, in this case, the Divisional Court did consider that it was appropriate *a* and relevant to look at what had happened before the child was born. However, it seems to me that the Divisional Court fell into error in not applying the result of that view to the case because, in effect, it appears that it did restrict consideration of the development of the child to events which had taken place since its birth. In my view, that is too narrow an approach.

Counsel for the child has argued that one should not have regard to what has taken *b* place before the birth of the child. That seems to me to be the result of his submissions. He further argues that, in point of fact, an appropriate procedure in a case of this nature is for the wardship jurisdiction of the court to be invoked. However, having regard to the recent decisions of the House of Lords in *A v Liverpool City Council* [1981] 2 All ER 385, [1982] AC 363 and *W v Hertfordshire CC* [1985] 2 All ER 301, [1985] AC 791, that is only appropriate if the statutory scheme provided by the 1969 Act is not applicable. In *c* my judgment, bearing in mind that what one has to have regard to is the continuing process of the development of the child, s 1(2)(*a*) is apt to cover the facts of the present case.

Accordingly, I have come to the conclusion that the Divisional Court was wrong in the decision to which it came and that the justices were in fact correct when they stated in para 7(b) of the case: *d*

'However, we took the view that a child's development is a continuing process which encompasses the past and the present and we considered that events in the past life of this child, even during the time when it was a foetus in the womb, were relevant.'

Those events, which had the effect of preventing the proper development, and *e* impairing the health, of this child, were avoidable and that, as a part of a continuing process, they could and should have been in the contemplation of the court. Accordingly, they were entitled to find the primary condition of the section fulfilled and to proceed to make a care order, it not being disputed that the child was in need of care or control.

In my judgment, the appeal should be allowed and the decision of the justices restored. *f*

WOOLF LJ. I agree that this appeal should be allowed and I gratefully adopt the facts as set out by Stephen Brown LJ.

In my view, it is most important, when answering the questions posed by the justices in the case stated, to look at the statutory provisions with which the justices were concerned and determine their proper interpretation. Section 1 of the Children and Young Persons Act 1969 contains a most important and valuable power giving a local *g* authority the ability to go before a juvenile court and to obtain from that court orders for the care and protection of children. It is, however, to be noted that, as counsel for the parents submitted, the procedure which flows from that section does in some degree interfere with the mother's rights which would exist in wardship proceedings, and it is, therefore, important from her point of view that, in cases which do not fall properly *h* within s 1, that procedure should not be invoked.

In my view, this case raises a question that has not previously come before the court as to whether or not matters which flow from what was done to a child prior to its birth justify an order being made under s 1 subsequent to its birth. If there was any doubt as to whether a child includes an unborn child for the purposes of s 1 of the 1969 Act, in my view that doubt is removed by s 70(1) of the 1969 Act, which defines a 'child' as *j* meaning 'a person under the age of 14'. A 'person' denotes someone who is living, not someone who has yet to be born.

It follows, in my view, from that approach to the interpretation of s 1 that what has to be considered in deciding whether the requirements of s 1(2)(*a*) of the 1969 Act have been met in any particular case is whether a living child's proper development is being prevented or neglected or a living child's health is being impaired or neglected or a living child is being ill treated. However, the fact that the question has to be posed in that way

does not mean that what happened before the birth of the child has to be ignored for all
a purposes. In my view, the proper approach to the interpretation of s 1(2)(*a*) involves
asking two questions, the first being 'Is the living child's proper development etc being
prevented or neglected?' and the second question being whether that was avoidable.

In considering those questions in relation to this case there was no doubt that the
child's health was being impaired and, because of that, the answer to the first question
must be in the affirmative. The next question is: was that avoidable? Again, in my view,
b the answer must be in the affirmative because the mother, prior to the birth of the child,
should have taken steps to avoid the consequences to that child after its birth. Whereas
in asking the first question I do not regard it as proper to look at what occurred before
birth, in asking the second question it is, in my view, perfectly permissible to consider
what happened before birth. The only matter with which the court is concerned in
relation to the second question is: was it avoidable or not?
c So far as the use in s 1(2) of the word 'being' is concerned, I would respectfully adopt
the approach of the Family Division in M v Westminster City Council [1985] FLR 325 in
the passage from the judgment of Butler-Sloss J, to which Stephen Brown LJ referred,
subject to one qualification. In that passage the judge said (at 336):

> 'Therefore, the magistrates' approach to this case, whereby they said that you look
d > at the position when the proceedings were started and are entitled to interpret it in
> the light of anything relevant which has happened since, was an entirely proper way
> for them to consider this matter . . .'

The judge, when the whole passage which Stephen Brown LJ cited from her judgment is
looked at, may not have been intending to limit her approach to a consideration of the
situation at the time when the proceedings were started. If she was intending to limit
e consideration to that time or a consideration from that time, then I would respectfully
disagree with her approach because, in my view, it is at the time of the hearing with
which the justices are primarily concerned although, in accordance with what Butler-
Sloss J said, in approaching the matter you look at the continuing situation. I would
respectfully, on this aspect, prefer the approach of Bush J in the same case (at 340–341).
f [His Lordship then quoted the extract from Bush J's judgment set out in the judgment
of Hollings J (p 24 *j* to 25 *c*, ante) and continued:] Applying that approach, I would say,
on the findings of fact made by the justices in this case, that, so far as the questions posed
in the Divisional Court are concerned, the answers would be as follows.

In relation to question (1), which is:

> 'Is it wrong in law for the Juvenile Court to find that the condition under
g > Section 1(2)(*a*) of the Children and Young Persons Act 1969 is satisfied in
> circumstances where the child has never been in the care of either parent or out of
> the care of responsible agencies?'

I would answer that it is possible, as a matter of law, for the juvenile court to find that
the conditions under that section are satisfied in those circumstances.
h In relation to question (2), which is:

> 'Is the condition in Section 1(2)(*a*) of the Children and Young Persons Act 1969
> satisfied in respect of a child when the evidence of the child's proper development
> being avoidably prevented or neglected or its health being avoidably impaired or
> neglected or its being ill-treated relates to when the child was "en ventre sa mere"?'

j I would answer that question by saying that what the court is concerned with is the
condition of the child after its birth, but matters occurring before the child was born can
give rise to its being in a condition which satisfies the requirements of the section.

In relation to question (3), which is:

> 'On the facts found could the Juvenile Court properly find that the proper
> development of the child is being avoidably prevented or neglected or her health is
> being avoidably impaired or neglected or she is being ill-treated?'

I would answer that question in the affirmative, but I would say, on the facts of the particular case which was before the juvenile court, that the primary provision of the *a* subsection with which the justices should have been concerned related to the question of the health of the child. It was that which was being impaired as a result of what had occurred before its birth.

I do not consider that it is necessary for me to deal specifically with the fourth question because, clearly, this was, in my view, a matter falling within the juvenile court's jurisdiction under the 1969 Act.   *b*

It is for those reasons that I agree that this appeal should be allowed.

DILLON LJ. I agree that this appeal should be allowed. I would stress that there is no question whatever in this case of giving this child back to a mother who is a drug addict. There is no doubt that the child is in need of care and it is essentially a question of which is the appropriate procedure to ensure that that care is provided. Is it the procedure of a *c* care order made by the juvenile court in favour of the local authority under s 1 of the Children and Young Persons Act 1969 or is it the procedure of wardship in the Family Division?

It has been pointed out by Lord Scarman in *W v Hertfordshire CC* [1985] 2 All ER 301 at 303, [1985] AC 791 at 795 that Parliament has, by a series of statutes, including in particular the 1969 Act, entrusted the responsibility for the care of children received into *d* care by a local authority to the local authorities, subject to the safeguards specified in the legislation. It has been said by Lord Scarman and the other members of their Lordships' House that the purpose of the statutory scheme is clear, whatever difficulties may arise in the interpretation of some of the detailed provisions. It follows that where the statutory scheme applies, there is no scope for wardship.

In the circumstances of this case, I have no doubt that, on the findings of the juvenile *e* court, they were fully entitled to be satisfied that the primary condition in s 1(2)(*a*) of the 1969 Act was satisfied. The development of the child is, as has been pointed out, a continuing process. I have, for my part, sympathy with the view expressed by Butler-Sloss J in *M v Westminster City Council* [1985] FLR 325 at 336 that the primary conditions should not be looked at as alternatives but should be looked at as a whole. I do not see *f* any antithesis between proper development and health. Here there is the continuing process that the mother was a taker of methadone, both throughout the pregnancy and thereafter up to the conclusion of the hearing in the juvenile court. The child was therefore born affected by the drug and suffering from drug abuse symptoms which needed intensive special care for several weeks; and equally, because the drug abuse would have continued, the mother was unable to breast feed the child or look after the *g* child. The whole process has to be looked at as a whole and, in my view, the primary condition in s 1(2)(*a*) was satisfied. The proper development of the child was avoidably prevented and her health was avoidably impaired.

That being so, this appeal should be allowed and the care order of the justices should be restored.

h

Appeal allowed. Care order restored. Leave to appeal to the House of Lords refused.

Solicitors: *D C H Williams*, Reading (for the local authority); *Rowberry Morris & Co*, Reading (for the child); *Blandy & Blandy*, Reading (for the parents).

Celia Fox   Barrister. *j*

Appeal
The child, by her guardian ad litem, appealed, with leave of the Appeal Committee of the House of Lords granted on 8 May 1986.

James Townend QC and *Christopher Critchlow* for the child.
Nicholas Medawar QC and *Barbara Slomnicka* for the local authority.
T Scott Baker QC and *Paul Reid* for the parents.

Their Lordships took time for consideration.

a

4 December. The following opinions were delivered.

LORD KEITH OF KINKEL. My Lords, I have had the opportunity of considering in draft the speech to be delivered by my noble and learned friend Lord Brandon. I agree with it, and for the reasons he gives would dismiss the appeal.

b

LORD BRANDON OF OAKBROOK. My Lords, on 1 August 1985 the justices of the petty sessional division of Reading, sitting as a juvenile court at the Civic Centre, Reading, made an order (the care order) committing the case of a baby girl (the child) to the care of the Berkshire County Council (the local authority). The original parties to the proceedings consisted only of the local authority and the child, for whom a guardian ad *c* litem was appointed. The child's parents, however, were subsequently allowed to intervene and take part in the proceedings. The care order having been made, the child by her guardian ad litem appealed by way of case stated against it to the Divisional Court of the Family Division of the High Court (Hollings and Waite JJ). An order was made before the hearing of the appeal that the parents should be parties to it as second respondents, and at the hearing of the appeal they were separately represented by counsel, *d* who supported the child's appeal. By an order made on 4 February 1986 the Divisional Court allowed the appeal and discharged the care order. The local authority, with the leave of the Divisional Court, appealed to the Court of Appeal (Dillon, Stephen Brown and Woolf LJJ), and that court by an order made on 19 March 1986 allowed the appeal, setting aside the order of the Divisional Court and restoring the care order. The child by her guardian ad litem now brings a further appeal to your Lordships' House with the *e* leave of this House. The parents appear again separately by counsel as second respondents supporting the child's appeal. The sole question to be decided by your Lordships, as it was in both the Divisional Court and the Court of Appeal, is whether, having regard first, to the terms of the relevant statutory provisions, and secondly, to the facts of the particular case, the juvenile court had jurisdiction to make the care order. It is not *f* contended for the child or the parents that, if the juvenile court had jurisdiction to make the care order, they were wrong to exercise it.

The relevant statutory provisions are to be found in the Children and Young Persons Act 1969 as later amended and are in these terms:

'PART I

CARE AND OTHER TREATMENT OF JUVENILES THROUGH COURT PROCEEDINGS

Care of children and young persons through juvenile courts

g

1.—(1) Any local authority . . . who reasonably believes that there are grounds for making an order under this section in respect of a child . . . may . . . bring him before a juvenile court.

h
(2) If the court before which a child . . . is brought under this section is of opinion that any of the following conditions is satisfied with respect to him, that is to say— (*a*) his proper development is being avoidably prevented or neglected or his health is being avoidably impaired or neglected or he is being ill-treated; or (*b*) it is probable that the condition set out in the preceding paragraph will be satisfied in his case, having regard to the fact that the court or another court has found that that *j* condition is or was satisfied in the case of another child . . . who is or was a member of the household to which he belongs; or (*bb*) it is probable that the condition set out in paragraph (*a*) of this subsection will be satisfied in his case, having regard to the fact that a person who has been convicted of an offence mentioned in Schedule 1 to the [Children and Young Persons Act 1933] is, or may become, a member of the same household as the child . . . and also that he is in need of care or control which he is unlikely to receive unless the court makes an order under this section in respect of him, then . . . the court may if it thinks fit make such an order.

(3) The order which a court may make under this section in respect of a child . . .
is . . . (c) a care order (other than an interim order) . . .   *a*

Detention

28.—(1) If, upon an application to a justice by any person for authority to detain
a child . . . and take him to a place of safety, the justice is satisfied that the applicant
has reasonable cause to believe that—(a) any of the conditions set out in section   *b*
1(2)(a) to (e) of this Act is satisfied in respect of the child . . . the justice may grant
the application; and the child or young person in respect of whom an authorisation
is issued under this subsection may be detained in a place of safety by virtue of the
authorisation for twenty-eight days beginning with the date of authorisation, or for
such shorter period beginning with that date as may be specified in the
authorisation . . .   *c*
(6) If while a person is detained in pursuance of this section an application for an
interim order in respect of him is made to a magistrates' court or a justice, the court
or justice shall either make or refuse to make the order . . .

Part III

                                    . . .   *d*

Supplemental

70.—(1) In this Act, unless the contrary intention appears, the following
expressions have the following meanings . . .

"child" . . . means a person under the age of fourteen . . .'   *e*

The particular facts of the case as found by the juvenile court and set out in the case
stated, are as follows. (a) The child was born to her mother, who was then aged 29, on 12
March 1985 at the Royal Berkshire Hospital in Reading. (b) At the time of her birth the
child was suffering from symptoms caused by withdrawal from narcotics. (c) The mother
had been a registered drug addict since 1982 and had been takings drugs for approximately   *f*
ten years. (d) The mother had continued to take drugs, both by oral means and by
injection, from the time that she knew that she was pregnant to the time when the child
was born. (e) During the pregnancy the mother took drugs in excess of those which were
prescribed for her by her registered medical practitioner. (f) The mother knew that by
taking drugs while pregnant she could be causing damage to her child. (g) The child was
kept in intensive care in hospital for several weeks immediately following the birth,
indeed until 19 May. A place of safety order was obtained by the Berkshire social services   *g*
on 23 April and successive interim care orders were in force from 13 May 1985 to the
date of the hearing. (h) The child had never been in the care or control of the mother or
father since her birth. (i) The medical condition in which the child was born was a direct
result of deliberate and excessive taking of drugs by the mother during pregnancy. (j)
The mother, and the father too, continued to be addicted to drugs and remained so on   *h*
the final day of the hearing of the case.
The question whether the juvenile court had jurisdiction to make the care order
depends on whether the particular facts of the case brought it within para (a) and the
latter part of s 1(2) of the 1969 Act. This in turn means that the only basis on which the
juvenile court could have had such jurisdiction was that two conditions were satisfied.
The primary condition, arising from para (a) of s 1(2), is that (i) the proper development   *j*
of the child was being avoidably prevented or neglected, or (ii) the health of the child
was being avoidably impaired or neglected, or (iii) the child was being ill-treated. The
secondary condition, arising from the latter part of s 1(2), is that the child was in need of
care and control which she was unlikely to receive unless the court made a care order. It
has never been in dispute that the secondary condition was satisfied; but there is and has

been a dispute between the local authority on the one hand, and the child and the parents
a on the other hand, whether the primary condition was satisfied.

In the case stated the juvenile court, after reciting the submissions made to them on
behalf of the local authority, the child and the parents, expressed this opinion:

> 'We accepted that the particular circumstances on which the primary condition
> was based would not recur since the child had now been born. However, we took
b the view that a child's development is a continuing process which encompasses the
> past and the present and we considered that events in the past life of this child, even
> during the time when it was a foetus in the womb, were relevant. For this reason
> we considered that we were entitled to have regard to the mother's abuse of her own
> bodily health during pregnancy when deciding whether the condition in
> Section 1(2)(a) Children and Young Persons Act 1969 was proved in respect of the
c child born of that pregnancy. We were satisfied that the child's proper development
> was being avoidably prevented or neglected or her health was being avoidably
> impaired or neglected or she was being ill-treated. In so deciding we accepted that
> we should not look at the future development of the child.'

The juvenile court went on to state four questions for the opinion of the High Court:

d '1. Is it wrong in law for the Juvenile Court to find that the condition under
> Section 1(2)(a) of the Children and Young Persons Act 1969 is satisfied in
> circumstances where the child has never been in the care of either parent or out of
> the care of responsible agencies? 2. Is the condition in s 1(2)(a) of the Children and
> Young Persons Act 1969 satisfied in respect of a child when the evidence of the
> child's proper development being avoidably prevented or neglected or its health
e being avoidably impaired or neglected or its being ill-treated relates to when the
> child was "en ventre sa mere"? 3. On the facts found could the juvenile court
> properly find that the proper development of the child is being avoidably prevented
> or neglected or her health is being avoidably impaired or neglected or she is being
> ill-treated? 4. In considering Section 1(2)(a) of the Children and Young Persons Act
> 1969 should the Juvenile Court have considered the availability of Wardship
f proceedings and/or proceedings under the Child Care Act 1980 and/or any other
> powers and procedures available to the local authority?'

Before examining the way in which first the Divisional Court and second the Court of
Appeal dealt with the case stated, it will be convenient to refer to three reported cases on
the meaning of the expression 'is being' in s 1(2)(a), all of which were cited to the juvenile
g court and the Divisional Court, and the last two of which were cited to the Court of
Appeal.

In *Essex CC v TLR and KBR* (1978) 143 JP 309 the custody of two children, the marriage
of whose parents had broken down, was early in 1974 granted to their father, a soldier
then serving in England. In March 1974, at the request of the father on his being posted
to Hong Kong, the children were voluntarily received into the care of the Essex County
h Council, which placed them with foster-parents in Colchester. In 1976 the county council
received information that the father, who was by that time serving in Northern Ireland,
intended to go to Hong Kong to marry a Chinese woman, and then to come to Colchester
to collect the children and take them to live with him in Northern Ireland. The county
council, in order to prevent the removal of the children, sought a care order from a
juvenile court at Colchester under s 1(2)(a), and, as a preliminary to those proceedings,
j applied for and was granted authority to detain the children temporarily in a place of
safety. Up to and at the time of the hearing the fostering of the children was entirely
satisfactory, in that their proper development was being promoted, their health was
being safeguarded and they were being well treated. The juvenile court having refused
to make a care order, the county council appealed by way of case stated to the Divisional
Court of the Queen's Bench Division (Lord Widgery CJ, Kilner Brown and Robert Goff

JJ). That court held, upholding the decision of the juvenile court, that there was no
material on which that court could have found that any of the conditions specified in *a*
s 1(2)(*a*) was satisfied.

Robert Goff J, with whom Lord Widgery CJ and Kilner Brown J both agreed, said (at
311–312):

> 'In my judgment, the conclusion of the justices was right in law, and, not only
> that, it was right for the correct reasons. It is clear that they approached the statute *b*
> in accordance with the correct legal principles. They first looked at the relevant part
> of the subsection (subparagraph (*a*)) in its context in the Act and ascertained its
> natural and ordinary meaning, and concluded, in my judgment correctly, that on
> its natural and ordinary meaning it refers only to events presently in existence. They
> then asked themselves the question: Does the context require any different
> construction? On examining the context, they saw from the statute that the *c*
> immediately following part of the subsection (subparagraph (*b*)) dealt with the
> probability that the condition set out in the preceding paragraph would be satisfied
> and limited by its words the circumstances in which such a probability could be
> considered. I can add that there appears to have been added to the statute another
> subparagraph, (*bb*), wherein a further specific circumstance can be taken into account
> which may give rise to a probability that the condition set out in subparagraph (*a*) *d*
> of that subsection will be satisfied. These two subparagraphs—(*b*) and (*bb*)—show
> that the words of subparagraph (*a*) should be given their natural and ordinary
> meaning, viz., that it is only concerned with presently existing events and not with
> future or probable events, the latter being specifically dealt with in the succeeding
> subparagraphs. Counsel for the appellants has urged upon us that to adopt what she
> has called "a literal interpretation" would have the effect that courts cannot take *e*
> account of future events when it is highly desirable that they should be able to do
> so. As to that, I would say only this. The construction adopted by the magistrates is,
> in my judgment, the only possible construction one can place upon the clear
> wording of the statute, having regard to the words used and the context in which
> these words are found, and, however desirable it may be that the court should have
> wider powers than those conferred upon it by the statute, it is the duty of this court *f*
> to give effect to the clear words of the statute.'

In *F v Suffolk CC* (1981) 2 FLR 208 McNeill J, hearing the Crown Office list, had before
him an appeal by way of case stated against a care order in respect of a child made by a
juvenile court at Lowestoft on the ground that the proper development of the child was
being avoidably prevented or neglected. In the course of a judgment upholding the care *g*
order he said (at 213):

> 'What the court has to consider, as I see it, is this: is there present avoidable neglect
> or prevention? That is the present tense application to these words. Is that something
> which is happening now, or it may be has happened, with the result that the proper
> development of the child is affected in those ways? The proper development of the
> child is a continuing process, past, present, and future, and what the court has to *h*
> look at, in my view, is the present conduct and its effect on the development of the
> child in the past, at the present time and at any rate in the foreseeable future.
> Development being a continuing matter, I do not think this section is intended to
> rule out of consideration either mental development or development in its broadest
> and continuing sense.'
> *j*

In *M v Westminster City Council* [1985] FLR 325 the Divisional Court of the Family
Division (Bush and Butler-Sloss JJ) had before it an appeal by way of case stated against a
care order made in respect of a child by the Westminster North Juvenile Court. It had
been contended by counsel for the appellant that, because of the use of the expression 'is
being' in s 1(2)(*a*), the justices were only entitled to look at the situation of the child as at

the date of the hearing before them and were not entitled to look at its previous situation.

a   Butler-Sloss J, delivering the first judgment at the request of Bush J, rejected this contention. She referred to the passage in the judgment of McNeill J in F v Suffolk CC which I have cited above, and, subject to some possible qualification as to how far in the future the court should look, expressed her complete agreement with it. She went on to say (at 336):

b   'For my part, I find it impossible to find that for the primary condition to be established the child's proper development can only be considered as being avoidably prevented at the time of the hearing. A child's development is a continuing process. The present must be relevant in the context of what has happened in the past and it becomes a matter of degree as to how far in the past you go. . . I take the view that this very restrictive approach, put forward . . . by counsel for the appellant, is quite inappropriate to the way in which one should look at the proper development of a

c   child. Therefore, the magistrates' approach to this case, whereby they said that you look at the position when the proceedings were started and are entitled to interpret it in the light of anything relevant which has happened since, was an entirely proper way for them to consider this matter, and it leaves out any problems there may be as to the future because it is clear from their case that they did not consider the

d   future in respect of the primary condition. It is right, it seems to me, looking at the primary conditions, that they should not be looked at as alternatives but looked at as a whole.'

Bush J, delivering the second judgment, said (at 340–341):

e   'If the strict interpretation urged by [counsel for the mother] were accepted, then there never could be a care order made, for example, in the case [of] a child who had recovered from the injury done to him and who was in the benign care of foster parents or a children's home. I cannot think that that was the intention of Parliament. It is clear, of course, that in using the present tense Parliament was expressly ruling out a care order because of fear of future harm where there was nothing presently in the condition or treatment of the child whereby his proper

f   development was being avoidably prevented or neglected or his health avoidably impaired or neglected. This must be the basis of the decision in the Divisional Court in Essex County Council v TLR and KBR (1979) 9 Fam. Law 15 though, of course, the report we have for our purposes is wholly inadequate. The development of a child is a continuing matter and encompasses the past, present and, to a certain extent, the future. The magistrates, in determining the primary condition, must have

g   regard to the past treatment of the child as well as to the present. They must ask themselves on the day of the hearing: "Are we satisfied that his proper development is being avoidably prevented or neglected, or his health is being avoidably impaired or neglected?" They are not bound to answer the question in the negative if, for example, there has been a temporary respite in the condition or treatment of the child. In my view "is being" is not temporal in the sense that it means "now", "this

h   minute"; it is descriptive of the child, that is the child must fall into the category mentioned in the section. If the words used had been different then different considerations would apply. "Has been" would indicate some time in the past; "will be" would indicate some time in the future; "is being" would indicate a situation over a period, not now at this precise moment but over a period of time sufficiently proximate to the date of the inquiry to indicate that it is the present, not history and

j   not the days to come. It is the description of a continuing set of circumstances which may not obtain on the particular day on which the matter is being considered but represents a category which the description of the child fits.'

I now turn to examine the way in which first the Divisional Court, and later the Court of Appeal, dealt with the problems which arise in the present case. Hollings J delivered

the leading judgment in the Divisional Court. He referred to the last two of the three
reported cases to which I have drawn attention and it seems clear that he accepted the   *a*
general correctness of the views expressed by McNeill J in the one case and by Butler-
Sloss and Bush JJ in the other. Despite this, he said (at p 26, ante):

> 'The difficulty which, however, I have found is this: that unlike M *v Westminster
> City Council* [1985] FLR 325 and F *v Suffolk CC* (1981) 2 FLR 208 the whole of the
> conduct, if I may so describe it, of the mother vis-à-vis the child relates to the period   *b*
> before birth. The mother's present conduct vis-à-vis the child has never been tested,
> and of its very nature her previous conduct vis-à-vis this child can never be repeated.
> It is that circumstance which to my mind distinguishes this case from that of M *v
> Westminster City Council*, and indeed from F *v Suffolk CC*. The only evidence before
> the justices as to the situation after the birth of the child was that this mother and
> father (we are of course concerned chiefly with the mother) continue, or continued   *c*
> at least until the hearing before the magistrates, to take class A drugs. There was no
> evidence before the magistrates as to the effect that had or might have on her caring
> for the child. There was no evidence to suggest that her use or abuse of drugs would
> affect the child or that the parents would administer drugs to the child. Indeed no
> one has suggested that the mother would seek to do so, I hasten to add. As counsel
> for the local authority submitted in M *v Westminster City Council*, in the case of a   *d*
> battered child who is now in the care of a local authority one cannot say that this
> condition does not apply, because the child is now in care. That is because the child
> was battered when in the care of the mother and alive, and it is only because of the
> intervention of the social services and the care application that the child is no longer
> with the mother. What the justices have realistically to be concerned with is not the
> situation technically as it is before them at the time but the situation in the   *e*
> continuum, as it has been described by Butler-Sloss and Bush JJ. They had to look at
> the ability of the mother and the risk to the child in the light of the past, with some
> thought to the future, though not so far into the future. In the present case there is
> a notable absence of any such state of affairs. That this child is in need of care and
> control is, as I said at the outset, conceded. However, in my judgment the justices,
> confined as they were to the provisions of that section of the 1969 Act, as interpreted   *f*
> by the two cases to which I have referred, even though they were entitled to look at
> what happened during the pregnancy, ought not . . . to have come to the conclusion
> that this condition has been satisfied in any of its respects, for the reasons I have
> already stated.'

Hollings J went on to deal with the four questions of law posed by the juvenile court   *g*
in the case stated. With regard to question 1, whether it was wrong in law for the juvenile
court to find that the condition under s 1(2)(*a*) was satisfied in circumstances where the
child had never been in the care of either parent, or out of the care of responsible agencies,
Hollings J said that there might be cases in the future in which it might be right to find
that condition proved, even though the child was never in the care of either parent, but
it was wrong in this case. To question 2, whether the condition in s 1(2)(*a*) was satisfied   *h*
in respect of the child when the evidence (which he emphasised was the *only* evidence)
that the child's proper development was being avoidably prevented or neglected or her
health was being avoidably impaired or neglected or she was being ill-treated related to
when the child was en ventre sa mère, Hollings J gave a negative answer. To question 3,
whether on the facts found the juvenile court could properly find that the proper
development of the child was being avoidably prevented or neglected or her health was   *j*
being avoidably impaired or neglected or she was being ill-treated, and also to question
4, whether in considering s 1(2)(*a*) the juvenile court should have considered the
availability of wardship proceedings and/or any other powers or procedures available to
the authority, Hollings J again gave negative answers. Waite J agreed with the judgment
of Hollings J.

The first judgment in the Court of Appeal was delivered by Stephen Brown LJ. He
a referred to the passage in the judgment of Butler-Sloss J in M *v Westminster City Council*
[1985] FLR 325, 336, which I cited earlier and continued (at p 30, ante):

'The facts of that case were different from the particular facts of the present case,
but it is significant that, in this case, the Divisional Court did consider that it was
appropriate and relevant to look at what had happened before the child was born.
However, it seems to me that the Divisional Court fell into error in not applying
b the result of that view to the case because, in effect, it appears that it did restrict
consideration of the development of the child to events which had taken place since
its birth. In my view, that is too narrow an approach ... Accordingly, I have come
to the conclusion that the Divisional Court was wrong in the decision to which it
came and that the justices were in fact correct when they stated in para 7(b) of the
case: "However, we took the view that a child's development is a continuing process
c which encompasses the past and the present and we considered that events in the
past life of this child, even during the time when it was a fetus in the womb, were
relevant." Those events, which had the effect of preventing the proper development,
and impairing the health, of this child, were avoidable and, as a part of a continuing
process, they could and should have been in the contemplation of the court.
d Accordingly, they were entitled to find the primary condition of the section fulfilled
and to proceed to make a care order, it not being disputed that the child was in need
of care or control.'

Woolf LJ, who delivered the second judgment, said (at pp 30, 31, ante):

'In my view, this case raises a question that has not previously come before the
e court as to whether or not matters which flow from what was done to a child prior
to its birth justify an order being made under s 1 of the 1969 Act subsequent to its
birth. If there was any doubt as to whether a child includes an unborn child for the
purposes of s 1, in my view that doubt is removed by s 70(1) of the 1969 Act, which
defines a "child" as meaning "a person under the age of 14". A "person" denotes
someone who is living, not someone who has yet to be born. It follows, in my view,
f from that approach to the interpretation of s 1 that what has to be considered in
deciding whether the requirements of s 1(2)(*a*) of the 1969 Act have been met in
any particular case is whether a living child's proper development is being prevented
or neglected or a living child's health is being prevented or neglected or a living
child is being ill-treated. However, the fact that the question has to be posed in that
way does not mean that what happened before the birth of the child has to be
g ignored for all purposes. In my view, the proper approach to the interpretation of
s 1(2)(*a*) involves asking two questions, the first being "Is the living child's proper
development etc being prevented or neglected?" and the second question being
whether that was avoidable. In considering those questions in relation to this case
there was no doubt that the child's health was being impaired and, because of that,
the answer to the first question must be in the affirmative. The next question is:
h was that avoidable? Again, in my view, the answer must be in the affirmative
because the mother, prior to the birth of the child, should have taken steps to avoid
the consequences to that child after its birth. Whereas in asking the first question I
do not regard it as proper to look at what occurred before birth, in asking the second
question it is, in my view, perfectly permissible to consider what happened before
birth. The only matter with which the court is concerned in relation to the second
j question is: was it avoidable or not?'

Later, Woolf LJ indicated how he would answer the four questions of law posed in the
case stated (see pp 31–32, ante). With regard to question 1 he said that it was possible, as
a matter of law, for the juvenile court to find that the conditions under s 1(2)(*a*) were
satisfied in the circumstances set out. With regard to question 2 he said that what the

court was concerned with was the condition of the child after its birth, but matters occurring before the child was born could give rise to its being in a condition which *a* satisfied the requirements of the section. With regard to question 3, he said that he would answer it affirmatively, but stressed that the main matter with which the justices should have been concerned was the child's health. He did not consider it necessary to answer question 4.

Dillon LJ, who delivered the third judgment, said (at p 32, ante):

> 'In the circumstances of this case, I have no doubt that, on the findings of the *b* juvenile court, they were fully entitled to be satisfied that the primary condition in s 1(2)(a) of the 1969 Act was satisfied. The development of the child is, as has been pointed out, a continuing process. I have, for my part, sympathy with the view expressed by Butler-Sloss J in M v *Westminster City Council* [1985] FLR 325 at 336 that the primary conditions should not be looked at as alternatives but should be *c* looked at as a whole. I do not see any antithesis between proper development and health. Here there is the continuing process that the mother was a taker of methadone, both throughout the pregnancy and thereafter up to the conclusion of the hearing in the juvenile court. The child was therefore born affected by the drug and suffering from drug abuse symptoms which needed intensive special care for several weeks; and equally, because the drug abuse would have continued, the *d* mother was unable to breast feed the child or look after the child. The whole process has to be looked at as a whole and, in my view, the primary condition in s 1(2)(a) was satisfied. The proper development of the child was avoidably prevented and her health was avoidably impaired.'

The appeal raises a number of questions with regard to the meaning and effect of s 1(2)(a) of the 1969 Act. The first question is whether the three situations (I prefer to call *e* them 'situations' rather than 'conditions') described in s 1(2)(a) are to be regarded as alternatives or are to be looked at as a whole. Butler-Sloss J in M v *Westminster City Council* [1985] FLR 325 expressed the view that the three situations should be looked at as a whole, on the ground, as I understand it, that there was no necessary antithesis between them. Dillon LJ in the Court of Appeal in the present case expressed sympathy with that view. With respect to both Butler-Sloss J and Dillon LJ, I cannot agree with them on this *f* point. It seems to me that, on the ordinary and natural meaning of the words used, the three situations are to be regarded as alternatives. So to regard them is in no way inconsistent with the likelihood that, in many cases, any two of the three situations, or indeed all three of them, may coexist.

There follows a series of questions relating to the meaning and effect of the expression *g* 'is being', as used in the description of each of the three situations. First, does the expression refer to an instant, or to a continuing, situation? Second, if it refers to a continuing situation, as at what point of time should the court consider whether that continuing situation exists? Third, how far back and how far forward, if at all, from that point of time should court look? Fourthly, can the court look back to the time before the child concerned was born? *h*

With regard to the first of these questions relating to the expression 'is being', there are in my view two compelling reasons for concluding that what is being referred to is a continuing, rather than an instant, situation. The first reason is that the use of the present continuous of itself indicates a reference to a continuing situation or state of affairs. The second reason is that the concepts of development, health and treatment of a child, which are the three alternative concepts dealt with in s 1(2)(a), are themselves continuing *j* concepts. It follows that I agree broadly with the views expressed on the matter by McNeill J in F v *Suffolk CC* and by Bush and Butler-Sloss JJ in M v *Westminster City Council*, as did both the Divisional Court and the Court of Appeal in the present case.

With regard to the second question relating to the expression 'is being', it is in my opinion necessary to have in mind the purpose sought to be achieved not only by s 1 but also by s 28 of the 1969 Act. The effect of s 28, when combined with that of s 1, is to

create a process for the protection of children which may often include three separate but
a connected stages. The first stage is the grant by a justice to an applicant under s 28(1) of
authority to detain a child and take it to a place of safety for up to 28 days. Where the
ground of the application is concern about the present development, health or treatment
of a child, the justice can only accede to it if he or she is satisfied that the applicant has
reasonable cause to believe that one or more of the three situations described in s 1(2)(a)
exists in respect of the child. The second stage is the making by a magistrates' court or a
b justice of one or more interim care orders under s 28(6). The purpose of such an order or
orders is to preserve, for the protection of the child, the temporarily safe situation created
by the original authority to detain the child and keep it in a safe place granted under
s 28(1) until the third stage is reached. That third stage is the hearing and determination
of proceedings for a full care order (by which I mean a care order which is not an interim
one) to be made under s 1.
c All these three stages were gone through in the present case. Authority to detain the
child and take it to a place of safety was granted on 23 April 1985. Then, proceedings for
a full care order having been begun on 25 April 1985, successive interim care orders were
made on 13 May, 10 June and 8 July 1985. Finally, the hearing of the proceedings for
the making of a full care order took place on 23 and 25 July and 1 August 1985, the order
being made on the last of these dates. In the result a period of just over 14 weeks elapsed
d between the original authority to detain and take to a place of safety being granted and a
full care order being made, and throughout that period the child was in the safe care of
foster parents chosen by the local authority.
Against the background of these three possible stages in the process of protecting a
child under ss 1 and 28 it is, in my view, clear that the court, in considering whether a
continuing situation of one or other of the kinds described in s 1(2)(a) exists, must do so
e as at the point of time immediately before the process of protecting the child concerned
is first put into motion. To consider that matter at a point of time when the child has
been placed under protection for several weeks, first by a place of safety order and then
by one or more interim care orders, would, as pointed out by Bush J in M v Westminster
City Council, defeat the purpose of Parliament. I would answer the second question
relating to the expression 'is being' accordingly.
f With regard to the third question relating to the expression 'is being', it seems to me
that the court, in considering, as at the point of time immediately before the process of
protecting the child concerned is first put into motion, whether a continuing situation
of any of the three kinds described in s 1(2)(a) exists, must look both at the situation as it
is at that point of time and also at the situation as it has been in the past; how far back in
the past must depend on the facts of any particular case. Should the court look at the
g future as well? In my view it should, but only in a hypothetical way by looking to see
whether the situation which began earlier and was still continuing at the point of time
immediately before the process of protecting the child was put into motion would, if
that process had not been put into motion, have been likely to continue further. I would
not think it right for the court to look at the future alone: only at the hypothetical future
h in conjunction with the actual present (in the sense in which I have defined that concept)
and the actual past. It follows that I agree with the decision in Essex CC v TLR and KBR
143 JP 309 on its facts, for in that case the court was being asked to look at the future
alone without any connection with the present or the past. The case must not, however,
be regarded as good authority for the wider proposition that it is never permissible for
the court to look at the hypothetical future, so long as it does so in conjunction with the
j present and the past.
It is with regard to the fourth question relating to the expression 'is being', namely
whether the court, in viewing the past, can look back to the time before the child
concerned was born, that the division of opinion between the Divisional Court and the
Court of Appeal has arisen. The view of the Divisional Court can be summarised in this
way. First, the expression 'child' in s 1(2)(a) must be interpreted, in accordance with the
definition of it contained in s 70(1), as meaning a person under the age of 14. Second, a

child does not become a person until it is born. Third, that being so, it was not permissible for the juvenile court, in considering whether any of the three continuing situations in respect of the child described in s 1(2)(a) existed, to look back to the time before it was born and before, therefore, it had become a person. Fourth, without looking back at that earlier time, there was no material on which the juvenile court could find that any of the three continuing situations referred to existed.

The three members of the Court of Appeal, while arriving at the same result, did not, as I understand their judgments, proceed on precisely the same grounds. Stephen Brown and Dillon LJJ, on the one hand, appear to have founded their decision on the broad ground that to exclude consideration of the time before the child was born involved adopting too narrow an approach to the question whether any of the three continuing situations in respect of the child described in s 1(2)(a) existed. It was permissible for the juvenile court to look at that earlier time and, having done so, it had ample material on which it could find that both of the first two continuing situations referred to existed. Woolf LJ, on the other hand, took the view that the juvenile court, in considering whether either of the first two continuing situations existed, had to ask itself two separate questions. The first question was, in the case of the first situation, whether the proper development of the child was being prevented or neglected and, in the case of the second situation, whether the health of the child was being impaired or neglected. The second question in either case, assuming an affirmative answer to the first, was whether that situation was avoidable, that is to say, whether it could have been avoided. In the view of Woolf LJ it was not permissible for the juvenile court to look back at the time before the child was born in order to answer the first question; but it was permissible for it to do so in answering the second question. Proceeding in this way the juvenile court had material before it on which it could give affirmative answers to both questions.

In my opinion the provisions contained in s 1(2)(a) must be given a broad and liberal construction which gives full effect to their legislative purpose. That purpose is to protect, among other ways through the medium of a care order, any child of whom it can be said, in the ordinary and natural meaning of the words used, either (i) that its proper development is being avoidably prevented or neglected or (ii) that its health is being avoidably impaired or neglected or (iii) that it is being ill-treated. Children for whom such protection is provided include children who are only a few weeks or even a few days old.

The child in the present case, having been born on 12 March 1985, was in hospital (for part of the time at least, in intensive care) from that date until 19 May 1985 because she was suffering from symptoms caused by withdrawal from narcotic drugs. The point of time at which the process of protecting her was first put in motion was 23 April 1985, when the local authority's social services department was granted authority to detain the child and take her to a place of safety, and that was accordingly the point of time as at which the juvenile court had to consider whether any of the continuing situations described in s 1(2)(a) existed. The court found, and had ample material on which to find, that at that point of time, when the child was still in hospital, both the first and the second of those situations existed, that is to say (i) her proper development was being avoidably prevented and (ii) her health was being avoidably impaired. Each situation could have been avoided if the mother had not persisted in taking excessive narcotic drugs throughout her pregnancy. I see no reason why the juvenile court, in considering whether those situations existed, should not have looked back at the time before the child was born. At the relevant point of time for such consideration the child was six weeks old and, accordingly, a person under the age of 14 years, within the meaning of the expression 'child' in s 70(1). The circumstance that the cause of the two situations in which the child was at that point of time, and the possibility of their having been avoided, dated back to the time before she was born appears to me to be immaterial. I can find nothing in s 1(2)(a) which would exclude taking into account those matters. Further, it seems to me that the legislative purpose of s 1(2)(a) is best furthered by allowing such matters, in a case of this kind, to be taken into account.

It follows that I agree with the broad grounds of decision relied on by Stephen Brown
a and Dillon LJJ in the Court of Appeal and would dismiss the appeal.

There is one further matter with which I should deal before parting with this case. It
may seem curious at first sight that, since both the child's guardian ad litem and the
parents agree that a care order is necessary, they should have fought such a prolonged
battle against its being made by the juvenile court. The explanation, however, is that all
three believe that it would be better for the order to be made by the Family Division of
b the High Court in wardship proceedings under s 7 of the Family Law Reform Act 1969
than by the juvenile court under s 1 of the Children and Young Persons Act 1969. The
reason why they believe that it would be better for the order to be made in wardship
proceedings is that the High Court would then be able to exercise control over the local
authority in respect of the manner in which it implemented the order, whereas if the
order is made by the juvenile court, the High Court would not have that power: see *A v*
c *Liverpool City Council* [1981] 2 All ER 385, [1982] AC 363 and *W v Hertfordshire CC* [1985]
2 All ER 301, [1985] AC 791. In particular they fear that the local authority, if left to
itself, may decide to programme the child for early adoption without their having an
adequate opportunity to resist such a course being taken. I do not consider that it would
be appropriate for your Lordships to express any view whether these beliefs and fears are
justified or not. The only question for decision on this appeal is whether the juvenile
d court had jurisdiction to make the care order which it did make, and I think that your
Lordships should confine yourselves to the decision of that question.

LORD GRIFFITHS. My Lords, I have had the advantage of reading in draft the
speeches proposed by my noble and learned friends Lord Brandon and Lord Goff. I agree
with both of them that this appeal should be dismissed and with the reasons they have
e given for reaching this conclusion.

LORD MACKAY OF CLASHFERN. My Lords, I have had the advantage of reading
in draft the speeches proposed by my noble and learned friends Lord Brandon and Lord
Goff. I agree with both of them that this appeal should be dismissed and with the reasons
f they have given for reaching this conclusion.

LORD GOFF OF CHIEVELEY. My Lords, in cases under s 1(2)(*a*) of the Children
and Young Persons Act 1969 the magistrates have to ask themselves the questions: is the
proper development of the child being avoidably prevented or neglected? or is its health
being avoidably impaired or neglected? or is it being ill-treated? If any one of these
questions can properly be answered by them in the affirmative, at the time when they
g are asked to make their order, the primary condition for the making of the order is
fulfilled.

The problem in the present case arises from the fact that the child suffered from
withdrawal symptoms which necessitated her immediate admission to intensive care
when she was born, because her mother took drugs before her child was born, during
h the period of her pregnancy. The question has therefore arisen whether, in such
circumstances, it could be said that, at the time when the justices made their order, the
child's proper development was being avoidably prevented or her health was being
avoidably impaired. The submission that these questions must be answered in the
negative was founded on the allegation that the time when the child's proper development
was being avoidably prevented or her health was being impaired was when her mother
j was taking drugs during her pregnancy, and that this had ceased when the child was
born, with the consequences (1) that the condition no longer existed when the order was
made and (2) during the time when the child's proper development was being avoidably
neglected or her health was being avoidably impaired she was unborn and not therefore
a 'child' within the meaning of that word as used in s 70(1) of the 1969 Act.

There is, I think, considerable force in this argument, as is demonstrated by the
differing views taken by the courts below. In particular, we must avoid a construction of

the Act which produces the result that any child born suffering from the symptoms or
effects of some avoidable antenatal affliction could be described, after its birth, as being a   *a*
child whose proper development *is being* avoidably prevented or whose health *is being*
avoidably impaired. The mere fact of a past avoidable prevention of proper development
or impairment of health is not, in my opinion, sufficient to fulfil the condition, even if
there are symptoms or effects which persist or manifest themselves later.

I approach the matter as follows. The words 'is being' are in the continuous present.
So there has to be a continuum in existence at the relevant time, which is when the   *b*
justices consider whether to make a place of safety order. In cases under the subsection,
this may not be established by proof of events actually happening at the relevant time.
In the nature of things, it may well have to be established, as continuing at that time, by
evidence that (1) the relevant state of affairs had existed in the past and (2) there is a
likelihood that it will continue into the future. So it can be said that a child is being ill-
treated if it has been cruelly beaten in the past, and there is a likelihood that it will   *c*
continue to be cruelly beaten in the future. It is not enough that something has avoidably
been done or omitted to be done in relation to the child in the past which has, for
example, impaired its health, and that the symptoms or effects still persist at the relevant
time; for it cannot be said in such circumstances that, at the relevant time, the child's
health *is being* avoidably impaired: all that can be said is that its health has been avoidably
impaired in the past.   *d*

I turn to the present case. Could it properly be said, at the time when the justices had
to consider whether to make an order, that the proper development of the child was
being avoidably prevented or that her health was being avoidably impaired? The justices
could, first of all, look to the past and see that, by reason of the mother taking drugs
during her pregnancy, the proper development of the child had been avoidably prevented
or that her health had been avoidably impaired. In drawing this conclusion, I can see no   *e*
reason why the justices should not be entitled to have regard to events which occurred
before the child was born. They have, of course, to consider the question whether the
relevant continuum exists, at the date when they are asked to make their order, with
reference to a living child. But in looking for evidence whether such continuum then
exists, there is no reason why they should not look at events which occurred while the   *f*
child was still unborn or at the state of affairs at the child's birth, and it is contrary to
common sense that they should be inhibited from doing so. Second, they could also say
that, at the time when they considered whether to make an order, there was a likelihood
that, by reason of the mother's drug addiction, the child's proper development would
continue to be prevented or her health would continue to be impaired in the future,
because the mother (and indeed the child's father, whom the mother has now married)
were both still drug addicts, and parents suffering from that most unfortunate affliction,   *g*
particularly a mother so addicted that she continued to take drugs throughout her
pregnancy in the knowledge of the effect which this might have on her unborn child,
could be said to be unlikely to be able to care for their child, so that there was a likelihood
that, by reason of her mother's addiction to drugs, the child's proper development would
continue to be avoidably prevented or her health would continue to be avoidably   *h*
impaired in the future.

But let us take a different case. Suppose that a mother conceives a child when she is an
alcoholic and is unable at first to give up drinking, despite the fact that she knows that
this may have an adverse effect on her unborn child. Shortly before the child is born, the
full effect of her conduct is brought home to her, and she becomes a confirmed teetotaller.
The child is born. Its proper development has indeed been prevented, or its health has   *j*
indeed been impaired, by its mother's drinking. But, if the case then came before the
justices, I do not think that they could then properly conclude that, at the time when
they were asked to make the order, the child's proper development was then *being*
avoidably prevented, or that its health was then *being* avoidably impaired. By then, the
damage had been done: and there was no likelihood of any further avoidable prevention

of the child's development or impairment of its health. The same would have been true
a in the present case if the mother had, before the child was born, irrevocably given up the
taking of drugs.

In the present case the justices looked only to the past history of the child, and
studiously avoided considering the likelihood of prevention of the child's proper
development or impairment of her health continuing into the future. I have little doubt
that, in so doing, they misunderstood a judgment of my own in *Essex CC v TLR and KBR*
b (1978) 143 JP 309. In that case, justices were asked to make a care order under s 1(2)(a) of
the 1969 Act solely on the basis of an event which was said to be going to happen in the
future, ie that the father was going to take the children away from foster parents to live
with him in Northern Ireland after he had married a Chinese woman in Hong Kong.
The justices refused to make an order, and a Divisional Court held that they were right
to do so, because there was no relevant state of affairs then in existence which justified
c the making of an order, and the case fell within neither of the subsections of s 1 which
specifically refer only to future events. However, when justices are considering whether
there is a presently existing state of affairs, and there is evidence before them of events
which indicate the existence of such a state of affairs in the past, the justices are entitled
and, indeed, bound to consider whether at the time when they are considering making
an order, there is an existing likelihood that the state of affairs revealed by those past
d events will continue into the future, in order to decide whether the necessary continuum
exists at the relevant time.

Even so, since the justices held, and indeed there was no dispute, that the child in the
present case was in need of care and control which she was unlikely to receive unless the
court made a care order, it is, I consider, an inevitable inference that the justices
considered that prevention of the child's proper development or impairment of her
e health was likely to continue into the future. Accordingly, I am of the opinion that the
justices were entitled to make the order which they made. I too would therefore dismiss
the appeal.

Appeal dismissed.

f
Solicitors: *Kingsford Dorman*, agents for *Rowberry Morris & Co*, Reading (for the child);
Sharpe Pritchard & Co, agents for *D C H Williams*, Reading (for the local authority);
Gregory Rowcliffe & Co, agents for *Blandy & Blandy*, Reading (for the parents).

Mary Rose Plummer   Barrister.

R v Fairhurst
and other appeals

COURT OF APPEAL, CRIMINAL DIVISION
LORD LANE CJ, NOLAN AND MACPHERSON JJ
25, 31 JULY 1986

Sentence – Juvenile – Detention – Punishment of grave crimes – Guidelines on appropriate sentences for grave crimes committed by juveniles – Children and Young Persons Act 1933, s 53(2) – Children and Young Persons Act 1969, s 23(1).

A juvenile may be sentenced to detention under s 53(2)[a] of the Children and Young Persons Act 1933 for a grave crime even though it is not of such exceptional gravity as attempted murder, manslaughter, wounding with intent, armed robbery or similar crimes, but should not be sentenced to s 53(2) detention simply because a sentence of 12 months' youth custody seems to be too low for the particular offence committed. Where the offence committed by a juvenile would merit more than 12 months' but less than two years' custody for an offender aged 17 or over the sentence should normally be 12 months' youth custody rather than s 53(2) detention. However, where the offence is so serious that it would have called for a sentence of two years' youth custody or more for an offender aged 17 or over, the proper sentence for a juvenile is a similar term of s 53(2) detention. Where more than one offence is involved for which the juvenile could be sentenced to s 53(2) detention but the offences vary in seriousness, then, if at least one of the offences is sufficiently serious to warrant s 53(2) detention, detention sentences of under two years' duration, whether concurrent or consecutive, may properly be imposed in respect of the other offences. Where an offender is aged under 15 and thus ineligible for youth custody, a detention sentence of less than two years may be appropriate (see p 49 *b* to *f*, post).

Where there are two offences committed by a 15- or 16-year old and the first offence carries a maximum sentence of 14 years and the second carries a lower maximum, it is generally not proper to pass a sentence of s 53(2) detention in respect of the first offence, if it would not otherwise merit it, in order to compensate for the fact that 12 months' youth custody is grossly inadequate for the second offence. Where, however, the defendant's behaviour giving rise to the second offence is truly part and parcel of the events giving rise to the first offence, such a sentence may properly be imposed (see p 49 *f* to *g*, post.)

It is undesirable that sentences of s 53(2) detention and youth custody should be passed on an offender to run either consecutively or concurrently with each other. Where that is unavoidable, however, the court may feel it right to impose no separate penalty for the offence for which s 53(2) detention is not available (see p 50 *a b*, post).

When deciding on the proper length of detention under s 53(2) allowance should be made for time spent on remand in custody prior to sentence. However, time spent on remand by a juvenile who is committed to the care of a local authority under s 23(1)[b] of the Children and Young Persons Act 1969 does not count against the length of the eventual sentence, including s 53(2) detention. On the other hand, allowance should be

---

a   Section 53(2), so far as material, is set out at p 48 *b c*, post
b   Section 23(1) provides that: 'Where a court—(*a*) remands or commits for trial a child charged with homicide or remands a child convicted of homicide; or (*b*) remands a young person charged with or convicted of one or more offences or commits him for trial or sentence, and he is not released on bail, then, subject to the following provisions of this section, the court shall commit him to the care of a local authority in whose area it appears to the court that he resides or that the offence or one of the offences was committed.'

made for time spent on remand in care where the offender is held under a regime
a comparable to a remand in custody, e g where he is placed in secure accommodation or is
held under highly structured and closely supervised conditions. Where such allowance is
made in respect of a remand either in custody or in care that fact should be stated by the
court when passing sentence (see p 50 *g* to *j*, post).

Notes

b For custodial sentences on youthful offenders, see 11 Halsbury's Laws (4th edn) paras
551–559.

For the Children and Young Persons Act 1933, s 53, see 6 Halsbury's Statutes (4th edn)
55.

For the Children and Young Persons Act 1969, s 23, see ibid 265.

c **Cases referred to in judgment**

R v Butler (1984) 6 Cr App R(S) 236, CA.
R v Dolan (1976) 62 Cr App R 36, CA.
R v Gaskin (1985) 7 Cr App R(S) 28, CA.
R v McKenna [1986] Crim LR 195, CA.
R v Murphy and Duke [1986] Crim LR 571, CA.
d R v Nightingale (1984) 6 Cr App R(S) 65, CA.
R v Oakes (1983) 5 Cr App R(S) 389, CA.
R v Standing and Ealand (1986) 83 Cr App R 241, CA.

Appeals against sentence

e Jonathan Fairhurst and six other appellants were convicted in the Crown Court at various
places of indecent assault, rape, theft, burglary and associated offences and were sentenced
to varying terms of youth custody or detention under s 53(2) of the Children and Young
Persons Act 1933. The appellants all appealed against their sentences. The appeals were
listed for hearing together. The case is reported solely on the principles of sentencing to
be followed in sentencing to detention under s 53(2) of the 1933 Act and to youth custody
f under ss 6 and 7 of the Criminal Justice Act 1982.

Franz J Muller QC (assigned by the Registrar of Criminal Appeals) for the appellant
Fairhurst.
J J Walker-Smith (assigned by the Registrar of Criminal Appeals) for the appellant
Hippolyte.
g Kathryn Brown (assigned by the Registrar of Criminal Appeals) for the appellant Wilson.
Michael J Taylor (assigned by the Registrar of Criminal Appeals) for the appellants Narey
and Hardman.
John H Muir (assigned by the Registrar of Criminal Appeals) for the appellants Ellis and
Mawson.

h   *Cur adv vult*

31 July. The following judgment of the court was delivered.

LORD LANE CJ. A number of cases involving sentences of detention under s 53(2) of
the Children and Young Persons Act 1933 and of youth custody under the provisions of
j the Criminal Justice Act 1982 have been listed for consideration by the court. The reason
is that points of difficulty have arisen which we wish to try to resolve for the benefit of
sentencing courts in the future.

The first and principal problem is the interrelation between ss 6 and 7(8) and (9) of the
1982 Act on the one hand and s 53(2) of the 1933 Act on the other. Section 6 of the 1982
Act introduces the concept of youth custody. Section 7(8) provides as follows:

'An offender aged less than 17 years shall not be sentenced to a term of youth custody which exceeds 12 months at a time; and accordingly—(a) a court shall not pass a youth custody sentence on such an offender whose effect would be that he would be sentenced to a total term which exceeds 12 months; and (b) so much of any such term for which such an offender is sentenced as exceeds 12 months shall be treated as remitted.'

Section 53(2) of the 1933 Act provides:

'Where a child or young person is convicted on indictment of any offence punishable in the case of an adult with imprisonment for fourteen years or more, not being an offence the sentence for which is fixed by law and the court is of opinion that none of the other methods in which the case may legally be dealt with is suitable, the court may sentence the offender to be detained for such period not exceeding the maximum term of imprisonment with which the offence is punishable in the case of an adult as may be specified in the sentence . . .'

Three points are of particular importance: (1) the 'fourteen years' requirement; (2) the requirement that no other method of disposal is suitable; (3) the conviction must be on indictment.

As to the occasion on which a sentence of s 53(2) detention can properly be imposed, there are two poles of judicial opinion. They can perhaps be exemplified by the cases of *R v Oakes* (1983) 5 Cr App R(S) 389 on the one hand and *R v Butler* (1984) 6 Cr App R(S) 236 on the other.

In *R v Oakes* the offender was aged 16 and fell to be dealt with for two offences of burglary and two other offences with 12 offences to be taken into consideration. He, in company with his brother, had gone to the house of a woman of 87 and, while he had engaged her in conversation at the front door, his brother broke in at the back and stole property valued at £1,200. The other offences were of a similar type. He was sentenced to 30 months' detention under the provisions of s 53(2) of the 1933 Act. On appeal it was held that the court had in law the power to pass the sentence it in fact passed, but that the choice of sentence was not appropriate to the circumstances of the case. Section 53(2) was not to be used as a means of escaping from the very specific limitations imposed by the 1982 Act. It was designed to give the courts exceptional powers to deal with young people in exceptionally serious cases. The burglaries in that case were not, so it was held, in the province of the very serious crime with which s 53(2) was designed to deal. The offences were serious and unpleasant, but not of the gravity of those with which s 53(2) was intended to deal. The court varied the sentence to 12 months' youth custody.

At the other end of the scale from *R v Oakes* is the decision of this court in *R v Butler* to which I was a party. *R v Butler* was a case in which the appellant was aged 16. He pleaded guilty to six counts of burglary and asked for no less than 23 other offences, mostly of the same type, to be taken into consideration. In some cases damage was done to the houses and the amount of the damage involved was substantial. He was sentenced to a total of two years' detention, which was left unaltered on appeal to this court. Boreham J, giving the judgment of the court, said (6 Cr App R(S) 236 at 243):

'It seems to us, in the light of the decision in *R v Nightingale* (1984) 6 Cr App R(S) 65, that the crucial question in circumstances such as these is: were there other methods which were suitable and adequate for disposing of the matter? Narrowing that question to the particular circumstances of this case, was 12 months' youth custody adequate to reflect the gravity of the offences? No doubt in considering that question the court will hesitate before making use of section 53(2) and will confine itself, if it properly can, to 12 months' youth custody. But where such a sentence is clearly inadequate, then in our judgment the court should take advantage of section 53(2) and pass the appropriate term of custodial sentence.'

We find it unnecessary to cite the further authorities which are all usefully set out in the judgment given by Mustill LJ in *R v Standing and Ealand* (1986) 83 Cr App R 241.

a   It seems to us, with the benefit of hindsight, that the decision in *R v Oakes* on the one hand and *R v Butler* on the other may have gone too far, each of them in opposite directions. On the one hand there exists the desirability of keeping youths under the age of 17 out of long terms of custody. This is implicit in the provisions of the 1982 Act already referred to. On the other hand it is necessary that serious offences committed by youths of this age should be met with sentences sufficiently substantial to provide both the appropriate punishment and also the necessary deterrent effect, and in certain cases

b   to provide a measure of protection to the public. A balance has to be struck between these objectives.

        In our view (1) it is not necessary, in order to invoke the provisions of s 53(2) of the 1933 Act, that the crime committed should be one of exceptional gravity, such as attempted murder, manslaughter, wounding with intent, armed robbery or the like, (2) on the other hand it is not good sentencing practice to pass a sentence of detention under

c   s 53(2) simply because a 12 months' youth custody sentence seems to be on the low side for the particular offence committed, (3) where the offence plainly calls for a greater sentence than one of 12 months' youth custody and is sufficiently serious to call for a sentence of two years' youth custody or more had the offender been aged 17 or over, then it will be proper to sentence to a similar term of s 53(2) detention. If the offence would merit a sentence of less than two years' but more than 12 months' youth custody for an

d   offender aged 17 or over, then the sentence should normally be one of youth custody and not of s 53(2) detention. It cannot be said that the difference between a sentence of, say, 21 months' and one of 12 months' youth custody is so great that the 12 months could be regarded as an inappropriate term, (4) where more than one offence is involved for which s 53(2) detention is available, but the offences vary in seriousness, provided that at least one offence is sufficiently serious to merit s 53(2) detention, detention sentences of under

e   two years' duration, whether concurrent or consecutive, may properly be imposed in respect of the other offences (see *R v Gaskin* (1985) 7 Cr App R(S) 28), and (5) where an offender is aged under 15 and thus ineligible for youth custody, a detention sentence of less than two years may well be appropriate.

        Where there are two offences committed by a 15- or 16-year old and one of them, A,

f   carries a maximum sentence of 14 years, and the other, B, carries a lower maximum, then generally speaking it is not proper to pass a sentence of s 53(2) detention in respect of offence A, which would not otherwise merit it, it order to compensate for the fact that 12 months' youth custody is grossly inadequate for offence B. Where however it can truly be said that the defendant's behaviour giving rise to offence B is part and parcel of the events giving rise to offence A, such a sentence may properly be passed.

g   A further matter which has particularly exercised the court in this area is the desirability or otherwise of passing consecutive or concurrent sentences of s 53(2) detention and youth custody. The difficulty arises where one of the offences carries a maximum penalty of 14 years or more but where the other carries a maximum penalty of *less* than 14 years, or equally where the other offence comes before the Crown Court on committal for sentence under s 37 of the Magistrates' Courts Act 1980. What is the

h   court to do if it determines that a s 53(2) detention sentence is appropriate for the first offence and wishes to pass a sentence of youth custody in respect of the other? There are great differences between the procedures applicable to the two types of sentence. For example the offender serving a youth custody sentence is eligible for release after serving two-thirds of his sentence. He will then be subject to supervision for the remainder of the original term. There is no power of recall, but failure to comply with the requirements

j   of s 15 of the 1982 Act is a summary offence punishable with not more than 30 days' custody. On the other hand a juvenile subject to a s 53(2) detention sentence has no entitlement to release after any particular part of his sentence has been served. The question of release before the end of the term imposed by the court is a matter for the Home Secretary to decide on the advice of the Parole Board. If the youth is so released, he will be on licence for the whole of the rest of the term imposed by the court.

        It is plain from this that to pass such sentences, either to run consecutively or concurrently, would produce complications. As this court has said in *R v Gaskin* (1985) 7 Cr App R(S) 28 and *R v McKenna* [1986] Crim LR 195, it is undesirable that sentences of s 53(2) detention and of youth custody should be passed to run either consecutively to or concurrently with each other. It is not however always possible to avoid this. The only way out of the problem in general may be to impose no separate penalty for the offences for which s 53(2) detention is not available. Although that solution is not altogether satisfactory, it seems to us that it provides less difficulties than any other possible method.

If that is done, and the offender successfully appeals against conviction on the count carrying the s 53(2) detention, he does not automatically walk free. This is by reason of s 4 of the Criminal Appeal Act 1968, which provides as follows:

> '(1) This section applies where, on an appeal against conviction on an indictment containing two or more counts, the Court of Appeal allow the appeal in respect of part of the indictment.
> (2) Except as provided by subsection (3) below, the Court may in respect of any count on which the appellant remains convicted pass such sentence, in substitution for any sentence passed thereon at the trial, as they think proper and is authorised by law for the offence of which he remains convicted on that count.
> (3) The Court shall not under this section pass any sentence such that the appellant's sentence on the indictment as a whole will, in consequence of the appeal, be of greater severity than the sentence (taken as a whole) which was passed at the trial for all offences of which he was convicted on the indictment.'

In *R v Dolan* (1976) 62 Cr App R 36 at 39 this court held that where a conviction was quashed leaving in existence convictions on other counts in respect of which no penalty was imposed, the court was entitled under s 4(2) to pass such sentence as seemed to them appropriate on the latter counts. Problems will still arise however where, for example, the convictions have been in respect of two separate indictments.

Finally, courts should be aware of an anomaly which exists in this area as to the extent to which time spent on remand in custody or on remand in care counts towards the eventual sentence. Section 10 of the 1982 Act extends to detention centre orders and youth custody sentences the provisions relating to imprisonment in s 67 of the Criminal Justice Act 1967, so that those custodial sentences are reduced by any period spent in custody in connection with the offence for which the sentence was passed. These provisions do not, however, apply to sentences of detention under s 53(2). It follows that courts should bear in mind when deciding on the proper length of a sentence under s 53(2) that allowance should be made for time spent on remand in custody prior to sentence. It should equally be noted that time spent by a juvenile committed on remand to the care of a local authority under s 23(1) of the Children and Young Persons Act 1969 does not count against the length of an eventual sentence, including s 53(2) detention (see s 67(6) of the 1967 Act and Home Office Circular 42/1983, para 26).

We consider that allowance should also be made for time spent on remand in care where the offender is held under a regime comparable to a remand in custody, for example where he is placed in secure accommodation (see *R v Murphy and Duke* [1986] Crim LR 571), or where he is held under highly structured and closely supervised conditions. Where such allowance is made either in the case of a remand in custody or in the case of a remand in care, that fact should be stated by the court when passing sentence.

Against this background we now turn to examine the individual cases which are before us.

[The court then considered the facts of the appeals; all were allowed in part, the appeals of Naray and Hardman having been relisted to 16 October 1986.]

Appeals allowed in part.

N P Metcalfe Esq   Barrister.

a # Debenhams plc v Westminster City Council

HOUSE OF LORDS

LORD KEITH OF KINKEL, LORD TEMPLEMAN, LORD GRIFFITHS, LORD MACKAY OF CLASHFERN AND LORD ACKNER

27, 29, 30 OCTOBER, 4 DECEMBER 1986

b
Rates – Exemption – Listed building – Structure fixed to building – Hereditament included in list of buildings of architectural or historic interest – Unoccupied property – Hereditament comprising two buildings connected by a footbridge and tunnel – One building listed but the other not – Buildings used together as commercial unit – Buildings becoming unoccupied – Whether unlisted building part of listed building – Whether unlisted building a structure fixed to listed building –
c Whether exemption available if only part of hereditament listed – General Rate Act 1967, Sch 1, para 2(c) – Town and Country Planning Act 1971, s 54(9).

The respondents were the owners of a hereditament which comprised two separate buildings (the Regent Street building and the Kingly Street building) on opposite sides of a street but joined by a footbridge over and a tunnel under the street. In 1973 the
d Secretary of State for the Environment included the Regent Street building in a list of buildings of special architectural or historical interest compiled under s 54ᵃ of the Town and Country Planning Act 1971. The respondents used the two buildings as a single commercial unit, the Kingly Street building being treated as an annexe of the Regent Street building. In October 1981 the respondents vacated the hereditament and it remained unoccupied throughout the 1982–83 rating year. The respondents claimed
e listed building exemption from rates under para 2(c)ᵇ of Sch 1 to the General Rate Act 1967 for the period the hereditament was unoccupied but the rating authority refused to allow such an exemption and brought proceedings against the respondents for non-payment of rates. The magistrate held that the respondents were not entitled to listed building exemption because part of the rated hereditament, namely the Kingly Street building, was not a listed building. The respondents appealed, contending that the whole
f premises was a listed building because the Kingly Street building was a 'structure fixed to a building' which was listed, and was therefore to be treated, by virtue of s 54(9) of the 1971 Act, as part of the listed building The judge allowed the appeal, and his decision was upheld by the Court of Appeal. The rating authority appealed to the House of Lords.

Held (Lord Ackner dissenting) – The appeal would be allowed for the following
g reasons—

(1) For the purposes of s 54(9) of the 1971 Act a 'structure fixed to a [listed] building' only encompassed a structure which was ancillary and subordinate to the listed building itself and which was either fixed to the main building or within its curtilage, e g the stable block of a listed mansion house or the steading of a listed farmhouse. The fact that one building was subordinated to another for the commercial purposes of the occupier
h or that a completely distinct building was connected to a listed building to which it was not subordinate did not make the building a structure fixed to a listed building. Since the Regent Street and Kingly Street buildings were historically completely independent the Kingly Street building was not a listed building under s 54(9) of the 1971 Act (see p 55 *e* to p 56 *b*, p 57 *e* to *h*, p 59 *e* to *g* and p 60 *d* to *h*, post); A-G (ex rel Sutcliffe) v
j Calderdale BC (1982) 46 P & CR 399 considered.

(2) Having regard to the fact that the rating exemption in para 2(c) of Sch 1 to the 1967 Act related to hereditaments and not buildings whereas listing under s 54 of the 1971 Act related to buildings rather than hereditaments, where a hereditament comprised two independent buildings, of which one was listed and the other was not, listed building

---

a   Section 54, so far as material, is set out at p 54 *d* to *g*, post
b   Paragraph 2(c) is set out at p 53 *j* to p 54 *b*, post

exemption from rates could not be claimed under para 2(c) in respect of the hereditament (see p 56 d to h, p 57 c e to h and p 60 d to h, post).

Per curiam. If a structure is by virtue of the 1971 Act to be treated as a part of a building which has been listed under s 54 of the 1971 Act, it must be so treated for the purposes of any other Act which makes special provision for listed buildings, e g exemption from rates in certain circumstances (see p 56 c, p 57 f to h and p 61 j, post).

Notes

For exemptions from rating generally, see 39 Halsbury's Laws (4th edn) para 84, and for a case on the subject of exemption from rating of listed buildings, see 38 Digest (Reissue) 331, 2268.

For the General Rate Act 1967, Sch 1, para 2, see 27 Halsbury's Statutes (3rd edn) 210.

For the Town and Country Planning Act 1971, s 54, see 41 ibid 1651.

Cases referred to in opinions

A-G (ex rel Sutcliffe) v Calderdale BC (1982) 46 P & CR 399, CA.
Corthorn Land and Timber Co Ltd v Minister of Housing and Local Government (1965) 17 P & CR 210.
Providence Properties Ltd v Liverpool City Council [1980] RA 189, DC.

Appeal

Westminster City Council (the rating authority) appealed by leave of the Appeal Committee of the House of Lords granted on 8 May 1986 against the decision of the Court of Appeal (Fox, Neill and Ralph Gibson LJJ) ([1986] RA 114) on 25 March 1986 dismissing an appeal by the rating authority against the decision of Hodgson J ([1985] RA 265) hearing the Crown Office list on 7 February 1985 whereby he allowed an appeal by the respondents, Debenhams plc, by way of case stated from a decision of John Quentin Campbell Esq, a metropolitan stipendiary magistrate, in respect of his adjudication at Horseferry Road Magistrates' Court, on 29 March 1983 whereby he determined that a hereditament comprising shop and premises at 200–202 Regent Street and 50–52 Kingly Street owned by the respondents was not exempt from rating under Sch 1, para 2(c) of the General Rate Act 1967 during a period from 1 February 1982 to 31 March 1983 when it was unoccupied and he directed that a distress warrant in respect of the unpaid rates on the premises during that period should be issued on the application of the rating authority. The facts are set out in the opinion of Lord Keith.

Graham Eyre QC and *Richard Hone* for the rating authority.
Matthew Horton and *Michael Humphries* for the respondents.

Their Lordships took time for consideration.

4 December. The following opinions were delivered.

LORD KEITH OF KINKEL. My Lords, this appeal raises difficult questions as to the proper construction of certain of the unoccupied rates provisions of the General Rate Act 1967, as amended in their application to buildings listed by the Secretary of State, under s 54 of the Town and Country Planning Act 1971, as being of special architectural or historic interest. The proper construction of certain provisions of s 54 is also in issue.

The appellants are the rating authority for the City of Westminster and the respondents were at the material time owners of a hereditament described in the valuation list which came into force on 1 April 1973 as '200/202 Regent Street (and 50/52 Kingly Street)'. This hereditament was formerly Hamleys toy shop. It comprised premises fronting onto Regent Street and running back to the west side of Kingly Street at the rear, and also (notwithstanding the description in the list) further premises on the east side of Kingly Street and known as 27–28 Kingly Street. The back part of the former premises (50–52 Kingly Street) was formerly connected to the latter premises by a footbridge passing over *a* Kingly Street at second floor level and by a tunnel passing underneath it. The tunnel was filled in by operations which concluded in January 1983 and the footbridge was removed in March 1983. These works were done to enable 27–28 Kingly Street (the Kingly Street building) to be sold separately. No physical demarcation existed between 200–202 Regent Street and 50–52 Kingly Street (the Regent Street building).

b In 1973 the Secretary of State for the Environment compiled, under s 54 of the 1971 Act, a list of buildings of special architectural or historic interest which included a number of properties in Regent Street. Under the heading 'Regent Street, W1 (East Side)' there appeared, inter alia, 'Nos. 172 to 206 (even)'.

c The respondents occupied the hereditament and carried on Hamleys toy shop there until 31 October 1981, when they vacated it, and it remained unoccupied when, on 22 July 1982, the rating authority made a complaint against the respondents for nonpayment of rates amounting to £68,696·91 on the hereditament in respect of the period from 1 February 1982 to 31 March 1983. At the same time it issued a summons applying for a distress warrant, which was heard by Mr J Quentin Campbell, a metropolitan stipendiary magistrate, on 29 March 1983. The respondents claimed exemption from unoccupied rates under para 2(c) of Sch 1 to the 1967 Act, but the magistrate rejected the claim and issued a distress warrant, holding that the exemption for listed buildings there provided for was not available when, as he found to be the case, part only of the hereditament was listed. He found that the Regent Street building was listed but that the Kingly Street building was not. At the request of the respondents the magistrate stated a case for the opinion of the High Court, in which he made findings of fact, on which the foregoing account is based, and posed the following questions of law:

e '(i) Did I err in law in holding that only part of the hereditament was listed? (ii) Did I err in law in holding that the listed part was 200/202 Regent Street and 50–52 Kingly Street?'

The respondents' appeal by stated case was heard by Hodgson J who allowed it and answered the questions of law in the affirmative (see [1985] RA 265). On appeal by the rating authority the Court of Appeal (Fox, Neill and Ralph Gibson LJJ) affirmed that decision (see [1986] RA 114). The rating authority now appeals to your Lordships' House.

f Section 17 of the 1967 Act provides that a rating authority may resolve that the provisions of Sch 1 to the Act shall apply to their area, and the appellants have done so. Paragraph 1(1) of Sch 1 provides that in these circumstances where any relevant hereditament in the area is unoccupied for a continuous period exceeding three months—

g 'the owner shall, subject to the provisions of this Schedule, be rated in respect of that hereditament for any relevant period of vacancy; and the provisions of this Act shall apply accordingly as if the hereditament were occupied during that relevant period of vacancy by the owner.'

By para 15—

h '"relevant hereditament" means any hereditament consisting of, or of part of, a house, shop, office, factory, mill or other building whatsoever, together with any garden, yard, court or other land ordinarily used or intended for use for the purposes of the building or part.'

Paragraph 2, as amended by s 291 of and Sch 23 to the 1971 Act, provides:

j 'No rates shall be payable under paragraph 1 of this Schedule in respect of a hereditament for, or for any part of the three months beginning with the day following the end of, any period during which—(a) the owner is prohibited by law from occupying the hereditament or allowing it to be occupied; (b) the hereditament is kept vacant by reason of action taken by or on behalf of the Crown or any local or public authority with a view to prohibiting the occupation of the hereditament or to acquiring it; (c) the hereditament is the subject of a building preservation notice as defined by section 58 of the Town and Country Planning Act 1971 or is included in a list compiled or approved under section 54 of that Act, or is notified to the rating authority by the Minister as a building of architectural or historic interests; (d) the hereditament is the subject of a preservation order or an interim preservation *a* notice under the Ancient Monuments Acts 1913 to 1953, or is included in a list published by the Minister of Public Building and Works under those Acts; (e) an agreement is in force with respect to the hereditament under section 56(1)(a) of this Act; or (f) the hereditament is held for the purpose of being available for occupation by a minister of religion as a residence from which to perform the duties of his office.'   *b*

It is sub-para (c) of that paragraph which is directly in point here. If it be a correct conclusion that the whole of the hereditament is to be regarded as included in the list compiled by the Secretary of State in 1973, notwithstanding that only part of it is specifically mentioned in that list, then exemption from unoccupied rates will be available. Counsel for the respondents argued that, on a proper construction and *c* application of the relevant provisions of the 1971 Act as regards listing, this was indeed the position.

Section 54(1), (2) and (9) of the 1971 Act is in these terms:

'(1) For the purposes of this Act and with a view to the guidance of local planning authorities in the performance of their functions under this Act in relation to *d* buildings of special architectural or historic interest, the Secretary of State shall compile lists of such buildings, or approve, with or without modifications, such lists compiled by other persons or bodies of persons, and may amend any list so compiled or approved.

(2) In considering whether to include a building in a list compiled or approved under this section, the Secretary of State may take into account not only the building *e* itself but also—(a) any respect in which its exterior contributes to the architectural or historic interest of any group of buildings of which it forms part; and (b) the desirability of preserving, on the ground of its architectural or historic interest, any feature of the building consisting of a manmade object of structure fixed to the building or forming part of the land and comprised within the curtilage of the building.   *f*

(9) In this Act "listed building" means a building which is for the time being included in a list compiled or approved by the Secretary of State under this section; and, for the purposes of the provisions of this Act relating to listed buildings and building preservation notices, any object or structure fixed to a building, or forming part of the land and comprised within the curtilage of a building, shall be treated as part of the building.'   *g*

The argument for the respondents, which was accepted by Hodgson J and the Court of Appeal, was that the Kingly Street building, not mentioned in the list compiled by the Secretary of State, was, within the meaning of s 54(9), a 'structure' which by the footbridge and the tunnel was fixed to the Regent Street building, which was mentioned in that list, or, alternatively, formed part of the land and was within the curtilage of the *h* latter building. Accordingly, it fell to be treated as part of the listed building. The argument was supported by reliance on A-G (ex rel Sutcliffe) v Calderdale BC (1982) 46 P & CR 399. That case concerned a disused mill and a terrace of cottages with a bridge linking the two, the cottages having been formerly owned by the millowners and occupied by their workers, though they had later come to be in separate ownership. The mill was listed but the cottages were not. The Court of Appeal held that, within the meaning of *j* s 54(9), the terrace of cottages was a structure fixed to the mill, and further, was one which formed part of the land and was comprised within the curtilage of the mill. The cottages could not, therefore, be demolished without the consent of the Secretary of State.

In my opinion, the success or failure of the argument must turn on the meaning to be attributed to the word 'structure' in s 54(9). In its ordinary significance the word certainly embraces anything built or constructed and so would cover any building. The question is whether its context here requires a narrower meaning to be attributed to it. The wider

meaning could lead to some strange results. For example, if one house in an architecturally
a undistinguished terrace was listed as having once been the birthplace of an historically
famous personage it appears that all the houses in the terrace, being fixed to the listed
building either directly or through each other, would require to be treated as part of it,
as, indeed, might many other terraces connected to that one. Many other such examples
may be figured. Notice of listing, under s 54(7), is required to be given only to the owner
and occupier of the listed building itself, so the owner of some quite remote building
b might unwittingly undertake its demolition and become liable to penalties under s 55(1).

The incongruous results which might follow from the decision in the *Calderdale* case
were recognised by Stephenson LJ (at 405), giving the leading judgment in the Court of
Appeal, but he took the view that the argument from incongruity was met by the fact
that the listing building code of control did not prevent demolition or alteration, but
merely required consent to it. It is to be observed that the words in s 54(9) 'any object or
c structure fixed to a building, or forming part of the land and comprised within the
curtilage of a building' echo similar words in s 54(2), where, however, the words are
prefaced by 'man-made', and the relevant object or structure must be a feature of the
building. It is, I think, clear that in the context of sub-s (2) the word 'structure' is not
intended to embrace some other complete building in its own right. This indicates that
the draftsman of the relevant part of the 1971 Act has thought it appropriate to use the
d word in a narrow sense the first time that he introduced the quoted phrase, and it is a
reasonable inference that he intended to use it in the same sense the second time. At all
events, the result is to introduce an ambiguity into sub-s (9), or perhaps more accurately,
to deepen the ambiguity which is there already. In resolving a statutory ambiguity, that
meaning which produces an unreasonable result is to be rejected in favour of that which
does not, it being presumed that Parliament did not intend to produce such a result. In
e my opinion to construe the word 'structure' here as embracing a complete building not
subordinate to the building of which it is to be treated as forming part, would, in the
light of the considerations I have mentioned, indeed produce an unreasonable result.
Stephenson LJ in the *Calderdale* case considered that objection to be offset by what he
regarded as part of the purpose of the listing provisions, namely that of protecting the
setting of an architecturally or historically important building. But if that was part of the
f purpose, it would have been expected that Parliament would not have stopped at other
buildings fixed to or within the curtilage of such a building, but would have subjected
to control also buildings immediately adjoining but not fixed to the listed building, or
on the opposite side of the street. All these considerations and the general tenor of the
second sentence of sub-s (9) satisfy me that the word 'structure' is intended to convey a
limitation to such structures as are ancillary to the listed building itself, for example the
g stable block of a mansion house or the steading of a farmhouse, either fixed to the main
building or within its curtilage. In my opinion the concept envisaged is that of principal
and accessory. It does not follow that I would overrule the decision in the *Calderdale* case,
though I would not accept the width of the reasoning of Stephenson LJ. There was, in
my opinion, room for the view that the terrace of cottages was ancillary to the mill.
h   The question thus comes to be whether the Kingly Street building was at the material
time ancillary to the Regent Street building. The former was not of its nature ancillary
the latter, in the sort of sense that a steading is ancillary to a farmhouse. It was historically
an independent building. It is true that for a very considerable period of time both
buildings were occupied and used together for the purposes of Hamleys toy shop, but
throughout the rating year 1982–83 neither of them was being used for any purpose
j whatsoever, and indeed it must have been in contemplation that there would be no
resumption of joint use, as is evidenced by the circumstance that in October 1982 steps
began to be taken to sever the links between the two buildings with a view to the Kingly
Street building being sold off separately. These considerations tend to show that on a
broad perspective the Kingly Street building was not ancillary to the Regent Street
building. The matter of listing or not listing cannot turn on the business purposes or
manner of use of adjoining properties of a particular occupier. Fox LJ, giving the leading
judgment in the Court of Appeal in this case, said that the Kingly Street building was

really an annexe fixed to the rest of the hereditament. From the point of view of the
occupier that may have been so, but the subordination of one building to another for the *a*
particular purposes of someone who happens for the time being to occupy both does not
mean that objectively speaking and for the purposes of the listing legislation one of the
buildings is ancillary to the other. In my opinion the Kingly Street building was an
independent building and does not fall within s 54(9).

A large part of the argument for the rating authority was directed to the proposition
that the words in s 54(9) 'for the purposes of the provisions of this Act relating to listed *b*
buildings and building preservation notices' had the effect that the enactment which
followed them was not to be taken into account for the purposes of Sch 1 to the 1967
Act. In my opinion that proposition is ill-founded. The quoted words have the effect, for
the purposes of the listed building provisions of the Act, of widening the definition of
'building' in s 290(1) of the 1971 Act. No other effect can properly be attributed to them.
It would be an absurd result, such as cannot have been intended by Parliament, if a *c*
structure subjected to listed building control by the 1971 Act were to be treated as not so
subjected for the purpose of some other Act dealing with the consequences of listing.

Having reached the conclusion that only the Regent Street building is listed and not
the Kingly Street building, it is necessary to consider whether or not para 2(*c*) of Sch 1 to
the 1967 Act applies to that situation. The construction of para 2(*c*) presents difficulty
owing to the draftsman, as it would appear, not having kept in view the distinction *d*
between a hereditament and a building. It is buildings, not hereditaments, which may
be the subject of building preservation notices (under s 58 of the 1971 Act), and which
are included in lists compiled under s 54. Although a hereditament may consist in a
building and no more, there are a great many hereditaments which comprise a building
and also something more, even if only a small garden or yard. Some hereditaments may
comprise more than one independent building, as is the position here. 'Hereditament' *e*
throughout para 2 of Sch 1 to the 1967 Act must, in my opinion, be read as 'relevant
hereditament' as defined in para 15. The schedule is, after all, dealing only with relevant
hereditaments. So it is clearly in contemplation that a hereditament which attracts the
exemption from rates afforded by para 2 may be not only one which is a building and no
more, but also one which is a building with a garden, yard, court or other land ordinarily *f*
used for the purposes of the building. It follows that the presence of such garden etc
would not deprive the hereditament of the exemption, notwithstanding that it is only
the building, and not the whole hereditament, which, for example, is included in a list
compiled under s 54 of the 1971 Act. Likewise, the presence of some ancillary structure
such as a garage or outhouse, either fixed to the main building or within its curtilage,
would not affect the exemption since by virtue of s 54(9) such ancillary structure would *g*
fall to be treated as part of the building.

The position in the present case is that the hereditament comprises two independent
buildings, one of which is listed and the other of which is not. In the event that one of
the buildings, but not the other, was the subject of a building preservation notice made
under s 58 of the 1971 Act, it could be said, without any undue straining of language,
that the hereditament as such was the subject of the notice, even though the notice *h*
applied to part only of it. If one only of two buildings on the hereditament was included
in a list compiled under s 54, it could surely not be said that the hereditament as such
was included in the list. On the other hand, it is not likely that Parliament would have
intended to treat the two cases differently. Paragraph 2 should be construed so as to
accord the same treatment to both. In making the choice between the stricter and the
more liberal constructions some assistance can, in my opinion, be derived from para 3 of *j*
Sch 1 to the 1967 Act, which provides:

'The Minister may by regulations provide that rates shall not be payable under
paragraph 1 of this Schedule in respect of hereditaments of such descriptions as may
be prescribed by the regulations or in such circumstances as may be so prescribed
and the regulations may make different provision for hereditaments of different
descriptions and for different circumstances.'

The provision enables the minister to enlarge the classes of hereditaments in respect of

a which the exemption is afforded. It does not enable him to restrict it. There would seem to be nothing to prevent the minister, if so advised, from prescribing by regulations hereditaments comprising both a listed and unlisted building in relation to which the value of the listed building amounted to more than some specified proportion of the value of the whole hereditament. It might seem unfair that exemption should be denied where the value of the listed building accounted for a very large proportion of the value

b of the whole hereditament. Yet from the other point of view it might seem unreasonable that exemption should be afforded where the value of the listed building formed a very small proportion of the total value. The minister has been given power which would enable him to alleviate the former anomaly but not the latter. Accordingly, para 3 is an indication in favour of the view that Parliament intended the stricter construction of para 2(*c*) of Sch 1 to the 1967 Act.

c   In *Providence Properties Ltd v Liverpool City Council* [1980] RA 189 a Divisional Court consisting of Lord Lane CJ and Boreham J had occasion to consider the scope of the para 2(*c*) exemption in relation to a hereditament which comprised three warehouses, one of which was listed and the other two of which were not. It was decided that the exemption was not available to a hereditament part only of which was listed. The reasoning was that if Parliament had intended to afford the exemption to such a hereditament it would have

d done so in express terms. There is much force in that view of the matter, and taken in conjunction with the other considerations set out above it must, in my opinion, determine the issue in favour of the rating authority.

My Lords, for these reasons I would allow the appeal and restore the adjudication of the stipendiary magistrate and the distress warrant. The questions posed in the case stated do not deal exhaustively with the issues raised in the appeal. They should be answered in

e the affirmative, but in addition it should be found that on a true construction of para 2 of Sch 1 to the 1967 Act exemption from rates is not available to the respondents' hereditament in respect of the rating year 1982–83.

LORD TEMPLEMAN. My Lords, for the reasons given by my noble and learned

f friend Lord Keith, I agree that this appeal should be allowed and that this House should make the findings he has proposed.

LORD GRIFFITHS. My Lords, I have had the advantage of reading in draft the speeches prepared by my noble and learned friends Lord Keith and Lord MacKay. I agree with them, and for the reasons which they give I would allow the appeal.

g **LORD MACKAY OF CLASHFERN.** My Lords, I have the advantage of reading in draft the speeches prepared by my noble and learned friends Lord Keith and Lord Ackner.

I agree with both that the principal argument relied on by the rating authority in the present case is ill-founded. I agree with my noble and learned friend Lord Keith that this

h appeal should be allowed for the reasons which he has given. Since I differ from my noble and learned friend Lord Ackner on this aspect of the appeal and also from the unanimous judgment of the Court of Appeal I shall add some observations.

Although the question in this appeal arises in the context of relief from rates on unoccupied property, the point that has divided us is of considerable importance in the administration of the system of listed building control now governed by the provisions

j of the Town and Country Planning Act 1971.

By the first part of s 54(9), for the purposes of the 1971 Act 'listed building' means a building which is, for the time being, included in a list compiled or approved by the Secretary of State under the section. The list so compiled or approved is to be a list of buildings of special architectural or historic interest. Since it is obviously necessary that the list should identify the buildings contained in it, the question whether a particular physical entity is listed or not listed depends on whether on reading the list and taking account of the statutory provisions that entity is to be regarded as a building or part of a

building included in the list. In the present case the contention for the respondents is
that the entry in the list under the heading 'Regent Street, W1 (East Side) Nos. 172 to 206   *a*
(even)' meant not only that the building which has the address 200–202 Regent Street,
and, since it physically carries through to Kingly Street, also has the address 50–52 Kingly
Street and which I shall refer to as 'the Regent Street building', was included in the list,
but also that a building on the opposite side of Kingly Street, namely 27–28 Kingly
Street, which I shall refer to as 'the Kingly Street building', was in the list. If this
contention is correct, inevitably a considerable number of other buildings in Kingly   *b*
Street, in Foubert's Place, in Carnaby Street and in Fuch's Place, which were included in
the block of which the Kingly Street building formed part, were also included in the list.
If the intention of the Secretary of State in compiling or approving this list was to include
all these buildings in it one would have expected the entry to have clearly included them.
If the effect of the action taken by the Secretary of State was that all of these buildings
should be included, in my opinion the entry in the list is positively misleading.   *c*

The magistrate found that the entry in the list referred and referred only to the Regent
Street building and did not extend to the Kingly Street building. He has asked for the
opinion of the court whether he erred in law in so holding. The respondents urge that
he was wrong and the reason for this submission is the second part of s 54(9), which
provides:
    d

> '... for the purposes of the provisions of this Act relating to listed buildings and
> building preservation notices, any object or structure fixed to a building, or forming
> part of the land and comprised within the curtilage of a building, shall be treated as
> part of the building.'

Before considering this submission further I think it is necessary to refer to the   *e*
definitions of 'land' and 'building' provided in the interpretation section, s 290(1) of the
1971 Act:

> '"land" means any corporeal hereditament, including a building, and, in relation
> to the acquisition of land under Part VI of this Act, includes any interest in or right
> over land.'

and   *f*

> '"building" (except in sections 73 to 86 of this Act and Schedule 12 thereto)
> includes any structure or erection, and any part of a building, as so defined, but does
> not include plant or machinery comprised in a building.'

Cases under the Income and Corporation Taxes Act 1970 demonstrate that the word   *g*
'plant' is a word of very extensive import and it is obvious that plant or machinery could
be fixed to a building and might include structures so fixed.

The statutory provision which is now the latter part of s 54(9) first appeared in the
Town and Country Planning Act 1968. As an illustration of a question that had arisen
prior to that statutory provision which might throw light on the reason for its insertion
in the legislation in 1968 your Lordships were referred to the decision of Russell LJ   *h*
sitting as an additional judge in the Queen's Bench Division in *Corthorn Land and Timber
Co Ltd v Minister of Housing and Local Government* (1965) 17 P & CR 210. In that case a
building preservation order had been made in respect of a mansion of outstanding
architectural merit. The building preservation order provided, inter alia, that the
mansion should not, without the consent of the planning authority be demolished,
altered or extended and that the following items, inter alia, should not be altered or   *j*
removed: (1) 27 portrait panels in the King's Room being nineteenth century copies of
Tudor and Stuart kings and queens; (2) carved oak panels in the wall of the Oak Room
dating from the fifteenth to mid seventeenth centuries; (3) a large wood carving in the
Great Hall; (4) large wooden medieval equestrian figures on the main landing; (5) a pair
of painted wooden panels depicting the hall in the ornate mantlepiece in one of the
drawing rooms.

The owner applied to quash the building preservation order on the ground that the

above-mentioned items were not properly included in it. It was held that any chattel
a which was affixed definitely to a building became part of the building, that there was no
doubt that the items in dispute were all fixed and annexed in their places as part of an
overall and permanent architectural scheme and were intended in every sense to be
annexed to the freehold, and were accordingly part of the building, and that, in these
circumstances, the restriction on their removal was properly made. Russell LJ, after
saying that he did not propose to detail the effect of the evidence laid before him as to the
b methods of fixing employed in relation to the various items in dispute, said (at 213): '. . .
it suffices to say that all the items would properly be described as fixtures as that phrase
is commonly applied in law.' Russell LJ went on to quote from a number of authorities
which can be summarised by saying that the ancient rule of the common law was that
whatever is planted or built in the soil or freehold becomes part of the freehold or
inheritance, thus a house becomes part of the land on which it stands and anything
c annexed or affixed to any building (not merely laid on or brought into contact with the
building) was treated as an addition to the property of the owner of the inheritance in
the soil and was termed a 'fixture'. This rule of the common law was relaxed in favour of
trade to enable tenants to affix their machinery or plant to a building or to the land and
not thus make a present of it to the landlord, so that machinery or plant fixed to the
inheritance for the purposes of trade may be removed by the tenant during the tenancy
d under certain conditions.

In the 1971 Act the general definition of 'building' excludes from its scope plant and
machinery. Certain items that otherwise would be 'fixtures' and form part of the building
are therefore excluded. Against this background it appears to me that the word 'fixed' is
intended in s 54(9) to have the same connotation as in the law of fixtures and that what
is achieved by the latter part of s 54(9) is that the ordinary rule of the common law is
e applied so that any object or structure fixed to a building should be treated as part of it.
The provision is dealing with the question whether certain things, namely objects or
structures, are to be treated as part of a building, not whether what is undoubtedly a
building or part of a building is to be regarded as part of another building. The use of
the indefinite article in describing the subject matter of the provision tends to suggest
this in my opinion. The result would be to put beyond question the matter that was
f decided by Russell LJ in the case to which I have referred and I consider that in its context
this is the natural interpretation of the provision. I think it is not a natural use of
language to describe two adjoining houses in a terrace by saying that one is an object or
structure fixed to the other. It would, I think, be a perfectly appropriate provision in a
contract for the sale of a house that there was included in the sale any object or structure
fixed to the house but I think it highly unlikely that the purchaser would expect under
g the terms of such a contract to become the owner of the house next door, with which it
shared a mutual wall.

The respondents' contention involves reading the word 'structure' in its context as
including a completely distinct building which is connected structurally to the first
building. This reading seriously restricts the power of the Secretary of State in relation to
h listed buildings since on this view he could not select one out of a terrace of houses nor
could he select a part of a building to be listed. Part of a building necessarily is fixed, in
the sense contended for, to the rest of the building. It is suggested that having regard to
the purpose of the 1971 Act no harm is done by forcing the Secretary of State if he wishes
to list a building in a terrace to list the whole terrace since in respect of the buildings in
the terrace not of architectural or historic interest permission for alteration or demolition
j could readily be given. However, s 54(2)(*a*) gives ample power to the Secretary of State if
he chooses to list the whole terrace in respect of architectural or historic interest possessed
by the whole; and the suggestion involves a compulsory notification to the owners of the
whole terrace that their houses have been included in the list in view of the terms of
s 54(7). I consider the respondents' construction is hard to reconcile with the provisions
of s 190 of the 1971 Act dealing with the service of a purchase notice when listed building
consent has been refused, conditionally granted, or modified. In certain circumstances
the owner may require the listed building to be purchased. Section 190(3) provides:

'In this section and in Schedule 19 to this Act, "the land" means the building in respect of which listed building consent has been refused, or granted subject to *a* conditions, or modified by the imposition of conditions, and in respect of which its owner serves a notice under this section, together with any land comprising the building, or contiguous or adjacent to it, and owned with it, being laid as to which the owner claims that its use is substantially inseparable from that of the building and that it ought to be treated, together with the building, as a single holding.'

This seems to envisage that a listed building will normally constitute a single holding. *b*

In my opinion it is inconsistent with this provision to interpret s 54(9) as having the effect that if the Secretary of State lists one building in a terrace the consequence is that all the other buildings in the terrace which are distinct from the listed building and are owned separately from it and from one another and whose uses are completely independent from that of the listed building are to be treated as part of the listed *c* building.

I see no practical difficulty in the operation of the 1971 Act on the construction which appears to me to be correct. If a listed building is extended, the extension will form part of the listed building without any need to rely on s 54(9). So far as buildings are concerned which exist at the date of the listing, the Secretary of State will have the right to include or exclude without being constrained to include by reason of physical *d* connection between a building he wishes to include and one he wishes to exclude.

Applying these considerations to the present case leads me to the conclusion that the magistrate decided it correctly. He concluded that what is found in the list was intended to refer only to the Regent Street building and was not intended to include the Kingly Street building. I consider that he was not bound to hold that the Kingly Street building was a structure fixed to the Regent Street building. It was a completely distinct building *e* which, at the end of the period in respect of which exemption was in question, was completely separate from the Regent Street building and even when connected to it by footbridge and tunnel it was not a structure fixed to it within the meaning of s 54(9). The magistrate was not, in my opinion, in any way bound to hold that the Kingly Street building was within the curtilage of the Regent Street building as it was separated from that at ground level by a public street, although, for rating purposes, when the buildings *f* were in common occupation they were treated as a single hereditament. The effect of the respondents' contention, in my opinion, is to say that the list compiled or approved by the Secretary of State included not only the Regent Street building but also the Kingly Street building. The list so long as it remained unaltered therefore included the Kingly Street building even after the footbridge was demolished and the tunnel was closed and the two buildings were completely distinct and separated by a public road. If the *g* Secretary of State should now decide that the Kingly Street building should be deleted from the list it is not entirely clear to me what action he could take to achieve this purpose. The same consideration applies to all the other buildings in the block of which the Kingly Street building forms part. According to the respondents' contention, as I have already said, these were all listed when 200–202 Regent Street was inserted in the list and notice should have been served on the owners of all these properties in terms of *h* s 54(7) that they were so included. If this were truly the position the only proper course, in my opinion, would have been to include their addresses in the list along with 200–202 Regent Street. The concept of a building impliedly in the list when it consists of premises distinct from those whose addresses is given in the list seems to me calculated to lead only to confusion in a case where the list is a document which requires to be registered in the register of local land charges and which should, consequently, have the *j* precision necessary to enable a person inspecting that register to appreciate all the subjects to which it relates.

In my opinion A-G (ex rel Sutcliffe) v Calderdale BC (1982) 46 P & CR 399 is a very special case on its facts and I believe that it was possible to treat the terrace and the mill, having regard to the history of the properties, as a single unit. At the time the listing was made the whole property was in one ownership and therefore when the mill was included

a notice to that effect was served on the only person who was interested as owner in the
a terrace. For the reasons which I have already given, I cannot regard, with respect, the
reasoning by which the Court of Appeal in that case reached its conclusion as according
with the true construction of s 54(9) the 1971 Act.

LORD ACKNER. My Lords, when counsel for the rating authority opened this appeal,
b he submitted to your Lordships, consistent with the rating authority's written case, that
the appeal only raised one question and that this question, although wrongly answered
by the Court of Appeal, had been properly formulated by Fox LJ in the course of his
judgment ([1986] RA 114 at 122), with which Neill and Ralph Gibson LJJ concurred.
The question was:

c 'Can a building which is treated as part of the listed building by the provisions of
s 54(9) be properly regarded as "included in a list compiled or approved under s 54
of the Town and Country Planning Act 1971"?'

Neither in the Court of Appeal nor in his case nor before your Lordships' House did
counsel for the rating authority seek to suggest that if that question, contrary to his
submissions, was answered in the affirmative, the appeal could succeed on any other
d ground, or that it gave rise to any other issue. Until invited by your Lordships to consider
the matter, he did not suggest that the Court of Appeal was in error in their following
conclusions: (a) that 27–28 Kingly Street (the Kingly Street building) was a 'structure
fixed to' 200–202 Regent Street (the Regent Street building), the building expressly
included in the list, and (b) that the Kingly Street building was a 'structure forming part
of the land and comprised within the curtilage' of that listed building.
e And, accordingly, by reason of the provision of s 54(9) of the Town and Country
Planning Act 1971 the Kingly Street building was to be treated as part of the Regent
Street building.

Hodgson J and the Court of Appeal, in reaching their decisions on the above two
matters, derived assistance from *A-G (ex rel Sutcliffe) v Calderdale BC* (1982) 46 P & CR
399, in which the leading judgment was given by Stephenson LJ and with which Sir
f Sebag Shaw and I concurred. Counsel for the rating authority, neither in his case nor in
your Lordships' House, until invited to do so, sought to criticise that decision. He
submitted that the essential issue in the *Calderdale* case was whether the terrace in
question was subject to the statutory control of works of demolition, under s 55 of the
1971 Act. He submitted that the Court of Appeal in that case did not have any reason to
consider the provisions of Sch 1 to the General Rate Act 1967 relating to the exemption
g from rates in respect of an unoccupied hereditament included in a list compiled or
approved under s 54 of the 1971 Act. He maintained that there was no conflict between
that case and *Providence Properties Ltd v Liverpool City Council* [1980] RA 189. Counsel for
the rating authority contended that the question as to what is or is not a 'listed building'
or what is or is not to be treated as part of such a building for the purpose of the provisions
of the 1971 Act is wholly irrelevant to the question whether a hereditament is exempt,
h by virtue of para 2(c) of Sch 1 to the 1967 Act, as being 'included in a list compiled or
approved by the Secretary of State under [s 54 of the 1971 Act]'.

The contention of counsel for the rating authority was that the words in s 54(9) 'for
the purposes of the provisions of this Act relating to listed buildings' confined the effect
of what is provided in the subsection, namely the widening of the definition of 'listed
building', to the provisions of the 1971 Act. It could not be taken into account for the
j purposes of Sch 1 to the 1967 Act. I entirely agree with the view expressed by my noble
and learned friend Lord Keith, whose speech in draft I have had the privilege of reading,
that this proposition is ill-founded. If a structure is by virtue of the 1971 Act to be treated
as a part of a building which has been expressly included in the list, it cannot cease to be
so treated for the purposes of some other Act which itself makes special provision
(exemption from rates in certain circumstances) for buildings which are included in the
list.

The fact that the rating authority was willing to accept the Court of Appeal's construction of the words 'structure' as used in s 54(9) of the 1971 Act and its almost total *a* absence of enthusiasm in espousing the critical comments of that decision made by your Lordships during the course of argument, is not and cannot in any sense be decisive of the point. If the Court of Appeal in the *Calderdale* case and in the instant appeal has misinterpreted those words, then your Lordships must so declare. However, the course which the rating authority's argument took, particularly when it stressed at the outset of the appeal the importance of its success in the appeal, is not lightly to be dismissed. It *b* certainly suggests that if the Court of Appeal was in error in the *Calderdale* case and/or in this case, that error is not easily discernible. For the reasons which I now set out I am unable to discern the error and accordingly I would have dismissed this appeal.

1   *The literal interpretation of the words 'structure fixed to'*
It has at no time been disputed that 'structure' in its ordinary everyday sense includes *c* a building. Section 290 of the 1971 Act is the definition section. It does not define 'structure'. It provides, however, that except so far as the context otherwise requires, building 'includes any structure or erection and any part of a building, as so defined, but does not include plant or machinery comprised in a building'. Thus, the power given by s 54 of the 1971 Act to the Secretary of State to compile lists of buildings of special architectural or historic interest includes the power to list a part only of a building. Thus, *d* it is accepted that if the Secretary of State should include in the list only the facade of a building, as indeed we are told he does from time to time, then by virtue of s 54(9) the whole building, that is the structure of which the facade is but a part, falls to be treated as part of that which is expressly included in the list, ie the facade.
But in the example given above, what is the building? The facade, the 'listed building', may only extend across part of the face of the original building, let alone the original *e* building as subsequently extended. Clearly on a literal interpretation of the words of sub-s (9) every part of the building, original or extended, is 'a structure fixed to' the listed building, the facade, and is by virtue of the subsection to be treated as part of the facade. Thus far, I believe, there is no dispute. Yet to treat such a structure as ancillary or subordinate or as a feature of the facade would, to my mind, be quite unrealistic. *f*
Approaching the matter from another angle, one can well envisage a listed Georgian mansion, far too large to provide a convenient private residence, whose optimum, or most profitable use, bearing in mind its situation and the size of its grounds, is that of a high class hotel. However, for such a development considerable extensions and alterations are necessary to provide more bedroom accommodation, conference halls and other facilities. Clearly such alterations and extensions would affect the character of the *g* Georgian mansion and accordingly listed building consent would be required (see s 55). If the consent were to be given on terms, inter alia, that the extensions should be achieved by building two extensive wings onto the Georgian mansion, again quite clearly on a literal interpretation of the words of s 54(9) the wings, when built, would fall to be treated as part of the Georgian mansion.
However, assume that the extra accommodation which is contemplated as being *h* necessary to make the development a success would so dwarf the listed building, if it were to consist of two wings built onto the listed building, that listed building consent is only given on terms that two large buildings were erected on either side of the listed building, but each connected thereto with a bridge. Again, applying the ordinary meaning to the word 'structure', each of those new buldings would by reason of the terms of s 54(9) be treated as part of the listed building. *j*

2   *The purposive approach*
The purpose of 'listing' buildings is to ensure the protection and enhancement of the local heritage of buildings. This is achieved by making it an offence for a person to execute 'any works for the demolition of a listed building or for its alteration or extension

in any manner which would affect its character as a building of special architectural or
a historic interest' (s 55(1)). To confine this control to the building which is expressly
included in the list, because of its special architectural or historic interest, may be often
quite insufficient: the example of the Georgian facade referred to above is but one
obvious example. Hence the extended definition of 'listed building' contained in s 54(9).
If the two additional buildings connected to the Georgian mansion in the example given
above are not, when built, to be treated as part of the mansion, the purpose of the Act
b would be frustrated. Listed building consent would not have been necessary in the first
instance and demolition of *one* of the new buildings, thereby destroying the whole
harmony of the development, could take place at the whim of the owner. It is common
ground that no planning permission would be required for such demolition and that the
building bye-law control is only designed to ensure that the physical stability of the
remaining building is not affected, that control not being concerned with aesthetics.
c Thus, both the ordinary meaning of the words used in s 54(9) and the very purpose of
the legislation strongly supports the proposition that the word 'structure' covers any
building and therefore includes the Kingly Street building. It is not disputed that it was
'fixed to', that is joined onto, the Regent Street building both by the underground tunnel
and by the footbridge. Moreover, it formed part of the land and was comprised within
d the curtilage of the Regent Street building.

3 *Does the context require a different meaning from that normally associated with the ordinary*
use of the word?
In the *Calderdale* case 46 P & CR 399 there was a terrace of cottages, a mill and a bridge
which linked the two. The mill was expressly included in the list but the terrace was not.
The issue was whether listed building consent was necessary for the demolition of the
e terrace? Skinner J, dealing with the first limb of s 54(9) held that the terrace was not a
'structure fixed to' the mill, on the ground, not argued by counsel or put to them by the
judge, that the terrace could not be both fixed to the mill and comprised in the curtilage
of the mill and that the two alternative limbs of s 54(9) were mutually exclusive. He
then proceeded to give his reasons for holding that the terrace was within the curtilage
f of the mill. The Court of Appeal rejected this proposition, concluding that a structure
can be both fixed to a listed building and comprised within its curtilage, as indeed had
been common ground before the judge. No reliance was placed in your Lordship's House
on this aspect of Skinner J's decision.
Skinner J's interpretation of the first limb of the s 54(9) was designed to avoid what he
considered was the incongruity of deciding, in accordance with the ordinary sense of the
g words of the subsection, not only that the first of the cottages was fixed to the mill but so
was the whole terrace.
Stephenson LJ in the *Calderdale* case 46 P & CR 399 at 405 expressly accepted that the
literal construction could give rise to incongruity. He said:

h 'A multiple store adjacent to the birthplace of a statesman might have to be
treated as part of the birthplace because it was a structure fixed to it. A block of flats
replacing the stables of a mansion house might have to be treated as part of the
mansion because [they are] within the curtilage of the mansion.'

However, he concluded, rightly in my judgment, that the theoretical absurdities are
fairly met by the nature of the control imposed on listed buildings and all their parts,
actual and deemed. The code of listed building control does not *prevent* demolition or
j alteration or extension. It merely requires *consent* to such works. As counsel for the rating
authority emphasised, there is likely to be far less difficulty in obtaining permission to
demolish, alter or extend a structure fixed to a building which has not been expressly
referred to in the list, since ex hypothesi it is not of itself of sufficient architectural or
historic interest to merit specific mention.
In the *Calderdale* case a subsidiary argument, not taken before the judge, was raised in

the notice of appeal. This argument, which was rejected by the Court of Appeal and not in terms adopted by counsel for the rating authority in your Lordships' House has *a* apparently found some favour with your Lordships. As I understand it, it proceeds as follows. Section 54(2) of the 1971 Act provides:

> 'In considering whether to include a building in a list compiled or approved under this section, the Secretary of State may take into account not only the building itself but also . . . (*b*) the desirability of preserving on the ground of its architectural *b* or historic interest, *any feature of the building consisting of* a manmade object or structure fixed to the building or forming part of the land and comprised within the curtilage of the building.'

The submission in the *Calderdale* case was that the words which I have emphasised were intended by the draftsman to be included in s 54(9) immediately prior to the words 'any object or structure fixed to a building' thereby qualifying and very substantially *c* limiting the ordinary meaning, inter alia, of the word 'structure' to a mere feature or characteristic of the building which has been expressly listed. Thus the words in s 54(9), with which your Lordships are concerned, are said to be mere shorthand for the words in s 54(2)(*b*).

I cannot attribute to the draftsman of s 54 some invincible repugnance to repeat in s 54(9) some eight words which he had used in an earlier subsection of the same section. *d* The words in s 54(2)(*b*) are used in a quite different context, namely in the context of the factors, other than the building, which the Secretary of State may take into account when considering whether or not to include a building in the list. Section 54(2)(*b*) empowers the Secretary of State to list a building which may have little or no architectural or historic interest if it includes a special feature, e g a staircase, a painted ceiling or a seventeenth century folly within its grounds. That subsection is not concerned with *e* extending the definition of 'listed building'. If such a narrow construction is acceptable then it really defeats the purpose of the 1971 Act.

However, I do not understand your Lordships to limit 'structures' to mere features or characteristics of the building expressly included in the list. Your Lordships are prepared to accept that 'structure' has a wider meaning and includes a separate building providing *f* it is ancillary or subordinate or an accessory to the building expressly included in the list. Your Lordships would not therefore overrule the decision in the *Calderdale* case, that the terrace of cottages were a 'structure fixed to' the mill, but would not accept the width of the reasoning of Stephenson LJ.

The only support for this approach appears to me to be a combination of the language of s 54(2)(*b*) and the incongruity argument. With all proper respect, I cannot accept that *g* this provides sufficient justification for departing so radically from the ordinary meaning of the words in s 54(9) and the very purpose for which they were used.

However, to my mind, even on that interpretation, the Kingly Street building qualified to be treated as part of the Regent Street building. It was attached to the main shop in order to extend its shopping facilities. Understandably listed building consent was thought to be necessary for the removal of the connecting footbridge and this was *h* accordingly applied for and granted prior to its demolition in March 1983. The Kingly Street building was used as a subordinate part of the main shop and an ancillary thereto. It was, as Fox LJ aptly described it, an annexe. It is thus in no way surprising that it, together with the main shop in the Regent Street building, formed a single hereditament for rating purposes.

j

Appeal allowed.

Solicitors: *G Matthew Ives* (For the appellants); *Forsyte Kerman* (for the respondents).

Mary Rose Plummer   Barrister.

a # Rainey v Greater Glasgow Health Board

HOUSE OF LORDS

LORD KEITH OF KINKEL, LORD BRANDON OF OAKBROOK, LORD GRIFFITHS, LORD MACKAY OF CLASHFERN AND LORD GOFF OF CHIEVELEY

6, 7 OCTOBER, 27 NOVEMBER 1986

b

Employment – Equality of treatment of men and women – Variation between woman's and man's contracts due to material difference other than sex – Material difference – Circumstances to be considered – Employers forced to recruit particular employees at higher wage than other employees having similar qualifications and experience – Recruited employees all men – Whether circumstances in which recruited employees employed relevant – Whether 'material difference' relating only to personal circumstances or qualities of employees – Whether economic factors affecting efficient running of employer's business relevant – Equal Pay Act 1970, s 1(3).

In 1979 the Scottish health department decided to discontinue the specialist prosthetic service provided by private contractors and to engage full-time prosthetists to be employed within the national health service on the appropriate civil service pay scale. However, in order to recruit prosthetists from the private contractors for the new service the department offered to prosthetists employed by the private contractors the option of entering the national health service on the civil service scale or on the basis of the pay and conditions offered by the private contractors, such pay being considerably higher than that paid under the civil service scale. Twenty prosthetists, including C, all of whom happened to be men, employed by the private contractors opted to join the national health service on the private sector pay and conditions. The appellant, a woman, later entered the employment of the national health service direct as a prosthetist and was paid according to the appropriate civil service scale. Because of the disparity between her pay and that of C, whose qualifications and experience were broadly similar, the appellant applied to an industrial tribunal under the Equal Pay Act 1970 for a declaration that she was entitled to the same pay as C. At the date of the tribunal hearing C was being paid £10,085 and the appellant £7,295. The tribunal dismissed the appellant's application on the ground that the difference in salary between the appellant and C was 'genuinely due to a material difference (other than difference of sex) between her case and his' and therefore the equality requirements of the 1970 Act were excluded by s 1(3)ᵃ of that Act. On appeal, both the Employment Appeal Tribunal and the Court of Session upheld that decision. The appellant appealed to the House of Lords, contending that only a difference relating to the personal circumstances of the two employees, such as their respective skills, experience or training, could be a 'material difference' for the purposes of s 1(3).

Held – On the true construction of s 1(3) of the 1970 Act a 'material difference' between a male and a female employee which had the effect of excluding the equality requirements of the 1970 Act was not restricted to the circumstances or qualities personal to the employees concerned but embraced all the significant and relevant circumstances, including, where relevant, differences connected with economic factors affecting the efficient running of the employer's business. Since there had been sound reasons for offering C and other prosthetists employed by the private contractors more than the civil service rates of pay in order to attract them to enter national health service employment, effectively C was being paid more than the norm rather than the appellant being paid less. Furthermore, the fact that the appellant was a woman and C a man was fortuitous. It followed that there was a material difference between the appellant's case and C's for the purpose of s 1(3) of the 1970 Act and therefore the equality provisions of that Act did not apply. The appeal would accordingly be dismissed (see p 70 *a* to *c*, p 72 *f* to *j* and p 73 *d* to *f j* to p 74 *c*, post).

---

a   Section 1(3) is set out at p 68 *a*, post

Jenkins v Kingsgate (Clothing Productions) Ltd [1981] 1 WLR 972 and *Bilka-Kaufhaus GmbH v Weber von Hartz* [1986] IRLR 317 applied.   *a*

Notes

For equal treatment of men and women as regards terms and conditions of employment, see 16 Halsbury's Laws (4th edn) para 767.

For the Equal Pay Act 1970, s 1, see 16 Halsbury's Statutes (4th edn) 188.   *b*

Cases referred to in opinions

Bilka-Kaufhaus GmbH v Weber von Hartz Case 170/84 [1986] IRLR 317, CJEC.
Clay Cross (Quarry Services) Ltd v Fletcher [1979] 1 All ER 474, [1978] 1 WLR 1429, CA.
Jenkins v Kingsgate (Clothing Productions) Ltd Case 96/80 [1981] 1 WLR 972, [1981] ECR 911, CJEC; *subsequent proceedings* [1981] 1 WLR 1485, EAT.
Shields v E Coomes (Holdings) Ltd [1979] 1 All ER 456, [1978] 1 WLR 1408, CA.   *c*

Appeal

Mrs Elizabeth Anne Rainey, who was employed as a prosthetist by the respondents, the Greater Glasgow Health Board, appealed against the interlocutor of the First Division of the Inner House of the Court of Session in Scotland (the Lord President (Lord Emslie) and Lord Cameron, Lord Grieve dissenting) ([1985] IRLR 414) on 3 July 1985 dismissing   *d* her appeal against the decision of the Employment Appeal Tribunal (Lord McDonald and Mr W Barrie Abbott, Mr J S Bell dissenting) ([1984] IRLR 88) on 26 October 1983 dismissing her appeal against the decision of an industrial tribunal dated 11 April 1983 which had dismissed her application under the Equal Pay Act 1970 for a declaration that she was entitled to the same pay as Mr Alan Crumlin, who was employed by the respondents on like work. The facts are set out in the opinion of Lord Keith.   *e*

Anthony Lester QC and *David Pannick* for the appellant.
W A Nimmo Smith QC and *Ann Paton* (both of the Scottish Bar) for the respondents.

Their Lordships took time for consideration.   *f*

27 November. The following opinions were delivered.

LORD KEITH OF KINKEL. My Lords, this appeal from an interlocutor of the First Division of the Inner House, which affirmed the decisions of an industrial tribunal and of the Employment Appeal Tribunal, is concerned with the proper construction of   *g* certain provisions of the Equal Pay Act 1970.

The appellant, a woman, has since 1 October 1980 been employed by the respondents, the Greater Glasgow Health Board, at the Belvidere Hospital, Glasgow, as a prosthetist. A prosthetist is one who is concerned with the fitting of artificial limbs. Before 1980 no prosthetist was directly employed by any health authority in Scotland. The requisite   *h* services were provided by private contractors themselves employing qualified prosthetists who worked in a number of hospitals, including Belvidere Hospital. One of these was a Mr Alan Crumlin. In 1979 the Secretary of State for Scotland decided to establish a prosthetic fitting service within the national health service in Scotland, and to discontinue the arrangement under which the service was provided by private contractors. To achieve this object it was necessary that a sufficient number of qualified prosthetists should be   *j* recruited to the national health service en bloc. The only prosthetists then available were those employed by the private contractors. The remuneration of employees of the national health service is determined by negotiation and agreement in the Whitley Councils for the Health Services (Great Britain). It was decided by the Scottish Home and Health Department that, in general, the remuneration of employees in the new prosthetic

service should be related to the Whitley Council scale, and that the appropriate scale for
a them would be that for medical physics technicians. Since, however, it was appreciated
this might not be attractive to the prosthetists in the employment of private contractors,
whom it was desired to recruit en bloc, it was decided to offer them an option. That
option, as set out in a letter from the department to Mr Crumlin dated 11 January 1980,
was either to come into the national health service on national health service rates of pay
and conditions of service or to remain on the rates of pay and conditions of service which
b he presently received, subject to future changes as negotiated by his trade union, the
Association of Scientific, Technical and Managerial Staffs (the ASTMS), for the prosthetists
employed by contractors. It is to be observed that in England prosthetic services were to
continue to be provided through private contractors. Mr Crumlin and all the other
prosthetists who received the offer (about 20 in number, who all happened to be men)
opted for the second alternative. This meant that they retained their existing salaries, and
c that future increases were to be negotiated with the ASTMS and not the Whitley Council.
Mr Crumlin commenced employment with the national health service at Belvidere
Hospital in July 1980 at the salary of £6,680 per annum, the same as he had been
receiving from his former employer. At the time of the hearing before the industrial
tribunal, on 23 March 1983, it had increased to £10,085 per annum.
    The appellant entered the employment of the national health service as a prosthetist
d working at Belvidere Hospital on 1 October 1980. She did so direct, not having been
previously employed by a private contractor. Her qualifications and experience were
broadly similar to those of Mr Crumlin. The rates of pay and conditions of service offered
to and accepted by her corresponded to those of a medical physics technician at the
appropriate point on the Whitley Council scale. Her starting salary was £4,773, and at
the time of the hearing before the industrial tribunal it had increased to £7,295. A male
e prosthetist, Mr Davey, was engaged at the same time and on the same conditions. He has
since left his employment.
    No prosthetists have since 1980 transferred from private employment to national
health service employment, and no such transfers on special terms will be permitted in
the future. Any prosthetists engaged by the respondents in the future, whether male or
female, will do so on the national health service scale of remuneration. No arrangements
f have been made for phasing out the disparity between the prosthetists who transferred
from the private sector in 1980, such as Mr Crumlin, and those who entered the national
health service employment directly, such as the appellant.
    In these circumstances, the appellant applied to an industrial tribunal, under the Equal
Pay Act 1970, for a declaration that she was entitled to the same pay as Mr Crumlin.
    The appellant founded on s 1(1) and (2)(a) of the 1970 Act, which provide (as
g substituted by s 8(1) of the Sex Discrimination Act 1975):

    '(1) If the terms of a contract under which a woman is employed at an
    establishment in Great Britain do not include (directly or by reference to a collective
    agreement or otherwise) an equality clause they shall be deemed to include one.
h   (2) . . . (a) where the woman is employed on like work with a man in the same
    employment—(i) if, (apart from the equality clause) any term of the woman's
    contract is or becomes less favourable to the woman than a term of a similar kind in
    the contract under which that man is employed, that term of the woman's contract
    shall be treated as so modified as not to be less favourable, and (ii) if (apart from the
    quality clause) at any time the woman's contract does not include a term
j   corresponding to a term benefiting that man included in the contract under which
    he is employed, the woman's contract shall be treated as including such a term . . .'

    The respondents did not dispute that the appellant was employed on like work with
Mr Crumlin, nor that the term of her contract as regards remuneration was less
favourable than the corresponding term of Mr Crumlin's contract. They founded on

s 1(3) of the 1970 Act and undertook the burden of satisfying its provisions, which at the
material time were in these terms: *a*

> 'An equality clause shall not operate in relation to a variation between the
> woman's contract and the man's contract if the employer proves that the variation
> is genuinely due to a material difference (other than the difference of sex) between
> her case and his.'

The industrial tribunal dismissed the appellant's application. Having narrated the facts   *b*
of the case as found by them and the contentions of the parties they stated:

> 'Having considered the evidence the tribunal is satisfied that what has caused the
> difference in the salary scale of the applicant and Mr Crumlin is not market forces
> but is the fact that Mr Crumlin is paid on a scale negotiated and agreed between his
> trade union and the Scottish Home and Health Department whereas the [appellant]   *c*
> is paid according to a different scale. The scale on which the [appellant] is paid is an
> ad hoc scale and not one which has been negotiated between her trade union and
> the Scottish Home and Health Department. There was clear evidence that any male
> employees recruited at the same time as or after the recruitment of the [appellant]
> would be paid the same rate as the [appellant] was and subject to the same scale. We
> had no doubt on the evidence that had any of the prosthetists employed by the   *d*
> private contractors been female they would have been paid the same higher rate of
> pay as the male prosthetists transferred from the private contractor. The tribunal
> were therefore forced to the conclusion that the difference had nothing to do with
> the fact that the [appellant] was female. We were satisfied that the reason for the
> difference was because of the different method of entry and had nothing to do with
> sex. The application must therefore be dismissed.'   *e*

The appellant appealed to the Employment Appeal Tribunal, which, by a majority,
dismissed the appeal (see [1984] IRLR 88). A further appeal to the Court of Session was
also dismissed by the First Division of the Inner House (the Lord President (Lord Emslie)
and Lord Cameron, Lord Grieve dissenting) (see [1985] IRLR 414).

The facts found by the industrial tribunal make it clear that the Secretary of State for   *f*
Scotland decided, as a matter of general policy, that the Whitley Council scale of
remuneration and negotiating machinery, which applied throughout the national health
service in Scotland, was appropriate for employees in the prosthetic service. It was also
decided that the appropriate part of the scale for such employees was that applicable to
medical physics technicians, presumably because the nature of their work was considered
comparable to that of the prosthetists. So all direct entrants to the service, whether male
or female, were to be placed on that part of the scale and made subject to Whitley Council   *g*
negotiations. But it was apparent that the new service would not get off the ground
unless a sufficient number of the prosthetists in the employment of the private contractors
could be attracted into it. So the further policy decision was taken to offer these
prosthetists the option of entering the service at their existing salaries and subject to the
ASTMS negotiating machinery. As it happened, all the prosthetists privately employed   *h*
were male. In the result, Mr Crumlin had the benefit of the offer and so emerged with a
higher salary and better prospects for an increase than did the appellant, who did not
have that benefit.

The main question at issue in the appeal is whether those circumstances are capable in
law of constituting, within the meaning of s 1(3) of the 1970 Act, 'a material difference
(other than the difference of sex) between her case and his'.   *j*

Counsel for the appellant argued that nothing can constitute such a difference which
is not related to the personal circumstances of the two employees, such as their respective
skills, experience or training. Reliance was placed on the decision of the Court of Appeal
in *Clay Cross (Quarry Services) Ltd v Fletcher* [1979] 1 All ER 474, [1978] 1 WLR 1429. In
that case a woman sales clerk was employed at a lower wage than a male sales clerk who
had been engaged at a later date. The employers relied, as being the material difference

between her case and his, on the circumstance that the male clerk had been the only
a suitable applicant for the post and that he had refused to accept it unless he was paid the
same wage as he had received in his previous job. The Employment Appeal Tribunal had
accepted this as discharging the onus on the employers under s 1(3) of the 1970 Act, but
their decision was reversed by the Court of Appeal. Lord Denning MR said ([1979] 1 All
ER 474 at 477, [1978] 1 WLR 1429 at 1433):

> 'The issue depends on whether there is a material difference (other than sex)
b > between her case and his. Take heed to the words "between her case and his". They
> show that the tribunal is to have regard to *her* and to *him*, to the personal equation of
> the woman as compared to that of the man, irrespective of any extrinsic forces
> which led to the variation in pay. As I said in *Shields v E Coomes (Holdings) Ltd* [1979]
> 1 All ER 456 at 464, [1978] 1 WLR 1408 at 1418, the subsection applies when "the
> personal equation of the man is such that he deserves to be paid at a higher rate than
c > the woman". Thus the personal equation of the man may warrant a wage differential
> if he has much longer length of service; or has superior skill or qualifications; or
> gives bigger output or productivity; or has been placed, owing to down-grading, in
> a protected pay category, vividly described as "red circled"; or to other circumstances
> personal to him in doing his job. But the tribunal is not to have regard to any
d > extrinsic forces which have led to the man being paid more. An employer cannot
> avoid his obligations under the 1970 Act by saying: "I paid him more because he
> asked for more", or "I paid her less because she was willing to come for less". If any
> such excuse were permitted, the Act would be a dead letter. Those are the very
> reasons why there was unequal pay before the statute. They are the very
> circumstances in which the statute was intended to operate. Nor can the employer
e > avoid his obligations by giving the reasons why he submitted to the extrinsic forces.
> As for instance by saying: "He asked for that sum because it was what he was getting
> in his previous job", or "He was the only applicant for the job, so I had no option".
> In such cases the employer may beat his breast, and say: "I did not pay him more
> because he was a man. I paid it because he was the only suitable person who applied
> for the job. Man or woman made no difference to me." Those are reasons personal
f > to the employer. If any such reasons were permitted as an excuse, the door would
> be wide open. Every employer who wished to avoid the statute would walk straight
> through it.'

Lawton LJ said ([1979] 1 All ER 474 at 480, [1978] 1 WLR 1429 at 1437):

> 'What does s 1(3) in its context in both the Equal Pay Act 1970 and the Sex
g > Discrimination Act 1975 mean? The context is important. The overall object of
> both Acts is to ensure that women are treated no less favourably than men. If a
> woman is treated less favourably than a man there is a presumption of discrimination
> which can only be rebutted in the sphere of employment if the employer brings
> himself within s 1(3). He cannot do so merely by proving that he did not intend to
h > discriminate. There are more ways of discriminating against women than by
> deliberately setting out to do so: see s 1(1)(b) of the Sex Discrimination Act 1975. If
> lack of intention had provided a lawful excuse for variation, s 1(3) would surely
> have been worded differently. The variation must have been genuinely due to (that
> is, caused by) a material difference (that is, one which was relevant and real) between
> (and now come the important words) her case and his. What is her case? And what
j > is his? In my judgment her case embraces what appertains to her *in* her job, such as
> the qualifications she brought to it, the length of time she has been in it, the skill
> she has acquired, the responsibilities she has undertaken and where and under what
> conditions she has to do it. It is on this kind of basis that her case is to be compared
> with that of the man. What does not appertain to her job or to his are the
> circumstances in which they came to be employed. These are collateral to the jobs
> as such.'

In my opinion these statements are unduly restrictive of the proper interpretation of
s 1(3). The difference must be 'material', which I would construe as meaning 'significant *a*
and relevant', and it must be between 'her case and his'. Consideration of a person's case
must necessarily involve consideration of all the circumstances of that case. These may
well go beyond what is not very happily described as 'the personal equation', i e the
personal qualities by way of skill, experience or training which the individual brings to
the job. Some circumstances may on examination prove to be not significant or not
relevant, but others may do so, though not relating to the personal qualities of the *b*
employee. In particular, where there is no question of intentional sex discrimination,
whether direct or indirect (and there is none here), a difference which is connected with
economic factors affecting the efficient carrying on of the employer's business or other
activity may well be relevant.

This view is supported by two decisions of the Court of Justice of the European
Communities on the interpretation of art 119 of the EEC Treaty, requiring the application *c*
'of the principle that men and women should receive equal pay for equal work', and to
the implementation of which the Equal Pay Act 1970 is directed. The first of these
decisions is *Jenkins v Kingsgate (Clothing Productions) Ltd* Case 96/80 [1981] 1 WLR 972,
which originated in the Employment Appeal Tribunal in England. A company employed
full-time and part-time workers on like work, but paid the latter, almost all of whom
were female, less than the former, who were predominantly male. The company claimed *d*
that it did so in order to encourage full-time work and hence achieve fuller utilisation of
machinery, and this was accepted by an industrial tribunal as discharging the onus under
s 1(3). The Employment Appeal Tribunal referred to the European Court questions
directed to ascertaining whether the employers' policy constituted a contravention of art
119. The court's answer was (at 982–983):
e

'9. It appears from the first three questions and the reasons stated in the order
making the reference that the national court is principally concerned to know
whether a difference in the level of pay for work carried out part-time and the same
work carried out full-time may amount to discrimination of a kind prohibited by
article 119 of the Treaty when the category of part-time workers is exclusively or *f*
predominantly comprised of women. 10. The answer to the questions thus
understood is that the purpose of article 119 is to ensure the application of the
principle of equal pay for men and women for the same work. The differences in
pay prohibited by that provision are therefore exclusively those based on the
difference of the sex of the workers. Consequently the fact that part-time work is
paid at an hourly rate lower than pay for full-time work does not amount per se to
discrimination prohibited by article 119 provided that the hourly rates are applied *g*
to workers belonging to either category without distinction based on sex. 11. If
there is no such distinction, therefore, the fact that work paid at time rates is
remunerated at an hourly rate which varies according to the number of hours
worked per week does not offend against the principle of equal pay laid down in
article 119 of the Treaty in so far as the difference in pay between part-time work *h*
and full-time work is attributable to factors which are objectively justified and are
in no way related to any discrimination based on sex. 12. Such may be the case, in
particular, when by giving hourly rates of pay which are lower for part-time work
than those for full-time work the employer is endeavouring, on economic grounds
which may be objectively justified, to encourage full-time work irrespective of the
sex of the worker. 13. By contrast, if it is established that a considerably smaller *j*
percentage of women than of men perform the minimum number of weekly
working hours required in order to be able to claim the full-time hourly rate of pay,
the inequality in pay will be contrary to article 119 of the Treaty where, regard
being had to the difficulties encountered by women in arranging to work that
minimum number of hours per week, the pay policy of the undertaking in question

cannot be explained by factors other than discrimination based on sex. 14. Where
a   the hourly rate of pay differs according to whether the work is part-time or full-
time it is for the national courts to decide in each individual case whether, regard
being had to the facts of the case, its history and the employer's intention, a pay
policy such as that which is at issue in the main proceedings although represented
as a difference based on weekly working hours is or is not in reality discrimination
based on the sex of the worker. 15. The reply to the first three questions must
b   therefore be that a difference in pay between full-time workers and part-time
workers does not amount to discrimination prohibited by article 119 of the Treaty
unless it is in reality merely an indirect way of reducing the level of pay of part-time
workers on the ground that that group of workers is composed exclusively or
predominantly of women.'

c   The formal ruling of the court was (at 984):

'1. A difference in pay between full-time workers and part-time workers does not
amount to discrimination prohibited by article 119 of the Treaty unless it is in
reality merely an indirect way of reducing the pay of part-time workers on the
ground that that group of workers is composed exclusively or predominantly of
d   women. 2. Where the national court is able, using the criteria of equal work and
equal pay, without the operation of Community or national measures, to establish
that the payment of lower hourly rates of remuneration for part-time work than for
full-time work represents discrimination based on difference of sex the provisions
of article 119 of the Treaty apply directly to such a situation.'

e   When the case was again before the Employment Appeal Tribunal, Browne-
Wilkinson J, delivering judgment, accepted that the ruling of the European Court
established that a differential in pay between part-time workers, who are predominantly
women, and full-time male workers can be justified as being a material difference by
showing that the pay differential does in fact achieve economic advantages for the
employer (see [1981] 1 WLR 1485 at 1492). He found difficulty, however, in elucidating
f   whether the judgment and ruling of the European Court meant that it was sufficient for
the employer to show that he had no intention of discriminating because his pay practice
was directed to some legitimate economic objective, or that he must show that the
practice was in fact reasonably necessary in order to achieve that objective. In the result,
he took the view that if art 119 as construed by the European Court was satisfied if the
employer met the less demanding criterion, nevertheless s 1(3) of the 1970 Act went
g   further than that and required the employer to meet the more demanding one. This
view is encapsulated in this passage (at 1495):

'(4) If the industrial tribunal finds that the employer intended to discriminate
against women by paying part-time workers less, the employer cannot succeed
under section 1(3). (5) Even if the employers had no such intention, for section 1(3)
h   to apply the employer must show that the difference in pay between full-time and
part-time workers is reasonably necessary in order to obtain some result (other than
cheap female labour) which the employer desires for economic or other reasons.'

In the result, the case was remitted to the industrial tribunal to find whether the lower
rate of pay for part-time workers was in fact reasonably necessary in order to enable the
j   employers to reduce absenteeism and to obtain the maximum utilisation of their plant.
The European Court had occasion to consider the question afresh in *Bilka-Kaufhaus
GmbH v Weber von Hartz* Case 170/84 [1986] IRLR 317. A German department store
operated an occupational pension scheme for its employees, under which part-time
employees were eligible for pensions only if they had worked full-time for at least 15
years over a total period of 20 years. That provision affected disproportionately more

women than men. A female part-time employee claimed that the provision contravened
art 119 of the EEC Treaty. The employers contended that it was based on objectively *a*
justified economic grounds, in that it encouraged full-time work which resulted in lower
ancillary costs and the utilisation of staff throughout opening hours. The European Court
by its decision made it clear that it was not sufficient for the employers merely to show
absence of any intention to discriminate, saying (at 320–321):

> 'It is for the national court, which has sole jurisdiction to make findings of fact, to *b*
> determine whether and to what extent the grounds put forward by an employer to
> explain the adoption of a pay practice which applies independently of a worker's sex
> but in fact affects more women than men may be regarded as objectively justified
> economic grounds. If the national court finds that the measures chosen by Bilka
> correspond to a real need on the part of the undertaking, are appropriate with a view
> to achieving the objectives pursued and are necessary to that end, the fact that the *c*
> measures affect a far greater number of women than men is not sufficient to show
> that they constitute an infringement of Article 119. The answer to question 2(a)
> must therefore be that under Article 119 a department store company may justify
> the adoption of a pay policy excluding part-time workers, irrespective of their sex,
> from its occupational pension scheme on the ground that it seeks to employ as few
> part-time workers as possible, where it is found that the means chosen for achieving *d*
> that objective correspond to a real need on the part of the undertaking, are
> appropriate with a view to achieving the objective in question and are necessary to
> that end.'

It therefore appears that the European Court has resolved the doubts expressed by
Browne-Wilkinson J in *Jenkins v Kingsgate (Clothing Productions) Ltd* and established that
the true meaning and effect of art 119 in this particular context is the same as that there *e*
attributed to s 1(3) of the 1970 Act by the Employment Appeal Tribunal. Although the
European Court at one point refers to 'economic' grounds objectively justified, whereas
Browne-Wilkinson J speaks of 'economic or other reasons', I consider that read as a whole
the ruling of the European Court would not exclude objectively justified grounds which
are other than economic, such as administrative efficiency in a concern not engaged in *f*
commerce or business.

The decision of the European Court on art 119 must be accepted as authoritative and
the judgment of the Employment Appeal Tribunal on s 1(3) of the 1970 Act, which in
my opinion is correct, is in harmony with it. There is now no reason to construe s 1(3) as
conferring greater rights on a worker in this context than does art 119 of the Treaty. It
follows that a relevant difference for purposes of s 1(3) may relate to circumstances other *g*
than the personal qualifications or merits of the male and female workers who are the
subject of comparison.

In the present case the difference between the case of the appellant and that of Mr
Crumlin is that the former is a person who entered the national health service at Belvidere
Hospital direct while the latter is a person who entered it from employment with a
private contractor. The fact that one is a woman and the other a man is an accident. The *h*
findings of the industrial tribunal make it clear that the new prosthetic service could
never have been established within a reasonable time if Mr Crumlin and others like him
had not been offered a scale of remuneration no less favourable than that which they
were then enjoying. That was undoubtedly a good and objectively justified ground for
offering him that scale of remuneration. But it was argued for the appellant that it did
not constitute a good and objectively justified reason for paying the appellant and other *j*
direct entrants a lower scale of remuneration. This aspect does not appear to have been
specifically considered by either of the tribunals or by their Lordships of the First
Division, apart from Lord Grieve, who said ([1985] IRLR 414 at 425):

> 'I accept that the facts which provided the evidence before both Tribunals were
> sufficient to explain why Mr Crumlin (and his colleagues) were paid on a scale

a   equivalent to that which they had been receiving while employed in the private
    sector, but in my opinion that evidence is not sufficient to explain why, when the
    National [Health] Service door was opened to the appellant (and other prosthetists
    not previously employed in the private sector) the appellant (and her fellow
    prosthetists) were paid on a lower scale. In the absence of a reasonable explanation
    as to why the appellant was paid on a lower scale than Mr Crumlin I am of opinion
    that the respondents have not discharged the onus placed upon them by s. 1(3) of
b   the 1970 Act, and that the majority of the Employment Appeal Tribunal were not
    entitled on the facts before them to conclude that they had.'

    The position in 1980 was that all national health service employees were paid on the
    Whitley Council scale, and that the Whitley Council negotiating machinery applied to
    them. The prosthetic service was intended to be a branch of the national health service.
c   It is therefore easy to see that from the administrative point of view it would have been
    highly anomalous and inconvenient if prosthetists alone, over the whole tract of future
    time for which the prosthetic service would endure, were to have been subject to a
    different salary scale and different negotiating machinery. It is significant that a large
    part of the difference which has opened up between the appellant's salary and Mr
    Crumlin's is due to the different negotiating machinery. Accordingly, there were sound
d   objectively justified administrative reasons, in my view, for placing prosthetists in
    general, men and women alike, on the Whitley Council scale and subjecting them to its
    negotiating machinery. There is no suggestion that it was unreasonable to place them on
    the particular point on the Whitley Council scale which was in fact selected, ascertained
    by reference to the position of medical physics technicians and entirely regardless of sex.
    It is in any event the fact that the general scale of remuneration for prosthetists was laid
e   down accordingly by the Secretary of State. It was not a question of the appellant being
    paid less than the norm but of Mr Crumlin being paid more. He was paid more because
    of the necessity to attract him and other privately employed prosthetists into forming
    the nucleus of the new service.
        I am therefore of the opinion that the grounds founded on by the respondents as
    constituting the material difference between the appellant's case and that of Mr Crumlin
f   were capable in law of constituting a relevant difference for purposes of s 1(3) of the 1970
    Act, and that on the facts found by the industrial tribunal they were objectively justified.
        Counsel for the appellant put forward an argument based on s 1(1)(b) of the Sex
    Discrimination Act 1975 (with which the 1970 Act is to be read as one: see Shields v E
    Coomes (Holdings) Ltd [1979] 1 All ER 456 at 463, [1978] 1 WLR 1408 at 1416), which is
g   in these terms:

        'A person discriminates against a woman in any circumstances relevant for the
        purposes of any provision of this Act if . . . (b) he applies to her a requirement or
        condition which he applies or would apply equally to a man but—(i) which is such
        that the proportion of women who can comply with it is considerably smaller than
        the proportion of men who can comply with it, and (ii) which he cannot show to be
h   justifiable irrespective of the sex of the person to whom it is applied, and (iii) which
        is to her detriment because she cannot comply with it.'

    This provision has the effect of prohibiting indirect discrimination between women and
    men. In my opinion it does not, for present purposes, add anything to s 1(3) of the 1970
    Act, since, on the view which I have taken as to the proper construction of the latter, a
j   difference which demonstrated unjustified indirect discrimination would not discharge
    the onus placed on the employer. Further, there would not appear to be any material
    distinction in principle between the need to demonstrate objectively justified grounds of
    difference for purposes of s 1(3) and the need to justify a requirement or condition under
    s 1(1)(b)(ii) of the 1975 Act. It is therefore unnecessary to consider the argument further.
        My Lords, for these reasons I would dismiss the appeal with costs.

LORD BRANDON OF OAKBROOK. My Lords, I have had the advantage of reading in draft the speech prepared by my noble and learned friend Lord Keith. I agree *a* with it, and for the reasons which he gives I would dismiss the appeal.

LORD GRIFFITHS. My Lords, I have had the advantage of reading in draft the speech prepared by my noble and learned friend Lord Keith. I agree with it, and for the reasons which he gives I would dismiss the appeal.

b

LORD MACKAY OF CLASHFERN. My Lords, I have had the advantage of reading in draft the speech prepared by my noble and learned friend Lord Keith. I agree with it, and for the reasons which he gives I would dismiss the appeal.

LORD GOFF OF CHIEVELEY. My Lords, I have had the advantage of reading in draft the speech prepared by my noble and learned friend Lord Keith. I agree with it, *c* and for the reasons which he gives I would dismiss the appeal.

Appeal dismissed.

Solicitors: *Denise Kingsmill & Co* (for the appellant); *Lawrence Graham*, agents for *John R Griffiths WS*, Edinburgh (for the respondents). *d*

Mary Rose Plummer   Barrister.

e

R v Immigration Appeal Tribunal, ex parte Hassanin

f

COURT OF APPEAL, CIVIL DIVISION
SIR JOHN DONALDSON MR, DILLON AND CROOM-JOHNSON LJJ
2, 3, 6, 16 OCTOBER 1986

Immigration – Appeal – Evidence – Evidence of facts existing at time of Secretary of State's decision – Secretary of State deciding to deport applicant – Secretary of State unaware of facts when decision to deport made – Whether adjudicator or tribunal can admit evidence of facts not considered by Secretary of State – Immigration Act 1971, s 19.

g

Where an appellant appeals to an adjudicator or the Immigration Appeal Tribunal under s 19[a] of the Immigration Act 1971 against a deportation order issued by the Secretary of State on the grounds that the Secretary of State ought to have exercised his discretion *h* differently, the appellant is entitled to adduce evidence of any facts which existed at the time the decision was made, even if those facts were not then known to the Secretary of State. The credibility and the weight to be attached to such evidence is a question for the adjudicator or the tribunal (see p 78 *bc*, p 79 *a b g* and p 80 *c e*, post).

Notes *j*
For the procedure in immigration appeals, see 4 Halsbury's Laws (4th edn) paras 1024–1026.
  For the Immigration Act 1971, s 19, see 41 Halsbury's Statutes (3rd edn) 40.

---

a Section 19, so far as material, is set out at p 76 *e* to *g*, post

Cases referred to in judgments

a *R v Immigration Appeal Tribunal, ex p Kotecha* [1983] 2 All ER 289, [1983] 1 WLR 487, CA.

R v Immigration Appeal Tribunal, ex p Osei [1985] CA Transcript 584.

R v Immigration Appeal Tribunal, ex p Weerasuriya [1983] 1 All ER 195.

Cases also cited

b *R v Immigration Appeal Tribunal, ex p Singh* [1986] 1 WLR 910, HL.

R v Immigration Appeal Tribunal, ex p Zaman [1982] Imm AR 61.

R v Secretary of State for the Home Dept, ex p Husbadak [1982] Imm AR 8.

Appeal

Abed el Naby Mohamed el Nashouky el Hassanin appealed against the decision of Mann J
c hearing the Crown Office list on 16 October 1985 dismissing an application by the
appellant for judicial review of a decision of the Immigration Appeal Tribunal dated 21
June 1984 dismissing the appellant's appeal against the decision of an adjudicator (Mr M
Patey) dated 21 December 1983 dismissing the appellant's appeal from a decision made
by the Secretary of State on 2 February 1983 to deport the appellant. The facts are set out
d in the judgment of Dillon LJ.

Louis Blom-Cooper QC and *Nicholas Blake* for the appellant.
John Laws for the respondents.

Cur adv vult

e 16 October. The following judgments were delivered.

DILLON LJ (giving the first judgment at the invitation of Sir John Donaldson MR).
This appeal was heard together with other appeals which all raise the same point of law,
namely whether, in a deportation case, an appellant can, in an appeal to an adjudicator or
f to the Immigration Appeal Tribunal against a decision of the Secretary of State to make a
deportation order against him, rely on facts or circumstances which existed at the time
of the Secretary of State's decision but were not then known to the Secretary of State.

The present appellant is an Egyptian citizen. On 21 August 1979 he was granted leave
to enter the United Kingdom for one month as a visitor. That leave was subsequently
extended to 31 December 1979, but he remained here without authorisation beyond
g that date. In the course of 1980 he applied to remain as a student, but that application
was rejected. Then, on 10 February 1981, the United Kingdom Immigrants Advisory
Service wrote to the Home Office on his behalf claiming political asylum. The appellant
was interviewed by representatives of the Home Office on 1 December 1981 in
connection with his application for political asylum. That application was refused by the
Secretary of State in March 1982; against such a decision there is no appeal. Then, as the
h appellant had still not left the United Kingdom, the Secretary of State decided, on
2 February 1983, to deport him under s 3(5) of the Immigration Act 1971 as an
overstayer.

The appellant promptly appealed, as he was entitled to, against that decision to deport
him, but his appeal was dismissed by an adjudicator in December 1983. He appealed,
with leave, to the appeal tribunal, but his appeal was dismissed in June 1984. He then,
j with leave granted in November 1984 by Lloyd J, applied for judicial review of the
decision of the appeal tribunal. That application was refused by Mann J on 16 October
1985, and it is against that decision of Mann J that the present appeal is brought.

The main case for the appellant before the adjudicator and before the appeal tribunal
was that he was a political refugee who had a well-founded fear of the consequences if he
were to be deported to Egypt. That, however, was rejected on the facts both by the

adjudicator and by the appeal tribunal. Their conclusion on this point was not challenged
in the High Court (and could not be) or in this court.   *a*

In his notice of appeal to the adjudicator dated 15 February 1983, however, the
appellant had put his grounds of appeal more widely and had referred also to the
condition of his wife. The question of law for the High Court and for this court was
whether he was entitled to put evidence of compassionate family circumstances before
the tribunal.

All that the Secretary of State knew about the appellant's personal circumstances in the   *b*
United Kingdom was derived from the interview with the appellant on 1 December
1981 and was that the appellant was unmarried, and sharing a room with a Moroccan
friend. In fact he married the Moroccan friend, Lalifa El Khattari, on 5 April 1982 and
by 2 February 1983, when the Secretary of State made his decision, she was pregnant
with their child (a daughter in fact born on 23 March 1983). Although a Moroccan
citizen, the appellant's wife had in January 1981 been granted indefinite leave to remain   *c*
in the United Kingdom. She has an adoptive daughter, Nisrine Hassan, the child, born
in England in January 1978, of her (the appellant's wife's) sister, since deceased. It seems
that at the time of the interview with the appellant on 1 December 1981 Nisrine was in
Morocco with her natural father, but she was returned to England in August 1982 and
looked after by the appellant and his wife and admitted to a school in London, and there
is evidence that the home background provided by the appellant and his wife was giving   *d*
Nisrine stability and security, previously lacking in her life.

The determination of an appeal to an adjudicator against a decision of the Secretary of
State to make a deportation order is governed by s 19 of the 1971 Act, sub-ss (1) and (2)
of which provide as follows:

> '(1) Subject to sections 13(4) and 16(4) above, and to any restriction on the   *e*
> grounds of appeal, an adjudicator on an appeal to him under this Part of this Act (a)
> shall allow the appeal if he considers (i) that the decision or action against which the
> appeal is brought was not in accordance with the law or with any immigration rules
> applicable to the case; or (ii) where the decision or action involved the exercise of a
> discretion by the Secretary of State or an officer, that the discretion should have been
> exercised differently; and (b) in any other case, shall dismiss the appeal.   *f*
>
> (2) For the purposes of subsection (1)(a) above the adjudicator may review any
> determination of a question of fact on which the decision or action was based; and
> for the purposes of subsection (1)(a)(ii) no decision or action which is in accordance
> with the immigration rules shall be treated as having involved the exercise of a
> discretion by the Secretary of State by reason only of the fact that he has been
> requested by or on behalf of the appellant to depart, or to authorise an officer to   *g*
> depart, from the rules and has refused to do so.'

The present case is put entirely under s 19(1)(a)(ii) in that the Secretary of State
exercised a discretion in deciding to deport the appellant, and it is said that the discretion
should have been exercised differently. No reliance is placed on s 19(1)(a)(i).

Under r 29 of the Immigration Appeals (Procedure) Rules 1972, SI 1972/1682, which   *h*
were in force when the appeals to the adjudicator and to the appeal tribunal in this case
were heard, an appellate authority, whether an adjudicator or the appeal tribunal, had
power to receive oral documentary or other evidence of any fact which appeared to the
authority to be relevant to the appeal, and under r 18 the appeal tribunal had a discretion
to receive further evidence beyond the evidence received by the adjudicator.

The rules, in the relevant Statement of Changes in Immigration Rules (HC Paper   *j*
(1982–83) no 66) contain provisions as follows:

> '154. In considering whether deportation is the right course on the merits the
> public interest will be balanced against any compassionate circumstances of the case.
> While each case will be considered in the light of the particular circumstances, the

aim is an exercise of the power of deportation that is consistent and fair as between one person and another, although one case will rarely be identical with another in all material respects . . .

158. Deportation will normally be the proper course where the person . . . has remained without authorisation. Full account is to be taken of all the relevant circumstances known to the Secretary of State . . . before a decision is reached.'

Against that legislative framework, it was held by Webster J in *R v Immigration Appeal Tribunal, ex p Weerasuriya* [1983] 1 All ER 195 that facts coming into existence after a decision of the Secretary of State under the 1971 Act are not admissible in evidence, or to be considered, on an appeal before an adjudicator or the appeal tribunal in relation to that decision. *Ex p Weerasuriya* was approved by this court in *R v Immigration Appeal Tribunal, ex p Kotecha* [1983] 2 All ER 289, [1983] 1 WLR 487 and was applied by this court in *R v Immigration Appeal Tribunal, ex p Osei* [1985] CA Transcript 584. None of these cases is challenged on this appeal. The basis of the reasoning is that the decision appealed against, in immigration appeals such as the present, is an administrative decision of the Secretary of State, and the appellate structure under the 1971 Act is not an extension of the original administrative decision-making function, but simply a process for enabling the decision of the Secretary of State to be reviewed. Therefore, facts which happened after the date of the Secretary of State's decision are outside the scope or area of review of the appellate structure, whether before an adjudicator or before the appeal tribunal.

The law as decided in the cases just mentioned has now been taken a stage further by the decisions in the High Court in the present case and in the parallel cases of Ekrem Kandemir and Mohamed Farooq in that it has now been held that it is equally outside the scope or area of review of the appellate authorities under the 1971 Act to consider circumstances which existed at the time of the Secretary of State's decision, but were not then known to him. The argument in favour of such an extension relies particularly on the requirement in para 158 of HC Paper (1982–83) no 66 that full account is to be taken of all the relevant circumstances known to the Secretary of State. It is said that if the appellate structure under the Act is merely a process for enabling the decision of the Secretary of State to be reviewed, and if the Secretary of State is only required to consider the circumstances known to him, then equally the adjudicator and the appeal tribunal in the appellate structure should be limited to considering the circumstances known to the Secretary of State at the time he made his decision. Indeed, in *Ex p Weerasuriya* Webster J referred to the equivalent of para 158 as supporting his conclusion that facts which only happened after the Secretary of State had made his decision could not be considered by the appellate tribunals. Webster J accepted, however, as common ground between the parties in that case that an appellate tribunal may take into account evidence which was not available at an earlier stage of the proceedings in question provided that it was not evidence of any fact which was not in existence when the Secretary of State made his decision (see [1983] 1 All ER 195 at 201).

Whatever its effect on the admissibility of evidence before the appellate tribunals, para 158 serves a very useful purpose in protecting the Secretary of State from allegations that he ought to have made inquiries and found out all the relevant facts before making any decision to deport an overstayer; he is entitled to act merely on the relevant circumstances known to him. The significance of this is underlined by the facts in the parallel appeal of Mohamed Farooq. Mr Farooq entered the United Kingdom on 9 January 1976 as a short term visitor with permission to stay for one month only. He said he wanted to stay for three weeks only and knew no one in the United Kingdom. Within hours events happened which led the immigration officer to believe that Mr Farooq had lied in order to secure his admission to the United Kingdom. However, it was not then possible to find him and he was not found until he was denounced to the immigration authorities in July 1983. The Secretary of State then made the decision to deport Mr

Farooq and signed a detention order without any previous interview for fear that if Mr Farooq learned that he had been traced he would abscond from his then current address *a* and place of work, and again be lost elsewhere in the United Kingdom. For my part I see no objection to the Secretary of State deciding to deport an overstayer, without any interview of the person concerned to discover his current circumstances, if the Secretary of State fears that that person will abscond if approached; the Secretary of State is protected by para 158.

But if the Secretary of State is entitled to decide to make a deportation order without *b* interview of the person concerned and without knowledge of his personal circumstances, merely in the knowledge that that person has remained in the United Kingdom without authorisation, and if the appellate authorities under the 1971 Act are precluded from considering facts which were not known to the Secretary of State when he made his decision to deport, then the appeal to an adjudicator, which is given to the proposed deportee as of right by s 15(1) of the 1971 Act is rendered almost nugatory. He will never *c* be able to put before any appellate authority any compassionate circumstances of his case, because, ex hypothesi, those circumstances were not known to the Secretary of State. That, in my judgment, would be contrary to the scheme of the 1971 Act.

I turn to a further factor. Wherever there is an appeal to an adjudicator under Pt II of the 1971 Act, which includes ss 15 and 19, the respondent to the appeal is required by the 1972 rules to provide for the adjudicator a written explanatory statement of the facts *d* relating to the decision in question and the reasons therefor. That explanatory statement is admissible evidence on the hearing of the appeal by the adjudicator, but it is clearly not intended to be the only admissible evidence. I have already referred to the powers of the adjudicator and the appeal tribunal to receive evidence. It is normal practice for further oral or documentary evidence to be given before the adjudicator. The adjudicator is empowered by s 19(2) to review any determination of any question of fact, and if he *e* reaches a different conclusion on any question of fact that will almost always be because he has had fuller and better evidence than was available to the Secretary of State or his officer when the decision under appeal was made. That will regularly involve that the adjudicator has received evidence of facts, at any rate on points of detail, which were not known to the Secretary of State, or his officers, when the decision appealed against was *f* made.

Counsel for the respondents was disposed to accept, consistently with the concession made in *Ex p Weerasuriya*, that in considering whether 'the discretion should have been exercised differently', the adjudicator was entitled to consider facts given in evidence which were not known to the Secretary of State at the time of his decision if they were within the general ambit of the case which the Secretary of State knew before he made his decision that the proposed deportee was making. Counsel for the respondent objects *g* particularly to evidence being given on an appeal to support an entirely fresh case of which there was no hint in what was said on behalf of the proposed deportee before the decision to deport him was made. Apart from the difficulty already mentioned in cases like Mr Farooq's where there was no opportunity to make any representations before the decision to deport was made, I find great difficulty in seeing where any line is to be *h* drawn. Is there a difference, and if so what, between 'facts' which are put in evidence, and 'relevant circumstances' in para 158, which picks up the phrase 'relevant factors' in para 156 of HC Paper (1982–83) no 66? How far can the barest hint of a case, or even a fairly fully particularised case, be amplified by fresh facts and further particulars?

I do not read the requirement in para 158 that 'full account is to be taken of all the relevant circumstances known to the Secretary of State . . . before a decision is reached' as *j* imposing a negative duty on the adjudicator or the appeal tribunal, in reviewing the Secretary of State's exercise of his discretion, not to take account of circumstances which, though existing, were not known to the Secretary of State when he made his decision. To imply such a negative duty would be inconsistent with the powers of the adjudicator and the appeal tribunal under the rules to receive evidence on an appeal.

In view of the factors discussed above, I for my part accept the general submission of
a counsel for the appellant that on any appeal to an adjudicator where the question is
whether a discretion of the Secretary of State or an officer should have been exercised
differently, evidence of any facts which existed at the time the decision in exercise of the
discretion was made is admissible, even though those facts were not known to the
decision maker at the time of the decision. The credibility of such evidence and weight
to be attached to it are different matters. It may well be that if an appellant seeks to put
b forward a wholly new case to the adjudicator, which is different from and even
inconsistent with the case which, before the decision was made, he was urging on the
Secretary of State or his officers, the adjudicator will readily conclude that the new case is
spurious and untrue. In the present case, however, there is no question of credibility.
   I therefore respectfully disagree with Mann J's ruling on the law as to the admissibility
of the compassionate factors in relation to his wife and Nisrine on which the appellant
c relies.
   What then is the effect of his conclusion of law on the appellant's appeal? When the
appellant's appeal was before the adjudicator, the compassionate factors were considered
by the adjudicator, but he rejected them as a ground for setting aside the Secretary of
State's decision to deport the appellant, because he felt that no good cause had been shown
why the family should not go to Morocco, the country of the appellant's wife's nationality.
d That conclusion was, in my judgment, wrong because there was nothing to indicate that
the appellant would be admitted to Morocco, a country of which he is not a national.
   When the appellant appealed to the appeal tribunal, the tribunal held, in my judgment
wrongly, that it was precluded from taking the compassionate factors into consideration
because they had not been known to the Secretary of State when he made his decision.
e The appeal tribunal also stated, however, in its decision:

   'Even were those facts before us, we would not, in the circumstances generally be
   inclined to say that they constituted compassionate circumstances that outweigh the
   public interest served by enforcing the proposed order.'

   I read this as an alternative ground for the decision on the facts; it is a decision which on
f the facts cannot be challenged. Moreover, judicial review is a discretionary remedy.
Accordingly, notwithstanding that I differ from the judge and the appeal tribunal on the
law, I would on the facts dismiss this appeal.

SIR JOHN DONALDSON MR. I am in complete agreement with Dillon LJ as to the
law. I am equally in agreement with him that, notwithstanding this conclusion, the
g appeal should be dismissed for the reasons which he has given.
   Section 19(1) of the Immigration Act 1971 requires the adjudicator and, on appeal, the
Immigration Appeal Tribunal to consider whether 'the discretion should have been
exercised differently'. If the words are not to receive a restrictive construction, the
adjudicator is free to conclude that the discretion should have been exercised differently
if (a) the decision maker misdirected himself in law, (b) the decision maker misdirected
h himself in fact on the evidence available to him, (c) although the decision maker rightly
directed himself in law and rightly evaluated the evidence available to him, further
evidence shows that the facts were not as he believed them to be or (d) there were other
relevant circumstances which are unknown to the decision maker but which have
become known to the adjudicator. If Parliament had intended the adjudicator to confine
himself to (a) and (b), which involve self-misdirection by the decision maker, s 19(1)(a)(ii)
j would have read: '. . . that he should have exercised his discretion differently.' This is not
the wording of the subsection, and the adjudicator has therefore to extend the scope of
his inquiry at least to (c), whether, in the light of further evidence, the decision maker
correctly found the facts, irrespective of why he failed to do so. If the adjudicator is
required to make this inquiry, which involves evaluating the exercise of the discretion
in the context of a scenario different from that which confronted the decision maker

himself, I fail to see any reason why Parliament should have intended to exclude (d), construction of new facts, and, in the light of a situation such as that disclosed in the *a* *Farooq* appeal, every reason why it should not have so intended.

Similarly with para 158 of the Statement of Changes in Immigration Rules (HC Paper (1982–83) no 66). This has to be read in the light of para 154 of HC Paper (1982–83) no 66 with its requirement that the public interest has to be balanced against any compassionate circumstances. Such circumstances may or may not be known to the decision maker and in a *Farooq* situation probably will not be. It makes sense to construe *b* para 158 as requiring the decision maker to take account of *all* the relevant circumstances known to him thereby reminding him of the all-embracing character of the balancing operation called for by para 154. It does not make any sense to construe the paragraph as being intended, by implication, to limit the decision maker to a consideration of facts known to him, since unknown facts could not be taken into account by him in any event. Accordingly, in the light of the construction which I put on s 19(1)(*a*) of the 1971 *c* Act, I can see no reason why the paragraph should limit the adjudicator to a consideration of facts known to the decision maker. Circumstances arising after the moment when the decision was taken are logically in a quite different category and as to those we are bound by the decision of this court in *R v Immigration Appeal Tribunal, ex p Kotecha* [1983] 2 All ER 289, [1983] 1 WLR 487, with which I should in any event not be disposed to disagree. This view of para 158 not only takes account of the requirements of a Farooq situation, *d* but also is consistent with the Home Office practice of including in the statement of facts for consideration by the adjudicator issues raised and facts coming to the notice of the Secretary of State after the making of the decision and the results of his review of that decision in the light of those issues and facts.

CROOM-JOHNSON LJ. I agree with the judgments of Sir John Donaldson MR and *e* Dillon LJ.

Appeal dismissed. No order as to costs.

Solicitors: *Eaton Kellas* (for the appellant); *Treasury Solicitor.*

Frances Rustin   Barrister.

a Pagnan SpA v Tradax Ocean Transportation SA

QUEEN'S BENCH DIVISION (COMMERCIAL COURT)
STEYN J

b
7, 8 MAY, 24 JUNE 1986

Sale of goods – Duty of seller – Export licence – Absolute or qualified duty – Force majeure – Quota restrictions on export – Sellers required to 'provide for export certificate' – Quota exhausted and sellers unable to obtain certificate – Whether sellers under absolute obligation to provide export certificate – Whether sellers merely required to use best endeavours to obtain
c *export certificate.*

Force majeure – Sale of goods – Government intervention beyond seller's control – Contract containing force majeure clause and special condition imposing absolute obligation on sellers to provide export certificate – Quota system governing exports – Quota exhausted and sellers unable to obtain export certificate – Whether obligation to provide export certificate overriding force
d *majeure clause – GAFTA Form 119, cl 19.*

By a contract of sale dated 23 November 1982 the sellers agreed to sell to Italian buyers 35,000 tonnes of Thai tapioca. It was a special condition of the contract that the sellers would 'provide for [an] export certificate' thereby enabling the buyers to obtain the necessary import licence to enable the tapioca to be imported into the EEC. The contract
e also incorporated the terms of GAFTA Form 119, which included a standard force majeure clause, cl 19[a], providing that, in the case of, inter alia, the prohibition of export or any executive or legislative act done by the government of a country of origin restricting export, such restriction would be deemed by both parties to apply to the contract to the extent that the restriction prevented the fulfilment of the contract and to that extent the contract or any unfulfilled part of it would be cancelled. Shortly before
f the contract was made a quota system was introduced by agreement between Thailand and the EEC governing the export of tapioca from Thailand to the EEC and enforced by regulations promulgated in Thailand. Under the quota system the annual quota was divided into quarterly sub-quotas. By March 1983 the sub-quotas for the first two quarters of that year were exhausted and accordingly the sellers were unable to make agreed shipments in April and May 1983. The buyers declared the sellers in default and
g claimed damages. The claim was referred to arbitrators, who upheld the claim and awarded damages to the buyers. Subsequently, that award was set aside by the GAFTA Board of Appeal, which held that the buyers' claim failed on the ground that the sellers were relieved of liability by cl 19 of GAFTA Form 119, which operated to cancel both the April and May portions of the contract because fulfilment thereof was prevented by executive acts of the Thai government. The buyers appealed to the High Court. The
h questions arose (i) whether the special condition in the contract imposing the duty on the sellers to 'provide for' an export certificate imposed on the sellers an absolute obligation or merely an obligation to use their 'best endeavours' to obtain an export certificate and (ii) if the obligation was absolute in character, whether the special condition overrode the
. force majeure clause contained in cl 19 of GAFTA Form 119.

j **Held** – (1) The special condition in the contract requiring the sellers to provide for an export certificate expressly placed the burden of obtaining the export certificate on the sellers. Whether that duty was absolute or merely required the use of reasonable diligence was a matter of construction which was not governed by any technical rules. The court

---

a   Clause 19 is set out at p 83 *g h*, post

would therefore consider the ordinary meaning of the relevant words, read in the context
of the contract as a whole and against the contextual scene. It would therefore be wrong   *a*
to start with an a priori assumption that the parties were more likely to have in mind a
duty to use reasonable diligence only and, in the circumstances, the natural meaning of
the words 'sellers to provide for [an] export certificate' was more consistent with an
absolute obligation than with a duty to use reasonable diligence. It followed that the
special condition, properly construed, imposed an absolute obligation on the sellers to
obtain an export certificate, and accordingly there was a prima facie breach of that   *b*
condition (see p 87 *a* to *d f* to *j* and p 88 *j* to p 89 *b*, post); dictum of Lloyd J in *Coloniale
Import-Export v Loumidis Sons* [1978] 2 Lloyd's Rep at 562–563 considered.

(2) On balance the special condition was not inconsistent with cl 19 of GAFTA Form
119 since although there was an absolute obligation to obtain an export certificate, and
breach of that obligation gave rise to a prima facie liability for damages, the sellers were
excused from liability if they showed that the case was within the scope of cl 19.   *c*
Furthermore, although the words used in the special condition were sufficient to create
an absolute duty, they fell short of evincing a clear intention to override cl 19. It followed
that the question whether the sellers were excused by reason of the provisions of cl 19
was one of fact, which the GAFTA Board of Appeal had determined in favour of the
sellers. The appeal would therefore be dismissed (see p 89 *j* to p 90 *c h*, post).
   d

Notes

For force majeure clauses, see 9 Halsbury's Laws (4th edn) para 457, and for case on the
subject, see 12 Digest (Reissue) 502, 3505.

For contracts made subject to licence, see 9 Halsbury's Laws (4th edn) para 459, and
for cases on the subject, see 12 Digest (Reissue) 501, 3498–3500.
   e

Cases referred to in judgment

*Anglo-Russian Merchant Traders Ltd and John Batt & Co (London) Ltd, Re an arbitration
    between* [1917] 2 KB 679, CA.
Coloniale Import-Export v Loumidis Sons [1978] 2 Lloyd's Rep 560.
Czarnikow (C) Ltd v Centrala Handlu Zagranicznego 'Rolimpex' [1978] 2 All ER 1043, [1979]   *f*
    AC 351, [1978] 3 WLR 274, HL.
Gesellschaft Burgerlichen Rechts v Stockholms Rederiaktiebolag Svea, The Brabant [1966] 1 All
    ER 961, [1967] 1 QB 588, [1966] 2 WLR 909.
Partabmull Rameshwar v K C Sethia (1944) Ltd [1951] 2 All ER 352n, [1951] 2 Lloyd's Rep
    89, HL.
   g

Appeal

The plaintiffs, Pagnan SpA (the buyers), appealed with leave granted pursuant to s 1 of
the Arbitration Act 1979 against the award of the GAFTA Board of Appeal dated 23
September 1985 whereby they held that the buyers' claim for default against the
defendants, Tradax Ocean Transportation SA (the sellers), failed on the ground that the
sellers were relieved from liability by reason of cl 19 of GAFTA Form 119. The facts are   *h*
set out in the judgment.

David Johnson QC and *Christopher Hancock* for the buyers.
Bernard Rix QC and *Mark Havelock-Allan* for the sellers.

                                                                    Cur adv vult   *j*

24 June. The following judgment was delivered.

STEYN J. In 1983 a quota system, which had been negotiated between Thailand and
the EEC, governed the export of tapioca pellets from Thailand to the EEC. It was

enforced by regulations promulgated in Thailand. The regulations divided the annual
a quota into quarterly sub-quotas. By March 1983 the sub-quotas for the first two quarters
of 1983 were exhausted. The consequence was that the sellers, under a contract of sale
dated 23 November 1982, were unable to make agreed shipments in April and May
1983. The buyers declared the sellers to be in default and claimed damages in arbitration
proceedings under the Arbitration Rules of the Grain and Feed Trade Association
(GAFTA). The buyers succeeded in the first tier arbitration but the award was set aside
b on appeal by the GAFTA Board of Appeal. Pursuant to s 1 of the Arbitration Act 1979
leave to appeal against the award of the board of appeal was given. On the hearing of the
appeal the issues, and sub-issues, were numerous. Two principal issues were, however,
identified: (a) whether a special condition in a GAFTA 119 contract, which imposed the
duty on the seller 'to provide for' an export certificate is to be interpreted as imposing on
the seller an absolute obligation or only a 'best endeavours' obligation; (b) if, as the buyers
c contend, the obligation was absolute in character, whether the special condition 'overrides'
a standard form GAFTA 119 force majeure clause. Both issues are questions of
construction. If the buyers are successful on both issues, the buyers are in principle
entitled to recover substantial damages. The buyers contend that they are entitled to
damages in a sum in excess of $US500,000. On the other hand, if the buyers are not
successful on both these issues, it will be necessary to examine other ways in which the
d buyers wish to challenge the award of the board of appeal.

The background
Bearing in mind that one is dealing with questions of construction, it seems
unnecessary to set out the background in detail. Instead I propose to extract from the
award of the board of appeal that minimal recapitulation of events, as found by the board
e of appeal, which is necessary to render the commercial dispute intelligible. By a contract
dated 23 November 1982 Tradax Ocean Transportation SA, a Panamanian company, to
whom I shall refer as 'the sellers', sold to Pagnan SpA, an Italian company, to whom I
shall refer as 'the buyers', 35,000 tonnes, 5% more or less at the buyers option, of Thai
tapioca pellets at a price of $US109 per tonne FOB stowed/trimmed Sriracha for shipment
f as follows: (i) February 1983: 10,000 tonnes more or less; (ii) April 1983: 10,000 tonnes
more or less; (iii) May 1983: 15,000 tonnes more or less. The contract contained the
following provision under the heading special conditions:

'Sellers to provide for export certificate enabling Buyers to obtain import licence
into EEC under tariff 07.06 with 6% import levy.'

g Clause 19 of GAFTA Form 119 provides as follows:

'Prohibition—In case of prohibition of export, blockage or hostilities or in case of
any executive or legislative act done by or on behalf of the government of a country
of origin, or of the territory where the port or ports of shipment named herein is/
are situate, restricting export, whether partially or otherwise, any such restriction
shall be deemed by both parties to apply to the Contract to the extent of such total
h or partial restriction to prevent fulfilment whether by shipment or by any other
means whatsoever and to that extent this contract or any unfulfilled portion thereof
shall be cancelled. Sellers shall advise Buyers without delay with the reasons therefor,
and if required, Sellers must produce proof to justify the cancellation.'

It is necessary to put this contract in its contextual scene. The sellers are a company in
j the Cargill Group, one of the largest amongst the great grain merchants of the world.
They had through an associated company a considerable presence in Thailand. The
buyers are major traders in constituents for animal feeding stuffs. The buyers regularly
purchase large quantities of Thai tapioca pellets for import into the EEC.
Thai tapioca pellets are used exclusively as a component of animal feeding stuffs in the
EEC and competes as such with grain. There is virtually no market for Thai tapioca

pellets anywhere else in the world; the reason is largely that the price obtainable in the EEC, where grain prices are supported, is much higher than the price obtainable outside *a* the EEC. By the time the contract was made between the parties on 23 November 1982 there was already in place, to the knowledge of both parties, a quota system restricting the export of Thai tapioca pellets to the EEC. By a co-operation agreement between the EEC and Thailand, which came into effect in July 1982, Thailand, inter alia, undertook to limit by a system of export certificates its exports of tapioca pellets to the Community as follows: 5m tonnes per year for 1983 and 1984 with an additional quantity of 10% of *b* the annual quantity for the two-year period, which might be used in full in one year or partially in both years. The EEC in turn agreed to classify Thai tapioca under tariff 07.06A of the EEC Common Customs Tariff, and to limit the levy applicable to the agreed quantities to a maximum of 6% ad valorem, instead of the barley levy which would otherwise be applicable to tapioca. The latter levy varied from time to time but at that time stood at $US100 per tonne. There was no embargo on non-certificated goods coming *c* into the Community, but the barley levy, which would in effect double the price of the goods, was a sufficient disincentive.

When the contract was concluded Thailand had already brought the quota system into force by regulations. The first regulations were promulgated on 30 September 1982. These regulations divided the year into four quarters, and, in so far as material to the present dispute, stipulated the following sub-quotas: 1 January–31 March 1983: 1·6m *d* tonnes; 1 April–30 June 1983: 1·35m tonnes; 1 July–30 September 1983: 1m tonnes. The regulations provided for the administration of the system. In particular it is relevant to observe that an exporter had to be registered and had first to obtain, inter alia, an export licence before he could obtain an export certificate. A notice from the Foreign Department, which was published on 9 November 1982, further explained the administration of the system. The board expressly found that both parties were well *e* aware of all the regulations and notices *as and when issued*, ie both parties were aware of the essentials of the quota system when they concluded the contract on 23 November 1982. It irresistibly follows from these primary facts, as found by the board of appeal, that both parties must have been aware that contracts for the sale of Thai tapioca could conceivably be affected by the exhaustion of the applicable quotas. Against this background they concluded the contract in November 1982 for three deliveries, *f* respectively in February, April and May 1983.

In the result the first delivery under the contract duly took place. There was no dispute regarding that delivery. The dispute centred on the deliveries due in April and May 1983. It is unnecessary to trace in detail the regulations and notices, which were issued after the conclusion of the contract. The board of appeal found that the situation started to get out of control. The 1982 quota had been exceeded in December 1982. The excess *g* was taken out of the first quarter for 1983. Large numbers of vessels arrived with a lifting capacity far in excess of the quota. The amount to be loaded for the first quarter of 1983 was again exceeded. The board found that the Thai authorities made it clear to all exporters that from 16 March to the end of May 1983 they were not going to allow any tapioca products at all to be loaded for export to the EEC. It was common ground *h* that the buyers nominations of vessels to lift the April and May instalments complied with the contract. It was not, however, possible for the sellers to obtain export certificates in order to enable the goods to be imported into the EEC at a 6% levy.

The history of the dispute, and in particular the positions adopted by the parties, is set out in the award. For the purposes of this judgment it is sufficient to say the buyers contended that the sellers were in default, whereas the sellers contended that they had *j* done all that was required of them and that, in any event, they were protected by cl 19, the force majeure provision under GAFTA 119.

This dispute led to arbitration proceedings under the GAFTA arbitration rules.

The first tier arbitration
By a unanimous award dated 9 January 1985 the arbitrators held that the sellers were

in default, and awarded $US562,500 to the buyers by way of damages, together with
interest. Since the appeal against this award involved a complete rehearing, the findings
in the first award are strictly not material on this appeal. By way of narrative I note,
however, that in para 22 of the award the arbitrators found:

> '. . . there was not a prohibition of Export of Thai Tapioca Pellets and the fact that
> sellers could not obtain an export certificate enabling Buyers to obtain an import
> licence allowing import into the EEC at 6% import levy, did not alter Sellers
> obligations under the FOB contract between the parties for the sale of the goods.'

The award of the board of appeal

By an award dated 23 September 1985 the board of appeal set aside the first award and
directed that the buyers' claim for default fails on the ground that the sellers were
relieved from liability by reason of cl 19 of GAFTA Form 119 which operated to cancel
both the April and May 1983 portions of the contract because fulfilment thereof was
prevented by executive acts of the Government of Thailand. The board made no express
rulings on the questions whether the special condition imposed an absolute obligation
on the sellers to provide an export certificate and, if so, whether the special condition
overrides cl 19. It is necessary to set out in extenso how the board of appeal approached
the matter:

> '37. The Buyers' contention was that there was no de jure prohibition of export
> by the Thai authorities and that if an exporter wished to ship Thai tapioca products
> to the E.E.C. without an export certificate, that was his affair and that nothing was
> done either by the Government of Thailand, or by the E.E.C. to prevent the export
> from Thailand and the import into the E.E.C. of such uncertificated goods. The
> Buyers insisted that the Sellers had an absolute obligation "to provide for export
> certificate enabling Buyers to obtain import licence into E.E.C. under tariff 07.06
> with 6% import levy" and that this obligation was an essential term of the contract,
> breach of which would render the Sellers liable in damages, and the Buyers pointed
> to a number of cases decided in the courts on the question of liability for the
> provision of export licences. Since, said the Buyers, there was no actual prohibition
> of export, the Sellers were not relieved of their obligations under the contract by
> Clause 19 of GAFTA 119, which Clause did not, in any event, override the Special
> Condition.
>
> 38. The Sellers' view, however, was that there was a de facto prohibition of export
> in that: (a) No further goods could be loaded on any vessels whatsoever after
> midnight on the 13th March 1983 until the end of May 1983 (and nor were any
> such loaded). (b) The Thai authorities interpreted the Thai regulations by making it
> clear that no exporter should in fact apply for an export licence to load goods,
> because even an export licence would not be granted, let alone an export certificate,
> which certainly would not be granted. (c) The Contract was a contract for the sale of
> certificated goods to the E.E.C., so that if the Government of Thailand ordered that
> no such goods were to be available for shipment within the shipment months of the
> Contract, namely April and May 1983, then there was in effect a prohibition of
> export within clause 19 of GAFTA 119.
>
> 39. There is no doubt in our minds that the Contract was one for certificated
> goods, and was not merely one for goods to be shipped on the basis that the Sellers
> were to be liable for getting an export certificate, or be liable in damages if they
> failed to obtain an export certificate. We find that in fact not only the Sellers, but
> also the Buyers knew perfectly well that no goods at all could be either loaded or
> certified for export to the E.E.C. from after midnight on 13th March 1983 until the
> end of May 1983, this being clear from the Buyers' nomination of the "KERVAN"
> (chartered subject to stem), as set out at Paragraph 24 above, showing that the Buyers
> understood perfectly well that the vessel could not be accepted and loaded, so that
> the nomination was only made subject to stem, which could not be made available.
>
> 40. The Buyers complained that the Sellers never actually made application for

export licences following the nominations for the April and May deliveries (q.v. supra) and that they should have been able to demonstrate that they used their "best endeavours" to obtain both an export licence and then an export certificate for those deliveries. However, in our view, the question never arose. By the time the Buyers made their nomination for the April delivery on 1st April 1983 (see paragraph 24 above), it had already been made abundantly clear to the Sellers by the Thai Authorities, and by Mr. Danai of the Foreign Trade Department in particular, that no applications for an export licence for E.E.C. destination would be entertained by the Foreign Trade Department. The Thai Government did not want to permit even uncertificated goods to be exported to the E.E.C. (the application for an export licence had to show the country of destination). *A fortiori*, the Thai Government position was even clearer by the time of the nomination for the May portion on 29th April 1983, and in neither case do we feel that any purpose would have been served by the Sellers making an application for an export licence. The Foreign Trade Department's position remained throughout April and May 1983 that no applications would be entertained. The Buyers knew this (we find) and lost no time in declaring the sellers in default in each instance, on 11th April 1983 for the April delivery (see paragraph 25(7) above) and on 6th May 1983 for the May delivery (see paragraph 26 above), from which dates respectively the Sellers' obligations for the respective portions were terminated by the Buyers' declarations of default.

41. Thus the Sellers had only to show that, between 1st April and 11th April 1983 for the April portion and between 29th April and 6th May 1983 for the May portion, fulfilment of the contract was prevented by an executive or legislative act done by or on behalf of the Government of Thailand (being both the country of origin and of shipment) as provided for in Clause 19 of GAFTA 119.

WE FIND that fulfilment was so prevented and that notwithstanding the contractual obligation imposed on the Sellers "to provide for export certificate enabling Buyers to obtain import licence into E.E.C. under tariff 07.06 with 6% import levy", the provisions of Clause 19 of GAFTA 119 nevertheless operated to cancel the contract so far as the April and May 1983 portions were concerned as a result of the actions of the Thai Government.'

It will be observed that it was argued that, if the special condition created a 'best endeavours' obligation only, the sellers were in breach of that obligation. The board of appeal found on the facts that this contention could not succeed. The buyers attempted to revive this argument in this court but eventually abandoned it.

The first question: did the special condition create an absolute obligation?

If an overseas sale does not expressly provide whether the seller or buyer is bound to obtain a necessary export licence, the task of the court may be to derive from the terms of the contract, and the circumstances in which it was concluded, an implied term placing on the seller or the buyer the duty to obtain the export licence. Often the decisive factor in such a case will be the relative strengths of the parties' positions in seeking to obtain such a licence. Having determined the necessary implication placing the duty on one of the parties, the question will arise whether the relevant duty is absolute or one of exercising reasonable diligence only. If such a contract does not expressly place the burden to obtain an export licence on one of the parties, it will almost invariably also be silent on the question whether the duty is absolute or one of exercising reasonable diligence only. The gap as to the extent of the duty will also be filled by a process of implication. In accordance with the principles governing the implication of terms, the court will usually incline towards implying the minimal provision necessary to give business efficacy to the contract, viz that the duty is one of reasonable diligence only: *Re*

an arbitration between Anglo-Russian Merchant Traders Ltd and John Batt & Co (London) Ltd
a [1917] 2 KB 679.

In the present case, however, a wholly different approach is required. The special condition expressly placed the burden of obtaining the export certificate on the seller. It is a matter of construction whether that duty is an absolute one or only one of using reasonable diligence. Indeed it is not contended in this case that there is any room for an implication. If the matter were not governed by any technical rules my approach would
b be as follows: one is simply concerned with the ordinary meaning of the relevant words, read in the context of the contract as a whole, and against the contextual scene. It is wrong therefore to start with an a priori assumption that the parties are more likely to have in mind a duty to use reasonable diligence only. The risk that an export certificate may not be available was known to both parties: they were free to impose an absolute obligation to obtain an export certificate, or a duty to use reasonable diligence. How they
c wished to approach the matter of allocation of risk is therefore entirely a matter for them, and should not be approached with any preconceptions. Neither construction is implausible or unreasonable. I approach the matter in this way.

Prima facie the words 'sellers to provide for export certificate' mean that the sellers undertake responsibility for obtaining or supplying the relevant certificates. The natural
d meaning of these words are more consistent with an absolute obligation than with a duty to use reasonable diligence only. Indeed, a process of implication rather than construction seems necessary to arrive at the opposite conclusion. It was suggested on behalf of the sellers that it is significant that the parties used the word 'guarantee' in other contexts in the contract. Specifically, it was contended that the parties eschewed the use of language in the special condition which might indicate an absolute obligation. In my judgment
e these are differences in terminology, which in a contract such as the present throws no light on the meaning of the relevant words.

A more weighty point made on behalf of the sellers was that one is dealing with an FOB contract in terms of which the buyers could select the date of nomination of the ship. It is implausible, it was argued, that in such a contract the sellers would undertake an absolute obligation to obtain an export certificate on uncertain future dates. It must
f be borne in mind that the buyers' option was strictly circumscribed by the provision for shipment of instalments in February, April and May 1983. Nevertheless, this is a relevant point. It is insufficient, however, to persuade me that the ordinary meaning of the words of the special condition should not prevail. Moreover, it is outweighed by another factor: while both parties were aware of the existence of the quota system and indeed its details, it is relevant in my judgment that the sellers had a substantial business presence in
g Thailand, whereas the buyers did not. Looking at the position at the time of the conclusion of the contract, it would therefore have been in the minds of the parties that in relation to the potential exhaustion of the quota the sellers would have been in a markedly better position to assess the risks. It was argued that the board of appeal made no express finding to this effect. In my judgment, however, it is an irresistible inference from the primary facts as to the sellers' presence in Thailand, which are set out in the
h award. Moreover, *Partabmull Rameshwar v K C Sethia (1944) Ltd* [1951] 2 All ER 352n, [1951] 2 Lloyd's Rep 89, although a very different case, shows that the knowledge of the parties can be relevant to the question what the standard of the duty to obtain an export licence is (see also Benjamin *Sale of Goods* (2nd edn, 1981) para 1577). So if matters stood there, my conclusion would be that the special condition imposes an absolute obligation.

On behalf of the sellers it was submitted that the foregoing approach is wrong. It was
j said that there is a general rule that the duty to obtain a licence is one of reasonable diligence only, unless the term imposing that duty expressly or by necessary implication imposes an absolute duty to obtain an export licence. During the argument a number of cases were cited but only *Coloniale Import-Export v Loumidis Sons* [1978] 2 Lloyd's Rep 560 appeared to throw any light on the question of construction under consideration. In that

case the buyers failed to obtain an import licence. The sellers claimed damages. The
relevant contractual provisions were as follows: *a*

> '30. Authority to Export/Import: The responsibility in connection with the
> authority . . . to import into the country of destination shall be that of the buyers . . .
> 37. Force majeure: Total or partial non-performance, or tardy performance of
> the contract can only be justified by a case of force majeure.'

Lloyd J came to the following conclusion (at 562–563):   *b*

> 'The phrase "responsibility in connection with the authority to import" is far
> from precise; it could bear a number of different meanings. But bearing in mind
> that these are standard conditions intended to be incorporated in a variety of
> different contracts, governed by a variety of different municipal legal systems, and
> that art. 30 in particular is dealing with both import and export licences, I regard it *c*
> as more likely, and therefore the better construction, that art. 30 was intended to
> establish whose duty it was to get the licence in question and to leave open the
> nature of the obligation. If that is right, then it is conceded that the nature of the
> obligation here must depend on implication; and the only term that can be implied
> is the more limited obligation in accordance with *Re Anglo-Russian Merchant Traders
> Ltd. v. John Batt & Co. (London) Ltd.* But if I am wrong in what I have just said and if *d*
> art. 30 is concerned with the nature of the obligation to obtain a licence as well as
> whose duty is was, then it seems to me that on its true construction it imposes only
> the more limited obligation, and not an absolute warranty. On that view alone one
> reaches the same result but by a different route. My reasons for that view are, first,
> that it requires clear words to impose an absolute warranty in a commercial contract
> against the background of the decision of the Court of Appeal in *Anglo-Russian* *e*
> *Merchant Traders Ltd. v. John Batt & Co. (London) Ltd.*, and the word "responsibility"
> standing on its own is not, in my judgment, clear enough. Secondly, it seems to me
> that the limited obligation is more consistent with the presence of the force majeure
> clause in the same contract.'

In the present case it was conceded, and rightly so, that the only question is whether the *f*
special condition on its proper construction imposes an absolute obligation or not. No
question of an implication arises.
    The alternative ground on which Lloyd J based his conclusion involved the construction
of the relevant contractual provisions before him. He was, of course, dealing with a
differently worded contract, and he was influenced by the fact that he was dealing with
standard conditions. In no sense can the decision be said to be directly in point. Moreover, *g*
as Lloyd J recognised, the decision in *Re an arbitration between Anglo-Russian Merchant
Traders Ltd and John Batt & Co (London) Ltd* [1917] 2 KB 679 was directed to the type of
term *to be implied*. The *Anglo-Russian* decision does not in my judgment assist in the task
of interpreting the clause in the present case. In my judgment too much was made in
argument of Lloyd J's alternative observations. The task of the court is to construe the
meaning of the special condition without any preconception as to what the parties *h*
intended. In other words, it is wrong to introduce uncertainty by starting from the
viewpoint of a general rule governing such clauses, and then to resolve the question of
construction by reference to it. The court's task is simply to determine the meaning of
the provision, against its contractual and contextual scene. In the unlikely event of both
interpretations being equally open for selection, a court will select the less burdensome
obligation. That must, however, be an aid of last resort, and it does not apply in the *j*
present case.
    In my judgment the special condition, properly construed, imposed an absolute
obligation on the sellers to obtain an export certificate. And, I would add, that a similar
obligation rested on them to obtain an export licence, since the possession of the latter
was a precondition to obtaining an export certificate.

Does cl 19 override the special condition?

a   It follows from the conclusion that the special condition imposed an absolute obligation to obtain an export certificate that there was a prima facie breach of this obligation, because it is common ground that no export certificate was obtained. The question is whether the sellers are excused from liability by the provisions of cl 19. The buyers conceded that if the special condition only imposed a duty of reasonable diligence, its language would not be apt to override cl 19. Having determined, however, that the

b   special condition imposed an absolute obligation to obtain an export certificate, it was submitted on behalf of the buyers that the typed special condition and the printed cl 19 are in conflict. The contract provided as follows:

'Special terms and conditions contained herein and/or attached hereto shall be treated as if written on such contract form and shall prevail in so far as they may be inconsistent with the printed clauses of such Contract Form.'

c

Accordingly, the buyers submitted that the special condition must prevail, or, as it was put in argument, the special condition overrides cl 19. The sellers, on the other hand, contended that, even if the special condition imposed an absolute obligation, its language does not evince an intention to override cl 19.

This is a question on which I have found the arguments finely balanced. Ultimately,

d   the answer must be sought in the particular language of the two contractual provisions contained in this contract. Sometimes, contracts for overseas sales contain express language making clear that the obligation to obtain an export licence is not subordinated to the force majeure clause. An example of such a provision is to be found in *C Czarnikow Ltd v Centrala Handlu Zagranicznego 'Rolimpex'* [1978] 2 All ER 1043, [1979] AC 351. In

e   that case r 18(a) of the Rules of the London Refined Sugar Association provided, inter alia, that if delivery was prevented by 'government intervention . . . beyond the Sellers' control' the contract would be void without penalty. Rule 21 made the seller 'responsible for obtaining any necessary export licence'. It further provided that 'the failure to obtain such licences shall not be sufficient grounds for a claim of force majeure if the regulations in force . . . when the contract was made, called for such licences to be obtained'. The

f   present case is quite different: there is no express provision making clear that the special condition overrides cl 19.

The premise of the buyers' argument is that the special condition and cl 19 are inconsistent. If that premise is established, the conclusion contended for by them follows. That is so because the contract expressly provides that, if the specially negotiated terms are inconsistent with the printed conditions the former prevail. The rationale of this

g   clause is obvious: in the event of inconsistency the typed words, specially selected by the parties to regulate their commercial dealings, ought to carry greater weight than a standard form provision, devised for the generality of cases involving users of the standard form. Indeed, even in the absence of such a provision, that would be the way in which a court would approach the matter in the event of a genuine inconsistency between contractual provisions: *Gesellschaft Burgerlichen Rechts v Stockholms Rederiaktiebolag*

h   *Svea, The Brabant* [1966] 1 All ER 961, [1967] 1 QB 588. The question is therefore whether the special condition and cl 19 are inconsistent. This question must be approached on the basis that the court's duty is to reconcile seemingly inconsistent provisions if that result can conscientiously and fairly be achieved. It follows that the critical question is whether the special condition and cl 19 are manifestly inconsistent.

On balance I have come to the conclusion that the special condition is not inconsistent

j   with cl 19. The starting point must be that there is an absolute obligation to obtain an export certificate. Breach of this obligation gives rise to a prima facie liability for damages. On the other hand, the sellers will be excused from liability if they can prove the necessary facts to bring the case within the scope of cl 19. Viewed from the buyers' point of view this conclusion no doubt detracts from the value to them of the absolute contractual duty placed on the sellers to obtain an export certificate. It is, however, a

construction which assigns a meaningful interpretation to both clauses, and does not
treat them as in conflict. In my view it is to be preferred to a construction which treats *a*
them as in conflict. Moreover, and looking at the matter from the point of view of the
particular words used in the special condition, the language (viz the sellers' duty 'to
provide for' export certificate), although sufficient to create an absolute duty, falls short
of evincing a clear intention to override cl 19.

In my judgment therefore the special condition does not override cl 19. The question
whether the sellers were excused by reason of the provisions of cl 19 was one of fact. The *b*
board of appeal answered that question in favour of the sellers. Prima facie that is the
end of the matter.

The remaining issues

At one stage counsel for the buyers argued that, on the findings of the board of appeal,
the sellers had not succeeded in establishing the necessary facts to bring the case within *c*
the scope of cl 19. The board of appeal found that fulfilment of the contract was
prevented by executive acts done by the government of Thailand. That is sufficient to
bring the case within the scope of cl 19. In so far as this argument was still alive at the
end of the hearing, I conclude that in the light of the board's findings it is devoid of
merit.

On behalf of the buyers one further argument was advanced. It was submitted that *d*
the sellers were, in any event, in breach because export to a non-EEC destination was
possible. At the hearing a question arose whether this argument was open to the buyers,
having regard to the issues in the arbitration. By letters dated 13, 14 and 15 May, further
submissions were placed before me. In addition an agreed statement of facts was placed
before me, which helpfully described what happened at the hearing before the board of *e*
appeal. In my judgment there is no doubt that counsel for the sellers and the board of
appeal were given the clear impression that the argument now sought to be advanced
was not being put forward. Counsel for the buyers said that goods without an EEC
certificate were 'worse than useless'; he accepted that the contract was for certificated
goods, and he did not advance the arguments now sought to be put forward. On behalf
of the sellers it was submitted before the board of appeal that the buyers were not *f*
advancing a claim for damages for failure to step to a non-EEC destination. Counsel for
the buyers did not demur. In my judgment is is quite clear that this question was not an
issue which the board of appeal was called on to decide. That is the end of the matter. It
is right, however, to add that the position adopted at the arbitration by counsel for the
buyers was plainly right: the contract was to supply certificated goods, and, in any event,
the buyers did not want uncertificated goods. The contrary arguments were not *g*
sustainable.

Conclusion

It follows that the appeal must fail.

Appeal dismissed.   *h*

Solicitors: *Middleton Potts & Co* (for the buyers); *Sinclair Roche & Temperley* (for the sellers).

K Mydeen Esq   Barrister.

a

Cooper and another v Coles

QUEEN'S BENCH DIVISION
STEPHEN BROWN LJ AND OTTON J
9 JULY 1986

b *House to house collection – Collection – Sale of goods – Sale by means of visits from house to house on representation that part of proceeds would go to charity – Whether a 'collection' – Whether such sales required to be licensed – House to House Collections Act 1939, s 1.*

For the purpose of s 1[a] of the House to House Collections Act 1939 a 'collection' includes an inducement to purchase an article on the representation that part of the proceeds will *c* go to charity, and accordingly going from house to house selling goods on that basis requires a licence under s 1 (see p 93 *e* to *g*, p 94 *g* to *j* and p 95 *a*, post).

    Emanuel v Smith [1968] 2 All ER 529 followed.
    Dictum of Forbes J in *Murphy v Duke* [1985] 2 All ER at 280 disapproved.

Notes
d For house to house collections, see 5 Halsbury's Laws (4th edn) paras 860–869, and for cases on the subject, see 8(1) Digest (Reissue) 481–482, 2499–2502.
    For the House to House Collections Act 1939, s 1, see 5 Halsbury's Statutes (4th edn) 664.

Cases referred to in judgments
e *Emanuel v Smith* [1968] 2 All ER 529, sub nom *Carasu Ltd v Smith* [1968] 2 QB 383, [1968] 2 WLR 1354, DC.
Murphy v Duke [1985] 2 All ER 274, [1985] QB 905, [1985] 2 WLR 773.

Case stated
f Brian George Cooper and John McGee Mason appealed by way of case stated by the justices for the county of Nottinghamshire acting in and for the petty sessional division of the City of Nottingham in respect of their adjudication as a magistrates' court sitting at Guildhall, Nottingham on 21 January 1985 whereby on informations laid by the respondent, Edward James Coles, an inspector of the Nottingham Constabulary, the appellants were found guilty of promoting a collection for charitable purposes between *g* 2 May and 30 June 1984 in Nuthall Road, Nottingham during a period for which there was no licence in force authorising such collection, contrary to s 1(2) of the House to House Collections Act 1939. The facts are set out in the judgment of Otton J.

Peter Ralls for the appellants.
Lynn Tayton for the respondent.
h

OTTON J (delivering the first judgment at the invitation of Stephen Brown LJ). This matter comes before the court by way of case stated by the justices for the county of Nottinghamshire, acting in the petty sessional division of the City of Nottingham in respect of their adjudication on 21 January 1985.
j   On 1 November 1984 an information was laid by the respondent, an inspector of the Nottinghamshire Constabulary, against the first appellant stating that he, between 2 May and 30 June 1984 in the city of Nottingham, did promote a collection for charitable purposes in Nuthall Road, Nottingham, during a period for which there was no licence

---

a   Section 1, so far as material, is set out at p 92 *g h*, post

in force authorising any such collection, contrary to s 1(2) of the House to House
Collections Act 1939. There was a second information in identical terms against the *a*
second appellant.

The facts heard by the justices were not in dispute, and they can be summarised as
follows. Some time between the end of May and the beginning of June 1984 a Mr
Brooks, who lives at 9 Nuthall Road, purchased at his home an ironing board cover for
the sum of £3·99 from an unknown woman who purported to represent the 'St Mary's
Charity Aid'. She produced an identity card stating 'St Mary's Charity Aid', on the reverse *b*
of which it was stated that a donation had been made to a Jimmy Saville Appeal. The
precise nature of that appeal was not before us, but we proceed on the basis that that was
a thoroughly good and worthy cause. No doubt the magistrates did also. The woman
stated that St Mary's was a registered charity. The magistrates found as a fact that Mr
Brooks would not have purchased the item if he had known that the St Mary's Charity
Aid was not in fact a registered charity. At the material time, the appellants were the *c*
principals involved in the running of the organisation known as St Mary's Charity Aid.
This was not a registered charity but a private company who supplied goods and identity
cards to people who then went selling door to door representing themselves as being
from St Mary's Charity Aid. The magistrates found as a fact that St Mary's Charity Aid
do make donations to charity.

It was conceded by the appellants before the magistrates, and before this court, that *d*
their acts amount to a promotion and that it was for a charitable purpose within the 1939
Act. It was contended on behalf of the appellants that the activity complained of did not
fall within the definition of a collection, since the exchange of goods for money amounted
to a sale of goods. The magistrates, having been referred to several authorities, came to
the conclusion that there was a collection within the meaning of the Act and they
convicted the appellants. *e*

The question which has been referred to the court is as follows, with a slight
amendment: were the magistrates correct in convicting the appellants of providing a
collection for charitable purposes during a period for which there was no licence in force,
contrary to s 1(2) of the 1939 Act, on finding that the activities of the appellants fell
within the ambit of a collection as defined by s 11(1) of the Act? *f*

It is necessary to look at the Act in question. It is 'An Act to provide for the regulation
of house to house collections for charitable purposes; and for matters connected
therewith'. Section 1 provides, so far as material:

> '(1) Subject to the provisions of this Act, no collection for a charitable purpose
> shall be made unless the requirements of this Act as to a licence for the promotion
> thereof are satisfied. *g*
> (2) If a person promotes a collection for a charitable purpose, and a collection for
> that purpose is made in any locality pursuant to his promotion, then, unless there is
> in force, throughout the period during which the collection is made in that locality,
> a licence authorising him, or authorising another under whose authority he acts, to
> promote a collection therein for that purpose, he shall be guilty of an offence . . .'

h

Section 11 is an interpretation section and states:

> '. . . "charitable purpose" means any charitable, benevolent or philanthropic
> purpose, whether or not the purpose is charitable within the meaning of any rule of
> law; "collection" means an appeal to the public, made by means of visits from house
> to house, to give, whether for consideration or not, money or other property; and *j*
> "collector" means, in relation to a collection, a person who makes the appeal in the
> course of such visits as aforesaid . . .'

Counsel for the appellants, in directing our attention to the 1939 Act, draws our
attention specifically to the words 'to give', and has sought to make a distinction between
them and the words 'to sell'.

We have been referred to *Emanuel v Smith* [1968] 2 All ER 529, [1968] 2 QB 383. The
a headnote reads (sub nom *Carasu Ltd v Smith* [1968] 2 QB 383):

> 'A company and its managing director promoted an activity in respect of which
> they employed a collector who visited house to house and offered toilet and other
> articles, saying, "Would you like to buy something in aid of the ——— fund?"
> showing a pamphlet describing the fund as a national charity. Part of the proceeds
> were given to a certain charity. No licence authorising the promotion was in force,
b and the company, its managing director and the collector were convicted of offences
> contrary to section 1 of the House to House Collections Act, 1939. On appeal, on the
> contention that the activity promoted was not a collection within section 11 of the
> Act of 1939:—*Held*, dismissing the appeal, that an activity was a "collection" within
> section 11(1) of the House to House Collections Act, 1939, if a person was induced
c to purchase an article on the representation that part of the proceeds would go to a
> charitable purpose.'

Lord Parker CJ said ([1968] 2 All ER 529 at 531–532, [1968] 2 QB 383 at 388–389):

> 'There is no doubt here that the appellant company and the appellant Emanuel
> were promoting an activity and that the appellant Hird was acting as a collector in
d the course of that activity. The sole question here is whether in each of these cases
> the activity promoted was a collection . . . Counsel for the appellants has argued that
> the appellant company's activities here do not amount to a collection within the
> meaning of the Act of 1939. He says that to say to somebody, "If you will buy our
> toothpaste some of the proceeds will find its way to the fund", is not a collection
> within the meaning of the Act of 1939. More strictly, he should say, so it seems to
e me, that to say, "Would you like to buy something in aid of the Children's Research
> Fund?", is not a collection within the meaning of the Act of 1939. In my judgment,
> it plainly comes within the definition. A collection is not confined to an appeal by
> way of house to house visits "to give", but extends to such an appeal "to give,
> whether for a consideration or not"; and, if a person is induced to purchase an article
> on the representation that part of those proceeds will go to a charitable purpose,
f then, as it seems to me, the activity is plainly a collection within the meaning of the
> Act of 1939. I would dismiss each of these appeals.'

Ashworth and Blain JJ both agreed.
In my judgment, the facts of that case are identical to the facts as found by the
magistrates and which this court has to consider. Counsel for the appellants, who is
g clearly well versed in this particular aspect of the law, seeks to advance the same argument
as was advanced by counsel for the appellants in *Emanuel v Smith*. In so doing he relies
heavily on the subsequent decision of *Murphy v Duke* [1985] 2 All ER 274, [1985] QB
905. I do not propose to go into the details of that case, which was a decision of Forbes J,
save only to record that in the headnote it is shown that the judge held, in allowing the
appeal—
h

> '(1) that a person was to be regarded as carrying on the trade of a pedlar for the
> purposes of section 5 of the Pedlars Act 1871 if he regularly earned a part of his
> living from peddling, and that, accordingly, the applicant's intention to earn about
> £10 a week from selling the association's goods as a supplement to his income, was
> an intention to trade as a pedlar. (2) That having regard to the provisions of section
j 1 of the Trading Representations (Disabled Persons) Act 1958, the definition of a
> house to house collection in section 11(1) of the House to House Collections Act
> 1939 as an appeal to the public to give money or other property "whether for
> consideration or not" did not include the activity of going from house to house
> selling goods; that, accordingly, since the House to House Collections Act 1939 did
> not apply to the activity of selling the association's goods and the applicant satisfied

all the requirements of section 5 of the Pedlars Act 1871, he was entitled to a
certificate under the latter Act.'

a

(See [1985] QB 905 at 906.)

In the course of his judgment Forbes J cast some doubt on *Emanuel v Smith*, by saying
([1985] 2 All ER 274 at 280, [1985] 1 QB 905 at 918–919):

'It is plain to me that in dealing with *Emanuel v Smith* the Divisional Court
considered that the words "to give, whether for consideration or not" were apt to *b*
cover sales and it seems to me that they did so because the provisions of the 1958
Act had not been drawn to their attention. It is quite clear from a perusal of the case,
as reported, that there is no mention of that Act at all. Counsel for the respondent
says that perhaps it is remarkable that there should have been that amount of
incuriosity both in the court and in counsel in the case, but I do not find that
difficult to understand at all. This particular Act has been brought to my attention *c*
simply because the appellant in this case is employed by an association which has a
certificate of exemption under the 1958 Act. It would, therefore, have been well
aware of the existence of the 1958 Act and its provisions and sensibly would have
instructed its solicitors and counsel about them. The activities carried out by Mr
Emanuel would not have been covered by the 1958 Act at all. He was selling
commercially produced toothpaste, he was not selling toothpaste produced by a *d*
blind or partially sighted person, nor was he representing that he was doing so, and
the 1958 Act, therefore, had no application to him. He and his solicitors and counsel
can, it seems to me, be excused, having regard to the multiplicity of statutes which
exist, for not recalling the existence of this particular statute. In any event, it seems
to me that the Divisional Court in *Emanuel v Smith* was not provided with the
arguments with which I have been provided and I feel quite satisfied that if those *e*
arguments, including in particular the argument drawn from the 1958 Act, had
been put before the Divisional Court it would not have come to the conclusion
which it did. It seems to me, therefore, that I am justified in treating that decision
as a decision given per incuriam and therefore one which I need not follow and I do
not intend to follow it.'

f

I have listened very carefully to the submissions made by counsel for the appellants.
However, I regret to say that I am not persuaded that *Emanuel v Smith* was decided per
incuriam. It seems to me that Forbes J in *Murphy v Duke* was construing and dealing with
the 1958 Act. In *Emanuel v Smith* the Divisional Court was construing the very Act which
is now before us, and in circumstances which were identical. Accordingly, in my
judgment, it is necessary to construe the 1939 Act within its own four corners. With *g*
respect to Forbes J, it is not necessary to construe the two Acts together or to construe the
earlier Act in the light of the subsequent Act. The later Act does not specifically or by
implication seek to amend the earlier Act. Accordingly, the situation is, in my judgment,
on all fours with the situation considered by the Divisional Court in *Emanuel v Smith*.

This court is bound by the decision of the Divisional Court in *Emanuel v Smith*, and
even if we were not I see no reason to depart from that decision. Accordingly, in my *h*
judgment, this appeal should be dismissed.

STEPHEN BROWN LJ. I agree, and I would add that *Emanuel v Smith* [1968] 2 All ER
529, [1968] 2 QB 383 is a very clear decision on the construction of the House to House
Collections Act 1939. The facts in that case were on 'all fours' with the facts of this case. *j*
The judgment of Lord Parker CJ, with whom the other two judges agreed, plainly
interpreted the provisions of s 11 of the 1939 Act. I am surprised that Forbes J should
have felt it appropriate to say in *Murphy v Duke* [1985] 2 All ER 274 at 280, [1985] QB
905 at 919 that he regarded that decision as having been made per incuriam. In so far as
that view is recorded in the headnote of the reports of *Murphy v Duke* I regard it as

a   important that it should be dissented from. In my judgment Forbes J was not construing the same Act. If he was purporting to construe the provisions of s 11 of the 1939 Act he was, in my judgment, wrong in the conclusion to which he came. The authority of *Emanuel v Smith* should be indorsed. It is binding on us, but in addition I take the view that that judgment is one with which I would agree even if I were not bound by it. For the reasons Otton J has given I too would dismiss this appeal.

b   *Appeal dismissed.*

Solicitors: *Temple Wallis*, Nottingham (for the appellants); *D W Ritchie*, Nottingham (for the respondent).

Raina Levy   Barrister.

c

Orchard v South Eastern Electricity Board

COURT OF APPEAL, CIVIL DIVISION

SIR JOHN DONALDSON MR, DILLON AND CROOM-JOHNSON LJJ

d   3, 4, 13 NOVEMBER 1986

Solicitor – Costs – Payment by solicitor personally – Legally-aided plaintiff bringing unsuccessful action against defendants – Defendants seeking order for costs against solicitor personally on ground that plaintiff's claim so hopeless that solicitor by inference guilty of serious misconduct in allowing action to continue – Plaintiff not waiving client's privilege – Whether order for costs
e   *against solicitor appropriate – RSC Ord 62, r 8(1).*

The plaintiff instructed solicitors and obtained legal aid to bring an action against the defendant electricity board claiming damages for negligence and/or breach of statutory duty and alleging, inter alia, that faults in the electricity supply provided by the defendants to his house had caused substantial quantities of water to appear in parts of
f   the property, such as the floor, ceilings and light sockets. The defendants by their defence alleged that the damage was self-inflicted. Prior to the trial the defendants' solicitors wrote to the plaintiff's solicitors warning that in their view the action was misconceived and if it was proceeded with and was unsuccessful they intended to apply for an order under RSC Ord 62, r 8(1)[a] making the solicitor personally liable for their costs. They also wrote to the legal aid committee which had granted the plaintiff legal aid suggesting that
g   it discharge the legal aid certificates, but the committee declined to do so. The action proceeded to trial, where the plaintiff's claim was supported by expert witnesses. The judge found that the damage to the plaintiff's house had been deliberately caused by the plaintiff's son and that the plaintiff and his family must have been aware of that. The judge accordingly dismissed the claim. The defendants then applied for an order under
h   Ord 62, r 8(1) that the plaintiff's solicitors be personally liable for their costs, contending that the plaintiff's claim was so obviously bizarre and unlikely to succeed that the solicitors had been guilty of serious misconduct in bringing and continuing the litigation. The plaintiff refused to waive the solicitor/client privilege with the result that the plaintiff's solicitors were unable in their defence to disclose any matters passing between them and their client. The judge refused to make the order against the solicitors. The
j   defendants appealed.

Held – Although the court had jurisdiction under RSC Ord 62, r 8(1) to order an unsuccessful party's solicitor to pay personally the costs of the opposing successful party,

---

a   Rule 8(1) is set out at p 97 *g h*, post

that power would be exercised with great care and only where there was clear evidence
that the solicitor had allowed to proceed an action which was so inappropriate that it
could only be mala fide or amount to an abuse of the process of court, since in rebutting
a complaint a solicitor might be restricted by his duty of confidentiality to his client. In
the circumstances, since there was no evidence of matters passing between the plaintiff's
solicitors, their client and the legal aid committee, it could not be inferred that the
solicitors had misled the committee, or that they had supported a claim which they
thought to be inappropriate. Furthermore, the plaintiff's case had been supported by
expert evidence and the trial judge who had heard that and the other evidence had
declined to make an order against the solicitors. The appeal would therefore be dismissed
(see p 100 b to e, p 101 g h, p 102 a b, p 104 d and p 105 h to p 106 c h j, post).

Edwards v Edwards [1958] 2 All ER 179, Kelly v London Transport Executive [1982] 2
All ER 842, and Davy-Chiesman v Davy-Chiesman [1984] 1 All ER 321 considered.

Per curiam. (1) There is no basis for suggesting that counsel owes any duty to his
client's opponent in litigation or that the public interest immunity protecting members
of the Bar only relates to claims by their own lay clients, leaving them unprotected from
claims by the other side (see p 99 e to g and p 106 f g, post); Rondel v Worsley [1967] 3 All
ER 993 explained; dictum of Lord Denning MR in Kelly v London Transport Executive
[1982] 2 All ER at 851 disapproved.

(2) Threats made prior to, or during the hearing of, an action that an application will
be made for costs against the other party's solicitor personally are objectionable as being
contrary to the interests of justice and the proper conduct of a case and (per Dillon LJ)
might in certain circumstances amount to contempt of court (see p 104 b c and p 106 f j,
post).

Per Dillon and Croom-Johnson LJJ. RSC Ord 62, r 8 is not apt to cover an application
for an order for costs to be made against counsel (see p 106 g j, post); dictum of May LJ in
Davy-Chiesman v Davy-Chiesman [1984] 1 All ER at 328 applied.

Cases referred to in judgments

Blundell v Blundell (1822) 5 B & Ald 533, 106 ER 1286.
Carl-Zeiss-Stiftung v Herbert Smith & Co (a firm) (No 2) [1968] 2 All ER 1233; affd on different
   grounds [1969] 2 All ER 367, [1969] 2 Ch 276, [1969] 2 WLR 427, CA.
Davy-Chiesman v Davy-Chiesman [1984] 1 All ER 321, [1984] Fam 48, [1984] 2 WLR 291,
   CA.
Edwards v Edwards [1958] 2 All ER 179, [1958] P 235, [1958] 2 WLR 956.
Jones, Re (1870) LR 6 Ch App 497, LC.
Kelly v London Transport Executive [1982] 2 All ER 842, [1982] 1 WLR 1055, CA.
Myers v Elman [1939] 4 All ER 484, [1940] AC 282, HL.
Rondel v Worsley [1967] 3 All ER 993, [1969] 1 AC 191, [1967] 3 WLR 1666, HL.
Whitehouse v Jordan [1981] 1 All ER 267, [1981] 1 WLR 246, HL; affg [1980] 1 All ER
   650, CA.

Cases also cited

Dawson v Ramoneur Co Ltd (1976) 120 SJ 838.
Hanning v Maitland (No 2) [1970] 1 All ER 812, [1970] 1 QB 580, CA.
Holmes v National Benzole Co Ltd (1965) 109 SJ 971.
Kyle v Mason (1963) Times, 3 July, CA.

Appeal

The defendants, South Eastern Electricity Board, appealed against that part of the
judgment of Steyn J dated 18 March 1985 whereby, having dismissed the action brought
by the plaintiff, Joseph William Alexander Orchard, against the board for negligence
and/or breach of statutory duty in respect of damage to the plaintiff's property, known
as 3 Church Lane, Adisham, Kent, by faults in the electrical supply provided by the
board, the judge refused the board's application for an order pursuant to RSC Ord 62,

r 8(1)(c) that the plaintiff's solicitors, Messrs Roderick O'Driscoll & Partners, should pay
personally the costs of the board in their defence of the action. The facts are set out in the
judgment of Sir John Donaldson MR.

Dermod O'Brien QC and *Andrew Collender* for the board.
Jonathan R Playford QC and *Roger Eastman* for the plaintiff and the solicitors.

Cur adv vult

13 November. The following judgments were delivered.

SIR JOHN DONALDSON MR. The plaintiff, assisted by solicitors and counsel under
the Legal Aid Act 1974, brought proceedings against the South Eastern Electricity Board
claiming damages for negligence and breach of statutory duty. After a hearing which
lasted for 12 days, Steyn J dismissed the plaintiff's claim with costs but, in the light of the
fact that his means were such that he had not been required to make any contribution
under the legal aid scheme, stayed execution of that part of the order which related to
costs until further order.

In the light of s 13(3)(b) of the 1974 Act and of the decision of this court in *Kelly v
London Transport Executive* [1982] 2 All ER 842, [1982] 1 WLR 1055, it was appreciated
by the board and their professional advisers that an application for an order that the costs
of the board should be paid out of the legal aid fund was doomed to failure.
Notwithstanding that they had incurred substantial costs (the plaintiff's own costs were
taxed at £54,000 and the boards costs were likely to have been comparable) they could
not realistically submit that this would cause them 'serious financial hardship'. The board
had from the outset contended that the plaintiff's claim was wholly without foundation.
In default of being able to look to the legal aid fund for reimbursement, they applied for
an order under RSC Ord 62, r 8 that the plaintiff's solicitors be required to pay their costs
of defending themselves against the claim. The judge dismissed this application and the
board now appeal.

Before turning to the appeal itself, it is desirable that I should say a word about RSC
Ord 62, r 8. Rule 8(1) merely confirms the ancient jurisdiction of the court to exercise
control over its own officers, who include all who are admitted to the roll of solicitors.
Their full title is indeed 'Solicitor of the Supreme Court'. Rule 8(1) is in the following
terms:

'Subject to the following provisions of this rule, where in any proceedings costs
are incurred improperly or without reasonable cause or are wasted by undue delay
or by any other misconduct or default, the Court may make against any solicitor
whom it considers to be responsible (whether personally or through a servant or
agent) an order—(a) disallowing the costs as between the solicitor and his client; and
(b) directing the solicitor to repay to his client costs which the client has been ordered
to pay to other parties to the proceedings; or (c) directing the solicitor personally to
indemnify such other parties against costs payable by them.'

In making the application in the court below counsel for the board comprehensively
condemned not only the plaintiff's leading and junior counsel, but 'anybody else who
has been involved in the handling of the plaintiff's case'. In terms he claimed to make no
distinction between them and submitted that it would be invidious for the court to do
so. He continued:

'I ask that the solicitor be ordered to pay the costs of this case, the court recognising
that he may have claims over which he may see fit to exercise. Whether these are
against counsel, against Mr Saunders [a witness] or against others that have been
engaged in this matter is not for me to say.'

It is not clear to me what rights the solicitor would have against a witness, whether

expert or otherwise, in respect of evidence given in court and the assertion of such a
right, other than rhetorically, would raise an issue of considerable public interest and *a*
importance. When I inquired what rights the solicitor would have against counsel, I was
referred to the judgment of Lord Denning MR in *Kelly v London Transport Executive*
[1982] 2 All ER 842 at 850–851, [1982] 1 WLR 1055 at 1064–1065. He said:

'Over the weekend I have looked at the authorities in this matter. As a result, the
principle is clear that a solicitor is under a duty, not only to his own client who is
legally aided, but also to the unassisted party who is not legally aided. If the solicitor *b*
fails in that duty, the unassisted party is at liberty to call him before the court,
whereupon the court can make an order that he is to make good any loss or expense
caused to the unassisted party by any breach of it. This is well established. It is not
confined to legally-aided cases, but to all cases, an order to make the solicitor pay the
costs of the other side. As Abbott CJ said as long ago as 1822 in *Blundell v Blundell* 5
B & Ald 533 at 534, 106 ER 1286: ". . . it will be a wholesome lesson to others . . ." *c*
Lord Hatherley LC said in *Re Jones* (1870) LR 6 Ch App 497 at 499 that solicitors
must—"not only perform their duty towards their own clients, but also towards all
those *against* whom they are concerned, and that care should be taken to see that the
litigation is the *bonâ fide* litigation of the client who instructs the solicitor, and not a
litigation carried on altogether on the solicitor's account." [Lord Denning MR's *d*
emphasis.] This principle was emphatically affirmed by the House of Lords in *Myers
v Elman* [1939] 4 All ER 484 at 489, [1940] AC 282 at 290, where Viscount Maugham
said: "These cases did not depend on disgraceful or dishonourable conduct by the
solicitor, but on mere negligence of a serious character, the result of which was to
occasion *useless costs to the other parties*." [Lord Denning MR's emphasis.] These then
are the duties of solicitors who act for legally-aided clients. They must inquire *e*
carefully into the claim made by their own legally-aided client so as to see that it is
well founded and justified, so much so that they would have advised him to bring
it on his own if he had enough means to do so, with all the risks that failure would
entail. They must consider also the position of the other side. They must not take
any advantage of the fact that their own client is legally aided and so not able to pay
any costs. They must not use legal aid as a means to extort a settlement from the *f*
other side. They must remember the position of the defendant and that he is bound
to incur a lot of costs to fight the case. If a reasonable payment is made into court, or
a reasonable offer is made, they must advise its acceptance. They must not proceed
with the case on the chance of getting more. They must put out of their minds
altogether the fact that, by going on with the case, they will get more costs for
themselves. They must not run up costs by instructing endless medical experts for *g*
endless reports or by any unnecessary expenditure. They must not ask a medical
expert to change his report, at their own instance, so as to favour their own legally-
aided client or conceal things that may be against him. They must not "settle" the
evidence of the medical experts as they did in *Whitehouse v Jordan*, which received
the condemnation of this court (see [1980] 1 All ER 650 at 655) and the House of
Lords. As Lord Wilberforce said ([1981] 1 All ER 267 at 276, [1981] 1 WLR 246 at *h*
256–257): "Expert evidence presented to the court should be, and should be seen to
be, the independent product of the expert, uninfluenced as to form or content by
the exigencies of litigation." All this is not only in regard to solicitors but also to
counsel as well. We all know that the area committees depend largely on the opinion
of counsel, whether legal aid should be given for the purpose or not, and whether
the case should proceed further or not. So much so that counsel have a special *j*
responsibility in these cases. They owe a duty to the area committees who rely on
their opinions. They owe a duty to the court which has to try the case. They owe a
duty to the other side who have to fight it and pay all the costs of doing so. If they
fail in their duty, I have no doubt that the court can call them to account and make

them pay the costs of the other side. They will not be able to escape on the ground
that it was work done by them in the course of litigation. They cannot claim the
immunity given to them by *Rondel v Worsley* [1967] 3 All ER 993, [1969] 1 AC 191.
That only avails them in regard to their own client. They have no immunity if they
fail to have regard to their duty to the court and to the other side. If these precepts
are observed, I hope we shall in future have no more disgraces such as have attended
this case. But for the reasons I have given, I would dismiss this appeal.'

The circumstances in which these remarks came to be made were unusual. The issue
in the appeal appears to have been confined to whether the LTE could make good its
claim to have its costs paid out of the legal aid fund. Certainly there is no trace in the
report of any application by LTE for an order against the solicitor. This part of the
judgment was therefore obiter. Furthermore, it appears that the argument was concluded
on a Friday and judgment given on the Monday, these remarks being based on personal
research conducted 'over the weekend' without the benefit of argument from counsel.
Neither Ackner nor O'Connor LJJ adverted to the topic in terms and I do not construe
the introductory words of the judgment of Ackner LJ ('I agree') as conveying anything
more than his agreement that the appeal should be dismissed.

I have quoted from the judgment at some length for two reasons. First, because it
provides a useful summary of the duties of a solicitor acting for a legally-aided client.
Whether that duty is owed to the opposing party is open to considerable doubt, at least
where the solicitor is acting with the authority of his client and is not carrying on the
litigation on his own account. However, the duty is undoubtedly owed to the court (see
Myers v Elman [1939] 4 All ER 484 at 497, [1940] AC 282 at 302 per Lord Atkin), the
duty being to conduct the litigation with due propriety, and the court may, in the
exercise of its traditional jurisdiction over its own officers, order the solicitor to
compensate the opposing party where the solicitor is in breach of that duty to the court.
Second, because, whilst there is no doubt that members of the Bar owe a duty to the
court as well as to their lay client, I know of no basis for a contention that they owe any
independent duty to their lay client's opponent. Furthermore, so far as I am aware, the
courts have never asserted any jurisdiction over members of the Bar, apart from their
general jurisdiction to control the conduct of all who appear before them and apart from
their appellate jurisdiction as visitors of the four Inns of Court, and it would seriously
undermine the independence of the Bar if they did so. Equally, I can find no basis in
logic or authority for holding that the essential public interest immunity affirmed in
Rondel v Worsley [1967] 3 All ER 993, [1969] 1 AC 191 protects the Bar only in relation
to claims by their own lay clients, leaving them unprotected in respect of the far greater
risk of claims by disgruntled litigants on the other side.

For the sake of completeness, I should draw attention to the fact that the only order
made by the court in relation to the solicitor concerned was that he should attend before
the court *for consideration* of whether he should pay the LTE's costs. This was an order
which it was within the court's competence to make of its own motion, but in fact it was
subsequently rescinded in chambers in the light of representations by the solicitor with
the concurrence of the LTE. The liability of the solicitor and the correctness of Lord
Denning MR's opinion never therefore received further consideration.

One of the earlier cases in which the court was asked to exercise this jurisdiction in the
context of legally-aided litigation was *Edwards v Edwards* [1958] 2 All ER 179, [1958] P
235. Two matters were in issue. First, it was said that the wife's solicitors had run up the
costs of documentation without regard to propriety. Second, and more relevant to the
present application, it was said that the wife's solicitor continued with a claim for
maintenance without seeking the advice of counsel and after becoming aware on
discovery that there was no basis for any allegation that the husband had wilfully
neglected to maintain the wife.

Sachs J examined the authorities and stated that it was axiomatic that the mere fact

that the litigation failed was no reason for invoking the jurisdiction, nor was an error of
judgment, nor even the mere fact that an error was of an order which constituted or was *a*
equivalent to negligence. There had to be something which amounted to a serious
dereliction of duty (see [1958] 2 All ER 179 at 186, [1958] P 235 at 248). The decision of
this court in *Davy-Chiesman v Davy-Chiesman* [1984] 1 All ER 321, [1984] Fam 48 was to
the like effect. The jurisdiction could only be invoked in the case of serious misconduct,
and the initiation or continuance of an action when it had no or substantially no chance
of success might constitute such misconduct (see [1984] 1 All ER 321 at 334, [1984] Fam *b*
48 at 67 per Dillon LJ).

That said, this is a jurisdiction which falls to be exercised with care and discretion and
only in clear cases. In the context of a complaint that litigation was initiated or continued
in circumstances in which to do so constituted serious misconduct, it must never be
forgotten that it is not for solicitors or counsel to impose a pre-trial screen through which
a litigant must pass before he can put his complaint or defence before the court. On the *c*
other hand, no solicitor or counsel should lend his assistance to a litigant if he is satisfied
that the initiation or further prosecution of a claim is mala fide or for an ulterior purpose
or, to put it more broadly, if the proceedings would be, or have become, an abuse of the
process of the court or unjustifiably oppressive.

There is one other aspect of which sight must not be lost. Justice requires that the
solicitor shall have full opportunity of rebutting the complaint, but circumstances can *d*
arise in which he is hampered by his duty of confidentiality to his client, from which he
can only be released by his client or by overriding authority, such as that contained in
reg 74 of the Legal Aid (General) Regulations 1980, SI 1980/1894. In such circumstances
justice requires that the solicitor be given the benefit of any doubt.

The plaintiff's complaints were weird in the extreme. In the autumn of 1977 he was
living with his wife and 15-year-old son at 3 Church Lane, Adisham, near Canterbury in *e*
Kent. This was a semi-detached cottage. Substantial quantities of water were found on a
number of occasions in different parts of the cottage, such as the floor, ceilings and near
light sockets. The plaintiff was an employee of the water authority and was well placed
to satisfy himself that this was not of its doing. He then conceived the idea that the
defendant electricity board must be responsible. In fairness to the board, it must be said *f*
that they investigated this surprising claim quickly and thoroughly and reached the
conclusion, which proved right in the event, that someone in the household was spilling
or throwing water about. The phenomenon continued and indeed spread to such bizarre
happenings as the uncovenanted and unexplained movement of physical objects within
the rooms and damage to the ceilings and pipework to an extent which caused the cottage
to become uninhabitable and the plaintiff and his family to leave for rented *g*
accommodation.

If matters had stopped there, I should have had considerable doubts about the propriety
of assisting the plaintiff to launch an action against the board and I am confident that he
would not have obtained legal aid. However, they did not stop there. The plaintiff
consulted solicitors who took expert advice which led to the evolution of the theory that
the cause might lie in defects in the board's system of earthing and/or some discontinuity *h*
in the neutral electricity line serving the cottage. The details do not matter for present
purposes. Suffice it to say that these solicitors, who were a different firm from those who
carried the matter through to trial, applied for and were granted an unconditional legal
aid certificate to prosecute the plaintiff's claim. It must be inferred that this application
was supported by counsel's opinion. Immediately thereafter, the plaintiff changed his
solicitors, or vice versa, and Messrs Roderick O'Driscoll & Partners of Maidstone took *j*
over the conduct of the proceedings. It is in relation to that firm that the application is
made.

The plaintiff's case at the trial was that all the water phenomena were caused by an
escape of electricity through the earth under the cottage, thereby heating water in the
soil to a point at which it became steam and/or causing the water to change into hydrogen

and oxygen gases, the latter being responsible explosively for some of the so-called 'dynamic' incidents, ie the movement of physical objects. In fact, on the advice of counsel, reliance on the 'dynamic' phenomena was abandoned some time before the trial. All this may sound ludicrous, but there is no doubt that it was supported by expert advice. Furthermore, the alternative was prima facie even more ludicrous. It was that someone in the plaintiff's household, to the knowledge of the other members, was deliberately and systematically destroying their home for no apparent purpose other than to mount a claim against the board, notwithstanding that no member of the family appeared to have any grudge against the board. It was a quite astonishing situation, in which the truth, as eventually determined by the judge, namely that it was probably all the work of the son, but that the plaintiff and his wife must from an early stage have realised what was going on, was even stranger than the fiction propagated by the plaintiff, supported in all innocence as he was by experts, some of whom were highly qualified.

The initial basis of the application under RSC Ord 62, r 8, and of the appeal, was that the solicitors were guilty of serious misconduct in failing to inform the legal aid authorities of the circumstances and prospects for success of the plaintiff's claim, contrary to their duty under s 7(5) of the Legal Aid Act 1974. There was no evidence of any such failure, but counsel for the board invited the court to infer it on the basis that, if this duty had been complied with, the legal aid authorities could not possibly have failed to discharge the plaintiff's legal aid certificate. This view was based on a very large number of arguments and a body of evidence on which the board successfully relied at the trial, the substance of which had been communicated to the plaintiff's solicitors some time beforehand. However, it is not clear to me why it necessarily follows that the legal aid authorities would have discharged the plaintiff's certificate if this information had been passed to them. After all, counsel may have advised on the basis of the opinions of the plaintiff's experts that there was some answer and that a reasonable chance of success still remained. And it must never be forgotten that what the board were alleging was that this damage was self-inflicted. This is not something which the legal aid authorities could be expected to accept lightly.

In point of fact there were at least two contra-indications to drawing any such inference. The first was that the board's solicitors had themselves at an early state written to the legal aid authorities giving reasons why the certificates should be discharged. Whatever else might be expected, it could hardly be said that the authorities had not been put on inquiry and I infer, in the absence of evidence to the contrary, that they made inquiries of the plaintiff's solicitors and counsel and were satisfied by the answers which they received. This, of course, leaves open the possibility that they were misled by solicitors and counsel. This is certainly not something which I should be prepared to assume. In any event, in this context, it has to be remembered that the plaintiff's solicitors, and for that matter counsel, are unable to give evidence of what they were asked, what they replied and what information they volunteered. All this must remain under the seal of professional privilege, in the absence of a waiver by the plaintiff or, since he is now dead, his personal representatives. We were told, and I accept, that no such waiver has been forthcoming. The second contra-indication is that, despite what emerged at the trial, details of which can scarcely have escaped the attention of the legal aid authorities, they have themselves taken no action whatever against the plaintiff's solicitors or counsel or, so far as I am aware, given any indication that they were dissatisfied with the way in which solicitors and counsel discharged their duties to the fund.

However that may be, this basis for the board's claim wholly disappears when leading counsel for the plaintiff at the trial (not Mr Jonathan Playford QC) told the judge, on instructions, and the judge accepted, that the legal aid committee were informed of all the summonses and of all the reports and of all the advices of counsel. The board in their notice of appeal alleged that 'The learned Judge misinterpreted the assurance of Counsel as to the extent to which the committee was informed of the course and prospects of the claim', but, having subsequently read the transcript, counsel for the board quite rightly

did not press this contention. Instead he relied on what he characterised in his skeleton
argument as the duty of the plaintiff's solicitors so to act as to protect the board from the　*a*
expenses of defending a hopeless claim.

I am bound to say that, so stated, I do not believe that such duty exists. However, I do
accept that the plaintiff's solicitors had a duty not to further a claim which could be
characterised as an abuse of the process of the court and this, I think, is what counsel
really meant. In support of it he contended that no competent counsel, whether leader
or junior, no competent solicitor and no competent expert could possibly have supported　*b*
the plaintiff's claim.

The basis of this somewhat sweeping assertion was that, in order to make good his
claim, the plaintiff would have to explain how it was that water ran uphill under this
cottage, leaving the footings dry, through a layer of bitumen, and in some cases also
through a damp-proof membrane, and then through a layer of thermoplastic tiles leaving
them undisturbed. He would also have to explain this phenomenon in the face of　*c*
evidence that his experience was unique in the 65-year history of the electricity supply
industry and why the other semi-detached cottage was not also similarly affected. In
addition there were other problems facing the plaintiff. To boil the moisture in the soil
under the cottage would require enormous energy and this simply was not available and,
if it had been available, the water would not have arrived in the cottage cold, ie at the
ambient temperature. Finally, confining myself to the major points made by counsel for　*d*
the board, the plaintiff had to overcome the damage to his credibility arising out of the
abandoned claims based on the so-called dynamic incidents.

Whilst I have to agree that all this takes some swallowing, I am far from convinced
that it would necessarily have looked like this to the plaintiff's solicitors, counsel and
experts preparing for the trial or earlier. The conclusive element, which counsel for the
board quite rightly omits from his catalogue, is hindsight, knowledge that all these　*e*
factors were proved at the trial and the plaintiff was quite unable to overcome them. In
the end what matters is what the judge thought. He lived with this saga for 12 days. He
had unrivalled opportunities for hearing the plaintiff's case put and knowing what it
looked like before it was destroyed by cross-examination and the deployment of the
board's evidence. Forewarned of this application, the following interchange took place　*f*
between him and counsel for the board during the latter's final speech:

> '*Steyn J*. There is one last matter I want to mention to you, and perhaps it is not
> strictly relevant to the merits, and I am giving no indication of which way I am
> thinking at the moment. But assume for the sake of argument I were in your
> favour, I did notice that your solicitors expressed extremely strong views about this
> case, and in a certain eventuality it is something I ought perhaps to refer to, because　*g*
> it struck me that the legal aid authorities were absolutely correct in granting legal
> aid in this case, and indeed that the solicitors and counsel involved acted perfectly
> properly, and I would have been disappointed in all of them if they had not acted as
> they had. It is only in a certain eventuality that I will refer to that, but I thought I
> would put it to you. *Mr O'Brien*: My Lord, I am saving my argument on that until I
> have heard your Lordship's judgment. I would ask your Lordship to, as it were,　*h*
> reserve your Lordship's observations until that matter came to arise.'

Later, when counsel for the board had deployed his arguments in full, the judge gave
a judgment in which he reviewed the authorities and expressed his conclusion as follows:

> 'I do not therefore disagree with the legal submissions advanced on behalf of the　.
> board. In my judgment, however, the matter raises no issue of principle. It simply　*j*
> involves the application of well-known principles to the facts of this case. While it
> was not positively submitted that the area committee had been misled, leading
> counsel for the board issued what he described as a number of challenges, thereby
> seeking to elicit information as to what the committee was told on various aspects

of the case. I have been informed by leading counsel for [the plaintiff] that the
committee was kept informed of the advice of counsel, the interlocutory proceedings
and all reports received. I accept this assurance, and proceed to consider the matter
on the basis that the committee was fairly informed of the circumstances of the case.
It is, however, submitted that the proceedings were doomed to fail, and that any
competent lawyer would have so advised. This submission came as something of a
surprise to me. When it was made I inquired why it was then considered necessary
on behalf of the board not only to call 11 witnesses and an expert but also to cross-
examine [the plaintiff] and some of his witnesses at very great length. The answer
was, and this is understandable, that it was done out of excess of caution. So be it. I
must now consider the submission on its merits. I have, of course, in my judgment
decisively rejected [the plaintiff's] claim on a number of grounds. I did so on the
basis of a detailed consideration of the evidence and counsel's speeches. I must now
ignore hindsight, and consider the position as it would have appeared to counsel and
solicitors when they were called on to advise. While I have taken into account all
the submissions made on behalf of the board, I will simply record the principal
considerations which influenced my decision on this application. Looking at the
broad picture of this case, I take the view that the conduct of counsel and solicitors
was entirely proper, and that their decisions were reached on reasonable grounds. It
is important to bear in mind the following considerations. (a) [The plaintiff's] case
that water was seen to rise (and particularly from the area near the skirting boards)
was supported by a number of witnesses, some of them being entirely independent.
(b) An explanation for this phenomenon was advanced by Mr Bowie, an electrical
engineer, whom I described as a responsible and fair-minded expert, despite the fact
that I preferred the evidence of the board's expert. (c) Admittedly, Mr Bowie's
evidence was based on the test results of an electrician whose evidence I rejected as
wholly unreliable. Odd as his behaviour had been, I consider that counsel and
solicitors were entitled to accept his test results as a foundation for [the plaintiff's]
case. I have not lost sight of the change in [the plaintiff's] case when he abandoned
the allegation that the so-called dynamic incidents were caused by electricity.
Eventually, I attached great importance to this aspect. However, in my judgment
counsel and solicitors were conscientiously entitled to take the view that there was a
genuine claim in respect of water damage, which the plaintiff and his family had
attempted to support by the fabrication of other incidents. Finally, in so far as
emphasis has been placed on the fact that special damages were only of the order of
£2,702, and that I assessed general damages at £4,000, I should say that in my
judgment counsel could quite fairly have taken the view that if the claim succeeded
the award of general damages would be much higher. Inevitably I was influenced
by my impression that even if the claim was established the importance of the water
damage was overstated. Looking at the whole picture as revealed by the hearing of
many witnesses, I am of the opinion that the application should fail. In my view
leading counsel, his junior and solicitors acted entirely properly.'

Counsel for the board's principal attack on this judgment was directed to trying to
satisfy us that the judge should not have reached conclusions (a), (b) and (c). This
necessarily involves something in the nature of a full appeal on the facts by the successful
party to litigation on the basis of a new standard of proof, namely not the balance of
probabilities but whether the plaintiff's case reached the level of credibility at which it
could not be characterised as an abuse of the process of the court. As the rules stand, the
board may have been within their rights, but it is intriguing to speculate whether, if the
board had been of lesser financial stature and had attempted such an appeal, the plaintiff's
solicitors might not themselves have counter-attacked the board's solicitor by seeking an
order under RSC Ord 62, r 8 on the grounds that the board's appeal was itself an abuse of
the process of the court and that no solicitor should have assisted with it. I am not

suggesting that such a cross-application would necessarily have succeeded, but it is certainly a theoretical possibility and an unattractive one. Suffice it to say that none of *a* the board's submissions caused me to have the slightest doubts about the unassailability of the judge's conclusions.

There is one final matter which cannot be ignored. Whilst there can be no objection to an application under RSC Ord 62, r 8 at the conclusion of a hearing, given appropriate facts, it is quite another matter where such an application is threatened during or prior to the hearing. Objectivity is a vital requirement of professional advisers. Hence, for *b* example, the rejection of contingency fees and the impropriety of a solicitor acting for co-defendants. Threats to apply on the basis that the proceedings must fail not only make the solicitor something in the nature of a co-defendant, but they may well, and rightly, make him all the more determined not to abandon his client, thereby losing a measure of objectivity. Whilst a solicitor who has been subjected to an order making him personally liable for the costs of an action should certainly have a right of appeal, it is for *c* consideration by the Supreme Court Rule Committee whether the applicant for such an order should be able to appeal a refusal without the leave of the trial judge (cf the Supreme Court Act 1981, s 18(1)(*f*)).

I would dismiss the appeal.

DILLON LJ. The law as to the court's power under RSC Ord 62, r 8 to order a solicitor, *d* and in particular a solicitor acting for a legally-aided client, to bear the costs of litigation personally has been clearly laid down in such cases as *Edwards v Edwards* [1958] 2 All ER 179, [1958] P 235 and *Davy-Chiesman v Davy-Chiesman* [1984] 1 All ER 321, [1984] Fam 48. The only question in this appeal is as to the application of that law to the circumstances of this case.

The case is bizarre. It is now clear from the judgment of Steyn J at the trial that all the *e* 'incidents' of which the plaintiffs complained, both the so-called 'water phenomena' and the so-called 'dynamic phenomena' came about, in so far as they happened at all, by human agency, and were fabricated by the plaintiff and his wife, or by their teenage son with the knowledge of this parents, in fraud of the defendant board. The claim was entirely bogus. It does not, however, automatically follow that the plaintiff's solicitors *f* were guilty of 'a serious dereliction of duty' or 'serious misconduct' (the criteria for liability) in allowing the case to come on for trial or in their dealings with the legal aid area committee.

Certainly the relevant entries in the diary kept by the plaintiff and his wife, which came to constitute the further and better particulars of the incidents relied on in the statement of claim, make strange reading, and any lawyer might readily have concluded that it would be a difficult task to establish the board's liability on the balance of *g* probabilities, which is the standard of proof required in civil litigation. But the plaintiff and his wife were elderly people of excellent previous character, apparently sane, and not the sort of people one would readily suspect of fabricating such a case, especially as that involved wrecking their own home as the preliminary to moving out to temporary rented accommodation elsewhere. Indeed, the judge himself referred to his own *h* conclusion as extraordinary, even though he held it to be the only possible finding on the evidence. In addition, there were independent witnesses from the neighbourhood, whose good character was not in question, who believed that they had seen water appearing on the floors and elsewhere in the plaintiff's house and gave evidence to that effect. There was Mr Saunders, apparently independent of the plaintiff, who put forward pseudo-scientific theories to explain how what the plaintiff said had happened could have *j* happened, and who was apparently sufficiently qualified to take the measurements and readings which he took, although in truth they were wholly unreliable, and there was also Mr Bowie, with the qualifications to speak as an independent expert witness, who endeavoured in his report and in the witness box to show that the water phenomena could have happened as spoken to by the plaintiff and could have been due to the board's breach of duty.

a Against that background, when the board asked after judgment at the end of the trial for an order against the plaintiff's solicitors to pay the defendants' costs, the onus must have been on the board to satisfy the judge on at least the balance of probabilities that the plaintiff's solicitors had been guilty of the requisite serious dereliction of duty or serious misconduct. The board's difficulty, in endeavouring to discharge that onus, is that they do not know what passed between the plaintiff's solicitors and their client or his counsel or between the plaintiff's solicitors and the legal aid authorities: everything in those *b* fields is privileged and the privilege is the privilege of the plaintiff, not of his solicitors and still less of the board. The board have therefore to ask the court to draw inferences from the weaknesses in the plaintiff's case, as formulated from time to time, to which the board's solicitors repeatedly drew the plaintiff's solicitors' attention from the outset of the proceedings.

But the board's difficulties do not stop there. In the discussion, after the judgment as *c* between the parties, when the order for costs as against the plaintiff's solicitors was sought, the judge was told, on instructions, by leading counsel (not Mr Playford QC) then acting for the plaintiff, that matters were fairly put before the legal aid committee, that that committee was regularly kept informed of all the developments and that it was advised of all the summonses and all of the reports and of the advices of counsel. We are now asked by the defendants to say, as a matter of inference and without any evidence, *d* that all those assurances, which the judge apparently accepted, were wrong.

We are asked to conclude that the legal aid committee cannot have been kept properly informed, even though there is no indication that the legal aid authorities have ever complained or sought costs against the plaintiff's solicitors. Furthermore, in so far as it was recognised in *Davy-Chiesman v Davy-Chiesman* [1984] 1 All ER 321, [1984] Fam 48 that a solicitor is in very many circumstances protected from personal liability if he has *e* acted on the advice of experienced counsel properly instructed, the board ask us to draw an inference in the alternative from the improbability, or, as they put it, impossibility of proof, of the plaintiff's complaints, viz either that leading counsel cannot have been properly instructed when he wrote whatever opinions he did write for the legal aid authorities or his opinions were so inept and fell so far short of proper discharge of his *f* duty that no competent solicitor, exercising common sense, could have paid any attention to them.

So far as those alternatives are concerned, there is no material whatsoever from which this court could make a finding that counsel was not properly instructed. As to the shortcomings of counsel's opinions, we have not seen those opinions. It may well be the duty of counsel primarily, but also of the solicitor with due regard to the views expressed *g* by experienced counsel, to weigh the evidence available to his client, if a plaintiff, to see whether the plaintiff's claim raises a triable issue. It is not the duty of the solicitor to endeavour to assess the result where there is a likelihood of a conflict of evidence between his client's witnesses and those of the other side: see *Carl-Zeiss-Stiftung v Herbert Smith & Co (a firm) (No 2)* [1969] 2 All ER 367 at 378, [1969] 2 Ch 276 at 297 per Sachs LJ. In the light of the apparent integrity of the plaintiff, the apparent evidence of his supporting *h* witnesses from the neighbourhood and the reports of Mr Bowie as a qualified expert witness, I would not be prepared to hold, without ever knowing what the solicitors and counsel did advise their client and the legal aid committee, that the solicitors and counsel must have so fallen short of the proper discharge of their duty that the solicitors ought to be found guilty of a serious dereliction of duty or serious misconduct in allowing the case to proceed with the benefit of legal aid.

j In a case such as the present, the charge against a solicitor of misconduct or dereliction of duty, which would have to be made out before the court could impose personal liability for the costs of the action on the solicitor, is a serious charge, with very serious consequences. Such a charge ought not to rest solely on inference without evidence. I appreciate that, as already mentioned, defendants who wish to make such a charge against solicitors for the plaintiff have a difficulty in getting evidence because of the rules of legal professional privilege. Those rules of privilege also, however, hamper the solicitor in seeking to justify his own conduct of the case. The justification of privilege lies in the field of public policy; that a defendant may thereby be precluded from making out a *a* claim that his costs should be paid by the plaintiff's solicitor personally is part of the price which has to be accepted from rules designed to ensure that a litigant has freedom to consult with his lawyers before his case comes before the court.

This public policy aspect does, however, have further implications. The power of the court to order a solicitor to pay the costs personally where litigation has been initiated or continued unreasonably when it has no or substantially no chance of success is, in an *b* appropriate case, a very salutary power. I do not, however, regard it as at all salutary that a practice should develop whereby solicitors for defendants endeavour to browbeat solicitors for legally-aided plaintiffs into dropping their clients' cases, or into procuring revocation of the relevant legal aid certificates, by threats that the defendants will seek to hold the plaintiffs' solicitors personally liable for the costs of the litigation. In *Carl-Zeiss-Stiftung v Herbert Smith & Co (a firm) (No 2)* [1968] 2 All ER 1233 at 1236 Pennycuick J *c* said in relation to an attempt by a plaintiff to harass the solicitors for the defendant (by a claim that all funds in the solicitors' hands were subject to a constructive trust):

'The prospect of this personal liability would be a grave deterrent to a responsible solicitor undertaking the conduct of such an action at all, for ... the conduct of the action would represent a gamble on his client's success, a highly undesirable state of *d* affairs. If he did undertake the defence, the fact that he was at risk in regard to this liability might, and in many circumstances almost inevitably would, tend to influence and hamper him at various stages in the action ... He might even find that his interest was in conflict with his duty to his client, for example, in connexion with some suggested compromise. There can I think be no doubt that such a claim would represent a very serious obstruction in the course of justice.' *e*

These words can readily be applied to any such browbeating practice as I have mentioned on the part of defendants or their solicitors, should such a practice develop; indeed, such conduct might be contempt of court.

Finally I agree entirely with the comments of Sir John Donaldson MR on the dicta of Lord Denning MR in *Kelly v London Transport Executive* [1982] 2 All ER 842 at 851, *f* [1982] 1 WLR 1055 at 1065 where he suggested that an unassisted defendant who had no claim against the legal aid fund might have a claim for his costs against counsel for the unsuccessful assisted party. I do not see how it can be said that the immunity given to counsel by *Rondel v Worsley* [1967] 3 All ER 993, [1969] 1 AC 191 only applies to claims against counsel by their own clients and not to claims by the other side. I note also that in *Davy-Chiesman v Davy-Chiesman* [1984] 1 All ER 321 at 328, [1984] Fam 48 at 58 *g* per May LJ it was accepted, rightly in my view, on the wording of the rule that an application for costs under RSC Ord 62, r 8 could not be made against counsel.

In the present case counsel for the board submitted that the solicitors were liable under Ord 62, r 8 for any costs wasted by the misconduct of default of counsel instructed by the solicitors, because counsel was an 'agent', within the meaning of the rule, of the solicitors. That submission rests on a misconception of the position of counsel, vis-à-vis *h* his instructing solicitor.

I too would dismiss this appeal.

CROOM-JOHNSON LJ. I agree with the judgments of Sir John Donaldson MR and of Dillon LJ.

Appeal dismissed. Leave to appeal to the House of Lords refused. *j*

Solicitors: *L Watmore & Co* (for the board); *Barlow Lyde & Gilbert* (for the plaintiff and the solicitors).

Diana Procter   Barrister.

Practice Direction

COMPANIES COURT

Practice – Companies Court – Applications – Applications which are to be made to judge in open court – Applications which are to be made to registrar – Applications which may be dealt with by chief clerk – Insolvency Act 1986, ss 5(3), 14(3), 18(3), 127 – Insolvency Rules 1986, rr 4.3, 4.8(6), 4.15. 4.19, 4.22(2), 4.35, 4.47, 4.59, 4.74(4), 4.85, 4.102, 4.103, 4.111, 4.221, 7.11, 13.2(2).

1. As from 29 December 1986 the following applications shall be made direct to the judge and, unless otherwise ordered, shall be heard in open court:

    (i) applications to commit any person to prison for contempt;

    (ii) applications for urgent interlocutory relief (e g applications pursuant to s 127 of the Insolvency Act 1986 prior to any winding-up order being made);

    (iii) applications to restrain the presentation or advertisement of a petition to wind up;

    (iv) petitions for administration orders or an interim order on such a petition;

    (v) applications after an administration order has been made pursuant to s 14(3) of the 1986 Act (for directions) or s 18(3) of the Act (to vary or discharge the order);

    (vi) applications pursuant to s 5(3) of the 1986 Act (to stay a winding up or discharge an administration order or for directions) where a voluntary arrangement has been approved;

    (vii) appeals from a decision made by a county court or by a registrar of the High Court.

2. Subject to para 4 below all other applications shall be made to the registrar in the first instance, who may give any necessary directions and may, in the exercise of his discretion, either hear and determine it himself or refer it to the judge.

3. The following matters will also be heard in open court:

    (i) petitions to wind up (whether opposed or unopposed);

    (ii) public examinations;

    (iii) all matters and applications heard by the judge except those referred by the registrar to be heard in chambers or so directed by the judge to be heard.

4. In accordance with directions given by the Lord Chancellor the registrar has authorised certain applications to be dealt with by the chief clerk of the Companies Court pursuant to r 13.2(2) of the Insolvency Rules 1986, SI 1986/1925. The applications are:

    (a) to extend or abridge time prescribed by the rules in connection with winding up (r 4.3);

    (b) for substituted service of winding-up petitions (r 4.8(6));

    (c) to withdraw petitions (r 4.15);

    (d) for the substitution of a petitioner (r 4.19);

    (e) for directions on a petition presented by a contributory (r 4.22(2));

    (f) by the Official Receiver for limited disclosure of a statement of affairs (r 4.35);

    (g) by the Official Receiver for relief from duties imposed on him by the rules (r 4.47);

    (h) by the Official Receiver for leave to give notice of a meeting by advertisement only (r 4.59);

    (i) by a liquidator for relief from the requirement to send out forms of proof of debt (r 4.74(4));

    (j) to expunge or reduce a proof of debt (r 4.85);

    (k) to appoint a liquidator in either a compulsory or a voluntary winding up (rr 4.102 and 4.103);

    (l) for leave to a liquidator to resign (r 4.111);

(m) by a liquidator for leave to make a return of capital (r 4.221);

(n) to transfer proceedings from the High Court to the county courts (r 7.11);

(o) for leave to amend any originating application.

5. The Practice Directions dated 15 October 1979 ([1979] 3 All ER 613, [1979] 1 WLR 1416) and 3 March 1982 ([1982] 1 All ER 846, [1982] 1 WLR 389) are hereby revoked.

By the direction of the Vice-Chancellor.

10 December 1986

29 Equities Ltd v Bank Leumi (UK) Ltd

COURT OF APPEAL, CIVIL DIVISION
DILLON, CROOM-JOHNSON AND BALCOMBE LJJ
9, 10 OCTOBER 1986

Sale of land – Rescission of contract – Contract for sale of leasehold interest – Purchaser entitled to rescind if reversioner's licence to assign 'cannot be obtained' – Vendor unable to obtain licence because of purchaser's fault – Vendor purporting to rescind contract – Whether right to rescind arising on contractual date for completion – Whether question whether licence 'cannot be obtained' a question of fact – National Conditions of Sale (20th edn), condition 11(5).

By a contract dated 10 July 1985 the purchaser agreed to buy a leasehold flat from the vendor. The contract incorporated the National Conditions of Sale (20th edn), condition 11(5)[a] of which provided that the sale was subject to the reversioner's licence to assign being obtained, that the vendor would use its best endeavours to obtain the licence and that if the licence 'cannot be obtained' the vendor could rescind the contract. As a prerequisite to granting a licence the landlords (ie the reversioner) required the purchaser to provide a bank reference and two personal guarantors. On 28 November, the day before completion, the purchaser provided the names of the guarantors stating that bank references for them would follow in due course. On the same day the vendor warned the purchaser that unless the licence was procured by 29 November it would exercise its right to rescind the contract under condition 11(5). As a result the purchaser lodged a caution at the Land Registry. On 2 December, the licence to assign still not having been obtained, the vendor notified the purchaser of its intention to rescind and subsequently sought an order that the caution be vacated. The purchaser, on the other hand, sought specific performance of the contract, contending (i) that the vendor could not say that the licence 'cannot be obtained' under condition 11(5) because there were indications to the contrary and (ii) that the vendor's right to rescind under condition 11(5) did not arise at the contractual date for completion but only when specific performance would no longer be available to the purchaser. The judge held that the vendor's right to rescind under condition 11(5) arose at the date for completion of the contract and that since the landlords' licence to assign had not been forthcoming on the date for completion the vendor had been entitled to rescind on that date. He accordingly dismissed the purchaser's summons for specific performance and granted an order vacating the caution. The purchaser appealed.

Held – Condition 11(5) of the National Conditions of Sale did not require a licence to assign to be obtained by the contractual date for completion. Instead, since the precondition to the vendor's exercising his right to rescind under condition 11(5) was that the licence to assign could not be obtained, the court would consider whether at the date when the vendor purported to rescind it could fairly be said as a question of fact to be decided in the light of common sense that the licence could not be obtained. Since by

---

a   Condition 11(5) is set out at p 110 e, post

a the time the notice of rescission was given the purchaser had met the landlords' requirements for guarantors and there was every indication that the licence would be granted, the vendor had not been entitled to rescind the contract under condition 11(5). The notice of rescission was accordingly ineffective and the purchaser's appeal would be allowed (see p 113 b d f j to p 114 b, post).

Decision of Knox J [1986] 2 All ER 873 reversed.

b **Notes**

For the vendor's duty to obtain the reversioner's consent to an assignment of leasehold, see 42 Halsbury's Laws (4th edn) para 250, and for cases on the subject, see 40 Digest (Reissue) 425–426, 3772–3778.

For the right of rescission, see 42 Halsbury's Laws (4th edn) para 111, and for cases on the subject, see 40 Digest (Reissue) 311–316, 2693–2744.

c

Cases referred to in judgments

Jneid v Mirza [1981] CA Transcript 306.
Lipmans Wallpaper Ltd v Mason & Hodghton Ltd [1968] 1 All ER 1123, [1969] 1 Ch 20, [1968] 2 WLR 881.
d *Shires v Brock* (1977) 247 EG 127, CA.

Cases also cited

Aberfoyle Plantations Ltd v Cheng [1959] 3 All ER 910, [1960] AC 115, PC.
Bickel v Courtenay Investments (Nominees) Ltd [1984] 1 All ER 657, [1984] 1 WLR 795.
Day v Singleton [1899] 2 Ch 320, CA.
e *Property and Bloodstock Ltd v Emerton* [1967] 3 All ER 321, [1968] Ch 94, CA.

Appeal

The plaintiff, 29 Equities Ltd (the purchaser), appealed against the judgment of Knox J ([1986] 2 All ER 873, [1986] 1 WLR 950) given on 11 March 1986 whereby he *f* (i) dismissed the purchaser's summons for summary judgment against the defendant, Bank Leumi (UK) Ltd (the vendor), pursuant to RSC Ord 86 and refused an order for specific performance of an agreement for the sale of leasehold property known as Flat 47, 27–29 Abercorn Place, London NW8, dated 10 July 1985 made between the purchaser and the vendor, and (ii) ordered that the caution against dealings registered at Her Majesty's Land Registry on the purchaser's application of 10 December 1985 be vacated. *g* The facts are set out in the judgment of Dillon LJ.

Terence Etherton for the purchaser.
T W E Evans for the vendor.

h **DILLON LJ.** This is an appeal against a decision of Knox J given on 11 March 1986 (see [1986] 2 All ER 873, [1986] 1 WLR 1490). It raises a question as to the construction and effect of a provision in the National Conditions of Sale (20th edn) where there is a sale of leasehold property and the landlord's consent to assignment is necessary.

As to the facts, the appellant company was the purchaser and the respondent bank was the vendor of the property in question, a leasehold flat, Flat 47, 27–29 Abercorn Place, *j* London NW8, held at a ground rent for a term of 99 years from 29 September 1970. The only term of that lease which I need mention is that it included the usual covenant that the term should not be assigned without the landlords' licence which was not to be unreasonably withheld.

The contract for sale by the vendor to the purchaser was entered into on 10 July 1985. I should mention briefly certain points on the title to the flat because they explain the provision in the contract as to the completion date and they explain certain observations of the landlords later when the question of their licence to assign had arisen. The flat at

some time before March 1982 had become vested in a Mr Rozner. In March 1982 he had
assigned the lease to a company called Gallithorn Ltd which he controlled. That company   *a*
had charged the lease to the vendor by an all moneys charge. Some time later Gallithorn
Ltd went into liquidation and, with the leave of the court, in June 1984 the liquidator of
Gallithorn Ltd disclaimed the lease. Thereafter on 6 August 1984 the term of the lease
had been vested in the vendor, the mortgagee, by an order of the Companies Court under
the Companies Act 1948. That was a vesting order, and, in order that the title should be
accepted by the Land Registry, the title being registered, the stamp duty on the vesting   *b*
order had to be submitted for adjudication. Accordingly, the contract for the sale of the
lease provided that the completion should take place on the seventh day after receipt by
the vendor's solicitors of the vesting order duly adjudicated. In point of fact, the vesting
order was received by the vendor's solicitors duly adjudicated on Friday, 22 November
1985, so that the contractual completion date became Friday, 29 November 1985.

The contract for sale incorporated the National Conditions of Sale with amendments,   *c*
most of which are immaterial. Under condition 5 of the National Conditions of Sale time
was not to be of the essence of the contract. As the property was leasehold, condition 11
of the National Conditions of Sale applied. Condition 11(1) provides:

> 'Where the interest sold is leasehold for the residue of an existing term the
> following provisions of this condition shall apply.'   *d*

Condition 11(5), which is the crucial provision in this case, provides:

> 'The sale is subject to the reversioner's licence being obtained, where necessary.
> The purchaser supplying such information and references, if any, as may reasonably
> be required of him, the vendor will use his best endeavours to obtain such licence
> and will pay the fee for the same. But if the licence cannot be obtained, the vendor   *e*
> may rescind the contract on the same terms as if the purchaser had persisted in an
> objection to the title which the vendor was unable to remove.'

The effect of those last words is that, if the contract is rescinded by the vendor under
condition 11(5), the vendor is to return the deposit without interest, without the costs of
investigating the title or other compensation or payment, and the purchaser is to return   *f*
the abstract and other papers furnished to him; in other words, the matter is called off.

The vendor's right to rescind where the purchaser persists in an objection to the title
which the vendor is unable to remove is conferred by general condition 10 of the
National Conditions of Sale. Condition 10(1) provides:

> 'If the purchaser shall persist in any objection to the title which the vendor shall
> be unable or unwilling, on reasonable grounds, to remove, and shall not withdraw   *g*
> the same within 10 working days of being required so to do, the vendor may,
> subject to the purchaser's rights under Law of Property Act 1925, ss. 42 and 125, by
> notice in writing to the purchaser or his solicitor, and notwithstanding any
> intermediate negotiation or litigation, rescind the contract.'

We were also referred to the well-known condition 22 of the National Conditions of Sale.   *h*
That provides in the 20th edition:

> '(1) At any time on or after the completion date, either party, being ready and
> willing to fulfil his own outstanding obligations under the contract, may (without
> prejudice to any other right or remedy available to him) give to the other party or
> his solicitor notice in writing requiring completion of the contract in conformity
> with this condition.   *j*
> (2) Upon service of such notice as aforesaid it shall become and be a term of the
> contract, in respect of which time shall be of the essence thereof, that the party to
> whom the notice is given shall complete the contract within 16 working days after
> service of the notice (exclusive of the day of service); but this condition shall operate

a without prejudice to any right of either party to rescind the contract in the meantime . . .'

In fact, by the special conditions of this particular contract, 10 working days were substituted for 16 working days for the purposes of condition 22(2).

b As to the facts in relation to the grant of the landlords' licence to assign, they are set out with great care and in full detail in the judgment of Knox J ([1986] 2 All ER 873 at 876–881, [1986] 1 WLR 950 at 953–960), and I do not need to repeat them. It is sufficient for present purposes to say that the purchaser is a company incorporated in the Channel Islands, and it seems that it is a company which at the time of the contract had only fairly recently been established and which did not then have any bank account in this country.

c When the contract had been entered into, the vendor's solicitors on the following day, 11 July 1985, sent to the landlords' managing agents, Messrs Keith Cardale Groves, somewhat rudimentary references which had previously been supplied by the purchaser's solicitors.

One of the difficulties that arose in this case and arises in many cases where there is a sale of leasehold property subject to the landlord's consent to assign is that neither the vendor nor the purchaser has any real leverage on the landlord to give his consent or even to act speedily in going through any necessary formalities. What so often happens is that d the landlord takes a very long time before giving his mind to the matter. Surveyors or managing agents have other things to do and are in no hurry. Ultimately the matter is passed to the landlord's solicitors to prepare a formal deed of licence or consent, and rather a large meal is made of it over a considerable period of time at the expense ultimately of the vendor or purchaser of the leasehold interest.

In this case, although the information, such as it was, had been promptly sent to the e landlords' agents on 11 July they did not reply until 28 August. They then wrote, saying that they understood that Mr Rozner was a director of the purchaser company and they said that they had had difficulties before with Mr Rozner and Gallithorn Ltd. So they were going to seek the landlords' instructions as to their requirements. That produced ultimately on 18 September a letter requiring, among other things, a satisfactory bank reference, full details of the company (the purchaser) and two personal guarantors, both f of whom should be British based. In the circumstances, it has not been suggested that the landlords were unreasonable in saying that they required British-based personal guarantors. The letter of 18 September from Keith Cardale Groves ends up with the statement: 'Once we have received satisfactory replies to the above we will consider this matter further and recommend to our client that consent to the proposed assignment be granted.' The bank reference was supplied to the satisfaction of Keith Cardale Groves, g and it was pointed out that Mr Rozner was not, at any rate by that time, a director of the purchaser company. The correspondence did not indicate whether he had any interest in the purchaser company, but a letter was sent by a firm called Youngstein & Gould, who we were told are international law consultants, naming two other persons, both non-residents of the United Kingdom, as having been the only directors of the purchaser company since 1 June 1985.

h That letter was passed on to the landlords with the hope expressed by the purchaser's solicitors that it would deal with all the points raised by the landlords, which it palpably did not. On 29 October 1985 Keith Cardale Groves came back with a restatement that their requirement was that there be two British-based guarantors as the flat was being assigned to a company based outside mainland Britain. That letter also said:

j 'We would confirm that as soon as we have received details of suitable guarantors we will be in a position to recommend to our clients that licence be granted. The matter will then be handed over to our clients' solicitors, Messrs. Pickering Kenyon for their attention.'

On 21 November Keith Cardale Groves confirmed that a reference from the National

Westminster Bank was satisfactory. They said again: 'We look forward to receiving in due course details of the two guarantors who have been appointed.' On Monday, 25 *a* November the adjudicated stamped vesting order having by then been received by the vendor's solicitors, the vendor's solicitors wrote intimating that unless the licence to assign could be obtained by Friday, 29 November (by then fixed as the contractual completion date), the vendor proposed to rescind the contract in accordance with condition 11(5).

On 28 November (the Thursday before) the purchaser's solicitors wrote putting *b* forward the names of two individuals in London as the proposed guarantors, and they stated that they were obtaining a bank reference of each of them and would let the vendor's solicitors have that. They also sent that to Keith Cardale Groves.

That, therefore, was the state of play on 29 November. On Monday, 2 December the vendor's solicitors, in purported exercise of the power under condition 11(5) of the National Conditions of Sale, purported to rescind the contract because the landlords' *c* consent had not been obtained. In fact, shortly thereafter two different individual guarantors were suggested by the purchaser's solicitors and they and their references were accepted by Keith Cardale Groves on 22 January 1986. So far as the landlords were concerned, the matter would then have gone to their solicitors for the preparation of the formal licence to assign, but it did not because the vendor was maintaining, as it has maintained ever since, that the contract had been validly rescinded by the notice of 2 *d* December 1985 under condition 11(5).

In consequence, a caution was registered against the title by the purchaser on 10 December 1985, and it issued the writ in this action claiming specific performance of the contract on 14 January 1986. The purchaser followed that up by a summons for summary judgment under RSC Ord 86 on the footing that there is no defence to the action. The vendor countered with a motion to vacate the caution, which is merely the other side of *e* the coin. By sensible co-operation between the parties, both came on for effective hearing before Knox J on 7 March 1986, and he delivered judgment on 11 March. He held that the notice of rescission was valid. He accordingly dismissed the purchaser's summons for summary judgment under RSC Ord 86 and granted the vendor an order vacating the caution. That, by orders which I need not mention, has been stayed pending the hearing *f* of this appeal in which we have to consider the validity of the judge's conclusions in the circumstances of this case.

The judge was persuaded by the arguments that were put to him, and I perhaps ought to mention that counsel who has appeared for the purchaser in this court did not appear before Knox J. On the arguments put to him, the judge held that the question which he had to consider was whether the vendor's right to rescind under condition 11(5) arose at *g* the contractual date for completion or whether it arose only at whatever later date was the one when the purchaser was entitled to treat the contract as at an end, time not being of the essence, or, alternatively, at the date when specific performance was no longer available. When the judge said 'arose' he may have meant 'fell to be considered'. He went on from there to consider whether the vendor would have been entitled, where the landlords' consent to assignment had not been obtained, to serve a notice to complete *h* under condition 22, and inclined to the view that the vendor was in no safe position to do so: he had not yet obtained the landlords' licence to assign. He then considered the words of condition 11(5) and said that 'cannot be obtained' does not mean 'cannot ever be obtained'. He commented that various other forms of tense or mood could be used but ultimately concluded that the expression 'cannot be obtained' was equivalent to 'is not forthcoming'. Looking at the matter, as he held he ought to, at the contractual date *j* for completion, 29 November 1985, he considered that, as the landlords' licence to assign was not then forthcoming, the vendor's right to rescind under condition 11(5) was exercisable and so was validly exercised on 2 December.

The trouble I feel about that, with respect to the judge, is that it involves a drastic rewriting of the condition and a concentration on a contractual date for completion

which is not mentioned in the clause at all. Under condition 10(1) the vendor is given a
a right to rescind if certain events have happened:

> 'If the purchaser shall persist in any objection to the title which the vendor shall
> be unable or unwilling, on reasonable grounds, to remove, and does not withdraw
> [it within a specified period] of being required so to do . . .'

If that happens, the vendor has a right to rescind whether before or after the contractual
b date for completion. Under condition 11 the vendor is given a right to rescind if the
licence cannot be obtained. It seems to me that the natural construction of that clause
requires one to look at the date when the vendor has purported to exercise his right to
rescind. The court has to consider whether at that date it can fairly be said as a question
of fact that the licence cannot be obtained.

As Goff J pointed out in *Lipmans Wallpaper Ltd v Mason & Hodghton Ltd* [1968] 1 All
c ER 1123 at 1128, [1969] 1 Ch 20 at 34, the vendor could not escape under the clause by
rescinding on the ground that consent was not obtainable without first using his best
endeavours to get it; but that is not in question here. As Goff J equally pointed out, if the
facts are that there has been a categorical refusal of consent by the landlord, then it is not
incumbent on the vendor to make further or yet further attempts to persuade the
landlord to change his mind or to give the purchaser an opportunity of trying his powers
d of persuasion on the landlord or taking various other steps which hypothetically might
equally well, or might not, have any effect in persuading the landlord to change his mind
(see [1968] 1 All ER 1123 at 1129, [1969] 1 Ch 20 at 34–35). But the question is a simple
question of fact to be decided in the light of common sense.

In the present case there is no doubt at all that it is impossible to say at 2 December
1985 that 'the licence cannot be obtained' unless you put the complete gloss on those
e words that the judge did and ask yourself instead whether it was forthcoming by 29
November. It is impossible to say on the facts that 'it cannot be obtained', because at long
last the purchaser's solicitors had put forward the names of guarantors in response to the
landlords' requirements, the bank reference had been supplied satisfactorily and the
landlords' agents had several times intimated that, if the guarantors put forward were
satisfactory, they would recommend that the licence to assign should be granted by the
f landlords.

On the facts of this case, therefore, I have no doubt that the vendor was not in a
position to serve its condition 11(5) notice when it served it. The notice was thus
ineffective to bring the contract to an end.

The judge sought to produce a result which is in harmony with the vendor's position
under condition 22, and he was frightened of a position that the vendor might be locked
g in where the landlords' consent was required for completion but, through no fault of the
vendor, was not forthcoming. We have been referred to certain unreported decisions of
this court in which there is comment on this position. In *Jneid v Mirza* [1981] CA
Transcript 306 Fox LJ, giving the leading judgment in this court, said:

h > '. . . if the vendors [on whom there was the obligation to provide licences to
> assign] were never in a position before, during or on the expiration of the notice to
> complete to produce the [licences] at any time, then the vendors were quite plainly
> never ready at any material time to fulfil their obligations under this contract . . .'

In *Shires v Brock* (1977) 247 EG 127 at 129 Goff LJ said that it was misconceived for
j vendors' solicitors to give a notice pursuant to condition 22 of the National Conditions of
Sale at a time when the vendors, not having been able to get the reversioner's licence to
assign, were not in a position to perform their part of the contract. However, I do not
find it necessary to consider what the position would have been in this case under
condition 22 because the vendor never gave a notice under condition 22.

For my part, I would allow this appeal and set aside the order of Knox J. I would dismiss the vendor's motion to vacate the caution and, subject to any further submissions that may be made, on the purchaser's summons under RSC Ord 86 I would make an order for specific performance.

CROOM-JOHNSON LJ. I agree.

BALCOMBE LJ. I agree that this appeal should be allowed for the reasons given by Dillon LJ, and I too would wish to reserve for another occasion, should the point arise, whether a vendor in the position of this vendor, who might be, so it is said, locked into the contract, where the landlords are not refusing to grant their licence but are being dilatory in granting it, is able to serve a notice under condition 22 notwithstanding the remarks of Goff LJ in *Shires v Brock* (1977) 247 EG 127 at 129 and Fox LJ in *Jneid v Mirza* [1981] CA Transcript 306.

Appeal allowed.

Solicitors: *William Stockler & Co* (for the purchaser); *Isadore Goldman & Son* (for the vendor).

Diana Procter   Barrister.

Winkworth v Edward Baron Development Co Ltd and others

HOUSE OF LORDS

LORD KEITH OF KINKEL, LORD TEMPLEMAN, LORD GRIFFITHS, LORD MACKAY OF CLASHFERN AND LORD ACKNER

30 OCTOBER, 3, 4 NOVEMBER, 4 DECEMBER 1986

Mortgage – Possession of mortgaged property – Adverse interest – Equitable interest – Wife's equitable interest – Matrimonial home purchased and owned by company – Wife a director of company – Husband arranging for company to mortgage property without wife's knowledge – Company incurring overdraft – Wife making contribution to reduce company overdraft – Mortgagee seeking possession of property from company – Whether any connection between contribution and acquisition of matrimonial home – Whether wife's contribution giving her equitable interest in home – Whether wife acting in breach of duty as director.

A husband and wife purchased for £115,000 the two issued shares of the respondent company using money withdrawn from the company's bank account. One share each was transferred to the husband and the wife, who then became the company's sole directors. The company then purchased for some £82,000 a freehold property which the husband and wife occupied as their home. After the purchase and other expenditure the company's bank account was overdrawn and, on the husband's instructions, the company's solicitors gave an undertaking to the bank to hold the deeds of the property to the order of the bank. The husband and wife subsequently sold their former matrimonial home and paid the proceeds of £8,600 into the company's bank account thereby reducing the overdraft to £8,160. Some months later, without the wife's knowledge or consent, the company mortgaged the property to the appellant for £70,000, the wife's signature on the legal charge and other documents having been forged by the husband. The company subsequently became insolvent and went into liquidation, and when it defaulted in paying the mortgage the appellant brought an action for possession. The company and

the husband did not resist the appellant's claim but the wife, who was in occupation of
a the property, claimed that the payment of the £8,600 into the company's bank account
from the proceeds of the sale of the former matrimonial home prior to the legal charge
executed in favour of the appellant had given her an equitable interest in the property
which overrode the appellant's interest. The judge held that the wife had not acquired
an equitable interest in the property and ordered her to give up possession to the
appellant. On appeal by the wife, the Court of Appeal held that she had acquired an
b equitable interest and discharged the order. The appellant appealed to the House of
Lords.

Held – The appeal would be allowed for the following reasons—
    (1) The equitable doctrine that a legal owner of property held in trust for those who
contributed to the purchase price of the property or made contributions referable to its
c acquisition did not apply to give the wife an equitable interest in the property because
the payment of the £8,600 was not referable to the acquisition of the property, since the
purchase price of the property had already been paid in full by the company by the time
the £8,600 was paid in to the company's bank account and there was no connection
between the payment for the property and the incurring of the overdraft (see p 116 *a*,
d p 117 *f g*, p 118 *b* and p 119 *d* to *g*, post).
    (2) Having regard to the facts (*a*) that when the £115,000 was withdrawn from the
company's bank account to pay for their shares and when the company's overdraft was
incurred and increased for their benefit the husband and wife had breached the duty
which they as directors owed to the company and its creditors to ensure that the affairs
of the company were properly administered, and (*b*) that the wife had failed to discover
and exercise her powers as a director, equity would not compel or even allow the
e company to hold part of its property on trust for the wife to the detriment of and in
priority to the claims of its creditors (see p 116 *a*, p 118 *e* to *g* and p 119 *d* to *g*, post).

Notes
For priority between mortgagees of land and of persons claiming equitable interests in
f that land, see 32 Halsbury's Laws (4th edn) paras 551–554, and for cases on the subject,
see 35 Digest (Reissue) 318–325, 2707–2740.

Cases referred to in opinions
Burns v Burns [1984] 1 All ER 244, [1984] Ch 317, [1984] 2 WLR 582, CA.
Campbell v M'Creath 1975 SC 81.
g *Williams & Glyn's Bank Ltd v Boland* [1980] 2 All ER 408, [1981] AC 487, [1980] 3 WLR
    138, HL.

Appeal
The plaintiff, Peter William Francis Henry Winkworth, appealed with leave of the Court
of Appeal granted on 11 December 1985 against the decision of that court (Neill and
h Nourse LJJ, Kerr LJ dissenting) on 5 December 1985 whereby it allowed an appeal by the
third defendant, Joy Evelyn Wing, against the order of Mr Gerald Godfrey QC sitting as
a deputy judge of the High Court dated 26 July 1984 that, inter alia, Mrs Wing deliver
to Mr Winkworth by 26 October 1984 possession of the property known as 75 Hayes
Lane, Beckenham, Kent. The first defendant, Edward Baron Development Co Ltd, and
the second defendant, Colin Douglas Wing, took no part in the appeal. The facts are set
j out in the opinion of Lord Templeman.

Andrew Morritt QC and *David Parry* for Mr Winkworth.
Alan Ward QC and *Peter Ralls* for Mrs Wing.

Their Lordships took time for consideration.

4 December. The following opinions were delivered.

                                                                         a

LORD KEITH OF KINKEL. My Lords, I have had the opportunity of considering in draft the speech to be delivered by my noble and learned friend Lord Templeman. I agree with it, and for the reasons he gives would allow the appeal.

LORD TEMPLEMAN. My Lords, the issued share capital of the respondent company, Edward Baron Development Co Ltd, consisted of two shares. On 23 July 1980 the sum   *b* of £200,000 was paid into the company's bank account, being part of the proceeds of sale of a venture by the company. A potential liability to corporation tax exceeding £100,000 had been incurred. One of the shares in the company was transferred to the respondent, Mr Wing, and the other to his wife, the respondent, Mrs Wing, for £115,000. The purchase price was extracted from the company's bank account. Mr and Mrs Wing became the sole directors of the company. Mrs Wing was appointed secretary. The   *c* company acquired the registered freehold property, 75 Hayes Lane, Beckenham, Kent. The company paid £70,000 for the property, £12,000 for fixtures and fittings, and incidental costs and expenses. On 31 July 1980 all these sums had been paid in full and the company's bank balance had been reduced to £271·03. Mr and Mrs Wing went into occupation of Hayes Lane, which they regarded as their matrimonial home and which they intended to transfer to themselves if and when but not before the company had   *d* been reimbursed in full for its expenditure. Nevertheless in August 1980 Hayes Lane belonged absolutely to the company in law and in equity.

    The appellant, Mr Winkworth, claims to be a mortgagee of Hayes Lane from the company. His claim is not disputed by the company or by Mr Wing but is resisted by Mrs Wing. In these proceedings, the trial judge ordered Mrs Wing to deliver up   *e* possession to Mr Winkworth. By a majority (Nourse and Neill LJJ) the Court of Appeal reversed the trial judge and discharged his order on the grounds that in November 1980 Mrs Wing obtained an equitable interest in Hayes Lane prior to the legal charge subsequently acquired by Mr Winkworth. Kerr LJ, the third member of the Court of Appeal, agreed with the trial judge that Mrs Wing did not acquire an equitable interest in Hayes Lane. Mr Winkworth now appeals against the majority decision of the Court of   *f* Appeal.

    Mrs Wing knew nothing about business and left the management of the company's affairs in the hands of her husband. After taking control of the company and paying the purchase price for the shares out of the company's bank account, Mr Wing drew further cheques on the company's bank account to finance the purchase of a washing machine for Hayes Lane, a motor car and jewellery for his wife, and other items of expenditure   *g* appropriate to an establishment in Beckenham. By a letter dated 8 August 1980 the company's solicitors, on the instructions of Mr Wing, undertook to hold the title deeds of Hayes Lane to the order of the bank. Mr Wing intended that the company would raise £70,000 on the security of a fixed mortgage of Hayes Lane to a commercial lender, and would then pay off the bank overdraft out of the mortgage money. Mr Wing did not confide this intention to his wife because she would not have agreed to a mortgage of the   *h* matrimonial home. The overdraft exceeded £16,000 when, in November 1980, Mr and Mrs Wing sold their former matrimonial home, The Drive, Beckenham, which they held as joint tenants. After redemption of two charges on The Drive, the balance of the proceeds of sale of The Drive, amounting to £8,600·91, were paid into the company's bank account, thus reducing the overdraft from £16,760·75 to £8,159·84. Mrs Wing authorised the payment of £8,600·91 from the proceeds of sale of The Drive into the   *j* company's bank account. She did not say in evidence whether she knew that the account was overdrawn. She did not know of the undertaking to the bank which secured the overdraft on the title deeds of Hayes Lane. On 26 August 1981 Mr Winkworth advanced £70,000 to the company. The advance was paid to the company's solicitors in consideration of a legal charge on Hayes Lane. The company's solicitors, who were also

Mr Winkworth's solicitors, received and registered the legal charge affixed with the seal
a of the company, and appearing to be signed by both Mr and Mrs Wing. The solicitors
also received three letters which appeared to be signed by Mr and Mrs Wing, and which
acknowledged, inter alia, that Mr and Mrs Wing occupied Hayes Lane as bare licensees
of the company and not by virtue of any tenancy or lease. That acknowledgment was
accurate. But the signature of Mrs Wing on the legal charge and on the letters had been
forged by Mr Wing. The company, having been stripped, declined into insolvency and
b went into liquidation, probably belatedly, in 1983.

It is now contended on behalf of Mrs Wing that the payment of £8,600·91 into the
company's bank account in November 1980 obtained for Mrs Wing an equitable interest
in Hayes Lane in the proportion that £8,600·91 bears to £70,000, and that her equitable
interest takes priority over the claims of the company's creditors, secured and unsecured.
This bold and astonishing proposition would enable Mrs Wing to continue in occupation
c of Hayes Lane, without any contribution to its expenses until a court, on the application
by the company under s 30 of the Law of Property Act 1925, thought fit to order Hayes
Lane to be sold with vacant possession for the benefit of the company and Mrs Wing as
tenants in common in equity. Mr Wing has not had the effrontery to raise on his own
behalf a similar contention in respect of any part of the sum of £8,600·91 which he and
Mrs Wing provided out of the proceeds of the sale of The Drive. No doubt he is pleased
d to have maintained a matrimonial home for over six years without cost to himself and at
the expense largely of the Inland Revenue. Responsibility for the last three years, and for
the six-figure litigation costs borne by the legal aid fund, is shared by the decision of this
House in *Williams & Glyn's Bank Ltd v Boland* [1980] 2 All ER 408, [1981] AC 487.

The argument on behalf of Mrs Wing exploits the equitable doctrine that a legal owner
holds in trust for the persons who contribute to the purchase price of the property or
e make contributions referable to the acquisition of the property. The doctrine was
discussed in *Burns v Burns* [1984] 1 All ER 244, [1984] Ch 317 and other authorities
mentioned in the judgment of Nourse LJ in the present case. The sum of £8,600·91,
paid into the company's bank account from the proceeds of sale of The Drive belonging
to Mr and Mrs Wing, reduced the company's overdraft which was secured by the
solicitors' undertaking to hold the title deeds of Hayes Lane to the order of the bank.
f Therefore, it is said, the payment of £8,600·91 was referable to the acquisition of Hayes
Lane by the company, and equity requires the company to hold Hayes Lane in trust for
the company and Mr and Mrs Wing or one of them. The simple answer to this tortuous
argument is that the payment of £8,600·91 was not referable to the acquisition of Hayes
Lane, which had already been bought and paid for in full. There was no connection
between the payment for Hayes Lane and the incurring of the overdraft. There was no
g connection between the acquisition of Hayes Lane and the payment of £8,600·91. The
proper inference to be drawn from the admitted facts is that Hayes Lane, acquired by the
company, and the sum of £8,600·91, paid into the company's bank account, became
assets of the company, managed by Mr Wing for the benefit of himself and Mrs Wing, as
sole and equal shareholders and not as owners of equitable interests. Counsel for Mrs
h Wing urged that this inference does not take account of the fact that Mr and Mrs Wing
intended that Hayes Lane should be their matrimonial home, and does not take account
of the fact that Mr and Mrs Wing intended to purchase Hayes Lane from the company.
But these intentions cannot affect the mortgagee of Hayes Lane or the liquidator of the
company. There was no contract by the company to sell Hayes Lane to Mr and Mrs Wing
or either of them by instalments or at all. Even if the £8,600·91 could be construed as an
j optimistic deposit towards an unrealised purchase, such a deposit would not create an
equitable interest in Hayes Lane which entitled Mrs Wing to remain in occupation. The
claim now put forward by Mrs Wing is in reality a claim that in November 1980 the
company sold to Mrs Wing a part interest in Hayes Lane (ignoring the fixtures and
fittings) of a size and at a price calculated by reference to the accidental balance of the
proceeds of sale of The Drive (ignoring her husband's claim to share in that balance) and

by reference to the price originally paid by the company (ignoring costs and expenses). In my opinion, the payment of £8,600·91 into the company's bank account did not *a* manifest an intention on the part of Mrs Wing to offer to buy a part interest in Hayes Lane. By submitting to a reduction in its overdraft, the company did not manifest an intention to sell to Mrs Wing a bizarre proportion of Hayes Lane at a price which had never been negotiated and could never have been justified.

Moreover, equity will not intervene to confer on Mrs Wing an interest in priority to creditors because her husband, without her knowledge, impliedly agreed to charge the *b* title deeds of Hayes Lane with the repayment of debts improperly incurred by Mr Wing for the benefit of himself and his wife. Equity is not a computer. Equity operates on conscience but is not influenced by sentimentality. When a man (it usually is a man) purchases property and his companion (married or unmarried, female or male) contributes to the purchase price, or contributes to the payment of a mortgage, equity treats the legal owner as a trustee of the property for himself and his companion in the *c* proportions in which they contribute to the purchase price because it would be unconscionable for the legal owner to continue to assert absolute ownership unless there is some express agreement between the parties, or unless the circumstances in which the contributions were made established a gift or loan or some relationship incompatible with the creation of a trust. But a company owes a duty to its creditors, present and future. The company is not bound to pay off every debt as soon as it is incurred and the *d* company is not obliged to avoid all ventures which involve an element of risk, but the company owes a duty to its creditors to keep its property inviolate and available for the repayment of its debts. The conscience of the company, as well as its management, is confided to its directors. A duty is owed by the directors to the company and to the creditors of the company to ensure that the affairs of the company are properly administered and that its property is not dissipated or exploited for the benefit of the *e* directors themselves to the prejudice of the creditors. Both Mr and Mrs Wing committed a breach of their duty to the company and its creditors when £115,000 was withdrawn from the company to pay for their shares and when the company's overdraft was incurred and increased at least partly for their benefit. When Mr and Mrs Wing paid £8,600·91 to the company, their liability to the company and its creditors far exceeded that sum. *f* These breaches of duty would not have mattered if Mr and Mrs Wing had been able to maintain the solvency of the company and to see that all its creditors were paid in full. But in that case it would have been unnecessary for equity to insist that the company hold Hayes Lane as a trustee, because Mr and Mrs Wing were the only shareholders and could, without the assistance of equity, compel the company to treat Hayes Lane as though it belonged to Mr and Mrs Wing. When the company received £8,600·91 from *g* Mr and Mrs Wing in the circumstances which existed, the conscience of the company did not require the company to confer on Mrs Wing an interest ranking in priority to the claims of creditors. On the contrary, the company was under a duty to apply the sum of £8,600·91 (as it did) for the benefit of the creditors of the company and in part repair of the damage inflicted by the directors. Mr Wing was responsible for the insolvency of the company. Mrs Wing was not aware that, as a director, she owed any duty to the *h* company or its creditors. But in the circumstances of this case and in view of Mrs Wing's failure to discover and exercise her powers as a director so as to ensure that the affairs of the company were properly conducted, equity will not, in my opinion, compel, or even allow, the company to hold part of its property on trust for Mrs Wing to the detriment of creditors and in priority to the claims of creditors.

Counsel for Mrs Wing submitted that, even if Mrs Wing had no equitable interest, she *j* could only be evicted by the company or by a mortgagee claiming under a valid legal charge. Counsel submitted that Mr Winkworth could not enforce a forged legal charge. But the company has admitted the validity of the legal charge by submitting in these proceedings to orders for possession and payment in favour of Mr Winkworth. That admission is clearly correct because Mr Winkworth agreed to advance and did advance

a £70,000 at the request of Mr Wing, the effective managing director of the company, and paid his money to the solicitors of the company on the promise of a legal charge. The company must either admit the validity of the existing legal charge or provide a new, valid legal charge to which Mr Winkworth is clearly entitled. The liquidator has sensibly conceded the validity of the existing legal charge. The legal charge is now binding on the company and enables Mr Winkworth to exercise the powers conferred by the legal charge so as to obtain possession against Mrs Wing. Finally, counsel for Mrs Wing
b submitted that the legal charge is not enforceable by Mr Winkworth because, so it is claimed, £20,000 out of the £70,000 advanced by Mr Winkworth were applied by the company for the benefit of Mr Wing. This misapplication was said to be known of by the solicitor who acted for the company but not by the solicitor in the same firm who, in different premises, acted separately for Mr Winkworth. Nevertheless it is said that 'the firm' had notice of the misapplication and this notice affected Mr Winkworth. Mr
c Winkworth had no knowledge of any misapplication. In the first place, Mrs Wing had no right to complain on behalf of the company and in the second place *Campbell v M'Creath* 1975 SC 81 is clear authority against the proposition that Mr Winkworth had notice through a solicitor who acted separately for him, because the solicitor was a member of the same firm which advised the company.

I agree with the views expressed by the trial judge and by Kerr LJ and would allow the
d appeal and restore the order made by the trial judge. Mrs Wing must give vacant possession of Hayes Lane not later than 8 January 1987.

LORD GRIFFITHS. My Lords, I have had the advantage of reading in draft the speech prepared by my noble and learned friend Lord Templeman. I agree with him that this appeal should be allowed and with the reasons he has given for reaching this conclusion.
e

LORD MACKAY OF CLASHFERN. My Lords, I have had the advantage of reading in draft the speech proposed by my noble and learned friend Lord Templeman. I agree with him that this appeal should be allowed and with the reasons he has given for reaching this conclusion.

f **LORD ACKNER.** My Lords, I have had the advantage of reading in draft the speech prepared by my noble and learned friend Lord Templeman, and for the reasons he gives I would allow the appeal.

Appeal allowed.

g Solicitors: *Parlett Kent & Co* (for Mr Winkworth); *Clemence Turner & Henry,* Bromley (for Mrs Wing).

Mary Rose Plummer   Barrister.

R v Court

a

COURT OF APPEAL, CRIMINAL DIVISION
RALPH GIBSON LJ, HIRST AND OTTON JJ
31 JULY, 17 OCTOBER 1986

Criminal law – Indecent assault – Mental element – Motive – Secret motive – Assault on young *b*
girl by spanking – Accused having secret indecent motive – Whether evidence of secret motive
admissible – Whether prosecution required to adduce evidence of indecent motive – Sexual Offences
Act 1956, s 14(1).

The appellant, a shop assistant, pulled a 12-year-old girl visitor to the shop across his
knees and smacked her with his hand 12 times on her buttocks outside her shorts for no *c*
apparent reason. When asked by the police why he had done so he said that it was
'buttock fetish' and that although he had experienced the urge to do it on rare occasions
in the past he had never before done so. He pleaded guilty to assault, but denied that it
was indecent and contended that his statement about his 'buttock fetish' should be
excluded as being merely a secret motive which was not communicated to the victim
and which could not make indecent an act which was not overtly indecent. The judge *d*
refused to exclude the evidence and directed the jury that the prosecution had to prove
(i) that the appellant's conduct was such that it would appear to an ordinary observer as
an affront to modesty and (ii) that the appellant had an indecent intention in doing what
he did. The appellant was convicted of indecent assault contrary to s 14(1)[a] of the Sexual
Offences Act 1956. He appealed against his conviction on the ground that the judge had
been wrong in law to admit evidence of a secret motive and to allow the jury to consider *e*
it in deciding whether the assault had been committed in circumstances of indecency.

Held – The appeal would be dismissed for the following reasons—
  (1) The essential mental element of an indecent assault under s 14(1) of the 1956 Act
was that the accused knew or was reckless about the existence of circumstances which *f*
were indecent, in the sense of contravening standards of decent behaviour in relation to
sexual modesty or privacy, and no proof of any further indecent intention or motive was
required. If evidence of such motive did exist, however, it did not have to be excluded as
irrelevant, but could be admitted in evidence as being of direct relevance in proving the
offence charged, subject to the court's discretion to exclude prejudicial evidence which
was of little or no probative value. In the circumstances, the evidence as to the appellant's *g*
secret motive was admissible (see p 121 f, p 124 d g to p 125 a f g, p 126 a b e and p 127 d,
post); *R v Kimber* [1983] 3 All ER 316 considered; *R v Pratt* [1984] Crim LR 41 overruled.
  (2) The judge should have directed the jury that the secret motive of the appellant
could not have turned into circumstances of indecency circumstances which without
that motive the jury would not have regarded as indecent. On the facts, however, the
jury had considered the two parts of the judge's direction separately and had accepted *h*
that the assault was committed in circumstances of indecency. It followed therefore that,
notwithstanding the judge's misdirection, the jury's verdict was not unsafe or
unsatisfactory, the appeal would accordingly be dismissed (see p 121 f, p 125 j, p 126 f g
and p 127 c d, post).

j

Notes
For the offence of indecent assault, see 11 Halsbury's Laws (4th edn) para 1241, and for
cases on the subject, see 15 Digest (Reissue) 1233–1234, 10521–10542.
  For the Sexual Offences Act 1956, s 14, see 12 Halsbury's Statutes (4th edn) 281.

---

a   Section 14(1), so far as material, is set out at p 123 f, post

Cases referred to in judgment

a   *DPP v Morgan* [1975] 1 All ER 8, [1976] AC 182, [1975] 2 WLR 913, HL.
      R v Donovan [1934] 2 KB 498, [1934] All ER Rep 207, CCA.
      R v George [1956] Crim LR 52, Assizes.
      R v Kilbourne [1972] 3 All ER 545, [1972] 1 WLR 1365, CA.
      R v Kimber [1983] 3 All ER 316, [1983] 1 WLR 1118, CA.
      R v Leeson (1968) 52 Cr App R 185, CA.
b   *R v May* [1912] 3 KB 572, CCA.
      R v Pratt [1984] Crim LR 41, Crown Ct.
      R v Venna [1975] 3 All ER 788, [1976] QB 421, [1975] 3 WLR 737, CA.

Case also cited

      R v Thomas (1985) 81 Cr App R 331, CA.
c

Appeal against conviction

Robert Christopher Court appealed against his conviction on 19 February 1986 in the Crown Court at Caernarfon before Mars-Jones J and a jury on a charge of indecent assault on a girl under the age of 13, contrary to s 14 of the Sexual Offences Act 1956, in respect of which he was sentenced to probation for three years on condition that he received *d* psychiatric treatment for 12 months. The facts are set out in the judgment of the court.

T A Halbert (assigned by the Registrar of Criminal Appeals) for the appellant.
Robin Spencer for the Crown.

At the conclusion of the argument Ralph Gibson LJ announced that the appeal would be
e dismissed for reasons to be given later.

17 October. The following judgment of the court was delivered.

RALPH GIBSON LJ. On 19 February 1986 in the Crown Court at Caernarfon before
f Mars-Jones J the appellant, who is aged 27, was convicted of an indecent assault on a girl under the age of 13. On 20 February he was made the subject of a probation order for three years with a condition that he should receive psychiatric treatment for 12 months. He appealed against conviction on a point of law and his appeal was heard by this court on 17 July. We announced on 31 July 1986 that his appeal was dismissed for reasons to be given at a later date. They are as follows.

g   The appellant was an assistant in his family's gift shop in Abersoch. The victim of the assault was aged 12. She and her family were on holiday and she had visited the shop on several occasions. On two of those occasions the appellant had asked her if she had ever been spanked. When she said, 'No,' he had replied, 'That's the kind of girl I like.' On 13 September 1985 the girl again went into the shop with her brother. The appellant again asked her if she had ever been spanked. She said, 'No.' He asked her if she would let him
h spank her. She said, 'No,' and walked away to another part of the shop. A little later when she passed him to get to the front of the shop he seized her arm, pulled her across his knees and struck her 12 times on her buttocks outside her shorts. He stopped when her brother appeared. He got up and gave the children some items on sale in the shop, saying, 'If you don't tell you can have these.'

      The girl went home and told her mother that the appellant had spanked her for no
j apparent reason and scared her. When her father went to the shop the appellant apologised profusely. The father complained to the police and the appellant was arrested and interviewed. He admitted spanking the girl and when asked why said: 'I don't know; buttock fetish.' He went on to say that it was something he had experienced over the past nine years, but that the urge came over him 'only once in a blue moon'. This was the first time he had ever done it.

      At the trial the appellant admitted assault and pleaded guilty thereto. He denied that the assault was indecent. His counsel invited the judge to rule that the evidence of the appellant's admission of having a 'buttock fetish' should be excluded on the ground that, being a secret uncommunicated motive, it could not make indecent an assault which by reference to the overt circumstances was not indecent. The judge refused to exclude the evidence. We have no transcript of the submission or ruling. The appellant did not give evidence.

The submissions for the appellant in this court were that the judge was wrong in law in admitting evidence of the appellant's secret motive, and in directing the jury that they could consider that secret motive in considering whether the assault was committed in circumstances of indecency. The judge should, it was said, have directed the jury to decide objectively whether or not the assault was indecent on the basis of what was revealed to or apprehended by the victim at the time and without regard to any secretly held motive.

The directions of the judge on the law as to what was required to be proved for conviction were as follows. After telling the jury that the accused admitted assaulting the girl he continued:

'Indecent assault has been defined as an assault accompanied by circumstances of indecency on the part of the defendant towards the girl, and "indecent" has been defined as overtly sexual. What has the prosecution got to prove to establish the defendant's guilt on this charge of indecent assault? They must prove two things. Firstly, that the defendant's conduct was such that it would appear to an ordinary observer as an affront to modesty; conduct which contravened right-thinking people's ideas of standards of decent behaviour. Secondly, that the defendant had an indecent intention in doing what he did. So first you must have conduct which would appear to the ordinary observer as an affront to modesty, and second you must have an indecent intention on the part of the defendant in doing what he did. The prosecution do not have to prove that the girl . . . realised that this was an indecent assault.'

The judge thus told the jury that proof of the indecent intention of the accused was a requirement additional to and separate from proof of objectively indecent conduct but there was no direction at that point on the relevance if any of a proved indecent intention to the consideration by the jury of the question whether the conduct was objectively indecent.

For the Crown in this court it was accepted that, if the circumstances of the assault were incapable of being regarded as indecent, then the secret motive of the accused could not make an assault indecent. The secret motive or intention of the accused would then be irrelevant. If, however, the circumstances of the assault were such that the jury could hold them to be indecent, then the secret motive of the accused could be taken into account by the jury in deciding whether the circumstances were in fact indecent. The offence of indecent assault included both a battery, or touching, and the psychic assault without touching. If there was touching, it was not necessary to prove that the victim was aware of the assault or of the circumstances of indecency. If there was no touching, then to constitute an indecent assault the victim must be shown to have been aware of the assault and of the circumstances of indecency.

In the view of this court the first concession by the prosecution was rightly made: if the circumstances of the assault are incapable of being regarded as indecent, they cannot become indecent because of a secret motive of the accused. Streatfeild J so held in *R v George* [1956] Crim LR 52, where the accused attempted to remove a girl's shoe from her foot because it gave him some sexual gratification, but there were not overt circumstances of indecency towards the victim. Further, in *R v Kilbourne* [1972] 3 All ER 545 at 551, [1972] 1 WLR 1365 at 1372 Lawson J had directed the jury that an indecent assault meant—

'a deliberate touching of somebody else's body, clothed or unclothed, with an a indecent intention. That is to say, a deliberate touching which is activated by some indecent purpose.'

The Court of Appeal (Lawton LJ, MacKenna and Swanwick JJ) held that direction to be much too wide because it could cover acts which were nothing more than preliminary steps towards committing an indecent assault as for example in touching a woman's hand.

b This principle, however, provides no answer to the issue raised in this case. The rejection by the court in *R v Kilbourne* of the definition proposed by Lawson J establishes that indecent purpose by itself is not enough. It does not decide whether or not an indecent purpose or intention is an essential ingredient of the offence, which is the key question in the present case. We should first note that the words 'indecent intention' or 'indecent purpose' in our view appear at first sight to have greater precision of meaning than they retain on closer examination. So far as the indecent circumstances of an assault

c are overt, the intention of the accused may, of course, be regarded as indecent if, knowing of those circumstances, he makes the assault. But if 'indecent intention' or 'indecent purpose' were to be taken to mean the ulterior intention or motive of the accused, then it would be necessary to determine whether such motive need relate only to the gratification which the accused seeks from his act, or also to the desired effect on the

d victim, or whether either would suffice. A man might make an assault in circumstances which were known to him, and which were objectively indecent, but entirely without prurient interest on his own part and solely from anger or with the purpose of chastising. Further, on the same assumption, would it be sufficient that the accused was proved to have an intention or purpose which the jury regards as indecent, or must the accused also be shown to have realised that his purpose was indecent? Such questions, and the

e difficulty of answering them, cannot lead the court to answer the key question in the negative if it is clear that the law otherwise requires an affirmative answer, but they are, in our view, relevant to consideration of the construction of what Parliament is to be taken as having intended by the words of its enactments.

The offence of indecent assault is now contained in s 14(1) of the Sexual Offences Act 1956. It provides, omitting words which are irrelevant: 'It is an offence . . . for a person

f to make an indecent assault on a woman.' The section is silent as to the necessary mental element in the offence. In *R v Kimber* [1983] 3 All ER 316, [1983] 1 WLR 1118 the appellant was charged with indecent assault on a woman who was a patient in a mental hospital. The recorder ruled that a defendant charged with an indecent assault on a woman could not raise the defence that he believed that the woman had consented to what he did. This court (Lawton LJ, Michael Davies and Sheldon JJ) held the ruling of

g the recorder was wrong. In giving the judgment of the court, and in applying *DPP v Morgan* [1975] 1 All ER 8, [1976] AC 182, Lawton LJ said ([1983] 3 All ER 316 at 319, [1983] 1 WLR 1118 at 1121–1122):

'The Crown had to prove that the appellant made an indecent assault on Betty. As there are no words in the section to indicate that Parliament intended to exclude

h mens rea as an element in this offence, it follows that the Crown had to prove that the appellant intended to commit it. This could not be done without first proving that the appellant intended to assault Betty. In this context assault clearly includes battery. An assault is an act by which the defendant intentionally or recklessly causes the complainant to apprehend immediate, or to sustain, unlawful personal violence: see *R v Venna* [1975] 3 All ER 788 at 793, [1976] QB 421 at 428–429. In this case the

j appellant by his own admission did intentionally lay his hands on Betty. That would not, however, have been enough to prove the charge. There had to be evidence that the appellant had intended to do what he did unlawfully. When there is a charge of indecent assault on a woman, the unlawfulness can be proved, as was sought to be done in *R v Donovan* [1934] 2 KB 498, [1934] All ER Rep 207, by evidence that the defendant intended to cause bodily harm. In most cases, however, the prosecution tries to prove that the complainant did not consent to what was done. The burden of proving lack of consent rests on the prosecution: see *R v May* [1912] 3 KB 572 at 575 per Lord Alverstone CJ. The consequence is that the prosecution has to prove that the defendant intended to lay hands on his victim without her consent. If he did not intend to do this, he is entitled to be found not guilty; and if he did not so intend because he believed she was consenting, the prosecution will have failed to prove the charge. It is the defendant's belief, not the grounds on which it was based, which goes to negative the intent.'

Later, in finding that despite the misdirection there had been no miscarriage of justice, the court held that the appellant had not cared whether the victim was consenting, that he had been accordingly reckless as to consent and that recklessness was also sufficient to support a conviction of indecent assault. There was in that case no issue with reference to the indecency of the assault: the accused had attempted to have sexual intercourse with the victim who was only partly clothed. The question for this court in this case, as already noted, centres on the mental element required for proof of the offence of indecent assault with reference to the alleged indecency of a proved intentional assault.

On any view the submission for the appellant that no mental element is required with reference to indecency is impossible of acceptance having regard not least to *R v Kimber* [1983] 3 All ER 316, [1983] 1 WLR 1118. An indecent assault is an assault committed in circumstances of aggravation. It seems to us that at least it must be proved that the accused intentionally assaulted the victim with knowledge of the indecent circumstances or being reckless as to the existence of them. Thus in *R v Leeson* (1968) 52 Cr App R 185 (Diplock LJ, Ashworth and Lyell JJ) the assault involved the kissing of a girl against her will accompanied by suggestions that sexual intercourse should take place. The court held that spoken words constituted circumstances of indecency on the part of the accused towards the person assaulted. If, on the other hand, the person had used such words in a foreign language, not knowing their meaning or that they were indecent, as a result of a malicious trick by a third party, and without recklessness, he could surely not be convicted of indecent assault, even though the words were, and were understood by the victim to be, indecent as an affront to her modesty.

But must it be proved further that the accused not only knew or was reckless as to existence of the circumstances which are ruled by the judge to be capable of being indecent and held by the jury to be indecent, but also that the accused had an 'indecent intention' in doing what he did?

We are in this case concerned with an assault by touching, or a battery. In our view the judge was right to direct the jury that it was not necessary for the prosecution to prove that the girl knew or thought the assault on her to be indecent. It is sufficient if the circumstances are capable in law of being held to be indecent and the jury holds them to be so. The judge directed the jury that the assault on this girl was indecent if—

'it would appear to an ordinary observer as an affront to modesty: conduct which contravened right thinking people's ideas of standards of decent behaviour.'

Professor Glanville Williams in his textbook *Criminal Law* (2nd edn, 1985) p 231 has written:

'"Indecent" may be defined as "overtly sexual", though it covers homosexual as well as heterosexual assaults.'

We agree that the offence is concerned with contravention of standards of decent behaviour in regard to sexual modesty or privacy. The prosecution must prove an intentional assault in circumstances known to the accused, or as to the existence of which he is shown to have been reckless, which circumstances are shown to be indecent in the sense described. This is the essential mental element in the offence and, in our judgment, no proof of any further indecent intention or motive is required. We have reached that

conclusion because the statute does not by express words require such proof and we see
a no reason to attribute to Parliament an intention to include such an additional requirement.

Our attention was drawn to *R v Pratt* [1984] Crim LR 41 and to the cases there mentioned, in which the recorder ruled that an assault (not a battery or touching) in circumstances of indecency known to and intentionally brought about by the accused was not an indecent assault in law unless the prosecution also proved an ·indecent
b intention. The facts were unusual. The accused at night threatened two boys aged 13 by pretending to have a gun and thus forced them to undress so as to reveal their private parts. As each undressed the other was forced to shine a torch on him. The accused stood some five yards away. The defendant gave evidence that his sole motive in causing the two boys to reveal their private parts was to search for cannabis which he thought the boys had taken from him. The report is followed by the comment of Professor J C Smith
c QC as follows:

'It is respectfully submitted that the ruling was clearly correct. The act must be objectively indecent but the essence of the offence is the indecent intention with which it is done. An examination of a 15 year old girl by a midwife for medical purposes is clearly not an indecent assault, but precisely the same acts done solely for
d the purpose of the sexual gratification of the person doing the acts would be.'

A similar comment is made by Professor Glanville Williams in *Criminal Law* p 231, where the following appears:

'An assault is not indecent if it is neither intended by the defendant nor interpreted by the other party as having a sexual purpose. A doctor who makes an intimate
e examination of a girl of 15 for medical reasons is not guilty of indecent assault because he acts from a non-sexual motive, though if it were an indecent assault the consent of the girl would be no defence.'

We have considered the comments of Professor Smith and of Professor Glanville Williams with the care which comes from our great respect for their learning, but we are
f not, however, persuaded by them to take a different view. In our judgment, the ruling in *R v Pratt* was wrong. The references in the comments cited by us to the examination of a 15-year-old girl by a midwife or doctor for medical purposes are references to the rule in s 14(2) of the 1956 Act that a girl under the age of 16 cannot in law give any consent which would prevent an act being an assault for the purposes of the section. In our judgment it is not necessary to infer a requirement of proof of a sexual purpose, or
g of an indecent intention, for proof that a person has made an indecent assault, in order to protect from the theoretical risk of conviction for indecent assault the midwife or doctor who intimately examines a girl under the age of 16 without effective consent. If consent has been given by the parent or guardian there is, of course, no assault. If no such consent has been given, an intimate examination carried out for genuine medical purposes is, in
h our view, not indecent. Neither the girl examined, nor the right thinking members of society, would regard such an examination as an affront to the modesty of the girl or conduct which contravened normal standards of decent behaviour. So long as the examination is carried out for genuine medical purposes in a manner and in circumstances consistent with those purposes, then in our view the fact that the doctor or midwife happens to have some secret indecent motive, or happens to obtain some sexual
j gratification known only to himself from carrying out his legitimate work, cannot in our view render the circumstances indecent.

How then stands this conviction? The judge directed the jury that the prosecution had to prove that the accused had an indecent intention in doing what he did. If our view is right, that was a misdirection. In most cases it would be a misdirection in favour of the defence. On the special facts of this case, it is said to have been the cause of the admission

of damaging evidence which either was inadmissible in law, or which the judge in the
exercise of his discretion should have excluded as prejudicial and not probative.   *a*

We reject this submission. The fact that on our view of the construction of s 14
positive proof of indecent intention is not required, additional to proof of knowledge of
the circumstances of indecency, does not mean that, if evidence of such purpose or
motive exists, it must be excluded as irrelevant. Motive is normally of direct relevance
in proof of an offence charged even when proof of the motive is not necessary to prove
the offence. Counsel for the appellant conceded, and rightly in our view, that the acts of   *b*
the appellant in this case were capable of being regarded by the jury as an indecent
assault. The acts were to be described by this 12-year-old girl who was assaulted. It seems
to us that the grabbing of a 12-year-old girl by a 27-year-old man, who placed her in his
lap, face down, in order to smack her bottom over her shorts, is likely to vary in the
nature of the act as it is done, and as it will seem to the child who suffers it, according to
the purposes of the man. It may be the ordinary innocent rough play of an uncle and   *c*
niece in which nothing indecent obtrudes. If the man is actuated by an indecent motive,
it is likely in our view to affect the way in which he takes hold of the child and restrains
her and then strikes her. The man may well explain that his secret motive in fact had no
effect on his actions. In our view, in the rare case in which the prosecution has available
evidence of an admitted secret motive which actuated the accused to commit the
particular offence charged, it is open to the prosecution to call that evidence. It was in   *d*
our view admissible in this case and we see no reason why the judge should have excluded
it.

In a case in which the secret sexual motive of the accused could not affect the manner
in which he did the acts complained of, and in which the evidence of motive is not
relevant on any other issue in the case, the court's discretion to exclude prejudicial
evidence of little or no probative value would arise and be exercised. We do not accept   *e*
the submission for the Crown that the existence of such a motive is always admissible as
a makeweight on the issue of objective indecency.

The last point is this: it is contended for the appellant that, since a secret indecent
motive cannot by itself make the circumstances of an assault indecent, which without it
are not indecent, the jury should be directed that, after assessing what happened and   *f*
what the accused is proved to have done, having regard to any evidence of motive, they
must not use the evidence of secret motive again in deciding whether the circumstances
were in fact indecent. No such direction was given to the jury in those terms in this case.
As already stated, the judge distinguished clearly between proof of the indecent intention
and of the 'conduct of the defendant such that it would appear to an ordinary observer as
an affront to modesty'. On the view which we hold of the law, the jury should be directed   *g*
in such a case that the secret motive cannot turn into circumstances of indecency
circumstances which without it the jury would not regard as indecent.

The judge fairly and accurately described the conduct of the appellant in this case thus:

'Now what of the defendant's conduct, putting this young girl across his lap and
spanking her about 12 times across her bottom with his open hand, repeated
physical contact in an area immediately adjacent to that girl's private parts? Could   *h*
that be described as conduct which was not an affront to modesty, or was it patently
conduct which contravened any right-thinking person's idea of what is decent?'

The jury were, as we have said, entitled to assess the nature of the appellant's acts by
reference to his proved purpose. The jury took great care. They did not regard proof of
this appellant's indecent intention as conclusive of the issue of objective indecency. The   *j*
jury retired at 11.00 am. At 12 noon they sent a note to the judge. The note read: 'We
have agreed that his intentions were indecent but cannot agree on whether the actual act
of spanking was indecent. May we have some guidance?' The judge answered their
question thus:

a
> 'The prosecution have to prove that the defendant's conduct was such that it would appear to the ordinary observer as an affront to modesty, something which falls very far short of the customary standards of decent behaviour . . . It is for you to decide whether in fact it was an indecent assault.'

The jury had one further question: they were dealing with analogies and had considered the examination of a patient by a doctor which they knew to be permitted by virtue of the fact that we go to the medical practitioner. The further direction of the
b
judge was as follows:

> 'In that situation what is vital is whether the examination was necessary or not. If it wasn't necessary but indulged in by the medical practitioner it would be an indecent assault. But if it was necessary, even though he got sexual satisfaction out of it, that wouldn't make it an indecent assault.'

c
The course of the trial, as we have set it out, shows, in our judgment, that the jury clearly regarded as separate the two aspects of the case as left to them by the judge. At the end they were not directed to have regard to the secret motive in deciding whether the circumstances were indecent. On the analogous case raised by them they were directed, in our view correctly, that a secret motive would not itself make an assault, which was in
d
all other respects not indecent, an indecent assault.

There was in this case evidence of circumstances of indecency. The jury accepted that this assault was committed in circumstances of indecency. We see no ground for regarding this verdict as unsafe or unsatisfactory, and the appeal is therefore dismissed.

Appeal dismissed.

e
Solicitors: *Crown Prosecution Service.*

Sophie Craven   Barrister.

Practice Note

a

QUEEN'S BENCH DIVISION

LORD LANE CJ, WATKINS LJ AND SIMON BROWN J

19 DECEMBER 1986

Criminal law – Bail – Absconding from bail – Procedure for dealing with allegations of failure to surrender to custody – Procedure where bail granted by court – Procedure where bail granted by police – Bail Act 1976, s 6.

b

LORD LANE CJ gave the following direction at the sitting of the court.

1. This Practice Direction is issued with a view to clarifying any misunderstandings as to the effect of the decision in *Schiavo v Anderton* [1986] 3 All ER 10, [1986] 3 WLR 176, in which, inter alia, the Divisional Court provided guidance on the procedure to be adopted in magistrates' courts when dealing with allegations of failure to surrender to custody contrary to s 6 of the Bail Act 1976.

c

2. *Bail granted by a magistrates' court*

Where a person has been granted bail by a court and subsequently fails to surrender to custody as contemplated by s 6(1) or (2) of the Bail Act 1976, on arrest that person should be brought before the court at which the proceedings in respect of which bail was granted are to be heard. It is neither necessary nor desirable to lay an information in order to commence proceedings for the failure to surrender. Having regard to the nature of the offence, which is tantamount to the defiance of a court order, it is more appropriate that the court itself should initiate the proceedings by its own motion, following an express invitation by the prosecutor. The court will only be invited so to move if, having considered all the circumstances, the prosecutor considers proceedings are appropriate. Where a court complies with such an invitation, the prosecutor will naturally conduct the proceedings and, where the matter is contested, call the evidence. Any trial should normally take place immediately following the disposal of the proceedings in respect of which bail was granted.

d

e

f

3. *Bail granted by a police officer*

Where a person has been bailed from a police station subject to a duty to appear before a magistrates' court or to attend a police station on an appointed date and/or time, a failure so to appear or attend cannot be said to be tantamount to the defiance of a court order. There does not exist the same compelling justification for the court to act by its own motion. Where bail has been granted by a police officer, any proceedings for a failure to surrender to custody, whether at a court or a police station, should accordingly be initiated by charging the accused or by the laying of an information.

g

N P Metcalfe Esq   Barrister.

a   # R v Crown Court at Maidstone, ex parte Gill

QUEEN'S BENCH DIVISION
LORD LANE CJ, NOLAN AND MACPHERSON JJ
14 JULY 1986

b   *Crown Court – Supervisory jurisdiction of High Court – Trial on indictment – High Court having no supervisory jurisdiction in matters relating to trial on indictment – Relating to trial on indictment – Forfeiture order following conviction for drug offence – Whether forfeiture order a 'matter relating to trial on indictment' – Whether High Court having jurisdiction to hear application for certiorari to quash order – Supreme Court Act 1981, s 29(3).*

c   *Sentence – Forfeiture order – Forfeiture of property – Cars used in drug offences – Owner's two cars used by his son to transport drugs – Owner not aware of purpose for which son used cars – Charge concerning one car not proceeded with – Whether cars 'shown to relate to offence' – Whether cars properly forfeited when owner unaware of criminal use – Misuse of Drugs Act 1971, s 27.*

d   The applicant lent two cars to his son who, without his father's knowledge, used the cars for two separate journeys to supply prohibited drugs. The son was later charged with two offences of supplying heroin. He pleaded guilty to one charge and was sentenced to four years' imprisonment. The other charge was not proceeded with. After passing sentence the trial judge made a forfeiture order under s 27[a] of the Misuse of Drugs Act 1971 forfeiting the two cars. The applicant applied for certiorari to quash the forfeiture order. The Crown contended that the forfeiture order was a matter 'relating to trial on indictment' and therefore under s 29(3)[b] of the Supreme Court Act 1981 the court had no jurisdiction to consider the application.

Held – The application would be allowed and the forfeiture order quashed for the following reasons—

f   (1) The forfeiture order in respect of the applicant's cars was not a matter 'relating to trial on indictment' for the purposes of s 29(3) of the 1981 Act because it was not an order which affected the conduct of the trial of the applicant's son in any way. Accordingly, the court was not excluded by s 29(3) from considering the application (see p 133 *b d h j* and p 134 *h*, post); *Smalley v Crown Court at Warwick* [1985] 1 All ER 769 applied; *R v Crown Court at Cardiff, ex p Jones* [1973] 3 All ER 1027 and *R v Smith (Martin)* [1974] 1 All ER 651 doubted.

g   (2) Since one of the cars had not been used in the transaction to which the son had pleaded guilty that vehicle had not been 'shown to relate to the offence' and therefore the trial judge had had no jurisdiction under s 27(1) of the 1971 Act to make a forfeiture order in respect of that vehicle. In respect of the vehicle which had been used in the offence to which the son had pleaded guilty the judge ought not to have made the forfeiture order because the applicant had had no reason to suspect that the son would use the car to transport prohibited drugs and the order would not, contrary to the judge's view, act as any form of deterrent to the son or to others (see p 134 *e* to *h*, post).

Per curiam. There may well be cases where a person who lends a motor car to another should have been put on notice or suspicion that the car was going to be used for some illegal purpose and in such a case it may be perfectly proper for a forfeiture order to be made by the judge in order to mark his disapproval of the failure to take the necessary precautions (see p 134 *d e h*, post).

---

a   Section 27 is set out at p 130 *j* to p 131 *a*, post
b   Section 29(3) is set out at p 131 *d e*, post

Notes

For forfeiture orders, see 11 Halsbury's Laws (4th edn) para 1092.   *a*

   For the Misuse of Drugs Act 1971, s 27, see 41 Halsbury's Statutes (3rd edn) 905.

   For the Supreme Court Act 1981, s 29, see 11 Halsbury's Statutes (4th edn) 780.

Cases referred to in judgments

R v Central Criminal Court, ex p Raymond [1986] 2 All ER 379, [1986] 1 WLR 710, DC.

R v Crown Court at Cardiff, ex p Jones [1973] 2 All ER 1027, DC.   *b*

R v Crown Court at Sheffield, ex p Brownlow [1980] 2 All ER 444, [1980] QB 530, [1980] 2
   WLR 892, CA.

R v Cuthbertson [1980] 2 All ER 401, [1981] AC 470, [1980] 3 WLR 89, HL.

R v Menocal [1979] 2 All ER 510, [1980] AC 598, [1979] 2 WLR 876, HL.

R v Smith (Martin) [1974] 1 All ER 651, [1975] QB 531, [1974] 2 WLR 495, CA.

Smalley v Crown Court at Warwick [1985] 1 All ER 769, [1985] AC 622, [1985] 2 WLR   *c*
   538, HL.

Application for judicial review

Dara Singh Gill applied, with the leave of Mann J granted on 27 September 1985, for
judicial review by way of an order of certiorari to quash the order made by his Honour   *d*
Judge Russell Vick in the Crown Court at Maidstone on 5 July 1985 ordering that two
motor vehicles belonging to the applicant, namely a Volvo motor car reg no YYN 2T and
a Triumph motor car reg no SGK 714R, be forfeited to the Crown following the
conviction of the applicant's son, Sarjit Gill, on a charge of supplying heroin. The facts
are set out in the judgment of Lord Lane CJ.

                                                                                           e

Tudor Owen for the applicant.
Keith Simpson for the Crown.
Alan Moses as amicus curiae.

LORD LANE CJ. This is an application for judicial review by way of certiorari, to   *f*
remove into this court and quash an order made by his Honour Judge Russell Vick on 5
July 1985 in the Crown Court at Maidstone.

   The applicant is a man called Dara Singh Gill. He has a son called Sarjit. Sarjit stood
trial before Judge Russell Vick in June 1985 on an indictment containing five counts.
We are only concerned with two of those counts. The first of the two alleged that on 8
November 1984 Sarjit supplied a small quantity of heroin, a Class A drug. The second   *g*
charge with which we are concerned alleged that on 13 November, five days later, Sarjit
supplied something like a kilogram of heroin. In both cases the supply was to an
undercover policeman.

   Initially Sarjit pleaded not guilty to all five counts. However, during the course of the
trial and before he, Sarjit, had given evidence, he asked for the charge in respect of the
kilogram of heroin to be put to him again, and he then pleaded guilty to that count. He   *h*
was sentenced to four years' imprisonment. The first count relating to the small quantity
of heroin was ordered to remain on the file on the usual terms, not to be proceeded with
without the leave of the court.

   Sarjit had used two motor cars in the course of his activities in these matters. On the
first occasion it was a Volvo motor car which he used and on the second occasion, because
the Volvo apparently would not start, he used a Triumph motor car. Each of those   *j*
vehicles belonged to the applicant.

   The judge was minded to order the forfeiture of those vehicles under the terms of the
Misuse of Drugs Act 1971, s 27, which provides:

   '(1) Subject to subsection (2) below, the court by or before which a person is
   convicted of an offence under this Act may order anything shown to the satisfaction

a
of the court to relate to the offence, to be forfeited and either destroyed or dealt with in such other manner as the court may order.

(2) The court shall not order anything to be forfeited under this section, where a person claiming to be the owner of or otherwise interested in it applies to be heard by the court, unless an opportunity has been given to him to show cause why the order should not be made.'

b
As the applicant was not in court at the hearing in June the matter was adjourned in the light of sub-s (2) to 5 July for representations, if any, to be made by or on behalf of the applicant as to why the forfeiture order should not be made. Sarjit was not present at this hearing on 5 July. Representations were duly made to Judge Russell Vick, but the judge was unmoved by those representations, and he made orders in respect of both cars that they should be forfeited. The terms of his judgment in which he said that will have
c
to be considered in a little more detail at a later stage.

The first problem is one of jurisdiction. It is the contention of the Crown put forward in this court that the Divisional Court has no jurisdiction to entertain this application for the reasons of the terms of the Supreme Court Act 1981, s 29(1) and (3), which provides:

d
'(1) The High Court shall have jurisdiction to make orders of mandamus, prohibition and certiorari in those classes of cases in which it had power to do so immediately before the commencement of this Act.

(3) In relation to the jurisdiction of the Crown Court, other than its jurisdiction in matters relating to trial on indictment, the High Court shall have all such jurisdiction to make orders of mandamus, prohibition or certiorari as the High Court possesses in relation to the jurisdiction of an inferior court.'

e
The argument of the Crown is this: that the forfeiture order was clearly a matter relating to trial on indictment, and that accordingly this court has no power to consider the application.

If indeed one takes the words at their face value, namely the words 'in matters relating to trial on indictment', that is probably correct. It would mean that the applicant would
f
have no remedy if the judge had made an order which was plainly unjust. The reason for that is that he would have no right to pursue an appeal in the Criminal Division of the Court of Appeal, because he would not be a convicted person and had not been sentenced. The result of no remedy would, of course, be highly unfortunate, but, if that is the result of the statutory provision, then that would be the end of the matter.

However, a recent decision by the House of Lords, *Smalley v Crown Court at Warwick*
g
[1985] 1 All ER 769, [1985] AC 622, makes it clear that the words of s 29(3) of the 1981 Act are not to be read in their widest sense. This particular case differed sharply from the facts in the instant case, because it involved an order to estreat a recognisance. But Lord Bridge in his speech said ([1985] 1 All ER 769 at 779, [1985] AC 622 at 642):

'Beyond this it is not difficult to discern a sensible legislative purpose in excluding appeal or judicial review of any decision affecting the conduct of a trial on
h
indictment, whether given in the course of the trial or by way of pre-trial directions. In any such case to allow an appellate or review process might, as Shaw LJ pointed out in *R v Crown Court at Sheffield, ex p Brownlow* [1980] 2 All ER 444 at 455, [1980] QB 530 at 544–545, seriously delay the trial. If it is the prosecutor who is aggrieved by such a decision, it is in no way surprising that he has no remedy, since prosecutors have never enjoyed rights of appeal or review when unsuccessful in trials on
j
indictment. If, on the other hand, the defendant is so aggrieved, he will have his remedy by way of appeal against conviction under the Criminal Appeal Act 1968 if he has suffered an injustice in consequence of a material irregularity in the course of the trial, which, I apprehend, may well result not only from a decision given during the trial, but equally from a decision given in advance of the trial which affects the conduct of the trial, eg a wrongful refusal to grant him legal aid.

I can, however, discover no intelligible legislative purpose which would be served by giving to the words "relating to trial on indictment" a wider operation than indicated in the foregoing paragraph. An order estreating the recognisance of a surety for a defendant who fails to surrender to his bail at the Crown Court to which he was committed for trial cannot affect the conduct of any trial on indictment in any way. If such an order is wrongly made, for example by denying the surety the right to be heard, I can see no sensible reason whatever why the aggrieved surety should not have a remedy by judicial review. Still less can I see any reason for distinguishing in this respect between the position of a surety, on the one hand, for a defendant committed on bail to the Crown Court for trial and a surety, on the other hand, for a defendant committed on bail to the Crown Court either for sentence after conviction by a magistrates' court, or on appeal to the Crown Court against conviction and sentence by a magistrates' court. If, therefore, the phrase "relating to trial on indictment" may be construed broadly or narrowly, a purposive approach points, to my mind, unmistakably to a construction sufficiently narrow, at all events, to avoid the exclusion of judicial review in such a case as this . . .

I think the decision of the majority in that case [ie *Brownlow*'s case] was right that the order in question, potentially affecting, as it did, the composition of a jury for a forthcoming trial, was, as Shaw LJ put it, "closely related to trial on indictment", or as I would prefer to say, was an order affecting the conduct of the trial . . .

It must not be thought that in using the phrase "any decision affecting the conduct of a trial on indictment" I am offering a definition of a phrase which Parliament has chosen not to define. If the statutory language is, as here, imprecise, it may well be impossible to prescribe in the abstract a precise test to determine on which side of the line any case should fall and, therefore, necessary to proceed, as counsel for the appellant submitted that we should, on a case basis. But it is obviously desirable that your Lordships' House should give a clear guidance as the statutory language permits, and I hope the criterion I have suggested may provide a helpful pointer to the right answer in most cases.'

Was this an order in the present case affecting the conduct of the trial? Of course the sentence of the court, or a penalty imposed on a defendant, is part of the actual trial process and is plainly within the narrow meaning of the statutory words which Lord Bridge suggested.

We were referred to the decision of the House of Lords in *R v Menocal* [1979] 2 All ER 510 at 515, [1980] AC 598 at 606, where Lord Salmon said:

'The fact that s 27(1) is wide enough to empower the Crown Court (subject to the conditions set out in s 27(2)) to order persons other than the offender to forfeit anything relating to the offence and that such an order could not, in the nature of things, be regarded as a sentence or order against the offender is entirely irrelevant in the present case.'

That plainly is an obiter dictum but it points sharply to the view taken by Lord Salmon as to the circumstances of this case.

The fate of the motor cars, the Volvo and the Triumph, in the present case was a matter of indifference to the defendant Sarjit who, as I say, was not even present on 5 July at Maidstone when this order was made against the applicant. It was an order which, as a matter of practical politics, affected only the applicant.

We have also had our attention drawn to two earlier cases, I mention them in passing out of courtesy to counsel, *R v Crown Court at Cardiff, ex p Jones* [1973] 3 All ER 1027, which was a case of an order for contributions towards legal aid costs, and *R v Smith (Martin)* [1974] 1 All ER 657, [1975] QB 531. Both of those cases, in the light of their Lordships' decision in *Smalley v Crown Court at Warwick* must be of doubtful authority.

But more recently, in *R v Central Criminal Court, ex p Raymond* [1986] 2 All ER 379, a [1986] 1 WLR 710, another division of this court had reason to examine the *Smalley* speeches in depth. That was the case of an order by the judge at trial that an indictment should remain on the file not to be proceeded with without the leave of the court. That was held to be an order affecting the conduct of the trial, because it quite plainly affected whether the trial should take place at all.

The present order, in my judgment, did not affect the conduct of the trial. It did not affect this defendant at all as a matter of practical politics. So far as the defendant was
b concerned, the proceedings had ended at the hearing in June, before the applicant had been asked to attend to show cause why the cars should not be forfeited. No appeal or application by the applicant could have had the effect of holding up the trial, for obvious reasons.

We have been referred by counsel as amicus curiae to two definitions: first of all the definition of sentence in the Courts Act 1971, s 57:
c
'In this Act, unless the context otherwise requires . . . "sentence", in relation to an offence, includes any order made by a court when dealing with an offender . . .'

Counsel's submission, which I accept, is that this order was not an order dealing with an offender. There is a similar provision in almost identical terms in the Criminal Appeal Act 1968.
d
For those reasons, in my judgment, we have jurisdiction to entertain this application.

I now therefore turn to the merits. There are two aspects: one relates to the Volvo motor car alone, and the other aspect relates to both motor cars.

From what has already been said, it is plain that the Volvo motor car was not used in the second transaction to which a plea of guilty was entered, namely the 13 November transaction when a kilogramme of heroin was handed over to the policeman. It was used
e in the earlier transaction, namely the allegation that the defendant had handed a small quantity of heroin to the same recipient at the earlier date. In respect of that count the plea of not guilty entered by the defendant Sarjit at the outset of the trial remained unaltered. It is a question therefore whether the words 'anything shown to relate to the offence' were satisfied in those circumstances. I think that they were not.

f We were referred helpfully to a further decision of the House of Lords in *R v Cuthbertson* [1980] 2 All ER 401 at 406, [1981] AC 470 at 483 (the famous case of Operation Julie) where Lord Diplock said:

'Where it is possible to identify something tangible that can fairly be said to relate to any such transaction, such as the drugs involved, apparatus for making them, vehicles used for transporting them, or cash ready to be, or having just been, handed
g over for them, then if it is desired to forfeit it the transaction must be made the subject of a charge of the substantive offence. There does not seem to me to be anything unreasonable in requiring this to be done. Forfeiture is a penalty; justice requires that it should not be imposed by a court in the absence of a finding or an admission of guilt.'

h Counsel for the Crown submits to us that the earlier occasion of 8 November was really all part and parcel of the main transaction. The smaller transaction was simply handing a sample to the proposed purchaser, and therefore it can properly be said that the Volvo motor car was so to speak used or related to the charge to which the plea of guilty had been entered.

I disagree. I think that the matter was unresolved, namely whether the Volvo motor
j car had in fact been used for the purpose of the count to which the defendant pleaded guilty. That was a matter which the jury would have had to decide. They did not. So it remains a matter undecided. Accordingly so far as the Volvo was concerned at any rate, this forfeiture order should not have been made.

In fairness to everyone, may I add this? It was not until this morning that this point raised its head at all. Consequently neither the judge, nor anyone else in the case, needs to feel guilty about having failed to spot it. It was only the skill of counsel for the applicant which brought the matter to light.

That leaves the Triumph. It is important to see what it was that the judge had to say. This was of course on the occasion when representations were made to him on behalf of the applicant that a forfeiture order should not be made. This is what he said:

> '[Counsel for the applicant's] further point is that had the defendant [Sarjit] gone to a car hire firm they would not be at risk of forfeiture. That is not this case. It is not the case of a car hire. This is the case of a father who made available both vehicles to his son, apparently with no inquiry as to what use the son was making of the vehicle. The Volvo had broken down on the day the drugs were to be handed over and the Triumph motor vehicle was made available for him. I have heard the evidence of [the applicant] and I am satisfied that he was clearly a person not aware that his son was, in fact, a drug dealer or involved with them in any way. He said he disassociates himself wholly from what his son did and has not yet visited him in prison although he expects that he will have to do so, and what has happened has embarrassed the family. But, as [counsel for the Crown] rightly points out, if people are in the vile trade of pushing and peddling drugs to others the fear that they may lose a vehicle will encourage them, it seems to me, [to] make use of vehicles of other people. This is a case in which I exercise my discretion to order that both vehicles be forfeited in relation to these offences.'

It may be that there will be cases where a man who lends a motor car should have been put on notice or on suspicion that the car was going to be used for some illegal purpose, and in those cases it may be perfectly proper for a judge to make orders of forfeiture in order to mark his disapproval of the failure to take the necessary precautions.

But this case was not such a case at all, because on the judge's findings, the applicant, had no reason to suppose that the car was going to be used for anything other than legitimate purposes. Both these cars apparently were used as family cars, sometimes for taking children to and fro from school, other times for ordinary family business. There was no reason, on the judge's findings, for the applicant to be under any sort of suspicion about what was going on. It certainly would not have prevented the offence if the applicant had said, 'Son, you may not use this car for illegal purposes.' It certainly would not have helped if he had asked the defendant, 'Are you going to use the car for ferrying heroin?' because the answer would obviously have been, 'No.'

It is difficult therefore to follow the judge's reasoning in the passage read. It is difficult to understand how forfeiture in the circumstances of this case could act as a deterrent to the man convicted or how in the future, by forfeiting cars in these circumstances, anyone would be deterred.

For those reasons I think the conclusion to which the judge came was one which was clearly not open to him on the facts, and I would allow the application and quash the forfeiture order.

NOLAN J. I agree.

MACPHERSON J. I agree.

Certiorari granted. Forfeiture orders quashed.

Solicitors: *Wilson Houlder & Co,* Southall (for the applicant); *R A Crabb,* Margate (for the Crown).

N P Metcalfe Esq   Barrister.

a

Aswan Engineering Establishment Co v Lupdine Ltd and another (Thurgar Bolle Ltd, third party)

COURT OF APPEAL, CIVIL DIVISION

b

FOX, LLOYD AND NICHOLLS LJJ

19, 20, 21, 22 MAY, 3, 4 JUNE, 16 JULY 1986

Sale of goods – Implied condition as to merchantable quality – Suitability for purpose – Purpose for which goods might reasonably be expected to be used – Whether goods required to be suitable for every purpose for which they were normally bought – Sale of Goods Act 1979, s 14(6).

c

Sale of goods – Implied condition as to fitness – Reliance on seller's skill and judgment – Stated purpose not materially different from purpose for which the goods commonly bought – Whether condition as to fitness for purpose different from condition as to merchantable quality – Sale of Goods Act 1979, s 14(3).

d

Negligence – Duty to take care – Manufacturer's liability – User of manufacturer's product – Proximity – Plaintiff's goods shipped to Kuwait in pails – Pails collapsing under heat when left in sun on quayside – Whether manufacturer of pails owing duty of care to plaintiff.

The plaintiff was a construction company carrying on business in Kuwait. In 1980 it

e

bought a quantity of liquid waterproofing compound from the first defendants for shipment to Kuwait. The waterproofing compound was packed in heavy duty plastic pails manufactured and supplied by the second defendants. On arrival in Kuwait the pails were stacked five or six high in containers and left in the sun on the quayside. The pails collapsed under the intense heat and the entire consignment of waterproofing compound was lost. The pails could only have withstood the extremely high temperatures

f

if they had been packed into the containers in a particular way. The plaintiff brought an action against the first defendants claiming damages for the loss and the first defendants joined the second defendants as third parties. The first defendants alleged that the pails manufactured and supplied by the second defendants were not of merchantable quality since they were not fit for export to Kuwait, and since the second defendants knew the purpose for which the pails were required there was an implied term that the pails would be fit for that purpose. The first defendants subsequently went into liquidation and the

g

plaintiff then claimed damages against the second defendants in negligence in respect of the loss of the waterproofing compound, alleging that the second defendants owed the plaintiff a duty of care to provide pails suitable for the journey to Kuwait which would preserve the plaintiff's property (ie the waterproofing compound). At the trial of the action the questions arose (i) whether the pails were of merchantable quality within

h

s 14(6)[a] of the Sale of Goods Act 1979, (ii) whether there was an implied condition under s 14(3)[b] that the pails were reasonably fit for the purpose for which they were to be used, and (iii) whether the second defendants owed a duty of care to the plaintiff in respect of the loss of the waterproofing compound. The judge held that the plaintiff was entitled to succeed against the first defendants in contract and accordingly awarded the plaintiff damages. However, he found on the facts that the pails had been of merchantable quality

j

and also that there had been no implied term that they would be fit for the journey to Kuwait. He therefore dismissed the first defendants' claim against the second defendants.

---

a   Section 14(6) is set out at p 140 *c*, post

b   Section 14(3) is set out at p 145 *g*, post

He also dismissed the plaintiff's claim against the second defendants, on the ground that, as manufacturers, they did not owe a duty of care to the plaintiff because there was not the requisite degree of proximity between the parties. The plaintiff and the first defendants appealed.

Held – (1) On the true construction of s 14(6) of the 1979 Act goods were of merchantable quality if they were suitable for one or more purposes for which they might, without abatement of price, reasonably be expected to be used but they were not required to be suitable for every purpose within such a range of purposes for which such goods were normally bought. The pails were thus of merchantable quality as heavy duty pails suitable for export because, although the pails were not suitable for use in all parts of the world when stacked five or six high, they were suitable for use when so stacked in many parts of the world and they were suitable for export to the Middle East if the particular packing method was used. Furthermore, there was no evidence that a buyer who wanted pails for export and knew that they could not withstand very high temperatures unless they were packed in a particular way would ask for an abatement of price (see p 145 c to e, p 147 g j to p 148 a, p 156 h and p 159 f, post).

(2) (Per Fox and Lloyd LJJ) There was no evidence to show that the first defendants had relied on the second defendants' skill and judgment in providing the pails and accordingly a condition as to fitness for the particular purpose for which the first defendants required the pails could not be implied under s 14(3) of the 1979 Act, or (per Nicholls LJ) if there had been reliance on the part of the first defendants the purpose stated by the first defendants was not materially different from the relevant purpose for which the pails were commonly bought, so that the fitness for purpose condition, if it applied, added nothing to the merchantable quality condition. The first defendants' appeal would therefore be dismissed (see p 149 b to e, p 157 f g and p 159 f, post); *Henry Kendall & Sons (a firm) v William Lillico & Sons Ltd* [1968] 2 All ER 444 and dictum of Lord Diplock in *Ashington Piggeries Ltd v Christopher Hill Ltd* [1971] 1 All ER at 886 considered.

(3) (Per Fox and Lloyd LJJ) The scope of a manufacturer's duty of care did not extend beyond consequences that were reasonably foreseeable and since in all the circumstances the damage suffered by the plaintiff was not of a type which the second defendants could reasonably have been expected to foresee, or (per Nicholls LJ) since the pails were as fit for the purposes for which goods of that kind were commonly bought as it was reasonable to expect, the second defendants were not in breach of any duty to the plaintiff to take reasonable care. It followed that the plaintiff's appeal would be dismissed (see p 153 c d f, p 158 a b c f and p 159 f, post); *Donoghue v Stevenson* [1932] All ER Rep 1, *Junior Books Ltd v Veitchi Co Ltd* [1982] 3 All ER 201 and *Muirhead v Industrial Tank Specialities Ltd* [1985] 3 All ER 705 considered.

Quaere. What degree of physical proximity is required between goods which are purchased by a plaintiff from their manufacturer and which prove to be defective or dangerous and the plaintiff's 'other property' if the manufacturer is to be liable to the plaintiff for the loss of or damage to the 'other property' (see p 152 g to p 153 a and p 158 g to p 159 f, post).

Notes

For implied terms as to quality or fitness, see 41 Halsbury's Laws (4th edn) paras 691–695, and for cases on the subject, see 39(2) Digest (Reissue) 202–217, 224–230, 1546–1655, 1739–1801.

For claims in negligence for economic loss, see 34 Halsbury's Laws (4th edn) para 6.

For the Sale of Goods Act 1979, s 14, see 49 Halsbury's Statutes (3rd edn) 1115.

Cases referred to in judgments

Anderton v Ryan [1985] 2 All ER 355, [1985] AC 560, [1985] 2 WLR 968, HL.

a *Anns v Merton London Borough* [1977] 2 All ER 492, [1978] AC 728, [1977] 2 WLR 1024, HL.

Ashington Piggeries Ltd v Christopher Hill Ltd, Christopher Hill Ltd v Norsildmel [1971] 1 All ER 847, [1972] AC 441, [1971] 2 WLR 1051, HL.

Bristol Tramways etc Carriage Co Ltd v Fiat Motors Ltd [1910] 2 KB 831, [1908–10] All ER Rep 113, CA.

Brown (B S) & Son Ltd v Craiks Ltd [1970] 1 All ER 823, [1970] 1 WLR 752, HL.

b *Cammell Laird & Co Ltd v Manganese Bronze and Brass Co Ltd* [1934] AC 402, [1934] All ER Rep 1, HL.

Canada Atlantic Grain Export Co v Eilers (1929) 35 Ll L Rep 206.

Candlewood Navigation Corp Ltd v Mitsui OSK Lines Ltd, The Mineral Transporter, The Ibaraki Maru [1985] 2 All ER 935, [1986] AC 1, [1985] 3 WLR 381, PC.

Cehave NV v Bremer Handelsgesellschaft mbH, The Hansa Nord [1975] 3 All ER 739, [1976]
c QB 44, [1975] 3 WLR 447, CA.

Donoghue (or M'Alister) v Stevenson [1932] AC 562, [1932] All ER Rep 1, HL.

Drummond (James) & Sons v E H Van Ingen & Co (1887) 12 App Cas 284.

Gardiner v Gray (1815) 4 Camp 144, 171 ER 46.

Grant v Australian Knitting Mills Ltd [1936] AC 85, [1935] All ER Rep 209, PC; *rvsg* (1933) 50 CLR 387, Aust HC.

d *Jones v Bright* (1829) 5 Bing 533, 130 ER 1167.

Jones v Just (1868) LR 3 QB 197.

Jones v Padgett (1890) 24 QBD 650, DC.

Junior Books Ltd v Veitchi Co Ltd [1982] 3 All ER 201, [1983] 1 AC 520, [1982] 3 WLR 477, HL.

Kendall (Henry) & Sons (a firm) v William Lillico & Sons Ltd [1968] 2 All ER 444, sub nom
e *Hardwick Game Farm v Suffolk Agricultural Poultry Producers Association* [1969] 2 AC 31, [1968] 3 WLR 110, HL.

Leigh & Sillavan Ltd v Aliakmon Shipping Co Ltd, The Aliakmon [1986] 2 All ER 145, [1986] AC 785, [1986] 2 WLR 902, HL; *affg* [1985] 2 All ER 44, [1985] QB 350, [1985] 2 WLR 289, CA.

f *Muirhead v Industrial Tank Specialities Ltd* [1985] 3 All ER 705, [1986] QB 507, [1985] 3 WLR 993, CA.

Niblett Ltd v Confectioners' Materials Co Ltd [1921] 3 KB 387, [1921] All ER Rep 459, CA.

R v Shivpuri [1986] 2 All ER 334, [1986] 2 WLR 988, HL.

Cases also cited

g *BSC Footwear Ltd (formerly Freeman Hardy & Willis Ltd) v Ridgway (Inspector of Taxes)* [1971] 2 All ER 534, [1972] AC 544, HL.

Clay v A J Crump & Sons Ltd [1963] 3 All ER 687, [1964] 1 QB 533, CA.

Ingham v Emes [1955] 2 All ER 740, [1955] 2 QB 366, CA.

Lambert v Lewis [1978] 1 Lloyd's Rep 610; *rvsd in part* [1980] 1 All ER 978, [1982] AC 225, CA; *rvsd in part* [1981] 1 All ER 1185, [1982] AC 225, HL.

h *Tai Hing Cotton Mill Ltd v Liu Chong Hing Bank Ltd* [1985] 2 All ER 947, [1986] AC 80, PC.

Teheran-Europe Co Ltd v S T Belton (Tractors) Ltd [1968] 2 All ER 886, [1968] 2 QB 545, CA.

Appeals

The plaintiff, Aswan Engineering Establishment Co (Aswan), appealed against that part
j of the judgment of Neill J given on 1 August 1984 whereby he dismissed its claim against the second defendants, Thurgar Bolle Ltd, for damages of £188,811·40 and interest, and held that Thurgar Bolle did not owe a duty of care to Aswan to ensure that V20 plastic pails manufactured and supplied by Thurgar Bolle were of merchantable quality and/or were suitable for holding safely and securely for a sea journey from the United Kingdom to Kuwait waterproofing compound known as Lupguard manufactured by the first

defendants, Lupdine Ltd, and purchased by Aswan. The grounds of the appeal were,
inter alia, that (i) the judge erred in law in holding that there was not the requisite degree
of proximity between Aswan and Thurgar Bolle so as to place a duty of care on Thurgar
Bolle and (ii) the judge ought to have held that Thurgar Bolle owed a duty of care to
Aswan because Thurgar Bolle knew and intended that the pails would be used to hold
liquids (including Lupguard) and appreciated that export shipments could be stored on
quaysides and could be in transit for a total of several weeks, and Thurgar Bolle realised
or ought to have realised that if the pails failed their contents would be lost or damaged,
with consequent loss to Aswan. Lupdine also appealed against that part of the judgment
of the judge whereby he dismissed their claim against Thurgar Bolle for indemnity in
the sum claimed by Aswan against Lupdine and ordered them to pay to Thurgar Bolle
the sum of £5,994·51 on a counterclaim brought by Thurgar Bolle. The grounds of the
appeal were, inter alia, that (i) the judge erred in fact or in law in holding that the pails
were of merchantable quality and (ii) that the judge erred in holding that the liability of
Lupdine to Aswan was not caused by any breach by the Thurgar Bolle of the contract
between Lupdine and Thurgar Bolle. Thurgar Bolle were joined as third parties in the
action by Lupdine and were later sued as second defendants by Aswan. The facts are set
out in the judgment of Lloyd LJ.

Richard Aikens QC for the appellants.
A W Stevenson and *Steven Coles* for Thurgar Bolle.

Cur adv vult

16 July. The following judgments were delivered.

LLOYD LJ (giving the first judgment at the invitation of Fox LJ). The facts of this
appeal are simple enough. But they have given rise to two difficult questions of law. The
first, on which there is said to be no authority, is the meaning of merchantable quality,
as now defined by s 14(6) of the Sale of Goods Act 1979. That question arises in third
party proceedings between Lupdine Ltd and Thurgar Bolle Ltd, the first and second
defendants.

The second question concerns the scope of the manufacturer's duty of care in tort.
That question arises between Thurgar Bolle and Aswan Engineering Establishment Co
(Aswan), the plaintiffs. As so often happens, the second question only arises because
Aswan's primary remedy is not available or, rather, is unlikely to prove fruitful; for
Lupdine, the intermediate sellers, are now in liquidation.

Lupdine are (or were) manufacturers of a waterproofing compound known as
'Lupguard'. Aswan is a construction company carrying on business in Kuwait. In June
1980 it bought a quantity of about 35,100 kg of Lupguard for shipment to Kuwait. The
Lupguard was packed in plastic pails manufactured and supplied by Thurgar Bolle. Each
pail held about 25 kg of Lupguard. The pails were stacked five or six high in 20-foot
containers, 702 pails per container. The first container was shipped on 13 July 1980. Four
more containers were shipped on various days between 28 July and 19 September 1980.
When the containers arrived, they were left standing on the quayside in full sunshine.
As a result the temperature inside the containers reached 70°C or 158°F. It was as if the
plastic pails had been put in an oven. Not surprisingly the plastic pails collapsed, and
there was a total loss of the Lupguard. Thurgar Bolle say that some of the Lupguard
could have been salvaged, but I was not persuaded that that would have been practicable.

Aswan brought a claim against Lupdine. Lupdine brought in Thurgar Bolle as third
parties. Aswan then amended its claim so as to join Thurgar Bolle as second defendants.
Neill J held that Aswan was entitled to succeed against Lupdine in contract. Damages
were agreed at £118,881·40, but he dismissed Lupdine's claim against Thurgar Bolle. He
held that the pails were of merchantable quality within the meaning of s 14(6) of the
1979 Act. He held further that there was no express or implied term that they were to
be fit for the journey to Kuwait.

As for Aswan's claim against Thurgar Bolle, Neill J reviewed the recent cases on a
a manufacturer's liability in tort, including *Anns v Merton London Borough* [1977] 2 All ER
492, [1978] AC 728 and *Junior Books Ltd v Veitchi Co Ltd* [1982] 3 All ER 201, [1983] 1 AC
520. He held that Aswan had, in the words of Lord Roskill ([1982] 3 All ER 201 at 213,
[1983] 1 AC 520 at 546), failed to show 'the requisite degree of proximity so as to give
rise to the relevant duty of care'. Accordingly, he dismissed Aswan's claim against
Thurgar Bolle. It was unnecessary for him to consider whether, if Thurgar Bolle had
b been under a relevant duty of care, they were in breach of that duty.

There is now an appeal to this court. Aswan appeal against the judge's decision in
favour of Thurgar Bolle on the second question, namely the scope of the manufacturer's
duty of care in tort. Its case has been presented by Mr Aikens QC and presented, if I may
so so, with his usual skill. He accepts that if this were a case of what he called 'pure
economic loss' then Aswan could not recover damages from Thurgar Bolle. The decision
c in *Muirhead v Industrial Tank Specialities Ltd* [1985] 3 All ER 705, [1986] QB 507 precludes
that argument so far as this court is concerned, though counsel reserves the point in case
this matter should go to the House of Lords. But this is not, says counsel, a case of pure
economic loss. Aswan has suffered physical damage to its goods, namely the Lupguard
which it has lost by reason of the negligence of Thurgar Bolle in manufacturing the pails.
That brings the case within the ordinary principles established in *Donoghue v Stevenson*
d [1932] AC 562, [1932] All ER Rep 1.

In addition to representing Aswan, Mr Aikens is also instructed on behalf of the
liquidator of Lupdine to pursue Lupdine's appeal in the third party proceedings. It is, of
course, unusual for the same solicitors and counsel to be appearing for both plaintiff and
defendant. But no doubt the liquidator has been advised that the judge's decision in
favour of Aswan against Lupdine is unappealable. In those circumstances, Aswan and the
e liquidator of Lupdine have a common interest in securing the maximum recovery from
Thurgar Bolle. Counsel for Thurgar Bolle did not suggest any reason why Mr Aikens
should not appear for both parties (whom I will call 'the appellants'), and I see no objection
myself.

It is convenient to take Lupdine's appeal first. As already mentioned, Neill J found that
the pails were of merchantable quality. There was therefore no breach of the condition
f to be implied by virtue of s 14(2) of the 1979 Act. He also found, inferentially, that no
particular purpose was made known to Thurgar Bolle so as to attract the condition to be
implied by virtue of s 14(3) of the Act. Counsel for the appellants attacked both findings.

I take first the judge's finding that the pails were merchantable. As to the cause of
failure, experts were instructed on both sides. Shortly before the trial, the experts were
able to reach agreement on all important issues of primary fact. They incorporated their
g agreement into a joint memorandum which was put before the court. In particular they
agreed that the pails were bound to fail at 60°C (140°F) or above when stacked five or six
high with a load of 25 kg per pail, so that the lid of the lowest pail was bearing a weight
of 100 or 125 kg. However, the pails would not have failed if the temperature had been
52°C (122°F) or below. Nor would they have failed, even at 70°C if the rows had been
h separated horizontally with wooden battens (a method of stuffing containers which
became known as the 'eggbox' method), so that the weight of each row of pails was taken,
not by the row below, but directly by the floor of the container through vertical supports.
There was no agreement whether the pails would have survived 70°C and if so, for how
long, if stacked two, three or four rows high *without* horizontal separation and vertical
supports. But one of the experts gave evidence, on which counsel for the appellants
j relied, that a stack of three would have been in trouble, and even a stack of two if left
long enough. There was evidence that pails had been used for export to other parts of the
world without mishap.

On those primary facts, the judge stated his conclusion as follows:

'It was nevertheless necessary for the V20 pails to be merchantable as heavy duty
pails suitable for export. Having heard and read the expert evidence, however, I am
satisfied that these pails were merchantable within the meaning ascribed to that

term by s 14(6) of the 1979 Act. They were very strong pails and they were nearly
able to withstand the high temperature of the Gulf.'   *a*

That conclusion would have been unassailable on the law as it stood before the Supply
of Goods (Implied Terms) Act 1973. As I shall hope to show in a moment, the law had
developed to a point where the dividing line, and overlap such as it was, between s 14(1)
and s 14(2) of the Sale of Goods Act 1893, and the meaning to be attached to the words
'merchantable quality' in the latter subsection, then undefined, had become tolerably
clear. But counsel for the appellants submits that that state of affairs has been changed by   *b*
the definition of 'merchantable quality' introduced by the 1973 Act, and now contained
in s 14(6) of the 1979 Act, which provides:

'Goods of any kind are of merchantable quality within the meaning of subsection
(2) above if they are as fit for the purpose or purposes for which goods of that kind
are commonly bought as it is reasonable to expect having regard to any description   *c*
applied to them, the price (if relevant) and all the other relevant circumstances.'

It is not possible to appreciate the change which that definition is said to have brought
about without first looking at the law as it stood before the 1973 Act. But, if I may
anticipate counsel for the appellants' argument, he submits that the reference to 'the
purpose or purposes' (in the plural) as distinct from 'a purpose' (in the singular) has
brought about a fundamental shift in the relationship between the old s 14(1) and s 14(2),   *d*
by very largely extending the scope of s 14(2) at the expense of s 14(1). He concedes that,
unless he is right on his construction of s 14(6), then his argument on s 14(2) must fail.

The starting point of the development of the modern law as to merchantable quality
is often taken to be *Gardiner v Gray* (1815) 4 Camp 144 at 145, 171 ER 46 at 47, where
Lord Ellenborough CJ said: *e*

'He cannot without a warranty insist that it shall be of any particular quality or
fineness, but the intention of both parties must be taken to be, that it shall be
saleable in the market under the denomination mentioned in the contract between
them. The purchaser cannot be supposed to buy goods to lay them on a dunghill.'

Among the nineteenth century milestones were *Jones v Bright* (1829) 5 Bing 533, 130 ER
1167, *Jones v Just* (1868) LR 3 QB 197, *James Drummond & Sons v E H Van Ingen & Co*   *f*
(1887) 12 App Cas 284 and *Jones v Padgett* (1890) 24 QBD 650. In *Jones v Padgett*, decided
shortly before the Sale of Goods Act 1893 was passed, the facts were that the plaintiff was
a wool merchant who ordered a quantity of indigo blue cloth. He also had a tailor's
business. He intended to use the cloth for making servants' liveries. It was not strong
enough for that purpose. He sued for breach of an implied term that the cloth should be
merchantable. He failed, since the cloth was suitable for other purposes for which cloth   *g*
of that description was ordinarily used.

The twentieth century cases start with *Bristol Tramways etc Carriage Co Ltd v Fiat Motors
Ltd* [1910] 2 KB 831 at 841, [1908–10] All ER Rep 113 at 117–118, where Farwell LJ
said:

'The phrase in s. 14, sub-s. 2, is, in my opinion, used as meaning that the article is   *h*
of such quality and in such condition that a reasonable man acting reasonably would
after a full examination accept it under the circumstances of the case in performance
of his offer to buy that article whether he buys for his own use or to sell again.'

Next came two cases containing well-known dicta of Lord Wright. In *Canada Atlantic
Grain Export Co v Eilers* (1929) 35 Ll L Rep 206 at 213 he said: *j*

'... if goods are sold under a description which they fulfil, and if goods under
that description are reasonably capable in ordinary user of several purposes, they are
of merchantable quality within s. 14(2) of the Act if they are reasonably capable of
being used for any one or more of such purposes, even if unfit for use for that one
of those purposes which the particular buyer intended.'

In *Cammell Laird & Co Ltd v Manganese Bronze and Brass Co Ltd* [1934] AC 402 at 430,
a [1934] All ER Rep 1 at 14 he said:

'In earlier times, the rule of caveat emptor applied, save only where an action
could be sustained in deceit on the ground that the seller knew of the defect, or for
breach of express warranty (warrantizando venditit). But with the growing
complexity of trade, dealings increased in what are now called "unascertained or
b future goods," and more generally "goods sold by description." As early as 1815 in
Gardiner v. Gray (4 Camp 144 at 145, 171 ER 46 at 47) Lord Ellenborough stated
the rule. Goods had been sold as waste silk; a breach was held to have been
committed on the ground that the goods were unfit for the purpose of waste silk
and of such a quality that they could not be sold under the denomination. What
sub-s. 2 now means by "merchantable quality" is that the goods in the form in
c which they were tendered were of no use for any purpose for which such goods
would normally be used and hence were not saleable under that description.'

The dictum of Farwell LJ in the *Bristol Tramways* case, and the dicta of Lord Wright in
the two cases to which I have just referred, are sometimes thought to have illustrated
different approaches. But the diversity, if any, was resolved by the decision of the House
d of Lords in *Henry Kendall & Sons (a firm) v William Lillico & Sons Ltd* [1968] 2 All ER 444,
[1969] 2 AC 31, and in particular by the speech of Lord Reid. Before coming to that
speech, I should first mention the judgment of Dixon J in *Grant v Australian Knitting Mills
Ltd* (1933) 50 CLR 387 at 418, where he said:

'The condition that goods are of merchantable quality requires that they should
be in such an actual state that a buyer fully acquainted with the facts and, therefore,
e knowing what hidden defects exist and not being limited to their apparent condition
would buy them without abatement of the price obtainable for such goods if in
reasonably sound order and condition and without special terms.'

Dixon J's definition is clearly an adaptation and extension of Farwell LJ's dictum in the
Bristol Tramways case. It is important because of its reference to price as a necessary
f element in the concept of merchantable quality.

In *Henry Kendall & Sons v William Lillico & Sons Ltd* [1968] 2 All ER 444, [1969] 2 AC
31 the facts, so far as are relevant for present purposes, were as follows. The plaintiffs,
game farmers in Suffolk, bought a compound meal from the defendants, SAPPA, for
feeding to their pheasants and partridges. The compound meal contained a proportion
of Brazilian groundnut extractions. The defendants bought the groundnuts from the
g third parties, and the third parties from the fourth parties. Unknown to any of the parties
at the time of the sale, the groundnuts were contaminated by a substance known as
aflatoxin. The compound meal, when fed to the pheasants and partridges, was fatal. But
the groundnuts could be fed safely to cattle and other animals, provided the proportion
of groundnuts in the compound feed was kept below a certain level. The defendants
claimed against the third parties and the third parties against the fourth parties for
h breach, inter alia, of s 14(2) of the 1893 Act. Havers J held that the groundnuts were of
merchantable quality. He found that the goods 'were capable in their ordinary user of
being ultimately compounded into food for cattle (including a wide variety of animals
under that description) or into food for poultry (including a wide variety of birds under
that description)'. However, as a compound food for poultry, the goods had proved fatal
to very young birds such as day-old ducklings, turkey poults and pheasant chicks. Havers
j J concluded:

'Though the meal was unfit for use for one purpose, as a compound food for
poultry, I cannot find that the meal in the form in which it was tendered was of no
use for any purpose for which the meal would normally be used and hence was
unsaleable under that description.'

It is clear that Havers J was directing himself according to the dictum of Lord Wright in the *Cammell Laird* case. Lord Pearce, in a dissenting speech in the House of Lords on this point, held that the judge had misdirected himself. Lord Pearce preferred the approach of Farwell LJ and Dixon J with its emphasis on price. On that approach, and by reason of another factor to which I shall refer later, he would have held that the groundnuts were unmerchantable. But the majority took a different view. Lord Morris said ([1968] 2 All ER 444 at 468, [1969] 2 AC 31 at 97):

'Some goods which are bought by description may be capable of being used in many different ways. It can happen, therefore, that, if a buyer just orders goods generally by description, he may want them for only one or possibly for more than one of several uses. It would not be reasonable to require the seller to deliver goods which would do for all the possible purposes. If the buyer wants goods that are suitable for each one of several purposes, he must make that clear to the seller and make it clear that he is relying on the seller to let him have goods that would be suitable for each one of the purposes. If the buyer merely orders goods by description, all that he can expect is that he will get goods that correspond with the description and goods of such a quality that they could be used for one of the purposes for which such goods are normally used.'

Later, after referring to a passage in Atkin LJ's judgment in *Niblett Ltd v Confectioners Materials Co Ltd* [1921] 3 KB 387 at 404, [1921] All ER Rep 459 at 465, he said ([1968] 2 All ER 444 at 468, [1969] 2 AC 31 at 97):

'This passage brings out the point that in deciding whether goods are merchantable it has to be considered whether some buyer or buyers could reasonably be contemplated who would wish to buy goods which were in the actual condition of the goods tendered and who had knowledge of defects in them which might be hidden. The goods must of course comply with the description. If, therefore, goods of the contract description are tendered and if the tendered goods though having certain defects are reasonably capable of being put to a use for which a buyer knowing of the defects would be likely to buy them, then they are of merchantable quality.'

Lord Morris then expressly approved and applied the passage which I have already cited from Lord Wright's judgment in *Canada Atlantic Grain Export Co v Eilers* (1929) 35 Ll L Rep 206 at 213. Lord Guest, like Lord Pearce and Lord Wilberforce, preferred Dixon J's approach because of his inclusion of price as an essential element in the definition. He said ([1968] 2 All ER 444 at 477, [1969] 2 AC 31 at 108):

'The test under s. 14(2) must be whether the article is saleable in the ordinary market for such goods under that description. The test put forward by Lord Wright ([1934] AC 402 at 430, [1934] All ER Rep 1 at 14) may be one factor or one guide in the determination of merchantability, but it cannot be the determining factor since purpose is not the sole test of merchantability and the test omits all reference to price. If the test of unmerchantability is that the article is fit for no use, few goods would be unmerchantable because use can always be found for goods at a price.'

As Lord Pearce said ([1968] 2 All ER 444 at 486, [1969] 2 AC 31 at 118):

'In return for a substantial abatement of price a purchaser is ready to put up with serious defects, or use part of the price reduction in having the defects remedied. In several classes of goods there is a regular retail market for "seconds", that is, goods which are not good enough in the manufacturer's or retailer's view to fulfil an order and are therefore sold off at a cheaper price. It would be wrong to say that "seconds" are necessarily merchantable.'

But, unlike Lord Pearce, Lord Guest upheld the judge's conclusion that the goods were

merchantable, because there was no evidence that the price at which the ground nuts
a were sold after the defect had been discovered, namely the presence of aflatoxin, was
other than the ordinary price for the goods.

It is in Lord Reid's speech that the clearest guidance is to be found as to the state of the
law before the 1973 Act was passed. 'Merchantable,' he said, 'can only mean commercially
saleable.' He continued ([1968] 2 All ER 444 at 449–450, [1969] 2 AC 31 at 75):

b 'If the description is a familiar one, it may be that in practice only one quality of
goods answers that description—then that quality and only that quality is
merchantable quality. Or it may be that various qualities of goods are commonly
sold under that description—then it is not disputed that the lowest quality
commonly so sold is what is meant by merchantable quality; it is commercially
saleable under the description.'

c There was clear evidence in the case that Indian ground nut extractions, which were
known to be contaminated with aflatoxin, were nevertheless sold, presumably for use in
cattle food, without abatement of price. Lord Reid concluded ([1968] 2 All ER 444 at
453, [1969] 2 AC 31 at 79):

d 'I think that it must be inferred from the evidence that buyers who include
ground nut extractions in their cattle foods are prepared to pay a full price for goods
which may be contaminated; but buyers who only compound poultry foods would
obviously not be prepared to buy contaminated goods at any price. Nevertheless
contaminated ground nut extractions are merchantable under the general description
of ground nut extractions because, rather surprisingly, some buyers appear to be
ready to buy them under that description and to pay the ordinary market price for
e them.'

As for the authorities, Lord Reid was unwilling to accept either Lord Wright's
definition or Dixon J's definition as they stood. But he was able to bring about a synthesis
by a slight adaptation of both definitions. As for Lord Wright's definitions, Lord Reid
pointed out that, whereas in some cases, such as the *Cammell Laird* case itself, there is only
f one use to which the goods can be put, so that if the goods are of no use for that purpose
they are of no use for any other purpose, in other cases different qualities of the same
kind of goods are commonly sold under different descriptions. He said ([1968] 2 All ER
444 at 451, [1969] 2 AC 31 at 77):

g 'Suppose goods are sold under the description commonly used to denote a high
quality and the goods delivered are not of that high quality but are of a lower quality
which is commonly sold under a different description, then it could not possibly be
said that the goods in the form in which they were tendered were of no use for any
purpose for which those goods would normally be used. They would be readily
saleable under the appropriate description for the lower quality. But surely LORD
WRIGHT did not mean to say that therefore they were merchantable under the
h description which was appropriate for the higher quality. They plainly were not.
LORD WRIGHT said: "no use for any purpose for which *such goods* would normally be
used." Grammatically "such goods" refers back to "the goods in the form in which
they were tendered"; but what he must have meant by "such goods" were goods
which complied with the description in the contract under which they were sold.
Otherwise the last part of the sentence "and hence were not saleable under that
j description" involves a non sequitur. If I now set out what I am sure that he meant
to say, I think it would be accurate for a great many cases though it would be
dangerous to say that it must be universally accurate. The amended version would
be "What sub-s. (2) now means by 'merchantable quality' is that the goods in the
form in which they were tendered were of no use for any purpose for which goods
which complied with the description under which these goods were sold would

normally be used, and hence were not saleable under that description." This is an
objective test: "were of no use for any purpose ..." must mean "would not have   *a*
been used by a reasonable man for any purpose ..."' (Lord Reid's emphasis.)

As for Dixon J's definition, Lord Reid was unwilling to accept the reference to 'a buyer',
since 'a buyer' might be taken to mean 'any buyer', or 'all buyers'. Yet for *some* buyers the
defective goods might be useless, while not so for other buyers. So Lord Reid substituted
'some buyers' for 'a buyer' in Dixon J's definition. Applying that amended definition,   *b*
Lord Reid concluded that the groundnuts, though contaminated, were merchantable.

In *B S Brown & Son Ltd v Craiks Ltd* [1970] 1 All ER 823, [1970] 1 WLR 752, a Scottish
appeal decided the following year, the facts were that the pursuers bought cloth by
description at 36d per yard intending to resell it as dress material. It was unsuitable for
that purpose but was suitable for various industrial purposes. The price of the cloth was
high for the industrial use, but low for the dress use. The price which the pursuers   *c*
eventually obtained, or should have obtained, on resale of the cloth was 30d per yard.
The House of Lords held that the cloth was merchantable, since it could be used in
normal course for the industrial use, and was suitable for that purpose. The discrepancy
in the price, that is to say, the difference between 30d and 36d yard, was not such as to
show that the cloth was unmerchantable.

The only other case to which I need refer is *Ashington Piggeries Ltd v Christopher Hill Ltd*   *d*
[1971] 1 All ER 847, [1972] AC 441, though there is nothing of direct relevance to the
present point except in the dissenting speech of Lord Diplock. The facts of the case
(which I shall have to return to later when I come to the argument under s 14(3) of the
1979 Act) are that the plaintiffs sold a compound food containing Norwegian herring
meal to the defendants, who were mink breeders. The plaintiffs bought the herring meal
from Norsildmel, the Norwegian exporters. Unknown to any of the parties, the herring   *e*
meal was contaminated with a minute quantity of DMNA, a substance which was fatal
to mink. The plaintiffs claimed the price of the compound food sold to the defendants.
The defendants counterclaimed damages for loss of their mink relying, inter alia, on
s 14(2) of the 1893 Act. The plaintiffs joined Norsildmel as third parties to the
counterclaim. Milmo J found that the herring meal was merchantable. There was no
evidence, he said, to prove that any part of the shipment was unfit for other animals such   *f*
as pigs or poultry. Accordingly, there was no evidence to support a finding that the
herring meal was unmerchantable. There was no appeal to the House of Lords against
that finding.

The contest in the Court of Appeal and in the House of Lords centred around s 14(1),
on which the plaintiffs ultimately succeeded. As to the dividing line between s 14(1) and
s 14(2), there is a passage in Lord Diplock's speech, to which Neill J referred in his   *g*
judgment and which is worth quoting in full ([1971] 1 All ER 847 at 886, [1972] AC
441 at 506):

> 'To attract the condition to be implied by sub-s (1) the buyer must make known
> the purpose for which he requires the goods with sufficient particularity to enable a
> reasonable seller, engaged in the business of supplying goods of the kind ordered, to   *h*
> identify the characteristics which the goods need to possess to fit them for that
> purpose. If all that the buyer does make known to the seller is a range of purposes
> which do not all call for goods possessing identical characteristics and he does not
> identify the particular purpose or purposes within that range for which he in fact
> requires the goods, he does not give the seller sufficient information to enable him
> to make or to select goods possessing a characteristic which is needed to make them   *j*
> fit for any one of those purposes in particular, if the same characteristic either is not
> needed to make them fit, or makes them unfit, for other purposes within the range.
> A "range of purposes" case thus poses a stark question of legal policy as to whether
> the seller's responsibility ought to be to supply goods which are fit for at least one of
> the purposes within the range or to supply goods which are fit for all of those

purposes unless he expressly disclaims responsibility for their fitness for any one or more of them. The answer to this question of policy has, in my view, been pre-empted by s 14(2) of the Sale of Goods Act 1893. The commonest way in which a buyer makes known to the seller a range of purposes for which the goods are required is by the description by which he buys them and by nothing more. This is the case that is contemplated by sub-s (2). This, as it has been authoritatively construed by the courts, provides that the only condition to be implied as to the responsibility of the seller is that the goods should be reasonably fit for one of the purposes within the range.'

Although, as I have said, Lord Diplock would have found in favour of Norsildmel in the third party proceedings, and therefore dissented in the result, there is no reason to suppose that the last sentence which I have quoted does not represent an accurate distillation of the law as it stood when the 1973 Act was passed.

I will now attempt to summarise the position as it was in my own words. To bring s 14(2) into operation, a buyer had to show that the goods had been bought by description from a seller dealing in goods of that description. If so, then, subject to a proviso which is immaterial for present purposes, the goods were required to be of merchantable quality. In order to comply with that requirement, the goods did not have to be suitable for every purpose within a range of purposes for which goods were normally bought under that description. It was sufficient that they were suitable for one or more such purposes without abatement of price since, if they were, they were commercially saleable under that description.

Counsel for the appellants submits that the direction in which the law has developed over the last century and a half, and which I have attempted to describe, has been radically changed by s 14(6) of the 1979 Act. There is, of course, no reason why Parliament should not have intended to bring about such a change. But it prompts careful consideration. Since one of his arguments on s 14(2) depends on the language of s 14(3), it is convenient at this point to set out both subsections:

'(2) Where the seller sells goods in the course of a business, there is an implied condition that the goods supplied under the contract are of merchantable quality, except that there is no such condition—(a) as regards defects specifically drawn to the buyer's attention before the contract is made; or (b) if the buyer examines the goods before the contract is made, as regards defects which that examination ought to reveal.

(3) Where the seller sells goods in the course of a business and the buyer, expressly or by implication, makes known—(a) to the seller, or (b) where the purchase price or part of it is payable by instalments and the goods were previously sold by a credit-broker to the seller, to that credit-broker, any particular purpose for which the goods are being bought, there is an implied condition that the goods supplied under the contract are reasonably fit for that purpose, whether or not that is a purpose for which such goods are commonly supplied, except where the circumstances show that the buyer does not rely, or that it is unreasonable for him to rely, on the skill or judgment of the seller or credit-broker.'

Counsel for the appellants' argument is that the definition in s 14(6) refers to the purpose or purposes for which goods of any kind are commonly bought. Therefore the goods are not merchantable unless they are as fit as it is reasonable to expect for all the purposes for which those goods are commonly bought. It is no longer sufficient that they should be fit for one such purpose. Counsel for Thurgar Bolle, on the other hand, submits that the definition has changed little if anything. It enacts the common law definition proposed by Lord Reid in Henry Kendall & Sons v William Lillico & Sons Ltd [1968] 2 All ER 444, [1969] 2 AC 31.

The argument of counsel for the appellants is undoubtedly attractive at first sight. If

Parliament had intended to enact Lord Reid's formulation, it might have been expected that the definition would have referred to *one* of the purposes for which goods are *a* commonly bought. But there is an equally strong, and perhaps even stronger, argument the other way. If Parliament had intended to enact what counsel for the appellants submits is the meaning of s 14(6), then the definition would surely have referred specifically to all purposes, not just the purpose or purposes. The reason why Parliament did not adopt either of those courses is, I think, to be found in the speech of Lord Reid in *Henry Kendall & Sons v William Lillico & Sons Ltd*. In the passage which I have already *b* quoted, Lord Reid points out that goods of any one kind may be sold under more than one description, corresponding to different qualities.

To take the facts of the present case, heavy duty pails are no doubt of higher quality than ordinary pails, and for that reason no doubt command a higher price. Pails which are suitable for the lower quality purpose may not be suitable for the higher quality purpose. It would obviously be wrong that pails sold under a description appropriate to *c* the higher quality should be held to be merchantable because they are fit for a purpose for which pails are sold under the description appropriate to the lower quality. Since the definition presupposes that goods of any one kind may be sold under more than one description, it follows that the definition had, of necessity, to refer to more than one purpose. In my opinion, this is the true and sufficient explanation for the reference to 'purposes' in the plural. The reference to *the* purpose in the singular was required in order *d* to cover one-purpose goods, such as the pants in *Grant v Australian Knitting Mills Ltd*. It would be wrong to infer from the use of the phrase 'purpose or purposes' that Parliament intended any such far-reaching change in the law as that for which counsel for the appellants contends. On the contrary, I agree with counsel for Thurgar Bolle that the definition is as accurate a reproduction of Lord Reid's speech in *Henry Kendall & Sons v William Lillico & Sons Ltd* as it is possible to compress into a single sentence. *e*

We were told that there is no reported case in which it has fallen to a court to construe and apply the definition in s 14(6). But the definition was considered by Lord Denning MR in *Cehave NV v Bremer Handelsgesellschaft mbH, The Hansa Nord* [1975] 3 All ER 739 at 748, [1976] QB 44 at 62. That was a case which fell to be decided under the old law. But Lord Denning MR clearly regarded the statutory definition as encapsulating the *f* existing common law. He said:

'For myself, I think the definition in the latest Act is the best that has yet been devised . . . The Act itself only applies to contracts made after 18th May 1973. But the definition seems to me appropriate for the contracts made before it.'

The textbook writers are divided. Professor Goode, in *Commercial Law* (1982, rev 1985) *g* p 261, expresses the tentative view that the definition appears to change the law by requiring the goods to be fit for *all* their normal purposes, whereas previously it was considered sufficient if the goods were suitable for any one normal purpose, even though unfit for other purposes. Professor Atiyah, on the other hand, in *The Sale of Goods* (7th edn, 1985) p 133, can see little, if any, difference between the new law and the old. It seems to him improbable that the new statutory definition will have much effect on the *h* law. In *Benjamin's Sale of Goods* (2nd edn, 1981) para 801 Mr Francis Reynolds takes the same view as Professor Atiyah. He regards the statutory definition as largely declaratory. The suggestion to be found in the Ontario Law Reform Commission's Report on the Sale of Goods (1979) that the reference to 'purpose or purposes' means that goods are unmerchantable unless they are fit for all purposes which can reasonably be contemplated is rejected. It is described as being at the extreme end of the spectrum. The author *j* concludes that the new definition makes no substantial difference. For the reasons I have given, I prefer the views of Professor Atiyah and Mr Francis Reynolds to that, tentatively expressed, by Professor Goode.

We invited counsel for Thurgar Bolle to refer us to the Law Commission Report on Exemption Clauses in Contracts (Law Com no 24 (1969)), which preceded the enactment of the 1973 Act, and also to the Law Commission working paper on the Sale and Supply

a of Goods (no 85 (1983)). But counsel for the appellants objected. I can see no conceivable reason why we should not have been referred to the Law Commission papers, and good reasons why we should. I note that in *R v Shivpuri* [1986] 2 All ER 334 at 343, [1986] 2 WLR 988 at 1000 Lord Bridge, giving the leading speech in the House of Lords, regretted that the House had not taken due note of the Law Commission's report which preceded the enactment of the Criminal Attempts Act 1981 in reaching their decision in *Anderton*

b *v Ryan* [1985] 2 All ER 355, [1985] AC 560, now held to have been wrongly decided. In my judgment it is not only legitimate but highly desirable to refer to Law Commission reports on which legislation has been based. But since counsel for Thurgar Bolle concurred in counsel for the appellants' objection, I say no more about it.

Counsel for the appellants had a further argument in relation to s 14(2) based on the language of s 14(3). I will come back to his main argument on s 14(3) at a later stage. On

c s 14(2) he submits that the inclusion in s 14(3) of the phrase 'whether or not that is a purpose for which such goods are commonly supplied' shows that Parliament did indeed intend to bring about a fundamental shift of emphasis between s 14(2) and s 14(3). Hitherto, as Lord Reid pointed out in *Henry Kendall & Sons v William Lillico & Sons Ltd* [1968] 2 All ER 444 at 453, [1969] 2 AC 31 at 79, there has been a tendency to confine the scope of s 14(2) and extend the scope of s 14(3). The inclusion in s 14(3) of the words

d to which I have referred shows, says counsel for the appellants, that in future s 14(2) is intended to cover use for all normal purposes, thus very greatly extending the scope of that subsection, whereas s 14(3) is to be confined to use for special or abnormal purposes.

I cannot accept that argument for three reasons. In the first place it is not what the words say. Section 14(3) is clearly intended to cover normal as well as abnormal purposes. In those circumstances, if s 14(2) is also to cover use for all normal purposes, in the sense

e that goods are to be regarded as unmerchantable unless they are fit for all normal purposes, then the distinction between the two subsections would be largely obliterated. Secondly, it would mean that Parliament had enacted a consequence which Lord Morris, in a passage which I have already quoted from his speech in *Henry Kendall & Sons v William Lillico & Sons Ltd* [1968] 2 All ER 444 at 468, [1969] 2 AC 31 at 97, described as

f being unreasonable. Thirdly, it would mean that the law had gone even further in the direction of caveat venditor than it did in that case, past a point which Lord Diplock, in his dissenting speech in *Ashington Piggeries Ltd v Christopher Hill Ltd* [1971] 1 All ER 847 at 888, [1972] AC 441 at 509, regarded as already too far. Of course, all these things are possible, but I would require clearer words in s 14(3) and (6) to persuade me that that is what Parliament has done.

g So I would reject counsel for the appellants' argument on the construction of s 14(6). The definition has not revolutionised the law. As mentioned earlier, he conceded that if he were wrong on s 14(6) he could not successfully attack the judge's finding that these pails were merchantable. But it is as well to mention why, in my view, that concession was properly made. I can well understand an argument that goods should be regarded as unmerchantable if they contain a hidden defect which, while leaving the goods suitable

h for some purposes, renders them unsuitable for others. If the buyer does not know, and cannot find out, for what purposes the goods are unsuitable, they are no more than a trap. That was the argument which appealed to Lord Pearce in *Henry Kendall & Sons v William Lillico & Sons Ltd*, and was one of the two reasons why he dissented on the point. But the majority took the opposite view. One must assume that the hypothetical buyer knows not only that the goods on offer are defective but also what the nature of the

j particular defect is; so that in the present case one must assume that the hypothetical buyer knows that the pails are incapable of withstanding temperatures in excess of 60°C when stacked five or six high, or perhaps two or three high, without separation. Does that make them unmerchantable within the meaning of s 14(6)? Clearly not. I will assume, as was conceded by counsel for Thurgar Bolle, that the 'description applied' to the pails was that they were to be heavy duty pails for export shipment. There was no evidence that a hypothetical buyer who wanted the pails for export, say, to Europe, and who knew of the particular defect, would insist on an abatement in the price. I would be   *a* astonished if he had. The pails were perfectly suitable for that purpose, and therefore of merchantable quality within the definition. Indeed, they were suitable for export to the Middle East as well as Europe. For if the eggbox method of stuffing had been used, the pails would have survived despite the temperature.

The evidence was that the additional cost of adopting the eggbox method was £250 per container, amounting to less than 35p per pail. Even if the additional cost had been   *b* reflected in a diminution in the price (which I very much doubt) the difference would not in my judgment have been such as to render the pails unmerchantable: see *B S Brown & Son Ltd v Craiks Ltd* [1970] 1 All ER 823, [1970] 1 WLR 752.

Before leaving s 14(2), I should mention the so-called data sheet, which was the subject of much argument in the court below, and before us. The data sheet is a document produced by Thurgar Bolle. It gives the dimensions and capacity of the pail, namely 23   *c* litres 650 cc. It states the material and the chemical resistance. Then, at the bottom, against 'Stackability', appear the words '6 high'. Immediately below are the words 'Based on S.G. of 1·4 at 68–78°F'. It was argued in the court below that the reference to 'six high' constituted an express contractual warranty between Thurgar Bolle and Lupdine. But that argument was rejected by the judge and abandoned before us. Instead counsel for the appellants argued, as I understood him (though his main argument on the data sheet   *d* was advanced in relation to another part of the case), that 'six high' was part of the description of the goods and, since the pails were incapable of being stacked six high at temperatures above 60°C without horizontal separation and vertical supports, the pails were not as fit as it was reasonable to expect 'having regard to [the] description applied ... and all the other relevant circumstances' of the case, and were therefore unmerchantable.   *e*

There are a number of answers to that argument. But it is sufficient to refer to the answer given by Neill J. The reference to 'six high' cannot stand on its own. Stackability must obviously depend on the weight of the material contained in the pails above. Instead of giving a weight per pail, the data sheet gives a specific gravity within a temperature range. I see no reason not to take that information at its face value. The data   *f* sheet is informing the buyer that the manufacturer has tested the pails, and that they stack six high with contents having a specific gravity within the stated range. The data sheet is saying nothing about stackability with contents having a higher specific gravity, or at temperatures outside the range. If that is the right construction of the data sheet, as I believe it to be, then it is clear that it cannot help counsel for the appellants in his argument on s 14(2).

I come now to s 14(3). I can deal with the point much more shortly, since no question   *g* of law is involved. In the court below counsel for the appellants relied on an express term that the pails were to be suitable for export to Kuwait. But the judge rejected Lupdine's evidence on the point, and the argument was not pursued in this court. Instead, counsel relied on an implied term under s 14(3). It was said that Lupdine made known to Thurgar Bolle that the pails were wanted for export, that this was a stated purpose,   *h* distinct from, for example, use for domestic purposes, and that the purpose was sufficiently defined to be a 'particular purpose' within s 14(3). A particular purpose need not be a narrow purpose.

Counsel for the appellants relied on the two decisions in the House of Lords to which I have already referred, namely *Henry Kendall & Sons v William Lillico & Sons Ltd* [1968] 2 All ER 444, [1969] 2 AC 31 and *Ashington Piggeries Ltd v Christopher Hill Ltd* [1971] 1 All   *j* ER 847, [1972] AC 441. In the former case the purchase of groundnut extractions for compounding into food for cattle and poultry and in the latter case the purchase of herring meal for inclusion in animal feeding stuffs, though wide purposes, were nevertheless held to be particular purposes within the meaning of what is now s 14(3). In *Ashington Piggeries Ltd v Christopher Hill Ltd* the narrow purpose for which the herring

meal was required was compounding into mink food. That purpose was never made
a known to the sellers. But the sellers were held liable under what is now s 14(3), since
feeding to mink was found to be a normal use within the wider stated purpose of
compounding into food for cattle and poultry. In the same way, submitted counsel for
the appellants, exporting to the Middle East is a normal use within the wider stated
purpose of exporting generally. There is no finding that the conditions on the voyage, or
after arrival, were abnormal in any way. Since the pails were not suitable for exporting
b to the Middle East, Thurgar Bolle are in breach of s 14(3). So ran the argument. I see
the force of that argument, but it fails, for a reason which I have not so far mentioned.
Section 14(3), like the old s 14(1), depends on reliance. Unless the buyer relies on the
seller's skill or judgment in selecting the appropriate goods for the stated purpose, there
is no implied condition. In many cases reliance can be inferred. But in the present case
the circumstances show quite clearly that Lupdine never relied on Thurgar Bolle's skill
c or judgment in any relevant sense at all.

In September 1979 Mr Hamilton, of Lupdine, saw a description of the pail in a
catalogue. He made inquiries of Thurgar Bolle and was sent a sample. The following
June Lupdine wrote: 'We are currently involved in considerable export of our
waterproofing compound and feel that this V20 container will be more suitable and
robust than the ones we are currently using.' A week later they placed a trial order.
d Neill J concluded that this was not a case where any special characteristics had been made
known to the sellers in circumstances which showed that the buyers relied on their skill
and judgment. It would require a strong case for us to go behind that finding of fact. I
would, however, go further than the judge. In my judgment the circumstances showed
positively that the buyers did *not* rely on the sellers' skill or judgment in any relevant
sense. In those circumstances there can be no question of an implied condition under
e s 14(3).

Moreover, even if there had been an implied condition, I should have declined to hold
that Thurgar Bolle were in breach. In *Henry Kendall & Sons v William Lillico & Sons Ltd*
[1968] 2 All ER 444 at 482–483, [1969] 2 AC 31 at 114 Lord Pearce said:

'It was argued that such a purpose was too wide and had not enough particularity
f   to constitute a particular purpose. I do not accept this contention. Almost every
purpose is capable of some sub-division, some further and better particulars . . . A
purpose may be put in wide terms or it may be circumscribed or narrowed . . . The
less circumscribed the purpose, the less circumscribed will be, as a rule, the range of
goods which are reasonably fit for such purpose.'

To the same effect is an observation of Lord Wilberforce in *Ashington Piggeries Ltd v*
g *Christopher Hill Ltd* [1971] 1 All ER 847 at 878, [1972] AC 441 at 497 that width of
purpose is compensated, from the seller's point of view, by the dilution of his
responsibility. If making known that the pails were wanted for export is a particular
purpose within s 14(3), as counsel for the appellants contends, then the purpose could
hardly be wider. A very wide range of goods must be regarded as reasonably fit for that
h purpose. On the facts, these pails fell within that range. Indeed, so wide is the purpose
that it could be said that the pails needed to be little, if anything, more than merchantable.

For the reasons I have given, I would dismiss Lupdine's appeal in the third party
proceedings.

I now come to Aswan's appeal in the main action. It raises the second difficult point of
law to which I referred earlier, relating to the scope of a manufacturer's duty of care in
j tort. Aswan's case against Thurgar Bolle was pleaded in November 1983, shortly after the
decision in *Junior Books Ltd v Veitchi Co Ltd* [1982] 3 All ER 201, [1983] 1 AC 520 but
before the decision of this court and the House of Lords in *Leigh & Sillavan Ltd v Aliakmon*
Shipping Co Ltd, The Aliakmon [1985] 2 All ER 44, [1985] QB 350, CA; *affd* [1986] 2 All
ER 145, [1986] AC 785, HL, the decision of this court in *Muirhead v Industrial Tank*
Specialities Ltd [1985] 3 All ER 705, [1986] QB 507, and the decision of the Privy Council

in *Candlewood Navigation Corp Ltd v Mitsui OSK Lines Ltd, The Mineral Transporter, The Ibaraki Maru* [1985] 2 All ER 935, [1986] AC 1. Not surprisingly, perhaps, in view of *a* certain observations of Lord Roskill in *Junior Books*, the case against Thurgar Bolle in tort is pleaded almost as if it were a case in contract.

I will quote three paragraphs from the amended statement of claim:

'10. At all material times [Thurgar Bolle] well knew that the pails were to be used to hold the Lupguard which was to be carried from the UK to Kuwait. Further, *b* [Thurgar Bolle] knew that the pails would be stowed up to six tiers high in containers during the sea journey from the UK to Kuwait.

11. In the premises [Thurgar Bolle] owed a duty of care to [Aswan] to ensure that the pails to be supplied by them would be of merchantable quality and suitable for holding safely and securely material manufactured by [Lupdine] for the sea journey from UK to Kuwait ...

13. In breach of duty, [Thurgar Bolle] provided pails which were not of *c* merchantable quality and/or were not suitable to withstand the voyage to Kuwait. [Aswan] repeat the Particulars given under Head (1) of paragraph 6 above.'

The particulars referred to in para 13 are the same particulars that had been pleaded in support of Aswan's claim in contract against Lupdine. Thurgar Bolle asked for further particulars of the allegation that they, Thurgar Bolle, knew that the pails were intended *d* for shipment six high to Kuwait. In answer Aswan relied on conversations between representatives of Thurgar Bolle and Lupdine.

When the matter came before the judge in July 1984, the case was put on a broader basis. It was argued that the pails were not only defective in a contractual sense, in other words unmerchantable or unfit for the particular purpose made known to the manufacturer, but also dangerous in a tortious sense. The argument was summarised by *e* the judge as follows:

'I come finally to the claim by Aswan against Thurgar Bolle. [Counsel for Aswan] contended in the first place that Aswan could recover in accordance with the general principle in *Donoghue v Stevenson* [1932] AC 562, [1932] All ER Rep 1. The Lupguard, he said, had been damaged by the defective pails. He drew my attention to the *f* formulation of this general principle in *Junior Books Ltd v Veitchi Co Ltd* [1982] 3 All ER 201 at 216, [1983] 1 AC 520 at 549, where Lord Brandon in his dissenting speech said: "... a person who manufactures goods which he intends to be used or consumed by others is under a duty to exercise such reasonable care in their manufacture as to ensure that they can be used or consumed in the manner intended without causing physical damage to persons or their property." In the alternative, *g* said [counsel], Aswan could recover on the basis that the pails themselves had suffered damage and he relied on the speeches of the majority in *Junior Books*.'

The judge then turned to consider the nature and extent of the duty of care owed by Thurgar Bolle to Aswan. The judgment contains this illuminating passage:

'In answer to this question and in evaluating the degree of proximity between *h* Aswan and Thurgar Bolle I must take account of all the facts and circumstances. I must also look at the position from the standpoint of each of the two parties. The actual or implicit reliance of the consumer or user on the skill and experience of the manufacturer or the supplier is a relevant factor in most cases of this kind. The question, "Who is my neighbour?" may invite the preliminary response, "Consider first those who would regard you as their neighbour."' *j*

On the facts, the judge was not persuaded that the conversation referred to in the particulars of the points of claim had ever taken place. So there was no evidence that Thurgar Bolle knew that the pails were intended for export to the Middle East. Even if there had been such evidence, the judge would have rejected any duty of care. He stated

a his conclusion as follows:

'I am satisfied that a sufficient degree of proximity has not been shown. Aswan relied on Lupdine to provide proper packaging and proper stowage. They did not rely on Thurgar Bolle and had no contact with them. As far as I am aware they never saw any of the Thurgar Bolle advertising material nor was there any evidence that they placed any reliance on Thurgar Bolle. The pails were strong pails without

b any hidden defects. Moreover, even if I had come to the conclusion that Mr Hamilton had made known to Thurgar Bolle that the pails were required for the Middle East, I would still not have been satisfied that there was a sufficient degree of proximity between Thurgar Bolle and Aswan to establish the *relevant* duty of care.' [Neill J's emphasis.]

c   Before us, counsel for the appellants did not seek to argue that Aswan can recover on the basis that it had suffered economic loss, though, as already mentioned, he reserved that point for the House of Lords if necessary. He argued instead that what Aswan suffered was physical loss or damage to the Lupguard. If this should have been foreseen, as he submits it should, then Aswan can recover on the narrower principle stated in *Donoghue v Stevenson* [1932] AC 562, [1932] All ER Rep 1, namely the manufacturer's

d duty of care not to put into circulation products which are liable to cause foreseeable damage to person or property. So the case raises once again the difficult borderline between 'pure' economic loss, which counsel for the appellants concedes is not recoverable in this court, and loss resulting from physical damage to other property of the plaintiff.

Counsel for Thurgar Bolle dealt briefly with this aspect of the case. He argued in passing that it was not reasonably foreseeable that the pails would be stacked six high in

e temperatures of 70°C; but his main argument consisted largely of forensic apostrophe: if Thurgar Bolle are not liable to their immediate purchaser, Lupdine, on the ground that the pails were merchantable, how can they possibly be liable to the ultimate consumer? He might perhaps have argued that, on the case as pleaded, the appeal could not succeed if the contractual issues were to be decided in favour of Lupdine. But he forbore to take any pleading point. He put the point more generally. Remedies in contract and in tort

f must be harmonised. If, despite the alleged defect, the pails were merchantable in the contractual sense, it would be absurd to regard them as dangerous in the tortious sense.

The most recent case in the field of tortious liability for dangerous products is *Muirhead v Industrial Tank Specialities Ltd* [1985] 3 All ER 705, [1986] QB 507, the case on which, together with Lord Brandon's dissenting speech in *Junior Books Ltd v Veitchi Co Ltd* [1982]

g 3 All ER 201, [1983] 1 AC 520, counsel for the appellants relied most strongly. The facts were that the plaintiff, a wholesale fish merchant, engaged the first defendants to install a tank for the storage of lobsters. The second defendants manufactured and supplied pumps which circulated the seawater through the tank. The third defendants, who carried on business in France, supplied the electric motors for the pumps. The voltage of the motors was not the same as in England. As a result the motors cut out, and the

h lobsters died. The plaintiff recovered judgment against the first defendants, but the judgment was not satisfied because the first defendants, as here, had gone into liquidation. Against the second and third defendants the plaintiff claimed damages in tort under various heads, including (i) the cost of the pumps, (ii) the loss of profits on the operation as a whole and (iii) the death of the lobsters. The judge dismissed the claim against the second defendants, but he gave judgment against the third defendants for damages to be

j assessed under each of the various heads claimed. The judge approached the case as one in which the plaintiff was claiming to recover pure economic loss. Applying *Anns v Merton London Borough* [1977] 2 All ER 492, [1978] AC 728 and *Junior Books Ltd v Veitchi Co Ltd*, he held that the plaintiff was entitled to recover. But this court took a different view. The plaintiff was entitled to recover for the physical damage to the lobsters and for the financial loss suffered as a consequence of that physical damage. But he was not entitled to recover loss of profit on the operation as a whole, since such loss was pure economic loss, and the facts were not such as to bring the case within the very limited extension of the law effected by the *Junior Books* case. It is the latter aspect of the decision which has made it impossible for counsel for the appellants to found a case on pure economic loss in this court. But he relies strongly on the former aspect of the decision.

There are two straightforward factual distinctions between *Muirhead*'s case and the present case. The first is that the physical damage to the lobsters, which it was held that the manufacturer of the motors ought to have foreseen, was physical damage to *other* property of the plaintiff. The second is that in *Muirhead*'s case the judge found that the defendants knew that the motors were going to be incorporated in pumps for use on fish farms in the United Kingdom, whereas in the present case the judge has found that Thurgar Bolle did not know that the pails were going to be used for export to the Middle East, where they would be stacked six high at temperatures of 70°C. I shall deal with each of these points of distinction in turn. But in passing, it may be noted that if, in *Muirhead*'s case, third party proceedings had been brought by the manufacturer of the pumps against the manufacturer of the motors it might well have been held that the motors were merchantable, since they were perfectly suitable for use in France. So it does not necessarily follow in every case, as counsel for Thurgar Bolle submitted, that because a product is merchantable that it may not be dangerous.

The distinction between a defective product which renders the product itself less valuable and a defective product which creates a danger to *other* property of the plaintiff was the corner-stone of Lord Brandon's dissenting speech in the *Junior Books* case. It is a distinction which is well established both in English and American law. Where the defect renders the product less valuable, the plaintiff's remedy (if any) lies in contract. Where it creates a danger to other property of the plaintiff, the remedy (if any) lies in tort, although it may also lie in contract if the manufacturer is also the seller, as in *Grant v Australian Knitting Mills Ltd* [1936] AC 85, [1935] All ER Rep 209. The *Junior Books* case was the first case to cross the line, as it were, between tort and contract. That step was justified because the relationship between the parties was such that it could be regarded as equivalent to contract. In the great majority of cases the question whether the danger created is danger to *other* property of the plaintiff admits of an obvious answer.

The peculiarity of the present case is that the position is not so clear. If Aswan had bought empty pails from a third party and then used the pails for exporting the Lupguard, clearly there would have been damage to other property of the plaintiff. But in the present case the property in the pails and the property in the Lupguard passed to the plaintiff simultaneously. Indeed, it is rather artificial to think of the property in the pails passing at all. Aswan was buying Lupguard in pails. It was not buying Lupguard *and* pails. One can think of other cases by way of illustration without difficulty. If I buy a defective tyre for my car and it bursts, I can sue the manufacturer of the tyre for damage to the car as well as injury to my person. But what if the tyre was part of the original equipment? Presumably the car is *other* property of the plaintiff, even though the tyre was a component part of the car, and property in the tyre and property in the car passed simultaneously. Another example, perhaps even closer to the present case, would be if I buy a bottle of wine and find that the wine is undrinkable owing to a defect in the cork. Is the wine other property, so as to enable me to bring an action against the manufacturer of the cork in tort? Suppose the electric motors in *Muirhead*'s case had overheated and damaged the pumps. Would the plaintiff have recovered for physical damage to the pumps as well as the lobsters?

I do not find these questions easy. There is curiously little authority on the point in England, compared with America, where the law as to product liability is more highly developed. My provisional view is that in all these cases there is damage to other property of the plaintiff, so that the threshold of liability is crossed. Whether liability would be established in any particular case is, of course, another matter. So while I recognise the

existence of the first ground of distinction between *Muirhead's* case and the present case,
a and while I accept that the purchase of the pail was only incidental to the purchase of the
Lupguard, I am not prepared to decide this case in favour of Thurgar Bolle on that
ground.

I come now to the second ground of distinction. Here Thurgar Bolle's case rests on
firmer foundations. In *Muirhead's* case there was, as already mentioned, a finding of fact
that the third defendant, the manufacturer of the motors, knew that the motors were to
b be incorporated in pumps for use on fish farms in the United Kingdom. The whole
purpose of the pumps was to preserve the health of the lobsters. If the pumps failed,
through a defect in the motors, physical harm to the lobsters was liable to occur. Of
course the lobsters would not necessarily be killed. That would depend on how soon the
failure of the pumps was remedied. But physical damage of the relevant type was plainly
foreseeable. On that basis the Court of Appeal held that the third defendants were liable.
c One only has to state the chain of reasoning in *Muirhead's* case to see how far it is removed
from the facts of the present case. In one sense, of course, almost anything can be
foreseen. But that is not the test. The question is not whether the consequence was of a
type which was foreseeable, but whether it was of a type which was *reasonably* foreseeable.
The scope of the manufacturer's duty of care does not extend beyond that point.

In the present case the Lupguard suffered damage because the pails were stacked six
d high and left for many days in temperatures of 70°C. Was that damage of the type which
was reasonably foreseeable? In my opinion the answer is a categoric No. Counsel for the
appellants relied on the absence of any evidence that either the voyage to Kuwait or the
leaving of the containers on the quayside were abnormal in any way. Indeed, the judge
found by inference that the transit was normal. Counsel for the appellants also relied, in
this connection, on the data sheet. At the very least, he said, the data sheet should have
e contained a warning that the pails could not be stacked six high at temperatures in excess
of the stated range.

I accept that the voyage to Kuwait may not have been abnormal for a voyage to
Kuwait. But it by no means follows that the conditions to which the pails were subjected
were conditions which Thurgar Bolle should reasonably have foreseen. Nor was I
persuaded that the data sheet assists counsel for the appellants' argument on foreseeability.
f Thurgar Bolle were obliged, as manufacturers, to exercise reasonable care to ensure that
the pails were robust enough to withstand the ordinary stresses and strains of an export
transaction, without the lid coming off and without leaking. But the type of damage
which occurred and the conditions in which it occurred were altogether outside the
range of what was reasonably foreseeable, and therefore outside the scope of their duty
of care. To hold otherwise on the facts of the present case would be to impose on the
g manufacturers a liability not far short of that of an insurer.

There is another approach which leads to the same result. Lord Atkin's formulation in
Donoghue v Stevenson [1932] AC 562, [1932] All ER Rep 1 of the manufacturer's duty of
care excludes the case where there has been a reasonable opportunity of intermediate
examination. Those words have been the subject of much subsequent analysis, almost as
h if they formed part of a statute. Sometimes they are treated as if they impose on the
plaintiff an independent requirement which he must satisfy, a hoop through which he
must pass, before his action in tort can succeed. Counsel for the appellants argues that
the plaintiff here can pass through that hoop without difficulty, because no intermediate
examination would have revealed the defect in the pails, other than a test to destruction.
This cannot have been what Lord Atkin had in mind. I agree that it is unlikely that Lord
j Atkin had such a test in mind when he referred to intermediate examination. But that
does not dispose of the difficulty. The words 'no reasonable possibility of intermediate
examination' take colour from the preceding words 'which he sells in such a form as to
show that he intends them to reach the ultimate consumer in the form in which they
left him' (see [1932] AC 562 at 599, [1932] All ER Rep 1 at 20). They do not impose an
independent requirement which the plaintiff must satisfy. They are factors, usually very

important factors, which the court has to take into account in determining whether the
damage to person or property was reasonably foreseeable.   *a*

In the present case it was not contemplated (to use Lord Wright's expression in *Grant
v Australian Knitting Mills Ltd* [1936] AC 85 at 105, [1935] All ER Rep 209 at 218) that the
pails would be tested to destruction. But that some further testing was contemplated is
clear from the fact that the first order was a trial order. At the very least, Thurgar Bolle
were entitled to assume that there would be some further discussion between Thurgar
Bolle and Lupdine if the pails were going to be put to some special use. If a manufacturer   *b*
sells a defective tyre which is fitted as original equipment to a car, he owes a duty of care
to the ultimate consumer, because the consequence of the defect does not depend in any
way on the type of car to which the tyre is fitted. But, if a sound tyre intended for use on
a car is fitted not to a car but to a bus, the manufacturer owes no duty of care, not because
there was an opportunity of intermediate examination in any ordinary sense, but because
the use to which the tyre was put was not reasonably foreseeable. Indeed, in such a case   *c*
it is artificial to think of the tyre as being defective or dangerous at all. The danger arises
not from any defect in the tyre, but solely as a result of the use to which the tyre is put.
That is essentially the same as the position here.

So whether one approaches the present case as one in which Lupdine had an
opportunity of intermediate examination in a rather loose sense or whether (as I would
prefer) one asks the simple question: Whether the damage was reasonably foreseeable? I   *d*
would reach the same conclusion. Of course, even if the damage had been reasonably
foreseeable, that would not of itself have established that Thurgar Bolle were under a
duty of care. There would be a second question to be answered, as is shown by the
decision of the House of Lords in *Leigh & Sillavan Ltd v Aliakmon Shipping Ltd, The Aliakmon*
[1986] 2 All ER 145, [1986] AC 785, and in particular by the judgment of Oliver LJ in
the Court of Appeal in that case ([1985] 2 All ER 44, [1985] QB 350). But in the present   *e*
case that second question does not call for an answer.

For the reasons I have given, I would hold that the damage which Aswan suffered in
this case, namely physical loss of the Lupguard, was not damage of a type which was
reasonably foreseeable by Thurgar Bolle, and was therefore outside the scope of Thurgar
Bolle's duty of care as a manufacturer. In reaching that conclusion, I am assuming in   *f*
Aswan's favour that the damage was damage to other property, and not a defect in the
property itself. In those circumstances it is unnecessary to go on to consider whether
Thurgar Bolle were in breach of duty, and, if so, whether the breach caused the damage,
and whether the consequences were too remote. It is sufficient to say that the answer to
all those questions would, I suspect, have been favourable to Thurgar Bolle, and for much
the same reasons. It is also unnecessary to consider counsel for Thurgar Bolle's argument   *g*
that part of Aswan's loss was caused not by Thurgar Bolle's negligence but by the failure
of Lupdine to stop the last consignment before it was shipped on 19 September 1980.

That leaves only counsel for the appellants' specific criticism of the judgment below.
The emphasis which the judge placed on Aswan's reliance on Lupdine and on the absence
of any reliance on Thurgar Bolle shows, in counsel's submission, that the judge was
applying the wrong test. He was applying the test of very close proximity appropriate to   *h*
Junior Books liability, instead of the test appropriate to ordinary liability in tort. If he had
applied the latter test, he would, so it is said, have reached a different result.

I do not accept that criticism. It is true that the concept of reliance appears as an
important element of liability in the *Junior Books* case. But that does not mean that it is
inappropriate in other contexts. In one of the passages which I have already quoted,
Neill J said: 'The actual or implicit reliance of the consumer or user on the skill and   *j*
experience of the manufacturer or the supplier is a relevant fact in most cases of this
kind.' As a general statement, that is unexceptionable. Robert Goff LJ was referring to
that use of the word when, in the course of his judgment in *Muirhead's* case [1985] 3 All
ER 705 at 714, [1986] QB 507 at 527, he said:

a

'There is also a sense in which a purchaser of goods relies on the manufacturer to have manufactured goods which are not defective, and so decides to order goods, made by the particular manufacturer, from his immediate supplier.'

In finding that Aswan relied on Lupdine but not on Thurgar Bolle, the judge may perhaps have been using the word with two slightly different shades of meaning. But I am wholly unwilling to infer that he applied the wrong test.

b

I said at the outset that the main appeal raises a difficult question of law. Counsel for the appellants described it as an important question. On reflection, I am not persuaded that the case involves any more than a relatively simple question of fact. The judge found that there was an insufficient degree of proximity between Thurgar Bolle and Aswan to establish the relevant duty of care. Another way of saying the same thing in a case such as the present, that is to say a case of physical damage to person or property, is that the type of damage was not reasonably foreseeable.

c

In my judgment Neill J applied the right test and reached the right conclusion in the main action as well as the third party proceedings. I would dismiss both appeals.

NICHOLLS LJ. The arguments presented to the court were wide ranging, but as I see it, these appeals fall to be decided on comparatively narrow points.

d

Implied conditions

Lupdine's appeal turns on whether Thurgar Bolle were in breach of the implied conditions set out in s 14(2) and s 14(3) of the Sale of Goods Act 1979. Considering s 14(2) first, it is not in dispute that the implied condition as to merchantable quality applied to the contracts under which the plastic pails were sold by Thurgar Bolle to Lupdine. Thus,

e

on the wording of s 14(6), three questions arise. (i) What 'kind' of goods were these, within the meaning of s 14(6)? (ii) What was the purpose, or what were the purposes, for which goods of that kind were commonly bought? (iii) Were the goods as fit for that purpose (or those purposes) as it was reasonable to expect having regard to any description applied to them, the price (if relevant) and all the other relevant circumstances? Each of these questions is one of fact.

f

As to question (i), the starting point is that the goods were plastic pails. But from there it is necessary to go on to consider whether these pails were of any particular type, so that some additional description is to be included in the statement of what kind of goods these comprised. In Thurgar Bolle's advertising literature, the V20 pail was described as a 'shipping container' and a 'heavy duty container'. The test applied by the judge was whether the pails were merchantable as 'heavy duty pails suitable for export'. I did not

g

understand counsel for Thurgar Bolle to demur at the goods being so classified, and I draw no distinction between these different expressions. Furthermore, the data sheet issued by Thurgar Bolle's concerning the V20 pail stated, as one of the attributes of the pails: 'Stackability—V20 6 high'. For my part I would be inclined to decide that this attribute also is to be imported into the classification of the 'kind' of goods in question in

h

this case. I do not see why, if it is appropriate (based on the description in Thurgar Bolle's literature) to describe the pails as heavy duty shipping containers, it is not equally appropriate in this case to import from the same literature the further description concerning use for stacking purposes. Thus the goods comprised heavy duty, plastic pails, suitable for export and stacking up to six high. On this footing, it follows that the answer to question (ii) must be taken to be that one of the purposes for which this kind

j

of goods was commonly bought was for use in the export trade as heavy duty plastic pails, stacked up to six high.

Turning to question (iii): were the pails supplied by Thurgar Bolle as fit for that purpose as it was reasonable to expect having regard to all the relevant circumstances? Two particular points arise here. The first is this: although a reasonable purchaser would expect that these plastic pails, when filled, would be able to cope with the stress of being stacked six high, I think that, despite the reference to 'export', he would not expect them a to be able to do so in all climatic conditions and in all temperatures, however extreme, either of heat or of cold. The latter expectation would be unreasonable. This, I add, is a conclusion I reach against the background that there was no specific evidence on this point at the trial.

I should here refer to the phrase 'Based on S.G. of 1·4 at 68–78°F' appearing at the foot of the data sheet immediately below the statement regarding stackability. Clearly that b statement does not help Lupdine. On the one hand, I am unable to accept that this phrase indicates, by reference to a temperature range, the limits of the manufacturer's claim that filled pails can be stacked six high; that would be an unnatural construction of the language, and would also yield an absurd result, because the stated, narrow temperature range does not even embrace normal temperatures found for all or part of most days and nights in this country. But, on the other hand, rejecting that construction which would c assist Thurgar Bolle, and reading this phrase (as I think it has to be read) as indicating only that the statement of the stackability performance of the V20 pail is based on the contents of the stacked pails not having a specific gravity exceeding 1·4 in the stated temperature range, does not mean that this statement assists Lupdine. To my mind this statement of specific gravity, measured by reference to a narrow range of moderate temperatures, would not serve to cause or encourage a reasonable purchaser of these d plastic pails to believe that the stated stackability performance would apply to every extreme of temperature, however high or low, and however far removed from the 68–70°F range.

The second point on question (iii) concerns the strength of the pails. The evidence of the expert witness called by Aswan was that he had not come across a better pail purely as a pail. The failure of the pails was caused by 'creep' produced by a combination of e weight, time and temperature. The experts agreed that the pails were bound to fail when filled and stacked five or six high directly on one another at temperatures in the region of 60°C. What happened was that the pails were stacked five high (or, in some places, six high) with each pail containing 25 kg of Lupguard, and they were packed in shipping containers. The immediate cause of the failure, as found by the judge, was that on arrival in Kuwait the shipping containers were left on the dockside or in a customs area for f periods of several days. In consequence, the inside temperature of the containers reached between 60°C (140°F) and 70°C (158°F). Even in the context of a heavy duty shipping pail, these are very high temperatures indeed. The expert evidence also established that the failure would probably not have occurred if the temperatures had not exceeded 50°C (122°F). This latter temperature is itself a very high one. Thus, although the pails were not suitable for use in all parts of the world when stacked five or six high, they were g suitable for use so stacked in many parts of the world. They could cope with the combined stress of weight, time and temperatures up to 122°F. As the judge concluded, the pails were very strong and they were nearly able to withstand the high temperature of the Gulf.

With the pails having this quality and achieving this level of performance, I think that h the answer to question (iii) must be Yes. I agree with the judge that the pails were of merchantable quality: they were as fit for export purposes, even when stacked five or six high, as it was reasonable to expect.

I turn to the 'fitness for purpose' condition. The judge expressed his conclusion on this point as follows:

'Furthermore, in the light of my finding that Mr Hamilton did not disclose the j destination of the pails to Mr Riley or to anyone else in the course of a telephone conversation in June 1980, this is not a case where any special characteristics which were required for the pails were made known to the sellers in circumstances which showed that the buyers relied on their skill and judgment.'

I read this conclusion of fact as one based on the judge's finding that Mr Hamilton did not disclose the intended destination of the pails over the telephone in June 1980. But Mr Hamilton had read Thurgar Bolle's advertising literature, and knew about the stackability claim of Thurgar Bolle made in the literature. His evidence was that this was why he went to Thurgar Bolle in the first place. On 17 June 1980 Lupdine sent a letter to Thurgar Bolle which, after mentioning trade and bank references, concluded in these terms:

'. . . we trust that when we again contact you to place a firm order at the end of this week for your V20 containers a credit account in our name will have been opened. We are currently involved in considerable export of our waterproofing compound and feel that this V20 container will be more suitable and robust than the ones we are currently using. Our current usage of up to 2,000 pails per month is expected to rise to over 3,000 before too long and it is this size of credit facility we are looking for.'

A week later Lupdine placed with Thurgar Bolle a trial order for a quantity of the V20 pails, and thereafter further orders followed. On these facts I would be prepared to decide that Lupdine did make known to Thurgar Bolle a particular purpose for which the V20 pails were required, 'particular purpose' in this section meaning little more than 'stated' or 'defined': see Lord Wilberforce in *Ashington Piggeries Ltd v Christopher Hill Ltd* [1971] 1 All ER 847 at 877, [1972] AC 441 at 496.

Furthermore, I doubt whether the circumstances do show that, in deciding to buy the V20 pail for the use stated in the letter of 17 June 1980, Lupdine did not rely on Thurgar Bolle's skill. Lord Reid pointed out in *Henry Kendall & Sons (a firm) v William Lillico & Sons Ltd* [1968] 2 AC 444 at 456, [1969] 2 AC 31 at 82 that, in the case of goods being bought from the manufacturer, it can only be in unusual circumstances that a buyer does not rely in part, at least, on the skill or judgment of the manufacturer. Lupdine no doubt formed a view on the suitability of the V20 pails, having seen and examined those supplied initially, but I doubt if that establishes that Lupdine placed no reliance at all on the published claims made for the product by the manufacturer, Thurgar Bolle, or that any such reliance would have been unreasonable.

In my view, however, nothing turns on this because, even if Lupdine were to suceed on this point, their claim based on s 14(3) must still fail. The particular purpose made known was not materially different from, or more precise than, the export purpose stated and considered above in the context of merchantable quality. This being so, in my view, on the facts of this case, if the merchantable quality claim fails, so also does the fitness for purpose claim: the pails were reasonably fit for use in the export trade, even though they were not able to withstand the high temperature of the Gulf when stacked five or six high for several days. Given that the particular purpose made known was not materially different from, or more precise than, the relevant purpose for which the goods were commonly bought, I see nothing surprising in the conclusion that in this case the fitness for purpose condition adds nothing to the merchantable quality condition.

Negligence

Aswan's claim in tort against Thurgar Bolle is that the loss suffered by Aswan when the pails failed is recoverable under the principle enunciated in *Donoghue v Stevenson* [1932] AC 562 at 599, [1932] All ER Rep 1 at 20 in the celebrated statement by Lord Atkin:

'. . . a manufacturer of products, which he sells in such a form as to show that he intends them to reach the ultimate consumer in the form in which they left him with no reasonable possibility of intermediate examination, and with the knowledge that the absence of reasonable care in the preparation or putting up of the products

will result in an injury to the consumer's life or property, owes a duty to the
consumer to take that reasonable care.'   *a*

In my view, the short and narrow answer to this claim lies in the factual conclusion
already referred to above concerning the merchantability of the pails. The pails were as
fit for the purposes for which goods of the appropriate kind are commonly bought as it
was reasonable to expect, having regard to all the relevant circumstances. The relevant
circumstances here included no special or unusual circumstance. Nor were Thurgar Bolle   *b*
aware that their customer intended to stack the pails five and six high for some days at
temperatures over 50°C. That being so, on the facts of this case, it seems to me that this
claim, that the manufacturer was in breach of a duty to take 'reasonable' care, is hopeless.

Aswan sought to rely on the summary of the duty of care propounded by *Donoghue v
Stevenson* contained in the speech of Lord Brandon in *Junior Books Ltd v Veitchi Co Ltd*
[1982] 3 All ER 201 at 216, [1983] 1 AC 520 at 529:   *c*

'. . . a person who manufactures goods which he intends to be used or consumed
by others is under a duty to exercise such reasonable care in their manufacture as to
ensure that they can be used or consumed in the manner intended without causing
physical damage to persons or their property.'

In particular it was submitted that the use of the pails 'intended' by Thurgar Bolle was   *d*
for export, worldwide, in shipping containers, stacked five or six high, without horizontal
or vertical supporting boards, carrying loads of up to 25 kg per pail. The use actually
made was within that intended use. I cannot accept this.

Counsel for the appellants accepted (in my view rightly) that in this context intention
is to be judged objectively, and that the test in this case is what a reasonable purchaser
would understand to be the intended use of the pails. This seems to me to yield the result   *e*
that in this case, in considering the extent of the duty of care, the test applicable regarding
intended use is not materially different from that prescribed by s 14(6), namely the
purposes for which heavy duty pails suitable for export and for being stacked up to six
high are commonly bought. I can see no ground for concluding that a reasonable
purchaser would understand that such pails were intended to be used for purposes other
than those for which they are commonly bought. If, as here, the pails were reasonably fit   *f*
for those purposes, that seems to me sufficient to show also that there was no breach of
duty by Thurgar Bolle in manufacturing and selling the V20 pails as they did.

Accordingly, what the position would be if these pails had not been of merchantable
quality because of carelessness in the manufacturing process does not fall to be decided.
But, in deference to the arguments addressed to us, I will add that at present I am not
persuaded that, even in that event, Aswan would have been entitled to recover from   *g*
Thurgar Bolle the value of the wasted Lupguard.

The corner-stone of Aswan's claim was that the Lupguard solution and the pails were
different items of property, so that the failure of the pails caused physical damage to
Aswan's property in that the failure of the pails resulted in the Lupguard being spilled
and wasted. In strict legal analysis, this must be correct, although in this case the
Lupguard, whilst in the ownership of Aswan up to the time when the pails failed, was   *h*
always in very close physical proximity to the pails. When Aswan acquired ownership,
the Lupguard being bought was already in the pails, and the pails were already stacked
five or six high in the shipping containers on board ship.

But quite apart from this, I have found the submission surprising and unattractive,
having regard to the nature of the goods, the nature of the defect and the nature of the   *j*
damage sustained. The goods consisted of strong, but simple, plastic pails with lids, the
defect was that they were not sufficiently robust, and the damage sustained consisted of
the loss of the value of the contents of the pails when the lids and sides gave way. If
Aswan's argument is correct, it seems to follow that with the simplest containers, such as
bags and cartons and buckets, the duty of care owed by a manufacturer under the

principle of *Donoghue v Stevenson* would give rise to liability if, through carelessness in manufacture, those containers (not otherwise harmful) failed when used as intended, and the contents (whatever they might be) were lost. To my mind that, as a general proposition, would be to press the extent of the duty of care under *Donoghue v Stevenson* unacceptably far. If a customer buys a light and fragile piece of jewellery in a jeweller's shop, and the assistant hands the jewellery to the customer inside an elegant carrier bag, is the carrier bag manufacturer liable to the customer if, through carelessness in manufacture, the bag tears open outside the shop and the expensive piece of jewellery falls out and is broken? A similar question can be asked with regard to plastic bags provided in a supermarket and filled with household shopping. Again, I question whether the purchase of a household galvanized iron bucket which leaks when used is to be expected to have a remedy against the manufacturer in respect of the loss of the contents. Although normally the value of the lost contents in this type of case will be small, that will not always be so.

I have referred to these simple instances because they illustrate the length to which the duty of care of a manufacturer contended for by Aswan would extend. They illustrate this, because I can see no material difference between the ultimate user of a household carrier bag or bucket and the ultimate user of an industrial plastic pail. In each case it seems to me that there is much to be said for the view that, in the absence of facts giving rise to a very close proximity between manufacturer and user, as in the *Junior Books* case, the manufacturer's duty of care does not give rise to liability in respect of lost contents. In such a case the customer can normally proceed for breach of contract against his supplier, as Aswan has done in this case against Lupdine. That the supplier may not have adequate financial resources to meet the claim in full is the usual risk inherent in contractual dealings between parties. As between manufacturer and ultimate consumer, it may be that in this type of case, and leaving aside any limited guarantee given by the manufacturer, it is for the ultimate consumer to satisfy himself that the container is strong enough to hold what he wishes to place therein when used in the way he has in mind. But, since the matter does not need to be decided on the facts of this case, I will not pursue this or other possibilities.

For these reasons I, too, agree that the appeals should be dismissed.

FOX LJ. I have had the advantage of reading in draft the judgment of Lloyd LJ. I agree with it, and would dismiss these appeals.

Appeals dismissed. Leave to appeal to the House of Lords refused.

Solicitors: *Ince & Co* (for the appellants); *Kennedys* (for Thurgar Bolle).

Diana Procter   Barrister.

Practice Direction

a

QUEEN'S BENCH DIVISION

Practice – Service out of the jurisdiction – Defendant resident in EEC, Scotland or Northern Ireland – Leave to serve abroad not required – Indorsement of writ – Writs not indorsed not to be served out of jurisdiction without leave – Countries to which practice applies – Default *b* *judgments – Civil Jurisdiction and Judgments Act 1982 – RSC Ord 6, r 7, Ord 11, r 1(1)(2)(a), Ord 13, r 7B.*

1. The Civil Jurisdiction and Judgments Act 1982 comes into force on 1 January 1987.

2. One of the purposes of the 1982 Act is to waive the need to obtain leave to serve abroad where the defendants are resident in the EEC, Scotland or Northern Ireland.   *c*

3. If the plaintiff wishes to avail of this facility the writ must be indorsed, before issue, with a statement that the High Court of England and Wales has the power under the Civil Jurisdiction and Judgments Act 1982 to hear and determine this claim and that no proceedings are pending between the parties in Scotland, Northern Ireland or another convention territory of any contracting state as defined by s 1(3) of the said Act (RSC Ord 6, r 7, Ord 11, r 1(2)(a)).   *d*

4. If the writ is not so indorsed then the writ must be marked 'Not for service out of the jurisdiction' unless an order giving leave to issue is produced. Leave cannot be given under Ord 11, r 1(1) if the writ could be served without leave under Ord 11, r 1(2).

5. The countries to which the Act currently applies are as follows:

> Belgium   *e*
> Denmark
> France
> Federal Republic of Germany (West Germany)
> Italy
> Luxembourg
> Netherlands   *f*
> United Kingdom.

6. Where the writ is to be served abroad the number of days for acknowledging service under the extra-jurisdiction table (see *The Supreme Court Practice 1985* vol 2, para 902) should be stated on the writ.

Default judgments   *g*

7. Where the writ has been served out of the jurisdiction under the provisions of Ord 11, r 1(2) above, a judgment in default of notice of intention to defend can only be entered by leave of the court (Ord 13, r 7B). The leave may be given ex parte, on affidavit. The leave must be drawn up and attached to the judgment.

J R BICKFORD SMITH
Senior Master.

17 December 1986

a

R v Secretary of State for Transport, ex parte Gwent County Council

COURT OF APPEAL, CIVIL DIVISION

MAY, WOOLF LJJ AND SIR ROUALEYN CUMMING-BRUCE

6, 7, 31 OCTOBER 1986

b

Natural justice – Public inquiry – Duty to hear parties – Effect of government policy – Secretary of State wishing to increase tolls levied on users of bridge – Public inquiry held to consider objections to proposed increase – Inspector deciding certain objections falling within matters of government policy – Inspector not considering or evaluating objections – Whether inspector entitled to ignore objections because of policy – Whether public inquiry and order increasing tolls invalid – Severn
c *Bridge Tolls Act 1965, ss 1(1), 3(3), 4, Sch 2 – Severn Bridge Tolls Order 1985.*

In 1966 the Severn Bridge was opened as a toll bridge. By s 1(1)[a] of the Severn Bridge Tolls Act 1965 the Secretary of State for Transport was empowered to levy tolls on users of the bridge subject, under s 3(3)[b], to holding a local inquiry to consider objections to a
d proposed toll and, under s 4[c], to the revenue produced by the tolls not exceeding the amount required to meet the expenses set out in Sch 2[d] to the Act, being capital expenses in providing the bridge and additions and improvements thereto, and maintenance, repair and running costs. In 1981 the Secretary of State proposed to make an order increasing the tolls by 150%. Six local authorities, including the applicant authority, objected to the proposed order and a local inquiry was held to consider the objections. At
e the inquiry the local authorities called evidence to the effect that it would be inequitable for users of the Severn Bridge to have to bear the full cost of the bridge and associated roads and bridges. The Department of Transport stated in its submission to the inquiry that it was government policy that the cost of crossings of estuaries should be met by users rather than the general public and that tolls levied on the users of the Severn Bridge should therefore be sufficient to cover the total cost of the bridge and certain other
f associated roads and bridges. In his report recommending that the proposed order be implemented the inspector summarised the local authorities' objections, but did not evaluate them or give his own conclusions on them because he regarded them as falling within matters of government policy on which he was not permitted to express an opinion. The Secretary of State, by the Severn Bridge Tolls Order 1985, increased the tolls as originally proposed. The applicant authority sought judicial review of the order
g by way of a declaration that the Secretary of State had acted ultra vires because the

---

a Section 1(1), so far as material, provides: 'The Minister of Transport . . . shall have power, subject to and in accordance with the . . . provisions of this Act, to levy tolls in respect of vehicles using the specified carriageways.'

b Section 3(3), so far as material, provides: 'If, within six weeks from the latest date of publication of the notice [of the proposed toll], any objection to the proposed order is received by the Minister
h and the objection is not withdrawn, then—(a) if the objection is . . . from any . . . local authority in England or Wales . . . the Minister shall cause a local inquiry to be held . . .'

c Section 4, so far as material, is set out at p 164 *b c*, post

d Schedule 2, so far as material, provides:

'1. Reimbursement with interest of all expenses properly chargeable to capital account which have . . . been, or may . . . be, incurred . . . in providing the relevant works.

2. Reimbursement with interest of all expenses properly chargeable to capital account which
j may . . . be incurred . . . in providing additions to, or improvements of, the relevant works.

3. Defraying all expenses . . . which are properly chargeable to revenue account and are incurred during the toll period . . . in, or in connection with, the maintenance, repair or renewal of the relevant works, or of any such addition or improvement as is mentioned in paragraph 2 of this Schedule, or the operation during the toll period of services of facilities provided by the Minister in connection with the relevant works or any such addition or improvement . . .'

inspector's refusal to make any findings on matters which were covered by government *a*
policy had invalidated the inquiry, with the result that the Secretary of State had not
considered the local authorities' objections, as he was required to do by the 1965 Act,
before making the order. The judge held that there had been a procedural impropriety
which had not been cured and declared the order invalid. The Secretary of State appealed,
contending that the inspector was not obliged to evaluate the objections of the local
authorities and that in any event there had not been any unfairness caused to the
objectors. *b*

Held – The court would not intervene to grant relief by way of judicial review of a
decision of the Secretary of State merely because there had been some procedural
impropriety in the conduct of a public inquiry unless an objector could show that the
impropriety had resulted in a breach of the law, eg by showing that he had been
prejudiced by a failure to conduct the proceedings fairly. The crucial issue was therefore *c*
not whether there had been any procedural impropriety and whether it had been cured
but whether the objectors had been treated fairly, and in determining that issue the court
would look at the whole procedure leading to the making of the order, namely the
conduct of the inquiry and the subsequent decision of the Secretary of State. On the facts,
there had been no procedural impropriety because the inspector had a discretion whether
to express his conclusions on matters raised by the objectors and on the question whether *d*
there should be a departure from government policy in the case of the Severn Bridge the
inspector's opinion would be of no more value than that of any other member of the
public. Furthermore, looking at the whole procedure for making the order, since the
Secretary of State had fully considered and evaluated on the merits those points on which
the inspector had declined to comment the objectors had not been treated unfairly. The
appeal would accordingly be allowed (see p 165 h to p 166 a d to f, p 172 f to g and p 173 *e*
e to p 174 a f g, post).
Bushell v Secretary of State for the Environment [1980] 2 All ER 608 considered.
Decision of Webster J [1986] 2 All ER 18 reversed.

Notes
For public inquiries, procedural requirements and the fettering of discretion, see 1 *f*
Halsbury's Laws (4th edn) paras 15, 25, 33.
For the rules of natural justice, see ibid paras 64–69, 74–77.

Cases referred to in judgment
Bushell v Secretary of State for the Environment [1980] 2 All ER 608, [1981] AC 75, [1980] 3
WLR 22, HL. *g*
Council of Civil Service Unions v Minister for the Civil Service [1984] 3 All ER 935, [1985] AC
374, [1984] 3 WLR 1174, HL.
Johnson (B) & Co (Builders) Ltd v Minister of Health [1947] 2 All ER 395, CA.

Cases also cited
Associated Provincial Picture Houses Ltd v Wednesbury Corp [1947] 2 All ER 680, [1948] 1 *h*
KB 223, CA.
British Oxygen Co Ltd v Minister of Technology [1970] 3 All ER 165, [1971] AC 610, HL.
Deasey v Minister of Housing and Local Government (1970) 214 EG 415.
East Hampshire DC v Secretary of State for Environment [1978] JPL 182, DC; affd [1979] JPL
533, CA.
Padfield v Minister of Agriculture Fisheries and Food [1968] 1 All ER 694, [1968] AC 997, *j*
HL.
R v Monopolies and Mergers Commission, ex p Matthew Brown plc (17 July 1986, unreported),
DC.
R v Secretary of State for Environment, ex p Brent London BC [1983] 3 All ER 321, [1982] QB
593, DC.

Appeal

a The Secretary of State for Transport appealed against the decision of Webster J ([1986] 2 All ER 18, [1986] 1 WLR 1055) hearing the Crown Office list on 12 December 1985 whereby on the application of Gwent County Council, acting on its own behalf and on behalf of the South Glamorgan, Mid-Glamorgan, West Glamorgan, Dyfed and Avon County Councils, and supported by certain other bodies, the judge granted a declaration that in making the Severn Bridge Tolls Order 1985, SI 1985/726, the Secretary of State

b acted ultra vires his powers under the Severn Bridge Tolls Act 1965 and that that order was null and void. The facts are set out in the judgment of Woolf LJ.

John Laws for the Secretary of State.
Malcolm Pill QC and *Keith Bush* for the applicant.

c   *Cur adv vult*

31 October. The following judgments were delivered.

WOOLF LJ (giving the first judgment at the invitation of May LJ). This appeal by the Secretary of State for Transport arises out of a decision of Webster J ([1986] 2 All ER 18,

d [1986] 1 WLR 1055) given on 12 December 1985 on an application for judicial review by the Gwent County Council acting on its own behalf and on behalf of the county councils of South Glamorgan, Mid-Glamorgan, West Glamorgan, Dyfed and Avon and which was supported by the Welsh Counties Committee, the Association of District Councils in Wales, the Gwent Association of District Councils, the Trades Union Council (Wales), the Freight Transport Association, the Road Haulage Association, the Automobile

e Association and the South Glamorgan Chamber of Trade. Webster J decided that in making the order known as the Severn Bridges Tolls Order 1985, SI 1985/726, the Secretary of State for Transport acted ultra vires his powers under the Severn Bridge Tolls Act 1965 and that the order was null and void and the applicants were entitled to a declaration to this effect.

The appeal raises a question of some importance in relation to local inquiries since

f Webster J came to his decision on the basis that there was procedural impropriety by the inspector who conducted the inquiry into the 1985 order as a result of his failure to evaluate and report his conclusions on certain issues which the Secretary of State had argued raised questions of policy on which an inspector was not required to express his views. Webster J also decided that this procedural impropriety by the inspector was not cured by the subsequent decision of the Secretary of State to make the order.

g
The law

By s 1 of the Severn Bridge Tolls Act 1965 the Secretary of State is given the power, but is not placed under a duty, to levy tolls. The power can be exercised in respect of the whole of the carriageway between the last junction to the east of the River Severn and the last junction to the west of the River Wye with a special road and therefore includes

h the bridges over both those rivers.

Section 2 gives the Secretary of State power to provide different rates of tolls for different classes of vehicles.

The procedure for making an order is contained in s 3. This section requires a draft order to be prepared, the draft order to be published, and that there should be a right of objection and if objections are made and not withdrawn, in the case of objections by local

j authorities and certain other specified bodies, the Secretary of State shall, and in the case of other objections the Secretary of State may, hold a local inquiry.

Section 3(4) is important and states:

'After considering any objections to the proposed order which are not withdrawn, and, where a local inquiry is held, the report of the person who held the inquiry, the Minister may make the order either without modification or subject to such modifications as he thinks fit.'

Although s 3 does not expressly require the Secretary of State to issue a decision letter, s 12 of the Tribunals and Inquiries Act 1971 requires him to give reasons for his decision and the issue of a decision letter is a convenient way of complying with this obligation. Pursuant to s 19 the order is made by statutory instrument and is subject to annulment by or a resolution of either House of Parliament.

The amount of toll which the Secretary of State can levy is limited by the provisions of s 4 of and Sch 2 to the 1965 Act. Section 4(2) provides that he cannot specify—

'scales of tolls exceeding those which in his opinion would be requisite to secure that, taking one year with another, the revenue produced by the tolls during the toll period [here 40 years] ... would be sufficient [to reimburse with interest the expenses specified in Sch 2 incurred in connection with providing the carriageway].'

It is not necessary to go into detail as to what those expenses are since it is not contended that the Secretary of State in making the 1984 order exceeded the limitations contained in s 4 and Sch 2.

The provisions requiring a local inquiry to be held contained in s 3 of the 1965 Act are now a common feature of many statutory procedures governing administrative decisions by ministers. The purpose of such a local inquiry was clearly spelt out in the speeches of the House of Lords in *Bushell v Secretary of State for the Environment* [1980] 2 All ER 608, [1981] AC 75. Lord Diplock said ([1980] 2 All ER 608 at 612, [1981] AC 75 at 94):

'The essential characteristics of a "local inquiry", an expression which when appearing in a statute has by now acquired a special meaning as a term of legal art, are that it is held in public in the locality in which the words that are the subject of the proposed schemes are situated by a person appointed by the minister on whom the statute has conferred the power in his administrative discretion to decide whether to confirm the scheme. The subject matter of the inquiry is the objections to the proposed scheme that have been received by the minister from local authorities and from private persons in the vicinity of the proposed stretch of motorway whose interests may be adversely effected, and in consequence of which he is required by Sch 1, para 9, to hold the inquiry. The purpose of the inquiry is to provide the minister with as much information about those objections as will ensure that in reaching his decision he will have weighed the harm to local interests and private persons who may be adversely affected by the scheme against the public benefit which the scheme is likely to achieve and will not have failed to take into consideration any matters which he ought to have taken into consideration.'

Viscount Dilhorne, referring to the Franks Committee's Report on Administrative Tribunals and Enquiries of 1957 (Cmnd 218, para 269) stated ([1980] 2 All ER 608 at 621, [1981] AC 75 at 107):

'... the primary purpose of a local inquiry must be—"to ensure that the interests of the citizens closely affected should be protected by the grant to them of a statutory right to be heard in support of their objections, and to ensure that thereby the Minister should be better informed of the facts of the case".'

Unlike the inquiry to which Lord Diplock was referring, the inquiry into the 1985 order was conducted by an independent inspector appointed by the Lord Chancellor. Subject to any statutory procedural rules which apply to the inquiry and the requirements in the statute creating the power to hold the inquiry, the inspector has a wide discretion as to the procedure which he follows. But he must not use that discretion to frustrate the purpose of the inquiry and he must therefore give the objectors an adequate opportunity properly to present their objections to the proposal. It has to be remembered that this may be the only opportunity which persons in the locality have of expressing their views about a proposal of central government which can have a very material impact on the area in which they live. However, as well as bearing in mind the importance of a local inquiry to the process of consulting and informing local opinion and gleaning local information the inspector has to take into account the undesirability of a local inquiry being unduly extended. Unnecessary expense and delay can be caused if an inquiry becomes a forum for the discussion or irrelevant matters. It was for this reason that the House of Lords in *Bushell's* case upheld the decision of the inspector not to allow cross-examination of the department's witnesses as to the reliability and statistical validity of the methods for traffic prediction used by the department in order to assess traffic needs for the purpose of applying the government's policy with regard to the national motorway network. This refusal to allow cross-examination could be justified either on the basis that the local inquiry was not the appropriate forum in which to discuss such policy matters or because the departmental witnesses were just unqualified to answer questions on that subject. Lord Diplock dealt with what is meant by policy for this purpose. He said ([1980] 2 All ER 608 at 614–615, [1981] AC 75 at 98):

> '"Policy" as descriptive of departmental decisions to pursue a particular course of conduct is a protean word and much confusion in the instant case has, in my view, been caused by a failure to define the sense in which it can properly be used to describe a topic which is unsuitable to be the subject of an investigation as to its merits at an inquiry at which only persons with local interests affected by the scheme are entitled to be represented. A decision to construct a nationwide network of motorways is clearly one of government policy in the widest sense of the term. Any proposal to alter it is appropriate to be the subject of debate in Parliament, not of separate investigations in each of scores of local inquiries before individual inspectors up and down the country on whatever material happens to be presented to them at the particular inquiry over which they preside. So much the respondents readily concede. At the other extreme the selection of the exact line to be followed through a particular locality by a motorway designed to carry traffic between the destinations that it is intended to serve would not be described as involving government policy in the ordinary sense of that term. It affects particular local interests only and normally does not affect the interests of any wider section of the public, unless a suggested variation of the line would involve exorbitant expenditure of money raised by taxation. It is an appropriate subject for full investigation at a local inquiry and is one on which the inspector by whom the investigation is to be conducted can form a judgment on which to base a recommendation which deserves to carry weight with the minister in reaching a final decision as to the line the motorway should follow.'

Later Lord Diplock added ([1980] 2 All ER 608 at 616, [1981] AC 75 at 100):

> 'But whether the uniform adoption of particular methods of assessment is described as policy or methodology, the merits of the methods adopted are, in my view, clearly not appropriate for investigation at individual local inquiries by an inspector whose consideration of the matter is necessarily limited by the material which happens to be presented to him at the particular inquiry which he is holding.'

However, whether it is sought to justify an inspector's decision to restrict the investigation of a line of inquiry on the basis that the issue is one of policy or on the basis that it is not a matter which it is appropriate for examination at a local inquiry or on the basis that the investigation would not be able to assist in achieving the object of the inquiry, all the speeches in the House of Lords in the *Bushell* case make it clear that in the end the propriety of the decision will depend on whether or not it resulted in unfairness to those taking part in the inquiry.

Although it is convenient to categorise what is complained of in this case as procedural impropriety, adopting one of the labels listed by Lord Diplock in his speech in *Council of Civil Service Unions v Minister for the Civil Service* [1984] 3 All ER 935, [1985] AC 374, it is important to remember that it is not sufficient in order to obtain relief from the courts, whether by way of judicial review or otherwise, merely to identify some action on the part of the inspector which can be justifiably criticised from a procedural point of view. *a* The courts will only interfere if a procedural impropriety results in a breach of the law which will most frequently be based on an allegation that the objectors were being treated unfairly.

In relation to this case a procedural decision of the inspector could have the result that the minister had no power to make the order because it involved a breach of the law. However, for this to be the position the procedure at the local inquiry would have to be *b* so flawed that it could be said that for practical purposes there had been no local inquiry or there would have to be a wholly inadequate report to be considered by the minister. Then the minister could not perform his obligation to consider objections and the report of the person who held the inquiry which s 3(4) of the 1965 Act makes a condition precedent to the Secretary of State exercising his power. If the procedure falls down in this extreme manner, then there can be no question of the Secretary of State being able *c* to cure the inspector's default. The procedure would have to start again.

Usually it will not however be necessary for an objector seeking relief in the courts to go so far as to establish that there has been a failure to fulfil the express requirements of the 1965 Act. It will be sufficient to show that he has been prejudiced by a failure to conduct the proceedings fairly which is inevitably an implied statutory requirement arising out of an obligation to hold an inquiry. In considering the question of the fairness *d* of the proceedings it is necessary to examine the proceedings as a whole: not only what has happened before the inspector but also what has happened before the minister, and it is only if the procedure as a whole is unfair that the courts can intervene. Approaching the matter in this way in my view it is preferable for the court not to ask itself two questions, as Webster J was invited to do in the court below; the first question being whether there was a procedural impropriety by the inspector, the second being whether *e* or not this procedural impropriety was cured by the Secretary of State when he came to give his decision. The court should focus on answering the one question as to the fairness of the proceedings as a whole. What Lord Diplock said in *Bushell's* case [1980] 2 All ER 608 at 613, [1981] AC 75 at 96 in relation to an inquiry under the Highways Act 1959 can be applied generally. He said: *f*

'If the minister is to give proper consideration to objections to the scheme by persons in the vicinity of the proposed stretch of motorway . . . fairness requires that the objectors should have an opportunity of communicating to the minister the reasons for their objections to the scheme and the facts on which they are based. The Highways Act 1959 requires that the form in which that opportunity is to be afforded to them is at a local inquiry. Fairness, as it seems to me, also requires that *g* the objectors should be given sufficient information about the reasons relied on by the department as justifying the draft scheme to enable them to challenge the accuracy of any facts and the validity of any arguments on which the departmental reasons are based.'

However, it is not be ignored that Lord Diplock added ([1980] 2 All ER 608 at 613–614, *h* [1981] AC 75 at 96–97):

'It is evident that an inquiry of this kind and magnitude is quite unlike any civil litigation and that the inspector conducting it must have a wide discretion as to the procedure to be followed in order to achieve its objectives. These are to enable him to ascertain the facts that are relevant to each of the objections, to understand the *j* arguments for and against them and, if he feels qualified to do so, to weigh their respective merits, so that he may provide the minister with a fair, accurate and adequate report on these matters.'

Having regard to the nature of the challenge made by the objectors in this case to the validity of the order it is important to note what Lord Diplock says with regard to the *a* inspector feeling qualified to evaluate the merits. This was a matter also considered by Lord Lane in dealing with an argument of counsel for the objectors. Lord Lane said ([1980] 2 All ER 608 at 632, [1981] AC 75 at 122):

> *b* 'The inspector, he submitted, was under a duty not merely to report but also to recommend. By treating the question of need for the motorway as irrelevant he excluded from his mind considerations which might have resulted in a recommendation favourable to the objectors. This is said to be a breach of the rules of natural justice and consequently a failure to comply with the provisions of the 1959 Act requiring the intervention of the court. I disagree. It would have been inappropriate for the inspector to have made recommendations as to the need for the motorway as a whole. He properly fulfilled his duties by presenting all the material evidence to the minister in his report.'

c After describing how the matter could be tested in a practical way Lord Lane went on ([1980] 2 All ER 608 at 633, [1981] AC 75 at 123):

> 'In short, the question of need is a matter of policy or so akin to a matter of policy that it was not for the inspector to make any recommendation.'

d I have sought to stress the paramount importance of the question whether the results achieve fairness, because on the different arguments which were advanced before him Webster J was, on the facts of this case, concerned to ascertain whether or not the matters in respect of which the complaints were made were properly describable as policy or broad policy. I suggest that in most cases a proper assessment of the validity of the decision is unlikely to be provided by approaching the matter in this way. Where the inquiry is into a scheme promoted by a minister, it is inevitable that what is proposed *e* will to some extent reflect the policy of the department over which he presides. That is the result of an administrative procedure which starts with the department publishing a draft order. The proposal may be one-off and in that sense there may be no question of national policy involved. On the other hand the draft order may only relate to a small part of some national scheme where there is a clearly defined national policy. However, *f* even in a case which falls within the latter category, the fact of the national policy does not necessarily inhibit the objectors. They are still perfectly entitled to have investigated all matters on which they rely for saying that the national policy should be departed from within their locality. While the minister is entitled to have a policy, he must always be prepared to consider, having regard to special circumstances, departing from that policy. In practice therefore, from the objectors' point of view, the position is not going *g* to be that different whether the minister is relying on 'a broad' or 'a national' or 'local' policy. In most cases it can be contended that the policy should not be applied in the particular locality.

In relation to many local inquiries there are now statutory rules of procedure which give guidance as to what will be a fair procedure in the circumstances. No such rules have been made in relation to the 1965 Act. However, at the pre-inquiry meeting which *h* the inspector held on 11 June 1984 he indicated that he intended to follow the rules set out in the Highways (Inquiries Procedure) Rules 1976, SI 1976/721, so far as these were appropriate. Counsel for the applicant therefore relies on these rules. It is therefore necessary to refer to certain of them.

The 1976 rules do not expressly deal with the question of whether or not the inspector is under an obligation to evaluate and report on matters of government policy. However, *j* there are references in the rules which make it clear that a local inquiry has a limited role in relation to government policy. For example r 11(2) provides that the appointed person shall disallow any question which in his opinion is directed to the merits of government policy and at the pre-inquiry meeting the inspector made it clear that he was not going to allow questions to be directed to the department's witnesses on this subject. (Though he qualified this by saying that discussion would be permissible as to the accuracy as a matter of fact of any statement made about what that policy was.)

Rule 13(1) underlines the extent of the inspector's discretion since it states that, except
as otherwise provided in the rules, the procedure of the inquiry shall be such as the *a*
appointed person shall in his discretion determine.

Rule 15 deals with the contents of the inspector's report and requires that it shall
'include the appointed person's findings of facts, his conclusions and his recommendations,
if any, or his reasons for not making any recommendations'. Rule 15 should not be
regarded as requiring the inspector to include in his report conclusions on every issue at
the inquiry. He may, for example, perfectly properly decide (as this inspector at the pre- *b*
trial meeting decided he would do without objection) not to express conclusions on
matters of law but to refer those for decision by the minister. If the inspector decides not
to express a conclusion on a particular matter, then this exercise of his discretion can only
be criticised by the objectors if the absence of the inspector's conclusion may prejudice
the evaluation by the Secretary of State of the case for the objectors. If this is the position,
the objectors can complain they have not been dealt with fairly and in an appropriate *c*
case the court can intervene.

The facts

Since the Severn Bridge opened in 1966 tolls have been levied on vehicles using this
part of the M4 motorway. Originally the rate was 1s for motor cycles and 2s 6d for all
other vehicles. From time to time the rates increased so that when the draft order which *d*
led to these proceedings was published on 30 September 1983 the existing rates were 10p
for two-wheeled motor cycles, 20p for three-wheeled motor cycles and other motor
vehicles other than goods vehicles having an unladen weight exceeding 30 cwt or
passenger vehicles adapted to carry more than 16 passengers, the rate for which was 40p.
The draft order proposed that there should be no toll for two-wheeled motor cycles but
that the 20p rate should increase to 50p and the 40p rate should increase to £1. *e*

In relation to the draft order in the House of Commons on 28 October 1983 the
Minister of State for Transport made a statement with regard to the proposed order
which Webster J accurately stated indicated that the—

> 'maker of it was under the mistaken impression that ss 1 to 4 of the Act obliged
> the Secretary of State to recover from tolls the full cost of the bridge as specified in *f*
> s 2 of the Act, whereas, in fact, those sections give him a discretion as to the amounts
> to be levied by tolls . . .'

(See [1986] 2 All ER 18 at 21, [1986] 1 WLR 1055 at 1058.)

However, during the inquiry, which was held between 17 July and 1 August 1984,
this ministerial misstatement was drawn to the attention of the inspector and it is clear *g*
that the department conducted its case at the inquiry on the correct basis, the inspector's
report correctly sets out the position as to the Secretary of State's powers, and the Secretary
of State's decision contained in the decision letter is expressed in terms which are only
consistent with his recognising that he had the discretion which the Act in fact gives
him.

The objectors make no complaints about the manner in which the inquiry was *h*
conducted or as to the way in which their case was summarised by the inspector in his
report which is dated 31 October 1984. Indeed in an affidavit sworn on 22 August 1985
in support of their application for judicial review, a solicitor in the firm acting for the
applicants acknowledges that no restrictions were placed on the objectors in the
presentation of their case as to the proposed tolls.

The form of the inspector's report follows that contemplated by r 15 and, as now is *j*
almost the invariable practice, includes sections containing summaries of the cases for
the various parties, a section dealing with legal submissions, a section setting out the
inspector's findings of fact, a section dealing with the inspector's conclusions and finally
the inspector's recommendations. The first section to which I have referred includes a
statement of the department's case followed by a statement of each objector's case and in
relation to the principal objectors cases the department's reply.

The criticisms of the inspector's report are confined to his failure to express conclusions
a on those parts of the objectors' case which the department contended were the subject of
a specific policy of the Secretary of State as to the Severn Bridge. Throughout, that is
before the inspector, Webster J and this court, the objectors have drawn a distinction
between the general policy which the Secretary of State has as to charging tolls and the
specific policy which he suggested he has in relation to the Severn Bridge. In order to
understand this distinction and the case for the objectors it is necessary to refer to various
b passages in the inspector's report.

The case for the Department of Transport as recorded by the inspector includes the
following:

'9.1 The Government's policy since the Severn Bridge had been built was that the
cost of estuarial crossings should be paid for by the users of such crossings. This has
c been applied to other crossings, e.g. the Dartford Tunnel and the Humber Bridge.
The principle of levying tolls was outside the scope of the inquiry and the merits of
the Government's policy were not matters with which the Department's witnesses
would deal . . .

9.3 Successive Governments had taken the view that tolls were justified because
users of estuarial crossings benefited from the exceptional savings in time and
d money which such costly facilities afforded.'

In setting out in his report the case of the Welsh authorities, the inspector included
reference to the fact that their case was that there should be no tolls at all but they
accepted that the merits of the government policy on this question was not within the
scope of the current inquiry. He also summarised the Welsh authorities' case as having
e four aspects. (1) There was no clear and consistent government policy with regard to tolls
on estuarial crossings. (2) The method of accounting was unrealistic; the expenses and
payments were notional and it is unfair to impose on users the entire notional cost for 40
years, including new strengthening work. (3) The probability of the construction of a
second crossing within the toll period must invalidate the predictions about tolls made
by the department. (4) The bridge had an unfavourable image in the minds of those
f whose decision were vital to the economic future of South Wales.

The inspector then records, as being part of the department's reply to this case of the
Welsh authorities:

'The Government's policy was that the Severn Bridge should be tolled; that all the
Schedule 2 costs should be recovered and this should be done within the 40 years
toll period. Various items which the South Wales authorities claimed should not be
g recovered from tolls must, according to Government policy, be so recovered . . .'

(See para 10.1.56.)

Included in the inspector's summary of the department's reply to legal submissions
was a statement by counsel:

'The Secretary of State would reach a decision on the level of tolls only after
h considering objections. His decision would be made when, in the light of the
Inspector's report, he confirmed the draft Order or modified it or did not confirm
it. Successive Governments had adopted the policy that the tolls should meet
expenditure over a 40 year period. No statement has been made that this period
would be extended. The Secretary of State could alter his policy at any time and, in
the light of the Inspector's report, he could consider whether to adhere to his policy
j or change it. He could set tolls at a level which would make an extension of the 40
year period likely. Therefore the Secretary of State had not taken a decision on the
draft Order nor fettered his discretion in advance.'

(See para 12.7.)

It is next necessary to refer to the following paragraphs in the section of the inspector's
report containing his conclusions:

'14.2 The present policy of the Government with regard to the imposition of tolls on estuarial crossings is quite clear though, at different times, different terminology has been employed by Ministers to express that policy; its application varies if the full implementation of policy is not possible because of economic and social constraints in the immediate area served by the crossing. That policy, so far as the Severn Crossing is concerned, is that those driving over it should meet the total costs set out in Schedule 2 of the 1965 Act over the 40 year period from its opening. In effect, the expenses are treated as if a loan had been raised . . .

14.5 It is not part of my function to express any opinion upon the merits of government policy; once I know what it is, I must pay regard to it in making my recommendation upon the draft Order . . .

14.6 I cannot agree that the items which they [the South Wales authorities] seek to exclude from the expenses can be so excluded without conflicting with the Government policy . . .'

In para 14.16 the inspector deals with the question of the total abolition of tolls. He records the advantages but points out that this would conflict directly with government policy. He adds that he has reported the evidence given at the inquiry for the information of the Secretary of State but that he does not propose to make any further comments.

The inspector then, in paras 14.17 to 14.22, deals with a series of arguments and as these are the paragraphs on which the outcome of this appeal principally revolves I should set them out in full:

'14.17 It was claimed by the South Wales Authorities that, even if abolition were not possible, some items should not be debited in the accounts and be met by tolls. Many other crossings had been built with aid from the Government, typically of 25%, and this sum should be deducted from the capital cost. Whilst there is no doubt that prior to the mid-1960's, grants of one sort or another were given to local authority bridges and tunnels; according to the evidence, the more modern crossings, e.g. the Humber bridge and second Mersey tunnel have, generally speaking, not had such aid (Doc. 4/2). This, again, is a matter of policy and apart from drawing attention to what seems to be a change in the method of financing, I do not see it as part of my function to express a view on whether the earlier or later system ought to be followed. It is, however, interesting to note that a grant of as much as 75% was envisaged in 1935/36 (para. 10.1.38 hereof).

14.18 The Wye bridge was very similar to other bridges on motorways and other roads and its cost ought not to be counted in the tolls account, so it was said. Again, the £943,000 for approach roads should be excluded. The Department replied that these were items which must be charged in accordance with the Government's policy and I accept this.

14.19 The value of the length of bridge itself ought to be deducted; it would have cost about £1m. at 1966 prices as a length of motorway. Again, to omit this would conflict with the policy adopted by the Secretary of State, in my view.

14.20 Whilst the £19·6m ought to be spent, much of it was due to higher standards and increases in the numbers and weight of HGVs; these were extraordinary items and should be met by taxation, not tolls. My opinion on this suggestion is the same; to adopt it would conflict with Government policy.

14.21 Another claim of the Welsh Authorities was that as there were beneficiaries other than persons using the bridge, e.g. those on roads relieved by it, the imposition of tolls to cover 100% of the cost was unfair; once more, I believe that, apart from the impossibility of charging such beneficiaries directly, to charge a proportion of the costs to the Exchequer would conflict with the policy laid down.

14.22 To charge deficits each year to the Consolidated Fund, as suggested by Mr. Heycock (para. 10.1.36) hereof) would not accord with Government policy.'

a   In para 14.23 the inspector deals with one of the main grounds of objection formulated by the Welsh authorities, namely the adverse effect which the increase in tolls would have on the economy of South Wales and the similar argument advanced on behalf of the County of Avon. With regard to this argument he does express his conclusion that the effect would not be significant. He also expresses his conclusions about the fairness of the proposed division between the different types of vehicle and the fact that the amount which it is proposed to raise comes within the powers given by the Act. Finally the

b   inspector sets out his recommendation that the proposed order should be made subject to a minor modification.

      On 23 May 1985 the Secretary of State issued his decision letter and laid the order before Parliament. In the decision letter in addition to indicating that he accepts the inspector's findings of fact, agrees with his conclusions and accepts the inspector's recommendation, the Secretary of State deals with the question of policy in two

c   paragraphs which it is also necessary to set out. The paragraphs are in the following terms:

      '5. The Secretary of State has also considered the objections to Government policy on the merits of which the Inspector felt it was not his function to express an opinion. The objectors argued against tolls in general and against tolls at the Severn

d   Bridge in particular. In relation to tolls in general, Government policy towards estuarial crossings is that they should be paid for by the user rather than the taxpayer. The Government remains convinced that this policy is justified where users benefit from the exceptional savings in time and money which these expensive facilities make possible and there are no counter arguments on grounds of traffic diversion or congestion. Parliamentary agreement to the charging of tolls has

e   enabled crossings to be built which might not otherwise have been provided.

      6. With regard to policy as it affects the Severn Bridge, the main additional arguments were that tolls had an adverse effect on the local economy, that certain items should be disregarded in assessing the tolls to be charged, that credit should be given for Government grant not made, that the toll period should be extended, and that it was inopportune to raise tolls when the service provided was likely to

f   suffer on account of the need to execute repair and strengthening works. On the last point, the Secretary of State has shown himself ready to abandon tolls as a temporary expedient when circumstances warranted it, as appears from his statement of 31 October 1983 (noted in Inquiry Document 6/15), but it appears to him that he ought not to forego a permanent tolls increase amply justified by the financial evidence when it is not yet apparent that the operation of the bridge will necessarily

g   be significantly affected by remedial works. For the rest, it seems to the Secretary of State that the different bases of accounting suggested were but means to an end— the elimination or reduction of tolls—which he could justify only on grounds of traffic diversion or congestion or by reason of the effect of tolls on the local economy. It does not appear to the Secretary of State that the tolls proposed would be likely to cause sufficient traffic to divert to alternative routes so as to render tolling

h   impracticable or to generate unacceptable congestion on other roads. On the economic point, the Inspector found (paragraph 13.5) that in the application of the policy to estuarial crossings generally the Government has regard to the economic needs of the area served, but the Inspector also concluded (paragraph 14.23) that the tolls proposed would not deter a serious developer or have significant effect on the economy of South Wales or cause any real harm to the economy of Avon or the

j   Forest of Dean. The Secretary of State agrees with the Inspector's opinion and concludes that there is no convincing reason to modify policy in relation to the Severn Bridge.'

      It will be noted that in these paragraphs the Secretary of State deals specifically with the principal arguments advanced by the objectors.

The issues

Both before Webster J and on this appeal counsel for the applicants has relied on the   *a* statement which the minister made in the House of Commons to which reference has already been made. Webster J took the view that this statement of the position did not in itself invalidate the order since having regard to the decision letter he was unable to conclude that the Secretary of State was misdirecting himself when the order was made. Webster J did, however, indicate that this point might have some relevance when considering the objectors' principal ground of complaint. In my view, while it was   *b* unfortunate that the minister should have made this error and it is appropriate that it should have been investigated as the error was clearly identified and accepted, it does not affect the validity of the order or the merits of the other issues argued before Webster J and this court.

Turning therefore to the principal issue, that is whether the Secretary of State had power to make the order having regard to the failure of the inspector to express   *c* conclusions in respect of the matters dealt with by him in paras 14.17 to 14.22, Webster J came to the conclusion that this constituted a procedural impropriety such as to invalidate the order unless the impropriety was cured between the time it occurred and the time when the order was made. He came to this conclusion because he considered that the inspector was dealing with matters which were appropriate for full investigation at a local inquiry, they were not necessarily inconsistent with matters of broad policy and   *d* it would not have been inappropriate for an inspector to report his conclusions on them since they would, and should in his view, have assisted the Secretary of State in the exercise of his discretion. Webster J added that, even if the inspector had felt it necessary to recommend the making of an order which would affect the recovery of the maximum amount recoverable under the 1965 Act he could usefully have expressed his conclusions about whether in relation to each point raised the expense in question was or was not one   *e* which could properly be brought within Sch 2 to the Act.

With regard to this conclusion of Webster J it is important to emphasise that the arguments which were advanced by counsel who then appeared on behalf of the Secretary of State were different from the arguments which counsel advanced before this court. On the arguments we have heard, I am quite satisfied that there was no procedural   *f* impropriety. I have already indicated that, even if the rules applied, there still remained a discretion in the inspector whether to express his conclusion on any particular matter and in my view it would be wholly appropriate for an inspector to take the view that in relation to the matters dealt with in the paragraphs of which complaint is made no purpose could be served by his expressing his opinion further than he had. In respect of each matter he had found the facts which were necessary for the Secretary of State to   *g* come to a conclusion and clearly indicated that he regarded them as being covered by the policy. Apart from the question of whether or not an exception should be made to the policy, there was nothing further for the inspector to evaluate. These issues were distinct from the issue whether the imposition of tolls or increased tolls would cause damage in the locality, which was an issue which the inspector could evaluate and on which he could and did express an opinion. As to whether there should or should not be a   *h* departure from the policy, the inspector's opinion would be of no more value than that of any other member of the public and his opinion would not be one which could be expected to carry any particular weight with the Secretary of State, who has to exercise a political judgment, in deciding whether or not to apply the policy. Furthermore, although a distinction can be made between the Secretary of State's policy with regard to tolls in general and his so-called specific policy in respect of the Severn crossing, the   *j* specific policy was no more than an application of the 'broad policy' to the Severn crossing and the same case could have been made on behalf of the department without referring to a specific policy in relation to the Severn Bridge. Though the reliance on a specific policy was not surprising and could well be due to the fact that on the last occasion the tolls had been increased there had also been an inquiry where much the same arguments

had been advanced and the Secretary of State had applied the policy in the same way, this
a specific policy did not prevent the inspector evaluating any evidence or properly
performing his functions.

With regard to the reference by Webster J to the desirability of the question of whether
or not the expenses fell within Sch 2 being dealt with by the inspector, in fact this was
dealt with quite clearly by him and it is accepted that all the expenses could properly be
brought within Sch 2 to the Act.

b No doubt because of the argument which was advanced before him, Webster J did not
consider whether there was any unfairness to the objectors which, as I have already
indicated, I regard as being the critical question. Instead Webster J, as he was invited to
do, considered whether or not the procedural impropriety had been 'cured'. This is an
approach which has been applied to situations where there is an initial hearing followed
by an appeal, which is quite a different situation. Webster J decided that the procedural
c impropriety had not been cured because he was not satisfied that the Secretary of State
had considered or evaluated on its merits each of the points about which the inspector
had not expressed his conclusion. If there had been a failure in this regard this could in
itself be a ground for challenging the validity of the order. However, Webster J went on
to say:

d   '... if there had been no prior procedural impropriety I would reject the
submission of counsel for the applicants that this letter, read in conjunction with
the report, was evidence of a failure on the part of the Secretary of State to give
genuine or adequate consideration to the objections.'

(See [1986] 2 All ER 18 at 31, [1986] 1 WLR 1055 at 1071.)

e I am therefore not sure what view Webster J was in fact taking. However, having
regard to the passages in the decision letter which I earlier cited in this judgment, I am
quite satisfied that the points on which the inspector did not express conclusions were
fully considered and evaluated by the Secretary of State on their merits and that, even if
there was a procedural impropriety, there would be no question of the objectors being
treated unfairly in consequence of this. It follows that in my view this appeal must be
f allowed and the application for judicial review dismissed. It only remains for me to
express my indebtedness to counsel for their very helpful arguments.

SIR ROUALEYN CUMMING-BRUCE. I have read the judgment just delivered
and the one about to be delivered by May LJ. I agree with each of them and have nothing
to add.

g
MAY LJ. I respectfully agree with the judgment which has been delivered by Woolf LJ,
which I had the advantage of reading in draft and with the reasons he gives for allowing
this appeal. I only add a few words of my own because we are differing from the judge
below. As Woolf LJ has pointed out, the argument on behalf of the Secretary of State
addressed to us followed a different path from that addressed to Webster J. The latter
h argument, founded specifically on the submission that the Secretary of State was under
no duty to consider objections to a ministerial policy which he had power to pursue or
objections raising points which were inconsistent with it, led the judge into too narrow a
consideration of the contentions of the applicant for judicial review that in making the
Severn Bridge Tolls Order 1985, SI 1985/726, the Secretary of State acted ultra vires. It
was for this reason that the judge derived from the speeches in *Bushell v Secretary of State*
j *for the Environment* [1980] 2 All ER 608, [1981] AC 75 certain limited principles relating
to matters which can properly be withdrawn from consideration and conclusion at a local
inquiry on the ground that they relate to or are governed by a policy on which the
relevant minister has already decided. However, although *Bushell's* case was principally
concerned with the impact of policy matters on the conduct of a highway inquiry and
subsequent judicial review proceedings, the underlying consideration governing their

Lordships' decision in that case was whether the conduct of the inquiry and the subsequent decision of the Secretary of State had been fair to those who wished to object *a* to the draft schemes which the former had published. In his speech Lord Diplock pointed out that the procedure at a local inquiry (in *Bushell's* case it was under the Highways Act 1959 but the principle applies to all local inquiries) had necessarily to be left to the discretion of the minister or the inspector appointed by him to hold the inquiry. Lord Diplock continued ([1980] 2 All ER 608 at 612–613, [1981] AC 75 at 95):

'In exercising that discretion, as in exercising any other administrative function, *b* they owe a constitutional duty to perform it fairly and honestly and to the best of their ability, as Lord Greene MR pointed out in his neglected but luminous analysis of the quasi-judicial and administrative functions of a minister as confirming authority of a compulsory purchase order made by a local authority which is to be found in *B Johnson & Co (Builders) Ltd v Minister of Health* [1947] 2 All ER 395 at 399– *c* 400. The judgment contains a salutary warning against applying to procedures involved in the making of administrative decisions concepts that are appropriate to the conduct of ordinary civil litigation between private parties. So rather than use such phrases as "natural justice", which may suggest that the prototype is only to be found in procedures followed by English courts of law, I prefer to put it that in the absence of any rules made under the Tribunals and Inquiries Act 1971 the only *d* requirement of the Highways Act 1959 as to the procedure to be followed at a local inquiry held pursuant to Sch 1, para 9 is that it must be fair to all those who have an interest in the decision that will follow it whether they have been represented at the inquiry or not. What is a fair procedure to be adopted at a particular inquiry will depend on the nature of its subject matter.'

In the instant case I think that the judge was led to consider too particularly questions *e* concerning ministerial policy, with the result that he failed to consider whether overall the whole procedure which led to the making of the 1985 order, that is the one adopted by the minister, by the inspector and thereafter by the minister again looked at in the whole, had been fair to the local objectors. The basis of the challenge to the 1985 order was 'procedural impropriety': it was not contended that either the inspector or the *f* minister had failed to comply with any statutory requirements relating to the conception and making of the order; thus the question for the court was and is whether the whole process had by the end been fair to those who wished to object to it. In judicial review proceedings, except for some founded on alleged illegality, I think that the courts should try to take a wide view of the whole transaction impugned rather than become enmeshed, and perhaps thus led into error, in and by particular details of that transaction. *g* For the reasons given by Woolf LJ I am satisfied that the relevant transaction here, that is the conception of, necessary investigation into, and making of the 1985 order was fair to all those concerned. Accordingly I too would allow this appeal.

Appeal allowed. Leave to appeal to the House of Lords refused.

h
16 December. The Appeal Committee of the House of Lords (Lord Brandon of Oakbrook, Lord Oliver of Aylmerton and Lord Goff of Chieveley) refused leave to appeal.

Solicitors: *Treasury Solicitor*; M D Boyce, Cardiff (for the applicant).

Carolyn Toulmin   Barrister.

SCF Finance Co Ltd v Masri and another (No 2)

COURT OF APPEAL, CIVIL DIVISION

SLADE, RALPH GIBSON LJJ AND SIR JOHN MEGAW

3, 4, 5, 6, 9, 10 JUNE, 16 JULY 1986

Commodities market – Broker – Indemnity – Sums received by broker on behalf of client trading in commodity and financial futures – Broker extending credit to client to finance transactions – Client incurring substantial losses – Broker claiming reimbursement of losses incurred on client's behalf – Whether broker claiming for repayment of loans or for repayment of 'deposit' made by client – Banking Act 1979, s 1(1).

Bank – Deposit-taking business – Commodity broking – Sums received by broker on behalf of client trading in commodities and financial futures – Whether sums constituting 'deposits' – Whether broker holding himself out to 'accept deposits on a day-to-day basis' – Whether deposits accepted only on 'particular occasions' – Whether broker required to be licensed deposit-taker – Whether client's civil liability to broker affected by taking deposit in contravention of legislation – Banking Act 1979, s 1(1)(2)(3)(4)(b)(6)(b)(8).

The plaintiffs carried on business as licensed dealers in commodity and financial futures and held themselves out as willing to deal on a client's behalf in the market on a day-to-day basis on the terms of the plaintiffs' customer agreement, which provided that the plaintiffs, as the client's agent, would from time to time enter into transactions on the client's behalf and would from time to time demand from the client 'deposits' to cover the transactions and 'margins' to cover the risk of loss on the transactions. The agreement entitled the plaintiffs to place deposits thus received in their general account and to mix the deposits with other moneys in the account, from which the plaintiffs made loans to their clients. The agreement also served the purpose of affording the plaintiffs primary security for a client's default in indemnifying them by authorising them to sell the client's property and to close his accounts. The plaintiffs charged commission for buying and selling commodities and futures on behalf of clients and charged interest for providing finance for clients in the form of credit. The plaintiffs accepted primary liability under contracts of sale and purchase entered into on a client's behalf and assumed the risk of loss under those contracts and were themselves required to put up margins to brokers with whom they dealt. In April 1983 the defendant opened an account with the plaintiffs and agreed that they should act for him in dealings on the commodity and futures market on the terms of the plaintiffs' customer agreement. Between April and November 1983 the defendant, as required by the plaintiffs, deposited $US949,108 with them. From time to time the sums deposited fell short of the amount required to finance transactions on the defendant's behalf and when that occurred the plaintiffs extended substantial credit to the defendant to finance his transactions. By January 1984 there was an equity deficit exceeding $1m on the defendant's account with the plaintiffs. When the defendant failed to settle the account it was closed leaving losses outstanding of $910,000. The plaintiffs brought an action against the defendant to recover that amount. The defendant contended, inter alia, that the agreement between himself and the plaintiffs was illegal because it contravened s 1(1)[a] of the Banking Act 1979 in that the plaintiffs intended to accept and had accepted 'deposits' from the defendant in the course of carrying on an unauthorised 'deposit-taking business', and accordingly the plaintiffs were not entitled to recover any sums from him under the agreement between the parties. The plaintiff also counterclaimed to recover sums already paid under the

_____
a Section 1 is set out at p 185 c to p 186 a, post

agreement. The judge rejected the plea of illegality and gave judgment for the plaintiffs on their claim and the defendant's counterclaim. The defendant appealed.

a

Held – The appeal would be dismissed for the following reasons—

(1) The amounts paid by the defendant to the plaintiffs had been 'paid by way of security for payment for the provision of property or services . . . to be provided' by the plaintiffs within s 1(6)(b) of the 1979 Act, rather than by way of security for the repayment of loans made to him by the plaintiffs or for the repayment of any deficiency which the primary security afforded by the customer agreement was insufficient to cover, since if a futures contract resulted in actual delivery of the physical commodity the plaintiffs had provided 'property' and if, as was usual, it did not the plaintiffs had provided 'services' in the form of incurring the relevant risks and consequent losses and the extension of incidental credit in the course of their dealings. In either case, the money had been paid by the defendant as security to protect the plaintiffs against the risk that the defendant might default in reimbursing them for expenses properly incurred in carrying out their contractual duty to buy property in order to provide it to the defendant or in carrying out their contractually agreed services, which included the obligation to be primarily responsible for making payments under the futures contracts in respect of which the defendant was contractually bound to indemnify the plaintiffs. Accordingly, since the amounts paid by the defendant to the plaintiffs had been paid by way of security for payment for the provision of property or services by the plaintiffs, within s 1(6)(b), it followed that under s 1(4)(b) they were not 'deposits' for the purposes of the 1979 Act (see p 188 *e* to p 189 *c*, post).

b

c

d

(2) Even if the sums paid by the defendant were 'deposits' they had not been accepted in the course of 'carrying on . . . a deposit-taking business' by the plaintiffs, within s 1(1) of the 1979 Act, because even if the plaintiffs lent the money deposited to others or used it to finance other business activities, thereby satisfying the conditions for a 'deposit-taking business' laid down in s 1(2)(a) and (b), their business was exempted by s 1(3) from being a 'deposit-taking business' because (a) the plaintiffs did not in the normal course of their business 'hold [themselves] out to accept deposits on a day to day basis', within s 1(3)(a), since such holding out could only occur where a person by express or implied invitation held himself out as being generally willing on any normal working day to 'accept' deposits from the persons invited to make deposits, whereas the plaintiffs, instead of accepting deposits, themselves initiated the payment of deposits from their clients as and when it became necessary for them to do so, and (b) the occasions on which the plaintiffs accepted deposits from clients were properly to be regarded as 'particular occasions' within s 1(3)(b), since such occasions occurred only when they found it necessary for their own protection to demand deposits from their clients, and the mere fact that such occasions were numerous did not render them any less 'particular' for the purposes of s 1(3)(b) (see p 190 *c* to *f*, post).

e

f

g

(3) Furthermore, even where a deposit was taken in contravention of s 1(1) of the 1979 Act, s 1(8) made it plain that the rights of both the depositor and the depositee under the law of contract remained unaffected. It followed that even if the plaintiffs had accepted deposits from the defendant in contravention of s 1(1) the defendant remained liable in contract to them and was thus liable for the sums claimed by the plaintiffs and unable to recover the sums he had already paid to them (see p192 *h* to p 193 *b h*, post); *St John Shipping Corp v Joseph Rank Ltd* [1956] 3 All ER 683 applied.

h

Decision of Leggatt J [1986] 1 All ER 40 affirmed.

j

Notes

For deposit-taking business, see Supplement to 3 Halsbury's Laws (4th edn) para 200.
For the Banking Act 1979, s 1, see 4 Halsbury's Statutes (4th edn) 407.

Cases referred to in judgment

a *Bedford Insurance Co Ltd v Instituto de Resseguros do Brasil* [1984] 3 All ER 766, [1985] QB 966, [1984] 3 WLR 726.
Cope v Rowlands (1836) 2 M & W 149, 150 ER 707.
Jackson v Hall [1980] 1 All ER 177, [1980] AC 854, [1980] 2 WLR 118, HL.
Marles v Philip Trant & Sons Ltd (MacKinnon, third party) (No 2) [1953] 1 All ER 651, [1954] 1 QB 29, [1953] 2 WLR 564, CA.
b *Phoenix General Insurance Co of Greece SA v Halvanon Insurance Co Ltd* [1986] 1 All ER 908.
St John Shipping Corp v Joseph Rank Ltd [1956] 3 All ER 683, [1957] 1 QB 267, [1956] 3 WLR 870.
Stewart v Oriental Fire and Marine Insurance Co Ltd [1984] 3 All ER 777, [1985] QB 988, [1984] 3 WLR 741.
Vita Food Products Inc v Unus Shipping Co Ltd [1939] 1 All ER 513, [1939] AC 277.

c
Cases also cited

Britt v Buckinghamshire CC [1963] 2 All ER 175, [1964] 1 QB 77, CA.
Hales v Bolton Leathers Ltd [1951] 1 All ER 643, [1951] AC 531, HL.
Kiriri Cotton Co Ltd v Dewani [1960] 1 All ER 177, [1960] AC 192, PC.
Samson v Frazier Jelke & Co [1937] 2 All ER 588, [1937] 2 KB 170.
d *Waugh v Morris* (1873) LR 8 QB 202, [1861–73] All ER Rep 941.

Appeal

The first defendant, Khalil Said Masri, appealed against the judgment of Leggatt J given on 4 July 1985 ([1986] 1 All ER 40) giving judgment for the plaintiffs, SCF Finance Co Ltd (SCF), for the sum of $US910,031·70 with interest on the plaintiffs' action against Mr
e Masri and the second defendant, Ina'am Masri (otherwise Ina'am Mahmoud El Khatib) (Mr Masri's wife), and dismissing Mr Masri's counterclaim against the plaintiffs for repayment of the sum of $949,108·08 he had paid to SCF. The grounds of the appeal were: (1) that the judge was wrong in law in holding that the acceptance of deposits in breach of s 1 of the Banking Act 1979 pursuant to a contract to carry out trading in commodity futures did not render the contract unenforceable by SCF; (2) that the judge
f ought to have held (a) that at all material times SCF were carrying on a deposit-taking business within s 1(2) of the Act, (b) that at the date of the contract between SCF and Mr Masri, SCF intended that Mr Masri should from time to time pay SCF deposits within s 1(4) of the Act, (c) that pursuant to the contract SCF accepted from Mr Masri deposits in the course of their deposit-taking business in contravention of s 1(1) of the Act, (d) that at all material times it was SCF's intention and purpose that the contract should be
g performed in an illegal manner, and (e) that, accordingly, the contract was unenforceable by SCF and they were not entitled to recover any sum from Mr Masri; (3) that the judge ought to have held that pursuant to the contract SCF had received from Mr Masri the sum of $949,108·08 as agent on his behalf and accordingly, by reason of s 1(8) of the Act, Mr Masri was entitled to repayment of that sum. The facts are set out in the judgment of
h the court.

Stanley Brodie QC and *Christopher Moger* for Mr Masri.
Nicholas Lyell QC, Richard Aikens QC and *Richard Lord* for SCF.
Mrs Masri did not appear.

Cur adv vult

j
16 July. The following judgment of the court was delivered.

SLADE LJ. This is an appeal by Mr K S Masri, the first defendant, from a judgment of Leggatt J delivered on 4 July 1985 in favour of the plaintiffs, SCF Finance Co Ltd (SCF) (see [1986] 1 All ER 40). The second defendant is his wife. She has taken no part in this appeal.

SCF, whose parent company is Socofi AG of Geneva, are licensed dealers under the Prevention of Fraud (Investments) Act 1958. At all material times they carried on business at Winchester House in the City of London as brokers dealing in commodity and financial futures, bullion and foreign exchange. Between 6 April 1983 and 27 January 1984 the appellant, Mr Masri, a Jordanian investor, was a client of SCF and through them traded extensively in these various items. Between April 1983 and January 1984 Mr Masri paid to SCF seven sums totalling $US949,108·08, which SCF required if they were to continue trading on his behalf. On 30 January 1984 SCF liquidated his positions on his account with them. By that time, in the course of carrying out their duties or functions for him over this period, SCF had themselves incurred further liabilities or losses in the market amounting to $910,031·80, which were not covered by the sums paid to them by Mr Masri.

SCF then brought these proceedings to recover the sum of $US910,780·80, a claim which, having regard to an accountant's investigation, they subsequently reduced to $910,031·80. The latter was a figure which, as a matter of accountancy, counsel for Mr Masri did not challenge at the trial. As the judge observed in his judgment, the main part of Mr Masri's defence in the proceedings consisted of criticisms of the way in which SCF conducted their business (see [1986] 1 All ER 40 at 45). He complained, inter alia, that SCF had traded on their own account in conflict with his interests, that they had delayed in carrying out his business, that they had failed to account properly and had given him bad advice. All these criticisms the judge dealt with and rejected (at 46–47). He dealt with and rejected submissions that SCF were not entitled to liquidate Mr Masri's position at the end of January 1984, and that the contract pursuant to which they acted for him was governed by Jordanian rather than English law (at 47). Finally, he considered and rejected a defence introduced by his leave on the second day of the trial by way of re-amendment of the points of defence and counterclaim (at 47–53). This was a plea to the effect that it was at all material times the intention and purpose of SCF, unknown to Mr Masri, that the agreement should be performed in an illegal manner, contrary to s 1 of the Banking Act 1979. This illegality was said to involve a twofold consequence, namely that SCF could not recover all or any part of the sum of $US910,031·80, while, secondly, Mr Masri himself could recover the sums which he had paid to SCF. The amended counterclaim included a claim for the repayment of those sums, which SCF admit and assert amount to $949,108·08.

The judge rejected the plea of illegality no less decisively than he had rejected the other pleas advanced on behalf of Mr Masri. He accordingly gave judgment for SCF for a sum of $US910,031·70 together with interest in the action and also gave judgment for SCF on the counterclaim.

Before this court Mr Masri's grounds of appeal are confined exclusively to the illegality point. The judge himself had no doubt where the merits lie in this case. He observed (at 53–54):

'Try as I may, I can see no ground for sympathy with [Mr Masri] in being required to pay for the losses which he incurred through unsuccessful speculation in the commodity market. There appears to me to be no reason why he should not pay and every reason why he should. No doubt it was a reflection of his discontent that he appeared ready to say in evidence whatever he thought might suit his attempt to thwart [SCF's] claim. Shorn of any commercial reason for not paying, he has sought to dub [SCF's] business illegal on account of matters of which he was oblivious and which are not shown to have caused him any harm. That these attempts have failed is due not to any lack of skill on the part of [Mr Masri's] lawyers, but to the intrinsic lack of merit in the argument.'

Counsel on behalf of Mr Masri has not attempted to suggest to us that his case deserves sympathy. However, he has submitted, without doubt correctly, that if the plea of illegality is well founded in law, his client is entitled to take his stand on it.

The judge set out the facts of the case in detail in his very full and careful judgment. A number of the matters of fact to which he referred are not material on this appeal. We will, however, gratefully adopt and incorporate in this judgment more or less verbatim, without further acknowledgment, many passages in his judgment which relate to those facts which are material. We will begin by referring to the commercial background to SCF's trading, which the judge himself derived from the expert evidence of Mr P E Thompson, a consultant to the London Commodity Exchange Co Ltd, who has had wide experience in this field.

A futures contract is a legally binding commitment to deliver at a future date, or take delivery of, a given quantity of a commodity, or a financial instrument, at an agreed price. The contract is standardised in all respects, except with regard to price and terms of delivery. Standardisation of contracts allows interchangeability with all other contracts of the same delivery period. This allows buyers and sellers to offset or liquidate any of their open positions with an equal and opposite transaction of a futures contract. Less than 2% of futures contracts culminate in the actual delivery of the physical commodity.

The trading of future contracts takes place on recognised exchanges, such as the Commodity Exchange Inc of New York (Comex), and is effected through a member of the exchange. Orders to buy and sell are passed to the exchange floor by telephone or telex whence they are taken by messenger to a relevant trading ring or pit for execution by a floor broker. Contracts entered into in this way are cleared by the clearing house. Its prime function is to guarantee the performance of the contracts executed on the floor of the exchange. This it does by interposing itself as principal between the parties, becoming the seller to every buyer and the buyer to every seller, and thus a party to every trading transaction.

Clearing houses are membership organisations, like the commodity exchanges which they serve. Membership of an exchange is a prerequisite for membership of a clearing house, though not all exchange members are members of the relevant clearing house. Every broker on the floor of the exchange must have an arrangement with a clearing house member to be responsible to the clearing house for that broker's trading. Membership of a clearing house entails the assumption of substantial contingent liability to the clearing house, which will only accept contracts for clearance from or to the account of its members. Since its members are liable for the full performance of all contracts which they submit for clearance, a clearing house member acting as a broker for a customer assumes the risk or default by its customer.

By contrast with commodity markets, trading in foreign currency on the Interbank Forex and in the gold and silver bullion markets does not take place at a particular exchange. Instead business is conducted between offices by telephone, except for fixings on the bullion markets. There are no standardised contracts and most deals are done on a spot or cash basis, although it is possible to deal on a forward basis.

In the United States the public interest is protected by the Commodity Futures Trading Commission (CFTC). It has regulatory powers which apply to exchanges in the United States, their floor members and American brokerage houses, known as futures commission merchants (FCM's), who transact futures contracts for their customers. Since in the United States the clearing house interposes itself as a principal between buyer and seller in futures contracts, the floor members and FCM's normally act as agents for their customers.

SCF gave voluntary particulars of their modus operandi which were accepted by the judge as accurate. The following summary of the way in which they conduct their business will suffice for present purposes, even though it does not refer to every stage in the process of carrying out a transaction.

After an order has been received by SCF, one of its dealers will fill in details of the order on a dealing ticket. The order is then placed by telephone with brokers having access to the floor of the relevant exchange (eg Comex for futures). The dealer identifies on the dealing ticket the broker with whom the order is placed, the client number and the number of the day's transaction with the broker concerned. Upon confirmation by telephone from the broker that the order has been filled, the dealer will insert the 'execution price' on the dealing ticket. The execution of the order is then confirmed to the client by telex which will inform him of the price paid or obtained on execution.

Normally SCF will have with brokers separate accounts respectively for futures, bullion and foreign exchange. SCF's account number with the broker will be shown on the dealing ticket.

Following each day's trading, brokers will send to SCF a telex recap of all sales and purchases done for SCF by them. They also send to SCF printed daily statements of account, which show, inter alia, the consolidated position between the brokers and SCF and the amounts due to the broker or to SCF, together with amounts received from SCF and the opening of the day's account.

SCF's computer produces a daily recap client by client. The daily recaps set out the quantity and type of lots dealt in for that day and the prices at which they were bought or sold and details of the client's 'open' positions. They also give the client's 'cash position', his 'margin' and 'maintenance' and his 'equity'. ('Cash position' represents cash remitted plus realised profit and interest on cash and on realised profits, minus realised losses and interest on realised losses. The judge explained that 'margin' in its narrowest meaning is a sum paid by a client to his broker to cover the risk of loss on a transaction on his account (see [1986] 1 All ER 40 at 44). 'Maintenance' is a sum paid by a client to his broker to cover a shortfall between the price of a commodity bought and its current market value. A call for maintenance is in effect a call to maintain the margin by supplementing it. 'Equity' is the amount standing to his credit after the deduction from cash of margin and maintenance.) The information in the daily recap is sent by telex to the client.

We now quote from paras 4, 5, 6 and 7 of SCF's voluntary particulars:

> '4(d) The computer also produces daily "Trial Balances" . . . and daily "Edit Lists" . . . listing all transactions for all clients and all brokers concerned. The former produces the cumulative effect of every transaction as between SCF and the client and SCF and the broker. The latter records the details of each transaction effected as between SCF and the client and SCF and the broker. (e) Brokers telex SCF with the total cash due to or from SCF on a consolidated basis. If due to the broker cash is then remitted to the broker on instructions to SCF's bank. However, where SCF had a deposit account with a broker, the broker would credit any sums due directly to SCF without sending a daily telex advice. These sums appear both on the daily and the Monthly Statements from the broker . . .
>
> 5. At the end of each month, SCF receives Monthly Statements of Account from brokers . . . These are then reconciled on a consolidated basis . . . SCF produces by computer Monthly Statements of Account . . . for each client. These accounts show the month's trading commodity by commodity and commissions thereon, the monthly figures for Margin and Maintenance, and the client's "Call Accounts". The "Call Accounts" show the client's overall position. They show cash received, profit and loss commodity by commodity, interest, and the net balance at the end of that month's trading.
>
> 6. SCF will request payments of money from the client in the daily telex confirmations of trade. In those telexes, SCF will state that the account is now "on call" for a certain figure. Interest is worked out on a monthly basis and monthly statements of interest are compiled . . . and those figures are incorporated on the client's monthly Call Account . . .
>
> 7. During the early months of Mr Masri's trading with SCF, it was SCF's practice to produce daily Margin and Maintenance print-outs . . . The information that is contained in these print-outs is contained in condensed form on the Daily Recaps . . .'

The judge found that SCF's procedure ensured that each order was given a properly
a identifiable execution and that the check conducted at the end of each trading day
enabled SCF to ensure that each execution was correlated with a specific order placed by
a specific client (at 46–47).

As is normal, so the judge found, where a London broker trades on behalf of clients
into futures markets in the United States, any FCM through whom SCF carry out their
trading identifies SCF as their client and does not know or recognise SCF's own individual
b clients, although the FCM can distinguish transactions by the numbers allocated to them
(at 47).

Finally, in his summary of SCF's mode of conduct of their business, the judge made
these findings (at 47):

c
'I accept and adopt Mr Thompson's conclusions that many London commodity
brokers and FCM's in the United States trade for their own account as well as for
their clients, and that this dual capacity has always been acceptable in the
international futures industry. The procedure and methods of business used by
[SCF] conformed with the standard of conduct and market practice which is
expected of London futures brokers and gave rise to no conflict of interest between
[Mr Masri] and themselves. Because futures exchanges in the United States attract a
d very substantial volume of business, errors inevitably occur in the handling of it,
and it would have been unusual for [SCF] not to have received any price adjustments
in respect of business done on these futures exchanges. In the United States price
adjustments of this kind are normally passed to clients.'

Most of SCF's more important clients had been introduced to them by a Mr El Fadl. In
early 1983 he procured a request by Mr Masri to help him open an account with SCF. Mr
e Masri was satisfied that dealing through them would enable him to preserve his
anonymity, which he wished to do. The trading relationship between Mr Masri and SCF
began on 6 April 1983 when a telex exchange took place between the office of Mr Masri
in Amman, where Mr El Fadl was with him, and SCF. The gist of this exchange was that
Mr Masri requested SCF, and SCF agreed, to open an account for him and carry out a
transaction in bullion. Mr Masri also agreed to send a cheque for $50,000 to SCF.
f The judge found that Mr Masri received a copy of SCF's form of customer agreement
at the outset of his dealings with them; that he did so without demur and with a promise
to sign it; and that he continued to deal with SCF without giving any reason for not
signing it. He therefore found that Mr Masri's dealings were subject to the terms of the
customer agreement. Though any such inference was strenuously disputed on behalf of
Mr Masri at the trial, it was not challenged in this court.
g The form of customer agreement was addressed to SCF, and, so far as material,
provided as follows:

'Gentlemen:
In consideration of your accepting one or more accounts of the undersigned
(whether designated by name, number or otherwise) and your agreeing to act as
h broker/dealer for the undersigned in the purchase or sale of commodity futures,
commodity options, actuals or cash commodities, purchase or sale of bullion and
purchase or sale of currencies, the undersigned agrees as follows:
1 All transactions for the accounts of the undersigned and all rights of the
undersigned with respect thereto shall be subject to the laws of any applicable
jurisdiction and to the constitution, rules, regulations, customs and usages of the
j exchange or market, and its clearing house, if any, where the transactions are
executed by you or your agents. Actual deliveries are intended on all transactions.
The undersigned also agrees not to exceed the position limits set by any governmental
agency as well as limits established [by] exchanges and boards of trade for the
account of the undersigned acting alone or in concert with others and to promptly
advise you if the undersigned is required to file reports of commodity positions with

the United States Commodity Futures Trading Commission or other authority
having jurisdiction in the circumstances . . .

    4 The undersigned promptly will furnish and maintain such deposits and
margins for said accounts as you may require in your own discretion from time to
time.'

Clause 6 gave SCF authority, inter alia, to carry in their general account any moneys of
the customer from time to time in their possession and to commingle it with their
property and with property held for others without necessarily keeping it in segregated
accounts.

Clause 8 authorised SCF in any one or more of three specified contingencies to—

    'sell any or all of the property which may be in your possession or in the possession
of any affiliate of yours or any clearing house or clearing broker or any bank
pursuant to authority granted by you or to which you have been granted access by
the undersigned, or which you or any of such entities may be carrying for the
undersigned (either individually or jointly with others), or to buy in any property
of which the account or accounts of the undersigned may be short, or cancel any
outstanding orders in order to close out the account or accounts of the undersigned
in whole or in part, or in order to close out any commitment made on behalf of the
undersigned.'

The three contingencies were:

    '(i) should the undersigned die or default in any payment, (ii) should the
undersigned fail to fully and timely comply with any obligations the undersigned
may have to you, to any of your affiliates or to any clearing broker, clearing house
or bank through you, or (iii) should you for any reason whatsoever deem it necessary
for your protection of any of your affiliates.'

Clause 8 further provided that, following any such sale, purchase or cancellation the
customer would 'remain liable for any deficiency'.

Clause 10 provided:

    'The undersigned undertakes, at any time upon your demand, promptly to
discharge obligations of the undersigned to you, or in the event of a closing of any
account of the undersigned in whole or in part, promptly to pay you the deficiency,
if any, and no oral agreement or instructions to the contrary shall be recognized or
enforceable.'

The substantive part of the customer agreement was followed by 'RISK DISCLOSURE
STATEMENT – Please Read Carefully'. This began:

    'In connection with trading commodity futures contracts on exchanges located in
the United States, the following statement is provided to you in accordance with
Regulation 1.55 of the Commodity Futures Trading Commission. The risk of loss
in trading commodity futures contracts can be substantial. You should therefore
carefully consider whether such trading is suitable for you in light of your financial
condition. In considering whether to trade, you should be aware of the following:
1. You may sustain a total loss of the initial margin funds and any additional funds
that you deposit with your broker to establish or maintain a position in the
commodity futures market. If the market moves against your position, you may be
called upon by your broker to deposit a substantial amount of additional margin
funds, on short notice, in order to maintain your position. If you do not provide the
required funds within the prescribed time, your position may be liquidated at a loss,
and you will be liable for any resulting deficit in your account . . .'

Mr Masri was thus given clear warning of the risks of trading in a futures market and
a that he might lose the funds deposited with SCF to secure margin and maintenance
requirements during the course of trading if the market moved against him.

From April 1983 to November 1983 Mr Masri deposited sums with SCF from time to
time to secure margin and maintenance requirements notified to him by SCF by telex.
Seven such sums totalling $949,109 were deposited between April 1983 and November
1983. They were credited to an account in the name of Mr Masri designated the 'U.S.
b Dollar Call Account'. These began with sums of $50,000, $76,409 and $101,000,
deposited respectively on or shortly after 6 April 1983, 29 April 1983 and 25 May 1983.
Mr Masri's equity positions fluctuated between April 1983 and the end of December
1984 and, while his position was in credit from time to time during April and May 1983,
his trading thereafter was very unsuccessful. Between June and December 1983 his
equity position was in credit on only two days and was on all other dates substantially in
c debit.

Though these seven deposits were made, the evidence shows that SCF treated Mr Masri
as a favoured client in the same manner as they treated a number of other important
clients. For on frequent occasions during their trading relationship they did not demand
actual payment of the further sums which they would have been entitled to demand by
d way of deposit for the purpose of financing the market requirements for margin and
maintenance calls in respect of his dealings when there was a shortfall in the funds which
he had deposited. Instead, without objection from him, they merely debited his US
dollar call account with these further sums and with interest thereon, on the footing that
they represented advances to him. At the same time they credited to this account interest
on the moneys which had been deposited. The evidence of Mr Hussein Chalabi, SCF's
managing director, was that SCF put up substantial credit for their more important
e trading clients in relation to their dealings when the clients could not conveniently do
so. This was no doubt one reason why Mr Masri and other similar clients found it more
attractive to deal through SCF than through ordinary brokers who would have offered
no such credit in respect of margin and maintenance. If, as did not in the event happen,
Mr Masri's position had been closed with losses which did not exhaust his deposits, he
f would have been entitled to have repaid to him the unexhausted balance.

SCF, at the request of their parent company, Socofi AG, also held for safe keeping a few
sums of money, of a relatively small amount, for nine Iraqi customers of Socofi, who did
not wish to take the moneys back to Iraq. The moneys so held were relatively small in
amount, never in the aggregate exceeding $US165,000. They were deposited with the
Trade Development Bank by SCF, which allowed to the customers a rate of interest
g calculated at the mean of the bank's interest rates for debit and credit, less $\frac{1}{2}\%$, with the
result that SCF lost interest in respect of such deposits. Mr Chalabi, not surprisingly in
the judge's view, asserted that this was not done by way of business.

At the material time clients' moneys were not kept separately from SCF's general
funds. SCF maintained a current account with the Manufacturers Hanover Trust Co
(called the special US dollar demand deposit account), which was their main operating
h account and attracted interest. At least in the first instance all moneys received by SCF
from Mr Masri and from other clients, and also moneys received from Socofi and others
to finance their operations, went into this account, as did the moneys received from the
Iraqi clients for safe keeping. The funds in this commingled account were used by SCF
to provide margin and maintenance deposits to their own brokers in respect of their
accounts with them, to lend money to their own clients, to place from time to time sums
j on interest-bearing deposits with institutions and for the general purposes of their
business.

Mr Chalabi acknowledged that what were described in SCF's documents as 'clients'
deposits' represented amounts paid by clients to secure or collateralise their transactions
against losses, actual or anticipated. He agreed that in the commodity markets only about

2% of operators take delivery of the commodity in question, though many of those dealing in foreign exchange take actual delivery. The judge summarised the services *a* provided by SCF for their clients as follows ([1986] 1 All ER 40 at 50):

> 'The services afforded by [SCF] consisted essentially of buying and selling commodities on behalf of trading clients for which they charged commission and providing finance for which they charged interest.'

From 1 December 1983 Mr Masri's equity position was never in debit for less than *b* $690,000 and by the end of the month the debit exceeded $1m. SCF called for further funds from him at the beginning of December. Thereafter he agreed that his deficit balance as at 31 December 1983 would be cleared by 17 January 1984, but he did not perform this agreement. By 17 January his equity deficit had risen to well over $1m. By telexes of 23 and 26 January 1984 SCF demanded payment of further sums. On 27 January 1984 Mr Masri informed Mr El Fadl for SCF that he would not make a cash *c* payment. On, or very shortly after, 28 January 1984, he received a telegram threatening to liquidate his positions on his accounts unless he paid in full all funds needed to support them by the opening of the New York Exchange on 30 January 1984. Mr Masri did not respond. On 30 January 1984 SCF therefore liquidated his positions on his account, as, at least prima facie, they were entitled to do by virtue of cl 8 of the customer agreement.

On the closing of this account SCF called on him to pay the balance due on his account *d* as (at least prima facie) they were entitled to do by virtue of cl 10 of the customer agreement. On Mr Masri's failure to pay all or any part of this balance, SCF brought the present proceedings. The writ was issued on 7 February 1984.

The original points of defence served on behalf of Mr Masri on 20 August 1984 put forward a wide variety of pleas, all of which were either rejected by the judge or not proved at the trial. The only plea on which this appeal is based, which was introduced on *e* 19 June 1985 at the trial by way of reamendment of the points of defence, reads as follows:

> '17A. Further or alternatively the Plaintiffs were at all material times carrying on a deposit-taking business within the meaning of Section 1(2) of the Banking Act 1979 ("the Act"). *f*
>
> 17B. At the date of the agreement referred to in paragraph 2 hereof it was intended by the Plaintiffs that the First Defendant should from time to time pay to the Plaintiffs deposits in relation to his trading within the meaning of Section 1(4) of the Act.
>
> 17C. Between about April 1983 and January 1984 the First Defendant paid to the Plaintiffs deposits amounting to the sum of U.S. $809113.20 as alleged in paragraph *g* 16 hereof alternatively U.S. $949108.08 as alleged by the Plaintiffs in paragraph 1 of the Schedule to the Further and Better Particulars of the Points of Claim served on 26th October 1984.
>
> 17D. The Plaintiffs accepted those deposits in the course of the business mentioned under paragraph 17A above and in contravention of Section 1(1) of the Act.
>
> 17E. In the premises it was at all material times the intention and purpose of the *h* Plaintiffs (unknown to the First Defendant) that the agreement should be performed in an illegal manner as aforesaid.
>
> 17F. Accordingly the Plaintiffs are not entitled to recover the sum claimed or any sum from the First Defendant.'

The agreement referred to in para 2 was the agreement concluded on or about 6 April *j* 1983 whereby it was agreed that SCF would act for Mr Masri in regard to his contemplated dealings in bullion and bonds and the financial futures market.

The broad purpose of the 1979 Act is described in its title as follows:

> 'An Act to regulate the acceptance of deposits in the course of a business; to confer functions on the Bank of England with respect to the control of institutions carrying

on deposit-taking businesses; to give further protection to persons who are depositors with such institutions; to make provision with respect to advertisements inviting the making of deposits; to restrict the use of names and descriptions associated with banks and banking; to prohibit fraudulent inducement to make a deposit; to amend the Consumer Credit Act 1974 and the law with respect to instruments to which section 4 of the Cheques Act 1957 applies; to repeal certain enactments relating to banks and banking; and for purposes connected therewith.'

One of the particular purposes of the Act (by a prohibition contained in s 1(1)) is to restrict the circumstances in which persons may accept 'deposits' within the meaning of the Act and to limit the classes of persons who may accept them.

Section 1 of the Act provides:

'*Control of deposit-taking and meaning of "deposit"*.—(1) Except as provided by section 2 below, no person may accept a deposit in the course of carrying on a business which is a deposit-taking business for the purposes of this Act.

(2) Subject to subsection (3) below, a business is a deposit-taking business for the purposes of this Act if—(a) in the course of the busines money received by way of deposit is lent to others, or (b) any other activity of the business is financed, wholly or to any material extent, out of the capital of or the interest on money received by way of deposit.

(3) Notwithstanding that paragraph (a) or paragraph (b) of subsection (2) above applies to a business, it is not a deposit-taking business for the purposes of this Act if, in the normal course of the business,—(a) the person carrying it on does not hold himself out to accept deposits on a day to day basis; and (b) any deposits which are accepted are accepted only on particular occasions, whether or not involving the issue of debentures or other securities.

(4) Subject to subsection (5) below, in this Act "deposit" means a sum of money paid on terms—(a) under which it will be repaid, with or without interest or a premium, and either on demand or at a time or in circumstances agreed by or on behalf of the person making the payment and the person receiving it; and (b) which are not referable to the provision of property or services or to the giving of security; and references in this Act to money deposited and to the making of deposits shall be construed accordingly.

(5) Except in so far as any provision of this Act otherwise provides, in this Act "deposit" does not include—(a) a loan made by the Bank, a recognised bank or a licensed institution; or (b) a loan made by a person for the time being specified in Schedule 1 to this Act; or (c) a loan made by a person, other than a person falling within paragraph (a) or paragraph (b) above, in the course of a business of lending money carried on by him; or (d) a sum which is paid by one company to another at a time when one is a subsidiary of the other or both are subsidiaries of another company; or (e) a sum which is paid to an institution by a person who at the time it is paid is a director, controller or manager of the institution or the wife, husband, son or daughter of such a person.

(6) For the purposes of subsection (4)(b) above, money is paid on terms which are referable to the provision of property or services or to the giving of security if, and only if,—(a) it is paid by way of advance or part payment for the sale, hire or other provision of property or services of any kind and is repayable only in the event that the property or services is or are not in fact sold, hired or otherwise provided; or (b) It is paid by way of security for payment for the provision of property or services of any kind provided or to be provided by the person by whom or on whose behalf the money is accepted; or (c) it is paid by way of security for the delivery up or return of any property, whether in a particular state of repair or otherwise.

(7) Any person who accepts a deposit in contravention of subsection (1) above shall be liable—(a) on summary conviction to a fine not exceeding the statutory

maximum; and (b) on conviction on indictment to imprisonment for a term not exceeding two years or to a fine or both.

(8) The fact that a deposit is taken in contravention of this section shall not affect any civil liability arising in respect of the deposit or the money deposited.'

However, s 2 exempts from the prohibition the Bank of England, banks 'recognised' under the Act and other institutions 'licensed' thereunder and also persons for the time being specified in Sch 1. It enables the Treasury to add or remove persons to or from the Sch 1 list by statutory instrument. So far as material, s 2 provides:

'(1) The prohibition in section 1(1) above on the acceptance of a deposit does not apply to—(a) the Bank; or (b) a recognised bank; or (c) a licensed institution; or (d) a person for the time being specified in Schedule 1 to this Act; and does not apply to a transaction prescribed for the purposes of this section by regulations made by the Treasury.

(2) The Treasury may from time to time by order made by statutory instrument— (a) add a person to the list set out in Schedule 1 to this Act, or (b) remove a person from that list (whether that person was included in the list as originally enacted or was added to it by virtue of this subsection) . . .

(5) Regulations under subsection (1) above may prescribe transactions by reference to any factors appearing to the Treasury to be appropriate and, in particular, by reference to all or any of the following, namely—(a) the amount of the deposit; (b) the total liability of the body concerned to its depositors; (c) the circumstances in which or the purpose for which the deposit is made; and (d) the identity of the person by whom the deposit is made or accepted . . .'

Section 3 of the Act and Sch 2 set out the criteria for recognition and licensing. Schedule 1 contains 14 multifarious exemptions, of which we merely mention two by way of example: 'A member of the Stock Exchange in the course of business as a stockbroker or stock jobber' and 'A local authority'.

The Treasury, in the exercise of the powers conferred on them by s 2(1) and (5), have made a number of sets of regulations. The first were the Banking Act 1979 (Exempt Transactions) Regulations 1979, SI 1979/1204. However, they have been added to and amended by, inter alia, the Banking Act 1979 (Exempt Transactions) (Amendment) Regulations 1983, SI 1983/510. These were made on 30 March 1983, laid before Parliament on 5 April 1983 and came into operation on 26 April 1983 (shortly after the trading relationship between SCF and Mr Masri began). They inserted in the principal regulations a new reg 14 and Sch 3. The new reg 14 provided, inter alia:

'(1) The acceptance by a member of a market organisation listed in Part 1 of Schedule 3 to these Regulations (in this Regulation described as a "broker") of a deposit from a client is an exempt transaction if the deposit is taken either:—(a) as security in respect of any loss which the broker may incur as a result of entering into a contract to which this paragraph applies or of the client's failure to perform an obligation under such a contract; or (b) on terms that it will be repaid on demand if it is not applied by the broker:—(i) as security as described in sub-paragraph (a) above, or (ii) on behalf of the client, as consideration under a contract to which this paragraph applies . . .

(4) The acceptance by a body listed in Part 2 of Schedule 3 to these Regulations of a deposit by a member of that body is an exempt transaction.'

Part 1 of the new Sch 3 included 16 large and important market organisations (but not SCF). Part 2 included the Grain and Feed Trade Association Ltd and the International Commodities Clearing House Ltd. Finally, the Treasury, on 14 December 1983, made the Banking Act 1979 (Exempt Transactions) Regulations 1983, SI 1983/1865, which repealed all the previous regulations referred to and consolidated them with amendments.

These regulations reproduced reg 14 referred to above. We will henceforth refer to it
a simply as 'reg 14'.

We pause to make these general comments on s 1 of the Act. It does not render
unlawful the carrying on of 'a deposit-taking business' as such. What sub-s (1) of s 1 does
is to render unlawful a specific act, that is to say, the acceptance of 'a deposit in the course
of carrying on a business which is a deposit-taking business for the purposes of this Act'.
If, therefore, the transactions between SCF and Mr Masri have not involved the acceptance
b of any 'deposit' in the relevant sense by SCF, it matters not whether the business of SCF is
(or is not) a 'deposit-taking business' within the relevant meaning.

Have SCF accepted 'deposits' from Mr Masri?

The first inquiry must therefore be whether SCF have accepted from Mr Masri
c 'deposits' in the relevant sense. In view of s 1(4)(b) of the 1979 Act, a sum of money paid
to SCF on terms which *are* 'referable to the provision of property or services or to the
giving of security' is incapable of constituting a 'deposit' in the relevant sense. In view of
s 1(6)(b) of the Act, a sum of money 'paid by way of security for payment for the provision
of property or services of any kind provided or to be provided by the person by whom or
on whose behalf the money is accepted' is incapable of constituting a 'deposit' within the
d meaning of the section. SCF submit that on the evidence the so-called deposits on which
Mr Masri relies for the purpose of his argument are 'paid by way of security for payment
for the provision of property or services . . . provided or to be provided by [SCF]'. If this
contention is well founded, it must by itself dispose of this appeal. We therefore begin
by considering it.

It is common ground between counsel that the sums in question were paid to SCF on
e terms which were referable to the giving of security. If, therefore, s 1(4)(b) stood alone, it
would dispose of the plea of illegality. However, the crucial question is, security for
what? For the exemption apparently conferred by the wider general words of s 1(4)(b) is
circumscribed by the limiting provisions of s 1(6). Though at one stage in his argument
counsel for SCF placed some reliance on para (a) of s 1(6), that paragraph in our judgment
cannot apply on the facts of the present case, if only because of the presence in the
f paragraph of the word 'only'. If SCF are successfully to invoke s 1(4)(b) for the purpose of
establishing that the relevant sums were not deposits, they must show that the payments
fall within s 1(6)(b).

Counsel for Mr Masri forcefully submitted that it could not properly be said that these
sums had been paid 'by way of security for payment for the provision of property or
services of any kind provided or to be provided by [SCF]'. He stressed that the particular
g arrangements made between SCF and Mr Masri involved SCF giving him substantial
continuing credit, and thus, in his submission, the making of loans. He also pointed out
(correctly in our judgment) that the benefit of the contracts of sale and purchase into
which SCF entered on behalf of Mr Masri would themselves constitute the *primary*
security for the repayment of any moneys which might be due from him to SCF on the
closing out of his account, since these contracts would be included in the property
h charged to SCF by virtue of cl 8 of the customer agreement and SCF would have the right
to enforce their security under that clause for the purpose of wholly or partially
recovering any such sums which might be due to them. In these circumstances, he
submitted, on a true analysis the sums in question were paid as security for the repayment
to SCF (a) of the moneys lent by them to Mr Masri and (b) of any deficiency which the
primary security afforded by cl 8 of the customer agreement might be insufficient to
j cover. Essentially, he submitted, the sums in question had been paid to secure repayment
of the loans made by SCF and to secure them against shortfall losses. Accordingly, in
counsel's submission, the sums could not properly be said to have been 'paid by way of
security for the provision of property or services of any kind provided or to be provided
by [SCF]'.

Counsel for Mr Masri sought to draw support for his submissions on the construction and effect of s 1(6)(b) from the provisions of the new reg 14. In his submission, that *a* regulation demonstrated the opinion of the legislature that, in default of the new regulation, the acceptance by a broker of a deposit in respect of a loss which he might incur as a result of entering into a contract on behalf of his client would otherwise constitute a 'deposit' for the purpose of s 1(1) of the Act.

We think there are two answers to the latter submission. First, the decision of the House of Lords in *Jackson v Hall* [1980] 1 All ER 177, [1980] AC 854 appears to establish *b* that rules made in the exercise of a statutory power, at least where not affirmatively approved by Parliament (as the regulations in the present case were not) cannot be relied on as an aid to the construction of the statute. Second, we agree with the judge that the purpose of the regulation may well have been merely the unequivocal validation, for the avoidance of doubt, of the acceptance of deposits in the course of transactions on recognised commodity markets (see [1986] 1 All ER 40 at 52), so that on any footing the *c* regulations would have afforded no sure guide to the construction of s 1.

However, the primary submissions of counsel for Mr Masri in relation to s 1(6)(b) require and deserve careful consideration. First, it is necessary to identify the nature of the services which SCF afforded to Mr Masri. On every occasion when on his instructions they entered into a contract of purchase or sale, SCF themselves assumed the liability under such contract to the broker. They themselves were immediately on risk as soon as *d* it was concluded. Furthermore, even though they allowed Mr Masri credit in respect of margins, they themselves were obliged, in accordance with accepted custom, immediately to put up a margin to the broker with whom they dealt (who would not allow them credit), and thereafter, so far as necessary, to put up further sums by way of maintenance. In these circumstances, we think that counsel for SCF was right in submitting that, on their true analysis, essentially the services which SCF afforded to Mr Masri comprised *e* three constituents, that is to say (i) the entering into the various contracts of sale and purchase (for which they were entitled to commission), (ii) the extending of credit (for which they were entitled to interest) and (iii) the acceptance of the risk of loss and of primary liability to the broker (in respect of which they were entitled to be indemnified). On the rare occasions when the contracts of purchase entered into by SCF for Mr Masri *f* resulted in the actual delivery of the physical commodity, SCF were, in our judgment, 'providing property' for Mr Masri and to this extent the sums in question were paid by Mr Masri 'by way of security for payment for the provision of property . . . to be provided' by SCF. However, in the usual case of a contract of sale or purchase which had no such result, SCF were, in our opinion, 'providing services' for Mr Masri so that the large balance of the sums paid were paid 'by way of security for payment for the provision of *g* services . . . to be provided' by SCF. Counsel for Mr Masri sought to draw a distinction between the payment for services or property on the one hand and reimbursement of losses or interest payments on the other hand. In the present case the distinction does not, in our judgment, exist. The incurring of the relevant risks and consequent losses and the extension of incidental credit in the course of their dealings were parts of the services which SCF offered to, and were accepted by, Mr Masri. In our judgment, *h* therefore, SCF are right in submitting that the moneys in question were paid 'by way of security for payment for the provision of property or services . . . to be provided' by SCF within the meaning of s 1(6)(b) of the Act.

The purpose and effect of the section is to impose criminal liability on any person who accepts a deposit in breach of its provisions. Though civil liability alone is an issue in the present case, Mr Masri's argument inevitably involves the contention that SCF have been *j* in breach of the criminal law. If the construction of the section gave rise to any real doubt or ambiguity, the court should in our judgment, in accordance with established principles, lean against a construction which involved the imposition of criminal liability. However, we do not think the section does give rise to ambiguity in the present instance. Whatever canon of construction is applied, we regard the words of s 1(6)(b) as capable of

only one sensible meaning in relation to the facts of this case. Putting the matter very
shortly, the words 'paid by way of security for payment for the provision of property'
must on any footing include moneys paid to SCF which could be used by way of security
to protect them against the risk that Mr Masri might default in reimbursing them for
any expense which they had properly incurred in carrying out their contractual duty to
buy property in order to provide it to Mr Masri. So, equally, the words 'payment for the
provision of services' cannot sensibly bear any meaning other than that they include any
expense which SCF have incurred in carrying out their contractually agreed services.
Those services included making payments as required by the contractually accepted rules
and regulations of the futures market, in respect of which (as part of the consideration
for providing those services) Mr Masri is contractually bound to indemnify them. Default
by Mr Masri in performing that contractual obligation is a risk in respect of which the
security is given.

It follows that the moneys in question were not 'deposits' within the definition
contained in s 1(4). On this ground, if no other, Mr Masri's defence to the proceedings
based on s 1(1) of the 1979 Act must fail.

Is the business of SCF a deposit-taking business?

However, in case this conclusion should be wrong, we will proceed to consider the two
further or alternative principal grounds on which SCF submit that the same result must
ensue, even if, contrary to their submission and our conclusion, the sums received by
them from Mr Masri constituted 'deposits' as defined by s 1(4) and (6) of the Act. The
first of these two points arises as follows.

The prohibition imposed by s 1(2) is against the acceptance of a deposit 'in the course
of carrying on a business which is a deposit-taking business for the purposes of this Act'.
By virtue of sub-s (2) and subject to sub-s (3), a business is a deposit-taking business for
the purposes of this Act if—

> '(a) in the course of the business money received by way of deposit is lent to
> others, or (b) any other activity of the business is financed, wholly or to any material
> extent, out of the capital of or the interest on money received by way of deposit.'

The conditions in paras (a) and (b) are alternative conditions. Though counsel for SCF did
not accept this, we think that on the assumption that the receipts in question and the
other similar receipts from SCF's other customers constituted moneys 'received by way
of deposit', the condition in para (a) at least is satisfied. The evidence shows that the
deposits received, being commingled in SCF's general account with other moneys, were
from time to time lent to others.

However, even if the condition in para (a) or that in para (b) applies to a business, sub-s
(3) exempts it from being a 'deposit-taking business' if in the normal course of the
business—

> '(a) the person carrying it on does not hold himself out to accept deposits on a day
> to day basis; and (b) any deposits which are accepted are accepted only on particular
> occasions, whether or not involving the issue of debentures or other securities.'

SCF submits that, if the sums in question constitute 'deposits', the words just quoted
are a precisely accurate description of the normal course of their business. This is the
second of the three principal grounds on which they reply to the defence based on s 1(1).

In the context of s 1(3), the submissions of counsel for Mr Masri to the contrary were
essentially to the following effect. He pointed out that SCF unquestionably carry on their
business as commodity brokers on a day-to-day basis and hold themselves out as so doing.
Furthermore, as cl 4 of the customer agreement illustrates, the terms on which they offer
their services to their clients require the clients (unless they are given credit) to furnish
and maintain such deposits as SCF may require. More or less daily they will be demanding
and accepting deposits from one client or another. In these circumstances, he submitted,

SCF are 'holding themselves out to accept deposits on a day-to-day basis' in the sense of s 1(3)(a). In the context of s 1(3)(b), he pointed out that, according to the evidence, SCF at the material time had thirty small clients, five large clients and, in addition, the clients represented by two banks. There has, he suggested, been a regular flow of deposits from one or more of these clients, in such a way as to render the receipt of deposits part of the ordinary course of SCF's business; in view of SCF's mode of trading, the possibility of a demand and receipt of a deposit from any client arises every working day. In the submission of counsel for Mr Masri, it cannot therefore be said that any deposits which are accepted are accepted 'only on particular occasions' within s 1(3) of the Act.

The Act gives no guidance as to the construction of s 1(3) beyond that afforded by the wording of the subsection itself. In our judgment, however (without attempting any comprehensive definition of the phrase), on the ordinary meaning of the words, a person 'holds himself out to accept deposits on a day to day basis' only if (by way of an express or implicit invitation) he holds himself out as being generally willing on any normal working day to accept such deposits from those persons to whom the invitation is addressed who may wish to place moneys with him by way of deposit. There is no evidence that SCF have done this in the present case. They have held themselves out as being willing on a day-to-day basis to enter into customer agreements with customers whom they regard as suitable, the terms of these agreements being such that SCF as agents will enter into transactions on behalf of the clients and will from time to time demand deposits as they may be required, having regard to the clients' instructions. However, the initiative leading to the payment of the several deposits will in each case come from SCF rather than the customer. This, it seems to us, does not involve any 'holding out' by SCF in the sense of s 1(3)(a).

For similar reasons, in our judgment the occasions on which SCF accept deposits from their trading customers are properly to be regarded as 'particular occasions' within the meaning of s 1(3)(b). The particular occasions will be those occasions on which SCF find it necessary or advisable for their own protection to demand deposits, having regard to the course of the trading carried out and to be carried out by them in accordance with their clients' instructions. The mere fact that these occasions may be numerous does not render them any less 'particular' within the meaning of s 1(3)(b).

The deposits received by the Iraqi customers, in our view, cannot possibly deprive SCF of any exemption to which they may be otherwise entitled under s 1(3). They were indubitably accepted on particular occasions, when they parent company requested them to accept them. They involved no 'holding out'.

Counsel for Mr Masri submitted that the burden of proof falls on SCF to show that they are entitled to the exemption afforded by s 1(3) and that they have not discharged this onus. We believe that no evidence called on behalf of SCF at the trial was specifically directed to the provisions of s 1(3). Nevertheless, a lot of evidence was given, in particular by Mr Chalabi, as to the manner in which SCF carried on their business and Mr Masri of course had the opportunity to test this evidence by cross-examination. On the construction which we place on s 1(3), and on the balance of probabilities, we hold that SCF's business is not a deposit-taking business for the purposes of the 1979 Act.

The effect of any relevant illegality

This conclusion, if correct, must again dispose of this appeal. Nevertheless, in case it be wrong, we turn to the last of the three principal grounds on which SCF answer the defence of illegality, which was ultimately the only ground relied on by the judge in dismissing Mr Masri's claim. He considered that there was 'much to be said' for the arguments advanced on behalf of SCF to the effect that they were not in contravention of s 1 of the 1979 Act. He said that if he were obliged to resolve these issues, he would have been disposed to do so in SCF's favour (see [1986] 1 All ER 40 at 52). However, he preferred to decide the case on a simpler ground.

For present purposes, let it be assumed against SCF that they have unlawfully accepted

deposits in the course of carrying on a business which is a deposit-taking business in
a breach of s 1 of the Act. Nevertheless, in SCF's submission, while on the stated assumption
s 1(7) would expose them to certain statutory penalties, the Act does not affect any civil
liability arising in respect of the deposit or the money deposited; still less does it affect
the validity of the contracts for commodity and financial futures in respect of which SCF
claim against Mr Masri.

On the same assumption, however, counsel for Mr Masri made contrary submissions
b on the following lines. The contract between the parties (cl 4 of the customer agreement)
provided for the commission by SCF (though Mr Masri was unaware of this) of the very
thing which s 1(1) expressly prohibited, namely the acceptance of deposits by a person
carrying on a deposit-taking business. SCF were thus committing an unlawful act in
entering into the contract. Since the illegality derived from the conduct of one party
only, namely SCF, and the ultimate intention of the Act is to protect the customer, there
c is no warrant for reading into the Act any intention to deprive customers such as Mr
Masri of his rights and remedies under the contract. His rights and remedies would be
preserved. However, the illegality on the part of SCF in effecting and carrying out the
contract, so it was submitted, deprived SCF themselves of any right to enforce it. In this
context counsel for Mr Masri particularly relied on the recent decision of Hobhouse J in
Phoenix General Insurance Co of Greece SA v Halvanon Insurance Co Ltd [1986] 1 All ER 908,
d whose reasoning, mutatis mutandis, he adopted.

Further, or alternatively, counsel for Mr Masri pointed out that SCF's claim to the right
under cl 8 of the customer agreement to close down Mr Masri's account and hold him
liable for the deficiency arose because he had declined to put up the further deposits
which had been demanded of him under cl 4. The result, in his submission, must be that
SCF have no cause of action. In this context he invoked the statement of the law by
e Denning LJ in *Marles v Philip Trant & Sons Ltd (MacKinnon, third party) (No 2)* [1953] 1
All ER 651 at 658, [1954] 1 QB 29 at 38:

'So far as the cause of action itself is concerned, the principle is well settled that, if
the plaintiff requires any aid from an illegal transaction to establish his cause of
action, then he shall not have any aid from the court.'

The *Phoenix* decision was given after Leggatt J had given judgment in the present case.
It was the last of a line of three recent decisions which all concerned the effect of contracts
entered into with persons carrying on business in breach of the provisions of the
Insurance Companies Act 1974. The two earlier decisions were those of Parker J in
g *Bedford Insurance Co Ltd v Instituto de Resseguros do Brasil* [1984] 3 All ER 766, [1985] QB
966 and of Leggatt J, who declined to follow that decision, in *Stewart v Oriental Fire and
Marine Insurance Co Ltd* [1984] 3 All ER 777, [1985] QB 988, but, at the invitation of
SCF's counsel, followed his own decision in *Stewart* in the present case. In the *Phoenix*
decision, which we understand is now under appeal, Hobhouse J in effect followed a
middle course between the two earlier, conflicting decisions.

h All these three recent cases contain a helpful review of some of the earlier authorities.
Nevertheless, we think, with respect, that for the purposes of the present appeal we can
derive only very limited assistance from their rationes decidendi, and that detailed
discussion of them would achieve no useful purpose. For the facts of these cases were
very different. The statute, or statutes, there under consideration rendered unlawful not
a specific class of act or transaction, but the carrying out of a specific class of (insurance)
j business.

In considering the effect of any illegality which may have been involved in the
acceptance of moneys by SCF from Mr Masri, in our opinion, it is sufficient for us to
follow the now well-established principles which are stated by Devlin J in *St John Shipping
Corp v Joseph Rank Ltd* [1956] 3 All ER 683 at 690, [1957] 1 QB 267 at 288, and were cited
by the judge in his judgment ([1986] 1 All ER 40 at 52–53):

'A court should not hold that any contract or class of contracts is prohibited by statute unless there is a clear implication, or "necessary inference", as PARKE, B., put *a* it [in *Cope v Rowlands* (1836) 2 M & W 149 at 159, 150 ER 707 at 711], that the statute so intended. If a contract has as its whole object the doing of the very act which the statute prohibits, it can be argued that you can hardly make sense of a statute which forbids an act and yet permits to be made a contract to do it; that is a clear implication. But unless you get a clear implication of that sort, I think that a court ought to be very slow to hold that a statute intends to interfere with the rights *b* and remedies given by the ordinary law of contract. Caution in this respect is, I think, especially necessary in these times when so much of commercial life is governed by regulations of one sort or another which may easily be broken without wicked intent. Persons who deliberately set out to break the law cannot expect to be aided in a court of justice, but it is a different matter when the law if unwittingly broken. To nullify a bargain in such circumstances frequently means that in a *c* case—perhaps of such triviality that no authority would have felt it worth while to prosecute—a seller, because he cannot enforce his civil rights, may forfeit a sum vastly in excess of any penalty that a criminal court would impose; and the sum forfeited will not go into the public purse but into the pockets of someone who is lucky enough to pick up the windfall or astute enough to have contrived to get it. It is questionable how far this contributes to public morality. In *Vita Food Products,* *d* *Inc. v. Unus Shipping Co., Ltd.* ([1939] 1 All ER 513 at 523, [1939] AC 277 at 293), LORD WRIGHT said: "Nor must it be forgotten that the rule by which contracts not expressly forbidden by statute or declared to be void are in proper cases nullified for disobedience to a statute is a rule of public policy only, and public policy understood in a wider sense may at times be better served by refusing to nullify a bargain save on serious and sufficient grounds."' *e*

Even if the Act did not contain s 1(8), the court therefore should be very slow to hold that the Act intended to interfere with the rights and remedies given to the parties by the ordinary law of contract. However, s 1(8), in our judgment, provides a conclusive answer to Mr Masri's arguments that the (assumed) illegal conduct of SCF deprives them of any right to enforce the contract with Mr Masri. In this context we found convincing *f* the following submissions made by junior counsel on behalf of SCF. While s 1(1) and (7) renders it a statutory offence to accept deposits in the course of carrying on a deposit-taking business, s 1(1) conspicuously does not expressly render unlawful the contract pursuant to which deposits are taken. Section 1(8) expressly demonstrates the intention of the legislature that the fact that a deposit taken in contravention of the section 'shall not affect any civil liability arising in respect of the deposit or the money deposited'. A *g* fortiori the legislature cannot have intended that this fact should affect any civil liability arising in respect of the contract pursuant to which the deposit is taken, particularly when that contract does not have as its *object* the taking of deposits, but the taking of the deposits is a merely incidental feature (compare *St John Shipping Corp v Joseph Rank Ltd* [1956] 3 All ER 683 at 692, [1957] 1 QB 267 at 291 per Devlin J). In these circumstances, in the submission of junior counsel for SCF, s 1(8) throws the clearest light on the *h* construction of the Act; it makes plain the legislature's intention that the respective rights and remedies of the parties under the ordinary law of contract should not be affected even though a deposit had been taken in contravention of the section.

We think these submissions are well founded. We are unable to accept the submission of counsel for Mr Masri that s 1(8) refers only to the civil liability *of the depositee* 'in respect of the deposit or the money deposited'. While more often than not such liability would *j* be that of the depositee, civil liability on the part of the depositor could also arise in respect of the deposit and we can see no sufficient grounds for excluding such liability from the operation of the section. If the legislature had intended to refer only to civil liability on the part of the depositee, it would surely have said so.

Our conclusion on the issue of illegality is thus the same as that stated by the judge
([1986] 1 All ER 40 at 53):

> '. . . even assuming that [SCF] were in contravention of s 1 of the 1979 Act, [Mr
> Masri's] civil liability to them is unaffected by it. This defence therefore fails.
> Similarly, the payments which [Mr Masri] has already made have been lawfully
> applied by [SCF] on his behalf as consideration under the contracts entered into for
> him. Even if those payments were made in contravention of s 1 of the Act, civil
> liability in respect of the money paid is not affected. It is irrecoverable, and the
> counterclaim fails under this head.'

Before leaving the case we should say that we wish to leave open any consideration of
the legal effect (in particular as to the applicability of s 1(8)) if parties were to enter into a
transaction in contravention of s 1 of the Act and one or both parties in so doing were
well aware that illegality was involved. In this context, we should perhaps refer briefly
to a piece of history on which some reliance was placed by counsel for Mr Masri in
argument. On 18 May 1983 the Bank of England wrote a circular letter to all licensed
dealers in securities, including SCF, who are not recognised banks or licensed institutions
under the Act. The purpose of the letter was to remind such licensed dealers of the
implications of the Act for the conduct of their securities' business. It enclosed an 'aide-
memoire' which suggested, inter alia, that any deposits accepted might be placed,
without first having been used in any way, in a segregated account with the dealers' usual
bankers. On 13 January 1984 a meeting took place between respective representatives of
SCF and the Bank of England. Notes of the meeting record Mr Chalabi as saying:

> 'Mr Chalabi pointed out that we passed on to the broker the margin moneys we
> received from the client; however the fact that we paid into our account the margin
> money and paid it out to the broker showed we were acting as principal and were
> caught by the Act.'

Following this meeting, however, SCF took advice from their then solicitors, Messrs
Coward Chance, who apparently advised them that the payment in question could fairly
be regarded as falling within the class of payments which under s 1(6) of the Act do not
fall within the definition of 'deposit'. Notwithstanding this advice, SCF agreed with the
Bank of England that moneys received by them from clients in respect of commodity
transactions would in the future be paid into a segregated account with SCF's bankers.

Counsel for Mr Masri submitted that the notes of the meeting of 13 January 1984
show that as at that date SCF thought they were in breach of the Act. We are not
convinced that the evidence establishes this much, still less that they thought this at any
earlier date than that. Even if it does, however, in our judgment this is irrelevant to the
issues which we have to decide. The opinion as to the legal position attributed to Mr
Chalabi was, in our judgment, erroneous. The advice subsequently given by Coward
Chance as to the application of s 1(6) of the Act was correct. There is no possibility of Mr
Chalabi's statement giving rise to any binding admission or estoppel.

For the reasons stated above, we conclude that Mr Masri's defence based on s 1 of the
1979 Act is ill-founded for each of the three reasons principally relied on by SCF and that
his counterclaim must inevitably fail likewise. We dismiss this appeal.

Appeal dismissed. Leave to appeal to the House of Lords refused.

Solicitors: *Herbert Oppenheimer Nathan & Vandyk* (for Mr Masri); *Elborne Mitchell & Co*
(for SCF).

Wendy Shockett   Barrister.

SCF Finance Co Ltd v Masri and another   *a* (No 3) (Masri, garnishee)

COURT OF APPEAL, CIVIL DIVISION

SLADE, RALPH GIBSON LJJ AND SIR JOHN MEGAW

11, 12, 13 JUNE, 16 JULY 1986

b

Estoppel – Issue estoppel – Dismissal of application – Applicant not proceeding with application – Applicant not conceding issue but acknowledging that application would be dismissed – Whether applicant estopped from raising issue in subsequent garnishee proceedings.

Execution – Garnishee order – Person within jurisdiction indebted to judgment debtor – Plaintiff   *c* *seeking to attach debt due to defendant in Jordan – Garnishee out of jurisdiction when order nisi made – Garnishee instructing solicitors to accept service of proceedings – Whether garnishee a 'person within jurisdiction' – Whether garnishee 'indebted' to defendant – RSC Ord 49, r 1(1).*

In an action in which the plaintiffs claimed $US910,031 from the defendant, a Jordanian national, the plaintiffs obtained a Mareva injunction pending trial of the action. The *d* assets made subject to the injunction included a dollar bank account in the name of the defendant's wife, who applied to have the injunction set aside so far as it related to the dollar account, on the ground that she and not the defendant was the beneficial owner. The sole issue raised by the wife's application was, as she conceded, the ownership of the dollar account. The hearing of the wife's application on the merits was fixed for 8 July 1985. On 4 July judgment was given for the plaintiffs in their action against the *e* defendant. In the course of his judgment the judge rejected the defendant's evidence and when the wife's application came on for hearing on 8 July before the same judge she decided, without formally withdrawing it, not to proceed with the application because of the judge's attitude towards her husband's evidence in the plaintiffs' action and because he intended to appeal. She stated through counsel that she did not concede the issue of ownership of the dollar account and expressly reserved that issue but she acknowledged *f* that the consequence of not proceeding would be that her application would be dismissed. Her application was then dismissed. On the same day, while the husband and wife and their advisers were still in court, the plaintiffs applied ex parte under RSC Ord 49, r 1[a] for a garnishee order against the wife to attach the dollar account. The plaintiffs contended that the dismissal of the wife's application raised an issue estoppel which precluded her from further contesting the issue of ownership of the dollar account and *g* that the dismissal accordingly established that the account belonged to the defendant and was therefore available for execution to satisfy the plaintiffs' judgment against the defendant. The wife's counsel invited the court not to make any order that day and informed the court that the wife had instructed her solicitors to accept service of any garnishee proceedings. The application was served on the wife and adjourned to the following day, 9 July, but on the morning of 9 July the wife left England for Jordan and *h* was not in the jurisdiction when the garnishee application came on for hearing. The judge made an order nisi against the wife attaching the dollar account and at a subsequent hearing made the order absolute on the grounds (i) that the wife was a 'person within the jurisdiction [who was] indebted to the judgment debtor' for the purposes of Ord 49, r 1(1) despite not being within the jurisdiction when the order nisi was made, because *j* she had agreed to service of the garnishee proceedings on her solicitors, and (ii) the wife was precluded by issue estoppel arising out of the dismissal of her application from raising the issue of ownership of the dollar account in the garnishee proceedings. The wife appealed.

***

a   Rule 1, so far as material, is set out at p 201 *h j*, post

Held – The wife's appeal would be dismissed for the following reasons—

a (1) An order dismissing proceedings, even where there had been no argument or evidence directed to the merits of the case, was capable of giving rise to an issue estoppel if the litigant had put forward a positive case as the basis for applying for the relief sought in the proceedings but at trial had declined to continue with the proceedings and had submitted to the order dismissing them. Furthermore, the fact that on the dismissal of the proceedings the litigant had expressly reserved the very issue that was to have been

b tried did not necessarily prevent the general rule of res judicata applying, namely that it was an abuse of process to raise in subsequent proceedings an issue which could have been litigated in earlier proceedings. In all the circumstances, the wife's fear of the judge being adversely disposed to her had been irrational and she knew the consequences of not proceeding with her application to vary the injunction. Accordingly, the res judicata rule applied, notwithstanding the wife's reservation of the issue of ownership of the

c dollar account. It followed that the wife was prevented by issue estoppel from contending in the garnishee proceedings that the dollar account belonged to her and thus was not available for attachment, and accordingly in the garnishee proceedings the account was to be treated as belonging to the defendant (see p 208 e g j to p 209a, post); *Yat Tung Investment Co Ltd v Dao Heng Bank Ltd* [1975] AC 581 and *Khan v Goleccha International Ltd* [1980] 2 All ER 259 applied.

d (2) The wife was a 'person within the jurisdiction' for the purposes of RSC Ord 49, r 1(1) even though she was not within the jurisdiction when the order nisi was made, since her voluntary submission to the jurisdiction by agreeing to accept service of the garnishee proceedings on her solicitors was sufficient to make her, as garnishee, 'a person within the jurisdiction' within r 1(1) (see p 204 b to f, post); dictum of Mustill LJ in *Rothmans of Pall Mall (Overseas) Ltd v Saudi Arabian Airlines Corp* [1980] 3 All ER at 364

e applied.

(3) The wife was a person 'indebted' to the defendant as the judgment debtor for the purposes of RSC Ord 49, r 1(1) because the effect of the issue estoppel arising out of the dismissal of the wife's application was that as between the wife and the defendant the debt due from the bank to the wife in respect of the dollar account was a debt due to the defendant. Furthermore, if such indebtedness was in Jordan and therefore outside the

f jurisdiction that only went to discretion rather than jurisdiction to make the garnishee order. The account was accordingly available for attachment against the wife in the garnishee proceedings to satisfy the judgment debt due from the defendant to the plaintiffs (see p 205 b c g to p 206 f j, post); *Swiss Bank Corp v Boehmische Industrial Bank* [1923] 1 KB 673 applied; *Richardson v Richardson* [1927] All ER Rep 92 considered.

g **Notes**

For issue estoppel, see 16 Halsbury's Laws (4th edn) para 1530, and for cases on the subject, see 21 Digest (Reissue) 43–50, 287–316.

For the requirement that the garnishee be within the jurisdiction, see 17 Halsbury's Laws (4th edn) para 526, and for a case on the subject, see 21 Digest (Reissue) 456, 3609.

h **Cases referred to in judgment**

Carl-Zeiss-Stiftung v Rayner and Keeler (No 2) [1966] 2 All ER 536, [1967] 1 AC 853, [1966] 3 WLR 125, HL.

Khan v Goleccha International Ltd [1980] 2 All ER 259, [1980] 1 WLR 1482, CA.

Martin v Nadel (Dresdner Bank, garnishees) [1906] 2 KB 26, [1904–7] All ER Rep 827, CA.

j *Ord v Ord* [1923] 2 KB 432, [1923] All ER Rep 206, DC.

Richardson v Richardson [1927] P 228, [1927] All ER Rep 92.

Rothmans of Pall Mall (Overseas) Ltd v Saudi Arabian Airlines Corp [1980] 3 All ER 359, [1981] QB 368, [1980] 3 WLR 642, QBD and CA.

SCF Finance Co Ltd v Masri (No 2) [1987] 1 All ER 175, CA; *affg* [1986] 1 All ER 40.

Swiss Bank Corp v Boehmische Industrial Bank [1923] 1 KB 673, CA.

Yat Tung Investment Co Ltd v Dao Heng Bank Ltd [1975] AC 581, [1975] 2 WLR 690, PC.

Appeal

Mrs Ina'am Masri, the garnishee, appealed with the leave of the judge against a garnishee   *a*
order absolute made by Leggatt J on 25 July 1985 ordering that Mrs Masri pay the
judgment creditor, SCF Finance Co Ltd (SCF), the sum of $US400,000 and costs of the
garnishee proceedings, and sought an order that the order of 25 July be set aside and the
garnishee order nisi made by the judge on 9 July 1985 be discharged or, alternatively,
that the matter be remitted to the court below for trial of such question as might be
appropriate and for consideration whether a garnishee order absolute should be made.   *b*
The principal grounds of appeal were (i) that the judge was wrong in law in holding that
Mrs Masri was a person within the jurisdiction for the purposes of RSC Ord 49, r 1(1), (ii)
that the judge had failed to consider whether she was indebted, if at all, within the
jurisdiction as required by Ord 49, r 1(1), (iii) that the judge was therefore wrong in law
in holding that the court had jurisdiction pursuant to Ord 49, r 1 to make a garnishee
order against her and (iv) that the judge was wrong in law in holding that she was   *c*
estopped from contending that the sum of $US400,000 held in an account in her name
with Arab Bank Ltd belonged to her and consequently that she was indebted to the
judgment debtor, her husband, Mr Khalil Said Masri, within Ord 49, r 1(1). The facts are
set out in the judgment of the court.

Stanley Brodie QC and *Christopher Moger* for Mrs Masri.   *d*
Nicholas Lyell QC, Richard Aikens QC and *Richard Lord* for SCF.

Cur adv vult

16 July. The following judgment of the court was delivered.
      e
RALPH GIBSON LJ. On 4 July 1985 Leggatt J gave judgment for SCF Finance Co Ltd
(SCF) for $910,031·70, together with interest thereon, as sums due from the first
defendant (Mr Masri) and rising out of transactions conducted for Mr Masri by SCF (see
SCF Finance Co Ltd v Masri (No 2) [1986] 1 All ER 40). Mr Masri's appeal against that
judgment, based on the contention that the taking of deposits by SCF under the terms of
their customer agreement was in breach of s 1 of the Banking Act 1979, has been   *f*
dismissed for the reasons set out in the judgment of this court (see [1987] 1 All ER 175).
This second appeal was brought by the second defendant (Mrs Masri), the wife of Mr
Masri, against the order made by Leggatt J on 25 July 1985 whereby he directed Mrs
Masri to pay to SCF the sum of $400,000 and the costs of the garnishee proceedings
against her in which that order was made. At the request of both sides the court heard
the argument on the second appeal immediately following, and before the decision of,   *g*
the first appeal.
      The garnishee proceedings were concerned with the sum of $400,000 or thereabouts
standing in an account (we refer to the relevant account or accounts as one) in Mrs Masri's
name with the United Arab Bank Ltd at their branch at St Martin's le Grand in London.
The decision of the judge was that, since that sum of money (the dollar account) was in
truth the property of Mr Masri, although in the name of Mrs Masri and claimed by her   *h*
to be her own property, it was a debt due from Mrs Masri to her husband and available
to be attached in garnishee proceedings under RSC Ord 49 towards payment of Mr
Masri's judgment debt to SCF. The decision of the judge was made without there having
been any trial on the merits of the issue whether Mrs Masri or her husband was the
beneficial owner of the dollar account. The decision was based on issue estoppel: in the
events which had happened Mrs Masri was held to be estopped from asserting that the   *j*
beneficial ownership of the dollar account was other than in her husband. The estoppel
was held to have arisen against Mrs Masri because she had made an application to the
court for the setting aside of a Mareva injunction, in so far as it affected her, on the
ground that the dollar account was her own separate property and not that of her
husband; and then, when her application was called on for trial, she had declined to

proceed with it and had accepted that it be dismissed. By her appeal Mrs Masri has
a contended that the garnishee proceedings against her were entertained by the court, and
judgment given in those proceedings, without jurisdiction; and that, in any event,
Leggatt J was wrong to hold that the estoppel had been raised against her. Before
considering the submissions of the parties it is necessary to state the sequence of the
events which happened. This must be done in detail as to some aspects of the story, and,
in particular, for the purpose of examining what issue or issues, if any, was or were
b conclusively resolved against Mrs Masri when her application was dismissed, and whether
at the relevant time Mrs Masri was 'within the jurisdiction' for the purposes of Ord 49.

The course of the proceedings

(i) The proceedings against Mr Masri were begun by writ issued on 7 February 1984.
Leave had been obtained on 6 February 1984 to serve the writ on Mr Masri in Amman
c in Jordan. At the same time SCF applied for relief by way of Mareva injunction. By order
of 6 February it was ordered that, on the usual undertakings as to damages, Mr Masri 'be
restrained . . . from removing from the jurisdiction . . . or otherwise dealing with any of
[his] assets within the jurisdiction . . . so as to reduce the value of his assets . . . below the
sum of £700,000 . . .', and the order was to apply to 'any . . . accounts held by or on
behalf of [Mr Masri] by Arab Bank Limited' at two named branches in London.
d (ii) The response of Mr Masri on affidavit to the making of the Mareva injunction was
to the effect that there were then in his London accounts no more than $US28,011 and
£6·11. Shortly thereafter SCF obtained evidence from which, as they have submitted, it
should be inferred that Mr Masri had in an account in the name of Mrs Masri with the
United Arab Bank in London a sum of about $400,000 (the dollar account), by means of
which he was carrying out deals in foreign currencies. The evidence (which need not be
e set out in detail), included the description of a transaction between Mr Masri and Mr El
Qader on 8 April 1984 in Mr Masri's office in Amman which Mr Masri completed by
handing to Mr El Qader a cheque for £20,000 sterling. The cheque was filled out there
and then with Mr El Qader's name as payee, the amount payable and the date, but the
cheque had previously been signed by Mrs Masri, who was not present, in her maiden
f name of El Khatib.
(iii) On 10 April 1984 on the application of SCF based on the evidence mentioned,
Webster J amended the Mareva injunction so as to apply it to 'accounts held by or on
behalf of [Mr Masri] or in the names of [Mrs Masri]' by the United Arab Bank, thereby
including the dollar account.
(iv) On 18 April 1984 Mrs Masri applied to the court for the Mareva injunction, in so
g far as it applied to any account in her name, whether her maiden or married name, to be
set aside or varied on the ground that the money in the accounts in her name was her
own beneficial property and not that of Mr Masri. Her affidavit evidence included
assertions that since their marriage in 1959 her money (then the sterling equivalent of
about £4,400) had always been kept separate from her husband's; that she had made
large profits by dealing in real estate; and that in about 1964 to 1965 she had begun
h dealing in foreign currencies through several accounts in her sole name with banks,
including the Arab Bank. As to the account of the transaction with Mr El Qader, in so far
as it referred to Mr Masri producing a cheque form from his desk which already bore
Mrs Masri's signature and asserted that Mrs Masri was not present at the time, that
account was described as a 'complete fabrication' on the part of SCF. Mrs Masri had, she
claimed, gone to Mr Masri's office and concluded the transaction with Mr El Qader.
j (v) Her application came before Hirst J on 3 September 1984. By that date a number
of affidavits had been filed on both sides. Counsel for Mr Masri argued that in law, for
the purposes of a Mareva injunction, if Mrs Masri, as a third party not concerned in the
proceedings between SCF and Mr Masri, claimed that the dollar account was beneficially
her own money, the court was bound to give effect to that claim and to discharge the
Mareva injunction so far as it affected that account, without conducting an inquiry into

the ownership of the money in the account. The submission, in brief, was that SCF must first get judgment against Mr Masri, if they could, and then in execution proceedings *a* take such property as could be proved to be that of Mr Masri. Hirst J rejected that submission. He held that in order for the court to deal with Mrs Masri's application to discharge the injunction so far as concerned the dollar account it was necessary to investigate the issue on the merits, including the allegations of SCF and of Mrs Masri and the evidence relied on by them. The Mareva injunction was accordingly continued pending the further hearing of Mrs Masri's application which was adjourned. SCF were *b* given leave to join Mrs Masri as second defendant in the main action, and she was so joined; but no relief has been claimed against her other than with reference to the claim of SCF that the dollar account is the property of Mr Masri. Hirst J's order was the subject of an appeal (see [1985] 2 All ER 747, [1985] 1 WLR 876) as set out in paragraph (viii) hereunder.

(vi) On 3 November 1984 directions were given by Hirst J for trial of the main action *c* and of Mrs Masri's application. First, it was ordered that trial of the main action be expedited. That order meant that the trial was likely to take place in June 1985. It was expected to take 10 days. Next, for the hearing of Mrs Masri's application, it was ordered that SCF be given leave to cross-examine both Mr Masri and Mrs Masri on their affidavits filed in support of her application; and that similar leave be given to Mr and Mrs Masri to cross-examine six witnesses who had sworn some of the affidavits on which SCF relied *d* in support of their case that the dollar account was the beneficial property of Mr Masri. Included among those witnesses was Mr El Qader who had received the cheque for $20,000 in Amman. The consequence of the orders for cross-examination, made under RSC Ord 38, r 2, was that if any of the witnesses named therein did not attend for cross-examination the affidavit of that person 'shall not be used as evidence without the leave of the court'. Further, provision was made for discovery of documents directed to the *e* issues raised both in the main action and in the application. The hearing of the application was estimated by the parties also to require ten days, including cross-examination of deponents. Lastly, it was directed that the hearing of Mrs Masri's application take place immediately after the trial of the main action.

(vii) It is necessary to draw attention to one aspect of the proceedings which were *f* before Hirst J for directions in September and November 1984. The Mareva injunction, of which notice had been given to the Arab Bank, caught within its terms the dollar account in the name of Mrs Masri, and it prevented both Mr Masri and Mrs Masri from removing that money from the account. Such an injunction is made by the court 'pending trial': if SCF failed in their action against Mr Masri the injunction would lapse, subject only to any power in the court to continue the injunction pending an appeal by *g* SCF. If SCF succeeded in their action against Mr Masri the injunction would have served its purpose in preserving, pending trial of the action, assets within the jurisdiction said to be the property of Mr Masri so as to make them available to satisfy the judgment against him if shown to be his; and any continuation of the injunction (again subject to the power of the court to continue the injunction pending any appeal by Mr Masri) would be for the purposes of preserving the account only while the necessary proceedings were *h* completed which would establish whether the money in the account belonged to Mr Masri as SCF claimed, or to Mrs Masri as she and Mr Masri asserted.

(viii) Mrs Masri appealed to the Court of Appeal against the order of Hirst J as set out in para (v) above. She contended that, on the argument presented to Hirst J, the Mareva injunction so far as it affected the account at the Arab Bank in the name of Mrs Masri, should have been set aside. On 2 April 1985 her appeal was rejected by this court for *j* reasons given by Lloyd LJ in a judgment with which Sir George Waller agreed (see [1985] 2 All ER 747, [1985] 1 WLR 876). Lloyd LJ said ([1985] 2 All ER 747 at 753, [1985] 1 WLR 876 at 884):

'For the reasons that I have given I would hold that there is no such rule or principle as that for which counsel for [Mrs Masri] contends. It follows that this appeal must be dismissed. For convenience I would summarise the position as follows. (i) Where a plaintiff invites the court to include within the scope of a Mareva injunction assets which appear on their face to belong to a third party, eg a bank account in the name of a third party, the court should not accede to the invitation without good reason for supposing that the assets are in truth the assets of the defendant. (ii) Where the defendant asserts that the assets belong to a third party, the court is not obliged to accept that assertion without inquiry, but may do so depending on the circumstances. The same applies where it is the third party who makes the assertion, on an application to intervene. (iii) In deciding whether to accept the assertion of a defendant or a third party, without further inquiry, the court will be guided by what is just and convenient, not only between the plaintiff and the defendant, but also between the plaintiff, the defendant and the third party. (iv) Where the court decides not to accept the assertion without further inquiry, it may order an issue to be tried between the plaintiff and the third party in advance of the main action, or it may order that the issue await the outcome of the main action, again depending in each case on what is just and convenient. (v) On the facts of the present case the judge was in my view plainly right to hold that he could not decide the matter without further inquiry; for the reasons I have already mentioned he was not obliged to decide in favour of [Mrs Masri], without further inquiry, by any rule or principle such as that suggested by counsel for [Mrs Masri].'

Earlier in his judgment Lloyd LJ described what 'the matter' was which the judge could not decide without further inquiry; the judge had 'held that it will be necessary to have a lengthy hearing to determine the beneficial ownership' of the dollar account (see [1985] 2 All ER 747 at 749, [1985] 1 WLR 876 at 879).

(ix) The main action came on for trial before Leggatt J in June 1985. On 4 July 1985 judgment was given for SCF for $910,031 plus interest as stated above, and Mr Masri's counterclaim was dismissed (see [1986] 1 All ER 40). Leggatt J rejected the evidence of Mr Masri where it conflicted with that of other witnesses. Immediately on judgment being given, counsel for SCF applied for an 'extension of the Mareva injunction . . . until after the hearing of the second part of this action', ie the hearing of Mrs Masri's application. An order was made to that effect without opposition. The hearing of Mrs Masri's application was fixed for 8 July 1985. There was by then a large volume of 27 affidavits together with exhibited documents including bank statements. In the course of the brief discussion in court counsel who appeared for Mr and Mrs Masri referred to the remaining part of the proceedings as 'an exceedingly simple issue: it is really a question of who owns the money'.

(x) On 8 July 1985 Mrs Masri's application was called on before Leggatt J. Mr and Mrs Masri were both present. SCF had arranged for the attendance in London from abroad of the witnesses ordered to attend for cross-examination. Counsel for Mrs Masri at once announced that Mrs Masri had decided not to proceed with 'her application to discharge the Mareva injunction' and that 'the obvious result is that the application must be dismissed with costs'. SCF had been informed of Mrs Masri's intention not to proceed some 30 minutes before. The events which followed, and the submissions made, reflected to some extent the surprise thereby caused and the inevitable lack of prior consideration by both sides.

(xi) The position adopted on behalf of Mrs Masri was described in this court by her counsel as follows: (a) the issue which in practical terms the judge would have had to decide would have been the ownership of the dollar account; (b) Mrs Masri did not wish on that day to pursue the issue as to who owned the dollar account; (c) Mr Masri was intending to appeal against the judgment but only on the issue of illegality under the Banking Act 1979 and, if his appeal was successful, no issue would remain with reference to the Mareva injunction; (d) Mrs Masri did not concede that the dollar account was beneficially the property of Mr Masri.

(xii) As to why Mrs Masri was on that day adopting the position described, her counsel gave an explanation, which he has told this court was inept and not intended to mean *a* what on its face it appeared to mean. He said:

'Mrs Masri has had explained to her the effect of your Lordship's judgment last Thursday, and in the light of the observations that your Lordship has made, she takes the position that it would be less than forthcoming on her part as Mrs Masri were she not to assist her husband by leaving the moneys within the jurisdiction to *b* be able to satisfy, at least in part, any judgment which is finally confirmed against her husband. So the obvious result is that the application must be dismissed with costs.'

Counsel for SCF has not argued that Mrs Masri is to be treated by those words of her counsel as having made any effective concession. Before this court counsel for Mrs Masri has added to that explanation by reference to what he called the 'emotional element'. *c* Given the disapproval of Mr Masri expressed by the judge, it was not wished to expose Mrs Masri to cross-examination before that judge. It was preferred not to proceed, but to submit to pay the costs of the application and to let the dollar account remain where it was, leaving SCF to establish later, if they could, that it belonged to Mr Masri.

(xiii) It is thus clear that SCF had done nothing to cause Mrs Masri to do what she did. It is also clear that SCF did nothing to lead Mrs Masri or her advisers to believe that she *d* was, or would be, free to cause her application to be dismissed on 8 July 1985, when it had been directed by the court to be heard, and later to raise again the issues which were raised for trial in that application. Counsel for SCF immediately contended that, on Mrs Masri not pursuing her application, the dollar account was established to be the property of Mr Masri and therefore available to SCF in execution. To Leggatt J, it did not at first so appear: he said that Mrs Masri had not conceded that the dollar account was the *e* property of Mr Masri and that what she had done was not to pursue her application to discharge the Mareva injunction. Counsel for SCF replied that, on inviting the dismissal of her application, it was no longer open to Mrs Masri to contend that the beneficial ownership of the dollar account was in her and that the true position was, or would be, one of issue estoppel. Leggatt J observed that such consequences were matters for the *f* parties and not for the court on that occasion. Warned thus expressly of the contention which would be made by SCF as to the consequences of not proceeding with her application, Mrs Masri, through her counsel, persisted, and her application was dismissed.

(xiv) On 8 July 1985 on the occasion of Mrs Masri not proceeding with her application, a number of separate matters were discussed and disposed of by Leggatt J. They included continuation of the Mareva injunction originally imposed by order of Webster J of 6 *g* February 1984 as against Mr and Mrs Masri with amendment of the terms, and applications by Mr and Mrs Masri for stay of execution which were refused. During the course of this series of applications and submissions, and while Mr and Mrs Masri were still in court with their counsel and solicitors, counsel for SCF made an ex parte application pursuant to RSC Ord 49 for leave to serve a garnishee order on Mrs Masri. He put before the judge a draft affidavit written out by Mr Brentnall, a partner in Messrs *h* Elborne Mitchell & Co, solicitors for SCF, with an undertaking that it would be duly sworn. It provided evidence, inter alia, of the existence of US$400,000 held by Mrs Masri in the dollar account as nominee of Mr Masri; alternatively, of Mrs Masri being on that day in Court 47, of being last seen in the precincts of the court at about 1.45 pm, and of the deponent's belief that she was still within the jurisdiction. The grounds of belief that Mrs Masri held the dollar account as nominee of Mr Masri, or was indebted to him in *j* that sum, were stated to be set out in the affidavits filed in Mrs Masri's application. Counsel for SCF explained that garnishee proceedings were needed in order to execute against the assets. He added that what was important to SCF, and the reason for haste, was that they should be able to serve Mrs Masri with the order while she was in the jurisdiction.

a (xv) Since counsel for Mrs Masri was in fact present the judge asked him if he wanted to say anything about the making of a garnishee order nisi and a suitable return date for it. As to the garnishee application, counsel submitted, firstly, that the matter was not properly before the court because the affidavit, being unsworn, did not satisfy Ord 49, r 2. There was no sufficient urgency to justify such a course. Secondly, Mrs Masri had given instructions to her solicitors to accept service of any garnishee order nisi, or other proceedings which SCF might obtain, so that there was absolutely no need for the judge *b* to deal with the matter on that day. Mrs Masri would have to return to England from Jordan if there was to be a hearing. Counsel for Mrs Masri said that time was required to enable the matter to be considered by her advisers before a convenient return date could be proposed. He repeated that there was no question of Mrs Masri in any way evading the consequences of the proceedings (ie the garnishee proceedings) which SCF wished to pursue.

c (xvi) Leggatt J then announced that he was not disposed to deal with the garnishee application until the next day, 9 July 1985, for the reason that, even if Mrs Masri were to leave the jurisdiction, she had given instructions for acceptance of service and if she revoked those instructions SCF would be entitled to substituted service.

(xvii) On 9 July 1985 SCF submitted to Leggatt J a sworn affidavit which was substantially in the form put in on 8 July, but the reference to the presence of Mrs Masri *d* within the jurisdiction was shortened to a statement that she was 'present at Court 47 . . . on 8 July 1985 at the hearing of this application'. An order was made as follows:

'That all debts due or accruing due from [Mrs Masri as] garnishee to [Mr Masri as] judgment debtor in the sum of US$400,000 . . . now standing to the Credit of [Mrs Masri] the garnishee at United Arab Bank Limited St Martins Le Grand Branch, be *e* attached to answer [the] judgment recovered against [Mr Masri] in the High Court of Justice on the 4th day of July 1985 for the sum of $910,031·70 . . . and the costs of the action [etc].'

The order directed Mrs Masri to attend on 22 July 1985 on an application by SCF that she be ordered to pay to SCF the amount of the debt. The return date was later changed to *f* 24 July to comply with Ord 49, r 3. Mrs Masri did not attend on that date, but a draft affidavit was received by the judge in which she repeated her claim to ownership of the dollar account. Before this court, among other submissions, it has been contended for Mrs Masri that Leggatt J had no jurisdiction to make any order in garnishee proceedings because Mrs Masri asserts that she left England on the morning of 9 July 1985 at about 9.00 a m and thus before Leggatt J on that day made the garnishee order nisi.

g
The provisions of RSC Ord 49

Before stating the grounds of decision of Leggatt J it is necessary to set out the provisions of Ord 49 from which any jurisdiction to make the order under appeal must be derived. Omitting words not relevant for these purposes, and adding the names of the parties, Ord 49, r 1(1) reads as follows:
h
'Where . . . "the judgment creditor" [SCF] . . . has obtained a judgment . . . for the payment by . . . "the judgment debtor" [Mr Masri] . . . of a sum of money . . . and any other person within the jurisdiction . . . [ie] "the garnishee" [Mrs Masri] . . . is indebted to the judgment debtor, the Court may . . . order the garnishee to pay the judgment creditor the amount of any debt due or accruing due to the judgment *j* debtor from the garnishee, or so much thereof as is sufficient to satisfy that judgment . . . and the costs of the garnishee proceedings.'

Then, by Ord 49, r 1(2) it is provided:

'An order under this rule shall in the first instance be an order to show cause, specifying the time and place for further consideration of the matter, and in the

meantime attaching such debt as is mentioned in paragraph (1) . . . to answer the
judgment . . . and the costs of the garnishee proceedings.'   *a*

By Ord 49, r 2 it is provided:

'An application for an order under rule 1 must be made *ex parte* supported by an
affidavit—(*a*) stating the name and last known address of the judgment debtor, (*b*)
identifying the judgment or order to be enforced . . . (*c*) stating that to the best of
the information or belief of the deponent the garnishee . . . is within the jurisdiction   *b*
and is indebted to the judgment debtor . . . '

Order 49, r 3(1) deals with service of the 'order to show cause' on the garnishee and the
judgment debtor, and, by r 3(2), it is provided 'that such an order shall bind in the hands
of the garnishee as from the service of the order on him any debt specified in the order
. . .'   *c*

Order 49, r 6 deals with claims of third persons: if some other person than the
judgment debtor claims to be entitled to the debt sought to be attached, the court may
order that person to attend before the court and state the nature of his claim. After
hearing any such person the court may summarily determine the question at issue or
make such other order as it thinks just, including an order for trial of the validity of the
third person's claim.   *d*

Finally, by Ord 49, r 8 it is provided:

'Any payment made by a garnishee in compliance with an order absolute under
this Order, and any execution levied against him in pursuance of such an order,
shall·be a valid discharge of his liability to the judgment debtor to the extent of the
amount paid or levied notwithstanding that the garnishee proceedings are
subsequently set aside or the judgment or order from which they arose reversed.'   *e*

The judgment of Leggatt J

The submissions before the judge were as follows. For Mrs Masri it was submitted that
the garnishee proceedings were misconceived and outside the jurisdiction of the court.
On behalf of SCF it was said that Mrs Masri was prevented by issue estoppel from
contending that the beneficial ownership of the dollar account was other than in Mr   *f*
Masri and that, accordingly, the case should be summarily determined under Ord 49,
r 5. If SCF had failed on the estoppel issue, but succeeded on jurisdiction, the matter
would have had to go for trial.

As to jurisdiction, Leggatt J held that, since Mr Masri was to be treated as the owner of
the dollar account (by reason of issue estoppel), notwithstanding the absence of proof of
any prior demand for the money, Mrs Masri was to be treated as being indebted to him,   *g*
and there was, therefore, a debt which under Ord 49 the court could direct to be paid by
Mrs Masri to SCF in part payment of the sums due from Mr Masri under the judgment.
Further, Leggatt J held that the requirement under Ord 49, r 1 that the garnishee be 'a
person within the jurisdiction' indebted to the judgment creditor was satisfied
notwithstanding her contention that, despite her presence when the order was applied   *h*
for, she was on an aircraft bound for Jordan when the order nisi was made on the
morning of 9 July 1985. The judge held that, under the rule, and having regard to the
procedure prescribed by Ord 49, r 2 for applying for an order of this nature, the moment
at which the garnishee must be within the jurisdiction is the 'moment at which either
the supporting affidavit is made or, more realistically, when the application is made in
support of which the affidavit is sworn'. Mrs Masri was in the court when the application *j*
was made.

As to the issue estoppel, the findings of the judge were as follows: In the proceedings
between SCF and Mrs Masri, with reference to the application of the Mareva injunction,
it was implicit in the case of SCF that the dollar account was in truth the property of her
husband. When Mrs Masri, for the purposes of her application, contended that the

Mareva injunction should be discharged so far as it affected the dollar account, she alleged
a that she beneficially owned the money in it. It was plain from the judgment of the Court
of Appeal (see [1985] 2 All ER 747, [1985] 1 WLR 876), on her appeal from Hirst J, that
it would be necessary for a hearing to take place to determine the issue of the beneficial
ownership of the dollar account. To that end directions had been given by Hirst J for the
hearing of the issue immediately after the hearing of the action and 'as a matter of form'
that was to occur on her application to discharge the Mareva injunction so far as it
b affected her. The issue for determination on the hearing of the application was: which
assertion with reference to the dollar account, ie that of SCF or that made by Mrs Masri,
was correct? There was a decision of the court on that issue in the form of a dismissal of
her application, and that decision was final in that it determined the issue. Mrs Masri had
'deliberately refrained from taking' the opportunity to establish that the dollar account
belonged to her; and that to allow her to avail herself of that argument in the garnishee
c proceedings would be to permit her to abuse the process of the court. Accordingly Mrs
Masri was by reason of issue estoppel precluded from asserting that the dollar account
was her property.

Jurisdiction
    Before this court, for Mrs Masri three points were taken on jurisdiction. The first turns
d on her departure by air from London Airport at about 9.00 am on 9 July 1985. The
order nisi was made some time after the court sat at 10.30 am. Junior counsel who dealt
very ably with this part of Mrs Masri's case, gave to this point as much force as it could
possibly attain, and made it seem less unattractive, by candid acknowledgment of its lack
of merits in the events which happened. His submission was that the rule requires the
physical presence of the garnishee within the territorial limits of England and Wales at
e the relevant time. The rule does not define what that time is. Since the effect of attaching
the debt is achieved by service of the order nisi (Ord 49, r 3(2)), the relevant time, on
construction of the order, should be taken as service of that order at the earliest;
alternatively, it should be the making of the order absolute. The requirement of presence
within the jurisdiction was intended to secure that the process of attachment is made
available only against persons of sufficient connection with this country. There had been
f no intention by Mrs Masri, or her advisers, to mislead either SCF or the court. She had
said that she would submit to service on her solicitors and she had been duly served. If
the requirement of presence within the jurisdiction was not satisfied, the court could not
acquire jurisdiction by concession of Mrs Masri.
    The requirement of Ord 49, r 1(1) that a garnishee shall be a person 'within the
jurisdiction' would in some cases be capable of giving rise to one or both of two difficult
g questions, as junior counsel's argument clearly demonstrated. Would merely temporary
physical presence of the garnishee within the territorial limits of England and Wales at
the relevant time suffice to render him 'within the jurisdiction'? At what stage or over
what stages of the proceedings does physical presence of the garnishee found jurisdiction?
Contrary to junior counsel's submission, we strongly incline to the view that the answer
to the first of these two questions is Yes, though the court, in the exercise of its discretion,
h would no doubt decline to make the order if it were not just and convenient for the
issues to be tried here. As to the second question, we would without hesitation reject
junior counsel's submissions that for physical presence to found jurisdiction it must exist
at the time of service of the order nisi, or of the making of the final order. We have no
doubt that physical presence of the garnishee in this country at the time of the making
j of the order nisi is sufficient to found jurisdiction which would not be lost by subsequent
departure of the garnishee. That conclusion is securely based on the language of Ord 49,
r 1, which provides that 'Where . . . any other person within the jurisdiction . . . is
indebted . . . the Court may . . . order [etc]'. The procedure from order nisi to final order
is to be treated as one procedure, and jurisdiction at the start must have been intended to
endure until the end. As to whether physical presence at the time of the making of the

application is sufficient, there is much to be said in favour of Leggatt J's conclusion that it is. Nevertheless, r 1 itself in words says not that the judgment creditor 'may apply', but *a* that the 'Court may . . . order'; and such language points to the order nisi rather than to the application as to the relevant moment for jurisdiction. Moreover, in some cases, though not the present, there could be uncertainty as to when the application is to be treated as effectively made.

In the end, we do not find it necessary to decide either of the two last-mentioned questions relating to the meaning of the phrase 'other person within the jurisdiction', *b* since, whatever the answers to them may be, we are of the clear opinion that a person must be 'within the jurisdiction' for the purpose of Ord 49, r 1(1) if, before the order nisi is made, he or she has agreed to submit to the jurisdiction of the English court for the purpose of the relevant garnishee proceedings. In the present case, in our judgment, at the time when the order nisi was made, Mrs Masri was a 'person within the jurisdiction' within the meaning of that rule because she agreed to submit to it. She had, by her *c* counsel, as described above, invited SCF not to press the court on 8 July to make the order nisi on that day, when she was present in court, on the ground that she had instructed her solicitors to accept service of garnishee proceedings; and that she did not intend to evade the consequences of the garnishee proceedings which SCF wished to purue. SCF acted on that invitation. We accept that this is not a case of an intention to deceive. The point was not present to anyone's mind. It is no more than a willingness on the part of *d* Mrs Masri to take the benefit of having by her advisers helped to lead the advisers of SCF into the alleged error. The point, however, cannot help her. She anounced her willingness to submit to the jurisdiction of the court for the purposes of the garnishee proceedings. Order 49, in our judgment, is not to be construed so as to require the court to decline to exercise jurisdiction, where a party voluntarily submits to that jurisdiction, on the ground only that the garnishee was not physically present: see *Rothmans of Pall Mall* *e* *(Overseas) Ltd v Saudi Arabian Airlines Corp* [1980] 3 All ER 359 at 364, [1981] QB 368 at 375 per Mustill J. Mrs Masri is to be treated in this case as having agreed to submit to the jurisdiction of the court. It would not be just to permit her to resile from that agreement. In those circumstances she must be treated as 'within the jurisdiction' for the purposes of the garnishee proceedings.

The next point raises questions concerned both with jurisdiction and with the *f* discretion of the court. Counsel for Mrs Masri submitted that the application in these garnishee proceedings was misconceived in that there was at no time evidence of any debt due from Mrs Masri to Mr Masri on the case made by SCF: the advisers of SCF had, said counsel, made in their haste a pardonable but fatal error. There was, without question, a debt due from the Arab Bank in respect of the amount in the dollar account. If the bank had been named as garnishee, owing a debt to Mr Masri, then, on Mr and *g* Mrs Masri, and no doubt the bank, asserting that the dollar account was the beneficial property of Mrs Masri, that issue could have been tried between the parties by directions for trial given under Ord 49, r 6. The court should not, it was submitted, find a 'debt' due, where in truth there was none, in order to save the proceedings.

Counsel for Mrs Masri contended that the error made by the advisers of SCF was made *h* the more apparent by the course of further garnishee proceedings which SCF took against the Arab Bank (naming Mr Masri as judgment debtor), with the object of obtaining payment under the earlier order that the dollar account be paid to them by Mrs Masri. This further application of SCF was ultimately dismissed by Webster J. Though the course of these further proceedings was examined with some care and in some detail in argument before us, we do not find it necessary to do the same in this judgment. Even *j* assuming in favour of Mr Masri that the order dismissing the application and the reasoning on which it was based were correct, it does not, in our judgment, follow that the original garnishee proceedings in which Leggatt J made his order against Mrs Masri were misconceived.

On the assumption that the judge was right in finding issue estoppel against Mrs Masri

(which we think a correct assumption for the reasons stated below), Mrs Masri, albeit
a apparently without the knowledge of the Arab Bank, must at all times have held the
moneys in the dollar account as nominee or trustee for Mr Masri. Mr Masri is equally
bound by this estoppel because he was a party to these proceedings and was present and
represented when they were dismissed. We accept that the existence of this trust would
not by itself necessarily have given rise to the existence of any 'debt' in the relevant sense
owed by Mrs Masri to Mr Masri. However, it did mean that it was open to him to
b demand payment to himself of these moneys at any time. When, in the application to
set aside the Mareva injunction and the garnishee proceedings brought against her, Mrs
Masri (albeit apparently in concert with Mr Masri) claimed these moneys as her own, she
must be treated for present purposes as thereby denying Mr Masri's right to them and as
repudiating the trust. Such repudiation, in our judgment, for the purposes of the
garnishee proceedings gave rise to the existence of an indebtedness on the part of Mrs
c Masri to Mr Masri in the amount of these moneys. If the relevant issue estoppel applies,
it is not open to Mr or Mrs Masri to deny the existence of the debt which is asserted for
the purpose of Ord 49.
    The last challenge to the validity of the order, also on the grounds both of jurisdiction
and of discretion, was based on the submission advanced by junior counsel for Mrs Masri
that the law requires not only that the garnishee be within the jurisdiction but also that
d the debt be situated and payable within the jurisdiction. This argument was primarily
based on the decision of Hill J in *Richardson v Richardson* [1927] P 228 at 235, [1927] All
ER Rep 92 at 96, where it was held that the words 'any other person is indebted to the
judgment debtor and is within the jurisdiction' then contained in what was RSC Ord 45,
in principle and on authority, meant 'is indebted within the jurisdiction and is within
the jurisdiction'. In this context junior counsel pointed to the facts that both Mr and Mrs
e Masri live in Amman in Jordan, and that, on the assuption that Mr Masri caused the fund
in the dollar account to be paid to that account in his wife's name out of his assets, the
relevant acts must in probability all have taken place in Amman. Mr Masri could not, he
said, have sued for the alleged debt in this country except during the time when Mrs
Masri was in England for the hearing of the action. Mrs Masri should, accordingly, be
f treated as owing any debt only in Jordan. Alternatively, the court should in the exercise
of its discretion decline to make any order.
    The decision in *Richardson v Richardson* is not binding on us and it seems to us that the
relevant words in Ord 49, r 1, which were in 1923 to 1927 contained in the then Ord 45,
are not to be read as proposed by Hill J in that case. Order 49, r 1 contains no express
requirement that the garnishee be indebted within the jurisdiction and we see no reason
to read in words to that effect. We accept that in a case where the garnishee is not
g 'indebted within the jurisdiction' this may be relevant to the exercise of the court's
discretion. Thus Scrutton LJ in *Swiss Bank Corp v Boehmische Industrial Bank* [1923] 1 KB
673 at 680–681 referred to the earlier decision of this court in *Martin v Nadel (Dresdner
Bank, garnishee)* [1906] 2 KB 26, [1904–7] All ER Rep 827 (on which Hill J had relied in
Richardson v Richardson) as a—

h   'decision . . . that the Court will not make absolute a garnishee order where it will
       not operate to discharge the garnishee in whole or pro tanto from the debt; it will
       not expose him to the risk of having to pay the debt or part of it twice over. That is
       well established as a principle of discretion on which the Court acts.'

    On the facts of the present case, we accept the submission of counsel for SCF that, on
j the basis of the principles stated by Bankes LJ in the *Swiss Bank* case [1923] 1 KB 673 at
678, the debt which has been shown to be due from Mrs Masri to Mr Masri should be
treated as properly recoverable in England and capable of being discharged under English
law. By virtue of the doctrine of issue estoppel (as to which see below) the order of the
court dismissing Mrs Masri's application to discharge the Mareva injunction, made in
proceedings to which Mr and Mrs Masri were parties, has established that, as between the

two of them and as a matter of English law, the debt due from the Arab Bank, which is a debt arising in this country, is due to Mr Masri and therefore available to be attached in satisfaction of the judgment debt due from him to SCF. Nothing put forward in evidence or in argument has given us the least reason to suppose that Mrs Masri could be at any risk of being ordered to pay the debt a second time to her husband.

For all these reasons, we conclude that if his decision was correct on the question of issue estoppel, there was no reason why, as a matter of jurisdiction or discretion, Leggatt J should have refused to make absolute the garnishee order against Mrs Masri.

Issue estoppel

The remaining question is whether the judge was right in his finding that Mrs Masri was prevented by issue estoppel from contending in the garnishee proceedings that the dollar account was her property. The submissions of counsel for Mrs Masri were, in summary, as follows. (i) On 8 July 1985 Mrs Masri withdrew her application to vary or to discharge the Mareva injunction, so far as it affected her; and, since she expressly did not concede that the dollar account belonged to Mr Masri, the withdrawal of the application can be treated only as a decision to leave the dollar account as it was, subject to the injunction, pending the appeal by Mr Masri against the decision of Leggatt J. (ii) Since she had withdrawn her application, there were no proceedings before Leggatt J on 8 July in which any issue was, or could have been, determined against her; and for the same reason she did not fail, and could not have failed, to take in proceedings an opportunity to establish that the dollar account was her property. (iii) If there were proceedings before Leggatt J in which any issue was decided, the issue in those proceedings was not, or was not necessarily, the beneficial ownership of the dollar account, but whether the Mareva injunction should be continued or varied.

As to the first point it is, we think, clear that Mrs Masri did not withdraw her application and, moreover, never applied to withdraw it. She announced that she was not proceeding with it and acknowledged that the consequence must be that it be dismissed. It was dismissed. The application by Mrs Masri to set aside the Mareva injunction was not itself an action but was a summons in the action brought by SCF against Mr Masri; and, as such, by RSC Ord 21, r 6, it could not be withdrawn save by leave of the court. There was no application for leave to withdraw. If made, such an application would, in our judgment, have been refused. There were no grounds advanced on which it would have been just to permit Mrs Masri to withdraw her application on terms that she should be free to raise again against SCF such issues as were raised for decision in her application. Similarly, if on behalf of Mrs Masri application had been made for her application to be adjourned for hearing until after decision of the appeal by Mr Masri, we see no reason why it should have been granted. No convincing reason could be advanced other than the desire to avoid incurring the costs of a hearing which would be unnecessary if the appeal succeeded. As to that, if Mrs Masri had wished to avoid that risk in costs she should not have applied to set aside the injunction before final disposal of the main action. She had sought and obtained a date for the hearing of her application. SCF had been able to secure the attendance in London from overseas of the deponents ordered to attend for cross-examination and SCF were ready to proceed. In the event no application for an adjournment was made. Mrs Masri is to be treated as a litigant who, for her own reasons, decided not to pursue an application which was ready for trial and which in consequence was dismissed.

Was any issue decided by the dismissal of the application, and, if Yes, what was it? It seemed to Leggatt J, as stated above, that the issue for determination on the hearing of her application was whether SCF or Mrs Masri were right in their respective contentions as to the beneficial ownership of the dollar account. He said:

'The issue falling to be determined in the proceedings ... [was] not formally drawn up: but that can only have been because the issue was so obvious and so certain that formal drafting appeared to all parties to be unnecessary.'

That finding of the judge is, in our view, right. The order of Hirst J made on 30
a November 1984, whereby he directed that the hearing of Mrs Masri's application to
discharge the Mareva injunction should be heard immediately after the trial of the main
action, must be treated as a direction for the hearing of the issue as to the ownership of
the dollar account. He clearly contemplated that if SCF succeeded in the main action, the
fate of Mrs Masri's application would depend on whether SCF succeeded in proving that
Mr Masri was the beneficial owner of the moneys in that account.

b But is that issue to be treated as having been decided by virtue of the order dismissing
Mrs Masri's application to discharge the Mareva injunction? Before Leggatt J and on this
appeal counsel for SCF relied on the principles restated in this court in *Khan v Goleccha
International Ltd* [1980] 2 All ER 259, [1980] 1 WLR 1482. In that case an order by
consent had been made by the Court of Appeal on the basis of an express acceptance by
counsel for the plaintiff borrower that a transaction was not one of moneylending and
c was outside the scope of the Moneylenders Act 1929. Later the plaintiff brought an
action against the defendant company claiming that the debt was statute-barred by
s 13(1) of that Act. In his judgment, with which Cumming-Bruce and Bridge LJJ agreed,
Brightman LJ referred to the express acceptance by counsel before the Court of Appeal
that the transaction was not a lending of money, and to the dismissal of the appeal on
that basis, and asked 'Does that admission and the consent order so made give rise to
d estoppel, more particularly to the brand of estoppel sometimes called issue estoppel?' He
then continued ([1980] 2 All ER 259 at 264–265, [1980] 1 WLR 1482 at 1488–1489):

'First, for the general principle (*Ord v Ord* [1923] 2 KB 432 at 439, [1923] All ER
Rep 206 at 210 per Lush J; I need not narrate the facts): "The words 'res judicata'
explain themselves. If the res—the thing actually or directly in dispute—has been
e already adjudicated upon, of course by a competent Court, it cannot be litigated
again. There is a wider principle, to which I will refer in a moment, often as covered
by the plea of res judicata, that prevents a litigant from relying on a claim or defence
which he had an opportunity of putting before the Court in the earlier proceedings
and which he chose not to put forward . . ." I turn straight to the wider principle
([1923] 2 KB 432 at 443, [1923] All ER Rep 206 at 212): "The maxim 'Nemo debet
f bis vexari' prevents a litigant who has had an opportunity of proving a fact in
support of his claim or defence and chosen not to rely on it from afterwards putting
it before another tribunal. To do that would be unduly to harass his opponent, and
if he endeavoured to do so he would be met by the objection that the judgment in
the former action precluded him from raising that contention. It is not that it has
been already decided, or that the record deals with it. The new fact has not been
g decided; it has never been in fact submitted to the tribunal and it is not really dealt
with by the record. But it is, by reason of the principle I have stated, treated as if it
had been".'

After a reference to the opinion of Lord Wilberforce in *Carl-Zeiss-Stiftung v Rayner &
Keeler Ltd (No 2)* [1966] 2 All ER 536 at 584, [1967] 1 AC 853 at 964–965 as to the
h material at which the court may look in order to identify the issue—

'not merely at the record of the judgment relied on, but at the reasons for it, the
pleadings, the evidence . . . and if necessary other material to show what was the
issue decided . . .'

j Brightman LJ continued ([1980] 2 All ER 259 at 266, [1980] 1 WLR 1482 at 1490):

'Looking at the matter broadly, the issue of "lending of money" was raised in the
Queen's Bench action. The judge decided that there was a lending of money within
the meaning of the Act. The plaintiff appealed. The Court of Appeal gave judgment
dismissing the appeal. The judgment was given by consent and the consent was
given because the company claimed, and the plaintiff accepted, that there was no

lending of money. In my view, that admission by the plaintiff, given to the court
and founding the judgment by consent, was just as efficacious for the purpose of
issue estoppel as a judicial decision by the court after argument founding a similar
judgment. The only sensible approach of the law, in my view, is to treat an issue as
laid at rest, not only if it is embodied in the terms of the judgment, or implicit in
the judgment because it is embodied in the spoken decision, but also if it is
embodied in an admission made in the face of the court or implicit in a consent
order.'

Finally, Brightman LJ dealt with an argument put forward that, while an order by
consent at first instance founded on an admission made by one party could lead to res
judicata, an order by consent on appeal dismissing the appeal could not on the ground
that an appellate court could not properly interfere with the decision of an inferior court
without proper judicial consideration. Brightman LJ continued ([1980] 2 All ER 259 at
267, [1980] 1 WLR 1482 at 1491):

'I refer back to what Lush J said in Ord v Ord [1923] 2 KB 432 at 443, [1923] All
ER Rep 206 at 212: "The maxim 'Nemo debet bis vexari' prevents a litigant who
has had an opportunity of proving a fact in support of his claim or defence and
chosen not to rely on it from afterwards putting it before another tribunal." In this
case [the plaintiff] had his opportunity, in support of his appeal on the previous
occasion, of establishing that money was lent. He chose not to establish that position.
His counsel got up in court and deliberately abandoned it. So it seems to me that he
loses his right of establishing that same position before another tribunal.'

The decision in Khan's case makes it clear that an order dismissing proceedings is
capable of giving rise to issue estoppel even though the court making such order has not
heard argument or evidence directed on the merits. If in the present case there had been
no attempt expressly to preserve the issue of the beneficial ownership of the dollar
account by not conceding it, the effect of Mrs Masri declining to proceed with the hearing
and acknowledging that her application must be dismissed, must in our judgment have
been finally to determine the issue against Mrs Masri. That effect must have followed
because decision of the issue, one way or the other, was the 'necessary step' to the decision
which the court would have had to make if the court had proceeded to hear Mrs Masri's
application on the merits (see per Lord Wilberforce in Carl-Zeiss-Stiftung v Rayner & Keeler
Ltd (No 2) [1966] 2 All ER 536 at 584, [1967] 1 AC 853 at 964 cited by Brightman LJ in
Khan's case). If a party puts forward a positive case, as the basis of asking the court to
make the order which that party seeks, and then at trial declines to proceed and accepts
that the claim must be dismissed, then that party must, in our view, save in exceptional
circumstances, lose the right to raise again that case against the other party to those
proceedings.

Counsel for Mrs Masri, in seeking to distinguish Kahn's case, relied principally on the
fact that, on behalf of Mrs Masri, he had expressly stated that she did not concede that
her husband owned the dollar account. It was the admission in Khan's case which made
the consent order effective to create an issue estoppel. Here there was no admission and
therefore, he argued, there could be no estoppel from the consent order. He argued that
on his stating to Leggatt J that Mrs Masri did not concede that this dollar account was her
husband's property, it was for SCF, if they wanted a decision on the merits then and
there, to persuade the judge not to dismiss Mrs Masri's application but to hear the case
out; if they had taken that course it is a matter of speculation whether Mrs Masri would
have taken part in the hearing.

It seems that the effect of an express reservation by counsel of an issue ordered to be
tried has not been previously decided. It is not possible, in our view, to decide that such
a reservation is to be given in all such cases some defined effect. The court is applying
principles which are intended to 'treat an issue as laid to rest' ([1980] 2 All ER 259 at 267,
[1980] 1 WLR 1482 at 1490 per Brightman LJ) where it would be unfair and unjust

between the parties to treat it otherwise; and, in particular, the court is concerned to
a prevent abuse of the court's procedure by any party. At the time at which the court had
directed trial of the issue, Mrs Masri decided in seeking her own advantage and
convenience, not to proceed with her application. It is probable that she and her husband
feared that the poor showing of Mr Masri as a witness of fact in the main action damaged
their prospects of success on the issue of ownership of the dollar account. Such a fear, in
so far as it related to Mr Masri's credibility as a witness of fact, was a rational consequence
b of the expression by the judge of the grounds of that part of his judgment from which
no appeal was, or usefully could have been, brought; but that fear afforded no ground
for permitting Mrs Masri in effect to withdraw her application in order to start again at a
time which she judged more propitious. She had no rational ground for fearing that the
judge would be unfairly disposed against her on her evidence because of the view which
the judge had been compelled to hold of Mr Masri's credibility on other issues. The
c conduct of her counsel, of course, can in no way be criticised. He had received instructions
that Mrs Masri would not proceed with her application which entailed, if her affidavit
was to be available in evidence, that she submit to cross-examination. He stated the fact
that Mrs Masri did not concede that her husband owned the dollar account. We would
hold, however, that to allow effect, on the facts of this case, to that statement by counsel,
namely that his client did not concede the issue which she declined to have tried, would
d be to permit the process of the court to be abused by Mrs Masri for her own advantage.

Examination of the proceedings before Leggatt J shows that Mrs Masri cannot have
been misled as to the consequences of her action by anything said or done by SCF or by
the court. It has not been submitted that she was misled. At one stage the judge expressed
a view, consistent with the non-concession being treated as effective, but on behalf of SCF
counsel at once asserted that issue estoppel would be raised against her and the judge
e observed that the consequences were matters for the parties: see para (xiii) above.

The principle of the decision of this court in *Khan's* case is, in our judgment, applicable
to this case: a litigant who has had an opportunity of proving a fact in support of his
claim or defence and has chosen not to rely on it is not permitted afterwards to put it
before another tribunal. In this case Mrs Masri had her opportunity to establish the case
on which her application was based; and she chose not to establish her alleged ownership
f of the dollar account. Her counsel on her instructions acknowledged that her application
must be dismissed. His attempt to reserve the issue was, in our judgment, ineffective.

In *Yat Tung Investment Co Ltd v Dao Heng Bank Ltd* [1975] AC 581 the Privy Council
upheld the application by the Supreme Court of Hong Kong of the doctrine of res
judicata in the wider sense, namely that it would be an abuse of the process of the court
to raise in subsequent proceedings matters which could and should have been litigated
g in earlier proceedings. Lord Kilbrandon, giving the judgment of their Lordships, gave
warning (at 590):

'The shutting out of a "subject of litigation" [was] a power which no court should
exercise but after scrupulous examination of all the circumstances [the exercise of
such a power] is limited to cases where reasonable diligence would have caused a
h matter to be earlier raised; moreover, although negligence, inadvertence or even
accident will not suffice to excuse, nevertheless "special circumstances" are reserved
in case justice should be found to require the non-application of the rule.'

In this case, in our judgment, there is no reason for the rule not to be applied. We
dismiss the appeal.

j
Appeal dismissed. Leave to appeal to the House of Lords refused.

Solicitors: *Herbert Oppenheimer Nathan & Vandyk* (for Mrs Masri); *Elborne Mitchell & Co*
(for SCF).

Wendy Shockett   Barrister.

Hotson v East Berkshire Area Health Authority

COURT OF APPEAL, CIVIL DIVISION
SIR JOHN DONALDSON MR, DILLON AND CROOM-JOHNSON LJJ
28, 29 OCTOBER, 14 NOVEMBER 1986

Damages – Personal injury – Loss of chance of better medical result – Increased chance of adverse medical result developing – Hospital's breach of duty – Plaintiff injured and having 75% chance of a permanent disability developing – Hospital wrongly diagnosing injury for five days – Wrong diagnosis making permanent disability inevitable – Whether plaintiff entitled to damages for loss of 25% chance of full recovery.

In 1977 the plaintiff, then 13 years old, injured his hip in an accident at school. When he went to a hospital run by the defendant health authority his hip was not examined but instead his knee was X-rayed and he was sent home with a knee bandage. It was not until five days later that the nature and extent of his hip injuries was discovered and he was given emergency treatment at the hospital. The nature of the hip injury was such that a severe medical condition causing deformity of the hip joint, restricted mobility and general disability was likely to develop and did indeed develop, leaving the plaintiff with a major permanent disability at the age of 20. The plaintiff claimed damages for negligence against the hospital authority, which admitted that there had been a breach of duty when the plaintiff was first examined but denied that the resulting delay had adversely affected the plaintiff's long-term future. At the trial of the action the judge found as a fact that even if the hospital's medical staff had correctly diagnosed and treated the plaintiff when he first attended the hospital there was still a 75% risk of the plaintiff's disability developing, but the medical staff's breach of duty had turned that risk into an inevitability, thereby denying the plaintiff a 25% chance of a good recovery. The judge awarded the plaintiff damages which included an amount of £11,500 representing 25% of the full value of the damages awardable for plaintiff's disability, which were assessed at £46,000. The health authority appealed, contending that since the plaintiff had not shown on the balance of probabilities that their admitted breach of duty had caused his permanent disability he was not entitled to any award of damages and that although damages in respect of a lost chance were recoverable in contract they were not recoverable in tort.

Held – Where the court was satisfied on the balance of probabilities (a) that the defendant owed a duty of care to the plaintiff, (b) that the defendant had breached that duty and (c) that the loss or damage occasioned by the breach was the loss of a chance or benefit which was capable of being identified and valued, the plaintiff was entitled to recover damages in tort for the loss of the chance or benefit which the defendant's negligence had deprived him of. Accordingly, damages for such a lost chance were not limited to cases in which the action was founded in contract. Since the hospital authority's admitted breach of duty had, on the balance of probabilities, resulted in an increased risk that the plaintiff would develop a permanent disability and since the benefit lost by the plaintiff was a one-in-four chance of avoiding the disability, the plaintiff was entitled to the award made by the judge of one-quarter of the damages awardable for the permanent disability. The appeal would therefore be dismissed (see p 215 j to p 216 e h to p 217 e, p 218 d, p 219 d to g, p 220 d e and p 222 g to p 223 c, post).

Per Sir John Donaldson MR and Croom-Johnson LJ. Loss of a chance of recovery or exposure to the chance of an injury will not of themselves give rise to more than nominal damages if in the event the plaintiff remains uninjured and unaffected by the loss of the chance (see p 218 a b and p 224 b, post).

Decision of Simon Brown J sub nom *Hotson v Fitzgerald* [1985] 3 All ER 167 affirmed.

a

Notes

For the burden of proving negligence, see 34 Halsbury's Laws (4th edn) paras 54, and for cases on the subject, see 36(1) Digest (Reissue) 223–227, 871–879.

For the measure of damages in tort generally, see 12 Halsbury's Laws (4th edn) paras 1138, 1141, and for cases on the subject, see 17 Digest (Reissue) 113–119, *168–208.*

b

Cases referred to in judgments

Barnett v Chelsea and Kensington Hospital Management Committee [1968] 1 All ER 1068, [1969] 1 QB 428, [1968] 2 WLR 422.

Bonnington Castings Ltd v Wardlaw [1956] 1 All ER 615, [1956] AC 613, [1956] 2 WLR 707, HL.

c *Chaplin v Hicks* [1911] 2 KB 786, [1911–13] All ER Rep 224, CA.

Cummings (or McWilliams) v Sir William Arrol & Co Ltd [1962] 1 All ER 623, [1962] 1 WLR 295, HL.

Davies v Taylor [1972] 3 All ER 836, [1974] AC 207, [1972] 3 WLR 801, HL.

Kenyon v Bell 1953 SC 125, Ct of Sess.

d *Kitchen v Royal Air Force Association* [1958] 2 All ER 241, [1958] 1 WLR 563, CA.

Kranz v M'Cutcheon (1920) 18 OWN 395.

McGhee v National Coal Board [1972] 3 All ER 1008, [1973] 1 WLR 1, HL.

Mallett v McMonagle [1969] 2 All ER 178, [1970] AC 166, [1969] 2 WLR 767, HL.

Marbe v George Edwardes (Daly's Theatre) Ltd [1928] 1 KB 269, [1927] All ER Rep 253, CA.

e *Robinson v Post Office* [1974] 2 All ER 737, [1974] 1 WLR 1176, CA.

Seward v Vera Cruz (owners), The Vera Cruz (1884) 10 App Cas 59, [1881–5] All ER Rep 216, HL.

Sykes v Midland Bank Exor and Trustee Co Ltd [1970] 2 All ER 471, [1971] 1 QB 113, [1970] 3 WLR 273, CA.

Vyner v Waldenberg Bros Ltd [1945] 2 All ER 547, [1946] KB 50, CA.

f

Cases also cited

Cook v Swinfen [1967] 1 All ER 299, [1967] 1 WLR 547, CA.

Cork v Kirby Maclean Ltd [1952] 2 All ER 402, CA.

Cutler v Vauxhall Motors Ltd [1970] 2 All ER 56, [1971] 1 QB 418, CA.

Eyre v Measday [1986] 1 All ER 488, CA.

g *Fraser v B N Furman (Productions) Ltd (Miller Smith & Partners, third parties)* [1967] 3 All ER 57, [1967] 1 WLR 898, CA.

Gauntlett v Northampton Health Authority [1985] CA Transcript 835.

Lim Poh Choo v Camden and Islington Area Health Authority [1979] 2 All ER 910, [1980] AC 174, HL.

h *Mulvaine v Joseph* (1968) 112 SJ 927.

Saif Ali v Sydney Mitchell & Co [1978] 3 All ER 1033, [1980] AC 198, HL.

Wathen v Vernon [1970] RTR 471, CA.

Appeal

j The East Berkshire Area Health Authority (the defendants) appealed against the decision of Simon Brown J on 15 March 1985 ([1985] 3 All ER 167, [1985] 1 WLR 1036) allowing the claim of the plaintiff, Stephen John Hotson (an infant suing by Cyril Arthur Hotson, his father and next friend), in an action for damages for breach of duty and negligence brought against M V J Fitzgerald, D Goldstein, R J Habershon and the health authority. By a respondent's notice dated 23 April 1985 the plaintiff cross-appealed on quantum. By a notice dated 1 May 1985 the plaintiff discontinued the action against the first, second

and third defendants in respect of the claim for damages. The facts are set out in the
judgment of Sir John Donaldson MR.   *a*

Adrian Whitfield QC, Kieran B Coonan and *Andrew Grubb* for the defendants.
Graeme Williams QC and *David Ashton* for the plaintiff.

Cur adv vult
b

14 November. The following judgments were delivered.

SIR JOHN DONALDSON MR. This appeal appears to raise a novel point on damages
in the law of tort. More specifically: can a plaintiff recover damages in negligence for the
loss of a chance or loss of opportunity? In this case the problem arises in the context of
medical negligence, but it could arise in many other contexts.   *c*
    The facts can be briefly stated. Stephen Hotson, then aged 13, was at school on 26
April 1977. He fell from a rope on which he had been swinging. He dropped some 12 ft
onto muddy ground, landing on his seat. Despite the softness of the ground, the shock
was sufficient to cause him to suffer an acute traumatic fracture separation of the left
femoral epiphysis. This is a very serious injury in a child of this age, as the judge (Simon
Brown J) explained ([1985] 3 All ER 167 at 169–170, [1985] 1 WLR 1036 at 1038–1039): *d*

> 'The femoral epiphysis (the epiphysis as I shall refer to it henceforth) is the spongy
> extremity of the upper femur, its surface being covered with cartilage, which slots
> into the cavity of the acetabulum to form the hip joint. In a child the epiphysis is
> connected to the neck of the femur by an epiphysial plate (sometimes called a
> growth plate) which is essentially a sandwich filling of cartilage between, on the *e*
> upper side, the epiphysis and on the lower side the bony femoral neck. The plate
> exists only in a growing skeleton and indeed it enables the bone to grow; in maturity
> it forms bone across the gap. The major threat created by an injury such as the
> plaintiff's is that it will so interfere with the blood supply to the epiphysis that
> avascular necrosis will develop. This is a condition whereby through lack of
> sufficient blood the epiphysis becomes demineralised, weakened and softened and *f*
> thus denser, distorted and deformed. When that occurs, not only does it cause
> misshapenness of the joint with associated pain, restriction in mobility and general
> disability, but it also carries with it the virtual certainty that osteo-arthritis will
> develop within the joint.'

The unfortunate plaintiff has indeed suffered avascular necrosis of the epiphysis with *g*
consequential serious disabilities which will become more serious over the years. In
money terms the judge has assessed these disabilities as £46,000. Since this figure is not
now in dispute, I need not detail the disabilities or how the sum is made up.
    I now come to the admitted negligence of the East Berkshire Area Health Authority
(the defendants). Shortly after the accident the plaintiff was taken to St Luke's Hospital,
Maidenhead, and examined. His left knee was X-rayed and showed no injury. For some *h*
unexplained reason, there was no X-ray examination of his femur or hip. He was given
an elastic knee bandage and told to return in ten days, if necessary. I draw a veil over the
next five days, during which the plaintiff suffered excruciating pain and received scant
sympathy and no real treatment from his general practitioner. That doctor and his
partners were additional defendants, but that aspect of the matter was settled. Happily,
on 1 May 1977 the plaintiff was taken back to St Luke's, where he was re-examined and *j*
his hip X-rayed. This revealed the true nature and extent of the injury and led to
emergency treatment by traction and by manipulation under general anaesthetic, coupled
with the reduction and pinning of the fracture.
    It was common ground that the neglect to diagnose and treat the plaintiff's injury

caused him avoidable pain and suffering for the five days between 26 April and 1 May.
For this the judge awarded the very modest sum of £150, in respect of which there is no
appeal. What is in dispute is whether he is entitled to any further damages. This turns
on the long-term effects of the delay in diagnosis and treatment. On this there was a
conflict of medical evidence which reflects the fact that, whilst all or most surgeons
would regard immediate treatment as essential, if only to relieve pain, there is no
certainty that immediate treatment will avoid avascular necrosis with consequential
disability.

The judge made four findings of fact, which are accepted by the defendants. They are
as follows (see [1985] 3 All ER 167 at 171, [1985] 1 WLR 1036 at 1040–1041):

'1. Even had the defendants diagnosed and treated the plaintiff on 26 April there
is a high probability, which I assess as a 75% risk, that the plaintiff's injury would
have followed the same course as it in fact has, ie he would have developed avascular
necrosis of the whole femoral head with all the same adverse consequences as have
already ensured and with all the same adverse future prospects. 2. That 75% risk
was translated by the defendants' admitted breach of duty into an inevitability.
Putting it the other way, the defendants' delay in diagnosis denied the plaintiff the
25% chance that, given immediate treatment, avascular necrosis would not have
developed. 3. Had avascular necrosis not developed, the plaintiff would have made
a very nearly full recovery. 4. The reason why the delay sealed the plaintiff's fate
was because it allowed the pressure caused by haemarthrosis (the bleeding of
ruptured blood vessels into the joint) to compress and thus block the intact but
distorted remaining vessels with the result that even had the fall left intact sufficient
vessels to keep the epiphysis alive (which, as finding no 1 makes plain, I think
possible but improbable) such vessels would have become occluded and ineffective
for this purpose.'

Having reviewed the authorities, the judge reached four conclusions of law ([1985] 3
All ER 167 at 180, [1985] 1 WLR 1036 at 1050):

'(1) If the plaintiff proves both medical negligence and that he has thereby (a) lost
a substantial chance of achieving a better medical result, alternatively, (b) incurred a
substantial risk of an adverse medical result developing, he is entitled to damages.
(2) If the extent of that proved loss of chance or risk is clearly unascertainable, then
the plaintiff is entitled to recover damages in full. (3) The extent of the loss of chance
or risk should, however, be ascertained if possible and the plaintiff's damages be
calculated and discounted accordingly. (4) Generally speaking the plaintiff will be
required to establish a higher degree of substantiality in order to succeed on basis (2)
than on basis (3); even on basis (3) the court will look for a higher degree of
substantiality when the claim is not attached to a directly provable period of
suffering or disability, particularly a serious one, than when it is.'

These conclusions are not accepted.

Combining fact and law, Simon Brown J awarded the plaintiff £11,650, being the
£150 for pain and suffering together with £11,500 or 25% of the full liability figure of
£46,000. The defendants now appeal.

The essence of the defendants' argument is that the standard of proof in civil
proceedings is the balance of probabilities. In percentage terms, where it is alleged that
an event, act or omission has occurred, he who alleges it must satisfy the court that it is
more than 50% likely that it occurred. In the instant case the plaintiff only proved that it
was 25% likely that the delay in diagnosing and treating his injury permitted the
avascular necrosis to occur. Accordingly, he cannot establish that *any* loss flowed from
the delay and cannot recover damages based on it. As a subsidiary argument, the

defendants contend that, even though, as is the case, it is possible to sue in contract for the loss of a chance, no such claim in tort has ever been recognised.

The principal argument has a superficial attraction. This attraction stems from its simplicity and the fact that it is undoubtedly based on well-settled principles of law. So far as past happenings are concerned, the court does indeed approach the matter on the basis that, if it is 50% or less likely to have happened, it did not happen and that, if it is more than 50% likely, it did. In general it is only in relation to future happenings, its view of which must inevitably be more or less speculative, that it translates likelihood into what might be described as partial or discounted findings of fact.

If authority for these principles were needed, it is to be found in the speech of Lord Diplock in *Mallett v McMonagle* [1969] 2 All ER 178 at 190–191, [1970] AC 166 at 176:

> 'The role of the court in making an assessment of damages which depends on its view as to what will be and what would have been is to be contrasted with its ordinary function in civil actions of determining what was. In determining what did happen in the past a court decides on the balance of probabilities. Anything that is more probable than not it treats as certain. But in assessing damages which depend on its view as to what will happen in the future or would have happened in the future if something had not happened in the past, the court must make an estimate as to what are the chances that a particular thing will or would have happened and reflect those chances, whether they are more or less than even, in the amount of damages which it awards.'

This is supported by a passage from the speech of Lord Reid in *Davies v Taylor* [1972] 3 All ER 836 at 838, [1974] AC 207 at 212–213 where he said:

> 'When the question is whether a certain thing is or is not true—whether a certain event did or did not happen—then the court must decide one way or the other. There is no question of chance or probability. Either it did or it did not happen. But the standard of civil proof is a balance of probabilities. If the evidence shows a balance in favour of it having happened then it is proved that it did in fact happen. But here we are not and could not be seeking a decision either that the wife would or that she would not have returned to her husband. You can prove that a past event happened, but you cannot prove that a future event will happen and I do not think that the law is so foolish as to suppose that you can. All that you can do is to evaluate the chance. Sometimes it is virtually 100 per cent; sometimes virtually nil. But often it is somewhere in between. And if it is somewhere in between I do not see much difference between a probability of 51 per cent and a probability of 49 per cent.'

Applying that approach to the judge's findings of fact, counsel for the defendants submits that no causal connection between the negligence and the development of avascular necrosis and consequent disability has been established, since a 25% likelihood fails to achieve the requisite standard of proof. Without that causal connection, there can be no liability in damages based on that development. In more concrete terms, it is all, ie £46,000, or nothing, £46,000, if the likelihood of the connection exceeds 50% cent and otherwise nothing. In the instant case it is nothing.

In counsel's submission, damages in respect of a lost chance are recoverable only where the defendant breaks a contract under which the plaintiff was entitled to a chance or where chances are relevant to *valuing* an injury proved to result from the defendant's breach of duty. An example of a successful contractual claim for damages for the loss of a chance is provided by *Chaplin v Hicks* [1911] 2 KB 786, [1911–13] All ER Rep 224, where an entrant in a beauty competition was not notified of the date of the final and so lost the chance of a prize. Examples of valuing an injury on the basis of the chance of its proving more or less severe are, of course, legion.

The only authority directly in point is *Kenyon v Bell* 1953 SC 125, where Lord Guthrie
a held, in preliminary proceedings as to the relevancy, that an averment that negligent
medical treatment caused the loss of an eye was a good plea, but that an alternative
averment that the treatment led to the loss of the chance of saving an eye was not. Lord
Guthrie considered various reported decisions but, holding that they did not assist,
expressly based his decision on 'the general principles of the law of reparation' and quoted
with approval a dictum of Master J in *Kranz v M'Cutcheon* (1920) 18 OWN 395:
b
'The rule against the recovery of uncertain damages is directed against uncertainty
as to cause rather than as to the extent or measure.'

(See 1953 SC 125 at 128.)
This authority certainly supports the defendant's argument, but is not binding on this
court. As will appear, I do not think that it represents the law of England.
c Mention must also be made of another Scottish authority, this time in the House of
Lords. In *McGhee v National Coal Board* [1972] 3 All ER 1008, [1973] 1 WLR 1 a workman
was necessarily exposed to brick dust in the course of his employment. His employers
were in breach of a statutory duty to provide adequate washing facilities at his place of
work. The brick dust caused damage to the skin and the extent of the damage, and the
seriousness of the consequences, depended in part on how long the dust was allowed to
d remain in contact with the skin. The Scottish courts held that the workman could not
succeed unless he could prove, on the balance of probabilities, that the provision of
washing facilities at the work place and their use by him would have prevented him
being afflicted with dermatitis. The House of Lords held that it sufficed if the workman
could show that, on the balance of probabilities, the lack of washing facilities contributed
materially to the occurrence of the dermatitis and followed its own decision in *Bonnington
e* *Castings Ltd v Wardlaw* [1956] 1 All ER 615, [1956] AC 613. However, the decision in
McGhee v National Coal Board is remarkable, in the literal sense of the word, for passages
in the speeches of Lord Reid, Lord Wilberforce, Lord Simon and Lord Salmon which
might suggest that where an employer is in breach of statutory duty and injury is
suffered which that duty was designed to avoid, but, in the current state of medical
f knowledge it is impossible to prove how effective the statutory precaution would have
been in a particular case, the burden of proof is reversed and it is for the employer to
prove that there was no causal connection (see [1972] 3 All ER 1008 at 1011, 1013, 1014–
1015, 1018, [1973] 1 WLR 1 at 4–5, 7, 8–9, 12–13). Perhaps a more orthodox
interpretation of this decision is that, where a statutory duty is admittedly aimed at a
particular mischief, the duty is broken and the mischief occurs, there is a prima facie
g inference of causation. However that may be, it is clear that no one suggested that it was
possible to assess the likelihood that the provision of washing facilities would have
prevented or reduced the severity of the dermatitis and that damages should be awarded
on the basis of a discount reflecting such likelihood.
In the instant appeal the plaintiff gave notice of a contention that the award of damages
should be increased to £27,750, being 60% of full liability, but at no time has he
h abandoned his basic claim that the delay in diagnosis and treatment deprived him of a
chance of avoiding the disability from which he suffers and that any award of damages
should reflect this chance. Nor has he put forward an alternative claim for full liability
based on (a) accepting the defendants' arguments and contending that the likelihood of
avoiding the disability exceeded 50% or (b) claiming that on some reasoning based on, or
analogous to, that of *McGhee v National Coal Board*, it should be held that the delay made
j a material contribution to the disability. Having mentioned the plaintiff's respondent's
notice, albeit in a different context from pure quantum, it may be convenient to say that
I can see no basis on which we could differ from the judge's assessment of the likelihood
of timeous treatment having been successful and I would dismiss the cross-appeal.
I return therefore to the problem of liability. As a matter of common sense, it is unjust

that there should be no liability for failure to treat a patient, simply because the chances of a successful cure by that treatment were less than 50%. Nor, by the same token, can it *a* be just that, if the chances of a successful cure only marginally exceed 50%, the doctor or his employer should be liable to the same extent as if the treatment could be guaranteed to cure. If this is the law, it is high time that it was changed, assuming that this court has power to do so.

Equally I am quite unable to detect any rational basis for a state of the law, if such it be, whereby in identical circumstances Dr A who treats a patient under the national *b* health service, and whose liability therefore falls to be determined in accordance with the law of tort, should be in a different position from Dr B who treats a patient outside the service, and whose liability therefore falls to be determined in accordance with the law of contract, assuming, of course, that the contract is in terms which impose on him neither more nor less than the tortious duty.

The answer I think lies in examining precisely what the plaintiff has to allege and *c* prove. First, he has to prove a duty. This is no problem in this case, since it is admitted. But for that admission, it would have been necessary to establish the duty, the necessary factual basis being proved on the balance of probabilities. I say that because there is no room in either justice or law for holding a defendant liable on the basis that he *may* have been subject to a duty. Either he was or he was not. Second, the plaintiff has to prove a breach of that duty. Here again there is no problem, since the failure to treat the plaintiff *d* properly on the occasion of his first visit to the hospital admittedly constituted a breach of that duty. But, if this breach had had to be established, any necessary facts would have had to have been proved on the balance of probabilities. Again I say this because there is no room in justice or law for holding a defendant liable on the basis that there is a significant possibility, not amounting to a probability, that he was in breach of his duty. Third, in the case of tort but not of contract, the plaintiff has to prove some loss or *e* damage and must do so on the balance of probabilities. It is this third requirement which requires further analysis. Hereafter, for simplicity, I will refer to 'loss or damage' simply as 'loss'.

The distinction between what must be proved in contract and what must be proved in tort in order to establish a cause of action may be regrettable, but it does not lie within *f* the power of this court to do anything about it. In any event, it is not usually of practical importance, save perhaps in the context of limitation, where the loss necessary to complete the cause of action in tort occurs a significant time after the breach of duty. Even in contract, if more than a bare right of action is to be established, the plaintiff must prove a loss of substance and, once again, this must be proved on the balance of probabilities. Having identified and proved that loss, the loss has then to be valued. *g* Identification and valuation are distinct and separate processes, but, pace *McGhee's* case, it is for the plaintiff to prove both the identified loss and its value and to do so in each case on the balance of probabilities.

In the instant case the plaintiff has no difficulty in identifying the loss on which he relies. It has been described by the judge as 'a substantially increased risk that avascular necrosis would develop and long term disability result' (see [1985] 3 All ER 167 at 171, *h* [1985] 1 WLR 1036 at 1040) and in argument as 'the chance of avoiding avascular necrosis and its consequences'. I think it is the use of the latter description, with its reference to *chances*, which has complicated what is essentially a simple claim. I say that because the use of the word 'chance' imports probabilities and opens the way to the argument put forward by the defendants. I also think that it is inaccurate, because it elides the identification of the loss with the valuation of that loss, and they are distinct *j* processes.

In my judgment the essence of the plaintiff's claim is that he has lost any *benefit* which he would have derived if, on the occasion of his first visit to the hospital, he had received the treatment which he in fact received on the occasion of his second visit. This loss of benefit is, of course, admitted, since it flows inexorably from the admission of negligence. Furthermore, it is admitted that it had some value, namely that earlier treatment would have reduced the period over which the plaintiff would have been in pain. Whether it had any further value was in issue. However, if it had been necessary to prove that earlier treatment constituted any benefit, this would have had to have been done on the balance of probabilities.

Counsel for the defendants seeks to escape from the consequences of this analysis by submitting that it really cannot make any difference that, in this particular case, the plaintiff can prove that loss of the benefit of early treatment undoubtedly led to pain and suffering, which is a proper subject matter for damages in tort. The real issue is whether, viewed in isolation, the loss of the benefit of early treatment in relation to avascular necrosis and its consequences sounds in damages, when all that can be proved is that there was a chance that it would have been successful. With this I agree. In counsel's submission it does not sound in damages because damages in tort are confined to compensating proved financial or physical losses and the loss of a chance is neither.

It has been said times without number that the categories of negligence are never closed and, subject to the rules relating to remoteness of damage, which are not material in the instant case, I can see no reason why the categories of loss should be closed either.

If the plaintiff can rely on the loss of the *benefit* of timeous treatment, he has still to satisfy the court as to the value of this benefit, and once again he must do this on the balance of probabilities. He did this in three stages. First, he identified, and proved to this standard, that the benefit which he had lost was a one in four chance of avoiding avascular necrosis. Second, he established, again on the balance of probabilities, that the long-term disability from which he is suffering was to be valued at £46,000. Third, he submitted, and the judge accepted, that a one-in-four chance of avoiding this loss was worth one-quarter of the value of the loss itself. I am not sure that this necessarily follows, although it is no doubt a convenient approach. There could, I think, be circumstances in which the 'worst case' was either relatively trivial or, alternatively, was so dire that in the first case a one-in-four chance of avoidance would be worth less than, and in the second case would be worth far more than, 25% of the 'worst case' value. However, there was no challenge to this proportionate approach either here or below.

Counsel for the defendants also submitted that this approach leads to a number of anomalous results.

(a) *Damages for a lost chance or increased risk will be recoverable in all negligence actions*

By this I think counsel meant that proportionate awards of damages will be recoverable in all negligence actions. Not so. Usually the duty will not confer on the plaintiff the benefit of a chance, but of a certainty. And, even when it confers a chance, breach of that duty will only lead to a proportionate award where it is impossible to determine what would have been the consequences of the plaintiff being given that chance, although possible to determine the likelihood of particular consequences. Take the case of a solicitor who fails to advise his client that the property which he is about to purchase is subject to a right of way. If the client had been told, he would or he would not have gone ahead with the transaction. That would have been *his* choice, not the choice of fate. Ascertaining what his choice would have been is possible, whereas the prospects for a cure of a particular patient are sometimes not. The damages recoverable by the solicitor's client would therefore be all or nothing, depending on whether he could prove, on the balance of probabilities, that he would have abandoned the transaction.

(b) *Time will start to run when a chance is lost or a risk is increased, not when physical injury is sustained*

This is no more anomalous than the difference between limitation where the claim is founded in contract and where it is founded in tort. In any event, it is not a case of the cause of action being brought forward in point of time. All that is involved is that different causes of action may have different starting points when calculating periods of limitation.

(c) *Plaintiffs who are deprived of a chance of recovery or exposed to a chance of injury will have a right of action even if they remain uninjured in the event*
This may be correct, but it is not of practical consequence, since the loss suffered will be nil and, at best, only nominal damages will be recoverable.

(d) *Where there is a negligent failure to diagnose and treat in a way which would have given a 25% increased chance of survival, the patient would recover damages subject to a 75% discount, but his dependants would obtain no award under the Fatal Accidents Act 1976 because they could not prove that the negligence caused the death*
This may be regarded as an anomaly, but it stems from the wording of the statute: 'If death is caused by any wrongful act, neglect or default . . .' I do not regard this anomaly, if such it be, as throwing any light on the problem with which we are concerned.

It will be seen that I entirely agree with the judge's first conclusion of law, but have reservations about the remainder which are, I think, based on *McGhee v National Coal Board*, an authority which I have had some difficulty in understanding.

For the reasons which I have sought to express, I agree that the plaintiff was entitled to the award of damages made by the judge and I would dismiss the appeal.

DILLON LJ. It is well established that in an appropriate factual and legal context a plaintiff can recover damages for the loss of a chance, where the wrongful act of the defendant has deprived the plaintiff of a chance of achieving some benefit, even though the chance was less than a 50% chance, provided that it was not minimal or, as it has been put, a mere speculative possibility: see for instance *Chaplin v Hicks* [1911] 2 KB 786, [1911–13] All ER Rep 224, where the defendant had contracted that the plaintiff should have a chance of competing for a theatrical engagement and he broke his contract, and *Davies v Taylor* [1972] 3 All ER 836, [1974] AC 207, where the court considered what expectation of financial benefit had to be shown by a dependant claiming under the Fatal Accidents Acts 1846 to 1959.

In *Chaplain v Hicks* no one could ever know whether, but for the defendant's wrongful act, the plaintiff would have been successful in the competition. But for his act, however, she would have had the chance of competing; by his act she was deprived of that chance and for that chance, and not for any probability of success, she was compensated by an award of damages. In the present case, when the plaintiff was taken to St Luke's Hospital on 26 April 1977 he had, on the judge's findings, a 25% chance that by prompt treatment the development of avascular necrosis of the left femoral epiphysis, with all its serious consequences, could be avoided. When he left the hospital to return home that day he had lost that chance as a result of the breach of duty on the part of the doctor, for whom the defendants are responsible, in conducting his examination of the plaintiff that day. As a result of the doctor's negligence, there was no prompt treatment and so we can never know how the chance would have turned out had the examination of the plaintiff not been negligent. Why then should not the plaintiff be compensated by damages for the loss of that chance?

The answer given by counsel for the defendants is that the plaintiff's cause of action lies in tort and not in contract, and in tort, unlike contract, damage caused to the plaintiff by the defendant's wrongful act is an essential ingredient of the cause of action. Counsel referred to various statements of principle of high authority, such as the reference by Viscount Kilmuir LC in *Cummings (or McWilliams) v Sir William Arrol & Co Ltd* [1962] 1 All ER 623 at 626, [1962] 1 WLR 295 at 299 to the necessity, in actions of negligence, of establishing not only the breach of duty but also the causal connection between the

breach and the injury complained of, and the statement by Lord Diplock in *Mallett v*
a *McMonagle* [1969] 2 All ER 178 at 190–191, [1970] AC 166 at 176 that the court decides
questions of fact on the balance of probabilities and treats as certain anything that is more
probable than not. Adding these two together, counsel submits that the plaintiff cannot
recover anything against the defendants because, on the judge's findings, he does not
show that but for the doctor's negligence there was a more than 50% chance, a balance of
probabilities, that avascular necrosis would have been avoided by prompt treatment on
b 26 April.

Medicine does not deal only in certainties. In that, no doubt, medicine is not unique,
but there are very many cases in which the patient who goes to a doctor has only a
chance, be it greater or less, of being cured of his ailment, or only a chance of avoiding a
further deterioration in his condition. If counsel is right, and the chance is lost through a
negligent failure of the doctor to examine the patient properly or to diagnose correctly,
c with the result that the treatment which alone might have saved the patient is not
undertaken, the patient will have no remedy unless he can show that the chance of the
treatment, if undertaken, proving successful was more than 50%. That to my mind is
contrary to common sense.

The fundamental question is: what is the damage which the plaintiff has suffered? Is
it the onset of the avascular necrosis or is it the loss of the chance of avoiding that
d condition? In my judgment, it is the latter. I see no reason why the loss of a chance
which is capable of being valued should not be capable of being damage in a tort case just
as much as in a contract case such as *Chaplin v Hicks*. If that is right, there is no difficulty
over causation. Causation (that the damage was caused by the wrongful act of the
defendant) has to be proved on the balance of probabilities, but by that standard of proof
it was amply proved in the present case that the chance which the plaintiff on the judge's
e findings had had was lost by the admitted negligence of the doctor.

The position would have been different if, as in *Barnett v Chelsea and Kensington Hospital*
Management Committee [1968] 1 All ER 1068, [1969] 1 QB 428 the finding on the facts on
the balance of probabilities had been that had all care been taken still the patient would
have suffered the same result. In that event there would, on the facts, have been no lost
chance and the plaintiff would thus have suffered no damage from the negligence. The
f defendants' witness, Mr Bonney, said in part of his evidence that there was no chance and
that in this plaintiff's case, whatever statistics may show, avascular necrosis was inevitable.
But the judge did not accept that evidence of Mr Bonney. The judge found that there
was a significant chance, though less than 50%. That chance the plaintiff has lost through
the negligence of the doctor for whom the defendants are responsible. The plaintiff has
thereby suffered damage for which he is entitled to be compensated. I would accordingly
g dismiss this appeal.

As to the cross-appeal, whereby the plaintiff seeks to establish that the chance which
he lost of avoiding avascular necrosis was a 60%, and not merely a 25%, chance, I see no
justification for interfering with the judge's finding, much as I sympathise with the
plaintiff. The judge had before him two expert witnesses, Mr Bonney and Mr Bucknill,
h neither of whose evidence was very satisfactory on this point. There were internal
inconsistencies in Mr Bonney's evidence on the point, while Mr Bucknill's, which was
difficult to follow because it did not appear until a late stage that he drew a fundamental
distinction between a probability and a likelihood, did not persuade the judge. The judge
had to form his own view, and this court, which has not seen either witness, could not
reach any different conclusion.

j
CROOM-JOHNSON LJ. On 26 April 1977 the plaintiff, then aged 13, suffered an
injury to his hip joint when he fell from a rope at school. He suffered from an acute
fracture separation of the left femoral epiphysis. He was taken to St Luke's Hospital,
Maidenhead. His left knee was X-rayed, but not the hip. He was sent home. On 1 May,

after several days of intense pain, he was sent back to St Luke's, where further X-rays were taken, this time of the hip. The fracture was diagnosed, and he was put on traction. On 2 May the hip was operated on. The defendants admitted that the failure to diagnose the fracture on 26 April and to treat it until 2 May was a breach of duty. For the five days' pain and suffering the judge awarded £150. The whole question in this appeal has concerned the long-term results.

The plaintiff's injury was undoubtedly serious, particularly in a growing boy, and a serious one of its type. It was one from which the prospects of recovery are poor. He now has a grievously and permanently disabled leg, which is shortened. There were agreed medical reports from a Mr Westcombe which describe the present condition and the deterioration both of his leg and back which may be expected to take place in the future. These reports formed the ground on which damages for the leg injury were assessed on a full liability basis.

The East Berkshire Area Health Authority became the only effective defendants. The other defendants were the doctors in the partnership practice who attended to the plaintiff during the six days between the hospital visits. The plaintiff discontinued against them, and they fall out of the story.

The case was brought in negligence. The amended statement of claim alleged that the present injuries to the plaintiff resulted from the negligence in failing to carry out a proper diagnosis on 26 April 1977. In view of the course which the case took at trial, it is necessary to set out what needed to be proved.

This is an action on the case. The plaintiff, in order to succeed, had first to establish a breach of duty. This was admitted by the defendants. He then had to prove damage, which was the gist of the action, and that each of the heads of damage was caused by the breach of duty. All these had to be proved by the normal standard of proof in civil liability, on at least a balance of probabilities. In *Bonnington Castings Ltd v Wardlaw* [1956] 1 All ER 615, [1956] AC 613 it was held that the breach of duty must be proved to have caused or contributed to the damage, and if there is more than one cause the contribution may be less than half so long as it is material. That case also overruled *Vyner v Waldenberg Bros Ltd* [1945] 2 All ER 547, [1946] KB 50 in so far as it laid down that in actions based on breaches of statutory duty the onus of proof is reversed.

How the onus of proof is discharged will vary. It may depend on direct oral evidence, on inferences to be drawn from proved facts, on expert opinion or in other ways. In appropriate cases, where a recognised precaution is not taken and injury is suffered of the kind which that precaution is designed to prevent, the court may draw the inference of cause and effect: see *McGhee v National Coal Board* [1972] 3 All ER 1008, [1973] 1 WLR 1. I do not read that case as departing from *Bonnington Castings Ltd v Wardlaw* and reversing the onus of proof. But in the end the judge decides as a question of fact whether the case is made out or not, on a balance of probability, taking all the facts into account.

In cases brought under the Fatal Accidents Act 1976 the executor or administrator of the deceased (who for technical reasons is the plaintiff) has to prove that the deceased would have succeeded in an action if he had not died. The proof of liability is thus the same as in actions for personal injuries, save in fatal accident cases the death is essentially the cause of action: see *Seward v Vera Cruz (owners), The Vera Cruz* (1884) 10 App Cas 59 at 67, [1881–5] All ER Rep 216 at 220 per the Earl of Selborne LC. The death is the equivalent of the 'damage' which in an action for personal injuries completes the cause of action.

Once the 'damage' has been proved, the loss and compensation must be assessed as money damages. In fatal accident cases, where there must be dependants of the deceased before the action will lie, the damages must be 'proportioned to the injury resulting from the death to the dependants respectively' (see s 3(1) of the 1976 Act). The 'injury' is financial injury only, and is the equivalent in a fatal accident case to the 'loss' in an action for personal injuries. The onus of proving these is less strict than in the primary proof of liability. In both the proof of liability and the assessment of loss, consideration of chances may enter into it. In proof of liability the chances that a particular cause will produce a particular effect are often relevant. They may range from being certain on the one hand to being negligible or non-existent on the other, but at this stage of the case they are an element, and no more, in the proof of the cause of action. In the assessment of loss the future may have to be looked at, and again chances may be taken into account. Typical examples are the chances that epilepsy may supervene after a head injury. A plaintiff with a 30% chance of developing epilepsy will recover more damages than one with a 5% chance. In fatal accident cases the question is whether the dependant had a reasonable expectation of financial support from the deceased, not whether it is proved on a balance of probabilities that such support would have been received: see *Davies v Taylor* [1972] 3 All ER 836, [1974] AC 207. In that case a wife had left her husband five weeks before his death. She had refused to return to him, so the husband instructed his solicitor to begin divorce proceedings. When the husband was killed, she began proceedings under the Fatal Acidents Acts 1846 to 1959 alleging that there was a prospect of reconciliation, in which case she would have been able to recover as a dependant. She was not believed and the action failed at the proof of 'injury' stage, but it was the test of 'reasonable expectation' which was adopted.

In the present case, apart from the agreed reports of Mr Westcombe, medical reports were not exchanged. It must have been apparent to the plaintiff's advisers that his leg had a poor chance of recovery in any event, and that he was at risk of losing the case altogether (apart from the five days' pain and suffering) if he could not prove that the delay in diagnosis had had a material adverse effect on him. In other words, he would not have proved the 'damage' necessary to establish that part of his cause of action. Counsel for the plaintiff accordingly opened the case on the basis that he was asking for a finding that the plaintiff had suffered a loss of his chance of recovering from his broken hip and that he should receive only a proportion of the damages which would be appropriate if his eventual condition could be blamed entirely on the defendants. Counsel for the defendants submitted that the proper approach would be to try to prove causation on a balance of probabilities and thereafter, if appropriate, assess damages on the usual basis taking chances into account.

In my opinion this exchange led to a misunderstanding which persisted right up to this court. The plaintiff's medical witness was Mr Bucknill, a consultant orthopaedic surgeon. He gave evidence that the effect of an injury such as the plaintiff's is to interfere with the blood supply to the epiphysis so that avascular necrosis may develop. There may be haemarthrosis, which means bleeding from ruptured blood vessels into the hip joint. Delay in treating and pinning the damaged bone causes the blood in the haemarthrosis to compress and block the further supply of blood from any undamaged vessels. The result would be adverse. Mr Bucknill's evidence was that timely surgical intervention would have given the plaintiff a 40% chance of recovery. The defendants' expert witness was Mr Bonney. His evidence was that the very nature of this operation on someone so badly injured as the plaintiff was the cause of his final disability because of the manipulation of the limb which it necessarily entailed. The delay did not affect that, and therefore did not cause any additional incapacity.

Both witnesses had seen the hospital records, X-rays and operation notes.

The plaintiff's approach to the claim, as being one for the loss of a chance, resulted in a great deal of the medical evidence being taken up with the question: was there a chance and, if so, what was it? It was dealt with in a somewhat general manner, with some reliance on medical papers and the statistics to be extracted from them. In the end the judge accepted the evidence of neither surgeon in its entirety. He found that the operation ought to have been carried out at once. As to the effects of the delay, he made the following findings of fact ([1985] 3 All ER 167 at 171, [1985] 1 WLR 1036 at 1040–1041):

'1. Even had the defendants correctly diagnosed and treated the plaintiff on 26
April there is a high probability, which I assess as a 75% risk, that the plaintiff's *a*
injury would have followed the same course as in fact it has, ie he would have
developed avascular necrosis of the whole femoral head with all the same adverse
consequences as have already ensued and with all the same adverse future prospects.
2. That 75% risk was translated by the defendants' admitted breach of duty into an
inevitability. Putting it the other way, the defendants' delay in diagnosis denied the
plaintiff the 25% chance that, given immediate treatment, avascular necrosis would *b*
not have developed. 3. Had avascular necrosis not developed, the plaintiff would
have made a very nearly full recovery. 4. The reason why the delay sealed the
plaintiff's fate was because it allowed the pressure caused by haemarthrosis (the
bleeding of ruptured blood vessels into the joint) to compress and thus block the
intact but distorted remaining vessels with the result that even had the fall left intact
sufficient vessels to keep the epiphysis alive (which, as finding no 1 makes plain, I *c*
think possible but improbable) such vessels would have become occluded and
ineffective for this purpose.'

These findings mean that in any event the plaintiff had only a 25% chance of recovery,
but that the delay removed that chance and made his condition that much worse. The
judge assessed the damages at £46,000 and awarded him 25%, £11,500, plus the £150. *d*

The defendants accept those findings. Their argument before the judge and in this
court was that to find for the plaintiff for the loss of a chance which was itself an
improbability was to depart from the rule that liability must be established on a balance
of probabilities. In support of that they also submitted that authorities under the Fatal
Accidents Act, such as *Davies v Taylor* [1972] 3 All ER 836, are special to cases brought
under that Act and have no application to actions at common law, and that damages *e*
awarded for the loss of a chance should be restricted to actions for breach of contract such
as *Chaplin v Hicks* [1911] 2 KB 786, [1911–13] All ER Rep 224 and *Marbe v George
Edwardes (Daly's Theatre) Ltd* [1928] 1 KB 269, [1927] All ER Rep 253. Counsel for the
defendants referred us to a number of cases where actions for negligence have failed on
the issue of causation in spite of there having been a breach of duty, such as *Barnett v
Chelsea and Kensington Hospital Management Committee* [1968] 1 All ER 1068, [1969] 1 QB *f*
428, *Sykes v Midland Bank Exor and Trustee Co Ltd* [1970] 2 All ER 471, [1971] 1 QB 113
and *Robinson v Post Office* [1974] 2 All ER 737, [1974] 1 WLR 1176. All of those cases
were decided on their own facts. On the other hand, in *Kitchen v Royal Air Force Association*
[1958] 2 All ER 241, [1958] 1 WLR 563 a claim against a firm of solicitors was clearly
based on negligence and resulted in damages being awarded against them for the loss of a
chance of conducting successful litigation against a third party. *g*

There is nothing in the proposed distinction between contract and tort. There would
be no sense in a distinction which allowed damages to be recovered from a private doctor
but not against a national health service doctor.

Nor is the distinction between common law and the Fatal Accidents Act valid. Once
the cause of action has been completed, in the one case by proof of 'damage' and in the
other by proof of death, the assessment of loss which may depend on chances in the *h*
future must proceed on similar lines.

The misunderstanding which arose in the present case came from two sources. One
was the presentation of the plaintiff's case and the other was the concentration in the
medical evidence on what would have been the plaintiff's chance of recovery but for the
delay in diagnosis. This created the impression that it was the loss of that chance alone
which was to be regarded as the 'damage' which completed the plaintiff's cause of action *j*
entitling him to money compensation for the injury to his leg, rather than a way of
computing a loss to which he was already entitled. This ignored the fact that the
estimation of chances may enter into consideration at every stage in a case, both in proof
of liability and in assessing damages.

In his closing speech, the plaintiff's counsel said:

'It is our submission, first of all, that the loss of a chance, even a less than 50% chance, is enough to found a claim for damages in tort ... damage is proved by proving on the balance of probabilities the loss of a 25% chance.'

Put simply that way, the proposition is unsustainable. If it is proved statistically that 25% of the population have a chance of recovery from a certain injury and 75% do not, it does not mean that someone who suffers that injury and who does not recover from it has lost a 25% chance. He may have lost nothing at all. What he has to do is prove that he was one of the 25% and that his loss was caused by the defendant's negligence. To be a figure in a statistic does not by itself give him a cause of action. If the plaintiff succeeds in proving that he was one of the 25% and that the defendant took away that chance, the logical result would be to award him 100% of his damages and not only a quarter, but that might be left for consideration if and when it arises. In this case the plaintiff was only asking for a quarter.

Even the judge at one point in his judgment said ([1985] 3 All ER 167 at 178, [1985] 1 WLR 1086 at 1047):

'The defendants' breach of duty here (a) denied the plaintiff the 25% chance of escaping, and thus (b) *may have caused* the very disability which occurred.' (My emphasis.)

In the end he decided that the 25/75% split in the chances was something which went to quantification of damages and not to causation.

The role of the 25/75% split as no more than part of the evidentiary material going to proof of liability seems to have been largely lost sight of. The judge, in the commendable interest of brevity, did not give a detailed analysis of the medical evidence on causation. What he did was to make the findings of fact which I have set out earlier. There was evidence to support them in that of Mr Bucknill. After stating that the plaintiff's femur was displaced and displacement increases bleeding, he went on to say that the longer the displacement continued the greater the increase in the bleeding. The consequence of that would be compression of the blood vessels leading directly to impaired blood supply to the epiphysis. Even though the chance of that happening was less than 50% or (as the judge found) 25%, that evidence justified the judge in finding the facts that he did. He clearly did not accept Mr Bonney's evidence that in the plaintiff's case the six days' delay had made no difference at all.

That is sufficient to dispose of this appeal. But the judge dealt with an alternative ground. This was that the loss of the statistical chance could be attached parasitically to the undoubted injury of five days' pain and suffering. He held that it could. This argument really stands or falls with the main one whether the loss of a statistical chance can itself found a claim in law unless causation is properly proved.

It is not the case that in no circumstances can the loss of a chance ever found an action in tort. But it must be where the chance is one personal to the plaintiff and not to the world at large, or even, if I may coin a phrase, the world at little. The plaintiff is only entitled to compensation for the loss of his own chance and not someone else's. In the actions for breach of contract, for example, such as *Chaplin v Hicks* [1911] 2 KB 786, [1911–13] All ER Rep 224 and *Marbe v George Edwards (Daly's Theatre) Ltd* [1928] 1 KB 269, [1927] All ER Rep 253 there is no problem, the contract was with the plaintiff. In *Kitchen v Royal Air Force Association* [1958] 2 All ER 241, [1958] 1 WLR 563 the chance of success was the plaintiff's and no one else's. The imaginary case was put to us in argument of a horse being negligently prevented from arriving at a racecourse in time for the start of the race. Assuming that an action was brought in tort (no breach of contract being committed) it might be that the loss of his chance of winning might avail the owner.

The assessment of damages would clearly present a problem, possibly depending on evidence from bookmakers. But that case may be left until it arises.

The defendants in this case are alarmed at the thought that if the loss of a chance of getting better should be capable of being 'damage' sufficient to found a cause of action based on medical negligence it will open the floodgates to many actions where in the end no harm has followed. I do not think that alarm is justified. In the first place, a mere statistical chance will not be enough. The chance must be something lost to the individual patient. Secondly, the chance that something may go wrong is normally subsumed in the eventual result. If no harm is caused in the end the plaintiff will have suffered no damage, even if at one stage in his treatment there was a risk that things might go wrong.

In my view the findings of fact conclude this appeal once they are accepted by the defendants. I would therefore dismiss the appeal.

The plaintiff cross-appealed, arguing that the 25% figure ought to have been 60%. This was based on one answer given by Mr Bonney in cross-examination. The meaning of the answer, in the context in which it was given, was and is by no means clear. It is insufficient to justify an alteration of the figure. I would also dismiss the cross-appeal.

Appeal dismissed. Leave to appeal to the House of Lords refused. Cross-appeal dismissed.

Solicitors: *Hempsons* (for the defendants); *Lloyd Howorth & Partners*, Maidenhead (for the plaintiff).

Frances Rustin   Barrister.

Taylor v Chief Constable of Cheshire

QUEEN'S BENCH DIVISION
RALPH GIBSON LJ AND McNEILL J
27 OCTOBER 1986

Criminal evidence – Video recording – Offence viewed on visual display unit – Admissibility of what was seen on visual display unit or video recording – Recording not available at trial – Whether evidence of contents of video recording inadmissible as hearsay – Whether evidence of what was seen on visual display unit or video recorder admissible as direct evidence of what was seen to be happening.

The appellant was charged with the theft of a packet of batteries from a shop. The prosecution evidence rested in part on what three police officers had seen in a video recording which allegedly showed the appellant committing the offence. The video recording was mistakenly erased before the trial and was therefore not available to be viewed by the justices, who nevertheless regarded the officers' evidence of what they had seen on the video recording as admissible and convicted the appellant. The appellant appealed, contending that the officers' evidence should have been excluded as hearsay.

Held – There was no effective distinction, for the purpose of admissibility, between a direct view of the actions of an alleged offender by a witness and a view of those actions on a visual display unit of a camera or on a video recording of what the camera recorded, provided that what was seen on the visual display unit or video recording was connected by sufficient evidence to the alleged actions of the accused at the time and place in question. Evidence as to the contents of a film or video recording was not inadmissible because of the hearsay principle, but was direct evidence of what was seen to be happening in a particular place at a particular time. The fact that the video recording was not available at the trial did not of itself render the evidence of the police officers inadmissible, although the court had carefully to assess the weight and reliability of that evidence. Since the evidence of the police officers had been rightly admitted and since the justices had correctly directed themselves as to its weight and reliability, the appeal would be dismissed (see p 227 *e f*, p 228 *h*, p 230 *b* to *g*, p 231 *e* and p 232 *a e* to *g*, post).

R v Kajala (1982) 75 Cr App R 149, *R v Maqsud Ali* [1965] 2 All ER 464, *R v Fowden and White* [1982] Crim LR 588 and *R v Grimer* [1982] Crim LR 674 considered.

Per McNeill J. Where the identification of an offender depends wholly or largely on the evidence of a witness describing what he saw on a visual display unit contemporaneously with the events which he describes or on a video recording of that display, or on what the tribunal of fact sees from such a recording, that evidence is necessarily subject to the appropriate directions as to identification evidence (see p 232 *b c*, post); *R v Turnbull* [1976] 3 All ER 549 applied.

Notes

For the hearsay rule and exceptions to it, see 11 Halsbury's Laws (4th edn) paras 437–438, and for cases on the subject, see 14(2) Digest (Reissue) 596–598, 4841–4862.

Cases referred to in judgments

Garton v Hunter [1969] 1 All ER 451, [1969] 2 QB 37, [1969] 2 WLR 86, CA.
Morgan v Lee [1985] RTR 409, DC.
Owen v Chesters [1985] RTR 191, DC.
R v Fowden and White [1982] Crim LR 588, CA.
R v Grimer [1982] Crim LR 674, CA.
R v Kajala (1982) 75 Cr App R 149, CA.
R v Maqsud Ali [1965] 2 All ER 464, [1966] 1 QB 688, [1965] 3 WLR 229, CA.
R v Turnbull [1976] 3 All ER 549, [1977] QB 224, [1976] 3 WLR 445, CA.

Case stated

Douglas Andrew Taylor appealed by way of case stated by the justices for the county of   *a*
Cheshire acting in and for the petty sessional division of Halton in respect of their
adjudication as a juvenile court sitting at Runcorn on 11 March 1986 whereby they
convicted the appellant of theft of a packet of batteries, contrary to s 1 of the Theft Act
1968, and fined him £50. The facts are set out in the judgment of Ralph Gibson LJ.

Timothy King for the appellant.   *b*
Jane Hayward for the prosecutor.

RALPH GIBSON LJ. This is an appeal by case stated from a decision of justices for the
county of Cheshire in the petty sessional division of Halton, in respect of their decision
whereby they convicted the appellant of theft contrary to s 1 of the Theft Act 1968. The
information alleged that the appellant on 3 December 1985 at Runcorn stole one packet   *c*
of Duracell batteries to the value of £1·89, the property of W H Smith Ltd.

The evidence for the prosecution rested in part on what witnesses had seen in a video
recording. At the trial a copy of that video recording was not available to be viewed by
the justices. Objection was therefore taken that the evidence which was to be tendered
by the prosecution witnesses as to what they had seen was not admissible. The matter
was argued, and the justices made a preliminary ruling that the evidence was not on the   *d*
grounds put forward inadmissible. The trial proceeded.

The facts found by the justices were as follows. On 3 December 1985 Brian
Hitchmough, a security officer at W H Smith, was on duty at this shop. He was observing
customers in the store on two television screens, which were in turn linked to two remote
control cameras which he could control. One of those screens was linked to a video
recording. The recorder was switched on, and a recording was made of an incident which *e*
lasted for a few seconds only and showed the back view of a person who, it was alleged,
picked up a pack of batteries in his right hand and placed them inside his jacket. He then
glanced up at the camera full face and walked out of camera range.

That recording was seen by Mr Glen Denson, the manager of the store, within a few
minutes of it being made. About half an hour after the recording was made, Wpc
Jennings and Det Con Holian viewed the recording and identified the appellant as the   *f*
person who was shown in it.

Some time after Christmas 1985 that recording was viewed by Det Con Baker and
again by Det Con Holian, and Det Con Baker also identified the appellant. The recording
was later taken to Runcorn police station to be viewed by Mr Brian de Haas, who was
then the appellant's solicitor. In the event it could not be played on the police video, so it
was returned to W H Smith and later arrangements were made for it to be viewed by Mr   *g*
de Haas.

The case next records the following, that after viewing the recording Mr de Haas
formed the opinion that no offence was disclosed, and also that he could not be sure that
it was the appellant who was depicted. I break off reciting the facts to say that that is in
fact a reference to evidence which Mr de Haas gave at the trial.   *h*

Returning to the findings, the video recording was left at W H Smith's for safe
keeping, as it was intended that the justices should view the recording. Shortly before
the hearing on 11 March 1986, it was discovered that the recording had been erased from
the video cassette by new security officers who had used the cassette.

As I have said, objection was taken to the admissibility of that evidence in advance,
and the grounds on which the objection was argued are recorded as follows. It was said   *j*
for the appellant that, although the video recording itself would have been admissible
evidence, the evidence of the three police officers as to what they had seen depicted by
the video recording was hearsay evidence and therefore inadmissible; the reason being
that they would not be giving evidence of what they had seen directly.

It was also contended that, although previously the evidence of a police officer as to

what he had seen displayed on the screen of a Lion intoximeter had been held not to be
a hearsay evidence, that could be distinguished from the present case in that the
intoximeter was an approved device, whereas here no device had been approved. I have
read that now to put it out of the case. The cases referred to before the magistrates were
Morgan v Lee [1985] RTR 409 and *Owen v Chesters* [1985] RTR 191, and neither side has
in the hearing before this court submitted that any assistance can be derived from those
authorities.

b Returning to the contentions for the appellant before the justices, it was next alleged
that to allow such evidence to be given made the prosecution evidence stronger, since
each police officer would positively identify the appellant and say that he had committed
an offence, whereas it should be for the court, after viewing a video recording, to
determine whether or not an offence had been committed, and if so, whether it was the
appellant who had committed such offence. It will be necessary to return to these aspects
c of the submission later in this judgment.

The submissions made by counsel for the appellant have been in summary as follows.
Without production of the original recording, or of a proven copy, no evidence, he said,
could be given of what any witness says he saw on the recording. Where evidence is
given by production of a recording for viewing by the court, a witness, it was conceded,
may give evidence to supplement it by giving evidence of identification, but such
d evidence of identification is inadmissible if the recording is not produced and viewed by
the court. Finally, it was submitted that, even if there is no demonstrably applicable
principle of law by reference to which evidence of what is seen on a recording can be
treated as inadmissible if the recording is not produced, this court should nevertheless as
a matter of policy pronounce such a principle because, if the recording is not produced,
there is no possibility of the court assessing what counsel referred to as the only real
e evidence, which was the recording itself.

I for my part am unable to accept those submissions. In my judgment the evidence
tendered was not inadmissible in law, whether by reference to the hearsay rule or any
other principle in law. I would start with *R v Kajala* (1982) 75 Cr App R 149. The nature
of that case was that there had been a public disturbance in Southall. Parts of what
f occurred were filmed by BBC cameras. A prosecution witness saw the BBC broadcast and
recognised the appellant as one taking part in the disturbance. That witness gave evidence
of what he saw on the recording and said that he confidently recognised the appellant.
There was evidence to prove that the film depicted some of the events of the disturbance
at the time and place at which it had occurred. In that case a copy of the original
recording which had been seen by the witness was shown to the court. Because what was
tendered was not the original, objection was taken to it, and to evidence given by
g reference to it. In rejection the submission that the evidence was inadmissible, Ackner
LJ, giving the judgment of the court, said (at 152):

'The old rule, that a party must produce the best evidence that the nature of the
case will allow, and that any less good evidence is to be excluded, has gone by the
board long ago. The only remaining instance of it is that, if an original document is
h available on one's hands, one must produce it; that one cannot give secondary
evidence by producing a copy. Nowadays we do not confine ourselves to the best
evidence. We admit all relevant evidence. The goodness or badness of it goes only
to weight, and not to admissibility. *Garton v. Hunter* ([1969] 1 All ER 451, [1969] 2
QB 37), per Lord Denning. See also Archbold, *Criminal Pleading, Evidence and Practice*
((40th edn, 1979) para 1001).'

j The next case to which I would refer is the case of *R v Fowden and White* [1982] Crim
LR 588. There two persons, the appellants, were alleged to have been photographed on a
video film carrying out acts of theft. At their trial the Crown sought to call evidence
from a police officer and a store detective who knew Fowden and White to say that the
persons on the film were the accused. The judge admitted that evidence of identity,

against the contention for the defence that it was purely a matter for the jury, looking at the film, to determine the question of identity. On appeal it was held (at 589)—

'there was no difference in principle between a video film and a photograph or tape recording. Although it was not strictly necessary to decide the point the Court was of the opinion there was no reason in principle why the Crown should not be able to call a witness who knows someone to look at a photograph and give evidence to the effect that he knows the person, and it is the accused.'

However, in the circumstances of that particular case the court held (at 589):

'... the evidence should not have been admitted as the prejudicial value outweighed its probative effect, because the identifying witnesses knew the accused from a similar shoplifting case a week later, and accordingly the defence were deprived from testing the accuracy of the identification without causing prejudice and embarrassment.'

It is to be noted therefore, in my judgment, that the court was proceeding on the basis that the evidence called was admissible in law, but subject to the discretionary power of the court to exclude it on well-known principles.

I would now go back to the case to which we were referred of *R v Maqsud Ali* [1965] 2 All ER 464, [1966] 1 QB 688. There evidence of murder was tendered against two accused based on admissions recorded in Punjabi dialect on a tape recorder concealed in a room in a police station. The evidence tendered was of translators who had listened to the tape and a transcript of their translations in translation. The evidence was ruled to be admissible. Marshall J, giving the judgment of the Court of Criminal Appeal, said ([1965] 2 All ER 464 at 469, [1966] 1 QB 688 at 701):

'For many years now photographs have been admissible in evidence on proof that they are relevant to the issues involved in the case and that the prints are taken from negatives that are untouched. The prints as seen represent situations that have been reproduced by means of mechanical and chemical devices. Evidence of things seen through telescopes or binoculars which otherwise could not be picked up by the naked eye have been admitted, and now there are devices for picking up, transmitting, and recording, conversations. We can see no difference in principle between a tape recording and a photograph. In saying this we must not be taken as saying that such recordings are admissible whatever the circumstances, but it does appear to this court wrong to deny to the law of evidence advantages to be gained by new techniques and new devices, provided the accuracy of the recording can be proved and the voices recorded properly identified; provided also that the evidence is relevant and otherwise admissible, we are satisfied that a tape recording is admissible in evidence. Such evidence should always be regarded with some caution and assessed in the light of all the circumstances of each case. There can be no question of laying down any exhaustive set of rules by which the admissibility of such evidence should be judged.'

In my judgment that passage indicates that the evidence of the tape recording is to be viewed as any other evidence and subject to all other considerations of weight etc. I refer to another passage in this judgment because of reliance placed on it by counsel for the appellant. The passage in the judgment is as follows ([1965] 2 All ER 464 at 469–470, [1966] 1 QB 688 at 702):

'It is next said that the recording was a bad one, overlaid in places by street and other noises. This obviously was so and, and a result much of the conversation was inaudible or undecipherable. In so far as that was so, much of the conversation was never transcribed, but there still remained much that was transcribed, and the judge after full argument ruled that what was deciphered should be left for the jury to assess. We think that he was right. Lastly, it was said that the difficulties of language

a   were such as to make any transcription unreliable and misleading. This argument
    the judge treated with great care and circumspection. [Marshall J then referred to
    the warning given by the trial judge in his summing up and set out the facts in
    respect of those passages common to the translations and continued:] The court does
    not feel it necessary to go in detail into the common passages. Suffice it to say that,
    if they are accurate, there are phrases on the tape recording in which words said by
    both of these appellants on their face value amount to, or come very near to, a
b   confession of guilt in this particular case. In the matter of the transcripts the court
    desires only to say this. Having a transcript of a tape recording is, on any view, a
    most obvious convenience and a great aid to the jury, otherwise a recording would
    have to be played over and over again. Provided that a jury is guided by what they
    hear themselves and on that they base their ultimate decision, we see no objection
    to a copy of a transcript, properly proved, being put before them. Here all the
c   translations [I think that must be 'translators'] were submitted to detailed and
    searching cross-examination, and it should be stated also that one of the translators
    called on behalf of the defence in the final part of his evidence came very close to
    agreeing with Rahmet Khan's translation and Changuz's translation, particularly on
    the one sentence that involved the appellant Maqsud.'

d   Counsel for the appellant fastened on the words in that passage 'provided that a jury is
    guided by what they hear themselves and on that they base their ultimate decision', and
    submitted that that should be treated as an authority, or at least an indication, that unless
    the tape is available to be played, no evidence would be admissible as to what anyone had
    heard on the tape. For my part I do not accept that submission. The court was referring
    to all the evidence. As we know, the tape was in Punjabi. The jury, I am sure, would
e   have great difficulty in assessing the validity of the translators' text by reference to the
    original Punjabi, and the point in my view was that the jury had to act on the evidence
    of the translators as tested in cross-examination as with reference to any similar issue.
    They would of course be entitled to take into account the audibility of the tape played to
    them, even if they were unable to understand the audible parts in Punjabi. I find no
    foundation in that case for the submission that in the absence of a tape, evidence as to
f   what was on the tape must be treated as inadmissible.
        I go next to the last authority to which we were referred, which is R v Grimer [1982]
    Crim LR 674. In that case—

        'The theft of a bottle of spray cologne from a shop was recorded on video tape.
        This was seen later by a security officer who recognised the thief as the appellant, a
        man he had known socially for a number of years. The appellant was arrested and
g   charged with theft. The judge at the trial ruled that the security officer's evidence
        was admissible. The jury also saw the video tape. The appellant was convicted. He
        appealed on the ground . . . that the judge erred in admitting the security officer's
        evidence.'

    The report reads that the Court of Appeal, Criminal Division, in its judgment held—
h
        'that there was no distinction between the evidence of a man who looked at a
        video tape (provided there was no challenge to the validity of the tape itself) from
        that of a bystander who observed the primary facts, saw someone with whom in the
        past he was acquainted and could say so to the jury.'

    This court has obtained the transcript of the judgment of Purchas J giving the judgment
j   of the court, and accepts that that is an accurate summary of the main part of the decision.
        We were referred by counsel for the appellant to other parts of the transcript. It is clear
    that one of the main objections was that the evidence of the witness was in fact that of an
    expert witness giving opinion evidence. The court rejected that submission, and in so
    doing founded on the fact that he, having known this witness for many years, was doing
    no more than that which any witness does who claims to identify someone well known

to him on having seen him in another incident and then identifying him later. Again
the fact that that was referred to in a case in which the tape was produced, in my *a*
judgment founds no basis for saying that the evidence tendered if the tape has been lost
becomes inadmissible as opposed to becoming subject to the comments as to weight and
persuasiveness which naturally follow from the loss of the tape.

As to the submission for the prosecutor, counsel submitted that once it is proved that
a video recording was a recording of what a machine detected and reproduced at the time
and place in question, evidence of witnesses of what they say they saw on the recording *b*
is not different in law in point of principle from evidence of witnesses who claim to have
seen the events by direct vision. She contended that all the arguments advanced on behalf
of this appellant are in truth arguments properly directed at weight and not at
admissibility. I think she adds that they were present to the mind of the justices, and that
they were fully taken into account. She has referred the court to no further authority.

In substance I accept the contention made for the prosecutor. For my part I can see no *c*
effective distinction so far as concerns admissibility between a direct view of the action
of an alleged shoplifter by a security officer and a view of those activities by the officer
on the video display unit of a camera, or a view of these activities on a recording of what
the camera recorded. He who saw may describe what he saw because, as Ackner LJ said
in *R v Kajala*, to which I have referred, it is relevant evidence provided that that which is
seen on the camera or recording is connected by sufficient evidence to the alleged actions *d*
of the accused at the time and place in question. As with the witness who saw directly, so
with him who viewed a display or recording, the weight and reliability of his evidence
will depend on assessment of all relevant considerations, including the clarity of the
recording, its length and, where identification is in issue, the witness's prior knowledge
of the person said to be identified, in accordance with well-established principles.

Where there is a recording, a witness has the opportunity to study again and again *e*
what may be a fleeting glimpse of a short incident, and that study may affect greatly both
his ability to describe what he saw and his confidence in an identification. When the film
or recording is shown to the court, his evidence and the validity of his increased
confidence, if he has any, can be assessed in the light of what the court itself can see.
When the film or recording is not available, or is not produced, the court will, and in my *f*
view must, hesitate and consider very carefully indeed before finding themselves made
sure of guilt on such evidence. But if they are made sure of guilt by such evidence,
having correctly directed themselves with reference to it, there is no reason in law why
they should not convict. Such evidence is not, in my view, inadmissible because of the
hearsay principle. It is direct evidence of what was seen to be happening in a particular
place at a particular time and, like all direct evidence, may vary greatly in its weight, *g*
credibility and reliability.

One particular aspect of this case is to be noted. The lost recording was made available
to the appellant's representative before the hearing. That was Mr de Haas. In the event
he gave evidence as to what he had seen. The point is made by counsel for the appellant
that, where this occurs, the making available of the recording to the advisers of the
defence, and there is then a loss or accidental destruction of the recording, the defendant *h*
could be put in difficulty because he might want to call his representatives as witnesses
in order to say what they saw on the recording, and they could not conveniently in the
ordinary course of trial do that and act as advocate or representative for the accused. I see
the force of that complaint. In my judgment it is one of the matters to which the court
would have regard if, on the tendering of this evidence, or evidence of this nature, which
if I am right is admissible, the court will have regard to in exercising its descretion to *j*
exclude evidence in a criminal case.

That is sufficient to dispose of the point raised in the case. I would answer the question
by saying that the evidence was admissible, and the justices were right so to treat it.

It is necessary to mention some other aspects of this case. The objection to the
admission of the evidence included, as I have already read out, reference to a contention

that the witnesses, if called, would say that the appellant had committed an offence,
a whereas it was contended that it should be the court, after viewing the video recording,
who should determine whether or not an offence had been committed. There can be no
doubt that a witness cannot be called to give his view, on what he has seen in a recording,
or indeed on what he saw direct, that in his opinion an offence of any sort has been
committed. All he can do is to describe what he saw, and matters of inference from the
primary facts are for the court.

b Some concern about the course of the trial, indicated by what was there said for the
appellant, arose because it might have reflected the submission that had been made for
the prosecution, and also because, as I have already read out, the findings of fact include
that Mr de Haas, the solicitor previously acting for the appellant, had formed the opinion
that no offence was disclosed, and appears to have been allowed to give that evidence.

Having heard counsel, neither of whom appeared in the court below, but who have
c obtained instructions, it appears to me that although there are some aspects of this case
which gave rise to some anxiety, I am left, after considering the matter, confident that
after ruling that this evidence was admissible, the trial thereafter followed a perfectly
proper and normal course in all respects. The fact is that the case is directed to the one
matter raised, namely the admissibility of the evidence, and it did not include other
matters of evidence which were relevant to the conclusion which the court reached on
d the guilt of the accused. He did not give evidence, although his former solicitor did, to
the effect to which I have referred.

The next matter to be mentioned is that counsel for the appellant submitted that if
this court formed the view that the evidence was admissible, nevertheless it was not clear
that the court had correctly directed itself with reference to the assessment of the weight
and reliability of the evidence tendered by reference to the lost tape. I have considered
e his submissions and what appears in this case, and I am unable to accept that there is any
reason to think that the court did misdirect itself or fail to appreciate all matters which
went to weight of this evidence.

It is to be noticed that the justices stated that all there was in the recording was a matter
of a few seconds only showing the back view of a person who was alleged to have picked
f up a pack of batteries in his right hand and placed them inside his jacket. It seems to me
clear that their attention was directed to the summary of the totality of what these
witnesses had seen. It is clear, because we inquired about this, that there was other
evidence not relevant to this issue raised in the case, which was relevant to their
conclusion that the evidence of what the man in the recording was seen to have done,
coupled with the other evidence, was such that they could from it conclude that the
g offence of theft had been made out. It is not a case of the witnesses saying they thought
it was theft. I mention it so that it will be clear that it has been examined, that the other
evidence included evidence about the appellant being seen in the vicinity and his passing
over something to another person, which was alleged to have appeared to be a battery,
and also of his interview which contained an admission that he had been at the time and
place in question.

h That evidence which is not in the case has not been relevant at all to the consideration
of the issue raised, but has gone to the question which counsel for the appellant asked
leave to raise, and which we allowed him to raise, namely whether, quite apart from that
issue there was any reason for supposing that there had in this case been a misdirection
by the justices of themselves. I have already dealt with the evidence about Mr de Haas
expressing an opinion that no offence was disclosed.

j At the end of the day I look at para 6 of the case, which records the opinion of the
justices that because the prosecution witnesses would be giving evidence of what they
had actually seen depicted by the video recording, the evidence of the police officers was
to be admitted and was not hearsay. They go on to record that, having allowed their
evidence to be given on that, as I think entirely proper basis, they found the appellant
guilty of the offence with which he was charged.

Having thus correctly, as I think, admitted the evidence, there being nothing to indicate that they had misapprehended it or misdirected themselves with reference to *a* the other evidence in the case, for my part I would dismiss this appeal.

McNEILL J. Where the identification of an offender depends wholly or in major part on the evidence of a witness describing what he saw on a visual display unit, contemporaneously with the events which he describes, or which a tribunal of fact sees from the recorded copy of that display, or what a witness says he saw on a recorded copy *b* of that display, whether or not that copy is available to be seen by the tribunal of fact, and any combination of one or more of those circumstances, that evidence is necessarily subject to the directions as to identification evidence laid down in *R v Turnbull* [1976] 3 All ER 549, [1977] QB 224 and juries will be directed, and justices must direct themselves, to approach the evidence in accordance with that authority.

The matter is more complicated because the tribunal of fact has to apply the *R v* *c* *Turnbull* direction first of all to the camera itself, that is to say, as to its position, its opportunity for viewing that which it depicts, to the visual display unit or recorded copy, and to the witness. In other words, each of the three had to be subjected to the *R v* *Turnbull* test.

It is the more important that that test should be complied with strictly where, as here, in the absence of a copy which the justices could see, there is conflicting evidence on the *d* one side and the other as to what actually appeared on the copy, and as to the certainty of identification of the offender.

Ralph Gibson LJ has referred to the facts here, and in particular to the evidence which the solicitor gave to the justices, and he has also pointed out that the appellant himself did not give evidence.

It does not seem to me, either on the question as posed, which should be answered in *e* the terms that Ralph Gibson LJ has propounded, or on the subsidiary point raised by counsel for the appellant that it may be that the justices did not apply as strict a test as is required, that it can be said on the material before the court that they were in error. Indeed, it seems to me that the justices' finding at para 6, which Ralph Gibson LJ has referred to, makes it clear that not merely was the material admissible in the form in *f* which it was proffered, that is to say the oral evidence without the copy being available, but that the justices applied themselves to the facts and came to a conclusion of fact which was justified on the evidence, that is to say that they were satisfied on the proper standard of proof that this appellant was the person concerned and that he was guilty of theft as charged.

I agree with the order proposed by Ralph Gibson LJ. *g*

Appeal dismissed.

The court refused leave to appeal to the House of Lords but certified, under s 1(2) of the Administration of Justice Act 1960, that the following point of law of general public importance was involved in the decision: whether it is lawful for a court in a criminal trial to admit in evidence oral evidence as to the contents of a video recording for the purpose of showing that the defendant *h* *committed acts allegedly amounting to an offence or allegedly implicating the defendant in an offence, including evidence as to identity, when the video recording is not produced to the court and when each of the witnesses is giving evidence as to what each has seen on the video recording viewed after the commission of the alleged offence.*

11 December. The Appeal Committee of the House of Lords (Lord Bridge of Harwich, Lord *j* *Brandon of Oakbrook and Lord Oliver of Aylmerton) refused leave to appeal.*

Solicitors: *Byrne Frodsham & Co*, Widnes (for the appellant); *E C Woodcock*, Chester (for the respondent).

Sophie Craven   Barrister.

Simister v Simister

a

FAMILY DIVISION
WAITE J
9, 10 APRIL 1986

b *Divorce – Financial provision – Application – Locus standi – Maintaining spouse – Maintenance agreement in force between spouses – Application by maintaining spouse for order against himself for periodical payments in favour of maintained spouse – Whether concept of ancillary relief wide enough to permit application to be made by spouse who will not gain direct financial benefit from order – Whether court should make such order.*

c The concept of 'ancillary relief' in the Matrimonial Causes Act 1973 and the Matrimonial Causes Rules 1977 is not restricted to applications by the party standing to gain direct financial benefit from the making of an order for financial provision but is wide enough to permit a spouse who is already obliged to maintain the other spouse under a maintenance agreement to claim, on his own application alone and for genuine and good cause, an order that he be made liable for periodical payments in favour of the maintained d spouse, notwithstanding that the latter has made no application for such an order and may, in fact, oppose the making of it. Whether the court will make such an order in a particular case will depend on the merits (see p 236 g to j, post).

Dictum of Booth J in *Peacock v Peacock* [1984] 1 All ER at 1071 applied.

Notes
e For periodical payments orders in matrimonial proceedings and applications therefor, see 13 Halsbury's Laws (4th edn) paras 1051–1095.

For the Matrimonial Causes Act 1973, see 43 Halsbury's Statutes (3rd edn) 539.

For the Matrimonial Causes Rules 1977, see 10 Halsbury's Statutory Instruments (5th reissue) 216.

f **Case referred to in judgment**
Peacock v Peacock [1984] 1 All ER 1069, [1984] 1 WLR 532.

Appeal
David Albert Simister (the husband) appealed against the order of Mr Registrar Berkson in the Liverpool County Court dated 10 October 1984 dismissing his application dated 8 g August 1984 for, inter alia, an order for a periodical payments order for Lilian Simister (the wife). The appeal was heard and judgment was given in chambers. The case is reported by permission of Waite J. The facts are set out in the judgment.

Thomas Coningsby QC for the husband.
h *Martyn Bennett* for the wife.

WAITE J. This is an appeal from an order of the registrar in the county court striking out in limine a husband's application for an order, purportedly by way of ancillary relief, that he should make periodical maintenance payments to his divorced wife. The striking out order was made on the ground that the application was misconceived in law in that the order requested by the husband was one which the court had no jurisdiction to grant. j The appeal thus raises, as with most issues derived from a plea in bar or demurrer, a pure question of law; and I am therefore dealing with it as a preliminary issue before any investigation is made into the merits of the further applications, one by each side, which have been consolidated with this appeal but which give rise to issues of discretion rather than of law.

The question, bluntly expressed, is this: can a maintaining spouse be heard, on his own application alone, to claim an order that he be made liable for periodic maintenance in *a* favour of the maintained spouse, notwithstanding that the latter has made no application for such an order and indeed opposes the making of it at all? Counsel say that this question is not covered by any direct authority. That is not, when one comes to think of it, surprising. Maintenance is normally very much a dunning process, with one side pressing for as much, and the other side holding out for as little, as each can fairly get or give. The maintaining spouse who insists on an order against himself in the face of *b* opposition from his former partner must therefore be a rare bird. The issue on this appeal is whether such a bird can be permitted to fly at all.

The facts, as one would expect if such an unusual question is to arise at all, are somewhat out of the ordinary. Following the breakdown of their marriage, the parties were at first formally separated. They executed a maintenance agreement under which, in the event (which happened) of an agreed sale and shared distribution of the sale *c* proceeds of the matrimonial home, the husband became liable thereafter to pay the wife a sum equivalent to one-third of his income from all sources, howsoever derived and regardless of any income to which the wife herself might become entitled. The husband, whose earnings have increased dramatically as a result of changes of employment experienced in the mean time, now very much regrets the generosity of that agreement *d* and is strongly critical of his former solicitors for having hung such an albatross around his neck.

The maintenance agreement did, however, contain one safeguard. The husband's liability thereunder was expressed to continue until the death or remarriage of the wife or (and I quote from the agreement) 'the making of a court order whereby the husband is ordered to make any payment to or for the benefit of the wife'.

Ten months after the execution of the maintenance agreement the wife petitioned for *e* divorce. Her petition included, in the usual way, a prayer in general terms for ancillary relief. The husband filed no answer. The cause proceeded as undefended, was dealt with under the special procedure and resulted in a decree nisi four months later in which no reference at all was made to ancillary relief. The marriage was dissolved in due course by decree absolute six weeks later.

Financial matters had thus been untouched up to that point by the divorce proceedings, *f* and the parties continued, after the dissolution of the marriage, to treat themselves as subject to the terms of the maintenance agreement.

That agreement was one to which the husband, however, took increasing objection with the passing of time as his circumstances improved and its onerous nature thus became clearer. He developed a reluctance to comply with the letter and to some extent *g* with the substance of the maintenance agreement, to the point at which the wife found it necessary in due course to bring enforcement proceedings against him to compel the discharge of the various obligations for discovery and payment incorporated within it. Her proceedings were started originally in the Chancery Division, but were later transferred to the Family Division, where the husband, having for that purpose instructed new solicitors, had by then launched an application under s 35 of the Matrimonial Causes *h* Act 1973 to vary the maintenance agreement on the ground of changed circumstances. Before that application by the wife and cross-application by the husband had been taken very much further, the husband and his new professional advisers became attracted to an approach more radical than a mere application to vary the terms of the maintenance agreement. If the court could be persuaded to make an order for periodical payments by the husband to the wife, then the maintenance agreement would, arguably at least, *j* become wholly discharged by virtue of the provision which I have already quoted. The husband's advisers thought that there would, moreover, be attractions in obtaining an order in that form for the following reason. The husband hoped that the time would come (though it had not then and has not yet arrived) when he would be in a position to

offer a capital settlement to the wife to achieve a clean break. According to the advice of
a his experienced counsel, the changes in s 25 of the 1973 Act introduced by the
Matrimonial and Family Proceedings Act 1984 had the consequence that, if a time should
ever come in future when the husband was in a position to make a capital proposal which
the wife was unwilling to accept, then he would be in a stronger position to compel her
to do so if there was then in force a periodical payments order under the ancillary relief
jurisdiction than would be the case if she was receiving the equivalent payments merely
b under the terms of some variation of the maintenance agreement directed by the court
under s 35.

It is neither relevant nor necessary for me to express any view one way or the other on
that aspect of the case. I mention it only to demonstrate what has never been challenged,
namely the bona fides of the application for ancillary relief which has resulted in this
current appeal.
c   Such were the motives which led the husband in due course to give notice in the
divorce proceedings in a form complying with Matrimonial Causes Rules 1977, SI 1977/
344, r 68 of his intention to apply to the court for a periodic payments order for the wife
petitioner and a corresponding order for the maintenance of a named child of the family.

The wife responded with a summons to strike out that notice, at all events so far as it
related to the claim for a periodical payments order in her own favour, on the ground,
d among other things, that it was misconceived in law. Such an application, it was said, is
simply a legal impossibility. The county court registrar (the divorce proceedings being
still at that stage in his court) acceded to the striking out application, holding that an
application by a maintaining spouse that he should voluntarily be placed under
compulsion to maintain the other spouse was not one which he was competent in law to
be heard to make.
e   The husband's appeal against that striking out decision came in due course to the High
Court (to which the divorce proceedings had in the interval been transferred) and was
there consolidated with the two existing sets of proceedings already mentioned, that is to
say the wife's original claim to enforce the maintenance agreement and the husband's
cross-claim to vary it.
f   Notwithstanding the consolidation, I am giving judgment independently on the
appeal as a preliminary issue of law for the reasons already indicated.

Counsel for the wife, arguing in support of the view taken by the registrar, points to
the way in which the scheme of the legislation embodied in the 1973 Act and the rules
of court contemplates a procedure of the most adversarial kind. He instanced in particular
the numerous references to orders 'in favour of' the maintained spouse and the adversarial
g connotation of expressions such as the party 'against whom' an order has been made to
be found in the amended s 31(7) of the 1973 Act. He further prays in aid the views of
the editor of *Butterworths Family Law Service* division D, para 621, who, in commenting
on the decision in *Peacock v Peacock* [1984] 1 All ER 1069, [1984] 1 WLR 532 (to which
reference will be made in a moment), observes that there is something intrinsically odd
about the machinery of the ancillary relief procedure being brought into play by a person
h wishing the court to make an order against himself.

Counsel for the husband points, on the other hand, to the breadth of the conception
involved in the expression 'ancillary relief'. It is a term, he submits, going wider than the
mere movement of cash from the wallet of one to the purse of another. A party, he
contends, who is made liable under an order for periodical payments, punitive though
such an order may at first sight appear to be, is not necessarily precluded from obtaining
j relief by means of such an order. It may only be a fiscal relief or it may represent no
more than peace of mind resulting from the substitution of definition for uncertainty;
but it is, so counsel submits, a measure of relief all the same.

He relies also on the facts that the sections of the 1973 Act dealing with financial relief
in Pt II are based on the underlying concept of financial provision orders of various kinds,

and the fact that, in all that group of sections, there is not to be found any specific statutory requirement that the relevant prohibition may only be granted at the request *a* of the party standing to gain direct financial benefit from it. In support of that interpretation of the statute, as recently amended, he relies on the observations, obiter though he acknowledges them to have been, of Booth J in *Peacock v Peacock* [1984] 1 All ER 1069 at 1071, [1984] 1 WLR 532 at 535. The immediate issue in that case was far away from the facts with which the present issue is concerned and it turned on the impact of social security on a husband's liability for maintenance. The registrar had *b* refused an order for maintenance pending suit in a wife's favour and interim periodical payments for the children of the marriage solely on the ground that such an order would not benefit the applicant because it would not take her outside the limit of her entitlement to supplementary benefit. The judge held that such an approach was wrong; the fact that the wife was receiving supplementary benefit was a matter properly to be taken into account in assessing maintenance pending suit, but only as part of the court's general *c* discretion. There still remained a duty on the court to assess what in all the circumstances the husband, on his income, could reasonably afford to pay. That was sufficient to dispose of the decision, but the judge made the following further observation in its support ([1984] 1 All ER 1069 at 1071, [1984] 1 WLR 532 at 535):

'A further point in this matter is that the husband himself is entitled to ask the *d* court for appropriate orders, and to ask the court to assess the amount he should pay. The court is not bound by the assessment of the Department of Health and Social Security, and I do not think that the husband is necessarily bound by any such assessment. He has got the right to come to court and to ask the court to make its own assessment, which it will probably do on a much broader principle, as in fact is the situation in this case. The court has a duty to make an order which is reasonable *e* in all the circumstances, and to take into account all the needs and obligations of the husband, and, as counsel has argued on his behalf today, to take into account his future liabilities and problems in setting himself up as he has recently left the matrimonial home. The figure that the court may think proper to order may not be that at which the Department of Health and Social Security assesses as the husband's obligations. Therefore, it seems to me that not only the wife but also the *f* husband is entitled to ask the court for a proper assessment.'

I am grateful to both counsel for their helpful submissions. Those of counsel for the husband, in my judgment, should prevail. It is true that the 1973 Act and the 1977 rules are both expressed in language more apt to deal with the everyday case of the pursuer and the pursued than with the maverick instance of the spouse who seeks a self-inflicted order. Nevertheless, I am satisfied that the concept of ancillary relief is wide enough to *g* include the case of a maintaining spouse who genuinely and for good cause wishes to obtain an order against himself. Such a spouse may not indeed be such a maverick figure as at first sight appears. There may be sound fiscal reasons for the order sought or there may be family reasons, such as the fact that the maintained spouse is under disability. In such a case there would be very little distinction in principle to be drawn between a *h* maintained spouse under disability on the one hand and a child of the family on the other. Counsel for the wife concedes that a voluntary requested order for the periodic maintenance of a child of the family would be unobjectionable. Indeed, he takes no objection to the making of such an order in favour of the child of the family in the present case. This construction of the statute is, moreover, authoritatively supported by the observations obiter of Booth J in *Peacock*'s case. *j*

I therefore allow the appeal, holding that the husband's application for a periodic payments order is one which he is competent in law to maintain. Whether he should be allowed to maintain it on the merits of the case so as to lead to such an order being actually made in his favour is, of course, an entirely different question, which cannot be answered until the court has received evidence and heard argument on the two

applications with which this appeal has been consolidated, to the hearing of which
a applications I shall now turn.

Appeal allowed; proceedings continued on merits.

Solicitors: *Broomheads*, Sheffield (for the husband); *Davis Campbell & Co*, Liverpool (for
the wife).
b

Bebe Chua   Barrister.

Morrow v Nadeem

c
COURT OF APPEAL, CIVIL DIVISION
SLADE, NEILL AND NICHOLLS LJJ
7 JULY 1986

Landlord and tenant – Business premises – Notice by landlord to terminate tenancy – Validity –
d *Notice failing to identify landlord correctly – Whether notice valid – Landlord and Tenant Act*
1954, s 25(1).

Landlord and tenant – Business premises – Notice by landlord to terminate tenancy – Waiver by
tenant of invalidity of notice – Notice failing to identify landlord correctly – Notice given by
'solicitors and agents of' person who controlled landlord company – Tenant serving counter-
e *notice on solicitors – Whether tenant waiving invalidity of notice – Landlord and Tenant Act*
1954, s 25(1).

By two tenancy agreements dated 14 May 1980 the appellant rented a suite of consulting
rooms for three years from the landlord, a company controlled by one AD. In June 1982
notices were served on the appellant under s 25(1)[a] of the Landlord and Tenant Act 1954
f terminating the tenancies. The notices were signed by a firm of solicitors as 'Solicitors
and Agents for' AD. In July the appellant served counter-notices on the solicitors stating
that she was unwilling to give up possession, and in October she applied to the county
court for the grant of new tenancies, naming AD as the landlord in each application. The
landlord company subsequently sold its interest to the respondent, who applied to be
substituted as respondent in the proceedings in succession to the company. The appellant
g then amended her application for a new tenancy to challenge the validity of the notices
served on her in June 1982, claiming that they had failed to identify the landlord
correctly. The judge held that the notices were valid or, alternatively, that any invalidity
had been waived by the appellant.

Held – A notice under s 25(1) of the 1954 Act was required to give the tenant sufficient
h information to enable him if he so wished to avail himself of his statutory rights to serve
a counter-notice on the landlord and thereafter apply to the court for a new tenancy, and
in order that he could do that it was necessary for the notice to state correctly the name
of the landlord. Since the notices served on the appellant had failed to name the correct
landlord they were invalid. Furthermore, that invalidity had not been waived because
the error in the notices was not such as to put the appellant on inquiry regarding who
j was the landlord. The appeal would therefore be allowed (see p 241 *e* to *g j*, p 242 *j*, p 243
h and p 244 *h* to p 245 *c f* to p 246 *c e g h*, post).
   Dictum of Barry J in *Barclays Bank Ltd v Ascott* [1961] 1 All ER at 786 applied.
   Tennant v London CC (1957) 121 JP 428 considered.

a   Section 25(1), so far as material, is set out at p 239 *a*, post

Notes
For a landlord's notice to terminate a business tenancy, see 27 Halsbury's Laws (4th edn) *a*
para 485, and for cases on the subject, see 31(2) Digest (Reissue) 945–949, 7725–7741.
    For the Landlord and Tenant Act 1954, s 25, see 23 Halsbury's Statutes (4th edn) 143.

Cases referred to in judgments
Barclays Bank Ltd v Ascott [1961] 1 All ER 782, [1961] 1 WLR 717.
Boltons (House Furnishers) Ltd v Oppenheim [1959] 3 All ER 90, [1959] 1 WLR 913, CA. *b*
Harmond Properties Ltd v Gajdzis [1968] 3 All ER 263, [1968] 1 WLR 1858, CA.
London CC v Vitamins Ltd, London CC v Agricultural Food Products Ltd [1955] 2 All ER 229,
    [1955] 2 QB 218, [1955] 2 WLR 925, CA.
Piper v Muggleton [1956] 2 All ER 249, [1956] 2 QB 569, [1956] 2 WLR 1093, CA.
Tegerdine v Brooks (1977) 36 P & CR 261, CA. *c*
Tennant v London CC (1957) 121 JP 428, CA.

Cases also cited
Airport Restaurants Ltd v Southend-on-Sea Corp [1960] 2 All ER 888, [1960] 1 WLR 880,
    CA.
Bristol Cars Ltd v RKH Hotels Ltd (in liq) (1979) 38 P & CR 411, CA. *d*
Evans Construction Co Ltd v Charrington & Co Ltd [1983] 1 All ER 310, [1983] QB 810, CA.
Peyman v Lanjani [1984] 3 All ER 703, [1985] Ch 457, CA.
Smith (A J A) Transport Ltd v British Rlys Board (1980) 257 EG 1257, CA.

Appeal
Carol Stuart Morrow appealed against the order made by his Honour Judge Martin QC *e*
in the Bloomsbury County Court on 14 February 1986 whereby he declared that two
notices dated 16 June 1982 terminating the appellant's tenancies of a suite of rooms at 59
Wimpole Street, London W1, were valid. The respondent was Mahmud Nadeem
following an order made on 20 November 1985 substituting him as respondent in
succession to Alfred Danzig. The facts are set out in the judgment of Nicholls LJ. *f*

Gavin Lightman QC and *David Iwi* for the appellant.
R W Kirk for the respondent.

NICHOLLS LJ (giving the first judgment at the invitation of Slade LJ). This is an
appeal from a decision of his Honour Judge Martin QC sitting in the Bloomsbury County *g*
Court on 14 February 1986. The matter in contention is the validity of two notices served
under s 25 of the Landlord and Tenant Act 1954 on the appellant, Dr Carol Morrow,
who is the applicant in the present proceedings.
    The facts lie in a very small compass. By an agreement dated 14 May 1980 a company
called GD Investments Ltd, demised to the appellant accommodation in 59 Wimpole
Street, London W1 for use by her as professional consulting rooms. The property demised *h*
comprised, first, a front room and a middle room situate on the ground floor of 59
Wimpole Street, for a term of three years from 29 September 1979, and, second, a small
room on the second floor at the same address for a term of three years from 1 February
1980. I need not refer to any of the other provisions in the agreement. It is not in dispute
that Pt II of the 1954 Act applied to that tenancy (or those tenancies, whichever may be
the correct legal description). *j*
    On 16 June 1982, or shortly thereafter, a firm of solicitors, Messrs Philip Ross & Co,
served on the appellant two notices. Both were on a standard printed form corresponding
to Form 7 in the schedule to the Landlord and Tenant (Notices) Regulations 1957, SI
1957/1157, as amended. Under those regulations at that time this form, or one
substantially to the like effect, was required to be used for a landlord's notice to terminate
a business tenancy under s 25 (see s 66(1) of the 1954 Act and reg 4).

The need for such a notice to be in a particular form stems from s 25 itself, s 25(1)
a providing:

> 'The landlord may terminate a tenancy to which this Part of this Act applies by a
> notice given to the tenant in the prescribed form specifying the date at which the
> tenancy is to come to an end . . .'

The notice given with regard to the two ground floor rooms reads as follows:

b
> 'To Dr. Carol Morrow of 59, Wimpole Street, London, W.1., tenant of premises
> known as Front and Middle Rooms on the Ground Floor of 59, Wimpole Street,
> London, W.1.
>
> 1. We, Philip Ross & Co., of 77, Wimpole Street, London W1A 3BQ, Solicitors and
> Agents for your landlord (*Note* 7) of the above-mentioned premises, hereby give you
c notice terminating your tenancy on the 25th day of December, 1982 (*Note* 1).
>
> 2. You are required within two months after the giving of this notice to notify
> me in writing whether or not you will be willing to give up possession of the
> premises on that date (*Note* 2).
>
> 3. The Landlord would not oppose an application to the court (*Note* 3) under Part
> II of the Act for the grant of a new tenancy (*Note* 6).
d 4. This notice is given under the provisions of section 25 of the Landlord and
> Tenant Act 1954. Your attention is called to the Notes overleaf. Dated this 16th day
> of June 1982 Signed (Philip Ross & Co.)'

Then the printed reference to 'landlord' was struck out. 'Address . . . 77, Wimpole Street,
London, W1A 3BQ'. To the left of the signature appeared the rubric: 'Solicitors and Agents
for Alfred Danzig.'
e
The material part of Note 7, appearing overleaf, reads:

> 'The term "landlord" in this Notice does not necessarily mean the landlord to
> whom the rent is paid: it means the person who is the landlord for the purposes of
> Part II of the Act . . .'

f Note 2 provides as follows:

> 'Part II of the Act enables the tenant on being served with a notice in this form, to
> apply to the court for an order for the grant of a new tenancy. Such an application,
> however, will not be entertained unless the tenant has within 2 months after the
> giving of the Notice terminating the tenancy notified the landlord in writing that
> he will not be willing to give up possession of the premises on the date specified in
g the Notice. The application must be made not less than 2 nor more than 4 months
> after the giving of the notice.'

Note 6, so far as material, states:

> 'If the landlord states in this Notice that he will not oppose an application to the
> court for the grant of a new tenancy, it will be open to the tenant and the landlord
h to negotiate on the terms of the tenancy . . .'

The notice relating to the small room on the second floor was to the same effect as the
notice I have read, save that it referred to that room as the property demised and 1
February 1983 as the date of termination of the tenancy. It will be observed that nowhere
in either notice was there any mention of GD Investments Ltd.
j On 7 July 1982 solicitors acting for the appellant gave counter-notices on her behalf
that she was unwilling to give up possession on the dates specified. The notices were
addressed to Philip Ross & Co, who were described, following the form used by them in
their s 25 notices, as 'Solicitors and Agents for Alfred Danzig'. Subsequently, on 6 October
1982 the appellant commenced the present two sets of proceedings in the county court,
applying in the normal way for the grant to her of new tenancies, in the one case of the
ground floor accommodation and, in the other case, of the small room on the second

floor. The applications contained the usual particulars, including a reference to the tenancy agreement of 14 May 1980 made between GD Investments Ltd and the appellant. The respondent to each application was Alfred Danzig, and his address was given as 'c/o Messrs. Philip Ross & Co.' and their address was then stated.

Three years later, on 11 November 1985, solicitors acting for Mr Mahmud Nadeem issued a summons for an order in each set of proceedings substituting himself as the respondent on the ground that he—

'is now the landlord of [the appellant] within the meaning of section 44 of the said Act in respect of both the said actions as successor in title to the above-mentioned Alfred Danzig and G.D. Investments Limited respectively.'

An order substituting Mr Nadeem was made on 20 November 1985, and hence Mr Nadeem is now the respondent in the proceedings and the respondent to this appeal.

On 9 December 1985 the appellant's two applications were amended by her to add the following paragraph as the primary relief sought, namely 'an Order that a Notice dated 16th June 1982 purporting to determine my tenancy of the above property was invalid'. An order for the grant of new tenancies then became relief sought in the alternative.

The circumstance in which that amendment came to be made was that on 12 November 1985 a firm of solicitors, Messrs Maurice Nadeem & Co, wrote to the appellant's solicitors a letter which included the following passage:

'Since Mr. Nadeem has now become by purchase the immediate landlord of Dr. Morrow, you will know that he is required by the rules to be a party to the proceedings. He became landlord as successor in title to G.D. Investments Limited, but has no knowledge of Mr. Danzig, the Respondent. Nevertheless, since you have served a counter-notice to the notice apparently served by Mr. Danzig, and made applications under Section 25 which name him as Respondent, we take it that there is no question but that you accept that he was the competent landlord at the time the counter-notice and application were issued by you on Dr. Morrow's behalf. Please be good enough to inform us immediately if this is not the case.'

On receiving that letter the appellant's solicitors consulted counsel, and shortly thereafter the applications were amended.

The only further facts I need mention at this stage are that it was on 10 September 1985 that the respondent became landlord in succession to GD Investments Ltd. Prior to that, the appellant's landlord for the purposes of the 1954 Act was at all times GD Investments Ltd. Mr Danzig never was the landlord at any material time. His involvement was that he was the controlling shareholder and the sole director of GD Investments Ltd. Of the 1,000 shares issued by the company, 999 were held by him, and the remaining share was held jointly by him and his wife.

As I have indicated, the matter in contention now is the primary relief sought in the two sets of proceedings. On 14 February 1986 the judge heard this issue as a preliminary point. At the hearing there was no oral evidence adduced. Having heard argument, he rejected the appellant's contention that the notices were invalid.

After setting out the rival submissions made to him, Judge Martin expressed his conclusion succinctly in these terms:

'I find, and I think it is inescapable, that Alfred Danzig was authorised to act on behalf of GD Investments Ltd as its general agent, indeed GD Investments Ltd was Alfred Danzig in all but name. I hold that he had express or at least implied authority to serve notices with his name on them and not that of his company. I hold that the proceedings thereafter were properly constituted and that the company would have been bound by the proceedings. [The respondent] has become the landlord in succession to Mr Danzig. In these circumstances, the tenant has in no way been prejudiced or misled.'

He also decided that, if he were wrong on this and if it were necessary so to decide, the
a appellant had waived any objection she might have had to the validity of the notices.
The landlord, GD Investments Ltd, whom she knew was the landlord named in the lease,
was not 'on the notices' and there was ample material that there might be a case for
investigation, but no inquiries or investigation had been made, and objection was not
taken to the validity of the notices until December 1985. I add, however, that the judge
accepted that there was no evidence that the appellant knew who Mr Danzig was prior
b to receipt of the letter from the respondent's solicitors in November 1985.

I come, first, to the question of the validity of the notices. It is to be observed at once
that the question is not one concerning the validity of a common law notice to quit or
the essential ingredients of such a notice. We were referred to the decision of this court
in *Harmond Properties Ltd v Gajdzis* [1968] 3 All ER 263, [1968] 1 WLR 1858 as authority
for a proposition to the effect that a common law notice to quit is valid if it is given by a
c duly authorised general agent, even though the name of the person on whose behalf the
notice is given is not named. The question arising on this appeal is a different one: it is
whether the form prescribed under the 1954 Act requires the name of the landlord to be
stated. In my view it does. The question falls to be answered according to the proper
construction of the statutory provisions including the prescribed form. Form 7 starts by
leaving a blank for the name and address of the person to whom the notice is addressed
d as tenant of premises which are then to be identified. Immediately below that the format
of the opening paragraph, para 1, is such as to show that what is envisaged is that the
name and address of the relevant landlord will be inserted. Paragraph 1 of the prescribed
form reads: 'I ... of ... landlord of the above-mentioned premises ...' That form
predicates that the blank spaces preceding the phrase 'landlord of the above-mentioned
premises' will be duly completed with the name and address of the person who is
e correctly so described.

This impression is confirmed by a reading of the notice as a whole in conjunction with
the notes which are required to accompany the form. When the notice is so read, it is
apparent that what is contemplated is that by the form the tenant will be given the
information sufficient to enable him, if he so wishes, to avail himself of his statutory
f rights by serving the requisite counter-notice on the landlord within two months and
thereafter applying to the court for a new tenancy between two and four months after
service of the s 25 notice. To such an application the relevant landlord would be a
necessary party (see *Piper v Muggleton* [1956] 2 All ER 249, [1956] 2 QB 569). The
information needed by the tenant for those purposes will include information as to the
identity of the landlord for the purposes of Pt II of the 1954 Act, who may not be the
g same person as the person who granted the tenancy to the tenant, or the person to whom
the tenant pays his rent (see s 44 of the 1954 Act). In line with this, para 2, which reads
in part, 'You are required within two months after the giving of this notice to notify me
in writing whether or not you will be willing to give up possession ...', is a reflection of
s 25(5). Section 25(5) provides that:

h   'A notice under this section shall not have effect unless it requires the tenant,
within two months after the giving of the notice, to notify the landlord in writing
whether or not, at the date of termination, the tenant will be willing to give up
possession of the property comprised in the tenancy.'

'Me' in para 2 contemplates that the landlord will have been named in para 1 of the
notice.
j In this case the notices did not include the name or address of the competent landlord.
What is more, the notices misstated the name of the landlord, in that the natural
implication to be drawn from the language used in these notices was that the landlord
was Alfred Danzig, for whom Philip Ross & Co were expressed to be acting as solicitors
and agents. Accordingly, in my judgment these notices did not comply with the statutory
requirements.

The conclusion I have reached on this question is in accord with the authorities to which we were referred. We were referred to the decision of Barry J in *Barclays Bank Ltd v Ascott* [1961] 1 All ER 782, [1961] 1 WLR 717. There the landlords had stated in their notice of termination that they would not oppose the grant of a tenancy if the tenant could find a guarantor, but they did not state expressly whether they were otherwise opposing the grant of a new tenancy and did not indicate, as required, if opposing, on what ground under s 30 of the 1954 Act they were opposing. Barry J said ([1961] 1 All ER 782 at 786, [1961] 1 WLR 717 at 722):

'A number of very useful authorities have been cited to me, but, as I see it, none of them is directly in point, and I do not think that any useful purpose would be served if I were to refer to them in detail. It appears to me that the real gist of these decisions was summarised by HODSON, L.J., in *Bolton's (House Furnishers), Ltd.* v. *Oppenheim* ([1959] 3 All ER 90, [1959] 1 WLR 913). As I understand HODSON, L.J.'s judgment, the question which the court really has to consider is whether the notice given by the landlord has given such information to the tenant as will enable the tenant to deal, in a proper way, with the situation (whatever it may be) referred to in the notice. It is clear, I think, from the authorities which have been cited to me that this notice should be construed liberally, and provided that it does give the real substance of the information required, then the mere omission of certain details, or the failure to embody in the notice the full provisions of the section of the Act referred to, will not in fact invalidate the notice. However, no authority has been cited to me which indicates, or which would even tend to indicate, that a notice should be construed otherwise than in accordance with the ordinary rules of construction, or that the court would be entitled to give to it a meaning which it does not in fact bear under the ordinary rules of grammar or construction.'

The validity of a s 25 notice came before this court in *Tegerdine v Brooks* (1977) 36 P & CR 261. In that case some of the prescribed notes had been omitted from the s 25 notice, but on the particular facts of that case the omitted notes were immaterial. The court decided that in those circumstances the notice given was valid as one substantially to the like effect as the form set out by the regulations; but (and this is the relevance of this decision for the present purposes) all three members of the court, namely Cairns, Roskill and Bridge LJJ, expressly adopted the statement of Barry J as correct. With that I contrast the present case, where the notices did not give the real substance of the information required by the tenant; indeed, they misstated a relevant and important piece of that information.

There might perhaps be an exceptional case in which, notwithstanding the inadvertent misstatement or omission of the name of the landlord, any reasonable tenant would have known that that was a mistake and known clearly what was intended. But that is not this case. Accordingly, whether in such a case the notice would be valid or not is not a matter arising for decision, and I do not pause to consider what the legal position would be in such a case. Indeed in this case the judge concluded that the appellant had not been prejudiced or misled. But through her advisers she served counter-notices addressed to Mr Danzig and commenced proceedings against Mr Danzig, and there is no reason to doubt that those steps were taken with regard to Mr Danzig in good faith. Accordingly, I do not think that, with all respect to the judge, there was material on which he could conclude that the tenant had in fact in no way been misled in this case.

Moreover, although it seems very likely that Mr Danzig was authorised to act on behalf of GD Investments Ltd, that is nothing to the point. The fact that the notices were served with the authority of the landlord does not cure the defect in the form of the notices or enable the landlord to escape from the consequences which would otherwise flow from the notices not being in due form.

For the respondent it was submitted that, since Mr Danzig was the company in all but name and since he had authority to serve the notices, that was sufficient to comply with

the statutory requirements, and reliance was placed on the decision of this court in
a   *Tennant v London CC* (1957) 121 JP 428. That case concerned the adequacy of the signature
of a s 25 notice. Jenkins LJ said, referring to the 1954 Act (at 438–439):

> 'In that Act the only provision as to signature of the landlord's notice to terminate
> the tenancy consists of the words in s. 25(1), that the notice is to be "in the prescribed
> form", coupled with the occurrence of the word "landlord" alongside the space for
b   > signature in the prescribed form itself. There is no imperative requirement in the
> body of the Act or anywhere else that the notice shall be signed by the landlord. The
> nearest to it is simply a space in the prescribed form designed for signature by
> somebody designated as the landlord. On the authorities to which I have referred, I
> cannot think that these few words to be collected from s. 25 and from the prescribed
> form can be sufficient to oust the common law rule. I therefore conclude that a
c   > landlord's notice to terminate a tenancy under s. 25(1) is a good notice if it is signed
> by the landlord personally or by his duly authorised agent or if the landlord's name
> is affixed to the notice by someone writing the landlord's signature for him with
> due authority per procurationem.'

In that case the landlord, the London County Council, was named in the s 25 notice as
the landlord. The common law rule to which Jenkins LJ was referring was expressed by
d   him as follows (at 438):

> 'The principle to be deduced from these cases, other than *London County Council* v.
> *Agricultural Food Products* which was concerned with a contractual provision, seems
> to me to be this, that prima facie when there is a provision in a statute requiring a
> document to be signed, with nothing in the subject-matter or context of the
e   > legislation to indicate that personal signature is necessary, then the common law
> rule prevails and a signature duly authorised by a person affixed to a document by
> another person is the signature of the person giving the authority.'

With that in mind, I do not think the first passage cited above from the judgment of
Jenkins LJ was directed at all at what the position would be if the landlord had not been
f   named in the s 25 notice. Whether the signature by an authorised agent is sufficient is
one matter: whether the landlord needs to be named, and a fortiori if a person is named
as landlord whether that needs to be a correct statement of the name of the competent
landlord, is an altogether different matter.

In the alternative counsel for the respondent relied on the words in reg 4 which permit
the degree of latitude inherent in the phrase that the notice is to be in the prescribed
g   form or one substantially to the like effect. Here, it was said, it was the merest technicality
that Philip Ross, who were the landlord's solicitors, did not name GD Investments Ltd. I
cannot accept this. I have already concluded that the notices did not give the real
substance of the information required by the statute. A form made out in such a way as
not to give the real substance of the information required is not a form substantially to
the like effect as the statutory form of notice.

h   For these reasons I conclude that the notices when given were invalid.

The second issue raised concerns waiver. On this we were supplied with an agreed
statement of facts, to the effect that protracted correspondence passed between solicitors
in the period from 1982 to 1985 on the basis that there were live and valid applications
on foot in the Bloomsbury County Court under Pt II of the 1954 Act, which applications
arose out of the notices which are the subject of this appeal, and that no suggestion was
j   made in that correspondence that the validity of the notices was being or would be
challenged. Further, between the date of the notices in 1982 and the date of the
amendment of the originating applications in December 1985, no further facts came to
light, or were suggested or disclosed in the correspondence between the solicitors, to
affect the appellant's mind or to give any indication as to what she thought about the
identity of her landlord, apart from the respondent's solicitors' letter of 12 November

1985. Prior to that letter nothing in the correspondence indicated that Mr Danzig was
not the landlord.   *a*

Those being the facts, I can deal more shortly with the question of waiver. On those
particular facts, on the face of the notices and in the light of the facts known to the
appellant, there was nothing to indicate to her or her advisers that the notices contained
an erroneous statement so that they were, or might be, invalid. Nor was there anything
so strange about the statement implicit in the notices served in 1982 in respect of the
lease granted in 1980 that Mr Danzig was the landlord to cause the appellant's solicitors   *b*
to make further inquiry. What they did was to serve counter-notices and commence
applications for new tenancies. On the evidence, the landlord's solicitors never demurred
at Mr Danzig being made the respondent, nor did they ever tell the appellant's solicitors
of the true position. The appellant's solicitors were never disabused of their belief that
Mr Danzig was indeed the competent landlord until the middle of November 1985, at
which stage the invalidity point was taken with reasonable promptness.   *c*

We were referred on this to another passage in the judgment of Jenkins LJ in *Tennant
v London CC*. The issue in that case, as I have already indicated, was whether a s 25 notice
signed by a person on behalf of the council had been duly signed by the landlord. There
the court held that the notice was valid as having been duly signed, but Jenkins LJ added
this on the question whether in any event the tenant had waived the objection to the
signature of the notice (121 JP 428 at 441):   *d*

> 'I do regard it as most desirable in cases under the Landlord and Tenant Act, 1954,
> where time may be an important consideration, that parties who wish to take
> objection to the form or the validity of the proceedings should act promptly and not
> reserve objections of this sort until the proceedings have been on foot for a matter
> perhaps of months. Accordingly, had it been necessary for me to arrive at a   *e*
> conclusion on this part of the case, I would have been prepared to hold that any
> otherwise well-found objection there might be to the notice was, on the facts to
> which I have briefly referred, waived, so that the objection is no longer available to
> the tenant as a bar to the proceedings.'

I respectfully agree that parties who wish to take objections of the nature of those   *f*
taken in that case and in this case should act promptly. On the particular facts, however,
that was a case where from the outset, from service of the notice, the tenant knew of the
matter of which he subsequently complained; and thus he knew for some considerable
time of the facts which were subsequently relied on by him as founding the objection.
That is not this case: rather this is a case within the passage in the judgment of Romer LJ
in *Tennant v London CC* 121 JP 428 at 443 where he said: *g*

> 'I can imagine a case where a notice terminating a tenancy might be subject to a
> latent or concealed defect which did not come to light and was not apprehended by
> the tenant until after he had taken some step which might be construed as accepting
> the validity of the notice. In such a case I do not myself think that he would be
> subject to the operation of the principle.'
>   *h*

In the present case the steps taken by the appellant, in serving counter-notices and
commencing proceedings and not objecting to the validity of the notices, were all taken
in ignorance of the fact that Mr Danzig was not the competent landlord.

Whether a failure to make inquiries could in appropriate circumstances give rise to a
party wishing to challenge the validity of a notice being estopped from doing so or being
held to have waived his right of challenge, is also not a matter which needs to be   *j*
considered in this case, and so I say nothing on that. Here, on the very limited evidence
before the court about the history of the transactions, there was no cause why the
appellant, acting reasonably, should not have taken the notices at their face value and
acted (and over the next four years continued to act) on that footing, as she did without
dissent from the landlord's solicitors.

a   It is suggested that the appellant, on receiving the notices from a person of whom she did not know, should have taken the point about possible invalidity there and then and made this point when serving the counter-notices. On matters involving waiver, or estoppel, or election each case turns on its own particular facts, and on the facts of this case I can see no basis on which the appellant was obliged so to act, so that her failure to do so precluded her from taking the point thereafter.

b   I should add, finally, that counsel for the appellant submitted en passant that the defect in these notices was a defect which in any event was not capable of being waived. I do not accept this. I can see no reason why this particular type of defect should be accorded some particular immunity regarding waiver.

For these reasons for my part I would respectfully disagree with the judge's decision and hold that both notices were invalid and that the appellant is not precluded from asserting the invalidity of the notices as she now seeks to do, and would accordingly allow
c   this appeal.

NEILL LJ. The first question which arises for decision in this appeal is whether the notices served on the appellant on 16 June 1982 were valid notices under the provisions of s 25 of the Landlord and Tenant Act 1954. Section 25(1) is in these terms:
d
'The landlord may terminate a tenancy to which this Part of this Act applies by a notice given to the tenant in the prescribed form specifying the date at which the tenancy is to come to an end . . .'

Section 66(1) provides:
e
'Any form of notice required by this Act to be prescribed shall be prescribed by regulations made by the Secretary of State by statutory instrument.'

The regulations made under the 1954 Act, the Landlord and Tenant (Notices) Regulations 1957, SI 1957/1157, prescribe that a notice to be given under s 25 shall be in
f   Form 7 set out in the schedule to the regulations, or in a form substantially to the like effect. In my view it is clear that a notice under s 25 must include all the matters prescribed or indicated in Form 7 in so far as they may be relevant, so as to give proper information to the tenant to enable him to deal with the situation referred to in the notice. So much appears from the judgment of Barry J in *Barclays Bank Ltd v Ascott* [1961] 1 All ER 782 at 786, [1961] 1 WLR 717 at 722, in a passage which has been approved in
g   this court.

In *Tegerdine v Brooks* (1977) 36 P & CR 261 the Court of Appeal had to consider a case where the notice omitted some of the notes set out in Form 7. The court held that in the circumstances of that particular case the notes were irrelevant, so that the omission of the notes did not invalidate the notice. But it seems quite clear from the judgments in that case that a notice which is incomplete or inaccurate in a relevant respect is a bad notice.
h   The question then arises: is the name and identity of the landlord a relevant piece of information to be included in the statutory notice and to be imparted to the tenant so that he or she may be in a position to deal with the situation referred to in the notice? I have no doubt that, save perhaps in an exceptional case, this information is relevant and that a notice under s 25 should include the name of the landlord. This requirement of the regulations is in my judgment a quite different matter from the question whether
j   persons other than the landlord may be entitled to sign a notice in the name, or on behalf, of the landlord. I would therefore answer this first question by saying that in my view the judge came to the wrong conclusion and that the notices served in this case were not valid notices.

I turn to the second question: if the notices were invalid, is the appellant now debarred, either by reason of the doctrines of election or waiver or by reason of some estoppel, from relying on their invalidity? On this aspect of the case I do not consider that I can usefully add to what has already been said by Nicholls LJ.   *a*

In these circumstances I agree that this appeal should be allowed.

SLADE LJ. I agree with both judgments that have been delivered and only wish to add a few observations on the first issue, out of deference to the judge with whom we are differing and to counsel's well-sustained argument on behalf of the respondent.

I agree with Neill and Nicholls LJJ that the fact that Mr Danzig was authorised to act *b* on behalf of GD Investments Ltd as its general agent has no relevance to the question whether the notices purportedly given on behalf of the landlord in the present case were valid. For this is not a case of a notice to quit given at common law but a notice given under the particular statutory framework laid down by the Landlord and Tenant Act 1954.

For my part, I think that the notices of 16 June 1982 were clearly not in the form *c* prescribed by that Act, since they did not specify the name and address of the landlord as the prescribed form contemplates. Regulation 4 of the Landlord and Tenant (Notices) Regulations 1957, SI 1957/1157, permits the use of the forms in the appendix to the regulations, or 'forms substantially to the like effect'. The relevant test to be applied in determining the sufficiency or otherwise of a notice given by the landlord under the Act which is not in the prescribed form is, I think, that stated by Barry J in *Barclays Bank v* *d* *Ascott* [1961] 1 All ER 782, [1961] 1 WLR 717. This test, which was approved by this court in *Tegerdine v Brooks* (1977) 36 P & CR 261, has already been quoted by Nicholls LJ in his judgment and I will not repeat it. Applying it to the present case, I am satisfied that the landlord's notices of 16 June 1982 did not give such information to the appellant as would enable her to deal in a proper way with the situation referred to in the notices. The situation with which those notices confronted her was one in which she was *e* required, within two months after the giving of the notices, to notify 'the landlord' whether or not she would be willing to give up possession of the premises on the dates of termination of her tenancies. She needed to know the true identity of the landlord for this purpose. She also needed to know the landlord's true identity for the purpose of properly constituting any proceedings which she might wish to institute for the purpose *f* of applying for a new tenancy. In view of the decision in *Piper v Muggleton* [1956] 2 All ER 249, [1956] 2 QB 569, I respectfully disagree with the view of the judge that the proceedings which she launched against Mr Danzig following the receipt of the notices were properly constituted.

The notices of 16 June 1982 both failed to name the correct landlord and, in addition, incorrectly represented that Mr Danzig was the landlord. They were not merely non- *g* informative, but also, albeit no doubt quite innocently, misleading in a most material respect. I think that these errors must have invalidated them. They cannot be said to have been in a form 'substantially to the like effect' as the prescribed forms.

For these reasons, in agreement with Neill and Nicholls LJJ, I am of opinion that the judge erred in his views on the first of the two main questions which arise on this appeal. I am also of opinion that he erred on the second issue. On this aspect I do not wish to add *h* anything of my own. I too would allow this appeal.

Appeal allowed.

Solicitors: *G Lebor & Co* (for the appellant); *Maurice Nadeem & Co* (for the respondent).

Celia Fox   Barrister.

a

Re St Mary's, Banbury

ARCHES COURT OF CANTERBURY
DEAN SIR JOHN OWEN
21 MARCH, 4 OCTOBER 1986

b *Ecclesiastical law – Faculty – Pews – Removal of pews – Pews allotted to particular parishioners – Extent of allottees' interest in pews allotted – Act for rebuilding parish church providing for pews to be sold and disposed of – Freehold of church vested in incumbent – Petition for faculty to remove pews from nave and replace them with chairs – Whether successors in title to allottees of numbered pews entitled to insist that pews remain in nave – Whether successors in title having freehold interest in pews and soil thereunder – Whether right of access to pews and to exclusive*

c *use of pews for worship preventing grant of faculty to remove pews.*

Ecclesiastical law – Faculty – Alterations to church – Church listed as being of special architectural or historic interest – Restriction on alterations to listed buildings not applying to ecclesiastical buildings – Whether fact of listing relevant in considering whether to allow alterations.

d *Ecclesiastical law – Faculty – Reordering of church – Conflicting claims of worship and of conservation – Circumstances in which reordering should normally be allowed – Guidelines on how court will balance conflicting interests.*

Ecclesiastical law – Faculty – Evidence – Alterations to historic churches – Necessity for evidence from Department of the Environment, local planning authority and relevant architectural and

e *historical bodies – Form of evidence – Need to amend rules to allow reception of such evidence – Faculty Jurisdiction Rules 1967.*

In 1790 an Act was passed to enable a parish church to be pulled down and rebuilt. Under the Act the freehold of the nave and aisles remained vested in the rector but trustees appointed under the Act were empowered to 'allot and appoint' one pew to each person

f who subscribed £10 or more towards the rebuilding costs, and the trustees were given a residual power to 'sell and dispose' of any surplus pews to purchasers in such manner as the trustees thought fit. The Act provided that when a pew was 'allotted' to a subscriber or to a purchaser the pew was to be 'vested in the said Subscribers and Purchasers thereof respectively, his and her Heirs and Assigns, immediately upon the allotting of the same'. The Act did not provide for the repair of pews allotted but did provide that in order to

g preserve uniformity of pews no person was entitled to affix linings to or to paint a pew. In 1983 the rector and churchwardens petitioned for a faculty to carry out works in the church, including the removal of pews in the nave (which were original pews) and their replacement by chairs for the purpose of bringing the celebrant and choir nearer to the congregation and facilitating the use of the church as a concert hall. The petition was opposed by, inter alios, three persons who each proved title to a numbered pew in the

h nave derived from the title of a person who had originally been allotted a pew under the trustees' residual power to allot surplus pews to purchasers. The chancellor held that the parties opponent had neither any freehold interest in their respective pews or the soil thereunder nor any proprietary interest in the woodwork of the pews, but that they had a right to exclusive use of their respective pews for the purpose of worship and a right of access to those pews which could not be replaced by a right to use chairs in substitution

j for the pews. The chancellor accordingly held that there was no jurisdiction to grant the faculty sought. The petitioners appealed.

Held – On its true construction the 1790 Act contemplated statutory rights to the use on religious occasions of specific fixed numbered pews, because the power given to the

trustees by the Act 'to sell' pews or seats was only consistent with a perpetual right, and
the provision in the Act that 'all such Pews or Seats shall be vested in the said Subscribers   *a*
and Purchasers thereof respectively, his or her Heirs and Assigns' was likewise only
consistent with a perpetual right, since before 1822 the only way of creating a fee simple
by a direct grant inter vivos was by such a limitation to the grantee and his or her heirs.
The chancellor had therefore been correct to hold that each existing pew right was a right
to use the existing relevant numbered pew during divine service and other religious
observances at times when the church was open for worship, subject to the regulations   *b*
of the church. Furthermore, the pews could not be permanently removed without the
consent of the owners, and no faculty could destroy the statutory rights created by the
1790 Act. It followed therefore that, since the petition was for a faculty to remove all the
pews, and to remove all but three would be absurd, the petitioners' appeal would be
dismissed (see p 253 *f* to p 254 *a* and p 255 *d*, post).

Per curiam. (1) Although the exemption in respect of ecclesiastical buildings on the   *c*
restriction on alterations to listed buildings is necessary so that the dead hand of the past
does not prevent the proper use of a building consecrated to the worship of God, the
listing of a church as a building of special architectural or historic interest indicates that
a faculty which might affect the special nature of that interest should be allowed only in
cases of proved necessity (see p 250 *d e*, post).

(2) When the incumbent and the parochial church council desire a reordering of a   *d*
church it should normally be allowed if the church is not listed and if it can be done
without necessitating any permanent and irreversible change to the building. Where,
however, such a change would be necessitated and the church is listed it will be necessary
to balance the claims of the congregation against the claims of conservation (see p 250 *h*
and p 254 *f g*, post).

(3) If proper and informed decisions are to be made in relation to alterations to historic   *e*
churches where there are valid, concerned and yet conflicting interests, it is vital that the
Department of the Environment, the local planning authority and the various voluntary
historical and architectural bodies concerned with such matters should be able to give
evidence in faculty proceedings, preferably orally but, if that is impossible, in writing.
The Faculty Jurisdiction Rules 1967 require speedy amendment to allow the reception of   *f*
such evidence (see p 251 *j* to p 252 *a*, post).

Guidelines on how the court will balance the interests of worship and the interests of
conservation when exercising its faculty jurisdiction over the reordering of a church (see
p 254 *j* to p 255 *d*, post).

Decision of Chancellor Peter Boydell QC [1985] 2 All ER 611 affirmed.

Notes   *g*

For pews in churches, see 14 Halsbury's Laws (4th edn) paras 1086–1091, and for cases
on the subject, see 19 Digest (Reissue) 384–394, 3018–3144.

For the exemption in respect of ecclesiastical buildings on the restriction on alterations
to listed buildings, see 34 Halsbury's Laws (4th edn) para 660.

For the principles and practice of the faculty jurisdiction, see 14 ibid para 1310, and   *h*
for cases on the subject, see 19 Digest (Reissue) 452–461, 3564–3622.

For evidence in faculty proceedings, see 14 Halsbury's Laws (4th edn) para 1326, and
for cases on the subject, see 19 Digest (Reissue) 441–442, 3504–3511.

Cases referred to in judgment
Brumfitt v Roberts (1870) LR 5 CP 224.   *j*
Holy Innocents, Fallowfield, Re [1982] Fam 135, [1982] 3 WLR 666, Con Ct.
Nickalls v Briscoe [1892] P 269, Arches Ct.
Peek v Trower (1881) 7 PD 21, Arches Ct.
Philipps v Halliday [1891] AC 228, HL.

Appeal

a By a notice of appeal dated 7 November 1985 the team rector of the parish church of St
Mary's, Banbury, the Rev Ronald Mitchinson, and the churchwardens, Jim Church,
William Yarnold and Jack Billington, appealed to the Arches Court of Canterbury from
so much of the judgment of the Oxford Consistory Court (Chancellor Peter Boydell QC)
([1985] 2 All ER 611, [1986] Fam 24) on 21 February 1985 whereby the petitioners were
refused a faculty for the removal of the main block of pews in the nave of the church and
b for certain related works. The respondents to the appeal were Mr K H Bolton, Mrs G M
Jakeman, Mr C D Hone, Mrs A Hopcraft, Mr C F Herbert, Mr J Williamson, Mr M S
Hedges and Mrs E Palmer. The facts are set out in the judgment.

Sheila Cameron QC for the petitioners.
Jonathan Henty for the respondents Mr Bolton and Mrs Jakeman.
c The other respondents did not appear.

Cur adv vult

4 October. The following judgment was delivered.

d **THE DEAN OF THE ARCHES.** On 21 February 1985 Chancellor Peter Boydell QC
gave judgment in the Oxford Consistory Court ([1985] 2 All ER 611, [1986] Fam 24).
His judgment was a model of clarity of thought and expression and fully revealed his
learning and industry.

This is an appeal from that part of the judgment which provided that the petitioners,
they being the team rector and the three churchwardens of the parish of Banbury, should
e be refused a faculty for (1) the removal of the main block of pews in the nave of St Mary's
Church and for the provision of a circular carpeted area in the nave beneath the dome
and consequential work and (2) the provision of a mobile altar and platform in the nave.

The Chancellor found against the petitioners on two main grounds: (1) that two of the
parties opponent, namely Mr Bolton and Mrs Jakeman, and also Mr Strange, are entitled,
f by statutory rights now vested in them but originally created by an Act of Parliament of
1790 (30 Geo 3 c 72), to the use in perpetuity 'during divine service and other religious
observances at times when the church is open for worship, subject to regulations of the
church', of enclosed pews in the main block, those pews being of the same nature and in
the same position as those constructed in 1797; these rights he found to be not removable
by faculty and in practice to be such as to make the whole proposed scheme impractical;
g (2) that, even if there had been power to remove such pew rights by faculty, in his
discretion he would have found against the petitioners and, even if there had been no
established rights to pews, as to which there is no doubt, he would probably have refused
the faculty on the basis that on a consideration of all the factors relevant the petitioners
had not persuaded him that it would be right at this stage to authorise the removal of
such pews.

h By their notice of appeal the petitioners raised a number of objections. As a result of
the way in which the appeal has been argued it is possible to say that there are two main
questions: (A) what are the present pew rights of Mr Bolton, Mrs Jakeman and Mr
Strange? (B) if there was a discretion to grant the faculty, was the chancellor right in
exercising it against the petitioners?

The chancellor, in his judgment, dealt with the essential history of the church. It is not
j necessary for me to repeat all of this. Certain aspects are, however, crucial to a proper
consideration of the two questions.

Under the provisions of the 1790 Act of Parliament the existing medieval Banbury
Parish Church was demolished, in part by gunpowder, in that year. The Act was necessary
to raise the money required for rebuilding; a main source was to be the sale of pews or

seats. Samuel Pepys Cockerell designed the replacement church, which was opened, before completion, in 1797. The replacement was completed in 1822 to the further design of his son, Charles Robert Cockerell. The original and completion designs, which included box pews, if not those at present in situ, then others of a similar nature and location, have led to the construction of a church which has been described as neo-classical. In 1864 the interior was remodelled by A W Blomfield, who added a chancel and may well have had the existing box pews cut down in size. I see no reason to differ from the chancellor's conclusion in his judgment that 'The present pews are the pews of 1797 which were remodelled in the 1870s' (see [1986] Fam 24 at 30). I also agree with the chancellor that the date of the existing pews is not of great importance in determining whether they should now be removed. It is to be noted that Blomfield, at a time when they were not well regarded, still retained these box pews. It seems likely that he regarded them as a necessary and integral part of the Cockerells' building. On 9 April 1952 the church was listed as a building of special architectural or historic interest. It is now listed as a building Grade A. If it were not for the ecclesiastical exemption s 56(1)(*a*) of the Town and Country Planning Act 1971 the effect of this listing would be to make it a criminal offence to execute any works *to the building* which would affect its character as a building of special architectural or historic interest. By s 54(9) of the 1971 Act 'any object or structure fixed to a building . . . shall be treated as part of the building'. An argument based solely on this consideration was not developed at the hearing of the appeal and it is sufficient to state that, although the exemption is necessary so that in such cases the dead hand of the past shall not prevent the proper use of a building consecrated to the worship of God, a listing does indicate that a faculty which might affect the special nature of the architectural or historic interest (and certainly the removal of all the pews from this church would do this) should only be allowed in cases of clearly proved necessity. The faculty jurisdiction must and does treat churches such as St Mary's, Banbury as treasures not only for the people of the parish, whether churchgoing or not, not only for the Anglican Church, but also for the country at large. When, as here in 1977–81, the church has received some £80,000 of public money towards repairs, there must be an obligation to consult the Department of the Environment, which it is now clear, although this played no part in the decision of either the chancellor or this court, was at first favourable to the petitioners but subsequently was not. As I shall make it clear I do not agree with this original but subsequently changed attitude.

The arguments used by the petitioners to support the petition are both liturgical and secular.

The liturgical argument, as I understand it, is that the priest and choir and congregation should be much closer together than is possible at present and that there should be a central altar around which the priest and congregation should be able to worship together, the priest in a westward-facing position and the congregation gathered around and close to the altar. The churchmanship which supports such an approach to worship is perfectly reasonable and by no means uncommon; when, as here, it is desired by the incumbent and the parochial church council it should normally lead to a reordering, if there is no listing and if this can be done without necessitating any permanent *and* irreversible change to the building. Where such a change would be necessitated and the church is listed it will be necessary to balance the claims of the congregation against the claims of conservation.

The secular argument is that the removal of the pews would facilitate the provision of important public musical concerts which have been held in the church, at an average annual rate of eight concerts, for many years but which could more economically, more effectively and more comfortably be provided if the faculty were to be granted and all the pews were to be removed. It is apparent from the team rector's evidence that the plans on which the petition is based came into existence as a result initially of a desire to act in accordance with a recommendation, made by the director of a fund-raising campaign in 1977 to raise money for roof repairs, that the work necessary to make it possible to use the church as a top class concert hall should be completed. Whilst this

a again is an interest to be considered it can only be considered in the light of the undoubted fact that the primary purpose of a church is as a place of worship.

The diocesan advisory committee report dated 12 September 1983 enthusiastically supported the present proposals. Some might think the language of the report rather extreme and hard to justify. The passage I have in mind states:

b   'This unique baroque church, designed by the Cockerells, was more a theatre than a church, though later alterations added a chancel and removed the E. section of the 4 galleries. It was further marred by the huge blocks of pews, cramped and uncomfortable. The boards beneath them were apparently laid on bare earth and are now rotting. We thought Mr. Gotch's plans most commendable, creating a central carpeted space under the dome, with 3 groups of chairs, restoring the

c   baroque appearance of the church. Cockerell père et fils would surely be delighted by these proposals . . .'

I merely note that the church is not a baroque church and far from the church being marred by a later addition of pews they were a necessary and integral part of the original Cockerell design.

At the hearing before the chancellor there was no evidence from the Council for Places

d of Worship: this was because no witness could attend on the days fixed for the hearing. Criticism was made of the chancellor because he did not take into account letters written on behalf of the council. Counsel for the petitioners says that because the council is a body entitled by r 6(2) of the Faculty Jurisdiction Rules 1967, SI 1967/1002, to appear and give evidence the chancellor should not have insisted on rejecting the written representations unless the other side agreed, which they did not, but should have received

e those letters whilst rejecting written representations from the Department of the Environment and the various interested specialist bodies. The chancellor was told that both the Department of the Environment, whose representations he did not see although I have now seen the original letter, and the council, whose representations he did see, changed their attitudes to the proposals (but in different directions from each other) between their earlier and later written submissions. In these circumstances the chancellor

f decided that—

'in the absence of witnesses from those, and the other, bodies whose evidence could be tested it would have been neither just nor helpful to have regard to their various and diverse written representations.'

g (See [1986] Fam 24 at 27.)

Rule 6(1) of the Faculty Jurisdiction Rules 1967 provides that the evidence at the hearing shall, unless the judge otherwise orders, be given orally. At the outset the chancellor made it clear that he would not otherwise order. He was, in my judgment, entitled and correct in the circumstances to exclude the council's written representations. I am able to add that having seen the written representations it seems clear that they

h would not, even if received in evidence, have affected the chancellor's decision or shaken his acceptance of much of the evidence of Mr Peter Howell, a distinguished member of both the Victorian Society and the Oxfordshire Architectural and Historical Society, who was called as a witness by one of the parties opponent.

There was also no evidence from the Department of the Environment or from the Georgian Group, the Oxford Architectural and Historical Society or other such societies.

j Such evidence would not, under the rules, have been receivable. The rules require speedy amendment. If proper and informed decisions are to be made in cases such as this where there are valid, concerned and yet conflicting interests, it is in my judgment vital that the department, the local planning authority and the various splendid voluntary bodies should be able to give their evidence, preferably orally, but, if that is impossible, in writing. The Report of the Faculty Jurisdiction Commission (1984) para 191 recommends

a change in the rules which would allow the reception of such evidence. I trust and hope
that this change will soon be made.   *a*

I now turn to the two questions raised by the notice of appeal.

1   *What are the present rights of pew holders?*

It is common ground between the petitioners and the respondents that each of the
three named pew holders, two of whom are respondents whilst the third is not, has good
title by succession to whatever was initially passed to his or her original predecessor in   *b*
title.

A convenient starting point for the consideration of the extent of those rights is the
proposition that, although a right to use a particular seat or pew may have been acquired
by a faculty or presumed faculty, there is no right at common law to buy or sell a seat or
pew. There is no question here of faculty rights. Although the common law is so   *c*
restricted Parliament is not. Acts of Parliament conferring pew or seat rights have not
been uncommon. The two respondent pew holders claim rights under the 1790 Act.
Counsel for the petitioners argues that on a proper construction of the Act each pew right
holder is entitled to no more than to be seated for divine services and other religious
observances in a position in the church which is no less advantageous in relation to other
seats and to the altar than the pew allotted to his or her predecessor in title. If she is right   *d*
the pew right holder's property rights can present no absolute bar to the grant of the
faculty now sought by the appellant petitioners. Counsel for the respondents argues that
the pew holders are entitled to the use for divine services and other religious observances
of their allotted and numbered pews as and where they now are. A faculty cannot
overrule a statutory right and it is clear that if counsel for the respondents is right the
petition must, in all common sense, fail.   *e*

Both counsel agree that the Act created interests, each in the nature of an easement,
and that to ascertain the nature and extent of that right it is necessary to construe the Act.
In *Brumfitt v Roberts* (1870) LR 5 CP 224 at 232–233 Bovill CJ, having stated that—

'The right in a pew is essentially a right to use it for the services of the Church,
and at times when it is open for use, subject to the regulations of the church; and   *f*
there is no right of access to it or to use it for other purposes or in any other manner,'

further stated that the interest which passed by the statutes considered in that case was—

'not an interest in land, but an interest of a peculiar nature created by the Act of
Parliament, and more in the nature of an easement, though there are attached to it
incidents of perpetuity of possession which could only be attached to such a right by   *g*
the power of legislation. The statute has created a special interest in the pews and
seats not known to the common law, and such interest exists by force of the
statute . . .'

On all of this there is agreement. The difference, as I understand it, between the
contention of counsel for the petitioners and that of counsel for the respondents is that
whereas counsel for the petitioners claims that the right is not in an individual   *h*
geographically fixed pew or seat but in a seat or seats of some kind in an area from which
the originally allotted pew and its geographical location may have been excluded, counsel
for the respondents claims that the pew rights originally conferred were, as are the
present rights, in specific pews, whether similarly constituted or not, in specific
permanent, originally allotted locations.

Under the description 'Allotment of Pews' the Act provides that the trustees—   *j*

'shall allot and appoint to and for the Use of each Person who shall subscribe Ten
Pounds or upwards towards the Expenses of taking down and rebuilding the said
Church, Chancel, and Tower, such One Pew or Seat as shall be sufficient to contain
commodiously such Subscriber, and his or her Family; and the said Trustees are

a

hereby directed, at any Time or Times after such Allotments and Dispositions of such Pews or Seats as aforesaid shall have been made to or for the Use of the Subscribers as aforesaid, to sell and dispose of all or any of the Residue of such Pews or Seats, and allot the same to any Person or Persons, and in such Manner as they shall think fit and proper . . .'

The same section then continues:

b

'and all such Pews or Seats shall be vested in the said Subscribers and Purchasers thereof respectively, his and her Heirs and Assigns, immediately upon the allotting of the same . . .'

The Act further provides:

c

'That when the Pews and Seats are allotted or appointed as aforesaid, the said Trustees . . . shall cause them to be numbered, and such Numbers to be entered in a Book, with the Names of the Persons to whom the Pews or Seats shall be allotted or appointed . . . Provided always, that for the better Preservation of Uniformity in the Pews or Seats of the said Church, no Person entitled to any Pew or Seat therein, shall be permitted to affix any Lining thereto, or to paint the same, under a Penalty of Ten Pounds . . .'

d

Accordingly the Act empowered the trustees of the scheme to create pew or seat rights to individual and identifiable pews or seats. It is common ground that the Cockerell design provided for pews such as those which the petitioners now seek to remove and that the original allocations were to pews, ie not to movable chairs but to enclosed seats affixed to the floor of the building and 'vested' in the purchasers or subscribers.

e

I have to gather the effect of the statute by considering it in its entirety. I cannot accept that it was ever contemplated by the original purchasers and subscribers that the rights created by the Act were not tied to the geographical locations of those pews as originally sited. I have no hesitation in finding that the Act, the original trustees and the original subscribers and purchasers contemplated statutory rights to the use on religious occasions of specific fixed numbered pews: the purchasers would not have paid for uncertainly located seats.

f

Indeed, there being an undoubted right to grant a faculty for the exclusive use of a specific identified pew I see no reason to think that the scheme contemplated by the Act contemplated any less. In this connection counsel for the respondents submits that the nature and the extent of the rights created may be appreciated by a consideration of the remedy for interference. *Philipps v Halliday* [1891] AC 228 is authority for saying that, where, by means of a faculty, there is an exclusive right to the use of a numbered pew, the destruction of that pew will entitle the faculty holder to bring an action of disturbance in order to maintain it. I see no reason why the sale of a pew should pass a lesser right.

g

Counsel for the petitioners argues that the Act could not have contemplated perpetual rights, but in my judgment the Act did confer perpetual rights just as was done by the Act considered in *Brumfitt v Roberts*. The use of the term 'sale' is only consistent with a perpetual right and so also is the provision that 'all such Pews or Seats shall be vested in the said Subscribers and Purchasers thereof respectively, his and her Heirs and Assigns', for before 1822 the only way of creating a fee simple by a direct grant inter vivos was by such a limitation to the grantee and his or her heirs.

h

I am sure that the chancellor was correct when he held that each existing pew right is a right to use the existing relevant numbered pew during divine service and other religious observances at times when the church is open for worship, subject to the regulations of the church.

j

Further, I am satisfied that the pews cannot be permanently removed without the consent of the owners (any other decision would be inconsistent with any form of ownership) and that no faculty may destroy the statutory rights created by the Act.

This is sufficient to decide the appeal against the petitioners, for the petition is for a faculty to remove all the pews and to remove all but three would be absurd.

I shall, however, also consider the second question.

2   Assuming a discretion in the chancellor to grant a faculty, was he right in exercising it against the petitioners?

Sitting as I now do as the appellate judge, I may draw any inferences of fact which might have been drawn by the chancellor. I may give any judgment or direction which the chancellor ought to have given. I may remit the matter with a direction for rehearing and determination by the chancellor's court or I may allow the appeal substituting my own discretion if the chancellor's exercise of discretion was based on an erroneous evaluation of the facts taken as a whole.

I intend to take none of these courses since I am satisfied that the chancellor was correct in his decision that even if such discretion had been available to him he would not have exercised his discretion in favour of the petitioners.

I am satisfied that the chancellor gave full and proper weight to the evidence of the team rector, to the almost unanimous support of the parochial church council and to the favourable report of the diocesan advisory committee. These factors are important. They were clearly in the chancellor's mind and were evaluated by him. However, it was necessary also to have in mind the law as stated by Lord Penzance in *Nickalls v Briscoe* [1892] P 269 at 283:

> 'The notion that the matter here in question should be decided by the wishes of the majority of the parishioners proceeds, in my opinion, upon an entirely mistaken view of the law. The appellants have put forward their attachment to the old church and its interesting connection with times gone by; but they seem to forget that the sacred edifice has a future as well as a past. It belongs not to any one generation, nor are its interests and condition the exclusive care of those who inhabit the parish at any one period of time. It is in entire conformity with this aspect of the parish church that the law has forbidden any structural alterations to be made in it, save those which are approved by a disinterested authority in the person of the Ordinary, whose deputed discretion and judgment we are here to exercise to-day.'

It is accordingly apparent that a chancellor cannot only consider the views, especially liturgical views which are notoriously subject to change, of the incumbent and congregation; he cannot only consider the views of conservationists. He is appointed by law to be a disinterested but informed and committed guardian of all interests and he must consider all relevant factors. Then bearing in mind that the burden is on those who propose changes (per Lord Penzance, Dean of the Arches, in *Peek v Trower* (1881) 7 PD 21 at 27) he must decide whether or not there should be a faculty for change.

Nothing would be gained by my setting out all the other factors which Chancellor Boydell rightly took into account in this case. The comfort or discomfort of pews and especially these pews, the aesthetic acceptability of carpeting, the fact that the chancellor has given permissions which will allow the petitioners to construct a permanent platform, which can be used for divine services and for concerts, and to have an altar at the top of the chancel steps, the fact that there are three pew holders whose rights would be gravely affected and others were no doubt all considered by the chancellor, but in my opinion these are all minor when weighed against the fact that St Mary's is a building of special architectural and historic interest and the removal of the pews, which were an integral part of the design of the church and which have been there since the church was built, would gravely damage those interests.

That and the further fact that there is no clearly proved necessity for change are sufficient to decide the second question against the petitioners, but it will be helpful to add a few general observations which will indicate the attitude of this court to these problems when there is a conflict, as here, between the interests of worship and the interests of conservation. The following principles may act as guidelines: (a) it must

never be forgotten that a church is a house of God and a place for worship. It does not
a belong to conservationists, to the state or to the congregation but to God; (b) in deciding
whether to allow a reordering the court will not only have in mind the matters listed, for
example, by Chancellor Spafford in *Re Holy Innocents, Fallowfield* [1982] Fam 135 at 137–
138 but also these other matters: (i) the persons most concerned with the worship in a
church are those who worship there regularly although other members of the church
may also be concerned; (ii) when a church is listed as a building of special architectural
b or historic interest a faculty which would affect its character as such should only be
granted in wholly exceptional circumstances, those circumstances clearly showing a
necessity for such a change. When the Faculty Rules have been amended it should be
possible to add 'and should never be granted unless the evidence, oral or written, of every
concerned body has been invited and, if tendered, considered'. A reordering of such a
church solely to accommodate liturgical fashion is likely never to justify such a change;
c (iii) whether a church is so listed or not a chancellor should always have in mind not only
the religious interests but also the aesthetic, architectural and communal interests
relevant to the church in question; (iv) although the faculty jurisdiction must look to the
present as well as to the future needs of the worshipping community a change which is
permanent and cannot be reversed is particularly to be avoided.

In the circumstances the appeal fails. I shall, if necessary, hear arguments as to costs at
d a later date.

Appeal dismissed.

Solicitors: *Hancocks*, Banbury (for the petitioners); *Aplin Stockton*, Banbury (for the
e respondents Mr Bolton and Mrs Jakeman).

N P Metcalfe Esq   Barrister.

f # R v Weston-super-Mare Justices, ex parte Shaw

QUEEN'S BENCH DIVISION
WATKINS LJ, MANN AND NOLAN JJ
14, 22 OCTOBER 1986

g
*Magistrates – Procedure – Court list – Court list listing all charges against defendant for hearing
on same day – Whether practice of putting court list containing list of all charges before
magistrates wrong in law.*

The applicant was charged with causing wasteful employment of police time by making
h a false report, contrary to s 5(2) of the Criminal Law Act 1967, and with six charges
relating to the use of a motor scooter. On the day of his appearance before the magistrates
all seven charges were listed in the court list and a copy of the list was placed before each
justice. The applicant was found guilty of the s 5(2) charge and pleaded guilty to the
other six charges. He applied for, inter alia, a declaration that the practice of producing a
court list for the justices with a listing of all the charges against a defendant was contrary
j to law because in hearing the s 5(2) charge the justices could have been prejudiced by
knowing that the applicant was charged with other offences.

Held – It was not unlawful to list all charges, whether related or unrelated, against a
single defendant which were set down for hearing on the same day or for the justices to
see that list. It followed that the application would be dismissed (see p 259 *e* to *g j*, post).

R v Liverpool City Justices, ex p Topping [1983] 1 All ER 490 not followed.

Per curiam. There may be occasions when it would be most undesirable for unrelated
charges against a defendant to be listed together, and the good sense of the justices' clerk   *a*
should enable him to identify those occasions. Should in any case there be a complaint,
the justices should themselves determine whether their knowledge of the other charges
in the list should cause them to disqualify themselves by reference to the test of ostensible
bias (see p 259 *h j*, post).

Notes

b

For test of disqualification of justices by bias, see 29 Halsbury's Laws (4th edn) para 257,
and for cases on the subject, see 33 Digest (Reissue) 73–75, 259–271.

For the duty of the clerk to keep the court register, see 29 Halsbury's Laws (4th edn)
para 503.

For the Criminal Law Act 1967, s 5, see 12 Halsbury's Statutes (4th edn) 364.

c

Cases referred to in judgments

R v Gould [1968] 1 All ER 849, [1968] 2 QB 65, [1968] 2 WLR 643, CA.
R v Liverpool City Justices, ex p Topping [1983] 1 All ER 490, [1983] 1 WLR 119, DC.
R v McLean, ex p Aikens (1974) 139 JP 261, DC.
R v Uxbridge Justices, ex p Burbridge (1972) Times, 21 June, DC.
R v Weston-super-Mare Justices, ex p Stone (19 November 1984, unreported), DC.   *d*
Young v Bristol Aeroplane Co Ltd [1944] 2 All ER 293, [1944] KB 718, CA; *affd* [1946] 1 All
ER 98, [1946] AC 163, HL.

Application for judicial review

Phillip Anthony Shaw applied, with leave of Taylor J granted on 8 November 1985, for,
inter alia, (i) an order of certiorari to quash the decision of the Weston-super-Mare justices   *e*
to continue to hear a charge against the applicant of wasting police time having been
made aware by the court sheets placed in front of them of six other charges against him
and (ii) a declaration that the practice of producing for a bench of justices court sheets
being part of the court register showing in addition to the charge that the bench were
about to try all other outstanding charges and all outstanding convictions on which the   *f*
defendant awaited sentence was wrong in law. The facts are set out in the judgment of
Mann J.

Louis Blom-Cooper QC and *Heather Williams* for the applicant.
Ian Dixey for the justices.

Cur adv vult   *g*

22 October. The following judgments were delivered.

MANN J (giving the first judgment at the invitation of Watkins LJ). There is before the
court an application for judicial review. The applicant was given leave to move by Taylor   *h*
J on 8 November 1985. The respondents are the Weston-super-Mare justices and the
decision impugned is a decision of the justices made on 25 November 1985.

The circumstances giving rise to this application are as follows. On 25 November 1985
the applicant, who was then aged 20, appeared before the justices to answer seven charges.
One was of causing certain wasteful employment of the police by knowingly making a
false report tending to show that an offence of assault had been committed contrary to   *j*
s 5(2) of the Criminal Law Act 1967. To that charge a plea of not guilty had been entered
on 14 November. The other six charges involved an escapade with a motor scooter over
the period 29–30 September 1985. Another youth was involved in that escapade and he
was the subject of three charges. The applicant was represented by his solicitor, who is
Mrs Rosemary Gordon. When she arrived at the court, she observed the court list which
was posted on the notice board. All seven charges against the applicant were listed. Mrs

Gordon also observed that copies of the list had been placed on the bench in front of the
a places where each justice would sit.

On the sitting of the court, Mrs Gordon submitted that the justices should not try the
charge of causing wasteful employment of the police because a reasonable and fair-
minded person sitting in the court and knowing that the justices knew of the six other
charges would have a reasonable suspicion that a fair trial was not possible on that charge.
The justices retired to consider this submission. On their return the chairman announced:
b 'The application made by your solicitor is not granted. We feel there would be no
prejudice to you.' The trial proceeded. The applicant was found guilty. The applicant
next pleaded guilty to the remaining six charges and was given a custodial sentence on
all seven. The applicant appealed against sentence to the Crown Court, but this appeal
stands adjourned pending the result of these proceedings. The Crown Court released the
applicant on bail.

c The relief sought is, first, an order of certiorari to quash the decision to try the charge
of wasteful employment of the police and, second, a declaration that the practice of
producing for the justices a court list such as was here produced is a practice which is
contrary to law. A claim for relief in respect of an incident which occurred during the
trial was not pursued before this court.

Counsel for the applicant submitted that the formulation of the decision on Mrs
d Gordon's submission indicates that the justices either misunderstood or misapplied the
proper test. The proper test, he said, is to be found in the decision of this court in *R v
Liverpool City Justices, ex p Topping* [1983] 1 All ER 490, [1983] 1 WLR 119. I agree that
that is where the proper test is to be found. Ackner LJ said ([1983] 1 All ER 490 at 494,
[1983] 1 WLR 119 at 123):

e   'We conclude that the test to be applied can conveniently be expressed by slightly
        adapting the words of Lord Widgery CJ in a test which he laid down in *R v Uxbridge
        Justices, ex p Burbridge* (1972) Times, 21 June and referred to by him in *R v McLean,
        ex p Aikens* (1974) 139 JP 261 at 266: would a reasonable and fair-minded person
        sitting in court and knowing all the relevant facts have a reasonable suspicion that a
        fair trial for the applicant was not possible?'

f
If then the justices simply asked themselves, 'Do we feel prejudiced by reason of our
knowledge of the other six charges?' then they would have applied the wrong test and
exercised their discretion on an erroneous basis. Did the justices pose to themselves so
simple a question? They did not lack instruction. Mrs Gordon has deposed that she
addressed the bench 'on the principles outlined in ex parte Topping'. Her contempora-
g neous note records the advice which the court clerk (Mr Ray) proposed to give to the
justices, that is to say: 'The test is whether ordinary members of public would feel that
defendant not receiving a fair trial.' The three justices concerned have deposed as follows:

        'We confirm that at the commencement of proceedings on the 25th November,
        1985, Mrs. Gordon raised an objection to the list of offences alleged to have been
        committed by her client which we then had before us. Her objection was, in
h   substance, that we might in fact be prejudiced, or be thought by an observer to be
        prejudiced, in the trial of the allegations of wasting police time by knowledge of the
        fact that the Defendant was charged with other matters. We retired and considered
        whether or not we were in fact, or were likely to be seen to be prejudiced. In
        retirement our Clerk Mr. A. Ray advised us about the effect of R v Liverpool Justices
        ex parte Topping, and also a recent decision involving our own Bench R v Weston-
j   super-Mare Justices ex parte Stone. We considered we were not prejudiced in fact
        and did not believe we could be seen to be prejudiced and decided to exercise our
        discretion to proceed with the trial.'

In the light of that passage I find it impossible to say that the justices applied the wrong
test. True it is that the announcement of the decision in court was couched in less than
felicitous language, but the correct test having in fact been applied, I would not flaw the

decision by reference to the language employed. Nor does it seem to me to be material
that the justices asked themselves in addition and perhaps gratuitously whether they   *a*
were actually prejudiced in fact. If the justices applied the correct test, then it was not
suggested on behalf of the applicant that the exercise of their discretion could be faulted
in this court. I would refuse an order or certiorari.

I turn to the claim for declaration. The court list was typed on a printed sheet headed
'REGISTER OF THE MAGISTRATES' COURT SITTING AT THE COURT HOUSE, WALLISCOTE ROAD,
WESTON-SUPER-MARE'. The printed sheet is a sheet in the form prescribed by the Magistrates'   *b*
Courts (Forms) Rules 1981, SI 1981/533, for the register to be kept pursuant to r 66 of
the Magistrates' Courts Rules 1981, SI 1981/552 (see Form 148). Typed on the sheet are
the name of the informant, the name of the defendant, the nature of the offences alleged
against the defendant and the date of the offence. The clerk to the justices has deposed
that the court list as prepared and made available on 25 November 1985 was prepared
and made available in accordance with the usual practice of the justices.   *c*

Counsel for the applicant asserted that the practice is wrong in law. He relied on the
decision in *R v Liverpool City Justices, ex p Topping* [1983] 1 All ER 490 at 495–496, [1983]
1 WLR 119 at 124–125, where Ackner LJ said:

'We are asked to make a declaration that the practice of producing for a bench of
magistrates computerised court sheets, showing all charges and convictions (in   *d*
respect of which convictions the defendant is awaiting sentence by the court) then
outstanding and including the charge which the bench is about to try, is wrong in
law . . . [The computer] is apparently programmed in such a way that it produces in
relation to each defendant one list which shows not only the charge which is to be
heard, but all other charges, related or unrelated, which are outstanding and all
convictions, whether the result of a plea of guilty or a conviction, which are awaiting   *e*
sentence. This is no doubt very convenient for the administration and may be of
great advantage for the office staff. In our judgment it is most undesirable that such
a document should be put before the magistrates and for these reasons. (1)
Defendants in person will [not] know what other charges or convictions have thus
been drawn to the magistrates' attention, and will therefore be deprived of any
opportunity to make the appropriate application. (2) Even those who are represented   *f*
may be unaware of the material which has been put before the magistrates. (3)
Having arrived at court prepared for the trial, the expense of witnesses being
incurred, a defendant or his advocate may well be very averse to making an
application which will result in an adjournment, and thereby obliged to run the
risk of prejudice, to which risk he should not be subjected. (4) While on occasions it
may be necessary to make an application for the trial by another bench of magistrates,   *g*
the system should be such that such occasions are as rare as possible. A system which
is calculated to make this a regular event must be a bad system . . . In the affidavits
put in on behalf of the justices, there is no suggestion that they are incapable of
controlling their computer. The chief constable, who was represented on this
application, provided us with no information to suggest that there cannot be put
before the justices the limited material as occurred in the pre-computer era. To our   *h*
mind there is a real danger that administrative convenience is being given greater
priority than the requirements of justice. We therefore repeat that in our judgment
the practice of putting before the justices court sheets expressed in this fashion is
most undesirable. Can it also be said to the wrong in law? It was common ground
between counsel who appeared on this application that the "court sheets" referred to
in it are in fact the court register; this we were able to confirm by our own   *j*
inspection. The authority for the keeping of the court register is contained in r 66
of the Magistrates' Courts Rules 1981, SI 1981/552. It is sufficient for present
purposes to note that neither that rule, nor the form prescribed in it (Form 148 in
Stone's Justices' Manual 1982, vol 3, p 7625) contains provision for the entry in the
register, or in any particular sheet of it, of any offence or matter of complaint other
than that (or, where associated offences or complaints are heard together, those) in

a respect of which the court is to adjudicate. For this reason, therefore, we grant the declaration sought, that the practice complained of by the applicant is wrong in law.'

It is at once to be observed that it was agreed that the court sheets were in fact the court register and that this court confirmed that agreement by its own inspection. The register was not in the prescribed form in that it contained matters other than those required by the rules. It was therefore not kept in accordance with law. That however is not this case.

b In this case the court is not concerned with the court register. It is concerned with the daily list which, presumably, for reasons of convenience is typed up on the form prescribed for the register. Such a case was considered by this court in *R v Weston-super-Mare Justices, ex p Stone* (19 November 1984, unreported). The case concerned the bench and practice with which the court is now concerned. After referring to *R v Liverpool City Justices, ex p Topping*, Robert Goff LJ said:

c
'Here the situation is simply that a list had been drawn up in advance of the hearing, setting out all the matters that were to be dealt with on that particular day. Among the matters that were to be dealt with on that particular day were these two charges laid against the applicant, Mr Stone. It must often be the case in a magistrates' court that on one particular day more than one charge is listed to be dealt with

d against one particular person. We have only to think of such everyday matters as motoring offences and thefts to realise that that must frequently be the case. Sometimes those matters may arise out of the same episode, as, for example, where there are a number of motoring offences charged against a particular defendant, driving whilst uninsured, driving without a licence and so on. But that will by no means always be the case; for example, more than one charge of theft may be listed

e for hearing on the same day against a particular person. The preparation of the list setting out all the matters to be dealt with on a particular day cannot, in my judgment, be wrong in law; indeed I cannot see anything wrong in law in preparing such a list even if the list consists of a photocopy of an uncompleted page of what will ultimately become the complete court register. It simply lists the matters which are to be dealt with in the court on that particular day. I cannot see, for my part,

f that the preparation of such a list and the publication of it to justices in advance can be said to be of itself wrong in law.'

Counsel for the applicant said that this decision is in direct conflict with *R v Liverpool City Justices, ex p Topping*, is wrong and should not be followed. If there is a conflict between two decisions of the court, then this court must prefer one to the other (see by

g analogy *Young v Bristol Aeroplane Co Ltd* [1944] 2 All ER 293 at 300, [1944] KB 718 at 729 and *R v Gould* [1968] 1 All ER 849, [1968] 2 QB 65). If and in so far as *R v Liverpool City Justices, ex p Topping* decides that as a general proposition it is unlawful to list all charges related or unrelated against a single defendant which are for hearing on the same day and for the justices to see the list, then I prefer *R v Weston-super-Mare Justices, ex p Stone* and would respectfully adopt what Robert Goff LJ there said. There may well be some

h occasions when it would be most undesirable for unrelated charges to be listed together. The good sense of a clerk to justices should enable him to identify those occasions. Should in any case there be complaint, then the justices themselves have to determine whether their knowledge of other charges in their list should cause them to disqualify themselves by reference to the test of ostensible bias.

I would refuse the declaration which is sought.

j
NOLAN J. I agree.

WATKINS LJ. I agree with the judgment of Mann J. I add some words of my own solely because we were asked to resolve the clash of judicial opinion said to be reflected in the contrasting opinions expressed in *R v Liverpool City Justices, ex p Topping* [1983] 1 All ER 490, [1983] 1 WLR 119 and *R v Weston-super-Mare Justices, ex p Stone* (19

November 1984, unreported). That these opinions conflict in an important respect cannot be doubted in my view. The reason why they do is, I think, not difficult to find. It has its genesis in the status attributed to the 'court sheets' placed on the bench before justices informing them of the charges laid against a defendant which they are about to try.

In *R v Liverpool City Justices, ex p Topping* it was said to be common ground between counsel on both sides that the 'court sheets' referred to in the evidence setting out the charges laid against the defendant were the court register, a fact which Ackner LJ said 'we were able to confirm by our own inspection'.

On that basis of fact he went on to declare ([1983] 1 All ER 490 at 496, [1983] 1 WLR 119 at 125):

'It was common ground between counsel who appeared on this application that the "court sheets" referred to in it are in fact the court register; this we were able to confirm by our own inspection. The authority for the keeping of the court register is contained in r 66 of the Magistrates' Courts Rules 1981, SI 1981/552. It is sufficient for present purposes to note that neither that rule, nor the form prescribed in it (Form 148 in *Stone's Justices' Manual* 1982, vol 3, p 7625) contains provision for the entry in the register, or in any particular sheet of it, of any offence or matter of complaint other than that (or, where associated offences or complaints are heard together, those) in respect of which the court is to adjudicate. For this reason, therefore, we grant the declaration sought, that the practice complained of by the applicant is wrong in law.'

If the basis of fact was well founded it may well be that, for the reasons Ackner LJ gave, the practice complained of in *R v Liverpool City Justices, ex p Topping* was wrong in law.

I have the feeling, however, that the factual basis was probably unsound. As I understand what we were told by counsel in the present case, the 'court sheets' before us are similar to those in *R v Liverpool City Justices, ex p Topping* [1983] 1 All ER 490, [1983] 1 WLR 119. Counsel who appeared for the applicant in that case and who appears for the applicant in this maintains they are the court register. I think he is wrong. At the head of each sheet it is the fact that the words 'REGISTER OF THE MAGISTRATES' COURT SITTING AT THE COURT HOUSE' etc appear, but they are loose sheets which provide no further information until conviction and sentence or acquittal than the name of the defendant and the nature of the offence charged. When the charge or charges have been dealt with, the minute of adjudication and other details relating to, among other things, costs and legal aid are entered on the sheet which, when complete, is placed in the court register.

It is, counsel for the justices informed us (this is consistent with what I have always understood), only when the sheet is completed and placed in the register that it comes properly to be described as part of the court register. Prior to that, it is rightly described as a court sheet bearing a charge or charges.

If that be right, then the premise on which the practice referred to in *R v Liverpool City Justices, ex p Topping* was declared to be unlawful is obviously factually erroneous.

I accept that the sheets in the present case truly were court sheets and would not have become part of the court register unless and until the charges on them had been disposed of and all details of disposal and so forth entered and the sheet placed in the register.

I see nothing unlawful about that or any other part of the process complained of. I agree with the observations of Robert Goff LJ in *R v Weston-super-Mare Justices, ex p Stone*.

It follows, therefore, that the declaration sought is refused.

Application refused.

Solicitors: *Gordon & Penney*, Weston-super-Mare (for the applicant); *A M Roost*, Weston-super-Mare (for the justices).

Dilys Tausz   Barrister.

Leary v Leary

a

COURT OF APPEAL, CIVIL DIVISION
MAY AND PURCHAS LJJ
2, 11 SEPTEMBER 1986

b
Costs – Gross sum in lieu of taxed costs – Award reflecting conduct of party – Divorce – Ancillary proceedings – Husband refusing to disclose financial situation in ancillary relief proceedings – Judge making fixed award of costs against husband without warning – Whether husband should have been given opportunity to make representations before award made – Whether breach of natural justice – RSC Ord 62, r 9(4)(b).

c
Following the dissolution of the parties' marriage the wife applied for ancillary relief. The husband persistently failed to disclose his financial position, thereby causing the proceedings to be unduly protracted. In the course of the several hearings of the wife's application her solicitors prepared an itemised but estimated schedule of the costs of the suit amounting to £33,513. The schedule was made available to the husband and a bill of costs in equivalent terms was delivered to him after the hearing had been concluded.
d
In delivering judgment, in which she granted the wife ancillary relief, the judge, without prior warning to the husband, made an order under RSC Ord 62, r 9(4)(b)[a] directing him to pay to the wife a fixed amount of £31,000 costs instead of having the costs of the proceedings taxed. The judge stated when making the award that the order for costs should reflect the true position, which was that the husband's failure to disclose his financial position had necessitated an inquiry quite out of proportion to the end result,
e
that the wife should in no way be in debt as the result of the husband's actions and that the possibility of further litigation arising out of a taxation should be forestalled. The husband appealed against the award of costs.

Held – When determining an application for ancillary relief a judge was entitled to exercise his discretion under RSC Ord 62, r 9(4) to award a fixed sum of lieu of taxed
f
costs if he considered such an award was required to reflect the failure of a party to disclose his or her financial situation. The powers exercisable under r 9(4) were not confined to modest and simple cases and nor was the judge required, before making the award, to conduct an inquiry in the nature of a preliminary taxation in which there was a detailed investigation of the figures, since the whole purpose of an award under r 9(4) was to avoid the expense, delay and aggravation involved in protracted litigation arising
g
out of a taxation. The discretion was, however, required to be exercised judicially and the judge was required to give proper consideration to all relevant factors. Furthermore, it depended on the circumstances of the case whether the rules of natural justice required the judge to give prior warning of his intention to make a fixed award and to give the affected party the opportunity of making submissions before doing so; but where the judge assessed a gross sum without warning it was open to the parties or their
h
representatives to apply to him for an opportunity to make submissions on the matter in case certain aspects had been overlooked. Having regard to the circumstances, the judge's decision to make an award under Ord 62, r 9 without giving prior warning to the husband could not be challenged as an exercise of discretion and the husband had not been prejudiced by being deprived of the opportunity to contest the costs submitted by the wife's solicitors. Accordingly, the appeal would be dismissed (see p 264 h to
j
265 b d e g h and p 266 d to p 267 b, post).

Notes

For costs to which a person is entitled, see 37 Halsbury's Laws (4th edn) para 725, and for cases on the subject, see 37(3) Digest (Reissue) 284–285, 4613–4621.

---

a   Rule 9, so far as material, is set out at p 262 *f* to *h*, post

For orders for costs in matrimonial proceedings generally, see 13 Halsbury's Laws (4th   *a*
edn) paras 958–959, and for cases on the subject, see 27(2) Digest (Reissue) 744–747,
5845–5884.

Cases referred to in judgments
Alltrans Express Ltd v CVA Holdings Ltd [1984] 1 All ER 685, [1984] 1 WLR 394, CA.
Practice Direction [1982] 2 All ER 800, [1982] 1 WLR 1082.
Silva v C Czarnikow Ltd (1960) 104 SJ 369.   *b*
Singer (formerly Sharegin) v Sharegin [1984] FLR 114, CA.

Cases also cited
EMI Records Ltd v Ian Cameron Wallace Ltd [1982] 2 All ER 980, [1983] Ch 59.
Project Development Co Ltd SA v KMK Securities Ltd (Syndicate Bank intervening) [1983] 1 All
  ER 465, [1982] 1 WLR 1470.   *c*

Interlocutory appeal
The respondent, Martin Paul Leary (the husband), appealed pursuant to leave of the
judge granted on 9 May 1986 against the order of Booth J in chambers dated 26 March
1986 on the hearing of two applications by the petitioner, Diane Susan Leary (the wife),
for ancillary relief following on the dissolution of her marriage with the husband   *d*
whereby the judge ordered the husband to pay the wife on or before 3 April 1985 the
sum of £31,000 assessed by the judge as the costs recoverable by the wife from the
husband in respect of the proceedings in the suit. The facts are set out in the judgment
of the court.

Andrew McDowall for the husband.   *e*
Peter Singer for the wife.

Cur adv vult

11 September. The following judgment of the court was delivered.

PURCHAS LJ. This is an appeal with leave of the judge from part of an order made by   *f*
Booth J on 26 March 1986. The appeal raises a short but important point relating to the
powers of the court to award a fixed sum in costs under the provisions of RSC Ord 62,
r 9. It is convenient at the outset to recite the relevant portions of this rule:

'(1) Subject to this Order, where by or under these rules or any order or direction
of the Court costs are to be paid to any person, that person shall be entitled to his
taxed costs.   *g*
(2) Paragraph (1) shall not apply to costs which by or under any order or direction
of the Court . . . (b) are to be assessed or settled by a master; but rules 28, 28A, 31 and
32 shall apply in relation to the assessment or settlement by a master of costs which
are to be assessed or settled as aforesaid as they apply in relation to the taxation of
costs by a taxing officer . . .
(4) The Court in awarding costs to any person may direct that, instead of taxed   *h*
costs, that person shall be entitled . . . (b) to a gross sum so specified in lieu of taxed
costs . . .'

The part of the judge's order against which the appeal is brought provided:

'9. The Respondent do on or before the 3rd April 1986 pay to the Petitioner the
sum of £31,000 assessed as the costs recoverable by her from the Respondent in   *j*
respect of the proceedings in this suit, to include all costs reserved and all costs
hitherto ordered to be paid by him to her and to take account of the costs hitherto
ordered to be paid by her to him; and it is directed that interest at the judgment
debt rate for the time being shall be payable on any outstanding balance of the said
costs from the 24th April 1986 until payment is made.'

a The respondent, Martin Paul Leary, to whom we shall refer as 'the husband' notwithstanding the dissolution of the marriage, appeals against this provision made in favour of the petitioner, Diana Susan Leary, to whom we shall refer as 'the wife'.

The background to the appeal can be shortly stated. Paragraph 9 was one paragraph of an order dealing comprehensively with the disposition of the family assets and the future maintenance of the wife and two children of the family made after a protracted hearing of two applications for ancillary relief in the matrimonial suit made by the wife and b dated 5 November 1984 and 16 October 1985. The judgment refers to an application for ancillary relief filed by the wife on 2 June 1983 following on the filing of her petition on 11 January 1983 and the husband's answer of 3 February 1983 on the cross-allegations of adultery alleged in which the suit was eventually compromised and a decree nisi pronounced on 24 November 1983 which was made absolute on 30 July 1984. As counsel for the wife mentioned during argument, the litigation on the ancillary matters arising c from the dissolution of this marriage had, by the hearing before the judge, been on foot for more than three years. That the investigation of the husband's assets took a long time and involved an adjournment of the hearing of the applications was due to the attitude taken by the husband. This is commented on by the judge in her judgment in the following terms:

d   'There then comes the question of costs. I have considered whether I ought to deal with this as part and parcel of the wife's lump sum payment. I have come to the conclusion that I should not, and that I should deal with the question of costs separately. Because this case has been of such particular complexity and difficulty, it is right that the order for costs should reflect what I feel to be the true position. It has been an inquiry which has been quite out of proportion to the end result, but it e   has been necessitated entirely by the husband's approach and unfortunately by the approach of those with whom he has been associated, including, I have no doubt whatever, Mr Bousfield [the husband's financial adviser]. His failure to disclose his financial situation has persisted to the last, as I have found, so that I have still been quite unable to quantify in any terms what his assets and wealth amount to. In f   those circumstances no legal adviser acting on behalf of the wife could properly have advised the wife to settle her financial claim. It is a responsibility which in the circumstances had to be taken by the court itself. As a result of that the wife should in no way be in debt as a result of the husband's actions. Therefore I have come to the conclusion without hesitation that it is right for me to assess the costs on the basis that the wife should be indemnified against the costs incurred as a result of the g   husband's actions.'

It is only necessary to add that we understand from counsel that the husband appeared in person on the hearing of the application having dispensed with the services of his legal and financial advisers, who were in fact called on subpoena in support of the wife's case. On any footing it has correctly been described as a complex and difficult case.

h During the course of the hearings which took place between 14 October 1985 and 26 March 1986 in pursuance of the practice direction relating to estimated costs of the suit (see [1982] 2 All ER 800, [1982] 1 WLR 1082) the wife's solicitors had prepared an itemised schedule of costs which amounted in total to £33,513. We have been told that since the hearing a bill of costs has been delivered in equivalent terms and that accordingly the wife's solicitors are bound in practice to that figure. The schedule had been available j in October 1985 and was brought up to date in March 1986 to include the completion of the final hearing. There is some dispute as to how and at what stage it came into the hands of the husband who, it is to be remembered, was appearing in person. Certainly it was in his possession during the adjourned hearing of the applications in March 1986 and may well have been available to him at an earlier date. That there was some discussion on one item, namely counsel's fees, counsel for the wife recalls but, as one would expect, he frankly acknowledges that he has no detailed personal recollection of the extent to which reference was made to the schedule or as to any discussion on it which may have taken place before the judge delivered her judgment.

The judge, without, it appears, giving any indication that it was her intention so to do during the hearing of the application or the submissions of counsel and the husband, elected to assess a figure for costs under the provision of the order which we have already cited and reached the figure of £31,000. Her reasons for doing this appear from the passage in the transcript of her reserved judgment:

'In order to prevent any further litigation between these parties, any question of taxation with regard to that, I propose to order the husband to pay a fixed sum as regards the wife's costs. Having regard to the element in the figure of £33,500 submitted by the wife's solicitors of the husband's own costs which the wife has to bear and the element of costs other than those relating to the financial matters which are the costs before me, I have come to the conclusion that the proper order to make would be an order of £31,000. That will be payable by way of costs and not by way of the lump sum order for the wife.'

In doing this the judge was acting under the provisions of Ord 62, r 9 already cited.

In his notice of appeal prepared personally the husband gives three grounds:

'1. That I have been denied Natural Justice to consider the reasonableness or otherwise of a fair and proper assessment of the Petitioner's Solicitors' costs and disbursements. 2. That I should have an opportunity to challenge each and every item and/or their rates of charges. 3. That the Petitioner be ordered to pay the costs of this appeal.'

In support of the appeal counsel for the husband submitted the following points. (1) The powers granted by Ord 62, r 9 ought primarily to be used in modest and simple cases. (2) When the power is used it ought to be (to quote his words) 'on a not less than' figure as a basis of assessment. By this we understand him to mean that the judge ought to take the lowest reasonable figure which might have been achieved if the costs were taxed. (3) In practice, in assessing costs against a submitted account, in carrying out the exercise in (2) above the judge invariably makes a discount from the figure claimed rather in the way of taxing down a charge. Inasmuch as the judge here merely excluded extraneous or irrelevant items but otherwise accepted the figures at their face value, counsel for the husband submitted that she committed an error in law, on which he is entitled to rely on appeal. (4) Before exercising the power given to her under Ord 62, r 9 the judge should have given some warning to the parties, particularly the party against whom the order was to be made, so that a specific attack on the figures in the schedule could be made. This contention echoed ground 2 in the notice of appeal. In support of this counsel for the husband referred us to a case in which Streatfeild J acted under Ord 62, r 9 but after hearing oral evidence of a representative of the solicitors for the party in whose favour the order was to be made (see *Silva v C Czarnikow Ltd* (1960) 104 SJ 369).

Dealing with the last of the submissions of counsel for the husband first, in our judgment the suggestion that there ought to be an inquiry in the nature of proceedings before a taxing master at the trial seems to us to be ill-founded. Counsel for the wife told us that in practice in the Family Division in his own experience judges on a number of occasions have made orders in very substantial cases without making any formal inquiry by way of hearing evidence other than receiving schedules of estimated costs in accordance with *Practice Direction* [1982] 2 All ER 800, [1982] 1 WLR 1082 and the judgments delivered by Cumming-Bruce and May LJJ in *Singer (formerly Sharegin) v Sharegin* [1984] FLR 114. We have not been referred, however, to any case in which the principles on which the powers granted by Ord 62, r 9 in a matrimonial suit should be exercised have been considered in this court.

The terms of Ord 62, r 9 themselves give assistance to the solution of this problem.
a Rule 9(4) clearly imports that the gross sum so specified by the court is 'instead of taxed costs' (see the introductory words) and under sub-para (*b*) 'to a gross sum so specified in lieu of taxed costs'. The purpose of this rule is to achieve exactly the objectives mentioned by the judge, namely the avoidance of expense, delay and aggravation involved in a protracted litigation arising out of taxation. This would be achieved especially in complex cases. The order, therefore, does not envisage that any process similar to that involved in
b 'taxation' should take place. Although Streatfeild J in *Silva v C Czarnikow Ltd* received evidence from a managing clerk estimating the costs, there was another reason for assessing a figure on established evidence since we notice from the report that counsel for the defendants thereupon made an immediate application for a garnishee order against the plaintiff's bank and produced the affidavit required under the then Ord 45, r 1. The circumstances, therefore, in that case were exceptional and the judgment is not an
c authority, persuasive or otherwise, that before assessing a gross figure in lieu of taxed costs under Ord 62, r 9 a judge is obliged to receive evidence on oath or anything more than some evidence as to the estimated costs. For these reasons, therefore, we have formed the view that the ground of appeal in so far as it may have been based on any formal restriction in the operation of the powers granted under Ord 62, r 9 is ill-founded. However, the matter does not end there.
d   The unlimited discretion given by Ord 62, r 9 must be exercised in a judicial manner. How the powers are to be used varies widely from case to case and each case must be considered on its own merits. It is easy to envisage cases where a judge could be said to have acted unjudicially: eg by clutching a figure out of the air without having any indication as to the estimated costs; receiving such an estimate without the details being made available to the other side; or refusing a request to hear submissions on such a
e schedule if the party against whom the order is to be made makes, on reasonable grounds, an application to be heard. There will be many cases in which the judge may well feel that he or she would be assisted by submissions from counsel on whether (a) a gross figure should be assessed under Ord 62, r 9 at all, and (b) if so, at what figure. There is, however, no statutory obligation on the judge to receive such submissions provided that
f he observes the rules of natural justice. Again, as counsel for the husband submitted, there may well be occasions on which the judge will make a discount on the figures produced in the schedule on a fail-safe or 'not less than' basis. Again there is no statutory obligation for him to do this; and, indeed, unless there appears some reasonable ground to invite inquiry into the actual figures an arbitrary reduction of the kind suggested by counsel for the husband could well cause an injustice to the successful party. As we have
g mentioned earlier in this judgment, once the estimate is produced the solicitors are more or less fixed to that amount or something less. There is, in our judgment, no justification either in law or in precedent for the contentions of counsel for the husband that the process provided in Ord 62, r 9 should only be used in simple cases, or cases involving small amounts; indeed, from the information provided by counsel for the wife rather the contrary.
h   There remains only the question whether the judge was entitled to fix a gross sum without indicating to the husband that she proposed to do this, when reserving judgment; or to give the husband an opportunity to make submissions before proceeding to that part of her judgment in which she dealt with costs. This raises a number of questions. (a) Did the judge give proper consideration to matters before assessing the gross sum? (b) Was the figure so plainly wrong that she must have erred in law in the exercise of her
j discretion? (c) Was she under any obligation to warn the husband specifically of her powers under Ord 62, r 9? (d) Was she under any obligation to permit a detailed investigation of the figures in the schedule as sought in ground 2 of the notice of appeal? (e) Has the husband been prejudiced by being deprived of the opportunity to attack the figures?

That the judge gave careful consideration to the question of costs before assessing the gross sum appears from the judgment:

'So far as her debts are concerned, the one debt that I have heard about, and, of course, it is a very heavy debt, is with regard to the costs of these proceedings. Very properly her solicitors have broken down those costs and have shown quite clearly how they now add up in total, including the costs of today, to a sum of £33,500. It has to be said that they include costs incurred by the husband in an application with regard to the children which were ordered to be paid by the wife and also include costs relating to injunction proceedings that have taken place between the parties. The solicitors hold £1,000 on account but otherwise they look to the wife for the payment of those substantial costs. This has obviously not been an easy case with which to deal. The documents have been massive. The hearing has properly occupied very much time. The approach of the court, as again I think I have made clear throughout the course of this hearing, where there has not been full disclosure must be to draw inferences on the evidence available to it.'

Indeed, as we have understood the submissions of counsel for the husband, he does not attempt to show that the figures in the schedule can be attacked in detail in any way apart from the general principles to which we have already made reference in this judgment.

It must be borne in mind that the judge is perhaps one of the most experienced authorities on the question of costs in general as a result of her wide experience in this field. We would therefore answer the questions posed in paras (a) and (b) above in the affirmative and the negative respectively.

We now turn to the questions posed in paras (c) and (d) above. The basic proposition is that the conduct of a trial is essentially within the discretion of the judge. There is no statutory obligation to give any indication of the powers or their proposed exercise under Ord 62, r 9. To allow a detailed investigation of the figures, as suggested in the second ground of the notice of appeal, would, as we have already indicated, fly in the teeth of the provisions and objective of Ord 62, r 9 itself. Clearly to allow at trial what would in effect be a preliminary taxation would be an affront to the process. At the very most it could be said that a party by reference to a schedule of costs might submit, and submit successfully in certain circumstances, that in the particular case concerned it would be wrong to assess a gross figure because of questions possibly arising out of the individual items disclosed in the schedule. Judges frequently extend, as a matter of courtesy and discretion and in order to achieve justice in the case of illiterate or ill-informed litigants in person, considerable help in the conduct of their cases. Whether this should be done, and the degree to which it should extend, again must depend on the circumstances of the case and be entirely in the discretion of the trial judge. In the case of a sophisticated and educated man who has deliberately deprived himself of professional assistance the resolution of these matters by the trial judge may well differ from the course adopted in a case of a litigant not so privileged. This court would in any event only interfere if the exercise by the trial judge of his discretion in these matters demonstrated in the ordinary sense detailed in the judgment in *Alltrans Express Ltd v CVA Holdings Ltd* [1984] 1 All ER 685, [1984] 1 WLR 394 that the judge had erred or was plainly wrong. In our judgment, on the facts of this case, the decision by the judge not to warn the husband of his rights under Ord 62, r 9 is impossible to challenge as an exercise of discretion. Finally, turning to para (e) above, we have no hesitation at all in saying that the husband has in no way been prejudiced by being deprived of the opportunity to deal with the exercise of the powers under Ord 62, r 9. Even in the case where a judge assesses a gross sum without warning it is open to the parties, or their representatives, to apply to the judge for an opportunity to make submissions on the matter in case certain relevant aspects have been overlooked, and on the receipt of such submissions before the order has been drawn up for the judge to make any adjustment appropriate to the order he or she proposes to

make. In this case there has been no suggestion that the figures in the schedule are in any
a way excessive.

In all the circumstances, therefore, we are satisfied that there has been no miscarriage
of justice in this case, that the judge exercised her discretion in a perfectly proper manner
and that none of the grounds adumbrated in the notice of appeal or developed by counsel
for the husband in argument have been established. Accordingly, this appeal is dismissed.

b *Appeal dismissed.*

Solicitors: *Birkbeck Montagu's* (for the husband); *Bernard Sheridan & Co* (for the wife).

Mary Rose Plummer   Barrister.

c

Lombard North Central plc v Butterworth

d COURT OF APPEAL, CIVIL DIVISION
LAWTON, MUSTILL AND NICHOLLS LJJ
27 JUNE, 31 JULY 1986

*Hire – Damages for breach of contract of hiring – Repudiation of contract by hirer – Contract
providing that owner entitled to all arrears and future instalments on termination – Contract
further providing that punctual payment of each instalment of essence of contract – Hirer
e breaching contract by not paying instalments punctually – Owner terminating contract – Whether
hirer's breach in failing to pay punctually amounting to repudiation of contract by hirer – Whether
breach of time of essence provision amounting to repudiation – Whether provision entitling owner
to all arrears and future instalments a penalty – Whether owner entitled to recover damages for
loss of whole transaction.*

f
The plaintiffs, a finance company, leased a computer to the defendant for a period of five
years on payment of an initial sum of £584·05 and 19 subsequent quarterly instalments
of the same amount. Clause 2(a) of the hiring agreement made punctual payment of
each instalment of the essence of the agreement and under cl 5 failure to make due and
punctual payment entitled the plaintiffs to terminate the agreement. By cl 6 the plaintiffs
g were entitled on termination to all arrears of instalments and all future instalments
which would have fallen due had the agreement not been terminated. Although the
defendant paid the first two instalments promptly, the next three were paid very
belatedly, and on four occasions payment made by direct debit was recalled by the bank.
When the sixth instalment was six weeks overdue the plaintiffs wrote to the defendant
terminating the agreement. Subsequently the plaintiffs recovered possession of the
h computer and sold it for only £172·88. The plaintiffs brought an action against the
defendant claiming the amount of the unpaid sixth instalment and the 13 future
instalments or, alternatively, damages for breach of contract. They then applied for and
obtained summary judgment under RSC Ord 14 for damages to be assessed. In assessing
the damages the master held that the defendant had by his conduct repudiated the
contract and accordingly the plaintiffs were entitled to recover damages in respect of all
j future instalments less certain credits. The defendant appealed, contending that he ought
not to be held liable for more than the amount due and unpaid at the date of termination,
because (i) cl 6 of the agreement created a penalty and was therefore unenforceable and
(ii) the defendant's conduct had not amounted to a repudiation of the contract. The
plaintiffs sought to uphold the judgment on the alternative ground that cl 2(a) of the
agreement, which made punctual payment of each instalment of the essence, entitled

them to treat default in one payment as a repudiation by the defendant of the agreement and thus enabled them to recover their loss in respect of the whole transaction.

Held – (1) In the absence of a repudiatory breach, cl 6 created a penalty in so far as it purported to require the defendant to make payment in respect of rental instalments which had not accrued at the date of termination regardless of the seriousness or triviality of the breach which resulted in the plaintiffs terminating the agreement. Consequently cl 6 was unenforceable (see p 271 *f*, p 277 *e f* and p 280 *f*, post); *Financings Ltd v Baldock* [1963] 1 All ER 443 applied.

(2) The repeated failure of the defendant to pay the instalments punctually did not justify the court drawing the inference that he had thereby evinced an intention not to adhere to his obligation under the agreement to make punctual payment and therefore, even bearing in mind the commercial objective of the agreement so far as it concerned the plaintiffs, the defendant's conduct in failing to make punctual payment did not amount to a repudiation by him of the agreement (see p 271 *f*, p 277 *j*, p 279 *d* to *e* and p 280 *f*, post).

(3) However, the provision in cl 2(*a*) of the agreement that punctual payment of the instalments was of the essence of the agreement made prompt payment a condition, and when cl 2(*a*) was read with cll 5 and 6 it had the effect of making default in punctual payment a breach of the agreement going to the root of the contract and accordingly, even though that breach on its own was not sufficient to constitute repudiation, it entitled the plaintiffs to terminate the contract, independently of cl 6, and to recover damages for the loss of the whole transaction. It followed therefore that the appeal would be dismissed (see p 271 *g* to p 272 *c*, p 273 *d* to *f j* to p 274 *a*, p 275 *c d*, p 279 *g* to *j* and p 280 *d f*, post); *Financings Ltd v Baldock* [1963] 1 All ER 443 considered.

Notes

For a hirer's obligations to pay rental, see 2 Halsbury's Laws (4th edn) paras 251–252, and for cases on the subject, see 3 Digest (Reissue) 464, *3084–3085*.

For repudiation of a contract, see 9 Halsbury's Laws (4th edn) paras 546–550, and for cases on the subject, see 12 Digest (Reissue) 413–416, *3040–3049*.

Cases referred to in judgments

Bettini v Gye (1876) 1 QBD 183, [1874–80] All ER Rep 242.
Brady v St Margaret's Trust Ltd [1963] 2 All ER 275, [1963] 2 QB 494, [1963] 2 WLR 1162, CA.
Bridge v Campbell Discount Co Ltd [1962] 1 All ER 385, [1960] AC 600, [1962] 2 WLR 439, HL.
Bunge Corp v Tradax SA [1981] 2 All ER 513, [1981] 1 WLR 711, HL; *affg* [1981] 2 All ER 513, CA.
Capital Finance Co Ltd v Donati (1977) 121 SJ 270, CA.
Charterhouse Credit Co Ltd v Tolly [1963] 2 All ER 432, [1963] 2 QB 683, [1963] 2 WLR 1168, CA.
Financings Ltd v Baldock [1963] 1 All ER 443, [1963] 2 QB 104, [1963] 2 WLR 359, CA.
Hong Kong Fir Shipping Co Ltd v Kawasaki Kisen Kaisha Ltd [1962] 1 All ER 474, [1962] 2 QB 26, [1962] 2 WLR 474, CA.
Photo Production Ltd v Securicor Transport Ltd [1980] 1 All ER 556, [1980] AC 827, [1980] 2 WLR 283, HL.
Steedman v Drinkle [1916] 1 AC 275, [1914–15] All ER Rep 298, PC.
United Dominions Trust (Commercial) Ltd v Ennis [1967] 2 All ER 345, [1968] 1 QB 54, [1967] 3 WLR 1, CA.

Cases also cited

Dunlop Pneumatic Tyre Co Ltd v New Garage and Motor Co Ltd [1915] AC 79, [1914–15] All ER Rep 739, HL.

Interoffice Telephones Ltd v Robert Freeman Co Ltd [1957] 3 All ER 479, [1958] 1 QB 190,
CA.
Robophone Facilities Ltd v Blank [1966] 3 All ER 128, [1966] 1 WLR 1428, CA.

Appeal

The defendant, Lawrence Arthur Butterworth, appealed against the order of Master
Lubbock made on 18 December 1985 whereby he ordered the defendant to pay the
plaintiffs, Lombard North Central plc, damages and interest in the sum of £7,694·34,
such damages having been assessed by the master as appropriate after judgment had been
given for the plaintiffs under RSC Ord 14, r 3 by Master Waldman on 14 December 1984
in an action in which the plaintiffs claimed against the defendant the sum of £6,869·97
and interest in respect of rentals under a hiring agreement or, alternatively, as damages
for breach of contract. The facts are set out in the judgment of Mustill LJ.

William Hart for the defendant.
Andrew Onslow for the plaintiffs.

Cur adv vult

31 July. The following judgments were delivered.

MUSTILL LJ (giving the first judgment at the invitation of Lawton LJ). The respondent
plaintiffs are a finance company. The defendant appellant is an accountant. The defendant
wished to buy a computer to improve his business, and enlisted the help of the plaintiffs.
They purchased a particular model, and then entered into an agreement of hiring
whereby they agreed to lease the computer to the defendant for a period of five years.
There was to be an initial payment of £584·05 and 19 subsequent instalments of the
same amount, payable at intervals of three months. In addition, value added tax was to
be paid.

The hiring agreement contained the following material provisions:

'THE LESSEE . . . AGREES . . .

2 (a) to pay to the lessor: (i) punctually and without previous demand the rentals
set out in Part 3 of the Schedule together with Value Added Tax thereon punctual
payment of each which shall be of the essence of this Lease . . .

5. IN THE EVENT THAT (a) the Lessee shall (i) make default in the due and punctual
payment of any of the rentals or of any sum of money payable to the Lessor
hereunder or any part thereof . . . then upon the happening of such event . . . the
Lessor's consent to the Lessee's possession of the Goods shall determine forthwith
without any notice being given by the Lessor, and the Lessor may terminate this
Lease either by notice in writing, or by taking possession of the Goods . . .

6. IN THE EVENT that the Lessor's consent to the Lessee's possession of the goods
shall be determined under clause 5 hereof (a) the Lessee shall pay forthwith to the
Lessor: (1) all arrears of rentals; and (ii) all further rentals which would but for the
determination of the Lessor's consent to the Lessee's possession of the Goods have
fallen due to the end of the fixed period of this Lease less a discount thereon for
accelerated payment at the rate of 5 per cent per annum; and (iii) damages for any
breach of this Lease and all expenses and costs incurred by the Lessor in retaking
possession of the Goods and/or enforcing the Lessor's rights under this Lease together
with such Value Added Tax as shall be legally payable thereon; (b) the Lessor shall
be entitled to exercise any one or more of the rights and remedies provided for in
clause 5 and sub clause (a) of this clause and the determination of the Lessor's consent
to the Lessee's possession of the Goods shall not affect or prejudice such rights and
remedies and the Lessee shall be and remain liable to perform all outstanding

liabilities under this Lease notwithstanding that the Lessor may have taken possession of the Goods and/or exercised one or more of the rights and remedies of *a* the Lessor. (*c*) any right or remedy to which the Lessor is or may become entitled under this Lease or in consequence of the Lessee's conduct may be enforced from time to time separately or concurrently with any other right or remedy given by this Lease or now or hereafter provided for or arising by operation of law so that such rights and remedies are not exclusive of the other or others of them but are cumulative.'   *b*

The letting under this agreement did not go well. The instalments were due to be paid by direct debit. The first two were effected satisfactorily but the third was twice recalled by the bank and remained unpaid for a period of four months. The fourth was paid two weeks late. The fifth was two months late. The sixth was paid on time, but was recalled by the bank. It was paid again one month later, and again recalled by the bank. Two *c* weeks later the plaintiffs lost patience and sent to the defendant a letter in the following terms:

'We regret that in spite of our previous reminders you are still in arrear with your payments. Please take notice that pursuant to the terms of the lease our consent to your possession of the goods is now withdrawn and you are required to make them available for collection. Your liability under the terms of the lease will not cease *d* upon the return of these goods as we are entitled to call upon you to make payment of the balance of the rentals due under the remaining period of the lease. If payment of the arrears has been made within the last 7 days please ignore this notice.'

Subsequently, the plaintiffs recovered possession of the computer and sold it. The instrument fetched very little by comparison with its purchase price, and the net proceeds *e* of sale were only £172·85.

On 18 May 1984 the plaintiffs commenced the present action by specially indorsed writ. The material parts read:

'4. Pursuant to Clause 5 of the said Lease Agreement the Plaintiff terminated its consent to the Defendant's possession of the said Computer and Printer by a notice *f* in writing dated the 20th day of December 1982 and by virtue of the Defendant's default under the said Lease Agreement the same has been determined.

5. Pursuant to Clause 6 of the said Lease Agreement and by virtue of the determination of consent to possession pursuant to Clause 5 thereof the Plaintiff is entitled to claim (a) all of his rentals (b) all further rentals which would have been payable had the Lease Agreement continued for the full period and (c) damages for *g* breach of the Lease Agreement.

6. The Plaintiff has recovered possession of the said Computer and Printer in accordance with its entitlement to do so under Clause 5 of the said Lease Agreement and the net proceeds of sale amounted to £172·85. Calculating the amounts due to the Plaintiff the Defendant will be given credit for this sum and an allowance will be made for accelerated receipt of the payment due under the said Lease Agreement *h* as provided in Clause 6 thereof.

7. The Defendant has failed to pay the sums referred to in paragraph 5 hereof and the Plaintiff is entitled under the Lease or alternatively as damages for breach of the Lease, the sum of £6,869·97.'

The sum of £6,869·97 was arrived at by adding the amount of the unpaid instalment *j* and value added tax, and the 13 rentals due after termination, and then giving credit for the net proceeds of sale and an allowance of £1,221·49 for accelerated receipt. The pleading concluded with claims for £6,869·97 under para 7, interest and 'damages for breach of contract'.

The plaintiffs then issued an application for summary judgment under RSC Ord 14.

An affidavit in reply was sworn on behalf of the defendant. This did not put in issue the
a   plaintiffs' right to terminate the contract, or to recover a sum attributable to the future
instalments, but complaint was made about the low price obtained on the resale. The
affidavit concluded by asserting that the defendant had a partial defence on the merits,
and asking that he should have leave to defend sufficient to enable him to dispute the
calculations in the statement of claim.

Precisely what happened thereafter is not clear, but it appears that the plaintiffs did
b   not go to judgment for their claim in debt under cl 6 of the agreement, but instead
obtained a judgment for damages to be assessed. The matter was then referred to Master
Lubbock, who heard evidence on the resale value of the computer. He decided this issue
in favour of the plaintiffs. Argument was also addressed on the measure of recovery.
Notwithstanding that the plaintiffs had recovered judgment for damages to be assessed,
they continued to rely on cl 6. The defendant replied that this was a penalty. In the
c   event, the master found it unnecessary to reach a conclusion on this question, since he
found that the defendant had repudiated the contract, and that accordingly damages
were recoverable in respect of the future instalments, subject to the credits allowed in the
statement of claim. He gave judgment accordingly. The defendant now appeals,
maintaining that he should not be held liable for more than the amount due and unpaid
at the date of termination.
d   Three issues were canvassed before us. (1) Is cl 6 of the agreement to be disregarded,
on the ground that it creates a penalty? (Strictly speaking, this issue does not arise, since
the judgment was for damages to be assessed, but cl 6 was relied on by the plaintiffs
before the master and in this court, without objection.) (2) Apart from cl 2(*a*) of the
agreement, was the master correct in holding that the conduct of the defendant amounted
to a wrongful repudiation of the contract, and that the sum claimed was recoverable in
e   damages? (3) Does the provision in cl 2(*a*) of the agreement that time for payment of the
instalments was of the essence have the effect of making the defendant's late payment of
the outstanding instalment a repudiatory breach?

As to the first two issues, I need say only that I have had the advantage of reading in
draft the judgment to be delivered by Nicholls LJ, and that I am in such entire agreement
f   with his conclusions and reasons that it is unnecessary to add any observations of my
own.

I would, however, wish to deal with the third point. Important as it is, this point has
played only a minor part in the proceedings. There is no explicit reference to it in the
pleadings, although it is just open to the plaintiffs through their claim for damages. We
are told that it was argued before the master, yet there is no reference to it in his
g   judgment. The matter received little prominence during the argument before us, nor
were submissions directed at any stage to the possibility that the plaintiffs had by their
prior conduct waived their right to insist on the stipulation that time was of the essence.

The reason why I am impelled to hold that the plaintiffs' contentions are well-founded
can most conveniently be set out in a series of propositions. (1) Where a breach goes to
the root of the contract, the injured party may elect to put an end to the contract.
h   Thereupon both sides are relieved from those obligations which remain unperformed.
(2) If he does so elect, the injured party is entitled to compensation for (a) any breaches
which occurred before the contract was terminated and (b) the loss of his opportunity to
receive performance of the promisor's outstanding obligations. (3) Certain categories of
obligation, often called conditions, have the property that any breach of them is treated
as going to the root of the contract. On the occurrence of any breach of condition, the
j   injured party can elect to terminate and claim damages, whatever the gravity of the
breach. (4) It is possible by express provision in the contract to make a term a condition,
even if it would not be so in the absence of such a provision. (5) A stipulation that time
is of the essence, in relation to a particular contractual term, denotes that timely
performance is a condition of the contract. The consequence is that delay in performance
is treated as going to the root of the contract, without regard to the magnitude of the

breach. (6) It follows that where a promisor fails to give timely performance of an obligation in respect of which time is expressly stated to be of the essence, the injured *a* party may elect to terminate and recover damages in respect of the promisor's outstanding obligations, without regard to the magnitude of the breach. (7) A term of the contract prescribing what damages are to be recoverable when a contract is terminated for a breach of condition is open to being struck down as a penalty, if it is not a genuine covenanted pre-estimate of the damage, in the same way as a clause which prescribes the measure for any other type of breach. No doubt the position is the same where the clause *b* is ranked as a condition by virtue of an express provision in the contract. (8) A clause expressly assigning a particular obligation to the category of condition is not a clause which purports to fix the damages for breaches of the obligation, and is not subject to the law governing penalty clauses. (9) Thus, although in the present case cl 6 is to be struck down as a penalty, cl 2(*a*)(i) remains enforceable. The plaintiffs were entitled to terminate the contract independently of cl 5, and to recover damages for loss of the future *c* instalments. This loss was correctly computed by the master.

These bare propositions call for comment. The first three are uncontroversial. The fourth was not, I believe, challenged before us, but I would in any event regard it as indisputable. That there exists a category of term, in respect of which any breach whether large or small entitles the promisee to treat himself as discharged, has never been doubted in modern times, and the fact that a term may be assigned to this category by express *d* agreement has been taken for granted for at least a century: see, by way of example only, *Bettini v Gye* (1876) 1 QBD 183 at 187, [1874–80] All ER Rep 242 at 244, *Hong Kong Fir Shipping Co Ltd v Kawasaki Kisen Kaisha Ltd* [1962] 1 All ER 474 at 487, [1962] 2 QB 26 at 70, *Financings Ltd v Baldock* [1963] 1 All ER 443, [1963] 2 QB 104, *Photo Production Ltd v Securicor Transport Ltd* [1980] 1 All ER 556 at 567–568, [1980] AC 827 at 849, *Bunge Corp v Tradax SA* [1981] 2 All ER 513 at 541, 544, [1981] 1 WLR 711 at 715, 719 and Cheshire *e* and Fifoot *Law of Contract* (10th edn, 1981) p 137.

The fifth proposition is a matter of terminology, and has been more taken for granted than discussed. That making time of the essence is the same as making timely performance a condition was, however, expressly stated by Megaw and Browne LJJ in *Bunge Corp v Tradax SA* [1981] 2 All ER 513 at 532, 536, 539, and the same proposition *f* is implicit in the leading speeches of Lord Wilberforce and Lord Roskill in the House of Lords.

The sixth proposition is a combination of the first five. There appears to be no direct authority for it, and it is right to say that most of the cases on the significance of time being of the essence have been concerned with the right of the injured party to be discharged, rather than the principles on which his damages are to be computed. *g* Nevertheless, it is axiomatic that a person who establishes a breach of condition can terminate and claim damages for loss of the bargain, and I know of no authority which suggests that the position is any different where late performance is made into a breach of condition by a stipulation that time is of the essence.

In this connection, it is useful to refer to *Bunge Corp v Tradax SA*. An f o b contract for the sale of goods required the buyers to give notice of the probable readiness of the ships *h* on which the goods were to be carried. The notice was given four days too late. The sellers declared the buyers in default and claimed damages for default on the basis that the term as to notice was a condition. The damages claimed were the difference between the contract price and the market price, the classical measure for wrongful non-acceptance, by which the seller recovers on the basis that the buyer's repudiation has cost him the benefit of the buyer's future obligation to pay the price. The sellers did not *j* contend that, if the term was not a condition, the delay of four days amounted to a repudiation (see [1981] 2 All ER 513 at 531). Most of the attention given to the dispute, in its passage through two levels of arbitration and three hearings in the courts, was devoted to consideration of whether the term was a condition. There was, however, a subsidiary question whether the damages should be computed in accordance with a particular contractual term (which the House of Lords held that they should not), and if not, whether at common law they should be computed on the basis of the contract quantity. If the defendant's argument in the present case is right, the whole of this discussion was misconceived. Yet it was never suggested by counsel or by any of the arbitrators and judges who heard the case that the comparative triviality of the breach made any difference to the seller's right, if the term was properly to be regarded as a condition, to recover damages in respect of the buyer's unperformed obligations. If they were right in making this assumption, in a case where time was of the essence by implication, how much more should this be so where the parties have made an express stipulation to this effect.

I return to the propositions stated above. The seventh is uncontroversial, and I would add only the rider that when deciding on the penal nature of a clause which prescribes a measure of recovery for damages resulting from a termination founded on a breach of condition, the comparison should be with the common law measure, namely with the loss to the promisee resulting from the loss of his bargain. If the contract permits him to treat the contract as repudiated, the fact that the breach is comparatively minor should in my view play no part in the equation.

I believe that the real controversy in the present case centres on the eighth proposition. I will repeat it. A clause expressly assigning a particular obligation to the category of condition is not a clause which purports to fix the damages for breach of the obligation, and is not subject to the law governing penalty clauses. I acknowledge, of course, that by promoting a term into the category where all breaches are ranked as breaches of condition, the parties indirectly bring about a situation where, for breaches which are relatively small, the injured party is enabled to recover damages as on the loss of the bargain, whereas without the stipulation his measure of recovery would be different. But I am unable to accept that this permits the court to strike down as a penalty the clause which brings about this promotion. To do so would be to reverse the current of more than 100 years' doctrine, which permits the parties to treat as a condition something which would not otherwise be so. I am not prepared to take this step.

It remains to mention two reported cases. The first is *Steedman v Drinkle* [1916] 1 AC 275, [1914–15] All ER Rep 298. Land in Canada was purchased under an agreement, whereby the price was payable by one initial payment followed by annual instalments. The agreement stipulated that if the purchaser should make default in any of the payments, the vendor should be at liberty to cancel the agreement and to retain, as liquidated damages, the payments already made. It was also provided that time was to be considered as of the essence of the contract. The first deferred payment was not made on the due date. The vendor gave notice cancelling the agreement. Three weeks after the due date the purchaser tendered the amount due, which was refused. He thereupon brought an action claiming specific performance and relief from forfeiture of the amount already paid. The Judicial Committee of the Privy Council upheld the decision of the Canadian court, that the stipulation as to the retention of the sums already paid was a penalty. But the Board declined to grant specific performance. Viscount Haldane said ([1916] 1 AC 275 at 279, [1914–15] All ER Rep 298 at 300):

'Courts of Equity, which look at the substance as distinguished from the letter of agreements, no doubt exercise an extensive jurisdiction which enables them to decree specific performance in cases where justice requires it, even though literal terms of stipulations as to time have not been observed. But they never exercise this jurisdiction where the parties have expressly intimated in their agreement that it is not to apply by providing that time is to be of the essence of their bargain.'

This authority would, of course, have been decisive of the present case if the vendor had gone on to claim damages for loss of the contract. He did not do so. Nevertheless, it does,

in my view, show quite clearly that a clause making time of the essence, and hence
making prompt performance a condition, is not to be struck down merely because a *a*
breach of the obligation is not sufficient on its own to constitute a repudiation.

Secondly, there is *Photo Production Ltd v Securicor Transport Ltd* [1980] 1 All ER 556,
[1980] AC 827. This case is of great importance, for giving the quietus to the doctrine of
fundamental breach. Its significance in the present instance lies in a passage from the
speech of Lord Diplock. In order to place this in context, I must first quote from that
part of the speech in which Lord Diplock develops a system of primary and secondary *b*
obligations, foreshadowed in earlier pronouncements ([1980] 1 All ER 556 at 566–567,
[1980] AC 827 at 849):

> 'Every failure to perform a primary obligation is a breach of contract. The
> secondary obligation on the part of the contract breaker to which it gives rise by
> implication of the common law is to pay monetary compensation to the other party *c*
> for the loss sustained by him in consequence of the breach; but, with two exceptions,
> the primary obligations of both parties so far as they have not yet been fully
> performed remain unchanged. This secondary obligation to pay compensation
> (damages) for non-performance of primary obligations I will call the "general
> secondary obligation". It applies in the cases of the two exceptions as well. The
> exceptions are: (1) where the event resulting from the failure by one party to *d*
> perform a primary obligation has the effect of depriving the other party of
> substantially the whole benefit which it was the intention of the parties that he
> should obtain from the contract, the party not in default may elect to put an end to
> all primary obligations of both parties remaining unperformed (if the expression
> "fundamental breach" is to be retained, it should, in the interests of clarity, be
> confined to this exception); (2) where the contracting parties have agreed, whether *e*
> by express words or by implication of law, that *any* failure by one party to perform
> a particular primary obligation ("condition" in the nomenclature of the Sale of
> Goods Act 1893), irrespective of the gravity of the event that has in fact resulted
> from the breach, shall entitle the other party to elect to put an end to all primary
> obligations of both parties remaining unperformed (in the interests of clarity, the
> nomenclature of the Sale of Goods Act 1893, "breach of condition", should be *f*
> reserved for this exception). Where such an election is made (a) there is substituted
> by implication of law for the primary obligations of the party in default which
> remain unperformed a secondary obligation to pay monetary compensation to the
> other party for the loss sustained by him in consequence of their non-performance
> in the future and (b) the unperformed primary obligations of that other party are
> discharged. This secondary obligation is additional to the general secondary *g*
> obligation; I will call it "the anticipatory secondary obligation".' (Lord Diplock's
> emphasis.)

A little later comes the passage relied on ([1980] 1 All ER 556 at 567, [1980] AC 827 at
850):

> 'Parties are free to agree to whatever exclusion or modification of all types of *h*
> obligations as they please within the limits that the agreement must retain the legal
> characteristics of a contract and must not offend against the equitable rule against
> penalties, that is to say, it must not impose on the breaker of a primary obligation a
> general secondary obligation to pay to the other party a sum of money that is
> manifestly intended to be in excess of the amount which would fully compensate
> the other party for the loss sustained by him in consequence of the breach of the *j*
> primary obligation.'

I do not read this passage as being concerned with anything other than penalty clauses in
their ordinary sense, viz clauses which purport to fix the damages recoverable for breach
of a primary obligation in a manner which does not reflect those which would be

recovered at common law. The reference is to clauses which, in the terminology established by Lord Diplock, fix the extent of the general secondary obligation (not, it may be noted, the 'anticipatory secondary obligation') to pay damages for breach of the primary obligation. I cannot see anything to suggest that Lord Diplock was putting in question the right of the parties to decide on the character of the primary obligation. Put in language perhaps more familiar, Lord Diplock was speaking of clauses which restrict the rights of the parties to recover the appropriate measure of damages; he was not concerned with the right of the parties to decide that all breaches of contract should be treated as breaches of condition. Nor am I able to accept that Lord Diplock, who had been concerned for nearly 20 years with explaining the consequences of a breach of contract, should at this very late stage introduce the law of penalties so as to produce a result quite different from anything which he had said before.

For these reasons I conclude that the plaintiffs are entitled to retain the damages which the master has awarded. This is not a result which I view with much satisfaction, partly because the plaintiffs have achieved by one means a result which the law of penalties might have prevented them from achieving by another and partly because if the line of argument under cl 2 had been developed from the outset, the defendant might have found an answer based on waiver which the court is now precluded from assessing, for want of the necessary facts. Nevertheless, it is the answer to which, in my view, the authorities clearly point. Accordingly, I would dismiss the appeal.

NICHOLLS LJ. Shortly stated, the two issues raised on this appeal are whether the sums payable under cl 6 of the lease agreement constituted a penalty and, if so, whether the conduct of the hirer (the defendant) amounted to a repudiation of the agreement that was accepted by the owner (the plaintiffs).

The claim under cl 6

On the first issue, the criticism of cl 6 advanced on behalf of the defendant was confined to the absence of provision giving credit for the net amount of the price obtained by the plaintiffs on any resale of the goods effected by it after retaking possession. Argument in this court took place on the footing that the presence or absence of such a provision, which I shall call a 'resale price allowance', was crucial on the penalty point, counsel for the defendant putting forward the omission of such an allowance as the fundamental objection to the clause.

If this were right, and cl 6 would be unobjectionable if it included a resale price allowance, it could only be because cl 6, with the addition of a provision for such an allowance, would represent a genuine estimate of the loss likely to be suffered in this case by the plaintiffs. It is on this footing that the clause would be enforceable. In that event the sum of £6,869·97 claimed in the action with interest, would have been payable by the defendant (because in arriving at that sum the plaintiffs in fact gave credit for the net resale price of the computer, even though cl 6 did not require this). The sum of £6,869·97 is made up of one instalment in arrear (£585·05, plus £87·61 value added tax) and 13 future instalments (£7,592·65) less the net proceeds of sale (£172·85) and less also an allowance for accelerated receipt of the future instalments (£1,221·49). But, on the other hand, according to this argument advanced for the defendant, if cl 6 is struck down as a penalty because of the absence of a resale price allowance, the consequence in law is that nothing is recoverable by the plaintiffs except the one unpaid instalment (£585·05 plus value added tax) and interest thereon.

In my view these two alternative conclusions have only to be set beside each other for their mutual incompatability to be evident. As Lord Denning pointed out in *Bridge v Campbell Discount Co Ltd* [1962] 1 All ER 385 at 401, [1962] AC 600 at 632, when equity granted relief against a penalty it always required the recipient of its favours, as a condition of relief, to pay the damage which the other party had really sustained. If a genuine estimate of the damage really sustained by the plaintiffs here produces the sum

of £6,869·97, how can the striking down of cl 6 as a penalty because of the omission of a
resale price allowance somehow result in him recovering only £585·05?

    As I see it, the answer to this question is to be found in the assumption underlying the
argument of the defendant that cl 6 with the addition of a resale price allowance would
not be a penalty. In my view, in the absence of a repudiatory breach that assumption is
misconceived. The ratio of the decision of this court in *Financings Ltd v Baldock* [1963] 1
All ER 443, [1963] 2 QB 104 was that when an owner determines a hire-purchase
agreement in exercise of a right so to do given him by the agreement, in the absence of
repudiation he can recover damages for any breaches up to the date of termination but
not thereafter, and a 'minimum payment' clause which purports to oblige the hirer to
pay larger sums than this is unenforceable as a penalty. Lord Denning MR said ([1963] 1
All ER 443 at 445, [1963] 2 QB 104 at 110):

> 'Undoubtedly the cases in the past give rise to some conflict, and, therefore, I will
> try to state the matter on principle. It seems to me that, when an agreement of
> hiring is terminated by virtue of a power contained in it and the owner retakes the
> vehicle, he can recover damages for any breach up to the date of termination, but
> not for any breach thereafter, for the simple reason that there are no breaches
> thereafter.'

He added ([1963] 1 All ER 443 at 445, [1963] 2 QB 104 at 111):

> 'Seeing that they can no longer rely with any confidence on the "minimum
> payment" clause, the owners have reverted recently to a claim for damages under
> the general law. But they can only do so, it seems to me, subject to the general
> principle which I have already stated, namely, that when they terminate the hiring
> and retake the vehicle, they can only get damages for any breaches up to the date of
> termination but not thereafter.'

Diplock LJ said ([1963] 1 All ER 443 at 452, [1963] 2 QB 104 at 121):

> 'In the present contract cl. (8) itself merely defines a number of events, the
> occurrence of any one of which gives the plaintiffs an option to bring the contract
> to an end. Clause (11) purports to confer on the plaintiffs other rights on exercising
> their option to bring the contract to an end, but this clause is void as a penalty clause,
> at any rate in so far as it purports to confer rights on the plaintiffs in the events
> which in fact gave rise to their right to bring the contract to an end, namely, the
> defendant's breach of contract in failing to pay two instalments of hire. The plaintiffs
> are, therefore, in my opinion, forced to rely on their ordinary remedies for those
> breaches of contract which had accrued at the date when the contract was
> determined, viz., Apr. 7, 1960. I have already expressed my opinion that, on that
> date, the only causes of action which had accrued to the plaintiffs were for the two
> instalments due on Feb. 25 and Mar. 22, 1960, then in arrear. There had, on Apr. 7,
> 1960, been no repudiation by the defendant of his contract and no fresh breach by
> him which went to the root of the contract so as to evince his intention no longer to
> be bound by it. The plaintiffs' remedy is, accordingly, limited to recovery of the two
> instalments, together with interest thereon at the agreed rate of ten per cent. per
> annum from the dates they respectively fell due.'

    This principle has since been applied in several decisions of this court, including *Brady
v St Margaret's Trust Ltd* [1963] 2 All ER 275, [1963] 2 QB 494, *Charterhouse Credit Co Ltd
v Tolly* [1963] 1 All ER 432, [1963] 2 QB 683, *United Dominions Trust (Commercial) Ltd v
Ennis* [1967] 2 All ER 345, [1968] 1 QB 54 and *Capital Finance Co Ltd v Donati* (1977) 121
SJ 270.

    Of these I refer to one only, *Capital Finance Co Ltd v Donati*. There the court applied the
principle in a hire-purchase case where on determination of the hiring, the owner having
power to determine the hiring if the hirer made default in the punctual payment of any

instalment, a minimum payment clause came into operation that was substantially similar to cl 6 save that, unlike cl 6, it did give credit to the hirer for any sum recovered on the sale of the Fiat car subject to that agreement. The sum expressed to be payable comprised the arrears of hire rent up to the date of termination, any expenses incurred by the owner in recovering possession of the car, and also the amount of the owner's loss on the transaction which was agreed as being the difference between the hire-purchase price and the total of (i) the net proceeds of sale of the car, (ii) the initial payment and the instalments paid by the hirer and (iii) a sum representing a reasonable proportion of the charges shown in the schedule applicable to that part of the hire-purchase price which the owner would by operation of the clause receive prematurely. Cairns LJ pointed out that while there was a difference of opinion in *Financings Ltd v Baldock* as to the proper measure of damages in a case of repudiation, all members of the court held that in the absence of repudiation the common law measure of damages was limited to the overdue instalments and interest thereon and that the provision for additional damages was a penalty clause. He said (I read from the transcript):

> 'The clause in the present case does differentiate between an early and a late breach by providing for the deduction of a reasonable proportion of the charges, but it makes no distinction between the most trivial breach (for example, delay of a few days in the payment of one instalment) and a repudiatory breach. It purports to assess "the owners' loss on the transaction" and the method of assessment shows that what is meant is that the owners are to be recompensed for all the consequences of the hirer's breach and of their own election to determine the hiring. This could only be free from the element of penalty if the whole of this loss could be said to result from the breach, which would be contrary to the ratio decidendi of *Financings Ltd v Baldock*.'

In my view, applying the principle enunciated in *Financings Ltd v Baldock* to this case leads inescapably to the conclusion that in the absence of a repudiatory breach cl 6(a) is a penalty in so far as it purports to oblige the defendant, regardless of the seriousness or triviality of the breach which led to the plaintiffs terminating the agreement by retaking possession of the computer, to make a payment, albeit a discounted payment, in respect of rental instalments which had not accrued due prior to 20 December 1982.

From what I have said it will be apparent that I consider that, in the absence of a repudiatory breach, the outcome of this issue is not dependent on the inclusion or exclusion of a resale price allowance, and indeed the legal result would have been the same if cl 6 had contained a resale price allowance.

I consider below whether there was a repudiatory breach in this case, but for completeness I add here that it was accepted by counsel for the plaintiffs (and, in my view, rightly so) that if cl 6(a) was unenforceable as a penalty, the provisions in cl 6(b) would not assist the plaintiffs in this case.

The claim for damages

I turn to the second issue, which is whether the loss really sustained by the plaintiffs in this case by reason of the defendant's defaults in payment of the instalments amounted to loss of the whole hiring transaction. It would have so amounted if, but only if, the defendant's conduct amounted to a repudiation of the lease agreement and that repudiation was accepted by the plaintiffs.

I preface this issue with a reminder of the commercial realities of this lease transaction. In so doing I do not seek to ascribe to the transaction any legal characteristics other than those set forth in the lease agreement entered into by the parties. But in considering whether a hirer's conduct amounts to repudiation the commerical setting and objective of the agreement must be of prime importance. The plaintiffs are a well-known finance company. Their business is to provide finance for, amongst other matters, the acquisition by customers of goods, whether by hire purchase or lease or otherwise. They do not themselves supply the goods. They adopt the normal practice of finance companies: they purchase the goods chosen by the customer from the supplier and pay for them, and then let them to the customer on hire purchase or hire or as the case may be.

It is in these circumstances that the plaintiffs became the owner of a Lomactina computer. When entering into the present lease agreement the objective of the plaintiffs was the unexceptional one of obtaining over the agreed period of hire a rate of return, which would yield for them a commercial profit, on the money paid out by them on the acquisition of the computer being hired. I pause to observe that although the agreement was one of lease (or hire) and not of hire purchase, and the defendant was not given the right to buy the hired goods at the end of the hire period, the defendant was given the right (by cl 10(a)) at the expiration of that period to receive as a rebate of rentals paid a sum equal to 95% of the net proceeds of sale if the plaintiffs were successful in selling the goods, up to a maximum rebate of 80% of the rentals paid. Under cl 10(c), if the defendant introduced a prospective cash purchaser for the goods within seven days after the termination of the lease at a price in excess of the best price otherwise obtainable by the plaintiffs, the plaintiffs agreed to offer to sell the goods to him at the offered price. Thus in practice a route was open to the defendant to buy the goods at the end of the hire period for 5% of their then value (the maximum rebate provision being unlikely to be material in the case of quickly depreciating goods such as a computer). In the case of this agreement, so far as the plaintiffs were concerned its commercial interest in the goods, if they were repossessed, would be confined to reselling them for what they would fetch.

In these circumstances, it was a matter of importance to the plaintiffs that the agreed instalments should be paid, and should be paid promptly. I can see no reason to doubt that the interest charges were calculated by reference to the agreed hire instalment dates, on the footing that the instalments would be paid regularly and with reasonable promptness. To the plaintiffs a hirer who is repeatedly and significantly late with his payments, and who has to be chased with reminders and warnings, time after time, is an unattractive hirer whose transaction may eventually become an unprofitable one, in which event the plaintiffs will lose substantially the whole benefit intended to be acquired by it under the agreement.

For his part the defendant's objective was to have the use of the hired goods whilst making the instalment payments and at the end of the hire period, when he had paid all the instalments, to have the opportunity in practice to acquire ownership of the goods on payment of a small or nominal sum.

I now turn to the detailed facts.

The plaintiffs' outlay on the computer in May 1981 was £8,955. Interest charges over the five-year period were fixed at £2,726, making a total of £11,681. This was the sum payable by the defendant by 20 quarterly instalments of £584·05 (plus value added tax), starting on 19 May 1981. Unfortunately and regrettably the evidence before the court on the payments history is sparse, consisting only of the defendant's statement of account with the plaintiffs and the notice of termination dated 20 December 1982. The statement of account shows that the first three of the quarterly payments, those accruing in May, August and November 1981, were duly made. However, 1982 was a different story. The direct debit of the instalment payable on 19 February 1982 was recalled by the bank twice, on 24 February and again on 29 March. The next instalment was due on 19 May, but on that date neither that instalment nor the February instalment was paid. On 3 June (that is some 3½ months late in the case of the February instalment and three weeks late in the case of the May instalment) the February and May instalments were paid. Thereafter the August instalment was not paid until 28 October, which was ten weeks late. Payment by direct debit of the next instalment due, on 19 November, was recalled by the bank twice, on 24 November and again on 3 December 1982.

It was against this background that, the November instalment remaining unpaid, the plaintiffs gave notice of termination on 20 December. I add that no interest had been paid by the defendant in respect of any of his late payments.

In these proceedings no explanation has been put forward by the defendant, or on his behalf, concerning these events in 1982. The explanation for the repeated recall of the direct debits which immediately springs to mind is financial difficulty, temporary or otherwise, but no such explanation has been advanced for the defendant. The affidavit evidence filed on his behalf in answer to the application for summary judgment under RSC Ord 14 was limited to contesting the adequacy of the price obtained when the computer was resold, and the oral evidence adduced on his behalf on the inquiry as to damages was similarly limited. On the other hand, it is for the plaintiffs, as the party asserting that the defendant's conduct amounted to repudiation, to plead and prove this. In particular, there must have been further communications between the plaintiffs and the defendant over the latter's repealed failure to make prompt payment. The plaintiffs are asking the court to find that by his conduct the defendant committed a repudiatory breach of the agreement, but they have not produced any of these communications or given any evidence of the defendant's response, or lack of response, to any reminders or warnings given to him. The court has been left in the dark over what was going on between the parties.

In these circumstances I have come to the conclusion that the court is not entitled to draw the inference that by 20 December 1982 the defendant had evinced an intention not to adhere to, not to be bound by, his obligation under the lease agreement to pay the instalments and to do so promptly and regularly. In reaching this conclusion I have in mind the commercial objective of this agreement as far as the plaintiffs were concerned, as described above. But, given the bare facts I have mentioned, the plaintiffs' action was too hasty. The three 1981 instalments had been paid promptly, the first three of the 1982 instalments had been paid belatedly or very belatedly but they had been accepted, and when notice of termination was given on 20 December 1982 only one instalment, the one due on 19 November, was outstanding. Without more I do not think those facts justify a finding of repudiation by 20 December 1982.

Thus far I have reached my conclusion regarding repudiation without giving any weight or effect to the provision in cl 2(a) of the lease, that punctual payment of each rental instalment was of the essence of the lease.

I must now consider a further submission advanced by the plaintiffs that, time of payment having been made of the essence by this provision, it was open to the plaintiffs, once default in payment of any one instalment on the due date had occurred, to treat the agreement as having been repudiated by the defendant, and claim damages for loss of the whole transaction, even though in the absence of this provision such a default would not have had that consequence. On this, the question which arises is one of construction: on the true construction of the clause, did the 'time of the essence' provision have the effect submitted by the plaintiffs? In my view, the answer to that question is Yes. The provision in cl 2(a) has to be read and construed in conjunction with the other provisions in the agreement, including cll 5 and 6. So read, it is to be noted that failure to pay any instalment triggers a right for the plaintiffs to terminate the agreement by retaking possession of the goods (cl 5), with the expressed consequence that the defendant becomes liable to make payments which assume that the defendant is liable to make good to the plaintiffs the loss by them of the whole transaction (cl 6). Given that context, the 'time of the essence' provision seems to me to be intended to bring about the result that default in punctual payment is to be regarded (to use a once fashionable term) as a breach going to the root of the contract and, hence, as giving rise to the consequences in damages attendant on such a breach. I am unable to see what other purpose the 'time of the essence' provision in cl 2(a) can serve or was intended to serve or what other construction can fairly be ascribed to it.

If that construction of the agreement is correct then, as at present advised, it seems to me that the legal consequence is that the plaintiffs are entitled to claim damages for loss of the whole transaction. I say 'as at present advised', because on this no argument to the contrary was advanced on behalf of the defendant, and Mustill LJ's illuminating analysis

leaves no escape from the conclusion that parties are free to agree that a particular
provision in their contract shall be a condition such that a breach of it is to be regarded as   *a*
going to the root of the contract and entitling the innocent party (1) to accept that breach
as a repudiation and (2) to be paid damages calculated on that footing.

I have to say that I view the impact of that principle in this case with considerable
dissatisfaction, for this reason. As already mentioned, the principle applied in *Financings
Ltd v Baldock* was that when an owner determines a hire-purchase agreement in exercise
of a power so to do given him by the agreement on non-payment of instalments, he can   *b*
recover damages for any breaches up to the date of termination but (in the absence of
repudiation) not thereafter. There is no practical difference between (1) an agreement
containing such a power and (2) an agreement containing a provision to the effect that
time for payment of each instalment is of the essence, so that any breach will go to the
root of the contract. The difference between these two agreements is one of drafting
form, and wholly without substance. Yet under an agreement drafted in the first form,   *c*
the owner's damages claim arising on his exercise of the power of termination is confined
to damages for breaches up to the date of termination, whereas under an agreement
drafted in the second form the owner's damages claim, arising on his acceptance of an
identical breach as a repudiation of the agreement, will extend to damages for loss of the
whole transaction.

Nevertheless, as at present advised, I can see no escape from the conclusion that such is   *d*
the present state of the law. This conclusion emasculates the decision in *Financings Ltd v
Baldock*, for it means that a skilled draftsman can easily side-step the effect of that decision.
Indeed, that is what has occurred here.

I add only that I can see nothing in *Financings Ltd v Baldock* itself that would assist the
defendant on this point. Each member of the court emphasised that in that case there
had been no repudiation of the agreement, and Diplock LJ observed that in that case   *e*
time of payment was not of the essence of the contract (see [1963] 1 All ER 443 at 450,
[1963] 2 QB 104 at 118–119) and that 'in the absence of any express provision to the
contrary in the contract' the failure to pay two instalments on the due date did not of
themselves go to the root of the contract (see [1963] 1 All ER 443 at 451, [1963] 2 QB
104 at 120).

For these reasons, I too would dismiss this appeal.   *f*

LAWTON LJ. I have read in draft the judgments of Mustill and Nicholls LJJ; I agree
and have nothing to add.

Appeal dismissed. No order as to costs.
    g

Solicitors: *Gordon & Penney*, Weston-super-Mare (for the defendant); *Wilde Sapte* (for the
plaintiffs).

Mary Rose Plummer   Barrister.

Rosemary Simmons Memorial Housing Association Ltd v United Dominions Trust Ltd (Bates & Partners (a firm), third party)

CHANCERY DIVISION

MERVYN DAVIES J

1, 2 10 JULY 1986

Charity – Power – Power to fulfil objects – Advancement of charity's objects – Charity set up with object of providing housing for persons in need – Non-charitable company building housing which charity intended to build – Charity guaranteeing company's debts in order to ensure houses built – Whether charity acting ultra vires – Whether guarantee void.

The plaintiff was a charitable housing association which had nine members. It was set up to provide housing for persons in need and had power under its rules 'to do all things necessary or expedient for the fulfilment of its objects'. In 1981 the plaintiff wished to provide housing accommodation for the elderly on certain land and entered into negotiations with the defendant finance company for the provision of finance for the purchase of that land and the building of flats thereon, but the parties were unable to reach agreement. In 1982 the defendant made an offer of finance to R Ltd, a non-charitable company, to enable it to purchase the land and build the flats. R Ltd was controlled by virtually the same persons that controlled the plaintiff. The defendant's offer of finance to R Ltd was conditional on, inter alia, security being given by the plaintiff by a legal charge by way of a mortgage over its leasehold interest in another property and by a continuing unlimited guarantee. The offer was accepted by R Ltd and subsequently the plaintiff executed a mortgage over its leasehold property and entered into a guarantee, the terms of which provided that in consideration of the defendant at the request of the plaintiff giving credit to R Ltd, the plaintiff covenanted with the defendant in wide terms that it would repay on demand all money which became payable by R Ltd to the defendant. The plaintiff later purchased the freehold interest of the property it had mortgaged to the defendant and executed a further mortgage over the freehold. Subsequently the plaintiff sought, inter alia, declarations that the guarantee and the mortgages were invalid on the ground that it had no express or implied power to guarantee the obligations of a non-charitable body such as R Ltd. The defendant conceded that if the guarantee was invalid the mortgages were also invalid, but contended that there was a distinction between a transaction which was ultra vires in the strict sense in that the plaintiff had no capacity to carry it out and a transaction which had merely been improperly exercised.

Held – Although the plaintiff had implied powers to buy, sell, lease, build or contract if to do so was necessary or expedient for the fulfilment of its objects, it could not be implied that the plaintiff had any power to give away its assets, at any rate to a non-charitable body, since that was beyond its corporate capacity and ultra vires in the strict sense. The giving away of a gratuitous guarantee was on the same footing, since the plaintiff received no right or benefit in law in return for the guarantee albeit that there was detriment to the defendant. The plaintiff had merely obtained the satisfaction of knowing that work which it desired to see carried out would be carried out by a third party, but that was irrelevant since the plaintiff had to advance its own charitable purposes either by its own actions or through its agents or subsidiaries, and in guaranteeing R Ltd's obligations it was not advancing its own interests in that way. Furthermore, it could not be implied that a charitable housing association had corporate capacity 'gratuitously' to guarantee the liabilities of a third party with whom it had no legal tie.

Although the plaintiff members and the shareholders of R Ltd were almost entirely the same persons, the fact remained that the plaintiff and R Ltd were separate corporate bodies which were not associated together in any legal sense. It followed that it was beyond the corporate capacity of the plaintiff to give the guarantee to the defendant and accordingly the guarantee and mortgages were void (see p 286 *e* to p 287 *b*, post).

Baldry v Feintuck [1972] 2 All ER 81 and Rolled Steel Products (Holdings) Ltd v British Steel Corp [1985] 3 All ER 52 considered.

Notes

For powers to deal with charity land, see 5 Halsbury's Laws (4th edn) paras 806–810.

Generally for the liability of trustees in respect of the misapplication of charity property, see ibid para 842, and for cases on the subject, see 8(1) Digest (Reissue) 444–446, 1901–1933.

Cases referred to in judgment

Baldry v Feintuck [1972] 2 All ER 81, [1972] 1 WLR 552.
Rolled Steel Products (Holdings) Ltd v British Steel Corp [1985] 3 All ER 52, [1986] Ch 246, [1985] 2 WLR 908, CA.

Originating summons and counterclaim

By a summons dated 16 August 1985 the plaintiff, Rosemary Simmons Memorial Housing Association Ltd (Rosemary), sought, inter alia, as against the defendant, United Dominions Trust Ltd (UDT): (1) a declaration that the deed of mortgage dated 22 March 1982 made between Rosemary and UDT whereby Rosemary's leasehold interest in Gunters Mead, Copsem Lane, Oxshott, Surrey registered in the Land Registry with title absolute under title no SY 416675 held under a lease dated 14 February 1972 made between The Queen's Most Excellent Majesty and the Crown Estate Commissioners and Rosemary's leasehold interest in the land adjoining Gunters Mead and registered at the Land Registry with title absolute under title no 416676 held under a lease dated 14 February between the same parties as the lease for Gunters Mead were charged by way of legal mortgage to UDT to secure all money advanced to Roger Simmons Memorial Housing Ltd and guaranteed by Rosemary was null and void and of no effect; (2) a declaration that the mortgage dated 6 May 1982 made between Rosemary and UDT whereby the piece or parcel of land situate in and having a frontage to the east side of Copsem Lane, Oxshott, Surrey together with the buildings erected or in the course of erection thereon and which was more particularly described and contained in a transfer dated 6 May 1982 made between the Crown Estate Commissioners, Birds Hill Oxshott Estate Co Ltd and Rosemary together with all rights and privileges appurtenant thereto was charged by way of legal mortgage to UDT to secure the moneys and liabilities therein described owing from or incurred by Rosemary was null and void and of no effect; (3) an order for the delivery up of those mortgages to be cancelled; and (4) a declaration that Rosemary was entitled to the mortgaged properties discharged from all claims under the respective mortgages. UDT by counterclaim against Rosemary and Wiggins Group plc (Wiggins) sought, inter alia: as against Rosemary alone (i) possession of the properties charged by the deeds of mortgage, (ii) a declaration that the guarantee dated 22 March 1982 made between Rosemary and UDT was valid and binding on Rosemary and payment by Rosemary of all sums due under the guarantee; as against Wiggins alone (iii) a declaration that a guarantee dated 22 March 1982 entered into between Wiggins and UDT was valid and binding on Wiggins (even in the event of the guarantee entered into by Rosemary being determined to be invalid) and payment by Wiggins of all sums due under the guarantee; and as against both Rosemary and Wiggins (iv) all further accounts, inquiries and directions. UDT also issued a third party notice against a firm of solicitors, Messrs Bates & Partners, to determine as between UDT and Bates & Partners the question whether the mortgages and the guarantee given by Rosemary were void. The facts are set out in the judgment.

Hubert Picarda for Rosemary.
Alan Steinfeld for UDT.
Benjamin Levy for Bates & Partners.
Wiggins was not represented.

Cur adv vult

10 July. The following judgment was delivered.

MERVYN DAVIES J. The principal question I have to decide is whether or not a gratuitous guarantee by a charitable housing association is valid. The question arises in the course of an originating summons, a counterclaim and a third party notice.

The plaintiff in the originating summons is the Rosemary Simmons Memorial Housing Association Ltd (Rosemary). The defendant is United Dominions Trust Ltd (UDT). Rosemary claims: (1) a declaration that a mortgage dated 22 March 1982 and made between Rosemary and UDT relating to leasehold interests in property called Gunters Mead and some adjoining property is void; (2) a similar declaration as respects another mortgage between the parties dated 6 May 1982, being over the freehold interest in the same land (Rosemary having, as I understand, in the mean time acquired the freehold); (3) delivery up of the mortgage deeds; and (4) a declaration that Rosemary is entitled to the mortgaged properties discharged from the mortgages.

The counterclaim by UDT against Rosemary asks for possession of the mortgaged properties and as well a declaration that a guarantee dated 22 March 1982 and made between Rosemary and UDT is valid and binding (with payment of the sums due). UDT then bring in Wiggins Group plc (Wiggins) as second defendant to the counterclaim. Against Wiggins there is sought a declaration that a guarantee dated 22 March 1982 made between Wiggins and UDT is binding on Wiggins (even if the Rosemary guarantee is determined to be invalid). Wiggins was not represesented before me.

The third party notice is by UDT against Messrs Bates & Partners, a firm of solicitors. There UDT desires to have determined not only as between Rosemary but also as between UDT and Bates & Partners the question whether the mortgages and the Rosemary guarantee are void.

Rosemary is a charitable housing association. In 1959 it was registered under the Industrial and Provident Societies Act 1893, and so became a body corporate (see s 21). Its registration and incorporation now continue under the Industrial and Provident Societies Act 1965 (see ss 1 to 4). Rosemary is also registered with the Housing Corp under s 13 of the Housing Act 1974. It is an exempt charity for the purposes of s 29 of the Charities Act 1960. Rules 2 and 3 of its rules are as follows:

'2. The objects of the Association shall be (a) to carry on for the benefit of the community, the business of providing housing and any associated amenities for any persons in necessitous circumstances upon terms appropriate to their means, and (b) to provide for aged persons in need thereof housing and any associated amenities specially designed or adapted to meet the disabilities and requirements of such persons.

3. The Association shall have power to do all things necessary or expedient for the fulfilment of its objects.'

Rule 18 confers borrowing powers up to £5m, with certain provisions as to the interest that may be paid.

In 1981 Rosemary wished to provide housing accommodation for the elderly by

building 36 flats on 3·7 acres of land at Sunningdale. On 22 June 1981 UDT wrote to
Rosemary stating that it was prepared to lend Rosemary £1,088,850 for that purpose on   *a*
certain terms and conditions. That money was for buying the Sunningdale land and
building thereon. As well the letter offers a loan of £30,000 to buy the freehold of the
Gunters Mead land that I have already mentioned. The terms and conditions included
the giving of mortgages over the Sunningdale land and Gunters Mead. These offers of
loan were not taken up. However, in circumstances I will mention later, UDT on 18
January 1982 again offered a loan of the same sum of £1,088,850 for the Sunningdale   *b*
project. On 4 March 1982 the offer was increased to £1,200,000.

The January 1982 offer was addressed to Regentgable Ltd. That company was
incorporated under the Companies Act 1948 under that name. Its memorandum was
altered by a special resolution on 11 December 1981. Its name was changed to Roger
Simmons Memorial Housing Ltd (Roger) on 11 February 1982. Roger's objects include
buying and trafficking in land. Its income is to be applied towards the promotion of its   *c*
object and is not to be paid to its members by way of dividend, bonus or otherwise. The
directors are to receive no fees. On dissolution its assets are to go to some company with
similar objects or to charity. But although Roger in this way affords no benefits to its
members it is admittedly not a charity. During the time with which I am concerned, ie
January to June 1982, there were nine members of Rosemary. Seven of them were
shareholders in Roger and six of them were members of the Roger board. Thus Rosemary   *d*
and Roger were at all material times under the control of virtually the same body of
persons.

As I have said, UDT on 18 January 1982 made an offer of a loan concerning the
Sunningdale land to Regentgable (now Roger). The offer was conditional on security
being given. The letter states that the 'security' shall be constituted by, inter alia:
          e

'(A). A first legal charge on the site [(ie the Sunningdale land]; (B). The continuing
non-determinable unlimited guarantee of [Rosemary]; (C). A first legal charge on
the leasehold interest in Gunters Mead, Copsem Lane, Oxshott in the ownership of
[Rosemary]. [Roger] will procure and [Rosemary] undertakes to execute a first legal
charge on the freehold reversion immediately it has been acquired by [Rosemary].'

On the copy letter before me it appears that this offer was accepted by Rosemary and   *f*
by Roger, Mr D L Jones signing as a director of Rosemary and again as a director of
Roger.

So UDT's offer of loan to Roger was accepted. On 22 March 1982 Rosemary gave the
required guarantee. The deed of guarantee witnesses that, in consideration of UDT at the
request of Rosemary giving credit to Roger, Rosemary covenanted with UDT in wide
terms to the effect that Rosemary would pay on demand all money which could at any   *g*
time thereafter be due from Roger to UDT. I note that in a proviso about interest payable
there is a reference to 'the rules of the guarantor [Rosemary]'. That suggests that UDT
had seen the Rosemary rules, since r 18 has the provisions about interest that I have
referred to. On the other hand in the mortgage deed I am about to mention there is a
reference in cl 17 to Rosemary's 'Memorandum and Articles of Association'.   *h*

On the same day, 22 March 1982, Rosemary executed a mortgage in favour of UDT.
It was expressed to be supplemental to the deed of guarantee. The mortgage was given
over the Rosemary leasehold interest in the Gunters Mead land. It was recited that the
mortgage was given further to secure Rosemary's obligations under the guarantee and as
well to secure the future obligations of Rosemary to UDT.

On 6 May 1982 Rosemary acquired the freehold of the Gunters Mead land. On the   *j*
same day the freehold was mortgaged to UDT with Rosemary covenanting to pay on
demand all money which should be owing by Rosemary as principal, guarantor or surety
on any account including any guarantee already given.

Thus it was that by 6 May Rosemary was guaranteeing the liabilities of Roger and
giving security to support such guarantee, with Roger carrying out the housing project

on the Sunningdale land that had originally been proposed by Rosemary for itself. In an
affidavit sworn on 25 November 1985 Mr C P Joseph, a senior manager with UDT, says
that the Sunningdale scheme was to have been undertaken exclusively by Rosemary. He
says:

> 'It was only at a subsequent stage that for what was said to be technical reasons it
> was decided that the project should be undertaken by a newly formed separate
> association, namely Roger, whose officers were or appeared to be the same officers
> as those of Rosemary. UDT were prepared to agree to this change of plan provided
> that it received, in effect, the same security (in the shape of Rosemary's personal
> covenant and the charges over its said property) as it would have received had the
> project been undertaken by Rosemary directly. Accordingly UDT insisted, and the
> officers of Rosemary agreed, that, if it was to finance the project, it should be granted
> a personal guarantee by Rosemary and the said charges.'

In this situation it was agreed by counsel that the first question for decision was the
question in the counterclaim whether or not the Rosemary guarantee is valid. Counsel
for UDT said that if the guarantee was invalid then so were the two mortgages; so that if
I were against him on the counterclaim then Rosemary would succeed on paras 1 and 2
of the originating summons. Counsel for UDT also intimated that he would, at any rate
for the time being, not be seeking any order of possession. If the guarantee is valid, a
second question arises in that counsel for Rosemary then contends that nevertheless the
mortgages are void under the provisions of s 137 of the Housing Act 1980.

I turn to the question whether or not the guarantee is valid. The only cases to which I
was referred in this connection were *Rolled Steel Products (Holdings) Ltd v British Steel Corp*
[1985] 3 All ER 52, [1986] Ch 246 and *Baldry v Feintuck* [1972] 2 All ER 81, [1972] 1
WLR 552. Counsel for Rosemary submitted that the guarantee was void for the reason
that Rosemary had no express or implied power to guarantee the obligations of a non-
charity such as Roger. He referred to the words of Brightman J in *Baldry v Feintuck* [1972]
2 All ER 81 at 85, [1972] 1 WLR 552 at 558:

> 'In my opinion it is not open to one charity to subscribe to the funds of another
> charity unless the recipient charity is expressly or by implication a purpose or object
> of the donor charity. That must be a correct conclusion, because otherwise any
> charity could, by a sidewind, defeat and supplant its own particular objects. I turn
> to the proposed milk campaign fund. That is, admittedly, according to the literature,
> a political purpose. It is, therefore, inevitably not a charitable purpose, educational
> or otherwise, because political purposes are not charitable. It follows on that count
> alone that charitable funds cannot lawfully be used for setting up such a fund.
> Charitable funds cannot be applied to non-charitable purposes.'

In line with those sentiments counsel for Rosemary said that Rosemary's charitable
funds could not be applied actively or prospectively for the non-charitable purposes of
Roger. Counsel for UDT, with the support of counsel for Bates & Partners sought to
distinguish the *Baldry* case on the ground that *Baldry* was a case of giving away money
whereas here Rosemary is not giving but simply incurring an obligation with a view to
furthering its own objects albeit on the basis that those objects were being advanced by
the third party. That argument was put against the background of the principal
submission of counsel for UDT, which was that it is within the corporate capacity of
Rosemary to give guarantees and UDT was entitled to assume that the giving of the
guarantee was a proper exercise of the power by Rosemary's officers.

I interrupt further explanation of the submission to say that s 9 of the European
Communities Act 1972 does not fall for consideration because that section appears not to
apply to such an incorporated body as a registered housing association.

Reverting to the submission it is said: (1) one has to distinguish between ultra vires in
the strict sense (see e g the *Rolled Steel Products (Holdings) Ltd v British Steel Corp* [1985] 3

All ER 52 at 92, [1986] Ch 246 at 304) and an improper exercise of powers; (2) for the purpose of determining whether or not an act is ultra vires or merely done by an *a* improper exercise of powers, one should in the present case pose the question: did Rosemary have power in any circumstances to enter into a guarantee in respect of the liabilities of a third party, or are there no circumstances in which Rosemary had such a power?; (3) if the answer to the question is that there are circumstances where Rosemary does have power to give a guarantee then one is here not dealing with any problem of ultra vires in the strict sense: one is dealing with an improper exercise of a power; (4) if *b* Rosemary has merely had its powers improperly exercised, then UDT as against Rosemary is entitled to enforce the guarantee since UDT acted in good faith and had no express notice that there was any impropriety in the giving of the guarantee; (5) finally, so the argument goes, Rosemary had power to enter into the guarantee because the giving of the guarantee may be 'necessary or expedient for the fulfilment of its objects' (see rr 1 and 3).   *c*

Counsel for UDT instanced occasions when guarantees might be expected to be given, e g to procure delivery of building materials in the course of a building contract when the contractor is in difficulties in being unable without such a guarantee to get building supplies from his supplier.

I do not accept counsel for UDT's persuasive argument. I agree with him to the extent that the first question arising is to decide whether or not what Rosemary has done (giving *d* the guarantee) is ultra vires in the sense that the transaction is a transaction which Rosemary has no capacity to carry out, as opposed to a transaction which it cannot properly do (see [1985] 3 All ER 52 at 92, [1986] Ch 246 at 304 per Browne-Wilkinson LJ). This question of corporate capacity depends on the construction of the 'objects' provisions in the Rosemary rules (see [1985] 3 All ER 52 at 85, [1986] Ch 246 at 295 per Slade LJ). Those rules are rr 2 and 3 which are set out above.   *e*

There is of course no express reference to guaranteeing either as an object or as a power. So one considers what if any power to guarantee may be implied, bearing in mind that r 3 says that Rosemary has power 'to do all things necessary or expedient for the fulfilment of its objects'. I accept that it is to be implied that Rosemary has, with or without r 3, many and varied powers. The rules are largely silent on the topic of powers, *f* save as to borrowing. Thus it must be understood that Rosemary has power to buy, or sell, or lease, or build, or contract, if to do so is necessary or expedient for the fulfilment of its objects. On the other hand I do not see that there can be implied any power in Rosemary to give away its assets, at any rate to a non-charitable body. Such a giving away is beyond the corporate capacity, ie ultra vires in the strict sense. To my mind the giving of a gratuitous guarantee is on the same footing. I say 'gratuitous' in the sense that *g* Rosemary received no right or benefit at law in return for the guarantee albeit that there was detriment to UDT; so that technically the guarantee was supported by consideration (see *Chitty on Contract* (25th edn, 1983) vol 1, pp 80–81, paras 144–145).

Rosemary merely received the satisfaction of knowing that work it desired to see carried out would be carried out by a third party. But Rosemary must advance its own charitable purposes either by its own actions or through its agents or subsidiaries. In *h* guaranteeing Roger it was not advancing its interests in that way. It may well be that a power to guarantee can be implied as to transactions in which Rosemary itself is involved, e g the building example referred to above. But I do not see how one can sensibly suppose that by implication a registered charitable housing association is to be regarded as having the corporate capacity 'gratuitously' to guarantee the liabilities of a third party with whom it has no legal tie.   *j*

Counsel for UDT stressed that Roger was providing housing so that Rosemary was in that sense seeing its objects (as in r 2) promoted as a consequence of the giving of the guarantee. I see the superficial attraction of that assertion, but it does not remove the difficulty, as I see it, of Rosemary committing itself gratuitously to bear the liabilities of a third party. I appreciate that the Rosemary members and the Roger shareholders are a almost wholly the same persons, but that does not avoid the fact that Rosemary and Roger are separate corporate bodies not associated together in any legal sense. Had Roger been a subsidiary of Rosemary the situation might be otherwise. But it is not, so the matter cannot be considered on that footing. Accordingly I hold that it was beyond the corporate capacity of Rosemary to give the guarantee given to UDT. The guarantee is therefore void. Since that is so counsel for UDT accepts, as I have said, that, as well, the mortgages are void.

b Since I regard the guarantees void, the second question I have mentioned, i e as to s 137 of the Housing Act 1980, does not arise. However I feel I should briefly express my views on the question. It is said by counsel for Rosemary that the mortgages (not the guarantee) are void as having been executed without the consent of the Housing Corp. The origin of this submission is s 2 of the Housing Act 1974. I set out s 2 of the Housing Act 1974, so far as now material:

c *'Control by Corporation of dispositions of land by housing associations.*—(1) Subject to the following provisions of this section,—(a) a registered housing association may not sell, lease, mortgage, charge or otherwise dispose of any land, and (b) an unregistered housing association may not sell, lease, mortgage, charge or otherwise dispose of any grant-aided land, as defined in Schedule 2 to this Act, except with d consent of the Corporation.

(2) Subsection (1) above shall not apply to a disposition by a housing association which is a registered charity if—(a) the disposition is *one which*, by virtue of subsection (1) or subsection (2) of section 29 of the Charities Act 1960 (certain disposals not to take place without an order of the court or of the Charity Commissioners), *cannot* be made without such an order as is mentioned in that e section; or (b) the disposition is of land which is not grant-aided land, as defined in Schedule 2 to this Act, and is one for which the sanction of an order under the said section 29 is not required by virtue of subsection (3) thereof (certain dispositions excluded from the requirements of that section) . . .

(6) Any reference in this section to the consent of the Corporation is a reference to an order under the seal of the Corporation giving their consent.'

f Subsection (1) indicates that Rosemary may not mortgage without the consent of the Housing Corp. It was common ground that Rosemary was not exempted by sub-s (2) and, further, that there were no consents under seal (see sub-s (6)).

One then goes to s 123 of the Housing Act 1980, which makes certain amendments to s 2 of the 1974 Act. In particular s 123(6) enacts as follows:

g 'After subsection (5) there is inserted the following subsection—"(5A) Where a housing association has, at any time, made a disposition requiring the consent of the Corporation under this section, then—(a) in favour of any person claiming under the association, the disposition shall not be invalid by reason that any consent of the Corporation which is required has not been given; and (b) a person dealing with the h association or a person claiming under the association shall not be concerned to see or inquire whether any such consent has been given.".'

With that subsection in mind, it appears that UDT would not be prejudiced by the absence of consents. But there is yet another provision of the 1980 Act which bears on the topic. Section 137 reads as follows:

j *'Avoidance of certain unauthorised disposals.*—(1) If—(a) at any time after 18th July 1980 a local authority or a housing association has disposed of a house; and (b) the disposal was one which, under section 104 of the 1957 Act or section 2 of the 1974 Act, required the consent of the Secretary of State or of the Housing Corporation (or would have required it had the relevant provisions been in force) but was made without that consent; then, unless the disposal was to an individual (or to two or more individuals) and did not extend to any other house, it shall be void (and, if made before the passing of this Act, be deemed always to have been void) and section 128(2) of the Local Government Act 1972 or, as the case may be, subsection (5A) (inserted by section 123(6) of this Act) of section 2 of the 1974 Act (protection of purchasers) shall not apply.

(2) In this section "house" includes a flat and "the relevant provisions" means Part I and sections 91 and 123 of this Act.'

Relying on s 137, counsel for Rosemary submitted that Rosemary, in granting each mortgage, 'disposed of a house' and that the disposal, not being to an individual, the mortgages were void by the terms of the subsection. An affidavit of Mr Robert Southcott, the chairman of Rosemary, states, as to the land comprised in the mortgages, that a house known as Gunters Mead was built in 1928. However Mr Southcott goes on to say that when the guarantee was completed, ie on 22 March 1982, the accommodation existing at the Gunters Mead development was (i) the house, (ii) a staff flat (located within the house), (iii) 40 self-contained units of accommodation for elderly persons, (iv) a gardener's bungalow, (v) a garage block with a staff flat above and (vi) 16 lock-up garages.

I cannot regard a disposal of property comprising items (i) to (vi) as the 'disposal of a house' within s 137. Accordingly, were it necessary to make a finding, I should find against counsel for Rosemary in saying that the UDT mortgages were not void for a lack of consent under seal given by the Housing Corp.

Declaration accordingly. Counterclaim dismissed.

Solicitors: *Hamlins Grammer & Hamlin* (for Rosemary); *Berwin Leighton* (for UDT); *Barlow Lyde & Gilbert* (for Bates & Partners).

Jacqueline Metcalfe   Barrister.

County Personnel (Employment Agency) Ltd v Alan R Pulver & Co (a firm)

COURT OF APPEAL, CIVIL DIVISION

SIR NICOLAS BROWNE-WILKINSON V-C, STEPHEN BROWN AND BINGHAM LJJ

14, 15, 16, 17 OCTOBER 1986

Solicitor – Negligence – Duty to exercise reasonable skill and care – Unusual clause in lease – Duty to explain clause to client and alert client to risk of entering into unusual lease.

Solicitor – Negligence – Damages – Assessment of damages – Date of assessment – Solicitor's negligence causing client to enter into unfavourable lease – Client unable to sell lease and surrendering it on payment of premium – Diminution in value principle not appropriate in assessing client's damages – Whether court could make general assessment of damages – Whether damages required to be assessed as at date of breach.

In December 1978 the plaintiff entered into negotiations with the head lessee of a property for a 15-year underlease of two ground floor rooms to be used as business premises and instructed the defendant firm of solicitors to act in connection with the proposed underlease. The headlease provided for five-yearly rent reviews. The terms of the proposed underlease were that the initial rent was to be £3,500 per year subject to the rent being increased every five years on the same dates and by the same percentage increase as the head lessee's rent was increased on the headlease's five-yearly rental reviews. The solicitors did not ascertain the rent payable under the headlease and did not advise the plaintiff to do so or to have the property valued before entering into the underlease. In 1983 the plaintiff received an offer of £17,000 for the underlease and goodwill of its business but the sale fell through, partly because the position regarding rent reviews was uncertain. The rent payable under the headlease was £2,250, which was increased to £5,800 on the first rent review in 1984 with the result that, applying the same percentage increase, the rent under the underlease was increased from £3,500 to £9,022, compared with an open market rent of £2,600. The plaintiff refused to pay the increase and later surrendered the underlease on payment of £16,000 and £2,761 increased rent. The plaintiff brought an action against the solicitors claiming as damages for negligence the amount required to surrender the underlease, the increased rent and the £17,000 lost on the prospective sale. The judge found that in regard to the rent review clause the solicitors had not been negligent and dismissed the action. The plaintiff appealed.

Held – (1) On the issue of liability and applying the principle that a client was entitled to expect his solicitor to exercise reasonable professional judgment, a solicitor ought to be put on inquiry when faced with an unusual clause in a lease and was required in the proper discharge of his duty of care to alert the client to the effect of such a clause and the risks inherent in entering into such a lease. Since the rent review clause in the underlease was very unusual in that the more the head lessee's rent was increased on his rent reviews the greater the profit he could exact from the plaintiff because the same percentage uplift applied to the plaintiff's rent, the solicitors had been negligent in failing to ascertain the rent payable under the headlease and in failing to explain the effect of the rent review clause to the plaintiff before the plaintiff entered into the underlease (see p 295 *b* to p 296 *c e* and p 298 *h* to p 299 *c*, post); dicta of Harman and Salmon LJJ in *Sykes v Midland Bank Exor and Trustee Co Ltd* [1970] 2 All ER at 475, 477 applied.

(2) On the issue of damages, the court would not invariably assess the damages for a solicitor's negligence by applying the diminution in value principle (ie the difference between (a) the open market value of the asset acquired as it actually was and (b) the

lower of the price paid and the open market value of the asset as it was thought to be),
nor would it invariably assess the damages as at the date of breach. Where the mechanical   *a*
application of those principles was inappropriate the court could make a more general
assessment and at a date other than the date of breach. Adopting such an approach, the
plaintiff appeared to be entitled to what it had cost to surrender the underlease and
possibly to the value of a saleable lease and goodwill, depending on whether the plaintiff
could have negotiated such a lease and if so where, and to what extent that would have
affected its goodwill. The appeal would accordingly be allowed and the case would be   *b*
remitted for the assessment of damages (see p 297 *f* to p 298 *h* and p 299 *d* to *g*, post);
dictum of Lord Blackburn in *Livingstone v Rawyards Coal Co* (1880) 5 App Cas at 39 and
Dodd Properties (Kent) Ltd v Canterbury City Council [1980] 1 All ER 928 applied.

Notes
For solicitor's negligence in non-contentious matters, see 44 Halsbury's Laws (4th edn)   *c*
paras 135, 138, and for cases on the subject, see 44 Digest (Reissue) 132–133, 144–160,
1306–1334, 1468–1605.

Cases referred to in judgments
Bowdage v Harold Michelmore & Co (1962) 183 EG 233.
Braid v W L Highway & Sons (1964) 191 EG 433.   *d*
Dodd Properties (Kent) Ltd v Canterbury City Council [1980] 1 All ER 928, [1980] 1 WLR
433, CA.
Ford v White & Co [1964] 2 All ER 755, [1964] 1 WLR 885.
Hadley v Baxendale (1854) 9 Exch 341, [1843–60] All ER Rep 461.
Ladenbau (G & K) (UK) Ltd v Crawley & de Reya (a firm) [1978] 1 All ER 682, [1978] 1
WLR 266.   *e*
Livingstone v Rawyards Coal Co (1880) 5 App Cas 25, HL.
Midland Bank Trust Co Ltd v Hett Stubbs & Kemp (a firm) [1978] 3 All ER 571, [1979] Ch
384, [1978] 3 WLR 167, CA.
Miliangos v George Frank (Textiles) Ltd [1975] 3 All ER 801, [1976] AC 443, [1975] 3 WLR
758, HL.
Perry v Sidney Phillips & Son (a firm) [1982] 3 All ER 705, [1982] 1 WLR 1297, CA.   *f*
Philips v Ward [1956] 1 All ER 874, [1956] 1 WLR 471, CA.
Pilkington v Wood [1953] 2 All ER 810, [1953] Ch 770, [1953] 3 WLR 522, CA.
Simple Simon Catering Ltd v J E Binstock Miller & Co (1973) 228 EG 527, CA.
Sykes v Midland Bank Exor and Trustee Co Ltd [1970] 2 All ER 471, [1971] 1 QB 113,
[1970] 3 WLR 273, CA.
   g
Cases also cited
Boyce v Rendells (1983) 268 EG 268.
Bwllfa and Merthyr Dare Steam Collieries (1891) Ltd v Pontypridd Waterworks Co [1903] AC
426, [1900–03] All ER Rep 600, HL.
Carradine Properties Ltd v D J Freeman & Co (a firm) (1982) Times, 19 February.   *h*
Foster v Outred & Co (a firm) [1982] 2 All ER 753, [1982] 1 WLR 86, CA.
Goody v Baring [1956] 2 All ER 11, [1956] 1 WLR 448.
Lake v Bushby [1949] 2 All ER 964.

Appeal
The plaintiff, County Personnel (Employment Agency) Ltd, appealed from the judgment   *j*
of Robert Wright QC sitting as a deputy judge of the High Court on 15 July 1985
whereby he dismissed the plaintiff's action for negligence against the defendants, Alan R
Pulver & Co (a firm) (Pulvers). The facts are set out in the judgment of Bingham LJ.

Jonathan Gaunt for the plaintiff.
Ivan Krolick for Pulvers.

BINGHAM LJ (delivering the first judgment at the invitation of Sir Nicolas Browne-
a Wilkinson V-C). This is an appeal against a decision of Mr Robert Wright QC sitting as a
deputy judge of the High Court in the Chancery Division. On 15 July 1985 he dismissed
the claim made by the plaintiff against its former solicitors, Messrs Alan R Pulver & Co
(Pulvers), for damages for negligence. The plaintiff challenges that decision, although
the live issues have been considerably narrowed on appeal.

The facts can for present purposes be summarised relatively briefly. Mrs Valerie
b Feldman and Mrs Kathleen Balfe had worked together in an employment agency in
Windsor. They decided to go into business on their own account through the medium
of a company to be incorporated. For this purpose they required business premises.
Having answered a newspaper advertisement, they were shown, by a Mr Cook, who was
trading as Home Counties Businesses, two rooms on the ground floor of 109 Queen
Street, Maidenhead. For these rooms Mr Cook asked for an annual rent of £3,500
c inclusive. Mrs Feldman and Mrs Balfe expected that their business would cover such a
rent, and informally agreed to take a lease of the rooms at that rent for a 15-year term
with five-yearly rent reviews. It does not appear that Mr Cook had, initially, any interest
in the premises at 109 Queen Street, but he set about negotiating the terms of a headlease
of the whole building to himself with a view to subletting the ground floor rooms to
Mrs Feldman and Mrs Balfe or their company when formed.

d On 21 December 1978 Mrs Feldman instructed Mr Rose of Pulvers to act in the
matter. He was a managing clerk employed by Pulvers, and a trusted friend and adviser
of Mrs Feldman. She told him of her plans and asked him to act in connection with the
grant of a proposed underlease of the ground floor rooms. He accepted those instructions.

Either on that day or 22 December, Mrs Feldman collected from Mr Cook's solicitors
and delivered to Mr Rose for his consideration a draft of the underlease proposed by Mr
e Cook. Unfortunately no copy of that document in its original form is still extant, and Mr
Rose died in February 1979. It is common ground that the draft underlease was for a
term of 15 years with provision for rent reviews (upwards only) in the fifth and tenth
years, but the evidence before the deputy judge and before us leaves unclear the precise
effect of the rent review clause at that stage. Two pieces of evidence suggest that the
underlessee's proposed rent may have been tied to a percentage of the mesne lessor's rent
f under the headlease. The first piece of evidence is a manuscript note of Mr Rose in these
terms:

'£3,500 comm'c'ng rent, 5 years. Thereafter %age of whole rent + rates + w.r.
and ins'ce and cl'ng and lighting stairs & passageway.'

g The other is an inquiry made by Mr Rose of Mr Cook's solicitors on 9 January 1979:

'What is to be the percentage of the landlord's rent of the whole building, as
reviewed in due course, which the tenant will pay? It must be borne in mind that
the rental payable pursuant to the underlease includes general and water rates. It
therefore seems relevant that the underlessees should know the present rent payable
h under the headlease (which knowledge cannot affect this transaction) so that they
might be advised fully as to their position under clause 1 of the underlease.'

Before the date of this inquiry Mr Rose had received a copy of the headlease of the
whole building from Mr Cook's solicitors. This was for a 15-year term with rent reviews
in the fifth and tenth years. The clause was in a familiar form with provision for notice
j and counter-notice and independent determination in default of agreement. The rent
could be revised upwards only, so as to accord with the open market rental value of the
premises on the review dates.

Only three points need be noted on the headlease. First, the rent payable under the
headlease was cut out from the copy sent to Mr Rose. This is why he inquired what the
rent was. Second, there was a covenant against assigning or subletting without the head
lessor's written licence, such licence not to be unreasonably withheld. Third, the lessee

covenanted that on any subletting the sublessee's right to security of tenure under the
Landlord and Tenant Act 1954 should be effectively excluded.

On 10 January Mr Rose wrote to Mrs Feldman concerning the draft underlease, of
which Mrs Feldman as well as he had copies. He told her that he had received a copy of
the headlease with the rent cut out and he advised her on the rent review clause in the
underlease, indicating that in one respect (not now material) it appeared to be favourable
to her. He suggested that he should take Mrs Feldman through the headlease and the
underlease 'so that you might clearly understand your obligations in the matter both on
behalf of the [plaintiff] and so far as concerns Kathy and yourself, as guarantors'. He
thought that a suitable time for such a meeting might be after the result of inquiries and
searches had been received.

Mr Cook's solicitors answered the inquiry I have quoted above by saying: 'The wording
has now been revised.' This was, it seems, a reference to a revised draft underlease which
Mr Cook's solicitors sent to Mr Rose on 9 January, their letter crossing with Mr Rose's
inquiries. Whatever the rent clause may have said before, it now provided for a—

> 'yearly rent of £3,500 inclusive of General Rates and Water Service charges ("the
> initial rent") for the first five years of the term created by the Head Lease (or such
> lesser period thereof as shall remain at the commencement of the term hereby
> created) and thereafter paying for the periods set out in the Head Lease an amount
> equivalent to the initial rent increased by the same percentages as the Landlord's
> rent has been increased under the terms of the Head Lease.'

On 24 January Mrs Feldman and Mr and Mrs Balfe attended at Pulvers' offices. Mr
Rose went through the underlease and the headlease with them. He dictated a letter to
Mr Cook's solicitors in their presence. The attendance lasted about one hour. What Mr
Rose said on that occasion, and whether it was sufficient to discharge the duty of care
which Pulvers by Mr Rose owed to the plaintiff, are the questions which lie at the heart
of this appeal. But before considering those matters in detail I should briefly complete
the narrative.

The plaintiff was allowed into possession of the ground floor rooms on 19 February
and the lease and counterpart were exchanged very shortly thereafter. In May Pulvers
received from Mr Cook's solicitors a certified copy of the headlease, showing the rent of
the whole building under the headlease to have been £2,250 per year exclusive of rates
(as compared with £3,500 inclusive for the ground floor rooms only in the underlease).
Problems then arose because the head lessor had not given consent to the subletting of
the ground floor rooms, his sticking point being that Mr Cook had not excluded the
right to security under the 1954 Act in the underlease. The subletting was therefore in
breach of covenant and rendered Mr Cook's interest under the headlease (and thus the
plaintiff's interest under the underlease) liable to forfeiture. Resolution of these problems
took a very long time, during which the plaintiff was advised by Pulvers in a manner of
which no complaint is now made. Eventually a new underlease (running from the same
date and otherwise unchanged) was executed, security having been excluded and the
head lessor having given his consent. This was in July 1982. By that time the plaintiff,
despairing at the time taken to finalise the new underlease and other matters, had
instructed other solicitors, Messrs Aubrey Croysdale & Stern, to act for it.

Towards the end of 1983 the plaintiff wished to dispose of its sublease and the goodwill
of its business. An offer of £17,000 was obtained. But this offer fell through, partly
because there was no security and partly (it seems) because of uncertainty surrounding
the whole question of rent review.

In the spring of 1984 the first rent reviews were negotiated. The rent under the
headlease, originally fixed at £2,250 exclusive (found to be the true open market rental)
was by agreement increased to £5,800. The yearly rent payable pursuant to the underlease,
originally agreed at a level at least three times higher than the market rent for the two
ground floor rooms, rose 'by the same percentages as the Landlord's rent has been

increased under the terms of the Head Lease' to £9,022. At open market value the yearly rent would, on the evidence, have been £2,600 inclusive. The plaintiff refused to pay this rent, and eventually the mesne lessor (an assignee of Mr Cook) accepted a surrender of the sublease on payment of £16,000 plus a sum of £2,761 representing the increased rent payable since the rent review date under the headlease. The plaintiff claims that sum, plus £17,000 lost on the prospective sale of the underlease and goodwill, as damages for negligence against Pulvers.

The deputy judge concluded that Pulvers, by Mr Rose, had been negligent in failing to advise the plaintiff that the security provisions of the 1954 Act would have to be excluded and on the consequences of that exclusion, and in failing to advise the plaintiff not to enter into the original underlease until the licence of the head landlord had been obtained. But he held that no damage flowed from those failures. These conclusions have not been challenged on this appeal. It is, therefore, enough to say that they appear to be plainly correct, as the parties have accepted.

The plaintiff's allegations of negligence (so far as relevant to this appeal) were that Pulvers, through Mr Rose, (1) failed to ascertain the initial rent under the headlease or warn the plaintiff of the risks entailed in taking the original sublease without knowing the amount of that rent, (2) failed to advise the plaintiff to obtain valuation advice on the initial rent under the headlease and under the underlease compared with market value, and (3) failed to advise the plaintiff about the operation of the rent review clause in the underlease and the undesirability of entering into such a clause. These allegations were directed to the period January to February 1979, before the plaintiff entered into the underlease, and in particular to the meeting on 24 January 1979 when Mr Rose took Mrs Feldman and Mrs Balfe through the headlease and the underlease.

The deputy judge found that the rent review clause in the underlease was most unusual, a finding on which the plaintiff strongly relies. He then continued in these terms:

'What I have to decide is whether, in the light of what he was instructed to do and without the benefit of hindsight, Mr Rose fell short of the standard of what a reasonably competent practitioner would do having regard to the standards normally adopted in his profession, and the authority for that is the case I have just cited, *Midland Bank Trust Co Ltd v Hett Stubbs & Kemp (a firm)* [1978] 3 All ER 571, [1979] Ch 384. I have to bear in mind that a solicitor is not obliged to advise on value (*Bowdage v Harold Michelmore & Co* (1962) 183 EG 233) but is obliged to explain any unusual clauses in a document on which he is asked to advise (*Sykes v Midland Bank Exor and Trustee Co Ltd* [1970] 2 All ER 471, [1971] 1 QB 113). On these principles I have come to the conclusion that Mr Rose was not negligent in any of the respects pleaded above in relation to the rent review clause. I find as a fact that Mr Rose did explain the rent review clause to Mrs Feldman at least, despite her assertion that he did not. Mrs Feldman is far more businesslike and intelligent in business matters than she would have had me believe. I do not criticise her for this. In the light of the financial disaster which has taken place and her belief that it was Mr Rose's fault, she has convinced herself that the matter was not explained to her. The same applies to Mrs Balfe with the additional factor that Mrs Feldman was clearly the leader in business matters. Mr Rose cannot give evidence. The documentary evidence supports my conclusion that he did explain the clause. First, it is clear from the inquiries before contract that Mr Rose was concerned over the rent review clause. He wanted to know what was the percentage of the rent of the whole premises which the plaintiff would have to pay and asked for particulars of the landlord's rent having regard to the fact that the rent under the underlease included general and water rates. He asked for the rent under the headlease. The answer simply records that the wording had been altered. I infer therefore that, whatever was in the original clause, it was altered simply to provide, as does the present underlease, that the original rent would vary in proportion to the increases in market value. On 10 January 1979 Mr Rose wrote to Mrs Feldman saying that he would like an early opportunity of going through the headlease and underlease with her. As a preliminary point Mr Rose wrote that the rent review clause was favourable to her in that it would or might take effect from 19 February instead of at the date of the earlier lease. Mrs Feldman told me that she had met Mr Rose for this purpose at his office and had the draft underlease with her. Mrs Feldman says that that is all he ever said about the rent review clause. Mr Rose knew Mrs Feldman very well. I am sure he would have been concerned to do his best for her. Further I believe and find that he would have carried out his intention of going through the underlease. He may not have spent much time on the rent review clause. It is short and as a matter of English it is clear. Mrs Feldman said that all Mr Rose said was that it was favourable because of the later date which might defer the review for a time and that she did not read it. If it was mentioned I infer from the documents and circumstances that Mr Rose would have explained its effect, namely that the original rent would be reviewed upwards in step with the increases in market value in the headlease. Alternatively, the burden of proof was on the plaintiff to establish that Mr Rose did not give this explanation and in my judgment it has not been discharged. Mr Rose did not give any further or fuller explanation, pointing out that much might depend on the extent to which each rent was at market value at the outset, nor did he suggest that valuation advice should be obtained. But on the standards of competence required I do not think that he was bound to do so. The plaintiff relied on *Sykes v Midland Bank Exor and Trustee Co Ltd*, to which I have referred, to establish that Mr Rose was under a duty to explain the unusual clause and that this was an unusual clause and that the explanation should have extended to the valuation implications. I do not accept that this was so. *Sykes's* case is authority for the proposition that a solicitor must explain the legal consequences of an unusual clause. I do not think that it requires him to explain the financial implications at any rate on the retainer given and in the light of the fact that the rent had been agreed before Mr Rose was consulted. It was suggested that Mr Rose should have been put on inquiry by the fact that the rent was cut out of the copy of the headlease supplied to him. That should have made him so suspicious that he should have advised the taking of valuation advice or insisted on being told the amount of the rent under the headlease. The point is one on which my mind has been inclined to one side and the other in considering the evidence and the arguments, but I have come to the conclusion that Mr Rose need not have done more than he did. The rent of the underlease had been agreed at arm's length before he was consulted. The ground floor would be much the more valuable part of the premises and the rent was inclusive of rates. I can well see good reasons why the underlessor would not want to give the rent he was paying, lest it lead to arguments for which there was no foundation. I do not think that the inference could be drawn that the purpose was to conceal an excessive rent for the underlease, or, alternatively, that it should have drawn Mr Rose's attention to it so strongly as to put him on inquiry.'

The principles of law governing the decision on liability in this case were not in serious issue between the parties. The starting point is Salmon LJ's observation in *Sykes v Midland Bank Exor and Trustee Co Ltd* [1970] 2 All ER 471 at 477, [1971] 1 QB 113 at 125:

'In my view, it is quite impossible to lay down any code setting out the duties of a solicitor when advising his client about a lease. A great deal depends on the facts of each particular case. A solicitor's duty is to use reasonable care and skill in giving such advice as the facts of the particular case demand.'

Attention was also drawn to a sentence in the judgment of Harman LJ ([1970] 2 All ER 471 at 475, [1971] 1 QB 113 at 125):

a
'When a solicitor is asked to advise on a leasehold title it is, in my judgment, his duty to call his client's attention to clauses in an unusual form which may affect the interests of his client as he knows them.'

It seems obvious that legal advice, like any other communication, should be in terms appropriate to the comprehension and experience of the particular recipient. It is also, I think, clear that in a situation such as this the professional man does not necessarily discharge his duty by spelling out what is obvious. The client is entitled to expect the

b exercise of a reasonable professional judgment. That is why the client seeks advice from the professional man in the first place. If in the exercise of a reasonable professional judgment a solicitor is or should be alerted to risks which might elude even an intelligent layman, then plainly it is his duty to advise the client of these risks or explore the matter further.

Counsel for Pulvers quite rightly emphasised two matters, which should be constantly

c borne in mind. The first is that Pulvers, through no fault of their own, have lost the benefit of Mr Rose's evidence, and have had to conduct their defence to this claim without access to all the relevant documents. This being so, and with the relevant oral evidence of fact relating to matters six years earlier, much has had to depend on inference. The second is the danger of hindsight. It is easy to be mesmerised by the figures which resulted from the rent review in 1984. That would be wrong. The correct approach is to

d view matters as they should have presented themselves to a reasonably careful and competent solicitor in January and February 1979.

There were, on the facts of the present case, three things which should have impinged on the mind of a reasonably careful and competent solicitor practising in this field. First, Mr Cook or his solicitors did not wish the plaintiff and Pulvers to know the rent being

e paid for the whole building under the headlease. This was not in itself shocking or sinister. There could have been a perfectly good reason for it. It did, none the less, appear to be a fact. Second, Mr Cook (trading as Home Counties Businesses) was taking a headlease of the whole premises with a view to subletting part. That again was not in itself surprising. He may simply have wanted the use of the upper part of the building. But he was likely to try and make a profit if he could. Third, this was a most unusual

f clause. These things, and particularly the third, should (I think) have caused a reasonably careful and competent solicitor to think about this clause rather more carefully than would have been appropriate had the clause been in a familiar standard form. It would have been appropriate to consider whether there was anything in the terms of this clause which might prove disadvantageous to the client.

On such consideration it should have been obvious that the clause required the client,

g on both rent reviews, to pay the same percentage increase as was made between two other parties to a figure of which Mr Rose and the plaintiff were unaware. If it were safe to assume that the initial levels of both the (unkown) headlease rent and the underlease rent were in accord with open market levels that arrangement might just be acceptable. The headlease rent would necessarily be higher than the underlease rent. The mesne lessor would therefore have an incentive to hold out for the lowest percentage increase

h possible. He could never make an increased profit by allowing his own rent to rise. But very little reflection would show that the position might be very different if either of these assumptions could not be safely made. If the headlease rent were below the market level, the percentage uplift to be applied to it at the first rent review would be greater than the percentage uplift experienced in rents generally, with the result that the company's rent would be increased by more than any general increase in rents warranted.

j If the agreed underlease rent were above the open market level, the excess might be exponentially increased during the 15-year term of the lease, even if the initial headlease rent were at the open market level. If perchance the initial headlease rent for the whole building were below the underlease rent for the ground floor rooms, then the mesne lessor would have no incentive to hold out at the rent reviews for the lowest rent increase obtainable because the greater his own rent the greater the profit rental he could exact from the plaintiff. These reflections involve no element of valuation, on which a solicitor is plainly unfitted to advise. They are reflections which, in my judgment, would and should occur to a reasonably careful and competent solicitor called on to consider and advise on this clause against the background I have described. Having done so, he would and should have advised the plaintiff that it was, on existing information, impossible to say how the clause would operate in practice, but that its operation might to a greater or lesser extent be disadvantageous to the plaintiff, that unless both initial rents were known and investigated and found to be at open market levels the risk of disadvantage could not, on the proposed wording, be eliminated and that, as matters stood, the plaintiff should not consider entering into a lease which contained this clause. Distasteful though it is to make a finding of negligence against a dead man who cannot defend himself, the inescapable fact is that Mr Rose did not give this advice or anything like it and, in my view, he was negligent in failing to do so.

It follows that I cannot agree with the approach of the deputy judge to this matter. I accept the inference which he drew 'that Mr Rose would have explained its effect, namely that the original rent would be reviewed upwards in step with the increases in market value in the headlease'. This explanation was not itself entirely accurate, if the headlease rent was below the open market level, but, more importantly, it did nothing to alert Mrs Feldman to the possible risks I have mentioned. The deputy judge found that Mr Rose gave no further or fuller explanation, but I (unlike the judge) think he was bound in law to do so. I cannot accept the distinction drawn between legal consequences and financial implications, because in this case the significance of the legal consequences lay in the financial implications. Even accepting that Mrs Feldman was not a naive innocent in the commercial world, I regard this as a classic case in which the professional legal adviser was bound to warn his client of risks which should have been apparent to him but would, on a simple reading of the clause, have been most unlikely to occur to her.

It was argued for Pulvers that if, contrary to their primary submission, Mr Rose was negligent at all, no damage flowed from that negligence. This submission rested on the conduct of the plaintiff in instructing other solicitors, Aubrey Croysdale & Stern, before the second underlease was granted. That, it was said, broke the chain of causation: any damage which the plaintiff may be shown to have suffered flowed from the negligence of these new solicitors and not Pulvers. It is quite true that when the new solicitors were instructed they knew, as Pulvers in February 1979 had not known, the rent under the headlease. But Pulvers had known that rent in May 1979, 2½ years before they ceased to act. They advised on the new underlease in October 1980. The deputy judge held that Pulvers were not at that stage at fault in failing to review the whole transaction. That finding was not challenged on appeal. The decision was then made to seek a new underlease, the head lessor's consent having been obtained and the security of tenure provisions excluded. The new solicitors were instructed to implement that decision, not to review it. There is nothing in the facts as found to support the conclusion that anything done or omitted by the new solicitors broke the chain of causation between Pulvers negligence and whatever damage the plaintiff suffered.

The deputy judge accepted Mrs Feldman's evidence that if she and Mrs Balfe had known of the financial implications of the rent review clause the plaintiff would not have proceeded. Having, however, concluded that there was no effective negligence by Mr Rose, the deputy judge made no finding on damages. In this court it is accepted that we cannot carry out a detailed inquiry into damages. But we have been asked to rule on the principles to be applied in assessing damages and this we agreed to do.

The plaintiff claims as damages the three sums which I have already mentioned: the capital sum of £16,000 paid to the mesne lessor in consideration of his accepting a surrender of the underlease in June 1984; £2,761 arrears of rent paid to the mesne landlord as part of that settlement; and £17,000 lost on the prospective sale of the underlease and the goodwill of the plaintiff's employment agency business. It is to be observed that these figures exclude any element attributable to the first five-year period of the underlease, during which it may fairly be said that the rent paid by the plaintiff in excess of the open market rent was the result of the plaintiff's willingness to pay the rent asked. It plainly had nothing to do with the operation of the rent review clause.

Pulvers attacked this method of calculating the claim as being bad in principle. It was said that the correct measure of damage (whether in contract or in tort) for negligent advice is the difference between (a) the open market value of the asset acquired as it actually was and (b) whichever is lower of the price paid and the open market value of the asset in the state in which, as a result of the negligent advice, it was thought to be. I shall for convenience call this 'the diminution in value rule'. In Pulvers' submission the diminution in value rule is to be applied as at the date of breach of contract or entry into the transaction and account should not in general be taken of events which occur later.

The principles to be applied in assessing damages in this case are, in my judgment, these.

(1) The overriding rule was stated by Lord Blackburn in *Livingstone v Rawyards Coal Co* (1880) 5 App Cas 25 at 39 and has been repeated on countless occasions since: the measure of damages is—

'that sum of money which will put the party who has been injured, or who has suffered, in the same position as he would have been in if he had not sustained the wrong for which he is now getting his compensation or reparation.'

As Megaw LJ added in *Dodd Properties (Kent) Ltd v Canterbury City Council* [1980] 1 All ER 928 at 934, [1980] 1 WLR 433 at 451:

'In any case of doubt, it is desirable that the judge, having decided provisionally as to the amount of damages, should, before finally deciding, consider whether the amount conforms with the requirement of Lord Blackburn's fundamental principle. If it appears not to conform, the judge should examine the question again to see whether the particular case falls within one of the exceptions of which Lord Blackburn gave examples, or whether he is obliged by some binding authority to arrive at a result which is inconsistent with the fundamental principle.'

(2) On the authorities as they stand the diminution in value rule appears almost always, if not always, to be appropriate where property is acquired following negligent advice by surveyors. Such cases as *Philips v Ward* [1956] 1 All ER 874, [1956] 1 WLR 471, *Pilkington v Wood* [1953] 2 All ER 810, [1953] Ch 770, *Ford v White & Co* [1964] 2 All ER 755, [1964] 1 WLR 885 and *Perry v Sidney Phillips & Son (a firm)* [1982] 3 All ER 705, [1982] 1 WLR 1297 lay down that rule and illustrate its application in cases involving both surveyors and solicitors.

(3) That is not, however, an invariable approach, at least in claims against solicitors, and should not be mechanically applied in circumstances where it may appear inappropriate. In *Simple Simon Catering Ltd v J E Binstock Miller & Co* (1973) 228 EG 527 the Court of Appeal favoured a more general assessment, taking account of the 'general expectation of loss'. In other cases the cost of repair or reinstatement may provide the appropriate measure (see *Dodd Properties (Kent) Ltd v Canterbury City Council* [1980] 1 All ER 928 at 938, [1980] 1 WLR 433 at 456 per Donaldson LJ). In other cases the measure of damages may properly include the cost of making good the error of a negligent adviser: examples are found in *Braid v W L Highway & Sons* (1964) 191 EG 433 and *G & K Ladenbau (UK) Ltd v Crawley & de Reya (a firm)* [1978] 1 All ER 682, [1978] 1 WLR 266.

(4) While the general rule undoubtedly is that damages for tort or breach of contract are assessed as at the date of the breach (see, e g, *Miliangos v George Frank (Textiles) Ltd* [1975] 3 All ER 801 at 813, [1976] AC 443 at 468 per Lord Wilberforce), this rule also should not be mechanically applied in circumstances where assessment at another date may more accurately reflect the overriding compensatory rule. The *Dodd Properties* case both affirms this principle and illustrates its application.

(5) On the facts of the present case the diminution in value rule would involve a somewhat speculative and unreal valuation exercise intended to reflect the substantial negative value of this underlease. It would also seem likely to lead to a total claim well above the figure the plaintiff claims. By contrast, there is firm evidence that £18,761 is what it actually cost the plaintiff, as a result of an arm's length negotiation after expiry of the first five years of the underlease, to extricate itself from the consequences of the negligent advice it had received. Unless (which seems unlikely) it can be shown that payment of this sum did not represent a reasonable attempt by the plaintiff to mitigate the loss it had suffered, this figure would represent a fair assessment of one head of the plaintiff's loss.

(6) Even after an appropriate measure has been found to reflect damage recoverable under the first limb of the rule in *Hadley v Baxendale* (1854) 9 Exch 341, [1843–60] All ER 461, there will be cases in which a plaintiff will not be adequately compensated unless he receives damages to reflect his loss under the second limb also. In claiming £17,000 for loss of its prospective sale of the lease and the goodwill of the business the plaintiff advances the present as such a case. It must, however, be accepted on the findings of the deputy judge that if it had not been negligently advised the plaintiff would not have entered into this underlease at all. This being so, damage cannot be assessed with reference to a specific gain which the plaintiff would only have made if it had entered into this underlease, unless it be proper on the facts to conclude that, properly advised, the plaintiff would probably have been able to negotiate the grant of this underlease but without the offending clause. Even then the offer of £17,000 would call for closer scrutiny.

(7) It may alternatively be proper to conclude when the facts are investigated that even if the plaintiff, properly advised, would not have taken an underlease of 109 Queen Street, it would none the less have taken a lease of other premises from which to conduct its employment agency business. On their initial introduction to Mr Cook, Mrs Feldman and Mrs Balfe were shown other premises in Maidenhead and it may be that they would have accepted the other premises had the Queen Street transaction fallen through. Had they done so and had the plaintiff conducted its business from the other premises, it may be correct to infer that goodwill would have been established and (perhaps) a saleable lease obtained. But it would be proper to approach this assessment in a cautious and conservative manner: the premises chosen were clearly thought to be the more promising for purposes of the business it was proposed to conduct; it does not follow that the business could have been conducted as successfully from other premises; the value of the plaintiff's potential goodwill would have to be looked at in the light of its accounts; there might be no prospect of obtaining a significant premium on sale of a lease at open market rent; and the speculative nature of the assessment should be borne in mind.

(8) Any damages awarded would no doubt attract an award of interest in the usual way.

I would accordingly allow the appeal and remit the case to a Chancery master for the assessment of damages in accordance with the principles stated.

STEPHEN BROWN LJ. I agree that the appeal should be allowed for the reasons given by Bingham LJ, and I further agree that the issue of damages should be remitted to a Chancery master for assessment in accordance with the principles which he was stated.

SIR NICOLAS BROWNE-WILKINSON V-C. I also agree and only add a few remarks on two points.

First on the issue of liability for negligence. In addition to those matters referred to by Bingham LJ, in my judgment the rent review clause was in itself so unusual that any careful solicitor would have considered its repercussions very carefully. Its effect was to make the rent payable under the underlease wholly dependent on the proper operation

of the rent review clause in the headlease. The rent review clause in the headlease
required the service of a counter-notice by the tenant, time being of the essence, if the
revised rent proposed by the head landlord in his notice was not to become binding. The
hazards involved in the operation of such rent review machinery are notorious. Even if
the machinery were properly operated, under this clause the underlessee had no say
whatsoever in the negotiation or fixing of the rent payable under the headlease on a
review.

Faced with such a clause, a solicitor properly discharging his duty to his client would
have had to consider very carfully its repercussions. If very careful consideration had
been given to this clause, Mr Rose would very soon have discovered the actual hazard
which has caused damage in this case, which Bingham LJ has illustrated. Having
discovered that, he would have had to warn the client (the plaintiff) of the risks involved
in accepting such a clause, at least without knowing the rent payable under the headlease.

In the circumstances, it seems to me that Mr Rose was most clearly put on inquiry as
to the effect of this clause. He neither pursued the necessary inquiries nor gave adequate
warning of the hazards to the client.

As to measure of damages, in my judgment the diminution in value rule is wholly
inappropriate to the quantification of damages in this case. The diminution in value rule
is concerned with a case where the client has purchased for a capital sum a property
having a capital value. Such client thinks that it has certain features which render it more
valuable. Due to the shortcomings of his professional adviser he is not aware of the fact
that it lacked these features. The measure of damage is the difference, put broadly,
between its actual value and the value it would have had had it possessesd the features
which he thought it had. The essence of such a rule is to compare two actual values. In
the present case the plaintiff was buying an asset which, as it thought, could have no
capital value; it was buying an underlease at a rack market rent which would have no
capital value. As a result of the negligence by the solicitors the plaintiff has exposed itself
to a long-standing liability requiring it to pay substantial sums out of pocket. To apply
any test of capital diminution in such circumstances would be wholly artificial. The loss
suffered is the liability to pay a sum over a period of time. The plaintiff managed to
extricate itself from such liability by the down payment of a capital sum. In my
judgment, the capital sum it had to pay is the true measure of damage under that head.

I agree with Bingham LJ in saying that the price paid to the landlord to accept a
surrender is the right measure of damage under that head.

For those reasons, and for all the other reasons given by Bingham LJ, I agree that the
appeal should be allowed on liability and the case remitted to a Chancery master for
assessment of damages in accordance with the principles stated in Bingham LJ's
judgment.

Appeal allowed. Case remitted to a Chancery master for assessment of damages. Costs reserved.

Solicitors: *Fairchild Greig & Wells* (for the plaintiff); *Reynolds Porter Chamberlain* (for
Pulvers).

Vivian Horvath   Barrister.

Pritchard v J H Cobden Ltd and another   *a*

COURT OF APPEAL, CIVIL DIVISION

O'CONNOR, CROOM-JOHNSON LJJ AND SIR ROGER ORMROD

23, 24, 25, 26, 27, 30 JUNE, 1, 30 JULY 1986

Damages – Personal injuries – Loss of future earnings – Multiplier – Date at which multiplier to   *b*
be calculated – Whether multiplier to be calculated at date of trial or date of accident.

Damages – Personal injuries – Divorce – Divorce caused by injury – Loss arising from plaintiff's
liability in divorce proceedings to make financial provision for spouse and children – Plaintiff
severely injured as result of defendant's negligence – Plaintiff's marriage breaking up because of
his injuries – Order in divorce proceedings requiring plaintiff to make periodical payments to wife   *c*
and children – Whether financial orders in matrimonial proceedings representing 'loss' to plaintiff
– Whether court should refuse to make award for loss consequent on break-up of marriage as
matter of policy or as indirect economic loss.

In June 1976 the plaintiff, then aged 30, suffered serious and permanent brain damage
and other injuries as the result of a motor accident caused by negligence for which the   *d*
defendants were liable. Subsequently the plaintiff's marriage broke down and a decree
nisi of divorce was granted in December 1984. In his claim for damages for personal
injuries against the defendants the plaintiff claimed as a head of damage the extra expense
he would incur as a result of the divorce, on the ground that the marriage had broken
down as a result of his injuries. In order to accommodate that claim the wife's claim for
financial relief in the matrimonial proceedings was heard together with the plaintiff's   *e*
claim against the defendants in September 1985. The judge dealt with the usual heads of
damage in the plaintiff's claim and reached a figure of £381,126. He then dealt with the
matrimonial proceedings and made orders for financial provision representing
expenditure by the plaintiff of £53,000. He added that sum to the figure already assessed,
and held the defendants liable for the sum of £434,126 plus interest. The defendants
appealed, contending that the assessment of damages was excessive on the grounds (i) *f*
that the practice of calculating a multiplier in personal injury cases as at the date of the
trial led to results which were inconsistent with those in fatal accident cases where the
assessment was made at the date of death, and led also to excessive awards for future loss
of earnings as well as putting a premium on delay, and (ii) that the proposition that
expenditure arising out of divorce was recoverable as part of the damages in an action for
personal injuries was wrong in law.   *g*

Held – (1) In a personal injury case the date of trial was the appropriate date on which to
determine (a) the actual loss of earnings up to that date and (b) the future loss of earnings
based on a multiplier and multiplicand ascertained from the facts as they were at that
date. There was no good reason for reducing the multiplier by the period of time that   *h*
had elapsed since the accident, since a measure of delay was often justifiable, and undue
delay could be dealt with by other means. It followed that the multiplier fixed by the
judge and the sum calculated therefrom for the loss of future earnings would not be
reduced. Accordingly, the appeal against that part of the award would be dismissed (see
p 306 *h* to p 307 *c h j*, p 308 *a* and p 314 *b c*, post).

(2) The expenditure arising out of the divorce was not recoverable against the   *j*
defendants as part of the damages, because financial orders made in matrimonial
proceedings did not represent a 'loss' in any ordinary sense but were rather a redistribution
of the parties' combined assets. In any event, the financial consequences of divorce were
too remote to be recoverable, or alternatively would be excluded as being an indirect
economic loss or as a matter of policy. Accordingly, the sum of £53,000 awarded under
that head would be disallowed, and, after taking into account the awards for general

damage and the costs of care and attention, which had been excessive, the damages awarded to the plaintiff would be reduced to £363,126. The appeal would accordingly be allowed to that extent (see p 309 j to p 310 c f g j to p 311 a, p 314 a, p 315 j to p 316 c f to j and p 317 j to p 318 a, post); *Jones v Jones* [1984] 3 All ER 1003 not followed.

Notes

For the general principles of damages for personal injuries, for damages for pecuniary loss and for damages for future loss of earnings, see 12 Halsbury's Laws (4th edn) paras 1146, 1151, 1155–1156.

Cases referred to in judgments

Birkett v Hayes [1982] 2 All ER 710, [1982] 1 WLR 816, CA.
British Transport Commission v Gourley [1955] 3 All ER 796, [1956] AC 185, [1956] 2 WLR 41, HL.
Cookson v Knowles [1978] 2 All ER 604, [1979] AC 556, [1978] 2 WLR 978, HL; *affg* [1977] 2 All ER 820, [1977] QB 913, [1977] 3 WLR 279, CA.
Daubney v Daubney [1976] 2 All ER 453, [1976] Fam 267, [1976] 2 WLR 959, CA.
George v Pinnock [1973] 1 All ER 926, [1973] 1 WLR 118, CA.
Graham v Dodds [1938] 2 All ER 953, [1983] 1 WLR 808, HL.
Housecroft v Burnett [1986] 1 All ER 332, CA.
Jones v Jones [1984] 3 All ER 1003, [1985] QB 704, [1984] 3 WLR 862, CA; *varying* [1983] 1 All ER 1037, [1983] 1 WLR 901.
Mallett v McMonagle [1969] 2 All ER 178, [1970] AC 166, [1969] 2 WLR 767, HL.
Overseas Tankship (UK) Ltd v Morts Dock and Engineering Co Ltd, The Wagon Mound (No 1) [1961] 1 All ER 404, [1961] AC 388, [1961] 2 WLR 126, PC.
Taylor v O'Connor [1970] 1 All ER 365, [1971] AC 115, [1970] 2 WLR 472, HL.

Cases also cited

Anns v Merton London BC [1977] 2 All ER 492, [1978] AC 728, HL.
Candlewood Navigation Corp Ltd v Mitsui OSK Lines Ltd, The Mineral Transporter, The Ibaraki Maru [1985] 2 All ER 935, [1986] AC 1, PC.
Fitzpatrick v Batger & Co Ltd [1967] 2 All ER 657, [1967] 1 WLR 706, CA.
Home Office v Dorset Yacht Co Ltd [1970] 2 All ER 294, [1970] AC 1004, HL.
Jefford v Gee [1970] 1 All ER 1202, [1970] 2 QB 130, CA.
Lamb v Camden London Borough [1981] 2 All ER 408, [1981] QB 625, CA.
Lambert v Lewis [1981] 1 All ER 1185, [1982] AC 225, HL.
Lim Poh Choo v Camden and Islington Area Health Authority [1979] 2 All ER 910, [1980] AC 174, HL.
Lodge Holes Colliery Co v Wednesbury Corp [1908] AC 323, HL.
McLoughlin v O'Brian [1982] 2 All ER 298, [1983] 1 AC 410, HL.
Muirhead v Industrial Tank Specialities Ltd [1985] 3 All ER 705, [1986] AC 507, CA.
Spartan Steel and Alloys Ltd v Martin & Co (Contractors) Ltd [1972] 3 All ER 557, [1973] QB 27, CA.
Weld-Blundell v Stephens [1920] AC 956, [1920] All ER Rep 32, HL.

Appeal

The defendants, J H Cobden Ltd and Malcolm Cyril Parrott, appealed against the judgment of Swinton Thomas J given on 1 October 1985 awarding the plaintiff, Vivian John Pritchard (by his next friend Philip James Pritchard), £450,932 plus interest in an action for damages for personal injuries caused by the defendants' negligence. The facts are set out in the judgment of O'Connor and Croom-Johnson LJJ.

Piers Ashworth QC and *Benjamin Browne* for the defendants.
W R H Crowther QC and *Rosalind Foster* for the plaintiff.

Cur adv vult

30 July. The following judgments were delivered.

O'CONNOR LJ. This judgment has been prepared jointly by Croom-Johnson LJ and myself and is to be read as our judgment.

On 28 June 1976 the plaintiff sustained serious injuries when his motor car was in collision with the defendants' vehicle. At that time the plaintiff was not quite 30 years of age and was married with a 6½-year-old daughter. He was employed by the Ministry of Defence as a professional technical officer. As a result of his injuries including brain damage the plaintiff is unemployable.

The case did not come on for trial until September 1985. By that time much had happened. In January 1977 the wife gave birth to twins and the plaintiff returned home from hospital. Unfortunately, despite a move of house in 1983, the marriage did not survive, the wife petitioned for divorce and the decree nisi was pronounced in December 1984. The plaintiff amended his statement of claim alleging that his marriage had broken down as a result of the injuries he had sustained and claiming as a head of damage any extra expense that he might incur as a result of the divorce. In order to accommodate this unusual claim the wife's claim for financial relief in the matrimonial proceedings was ordered to be tried by the same judge who heard the personal injury case. The trial took on a most unusual form: in addition to the plaintiff and the defendants the wife was represented and the quantification of the plaintiff's claim against the defendants and the wife's claim for financial provision were all heard together over a period of five days. In his judgment the judge first of all dealt with all the usual heads of damage in the plaintiff's claim and arrived at a figure of £381,126. He then dealt with the matrimonial proceedings and imposed a 'clean break' solution. He ordered that the wife should receive £50,000, that her interest in the matrimonial home when it came to be sold after the twins attained majority should be increased from one-half to two-thirds and he ordered periodic payments in favour of the children totalling £50 per week. The plaintiff was to move out of the matrimonial home into another house which had been bought for him out of an interim payment made by the defendants. The judge now turned back to the claim against the defendants and decided that as a result of the divorce and as a result of the orders that he had just made the plaintiff had suffered damage which he assessed in the sum of £53,000, added to this the sum which he had already assessed and held that the defendants were liable in the sum of £434,126.

By their appeal the defendants challenge the judge's assessment of damage under some of the customary heads and the whole of his assessment flowing from the divorce. We propose to deal with the customary heads of damage first.

Loss of earnings

The net loss of earnings to the date of trial was agreed in the sum of £46,478. This was an accurate figure calculated by accountants taking the year by year earnings that the plaintiff would have earned in his post and applying the appropriate tax deductions for his financial situation.

The parties agreed that for future loss the judge should use as a multiplicand the net figure of £9,000 per annum. The judge took a multiplier of 14 and produced an award of £126,000, so that the total award for loss of earnings past and future came to £172,478. Counsel on behalf of the defendants has submitted that the long delay in bringing the case to trial has led to an award which is much greater than it would have been had the case come to trial say three, or even four, years after the accident. He submitted that this was a good ground for this court to re-examine the present practice for assessing damage for loss of earnings past and future in the case of a living plaintiff. The present practice is not in dispute and although invited to depart from it the judge refused to do so. Loss of earnings between the date of accident, when the cause of action accrued, and the date of trial have always been claimed as special damage. Since the decision of the House of Lords in *British Transport Commission v Gourley* [1955] 3 All ER 796, [1956] AC 185 it is the loss of wages net of income tax that has to be ascertained. This has always been done as a straight calculation and no one has suggested that, when the total figure has been ascertained as best the court can in an individual case, any deduction should be made for the mere chance that during that period the plaintiff might not have earned his wages because, for example, he might have fallen ill or lost his job and been unable to get one as remunerative as the one that he held.

Until 1970 the element of future loss of earnings was hidden in a single award for general damages which included the award for pain, suffering and loss of amenity and it was only the introduction of interest that required the judges to separate the award for future loss in the award for general damages. The judges were familiar with the practice of finding a multiplicand and applying a multiplier in order to assess the loss of dependency in Fatal Accidents Act cases. It so happened that at that precise time the House of Lords in two cases laid down exactly how the exercise should be performed in Fatal Accidents Act cases: *Mallett v McMonagle* [1969] 2 All ER 178, [1970] AC 166 and *Taylor v O'Connor* [1970] 1 All ER 365, [1971] AC 115.

The fall in the value of money coupled with the real increase in earnings has meant that the award for loss of earnings has come to play a very large part in the awards for damages for personal injuries. As far as interest is concerned the rule is that interest is awarded on the award for past loss of earnings but not on that for future loss of earnings. There was some dispute as to how this should be done in Fatal Accidents Act cases and that dispute was finally settled in *Cookson v Knowles* [1978] 2 All ER 604, [1979] AC 556. The House of Lords held (as the Court of Appeal had done: see [1977] 2 All ER 820, [1977] QB 913) that the award should be split into two parts. The number of years' purchase of the annual dependency, that is the multiplier, should be calculated as heretofore from the date of death but, instead of a simple multiplicand for the whole period, a multiplicand or multiplicands appropriate for the period between death and trial should be used in order to ascertain a sum upon which interest would be payable and the balance of the multiplier applied to a single multiplicand for future loss on which no interest is payable. In the vast majority of Fatal Accidents Act cases the amount of the dependency of the dependents is directly linked to the notional earnings that the deceased would have earned but for his death. Seeking support from the speeches in *Mallett v McMonagle* and in *Cookson v Knowles*, counsel for the defendants has submitted that in principle there should be no difference between the calculation of the value of the dependency in Fatal Accidents Act cases and the valuation of the loss of earnings element in a personal injury case.

In *Mallett v McMonagle* the deceased was 25 at the date of his death, the net dependency of his widow and children was £520 per annum, and there was evidence that he would have got a job that would have produced a little more money, say £100 per annum. A jury in Northern Ireland assessed the Fatal Accidents Act damages in the sum of £21,500, that is about 40 years' purchase. Not surprisingly the Court of Appeal in Northern Ireland set aside the award on the ground that it was wholly excessive and ordered a new trial. The plaintiffs came to the House of Lords and, in trying to show that the jury's award was not wholly excessive, it was submitted that inflation should be taken into account in assessing the notional earnings of the deceased and indeed a rate of $3\frac{1}{2}\%$ compound was put forward. Lord Diplock was the only one of their Lordships who dealt with this topic in his speech. He rejected the argument on inflation, saying ([1969] 2 All ER 178 at 190, [1970] AC 166 at 176):

'In my view, the only practicable course for courts to adopt in assessing damages awarded under the Fatal Accidents Acts is to leave out of account the risk of further inflation on the one hand and the high interest rates which reflect the fear of it and capital appreciation of property and equities which are the consequence of it on the other hand. In estimating the amount of the annual dependency in the future, had the deceased not been killed, money should be treated as retaining its value at the date of the judgment, and in calculating the present value of annual payments which would have been received in future years, interest rates appropriate to times of stable currency such as 4 per cent. to 5 per cent. should be adopted.'

Lord Diplock then went on to consider the problem of assessing a multiplier and said ([1969] 2 All ER 178 at 191, [1970] AC 166 at 176–177):

'The starting point in any estimate of the number of years that a dependency would have endured is the number of years between the date of the deceased's death and that at which he would have reached normal retiring age. That falls to be reduced to take account of the chance not only that he might not have lived until retiring age but also the chance that by illness or injury he might have been disabled from gainful occupation. The former risk can be calculated from available actuarial tables. The latter cannot. There is also the chance that the widow may die before the deceased would have reached the normal retiring age (which can be calculated from actuarial tables) or that she may remarry and thus replace her dependency from some other source which would not have been available to her had her husband lived. The prospects of remarriage may be affected by the amount of the award of damages. But insofar as the chances that death or incapacitating illness or injury would bring the dependency to an end increase in later years when, from the nature of the arithmetical calculation their effect on the present capital value of the annual dependency diminishes, a small allowance for them may be sufficient where the deceased and his widow were young and in good health at the date of his death. Similarly even in the case of a young widow the prospect of remarriage,may be thought to be reduced by the existence of several young children to a point at which little account need be taken of this factor. In cases such as the present where the deceased was aged 25 and the appellant, his widow, about the same age, courts have not infrequently awarded 16 years' purchase of the dependency. It is seldom that this number of years' purchase is exceeded. It represents the capital value of an annuity certain for a period of 26 years at interest rates of 4 per cent., 29 years at interest rates of 4½ per cent. or 33 years at interest rates of 5 per cent. Having regard to the uncertainties to be taken into account 16 years would appear to represent a reasonable maximum number of years' purchase where the deceased died in his twenties.'

In *Cookson v Knowles* [1978] 2 All ER 604 at 607, [1979] AC 556 at 567 Lord Diplock said:

'Two separate though related questions are involved in the appeal to your Lordships' House. The first is whether and, if so, how should the prospect of continued inflation after the date of trial be dealt with in assessing the capital sum to be awarded by way of damages in fatal accident and personal injury cases.'

In dealing with this issue he reiterated much of what he had said in *Mallett v McMonagle*. It is, however, in the speech of Lord Fraser that we find the difference between the assessment of damages under the Fatal Accidents Acts and in personal injury cases contrasted and considered. We must cite what he said at some length, starting at the beginning of his speech ([1978] 2 All ER 604 at 613–615, [1979] AC 556 at 574–576):

'My Lords, three questions are raised in this appeal. The first relates to the basis on which damages under the Fatal Accidents Acts 1846 to 1959, and now under the Fatal Accidents Act 1976, ought to be assessed, and in particular whether it should be similar to the basis used for assessing damages for personal injuries. The second is whether the prospect of future inflation should be taken into account in assessing damages under the Acts and, if so, how that should be done. The third question relates to the principles on which the discretionary power of the court to award interest on the principal sum of damages under the Acts ought to be exercised. The questions are separate but to some extent are related to one another. On the first question the most important point is whether the damages ought to be assessed as at the date of death or as at the date of trial. In strict theory I think there is no doubt that they should be assessed as at the date of death, just as in theory they are assessed at the date of injury in a personal injury case. But the damages awarded to dependants under the Fatal Accidents Acts for loss of support during what would (but for the fatal accident) have been the remainder of the deceased person's working life have to be based on estimates of many uncertain factors, including the length of time during which the deceased would probably have continued to work and the amount that he would probably have earned during that time. The court has to make the best estimates that it can having regard to the deceased's age and state of health and to his actual earnings immediately before his death, as well as to the prospects of any increases in his earnings due to promotion or other reasons. But it has always been recognised, and is clearly sensible, that when events have occurred, between the date of death and the date of trial, which enable the court to rely on ascertained facts rather than on mere estimates, they should be taken into account in assessing damages. Thus if a dependant widow has died between the date of the injured man's death and the date of the trial or if (before the Fatal Accidents Act 1976, s 3(2) became law) she had remarried, the fact would be taken into account, just as medical evidence of facts relating to the injuries of an injured person up to the date of trial is taken into account in preference to prognosis made immediately after the accident. Similarly if the rate of wages paid to those in the same occupation as the deceased person has increased between the date of death and the date of trial the increase is rightly taken into account in assessing damages due to his dependants under the Fatal Accidents Acts. Assessment of damages in this way requires the pecuniary loss to be split into two parts, relating respectively to the period before the trial and the period after the trial, in the same way as it is split in a personal accident case. To that extent the same method of assessment is used in both classes of case. The loss of support between the date of death and the date of trial is the total of the amounts assumed to have been lost for each week between those dates, although as a matter of practical convenience it is usual to take the median rate of wages as the multiplicand. In a case such as this, where the deceased's age was such that he would probably have continued to work until the date of trial, the multiplier of this part of the calculation is the number of weeks between the date of death and the date of trial. That is convenient, although it is strictly speaking too favourable to the plaintiff, because it treats the probability that, but for the fatal accident, the deceased would have continued to earn the rate for the job and to apply the same proportion of his (perhaps increased) earnings to support his dependants as it it were a certainty. I mention that in order to emphasise how uncertain is the basis on which the whole calculation proceeds. That was the method employed by the Court of Appeal, which calculated the dependency at date of death as £1,614, and at date of trial as £1,980, giving a median of £1,797 per annum as the multiplicand for the period of $2\frac{1}{2}$ years between the two dates. For the period after the date of trial, the proper multiplier is, in my opinion, based on the rate of wages for the job at the date of trial. The reason is that that is the latest available information, and, being a hard fact, it is a more reliable starting point for the calculation than the rate of wages at the time of death. The appropriate multiplier will be related primarily to the deceased person's age and hence to the probable length of his working life at the date of death. In the present case the deceased was aged 49 at the date of his death and the trial judge and the Court of Appeal used a multiplier of 11. That figure was not seriously criticised by counsel as having been inappropriate as at the date of death, although I think it is probably generous to the appellant. From that figure of 11, the Court of Appeal deducted $2\frac{1}{2}$ in respect of the $2\frac{1}{2}$ years from the date of death to the date of trial, and they used the resulting figure of $8\frac{1}{2}$ as the multiplier for the damages after the date of trial. In so doing they departed from the method that would have been appropriate in a personal injury case and counsel for the appellant criticised the departure as being unfair to the appellant. The argument was that if the deceased man had had a twin brother who had been injured at the same time as the deceased man was killed, and whose claim for damages for personal injury had come to trial on the same day as the dependant's claim under the Fatal Accidents Acts, the appropriate multiplier for his loss after the date of trial would have been higher than 8½. On the assumption, which is probably correct, that that would have been so, it does not in my opinion follow that the multiplier of 8½ is too low in the present claim under the Fatal Accidents Acts where different considerations apply. In a personal injury case, if the injured person has survived until the date of trial, that is a known fact and the multiplier appropriate to the length of his future working life has to be ascertained as at the date of trial. But in a fatal accident case the multiplier must be selected once and for all as at the date of death, because everything that might have happened to the deceased after that date remains uncertain. Accordingly having taken a multiplier of 11 as at the date of death, and having used 2½ in respect of the period up to the trial, it is in my opinion correct to take 8½ for the period after the date of trial. That is what the Court of Appeal did in this case.'

This part of Lord Fraser's speech was expressly approved by the House of Lords in *Graham v Dodds* [1983] 2 All ER 953, [1983] 1 WLR 808. In that case the majority in the Court of Appeal in Northern Ireland had concluded that there was a conflict between the speeches of Lord Diplock and Lord Fraser in *Cookson v Knowles* and that Lord Diplock must be understood to have been saying that the future loss element should be assessed by applying a multiplier appropriate to the age that the deceased would have been had he survived to the date of trial. Lord Bridge, with whose speech the other members of the House including Lord Diplock agreed, citing the passage from Lord Fraser, said ([1983] 2 All ER 953 at 958, [1983] 1 WLR 808 at 815):

'If I may say so respectfully, I find the reasoning in this passage as cogent as it is clear. But, what is perhaps more important, I can find nothing in the speech of Lord Diplock which conflicts in any way with Lord Fraser's reasoning or with his conclusion. The two passages cited by Gibson LJ from Lord Diplock's speech dealing with the assessment of the dependants' future loss from date of trial are not directed to the question of the appropriate multiplier and certainly lend no support to the doctrine that this can be calculated on the assumption that the deceased, if he had survived the accident, would certainly have remained alive and well and in the same employment up to the date of trial. Such a doctrine, ignoring the uncertainty which, as Lord Fraser pointed out, affects everything that might have happened to the deceased after the date of his death, is clearly contrary to principle and would lead to the highly undesirable anomaly that in fatal accident cases the longer the trial of the dependants' claims could be delayed the more they would eventually recover.'

Counsel for the defendants relies strongly on the last sentence in that passage from Lord Bridge's speech. He submits that delay between the date of the accident and the date of trial in a personal injury case produces the same anomaly and that it is as undesirable in that context as it is in cases under the Fatal Accidents Acts. He submitted that the figures in the present case show that the plaintiff thas been awarded 23 years' purchase of his loss of earnings, the nine years between accident and trial being separately calculated for interest purposes just as in the Fatal Accidents Act computation and 14 years' purchase for future loss beyond trial is added. He produced a table to show that a fund of £172,478 subjected to a 4½% discount rate would provide annual drawings of £9,000 for no less than 45 years and he submitted for a man of 39 that was manifestly wrong.

We cannot agree with the submission of counsel for the defendants. In the first place we think it quite plain that the House of Lords recognised this difference in *Cookson v*

Knowles and in *Graham v Dodds*. Lord Fraser was, as indeed were all of their Lordships,
well aware that actions for personal injuries take time to come on for trial. This is not a
delay problem because the choice must be, should future loss of earnings be assessed as
from the date of trial or as from the date of the accident? The actual assessment has to be
done at the date of trial: it is at that date that all the factors affecting the future have to be
considered; from that consideration an appropriate multiplicand and an appropriate
multiplier emerge. We can see no good reason for artificially reducing the multiplier by
the period of time that has elapsed from the date of the accident. It seems to me that in
the case of a live plaintiff future loss of earnings is a different head of damage to past loss
of earnings. In my judgment there are good reasons for preserving this distinction. The
great majority of injured wage-earners need their wages to defray their current expenses
in the period between accident and trial. In so far as the injury produces a shortfall in
earnings, that shortfall is made up by drawing on savings or alternatively by borrowing
the money. It is for this reason that interest is awarded on this part of the award: it is the
assessment of money actually lost and the award replaces the loss. That is quite different
to assessing a capital sum to compensate for future loss of earnings and it is only to the
latter exercise that the machinery of multiplier and multiplicand has any relevance.

In the present case it is quite wrong to add the £46,478 awarded for past loss to the
sum of £126,000 awarded for future loss and carry out the exhaustion exercise on a
capital sum of £172,478. If the defendant's submission were upheld the plaintiff would
receive the £46,478 for past loss and only five years' purchase for future loss of £9,000 pa,
that is £45,000. That is manifestly inadequate compensation for a man of 39.

If the defendants were right in their argument in respect of loss of earnings, it would
have to apply equally to other forms of expense where appropriate, such as continuing
expense on special nursing care or domestic help. By the time the trial takes place, a
tetraplegic plaintiff may have spent a great deal of money on several years' special nursing
care, say five or six years. If all he can then recover is the balance of the total number of
years' purchase, that money will not be enough for his legitimate future needs.

In his submissions to us, counsel pointed out some practical results of the defendants'
submission. A plaintiff might be the victim of an industrial disease (unknown to him)
and be off work with it for many years. Then he might learn that it was caused in
circumstances giving rise to a remedy against his previous employers. His total sum of
compensation for lost earnings might provide little or nothing for the future. Similar
complications may be envisaged where infants require long periods of special nursing, or
where the injured plaintiff has only a very short expectation of life at the time of the
accident.

The defendants have advanced their argument in another way. It is based on the delay
which has occurred in the present case in bringing it to trial, and the argument is that
where there is such a long period policy requires that there should be a reduction in the
multiplier. Otherwise, delay means larger damages, and injustice to the defendant. But
the whole of the time occupied before trial is not 'delay'. In every contested action there
is an interval of time between the arising of the cause of action and trial. That interval
may in some cases be lengthened by unnecessary delay, which should be prevented
wherever possible. Sometimes a longer interval works in favour of justice, as where what
was only a risk of epilepsy becomes a fact of epilepsy. But the plaintiff is not to be
deprived of his proper sum of compensation because his case takes a long time, even an
unnecessarily long time, to come to trial. The weapons to be used against too long an
interval of time are striking out for want of prosecution, or in some cases depriving the
plaintiff of part of the interest on his special damage, or in bringing on the hearing in
good time.

The last point taken by the defendants on this part of the case was that in any event
the multiplier of 14 used by the judge was too great. It was certainly above that normally
used where the age at the date of assessment is 39. In such cases a multiplier of 12 is
normally the maximum and in many cases less than that. However, although it was

high, it was a matter within the range of the judge's discretion, and not so high that it
would be interfered with.

    The conclusion is that the judge's award of £126,000 for the plaintiff's loss of future
earnings should not be reduced.

[Their Lordships then considered the awards of £60,000 general damages for pain,
suffering and loss of amenity, and the award for the costs of care and attention which
included £18,000 representing the value to the plaintiff of the additional services given
to him by his wife during the nine years which elapsed after he came home from hospital
and, after considering the medical reports on the plaintiff and the award made in
Housecroft v Burnett [1986] 1 All ER 332, reduced the damages for pain suffering and loss
of amenity to £50,000 and for loss of the wife's additional services to £9,000. Their
Lordships continued:]

The divorce

    Before dealing with the next heads of damages it is convenient to set out the procedure
which was followed in the present case. The marriage took place in 1969 and following
that a daughter, Louise, was born. The plaintiff's accident occurred on 28 June 1976. In
January 1977 the twin girls were born. At that time the family was living at 20 Twynham
Close, Downton in a house which was by now too small for it. The family needed a larger
house, and in 1983 20 Twynham Close was sold for £27,500 and Brindle Lodge, Nunton
was bought in joint names for £77,500. Owing to the plaintiff's injuries the marriage
had finally broken down. In June 1984 the wife filed a petition for divorce in the
Winchester County Court. The decree nisi was granted on 10 December 1984, with care
and control to her of the three daughters. On 22 February 1985 her claims for ancillary
relief were transferred to the Family Division of the High Court to be heard before a
judge of that division at the same time as the trial of the personal injuries action. That
was done in order to take advantage of *Jones v Jones* [1984] 3 All ER 1003, [1985] QB 704,
which had been decided in June 1984. In July 1985 an up-to-date valuation of Brindle
Lodge was obtained at £92,000. Also in July 1985 a second house was bought for the
plaintiff to move to on his own. This was 31 Weavills Road, Bishopstoke. It cost £57,950.
Both the houses were bought with the help of interim payments made by the defendants.

    Thus it was that in July 1985 both the personal injury action and the Family Division
proceedings were heard together at Winchester.

    After assessing most of the damages in the personal injuries action, the judge
interpolated his orders in the maintenance proceedings. At the beginning of his judgment
he said:

> 'Accordingly, following the decision of the Court of Appeal in *Jones v Jones* [1984]
> 3 All ER 1003, [1985] QB 704, the plaintiff is entitled to recover as damages in his
> action against the defendants any financial loss which he may be able to prove that
> he has sustained by reason of the dissolution of the marriage. This claim, together
> with the claim in respect of the acquisition of Brindle Lodge and 31, Weavills Road,
> presents problems both in relation to principle and in relation to calculation.'

Later he said:

> 'The claims in respect of Brindle Lodge and Weavills Road are to an extent inter-
> dependent and dependent on my decision in relation to the matrimonial proceedings.
> The claim in respect of the extra cost of maintaining two households is wholly
> dependent on the decision in the matrimonial proceedings.'

Jones v Jones was tried by Stocker J. By that time the Joneses' marriage had broken up
due to a motor cycle accident. There were the claims of a usual nature in cases of serious
injury including as an element in his general damages the distress caused by the loss of
his marriage. It was also submitted that 'the sums which are likely to be awarded to the
wife and children in the Family Division in proceedings in ancillary claims to the

matrimonial proceedings, the wife having claimed all the appropriate relief, such as
a secured maintenance and a lump sum' could be recovered by the plaintiff from the
tortfeasor. No such proceedings had by then taken place. Stocker J made no award on
that part of the claim. He agreed that if the break-up of the marriage could be proved to
have been brought about by the defendant's negligence such damages could be recovered
in principle, although it was a novel point, but without any evidence of the kind which
would be required in the Family Division for the purpose of deciding questions of
b ancillary relief he declined to speculate on the award which that Division might make.
He pointed out that in awarding (as he did) a large sum for the plaintiff's loss of future
earnings he was awarding the money out of which the plaintiff would have maintained
his wife and family had there been no accident. The husband and wife later obtained a
consent order in the Hereford County Court by which periodical payments were to be
made to the wife and the children of the marriage. In addition a lump sum of £25,000
c was to be paid to the wife to buy a house for herself and the children.
     The husband then appealed in the personal injuries action, asking for his damages to
be increased because there was now evidence of loss to himself to support his claim to
pass on to the tortfeasor the moneys which the county court ordered him to pay to his
family. The plaintiff's counsel appears to have advanced an additional argument. Not
only did he put his claim on the basis that what the court had ordered was a loss to his
d client, but that the extra cost of paying for two households instead of one was recoverable.
He submitted that not only was the lump sum recoverable but also the cost to the
plaintiff of being kept out of that amount of money: what he termed 'the income
element'. Thirdly, he claimed the additional cost of providing maintenance to a separate
family unit. The Court of Appeal ordered that the £25,000 lump sum (subject to an
immaterial deduction which seems to have had no evidential basis) was a loss to the
e husband and could be passed on to the tortfeasor. The 'income element' it did not deal
with at all. With regard to the periodical payments it was held that there were so many
imponderables in the calculations which would have to be made that it could not be said
that the sums payable under those payments were greater than those which the plaintiff
would have had to pay for the maintenance of his wife and children if they had continued
to live with him. It rejected that head of claim. The Court of Appeal therefore dealt with
f the claim in the way in which it had been presented to Stocker J, as a question of principle
tied to the court order.
     The respondent did not appeal Stocker J's finding on the question of principle, but
conceded that the issue was only one of quantification. The matter on which the court
decided the appeal does not seem to have been contested by the respondent save that the
quantification was opposed on grounds of policy. Since that point was not argued, *Jones v*
g *Jones* is not an authority binding on us. As it is a matter of law, we have heard argument
afresh. With great respect to that court, for the reasons set out in the judgment in this
case of Sir Roger Ormrod, sums ordered to be paid or expended in maintenance
proceedings in matrimonial cases are not to be regarded as 'loss' caused to someone like
the present plaintiff.
h Counsel for the plaintiff submits that once it is established that the divorce is proved
to have been caused by the plaintiff's injuries and that it was a foreseeable consequence
of them, then the financial provisions made for the wife and children in proceedings for
ancillary relief are a loss to the plaintiff for which the tortfeasor must reimburse him. He
relies on *Overseas Tankship (UK) Ltd v Morts Dock and Engineering Co Ltd, The Wagon Mound*
(No 1) [1961] 1 All ER 404, [1961] AC 388. Counsel for the defendants concedes that the
j injuries caused the divorce, at least in part, and that it was foreseeable as a possible
consequence. He submits, however, firstly that orders made under Matrimonial Causes
Act 1973, ss 23, 24 and 25, as amended by Matrimonial and Family Proceedings Act
1984, s 3, do not produce or quantify any losses suffered by the plaintiff. He submits that
those sections provide a statutory procedure whereby the court has to exercise its
discretion in accordance with stipulated guidelines and to redistribute the finances and

property of both spouses by making orders for financial provision and by property
adjustment orders. Priority is given to the welfare of children while they are minors. *a*
Particular regard is to be paid to a wide range of circumstances, one of them being (where
appropriate) the conduct of each of the parties. What is redistributed are the total assets
and potential assets of the spouses, and that to use the word 'loss' is inapt. This is the same
whether the provision made is (for example) by a lump sum or periodical payment under
s 23 or by an property adjustment under s 24. It is common ground that damages for
personal injuries recovered by a spouse shall be included in the 'pot' which is to be shared: *b*
see *Daubney v Daubney* [1976] 2 All ER 453, [1976] Fam 267. Such money is available
from damages whether awarded for loss of future earnings or damages for pain and
suffering and loss of amenity. It is submitted that to hand on to the tortfeasor the liability
for a lump sum which may itself have come out of the 'pot' is only to increase again the
size of the 'pot'.

Consequently, it is submitted, the order of the court is independent of any claim *c*
which the plaintiff may have for loss or damage directly attributable to his injuries.

This submission is right, and is supported also on grounds of policy. In the present
case the hearings in the Queen's Bench action and the family proceedings were
deliberately fixed to take place together, nine years after the accident and one year after
the petition was filed. That would not always be so. The Queen's Bench action might
come on first. The judge would find himself trying to foresee what a family judge might *d*
decide several years later, if at all. He would require evidence of the finances of the other
spouse, the relationship of the parties, an assessment of their characters and financial
needs, the chances that they might separate and divorce, and what those chances would
have been even if there had been no injury to the plaintiff. If family proceedings did
come on, some time afterwards, all that evidence might turn out to be wrong or
inappropriate. There would be a breeding ground not only for differences between the *e*
two divisions of the High Court but also for dissatisfaction by the parties to the marriage.
On the other hand, if the family proceedings came on first, the defendant in the personal
injury action might complain that if he was to be bound by the outcome of those
proceedings he should be entitled to take part.

Owing to the special nature of the matrimonial proceedings, a head of damages based *f*
on them is too remote. On grounds of policy, it is also undesirable to bring into the
personal injury litigation the considerations which are relevant to the matrimonial relief.
They would increase evidentiary difficulties (as was foreseen by Stocker J in *Jones v Jones*)
and tend to lengthen litigation. As will become apparent when the orders made by the
judge in this case are later considered, investigations as to the tax positions of the parties
to the marriage would become necessary.

We have had cited to us many cases in which there has been decision and discussion *g*
on what is and what is not to be regarded as 'reasonably foreseeable'. It has also been
urged that the effect of allowing a claim on this basis would be to award damages for
economic loss. It is not necessary to come to any conclusion on either of those grounds.

It is enough to say that damages are not to be assessed simply on the basis of the results
of financial provisions and property adjustments in maintenance proceedings arising *h*
from a divorce. It follows also that if a court order cannot be used in that way, neither
can a voluntary agreement made between the parties to the same effect. That would
certainly be an intervening cause.

We have had the advantage of reading the judgment prepared by Sir Roger Ormrod;
for the reasons given by him and for those that we have set out above we agree that any
alteration of the plaintiff's financial position as a result of divorce or breakdown of *j*
marriage should be wholly disregarded when it comes to assessing the damages
recoverable by him from the defendants. We consider that this should be so despite the
fact that the divorce has resulted from the injuries caused to the plaintiff by the negligence
of the defendants. We think that in the public interest the court should not include this
head of damage, the investigation of which involves the conflict and expense to which

we and Sir Roger Ormrod have referred and is not only of its nature highly speculative
a but, in an age where breakdown of marriage is all too common, is also open to abuse. We
conclude that the sum of £53,000 awarded under this head should be disallowed.

If we are wrong in holding that this head of damage must be excluded as a matter of
public policy, we go on to consider how it ought to be approached in the present case.
The actual decision in *Jones v Jones* [1984] 3 All ER 1003, [1985] QB 704 did not apply
all the arguments which were addressed to the Court of Appeal. In the present case one
b such was addressed to the trial judge. It was based on *George v Pinnock* [1973] 1 All ER
926, [1973] 1 WLR 118. The trial judge followed *Jones v Jones* but in relation to 31
Weavills Road placed some reliance on *George v Pinnock*. That case had nothing to do with
divorce or breakdown of marriage but decided the proper approach to a claim that, as a
result of being confined to a wheelchair, the plaintiff had to move from a house to a
bungalow. In the present case, as Sir Roger Ormrod has pointed out, the need for a
c second house arose out of the divorce and the plaintiff's equity in the matrimonial home
was sufficient to enable him to purchase one. The only reason he could not use it for that
purpose was the order of the court in the matrimonial proceedings.
In *George v Pinnock* ([1973] 1 All ER 926 at 933, [1973] 1 WLR 118 at 124–125 Orr LJ
said):

d   'For the plaintiff it has been contended in the first place that she should receive as
       additional damages either the whole or some part of the capital cost of acquiring the
       bungalow, since it was acquired to meet the particular needs arising from the
       accident. But this argument, in my judgment, has no foundation. The plaintiff still
       has the capital in question in the form of the bungalow. An alternative argument
       advanced was, however, that as a result of the particular needs arising from her
e   injuries, the plaintiff has been involved in greater annual expenses of accommodation
       than she would have incurred if the accident had not happened. In my judgment,
       this argument is well founded, and I do not think it makes any difference for this
       purpose whether the matter is considered in terms of a loss of income from the
       capital expended on the bungalow or in terms of annual mortage interest which
       would have been payable if capital to buy the bungalow had not been available. The
f   plaintiff is, in my judgment, entitled to be compensated to the extent that this loss
       of income or notional outlay by way of mortgage interest exceeds what the cost of
       her accommodation would have been but for the accident. She would also, in my
       judgment, have been entitled to claim the expenses of a move to a new home
       imposed by her condition and the expense of any new items of furniture required
       because of that condition, but there was no evidence before the learned judge under
g   either of those headings. As to the increased cost of accommodation, if any, it was,
       as I have said, agreed that we should make the best estimate we could on the
       available material, and the matter can only be approached on a broad basis.

The relevant terms of the orders made by the judge in the family proceedings and
their effect as applied by him were as follows.
h   (1) *Periodical payments to the children*: £18 per week to the eldest daughter Louise until
the age of 17 years on completion of her education, and £16 per week to each of the
twins, on like terms.
(2) *Payment of a lump sum to the wife*: out of the plaintiff's damages, but ignoring certain
elements of them, a lump sum of £50,000. This was to be regarded as capitalised
periodical payments providing her with an income for life. The £18,000 award to the
j   plaintiff as the total value of his wife's services to him was regarded as going straight to
her and then being a capital sum in her hands for the purpose of making that assessment.
On payment of that sum, her claim for periodical payments and any claim under the
Inheritance (Provision for Family and Dependants) Act 1975 would be dismissed. The
lump sum was not ordered to be paid by the defendants, as happened in *Jones v Jones*
[1984] 3 All ER 1003, [1985] QB 704.

(3) *Brindle Lodge*: to be held on trust for sale, not to be sold for 9½ years until the twins reached the age of 18. Two-thirds of the proceeds to go to the wife and one-third to the *a* plaintiff. In the meantime the wife was to occupy it and be responsible for its maintenance and all its outgoings. The furniture and contents were to vest in her.

The current value of the house was taken as £90,000. The effect of this order regarding Brindle Lodge was that the plaintiff's existing half share in the house, now worth £45,000, was changed to one-third, worth £30,000, representing 'an immediate loss to him of £15,000'. In addition, he held that the plaintiff thereby lost the use of his £30,000 *b* interest for 9½ years, to that he applied an interest rate of 4½% net, making an annual sum of £1,350 lost. Giving that sum a multiplier of six years, the plaintiff was deprived of £18,100. The judge added to that the 'immediate loss' of £15,000, making the plaintiff's 'loss' on Brindle Lodge £23,100. This was held to be recoverable from the defendant, applying *Jones v Jones*, as losses stemming from the divorce.

(4) *31 Weavills Road*: it was held that the purchase of this house for the plaintiff was *c* reasonable. The defendants do not contest that a second house is necessary, but say this house was too large and (at £57,950) unreasonably expensive. The whole cost of purchase could not be recovered from the defendants. The judge applied the approach used in *George v Pinnock* [1973] 1 All ER 926, [1973] 1 WLR 118 and awarded the plaintiff 14 years' purchase of the loss of the use of that money at 4½% amounting to £36,500. Against that he set off the £23,100 representing the plaintiff's 'loss on the transfer of his *d* interest in Brindle Lodge to [the wife]' which could be utilised towards the purchase of his new home.

Alternatively, the sum of £36,500 represented the totality of his losses in relation to the two properties. In addition, £6,000 was awarded for additional costs of moving to and furnishing Weavills Road, and this sum is not now challenged.

There was a third element of cost relating to Weavills Road which was passed on as a *e* liability to the defendants. This was a sum of £10,500, representing a capitalised annual sum of £750 per annum, being the additional cost to the plaintiff of running the second house. It was not properly pleaded, nor was there any clear evidence directed to it, but there was enough to show that it does represent an expense that must be incurred by him. It was not excessive and ought not to be interfered with.

The result was that, by adding the three sums of £36,500 (the two houses), £6,000 *f* (removal costs) and £10,500 (additional cost of Weavills Road), £53,000 was added to the plaintiff's damages to be recovered from the defendants.

The defendants challenge this sum in several ways. First, it is said that the figures relating to Brindle Lodge are irrelevant. Whatever the size of the plaintiff's equity in Brindle Lodge, it was money which would have been locked up in that house in any event if there had been no divorce. Adjusting the sizes of the shares of the two spouses *g* from fifty-fifty to two-thirds, one-third did not create an 'immediate loss' of £15,000 to the plaintiff. For the same reason, he was not deprived of the use of his £30,000 either for 9½ years or at all. There was no 'loss' on Brindle Lodge of £23,100. This figure was an application of *Jones v Jones* and, for reasons which have been given already, an erroneous one. Moreover, the £30,000 which will be locked up in Brindle Lodge for 9½ years will *h* be released to him in 1995 and should be taken into credit, as counsel for the plaintiff has conceded.

The defendants' second objection is in the cost of £57,950 for Weavills Road. What was needed was a house big enough for the plaintiff and a housekeeper in the area of Chandlers Ford, which is where the Hexagon Centre is at which the plaintiff is to attend for work. The justification for the purchase of Weavills Road was that it contained an *j* extra bedroom in case the plaintiffs father or other relative wished in the future to spend the night there. On the other hand the defendants point out that there was evidence of plenty of suitable houses available in the neighbourhood at prices of not more than £40,000 which would have been a reasonable price to pay. The plaintiff's father lives no

a further away than Salisbury. The criticism of the £57,950 purchase price is justified, and £40,000 should be substituted in the Weavills Road calculations. Applying the reasoning of *George v Pinnock* it is right that since, because of his injuries, it has been necessary for the plaintiff to buy a second house, he is entitled to pass on to the defendants what it will cost him to be kept out of the use of the purchase price of that house. An annual loss of income from £40,000, based on 4½% and using the judge's multiplier of 14 years, produces a capital sum of £25,200. If one adds to that the cost of the move and furniture
b (£6,000) and the extra cost of running Weavills Road (£10,500) one gets a figure of £41,700.

From that sum, certain deductions must be made. The first is the plaintiff's concession that in 1995 he will be entitled to his £30,000 on the sale of Brindle Lodge. Therefore, for 9½ years Weavills Road will cost the income on £40,000, totalling £16,100. After 1995 Weavills Road will cost the income on £10,000 for another 4½ years, or £2,045.
c The loss of Weavills Road is therefore £18,145. To that must be added the sums of £6,000 and £10,500. The total loss to the plaintiff is now £34,645.

Tax savings

The other major question is that of tax savings. These were not applied by the judge.
d The defendants point out that the break-up of the family will produce considerable tax savings and if loss such as the cost of the purchase of 31 Weavills Road is to be charged to him there should be brought into account on the credit side what those savings will be to the plaintiff. We have been given the figures, without objection. They are substantial.

In future, instead of maintaining his children out of taxed income, he will do so out of gross income. In round figures, the tax saving to him will be £750 a year. If capitalised
e at six years' purchase until 1995, it will amount to £4,500.

Another tax saving is that he will not receive income from the £50,000 lump sum. Assuming a gross 10% return would have been received from that sum if left in the plaintiff's hands, the tax on that would be £1,450 per annum. Fourteen years' purchase of that is £20,300.

Thus far, tax savings to the plaintiff total £24,800.
f Against that must be set a new tax liability. The plaintiff will now receive a single person's allowance instead of a married man's allowance. The difference at present rates is £1,320. The tax on £1,320 is £382 per annum, which given by 14 years' purchase is £4,508. If that figure is deducted from the £24,800 saved, it means that the net tax savings capitalised over the appropriate periods come to £20,292.

This sum then requires to be substracted from the cost to the plaintiff of having to buy
g 31 Weavills Road. The sum is £34,645 minus £20,292, which is £14,353. In round figures that is £15,000.

The result would be that the award of £53,000 would be reduced to £15,000.

Interest

The defendants' last submission was that the award of interest on the special damage
h was too great.

They asked the trial judge to make a reduction in the 9½-year period, because the delay in bringing the case to trial was unjustified, as had been suggested in *Birkett v Hayes* [1982] 2 All ER 710, [1982] 1 WLR 816.

The judge acceded to that submission. He disallowed interest for two years, which reflected a period during which the plaintiff's solicitors had let the action go to sleep.
j The defendants now submit that the disallowance was not enough, and that the case ought to have been ready for trial even earlier than 7½ years after the accident. There is some justification for that submission, but the matter was one for the judge's discretion, and it has not been shown that he exercised it wrongly. Accordingly the reduction in interest will not be altered.

In the result, the appeal will be allowed in the manner indicated. The damages will be reduced to £362,126.

       a

SIR ROGER ORMROD. I agree that on the first ground this appeal fails, namely that the years' purchase should be counted from the date of the injury and not from the date of trial. Counsel for the defendants conceded that the judge had followed the general practice in personal injury cases but argued tenaciously that the practice should be changed and brought into line with that adopted in Fatal Accident Act cases. He put *b* forward two principal reasons: first, that the longer the time which elapses between accident and trial, the larger the overall amount of the award for loss of wages or salary; and, second, that the present practice produces higher awards than would the Fatal Accidents Act practice if applied to personal injury cases. The first puts a premium on delay, the second creates an anomaly between two cases identical in all respects except that in one case the man is gravely injured and in the other killed. With respect to the *c* careful argument of counsel for the defendants, I have not found that these are sufficiently convincing reasons for upsetting the established practice which would, inevitably, cause widespread confusion, and, as counsel for the plaintiff was able to demonstrate, produce some unacceptable results.

In my judgment, the only valid reason for changing the practice would be that it was producing awards which were unjustifiably high in that the sums awarded exceeded *d* those which were reasonably required to restore plaintiffs, so far as money can do so, to the position they would have been in if the accident had not happened. It is not enough to demonstrate that lapse of time has led to an award which is probably higher than it would have been had it been made within two or three years of the accident. Experience is a more reliable guide than hypothesis and a late award may be fairer than an earlier one. In any event, it is an inappropriate way of punishing or discouraging delay. *e* Similarly, it is not enough to point to the discrepancy with Fatal Accidents Act cases without showing that the Fatal Accidents Act practice is the fairer of the two.

The second main ground of appeal relates to those items which arise out of the divorce between the plaintiff and his wife, allowed by the judge on the authority of *Jones v Jones* [1984] 3 All ER 1003, [1985] QB 704. These items were characterised by the judge as *f* 'Loss arising in respect of the purchases of properties and in relation to the orders for financial relief made in divorce proceedings'. He quantified this under three heads as follows:

(1) In respect of Brindle Lodge and 31 Weavills Road, Bishopstoke   £36,500
(2) Legal and removal costs   £6,000   *g*
(3) Additional costs of maintaining two households   £10,500

                                          £53,000

The figure of £36,500, it is agreed, should be £25,750, making the total £42,250.   *h*

Counsel for the defendants has attacked the award of these items in two ways. First, he submits that *Jones v Jones* (which is the only authority for the proposition that expenditure arising out of a divorce is recoverable as part of the damages in an action for personal injuries) is wrong in law and ought not to be followed. He further contends that although it is a decision of this court, it is not binding on us because the question of principle was not argued and was, therefore, not decided. In any event the judge went *j* wrong in his assessment of the loss sustained by the plaintiff under this head.

It is useful to record at this stage some of the relevant facts and dates. The accident occurred on 28 June 1976. At that time the plaintiff was married with one child but his wife was pregnant. Twins were born on 18 January 1977. Up to the summer of 1983 the

family lived at 20 Twynham Close, Downton, a modest house in the joint names of the
a plaintiff and his wife. At this stage an interim payment of damages was made by the
defendant and it was used in part to finance the purchase of Brindle Lodge, Nunton, a
bigger and better house. Twynham Close was sold for £27,500 and Brindle Lodge was
bought in joint names for £77,500. On 6 June 1984, the wife filed a petition for divorce,
and a decree nisi was pronounced on 10 December 1984. Another interim payment was
made, and in July 1985 another house was bought for the plaintiff, 31 Weavills Road,
b Bishopstoke, for £57,950. Brindle Lodge was valued at £92,000 at this time. The
plaintiff's claim for damages and the wife's claims for financial provision for herself and
the children were ordered to be heard together by a judge of the Family Division and,
pursuant to that order, Swinton Thomas J gave judgment in both proceedings on 26
September 1985.

His judgment falls into three stages, reflecting the intrinsic difficulties of dealing with
c these two aspects of the case together, which are referred to in more detail later in this
judgment. In stage 1, the judge assessed the damages in the ordinary way and arrived at
a total figure of £381,126. Stage 2 was the determination of the wife's claim for ancillary
relief in the divorce proceedings. Basing himself presumably on the figure of £381,126
as the total resources to be taken into account and applying the criteria of s 25 of the
Matrimonial Causes Act 1973 as amended he made the following orders: periodical
d payments for the children: 1 × £18 per week, 2 × £16 per week less tax, payable direct
to the children: £2,600 per annum; lump sum for wife: £50,000 (wife's claim for
periodical payments and under the Inheritance Act dismissed); wife to occupy Brindle
Lodge until twins attain the age of 18 years; house then to be sold and net proceeds of
sale divided as to 66% to the wife and 33% to the husband.

At stage 3 the judge returned to the assessment of the claim for damages and added a
e further £53,000 representing the 'recoverable loss' from the divorce, as already set out.

It is not possible to decide whether Jones v Jones is binding on us without first examining
the argument that it was wrongly decided, because the case of counsel for the defendants
is that none of the grounds on which he relies were put before the court in Jones v Jones.
So, without disrespect to that court, it will be convenient first to approach the question
f of principle de novo.

In my judgment, the first question is whether orders made under ss 23 and 24 of the
Matrimonial Causes Act 1973, that is orders for financial provision and property
adjustment orders, can cause a 'loss' to a spouse who is plaintiff in an action for damages
for personal injuries.

Orders under these sections are different from the orders which the court used to make
g under the previous divorce legislation, and the philosophy underlying them is different.
Under the previous regime husbands were ordered to make periodical payments
(permanent maintenance) out of their own resources to discharge their legal obligations
to support their former wives and children. The reforms of 1969–70 abolished the
matrimonial offence as the basis for divorce and substituted the concept of 'irretrievable
breakdown of marriage', and at the same time changed the basis for post-divorce financial
h and property settlements from 'support' to 'adjustment' of property rights and obligations
to meet the new situation. The court now has jurisdiction over all the assets or resources
of the couple and has unfettered powers over both capital and income. Section 25 requires
the court to have regard to all the 'resources' of the parties and to take into account their
needs and liabilities and their contributions both past and future to the welfare of the
family.

j The effect of these orders is, essentially, to adjust the availability of resources to needs
in the post-divorce situation. This means that both resources and obligations formerly
enjoyed or/and discharged jointly must now be separated, which means quantified and
identified.

It follows that these orders neither add to nor reduce the total of the assets available to

the spouses before the divorce: they merely redistribute them. This process can be most
clearly demonstrated in relation to the order for periodical payments for the children.
Before the divorce both parents were jointly responsible for providing a home for the
children, supporting them and bringing them up. This liability was not quantified or
identified but though inchoate it was a real liability. Under the order the husband's
obligation is now defined, quantified and limited to £2,600 per annum less tax unless
and until the order is varied. It is not possible to quantify the effect of the order on the
husband's financial position so that no 'loss' can be proved; quantification of an inchoate
obligation cannot in any event produce a 'loss' in any ordinary sense.

The £50,000 lump sum was intended as a capitalisation of the wife's periodical
payments but might equally well have been a simple transfer of capital. There again
during the marriage the wife is entitled to look to the resources of the family for all her
normal needs. Her claim on, or her share of, the joint resources was inchoate but none
the less real. On divorce, it has to be quantified and, as the funds are in the name of the
husband, he has to make the appropriate transfer. Here again no 'loss' is involved and
thereafter the husband has the enjoyment of the balance of the capital unencumbered by
inchoate claims by the wife or the children.

The position in relation to Brindle Lodge is slightly different. It is owned jointly by
husband and wife in equal shares. it would have been feasible for the judge to order it to
be sold and the proceeds divided equally. On the evidence, each share would have been
worth about £45,000, and each party could have bought a house for himself and herself
for about £40,000. If this had been done no 'loss' would have been caused to the husband
except in standard of housing. Instead, the judge decided in the interest of the children
to defer the sale for nine years or so. This entails a loss of interest on the husband's share
but it is part of his contribution to the maintenance and upbringing of his children. Had
the house been sold immediately the orders for periodical payments might have been
increased. The judge also reduced the husband's interest in the house from one-half to
one-third and increased the wife's accordingly. This does no more than to adjust their
respective interests to take account of the assumption by the wife of the full responsibility
for making a home and a life for the children, and of the corresponding relief to the
husband.

For these reasons, financial and property adjustment orders made after a divorce should
not in my judgment be regarded as producing a loss vis-à-vis third parties. They should
be regarded as a distribution of a previously undistributed whole, providing each party
with a separate fund out of which to provide for himself and herself and for their
obligations to the children, if any. It follows, if this reasoning be right, that the three
items allowed by the judge as additions to his figure of £381,126 are not recoverable
against the defendants as part of the damages.

If, however, this part of the claim cannot be disposed of in this way, the other criticisms
of counsel for the defendants must be considered. It was conceded in this case, as it was
in *Jones v Jones* [1984] 3 All ER 1003, [1985] QB 704, that it was 'foreseeable' that if a
person were injured by the negligence of the defendant he might sustain severe head
injuries, which might produce a personality change, which might lead to breakdown of
marriage, divorce, and presumably financial and property adjustment orders. Rightly or
wrongly this seems to me to attenuate the concept of 'foreseeability' to the point when
its value as a measure of damage is greatly diminished. In fact, it is conceded that not all
'foreseeable' loss is recoverable and that there must be some limits.

Subject to *Jones v Jones*, there is, in my judgment, a strong case for holding that the
limit should be set at a point which excludes the consequences of divorce from the
assessment of damages in personal injury actions. It is not particularly important to
decide which label to apply, though 'remoteness', 'novus actus interveniens' or 'indirect
economic loss' are possibilities. The fact remains that from a pragmatic point of view the
inclusion of such a head of damage leads to great difficulties. It is significant that no
attempt to include it had ever been made before *Jones v Jones*.

These difficulties were present in both *Jones v Jones* and in this case. At first instance in
Jones v Jones Stocker J was able to avoid the difficulties by holding that there was no
evidence of loss arising out of the divorce in that case. But the plaintiff overcame that by
obtaining a consent order in the county court after Stocker J's judgment for payment to
the wife of a lump sum of £25,000. Additional evidence was admitted in the Court of
Appeal, the appeal was allowed and the award of damages increased by £15,000. In this
case, the action and the claim for financial provision in the divorce were heard by the
same judge, simultaneously. But this is only an apparent solution. The judge, as has been
pointed out already, had to split his judgment into three stages: damages, financial
provision, and more damages. This means that it is impossible to avoid circularity and to
reach finality because the financial provision depends on the damages and the damages
on the financial provision and so on.

The next difficulty is that the divorce orders are wholly discretionary. If it is permissible
to pass on the cost of these orders in whole or part to the defendants in the civil action,
they ought to have a sufficient interest to be represented in the proceedings for financial
provision etc.

An order might be reasonable between husband and wife but quite unreasonable vis-
à-vis the defendants. The order in relation to Brindle Lodge is a case in point.

There are other anomalies. If the marriage breaks down after judgment has been
entered in the civil action the so-called loss from the divorce will be irrecoverable. So
people will be well advised to get a decree nisi before judgment in the action. Other
possibilities are that judges will be asked to assess the chances of breakdown of marriage
and make an allowance for it in their assessments of damage. Further difficulties arise
over quantification. The cliche 'It always costs more to keep two homes' is not by any
means universally true. With social security benefits at one end of the scale and tax
savings at the other, it may actually be cheaper. Junior counsel for the defendants'
interesting calculations of the tax effects of the orders in this case revealed surprising
advantages for the husband.

These considerations suggest to my mind that the financial consequences of divorce
should be regarded as too remote to be recoverable or alternatively excluded as indirect
economic loss or, failing both of these, excluded as a matter of policy.

I turn now to the question of whether any of these arguments can be allowed to affect
our minds in the light of the decision of this court in *Jones v Jones*. I am satisfied that we
can and should re-examine this important issue of principle. Counsel for the defendants
in that case virtually conceded that damages were recoverable for the financial
consequences of divorce, subject to his submission that as a matter of policy it should not
be permitted, but he advanced only one reason for this, namely the 'floodgates' argument.
This was rejected by Dunn LJ, in giving the judgment of the court, as it usually is. It is
clear, however, that none of the arguments put to us by counsel for the defendants were
put to the court in *Jones v Jones* and there is nothing to indicate that they or any of them
were in the mind of the court when it reached its decision. In my view, therefore, we
are not bound to hold as a matter of principle that damages are recoverable under this
head.

Finally, I do not think that the three items awarded under this head of damages
were adequately proved. So far as the loss ascribed to the property transactions (£36,500
now reduced to £25,750) is concerned, this, in my opinion, was caused by the decision
that Brindle Lodge was not to be sold immediately but was to be retained until the
children were 18 years of age. As I have said, both parties could have rehoused
themselves adequately without loss out of the proceeds of sale of Brindle Lodge. The
legal and removal costs are largely speculative. As for the additional cost of maintaining two households, I think, in view of the tax advantages, that this may be an
illusory loss.

I would therefore allow this appeal in regard to the items arising out of the divorce
and reduce the judge's award of damages by £53,000. I also agree that the general

damages should be reduced to £50,000 and the item for the plaintiff's services should be reduced to £9,000.

Appeal allowed. Damages reduced to the sum of £362,126 plus interest. No order as to costs. Leave to appeal to the House of Lords refused.

Solicitors: Sharpe Pritchard & Co, agents for C A Norris, Ringwood (for the defendants); Trethowans, Salisbury (for the plaintiff).

Patricia Hargrove   Barrister.

Chief Constable of Avon and Somerset v Fleming

QUEEN'S BENCH DIVISION
GLIDEWELL LJ AND OTTON J
30 OCTOBER 1986

Road traffic – Motor vehicle – Motor cycle – Motor cycle manufactured for road use but adapted for use in scrambling on private land – Whether motor cycle a 'motor vehicle' – Road Traffic Act 1972, s 190.

The respondent was stopped by police when pushing his motor cycle on a public road. The motor cycle had been manufactured for road use but had been adapted for the sport of 'scrambling' on private land by the removal of its registration plate, reflectors, lights and speedometer. The respondent did not have a driving licence, insurance or protective headgear when he was stopped. He was charged under the Road Traffic Act 1972 with various offences relating to the driving and use of a 'motor vehicle'. The court found that the description of the vehicle proffered by the police was vague and unsatisfactory and held that the police had not proved that the motor cycle was a 'motor vehicle' within s 190[a] of the 1972 Act. On appeal by the prosecution by way of case stated, the question arose whether the respondent's motor cycle had lost its status as a 'motor vehicle'.

Held – The test of whether a vehicle was a 'mechanically propelled vehicle intended or adapted for use on roads' and therefore a 'motor vehicle' for the purposes of s 190 of the 1972 Act was whether a reasonable person, looking at the vehicle, would say that its general use encompassed possible general road use, and the particular user to which a particular person put a vehicle was irrelevant. A vehicle originally manufactured for use on a road could cease to be a 'motor vehicle' for the purposes of s 190 if it was subsequently altered but only if such alterations were very substantial. Because the exact description of the vehicle was vague and unsatisfactory the court had been entitled to find that the police had not proved that the motor cycle was a motor vehicle and the prosecution's appeal would accordingly be dismissed (see p 322 d e h j and p 323 c to f, post).

Burns v Currell [1963] 2 All ER 297 applied.

Notes
For the meaning of motor vehicle, see 40 Halsbury's Laws (4th edn) para 76, and for cases on the subject, see 39(1) Digest (Reissue) 415–417, 3297–3305.

For the Road Traffic Act 1972, s 190, see 42 Halsbury's Statutes (3rd edn) 1829.

---

a   Section 190, so far as material, is set out at p 320 c, post

Cases referred to in judgments

a   *Burns v Currell* [1963] 2 All ER 297, [1963] 2 QB 433, [1963] 2 WLR 1106, DC.
   Daley v Hargreaves [1961] 1 All ER 552, [1961] 1 WLR 487, DC.
   O'Brien v Anderton [1979] RTR 388, DC.

Case stated

The Chief Constable of Avon and Somerset Constabulary appealed by way of case stated
b   by justices for the county of Avon acting in and for the petty sessional division of Bristol
in respect of their adjudication as a juvenile court sitting at Bristol on 7 February 1986
whereby they dismissed informations laid by the appellant charging the respondent,
Andrew Fleming, with the offences of (1) driving a motor vehicle when not the holder
of a driving licence authorising him to drive that vehicle, contrary to s 84(1) of the Road
Traffic Act 1972, (2) using a motor vehicle without insurance in force to cover his use,
c   contrary to s 143 of the 1972 Act, (3) using a motor vehicle with no test certificate in
force, contrary to s 44 of the 1972 Act, (4) using a motor vehicle not equipped with
obligatory lights, contrary to reg 16(1) of the Road Vehicles Lighting Regulations 1984,
SI 1984/812, and s 40 of the 1972 Act, (5) driving a motor vehicle on a road when not
wearing protective headgear, contrary to ss 32 and 78 of the 1972 Act and reg 4 of the
Motor Cycles (Protective Helmets) Regulations 1980, SI 1980/1279, (6) using a motor
d   vehicle not fitted with a speedometer, contrary to reg 18 of the Motor Vehicles
(Construction and Use) Regulations 1978, SI 1978/1017, and s 40 of the 1972 Act, and (7)
using a motor vehicle not equipped with reflectors on a road, contrary to reg 16(1) of the
1984 regulations and s 40 of the 1972 Act. The questions for the opinion of the court
were: (1) whether if a motor bicycle was originally constructed and intended for use on
roads at the time of its manufacture, its status as a 'motor vehicle' for the purposes of
e   s 190 of the Road Traffic Act 1972 (and hence also s 136 of the Road Traffic Regulation
Act 1984) could be altered by a person making modifications to that motor cycle, and (2)
if so, whether the removal of the lights, speedometer, number plates and reflectors was
sufficient adaptation of a motor cycle so that it ceased to be a 'motor vehicle' within the
meaning of s 190. The facts are set out in the judgment of Glidewell LJ.

f   *Richard Stead* for the appellant.
   Richard Bromilow for the respondent.

GLIDEWELL LJ. This is an appeal by way of case stated by justices for the county of
Avon sitting as a juvenile court at Bristol. Appeals from the juvenile court to this court
g   are relatively rare and even rarer in motoring cases, such as this is. It is a case in which
the appellant is concerned about the dangers inherent in the use by young men of motor
cycles which they normally use off the highway but which from time to time they may
be tempted to use on the highway.

What the appellant, we are told, is really seeking is some guidance. Whether this case
is one which provides a useful vehicle for such guidance I very much doubt, as will
h   emerge from the way in which the justices stated the case.

The respondent, whose age we do not know precisely save that he is a juvenile, was
charged on informations alleging no less than seven offences arising out of his alleged use
of a motor vehicle on 12 June 1985 on a road in the St Annes district of Bristol. One of
the alleged offences was driving a motor vehicle when not the holder of a driving licence.
The others all related to the alleged user of the motor vehicle: in the first case without
j   insurance; in the second case with no test certificate and, in the other cases, in relation to
the absence of various parts of the vehicle or of safety equipment for himself, all of which
are required by regulations.

The facts found by the justices are that on the day in question, on Ripon Road, St
Annes, Bristol, the respondent was moving a mechanically propelled two-wheeled vehicle
on a road. He was pushing it. The justices make it quite clear that they did, in view of

the conclusion to which they came, consider whether he was driving it. The conclusion
to which they came was that the vehicle was not a 'motor vehicle' within the meaning of
s 190 of the Road Traffic Act 1972 and thus that none of the offences were made out.
They found that the vehicle had been manufactured for road use. It had not been
registered, although the engine fitted to it was from a registered motor cycle. On the day
in question the vehicle had no registration plate, no reflectors, no lights and no
speedometer. It was acquired by the respondent in that condition. It had not been altered
or adapted by him in any way. Not unnaturally the respondent did not have a driving
licence or any insurance. He had not passed a driving test and he was not wearing
protective headgear. They found that he had been riding the vehicle on land not forming
part of the road and that he was moving the vehicle from that land to his home when he
was seen by police officers. They do not say this in terms, but it seems a clear inference
that he had been involved in the sport of scrambling on private land and was pushing
this motor bicycle back from the field where he had been scrambling to his home when
he was stopped.

The definition in s 190 of the 1972 Act of a motor vehicle is 'a mechanically propelled
vehicle intended or adapted for use on roads'. Section 190 also defines a motor cycle as 'a
mechanically propelled vehicle, not being an invalid carriage, with less than four wheels
and the weight of which unladen does not exceed 410 kilograms'.

Those two definitions taken together mean that something may be a motor cycle but
not a motor vehicle if it is mechanically propelled and has less than four wheels, but is
not intended or adapted for use on roads. It may be, for instance, that some motor cycles
used at speedway tracks come into that category.

The contention on behalf of the appellant was that the vehicle was a motor vehicle
because it had been manufactured for use on the roads and that taking some parts off it
could not change that status. The respondent, who represented himself we are told, said
that the vehicle had been adapted not to be used on the roads before he acquired it and
that it was in that state when he was seen by police officers. The justices unfortunately
were not referred to any cases. Perhaps in the circumstances in the juvenile court it was
understandable but it was unfortunate, because there is in the authorities a certain
amount of learning, to which I will come in a moment, on what constitutes a motor
vehicle within the definition of the 1970 Act. Before I do that, it is right that I should go
on to read out the way in which the justices set out their opinion. They said this:

> 'We were of opinion that Section 190 of the Road Traffic Act, 1972 which defines
> a "motor vehicle" for the purposes of that Act as "a mechanically propelled vehicle
> intended or adapted for use on roads" contemplates the possibility of an alteration
> to the status of a vehicle to or from that of a "motor vehicle" during its life. The
> words do not import, as would words such as "manufactured", "constructed" or
> "designed" for use on roads, that the manufacturer of a vehicle can fix its status
> forever. We considered that it was a question of fact and degree in any particular
> case whether a particular vehicle, which had started life as a "motor vehicle" had
> ceased to be "intended or adapted for use on roads." The evidence before us as to the
> exact description of the vehicle in question was vague and unsatisfactory and, the
> Respondent having raised the issue of whether it was a "motor vehicle" or not, we
> were conscious of the burden on the Appellant to prove beyond reasonable doubt
> that it was such. We were not satisfied on the evidence presented, so as to be sure of
> the status of the vehicle. Accordingly, as each of the informations before us required
> proof that the vehicle used or driven (as the case may be) was a motor vehicle, we
> dismissed all seven informations.'

They then posed two questions for this court. The first is:

> 'if a motor bicycle is originally constructed and intended for use on roads at the
> time of its manufacture, can its status as a "motor vehicle" for the purposes of Section

a   190 of the Road Traffic Act, 1972 (and hence, also Section 136 of the Road Traffic
Regulation Act, 1984) be altered by a person making modifications to that motor
cycle?'

The second question is:

b   'if the above question is answered in the affirmative, is the removal of the lights,
speedometer, number plates and reflectors sufficient adaptation of the motor cycle
so that it ceases to be a "motor vehicle" within the meaning of the sections
mentioned?'

I have already said that the appellant brings this case because he is asking for guidance
and, of course, he is entitled to the guidance of this court. He has also made it clear in
correspondence and through counsel acting on his behalf this morning, that if we allow
the appeal he is not asking us to send this particular case back to the magistrates. The
c   respondent is in no danger of being convicted. The matter does, however, go somewhat
further than that because the appellant is coming close to posing a theoretical question
for the court. However, we will do our best to give some guidance.

The principal authority to which we were referred on this branch of the law is the
decision of this court in *Burns v Currell* [1963] 2 All ER 297, [1963] 2 QB 433. That was a
d   case in which the vehicle in question was a go-kart, that is to say a self-propelled vehicle
mounted on four small wheels with a single seat and a steering wheel and column. It had
a silencer and brakes but it was not fitted with a horn, mirrors, springs or various other
requirements of the Motor Vehicles (Construction and Use) Regulations 1955, SI 1955/
482. The driver was seated on the vehicle on a public road. He was not insured against
third party risks. Various informations arising out of that use were preferred against
e   him. He contended that the go-kart was not intended or adapted for use on the roads
within the appropriate section of the then legislation, the Road Traffic Act 1960. The
justices were of the opinion that the go-kart was a motor vehicle and convicted him. He
appealed. The headnote reads ([1963] 2 QB 433 at 434):

'. . . in determining whether a vehicle was "intended" for use on roads, the test to
f   be applied was whether a reasonable person, looking at the vehicle, would say that
one of its users was a road user; the question was not whether there was an isolated
user, or a user in an emergency, but whether some general use on the road was
contemplated as one of the users.'

The court took the view that there was no evidence before the justices to satisfy them
beyond reasonable doubt that any reasonable person would say of this go-kart that one of
g   its users would be a use on the road. Accordingly, the appeal was allowed.

The main passage is contained in the judgment of Lord Parker CJ where he said
([1963] 2 All ER 297 at 300, [1963] 2 QB 433 at 440–441):

'Thus, in the ordinary case, it seems to me that there will be little difficulty in
saying whether a particular vehicle is a motor vehicle or not. But to define exactly
h   the meaning of the words "intended or adapted" is by no means easy. For my part, I
think that the expression "intended", to take that word first, does not mean
"intended by the user of the vehicle either at the moment of the alleged offence or
for the future". I do not think that it means the intention of the manufacturer or
the wholesaler or the retailer; and it may be, as SALMON, J., said in *Daley's* case [see
Daley v Hargreaves [1961] 1 All ER 552, [1961] 1 WLR 487] that it is not referring
j   to the intention as such of any particular purpose. SALMON, J., suggested that the
word "intended" might be paraphrased as "suitable or apt". It may be merely a
difference of wording, but I prefer to make the test whether a reasonable person
looking at the vehicle would say that one of its users would be a road user. In
deciding that question, the reasonable man would not, as I conceive, have to envisage

what some man losing his senses would do with a vehicle; nor an isolated user or a
user in an emergency. The real question is: is some general use on the roads *a*
contemplated as one of the users? Approaching the matter in that way at the end of
the case, the justices would have to ask themselves: has it been proved beyond a
reasonable doubt that any reasonable person looking at the Go-Kart would say that
one of its uses would be use on the road? For my part, I have come to the conclusion
that there really was no such evidence before them as to satisfy them on that point
according to the ordinary standard of proof. The evidence was that the appellant *b*
had used this vehicle on this day alone and that he had never used it before. There
was no evidence that other people used these vehicles on the road, nor is it suggested
by the justices that they came to their conclusion, as they would be entitled to up to
a point, on their own experience and knowledge. As I have said, all that they had
before them was that a Go-Kart had been used on a road to which the public had
access on this one occasion. Looked at in that way, so far as this matter of "intended" *c*
is concerned, I do not think that the justices had any material on which they could
feel sure so as to be able to convict.'

I emphasise that that test is what would be the view of the reasonable man as to the
general user of this particular vehicle, not what was the particular user to which this
particular appellant put it, either at the time in question or, indeed, generally. In other *d*
words, if a reasonable man were to say, 'Yes, this vehicle might well be used on the road',
then, applying the test, the vehicle is intended or adapted for such use. If that be the case,
it is nothing to the point if the individual defendant says: 'I normally use it for scrambling
and I am only pushing it along the road on this occasion because I have no other means
of getting it home', or something of that sort.

Another decision of this court to which we were referred, though counsel for the *e*
appellant accurately told us that it did not lay down any further principle than that
contained in *Burns v Currell* is *O'Brien v Anderton* [1979] RTR 388. In that case the
defendant, who was also a juvenile of 14, was riding what is described as an 'Italget'
motor cycle on a road. He was not wearing a crash helmet. He was uninsured. There was
no excise licence for the vehicle. He was charged with a variety of offences arising out of
that. The justices found that the 'Italget' was a mechanically propelled vehicle within the *f*
definition of a motor vehicle in s 190 of the 1970 Act. It was a two-wheeled vehicle
propelled by a 22 cc internal combustion engine with a seat and handle bars for carrying
its rider. It was the defendant who appealed. The Divisional Court said that the justices
had applied the right test, that it was a matter of fact for them and that there was plenty
of material on which they could conclude that that vehicle was a motor vehicle. That
vehicle, it seems, was in its original state. *g*

There may in practice be a difference, and it may be a difference which is very often of
importance in a case such as this, between a vehicle which is in its original state and a
vehicle which has been altered since it was first constructed. If a vehicle such as a go-kart
in its original state does not have many of the attributes of a vehicle which is normally
going to be used on a road, it may be that justices will have no great difficulty in
concluding that the vehicle is not intended or adapted for use on a road. But if a vehicle *h*
was originally manufactured for use on a road and thereafter is altered, then the approach
may properly be to consider whether the degree of alteration is so great as to bring the
vehicle outside the definition of 'motor vehicle' in s 190. In my view, once a vehicle has
been manufactured as one which is intended or adapted for use on a road, it would
require very substantial, indeed dramatic, alteration, if it could be said no longer to be a
'motor vehicle'. Counsel for the appellant gave an example, which may well be *j*
appropriate, of a motor vehicle being fitted with spiked or studded tyres on wheels which
meant that it could not be driven on a public road but only on soft ground. It may be
that justices confronted with a vehicle of that sort would be justified in finding that it
was not intended or adapted for use on the road. But, short of some major alteration of

that kind, it seems to me improbable that a vehicle originally manufactured as a motor
a vehicle would lose that character.

Whether the detachment of parts of a vehicle which are required by the relevant
regulations on a motor vehicle if it is to be used on a public road would turn that vehicle
into one which any reasonable person would say was no longer intended or adapted for
use on a road, is of course a question of fact for the justices. I will go so far as to venture
the opinion that it is improbable that the mere omission of the items referred to in the
b second question without more would suffice to change the status of a vehicle which
originally was a motor vehicle into one which was not. But the difficulty with this case,
so far as this court is concerned, is the difficulty that the justices themselves found, that
is to say, they make the point very firmly that the evidence before them as to the exact
description of the vehicle in question was vague and unsatisfactory. In *O'Brien v Anderton*
the justices had, and indeed it is clear from the report that the Divisional Court had,
c photographs of the vehicle in question and a fairly detailed description of it. These
justices did not. In the end, they decided that since the onus of proof was on the
prosecution to prove that the vehicle was indeed a motor vehicle, they could not be
satisfied that it was within the definition.

For myself, I cannot find that they were in any sense wrong or perverse in taking that
attitude. Indeed, the questions posed in the case do not ask us to say that they were. They
d go only part of the way towards dealing with the problem that the justices had to deal
with.

The first question, 'if a motor bicycle is originally constructed and intended for use on
roads at the time of its manufacture, can its status as a "motor vehicle" . . . be altered by a
person making modifications to that motor cycle', it is conceded, can only be answered
Yes. As to the second question, since the facts in relation to this matter are so unclear, I
e would decline to answer it in this case, but I hope that in what I have already said I have
given guidance that may be of assistance in the future. In the light of what I have said
about the justices' finding, my view is that this appeal should be dismissed.

OTTON J. I agree, and for all the reasons given by Glidewell LJ.

f *Appeal dismissed.*

Solicitors: *Blyth Dutton*, agents for *R O M Lovibond*, Bristol (for the appellant); *Sansbury Hill
& Co*, Bristol (for the respondent).

Raina Levy   Barrister.

R v Secretary of State for the Home Department and another, ex parte Herbage (No 2)

COURT OF APPEAL, CIVIL DIVISION

MAY, PURCHAS LJJ AND SIR DAVID CAIRNS

2, 3 SEPTEMBER, 5 NOVEMBER 1986

Judicial review – Leave to apply for judicial review – Procedure for challenging grant of leave – Applicant granted discovery pending hearing of application for judicial review – Respondents appealing against order for discovery – Respondents seeking on appeal to challenge grant of leave to apply for judicial review – Whether court having jurisdiction on discovery appeal to set aside grant of leave to apply for judicial review – Supreme Court Act 1981, s 16(1) – RSC Ord 53, r 3.

Prison – Prison conditions – Cruel and unusual punishments – Prisoner housed in psychiatric wing of prison hospital although not suffering any psychiatric illness – Prisoner disturbed at night by mentally disturbed patients – Prisoner complaining that conditions amounted to infliction of 'cruell and unusuall punishments' contrary to Bill of Rights – Whether governor's care of prisoner open to judicial review – Bill of Rights.

The applicant was detained in prison awaiting an extradition warrant for his surrender to the United States of America in respect of 25 charges of dishonesty. Because of his medical condition (he was obese and unable to walk upstairs) the applicant was accommodated on the ground floor of the hospital wing of the prison where psychiatric patients were kept. The applicant complained that he was unable to sleep at night because of shouting, screaming and banging from mentally disturbed patients and he made other specific complaints about the conditions in which he was detained. He contended that such conditions amounted to the infliction of 'cruell and unusuall punishments' contrary to the Bill of Rights[a] and that because they had carried out their duties under the Prison Act 1952 and the Prison Rules 1964 in a manner which was in breach of the Bill of Rights and the Convention for the Protection of Human Rights and Fundamental Freedoms the Secretary of State for the Home Department and the prison governor had acted and were acting illegally. The applicant was granted leave ex parte under RSC Ord 53, r 3[b] to apply for judicial review by way of an order of mandamus directing the prison governor and the Secretary of State to detain him according to law. Pending the hearing of the application the applicant obtained an order for discovery of all medical and psychiatric reports on him during his remand in custody. The Secretary of State and the governor appealed against the order for discovery, contending (1) that the order for discovery should not have been made because as a matter of law leave to apply for judicial review ought not to have been granted, since judicial review could not go to control the prison governor's exercise of his managerial function in the prison and there was nothing for the court to review in regard to the Secretary of State's actions because he had not given any instructions or reached any decision about the circumstances of the applicant's detention, and (2) that it was open to the respondents to challenge the grant of leave to

---

a The Bill of Rights, so far as material, provides: '. . . That excessive baile ought not to be required nor excessive fines imposed nor cruell and unusuall punishments inflicted . . .'

b Rule 3, so far as material, provides:
  '(1) No application for judicial review shall be made unless the leave of the Court has been obtained in accordance with this rule.
  (2) An application for leave must be made *ex parte* to a judge . . .'

apply for judicial review on the appeal because the application for discovery was the first
time that the argument against leave could be rehearsed inter partes.

Held (May LJ dissenting) – The appropriate procedure for challenging leave granted ex
parte under RSC Ord 53, r 3 to apply for judicial review was either by an application
under the inherent jurisdiction of the court to the judge who granted the leave or by way
of an appeal under the general appellate jurisdiction conferred by s 16(1)[c] of the Supreme
Court Act 1981. Accordingly, having regard to the availability of those remedies, the
grant of such leave could not be challenged on an application for discovery in the judicial
review proceedings or on an appeal against the order for discovery, and it was therefore
not open to the court in the present proceedings to set aside the order giving leave to
apply for judicial review. The appeal would accordingly be dismissed (see p 335 *c* to *g j*
to p 336 *d*, p 337 *h* and p 339 *e* to *h*, post).

Per Purchas LJ and Sir David Cairns. The right under the Bill of Rights not to be
inflicted with 'cruell and unusuall punishments' is a fundamental right going beyond
the ambit of the 1964 rules and accordingly the court has jurisdiction to grant relief
under RSC Ord 53 if it is established that a prison governor has been guilty of such
conduct (see p 337 *d j* to p 338 *b* and p 339 *e j*, post); *Congreve v Home Office* [1976] 1 All
ER 697 and *A-G v Wilts United Dairies* (1922) 91 LJKB 897 applied; *R v Deputy Governor of
Camphill Prison, ex p King* [1984] 3 All ER 897 distinguished.

Notes

For officials and bodies amenable to mandamus, see 1 Halsbury's Laws (4th edn) para
100, and for cases on the subject, see 16 Digest (Reissue) 365–366, 3866–3874.

For liberties guaranteed by the Bill of Rights and enforcement of those rights, see 8
Halsbury's Laws (4th edn) paras 830, 838.

For the Bill of Rights, see 10 Halsbury's Statutes (4th edn) 44.

For the Prison Act 1952, see 25 Halsbury's Statutes (3rd edn) 828.

For the Supreme Court Act 1981, s 16, see 11 Halsbury's Statutes (4th edn) 772.

For the Prison Rules 1964, see 18 Halsbury's Statutory Instruments (4th reissue) 10.

f Cases referred to in judgments

A-G v Wilts United Dairies (1922) 91 LJKB 897, HL; *affg* 37 TLR 884, CA.
Becker v Noel [1971] 2 All ER 1248, [1971] 1 WLR 803, CA.
Congreve v Home Office [1976] 1 All ER 697, [1976] QB 629, [1976] 2 WLR 291, CA.
Council of Civil Service Unions v Minister for the Civil Service [1984] 3 All ER 935, [1985] AC
374, [1984] 3 WLR 1174, HL.
IRC v National Federation of Self-Employed and Small Businesses Ltd [1981] 2 All ER 93,
[1982] AC 617, [1981] 2 WLR 722, HL.
Khawaja v Secretary of State for the Home Dept [1983] 1 All ER 765, [1984] AC 74, [1983] 2
WLR 321, HL.
O'Reilly v Mackman [1982] 3 All ER 1124, [1983] 2 AC 237, [1982] 3 WLR 1096, HL.
R v Deputy Governor of Camphill Prison, ex p King [1984] 3 All ER 897, [1985] QB 735,
[1985] 2 WLR 36, CA.
R v Hull Prison Board of Visitors, ex p St Germain [1979] 1 All ER 701, [1979] QB 425,
[1979] 2 WLR 42, CA.
WEA Records Ltd v Visions Channel 4 Ltd [1983] 2 All ER 589, [1983] 1 WLR 721, CA.

Cases also cited

Buckley v Law Society [1983] 2 All ER 1039, [1983] 1 WLR 985.
Hunter v Chief Constable of West Midlands [1981] 3 All ER 727, [1982] AC 529, HL.

---

c   Section 16(1), so far as material, provides: 'Subject as otherwise provided . . . the Court of Appeal
shall have jurisdiction to hear and determine appeals from any judgment or order of the High
Court.'

R v East Berkshire Health Authority, ex p Walsh [1984] 3 All ER 425, [1985] AC 154, HL.
R v Governor of Brixton Prison, ex p Anderson (1 May 1986, unreported), QBD.
R v Lancashire CC, ex p Huddleston [1986] 2 All ER 941, CA.
R v Secretary of State for the Environment, ex p Greater London Council [1985] CA Transcript 67.
R v Secretary of State for the Home Dept, ex p McAvoy [1984] 3 All ER 417, [1984] 1 WLR 1408.
Smiths Ltd v Middleton [1986] 2 All ER 539, [1986] 1 WLR 598, CA.

Interlocutory appeal

The Secretary of State for the Home Department and the governor of HM Prison, Pentonville, where the applicant, Alex William Herbage, was detained while awaiting extradition to the United States of America, appealed with leave against the order of Hodgson J, hearing the Crown Office list on 22 May 1986, that the Secretary of State and the governor disclose whether they had at any time in their possession, custody or power any medical or psychiatric reports concerning the applicant since his remand in custody on 1 August 1985 and in particular disclose all reports concerning the applicant written and submitted by Dr Rees, a psychiatrist and medical officer at Pentonville Prison and/or arising out of any observations by Dr Rees concerning the applicant. The facts are set out in the judgment of May LJ.

John Laws for the Secretary of State and the governor.
Alan Newman and *Delroy Duncan* for the applicant.

Cur adv vult

5 November. The following judgments were delivered.

MAY LJ. In this case we are concerned with an appeal against an order for discovery in judicial review proceedings. The latter comprised an application for an order of mandamus directed to the governor of HM Prison Pentonville and the Secretary of State for the Home Department directing them to detain the applicant according to law.

The applicant, Alex William Herbage, is the subject of extradition proceedings at the instance of the United States government in respect of a total of 25 charges of obtaining by deception, false accounting and handling stolen goods. A metropolitan stipendiary magistrate sitting at Bow Street made an order on 25 March 1986 committing the applicant in custody to await the extradition warrant of the Secretary of State for his surrender to the United States of America in respect of those charges. An application for an order of habeas corpus by way of appeal against the magistrates' order was dismissed by the Divisional Court (Stephen Brown LJ and Otton J) on 30 July 1986. There is a petition by way of further appeal to the House of Lords pending[1].

The applicant himself is greatly overweight. He is aged 56 and at one point was at least 35 stones. His condition prevented him from walking upstairs. From August until October 1985 he was held in Winchester Prison. He was then transferred to Pentonville Prison, which is the one which holds male prisoners who are the subject of extradition proceedings. On his transfer, the applicant was immediately referred to the prison medical authorities at Pentonville and they directed that having regard to his condition he should be kept in the hospital wing of that establishment. That wing extends to two floors. The ground floor contains offices and accommodation reserved for prisoners who are mentally disturbed in varying degrees. The quieter patients are housed in cells nearest the administration offices. The first floor of the hospital wing houses prisoners who are

---

1 The Appeal Committee of the House of Lords (Lord Keith of Kinkel, Lord Templeman and Lord Griffiths) refused the applicant leave to appeal on 6 November 1986

medically ill and comprises cells, a ward and further offices. Access to the first floor is by
a two flights of stairs. There is no lift. The mentally disturbed patients have to be housed
on the ground floor where they are closer to the protective rooms and the prison staff are
not thereby required to negotiate stairs with them. As the applicant is unable to walk
upstairs, it was not possible to accommodate him on the first floor in the medical wards.
The governor at Pentonville therefore arranged for him to be accommodated in a cell on
the ground floor, near the staff quarters and at the quietest end of that floor. A specially
b reinforced bed that he had used at Winchester was provided for him.

However, the applicant complains that in his cell on the ground floor he is constantly
subjected throughout the night to shouting, screaming and banging from the other
mentally disturbed inmates. He contends that although he himself is wholly sane, he is
surrounded by schizophrenics, psychopaths, mental depressives and other mentally
disturbed persons with the result that he finds himself unable to sleep. He makes other
c specific complaints about the conditions in which he is presently detained at Pentonville,
but it is unnecessary for present purposes to go into these in any detail. The applicant's
overall contention is that in these circumstances he is subjected to 'cruell and unusuall
punishment' contrary to the Bill of Rights (1688). His case is, further, that not only have
there been breaches of that statute, but also that in purporting to carry out their duties
under the Prison Act 1952 and the Prison Rules 1964, SI 1964/388, in breach of the
d seventeenth century statute and, indeed, of the provisions of the European Convention
on Human Rights (Convention for the Protection of Human Rights and Fundamental
Freedoms (Rome, 4 November 1950; TS 71 (1953); (Cmd 8969)), both the Secretary of
State and the prison governor have been and are acting illegally. The applicant's
contention is that such illegality in their performance of their statutory powers or duties
is judicially reviewable by the courts.
e In those circumstances the applicant applied for and obtained the leave of Hodgson J
to move for the order of mandamus to which I have referred. The substantive proceedings
are still pending.

However, in para 4 of the applicant's second affidavit, which was filed in support of an
application for leave to administer interrogatories and for discovery of documents in
f those pending judicial review proceedings, the applicant swore:

> 'In conversations which I have had with Dr. Rees, a Medical Officer on the
> permanent staff at H. M. Prison Pentonville, and, I verily believe, fully qualified as a
> registered medical practitioner, I am led to believe that he has submitted a number
> of medical reports expressing concern at the conditions under which I am being
> kept, and recommending that I be transferred back to Winchester. Such documents
g > would appear to give the lie to the passages from [paragraphs of the affidavit sworn
> by the governor quoted elsewhere in the applicant's second affidavit].'

The application for interrogatories and discovery came before Hodgson J on 22 May
1986. He refused leave to administer the interrogatories but made an order that the
h respondents to that application (the Secretary of State and the prison governor) should
file a list of documents stating whether they have or have at any time had in their
possession, custody or power any medical and or psychiatric reports concerning the
applicant since his remand in custody on 1 August 1985 and in particular (but without
prejudice to the generality of the foregoing) all reports concerning the applicant written
and submitted by Dr Rees, and/or arising out of any observations by Dr Rees concerning
j the applicant.

The Secretary of State and the prison governor now appeal against that interlocutory
order by the judge.

Leave is required to start judicial review proceedings by virtue of s 31(3) of the
Supreme Court Act 1981 and RSC Ord 53, r 1. If leave is granted, discovery is not
automatic as it is in actions begun by writ, by virtue of Ord 24, r 2. Discovery may,

however, be ordered in judicial review proceedings by virtue of the interoperation of
Ord 53, r 8(1) and Ord 24, r 3(1). Order 53, r 8(1) provides:

a

> 'Unless the Court otherwise directs, any interlocutory application in proceedings
> on any application for judicial review may be made to any judge or a master of the
> Queen's Bench Division, notwithstanding that the application for judicial review
> has been made by motion and is to be heard by a Divisional Court. In this paragraph
> "interlocutory application" includes an application for an order under Order 24 or
> 26 or Order 38, rule 2(3) or for an order dismissing the proceedings by consent of
> the parties.'

b

Order 24, r 3(1) provides:

> 'Subject to the provisions of this rule and of rules 4 and 8, the Court may order
> any party to a cause or matter (whether begun by writ, originating summons or
> otherwise) to make and serve on any other party a list of the documents which are
> or have been in his possession, custody or power relating to any matter in question
> in the cause or matter, and may at the same time or subsequently also order him to
> make and file an affidavit verifying such a list and to serve a copy thereof on the
> other party.'

c

On the hearing of an application for an order for discovery under Ord 24, r 3 the court,
by virtue of r 8—

d

> 'if satisfied that discovery is not necessary, or not necessary at that stage of the
> cause or matter, may dismiss or, as the case may be, adjourn the application and
> shall in any case refuse to make such an order if and so far as it is of opinion that
> discovery is not necessary either for disposing fairly of the cause or matter or for
> saving costs.'

e

A party who has served a list of documents pursuant, inter alia, to an order under r 3
must allow the other party to inspect the documents referred to in the list, subject always
to a valid claim to privilege and to the provisions of r 13(1), which is in these terms:

> 'No order for the production of any documents for inspection or to the Court
> shall be made under any of the foregoing rules unless the Court is of opinion that
> the order is necessary either for disposing fairly of the cause or matter or for saving
> costs.'

f

On the facts of this case and in the procedural context I have outlined, counsel for the
Secretary of State and the governor accepted that if leave had been justifiably given to
bring these judicial review proceedings in the first place, then he could not challenge the
order for discovery now appealed against. He argued, however, that leave should never
have been given in the first place, that so soon as these proceedings reached an inter partes
hearing on the merits it would quickly become apparent that they could not be
maintained and that consequently it could not be said that either discovery or inspection
were necessary either for fairly disposing of the matter or for saving costs.

g

Counsel's argument was twofold. He contended, first, that on the authority of *R v
Deputy Governor of Camphill Prison, ex p King* [1984] 3 All ER 897, [1985] QB 735 judicial
review would not go to the governor of one of Her Majesty's prisons to control his
exercise of his management function in his prison. Further, in so far as the Secretary of
State is concerned, counsel argued that as it has not been alleged that he or officers of his
department had given any instruction or reached any decision about the circumstances
or nature of the applicant's incarceration, there is, as yet at any rate, nothing for the court
to review in these proceedings.

h

j

Counsel's second argument was based on the premise that, before the court could be
in any position to decide whether to grant judicial review, it would itself have to
investigate the primary facts relating to the applicant's detention. This, however, was the

a duty of the Secretary of State and the board of visitors and it would be wrong for the court to usurp their functions.

Counsel for the Secretary of State and the governor accepted that the present appeal, although in substance one against the order for discovery, was in effect an appeal against the grant of leave in the first place. However, he submitted that the court should not be thereby inhibited from considering and, if it thought right, allowing the appeal for a number of reasons. First, the application for leave was made, as is usual, ex parte. Thus it *b* was not until the hearing of the application for discovery that the arguments against the grant of leave in any event could be rehearsed inter partes. Second, although at an early stage of his judgment which is now being appealed the judge referred at least to the possibility that as a matter of law it would not be right for the court to consider in judicial review proceedings whether there has been a breach of the Bill of Rights in this case, nevertheless he ultimately granted the application for discovery because leave to move *c* had in fact been given. Thus the question of whether or not leave had been rightly given at the start was clearly one to be considered in the instant appeal. Third, as I have already pointed out, discovery in judicial review proceedings is discretionary; such proceedings are intended to provide a relatively speedy remedy, thus interlocutory applications should not be encouraged unnecessarily; it follows that when interlocutory applications are made, as in the instant case, it should be open to the other party to challenge the need for *d* any interlocutory order on the basis that the whole proceedings were misconceived in any event.

I therefore consider, first, the application for leave to bring judicial review proceedings and whether, once granted, it is to be considered as not substantially open to challenge until the formal hearing inter partes of the proceedings themselves. When discussing the requirement to obtain leave in his speech in *O'Reilly v Mackman* [1982] 3 All ER 1124 at *e* 1130, [1983] 2 AC 237 at 280 Lord Diplock said: 'The application for leave, which was ex parte but could be, and in practice often was, adjourned in order to enable the proposed respondent to be represented . . .' Speaking for myself, my recent experience is that adjournments to enable potential respondents to judicial review proceedings to appear on the application for leave are infrequent, a tendency no doubt enhanced by the modern *f* practice by which leave may be granted without any hearing at all on the documents.

The next point to make is that although an appeal does lie to this court against an ex parte order made by a judge of the High Court by virtue of s 16(1) of the Supreme Court Act 1981 (see *WEA Records Ltd v Visions Channel 4 Ltd* [1983] 2 All ER 589, [1983] 1 WLR 721) nevertheless in his judgment in that case Sir John Donaldson MR said ([1983] 2 All ER 589 at 593, [1983] 1 WLR 721 at 727):

g 'As I have said, ex parte orders are essentially provisional in nature. They are made by the judge on the basis of evidence and submissions emanating from one side only. Despite the fact that the applicant is under a duty to make full disclosure of all relevant information in his possession, whether or not it assists his application, this is no basis for making a definitive order and every judge knows this. He expects at a later stage to be given an opportunity to review his provisional order in the light *h* of evidence and argument adduced by the other side and, in so doing, he is not hearing an appeal from himself and in no way feels inhibited from discharging or varying his original order. This being the case it is difficult, if not impossible, to think of circumstances in which it would be proper to appeal to this court against an ex parte order without first giving the judge who made it or, if he was not available, another High Court judge an opportunity of reviewing it in the light of *j* argument from the defendant and reaching a decision.'

In these circumstances I see no reason why, on an application for discovery in judicial review proceedings and on an appeal against any order made on such an application, it should not be open to the respondent to the review proceedings to contend that as a matter of law it had been wrong to grant the original leave and that consequently no order for discovery should be made. If, on the material then before the judge or this court, and having heard argument inter partes, either were to come to the conclusion that the review proceedings were misconceived, then in my opinion no order for discovery should be made and the respondent should then apply on notice to the judge who originally granted leave asking him to rescind it. On the other hand if the respondent cannot satisfy the judge or this court that leave should never have been given, then ex hypothesi it stands and is at least a very important consideration to have in mind in exercising one's discretion whether or not to make an order for discovery. Indeed, in the instant appeal, as I have said, counsel for the Secretary of State and the governor conceded that if he did not satisfy us that the original leave to bring the review proceedings had been wrongly granted, then he could not otherwise succeed on his appeal against the order to give discovery.

I turn therefore to consider the challenge of counsel for the Secretary of State and the governor, to the original grant of leave. In so far as the proceedings against the governor of Pentonville Prison are concerned, in my opinion the position is clear. In *Ex p King*, to which I have already referred, the question was whether judicial review would go to the governor of Camphill Prison in respect of an adjudication of his on a prisoner which, it was contended, had been based on a misconstruction of one of the Prison Rules 1964. On appeal from the refusal of the Divisional Court to grant judicial review this court held, first, that the governor had, indeed, misconstrued the rule but, second, that judicial review would not be granted to regulate the exercise by a prison governor of his managerial function of governing his own prison. In my opinion the instant case is a fortiori. In *Ex p King* what it was sought to challenge was an adjudication by the deputy governor; in *R v Hull Prison Board of Visitors, ex p St Germain* [1979] 1 All ER 701, [1979] QB 425 this court has held that an adjudication under the 1964 rules by a board of visitors was subject to judicial review; thus in *Ex p King* there was clearly a strong argument available to the applicant that an adjudication by a deputy governor should similarly be subject to judicial review. However, this court held that he was not, principally because the task of managing and maintaining discipline in a prison is that of the governor, that it is already an extremely difficult one, particularly in modern conditions, and that to allow prisoners to challenge in the courts the disciplinary decisions of the governor would make his task wellnigh impossible. If a governor's decision on an adjudication on a prisoner is not subject to judicial review, then in my opinion it is clear that neither, for instance, is his decision about in which cell a particular prisoner is to be housed. For these reasons I respectfully think that the judge was wrong to grant leave to bring these judicial review proceedings against the governor of Pentonville Prison.

In so far as the Secretary of State is concerned, the members of this court in their judgments in *Ex p King* pointed out that in appropriate circumstances instances of mismanagement in prisons could be controlled by the courts by way of judicial review proceedings against the Secretary of State. In his judgment Lawton LJ held that since the enactment of the Prison Act 1952 the Secretary of State has had the duty to ensure that the Act and all rules made under it are complied with. He said ([1984] 3 All ER 897 at 901, [1985] QB 735 at 749):

'If he fails to perform this duty, he will be answerable to the law just as any other minister who fails to perform his statutory duties or uses his statutory powers unlawfully.'

Later in his judgment Lawton LJ said ([1984] 3 All ER 897 at 902, [1985] QB 735 at 749):

'All prisons are likely to be have within them a few prisoners intent on disrupting the administration. They are likely to have even more who delude themselves that they are the victims of injustice. To allow such men to have access to the High Court whenever they thought that the governor abused his powers, failed to give them a fair hearing or misconstrued the prison rules would undermine and weaken his authority and make management very difficult indeed. In prisons, as in the armed services, those who have grievances can, and should, follow the way laid down for getting them dealt with. Prisoners can make complaints to the visiting committee or board of visitors (see r 95) and petition the Secretary of State. If a prisoner has a well-founded complaint that a governor has misconstrued a prison rule and the Secretary of State has rejected his petition inviting attention to the misconstruction, he may be entitled to apply for judicial review of the Secretary of State's decision, the relief being in the form of a declaration as to what is the correct construction.'

In his judgment on the same point Griffiths LJ, after referring to the duties vested in the Secretary of State in respect of prisons by s 4 of the 1952 Act, continued ([1984] 3 All ER 897 at 904, [1985] QB 735 at 752):

'In these circumstances the court should, in the first instance, be prepared to assume that the Home Secretary will discharge the duty placed on him by Parliament to ensure that the prison governor is doing his job properly. If it is shown that the minister is not discharging this duty and allowing a prison governor to disregard the prison rules then judicial review will go to correct that situation by requiring the minister to perform his statutory duty. I regard this as the route by which the court in the present case could legitimately have been called on to construe r 47(7). If the prisoner had petitioned the Home Secretary and made clear that his complaint was that he had lost remission because the governor had wrongly construed the rule it would have been the duty of the Home Secretary to consider the construction of the rule. If the Home Secretary had then misconstrued the rule and thus rejected the petition it would then have been open to the prisoner to seek judicial review of the Home Secretary's decision on the ground that he had rejected his petition because he had misdirected himself in law'.

Finally, Browne-Wilkinson LJ said ([1984] 3 All ER 897 at 905, [1985] QB 735 at 753–754):

'By s 4(2) of the Prison Act 1952 Parliament imposed on the prison commissioners the duty to ensure that the provisions of the Act and any rules made under it are complied with. On the dissolution of the prison commissioners on 1 April 1963 (by the Prison Commissioners Dissolution Order 1963, SI 1963/597) this duty became vested in the Home Secretary. Parliament has therefore by express enactment imposed on someone other than the courts a specific obligation to ensure compliance with the statutory provisions. In my judgment, where Parliament has so provided it would not normally be appropriate for the court to take jurisdiction to ensure compliance with such statutory provisions, at least in cases where the person entrusted with the duty has adequate powers to ensure that the statutory provisions are in fact complied with. In the present case, therefore, the primary obligation to ensure that prison discipline is administered in accordance with the statutory provisions is vested, not in the court, but in the Secretary of State. He has adequate powers to ensure compliance with the law by prison governors since they are his servants or agents and must comply with his instructions. If, as in the present case, a disciplinary award has been made by the prison governor in excess of his powers under the rules, the Home Secretary can, and no doubt will, remit that disciplinary award under r 56 and can, no doubt, ensure that there is entered on the prisoner's record a statement that the original award should be disregarded. In my judgment in such a case as this the jurisdiction on the court is limited to ensuring compliance by the Home Secretary with *his* statutory obligations under s 4(2). If the Home Secretary were to fail to ensure compliance with the rules, he would himself be in breach of his statutory duty and the court could, and would, require him to remedy that breach.'

The difficulty about this approach in the instant case, however, is that there is no evidence before the court of any act or omission by the Secretary of State or his department which could be said to be a breach of his duties under the 1952 Act. We were told that the applicant has petitioned the Secretary of State with regard to the conditions of his detention, that this is presently being considered, but that no decision has yet been reached on the petition. Further, there is no evidence before us that the Secretary of State is allowing the state of affairs of which the applicant complains to continue to exist. In his speech in *Council of Civil Service Unions v Minister for the Civil Service* [1984] 3 All ER 935 at 949, [1985] AC 374 at 408 Lord Diplock said:

'Judicial review, now regulated by RSC Ord 53, provides the means by which judicial control of administrative action is exercised. The subject matter of every judicial review is a decision made by some person (or body of persons) . . . or else a refusal by him to make a decision.'

I have found this a difficult point in the instant case. In the most unlikely event that an individual prison officer, unknown to his governor and to the Secretary of State, were to maltreat prisoners, would judicial review go, with nothing more, to the Secretary of State? I cannot think so. If the situation were not swiftly put right after a telephone call to a responsible official in the Home Office, then the position would be very different. On the other hand, the wording of ss 1 and 4 of the 1952 Act is wide and effectively imposes a continuing duty on the Secretary of State with regard to the welfare of prisoners. However, it is on the Secretary of State that Parliament has by this statute imposed the duty of running Her Majesty's prisons and in my opinion it is not for the court to intervene unless it is shown that by taking some decision or failing to take a decision which he ought to have taken the Secretary of State has failed to carry out that duty in accordance with the statute and the rules made thereunder.

In the result I respectfully think that leave ought not to have been granted to apply for judicial review directed to the Secretary of State in the circumstances of the instant case on the material then and now before the court.

The appeal presently before us, however, is not against the original grant of leave but against the order for discovery. Nevertheless, for the reasons I have given, in my opinion the applications for judicial review against both the Secretary of State and the governor as at present constituted are bound to fail. In exercising his discretion to order discovery I think the judge ex hypothesi acted on an erroneous view of the law and thus that it is open to this court to exercise its own discretion. If, as I think, the applications for judicial review, when heard inter partes are bound to fail in limine, then clearly discovery is not necessary either for disposing fairly of them or for saving costs.

Nevertheless, I should add that I find myself unable to accept the alternative contention of counsel for the Secretary of State and the governor that the order for discovery should be set aside because the basis on which it was made was that the court would have to investigate the primary facts of the applicant's detention, that discovery would be necessary for that investigation, and that a court should not constitute itself a fact-finding tribunal in this type of matter. In the majority of applications for judicial review the underlying facts are agreed, or appear in documentary form, and the issues for the court are largely, if not entirely, questions of law. However, although the court's function is supervisory, it may well involve some investigation of the facts of a case. As Lord Wilberforce said in *Khawaja v Secretary of State for the Home Dept* [1983] 1 All ER 765 at 777–778, [1984] AC 74 at 105:

'The court's investigation of the facts is of a supervisory character and not by way of appeal (it should not be forgotten that a right of appeal as to the facts exists under s 16 of [the Immigration Act 1971] even though Parliament has thought fit to impose conditions on its exercise). It should appraise the quality of the evidence and decide whether that justifies the conclusion reached, eg whether it justifies a

conclusion that the applicant obtained permission to enter by fraud or deceit. An
a   allegation that he has done so being of a serious character and involving issues of
personal liberty requires a corresponding degree of satisfaction as to the evidence. If
the court is not satisfied with any part of the evidence it may remit the matter for
reconsideration or itself receive further evidence. It should quash the detention
order where the evidence was not such as the authorities should have relied on or
where the evidence received does not justify the decision reached or, of course, for
b   any serious procedural irregularity.'

There are dicta to the same effect in the speeches of Lord Fraser and Lord Scarman in the
same case. Further, the power given to the court by Ord 53, r 8(1) read with Ord 38,
r 2(3) to permit cross-examination of the deponents of affidavits filed in judicial review
proceedings is clearly only consistent with some fact-finding role of the court in such
c   proceedings. It should not be often that this power need be exercised, but in the instant
case I agree with the judge that if the merits of the judicial review proceedings and
allegations were to be gone into, then clearly the discovery ordered would be necessary
and proper.
    I have had the advantage of reading in draft the judgments which Purchas LJ and Sir
David Cairns are about to deliver. I differ from them with regret. Nevertheless, for the
d   reasons I have given earlier, I, for my part, respectfully think that the judge was wrong
to order discovery herein and I would have allowed this appeal.

PURCHAS LJ. I have had the privilege of reading the judgment to be delivered by
May LJ in draft and have discovered that I have the misfortune to have reached a
conclusion that differs from his. The full facts and circumstances of the appeal have
e   already been set out in the judgment delivered by May LJ. I merely repeat certain salient
matters for ease of reference in his judgment. The applicant as May LJ has already said,
is urgently sought by the law enforcement authorities of the United States of America in
connection with alleged massive and numerous frauds on the citizens there. Extradition
proceedings are on foot which are contested by the applicant. His objections to an
extradition order were recently dismissed by the Divisional Court (Stephen Brown LJ
f   and Otton J) on 30 July 1986. The applicant, at the time of the hearing of this appeal,
was intending to petition to the House of Lords for leave to appeal, such leave having
been refused by the Divisional Court. If the petition is successful the appeal is unlikely
to be determined for several months at the least[1]. In the mean while bail has been
refused. The applicant is possessed of substantial assets abroad in countries other than the
United States of America, which makes it probable that conditions of bail would not be
g   observed. The applicant has been in custody since August 1985. In the early stages he
was detained in Winchester Prison where he raised no objection to the conditions to
which he was subjected.
    He has now been transferred to Pentonville Prison. The applicant raises substantial
complaints about the conditions under which he is being detained. These have caused
anxiety to the High Court (see the application for bail and the judgment of Woolf J
h   hearing the Crown Office list on 20 December 1985). He suffers from considerable
physical disabilities, namely gross overweight leading to immobility. Apart from some
degree of depression associated with his failure to be able to cope with this condition and
also, no doubt, in connection with his present position vis-à-vis the extradition
proceedings, there is no evidence in the reports available to the court of any psychiatric
illness. Nevertheless, because of his immobility, for the reasons already described by May
j   LJ the applicant is detained in the hospital wing of Pentonville Prison. He is, for practical
purposes, unable to mount stairs and this means that he has to be in a cell on the ground

---

1 The Appeal Committee of the House of Lords (Lord Keith of Kinkel, Lord Templeman and Lord
Griffiths) refused the applicant leave to appeal on 6 November 1986

floor which is the psychiatric wing of the hospital which, for reasons already described by May LJ, has also to be on the ground floor. The applicant objects to the limited amount of association he is permitted; to the fact that meals are served in his cell and to the disturbances which are caused by other inmates detained in adjoining cells.

The applicant's application for leave to apply for judicial review under RSC Ord 53, r 3(2) was dated 9 May 1986. He seeks an order of mandamus directed to the governor of Pentonville Prison and to the Secretary of State for the Home Department directing them to detain him according to law. The application also sought interlocutory relief by way of injunction, declaration or otherwise. Hodgson J on the ex parte application made by counsel for the applicant on 13 May 1986 granted leave to apply for judicial review and leave to amend the form of the application to include, inter alia, grounds based on alleged breaches of the provisions of the Bill of Rights (1688). Notice of the application had been served on the Treasury Solicitor representing the two proposed respondents and a representative was present in court. No action was taken to invite the judge to adjourn the application so that the Treasury Solicitor could be heard on an inter partes hearing before granting or refusing leave. The judge gave leave to serve short notice of motion for a hearing inter partes of an application for interlocutory relief as claimed in the application. This was heard by Hodgson J on 19 May 1986 (see [1986] 3 All ER 209, [1986] 3 WLR 504). Although the judge held that as a matter of jurisdiction he was able to grant an interim injunction in the mandatory form sought against an officer of the Crown, he had no hesitation in refusing to do so as a matter of discretion. On this occasion it is clear from the judgment that counsel for the Secretary of State and the governor in that case directed much of his submissions to the merits of the substantive case alleging that there was no basis in law on which an order could issue and that leave should not have been granted in the first place (see [1986] 3 All ER 209 at 216, [1986] 3 WLR 504 at 513). This is the course he has adopted also in this court.

On 19 May 1986 when refusing the application for interlocutory relief the judge gave further leave to counsel for the applicant to serve short notice on an application to administer interrogatories and for an order for discovery of specific documents (medical reports) returnable on 22 May 1986. On that occasion the judge refused the application for interrogatories. There is no appeal against this refusal. He did, however, order against both the Secretary of State and the governor discovery of documents by lists, to include all medical and/or psychiatric reports concerning the applicant since his remand in custody on 1 August 1985 etc. Against this order counsel now appeals on behalf of both the Secretary of State and governor of the prison. If the leave to move for judicial review granted on 13 May 1986 was properly granted, then counsel does not seek to oppose the order for discovery made by Hodgson J on 22 May 1986. He concedes that if the leave to move was properly given, the judge properly exercised his discretion to order discovery against both the Secretary of State and the prison governor under RSC Ord 53, r 8 and Ord 24. But, he says, it is open to him on this appeal, and he has in fact been permitted by the court so to do, to argue the full merits of whether or not leave should have been granted on the application made ex parte to Hodgson J on 13 May.

Counsel for the Secretary of State and the governor submitted that if, as a matter of law, there was no ground on which an application for judicial review could possibly succeed (ie that leave should in fact not have been given in the first place) then it would be an abuse of the process of the court to apply for discovery in such circumstances and that, therefore, discovery should not have been ordered.

On 19 May 1986, although Hodgson J in the event refused interlocutory relief, he did this as a matter of discretion and not on the ground that he would not or should not have granted leave in the first place had evidence and/or argument from both sides been available to him on that occasion.

When analysed the submissions of counsel for the Secretary of State and the governor amounted to an appeal against the original granting of leave to seek relief under Ord 53, r 3 and indirectly supporting on different grounds (in the form of an affirming respondent's notice) the decision of Hodgson J refusing to grant interim relief on 19 May 1986, but not an appeal on the merits of the individual applications for discovery as against either the Secretary of State or the prison governor. Counsel for the Secretary of State and the governor did not condescend to argue on the basis that, for instance, as against the Secretary of State there was no prima facie evidence that there were documents in respect of which an order for discovery ought to be made. I can see grounds for distinguishing between the application in relation to the governor of the prison and the Secretary of State. In his affidavit, sworn on 19 May 1986, the applicant refers to reports by Dr Rees, a psychiatrist and medical officer on the permanent staff of the prison, relating to the applicant, whereas there is no evidence of any such documents being in the power or control of the Secretary of State. However, since these distinctions in detail were not argued by counsel for the Secretary of State and the governor, it is not necessary for me to deal with this aspect of the matter. Counsel frankly argued his case on the basis of the merits of the original application as they affect, or should have affected, Hodgson J on 22 May 1986 and the appeal from that order on the present occasion.

In considering whether this is an appropriate course to adopt, it is relevant to observe what other courses were open to the Secretary of State and the governor in this case. From the transcript of the proceedings on 13 May 1986 it is clear that both counsel for the Secretary of State and the governor and the Treasury Solicitor had been given full notice of the nature of the application and that the latter had a representative as observer present in court. It was open to the Treasury Solicitor to have instructed counsel for the Secretary of State and the governor or a substitute, to attend so as to request an adjournment of the application for an inter partes hearing (see the speech of Lord Diplock in *IRC v National Federation of Self-Employed and Small Businesses Ltd* [1981] 2 All ER 93, [1982] AC 617 (the *Fleet Street Casuals* case) to which reference is made subsequently in this judgment). Subsequently, it was open to the Secretary of State and the governor to apply to set the leave, which had been granted ex parte, aside under the inherent jurisdiction of the court as recognised in the case of leave granted in chambers by RSC Ord 32, r 6. That this is a general inherent jurisdiction and not confined to leave granted ex parte in chambers is clear from the practice direction given by Lord Denning MR in *Becker v Noel* [1971] 2 All ER 1248, [1971] 1 WLR 803. Finally, if the Secretary of State and the governor, or either of them, could bring themselves within the provisions of Ord 18, r 19(1)(a) they could have applied to strike out the originating motion issued by the applicant pursuant to Ord 53, r 5. In view of the remedies which were available, I doubt whether it would have been appropriate to appeal against the granting of leave although this course would also appear to have been open by virtue of s 16(1) of the Supreme Court Act 1981 (see the passage cited in the judgment of May LJ from *WEA Records Ltd v Visions Channel 4 Ltd* [1983] 2 All ER 589 at 593, [1983] 1 WLR 721 at 727). However, a little earlier in the judgment Sir John Donaldson MR says:

'In terms of jurisdiction, there can be no doubt that this court can hear an appeal from an order made by the High Court on an ex parte application. This jurisdiction is conferred by s 16(1) of the Supreme Court Act 1981. Equally there is no doubt that the High Court has power to review and to discharge or vary any order which has been made ex parte. This jurisdiction is inherent in the provisional nature of any order made ex parte and is reflected in RSC Ord 32, r 6.'

In the context of this passage, the second paragraph of the extract cited by May LJ must be taken as a strong indication that the Court of Appeal will not readily accept a motion where the appellant ought to have applied to the judge at first instance to set the leave granted ex parte aside.

Therefore, I approach the submissions of counsel for the Secretary of State and the governor with some degree of caution since he is attempting to achieve on appeal relief which he should have obtained at first instance. The purpose of the provisions of RSC Ord 53, r 3 is clearly established as being—

> 'to prevent the time of the court being wasted by busybodies with misguided or trivial complaints of administrative error, and to remove the uncertainty in which public officers and authorities might be left whether they could safely proceed with administrative action while proceedings for judicial review of it were actually pending even though misconceived.'

(See per Lord Diplock in the *Fleet Street Casuals* case [1981] 2 All ER 93 at 105, [1982] AC 617 at 643.) Lord Diplock envisaged the stage which he described as 'threshold' involving in certain circumstances an adjournment for the persons or bodies against whom relief is sought to be represented.

This authority would have supported an application in this case for an adjournment to an inter partes hearing. Of course, in many cases, where notice has not been given to the proposed respondent, this course would not be available, unless taken by the judge of his own motion. The proper remedy then lies in an application to set the leave granted ex parte aside and not by way of an appeal under s 16(1) of the Supreme Court Act 1981.

But counsel for the Secretary of State and the governor boldly asserts that the Secretary of State and the governor were entitled to adopt 'a passive role' in the hope that if and when some application for interlocutory relief should be made by the applicant they could then use this as a vehicle to test the issues which should have been raised immediately before the judge at first instance to oppose or set aside the granting of leave under Ord 53, r 3. As a matter of procedure alone, I must confess to having serious doubts about the propriety of such a course being taken by a respondent who has not availed himself of the opportunities provided under statute and the rules to challenge the position in which he finds himself as respondent to an application under Ord 53. Such a course is alien to the sense of expedition referred to by Lord Diplock in the *Fleet Street Casuals* case. However, the matter does not end there. It is necessary to consider the submissions on which counsel for the Secretary of State and the governor relies in his attempt to pursue this forensically dubious course.

Counsel for the Secretary of State and the governor submitted that as regards the order sought against the prison governor, this court was bound by *R v Deputy Governor of Camphill Prison, ex p King* [1984] 3 All ER 897, [1985] QB 735 as the applicant's complaints really related to matters of management and these fell within the provisions of the Prison Rules 1964, SI 1964/388. He submitted that this case established that judicial review was not available where the complaint concerned a breach of the 1964 rules or a misconstruction or misapplication of the powers granted to the governor thereby (see [1984] 3 All ER 897 at 904, [1985] QB 735 at 752 per Griffiths LJ):

> 'If a governor was a law unto himself it would be a powerful reason for having judicial review available to curb any excesses or abuse of his powers. But the governor is not a law unto himself, he is appointed by and responsible to the Home Secretary and Parliament has placed a special responsibility on the Home Secretary to supervise governors and other prison officers to ensure that they discharge their duties properly and to report annually to Parliament on the state of the prisons including all punishments inflicted therein: see Prison Act 1952, ss 4 and 5, which set out the duties of the prison commissioners now vested in the Home Secretary, and in particular s 4(2): "The Prison Commissioners, by themselves or their officers, shall visit all prisons and examine the state of buildings, the conduct of officers, the treatment and conduct of prisoners and all other matters concerning the management of prisons and shall ensure that the provisions of this Act and of any rules made under this Act are duly complied with."'

Griffiths LJ continues in the passage immediately following to indicate that:

a
    'If it is shown that the minister is not discharging this duty and allowing a prison governor to disregard the prison rules then judicial review will go to correct that situation by requiring the minister to perform his statutory duty.'

We have been told that the applicant has in fact sent a petition to the Secretary of State but it is not known with what result. I understand the matter is still under consideration by the minister.

b
    As May LJ has pointed out, the decision in *R v Hull Prison Board of Visitors, ex p St Germain* [1979] 1 All ER 701, [1979] QB 425 was considered in *Ex p King*. *Ex p St Germain* is authority for the proposition that an adjudication by a board of visitors under the 1964 rules is subject to judicial review. A complaint, therefore, relating to an alleged breach of the 1964 rules must, in the first instance, be made to the prison governor whose adjudication thereon is to be considered on complaint to the board of visitors. It is only

c
at this stage that the courts will assume powers of review of the decision. This is not an unusual position where the court will not interfere until the subsidiary avenues of review have been exhausted. For the reasons given by May LJ, adverting to matters of public policy and the difficulty of managing a prison and maintaining discipline therein, this is clearly a convenient and salutary position. However, the instant case is not restricted to alleged breaches of the 1964 rules and, therefore, in my judgment, with great respect to

d
May LJ and notwithstanding the arguments of counsel for the Secretary of State and the governor to the contrary, is clearly distinguishable from *Ex p King*. Furthermore, the applicant asserts that approaches to the board of visitors which he made were met with a response that they were not concerned with events occurring in the hospital wing. It is, I think, common ground that in taking this line the board of visitors were wrong; but this would not found a complaint against the prison governor.

e
    The submissions of counsel so far as the Secretary of State is concerned have been fully reviewed in the judgment of May LJ. I need not repeat those submissions in this judgment and gratefully adopt May LJ's analysis of them. It is clear from the extracts from *Ex p King* and the speech of Lord Diplock in *Council of Civil Service Unions v Minister for the Civil Service* [1984] 3 All ER 935, [1985] AC 374 that the courts will review under RSC Ord 53 administrative action exercised or failure to exercise administrative duties

f
by the minister under the provisions of the Prison Act 1952, s 4(2) if it is established that the minister has failed to perform those statutory duties or uses his statutory powers unlawfully. In the present case, although the original application for leave to move for judicial review was directed both to the prison governor and the Secretary of State, I have not so far detected immediately from the evidence filed in accordance with Ord 53, r 3 any specific aspect in which it is alleged that the minister has so failed. The argument is,

g
however, that if in a notorious case, as the applicant's case is, it were to be established that serious breaches of the Bill of Rights were occurring then there is a foundation of an allegation that the Secretary of State had failed to perform his duties of supervision imposed generally on him by the 1952 Act, s 4(2). This would be an issue to be argued inter partes before the judge at first instance rather than as an issue introduced more or less by a side wind on an appeal in interlocutory proceedings.

h
    Counsel for the applicant submitted that the appeal was misconceived because it was in fact an attempt to reopen the question of the granting of leave under Ord 53, r 3. For the reasons already appearing in this judgment I am impressed by this submission. The judge was clearly well aware of the authority of *Ex p King*, but nevertheless granted leave. Counsel for the applicant emphasised that the case against the governor, however, was not based merely on breaches of the 1964 rules but on an alleged breach of the provision

j
of the Bill of Rights, namely that the applicant was entitled not to be inflicted with 'cruell and unusuall punishments'. This is a fundamental right which, in my judgment, goes far beyond the ambit of the 1964 rules. For my part, if it were established that a prison governor was guilty of such conduct, it would be an affront to common sense that the court should not be able to afford relief under Ord 53. There is authority for this in the

judgments of this court in *Congreve v Home Office* [1976] 1 All ER 697 at 710, [1976] QB 629 at 652, 655, a case which concerned the right not to be subjected to an unauthorised levy, per Lord Denning MR:

> 'There is yet another reason for holding that the demands for £6 to be unlawful. They were made contrary to the Bill of Rights. They were an attempt to levy money for the use of the Crown without the authority of Parliament; and that is quite enough to damn them: see *Attorney-General v Wilts United Dairies* (1921) 37 TLR 884; (1922) 91 LJKB 897.'

and per Roskill LJ, referring also to *A-G v Wilts United Dairies*.

Of course, merely making an allegation without any foundation would not necessarily invoke the relief afforded under Ord 53 for there is the initial or 'threshold' necessity to obtain leave referred to by Lord Diplock (in the *Fleet Street Casuals* case) and even if leave were obtained by fraud or as a result of an error of law the protection of Ord 18, r 19 and the inherent jurisdiction of the court to set aside leave granted ex parte to which I have already referred. In this case, however, Hodgson J, acting on the uncontroverted evidence of the applicant concluded that there was some ground to justify an investigation. There are unusual features in this case which, in my judgment prima facie call for further investigation. This is far from saying that every prisoner who complains about the management of the prison can apply to the court under Ord 53 alleging a breach of the Bill of Rights. Unjustified complaints of this nature will be readily detected by the judge hearing the application.

Once the central issue is divested of the encumbrance of considerations of breaches of 1964 rules or duties under the 1952 Act and is viewed as a case involving a breach of the Bill of Rights alone, then the matter, in my judgment, becomes easier to comprehend. Two questions arise. The first is: what are the conditions in fact in which the applicant is presently detained at Pentonville? The second is: do these conditions amount to 'cruell and unusuall punishment'? By way of example, and not wishing to indicate any view of the actual conditions existing, it is generally held to be unacceptable that persons supposedly of normal mentality should be detained in psychiatric institutions as is said to occur in certain parts of the world. Coming close to the alleged facts of this case, if it were to be established that the applicant as a sane person was, for purely administrative purposes, being subjected in the psychiatric wing to the stress of being exposed to the disturbance caused by the behaviour of mentally ill and disturbed prisoners, this might well be considered as a 'cruell and unusuall punishment' and one which was not deserved. This raises issues quite different from compliance or non-compliance with the 1964 rules; although they may well involve breaches on the part of the Secretary of State of the 1952 Act.

The questions involved have not so far been properly investigated. Counsel for the Secretary of State and the governor does not appear to have condescended to refer to them before Hodgson J and, before us, merely argued *Ex p King*. The existence of medical reports going to the resolution of this matter cannot be ignored in limine. If it were to be established that medical opinion supported the contention that the applicant's detention was inflicting a 'cruell and unusuall punishment' on him, then, in my judgment, the court has power, and ought, to intervene. Certainly leave for a proper investigation should be granted. If in order to determine whether a case that 'cruell and unusuall punishment' has been inflicted is established, it is necessary to investigate conflicts of testimony; then, if there are documents which will assist in the resolution of these issues known to be in existence, it is unarguable that they should not be made available to the court. In this case the course adopted by counsel for the Secretary of State and the governor acknowledges the existence of such documents, otherwise he would not have restricted his argument to attacking the granting of leave in the first instance but would have better perhaps directed his efforts to attacking the order for discovery on a the merits which, let it be remembered, remains a matter of discretion in the judge under Ord 53.

For these reasons I have come to the conclusion that counsel for the Secretary of State and the governor fails in his submission as against the prison governor on two grounds: first, that he has adopted the wrong procedure having failed to avail himself of the opportunity to challenge the original granting of leave; and, second, as he did not specifically attempt to deal with the separate incidents of the alleged breach of the Bill of

b Rights and because indeed, in the absence of specific evidence as to the effect on the applicant of the conditions of his detention, it would be impossible for him so to do. As against the Secretary of State, he fails only on the first of the two grounds on which he failed as against the governor of Pentonville Prison; but in the practical circumstances of the order for discovery and the appeal against it, this refinement is probably academic in any event.

c Finally, I turn to the alternative contention of counsel for the Secretary of State and the governor, namely that the order for discovery should be set aside because the basis on which it was made was that the court would have to investigate the primary facts of the applicant's detention. As already appears from this judgment, like May LJ, I find myself unable to accept this submission. There is nothing that I wish to add to the reasons given by May LJ for my attitude on this aspect of the case.

d For these reasons I would dismiss this appeal.

SIR DAVID CAIRNS. In my opinion this appeal should be dismissed. I can state quite briefly the reasons which led me to that conclusion. I have, however, had the advantage of seeing in draft the judgment of Purchas LJ and I entirely agree with it.

e It is accepted by counsel for the Secretary of State and the governor that the only basis on which the appeal could succeed is that leave to appeal for judicial review should never have been granted.

Once leave to apply for judicial review has been given, then unless and until that leave has been set aside it must remain valid until the hearing of the application. It appears to

f me that in proceedings by way of an application for discovery, or by way of an appeal from an order for discovery, it is wholly inappropriate for the court to embark on any inquiry as to whether leave was rightly given.

If under s 16(1) of the Supreme Court Act 1981 there is a right of appeal against the leave, then, in the absence of fraud, or an application under the inherent jurisdiction to the judge who made the ex parte order, such an appeal must be the only appropriate way

g of getting rid of the leave. If that subsection is not applicable and there is no right of appeal, then that must be because it is thought undesirable that delay and expense should be caused by appeals which would rarely have any chance of success. The necessity to have to apply for judicial review is somewhat analogous to the necessity in some types of case to apply for leave to appeal. I have never heard of an appeal being instituted against leave to appeal and I should be surprised if such an appeal would be countenanced.

h However that may be, I am satisfied that it is not open to this court at the hearing of this appeal to set aside the order giving leave to apply for judicial review and that while that order stands it cannot be treated as a nullity.

If, contrary to my opinion, it is open to this court to consider whether leave to apply for judicial review was rightly given, I should not be disposed to hold that it was not. The decision in *R v Deputy Governor of Camphill Prison, ex p King* [1984] 3 All ER 897,

j [1985] 1 QB 735 may be distinguishable on the ground that that was a case of alleged breach of prison regulations, whereas the allegation in the instant case is of breach of statutory duties. As against the Secretary of State *Ex p King* is not applicable and I am not persuaded that the case against him is so weak that on the material before us it is bound to fail.

For these reasons, with great respect for the views of May LJ, who has reached a
contrary conclusion, I am of opinion that the decision of Hodgson J was right and I would   *a*
dismiss this appeal.

Appeal dismissed. Leave to appeal to the House of Lords refused.

Solicitors: *Treasury Solicitor; Barker Austin* (for the applicant).

  b

Mary Rose Plummer   Barrister.

  c

South Shropshire District Council v Amos

COURT OF APPEAL, CIVIL DIVISION
PARKER AND BALCOMBE LJJ
7, 25 JULY 1986

  d

*Evidence – Without prejudice correspondence – Correspondence forming part of negotiations –
Privilege from admission in evidence – Whether 'without prejudice' letter which merely initiates
negotiations privileged – Whether letter which does not contain offer can be privileged.*

The fact that a document is headed 'without prejudice' does not conclusively or   *e*
automatically render it privileged from admission in evidence in any subsequent
proceedings, and if a claim for such privilege for the document is challenged the court
will look at the document to determine its nature. However, all documents which form
part of negotiations between the parties are prima facie privileged from admission in
evidence if they are marked 'without prejudice', even if the document in question merely
initiates the negotiations and even if the document does not itself contain an offer (see   *f*
p 344 *e f*, post).
    Re Daintrey, ex p Holt [1891–4] All ER Rep 209 and dictum of Fox LJ in *Cutts v Head*
[1984] 1 All ER at 611 applied.

Notes
For communications 'without prejudice', see 17 Halsbury's Laws (4th edn) paras 212–   *g*
213, and for cases on the subject, see 22 Digest (Reissue) 407–410, 4082–4108.

Cases referred to in judgment
Cutts v Head [1984] 1 All ER 597, [1984] Ch 290, [1984] 2 WLR 349, CA.
Daintrey, Re, ex p Holt [1893] 2 QB 116, [1891–4] All ER Rep 209, DC.
Norwich Union Life Insurance Society v Tony Waller Ltd (1984) 270 EG 42.   *h*
Walker v Wilsher (1889) 23 QBD 335, CA.

Interlocutory appeal
By an originating summons dated 10 June 1985 the respondents, South Shropshire
District Council, applied for an order that two documents prepared by solicitors for the
appellant, Lionel Amos, namely a claim for compensation made in October 1981 in   *j*
respect of a discontinuance order made by the respondents under s 51 of the Town and
Country Planning Act 1971 and an amended claim for compensation made in May 1982,
both of which were marked 'without prejudice', should be admitted in evidence in
proceedings before the Lands Tribunal to determine the amount of the compensation.

On 21 January 1986 Gatehouse J ordered that the documents be admitted in evidence.
a Mr Amos appealed against that order. The facts are set out in the judgment of the court.

Gerard Ryan QC and *Keith Lindblom* for Mr Amos.
Jeremy M Sullivan QC and *Brian Ash* for the respondents.

At the conclusion of argument the court announced that the application would be
b dismissed for reasons to be given later.

25 July. The following judgment of the court was delivered.

PARKER LJ. On 8 November 1986 the respondents made a discontinuance order
under s 51(1) of the Town and Country Planning Act 1971 in respect of the business use
c by the appellant, Mr Amos, of premises known as The Forge, Middleton, in the county
of Shropshire. That order was duly confirmed by the Secretary of State under s 51(4) of
the 1971 Act on 13 July 1977. On 13 December 1977 Mr Amos made a written claim
for compensation pursuant to s 170(2) of the 1971 Act. That claim consisted in a single
page document specifying the heads under which compensation was claimed. It did not
contain any quantification of the amount claimed. It stated, inter alia, 'The Claimant
d wishes the amount of compensation to be negotiated with his agent . . .'
    Although correspondence ensued, it is common ground that no figures or particulars
were submitted on behalf of Mr Amos until October 1981.
    On 14 October 1981 Messrs David Allberry & Co, chartered surveyors who had then
been appointed Mr Amos's agents, wrote to the respondents' district valuer advising him
of their appointment. Their letter included the following paragraph:
e
    'A meeting with the District Council has been arranged, as you know, for Tuesday
    next, 20 October, at which we shall be present. It is our intention at that meeting to
    submit a detailed claim on our client's behalf, the intention being that such a claim
    will be full and final under all heads and which will be included in the reference to
    the Lands Tribunal, the papers for which are currently in course of preparation.'
f
This letter was not headed 'Without Prejudice'.
    Despite what was said in that letter, however, what the agents in fact produced at the
meeting was a 20-page document headed 'Without Prejudice'. It contained full particulars
of the claim then being advanced together with submissions in support of the claim. We
shall hereafter refer to it as document A.
g   It did not result in the acceptance of the claim as put, to an agreed compromise figure
or to a reference to the Lands Tribunal, to which disputed questions of compensation are
by s 179 of the 1971 Act to be referred. It was, after some correspondence, later
superseded by an amended document in similar form and of similar length also marked
'Without Prejudice' to which we shall refer as document B. This was sent by David
Allberry & Co to the district valuer under cover of a letter dated 21 May 1982. That letter
h was itself marked 'Without Prejudice' and was in the following terms:

    'Further to our letter of 2 February we now enclose our client's claim in the above
    matter together with supporting documents. We would be glad to have the
    opportunity of a meeting in order to discuss this claim with a view to negotiating a
    settlement and once you have studied the documents, we will be grateful if you
    could suggest a date for such a meeting.'
j
    Negotiations ensued but were unsuccessful, and on 20 October 1983 the matter was
referred to the Lands Tribunal under s 179 of the 1971 Act.
    In the course of correspondence relating to the reference between solicitors, the
respondents' solicitors wrote to Mr Amos's solicitors on 17 February 1984:

'I refer to previous correspondence and to your client's "Without Prejudice" claims of 20th October 1981 and 21st May 1982. The Council does not accept that a claim *a* for statutory compensation can be made on a "without prejudice basis", particularly in view of the provisions of section 4 of the Land Compensation Act 1961 relating to costs. Would you please confirm that the claims are to be treated as "open" claims; if not will you please submit an open claim, including full details of professional fees and earlier items previously omitted. If you adopt the latter course the Council will contend that its liability for costs (if any) should only run from the date of *b* delivery of an open, particularised claim.'

Mr Amos's solicitors were not prepared to agree to the two documents, being documents A and B, being treated as 'open' claims and the question whether they should be admitted in evidence came before a member of the Lands Tribunal, Mr W H Rees FRICS, for determination on a pre-trial review on 15 March 1985. He determined that the *c* two documents should not be admitted in evidence and so ordered on 10 April 1985.

By originating summons issued pursuant to s 12(6) of the Arbitration Act 1950 and r 38 of the Lands Tribunal Rules 1975, SI 1975/299, and dated 10 June 1985, the respondents applied in the Queen's Bench Division of the High Court for an order that the two documents be admitted in evidence. On 21 January 1986 the matter was heard before Gatehouse J. The application succeeded. *d*

The judge was referred to two authorities, *Re Daintrey, ex p Holt* [1893] 2 QB 116, [1891–4] All ER Rep 209 and *Norwich Union Life Insurance Society v Tony Waller Ltd* (1984) 270 EG 42. In the first of these cases it was held that a letter headed 'Without Prejudice', which clearly contained an offer to settle pending litigation but which was also a clear act of bankruptcy, could be put in evidence on the hearing of a bankruptcy petition on the ground that it was 'one which, from its character, might prejudicially affect the recipient *e* whether or not he accepted the terms offered thereby' (see [1893] 2 QB 116 at 120, [1891–4] All ER Rep 209 at 212). In the course of giving the judgment of the court Vaughan Williams J said ([1893] 2 QB 116 at 119–120, [1891–4] All ER Rep 209 at 211–212):

'In our opinion the rule which excludes documents marked "without prejudice" has no application unless some person is in dispute or negotiation with another, and *f* terms are offered for the settlement of the dispute or negotiation, and it seems to us that the judge must necessarily be entitled to look at the document in order to determine whether the conditions, under which alone the rule applies, exist. The rule is a rule adopted to enable disputants without prejudice to engage in discussion for the purpose of arriving at terms of peace, and unless there is a dispute or negotiations and an offer the rule has no application. It seems to us that the judge *g* must be entitled to look at the document to determine whether the document does contain an offer of terms.'

In the second of the two cases Harman J said (270 EG 42 at 43):

'The rule is, as [counsel for the landlords], in my view, absolutely correctly submitted, a rule of public policy based upon the proposition that it is better to *h* settle than to fight—I paraphrase [counsel for the landlords], but I think that is not unfair as a way of putting what he was submitting. It is, in my judgment, an accurate description of the purpose of the rule, and it also, in my judgment, illuminates the occasions on which the rule arises, and they are entirely in accordance with Vaughan Williams J's formulation. The rule has no application unless some other person is in dispute or negotiation with another. Here, the letter of August 4 *j* 1982 was written, not quite out of the blue, because there had been that rather inept inspection letter written eight months earlier, but written at a time when there was, so far as anything before me goes, no view, position, attitude or anything else emanating from or evidenced by the tenant. The matter at that stage was, in my view, entirely an opening shot, and an opening shot in a situation where no war had been declared and no dispute had arisen. Indeed "shot" may be an inapt word to apply to it. As it seems to me, this letter was not written in the course of negotiation, which must imply that each side has expressed a view and that a *modus vivendi* between them is being proposed, nor had a dispute been constituted, whether by litigation, arbitration or mere verbal or oral threats over the back fence of two neighbouring properties. It seems to me beyond any question that this rubric "Without Prejudice" can only be effectively used where one has an extant disagreement—dispute, issue, call it what you will—or extant negotiations with both sides having set up their own position in them. As it seems to me, this letter, being the initiating letter, could not appropriately be so headed, and I therefore hold against [counsel for the landlords'] first argument. In my view, it is not governed by the rubric attached to it "Without Prejudice", which words remain part of it and are material as part of its writing for the purpose of understanding what it really says but which do not have the effect of validly claiming privilege.'

The judge in our view quite correctly concluded that in holding that an initiating letter could not effectively or appropriately be headed 'Without Prejudice' Harman J erred. If this were so no one could safely proceed directly to an offer to accept a sum in settlement of an as yet unquantified claim. He accordingly proceeded on the basis stated by Vaughan Williams J and considered whether the two documents were offers to settle a dispute, which it was conceded had been in existence since December 1977 when Mr Amos had put in his original claim. He concluded that they were not, but were particulars of the original unspecified claim to compensation. In reaching his conclusion he did not however have before him the letters of 14 October 1981 and 21 May 1982; nor did he have the benefit of being referred to the judgment of Fox LJ in *Cutts v Head* [1984] 1 All ER 597 at 611, [1984] Ch 290 at 313–314, where, having referred to *Walker v Wilsher* (1889) 23 QBD 335 and *Re Daintrey, ex p Holt* [1893] 2 QB 116, [1891–4] All ER Rep 209, he said:

'Those cases, I think, emphasise two things. First, that the purpose of the rule is to facilitate a free discussion of compromise proposals by protecting the proposals and discussion from disclosure in the proceedings. The ultimate aim appears to be to facilitate compromise. Second, whilst the ordinary meaning of "without prejudice" is without prejudice to the position of the offeror if his offer is refused, it is not competent to one party to impose such terms on the other in respect of a document which, by its nature, is capable of being used to the disadvantage of that other. The expression must be read as creating a situation of mutuality which enables both sides to take advantage of the "without prejudice" protection. The juridical basis of that must, I think, in part derive from an implied agreement between the parties and in part from public policy. As to the former, Bowen LJ in *Walker v Wilsher* 23 QBD 335 at 339, after the passage which I have already cited to the effect that it is important that the door should not be shut against compromises, went on to say: "The agreement that the letter is without prejudice ought, I think, to be carried out in its full integrity." As to public policy it obviously is desirable to facilitate compromise rather than forcing the parties to litigate to the end. But to achieve a compromise one of them has to make an offer. He might be apprehensive that his offer might be used against him if the negotiations failed. So he would make his offer without prejudice to his position if the offer was refused. But that was unfair to the other party. It was one-sided. So it was necessary to extend the without prejudice umbrella to cover both parties.'

That passage is important for two reasons. First it shows that the rule depends partly on public policy, namely the need to facilitate compromise, and partly on implied agreement. Second it shows that the rule covers not only documents which constitute offers but also documents which form part of discussions on offers, ie negotiations.

In the present case Mr Amos had indicated from the very outset that he wished, through his agents, to negotiate. There was then correspondence leading up to the letter *a* which preceded document A. That letter certainly indicated that the document when submitted was intended to be 'open' but when produced it was marked 'Without Prejudice'. This prima facie means that it was intended to be a negotiating document. The prima facie inference, therefore, is that the agents had changed their intention. This might have been displaced had there been evidence that, when tendered, it was so tendered on the same basis as originally indicated, but there was no such evidence and it *b* is not without significance that when the question was first raised by the respondents' solicitors in their letter of 17 February 1984 they did not say that the document or its successor *were* 'open'. It was contended merely that it was impossible to make an effective 'without prejudice' offer. That contention was not pursued before us, in our view rightly. It is without foundation. Bearing in mind the original expressed intention to negotiate, the fact that there was a dispute in existence, that it is common practice for such claims *c* to be the subject of negotiation before the parties resort to a reference to the Lands Tribunal, and that the document was clearly marked 'Without Prejudice', we have no hesitation in concluding that those words should be given their ordinary effect. The position with regard to document B is in our view plainer. It was clearly written in the course of negotiation and was accompanied by a letter which was itself headed 'Without Prejudice'. Both documents are in our view inadmissible. *d*

It was for these reasons that we allowed the appeal on the conclusion of the argument. The order of the judge must be set aside and an order made that neither document A nor document B be admitted in evidence on the hearing by the Lands Tribunal of the Mr Amos's claim to compensation.

In order to avoid any possibility of future unnecessary disputes about such matters we conclude by stating that we agree with the judge (a) that the heading 'Without Prejudice' *e* does not conclusively or automatically render a document so marked privileged, (b) that, if privilege is claimed but challenged, the court can look at a document so headed in order to determine its nature and (c) that privilege can attach to a document headed 'Without Prejudice' even if it is an opening shot. The rule is, however, not limited to documents which are offers. It attaches to all documents which are marked 'without *f* prejudice' and form part of negotiations, whether or not they are themselves offers, unless the privilege is defeated on some other ground as was the case in *Re Daintrey, ex p Holt* [1893] 2 QB 116, [1891–4] All ER Rep 209.

Appeal allowed.

Solicitors: *Thompsons*, agents for *Morgans*, Ludlow (for Mr Amos); *Edge & Ellison Hatwell* *g* *Pritchett & Co*, Birmingham (for the respondents).

Wendy Shockett   Barrister.

Simaan General Contracting Co v Pilkington Glass Ltd

QUEEN'S BENCH DIVISION (OFFICIAL REFEREES' BUSINESS)
HIS HONOUR JUDGE JOHN NEWEY QC
18, 31 JULY 1986

Evidence – Without prejudice correspondence – Application for security for costs – Without prejudice correspondence concerning negotiations between parties – Whether admissible in evidence at hearing of application.

On the hearing of a summons for security for costs the general rule relating to 'without prejudice' correspondence applies, namely that without prejudice correspondence concerning negotiations between the parties is not admissible in evidence without the consent of all parties concerned (see p 347 *c* and p 348 *d e h*, post).

Notes

For communications 'without prejudice', see 17 Halsbury's Laws (4th edn) paras 212–213, and for cases on the subject, see 22 Digest (Reissue) 407–410, 4082–4108.

Cases referred to in judgment

Calderbank v Calderbank [1975] 3 All ER 333, [1976] Fam 93, [1975] 3 WLR 586, CA.
Chocoladefabriken Lindt & Sprungli AG v Nestlé Co Ltd [1978] RPC 287.
Cutts v Head [1984] 1 All ER 597, [1984] Ch 290, [1984] 2 WLR 349, CA.
Parkinson (Sir Lindsay) & Co Ltd v Triplan Ltd [1973] 2 All ER 273, [1973] QB 609, [1973] 2 WLR 632, CA.
Walker v Wilsher (1889) 23 QBD 335, CA.

Application

The plaintiffs, Simaan General Contracting Co, a company incorporated in and under the laws of the United Arab Emirates, issued a writ on 4 March 1986 against the defendants, Pilkington Glass Ltd, a company incorporated in England, claiming damages for negligence in supplying coated glass units. The defendants issued a summons dated 8 May 1986 under RSC Ord 23, r 1(1)(a) seeking security for costs from the plaintiffs on the grounds that the defendants were ordinarily resident out of the jurisdiction. The summons was heard in chambers but judgment was given by his Honour Judge John Newey QC in open court. The facts are set out in the judgment.

Romie Tager for the plaintiffs.
D M Harris for the defendants.

Cur adv vult

31 July. The following judgment was delivered.

HIS HONOUR JUDGE JOHN NEWEY QC. In this case the plaintiffs, Simaan General Contracting Co, a company incorporated under the laws of the United Arab Emirates, whose address is in Abu Dhabi, have brought an action against the defendants, Pilkington Glass Ltd, a company incorporated in England, claiming damages for negligence in the supply of coated glass units.

The glass units were for installation in an office building which the plaintiffs were building as contractors. ICA Group Feal, an Italian company, were sub-contractors for curtain walling, nominated by the employer's supervising officer, and the defendants were suppliers to them. There was no contract between the plaintiffs and the defendants.

The plaintiffs issued and served their writ on 4 March 1986 and delivered their statement of claim on 30 April. The defendants have, or are about to deliver, a defence denying liability, and I have given directions ending with a hearing date 15 June 1987, and an estimated length of 12 days. On 8 May 1986 the defendants issued a summons under RSC Ord 23, r 1(1)(a) seeking security for costs from the plaintiffs on the grounds that they are ordinarily resident out of the jurisdiction.

The summons came before me on 18 July, when affidavit evidence was relied on by both parties. To an affidavit of Mr David Rose, a partner in the firm of solicitors acting for the plaintiffs, was exhibited a letter from Mr C R Bayley, a solicitor for the defendants, dated 14 February 1986, part of which reads:

'Without prejudice, having seen the correspondence you will no doubt be aware that [the defendants have] offered to supply, without charge, up to a total of 50 replacement units for the building. The supply of such units would be subject to a formal agreement in full and final settlement of the various parties' claims arising out of this matter.'

Mr Rose deposed in his affidavit that since receipt of the letter he had been supplied by the plaintiffs with further documents—

'which make it clear that there had been negotiations between all relevant parties . . . for the compromise of the claims relating to the defective glass supplied . . . with the defendant offering to replace 50 glazing units on the basis which was understood to include their delivery to Abu Dhabi.'

Assuming that the plaintiffs have a valid claim and that the number of defective units does not exceed 50, their replacement by new units would not be sufficient to compensate the plaintiffs, for, according to para 14 of the statement of claim, the supervising officer is requiring that the whole of the curtain walling be taken down and replaced.

Counsel for the plaintiffs submitted that on a summons for security for costs the court may properly take into account evidence of offers in settlement made by the defendants, even if they were made 'without prejudice', in order to decide whether the plaintiffs are likely to succeed in the action and whether it would be just to them to require them to provide security. Counsel for the defendants submitted that evidence of 'without prejudice' offers is wholly inadmissable on applications for security.

Both counsel agreed that there is no reported case in which it has been decided whether evidence of 'without prejudice' offers may be given on summonses for security for costs. I was referred to cases and to notes in *The Supreme Court Practice 1985* concerning the circumstances in which security should be ordered and those in which 'without prejudice' offers may be mentioned. I decided to reserve judgment and at counsel's request I am giving it in open court.

Sir Lindsay Parkinson & Co Ltd v Triplan Ltd [1973] 2 All ER 273, [1973] QB 609 concerned an application for security for costs against a plaintiff company, which was believed to be unable to pay the defendant's costs if unsuccessful, under s 447 of the Companies Act 1948 by a defendant who had made an open offer in settlement. Lord Denning MR said that the Court had a discretion whether to order security which it would exercise 'considering all the circumstances of the particular case' (see [1973] 2 All ER 273 at 285–286, [1973] QB 609 at 626–627). He listed circumstances suggested by counsel, including whether the company had a good prospect of success, whether there was an admission by the defendant, on the pleadings or elsewhere, that money was due and whether the application for security was being used oppressively so as to try to stifle a genuine claim. He then said ([1973] 2 All ER 273 at 286, [1973] QB 609 at 627):

'I am quite clear that a payment into court, or an open offer, is a matter which the court can take into account. It goes to show that there is substance in the claim: and that it would not be right to deprive the company of it by insisting on security for costs.'

Cairns LJ agreed with Lord Denning MR. He thought that on the information
available to the court the plaintiff was likely to recover more than had been offered by
the defendant in an open letter. He thought that the proper view was that the defendant
had in effect got security to the extent of the offer. Cairns LJ said ([1973] 2 All ER 273 at
287, [1973] 1 QB 609 at 628):

> 'I am not impressed by the argument that this would be likely to hinder parties
> from paying into court or making an offer ... In any case where the plaintiff ...
> has a prospect of recovering some sum in proceedings, it is a matter of simple
> prudence on the part of defendants ... to make a payment in or an offer which will
> relieve them of having to pay in the long run what may be a heavy bill of costs
> resulting from a comparatively small award in favour of the plaintiff ...'

It is public policy to encourage litigants to settle their differences and, since they are
most unlikely to negotiate satisfactorily if every word which they utter and every offer
which they make can be quoted against them later, the general rule has long been that
nothing which is written or said 'without prejudice' can be referred to in court
subsequently without the consent of all parties concerned.

To the general rule there are exceptions. In *Walker v Wilsher* (1889) 23 QBD 335 at
338 Lindley LJ referred to letters written without prejudice being considered in a case in
which a question of laches was raised and, at least in my experience, they are referred to
freely without protest on applications to strike out for want of prosecution.

In *Chocoladefabriken Lindt & Sprungli AG v Nestlé Co Ltd* [1978] RPC 287 at 289–290
Megarry V-C, while recognising that a result of the 'without prejudice' rule might be to
prevent the true case coming before the judge, left open the question of whether it could
be relied on in 'any case in which there are grounds for believing that the rule is going to
be used to perpetrate some fraud or dishonesty'.

In *Calderbank v Calderbank* [1975] 3 All ER 333, [1976] Fam 93, a case in which a
husband had applied for financial provision or a property adjustment order under the
Matrimonial Causes Act 1973, the Court of Appeal held that the wife's offer of a home to
the husband before the proceedings were heard could be taken into account on the issue
of costs. Cairns LJ referred to types of proceedings where protection as to costs has been
afforded to parties who wish to compromise and for whom payment into court is not an
appropriate method, such as a sealed offer in the Lands Tribunal. He said ([1975] 3 All
ER 333 at 342, [1976] Fam 93 at 106):

> 'Counsel for the husband drew our attention to a provision in the Matrimonial
> Causes Rules 1968, SI 1968/219, with references to damages which were then
> payable by a co-respondent, provision to the effect that an offer might be made in
> the form that it was without prejudice to the issue as to damages but reserving the
> right of the co-respondent to refer to it on the issue of costs. It appears to me that it
> would be equally appropriate that it should be permissible to make an offer of that
> kind in such proceedings as we have been dealing with and I think that that would
> be an appropriate way in which a party who was willing to make a compromise
> could put it forward.'

In *Cutts v Head* [1984] 1 All ER 597, [1984] Ch 290 the Court of Appeal held that an
offer of settlement made before the trial of an action in a letter expressed to be 'without
prejudice' but reserving the right to bring the letter to the attention of the judge on the
issue of costs after judgment if the offer is refused is admissible on the question of costs
without the consent of all parties, in all cases in which a payment into court would not
be appropriate. Oliver LJ said ([1984] 1 All ER 597 at 605, [1984] Ch 290 at 306):

> '(1) The protection from disclosure of without prejudice negotiations rests in part
> on public policy and in part on convention (ie an express or implied agreement that
> the negotiations shall be protected). (2) There is no public policy which precludes a
> conventional modification of the protection to the extent suggested in *Calderbank v*

Calderbank . . . As a practical matter, a consciousness of a risk as to costs if reasonable offers are refused can only encourage settlement . . .'

The effect of *Calderbank v Calderbank* and *Cutts v Head* has now been given statutory effect by a new r 14 inserted in RSC Ord 22.

It is obvious that the same considerations should be taken into account by a court hearing a summons under Ord 23, r 1 as one under s 447 of the 1948 Act (now s 726(1) of the Companies Act 1985). They include, therefore, the plaintiffs' prospects of success, any admission by the defendant and whether the application is made oppressively. In *Sir Lindsay Parkinson & Co Ltd v Triplan Ltd* [1973] 2 All ER 273 at 286, [1973] QB 609 at 627, Lord Denning MR said that payments into court and open offers were matters which the court could take into account. No doubt he would today add 'Calderbank letters', which are the equivalent of payments in. Lord Denning MR did not mention 'without prejudice' offers and possibly he meant to exclude them by implication. Cairns LJ referred to 'offers' without classification, but in the case before the Court of Appeal the offer was an 'open' one.

Evidence as to 'without prejudice' negotiations could assist a court in forming views as to a plaintiff's prospects of success and whether a defendant is endeavouring to stifle an action. Because of its qualified nature a 'without prejudice' offer could not, I think, constitute an admission.

To allow one party to give evidence of 'without prejudice' communications without the consent of another would be in direct conflict with the general rule excluding such evidence and with the public policy which supports it. Defendants sued by plaintiffs resident abroad or by companies likely to get into financial difficulties would be deterred from exploring possibilities of settlement and making sensible offers for fear of prejudicing their prospects of being able to obtain security for costs. In particular a defendant who has obtained an order for security intended to relate to preparations for trial only would be most unwilling to take any action which might prevent him from obtaining a second order for security in respect of trial costs.

To the extent that the general rule is based on convention, as Oliver LJ stated in *Cutts v Head* that it is, for a party to adduce evidence of 'without prejudice' matters would be a breach of convention by him.

In striking-out applications, it is not the content of 'without prejudice' negotiations but the fact that they took place which may be material as excusing delay. Defendants who make payments into court or who write Calderbank letters are making offers, which they intend should be mentioned in open court in appropriate circumstances. They do so, instead of making fully 'without prejudice' offers, for tactical reasons and because of possible costs advantages. A defendant who has the misfortune to be sued by a plaintiff against whom it may be difficult to enforce an order for costs should not be at a disadvantage in obtaining security because he has, for whatever reason, made attempts to settle the case.

In my opinion, evidence of 'without prejudice' negotiations is not admissible on summonses for security for costs and the passages in Mr Rose's affidavit and in Mr Bayley's letter relating to such negotiations should be disregarded. For reasons which I gave on 18 July, I think that the plaintiffs should give the defendants security for costs in the sum of £20,000.

Order accordingly.

Solicitors: *Michael Conn & Co* (for the plaintiffs); *C R Bayley*, St Helens (for the defendants).

K Mydeen Esq   Barrister.

R v Newcastle upon Tyne City Justices, ex parte Skinner

QUEEN'S BENCH DIVISION
GLIDEWELL LJ AND OTTON J
21 OCTOBER 1986

Case stated – Magistrates' courts – Recognisance – Applicant required to enter recognisance as condition of justices stating case – Means of applicant – Justices requiring defendant to enter into recognisance based on time and work involved in preparing case – Whether justices required to take into account defendant's means when setting recognisance – Magistrates' Courts Act 1980, s 114.

The applicant was found guilty of burglary by justices. When he requested the justices to state a case for the opinion of the High Court he was informed by their clerk that he would be required to enter into a recognisance under s 114[a] of the Magistrates' Courts Act 1980 in the sum of £500 before the matter could be taken further. The sum proposed related to the amount of time and work required of the magistrates' court staff in preparing the case. The applicant, who was receiving supplementary benefit and had no capital, applied for an order of mandamus requiring the justices to state the case without first requiring him to enter into a recognisance, contending that his means should have been taken into account in considering whether he should be required to enter into a recognisance.

Held – Although justices were entitled to require an applicant for a case to be stated to enter into a recognisance under s 114 of the 1980 Act in order to ensure that the applicant genuinely intended to pursue his appeal, they were required to have regard to his means before deciding whether to require any recognisance and, if so, the amount. Since the justices had clearly not taken the applicant's means into account when they required him to enter into a recognisance of £500, the appeal would be allowed and the case referred back to the justices to decide whether in all the circumstances a recognisance was required of the applicant as a condition of their stating a case for appeal (see p 351 *g h* and p 352 *e g*, post).

Notes

For the requirement of a recognisance when magistrates state a case, see 29 Halsbury's Laws (4th edn) 479, and for cases on the subject, see 33 Digest (Reissue) 180, 1392–1396.

For the Magistrates' Courts Act 1980, s 114, see 50(2) Halsbury's Statutes (3rd edn) 1542.

Application for judicial review

Paul Anthony Skinner applied, with the leave of Mann J given on 28 May 1986, for judicial review by way of an order of mandamus requiring the Newcastle upon Tyne city justices to state a case on reasonable terms having regard to the means and circumstances of the applicant. The facts are set out in the judgment of Glidewell LJ.

Simon Wood for the applicant.
The justices did not appear.

GLIDEWELL LJ. This is an application, by leave of the single judge, for an order of mandamus requiring the justices for the county of Tyne and Wear, sitting at Newcastle upon Tyne, to state a case. That, in form, is the remedy which is sought, but in substance

---

a   Section 114, so far as material, is set out at p 351 *d*, post

the application is to require the justices to consider properly the applicant's means before fixing a recognisance into which they required him to enter as a condition of stating a case.

The matter has been argued with commendable brevity and clarity by counsel for the applicant and I say at once that we propose to grant his application. I should explain shortly how it comes about. On 8 January 1986 the applicant appeared in front of the Newcastle city magistrates charged with burglary. He pleaded not guilty and was represented by Mr Hodgson, a solicitor. The magistrates tried the question of his guilt and no complaint is made about anything that occurred during that process. They found the case proved.

Mr Hodgson then addressed the magistrates in mitigation on behalf of the applicant. Having considered that mitigation, the chairman of the magistrates, according to an affidavit made by Mr Hodgson and another affidavit made by a Mr Bynoe, who is a partner in another firm of solicitors in Newcastle-upon-Tyne, who was in court waiting for the next case, uttered words which both Mr Hodgson and Mr Bynoe took to indicate doubt in the minds of the justices whether this defendant had the necessary intention for him to be guilty of the crime of burglary.

On the question whether those words, which I do not propose to set out in detail in this judgment, if they were said by the chairman, did demonstrate that the applicant did not have that intention, the justices were asked to state a case for the opinion of this court. The application was duly made on 28 January and in reply Mr Gane, the clerk to the city justices (not the clerk who was sitting in court), replied by a letter of 29 January 1986. That letter reads:

> 'In the event of this matter proceeding in accordance with Rule 76 to 81 of the Magistrates' Courts' Rules, 1981, it will first be necessary for your client to enter into a recognizance in the sum of £500·00 to prosecute the appeal, and I should be grateful if you would inform Mr. Legard of my office when it will be convenient for your client to attend this court for that purpose.'

In reply to that, the applicant's solicitors wrote on 26 February, saying:

> 'Our above-named client is unemployed. He is in receipt of Supplementary Benefit and has no capital whatsoever. He has been granted Emergency Legal Aid to pursue this appeal and we anticipate a nil contribution. In view of the above information we shall be grateful if you would reconsider whether there should be a recognizance at all in this case and if so the size of such recognizance.'

The facts set out in that letter are supported by an affidavit by the applicant himself, sworn on 13 May 1986, which is before us and which indeed says that he is on supplementary benefit. He details his modest income and his outgoings. It is right to say that it must be obvious that, on the face of it, he would not be able, if called on to do so, to meet a recognisance in the sum of £500 unless he was required to pay it over an inordinately long period of time.

The letter from the solicitors of 26 February received an immediate response from Mr Gane on 27 February. He said:

> 'Thank you for your above quoted letter dated 26th February 1986, giving personal particulars concerning your above-named client. It is the recognised practice of this court to require an applicant who has requested a case to be stated to enter into a recognizance to pursue that appeal, and the sum of £500 is indeed a comparatively small amount having regard to the considerable amount of work and expertise that is involved for my office and myself; in the same way as you have been covered by a certificate to cover your professional costs, there requires to be a token of your client's bona fides that he intends to pursue this appeal to its conclusion. Unfortunately, it is common-place that appellants both when appealing

by notice of motion and when appealing by case stated, and after putting my office and myself to many many hours of work, then withdraw or abandon the appeal. Accordingly, I should be grateful if your client would attend this office to enter into a recognizance as soon as possible."

The submission of counsel for the applicant is that, while the justices undoubtedly have power to require a recognisance before they state a case, one of the factors which must be taken into account when deciding whether to require a recognisance at all, and if so the amount of it, is the means of the applicant. He submits further that it appears from the correspondence I have quoted that these justices have not considered the means of the applicant, but that the recognisance has been fixed at a sum which is related more to the amount of time and work which will be required of the magistrates' court staff than to the personal characteristics of the applicant. He submits that that is wrong and that the magistrates should now be required to reconsider the matter.

The power in magistrates to require a recognisance is quite clear. It is to be found in s 114 of the Magistrates' Courts Act 1980, which, so far as is material, reads:

'Justices to whom application has been made to state a case for the opinion of the High Court on any proceeding of a magistrates' court shall not be required to state a case until the applicant has entered into a recognizance, with or without sureties, before the magistrates' court, conditioned to prosecute the appeal without delay and to submit to the judgment of the High Court and pay such costs as that Court may award . . .'

The section does not say in terms that the magistrates must consider the applicant's means when deciding on the amount of the recognisance. Apparently, the matter has never previously been considered by this court. Counsel for the applicant tells us that he knows of no authority and there is none referred to in the notes in *Stone's Justices' Manual 1986*. Counsel for the applicant, however, does refer us to the analogous passage in relation to a case stated by a Crown Court after appeal to it from the magistrates' court. That is to be found not in the statute, but in the Crown Court Rules 1982, SI 1982/1109, r 26. That rule deals generally with an application to a Crown Court to state a case. Paragraph (11) provides:

'If the Crown Court so orders, the applicant shall, before the case is stated and delivered to him, enter before an officer of the Crown Court into a recognizance, with or without sureties and in such sum as the Crown Court considers proper, having regard to the means of the applicant, conditioned to prosecute the appeal without delay.'

One finds there the requirement that the Crown Court shall have regard to the means of the applicant. In our view, although the same phrase is not to be found in s 114 of the 1980 Act, the same principle must necessarily apply to magistrates as it does to the stating of a case by the Crown Court. In other words, while magistrates are perfectly entitled to take the view that, in order to ensure that an applicant in a case stated intends genuinely to pursue the appeal, they can require a recognisance, they must have regard to his means in fixing the amount of that recognisance and in deciding whether or not to require any recognisance at all in the particular case.

For my part, I go further and suggest this. If an applicant on supplementary benefit is granted legal aid with a nil contribution, when the matter comes before this court, if he fails in his appeal, he will normally not have any order for costs made against him. Certainly, if an order were to be made, it would be one not to be enforced without leave of the court. However, if magistrates require a recognisance which is well outside any possibility of the applicant satisfying it, when they have not had regard to the applicant's means, that may put pressure on an applicant to pursue an appeal which, in the end, the stated case shows to be absolutely hopeless. If he does pursue his appeal, he will not forfeit his recognisance and he will not have to meet the penalty of costs. That clearly is an undesirable situation. That is not the only reason, but certainly it is a reason which supports the view that the magistrates must take the applicant's means into account.

Is it clear that these magistrates have not done so? The magistrates have indicated that they do not, at this stage, wish to file any affidavits themselves in opposition to this application. We do have the affidavit of their clerk and also an affidavit from Mr Legard, the court clerk who was sitting in court on the occasion when the applicant was convicted. Mr Legard, with respect to him, does not really deal with the question of the applicant's means at all, save to say that in his view the applicant is in no way inhibited by the recognisance in attempting to achieve an acquittal.

Mr Gane makes it clear in his affidavit that—

> 'the recognizance . . . is simply an earnest of the bona fides of the Appellant, and that in the event of the matter proceeding to appeal, there would be no question of any financial impost or penalty.'

Later on, he says: 'It is feared that the Appellant's solicitors totally misunderstand the effect of the section . . .'

It may be (I make no comment about this) that the applicant's solicitors may not be wholly familiar with all the requirements of stating a case, but it must be envisaged that when they receive the case stated they would then have to consider, with counsel, whether to advise their client to proceed with the appeal or not. If they concluded that the appeal ought not to be proceeded with, the applicant would then be at risk of his recognisance being forfeited. Clearly, at that stage, the magistrates would have to consider his means whether they should forfeit any or part of it. It does not seem from what Mr Gane says in his affidavit or in his letters, to which I have referred, that the magistrates have taken that into account at the present stage. Accordingly, for my part, I would grant the application and order not that the magistrates do state a case, because they are willing to do so, but that they do now consider whether they should require a recognisance from this applicant as a condition of stating a case and, if so, the amount of that recognisance, having regard to the applicant's means and assets.

OTTON J. Section 114 of the Magistrates' Courts Act 1980 clearly gives the justices the power to require a recognisance. I agree with Glidewell LJ, that they should take into account the means of the applicant. By the two letters from their clerk, to which reference has been made, they appear not to have had regard to this applicant's means. They clearly should have done so.

I wish only to emphasise one practical matter. If justices require a recognisance which is unreasonable having regard to the applicant's means, this may prove to be counter-productive. Instead of discouraging the applicant from prosecuting his application, he may be encouraged to prosecute his application even though his prospects of success are remote. If he loses before the Divisional Court, then the court, having regard to his means, is unlikely to make any order for costs against him. I therefore agree that the order should be made in the terms adumbrated by Glidewell LJ.

Order for mandamus granted. Case remitted to magistrates to consider whether recognisance required from the applicant.

Solicitors: *Harvey & Marron*, Newcastle upon Tyne (for the applicant).

Dilys Tausz   Barrister.

a   # R v Rushmoor Borough Council, ex parte Barrett and another

QUEEN'S BENCH DIVISION (CROWN OFFICE LIST)

REEVE J

b   2 JULY, 4 SEPTEMBER 1986

Housing – Local authority houses – Tenant's right to buy – Early disposal – Repayment of discount – Exempted disposals – Disposal pursuant to property adjustment order in connection with matrimonial proceedings – Matrimonial home purchased at discount pursuant to right to buy – Parties divorced a year after purchase – Property sold and proceeds divided equally between parties pursuant to consent order made in proceedings for financial relief – Whether sale a

c   *'disposal . . . in pursuance of' property adjustment order – Whether sale an exempted disposal – Whether discount required to be repaid – Matrimonial Causes Act 1973, ss 24, 24A – Housing Act 1985, s 160(1)(c).*

In 1984 the applicants, who were husband and wife, exercised the right granted to them by the Housing Act 1980 as secure tenants to buy the freehold of the local authority

d   house which they occupied as their matrimonial home. The amount they were required to pay was reduced by a discount from the purchase price calculated in accordance with the 1980 Act, and the conveyance to them of the freehold contained the covenant stipulated by that Act to repay to the local authority the discount or a proportion thereof in the event of their disposing of the property within five years of the conveyance. In 1985 a decree absolute was pronounced dissolving the applicants' marriage, and in 1986,

e   in proceedings between the applicants for financial relief, the registrar made a consent order that the matrimonial home be sold and the proceeds divided equally between the parties. On the sale of the property the local authority demanded the payment of £10,120 in accordance with the covenant in the conveyance. The applicants sought a declaration that the local authority's demand was wrong in law, on the ground that the sale of the property had been ordered pursuant to the court's power under s 24 of the

f   Matrimonial Causes Act 1973 to make property adjustment orders, and was therefore an exempted disposal by virtue of s 160(1)(c)[a] of the Housing Act 1985, with the result that the discount did not fall to be repaid.

Held – On the true construction of s 160(1)(c) of the 1985 Act a 'disposal . . . in pursuance of an order made under section 24 of the Matrimonial Causes Act 1973' contemplated a

g   transfer or settlement of property under s 24 which involved continued occupational enjoyment of the property by a spouse and/or children of the family and whereby no liquid cash advantage was gained. Accordingly, such a disposal did not include the sale of a matrimonial home by order of the court in proceedings for financial relief after divorce, since in making such an order the court was exercising the power conferred on it by s 24A of the 1973 Act to order the sale of property. It followed therefore that the

h   applicants were obliged to pay the £10,120 to the local authority (see p 357 h to p 358 b, post).

Dicta of Ormrod LJ in *Ward v Ward and Greene* [1980] 1 All ER 176 and of Goff LJ in *Re Holliday (a bankrupt), ex p the trustee of the bankrupt v The bankrupt* [1980] 3 All ER at 393–394 explained.

j   *Practice Note* [1980] 1 WLR 4 criticised.

Notes

For repayment of the discount given to a person exercising as a secure tenant the right to buy the freehold of a dwelling house, see 27 Halsbury's Laws (4th edn) para 895.

---

a   Section 160(1), so far as material, is set out at p 355 d, post

For the Matrimonial Causes Act 1973, ss 24, 24A, see 27 Halsbury's Statutes (4th edn) 726, 728.

As from 1 April 1986 Pt V (ss 118–188) (The Right to Buy) of the Housing Act 1985 replaced Ch I of Pt I of the Housing Act 1980. For s 160 of the 1985 Act, see 21 Halsbury's Statutes (4th edn) 169.

Cases referred to in judgment

Holliday (a bankrupt), Re, ex p the trustee of the bankrupt v The bankrupt [1980] 3 All ER 385, [1981] Ch 405, [1981] 2 WLR 996, CA.
Practice Note [1980] 1 WLR 4.
Thompson v Thompson [1985] 2 All ER 243, [1986] Ch 38, [1985] 3 WLR 17, CA.
Ward v Ward and Greene [1980] 1 All ER 176n, [1980] 1 WLR 4n, CA.
Williams v Williams [1977] 1 All ER 28, [1976] Ch 278, [1976] 3 WLR 494, CA.

Case also cited

Norman v Norman [1983] 1 All ER 486, [1983] 1 WLR 295.

Application for judicial review

Carol Ruth Barrett and Thomas Herbert John Barrett applied, with the leave of McNeill J given on 9 April 1986, for judicial review by way of a declaration that the decision of the respondent, Rushmoor Borough Council, contained in a letter dated 24 February 1986 adopting a letter from the Department of the Environment dated 17 February that the discount obtained on the purchase of 2 Beech Road, Hawley Estate, Farnborough, Hampshire from the council under the Housing Act 1980 be repaid, following the order made by consent by Mr Registrar Fuller in the Aldershot and Farnham County Court on 18 February 1986 directing the sale of 2 Beech Road with the proceeds to be divided equally between the applicants, on the grounds that such a disposal was pursuant to an order under s 24A of the Matrimonial Causes Act 1973 and not s 24 and was therefore not an exempted disposal for the purposes of s 160 of the Housing Act 1985, was wrong in law. The facts are set out in the judgment.

Nicholas Paul for the applicants.
Timothy Straker for Rushmoor Borough Council.

Cur adv vult

4 September. The following judgment was delivered.

REEVE J. The question which falls for decision in this application by way of judicial review is whether the sale of a matrimonial home by order of the court in proceedings for financial relief after divorce, being a 'disposal', is, or is not, a disposal 'in pursuance of an order under section 24 of the Matrimonial Causes Act 1973' on the true construction of those words as they appear in s 160(1)(c) of the Housing Act 1985. The answer to that question is of importance to the present applicants because, if it is in the affirmative, they will be exempted from the obligation to pay the sum of £10,120 to the local authority from which the home was purchased; whereas, if the answer is in the negative, they will be obliged to pay the whole of that sum. The facts, so far as material, are simple and are as follows.

In January 1982 Carol Ruth Barrett moved in to live as man and wife with Thomas Herbert John Barrett at 2 Beech Road, Farnborough, Hampshire which he was occupying as a tenant of Rushmoor Borough Council. They continued to live there together until about January 1983 when Mr Barrett moved out. Mrs Barrett remained in the property and the tenancy was transferred into her sole name. Mr Barrett returned to her in January *a* 1984 and the tenancy was thereupon transferred into their joint names. They then married on 6 March 1984. There are no children of the family.

In October 1984 Mr and Mrs Barrett, the present applicants, as secure tenants availed themselves of the right granted to them by ss 1 and 4 of the Housing Act 1980 to acquire the freehold of 2 Beech Road from Rushmoor Borough Council. The amount which they were required to pay was reduced by the discount of 44% from the purchase price calculated in accordance with s 7 of the 1980 Act. In this case the discount amounted to
b £12,650. The conveyance to them of the freehold contained the covenant, stipulated by s 8 of the Act, to pay to the local authority on demand the amount calculated in accordance with s 8(2) in the event of their disposing of the property within five years of the conveyance. On 4 December 1985 a decree absolute was pronounced dissolving the marriage between the applicants. Subsequently, on 18 February 1986, in proceedings between them for financial relief, it was ordered by consent by Mr Registrar Fuller sitting
c at Aldershot and Farnham County Court that 'The property known as 2 Beech Road, Hawley Street, Farnborough, Hampshire be sold, and the proceeds of sale divided equally between the parties'. In consequence of that order, the house was sold on 11 April 1986 and 80% of the discount of £12,650 (namely £10,120) falls to be paid by the applicants to the local authority in accordance with the covenant unless exemption can be claimed by them under the provisions of s 160 of the Housing Act 1985. That section, so far as
d relevant to the facts of this case, reads as follows:

> '(1) A disposal is an exempted disposal . . . if . . . (c) it is a disposal of the whole of the dwelling-house in pursuance of an order made under section 24 of the Matrimonial Causes Act 1973 (property adjustment orders in connection with matrimonial proceedings) . . .'

e Counsel for the applicants accepts that the sale of the house in April 1986 amounts to a disposal. However, he submits that it was a disposal 'in pursuance of an order made under section 24.' That section undoubtedly does not expressly confer on the court the power to order a sale. Such a power is, however, now expressly conferred by s 24A(1), which was inserted in the 1973 Act by s 7 of the Matrimonial Homes and Property Act
f 1981. Section 24A came into force as from 1 October 1981. Prior to October 1981, while there was still no express power in the Matrimonial Causes Act 1973 to order a sale, the courts frequently did order a sale of property in proceedings for financial relief. Counsel for the applicants has submitted that they did so exercising a power which was impliedly contained in s 24. He referred to a number of cases in support of that proposition. In *Williams v Williams* [1977] 1 All ER 28, [1976] Ch 278 a house had been purchased in
g 1970 in the joint names of the husband and the wife. They had four children. In 1971 the marriage was dissolved. In 1973 the husband applied by originating summons in the Chancery Division under s 30 of the Law of Property Act 1925 and s 57 of the Trustee Act 1925 for an order that the wife should concur in the sale of the house so that he could have his half share of the proceeds of sale. Foster J made the order for sale. On appeal it was held that, since the primary object in acquiring the property was to provide a home
h for the family, and it was still being used as a family home, the case should be sent back to be dealt with in the Family Division as part of a claim for financial relief in matrimonial proceedings. It seems clear to me from that case that if the court in the Family Division had thought it appropriate, in conjunction with proceedings under s 24 of the 1973 Act, to order a sale of the property, it would have had power to do so not under s 24 but under the s 30 application which was expressly remitted to it.

j Counsel further relied on a dictum of Goff LJ in *Re Holliday (a bankrupt), ex p the trustee of the bankrupt v The bankrupt* [1980] 3 All ER 385 at 393–394, [1981] Ch 405 at 418–419, where he is reported as saying:

> 'Where then the matrimonial jurisdiction is available I would agree that today a spouse wishing to obtain an order for sale should apply to the Family Division and if he or she applies in the Chancery Division the other spouse should apply for an

order for transfer to that division and for any ancillary relief he or she may wish to
seek under ss 23 and 24 of the Matrimonial Causes Act 1973. That division may   *a*
then dispose of the problem by a transfer of property order, or may consider the
question of sale in combination with an exercise of its powers under ss 23 and 24
. . .'

I cannot infer from that passage that Goff LJ was suggesting that the court had the powers
to order a sale under s 24. Had he meant to say that, instead of referring to 'the question   *b*
of sale in combination with an exercise of its powers under . . . s 24 . . .', he would have
said 'the question of sale in the exercise of its powers under s 24'.

In *Ward v Ward and Greene* [1980] 1 All ER 176n, [1980] 1 WLR 4n, which was an
appeal from a decision of Dunn J, Ormrod LJ concluded his judgment as follows:

'At the outset of his judgment the learned judge referred to the fact that he had
suggested that the husband should issue a pro forma summons under s 17 of the   *c*
Married Women's Property Act 1882 asking for the sale of the former matrimonial
home. This is a point which has been raised from time to time, which I know is
concerning the Law Commission at the moment. I have heard it suggested on a
number of occasions that in order for the court to make an order for a sale under the
Matrimonial Causes Act 1973, ss 23 and 24, it is necessary to issue proceedings either
under s 17 of the 1882 Act or, in appropriate cases, under s 30 of the Law of Property   *d*
Act 1925. For my part, I have never understood the advantages of multiplying
pieces of paper intituled in particular statutes named at the head of the summons.
It seems to me to be quite clear that s 17 of the 1882 Act gives the court power to
order a sale (certainly as clarified by the Matrimonial Causes (Property and
Maintenance) Act 1958) in proceedings between husband and wife in connection
with property. Section 30 of the Law of Property Act 1925 gives the court power to   *e*
order a sale where there is a trust for sale, and to my mind it cannot matter what the
nature of the proceedings are; what matters is whether the circumstances are such
as to bring the case within one or other of those Acts which give the necessary power
to the court to order the sale. So I think it may be helpful if we were to say that it is
not necessary to intitule proceedings as being under the Married Women's Property   *f*
Act 1882 or the Law of Property Act 1925, or to issue pro forma summonses to
enable the court to exercise its powers to order a sale where the circumstances justify
it under one or other of those Acts.'

Sir David Cairns expressly agreed with those observations.

Judgment in *Ward*'s case was given on 1 May 1979. On 4 December 1979 a Practice
Note ([1980] 1 WLR 4) was issued by the Senior Registrar of the Family Division as   *g*
follows:

'On May 1, 1979, in an unreported case of *Ward* v. *Ward and Greene* . . . the Court
of Appeal held that judges and registrars have power to order sale of property under
section 24 of the Matrimonial Causes Act 1973 and without specific application
under section 17 of the Married Women's Property Act 1882 or section 30 of the   *h*
Law of Property Act 1925 . . .'

With great respect to the draftsman of that practice note, I do not find to be accurate
the statement that 'judges and registrars have power to order sale of property under
section 24 of the Matrimonial Causes Act 1973'. What in fact *Ward*'s case suggested was
that in proceedings under s 24 (or s 23) of the 1973 Act the court, in appropriate   *j*
circumstances, might exercise its power to order a sale conferred on it by the 1882 Act or
the 1925 Act without observing the technicality of issuing a pro forma summons under
either of those two latter Acts. Oliver LJ in *Thompson v Thompson* [1985] 2 All ER 243 at
250, [1986] Ch 38 at 49 drew attention to the way in which the Court of Appeal decision
had been not entirely correctly translated in the Practice Note.

a As I have said, on 1 October 1981, s 7 of the Matrimonial Homes and Property Act 1981 was brought into force whereby there was inserted, after s 24 of the Matrimonial Causes Act 1973, s 24A. By s 24A(1) the court was expressly given jurisdiction to order a sale of property. Section 24A(1) reads as follows:

b 'Where the court makes under section 23 or 24 of this Act a secured periodical payments order, an order for the payment of a lump sum or a property adjustment order, then, on making that order or at any time thereafter, the court may make a further order for the sale of such property as may be specified in the order, being property in which or in the proceeds of sale of which either or both of the parties to the marriage has or have a beneficial interest, either in possession or reversion.'

It is to be noted that, when making an order for sale under s 24A(1), the court is making a further order to such order as it makes under s 23 or s 24. Counsel for the *c* applicants sought to argue variously that s 24A is no more than a procedural section to enable s 24 to be implemented, or is an amendment to s 24, or is to be treated as being swallowed up by, or merged in, s 24. To dispose of those arguments, it is sufficient to state, first, that s 24A is far more than merely procedural in that it expressly confers jurisdiction on the court, second, that s 24 is not in any way amended in that it remains wholly intact in its original form and, third, that s 24A is a section entirely separate from *d* s 24 and is quite capable of standing by itself in the context of the other sections of the 1973 Act.

Of course, if counsel's arguments on this aspect were sound, they would apply to s 23 as well as to s 24. It would only be where the court was making a property adjustment order that the order for sale could be said to be in pursuance of an order under s 24; whereas, where the court was making a secured periodical payments order or an order *e* for the payment of a lump sum, the order for sale would necessarily be in pursuance of an order under s 23. And yet s 160(1)(c) of the Housing Act 1985 refers only to exemptions in respect of disposals in pursuance of s 24, and makes no mention of s 23. In the result, Parliament would have produced a quite inexplicable anomaly. It would be an absurdity if, when the court orders a sale and directs that the proceeds of sale be used for the payment of a lump sum or for the purpose of a secured periodical payments *f* order, there should be no exemption under s 160(1)(c), whereas, if the manner in which the proceeds of sale are to be dealt with can be fitted into the provisions of s 24, exemption could be claimed. But that, clearly, is the logical outcome of counsel's submissions.

Moreover, it is necessary to consider the actual words of the order made by the registrar, which were that 'the property known as 2 Beech Road . . . be sold, and the proceeds of sale divided equally between the parties'. That part of the order which *g* directed that the property be sold is clearly exercising the power conferred on the court by s 24A. But it is less clear whether the equal division of the proceeds of sale is an order made under s 23 or under s 24. It is not a transfer of property under s 24(1)(a), nor is it a settlement of property under s 24(1)(b), nor an order concerned with a marriage settlement under s 24(1)(c) or (d). It is, presumably, a cross-order for the payment of a *h* lump sum under s 23(1)(c).

It follows from what I have said, that I hold that the sale of 2 Beech Road was not a disposal 'in pursuance of an order made under section 24 of the Matrimonial Causes Act 1973'.

It is not difficult to understand what was presumably in the mind of Parliament when enacting s 160 of the Housing Act 1985 in the words that it did. None of the categories *j* of exempt disposal contained in s 160, leaving aside for the moment s 160(1)(c), contemplates the discount from the purchase price being realisable in cash. That can hardly be described as an inequitable provision. If the argument for the applicants in this case were right, s 160(1)(c) would be wholly at variance with that principle. But on its true construction it is not. A sale, as is conceded, can be comprehended in the word 'disposal'. What is contemplated in s 160(1)(c) is a transfer or settlement of property

under s 24 which involves continued occupational enjoyment of the property by a spouse
and/or children of the family and whereby no liquid cash advantage is gained.

I therefore hold that, in the circumstances of this case, the sale of 2 Beech Road,
Farnborough, consequent on the order of the registrar was not a disposal in pursuance of
an order under s 24 of the Matrimonial Causes Act 1973, so that Rushmoor Borough
Council were correct in law in their letter of 24 February 1986 in insisting that the sum
of £10,120 (being 80% of the original discount) be repaid by the applicants.

Application dismissed.

Solicitors: *Tanner & Taylor*, Aldershot (for the applicants); *Sharpe Pritchard & Co*, agents
for *R G S Foster*, Farnborough (for Rushmoor Borough Council).

Bebe Chua   Barrister.

Monsanto plc v Transport and General Workers' Union

COURT OF APPEAL, CIVIL DIVISION
DILLON AND NEILL LJJ
8 JULY 1986

*Trade dispute – Acts done in contemplation or furtherance of trade dispute – In contemplation or
furtherance of – Industrial action taken as result of union ballot – Suspension of industrial action
pending negotiations – Negotiations unsuccessful – Resumption of industrial action – Whether
industrial action in furtherance of continuing dispute or fresh dispute – Whether fresh ballot
required – Trade Union Act 1984, s 10.*

A dispute arose between a company and a union over the engagement of temporary
labour and as a result industrial action was taken between 22 and 30 April 1986. The
action was then suspended pending the result of a ballot which resulted in a vote in
favour of industrial action short of strike action and the industrial action, in the form of
disruption, recommenced on 7 May. On 30 May five temporary workers were dismissed.
On 10 June a meeting of the local branch of the union resolved that the industrial action
should be suspended pending negotiations but should be reimposed if the negotiations
broke down. Normal working conditions continued until 23 June when a negotiating
meeting proved unsuccessful and the industrial action was reimposed. The company
issued a writ seeking an injunction requiring the union to withdraw official recognition
of the industrial action, on the ground that s 10ᵃ of the Trade Union Act 1984 required
the union to hold a fresh ballot before the industrial action was resumed. The judge
granted the injunction and the union appealed.

Held – On the true construction of s 10 of the 1984 Act a trade union was not required
to hold a fresh ballot before it could lawfully resume industrial action which had been
suspended pending negotiations provided the dispute continued to be the same dispute
as that in respect of which the ballot had been held and the original industrial action had
been commenced within four weeks of the ballot. In the circumstances, the industrial
action taken on and after 23 June had the support of a ballot, since the matters which led
to the outbreak of the further industrial action were matters within the scope of the

---

a   Section 10, so far as material, is set out at p 362 *h*, post

settlement of the original dispute, namely the company's right to employ temporary
a labour. Accordingly, the injunction would be discharged and the appeal allowed (see
p 364 *d* to p 365 *b g*, p 366 *d* to *g* and p 367 *b* to *d*, post).

Notes

For the immunity of trade unions from suit in tort, see 47 Halsbury's Laws (4th edn)
para 574.
b   For the Trade Union Act 1984, s 10, see ₁6 Halsbury's Statutes (4th edn) 723.

Case referred to in judgments

American Cyanamid Co v Ethicon Ltd [1975] 1 All ER 504, [1975] AC 396, [1975] 2 WLR
316, HL.

c
Cases also cited

Duport Steels Ltd v Sirs [1980] 1 All ER 529, [1980] 1 WLR 142, QBD, CA and HL.
Hadmor Productions Ltd v Hamilton [1982] 1 All ER 1042, [1983] 1 AC 191, HL.
NWL Ltd v Woods, NWL Ltd v Nelson [1979] 3 All ER 614, [1979] 1 WLR 1294, HL.

Interlocutory appeal

d The defendants, the Transport and General Workers' Union (the union), appealed against
the order of Gatehouse J sitting in Manchester on 4 July 1986 whereby he continued
inter partes an ex parte injunction which he had granted to the plaintiffs, Monsanto plc
(the company), on 2 July restraining the union from doing any act which directly or
indirectly induced employees of the company to break their contracts of employment
with the company and from otherwise interfering with the performance of those
e contracts of employment and requiring the union to withdraw official recognition of
industrial action which commenced on 23 June 1986. The facts are set out in the
judgment of Dillon LJ.

Alexander Irvine QC and *Alan Wilkie* for the union.
James Goudie QC and *Charles Garside* for the company.

f **DILLON LJ.** This is an appeal by the defendants in the action, the Transport and
General Workers' Union, against an order of Gatehouse J made on 4 July 1986, that is to
say last Friday, whereby with a minor variation he continued inter partes an ex parte
injunction against the union which he had granted to the plaintiffs, Monsanto plc, on 2
July 1986. That injunction restrains the union from doing any act which directly or
g indirectly induces employees of the plaintiffs to break their contracts of employment
with the plaintiffs and from otherwise interfering with the performance of those
contracts of employment and requires the union to withdraw official recognition of
industrial action which began, it is said, on 23 June 1986. The appeal raises a question of
the extent to which industrial action is franked by a ballot held in accordance with the
Trade Union Act 1984.
h   The history of the matter is as follows. The plaintiffs, Monsanto plc, are a chemical
company who have several plants in this country, one at Ruabon. There are some 500
employees at the Ruabon plant and somewhat over 250 of them are members of the
appellant union. These are the production workers at the plant. In the early months of
1986 the plaintiffs employed five production workers as temporary workers on three-
month contracts and not on permanent contracts. This was apparently an increase in the
j numbers employed at that time. A dispute between the union and the company arose as
a result of this in March and April 1986 and the union without any ballot imposed an
overtime ban which began on 22 April. The union had no justification for doing that
without a ballot and consequently an ex parte injunction was obtained against the union
from Macpherson J on 30 April. That was to extend over 6 May. On the injunction being
granted it is common ground that normal working was resumed.

The union then held a ballot of the relevant members. I shall have to come later to examine the precise terms of the ballot and the authority thereby conferred. It appears, *a* however, that a total of 257 ballot papers were issued; 193 were completed in favour of industrial action short of strike action; 58 were completed against such action. A mandate for strike action was not sought. There were no void papers but there were apparently a small number not handed in. The effect of that ballot was that on the day after the result was announced industrial action short of strike action began. It began initially with an overtime ban, but at 29 May the range of industrial action was considerably increased to *b* cover matters like a ban on training in certain areas, a ban on loading or unloading of trailers, a ban on the use of computers in plants and a direction that members should work without enthusiasm.

Whether or not as a consequence of that stepping up of the industrial action, the five temporary production workers were dismissed by the company on 30 May 1986. A meeting was then held between representatives of the company and representatives of *c* the union on 4 June. Apparently national officials of the union were involved and also members of the company's employers association. A statement was given to the union representatives on that occasion. It sets out under para 1 under the heading 'Temporary workers in production and manning':

> 'The Company cannot agree to negotiate on manning levels. As stated in previous *d* meetings, we are prepared to discuss these issues but the central issue is temporaries and we would want to resolve this at an early date. On the question of manning, we will listen to the views of employee representatives.'

Then there is a further heading, 'sanctions' in which the company states that it regrets 'that we are unable to consider the claim for reimbursement of sick pay benefits *e* withdrawn during the period of industrial action'.

There is also a reference to loss of pay and it is said that no one could have been under any misapprehension as a result of certain notices about the consequences of industrial action as it affects their pay.

The position is that the company had imposed what have been referred to as counter-sanctions in response to the union's industrial action. These involved the suspension of *f* the company's sick pay scheme, the suspension of a guaranteed week and of the company's early retirement scheme and apparently a suspension of the practice of allowing time off for personal reasons and public duties.

Following that meeting there was a branch meeting of the union on 10 June 1986 and the decision was then taken, as it is put by the union's district representative, to suspend the industrial action pending further negotiations, but that the action should be *g* reimposed should the negotiations break down. Meetings between the union and the company were therefore arranged for 12 and 13 June which were a Thursday and Friday. Before these meetings were held a notice was issued by the company on 12 June. It is headed 'Industrial action/Scheduled meetings'. It says this, so far as material:

> 'Following informal discussions between Management and Union Representatives, *h* two meetings have been arranged to clarify and discuss the background to the current dispute. These meetings take place as follows:—
> 2.00 p.m. Thursday – Management and TGWU representatives
> 3.00 p.m. Friday – Management, Senior TGWU representatives and M. Jeffreys.
> The range of industrial sanctions will be lifted with effect from 2.00 p.m. Friday, 13th June.'

j

I interject that that is of course after the first proposed meeting, but before the second. The notice goes on:

> 'As a result of the lifting of these sanctions the protective measures taken by the Company which have been in force for several weeks i.e.

a   – suspension of the sick pay scheme
     – suspension of early retirement scheme
     – time off for personal reasons, public duties etc.
     – suspension of guaranteed week
   are lifted, also with effect from 2.00 p.m. Friday, 13th June.

b   Furthermore, in a genuine effort to promote a constructive atmosphere for the discussions and to demonstrate the Company's willingness to ensure a permanent return to normality, any salary adjustments for failure to work normally during the dispute will be shelved as long as some means of compensation can be achieved, e.g. adjustment of balance hours etc. The position on sick pay scheme entitlements has already been made clear.'

c   Then, after a sentence which I need not read, the hope was expressed that the discussions would be constructive and that the company could plan forward on a permanent basis without the threat of a return to the previous situation which only caused difficulties for everybody.

The meetings on 12 and 13 June 1986 were duly held. We do not have any direct evidence as to what was said, done, achieved or not achieved at those meetings, but we have a joint statement issued after the meeting on 13 June signed by a representative of *d* the company and the branch secretary of the union which refers to the meeting of 13 June as a constructive meeting. It says that a series of meetings were agreed at that meeting and the first of these is a meeting covering the annual pay agreement which was planned for 23 June. Two other meetings are then referred to, the dates for which had yet to be agreed, and it was said: 'In the light of these discussions both sides confirm that normal working will continue.' Normal working did continue until the meeting of 23 *e* June which had been announced in that notice of 13 June to which I have just referred.

Unfortunately, that meeting did not prove successful. A short summary of what happened appears from a notice from the company to the workforce issued later on the same day. The relevant paragraph says this:

f   'A meeting arranged for this morning to discuss the 1986/7 pay settlement did not in fact cover this topic to any degree. The talks foundered on the question of pay and balance hours adjustments for walkouts, loss of production due to sanctions and sickness absences during the recent months of industrial action.'

This is amplified in minutes prepared by the company of that meeting of 23 June. These record firstly that Mr Jeffreys, having said that the meeting had been called to discuss pay, said there were also a number of other issues to cover:

g   'He had understood that no deductions of sick pay or adjustments of balance hours were to be made. He did, however, accept that some adjustment for walkouts was necessary although he maintains there had been a management "lock-out".'

Then the company said that it had not abandoned all deductions because otherwise there *h* would be no disincentive to continuing or recurring industrial action. The company claimed to have commuted disciplinary suspensions and said that individuals who walked out or who failed to work normally would have balance hours adjusted instead of pay being stopped. It was said that this had been made clear at the meetings on 12 and 13 June to which Mr Jeffreys riposted that the management had locked employees out and the employees should not lose money. In the upshot Mr Jeffreys said that if this was *j* the company's position then they would reimpose the previous industrial sanctions, because they were not prepared to accept any losses. There is a suggestion in the minutes that Mr Jeffreys had said he had misunderstood the company's position. They were still in dispute.

The result was that the union reimposed as from 2 pm on Monday 23 June 1986 all the bans listed in the union's notice of 29 May to which I have already referred. There

was beyond that a further stepping up of the industrial action short of strike action by a
further notice from union representatives to have effect from 10 pm on Tuesday 24 June *a*
to the effect that not only would the employees not work enthusiastically but instructions
for cutting production by 50% would come into force. Industrial action has consequently
continued and I do not need to go into the details any further. It has continued short of
strike action officially with the authority of Mr Jeffreys. I will have to come later to a
question that has been raised about there possibly having been at a later stage strike
action.   *b*

It is against that background that the company issued the writ in this action on 1 July
1986 and applied first for the ex parte injunction and then for the inter partes injunction.
It is quite clear that if the matter had to be decided solely on grounds of balance of
convenience as set out in the well-known case of *American Cyanamid Co v Ethicon Ltd*
[1975] 1 All ER 504, [1975] AC 396, the answer would be unhesitatingly in favour of the
grant of the injunction because the industrial action is causing the company unquantifiable *c*
damage and because, the issue being whether it is franked by the ballot which I have
already mentioned, it would be a simple matter for the union over a very few days to
hold a further ballot to get a fresh mandate.

However, the court in considering applications for interlocutory injunctions in matters
involving industrial action has to consider the provisions of ss 13 and 17 of the Trade
Union and Labour Relations Act 1974 (as amended). Section 13(1) of the 1974 Act (as *d*
substituted by the Trade Union and Labour Relations (Amendment) Act 1976, s 3(2))
provides:

'An act done by a person in contemplation or furtherance of a trade dispute shall
not be actionable in tort on the ground only—(a) that it induces another person to
break a contract or interferes or induces any other person to interfere with its *e*
performance . . .'

That has to be read with the Trade Union Act 1984 to which I will come. Section 17 of
the 1974 Act then provides by sub-s (2) (as inserted by the Employment Protection Act
1975, s 125, Sch 16, Pt III, para 6):   *f*

'It is hereby declared for the avoidance of doubt that where an application is made
to a court, pending the trial of an action, for an interlocutory injunction and the
party against whom the injunction is sought claims that he acted in contemplation
or furtherance of a trade dispute, the court shall, in exercising its discretion whether
or not to grant the injunction, have regard to the likelihood of that party's succeeding
at the trial of the action in establishing the matter or matters which would, under *g*
any provision of section 13 . . . afford a defence to the action.'

There is no doubt at all that so far as s 13 of the 1974 Act goes, apart from the 1984
Act, all the union's acts were done in contemplation or furtherance of a trade dispute.
But s 10 of the Trade Union Act 1984 qualifies the protection available to trade unions if
they act without the support of a ballot. Section 10(1) provides: *h*

'Nothing in section 13 of the 1974 Act shall prevent an act done by a trade union
without the support of a ballot from being actionable in tort (whether or not against
the trade union) on the ground that it induced a person to break his contract of
employment or to interfere with its performance.'   *j*

If therefore the industrial action taken by the union on and since 23 June is without the
support of a ballot the union has no defence to this action and the injunction must clearly
go. The only ballot there has been is the ballot declared on 6 May 1986.

Whether an act is to be taken as having been done with the support of a ballot is dealt
with by s 10(3) which provides:

a

'For the purposes of subsection (1) above, an act shall be taken as having been done with the support of a ballot if, but only if [four conditions are satisfied]'.

The first and most important of these conditions is:

'(a) the trade union has held a ballot in respect of the strike or other industrial action in the course of which the breach or interference referred to in subsection (1) above occurred.'

b

I shall come back to that. The only other condition in sub-s (3) that needs mention is:

'(c) the first authorisation or endorsement of any relevant act, and in the case of an authorisation the relevant act itself, took place after the date of the ballot and before the expiry of the period of four weeks beginning with that date . . .'

c

'Authorisation or endorsement' means by special definition (see s 10(5))—

'authorisation or endorsement of an act which, by virtue of section 15 of the Employment Act 1982, causes the act to be taken, for the purposes mentioned in that section, to have been done by the trade union.'

Here there is no doubt that the first authorisation of any relevant act took place, so far as regards industrial action beginning after the resumption of work after Macpherson J's

d order, after the date of the ballot and before the expiry of four weeks beginning with that date.

The intermediate words in the condition in para (c) say: 'and in the case of an authorisation the relevant act itself'. The relevant act is defined as meaning an act done in the course of the action mentioned in sub-s (3)(a) above of inducing a person to break his contract of employment or to interfere with its performance. It seems to me that it

e would be contrary to the scheme of the Act to construe the words 'the relevant act itself' as referring to any act done by the union in the course of the action mentioned in sub-s (3)(a) of inducing a person to break his contract of employment or to interfere with its performance, with the result that if the industrial action went on for more than four weeks from the date of the ballot a fresh ballot would be necessary before there could be any further inducement to a person to interfere with the performance of his contract of

f employment. Therefore I prefer to construe the words 'the relevant act itself' as meaning the relevant act the subject of the first authorisation. On that construction the condition in para (c) was satisfied so far as the ballot of 6 May is concerned and the whole case turns on the condition in para (a).

Those are the relevant statutory provisions, but of course we have very much in mind, because it has been pointed out many times by the House of Lords, that the discretion to

g be exercised on these applications for interlocutory relief is the discretion of the judge at first instance and not the discretion of the Court of Appeal. In the present case Gatehouse J did not give any detailed judgment, apparently for the very good reason that the hearing before him lasted until after 6 o'clock in the evening. He just expressed his conclusion in a very few sentences and the note of them sets it out as follows:

h

'I find this matter legally very difficult. Although I may have got the law completely wrong (I do not think I have) I do not think that it would be right to discharge the injunction. A sensible solution would be for the union to hold another ballot. The balance of convenience is served best if it is restrained over the period to hold a ballot. The status quo should be preserved.'

j The reference to finding the matter legally very difficult and thinking that he has not got the law completely wrong indicate to my mind that he was not merely deciding this case on the balance of convenience because it would be a sensible solution for the union to hold another ballot; he was addressing his mind, as required by s 17 of the 1974 Act, to the question whether the union was likely to make out its defence under s 13 of that Act as qualified by s 10 of the 1984 Act and he was reaching the conclusion that prima facie or on the balance of probabilities the union would not succeed in making out that defence. That at any rate is the interpretation which I put on the note of Gatehouse J's *a* reasons for his order.

The argument put before us by counsel for the company rests really on two points. There is a third point about strike action which I shall have to come to later. Counsel for the company says firstly that once industrial action is discontinued, for whatever reason and even if it is only pending negotiations, it is spent and there must be a further ballot before it can legitimately be resumed. He says secondly that the initial ballot was in *b* relation to the engagement of temporary employees, but that is no longer the issue causative of the industrial action from 23 June onwards, because the five employees have gone and so the ballot has been overtaken by subsequent events.

In considering that second submission I find it necessary first to look at the wording of s 10 of the 1984 Act. An act done by a trade union is actionable in tort on the ground that it induced a person to break his contract of employment or to interfere with its *c* performance if the act was done without the support of a ballot. An act is to be taken as having been done with the support of a ballot if, and only if, the union has held a ballot in respect of the industrial action in the course of which the breach or interference occurred. So the instruction to break the contract or interfere with its performance and the obedience to that instruction are industrial action and one has to consider whether the course of industrial action in which they occurred was a course of industrial action in *d* respect of which a ballot has been held. I look to see therefore what this ballot was about, and I find that in the heading to the announced return, which says:

'T & G W U Ballot in respect of Industrial Action in pursuit of a settlement of the dispute with Monsanto Ltd over the employment of Temporary Labour.'

Counsel for the company says that the industrial action was over the five temporary *e* employees, but for the purposes of this interlocutory appeal I could not accept that because the employees were dismissed on 30 May and in the memorandum of 4 June the company was treating the dispute as still continuing, the central issue being temporaries which the company wished to resolve at an early stage. Therefore I do not read it for present purposes as limited to the employment of five individuals. It is also a ballot in respect of industrial action in pursuit of a settlement of the dispute. The matters which *f* have led to the further outbreak of industrial action at 23 and 24 June are the arrangements in respect of pay during the time that the employees were acting in accordance with the union's instructions for industrial action, sick pay as a result of the counter-sanctions by the company and so forth and all that, as it seems to me, is part of the process covered by settlement of the dispute with the company over the employment of temporary labour, at any rate prima facie. We are not required on this appeal to *g* express a concluded view, but we are required by s 17 to have regard to the likelihood of the union succeeding at the trial.

In relation to counsel for the company's first submission it seems to me that in the normal course of industrial relations where industrial action has been begun the employer is likely to say that he will not negotiate while the industrial action is continuing. The *h* union may be prepared to suspend industrial action while negotiations take place, but the intention throughout would be that that is not a discontinuance of the industrial action but a temporary suspension for the purposes of negotiation so that the industrial action will be resumed if the negotiations fail. I do not for my part see that in such circumstances the statute or good industrial relations require a further ballot at each stage if there is a suspension for negotiations. *j*

Proceeding from there it seems to me that as the matters which led to the outbreak of the further industrial action or the reimposition of it are matters within the scope of the settlement of the original dispute, the principle of which has not been answered either way, that is to say, the principle of the company's power as manager to employ temporary labour, this is a case in which on the facts, so far as we can discern them from the affidavit

evidence in advance of the trial, the union is considerably more likely than not to succeed
a at the trial of the action.

That being so, I disagree with the view which I take Gatehouse J to have formed in
relation to s 17. Having to balance the important factor of the union's prospects of success
against the balance of convenience factors affecting the company which I mentioned
earlier, I reach the conclusion feeling free to exercise a discretion having regard to the
judge's approach to s 17, that in the circumstances of this case the injunction ought not
b to be granted.

I refer finally to the strike question. It is said that in the course of the industrial action
after 23 June the union's shop stewards gave a strike direction for which of course they
have no ballot authority at all. This depends in part on the evidence of the company's
witness, Mr Pritchard, who says:

c
'As from the commencement of the afternoon shift at 2 p.m. on Thursday the
26th June 1986, employees who were members of the T.G.W.U. were instructed to
resume normal working in accordance with the terms of their contract. Any
employee who refused to resume normal working was suspended . . . As individual
employees were suspended in the circumstances set out in paragraph 13 above, other
employees who were members of the T.G.W.U. walked out in sympathy and the
d remainder of T.G.W.U. employees on the particular shifts were then ordered to
walk out by the T.G.W.U. stewards. By the morning of Monday the 30th June 1986
all T.G.W.U. production staff had ceased to work, whether as a result of having been
suspended, having walked out in sympathy or being ordered not to continue their
duties by the T.G.W.U. stewards.'

Mr Jeffreys in his affidavit disputes that any instruction has been given by the union
e ordering the members to walk out. The union's position is that there is no official strike
and they have no desire at the moment for any official strike. At the time, however,
when the employees ceased work the company's position was that it was suspending all
employees who refused to give an undertaking to resume normal working. Therefore it
would seem that those members of the union who walked out in sympathy or were
f ordered to walk out, if they were so ordered by the shop stewards, were merely
anticipating by a pretty brief interval of time their suspension by the company.

I can see nothing in this to merit the interference of the court by a form of injunction
against official strike action. The present position, as I have said, is that the union holds
that there is no official strike. The company says that its suspension policy has been lifted.
So far as those two aspects of the case at any rate are concerned, there might even be a
g prospect of common ground between the parties. For these reasons for my part I would
allow this appeal and discharge the order of Gatehouse J.

NEILL LJ. I agree. I only add a few words of my own, because we are differing from
the decision of the judge. The facts of this case have been set out in the judgment of
Dillon LJ and I need not repeat them. It is central, however, to a consideration of this
h appeal to have regard to the terms of s 17(2) of the Trade Union and Labour Relations
Act 1974 as amended, which is in these terms:

'It is hereby declared for the avoidance of doubt that where an application is made
to a court, pending the trial of an action, for an interlocutory injunction and the
party against whom the injunction is sought claims that he acted in contemplation
or furtherance of a trade dispute, the court shall, in exercising its discretion whether
j or not to grant the injunction, have regard to the likelihood of that party's succeeding
at the trial of the action in establishing the matter or matters which would, under
any provision of section 13 . . . afford a defence to the action.'

In the present case, therefore, it is necessary for the court to form a view about what
can conveniently be described as the ballot defence, because as I read the notes of the

judgment of Gatehouse J, he appears to have been of the opinion that the chances of that
defence being established were not good. The relevant provisions concerning a ballot are   *a*
set out in s 10(3) of the Trade Union Act 1984. I need not refer further to paras (b), (c)
and (d) of that subsection, but I should repeat the provisions of sub-s (3)(a) with the
introductory words:

> 'For the purposes of subsection (1) above, an act shall be taken as having been
> done with the support of a ballot if, but only if—(a) the trade union has held a ballot   *b*
> in respect of the strike or other industrial action in the course of which the breach
> or interference referred to in subsection (1) above occurred.'

The crucial question therefore and the matter which was particularly argued on behalf
of the company is whether the trade union has held a ballot in respect of the industrial
action which is in issue in these proceedings, namely the action taken after 24 June 1986.
Counsel for the company suggested that the industrial action that was taken was not   *c*
covered by the ballot for at least three reasons. Firstly, he said that the ballot was only
directed to the particular dispute which had arisen in regard to the employment of five
men as temporary workers on a particular kind of work at the company's plant. That
point, it seems to me, is quite impossible to maintain in the light of the statement which
was given on behalf of the employers to the union at the meeting on 4 June. That
statement, which has been exhibited to a recent affidavit by Mr Jeffreys sworn on 8 July,   *d*
establishes that, certainly in the eyes of the company, the dispute was still in being and
unresolved at the date of the meeting on 4 June. It seems to me to follow from that that
there was a dispute as to the question of principle as to how far it was right for the
company to employ temporary employees rather than to put people on the permanent
pay roll.
Counsel for the company's second argument was that even if the dispute related to the   *e*
question of the principle of employing temporary staff the ballot could only be relied on
up to 13 June because, he suggested, once the action had been suspended or had come to
an end the force of the ballot ran out and any subsequent industrial action such as the
action which took place on 24 June was an entirely new action which would have
required the imprimatur of a new ballot.
In my view both as a matter of principle and on the facts of this case that submission   *f*
cannot be sustained, certainly not in this case. To my mind it would be quite wrong not
to allow to union officials the flexibility of being able to call off strike action or other
action temporarily so that negotiations can continue and then reimpose it if after a short
period the discussions fail to reach any fruitful result. On the facts of this case what
happened is made plain in para 10 of Mr Jeffreys' first affidavit where he said this: *g*

> 'On the 10th June 1986 at a branch meeting, at which I was present, a decision
> was taken to suspend the industrial action pending further negotiations, but that
> the action should be re-imposed should the negotiations break down. The industrial
> action was suspended on 2.00 p.m. on Friday, the 13th June.'

It seems to me that the original action was suspended but then was reimposed as indeed   *h*
both parties recognised in their documents when following the abortive negotiations on
23 June the action started up once more.
Counsel for the company's third argument was that the action which took place as
from 24 June had nothing to do with the dispute on the question of principle, even if
that was the original dispute. The dispute which led to the action and the breakdown of
the talks was a dispute about questions of sick pay and other aspects of what have been   *j*
called the counter-sanctions imposed by the company during the period in May and up
to the middle of June when the industrial action was first called off. As to that, it seems
to me, as Dillon LJ has already pointed out, the matter is really answered by the terms of
the ballot. The ballot paper which was signed by each of the individual people who voted
on it was headed as follows:

a   'T & G W U Ballot in respect of Industrial Action in pursuit of a settlement of the dispute with Monsanto Ltd over the employment of Temporary Labour.'

In my judgment, a dispute of this nature includes the working out of the financial consequences for members of the union. It seems to me therefore that while a matter such as sick pay payable during the period of the dispute remains in issue and unresolved the settlement of the dispute has not been achieved and that industrial action in pursuit of such a settlement is still covered by the ballot.

b

For these reasons therefore it seems to me that none of the arguments which counsel for the company put forward to suggest that this ballot did not cover the industrial action of 24 June 1986 and afterwards has any very real likelihood of success, at any rate on a prima facie view. Accordingly, what I have described as the ballot defence seems to me on the present state of the evidence (it may of course look very different at any hearing) to have at any rate a more than 50% chance of success. That is an important point to take

c into account in accordance with s 17(2) of the 1974 Act. Accordingly, I do not consider that it would be right to continue the injunction which Gatehouse J granted last Friday, 4 July 1986. For those reasons, as well as those given by Dillon LJ, I too would allow this appeal.

d   *Appeal allowed Injunction discharged.*

Solicitors: *Pattinson & Brewer* (for the union); *Alexander Tatham & Co*, Manchester (for the company).

Celia Fox   Barrister.

Practice Note

QUEEN'S BENCH DIVISION

LORD LANE CJ, CAULFIELD AND McCOWAN JJ

3 FEBRUARY 1987

Practice – Crown Office list – Arrangement of list – Cases not ready to be heard – Cases ready to be heard – Cases stood out – Expedited list – Cases listed for hearing.

LORD LANE CJ gave the following direction at the sitting of the court. This Practice Direction applies to the Crown Office list, the elements of which are described in the directions for London given on 31 July 1981 ([1981] 3 All ER 61, [1981] 1 WLR 1296).

1. As from 2 March 1987 the following arrangements will apply to the listing of cases included in the Crown Office list.

2. The Head Clerk, under the direction of the Master of the Crown Office, will arrange the Crown Office list into the following parts.

3. *Part A: cases not ready to be heard*
   Cases where leave has yet to be obtained, or the time limits for the filing or lodging of notices, affidavits or other documents have not expired and where, in consequence, a case is not yet ready to be heard.

4. *Part B: cases ready to be heard*
   In cases where the time limits mentioned in Part A have expired it will be assumed that all parties are ready to be heard. When a case enters Part B the applicant or his solicitors will be informed by letter. It will be the responsibility of the applicant or his solicitors to forward a copy of that letter to (i) the clerk to counsel instructed by the applicant and (ii) any respondent to the case or his solicitor, who should inform the clerk to counsel instructed by him. It will be the responsibility of counsels' clerks to inform the Head Clerk, *in writing*, of counsel's time estimate for the case and of any alteration thereto.

5. The Head Clerk will make arrangements for hearing dates to be fixed, drawing cases from Part B in order of entry so far as is practicable. While the Head Clerk will give as much notice as possible of the date fixed for hearing he cannot undertake to accommodate the wishes of applicants, respondents, their solicitors or counsel. The occasional need to list cases at short notice may mean that parties are unable to be represented by the counsel of their first choice. In particular it should be remembered that the cases listed in the Crown Office list take precedence, so far as the attendance of counsel is concerned, over cases listed for hearing in the Crown Court unless a Divisional Court or a judge otherwise directs.

6. *Part C: cases stood out*
   Where a case appears in Part B, or Part E (see post), and any party to the case is of the opinion that he is not ready to be heard he may apply to the Master of the Crown Office to have the matter stood out into Part C. Where the Master of the Crown Office accedes to such an application he may do so on such terms as he thinks fit. Where he declines to direct that the matter be stood out into Part C application may be made to a Divisional Court or a judge, as the case may be, by way of notice of motion.

7. *Part D: the expedited list*
   Cases entered in this list will be listed for hearing as soon as practicable. In cases other than those where a Divisional Court or a judge has directed that a case be considered for expedition, application for inclusion in Part D should be made in the first instance to the

a Master of the Crown Office, but, where he declines to direct its inclusion in Part D, application may be made to a Divisional Court or a judge, as the case may be, by way of notice of motion.

8. *Part E: cases listed for hearing*
This part of the list will contain those cases where a date for hearing has been fixed.

b 9. As from 2 March 1987 the Daily Cause List will, in relation to the Crown Office list, contain only such cases as are to be heard on the next sitting day.

10. A copy of Parts B, C, D and E of the Crown Office list may be inspected in the Crown Office.

11. In this Practice Direction the expression 'applicant' includes 'appellant' where the context so requires and the expression 'judge' means a judge hearing cases in the Crown *c* Office list.

N P Metcalfe Esq   Barrister.

d # R v Hammersmith and Fulham London Borough Council, ex parte Beddowes

COURT OF APPEAL, CIVIL DIVISION
FOX, KERR LJJ AND SIR DENYS BUCKLEY
e 25, 26, 30 JUNE, 1, 2, 3, 31 JULY 1986

Public authority – Statutory powers – Fettering future exercise of statutory powers – Exercise of existing powers fettering future exercise of powers – Alternative or overlapping powers – Restriction of user – Restrictive covenant controlling future use of land held by authority – Covenant by authority not to create lettings of flats on estate owned by authority except by long *f* *leases at a premium – Whether covenant a fetter on authority's duty to provide housing accommodation in its district – Housing Act 1957, s 104.*

The respondent council owned a housing estate, composed of nine blocks of flats (Blocks A to J), which was in a very bad state of repair and in much need of renovation and improvement. In June 1984, having considered the various options open to it to effect *g* such modernisation, the council, acting under its power under s 104ᵃ of the Housing Act 1957 to dispose of land held for housing purposes, resolved to authorise a phased redevelopment of the estate as a joint venture with one or more private developers with a view to the whole estate eventually being sold to owner-occupiers. It was proposed that the first step would be the sale of Block A to a housing association for £480,000. To provide the continuity required for a lengthy process of redevelopment the council *h* proposed to enter into a series of negative covenants with interested developers, which covenants would effectively prevent the council from creating any new lettings on that part of the estate retained by them, save by long leases at a premium. The purpose of the covenants was to guarantee completion of the development of the estate and its conversion to owner-occupation and, by barring the council from letting flats on normal council tenancies when they fell vacant, to prevent termination of the project by a future council *j* when it was only partially completed. In January 1986 the housing association refused to proceed with the purchase of Block A because it did not wish to be a party to covenants which would have the effect of preventing the rest of the estate from being used for rented housing. In March an offer was made by a private development company to

---

a Section 104, so far as material, is set out at p 378 *h j*, post

purchase Block A subject to the covenants. This was accepted by a majority of the council shortly before elections were due to take place which were likely to alter the political *a* complexion of the council. The appellant, a resident of a flat on the estate, applied for judicial review to quash the council's resolution accepting the developer's offer of purchase. The application was refused and the appellant appealed, contending, inter alia, (i) that the negative covenants imposed an unlawful fetter on the council's power as a housing authority to provide public housing accommodation under the 1957 Act, and (ii) that the council's housing policy as formulated was unreasonable. *b*

Held – (1) If a statutory power was honestly and reasonably exercised in order to achieve a statutory object, then its exercise for that purpose could not be regarded as a fetter on another power given for the same purpose. The power under s 104 of the 1957 Act to dispose of land held for housing purposes contained an implied power to impose covenants which restricted the council's use of the retained land, and therefore that *c* power overlapped with the council's statutory powers under the 1957 Act relating to use of the retained land for housing purposes. Applying the principle that all other powers were subordinate to the main power to carry out the primary purpose, it became necessary to ascertain the purpose for which the retained land was held. That purpose was the provision of 'housing accommodation' in the district and the council's policy in relation to the estate was consistent with that purpose, even though it was designed to *d* produce owner-occupation of flats rather than rented accommodation. Accordingly (Kerr LJ dissenting), the purpose for which the power to create restrictive covenants had been exercised by the council could reasonably be regarded as the furtherance of the statutory object of the provision of public housing accommodation, with the result that the creation of the restrictive covenants did not constitute an impermissible fetter on the council's powers (see p 378 *g*, p 379 *b g* to p 380 *a c* to *e j* to p 381 *a*, p 386 *f g*, p 387 *a d e* *e* and p 388 *b c*, post); *Blake (Valuation Officer) v Hendon Corp* [1961] 3 All ER 601 applied.

(2) The council's policy in relation to the modernisation of the estate was a rational and coherent policy which it was reasonably entitled to adopt and which could not be struck down as unreasonable even (Kerr LJ dissenting) with the addition of the restrictive covenants. The appeal would accordingly be dismissed (see p 378 *b c e*, p 382 *j*, p 387 *d e* and p 388 *e*, post); *Associated Provincial Picture Houses Ltd v Wednesbury Corp* [1947] 2 All *f* ER 680 applied.

Notes

For fettering by a public body of its own discretion, see 1 Halsbury's Laws (4th edn) paras 33–34, and for cases on the subject, see 1(1) Digest (Reissue) 96–97, 574–576.

As from 1 April 1986 s 104 of the Housing Act 1957 was replaced by s 32 of the *g* Housing Act 1985. For s 32 of the 1985 Act, see 21 Halsbury's Statutes (4th edn) 68.

Cases referred to in judgments

Associated Provincial Picture Houses Ltd v Wednesbury Corp [1947] 2 All ER 680, [1948] 1 KB 223, CA.

Ayr Harbour Trustees v Oswald (1883) 8 App Cas 623, HL.

Blake (Valuation Officer) v Hendon Corp [1961] 3 All ER 601, [1962] 1 QB 283, [1961] 3 WLR 951, CA.

Council of Civil Service Unions v Minister for the Civil Service [1984] 3 All ER 935, [1985] AC 374, [1984] 3 WLR 1174, HL.

Dowty Boulton Paul Ltd v Wolverhampton Corp [1971] 2 All ER 277, [1971] 1 WLR 204.

Short v Tower Hamlets London Borough (1985) 18 HLR 171, CA.

Stourcliffe Estates Co Ltd v Bournemouth Corp [1910] 2 Ch 12, [1908–10] All ER Rep 785, CA.

Cases also cited

Birkdale District Electric Supply Co Ltd v Southport Corp [1926] AC 355, HL.

British Transport Commission v Westmorland CC [1957] 2 All ER 353, [1958] AC 126, HL.

Manchester City Council v Greater Manchester CC (1980) 78 LGR 560, HL.

Appeal

a Doreen Beddowes appealed from the decision of Schiemann J hearing the Crown Office list on 7 May 1986 whereby he dismissed her application for judicial review by way of (i) an order of certiorari to quash a decision of the housing policy committee of the Hammersmith and Fulham London Borough Council on 19 March 1984 authorising the borough valuer to conclude the sale of Block A, Fulham Court, Fulham Road, London SW6, to the respondents, Barratt Urban Renewals (Central London) Ltd (Barratts), on *b* terms which included covenants restricting the future use of Blocks B to J, Fulham Court by the council, and (ii) an injunction restraining the council from entering into a contract for the sale of Block A on those terms. The facts are set out in the judgment of Fox LJ.

Andrew Arden and *Clare Hunter* for the appellant.
Raymond Kidwell QC and *Joseph Harper* for Barratts.
c The council was not represented.

Cur adv vult

31 July. The following judgments were delivered.

d **FOX LJ.** This is an appeal from a decision of Schiemann J, who dismissed an application by Doreen Beddowes for (1) an order of certiorari to quash a decision of the housing policy committee of the Hammersmith and Fulham London Borough Council on 19 March 1984, which authorised the borough valuer to conclude the sale of Block A, Fulham Court, Fulham Road, London SW6 on terms which included covenants restricting the future use of Blocks B to J, Fulham Court, and (2) an injunction restraining the *e* council from entering into a contract for the sale of Block A on those terms.

Fulham Court was built in 1933 and is owned by the council. It consists of a total of 372 flats in a number of blocks (Blocks A to J) together with an open space. All the blocks are in a very bad state of repair and are much in need of renovation and improvement. For the purposes of this case the estate can be divided into two parts, namely Block A and *f* the remainder of the estate. Fulham Court has been the subject of much dispute in the council for several years. The council consists of some 50 members. Prior to the local government elections on 8 May 1986, the council was controlled by a group which politically was predominantly Conservative, and which was in favour of selling Fulham Court for development for owner-occupation. The Labour councillors (24 in number) were opposed to that. Their opposition was based, principally, on the grounds that a sale *g* would involve the destruction of an entire community on the estate, and that the local shortage of rented housing was such that the loss of 372 council rented flats was unacceptable.

I come to the history of the matter in more detail. On 22 November 1983 the housing policy committee of the council had before it a budget review for 1984–85 in relation to the housing programme. The review noted that the council's financial position had *h* prevented it from proceeding with its improvement scheme at Fulham Court, and stated that an alternative mode of funding the improvements would be necessary. The review continued in para 6.1 as follows:

'The Committee has considered the difficult financial position affecting Fulham Court modernisation on several occasions during the year. Not only the capital cost (estimated at over £8 million between 1984/9) but also the full year costs of the *i* improvement works (at nearly £400,000) must now mean that other options need to be considered. The following options are listed for consideration.'

The options (and the committee's view on them) were as follows. (i) Continued day-to-day repairs. This was not cost-effective, and would not produce sufficient improvement. (ii) Rehousing of all tenants with disposal of the whole estate to a developer. This would *j* involve rehousing all the tenants and eventual sale with vacant possession. This was thought to involve too large a loss of council dwellings at a time of acute shortage. (iii) A joint venture for rehabilitation by a developer with a part buy-back package. (iv) Demolition and redevelopment. It was thought that the cost would make this unattractive to a developer. (v) Demolition and redevelopment with part buy-back. This option was thought to be unlikely to be attractive in the development market and, in addition, the council did not have sufficient financial resources to fund the buy-back part of the scheme.

The committee's preliminary view was that option (iii) was the most advantageous. The council would rehouse all tenants and enter into a joint venture scheme for the rehabilitation of the estate, incorporating a buy-back agreement for a scheme for sheltered housing for elderly people, and flats for shared ownership. Such a scheme would provide much needed housing for older people, and the shared ownership part of the scheme would provide capital receipts.

The committee resolved to recommend to the council that subject to the required consultation with tenants taking place, the housing policy committee be authorised 'to dispose of Fulham Court on terms to be approved by that committee and to take any necessary decisions on behalf of the council in that respect'.

On 23 November 1983 the matter came before a full meeting of the council. At that meeting the council had before it a report by the director of housing which stated that it would be possible to decant the whole of the Fulham Court estate over a period of three years. It was assumed that Fulham Court 'voids' would not be available for allocation, but that voids 'would be kept to the present low level during the three years'.

The Labour councillors were not happy with the recommendation of the committee, and Councillor Harrison moved an amendment to the effect that Fulham Court should remain the property of the council and that the council should undertake the full modernisation of the estate in the capital programme for 1984–85. That amendment was, however, defeated, and the committee's report was adopted by a narrow margin.

In March 1984 Councillor Harrison presented to the council a petition by some residents in the borough objecting to the sale of Fulham Court. The committee, in response to that in April 1984, resolved to inform the petitioners of the council's intentions to hold full consultation regarding the future of Fulham Court. A meeting of tenants was convened for 25 April 1984. The report of an inter-departmental committee of the council of June 1984 contains the following statement regarding tenant consultations:

> '8.4 *Tenant Consultation* As part of the normal consultation process all tenants on the Fulham Court Estate have been advised in writing concerning i) the council's decision in principle for a joint venture for the rehabilitation of Fulham Court by (a) developer(s) with a part buy-back package and ii) the proposal under consideration which would involve the rehousing of all tenants living on the estate and the sale with vacant possession to a selected developer who would undertake the improvement package.
> 8.5 A tenants' consultation meeting was held on Wednesday 25 April 1984 in Fulham Town Hall to which all tenants received a written invitation. The meeting, which was chaired by Councillor David Clark, Chairman, Housing Policy Committee, was held in order to give tenants full clarification about the Council's proposals and to hear what the tenants themselves wanted.
> 8.6 Furthermore, a questionnaire was circulated to all tenants prior to the consultation and further copies were available at the meeting inviting tenants to give their view on the proposals, including rehousing. Of the 372 dwellings on the estate 327 are currently occupied by secure tenants and 132 replies were received from these tenants. Of these 121 (91·6%) were in favour of the Council's proposals whilst only 10 (7·6%) were against, with 1 ambiguous response. Notwithstanding this, 129 of the replies indicated rehousing preferences of which 109 expressed a

preference for Fulham, 11 for Hammersmith and 9 for elsewhere outside the Borough. The overwhelming majority of tenants expressing an opinion on the Council's proposals which entail the rehousing of the tenants resident on the estate were in favour.'

In the spring of 1984 officers of the council entered into discussions with the Abbey Housing Association and the Nationwide Housing Trust and Woolwich Homes Ltd. These discussions led the council's officers to the conclusions (a) that the Fulham Court development was beyond the resources of a single non-profit-making association and (b) that the project would have to be phased in order to facilitate rehousing and participation by separate developers. Further, the council's officers also formed the view that the council would have to furnish guarantees on the future of the remainder of the estate for each participant, as uncertainty or termination of the project when it was only partially completed would have serious implications for the viability of the project.

On 24 June 1984 the housing policy committee had before it the report of the inter-departmental committee to which I have already referred. That contemplated the sale by the council of Blocks A to H (and possibly J) to a non-profit-making developer or developers to rehabilitate the estate. The scheme would involve either the buy-back by the council of one block for sheltered housing (for elderly people) with community rooms, or the retention of a block by the council for the same purpose, and the buy-back by the council of another block which could be made available to purchasers of flats on a shared-ownership basis with the council (which in effect consists of flats owned by the council, but the ownership of which is gradually purchased by the tenants). The remaining blocks would be rehabilitated for low-cost home ownership by, in the main, first-time buyers. The estate would therefore largely cease to consist of rented accommodation.

The inter-departmental report emphasised the need for a phased scheme of disposal by the council of the blocks to be sold. The relevant section of the report stated:

'8.21: A phased approach enables an earlier sale of blocks by the Council to the developer and thereby generation of capital receipt, reduces the potential for revenue loss through the retention of void units and vandalism, and with an earlier start on site results in a phased release of dwellings for sale and buy-back with consequential benefits for management of the implementation of capital and revenue expenditure.

8.22: Without the phased approach and recognising that full decanting of Fulham Court would require three years, with the majority of tenants being readily rehoused (75%) and the remaining tenants proving more difficult to rehouse, many of the dwellings would be void for most of the three year decant period. This not only increases the potential for vandalism and squatting, and the requirement of extended maintenance, but also results in considerable loss of rental income together with increased costs for security and caretaking etc. The phased decant and sale of blocks approach minimises both the loss of income and the expenditure associated with the void units whilst enabling an earlier capital receipt to be generated.

8.23: Critical to the concept of the scheme is that out-turn prices should be as low as possible for both the buy-back by the Council and the dwellings for sale to the Council's priority purchasers.'

The report recognised that it would be unlikely that any non-profit-making developers would be able to buy the estate outright or even on a phased basis, and that accordingly proposed negotiations be put in hand with two or three developers.

At the meeting of the housing policy committee on 26 June 1984 Councillor Harrison moved that negotiations be restricted to non-profit-making developers. That was defeated, and it was resolved to authorise—

'(1) the re-housing as soon and in the most sensitive manner possible of tenants from Blocks A–J inclusive with priority being given to those in the earlier phases.

(2) the Director of Housing and the Borough Valuer to negotiate for the
rehabilitation of the estate on a joint venture with one or more private developers
and conversion of the dwellings and blocks so as to provide 111 dwelling units for
sale at the lowest possible cost, 50% to Council nominees (who will be private
purchasers) and preference for the remaining units to be given to first-time buyers
who are residents of the Borough.'

The committee also resolved 'to make use of voids where that could be done without
putting the rehabilitation of the estate at risk'.

The restrictive covenants, which are at the centre of the present dispute, were conceived
by Councillor Howe, who is a member of the Bar. In para 24 of his affirmation of 22
March 1986, after saying that the need for continuity in the development of the estate
was obvious from an early stage, he continued as follows:

'24. I cannot now recall at what point in time Mr Marten first mentioned to me
that the building society housing association had expressed concern about the
question of continuity, but it would certainly have been before the end of 1984.
Quite apart from the specific indications given by those organisations, it was quite
obvious in the circumstances that the prospect of the modernisation scheme halting
after a particular phase, leaving the newly modernised flats in a largely unmodernised
Council estate in the present condition of Fulham Court, could hardly fail to be a
matter of concern to potential developers and even more so to potential purchasers
who would be going to live there.
25. The need for the Council to be able to give assurance of the continuity of the
scheme was aggravated by the bitter opposition of the Labour group on the Council,
and in particular Mr Harrison, to the whole scheme. This led to approaches being
made to potential developers in order to dissuade them from participating (we heard
that the first such approaches had been made to the Abbey and the Woolwich
Building Societies as early as February 1984), and it seemed reasonable to assume
that such efforts to dissuade potentially participating developers would be repeated
and intensified the closer any developer came to embarking on actual participation
in the scheme . . . Quite apart from approaches to developers, there also seemed a
strong likelihood that similar efforts would be made to dissuade potential purchasers
from buying the completed flats. Clearly such efforts could seriously interfere with
the sale of completed flats to priority purchasers (who are generally people on the
margin of being able to buy their homes at all) unless such purchasers could be
assured that the modernisation of the later phases of the estate would continue.
26. Because of my legal background, I naturally turned my mind (I believe
during late 1984 or very early 1985) to whether there was a legal mechanism by
which an assurance of continuity could be given to participating developers and
purchasers alike. Had there been a single suitable developer with the resources to
modernise the whole estate, a single contract of sale with deferred completion of the
later blocks in line with the phases of rehousing would have been the obvious
answer. However, as there was no such suitable single developer, it occurred to me
that a scheme of covenants linking together the successive phases of the development
might provide a similar assurance of continuity. Positive covenants to carry out the
modernisation scheme would by themselves be difficult or impossible to enforce
(mainly because of the difficulties of securing effective enforcement of an obligation
to carry out a necessarily delicate operation of rehousing), and would therefore not
be sufficient to provide the necessary degree of assurance of continuity to developers
or purchasers. It therefore seemed to me to couple such covenants with negative
covenants against re-letting, which would in practice be enforceable and therefore
provide the necessary degree of assurance.'

The result is that early in 1985 the borough solicitor's department was asked to consider whether a scheme of covenants would provide a satisfactory legal mechanism for assuring the continuity of the modernisation scheme.

Early in 1985 it became apparent that the building societies (or their housing subsidiaries) with which the council had been in negotiation regarding the requisition of the estate did not wish to proceed. A housing association was approached, but it appeared that the cost of renovating Block A was such that low-cost flats could not be made available without a subsidy. Negotiations for an urban development grant took place, but proved difficult. As a result, the council entered into negotiations with the Addison Housing Association (Addison) for the purchase of Block A with the assistance of funding from the Housing Corporation. Negotiations continued during the summer and autumn of 1985, and agreement was reached in principle for the purchase by Addison of Block A for the sum of £480,000. Precisely how much was known during the negotiations to the officers of Addison regarding the covenants which the council desired to include in the conveyances, and what was their attitude to them, I need not consider. The covenants themselves were not finalised by the council until the end of October 1985.

At that point I come to the terms of the covenants. They are covenants by the council and they restrict the future use by the council of Blocks B to J. They are as follows (the red land referred to is Blocks B to H):

'1. No part of the red land shall be used otherwise than as a residence for occupation by any or the following persons: (a) a person who at the date hereof occupies a dwelling forming part of the red land under a secure tenancy, for so long as such person continues as against the Transferor to have the right in law to occupy that dwelling and such right is incapable of being terminated by the Transferor by service of a notice, enforcement or any rights arising from breach of covenant, or otherwise; (b) a person who is in law as against the Transferor entitled to require the transfer to him of a secure tenancy in a dwelling forming part of the red land and such right is incapable of being terminated by the Transferor by service of notice, enforcement of any rights arising from breach of covenant, or otherwise; (c) a person to whom the Transferor has granted or shall have granted a lease pursuant to the provisions of Part I of the Housing Act 1980 and his heirs assigns successor in title and those lawfully deriving title under him; (d) a person to whom the Transferor or its successors in title or those deriving title under them has granted a lease of a dwelling forming part of the red land for use as his only or principal home being a lease for a term of not less than 99 years and granted at an initial premium of at least £10,000 at a ground rent not exceeding £100 per annum for the first 25 years and taking any service charges which are usual for such dwellings disposed of on long leases, save that in respect of dwellings contained in the block edged green on Plan A attached hereto the grant may be of an equity sharing lease in respect of which the grantee has an equity share of at least 25%; (e) the heirs assigns successors in title and those lawfully deriving title under a person referred to in paragraph (d) above.

2. No estate, interest or licence shall be created, granted, dealt in or disposed of in respect of the red land or any part thereof including any dwelling therein nor shall the Transferor part with control of any part or parts thereof otherwise than: (a) for the purposes of the residents in the red land of those referred to in paragraph 1 (b) to (e) above; or (b) for the purpose of effecting the modernisation and refurbishment of the red land or the part or parts thereof to which the transaction relates and the disposal thereof as modernised and refurbished individual dwellings to those permitted to reside there pursuant to paragraph 1(c) to (e) above, and no such transaction shall take place unless the conveyance shall contain covenants requiring modernisation and refurbishment works to be carried out requiring the disposal of the individual dwellings as aforesaid and imposing stipulations and restrictions in like form to those set out in the Third Schedule hereto.

3. The Transferor shall take all reasonable steps to bring about the disposal of the red land and the various part or parts thereof for the purposes described in paragraph *a* 2(b) above.'

With limited exceptions, these provisions would prevent the creation of any new lettings of any part of the red land, save by long leases at a premium and, in particular, would prevent temporary letting of voids. The basis of the council's view as to the need for the covenants was that the sale of Block A was the first phase in the implementation *b* of the scheme in relation to the whole estate which, because of the need for decanting, could not be done all at once. It was, in the council's view, necessary for the satisfactory implementation of phase 1 and then of the scheme as a whole that the successful continuation and completion of the other phases could, to some extent, be assured at this stage. I should add that the advice of counsel had been taken; he advised that the covenants could properly be entered into. *c*

On 19 November 1985 the housing policy committee resolved that the borough solicitor be authorised to include the covenants in the transfer documentation of Block A, and the subsequent transfers of Blocks B to H, 'in order to facilitate the implementation of the Fulham Court venture'.

At this stage it was assumed that the sale to Addison was proceeding. At the meeting on 16 December 1985 between representatives of the council and Mr Taussig, the *d* chairman of Addisons, and the chairman of the Notting Hill Housing Trust (with which Addison is associated) the council's representatives were informed that Addison were unhappy with the proposed covenants because, as a housing association and a charity, they felt that it would be contrary to their objects to be party to covenants which would have the effect of preventing the rest of the estate from being used for rented housing.

On 9 January 1986 Addison formally resolved to inform the council that Addison *e* would only wish to proceed with the purchase of Block A if it could do so without being a party to the scheme of covenants. The resolution reiterated Addison's 'enthusiasm for and interest in the scheme if the problem of the unacceptable covenants can be overcome'.

On 28 January 1986 there was a meeting of the housing policy committee. The events at that meeting gave rise to a question (which is no longer in issue) whether the committee had been fully informed of the reasons for Addison's withdrawal. The *f* committee resolved to approve the continuation of test marketing with commercial developers.

The majority group on the council were not prepared to proceed with the sale to Addison without the covenants. The minority were opposed to any sale to commercial developers.

The next meeting of the housing policy committee was on 19 March 1986. The *g* committee had before it a report stating that (i) Addison was willing to proceed with the purchase of Block A at the sum of £480,000 provided the covenants were omitted, (ii) Barratts, a firm of private developers, offered £670,150 for Block A, (iii) Barratts had offered to sell half the flats at a low cost price of £40,000, as opposed to Addison, which proposed to sell at £41,000; (iv) Barratts proposed to offer the other half of the flats at market price, which would be about 25% higher than the low cost price. Addisons, on *h* the other hand, intended to sell *all* the flats at £41,000 (and in consequence made a lower bid for the freehold). Barratts were willing to accept the covenants.

The committee resolved that Barratts' offer be accepted. It is that resolution of 19 November 1985 of which judicial review is now sought.

The case has been argued in this court by counsel for the appellant who resides at Fulham Court, and counsel for Barratts. In the High Court Barratts were not a party, and *j* the council appeared and were represented. Political control of the council changed after the local government elections in May 1986. The council took no part in the argument in this court.

Before Schiemann J, the appellant raised four grounds of challenge. These were (1) bad faith, (2) lack of proper consultation, (3) failure to have regard to relevant considerations

and (4) irrationality. The judge, on 7 May 1986, rejected all these contentions and
a dismissed the application.

On 7 May 1986 the council gave an undertaking to Woolf LJ not to enter into any
contract for the sale of Block A which did not contain a provision that, in the event of the
present appeal succeeding, the contract should be null and void. The council entered into
a contract with Barratts accordingly. The sale under the contract would be subject to the
covenants.

b   The appellant's principal argument in this appeal has been that the covenants impose
an unlawful fetter on the council's powers as a housing authority.

As a preliminary to the consideration of that matter, I think it is necessary to be clear
about what the council was doing and why. The covenants restrict the future use of the
retained land (ie Blocks B to H) to residence or occupation by, broadly, (a) persons who
were secure tenants under the Housing Act 1985 at the date of the contract, and persons
c entitled to have secure tenancies transferred to them (in both cases so long as the rights
of such persons cannot be terminated by the council), (b) holders of leases compulsorily
granted by the council under Pt I of the Housing Act 1980 and its successors, (c) persons
holding leases granted by the council or its successors for terms of not less than 99 years
at a premium of not less than £10,000 at a small ground rent.

There is also a covenant that the council will not make any disposition of any estate or
d interest in Blocks B to H except (i) for the purposes of residences for the persons referred
to in (a) to (c) above, (ii) for the purposes of modernising and refurbishing Blocks B to H,
or the part to which the transaction relates, and the disposal thereof to those permitted to
reside therein under (b) and (c) above. The result, therefore, is that apart from persons
having statutory rights of occupancy, the dwellings in the blocks were only to be let on
long leases at premiums of not less than £10,000 at a low ground rent. The transfer of
e Block A would contain a covenant not to use Block A otherwise than as residences for
persons holding a lease of not less than 99 years at a premium of not less than £25,000 at
a low ground rent.

The problem with which the council was faced was the modernisation of an estate,
laid out in blocks. The estate was 50 years old, and in bad repair. It was no longer possible
f to limp along with day-to-day repairs which were not cost effective, or indeed adequate.
A major programme of modernisation was necessary, and the cost was high. It was
estimated in November 1983 to be about £8m, and was an amount which the council
felt was too large for its own finances to sustain. The council, therefore, over a period
developed a policy for dealing with the problem. The essential features of that policy in
their final form were as follows.

g   (1) All the blocks should be sold to a developer for modernisation.

(2) The blocks, when modernised, should then be sold off as flats to the ultimate
purchasers. The whole of Blocks A to G would eventually pass into the hand of owner-
occupiers in this way.

(3) The preferred developers would be non-profit organisations, but the use of
h commercial developers was left open.

(4) The first block to be dealt with would be Block A, because it was different from
the others in that it faced the Fulham Road, and it included a number of shops and it had
a very ugly rear elevation which needed improvement for the benefit of the other blocks.
In general, its attractive renovation was a matter of some importance in relation to the
saleability of the other blocks.

j   (5) The council formed the view that persons buying owner-occupier flats in Block A
(and in the other blocks as the development proceeded) should have a guarantee as to the
user of the rest of the estate for owner-occupation. The individual purchasers of flats
would be expending a substantial capital sum by way of premium, and would want
binding assurances as to the user of the rest of the estate, since that would materially
affect their own dwellings. The council indeed felt that if it was adopting a policy of

owner-occupancy and encouraging sales of the individual flats on that basis, it was morally bound to give appropriate guarantees as to the effective implementation of what a it believed to be a suitable housing policy. In the absence of certainty as to the development of the whole estate, marketing might be difficult and the whole project might flop. Although the flats were being sold at comparatively modest prices, for most purchasers the acquisition would be an important financial step.

(6) The council would not have to spend its own overstretched resources, and would indeed receive substantial capital sums which could be applied to housing purposes.

That, it seems to me, is a coherent policy which is not manifestly unreasonable. I appreciate that there may be sharp differences of opinion as to the respective merits of owner-occupation and municipally rented housing, but the council's policy, as formulated, could not I think be struck down as 'unreasonable' within *Wednesbury* principles (see *Associated Provincial Picture Houses Ltd v Wednesbury Corp* [1947] 2 All ER 680, [1948] 1 KB 223).

Lord Diplock said in *Council of Civil Service Unions v Minister for the Civil Service* [1984] 3 All ER 935 at 951, [1985] AC 374 at 410:

> 'By "irrationality" I mean what can now be succinctly referred to as "*Wednesbury* unreasonableness" . . . It applies to a decision which is so outrageous in its defiance of logic or of accepted moral standards that no sensible person who had applied his d mind to this question to be decided could have arrived at it.'

The council's policy is not open to attack on that principle. The fact that Addison was willing to complete without the covenants makes no difference in my opinion. Whatever Addison's attitude the policy, in my view, is defensible as it stands since it was a rational policy for the development of the entire estate, with guarantees by way of restrictive e covenants as to future user of the various properties. That is quite usual in relation to a development of a single estate. I should add that although Addison was willing to complete without the covenants, we do not know the view of the Housing Corporation (which was financing Addison). The corporation was informed in the letter of 22 July 1985 that Block A would be sold in conjunction with 'an agreement designed to safeguard f participating developers and investment alike'.

The attack, as developed on the appeal, is, as I have indicated, really based on the contention that the covenants fetter the council's discretion to deal with the retained land and are accordingly bad.

The first question, I think, in relation to that contention is whether the council is entitled to impose on its retained land covenants which were restrictive of its user of that g land. In my opinion it is. Fulham Court was 'land acquired or appropriated by the council' for the purposes of Pt V of the Housing Act 1957 (as amended). It is now held by the council for the purposes of Pt II of the Housing Act 1985. Section 104 of the 1957 Act (now incorporated in s 32 of the 1985 Act) provided as follows:

> '(1) Without prejudice to the provisions of Chapter I of Part I of the Housing Act h 1980 (right to buy public sector houses) a local authority shall have power by this section, but not otherwise, to dispose of any land which they have acquired or appropriated for the purposes of this Part of this Act.
> (2) A disposal under this section may be effected in any manner but is not to be made without the consent of the Minister except in one falling within sub-section (3) below. j
> (3) No consent is required for the letting of land under a secure tenancy . . .
> (5) Subject to section 104A of this Act, on any disposal under this section, a local authority may impose such covenants and conditions as they think fit but a condition of the kinds mentioned in sub-section (b) below may only be imposed with the consent of the Minister . . .'

A restrictive covenant does not operate merely in contract. It is an equitable interest in
a the burdened land. Sections 104(1) and 32 (to which I have referred above) authorise a
local authority to dispose of 'land' held for housing purposes. Under the Interpretation
Act 1978, Sch 1, 'land' includes 'any estate interest easement servitude or right in or over
land'. It seems to me, therefore, that a local authority could, with the consent of the
minister, create restrictive covenants over its Pt V and Pt II land. The nature of a
restrictive covenant was referred to in argument, but no question of absence of necessary
b consents has been raised in this case. Subject to consent, it seems to me that the council
had power to create restrictive covenants under s 104(1) and (2).

In general, I do not understand it to be disputed that there was power in the council
(as the judge held) to create restrictive covenants under the Housing Acts, or otherwise.
Power to create restrictive covenants does not, however, resolve the question whether the
covenants constitute an unlawful fetter. There might, possibly, be an argument that if
c the minister gave consent to the covenants under s 104 or s 32, and a contract was made
accordingly, that is a complete and lawful disposition under the Housing Act itself, and
no further question could arise as to its enforceability, but the point has not been
investigated before us, and I disregard it altogether.

It is clear that a local authority cannot, in general, make declarations of policy which
are binding in future on the council for the time being. A council cannot extinguish
d statutory powers in that way. But it may be able to do so by the valid exercise of other
statutory powers. If a statutory power is lawfully exercised so as to create legal rights and
obligations between the council and third parties, the result will be that the council for
the time being is bound, even though that hinders or prevents the exercise of other
statutory powers.

Thus in *Dowty Boulton Paul Ltd v Wolverhampton Corp* [1971] 2 All ER 277, [1971] 1
e WLR 204 the corporation in 1936 granted the plaintiff a right to use the municipal
airport for 99 years, or for so long as the corporation should maintain it as a municipal
airport (whichever should be the longer). In 1970 the corporation announced its intention
to develop the site under its statutory powers as a housing authority. Pennycuick V-C
granted an interlocutory injunction to restrain the corporation from preventing the
plaintiff, pending trial, from using the airport. He said ([1971] 2 All ER 277 at 282,
f [1971] 1 WLR 204 at 210):

'The cases are concerned with attempts to fetter in advance the future exercise of
a statutory powers otherwise than by the exercise of a statutory power. The cases are
not concerned with the position which arises after a statutory power has been validly
exercised.'

g
Stourcliffe Estates Co Ltd v Bournemouth Corp [1910] 2 Ch 12, [1908–10] All ER Rep 785
is an example of the same principle.

What we are concerned with in the present case are overlapping or conflicting powers.
There is a power to create covenants restrictive of the use of the retained land and there
are powers in relation to the user of the retained land for housing purposes. In these
h circumstances, it is necessary to ascertain for what purpose the retained land is held. All
other powers are subordinate to the main power to carry out the primary purpose (see
Blake (Valuation Officer) v Hendon Corp [1961] 3 All ER 601 at 609, [1962] 1 QB 283 at
302).

Now the purpose for which the Fulham Court estate is held by the council must be
the provision of housing accommodation in the district. The council's policy in relation
j to the estate, as I have set it out above, seems to me to be consistent with that purpose.
The estate is in bad repair, and the policy is aimed at providing accommodation in the
borough of higher quality than at present by means of a scheme of maintenance and
refurbishment. The policy, it is true, is designed to produce owner-occupancy and not
rented accommodation. Historically, local authority housing has been rented. But a
substantial inroad on that was made by Pt I of the Housing Act 1980, which gave

municipal tenants the right to purchase their dwellings. In the circumstances it does not seem to me that a policy which is designed to produce good accommodation for owner-occupiers is now any less within the purposes of the 1957 and 1985 Acts, than the provision of rented housing. We are not dealing with a policy for providing highly expensive housing, but of owner-accommodation at apparently reasonable prices.

It is stressed on behalf of the appellant that Addison was prepared to complete the proposed contract which was at a lower price, without the covenants. I do not think that is relevant. The question, in effect, is whether the Barratt contract would be unlawful, not whether some other contract would have been lawful. What Addison was seeking was a contract which omitted a fundamental part of the council's policy, and it is that policy which is now in issue.

On the other hand, I do think it is of assistance to say that the council's object could plainly be achieved by sale of the whole estate, with the covenants in the form proposed, or by the granting of options over the whole estate for a purchase, subject to the covenants. The council did not do either of those things, and what it actually did do must be judged on its merits.

It seems to me that if the purpose for which the power to create restrictive covenants is being exercised can reasonably be regarded as the furtherance of the statutory object, then the creation of the covenants is not an unlawful fetter. All the powers are exercisable for the achieving of the statutory objects in relation to the land, and the honest and reasonable exercise of a power for that purpose cannot properly be regarded as a fetter on another power given for the same purpose.

We were referred to the decision in *Ayr Harbour Trustees v Oswald* (1883) 8 App Cas 623. But that was a case where the trustees simply 'renounced part of their statutory birthright'. There was an incompatibility between what they were proposing to do and the actual statutory purpose.

In the present case, as it seems to me, the purpose of the contract is the same as the statutory purpose. Devlin LJ said in *Blake (Valuation Officer) v Hendon Corp* [1961] 3 All ER 601 at 609, [1962] 1 QB 283 at 303:

'For example, a man selling a part only of his land might object to a refreshment pavilion on his boundary. Provided that the erection of a refreshment pavilion on that spot was not essential to the use of the land as a pleasure ground, the local authority could properly covenant not to erect one, notwithstanding that it had statutory power to do so. This illustrates the proper application of the principle in *Ayr Harbour Trustees v. Oswald* ((1883) 8 App Cas 623); see *Stourcliffe Estates Co., Ltd. v. Bournemouth Corpn.* ([1910] 2 Ch 12).'

I can see that there is something to be said for the view that so long as the council retains Pt V land it should retain all the powers which the statute gives in relation to that land. That is simple and logical. But I think it is too inflexible and takes insufficient account of the practical difficulties of administering such an estate as Fulham Court. To bring it up to standard, money has to be found and compromises have to be made. It is not practicable to sell the whole estate at once. It has to be phased in order to prevent excessive voids and high loss of income. On 21 March 1986 only Block A (32 flats) was totally empty. But the scheme was quite far advanced. Out of a total of 372 flats, 189 were empty. The policy having been decided on it was necessary to press ahead with it.

I should add that it is not suggested that there was bad faith in the timing of the scheme, as to implementation or otherwise. The idea of assurances of continuity was not new. In 1984 the council's officers had formed the view that the council would have to furnish guarantees on the future of the remainder of the estate. And in July 1985 the letter to the Housing Corporation stated that Block A would be sold in conjunction with an agreement 'safeguarding the developers and investment alike'.

In general, it seems to me that we are concerned with a rational scheme which the council could reasonably say that they were entitled to adopt as part of the housing policy *a* of the borough. In saying that, I do not mean that a scheme for rented housing would have been irrational. Either could be defensible. But it is the function of politicians to choose policies. The court is not concerned with their merits but their legality.

It is said that the covenants impose on the council an obligation to seek to eject any secure tenant who is in breach (however trivial) of his or her obligations under the tenancy agreement, and that this is quite contrary to accepted standards of public administration in so sensitive a field as housing. The point arises in this way. Paragraph
b 1(a) of the covenants refers to—

'A person who at the date hereof occupies a dwelling forming part of the red land under a secure tenancy, for so long as such person continues as against the Transferor (i.e. the Council) to have the right in law to occupy that dwelling and such a right is incapable of being terminated by the Transferor by service of a notice, enforcement
c of any rights arising from breach of covenant, or otherwise.'

There is a similar provision relating to the persons specified in para 1(b).

As I read s 82 of the 1985 Act, however, a periodic tenancy (which I assume Fulham Court tenancies to be, or mostly to be) cannot be brought to an end by the landlord except by obtaining an order of the court for possession. The tenancy only ends on the
d date on which the tenant is to give up possession under the order. The landlord must serve notice seeking possession but, in the case of a periodic tenancy, the notice does not determine the tenancy. In cases where grounds 1 to 8 in Sch 2 are applicable, the court must, in any event, be satisfied that it is reasonable to make an order. It is these grounds which cover the breaches of normal provisions in tenancy agreements.

The covenants, as drawn, do not seem to me to impose a positive obligation on the
e council to serve a notice seeking possession simply because a technical ground for seeking possession has arisen. It merely imposes an obligation to obtain possession when the tenancy is at an end. I see no necessity to read in the wider obligation which is not expressed.

That matter apart, the restrictions imposed by the covenants are, in effect, as follows.
f (i) The restriction of new lettings to long leases. That is central to the policy which the council had adopted in order to resolve the problems of this estate. For the reasons which I have indicated it seems to me a rational policy which a reasonable council could properly adopt. I appreciate that if the remaining blocks failed to sell, the council would be left with property which it could only put to a restricted use, ie direct owner-occupier sales. But there is nothing to indicate that such property, in London, will fail to sell.
g (ii) It produces some degree of inflexibility in providing accommodation for tenants who do not wish to leave the estate, or to leave quickly, but would be prepared to move to another block so as to free their own block for the modernisation works. The council's hands are tied. That may be an inconvenience, but if the scheme generally is an effectuation of the Pt V purposes, I cannot see that it invalidates the whole.
(iii) Flats are left empty while the 'decanting' is taking place and loss of revenue results.
h But that is inherent in the policy and it is clear that the question of voids was raised on a number of occasions at both committee and council meetings, including the housing policy committee in June 1984 and February 1985. It was accepted because of what was regarded, not unreasonably, as the wider benefits of the scheme.

On the wider aspects of the matter, it was suggested on behalf of the applicant that if this scheme was valid, a council could, on the sale of a single flat, tie the hands of its
j successors by covenants in relation to the rest of a large estate. I do not think that is a valid argument. We are dealing with a long considered and rational scheme which was substantially advanced in its operation so that half the flats were vacant. It bears no resemblance to artificial devices based on single flats.

For the reasons which I have indicated, I would reject the argument based on fetters.

It is further submitted that the council did not comply with its statutory obligations

as to consultation. Section 43 of the 1980 Act (now s 105 of the 1985 Act) provides as
follows:

> '(1) Every landlord authority shall, within 12 months of the commencement of
> this Chapter, make and thereafter maintain such arrangements as it considers
> appropriate to enable those of its secure tenants who are likely to be substantially
> affected by a matter of housing management—(a) to be informed of the authority's
> proposals in respect of that matter; and (b) to make their views known to the
> authority within a specified period . . .
> (2) It shall be the duty of a landlord authority, before making any decision on a
> matter of housing management, to consider any representation made to it in
> accordance with arrangements made by the authority under this section . . .'

The concept of 'housing management' is defined by s 42(2) as follows:

> 'A matter is one of housing management for the purposes of this Chapter if, in
> the opinion of the landlord authority concerned, it—(a) relates to the management,
> maintenance, improvement or demolition of dwelling-houses let by the authority
> under secure tenancies, or to the provision of services or amenities in connection
> with such dwelling houses, and (b) represents a new programme of maintenance,
> improvement or demolition or a change in the practice or policy of the authority:
> and (c) is likely substantially to affect its secure tenants as a whole or a group of
> them.'

It is not in doubt that there was appropriate consultation in 1984. It is said, however,
that there should have been further consultation in 1986 in consequence of the March
resolution. The position, it is said, thereby changed in consequence of (1) the fact that
Block A was now to be sold to a commercial (and not a non-commercial) developer and
(2) the introduction of the covenants. Consultation, it is said, must be on the proposal
actually to be implemented.

It does not seem to me that the identity of the developer (ie whether the developer is a
commercial developer or non-profit-making) is 'likely substantially to affect' the secure
tenants. Certainly the council would not be acting in a way which was *Wednesbury*
unreasonable if it was of that opinion. The circumstances which could be said seriously
to affect the tenants was the decision to dispose for improvement and owner-occupation.
That affected the tenants because of the need to rehouse. But at the time of the 1986
resolution, the estate was already half empty in consequence of the previous consultation.
There was no doubt about the rehousing policy.

We were referred to the decision in *Short v Tower Hamlets London Borough* (1985) 18
HLR 171, but I do not think that advances the matter. The proposal under challenge was
insufficiently formed to require consultation. It was too early. In the present case,
looking at the position in March 1986, there is still, it seems to me, no basis for a
contention that there was any failure to comply with the statutory consultation
requirements. The 'too early' argument does not apply. The material matters were settled
in 1984.

As to the covenants, it seems to me that they are merely an implementation of the
council's owner-occupier policy. That policy was apparent in the 1984 consultation.

There was advanced before the judge (though in the end it was not much pressed in
this court) the argument that the tenants had, at common law, a legitimate expectation
of further consultation to which the courts will give effect. The judge rejected that on
the ground that there is no case where the courts have added a common law duty where
there is already a statutory one. I see no reason to disagree with the judge's view.

In the circumstances, no valid ground of challenge is made out based in failure to
consult.

I would dismiss the appeal.

KERR LJ. I have come to a different conclusion on that part of the arguments which
a were presented under the heading 'unlawful fettering'. But since this does not affect the
fate of this appeal I will state my reasons fairly shortly.

The relevant history concerning the policy for Fulham Court shows opposing political
views within the housing policy committee and the council which were held throughout
with passionate intensity. These clearly increased with the approach of the local elections
on 8 May 1986, which were expected to result, as they did, in a change of the governing
b majority on the committee and council. The fact that this was in the mind of everyone
concerned at the time of the meeting of the committee on 19 March 1986, when the
decision was taken to sell Block A to Barratts subject to the restrictive covenants, is clear
from the affidavits which were sworn immediately thereafter in support and opposition
to the application for judicial review. That the date of 8 May 1986 was critical is also
apparent from the fact, as we were told, that the hearing was thereupon expedited so that
c Schiemann J was able to deliver his extempore judgment, a tour de force in the
circumstances and by any standard, on the afternoon of Wednesday, 7 May. In the light
of his decision the contract between the council and Barratts was then signed on the
following day, subject to the outcome of any appeal. By that evening the political control
of the council had changed.

Against that background, which represents only the final part of the history, it seems
d to me that the court must consider with the greatest care whether the decisions of the
committee and council, evidently taken by a majority of a single vote or so throughout,
were actuated by policy reasons based on the proper discharge of the authority's powers
and functions as a housing authority, or by extraneous motives. In saying this, I am of
course not suggesting that political considerations must not affect the decisions of local
authorities, which would plainly be absurd. The point in the present case, however, is
e that it concerns a decision which, consciously and indeed in my view quite deliberately,
fettered the freedom of action for the future of whoever might command a majority on
the committee and council in relation to Fulham Court as a whole. That this was the
intention is not really open to doubt, for the reasons explained hereafter. However, in
saying this I am of course not questioning the sincerity of the opposing convictions held
f on both sides. Nor am I in the least concerned with their respective merits. The court is
solely concerned with the question whether the decision under review was influenced by
irrelevant considerations which ought to have been excluded under the principles stated
by Lord Greene MR in the well-known passage in *Associated Provincial Picture Houses Ltd
v Wednesbury Corp* [1947] 2 All ER 680 at 682–683, [1948] 1 KB 223 at 229. In the
present case I have reluctantly come to the conclusion that the decision to sell Block A to
g Barratts subject to the covenants in question was so influenced by political considerations
designed to fetter the council's future policy that it should not be allowed to stand.

The legal position is succinctly stated in one paragraph of Wade *Administrative Law*
(5th edn, 1982) p 335 as follows, under the heading 'Contractual fetters on discretion'
and its correctness in principle was unchallenged:

h 'Just as public authorities must have policies, so they must make contracts. Like
policies, contracts may be inconsistent with the authorities' proper exercise of their
powers. But, unlike policies, contracts are legally binding commitments, and
therefore they present more difficult problems. The general principle is the same:
an authority may not by contract fetter itself so as to disable itself from exercising
its discretion as required by law. Its paramount duty is to preserve its own freedom
j to decide in every case as the public interest requires at the time. But at the same
time its powers may include the making of binding contracts, and it may be most
important that it should make them. Since most contracts fetter freedom of action
in some way, there may be difficult questions of degree in determining how far the
authority may legally commit itself for the future.'

In the present context I would only add that, when a local authority disposes of land adjacent or near to other land which it retains, it may of course act entirely properly in submitting itself to covenants which in some way fetter its otherwise unfettered use of *a* the retained land. A contractual fetter of this nature is not different in principle from any other fetter, as discussed in the foregoing passage.

What, then, is the evidence which assists in determining on which side of the line, as a matter of degree, the present case falls?

The political ingredient of the decision taken by the committee on 19 March appears clearly from paras 24 and 25 of an affidavit of 22 April 1986 of Mr P C Prince, the *b* chairman of the committee, sworn in opposition to the application for judicial review. (In drawing attention to this, I am not intending to detract one iota from the even more highly charged political content of Mr Harrison's evidence in support of the application. But he was not associated with the decision under review). Mr Prince stated:

'24. It would appear that Mr Harrison's prime ground of objection to the *c* proposed covenants is his desire, should his party be elected to control of the Council, to reverse the whole present policy for the sale for modernisation of Fulham Court. I would question the reasonableness, and indeed the rationality, of the Council taking such a step in future in view of the enormous amount of effort and resources which have been put into this project over the past two and a half years. 189 dwellings have been vacated, with all these vacations being on a voluntary basis. In *d* many cases the rehousing has been accomplished with extreme difficulty and after a great deal of work by officers in meeting tenants' requirements. The proposed phase 2 (blocks B, C and D) is now over two thirds empty, with block B (upon which work would be started in advance of C and D) now down to 9 out of 39 not yet rehoused or having accepted an offer. A decision to reverse this process would render all this work abortive, and immediately raise the question of how the social problems *e* of Fulham Court could be solved and how the Council could find the large capital resources needed to carry out the modernisation of the estate itself. I do not doubt that Mr Harrison would be capable of taking such a decision were he in a position to do so, but such a decision would in my view be one in which political considerations would outweigh any questions of reasonableness.

25. What Mr Harrison is effectively asking is that the Committee should take a *f* decision which is not in the belief of the Committee the best option available in the interests of good housing conditions in Fulham Court, specifically in order that he and his colleagues might be free to take in future what I would regard as an unreasonable decision which would run counter to a continuing policy which has now been pursued by the Council for two years.'

While this speaks for itself, it is clearly not determinative of the issue. But the decision *g* taken on 19 March 1986 was also taken against the background of a lengthy history during which policy decisions for the future of Fulham Court were considered and evolved. This appears to me to have taken a new turn shortly before the pending elections and with these in view. A great deal of this material will be found in the judgment of Fox LJ, and the judgment of Schiemann J recites it in even greater detail. I therefore *h* propose only to draw attention to those aspects of the history which have led me to the conclusion that the ultimate outcome, in the form of the committee's decision on 19 March 1986, was predominantly influenced by the political motive of fettering the political aspects of the future housing policy for Fulham Court rather than by any immediately necessary or relevant policy considerations. The various points are not listed in any order of importance, since I find it difficult to do so, and some are clearly weightier *j* than others. I am mainly concerned with their cumulative weight.

1. The original proposal was firmly in favour of a joint venture with a non-profitmaking developer. The circular which formed the basis of the consultation with the tenants in April 1984, the only consultation which took place, included the following under the heading *'Proposals for the future'*, and there are other similar references:

'On 23 November 1983, the Council made a decision in principle to fully
investigate the potential for a joint venture with a non-profit-making developer to
achieve the improvement of Fulham Court. The proposals currently under
consideration envisage the sensitive rehousing of all tenants resident in Fulham
Court in order to enable a joint venture proposal for the modernisation of the blocks
which will include a Sheltered Housing scheme by conversion, and flats for Shared
Ownership and Low cost home ownership for the Council's priority purchasers.'

2. Addision was a non-profit-making housing association and an entirely suitable
choice for the purposes of the first stage of this development, ie Block A. But for the
restrictive covenants, Addison was at all times willing to go ahead with the purchase and
development of Block A on terms acceptable to the committe and council. This is a
crucial point in the history. There was no evidence whatever, as first contended by
counsel for Barratts on this appeal, that the omission of the covenants would have
disabled Addison from obtaining the necessary finance from the Housing Corporation.

3. The original policy had envisaged 'sensitive rehousing' (see the passage quoted
above, and there were many others). But, whatever may be the legal effect of the
covenants in para 1(a) set out in the judgment of Fox LJ, these, to put it no higher, can
hardly claim to deserve this description.

4. The original policy had also envisaged the use of 'voids' to some extent. Thus, on
23 November 1983, the report by the director of housing to the council stated in para 8,
under *implications*: 'Some units becoming void on the Fulham Court Estate may become
usable as temporary accommodation for households needing them.' This obviously
became precluded when the restrictive covenants were put forward and adopted in
November 1985.

5. There was not a shred of evidence that Barratts, although of course developers for
profit, in fact required the covenants as a term of their participation in the development
of Block A. On the other hand, Addison had of course declined to proceed solely because
of them. While there are indications that the desirability and content of these remarkable
covenants gradually evolved in the minds of Councillor Howe and of some of the council
officials during 1985, the evidence suggests that, in effect, they were self-imposed. So far
as the committee and council appear to have been aware, they came out of the blue in
November 1985 without any evidence that they were an essential prerequisite for the
purpose of implementing the policy as it then stood. The joint report of the borough
solicitor and director of housing to the committee was based on the unqualified
assumption that the sale of Block A would proceed with Addison as the developer. The
relevant passages of the report introducing the restrictive covenants, were as follows:

'3.0 *Background*

3.1 Following full joint and individual consultation with the tenants of the
Fulham Court Estate, Members at a meeting of the Housing Policy Committee on
26th June 1984 determined to proceed with the joint venture for Fulham Court
involving the sale and rehabilitation of Blocks A to H inclusive. Housing Policy
Committee at its meeting of 12th February 1985 further determined that Block A
be sold to a housing association for an improvement for sale scheme as the first
phase of the joint venture, the shops being leased back to the Council.

3.2 Whilst a pre-requisite to the successful implementation was considered at the
time to be submission for Urban Development Grant (UDG) it was later determined
that a scheme could be devised on the basis of Housing Corporation finance which
would obviate the need for UDG. Housing Corporation finance for Improvement
for Sale schemes includes an element of subsidy in the form of the Housing
Association Grants (HAG).

3.3 Discussions have progressed with the Housing Corporation following which
Addison Housing Association has been invited to proceed with a scheme for the

improvement for sale of the residential part of Block A utilising Housing Corporation
funding. Addision Housing Association has sufficient allocation with the Corporation
to enable the acquisition and improvement of Block A in the current financial year.

3.4 Planning consent was granted for the scheme on 15th October 1985, and the
Housing Corporation has approved the funding for the scheme. Contracts can
therefore be exchanged within a very short time scale, with a view to an early
completion of the sale and a very early start on site.

4.0 *Special Conditions of Sale*

4.1 The key element of the Council's proposals for Fulham Court *and the
participation of non-profit maximising organisations (such as housing associations* and the
building society's sibling organisations) is that there should be continuity of
implementation. The joint venture package has been devised on this basis and
envisages the phased rehousing, sale and rehabilitation for sale of dwellings over a
three year plus period.' (My emphasis.)

6. Notwithstanding these explicit parts of this report, the covenants proposed in its
later passages were not withdrawn in January 1986, after it had become known that
Addison was ready, able and willing to proceed provided that these covenants were
dropped. Addison's rejection of these covenants, albeit notionally designed for its benefit,
demonstrated the inaccuracy (to put it no higher) of the words which I have emphasised
in para 4.1 of the report. Notwithstanding this, the option of thereupon simply dropping
these recently self-imposed covenants was never put before the committee in the report
of the chairman, Mr Prince, dated 28 January 1986 for the meeting of the committee on
that day. He merely reported that 'the Housing Association [Addison] would not sign
and it has subsequently confirmed its unwillingness to proceed'. Not a word about
Addison's reaction to the covenants. One is therefore bound to ask oneself why the
maintenance of these covenants was so relentlessly pursued at that stage. I find myself
unable to reach any credible conclusion other than that the predominant reason was the
approach of the elections and the desire to ensure, by means of the covenants, that no
alternative political housing policy could thereafter be adopted for Fulham Court without
a breach of contract on the part of the council.

7. In saying this, I would like to emphasise once again that in my view the overall
proposals for Fulham Court favoured by the bare majority of the committee and council
are not in themselves open to the slightest criticism from the point of view of a proper
development policy for adoption by a housing authority. Indeed, this was never
challenged by counsel for the applicant. But policies are liable to be reviewed, as the
result of events or political changes or both. They should remain open to review under
our democratic institutions, save to the extent that an immediate policy decision renders
it reasonably necessary to fetter future policy decisions. I can see no such necessity for the
covenants in the history of the present case.

8. In addition to the foregoing considerations, and without suggesting any criticism
of anyone concerned, it should also be borne in mind in this connection that by the end
of 1985 the original proposals for the development of Fulham Court had badly 'slipped'
in a number of respects. Thus, whereas in June 1984 it had been planned that Blocks B,
C and D might be empty by the end of 1985, by February 1985 this date had already
been reprojected to January 1987. At the same time, no progress of any kind had been
made with any further plans for the development of Fulham Court beyond the
development of Block A. No proposals, let alone possible developers, were in sight for
Blocks B to H. There were only 32 flats in Block A as against a total of 326 in Blocks B to
H. But the contractual terms for the development of Block A, admittedly the most
important one because of its frontal position, were nevertheless to govern the wholly
uncertain and possibly very distant future of all the remainder. In addition, no
reassessment of the overall housing implications of the original scheme for the borough
as a whole had been made since November 1983, and no further consultation with
anyone had taken place after April 1984.

In the upshot, I am left with the following clear conclusions on the evidence. (i) The
housing policies and aims for the development of Fulham Court as a whole pursued by
the majorities on the committee and council were in themselves perfectly proper and
open to no criticism whatever. (ii) But from about November 1985 onwards these
policies were deliberately underpinned by the scheme of the restrictive covenants, with
the predominant motive of seeking to ensure the continuation and irrevocable
maintenance of these policies in the event of a political change in the administration of
the borough after the elections in May 1986.

On that basis I feel bound to conclude that the decision to contract with Barratts for
the development of Block A on 19 March 1986, subject to these covenants, was an
unreasonable and impermissible exercise of the powers and functions of a housing
authority in the *Wednesbury* sense. Its predominant motivation was to fetter the political
aspects of the future housing policy for Fulham Court, and not the implementation of
the then (already modified) housing policy for reasons which were reasonably necessary
at the time. It follows that in my view the decision of 19 March 1986, and the recent
history which has preceded it, were predominantly motivated by purely political
considerations designed to fetter future policies and not by any presently required
contractual fetters.

Accordingly, I would quash the decision of 19 March 1986 and the consequent contract
with Barratts, and allow this appeal.

SIR DENYS BUCKLEY. I have had the advantage of reading in draft the judgments
of both Fox and Kerr LJJ. I agree with Fox LJ, and I do not really wish to add anything to
the reasons he has given, but in view of the fact that Fox and Kerr LJJ have differed, I will
add a few observations of my own.

It is true that the council's policy relating to Fulham Court only achieved any degree
of fulfilment on 8 May 1986, when the contract for the sale of Block A to Barratts was
signed. On the same day no doubt the council was in a state of political ferment on
account of the fact that the local government elections were to take place next day, with
a high possibility of a change occurring in the political control of the council. Doubtless
the majority party was determined to get the contract signed before any such change
could take place. But the policy which resulted in that contract had been in a state of
gestation at least since November 1983. The evidence indicates that as early as the spring
of 1984, the council's officers had formed the view that when the council sold the first
block of the property, which proved to be Block A, the council would have to give some
guarantee that the remainder of Fulham Court would be rehabilitated on similar lines in
accordance with the policy then adopted by the council. The inter-departmental report,
which was considered by the housing policy committee in June 1984, stressed the need
for a phased scheme for the rehabilitation of the whole of Fulham Court. It is, in my
view, clear that the intention throughout was that Fulham Court should be rehabilitated
in its entirety in accordance with one coherent scheme, although that scheme would
have to be carried out in phrases, and very possibly in collaboration with different
developers for the various phases, some at least of whom might not be non-profit-making
concerns.

The genesis of the restrictive covenants is dealt with by Mr Howe in his affirmation.
He was not cross-examined. His evidence clearly indicates that a primary purpose of
these covenants was to ensure continuity in the implementation of the scheme. I see
nothing to suggest that in 1984, even in its later months or early 1985, the possibility of
a change in the political control of the council in 1986 was exercising the minds of
members of the council in respect of the covenants.

The method of implementing the policy as regards Block A changed somewhat during
the period between the adoption of the policy and the contract with Barratts, partly on
account of financial considerations, and partly because Addison became disinclined at a
rather late stage to accept a contract incorporating the covenants. The policy, however,
remained consistent.

If, as the result of this appeal, the contract with Barratts proceeds, the restrictive covenants will probably prove to be of less significant importance to Barratts than to *a* prospective owner-occupiers who will acquire flats from Barratts, by whom individually the covenants will be enforceable against the council. Those prospective owner-occupiers will have a means to ensure that the remaining blocks of the estate will be developed in accordance with a consistent policy, and reasonably expeditiously.

I am clearly of the opinion that, if a statutory authority acting in good faith in the proper and reasonable exercise of its statutory powers undertakes some binding *b* obligation, the fact that such obligation may thereafter preclude the authority from exercising some other statutory power, or from exercising its statutory powers in some other way, cannot constitute an impermissible fetter on its powers. Any other view would involve that the doctrine against fettering would itself involve a fetter on the authority's capacity to exercise its powers properly and reasonably as it thinks fit from time to time. So, in my view, the decision of the present case depends primarily on *c* whether the council was acting properly and reasonably in proposing to covenant with Barratts in the terms of the restrictive covenants. For the reasons indicated by Fox LJ, I think this was so.

I would only add, with deference to Kerr LJ, that in my opinion those covenants do not involve insensitive rehousing. They may, it is true, involve some flats in Fulham Court being kept void for a time when they might otherwise be used for rehousing, but *d* this would not impede the sensitive rehousing elsewhere of tenants voluntarily vacating flats in Fulham Court. The council's policy clearly required the council's obtaining vacant possession of all the blocks. This must have been clear from the written information given to all tenants on the estate when they were consulted: see para 8.4 of the report of the inter-departmental committee of June, 1984, to which Fox LJ has referred.

I would dismiss the appeal. *e*

Appeal dismissed. Leave to appeal to the House of Lords granted.

Solicitors: *Alan Edwards & Co* (for the appellant); *Lewis Silkin* (for Barratts).

Frances Rustin   Barrister. *f*

a
Bass Holdings Ltd v Morton Music Ltd

CHANCERY DIVISION
SCOTT J
2, 3, 30 JULY 1986

b   Landlord and tenant – Lease – Option to renew – Observance of covenants – Condition of exercise
of option that 'all covenants ... have been observed' – Negative covenant – Breach of negative
covenant – Whether condition requiring performance and observance of all covenants could be
fulfilled once negative convenant broken – Whether tenant precluded from exercising option by
past breach of negative covenant.

c   By a lease dated 20 September 1982 the plaintiff demised certain premises to the
defendant for a term of 15 years from 1 April 1982. The lease reserved a yearly rent of
£15,000 payable quarterly for the first three years and thereafter the rent was subject to
periodic rent reviews. The lease contained tenant's covenants to pay the rent reserved at
the time and in the manner prescribed, to pay taxes and rates etc, to keep the premises in
good and substantial repair and not to apply for planning permission in respect of the
d   demised premises without the plaintiff's prior written consent. By cl 9 of the lease the
defendant was granted an option to apply for a further lease of the premises for a term of
125 years from the date of the term granted if it gave notice in writing to the plaintiff by
29 September 1985 and had paid the rent and performed and observed its obligations
under the lease. By a letter dated 19 September the defendant purported to exercise that
option, but the plaintiff refused to accept the letter as an effective exercise of the option
e   on the ground, inter alia, that the defendant was in breach of its tenant's covenants in
that it had been in arrears of rent and had previously applied for planning permission
without the plaintiff's consent. Before the purported exercise of the option the plaintiff
had forfeited the lease on account of arrears of rent and breach of the covenant concerning
planning permission but the defendant had been granted relief against forfeiture on
giving an undertaking to comply with the covenant not to apply for planning permission
f   without consent and on payment of rent arrears and rates, and it had complied with
those terms. The plaintiff sought declarations that the defendant's letter exercising the
option was invalid and that by reason of the breaches of covenant the defendant was not
entitled to exercise the option. The question whether the defendant was precluded from
exercising the option by virtue of its past breaches of covenant was tried as a preliminary
issue.

g
Held – Although a condition requiring performance and observance of a tenant's
covenants as a condition precedent to the tenant exercising a right under a lease did not
fail simply because there was a past but remedied breach of a positive covenant, once a
negative covenant was broken a condition requiring performance and observance of all
the covenants could not be fulfilled. Furthermore, a previous breach of a negative
h   covenant could not be ignored even if the state of affairs brought into existence by the
breach had come to an end, since the fact that the covenant had not been performed and
observed could not be altered by the payment of damages (which did not represent
performance of the covenant), or the effluxion of time making the cause of action statute-
barred, or the granting of relief from forfeiture (which was based on the fact that the
covenant had not been performed and observed). Although the defendant had paid the
j   arrears of rent and, for the purposes of cl 9 of the lease, the covenant for payment of rent
had accordingly been performed and observed, the defendant had committed breaches
of the covenant not to apply for planning permission without the plaintiff's consent and,
notwithstanding the grant of relief from forfeiture, the defendant could not claim to
have performed and observed that covenant. It followed therefore that a condition

precedent to the defendant's right to exercise the option in cl 9 had not been fulfilled (see
p 394 g, p 399 b c, p 400 h to 401 f j and p 402 b c, post).   a

Grey v Friar (1854) 4 HL Cas 565, Finch v Underwood (1876) 2 Ch D 310, Bastin v Bidwell
(1881) 18 Ch D 238, Simons v Associated Furnishers Ltd [1930] All ER Rep 427, Rugby School
(Governors) v Tannahill [1934] All ER Rep 187, Scala House and District Property Co Ltd v
Forbes [1973] 3 All ER 308 and Expert Clothing Service and Sales Ltd v Hillgate House Ltd
[1985] 2 All ER 998 considered.
                                                                                               b

Notes
For conditions precedent to exercise of options in a lease, see 27 Halsbury's Laws (4th
edn) para 116, and for cases on the subject, see 31(2) Digest (Reissue) 892–893, 7396–
7400.

Cases referred to in judgment   c
Bassett v Whiteley (1982) 45 P & CR 87, CA.
Bastin v Bidwell (1881) 18 Ch D 238.
Expert Clothing Service and Sales Ltd v Hillgate House Ltd [1985] 2 All ER 998, [1986] Ch
    340, [1985] 3 WLR 359, CA.
Finch v Underwood (1876) 2 Ch D 310, CA.
Grey v Friar (1854) 4 HL Cas 565, 10 ER 583.   d
Rugby School (Governors) v Tannahill [1935] 1 KB 87, [1934] All ER Rep 187, CA; affg,
    [1934] 1 KB 695.
Scala House and District Property Co Ltd v Forbes [1973] 3 All ER 308, [1974] QB 575,
    [1973] 3 WLR 14, CA.
Simons v Associated Furnishers Ltd [1931] 1 Ch 379, [1930] All ER Rep 427.
                                                                                               e

Cases also cited
Antaios Cia Naviera SA v Salen Rederierna AB, The Antaios [1984] 3 All ER 229, [1985] AC
    191, HL.
Carradine Properties Ltd v Aslam [1976] 1 All ER 573, [1976] 1 WLR 442.
Dyet Investments Ltd v Moore (1972) 223 EG 945.
Germax Securities Ltd v Spiegal (1979) 37 P & CR 204, CA.   f
Hankey v Clavering [1942] 2 All ER 311, [1942] 2 KB 326, CA.
Robinson v Thames Mead Park Estate Ltd [1947] 1 All ER 366, [1947] Ch 334.
United Dominions Trust (Commercial) Ltd v Eagle Aircraft Services Ltd [1968] 1 All ER 104,
    [1968] 1 WLR 74, CA.
United Scientific Holdings Ltd v Burnley BC [1977] 2 All ER 62, [1978] AC 904, HL.
West Country Cleaners (Falmouth) Ltd v Saly [1966] 3 All ER 210, [1966] 1 WLR 1485, CA.   g

Preliminary issues
By an originating summons dated 7 November 1985 the plaintiff, Bass Holdings Ltd,
sought as against the defendant, Morton Music Ltd, (1) a declaration that the defendant's
solicitors' letter of 19 September 1985 to the plaintiff was invalid and ineffective for the   h
purpose of exercising an option to obtain a further lease of premises known as the
Queen's Hotel, Westcliff-on-Sea, created by and contained in cl 9 of a lease of the premises
made 20 September 1982 between the plaintiff, Michael Clayton Collier and the
defendant, (2) further or alternatively a declaration that, by reason of breaches of covenant
committed by the defendant, the defendant was not entitled to the grant of a further
lease pursuant to cl 9, (3) a declaration that the option could no longer be exercised by   j
the defendant. On 9 May 1986 Master Cholmondeley-Clarke ordered that there be tried
as preliminary issues in the action, the questions (1) whether the option notice dated 19
September 1985 was a valid notice to exercise the option contained in cl 9 of the lease
and (2) whether the defendant was precluded from exercising the option by virtue of
past breaches of covenant. The facts are set out in the judgment.

Paul Morgan for the plaintiff.

a *Nicholas Dowding* for the defendant.

Cur adv vult

30 July. The following judgment was delivered.

b
SCOTT J. By a lease dated 20 September 1982 the plaintiff, Bass Holdings Ltd, demised to the defendant Morton Music Ltd, the Queen's Hotel, Hamlet Court Road, Westcliff-on-Sea, Essex. The term of the demise was expressed to be 'FIFTEEN . . . YEARS computed from the First day of April 1982'. A yearly rent of £15,000 payable on the usual quarter days was reserved 'for the first Three years of the said term'. Thereafter the rent was to be

c subject to upward adjustments in accordance with a rent review procedure. The Queen's Hotel included a public house as well as the accommodation usually associated with a hotel. The tenant's covenants included covenants obliging the tenant to keep the public house open during all lawful hours and to deal exclusively with the lessor for all beer sold or consumed on the demised premises. In short, the Queen's Hotel was let as a tied house.

The lease contained also tenant's covenants of a character commonly found in leases.

d There was a covenant to pay the rent reserved at the times and in manner prescribed; there was a covenant to pay taxes, rates, etc; there was a covenant to 'keep the demised premises and the painting papering and decoration thereof in good and substantial repair order and condition'; there was a covenant that the tenant would not apply for planning permission in respect of the demised premises without the lessor's prior written consent; there were many other covenants both of a positive and of a negative character that I

e need not detail. In addition, there were a number of tenant's covenants attributable to the Queen's Hotel's status as a tied house. The lease included a proviso for re-entry in the normal form.

Clause 9 of the lease contains the provision that has given rise to this litigation. It is in these terms:

f   'IF the Tenant shall be desirous of taking a further lease of the demised premises for a further term of One hundred and Twenty-five years . . . from the date of the term hereby granted and shall not later than the 29th September 1985 give to the Lessors notice in writing of such its desire and if it shall have paid the rent hereby reserved and shall have performed and observed the several stipulations on its part herein contained and on its part to be performed and observed up to the date thereof

g   then the Lessors will on payment to them by the Tenant of the sum of £300,000 let the demised premises to the Tenant for a further term of One hundred and Twenty-five years . . . from the date of the term hereby granted at a rent of one peppercorn per annum (if demanded) subject in all other respects to the same stipulations as are herein contained except this Clause for renewal and save for the alterations referred to in Part III of the Schedule hereto.'

h
By a letter dated 19 September 1985 written by Messrs Nutt & Oliver, the defendant's solicitors, the defendant purported to exercise its right under cl 9 of the lease to call for a new 125-year term. The letter was received by the plaintiff on 20 September 1985. It is in these terms:

j   'We act for Morton Music Limited the tenant of the above premises under a lease granted by you on the 20th September 1982. We hereby give you notice of our clients desire under clause 9 of the Lease to take a further term of the demised premises for 125 years from the 1st April 1982 and otherwise upon the terms referred to in the Lease. We are sending a copy of this letter to Messrs. Nabarro Nathanson your Solicitors and we look forward to hearing from them in connection with the new Lease accordingly.'

The plaintiff does not accept that this letter constituted an effective exercise of the cl 9 option. First, the plaintiff contends that the contents of the letter do not represent an exercise of the option. The commencement of the new term was expressed by the letter to be 1 April 1982. Clause 9 refers to 'a further term of One Hundred and Twenty-five ... years from the date of the term hereby granted ...' The plaintiff contends that 'the date of the term hereby granted' is either 20 September 1982, the date of the lease, or 31 March 1997, the date on which the 15-year term will expire and that, accordingly, the letter was an ineffective attempt to exercise the cl 9 option. Second, the plaintiff contends that in three respects the defendant was or is in brach of its covenants in the lease.

It is common ground that by September 1984 rent due under the lease was in arrears to an extent of £18,000, or thereabouts. In addition, the defendant was in default in payment of water rates.

On 11 September the plaintiff re-entered the demised premises and forfeited the lease on account of the rent arrears. On 9 October the defendant issued an originating summons seeking relief from forfeiture. In its answer to the defendant's application for relief from forfeiture, the plaintiff sought to maintain the forfeiture by relying alternatively on breaches by the defendant of its covenant not to apply for planning permission without the prior written consent of the plaintiff. It is not in dispute that in March 1984 and again in October or November 1984 applications were made on the defendant's behalf for outline planning permission. In neither case was the plaintiff's consent sought. Both applications were rejected by the local planning authority and it is common ground that neither has caused any quantifiable loss or damage to the plaintiff. But, none the less, each application represented a breach of covenant.

The defendant's response was to seek relief from forfeiture in respect not only of its rent arrears but also of its breaches of covenant.

The defendant's applications for relief from forfeiture were dealt with by an order made by Master Dyson on 12 March 1985 and slightly varied on 1 April 1985. The order recited an undertaking by the defendant at all times thereafter to comply with its covenant not to apply for planning permission without the plaintiff's written consent. The order granted the defendant relief from forfeiture both in respect of the rent arrears and in respect of the breaches of covenant to which I have referred. The relief was, however, granted on certain conditions. The conditions required payment by the defendant of the rent arrears and interest thereon, payment of rates and water rates in arrears and payment of the plaintiff's taxed costs. Each of these conditions was complied with. So the defendant's lease was reinstated. None the less rent had been in arrear and there had been breaches of covenant by the defendant.

The third matter relied on by the plaintiff relates to the defendant's repairing and decorating obligations under the lease. The plaintiff contends that over the period 20 September 1982 to 19 September 1985 the condition of the Queen's Hotel did not comply with those obligations. The defendant denies that this was so.

In the three respects that I have mentioned the plaintiff contends that the defendant failed to perform or observe its obligations under the lease and that in consequence the defendant was not entitled to exercise the cl 9 option. Of these three matters only the third, the alleged failure of the defendant to comply with its repairing and decorating obligations, raises any dispute of fact.

By an order made on 9 May 1986 by Master Cholmondeley-Clarke, two questions were directed (by para (2) of the order) to be tried as a preliminary issue, namely:

'(a) Whether the option notice dated 19th September 1985 is a valid Notice to exercise the option contained in clause 9 of the lease dated 20th September 1982 and (b) Whether the Defendant is precluded from exercising the said option by virtue of past breaches of covenant.'

The first of these two questions raises the point about the form of the letter of 19

September 1985. Was 'the date of the term hereby granted' 1 April 1982 or some other
a date? If it was some other date, does the error in the letter prevent the letter being treated
as an effective exercise of the cl 9 option?

The second question is whether the admitted previous breaches of covenant by the
defendant prevented the defendant from exercising the cl 9 option. The reference in sub-
para (b) of para (2) of the order of 9 May 1980 to 'past breaches of covenant' was not
intended to include the alleged breach of the repairing and decorating covenant. If the
b admitted breaches of covenant were fatal to the defendant's right to exercise the option,
there would be no point in wasting time and incurring considerable costs in trying to
resolve the substantial disputes of fact regarding the condition of the property.

So I turn to the two questions comprised in the preliminary issue.

(a) The question whether the letter of 19 September 1985 was appropriate in form to
constitute an exercise of the cl 9 option falls into two parts. One raises a point of
c construction of cl 9. What is the date referred to as 'the date of the term hereby granted'?
In the letter of 19 September 1985, 1 April 1982 was specified as the date of
commencement of the new term. Was that the right date? If it was not, a point of
construction of the letter itself arises. Was the letter, notwithstanding its reference to the
wrong commencement date, a sufficiently clear expression of intention to exercise the
cl 9 option?

d   On the first point there are three alternative dates which have been canvassed in
argument. One is 1 April 1982, the date from which the 15-year term granted by the
lease was expressed to be measured: '. . . FIFTEEN . . . YEARS computed from the First day
of April 1982 . . .' were the words in the habendum. The second date is 20 September
1982. That is the date borne by the lease. It is a fair inference that it was the date on
which the lease was executed. It that is right, it was the date on which the term granted
e by the lease came into existence. The third possibility is 31 March 1997, the date on
which the 15-year term will come to an end.

The third possibility, 31 March 1997, seems to me easy to reject. Clause 9 requires the
option to be exercised not later than 29 September 1985. The option is exercisable if the
tenant shall have performed and observed its obligations under the lease 'up to the date
thereof'. Both counsel for the plaintiff and counsel for the defendant agreed that 'up to
f the date thereof' meant up to the date of the exercise of the option, ie 29 September 1985
at the latest. There would be no sense whatever in requiring an option for a new 125-
year term from 31 March 1997 to be exercised some 12 years earlier and even less in
making the exercise conditional on observance of the tenant's obligations up to a date
some 12 years earlier than the commencement of the new term. I decline to attribute to
g the parties so eccentric and improbable an intention.

The date of the lease, 20 September 1982, was the date on which the term thereby
granted commenced. It was in a real sense 'the date of the term hereby granted'. But I
am not satisifed that it was the date the parties had in mind. If they had had 20 September
1982 in mind, the phrase used would be likely to have been the simple and commonly
used phrase 'from the date hereof'. The phrase 'the date of the term hereby granted'
h refers the reader back to the habendum in which the term is defined. It is there defined
as 'FIFTEEN . . . YEARS computed from the First day of April 1982'. A natural reading of
the phrase in cl 9 seems to me to lead to 1 April 1982 as being the date referred to. This
conclusion is supported by the language of the provisions dealing with the rent reserved
by the lease. Paragraph (A) of cl 3 of the lease reserves 'For the first Three years of the said
term the yearly rent of FIFTEEN THOUSAND POUNDS . . .' Paragraph (B) commences thus:

j
'During every period of Three years of the said term after the said first three years
that is to say during the three year periods commencing on the First day of April
One thousand nine hundred and eighty-five the First day of April One thousand
nine hundred and eighty-eight the First day of April One thousand nine hundred

and ninety-one and the First day of April One thousand nine hundred and ninety-
four . . .'   *a*

This language makes it clear that the 'first Three years of the said term' referred to in
cl 3(A) are the years from 1 April 1982 to 31 March 1985. It is consistent to construe the
phrase 'the date of the term hereby granted' in cl 9 as meaning 1 April 1982. It would be
inconsistent to construe the phrase as meaning 20 September 1982.

In my judgment, therefore, the letter of 19 September was correct in giving 1 April   *b*
1982 as the date from which the new 125-year term was to be computed. The question
whether, if the correct date of commencement of the cl 9 term had been 20 September
1982 or 31 March 1997, the letter of 19 September 1985 would none the less have
constituted an effective exercise of the cl 9 option does not now arise.

(b) The second question comprised in the preliminary issue is whether the defendant
was precluded from exercising the cl 9 option by virtue of what the order calls 'past   *c*
breaches of covenant'. The past breaches do not include the alleged breach of the repairing
covenant. The past breaches comprise the following admitted breaches of covenant: (i)
the failure to pay rent that led to the arrears of £18,000-odd referred to in the order dated
12 March 1985. The whole of the arrears and interest thereon were paid within 14 days
of the date of the order; (ii) the failure to pay water rates in respect of the period prior to
11 September 1984. The requisite sum was paid on or about 26 March 1985; (iii) the two   *d*
occasions, one in March 1984 and the other in October or November 1984, on which the
defendant made an application for outline planning permission without the consent of
the plaintiff. Relief from forfeiture of the lease on account of these breaches was granted
to the defendant under the order dated 12 March 1985.

Clause 9 expresses the right to exercise the option to be subject to two conditions
precedent. The first of these relates to the notice to be given exercising the option: *e*

'IF the Tenant . . . shall not later than the 29th September 1985 give to the Lessors
notice in writing of such its desire . . .'

Subject to the point that I have decided under question (a), it is not in dispute that this
condition was fulfilled. The second condition precedent is expressed thus:

'[If the tenant] shall have paid the rent hereby reserved and shall have performed   *f*
and observed the several stipulations on its part herein contained and on its part to
be performed and observed up to the date thereof . . .'

Did the admitted fact of the past breaches having occurred deprive the defendant of the
right to exercise the option? I have described the above provision as a condition precedent.
Its language requires it to be so construed. Authority, too, requires it to be treated as a   *g*
condition precedent (see *Grey v Friar* (1854) 4 HL Cas 565, 10 ER 583). It is also well
settled that fulfilment of the condition was necessary if the option was to be exercisable.
The difficulty, however, is in deciding exactly what it was that the condition required to
be done, or not to be done.

Counsel for the plaintiff has made three submissions. First, he has submitted that the
condition required the rent due under the lease to be paid at the times fixed by the lease   *h*
for payment. If rent were paid late, then, he submitted, the covenant for the payment of
rent would not have been 'performed and observed'. Late payment is made in order to
remedy a breach of covenant. It is not a performance of the covenant.

Second, he has submitted that the condition required all positive covenants in the lease
to be performed in the manner and at the times specified in the lease. This submission is   *j*
only different from the first in that the first relates specifically to rent and this relates to
positive covenants generally. Thus, counsel for the plaintiff submitted, there would be a
failure to perform and observe a covenant to keep demised property in repair if the
demised property were at any time during the term to be in disrepair. Subsequent repair
would remedy the past breach of covenant and would also, perhaps, discharge a

continuing obligation under the covenant, but it would not remove, and nothing could
a remove, the historical fact that the tenant had been in breach of the covenant to repair.
    Third, counsel for the plaintiff has submitted that the condition require that no breach
should have occurred of any negative covenant.
    In short, counsel's case for the plaintiff is that any breach, however slight, of any
covenant, whether positive or negative, prevents the defendant from claiming to have
performed and observed the convenants and bars exercise of the cl 9 option.
b   Counsel for the defendant, in answer, invites attention to the position at the time the
notice exercising the option is served. If by then, he submitted, all positive covenants
had been performed, at least in the sense that the acts required thereunder had been
done, and if at that time the negative covenants were being observed, the condition
would be fulfilled and the option would be exercisable.
    If the condition is to be construed literally according to its strict language, the
c submissions of counsel for the plaintiff are, in my view, correct. If a covenant has been
broken, the covenantee has not, strictly, performed and observed the covenant. But
counsel for the defendant, on the strength of a number of authorities, invited me to
adopt a more liberal construction of the condition precedent. So I must, I think, refer to
the authorities in order to see what, if any, principle they decide.
    I should start with *Grey v Friar* (1854) 4 HL Case 565, 10 ER 583. A 42-year mining
d lease contained a break clause giving liberty to the tenant, on giving 18 months' notice,
to put an end to the term. The provision was in these terms:

> 'Then and in such case (all arrears of rent being paid, and all and singular the
> convenants and agreements on the part of the said lessees having been duly observed
> and performed), this lease . . . shall . . . cease, determine, and be utterly void.'

e
The question was whether or not the provision made the performance of all the covenants
a condition precedent to the tenant's power to put an end to the lease. The Court of
Exchequer held that it did not. The Court of Exchequer Chamber held that it did. The
judges were summoned to advise the House of Lords. Eight of them thought that there
was a condition precedent; three thought there was not. The Lords themselves were
f divided. So the decision of the Exchequer Chamber stood. The ratio of the case is not
directly relevant since there is in my view no doubt but that the relevant part of cl 9
represents a condition precedent. But a number of the judgments contain pertinent
comments on the effect of the condition. Talfourd J said (4 HL Cas 565 at 592–593, 10
ER 583 at 594):

g   '. . . the truth probably is, that in the framing of the proviso in question, the
    parties did not intend to use the words "duly observed and performed" in their
    technical sense, as importing that no covenant during the eight years or longer
    period had ever been broken; in which sense they are certainly unreasonable; but in
    a sense in which they import a condition perfectly natural and just, namely, that
    before the expiration of the notice, the objects of the covenants should be attained,
h   that is, that the works should be put into repair, the water pumped out of the mine,
    and everything done which the lessees were bound to do in order that they might
    deliver up the premises in a proper condition to their landlord.'

Alderson B said (4 HL Cas 565 at 595, 10 ER 583 at 595):

j   'But I think that the condition precedent, even taking the words of it, may really
    mean that covenants broken, if the breach shall be compensated for before the
    expiration of notice, shall be considered as covenants duly performed within this
    proviso. For as rent in arrear, if paid before the expiration of the notice, clearly is
    within it, so the performance of the other covenants being found in conjunction
    with it, may bear the like interpretation.'

Erle and Coleridge JJ expressed the same opinion. Erle J said (4 HL Cas 565 at 599–600,
10 ER 583 at 596):   *a*

'It is said that there would be inconvenience in restricting the power of
determining it to the event of all the covenants having been performed, which
would be almost an impossibility. To this one answer is, that if the parties agree so
to stipulate, the law must give effect to the stipulation. It may also be answered, that
the stipulation does not mean that there should not have been any breach of   *b*
covenant during the term, but that when the notice expires there should not exist
any cause of action in respect of performance of covenants. The stipulation for
arrears of rent being paid, refers to a covenant which had been broken; but all cause
of action for the breach having been satisfied by subsequent accord, and the covenant
for rent would, within the meaning of this clause, be observed and performed, if all
arrears of rent were paid before the expiration of the notice. So the covenant for   *c*
repair, though broken during the term, would be observed if all repairs were at last
completed. So in respect of other breaches; if the damage had been settled by
arbitration and the amount paid, or if an action had been brought and the judgment
satisfied, the legal duty of the covenantor, by reason of his covenant, would have
been so far observed and performed, that all liability in respect thereof would be at
an end. In this sense, the stipulation would be free from any hardship towards the   *d*
lessee, as he might obtain the privilege if he did his duty. This construction does not
depend upon giving a peculiar effect to the words of this instrument, for it seems to
me that the same principle is applicable to all contracts. The legal effect of the
promise in every contract at common law is alternative, either to do the thing
promised or make compensation instead. In some contracts the alternative is
expressed when liquidated damages are stipulated for, in others the liability arises   *e*
by implication of law, either to do or to compensate for not doing, according as may
be settled by accord, or arbitration, or judgment. In all contracts the legal duty
thereunder has been performed, and so the contract may be said in one sense to be
performed, when either the thing contracted for has been done, or compensation
instead thereof has been made.'   *f*

Coleridge J said (4 HL Cas 565 at 608–609, 10 ER 583 at 600):

'The condition, thus expressed, I think it reasonable to understand as requiring
that the account between the parties must, both as to rent and covenants, be clear;
the rent need not have been always paid on the day; but all arrears, if any, must   *g*
have been paid up; the covenants must have been strictly kept, or, if broken, must
have been satisfied for. So understood, the words import a condition precedent
neither impossible nor unreasonable; and where that is clearly the case, the mere
difficulty of performance, from the number or nature of the covenants to be
performed,—a fact which must have been perfectly within the knowledge of the
party contracting,—seems to me a very unsatisfactory reason for holding it to be   *h*
otherwise.'

These views on the construction of the condition precedent in the case were all obiter.
They were, moreover, expressed in relation to the particular provision in the particular
lease before the court. None the less, they were expressed in response to the same
argument, broadly, as that which has been addressed to me, namely that to give a strict   *j*
literal construction to the condition precedent would be likely to render the option
unexercisable.
   Finch v Underwood (1876) 2 Ch D 310 concerned the lessor's covenant to grant the
tenants a new lease. The covenant was that the lessor—

a   'shall and will, at the expiration of the term hereby granted (in case the covenants
        and agreements on the said tenants' part shall have been duly observed and
        performed), grant unto the said tenants . . .'

the new lease (see at 311). At the expiry of the old lease, repairs to an amount of some
£13 required to be done. The question was whether this trifling breach of the repairing
covenant disentitled the tenants to the grant of the new lease. The Court of Appeal held
b   that it did. James LJ said (at 315):

        'No doubt every property must at times be somewhat out of repair, and a tenant
        must have a reasonable time allowed to do what is necessary: but where it is required
        as a condition precedent to the granting a new lease that the lessee's covenants shall
        have been performed, the lessee who comes to claim the new lease must shew that
        at that time the property is in such a state as the covenants require it to be. He can
c   easily send in his builder, get a report of what repairs are necessary, and do them
        before he applies for the lease. There is no hardship in requiring this of him, and I
        think he is not entitled to excuse himself by saying that the want of repair is trifling.
        The answer to that is, "No matter; your bargain was to leave the property in
        thorough repair." If he has not fulfilled his legal bargain, which is also his bargain
        in equity, he cannot sustain his claim for a lease.'
d
James LJ was, however, addressing himself to the state of the demised premises at the
expiry of the term. He was not addressing himself to the question whether trifling
breaches during the term but made good before the end of the term would have
disentitled the tenants to the grant of the new lease.
Mellish LJ did address himself to that question. He said (at 315–316):
e
        'Under the terms of the covenant in the present case the lease is to be granted only
        in case the covenants and agreements on the part of the tenants shall have been duly
        observed and performed. What does that mean? I think it does not mean that the
        tenants must have strictly observed and performed the covenants all through the
        term, for the expression is, "shall have been duly observed and performed;" and I
f   think that this is satisfied if they have been so observed and performed that there is
        no existing right of action under them at the time when the lease is applied for.'

The dicta I have cited from the judgments in *Grey v Friar* and from Mellish LJ's
judgment in *Finch v Underwood* all suggest that past breaches of covenant that have been
remedied do not prevent fulfilment of a condition cast in the terms that the conditions
g   in those two cases were cast.
        Bastin v Bidwell (1881) 18 Ch D 238 was a case on all fours with *Finch v Underwood*. The
lessor had covenanted that the tenant, on giving six months' notice before the expiry of
the current lease and 'upon paying the rent and performing and observing the covenants'
of his present lease, might have a new lease. Both at the time the notice was given and on
the expiry of the notice the tenant was in breach of his painting and repairing covenants.
h   Kay J held that the condition precedent had not been fulfilled and that the tenant was
not entitled to the new lease. He expressly avoided deciding whether, if the breaches at
the time that the notice was served had been remedied before its expiration, the condition
precedent would have been fulfilled.
        The point which Kay J had left undecided arose for decision in *Simons v Associated
Furnishers Ltd* [1931] 1 Ch 379, [1930] All ER Rep 427. This case involved a break clause.
j   The lessees were entitled to determine a 17-year term at the expiration of the first five or
ten years of the term. The right was subject to two conditions precedent. First, the tenant
had to give six months' previous notice. The second condition precedent required that
the lessee should 'up to the time of such determination pay the rent and perform and
observe the covenants and conditions on their part hereinbefore contained' (see [1931] 1

Ch 379 at 385, [1930] All ER Rep 427 at 429). The lessees served the six months' notice. At the date of the notice there were breaches of the repairing covenants in the lease. *a* These breaches were remedied before the expiration of the notice. Clauson J referred to *Grey v Friar* (1854) 4 HL Cas 565, 10 ER 583 and then said ([1931] 1 Ch 379 at 386, [1930] All ER Rep 427 at 429):

> 'The next question is, what does the clause mean? Upon a possible construction, it may make it essential that the tenant should comply with all the covenants *b* throughout the whole period of the five years or, in other words, that the tenant must be able to say that in no single instance during that period has rent been in arrear or a covenant broken. On that question there has been from time to time a certain amount of difference of judicial opinion. If the condition imports that it is unfulfilled if there has been any breach of covenant, even if it has been remedied, the condition may be a very hard one and such as can scarcely be supposed that *c* parties would enter into; but here I am bound by a very heavy weight of judicial opinion to hold that the true meaning of that clause is this, that it will have been complied with, if at the end of the five years "there should not exist any cause of action in respect of performance of covenants": or, I may put it this way, the condition must be understood as "requiring that the account between the parties must, both as to rent and covenants, be clear; the rent need not have been always *d* paid on the day; but all arrears, if any, must have been paid up; the covenants must have been strictly kept, or, if broken, must have been satisfied." In the language I have used I have ventured to quote the language in the first case of Erle J. (4 HL Cas 565 at 599–600, 10 ER 583 at 596) and in the second case the language of Coleridge J. (4 HL Cas 565 at 608–609, 10 ER 583 at 600) in advising the House of Lords in the case to which I have already referred.'   *e*

It was not argued in *Simons v Associated Furnishers Ltd* that a past breach of covenant would, notwithstanding that it had been remedied, be fatal to the lessees' right to exercise the break option. It was argued that the existence of breaches when the notice was served was fatal. Clauson J construed the relevant provision in the lease as directing attention to the state of affairs when the notice expired. He therefore rejected this argument and held *f* that the condition precedent had been fulfilled. The importance of the case for present purposes lies in the judge's acceptance of the dicta in the judgments of Erle and Coleridge JJ in *Grey v Friar*.

Finally, I should refer to *Bassett v Whiteley* (1982) 45 P & CR 87. The case concerned an option given to tenants to renew the lease for a further term provided that they—

> 'shall have paid the rent hereby reserved and shall have reasonably performed and *g* observed the several stipulations herein contained and on their part to be performed and observed up to the termination of the tenancy hereby created ...'

The tenants gave notice exercising the option. Between the date of the notice and of the expiry of the original term the tenants delayed on two occasions paying the rent due under the lease. They had, however, paid all the rent before the expiry of the original *h* term. The main argument in the case centred on the effect of the adverb 'reasonably' as qualifying the condition precedent. Waller LJ held that the tenants had reasonably performed and observed their obligations in payment of rent. Griffiths LJ rejected the suggestion that simply because all arrears of rent had been paid before the expiry of the original term, the condition precedent had necessarily been fulfilled, but agreed with Waller LJ that there had been a reasonable performance of the tenants' obligations. He *j* said at the end of his judgment (at 93):

> 'The word "reasonably" is clearly introduced in this clause to mitigate the great hardship that would flow from the possibility that a very trivial breach of the

a stipulations might result in the loss of the option. It gives a discretion to the court, and I have no doubt that it should, in this case, be exercised in favour of the tenants.'

Griffiths LJ commented in the course of his judgment that there was not much assistance to be derived from authorities dealing with the construction of different words in different leases.

b I would respectfully accept that, in the end, the questions raised in the present case turn on the construction of cl 9 of the lease. None the less, it does seem to me that the line of authorities to which I have referred do establish that a condition precedent which requires that there shall have been performance and observance of a tenant's covenants does not fail simply on account of there having been a past, but remedied, breach of covenant. It would be possible to formulate a condition precedent which did require that there should not at any time have been any breach of a tenant's covenants. But the fairly *c* common form of condition precedent that is to be found in cl 9, not materially different from the corresponding conditions precedent contained in the respective leases in *Grey v Friar, Finch v Underwood, Bastin v Bidwell* and *Simons v Associated Furnishers Ltd*, does not, in my judgment, fail on account of a past breach of covenant provided that the breach has been remedied.

It is a feature, however, of the authorities to which I have referred that none deals with *d* the case of a breach of a negative covenant. In each of the cases the breach relied on was an omission to comply with a positive obligation. A breach of a positive obligation is, in a real sense, capable of remedy. The act required to be done can be done late; the dilapidations can be repaired; the arrears of rent can be paid; the painting and decorations can be done. In all these cases the acts required by the positive covenant can be done; the breach can be remedied.

e But the position where there has been a breach of a negative covenant is more difficult. An act has been done that the tenant covenanted would not be done. If that has happened, how is it to be remedied? The act has been done. Premises may, in breach of a covenant not to use them for immoral purposes, be used for those purposes. The user may cease well before the time at which an option to take a new lease falls to be exercised. If the option is subject to the condition that all the tenant's obligations shall have been *f* performed and observed, how can that condition be held to have been fulfilled?

The question whether a breach of a negative covenant is capable of remedy has arisen often in cases concerning s 146 of the Law of Property Act 1925. *Rugby School (Governors) v Tannahill* [1934] 1 KB 695 was a case where demised premises had been used for immoral purposes. MacKinnon J said (at 701):

g 'A promise to do a thing, if broken, can be remedied by the thing being done. But breach of a promise not to do a thing cannot in any true sense be remedied; that which was done cannot be undone. There cannot truly be a remedy; there can only be abstention, perhaps accompanied with apology.'

The case went to appeal (see [1935] 1 KB 87, [1934] All ER Rep 187). In the Court of Appeal, Greer LJ agreed that the particular breach was not capable of remedy but reserved *h* his opinion whether a breach of a negative covenant was necessarily incapable of remedy. He said ([1935] 1 KB 87 at 90; cf [1934] All ER Rep 187 at 190):

'. . . but in some cases where the immediate ceasing of that which is complained of, together with an undertaking against any further breach, it might be said that the breach was capable of remedy.'

j Maugham LJ expressed the same reservation (see [1935] 1 KB 87 at 92–93, [1934] All ER Rep 187 at 191–192).

Scala House and District Property Co Ltd v Forbes [1973] 3 All ER 308, [1974] QB 575 was a case in which there had been a breach of a covenant not to assign, underlet or part

with possession. The Court of Appeal held that, for s 146 purposes, the breach was not
capable of remedy. Russell LJ said ([1973] 3 All ER 308 at 312, [1974] QB 575 at 585): *a*
'An unlawful subletting is a breach once and for all. The subterm has been created.' Later
he said ([1973] 3 All ER 308 at 315, [1974] QB 575 at 588): '... it is a complete breach
once for all: it is not in any sense a continuing breach.'

In *Expert Clothing Service and Sales Ltd v Hillgate House Ltd* [1985] 2 All ER 998, [1986]
Ch 340 Slade LJ distinguished between breaches of negative covenants and of positive
covenants so far as capability of remedy was concerned. He said ([1985] 2 All ER 998 at *b*
1008, [1986] Ch 340 at 354):

> 'While the *Scala House* decision is, of course, authority binding on this court for
> the proposition that the breach of a negative covenant not to assign, underlet or part
> with possession is never "capable of remedy", it is not, in my judgment, authority
> for the proposition that the once and for all breach of a positive covenant is never *c*
> capable of remedy.'

The s 146 authorities were dealing with a question of construction of s 146. But the
reasoning in the dicta to which I have referred bears, in my view, on the question of
construction of conditions precedent such as that with which I am concerned. It is easy
enough in relation to positive covenants to construe a requirement that the covenants be
'performed and observed' as requiring performance in the popular rather than in the *d*
legal sense of the expression (see Kay J in *Bastin v Bidwell* (1881) 18 Ch D 238 at 252). It is
quite another thing, to my mind, to try and extend that construction so as to cover
negative covenants as well.

Counsel for the defendant submitted initially that, if a negative covenant was being
observed at the relevant time, the fact that there had been an earlier breach or breaches
of the covenant was immaterial. The requirement of the condition precedent that the *e*
tenant 'shall have performed and observed' the covenant would, he said, be satisfied. This
proposition is far too wide to be acceptable. Counsel for the defendant then qualified his
submission by accepting that the tenant must show that any state of affairs brought into
existence by a previous breach of a negative covenant had ceased to exist. He instanced a
case of an assignment or subletting without consent where the assignee had reassigned *f*
the premises to the assignor or the subtenancy had been surrendered. An alternative
qualification of the primary submission was that the breach of a negative covenant
should be ignored if, at the relevant time, the lessor had no subsisting cause of action in
respect thereof. Support for counsel for the defendant's submission, thus qualified, was
found in some of the dicta from *Grey v Friar* that I have already cited. Erle J said (4 HL
Cas 565 at 600, 10 ER 583 at 596): *g*

> '... the contract may be said in one sense to be performed, when either the thing
> contracted for has been done, or compensation instead thereof has been made.'

And Coleridge J said (4 HL Cas 565 at 608–609, 10 ER 583 at 600):

> '... the covenants must have been strictly kept, or, if broken, must have been
> satisfied for.' *h*

I am, however, unable to accept the submissions of counsel for the defendant and can
see no escape from the conclusion that, once a negative covenant has been broken, a
condition that requires performance and observance of all covenants cannot be fulfilled.
The dicta in the cases to which I have referred and the general approach exemplified by
those cases make, if I may respectfully say so, very good sense where positive covenants *j*
are concerned. The requirement that a positive covenant be performed and observed can
easily and sensibly be read as a requirement that the acts necessary to be done for
compliance with the positive covenant should be done. This was what Kay J in *Bastin v
Bidwell* (1881) 18 Ch D 238 at 252 referred to as the popular meaning of performance of

a covenant. But a positive covenant requires an act to be done; breach of the covenant
a involves an omission. An omission can be remedied by doing late what should have been
done earlier. None of this applies to negative covenants. Negative covenants are broken
by the doing of some positive act. Once the act has been done, it has been done; the
covenant has not been performed and observed. The circumstance that the act effecting
the breach is not repeated and is an isolated act does not alter the fact that there has been
a breach of the covenant, that the covenant has not been observed and that a condition
b requiring the covenant to have been performed and observed, whether read strictly or in
a popular sense, has failed. The proposition that a previous breach of a negative covenant
can be ignored if the state of affairs brought into existence by the breach has come to an
end cannot, in my view, be accepted; nor am I able to accept that the breach can be
ignored if no existing right of action remains in respect thereof. I do not see how
payment of damages, or effluxion of time so that the cause of action has become statute-
c barred, or the granting of relief from forfeiture, can alter the fact that the covenant has
not been performed or observed. Payment of damages for breach does not represent the
performance of the covenant. The grant of relief from forfeiture is based on the fact that
the covenant has not been performed or observed. Neither inaction by a lessor so that a
cause of action for damages becomes statute-barred nor receipt of rent so that the right to
forfeit for breach of covenant is lost can rewrite history. The act representing a breach of
d covenant has been done. The covenant has not been observed. It is true, as counsel for
the defendant forcefully pointed out, that this conclusion has the result that relatively
trifling breaches of negative covenants will cause a condition precedent cast in the form
of the condition precedent in the present case to fail and the right to exercise the option
to be lost. I do not, however, accept that the consequence is to render the condition
e precedent virtually incapable of fulfilment. A negative covenant is not broken unless a
positive act is done. I do not see any reason why a tenant should not be able to desist from
a positive act that, if done, may place him in breach of a negative covenant. The parties
could, if they had wished, have rendered the condition precedent less onerous by
requiring, as the condition in *Bassett v Whiteley* (1982) 45 P & CR 87 required, merely
that the tenant's obligations be 'reasonably performed and observed'. The condition
f precedent in the present case contains no such qualification.

Certainty as to what will and what will not effect a failure of the condition precedent
is desirable in this, as in any other, lease. Coleridge J said in *Grey v Friar* (1854) 4 HL Cas
565 at 611, 10 ER 583 at 601:

> 'My answer, however, to your Lordships' question, does not rest on this
g explanation, but upon the broad principle of construing language which is
> unambiguous according to its plain meaning, and ascertaining the intention of
> parties from the language they use so construed; and I think it of the utmost
> consequence not to be diverted from that principle in any judicial decision, by the
> apparent inconvenience or hardships which may follow. It is far better that a known
> and certain and reasonable rule should bear hard on an individual now and then,
h who may thank his own incaution, or, it may be, his own dishonesty, for what he
> suffers, than that the whole public should labour under the intolerable grievance of
> having no certain rule at all by which their contracts are to be construed.'

Certainty would, in my view, be lost if I accepted the submissions of counsel for the
defendant.

I turn, therefore, to the breaches of covenant relied on by the plaintiff as disentitling
j the defendant to exercise the cl 9 option.

(i) It is common ground that the defendant allowed arrears of rent of £18,000-odd to
accumulate. The whole of the arrears, together with interest thereon was, however, paid
before the option was exercised. For the purpose of cl 9, the rent was paid and the
covenant for payment of rent was, in my judgment, performed and observed.

(ii) The defendant allowed water rates to fall into arrears. However, before the cl 9 option was exercised, the requisite amount had been paid by the defendant. For the purposes of cl 9, the covenant to pay water rates had, in my judgment, been performed and observed.

(iii) On two occasions the defendant committed a breach of its covenant not to apply for planning permission without the consent of the plaintiff. On two occasions, therefore, it failed to observe that covenant. By the order of 12 March 1985 the defendant was granted relief from forfeiture of the lease on account, inter alia, of those two breaches of covenant. But the grant of relief from forfeiture does not, in my judgment, enable the defendant to claim to have performed and observed that covenant. The condition precedent on which the defendant's right to exercise the cl 9 option depended was not, in my judgment, fulfilled.

I would, therefore, answer in the affirmative both questions comprised in the preliminary issue.

Determination accordingly. Leave to appeal granted.

Solicitors: *Nabarro Nathanson* (for the plaintiff); *Nutt & Oliver* (for the defendant).

Jacqueline Metcalfe   Barrister.

a

Practice Direction

Mental health – Patient's property – Receiver – Appointment of Public Trustee as receiver – Certain applications to be referred to Court of Protection – Form of order of appointment –
b   *Dealings with land – Execution of documents – Inquiries, applications and correspondence – Trustee Act 1925, ss 36(9), 54 – Variation of Trusts Act 1958, s 1(3) – Mental Health Act 1983, ss 96(1)(d)(e)(i)(k), 98, 99, 100, 104 – Enduring Powers of Attorney Act 1985 – Public Trustee and Administration of Funds Act 1986.*

1. The Public Trustee and Administration of Funds Act 1986 will come into force on 2
c   January 1987. From that date, the Public Trustee will be able to be appointed receiver under the Mental Health Act 1983.

2. However, in normal circumstances, the Public Trustee as receiver will refer to the Court of Protection any applications made in connection with any of the following: (1) paras (e), (i) and (k) of s 96(1) of the Mental Health Act 1983, or para (d) as regards substantial gifts; (2) applications under ss 98, 99, 100 and 104 of the Mental Health Act
d   1983; (3) applications under the Enduring Powers of Attorney Act 1985; (4) applications under s 1(3) of the Variation of Trusts Act 1958 and ss 36(9) and 54 of the Trustee Act 1925.

3. The Public Trustee will be appointed in all cases in which the Principal of the Management Division of the Court of Protection is at present receiver and a separate order will be pronounced in respect of each of those patients.

e   4. In the case of first general orders to be pronounced on or after 2 January 1987, the Public Trustee will be appointed in all cases in which the Principal of the Management Division would previously have been appointed.

5. The order appointing the Public Trustee in place of the Principal of the Management Division will be in the following form:

f

'COURT OF PROTECTION   No

Order dated [2 January 1987]

In the matter of [patient's name] (in this order referred to as the patient).

g   IT IS ORDERED

1. The Principal of the Management Division of the Court of Protection is discharged from the receivership and his final account as receiver is dispensed with.

2. The Public Trustee of Stewart House, 24 Kingsway, London WC2B 6HD is appointed receiver and in relation to the property and affairs of the patient is authorised generally for the purposes of Part VII of the Mental Health Act 1983 to
h   do or secure the doing of all such things as appear necessary or expedient.

3. The Public Trustee as receiver is authorised to carry into effect all or any contracts entered into by the Principal of the Management Division of the Court of Protection on behalf of the Patient.'

6. The first general order appointing the Public Trustee as receiver will be in the
j   following form:

'COURT OF PROTECTION   No

First General Order dated

In the matter of [patient's name] (in this order referred to as the patient)

On the application of

IT IS ORDERED

The Public Trustee of Stewart House, 24 Kingsway, London WC2B 6HD is appointed *a* receiver and in relation to the property and affairs of the patient is authorised generally for the purposes of Part VII of the Mental Health Act 1983 to do or secure the doing of all such things as appear necessary or expedient.'

7. The order which will be made where the Principal of the Management Division is at present receiver ad interim will be: *b*

'COURT OF PROTECTION   No

Supplemental order dated [2 January 1987]

In the matter of [patient's name]

    1. This order is supplemental to an order dated   (the interim order).

    2. The interim order shall be read and construed as if the name of the Public *c* Trustee were substituted therein as receiver in place of the Principal of the Management Division of the Court of Protection but in all other respects the interim order is confirmed.'

8. It has been agreed with HM Land Registry that no question will be raised as to the Public Trustee's power to dispose of or otherwise deal with land when he is acting under *d* an order in one of the above forms.

9. All documents to be executed by the Public Trustee pursuant to an order in one of the above forms will be sealed with his official seal.

10. From 2 January 1987 all inquiries, applications and correspondence concerning cases in which the Public Trustee has been appointed receiver should be sent to the Receivership Division, Stewart House, 14 Kingsway, London WC2B 6HD. All inquiries, *e* applications and correspondence in cases where any other person or body is receiver should continue to be sent to the Protection Division, Staffordshire House, 25 Store Street, London WC1E 7BP.

11. From 2 January 1987 the title 'Court of Protection' will apply only to what is at present entitled the Judicial Division of the Court of Protection. The Management Division (which will be known in future as the Receivership Division) and the Protection *f* Division will both become part of the new organisation, to be called the Public Trust Office. Until further notice, applications made to the Public Trust Office which concern matters solely within the province of the Court of Protection will be accepted as properly made, even if made in the wrong name, but time will be saved if the correct address is used. The address of the Court of Protection itself will remain Staffordshire House, 25 Store Street, London WC1E 7BP.   *g*

A B MACFARLANE
Master of the Court of Protection.

9 December 1986

a

Re Basham (deceased)

CHANCERY DIVISION

EDWARD NUGEE QC SITTING AS A DEPUTY JUDGE OF THE HIGH COURT

18, 19, 20 MARCH, 20 MAY 1986

b
Estoppel – Proprietary estoppel – Expectation of inheriting estate – Plaintiff working without payment and caring for stepfather – Plaintiff encouraged by stepfather to expect and believe that she would inherit his estate – Stepfather dying intestate – Whether proprietary estoppel applying only to existing right or particular property – Whether belief or expectation that future rights would be granted over estate capable of raising proprietary estoppel – Whether plaintiff entitled to estate.

c The deceased married the plaintiff's mother when the plaintiff was 15. From then until the deceased retired some 30 years later the plaintiff worked for the deceased without payment, helping him to run various public houses and a service station. The plaintiff, her husband and their children formed a very close-knit family with the deceased and the plaintiff's mother and always lived near by. On several occasions when the plaintiff and her husband considered moving away they were dissuaded by the deceased from *d* doing so. During his retirement and after the death of the plaintiff's mother the deceased was cared for by the plaintiff and her husband. The deceased owned a cottage and had on numerous occasions indicated to the plaintiff that she would get the cottage when he died in return for what she had done for the deceased. He reiterated that intention on his deathbed. His family also understood that the cottage would go to the plaintiff on his death. The deceased died intestate leaving an estate of some £43,000 comprising the *e* cottage valued at £21,000 and cash of £23,000, less funeral expenses and some small debts. His next of kin who were entitled to the estate on the intestacy were two nieces who were the administrators of the estate. The plaintiff brought an action against the nieces seeking a declaration that she was entitled to the deceased's estate because the deceased had induced and encouraged in her the expectation or belief that she would receive the estate on his death and she had acted to her detriment in reliance on that *f* expectation thereby raising a proprietary estoppel in her favour.

Held – Proprietary estoppel was a form of constructive trust which arose when A acted to his detriment on the faith of a belief known to and encouraged by B that he had or was going to be given a right in or over B's property, so that B was prevented by equity from insisting on his strict legal rights if to do so would be inconsistent with A's belief. *g* The belief on which A relied did not have to relate to an existing right nor to a particular property. It followed that a proprietary estoppel could be raised on a belief or expectation that future rights would be granted over a person's residuary estate. Since the plaintiff's belief that she would inherit the deceased's estate had been encouraged by the deceased and since the plaintiff and her husband had acted to their detriment in subordinating *h* their own interests to the wishes of the deceased in reliance of the plaintiff's belief that she would inherit, the plaintiff had established a proprietary estoppel and was entitled to the estate (see p 410 *a* to *c*, p 411 *c d g h*, p 413 *b c*, p 414 *e* to *h* and p 415 *a–f*, post).

Greasley v Cooke [1980] 3 All ER 710, *Taylor Fashions Ltd v Liverpool Victoria Trustees Co Ltd* [1981] 1 All ER 897 and *Re Cleaver (decd)* [1981] 2 All ER 1018 considered.

j **Notes**
For proprietary estoppel, see 16 Halsbury's Laws (4th edn) paras 1511, 1514, and for cases on the subject, see 21 Digest (Reissue) 5–7, 45–50.

Cases referred to in judgment
Birmingham v Renfrew (1937) 57 CLR 666, Aust HC.

Brikom Investments Ltd v Carr [1979] 2 All ER 753, [1979] QB 467, [1979] 2 WLR 737, CA. *a*

Cleaver (decd), Re, Cleaver v Insley [1981] 2 All ER 1018, [1981] 1 WLR 939.

Crabb v Arun DC [1975] 3 All ER 865, [1976] Ch 179, [1975] 3 WLR 847, CA.

Grant v Edwards [1986] 2 All ER 426, [1986] Ch 638, [1986] 3 WLR 114, CA.

Greasley v Cooke [1980] 3 All ER 710, [1980] 1 WLR 1306, CA.

Griffiths v Williams (1977) 248 EG 947, CA.

Hall-Dare, Re, Le Marchant v Lee Warner [1916] 1 Ch 272. *b*

Inwards v Baker [1965] 1 All ER 446, [1965] 2 QB 29, [1965] 2 WLR 212, CA.

Moorgate Mercantile Co Ltd v Twitchings [1975] 3 All ER 314, [1976] QB 225, [1975] 3 WLR 286, CA; *rvsd* [1976] 2 All ER 641, [1977] AC 890, [1976] 3 WLR 66, HL.

Ramsden v Dyson (1866) LR 1 HL 129.

Reynell v Sprye (1852) 1 De GM & G 660, 42 ER 710.

Smith v Chadwick (1882) 20 Ch D 27, CA; *on appeal* (1884) 9 App Cas 187, [1881–5] All *c* ER Rep 242, HL.

Spiers v English [1907] P 122.

Taylor Fashions Ltd v Liverpool Victoria Trustees Co Ltd [1981] 1 All ER 897, [1982] QB 133, [1981] 2 WLR 576.

Willmott v Barber (1880) 15 Ch D 96.
d

Cases also cited

Dillwyn v Llewelyn (1862) 4 De GF & J 517, [1861–73] All ER Rep 384, LC.

Plimmer v Mayor of Wellington (1884) 9 App Cas 699, PC.

Action

By a writ dated 4 October 1983 the plaintiff, Joan Eileen Bird, sought as against the *e* defendant, Robert Gerald Basham, the administrator of the estate of Henry Edward Basham deceased, (i) declarations that the plaintiff was absolutely and beneficially entitled or entitled to such extent as the court directed to the property known as Rosslyn, Vicarage Road, Great Hockham, Norfolk, and all other furniture, money and other property of the deceased, and (ii) such order directing the vesting of the property of the deceased in the plaintiff as may be appropriate on the grounds that the plaintiff acted to her detriment *f* and/or prejudiced herself in reliance on the expectation or belief induced and encouraged by the deceased that she had or would on the death of the deceased obtain beneficial ownership of all the deceased's property. On 2 April 1985 the defendant died, and letters of administration de bonis non were granted to Hazel Jean Tucker and Letty May Field, the nieces of the deceased, who became defendants to the action. The facts are set out in the judgment. *g*

William Henderson for the plaintiff.

Godfree Browne for the defendants.

Cur adv vult *h*

20 May. The following judgment was delivered.

EDWARD NUGEE QC. The plaintiff in this action, Mrs Joan Bird, is the stepdaughter of the late Mr Henry Basham, who died intestate on 13 April 1982 aged 86. The *j* defendants, Mrs Tucker and Mrs Field, are nieces of Mr Basham and are the administrators de bonis non of his estate. The plaintiff's mother married Mr Basham as her second husband in about 1936, when the plaintiff was aged about 15. From that time onwards the plaintiff's mother (until her death in 1976), the plaintiff and later her husband, son and daughter formed a very close-knit family with the deceased, and since about 1950 they have all lived within a few houses of one another in Vicarage Road, Great Hockham, Norfolk. They have, however, no blood relationship with the deceased, and the persons entitled to his estate on his intestacy are his brother, Mr Robert Basham, who was the original administrator of his estate and the original defendant in this action, but who died on 2 April 1985, and the children of his deceased sisters, of whom there are seven. Mrs Tucker is the daughter of Mr Robert Basham, and Mrs Field is the daughter of a deceased sister.

The deceased left a net estate of a little over £43,000, consisting of a cottage known as Rosslyn, Vicarage Road, Great Hockham, which was valued for probate at £21,000, cash on current account and deposit account and in the National Savings Bank amounting to nearly £23,000, and furniture and other chattels valued for probate at £100, from which funeral expenses and some modest debts fall to be deducted.

The plaintiff claims a declaration that she is absolutely and beneficially entitled to Rosslyn, and a declaration that she is absolutely and beneficially entitled to the deceased's furniture, money and other property, or alternatively a declaration that she is interested in Rosslyn and/or the deceased's furniture, money and other property to such an extent as the court may direct. Her claim is based on an allegation that she acted to her detriment or prejudiced herself in reliance on the expectation or belief, induced and encouraged by the deceased, that she had or would obtain beneficially on the death of the deceased ownership of Rosslyn and all the furniture and other property of the deceased. That is to say, it is based on the doctrine which has become known as proprietary estoppel.

The defendants accept that the plaintiff did a very great deal for the deceased, but they say that on the facts her acts were not done in reliance on any expectation she may have had but were attributable to her natural love and affection for the deceased, and that her expectation was not encouraged by the deceased and in any event did not extend to the whole of his estate. And they say that as a matter of law the doctrine of proprietary estoppel does not apply unless the expectation relates to a particular property in which the claimant has an existing right or of which the claimant has existing enjoyment, the principle being that where the doctrine applies equity intervenes to prevent the legal owner from disturbing such right or enjoyment. They accept that, if the necessary conditions were satisfied and if the plaintiff had been living at Rosslyn, an equity would have arisen which the court could have protected by giving her a life interest in the property or even by compelling the defendants to convey the property to her, but they say that such an equity cannot arise in the present case in relation to Rosslyn because the plaintiff was living in her own house a little way down the road, and that it cannot arise in any event in relation to the rest of the deceased's estate, of which he was free to dispose during his life.

The facts are not seriously in dispute. They were almost wholly within the knowledge of the plaintiff, her husband and her children, and not within the knowledge of the defendants or any other members of the family. The defendants therefore called no evidence, but confined themselves to testing the evidence called on behalf of the plaintiff by cross-examination and making submissions on the law. The plaintiff was an excellent witness, and I have no hesitation in accepting her evidence, which was to the following effect. When her mother married the deceased the plaintiff was training to be a hairdresser, but after their marriage she gave this up at their request in order to help them in running a cafe and boarding house at Sheringham, both of which belonged to the plaintiff's mother. When the war came the town became a restricted area and the business came to an end, and the plaintiff then helped her mother and the deceased at a public house known as the Eagle at Great Hockham. There she met her husband and married him in 1941. She continued to live at the Eagle for a time, and during this period the deceased told her that he had a tin box full of money and told her where it was hidden, and said that if anything happened to him and his wife it was hers. About a year after they married the plaintiff and her husband acquired their first home, a tenanted cottage at Great Hockham. The plaintiff proposed getting a regular job to supplement her husband's income, but the deceased wanted her to continue working for him, and said to her 'You don't have to worry about money, you'll be all right.' She continued to work at the Eagle during the six years that the deceased and her mother managed it, and then for two years they managed the Ship Inn at Weybourne, which was about two miles from Sheringham and over 40 miles from Great Hockham. Despite the distance the plaintiff used to go down to Weybourne to help them. Throughout the period to which I have been referring the deceased never paid the plaintiff for her work; her understanding was that when he died she would inherit his property, and on that understanding she did not ask for payment during his lifetime.

In about 1947 or 1948, when the deceased and his wife were still at Weybourne, the plaintiff and her husband were threatened with eviction from the house they occupied at Great Hockham. The plaintiff's husband worked in agriculture and contemplated moving from the house and taking a job with another employer which would carry with it a tied cottage. The deceased was opposed to such a move and wrote to the plaintiff with advice, ending by saying: 'You can rest assured that if this fails, which I don't think it will, I am always trying and willing to help you getting another suitable house.' Not long afterwards the deceased purchased Rosslyn, the purchase being completed by a conveyance dated 26 January 1949. The purchase money of £350 was provided largely, if not entirely, by the plaintiff's mother, and the plaintiff gave evidence of her mother coming to her and saying she had bought her a cottage. Rosslyn was, however, tenanted, and in June 1949 the deceased sought advice from solicitors in Norwich as to what was the best course to take for the benefit of the plaintiff and her husband. Their advice was that if Mr Bird was a service tenant he did not have security of tenure in his present house; but that if Rosslyn was transferred to him, as the deceased appears to have had it in mind to do, he would not be able to obtain possession of the property since the provision of the Rent Acts enabling a landlord to obtain possession for his own occupation applied only to cases where the property was purchased before 1 September 1939. In the event Rosslyn was never transferred to the plaintiff or her husband but remained in the name of the deceased.

Not long after this the deceased gave up the Ship Inn and moved to Great Hockham, where he bought a petrol station and a house known as Home Cottage. The plaintiff and her daughter helped in the petrol station from time to time; her son helped dig out the pits for the petrol tanks, for which he was paid a few pounds; and the plaintiff decorated Home Cottage from top to bottom and did a good deal of work in the garden, which extended to two acres. She described keeping the hedges in good order as a Forth Bridge job. The plaintiff's mother had a heart attack about six months after they moved into Home Cottage, and from then until her death about 25 years later the plaintiff spent an increasing amount of time looking after her. The deceased retired from keeping the petrol station in 1966 when he was 70, and he too required nursing attention from time to time, which the plaintiff gave. The plaintiff's husband, who had been farm manager for a local landowner for 15 years, lost his job when the landowner died and his heir put the management of the farm out to tender. He was offered a job in Lincolnshire, but the plaintiff's mother and the deceased would not hear of their leaving Great Hockham. It is fair to say that Mr Bird too had no wish to leave Norfolk; he was born in Vicarage Road, Great Hockham, and never wanted to move outside it. So he took a job making thermos flasks, though he would rather have been on a farm.

The plaintiff's mother died in 1976. At the time of her death the deceased was considering moving into Rosslyn, which was a smaller property than Home Cottage. He had obtained planning permission for building an additional room onto the ground floor. When the plaintiff's mother died he decided that he would nevertheless go ahead and build the additional room, saying to the plaintiff 'It's putting money on the property for you.' At the end of 1976 he sold Home Cottage for £16,700 and £16,000 of this was paid into his deposit account at the bank. About this time the plaintiff's husband, who owned a piece of land in Great Hockham, applied for planning permission with a view to selling it as building land. The deceased persuaded him not to sell, saying 'You don't have to sell that; keep it; you'll be all right; you'll have money on your own', referring, in the plaintiff's view, which I accept, to the deceased's intention to leave his money to the plaintiff on his death. As he was then 80, he did not expect this to be long delayed.

In 1978 a dispute arose between the deceased and his neighbour, a Mr Kenworthy, concerning the position of the boundary between their two properties and the use of a passageway between them. The deceased consulted solicitors but was deterred from taking further action by the thought of the costs that would be involved. He told the plaintiff to sort it out herself, as it was going to be her property. The plaintiff consulted her own solicitors, who advised her to exercise self-help and pull up the fence which Mr Kenworthy had erected and throw it back on to Mr Kenworthy's land, which she did. The plaintiff's evidence was quite clear that she was not acting for the deceased, whose own solicitors were not getting anywhere, but for herself; the deceased had told her that it was for her own benefit, the house was hers and it was up to her to see that it was put right. He was not willing to incur the costs of a court case.

During the remaining years of the deceased's life he used to lunch regularly with the plaintiff, and when he was not able to come she would take his lunch to him. Her husband and the deceased did not get on well together, but the plaintiff's husband would buy food for the three of them and also did all the work necessary to keep the garden of Rosslyn in order. In addition the plaintiff and he did work about the house and cleaned it, and the plaintiff bought carpets and laid them herself. The deceased never paid for any of this, but told them, 'You'll lose nothing for this, doing all these jobs,' and promised them that what was his would be theirs. At times the plaintiff's husband got quite upset at the amount of time and money the plaintiff was spending on the deceased, but she told him she had worked all her life for her parents, and if she did not she would not get what she had been promised. Mr Bird accepted this. As he himself disarmingly put it: 'I'm not very bright, but I'm not soft in the head. Anyone who worked like my wife and I did for him could expect a will leaving it to us: a promise is a promise.'

On Good Friday, 9 April 1982 the deceased had a severe stroke and he died four days later. During the four days he was hardly able to speak, but he indicated by signs that he wanted to make a will, leaving some money to the plaintiff's son Michael (which he did by writing a £ sign in the telephone book and pointing at Michael), and then he said in a long-drawn-out way, 'Joan, you're to have the house.' After his death the plaintiff telephoned the deceased's brother, Mr Robert Basham, to tell him. The telephone was answered by the defendant, Mrs Tucker, and almost her first words were: 'Oh Joan, what are you going to do with your cottage?' Mr Robert Basham was the one other member of the deceased's family who saw him from time to time during the later years of his life; and I consider that this reaction by his daughter affords strong confirmation of the understanding in the family that the plaintiff would inherit Rosslyn on the deceased's death.

Evidence was also given by the plaintiff's husband, that the deceased had always promised his property to the plaintiff, and that it was because of this that he was willing to do so much for the deceased. As I have already mentioned, he had expected the deceased to make a will in favour of the plaintiff. Further evidence was given by the plaintiff's daughter, Mrs Angela Hook, who was clearly deeply attached to the deceased, whom she referred to as Uncle Harry. The deceased had made gifts to her, amounting to at least £400, and a few days before his death he promised to give her £1,005 to help her establish a hairdressing salon, although he died before this gift could be effected. He also gave her his car when he ceased to drive himself. Her understanding was that her mother was to inherit everything for the benefit of the family. She too thought the deceased would have made a will. There was also some independent corroborative evidence from neighbours, some of it put in the form of statements under the Civil Evidence Act 1968. A Mrs Osborne, who had known the family for about 20 years, gave oral evidence of a conversation she had had with the deceased about a year before he died, in which, after they had been talking about a lady who had recently died and left quite a lot of money, the deceased said to her: 'Do you know what's going to happen to my money? It's all *a* going down the road to Joan.'

I turn then to the law. The plaintiff relies on proprietary estoppel, the principle of which, in its broadest form, may be stated as follows. Where one person (A) has acted to his detriment on the faith of a belief, which was known to and encouraged by another person (B), that he either has or is going to be given a right in or over B's property, B *b* cannot insist on his strict legal rights if to do so would be inconsistent with A's belief. The principle is commonly known as proprietary estoppel, and since the effect of it is that B is prevented from asserting his strict legal rights it has something in common with estoppel. But in my judgment, at all events where the belief is that A is going to be given a right in the future, it is properly to be regarded as giving rise to a species of constructive trust, which is the concept employed by a court of equity to prevent a person from relying on his legal rights where it would be unconscionable for him to do so. The *c* rights to which proprietary estoppel gives rise, and the machinery by which effect is given to them, are similar in many respects to those involved in cases of secret trusts, mutual wills and other comparable cases in which property is vested in B on the faith of an understanding that it will be dealt with in a particular manner, of which Nourse J said in *Re Cleaver (decd), Cleaver v Insley* [1981] 2 All ER 1018 at 1024, [1981] 1 WLR 939 at *d* 947:

> 'The principle of all these cases is that a court of equity will not permit a person to whom property is transferred by way of gift, but on the faith of an agreement or clear understanding that it is to be dealt with in a particular way for the benefit of a third person, to deal with that property inconsistently with that agreement or understanding. If he attempts to do so after having received the benefit of the gift *e* equity will intervene by imposing a constructive trust on the property which is the subject matter of the agreement or understanding.'

The factor which gives rise to the equitable obligation in the cases to which Nourse J is referring is B's receipt of the property on the faith of an understanding. In cases of proprietary estoppel the factor which gives rise to the equitable obligation is A's alteration *f* of his position on the faith of a similar understanding. A third situation in which the court imposes a constructive trust is where A and B set up house together in a property which is in the name of B alone, and A establishes a common intention between A and B, acted on by A to his (or more usually her) detriment, that A should have a beneficial interest in the property: see the statements of principle by Nourse LJ and Browne-Wilkinson V-C in *Grant v Edwards* [1986] 2 All ER 426, [1986] Ch 638. Here too, if the *g* two elements of common understanding or intention and detrimental acts on the part of A are established, they give rise to an equitable obligation enforceable against B which is in the nature of a constructive trust. A common theme can be discerned in each of these classes of case; and although different situations may give rise to differences of detail in the manner in which the court will give effect to the equity which arises in favour of A, one would expect the general principles applicable in the different situations to be the *h* same unless there is a sound reason to the contrary.

In the present case it is in my judgment clearly established by the evidence, first, that the plaintiff had a belief at all material times that she was going to receive both Rosslyn and the remainder of the deceased's property on his death, and secondly, that this belief was encouraged by the deceased. Counsel for the defendants submitted that the fact that the deceased made a number of gifts to Mrs Hook, the plaintiff's daughter, and had *j* promised her a further quite substantial gift, and the fact that on his deathbed he indicated a wish to make a will leaving an unspecified sum of money to Michael, the plaintiff's son, and that the plaintiff made no objection to such gifts, was inconsistent with a belief on her part that the whole of his estate was going to come to her. I do not think that these gifts or intended gifts detract from such a belief. As I have said, the plaintiff, her husband and her two children formed a close-knit family, and it is in my judgment quite consistent with the belief of the plaintiff, and of independent third parties such as Mrs Osborne, that the whole of the deceased's estate was to go to the plaintiff, that she should have raised no objection if, instead of it all going to her direct, some part of it was given to other members of her immediate family. As Mrs Hook put it, her understanding was that the plaintiff was to inherit everything for the benefit of the family; and, as counsel for the plaintiff submitted, the position was similar to that which would have existed had the deceased left a will giving everything to the plaintiff, hoping that she would do the right thing by Michael and Angela. Under such a will there would have been no obligation on the plaintiff to pass on any part of the estate to her children, but she might well have been expected to do so. Moreover, where a constructive trust affects the whole of the estate which the constructive trustee leaves at his death, as in *Re Cleaver*, it is only gifts which are calculated to defeat the intention of the persons involved (A and B) that are objectionable (see [1981] 2 All ER 1018 at 1024, [1981] 1 WLR 939 at 947 per Nourse J). I bear in mind that all claims to the property of a deceased person must be scrutinised with very great care; but I am satisfied that the deceased encouraged the plaintiff in the belief that all the property he possessed at the date of his death would pass to her, and I do not consider that the fact that he made certain gifts during his lifetime, and indicated a wish to make others, including the gift of a legacy to Michael, is inconsistent with such a belief. The gifts of which evidence was given were in favour of the plaintiff's children and in the circumstances did not in substance conflict, in my judgment, with his intention to benefit the plaintiff.

The third element that the plaintiff must prove in order to raise a constructive trust in a case of proprietary estoppel is that she acted to her detriment. Counsel for the defendants accepted that the plaintiff did a very great deal for the deceased, and it is clear that she did not receive any commensurate reward for this during his lifetime. There is some evidence, though not very much, of occasions when the plaintiff or her husband acted or refrained from acting in a way in which they might not have done but for their expectations of inheriting the deceased's property: I refer to the occasions when the plaintiff's husband refrained from selling his building land, and refrained from taking a job in Lincolnshire which would have made it impossible for the plaintiff to continue caring for her mother and the deceased, and the occasions when the plaintiff instructed solicitors at her own expense in connection with the boundary dispute between the deceased and Mr Kenworthy, and the expenditure of time and money on the house and garden and on carpeting the house, when the deceased had ample means of his own to pay for such matters. It may be that none of these incidents, taken by itself, would be very significant, but the cumulative effect of them supports the view that the plaintiff and her husband subordinated their own interests to the wishes of the deceased. Counsel for the defendant submitted that all this could be attributed to the plaintiff's natural love and affection for her stepfather; but in my judgment the plaintiff's acts went well beyond what was called for by natural love and affection for someone to whom she had no blood relationship, and both she and her husband made it very clear in their evidence that there was no great love and affection between her husband and the deceased, and that he was only willing to pay for meals that the plaintiff provided for the deceased and to work as he did in the garden of Rosslyn because of the expectation that the deceased's estate would in due course pass to the plaintiff.

The fourth element that the plaintiff has to prove is that the acts done by her were done in reliance on or as a result of her belief that she would become entitled to the deceased's property on his death. On this I derive some assistance from observations of Lord Denning MR in *Greasley v Cooke* [1980] 3 All ER 710, [1980] 1 WLR 1306. In that case the defendant came as a maid in 1938 to live in the house of a widower. He died in 1948 and after his death the defendant stayed on in the house looking after his son and daughter until their deaths in 1975, receiving no payment for doing so. She and the son lived as husband and wife throughout this period, and she was treated as one of the

family. The county court judge held that she believed, because of what was said to her
by the son, that she would be allowed to live and remain in the house as long as she   *a*
wished, though the judge said that she might have expected the son to make provision
for her to this effect in his will. However he held that she failed to prove that the reason
why she looked after the son and daughter without payment was because of her belief
that she would be entitled to live in the house as long as she wished, and he dismissed her
claim to be entitled to remain. The Court of Appeal reversed his decision. Lord Denning
MR said ([1980] 3 All ER 710 at 713, [1980] 1 WLR 1306 at 1311–1312):   *b*

'The first point is on the burden of proof. Counsel for the defendant referred us
to many cases, such as *Reynell v Sprye* (1852) 1 De GM & G 660 at 708, 42 ER 710 at
728, *Smith v Chadwick* (1882) 20 Ch D 27 at 44 and *Brikom Investments Ltd v Carr*
[1979] 2 All ER 753 at 759, [1979] QB 467 at 482–483 where I said that, when a
person makes a representation intending that another should act on it—"It is no   *c*
answer for the maker to say: 'You would have gone on with the transaction anyway.'
That must be mere speculation. No one can be sure what he would, or would not,
have done in a hypothetical state of affairs which never took place . . . Once it is
shown that a representation was calculated to influence the judgment of a reasonable
man, the presumption is that he was so influenced." So here. These statements to
the defendant were calculated to influence her, so as to put her mind at rest, so that   *d*
she would not worry about being turned out. No one can say what she would have
done if Kenneth and Hedley had not made those statements. It is quite possible that
she would have said to herself: "I am not married to Kenneth. I am on my own.
What will happen to me if anything happens to him? I had better look out for
another job now rather than stay here where I have no security." So, instead of
looking for another job, she stayed on in the house looking after Kenneth and   *e*
Clarice. There is a presumption that she did so relying on the assurances given to
her by Kenneth and Hedley. The burden is not on her but on them to prove that
she did not rely on their assurances. They did not prove it, nor did their
representatives. So she is presumed to have relied on them. So on the burden of
proof it seems to me that the judge was in error. The second point is about the need   *f*
for some expenditure of money, some detriment, before a person can acquire any
interest in a house or any right to stay in it as long as he wishes. It so happens that
in many of these cases of proprietary estoppel there has been expenditure of money.
But that is not a necessary element. I see that in Snell on Equity (27th Edn, 1973,
p 565) it is said that "A must have incurred expenditure or otherwise have prejudiced
himself". But I do not think that that is necessary. It is sufficient if the party, to   *g*
whom the assurance is given, acts on the faith of it, in such circumstances that it
would be unjust and inequitable for the party making the assurance to go back on
it (see *Moorgate v Twitchings* [1975] 3 All ER 314, [1976] 1 QB 225 and *Crabb v Arun
District Council* [1975] 3 All ER 865 at 871, [1976] 1 Ch 179 at 188). Applying those
principles here it can be seen that the assurances given by Kenneth and Hedley to
the defendant, leading her to believe that she would be allowed to stay in the house   *h*
as long as she wished, raised an equity in her favour. There was no need for her to
prove that she acted on the faith of those assurances. It is to be presumed that she
did so. There is no need for her to prove that she acted to her detriment or to her
prejudice. Suffice it that she stayed on in the house, looking after Kenneth and
Clarice, when otherwise she might have left and got a job elsewhere. The equity
having thus been raised in her favour, it is for the courts of equity to decide in what   *j*
way that equity should be satisfied. In this case it should be by allowing her to stay
on in the house as long as she wishes.'

Waller and Dunn LJJ agreed, and Waller LJ quoted a passage from the judgment of
Jessel MR in *Smith v Chadwick* (1882) 20 Ch D 27 at 44–45:

'Again on the question of the materiality of the statement, if the Court sees on the face of it that it is of such a nature as would induce a person to enter into the contract, or would tend to induce him to do so, or that it would be a part of the inducement, to enter into the contract, the inference is, if he entered into the contract, that he acted on the inducement so held out, and you want no evidence that he did so act . . . But unless it is shewn in one way or the other that he did not rely on the statement the inference follows.'

On the evidence in the present case I am satisfied that one reason why the plaintiff did so much for the deceased was her belief that, although she was not a blood relative of his, he would leave his estate to her on his death; but on the authority of *Greasley v Cooke*, if the evidence was not sufficient to establish this positively, the plaintiff would still be entitled to succeed on the fourth element in the absence of proof that she did not rely on the deceased's statements.

The four elements in the broad statement of principle with which I began this consideration of the law are thus in my judgment made out. Counsel for the defendants, however, submitted that there are two reasons why the plaintiff is not entitled to rely on proprietary estoppel in the present case. His main submission was that the representation or belief on which a plaintiff, A in the foregoing statement of principle, relies must be related to an existing right, that is to say unless there is a representation that A has a present right or interest, equity cannot intervene because there is nothing which equity can protect or make effective by the operation of an estoppel. What has to be shown, he submitted, is that A has been given an informal title, and equity will then prevent B, the owner of the property concerned, from taking it away from him. Linked to this submission, and deriving its main force from it, was his second submission, namely that proprietary estoppel must be related to a particular property and cannot extend to property as indefinite and fluctuating as the whole of a deceased person's estate.

In a number of leading cases the law is stated in a manner which is consistent with the submissions of counsel for the defendants. Thus in *Ramsden v Dyson* (1866) LR 1 HL 129 at 170 Lord Kingsdown states it as follows:

'The rule of law applicable to the case appears to me to be this: If a man, under a verbal agreement with a landlord for a certain interest in land, or, what amounts to the same thing, under an expectation, created or encouraged by the landlord, that he shall have a certain interest, takes possession of such land, with the consent of the landlord, and upon the faith of such promise or expectation, with the knowledge of the landlord, and without objection by him, lays out money upon the land, a Court of equity will compel the landlord to give effect to such promise or expectation.'

Similarly, in *Inwards v Baker* [1965] 1 All ER 446 at 449, [1965] 2 QB 29 at 37 Lord Denning MR said:

'It is an equity well recognised in law. It arises from the expenditure of money by a person in actual occupation of land when he is led to believe that, as the result of that expenditure, he will be allowed to remain there,'

I was also referred to *Moorgate Mercantile Co Ltd v Twitchings* [1975] 3 All ER 314 at 324, [1976] QB 225 at 242, where Lord Denning MR drew a parallel between the facts of that case, in which HP Information Ltd had held out the vendor of a car as the owner of it free from any hire-purchase agreement, and the cases in equity—

'when the owner of land, by his conduct, leads another to believe that he is not the owner, or, at any rate, that the other can safely spend money on it. It is held that he cannot afterwards assert his ownership so as to deprive him of the benefit of that expenditure: see *Ramsden v Dyson* (1866) LR 1 HL 129. The court of equity will look to the circumstances to see in what way the equity can be satisfied: see *Inwards v Baker* [1965] 1 All ER 446, [1965] 2 QB 29.'

Counsel for the defendants also relied on the five probanda set out in the judgment of
Fry J in *Willmott v Barber* (1880) 15 Ch D 96 at 105–106, and submitted, rightly, that　*a*
they were not all satisfied in the present case, and further submitted that it was necessary
that they should be satisfied in order that a claim based on proprietary estoppel should
succeed.

In this, as in other branches of the law, it is not difficult to find statements of principle
couched in terms which are broad enough to cover the facts of the particular case under
consideration, but which subsequent cases show to have been narrower than is necessary　*b*
to encapsulate the developed law. The law, in Lord Tennyson's words, 'slowly broadens
down from precedent to precedent', and in few areas is this more clear than that with
which I am concerned. The broadening process is brought out by Oliver J's consideration
of the authorities in *Taylor Fashions Ltd v Liverpool Victoria Trustees Co Ltd* [1981] 1 All ER
897 at 915–916, [1982] 1 QB 133 at 151–152, which is summed up as follows:

c

> '... the more recent cases indicate, in my judgment, that the application of the
> *Ramsden v Dyson* principle (whether you call it proprietary estoppel, estoppel by
> acquiescence or estoppel by encouragement is really immaterial) requires a very
> much broader approach which is directed to ascertaining whether, in particular
> individual circumstances, it would be unconscionable for a party to be permitted to
> deny that which, knowingly or unknowingly, he has allowed or encouraged another　*d*
> to assume to his detriment rather than to inquiring whether the circumstances can
> be fitted within the confines of some preconceived formula serving as a universal
> yardstick for every form of unconscionable behaviour.'

No case was cited to me, and I know of no case, which affords support for counsel's
main submission for the defendants, that the belief on which A relies must be related to
an existing right. Counsel for the defendants accepted that this suggested requirement　*e*
would have been satisfied if the plaintiff had been living with the deceased at Rosslyn,
but he contended that the fact that she lived a short distance down the road made all the
difference. In my judgment the question whether it is unconscionable for the deceased's
personal representatives to assert his legal title to his property cannot turn on a factor of
this kind. Although statements of principle such as those of Lord Kingsdown and Lord　*f*
Denning MR which I have quoted, and which were worded in broad enough terms to
cover the cases in which they were made, might suggest the contrary, it is in my
judgment established that the expenditure of A's money on B's property is not the only
kind of detriment that gives rise to a proprietary estoppel. *Greasley v Cooke* [1980] 3 All
ER 710, [1980] 1 WLR 1306 is an example of a case in which A was not shown to have
incurred any such expenditure: see in particular the second point referred to by Lord　*g*
Denning MR in the passage which I have quoted from his judgment. Nor in my
judgment is it necessary, notwithstanding the terms of such statements of principle, that
A should have been in occupation of B's land, or even in enjoyment of some right over
it. In *Crabb v Arun DC* [1975] 3 All ER 865, [1976] Ch 179, A acted to his detriment in
parting with part of his land without having secured for himself a right of way to his
remaining land, which was thereby rendered landlocked. But because he did so in the　*h*
belief, encouraged by B, that he would be granted a right of way over B's adjoining land,
the Court of Appeal held that an equity arose in his favour and that he was entitled to be
granted such a right of way. It appears from the judgments that A had not spent any
money on the access road over B's land, and that he had not even been using the access
road himself prior to parting with the portion of his own land that would have given
him direct access to the highway. The access road over which he was expecting to obtain　*j*
a right of way was being used by B's lorries (see [1975] 3 All ER 865 at 870, 878, [1976]
Ch 179 at 186, 197), but not by vehicles belonging to A, or at least, if it was being used
by A, this was a factor of so little importance in the minds of the members of the Court
of Appeal that none of them thought it necessary to refer to it. The important factors
were A's belief, B's encouragement of that belief and A's acts in reliance on that belief.

Moreover if, as in my judgment is the case, the equity which arises in favour of A in
a cases of proprietary estoppel is in the nature of a constructive trust, and is similar to the
equity which arises in cases of the kind referred to by Nourse J in the passage which I
have quoted from *Re Cleaver* [1981] 2 All ER 1018, [1981] 1 WLR 939, I can see no
ground for making what would appear to be an arbitrary distinction between the two
and holding that in cases of proprietary estoppel it is necessary for A to be in enjoyment
of B's property, when such a requirement is clearly not present in those other cases. If the
b proprietary estoppel were limited to cases in which A believed that he already had an
interest in B's property, such a requirement might make more sense. *Willmott v Barber*
was a case of this kind; and the use of the word 'estoppel' suggests such a limitation. But
as Oliver J indicated in the *Taylor Fashions* case, equitable doctrines cannot be confined
within a straitjacket by the labels which have become attached to them. It is clear that
the doctrine which bears the label 'proprietary estoppel' is not limited to cases of the
c *Willmott v Barber* kind, where A believes that he already has the interest which he asks
the court to confirm, but extends to cases in which A believes that he will obtain an
interest in the future; and this being so, I see no justification for importing a requirement
that he should in addition already be in enjoyment of some lesser interest.

Similar reasoning leads me to reject counsel's second submission for the defendants,
that the belief must relate to some clearly identified piece of property, movable or
d immovable, and that a claim cannot be based on proprietary estoppel where the
expectation is that A will inherit B's residuary estate. It is clear that in other cases of
constructive trust, such as those arising from mutual wills, the trust can bind the whole
of B's estate: see, for example, *Re Cleaver* and the leading Australian case of *Birmingham v
Renfrew* (1937) 57 CLR 666, to which Nourse J refers at length in his judgment. If the
belief that B will leave the whole of his estate to A is established by sufficiently cogent
e evidence, as in my judgment it is in the present case, I see no reason in principle or in
authority why the doctrine of proprietary estoppel should not apply so as to raise an
equity against B in favour of A extending to the whole of B's estate.

Accordingly, I hold that the plaintiff succeeds in this action and is entitled to relief in
relation to both the cottage Rosslyn and the remainder of the deceased's net estate. The
question then arises in what manner effect should be given to the equity which has arisen
f in the plaintiff's favour. The extent of the equity is to have made good, so far as may
fairly be done between the parties the expectations which the deceased encouraged: see
Griffiths v Williams (1977) 248 EG 947 at 949 per Goff LJ. Prima facie, therefore, the
plaintiff is entitled to a declaration that the defendants, as personal representatives of the
deceased, hold the whole of his net estate on trust for the plaintiff. However, the question
of costs arises. I have not heard argument on this, and I will give counsel an opportunity
g of addressing me further on costs; but it seems to me that the case is analogous to certain
other cases in which personal representatives or other parties, although unsuccessful in
the event, are not held personally liable for the costs of an action in which they have
acted reasonably. While costs are always a matter of discretion, there is a general principle
in a probate action that, where the cause of the litigation takes its origin in the fault of
h the testator, the costs of the unsuccessful parties are allowed out of the estate; and if the
circumstances lead reasonably to an investigation of the matter, then the costs may be
left to be borne by those who incurred them: see *Spiers v English* [1907] P 122. Similarly
in an administration action, where the difficulty to be solved is created by the testator
himself, the costs may be paid out of the estate, and in a proper case may be taxed as
between solicitor and client (though that basis of taxation has disappeared as a distinct
j basis under the new RSC Ord 62): see *Re Hall-Dare, Le Marchant v Lee Warner* [1916] 1 Ch
272. There is also the special rule now to be found in Ord 62, r 4(3) that in a probate
action, where a defendant has given notice with his defence that he merely insists on the
will being proved in solemn form and only intends to cross-examine the witnesses
produced in support of the will, no order for costs shall be made against him unless it
appears to the court that there was no reasonable ground for opposing the will.

The present case has arisen solely out of the failure of the deceased to make the will which was necessary, in view of the absence of any blood relationship, in order that indisputable legal effect should be given to the expectations which he had encouraged in the plaintiff. The defendants had little if any personal knowledge of some of the matters on which evidence has been given by or on behalf of the plaintiff, and were acting not only on their own behalf but on behalf of a number of other nephews and nieces of the deceased who would have been entitled to share in his estate had it passed on intestacy. In all the circumstances I do not think they acted unreasonably in testing the case put forward by the plaintiff which, while based firmly on established principles, on its facts went beyond the facts of any reported case. On learning of the plaintiff's claim they might, I think, have issued an originating summons making the plaintiff and one of the deceased's other next of kin defendants, to obtain the directions of the court as to how they should deal with the deceased's estate; and if they had done so it is reasonably clear that their costs would have been paid out of the deceased's estate. Doing the best that I can to act fairly between the parties, as I am enjoined to do by *Griffiths v Williams* (1977) 248 EG 947 and subject to anything that counsel for either party may say, I think that justice will be done if I order that the defendant's costs be paid out of the deceased's estate on the standard basis. I should perhaps add that, as the action is constituted, the case does not in my judgment fall within the new RSC Ord 62, r 6(2), so as to entitle them to costs on an indemnity basis, because although the defendants are personal representatives, the claim by the plaintiff is a claim against the estate and not a claim by a beneficiary under the trusts affecting the estate and, the claim having succeeded, the defendants no longer hold any fund in the capacity of personal representatives to which that rule can apply.

Judgment for plaintiff. Defendants' costs, on standard basis, to be paid out of estate other than cottage.

Solicitors: *Hood Vores & Allwood*, Dereham (for the plaintiff); *Block & Cullingham*, Ipswich (for the defendants).

Hazel Hartman   Barrister.

Hussain v New Taplow Paper Mills Ltd

COURT OF APPEAL, CIVIL DIVISION
KERR, LLOYD AND RALPH GIBSON LJJ
16, 17, 18 JUNE, 31 JULY 1986

Damages – Personal injury – Loss of earnings – Deduction of long-term sickness benefit payable under contract of employment – Employer insuring against contractual liability to pay long-term sickness benefit – Whether long-term sickness benefit in the nature of earnings and therefore to be brought into account in assessing damages – Whether benefit to be treated as proceeds of private insurance and thus not deductible from damages – Whether immediate ex gratia payment by employer to injured employee should be brought into account in assessing damages.

The plaintiff was employed as a machineman with the defendants under a contract of employment which provided that if he was incapacitated for work as the result of an accident occurring in the course of his employment he would receive his full pay for 13 weeks from the date of the injury and thereafter he would receive 50% of his pre-accident earnings by way of long-term sickness benefit payable under an insurance scheme run by the defendants, who had taken out a permanent health insurance policy to insure themselves against their contractual liability to pay long-term sickness benefit to employees. Under the terms of the plaintiff's contract it was clear that such long-term benefit was a continuation of earnings and was taxable. The entire cost of the insurance scheme was borne by the defendants, but there was no evidence that the plaintiff's wages would have been any higher if the defendants had not operated the scheme. The plaintiff was seriously injured in the course of his employment and brought an action for damages against the defendants in respect of his injury. The trial judge held that the defendants were two-thirds to blame for the accident and awarded the plaintiff damages on that basis for, inter alia, pre-trial and future loss of earnings without deducting the contractual long-term sickness benefit payable to the plaintiff. The defendants appealed against the judge's failure to bring into account and deduct the long-term sickness benefit from loss of earnings awards.

Held – Since the long-term sickness benefits contractually payable to the plaintiff were designed to compensate him for the loss of, or diminution in, his wages resulting from his injury, in the same way as the short-term benefits payable in the first 13 weeks after injury, and since the payments of long-term sickness benefits were in the nature of earnings, they were accordingly of the same nature as the earnings which the plaintiff claimed to have lost. Furthermore, the payments themselves were not the proceeds of private insurance even though the defendants had insured themselves against their contractual liability to pay the long-term benefits. Being in the nature of earnings, the plaintiff had already been compensated for his loss of earnings to the extent of such benefits, and since he could not show that he had paid for or bought those benefits, e g by receiving a lower wage than he would have if the defendants' insurance scheme had not been in operation, it followed that those benefits should be brought into account and deducted from the awards for the pre-trial and future loss of earnings. The defendants' appeal would therefore be allowed (see p 424 *d f h j*, p 428 *a b* and p 429 *a* to *d f g*, post).

Parry v Cleaver [1969] 1 All ER 555 applied.

Per curiam. Where an employee is injured in the course of his employment and his employer makes him an immediate ex gratia payment there is no reason why such a payment should not be taken into account in reduction of any damages for which the employer may ultimately be held liable. Employers should be encouraged to make ex gratia payments in such circumstances and such payments should be brought into

account on the grounds of justice, reasonableness and public policy (see p 428 *e f* and
p 429 *c d*, post); dictum of Lord Reid in *Parry v Cleaver* [1969] 1 All ER at 557 applied.   *a*

Notes
For deduction from damages for benefits received or receivable, see 12 Halsbury's Laws
(4th edn) para 1152 and 34 ibid para 83, and for cases on the subject, see 17 Digest
(Reissue) 117–118, 195–200 and 36(1) ibid 319–320, 1291–1295.
                                                                                              b

Cases referred to in judgment
Boarelli v Flannigan (1973) 36 DLR (3d) 4, Ont CA.
Bradburn v Great Western Rly Co (1874) LR 10 Exch 1, [1874–80] All ER Rep 195.
British Transport Commission v Gourley [1955] 3 All ER 796, [1956] AC 185, [1956] 2 WLR
    41, HL.
Browning v War Office [1962] 3 All ER 1089, [1963] 1 QB 750, [1963] 2 WLR 52, CA.   *c*
Chan v Butcher and Collins [1984] 4 WWR 363, BC CA.
Cunningham v Harrison [1973] 3 All ER 463, [1973] QB 942, [1973] 3 WLR 97, CA.
Dews v National Coal Board [1986] 2 All ER 769, [1987] QB 81, [1986] 3 WLR 227, CA.
Lincoln v Hayman [1982] 2 All ER 819, [1982] 1 WLR 488, CA.
Nabi v British Leyland (UK) Ltd [1980] 1 All ER 667, [1980] 1 WLR 529, CA.
Palfrey v Greater London Council [1985] ICR 437.   *d*
Parry v Cleaver [1969] 1 All ER 555, [1970] AC 1, [1969] 2 WLR 821, HL; *rvsg* [1967] 2
    All ER 1168, [1968] 1 QB 195, [1967] 3 WLR 739, CA.
Smith v Manchester Corp (1974) 17 KIR 1, CA.
Turner v Ministry of Defence [1969] CA Transcript 278A.

Cases also cited   *e*
Greenwood v Sparkle Janitor Service (1983) 145 DLR (3d) 711, BC SC.
Greenwood Shopping Plaza Ltd v Beattie (1980) 111 DLR (3d) 257, Can SC.
McKay v Camco Inc (1983) 2 DLR (4th) 688, Ont HC.
Mark Rowlands Ltd v Berni Inns Ltd [1985] 3 All ER 473, CA.

                                                                                           f
Appeal
By a writ issued on 7 April 1983 the plaintiff, Akhtar Hussain, claimed against the
defendants, New Taplow Paper Mills Ltd, his employers, damages for personal injury
and loss resulting from an accident on 17 March 1983 at the defendants' premises in the
course of the plaintiff's employment, due to the defendants' alleged negligence and
breach of statutory duty. On 4 July 1985 his Honour Judge Harris QC sitting as a judge   *g*
of the High Court, held that the plaintiff had established the defendants' liability in
negligence and for breach of statutory duty, but found that the plaintiff was one-third to
blame for the accident. On a full liability basis the judge awarded the plaintiff total
damages of £96,876·87, which included the sum of £59,250 for loss of past and future
earnings. In assessing sums awarded for loss of earnings the judge held that payments
made to the plaintiff under the defendants' permanent health insurance scheme,   *h*
amounting to £34,688, were not to be taken into account and were thus not deductible
from the awards for loss of earnings. By a notice of appeal dated 25 July 1985 the
defendants appealed, contending, inter alia, that the judge had erred in leaving out of
account the payments made under the defendants' insurance scheme, and instead those
payments fell to be deducted from the awards for loss of earnings. By a respondent's
notice dated 10 September 1985 the plaintiff contended that, inter alia, the judgment *j*
should be varied by substituting a finding that the accident was wholly the defendant's
fault and that there should be no apportionment. Before the hearing of the appeal the
parties came to terms on the issue of liability. The facts are set out in the judgment of
Lloyd LJ.

Michael Harvey QC and *Roger Ter Haar* for the defendants.
a *Gary Flather QC* and *Justin Fenwick* for the plaintiff.

Cur adv vult

31 July. The following judgments were delivered.

b **LLOYD LJ** (giving the first judgment at the invitation of Kerr LJ). On 17 March 1983 the plaintiff, Mr Akhtar Hussain, met with an accident at work, when his left arm became trapped between rollers in a paper-drying machine. The injury was very severe, necessitating an amputation through the middle of the forearm. The plaintiff brought an action against his employers, New Taplow Paper Mills Ltd, claiming damages for negligence and breach of statutory duty. His Honour Judge Harris QC, sitting as a judge *c* of the High Court, had a most difficult task in determining liability. After a hearing lasting six days, he found that the plaintiff had established liability under both heads. But he found that the plaintiff was himself one-third to blame for the accident. The damages which he awarded were reduced accordingly.

In addition to the difficult question on liability, there were difficult questions on damages. Under the heading of general damages, the judge awarded £27,500 on full *d* liability basis, for pain and suffering. For loss of earnings to the date of the trial he awarded £9,568. For loss of future earnings he awarded £49,682. I will return to the make-up of these figures later. For loss of earning capacity, commonly referred to as *Smith v Manchester* damages (see *Smith v Manchester Corp* (1974) 17 KIR 1), he awarded £5,000. For loss of pension rights he awarded £2,380. Finally, as special damages, he awarded £2,740, including £1,100 for prescription charges and the cost of replacing the *e* glove on the plaintiff's prosthesis from time to time as needed for the rest of the plaintiff's life. Thus total damages, on a full liability basis, came to £96,870.

Both parties appealed. Happily they came to terms on liability shortly before the appeal came on for hearing. That left only the defendants' appeal on damages. There is no appeal against the award of general damages for pain and suffering, or against the *f* damages for loss of pension rights; and the appeal against the *Smith v Manchester* damages was not pursued.

Thus almost the whole of the argument before us was taken up with damages for loss of earnings, and in particular with the question whether sums payable under the defendants' permanent health insurance scheme should be taken into account in calculating the plaintiff's loss. The judge took the view that those payments should not *g* be taken into account. On that basis, he arrived at a total of £59,250, on the agreed figures, for loss of earnings past and future. The payments left out of account amounted to £34,688. If, as the defendants submit, the judge was wrong to leave those payments out of account, the damages for loss of earnings would fall to be reduced by that amount.

There is thus a considerable sum involved in the outcome of this appeal on damages. In addition there is an important, and not altogether easy, question of principle to be *h* resolved, which has required us to consider closely the decision of the House of Lords in *Parry v Cleaver* [1969] 1 All ER 555, [1970] AC 1.

Before coming to the arguments advanced on either side, it is first necessary to set out in some detail the terms of the plaintiff's contract of employment, and the provisions of the permanent health insurance scheme, so far as relevant.

The contract of employment current at the time of the accident is dated June 1981. It *j* provides for the plaintiff's employment as a machineman at a rate of remuneration of £2·195 per hour. Against the heading 'Incapacity for work due to illness or injury' there appear the words 'See Works Rules under Sick Pay'. The works rules entitled 'Rules and Conditions of Employment' are contained in a booklet. I need only refer to paras 5, 6 and 8:

'5. SICK PAY—HOURLY RATED EMPLOYEES

SICK PAY		PERMANENT HEALTH INSURANCE PAY
	N H I SICKNESS BENEFIT	
4 days	2 weeks	13 weeks

(a) Sick pay is not paid for the first two weeks of absence. NHI Sickness Benefit must be claimed by the employee. After 2 weeks' absence sick pay is paid at one half of the previous calendar year's earnings for a further 11 weeks. At 13 weeks absence the Company Permanent Health Insurance Scheme takes over and pays the same amount . . .

6. INJURY PAY—HOURLY RATED EMPLOYEES If an employee is incapacitated for work as the result of an accident or illness arising out of and in the course of his employment, payments will be made as follows. (a) Injury pay will be paid at the rate of 100% of the previous calendar year's weekly earnings for a period of 13 weeks from the date of the injury, after which sick pay will apply except at the Company's discretion. *NHI Industrial Injury or Sickness Benefit must be claimed by the employee and refunded to the Company.* Employees are eligible for Injury Pay upon joining the Company, but eligibility for sick pay is unaltered by payment of Injury Pay, the higher of which will be paid. (b) A medical certificate must be in the Company's hands no later than the third day of absence and where necessary, further medical certificates must be delivered regularly to the Company throughout the total period of absence . . .

8. LONG TERM SICKNESS Any long term sickness is covered by an Insurance Scheme run by the Company, the conditions and payments through this Scheme are detailed in a separate book, issued with this book. Benefits under this scheme are subject to periodic check and/or medical examination. Abuse of the scheme will render the employee liable to disciplinary action.'

I need not refer to para 7, which deals with sick or injury pay for monthly paid employees.

It will have been noticed that paras 5(a) and 8 both refer to the company's permanent health insurance scheme. The scheme is described in a second booklet, which is issued to each employee. The booklet makes clear that the scheme is governed by rules and a policy.

The rules, as revised in 1981, are headed 'REVISED RULES OF THE NEW TAPLOW PAPER MILLS LTD. PERMANENT HEALTH INSURANCE SCHEME'. They contain the following definitions:

'(a) "Insurer" means N.E.L. Permanent Health Insurances Limited. (b) "Company" means The New Taplow Paper Mills Ltd. . . . (e) "Employer" means the Company or any associated or subsidiary company which has with the consent of the Insurer been included in the Scheme . . . (f) "Employee" means a person in the permanent full-time service of the Employer. (g) "Member" means an Employee who has been admitted to membership of the Scheme and remains in membership under the Rules . . . (k) "Deferred Period" means the first 13 weeks of any continuous period of Incapacity . . .'

The following are the most relevant provisions of the rules:

'3. BENEFIT (a) *Full Benefit.* A full benefit of 50% of Salary shall be payable to a Member within the provisions of these Rules following the Deferred Period and during such time before Terminal Date as Incapacity is admitted by the Employer and the Insurer. (b) *Reduced Benefit.* A proportionately reduced benefit shall be payable where full benefit would have been paid but for the adoption by the *a* Member of a different and less well paid occupation or the Member returning to his Occupation on a part-time basis with medical consent. The reduced benefit will be that proportion of the full benefit that loss of earnings calculated on the total earned income after Incapacity bears to Salary immediately before Incapacity . . .

4. LIMITS OF BENEFIT   (1) The maximum benefit payable under the Scheme in respect of each Member is subject to a normal maximum as provided below. The Insurer may agree to insure a benefit at a different level beyond the normal

b maximum for any Member subject to an overall maximum as provided below . . .

5. INCAPACITY   Incapacity shall mean a Member being totally incapacitated through illness or injury from following his Occupation and not following any other occupation except as provided under the proportionate benefit provisions of Rule 3 . . .

6. EVIDENCE OF HEALTH   The Employer's liability under the Scheme is insured

c with the Insurer and a Member's entitlement to benefit shall be that under Rule 3 provided insurance has been arranged. Any restriction on entitlement will be notified to the Member by the Employer. Before granting insurance on entry into the Scheme or any increase in benefit the Insurer may require evidence of good health . . .

7. THE COST   The whole cost of the Scheme will be borne by the Employer.

d 8. INCOME TAX   Payments made under this Scheme are a continuance of salary. They will, therefore, under present Inland Revenue practice, be taxed as earned income.

9. CESSATION OF MEMBERSHIP   An Employee will cease to be a Member:—(a) on reaching the Terminal Date, or (b) on leaving Service, or (c) on death.

10. OPTION ON LEAVING SERVICE   If a Member leaves the service of the Employer

e more than one year before Terminal Date and engages in a new employment within 31 days of leaving service he will have the right upon written notice to the Insurer within the 31 day period to obtain without medical evidence a new and individual Permanent Health Insurance Policy for benefits not exceeding those to which he was last entitled under the Scheme . . .

11. LEGAL LIABILITY OF EMPLOYER   Payments in respect of Incapacity are made

f without thereby admitting any legal liability on the part of the Employer.

12. TERMINATION OR AMENDMENT   The Employer reserves the right to terminate the Scheme or to amend the Rules at any time. Any such termination or amendment will not prejudice the potential payment of benefit where the Member is incapacitated under the provisions of Rule 5 but has not completed the Deferred Period or where benefit is already being paid under the Scheme. In the event of the

g termination of the Scheme for any reason the Insurer will issue policies of insurance to Employees who qualify for benefit. Such policies will provide an equivalent benefit to that which would have been paid by the Employer had the Scheme continued.'

The policy was issued in favour of the defendants, who are described as 'the Grantees'.

h 'Insured Employee' is defined as 'A Member whose benefits under the Scheme are insured hereunder'. The following are the most relevant provisions:

'2. (a) It is a condition of the Policy that (i) Employees become Members when they first become eligible under these Rules and (ii) their benefits under the Rules be offered to the Insurer for insurance. (b) Prior to acceptance and subsequent to

j payment of premium the benefit of a Member is covered for 2 months provided the Member is actively at work and following his normal employment on the date cover for benefit is due to commence.

3. BENEFITS   (a) *Benefit* The Benefit in respect of an Insured Employee is the same as the benefit payable under the Rules, subject to the limitations and conditions contained therein. (b) *When Benefit is payable* During such time following the

Deferred Period and prior to the Terminal Date as the Insured Employee is incapacitated from following his own occupation. (c) *To whom Benefit is payable* To *a* the Grantees to hold on trust for the Employer.

4. PREMIUMS (a) Rates . . . (d) Premiums are not payable in respect of an Insured Employee for periods in which he is receiving benefit. (e) Each Employer shall pay to the Grantees such premiums as are due in respect of his Employees . . .

5. OPTION ON LEAVING SERVICE An Insured Employee who leaves Service while the Scheme is in force may exercise the option available under the Rules. *b*

6. TERMINATION OF INSURANCE The insurance of an Insured Employee shall cease when he ceases to be a Member and (without prejudice to admitted claims or potential claims) that of all Insured Employees shall cease if premiums are not duly paid.'

I should now mention certain further facts which were not in dispute. The accident *c* occurred, as I have already said, on 17 March 1983. The plaintiff's payslip showed that he was then receiving basic pay, overtime pay and mill bonus amounting in all to a gross figure of £161. His net pay after deducting tax etc came to just over £100 per week. His payslip in the week after the accident shows that he received what is called 'Sick Pay' of £226, plus 'other' pay (which was not explained), giving a total gross figure of £292. The plaintiff's net pay, after deductions, came to £188, which was more than he was receiving *d* before the accident.

So it continued for 15 months until 18 June 1984, with sick pay constant at £226, and net pay varying between £70 and £125. Thereafter the plaintiff received half his pre-accident earnings until the date of trial in June 1985. The payslips continued to describe the payments as 'Sick Pay'. Under para 6(a) of the scheme, the plaintiff was entitled to 100% of pre-accident earnings for a period of 13 weeks only, after which he was entitled *e* to 50% of pre-accident earnings as sick pay. But the defendants continued to pay 100% for 15 months, as I have just mentioned, either as an act of benevolence or, as the defendants submit, by virtue of the discretion conferred on the defendants by para 6(a).

Shortly before the date of the trial, the defendants offered the plaintiff a job as a weighbridge attendant at a reduced wage which works out at £5,567 per annum, compared with pre-accident earnings as a machineman of £9,412 per annum. The judge *f* held, in effect, that the plaintiff would be acting unreasonably if he refused to accept that offer, and he awarded damages for loss of future earnings on that basis. We were invited to do the same.

I now return to the sums which the judge awarded. The plaintiff's total earnings to date of trial would have amounted to £20,123. His total receipts from the defendants amounted to £14,915. But that figure included £8,669 which the defendants recovered *g* from NEL Permanent Health Insurances Ltd (NEL) under the policy. £8,669 represents 50% of the plaintiff's pre-accident earnings from the end of the 'deferred period', ie from 13 weeks after the date of the accident until the date of trial. As already mentioned, the judge held that £8,669 should be left out of account. After deducting social security benefits to the date of trial, the judge arrived at the figure of £9,568 for pre-trial loss of earnings. If he had not left £8,669 out of account, the figure would have been £899. *h*

As for future loss of earnings, the judge took a net loss of salary of £3,845 a year (£9,412 less £5,567) to which he applied a multiplier of 14. After deducting half social security benefits over the balance of five years, he arrived at a figure of £49,682. It was agreed that the amount which the plaintiff would continue to receive from the defendants under the permanent health insurance scheme, and which the defendants will recover *⸱* from NEL under the policy, will amount to £1,858 a year, reducing the plaintiff's net *j* annual loss to £1,986. If those receipts had not been left out of account, the plaintiff's damages for loss of future earnings would have been £23,663, instead of £49,682.

The judge held that the plaintiff's receipts under the scheme, past and future, should be excluded for two interrelated reasons.

a   In the first place he held that the reference in the policy to the defendants' receiving sums 'on trust for the Employer' must be a misprint for 'on trust for the Employee'. Thus in the judge's view the plaintiff has, at the very least, an equitable right to sums payable under the policy.

I cannot accept that reasoning. Indeed, counsel for the plaintiff did not seek to support it. The definition of 'Employer' in the revised rules shows that more than one employer is intended to be covered. The defendants, as 'Grantees' of the policy, were insuring on
b   behalf of other employers in the same group, as well as themselves. The words 'on trust for the Employer' therefore mean exactly what they say. There is no warrant for holding that the plaintiff has any equitable interest in the policy proceeds; and counsel for the plaintiff expressly conceded, rightly in my view, that the plaintiff is not party to the policy in any other sense. Reading the scheme, the revised rules and the policy together, the position is quite clear. The plaintiff has a contractual right against the defendants to
c   certain benefits under the scheme and revised rules. The defendants have insured their liability to pay those benefits under the policy. It is true that the policy refers in various clauses to 'the Insured Employee', almost as if the employee were himself an insured person under the policy. But the definition of 'Insured Employee' shows that it is the employee's *benefits* that are insured, not the employee himself. The employee's benefits are the subject matter of the insurance. The persons insured are the employers, or rather
d   the grantees, namely the defendants.

I turn now to the second of the two arguments which led the judge to hold that the insurance proceeds should be left out of account. Even if the plaintiff is not a party to the policy, or entitled to the proceeds in equity, he has nevertheless paid his share of the premium; not directly, but indirectly, through his contract of employment. I will quote some passages from the judgment which give the flavour of the judge's reasoning. The
e   first passage reads:

'I am satisfied that the payments which the defendants made to the insurers form part of the attractive package deal of these paternalistic employers and, if they did not expend these large sums by way of premiums to insure the workers, that money would properly be paid to the workers rather than to the shareholders ... If they
f   left the company's employment they could continue to be covered ... If they remained, in my judgment it is quite clear that the premiums being paid were because the wages were kept lower than they would have been otherwise.'

The second passage reads:

'I consider the premiums paid by the defendants form part of the plaintiff's wage
g   structure and that if he had not been covered by that insurance he would have got more pay ... The purpose, as I understand it, of this permanent health insurance scheme was to benefit the employees and not to reduce the employer's liability should the employee be injured as a result of the employer's negligence or breach of statutory duty.'

h   In so far as the judge may be said to have found as a fact in those passages that the plaintiff would have got more pay but for the insurance, I am bound to say that the evidence to which we were referred does not support the judge's conclusion. Thus Mr Briggs, the defendants' commercial manager, was asked:

j   'Q. Well, look at it in this way. If you do not pay the insurance company the premium the company is saving itself X pounds, is it not?
Judge Harris (to the witness). If they do not pay the premium, they save that amount of money. That is what it is? A. Yes.
Q. And it would be reasonable to think that if they were not paying that premium for him, he would be receiving a higher wage? A. No.'

In truth the judge was, I think, resting his conclusion on a broader ground. Even if the plaintiff's wage would have been the same, he has nevertheless earned the benefits *a* payable under the scheme by working for the defendants. As counsel for the plaintiff put it, in language adopted by the judge, the benefits are part of the wage structure.

The difficulty I feel with that argument is that it would apply equally to sickness or injury benefit paid during the first 13 weeks of incapacity. It was never suggested that this payment should be left out of account. Yet those payments were 'earned' in exactly the same way as the subsequent payments. *b*

So some other reason must be found if the judge's conclusion is to be supported. Counsel for the plaintiff submits that there is a distinction to be drawn between short-term sickness or injury benefits which the plaintiff received during the first 13 weeks after the accident and the long-term benefits covered by the policy issued by NEL. The former benefits were like sick pay in the strict sense. They were paid in lieu of salary. The subsequent benefits, by contrast, though described as sick pay in the payslips, were *c* in reality the proceeds of private insurance. If that be their nature, then they ought to be excluded from the computation of damages, as was established as long ago as 1874 in *Bradburn v Great Western Rly Co* LR 10 Exch 1, [1874–80] All ER Rep 195. Counsel for the plaintiff relied, in particular, on the language of para 5(a) of the scheme, which provides for the 'Company Permanent Health Insurance Scheme' to 'take over' after 13 weeks. *d*

I cannot accept counsel for the plaintiff's suggested distinction. The nature of the payments did not change after 13 weeks; nor, indeed, did the source. The nature of the payments remained the same, namely sick pay. The source remained the same, namely the defendants. All that happened after 13 weeks was that the defendants were covered against their subsequent liability by the policy which they had taken out with NEL. I do not think it matters whether one regards that policy as a liability policy, an indemnity *e* policy or a policy to pay on a certain event. If there had been no policy at all, it could hardly have been argued that the long-term payments should be left out of account merely because they were long-term payments. The existence of the policy makes no difference. It did not change the nature of the payments. Furthermore, so far from the language of the scheme supporting counsel for the plaintiff's suggested distinction, it *f* points the other way. Paragraph 6(a) of the scheme in particular makes it clear that, in the case of injury, payments after the first 13 weeks are a continuation of sick pay. I see no reason to go behind that description. Similarly cl 8 of the revised rules makes it clear that payments under the scheme are a continuation of salary. Counsel for the plaintiff submits that this is for the purpose of taxation only. But again I see no reason not to take the words at their face value. Indeed, the very fact that the payments are taxable is at least some prima facie indication that they are not properly to be regarded as the proceeds *g* of insurance, though it is not, of course, conclusive: see *Parry v Cleaver* [1969] 1 All ER 555, [1970] AC 1.

There is no reason why an employer should not agree to make sick payments in lieu of salary, and to continue to do so indefinitely, so long as his employee is sick or otherwise incapacitated. In my view that is what the defendants agreed to do here. *h*

If that is right, then, with all respect to the judge, I find it impossible to agree that these payments should be left out of account. They went directly to reduce the plaintiff's loss of salary. If the plaintiff were to receive both sick pay in lieu of salary and damages for loss of the same salary, then, as a matter of ordinary common sense, he will be receiving double compensation. Counsel for the plaintiff asks what would have happened if the plaintiff had been injured by the negligence of a third party tortfeasor instead of *j* the defendants. Why should a third party tortfeasor take any benefit from the fact that the plaintiff is entitled to sick pay under his contract of employment? I will return to counsel's question when I come to deal with policy considerations. The simple answer at this stage is that no third party tortfeasor, however negligent, is liable to compensate a

plaintiff for more than he has lost. If the plaintiff has not in fact lost any salary, because
a he is entitled to sick pay, then the third party tortfeasor can count himself lucky. In this,
as in other respects, he takes his victim as he finds him.

I now turn to the authorities. In *Parry v Cleaver* [1969] 1 All ER 555 at 557, [1970] AC
1 at 13 Lord Reid identified two questions which arise in this type of case. First, what has
the plaintiff lost as a result of the accident? Second, what has he received which he would
not have received but for the accident? It has been laid down as a universal rule in *British*
b *Transport Commission v Gourley* [1955] 3 All ER 796, [1956] AC 185, if not before, that a
plaintiff cannot recover more than he has lost. But there is no such universal rule as to
what should be taken into account on the credit side. In two classes of case, it is well
established that receipts should be left out of account, namely the proceeds of private
insurance (to use the language of Lord Pearce in *Parry v Cleaver*) and sums coming to the
plaintiff by way of benevolence. The question which arose in *Parry v Cleaver* was whether
c a police disability pension payable under a statutory police pensions scheme should also
be left out of account. The House of Lords decided by a majority of three to two,
reversing a decision of the Court of Appeal ([1967] 2 All ER 1168, [1968] 1 QB 195), that
it should. Lord Reid, who gave the leading speech, rested his decision on two main
grounds. He held, first, that the question whether a receipt is to be taken into account
depends not on its source but on its nature. If the receipt is of the same nature as the
d wages which the plaintiff has lost, then, whatever be its source, that receipt is to be taken
into account. But if the receipt is of a different nature, then it is to be disregarded, even
though it comes from the same source as the wages that the plaintiff has lost. On the
facts Lord Reid held that payments under the police contributory pension scheme were
different in kind from wages. The pension scheme was a form of insurance. Accordingly
the payment should be left out of account up to the time when the plaintiff would have
e retired. But after the age of retirement the pension payments were to be brought into
account. The reasons for this apparent anomaly is made very plain by a paragraph at the
end of Lord Reid's speech ([1969] 1 All ER 555 at 563–564, [1970] AC 1 at 20–21):

f 'For a time after retirement from the police force he would still have been able to
work at other employment, so allowance must be made for that. As regards police
pension his loss after reaching police retiring age would be the difference between
the full pension which he would have received if he had served his full time and his
ill-health pension. It has been asked why his ill-health pension is to be brought into
account at this point if not brought into account for the earlier period. The answer
is that in the earlier period we are not comparing like with like. He lost wages but
g he gained something different in kind, a pension. But with regard to the period
after retirement we are comparing like with like. Both the ill-health pension and
the full retirement pension are the products of the same insurance scheme; his loss
in the later period is caused by his having been deprived of the opportunity to
continue in insurance so as to swell the ultimate product of that insurance from an
ill-health to a retirement pension. There is no question as regards that period of a
h loss of one kind and a gain of a different kind.'

The same reasoning underlies Lord Pearce's speech. He treated the question as
depending on whether the pension payments should be regarded as a substitute for the
capacity to earn. On the facts he held they were not.

Counsel for the plaintiff argued that the solution to the question cannot depend on
j whether the receipt is called sick pay or a pension. The sick pay in the present case is in
reality a form of disability pension, and therefore, applying *Parry v Cleaver*, is in reality a
form of insurance. It is therefore to be disregarded. I can see the force of that argument.
But I do not accept it. It is clear from *Parry v Cleaver* itself that there is indeed a
distinction between sick pay, strictly so called, and a pension. Lord Reid used the case of

sick pay to illustrate the very point he was making ([1969] 1 All ER 555 at 560, [1970]
AC 1 at 16):   *a*

> 'Then it is said that instead of getting a pension he may get sick pay for a time
> during his disablement—perhaps his whole wage. That would not be deductible, so
> why should a pension be different? But a man's wage for a particular week is not
> related to the amount of work which he does during that week. Wages for the
> period of a man's holiday do not differ in kind from wages paid to him during the   *b*
> rest of the year. And neither does sick pay; it is still wages. So during the period
> when he receives sick pay he has lost nothing. We never reach the second question
> of how to treat sums of a different kind which he would never have received but for
> his accident.'

So there is nothing in *Parry v Cleaver* which compels us to decide that sick pay in the   *c*
present case, if it is properly so described, should be left out of account. Indeed, counsel
for the defendants relies strongly on the paragraph I have just quoted in support of his
main argument.

The other ground on which Lord Reid rested his decision was one of public policy. I
will return to that ground later.

The next case which I shall mention is *Turner v Ministry of Defence* [1969] CA Transcript   *d*
278A. In that case the plaintiff had injured his little finger while working for the Ministry
of Defence. He brought a claim for damages against his employer. The question was
whether he should give credit for the sick pay which he received from the ministry. It
was held that he should. Lord Denning MR regarded that what he had said on the subject
of sick pay in *Browning v War Office* [1962] 3 All ER 1089, [1963] 1 QB 750 as being
entirely unaffected, and indeed supported, by what Lord Reid said in *Parry v Cleaver*.   *e*

The next case is *Cunningham v Harrison* [1973] 3 All ER 463, [1973] QB 942, another
decision of this court. The plaintiff, who had been employed by BP, was very severely
injured by the negligence of a third party. One of the questions was whether he should
give credit for an ex gratia payment, amounting to about half his salary, which he was
receiving from his former employers for life. It was held that the ex gratia payment   *f*
should be left out of account. The Court of Appeal treated the ex gratia payment as
analogous to sums coming to the plaintiff by way of benevolence, which, like the
proceeds of private insurance, have always been excluded. But it would have been
otherwise if BP had been obliged to make the payments under the plaintiff's contract of
employment.

The last case to which I wish to refer is *Palfrey v Greater London Council* [1985] ICR 437,   *g*
a decision of Mr Piers Ashworth QC sitting as a deputy judge of the High Court. The
judgment contains a most valuable summary of the existing law in this field. The
question for the judge's decision was whether statutory sick pay payable under the Social
Security and Housing Benefits Act 1982 should be taken into account in reduction of
damages. He held that it should. In his view there was no distinction between statutory
sick pay and sickness benefit, which it in part replaced (see s 10 and Sch 2), nor between   *h*
sickness benefit on the one hand and unemployment benefit, supplementary benefit and
other similar benefits on the other. Just as unemployment benefit and supplementary
benefit are taken into account (see the decisions of this court in *Nabi v British Leyland (UK)
Ltd* [1980] 1 All ER 667, [1980] 1 WLR 529 and *Lincoln v Hayman* [1982] 2 All ER 819,
[1982] 1 WLR 488), so also should statutory sick pay.

We were also referred to a very recent decision of this court in *Dews v National Coal*   *j*
Board [1986] 2 All ER 769, [1987] QB 81. But as Sir John Donaldson MR pointed out (see
[1986] 2 All ER 769 at 772, [1987] QB 81 at 89), the court was there concerned with the
first of the two questions identified by Lord Reid in *Parry v Cleaver* [1969] 1 All ER 555
at 557, [1970] AC 1 at 13, namely what had the plaintiff lost as a result of the accident?

The court was not concerned, as we are, with the second of the two questions. So I need
a not mention it further.

That leaves only a number of Canadian decisions which were put before the court as
persuasive authorities. It would appear that questions similar to the question before us
had been the subject of much litigation in the Supreme Court of Canada and other
Canadian courts. However, the one decision which I need mention in any detail is *Chan
v Butcher and Collins* [1984] 4 WWR 363, a decision of the British Columbia Court of
b Appeal referred to by Judge Harris in his judgment.

In that case the plaintiff was an employee of the Royal Bank of Canada. She was injured
in a motor accident by a third party tortfeasor. It is not clear how long she was away
from work; but it was less than six months. During that time she received from her
employer payments or benefits equal to 100% of her salary under 'a short term disability
program'. She could have recovered those payments by action if the bank had refused to
c pay. The question was whether they should be taken into account. The Court of Appeal,
reversing the judgment of the court below, held that they should not.

There are two strands in the court's reasoning. Firstly, it was said that though the
payments under the programme were measured by the wages payable to the particular
beneficiary, nevertheless the payments were not wages:

d   'They were benefits, promised in addition to wages to protect the employee
           against the risk of short-term unemployment caused by illness or accident.'

The court therefore characterised the benefits as being 'in the nature of insurance benefits
rather than in the nature of wages' (at 369). Secondly, it was said that the question
depended essentially on public policy. Why should the wrongdoer have the benefit of
the protection which the plaintiff had procured for herself 'by way of previous contractual
e arrangements made for her own benefit, not the tortfeasor's' (at 368)?

I shall return later to the question of public policy. As for the other ground of decision,
I am bound to say that I do not find the reasoning very compelling. Though there are
copious references to *Parry v Cleaver*, there is no reference to Lord Reid's view that sick
pay, as distinct from a disability pension, should be taken into account. The court passes
f straight from the statement that the payments received by the plaintiff while she was off
work were not wages to the conclusion that the payments were not in the nature of
wages. But that conclusion seems to beg the question. Moreover, it would appear from
Boarelli v Flannigan (1973) 36 DLR (3d) 4, which was not cited to us but which is referred
to in the judgment, that the Canadian courts may well have taken a different turning
from our courts on the question whether unemployment and welfare benefits should be
g deducted. We do not, of course, have the full facts of the case. Nor have we seen the
short-term disability plan. But I am left with the impression that, with all respect to the
British Columbia Court of Appeal, this court might well have reached a different
conclusion.

I now return briefly to the question whether the payments which the plaintiff has
been receiving, and will continue to receive, can properly be regarded as sick pay. I have
h already expressed a provisional view that they can and should be so regarded. Is there
anything in the cases to which I have referred which would persuade us to take the
opposite view? In *Parry v Cleaver* [1969] 1 All ER 555 at 560, [1970] AC 1 at 16 Lord
Reid refers to holiday pay and sick pay as being, like wages, a reward for contemporaneous
work, as distinct from the fruit of past work. I can see an argument that, once a plaintiff
has left the service of his employers, then any further payments, under whatever name
j the payments are made, cease to be in the nature of wages, and take on the nature of a
pension. But that is not this case. The plaintiff has remained throughout in the
employment of the defendants, and we are asked to approach the assessment of damages
on the basis that he will continue in the employment of the defendants, subject only to
the usual uncertainties of life which are covered by the *Smith v Manchester* element in the

award (see *Smith v Manchester Corp* (1974) 17 KIR 1). It is true that sickness is something
from which one hopes to recover. So is short-term disability. But there is no logical *a*
distinction between sickness and short-term disability on the one hand and long-term
disability on the other, so long as the employee remains in the service of the same
employer. The payments, whether for short-term or long-term disability, are, in the
words of Lord Pearce, a substitute for the capacity to earn. They are not, of course, wages
as such. But they are in my opinion in the nature of wages. I shall therefore hold that
they should be taken into account in reduction of damages. *b*

I come last to the question of public policy. There is much high authority for the view
that the question whether a receipt of a particular kind is deductible or not depends, in
the last resort, on 'justice, reasonableness and public policy' (see *Parry v Cleaver* [1969] 1
All ER 555 at 557), [1970] AC 1 at 13 per Lord Reid). Thus one of the grounds on which
Lord Reid based his decision in *Parry v Cleaver* was that Parliament had by s 2(1) of the
Fatal Accidents Act 1959 provided that pensions should be left out of account in actions *c*
under the Fatal Accidents Acts. Accordingly public policy required that they should also
be left out of account in common law actions. Similarly, Lord Denning MR said in
Cunningham v Harrison [1973] 3 All ER 463 at 468, [1973] QB 942 at 950–951:

'I can find no sound principle for saying what matters should or should not be
taken into account in reduction of damages. As each new point comes up, it is *d*
decided by the courts according to what is considered the best policy to adopt; and
thenceforward it governs subsequent cases.'

Arguments based on public policy tend to be somewhat imprecise, even, at times,
emotive. The present case was no exception. Why, says counsel for the plaintiff, should
third party tortfeasors reap the benefit of a scheme which was intended, not for their
benefit, but for the benefit of the employee? Why should a wrongdoer pay less than he *e*
would otherwise pay, or even nothing at all, when it is his victim who has earned the
benefit by his labour? I do not find such arguments on either side of much assistance.
But there is one consideration of public policy which is worth mentioning. If an
employee is injured in the course of his employment and his employers make him an
immediate ex gratia payment, as any good employer might, I see no reason why such a *f*
payment should not be taken into account in reduction of any damages for which the
employer may ultimately be held liable. Employers should be encouraged to make ex
gratia payments in such circumstances. If so, then public policy would seem to require
that such payments be brought into account.

It could, of course, be said that an ex gratia payment is like a sum coming to the
plaintiff by way of benevolence, and should therefore be disregarded. This is so where it *g*
is a third party who is ultimately held liable (see *Cunningham v Harrison* [1973] 3 All ER
463, [1973] QB 942). But there must surely be an exception to that general rule where
the ex gratia payment comes from the tortfeasor himself. So, if it is right that an ex gratia
payment by the employer should be brought into account where the employer is the
tortfeasor, why should it make any difference that the payment is one which he has
contracted to make in advance? So if counsel for the defendants is wrong in his main *h*
argument, that payments under the scheme are in the nature of wages and should be
brought into account on that score, there would be much to be said for his alternative
argument that such payments should in any event be brought into account on the
grounds of 'justice, reasonableness and public policy'. But it is unnecessary to decide the
case on that ground, since, on the facts of the present case, counsel for the defendants is
entitled to succeed on his first ground. *j*

At the outset, I mentioned that substantially the entire argument was taken up with
damages for loss of earnings. But there was one other very small point. The judge
awarded £1,100 special damages for prescription charges and replacement gloves for the
plaintiff's prosthesis. It would appear that in arriving at that figure he must have made

an arithmetical error. Possibly the judge took a multiplier of 30, being the number of
a years from the date of trial until the plaintiff's retirement, instead of a multiplier of 14.
But, whatever he did, it is clear that the figure under this head should not have exceeded
£576 and the total figure for special damages should have been £2,216 instead of £2,740.
The result of this appeal will be a substantial reduction in the plaintiff's damages.
Naturally we feel sympathy with the plaintiff, who has suffered a very severe injury. But,
if we left the judgment below as it stands, we are satisfied that the plaintiff would have
b been over-compensated.

The appeal will therefore be allowed, and the judgment below varied by substituting
£899 for pre-trial loss of earnings, £23,663 for loss of future earnings and £2,216 for
special damages.

c **RALPH GIBSON LJ.** I agree.

KERR LJ. I agree that this appeal should be allowed for the reasons stated in the
judgment of Lloyd LJ, which for my part I would summarise as follows.

First, since the plaintiff's claim is for loss of wages, earnings or salary, whatever term
d one uses, due to his injury, it is important to note that on the facts of this case the
payments of benefit which he received were designed precisely to compensate him for
the loss or diminution in his wages, earnings or salary which he sustained due to his
injury. The payments in question were accordingly of the same nature as those which he
claims to have lost, and therefore satisfy that aspect of the tests laid down by Lord Reid
in *Parry v Cleaver* [1969] 1 All ER 555, [1970] AC 1.

e Second, there is no evidence that the plaintiff's contractual right to these benefits had
been 'paid for', directly *or indirectly*, by the plaintiff by money, services or some detriment,
such as by foregoing some other advantage which he would have had but for his
contractual right to these payments. In particular, there was no evidence that the
plaintiff's wages would have been higher if the defendants had not operated this scheme
f for the benefit of their employees, of which the entire cost was borne by the defendants.
With all respect, as pointed out by Lloyd LJ, there is nothing which supports this
conclusion; indeed, the evidence is the other way.

In these circumstances the plaintiff has (a) already been compensated in relation to his
claim to the extent of the benefits received by him and (b) cannot show that he has in
some way already 'paid for' or 'bought' these benefits, as, for instance, by insurance, so
g that it would be wrong, as a matter of fairness, to require him to give credit for them.

I would stress point (b) and emphatically reserve my opinion in the event that the
plaintiff could have shown, to use the judge's phrase, that the benefits formed part of his
'wage structure', in the sense that he would have got more pay if his contract had not
provided for these benefits. If that had been the position, then I can see no difference in
principle between private sickness and accident insurance paid for out of the plaintiff's
h pocket on the one hand and benefits of this kind paid for by the plaintiff in some indirect
manner on the other hand, eg by being part of his 'wage structure' on the ground that
they involved the reduction of other advantages, or introduced other detriments, as the
'price' of these benefits.

Finally in this connection, I would not, as at present advised, draw any distinction in
relation to point (b) between cases where the tortfeasor is a third party and where it is the
j plaintiff's employer. If the plaintiff has been injured by the negligence of either, then it
seems to me that neither can claim credit for any alleviating benefit for which the
plaintiff has already 'paid', directly or indirectly. In relation to the employer/defendant,
it would require some express or implied term of the plaintiff's contract of employment,
or of his contractual rights to benefit, to have this effect, before the employer could claim

to be in a different position from a third party tortfeasor. But this would be extremely
unusual and in any event almost certainly void under s 3 of the Unfair Contract Terms   *a*
Act 1977.

Appeal allowed. Leave to appeal to the House of Lords refused.

16 December. The Appeal Committee of the House of Lords gave leave to appeal.
                                                                                          b
Solicitors: *William A Merrick & Co*, Maidstone (for the defendants); *Hubbard Wilton & Co*,
Reading (for the plaintiff).

                                                    Wendy Shockett   Barrister.

Hemens (Valuation Officer) v Whitsbury   *c*
Farm and Stud Ltd
and other appeals

COURT OF APPEAL, CIVIL DIVISION   *d*
LAWTON, LLOYD AND BALCOMBE LJJ
14, 15, 16 OCTOBER, 5 NOVEMBER 1986

*Rates – Exemption – Buildings occupied together with agricultural land and used solely in
connection with agricultural operations thereon – Thoroughbred racehorse stud – Thoroughbred
stud consisting of stud buildings and grazing paddocks – Whether grazing of thoroughbred horses*   *e*
*an 'agricultural operation' – Whether stud buildings used 'in connection with' agricultural
operation – Whether stud buildings used 'solely' in connection with agricultural operation –
General Rate Act 1967, s 26(3)(4)(a).*

Rates – Exemption – Agricultural buildings – Buildings used for the keeping and breeding of   *f*
*livestock – Livestock – Thoroughbred racehorses – Whether thoroughbred horses 'livestock' –
Rating Act 1971, ss 1(3), 2(1)(a).*

The appellants were the owners and occupiers of four separate hereditaments used as
studs for breeding thoroughbred racehorses. Each stud consisted of the stud buildings,
and paddocks which constituted 'agricultural land' within s 26(3)[d] of the General Rate   *g*
Act 1967 because they were used as pasture for the grazing of horses. Both the stud
buildings and the adjoining paddocks were essential for the running of the studs. The
buildings were used to house stallions, mares and foals and for breeding and foaling
while the paddocks were used for exercise and to enable the mares to feed on grass during
and after foaling. The appellants claimed exemption from rating in respect of the stud
buildings, submitting that they were 'agricultural buildings' because (i) they were   *h*
buildings 'used solely in connection with agricultural operations thereon', within
s 26(4)(a)[b] of the 1967 Act, since they were used solely in connection with the grazing of
horses in the paddocks, and (ii) they were buildings 'used for the keeping or breeding of
livestock', within s 2(1)(a)[c] of the Rating Act 1971. The local valuation court upheld the
appellants' claim but the Lands Tribunal reversed that decision, holding that thoroughbred
horses were not 'livestock' within the meaning of s 1(3)[d] of the 1971 Act and therefore   *j*
the buildings were not used for the keeping and breeding of 'livestock' within s 2(1)(a) of

---

a   Section 26(3), so far as material, provides: 'In this section the expression "agricultural land"—(*a*)
      means any land used as arable meadow or pasture ground only . . .'
b   Section 26(4), so far as material, is set out at p 433 *j*, post
c   Section 2(1), so far as material, is set out at p 434 *j*, post
d   Section 1(3), so far as material, is set out at p 449 *e*, post

that Act and also were not 'agricultural buildings' within s 26(4)(a) of the 1967 Act. The
a appellants appealed.

Held – The appeal would be dismissed for the following reasons—
(1) The appellants' stud buildings did not qualify for rating exemption as 'agricultural
buildings' for the purposes of s 26(4)(a) of the 1967 Act because they were not occupied
together with land on which 'agricultural operations' were carried out, since even though
b the appellants' paddocks were 'agricultural land' the purpose for which they used the
paddocks was not agricultural because the grazing of thoroughbred horses on paddocks
in the course of breeding and rearing was not an 'agricultural operation' (see p437 d to f,
p 440 h to p 441 c, p 443 h, p 445 a b d to f h and p 448 b c, post); Lord Glanely v Wightman
[1933] AC 618 distinguished.
(2) However, if the grazing of thoroughbred stock was an 'agricultural operation' for
c the purposes of s 26(4)(a) of the 1967 Act, then (Lawton LJ dissenting) although the stud
buildings were used 'in connection with' that agricultural operation because the use of
the buildings was complementary to the use of the paddocks, nevertheless (Lloyd LJ
dissenting) the stud buildings were not used 'solely' in connection with the grazing of
the paddocks, since the buildings were used for a number of purposes connected with
breeding, and grazing was merely one such purpose (see p 437 h, p 442 d h, p 448 f g j to
d p 449 c, post).
(3) The appellants' stud buildings did not qualify for rating exemption on the ground
that they were 'used for the keeping or breeding of livestock' within s 2(1)(a) of the 1971
Act, because thoroughbred horses were not 'livestock' as defined by s 1(3), since they did
not contribute to human subsistence and were not intended for use in the farming of
land (see p 437 a to c, p 443 h, p 449 f g j to p 450 a e, post); Belmont Farm Ltd v Minister of
e Housing and Local Government (1962) 13 P & CR 417 followed.

Notes
For exemptions of agricultural land and buildings from rating and the meaning of
agricultural buildings, see 39 Halsbury's Laws (4th edn) paras 62–64.
f   For the General Rate Act 1967, s 26, see 27 Halsbury's Statutes (3rd edn) 106.
For the Rating Act 1971, ss 1, 2, see 41 ibid 1169, 1170.

Cases referred to in judgments
Belmont Farm Ltd v Minister of Housing and Local Government (1962) 13 P & CR 417, DC.
Cresswell (Valuation Officer) v BOC Ltd [1980] 3 All ER 443, [1980] 1 WLR 1556, CA.
g *Crowe (Valuation Officer) v Lloyds British Testing Co Ltd* [1960] 1 All ER 411, [1960] 1 QB
592.
Derby (Earl) v Newmarket Area Assessment Committee (1930) 13 R & IT 59.
Eastwood (W & J B) Ltd v Herrod (Valuation Officer) [1970] 1 All ER 774, [1971] AC 160,
[1970] 2 WLR 775, HL.
Evans v Bailey (Valuation Officer) (1981) 260 EG 611, Lands Tribunal.
h *Forth Stud Ltd v East Lothian Assessor* [1969] RA 35, Lands Valuation Appeal Court,
Scotland.
Gilmore (Valuation Officer) v Baker-Carr [1962] 3 All ER 230, [1962] 1 WLR 1165, CA.
Glanely (Lord) v Wightman [1933] AC 618, HL.
Hardie v West Lothian Assessor 1940 SC 329.
Inland Revenue v Ardross Estates Co 1930 SC 487.
j *Kidson (Inspector of Taxes) v Macdonald* [1974] 1 All ER 849, [1974] Ch 339, [1974] 2 WLR
566.
Malcolm v Lockhart [1919] AC 463, HL.
McClinton v McFall (1974) 232 EG 707, CA.
Minister of Agriculture, Fisheries and Food v Appleton [1969] 3 All ER 1051, [1970] 1 QB
221, [1969] 3 WLR 755, DC.
Normanton (Earl) v Giles [1980] 1 All ER 106, [1980] 1 WLR 28, HL.

Peterborough Royal Foxhound Show Society v IRC [1936] 1 All ER 813, [1936] 2 KB 497.
Sargaison (Inspector of Taxes) v Roberts [1969] 3 All ER 1072, [1969] 1 WLR 951.   *a*

Cases also cited
Corser (Valuation Officer) v Gloucestershire Marketing Society Ltd [1981] RA 83, CA.
Maitland (William) & Sons v Aberdeenshire Assessor [1969] RA 289, Lands Valuation Appeal
   Court, Scotland.
Midlothian Assessor v Polton Pig Farm Ltd [1969] RA 96, Lands Valuation Appeal Court,   *b*
   Scotland.
Moon v London County Council, Potteries Electric Traction Co Ltd v Bailey [1931] AC 151, HL.
Parker-Jervis v Lane (Valuation Officer) [1973] RA 202, Lands Tribunal.
Rutherford v Maurer [1962] 1 QB 16, CA.
*Sykes v Secretary of State for the Environment, South Oxfordshire DC v Secretary of State for the
   Environment* (1980) 42 P & CR 19, DC.   *c*

Consolidated appeal
Whitsbury Farm and Stud Ltd appealed by way of case stated against the decision of the
Lands Tribunal (President V G Wellings QC) dated 28 November 1984 allowing
consolidated appeals by the valuation officer, Michael Arthur Hemens, from the decision
of the local valuation court for Hampshire South and Isle of Wight given on 8 February   *d*
1983 whereby the local valuation court determined that four groups of stud buildings
and premises at Whitsbury, Fordingbridge, Hampshire, all occupied by the appellants
for the purpose of breeding thoroughbred racehorses, were exempt from rating as being
agricultural buildings within the meaning of s 26(4) of the General Rate Act 1967. The
Lands Tribunal ordered that the hereditaments the subject of the appeals should be
entered in the valuation list with the description, gross values and rateable values   *e*
respectively set forth in the valuation officer's proposals relating thereto dated 25 March
1982. The facts are set out in the judgment of Lawton LJ.

William Glover QC and *Alun Alesbury* for the appellants.
Alan Fletcher QC and *Nicholas Huskinson* for the valuation officer.   *f*

Cur adv vult

5 November. The following judgments were delivered.

LAWTON LJ. This is an appeal by Whitsbury Farm and Stud Ltd, who are the owners   *g*
of a stud for the breeding of thoroughbred racing stock, against a refusal by the Lands
Tribunal to declare divers buildings on their land exempt from rating. The appeal raises
issues which have been discussed and litigated since at least 1930 and which are of interest
to all who are engaged in breeding thoroughbred racing stock.

The facts   *h*
   The facts set out in the case stated by the Lands Tribunal can be stated shortly. The
appellants occupy at Whitsbury in Hampshire four separate stud hereditaments. Each
stud lies within, or is attached to, land which is agricultural land within the meaning of
s 26(3) of the General Rate Act 1967. At all material times the stud buildings were in
excellent condition and were essential for accommodating and breeding thoroughbred
racing stock. The covering of mares by the stallions was usually accomplished in a   *j*
covering yard; but sometimes it took place outside in the adjoining paddocks. The
stallions were owned by a syndicate of 40 shareholders. The appellants were shareholders
in this syndicate. The syndicate made contracts with those owners who brought mares
to the stallions to be covered. The income from the service fees went to such of the
shareholders as sold the breeding rights. The appellants were paid by the syndicate the

cost of keeping the stallions. The mares which were covered were either the appellants'
a own property or visiting mares. Visiting mares were kept at the stud until such time,
usually 60 days, as it took to discover whether they were in foal. Some of the appellants'
mares were sent to other studs to be covered. Because of the Jockey Club's rules for
deciding the age of racehorses, covering took place between 15 February and 15 July each
year. Nearly all the mares produced their foals at night in the foaling boxes but a few did
so in the paddocks in daylight. All the mares and stallions had access to paddocks and,
b save in frosty weather, the mares spent most of each day in them. Paddocks were essential
for the running of the appellants' stud. They afforded space for exercise; and for mares
and foals the grass in them provided during the growing season, that is from March until
high summer, nourishment of a kind which mares required for providing milk for their
foals and bringing them into season and foals for growth. The paddocks were well looked
after because producing good quality grass was important for breeding. From time to
c time, sheep and cattle were put into the paddocks, the object of doing so being to keep
the grass down and to stop seeding. The appellants' stud was run in the way in which
studs are normally run. Lord Wright's description in *Lord Glanely v Wightman* [1933] AC
618 at 634–635 of how Lord Glanely's stud was run is much the same as that in the case
stated in this case. No more detail is necessary for providing the factual background to
d this appeal.

The issues

Broadly stated, this court has to ask itself this question: for rating purposes, should
breeding thoroughbred racing stock on premises with agricultural land attached or
adjoining be equated with the breeding of cattle and sheep on agricultural land? If it
should be, those who run studs should have the benefit of the same exemptions from
e rating as the occupiers of agricultural land enjoy. This broad question, however, has been
complicated by the statutory language in which Parliament has given the occupiers of
agricultural land their exemptions.

The legislative history

f Before 1896 farmers were rated just like other occupiers of land. The Agriculture
Rates Act 1896 gave for a period of five years a 50% exemption from rates to the occupiers
of 'agricultural land' which was defined in s 9 as follows:

g 'The expression "agricultural land" means any land used as arable, meadow, or
pasture ground only, cottage gardens exceeding one quarter of an acre, market
gardens, nursery grounds, orchards or allotments, but does not include land occupied
together with a house as a park, gardens, other than as aforesaid, pleasure-grounds,
or any land kept or preserved mainly or exclusively for purposes of sport or
recreation, or land used as a racecourse.'

Thereafter, other Acts extended the period and increased the percentage of the exemption.
The Local Government Act 1929 derated agricultural land fully. The General Rate Act
h 1967 consolidated various enactments relating to rating and valuation and by s 26
continued the policy of the earlier statutes of derating 'agricultural land' and 'agricultural
buildings'. Agricultural land was defined in the 1967 Act in substantially the same terms
as in the 1896 Act: see s 26(3). Such differences as there are have no relevance to this
appeal. The relevant part of the definition of 'agricultural buildings' in s 26(4) was as
follows:

j 'In this section, the expression "agricultural buildings"—(*a*) means buildings
(other than dwellings) occupied together with agricultural land or being or forming
part of a market garden, and in either case used solely in connection with agricultural
operations thereon . . .'

Farmers in Scotland were given the same kind of exemption from rating as those in

England and Wales; but, as the rating system there was different, as was the legal
terminology for describing interests in land, different wording had to be used. The first *a*
Scottish provision granting partial relief from rates was contained in the Agricultural
Rates, Congested Districts, and Burgh Land Tax Relief (Scotland) Act 1896. A relevant
modern provision was in s 7 of the Valuation and Rating (Scotland) Act 1956. Subsection
(2) was as follows:

> '... "agricultural lands and heritages" means any lands and heritages used for *b*
> agricultural or pastoral purposes only or as woodlands, market gardens, orchards,
> allotments or allotment gardens and any lands exceeding one quarter of an acre used
> for the purpose of poultry farming, but does not include any buildings thereon
> other than agricultural buildings, or any garden, yard, garage, outhouse or pertinent
> belonging to and occupied along with a dwelling-house, or any land kept or
> preserved mainly or exclusively for sporting purposes;
> "agricultural buildings" means buildings (other than dwelling-houses) occupied *c*
> together with agricultural lands and heritages, or being or forming part of a market
> garden, and in either case used solely in connection with agricultural operations
> thereon ...'

Since 1945, regulatory statutes have been passed which affect agricultural land, which
in the interests of precision and clarity has been defined. One such Act was the Town and *d*
Country Planning Act 1947. By s 12(2) it provided as follows:

> '... Provided that the following operations or uses of land shall not be deemed
> ... to involve development of the land ... (e) the use of any land for the purposes
> of agriculture ...'

'Agriculture' was defined in s 119(1): *e*

> 'In this Act ... "agriculture" includes ... dairy farming, the breeding and keeping
> of livestock (including any creature kept for the production of food, wool, skins or
> fur, or for the purpose of its use in the farming of land) ...'

The 1947 Act dealt with a subject matter different from rating; but it was concerned, *f*
just as the General Rate Act 1967 is, with the consequences which follow from carrying
on specified activities on land. It follows, in my judgment, that decisions on the
construction of s 7(2) of the 1956 Act and s 119(1) of the 1947 Act provide some, but not
conclusive, help in the construction of s 26(3) and (4) of the 1967 Act. I conclude the
legislative history relating to the derating of agricultural land and agricultural buildings
with the Rating Act 1971, which was, according to its long title, *g*

> 'An Act to extend the provisions relating to the exemption from rating of land
> and buildings used in connection with agriculture.'

This Act was passed following the decision in *W & J B Eastwood Ltd v Herrod (Valuation
Officer)* [1970] 1 All ER 774, [1971] AC 160. The House of Lords had adjudged that
broiler houses on a farm were not exempt from rating because they were not 'agricultural *h*
buildings' as defined by s 2(2) of the Rating and Valuation (Apportionment) Act 1928
which was the statute in force when the dispute arose, but which was superseded by
s 26(4) of the 1967 Act. The relevant part of the 1971 Act is in s 2 and is as follows:

> '(1) Subject to subsections (2) to (4) of this section, each of the following is an
> agricultural building by virtue of this section—(a) any building used for the keeping *j*
> or breeding of livestock ...
> (2) A building used as mentioned in subsection (1)(a) of this section is not an
> agricultural building by virtue of this section unless either—(a) it is solely so used;
> or (b) it is occupied together with agricultural land (as defined in the principal
> section) and used also in connection with agricultural operations on that land, and

a that other use together with the use mentioned in subsection (1)(a) of this section is its sole use.'

The English cases

Shortly after the Local Government Act 1929 derated agricultural land and agricultural buildings, seven occupiers of studs around Newmarket appealed to West Suffolk quarter sessions against the refusal of the Newmarket area rating assessment committee to regard them as exempt from rating on the ground that they were not occupying agricultural
b buildings within the meaning of s 2(2) of the 1928 Act. The appeals failed, the court finding that 'in the circumstances of this case, the breeding of livestock is not an agricultural operation': see *Earl of Derby v Newmarket Area Assessment Committee* (1930) 13 R & IT 59 at 60. We were told by counsel that quarter sessions in other parts of England followed this decision.

c Then came *Lord Glanely*'s case. It was not concerned with rating. The issue was whether the fees which Lord Glanely had derived in respect of a stallion he kept at stud should be assessed to income tax under Sch D of the Income Tax Act 1918, notwithstanding the fact that he had already been assessed under Sch B in respect of the occupation of land as occupied in part for husbandry purposes and in part for stud and racing purposes. The House of Lords adjudged that he should not be further assessed under Sch D because the
d fees were profits in respect of the occupation of land and were chargeable to income tax under Sch B. The decision turned on the construction of the Income Tax Acts and the effect of a number of cases on the issue in dispute (see [1933] AC 618 at 636–638 per Lord Wright). In the course of his speech Lord Wright said ([1933] AC 618 at 640):

e 'On these grounds I think that the service of the stallion is appurtenant to the soil and a profit of the occupation in every case, so that in this regard it is immaterial whether the service is to the appellant's own mares or whether it is sold to strangers; in the latter case the service is sold from the land and as a product of the land, just as much as bullocks, potatoes, fruit or eggs are sold from the land. Without the appellant's stud farm or some other such stud farm the stallions could not live or exercise their generating functions. The value of these functions is inseparably
f connected with the occupation of land.'

Rating authorities in England concluded that *Lord Glanely v Wightman* entitled the occupiers of stud farms of a similar kind to his to claim exemption from rating. The reasoning behind granting exemption must have been that, since the generative powers of stallions were, in Lord Wright's words, 'a product of the land', any land on which they grazed was agricultural land and any building in which they were stabled was an
g agricultural building. This reasoning would have made an enclosure in a zoo which accommodated any grazing animals agricultural land. From about 1933 until 1980 the occupiers of studs in England were not rated. Occupiers in Scotland were not so fortunate.

The Scottish cases

In *Forth Stud Ltd v East Lothian Assessor* [1969] RA 35 the Lands Valuation Appeal Court
h considered a number of cases which had been decided under s 9(11) of the Rating and Valuation (Apportionment) Act 1928, the wording of which had been similar to s 7(2) of the Valuation and Rating (Scotland) Act 1956. The court also considered the relevant English cases, including *Lord Glanely v Wightman*. The Forth Stud was run in much the same way as, but on a smaller scale than, the appellants' stud. The adjoining land was 25 acres in extent and was used for grazing, exercising and taking a crop of hay. In an earlier
j Scottish case, *Inland Revenue v Ardross Estates Co* 1930 SC 487 at 490, which was concerned with whether a silver fox farm was exempted from rating as agricultural land, Lord Sands had said:

'The use extends only to the breeding of such animals as are associated with an ordinary farm—horses, cattle, sheep, goats, pigs, and poultry.'

In yet another Scottish case, *Hardie v West Lothian Assessor* 1940 SC 329 at 334, Lord
Robertson had said:

a

> '... as I understand Lord Hunter's opinion, he expressed the view that the
> breeding of live stock might be an agricultural purpose although there was no
> pasturage of stock on the land ... In any event I am of the opinion that the rearing
> of stock is, or may be, an agricultural purpose, inferring an agricultural use of land
> within the meaning of the Act of 1928, without regard to the question whether the
> stock is reared to a material extent upon the crops raised on the land. But if the
> rearing of stock is to be regarded as in itself an agricultural purpose, the stock reared
> must be such as produces or directly contributes to produce "the means of human
> subsistence". I think that this is the ratio of the judgment in *Inland Revenue* v.
> *Ardross Estates Co.*'

b

Lord Fraser, in *Forth Stud Ltd v East Lothian Assessor*, adjudged that racehorses are not
animals associated with an ordinary farm and they did not produce or directly contribute
to produce the means of human subsistence. Lord Avonside referred to what Lord
Robertson had said in *Hardie v West Lothian Assessor* and went on as follows ([1969] RA
35 at 46):

c

> 'Further, the rearing of stock as an agricultural or pastoral operation must, on any
> proper view of the words, be rearing of stock which produces or contributes to
> produce the means of human subsistence. Animals reared for sport or entertainment
> or for their decorative qualities cannot, in my view, be regarded as being reared in
> the course of the activity of farming, which in its broad sense covers tillage and
> pasturing. The whole purpose of farming was and is, from the earliest times until
> now, to produce the means of human subsistence and there can be no doubt that
> that is why agricultural land, under legislation, enjoys the substantial financial
> privilege of being omitted from the valuation roll.'

d

e

The court adjudged that the Forth Stud was not entitled to exemption from rating as
agricultural land and heritages.

I find this case a most persuasive authority as to the overall legislative intention of
s 26(3) and (4) of the General Rate Act 1967. The question, however, remains whether
Parliament, by the words used in that Act and in the 1971 Act, intended either to qualify
or extend the overall intention. In *Evans v Bailey (Valuation Officer)* (1981) 260 EG 611,
which was concerned with a stud for breeding hunters, the Lands Tribunal treated *Forth
Stud Ltd v East Lothian Assessor* as a persuasive authority. That stud was not given
exemption from rating.

f

The construction of the 1967 and 1971 Acts

g

Since the intention of the 1971 Act was, inter alia, to extend the meaning of the words
'agricultural building', it is convenient to consider whether the buildings at the stud
come within the extended definition. The appellants, on the facts of this case, had to
prove first that the buildings were used for the keeping or breeding of livestock, as
defined in s 1(3), and, second that that use came within either para (*a*) or (*b*) of sub-s (2).

h

As I have already said, I have no doubt that the overall intention of Parliament in
providing for the derating of agricultural land and agricultural buildings was to help
farmers. But, since rating is concerned with the occupation of land, Parliament had to
define what kind of occupied land or buildings should be exempt from rating. This it
did in s 26(3) and (4) of the 1967 Act and ss 1 to 4 of the 1971 Act. The definitions are
more extensive than what in the ordinary usage of English would be meant by 'farm
land' or 'farm buildings'; but, with the exception of the inclusion of use for 'a plantation
or a wood or for the growth of saleable underwood', all the other uses relate to the
production of products directly connected with human subsistence. The words of
exclusion at the end of sub-s (3) strengthen this construction. Silviculture as a source of
fuel and building materials contributes indirectly, if not directly, to human subsistence.

j

In my judgment, the definition of 'agricultural land' in s 26(3) was intended to cover land used for purposes contributing to human subsistence. Since in both s 26(4) of the 1967 Act and s 2 of the 1971 Act the adjective 'agricultural' qualifies 'building' as well as land, it follows that a building to be exempt from rating must be one which is used for a purpose contributing to human subsistence and that 'livestock' in s 2(1)(a) means mammals or birds which also do so. I cannot accept the argument of counsel for the appellants that, because the statutory definition in s 1(3) of the 1971 Act starts with the words 'In this part of this Act "livestock" includes . . .', mammals such as thoroughbred racing stock, which contribute nothing to human subsistence, should come within the ambit of an exempting provision which is concerned with land used for purposes which do so contribute. If, as counsel for the valuation officer pointed out, the word 'livestock' in the 1971 Act included all mammals, a building in which zebras or giraffes were kept would be an agricultural building. In my judgment, the appellants' buildings at Whitsbury are not used for the keeping or breeding of livestock within the meaning of s 2(1)(a) of the 1971 Act. In *Belmont Farm Ltd v Minister of Housing and Local Government* (1962) 13 P & CR 417, which was a planning case, Lord Parker CJ construed a provision in the Town and Country Planning Act 1947, s 119(1), defining 'livestock' in an agricultural context, in the same sense as I have done.

The next question is whether the pasturing of racing stock in paddocks is an agricultural operation within s 26(4)(a) of the 1967 Act. As I understood the submission of counsel for the appellants, it was as follows. The valuation officer admitted that the paddocks were agricultural land. This was because horses were grazed in them. Putting horses out to graze so as to increase their breeding potential was an agricultural operation and the buildings were used in connection with it. All this brought the buildings within the ambit of s 26(4) of the 1967 Act. In my judgment, it does not. I accept the submission of counsel for the appellants that s 26(3) is concerned with the use of land, not the purpose for which it is used. The fact that the land is used in connection with the breeding of racing stock does not, as counsel for the valuation officer accepted, disqualify it from being 'agricultural land'. But, in order to qualify for exemption from rating, it is not enough that the buildings should be occupied together with agricultural land. They must be used solely in connection with agricultural operations thereon. The use of the word 'operation' is significant. It connotes action for a purpose. In this case, for what purpose? The answer is, the breeding of racing stock. This, in my judgment, in the context of the 1967 Act, is not an agricultural purpose and therefore grazing in connection with breeding is not an agricultural operation. This finding is fatal to the appellants' case.

I should, however, deal shortly with the other two issues in this appeal, namely if the grazing, as part of the breeding activities, was an agricultural operation on the land, were the buildings used in connection therewith? If yes, were they used solely in connection therewith? In what was an otherwise admirably clear and concisely stated case, the learned member of the Lands Tribunal did not ask himself the right question when considering whether the buildings were used in connection with the grazing for breeding purposes. He asked himself whether the grazing and the buildings, being, as he found, ancillary to each other, were ancillary to the entire stud operation. I am not satisfied that, in the ordinary use of English, it can be said that the buildings were used in connection with the grazing. The grazing was used in connection with the buildings. Nor am I satisfied that the buildings were used *solely* in connection with the grazing. The buildings were used for a number of purposes connected with breeding. Grazing was but one of them.

I would dismiss the appeal.

LLOYD LJ. In this case we have to determine whether certain buildings are agricultural buildings within the definition contained in s 26(4) of the General Rate Act 1967, as extended by s 1(1)(a) of the Rating Act 1971.

The outcome turns on two short questions of construction: first, whether the buildings, which were admittedly occupied together with agricultural land, were being used 'solely in connection with agricultural operations' on that land so as to bring the case within s 26(4) of the former Act; and, second, whether, if not, horses bred for riding, hunting or racing are 'livestock' so as to bring the case within s 2(1)(a) of the latter Act.

Before attempting to answer these questions, there are three preliminary observations worth making.

In the first place, I doubt if we get much help in a case such as the present by adopting what is now called a purposive approach. When the legislative purpose is clear, then it is always legitimate, and often very helpful, to have that purpose in mind when approaching questions of construction. But, where the legislative purpose is not so clear, it may be dangerous to speculate. In the present case we are concerned with the derating of agricultural land and buildings. The legislative history goes back nearly a hundred years. Partial relief was introduced by the Agricultural Rates Act 1896. Full relief was introduced by the Local Government Act 1929. The 1929 Act also introduced partial relief for industrial hereditaments. It may be that the legislative purpose of Parliament in derating agricultural land and buildings was to encourage the growing of food or the means of human subsistence. But it is not obvious that Parliament may not have had a wider purpose in mind, as is perhaps shown by the inclusion of woodland in the definition of agricultural land.

Second, I doubt if one gets much help by asking what would ordinarily be understood by an agricultural building, still less by asking what sort of building one would expect to find on an ordinary farm. On two occasions in recent years the courts have taken a narrow view of the exempting provisions. On both occasions Parliament has taken prompt action to extend the definition. I have in mind the 1971 Act itself, which was passed in the wake of *W & J B Eastwood Ltd v Herrod (Valuation Officer)* [1970] 1 All ER 774, [1971] AC 160. Broiler houses, which had been held not to fall within s 26 of the 1967 Act on the ground that they could not be said to have been used solely in connection with agricultural operations on agricultural land, are now included in the extended definition. So also are buildings used solely in connection with the keeping of bees. One would not perhaps normally think of such buildings as being agricultural buildings; nor would one expect to find such buildings on an ordinary farm. But they are now specifically included.

The second occasion on which Parliament has extended the definition in recent years followed a decision of this court in *Cresswell (Valuation Officer) v BOC Ltd* [1980] 3 All ER 443, [1980] 1 WLR 1556. In that case this court held that a fish farm was not exempt, on the ground that fish were not livestock within the 1971 Act. Within a year Parliament had, by the Local Government Planning and Land Act 1980, s 31, introduced a new s 26A in the General Rate Act 1967 so as to exempt land and buildings used solely for or in connection with fish farming.

So it would, I think, be dangerous in this case to ask what Parliament must have intended to include or exclude. Our task is to take the words that Parliament has actually used, to note what is in fact included and excluded, and then apply the result to this particular case.

The third general consideration is of a different kind. In 1933 the House of Lords decided *Lord Glanely v Wightman* [1933] AC 618. Although that case was concerned with the liability to income tax, nevertheless, the reasoning and, in particular, the speech of Lord Wright, was treated as being applicable in the rating field. Thereafter, for 50 years, it was accepted that stud farms were exempt. Stud buildings were not in fact rated. The courts are always reluctant to disturb such a long continued practice. Nevertheless, we are bound to do so, if we are persuaded that the practice is based on a misunderstanding of *Lord Glanely v Wightman*. It could not be argued, nor was it argued by counsel for the appellants, that, by consolidating the law in 1967 without reference to stud farms, and by extending the definition of agricultural land and buildings in 1971, and again in

1980, Parliament has, as it were, given its legislative approval to the practice based,
a rightly or wrongly, on the decision of the House of Lords in 1933.

With those preliminary observations, I turn to the language of the 1967 Act. The first
thing to notice is, of course, that 'agricultural operations' are not defined. But one thing
is beyond dispute. 'Agricultural' in the phrase 'agricultural operations' must have the
same meaning as it has in the phrase 'agricultural land'. So I would agree with counsel
for the appellants that the approach must be to ask: first, whether the land is agricultural
b land; second, what are the agricultural operations on that land; and, third, whether the
buildings which are occupied together with the land are used solely in connection with
those agricultural operations. If authority is needed for that approach it is to be found in
the speech of Lord Morris in *W & J B Eastwood Ltd v Herrod (Valuation Officer)* [1970] 1
All ER 774 at 782, [1971] AC 160 at 173. I do not myself regard it as helpful to split up
the third question into two sub-questions, ie were the buildings used in connection with
c agricultural operations on the land? If so, were they used *solely* in connection with such
operations? Both sub-questions are best considered together. Failure to do so led the
learned member of the Lands Tribunal to include a passage in the reasons for his decision
which is not altogether easy to understand.

Is the land agricultural land? Counsel for the valuation officer concedes that it is. But
it is necessary to examine the reasons for that concession in a little detail. For counsel for
d the appellants argues that the answer to the first question is crucial in answering the
second and the third.

The definition of agricultural land in s 26(3) of the 1967 Act is both positive and
negative. In the first half, the subsection tells us what agricultural land is, and in the
second half it tells us what it is not. The two halves of the definition are not altogether
easy to fit together. There is no difficulty in the case of land used for a plantation or a
e wood or for the growth of saleable underwood. Such land is agricultural land, unless it is
occupied together with a house as a park, or unless it is kept or preserved 'mainly or
exclusively for the purposes of sport or recreation'. So the occasional use of woodland for
shooting does not prevent it being agricultural land. But what about arable and pasture?
Unlike woodland, arable meadow and pasture are only included in the definition of
agricultural land if the land is used as arable meadow or pasture ground *only*. Does that
f mean that the occasional use of arable for shooting excludes it from the definition? If
woodland is included, in spite of it being used as cover for pheasants reared for sport, it
would seem artificial to exclude a field of kale on that ground. Occasional use of land as a
racecourse prevents it being agricultural land, unless the use is de minimis. But the
exclusion of land used as a racecourse is not qualified by the words 'mainly or exclusively'.
g So I would think that the occasional use of arable meadow or pasture for purposes of
sport or recreation would not prevent it being agricultural land within the definition,
despite the word '*only*'. But occasional use for other purposes would so prevent it.

I now come to the central issue in the case. Counsel for the valuation officer concedes
that the land is agricultural land, because it was used by horses for grazing. But he
submits that the breeding of horses, whether for use as hunters or in racing, is not an
h agricultural operation. When you are deciding whether the land is agricultural land, you
look only, he submits, at the use made of the land. But, when you are deciding whether
the operation is an agricultural operation, you look at the purpose of the occupier.

Counsel for the appellants, on the other hand, submits that there can be no distinction
between the use made of land, and the purpose for which land is used, whether as arable
or woodland, or for poultry farming or a market garden; and any distinction between
j the purposes for which land is used and the operations on that land would be highly
artificial, at any rate on the facts of this case. Since it is conceded that the use of *this* land
for grazing *these* horses made the land agricultural land, then it must follow that that use
is an agricultural operation. Of course, there may be operations on land which are not
agricultural operations. But here the operation in question, namely the grazing of horses
kept for breeding, is the very operation which makes the land agricultural land. It would

indeed be strange, he submits, if the operation which makes the land agricultural land is not itself an agricultural operation.

Throughout the hearing before us, I could see no answer to the argument of counsel for the appellants. It seemed to me that counsel for the valuation officer was in a dilemma. Either the operation carried out on the land which, for brevity, I will call the keeping of brood mares, is an agricultural operation or it is not. If it is, cadit quaestio. If it is not, then the land was not being used as arable meadow or pasture ground *only*, in which case the land is not agricultural land within the definition. But it is conceded that it is. So the operation must be an agricultural operation.

In *Peterborough Royal Foxhound Show Society v IRC* [1936] 1 All ER 813 at 815, [1936] 2 KB 497 at 500 Lawrence J seemed to regard it as self-evident that the breeding of hunters and racehorses takes place 'in the ordinary course of agriculture'. That dictum was quoted, without apparent disapproval, by Lord Wilberforce in *Earl of Normanton v Giles* [1980] 1 All ER 106 at 109–110, [1980] 1 WLR 28 at 32. Similarly, the Court of Appeal in *McClinton v McFall* (1974) 232 EG 707 held that land let for use as a stud farm was an agricultural holding within the meaning of the Agricultural Holdings Act 1948. Stamp LJ said (at 709):

'The activities in relation to the stud farm which I have described, so far as they consist of the grazing of horses, pasturing of cattle and making of hay, are clearly agricultural. So far as they consist of the breaking-in of horses for riding, the little schooling that is done, the showing of horses to customers, and the jumps and jumping on the five-acre field I have mentioned, they are not, in my judgment, inconsistent with the agriculture carried on.'

Moreover, the distinction between the use made of the land, and the purposes of the occupier, a distinction which lies at the heart of the argument of counsel for the valuation officer, is difficult to reconcile with land which is held for the *purposes* of poultry farming being included within the definition of agricultural land in s 26(3)(*a*) of the 1967 Act. It is also difficult to reconcile with the language of s 2 of the 1971 Act. Section 2(1)(*a*) provides that 'agricultural building' shall include any building used for breeding livestock. Section 2(1)(*b*) provides that it shall also include any building used solely in connection with the operations carried on in that building. This suggests that there is no distinction to be drawn between the *use* of the first building and the *operations* carried on in that building. If that is right, why should there be any distinction between the use of the land and operations on the land?

The argument of counsel for the appellants also appeared to be consistent with the approach adopted by the courts in construing other related provisions of the Rating and Valuation (Apportionment) Act 1928, namely those relating to industrial hereditaments. Thus, in *Crowe (Valuation Officer) v Lloyds-British Testing Co Ltd* [1960] 1 All ER 411, [1960] 1 QB 592, a majority of this court held that 'industrial purposes' in s 4(2) of the 1928 Act must mean those purposes which make the premises in question a factory within the meaning ascribed by s 3(2) of the Act. It is hard to believe that Parliament intended to draw a distinction between 'purposes' in the phrase 'industrial purposes' and 'operations' in the phrase 'agricultural operations'.

These are powerful arguments. But, in the end, I have come to the conclusion that they cannot succeed. There is no real dilemma. Parliament must clearly have envisaged that operations which are not agricultural operations might be carried out on land which nevertheless remains agricultural land. Otherwise, there would have been no point in including the reference to 'agricultural operations' in s 26(4)(*a*).

That being so, there are only two possible explanations of the apparent impasse. Either the reference to agricultural operations was intended to exclude, and exclude only, buildings used in connection with sport or recreation. For there is no other use of the land which is consistent with the land remaining agricultural land within s 26(3)(*a*). The alternative explanation is that Parliament did indeed intend to draw a distinction, as *a* counsel for the valuation officer submits, between the use to which land is put and the operations thereon. I do not find either explanation particularly satisfactory. But of the two I prefer the second. In other words, lands may be *used* as pasture land only, and so qualify as agricultural land; but the *operations* carried out on the land, looked at from another point of view, may be non-agricultural operations.

b If that be right, then the question whether the operation carried out on this land was an agricultural operation becomes largely, if not entirely, a question of fact. We cannot say, as a matter of law, that the operation was necessarily an agricultural operation by reason of the concession of counsel for the valuation officer that the land is agricultural land. It follows that I would reject, though not without considerable hesitation, the central submission of counsel for the appellants.

c The learned member of the Lands Tribunal has found, after carefully considering all the evidence, that the operation here was not an agricultural operation. I am not persuaded that there is any material on which we could or should disturb that finding.

Before leaving the second question, I should, however, deal briefly with *Lord Glanely v Wightman* [1933] AC 618, the case on which counsel for the appellants principally relied. The question in that case was whether the appellant, Lord Glanely, was liable to tax under Sch D on the stud fees earned by his stallion, Grand Parade. It was held by the House of Lords, reversing a majority of the Court of Appeal, that he was not so liable.
d There was no distinction to be drawn between the profits earned from the reproductive capacity of the appellant's stallion and the profits earned from the reproductive capacity of the appellant's mares. Since the latter were admittedly profits of the appellant's occupation of the land, and therefore assessable to tax under Sch B and not under Sch D, so also were the former. Counsel for the appellants relied in particular on a paragraph of
e Lord Wright's speech (at 638–639):

'If authority were needed, the provisions just quoted do at least show that profits of "occupation" include gains from the animal produce as well as the agricultural, horticultural or arboricultural produce of the soil. And the references to gardens, nurseries and woodlands show a scope of Schedule B beyond the use of the land and its products for the provision of food; equally it is obvious that the rearing of
f animals, regarded as they must be as products of the soil—since it is from the soil that they draw their sustenance and on the soil that they live—is a source of profit from the occupation of land, whether these animals are for consumption as food (such as bullocks, pigs or chickens), or for the provision of food (such as cows, goats or fowls), or for recreation (such as hunters or racehorses), or for use (such as draught or plough horses). All these animals are appurtenant to the soil, in the relevant sense
g for this purpose, as much as trees, wheat crops, flowers or roots, though no doubt they differ in obvious respects.'

But the question in *Lord Glanely v Wightman*, as counsel for the valuation officer pointed out, was whether the stud fees were severable from the profits of the breeding operation as a whole. There was no issue in the case whether the breeding operation was
h an agricultural operation. As Lord Wright himself pointed out (at 639), that question did not arise. Counsel for the appellants argued that, though Lord Wright left that question open, the whole tenor of his speech was consistent only with his view being that breeding racehorses is an agricultural operation. I do not agree. Indeed, it is significant that the ground on which Wilfrid Greene KC sought to distinguish *Malcolm v Lockhart* [1919] AC 463, a previous decision of the House of Lords, was that in *Malcolm v Lockhart* the farm
j was an agricultural farm (see [1933] AC 618 at 626):

'Supplying the services of a stallion is no part of the business of an agricultural farmer, and the fees for those services were easily severable from the profits of the farm. The case of a stud farm is quite different.'

That distinction is reflected in Viscount Buckmaster's speech. He said (at 631):

'The whole case [that is to say *Malcolm v Lockhart*] was based upon the occupation of the land being for ordinary farm purposes, and there was no reason to displace *a* the finding of the Courts that the sale of the services of the stallion when taken round the countryside formed no part of that business.'

So I do not consider that counsel for the appellants gets any assistance from *Lord Glanely v Wightman*. The case is authority for the proposition (i) that stud fees earned on a stud farm cannot be severed from the other receipts of the stud farm and (ii) that the profits of a stud farm are profits in respect of the occupation of land, and are therefore taxable *b* under Sch B. It is not authority for the proposition that stud farms are an agricultural operation within the meaning of s 26(4) of the General Rate Act 1967. If, therefore, the practice of exempting the buildings on stud farms was based, as I assume it was, on *Lord Glanely v Wightman*, then I am bound to conclude that it was based on a misunderstanding of that case.

I now turn to the third question. Assuming there were agricultural operations on the *c* land, were these buildings used solely in connection with those operations? If I am right on the second question, then the third question does not arise. But it was fully argued before us. So I mention it briefly.

I have no doubt that, if stud farming as carried on by these appellants was an agricultural operation, then these buildings were used solely in connection with that *d* operation. They serve no other purpose. It is unnecessary to inquire whether the buildings were more important than the land, or vice versa. I agree with the submission of counsel for the appellants that the relative importance of the buildings and the land is irrelevant. There may perhaps be cases where the use of the land is so insignificant compared with the use of the buildings that the proper conclusion on the facts would be that the building was not occupied solely in connection with agricultural operations on *e* the land, even though the buildings have no other use. *W & J B Eastwood Ltd v Herrod (Valuation Officer)* [1970] 1 All ER 774, [1971] AC 160 was such a case on the facts. But, in general, the question to be asked is not whether the buildings are more or less important than the land, but whether they serve any purpose other than the agricultural operations on the land. If not, then in the great majority of cases they will be used solely in connection with agricultural operations. *f*

Various expressions were suggested in *Eastwood v Herrod* as synonyms for the statutory language, including the word 'ancillary'. It may be that that word has led to the idea that the use of the buildings must be of minor importance only. That would be a misunderstanding. It would be inconsistent with what Lord Morris said in *Eastwood v Herrod* [1970] 1 All ER 774 at 783, [1971] AC 160 at 174:

g
'The words of the definition of "Agricultural buildings" suggest to my mind buildings that are needed as an adjunct or a necessary aid to agricultural operations taking place on agricultural land and used solely in connection with those operations. This does not necessarily involve that the use to which the buildings are put must be of minor or minimal importance but it does involve that no part of the use is unconnected with the agricultural operations on the land.' *h*

If a synonym is needed, then I would suggest 'complementary' rather than 'ancillary'. But it is better to apply the statutory language as it stands.

The member of the Lands Tribunal held that buildings were not occupied in connection with the agricultural operations on the land because, as he puts it, so far from the use of the buildings being ancillary to the use of the land, or the use of the land being *j* ancillary to the use of the buildings, each was ancillary to the enterprise as a whole. I find this hard to understand. If the enterprise as a whole had been an agricultural operation, then the fact that the use of the land was 'ancillary' to that operation would not have prevented the use of the buildings being ancillary to the operation on the land. So the learned member must, I think, have misdirected himself as to the correct test. This is

confirmed by the learned member's puzzling observation that, if he had found that the
a buildings were being used in connection with agricultural operations, then he would
have found they were being solely so used.

Since the member applied the wrong test, I should, had it been relevant, have felt free
to reach a different conclusion on the facts. Both counsel agreed that in those
circumstances, we should draw our own inference from the evidence. The evidence is
very well summarised in the case. It was hardly, if at all, in dispute. Having read the
b evidence, I am left in no doubt that the use of the buildings was not only essential to the
operations on the land, as the learned member himself has found, but was also confined
to those operations. In other words, the buildings served no other purpose.

It follows that, if I could have accepted the central submission of counsel for the
appellants on the first main question, I should have been in favour of allowing the appeal.

Finally, I turn to the second main question of construction, which I can deal with
c much more briefly. Sections 1 and 2 of the 1971 Act provide that 'agricultural buildings'
shall include any building which is used solely for the keeping or breeding of livestock.
It was accepted that the buildings were used solely for the keeping and breeding of
thoroughbred horses. The question is whether thoroughbreds are 'livestock'.

The dictionary meaning of 'livestock' is 'domestic animals generally'. This is clearly
too wide since it would presumably include cats and dogs. So the meaning must be
d confined to domestic animals in an agricultural context. This would cover all domestic
animals normally found on a farm, such as cattle, sheep and pigs, and might also include
deer other than ornamental deer. But does it include horses?

I have already referred to the dictum of Lawrence J in *Peterborough Royal Foxhound
Show Society v IRC* [1936] 1 All ER 813 at 815, [1936] 2 KB 497 at 500. He clearly
regarded horses as livestock. Others might share his view if the words stood alone. But,
e in the present case, we must have regard to the definition of livestock contained in s 1(3)
of the 1971 Act as including 'any mammal or bird kept for the production of food or
wool or for the purpose of its use in the farming of land'. It is not suggested by counsel
for the appellants that these horses fall within that definition. They are clearly not kept
for the production of food or wool, or for use in farming. But counsel for the appellants
points out that the definition is inclusive, not exclusive. It does not prohibit the inclusion
f of horses if they would otherwise be regarded as livestock.

A similar argument was advanced in *Cresswell (Valuation Officer) v BOC Ltd* [1980] 3 All
ER 443, [1980] 1 WLR 1556, to which I have already referred. In that case the question
was whether fish are livestock. It was argued that, though the fish were not mammals or
birds, they were certainly being kept for the production of food. They should therefore
be treated as livestock for the purposes of the Act. This court had no hesitation in
g rejecting that argument. Megaw LJ, in particular, made it clear that the meaning of
'livestock' must take colour from the definition, even if the definition is not exclusive. In
Belmont Farm Ltd v Minister of Housing and Local Government (1962) 13 P & CR 417 at 422–
423 Lord Parker CJ, after referring to Lawrence J's dictum in *Peterborough Royal Foxhound
Show Society v IRC*, held that thoroughbreds are not livestock. That decision was expressly
h approved by this court in *McClinton v McFall* (1974) 232 EG 707. Though I have doubt
on the first main question, for the reasons I have mentioned, I have no doubt on the
second. We are obliged to hold by authorities binding on this court that these horses are
not livestock within the meaning of the 1971 Act.

For the reasons I have mentioned, I too would dismiss the appeal.

j **BALCOMBE LJ.** It has at all times been conceded by the respondent valuation officer,
and rightly conceded, that the paddocks which constitute the land (as opposed to the
buildings) forming part of the appellants' premises at Whitsbury constitute 'agricultural
land' within the meaning of s 26(3)(a) of the General Rate Act 1967, as they are used as
pasture ground only, for the grazing of thoroughbred horses. The two questions which
arise on this appeal are: (1) are the stud buildings at Whitsbury used solely in connection

with agricultural operations on the paddocks? and (2) are the buildings used for the keeping or breeding of livestock?

    If either of these questions is answered in the affirmative, the appellants succeed on this appeal.

    I consider these questions in the order in which I have set them out above. In order to answer the first question it is necessary to answer the following subsidiary questions: (i) What are the operations which are being carried out on the paddocks? (ii) Are those operations agricultural? (iii) Are the stud buildings used 'in connection with' the operations on the paddocks? If so, (iv) are the buildings used 'solely' in connection with those operations?

The nature of the operations

    Counsel for the appellants submitted that the operations are either: (a) the grazing of thoroughbred horses in the course of breeding and rearing; or (b) the breeding of thoroughbred horses. In my judgment, his first submission is correct. It has been held by the House of Lords that, in considering what are the operations in question, one must look at what is being actually done on the land alone, and not at the combined purpose for which the land and buildings are being used: see *W & J B Eastwood Ltd v Herrod (Valuation Officer)* [1970] 1 All ER 774 at 782–783, 787, 788–789, [1971] AC 160 at 173–174, 178, 180–181. So I turn to consider the next question on the basis that the operations in question are the grazing of thoroughbreds for the purpose of breeding and rearing. (I prefer to use the word 'thoroughbreds' rather than 'racehorses', since, although the object of the breeding is to produce horses suitable for racing, that object is not achieved in every case.)

Are the operations agricultural?

    Although s 26 of the 1967 Act contains definitions of 'agricultural land' and 'agricultural buildings', it contains no definition of 'agricultural operations'. The phrase 'agricultural operations' occurs in both sub-ss (2) and (4) of s 26. Subsection (2) deals with the gross value for rating of a house—

    'occupied in connection with agricultural land and used as the dwelling of a person who—(a) is primarily engaged in carrying on or directing agricultural operations on that land; or (b) is employed in agricultural operations on that land in the service of the occupier thereof . . .'

Subsection (4) defines 'agricultural buildings' as meaning—

    '(a) buildings . . . occupied together with agricultural land . . . and . . . used solely in connection with agricultural operations thereon . . .'

    It is plain that not all operations carried out on agricultural land are themselves agricultural: indeed, if this were not so, it would have been sufficient simply to refer to 'operations on agricultural land'. Thus, pasture land, which is not preserved mainly or exclusively for purposes of sport, may from time to time be used for shooting. Shooting as such is not an agricultural operation and so a keeper's cottage would not come within sub-s (2), nor would any hut used for the purposes of the shooting be within sub-s (4): cf *Earl of Normanton v Giles* [1980] 1 All ER 106, [1980] 1 WLR 28. Nevertheless, the fact that not all operations carried out on agricultural land are themselves agricultural does not of itself meet the submission of counsel for the appellants that, if the operations in question (in this case the grazing of horses) are such as to make the land on which they are carried on agricultural land (as is here conceded), then they must of necessity be agricultural operations. There is an obvious attraction in this submission; however, I am not convinced that the reasoning behind it is sound.

    In the first place, sub-ss (2) and (4) of s 26 must be read together and in conjunction with the definition of 'agricultural land' in sub-s (3). When this is done, it is apparent

that, in considering whether *land* is agricultural, the court must look only at the actual
a use of the land, and not to the purpose of the occupier. On the other hand, in considering
whether the *operations* on that land are agricultural, there is no similar limitation, and
the references (in sub-s (2)) to a person engaged or employed 'in carrying on . . .
agricultural operations' and (in sub-s (4)) to a building used 'solely in connection with
agricultural operations', which, in its turn, contemplates the use of a building *partly* in
connection with agricultural operations, suggest to me that in this context the court
b should look at the facts from the point of view of the occupier of the land, and is not
limited merely to a consideration of the use to which the land is put.

The next submission of counsel for the valuation officer was that the most extensive
category of land included in the definition of agricultural land is land 'used as arable,
meadow or pasture ground *only*'. If operations involving the use of land for other
purposes are carried out, the land ceases to be agricultural and the question whether these
c operations are agricultural becomes irrelevant. Accordingly, the draftsman must have
envisaged that operations which were not agricultural might be carried out on land used
as arable, meadow or pasture ground only. I can see some force in this submission, but
its strength is weakened when one considers that other parts of the definition of
agricultural land, e g cottage gardens exceeding one quarter of an acre, market gardens,
nursery grounds, orchards or allotments, do not refer to the use of the land only for the
d specific purposes mentioned, and the draftsman was having to provide for operations
carried out on all types of agricultural land.

In the end, what persuades me that the meaning of 'agricultural' in relation to
operations is not confined to the use to which the land is put is a consideration of the
consequences of the more limited meaning in the light of the purpose which the section
was clearly intended to achieve. The section wholly exempts agricultural land and
e agricultural buildings from liability to be rated and follows on similar provisions in
earlier statutes dating back to 1896. The *Shorter Oxford English Dictionary* definition of
'agriculture' is:

> 'The science and art of cultivating the soil; including the gathering in of the crops
> and the rearing of live stock; farming (in the widest sense).'

f Although the definition of 'agricultural land' in s 26 includes land used for forestry and
horticulture, it expressly excludes park land, pleasure grounds, land kept or preserved
mainly or exclusively for purposes of sport or recreation, and land used as a racecourse. I
am left with the distinct impression that the object of the section is to benefit farming in
the widest sense.

If that is right, then in the case of land used as pasture only it is necessary to consider
g the kind of animals which are pastured on the land since, if they are not farm animals,
their grazing would not be an agricultural operation carried on on the land. In his
submissions counsel for the valuation officer gave as an example the use of land by the
occupier of a zoo for grazing zebras or bison; an unlikely, but no means impossible, use
of land. In my judgment, the grazing of such animals could not properly be described as
h an agricultural operation.

So in the present case the answer to the question turns on the nature of the animals
which graze the paddocks. Of course, some kinds of horse may properly be described as
farm animals, in which case their grazing would be an agricultural operation but, in my
judgment, a person who carries on the business of breeding thoroughbreds is not to be
described as a farmer, and the operation of grazing thoroughbreds for the purpose of
j breeding and rearing is not properly described as agricultural.

Thus far I have considered the question as if it were free from authority. The majority
of the cases support the conclusion at which I have arrived. In *Gilmore (Valuation Officer)
v Baker-Carr* [1962] 3 All ER 230 at 232, [1962] 1 WLR 1165 at 1172, a case which turned
on the same definitions of 'agricultural land' and 'agricultural buildings' in the Rating
and Valuation (Apportionment) Act 1928, Lord Denning MR said:

'The phrase "agricultural operations" is not defined but I should have thought
that it meant operations by way of cultivating the soil or rearing of livestock.'

In *Forth Stud Ltd v East Lothian Assessor* [1969] RA 35 the Lands Valuation Appeal Court
in Scotland was faced with the same question as we are: whether a commercial stud for
the breeding of thoroughbred horses was exempt from rating. This turned on the
definition of 'agricultural lands and heritages' in s 7(2) of the Valuation and Rating
(Scotland) Act 1956 as 'lands and heritages used for agricultural or pastoral purposes only'.
The court held that the stud was not exempt from rating, because land 'used for
agricultural or pastoral purposes only' meant, so far as the breeding of animals was
concerned, land used for animals which were associated with an ordinary farm. Although
the phrase which the court there had to construe was not the same as that which we have
to consider, I cannot identify any material difference. Further, I find myself in complete
agreement with the following passage from the judgment of Lord Avonside (at 46):

> 'Further, rearing of stock as an agricultural or pastoral operation must, on any
> proper view of the words, be rearing of stock which produces or contributes to
> produce the means of human subsistence. Animals reared for sport or entertainment
> or for their decorative qualities cannot, in my view, be regarded as being reared in
> the course of the activity of farming, which in its broad sense covers tillage and
> pasturing. The whole purpose of farming was and is, from the earliest times until
> now, to produce human subsistence and there can be no doubt that that is why
> agricultural land, under legislation, enjoys the substantial financial privilege of
> being omitted from the valuation roll.'

While this case is not strictly binding on us, it is of considerable persuasive authority
and, in considering the effect of statutes in similar terms which apply in different parts
of the United Kingdom, I adopt the approach of Foster J in *Kidson (Inspector of Taxes) v
Macdonald* [1974] 1 All ER 849 at 856–857, [1974] Ch 339 at 348, following Megarry J
in *Sargaison (Inspector of Taxes) v Roberts* [1969] 3 All ER 1072 at 1076, [1969] 1 WLR
951 at 957–958, viz to give the English statute a construction which looks at the realities
of the situation in the two systems of law (English and Scottish) at the expense of the
technicalities in any one system.

A similar association of 'agricultural' with farming in its ordinary sense is to be found
in the speeches in *W & J B Eastwood Ltd v Herrod (Valuation Officer)* [1970] 1 All ER 774
at 777, 788, [1971] AC 160 at 168, 180 per Lord Reid and Viscount Dilhorne.

Counsel for the appellants relies on the decision of the House of Lords in *Lord Glanely
v Wightman* [1933] AC 618, and in particular the speech of Lord Wright (at 638–639), as
leading to a conclusion in the opposite sense. To understand that case, it is necessary to
consider carefully what was the issue before the House. Lord Glanely owned and
occupied a stud farm near Newmarket for the breeding of thoroughbred racing stock.
Not only did he use the stallions he maintained for covering his own mares, but he also
charged fees for letting out the services on his stud farm of those stallions to the
thoroughbred mares of other owners. Under Sch B to the Income Tax Act 1918 tax was
chargeable in respect of all lands in the United Kingdom. The rate of tax chargeable
under Sch B depended on whether or not the land was used only or mainly for the
purposes of husbandry. The farm as a whole has been assessed to tax under Sch B: the
agricultural part at one rate, the land used purely for stud and racing purposes at a
different rate (at 634 per Lord Wright). So the issue whether that part of the land used
purely for stud and racing purposes was used only or mainly for the purposes of
husbandry was not before the House; it appears to have been accepted that it was not so
used. The Inland Revenue then sought to assess Lord Glanely under Sch D in respect of
the fees he received in respect of the services of his stallions in covering other owners'
mares on the stud farm. The question before the House was whether that additional
assessment was justified, 'that is, whether these fees are or are not covered by the general

assessment made on the lands under Schedule B' (at 634 per Lord Wright). It was held
a that the fees were part of the profits in respect of the occupation of the farm and
chargeable to income tax under Sch B, not Sch D. It was not disputed by the Crown that
the occupation of the land for the purposes of the stud farm was an occupation within
the meaning of Sch B (see at 629, 632 per Viscount Buckmaster and Lord Tomlin) and,
as I have already said, the question whether the land was used only or mainly for the
purposes of husbandry was not in issue. The reasoning of the majority can be found in
b the following passages from the speeches:

Viscount Buckmaster said (at 629):

'Now a stud farm is plainly an occupation of the land, and the breeding and sale
of foals arises from that occupation, and for that purpose the use of the stallion is as
indispensable as the use of the mare. The services, therefore, of the stallion upon the
land are as much a breeding operation as the production of the foal by the mare, and
c I find it difficult to see why, when other people's mares are sent on to the farm, and
kept there, the payment for the services of the stallion is not a normal part of the
purposes for which the land is occupied and inseparable therefrom.'

Lord Tomlin said (at 632):

d 'Looking at the matter apart from authority, I can see no reason in logic for
distinguishing between the profit derived from the reproductive capacity of the
female and the profit derived from the reproductive capacity of the male.'

Lord Russell said (at 633):

'It was conceded by the Crown, and necessarily conceded, that the normal receipts
e of a thoroughbred stud farm include stud fees received for the service by the stud
farm stallions of mares which belong to other people and which are brought on to
the stud farm for that purpose. Those stud fees are therefore in my opinion part of
the gains of the appellant in respect of his occupation of this land. By what right can
the Crown then claim to pick out one item from the various gains of the appellant
in respect of that occupation, and say that it is not covered with the other gains by
f the assessment under Schedule B but is available as a separate item for a separate
assessment under Schedule D? I can envisage no principle which would justify such
a course . . .'

Lord Wright delivered a long speech, and counsel for the appellants relies in particular
on the following passages (at 638–640):

g 'If authority were needed, the provisions just quoted do at least show that profits
of "occupation" include gains from the animal produce as well as the agricultural,
horticultural or arboricultural produce of the soil. And the references to gardens,
nurseries and woodlands show a scope of Schedule B beyond the use of the land and
its products for the provision of food; equally it is obvious that the rearing of
animals, regarded as they must be as products of the soil – since it is from the soil
h that they draw their sustenance and on the soil that they live – is a source of profit
from the occupation of land, whether these animals are for consumption as food
(such as bullocks, pigs or chickens), or for the provision of food (such as cows, goats
or fowls), or for recreation (such as hunters or racehorses), or for use (such as draught
or plough horses). All these animals are appurtenant to the soil, in the relevant sense
for this purpose, as much as trees, wheat crops, flowers or roots, though no doubt
j they differ in obvious respects . . . On these grounds I think that the service of the
stallion is appurtenant to the soil and a profit of the occupation in every case, so that
in this regard it is immaterial whether the service is to the appellant's own mares or
whether it is sold to strangers; in the latter case the service is sold from the land and
as a product of the land, just as much as bullocks, potatoes, fruit or eggs are sold

from the land. Without the appellant's stud farm or some other such stud farm the
stallions could not live or exercise their generating functions.'

Taken out of context, Lord Wright's remarks do undoubtedly support counsel's
submissions but, in my judgment, when properly understood, they are not authority for
the proposition that 'agricultural operations', in the context of a rating statute, includes
the rearing of animals for the purposes of recreation. We were told that, as a result of the
decision in *Lord Glanely v Wightman*, stud farms were considered to be exempt from
rating for nearly 50 years until the decision of the Lands Tribunal in *Evans v Bailey
(Valuation Officer)* (1981) 260 EG 611. I can only say that I find it surprising that the
misunderstanding of the decision in *Lord Glanely v Wightman* lasted so long.

Accordingly, I am of the view that the grazing of thoroughbreds for the purpose of
breeding and rearing was not, and is not, an agricultural operation within the meaning
of s 26(4) of the General Rate Act 1967.

If I am right in this view, the remaining subsidiary questions under the first question
do not arise but, as the matter was fully argued before us, and in case this case goes
further, I propose to deal with them.

Are the stud buildings used 'in connection' with the operations on the paddocks?

The member of the Lands Tribunal found the following facts as to the use of the stud
buildings:

'I have inspected the buildings and I find as a fact that they are of excellent quality
and that they are essential to the [appellants']activities. The buildings are particularly
important for reasons of security and safety of valuable animals, that is to say, the
stallions (in the public stud), the visiting mares and their foals (whether at foot or
born at Whitsbury), and for providing warmth in winter and coolness in summer
and protection from adverse weather, as premises providing facilities for covering
and for hay and concentrates to be dispensed, and for veterinary examinations,
weighing and measuring of foals, observation of pregnant mares and grooming of
yearlings to take place.'

In the light of these findings, it seems to me to be difficult, as a matter of ordinary
language, to say that the stud buildings are not partly used 'in connection with' the
operations on the paddocks, if these operations are, as I have said, the grazing of
thoroughbred horses in the course of breeding and rearing. In particular, it seems to me
that the use of the stud buildings for providing shelter to the grazing animals must be a
use in connection with the operations on the paddocks. However, this phrase has also
been the subject of judicial consideration. In *Gilmore (Valuation Officer) v Baker-Carr*
[1962] 3 All ER 230 at 234, [1962] 1 WLR 1165 at 1175 Donovan LJ said:

'But the clear impression which I receive from the statutory language is that the
buildings exempted were to be ancillary or complementary to the agricultural
purpose of the land, and not vice versa.'

This definition was approved by Viscount Dilhorne in *W & J B Eastwood Ltd v Herrod
(Valuation Officer)* [1970] 1 All ER 774 at 789, [1971] AC 160 at 181, who added:

'I think that the language of the definition requires that buildings to come within
it must be used as adjuncts to the agricultural operations on the land . . .'

In the same case Lord Reid said ([1970] 1 All ER 774 at 778, [1971] AC 160 at 168):

'I do not foresee serious difficulty if "used . . . in connection with" is held to mean
consequential on or ancillary to the agricultural operations on the land which is
occupied together with the buildings.'

I accept that it would be difficult in the present case to describe the use of the stud
buildings as ancillary to the grazing of the thoroughbreds on the paddocks, but I do not

see why it cannot properly be described as complementary to those operations. The
a Lands Tribunal's decision on this matter (that the stud buildings were not used in
connection with the operations on the paddocks) is not, as counsel for the valuation
officer submits, a decision of fact which cannot be challenged on appeal. It was an error
of law based on a misapplication of the statutory test to the primary facts as found by the
tribunal. As such, it is open to review by this court and, in my judgment, the stud
buildings are used in connection with the operations on the paddocks.
b

Are the stud buildings used 'solely' in connection with the operations?
    Here again, I have the misfortune to differ from the decision of the member of the
Lands Tribunal. I do not see how the use of the stud buildings as 'premises providing
facilities for covering' and 'for veterinary examinations' can be properly described as use
in connection with the operation of grazing the thoroughbreds. Accordingly, I would, if
c it were material, hold that the stud buildings are not used solely in connection with the
operations on the paddocks.
    I turn now to the second main question:

Are the buildings used for the keeping or breeding of livestock?
d   The *Shorter Oxford English Dictionary* definition of 'livestock' is: 'Domestic animals
generally; any animals kept or dealt in for use or profit.' If the question fell to be
answered without any indication that this dictionary meaning is to be qualified in any
way, it is clear that thoroughbred horses fall within the definition of 'livestock'. However,
the extension of the definition of 'agricultural buildings' in s 26 of the General Rate Act
1967 to include any building used for the keeping or breeding of livestock is contained
e in s 2(1)(*a*) of the Rating Act 1971 and s 1(3) of that Act defines 'livestock' for the
purposes, inter alia, of s 2 as including—

        'any mammal or bird kept for the production of food or wool or for the purpose
    of its use in the farming of land'.

f These words would be unnecessary if it were intended that 'livestock' should bear its
extensive dictionary meaning, and counsel for the appellants accepts that in this context
'livestock' does not include domestic animals of every description. He submits that it
does cover domestic animals found on agricultural premises or domestic animals in an
agricultural context. It will be apparent, from what I have already said in relation to
'agricultural operations', that, in my judgment, thoroughbred horses would not come
within this definition.
g   Again, the matter is not free from authority. In *Belmont Farm Ltd v Minister of Housing
and Local Government* (1962) 13 P & CR 417 a Divisional Court of the Queen's Bench
Division held that the breeding and keeping of horses, not intended for use in the
farming of land, did not amount to 'the breeding and keeping of livestock' and so was
not a use of land for the purposes of agriculture within the definition of 'agriculture'
h contained in s 119(1) of the Town and Country Planning Act 1947. We are not, of course,
bound to follow this decision, and I accept that it is a decision on a different definition of
'livestock' in a different Act. However, I find the reasoning of Lord Parker CJ in that case
relevant to the question we have to answer. There 'livestock' was defined as 'including
any creature kept for the production of food, wool, skins or fur, or for the purpose of its
use in the farming of land'. Apropos of this definition Lord Parker CJ said (at 421–422):
j
        'Granting that the word "including" has been used in an extensive sense, it seems
    to me nonsense for the draftsman to use those words "any creature kept for the
    production of food, wool, skins or fur, or for the purpose of its use in the farming of
    land", if the word "livestock" was intended to cover the keeping of any creature
    whether for its use in farming land or not. It seems to me that these words show a
    clear intention that "livestock," however it is interpreted, does not extend to the

breeding and keeping of horses unless it is for the purpose of their use in the farming of land.'

In my judgment, the same reasoning applies, mutatis mutandis, to the definition of 'livestock' in the 1971 Act.

Belmont Farm Ltd v Minister of Housing and Local Government was followed by another Divisional Court of the Queen's Bench Division in *Minister of Agriculture, Fisheries and Food v Appleton* [1969] 3 All ER 1051, [1970] 1 QB 221, again a case on the meaning of 'livestock' within a definition of 'agriculture', this time for the purposes of the Selective Employment Payments Act 1966. The *Belmont Farm* case was also approved by Russell LJ in *McClinton v McFall* (1974) 232 EG 707 at 709.

Counsel for the appellants seeks to rely on certain passages in the judgments of the Court of Appeal in *Cresswell (Valuation Officer) v BOC Ltd* [1980] 3 All ER 443, [1980] 1 WLR 1556. In that case the Court of Appeal held that fish were not livestock within the definition contained in the Rating Act 1971. That was the issue before the court and it is in that context that the passages on which counsel for the appellants relies are to be read. Thus, Eveleigh LJ said ([1980] 3 All ER 443 at 445, [1980] 1 WLR 1556 at 1560):

'For myself, I would be inclined, at a first look at s 2, to say that "livestock" there contemplates domestic animals or birds which are found on agricultural premises and which are supported by the land.'

It is clear that no member of the court in that case was considering the question whether thoroughbreds fell within the definition of 'livestock' (indeed, Watkins LJ cited the *Belmont Farm* case with apparent approval) and, in my judgment, that case does not support the contention of counsel for the appellants that 'livestock' in the 1971 Act includes thoroughbreds.

Accordingly, I answer the second main question also in the negative.

I would dismiss this appeal.

Appeal dismissed. Leave to appeal to the House of Lords granted.

Solicitors: *Ward Bowie*, agents for *Rustons & Lloyd*, Newmarket (for the appellant); *Solicitor of Inland Revenue.*

Mary Rose Plummer   Barrister.

a   # R v Monopolies and Mergers Commission,
        ## ex parte Elders IXL Ltd

QUEEN'S BENCH DIVISION (CROWN OFFICE LIST)

MANN J

b   22, 23, 24, 29 APRIL 1986

Monopolies and mergers – Monopolies and Mergers Commission – Commission's powers – Disclosure of confidential information – Disclosure to affected party in course of contested take-over – Commission acting 'for the purpose of facilitating the performance of [its] functions' – Commission receiving confidential information from bidder and disclosing it to company bid for – Whether commission acting fairly to bidder – Whether commission acting for purpose of facilitating
c   *performance of its functions – Whether commission entitled to disclose confidential information – Fair Trading Act 1973, s 133.*

The applicant company made a take-over bid for the second respondent, a company which had similar trading interests. The respondent company was hostile to the bid and
d   the proposed acquisition was referred to the first respondent, the Monopolies and Mergers Commission, by the Secretary of State for Trade and Industry acting under the Fair Trading Act 1973. In accordance with the terms of the applicant company's bid that bid automatically lapsed when it was referred to the commission, but the applicant company was interested in making a fresh bid if, after receiving the commission's report on the proposed merger, the Secretary of State allowed the applicant company to proceed. In
e   the course of investigating the proposed merger the commission requested both companies to provide extensive information concerning the proposed merger. The statement provided by the applicant company gave details of its intended new bid and how it would be financed and the applicant company requested that those details remain confidential to the commission and in particular be withheld from the respondent company. After considering representations from both companies the commission
f   decided to disclose to the respondent company the information provided by the applicant company, on the grounds (i) that the respondent company's comments, which would be made with special knowledge and authority, were necessary for the commission to be able to form an adequate view of whether the merger would operate against the public interest, (ii) that the commission's duty to conduct a full investigation into the proposed merger overrode any duty which it owed to the applicant company not to disclose
g   confidential information, and (iii) that natural justice required that the respondent company be given an opportunity to make fully informed representations about the information provided by the applicant company. The applicant company applied for certiorari to quash the commission's decision to disclose the information, contending (i) that the commission had not acted fairly towards the applicant company because its interest in non-disclosure had not been sufficiently taken into account, and (ii) that
h   disclosure would be contrary to s 133(1)[a] of the Act, which provided that information about an operating business obtained by the commission under the Act was not to be disclosed without the consent of that business, and that in the circumstances disclosure would not be 'for the purpose of facilitating the performance of [the] functions' of the commission and therefore permitted under s 133(2)(a).

j   **Held** – The application would be dismissed for the following reasons—
        (1) In performing its inquisitorial function of determining whether the prospective results of a merger would or could be expected to be against the public interest the commission was under a duty to act fairly to all parties who had a substantial interest in

---

a   Section 133, so far as material, is set out at p 454 *j* to p 455 *b*, post

the subject matter of the reference, but the concept of fairness was flexible and dependent on the particular situation and therefore the court had to decide what was fair in the particular situation. In the circumstances, the commission had been entitled to decide that the perceived detriment to the applicant which disclosure would cause should be subordinated to the commission's judgment of how best to perform its statutory function, which in the commission's view entailed disclosing the applicant's information to the respondent (see p 461 *a b f* to p 462 *a*, post); dictum of Sachs LJ in *Re Pergamon Press Ltd* [1970] 3 All ER at 542 applied.

(2) Since s 133(2) of the 1973 Act permitted the commission to disclose information obtained by it under the Act if the disclosure was for the 'purpose' of facilitating the performance of the commission's functions, the court was not required to conduct an objective examination of whether the disclosure would facilitate performance of the commission's functions but merely had to determine whether the commission had made the decision to disclose with the intention of facilitating its investigation. Since it had so decided, it was entitled to disclose the information (see p 462 *e f*, post); dictum of Lord Diplock in *Sweet v Parsley* [1969] 1 All ER at 364 applied.

Notes

For merger references, see 47 Halsbury's Laws (4th edn) para 89.

For the Fair Trading Act 1973, s 133, see 43 Halsbury's Statutes (3rd edn) 1735.

Cases referred to in judgment

Council of Civil Service Unions v Minister for the Civil Service [1984] 3 All ER 935, [1985] AC 374, [1984] 3 WLR 1174, HL.

Hoffmann-La Roche & Co AG v Secretary of State for Trade and Industry [1974] 2 All ER 1128, [1975] AC 295, [1974] 3 WLR 104, HL.

McInnes v Onslow Fane [1978] 3 All ER 211, [1978] 1 WLR 1520.

Nakkuda Ali v Jayaratne [1951] AC 66, PC.

Pergamon Press Ltd, Re [1970] 3 All ER 535, [1971] Ch 388, [1970] 3 WLR 792, CA.

R v Gaming Board for GB, ex p Benaim [1970] 2 All ER 528, [1970] 2 QB 417, [1970] 2 WLR 1009, CA.

Registrar of Restrictive Trading Agreements v W H Smith & Son Ltd [1969] 3 All ER 1065, [1969] 1 WLR 1460, CA.

Russell v Duke of Norfolk [1949] 1 All ER 109, CA.

Sweet v Parsley [1969] 1 All ER 347, [1970] AC 132, [1969] 2 WLR 470, HL.

Wiseman v Borneman [1969] 3 All ER 275, [1971] AC 297, [1969] 3 WLR 706, HL.

Cases also cited

Crofter Hand Woven Harris Tweed Co Ltd v Veitch [1942] 1 All ER 142, [1942] AC 435, HL.

Gammon (Hong Kong) Ltd v A-G of Hong Kong [1984] 2 All ER 503, [1985] AC 1, PC.

Khawaja v Secretary of State for the Home Dept [1983] 1 All ER 765, [1984] AC 74, HL.

Application for judicial review

Elders IXL Ltd (Elders) applied, with the leave of Mann J given on 26 March 1986, for judicial review by way of (i) an order for certiorari to quash the decision of the first respondent, the Monopolies and Mergers Commission, to disclose to the second respondent, Allied-Lyons plc (Allied), the contents of Chapter 7 of the applicant company's submission made to the commission in the course of the commission's investigation into a proposed merger of the two companies, (ii) a declaration that the commission was under no duty, whether under the Fair Trading Act 1973 or otherwise, to disclose to the respondent company the contents of Chapter 7, (iii) a declaration that it would not constitute a breach of the rules of natural justice or any duty to act fairly for the commission to refuse to disclose Chapter 7 to the respondent company, (iv) a declaration

that such disclosure would constitute a breach of s 133 of the 1973 Act and (v) an order
a of prohibition restraining such disclosure. The facts are set out in the judgment.

Robert Alexander QC, David Oliver QC and *Mark Howard* for Elders.
Mark Littman QC, John Mummery and *Adrian Hughes* for the commission.
J A Swift QC and *Stephen Richards* for Allied.

b
Cur adv vult

29 April. The following judgment was delivered.

MANN J. There is before the court an application for judicial review. I gave leave to
c move on 26 March 1986. The applicant is Elders IXL Ltd (Elders), which is a company
incorporated under the law of South Australia and which carries on business in brewing,
agriculture, finance and international trading in 23 countries. The first respondent is the
Monopolies and Mergers Commission. The commission now owes its existence to s 4(1)
of the Fair Trading Act 1973 and exists for the purpose of performing the functions
assigned to it by or under that Act. The second respondent is Allied-Lyons plc (Allied),
d which is a company incorporated in England and which carries on business in brewing,
wines and spirits and food in England and in other countries. The decision which is
impugned is a decision of the commission which is recorded in a letter from the chairman
dated 10 March 1986. I shall refer to the letter when I have set its context. Elders seek an
order to quash, together with declaratory relief.
I turn to the context in which the impugned decision was taken. In 1984 Elders
e became interested in acquiring Allied. On 21 October 1985 Elders announced a £1·8
billion cash offer for Allied's shares at £2·55 for each ordinary share. A formal offer
document was sent to Allied's shareholders on 18 November. Allied's board was hostile
to the offer. On 5 December the Secretary of State for Trade and Industry referred the
proposed acquisition to the commission in the exercise of his powers under s 75(1) of the
1973 Act, which entitles the Secretary of State to refer to the commission arrangements
f in contemplation which, if carried into effect, would result in the creation of a merger
situation qualifying for investigation. There is no dispute but that the acquisition, if
carried into effect, would result in the creation of a merger situation qualifying for
investigation (see s 64(8) of the 1973 Act). I need not recite the terms of the Secretary of
State's reference, but he issued a press notice of even date which contained this sentence:
'The Secretary of State considers that the financing of the proposed acquisition raises
g issues which deserve investigation by the Commission.'
I turn away from the context in which the impugned decision was taken in order to
look at the provisions of the 1973 Act which are relevant. I need not recite all of them in
terms. Under s 5(1) it is the duty of the commission to 'investigate and report' on any
question referred to it with respect to the possible creation of a merger situation
qualifying for investigation. On such a reference the commission must investigate and
h report on the question of whether the prospective result of the arrangements in
contemplation would, if those arrangements had been made and the results had occurred
before the date of the reference, give rise to a situation which 'operates, or may be
expected to operate, against the public interest' (see ss 69(1)(b), 75(2), (4)(c)).
It is to be observed and remembered that the commission's duty is thus to investigate
and report in regard to the public interest. It was agreed, and in my view rightly so, that
j the discharge of the duty involves the performance of an inquisitorial function. The
performance of the function is, as to procedure, dealt with in s 81 of the 1973 Act, which
provides, so far as is material:

'(1) ... the Commission, in carrying out an investigation on a reference made to
them under this Act ... (a) shall take into consideration any representations made

to them by persons appearing to them to have a substantial interest in the subject-matter of the reference, or by bodies appearing to them to represent substantial *a* numbers of persons who have such an interest, and (b) unless in all the circumstances they consider it not reasonably necessary or not reasonably practicable to do so, shall permit any such person or body to be heard orally by the ... the Commission ... or by a member of the ... Commission nominated by them for that purpose.

(2) Subject to subsection (1) of this section ... the Commission may determine their own procedure for carrying out any investigation on a reference under this *b* Act, and in particular may determine—(a) the extent, if any, to which persons interested or claiming to be interested in the subject-matter of the reference are allowed to be present or to be heard, either by themselves or by their representatives, or to cross-examine witnesses or otherwise take part in the investigation, and (b) the extent, if any, to which the sittings of ... the Commission are to be held in public.'

c

The matters which may be taken into account in the performance of the function are the subject of s 84(1), which provides, so far as is material:

'In determining for any purposes to which this section applies whether any particular matter operates, or may be expected to operate, against the public interest, the Commission shall take into account all matters which appear to them in the particular circumstances to be relevant and, among other things, shall have regard *d* to the desirability ...'

There then follows a list of matters concerning desirability.

The commission has at the outside nine months, beginning with the date of the reference, within which to make a report on the reference (s 70(1) of the 1973 Act). The provisions as to a report are in s 72. Subsection (1) provides: *e*

'In making their report on a merger reference, the Commission shall include in it definite conclusions on the questions comprised in the reference, together with— (a) such an account of their reasons for those conclusions, and (b) such a survey of the general position with respect to the subject-matter of the reference, and of the developments which have led to that position, as in their opinion are expedient for *f* facilitating a proper understanding of those questions and of their conclusions.'

A copy of any report is laid before Parliament (s 83(1)). Thereafter what is or is not to be done about the arrangements in contemplation is a matter for the Secretary of State (see s 73). In homely language, the minister decides whether the bid is or is not to proceed.

I must last refer to ss 82 and 133 of the 1973 Act. Section 82 enjoys the shoulder note *g* 'General provisions as to reports'. Subsection (1) provides:

'In making any report under this Act the ... Commission shall have regard to the need for excluding, so far as that is practicable,—(a) any matter which relates to the private affairs of an individual, where the publication of that matter would or might, in their opinion, seriously and prejudicially affect the interests of that *h* individual, and (b) any matter which relates specifically to the affairs of a particular body of persons, whether corporate or uncorporate, where publication of that matter would or might, in the opinion of the ... Commission ... seriously and prejudicially affect the interests of that body, unless in their opinion the inclusion of that matter relating specifically to that body is necessary for the purposes of the report.'

Section 133 is within the fascicle of sections described as 'Miscellaneous and *j* Supplementary Provisions'. It enjoys the shoulder note 'General restrictions on disclosure of information'. So far as is material, it provides:

'(1) Subject to subsections (2) to (4) of this section, no information with respect to any particular business which has been obtained under or by virtue of the provisions *a* (other than Part II) of this Act or under or by virtue of the Act of 1956 or the Act of 1968 shall, so long as that business continues to be carried on, be disclosed without the consent of the person for the time being carrying on that business.

(2) The preceding subsection does not apply to any disclosure of information which is made—(a) for the purpose of facilitating the performance of any functions of ... the Commission ... under this Act, the Restrictive Trade Practices Act 1956

b or the Restrictive Trade Practices Act 1968 ... or ... the Competition Act, 1980 ... or (b) in pursuance of a Community obligation within the meaning of the European Communities Act 1972 ...

(5) Any person who discloses any information in contravention of this section shall be guilty of an offence and shall be liable—(a) on summary conviction, to a fine not exceeding [the statutory maximum]; (b) on conviction on indictment, to imprisonment for a term not exceeding two years or to a fine or to both ...'

c

I return to the context in which the impugned decision was taken On 10 December 1985 the chairman of the commission wrote to the chairmen of Elders, Mr John Elliott, and of Allied, Sir Derrick Holden-Brown. The letters were in materially similar terms. Each requested the provision of extensive information in the form of a statement. The two chairmen were in particular each asked to cover the following matters:

d

'(a) Competition in the supply of beer in the United Kingdom; (b) Competition in the food industry, particularly if the Allied-Lyons Food Division is to be sold if the merger takes place; (c) The method proposed for financing the acquisition and the degree of risk to the financial stability of the merged group if the merger takes place (see the attached copy of a press notice by the Department of Trade and Industry); (d) The availability of finance for the future development of Allied-Lyons'

e business (or so much of it as would be retained); (e) Likely effects of the merger on employment, management and efficiency; (f) Any other matter which might be thought to affect the public interest.'

Each company submitted a statement: that of Elders was submitted on 16 January 1986 and that of Allied was submitted on 21 January. The submission of Elders contained

f in its Chapter 7 new financing arrangements in relation to a revised bid. The necessity for a revised bid appeared to Elders during the life of the first offer, which had lapsed in accordance with its terms on the Secretary of State's reference. Elders regarded and still regards Chapter 7 as confidential and believes that its revelation to Allied would 'frustrate or undermine' the further bid should the Secretary of State eventually allow it to be made. The necessity for confidentiality in regard to Chapter 7 was the subject of a

g covering note accompanying Elders' submission. Allied's submission also had a letter of even date, which was in these terms:

'In the meantime there is one matter which gives cause for concern. As the Commission will see from our Memorandum there is, on our part, considerable uncertainty as to what "arrangements" Elders has in contemplation for the purpose

h of acquiring control over Allied-Lyons: specifically, a bid price higher than 255 pence per share, disposal of business additional to those of Allied-Lyons' food division, perhaps the re-creation of the consortium which was originally intended? We are concerned that throughout the remainder of this Inquiry we may be dealing with a moving target. We would, therefore, urge the Commission to inform us as soon as possible if the arrangements in contemplation change in any of the above

j areas or other relevant areas so that we may make further submissions to the Commission on the changed position.'

The chairman of the commission gave Allied this reply on 24 January:

'I appreciate the difficulty in which your Company finds itself, in relation to the uncertainty about the precise future intentions of Elders IXL Ltd. To an extent this is a quandary which may arise whenever an attempted merger is referred to the Commission, but I recognise that this case has peculiar features. I am considering *a* whether we ought to take any practical steps on this account.'

On 27 January there was a meeting of the chairman of the commission, a representative of Elders and a representative of Elders' solicitors. The chairman said that he wished to disclose Chapter 7 to Allied and that if he did not do so Allied might seek to have any subsequent report set aside in the courts. The meeting was inconclusive. The question of *b* disclosure was returned to at a meeting on 31 January. The representatives of Elders re-emphasised the prejudice which the company would suffer should Chapter 7 be revealed to Allied. The representatives suggested that Chapter 7 should be submitted to the Bank of England for its independent advice on the financing arrangements and that questions to Allied could be formulated, which while not disclosing the arrangements would both enable the commission to have the benefit of Allied's views on those arrangements and *c* enable Allied to make representations on the factual matters which underlay the arrangements. The meeting was again inconclusive, but Elders agreed to send two draft letters and a list of suggested questions to the commission. The two letters were to explain why disclosure of Chapter 7 was regarded as prejudicial to Elders. One was to give reasons in full. The second was an expurgated version which could be disclosed to interested persons and in particular to Allied. The drafts and a list of questions were sent *d* on 5 February. The draft of the open letter was thereafter amended and on 12 February Elders sent to the commission both an open and a confidential letter, setting out objections to disclosure.

The open letter was, so far as material, in these terms:

'Our submission to the Monopolies Commission contains: details of how we *e* would finance a renewed bid for Allied; an indication of the price we might be willing to pay for Allied; and details of how we would re-finance the initial bank loans on a longer term basis. Clearly, none of this information had been publicly disclosed by us at the time our original bid for Allied was referred. In any take-over bid, an offeror will not, for tactical reasons, disclose details of its final offer until it is appropriate to do so. This applies not only in the UK market but in every other *f* market around the world of which we are aware. The need to keep our plans confidential until the appropriate time therefore continues to hold good for any renewed bid. We will not win a renewed offer for Allied if they or the public know in advance (let alone months in advance) what we intend to do. If some details of our plans became publicly available, Elders would be placed in an impossible position. Our plans would most likely be represented inaccurately but we would *g* not be in a position to rebuff or clarify our proposals without disclosing all the details. Apart from being damaging to Elders, there is the very real risk that a false market could be created in Elders' and Allied's shares which would clearly be of concern to the London and Australian Stock Exchanges. Disclosure now of our financing plans or even part of them would place Elders in a position which we and our advisers believe is unprecedented in any take-over situation in any major market *h* in the world. Disclosure would deny Elders the usual elements of surprise and timing in a take-over and this could seriously undermine Elders' ability successfully to bid for Allied. For example, disclosure of our plans will make it virtually impossible for us to choose for tactical reasons to mount a new offer below the level indicated in our submission. Allied would know that this new offer was below the price we ultimately intended to pay and would naturally use that information. This *j* could also have implications under the City Code on Take-overs and Mergers. Certain elements of Elders' financing arrangements are unique. Public knowledge of these plans might enable some other person to implement a similar financing proposal before Elders was free to do so itself. As a result, Elders' financing plans could be affected. We therefore believe that Allied should not have disclosed to it by

the Commission any details of our financing plans other than what is contained in
our offer document of 18th November 1985. Details of our arrangements will, of
course, be disclosed by us during the course of our renewed bid and the rules of the
City Code and The Stock Exchange provide for the timing and nature of such
disclosure. Allied will clearly have the required opportunity to comment on those
arrangements and its shareholders will have an opportunity to decide whether they
are acceptable to them. In conclusion, I would say that we believe that disclosure of
our plans now could prejudice our ability to mount a bid for Allied. Even if we did
succeed in mounting an offer, the vital tactical advantages referred to above would
have been lost. I am, however, willing for you to disclose full details of our current
financing plans to the Bank of England for the purposes of this inquiry so that they
can be in a position to offer comment and advice to the Commission on the
implications for the public interest.'

I need quote no further, save that the letter concludes: 'I am happy for you to show this
letter to third parties should you choose to do so.'

The chairman of the commission sent a copy of that letter to Allied. The chairman
and chief executive of that company replied in these terms on 17 February:

'We are of the view that the overriding consideration is the Commission's
performance of their statutory duties under Section 72 of the Fair Trading Act 1973.
The Commission are thus entitled, subject only to the provisions of Section 133 of
the Act, to disclose information of the kind which Mr. Elliott wishes to conceal to
any person whose evidence in relation to that information may be expected to be
relevant to the Commission's ability to discharge their statutory duties. We
appreciate that confidential business matters are disclosed to the Commission in the
course of a merger enquiry (including, in this reference, matters relating to the
future business plans of Allied-Lyons) but we think that it is clear, from analysis of
the relevant sections of the Fair Trading Act, that private interests relating to the
protection of confidential information must be subordinated to that of the wider
public interest. That applies most obviously to a case where the methods of financing
and refinancing an acquisition of this magnitude are at the very heart of the enquiry.
Moreover, Section 82 of the Act specifically contemplates that even information
which would "seriously and prejudicially affect the interests" of a company may be
included in the Report if "the inclusion of that matter relating specifically to that
body is necessary for the purposes of the Report". If we are right in that analysis,
Mr. Elliott's arguments for complete protection of confidentiality for his
arrangements are wholly irrelevant. Mr. Elliott argues that "we will not win a
renewed offer for Allied if they or the public know in advance (let alone months in
advance) what we intend to do"; but that, in addition to being a questionable
statement in itself, misses the point. The "public" is entitled to know what Mr.
Elliott and his bankers "intend to do" because what they intend to do and how they
intend to do it is now a matter of public interest—and will surely be included in the
Report. The issue therefore is, as we see it, whether the Commission can be satisfied
that they are carrying out their statutory duties under Section 72 of the Act if they
do not disclose to one of the principal parties involved the intentions of the other
party as to the arrangements in progress or contemplation, including the critical
area of financing. As to that issue "the arrangements in progress or contemplation"
now appear to be different in one important respect from those announced in the
Offer Document in that Elders "intend" to bid a price higher than 255p per share
but the methods of financing and refinancing the bid still remain wholly obscure.
Since the effect of the methods of financing the bid is likely to involve the dissolution
of the Allied-Lyons Group we believe that it would be unfair and unreasonable to
deny us the opportunity of submitting evidence in relation thereto which we cannot
effectively do without knowledge as to what the relevant arrangements are. May I

give you this assurance. Contrary to what Mr. Elliot suggests, any information
which you provided to us in relation to the arrangements would be treated as *a*
confidential throughout the remainder of the Enquiry and until the formation
entered the public domain at the time of publication of the Report. Each person
within Allied-Lyons and its advisors who received notice of this information would
be required to give appropriate undertakings to me in relation to this matter.'

Elders was afforded an opportunity in its turn to comment on that letter and its *b*
solicitors did so on 28 February. I should quote a passage from that letter:

'. . . we take the view that the MMC should obviously be provided with full
particulars of all matters which it requires for the purposes of its investigations. Our
clients have, accordingly, provided those particulars to the MMC and have been and
are willing to give such further explanations to the MMC as it may require.
Furthermore, Elders has invited the MMC to give to the Bank of England full *c*
particulars of Elders' financial proposals so that the MMC may (if it wishes to do so)
get the full benefit of the reaction of the Bank to those proposals. We understand
from the MMC that those details have been given to the Bank. In addition, the
MMC is, of course, free to test, check or verify the information provided to it by
Elders in whatsoever way it chooses but subject, of course, to the considerations as
to confidentiality referred to above. We believe that questions can be devised which *d*
will enable the MMC to perform its task in an entirely satisfactory fashion, i.e. one
which will enable it to do its statutory duty in a fair manner. Our concern is that
fairness in this context should include fairness to Elders. In our view it would be
quite unfair to Elders if those details were communicated to Allied-Lyons at this
stage, particularly where, as we believe to be the case, the MMC is obviously able to
carry out its responsibilities fairly and without making the detailed disclosures of *e*
Elders' plans to Allied-Lyons as Sir Derrick Holden-Brown contends.'

On 7 March, the chairman of the commission informed both Elders and Allied that
each had had an adequate opportunity of making representations on the issue of
disclosure. The decision of the commission was given in a letter of 10 March. It is that
decision which is the subject of the present proceedings. I must read it. It says: *f*

'I am now able to write to you further about the problem, first raised in your
letter to me of 16th January and the memorandum which accompanied it, of the
confidentiality of information supplied by Elders to the Commission about the
financing of Elders' bid. The information with which I am concerned in this letter
is that contained in Chapter 7 of your submission and the schedules to Chapter 7.
For convenience I refer to this information subsequently as "the financial
information". Elders' objections to the disclosure to Allied of the financial
information were amplified at two meetings (at the second of which you were
present) held with me, at Elders' request, on 27th and 31st January and in
correspondence in particular your two letters to me of 12th February and Freshfields'
letter of 28th February. As you know, Allied's views on the problem have also been *h*
sought; these were provided in their letter to me of 17th February, a copy of which
was sent to you and which received comment in Freshfields' letter. The Commission
attach the greatest concern to the protection of information supplied to them in
confidence in the course of any inquiry and have intervened before the courts in
order to secure this (the *Hoffmann-La Roche* case [*Hoffmann-La Roche & Co AG v
Secretary of State for Trade and Industry* [1974] 2 All ER 1128, [1975] AC 295], cited *j*
in Freshfields' letter, is the best known, but not the only instance). However,
important as such protection is, the prime duty of the Commission is the proper
performance of their statutory functions, in particular the proper conduct of their
investigations. Where the Commission are satisfied that that duty requires the
disclosure of information, they cannot regard the protection of its confidentiality as

a sufficient ground for withholding such disclosure. This is consistent with the Fair Trading Act, 1973, and in particular with section 133(2)(a). Having considered carefully the arguments which Elders have advanced for the protection of the financial information, the Commission have concluded that it is nevertheless their duty to disclose this to Allied. From the material available to the Commission and the positions adopted both by Elders and Allied (see, for example, the third paragraph of Allied's letter of 17th February) it seems inescapable that the financing aspect must be treated by the Commission as a significant part of their inquiry. Without full investigation of it they would be unlikely to be able to form an adequate view of the public interest. This has two consequences: (a) In order to obtain the necessary basis for eventually dealing in their report (in whatever sense) with all the matters set out in section 72(1) of the Act, the Commission consider that they must discover whether Allied can contribute data relevant to the financing aspect. The Commission appreciate the authority given to them by Elders to obtain expert comments on this aspect from the Bank of England. However, the potential effects of these financial arrangements on Allied and its future activities may also be relevant to the Commission's inquiry, and in this area Allied may reasonably be expected to comment with special knowledge and authority, which no outside expert could command. The Commission would not feel justified in depriving Allied of the opportunity of making such comments, nor in depriving themselves of the potential benefit to their enquiry of such comments; yet such comments cannot be made unless Allied have the necessary knowledge of the financing. (b) As is recognised in Freshfields' letter, it is the duty of the Commission to observe the requirements of natural justice and to act fairly in the conduct of any investigation. The Commission have taken into account the serious detriments which Elders anticipates might occur to it by reason of the disclosure to Allied of the financial information. Nevertheless, given the importance of the financial aspect to the inquiry the Commission do not consider that they would be fulfilling the duty to act fairly if they failed to give Allied the opportunity of making fully informed representations about the financial information. The Commission have been advised that, if they decided to withhold that opportunity and their ultimate decision were adverse to Allied, there would be a serious prospect that proceedings by Allied for judicial review based on that decision would succeed. The Commission therefore consider that they should supply Allied with the financial information. However, they do not overlook the serious detriments which Elders anticipates might occur to it if the financial information were disclosed to Allied. Their decision is therefore subject to the following points: (i) The Commission would be willing to consider any specific suggestions which might enable Allied, while not provided with the whole text of Chapter 7 and its Schedules, to receive the substance of the financial information. (ii) In its letter of 17th February, Allied has recognised the importance of the confidentiality of the financial information. Notwithstanding the comments on this aspect in Freshfields' letter, it would be the Commission's intention, before disclosing the financial information, to require that disclosure should be to the minimum number of individuals, each to be named in advance, and each to be required to give a personal undertaking to observe the confidentiality of the information and to use it only for the purpose of the inquiry. The Commission will refrain from providing Allied with the financial information until noon on Wednesday 19th March, to give Elders an opportunity of making suggestions under (i) above or of taking any action which Elders may wish meanwhile.'

On 20 March the commission agreed not to disclose any of the information in Chapter 7 to Allied until after the final determination of these present proceedings. Before that date, and after 10 March, there had been discussions with the object of determining whether it was possible to produce an amended and discloseable version of Chapter 7.

Elders found it impracticable to produce a version which did not reveal confidential details. There is no dispute now but that it is impracticable so to do.

I have before me an affirmation from the chairman of the commission and affidavits from the chairmen of Elders and Allied. I should quote from that part of the affirmation where the chairman of the commission draws attention to the particular features of the case:

'(1) The Commission considered it proper to proceed on the basis that the information about financial arrangements which was provided by Elders, particularly in chapter 7, was, as asserted by Elders, confidential and Allied were prepared to give undertakings to preserve that confidentiality... (2) The Commission also proceeded on the basis that consideration of the financial arrangements for the take-over was an important feature of the inquiry. (3) The Commission were prepared to consider and did in fact consider various methods suggested by Elders for disclosing to Allied the substance of the financial arrangements without disclosure of the whole of chapter 7. (4) After considering the various methods of dealing with the question of disclosure the Commission concluded that the procedures suggested by Elders would not provide Allied with an adequate opportunity to draw on their special knowledge in order to make comments or representations on those arrangements which would eventually assist the Commission in reaching their conclusions on this inquiry.'

I do not find it necessary to quote at any length from the affidavits, but in his second affidavit Mr Elliot explained that the arrangements set out in Chapter 7 involved unique financing concepts, which could be undermined by Allied should it learn of them and that disclosure of Chapter 7 would indicate the price that Elders might be prepared to pay for Allied. He expressed his belief that disclosure 'would give Allied a unique opportunity to forestall and frustrate the bid'.

Counsel for Elders attacked the decision of 10 March on two grounds. The grounds are separate, but their arguments overlap. The first ground is that the commission was guilty of a procedural impropriety in that the decision to disclose was a decision which was unfair to Elders, in that its interest in non-disclosure was not sufficiently taken into account.

The second ground was that disclosure would contravene s 133(1) of the 1973 Act and could not be justified under the exception contained in s 133(2)(a). Counsel did not suggest that the commission had failed to receive representations on the issue of disclosure, nor did he suggest that the decision of the commission was irrational, in the sense that it was 'a decision which is so outrageous in its defiance of logic or of accepted moral standards that no sensible person who had applied his mind to the question to be decided could have arrived at it' (per Lord Diplock in Council of Civil Service Unions v Minister for Civil Service [1984] 3 All ER 935 at 951, [1985] AC 374 at 410).

Counsel for the commission, whose submissions were adopted by counsel for Allied, submitted that the commission's decision was exposed to an attack only on the ground of irrationality and that as no such attack was made, the decision was flawless. I formed the view at an early stage of the argument that it was difficult to appreciate the commission's decision without reading Chapter 7. The interests of justice required that it should be disclosed to me in camera because disclosure in open court could have greater consequences than the limited disclosure that the present application is designed to prevent. No one objected to a disclosure or to it being in camera, but a difficulty arose in regard to the representatives of Allied. I would have permitted counsel and solicitors for Allied to attend on the court in camera, but attendance would have caused them embarrassment in that they are advising Allied generally on the reference to the commission. This practical difficulty was solved by an agreement between all counsel whereby Allied's representatives withdrew during the hearings in camera, of which there were two, but I was to be enabled to call on junior counsel for Allied for assistance on *a* matters revealed in camera, should I find it necessary to do so. Had I done so, junior counsel would have ceased to advise on the reference. I did not, in the event, find it necessary to call on him.

There was no dispute but that in the performance of its inquisitorial function the commission must act fairly to the parties concerned. By 'parties concerned' I mean at least those who have a 'substantial interest in the subject matter of the reference': see s 81(1)(a) of the 1973 Act. Elders and Allied are plainly such parties. Prima facie, then, *b* each of them is entitled to be treated fairly.

Fairness is a flexible concept, whose content is dependent on the situation which is under consideration. In *Re Pergamon Press Ltd* [1970] 3 All ER 535 at 542, [1971] Ch 388 at 403 Sachs LJ said:

c   'In the application of the concept of fair play, there must be real flexibility, so that very different situations may be met without producing procedures unsuitable to the object in hand. That need for flexibility has been emphasised in a number of authoritative passages in the judgments cited to this court. In the forefront was that of Tucker LJ in *Russell v Duke of Norfolk* [1949] 1 All ER 109 at 118, and the general effect of his views has been once again echoed recently by Lord Guest, Lord Donovan and Lord Wilberforce in *Wiseman v Borneman* [1969] 3 All ER 275 at 280, 283, 288, *d*   [1971] AC 297 at 311, 314, 320. It is only too easy to frame a precise set of rules which may appear impeccable on paper and which may yet unduly hamper, lengthen and, indeed, perhaps even frustrate (see per Lord Reid in *Wiseman v Borneman* [1969] 3 All ER 275 at 277, [1971] AC 297 at 308) the activities of those engaged in investigating or otherwise dealing with matters that fall within their proper sphere. In each case careful regard must be had to the scope of the proceeding, *e*   the source of its jurisdiction (statutory in the present case), the way in which it normally falls to be conducted and its objective.'

There is thus no set of rules of fairness which is applicable to all investigative procedures. There could not be such. In particular, there is no general rule that one party to an investigation should be given all of the material submitted by another: see *R v* *f* *Gaming Board for GB, ex p Benaim* [1970] 2 All ER 528, [1970] 2 QB 417, *Re Pergamon Press Ltd* and *McInnes v Onslow Fane* [1978] 3 All ER 211, [1978] 1 WLR 1520.

What is fair in relation to a particular process and to a particular situation which is subject to that process, is for determination by the court. The complaint by Elders is that the commission focused on fairness to Allied and sought to enable them to make representations on Elders' proposals, but did not sufficiently take account of the *g* disproportionate harm which could thereby be caused to Elders by a revelation of the financial arrangements. Elders recognises that there are competing considerations, but asserts that the balance struck was not a fair one.

Had the matter rested there, Elders' case would be a powerful one advanced on the basis that fairness to one party cannot involve the infliction of disproportionate unfairness to another. The matter does not, however, rest there because the considerations of fairness *h* arise in the course of a statutory investigation as to what is or is not in the public interest. It is plain to me from what I have heard in camera that the commission is of the view that it cannot perform this investigative function without knowing Allied's views on the consequences for Allied's business of the arrangements in Chapter 7. That view is not assailed as irrational. It is expressed, as was made plain in the letter of 10 March, with a full appreciation of the detriment which Elders apprehends it may suffer. The *j* commission has considered whether its objective could be achieved and the detriment avoided by means of a formulation of questions to Allied. For reasons given in camera and which I do not flaw as irrational, the commission has concluded that its objective could not be so achieved.

In my judgment, the commission was correct in subordinating a perceived detriment to Elders to its judgment of how best to perform its statutory function. I emphasise that there is no suggestion that the subordination was irrational or was done otherwise but in good faith.   *a*

I turn to the arguments founded on s 133. It is to be observed that s 133 is not confined to confidential information, but applies to any information obtained during, amongst other cases, a merger reference. The inhibition is absolute, subject to exceptions. The question is whether the exception in sub-s 2(*a*) applies. I remind myself that it provides:

'The preceding subsection does not apply to any disclosure of information which   *b*
is made (*a*) for the purpose of facilitating the performance of any functions of
the . . . Commission . . .'

Counsel for Elders submitted that the satisfaction of the exception was a matter for the objective determination of a court. On a prosecution under sub-s (5) the task would fall to a Bench or a jury. Counsel accepted that the commission must be allowed what he conveniently called 'a margin of appreciation'. As I understand him, the limits of the   *c* margin are determinable by the court. Thus, it was said to be outside the limits that a disclosure of information should be made which was severely prejudicial to an interested party when there is another practicable way of discovering what it is that the commission desires to know, that is to say, by the formulation of pertinent questions. It was also said to be outside the limits of disclosure if it would cause prejudice disproportionate to any advantage. I was referred to cases where the decision-maker had to have reasonable   *d* grounds for adopting a particular course, e g *Nakkuda Ali v Jayaratne* [1951] AC 66 and *Registrar of Restrictive Trading Agreements v W H Smith & Son Ltd* [1969] 3 All ER 1065, [1969] 1 WLR 1460.

I am unable to accept counsel's submission. The exception is not drawn as 'for facilitating', but as 'for the purpose of facilitating'. The former form would require an   *e* objective examination of whether disclosure did or did not facilitate. I agree with counsel for the commission that the latter form involves an inquiry as what the commission had in mind. I was referred to the speech of Lord Diplock in *Sweet v Parsley* [1969] 1 All ER 347 at 363–364, [1970] AC 132 at 165 where he said: '"Purpose" connotes an intention by some person to achieve a result desired by him.'

I would apply that connotation to the exception before me. I am satisfied from what I   *f* heard in camera that the commission's intention is to facilitate the performance of its functions. It was not suggested that the formation of that intention was either irrational or made in bad faith. I reach my conclusion without regret because it seems to me that it would be most unfortunate if the commission were to be in peril of exercises in objectivity by this court, magistrates or jurors during the course of discharging the difficult functions put on the commission by the 1973 Act. For the reasons I have   *g* endeavoured to give, this application is dismissed.

[The proceedings continued in camera.]

Application dismissed.   *h*

Solicitors: *Freshfields* (for Elders); *Treasury Solicitor*; *Ashurst Morris Crisp & Co* (for Allied).

Raina Levy   Barrister.

R v Monopolies and Mergers Commission, ex parte Matthew Brown plc

QUEEN'S BENCH DIVISION (CROWN OFFICE LIST)

MACPHERSON J

2, 3, 4, 17 JULY 1986

Monopolies and mergers – Monopolies and Mergers Commission – Commission's powers – Disclosure of confidential information – Refusal to disclose confidential information to affected party – Commission receiving submission from bidder in course of contested take-over bid – Commission not divulging information from bidder to company bid for – Whether commission acting fairly – Whether commission entitled to withhold information from company bid for.

The applicant company was the subject of a take-over bid by the second respondent, a rival brewing company. The proposed merger of the two companies was referred to the first respondent, the Monopolies and Mergers Commission, for investigation and report under the Fair Trading Act 1973. During the course of the commission's investigation the respondent company submitted additional evidence regarding the geographical concentration of licensed premises served by both companies together with comments on the effect the merger might have on competition in areas affected by the proposed take-over. The commission did not pass that evidence on to the applicant company. The commission's report concluded that the proposed merger would not be against the public interest. The applicant company applied for certiorari to quash the report, contending that the circumstances of its preparation showed manifest unfairness and procedural impropriety amounting to breach of the rules of natural justice because (i) the commission had not given the applicant company the opportunity of commenting on evidence submitted by the respondent company which was adverse to the applicant company's position, and (ii) the parties had not been given sufficient indication of the inferences which the commission had made or could make from the evidence so as to enable them to submit further evidence or argument, and (iii) the commission had taken into account irrelevant factors and had failed to take into account relevant factors in deciding that the proposed merger would not have an adverse effect on prices.

Held – The commission was under a duty to act fairly and, within the framework of the 1973 Act, had to establish its own procedure and approach to each reference made to it, but the concept of fairness was itself flexible and the question in each case was whether the commission had adopted a procedure so unfair that it could be said to have acted with manifest unfairness. Accordingly, the court would not lay down rules as to procedure in any particular inquiry and would not impose on the commission a requirement that every piece of material put before it which might in any way influence its report had to be put to all parties or to the opposing participants in a contested bid. Since the further evidence submitted by the respondent company merely amounted to a clearer statement of that company's original case, which had already been put to the applicant company and in respect of which it had had the opportunity of making representations, and since it was not incumbent on the commission to spell out the inferences it might draw or had drawn from the evidence before it, it could not be said that the commission had acted with manifest unfairness in the preparation of its report. The application would accordingly be dismissed (see p 469 c to f j to p 470 a e to h, p 471 g h, p 472 d e and p 473 d to f, post).

Board of Education v Rice [1911–13] All ER Rep 36, *Fairmount Investments Ltd v Secretary of State for the Environment* [1976] 2 All ER 865, *A-G of Hong Kong v Ng Yuen Shiu* [1983] 2 All ER 346 and *Mahon v Air New Zealand Ltd* [1984] 3 All ER 201 considered.

Notes

For merger references, see 47 Halsbury's Laws (4th edn) para 89.   *a*

Cases referred to in judgment

A-G of Hong Kong v Ng Yuen Shiu [1983] 2 All ER 346, [1983] 2 AC 629, [1983] 2 WLR 735, PC.

Board of Education v Rice [1911] AC 179, [1911–13] All ER Rep 36, HL.

Fairmount Investments Ltd v Secretary of State for the Environment [1976] 2 All ER 865,   *b* [1976] 1 WLR 1255, HL.

Hibernian Property Co Ltd v Secretary of State for the Environment (1973) 72 LGR 350, 27 P & CR 197.

Hoffmann-La Roche & Co AG v Secretary of State for Trade and Industry [1974] 2 All ER 1128, [1975] AC 295, [1974] 3 WLR 104, HL.

Mahon v Air New Zealand Ltd [1984] 3 All ER 201, [1984] AC 808, [1984] 3 WLR 884,   *c* PC.

Pergamon Press Ltd, Re [1970] 3 All ER 535, [1971] Ch 388, [1970] 3 WLR 792, CA.

R v Deputy Industrial Injuries Comr, ex p Moore [1965] 1 All ER 81, [1965] 1 QB 456, [1965] 2 WLR 89, CA.

R v Monopolies and Mergers Commission, ex p Elders IXL Ltd [1987] 1 All ER 451.

Wiseman v Borneman [1969] 3 All ER 275, [1971] AC 297, [1969] 3 WLR 706, HL.   *d*

Application for judicial review

Matthew Brown plc (Matthew Brown), applied, with the leave of Taylor J given on 9 January 1986, for judicial review by way of an order of certiorari to quash a report of the first respondent, the Monopolies and Mergers Commission, dated 18 October 1985 on a proposed merger between Matthew Brown and the second respondent, Scottish and   *e* Newcastle Breweries plc (Scottish and Newcastle). The facts are set out in the judgment.

Richard Buxton QC and *Peter Roth* for Matthew Brown.
John Mummery for the commission.
Anthony Graham-Dixon QC and *Kenneth Parker* for Scottish and Newcastle.   *f*

Cur adv vult

17 July. The following judgment of the court was delivered.

MACPHERSON J. This case concerns the report made by the Monopolies and Mergers   *g* Commission on 18 October 1985, on the proposed merger of Scottish and Newcastle Breweries plc (Scottish and Newcastle) and the applicant company, Matthew Brown plc (Matthew Brown). The reference to the commission arose from a bid made on 18 March 1985 by Scottish and Newcastle for the capital of Matthew Brown. On 24 April the Department of Trade and Industry referred the proposed merger to the commission and on 1 May a group of six members was appointed to handle the case. Mr D G Richards   *h* was to be the group chairman.

The group's conclusion was that the merger situation which would be created if the arrangements in contemplation were carried into effect might be expected not to operate against the public interest, so that the commission's report to the department was favourable to Scottish and Newcastle's bid.

In fact, the bid never went ahead after it had lapsed after the reference. A further bid   *j* later in 1985 was unsuccessful. An outside observer might thus ask, as I did myself, whether this court was being asked to deal with a dead issue. But both companies have their own reasons for the pursuit of their cases here before me. Matthew Brown would like to see the report impugned in case it should help to give the green light to any fresh bid which may be made after the 12-month period, which runs from the lapsing of the

last bid in December 1985. Scottish and Newcastle would like to see the report stand
a since if a fresh bid is made it could at least argue that in 1985 the arrangements then
proposed were probed and found by the commission not to be against the public interest.
Of course I see the point of both these attitudes. But I am bound to say that I wonder
whether the court should be asked to review by judicial process a report made on a dead
bid. Since I have heard full argument I propose to proceed to that review and not to be
influenced in that task by some lack of enthusiasm as to the vitality of the case. But as
b will be seen and heard at the end of this judgment, I reject this application and I would
not, even if Matthew Brown's arguments had appealed to me, have made any order in
this case in the exercise of my discretion. I am partly influenced in that respect by the
reservations I have about the application to which I have just referred. What would
happen in the event of a new bid I do not know. But judging by the pertinacity of
Matthew Brown's defence in 1985 and their persistence here, I suspect that all the present
c arguments would be advanced, even with some embellishment, in order to persuade the
Office of Fair Trading or the department that the matter should not be allowed to go
forward without further inquiry in the light of the circumstances surrounding any new
bid, which may well be different from those ruling in 1985.

That may be for the future. For the present, two parts of the report are attacked by
Matthew Brown, who say that they have been unfairly treated and that breaches of the
d rules of natural justice undermine the commission's report and its conclusions which
they seek to impugn. These are strong criticisms. And since a group of six members of
the commission and its advisory staff are concerned it is necessary to examine with care
the basis and grounds on which the matter is put forward, since it would be no light
matter to have to find that a public body carrying out an investigatory and reporting role
e had acted in a manifestly unfair manner.

North and West Cumbria was one of the battlegrounds of this conflict between these
Edinburgh and Blackburn based brewers. And our time has been particularly taken up
with an inquiry into the evidence and arguments advanced as to competition in that
area. To a lesser extent, we have considered the possible effect on prices of the merger
and the place or weight of that aspect of the matter in the commission's thinking. It
f seems to me to be quite unnecessary to go over in this judgment the timetable and
history of the commission's activities. They are set out in detail in the evidence which is
before me. Indeed the documents contain not only the facts on which each side relies but
much of their arguments as well.

Before coming to the two issues which the court faces I make some observations on
the commission's procedure and approach in so far as they concern this case. Counsel for
g Scottish and Newcastle and for the commission have both stressed that this must be an
important aspect of the case.

(1) The commission's duty is to investigate and to report. Its activities are inquisitorial
and it does not give judgment or reach the sort of conclusion required of a court. Its
conclusion in a case of this kind is a broad one, registering an opinion as to whether a
merger may or may not be against the public interest.

h (2) The commission has to consider, if a merger situation qualifying for investigation
has been created, whether the creation of that situation operates or may be expected to
operate against the public interest. The reference is framed under the provisions of
s 69(2) of the Fair Trading Act 1973 and the commission is not limited under s 69(4) in
its consideration of the elements or consequences of the merger.

(3) In determining the public interest issue the commission must take into account all
j matters which appear to it in the particular circumstances to be relevant, and it must
have particular regard to those matters set out in s 84 of the Act.

(4) The maintenance and promotion of effective competition and the interests of all
in respect of prices are obviously and specifically issues to be addressed by the commission.

(5) The commission has a discretion to regulate its own procedure (see s 81(2)). But in
so acting it must of course take into consideration any representations made by persons

having a substantial interest in the subject matter of the reference (s 81(1)). Many persons in addition to the protagonists were heard by the group in this case. Each person making *a* representations was heard separately and fully in accordance with the general and plainly acceptable procedure adopted by the commission.

(6) The commission is subject to the supervision of the High Court in its conduct of its affairs and duties under the relevant legislation.

(7) The rules of natural justice apply to the commission.

(8) If the commission adopted a procedure or took a step which was so manifestly *b* unfair as to be outside the area of its discretion to regulate its procedure, then its decision would be subject to judicial review.

That last statement of principle is really a distillation in terms of the present case of the dozen or so cases to which I was referred in argument.

Counsel for Matthew Brown relies particularly on four cases, *Board of Education v Rice* [1911] AC 179, [1911–13] All ER Rep 36, *Mahon v Air New Zealand Ltd* [1984] 3 All ER *c* 201, [1984] AC 808, *Fairmount Investments Ltd v Secretary of State for the Environment* [1976] 2 All ER 865, [1976] 1 WLR 1255 and *A-G of Hong Kong v Ng Yuen Shiu* [1983] 2 All ER 346, [1983] 2 AC 629.

He starts with Lord Loreburn's classic statement in *Board of Education v Rice* [1911] AC 179 at 182, [1911–13] All ER Rep 36 at 38: *d*

'Comparatively recent statutes have extended, if they have not originated, the practice of imposing upon departments or officers of State the duty of deciding or determining questions of various kinds. In the present instance, as in many others, what comes for determination is sometimes a matter to be settled by discretion, involving no law. It will, I suppose, usually be of an administrative kind; but sometimes it will involve matter of law as well as matter of fact, or even depend *e* upon matter of law alone. In such cases the Board of Education will have to ascertain the law and also to ascertain the facts. I need not add that in doing either they must act in good faith and fairly listen to both sides, for that is a duty lying upon every one who decides anything. But I do not think they are bound to treat such a question as though it were a trial. They have no power to administer an oath, and need not examine witnesses. They can obtain information in any way they think best, always *f* giving a fair opportunity to those who are parties in the controversy for correcting or contradicting any relevant statement prejudicial to their view. Provided this is done, there is no appeal from the determination of the Board under s. 7, sub-s. 3, of this Act. The Board have, of course, no jurisdiction to decide abstract questions of law, but only to determine actual concrete differences that may arise, and as they arise, between the managers and the local education authority. The Board is in the *g* nature of the arbitral tribunal, and a Court of law has no jurisdiction to hear appeals from the determination either upon law or upon fact. But if the Court is satisfied either that the Board have not acted judicially in the way I have described, or have not determined the question which they are required by the Act to determine, then there is a remedy by mandamus and certiorari.' *h*

Counsel for Matthew Brown stresses next the words of Lord Diplock in *Mahon v Air New Zealand Ltd* [1984] 3 All ER 201 at 210, [1984] AC 808 at 820–821:

'The rules of natural justice that are germane to this appeal can, in their Lordships' view, be reduced to those two that were referred to by the English Court of Appeal in *R v Deputy Industrial Injuries Comr, ex p Moore* [1965] 1 All ER 81 at 94–95, [1965] *j* 1 QB 456 at 488–490, which was dealing with the exercise of an investigative jurisdiction, though one of a different kind from that which was being undertaken by the judge inquiring into the Mt Erebus disaster. The first rule is that the person making a finding in the exercise of such a jurisdiction must base his decision on evidence that has some probative value in the sense described below. The second

a

rule is that he must listen fairly to any relevant evidence conflicting with the finding and any rational argument against the finding that a person represented at the inquiry, whose interests (including in that term career or reputation) may be adversely affected by it, may wish to place before him or would have so wished if he had been aware of the risk of the finding being made. The technical rules of evidence applicable to civil or criminal litigation form no part of the rules of natural justice. What is required by the first rule is that the decision to make the finding

b

must be based on *some* material that tends logically to show the existence of facts consistent with the finding and that the reasoning supportive of the finding, if it be disclosed, is not logically self-contradictory. The second rule requires that any person represented at the inquiry who will be adversely affected by the decision to make the finding should not be left in the dark as to the risk of the finding being made and thus deprived of any opportunity to adduce additional material of probative

c

value which, had it been placed before the decision-maker, *might* have deterred him from making the finding even though it cannot be predicated that it would inevitably have had that result.'

Counsel for Matthew Brown says that his clients did not have 'a fair crack of the whip', adopting Lord Russell's phrase used in *Fairmount Investments Ltd v Secretary of State for the*

d *Environment* [1976] 2 All ER 865 at 874, [1976] 1 WLR 1255 at 1266.

I have considered and taken into account all the points that have emerged from those cases. But it is important when considering the principles there set out to mark the submission of counsel for the commission that the concept of fairness is flexible and should never force the court to lay down over-rigid rules or steps which have to be followed as a matter of course, particularly in an investigation of this kind. As Lord Reid

e said in *Wiseman v Borneman* [1969] 3 All ER 275 at 277–278, [1971] AC 297 at 308:

'Natural justice requires that the procedure before any tribunal which is acting judicially shall be fair in all the circumstances, and I would be sorry to see this fundamental general principle degenerate into a series of hard-and-fast rules . . . Even where the decision is to be reached by a body acting judicially there must be a

f balance between the need for expedition and the need to give full opportunity to the defendant to see the material against him.'

Lord Morris, in the same case, said ([1969] 3 All ER 275 at 278, [1971] AC 297 at 308–309):

'We often speak of the rules of natural justice. But there is nothing rigid or

g mechanical about them . . . The principles and procedures are to be applied which, in any particular set of circumstances, are right and just and fair. Natural justice, it has been said, is only "fair play in action".'

The question, as Lord Morris posed it later, is—

'whether in the particular circumstances of a case, a tribunal acted unfairly so that

h it could be said that their procedure did not match with what justice demanded?'

Counsel for Scottish and Newcastle, in his turn, referred me to *Hoffman-La Roche & Co AG v Secretary of State for Trade and Industry* [1974] 2 All ER 1128, [1975] AC 295. Lord Diplock stressed, as does counsel for Scottish and Newcastle, that the Monopolies Commission does not adjudicate on a lis between contending parties. Lord Diplock went

j on to say ([1974] 2 All ER 1128 at 1156, [1975] AC 295 at 368):

'The adversary procedure followed in a court of law is not appropriate to its [the commission's] investigations. It has a wide discretion as to how they should be conducted. Nevertheless I would accept that it is the duty of the commissioners to observe the rules of natural justice in the course of their investigation—which means no more than that they must act fairly by giving to the person whose activities are being investigated a reasonable opportunity to put forward facts and arguments in justification of his conduct of these activities before they reach a   **a** conclusion which may affect him adversely.'

Similar principles are set out in *Re Pergamon Press Ltd* [1970] 3 All ER 535, [1971] Ch 388 where both Lord Denning MR and Sachs LJ stressed that 'fair play in action' must be applied with real flexibility. Sachs LJ said ([1970] 3 All ER 535 at 542, [1971] Ch 388 at   **b** 403):

'In each case careful regard must be had to the scope of the proceeding, the source of its jurisdiction . . . the way in which it normally falls to be conducted and its objective.'

I take into account also, of course, in my approach to the present case, the judgment of   **c** Diplock LJ in *R v Deputy Industrial Injuries Comr, ex p Moore* [1965] 1 All ER 81, [1965] 1 QB 456, to which counsel for Matthew Brown referred in his reply, and in particular Diplock LJ's specific list of requirements with which the deputy commissioner should, in that particular case, have complied (see [1965] 1 All ER 81 at 95, [1965] 1 QB 456 at 490). At the same time, it should be noted that Diplock LJ was there dealing with the case in point and he was saying what in that case was necessary in order to fulfil the   **d** requirements of the second rule of natural justice, namely, to give fair consideration to the contentions of all those involved and to listen fairly to all sides. In the end, as it seems to me, the question is whether I detect in this case manifest unfairness in all the circumstances, bearing in mind particularly the statutory framework and the commission's broad terms of reference. If there is any real risk that manifest unfairness may have tainted the commission's conclusion, then I would impugn its decision (see   **e** *Hibernian Property Co Ltd v Secretary of State* (1974) 27 P & CR 197).

Before leaving the law I refer finally to a useful case decided in this court by Mann J, which was *R v Monopolies and Mergers Commission, ex p Elders IXL Ltd* [1987] 1 All ER 451. The case concerned the disclosure of one side's financing plans and arrangements to another main party. Mann J referred to the commisson's duty to act fairly to the parties   **f** concerned in that case. I bear in mind Mann J's words and his conclusion when he said (at 461):

'What is fair in relation to a particular process and to a particular situation which is subject to that process, is for the determination by the court.'

As is so often the position each case depends on its own circumstances and its own facts.   **g**

In the light then of all these cases and of the questions distilled from them, Matthew Brown says that there was here manifest unfairness to them in that the commission relied on evidence put before it by Scottish and Newcastle which was not put before Matthew Brown. That evidence consisted of a number of maps which were photographed for me and which contained coloured pins showing the geographical concentration or spread of licensed premises in the relevant areas. With the maps there was submitted to   **h** the commission on 22 August 1985, as part of the Scottish and Newcastle submissions, comments concerning—

'the effect of increased share resulting from the merger, of tied and free trade outlets taken together in North and West Cumbria (and whether in practice any local concentration might subsequently be reduced by pub swaps).'   **j**

I quote those words from the comments which go on to address the question as to what effect the merger might have on competition in North and West Cumbria. The words come from what is termed 'the public interest letter' of 19 July 1985 which was sent by the commission to both main parties. There is incidentally and can be no challenge to the facts which the maps or pins portray or represent. The complaint is that that part of

the Scottish and Newcastle case as a whole was not specifically put before the applicants
a for their further comments.

Counsel for Matthew Brown has put the matter in a number of different and
cumulative ways. But in the end his submission takes the following course. He says that
all parties should have put to them the substance of any evidence which the commission
received which was adverse to the position adopted by the opposing party and on which
the commission would or might rely in making its report. Furthermore, he says that
b parties should be given sufficient indication of inferences which the commission think
do or may arise from evidence submitted to them so as to enable the opposing parties to
consider whether further evidence or argument should be submitted upon the relevant
point. In failing to give the applicants both a sight of those maps and submissions after
22 August and a right to comment upon them or indeed to call further evidence it is
thus said that there was manifest unfairness and procedural impropriety amounting to
c breach of the rules of natural justice. I am wholly unable to accept the applicant's
submissions for the following reasons.

(1) The timetable and conduct of the case by the commission must be looked at as a
whole. It is wrong in my judgment to seek to impose on the commission any such
uniform requirement that every piece of material put before the commission which may
in any way influence its report must go to all parties or even to the opposing main
d participants in the bid. The commission establishes, within the framework of the Fair
Trading Act 1973, its own procedure and its own approach to each individual reference.
Of course it must heed all representations made either way. But it has a discretion which
is broad and which should not be prescribed or inflexible. The concept of fairness is itself
flexible and should not be subject to the court laying down rules or steps which have to
be followed. The question in each case is whether the commission has adopted a
e procedure so unfair that no reasonable commission or group would have adopted it, so
that it can be said to have acted with manifest unfairness. Provided each party has its
mind brought to bear upon the relevant issues it is not in my judgment for the court to
lay down rules as to how each group should act in any particular inquiry. Of course
neither side must be faced with a bolt from the blue and no party may be kept in the
f dark and prevented from putting its case. But I am wholly unable to say that this
happened in the present case or that I can detect unfairness which approaches that which
might undermine this report.

(2) All parties knew perfectly well that competition in North and West Cumbria was
under review. Matthew Brown at all stages had their full opportunities to be heard on
that question. How they put their case was of course a matter for each applicant. From
g the very first letter of 26 April 1985 from the chairman of the commission the question
of competition was at large, and during the first oral hearing (on 21 June) it was and
must have been apparent that local concentration and specific local market considerations
were in the commission's minds. Indeed, as has been stressed in argument, the members
of the group were themselves focusing on that matter and it must have been apparent
that they were doubtful whether in view of already existing concentration the proposed
h merger would make much difference. Mr Townsend, the chairman and chief executive
of Matthew Brown, roundly disagreed, but the theme was there. Thereafter, in my
judgment, the correspondence shows that the whole question of concentration in North
and West Cumbria and of the local market was very much in the commission's mind. In
the 'public interest letter' of 19 July 1985, to which I have already referred, Mr MacTavish,
writing on behalf of the commission, indicated in terms the need to discuss 'the effect of
j increased share, resulting from the merger, of tied and free trade outlets taken together
in North and West Cumbria and whether in practice any local concentration might
subsequently be reduced by pub swaps'. Furthermore, Matthew Brown knew from the
Scottish and Newcastle submissions that it was their contention that it was necessary 'to
look in some detail at specific localities'. It is true that there was in that extract reference
specifically only to Carlisle, but the general message was to my mind plain. Counsel for
the commission rightly says in my judgment that nobody misled Matthew Brown into a

belief that local concentration was to be looked at in any particular manner and in particular in licensing division terms.   *a*

(3) Furthermore, no comfort can in my judgment be gained by Matthew Brown from the part played in the affair by Mr Jonathan Green. He was a senior economic adviser to the commission, whose assignment included responsibility for the investigation of 'facts relating to the question of concentration of supplies in North and West Cumbria'. He says in his affidavit that any remark that he made as to the evidence on the basis of which the commission would proceed related to his being satisfied as to the accuracy of the   *b* factual data supplied and did not relate to the nature of any conclusions which the group might reach. I see no reason to find that Matthew Brown were misled or lulled into any sense of false security by the part played by Mr Green. In so far as this was part of the argument in Matthew Brown's case I reject it.

(4) Then came Matthew Brown's second hearing on 1 August 1985. Counsel points of course particularly to the exchange which referred to the possibility of 'further points'   *c* being raised later in the month by Scottish and Newcastle 'which we [Matthew Brown] have not yet had an opportunity of dealing with'. Matthew Brown indicated that they would not be likely to put in any further submissions unless as a result of the commission's further discussions 'there appeared to be aspects of the merger which we have not dealt with'. The chairman then paid tribute to Mr Townsend and his clearly put case, and said that 'should anything fresh arise over the next few weeks which is of sufficient importance   *d* we will certainly come back to you for your comments'.

Between 25 September and 11 October 1985 there followed the exchange of letters on which (in addition to that indication) the applicants rely. It is argued that the commission misled Matthew Brown and held back information which 'objective fairness', to use the phrase of counsel for Matthew Brown, required them to put to Matthew Brown for   *e* comment.

The commission's answer to that charge is that the 22 August plans and papers were in truth no more than additional material by which Scottish and Newcastle sought to strengthen their already made point, namely that the 'market from the consumers' standpoint was very localized and much smaller than the licensing division'. The group indicated in terms on 11 October that this was so and that their view was that there was   *f* no need to seek further evidence from Matthew Brown. That is still the commission's standpoint and view and here again I cannot accept Matthew Brown's submission that the group's response was misleading.

Having decided to approach the matter on the licensing division basis, I do not believe that Matthew Brown were entitled to expect that the Scottish and Newcastle maps and papers should automatically be sent to them for further comment. The maps were new   *g* in the sense that they had not been put forward as such before, but the raw material for the information contained in them came from licensing records or from information which could be obtained by anybody. They were in reality simply a better effort to provide a model or display to illustrate the market as it existed and to highlight its local concentration.

(5) Furthermore, on 25 September 1985 Mr MacTavish, for the commission, told   *h* Matthew Brown's solicitors that since 1 August Scottish and Newcastle had put in a second submission and that there had been a second hearing with the company on 27 August. He then wrote as follows:

'The Group members have now considered the material thus presented and how it might fall to be included in their report. In this connection they have concluded   *j* that, while developing the Scottish and Newcastle case, it essentially covered ground which had already been gone over with Matthew Brown in sufficient detail for a correspondingly full account of Matthew Brown's position on these points to be included in the Commission's report. There was no need therefore for them to take up Mr Buxton's [counsel for Matthew Brown] offer.'

a Matthew Brown's solicitors came back on 4 October with their clients' comments on the draft of one section of the proposed report. In connection with the statement that consideration of concentration and its effect on competition requires detailed information on the location, ownership and supply characteristics of every on-licence outlet in the area, the solicitors wrote as follows:

b 'Matthew Brown has put statistics to the Commission on the basis of licensing divisions because it considers that those figures, together with the further information as to licensed and registered clubs, give a good general indication of local concentration. It has never been suggested in the course of the inquiry that that approach was inappropriate, or that a more detailed study of the kind mentioned in paragraph 25 of the draft was required, or was available to the Commission. Our clients assume that no such study has been undertaken, since nothing has been put c to Matthew Brown for comment, but they would be glad if you could confirm that that is the case.'

On 11 October 1985 Mr MacTavish replied. He said:

d 'Your letter also refers to the evidence presented by Matthew Brown on concentration of supply in North and West Cumbria. This has been very fully summarised in the draft chapter on the views of the main parties; and, as you will know from my letter of yesterday's date on this chapter, we have now accepted the inclusion of an additional table. As to the effect of increased concentration on competition this was raised in very specific terms by the Commission at the first hearing with Matthew Brown on 21 June 1985 ... It emerged from this, and from similar questioning of the Scottish and Newcastle representatives the previous day, e that the market from the consumers' standpoint was very localised and much smaller than the Licensing Division; and this along with the analytical implications is reflected in the passage referred to in your letter. Although not specifically requested to do so, Scottish and Newcastle subsequently elaborated on their earlier evidence on this point by producing detailed material to back up their contentions. The Group's consideration of this, and of whether there was need to seek further f evidence from Matthew Brown, is noted in my letter of 25 September to Mr. Paines [of Matthew Brown's solicitors].'

(6) In my judgment it was for the commission to decide whether, in the light of the submissions made already in detail to them, it was necessary to give Matthew Brown another bite at the cherry. I see no misleading of Matthew Brown by the commission. Indeed, in the letter of 11 October it was expressly stated that there was elaboration by g Scottish and Newcastle 'on their earlier evidence on this point by producing detailed material to back up their contentions'. So the commission did, in my judgment, indicate that Scottish and Newcastle had developed its argument in evidence.

But that does not in my judgment mean that the dozen pages, which can be seen to be substantially argument rather than fact when they are read in full, or the maps, necessarily had to be passed on in order that fair play should be seen to be in action. The h theme was not new at all. Matthew Brown had made its own case and its own theme. I do not impugn the commission for failing to submit those documents for comment or for further expansion of Matthew Brown's case.

(7) Finally, on this part of the case, I turn to the commission's report itself. The most relevant paragraphs, to which counsel for Matthew Brown referred, are paras 5.48 and j 7.9. It is perfectly true that para 5.48 contains a reference to the fact that—

'Detailed analysis of every full on-licensed outlet in the Petty Sessional Divisions where concentration was alleged had disclosed that, outside the main towns, there was only a handful of areas where the available outlets would be supplied with draught beers exclusively by the merged company at the time of the merger, and in every case at least one of these outlets was a free trade outlet.'

So the maps may well have been in the commission's mind, together with the other schedules and evidence about the numbers and concentration in Cumbria.

But in para 7.9 it is to be observed that the limit of the conclusion reached by the commission to which extra evidence may have contributed is stated as follows:

'Thirdly, from the point of view of the consumer and the effect on the consumer of increased concentration, it is not meaningful to consider an area the size of North and West Cumbria or even one the size of a licensing district within it. The relevant area for consumers is typically the individual town or even village. There are towns or villages where the preponderance of outlets is supplied either by Matthew Brown or by Scottish and Newcastle and there are a few villages where the only outlet is supplied by one or other of them; but on the information available to us we believe that there is no town or village big enough to support a number of pubs where, as a result of the merger, there would not still be an adequate number (having regard to the size of the population) of outlets supplied by brewers other than the merged company. Even where there would be a majority of outlets supplied by the merged company a substantial proportion of such outlets would be free houses or clubs, which could, as has been pointed out, change their supplier.'

We do not know exactly what material formed the basis for that third conclusion. But in any event I fail to see that any further comment by Matthew Brown would have altered the position at all. Their case and its stress was known. There were in truth no revelations in the new material. And certainly it was not in my judgment an outlandish or unreasonable view which the commission formed when it decided that further evidence or argument from Matthew Brown, in pursuance of the offer of counsel for Matthew Brown, was not necessary.

(8) It is not necessary for a tribunal always to spell out what inferences it may draw from evidence or what conclusions it may reach. All tribunals must watch and listen and make their respective findings. But in my judgment the approach of counsel for Matthew Brown is too rigid and goes further than the commission was required to go in the circumstances of this case.

(9) I do not find manifest, or indeed any, unfairness in this part of the case. And it is finally to be observed that although on 25 October 1985 Mr MacTavish told Matthew Brown that there had indeed been subsequent elaboration of Scottish and Newcastle's earlier evidence this did not at the time spur Matthew Brown into a request to see it. I refer to this aspect of the case again later.

I move then to consider the second complaint, namely that the commission took into account irrelevant factors and failed to take into account relevant factors in connection with prices, so that again the commission's conclusion is flawed. Matthew Brown in this connection proposed and made a survey of the prices charged for standard draught bitter beer in all its tied houses, in order to produce a weighted average price, by volume of beer sold in each house. The idea was that Scottish and Newcastle would perform a similar exercise. But they did not do so. Their contention was and is that a comparison based on weighted averages is invalid because considerations governing the general level of prices may vary markedly from area to area and from public house to public house.

In those circumstances it seems to me that provided the group had proper regard to such evidence as the parties did put before them as to prices it was a matter for the group to decide what weight, if any, or what reliance they should place on the arguments and method of comparison contended for by Matthew Brown. Counsel for Matthew Brown urges me to say that the group wrongly ignored Matthew Brown's survey and failed to press Scottish and Newcastle for a similar survey which might have produced a useful comparison, and that the group should have drawn adverse inferences from Scottish and Newcastle's failure to produce its own survey and figures.

I am unable to see any unfairness in this connection nor any basis on which I can detect a failure to consider relevant matters or a reliance upon irrelevant matters, within the

meaning of those phrases which are now familiar in RSC Ord 53 cases. In their conclusion
a section, para 7.19 is that which is attacked. And I am bound to say that I see nothing
whatsoever to complain about in that paragraph. At its heart is the conclusion that on
the evidence submitted it would be unsafe to reach any general conclusion about the
relative levels of the protagonists' prices. The paragraph goes on to consider what might
happen to prices and to conclude that in the group's opinion the merger would not be
likely to have any markedly adverse effect on prices once the forces of competition
b operated.

I cannot see force in Matthew Brown's arguments on this aspect of the case. And it is
right to say that counsel for Matthew Brown did not himself place much emphasis on it
at the end of the day.

I turn then to consider the question of the exercise of my discretion. Strictly perhaps
this is not germane since I reject Matthew Brown's substantive case. But even if I had
c seen force in their arguments I firmly believe that this would not have been a case in
which I would have come to Matthew Brown's aid.

First, because there was clear evidence of the existence of the material which counsel
for Matthew Brown so keenly urges me that his clients should have seen, and yet
Matthew Brown did not press for its disclosure after 25 October and before the report
was written.

d Secondly, because in spite of all that counsel for Matthew Brown says, I do not see what
further evidence or argument would have achieved. The maps simply set out in another
manner the known figures and nature of the licensed houses. And the dozen pages were
argument addressed to the already known point which Scottish and Newcastle were
making about markets and concentration, of which Matthew Brown in any event had
notice. Matthew Brown had had two long and full meetings with the commission.

e Thirdly, because, as I said at the outset, I am not at all happy that the court should be
asked to nullify the general conclusion reached in 1985 based on the facts and figures
then put before it of a report which stems from a reference of an extinct bid.

The future, as I have said, may disclose a further bid. Then the Secretary of State will
bear in mind Matthew Brown's protestations in this case. For the present I am bound to
f say that I think Matthew Brown protest too much, and that their application is not
soundly based and should be dismissed.

Application dismissed.

Solicitors: *Allen & Overy* (for Matthew Brown); *Treasury Solicitor*; *Slaughter & May* (for
Scottish and Newcastle).

Raina Levy   Barrister.

Six Arlington Street Investments Ltd v Persons unknown

CHANCERY DIVISION
KNOX J
25, 26 MARCH 1986

Execution – Possession – Writ of possession – Time of execution – Whether sheriff required to execute writ immediately or merely as soon as reasonably practicable.

The duty of a sheriff to execute a writ of possession, as with other writs of execution, is to execute it as soon as is reasonably practicable rather than immediately without the lapse of any interval of time whatever the circumstances (see p 477 *d f g*, post).

Dicta of Lord Abbott CJ in *Carlile v Parkins* (1822) 3 Stark at 167 and of Lord Denman CJ in *Mason v Paynter* (1841) 1 QB at 981 followed.

Notes

For delivery of possession, see 17 Halsbury's Laws (4th edn) para 501, and for cases on writ of possession, see 21 Digest (Reissue) 428–432, 3321–3376.

Cases referred to in judgment

Carlile v Parkins (1822) 3 Stark 163, 171 ER 809, NP.
Mason v Paynter (1841) 1 QB 974, 113 ER 1406.

Motion

By a motion dated 25 March 1986 the plaintiffs, Six Arlington Street Investments Ltd, sought a mandatory injunction ordering the Sheriff of Greater London forthwith to enter land and premises known as 15–17 Tramway Avenue, Stratford in the London borough of Newham and cause the plaintiffs to have vacant possession of the land and premises. The facts are set out in the judgment.

George Laurence for the plaintiffs.
Stephen Acton for the sheriff.

KNOX J. This is a motion, as originally issued, for a mandatory injunction ordering the Sheriff of Greater London forthwith to enter or cause to be entered certain land and premises known as 15–17 Tramway Avenue, Stratford, in the London borough of Newham, with an exception, on which nothing turns, and to cause the plaintiffs to have vacant possession of that land and premises.

Two questions, it is agreed, arise on this application. The first is whether it is right that I should grant a mandatory injunction, not quite in those terms, because in the course of the argument the plaintiffs who seek this injunction modified the precise terms and sought to obtain an injunction that the sheriff should use his best endeavours to obtain vacant possession before the close of business today. The second question, which has not been argued before me, and about which I say nothing revolves round the effect of the significance of the word 'vacant', and it is whether or not there is a duty on the sheriff to remove chattels from the premises in respect of which he has a writ of possession to execute.

The background to this case is that there was an application made under RSC Ord 113 by the plaintiffs to recover possession of land occupied by gipsies; I call them gipsies, although there is no clear evidence that they are such, but it is a convenient shorthand expression for these purposes. The land was first occupied, it appears, on the evening of 14 March, and some considerable number of caravans were taken onto the site. The

plaintiffs then had quite valuable property in the form of building materials, the evidence
a is of the order of £20,000-worth in value, and they discovered about this trespass on the
following Monday, 17 March, and with due expedition moved this court for abridgement
of the time for service, which is five days under Ord 113, and that application I granted
on the afternoon of that Monday 17. The matter came on before Falconer J on
Wednesday, 19 March, when he made an order for possession. So the process of execution
starts last Wednesday. The writ of possession was issued that day, and it was taken round
b to Messrs Burchell & Ruston, the office of the under-sheriff at 3.00 pm, on Wednesday,
19 March.

At that stage, all that reached that office was the writ of possession, which of course
describes the land in question and commands that the sheriff enter the said land and
cause the plaintiffs to have possession of it. That is the essential part of the writ. The
usual practice of including a plan had not been followed, although the plan followed the
c next day. Equally, there was at that stage no clear indication of any exceptional urgency
in relation to the matter, and a practice which is sometimes followed of supplying the
affidavit evidence on the basis of which the order has been made was not followed. There
is no obligation of course for it to be followed, but the fact is that there was no such
additional material provided at that stage. On that day the plaintiffs' solicitors contacted
the sheriff's officers, and there is in evidence a report of a conversation that took place on
d the telephone. It is contained in a letter from the plaintiffs' solicitors on the following
day, the Thursday, and they give this account of the telephone conversation:

'We asked you how quickly you would be able to execute the Writ of Possession
and you informed us that you would send one of your Officers round to the affected
site on Friday 21st March. If your Officer was unable to persuade the trespassers to
e leave those premises you said that the Writ would have to be entered on a "list and
it would be a case of first come first served".'

And then there was a further intimation that it would be necessary to have available an
alternative site to which the trespassers' caravans could be towed in the event of none of
f the trespassers actually being present when the officer performed the execution. That
was what happened on the Wednesday.

On the Thursday, the letter which I have just read an extract from, was actually sent.
That of course gave a brief outline of the history to date, including the fact that time for
service had been abridged by this court and that there was a grave risk of damage to
property, but no mention was made, because it was not then of course appreciated, that
g there was any risk to life and limb. Nevertheless, that letter sent and delivered on
Thursday, 20 March did show grounds of urgency. The warrant to the sheriff's officer
was delivered at 1.20 pm on that day, so that there was that interval of time between
3.30 the previous day when the writ of possession reached the under-sheriff's office and
1.20 the following day. At 3.00 pm on Thursday afternoon, the sheriff's officers did in
fact, one day earlier than they had prognosticated on the telephone the previous day, go
h to the premises and warn such occupants as they found that there was a writ of possession
which would be executed. At 5.30 that afternoon, there was a meeting with the police,
and it was made clear by the local superintendent to Mr Pedvin, the partner in the
sheriff's officers' firm, that a person described as the 'Queen of the Gypsies' had recently
died, and the travellers were coming into Newham to be present at her funeral. The
superintendent told Mr Pedvin that he was unable to obtain the services of sufficient
j policemen to be able to assist in the execution of the writ in view of the serious risk of
public disorder if it was sought to evict the travellers before the funeral. It was then
thought that the funeral would be taking place on the following Wednesday, which is
today. At that stage it was apparent that it was going to be very difficult indeed, and this
has not been criticised, to execute the writ before the funeral took place because of the
police view, formed no doubt on the basis of long experience.

The next day, which was the Friday, there was a letter written by the deputy sheriff of which some criticism has been made. He wrote to the plaintiffs' solicitors, and he said *a* very accurately, and properly no doubt, that most if not all writs of possession are matters of urgency and are certainly treated as such by his office. Then he pointed out certain other considerations. First of all, that there were numerous writs, and that a sheriff would be liable to criticism if without proper cause he preferred a later writ to an earlier one, but that in extreme cases, where there was physical danger not only to property but to individuals, that was a matter to be taken into account. Second, he pointed out the *b* necessity for police assistance where there was a risk of a disturbance, and he gave the information again regarding the prospective funeral. Then he said:

'As matters stand at present my officers have two further gypsy evictions scheduled for Thursday of next week, together with a number of other writs of possession during the course of that week. It is therefore unlikely that it will be possible both *c* from the point of view of my officers and the police, to mount the necessary full scale operation to execute your client's writ of possession until the following week. [That of course would have been the week after Easter.] It is possible that circumstances will alter and naturally should it prove possible to do so the execution of your client's writ will be brought forward to an earlier date.'
d

The weekend intervened, and on Monday, 24 March, having been alerted that the plaintiffs were proposing to take proceedings, the under-sheriff became directly involved himself. He wrote a letter on the Monday, which was delivered by hand to the plaintiffs at the hearing of the application that the plaintiffs launched on that Monday for leave to serve short notice. I do not think it necessary to read that letter in full. It does point out, amongst other things, the great influx of travellers in this particular area of London over *e* the last few days, and it repeats the advice of the superintendent that to enforce the writ of possession before the funeral would cause grave public disorder. It finishes by saying: '... the sheriff and this office are most anxious to obey the High Court Order as expeditiously as possible', and then it goes on with something in the nature of a cri de coeur by pointing out that in practical terms the number of writs and possessions in the year 1985 had increased by over 40%, and that there were gipsies who were being moved *f* round and round London. It is not suggested on any side that that particular aspect of the matter is something which this court ought to take into account in regard to whether a writ of possession has been properly executed.

I gave leave to serve short notice on Monday, and the matter came first before me yesterday and has been continued in argument today. The funeral was in fact arranged for yesterday and I understand, although this is not strictly in evidence, in fact did take *g* place yesterday.

Finally, so far as the facts are concerned, it is now established that the writ is to be executed this afternoon and arrangements have been made for that to be done in conjunction with the police. That was a matter that was only organised, I think, yesterday. It is set out in detail what the proposals are in Mr Black's affidavit which was sworn *h* yesterday, 25 March.

On those facts the question that I have to deal with is whether or not I should grant a mandatory injunction in the terms either in the notice of motion or as modified in the course of counsel's argument for the plaintiffs. The law in this regard seems to me clear on the authorities. Lord Denman CJ in *Mason v Paynter* (1841) 1 QB 974 at 981, 113 ER 1406 at 1408 said:
j

'It is now contended for the sheriff that he has a reasonable time to execute every writ. No doubt he has; but that does not excuse him in refusing to execute a writ, when he has the opportunity, is required to do it, and nothing occurs to prevent him.'

That was a case where, as the headnote states—

a

'The sheriff, having received notice that the landlord intended to apply to set aside the proceedings for irregularity, his officer did not execute the possession; and the proceedings were afterwards set aside by a Judge's order, but not for an irregularity . . .'

That was clearly a case where a sheriff had refused for a reason that he was not to know at
b the time when he refused whether it was good, bad or indifferent, and the court there held that he had no jurisdiction to refuse to execute a writ that had been issued to him.
    The references to reasonableness are based on the earlier decision of *Carlile v Parkins* (1822) 3 Stark 163 at 167, 171 ER 809 at 810, where Abbott CJ said: 'It has been objected that the action is not maintainable . . .' That was an action on the case against a sheriff for wilfully and without any reasonable or probable cause delaying to sell goods of the
c plaintiff, which he had seized by virtue of a writ of *levari facias*. Abbott CJ went on:

    '. . . but I am of opinion, that if the sheriff wilfully delays to sell for an unreasonable time, he is liable. If he abstains from pursuing the course of his duty, without any reasonable cause for the deviation, he is liable to an action; but if there be a reasonable and probable cause for what he does, he is not responsible: this I take
d   to be the law.'

    In my judgment, the law is perfectly clear. It can be formulated in a variety of different ways, but in my judgment the duty to execute a writ of possession, in common with other writs of execution, is to execute as soon as is reasonably practicable. Whether that is in any way different from the sheriff having a reasonable time in which to execute I very much doubt. The only passage in the textbooks that perhaps casts some doubt on
e that is to be found in 17 Halsbury's Laws (4th edn) para 501, which says, under the heading of 'Delivery of possession':

    'The sheriff must at once proceed to deliver to the plaintiff complete and vacant possession of the premises, turning out, by force if need be, all other persons, although if the person in possession attorns to the plaintiff this would appear to be
f   sufficient.'

The note to 'at once' is: 'If the sheriff delays, the plaintiff can bring an action for damages suffered as a result', and the authority for that is *Mason v Paynter*, from which I have read an extract. In my judgment the expression 'at once' is unfortunate and misleading in that it suggests that it must take place immediately without any interval of time, whatever the circumstances may be. That, in my judgment, is not only not in accordance
g with but contrary to what was said both in *Mason v Paynter* and in *Carlile v Parkins*. The test is what is 'reasonably practicable', not 'at once'.
    On those principles what I have to ask myself is whether there was a failure by the under-sheriff, or the sheriff's officers, such as to grant the application for a mandatory injunction. I have no doubt that there was no such justification. The highest that the
h case can be put is that the letter from the deputy sheriff indicated that there might well be a delay, but, of course, that was no more than the fact. There might indeed be delays, but the question is whether the delay was unreasonable, and I do not find, even in the paragraph which is perhaps the high-water mark of the plaintiffs' case in the deputy sheriff's letter of 21 March 1986, where it will be recalled it was said that there were two further gipsy evictions scheduled for Tuesday and Thursday of the next week and
j therefore it was unlikely that it would be possible to execute this writ until the following week, anything approaching a refusal, or a failure or an indication that there would be a refusal or failure on the sheriff's part to do what he recognised and his office recognised to be their duty. In the circumstances, therefore, I do not propose to grant a mandatory injunction.

There is still unresolved, and it may be that it will not need to be resolved by this court, the question of whether or not there is a duty on a sheriff to remove chattels, the chattels in question in this case, of course, being the caravans. I do not propose to say anything about that at this stage, but I decline to issue an injunction against the under-sheriff in the way asked.

Order accordingly.

Solicitors: *Baileys Shaw & Gillett* (for the plaintiffs); *Burchell & Ruston* (for the sheriff).

Evelyn M C Budd   Barrister.

R v Mara

COURT OF APPEAL, CIVIL DIVISION
PARKER LJ, HODGSON AND MACPHERSON JJ
14 OCTOBER, 5 NOVEMBER 1986

Health and safety at work – Employer's duties – Duty to other person's employees – Duty to conduct undertaking in such a way as to ensure other person's employees not exposed to risks to health and safety – Cleaning contractor cleaning company's premises – Cleaning contractor leaving cleaning machinery at company's premises with consent and agreeing to allow company's employees to use machinery – Company's employee electrocuted by faulty cable in cleaning machine – Whether company's employees persons who might be affected by contractor's conduct of its undertaking – Health and Safety at Work etc Act 1974, ss 2(2), 3(1).

The appellant was the director of a company which provided cleaning services. In December 1983 the company entered into a contract with IS to clean its premises on weekday mornings. It was agreed that the cleaning machines provided by the company would be left at IS's premises when not in use, and it was further agreed that IS's employees could use the machines to clean a loading bay at IS's premises. In November 1984 an employee of IS was electrocuted by a faulty cable on one of the company's machines while using it to clean the loading bay. The appellant was charged with failing to discharge an employer's duty contrary to ss 33(1)[a] and 37(1)[b] of the Health and Safety at Work etc Act 1974 by consenting to the breach by the company of its duty under s 3(1)[c] of that Act to conduct its undertaking in such a way as to ensure that persons not in its employment were not thereby exposed to risks to their health and safety. The appellant was convicted. He appealed.

_____

[a]   Section 33(1), so far as material, provides: 'It is an offence for a person—(a) to fail to discharge a duty to which he is subject by virtue of sections 2 to 7 . . .'

[b]   Section 37(1) provides: 'Where an offence under any of the relevant statutory provisions committed by a body corporate is proved to have been committed with the consent or connivance of, or to have been attributable to any neglect on the part of, any director, manager, secretary or other similar officer of the body corporate or a person who was purporting to act in any such capacity, he as well as the body corporate shall be guilty of that offence and shall be liable to be proceeded against and punished accordingly.'

[c]   Section 3(1) is set out at p 481 *b*, post

Held – The failure to remove or replace the unsafe cable was a breach by the company
a of its duty to its own employees under s 2(2)[d] of the 1974 Act, since it had not, so far as
reasonably practicable, provided and maintained plant which was safe and/or made
arrangements for ensuring safety in connection with the use and handling of articles.
Since the cable would or might have been used by IS's employees, it followed that they
too might be affected by, and exposed to, risks resulting from the way in which the
company carried out its undertaking, within the meaning of s 3(1) of the 1974 Act.
b Accordingly, the appellant had been rightly convicted and his appeal would be dismissed
(see p 481 g h and p 482 a to c, post).

Notes

For an employer's general duties to ensure the health and safety at work of his employees,
see 16 Halsbury's Laws (4th edn) para 773.
c   For an employer's duties to persons other than his employees, see ibid para 778.
For the Health and Safety at Work etc Act 1974, ss 2, 3, 33, 37, see 19 Halsbury's
Statutes (4th edn) 616, 618, 644, 650.

Cases referred to in judgment

d Aitchison v Howard Doris Ltd 1979 SLT (Notes) 22.
Carmichael v Rosehall Engineering Works Ltd 1984 SLT 40.
R v Swan Hunter Shipbuilders Ltd [1982] 1 All ER 264, CA.

Appeal

The appellant, John Joseph Mara, was convicted in the Crown Court at Warwick before
e his Honour Judge Harrison-Hall and a jury of failing to discharge an employer's duty
under ss 33(1) and 37(1) of the Health and Safety at Work etc Act 1974, in that on
10 November 1984 being a director of CMS Cleaning and Maintenance Services Ltd
(CMS) he consented to or connived at the breach by CMS of its duty as an employer
under s 3(1) of the 1974 Act to conduct its undertaking in such a way as to ensure that
persons not in its employment, namely employees of International Stores plc (IS) at High
f Street, Solihull, were not thereby exposed to risks to their health or safety or the breach
of duty by CMS was due to his neglect. The appellant was fined £200 and he appealed
against his conviction pursuant to a certificate granted by the trial judge under s 1(2) of
the Criminal Appeal Act 1965 on the question whether on 10 November 1984 any
employees of IS were on the evidence persons who might be affected by the conduct of
CMS of its undertaking within the meaning of s 3(1) of the 1974 Act. The facts are set
g out in the judgment of the court.

John R West (assigned by the Registrar of Criminal Appeals) for the appellant.
I H Foster for the Crown.

Cur adv vult

h 5 November. The following judgment of the court was delivered.

PARKER LJ. The appellant at all material times was a director of a company called
CMS Cleaning and Maintenance Ltd (CMS). It was a small company of which the
secretary and only other director was the appellant's wife.

j
_____

d   Section 2(2), so far as material, provides: 'Without prejudice to the generality of an employer's
duty under the preceding subsection, the matters to which that duty extends include in
particular—(a) the provision and maintenance of plant and systems of work that are, so far as is
reasonably practicable, safe and without risks to health; (b) arrangements for ensuring, so far as is
reasonably practicable, safety and absence of risks to health in connection with the use, handling,
storage and transport of articles and substances . . .'

In December 1983 CMS entered into a contract with International Stores plc (IS) to clean their premises at High Street, Solihull, for a consideration of £94 a week plus VAT. The work to be done by CMS was carried out on weekday mornings before the store opened. Their employees left the premises each morning at the latest by 9 am and did not return until about 7.30 the following morning or, in the case of Fridays, until about 7.30 am on Monday morning. The work involved the use of certain electrical cleaning machines provided by CMS, and these were left on the IS premises when CMS employees were not there. The machines included a polisher/scrubber.

Originally the contracted work involved the cleaning of the loading bay for the store, but the cleaning of such bay in the mornings was inconvenient because it was frequently interrupted by the arrival of delivery lorries. It was therefore agreed that cleaning of the loading bay should be removed from the ambit of the contract and the weekly charge reduced from £94 per week to £81·74 per week. At that time CMS agreed, at the request of IS, that their cleaning machines could be used by IS employees for cleaning of the loading bay and perhaps also other cleaning and to the knowledge of the appellant they were so used.

On Saturday afternoon, 10 November 1984 one Diarmid Cusack, an employee of IS, was using a CMS polisher/scrubber for cleaning the loading bay, when he was electrocuted due to the defective condition of the machine's cable. The cable had been damaged in a number of places revealing the insulation of the core conductors underneath. It had been repaired with insulating tape in many places. There was ample evidence that it was unsafe for general use and particularly unsafe if used in wet areas. The loading bay was ordinarily wet when the polisher/scrubber was used on it. The appellant admitted that he had last seen the cable some four to six weeks before the accident and that at that time there were two taped areas on it which he himself had placed there.

As a result of the accident IS, their manager, one Patrick Heaney, and the appellant were charged with offences under the Health and Safety at Work etc Act 1974 on an indictment containing ten counts. The first four related only to IS, the next five only to Patrick Heaney and the last to the appellant alone. IS pleaded guilty to one charge of failing to discharge the duty imposed by s 2(1) of the 1974 Act and for that offence was fined £5,000 and ordered to pay prosecution costs. The three other charges against it were not put. Patrick Heaney pleaded guilty to one charge of consenting to or conniving at a breach by IS of the duty imposed by s 2(2)(c) of the 1974 Act and for that offence was fined £1,000. He pleaded not guilty to the remaining charges against him and they were ordered to lie on the file.

The particulars of the sole offence charged against the appellant were as follows:

'On the 10th day of November 1984 being a director of C.M.S. Cleaning and Maintenance Services Limited consented to or connived at the breach by the said company of its duty as an employer under Section 3(1) of the Health and Safety at Work Act 1974 to conduct its undertaking in such a way as to ensure that persons not in its employment namely employees of International Stores PLC at High Street Solihull were not thereby exposed to risks to their health or safety or the said breach of duty by the company was due to his neglect.'

The appellant pleaded not guilty, but was on 27 February 1986 convicted of that offence after a two-day trial before his Honour Judge Harrison-Hall and a jury. He was fined £200.

He now appeals against conviction on the certificate of the trial judge that the case was fit for appeal on the question:

'Whether on the 10th day of November 1984 any employees of International Stores Limited were, on the evidence, persons who might be affected by the conduct by C.M.S. Limited of its undertaking within the meaning of section 3(1) of the 1974 Act.'

a   At the conclusion of the prosecution case it was submitted on behalf of the appellant that
there was no case for him to answer. That submission was rejected. Thereafter the
appellant neither gave nor called any evidence and was convicted on a unanimous verdict
after a short and admirable summing up, of which no criticism is or could be made.

The point arising on the appeal is, as appears from the foregoing, a short point of
construction. We therefore begin by setting out the terms of s 3(1):

b   'It shall be the duty of every employer to conduct his undertaking in such a way
as to ensure, so far as is reasonably practicable, that persons not in his employment
who may be affected thereby are not thereby exposed to risks to their health or
safety.'

It was first submitted, somewhat tentatively, that the subsection had no application to
undertakings consisting in the provision of services. There is no indication anywhere
c   that the undertakings referred to were intended to be restricted in any way and we have
no hesitation in rejecting this submission.

Next it was submitted that CMS was not, on Saturday morning, conducting its
undertaking at all and that the only undertaking then being conducted was the
undertaking of IS. Accordingly it was submitted that CMS was not in breach of the duty
d   imposed by s 3(1) and the appellant could not therefore have consented to or connived at
any such breach or caused any such breach by his neglect.

This submission has more force but, in our judgment, it is not permissible to treat the
section as being applicable only when an undertaking is in the process of being actively
carried on. A factory, for example, may shut down on Saturdays and Sundays for
manufacturing purposes, but the employer may have the premises cleaned by a contractor
over the weekend. If the contractor's employees are exposed to risks to health or safety
e   because machinery is left insecure, or vats containing noxious substances are left
unfenced, it is, in our judgment, clear that the factory owner is in breach of his duty
under s 3(1). The way in which he conducts his undertaking is to close his factory for
manufacturing purposes over the weekend and to have it cleaned during the shut down
period. It would clearly be reasonably practicable to secure machinery and noxious vats,
f   and on the plain wording of the section he would be in breach of his duty if he failed to
do so.

The undertaking of CMS was the provision of cleaning services. So far as IS is
concerned, the way in which CMS conducted its undertaking was to do the cleaning on
weekday mornings and leave its machines and other equipment on the premises in the
intervals with permission for IS employees to use the same and knowledge that they
g   would use the same.

That equipment included an unsafe cable. The failure to remove or replace that cable
was clearly a breach by CMS of its duty to its own employees imposed by s 2(2)(a) and (b)
of the 1974 Act. The manner in which it carried out its undertaking was such that it had
not provided and maintained plant which was, so far as reasonably practicable, safe, nor
had it made arrangements for ensuring, so far as reasonably practicable, safety in
h   connection with the use and handling of articles. Since the cable would or might be used
by IS employees, it follows that IS employees might be affected by, and exposed to, risks
by the way in which CMS carried out its undertaking.

It was contended that if s 3(1) was sufficiently wide to cover the present and other like
cases, there would be no need for s 6, and that ss 3, 4, 5 and 6 were in some way mutually
exclusive.

j   This contention is, in our judgment, untenable. To take a simple example, an employer
may provide for his own employees and the employees of others a piece of equipment
which he has leased from someone else. If that equipment is unsafe, he may be in breach
of s 2(2)(a) in regard to his own employees, for he may not have done all that was
reasonably practicable to see that it was safe. He may also be in breach of s 3, but, whether
or not he is in breach, the designer, manufacturer and lessor of the plant may also be in

breach of duty under s 6(1). It may well be that a person liable under one of the later sections will at the same time be liable under s 3, but this is the inevitable result of the wide wording of s 3 and should in practice cause no difficulty.

In our judgment there was a clear case for the appellant to answer and he was rightly convicted. The answer to the question in respect of which the judge certified that this was a proper case for appeal is that employees of IS were persons who might be affected by the way in which CMS conducted their undertaking within the meaning of s 3(1) of the 1974 Act.

We should mention in conclusion that the ambit of s 3(1) has been considered in *Aitchison v Howard Doris Ltd* 1979 SLT (Notes) 22, *Carmichael v Rosehall Engineering Works Ltd* 1984 SLT 40 and *R v Swan Hunter Shipbuilders Ltd* [1982] 1 All ER 264. We have however found little assistance from those cases in the determination of the question before us, although the last two lend some marginal support for the conclusion we have reached.

Accordingly this appeal is dismissed.

Appeal dismissed.

Solicitors: *J V Vobe & Co*, Birmingham (for the Crown).

N P Metcalfe Esq   Barrister.

a
Atkinson v Fitzwalter and others

COURT OF APPEAL, CIVIL DIVISION
MAY, PARKER AND STOCKER LJJ
1, 2, 31 JULY 1986

b
Libel and slander – Pleading – Amendment – Defence – Amendment to plead justification at a late stage – Amendment raising allegation of fraud – Whether late amendment alleging fraud should be allowed.

The plaintiff, a dentist, brought a libel action against the defendants in respect of comments contained in a television programme edited by the first defendant and transmitted by the second defendant. The plaintiff claimed the comments were
c
defamatory of him. The writ was served on 9 August 1984 and a defence in the form of a simple denial was served on 16 October 1984. After the writ had been served the defendants began to consider whether they could plead justification, and made inquiries to discover whether such a defence could be supported. By 14 January 1985 the action was set down for trial. By 11 September 1985 an amended defence pleading justification
d
was ready, but the defendants' solicitor mistakenly believed that the action had become dormant and no attempt was made to put in an amended defence until 16 April 1986, when the defendants successfully applied to the judge to stand the case out of the trial list and for leave to amend their defence to plead justification. The plaintiff appealed, contending (i) that the amendment amounted to an allegation of fraud and an amendment to pleadings to raise an allegation of fraud could not be allowed where fraud
e
had not been pleaded in the first place, (ii) the lengthy delay on the part of the defendants precluded them from amending their defence at such a late stage of the proceedings and (iii) the particulars in the amended plea of justification did not go to the real sting of the alleged libel and were too vague.

Held – The general principle to be applied in considering an amendment, however late,
f
was that it should be allowed if justice required it, provided the other party could be monetarily compensated for any inconvenience, and the fact that the amendment alleged fraud was not of itself reason to refuse to allow it to be made. On the facts, if the allegation of fraudulent conduct was true it ought to be investigated at the trial of the action, while any hardship caused to the plaintiff could be compensated for by the award of increased damages if the defence of justification failed. However, because so many of
g
the particulars in the plea of justification did not support the allegation of fraud the proposed amendment would be struck out but without prejudice to the defendants' right to make a further application for leave to amend. On that basis the appeal would be allowed (see p 487 *h j*, p 490 *b d* to *j*, p 491 *b c*, p 492 *j* to p 493 *a*, p 494 *b c g*, p 499 *f g* and p 502 *d* to *g*, post).

Associated Leisure Ltd v Associated Newspapers Ltd [1970] 2 All ER 754 applied.
h
Per May and Parker LJJ. Although when a properly drafted plea of justification is included in the defence in a defamation action it is permissible to rely on any facts that are proved in order to support it to reduce the damages, even though those facts by themselves are insufficient to make good the defence as a whole, nevertheless it is not permissible to plead, under the guise of particulars of justification, matters which do not go to a plaintiff's general reputation with a view to leading evidence about them solely
j
to support an argument that the damages should be reduced (see p 490 *j* to p 491 *a* and p 494 *d e*, post).

Per May LJ. The more serious the allegation that is made by an amended defence the more clearly must the court be satisfied that no prejudice is being caused to the plaintiff which cannot be compensated in some satisfactory way before allowing the amendment (see p 490 *c*, post).

Per Stocker LJ. A plea of justification should not be allowed by amendment in circumstances in which the statement alleged to be defamatory unequivocally involves *a* an assertion that a plaintiff has been fraudulent (see p 499 *h*, post).

Notes
For amendment to libel pleadings, see 28 Halsbury's Laws (4th edn) para 192, and for a case on the subject, see 32 Digest (Reissue) 202, *1732*.
  For the defence of justification, see 28 Halsbury's Laws (4th edn) para 185, and for *b* cases on the subject, see 32 Digest (Reissue) 201–202, *1722–1731*.

Cases referred to in judgments
Associated Leisure Ltd v Associated Newspapers Ltd [1970] 2 All ER 754, [1970] 2 QB 450, [1970] 3 WLR 101, CA.
Bentley & Co Ltd v Black (1893) 9 TLR 580, CA.   *c*
Bradford Third Equitable Benefit Building Society v Borders [1941] 2 All ER 205, HL.
Cropper v Smith (1884) 26 Ch D 700, CA.
Hendriks v Montagu (1881) 17 Ch D 638, CA.
Howe v Times Newspapers Ltd [1985] CA Transcript 1005.
Lever & Co v Goodwin Bros [1887] WN 107, CA.
Pamplin v Express Newspapers Ltd (1985) 129 SJ 190, [1985] CA Transcript 84.   *d*
Riding v Hawkins (1889) 14 PD 56, DC.
Symonds v City Bank (1886) 34 WR 364.

Interlocutory appeal
The plaintiff, John Atkinson, appealed with leave from orders made by Peter Pain J on 16 April 1986 standing the plaintiff's action for libel against the defendants, Ray *e* Fitzwalter and Granada Television Ltd, out of the jury list and granting an application by the defendants for leave to amend their defence to plead justification. The facts are set out in the judgment of May LJ.

Charles Gray QC and *Adrienne Page* for the plaintiff.
Richard L Hartley QC and *Richard Rampton* for the defendants.   *f*

Cur adv vult

31 July. The following judgments were delivered.

MAY LJ. This is an appeal with leave from orders of Peter Pain J made on 16 April 1986 *g* standing the case out of the jury list, in which it would shortly have come on for trial, and at the same time granting an application by the defendants for leave to amend their defence. On this appeal, the plaintiff seeks to have the order granting such leave set aside and the action tried as soon as practicable, if possible before the end of the current term.
  The plaintiff is a dentist practising in Coventry and he was referred to in a 'World in Action' programme in terms which he claims to have been defamatory. The programme *h* was about the very high level of fees said to have been earned by some dentists in the national health service and the way in which such dentists managed to do so. The libel alleged in para 4 of the statement of claim was that the words used referring to the plaintiff in the television programme, which was transmitted by the second defendants and of which the first defendant was the editor, meant and were understood to mean:
                                                                                                    j
  '(1) That the plaintiff deliberately and cynically performs unnecessary dental work on his patients; (2) That the plaintiff extorts from the N.H.S. substantial amounts of money for unnecessary work and for work that has not in fact been performed; (3) That the plaintiff is one of the most notable examples of a small minority of dentists who enjoy a luxurious lifestyle financed by such practices; (4) That the plaintiff is guilty of gross professional misconduct; (5) That the plaintiff is guilty or is reasonably suspected of being guilty of defrauding the N.H.S. and his

a patients; (6) That the plaintiff is deliberately damaging his patients' teeth for his own financial gain.'

The original defence served on 16 October 1984 merely denied that any words used in the television programme referred or were understood to refer to the plaintiff save in so far as he was expressly mentioned by name and that, where he was, such words were in their natural and ordinary meaning not defamatory of the plaintiff. The action proceeded
b with admirable rapidity. The writ was served on 9 August 1984 and by 14 January 1985 the action had been set down for trial. The plaintiff gave the defendants notice of this the following day. By April 1986 the case was in the jury list for that term and was likely to be reached. The defendants' application to the judge, if allowed, meant that the action was unlikely to be heard before next October at the earliest.

It appears from an affidavit sworn by the defendants' solicitors in support of the
c application for leave to amend the defence that the defendants have always felt, and indeed still feel, that their television programme was not defamatory of the plaintiff. Nevertheless, there was always the risk that the plaintiff might succeed in persuading the jury otherwise at trial. It should be remembered that although it was not expressly alleged in the programme that the plaintiff had been amongst those dentists who, in obtaining high incomes from the national health service, had broken the rules,
d nevertheless he was referred to as a high earner and it was clearly this class of dentist which the programme set out to criticise. However it is counsel's duty, as in cases of fraud, not to put a plea of justification on the record unless he has clear and sufficient evidence to support it. In the present case, after the writ and statement of claim had been served, the defendants set about substantial inquiries concerning the plaintiff and his dental practice and counsel was asked to advise whether the material which had been
e obtained would support such a defence. In the event, it was not until July 1985 that counsel was in a position finally to advise that a defence of justification was available and to settle an amended pleading raising that plea. An amended defence alleging justification and fair comment, in the terms which were before the judge and were sought to be supported before us, was not in fact ready until 11 September 1985.

At this point the defendants' solicitor erroneously formed the view that the action was
f dormant and with counsel's concurring advice decided that it was better for the time being to let sleeping dogs lie. As the judge pointed out in his judgment it is extremely difficult to understand why the defendants' solicitor did form this view, because not only had he been told by the plaintiff's solicitors that they had set the matter down, but he had repeated that information to his lay clients. In his affidavit he accepted that he had made a mistake. He had overlooked the true position and sought counsel's advice on the
g wrong basis. The judge came to the conclusion that although it was clear that in this respect the defendants' solicitor had blundered, he had not acted improperly.

The judge then referred to passages from the judgments of Lord Denning MR and Edmund Davies LJ in this court in *Associated Leisure Ltd v Associated Newspapers Ltd* [1970] 2 All ER 754, [1970] 2 QB 450. That was also a case in which at a late stage defendants to a libel action sought leave to amend their defence, theretofore comprising
h a mere general denial, to plead justification and fair comment. In his judgment Lord Denning MR referred to the well-settled principle that an amendment ought in general to be allowed, even if it comes late, if it is necessary to do justice between the parties, so long as any hardship done thereby can be compensated in money (see [1970] 2 All ER 754 at 757, [1970] 2 QB 450 at 455). Edmund Davies LJ expressed a similar view when he quoted the classic words from the judgment of Bowen LJ in *Cropper v Smith* (1884) 26
j Ch D 700 at 710–711:

'I know of no kind of error or mistake which, if not fraudulent or intended to overreach, the Court ought not to correct, if it can be done without injustice to the other party. Courts do not exist for the sake of discipline, but for the sake of deciding matters in controversy, and I do not regard such amendment as a matter of favour or of grace . . . It seems to me that as soon as it appears that the way in which a party has framed his case will not lead to a decision of the real matter in controversy, it is as much a matter of right on his part to have it corrected if it can be done without injustice, as anything else in the case is a matter of right.'   *a*

Just before this, Edmund Davies LJ had himself said ([1970] 2 All ER 754 at 758, [1970] 2 QB 450 at 457):

> 'These courts are here to administer justice. The concept of justice is not confined to the interests of the particular litigants; it embraces and extends to the protection *b* of the public weal. The issues involved in this litigation have an importance of direct concern to the community.'

Relying on these principles the judge in the instant case concluded that he ought to allow the amendment sought if any prejudice that this might cause to the plaintiff could be compensated for in money. Indeed, counsel who appeared for the plaintiff below *c* conceded that had the application for amendment been made in September 1985, she could hardly have resisted it. Having considered the question of prejudice, the judge in fact concluded that the scales came down heavily on this point in favour of the defendants and that therefore he ought to and did allow the amendment.

In seeking to challenge the judge's decision, counsel for the plaintiff in effect took four points before us. First, he referred to another passage from Lord Denning MR's judgment *d* in *Associated Leisure Ltd v Associated Newspapers Ltd* [1970] 2 All ER 754 at 758, [1970] 2 QB 450 at 456 to this effect:

> 'But when the defendant seeks to plead justification at a late stage, his conduct will be closely enquired into. The court will expect him to have shown due diligence in making his enquiries and investigations. The court may well refuse him *e* application if he has been guilty of delay or not made proper enquiries earlier.'

Counsel submitted that on the material to which I have referred and in all the circumstances of this case the judge had been wrong to reach the conclusion he did, as to the circumstances in which it came about that the application for leave to amend was not made until that very late stage.   *f*

Second, counsel submitted that a plea of justification, in particular the one sought to be made in the instant case, in truth raised an allegation of fraud and on general principles an amendment to allege fraud should not be allowed where this has not been pleaded in the first instance. He referred us to *The Supreme Court Practice 1985* vol 1, p 346, para 20/5–8/22 and to the various cases there mentioned. I shall consider these later in this judgment.   *g*

Third, counsel contended that the particulars in the plea of justification sought to be set up did not, when analysed, in truth go to the real sting of the alleged libel, namely that the plaintiff had been guilty of defrauding the national health service.

Finally and in any event counsel submitted that the particulars in the amended defence sought to be relied on were so vague as not to give the plaintiff any satisfactory indication of the case raised against him and that consequently the judge ought to have refused *h* leave to amend on this ground also.

In reply, counsel for the defendants first contended that the judge was not only entitled to reach the conclusions that he did about the circumstances in which the defendants' application for leave to amend came to be so delayed, but that indeed, having regard to the nature of the issues raised by the alleged libel and the plea of justification, justice would not be done if none of the facts comprising the plea of justification went before *j* the jury. In this connection he particularly referred to the passage in Edmund Davies LJ's judgment in *Associated Leisure Ltd v Associated Newspaperes Ltd* [1970] 2 All ER 754 at 758, [1970] 2 QB 450 at 457 which I have already quoted. Further, he submitted that quite clearly allowing the amendment could not cause any prejudice to the plaintiff which could not be compensated in money. The jury would be bound to take into a account the continuing injury up to verdict and if the plea of justification failed, their award of damages was likely to be substantially increased.

As to the contention that amendments to plead fraud should as a general rule not be allowed when the allegation is not made in the first place, counsel accepted that no doubt such amendments had to be looked at very closely. But in the instant case justice, in the sense to which I have referred, and indeed the concession by counsel for the plaintiff that but for the subsequent delay she could hardly have resisted the application, required that b leave to amend should be given.

In this connection, counsel also referred us to s 5 of the Defamation Act 1952, which can somewhat loosely be said to be concerned with the defence of 'partial justification'. He also referred us to passages from the judgment of Neill LJ in *Pamplin v Express Newspapers Ltd* [1985] CA Transcript 84 and in particular to where Neill LJ said:

c   'There may be many cases, however, where a defendant who puts forward a defence of justification will be unable to prove sufficient facts to establish the defence at common law and will also be unable to bring himself within the statutory extension of the defence contained in section 5 of the Defamation Act. Nevertheless the defendant may be able to rely on such facts as he has proved to reduce the damages, perhaps almost to vanishing point. Thus a defence of partial justification, d   though it may not prevent the plaintiff from succeeding on the issue of liability, may be of great importance on the issue of damages.'

On this basis also it was submitted that on the facts of the instant case it would be wrong not to allow a plea of justification by amendment unless it was apparent, which it was clearly not, that the amended plea sought to be made was wholly unparticularised e and without merit.

In so far as the intended plea itself was concerned, to the extent that it did not go to the allegation pleaded in the statement of claim that the programme meant and was understood to mean that the plaintiff had defrauded the national health service, nevertheless it was argued that it clearly went to the contention pleaded that the plaintiff had been guilty of gross professional misconduct.

f Finally, counsel for the defendants submitted that even though some criticism might be made of the form of the proposed amendment, there was nothing so wrong with the particulars of justification which a proper request for further and better particulars could not put right.

As to the first issue argued on this appeal, I am quite satisfied, as was the judge below, that there was good reason for the defendants not to seek leave to amend their defence g until at least September 1985. I also respectfully agree with the judge that though thereafter the defendants' solicitor blundered, that blunder was neither fraudulent nor intended to overreach in the sense referred to by Bowen LJ in the passage from his judgment in *Cropper v Smith* (1884) 26 Ch D 700 at 710–711 which I have already quoted. Further, it seems quite clear to me that to allow the amendment in this case would not cause any prejudice to the plaintiff which could not be compensated in money. Even h though some of the allegations in the particulars of justification relate to events some considerable time ago, it seems that at least adequate records are available and I have no doubt that in the instant case a substantial failure to make good the allegations contained in the intended plea of justification would rebound heavily against the defendants in so far as any award of damages by the jury was concerned.

As I have said, our attention was drawn to the note in *The Supreme Court Practice 1985* j vol 1, p 346, para 20/5–8/22 regarding late amendments to allege fraud and to the authorities referred to therein. I propose to consider such authorities seriatim but briefly. I preface my comments by saying that not only were we referred to no other authority by counsel in the course of hearing this appeal but also that my researches have not been able to discover any such. The content of the note is repeated almost verbatim in 36 Halsbury's Laws (4th edn) para 70, but no other authority is there referred to either.

In *Hendriks v Montagu* (1881) 17 Ch D 638 the proper officer of an insurance company
incorporated under its own Act of Parliament sought an interim injunction by motion   *a*
to restrain the defendants from applying for the registration of a joint stock company
with a name so like that of the insurance company as to be likely to mislead or deceive
the public into believing that the company was the same as the insurance company. The
motion was founded on s 20 of the Companies Act 1862, but that only applied to
someone attempting to take the name of a subsisting company already registered. The
insurance company was not such as it had been incorporated under its own statute. Faced   *b*
with this difficulty counsel for the plaintiff sought leave to amend the indorsement on
the writ and the terms of the motion so as to charge the defendants with the intention of
adopting the name and carrying on the business with the view of defrauding the plaintiff
company by unfairly, illegally and immorally appropriating a portion of the business of
the plaintiff company. Jessel MR refused leave to amend and said (at 642):

> 'Now, the only other point which I wish to advert to is the excuse which Mr.   *c*
> *Chitty* had for going on with his case after this point was taken and pointed out. He
> asked me for leave to amend his notice of motion, and to let the motion stand over.
> I cannot accede to that. There is no Judge more liberal, if I may use the expression,
> in allowing amendments, in order to try the real case, than I am, at any stage of the
> case; but I make one exception, that is as to charges of fraud. I do not, as a rule, allow   *d*
> amendments to make a charge of fraud at a time when the case is launched,
> independently of fraud. I generally stop there. To allow such an amendment as this
> would be to contravene that rule. Of course, like all my rules, it is not an absolute
> rule. I may make an exception to it if I see good ground for doing so, but generally
> it is my rule.'

In *Bentley & Co Ltd v Black* (1893) 9 TLR 580 a limited company sought to recover calls   *e*
in respect of shares which had been allotted to the defendant. At trial the defendant
sought to contend that he had been induced to enter into the contract to take the shares
by a fraudulent misrepresentation. This had not been pleaded in his original defence and
the necessary amendement was refused. Lord Esher MR said (at 580):

> 'It had for a long time been the universal practice, except in the most exceptional   *f*
> circumstances, not to allow an amendment for the purpose of adding a plea of fraud
> where fraud had not been pleaded in the first instance.'

However, a somewhat different view was taken by North J at first instance in *Symonds
v City Bank* (1886) 34 WR 364. That was an action brought by a shareholder for damages
for the fraudulent misrepresentations which it was alleged had induced her to take up   *g*
her shares, the company thereafter going into liquidation. The important point to note
is that the plaintiff's evidence had been taken before trial de bene esse and it was her
depositions that were intended to be used at the trial. The fraudulent misrepresentations
then sought to be relied on on her behalf were in some respects different from those
originally pleaded. Objection was taken on behalf of the defendants and counsel for the
plaintiff sought leave to make appropriate amendments. On this application North J said   *h*
(at 365):

> 'As to the other question whether an amendment should now be allowed, if it
> could be made without prejudicing the defendants I should make it, but no
> amendment could displace the fact that the now alleged misrepresentations were
> not originally put forward as material, and that there has been no opportunity of   *i*
> meeting these charges. But the objection taken by Mr. Kemp is fatal. The evidence   *j*
> of the plaintiff was taken *de bene esse*, and her depositions were intended to be used
> as evidence. Under these circumstances no amendment ought to be allowed unless
> it is so important as to justify ordering the whole matter to stand over, and evidence
> to be gone into afresh. I cannot allow an amendment which would allow of the

a   plaintiff's depositions being read when her cross-examination was not directed to
     the new points now brought forward.'

In this case there had on the one hand been an allegation of fraud in the original statement
of claim and indeed the particulars pleaded were not substantially different from those
sought to be made good at trial. In such circumstances the judge would have been
prepared to follow the general principle enunciated two years earlier by Bowen LJ in
b   *Cropper v Smith*, but for the fact that to have done so would have caused prejudice to the
     defendants because they would not have had the opportunity of cross-examining the
     plaintiff on her new case.

In my opinion the decision in *Lever & Co v Goodwin Bros* [1887] WN 107 does not
really help on the particular point with which we are presently concerned. In that case
the application to amend to allege fraud or the equivalent was made after the trial had
c   actually begun and in the course of the cross-examination of one of the plaintiffs. In such
     circumstances the Court of Appeal held that the trial judge had been right in refusing to
     allow the material questions to be put or the pleadings to be amended, saying (at 108):

d   '. . . the question was irrelevant to the issue raised on the pleadings, which was
     whether the defendants were passing off their soap as that of the plaintiffs; and it
     involved a charge of fraud, which should have been raised, if at all, in the defence,
     at the risk of costs, and could not be started in the middle of a cross-examination.'

I turn finally to *Riding v Hawkins* (1889) 14 PD 56. That was a probate action in which
the plaintiff as residuary legatee propounded a will and first codicil. The defendant
propounded the second and third codicils, in opposition to which the plaintiff pleaded
undue execution, testamentary incapacity, and that the execution of the codicils had
e   been obtained by the undue influence of the defendant. As the onus of establishing the
     two disputed codicils was on the defendant, his case was taken first. After this had been
     closed, counsel for the plaintiff indicated that he proposed to establish that the defendant
     had told deliberate untruths in the witness box. The trial judge then pointed out that
     that would amount to an allegation of fraud which was not then on the pleadings.
f   Counsel thereupon applied for leave to amend to add such a plea, limited, however, to
     the matters on which he had cross-examined the defendant. The defendant's counsel
     objected and continued his objection even after the trial judge offered an adjournment.
     In the end the judge allowed the pleadings to be appropriately amended. When the
     matter reached the Divisional Court on appeal counsel for the defendant (who was the
     appellant) took the point that at the stage at which the application was made it had been
g   far too late to permit an amendment to allege fraud. In reply the plaintiff's counsel
     pointed out that although there may be cases in which this is correct, his was one in
     which the facts from which the fraud could be concluded were not disclosed until the
     defendant had been cross-examined. The Divisional Court held that the trial judge had
     been justified in allowing the amendment under the circumstances and said (at 59):

h   'The charges made against the defendant, if established, would properly support
     a charge of fraud, and it was therefore the duty of the judge to allow the plaintiff to
     amend her pleadings, always taking care that the defendant was exposed to no
     hardship. This the learned judge did by offering to allow a postponement if the
     defendant wished it. The defendant's counsel had not availed themselves of this
     offer, but the Court was of the opinion that they were not thereby precluded from
j   arguing that their client was taken by surprise by the evidence given at the trial in
     support of the plea of fraud.'

The court consequently granted a new trial on the ground of surprise, but in regard to
the amendment of the pleadings held that the trial judge had been justified in allowing
it under the circumstances.

On this analysis I think that the note in *The Supreme Court Practice* to which we were **a**
referred correctly reflects the decisions in the cases there mentioned. Nevertheless,
particularly bearing in mind that Bowen LJ was a party to the decision in *Bentley & Co*
Ltd v Black (1893) TLR 580, I do not find it easy to reconcile Lord Esher MR's dictum in
that case with the 'all embracing principle' (as Edmund Davies LJ described it) of Bowen
LJ in *Cropper v Smith* (1884) 26 Ch D 700. In the end, I can see no logical reason why just
because an amendment seeks to raise an allegation of fraud for the first time this should
in most cases take the case outside the general principle that all amendments should be **b**
allowed so as to ensure that the real matters in controversy are before the court, provided
that can be done without injustice to the other side. On the other hand, it must be
remembered that fraud is a very serious allegation to make against a person, as for
instance would be an allegation of a criminal offence, and may, if not raised at the outset
be difficult, if not impossible, properly to investigate at a later stage in the proceedings.
Further, the more serious the allegation that is made, then the more clearly satisfied must **c**
a court be that indeed no prejudice is being caused which cannot be compensated for in
some satisfactory way or another before allowing the amendment.

In the instant case, for the reasons which I have sought to give and bearing in mind
the clear ratio behind the decision in *Associated Leisure Ltd v Associated Newspapers Ltd*,
namely that justice did require that the matters raised in the original publication, in the
ensuing writ and statement of claim and in the amended defence should be investigated **d**
in a court of law, I do not think that the fact that the plea of justification which it was
sought to add by way of amendment to the defence itself alleges fraud, at least in part
against the plaintiff, is of itself any reason not to allow an amendment to be made.

As to the third point taken by counsel for the plaintiff herein, I think that in the
circumstances the reasonable construction of the allegation in para 4(4) of the statement **e**
of claim is that the gross professional misconduct, which it is there alleged that the words
complained of meant and were understood to mean, comprised conduct of the nature
more particularly described in the other sub-paragraphs of that paragraph. It may be that
some professional negligence can amount to gross professional misconduct but it is not
lightly to be so described.

It follows that in my opinion the allegation in para 7(b) of the particulars of justification **f**
in the amendment sought and granted by the judge cannot with respect be allowed to
stand. It must then follow that those subsequent allegations in the particulars which
merely comprise allegations of negligent dentistry and nothing more, should also be
disallowed. For instance, in so far as the patient Owens is concerned who is dealt with in
para (8) of the particulars, only the allegation in the body of sub-para (c) that 'the plaintiff
had claimed fees for work which he had not carried out' and sub-sub-para (vi) thereunder, **g**
can be said to be proper. In so far as the patient Watson is concerned, who is dealt with
in para (9) of the particulars, on a correct analysis it will be apparent that the only
allegations made are allegations of negligence, albeit some of them serious negligence,
but not such as could be said to amount to gross professional misconduct. Similar analysis
of the allegations relating to the other named patients in my opinion necessarily leads
one to the conclusion that if there are any allegations which it is proper to allow to **h**
remain, they are very few and so entangled in many other allegations which should be
struck out that the particulars of justification are embarrassing. I should add that in my
view it is clear that neither para (10) nor para (15) of the particulars of justification relate
to any of the allegations in para (7) even as these presently stand.

For these reasons I do not think that the deficiencies in the particulars of justification
can be made good either by tightening up the language used or by answering any **j**
stringent request for further and better particulars. Indeed it is not easy, to say the least,
to see how such a request could be properly drafted.

To approach the matter from another angle: although, when a properly drafted plea
of justification is included in the defence in a defamation action it is permissible to rely
on any facts that are proved in order to support it to reduce the damages, even though

those facts by themselves are insufficient to make good the defence as a whole,
a nevertheless it is not permissible to plead, under the guise of particulars of justification,
matters which do not go to a plaintiff's general reputation, with a view to leading
evidence about them solely to support an argument that he should receive a smaller sum
by way of damages.

For the reasons which I have sought to give, I respectfully think that the judge reached
the wrong conclusion. I would allow this appeal and disallow the whole of the
b amendment for which leave was sought and obtained. Having regard, however, to the
guiding principle stated by Bowen LJ in *Cropper v Smith* and to what I think is the clear
ratio of this court's decision in *Associated Leisure Ltd v Associated Newspapers Ltd*, I do not
think that this should prevent the defendants from making a further attempt to obtain
leave to amend their pleadings to allege justification and fair comment. In deciding
whether or not to grant leave the master, as it will no doubt be, will be guided by the
c assistance which I trust our judgments on this appeal have given. For my part, I would
have no doubt that any application could properly be classed as vacation business, but it
must be made within a short fixed time. Further, having regard to the timescale, I think
that simultaneously with applying for such leave, if any application is indeed made, the
defendants should disclose all documents in their custody, possession or power relevant
to the fresh allegations which they seek to make.
d

PARKER LJ. The plaintiff, a dentist practising in Coventry, claims damages for libel
allegedly contained in a television programme 'Drilling for Gold' edited and published
by the first defendant and broadcast and published by the second defendants on 24 June
1984. The writ was issued on 9 August 1984 and the statement of claim was served on 4
September 1984. Having quoted extensively from the programme, para 4 of the
e statement of claim asserted:

'4. The said words in their natural and ordinary meaning meant and were
understood to mean (1) That the Plaintiff deliberately and cynically performs
unnecessary dental work on his patients; (2) That the Plaintiff extorts from the
N.H.S. substantial amounts of money for unnecessary work and for work that has
f not in fact been performed; (3) That the Plaintiff is one of the most notable examples
of a small minority of dentists who enjoy a luxurious life style financed by such
practices; (4) That the Plaintiff is guilty of gross professional misconduct; (5) That
the Plaintiff is guilty or is reasonably suspected of being guilty of defrauding the
N.H.S. and his patients; (6) That the Plaintiff is deliberately damaging his patients'
teeth for his own financial gain.'

g
If the words complained of bear the meanings alleged there is no doubt that they
contain very grave charges against the plaintiff. Paragraph 4(5) alleges directly that the
words used charge him with defrauding the national health service and his patients but
in my view sub-paras (1), (2), (3) and (6) also in substance allege that the words used
charge him with both civil and criminal fraud.
h The defence was delivered on 16 October 1984. It was brief indeed. It merely denied
that the words used referred or were understood to refer to the plaintiff save in so far as
he was expressly referred to by name and that the words used in their ordinary and
natural meaning bore or were understood to bear any of the meanings alleged or any
meaning defamatory of the plaintiff. It was thus a simple denial of the libel.

The summons for directions was heard in December 1984. Thereafter the action
j proceeded with speed and it was set down on 14 January 1985. On the following day the
plaintiff's solicitors so informed the defendants' solicitors. By that time lists of documents
had been exchanged. Thereafter, save for an inspection of the video film of the broadcast
on 13 February, nothing occurred inter partes until, the court having given notice on 4
April 1986 that the action was going into the warned list, the defendants' solicitors on 10
April (i) notified the plaintiff's solicitors that they intended to amend to plead justification

and fair comment, and (ii) requested consent for the case being stood out. This was
refused. A copy of the proposed amended defence was received by the plaintiff's solicitors   a
on 14 April and on 16 April applications for leave to amend and to stand the case out
until next October were heard by Peter Pain J. At that time the likelihood was that the
case would be heard before the end of the current term.

The judge allowed the amendment and stood the case out of the list for that term. The
plaintiff appeals to this court by leave of the judge.

Before considering the contentions advanced in support of and against the appeal it is   b
first necessary to mention briefly what had been going on on the defendants' side after
delivery of the original defence. This is revealed, or partially revealed, in an affidavit used
in support of the application to the judge. It explains (i) that justification was not raised
in the first instance because the defendants felt and still feel that the programme did not
make the allegations against the plaintiff which he alleges and were not defamatory of
him, and (ii) that justification could not be pleaded until counsel had before him   c
sufficient material and that this did not happen until July 1985. The defendants had
however from an early stage been seeking evidence on which to plead justification to
guard against the risk that the jury might hold that the words used were defamatory. I
see nothing wrong in this.

Although a draft amended defence was settled in July 1985 and finally approved by
the defendants early in September 1985, the defendants' solicitor for some wholly   d
unexplained reason considered that the action was dormant. After a discussion with
counsel, which was conducted on the basis of this wholly mistaken belief, it was decided
not to seek leave to serve the amended defence since this might re-activate the action.

The result is that although the defendants were in a position to apply for leave to
amend in early September 1985, they took no steps to obtain leave or warn the plaintiff
that he would or might be faced with such a plea until April 1986, when the trial on the   e
unamended pleadings was imminent. The result is also that, while from 16 October
1984 until April 1986 the plaintiff had every reason to suppose that he would not have
to face any actual charges he will now, if the amendment stands, have to face charges of
the most serious kind concerning details of dentistry allegedly done or not done by him,
statements made by him, and moneys charged by him going as far back as 1974. Such   f
charges are unquestionably charges of fraud and of criminal offences albeit that the
amended defence to which I now turn does not in terms so allege.

The amendment occupies no less than 19 pages. The first four such pages are occupied
with a description of the system of remuneration of dentists by the national health
service followed by: (i) a comparison of the plaintiff's gross earnings and the national
average expected gross earnings of a national health service dentist in the four years from   g
1980–81 to 1983–84; (ii) a comparison between the plaintiff's average cost per treatment
and national average cost per treatment in each of the three years 1982, 1983 and 1984;
(iii) a comparison between the average number of hours per year worked by national
health service dentists and the plaintiff's advertised surgery hours; (iv) an invitation to
the court to infer from the foregoing and the matters subsequently pleaded (a) that the
plaintiff performed treatments not justified by the patients' dental condition, (b) worked   h
too quickly and therefore badly and (c) claimed payment for work which he had not in
fact carried out.

The matters subsequently pleaded consist of allegations concerning the plaintiff's
treatment of eight individual patients and occupy the remaining pages. Many of the
details given do not in my view go to the charges sought to be justified at all. In many
instances it is impossible to ascertain quite what the defendants are alleging. Despite the   j
overall length of the pleading it cries aloud for particulars. With respect to the learned
pleader, I am bound to say that it is in my view prolix and embarrassing and one which
ought not to be allowed in its present form. If by some reasonable pruning and reasonable
request for particulars it could be cured it might, subject to considerations hereafter to
be mentioned, be allowed, but in my view its defects go beyond this and I would for my

part simply disallow it. If this course were taken without more the defendants would,
a however, then be free to rethink and apply hereafter to make an amendment in proper
form.

The question therefore arises whether they should be allowed to do so and it is this
which is in my view the real question which arises on the appeal. The plaintiff contends
that the defendants, having failed to justify allegations of fraud initially and having failed
to do so promptly when they were in a position to do so, cannot now be allowed to do so
b no matter how properly they plead.

In support of this contention the plaintiff relies on *The Supreme Court Practice 1985*
vol 1, p 346, para 20/5–8/22, which is in the following terms:

'Although it has been stated that it is "the universal practice, except in the most
exceptional circumstances, not to allow an amendment for the purpose of adding a
c plea of fraud where fraud has not been pleaded in the first instance" . . . yet such an
amendment is allowed at an early stage; and in special circumstances at the trial
though an adjournment would usually be granted . . .'

Reference to the cases cited in the note do not reveal any principle on which the
'almost universal practice' is based and do make it clear that even at the trial such an
amendment may be granted.
d I can see no reason why the same practice should not be applied where the allegation
of fraud which is introduced at a late stage appears in the form of justification in a libel
action but I do not consider that the practice, as such, is of much assistance to the plaintiff
for it recognises that there can be exceptions.

The plaintiff relies also on certain passages from the judgment of Lord Denning MR
in *Associated Leisure Ltd v Associated Newspapers Ltd* [1970] 2 All ER 754, [1970] 2 QB 450.
e In that case also there was an application at a very late stage to amend to plead justification.
It was not an allegation of fraud but the charge sought to be justified was just as serious.
It was in effect that the plaintiffs were associated with or acting for the American mafia.
The amendment was allowed by this court although refused by the master and the judge,
but in the course of his judgment Lord Denning MR said ([1970] 2 All ER 754 at 757,
f [1970] 2 QB 450 at 455):

'Counsel for the plaintiffs says, quite properly, that the pleading ought to be
scrutinised closely. The defendants ought to give proper particulars. They ought
not to be allowed to put in a loose, ineffective pleading at the last hour. I agree to
this extent: there are two sub-paragraphs (para 7(11) and (12)) which are not well
pleaded. They go, so far as I can see, to credit, not to justification. They must come
g out. The remaining paragraphs are not yet as complete in particulars as they might
be; but not so deficient as to require them to be struck out. Any deficiencies can be
made good by an application for further particulars.'

Later he said ([1970] 2 All ER 754 at 758, [1970] 2 QB 450 at 456):

'But when the defendant seeks to plead justification at a late stage, his conduct
h will be closely enquired into. The court will expect him to have shown due diligence
in making his enquiries and investigations. The court may well refuse him
application if he has been guilty of delay or not made proper enquiries earlier.'

Here, it is said, the case is one in which there has been great delay after the defendants
were in a position to plead justification and the amendment is a loose ineffective pleading.
j I agree, but it does not answer the question whether the defendants should be allowed,
even by proper amendment, to justify at all. The defendants submit that they should,
that the charges should be investigated, and that it would be quite unjust if the action
were tried without the amendment with the possible result that the plaintiff would
emerge without a stain on his character and enormous damages when the charges made,
if the jury were allowed to consider them, might have been found to be fully justified.

The defendants also rely on *Associated Leisure Ltd v Associated Newspapers Ltd* in particular on the statements of general principle in the judgments of Lord Denning MR and of Edmund Davies LJ (see [1970] 2 All ER 754 at 757, 758–759, [1970] 2 QB 450 at 455, 457). In addition they rely on the judgment of this court in *Howe v Times Newspapers Ltd* [1985] CA Transcript 1005.

In my view, apart from the general principle that amendments, however late, should be allowed if justice requires it provided that the other side can be compensated in money, the cases afford little assistance. I shall endeavour to apply that principle to the question whether a proper amendment should be allowed. This question can only be considered on the basis that the lengthy amendment proposed contains all facts from which the defendants might extract a proper plea. When I find that those facts comprise no more than an invitation to infer fraud from a comparison of the plaintiff's gross earnings, costs per treatment and hours of work with national averages, together with details of eight cases out of the great numbers which the plaintiff has treated over the period from 1974 to 1984, when six of those cases have already been investigated by the appropriate authorities and when the details given in large part do not go to justification of the charges, it appears to me unlikely that any pleading could be properly framed which, despite the delay and the inadequacy of the present amendment, ought in justice to be allowed.

A defendant is entitled to rely in mitigation of damages on any evidence which is properly before the jury and this can include evidence in support of an unsuccessful plea of justification (see Neill LJ in *Pamplin v Express Newspapers Ltd* [1985] CA Transcript 84). It therefore appears to me to be of considerable importance that defendants should be strictly limited to evidence which can truly be said to go to justification and should not be allowed, under the guise of justification, to lead evidence which does not in reality go to justification at all. The amendment as it stands would, if allowed, permit of just such evidence. If, from it, there is extracted and pleaded in a further proposed amendment only that which could properly go to justification, I doubt whether it would be of such substance that justice would require the amendment to be allowed. I readily accept the argument, already referred to, that it would be unjust for a plaintiff to emerge from a trial with enormous damages and without a stain on his character when the charges made might, had they been allowed to go to the jury, have been found to be justified. It is however, in my view, quite otherwise if at a very late stage a defendant seeks to set up matters which if established could not conceivably justify the real sting of the libel, but would or might be damaging to the plaintiff in other respects. I think it likely that any new proposed amendment would fall into the latter category but, since I cannot be entirely sure, I have come to the conclusion, after very considerable hesitation, that it would not be right to deprive the defendants of the right to apply for leave to make some different and properly-framed amendment. Accordingly, I would allow the appeal and disallow the whole of the amendment but leave the defendants free, on the terms proposed by May LJ, to apply, if so advised, for leave to make a new amendment.

STOCKER LJ. The words complained of as a libel occurred during the course of a television programme entitled 'Drilling for Gold' which was broadcast on 25 June 1984 and was one of a series of broadcasts called 'World in Action'. The first defendant was the editor and the second defendants were the broadcasters and publishers of this programme. The programme was concerned with the remuneration and earnings of dentists. A number of dentists were mentioned by name and their gross earnings stated. Part of the programme involved criticism of the method of remuneration of dentists for their work, a method which it was said encouraged dishonest malpractices such as claiming for work not in fact performed, or carrying out and charging for unnecessary work. Reference to the plaintiff was in these terms 'and John Atkinson whose car number plate led him into trouble with the General Dental Council for advertising grossed £105,315'. A picture of the plaintiff's car registered as 'JAW 900' appeared at the same time on the TV screen.

The plaintiff's case was that this reference to him carried the necessary implication that

a he was one of the dentists involved in the malpractices stated above. A substantial part of the broadcast programme was set out in the statement of claim served on 4 September 1984 and the plaintiff pleaded that the natural and ordinary meaning of the words quoted meant, and were understood to mean, one or more of the six defamatory meanings pleaded as fully set out in May LJ's judgment. The defence in its original unamended form was confined to the denials (1) that the words were or were understood

b to refer to the plaintiff save only in so far as he was referred to by name and (2) that the words in their natural and ordinary meaning bore, or were understood to bear any of the meanings pleaded in the statement of claim. The defence was served on 16 October 1984.

The action was set down for trial on 14 January 1985 and the plaintiff's solicitors, by letter of that date, notified the defendants' solicitors of that fact and on 4 April 1986 the

c court notified the plaintiff that the action was going into the warned list. The pleadings on this date were still in their original form. On 10 April 1986 the defendants, by telex, asked for consent that the action be stood out of the list and for the first time informed the plaintiff's solicitors of their intention to amend the defence to raise pleas of justification and fair comment. Consent was refused. A copy of the proposed amendments (which, with the particulars cover some 19 pages of pleadings) were received on the

d afternoon of 14 April and on 16 April the defendants' application was heard by Peter Pain J. In form, it was an application to stand the case out of the list but the substance was an application to amend, since this was the reason put forward in support of the application to stand the case out. The application was supported by an affidavit by a partner in the defendants' firm of solicitors in which he deposed to the fact that the defendants had not pleaded justification at the outset for the reason, inter alia, that the

e 'defendants felt, and still feel, that their programme did not make the allegations against the plaintiff of which he complains or that it was defamatory of him'. One of the bases for this assertion was that the programme was not concerned only with dishonest practices carried out by some dentists but covered other topics relevant to the system of remuneration and that some dentists could earn very large gross incomes by the proper

f exercise of their profession and that the plaintiff fell into this category. The affidavit also gave as a reason for not pleading justification at the outset the fact that before such a plea was put forward it was prudent and proper practice for counsel to be satisfied that what he proposed to plead as justification was sustainable in court.

The basis on which justification is pleaded in the defence is contained in para 7 of the pleading, which reads:

g   'The defendants will invite the court to infer from the foregoing and from the matters pleaded in sub-paragraphs 8 to 16(a) and (b) below that the plaintiff frequently: (a) performed unnecessary treatment on his patients (that is, treatment not justified by the patient's dental condition) and/or (b) worked too quickly, and badly; and/or (c) claimed payment from the NHS for treatments which he had not,

h   in fact, carried out.'

Sub-paragraphs (a) and (c) are clearly, and admittedly, allegations of fraud and dishonesty. It is contended on behalf of the defendants that sub-para (b) is also an allegation of fraud and dishonesty since it carried the implication that by working too quickly and badly the plaintiff was able to earn more fees than he would be able to do if he worked more slowly and carefully. I will consider further this aspect of the matter hereunder.

j The applications came before Peter Pain J on 16 April 1986 and after considering the arguments put forward on behalf of the respective parties he allowed the defendants to amend their pleadings to allege justification and stood the case out of the list.

In his judgment Peter Pain J, after quoting extensively passages from the judgment of Lord Denning MR and Edmund Davies LJ in *Associated Leisure Ltd v Associated Newspapers Ltd*, turned to consider whether or not the delay in putting forward the amendment was

culpable and he cited a further passage from the judgment of Lord Denning MR ([1970] *a*
2 All ER 754 at 758, [1970] 2 QB 450 at 456):

> 'But when the defendants seek to plead justification at a late stage, his conduct
> will be closely inquired into. The court will expect him to have shown due diligence
> in making his enquiries and investigations. The court may well refuse him
> application if he has been guilty of delay or not made proper enquiries earlier.'

He also referred to *The Supreme Court Practice 1985* vol 1, p 346, para 20/5–8/22: *b*

> '*Fraud, adding allegation of*—Although it has been stated that it is "the universal
> practice, except in the most exceptional circumstances, not to allow an amendment
> for the purpose of adding a plea of fraud where fraud has not been pleaded in the
> first instance" (*per* Lord Esher M.R. in *Bentley* v. *Black* ((1893) 9 TLR 580); *cf. Hendriks*
> v. *Montagu* ((1893) 17 Ch D 638 at 642); *Symonds* v. *City Bank* ((1885) 34 WR 364); *c*
> *Lever* v. *Goodwin* ([1887] WN 107)) yet such an amendment is allowed at an early
> stage; and in special circumstances at the trial though an adjournment would
> usually be granted, see *Riding* v. *Hawkins* ((1889) 14 PD 56). But such an amendment
> should not be allowed by the Court of Appeal (*Bradford, etc., Building Society* v.
> *Borders* ([1941] 2 All ER 205)).'

Having expressed his doubts as to whether it was right for the defendants to have *d*
delayed their application to amend in the way that they did the judge expressed his
conclusion on this factor of the defendants' delay and commented in these terms:

> 'In those circumstances I do not think it can be said that there was anything
> improper in the defendants' conduct although I am inclined to think it was ill- *e*
> advised, and it was especially ill-advised when they were to be so careless as to what
> the state of the action was. Now counsel for the plaintiff complains also that the
> affidavit of Mr Swaffer does not provide a very full explanation of the delay that
> took place up to September. The answer that is made to that is that if a plea of
> justification is to be made, one wants to assemble all the material particulars in that
> plea and not to do it bit by bit, and that while the defendant had substantial material *f*
> before him considerably earlier, his material was not complete until the time when
> it was done. That seems to me a proper way to go about matters. If one is to amend,
> one wants to have one amendment rather than a series of amendments. In any case,
> it seems to me that that delay really does not have any bearing on the present case
> because it is not the delay that has caused any difficulty here. It was the blunder as
> to the misunderstanding whether the case had been set down; and, indeed, counsel *g*
> for the plaintiff concedes that had the application to amend been made in September
> of last year, she could hardly have resisted it.'

On the issue whether or not the proposed particulars supported the general allegations
pleaded in the amendment in para 7, which I have cited above, the judge found that
though there was some force in this contention the matter could 'easily be put right by *h*
some adjustment to the wording'. He did not further consider what such adjustments
might involve or what modification to the wording was required. He expressed his
general conclusion on this aspect of the case in these terms:

> 'Counsel for the plaintiff took the point that the words pleaded do not support the
> general allegations made in para 7 of the amended defence. I think there is again
> some force in what she has to say there, but it seems to me a matter that could easily *j*
> be put right by adjustment of the wording. It is fairly clear what the defendants are
> driving at in their allegation, although the expression of it seemed to me to be
> required to be rather tightened. I refer to the words of Bowen LJ in *Cropper v Smith*
> (1884) 26 Ch D 700 at 710: "Courts do not exist for the sake of discipline, but for

a   the sake of deciding matters in controversy and I do not regard such amendment as a matter of favour or grace." So that it seems to me that counsel for the defendants succeeds in establishing the central point in his argument that in the light of the investigations which his clients have undertaken, the fruits of which appear in the amended defence, it would be quite artificial and therefore unjust to allow the plaintiff's claim to be tried without the matters set out in the amended defence being inquired into.'

b   The judge then proceeded to balance the prejudice to the plaintiff by the delay if the application were granted against the prejudice to the defendants if it were not. His balancing involved the factor of delay rather than any other factors of prejudice which he had considered in the earlier part of his judgment and he concluded:

c   'However, balancing the prejudice to the plaintiff against the prejudice to the defendants I am satisfied that the scales come down heavily in favour of the defendants and therefore that I ought to allow the amendment. I therefore allow the amendment. I direct that the case be taken out of the jury list for this term.'

   The grounds of appeal as reflected in the arguments before this court were:

d   '1. The judge ought to have rejected the application to amend on the grounds that the defendants had not shown that they had exercised due diligence and should have applied to amend sooner than they did. 2. He should in any event have found that the defendants' conduct was improper. 3. Before allowing the amendment the judge should have scrutinised it with care particularly as it contained an allegation of fraud. He ought to have rejected it as irrelevant to the plaintiff's case and that the *e*   allegation of fraud was improperly framed and particularised. 4. He ought to have found that the prejudice to the plaintiff if the amendment was allowed was greater to that of the defendants if the amendment was rejected. The plaintiff could not be adequately compensated in costs.'

f   Ground 3, as reflected in the argument before us, raises the question whether rules, in so far as they exist, which prohibit amendment to allege fraud in other classes of litigation extend also to libel actions where the amendments sought allege justification in terms which involve allegations of fraud. No consideration of the problem appears in the text books on the subject of defamation and no cases have been cited to us on this topic.

   It seems logical, therefore, at the outset to examine the question in the light of the note in *The Supreme Court Practice* above cited and the authorities cited thereunder.

g   The general proposition stated in the note, 'The universal practice except in the most exceptional circumstances not to allow amendment for the purpose of adding a plea of fraud where fraud has not been pleaded in the first instance' derives from the judgment in the Court of Appeal of Lord Esher MR (with which Bowen and Kay LJJ concurred), in *Bentley & Co Ltd v Black* (1893) 9 TLR 580. This was an action brought by the plaintiff company to recover calls in respect of shares allotted to the defendant. The defence was *h*   that the defendant had been induced to take up shares on the strength of misleading statements in a prospectus. The prospectus had set forth a certificate and report of a chartered accountant which was said to be misleading with regard to certain assets. The defendant did not allege that the prospectus itself contained any false statements nor that the directors acted otherwise than in good faith: the allegation was confined to the *j*   proposition that when the action was commenced the directors knew the certificate and report was misleading.

   The action was tried at first instance by Kennedy J. There is no report of any ruling made by him save that he directed a verdict and gave judgment for the plaintiff. The defendants then applied for a new trial. In the Court of Appeal, in the course of his judgment, Lord Esher MR said (at 580):

'He now said that he had been induced to enter into the contract to take the shares by a fraudulent misrepresentation. Two objections were taken to that defence. In the first place it was pointed out that fraud had not been pleaded, neither had any amendment been made for the purpose of setting up a plea of fraud. It had for a long time been the universal practice, except in the most exceptional circumstances, not to allow an amendment for the purpose of adding a plea of fraud where fraud had not been pleaded in the first instance. It was therefore clear that this defence could not now be relied on. The second objection to the defence was that there was no evidence of any fraudulent misrepresentation having been made.'

It seems clear from this passage that, in fact, no amendment to allege fraud had ever been made either before the action commenced or during the trial and it is not clear whether such an application was even made before the Court of Appeal. It was in this context that Lord Esher MR made the comments cited. For my part, I doubt if this passage made in a case in which it appears that no amendment had ever been made or even sought, does support the general proposition that fraud, if not pleaded initially, cannot be raised by subsequent amendment. No doubt it is a proposition which would apply in cases where the facts giving rise to the plea of fraud were all known at the time of the original pleading and certainly where the failure to plead such facts could amount to 'over reaching' or where the delay in pleading fraud was in connection with some tactical manoeuvre.

The other cases cited all relate to circumstances in which amendment to plead an alleged fraud was allowed. *Hendriks v Montagu* (1881) 17 Ch D 638 (the year seems misquoted in the note in *The Supreme Court Practice*) was a case in which an injunction was claimed to restrain the defendants from assigning to a company about to be formed a name strikingly similar to that of the plaintiffs. The claim was confined to, and founded on, an alleged breach of the Companies Act 1862. Jessel MR at first instance ruled that no right to relief was established on the cause of action pleaded. He then continued (at 642–643):

'Now, the only other point which I wish to advert to is the excuse which Mr. Chitty had for going on with his case after this point was taken and pointed out. He asked me for leave to amend his notice of motion, and to let the motion stand over. I cannot accede to that. There is no Judge more liberal, if I may use the expression, in allowing amendments, in order to try the real case, than I am, at any stage of the case; but I make one exception, that is as to charges of fraud. I do not, as a rule, allow amendments to make a charge of fraud at a time when the case is launched, independently of fraud. I generally stop there. To allow such an amendment as this would be to contravene that rule. Of course, like all my rules, it is not an absolute rule. I may make an exception to it if I see good ground for doing so, but generally it is my rule. Here is a plaintiff coming in under an Act of Parliament who says: "You shall not use a name so similar to mine as to be calculated to deceive." He asks me, having failed because his company was not registered, to change the whole complexion of the suit, and to turn it into a suit to charge the Defendants with the intention of adopting the name and carrying on the business with the view of defrauding the Plaintiff company by unfairly, illegally, and immorally appropriating a portion of the business of the Plaintiff company. Now I cannot allow any such case to be made.'

In *Symonds v City Bank* (1886) 34 WR 364 North J in an action for fraudulent misrepresentation refused to allow an amendment to permit evidence of fraud to be given outside the facts pleaded in support of the fraud alleged. With regard to the amendment he said (at 365):

'. . . if it could be made without prejudicing the defendants I should make it . . . I *a*   cannot allow an amendment which would allow of the plaintiff's depositions being read when her cross-examination was not directed to the new points now brought forward.'

This case, in my view, indicates that but for the reasons stated, North J would have allowed an amendment, at least to the particulars, in the course of the hearing itself.

b   *Riding v Hawkins* (1889) 14 PD 56, was a probate action in which the testator's daughter was the plaintiff. It concerned a will and three codicils. The third and fourth codicils made bequests to the defendant. As originally pleaded the plaintiff contested the codicils on the grounds of undue influence. After the defendant had been cross-examined an application was made to amend to allege fraud and misrepresentation confined to matters arising out of that cross-examination. The amendment was allowed. On appeal the court held that the judge was justified in allowing the amendment under the circumstances

c   since the charges made against the defendant, if established would properly support a charge of fraud and it was, therefore, the duty of the judge to allow the plaintiff to amend her pleadings, always taking care that the defendant was exposed to no hardship.

In *Lever & Co v Goodwin Bros* [1887] WN 107, which was an action by the plaintiffs to restrain the defendants from infringing a trademark, the judge refused an amendment to the effect that there had been an imitation calculated to deceive. On appeal the court

d   (Cotton, Lindley and Bowen LJJ) held that the judge was correct in refusing the amendment in the course of the trial and said (at 108):

'. . . it involved a charge of fraud, which should have been raised, if at all, in the defence, at the risk of costs, and could not be started in the middle of a cross-examination.'

e

In my view this case is no authority for the proposition that such an amendment cannot be made before a trial; indeed, the reference to the risk of costs suggests the contrary.

I am unable, for my part, to conclude from these authorities that there is any general rule that allegations of fraud must be pleaded at the outset and cannot be added by

f   amendment. Indeed, all the cases, except *Bentley & Co Ltd v Black*, clearly envisage that in a proper case such amendments are permissible, even at trial if justice so demands, and Lord Esher MR himself in *Bentley & Co Ltd v Black* adverted to 'exceptional circumstances' in which this might be so.

The general statement by Lord Esher MR, therefore, seems to me, on the authorities, to be confined to such circumstances as I have earlier indicated. In so far as such

g   circumstances exist in libel actions I see no grounds to distinguish cases where fraud is itself the cause of action or is the defence to the action, from libel actions in which fraud is the gist of a plea of justification. Save in so far as RSC Ord 82 contains special provisions for defamation actions, in my view defamation actions do not differ from any other so far as the rules of pleading are concerned and are subject to the same restraints imposed by the rules.

h   I should add that, in my opinion, a plea of justification should not be allowed by amendment in circumstances in which the statement alleged to be defamatory unequivocally involves an assertion that a plaintiff has been fraudulent. In such circumstances it behoves a defendant to be in possession of all the relevant facts in support of the contention before he makes the defamatory statement and cannot be allowed to amend on the basis that his statement was unsupported by evidence known to him at

j   that time. In the present case the defendants have not only pleaded but have supported by affidavit their belief that they were not intending to make any such allegation against the plaintiff. Their intention and belief is irrelevant to the jury's verdict as to their liability, but for the purpose of pleading an amendment it is, in my view, relevant and can justify departure from what might otherwise be the appropriate ruling.

The fact that, subject to the matters I have mentioned, there is no general rule inhibiting an amendment to plead justification where the gist of the plea is an allegation of fraud does not, in my view, render the fact irrelevant. It is certainly relevant to other issues posed in this appeal, a scrutiny of the conduct of the defence, delay and due diligence. These issues arise in any case where justification is pleaded by amendment to the original pleadings (vide Lord Denning MR in *Associated Leisure Ltd v Associated Newspapers Ltd* [1970] 2 All ER 754 at 758, [1970] 2 QB at 456). This fact was accepted by Peter Pain J and thus the issue raised on this appeal is whether or not he attached sufficient importance to it. The question of delay and due diligence seem to me largely to overlap and to be different aspects of the same conduct. Two distinct periods are involved, viz the period over which the collection and assessment of the material took place and the period between the collection and assessment of the material and the notification to the plaintiff of the intention to amend to plead justification and communication to him of the details of that plea.

Mr Prebble, a director of the defendants, in his affidavit stated that until the commencement of the proceedings by the plaintiff it was the belief by the defendants that the plaintiff did not fall into that category of dentist whose conduct was criticised in the programme, but, on the contrary, was one of the category mentioned in the programme who were not alleged to have acted improperly. Hence the defendants did not start to collect evidence until the action had been initiated by the plaintiff. He also deposed that the investigations were lengthy and difficult.

In my view, where a defendant has pleaded that the words complained of did not relate to or refer to the plaintiff and that the plea is genuinely put forward it can seldom, if ever, be a valid ground of criticism that the investigations are not put in hand until the proceedings have been initiated, a fortiori where that plea is supported by affidavit. The length and difficulty of the necessary investigations are not particularised, though it is clear that two of the parties concerned were unsuccessfully approached at an early stage. The information on which the particulars of justification are founded derive, except for two instances, from a statement of Mr Bailey, the dental officer of the Department of Health and Social Security, in which all the relevant records of the patients concerned are said to have been disclosed. This statement was taken on 22 February 1985. The propriety of these disclosures is not a matter for this court, but the defence had the substance of the information on which the plea of justification was based on this date. It may be that further inquiries were needed with regard to the plaintiff's income in various years, but it is not obvious to me why this information could not be derived from the same source and at the same time as the information regarding the plaintiff's income of £105,315 which was stated in the broadcast. The explanation may be put forward by the defendants that at that time they had no reason to investigate his income over other years. Assuming, therefore, that for practical purposes the defendants had acquired the relevant information by February 1985, it does not seem to me unreasonable that counsel did not finish the drafting of the amendment until July 1985 and that such draft did not receive the approval of the defendants' board until September 1985. In my view, these facts are capable of establishing that the defendants did exercise due diligence, up to this point, and I do not consider that the judge can be said to be in error in the conclusion that he reached on this aspect of the matter. Moreover, the plaintiff's counsel conceded that had the amendment been sought in September 1985, no objection could have been taken.

As to the failure of the defendants to apply for an amendment to be allowed or to notify the plaintiff of the nature of it sooner than they did it seems to me that this was plainly culpable. It was based on an error on the part of the defendants' solicitor who believed that the case had not been set down when in fact he had been told by letter of 15 January 1985 that it had and had so reported to his clients. Nor does it seem to me that quite apart from this error the defendants were entitled to assume that the case had 'gone to sleep' nor to refrain from prompt application even if it had. The question, therefore, to my mind is whether this culpable delay should override the interests of

justice that the whole of a plaintiff's character and history relevant to the issues raised by
a the plea of justification should be before a jury where he claims damages in respect of
injury to that character. In my view, it should not so override this factor. Apart from the
necessary postponement of the hearing of his claim the plaintiff would have been in no
better position had the amendment been made in September 1985. The judge said: 'I
have felt grave doubt as to whether it was right for the defendants to have delayed their
application to amend in the way they did.' But, having considered all the relevant factors
b in accordance with the dicta in *Associated Leisure Ltd v Associated Newspapers Ltd*, he came
to the conclusion that there was nothing improper in the defendants' conduct. In my
view he came to the conclusion he did on proper grounds and there is no basis on which
this court should interfere with his decision on this aspect of the matter. I should say that
if there were any reasonable basis for a belief that the defendants' delay in seeking leave
for their amendment was deliberate in order to overreach the plaintiff or to obtain some
c tactical advantage I should come to the opposite conclusion, but there is here evidence on
affidavit to the contrary sworn by a solicitor. For these reasons I have come to the
conclusion that on the issues of due diligence, delay and the conduct of the defendant,
this appeal fails.

There remains the further and important matter, mentioned but not dealt with in
detail by the judge in the court below, the form of the amended pleading itself. As Lord
d Denning MR said in *Associated Leisure Ltd v Associated Newspapers Ltd* [1970] 2 All ER
754 at 757, [1970] 2 QB 450 at 455: '. . . the pleading ought to be scrutinised closely. The
defendants ought to give proper particulars. They ought not to be allowed to put in a
loose, ineffective pleading at the last hour.'

The judge said:

e   'Counsel for the plaintiff took the point that the words pleaded do not support the
general allegations made in para 7 of the amended defence. I think there is again
some force in what she has to say there, but it seems to me a matter that could easily
be put right by adjustment of the wording. It is fairly clear what the defendants are
driving at in their allegation although the expression of it seemed to me to require
to be rather tightened.'

f I agree with this view, save that in my opinion it understates the case. The form of the
present pleading does not, in my opinion, fairly indicate what matters are relied on in
support of the plea said to be a justification of the real 'sting' of the words complained of
if the jury accepts that they were defamatory of the plaintiff. I accept that a defendant is
entitled to put forward a plea of justification in respect of any meaning which the jury
might find the words to bear. However, this court has been provided with a full transcript
g of the programme broadcast. It is clear that if the words relate to the plaintiff, and if the
jury finds them defamatory, the 'sting' of the libel is the allegation that unnecessary work
was done in order to receive unjustified fees and that claims were made for work not in
fact done. Both these allegations impute fraud and dishonesty. The broadcast is not
related to work badly done, nor could such an allegation per se support a claim of fraud.
h The only reference in the broadcast to bad, or incompetent, work is that a government-
sponsored dental strategy review group found that the payments system 'led to
unnecessary inept and ineffectual treatment', and there was a reference to a bad filling in
a tooth of one of the patients examined.

Apart from these two passing references nothing in the broadcast relates to poor or
negligent work. It all relates to unnecessary work and work paid for but not in fact
j carried out.

The general plea of justification is contained in para 7 of the amended defence. Its
terms have already been cited in this judgment. Sub-paragraph (b) of that paragraph
reads: 'Worked too quickly and badly.' It is contended on behalf of the defence that this
is capable of amounting to an allegation of fraud or dishonesty in that it implies that a
dentist by working too quickly, and thus, badly, can earn more fees than would be the

case if he worked properly. I doubt whether the wording of sub-para (b) is capable of
bearing this meaning, but in any event such an imputation does not, in my view, arise   *a*
from anything said in the broadcast or pleaded in para 4 of the statement of claim and is
not, therefore, a meaning which a jury could place on the words of which complaint is
made. Nor do I think it can be said to arise from the meanings pleaded in para 6 of the
statement of claim. It is said that sub-para (4) of this paragraph, 'that the plaintiff is guilty
of gross professional misconduct', can bear this interpretation. I do not agree that it can.
     Accordingly I would strike out sub-para (b) of para 7 of the amended defence.   *b*
     The purpose of pleading is to define clearly the issues to be decided by the court and
the jury and to make clear to the opposing party precisely what the case is that he has to
meet and to restrict the evidence to those issues. I find much of the amended defence, in
its present form, both confusing and ambiguous. For my part I do not see that any real
purpose is served by the descriptive matters contained in para 6(1), (2) and (3) of the
amended pleading. I do not go so far as to say these are embarrassing, but none of these   *c*
matters are likely to be disputed and, in my view, it is unnecessary to plead them. As to
para 6(4), I see no relevance in the recitation of the plaintiff's gross income as compared
with the average earnings and I consider that the whole of para 6(4) and (5) of the
amended pleadings should be struck out. No jury should be asked to infer fraud from
the fact alone that the plaintiff's income exceeded the national average.
     [His Lordship then considered the specific cases pleaded in paras 6(8) to (16) of the   *d*
amended pleading and continued:]
     In my view, however, once the particulars are limited to the matters pleaded by para
7(a) and (c) of the defence without sub-para (b), so much needs to be deleted and so little
is left that the appropriate course in my view is for the whole of the proposed amendment
to be struck out. What is required is that the pleadings should state in clear and precise
terms the particulars to be given under para 7(a) and (c) of the defence. I have indicated   *e*
the respects in which in my view the existing pleading is defective. I agree with May and
Parker LJJ that the whole of it should be struck out.
     Such radical alteration of the pleading gives rise to the argument put forward on behalf
of the plaintiff that the defendants should not be allowed to have a second chance to put
right a defective pleading, added at a fairly late stage. There is force in this contention   *f*
but, in my view, provided that the pleading, in its final form, properly and clearly
indicates to the plaintiff the case that is made against him, there is no reason in law why
he should be precluded from making a further application for leave to amend. Whether
this will be allowed will be a matter for the discretion of the master and, if need be, the
judge in the light of the guidance given in these judgments. There should be full
discovery at the time the application to amend it made.
     I have not found this an easy matter, but for the reasons I have given I would allow   *g*
this appeal.

Appeal allowed.

Solicitors: *Ward Bowie*, agents for *Foster Baxter Cooksey*, Willenhall (for the plaintiff);   *h*
Goodman Derrick & Co (for the defendants).

                                        Carolyn Toulmin   Barrister.

a
Hayward v Cammell Laird Shipbuilders Ltd

EMPLOYMENT APPEAL TRIBUNAL
POPPLEWELL J, MR J A POWELL AND MR H ROBSON
5 MARCH, 19 MAY 1986

b *Employment – Equality of treatment of men and women – Equal pay for equal work – Pay – Inequality of specific terms and conditions – Applicant employed as cook in shipyard – Applicant's work of equal value to male shipyard workers – Applicant paid less than male comparators – Whether equality provisions applying to terms and conditions as a whole or to specific terms – Whether female employee entitled to equality of particular term or condition of employment – Equal Pay Act 1970, s 1(2) – EEC Treaty, art 119.*

c
The applicant was a cook in a canteen at the employers' shipyard. A report of an independent expert stated that she was employed on work of equal value to that of male shipyard workers, who were relevant comparators. She was not paid the same basic wage or overtime rates as those comparators. The applicant applied to an industrial tribunal for a declaration that her basic pay and overtime pay should be the same as her male

d comparators. The tribunal refused to make such a declaration, on the grounds that for the purposes of awarding equal pay for work of equal value in accordance with s 1(2)[a] of the Equal Pay Act 1970 a term or condition relating to 'pay' was to be construed in accordance with the broad meaning given by art 119[b] of the EEC Treaty and therefore it was proper to consider the whole of the applicant's terms and conditions rather than specific terms which, taken on their own, were less favourable. The applicant appealed,

e contending that under s 1(2) of the 1970 Act once it was shown that she did do work of equal value she was entitled to point to specific terms in her contract which were less favourable than the comparators' terms and to have those terms amended in her favour to bring them into line.

Held – Since the terms of s 1(2) of the 1970 Act were ambiguous and capable of referring
f either to an employee's terms and conditions of employment as a whole or to specific terms only, s 1(2) was to be interpreted in the light of art 119 of the EEC Treaty, which clearly did not limit pay simply to wages or salary but involved any other consideration, whether in cash or in kind, received by the employee for his services. Accordingly, in deciding whether a female employee's conditions of employment were less favourable than those of an equivalent male employee for the purposes of a claim under the 1970

g Act, an industrial tribunal was entitled to consider her whole employment package and was not confined to considering specific terms of her contract of employment which might be less favourable. Since that was the approach adopted by the industrial tribunal the applicant's appeal would be dismissed (see p 509 j and p 512 c f, post).

Notes
h For equal treatment of men and women regarding terms and conditions of employment, see 16 Halsbury's Laws (4th edn) para 767.

For the Equal Pay Act 1970, s 1, see 16 Halsbury's Statutes (4th edn) 188–190.
For the EEC Treaty, art 119, see 42A Halsbury's Statutes (3rd edn) 779.

j **Cases referred to in judgment**
Bestuur der Sociale Verzekeringsbank v H J van der Vecht Case 19/67 [1967] ECR 345.
Bulmer (H P) Ltd v J Bollinger SA [1974] 2 All ER 1226, [1974] Ch 401, [1974] 3 WLR 202, CA.

---

a   Section 1(2), so far as material, is set out at p 505 *e* to *g*, post
b   Article 119 is set out at p 507 *j* to p 508 *a*, post

Clay Cross (Quarry Services) Ltd v Fletcher [1979] 1 All ER 474, [1978] 1 WLR 1429, CA.

Da Costa en Schaake NV v Nederlandse Belastingadministratie Cases 28, 29 and 30/62 [1963] *a* ECR 31.

EC Commission v UK Case 61/81 [1982] ECR 2601.

Garland v British Rail Engineering Ltd [1982] 2 All ER 402, [1983] 2 AC 751, [1982] 2 WLR 918, HL.

Haughton v Olau Line (UK) Ltd [1986] 2 All ER 47, [1986] 1 WLR 504, CA.

Jenkins v Kingsgate (Clothing Productions) Ltd Case 96/80 [1981] 1 WLR 972, [1981] ECR *b* 911, CJEC; *subsequent proceedings* [1981] 1 WLR 1485, EAT.

Magor and St Mellons RDC v Newport Corp [1951] 2 All ER 839, [1952] AC 189, HL.

Marshall v Southampton and South West Hampshire Area Health Authority (Teaching) Case 152/84 [1986] 2 All ER 584, [1986] QB 401, [1986] 2 WLR 780, CJEC.

Post Office v Crouch [1974] 1 All ER 229, [1974] 1 WLR 89, HL.

Roberts v Tate & Lyle Food and Distribution Ltd [1983] ICR 521, EAT; *subsequent proceedings* *c* [1986] 2 All ER 602, CJEC.

Sorbie v Trust Houses Forte Hotels Ltd [1977] 2 All ER 155, [1977] QB 931, [1976] 3 All WLR 918, EAT.

Tax on Imported Lemons, Re [1968] CMLR 1, Finanzgericht, Hamburg; *subsequent proceedings* sub nom *Firma August Stier v Hauptzollamt Hamburg-Ericus* Case 31/67 [1968] ECR 235.   *d*

Van Duyn v Home Office [1974] 3 All ER 178, [1974] 1 WLR 1107; *subsequent proceedings* [1975] 3 All ER 190, [1975] Ch 358, [1975] 2 WLR 760, [1974] ECR 1337, CJEC.

Worringham v Lloyds Bank Ltd Case 69/80 [1981] 2 All ER 434, [1981] 1 WLR 950, [1981] ECR 767, CJEC; *subsequent proceedings* [1982] 3 All ER 373, [1982] 1 WLR 841, CA.

Appeal   *e*

The applicant, Julie Ann Hayward, commenced employment with the respondents Cammell Laird Shipbuilders Ltd, on 19 August 1985 as an apprentice cook in a shipyard at the basic rate of pay applicable to all apprentices employed in the yard. After attending courses and obtaining appropriate certificates she qualified as a cook/chef and was paid as a canteen assistant at the rate of £4,976 pa. She applied to an industrial tribunal under s *f* 1(2)(c) of the Equal Pay Act 1970 claiming that she was entitled to the same pay as male tradesmen in the yard because her work was of equal value to theirs. By a decision dated 29 October 1984 the industrial tribunal (chairman Mr A M Coventry) found that she was employed on work of equal value to the comparators named in the report of an independent expert and accordingly an equality clause was deemed to operate in relation to any variation between the applicant's contract of employment and those of the male *g* comparators. On 4 April 1985 the applicant's solicitors requested a further hearing by the tribunal because it had not been possible to reach agreement on the applicant's terms of employment. By a decision dated 12 September 1985 the tribunal declined the applicant's request to make an unqualified declaration that her basic pay and overtime pay should be the same as her male comparators. The applicant appealed to the Employment Appeal Tribunal against that decision. The facts are set out in the judgment *h* of the appeal tribunal.

David Pannick for the applicant.
Charles James for the respondents.

Cur adv vult *j*

19 May. The following judgment of the appeal tribunal was delivered.

POPPLEWELL J. This is an appeal against the decision of an industrial tribunal sitting at Liverpool on 25 July 1985. It raises one point of construction. It is a difficult point. It

is this. The industrial tribunal had already determined that the applicant was employed
on work of equal value to the comparators named in the report of an independent expert.
She was a cook in a canteen at a shipyard. The comparators were shipyard workers. It
was accepted that she was not paid the same basic wage or overtime rates as the men who
did work of equal value to her. The employers' argument was that they did not have to
pay her the same basic wage or overtime rates because, considered as a whole, her terms
and conditions were not less favourable and they sought to introduce evidence to that
effect.

It was submitted on the applicant's behalf (1) that once it was shown that she did work
of equal value, she was entitled to point to specific terms in her contract which were less
favourable than the comparators' terms and to have those terms amended in her favour
to bring them into line, (2) it matters not if, when all her other terms or conditions are
considered, her position is better than the comparators'; the question which the tribunal
had to consider was whether it was open to them to hear evidence relating to it. There is
a factual dispute whether, even if all the terms are considered, she is better off than the
comparators: but this lies yet for decision depending on the result of the argument
presently put forward.

We turn first to the legislation which governs our decision. It may involve consideration
both of Community law and national law. The Equal Pay Act 1970 (which contains no
definition of 'pay') was 'An Act to prevent discrimination, as regards terms and conditions
of employment between men and women'. Section 1, so far as material, reads:

> '(1) If the terms of a contract under which a woman is employed at an
> establishment in Great Britain do not include (directly or by reference to a collective
> agreement or otherwise) an equality clause they shall be deemed to include one.
> (2) An equality clause is a provision which relates to terms (whether concerned
> with pay or not) of a contract under which a woman is employed . . . and has the
> effect that—(a) . . . (i) if (apart from the equality clause) any term of the woman's
> contract is or becomes less favourable to the woman than a term of a similar kind in
> the contract under which that man is employed, that term of the woman's contract
> shall be treated as so modified as not to be less favourable, and . . . (c) where a woman
> is employed on work which, not being work in relation to which paragraph (a) or
> (b) above applies, is, in terms of the demands made on her (for instance under such
> headings as effort, skill and decision), of equal value to that of a man in the same
> employment—(i) if (apart from the equality clause) any term of the woman's
> contract is or becomes less favourable to the woman than a term of a similar kind in
> the contract under which that man is employed, that term of the woman's contract
> shall be treated as so modified as not to be less favourable . . .'

The Act came into force at the end of December 1975 and sub-s (2)(c) was added by the
Equal Pay (Amendment) Regulations 1983, SI 1983/1794.

Counsel for the applicant made a number of submissions to us: firstly that the language
of the Act is unambiguous. He says that where *any* term is less favourable to the woman
than a term of a similar kind under which that man is employed, that term shall be
treated as modified as not to be less favourable; so that if a particular term is less
favourable it shall be modified. In the instant case the particular term has been identified;
it is less favourable, and it should be modified to accord with the term under which the
man is employed. There is no mention of any package and the other terms of the contract
are irrelevant. The section says nothing about when all the terms are taken together they
must be equal; it merely says that if *any* term is less favourable it shall be modified. And,
says counsel for the applicant, although no doubt the section could have been drafted
differently, it has been drafted in that way and it is quite unambiguous.

He drew our attention, as he had indeed drawn it to the industrial tribunal, to *Sorbie v
Trust Houses Forte Hotels Ltd* [1977] 2 All ER 155 at 158, [1977] QB 931 at 934–935,
where Phillips J, giving the decision of the Employment Appeal Tribunal, said:

'Counsel for the employers supports the decision of the industrial tribunal by saying that the effect of s 1(2)(a)(i) here is that the female employees [appellants] are to be remunerated at a rate of pay not less favourable than any man employed on like work, and that accordingly, if no man is employed on like work, the term can have no effect. Putting the same submission in a slightly different way, he says that the tribunal can have no jurisdiction to deal with matters arising after 5th January when there was no man employed on like work to that of the female employees. In our judgment that submission, and indeed the decision of the industrial tribunal, is wrong. It seems to us that the correct way to approach the matter is this: one looks to see, in accordance with s 1(2)(a)(i) (it for present purposes being common ground that the female employees are employed on like work with Mr Savvas) whether there is any term of the female employees' contract which is less favourable to them than a term of a similar kind in his contract. This requires one first to identify the term. If one does that in this case, the term in question is the term in the contract which specifies the remuneration. They did not, as far as we know, have any written contracts; but, if they had, there would have been a clause in it which would have said in the case of each of them that they would be paid at the rate of 85p an hour. That term is plainly less favourable than the similar term in Mr Savvas's contract, which would have provided that he was to be remunerated at 97½p an hour. One then goes on to see what the effect as prescribed is, and it is that that term, so identified, in the female employees' contracts shall be treated as so modified, as not to be less favourable.'

Counsel for the applicant made the further point that by looking at these specific terms a good number of practical problems are avoided, so that the tribunal does not have to weigh up the value of other parts of an applicant's contract which may have a monetary value; thus the problem of putting a value on sick pay, which may never be claimed, is readily avoided. Each term is analysed and identified and any term less favourable to a woman is to be modified. And he drew our attention to the decision of *Clay Cross (Quarry Services) Ltd v Fletcher* [1979] 1 All ER 474 at 479, [1978] 1 WLR 1429 at 1436, where Lawton LJ said:

'Consideration of the effect in law of these few facts has occupied this court for two and a half days. We have had to consider two decisions of this court, two of the Employment Appeals Tribunal, six of the United States federal courts, two of the United States Supreme Court, two of the European Court, art 119 of the EEC Treaty and a Community Council directive . . . I found all these complications disturbing. Parliament intended that industrial tribunals should provide a quick and cheap remedy for what it had decided were injustices in the employment sphere. The procedure was to be such that both employers and employees could present their cases without having to go to lawyers for help. Within a few years legalism has started to take over. It must be driven back if possible. If the wording of the relevant statutes has opened the door to legal subtleties, there is nothing the courts can do to stop what I regard as an unfortunate development. The remedy lies with Parliament. If, however, there are uncertainties in the statutes, when construing them the courts should, I think, lean in favour of a simplicity in meaning which will safeguard informality in procedure.'

We entirely indorse what Lawton LJ said about simplicity. As an aid to construction in the instant case, it has not provided us, unfortunately, with an immediate key to the solution.

The final point which counsel for the applicant made in his speech to us when dealing with the application of national law was in anticipation of an argument that was to be raised against him by counsel for the respondent employers, namely if his argument were to succeed so that each term individually and separately were looked at, there was a

very real risk of leap-frogging and Parliament could not have intended by this amendment
a that that should happen. To this counsel for the applicant answered shortly and succinctly
that if there were an anomaly it was for Parliament to rectify it by altering the terms of
the section and not to go behind the clear words of the Act of Parliament.

He then turned to the question of Community law. The industrial tribunal considered
this with obvious care. In their decision dated 12 September 1985 they said:

b '10 Another matter which we see as being of importance and likely to have a
significant bearing upon this problem is the interaction between the law of the
European Economic Community and our National Law, both generally, and in
relation to the particular problem with which we are dealing. Section 2(1) of the
European Communities Act 1972 provides that all the rights and obligations arising
under the Treaty of Rome [the EEC Treaty], to which we make further reference
below, are to be given legal effect in this country. That, of course, includes Article
c 119. Furthermore, our own Parliament enacted that, on joining the Community,
we should abide by certain fundamental principles laid down by the European
Court. Section 3(1) of the European Communities Act 1972 deals with that. The
principles, which are 2 in number, are:—(1) The supremacy of Community Law.
That is to say if there is a conflict or inconsistency between Community Law and
d our internal law, Community Law shall prevail. (2) The principle of direct
applicability, the effect of which is that if a member state has not legislated in
accordance with the requirements of Community Law an individual may bring
proceedings in his own national courts to enforce the rights and obligations
contained in the Treaty in relation to those Articles which are sufficiently clear,
precise, and unconditional, as not to require any further measure of implementation.
e Article 119 comes within that category; it seems probable, however, that the
principle does not apply to Directives.'

The question of directives has been considered by the European Court and by the
Court of Appeal since the industrial tribunal gave their decision. In *Marshall v Southampton
and South West Hampshire Area Health Authority (Teaching)* Case 152/84 [1986] 2 All ER
f 584 at 600, [1986] QB 401 at 422 the Court of Justice of the European Communities
held, inter alia, that an EEC directive may not of itself impose obligations on an
individual, and a provision of a directive may not be relied on as such against such a
person. According to art 189 of the EEC Treaty, the binding nature of a directive which
constitutes the basis for the possibility of relying on the directive before a national court
exists only in relation to each member state to which it is addressed.

g In *Haughton v Olau Line (UK) Ltd* [1986] 2 All ER 47 at 51, [1986] 1 WLR 504 at 508 Sir
John Donaldson said:

'However, [counsel for Miss Haughton] submitted that the directive [ie EC
Council Directive 76/207] could still be used to resolve ambiguities, since the 1975
Act [ie the Sex Discrimination Act 1975] was intended to give effect to the policy
enshrined in the directive . . . I do not find it necessary to pursue this aspect, because
h I do not regard the statute as being in the least ambiguous. The drafting may be
unusual, but that is a different matter.'

Article 119 of the EEC Treaty, which came into effect on 1 December 1961, reads (in
one translation with which we have been provided):

j 'Each Member State shall during the first stage ensure and subsequently maintain
the application of the principle that men and women should receive equal pay for
equal work.

For the purpose of this Article, "pay" means the ordinary basis or minimum wage
or salary and any other consideration, whether in cash or in kind, which the worker
receives, directly or indirectly, in respect of his employment from his employer.

Equal pay without discrimination based on sex means: (a) that pay for the same work at piece rates shall be calculated on the basis of the same unit of measurement; (b) that pay for work at time rates shall be the same for the same job.'

The industrial tribunal observed that these provisions worked perfectly well when those being compared did the same kind of work. But, as the industrial tribunal pointed out, difficulties arise when the work was not the same or the job different. As a result, on 10 February 1975 there was issued EC Council Directive 75/117. It observed—

'... Whereas implementation of the principle that men and women should receive equal pay contained in Article 119 of the Treaty as an integral part of the establishment and functioning of the common market; Whereas it is primarily the responsibility of the Member States to ensure the application of this principle by means of appropriate laws, regulations and administrative provisions; Whereas the Council resolution of 21 January 1974 concerning a social action programme, aimed at making it possible to harmonize living and working conditions while the improvement is being maintained and at achieving a balanced social and economic development of the Community, recognized that priority should be given to action taken on behalf of women as regards access to employment and vocational training and advancement, and as regards working conditions, including pay; Whereas it is desirable to reinforce the basic laws by standards aimed at facilitating the practical application of the principle of equality in such a way that all employees in the Community can be protected in these matters; Whereas differences continue to exist in the various Member States despite the efforts made to apply the resolution of the conference of the Member States of 30 December 1961 on equal pay for men and women and whereas, therefore, the national provisions should be approximated as regards application of the principle of equal pay.'

It then went on to adopt:

'*Article 1*
The principle of equal pay for men and women outlined in Article 119 of the Treaty, hereinafter called "principle of equal pay", means, for the same work or for work to which equal value is attributed, the elimination of all discrimination on grounds of sex with regard to all aspects and conditions of remuneration ...

Article 4
Member States shall take the necessary precautions to ensure that provisions appearing in collective agreements, wage scales, wage agreements or individual contracts of employment which are contrary to the principle of equal pay shall be, or may be declared, null and void or may be amended ...'

As a matter of history, the Equal Pay (Amendment) Regulations 1983 were introduced because the EEC Commission found that the United Kingdom had failed to fulfil its obligations under the EEC Treaty and had failed to implement art 1 of Directive 75/117 in relation to work of equal value (see *EC Commission v UK* Case 61/81 [1982] ECR 2601).

Counsel for the applicant makes a number of submissions on the application and effect of the Community law. He accepts as a correct proposition of law what was said by this tribunal in *Roberts v Tate & Lyle Food and Distribution Ltd* [1983] ICR 521 at 530, where Browne-Wilkinson J said:

'We were treated to an elaborate argument on Community law relevant to the cases before us. We accept that if the law of the E.E.C. on the subject is clear, we should so far as possible seek to construe the English statute so as to conform to the Community law. However, in our judgment the position in Community law is far from clear.'

In the instant case counsel for the applicant says the Community law is far from clear
a on the respondents' argument; it does not clearly establish that one should look at all
contractual terms of a woman compared with a man. Article 119 of the EEC Treaty, it is
true, does widely define 'pay' because the intention is to prevent employers giving the
same pay but different treatment as to other terms. But he goes further and says that
even if the Community law assists the employers and it is possible to look at the whole
of the conditions, there is no reason why domestic law should not provide greater rights
b for an employee so that this applicant has more rights under the domestic law than under
Community law. Our attention was drawn to the decision in *Jenkins v Kingsgate (Clothing
Productions) Ltd* [1981] 1 WLR 1485 at 1495, a decision of this tribunal where Browne-
Wilkinson J said:

c　　'We will assume, without deciding, that article 119 as construed by the European
Court of Justice does not apply to cases of unintentional indirect discrimination.
How then are we to construe the United Kingdom statute? Although we must
construe the United Kingdom legislation so as not to conflict with article 119 and so
far as possible to make it accord with article 119, it does not necessarily follow that
the United Kingdom legislation must in all respects have the same effect as article
d　　119. It would not contravene section 2 of the European Communities Act 1972 if
the United Kingdom statutes conferred on employees greater rights than they enjoy
under article 119. Since the Act of 1970 is an integral part of one code against sex
discrimination and the rest of the code plainly renders unlawful indirect
discrimination even if unintentional, it seems to us right that we should construe
the Equal Pay Act 1970 as requiring any difference in pay to be objectively justified
even if this confers on employees greater rights than they would enjoy under article
e　　119 of the E.E.C. Treaty.'

And finally, says counsel for the applicant, this is not a case where someone has come
to the tribunal basing their claim on the Community law. The applicant in the instant
case is entitled to rely on the clear terms of the 1970 Act.
f　　Counsel for the respondent employers has pointed out that this applicant's contract of
employment would very probably be different in a number of ways, as is the widespread
and long-established practice in British industry. He points out that she was a member
of staff, whereas the comparators were hourly paid, and, although her work may be of
equal value, the terms on which she is employed will be quite different so that there may
be entitlement to holidays, or entitlement to work overtime, which may be totally
g different from that of her comparators. Her hours of work may be different; her
conditions of work may be different. He approaches the 1970 Act in this way. He points
to the preamble, 'An Act to prevent discrimination as regards terms and conditions of
employment between men and women', and observes that the Act is intended to give
equal treatment as regards her conditions, 'equal treatment' meaning conditions looked
at overall.
h　　He next submits that when the 1970 Act was amended by the 1983 regulations to
include equal value, it had to be looked at in the light of art 119 of the EEC Treaty which
lay behind the directive and the judgment of the European Court. On this argument, s
1(1) of the 1970 Act means that men and women are entitled to equality, broadly
speaking, and s 1(2)(c), which refers to *any* term, can only mean, having regard to s 1(2),
any term concerned with pay and that the words 'of a similar kind' in s 1(2)(c)(i) mean
j that when the tribunal looks at the terms in a contract under which a man is employed,
those terms are terms concerning pay.
　　Article 119 of the Treaty clearly does not limit pay simply to wages or salary but
involves any other consideration whether in cash or in kind. It is also a very familiar
concept in the United Kingdom known in the industrial jargon as 'the total employment
package'.

Counsel for the respondent employers says that the English statute is ambiguous and that we should follow the approach of Lord Denning MR in *H P Bulmer Ltd v J Bollinger SA* [1974] 2 All ER 1226, [1974] Ch 401, and he drew particular attention to two passages, the first ([1974] 2 All ER 1226 at 1231–1232, [1974] Ch 401 at 418–419) reads:

'*4 The impact of the treaty on English law*
    The first and fundamental point is that the treaty concerns only those matters which have a European element, that is to say, matters which affect people or property in the nine countries of the Common Market besides ourselves. The treaty does not touch any of the matters which concern solely the mainland of England and the people in it. These are still governed by English law. They are not affected by the treaty. But when we come to matters with a European element, the treaty is like an incoming tide. It flows into the estuaries and up the rivers. It cannot be held back. Parliament has decreed that the treaty is henceforward to be part of our law. It is equal in force to any statute. The governing provision is s 2(1) of the European Communities Act 1972. It says: "All such rights, powers, liabilities, obligations and restrictions from time to time created by or arising under the Treaties, and all such remedies and procedures from time to time provided for by or under the Treaties, as in accordance with the Treaties are without further enactment to be given legal effect or used in the United Kingdom shall be recognised, and available in law, and be enforced, allowed and followed accordingly; and the expression 'enforceable Community right' and similar expressions shall be read as referring to one to which this subsection applies." The statute is expressed in forthright terms which are absolute and all-embracing. Any rights or obligations created by the treaty are to be given legal effect in England without more ado. Any remedies or procedures provided by the treaty are to be made available here without being open to question. In future, in transactions which cross the frontiers, we must no longer speak or think of English law as something on its own. We must speak and think of Community law, of Community rights and obligations, and we must give effect to them. This means a great effort for the lawyers. We have to learn a new system. The treaty, with the regulations and directives, covers many volumes. The case law is contained in hundreds of reported cases both in the European Court of Justice and in the national courts of the nine. Many must be studied before the right result can be reached. We must get down to it.'

The second passage ([1974] 2 All ER 1226 at 1236–1238, [1974] Ch 401 at 425–426) reads:

'*9 The principles of interpretation*
    In view of these considerations, it is apparent that in very many cases the English courts will interpret the treaty themselves. They will not refer the question to the European Court at Luxembourg. What then are the principles of interpretation to be applied? Beyond doubt the English courts must follow the same principles as the European Court. Otherwise there would be differences between the countries of the nine. That would never do. All the courts of all nine countries should interpret the treaty in the same way. They should all apply the same principles. It is enjoined on the English courts by s 3 of the European Communities Act 1972, which I have read. What a task is thus set before us! The treaty is quite unlike any of the enactments to which we have become accustomed. The draftsmen of our statutes have striven to express themselves with the utmost exactness. They have tried to foresee all possible circumstances that may arise and to provide for them. They have sacrificed style and simplicity. They have foregone brevity. They have become long and involved. In consequence, the judges have followed suit. They interpret a statute as applying only to the circumstances covered by the very words. They give them a literal interpretation. If the words of the statute do not cover a new

situation—which was not foreseen—the judges hold that they have no power to fill
the gap. To do so would be a "naked usurpation of the legislative function": see
Magor and St Mellons Rural District Council v Newport Corporation [1951] 2 All ER
839 at 841, [1952] AC 189 at 191. The gap must remain open until Parliament finds
time to fill it. How different is this treaty. It lays down general principles. It
expresses its aims and purposes. All in sentences of moderate length and
commendable style. But it lacks precision. It uses words and phrases without
defining what they mean. An English lawyer would look for an interpretation
clause, but he would look in vain. There is none. All the way through the treaty
there are gaps and lacunae. These have to be filled in by the judges, or by regulations
or directives. It is the European way. That appears from the decision of the Hamburg
court in *Re Tax on Imported Lemons* [1968] CMLR 1. Likewise the regulations and
directives. They are enacted by the Council of Ministers sitting in Brussels for
everyone to obey. They are quite unlike our statutory instruments. They have to
give the reasons on which they are based: see art 190 of the EEC Treaty. So they
start off with pages of preambles, "whereas" and "whereas" and "whereas". These
show the purpose and intent of the regulations and directives. Then follow the
provisions which are to be obeyed. Here again words and phrases are used without
defining their import. Such as "personal conduct" in the EEC Directive 64/221,
which was considered by Pennycuick V-C in *Van Duyn v Home Office* [1974] 3 All ER
178, [1974] 1 WLR 1107. In case of difficulty, recourse is had to the preambles.
These are useful to show the purpose and intent behind it all. But much is left to
the judges. The enactments give only an outline plan. The details are to be filled in
by the judges. Seeing these differences, what are the English courts to do when they
are faced with a problem of interpretation? They must follow the European pattern.
No longer must they examine the words in meticulous detail. No longer must they
argue about the precise grammatical sense. They must look to the purpose or intent.
To quote the words of the European Court in the *Da Costa* case [*Da Costa en Schaake
NV v Nederlandse Belastingadministratie* Cases 28, 29 and 30/62 [1963] ECR 31 at 38];
they must limit themselves to deducing from "the wording and the spirit of the
treaty the meaning of the Community rules . . ." They must not confine themselves
to the English text. They must consider, if need be, all the authentic texts, of which
there are now eight: see the *Sociale Verzekeringsbank* case [*Bestuur der Sociale
Verzekeringsbank v J H van der Vecht* Case 19/67 [1967] ECR 345]. They must divine
the spirit of the treaty and gain inspiration from it. If they find a gap, they must fill
it as best they can. They must do what the framers of the instrument would have
done if they had thought about it. So we must do the same. Those are the principles,
as I understand it, on which the European Court acts.'

The decision and arguments in *Worringham v Lloyds Bank Ltd* Case 69/80 [1981] 2 All
ER 434, [1981] 1 WLR 950 were relied on and also the decision of the House of Lords in
Garland v British Rail Engineering Ltd [1982] 2 All ER 402, [1983] 2 AC 751. Those
decisions and the terms of the article make it clear that if the interpretation of art 119
were the only question the answer would be clear. But counsel for the applicant by way
of reply argues that what has to be considered is how, in the light of art 119, s 1(2)(c) of
the 1970 Act came to be drafted in that way if it were intended that the overall picture
should be looked at. And it is pointed out that by s 1(3), if the variation is generally due
to a material factor which is not the difference of sex, an equality clause shall not operate
in relation to variation between the woman's contract and the man's contract. This, says
counsel for the applicant, will deal with the problem of leap-frogging. However, we have
to assume that Parliament intended to legislate an Act so as not to be inconsistent with
our treaty obligations. And in *Garland v British Rail Engineering Ltd* [1982] 2 All ER 402
at 415, [1983] 2 AC 751 at 771 Lord Diplock said:

'My Lords, even if the obligation to observe the provisions of art 119 were an
obligation assumed by the United Kingdom under an ordinary international treaty   *a*
or convention and there were no question of the treaty obligation being directly
applicable as part of the law to be applied by the courts in this country without need
for any further enactment, it is a principle of construction of United Kingdom
statutes, now too well established to call for citation of authority, that the words of a
statute passed after the treaty has been signed and dealing with the subject matter
of the international obligation of the United Kingdom, are to be construed, if they   *b*
are reasonably capable of bearing such a meaning, as intended to carry out the
obligation and not to be inconsistent with it. A fortiori is this the case where the
treaty obligation arises under one of the Community treaties to which s 2 of the
European Communities Act 1972 applies.'

We acknowledge that much of the argument of counsel for the applicant is legally   *c*
very persuasive, but we have come to the conclusion that the terms of s 1(2) are equally
capable of bearing the meaning ascribed to them by counsel for the respondent
employers. Accordingly we must apply art 119. Applying art 119 the tribunal must look
at the overall package. We reject the submission that this will pose any difficulty in
practice for an industrial tribunal which is quite capable of carrying out the inquiry. A
decision to the contrary, which would necessarily involve leap-frogging, would in the   *d*
view of the industrial members of this court result in widespread chaos in industry and
inflict grave damage on commerce. We are a pragmatic court, as are the industrial
tribunals, with members well versed in industrial practice. We should seek to interpret
an Act of Parliament with common sense applicable to industrial affairs and not in a way
which has precisely the opposite effect unless we were driven to it. To adopt and adapt
the words of Lord Reid in *Post Office v Crouch* [1974] 1 All ER 229 at 236, [1974] 1 WLR   *e*
89 at 96, when he said in relation to the Industrial Relations Act 1971:

'This in my judgment shows that the Act must be construed in a broad and
reasonable way so that legal technicalities shall not prevail against industrial relations
and common sense.'

We agree with the views of the industrial tribunal as an industrial jury. Accordingly,   *f*
the appeal is dismissed.

Appeal dismissed. Leave to appeal to Court of Appeal granted.

Solicitors: *Brian Thompson & Partners,* Manchester (for the applicant); *Davis Campbell &
Co,* Liverpool (for the respondents).   *g*

K Mydeen Esq   Barrister.

a

R v Andrews

HOUSE OF LORDS

LORD BRIDGE OF HARWICH, LORD BRANDON OF OAKBROOK, LORD GRIFFITHS, LORD MACKAY OF CLASHFERN AND LORD ACKNER

24, 25, 26 NOVEMBER 1986, 5 FEBRUARY 1987

b

Criminal law – Res gestae – Statement made as part of res gestae – Circumstances in which evidence admissible – Test to be applied – Statement made spontaneously and contemporaneously with event – Exception to hearsay rule – Victim seriously wounded in attack – Statement made by victim to police officer within minutes of attack – Victim identifying attackers – Victim dying two months later – Whether statement admissible as evidence of truth of facts asserted by victim – Factors to be considered by trial judge regarding admissibility of statement.

c

The appellant and another man knocked on the door of the victim's flat and when the victim opened it the appellant stabbed him in the chest and stomach with a knife and the two men then robbed the flat. The victim was found some minutes later. The police were called and they arrived very soon after. The victim, who was seriously wounded,

d told the police that he had been attacked by two men, and gave the name of the appellant and the name and address of the other man before becoming unconscious. He was then taken to hospital where he died two months later. At the trial of the appellant for murder the Crown sought to have the victim's statement to the police admitted in evidence. The trial judge ruled the statement was admissible. The appellant was convicted of manslaughter. He appealed to the Court of Appeal, contending that the victim's statement

e was inadmissible under the rule against the admission of hearsay evidence. The appeal was dismissed and the appellant appealed to the House of Lords.

Held – Hearsay evidence of a statement made to a witness by the victim of an attack describing how he had received his injuries was admissible in evidence, as part of the res gestae, at the trial of the attacker if the statement was made in conditions which were

f sufficiently spontaneous and sufficiently contemporaneous with the event to preclude the possibility of concoction or distortion. In order for the victim's statement to be sufficiently spontaneous to be admissible it had to be so closely associated with the event which excited the statement that the victim's mind was still dominated by the event. If there was a special feature, eg malice, giving rise to the possibility of concoction or distortion the trial judge had to be satisfied that the circumstances were such that there

g was no possibility of concoction or distortion. However, the possibility of error in the facts narrated by the victim went to the weight to be attached to the statement by the jury and not to admissibility. Since the victim's statement to the police was made by a seriously injured man in circumstances which were spontaneous and contemporaneous with the attack and there was thus no possibility of any concoction or fabrication of identification, the statement had been rightly admitted in evidence. The appeal would

h accordingly be dismissed (see p 514 f to h, p 519 j and p 520 c to p 521 a h, post).

Ratten v R [1971] 3 All ER 801 applied.

R v Bedingfield (1879) 14 Cox CC 341 overruled.

Notes

j For hearsay evidence and exceptions to the hearsay rule, see 11 Halsbury's Laws (4th edn) paras 437–439, and for cases on the subject, see 14(2) Digest (Reissue) 596–598, 4841–4862.

Cases referred to in opinions

Myers v DPP [1964] 2 All ER 881, [1965] AC 1001, [1964] 3 WLR 145, HL.

O'Leary v R (1946) 73 CLR 566, Aust HC.
R v Bedingfield (1879) 14 Cox CC 341, Assizes.
R v Blastland [1985] 2 All ER 1095, [1986] AC 41, [1985] 3 WLR 345, HL.
R v Boyle (6 March 1986, unreported), CA.
R v Nye and Loan (1978) 66 Cr App R 252, CA.
R v O'Shea (24 July 1986, unreported), CA.
R v Turnbull (1985) 80 Cr App R 104, CA.
Ratten v R [1971] 3 All ER 801, [1972] AC 378, [1971] 3 WLR 930, PC.
Subramaniam v Public Prosecutor [1956] 1 WLR 965, PC.

Appeal

Donald Joseph Andrews appealed with leave of the Appeal Committee of the House of Lords granted on 20 March 1986 against the decision of the Court of Appeal (Croom-Johnson LJ, Kenneth Jones J and Sir John Thompson) on 6 February 1986 dismissing his appeal against his conviction before the Common Serjeant (his Honour Judge Pigot QC) and a jury on charges of manslaughter and aggravated burglary. On 11 February the Court of Appeal refused the appellant leave to appeal to the House of Lords but certified under s 33 of the Criminal Appeal Act 1968 that a point of law of general public importance was involved in the decision to dismiss the appeal, namely: when the victim of an attack tells a witness what has happened and does that in circumstances which satisfy the trial judge that there was no opportunity for concoction, is the evidence of what the victim said admissible as truth of the facts recited as an exception to the hearsay rule? The facts are set out in the opinion of Lord Ackner.

Stephen Sedley QC and *S M Solley* for the appellant.
Michael Worsley QC and *Godfrey Carey* for the Crown.

Their Lordships took time for consideration.

5 February. The following opinions were delivered.

LORD BRIDGE OF HARWICH. My Lords, for the reasons given in the speech of my noble and learned friend Lord Ackner, with which I agree, I would dismiss this appeal.

LORD BRANDON OF OAKBROOK. My Lords, I have had the advantage of reading in draft the speech prepared by my noble and learned friend Lord Ackner. I agree with it, and for the reasons which he gives, I would dismiss the appeal.

LORD GRIFFITHS. My Lords, I have had the advantage of reading in draft the speech prepared by my noble and learned friend Lord Ackner. I agree with it, and for the reasons which he gives I would dismiss the appeal.

LORD MACKAY OF CLASHFERN. My Lords, I have had the advantage of reading in draft the speech prepared by my noble and learned friend Lord Ackner. I agree with it, and for the reasons he gives I would dismiss this appeal.

LORD ACKNER. My Lords,

The facts

On 13 September 1983 Alexander Morrow, who lived at flat 3, Rouple House, London, was attacked and stabbed with two different knives and robbed. Within minutes of the attack, and bleeding profusely from a deep stomach wound, he went downstairs to the

flat below for assistance. The police and ambulance were immediately telephoned, and
a again within a matter of minutes the police arrived, shortly followed by the ambulance.
Mr Morrow had been mortally wounded. He was kept alive on a life-support machine
but died two months after this attack. Both O'Neill and the appellant, Donald Joseph
Andrews, were charged with murder. O'Neill pleaded guilty to manslaughter, which
plea was accepted by the prosecution. The appellant pleaded not guilty and O'Neill was
the prosecution's main witness at the appellant's trial. O'Neill lived in flat 5, on the floor
b above that of the deceased. He and the appellant had been out drinking that day and
returned home in the evening about 8.30 pm to his, O'Neill's, flat. The substance of his
evidence was that as they were about to leave the flat a very short while later, the
appellant asked if O'Neill had any knives, and when O'Neill told him there were some in
the kitchen, the appellant helped himself to a large bread knife and a small potato knife.
He also took a blanket from O'Neill's daughter's cot. On the way out, the appellant
c stopped at the deceased's flat, put the blanket over his and O'Neill's head, handed O'Neill
the small potato knife and tried to force the lock of the flat using the bread knife. He
failed. He then knocked on the door and when the deceased answered, the appellant
shouldered the door open, lunging with the knife, and stabbing the deceased in his chest
and stomach. As the deceased fell down the appellant said: 'I am going to finish the old
bastard off.' O'Neill said he then dropped the potato knife, tried to save the deceased but
d in the process was stabbed twice in the leg. The cot blanket by this stage had come off
their heads. The appellant then ran into the room, came back with the deceased's stereo
player, told O'Neill to get the deceased's money and O'Neill took about £4. They then
returned to O'Neill's flat and put the blanket back. They then left, taking with them the
two knives and the stereo record player and went to the appellant's flat in Droitwich
House. Subsequently, O'Neill was taken by ambulance to hospital to have his wounds
e dealt with.

The hearsay evidence

There were effectively two trials, the first in January 1985 before the Recorder of
London. Counsel for the Crown considered that there was an adequacy of evidence
f capable of corroborating that of O'Neill, the appellant's accomplice. Without going
unnecessarily into detail, this consisted, inter alia, of the stolen stereo record player being
found on the bed in the appellant's flat, his lies to the police about how he had come by
it, evidence of the appellant being seen, after he returned to his flat, in possession of the
two knives, the appellant's own admission of his disposal of those knives and forensic
evidence with regard to blood stains on the appellant's clothing. However, in the event,
g the jury failed to agree.

On the retrial before the Common Serjeant, which began a week later, counsel for the
Crown wished to strengthen the case of the prosecution and he accordingly sought the
judge's ruling on the admissibility of the deceased's statement identifying his assailants
and made in the following circumstances. According to the neighbours' agreed witness
statements, the deceased was found on the landing on the floor below his flat between
h 8.35 pm and 8.45 pm. This must have been within a very few minutes of the stabbing,
bearing in mind O'Neill's evidence as to the time when he had returned to his flat and
the very nature of the stab wound in the deceased's stomach, from which blood was
pouring. The 999 call made by the neighbour was at 8.43 pm and Pc Worboys and Pc
Hanlon must have arrived a couple of minutes or so thereafter (Pc Worboys stated in
evidence that the ambulance arrived between 10 or 15 minutes after them and the
j uncontradicted evidence was that the ambulance arrived at 9.01 pm) Pc Worboys' main
preoccupation was in administering first aid, in particular in stopping blood pouring
from the stab wound in the stomach. While he was so doing he asked the deceased how
he had received his injuries. The deceased replied that he had been attacked by two men.
He gave the names of his attackers, as being Peter O'Neill from flat 5, Rouple House and
the other, as a man he knew as Donald. He said he had gone to the door of his flat,

opened the door and was attacked by these two men. Pc Worboys noticed that Pc Hanlon, who was making a note of this statement, had written down the name 'Donavon'. *a* Pc Worboys was convinced that the name was Donald and he told Pc Hanlon that he was wrong. Pc Hanlon was not as close to the deceased as Pc Worboys. In his evidence Pc Worboys confirmed that the deceased had said that he had been attacked by two persons, one of whom he knew as O'Neill and a person, whom Pc Hanlon thought the deceased had referred to as 'Donavon'. Pc Hanlon said that he heard 'Don' quite clearly but as he pronounced the rest of the word his voice 'mellowed and he got quieter'. He *b* said he did not notice that the deceased had any accent. The evidence was that the deceased spoke with a Scottish accent.

Counsel for the Crown sought to have the statement of the deceased admitted as evidence of the truth of the facts that he had asserted, namely that he had been attacked by both O'Neill and the appellant. Since evidence of this statement could only be given by a witness who had merely heard it, such evidence was clearly hearsay evidence. It was *c* not being tendered as evidence limited to the fact that an assertion had been made, without reference to the truth of anything alleged in the assertion. The evidence merely of the fact that such an assertion was made would not have related to any issue in the trial and therefore would not have been admissible. Had, for example, the deceased's state of mind been in issue and had his exclamation been relevant to his state of mind, then evidence of *the fact* that such an assertion was made, would not have been hearsay *d* evidence since it would have been tendered without reference to the truth of anything alleged in the assertion. Such evidence is often classified as 'original' evidence.

The res gestae doctrine

Counsel for the Crown based his submission that this hearsay evidence was admissible on the so-called doctrine of 'res gestae'. He could not submit that the statement was a *e* 'dying declaration' since there was no evidence to suggest that at the time when the deceased made the statement (two months before his ultimate death) he was aware that he had been mortally injured. Counsel for the Crown in support of his submission, both before the Common Serjeant, the Court of Appeal and in your Lordships' House, relied essentially on a decision of the Privy Council, *Ratten v R* [1971] 3 All ER 801, [1972] AC *f* 378, an appeal from a conviction for murder by the Supreme Court of the State of Victoria in which the opinion of the Board was given by Lord Wilberforce. Counsel for the Crown, for whose researches into this field of law I readily express my gratitude, invited your Lordships' attention to American, Canadian and Australian authorities in order to demonstrate their consistency with that decision and to support his contention, which is the real issue in this appeal, viz that your Lordships should accept the analysis, *g* reasoning and advice tendered by the Privy Council as being good English law.

I do not think it is necessary to burden this speech by travelling again over all the ground, which, if I may say so respectfully, was so admirably covered by Lord Wilberforce in his judgment. Before turning to the decision in *Ratten's* case, it is convenient at this stage to quote from *Cross on Evidence* (6th edn, 1985) p 585:

> 'Before Lord Wilberforce's important review of the authorities in *Ratten v R*, the *h* law concerning the admissibility of statements under this exception to the hearsay rule [the res gestae doctrine] was in danger of becoming enmeshed in conceptualism of the worst type. Great stress was placed on the need for contemporaneity of the statement with the event, but, what was far more serious, much attention was devoted to the question whether the words could be said to form part of the transaction or event with all the attendant insoluble problems of when the *j* transaction or event began and ended.'

Ratten v R

The appellant was charged with the murder of his wife by shooting her with a shotgun.

He accepted that he had shot her, but his defence was that the gun had gone off
a accidentally, whilst he was cleaning it. There was evidence that the deceased was alive
and behaving normally at 1.12 pm and less than ten minutes later she had been shot. To
rebut that defence, the prosecution called evidence from a telephone operator as to a
telephone call which she had received at 1.15 pm from the deceased's home. She said the
call came from a female who sounded hysterical and who said 'get me the police, please,'
gave her address, but before a connection could be made to the police station, the caller
b hung up. The appellant objected to that evidence on the ground that it was hearsay and
did not come within any of the recognised exceptions to the rule against the admission
of such evidence. The Judicial Committee held that the telephone operator's evidence
had been rightly received. They concluded that the evidence was not hearsay, but was
admissible as evidence of facts relevant to the following issues. First, as rebutting the
defendant's statement that his call for the ambulance after he had shot his wife was the
c only call that went out of the house between 1.12 pm and 1.20 pm, by which time his
wife was dead. Second, that the telephonist's evidence that the caller was a woman
speaking in an hysterical voice was capable of relating to the state of mind of the deceased
and was material from which the jury was entitled to infer that Mrs Ratten was suffering
from anxiety or fear of an existing or impending emergency. Lord Wilberforce said
d ([1971] 3 All ER 801 at 805, [1972] AC 378 at 387):

> 'The mere fact that evidence of a witness includes evidence as to words spoken by
> another person who is not called is no objection to its admissibility. Words spoken
> are facts just as much as any other action by a human being. If the speaking of the
> words is a relevant fact, a witness may give evidence that they were spoken. A
e > question of hearsay only arises when the words spoken are relied on "testimonially",
> ie as establishing some fact narrated by the words. Authority is hardly needed for
> this proposition but their Lordships will restate what was said in the judgment of
> the Board in *Subramaniam v Public Prosecutor* [1956] 1 WLR 965 at 970: "Evidence of
> a statement made to a witness by a person who is not himself called as a witness may
> or may not be hearsay. It is hearsay and inadmissible when the object of the evidence
f > is to establish the truth of what is contained in the statement. It is not hearsay and is
> admissible when it is proposed to establish by the evidence, not the truth of the
> statement, but the fact that it was made."'

Lord Wilberforce then proceeded to deal with the appellant's submission, on the
assumption that the words were hearsay in that they involved an assertion of the truth of
g some facts stated in them and that they may have been so understood by the jury. He
said ([1971] 3 All ER 801 at 806–807, [1972] AC 378 at 388–390):

> 'The expression "res gestae," like many Latin phrases, is often used to cover
> situations insufficiently analysed in clear English terms. In the context of the law of
> evidence it may be used in at least three different ways: 1. When a situation of fact
h > (eg a killing) is being considered, the question may arise when does the situation
> begin and when does it end. It may be arbitrary and artificial to confine the evidence
> to the firing of the gun or the insertion of the knife, without knowing, in a broader
> sense, what was happening. Thus in *O'Leary v Regem* (1946) 73 CLR 566 evidence
> was admitted of assaults, prior to a killing, committed by the accused during what
> was said to be a continuous orgy. As Dixon J said (at 577): "Without evidence of
j > what, during that time, was done by those men who took any significant part in the
> matter and specially evidence of the behaviour of the prisoner, the transaction of
> which the alleged murder formed an integral part could not be truly understood
> and, isolated from it, could only be presented as an unreal and not very intelligible
> event." 2. The evidence may be concerned with spoken words as such (apart from
> the truth of what they convey). The words are then themselves the res gestae or part

of the res gestae, ie are the relevant facts or part of them. 3. A hearsay statement is
made either by the victim of an attack or by a bystander—indicating directly or   *a*
indirectly the identity of the attacker. The admissibility of the statement is then
said to depend on whether it was made as part of the res gestae. A classical instance
of this is the much debated case of *R v Bedingfield* (1879) 14 Cox CC 341, and there
are other instances of its application in reported cases. These tend to apply different
standards, and some of them carry less than conviction. The reason why this is so is
that concentration tends to be focused on the opaque or at least imprecise Latin   *b*
phrase rather than on the basic reason for excluding the type of evidence which this
group of cases is concerned with. There is no doubt what this reason is: it is twofold.
The first is that there may be uncertainty as to the exact words used because of their
transmission through the evidence of another person than the speaker. The second
is because of the risk of concoction of false evidence by persons who have been
victims of assault or accident. The first matter goes to weight. The person testifying   *c*
to the words used is liable to cross-examination: the accused person (as he could not
at the time when earlier reported cases were decided) can give his own account if
different. There is no such difference in kind or substance between evidence of what
was said and evidence of what was done (for example between evidence of what the
victim said as to an attack and evidence that he (or she) was seen in a terrified state
or was heard to shriek) as to require a total rejection of one and admission of the   *d*
other. The possibility of concoction, or fabrication, where it exists, is on the other
hand an entirely valid reason for exclusion, and is probably the real test which
judges in fact apply. In their Lordships' opinion this should be recognised and
applied directly as the relevant test: the test should be not the uncertain one whether
the making of the statement was in some sense part of the event or transaction. This
may often be difficult to establish: such external matters as the time which elapses   *e*
between the events and the speaking of the words (or vice versa), and differences in
location being relevant factors but not, taken by themselves, decisive criteria. As
regards statements made after the event it must be for the judge, by preliminary
ruling, to satisfy himself that the statement was so clearly made in circumstances of
spontaneity or involvement in the event that the possibility of concoction can be   *f*
disregarded. Conversely, if he considers that the statement was made by way of
narrative of a detached prior event so that the speaker was so disengaged from it as
to be able to construct or adapt his account, he should exclude it. And the same
must in principle be true of statements made before the event. The test should be
not the uncertain one, whether the making of the statement should be regarded as
part of the event or transaction. This may often be difficult to show. But if the   *g*
drama, leading up to the climax, has commenced and assumed such intensity and
pressure that the utterance can safely be regarded as a true reflection of what was
unrolling or actually happening, it ought to be received. The expression "res gestae"
may conveniently sum up these criteria, but the reality of them must always be
kept in mind: it is this that lies behind the best reasoned of the judges' rulings.'

Lord Wilberforce then reviewed a number of cases in England, in Scotland, in Australia   *h*
and America and concluded that those authorities—

> 'show that there is ample support for the principle that hearsay evidence may be
> admitted if the statement providing it is made in such conditions (always being
> those of approximate but not exact contemporaneity) of involvement or pressure as
> to exclude the possibility of concoction or distortion to the advantage of the maker   *j*
> or the disadvantage of the accused.'

(See [1971] 3 All ER 801 at 808, [1972] AC 378 at 391.)
Applying that principle to the facts of the *Ratten* appeal there was in their Lordships'
judgment ample evidence of the close and intimate connection between the statement

ascribed to the deceased and the shooting which occurred very shortly afterwards. Lord
a Wilberforce commented ([1971] 3 All ER 801 at 809, [1972] AC 378 at 391–392):

> 'The way in which the statement came to be made (in a call for the police) and the
> tone of voice used, showed intrinsically that the statement was being forced from
> the deceased by an overwhelming pressure of contemporary event. It carried its
> own stamp of spontaneity and this was endorsed by the proved time sequence and
b the proved proximity of the deceased to the appellant with his gun.'

Thus, on the assumption that there was an element of hearsay in the words used, the
Privy Council concluded that they had been properly admitted.

In *R v Blastland* [1985] 2 All ER 1095 at 1103, [1986] AC 41 at 58 Lord Bridge regarded
the authority of *Ratten v R* as being of the highest persuasive authority. It was followed
and applied in the instant case by the Common Serjeant and by the Court of Appeal,
c Criminal Division and, accordingly, the appellant's appeal against his conviction for
manslaughter was dismissed. It had previously been applied in *R v Nye and Loan* (1978)
66 Cr App R 252 by the Court of Appeal, where a victim of a criminal assault, which had
occurred within a few yards of a police station, in a statement to police officers made
within minutes of the assault, identified the defendant as the man who had hit him in
the face. Lawton LJ in giving the judgment of the court put, as he described it, a gloss on
d Lord Wilberforce's test by adding as an additional factor to be taken into consideration
'was there any real possibility of error?' I will return to this particular point later. In *R v
Turnbull* (1985) 80 Cr App R 104 the Court of Appeal again applied the *Ratten* approach,
where a man who had been mortally wounded staggered into the bar of a public house
and in answer to questions put to him in the bar and in the ambulance on the way to
hospital he was understood to say that 'Ronnie Tommo' had done it. He died half an
e hour later in hospital. The victim had a Scottish accent and had consumed a great
quantity of alcohol and the name 'Ronnie Tommo' was said to constitute his attempt to
name the appellant. There have been two further decisions of the Court of Appeal in
1986 which have followed *Ratten's* case. *R v Boyle* (6 March 1986, unreported) involved
the theft of a grandfather clock from an old lady to whose home the appellant had
f obtained access by a false representation. When he took away the clock she came out of
the house with a piece of paper in her hand and when asked by a neighbour 'what is
happening' she said 'I am coming for his address'. This statement was admitted to support
the victim's account that the removal of the clock was against her will and to negative
the defence that it was being taken away by the defendant with her consent, to have it
repaired. I, for myself, would doubt whether this evidence was hearsay evidence. A clear
g issue in the case was the state of mind of the victim in relation to the removal of her
clock. Her statement in the circumstances, as the car drove off, was evidence from which
the jury could infer that she was not consenting to the clock being taken away. *R v O'Shea*
(24 July 1986, unreported) is a clearer case. The appellant was charged with burglary and
manslaughter. The prosecution case against the appellant was that he went to a second
floor flat and while he was battering down the door, the occupier of the flat, who was 79
h years of age, attempted to escape through the window, slipped and fell some 20 feet and
sustained bruising to his heart, which resulted in his death a week later. The statement
made by the deceased to two passers-by an hour or so later, when they found him lying
where he had fallen, that he had tried to get out of his flat because he was frightened that
two robbers who were trying to break down his door would kill him and that he had
therefore jumped from the window to escape, was admitted, as was a similar statement
j which he made to two police officers less than 20 minutes later.

Counsel for the appellant submitted, first, that there is no such exception to the rule
against the admission of hearsay evidence as that said to be covered by the res gestae
doctrine. Having regard to the authorities there is no substance in this proposition.
Second, he submitted that a hearsay statement cannot be admitted under the doctrine if
made after the criminal act or acts charged have ceased. He contended that the hearsay

statement must form part of the criminal act for which the accused is being tried. He
relied strongly on *R v Bedingfield* (1879) 14 Cox CC 341. In that case the accused was   *a*
charged with murder. The defence was suicide. The accused was seen to enter a house
and a minute or two later the victim rushed out of the house with her throat cut and said
to her aunt: 'See what Harry has done.' This exclamation was not admitted by
Cockburn CJ because 'It was something stated by her after it was all over, whatever it
was, and after the act was completed'. Counsel for the appellant submits that the decision
in *Ratten's* case involved an extension of the existing hearsay rule and so was in conflict   *b*
with the ruling of the majority in your Lordships' House in *Myers v DPP* [1964] 2 All ER
881, [1965] AC 1001 that it is now too late to add a further exception to the rule against
hearsay otherwise than by legislation. This submission is not assisted by the fact that
both Lord Reid and Lord Hodgson, who were party to the majority decision in the *Myers*
case, were also members of the Board in the *Ratten* case.

I do not accept that the principles identified by Lord Wilberforce involved any   *c*
extension to the exception to the hearsay rule. Lord Wilberforce clarified the basis of the
res gestae exception and isolated the matters of which the trial judge, by preliminary
ruling, must satisfy himself before admitting the statement. I respectfully accept the
accuracy and the value of this clarification. Thus it must, of course, follow that *R v
Bedingfield* would not be so decided today. Indeed, there could, as Lord Wilberforce
observed, hardly be a case where the words uttered carried more clearly the mark of   *d*
spontaneity and intense involvement.

The trial judge

My Lords, may I therefore summarise the position which confronts the trial judge
when faced in a criminal case with an application under the res gestae doctrine to admit
evidence of statements, with a view to establishing the truth of some fact thus narrated,   *e*
such evidence being truly categorised as 'hearsay evidence'. (1) The primary question
which the judge must ask himself is: can the possibility of concoction or distortion be
disregarded? (2) To answer that question the judge must first consider the circumstances
in which the particular statement was made, in order to satisfy himself that the event
was so unusual or startling or dramatic as to dominate the thoughts of the victim, so that
his utterance was an instinctive reaction to that event, thus giving no real opportunity   *f*
for reasoned reflection. In such a situation the judge would be entitled to conclude that
the involvement or the pressure of the event would exclude the possibility of concoction
or distortion, providing that the statement was made in conditions of approximate but
not exact contemporaneity. (3) In order for the statement to be sufficiently 'spontaneous'
it must be so closely associated with the event which has excited the statement that it can   *g*
be fairly stated that the mind of the declarant was still dominated by the event. Thus the
judge must be satisfied that the event which provided the trigger mechanism for the
statement was still operative. The fact that the statement was made in answer to a
question is but one factor to consider under this heading. (4) Quite apart from the time
factor, there may be special features in the case, which relate to the possibility of
concoction or distortion. In the instant appeal the defence relied on evidence to support   *h*
the contention that the deceased had a motive of his own to fabricate or concoct, namely
a malice which resided in him against O'Neill and the appellant because, so he believed,
O'Neill had attacked and damaged his house and was accompanied by the appellant, who
ran away, on a previous occasion. The judge must be satisfied that the circumstances
were such that, having regard to the special feature of malice, there was no possibility of
any concoction or distortion to the advantage of the maker or the disadvantage of the   *j*
accused. (5) As to the possibility of error in the facts narrated in the statement, if only the
ordinary fallibility of human recollection is relied on, this goes to the weight to be
attached to and not to the admissibility of the statement and is therefore a matter for the
jury. However, here again there may be special features that may give rise to the
possibility of error. In the instant case there was evidence that the deceased had drunk to

a excess, well over double the permitted limit for driving a motor car. Another example would be where the identification was made in circumstances of particular difficulty or where the declarant suffered from defective eyesight. In such circumstances the trial judge must consider whether he can exclude the possibility of error.

Croom-Johnson LJ in giving the judgment of the Court of Appeal, Criminal Division dismissing the appeal stated, in my respectful view quite correctly, that the Common Serjeant had directed himself impeccably in his approach to the evidence that he had b heard. It is perhaps helpful to set out verbatim how the judge stated his conclusions:

'I am satisfied that soon after receiving very serious stab wounds the deceased went downstairs for help unassisted and received some assistance. He was able to talk for a few minutes before he became unconscious. I am satisfied on the evidence, and not only the primary evidence but the inference of fact to which I am irresistibly c driven, that the deceased only sustained the injuries a few minutes before the police arrived and subsequently, of course, the ambulance took him to hospital. Even if the period were longer than a few minutes, I am satisfied that there was no possibility in the circumstances of any concoction or fabrication of identification. I think that the injuries which the deceased sustained were of such a nature that it would drive out of his mind any possibility of him being activated by malice and I d cannot overlook as far as the identification was concerned, he was right over Mr O'Neill who was a former co-defendant with the accused.'

Where the trial judge has properly directed himself as to the correct approach to the evidence and there is material to entitle him to reach the conclusions which he did reach, then his decision is final, in the sense that it will not be interfered with on appeal. Of course, having ruled the statement admissible the judge must, as the Common Sergeant e most certainly did, make it clear to the jury that it is for them to decide what was said and to be sure that the witnesses were not mistaken in what they believed had been said to them. Further, they must be satisfied that the declarant did not concoct or distort to his advantage or the disadvantage of the accused the statement relied on and where there is material to raise the issue, that he was not activated by any malice or ill-will. Further, f where there are special features that bear on the possibility of mistake then the jury's attention must be invited to those matters.

My Lords, the doctrine of res gestae applies to civil as well as criminal proceedings. There is, however, special legislation as to the admissibility of hearsay evidence in civil proceedings. I wholly accept that the doctrine admits the hearsay statements, not only where the declarant is dead or otherwise not available but when he is called as a witness. g Whatever may be the position in civil proceedings, I would, however, strongly deprecate any attempt in criminal prosecutions to use the doctrine as a device to avoid calling, when he is available, the maker of the statement. Thus to deprive the defence of the opportunity to cross-examine him, would not be consistent with the fundamental duty of the prosecution to place all the relevant material facts before the court, so as to ensure that justice is done.

h My Lords, I would accordingly dismiss this appeal.

Appeal dismissed.

Solicitors: *Fisher Meredith & Partners* (for the appellant); *Crown Prosecution Service.*

Mary Rose Plummer   Barrister.

Claydon and another v Bradley and another   *a*

COURT OF APPEAL, CIVIL DIVISION
DILLON, STEPHEN BROWN AND NEILL LJJ
13, 28 NOVEMBER 1986

Bill of exchange – Promissory note – Promise to pay at a fixed or determinable future time – *b*
Document stating payment to be made 'by 1st July 1983' – Document giving option to repay
before stated date – Whether promissory note – Bills of Exchange Act 1882, s 83(1).

The plaintiffs lent £7,600 to a company in which the defendant was the major
shareholder. The defendant signed a document which was headed with the company's
name and address and which acknowledged the loan, stating that it was 'to be paid back   *c*
in full by 1st. July 1983'. When the company went into liquidation the plaintiffs sought
to recover the £7,600 from the defendant personally, on the ground that the document
signed by the defendant was a promissory note within s 83(1)[a] of the Bills of Exchange
Act 1883 and that the defendant was personally liable, under s 26(1)[b], to pay it. Judgment
was given against the defendant in the county court. The defendant appealed to the
Court of Appeal.   *d*

Held – In providing that the loan was to be repaid 'by' 1 July 1983, the document signed
by the defendant contained an option to pay at an earlier date than the fixed date and the
uncertainty or contingency thereby created as to the time for payment meant that there
was not the unconditional promise to pay at a fixed or determinable future time which
was necessary to make a document a promissory note under s 83 of the 1882 Act.   *e*
Furthermore, the document was primarily a receipt for money containing the terms on
which it was to be repaid and was not intended to be negotiable or capable of being
enforced by a holder in due course. It followed that the appeal would be allowed (see
p 525 *f j*, p 526 *c d f g j*, p 527 *g h* and p 528 *b c*, post).
    Williamson v Rider [1962] 2 All ER 268 and *Akbar Khan v Attar Singh* [1936] 2 All ER   *f*
545 applied.

Notes

For promissory notes and time for payment, see 4 Halsbury's Laws (4th edn) paras 306,
337, and for cases on the subject, see 6 Digest (Reissue) 20–22, 114–137.
    For the Bills of Exchange Act 1882, ss 26, 83, see 5 Halsbury's Statutes (4th edn) 361,   *g*
393.

Cases referred to in judgments

Akbar Khan v Attar Singh [1936] 2 All ER 545, PC.
Burrows (John) Ltd v Subsurface Surveys Ltd [1968] SCR 607, Can SC.
Casborne v Dutton (1727) 1 Selwyn's NP (13th edn) 329.
Clayton v Gosling (1826) 5 B & C 360, 108 ER 134.   *h*
Creative Press Ltd v Harman [1973] IR 313, Ir HC.
Dagger v Shepherd [1946] 1 All ER 133, [1946] KB 215, CA.
Williamson v Rider [1962] 2 All ER 268, [1963] 1 QB 89, [1962] 3 WLR 119, CA.

                                                                                            j

---

a   Section 83(1) is set out at p 527 *b*, post
b   Section 26(1) provides: 'Where a person signs a bill as drawer indorser, or acceptor, and adds words
     to his signature, indicating that he signs for or on behalf of a principal, or in a representative
     character, he is not personally liable thereon; but the mere addition to his signature of words
     describing him as an agent, or as filling a representative character, does not exempt him from
     personal liability.'

Cases also cited

a *Brooks v Elkins* (1836) 2 M & W 74, 150 ER 675.
   Chadwick v Allen (1726) 2 Stra 706, 93 ER 797.
   Imperial Land Co of Marseilles, Re (1870) LR 11 Eq 478.

Appeal

b The first defendant, Pauline Bradley (Mrs Bradley), appealed against the order of Mr P J M Whiteman sitting as an assistant recorder in the Bristol County Court on 19 August 1985 whereby in an action brought by the plaintiffs, Terry John Claydon and Joan Elizabeth Claydon, against Mrs Bradley and the second defendant, Bradley Kitchens Ltd, he held that a document dated 23 December 1982 was a promissory note within the meaning of s 83 of the Bills of Exchange Act 1882 and gave judgment for the plaintiffs in the sum of £7,600 and interest. Proceedings against the second defendant were automatically stayed
c when it went into compulsory liquidation on 8 January 1985. The facts are set out in the judgment of Dillon LJ.

Mrs Bradley appeared in person.
James Wigmore for the plaintiffs.

d   *Cur adv vult*
   28 November. The following judgments were delivered.

DILLON LJ. This is an appeal by the first defendant, Mrs Bradley, against a decision of Mr P J M Whiteman sitting as an assistant recorder in the Bristol County Court on 19
e August 1985, whereby the plaintiffs were given judgment against Mrs Bradley for the sum of £7,600 with interest. The action had in fact been begun in the High Court, but was transferred to the county court by order of the district registrar in September 1984. At the trial before the assistant recorder Mrs Bradley was represented by solicitors and counsel, but in this court she has appeared in person.
   The action as against Mrs Bradley is founded on a document, which she admittedly
f signed, which bears the date 23 December 1982 and is in the following terms:

                                              'Bradley Kitchens Limited,
                                              10 Highlands Close,
                                              Rudloe,
                                              Wilts,
   Mr. T. Claydon,   23rd. December 1982.
g 27, The Land,
   Frampton Cotterel
   Nr. Bristol.
        Received from Mr. and Mrs. T. Claydon The Sum of £10,000 (Ten Thousand Pounds) as a loan to be paid back in full by 1st. July 1983 with an interest rate of
h 20% (Twenty Percent) per annum.
                                              Yours faithfully,
                                              P. M. Bradley.'

   Bradley Kitchens Ltd (the company) named at the head of that document was a company of which Mrs Bradley was the principal shareholder, a director and the secretary. The company was joined in the action as second defendant, and it was alleged that, if Mrs
j Bradley is not personally liable under the document above set out, then she signed it as agent for the company and the company is liable. However, the claim as against the company was automatically stayed when the company went into compulsory liquidation before the trial. It is not in doubt that the company is insolvent.
   The only issue on this appeal is whether the document dated 23 December 1982 above set out is a promissory note, within the meaning of s 83 of the Bills of Exchange Act

1882, on which Mrs Bradley is personally liable. The plaintiffs accepted by their counsel in this court that, if the document is not a promissory note, then their claim must fail as against Mrs Bradley. The main reason for this is that the plaintiffs rely on s 26 of the 1882 Act to establish the personal liability of Mrs Bradley under the document she signed, but they cannot pray that section in aid unless the document is a 'bill' within the meaning of that Act. Counsel for the plaintiffs candidly told us that the plaintiffs had thought that they were dealing with the company or with Mr Bradley, Mrs Bradley's husband. In fact, though this was not known to the plaintiffs, Mr Bradley was at the material time an undischarged bankrupt, and for that reason was not a director of, or shareholder in, the company.

The issue whether the document is or is not a promissory note depends entirely on issues of law. I should however first summarise the facts, which are carefully set out in the judgment of the assistant recorder.

In the latter part of 1982 there were discussions between Mr Claydon (the first plaintiff) and Mr Bradley with a view to making and marketing a form of jig, or 'butt and scribe kit', as it was called, for making kitchen worktops. The idea was that the kits would be marketed by the company, which Mr Claydon understood to be Mr Bradley's company, and would be made by another company which Mr Claydon acquired. Mr Bradley or the company were to buy the materials required for making the kits. According to Mr Claydon's evidence, which the judge accepted, Mr Bradley approached Mr Claydon towards the end of 1982 and asked Mr Claydon to put up finance to cover the purchase of materials for a short period of about a month. Mr Bradley had earlier told Mr Claydon that the company, or the Bradleys, were owed book debts of about £130,000, and the impression conveyed seems to have been that there was a temporary cash flow difficulty. Mr Claydon accordingly arranged a facility of £10,000 with his own bank. That is the origin of the figure of £10,000 in the document. £5,000 of that facility was drawn down just before Christmas 1982 and was thereupon handed by Mr Claydon to Mrs Bradley. Mr Bradley asked for further money after Christmas and Mr Claydon drew a further £2,600 from his bank on 6 January 1983 and handed it over to Mrs Bradley in a van outside the bank. Before they met at the bank on 6 January Mr Claydon had asked the Bradleys for a document to keep the bank happy, and Mrs Bradley prepared, signed and handed over on 6 January the crucial document, back-dated to 23 December 1982. Although that document refers to a loan of £10,000, it is common ground that no more than £7,600 (the £5,000 and the £2,600) was advanced.

The reason why no more was advanced was that Mr Claydon became suspicious, and dissatisfied with the failure of the Bradleys or the company to sell kits made or produce the proceeds of kits sold. On Mr Claydon's evidence, when Mrs Bradley gave him the document on 6 January 1983 he made a comment that it was signed by her, and she commented that it was no good Mr Bradley signing it.

When this appeal was launched, Mrs Bradley applied to the Registrar of Civil Appeals for leave to adduce further evidence on the hearing of the appeal. The registrar refused leave, but Mrs Bradley has appealed against the refusal and that appeal also is before us. Mrs Bradley has also slightly extended her application to adduce further evidence. I have no doubt that leave to adduce further evidence should not be granted. Part of what Mrs Bradley wants to put in would be the evidence of witnesses, and in particular Mr Bradley, who were available in the court below at the trial but whom her own counsel decided not to call. The rest consists of a statement and deposition by Mr Claydon in other proceedings. No doubt these documents have only recently come into Mrs Bradley's hands, but they contain nothing inconsistent with the evidence which Mr Claydon gave at the trial before the assistant recorder; it could not therefore be said that there is anything in this further part of the new evidence such that, if given, it would probably have an important influence on the result of the case.

What is, however, of more significance is that the Registrar of Civil Appeals, being a bit puzzled by the case and realising that Mrs Bradley was without legal advisers, made

some researches of his own into the law, as a result of which he has referred the members
_a_ of the court and counsel for the plaintiffs to two decisions, one of this court and the other
of the Privy Council, which were not cited to the assistant recorder. Both are highly
germane to the question whether the document with which we are concerned is a
promissory note within the statutory definition.

By the statutory definition in s 83 of the 1882 Act, a promissory note—

_b_   'is an unconditional promise in writing made by one person to another . . .
engaging to pay on demand or at a fixed or determinable future time, a sum certain
in money, to, or to the order of, a specified person or to bearer.'

In _Williamson v Rider_ [1962] 2 All ER 268, [1963] 1 QB 89 (the first of the cases to
which we were referred by the registrar) this court had to consider a document in the
following terms:

_c_   'In consideration of the loan of £100 . . . from Mr. S. J. Garrod . . . I John Rider
. . . agree to repay to Mr. S. J. Garrod the sum of £100 . . . on or before Dec. 31,
1956.'

The majority of this court, Willmer and Danckwerts LJJ, held that that document could
not be a promissory note within the meaning of s 83, because the words 'on or before
_d_ Dec. 31, 1956' gave the payer an option to repay on any day of his choosing before
31 December 1956, and so, in the view of the majority, there was no unconditional
promise to pay at a fixed future time as required by s 83. Ormerod LJ dissented. He
agreed that the words 'on or before Dec. 31, 1956' imported that, if the payer chose (it
being purely a matter for him) to pay at an earlier date than 31 December 1956, then the
holder of the bill was under an obligation to accept that payment, but he none the less
_e_ held, applying _Dagger v Shepherd_ [1946] 1 All ER 133, [1946] KB 215 (a decision on a
notice to quit), that there was a fixed date for payment, namely 31 December 1956, and
that the promisor had bound himself to pay on that date and could be sued if he failed
(see [1962] 2 All ER 268 at 276, [1963] 1 QB 89 at 102).

The words in the present case 'to be paid back in full by 1st. July 1983' are obviously
_f_ very similar to the words in _Williamson v Rider_. Indeed counsel for the plaintiffs accepted
that, if payment in full had been tendered at an earlier date, eg 1 April 1983, the plaintiffs
would have been bound to accept the tender. For my part, I am unable to distinguish the
present case from _Williamson v Rider_.

The decision of the majority in _Williamson v Rider_ was rejected and the dissenting
judgment of Ormerod LJ was preferred by the Supreme Court of Canada in _John Burrows
g Ltd v Subsurface Surveys Ltd_ [1968] SCR 607 and by the High Court of Ireland in _Creative
Press Ltd v Harman_ [1973] IR 313. In the Canadian case Ritchie J, who gave the judgment
of the court, followed the reasoning of Ormerod LJ in holding that a promise to pay a
sum in nine years and ten months from 1 April 1963 was an unconditional promise to
pay the sum at a fixed and determinable future time, despite a proviso which gave the
payer the option to pay the whole or any part of the sum at any earlier time on giving 30
_h_ days' notice of intention prior to such payment. In _Byles on Bills of Exchange_ (25th edn,
1983) p 18 the editors submit that the dissenting view of Ormerod LJ in _Williamson v
Rider_ is to be preferred to the majority view, and that is also the tenor of an article by
A H Hudson, 'Time and Promissory Notes' (1962) 25 MLR 593. In that article it is
suggested by reference to the judgment of Abbott CJ in _Clayton v Gosling_ (1826) 5 B & C
360, 108 ER 134 that a time of payment, in relation to a promissory note, is only
_j_ contingent if it is a 'time which may or may not arrive'.

In the present case the time for payment was bound to arrive; the money was payable
on 1 July 1983 if it had not been repaid, at the option of the payer, before. None the less,
we are bound by the decision of the majority in _Williamson v Rider_. As indicated already,
I cannot distinguish _Williamson v Rider_. I must therefore hold that the document which
Mrs Bradley signed was not a promissory note.

The second case to which the Registrar of Civil Appeals directed the court's attention is the decision of the Privy Council in *Akbar Khan v Attar Singh* [1936] 2 All ER 545. In *a* that case it was held that a particular document was merely a deposit receipt, setting out the terms on which an advance had been made, and not a promissory note. The actual question was one of stamp duty and involved considerations of the Indian Negotiable Instruments Act 1881. It seems that by that Act a promissory note was defined as an instrument in writing (not being a bank note or a currency note) containing an unconditional undertaking, signed by the maker, to pay a certain sum of money only to, *b* or to the order of, a certain person or to the bearer of the instrument. The definition included certain illustrations. One of these showed that a simple IOU was not a promissory note. Another showed that a note in the following term: 'I acknowledge myself to be indebted to B. in Rs. 1,000 to be paid on demand, for value received' was a promissory note; that form of words was derived from the early English case of *Casborne v Dutton* (1727) 1 Selwyn's NP (13th edn) 329, which was referred to by the assistant *c* recorder in his judgment in the present case.

In considering whether the document before them in *Akbar Khan v Attar Singh* was a promissory note, the Judicial Committee took the broad ground that that document was not, and could not have been intended to be, brought within a definition relating to documents which were to be negotiable instruments: the document was plainly merely a receipt for money containing the terms on which it was to be repaid. That approach is *d* directly applicable, in my judgment, to the present case. If the statutory definition of a promissory note in s 83 of the 1882 Act is applied literally, it would seemingly cover a range of documents which no one would ordinarily dream of regarding as promissory notes or bills of exchange or in any other way negotiable, such as four-year covenants in favour of charities, or legal charges on land containing the usual covenant by the mortgagor for payment on a fixed date or on demand. The document dated 23 December *e* 1982 is, in my judgment, like the document considered in *Akbar Khan v Attar Singh*, no more than a receipt for money containing the terms on which the money was to be repaid. That it cannot have been intended to be negotiable, and capable of being enforced according to its terms by a holder in due course, seems to be underlined by the peculiarity that it refers to a loan of £10,000 when in fact only £7,600 had been lent. *f*

In my judgment, therefore, this document is not a promissory note or a bill within the meaning of the 1882 Act. Consequently the plaintiffs cannot rely on s 26 of that Act in seeking to hold Mrs Bradley personally liable under the document. But, if s 26 is not available, there is nothing in the document to impose any personal liability on Mrs Bradley: it is merely a receipt for money lent given on behalf of the company.

Some play was made in argument of the fact that the address given under the *g* company's name on the document, '10 Highlands Close, Rudloe, Wilts', was the address of Mr and Mrs Bradley's home and not the registered office of the company. The registered office was at 20 The Circus, Bath. I do not, however, attach any importance to this, since on the documents in the bundle before the court both addresses seem to have been used indiscriminately.

For the foregoing reasons, I would allow this appeal, set aside the order of the assistant *h* recorder and dismiss this action as against Mrs Bradley. In so doing I would pay tribute to the care which the assistant recorder took over the case in his judgment. It is unfortunate that in a somewhat unfamiliar field of law he did not have the benefit of the citation of the authorities researched by the Registrar of Civil Appeals.

STEPHEN BROWN LJ. I agree with the judgment of Dillon LJ. I too would allow *j* this appeal.

NEILL LJ. The central issue in this appeal is whether the document dated 23 December 1982 and signed by Mrs Bradley is a promissory note. If it is a promissory note, the plaintiffs are entitled to rely on s 26 of the Bills of Exchange Act 1882 to establish the

personal liability of Mrs Bradley. If it is not a promissory note, the claim against Mrs
a Bradley will fail.

The Act was passed to codify the law relating to bills of exchange, cheques and
promissory notes. The definition of a promissory note is contained in s 83 of the Act.
Section 83(1) provides:

b 'A promissory note is an unconditional promise in writing made by one person
to another signed by the maker, engaging to pay, on demand or at a fixed or
determinable future time, a sum certain in money, to, or to the order of, a specified
person or to bearer.'

By s 89(1) of the 1882 Act the provisions of the Act relating to bills of exchange are
applied, subject to certain exceptions and with the necessary modifications, to promissory
notes. It follows, therefore, that 'An instrument expressed to be payable on a contingency'
c is not a promissory note (see s 11 of the 1882 Act).

The facts of the case have been set out by Dillon LJ. I need not repeat them. It is only
necessary to set out the relevant words of the document dated 23 December 1982:

'Received from Mr. and Mrs. T. Claydon The Sum of £10,000 (Ten Thousand
Pounds) as a loan to be paid back in full by 1st. July 1983 with an interest rate of
d 20% (Twenty Percent) per annum.'

Two arguments can be advanced in support of the proposition that this document is
not a promissory note: (1) that it is not a note because it is 'an instrument expressed to be
payable on a contingency'; and (2) that it is not a note because it is primarily a receipt
coupled with a promise to pay and is not intended to be negotiable.

e These arguments were not put forward in the court below, but as they raise questions
of law it is necessary for us to consider them, particularly as the appellant now appears in
person. The arguments are founded on two cases to which our attention has been drawn
by the Registrar of Civil Appeals.

In *Williamson v Rider* [1962] 2 All ER 268, [1963] 1 QB 89 the document provided for
the repayment of the loan 'on or before Dec. 31, 1956'. The majority of the Court of
f Appeal held that, as the document gave the borrower the option of paying at an earlier
date than the terminal date, there was a contingency as to the time of payment. Willmer
LJ said ([1962] 2 All ER 268 at 275, [1963] 1 QB 89 at 100): 'I find it difficult to resist the
conclusion that the introduction of the words ... "on or before" does introduce a
contingency'.

As has been pointed out by Dillon LJ, there is a decision of the Supreme Court of
g Canada and a decision of the High Court of Ireland in which the dissenting judgment of
Ormerod LJ in *Williamson v Rider* was preferred. This court, however, is bound by the
decision of the majority in *Williamson v Rider*, and I can see no valid basis for drawing a
distinction between the words of the document in that case and the words 'by 1st. July
1983' used in the document of 23 December 1982.

In both cases the signatory was given an option of paying at an earlier date than the
h terminal date. It follows therefore that the document sued on was not a promissory note
within the statutory definition in s 83 of the 1882 Act.

The second argument is based on the decision of the Privy Council in *Akbar Khan v
Attar Singh* [1936] 2 All ER 545, where consideration was given to the definition of a
promissory note in the Indian Negotiable Instruments Act 1881 and the Indian Stamp
Act 1899. The definition in the Indian statutes does not coincide with the definition in
j s 83 of the 1882 Act, but nevertheless the case is of direct relevance to the issue which
arises in the instant appeal. Lord Atkin (who delivered the judgment of the Privy
Council) said (at 550):

'Their Lordships prefer to decide this point on the broad ground that such a
document as this is not and could not be intended to be brought within a definition

relating to documents which are to be negotiable instruments. Such documents must come into existence for the purpose only of recording an agreement to pay money and nothing more, though of course they may state the consideration. Receipts and agreements generally are not intended to be negotiable, and serious embarrassment would be caused in commerce if the negotiable net were cast too wide. This document plainly is a receipt for money containing the terms on which it is to be repaid . . . Being primarily a receipt even if coupled with a promise to pay it is not a promissory note.'

It seems to me that the words of Lord Atkin can be applied to the document in question in the instant case. The document appears to be primarily a receipt. I would not regard it as a document which was intended to be negotiable or capable of being enforced by a holder in due course.

For these reasons as well as the reasons given by Dillon LJ I too would allow this appeal.

Appeal allowed.

Solicitors: *Brown & Partners*, Bristol (for the plaintiffs).

Celia Fox   Barrister.

Re Courage Group's Pension Schemes Ryan and others v Imperial Brewing and Leisure Ltd and others

CHANCERY DIVISION
MILLETT J
21, 24, 25, 26, 27 NOVEMBER, 10 DECEMBER 1986

Pension – Pension scheme – Company pension scheme – Variation of scheme – Alteration of rules – Removal of surplus in scheme by company – Company pension scheme managed by committee of management – Scheme having substantial surplus – Company taken over – New holding company wishing to substitute itself as 'the company' in the scheme and to remove surplus for own use – New company requesting committee of management to execute deeds amending trust deeds and rules of scheme – Whether amendments altering purposes of scheme and ultra vires – Whether committee of management at liberty or bound to execute amending deeds.

A company, IBL, and its subsidiary companies operated three similar contributory pension schemes for the benefit of employees of the group. Each scheme was governed by its own trust deed and rules made thereunder and each trust deed defined 'the company' whose employees could belong to the scheme as IBL. The trust deeds could be varied or altered provided that the alteration or variation did not 'have the effect of altering the main purpose of the Fund, namely the provision of pensions on retirement at a specified age for members'. The management of the schemes was entrusted to a committee of management. Two of the schemes provided that the rules could at any time be added to, deleted or varied by the company by deed 'and the Committee of Management shall concur in executing any such . . . deed'. The schemes made provision for 'the company', with the consent of the committee of management, to admit associated companies to participation in the scheme and for limited substitution of another company for IBL as 'the company'. In February 1986, in anticipation of a take-over bid

by H, the trust deeds were amended by the insertion of a new clause which had the effect
a of closing each of the schemes to new entrants if H acquired IBL and its subsidiaries. In
April 1986 H acquired control of IBL and would, but for the closure of the schemes in
February, have become a participating company and its employees entitled to become
participating employees in the schemes. In September H agreed to sell IBL and its
subsidiaries to E while retaining, if possible, the surplus in the schemes for its own
benefit or the benefit of its own employees. H accordingly proposed that the schemes
b would not form part of the sale to E, that H would be substituted for IBL as 'the company'
in the schemes, that employee members of the scheme would be transferred to a scheme
established by E and H would transfer £10m to the new scheme to top up their benefits,
and that H would either set aside sufficient funds for the pensioners and deferred
pensioners remaining in the schemes and remove the surplus (some £70m) for its own
use or reopen the schemes to new members and admit its own employees. IBL and its
c subsidiaries were sold to E and deeds amending the rules to enable the substitution of H
for IBL as 'the company' were executed by IBL. H requested the committee of
management to execute the deeds. The committee sought the determination of the court
on the questions (i) whether on the true construction of the trust deed for each scheme
the committee of management was at liberty to or was bound, at the request of H, to
execute the three deeds of variation enabling the substitution of H for IBL, and (ii)
d whether the committee of management was at liberty to or bound to concur in executing
any deed which H might request the committee to execute for the purpose of reopening
the schemes to new members.

Held – (1) There were no special rules of construction applicable to pension schemes
although a scheme's provisions would wherever possible be construed so as to give
e reasonable and practical effect to the scheme, bearing in mind that it had to be operated
against a constantly changing commercial background. The court would have regard to
the fact that it was important to avoid fettering unduly the power to amend the scheme,
thereby preventing the parties from making those changes which might be required by
the exigencies of commercial life, and that was particularly the case where the scheme
f was intended to benefit the employees of a group of companies and not just a single
company, since the composition of the group could constantly change. Furthermore, in
the case of an institution of long duration and gradually changing membership, such as
a club or pension scheme, each alteration in the rules had to be tested by reference to the
situation at the time of the proposed alteration and not by reference to the original rules
at the time of its inception (see p 537 f to h and p 538 c d, post); *Thellusson v Viscount
g Valentia* [1907] 2 Ch 1 considered.
(2) On the true construction of the rules, if the proposed amendments could properly
be made the committee nevertheless had a discretion whether or not to concur in
executing the necessary deeds (see p 535 g h and p 536 f to j, post).
(3) It was clearly desirable that some provision for substitution of 'the company' be
included in a group pension scheme, since otherwise the scheme would have to be wound
h up if the company was put into liquidation on a reorganisation or reconstruction of the
group. The need for provision to be made for substitution of 'the company' showed that
the identity of 'the company' was not of the essence or part of the main purposes of the
schemes. However, it did not follow from the need for a properly limited power of
substitution that an unlimited power of substitution could be validly introduced, or that
any company could be substituted in any circumstances and for any purposes. The
j validity of a power of substitution depended on the circumstances in which it was capable
of being exercised and the characteristics which had to be possessed by the company
capable of being substituted, while the validity of any purported exercise of such a power
depended on the purpose for which the substitution was made. Since H did not employ
and had never employed any of the employees for whose benefit the schemes had been
established and since H would have no remaining connection with the group and its

employees once the sale to E was completed, it followed that the amendment of the trust deeds and the rules to permit the substitution of H for IBL would manifestly alter the *a* main purpose of the scheme and be ultra vires (see p 537 *d*, p 541 *a b* and p 542 *e f*, post).

(4) In any event, irrespective of the sale to E, H could not have been substituted for IBL since, in order validly to exercise the power to substitute, the circumstances had to be such that substitution was necessary or at least expedient in order to preserve the scheme for those for whose benefit it was established, and the substituted company had *b* to be recognisably the successor to the business and workforce of the company for which it was substituted. It was not enough that it was a member of the same group as, or even the holding company of, the company for which it was substituted. It followed that the proposed power to substitute IBL's ultimate holding company for IBL in undefined circumstances was ultra vires because it was far too wide, because it would alter the main purposes of the schemes and because it was capable of defeating those purposes. Accordingly, the committee of management was not at liberty to execute the amending *c* deeds by which H was to be substituted for IBL (see p 542 *f g j*, post).

(5) However, in the absence of express provision entrenching the closure of any of the schemes against any future amendment of the trust deed and rules there was no reason to imply such a provision, since the company and the members of the closed schemes were both sufficiently protected against any unwelcome reopening of the schemes by the fact that both the company and the committee of management were necessary parties to *d* any amendments which were required to reopen the schemes. Furthermore, a purported restriction on the powers of the committee of management would not be effective since the powers conferred on the committee were vested in it in a fiduciary capacity, and even if the existing members of the committee could release, fetter or agree not to exercise any of the powers and discretions vested in the committee they could not deprive their successors of the right to exercise them. Accordingly, the committee of management *e* was at liberty, but not bound, to concur in executing any deeds amending the schemes for the purpose of reopening the schemes to new entrants (see p 536 *e f* and p 544 *e* to *j*, post); *Re Wills's Trust Deeds, Wills v Godfrey* [1963] 1 All ER 390 applied.

Notes

f

For occupational pension schemes generally, see 33 Halsbury's Laws (4th edn) paras 973–1012.

Cases referred to in judgment

Brooklands Selangor Holdings Ltd v IRC [1970] 2 All ER 76, [1970] 1 WLR 429.
Rhyl UDC v Rhyl Amusements Ltd [1959] 1 All ER 257, [1959] 1 WLR 465.
South African Supply and Cold Storage Co, Re, Wild v South African Supply and Cold Storage *g* *Co* [1904] 2 Ch 268.
Thellusson v Viscount Valentia [1907] 2 Ch 1, CA.
Whitmore-Searle v Whitmore-Searle [1907] 2 Ch 332.
Wills's Trust Deeds, Re, Wills v Godfrey [1963] 1 All ER 390, [1964] Ch 219, [1963] 2 WLR 1318.

h

Cases also cited

Anstis, Re, Chetwynd v Morgan (1886) 31 Ch D 596, CA.
Chelsea and Walham Green Building Society v Armstrong [1951] 2 All ER 250, [1951] Ch 853.
Cooke v New River Co (1888) 38 Ch D 56, CA.   *j*
Dingle v Turner [1972] 1 All ER 878, [1972] AC 601, HL.
Imperial Foods Ltd's Pension Scheme, Re [1986] 2 All ER 802, [1986] 1 WLR 717.
Jeffs (Inspector of Taxes) v Ringtons Ltd [1986] 1 All ER 144, [1986] 1 WLR 266.
Jones (Edward) Benevolent Fund Trusts, Re, Spink v Samuel Jones & Co Ltd (8 March 1985, unreported) Ch D.

McPhail v Doulton [1970] 2 All ER 228, [1971] AC 424, HL.

a Plumptre's Marriage Settlement, Re, Underhill v Plumptre [1910] 1 Ch 609.

Portland (Duke) v Lady Topham (1864) 11 HL Cas 32, [1861–73] All ER Rep 980, HL.

Wright's Trustees and Marshall, Re (1885) 28 Ch D 93.

Originating summons

By an originating summons dated 5 November 1986 the plaintiffs, (1) Bernard Joseph
b Ryan, (2) Peter Aikens, (3) Alan Wilson Jackson Holmes, (4) John Warwick Whitworth,
(5) Christopher Edward Montagnon, (6) Alan Moore and (7) John Edward Cregan, the
members of the committee of management under the Courage Retail Managers' Pension
Scheme, the Courage Staff Pension Scheme and the Courage Employees' Pension Scheme
(the schemes), sought the determination of the court on the following questions: (i)
whether on the true construction of the trust deeds and in the events which had happened
c the plaintiffs or their successors, as members of the committee of management under
each of the trust deeds of the schemes were (a) at liberty or (b) bound to concur, at the
request of the first defendant, Imperial Brewing and Leisure Ltd (IBL), in executing all
or any of three deeds of variation proposed by IBL relating to each of the schemes, (ii)
whether on the true construction of the trust deeds and three deeds dated 7 February
1986 executed thereunder and the events which had happened the plaintiffs or their
d successors as members of the committee of management were (a) at liberty or (b) bound
to concur in executing any deed which IBL might request them to execute for the
purpose of reopening the pension schemes, or any of them, to new members. The
defendants were (1) IBL, (2) Graham Horsford Griffin, (3) Imperial Group Pension Trust
Ltd and (4) Imperial Group Pension Investments Ltd. The facts are set out in the
e judgment.

Edward Nugee QC and Nicholas Warren for the plaintiffs.
Nigel Inglis-Jones QC and Geoffrey Topham for IBL.
Michael Hart for the second defendant.
Geoffrey Topham for the third and fourth defendants.

f
                                                                    Cur adv vult

10 December. The following judgment was delivered.

MILLETT J. In April 1986, following a hotly contested take-over battle, Hanson Trust
g plc (Hanson) acquired Imperial Group plc (Imperial Group). One of Imperial Group's
subsidiaries was Imperial Brewing and Leisure Ltd (IBL), the parent company of Imperial
Group's brewing and leisure division. After the sale during the summer of 1986 of part
of IBL's undertaking and the transfer of other subsidiary companies within the Hanson
Group, IBL and its remaining subsidiaries now consist only of those companies which
may be described as 'the Courage Group'.

h   On 17 September 1986 Hanson agreed to sell IBL and its subsidiaries to Elders IXL Ltd
(Elders), a company incorporated in South Australia, for a sum of approximately £1·4 bn.
The sale was subject to the fulfilment of a number of conditions. The last of those
conditions was fulfilled on 14 November 1986, and thereupon the sale became
unconditional. It was completed on 19 November 1986.

      IBL operates three contributory pension schemes for the benefit of employees within
j the Courage Group, namely the Courage Retail Managers' Pension Scheme, the Courage
Staff Pension Scheme, and the Courage Employees' Pension Scheme (the schemes). Each
is governed by its own trust deed and the rules made thereunder. The Courage Retail
Managers' Pension Scheme was established by a company then known as Barclay Perkins
& Co Ltd (Barclay Perkins) as a contributory pension scheme for the benefit of managers
of off-licences employed by that company or any of its associated companies. It was

constituted by an interim trust deed dated 30 November 1956, which provided for rules
to be made which would govern the scheme. The rules for which the interim trust deed *a*
provided were duly made by a trust deed dated 28 November 1957. In 1963 new rules
were substituted for the original rules, and IBL, which had absorbed the greater part of
the undertaking of Barclay Perkins, was substituted for that company for the purposes of
the scheme, which became a scheme for the benefit of managers of off-licences (and, by
other amendments to the rules introduced at the same time, of hotels, catering
establishments and public houses) employed by IBL or any of its associated companies. *b*
Barclay Perkins has long since been wound up. The rules currently in force are those
introduced by a further trust deed dated 5 April 1978 as amended from time to time.

The Courage Staff Pension Scheme and the Courage Employees' Pension Scheme,
which are in similar terms, were established by IBL originally as non-contributory
pension schemes for the benefit of different classes of employees of IBL and its associated
companies. These schemes, which are now contributory, were constituted by trust deeds *c*
dated 26 March 1959 and the rules made thereunder, which have been amended from
time to time. Since 1982 the three schemes have been reorganised so that the investments
are held by trustees while the active management of each scheme is entrusted to a
committee of management by which the various discretionary powers formerly vested
in the trustees are now exercisable. Each committee of management has power to act by
a majority. The seven plaintiffs constitute the committee of management of each of the *d*
three schemes.

At the time of the acquisition of Imperial Group by Hanson there were approximately
8,800 employed members and 12,400 pensioners and deferred pensioners altogether in
the three schemes. The total assets in the schemes at 5 April 1985 amounted to
approximately £252m. Taking the three schemes together, it is estimated that there is a
total surplus of assets over liabilities of £80m. This is due in part to overfunding in the *e*
past, and in part to the current buoyancy of the stock market. IBL and the members are
enjoying a 'contributions holiday': they are paying no contributions, and it is not
expected that there will be any need for contributions to be resumed for another ten
years.

On 7 February 1986, shortly after Hanson's unwelcome bid for Imperial Group was *f*
announced, the trust deeds of the three schemes were amended by the insertion of a new
clause which had the effect of closing each of the schemes to new entrants when Hanson
acquired control of Imperial Group. This action was taken by the committee of
management in order to protect the assets of the pension funds and the interests of
members, particularly in the surplus, from what was described as a 'predator'. On the
completion of Hanson's acquisition of Imperial Group, other companies in the Hanson
Group would automatically become associated companies of IBL within the meaning of *g*
the schemes and eligible to be admitted as participating companies therein, so that but
for this action by the committee of management their employees could have become
entitled to participate in the pension funds which had been built up by IBL and the
employees of companies in the Courage Group over many years. In addition to closing
the schemes to new entrants, the rules were amended to provide for an increase in the *h*
pensions and allowances, whether being paid or deferred, both immediately (by
amending r 21) and on a regular basis in the future (by amending r 19).

It has been alleged that the closure of the schemes to new entrants would make it more
difficult for an acquiring company to manage its acquisition, by creating within the
Courage Group a two-tier workforce, with existing employees entitled to participate in
the closed schemes and their surplus funds, and new employees excluded therefrom. The *j*
view has been expressed that this must be taken to have been the true purpose behind
the closure of the schemes. Before me, however, counsel for IBL disclaimed any
suggestion that in making the amendments in February 1986 the committee of
management had acted ultra vires, in bad faith or with an ulterior purpose or improper
motive, and accordingly the amendments must be treated as properly made for the stated
purpose.

Hanson has made no secret of its desire to remove for its own benefit, or for the benefit
a of employees of companies remaining in the Hanson Group, the greater part of the
surplus in the schemes. To achieve this, Hanson has formulated proposals, foreshadowed
in the agreement with Elders, which may be summarised as follows.

(i) Despite the sale of IBL and its subsidiaries to Elders, when they would cease to be
associated companies of Hanson, the schemes would remain with Hanson and would not
be transferred. This would be achieved by substituting Hanson for IBL as the principal
b company in each of the schemes, which would become a scheme for the employees of
Hanson and its associated companies.

(ii) Employed members of each of the schemes would be transferred to a new scheme,
or possibly an existing scheme, established by Elders. They would be offered the choice
of transferring their past service rights to the new scheme or leaving them as deferred
pensions in the existing schemes.

c (iii) In order to ensure that they would receive benefits substantially the same as or
better than under the existing schemes, there would be transferred with the employed
members sufficient of the funds to secure the benefits currently provided by the schemes
but disregarding the amendment to r 21 made in February 1986, together with an
additional £10m representing in effect that part of the £80m surplus which Hanson was
willing to make available to the employees of the companies being sold to Elders.

d (iv) Pensioners and deferred pensioners (including employed members who elected
not to transfer their past service rights to a new scheme) would remain in the existing
schemes, together with the balance of the funds. This would be greatly in excess of what
was required to fund their pensions, since it would include some £70m of the surplus. It
would be open to Hanson to agree to the pensioners and deferred pensioners being
transferred to the new scheme, and to agree to a greater part of the funds being
e transferred, but Hanson would not be under any obligation to agree to either course.

(v) The only members of the schemes then remaining would be the pensioners and
deferred pensioners, together with some 350 persons employed in what have been called
'the CTN businesses', which were formerly part of the IBL division but which have been
retained by Hanson, though Hanson is actively seeking a buyer for them.

f (vi) Hanson could then either run off the schemes as closed schemes, or seek to reopen them to new entrants and admit employees of companies within the Hanson Group
which, by virtue of the substitution of Hanson for IBL as the principal company for the
purpose of the schemes, would be eligible to become participating companies. In either
case, Hanson (rather than IBL) would be entitled to the benefit of any suspension of
employer's contributions or repayment of surplus to which the Occupational Pensions
g Board might agree.

The sale agreement with Elders required steps to be taken to procure that the
companies sold to Elders should cease to be participating employers in the schemes with
effect from 5 April 1987 at the latest and should become participating employers in
schemes established by Elders, and that their employees should cease to be members of
the schemes. This would require changes in the trust deeds and rules governing the
h schemes, and, if the deeds necessary to effect such changes were not executed by the date
on which the sale to Elders was completed, Elders undertook to procure the execution of
such deeds by the companies sold to it and to use its reasonable endeavours to procure
the execution or the concurrence in the execution of such deeds by the trustees and the
committee of management. It was recognised that it might not be possible to obtain the
substitution of Hanson for IBL as the principal company for the purpose of the schemes,
j and by a side letter bearing even date with the sale agreement Elders undertook that, if
the necessary deeds were not executed by 31 December 1986 and IBL remained the
principal company for the purpose of the schemes, then Elders would discuss what other
action might be taken to achieve the same objective, failing which Elders would pay
Hanson an additional sum of £50m by instalments over a period of six years. The sum
of £50m was to be increased or decreased in the proportion by which the surplus in the
schemes valued in 1986 was greater or less than £80m, and represented the estimated

value of the surplus less tax likely to be payable on any repayments of the surplus to the employer. Effectively, therefore, Hanson was selling Imperial Group to Elders, but was proposing to exclude the greater part of the surplus in the schemes from the sale. If it could not achieve this by 31 December 1986 then it was to receive additional consideration for the sale.

On 19 September 1986, two days after the conclusion of the sale agreement with Elders, drafts of nine deeds (the amending deeds), three for each of the schemes, were circulated to members of the committee of management, and on the same day a representative of Hanson attended a meeting of the committee to explain their purpose and effect, which was to implement the proposals I have summarised. Concern was expressed at the two principal features of the proposals: (i) the exclusion of the schemes from the sale, which would have the effect of expelling employed members from the schemes even though they continued to be employed by the same employers, and leaving pensioners and deferred pensioners in schemes which would be operated by Hanson despite the sale of the companies by which they had been employed, so that future discretionary increases in pensions would be determined by a company with which the pensioners enjoyed in most cases no, and in other cases only the most tenuous, past relationship; and (ii) the terms on which the estimated surplus of £80m was to be apportioned between the transferring employed members and the retained pensioners and deferred pensioners, which was not to be in proportion to the respective liabilities to the two classes of members, but was to leave all but £10m in the retained funds, so that transferring employed members could not expect to enjoy a contributions holiday of anything like the duration they might have hoped for had they remained members of the schemes. The committee of management took legal advice, and was advised that it was doubtful if the proposals could be lawfully implemented but that, even if they could, they would require the co-operation of the committee of management, which the committee had a discretion to give or withhold.

Hanson, by contrast, took the view that in the case of two of the schemes the committee of management had no discretion in the matter and, provided that the proposed amendments to the rules were intra vires, was bound to join in executing the amending deeds. Accordingly, on 5 November 1986 the plaintiffs issued the present originating summons asking whether they were (a) at liberty or (b) bound to execute the proposed amending deeds. That is the first question in the summons.

Hanson now became concerned that it might be too late to execute the amending deeds once the sale to Elders was completed. Accordingly, the amending deeds were engrossed and on 18 November 1986, four days after the sale to Elders had become unconditional and one day before it was completed, they were executed by IBL (and in the case of the Courage Retail Managers' Pension Scheme by each of the participating companies). They still remain to be executed by the plaintiffs.

Meanwhile, it was obviously necessary to make provision for new and prospective employees of IBL and the participating companies who began their employment with those companies after the closure of the schemes in April 1986. Accordingly, three interim deeds (one for each scheme) were executed on 17 October 1986 by IBL, the committee of management, the trustees, and in the case of the Courage Retail Managers' Pension Scheme each of the participating companies. These deeds recited that it was considered desirable to maintain uniformity among the various pension schemes, that it was intended to reopen the existing schemes to new entrants but that doubts had arisen whether the schemes could validly be reopened, that accordingly it was considered inappropriate to reopen the schemes at the present time, and that it was desirable to put interim arrangements into effect in the meantime. Each of the interim deeds then established an interim contributory pension scheme on the same terms (save for the amendment to r 21 made in February 1986) as those of the appropriate principal scheme, not as another retirement benefits scheme, but as a temporary annexure to the fund of the principal scheme. In each case it was provided that, if the principal scheme should be reopened or at the end of a period of two years from the date of the interim deed or such longer period as the Board of Inland Revenue might allow, the funds of the interim scheme should either be absorbed into the funds of the principal scheme and the new members should become full members thereof, or they should be transferred to another retirement benefits scheme.

In those circumstances, the plaintiffs have also sought a ruling from the court whether, once the schemes have been closed to new entrants, they can validly be reopened by an appropriate amendment to the trust deeds and rules. That is the second question in the summons. The two questions are mutually independent; for Hanson wishes to implement its proposals whether or not it is able subsequently to reopen the scheme, while the plaintiffs wish to know if the schemes can be validly reopened, whether or not Hanson's proposals are implemented.

Question 1: Hanson's proposals

It is convenient to take first the question whether, assuming the proposed amendments to be capable of being validly made, the committee of management has any discretion in the matter, or is bound to execute the amending deeds on request. With it goes another, closely connected question: whether, if the committee of management does hereafter execute the amending deeds, their validity will fall to be tested by reference to the situation on 18 November 1986, when they were executed by the other parties and Hanson was still IBL's ultimate holding company, or on the date of execution by the committee, when Hanson will no longer have any connection with IBL. The answers to these questions depend on the terms of the relevant rule-amending power.

The Courage Retail Managers' Pension Scheme

Clause 14 of the current trust deed is in the following terms:

'Subject as hereinafter provided the Committee of Management may from time to time and at any time with the consent of the Participating Companies by any deed or deeds executed by the Committee of Management and the Participating Companies alter cancel modify or add to all or any of the provisions of the Fund provided that no such alteration or cancellation modification or addition as aforesaid shall (i) except as provided in Clause [12] of this Deed have the effect of altering the main purpose of the Fund namely the provision of pensions on retirement at a specified age for members or if it would operate wholly to relieve the Participating Companies from making any contribution to the Fund . . .'

and then there are two further provisos which I need not read.

It is clear, and is common ground, that that clause vests the power to amend the rules in the committee of management acting with the consent of the participating companies, that any amending deed must be executed by the committee of management as well as by the participating companies, and that it has no effect until so executed. It follows, and is conceded by counsel for IBL, that the committee of management has a full discretion to exercise and that, if it does execute the amending deeds, their validity will fall to be tested by reference to the situation obtaining on the date when it does so.

The Courage Staff Pensions Scheme and the Courage Employees' Pension Scheme

In each case, cl 15 of the trust deed as amended is in the following terms:

'The Company may at any time by deed supplemental hereto add to delete or vary all or any of the provisions of this Deed or of the Rules and the Committee of Management shall concur in executing any such supplemental deed PROVIDED THAT no addition deletion or alteration shall be made which would (a) have the effect of altering the main purpose of the Fund namely the provision of pensions on retirement at a specified age for Members ...'

and again there follow two similar provisos which I need not read.

Counsel for IBL submitted that the clause is plain and unambiguous. Grammatically, he said, the clause has two limbs. The first vests the rule-amending power in the company alone. By the use of the word 'may', it authorises the company, by deed executed by the company alone, to amend the trust deed or the rules, subject only to the provisos set out in the clause. The second limb, which uses the mandatory word 'shall', then obliges the committee of management to concur. The contrast, he submitted, is clear: 'shall' means 'shall', it does not mean 'may'.

In my view, the clause does not raise the familiar question whether 'shall' is mandatory or permissive. Counsel for the members of the schemes who argued against the validity of Hanson's proposals agreed that in the present context the word is mandatory. The committee of management must concur. The question, counsel submitted, is: what is the nature of that requirement? Do the concluding words of the clause impose an obligation on the committee of management which the court would enforce? Or do they impose no such obligation, but rather add an essential requirement for the validity of any amending deed?

In my judgment, the clause is ambiguous. The concluding words of the clause are capable of meaning, as counsel for IBL would have them mean: 'and the Committee of Management shall [meaning 'must'] concur in executing any such supplemental deed [sc *or else equity will treat the committee as having done so*]', but they are equally capable of meaning: 'and the Committee of Management shall [meaning 'must'] concur in executing any such supplemental deed [sc *or else the deed will be invalid*]'.

Counsel for IBL submitted that the first is not only the more natural meaning, but the more appropriate in what were in their inception non-contributory schemes. I disagree. The company, whether as contributor or as employer, is sufficiently protected against alterations to the schemes by being made a necessary party to any amending deed. Even in a non-contributory scheme, however, the interests of the employed members, pensioners and deferred pensioners do not necessarily coincide with those of the company. They cannot be effectively protected at all if the all-important power to amend the trust deeds and rules is left to the company's sole discretion. The first of the two possible meanings of the clause is in fact a most improbable one.

I have no doubt that the second of the two possible meanings is the correct one. It is, indeed, the more natural meaning of the actual words used. The committee is required, not to concur 'in the execution of' the amending deed by the company, which it could do by passing a resolution to this effect, but to concur in 'executing' the amending deed itself. The word 'concur', however, denotes an act of voluntary agreement; the argument of counsel for IBL would be better served by the word 'join'. Moreover, the committee of management is on any view entitled to satisfy itself that the provisos are complied with; yet proviso (c), which I have not read, calls for an exercise of judgment on the part of the committee, which is hardly consistent with an overall absence of discretion.

In the end, however, these are peripheral matters. What I find decisive is that there is no readily apparent reason to require the committee of management to join in executing any amending deed if this is a mere formality, while to exclude any discretion in the committee would not only deny any effective protection to the members, but would make nonsense of the careful allocation of powers found elsewhere in the trust deeds and rules. What is the point of conferring a power on the committee, or requiring the committee's consent to be obtained, if the power can be assumed by the company or the committee's consent can be dispensed with by an amendment made by the company alone in which the committee is bound to concur? I conclude, therefore, that in the case of these two schemes also the committee of management has a discretion and is not bound to concur in executing the amending deeds.

a   Counsel for IBL submitted that, even so, the validity of the amending deeds will fall to be tested by reference to the situation obtaining on 18 November 1986, when they were executed by IBL, and not on the date when they are executed by the last of the necessary parties to do so; and he relied on *Whitmore-Searle v Whitmore-Searle* [1907] 2 Ch 332. In that case a disentailing assurance was held to be effective to create a fee simple although by the time the protector of the settlement gave his consent the tenant in tail was dead. I am not sure whether counsel's submission depended on the committee of

b   management being required only to concur in the execution of the amending deeds by IBL rather than, as I have held, being made necessary parties, but in any case I reject it. A disentailing assurance executed by a tenant in tail in reversion without the consent of the protector of the settlement is not without effect; it bars the entail, and creates a base fee. If the protector of the settlement gives his consent, the base fee is enlarged into a fee simple. The only question in *Whitmore-Searle v Whitmore-Searle* was whether the protector

c   of the settlement could give his consent after the death of the tenant in tail. That case has no relevance where the deed in question is altogether without effect until a necessary consent is given: see *Rhyl UDC v Rhyl Amusements Ltd* [1959] 1 All ER 257 at 271, [1959] 1 WLR 465 at 482. The trust deeds and rules of these schemes can be amended only by a deed executed both by the company and by the committee of management. Until so executed, it has no effect; and accordingly its validity must be tested by reference to the

d   circumstances obtaining at the date when the last of the necessary parties to execute it does so.

    The next question is whether the plaintiffs are entitled, if so minded, to join in executing the amending deeds. They may do so only if the proposed amendments are within the power to amend the trust deeds and rules, and can properly be made. They must not infringe the provisos to the rule-amending power, particularly the express

e   prohibition to be found in all three schemes against altering the main purpose of the schemes, namely the provision of pensions on retirement at a specified age for members. This is a restriction which cannot be deleted by amendment, since it would be implicit anyway. It is trite law that a power can be exercised only for the purpose for which it is conferred, and not for any extraneous or ulterior purpose. The rule-amending power is

f   given for the purpose of promoting the purposes of the scheme, not altering them.

    Before I consider this question, I should make some general observations on the approach which I conceive ought to be adopted by the court to the construction of the trust deed and rules of a pension scheme. First, there are no special rules of construction applicable to a pension scheme; nevertheless, its provisions should wherever possible be construed to give reasonable and practical effect to the scheme, bearing in mind that it

g   has to be operated against a constantly changing commercial background. It is important to avoid unduly fettering the power to amend the provisions of the scheme, thereby preventing the parties from making those changes which may be required by the exigencies of commercial life. This is particularly the case where the scheme is intended to be for the benefit not of the employees of a single company, but of a group of companies. The composition of the group may constantly change as companies are

h   disposed of and new companies are acquired; and such changes may need to be reflected by modifications to the scheme.

    Second, in the case of an institution of long duration and gradually changing membership like a club or pension scheme, each alteration in the rules must be tested by reference to the situation at the time of the proposed alteration, and not by reference to the original rules at its inception. By changes made gradually over a long period,

j   alterations may be made which would not be acceptable if introduced all at once. Even the main purpose may be changed by degrees. This is demonstrated by *Thellusson v Viscount Valentia* [1907] 2 Ch 1, which concerned the Hurlingham Club. The club was founded in 1868 for the purpose of providing a ground for pigeon-shooting and a place of resort for those who took part in pigeon-shooting, their families and friends. From time to time other activities were introduced without objection from members, and the rules were amended to reflect this. By 1904 the character of the club had changed, and it was described in the rules as being—

> 'instituted for the purpose of providing a ground for pigeon-shooting, polo, and other sports . . . as an agreeable country resort not only to members, but also to their families and friends.'

The committee then resolved to discontinue pigeon-shooting. The Court of Appeal upheld the resolution, commenting that, although the club was originally formed for the encouragement of pigeon-shooting, it had become a club for the encouragement of polo and other sports besides pigeon-shooting, and that none of those objects was a more fundamental object of the club in the sense that it could not be varied or excluded than any other. That case was strictly not concerned with the power to amend the rules, but once pigeon-shooting had been discontinued it would obviously be open to the members by the appropriate majority to delete the anachronistic reference to pigeon-shooting in the rules. So the main purpose of a club or pension scheme may be enlarged by appropriate amendments to the rules; and, once it becomes too late to challenge the amendments, the enlarged purposes become the new basis by reference to which any further proposed changes must be considered.

With those preliminary observations, I turn to the main question which has been argued before me, whether the proposed amendments to the trust deeds and the rules can properly be made; and I take first the proposed exclusion of the schemes from the sale to Elders by the substitution of Hanson for IBL as 'the company' for the purposes of each scheme.

It is a novel and startling proposition that a company and its associated companies participating with it in a pension scheme can be sold and continue to employ the whole or substantially the whole of the workforce for whose benefit the scheme was established, and yet the scheme itself can be excluded from the sale. My first reaction was to think that the substitution of one company for another as the principal company for the purpose of a pension scheme must necessarily be outside the rule-amending power, and that a scheme for the benefit of company A and its associated companies cannot be converted into a scheme for company B and its associated companies without inevitably effecting a change in the main purposes of the scheme. Such a conclusion, however, proves to be too sweeping. It is necessary to examine further the current provisions of the trust deeds and rules and the terms of the proposed amendments.

The Courage Retail Managers' Pension Scheme

It is not necessary to rehearse all the relevant provisions of the interim trust deed, the 1957 trust deed, and the original rules. It is sufficient to say that 'the company' was defined as Barclay Perkins, and that the scheme was from its inception a pension scheme for the employees of a group of companies, the group being identified as Barclay Perkins and its associated companies as defined in the rules. There was no provision for changing the identity of the group by substituting another company for Barclay Perkins. The sale of an associated company out of the group would cause a partial winding up of the scheme so far as regards members who were not transferred to the employment of the company or another of its associated companies remaining in the group. 'Associated company' was defined in the rules by reference to the definitions of holding and subsidiary company in the Companies Acts. The circularity created by leaving the definition of associated company, an element in the main purpose of the scheme, to be provided in the rules, which are incapable of altering the main purpose of the scheme, must be resolved by a restrictive interpretation of the power to define associated companies by the rules. The detailed definition is to be contained in the rules, and may be changed from time to time; but the definition must be one which includes only companies properly capable of being described as associated companies of the company.

On 1 April 1962 a substantial part of Barclay Perkins's undertaking was transferred to

and absorbed by its holding company, IBL, and eventually (though not until 1978)
Barclay Perkins was put into voluntary liquidation. Had nothing been done, this would
have effected a full dissolution of the scheme. In March 1963, however, at a time when
there was only one associated company of Barclay Perkins participating in the scheme,
steps were taken to substitute IBL for Barclay Perkins as 'the company' for the purposes
of the scheme. This was effected in two stages. First, the rules were amended by adding
a new provision in the following terms:

> '(iv) If the undertaking (or any substantial part of the undertaking) of the
> Company shall at any time have been absorbed or shall in the future be absorbed or
> acquired by or vested in any other body corporate and such body corporate shall in
> anticipation of or on or at any time after such absorption or acquisition by deed of
> declaration executed and delivered to the Trust undertake to perform all the
> obligations of the Company hereunder the Fund shall continue in operation and the
> Trust Deed and the Rules shall as from the date of such absorption or acquisition or
> as from such later date as such deed of declaration shall provide have effect as though
> such other body corporate had originally established the Fund and been a party to
> the Trust Deed and the Rules in place of the Company and the expression "the
> Company" as used throughout the Trust Deed and the Rules shall thenceforth mean
> such other body corporate.'

Second, IBL, Barclay Perkins and the trustees duly executed a deed in the terms
required by the new rule.

The Courage Staff Pensions Scheme and the Courage Employees' Pension Scheme

Again, it is not necessary to rehearse all the relevant provisions of the 1959 trust deeds
and the original rules. It is sufficient to say that in each case 'the company' was defined as
IBL, and that each of the schemes was from its inception a pension scheme for the
employees of a group of companies, the group being identified as IBL and its associated
companies as defined in the rules. The rules defined 'associated company' as:

> 'Any body whether corporate or unincorporate which is for the time being
> associated with the Company whether by shareholding or by regular trade dealings
> and which shall be admitted to participation in the Fund.'

I shall call this 'the current definition of associated company'. In each case, cl 10 of the
original trust deed provided for the possible substitution of another company for IBL in
the following terms:

> 'If the Company shall be wound up for the purpose of reconstruction or
> amalgamation with any other company the Trustees may make such arrangements
> and enter into such deeds and agreements as they may in their discretion think
> requisite for the substitution for the Company of such reconstructed or amalgamated
> company.'

I shall call this 'the current substitution clause'.

All three schemes

The current trust deeds and rules of the three schemes have been modernised and
assimilated. In each case 'the company' is defined as IBL; the current definition of
'associated company' and the current substitution clause are adopted, save that the
admission of an associated company to participate in the scheme now requires the prior
consent of the Commissioners of Inland Revenue; the functions of the trustees are now
exercisable by the committee of management; and the company is authorised with the
written consent of the committee of management to admit an associated company to
participation in the scheme. It is provided that an associated company which has been
admitted to participate shall cease to do so in certain specified circumstances, and in

particular if it is placed in liquidation otherwise than for the purpose of reconstruction or amalgamation, or if it ceases to be associated with the company either by shareholding or regular trade dealings. On an associated company ceasing to participate in the scheme there is to be a partial dissolution of that part (to be determined by the committee of management acting on actuarial advice) of the fund relating to the associated company. On a dissolution or partial dissolution any ultimate surplus may be applied in augmenting pensions up to the maxima permitted for the approval of the scheme by the Commissioners of Inland Revenue. In the Courage Staff Pensions Scheme and the Courage Employees' Pension Scheme any residual balance is to be paid to the company. No repayment to the company is permitted in the case of the Courage Retail Managers' Scheme.

Thus each of the three schemes is still a pension scheme for the employees of a group of companies, that group being defined as IBL and its associated companies. There is a limited right to substitute another company for IBL as 'the company' for the purpose of the scheme, but only if the company is wound up for the purpose of reconstruction or amalgamation, and the only company which may then be substituted is the reconstructed or amalgamated company. The sale of an associated company out of the group would still cause a partial dissolution of each scheme; but unless some other company were first substituted for IBL, the sale of IBL itself would not affect the scheme at all.

The current substitution clause would not permit the substitution of Hanson for IBL before or after the completion of the sale to Hanson. It is proposed to effect that substitution by the execution of two of the amending deeds for each of the three schemes. The first deed seeks to add a further substitution clause to the appropriate trust deed in the following terms:

'10B. If a Company ("the Founder") holds directly or indirectly a controlling interest in Imperial Group and decides that it should be "the Company" for the purposes of the Fund then the existing Company the Founder [in the case of the Courage Retail Managers' Scheme the participating companies] and the Committee of Management shall enter into a Deed whereby (a) the Founder becomes "the Company" for all the purposes of the Fund and assumes all the rights powers duties obligations discretions and liabilities of the Company under the Fund (b) the company that was formerly "the Company" is released from all its rights powers duties obligations discretions and liabilities as "the Company" and will continue to participate in the Fund as an "Associated Company".'

The second deed contains the requisite undertaking by Hanson to assume all the rights, powers, duties, obligations, discretions and liabilities of IBL in the place of IBL for the purposes of the relevant trust deed and rules as amended from time to time, a release of IBL from all the rights, powers, duties, obligations, discretions and liabilities it has or may have as 'the company' for the purposes of the relevant scheme, a statement that IBL shall be an associated company for all the purposes of the relevant scheme, and appropriate substitutions of Hanson in the definition of 'the company' in the relevant trust deed and rules.

These deeds were, of course, drafted on the assumption that they would be executed before the completion of the sale to Elders; but even on this assumption they were ill thought out. On the completion of the sale to Elders, Elders would become the holding company of Imperial Group and thus 'the founder', and could use the new clause to compel the further substitution of Elders for Hanson. It hardly needs to be said that this was far from the parties' intention. Now that the sale to Elders has been completed, however, the first deed can no longer serve the purpose for which it was intended. Elders, not Hanson, is now 'the founder', and is the only company which can be substituted for IBL under the provisions of the new clause. The second deed would simply be ineffective. It would not be right, however, to decide this case on the basis of the defective wording of the amending deeds, which I shall assume are capable of being redrawn to meet these criticisms, and I shall address the question more broadly.

It is obviously desirable that some provision for substitution should be included in a group pension scheme. It would be unfortunate if the whole scheme had to be wound up merely because, on some reorganisation of the group, the principal company was put into liquidation. A pension scheme is established not for the benefit of a particular company, but for the benefit of those employed in a commercial undertaking; and provision can properly be made for the scheme to continue for their benefit if, on a reconstruction of the group, the undertaking is transferred from one company to another within the group, and remains identifiably the same. The essential character of a corporate reconstruction is that substantially the same business is carried on and substantially the same persons continue to carry it on: see *Re South African Supply and Cold Storage Co, Wild v South African Supply and Cold Storage Co* [1904] 2 Ch 268 at 286, followed in *Brooklands Selangor Holdings Ltd v IRC* [1970] 2 All ER 76 at 87, [1970] 1 WLR 429 at 445. Where, on a reconstruction or amalgamation, substantially the same persons continue to be employed in the undertaking, then the substitution of the reconstructed or amalgamated company for the original principal company for the purpose of a group pension scheme is not only necessary and desirable but can properly be said to promote the main purpose of the scheme and not to alter it.

That, however, is not this case at all. The Courage Group has not been reconstructed but sold. There has been no transfer of the undertaking or any part thereof from one company to another. The employees for whose benefit the schemes were established continue to be employed by the same companies. There is no need to substitute another company for IBL in order to preserve the scheme for the benefit of those employees, for the sale of IBL to Elders has not affected the continuance of the schemes at all. The purpose of the proposed substitution of Hanson for IBL is not to preserve the schemes in existence for the benefit of those employed in the undertaking, but to prevent the schemes from continuing for their benefit and to bring about an unnecessary dissolution of the schemes which would not otherwise occur.

The need for some provision to be made for substitution shows that the identity of 'the company' is not of the essence or part of the main purpose of the schemes. In an emergency, and to preserve the schemes from premature dissolution, the trust deeds may properly be amended to allow a different company to be substituted for 'the company' and the definition of the group changed accordingly. But it does not follow from the need for a properly limited power of substitution that an unlimited power of substitution can be validly introduced, or that any company can properly be substituted in any circumstances and for any purposes. Counsel for IBL submitted that any company can properly be substituted provided only that the substitution is acceptable to the Commissioners of Inland Revenue. That submission confuses the advantages of retaining the approval of the Commissioners of Inland Revenue for any pension scheme which is operated in connection with a trade or undertaking carried on in the United Kingdom, with the objects or purposes of a pension scheme, which are to provide pensions for those employed in the undertaking, not tax benefits to other persons. In fact, the submission can be tested to destruction for, if correct, then had Hanson not excluded the schemes from the sale to Elders, Elders could now sell Imperial Group to a purchaser in the United Kingdom, exclude the schemes from the sale by substituting itself as 'the company', and make the schemes available to the employees of its Australian subsidiaries. In that situation, the attitude of the Inland Revenue in the United Kingdom would have no relevance.

The simple fact is that Hanson does not employ, and never has employed, any of the employees for whose benefit the schemes were established; and, now that the sale to Elders has been completed, Hanson has no remaining connection with IBL, its associated companies, or their employees at all. If the trust deeds and rules can be amended now to permit the substitution of Hanson for IBL, then they can be amended to permit the substitution of ICI or British Gas or the company which carries on the business of the local Chinese take-away. In my judgment, any such substitution would manifestly alter the main purpose of the schemes and be ultra vires.

I should, however, not like to leave it there, lest it be thought that Hanson could properly have been substituted for IBL if only the substitution had been effected in time *a* before the sale to Elders was completed. At that time, of course, Hanson was IBL's ultimate holding company, and the substitution of Hanson for IBL, while changing the definition of the group, would not by itself change its composition. The potential enlargement of the schemes by the addition of other companies in the Hanson Group as new associated companies occurred automatically on the acquisition of Imperial Group by Hanson and was not the result of any amendment to the schemes; while the spin-off *b* of employees of IBL and its associated companies would be the result, not of the substitution of Hanson for IBL alone (for IBL was to become and each of its associated companies was to remain an associated company), but of the combined effect of the substitution of Hanson for IBL and the sale of IBL to Elders. Counsel for IBL was, I think, minded to accept that the trust deeds and rules could not be amended for the purpose of expelling members from the schemes, but he submitted that there was nothing to *c* prevent Hanson from entering into commerial transactions which would have that result. Hanson was free to run down IBL's activities until it had no, or very few, employees, and then procure IBL to dispose of all its subsidiaries. By such means Hanson could bring about the dissolution of the whole, or virtually the whole, of each scheme without any change in the trust deeds or rules at all.

In my view, all this is beside the point. It does not matter that Hanson could have *d* achieved the same, or nearly the same, result by commercial transactions without any amendments to the schemes. It is one thing to remove members from the schemes by disposing of the companies by which they are employed. It is quite another to remove the schemes from the members by manipulating the trust deeds and rules, whether alone or in conjunction with a contemplated transaction.

In my judgment, the validity of a power of substitution depends on the circumstances *e* in which it is capable of being exercised and the characteristics which must be possessed by the company capable of being substituted; while the validity of any purported exercise of such a power depends on the purpose for which the substitution is made. The circumstances must be such that substitution is necessary or at least expedient in order to preserve the scheme for those for whose benefit it was established; and the substituted *f* company must be recognisably the successor to the business and workforce of the company for which it is to be substituted. It is not enough that it is a member of the same group as, or even that it is the holding company of, the company for which it is substituted. It must have succeeded to all or much of the business of the former company and have taken over the employment of all or most of the former company's employees. In my judgment, the proposed power to substituted IBL's ultimate holding company for *g* IBL in undefined circumstances is far too wide, alters and is capable of defeating the main purpose of the schemes, and is ultra vires.

Even if this were not the case, I would not uphold the proposed exercise of the power. The amending deeds are not an academic exercise designed to improve the constitution of the schemes for the future. They were occasioned by, and prepared in contemplation of, the impending sale to Elders. The whole object in substituting Hanson for IBL was to *h* bring about a dissolution or partial dissolution of the schemes on the completion of the sale to Elders which would otherwise not occur. The purpose of the amending deeds were frankly acknowledged by counsel for IBL to be—

'to retain within the control of Hanson a surplus which has been contributed by companies which Hanson has bought, and for which surplus Hanson has paid, *j* rather than allow it to be transferred to Elders.'

That purpose is foreign to the purpose for which the power to amend the trust deeds and rules is conferred, and invalidates any exercise of that power.

Accordingly, I hold that the committee of management is not at liberty to execute the six amending deeds by which Hanson is to be substituted for IBL. It remains to consider

the last three deeds, one for each scheme, by which the rest of Hanson's proposals were
to be carried into effect. These substitute a new provision in the event of a company
ceasing to be an associated company or ceasing for any reason to be a participating
company. This would, of course, have happened on the substitution of Hanson for IBL
and the completion of the sale to Elders. It may still happen on the sale by Elders of any
of IBL's subsidiaries, and the committee of management is entitled to know whether the
proposed amendments can properly be made.

Instead of the secession of a company causing a partial dissolution of the scheme, the
proposed new clause requires the trustees to set aside a portion of the fund, and either (i)
establish a new scheme and fund approved by the Commissioners of Inland Revenue as a
separate scheme on trusts corresponding as nearly as may be to the trusts of the existing
scheme, (ii) transfer the separated portion to an existing scheme or fund similarly
approved or (iii) hold the separated portion and deal with it for the benefit of the
employees and if applicable the pensioners and deferred pensioners of the seceding
company as if the scheme were being dissolved. The trustees are not to deal with the
separated portion in either of the first two ways unless satisfied after considering the
advance of the actuary that the benefits in the new or other schemes are 'equitable having
regard to the extent and amount of the separated portion'. There are elaborate provisions
for calculating the amount of the separated portion which, inter alia, require the
amendments made to r 21 in February 1986 to be ignored, and which are designed to
exclude any part of the surplus in the fund from being comprised in the separated
portion. On the company's secession, all employees of the seceding company who on
that date are members of the scheme and, if the trustees and the company so require and
the actuary agrees, the pensioners and deferred pensioners who have been employees of
the seceding company, are to accept rights in the new or other scheme or in the separated
portion, as the case may be, in lieu and satisfaction of their rights under the scheme.

The committee of management has strong reservations in regard to the proposed
amendments, and particularly in regard to the basis of valuing the separated portion. In
my judgment, there can be no objection in principle to the validity of such amendments
provided that they do not infringe the third proviso to the rule-amending power. In the
case of the Courage Retail Managers' Scheme they must not 'vary or affect any benefits
already secured by past contributions in respect of any Member without his consent in
writing'; and in the case of the other two schemes they must not 'reduce . . . the accrued
pension of any employed member' except in the circumstances specified. 'Accrued
pensions' is defined in the rules to mean pensions based on salary at the relevant date.
There was some dispute whether 'benefits already secured by past contributions' means
the same thing, or includes the prospective entitlement to pensions based on final salary.
In the absence of express definition, I see no reason to exclude any benefit to which a
member is prospectively entitled if he continues in the same employment and which has
been acquired by past contributions, and no reason to assume that he has retired from
such employment on the date of the employer's secession when he has not. The contrary
argument places a meaning on 'secured' which is not justified.

In my judgment, the proposed amending deeds as presently drawn suffer from serious
defects which take them outside the rule-amending power. In the first place, even if the
separated portion were to be calculated on a generous basis, there is no guarantee of the
benefits to be provided under the scheme to which the members are liable to be
transferred. All that is required is that those benefits must be 'equitable having regard to
the extent and amount of the separated portion'. That is not good enough. Instead of
remaining a member of the existing scheme, an employee is to be liable to be transferred
to a different scheme under which the rules and entitlements are unspecified. Even if the
separated portion is calculated on the footing that the valuable rights conferred by the
amendment made to r 19 in February 1986 are applicable, for example, there is no
requirement that the scheme to which he is to be transferred will contain a rule to similar
effect. There may simply be an augmentation to the surplus in the new scheme.

Moreover, the basis on which the separated portion is to be calculated does not recognise the entitlement of members under r 21 as amended in February 1986.

In my judgment, the proposed new clause does not contain the provisions and restrictions necessary to ensure that the powers conferred thereby cannot be exercised in a manner which would reduce the benefits currently secured by past contributions. Accordingly, I hold that these amending deeds, as presently drawn, are also outside the power to amend the trust deeds and rules. Whether, even if redrawn to meet the criticisms that have been made, it would be in the interests of members for them to be executed, is a matter for the committee of management to consider in its discretion.

The second question: reopening the schemes

Counsel for the second defendant submitted that the closure of the schemes to new entrants must be irrevocable, or it is meaningless. There was, he said, no difference between closure under the amendments introduced in February 1986 and closure under cl 12 of the trust deed (cl 11 in the case of the Courage Retail Managers' Scheme) which provides:

'The Company may by notice in writing to the Trustees at any time close the Fund so far as regards the admission of new Members and as from the date of such notice no person who is not then already a Member shall be admitted as a Member of the Fund.'

If the circumstances prevailing in February 1986 are considered, he said, the intention to close the schemes irrevocably in the event of Hanson's bid succeeding is obvious.

In my judgment, the question is not whether the closure of the schemes in February 1986 was, or was intended to be, irrevocable, but whether the closure of any of the schemes can be (and if it can, whether it has been) entrenched against the future exercise of the power to amend the trust deed and rules. There is no need to entrench the company's power to close the scheme by giving the appropriate notice: the company is sufficiently protected against any unwelcome reopening of the scheme by being a necessary party to the amendments required to reopen it. In like manner, the members of a closed scheme are sufficiently protected against any disadvantageous reopening of the scheme by the fact that the committee of management is a necessary party to the amendments which are required. Unless and until reopened, the scheme remains closed. Even if the closure is reversible, it is not meaningless.

There is, therefore, no reason to imply a provision, and there is certainly no express provision, to entrench the closure of any of the schemes against any future amendment of the trust deed and rules. I should add that I am far from persuaded that any purported restriction on the powers of the committee of management would be effective. The powers conferred on the committee are vested in it in a fiduciary capacity, and even if the present members of the committee can release or fetter or agree not to exercise any of the powers and discretions vested in the committee (as to which I decide nothing), they cannot deprive their successors of the right to exercise them: see *Re Wills's Trust Deeds, Wills v Godfrey* [1963] 1 All ER 390, [1964] Ch 219. They may, of course, defeat a future exercise of the power by exhausting the fund while the scheme remains closed, but that is a different matter. Whether the company could make the closure of the scheme irrevocable by releasing its own power to join in effecting the necessary amendments, a power which is not, I think, vested in the company in a fiduciary capacity, is a question which I need not decide.

In my judgment, whether or not the closure of the schemes could have been made proof against any future reopening, this has not been done; and accordingly I shall declare that the committee of management is (a) at liberty but (b) not bound to concur in executing any deeds amending the trust deeds or rules for the purpose of reopening the schemes to new entrants.

The wider issue

a   Hanson's proposals, which I have disallowed, were designed to remove for its own benefit, or for the benefit of employees in other companies in the Hanson Group, all but £10m of the surplus in the schemes. Its proposals would have had the effect of reducing or extinguishing the present expectation of employees of the Courage Group of companies of a continued suspension of their contributions. They thus raise the wider and controversial issue whether such surpluses should be regarded as available to the

b   employer or as belonging wholly or partly to the members. If I have not addressed that issue, it is not because I have overlooked it, but because it does not arise directly for decision. It is right, however, that I should explain why I have not based my decision on the ground that Hanson's proposals would deprive the employees of an accrued legal entitlement.

Such surpluses arise from what, with hindsight, can be recognised as past overfunding.

c   Prima facie, if returnable and not used to increase benefits, they ought to be returned to those who contributed to them. In a contributory scheme, this might be thought to mean the employer and the employees in proportion to their respective contributions. That, however, is not necessarily, or even usually, the case. In the case of most pension schemes, and certainly in the case of these schemes, the position is different. Employees are obliged to contribute a fixed proportion of their salaries or such lesser sum as the

d   employer may from time to time determine. They cannot be required to pay more, even if the fund is in deficit; and they cannot demand a reduction or suspension of their own contributions if it is in surplus. The employer, by way of contrast, is obliged only to make such contributions if any as may be required to meet the liabilities of the scheme. If the fund is in deficit, the employer is bound to make it good; if it is in surplus, the employer has no obligation to pay anything. Employees have no right to complain if,

e   while the fund is in surplus, the employer should require them to continue their contributions while itself contributing nothing. If the employer chooses to reduce or suspend their contributions, it does so ex gratia and in the interests of maintaining good industrial relations.

From this, two consequences follow. First, employees have no legal right to 'a

f   contributions holiday'. Second, any surplus arises from past overfunding not by the employer and the employees pro rata to their respective contributions but by the employer alone to the full extent of its past contributions and only subject thereto by the employees.

It will, however, only be in rare cases that the employer will have any legal right to repayment of any part of the surplus. Regulations shortly to be made under s 64 of the

g   Social Security Act 1973, as amended by para 3 of Sch 10 to the Social Security Act 1986, are expected to confer power on the Occupational Pensions Board to authorise modifications to pension schemes in order to allow repayment to employers. Repayment will, however, still normally require amendment to the scheme, and thus co-operation between the employer and the trustees or committee of management. Where the employer seeks repayment, the trustees or committee can be expected to press for

h   generous treatment of employees and pensioners, and the employer to be influenced by a desire to maintain good industrial relations with its workforce.

It is, therefore, precisely in relation to a surplus that the relationship between 'the company' as the employer and the members as its present or past employees can be seen to be an essential feature of a pension scheme. In the present case, the members of these schemes object to being compulsorily transferred to a new scheme of which they know

j   nothing except that it has a relatively small surplus. While they have no legal right to participate in the surpluses in the existing schemes, they are entitled to have them dealt with by consultation and negotiation between their employers with a continuing responsibility towards them and the committee of management with a discretion to exercise on their behalf, and not to be irrevocably parted from these surpluses by the unilateral decision of a take-over raider with only a transitory interest in the share capital of the companies which employ them.   *a*

Declarations accordingly.

Solicitors: *Linklaters & Paines* (for the plaintiffs); *Nabarro Nathanson* (for the IBL and the third and fourth defendants); *Lovell White & King* (for the second defendant).

b

Jacqueline Metcalfe   Barrister.

Practice Direction

c

FAMILY DIVISION

Affidavit – Filing – Practice – Family Division – Time for filing – Late filing – Effect – Effect on costs and consideration of affidavit.

Difficulties are being experienced because of the late filing of affidavits in cases proceeding   *d*
in the Principal Registry.

The President and judges of the Family Division require the attention of practitioners to be drawn to the practice set out in the Registrar's Direction of 7 February 1984 ([1984] 1 All ER 684, [1984] 1 WLR 306). Failure to comply with this practice may result in costs being disallowed or being ordered to be paid by the solicitor personally. Affidavits which are lodged in the Principal Registry within 14 days before the hearing date instead   *e*
of being lodged in the Clerk of the Rules' Department or with the clerk to the registrar may not be considered at all by the judge or the registrar as the case may be.

B P TICKLE
20 February 1987   Senior Registrar.

a

R v King and another

COURT OF APPEAL, CRIMINAL DIVISION
NEILL LJ, WATERHOUSE AND SAVILLE JJ
27 OCTOBER, 28 NOVEMBER 1986

b
  Criminal law – Obtaining property by deception – Deception – False representation – False inducement to be employed to do work – Appellants falsely claiming to be tree surgeons – Appellants inducing elderly widow to have trees cut down for payment – Whether appellants' deception operative cause of their obtaining payment from widow – Whether offence of obtaining property by deception established – Theft Act 1968, s 15(1).

c
  The appellants went to the house of an elderly widow, falsely claiming to be from a firm of tree surgeons. They informed her that four trees in her garden were dangerous and offered to fell them for £470 if it was paid in cash. While she was withdrawing the money, the police were informed and the appellants were arrested and charged with attempting to obtain property by deception, contrary to s 15(1)[a] of the Theft Act 1968. They were convicted. They appealed, contending that their conduct did not constitute
d
the offence of obtaining property by false pretences or by deception because, as a matter of causation, if the appellants had received the money for cutting down the trees they would have been paid by reason of the work they had done and not by reason of any representation they had made to secure the work.

  Held – Whether a person could be said to have obtained property by deception depended
e
on whether the deception was an operative cause of obtaining the property. That was an issue of fact to be decided by the jury applying their common sense. Since there was ample evidence on which a jury could have concluded that had the appellants succeeded in their scheme the money would have been paid to them as a result of the deception practised by them on the widow, the appeal would be dismissed (see p 550 *d e h j*, post).
f
  R v Martin (1867) LR 1 CCR 56 applied.

Notes
For obtaining property by deception, see 11 Halsbury's Laws (4th edn) para 1278, and for cases on the subject, see 15 Digest (Reissue) 1410–1413, 12343–12379.
  For the Theft Act 1968, s 15, see 12 Halsbury's Statutes (4th edn) 526.

g

Cases referred to in judgment
R v Lewis (January 1922, unreported), Somerset Assizes.
R v Martin (1867) LR 1 CCR 56.
R v Moreton (1913) 8 Cr App R 214, [1911–13] All ER Rep 699, CCA.

h
Cases also cited
R v Potger (1970) 55 Cr App R 42, CA.
Levene v Pearcey [1976] Crim LR 63, DC.

  Appeals
j David King and James Stockwell, appealed with leave of Russell J against their convictions in the Crown Court at Southampton before his Honour Judge Stock QC and a jury on

---

   a   Section 15(1), so far as material, provides: 'A person who by any deception dishonestly obtains property belonging to another, with the intention of permanently depriving the other of it, shall on conviction . . . be liable to imprisonment . . .'

19 February 1986 on a charge of attempting to obtain property by deception contrary to
s 15(1) of the Theft Act 1968 and s 1(1) of the Criminal Attempts Act 1981. The facts are   *a*
set out in the judgment of the court.

Nigel Cockburn (assigned by the Registrar of Criminal Appeals) for the appellants.
Keith Cutler for the Crown.

Cur adv vult   *b*

28 November. The following judgment of the court was delivered.

NEILL LJ. On 19 February 1986 in the Crown Court at Southampton the appellants,
David King and James Stockwell, were convicted of attempting to obtain property by   *c*
deception. They were each fined £100, with 30 days' imprisonment in default of
payment. They now appeal against conviction by leave of the single judge.
   The case for the prosecution at the trial can be stated quite shortly. On 5 March 1985
the appellants went to the house of Mrs Mitchell, in New Milton. Mrs Mitchell, who had
lived in the house all her life, was a widow of 68 years of age. The appellants told her that
they were from Streets, a firm of tree surgeons. She knew of the firm, and in answer to   *d*
her question one of the appellants claimed to be Mr Street. They told her that a sycamore
tree in her garden was likely to cause damage. They purported to carry out a test, with a
plastic strip placed against the tree, and one of the appellants then said that the tree was
dangerous.
   They told her that the roots of the tree were growing into the gas main and could
cause thousands of pounds in damage. They told her that it would cost £150 to fell the   *e*
tree, which Mrs Mitchell agreed to pay. They then looked at other trees and told her that
another sycamore was dangerous as well as one of her conifers. In addition they told her
that the roots of her bay tree were causing damage to the foundations of the house. Mrs
Mitchell asked the appellants about the cost of doing all the work, and they told her that
to remove the four trees including the bay tree would cost about £500. When Mrs
Mitchell told them that she was going to telephone her brother, one of the appellants   *f*
informed her that they would do the work for £470 if paid in cash. Mrs Mitchell then
said that she would have to go and get the money from the bank. In fact, she decided to
draw some money from her two building society accounts. From one account she
withdrew £100, and she was in the process of withdrawing £200 from her account with
a second building society, intending at that stage to go to her bank to draw the balance,
when the cashier at the second building society noticed that she seemed very distressed.   *g*
   Following a conversation between Mrs Mitchell and the cashier, the police were
informed. Police officers then went to Mrs Mitchell's house and found the appellants
there. The appellants were arrested, and on 17 February 1986 they appeared at the Crown
Court at Southampton on an indictment charging them with attempting to obtain
property by deception, contrary to s 1(1) of the Criminal Attempts Act 1981.
   At the outset of the trial counsel for the appellants moved to quash the indictment on   *h*
the ground that the conduct alleged did not constitute a criminal offence. As the
arguments advanced in support of the motion to quash the indictment were later
repeated in this court it is unnecessary for us to deal with the motion in detail. It is
sufficient to say (a) that after hearing argument the judge ruled that the count appeared
to him to be a good one and that he had no power to quash it and (b) that at the conclusion
of the evidence on 18 February counsel for the appellants submitted that there was no   *j*
case to answer. On that occasion some further argument on the same lines as on the
previous day took place. At the end of the argument the judge ruled that he proposed to
leave the case to the jury. At the same time, however, he allowed an unopposed
amendment to the indictment to add the word 'then' in the particulars of offence. We
shall have to set out the precise terms of the particulars of offence (as amended) a little
later in this judgment.

a   It may also be observed that, as the argument on the motion to quash required reference to be made to textbooks and other authorities, it was necessary to adjourn the case for a time so that research could be carried out in the local chambers and in the public library in Southampton. On Wednesday, 19 February 1986 the judge summed the case up to the jury. After a retirement of nearly three hours the jury returned verdicts of guilty against both men.

b   In support of the appeal against conviction counsel for the appellants argued that the judge erred in rejecting the motion to quash the indictment, or alternatively the submission that there was no case to answer. The argument was developed on the following lines: (1) that, as the appellants were charged with an attempt, it was incumbent on the prosecution to prove that if the relevant conduct had been completed it would have constituted a criminal offence; (2) that if the appellants had received £470 for cutting down the trees they would have been paid by reason of the work they had done, c   and not by reason of any representation they had made to secure the work; (3) that since the decision in R v Lewis (January 1922, unreported) it had been generally recognised that conduct of the kind complained of in the present case did not constitute the criminal offence of obtaining property by false pretences or by deception because, as a matter of causation, the relevant property was obtained by reason of the work carried out rather d   than by reason of any representation or deception. Our attention was directed to statements on the subject in some leading textbooks; (4) that the offence of obtaining a pecuniary advantage by deception contrary to s 16 of the Theft Act 1968 had no relevance in the present case (a) because the appellants were not given the opportunity to earn the remuneration 'in an office or employment'; on the facts of this case the appellants were independent contractors and (b) because during the course of the argument at the trial e   the prosecution stated in terms that they were not relying on the provisions of s 16.

In order to examine these arguments it is necessary to start by setting out the particulars of offence as stated in the indictment, as amended. The particulars read as follows:

f   'David King and Jimmy Stockwell on the 5th day of March 1985 in Hampshire, dishonestly attempted to obtain from Nora Anne Mitchell, £470 in money with the intention of permanently depriving the said Nora Anne Mitchell thereof by deception, namely by false oral representations that they were from J F Street, Tree Specialists, Pennington, that essential work necessary to remove trees in order to prevent damage to the gas supply and house foundations would then have to be carried out.'

g   It will be remembered that the word 'then' towards the end of the particulars was added by way of amendment on 18 February.

The argument advanced on behalf of the appellants on causation or remoteness was founded on the decision in R v Lewis, and on commentaries on that decision by academic writers. The report of the decision in R v Lewis is scanty and, as far as we are aware, is contained only in a footnote in Russell on Crime (12th edn, 1964) vol 2, p 1186, n 66).

In that case (which was a decision at Somerset Assizes in January 1922) a schoolmistress h   obtained her appointment by falsely stating that she possessed a teacher's certificate. She was held to be not guilty of obtaining her salary by false pretences, on the ground that she was paid because of the services she rendered, and not because of the false representation.

It was submitted on behalf of the appellants that the principle underlying the decision in R v Lewis could be applied in the present case. It was further submitted that the j   authority of R v Lewis was implicitly recognised by the enactment of para (c) of s 16(2) of the Theft Act 1968. Section 16 is concerned with the obtaining of a pecuniary advantage by deception; s 16(2) provides:

'The cases in which a pecuniary advantage within the meaning of this section is to be regarded as obtained for a person are cases where ... (c) he is given the opportunity to earn remuneration or greater remuneration in an office or employment ...'

It is to be observed, however, that Professor Glanville Williams in his *Textbook of Criminal Law* (2nd edn, 1983) p 792 has this to say of the decision in *R v Lewis*:   *a*

'Yet *Lewis* would not have got the job and consequently her salary, if it had not been for the pretence. Her object in making the pretence was to get the salary. Assuming, as is likely, that the employer would not have made her any payment of salary if a lie had not been operating on his mind, there was certainly a factual causal connection between the lie and the obtaining of salary. Why should it not be a *b* causal connection in law? We have seen that when the defendant produces a consequence intentionally, it is generally regarded as imputable to him. Why should it not be so here?'

Furthermore, the learned author of *Russell on Crime* p 1187 (immediately after the footnote already referred to) continued:

c

'But it is submitted that cases of this kind could be placed beyond doubt if the indictment were worded carefully. The essential point in this crime is that in making the transfer of goods the prosecutor must have been influenced by the false pretence as set out in the indictment.'

We have given careful consideration to the argument based on causation or remoteness, and have taken account of the fact that some support for the argument may be provided *d* by the writings of a number of distinguished academic lawyers. Nevertheless, we have come to the conclusion that on the facts of the present case the argument is fallacious.

In our view, the question in each case is: was the deception an operative cause of the obtaining of the property? This question falls to be answered as a question of fact by the jury applying their common sense.

Moreover, this approach is in accordance with the decision of the Court for Crown *e* Cases Reserved in *R v Martin* (1867) LR 1 CCR 56, where it was held that a conviction for obtaining a chattel by false pretences was good, although the chattel was not in existence at the time that the pretence was made, provided the subsequent delivery of the chattel was directly connected with the false pretence. Bovill CJ said:

'What is the test? Surely this, that there must be a direct connection between the *f* pretence and the delivery—that there must be a continuing pretence. Whether there is such a connection or not is a question for the jury.'

The decision in *R v Martin* was referred to with approval in *R v Moreton* (1913) 8 Cr App R 214, cf [1911–13] All ER Rep 699 at 700, where Lord Coleridge J said:

'Martin leaves the law in no doubt; it was held there that the fact that the goods *g* were obtained under a contract does not make the goods so obtained goods not obtained by a false pretence, if the false pretence is a continuing one and operates on the mind of the person supplying the goods.'

In the present case there was, in our judgment, ample evidence on which the jury could come to the conclusion that had the attempt succeeded the money would have *h* been paid over by the victim as a result of the lies told to her by the appellants. We consider that the judge was correct to reject both the motion to quash the indictment and the submission that there was no case to answer.

For the reasons which we have set out, we consider that the appellants were rightly convicted in this case, and the appeals must therefore be dismissed.

j

Appeals dismissed.

Solicitors: *Crown Prosecution Service.*

Dilys Tausz   Barrister.

a R v Felixstowe Justices, ex parte Leigh and another

QUEEN'S BENCH DIVISION
WATKINS LJ, RUSSELL AND MANN JJ
1, 8, MAY, 7 OCTOBER 1986

b

Magistrates – Anonymity – Policy of withholding names of justices – Bench adopting policy of withholding names of justices sitting on cases – Justices withholding names from newspaper reporter – Whether policy contrary to principle of open justice – Whether reporter entitled to declaration that policy contrary to law.

c A bench of magistrates adopted a policy of withholding the names of justices during the hearing of cases and from the public and press after cases were heard. In accordance with that policy the clerk to the justices refused to disclose to the applicant, a journalist who was writing an article on a case decided by the bench, the names of the chairman and other justices who had heard that case. The applicant applied for an order of mandamus *d* directing the clerk to disclose the identities of the justices and a declaration that the bench's policy of non-disclosure of justices' names was contrary to law.

Held – (1) The principle of open justice required that those who did justice should be known to the public and, accordingly, the power of magistrates to control their own proceedings did not entitle them to sit anonymously or to withhold their identity from *e* the public and press (see p 559 *c* to *e j* to p 560 *b* and p 561 *b* to *e*, post).

(2) The question whether a person had sufficient interest to bring an application for judicial review had to be decided by the court in its discretion on the facts of the particular application. In the circumstances the applicant had failed to show that he had a sufficient interest in the disclosure of the justices' names for the purpose of his article. It followed that he was not entitled on that ground to an order for mandamus. However, he had *f* sufficient interest because of the public interest in the maintenance and preservation of open justice in magistrates' courts, which was a matter of vital concern in the administration of justice, to seek a declaration. The declaration would accordingly be granted (see p 562 *g j* and p 563 *e* to *g*, post).

Notes

g For the reporting of criminal proceedings and the right of the public to attend, see 9 Halsbury's Laws (4th edn) para 13, and for cases on the subject, see 16 Digest (Reissue) 168–173, 1673–1724.

For locus standi necessary for persons seeking declarations, see 1 Halsbury's Laws (4th edn) 185–186.

h Cases referred to in judgments

A-G v Leveller Magazine Ltd [1979] 1 All ER 745, [1979] AC 440, [1979] 2 WLR 247, HL.
Gouriet v Union of Post Office Workers [1977] 3 All ER 70, [1978] AC 435, [1977] 3 WLR 300, HL.
IRC v National Federation of Self-Employed and Small Businesses Ltd [1981] 2 All ER 93, [1982] AC 617, [1981] 2 WLR 722, HL; *rvsg* [1980] 2 All ER 378, [1980] QB 407, *j* [1980] 2 WLR 579, CA.
R v Arundel Justices, ex p Westminster Press Ltd [1985] 2 All ER 390, [1985] 1 WLR 708, DC.
R v Central Criminal Court, ex p Crook (1984) Times, 8 November, DC.
R v Denbigh Justices, ex p Williams [1974] 2 All ER 1052, [1974] QB 759, [1974] 3 WLR 45, DC.

R v Horsham Justices, ex p Farquharson [1982] 2 All ER 269, [1982] QB 762, [1982] 2 WLR
430, DC and CA.
R v Reigate Justices, ex p Argus Newspapers and Larcombe (1983) 5 Cr App R (S) 181, DC.
Scott v Scott [1913] AC 417, [1911–13] All ER Rep 1, HL.

Cases also cited
Daubney v Cooper (1829) 10 B & C 237, 109 ER 438.
R v Altrincham Justices, ex p Pennington [1975] 2 All ER 78, [1975] QB 549, DC.
R v Lewes Prison Governor, ex p Doyle [1917] 2 KB 254, DC.
R v Russell, ex p Beaverbrook Newspapers Ltd [1968] 3 All ER 695, [1969] 1 QB 342, DC.
R v Sussex Justices, ex p McCarthy [1924] 1 KB 256, [1923] All ER Rep 233, DC.
Raybos Australia Pty Ltd v Jones [1985] 2 NSWLR 47, NSW CA.

Application for judicial review
By a notice of motion pursuant to RSC Ord 53 dated 17 July 1985 the applicants, David
Leigh and The Observer Ltd applied, with leave of Forbes J given on 19 July 1985, for
judicial review of a decision of the deputy clerk to the Felixstowe justices, made on
30 April 1985, to refuse to disclose to the applicants the identities of the justices who
heard the case of *R v Sangster and others* and the policy of the Felixstowe justices and their
clerk to withhold the names of justices during the hearing of cases from the public and
the press. The applicants sought (1) an order of mandamus directing the clerk to the
Felixstowe justices to disclose to the applicants the names of the chairman and of his or
her colleagues who tried the case of *R v Sangster* which concluded on 11 April 1985, (2) a
declaration that the policy of the Felixstowe justices and/or the clerk of the justices of
withholding as a matter of discretion or otherwise or exercising a discretion to withhold
from the press and the public the identity of justices hearing particular cases, was contrary
to law and (3) a declaration that the applicants were entitled to publish the identities of
the Felixstowe justices who heard the case of *R v Sangster*. The facts are set out in the
judgment of Watkins LJ.

Geoffrey Robertson for the applicants.
Andrew Marsden for the justices and their clerk.

Cur adv vult

7 October. The following judgments were delivered.

WATKINS LJ. The respondents to the application for judicial review which, with
leave, is before us, are the clerk and the deputy clerk respectively to the Felixstowe,
Ipswich and Woodbridge justices. It is made by the proprietors of one of the best-known
Sunday newspapers and the chief reporter on that newspaper, Mr David Leigh, who is a
very experienced and successful journalist, especially in the sphere of the criminal law,
about which he has written in books and reported on in countless cases heard in
magistrates' and higher courts in this country. The application is, he says, supported by
the National Union of Journalists which represents most court reporters in Great Britain,
and by the Guild of British Newspaper Editors which represents all editors of provincial
newspapers, and by the Society of British Editors which represents about 250 editors of
national newspapers and journals and editors working in television. For ease of reference
I shall refer to him hereafter as the applicant, on the understanding that he has his
employers with him in every sense in pursuit of the relief sought.
    That relief arises from a decision of the deputy clerk, on 30 April 1985, to refuse to
disclose to the applicant the identities of the justices who heard *R v Sangster* and the
policy of the justices who sit at Felixstowe, Ipswich and Woodbridge and their clerk to

withhold the names of justices during the hearing of cases, and afterwards, from the
a public and the press.

The applicant seeks an order of mandamus directing the clerk to disclose to him the
names of the chairman and the other justices who tried Sangster over two days ending
on 11 April 1985, and a declaration that the policy of the justices and the clerk as a matter
of discretion or otherwise to withhold from the public and the press the identity of
justices either hearing or who have heard cases is contrary to law.

b   The grounds relied on are (1) that the clerk was wrong in law in refusing to disclose to
the applicant in response to his bona fide inquiry the names of the justices who tried
Sangster so as to enable the applicant to exercise his right fully to report the case, (2) that
the policy of refusing to disclose the identities of justices is wrong in law and contrary to
the principle of open justice which, in the absence of statutory provision to the contrary,
requires the identity of justices as well as the proceedings over which they preside to be
c freely reportable, and (3) that the clerk's grounds set out in his letter to the applicant, of
3 May 1985, were unreasonable and not a justifiable departure from the 'open justice'
principle.

It is, I think, convenient to recite the contents of that letter now. It reads:

'Dear Mr. Leigh,
d   Thank you for your letter of 1st May. Mrs. Thew was perfectly correct in the
information that she gave you on the telephone recently.

It is, and has long been, the practice of each of the three Benches in this Clerkship
not to disclose the names of individual Magistrates who have adjudicated in a
particular case. I think perhaps you may have misunderstood Mrs. Thew when you
write that the decision was that of Captain Breene. It is not. It is merely an
e established practice of the Bench. I think also there is no law involved in the
decision. As far as I am aware there is no statute that says that names must be given
or that names may be withheld. It is a matter of practice.

The reason for the practice is twofold. Firstly, it protects the Magistrates from
unwanted approaches by members of the public. Magistrates as members of the
local community are particularly vulnerable. We have had cases locally where,
f following a decision where the Chairman's name has been reported, the Magistrate
concerned has been the subject of abusive telephone calls and letters.

It also protects Magistrates from approaches by the media. Magistrates take their
work seriously and are sensitive to attempts, often made, to turn their work into a
vehicle for media attention, trivialisation, sensationalism and the requirement of
instant wisdom. Magistrates would never comment on their decisions, their
g sentences or the reasons for them.

If, as in your newspaper's case, you are writing a serious article about some aspect
of the law, then the proper approach should be through the Clerk who is the
professional lawyer, and not through the lay Magistrate.

The second reason for the local practice of non disclosure is that a decision of a
Court is the collective decision of the Magistrates sitting. That being the case it is
h unnecessary to single out a particular Magistrate for attention. Each Bench of
Magistrates has its elected Chairman. He or she is the proper spokesperson for the
Magistrates and, certainly in the first instance, enquiries should be directed through
him or her if not the Clerk.

So far as the case to which you refer is concerned, I was approached by a reporter
from the Daily Telegraph who requested the name of the Chairman sitting in Court.
j I declined to give that information saying that it was a policy of the Felixstowe
Bench. I certainly did not say it was for security reasons, although that is how it was
reported. I am not aware, of course, what discussion he may have had with the
Court usher.

I hope this information is of assistance to you. If you think that I can be of further
help, please let me know.'

In his affidavit, the clerk contends that the applicant has no interest in the decision to withhold the names of justices in *R v Sangster* which entitles him to the relief sought and that this court is being asked to pronounce unlawful a matter on which the law is silent. The policy of the justices allows them a lawful discretion, taking account of circumstances, either to disclose or to withhold their names. Furthermore, it is not shown that anyone has been prejudiced by the decision not to reveal in *R v Sangster*.

The *Sangster* case was widely reported at the time it was heard, but not by the applicant. The facts were unusual. Six adults were accused of gross indecency with a 12-month-old child in a bath. Four of them were convicted and fined. During the hearing, when the justices were presumably advised by their clerk, an order was made under s 39 of the Children and Young Persons Act 1933 restricting publication of particulars calculated to lead to identification of the child. No one challenged the order during the proceedings. But a breach of it by two newspapers was suggested, if not alleged, by counsel appearing for the defendants at the beginning of the second day. He asked the press to exercise restraint in future reporting and for some sort of investigation by the police into newspaper reports already made. Whereupon the chairman of the bench, according to the clerk's affidavit, said:

> 'We take note of your remarks. We are concerned with the reporting. The Bench would expect a full investigation to take place.'

No one, says the clerk, asked for the names of the justices save one member of the press, a Daily Telegraph reporter we were told, who, when the justices were in their retiring room during the second day, asked the clerk for the name of the chairman. The clerk refused to give it, saying it was not the practice of the bench to disclose names. No more was heard of that. Reports in newspapers to the effect that it was for security reasons that the chairman declined to be named were, his clerk asserts, erroneous.

The applicant in his affidavit informs us that on reading reports of this extraordinary case he was struck by the wide variation in the interpretation of the effect of the order made under s 39. Obviously, newspapers had received contrasting legal advice on it from lawyers. So he decided to write an article about the case 'and the legal confusion surrounding the reporting of it'. He goes on in his affidavit to say:

> 'I wished to examine, inter alia, the appropriateness of the Magistrate's remarks on sentencing, the propriety of imposing a Section 39 Order in the first place, the differences of legal opinion as to its effect, the Chairman's decision to demand a police enquiry into the conduct of certain national newspapers, and the Chairman's reported decision to withhold his or her name "for security reasons" which plainly did not exist.'

On 1 May 1985 the applicant wrote to the clerk stating that the Observer proposed to publish an article in which reference would be made to the disputes over interpretation of the order made forbidding identification of the baby in the recent 'baby in the bath case'. He referred to what Mrs Thew, the deputy clerk, had told him over the telephone on 30 April about the policy of the bench not to disclose their own names. The reply was the letter of 3 May, the contents of which I have already read.

On 22 May the applicant wrote to the clerk stating that consideration was being given to testing the lawfulness of the practice of non-disclosure. He queried, inter alia, the origins of the policy. The respondents' solicitors replied to that in a later letter on 7 June, stating:

> 'Dear Mr. Leigh,
>
> RE:—FELIXSTOWE MAGISTRATES
> Thank you for your letter of 25th May. I have perused the correspondence and discussed the matter with the Clerk to the Felixstowe Bench. I hope that the following information answers the queries which you raise. (1) Mr. Wain has

a adopted a practice for himself and his staff that Magistrates' names, addresses and telephone numbers are not released to members of the public who make such requests to his office and staff. The reason for this is set out in Mr. Wain's letter of 3rd May. It is a practice which pre-dates Mr. Wain's clerkship. (2) It is an extension of the above practice that Magistrates' names are not exhibited outside the Court Rooms in which the Magistrates are sitting and are not endorsed upon Court lists.

b (3) If a party to any proceedings before the Court makes a request for release of the names of the individual Magistrates who are dealing with the case in which he or she is involved, the request is placed before the individual Magistrates concerned who decide whether to disclose their individual names to the party requesting it. Each request is dealt with on its own merits and frequently the names are disclosed. The most usual reason for a request in these circumstances is so that the person requesting the information can be satisfied that he does not know the individual

c Magistrates who are adjudicating. (4) Although individual Magistrates are aware of the practice of their Clerk's office, no policy decision has been made or recorded by the Bench. As the practice of the Court Clerks relating to the Felixstowe, Ipswich and Woodbridge Benches is being brought into question by your newspaper, the Clerk will suggest to each Bench that at their next meeting they consider whether the Clerk's present practice should continue or be changed. (5) It is fair to say that

d local reporters recognise individual Magistrates and on occasions in the local newspapers report the name of the Chairman sitting in Court. It is as a result of such a report that the example given in the third paragraph of Mr. Wain's letter of 3rd May arose. We trust that the above information answers the queries raised in your letter of 22nd May.'

e An extraordinary meeting of the Felixstowe bench took place on 5 August 1985. The clerk explained that the practice of non-disclosure was not absolute. The names of the adjudicating justices would frequently be given to defending advocates, and from time to time prosecuting solicitors and there were cases where they would be given to the press. It was a matter of discretion in every case.

It was there and then resolved:

f   '(a) to support the refusal to give the identities of the Justices adjudicating in the indecency case i) at the time of the hearing by Mr. Wain, ii) on the 30th April by Mrs. Thew. (b) to ratify the past practice that had been applied to the Felixstowe Bench for the last eight or nine years in exercising discretion in the disclosure of Justices' names. (c) The Justices further decided that if a request was made for the identity of the Justices *during the court hearing* the request should be conveyed to the

g   Justices who would communicate or answer either directly or through the clerk of the court. (d) If the request was made *before or after the court hearing* the decision would be within the discretion of the Clerk to the Justices, or in his or her absence, the Deputy Clerk to the Justices, or the Principal Assistant. In exercising that discretion the Clerk, or his Deputy, or Principal Assistant, would take into account all the surrounding circumstances, including the nature of the case, the length of

h time that had elapsed since the hearing, who made the request and the purpose to which the information was to be put. In exercising the discretion, the Clerk may refer the matter to the Justices concerned. (e) That the name of only the Chairman of the Court would not be disclosed. If disclosure was agreed, the names of all the Justices would be given. (f) The name of the Chairman of the Bench would be

j available to enquirers.'

The policy to withhold the names of justices originated in 1976 in circumstances explained in his affidavit by Mr Sharpe, the then clerk to the Ipswich justices. He became clerk in 1953. In 1978 he became clerk to the amalgamated benches of Ipswich, Felixstowe, Orwell and Woodbridge. He says that in 1976 one of the Ipswich justices was involved in an incident when sentencing a man. Afterwards the justice, whose affidavit fully explains the circumstances which appear not to merit any kind of criticism of him, *a* received abusive telephone calls which upset him very much. He discussed the matter with his fellow justices who agreed on a policy of their names not being disclosed. This policy was continued on the amalgamation of the benches.

This policy has been adopted in ten other magistrates' courts in various parts of the country and partially adopted in a few others. Adoption of it is said to be on the increase. The Law Society has expressed its apprehension about it. *b*

In July 1985 the Council of the Magistrates' Association passed the following resolution:

'It does not appear necessary, and will frequently be impracticable, for the names of adjudicating magistrates to be publicly listed before courts sit. The names of adjudicating magistrates should normally be available on request by persons having a bona fide interest (e.g. prosecutor or defendant or their legal representatives or *c* press representatives) during or after proceedings in court but there will be a small number of occasions when it will be in the interests of justice for the names to be withheld. Names should be withheld where there are substantial grounds for belief that the magistrates concerned, or members of their families, or other associates might in consequence of the proceedings be subject to violence or harassment. Examples are where defendants are believed to be members of terrorist groups, or *d* of other organisations habitually using violence or harassment to achieve or publicise their objectives.'

The Council of the Justices' Clerks' Society agrees broadly speaking with that. The Press Council has expressed the view that, except where there are substantial fears of harassment, the names of justices should be publicly known.

A large majority of clerks to justices say that it is the practice in their courts to follow *e* the guidance in the resolution of July 1985.

On 24 February 1981 the Secretary of Commissions, Lord Chancellor's Department, wrote to the National Council of Civil Liberties as follows:

'I am replying on behalf of the Lord Chancellor to your letter to him of 16 February, regarding a list of magistrates who serve on the County of Kent *f* Commission of the Peace. There is no statutory provision either prohibiting or requiring the publication of the names of Justices of the Peace. A general list of local justices is normally available at any courthouse, and the only reason why the identity of justices in a particular area might not be revealed to a person or organisation would normally be a risk that the information was required in order to facilitate harassment, intimidation or other threats or dangers to the magistrates concerned. *g* Such a problem sometimes arises in a particular case, where a dissatisfied litigant seeks personal retribution against the Bench concerned. In short, therefore, any person or body should be entitled to know the identity of the members of the local magistracy, unless there is some manifest reason in the public interest to refuse it in the particular case.'

h

On 9 April 1986 the applicant's solicitors wrote to the respondents' solicitors, stating:

'Our clients take the view that the resolution of the Magistrates' Association expresses a perfectly satisfactory principle which is consistent with the law and which, they feel, all magistrates should accept. If your clients were able to adopt the Magistrates' Association resolution it would seem that these proceedings would no longer serve any useful purpose. We are therefore instructed to write to ask you *j* whether you are able to confirm on behalf of your clients that they accept the policy contained in the Magistrates' Association resolution and are prepared to give an undertaking that they will continue to abide by it. On this basis we believe that the present proceedings could be terminated.'

In reply the respondents' solicitors took issue with the interpretation of the resolution and went on to state:

'It was quite clear that the Felixstowe Justices were unanimous in supporting the refusal to give the Justices' names in the *Sangster* case and that forms the substance of these proceedings. It is also fair to say that the Respondents to these proceedings are the Clerk and Deputy Clerk and they are not in a position themselves either to adopt the Magistrates' Association Resolution or reject it.'

So it is clear that the Felixstowe justices and their clerk are not going to be guided by the resolution of the Magistrates' Association.

Before turning to deal with the issues and the submissions of counsel on them, it is of interest to record what has been said by the Home Office Working Party on Magistrates' Courts on the subject of publication of justices' names. In their fifteenth report in September 1984, it is stated:

'The Working Party has been made aware of increasing pressures upon courts to publish the names of Justices who have adjudicated in particular cases. Although this may not present problems in certain rural areas where local justices are normally well known, it can lead to threats being made against justices in other areas. It is understood that the Lord Chancellor's policy is that if a bona fide press reporter requires a justice's name there is not normally any objection to it being given, but it should not be given to a defendant. It is felt by the Working Party that there is no general right to know the names and addresses of justices; if a person requires a justice, for instance to witness a signature, he should be advised to attend at the office of the justices' clerk.'

And in their sixteenth report in August 1985:

'In response to a question from a clerk as to whether the names and addresses of justices should be given to a solicitor with no particular legal reason for the information, the Working Party agreed the information should not be given. In discussion of this question attention was drawn to recent correspondence from the Law Society in which, whilst the justices' desire in view of recent events to remain anonymous was understood, it was maintained that there were cases where the names of the justices concerned should be known to solicitors for a number of reasons. In view of the conflicting opinions expressed both in the Working Party and elsewhere it is hoped that guidance will be given by the Home Office and/or Lord Chancellor's Department.'

No guidance on the subject has been given by the Home Office or the Lord Chancellor's Department.

There is no doubt in my mind that the policy of the Felixstowe justices as originally and most recently stated is highly controversial. It is of acute concern to the press, the more so because it is being adopted in an increasing number of other magistrates' courts and it introduces into the realm of public justice a previously unheard of anonymity of a number of those who have taken an oath to discharge it. It is a unique anonymity in discharge of the judicial function, in my experience.

The applicant contends that (1) the general rule that justice must be administered in public in order to allow of scrutiny of the behaviour of those who sit in judgment demands that their identity be known by notice outside the court room or made available on proper inquiry, (2) the right of the press to publish fair and accurate reports of proceedings cannot properly be exercised unless it includes a right to know the justices' names and their clerk has a duty to supply that information to bona fide members of the press, (3) justices have a statutory duty to sit in public at a known time and place, (4) the subordinate policy of the clerks to the Felixstowe justices to refuse to disclose the identity of justices was in this case unlawful, in that no reasonable clerk to justices could have made it and on the occasion in question there were no exceptional circumstances which *a* could be said to justify refusal, (5) the refusal to disclose and the general policy it arose from failed to take account of the open justice principle and public interest in court proceedings, and took account of such irrelevant matters as the possibility of personal embarrassment to the chairman, the standards of court reporting, the possibility of unwelcome approaches to justices and the desire to emphasise that decision-making is collective, (6) it cannot be a matter for the discretion of justices to decide whether or not *b* to disclose their identities. In so far as their clerk may have a discretion to decide on the bona fides of an inquirer that decision is reviewable on general principles by this court.

The basic proposition argued for by counsel for the respondents is that under the common law justices have power to control proceedings in their own courts: see *A-G v Leveller Magazine Ltd* [1979] 1 All ER 745, [1979] AC 440 and *R v Denbigh Justices, ex p Williams* [1974] 2 All ER 1052, [1974] QB 759. In controlling their own proceedings *c* justices may, for good reasons, choose to remain anonymous. No statute, rule or convention demands that they may not refuse to disclose identity. It would, he said, be irresponsible to deny this discretion to justices, seeing that some are exposed to improper behaviour by or on behalf of those they have adjudicated on and others, at times, wrongly approached by the press.

It is not, he maintains, the respondents' policy generally to refuse bona fide requests *d* for disclosure of the names of justices. If there is no discretion, how, he asks, is the request from the malicious or the malevolent inquirer to be dealt with? How can the fears of justices of wrongful approaches being made to them be allayed? The applicant has lost nothing by being denied the name of the chairman and has not, he submits, said what benefit to him or to anyone would arise from knowing it. Counsel also submitted, surprisingly I thought, that there was something to be said for withholding the names of *e* justices prior to a hearing so that the prosecution be denied the opportunity of choosing which court they would like to hear a particular case.

The role of the journalist and his importance for the public interest in the administration of justice has been commented on on many occasions. No one nowadays surely can doubt that his presence in court for the purpose of reporting proceedings *f* conducted therein is indispensable. Without him, how is the public to be informed of how justice is being administered in our courts? The journalist has been engaged on this task in much the same way as he performs it today for well over 150 years. In her work, *Justice and Journalism* (1971) p 24, Marjorie Jones, making a study of the influence of newspaper reporting on the administration of justice by magistrates, stated, having referred to a case decided in 1831: *g*

> 'The same ruling that excluded the attorney admitted the newspaper reporter. The journalist entered, and has remained, in magistrates' courts as a member of the public making notes. The constant presence of newspaper men in magistrates' courts provided not only a record of the proceedings but also a means of communication with the public. Through newspaper reports magistrates had access *h* to a wider audience beyond the justice room or the police office. Communication is particularly important for deterrent sentencing, which requires that potential offenders shall be aware of the punishment they are likely to incur.'

Later in her study, she recorded that in Dickens's time journalists were the only impartial observers who sat regularly in magistrates' courts, day after day, week after week, month after month. In the provinces, particularly, the same reporter might often *j* cover the local courts for year after year. These men regarded themselves as representing the absent public. And they were the first to concern themselves with the defence of the defenceless in the summary courts.

Lord Denning in *The Road to Justice* (1955) p 64 stated with regard to the free press:

a
'. . . a newspaper reporter is in every court. He sits through the dullest cases in the Court of Appeal and the most trivial cases before the magistrates. He says nothing but writes a lot. He notes all that goes on and makes a fair and accurate report of it. He supplies it for use either in the national press or in the local press according to the public interest it commands. He is, I verily believe, the watchdog of justice. If he is to do his work properly and effectively we must hold fast to the principle that every case must be heard and determined in open court. It must not take place

b
behind locked doors. Every member of the public must be entitled to report in the public press all that he has seen and heard. The reason for this rule is the very salutary influence which publicity has for those who work in the light of it. The judge will be careful to see that the trial is fairly and properly conducted if he realises that any unfairness or impropriety on his part will be noted by those in court and may be reported in the press. He will be more anxious to give a correct decision if

c
he knows that his reasons must justify themselves at the bar of public opinion.'

Those observations suffice to emphasise to the mind of anyone the vital significance of the work of the journalist in reporting court proceedings and, within the bounds of impartiality and fairness, commenting on the decision of judges and justices and their behaviour in and conduct of the proceedings. If someone in the seat of justice misconducts

d
himself or is worthy of praise, is the public disentitled at the whim of that person to know his identity?

It must ever be borne in mind that save on rare occasions when a court is entitled to sit in camera, it must sit in public. The principle of open justice has been well established for a very long time. This principle was commenced on by Lord Diplock in *A-G v Leveller Magazine Ltd* [1979] 1 All ER 745 at 749–750, [1979] AC 440 at 449–450 as follows:

e
'. . . prima facie the interests of justice are served by its being administered in the full light of publicity. As a general rule the English system of administering justice does require that it be done in public: *Scott v Scott* [1913] AC 417, [1911–13] All ER Rep 1. If the way that courts behave cannot be hidden from the public ear and eye this provides a safeguard against judicial arbitrariness or idiosyncrasy and maintains the public confidence in the administration of justice. The application of this

f
principle of open justice has two aspects: as respects proceedings in the court itself it requires that they should be held in open court to which the Press and public are admitted and that, in criminal cases at any rate, all evidence communicated to the court is communicated publicly. As respects the publication to a wider public of fair and accurate reports of proceedings that have taken place in court the principle requires that nothing should be done to discourage this. However, since the purpose

g
of the general rule is to serve the ends of justice it may be necessary to depart from it where the nature or circumstances of the particular proceeding are such that the application of the general rule in its entirety would frustrate or render impracticable the administration of justice or would damage some other public interest for whose protection Parliament has made some statutory derogation from the rule. Apart

h
from statutory exceptions, however, where a court in the exercise of its inherent power to control the conduct of proceedings before it departs in any way from the general rule, the departure is justified to the extent and to no more than the extent that the court reasonably believes it to be necessary in order to serve the ends of justice.'

j
It is particularly to be noted from those observations that not only must nothing be done to discourage the fair and accurate reporting of proceedings in court, but that no exercise of the inherent power of the court to control the conduct of proceedings must depart from the general rule of open justice to any greater extent than the court reasonably believes it necessary in order to serve the ends of justice. I do not myself see how it can properly be said that the ends of justice could in any respect be served by

justices withholding their names from the general public or at the very least from those
who essentially are concerned with the proceedings, namely the parties to them, their *a*
legal representatives and the press present in court to report those proceedings.

Whilst it is rightly said, as in this court one often hears it said, that justices have the
power to control the conduct of their own proceedings and to adopt policies with regard
to them, never before now, so far as I know, has it been suggested that such a power
includes so fundamental a matter as rendering anonymous the members of a magistrates'
court.   *b*

The function of justices and the importance they assume in the administration of
justice and our national life generally are too well recognised to require explanation in
this judgment. Suffice it to say that the office of justice of the peace is ancient and
honourable and indispensable to the needs of maintaining law and order and the doing
of justice generally. A justice of the peace is a known person. The Justices of the Peace
Act 1968, s 1(1) provided that with certain exceptions no one might become a justice *c*
unless appointed to the commission by name. Every justice using his or her name swears
on appointment an oath of allegiance and judicial oath. Section 121 of the Magistrates'
Courts Act 1980 makes provision for the constitution and place of sitting of magistrates'
courts. Justices must, it is provided, when conducting their business in a petty sessional
courthouse or on notice in an occasional courthouse, sit in open court subject to the
provisions of any enactment to the contrary.   *d*

It is well settled that a justice ought not to sit and adjudicate if some statutory
disqualification applies to him or he has some direct pecuniary interest in a case or is in
some way associated with a party to the proceedings or where he doubts his ability to be
impartial in the case to be heard or it be thought that a reasonable and a fair-minded
person knowing of the circumstances of the case might have a reasonable suspicion that
the justice was incapable of being impartial and of acting with appropriate detachment. *e*
Justices when they commence their duties are made aware of the likely situations in
which they should regard themselves as disqualified from sitting. But they cannot be
regarded as the only persons entitled to be judges of that. Others, including defendants
and their representatives, are entitled to object if it be felt that a justice who sits ought
not to because some element of disqualification exists. How can this right of objection *f*
be fully and properly exercised in all cases unless the identity of the justices is known at
least to all those taking part in the proceedings?

There is nowhere to be found any statutory provision or rule which entitles a justice
to anonymity in any circumstance. The naming of a justice is scarcely referred to in
legislation. I have found two instances of it. By s 8(4) of the Magistrates' Courts Act 1980
a report of committal proceedings may be published which contains the identity of the *g*
court and the names of the examining justices. Rule 36 of the Magistrates' Courts Rules
1981, SI 1981/552, provides that any record kept in pursuance of the rule in domestic
proceedings should indicate the names of the justices constituting the court by which a
decision was made.

So far as I have been able to ascertain, anonymity has never been claimed other than
by the number of justices I have mentioned by anyone who can be said to be a judicial or *h*
quasi-judicial person. This applies as much to High Court judges and circuit judges as to,
for example, members of tribunals. An inspector at a planning inquiry is by statutory
instrument disentitled from being anonymous. It would, I think, be thought outrageous
by trade unions and employers associations if they were not entitled to know the identity
of members of employment tribunals. Many of the persons I have mentioned are
subjected to criticism, vilification even at times, and suffer from being pestered by *j*
telephone and otherwise by persons who bear some grievance, and, moreover, occasionally
by being wrongly approached by the press. But such intrusions into their private lives
judges and others have inevitably to put up with as a tiresome if not worse incidence of
holding a judicial office. Consider too the position of jurors, interference with whom is

unhappily not unknown, especially these days. They are known persons. Their names
a are announced in open court before they take the oath.

I can easily understand that from time to time those justices who are subjected to
intolerable invasions of their privacy think that they ought to have some protection
against this form of unjustifiable behaviour.

However, whilst some forms of protection against intrusion into privacy are available
and often used where necessary, I do not see how in principle there can be any justification
b for a policy, the purpose of which is to keep secret the names of justices both when they
are sitting and afterwards. Collective responsibility is not, in my judgment, a good and
sufficient reason to defeat the principle which I believe to be that where open justice
prevails so shall those who do justice be known.

I would regard and I believe the general public likewise would regard a policy such as
that maintained by the Felixstowe justices and their clerk to be inimical to the proper
c administration of justice and an unwarranted and an unlawful obstruction to the right
to know who sits in judgment. There is, in my view, no such person known to the law
as the anonymous JP.

I do not for one moment suggest that the right to know involves the disclosure of any
more than the name of a justice. No one can demand the address and still less the
telephone number of a justice of the peace. Moreover, a clerk to justices would, it seems
d to me, act with justification in refusing during and after a hearing to give the name of
one of the justices to a person who the clerk reasonably believes requires that information
solely for a mischievous purpose. Save for such considerations as that, I would hold that
the bona fide inquirer is entitled to know the name of a justice who is sitting or who has
sat on a case recently heard.

I turn finally to the question of the applicant's locus standi. Leave to apply for judicial
e review was granted to the applicant by Forbes J at an ex parte hearing. His prima facie
view of standing is subject to a re-examination here of this question, in the light of the
fuller evidence and argument presented to us.

I take as my starting point the words of Lord Wilberforce in *IRC v National Federation
of Self-Employed and Small Businesses Ltd* (the *Fleet Street Casuals* case) [1981] 2 All ER 93 at
f 96, [1982] AC 617 at 630:

'There may be simple cases in which it can be seen at the earliest stage that the
person applying for judicial review has no interest at all, or no sufficient interest to
support the application; then it would be quite correct at the threshold to refuse
him leave to apply. The right to do so is an important safeguard against the courts
being flooded and public bodies harassed by irresponsible applications. But in other
g cases this will not be so. In these it will be necessary to consider the powers or the
duties in law of those against whom the relief is asked, the position of the applicant
in relation to those powers or duties, and the breach of those said to have been
committed. In other words, the question of sufficient interest cannot, in such cases,
be considered in the abstract, or as an isolated point: it must be taken together with
the legal and factual context. The rule requires sufficient interest *in the matter to
h which the application relates.*' (Lord Wilberforce's emphasis.)

Lord Scarman takes up the theme when he says ([1981] 2 All ER 93 at 113, [1982] AC
617 at 653):

'The sufficiency of the interest is, as I understand all your Lordships agree, a
mixed question of law and fact. The legal element in the mixture is less than the
j matters of fact and degree, but it is important, as setting the limits within which,
and the principles by which, the discretion is to be exercised.'

Later, Lord Scarman refers to the words of Lord Wilberforce in *Gouriet v Union of Post
Office Workers* [1977] 3 All ER 70 at 84, [1978] AC 435 at 482:

'. . . where he stated the modern position in relation to prerogative orders: "These are often applied for by individuals and the courts have allowed them liberal access *a* under a generous conception of locus standi." '

Lord Scarman goes on ([1982] 2 All ER 93 at 113, [1982] AC 617 at 653):

'The one legal principle, which is implicit in the case law and accurately reflected in the rules of court, is that in determining the sufficiency of an applicant's interest it is necessary to consider the matter to which the application relates. It is wrong in *b* law, as I understand the cases, for the court to attempt an assessment of the sufficiency of an applicant's interest without regard to the matter of his complaint.'

This applicant, I repeat, seeks from this court twofold relief, in the form of (1) an order for mandamus directing the clerk to reveal to the applicant the names of the justices who tried Sangster and (2) a declaration that the policy of the Felixstowe justices and/or of the *c* clerk (whether by discretion or otherwise) of withholding from the press and public the identity of the justices who hear particular cases is contrary to law. I should add here that at the hearing before us the applicant did not pursue, because of the staleness of the matter, a further declaration, originally sought, that he was entitled to publish the identities of the justices who tried Sangster.

The respondents' counsel did not dispute that in both the extant applications the *d* defendants, their legal representatives and press reporters in court at the time of the trial would have had locus standi. Indeed, we were referred by him, inter alia, to a number of recent applications for judicial review in which the press (under different guises) present in court were either held or assumed to have had sufficient interest in the challenge made by them to decisions of or rulings by justices in court (see *R v Horsham Justices, ex p Farquharson* [1982] 2 All ER 269, [1982] QB 762 (local newspaper proprietor and *e* journalist inter alios), *R v Reigate Justices, ex p Argus Newspapers and Larcombe* (1983) 5 Cr App R (S) 181 (newspaper publisher and editor) and *R v Arundel Justices, ex p Westminster Press Ltd* [1985] 2 All ER 390, [1985] 1 WLR 708 (newspaper proprietor whose deponents were a crime reporter and a news editor)). Also worthy of mention in this connection is the part played by a journalist in *R v Central Criminal Court, ex p Crook* (1984) Times, 8 November. *f*

How then is the sufficiency of the applicant's interest in the matter of each of the applications to be judged? I do not find it necessary for the purposes of this judgment to decide, as was urged on us by counsel for the respondents, whether or not a stricter test of sufficient interest still applies for the issue of mandamus, beyond saying that I am inclined to think it does not. The appropriate approach in this case, it seems to me, is for the court, in using what I regard as its undoubted discretion, to decide the question of *g* sufficient interest on each application primarily within its factual context.

It will be recalled that the applicant had not been present in court during the Sangster trial. His initial inquiry about the case to the clerk to the justices was made by telephone to his deputy on 30 April, some three weeks after the end of the trial. As I have already said, it was the applicant's intention to write an article for his newspaper commenting on certain aspects of the case, including the already reported decision by or on behalf of the *h* chairman of the Bench trying the case to refuse to divulge his name to a Daily Telegraph reporter at the court. The applicant's aim, it is clear, was not to report the case; it was to comment on various issues arising out of reports by others of the case. In particular, he wished to expose the apparent confusion amongst some newspapers over the effect of the court's order made under s 39 of the Children and Young Persons Act 1933 on the reporting of the case itself. *j*

It does not seem to me that within the ambit of that endeavour the identity of the justices themselves was essential, or even material. For these reasons the applicant, in my judgment, has failed to show that he has a sufficient interest in the disclosure of the justices' names for this purpose. It therefore follows that he is not entitled on that ground to the order for mandamus.

a Do different considerations apply to the application for the declaration in which it is sought to challenge the lawfulness of the policy of the justices and their clerk? I think they do. I have already emphasised the importance to the community at large of open justice and the role of the press as guardian and watchdog of the public interest in this matter, especially in magistrates' courts. Within the context of the administration of justice as a whole, the policy of routine non-disclosure adopted by the Felixstowe Bench and their clerk, shared in one form or another by a growing number of justices elsewhere,
b raises a matter of national importance.

Counsel for the respondents has argued vigorously that the class of interested persons in both these applications should be restricted at most to those persons present in court and that, since the applicant was not so present, he lacks the necessary standing before us. His position, it is argued, is comparable to that of a 'pressure group', a phrase employed in this context by Lord Diplock in the *Fleet Street Casuals* case [1981] 2 All ER 93 at 107,
c [1982] AC 617 at 644 in a much-quoted passage:

> 'It would, in my view, be a grave lacuna in our system of public law if a pressure group, like the federation, or even a single public spirited taxpayer, were prevented by outdated technical rules of locus standi from bringing the matter to the attention of the court to vindicate the rule of law and get the unlawful conduct stopped.'

d Counsel for the respondents, however, urges us not to be influenced by that view which, he says, is not characteristic of the more conservative stance of the majority of their Lordships' speeches in that case. I am conscious of that but nothing in those speeches, accepting all the cautionary words contained in them, opposes, I think, the view that the court has a large measure of discretion in determining whether sufficient interest has been established.

e The application before this court seems to me to be brought either by the applicant himself, or possibly by the press through him, as guardian of the public interest in the maintenance and preservation of open justice in magistrates' courts, a matter of vital concern in the administration of justice.

In the context of the unlawful use of power without jurisdiction, which I take the
f policy of the Felixstowe justices and their clerk to be, I feel that a 'public spirited citizen' (see Lord Denning MR in the *Fleet Street Casuals* case [1980] 2 All ER 378 at 390, [1980] QB 407 at 422, echoed by Lord Diplock in the passage quoted above), would have a sufficient interest in the matter of the declaration sought by this applicant. I would so regard him at the very least as such a person.

No one has contended that he has acted as a mere busybody in coming to this court to
g ask for the relief he seeks. The seriousness of his purpose is apparent. I think he has a sufficient interest in the matter of the application. Accordingly, I would grant him the declaration sought.

RUSSELL J. I agree.

h **MANN J.** I agree.

Declaration granted ; order of mandamus refused.

Solicitors: *Bindman & Partners* (for the applicants); *Westhorp Ward & Catchpole*, Ipswich (for the respondents).

j

Dilys Tausz   Barrister.

R v Panel on Take-overs and Mergers, ex parte Datafin plc and another (Norton Opax plc and another intervening)

COURT OF APPEAL, CIVIL DIVISION

SIR JOHN DONALDSON MR, LLOYD AND NICHOLLS LJJ

25, 26, 27 NOVEMBER, 1, 5 DECEMBER 1986

Judicial review – Availability of remedy – Take-over Panel – Panel on Take-overs and Mergers a self-regulating unincorporated association operating City Code on Take-overs and Mergers – Whether panel performing public duty – Whether panel amenable to public law remedies – Whether panel's decisions subject to judicial review.

The Panel on Take-overs and Mergers was a self-regulating unincorporated association which devised and operated the City Code on Take-overs and Mergers prescribing a code of conduct to be observed in the take-overs of listed public companies. The panel had no direct statutory, prerogative or common law powers, nor were its powers based solely on consensus, but they were supported and sustained by certain statutory powers and penalties introduced after the inception of the panel. In the course of a contested take-over for a company (M), the applicants and another company (NO) mounted rival bids and at a critical time in the bidding an investment institution (KIO) purchased shares in M at a price above the maximum which, under the terms of the code, NO was permitted pay. KIO subsequently committed those shares to NO's offer. The applicants complained to the panel that NO and KIO had acted 'in concert', contrary to the terms of the code, because KIO was one of the core underwriters to NO's bid and had a significant interest in the success of NO's bid because its underwriting fee was directly related to the success or failure of the bid. The panel rejected the applicants' complaint. The applicants sought leave to apply for judicial review of the panel's decision but leave was refused on the ground that the court had no jurisdiction to entertain the application. The applicants appealed to the Court of Appeal. On the hearing of the appeal, the panel contended (i) that the supervisory jurisdiction of the court was confined to bodies whose power derived solely from legislation or the exercise of the prerogative, and that therefore judicial review did not extend to a body such as the panel, and (ii) that applications to the court in the middle of take-over bids would create delay and uncertainty when it was essential that there should be speed, certainty and finality in rulings affecting financial dealings.

Held – (1) In determining whether the decisions of a particular body were subject to judicial review, the court was not confined to considering the source of that body's powers and duties but could also look to their nature. Accordingly, if the duty imposed on a body, whether expressly or by implication, was a public duty and the body was exercising public law functions the court had jurisdiction to entertain an application for judicial review of that body's decisions. Having regard to the wide-ranging nature and importance of the matters covered by the City Code on Take-overs and Mergers and to the public consequences of non-compliance with the code, the Panel on Take-overs and Mergers was performing a public duty when prescribing and administering the code and its rules and was subject to public law remedies. Accordingly, an application for judicial review of its decisions would lie in an appropriate case (see p 577 *a* to *d*, p 581 *h j*, p 582 *d e j*, p 583 *d f g*, p 584 *e h j*, p 585 *g* and p 587 *e f*, post); *R v Criminal Injuries Compensation Board, ex p Lain* [1967] 2 All ER 770, *O'Reilly v Mackman* [1982] 3 All ER 680, *R v BBC, ex p Lavelle* [1983] 1 All ER 241, *Council of Civil Service Unions v Minister for the Civil Service* [1984] 3 All ER 935 and *Gillick v West Norfolk and Wisbech Area Health Authority* [1985] 1 All ER 533 considered.

(2) Since an applicant for judicial review of a decision of the panel was required under
a RSC Ord 53 to obtain leave before applying, the court could, by refusing to entertain an
unmeritorious application made merely as a tactic in a take-over battle, ensure that its
jurisdiction was not used to frustrate the purpose for which the panel existed. The court
could meet the need for speed and finality by restricting the grant of certiorari and
mandamus to cases where there had been a breach of natural justice and by allowing
contemporary decisions of the panel to take their course in all other cases and considering
b the complaint and intervening, if at all, later and in retrospect by means of declaratory
orders which would enable the panel not to repeat any error and would relieve individuals
of the disciplinary consequences of any erroneous finding of breach of the code (see p 578
g h, p 579 *h* to p 580 *a*, p 581 *h*, p 582 *g* to *j* and p 585 *g*, post).
    (3) The applicants' application for leave to apply for judicial review would be refused
since on the facts there had been no illegality, irrationality or procedural impropriety in
c the decision of the panel, which had correctly approached the matter on the basis of the
code's definition of acting 'in concert' (see p 580 *g* to p 581 *b f* to *h*, p 585 *g* and p 587 *h j*,
post); dictum of Lord Diplock in *Council of Civil Service Unions v Minister for the Civil
Service* [1984] 3 All ER at 950–951 applied.
    Per curiam. The fact that the City Code on Take-overs and Mergers deals largely with
general principles means that it is unlikely that the panel could be accused of acting ultra
d vires (see p 579 *a* to *c*, p 581 *h* and p 585 *g*, post).

Notes
For the City Take-over Code and the Panel on Take-overs and Mergers, see 7 Halsbury's
Laws (4th edn) paras 790–794.

e **Cases referred to in judgments**
Council of Civil Service Unions v Minister for the Civil Service [1984] 3 All ER 935, [1985] AC
    374, [1984] 3 WLR 1174, HL.
Czarnikow v Roth Schmidt & Co [1922] 2 KB 478, [1922] All ER Rep 45, CA.
Gillick v West Norfolk and Wisbech Area Health Authority [1985] 3 All ER 402, [1986] AC
    112, [1985] 3 WLR 830, HL.
f *IRC v National Federation of Self-Employed and Small Businesses* [1981] 2 All ER 93, [1982]
    AC 617, [1981] 2 WLR 722, HL.
O'Reilly v Mackman [1982] 3 All ER 680, [1983] 2 AC 237, [1982] 3 WLR 604, QBD and
    CA; *affd* [1982] 3 All ER 1124, [1983] 2 AC 237, [1982] 3 WLR 1096, HL.
R v BBC, ex p Lavelle [1983] 1 All ER 241, [1983] 1 WLR 23.
R v Boycott, ex p Kearley [1939] 2 All ER 626, [1939] 2 KB 651.
g *R v Criminal Injuries Compensation Board, ex p Lain* [1967] 2 All ER 770, [1967] 2 QB 864,
    [1967] 3 WLR 348, DC.
*R v Disputes Committee of the National Joint Council for the Craft of Dental Technicians, ex p
    Neate* [1953] 1 All ER 327, [1953] 1 QB 704, [1953] 2 WLR 342, DC.
R v Industrial Court, ex p ASSET [1964] 3 All ER 130, [1965] 1 QB 377, [1964] 3 WLR
    680, DC.
h *R v Monopolies and Mergers Commission, ex p Argyll Group plc* [1986] 2 All ER 257, [1986]
    1 WLR 763, CA.
R v Postmaster General, ex p Carmichael [1928] 1 KB 291.

Cases also cited
Clifford and O'Sullivan, Re [1921] 2 AC 570, HL.
j *Law v National Greyhound Racing Club Ltd* [1983] 3 All ER 300, [1983] 1 WLR 1302, CA.
Nagle v Feilden [1966] 1 All ER 689, [1966] 2 QB 633, CA.
R v Barnsley Metropolitan BC, ex p Hook [1976] 3 All ER 452, [1976] 1 WLR 1052, CA.
R v East Berkshire Health Authority, ex p Walsh [1984] 3 All ER 425, [1985] QB 152, CA.
R v Electricity Comrs, ex p London Electricity Joint Committee Co (1920) Ltd [1924] 1 KB 171,
    CA.

R v Post Office, ex p Byrne [1975] ICR 221, DC.
R v Roupell (1776) 2 Cowp 458, 98 ER 1185.   *a*
R v Senate of University of Aston, ex p Roffey [1969] 2 All ER 964, [1969] 2 QB 538, DC.
Ridge v Baldwin [1963] 2 All ER 66, [1964] AC 40, HL.

Appeal and application for judicial review
The applicants, Datafin plc and Prudential-Bache Securities Inc of New York, appealed
against the decision of Hodgson J made on 25 November 1986 refusing the applicants *b*
leave to apply for judicial review of a decision of the respondent, the Panel on Take-overs
and Mergers, made on 24 November 1986 under the City Code on Take-overs and
Mergers to the effect that an offer by the intervener, Norton Opax plc, supported by the
second intervener, Samuel Montagu & Co Ltd, for the issued ordinary share capital of
McCorquodale plc had become unconditional. The Court of Appeal granted leave and
heard the substantive application for judicial review itself. The facts are set out in the *c*
judgment of Sir John Donaldson MR.

Jeremy Lever QC and *Derrick Turriff* for the applicants.
Robert Alexander QC, Timothy Lloyd QC and *Keith Rowley* for the panel.
Jonathan Sumption QC and *Stephen Richards* for Norton Opax plc and Samuel Montagu &
  Co Ltd.   *d*

Cur adv vult

5 December. The following judgments were delivered.

SIR JOHN DONALDSON MR. The Panel on Take-overs and Mergers is a truly
remarkable body. Perched on the 20th floor of the Stock Exchange building in the City *e*
of London, both literally and metaphorically it oversees and regulates a very important
part of the United Kingdom financial market. Yet it performs this function without
visible means of legal support.
  The panel is an unincorporated association without legal personality and, so far as can
be seen, has only about 12 members. But those members are appointed by and represent *f*
the Accepting Houses Committee, the Association of Investment Trust Companies, the
Association of British Insurers, the Committee of London and Scottish Bankers, the
Confederation of British Industry, the Council of the Stock Exchange, the Institute of
Chartered Accountants in England and Wales, the Issuing Houses Association, the
National Association of Pension Funds, the Financial Intermediaries Managers and
Brokers Regulatory Association, and the Unit Trust Association, the chairman and deputy
chairman being appointed by the Bank of England. Furthermore, the panel is supported *g*
by the Foreign Bankers in London, the Foreign Brokers in London and the Consultative
Committee of Accountancy Bodies.
  It has no statutory, prerogative or common law powers and it is not in contractual
relationship with the financial market or with those who deal in that market. According
to the introduction to the City Code on Take-overs and Mergers, which it promulgates: *h*

  'The Code has not, and does not seek to have, the force of law, but those who wish
  to take advantage of the facilities of the securities markets in the United Kingdom
  should conduct themselves in matters relating to take-overs according to the Code.
  Those who do not so conduct themselves cannot expect to enjoy those facilities and
  may find that they are withheld. The responsibilities described herein apply most
  directly to those who are actively engaged in all aspects of the securities markets, *j*
  but they are also regarded by the Panel as applying to directors of companies subject
  to the Code, to persons or groups of persons who seek to gain control (as defined) of
  such companies, and to all professional advisers (insofar as they advise on the
  transactions in question), even where they are not directly affiliated to the bodies

named in section 1(a). Equally, where persons other than those referred to above issue circulars to shareholders in connection with take-overs the Panel expects the highest standards of care to be observed. The provisions of the Code fall into two categories. On the one hand, the Code enunciates general principles of conduct to be observed in take-over transactions: these general principles are a codification of good standards of commercial behaviour and should have an obvious and universal application. On the other hand, the Code lays down a series of rules, some of which are no more than examples of the application of the general principles whilst others are rules of procedure designed to govern specific forms of take-over. Some of the general principles, based as they are upon a concept of equity between one shareholder and another, while readily understandable in the City and by those concerned with the securities markets generally, would not easily lend themselves to legislation. The Code is therefore framed in non-technical language (and is, primarily as a measure of self-discipline, administered and enforced by the Panel, a body representative of those using the securities markets and concerned with the observance of good business standards, rather than the enforcement of the law. As indicated above, the Panel executive is always available to be consulted and where there is doubt this should be done in advance of any action. Taking legal or other professional advice on matters of interpretation under the Code is not an appropriate alternative to obtaining a view or a ruling from the executive.'

'Self-regulation' is an emotive term. It is also ambiguous. An individual who voluntarily regulates his life in accordance with stated principles, because he believes that this is morally right and also, perhaps, in his own long-term interests, or a group of individuals who do so, are practising self-regulation. But it can mean something quite different. It can connote a system whereby a group of people, acting in concert, use their collective power to force themselves and others to comply with a code of conduct of their own devising. This is not necessarily morally wrong or contrary to the public interest, unlawful or even undesirable. But it is very different.

The panel is a self-regulating body in the latter sense. Lacking any authority de jure, it exercises immense power de facto by devising, promulgating, amending and interpreting the City Code on Take-overs and Mergers, by waiving or modifying the application of the code in particular circumstances, by investigating and reporting on alleged breaches of the code and by the application or threat of sanctions. These sanctions are no less effective because they are applied indirectly and lack a legally enforceable base. Thus, to quote again from the introduction to the code:

'If there appears to have been a material breach of the Code, the executive invites the person concerned to appear before the Panel for a hearing. He is informed by letter of the nature of the alleged breach and of the matters which the Director General will present. If any other matters are raised he is allowed to ask for an adjournment. If the Panel finds that there has been a breach, it may have recourse to private reprimand or public censure or, in a more flagrant case, to further action designed to deprive the offender temporarily or permanently of his ability to enjoy the facilities of the securities markets. The Panel may refer certain aspects of a case to the Department of Trade and Industry, The Stock Exchange or other appropriate body. No reprimand, censure or further action will take place without the person concerned having the opportunity to appeal to the Appeal Committee of the Panel.'

The unspoken assumption, which I do not doubt is a reality, is that the Department of Trade and Industry or, as the case may be, the Stock Exchange or other appropriate body would in fact exercise statutory or contractual powers to penalise the transgressors. Thus, for example, rr 22 to 24 of the Stock Exchange Rules provide for the severest penalties, up to and including expulsion, for acts of misconduct, and by r 23.1—

'Acts of misconduct may consist of any of the following . . . (g) Any action which has been found by the Panel on Take-overs and Mergers (including where reference *a* has been made to it, the Appeal Committee of the Panel) to have been in breach of The City Code on Take-overs and Mergers. The findings of the Panel, subject to any modification by the Appeal Committee of the Panel, shall not be re-opened in proceedings taken under Rules 22 to 24.'

The principal issue in this appeal, and the only issue which may matter in the longer *b* term, is whether this remarkable body is above the law. Its respectability is beyond question. So is its bona fides. I do not doubt for one moment that it is intended to and does operate in the public interest and that the enormously wide discretion which it arrogates to itself is necessary if it is to function efficiently and effectively. While not wishing to become involved in the political controversy on the relative merits of self-regulation and governmental or statutory regulation, I am content to assume for the *c* purposes of this appeal that self-regulation is preferable in the public interest. But that said, what is to happen if the panel goes off the rails? Suppose, perish the thought, that it were to use its powers in a way in which was manifestly unfair. What then? Counsel for the panel submits that the panel would lose the support of public opinion in the financial markets and would be unable to continue to operate. Further or alternatively, Parliament could and would intervene. Maybe, but how long would that take and who in the *d* meantime could or would come to the assistance of those who were being oppressed by such conduct?

A somewhat similar problem confronted the courts in 1922 when the Council of the Refined Sugar Association, a self-regulatory body for the sugar trade and no less respectable than the panel, made a rule which purported to preclude any trader from asking a trade arbitrator to state a case for the opinion of the court or from applying to *e* the court for an order that such a case be stated. The matter came before a Court of Appeal consisting of Bankes, Atkin and Scrutton LJJ in *Czarnikow v Roth Schmidt & Co* [1922] 2 KB 478, [1922] All ER Rep 45. The decision has no direct application to the present situation, because the court was concerned with the law of contract, but its approach was traditional, significant and, in the case of Scrutton LJ, colourful. This approach can be illustrated by brief quotations from the judgments. Bankes LJ said *f* ([1922] 2 KB 478 at 484, [1922] All ER Rep 45 at 48):

'To release real and effective control over commercial arbitrations is to allow the arbitrator, or the Arbitration Tribunal, to be a law unto himself, or themselves, to give him or them a free hand to decide according to law or not according to law as he or they think fit, in other words to be outside the law. At present no individual *g* or association is, so far as I am aware, outside the law except a trade union. To put such associations as the Refined Sugar Association in a similar position would in my opinion be against public policy. Unlimited power does not conduce to reasonableness of view or conduct.'

Scrutton LJ said ([1922] 2 KB 478 at 488, [1922] All ER Rep 45 at 50):

h

'In my view to allow English citizens to agree to exclude this safeguard for the administration of the law is contrary to public policy. There must be no Alsatia[1] in England where the King's writ does not run.'

Atkin LJ said ([1922] 2 KB 478 at 491, [1922] All ER Rep 45 at 51–52):

j

---

1   'Alsatias. The colloquial name (which first appears in Shadwell's plays in the time of Charles II) for recognized areas of sanctuary for criminals, survivals of the mediaeval sanctuaries, which lasted till the end of the seventeenth century in London. The one which gave its name to all the others was Alsatia or Whitefriars, between Fleet Street and the Thames, but the Southwark Mint, the Minories and other places were other convenient refuges for thieves . . .': *The Oxford Companion to Law* (1980) p 50

a
'I think that it is still a principle of English law that an agreement to oust the jurisdiction of the Courts is invalid . . . In the case of powerful associations such as the present, able to impose thier own arbitration clauses upon their members, and, by their uniform contract, conditions upon all non-members contracting with members, the result might be that in time codes of law would come to be administered in various trades differing substantially from the English mercantile law. The policy of the law has given to the High Court large powers over inferior

b
Courts for the very purpose of maintaining a uniform standard of justice and one uniform system of law . . . If an agreement to oust the common law jurisdiction of the Court is invalid every reason appears to me to exist for holding that an agreement to oust the Court of this statutory jurisdiction is invalid.'

Thus far I have made no mention of the facts underlying this application or of the
c parties, other than the panel. This is not accidental, but reflects the fact that the major issue of whether the courts of this country have any jurisdiction to control the activities of a body which de facto exercises what can only be characterised as powers in the nature of public law powers does not depend on those particular facts. Nor has the issue of jurisdiction vel non any connection with the quite distinct issue of how, in principle, the court should exercise any jurisdiction which it may have. The facts are only relevant to
d whether this is an appropriate case in which, in accordance with such general principles, to exercise any such jurisdiction. However, I should now remedy the deficiency.

The applicants for relief by way of judicial review are Datafin plc, an English company, and Prudential-Bache Securities Inc of New York. In addition there appear, as interveners, Norton Opax plc and Samuel Montagu & Co Ltd, their merchant bankers and financial advisers, both being English companies. Other members of the cast, albeit not parties to
e the proceedings, are Greenwell Montagu & Co Ltd, the stockbroking arm of Samuel Montagu. Laurence Prust, another stockbroker, the Kuwait Investment Office (KIO), a major investor in the United Kingdom financial market and McCorquodale plc, an English printing company, which was the target for the rival take-over bids which precipitated the present proceedings.

I can take the background facts from the paper prepared by the executive of the panel:

f
'2.1 In March 1986 Norton Opax made its original offer for McCorquodale, but the offer lapsed in April on reference to the Monopolies and Mergers Commission. On 24 September it was announced that the MMC had concluded that the acquisition would not operate against the public interest. Norton Opax was then free to proceed with its offer.

2.2 On 25 September 1986 Norton Opax announced its final offer for
g McCorquodale. The offer was two new Norton Opax ordinary shares for each McCorquodale ordinary share and, at that time, valued each McCorquodale ordinary share at 290p. In addition there was an underwritten cash alternative of 260p per McCorquodale share provided by Samuel Montagu. The Board of McCorquodale, advised by Kleinwort Benson, recommended shareholders to reject the offer.

h
2.3 On 1 November 1986 a competing offer was announced. The offerer was Datafin, a new company formed by certain executive directors and members of the management of McCorquodale and backed by a number of financial institutions, led by Prudential-Bache. The offer was 300p cash per McCorquodale share. Subsequently on 6 November 1986, Norton Opax announced an increased final offer of seven new Norton Opax ordinary shares for every three McCorquodale
j shares, valuing each McCorquodale share (on the basis of Norton Opax's share price at the time) at 340·7p, with an underwritten cash alternative of 303·3p per share. Datafin then increased its offer first to 310p and subsequently to 315p cash per share.

2.4 During the course of the offers Mr Robert Maxwell acquired a substantial shareholding in McCorquodale and by the time of the announcement of Datafin's final offer held some 22%. At that stage he undertook to commit his entire shareholding to Norton Opax's offer on the basis that if it failed both his shareholding *a* and Norton Opax's would be assented to Datafin's offer.

2.5 On 20 November 1986, Norton Opax declared its offer unconditional as to acceptances, having received acceptances representing 50·2% of the share capital of McCorquodale. At the request of the executive, Norton Opax has agreed not to declare its offer fully unconditional pending the result of this hearing.'

b

Both the alternative cash offers by Norton Opax were underwritten in a novel, but not unprecedented, form, involving core underwriters and core sub-underwriters as contrasted with traditional market underwriters. The executive reported:

'Under these arrangements in outline, a number of potential sub-underwriters are identified who are prepared to accept a lower commission if the offer fails, on the basis of a higher one if it is successful. This practice has recently developed and *c* its rationale is apparent in the case of companies bidding for others larger than themselves where there is a particular need to save costs if the bid is unsuccessful. It was first used in the Argyll/Distillers offer and was also seen as relevant for Norton Opax's bid for McCorquodale. Both core underwriters and market underwriters receive a greater commission if the bid is successful, but the difference is more marked in the case of the core underwriters. Full details of the commission *d* arrangements are set out in Samuel Montagu's submission, but they can be summarised as follows: (1) Market underwriters receive a commitment commission of $\frac{1}{2}$% together with a further $\frac{1}{8}$% for each period of 7 days (or part) in excess of 30 days. (2) Core underwriters receive a commitment commission of $\frac{1}{4}$%, increased to $1\frac{1}{2}$% if the bid is successful. (3) Both market and core underwriters receive a further $\frac{1}{4}$% based upon the value of Norton Opax shares allotted pursuant to the offer in *e* respect of acceptances received up to the time the cash alternative closes. Approximately 100 mn Norton Opax shares were involved in the initial underwriting on 25 September; of these KIO sub-underwrote some 11 mn as core underwriter and 8 mn as market underwriter. For the increased final offer announced on 6 November some 89 mn Norton Opax shares were underwritten, KIO taking *f* approximately 11 mn as core underwriter. In each case the proportion of shares underwritten by KIO was greater than that of other sub-underwriters although it is noteworthy that one other core sub-underwriter took 10 mn shares in the second underwriting. Moreover Greenwell Montagu have said that KIO's share was not disproportionately large, given that KIO are generally the greater participant in their underwriting list, owing to their substantial size.'

g

Consistently with the panel's declared intention of doing equity between one shareholder and another, the code contains rules which prevent an offeror from buying shares at prices higher than that contained in his offer without revising that offer upwards to match those prices and which also prevent him increasing any offer which has been made on the expressed basis that it would not thereafter be increased. These rules would *h* be ineffective if, while the offeror was subject to restrictions on his conduct, his servants, agents or those acting in collaboration with him remained wholly free to take whatever action they thought fit. Accordingly the rules contain restrictions on the freedom of action of persons acting in concert with the offeror, quaintly referred to as 'concert parties'. They are 'defined' in the rules as follows, although it should be noted that whilst part of the definition could be properly so described, the remainder involves a rebuttable *j* presumption that certain parties fall within the definition:

'**Acting in Concert**
This definition has particular relevance to mandatory offers and further guidance with regard to behaviour which constitutes acting in concert is given in the Notes on Rule 9.1.
Persons acting in concert comprise persons who, pursuant to an agreement or

understanding (whether formal or informal), actively co-operate, through the
acquisition by any of them of shares in a company, to obtain or consolidate control
(as defined below) of that company. Without prejudice to the general application of
this definition the following persons will be presumed to be persons acting in
concert with other persons in the same category unless the contrary is established:—

(1) a company, its parent, subsidiaries and fellow subsidiaries, and their associated
companies, and companies of which such companies are associated companies, all
with each other (for this purpose ownership or control of 20% or more of the equity
share capital of a company is regarded as the test of associated company status); (2) a
company with any of its directors (together with their close relatives and related
trusts); (3) a company with any of its pension funds; (4) a person with any investment
company, unit trust or other person whose investments such person manages on a
discretionary basis; (5) a financial adviser with its client in respect of the shareholdings
of: (a) the financial adviser; and (b) all the investment accounts which the financial
adviser manages on a discretionary basis, where the percentage of the client's equity
share capital held by the financial adviser and those investment accounts totals 10%
or more; and (6) directors of a company which is subject to an offer or where the
directors have reason to believe a BONA FIDE offer for their company may be
imminent.

Note: where the Panel has ruled that a group of persons is acting in concert, it will be
necessary for clear evidence to be presented to the Panel before it can be accepted that the
position no longer obtains.'

It is common ground that Datafin and Prudential-Bache, as the leading financial backer
of its bid, are concert parties. Accordingly, neither could seek to obtain further shares in
McCorquodale at a price in excess of 315p cash per share, the figure put forward in
Datafin's final offer. It is also common ground that Norton Opax and Laurence Prust/
Greenwell Montagu, the two brokers to the offer while acting as such were concert
parties, as were Norton Opax and Samuel Montagu, their merchant bankers. So too were
KIO and Greenwell Montagu, when acting on their behalf, but KIO was subject to no
relevant restrictions under the rules, provided that it was not acting in concert with one
or other of the rival bidders.

However, Datafin and Prudential-Bache maintained that KIO and Norton Opax were
concert parties and that KIO had acted in breach of the code in authorising Greenwell
Montagu to buy some 2·4 m McCorquodale shares on its behalf from Sun Life at a price
of 315·5p on 17 November 1986 immediately after Datafin had made a final offer of
315p and in assenting those shares to Norton Opax's offer.

The basic facts on which this charge was founded were as follows. (a) KIO had a
significant interest in the Norton Opax bid being successful, since, in that event under
the core underwriting arrangement, it would be paid about £350,000 in underwriting
fees, whereas it would only receive £35,000 if the bid failed. (b) The £350,000 would be
paid by Norton Opax through the principal underwriter, KIO being sub-underwriters.
(c) The purchase of the Sun Life shares was suggested to KIO by Greenwell Montagu, one
of the joint brokers to the Norton Opax bid. (d) KIO assented the shares to the Norton
Opax bid. (e) KIO could have bought McCorquodale shares on the market at a price
below 315·5p per share before the final Datafin offer was made at 315p per share and at
a time when Datafin might thereby have been induced to raise its earlier bid, but failed
to do so.

On these facts Datafin and Prudential-Bache concluded that there must have been
some agreement or understanding (formal or informal) between Norton Opax and KIO
actively to co-operate through the acquisition of shares in McCorquodale in order to
obtain control of that company. They further contended that KIO, as a concert party
with Norton Opax, had offered Sun Life more than 303·3p per share, the Norton Opax
cash alternative and that, reading the underwriting agreement and the offer together,

Norton Opax had agreed to acquire the ex-Sun Life McCorquodale shares from KIO at a price in excess of that on offer to other shareholders in McCorquodale, since the assent of these shares tipped the balance in favour of the success of the bid and entitled KIO to a bonus of the additional underwriting fee.

This complaint against Norton Opax and KIO was put to the panel and considered by the executive, which heard evidence and concluded:

'6   *The views of the executive*

6.1 In order that Norton Opax and KIO can be regarded as acting in concert, it must be established that there is an agreement or understanding, which provides for active co-operation between them; that such co-operation includes the purchasing of McCorquodale shares by one of them; and that any such purchasing is for the purpose of obtaining and consolidating Code control of McCorquodale.

6.2 To reach a conclusion of acting in concert, the executive considers there should be evidence that leads to that conclusion or circumstances must be such that it should on balance be inferred that the relevant parties were acting in concert. In this case, the executive has no reason to doubt the facts, and statements of intentions, as recounted by representatives of Norton Opax, Greenwell Montagu, Laurence Prust and KIO. The fact that people may act with similar intentions or that someone may purchase further shares with a view to becoming a substantial shareholder in the offeror will not of themselves amount to evidence of a concert party.

6.3 KIO is one of the most substantial investment institutions, in this country. For this reason it is generally offered a large share in underwritings by brokers, and deals with Greenwell Montagu on this basis. The particular type of underwriting arrangement entered into in connection with the Norton Opax offer, involving KIO's role as a "core" underwriter, although not the norm, is by no means extraordinary. The core underwriters were not approached before the day the offers were announced, did not know each other's identity and received no special presentations. Certain of them met the management for the standard presentation during the offer in the normal way but in fact KIO never met the management at all. The executive is therefore of the view that the underwriting arrangements do not provide evidence of any agreement or understanding providing for active co-operation between KIO and Norton Opax for the purpose of obtaining control of McCorquodale. The executive has discussed the subsequent purchases of Mc-Corquodale shares with KIO. As stated above, KIO have said that the purchase of McCorquodale shares was seen simply as an opportunity for acquiring a significant interest in the combined Norton Opax/McCorquodale group and was motivated solely by investment criteria. The executive see no reason to doubt KIO's motives in this respect. The fact that KIO sought to become a substantial shareholder in the combined group cannot of itself give rise to a presumption of concertedness. The purchase price of the McCorquodale shares is also worthy of note. At 315½p it was only ½p in excess of Datafin's offer. The exposure to KIO in the event that the Norton Opax offer lapsed was therefore minimal, since it would be able to realise 315p in accepting the Datafin offer. The executive has also discussed the purchases with the other investment institutions involved; again in each case the executive has been assured that the purchases were made solely with a view to investing in the combined group.

6.4 In conclusion, the executive is of the view that at no stage during the course of the offer has there been any agreement or understanding between KIO and Norton Opax which leads to their being held to be acting in concert.

7   *Consequences of the Panel's ruling*

7.1 If the Panel agrees with the executive's ruling the executive recommends that Norton Opax should be released from its undertaking not to declare the offer wholly unconditional.

7.2 If the Panel were to take the contrary view to the executive it would be necessary to address the question of how to deal with the consequences in the context of a final offer. On the one hand, to order an increased offer under either Rule 6 or Rule 11 would be problematic; as has been stated above, since the offer was expressed to be final, it could be argued that a concert party should not enable the offeror to increase his offer when he would otherwise be precluded from doing so. On the other hand, to require the bid to lapse might be equally inappropriate.'

The complaint was further considered by the panel itself, which also heard evidence. It dismissed the complaint, the chairman saying:

'The Panel have carefully considered the evidence laid before them in this case and I have to tell you that they are not convinced that a concert party did exist in Code terms in this instance; and they, therefore, uphold the ruling of the executive on that point. The Panel did go on to consider more generally the position of—the relationship of—core underwriting arrangements in circumstances such as these and they would wish to add a rider to the effect that the gearing effects core underwriting arrangements have could in their view, in particular circumstances, in particular cases, be such as to contribute appreciably towards the creation of a presumption of concerted action; and that, therefore, in cases where core underwriting arrangements are involved those concerned should have particular regard to the possibility of their being held, in the light of all the circumstances in a particular case, to be in concert. And they would further add that in such circumstances where there is core underwriting involved, one of the circumstances which would further intensify the degree of investigation which would be implied, would be the fact of purchases above the bid price. It is not of course to be seen as exclusively a feature that would necessarily be brought into examination; but the existence of purchases above the bid price is naturally one which would intensify the degree of examination which would be appropriate in such cases. It will clearly, I think, been apt for the Panel to issue a statement as soon as we can do so giving the announcement that a hearing on this subject has been held, that a concert party has not been found to exist and carrying also the rider points that I have mentioned.'

On the morning of 25 November 1986 Datafin and Prudential-Bache sought leave from Hodgson J to apply for judicial review of the panel's decision and for consequential relief. The judge refused the application without giving reasons, while indicating that in his view the court had no jurisdiction. The application was renewed to this court that afternoon and we began the hearing at once. In the course of the argument we decided to give leave and further determined to hear the substantive application ourselves. We gave leave because the issue as to jurisdiction seemed to us to be arguable and of some public importance and we retained seisin of the matter with a view to saving time in a situation of considerable urgency.

It will be seen that there are three principal issues.

(a) Are the decisions of the panel susceptible to judicial review? This is the 'jurisdictional' issue.

(b) If so, how in principle is that jurisdiction to be exercised given the nature of the panel's activities and the fact that it is an essential part of the machinery of a market in which time is money in a very real sense? This might be described as the 'practical' issue.

(c) If the jurisdictional issue is answered favourably to the applicants, is this a case in which relief should be granted and, if so, in what form?

As the new Norton Opax ordinary shares have been admitted to the Official Stock Exchange List and so can be traded, subject to allotment, any doubt as to the outcome of the present proceedings could affect the price at which these shares are or could be traded and thus the rights of those entitled to trade in them. Accordingly we thought it right to announce at the end of the argument that the application for judicial review would be refused. However, I propose to explain my reasons for reaching this conclusion by considering the three issues in the order in which I have set them out.

The jurisdictional issue

As I have said, the panel is a truly remarkable body, performing its function without visible means of legal support. But the operative word is 'visible', although perhaps I should have used the word 'direct'. Invisible or indirect support there is in abundance. Not only is a breach of the code, so found by the panel, ipso facto an act of misconduct by a member of the Stock Exchange, and the same may be true of other bodies represented on the panel, but the admission of shares to the Official List may be withheld in the event of such a breach. This is interesting and significant for listing of securities is a statutory function performed by the Stock Exchange in pursuance of the Stock Exchange (Listing) Regulations 1984, SI 1984/716, enacted in implementation of EEC Directives. And the matter does not stop there, because in December 1983 the Department of Trade and Industry made a statement explaining why the Licensed Dealers (Conduct of Business) Rules 1983, SI 1983/585, contained no detailed provisions about take-overs. It said:

> 1 . . . There are now no detailed provisions in these statutory rules about takeovers and the following paragraphs set out the provisions as regards public companies and private companies respectively. 2. As regards public companies (as well as private companies which have had some kind of public involvement in the ten years before the bid) the Department considers it better to rely on the effectiveness and flexibility of the City Code on Takeovers and Mergers, which covers bids made for public companies and certain private companies which have had some past public involvement. The City Code has the support of, and can be enforced against, professional security dealers and accordingly the Department expects, as a matter of course, that those making bids for public companies (and private companies covered by the Code) to use the services of a dealer in securities authorised under the Prevention of Fraud (Investments) Act, 1958 (such as a stock broker, exempt dealer, licensed dealer, or a member of a recognised association), in which case the Secretary of State's permission for the distribution of take over documents is not required. This is seen as an important safeguard for the shareholders of the public company (of which there may be several hundreds or thousands) and as a means of ensuring that such takeovers are conducted properly and fully in accordance with the provisions of the City Code. It would only be in exceptional cases that the Secretary of State would consider removing this safeguard by granting permission under Section 14(2) of the Act for the distribution of takeover documents in these circumstances.'

The picture which emerges is clear. As an act of government it was decided that, in relation to take-overs, there should be a central self-regulatory body which would be supported and sustained by a periphery of statutory powers and penalties wherever non-statutory powers and penalties were insufficient or non-existent or where EEC requirements called for statutory provisions.

No one could have been in the least surprised if the panel had been instituted and operated under the direct authority of statute law, since it operates wholly in the public domain. Its jurisdiction extends throughout the United Kingdom. Its code and rulings apply equally to all who wish to make take-over bids or promote mergers, whether or not they are members of bodies represented on the panel. Its lack of a direct statutory base is a complete anomaly, judged by the experience of other comparable markets world wide. The explanation is that it is an historical 'happenstance', to borrow a happy term from across the Atlantic. Prior to the years leading up to the 'Big Bang', the City of

London prided itself on being a village community, albeit of an unique kind, which
a could regulate itself by pressure of professional opinion. As government increasingly
accepted the necessity for intervention to prevent fraud, it built on City institutions and
mores, supplementing and reinforcing them as appeared necessary. It is a process which
is likely to continue, but the position has already been reached in which central
government has incorporated the panel into its own regulatory network built up under
the Prevention of Fraud (Investments) Act 1958 and allied statutes, such as the Banking
b Act 1979.

The issue is thus whether the historic supervisory jurisdiction of the Queen's courts
extends to such a body discharging such functions, including some which are quasi-
judicial in their nature, as part of such a system. Counsel for the panel submits that it
does not. He says that this jurisdiction only extends to bodies whose power is derived
from legislation or the exercise of the prerogative. Counsel for the applicants submits
c that this is too narrow a view and that regard has to be had not only to the source of the
body's power, but also to whether it operates as an integral part of a system which has a
public law character, is supported by public law in that public law sanctions are applied
if its edicts are ignored and performs what might be described as public law functions.

In *R v Criminal Injuries Compensation Board, ex p Lain* [1967] 2 All ER 770 at 778, [1967]
2 QB 864 at 882 Lord Parker CJ, who had unrivalled experience of the prerogative
d remedies both on the Bench and at the Bar, said that the exact limits of the ancient
remedy of certiorari had never been and ought not to be specifically defined. I respectfully
agree and will not attempt such an exercise. He continued:

'They have varied from time to time, being extended to meet changing conditions.
At one time the writ only went to an inferior court. Later its ambit was extended to
e statutory tribunals determining a lis inter partes. Later again it extended to cases
where there was no lis in the strict sense of the word, but where immediate or
subsequent rights of a citizen were affected. The only constant limits throughout
were that the body concerned was under a duty to act judicially and that it was
performing a public duty. Private or domestic tribunals have always been outside
the scope of certiorari since their authority is derived solely from contract, that is
f from the agreement of the parties concerned . . . We have, as it seems to me, reached
the position when the ambit of certiorari can be said to cover every case in which a
body of persons, of a public as opposed to a purely private or domestic character, has
to determine matters affecting subjects provided always that it has a duty to act
judicially. Looked at in this way the board in my judgment comes fairly and
squarely within the jurisdiction of this court. The board are, as counsel for the board
g said, "a servant of the Crown charged by the Crown, by executive instruction, with
the duty of distributing the bounty of the Crown". The board are clearly, therefore,
performing public duties.'

Diplock LJ, who was later to make administrative law almost his own, said ([1967] 2
All ER 770 at 779–780, [1967] 2 QB 864 at 884–885):
h
'The jurisdiction of the High Court as successor of the court of Queen's Bench to
supervise the exercise of their jurisdiction by inferior tribunals has not in the past
been dependent on the source of the tribunal's authority to decide issues submitted
to its determination, except where such authority is derived solely from agreement
of parties to the determination. The latter case falls within the field of private
j contract and thus within the ordinary civil jurisdiction of the High Court
supplemented where appropriate by its statutory jurisdiction under the Arbitration
Acts. The earlier history of the writ of certiorari shows that it was issued to courts
whose authority was derived from the prerogative, from royal charter, from
franchise or custom, as well as from Act of Parliament. Its recent history shows that
as new kinds of tribunals have been created, orders of certiorari have been extended

to them too and to all persons who under authority of government have exercised
quasi-judicial functions. True, since the victory of Parliament in the constitutional *a*
struggles of the seventeenth century, authority has been generally if not invariably
conferred on new kinds of tribunals by or under Act of Parliament and there has
been no recent occasion for the High Court to exercise supervisory jurisdiction over
persons whose ultimate authority to decide matters is derived from any other source.
I see no other reason, however, for holding that the ancient jurisdiction of the court
of Queen's Bench has been narrowed merely because there had been no occasion to *b*
exercise it. If new tribunals are established by acts of government, the supervisory
jurisdiction of the High Court extends to them if they possess the essential
characteristics on which the subjection of inferior tribunals to the supervisory
control of the High Court is based. What are these characteristics? It is plain on the
authorities that the tribunal need not be one whose determinations give rise directly
to any legally enforceable right or liability. Its determination may be subject to *c*
certiorari notwithstanding that it is merely one step in a process which may have
the result of altering the legal rights or liabilities of a person to whom it relates. It is
not even essential that the determination must have that result, for there may be
some subsequent condition to be satisfied before the determination can have any
effect on such legal rights or liabilities. That susbsequent condition may be a later
determination by another tribunal (see *R. v. Postmaster General, Ex p. Carmichael* *d*
([1928] 1 KB 291); *R. v. Boycott, Ex p. Keasley* ([1939] 2 All ER 626, [1939] 2 KB
651)). Is there any reason in principle why certiorari should not lie in respect of a
determination where the subsequent condition which must be satisfied before it can
affect any legal rights or liabilities of a person to whom it relates, is the exercise in
favour of that person of an excecutive discretion as distinct from a discretion which
is required to be exercised judicially?' *e*

Ashworth J, who, like Lord Parker CJ had served as junior counsel to the Treasury and
as such had vast experience in this field, said ([1967] 2 All ER 770 at 784, [1967] 2 QB
864 at 891–892):

'It is a truism to say that the law has to adjust itself to meet changing circumstances *f*
and although a tribunal, constituted as the board, has not been the subject of
consideration or decision by this court in relation to an order of certiorari, I do not
think that this court should shrink from entertaining this application merely
because the board have no statutory origin. It cannot be suggested that the board
have unlawfully usurped jurisdiction: they act with lawful authority, albeit such
authority is derived from the executive and not from an Act of Parliament. In the *g*
past this court has felt itself able to consider the conduct of a Minister when he is
acting judicially or quasi-judicially and while the present case may involve an
extension of relief by way of certiorari I should not feel constrained to refuse such
relief if the facts warranted it.'

The Criminal Injuries Compensation Board, in the form which it then took, was an
administrative novelty. Accordingly it would have been impossible to find a precedent *h*
for the exercise of the supervisory jurisdiction of the court which fitted the facts.
Nevertheless, the court not only asserted its jurisdiction, but further asserted that it was a
jurisdiction which was adaptable thereafter. This process has since been taken further in
O'Reilly v Mackman [1982] 3 All ER 680, [1983] 2 AC 237 by deleting any requirement
that the body should have a duty to act judicially, in *Council of Civil Service Unions v
Minister for the Civil Service* [1984] 3 All ER 935, [1985] AC 374 by extending it to a *j*
person exercising purely prerogative power, and in *Gillick v West Norfolk and Wisbech Area
Health Authority* [1985] 3 All ER 402 at 405, 415–416, [1986] AC 112 at 163, 177–178,
where Lord Fraser and Lord Scarman expressed the view obiter that judicial review
would extend to guidance circulars issued by a department of state without any specific

authority. In all the reports it is possible to find enumerations of factors giving rise to the jurisdiction, but it is a fatal error to regard the presence of all those factors as essential or as being exclusive of other factors. Possibly the only essential elements are what can be described as a public element, which can take many different forms, and the exclusion from the jurisdiction of bodies whose sole source of power is a consensual submission to its jurisdiction.

In fact, given its novelty, the panel fits surprisingly well into the format which this court had in mind in *R v Criminal Injuries Compensation Board*. It is without doubt performing a public duty and an important one. This is clear from the expressed willingness of the Secretary of State for Trade and Industry to limit legislation in the field of take-overs and mergers and to use the panel as the centrepiece of his regulation of that market. The rights of citizens are indirectly affected by its decisions, some, but by no means all of whom, may in a technical sense be said to have assented to this situation, eg the members of the Stock Exchange. At least in its determination of whether there has been a breach of the code, it has a duty to act judicially and it asserts that its raison d'être is to do equity between one shareholder and another. Its source of power is only partly based on moral persuasion and the assent of institutions and their members, the bottom line being the statutory powers exercised by the Department of Trade and Industry and the Bank of England. In this context I should be very disappointed if the courts could not recognise the realities of executive power and allowed their vision to be clouded by the subtlety and sometimes complexity of the way in which it can be exerted.

Given that it is really unthinkable that, in the absence of legislation such as affects trade unions, the panel should go on its way cocooned from the attention of the courts, in defence of the citizenry, we sought to investigate whether it could conveniently be controlled by established forms of private law, eg torts such as actionable combinations in restraint of trade, and, to this end, pressed counsel for the applicants to draft a writ. Suffice it to say that the result was wholly unconvincing and, not surprisingly, counsel for the panel did not admit that it would be in the least effective.

In reaching my conclusion that the court has jurisdiction to entertain applications for the judicial review of decisions of the panel, I have said nothing about the substantial arguments put forward by counsel for the panel based on the practical problems which are involved. These, in my judgment, go not to the existence of the jurisdiction, but to how it should be exercised and to that I now turn.

The practical issue

Counsel for the panel waxed eloquent on the disastrous consequences of the court having and exercising jurisdiction to review the decisions of the panel and his submissions deserved, and have received, very serious consideration. In his skeleton argument, he put it this way:

'Even if, which is not accepted, there is an apparent anomaly for an inability to challenge a patently wrong decision which may have important consequences, countervailing disadvantages would arise if the decision were open to review. Applications would often be made which were unmeritorious. The fact that the court could dismiss such applications does not prevent their having a substantial effect in dislocating the operation of the market during the pendency of proceedings, in creating uncertainty in areas where it is vital that there should be finality. That finality should more appropriately exist at the threshold stage, by denying the possibility of action, rather than at the subsequent stage when the court comes to exercise its discretion since by that time there will already have been a lack of finality for a period. The nature of the rulings of the take-over panel are particularly required to have speed and certainty: they may be given in the middle of a bid, and they clearly may affect the operation of the market, and even short-term dislocation could be very harmful. The present case illustrates the uncertainty within the

market which can be created by the mere bringing of an application. The issue is
important for self-regulation as a whole. It would create uncertainty if it were to be   *a*
said that each self-regulating body were to be considered in the context of the entire
factual background of its operation, and of the peculiar features of the take-over
panel which made it susceptible to judicial review. It would obviously have wide
ranging consequences if there were general statements that self-regulating bodies
carrying out important functions were susceptible to judicial review.'

I think that it is important that all who are concerned with take-over bids should have   *b*
well in mind a very special feature of public law decisions, such as those of the panel,
namely that however wrong they may be, however lacking in jurisdiction they may be,
they subsist and remain fully effective unless and until they are set aside by a court of
competent jurisdiction. Furthermore, the court has an ultimate discretion whether to set
them aside and may refuse to do so in the public interest, notwithstanding that it holds   *c*
and declares the decision to have been made ultra vires (see e g *R v Monopolies and Mergers
Commission, ex p Argyll Group plc* [1986] 2 All ER 257, [1986] 1 WLR 763). That case also
illustrates the awareness of the court of the special needs of the financial markets for
speed on the part of decision-makers and for being able to rely on those decision as a sure
basis for dealing in the market. It further illustrates an awareness that such decisions
affect a very wide public which will not be parties to the dispute and that their interests   *d*
have to be taken into account as much as those of the immediate disputants.

In the context of judicial review, it must also be remembered that it is not even
possible to apply for relief until leave has been obtained. The purpose of this provision
was explained by Lord Diplock in *IRC v National Federation of Self-Employed and Small
Businesses Ltd* [1981] 2 All ER 93 at 105, [1982] AC 617 at 642–643:

> 'The need for leave to start proceedings for remedies in public law is not new. It   *e*
> applied previously to applications for prerogative orders, though not to civil actions
> for injunctions or declarations. Its purpose is to prevent the time of the court being
> wasted by busybodies with misguided or trivial complaints of administrative error,
> and to remove the uncertainty in which public officers and authorities might be left
> whether they could safely proceed with administrative action while proceedings for   *f*
> judicial review of it were actually pending even though misconceived.'

In many cases of judicial review where the time scale is far more extended than in the
financial markets, the decision-maker who learns that someone is seeking leave to
challenge his decision may well seek to preserve the status quo meanwhile and, in
particular, may not seek to enforce his decision pending a consideration of the matter by
the court. If leave is granted, the court has the necessary authority to make orders   *g*
designed to achieve this result, but usually the decision-maker will give undertakings in
lieu. All this is but good administrative practice. However, against the background of
the time scales of the financial market, the courts would not expect the panel or those
who should comply with its decisions to act similarly. In that context the panel and those
affected should treat its decisions as valid and binding, unless and until they are set aside.   *h*
Above all they should ignore any application for leave to apply of which they become
aware, since to do otherwise would enable such applications to be used as a mere ploy in
take-over battles which would be a serious abuse of the process of the court and could not
be adequately penalised by awards of costs.

If this course is followed and the application for leave is refused, no harm will have
been done. If the application is granted, it will be for the court to decide whether to   *j*
make any and, if so, what orders to preserve the status quo. In doing so, it will have
regard to the likely outcome of the proceedings which will depend partly on the facts as
they appear from the information at that time available to the court, but also in part on
the public administrative purpose which the panel is designed to serve. This is somewhat
special.

Consistently with its character as the controlling body for the self-regulation of
a takeovers and mergers, the panel combines the functions of legislator, court interpreting
the panel's legislation, consultant and court investigating and imposing penalties in
respect of alleged breaches of the code. As a legislator it sets out to lay down general
principles, on the lines of EEC legislation, rather than specific prohibitions which those
who are concerned in take-over bids and mergers can study with a view to detecting and
exploiting loopholes.

b   Against that background, there is little scope for complaint that the panel has
promulgated rules which are ultra vires, provided only that they do not clearly violate
the principle proclaimed by the panel of being based on the concept of doing equity
between one shareholder and another. This is a somewhat unlikely eventuality.

When it comes to interpreting its own rules, it must clearly be given considerable
latitude both because, as legislator, it could properly alter them at any time and because
c of the form which the rules take, ie laying down principles to be applied in spirit as
much as in letter in specific situations. Where there might be a legitimate cause for
complaint and for the intervention of the court would be if the interpretation were so far
removed from the natural and ordinary meaning of the words of the rules that an
ordinary user of the market could reasonably be misled. Even then it by no means
follows that the court would think it appropriate to quash an interpretative decision of
d the panel. It might well take the view that a more appropriate course would be to declare
the true meaning of the rule, leaving it to the panel to promulgate a new rule accurately
expressing its intentions.

Again the panel has powers to grant dispensation from the operation of the rules: see,
eg, r 9.1. This is a discretionary power only fettered by the overriding obligation to seek,
if not necessarily to achieve, equity between one shareholder and another. Again I should
e be surprised if the exercise of this power could be attacked, save in wholly exceptional
circumstances and, even then, the court might well take the view that the proper form
of relief was declaratory rather than substantive.

This leaves only the panel's disciplinary function. If it finds a breach of the rules
proved, there is an internal right of appeal which, in accordance with established
f principles, must be exercised before, in any ordinary circumstances, the court would
consider intervening. In a case, such as the present, where the complaint is that the panel
should have found a breach of the rules, but did not do so, I would expect the court to be
even more reluctant to move in the absence of any credible allegation of lack of bona
fides. It is not for a court exercising a judicial review jurisdiction to substitute itself for
the fact-finding tribunal, and error of law in the form of a finding of fact for which there
g was no evidence or in the form of a misconstruction of the panel's own rules would
normally be a matter to be dealt with by a declaratory judgment. The only circumstances
in which I would anticipate the use of the remedies of certiorari and mandamus would
be in the event, which I hope is unthinkable, of the panel acting in breach of the rules of
natural justice, in other words, unfairly.

Nothing that I have said can fetter or is intended to or should be construed as fettering
h the discretion of any court to which application is made for leave to apply for judicial
review of a decision of the panel or which, leave having been granted, is charged with
the duty of considering such an application. Nevertheless, I wish to make it clear beyond
a peradventure that in the light of the special nature of the panel, its functions, the
market in which it is operating, the time scales which are inherent in that market and
the need to safeguard the position of third parties, who may be numbered in thousands,
j all of whom are entitled to continue to trade on an assumption of the validity of the
panel's rules and decisions, unless and until they are quashed by the court, I should expect
the relationship between the panel and the court to be historic rather than
contemporaneous. I should expect the court to allow contemporary decisions to take
their course, considering the complaint and intervening, if at all, later and in retrospect
by declaratory orders which would enable the panel not to repeat any error and would

relieve individuals of the disciplinary consequences of any erroneous finding of breach of the rules. This would provide a workable and valuable partnership between the courts *a* and the panel in the public interest and would avoid all of the perils to which counsel for the panel alluded.

The reasons for rejecting this application

There was some failure on the part of the applicants to appreciate, or at least to act in recognition of the fact, that an application for judicial review is not an appeal. The panel *b* and not the court is the body charged with the duty of evaluating the evidence and finding the facts. The role of the court is wholly different. It is, in an appropriate case, to review the decision of the panel and to consider whether there has been 'illegality', ie whether the panel has misdirected itself in law, 'irrationality', ie whether the panel's decision is so outrageous in its defiance of logic or of accepted moral standards that no sensible person who had applied his mind to the question to be decided could have *c* arrived at it, or 'procedural impropriety', ie a departure by the panel from any procedural rules governing its conduct or a failure to observe the basic rules of natural justice, which is probably better described as 'fundamental unfairness', since justice in nature is conspicuous by its absence. If authority be required for propositions which are so well established, it is to be found in the speech of Lord Diplock in *Council of Civil Service Unions v Minister for the Civil Service* [1984] 3 All ER 935 at 950–951, [1985] AC 374 at 410–411. *d*

In the course of the hearing before this court, the applicants sought and were given leave to amend their grounds of application. As so amended, they made three complaints of breaches of the code and of the panel's failure so to find: (a) in breach of the code, Norton Opax failed to increase its offer to McCorquodale shareholders, other than core sub-underwriters, to reflect the increased consideration paid to core sub-underwriters and the parent company of the principal core sub-underwriter for the McCorquodale *e* shares acquired by it from them; (b) in breach of the code, KIO acted in concert with Norton Opax in that, irrespective of the reasons for their conduct, they had an agreement with Samuel Montagu & Co Ltd, Norton Opax's merchant banker, which gave them an incentive to procure that Norton Opax's offer should become unconditional and they did so procure by purchasing shares at a price 12·2p in excess of the cash price offered by *f* Norton Opax and by assenting those shares to Norton Opax; (c) having regard to the timing and price paid by KIO for the McCorquodale shares, the fact that they were purchased through one of the brokers to Norton Opax's offer and the assenting of those shares to that offer, the panel could not properly have failed to find that KIO and Norton Opax were concert parties, unless it misdirected itself in law in the erroneous belief that a finding that there was communication between Norton Opax and KIO with regard to *g* those share purchases was necessary to support such a finding.

I can dispose of complaint (a) very quickly. Norton Opax never did pay an increased consideration for McCorquodale shares to core sub-underwriters or anyone else. The success of the bid brought with it an entitlement on the part of the core sub-underwriters to be paid an increased underwriting fee, but this was not part of the consideration for McCorquodale shares. It would have been payable to core sub-underwriters if the same *h* shares had been assented to Norton Opax by someone other than a core sub-underwriter. Furthermore, this point is not open, since it was not argued before the panel.

Complaint (b) essentially amounts to an allegation that an agreement which gives underwriters an interest in the success of a bid makes the underwriter a concert party if he purchases shares in the target company. The short answer to this is that 'concert party' could be so defined, but it is not and whether any alteration should be made is a matter *j* for the panel and not for the court.

Complaint (c) is no doubt based on the sentence in para 6.3 of the report of the panel's executive, which I have already quoted, reading: 'Certain of [the core underwriters] met the management for the standard presentation during the offer in the normal way, but in fact KIO never met the management at all'. Two assumptions are then made, namely

that the executive regarded this as conclusive of the absence of a concert party situation
and that the panel did likewise. We have in the event had the advantage of affidavit
evidence from the chairman which makes it clear that the panel made no such error. He
has deposed that the panel approached the matter on the basis of the definition of 'concert
party' which requires a finding of an agreement or understanding. It did not regard the
fact that there was no contact between KIO and Norton Opax as an absolute bar to a
finding of concerted action but rightly appreciated that, in the absence of such contact,
sufficient evidence to support an agreement or understanding had to be found elsewhere
if such a finding were to be made. There was no such evidence or none sufficient to
satisfy the panel and the evidence as a whole satisfied it that KIO's decision to purchase
the shares was made for genuine investment reasons which explained both the purchase
and when it was made.

While this is more than sufficient to dispose of complaint (c), the chairman's long,
detailed and helpful affidavit well illustrates the need for the court to avoid
underestimating the extent to which expert knowledge can negative inferences which
might otherwise be drawn from a partial knowledge of the facts and the extent to which
a greater knowledge of the facts can make a decision which at first might seem faintly
surprising, not only explicable, but plainly right. Thus the panel from its expertise knew
that no significance should be attached to the bare fact that KIO used Greenwell Montagu
as their brokers since—

'it is common for an investor who wishes to buy shares for which an offer is
current to use one of the brokers to the offer, because that broker's knowledge of the
market during such period is likely to be particularly good. Brokers to an offer are
regarded as free to continue their general broking business with other parties
throughout the offer, though they must be careful about disclosure of information.'

Again, the panel heard evidence from other institutional purchasers of McCorquodale
shares who bought at the same time and at substantially the same price as KIO, one of
whom was not a core sub-underwriter and could therefore only have been influenced by
investment considerations. They were also able to investigate in depth what were the
investment justifications of the purchases by both that institution and KIO.

In conclusion, I should like to make it clear that, but for the issue as to jurisdiction,
this is not a case in which leave to apply should ever have been given. All that could be
said at that stage was that there was a case for considering whether the advent of core
underwriting might not call for some reconsideration of the definition of 'concert party',
perhaps putting core underwriters in the category of persons in respect of whom there
was a rebuttable presumption of concerted action. That was plainly a matter for the panel
which was minded to add a rider to its decision pointing to the fact that core underwriting
arrangements might be subjected to close scrutiny, particularly where they were
associated with market purchases above the level of cash offers. The fact that the panel's
conclusion might at first have appeared surprising to someone who was not in day-to-day
contact with the financial markets and who had heard none of the evidence would not
have begun to justify the grant of leave to apply.

LLOYD LJ. I agree that this appeal should be dismissed for the reasons given by Sir
John Donaldson MR.

I add only a few words on the important question whether the Panel on Take-overs
and Mergers is a body which is subject to judicial review. In my judgment it is.

There have been a number of cases since the decision of the House of Lords in *O'Reilly
v Mackman* [1982] 3 All ER 1124, [1983] 2 AC 237 in which it has been necessary for the
courts to consider the new-found distinction between public and private law. In most of
them, objection has been taken by the defendant that the plaintiff has sought the wrong
remedy. By seeking a remedy in private law, instead of public law, the plaintiff has, so it
has been said, deprived the defendant of the special protection afforded by RSC Ord 53.

The formalism thus introduced into our procedure has been the subject of strong criticism by Sir Patrick Neill in his 1985 Child Lecture, and by other academic writers. The curiosity of the present case is that it is, so to speak, the other way round. The plaintiff is seeking a remedy in public law. It is the defendant who asserts that the plaintiff's remedy, if any (and counsel for the panel concedes nothing), lies in private law. Counsel for the panel has cast away the protection afforded by Ord 53 in the hope, perhaps, that the panel may, in the words of counsel for the applicants be subject to no law at all.

On this part of the case counsel for the panel has advanced arguments on two levels. On the level of pure policy he submits that it is undesirable for decisions or rulings of the panel to be reviewable. The intervention of the court would at best impede, at worst frustrate, the purposes for which the panel exists. Secondly, on a more technical level, he submits that to hold that the panel is subject to the supervisory jurisdiction of the High Court would be to extend that the jurisdiction further than it has ever been extended before.

On the policy level, I find myself unpersuaded. Counsel for the panel made much of the word 'self-regulating'. No doubt self-regulation has many advantages. But I was unable to see why the mere fact that a body is self-regulating makes it less appropriate for judicial review. Of course there will be many self-regulating bodies which are wholly inappropriate for judicial review. The committee of an ordinary club affords an obvious example. But the reason why a club is not subject to judicial review is not just because it is self-regulating. The panel wields enormous power. It has a giant's strength. The fact that it is self-regulating, which means, presumably, that it is not subject to regulation by others, and in particular the Department of Trade and Industry, makes it not less but more appropriate that it should be subject to judicial review by the courts.

It has been said that 'it is excellent to have a giant's strength, but it is tyrannous to use it like a giant'. Nobody suggests that there is any present danger of the panel abusing its power. But it is at least possible to imagine circumstances in which a ruling or decision of the panel might give rise to legitimate complaint. An obvious example would be if it reached a decision in flagrant breach of the rules of natural justice. It is no answer to say that there would be a right of appeal in such a case. For a complainant has no right of appeal where the decision is that there has been no breach of the code. Yet a complainant is just as much entitled to natural justice as the company against whom the complaint is made.

Nor is it any answer that a company coming to the market must take it as it finds it. The City is not a club which one can join or not at will. In that sense, the word 'self-regulation' may be misleading. The panel regulates not only itself, but all others who have no alternative but to come to the market in a case to which the code applies.

Counsel for the panel urged on us the importance of speed and finality in these matters. I accept that submission. I accept also the possibility that unmeritorious applications will be made from time to time as a harassing or delaying tactic. It would be up to the court to ensure that this does not happen. These considerations are all very relevant to the exercise of the court's discretion in particular cases. They mean that a successful application for judicial review is likely to be very rare. But they do not mean that we should decline jurisdiction altogether.

So long as there is a possibility, however remote, of the panel abusing its great powers, then it would be wrong for the courts to abdicate responsibility. The courts must remain ready, willing and able to hear a legitimate complaint in this as in any other field of our national life. I am not persuaded that this particular field is one in which the courts do not belong, or from which they should retire, on grounds of policy. And if the courts are to remain in the field, then it is clearly better, as a matter of policy, that legal proceedings should be in the realm of public law rather than private law, not only because they are quicker, but also because the requirement of leave under Ord 53 will exclude claims which are clearly unmeritorious.

So I turn to counsel for the panel's more technical argument. He starts with the speech

a of Lord Diplock in *Council of Civil Service Unions v Minister for the Civil Service* [1984] 3 All ER 935 at 949–950, [1985] AC 374 at 409:

'For a decision to be susceptible to judicial review the decision-maker must be empowered by public law (and not merely, as in arbitration, by agreement between private parties) to make decisions that, if validly made, will lead to administrative

b action or abstention from action by an authority endowed by law with executive powers, which have one or other of the consequences mentioned in the preceding paragraph. The ultimate source of the decision-making power is nearly always nowadays a statute or subordinate legislation made under the statute; but in the absence of any statute regulating the subject matter of the decision the source of the decision-making power may still be the common law itself, ie that part of the

c common law that is given by lawyers the label of "the prerogative". Where this is the source of decision-making power, the power is confined to executive officers of central as distinct from local government and in constitutional practice is generally exercised by those holding ministerial rank.'

On the basis of that speech, and other cases to which he referred us, counsel for the
d panel argues (i) that the sole test whether the body of persons is subject to judicial review is the source of its power, and (ii) that there has been no case where that source has been other than legislation, including subordinate legislation, or the prerogative.

I do not agree that the source of the power is the sole test whether a body is subject to judicial review, nor do I so read Lord Diplock's speech. Of course the source of the power will often, perhaps usually, be decisive. If the source of power is a statute, or subordinate
e legislation under a statute, then clearly the body in question will be subject to judicial review. If, at the other end of the scale, the source of power is contractual, as in the case of private arbitration, then clearly the arbitrator is not subject to judicial review: see *R v Disputes Committee of the National Joint Council for the Craft of Dental Technicians, ex p Neate* [1953] 1 All ER 327, [1953] 1 QB 704.

But in between these extremes there is an area in which it is helpful to look not just at
f the source of the power but at the nature of the power. If the body in question is exercising public law functions, or if the exercise of its functions have public law consequences, then that may, as counsel for the applicants submitted, be sufficient to bring the body within the reach of judicial review. It may be said that to refer to 'public law' in this context is to beg the question. But I do not think it does. The essential distinction, which runs through all the cases to which we referred, is between a domestic
g or private tribunal on the one hand and a body of persons who are under some public duty on the other. Thus in *R v Criminal Injuries Compensation Board, ex p Lain* [1967] 2 All ER 770 at 778, [1967] 2 QB 864 Lord Parker CJ, after tracing the development of certiorari from its earliest days, said:

'The only constant limits throughout were that the body concerned was under a
h duty to act judicially and that it was performing a public duty. Private or domestic tribunals have always been outside the scope of certiorari since their authority is derived solely from contract, that is from the agreement of the parties concerned.'

To the same effect is a passage from a speech of Lord Parker CJ in an earlier case, to which we were not, I think, referred, namely *R v Industrial Court, ex p ASSET* [1964] 3 All ER
j 130 at 136, [1965] 1 QB 377 at 389:

'It has been urged on us that really this arbitral tribunal is not a private arbitral tribunal, but that, in effect, it is undertaking a public duty or a quasi-public duty and, as such, is amenable to an order of mandamus. For my part, I am quite unable to come to that conclusion. It is abundantly clear that they had no duty to undertake the reference. If they had refused to undertake the reference they could not be

compelled to do so. I do not think that the position is in any way different once they
have undertaken the reference. They are clearly doing something which they were   *a*
not under any public duty to do, and, in those circumstances, I see no jurisdiction in
this court to issue an order of mandamus to the Industrial Court.'

More recently in *R v BBC, ex p Lavelle* [1983] 1 All ER 241, [1983] 1 WLR 23 Woolf J had
to consider an application for judicial review where the relief sought was an injunction
under Ord 53, r 1(2). The case was brought by an employee of the BBC. In refusing relief   *b*
Woolf J said ([1983] 1 All ER 241 at 249, [1983] 1 WLR 23 at 31):

'Paragraph (2) of r 1 of Ord 53 does not strictly confine applications for judicial
review to cases where an order for mandamus, prohibition or certiorari could be
granted. It merely requires that the court should have regard to the nature of the
matter in respect of which such relief may be granted. However, although   *c*
applications for judicial review are not confined to those cases where relief could be
granted by way of prerogative order, I regard the wording of Ord 53, r 1(2) and sub-
s (2) of s 31 of the [Supreme Court Act 1981] as making it clear that the application
for judicial review is confined to reviewing activities of a public nature as opposed
to those of a purely private or domestic character. The disciplinary appeal procedure
set up by the BBC depends purely on the contract of employment between the   *d*
applicant and the BBC, and therefore it is a procedure of a purely private or domestic
character.'

So I would reject counsel for the panel's argument that the sole test whether a body is
subject to judicial review is the source of its power. So to hold would in my judgment
impose an artificial limit on the developing law of judicial review. That artificiality is   *e*
well illustrated in the present case by reference to the listing regulations issued by the
Council of the Stock Exchange. As the foreword to the current edition makes clear, a
new edition of the regulations became necessary as the result of the Stock Exchange
(Listing) Regulations 1984, SI 1984/716. Those regulations were made as the result of a
requirement of an EEC Council directive. Counsel for the panel conceded that the listing
regulations are now the subject of public law remedies. By contrast (if his submission is   *f*
correct) the code, which is the subject not of a Council directive, but of a Commission
recommendation, is not.

I now turn to the second of the two arguments put forward by counsel for the panel
under this head. He submits that there has never been a case when the source of the
power has been other than statutory or under the prerogative. There is a certain
imprecision in the use of the term 'prerogative' in this connection, as Professor Sir   *g*
William Wade made clear in another Child Lecture, 'Procedure and Prerogative in Public
Law' (reprinted in (1985) 101 LQR 180). Strictly the term 'prerogative' should be
confined to those powers which are unique to the Crown. As Professor Wade pointed
out, there was nothing unique in the creation by the Government, out of funds voted by
Parliament, of a scheme for the compensation of victims of violent crime. Any foundation   *h*
or trust, given sufficient money, could have done the same thing. Nor do I think that the
distinction between the Criminal Injuries Compensation Board and a private foundation
or trust for the same purposes lies in the source of the funds. The distinction must lie in
the nature of the duty imposed, whether expressly or by implication. If the duty is a
public duty, then the body in question is subject to public law.

So once again one comes back to what I regard as the true view, that it is not just the   *j*
source of the power that matters, but also the nature of the duty. I can see nothing in *R v
Criminal Injuries Compensation Board, ex p Lain* which contradicts that view, or compels us
to decide that, in non-statutory cases, judicial review is confined to bodies created under
the prerogative, whether in the strict sense, or in the wider sense in which that word has
now come to be used. Indeed, the passage from Diplock LJ's judgment, which Sir John

Donaldson MR has already read, points in the opposite direction (see [1967] 2 All ER 770
a at 779, [1967] 2 QB 864 at 884).
   But suppose I am wrong; suppose that the courts are indeed confined to looking at the
source of the power, as counsel for the panel submits. Then I would accept the submission
of counsel for the applicants that the source of the power in the present case is indeed
governmental, at least in part. Counsel for the panel argued that, so far from the source
of the power being governmental, this is a case where the government has deliberately
b abstained from exercising power. I do not take that view. I agree with counsel for the
applicants when he says that there has here been an implied devolution of power. Power
exercised behind the schemes is power none the less. The express powers conferred on
inferior tribunals were of criticial importance in the early days when the sole or main
ground for intervention by the courts was that the inferior tribunal had exceeded its
powers. But those days are long since past. Having regard to the way in which the panel
c came to be established, the fact that the Governor of the Bank of England appoints both
the chairman and the deputy chairman, and the other matters to which Sir John
Donaldson MR has referred, I am persuaded that the panel was established 'under
authority of [the] government', to use the language of Diplock LJ in Lain's case. If in
addition to looking at the source of the power we are entitled to look at the nature of the
power, as I believe we are, then the case is all the stronger.
d   Before leaving counsel for the panel's second argument, I should mention one last
point. The jurisdiction of the court to grant relief by way of judicial review is now, of
course, recognised by s 31 of the Supreme Court Act 1981. Section 31(1)(a) refers
specifically to the old prerogative writs, namely mandamus, prohibition and certiorari.
Section 31(1)(b) and (2) provide that in an application for judicial review, the court may
grant a declaration or injunction if it is just or convenient to do so, having regard to
e various matters. I have already referred to the passage in Woolf J's judgment in R v BBC,
ex p Lavelle [1983] 1 All ER 241 at 249, [1983] 1 WLR 23 at 31 in which he says that
applications for judicial review under Ord 53 r 1(2) are not confined to those cases where
relief could be granted by way of prerogative order. As at present advised, I would agree
with that observation. I would only add as a rider that s 31(1) of the 1981 Act should not
f be treated as having put a stop to all further development of the law relating to the
prerogative remedies. I do not accept the submission of counsel for the panel that we are
here extending the law. But if we were, I would not regard that as an insuperable
objection. The prerogative writs have always been a flexible instrument for doing justice.
In my judgment they should remain so.

g **NICHOLLS LJ.** I entirely agree with the judgments of Sir John Donaldson MR and
Lloyd LJ which I have had the advantage of reading in draft. I add only a few
supplementary observations of my own.

Jurisdiction
   I take as my starting point R v Criminal Injuries Compensation Board, ex p Lain [1967] 2
h All ER 770 at 778, [1967] 2 QB 864 at 882 where Lord Parker CJ noted that the only
constant limits of the ancient remedy of certiorari were that the tribunal in question was
performing a public duty. He contrasted private or domestic tribunals whose authority
is derived solely from the agreement of the parties concerned.
   With that in mind, one looks at the Panel on Take-overs and Mergers. The panel
promulgates the City Code on Take-overs and Mergers. As its name implies, the code is
j concerned with takeover and merger transactions. Its ambit is very wide indeed. Among
the companies to which it applies are all listed public companies considered by the panel
to be resident in the United Kingdom.
   Despite the wide range of the companies and persons it directly affects, the panel
submitted that it is not performing a public duty and that none of its activities is
susceptible to judicial review. The only jurisdiction which the panel has is derived from

the consent of its members. It is, in the terms of Lord Parker CJ's dichotomy, a private or *a*
domestic tribunal whose authority is derived solely from the agreement of the bodies
concerned. It was submitted that the activities of the panel constitute self-regulation, and
self-regulation involves a voluntary submission of those who deal in the market to the
rules laid down by the panel and a commitment to accept the decisions of the panel.

I am unable to accept this as an accurate analysis of the panel's authority and functions.
The panel is an unincorporated association. Its members comprise a chairman and a
deputy chairman appointed by the Governor of the Bank of England, and representatives *b*
of the 12 bodies mentioned by Sir John Donaldson MR at the beginning of his judgment.
On a day-to-day basis the panel works through its executive, headed by the director
general. He also is appointed by the Governor of the Bank of England, and so is the
chairman of an appeal committee which hears appeals against rulings given by the
executive.

Beyond this the panel seems to have no formal constitution. Whether there is a *c*
contract between its members, or between the Bank of England and the bodies which
appoint representatives, and, if so, what are its terms were not matters in evidence or
explored before us. Presumably, therefore, the code and amendments to it require the
approval of all the members of the panel. However, it seems clear that, whether or not
there is a legally binding contract, there is an understanding between the bodies whose
representatives are members of the panel that they will take all such steps, by way of *d*
disciplinary proceedings against their members or otherwise, as are reasonably and
properly open to them to ensure that the code and the rulings of the panel are observed.
Similarly with the Bank of England: its weighty influence in the City of London is
directed to the same end. Indeed, the leading part played by the Bank of England in
setting up and running the panel is one of the matters which must be kept in mind if
the true role of the panel is to be evaluated. *e*

Another matter which must be noted is the involvement of the Stock Exchange, one
of the bodies appointing a representative on the panel. Since the code is concerned with
take-overs and many, if not most, of the important take-overs will be of companies whose
shares are listed on the Stock Exchange by companies whose shares are similarly listed,
the Stock Exchange is much concerned with the matters which the code seeks to regulate. *f*
In turn, a major element in the enforcement of these regulations is the sanctions which
the Stock Exchange possesses over listed companies.

In this regard it is important also to note that, whatever may have been the position in
the past, it is clear that today the Council of the Stock Exchange is performing a public
duty when deciding whether or not to admit a security to official listing and whether or
not to discontinue such a listing. There is no longer a formal listing agreement entered *g*
into by companies seeking a listing of their securities. The council now has all the powers
required or permitted to be conferred on 'the competent authorities' by, inter alia, the
admission directive of the Council of the European Communities of 5 March 1979 (EC
Council Directive 79/279): see the Stock Exchange (Listing) Regulations 1984, SI 1984/
716. Article 15 of that directive expressly provides that member states shall ensure that
decisions of the competent authorities refusing the admission of a security to official *h*
listing or discontinuing such a listing shall be subject to the right to apply to the courts.
Such an application, in this country, would take the form of an application for judicial
review.

From this it is evident that the activities of the Council of the Stock Exchange in laying
down requirements which a company must observe if it is to obtain and retain an official
listing, and in interpreting those requirements, and adjudicating on alleged breaches of *j*
those requirements, are activities which are subject to judicial review.

Today those requirements include observing the code. In para 6.15 of its official
publication 'Admission of Securities to Listing,' the council states that it attaches 'great
importance' to observance of the code.

The code contains a statement of general principles. For example, that all shareholders a   of the same class of an offeree company must be treated similarly by an offeror, and that during the course of a take-over or when one is in contemplation neither the offeror nor the offeree nor their advisers may furnish information to some shareholders which is not made available to all. The code also contains some detailed rules. Some of these are far-reaching. Thus a company can be compelled, in certain circumstances, to make an offer, or to increase the amount of an offer it has made. Under r 9 a person who acquires shares carrying 30% or more of the voting rights of a company is required to make an offer to

b   purchase all the equity capital of the company. Rule 6(2) provides that if while an offer is open the offeror or any person acting in concert with it purchases shares at above the offer price the offeror shall increase its offer to not less than the highest price paid for the shares so acquired. I do not suggest for one moment that these obligations are other than fair and reasonable and necessary. But, none the less, they are far-reaching, and the sanctions for their enforcement are also formidable: they include suspension of a listing

c   by the Council of the Stock Exchange, in performance of its public duty in that regard.

Thus the system which has evolved, on the point I am now considering, is indistinguishable in its effect from a delegation by the Council of the Stock Exchange to the panel, a group of people which includes its representative, of its public law task of spelling out standards and practices in the field of take-overs which listed companies must observe if they are to enjoy the advantages of a Stock Exchange listing and of

d   determining whether there have been breaches of those standards and practices. As is stated in the code, those who do not conduct themselves in matters relating to takeovers according to the code cannot expect to enjoy the facilities of the securities market in the United Kingdom.

In my view, and quite apart from any other factors which point in the same direction, given the leading and continuing role played by the Bank of England in the affairs of the

e   panel, the statutory source of the powers and duties of the Council of the Stock Exchange, the wide-ranging nature and importance of the matters covered by the code, and the public law consequences of non-compliance, the panel is performing a public duty in prescribing and operating the code (including ruling on complaints).

The particular facts

f   I am not without sympathy for the applicants. The Kuwait Investment Office (KIO) stood to receive about £300,000 in additional underwriting fees from Norton Opax plc if the Norton Opax bid for McCorquodale plc was successful and thus, depending on one's view of the likely trend in the price of Norton Opax shares, that might have given KIO a significant financial interest in the success of the Norton Opax bid. Then at a critical time in the course of the contest between the rival bids, when Datafin plc was

g   precluded from buying McCorquodale shares at above 315p per share and Norton Opax was precluded from buying McCorquodale shares at over 303·3p per share, KIO bought, through the brokers who were joint brokers to the Norton Opax offer, a substantial number of McCorquodale shares at 315·5p. I can well understand why the applicants felt aggrieved.

h   But the difficulties confronting the applicants on this judicial review application are manifestly insuperable. The panel, correctly, approached the matter on the basis of the code's definition of 'acting in concert'. The panel heard evidence from a KIO representative, and accepted that KIO treated investment and underwriting as separate businesses and that genuine investment reasons explained why KIO had not bought earlier and why it bought when it did. These, par excellence, were matters for the panel.

j   Any lingering concern about the scope for abuse of core underwriting agreements, and whether any steps should be taken to prevent a recurrence of this type of situation where suspicion and distrust are bound to breed, are matters for the panel. The evidence of the chairman shows that the panel have these considerations well in mind.

Leave to apply for judicial review granted. Substantive application dismissed.

Solicitors: *S J Berwin & Co* (for the applicants); *Freshfields* (for the panel); *Hepworth & Chadwick*, Leeds (for Norton Opax plc); *Ashurst Morris Crisp & Co* (for Samuel Montagu & Co Ltd).

Frances Rustin   Barrister.

Sharneyford Supplies Ltd v Edge (Barrington Black Austin & Co (a firm), third party)

COURT OF APPEAL, CIVIL DIVISION
KERR, PARKER AND BALCOMBE LJJ
28, 29, 30, 31 JULY, 14 OCTOBER 1986

Sale of land – Damages for breach of contract – Vendor's inability to show good title – Limitation on damages if vendor's inability to show good title not attributable to his default – Contract for purchase of farm with vacant possession on completion – Farm occupied by persons as business tenants – Vendor failing to serve notice terminating tenancy – Vendor failing to take proceedings against tenants – Whether vendor doing all he reasonably could to get vacant possession – Whether damages to be assessed in accordance with general law – Whether purchaser entitled to damages for loss of profits – Whether purchaser's damages limited to expenses incurred in abortive sale.

The defendant owned a maggot farm which he permitted two business tenants to occupy in return for supplying the defendant with maggots for his anglers' business. By a contract of sale the defendant agreed to sell the farm to the plaintiff for £8,500. It was a condition of the contract that vacant possession would be given on completion, but prior to completion the defendant did not serve notice terminating the tenants' tenancy and took no effective steps to remove them from the farm. After completion the tenants offered to vacate the farm on payment of £12,000 but the defendant did not accept that offer. The plaintiff, being unable to obtain vacant possession, brought an action for breach of contract against the defendant claiming as damages not only its expenses incurred in the abortive sale but also loss of profits. The issue whether the plaintiff's damages, if damages were to be awarded, would be limited to its expenses, under the rule that where the vendor of realty was unable to make good title the purchaser was not entitled to damages for the loss of his bargain but was limited to recovering his expenses, was tried as a preliminary issue. The judge held that the defendant was not obliged to take proceedings for possession against the tenants and that since he had done what he reasonably could, short of litigation, to obtain possession the damages payable to the plaintiff were limited to its expenses. The plaintiff appealed.

Held – A vendor who was unable to make good title and sought the protection of the rule limiting the purchaser's damages for breach of contract to the expenses incurred in the abortive sale had to prove that he had used his best endeavours to remove any defect in his title, and if he failed to prove that he had done so the rule did not apply. Since the defendant's tenants had a periodic tenancy which created a legal estate in the land that tenancy constituted a defect in the defendant's title. However, the defendant had failed to use his best endeavours to clear that defect since he had failed to give the tenants notice terminating the tenancy. Accordingly, the rule limiting the plaintiff's damages to its expenses did not apply and the plaintiff was entitled to recover damages for loss of profits. The appeal would accordingly be allowed (see p 595 *b c*, p 596 *a* to *e*, p 597 *d* to *g*, p 598 *h j*, p 599 *c d g h* and p 600 *d*, post).

Day v Singleton [1899] 2 Ch 320 and *Malhotra v Choudhury* [1979] 1 All ER 186 applied.
a Per curiam. The rationale of the rule limiting a purchaser's damages for breach of contract because of the vendor's inability to make a good title depended on the difficulties of making title to unregistered land, but now that registered title to land is general that rationale is no longer valid and the rule should be abolished (see p 594 *h j*, p 599 *h j* and p 600 *c d*, post); *Bain v Fothergill* [1874–80] All ER Rep 83 criticised.

Quaere. Whether before being allowed the protection of the rule limiting a purchaser's
b damages to his expenses, the vendor ought to be required, in the course of using his best endeavours to clear his title, to buy in any estate or incumbrance constituting a defect of title (see p 597 *j*, p 598 *a* to *c* and p 600 *h* to p 601 *a*, post).

Decision of Mervyn Davies J [1985] 1 All ER 976 reversed.

Notes
c For actions for damages by purchasers of realty, see 42 Halsbury's Laws (4th edn) para 267, and for cases on the subject, see 40 Digest (Reissue) 391–403, 3452–3579.

Cases referred to in judgment
Bain v Fothergill (1874) LR 7 HL 158, [1874–80] All ER Rep 83.
d *Braybrooks v Whaley* [1919] 1 KB 435, DC.
Daniel, Re, Daniel v Vassall [1917] 2 Ch 405, [1916–17] All ER Rep 654.
Day v Singleton [1899] 2 Ch 320, CA.
Engell v Fitch (1869) LR 4 QB 659, Ex Ch.
Flureau v Thornhill (1776) 2 Wm Bl 1078, [1775–1802] All ER Rep 91, 96 ER 635.
Hopkins v Grazebrook (1826) 6 B & C 31, 108 ER 364.
e *JW Cafés Ltd v Brownlow Trust Ltd* [1950] 1 All ER 894.
Malhotra v Choudhury [1979] 1 All ER 186, [1980] Ch 52, [1978] 3 WLR 825, CA.
Sikes v Wild (1861) 1 B & S 587, 121 ER 832; *affd* (1863) 4 B & S 421, 122 ER 517, Ex Ch.
Street v Mountford [1985] 2 All ER 289, [1985] AC 809, [1985] 2 WLR 877, HL.
Thomas v Kensington [1942] 2 All ER 263, [1942] 2 KB 181.
Watts v Spence [1975] 2 All ER 528, [1976] Ch 165, [1975] 2 WLR 1039.
f *Wroth v Tyler* [1973] 1 All ER 897, [1974] Ch 30, [1973] 2 WLR 405.

Cases also cited
Keen v Mear [1920] 2 Ch 574, [1920] All ER Rep 147.
Raineri v Miles (Wiejski and anor, third parties) [1980] 2 All ER 145, [1981] AC 1050, HL.
Ray v Druce [1985] 2 All ER 482, [1985] Ch 437.
g

Appeal
The plaintiff, Sharneyford Supplies Ltd (formerly Flinthall Farms Ltd), appealed from so much of the order of Mervyn Davies J ([1985] 1 All ER 976, [1986] Ch 128) made on 18 January 1985 on the trial of preliminary issues, as declared that the quantum of damages
h recoverable by the plaintiff for breach of an agreement made between the plaintiff and the defendant, Philip Michael Edge, for the purchase of a farm be assessed in accordance with the rule in *Bain v Fothergill* (1874) LR 7 HL 158, [1874–80] All ER Rep 83, and sought instead an order that damages for breach of the agreement should be assessed in accordance with the general law of contract. By an order dated 17 October 1985 the Registrar of Civil Appeals ordered that the third party, Barrington Black Austin & Co (a
j firm) (sued as Barrington Black & Co), Mr Edge's former solicitors, who were ordered by the judge to indemnify Mr Edge against the damages payable by Mr Edge to the plaintiff, be added as respondents to the plaintiff's appeal. By a respondent's notice dated 24 October 1985 the third party gave notice that on the hearing of the appeal it would contend that the declaration appealed from should be affirmed but that if the plaintiff's appeal should be allowed the judge's order should be varied by declaring either than Mr

Edge had been under a duty to mitigate his loss or that the third party was not liable to indemnify Mr Edge. The facts are set out in the judgment of Balcombe LJ.

a

Eben Hamilton QC and *Terence Mowschenson* for the plaintiff.
John M Collins for Mr Edge.
Peter Horsfield QC and *W D Ainger* for the third party.

Cur adv vult *b*

14 October. The following judgments were delivered.

BALCOMBE LJ (delivering the first judgment at the invitation of Kerr LJ). This appeal from an order dated 18 January 1985 of Mervyn Davies J on certain preliminary issues in the action (see [1985] 1 All ER 976, [1986] Ch 128) raises once again the question of the *c* application of the rule in *Bain v Fothergill* (1874) LR 7 HL 158, [1874–80] All ER Rep 83: in what circumstances can a purchaser of land recover damages for loss of bargain when the vendor is in breach of contract?

In 1970 the defendant, Philip Michael Edge (Mr Edge), agreed to buy a plot of land of just over half an acre at Monk Bretton, Barnsley, South Yorkshire, from a Mr Bywater. The land, with certain sheds erected on it, has at all material times been used as a maggot *d* farm. Mr Edge went into possession, paid the purchase price over a period (as agreed) of some six years, and on 8 December 1976 was registered at HM Land Registry as proprietor with absolute title to the freehold of the maggot farm. Mr Edge did not find his activities at the farm profitable and in April 1976 entered into negotiations with a Mr Brian Meek (who was subsequently joined by a partner, Mr Denis Holt) for the grant of a lease of the maggot farm for a term of ten years. The rent for the first five years was to *e* be 30 gallons of maggots per week delivered to Mr Edge's premises at 95 Kirkgate, Leeds, where he carried on business as Kirkgate Anglers. For the purposes of these negotiations Mr Edge was represented by a firm of solicitors then called Austin & Co (now Barrington Black Austin & Co, the third party to the action), and the partner who at all times dealt with Mr Edge's affairs was a Mr Roger Hill. The negotiations for a lease came to nothing, *f* but Mr Edge had allowed Messrs Meek and Holt to enter into possession of the maggot farm early in 1976, and from April 1976 they regularly supplied him with maggots and (save when he did not require the maggots, when the weather was bad) this supply has continued ever since. Mr Hill knew of the position of Messrs Meek and Holt and, when they (and a Mr Hughes who was then working with them) and Mr Edge were summonsed for causing a nuisance at the maggot farm, Mr Hill wrote a letter to the local council on *g* behalf of Mr Edge referring to the other defendants (ie Messrs Meek, Holt and Hughes) as Mr Edge's tenants.

So matters continued until the early summer of 1979 when Mr Edge entered into negotiations with the plaintiff company (then known as Flinthall Farms Ltd) for the sale to them of the maggot farm. For the purpose of these negotiations Mr Edge again instructed Mr Hill, and made it clear to Mr Hill (as also did the proposed purchasers' *h* solicitors) that the sale was to be with vacant possession and that in this connection there was concern about the position of Messrs Meek and Holt. Mr Hill did not give evidence at the trial and there has been no appeal by the third party against that part of the judge's order which declared that the third party was liable to indemnify Mr Edge in respect of all sums payable as damages in the action and in respect of his costs of the action and the third party proceedings. The judge accepted Mr Edge as a witness of truth; Mr Hill's acts *j* and omissions remain unexplained.

Inquiries before contact were duly submitted by the plaintiff's solicitors on 21 September 1979 and were answered by Mr Hill on behalf of Mr Edge on 25 September. The relevant questions and answers were as follows, all the answers being prefaced by the rubric:

a
'These replies on behalf of the Vendor are believed to be correct but their accuracy is not guaranteed and they do not obviate the need to make appropriate searches, enquiries and inspections.'

'8. *Adverse Rights.*' To the general question whether the vendor was aware of any adverse rights affecting the property, or of any other overriding interests under s 70(1) of the Land Registration Act 1925, Mr Hill gave the answer: 'No.'

b
'13. *Completion* How long after exchange of contracts will the Vendor be able to give vacant possession of the whole of the property? *Answer* Hopefully 4 weeks
Additional Enquiry 7 We believe that the premises are at present occupied. Vacant possession must be given at completion. Can you please say what steps the Vendor will take to obtain vacant possession and whether the present occupants come within the protection of Part II of the Landlord and Tenant Act 1954? *Answer* The Vendor
c
is already arranging for the property to be vacated and we are informed that the tenants cannot rely on the protection of the Act.'

The judge held that this answer was untrue in the sense that Mr Edge was not then arranging for a vacating of the property (see [1985] 1 All ER 976 at 981, [1986] Ch 128 at 139). No evidence was given to suggest that the second part of the answer was any
d more correct than the first part.

In due course on 14 November 1979 contracts were exchanged between Mr Edge and the plaintiff. The contract was in the form of the Law Society's Contract for Sale (1973 revision) and provided for the sale of the maggot farm by Mr Edge to the plaintiff at a price of £8,500 and for a covenant on the part of the purchaser to supply Mr Edge free of charge with 30 gallons of maggots every week for 20 years, determinable in certain
e circumstances. The judge found that the retail price of maggots was £3·25 a gallon in 1979, so that this part of the contract was worth about £100 per week to Mr Edge (see [1985] 1 All ER 976 at 979, [1986] Ch 128 at 136). A deposit of £850 was paid by the plaintiff. The date fixed for the completion was 12 December 1979 or earlier by arrangement. Under General Condition 3(1) the property was sold with vacant possession on completion.
f
When Mr Hill informed Mr Edge that contracts had been exchanged he asked him, in a letter dated 14 November 1979, to let him know 'the position regarding the tenants at the property'. This surprised Mr Edge. He had supposed that Mr Hill was getting the occupants out. Mr Edge spoke to Mr Holt. Mr Holt told him that he and Mr Meek were not leaving the farm. So Mr Edge again spoke to Mr Hill. Mr Hill said: 'Leave it to me.' So Mr Edge took no steps himself towards securing removal of the occupants. However,
g on 19 November 1979 Mr Edge telephoned Mr Hill's office and left a message which was recorded in the following terms: 'Can you write to people on Maggot Farm as Mr E. has had a word with them and they say they won't move out.' On 10 December 1979 Messrs Ray & Vials, the plaintiff purchaser's solicitors, inquired what steps were being taken to remove the occupants of the farm. On 11 December 1979 Mr Edge again tried to speak to Mr Hill. The completion date of 12 December 1979 came and went without
h completion and with Mr Meek and Mr Holt still in possession. On 28 December 1979 Mr Hill wrote to Mr Edge saying that he had sent papers to counsel for proceedings to be settled, and that the purchaser's solicitors had agreed to await the outcome of the proceedings. Papers were in fact sent to counsel on 2 January 1980. On 6 February 1980 Mr Hill wrote to Mr Holt in the following terms:

j
'We understand that you and a Mr. Meek occupy the property as Licensees of our client and have done so on an informal basis for some time. We believe you are aware that our client now requires possession of the property and have already written to you in this respect without having any reply from you. Will you please indicate as quickly as possible the earliest date on which you will be able to give vacant possession.'

The judge said that he did not see the letter said to have been written 'already' (see [1985] 1 All ER 976 at 982, [1986] Ch 128 at 139). Messrs Shaw & Ashton, solicitors acting for Messrs Meek and Holt, replied with a letter dated 15 February 1980, setting out what had happened in 1976 and since, and claiming that their clients were tenants and entitled to the protection of the Landlord and Tenant Act 1954. This letter was followed by an opinion of counsel dated 28 February 1980, in the course of which counsel said: 'I have settled pleadings but I hold out no hopes whatsoever for their success . . .' The substance of counsel's opinion was that there existed a business tenancy of the maggot farm.

No proceedings were launched, but attempts were made to negotiate a removal of the occupants of the farm. On 29 February 1980 Mr Hill wrote to Shaw & Ashton. It was stated that Mr Edge was willing to consider reimbursing the occupants with a sum of £1,000 said to have been spent by them on repairs and there was talk of a payment as well of twice the rateable value of the farm, a sum between £200 and £300 a year. The letter than itemised five complaints against the occupants for the purpose of suggesting that even if a tenancy existed there were grounds for having the tenants removed. (On this last point the judge commented that Mr Edge 'said in chief that he did not complain about the state of the farm to Mr Hill or to Mr Meek or to anyone' (see [1985] 1 All ER 976 at 982, [1986] Ch 128 at 141).) Shaw & Ashton replied on 4 March 1980:

'We have taken our clients' instructions in the matter and they do not accept as genuine any of the matters specified as breaches of the terms of the tenancy. They are, however, prepared to consider vacating the premises if compensated in the sum of £12,000·00. This is a figure which is not negotiable.'

In March 1980 Mr Edge was away on holiday. He did not see the letter of 4 March until 1984. However, Mr Hill communicated its contents to Mr Edge's father and was told by him that Mr Edge had not the means to pay £12,000. At the trial Mr Edge himself gave evidence to that effect. In any event no action was taken on the £12,000 offer.

The plaintiff's writ against Mr Edge, claiming specific performance of the contract of 14 November 1979 and damages for its breach, in addition to or in lieu of specific performance, was issued on 29 November 1980. A statement of claim and defence were duly served, and Mr Edge brought in Barrington Black Austin & Co as third party, he having by then instructed his present solicitors. Notwithstanding that the plaintiff was still claiming specific performance of the contract, in 1982 Mr Edge, through his new solicitors, entered into negotiations with Shaw & Ashton for the grant of an eight-year lease of the maggot farm to Messrs Holt and Meek, but these negotiations came to nothing. However, Mr Edge still continued, and continues, to receive his weekly supply of maggots from Messrs Meek and Holt. On 15 March 1984 the plaintiff was given leave to amend the statement of claim to abandon the claim for specific performance and to restrict the claim to damages and a return of the deposit. The damages were claimed under two heads: (a) the cost of investigating title and other expenses in the sum of £472·05; and (b) loss of profits from December 1979 to 30 June 1982, that being the date when the plaintiff found other premises at which to carry on the business of breeding maggots. The loss of profits claim is in the sum of £131,544 with interest. The plaintiff duly amended its statement of claim accordingly. By the same order of 15 March 1984 Master Dyson directed that there be tried as preliminary issues the following questions:

'(i) whether the Defendant [Mr Edge] is liable to the Plaintiff (ii) in the event that the Defendant is held to be so liable whether the quantum of damages recoverable by the Plaintiff is to be assessed in accordance with (a) the general law or (b) the rule in Bain v Fothergill ((1874) LR 7 HL 158, [1874–80] All ER Rep 83).'

On 4 July 1984 the master made another order. He directed that the third party be at liberty to appear at the trial of the preliminary issues and be bound by the result of the trial, and that the question of the liability of the third party be tried at the trial of the preliminary issues but subsequent thereto.

These matters came before Mervyn Davies J in December 1984. Liability was conceded
a by Mr Edge on the second day of the trial. By his order of 18 January 1985, after declaring
that the plaintiff was entitled to a return of the deposit with interest, on the preliminary
issues the judge declared (1) that Mr Edge was liable to the plaintiff for damages, and (2)
that the quantum of damages recoverable by the plaintiff for breach of contract be
assessed in accordance with the rule in *Bain v Fothergill* but so that the plaintiff might also
recover such further damages (if any) in tort for innocent misrepresentation as the court
b should determine. On the question of the liability of the third party to Mr Edge he
declared that the third party was liable to indemnify Mr Edge in respect of all sums
payable as damages in the action and in respect of his costs of the action and the third
party proceedings. The substance of the judge's judgment was that Messrs Meek and
Holt had a business tenancy of the maggot farm, that this constituted a defect in Mr
Edge's title and explained his inability to convey the farm with vacant possession
c according to his contract. Prima facie the rule in *Bain v Fothergill* applied, unless Mr Edge
had failed to do what he reasonably could to try to acquire vacant possession of the farm.
The judge held that Mr Edge had done what he reasonably could to try to acquire vacant
possession, so that the damages for breach of contract were limited by the rule in *Bain v
Fothergill*. He also held, declining to follow the decision of Graham J in *Watts v Spence*
[1975] 2 All ER 528, [1976] Ch 165, that innocent misrepresentation did not of itself
d take the case outside the rule in *Bain v Fothergill* so as to entitle the plaintff ipso facto to
damages for loss of bargain. The plaintiff has appealed against the order and on the
hearing of the appeal the substantive argument was between the plaintiff and the third
party. As argued before us, the appeal turns on the application of the rule in *Bain v
Fothergill* to the facts of the present case.

The rule in *Bain v Fothergill* stems from the eighteenth century case of *Flureau v*
e *Thornhill* (1776) 2 Wm Bl 1078 at 1078–1079, [1775–1802] All ER Rep 91 at 91–92. In
that case De Grey CJ said:

> 'Upon a contract for a purchase, if the title proves bad, and the vendor is (without
> fraud) incapable of making a good one, I do not think that the purchaser can be
> entitled to any damages for the fancied goodness of the bargain, which he supposes
f > he has lost.'

Blackstone J gave as the reason for the rule that:

> 'These contracts are merely upon condition, frequently expressed, but always
> implied, that the vendor has a good title.'

g As Lord Hatherley pointed out in *Bain v Fothergill* (1874) LR 7 HL 158 at 210, [1874–80]
All ER Rep 83 at 88, that reason cannot be right because, if there were such a condition,
then in the event of the title failing there could be no action for damages whatever. In
the period of 100 years which followed the decision in *Flureau v Thornhill* some judicial
doubts were expressed, both as to its soundness and as to whether there were any
exceptions to the rule. In *Hopkins v Grazebrook* (1826) 6 B & C 31, 108 ER 364 it was held
h that the rule did not apply when the vendor knew that he was offering a property the
title to which was defective, and his ability to sell it a matter beyond his own control.
When *Bain v Fothergill* came before the House of Lords, the House submitted some
questions for the consideration of the judges, and in answering these questions Denman J
said that mere inability to make a good title did not, of itself, bring a vendor within the
rule laid down in *Flureau v Thornhill* as to damages, but that it depended on the nature of
j the contract, and also on the reasons for the inability, whether he could avail himself of
that rule. A vendor who put up an estate for sale, contracting to make a good title, and
knowing he had no title, was responsible for his breach of contract in the same way and
to the same extent of damages as other persons breaking their contracts (see LR 7 HL 158
at 181–182). If Denman J's views had been accepted, the rule might have been limited to
those cases where the vendor's inability to make a good title was not the result of any act

or omission on his part. There would then have been a parallel with the vendor's usual
qualified covenants for title contained in a conveyance of land, which extend only to the   *a*
purchaser's disturbance by reason of some act, omission or incumbrance of the vendor
himself or any person through whom he derives title, otherwise than by purchase for
value. Unfortunately Denman J was in a minority of one; all the other judges favoured
an unqualified acceptance of the rule in *Flureau v Thornhill* and that was also the view of
the two members of the House, Lord Chelmsford and Lord Hatherley, who delivered
speeches in *Bain v Fothergill. Hopkins v Grazebrook* was overruled. Lord Chelmsford said   *b*
(LR 7 HL 158 at 207, [1874–80] All ER Rep 83 at 87):

> '... I think the rule as to the limits within which damages may be recovered
> upon the breach of a contract for the sale of a real estate must be taken to be without
> exception. If a person enters into a contract for the sale of a real estate knowing that
> he has no title to it, nor any means of acquiring it, the purchaser cannot recover   *c*
> damages beyond the expenses he has incurred by an action for the breach of the
> contract ...'

Lord Hatherley concurred, giving as the foundation of the rule that—

> 'having regard to the very nature of this transaction in the dealings of mankind
> in the purchase and sale of real estates, it is recognised on all hands that the purchaser   *d*
> knows on his part that there must be some degree of uncertainty as to whether,
> with all the complications of our law, a good title can be effectively made by his
> vendor; and taking the property with that knowledge, he is not to be held entitled
> to recover any loss on the bargain he may have made, if in effect it should turn out
> that the vendor is incapable of completing his contract in consequence of his
> defective title.'   *e*

(See LR 7 HL 158 at 210–211, [1874–80] All ER Rep 83 at 88.)
   The facts in *Bain v Fothergill* were that the vendor sold a leasehold interest where the
consent of the lessors was required to the assignment. That consent had not been obtained
at the time of the contract, as the vendor knew. It was held that this was a defect in his
title to which the rule in *Flureau v Thornhill* applied.
   The rule in *Bain v Fothergill* applies to the vendor's inability to complete because of a   *f*
defect in his title. 'Whenever it is a matter of conveyancing, and not a matter of title, it is
the duty of the vendor to do everything that he is enabled to do by force of his own
interest, and also by force of the interest of others whom he can compel to concur in the
conveyance': per Lord Hatherley in *Bain v Fothergill* LR 7 HL 158 at 209. This duty is an
absolute one: it is not enough for the vendor to maintain that he used his best endeavours
if these endeavours are unsuccessful. Examples of failure to take the necessary   *g*
conveyancing steps when it was within the vendor's power to do so are to be found in
Engell v Fitch (1869) LR 4 QB 659 (mortgagee's failure to recover possession from
mortgagor) and *Re Daniel, Daniel v Vassall* [1917] 2 Ch 405, [1916–17] All ER Rep 654
and *Thomas v Kensington* [1942] 2 All ER 263, [1942] 2 KB 181 (vendor's failure to redeem
a mortgage).
   But even limited in this way to defects in the vendor's title, the rule in *Bain v Fothergill*   *h*
is today impossible to justify. Its rationale depends, as has been seen, on the difficulties of
making title to land under English law. Now that registered title to land is the general
rule, this rationale is no longer valid, if indeed it ever was.
   Counsel for Mr Edge submitted to us that the rule still serves a useful purpose in
Yorkshire. In my judgment it serves no useful purpose anywhere within England or   *j*
Wales, and I note that this view is shared by the Law Commission in its Working Paper
no 98 (Transfer of Land: the Rule in Bain v Fothergill (1986)). The rule has been almost
universally condemned. In *Day v Singleton* [1899] 2 Ch 320 at 329 it was described by
Lindley MR as 'anomalous'; an expression repeated by Megarry J in *Wroth v Tyler* [1973]
1 All ER 897 at 918, [1974] Ch 30 at 56. In *Malhotra v Choudhury* [1979] 1 All ER 186 at

197, [1980] Ch 52 at 68 it was described by Stephenson LJ as 'exceptional' and 'anomalous'.
a For a convincing criticism of the rule see *McGregor on Damages* (14th edn, 1980) pp 497–498, para 702. Nevertheless the rule is binding on this court, unless and until the House of Lords declines to follow its own previous decision, or the law is altered by Parliament.

Notwithstanding Lord Chelmsford's statement in *Bain v Fothergill* LR 7 HL 158 at 207, [1874–80] All ER Rep 83 at 88 that the rule 'must be taken to be without exception', within a quarter of a century the Court of Appeal had introduced a most important
b exception to the rule. In *Day v Singleton* [1899] 2 Ch 320 the basic facts were the same as those in *Bain v Fothergill*, namely the sale of a leasehold interest when the lessor's consent to the assignment was required. The Court of Appeal held that the vendor was under a duty to use his best endeavours to procure the licence, and, in the event of a breach of that duty by the vendor, the purchaser was entitled to damages for loss of his bargain. It is true that on the facts of that case the vendor prevented the lessor's consent from being
c given (at 334 per Jeune P), and counsel for the third party submitted that that was the basis of the decision. However, the ratio decidendi of the majority (Lindley MR and Rigby LJ) is to be found in the following passages from the reserved judgment of Lindley MR (at 328–330):

'But if Singleton [the vendor] could have got the lessors' consent and would not—
d still more, if the refusal of that consent was procured by Singleton—Day would have had a right of action for damages against Singleton for a breach of his duty to obtain the lessors' consent, it being in his power to obtain it. In such an action (unless *Bain v. Fothergill* extends to it, which I will consider presently) the measure of damages would not be confined to the deposit and interest, and costs rendered useless; but the measure of damages would be the loss occasioned by not obtaining
e the lease . . . Singleton never asked the lessors to accept Day as their tenant . . . and consequently it would be for him, Singleton, to shew that if he had asked them they would have refused . . . there is no reason to suppose that Day would not have been accepted as a tenant . . . and it ought to be inferred as against Singleton that the lessors would have accepted Day if Singleton had asked them to do so. Having regard to this circumstance, we do not think that *Bain v. Fothergill* covers this case.
f There the vendors did all they could to obtain the lessors' consent to the assignment, and they failed to obtain it . . . If Dunn's representatives [the vendors] had tried to obtain the lessors' consent and had failed, Day could have obtained no more damages than those he has recovered [ie as limited by the rule in *Bain v Fothergill*]. The damage to him is occasioned by his not obtaining what he was entitled to by his contract; and so far as damages are concerned the reason why he fails to obtain what
g he bargained for is immaterial. The damage is the same whatever that reason may be. Why, then, should he obtain more damages if no attempt is made to obtain the lessors' consent than he would be entitled to if a proper effort to obtain such consent had been made and had failed? The only reason which can be assigned for deciding that he is entitled to more is that the rule which limits his damages in the first case is itself an anomalous rule based upon and justified by difficulties in shewing a good title to real property in this country, but one which ought not to be extended to
h cases in which the reasons on which it is based do not apply. This answer to the question with which we are dealing appears to us sufficient and satisfactory. The answer may possibly be difficult to reconcile with some of Lord Chelmsford's observations in *Bain v. Fothergill*, but the answer is, in our opinion, quite consistent with the decision in that case, and it has the merit of preventing the rule there
j upheld from leading to grievous injustice.'

It is apparent from this last passage that Lindley MR recognised the difficulty in distinguishing *Day v Singleton* from the reasoning on which *Bain v Fothergill* was decided. In *Bain v Fothergill* Lord Chelmsford had cited with approval the statement by Blackburn J in *Sikes v Wild* (1861) 1 B & S 587 at 594, 121 ER 832 at 835:

'I do not see how the existence of misconduct can alter the rule by which damages for the breach of a contract are to be assessed . . .'   *a*

Nevertheless, the decision in *Day v Singleton* relied on misconduct (the failure of the vendor to do his best to procure the lessors' licence) to decide the basis on which damages for breach of contract were to be assessed. Further, in so far as the court in *Day v Singleton* purported to follow *Engell v Fitch* (1869) LR 4 QB 659, it failed to draw the distinction, drawn by Lord Hatherley in *Bain v Fothergill*, between matters of conveyancing and *b* defects of title.

Fortunately, *Day v Singleton* [1899] 2 Ch 320 is a decision of the Court of Appeal which is binding on us, and has recently been followed and applied by this court in *Malhotra v Choudhury* [1979] 1 All ER 186, [1980] Ch 52. That was a case where one of two joint owners (who happened to be husband and wife) had entered into a contract for the sale of a house. When sued on his contract the husband claimed that he was unable to make *c* title because his co-owner, his wife, would not agree to the sale. The Court of Appeal (Stephenson and Cumming-Bruce LJJ) held that, where a vendor of real property sought to limit his liability for breach of contract under the rule in *Bain v Fothergill*, he had a duty to show that he had used his best endeavours to fulfil his contractual obligations, the onus being on him, both in the case of a defect of title and of conveyance. Since the defendant had given no evidence of an attempt by himself to obtain his wife's consent to *d* the sale, he had not discharged the burden of proof on him, even though there was evidence that the wife would not agree to the sale. Again counsel for the third party sought to distinguish that case on its facts, which undoubtedly suggested actual bad faith, almost amounting to collusion, on the part of the vendor. However, this court followed *Day v Singleton* and Stephenson LJ, while not suggesting that anything less than lack of good faith would exclude the rule in *Bain v Fothergill*, held that unwillingness to use best *e* endeavours to carry out a contractual promise is bad faith for this purpose ([1979] 1 All ER 186 at 200, [1980] Ch 52 at 72–73):

'. . . for there to be bad faith which takes the case out of this exceptional rule it is not necessary that there should be either a deliberate attempt to prevent title being made good or anything more than the unwillingness which I find it inevitable to *f* infer in this case. If a man makes a promise and does not use his best endeavours to keep it, it cannot take much and, in my judgment, may not need more to make him guilty of bad faith and to entitle the victim of his bad faith to his full share of damages to compensate him for what he has lost by reason of that breach of contract and bad faith.'

g

Cumming-Bruce LJ said ([1979] 1 All ER 186 at 204, [1980] Ch 52 at 77):

'. . . it is quite clear that on the ratio of *Day v Singleton* the vendor who seeks to avail himself of the protection afforded by what is described as the rule in *Bain v Fothergill* must go to the length of satisfying the court that he has done all that he reasonably can to mitigate the effects of his breach of contract by trying to remove *h* such fault on the title as appears.'

Another example of the application of the principle of *Day v Singleton* is to be found in *Braybrooks v Whaley* [1919] 1 KB 435: failure by a mortgagee vendor to make the necessary application to the court (under wartime legislation) for leave to realise his security.   *j*

These being the relevant legal principles, it remains to apply them to the facts of the present case. The finding of the judge that Messrs Meek and Holt had a periodic tenancy of the maggot farm, although the subject of one of the grounds in the notice of appeal, was not seriously challenged before us and in my judgment was clearly correct. This tenancy created a legal estate in the land (see *Street v Mountford* [1985] 2 All ER 289 at

291, [1985] AC 809 at 814) and was subject to the protection of Pt II of the Landlord and
a Tenant Act 1954. Since it could not be determined until long after the date fixed for
completion, it constituted a defect in Mr Edge's title which prevented him from carrying
out his contract to convey the farm with vacant possession. So, as the judge held, prima
facie the rule in Bain v Fothergill is applicable (see [1985] 1 All ER 976 at 986, [1986] Ch
128 at 143).

The question then arises: did Mr Edge establish that he had done all that he reasonably
b could to mitigate the effect of his breach of contract by trying to remove this defect on
his title? The judge held that he had (see [1985] 1 All ER 976 at 989, [1986] Ch 128 at
147). He summarised in numbered paragraphs what Mr Edge had done (see [1985] 1 All
ER 976 at 987–988, [1986] Ch 128 at 145–146). Of these numbered paragraphs, paras (i)
to (v) inclusive dealt with events up to and including the exchange of contracts. I fail to
see how these can have any relevance to the question at issue. Of the events subsequent
c to the date of contract, the only steps which it could be said that Mr Edge (or his solicitor,
whose acts or omissions for this purpose must be attributed to Mr Edge) took to try and
remove the defect on his title were the telephone conversation with Mr Hill between 14
and 19 November 1979 and the letters of 6 and 29 February 1980. The one striking
omission is that at no time did Mr Edge give to Messrs Meek and Holt notice to determine
their tenancy, either at common law or under s 25 of the Landlord and Tenant Act 1954.
d In the absence of such notices having been given, I find it impossible to say that Mr Edge
had done all that he reasonably could to try and remove the defect on his title and acquire
vacant possession of the farm. Counsel for the third party submitted that such notices
would have been to no avail, since under s 25 of the 1954 Act a notice of not less than six
months is necessary, and any such notice would necessarily have expired long after the
date fixed for completion; further, there was no likelihood that Mr Edge could have
e successfully resisted an application by Messrs Meek and Holt for a new tenancy. However,
it is by no means certain that Messrs Meek and Holt, if served with formal notice to
determine their tenancy, and thereby realising the seriousness with which Mr Edge
treated the matter, would have sought to resist giving up possession. It is significant that
neither Mr Meek nor Mr Holt was called to give evidence at the trial and, as has already
been said, the burden of proof to establish that he had taken all reasonable steps rested on
f Mr Edge. But in any event that argument is similar to that which was rejected in both
Day v Singleton and Malhotra v Choudhury: that it matters not that the attempt to clear the
title might have failed: it must at least have been tried. It follows that I am unable to
accept the judge's conclusion that Mr Edge had, by himself or his solicitor, done what he
reasonably could to try to acquire vacant possession of the farm (see [1985] 1 All ER 976
at 989, [1986] Ch 128 at 147). I also disagree with his conclusion that there was no bad
g faith on the part of Mr Edge (see [1985] 1 All ER 976 at 988, [1986] Ch 128 at 146), if
one adopts the definition of 'bad faith' in this context given by Stephenson LJ in Malhotra
v Choudhury [1979] 1 All ER 186 at 200, [1980] Ch 52 at 72–73. On this ground alone I
would allow this appeal.

However, it was argued before us, as it was before the judge, that Mr Edge's obligation
h to use his best endeavours to clear the defect on his title extended to an obligation on his
part to pay the £12,000 to buy out Messrs Meek and Holt, if that was a reasonable sum
in all the circumstances. It is not clear from his judgment whether the judge accepted
this submission as a matter of principle. He said that he had 'taken account' of the
suggestion that the £12,000 offer ought to have been pursued, at any rate in the sense
that there should have been negotiations to reduce that figure. However, he then went
j on to say that, in view of the intimation that the figure was not negotiable, he did not
think that Mr Edge was obliged to take that course (see [1985] 1 All ER 976 at 989,
[1986] Ch 128 at 147).

If a vendor is liable to use his best endeavours to clear any defect from his title, I can
see the logic of the argument that those endeavours could include, in an appropriate case,
the payment of a sum of money to a third party. However, logic has played little part in

the development of this particular branch of the law, and to apply it strictly in this instance would only serve to demonstrate the illogicality of some of the earlier *a* distinctions. The particular difficulty I find in following this argument to its logical conclusion is that the rule in *Bain v Fothergill* would then cease to exist, since there would be few cases in which a defect in title could not be removed if the sum offered were large enough. While I accept that it would be no bad thing if the rule were to cease to exist, I cannot believe that this is a valid way of removing it. Further, the practical problems would be great. How would the court determine, in any given case, whether the sum *b* which an incumbrancer might require to surrender the incumbrance which constituted a defect on the title was reasonable? In a case, such as *JW Cafés Ltd v Brownlow Trust Ltd* [1950] 1 All ER 894, when the defect consists of restrictive convenants affecting the title, how far would the vendor have to go in trying to procure the removal of these restrictive covenants, and at what price? To extend the principle of *Day v Singleton* [1899] 2 Ch 320 to this extent, logical though it might otherwise appear, could be productive of endless *c* litigation. Although there is no authority directly in point, I am fortified in my view by a passage in the leading textbook, *Williams on Vendor and Purchaser* (4th edn, 1936) p 1020:

> 'And where his [the vendor's] title is imperfect, he is of course not liable to pay *d* substantial damages if he declines to buy in any outstanding estate or incumbrance. Such an act as this would depend on others' consent, and does not lie entirely within his own power.'

It was also argued before us that the continued acceptance by Mr Edge of the supply of maggots from Messrs Meek and Holt, and the 1982 negotiations for the grant of a new *e* lease to them, in some way amounted to a failure by Mr Edge to use his best endeavours to clear the defect in his title. I am unable to follow this argument. While there appears to have been no evidence to justify the judge's finding (see [1985] 1 All ER 976 at 988, [1986] Ch 128 at 146) that the maggots were being produced and had to be used (impliedly by Mr Edge and no one else), so long as the tenancy had not been determined there was no reason why Mr Edge should not accept the rent payable under it; his failure *f* was to take the necessary steps to terminate the tenancy. Similarly, the 1982 negotiations were not of themselves of any significance; the most that can be said about them is that they were inconsistent with any attempt by Mr Edge to recover vacant possession from Messrs Meek and Holt.

The notice of appeal also included as a ground of appeal that the judge ought to have followed the decision of Graham J in *Watts v Spence* [1975] 2 All ER 528, [1976] Ch 165. *g* Counsel for the plaintiff very wisely did not attempt to argue this ground before us. In the circumstances I need only say that, like the judge, I find the criticism of *Watts v Spence* in *McGregor on Damages* (14th edn, 1980) pp 1000–1002, paras 1486–1489 entirely convincing.

In the circumstances I would allow this appeal and substitute for the second declaration made by the judge on the preliminary issues a declaration that the quantum of damages *h* recoverable by the plaintiff for breach of contract be assessed in accordance with the general law but so that the plaintiff may also recover such further damages (if any) in tort for innocent misrepresentation as the court shall determine.

KERR LJ. I have had the opportunity of reading the judgment of Balcombe LJ and *j* agree with his conclusion that the plaintiff's appeal should be allowed on the facts, because the defendant has failed to satisfy the requirement which has fortunately been engrafted on the rule in *Bain v Fothergill* (1874) LR 7 HL 158, [1874–80] All ER Rep 83 by this court in *Day v Singleton* [1899] 2 Ch 320 and followed in *Malhotra v Choudhury* [1979] 1 All ER 186, [1980] Ch 52. This qualification of the rule is that the vendor must

show that he did all that he reasonably could to perform the contract by removing any
a defect in the title which he agreed to transfer.

The judge clearly asked himself the correct question on the basis of these authorities.
He said ([1985] 1 All ER 976 at 986, [1986] Ch 128 at 144):

> 'In these circumstances it seems to me that the question for consideration is
> whether there were taken by the defendant or on his behalf those steps towards the
> *b* removal of the occupants of the farm which the law requires of him. More precisely,
> did the defendant by himself or his solicitor do what he reasonably could do to try
> to acquire vacant possession of the farm?'

However, with all due respect, I cannot accept that the facts listed in the following
passages of the judgment (see [1985] 1 All ER 976 at 987–988, [1986] Ch 128 at 145–
c 146) can possibly justify the affirmative answer which the judge gave to this question
(see [1985] 1 All ER 976 at 989, [1986] Ch 128 at 147). Neither Mr Edge nor, more
relevantly on the facts, Mr Hill took any steps to terminate whatever may have been the
rights of Messrs Meek and Holt in relation to the farm or took any steps to obtain vacant
possession. The service of a notice to quit was clearly the essential first step which had to
be taken by or on behalf of Mr Edge in any endeavour to comply with the requirements
d of the passage quoted above. But no such notice was ever given, and the judgment makes
no reference to this crucial and suprising omission. The history shows no real pressure,
let alone persistence, in any endeavour on the part of the vendor to perform this contract.
The fault clearly lay with Mr Hill, and Mr Edge has instituted third party proceedings
against his firm's insurers to which there can be no answer.

In my view the judge's review of the facts was far too lenient, from the point of view
e of the vendor, to justify his conclusion. The reason, I think, is that he applied an
insufficiently stringent test in answering the question which he correctly posed ([1985]
1 All ER 976 at 986, [1986] Ch 128 at 144). His language suggests that he may well have
taken the view that it was sufficient for Mr Edge to show that he was sincere in his wish
to obtain vacant possession and that he had manifested to Messrs Meek and Holt his
desire that they should go. This may have sufficed for the purposes of the original
f decision in *Bain v Fothergill* but not for the subsequent cases. Thus, the judge said that the
letter of 6 February 1980 was 'a plain indication of a wish to bring occupation to an end',
that Messrs Meek and Holt 'were in no way misled . . . into thinking that the defendant
was content that they should stay on the farm', and that both 'knew that at all times the
defendant was anxious to see their departure' (see [1985] 1 All ER 976 at 988, [1986] Ch
128 at 146). While he clearly accepted that the absolute nature of the rule in *Flureau v
g Thornhill* (1776) 2 Wm Bl 1078, [1775–1802] All ER Rep 91 and *Bain v Fothergill* had been
qualified by the subsequent decisions to which I have referred, he appears to have limited
their effect to the need for the vendor to show no more than some reasonable and sincere
manifestation of his desire to perform his contract by the removal of the relevant defect
in his title. However, it is clear from the passages cited by Balcombe LJ that the
h requirements imposed by these decisions, which a vendor must meet in order to obtain
the protection of the rule, go a great deal further, and, equally clearly, that on the facts of
this case the defendant is unable to show that he complied with these requirements.
That, fortunately, is sufficient to decide that, on the authorities binding on us, this appeal
must clearly be allowed, and it would be undesirable to say any more about the possible
legal consequences of hypothetically different facts.

j I would only add my entire concurrence, as at present advised, with the provisional
views expressed by the Law Commission in Working Paper no 98 (1986) on the
desirability of abolishing the rule in *Bain v Fothergill*, subject to the right of vendors to
stipulate expressly, if they wish to do so, for a limitation of their liability in damages to
compensate the purchasers for the loss of their bargain in the event of some defect in the
vendors' title. The history of the cases cited in the working paper and in the judgment of

Balcombe LJ in itself illustrates the basic injustice of the rule whenever a vendor is, or reasonably should be, aware of the defect in his title which causes the problem. Nowadays *a* this must surely be the position in virtually every case of a defective title. The decision of this court in *Day v Singleton* in 1899 was no doubt influenced by this consideration, since it is difficult, if not impossible, to square it with the apparently absolute nature of the rule in *Bain v Fothergill*. But fortunately it is binding on us, together with *Malhotra v Choudhury* [1979] 1 All ER 186, [1980] Ch 52, and marked the beginning of a lengthy series of cases, now including the present one, in which our courts have again and again *b* sought to escape from the clutches of the rule.

No case in which the rule was considered or applied has in fact involved any problem in ascertaining and fully understanding the defect of title in question. Admittedly this was also the position in *Bain v Fothergill* itself in 1874. But that case merely followed *Flureau v Thornhill* decided in 1776, a century earlier.

The explanation, as pointed out by Megarry J in *Wroth v Tyler* [1973] 1 All ER 897 at *c* 918, [1974] Ch 30 at 56 in a memorable phrase attributed to Lord Westbury, is no doubt that the rule was originally laid down for defects in title which lay concealed in title deeds 'difficult to read, disgusting to touch, and impossible to understand'. There seems to be no justification for its retention today.

PARKER LJ. I have had the opportunity of reading the judgments of both Kerr and *d* Balcombe LJJ. I agree with their conclusion that the appeal should be allowed and with their reasons for such conclusion. I also entirely agree that the rule in *Bain v Fothergill* (1874) LR 7 HL 158, [1874–80] All ER Rep 83 should be abolished at the earliest possible moment. It is not only anomalous and illogical. It is also unjust. If, for example, a vendor sells land, which he knows is subject to a tenancy, and contracts specifically to sell with vacant possession, he makes, in effect, a specific promise that he will get the tenants out. *e* If he breaks that promise I can see no reason in justice or logic or the original basis of the rule why he should not have to pay ordinary damages for breach of contract. It is not a question of it emerging after contract that there is a defective title, from the consequences of which the vendor should be relieved owing to the complexities of the law. The breach is no more excusable than is the breach by a seller of goods who has no title at the time of contract, who believes he will acquire one by the time of delivery but who fails to do *f* so. Where, as here, the purchaser has made it abundantly clear that vacant possession is vital to him there is, in my view, even less reason to relieve the vendor of liability for ordinary damages when he fails to honour a promise to give such possession.

I would add this. If it be right that the rule does not apply where the land sold is mortgaged and the vendor fails to redeem the mortgage (*Re Daniel, Daniel v Vassall* [1917] 2 Ch 405, [1916–17] All ER Rep 654 and *Thomas v Kensington* [1942] 2 All ER 263, [1942] *g* 2 KB 181), I can see no reason why it should apply where, for example, a tenant has offered to surrender his tenancy but the vendor fails to accept the offer or pay the price. It may be that the vendor does not want to pay the price but he will be faced with no more than the financial decision whether he should pay the price and honour his contract or break his contract and pay ordinary damages for the breach. Such a decision frequently *h* faces a seller of future goods when the market goes against him and buying in to honour his contract will result in the profit which he expected turning into a heavy loss. At present it appears to me that it is just as much in the power of a vendor who has an open offer, acceptance of which will enable him of his own motion to fulfil his contract, to do just that, as it is in the power of a mortgagor to fulfil his contract by redeeming a mortgage. *j*

It appears to me to follow from this that the rule ought also not to apply whenever the vendor could fulfil the promise to give vacant possession by payment of money. He may not wish to do so or may be without the resources to do so but, if he fails to do so, his inability to perform his contract is not in any real sense due to a defect in title but is due

to his unwillingness or financial inability to pay the price of performance. He is in the
a same position as the mortgagor who has not the resources to redeem the mortgage.

It is not in the present case necessary to decide the point but in the light of the above I
must express my doubts about the correctness of the statement from *Williams on Vendor
and Purchaser* (4th edn, 1936) p 1020 cited by Balcombe LJ that the vendor is not liable
to pay substantial damages if he fails to buy in any outstanding estate or incumbrance. If
in the present case, for example, the tenants had offered to vacate on payment of no more
b than their removal expenses I can see no principle which would justify the vendor being
relieved of the substantial damages which he was aware the purchaser would suffer if he
declined to pay and thus broke his promise to give vacant possession. If this be so it seems
to me also to follow that where there is no offer by the tenants the use of best endeavours
must involve at least an attempt to procure the result by negotiation.

c *Appeal by plaintiff allowed. Declaration on preliminary issues varied to declaration that quantum
of damages recoverable by plaintiff be assessed in accordance with the general law. Appeal by
third party dismissed. Leave to appeal to the House of Lords granted.*

Solicitors: *Ray & Vials*, Northampton (for the plaintiff); *Godlove Saffman Lyth & Goldman*,
Leeds (for Mr Edge); *Willey Hargrave*, Leeds (for the third party).

Wendy Shockett   Barrister.

Practice Direction

a

RESTRICTIVE PRACTICES COURT

Restrictive trade practices – Court – Practice – Variation of decision – Application – Contents of affidavit – Listing of proceedings – Evidence – Information to be provided to court – Restrictive Trade Practices Act 1976, s 4.

b

In circumstances where (a) a variation of a previous decision of the court is sought which would not in itself restrict or discourage competition to any material degree and (b) the director and any other party who appeared at the hearing of the previous proceedings consents to the variation, the application for leave together with the previous declaration or order of the court may be lodged with the proper officer of the court for consideration by the court.

c

The application for leave should be made by affidavit containing (i) (except in cases to which s 4(5) of the Restrictive Trade Practices Act 1976 applies) a statement of the material change in the relevant circumstances and (ii) a statement that the proposed variation would not in itself restrict or discourage competition, and exhibiting the signed consent of the director to the variation and any other party who appeared at the hearing of the previous proceedings.

d

The proper officer of the court will then put the application for leave before the court. If satisfied that leave may be given and that the application under s 4(1) of the 1976 Act should be granted the court may grant leave and cause the proceedings to be listed; the decision will be given in open court without the parties or their representatives being required to attend.

e

If on the evidence, and on any other evidence required by the court, the court is not satisfied that it is proper for the matter to be dealt with in this way the application under s 4(1) will be listed for hearing in the normal way.

Wherever possible, parties and their advisers are asked to ensure that sufficient information is provided to enable the court to be satisfied as to the propriety of making an order without hearing the parties since this direction is designed to save time and costs.

f

By direction of the President.

11 December 1986

Practice Direction

g

(Bankruptcy 3/86)

CHANCERY DIVISION

Bankruptcy – Petition – Creditor's petition – New form of petition – Completion of form – Title – Debt claimed – Date of service of statutory demand – Certificate at end of petition – Deposit on petition – Insolvency Act 1986, ss 267–269 – RSC Ord 65, r 7 – Insolvency Rules 1986, rr 6.1(4), 6.3, 6.6–6.12, Sch 4, Forms 6.7–6.9.

h

To help practitioners to complete the new forms of a creditor's bankruptcy petition (Insolvency Act 1986, ss 267 to 269; Insolvency Rules 1986, SI 1986/1925, rr 6.6 to 6.12, Sch 4, Forms 6.7 to 6.9), attention is drawn to the following points.

j

1. The petition does not require dating, signing or witnessing.

2. In the title it is only necessary to recite the debtor's name, eg Re John William Smith or Re J W Smith (male). Any alias or trading name will appear in the body of the

petition. This also applies to all other statutory forms other than those which require the
'full title'.

3. Where the petition is based on a statutory demand, only the debt claimed in the
demand may be included in the petition, except that interest or other charges which
have accrued since the date of the demand to the date of the petition may be added: see
r 6.8(1)(c) of the 1986 rules read with r 6.1(4).

4. When completing para 2 of the petition, attention is drawn to r 6.8(1)(a) to (c),
particularly where the 'aggregate sum' is made up of a number of debts.

5. Date of service of the statutory demand (para 4 of the petition): (a) In the case of
personal service, the date of service as set out in the affidavit of service should be recited
and whether service is effected *before/after* 1600 hrs on Monday to Friday or *before/after*
1200 hrs on Saturdays: see RSC Ord 65, r 7. (b) In the case of substituted service
(otherwise than by advertisement), the date alleged in the affidavit of service should be
recited. (As to the date alleged, see *Practice Direction (Bankruptcy 4/86)* [1987] 1 All ER
604.) (c) In the strictly limited case of substituted service by advertisement under r 6.3 of
the 1986 rules, the date to be alleged is the date of the advertisement's appearance or, as
the case may be, its first appearance: see rr 6.3(3) and 6.11(8).

6. There is no need to include in the preamble to or at the end of the petition details
of the person authorised to present the petition.

7. Certificates at the end of the petition: (a) the period of search for prior petitions has
been reduced to *three* years; (b) where a statutory demand is based wholly or in part on a
county court judgment the following certificate, which replaces the affidavit of county
court search, is to be added:

> 'I/We certify that on the   day of   19   I/we attended on the
>   County Court and was/were informed by an officer of the court that no
> money had been paid into court in the action or matter   v
> Plaint No   pursuant to the statutory demand.'

This certificate will not be required when the demand also requires payment of a
separate debt, not based on a county court judgment, the amount of which exceeds the
bankruptcy level (at present £750).

8. Deposit on petition. The deposit will now be taken by the court and forwarded to
the Official Receiver. The petition fee and deposit should be handed to the Supreme
Court Accounts Office, Fee Stamping Rooms, who will record the receipt and will
impress two entries on the original petition, one in respect of the court fee and the other
in respect of the deposit. Cheque(s) for the whole amount should be made payable to
'HM Paymaster General'.

JOHN BRADBURN
Chief Bankruptcy Registrar.

18 December 1986

Practice Direction

(Bankruptcy 4/86)

CHANCERY DIVISION

Bankruptcy – Statutory demand – Service – Substituted service – Circumstances in which substituted service permissible – Methods of substituted service – Substituted service by post – Substituted service by advertisement – Form of advertisement – Deemed time of service where substituted service by post – Insolvency Rules 1986, rr 6.3, 6.11.

Bankruptcy – Petition – Service – Substituted service – Evidence required to justify order for substituted service – Deemed time of service where substituted service by post – Insolvency Rules 1986, rr 6.14, 6.15.

Statutory demands

1. The creditor is under an obligation to do all that is reasonable to bring the statutory demand to the debtor's attention and, if practicable, to cause personal service to be effected. Where it is not possible to effect prompt personal service, service may be effected by other means such as first class post or insertion through a letter box.

2. Advertisement can only be used as a means of substituted service where: (a) the demand is based on a judgment or order of any court; (b) the debtor has absconded or is keeping out of the way with a view to avoiding service; and (c) there is no real prospect of the sum due being recovered by execution or other process.

As there is no statutory form of advertisement, the court will accept an advertisement in the following form:

'STATUTORY DEMAND

(Debt for liquidated sum payable immediately following a judgment or order of the court)

To (block letters)

of

TAKE NOTICE that a statutory demand has been issued by

Name of creditor

Address

The creditor demands payment of £   the amount now due on a judgment/ order of the High Court of Justice   Division [or   County Court] dated the   day of   19

The statutory demand is an important document and it is deemed to have been served on you on the date of the first appearance of this advertisement. You *must* deal with this demand within 21 days of the service on you or you could be made bankrupt and your property and goods taken away from you. If you are in any doubt as to your position, you should seek advice *immediately* from a solicitor or your nearest Citizens' Advice Bureau.

The statutory demand can be obtained or is available for inspection and collection from:

Name

Address

[Solicitor for] the creditor

Tel no   Reference

You have only 21 days from the date of the first appearance of this advertisement before the creditor may present a bankruptcy petition'

3. In all cases where substituted service is effected, the creditor must have taken all those steps which would suffice to justify the court making an order for substituted service of a petition. The steps to be taken to obtain an order for substituted service are set out below. Practitioners are reminded that failure to comply with the requirements of this Practice Direction may result in the court declining to file the petition (see r 6.11(5)(a)).

4. *Order for substituted service of a bankruptcy petition* In most cases, the following evidence will suffice to justify an order for substituted service:

(a) one personal call at the residence and place of business of the debtor where both are known or at either of such places as is known. Where it is known that the debtor has more than one residential or business address, personal calls should be made at all addresses;

(b) should the creditor fail to effect service, a first class prepaid letter should be written to the debtor referring to the call(s), the purpose of the same and the failure to meet with the debtor, adding that a further call will be made for the same purpose on the
day of   19   at   hours at [*place*]. At least two business days' notice should be given of the appointment and copies of the letter sent to all known addresses of the debtor. The appointment letter should also state that (i) in the event of the time and place not being convenient, the debtor is to name some other time and place reasonably convenient for the purpose, (ii) (statutory demands) if the debtor fails to keep the appointment the creditor purposes to serve the debtor by advertisement (see para 2) *or* post *or* insertion through a letter box *or* as the case may be, and that, in the event of a bankruptcy petition being presented, the court will be asked to treat such service as service of the demand on the debtor, (iii) (petitions) if the debtor fails to keep the appointment, application will be made to the court for an order for substituted service either by advertisement or in such other manner as the court may think fit;

(c) in attending any appointment made by letter, inquiry should be made whether the debtor has received all letters left for him. If the debtor is away, inquiry should also be made whether or not letters are being forwarded to an address within the jurisdiction (England and Wales) or elsewhere;

(d) if the debtor is represented by a solicitor, an attempt should be made to arrange an appointment for personal service through such solicitor. Practitioners are reminded that the rules provide for a solicitor accepting service of a statutory demand on behalf of his client but there is no similar provision in respect of service of a bankruptcy petition;

(e) the supporting affidavit should deal with all the above matters including all relevant facts as to the debtor's whereabouts and whether the appointment letter(s) has/ have been returned.

5. Where the court makes an order for substituted service by first class ordinary post, the order will normally provide that service be deemed to be effected on the seventh day after posting. Practitioners serving a statutory demand by post may consider using the same method of calculating service.

JOHN BRADBURN
Chief Bankruptcy Registrar.

18 December 1986

Practice Direction

(Bankruptcy 5/86)

CHANCERY DIVISION

Bankruptcy – Statutory demand – Service – Proof of service – Insolvency Rules 1986, r 6.11(3)(4)(5), Sch 4, Forms 6.11, 6.12.

1. The Insolvency Rules 1986, SI 1986/1925, r 6.11(3) provides that, if the statutory demand has been served personally, the affidavit of service must be made by the person who effected that service.

Rule 6.11(4) provides that, if service of the demand (however effected) has been acknowledged in writing, the affidavit of service must be made by the creditor or by a person acting on his behalf.

Rule 6.11(5) provides that, if neither r 6.11(3) nor r 6.11(4) applies, the affidavit must be made by a person having direct knowledge of the means adopted for serving the demand.

2. *Form 6.11 (affidavit of personal service of statutory demand)*
This form should only be used where the demand has been served personally and acknowledged in writing: see r 6.11(4).

If the demand has not been acknowledged in writing, the affidavit should be made by the process server and paras 2 and 3 (part) of Form 6.11 should be omitted: see r 6.11(3).

3. *Form 6.12 (affidavit of substituted service of statutory demand)*
This form can be used whether or not service of the demand has been acknowledged in writing. Paragraphs 4 and 5 (part) provide for the alternatives.

Practitioners are reminded, however, that the appropriate person to make the affidavit may not be the same in both cases.

If the demand has been acknowledged in writing, the appropriate person is the creditor or a person acting on his behalf. If the demand has not been acknowledged, that person must be someone having direct knowledge of the means adopted for serving the demand.

Practitioners may find it more convenient to allow process servers to carry out the necessary investigation whilst reserving to themselves the service of the demand. In these circumstances para 1 should be deleted and the following paragraph substituted:

'1. Attempts have been made to serve the demand, full details of which are set out in the accompanying affidavit of　　　　.'

31 December 1986

JOHN BRADBURN
Chief Bankruptcy Registrar.

Practice Direction

(Bankruptcy 1/87)

CHANCERY DIVISION

Bankruptcy – Statutory demand – Application to set aside statutory demand – Affidavit in support – Copies of documents to be lodged – Effect of not lodging required copies of documents – Circumstances in which statutory demand will be set aside – Extension of time to apply to set aside statutory demand – Insolvency Rules 1986, rr 6.4, 6.5, 7.4(1), Sch 4, Forms 6.4, 6.5.

1. The application (Insolvency Rules 1986, SI 1986/1925, Sch 4, Form 6.4) and affidavit in support (Form 6.5) exhibiting a copy of the statutory demand must be filed in court within 18 days of service of the statutory demand on the debtor. Where service is effected by advertisement in a newspaper the period of 18 days is calculated from the date of the first appearance of the advertisement: see *Practice Direction (Bankruptcy 4/86)* [1987] 1 All ER 604. Three copies of each document must be lodged with the application to enable the court to serve notice of the hearing date on the applicant, the creditor and the person named in Pt B of the statutory demand.

2. Where, to avoid expense, copies of the documents are not lodged with the application, any order of the registrar fixing a venue is conditional on copies of the documents being lodged on the next business day after the registrar's order, otherwise the application will be deemed to have been dismissed.

3. Where the statutory demand is based on a judgment or order, the court will not at this stage go behind the judgment or order and inquire into the validity of the debt nor, as a general rule, will it adjourn the application to await the result of an application to set aside the judgment or order.

4. When the debtor (a) claims to have a counterclaim, set-off or cross demand (whether or not he could have raised it in the action in which the judgment or order was obtained) which equals or exceeds the amount of the debt or debts specified in the statutory demand or (b) disputes the debt (not being a debt subject to a judgment or order), the court will normally set aside the statutory demand if, in its opinion, on the evidence there is a genuine triable issue.

5. *Applications for an extension of time to apply to set aside a statutory demand*
Each term two judges of the Chancery Division will sit to hear insolvency cases, one of whom (the bankruptcy judge) will be primarily concerned to hear cases affecting individual debtors.

After the expiration of 18 days from the date of service of the statutory demand, the debtor must apply for an extension of time if he wishes to apply to set aside the demand. The application for extension of time and (if necessary) to restrain the presentation of a bankruptcy petition should be made to the bankruptcy judge, but in cases of urgency and where the bankruptcy judge is not available the application may be made to the judge hearing ordinary motions. (This requirement will appear in a Practice Direction to be published.)

Paragraphs 1 and 2 of Form 6.5 (affidavit in support of application to set aside statutory demand) should be used in support of the application for extension of time with the following additional paragraphs:

'3. That to the best of my knowledge and belief the creditor(s) named in the demand has/have not presented a petition against me.

4. That the reasons for my failure to apply to set aside the demand within 18 days after service are as follows: . . .

5. Unless restrained by injunction the creditor(s) may present a bankruptcy petition against me.'

The fee on the application will be £15.

JOHN BRADBURN
6 January 1987   Chief Bankruptcy Registrar.

Practice Direction

(Chancery 1/87)

CHANCERY DIVISION

Trust and trustee – Counsel's opinion – Court's power to authorise action to be taken in reliance on counsel's opinion – Practice – Affidavits and documents required to support application to court – Consideration by judge – Service of notices – Costs – Administration of Justice Act 1985, s 48 – RSC Ord 15, r 13A, Ord 93, r 21.

1. In applications under s 48 of the Administration of Justice Act 1985 and RSC Ord 93, r 21 the ex parte originating summons shall be supported by an affidavit to which shall be exhibited: (a) copies of all relevant documents; (b) instructions to counsel; (c) counsel's opinion; (d) draft minutes of the desired order.

2. The affidavit (or the exhibits thereto) shall state: (a) the names of all persons who are, or may be, affected by the order sought; (b) all surrounding circumstances admissible and relevant in construing the document; (c) the date of call of counsel and his experience in the construction of trust documents; (d) the approximate value of the fund or property in question; (e) whether it is known to the applicant that a dispute exists and, if so, details of such dispute.

3. At the first hearing of the originating summons, if the evidence is complete, the master will refer the papers to the judge.

4. The judge will consider the papers and, if necessary, direct service of notices under RSC Ord 15, r 13A or request such further information as he may desire. If the judge is satisfied that the order sought is appropriate, the order will be made and sent to the applicant.

5. If following service of notices under Ord 15, r 13A any acknowledgment of service is received, the applicant shall apply to the master (on notice to the parties who have so acknowledged) for directions. If the applicant desires to pursue the application to the court, in the ordinary case the master will direct that the case proceeds as a construction summons.

6. If on the hearing of the construction summons the judge is of opinion that any party who has entered an acknowledgment of service has no reasonably tenable argument contrary to counsel's opinion, in the exercise of his discretion he may order such party to pay any costs thrown away, or part thereof.

SIR NICOLAS BROWNE-WILKINSON V-C
28 January 1987

Sampson v Crown Court at Croydon

HOUSE OF LORDS

LORD BRIDGE OF HARWICH, LORD BRANDON OF OAKBROOK, LORD GRIFFITHS, LORD ACKNER AND LORD GOFF OF CHIEVELEY

15 DECEMBER 1986, 11 FEBRUARY 1987

Crown Court – Supervisory jurisdiction of High Court – Trial on indictment – High Court having no jurisdiction in matters relating to trial on indictment – Relating to trial on indictment – Legal aid contribution order – Contribution order made prior to trial – Whether legal aid contribution order a 'matter relating to trial on indictment' – Whether High Court having jurisdiction to review order – Whether decision by Crown Court at end of trial indictment remitting sum payable under contribution order a 'matter relating to trial on indictment' – Whether High Court having jurisdiction to review decision – Supreme Court Act 1981, s 29(3) – Legal Aid Act 1982, ss 7(1), 8(5).

Crown Court – Supervisory jurisdiction of High Court – Trial on indictment – High Court having no jurisdiction in matters relating to trial on indictment – Relating to trial on indictment – Legal aid contribution order made prior to 1982 – Whether legal aid contribution order made prior to 1982 a 'matter relating to trial on indictment' – Whether High Court having jurisdiction to review order – Legal Aid Act 1974, s 32 – Supreme Court Act 1981, s 29(3).

A legal aid contribution order made by a magistrates' court or the Crown Court under s 7(1)*[a]* of the Legal Aid Act 1982 when granting legal aid to a defendant whose disposable income or capital exceeds the prescribed limits is not a matter 'relating to trial on indictment' for the purposes of s 29(3)*[b]* of the Supreme Court Act 1981 and accordingly the High Court is not excluded by s 29(3) from granting judicial review of the order. Where, however, at the conclusion of a trial on indictment the Crown Court makes a decision whether or not to exercise its discretion under s 8(5)*[c]* of the 1982 Act to remit any sums due from, or to order repayment of any sums paid by, the defendant under the contribution order, that decision is an integral part of the trial process and is not subject to judicial review (see p 613 *j* to 614 *d*, post).

Subsisting contribution orders which were made by the Crown Court under s 32(1)*[d]* of the Legal Aid Act 1974 prior to its repeal in 1982 are not subject to judicial review because such orders, in the circumstances in which they were made, are matters 'relating to trial on indictment' for the purposes of s 29(3) of the 1981 Act (see p 612 *b c*, p 613 *a b* and p 614 *b–d*, post); *R v Crown Court at Cardiff, ex p Jones* [1973] 3 All ER 1027 approved; *Smalley v Crown Court at Warwick* [1985] 1 All ER 769 considered.

Notes

For the supervisory jurisdiction of the High Court over the Crown Court, see 10 Halsbury's Laws (4th edn) paras 710, 870.

For the Supreme Court Act 1981, s 29, see 11 Halsbury's Statutes (4th edn) 780.

For the Legal Aid Act 1982, ss 7, 8 see 24 ibid 67, 69.

---

a   Section 7(1) provides: 'Where a court makes a legal aid order giving legal aid to a person whose disposable income or disposable capital exceeds the limits prescribed in relation to such income and capital respectively the court shall, subject to the provisions of this section, make an order ("a legal aid contribution order") requiring him to make a payment (in this Act referred to as "a contribution") in respect of the costs of the legal aid.'

b   Section 29(3) is set out at p 611 *b*, post

c   Section 8(5), so far as material, is set out at p 613 f g, post

d   Section 32(1), so far as material, is set out at p 612 c d, post

Cases referred to in opinions

Practice Direction [1981] 3 All ER 703, [1981] 1 WLR 1383.

R v Crown Court at Cardiff, ex p Jones [1973] 3 All ER 1027, [1974] QB 113, [1973] 3 WLR 497, DC.

R v Crown Court at Chichester, ex p Abodunrin (1984) 79 Cr App R 293, DC.

R v Hayden [1975] 2 All ER 558, [1975] 1 WLR 852, CA.

Smalley v Crown Court at Warwick [1985] 1 All ER 769, [1985] AC 622, [1985] 2 WLR 538, HL.

Appeal

Martin Thomas Sampson appealed, with leave of the Appeal Committee of the House of Lords granted on 18 December 1985, against the decision of the Divisional Court of the Queen's Bench Division (Ormrod LJ and Woolf J) on 17 November 1981 dismissing his application for judicial review by way of (i) a declaration that the order made by his Honour Judge Band QC in the Crown Court at Croydon on 7 May 1981 that the appellant pay a contribution of £250 at £10 per week to the cost of his legal aid defence pursuant to s 32 of the Legal Aid Act 1974, following the acquittal of the appellant on a charge of attempted arson, was wrong in law, and (ii) an order of prohibition restraining the justices of the peace for the Inner London Sessions area from enforcing the order. On 18 April 1985 the Divisional Court refused leave to appeal to the House of Lords but certified that a point of law of general public importance (set out at letter *j*, below) was involved in the decision to dismiss the application. The facts are set out in the opinion of Lord Bridge.

Nigal Ley and *Renée Calder* for the appellant.
John Laws as amicus curiae.

Their Lordships took time for consideration.

11 February. The following opinions were delivered.

LORD BRIDGE OF HARWICH. My Lords, on 22 March 1980 the appellant was tried in the Crown Court at Croydon charged with attempted arson. He was legally aided. At the close of the case for the prosecution the judge decided that there was no sufficient evidence to support a conviction and directed the jury to acquit. He nevertheless ordered that the appellant should contribute £250 to the cost of his legal aid defence pursuant to s 32 of the Legal Aid Act 1974. No appeal lies to the Court of Appeal Criminal Division against such an order. The appellant sought to challenge the order by way of an application for judicial review. On 17 November 1981 the application was dismissed by the Divisional Court (Ormrod LJ and Woolf J) on the ground that the order was made by the Crown Court in the exercise of 'its jurisdiction in matters relating to trial on indictment' and was not therefore subject to review by the High Court under s 10 of the Courts Act 1971. Although the attention of the Divisional Court was not directed to the case, their decision accorded with the earlier authority, by which they were bound, of *R v Crown Court at Cardiff, ex p Jones* [1973] 3 All ER 1027, [1974] QB 113. Nothing more would have been heard of the present case if the House had not recently voiced a doubt whether the *Cardiff* case was rightly decided: see *Smalley v Crown Court at Warwick* [1985] 1 All ER 769, [1985] AC 622. This, it may be assumed, prompted the belated grant in the present case of the necessary certificate by the Divisional Court and of leave to appeal by your Lordships' House. The certified question is:

'Whether a defendant who is acquitted on trial on indictment is entitled to seek judicial review of an order made at the trial that he should pay a contribution in respect of his own legal aid?'

Section 10(5) of the Courts Act 1971, now re-enacted by s 29(3) of the Supreme Court Act 1981, provides:

'In relation to the jurisdiction of the Crown Court, other than its jurisdiction in matters relating to trial on indictment, the High Court shall have all such jurisdiction to make orders of mandamus, prohibition or certiorari as the High Court possesses in relation to the jurisdiction of an inferior court.'

The scope of the exclusion intended by the words 'relating to trial on indictment' was considered in *Smalley's* case in relation to an order estreating the recognisances of a surety for a defendant committed for trial on indictment who failed to surrender to his bail. The decision was that such an order was not made in the exercise of the Crown Court's jurisdiction 'relating to trial on indictment'. In my speech in that case, with which all my noble and learned friends who were party to the decision indicated their agreement, I expressed the opinion that, in considering whether a decision sought to be challenged by judicial review was covered by the exclusion, it was useful to ask whether it affected the conduct of a trial on indictment. I pointed out that this phrase was not a statutory definition and added ([1985] 1 All ER 769 at 780, [1985] AC 622 at 643):

'If the statutory language is, as here, imprecise, it may well be impossible to prescribe in the abstract a precise test to determine on which side of the line any case should fall and, therefore, necessary to proceed . . . on a case by case basis.'

It is in any event clear, I apprehend, that certain orders made at the conclusion of a trial on indictment are excluded from judicial review as 'relating to trial on indictment' not because they affect the conduct of the trial, but rather because they are themselves an integral part of the trial process. This is obviously true of the verdict and sentence. It is equally true, according to the provisional view I expressed in *Smalley's* case, of certain orders for the payment of costs made under the Costs in Criminal Cases Act 1973. The doubt I expressed as to the correctness of the decision in the *Cardiff* case that a defendant tried on indictment cannot challenge by judicial review a legal aid contribution order made by the Crown Court arose from the consideration both that this, if correct, precludes any challenge to such an order and also that the statutory criteria governing the making of such an order are not the same as those which affect other decisions relating to the payment of costs of a criminal trial either out of central funds or inter partes. It is clear that a legal aid contribution order made by the Crown Court, if it cannot be questioned by a judicial review, is not open to any challenge. But whether there is a relevant distinction, for present purposes, between such an order and other orders relating to the costs of a trial on indictment is the issue presently calling for examination, which I can now undertake with the benefit of the full argument we have heard from counsel for the appellant and from counsel as amicus curiae.

A convenient starting point is a consideration of the orders which can be made under ss 3 and 4 of the Costs in Criminal Cases Act 1973. The relevant provisions are as follows:

'**3.**—(1) Subject to the provisions of this section, where a person is prosecuted or tried on indictment before the Crown Court, the court may—(*a*) order the payment out of central funds of the costs of the prosecution; (*b*) if the accused is acquitted, order the payment out of central funds of the costs of the defence . . .

4.—(1) Where a person is prosecuted or tried on indictment before the Crown Court, the court may—(*a*) if the accused is convicted, order him to pay the whole or any part of the costs incurred in or about the prosecution and conviction, including any proceedings before the examining justices; (*b*) if the accused is acquitted, order the prosecutor to pay the whole or any part of the costs incurred in or about the defence including any proceedings before the examining justices . . .'

An order that a convicted defendant pay the whole or any part of the costs of the prosecution under s 4(1)(*a*) is appealable under the Criminal Appeal Act 1968 as part of the sentence: see *R v Hayden* [1975] 2 All ER 558, [1975] 1 WLR 852. An order that the prosecutor pay the whole or any part of the costs of an acquitted defendant under s 4(1)(*b*) is not appealable, nor is any decision under s 3(1) either to make or to refrain from making an order for payment of costs out of central funds in favour of the prosecution or the defence. The common characteristic of all decisions made by the Crown Court under these provisions is that the court is exercising a discretion in the light of what it has learned in the course of the trial as to the nature of the case, both for the prosecution and the defence, and in the light of the conduct and the outcome of the trial itself: see the guidance given by the *Practice Direction* [1981] 3 All ER 703, [1981] 1 WLR 1383. It follows that all such decisions are so intimately bound up with the trial process that they must be treated as an integral part of it and thus must be considered as made in the exercise of the Crown Court's jurisdiction 'relating to trial on indictment' and accordingly are not subject to judicial review.

Section 32(1) of the Legal Aid Act 1974 provides:

'A person to whom legal aid has been ordered to be given for any purpose by a legal aid order may be ordered by a court having power to do so to make such contribution to the clerk of the collecting court in respect of the costs incurred on his behalf for that purpose as appears to the court making the order reasonable having regard to his resources and commitments or, if it so appears, to pay the whole amount of those costs to that clerk . . .'

By sub-s (4)(*b*) and (*c*) the power to make a legal aid contribution order under sub-s (1) in respect of legal aid costs incurred in proceedings on committal for trial and in the trial itself is vested in the Crown Court and is to be exercised after disposing of the case. The express requirement that in exercising this power the court is to have regard to the 'resources and requirements' of the legally aided defendant is accompanied by machinery, which the recipient of legal aid may himself invoke, for inquiry into his means by the Supplementary Benefits Commission, to whose report the court must have regard (see s 33) and by a power to make provision by regulation—

'as to the manner in which a person's resources and commitments are to be taken into account . . . for the purpose of determining the amount of the contribution which he may be required to make towards the costs of the legal aid.'

(See s 34(1).)

At first blush it might be thought that consideration of the resources and requirements of the defendant was the determining factor which should govern the court's decision to make a legal aid contribution order under s 32(1). But I am satisfied that this is not so. There are two facets of the decision. One is a consideration of what the defendant can afford to pay, determined in the light of whatever material relating to this means is available to the court. This will impose an upper limit on the contribution that can properly be ordered. But within that limit the court will also have to consider whether it is appropriate to order any contribution, having regard to the nature and conduct of the prosecution and defence and the outcome of the trial. The factors which should operate to determine this second facet of the decision must be, in the case of an acquitted defendant, indistinguishable from those which would apply to the decision whether or not to order payment out of central funds under s 3(1)(*b*) of the Costs in Criminal Cases Act 1973 of the costs of an unassisted defendant. In circumstances where it would be appropriate to award costs to the unassisted defendant, it would be inappropriate to order a contribution from the assisted defendant and vice versa. True it is that there is no power to order costs out of central funds to a defendant who has been convicted, whereas there is no obligation to order a contribution by a convicted defendant in receipt of legal aid. But this distinction does not affect the fundamental consideration that the court's discretion in deciding what, if any, legal aid contribution to make under s 32 of the Legal Aid Act 1974 must be influenced by the same factors, intimately related to the trial itself, as any decision made under s 3 or s 4 of the Costs in Criminal Cases Act 1973 and the nature of this discretion cannot, I think, be altered by the superimposed requirement to have regard to the defendant's 'resources and commitments'. For these reasons I am satisfied that a legal aid contribution order, like any other order with regard to costs which the Crown Court may make at the conclusion of a trial on indictment, is an integral part of the trial process, and thus belongs to the court's 'jurisdiction relating to trial on indictment' and is not subject to judicial review. *R v Crown Court at Cardiff, ex p Jones* [1973] 3 All ER 1027, [1974] QB 113 was rightly decided and the doubts I expressed about it in *Smalley v Crown Court at Warwick* [1985] 1 All ER 769, [1985] AC 622 were unfounded.

In a sense this conclusion is, save from the point of view of the present appellant, academic in view of the time that has elapsed since the relevant provisions of the Legal Aid Act 1974 were repealed and superseded by the new provisions of the Legal Aid Act 1982. In the course of argument your Lordships were invited to compare the old provisions with the new and in this process gave close consideration to the latter. In the circumstances it may not be inappropriate to express a view, even if obiter, as to how the statutory limitation on judicial review of Crown Court decisions, now embodied in s 29(3) of the Supreme Court Act 1981, may operate in relation to the relevant provisions of the 1982 Act which have replaced those I have been considering under the 1974 Act.

Under the old provisions the making of a legal aid contribution order, as we have seen, fell to be considered at the conclusion of the criminal proceedings in which the defendant had been legally aided. The radical change effected by the 1982 Act is to require, subject to certain exceptions, that the court which makes a legal aid order giving legal aid to a person whose disposable income and disposable capital exceed the respective limits prescribed by regulation shall also make a legal aid contribution order: see s 7(1). The amount of the contribution is to be determined in accordance with regulations made for the purpose and the amount may be required to be paid in one sum or by instalments: see s 7(2). Thus what will be, in effect, the maximum contribution which can be required from a defendant (subject to variation in the light of further information relating to, or a change in, his disposable income or disposable capital) will be determined at the outset of the proceedings in which he is legally aided. But the court by which the legally aided defendant is tried retains its discretionary control over costs by virtue of s 8(5), which provides:

'At the conclusion of the relevant proceedings the court in which those proceedings are concluded may, if it thinks fit—(a) remit any sum due under a legal aid contribution order from a legally assisted person which falls to be paid after the conclusion of those proceedings or, if that person has been acquitted, remit or order the repayment of any sum due from or paid by him under such an order . . .'

A legal aid order granting legal aid for the purposes of a trial on indictment may be made either by the magistrates' court before which the committal proceedings are conducted or by the Crown Court to which the defendant is committed: see s 28 of the 1974 Act, as amended by s 2 of the 1982 Act. It is established by *R v Crown Court at Chichester, ex p Abodunrin* (1984) 79 Cr App R 293, which the House affirmed in *Smalley,* that a decision of the Crown Court to refuse legal aid for trial on indictment is within the statutory exclusion from judicial review since it clearly affects the conduct of the trial. But, as at present advised, I see no reason why a legal aid contribution order under s 7(1) of the 1982 Act should not be subject to review on an appropriate ground, e g that the order was made in the face of unchallenged evidence that the defendant's disposable income and disposable capital did not exceed the prescribed limits. Such an order cannot affect the conduct of the trial and certainly cannot be regarded as an integral part of the trial process. On the other hand, a decision of the Crown Court at the conclusion of a trial whether or not to exercise its discretion under s 8(5) to remit or order repayment of any sums due from or paid by the defendant under a legal aid contribution order is in all respects comparable to the decisions relating to costs falling to be made under ss 3 and 4 of the Costs in Criminal Cases Act 1973 and s 32 of the 1974 Act which have been examined earlier in this opinion. It is, for the same reason, an integral part of the trial process and on that ground excluded from judicial review. I would dismiss the appeal and answer the certified question in the negative.

LORD BRANDON OF OAKBROOK. My Lords, I have had the advantage of reading in draft the speech prepared by my noble and learned friend Lord Bridge. I agree with it, and for the reasons which he gives I would answer the certified question in the negative and dismiss the appeal.

LORD GRIFFITHS. My Lords, I have had the advantage of reading in draft the speech prepared by my noble and learned friend Lord Bridge. I agree that the appeal should be dismissed and that the certified question should be answered in the negative.

LORD ACKNER. My Lords, I have had the advantage of reading in draft the speech prepared by my noble and learned friend Lord Bridge. I agree with it, and for the reasons he gives I would answer the certified question in the negative and dismiss the appeal.

LORD GOFF OF CHIEVELEY. My Lords, I have had the advantage of reading in draft the speech prepared by my noble and learned friend Lord Bridge. I agree with it, and for the reaons which he gives I would answer the certified question in the negative and dismiss the appeal.

Appeal dismissed.

Solicitors: *T W Mullaney*, Watford (for the appellant); *Treasury Solicitor.*

Mary Rose Plummer   Barrister.

a

Tilcon Ltd v Land and Real Estate Investments Ltd

COURT OF APPEAL, CIVIL DIVISION
DILLON AND CROOM-JOHNSON LJJ
22 OCTOBER 1986

b

Pleading – Amendment – New cause of action – Adding new cause of action – Cause of action accruing since original pleading – Plaintiffs seeking declaration entitling them to reject delivery of goods – Defendants counterclaiming for price of goods – Defendants subsequently seeking to amend counterclaim to plead repudiation – Whether repudiation a new cause of action accruing since counterclaim – Whether defendants entitled to amend counterclaim.

c

The plaintiffs entered into a 15-year contract with the defendants for the supply of a stipulated annual quota of clay suitable for the manufacture of facing bricks. The plaintiffs rejected the first delivery of clay, asserting that it did not satisfy the contractual requirements as to quality, and they issued a writ seeking a declaration that they were only required to accept clay of a particular quality. The defendants counterclaimed for the amount agreed to be paid under the contract for the first delivery. Subsequently, the defendants applied to amend their counterclaim to plead that the plaintiffs had repudiated the contract by their wrongful refusal to accept the first delivery and that the defendants had accepted the repudiation. The amendment was allowed by the master, and the plaintiffs appealed to the judge, contending that the defendants were seeking to add a fresh cause of action, namely repudiation, which arose out of an election to treat the plaintiff's alleged breach as repudiatory but which was made subsequent to the issue of the counterclaim and was therefore barred under the rule preventing the addition of a cause of action which had accrued since the original pleading. The judge dismissed the appeal and the plaintiffs appealed to the Court of Appeal.

d

e

f

Held – It had long been accepted that because an amendment related back to the date of the original pleading no new cause of action accruing since the original pleading would be allowed by amendment. Accordingly, an amendment to a counterclaim adding a new cause of action accruing since the date of the counterclaim would not be permitted. However, the assertion that the plaintiffs had repudiated the contract was not a new cause of action, since the facts giving rise to the claim had occurred before the issue of the counterclaim. Furthermore, the defendants' election to treat the contract as being repudiated was a result of those facts and went to the issue of remedy rather than constituting a fresh fact necessary to complete a new cause of action. It was accordingly unnecessary for the defendants to have made their election to repudiate before serving their counterclaim. The appeal would therefore be dismissed (see p 618 *c d* and p 620 *h* to p 621 *b*, *post*).

g

h

Eshelby v Federated European Bank Ltd [1931] All ER Rep 840 and dictum of Lord Wilberforce in *Johnson v Agnew* [1979] 1 All ER at 889–890 considered.

Notes

For leave to amend pleadings, see 36 Halsbury's Laws (4th edn) paras 68–72, and for cases on the subject, see 37(1) Digest (Reissue) 255–272, *1696–1781*.

j

Cases referred to in judgments

Eshelby v Federated European Bank Ltd [1932] 1 KB 254, [1931] All ER Rep 840, DC; *affd* [1932] 1 KB 423, [1931] All ER Rep 840, CA.
Johnson v Agnew [1979] 1 All ER 883, [1980] AC 367, [1979] 2 WLR 487, HL.
White & Carter (Councils) Ltd v McGregor [1961] 3 All ER 1178, [1962] AC 413, [1962] 2 WLR 17, HL.

Cases also cited

Distillers Co (Bio-Chemicals) Ltd v Thompson [1971] 1 All ER 694, [1971] AC 458, PC.
National Coal Board v Galley [1958] 1 All ER 91, [1958] 1 WLR 16, CA.
Yeoman Credit Ltd v Apps [1961] 2 All ER 281, [1962] 2 QB 508, CA.

Application for leave to appeal and interlocutory appeal

The plaintiffs, Tilcon Ltd, applied for leave to appeal against the judgment of his Honour Judge Paul Baker QC sitting as a judge of the High Court on 23 May 1986 whereby he dismissed the plaintiffs' appeal from the order of Master Barratt dated 6 May 1986 granting the defendants, Land and Real Estate Investments Ltd, leave to amend their defence and counterclaim in an action brought by the plaintiffs against the defendants in respect of an alleged breach of a contract made between the parties on 8 July 1983 for the supply by the defendants to the plaintiffs of a quantity of clay for manufacturing use. On 10 June 1986 Nicholls LJ adjourned the plaintiffs' application for leave to appeal and order that it should be heard by a two or three judge court and that if leave were granted, the appeal be heard immediately thereafter. The grounds of appeal were, inter alia, (i) that the judge was wrong in law in granting leave to the defendants to amend their defence and counterclaim, by reason of the fact that the cause of action which they sought to add thereby had not arisen or accrued at the date on which the original counterclaim was served, (ii) that the judge was wrong in law in giving the defendants leave to amend the pleadings to allege that the plaintiffs had acted in repudiatory breach of contract which had been accepted by means of the amendment when the repudiatory breach had not been accepted until after service of the original counterclaim. The facts are set out in the judgment of Dillon LJ.

Graham Platford for the plaintiffs.
John Harwood-Stevenson for the defendants.

DILLON LJ. The plaintiffs in this action, Tilcon Ltd, seek leave to appeal against a decision of his Honour Judge Paul Baker QC sitting as a judge of the High Court in the Chancery Division of 23 May 1986 whereby the judge dismissed the plaintiffs' appeal against an order made by Master Barratt slightly earlier that month granting leave to the defendants to amend their defence and counterclaim.

The application for leave to appeal came before Nicholls LJ, sitting as a single judge of this court on 1 July 1986 and he then adjourned the application to be heard by a two or three judge court which would be able to hear the appeal immediately afterwards if leave to appeal was then granted. The matter thus comes before us today. All the argument was directed to the substance of the appeal. We grant leave to appeal, and I proceed to consider whether the appeal should succeed or fail.

The dispute arises out of a contract between the plaintiffs and the defendants, Land and Real Estate Investments Ltd, in relation to the supply of clay or marl by the defendants from certain land they have near Tamworth in Staffordshire to the plaintiffs to carry on the business of manufacturing facing bricks. The contract is in writing and is dated 8 June 1983. It provided for the defendants to supply clay of a quality suitable for facing brick manufacture. The contract was to last for 15 years. The price payable by the plaintiffs for the clay was fixed at £4·20 per tonne of clay for the first year of the agreement with provision for review annually. The plaintiffs were required to pay for a minimum of 50,000 tonnes of clay in each year unless their failure to pay was due to the defendants' default. There was then in cl 12(2) a provision that, if the plaintiffs failed to remedy any breach after having received 14 days' written notice requiring them to do so, the defendants, while the default continued, could terminate the agreement forthwith by giving notice in writing to that effect. The disputes arose between the parties because the defendants offered a first delivery of clay which they said was of a suitable quality for manufacturing facing bricks, and the plaintiffs rejected it as not being of a suitable quality on the construction of the agreement which the plaintiffs put forward.

The writ in this action was issued on 22 June 1984. The plaintiffs claimed declarations
a as to the construction of the agreement to the effect that clay to be supplied by the
defendants to the plaintiffs pursuant to the agreement should be of a quality suitable for
facing brick manufacture of a particular quality and that the plaintiffs were required
only to accept delivery of clay of that quality, and they claimed by way of damages
certain sums in respect of testing the quality of the clay proffered by the defendants
under the agreement.

b The defendants served a defence and counterclaim on 7 September 1984. By the
defence they dispute the plaintiffs' construction of the agreement and assert that the clay
sought to be delivered and further clay which the defendants were ready and willing to
deliver accorded with the contract and that it was of a quality suitable for facing brick
manufacture. They say further that even if the contract were construed as referring to
clay of a quality suitable for the manufacture of Wilnecote facing bricks, this clay was
c and is so suitable.

The defendants proceeded to counterclaim. In their counterclaim they set out the 15-
year term of the agreement and the provisions for deliveries of 50,000 tonnes of clay a
year, the price to be paid and the minimum royalty, and in para 13 they plead:

d 'The Plaintiffs failed to pay to the Defendants any sum during the year ended
30th June 1983. In the premises and by virtue of Clause 6(2) as aforesaid the
Defendants were liable to pay to the Plaintiffs by the 14th July 1984 the sum of
£210,000 (£4·20 × 50,000), none of which sum has been paid.'

They further plead in para 14:

e '. . . by refusing to accept delivery of the said clay, the Plaintiffs have acted and are
acting in breach of the said contract, in consequence whereof the Defendants have
suffered and continue to suffer loss and damage in that they have incurred the cost
of the extraction of the said 20,000 tonnes, presently stockpiled on the said land and
have been deprived of the opportunity of profiting from a contract for the disposal
of waste in the areas which would, but for the Plaintiffs' said refusal, have been
f excavated . . .'

So they counterclaimed for the £210,000 and damages under para 14.
In 1986 the defendants applied to amend their counterclaim. That is the amendment
which the master allowed by his order which I have mentioned. The amendment does
two things. Firstly, it adds a further section to para 13 of the counterclaim:

g 'Further, by their wrongful refusal to accept delivery of the said clay the Plaintiffs
have in breach of the said Contract caused the Defendants further loss and damage
in that, repudiation having been accepted (paragraph 15 below), the Defendants
suffer continuing loss by virtue of their not receiving further minimum payments
in accordance with Clause 6 of the said Contract. Further or alternatively, the
Defendants have suffered loss and damage in that they have been deprived of the
h opportunity of profiting from sales of the said clay.'

Then they add a para 15:

'Further or alternatively, the Plaintiffs by their aforesaid conduct have acted in
repudiatory breach of the said contract which repudiation the Defendants hereby
j accept. In consequence of such repudiation the Defendants have suffered loss and
damage as aforesaid.'

So the relief sought is, apart from a consequential prayer which I need not mention, a
declaration that the plaintiffs have repudiated the contract, such repudiation the
defendants were entitled to accept, and have accepted, and damages in addition to the
£210,000 already claimed.

The plaintiffs object on somewhat technical grounds to that amendment being allowed. Their counsel has referred to *The Supreme Court Practice 1985* vol 1, para 20/5–8/2, pp 338–339. There it is correctly set out that:

'An amendment duly made ... takes effect, not from the date when the amendment is made, but from the date of the original document which it amends ... Thus, when an amendment is made to the writ, the amendment dates back to the date of the original issue of the writ and the action continues as though the amendment had been inserted from the beginning: "the writ as amended becomes the origin of the action, and the claim thereon indorsed is substituted for the claim originally indorsed". ...'

In relation to a counterclaim, the amendment is read back to the date of the counterclaim. The note continues:

'The rule as to the effect of an amendment is the reason why a plaintiff may not amend his writ by adding a cause of action which has accrued to him since the issue of the writ (see *Eshelby v Federated European Bank Ltd*. ([1932] 1 KB 254, [1931] All ER Rep 840; *affd* [1932] 1 KB 423, [1931] All ER Rep 840)) ...'

That practice has long pertained. How far it is wholly rational is a matter which we are not called on to consider. In *Eshelby v Federated European Bank Ltd* the plaintiff issued his writ claiming payment of one instalment of money under a particular contract. After the issue of the writ, the defendant defaulted in paying a further instalment under the same contract. The plaintiff sought leave to amend his pleading to claim in the same action the second instalment also. It was held that he could not do so. The non-payment of the second instalment was a separate cause of action which did not exist at the time when the writ was issued and would therefore have to be claimed, if at all, in a separate action.

Seeking to apply that to the present case, counsel for the plaintiffs says that a party to a contract who wants to treat the contract at an end has to elect to do so, it does not automatically happen, and the contract only comes to an end at the time when he so elects. Reference was made by the judge in his judgment to the statement by Lord Reid in *White & Carter (Councils) Ltd v McGregor* [1961] 3 All ER 1178 at 1181, [1962] AC 413 at 427 where he said:

'If one party to a contract repudiates it in the sense of making it clear to the other party that he refuses or will refuse to carry out his part of the contract, the other party, the innocent party, has an option. He may accept that repudiation and sue for damages for breach of contract whether or not the time for performance has come; or he may if he chooses disregard or refuse to accept it and then the contract remains in full effect.'

Counsel for the plaintiffs says that as the innocent party has to accept the repudiation before he can sue for damages on the footing of a repudiation, he cannot include his acceptance of the repudiation in an existing proceeding merely claiming damages for breach of contract, because he would be putting in evidence facts subsequent to the date of the original counterclaim, which he cannot do under the rule which has just been mentioned, and he would also not have a complete cause of action until the repudiation has been accepted in so far as he is seeking a cause of action in damages on the footing that the contract has been repudiated.

The defendants, on the other hand, draw a distinction between amendments which are really only options for a particular form of remedy or which crystallise a remedy as opposed to amendments which introduce new causes of action. We have been referred to various well-known definitions of the term 'cause of action'. They were not, however, directed to this particular problem, and I do not for my part find it necessary to set them

out. It is clear that there are many circumstances in which matters which would
a ordinarily fall to be pleaded and have happened since the pleading was originally
delivered may fall to be put before the court at the trial and may even be dealt with by
way of amendment of the pleadings. One obvious example is in the matter of special
damages in an action for damages for personal injuries. Special damages have to be
pleaded, and ordinarily the special damages down to the preparation of the statement of
claim would be pleaded in the statement of claim with perhaps some such words as 'and
continuing', and further details of the particulars of any additional matters of special
b damage or changes in the circumstances would have to be disclosed or pleaded, it does
not greatly matter which, up to the time of the trial. Again it would seem that if there
was an action against the defendant for breach of contract for failing adequately to repair
some article or machinery and further consequential damage was suffered by further
defects in the machinery being caused after the issue of the writ and the launching of the
c claim, it would be possible to amplify the plea by setting out the further damage.

There remains the question whether the acceptance of a repudiation stands in a
different category. Judge Baker held that it did not, but, beyond saying that he thought
the case was distinguishable from *Eshelby v Federated European Bank Ltd*, he did not go
into it in great detail on that aspect. In so far as it was asserted by the plaintiffs that the
defendants needed to assert and had not asserted the service of a notice of breach under
d cl 12 of the contract, the judge took the view that that was a matter for the plaintiffs to
raise, in pleading their amended defence to the counterclaim. It was not a matter which
arose on the application for leave to amend. It would then be seen at a later stage whether
the defendants were going to be forced into pleading something else or whether they
would be saying that there was a power to treat the contract as repudiated without
serving any notice, which was applicable in the circumstances which have happened. In
e this court counsel for the plaintiffs has not challenged that aspect, and accordingly I need
say no more about cl 12 of the contract.

Attention has, however, been drawn in this court to the decision of their Lordships'
House in the case of *Johnson v Agnew* [1979] 1 All ER 883, [1980] AC 367. That was a case
of a vendors' action for specific performance of a contract for the sale of land. The
f purchaser had defaulted and failed to complete. The vendors brought their action for
specific performance and obtained an order for specific performance, but the purchaser
failed to comply with that order. The vendors accordingly moved the court to discharge
the order for specific performance and make an order for damages against the purchaser
on the footing that the purchaser had repudiated the contract. It was held in their
Lordships' House, overruling a number of earlier decisions, that although a vendor had
g to elect at the trial whether to pursue the remedy of specific performance or that of
damages, if specific performance was ordered, the contract remained in effect and was
not merged in the judgment, so that, if the order was not complied with, he might apply
to the court to put an end to the contract and, if he did so, he was entitled to damages
appropriate to the breach of contract.

The leading speech in their Lordships' House was delivered by Lord Wilberforce. It is
h plain from his comments that he was concerned to dispel any mystification which had
been allowed to characterise contracts for the sale of land, as contrasted with other
contracts, and to apply the general rule of contract law. He then set out as follows ([1979]
1 All ER 883 at 889, [1980] AC 367 at 392–393):

> 'In this situation it is possible to state at least some uncontroversial propositions of
> law. First, in a contract for the sale of land, after time has been made, or has become,
j > of the essence of the contract, if the purchaser fails to complete, the vendor can *either*
> treat the purchaser as having repudiated the contract, accept the repudiation, and
> proceed to claim damages for breach of the contract, both parties being discharged
> from further performance of the contract; *or* he may seek from the court an order
> for specific performance with damages for any loss arising from delay in

performance . . . This is simply the ordinary law of contract applied to contracts capable of specific performance. Secondly, the vendor may proceed by action for the *a* above remedies (viz specific performance or damages) in the alternative. At the trial he will however have to elect which remedy to pursue. Thirdly, if the vendor treats the purchaser as having repudiated the contract and accepts the repudiation, he cannot thereafter seek specific performance. This follows from the fact that, the purchaser having repudiated the contract and his repudiation having been accepted, both parties are discharged from further performance. At this point it is important *b* to dissipate a fertile source of confusion and to make clear that although the vendor is sometimes referred to in the above situation as "rescinding" the contract, this so-called "rescission" is quite different from rescission ab initio, such as may arise for example in cases of mistake, fraud or lack of consent. In those cases, the contract is treated in law as never having come into existence. (Cases of a contractual right to rescind may fall under this principle but are not relevant to the present discussion.) *c* In the case of an accepted repudiatory breach the contract has come into existence but has been put an end to or discharged. Whatever contrary indications may be disinterred from old authorities, it is now quite clear, under the general law of contract, that acceptance of a repudiatory breach does not bring about "rescission ab initio".'

d

He then cites from a case on the general law of contract which has nothing to do with the sale of land, and adds ([1979] 1 All ER 883 at 890, [1980] AC 367 at 393–394):

'I can see no reason, and no logical reason has ever been given, why any different result should follow as regards contracts for the sale of land . . . [He then concludes finally as the fifth proposition:] . . . if the order for specific performance is not complied with by the purchaser, the vendor may *either* apply to the court for *e* enforcement of the order, *or* may apply to the court to dissolve the order and ask the court to put an end to the contract . . . It follows, indeed, automatically from the facts that the contract remains in force after the order for specific performance and that the purchaser has committed a breach of it of a repudiatory character which he has not remedied . . .'

f

Then the question was whether the vendor, who took the latter course of applying to the court to put an end to the contract, was entitled to recover damages for breach of the contract, and the answer was unquestionably that he was:

'If, as is clear, the vendor is entitled (after and notwithstanding that an order for specific performance has been made) if the purchaser still does not complete the contract, to ask the court to permit him to accept the purchaser's repudiation and to *g* declare the contract to be terminated, why, if the court accedes to this, should there not follow the ordinary consequences, undoubted under the general law of contract, that on such acceptance and termination the vendor may recover damages for breach of contract?'

(See [1979] 1 All ER 883 at 890, [1980] AC 367 at 394.)   *h*

That case was not directly concerned with points of pleading, which we are concerned with today, but it seems to me fundamental that their Lordships were recognising that the vendor's election to treat the contract as repudiated by what the purchaser had done did not have to be made before he issued his writ. He was entitled to elect in the course of the proceedings, at trial or even thereafter. That seems to me to be plainly inconsistent with the arguments which are put forward today by way of supposed application of *j* *Eshelby v Federated European Bank Ltd* or, indeed, by way of extension of *Eshelby*'s case. The facts which give rise to the cause of action happened before the counterclaim was served. The election to treat the contract as repudiated as a result of those facts is a matter going to remedy rather than a fresh fact necessary to complete a new cause of action.

Accordingly I agree with the conclusion of the judge, and I would dismiss this appeal.
a I would only add that both counsel who appeared before us today were only instructed at
a late hour yesterday, because this case was brought into the list at short notice. For my
part, I am extremely indebted to both for the excellence of their advocacy and the
thoroughness of the preparation of their cases.

CROOM-JOHNSON LJ. I agree.
b

Appeal dismissed.

Solicitors: *Alastair Thomson & Partners*, agents for *Sugden & Spencer*, Bradford (for the
plaintiffs); *Wragge & Co*, Birmingham (for the defendants).

c   Diana Procter   Barrister.

Jacques v Amalgamated Union of
d **Engineering Workers (Engineering Section)**

CHANCERY DIVISION
WARNER J
3, 4, 31 JULY 1985

e *Trade union – Rules – Alteration of rules – Validity – Requirement that 40% of affected members
vote in favour of change of rules – Union's rules revision committee passing resolution to abolish
40% vote requirement – Whether committee's resolution effective – Whether 40% requirement
could be abolished without 40% vote.*

A union's rules provided that they could not be changed to abrogate any of the principal
f benefits of the union, namely unemployment, sickness and superannuation benefits,
unless 40% of the members affected by the benefit voted in favour of abrogation. In 1979
the union's executive council was concerned about the state of its finances and, with a
view to decreasing the number of benefits paid to members, resolved that the rules be
amended by deleting the requirement that 40% of affected members had to vote in
favour of abrogating a benefit and that the provisions relating to unemployment and
g sickness benefit be replaced by new provisions which abrogated those benefits. Those
resolutions were passed at meetings of the union's rules revision committee. The
committee subsequently decided that there should be no new entrants to the
superannuation fund. None of the changes were put to a vote of affected members. The
plaintiff, a member of the union, brought proceedings against the union seeking, inter
alia, declarations that the purported amendment of the rules and the purported
h abrogation of the unemployment and sickness benefits and restriction on entry to the
superannuation fund were void.

Held – The rules of a trade union were not to be construed literally or by applying the
principles of statutory interpretation. Instead, the court would give the rules a reasonable
interpretation which accorded with what the court considered they must have been
j intended to mean, bearing in mind their authorship, their purpose and those who would
have to read and use them. Accordingly, since it was implicit in the union rules that the
requirement that there be a 40% vote of affected members could not be abolished without
the sanction of such a vote, the resolutions of the rules revision committee abrogating
the provisions relating to unemployment and sickness benefits were void, and declarations

to that effect would be granted. However, in relation to the decision to restrict entry to the superannuation fund, such a policy did not 'affect' existing members and accordingly *a* was not subject to the requirement of a 40% vote of affected members. That decision was accordingly valid and could not be challenged by the plaintiff (see p 628 *c d* and p 630 *a* to *e*, post).

Edwards v Halliwell [1950] 2 All ER 1064 followed.

Heatons Transport (St Helens) Ltd v Transport and General Workers Union [1972] 3 All ER 101 and *British Actors' Equity Association v Goring* [1978] ICR 791 applied. *b*

Watt v MacLaughlin [1923] 1 IR 112 not followed.

Notes

For alteration of the rules of a trade union, see 47 Halsbury's Laws (4th edn) para 512, and for cases on the subject, see s 47(1) Digest (Reissue) 419–420, 1846–1847. *c*

Cases referred to in judgment

Bonsor v Musicians' Union [1955] 3 All ER 518, [1956] AC 104, [1955] 3 WLR 788, HL; *rvsg* [1954] 1 All ER 822, [1954] Ch 479, [1954] 2 WLR 687, CA.

British Actors' Equity Association v Goring [1978] ICR 791, HL; *rvsg in part* [1977] ICR 393, CA. *d*

Edwards v Halliwell [1950] 2 All ER 1064, CA.

Faramus v Film Artistes' Association [1964] 1 All ER 25, [1964] AC 925, [1964] 2 WLR 126, HL.

Foss v Harbottle (1843) 2 Hare 461, 67 ER 189.

Heatons Transport (St Helens) Ltd v Transport and General Workers Union [1972] 3 All ER 101, [1973] AC 15, [1972] 3 WLR 431, HL. *e*

Porter v National Union of Journalists [1980] IRLR 404, HL.

Watt v MacLaughlin [1923] 1 IR 112, NI HC.

Action

By a writ indorsed with a statement of claim dated 10 February 1982 the plaintiff, Ernest Jacques, a member of the Amalgamated Union of Engineering Workers, sought, inter *f* alia, declarations against the union that the purported amendment of cl 14 of r 14 of the union's rules by the union's rules revision committee on 12 September 1979 and the purported deletion of rr 28 and 30 relating to unemployment and sickness benefits by the committee in May 1980 were void. The facts are set out in the judgment.

Brian Langstaff and *Timothy Owen* for the plaintiff. *g*
Jonathan Parker QC and *Patrick Elias* for the union.

Cur adv vult

31 July. The following judgment was delivered.

WARNER J. In this action, the plaintiff, Mr Jacques, who is a member of the *h* Amalgamated Union of Engineering Workers (Engineering Section), which I will call 'the union', challenges the validity of certain changes in the rules of the union made, or purportedly made, in 1979, 1980 and 1983.

The union started life on 1 July 1920 as the Amalgamated Engineering Union. It resulted from the amalgamation of ten previously existing unions. From the outset its objects included the provision of benefits for members such as unemployment, sickness, *j* superannuation and funeral benefits. The rules of the union in force at the time of the first of the changes that the plaintiff challenges were a set adopted at what is called in the union a 'rules revision meeting' held in May 1975. I will call that set of rules 'the 1975 rules'.

Rule 14 of the 1975 rules contained provisions for amending the rules. To understand

them one needs to know that whilst the general day-to-day government of the union is
vested in a small executive council, that council is answerable to a larger national
committee, which is elected annually and meets annually.

Clause 10 of r 14, which bore the side-heading 'Rules Revision', provided as follows:

'In 1980, and every fifth year thereafter, the National Committee after the
conclusion of the business dealing with the policy of the Union, shall consider
suggestions for alteration of rules and shall have power to make new or alter existing
rules on suggestions from branches, as herein provided. Such meeting shall be called
the Rules Revision meeting, at which no full-time official, except the President and
General Secretary of the Union, shall attend'.

There followed a paragraph with the side-heading 'Emergency Meetings', in these
terms:

'In the event of circumstances arising which in the opinion of the Executive
Council or National Committee necessitate an alteration to rule, they shall have
power to call together the Rules Revision meeting at any time for the purpose of
considering suggestions initiated by the Executive Council and making such
alterations as may be deemed necessary'.

Lastly, cl 10 contained a paragraph side-headed 'Delegates unable to attend', which was
in these terms:

'Should any member or provisional member of a Rules Revision meeting be
unable to attend any recalled meeting, the Executive Council shall call on the
representatives of the existing National Committee to replace any such delegate or
delegates.'

It was explained to me that the union's practice of holding quinquennial rules revision
meetings did not begin in 1980, but had existed before. Indeed the meeting at which the
1975 rules were adopted was itself such a meeting. It was also explained to me that, when
a rules revision meeting was recalled during the subsequent quinquennium, the delegates
attending it were not the members of the national committee elected for the year in
which the recalled meeting was held but those elected to the national committee for the
year in which the original rules revision meeting had been held. Hence the provision in
the last paragraph of cl 10 for the replacement of a delegate unable to attend by a member
of the current national committee. Thus, for instance, a recalled rules revision meeting
held in any year between 1975 and 1980 would be attended by members of the national
committee elected for 1975, supplemented by members of the national committee
elected for the current year called on to attend under the last paragraph of cl 10.

Clause 11 of r 14 provided, so far as material, that 'Any branch initiating an alteration
of rule must secure for it the support of two other branches'. It then went on:

'The Executive Council shall also at the same time have a right as if they were
acting as three branches, to put forward suggestions for the consideration of the
Rules Revision Committee.'

There followed, in cll 11 and 12, provisions requiring, in effect, all suggestions for the
alteration of rules to be published in the union's monthly journal not later than six
months prior to the rules revision meeting. Then came cl 13, the first paragraph of
which is central in this case. Clause 13 was renumbered 14 in 1977 when a new clause,
not relevant for present purposes, was added to r 14, and I propose from now on to refer
to it as cl 14. The first paragraph of it (which is the only material paragraph) had the side-
heading 'Abrogation of benefits' and read as follows:

'Whatever is agreed upon at the Rules Revision meeting shall be binding on all
the members, but no Rules Revision meeting or Council shall have the power to

abrogate any of the principal benefits of the Union, videlicet Unemployment, Sick, Permanent Disablement, Superannuation, or Funeral Benefits, except, thereafter, 40 *a* per cent of the members, affected by above benefit, vote in favour of the abrogation.'

That provision had existed in one form or another in the rules of the union ever since 1920. Indeed, as counsel for the plaintiff demonstrated to me, one can trace its origins as far back, at least, as the 1847 rules of the Journeymen Steam Engine, Machine Maker, and Millwrights' Friendly Society, which was one of the ancestors of the union. *b*

In 1974, in connection with proposals for the consolidation of the rules of the union with those of other unions with which it had amalgamated to form the Amalgamated Union of Engineering Workers, the question arose whether the benefits mentioned in the version of cl 14 then in force (which was, I think, identical to that in the 1975 rules) could be abrogated without a 40% vote of the members affected. It was thought that it would be impracticable to obtain such a vote. Indeed there is before me a table showing *c* the percentage of members of the union who have voted in ballots of the membership held since 1920. It seems that only once has that percentage exceeded 40%. That was on a ballot held in April 1926 in connection with the general strike of that year. Otherwise the highest polls achieved seem to have been around 30% and there have been occasions when fewer than 10% of the members have voted. Counsel (not either of the counsel who appeared before me on behalf of the union) was instructed to advise. On 21 April *d* 1974 he wrote an opinion, the relevant passage in which is as follows:

'Rule 14 Clause 13 of the AEU provides that a Rules Revision meeting called under Clause 10 of that Rule cannot "abrogate" any of the specified benefits without the required vote of 40 per cent of members affected. This means that a Rules Revision meeting cannot abrogate the benefits by amending the relevant Rules, i.e. Rules 28 (Unemployment Benefit), 30 (Sick Benefit), 31 (Permanent Disablement *e* Benefit), 33 (Superannuation Benefit) and 34 (Funeral Benefit). It does not mean, in my view, that a Rules Revision meeting cannot amend Rule 14, Clause 13 itself. That Clause does not provide that it is an "entrenched" Clause free from the power of amendment. Rule 37A Clause 6 is an example of an "entrenched" Clause (". . . no amendment shall be made to this Rule . . . which would have the effect of enabling *f* . . ." etc.). The contrast with Clause 13 of Rule 14 is clear, and—although the matter is not free from doubt—in my opinion a Rules Revision meeting can and should amend that Clause by deleting all the words in its first paragraph which follow the words ". . . shall be binding on all the members".'

It will be helpful, I think, if, as to that, I make two comments at once.

The first is that, as between the set of rules on which counsel was then advising and *g* the 1975 rules, there is, so far as I am aware, no material difference in the rules setting out members' rights to the benefits mentioned in cl 14 of r 14 (which he, of course, referred to as cl 13), viz rr 28, 30, 31, 33 and 34.

The second relates to r 37A, to which counsel referred. That rule, which was headed 'Protected Funds', was, so I was told, added as a result of the Industrial Relations Act 1971 *h* and was drafted by counsel. I was not told whether he was the same counsel as advised in 1974. Clause 6 of that rule was in these terms:

'Notwithstanding anything contained in Rule 14 or in any other provision of these rules or in any provision of the rules of the Amalgamated Union of Engineering Workers, no amendment shall be made to this Rule or to any other provision in *j* these rules and the National Committee shall not consent to any amendment of the rules of the Amalgamated Union of Engineering Workers which would have the effect of enabling part or all of any property which is or has been comprised in a Protected Fund to be transferred or appropriated to an unprotected Fund or otherwise to become available for financing strikes, lock-outs or other industrial *a*   action; and any purported amendment or consent which would have any such effect shall be void.'

As I understand it, nothing came of the 1974 proposals for consolidating the rules of the union with those of other unions, so that the opinion expressed by counsel in April of that year was not acted on in connection with those proposals. It appears that that opinion was simply filed by the union's solicitors.

b   Five years later, in 1979, the executive council of the union was worried about the union's finances. I have before me copies of the minutes of two meetings of that council held respectively on 3 and 24 July of that year.

At the first of those meetings the council agreed to submit to the rules revision committee a suggestion that members' contributions should be increased as from January 1980. The minutes continue:

c   'Discussion took place on the desirability of decreasing the number of benefits paid and in particular the reference in Rule 14, Clause 14 which required a ballot vote of the members concerned. AGREED: That we submit a suggested alteration to the Recalled Rules Revision Committee to amend Rule 14, Clause 14 to delete the necessity of holding a ballot vote of the members concerned to terminate payment of certain benefits, subject to legal advice being received on this issue.'

d
It seems that, as a result of that decision, the union's solicitors looked up the opinion that had been given by counsel in 1974. The minutes of the meeting of the executive council held on 24 July 1979 record:

'The General Secretary stated that he had received a reply from the solicitors in which they state they believe the Union would have a 50/50 chance of winning any
e   case brought against them by an aggrieved member should the Rules Revision Meeting agree with the suggested alteration to rule to delete the clause calling for a ballot of the membership concerned prior to any abrogation of benefits. They had also obtained the advice of a Q.C. who states that the Union had a 90% chance of winning of any case brought against it. AGREED: That we submit the suggested
f   alteration to Rule 14, Clause 14 to the forthcoming recalled meeting of the Rules Revision Committee.'

In the September 1979 issue of the union's monthly journal notice was given that the executive council had decided to recall the 1975 rules revision committee to discuss, among other issues, the suggestion that cl 14 of r 14 should be amended by, in effect, the deletion of everything in the first paragraph of that rule after the word 'members' where
g   it first appeared.

The recalled 1975 rules revision meeting was held on 12 September 1979. The report of its proceedings records that the suggested amendment to cl 14 of r 14 was carried by a majority of 27 votes to 24. Counsel for the plaintiff did not take the point that the six months' notice required by the rules had not been given.

Then came the 1980 rules revision meeting, which took place over a number of days
h   in May 1980. On 16 May resolutions were passed, in each case by a majority of 29 votes to 23, which had the effect, if they were effective, of abrogating unemployment and sickness benefit. The existing rr 28 and 30 were deleted. There was inserted a new r 28, which read:

'Any member of any section may, during a period of unemployment, be exempt
j   from paying contributions, providing he/she is not over 8 weeks in arrears at date of claim and the branch secretary is notified within seven days'.

There was also inserted a new r 30, which read:

'Any member unable to work due to sickness must inform the Branch Secretary in writing within 14 days, which shall entitle the member to exemption from

payment of contributions during the period of sickness. The member must inform
the Branch Secretary in writing immediately on returning to work.'   *a*

It was agreed that those changes in the rules should take effect as from 1 January 1981.
The executive council subsequently decided that any member already receiving either of
the benefits in question continuously prior to that date should continue to receive it in
accordance with the provisions of the deleted r 28 or r 30, as the case might be.

Some of the members of the union objected to what had been done and on 10 February   *b*
1982 the writ in this action was issued, claiming, among other relief, declarations that
the purported amendment of cl 14 of r 14 by the recalled 1975 rules revision committee
on 12 September 1979 and the purported deletion of rr 28 and 30 by the 1980 rules
revision committee in May 1980 were void. The statement of claim was indorsed on the
writ. A defence was served on 8 April 1982 and a reply on 24 May 1982.

On 28 April 1983 the 1980 rules revision committee was recalled to consider, not for   *c*
the first time, what should be done about superannuation benefit in view of the burden
that that imposed on the union's finances. The committee's decision was in these terms:

> 'As from 31st December 1983 there shall be no new entrants to this Fund.
> Executive Council will use the existing assets of the Fund in such a fashion as to
> sustain the payment of Superannuation Benefit at the levels laid down in Rule to all
> those members in receipt of same as at the 1st January 1984 and will further pay   *d*
> lump sums to those members currently in Sections 1 and 2 who are not in receipt of
> Superannuation Benefit as at the 31st December 1983. Executive Council will
> further ensure the viability of the Superannuation Fund by transfers from time to
> time from the General Fund to the Superannuation Fund as determined by our
> actuaries.'
                                                                                       e
On the first day of the trial before me the statement of claim was amended, with my
leave, so as to enable the plaintiff to challenge the validity of the first sentence of that
decision. It was too late for him to seek to challenge the remainder of it, because that
would have necessitated the introduction into the proceedings of a lot of new material.

There was little, if any, disagreement between counsel for the plaintiff and counsel for
the union as to the principles to be borne in mind when interpreting the rules of a trade *f*
union.

In *Heatons Transport (St Helens) Ltd v Transport and General Workers Union* [1972] 3 All
ER 101 at 110, [1973] AC 15 at 100–101 Lord Wilberforce, speaking on behalf of an
Appellate Committee of the House of Lords consisting of himself, Lord Pearson, Lord
Diplock, Lord Cross and Lord Salmon, said:
                                                                                       g
> 'But trade union rule books are not drafted by parliamentary draftsmen. Courts
> of law must resist the temptation to construe them as if they were; for that is not
> how they would be understood by the members who are the parties to the agreement
> of which the terms, or some of them, are set out in the rule book, nor how they
> would be, and in fact were, understood by the experienced members of the court.'

(That was a reference to the members of the National Industrial Relations Court.)   *h*

In *British Actors' Equity Association v Goring* [1977] ICR 393 at 396–397 Lord Denning
MR said:

> 'So when it comes to construing the rules, it seems to me that they should be
> construed, not literally according to the very letter, but according to the spirit, the
> purpose, the intendment, which lies behind them, so as to ensure—especially in a   *j*
> matter affecting the constitution—that they should be interpreted fairly, having
> regard to the many interests which its constitutional code is designed to serve. In
> *Bonsor* v. *Musicians' Union* ([1954] 1 All ER 822 at 826, [1954] Ch 479 at 485–486) I
> went too far when I suggested that the court might hold a rule to be invalid if it was
> unreasonable. That was pointed out in the House of Lords in *Faramus* v. *Film*

Artistes' Association ([1964] 1 All ER 25 at 33, [1964] AC 925 at 947). But although a rule cannot be held invalid if it is unreasonable, nevertheless, it seems to me that the courts, when called upon to construe the rules, must do all they can to construe them reasonably, fairly, broadly and liberally in the interests of all concerned in the association.'

In the same case Roskill LJ said (at 401–402):

'I confess that for myself I approach with caution any argument which involves reading or writing into a contract between an association and its members provisions which could perfectly easily have been but were not expressed had anyone thought about the problem, for it has often been said that it is not for the courts to rewrite contracts for the parties, least of all rules between a trade union and its members. On the other hand, as Lord Denning M.R. has pointed out, as often happens with rules of associations which have been evolved and amended sometimes over half a century as in this case and sometimes over much longer periods, it cannot fairly be expected that every eventuality which may occur with the passage of years will be foreseen by the draftsman of rules such as those. Like most rules these are imperfect; and, if a literal and arid legalistic construction of the language, however attractive at first sight to some lawyers, leads to results which one cannot believe the parties can have intended, a court should shrink from imposing such an interpretation upon the parties, and should, in my judgment, adopt a more sensible interpretation even though that other interpretation may require implying provisions because the parties did not express fully that which they must have intended. The rules of a trade union cannot be expected to cover every type of activity between that union and its members or between the governing body of that union and its members. The rules of a body such as this ought not, in my judgment to be too legalistically construed, and I respectfully agree on this with Lord Denning M.R.'

Lawton LJ, the third member of the court, emphasised the need to construe the rules in the light of their purpose and not to allow 'grammatical niceties' to frustrate it. That was particularly so, he said, with rules that were loosely worded (at 405–406).

When the case went to the House of Lords that tribunal went even further than the Court of Appeal had done in departing from the literal meaning of the rules. Viscount Dilhorne, in the course of his speech (with which Lord Pearson, Lord Salmon and Lord Scarman agreed) said ([1978] ICR 791 at 794–795):

'While it cannot be said that the rules are a fine example of legal drafting, I do not think that, because they are the rules of a union, different canons of construction should be applied to them than are applied to any written documents. Our task is to construe them so as to give them a reasonable interpretation which accords with what in our opinion must have been intended.'

In *Porter v National Union of Journalists* [1980] IRLR 404 at 407 Lord Diplock, with whose speech Lord Russell and Lord Keith agreed, said:

'I turn then to the interpretation of the relevant rules, bearing in mind that their purpose is to inform the members of the NUJ of what rights they acquire and obligations they assume vis-a-vis the union and their fellow members, by becoming and remaining members of it. The readership to which the rules are addressed consists of ordinary working journalists, not judges or lawyers versed in the semantic technicalities of statutory draftsmanship.'

Lord Diplock went on to quote what Lord Wilberforce had said in *Heatons Transport (St Helens) Ltd v Transport and General Workers Union* [1972] 3 All ER 101 at 110, [1973] AC 15 at 100–101. In *Porter v National Union of Journalists* [1980] IRLR 404 at 410 Viscount Dilhorne for his part said:

'In construing these rules I adhere to what I said in *British Actors' Equity Association v Goring*, namely that different canons of construction to those applied to any written *a* document are not to be applied to the rules of a union. I regard it as our task to construe them so as to give them a reasonable interpretation which accords with what in our opinion must have been intended. The more imprecise the language the greater may be the difficulty in deciding what was intended. I agree with my noble and learned friend Lord Wilberforce that the rules must not be construed as if drafted by parliamentary draftsmen ...'   *b*

There are, of course, in those dicta differences of emphasis and of formulation, but not, I think, diferences of principle. It is to be observed that Lord Pearson and Lord Salmon agreed both with what was said by Lord Wilberforce in the *Heatons Transport* case and with what was said by Viscount Dilhorne in the *British Actors' Equity* case. The effect of the authorities may I think be summarised by saying that the rules of a trade union are *c* not to be construed literally or like a statute, but so as to give them a reasonable interpretation which accords with what in the court's view they must have been intended to mean, bearing in mind their authorship, their purpose and the readership to which they are addressed.

In the present case two questions arise. The first is: was it open to the rules revision meeting to amend cl 14 of r 14 in the way that it purported to do in September 1979 *d* without the sanction of a 40% vote of the members affected? The second is: if not, was the decision of the rules revision meeting in April 1983 that, as from 31 December 1983, there should be no new entrant to the superannuation fund none the less effective?

On the first question counsel for the plaintiff's argument was, in a nutshell, that it was not open to the rules revision committee to do in two steps that which it could not do in one. It was implicit in r 14 that an amendment of cl 14 abolishing the requirement of a *e* 40% vote itself required the sanction of such a vote. Otherwise there was no point in having that safeguard in the rule. Counsel for the plaintiff referred me to a number of provisions in the rules which underlined the importance that their authors attached to the benefits referred to in cl 14, not least the tables of contributions and benefit that are to be found in a schedule to the rules. He also referred me to some authorities, to two of which I must expressly advert.   *f*

The first is *Watt v MacLaughlin* [1923] IR 112, a decision of Wilson J in the Chancery Division in Northern Ireland. In that case, the rules of a golf club adopted in 1895 included the following:

'Rule 24. No rule of the club shall be repealed or altered or new rule made except at a general meeting ... Rule 35. The clubhouse, with the exception of the bar and billiard-room, shall be open on Sundays. Rule 36. Golf shall not be played on the *g* links on Sundays. Rule 37. No future motion either to open the bar or billiard-room, or to open the links for play on Sundays, or to alter rule 35, shall be passed unless by a majority of two-thirds of those present and voting at such meeting.'

At a special general meeting of the club held on 8 July 1922 new rules were adopted which excluded the old r 37. A motion that that rule be still incorporated in the new *h* rules was rejected by a simple majority. Another special general meeting of the club was held on 5 August 1922 at which an attempt to bring about a reversal of that decision failed. At a third special general meeting of the club held on 26 August 1922 a motion was passed by a simple majority striking out the provision in the new rules that forbade the playing of golf on Sundays. Wilson J rejected an argument that the repeal of r 37 required a two-thirds majority. He said (at 119):   *j*

'Rule 37 only applies to future motions, 1, to open the bar or billiard-room on Sundays, or, 2, to open the links for play on Sundays, or, 3, to alter rule 35; and provides that such motions shall not be passed unless by a majority of two-thirds. No such motion was before the meeting of 8th July, 1922. There is no provision in

rule 37 or in any of the other old rules that a motion to repeal or alter rule 37 must
a be passed by a two-thirds majority. Unfortunately the framers of that rule did not
insert in that rule after the words "rule 35" the words "or this rule". It is contended
that this was the intention of those who passed it; but I cannot so construe rule 37
unless I add to that rule some such words. This rule duly passed is binding on all the
members of the club, whether present at the meeting or not. It can only bind them
to what it actually says in plain terms. No doubt the result is that the protection
intended for rule 36 has turned out illusory, but that cannot affect the proper
b construction of rule 37. I am therefore compelled to hold that the old rule 37 was
validly repealed at the meeting of 8th July, 1922, and the suggested rules as amended
were duly passed at that meeting, and were the only rules of the club binding on
the members on the 5th August and 26th of August, 1922.'

c Clearly, what Wilson J did was to construe the rules of the club literally. I do not think
that it would be consistent with the authorities to which I referred earlier if I were to
adopt the same approach in this case.

The other authority to which I must advert on the present question is a dictum of
Evershed MR in *Edwards v Halliwell* [1950] 2 All ER 1064. In that case (I quote from the
headnote):

d 'Rule 19 of the rules of the defendant trade union provided: "The regular
contributions of employed members shall be as per tables . . . and no alteration to
same shall be made until a ballot vote of the members has been taken and a two-
thirds majority obtained." In December, 1943, a delegate meeting of the union,
without taking any ballot, passed a resolution increasing the amount of the
contributions of employed members. The plaintiffs, two members of the union,
e claimed against two members of the executive committee of the union and the
union itself a declaration that the alteration adopted at the delegate meeting was
invalid.'

It was held that they were entitled to that declaration. Most of the argument and of
the judgments was about the rule in *Foss v Harbottle* (1843) 2 Hare 461, 67 ER 189, but
f Evershed MR said ([1950] 2 All ER 1064 at 1069):

'On the question of the construction of the rules, the point was debated whether
a delegate conference could validly by ordinary resolution of the conference revise
r. 19(1) by the abrogation or suspension of the words of prohibition on which the
plaintiffs' action has been founded and then proceed by a further ordinary resolution
to alter the rates of contribution payable, thereby avoiding any need to have a ballot
g or to obtain a two-thirds majority upon a ballot. I am not satisfied that, if a delegate
conference made such an alteration or revision of r. 19 as a mere prelude to the
alteration of the rates of contribution, such a procedure would successfully withstand
challenge. If it is the desire of those responsible for the administration of the affairs
of this union either to abrogate altogether the relevant provision in r. 19 or to make
h it inapplicable to an alteration of contribution rates by a delegate conference, I think
prudence would demand that such a revision should receive the confirmation of the
necessary two-thirds majority.'

One might infer from that that, if the alteration of r 19 was not 'a mere prelude' to an
alteration of the rates of contribution, Evershed MR would have had no doubt that it was
j valid. However, counsel for the union accepted, and in my opinion rightly, that, in the
present case, the alteration of cl 14 of r 14 in September 1979 was a 'mere prelude' to, at
least, the abrogation, or purported abrogation, of unemployment and sickness benefit in
May 1980. What counsel for the union relied on was the fact that the former step was
taken by the recalled 1975 rules revision meeting whilst the latter was taken by the 1980
rules revision meeting. Although the membership of those two meetings overlapped, it

was different. Thus each step was separately considered by a differently constituted rules revision meeting and the element of artificiality which would have existed if the two *a* steps had been taken at or by the same rules revision meeting was absent.

It seems to me, however, that the real question is whether it was implicit in cl 14 of r 14 that the rules revision meeting could not abolish the requirement of a 40% vote without the sanction of such a vote. Clearly, if one is to read r 14 literally, there is no room for such an implication. But, if one rejects that implication, is one giving to the rule a reasonable interpretation which accords with what must have been intended by its *b* authors? I think not, because, without that implication, the requirement of a 40% vote might as well not be there.

Quite rightly, in my view, counsel for the union did not rely on the contrast between cl 14 of r 14 and cl 6 of r 37A. To rely on that contrast would be to ignore the different authorship of the two rules.

I turn to the second question, which relates to the exclusion, or purported exclusion, *c* of new entrants to the superannuation fund as from 31 December 1983. Here the arguments, as it were, changed sides. It was counsel for the plaintiff who, in effect, sought to persuade me to construe the rule literally. He stressed that the relevant words were '40 per cent of the members, affected by above benefit' not '40% of the members affected by such abrogation'. Counsel for the union pointed out that existing members were not 'affected' in any reasonable sense, except beneficially, by the closure of the fund to new *d* entrants. That is manifestly so and I decline to attribute to the authors of the words 'affected by above benefit' an intention to describe by those words persons whose rights were not being abrogated.

In the result I will grant the plaintiff the declarations he seeks as to the purported amendment of cl 14 of r 14 in September 1979 and as to the purported deletion of rr 28 and 30 in May 1980, but I refuse him any declaration about the decision in April 1983 *e* concerning superannuation benefit.

Declarations accordingly.

Solicitors: *Howard Cohen & Co*, Leeds (for the plaintiff); *Lawford & Co* (for the union).

Vivian Horvath   Barrister.

a

Hamlet v General Municipal Boilermakers and Allied Trades Union

CHANCERY DIVISION
HARMAN J
27 FEBRUARY 1986

b

Trade union – Domestic tribunal – Review of decision – Jurisdiction of court – Adjudication by executive council on member's complaint – Provision for appeal to general council – Whether court having jurisdiction to review decision of executive council and general council.

c *Natural justice – Domestic tribunal – Appeal – Composition of appellate body – Appellate body hearing appeal from domestic tribunal – Whether member of domestic tribunal disabled from sitting on appeal from tribunal's decision.*

The plaintiff, who was a member of the defendant trade union, stood for election as an official of the union but was not elected. He made a complaint to the union's executive council that the election had been carried out in breach of the union's rules, but the complaint was dismissed as was an appeal by him to the union's general council. The plaintiff then brought an action against the union seeking declarations, inter alia, that the votes cast at two branch ballots were null and void and in breach of contract and that he had been duly elected. The union applied to strike out the statement of claim under RSC Ord 18, r 19 as disclosing no reasonable cause of action. The plaintiff applied for leave to amend his statement of claim to allege that the votes cast at the two branch *e* ballots were null and void, that the forms recording the result of the two ballots had not given the correct result and had been incorrectly signed, and that the plaintiff's appeal to the union's general council had been vitiated by bias and a breach of natural justice because four members of the executive council which had rejected the plaintiff's complaint had also sat on the general council at the hearing of his appeal. On the hearing *f* of both applications,

Held – The union's application to strike out the statement of claim would be allowed and the plaintiff's application to amend his statement of claim would be dismissed for the following reasons—

(1) The only duty of the court in considering questions of appeals and internal *g* machinery for resolving disputes within a union was to see that the machinery had been properly followed through. The court would not interfere with a decision of the union on such a dispute, even if it was said that the union in reaching its decision had taken into account matters it should not have taken into account. The court could upset a decision that was so perverse as to be properly described as a mere caprice, but unless the decision went to that length failure to take into account matters which were relevant or *h* the taking into account of matters which were irrelevant were not within the proper scope of a review of the decision by the court. In the circumstances, since all the irregularities complained of in the proposed amendments to the plaintiff's statement of claim were electoral irregularities, the remedy for which was a complaint to, and adjudication by, the executive council followed by an appeal to the general council, they were not matters which could found a cause of action in a court of law (see p 633 *j* to *j* p 634 *c h j* and p 636 *h*, post); dicta of James and Cotton LJJ in *Dawkins v Antrobus* [1881–5] All ER Rep at 129, 131 followed.

(2) There was no rule of natural justice that a member of a body which had sat at first instance was thereby disabled from sitting on appeal from that decision or that if such a person did sit on the appeal it was in some way vitiated. Furthermore, the union's rules, which was the very contract sued on, expressly provided that the general council, when

hearing an appeal from the executive council, should include the four members who had sat below. It followed that the plaintiff could not complain of a breach of natural justice *a* (see p 635 *j* and p 636 *e* to *h*, post); *Knox v Gye* (1872) LR 5 HL 656 and *R v Lovegrove* [1951] 1 All ER 804 followed.

Notes

For the court's jurisdiction to grant relief for breach of union rules, see 47 Halsbury's Laws (4th edn) paras 511, 517, and for cases on the subject, see 47(1) Digest (Reissue) *b* 418–419, *1842–1945*.

For the likelihood of bias, see 1 Halsbury's Laws (4th edn) para 69, and for a case on the subject, see 1(1) Digest (Reissue) 204, *1187*.

Cases referred to in judgment

Associated Provincial Picture Houses Ltd v Wednesbury Corp [1947] 2 All ER 680, [1948] 1 *c* KB 223, CA.
Dawkins v Antrobus (1881) 17 Ch D 615, [1881–5] All ER Rep 126, CA.
Ewert v Lonie [1972] VR 308, Vict SC.
King v University of Saskatchewan (1969) 6 DLR (3d) 120, Can SC.
Knox v Gye (1872) LR 5 HL 656.
R v Lovegrove [1951] 1 All ER 804, CCA.   *d*

Cases also cited

Leeson v General Council of Medical Education and Registration (1890) 43 Ch D 366, CA.
Maclean v Workers' Union [1929] 1 Ch 602, [1929] All ER Rep 468.

Adjourned summons

      e

The defendant, the General Municipal Boilermakers and Allied Trades Union, applied by a summons dated 18 November 1985 for an order pursuant to RSC Ord 18, r 19 striking out the statement of claim dated 30 November 1984 of the plaintiff, Alec Hamlet, in an action brought by the plaintiff against the union in which he sought, inter alia, declarations that the plaintiff was duly elected as the district delegate of the union for the South Coast and/or that the votes recorded by two branch ballots were null and void. By *f* a summons dated 20 December 1985 the plaintiff applied for leave to amend the statement of claim and reply. The facts are set out in the judgment.

T J Kerr for the plaintiff.
Brian Langstaff for the union.

      g

HARMAN J. I have before me two summonses: a summons issued by the defendant, the General Municipal Boilermakers and Allied Trades Union, on 18 November 1985 to strike out the statement of claim under RSC Ord 18, r 19 and the inherent jurisdiction on the ground that it discloses no reasonable cause of action, and a summons by the plaintiff, Mr Alec Hamlet, dated 20 December 1985, who sought leave to amend the *h* statement of claim and the reply in the terms of drafts annexed and consequential relief as to discovery thereafter.

     Counsel for the defendant union opened his summons on the assumption that leave to amend the statement of claim in the proposed form might be given, and on that he continued to submit, as he had always submitted, that there was no cause of action known to the law raised thereby.

     j

     The plaintiff's counsel, when he came to address me sought, as a result, I fear, of prompting from the bench, leave (and was granted leave) to amend his summons of 20 December by deleting the references to the reply and by adding references to two of the paragraphs in the reply: the proposed new para (3) to be added to the statement of claim as a new para (6)(a), and the proposed para (4) of the draft amended reply to be added as a

new para (6)(b). Counsel for the union did not object to the summons being amended in
a that form, and the matter has proceeded on the contention that, even if leave to make
those amendments to the statement of claim were granted, there would still be no
reasonable cause of action.

The matter arises out of the relationship between the plaintiff, who is a member of the
union, and the union based on the contract between them contained in the rule book of
the union. The statement of claim, as proposed to be amended, alleges the plaintiff's
b membership, alleges the rule book and alleges the plaintiff's candidature for election in
September 1982 for a particular post. It further alleges the announcement of the result
of the election, objections being lodged with certain results following and the final
allegation that a Mr Pratt was declared elected by the union and the plaintiff was not.
None of those allegations is in issue at all.

The pleading then goes on to allege in para (5) that the elections, or the votes at two
c particular branch ballots, Cosham and Gosport, were void and in breach of contract.
Then particulars are given, particulars, for example, that in breach of a particular rule a
ballot remained open for less than the one hour required by the rule, and such like
matters.

Paragraph (6) of the statement of claim alleges that objections in respect of the breaches
of rule were raised by the plaintiff with the union, and by amendment, that the executive
d council of the union rejected those objections. Mr Pratt assumed his office, and on 23
May 1983 the general council of the union rejected the plaintiff's appeals in respect of
the Cosham and Gosport branches. There was then sought to be added the new para
(6)(a):

e 'The plaintiff will contend at the trial that the voting result forms of Cosham and
Gosport branches did not record the correct result, nor were they correctly signed.'

The allegation is that the officials at the branches were 'out of benefit' and disentitled
from conducting the election voting, and that under cl (15)(j) of r 11 of the rule book the
executive council of the union had no power to count the votes recorded on the said
voting result forms.
f Paragraph (6)(b) goes on:

'The appeal to the general council [which had been pleaded in para (4) of the
amended statement of claim] was vitiated by a breach of natural justice and/or bias
or a reasonable suspicion thereof, in that four members of the executive council sat
on the appeal to the general council and accordingly the appeal was void.'

g The claim advanced by counsel for the union is that the whole of para (5) fails to raise
any cause of action at law by reason of the doctrine, well exemplified in the old decision,
but in my judgment still current in modern days, in *Dawkins v Antrobus* (1881) 17 Ch D
615 esp at 628, [1881–5] All ER Rep 126 esp at 129 per James LJ where that very
distinguished Lord Justice said:

'We have no right to sit as a Court of Appeal upon the decision of the members of
h a club duly assembled. All we have to consider is whether the notice was or was not
given according to the proper rules, whether the meeting was properly convened,
and whether the meeting, if properly convened, had come to the conclusion that
this gentleman ought to be expelled, having before it the fact that the committee
had, upon investigation of the matter, come to that conclusion, and expressed the
opinion, that his conduct was such as to entitle them to call upon him to resign.'

j Counsel for the union also cited Cotton LJ, who was very much to the same effect (17
Ch D 615 at 634, [1881–5] All ER Rep 126 at 131): 'We are not here to sit as a Court of
Appeal from the decision of the committee or of the general meeting.' That line of
thought, says counsel for the union, is entirely applicable today. The only duty of courts
in considering questions of appeals and internal machinery for resolving disputes in

unions is to see that the machinery has been properly followed through. The decision is
not one which the court has any business to go into. Indeed, counsel submitted (and he   *a*
may well be right in this) that it would not even be a proper contention, were it advanced,
to say that a club or trade union in reaching its decision had taken into account matters
it should not have taken into account, ie the administrative law rule exemplified in
Associated Provincial Picture Houses Ltd v Wednesbury Corp [1947] 2 All ER 680, [1948] 1
KB 223. He agreed and conceded that, if the decision was so perverse as to be described
properly as a 'mere caprice', then certainly the courts could upset it; but, unless it went   *b*
to that length, the failure to take account of matters that were relevant or the decision to
take into account matters that were irrelevant was not the proper scope of a review by
the courts of these sorts of decision. It was a machinery review, and perhaps a review of
decisions that were wholly unreasonable, but not more than that.

In my view that is indeed the correct analysis of the law. It follows that the allegations
in para (5), unless they amount to an allegation that the machinery of the union was not   *c*
properly followed through, cannot be heard in the court by way of appeal from that
decision. The machinery is set out in the rules, which are incorporated as part of the
pleading in the statement of claim and can of course be referred to as so incorporated; in
particular r 11, which sets out the electoral rule. That rule runs for several pages and
provides for various requirements. The rules go on, in r 17, to deal with the cross-heading
'Electoral Irregularities', and that rule provides: 'Any failure by any member of the   *d*
Society or any Branch to observe any of the provisions of Rule 11 shall constitute an
electoral offence', and it goes on in cl (18) to provide that if 'any member of the Society
alleges . . . an electoral offence . . . he shall make a complaint in writing to the Executive
Council . . .'; that complaint, by virtue of cl (18)(b), must be made within 28 days,
although there is a discretion in the executive council to receive complaints outside the   *e*
time limit. There is then a set of procedures as to how the executive council shall consider
and adjudicate on the matter and a provision in cl (19) that the executive council is
entitled to dismiss the same or, in cl (20), in its absolute discretion to decide what action
it may take. Clause (21) goes on to provide—

> 'that any person aggrieved by a decision of the Executive Council . . . may
> appeal . . . to the General Council who may hear and decide any such appeal in   *f*
> whatever manner they in their absolute discretion, may decide . . .'

Those provisions are not alleged in para (5) not to have been gone through so far as the
machinery is concerned. Paragraph (5) alleges, as I have already mentioned, various
express breaches of rr 11 and 28 and so on. All these appear to be plainly electoral
irregularities, and plainly matters requiring a complaint and an adjudication by the   *g*
executive council and an appeal to the general council. It is quite clear from para (4) that
there was what the plaintiff calls an 'objection' and what the rules call a 'complaint', and
from para (6) that the executive council considered and decided to reject that objection
and that the general council rejected an appeal from that decision of the executive
council. There is no suggestion at any point in those allegations that the machinery was
not properly followed through. Thus, if I were to permit this matter to go on, I would be   *h*
encouraging a plain breach of the rule in *Dawkins v Antrobus* and encouraging or
permitting the plaintiff to attempt to have the court sit in appeal on the decision of the
properly-constituted body before whom, by the rules, the plaintiff had agreed the
decision should be taken. It seems to me that that cannot be a matter raising a cause of
action proper for litigation in these courts, or, to use the old phrase, a reasonable cause of
action.

The next complaint in the proposed amendments is in para (6)(a), which asserts that   *j*
r 11, cl (15)(j) was broken. Clause (15)(j) is attended by some difficulty of construction.
The reason is that cl (15)(j) starts off by providing obligations on the branch president,
the member appointed, who is someone who assists in the management of the election,
and the secretary in entering the correct result on the voting result form, posting the

result form to the head office, a time limit on its receipt and requirements for the
a completion of it. It then goes on at the very end to say that any vote recorded shall be
disqualified if it is not correctly signed and 'this disqualification shall be obligatory. The
executive council shall have no power, by virtue of rule 11, paragraph (20) or otherwise,
to waive it'.

Counsel for the plaintiff argued that that raised a primary obligation on the executive
council (for which counsel for the union accepted that the union would be directly
b answerable), which primary obligation, says counsel for the plaintiff, was not a matter of
electoral irregularity requiring complaint under cl (18) of r 11, but was a free-standing
and independent obligation.

I have been convinced by counsel for the union that that is an impossible construction
of that clause. The clause is perhaps not drafted with the utmost skill; it may well be that
a careful draftsman, skilled in the art, would have made the last sentence of para (j) of
c cl (15) include a proviso to r 20, setting out the powers of the executive council dealing
with any electoral irregularity. But it has well been said that one must not construe trade
union rule books as if they were statutes: one must not look at them with the eye
accustomed to Income Tax Acts and strict settlements; one must consider them in a more
benign and loose way of reading. It seems to me that that mode of construction is one
which is entirely apt and desirable to apply to this rule.

d It would be the oddest sort of result if cl (15)(j) created in its first three sentences
electoral irregularities which were mandatorily under the rules to be the subject of a
complaint under cl (18), but in its last sentence created a different and free-standing
obligation on the executive council arising out of primarily the same facts as the
undoubted electoral irregularity. Further, as counsel for the union observed to me, one
must allow common sense to creep in, even in litigation over trade union rules, and how,
e in the name of fortune, counsel would have liked to express it, could the executive
council know that there had been an incorrect result entered on the face of the voting
form? They have, under cl (1), a duty to scrutinise the result of the election, but, if they
receive a form which apparently is properly created, how are they, sitting at head office,
to know that there is some voting irregularity underlying it? As it seems to me, that is a
f powerful reinforcement of the constructional view of the rule which I take, that the
addition of the last sentence to para (j) is in truth a proviso to the powers of the executive
council set out in cl (20), and is not a free-standing matter separate from all the other
obligations of cl (15), all of which are plainly matters raising electoral irregularities
within cl (17).

In my view the claim advanced by counsel for the plaintiff, which at one time did
g seem to me to have some force, could only have force if it were taken with a very strict,
wholly unrealistic (and unrelated to the true substance of that which one is construing),
view of the construction of this rule book. In my view the complaints in the proposed
para (6)(a), that the voting result forms were not correctly signed because some persons
were disentitled because they were out of benefit from conducting the voting in the
election, must have been complaints of electoral irregularities and must have come
h within the ambit of complaint to the executive council followed by appeal to the general
council. In fact, there was no complaint in this matter within the 28 days or at all, and,
as it seems to me, that matter is irretrievably water under the bridge and cannot be dug
up as a cause of action now.

Finally, there is the proposed para (6)(b). That alleges that the hearing by the general
council of the plaintiff's appeal was vitiated as contrary to natural justice by the fact that
j four members of the executive council sat on the general council. First, in my view of
the law, there is no rule of natural justice, or any justice, that a member of a body who
has sat at first instance is thereby disabled from sitting on appeal, or that, if an appeal is
heard on which such a person does sit, the appeal is in some way vitiated; that that was
the law, both at equity and in the common law courts, is in my view beyond any question
or doubt. *Knox v Gye* (1872) LR 5 HL 656, cited by counsel for the union, is a classic

illustration of it. There four members of the House of Lords were sitting, two of whom
had sat, one at first instance as the then Vice-Chancellor and one on appeal as the Lord *a*
Chancellor, and both were sitting in the House of Lords to try the final hearing. Nobody
regarded the House of Lords as improperly constituted on that ground. It was
commonplace in equity for a judge to sit on appeal on a matter where he had been
concerned below. The same applied to the common law courts. The court in banc
regularly and habitually included the judge who had tried the matter at nisi prius, from
whom a rule nisi had been obtained, which was then sought to be made absolute.   *b*

There is no sort of history of disablement of a judge, let alone of a court or tribunal,
from hearing a matter because one or two members have been concerned before. If a
modern instance is sought on the ground that these are all very old matters and we know
better than our grandfathers, a proposition I would venture to doubt in any event, one
can refer to what I would call the quite modern case of *R v Lovegrove* [1951] 1 All ER 804,
where that great judge Lord Goddard CJ laid down in plain terms the fact that the Court *c*
of Criminal Appeal, a purely statutory body constituted by the Criminal Appeals Act
1907, was entirely entitled to sit with Lynskey J as one of the three members, he having
been the judge who had tried the offence at first instance. Lord Goddard CJ observed in
flat and clear terms that there was no rule which prevented the judge who had heard the
matter sitting on the appeal, and it was quite contrary to all rules that he should be
disqualified. He said that there might be cases where it was desirable that the judge *d*
should not sit, but that was beside the point.

I was told that two Commonwealth decisions, one in Canada, *King v University of
Saskatchewan* (1969) 6 DLR (3d) 120, and one in Victoria, *Ewert v Lonie* [1972] VR 308,
have come to similar conclusions, and I am always glad to hear that the old learning has
been followed in far distant places.

The matter, however, goes further than that. Holding, as I would, that as a matter of *e*
the rules of natural justice there is no such rule as is contended by counsel for the
plaintiff, it goes further in the sense that the rule book here, which is the very contract
sued on, expressly provides that the general council hearing the appeal shall include the
four persons whom it is said sat: so they did; so they should; so the plaintiff by his
contract had agreed they should. They were not, it is clear, a majority of the general *f*
council. One of the four appears to have been a mere minute taker or recorder with no
voice or vote in the hearing in the general council. It is not on that sort of proposition
that I base the observations I am making. I base it on the proposition that, where a man
has expressly agreed by contract to accept a tribunal containing certain persons, he cannot
thereafter come bleating to the courts complaining of breach of natural justice when the
contract is carried out exactly according to its terms as he had always known, if he had *g*
read the rule book, he was bound to accept.

In my view there is no merit in para (6)(b), either as a general proposition of law or on
the particular contract here sued on. Thus, as it seems to me, none of the matters
advanced by counsel for the plaintiff amount to a reasonable cause of action, even if,
which I have not yet done, I were to allow him to amend to plead those inadmissible
matters. As it seems to me, it is probably the correct procedure (but I will listen to counsel *h*
about this), to rule on the summons for leave to amend by refusing leave to amend for
the reasons I have given, that is that the proposed amendments raised no reasonable cause
of action and therefore should not clutter up the pleading, and to strike out the original
pleading as it stands, which indeed counsel for the plaintiff would concede as it originally
stood would follow. The detail, as I say, I will consider. The application for discovery, of
course, does not arise at all on this view of the matter. *j*

Order accordingly.

Solicitors: *Bindman & Partners* (for the plaintiff); *Robin Thompson & Partners* (for the
union).

Evelyn M C Budd   Barrister.

a # Home Brewery plc v William Davis & Co (Loughborough) Ltd

QUEEN'S BENCH DIVISION AT NOTTINGHAM

PIERS ASHWORTH QC SITTING AS A DEPUTY JUDGE OF THE HIGH COURT

16, 17, 18, 21, 22, 23, 24, 25, 31 JULY 1986

b

Nuisance – Natural processes – Flooding – Percolation of water from higher land to lower land – Occupier of lower land filling in land and preventing free flow of water from higher land – Filling operations also squeezing water onto higher land – Filling operations causing flooding – Whether occupier of higher land entitled to passage of natural unconcentrated water from his land onto lower land – Whether occupier of lower land entitled to prevent water flowing onto his land from
c *higher land.*

In 1962 the plaintiffs purchased a plot of land. Water drained from that land onto adjoining lower land, which included two disused clay pits and an osier-bed. In 1969 the defendants bought the adjoining land for the purpose of developing it for housing and, in furtherance of that purpose, filled in the clay pits, which had the effect of producing a
d barrier which impeded the flow of water from the plaintiffs' land through the osier-bed thereby causing substantial flooding on the plaintiffs' land. The plaintiffs were forced to install pumps to overcome the flooding resulting from the blocked drainage. The defendants also filled in the osier-bed, which had the effect of squeezing out over a period of five years the water that was present in the bed, thereby causing additional flooding which was, however, controlled by the pumps which had been previously installed. The
e plaintiffs brought an action against the defendants claiming, inter alia, damages for nuisance.

Held – Although an occupier of lower land had no cause of action against an occupier of higher adjoining land for permitting the passage of natural unconcentrated water over
f or through the higher to the lower land, he was under no obligation to receive such water onto his land and was entitled to take steps consistent with the reasonable user of his land to prevent such water entering onto his land even if by doing so he occasioned damage to the higher land. However, if such steps involved unreasonable user resulting in damage to the land of the higher occupier, the occupier of the lower land was liable in nuisance. Applying those principles, the defendants had acted reasonably in filling
g clay pits and the land generally with a view to developing the area as a residential estate and accordingly the plaintiffs had no cause of action against the defendants with regard to the damage caused by filling the clay pits. However, on the facts, the temporary additional flooding caused by the in-filling of the osier-bed was reasonably foreseeable and therefore the defendants were liable to the plaintiffs in either nuisance or trespass for the damage thus occasioned, namely the additional cost of pumping and maintenance
h during the five-year period during which water was squeezed out (see p 641 g, p 642 a b, p 643 d, p 644 b c, p 646 c d g to p 647 b, p 648 c j and p 649 b e to g, post).

Gartner v Kidman (1962) 108 CLR 12 followed.

Leakey v National Trust for Places of Historic Interest or Natural Beauty [1980] 1 All ER 17 applied.

Smith v Kenrick [1843–60] All ER Rep 273, *Rylands v Fletcher* [1861–73] All ER Rep 1
j and *Gibbons v Lenfestey* (1915) 84 LJPC 158 considered.

Notes

For nuisances between neighbouring properties, see 34 Halsbury's Laws (4th edn) paras 315 et seq, and for cases on the subject concerning water, see 36(1) Digest (Reissue) 456–457, 461, 384–394, 414–417.

Cases referred to in judgment

Baird v Williamson (1863) 15 CBNS 376, 143 ER 831.   a

Bradford (Mayor) v Pickles [1895] AC 587, [1895–9] All ER Rep 984.

Broadbent v Ramsbotham (1856) 11 Exch 602, 156 ER 971.

Chasemore v Richards (1859) 7 HL Cas 349, [1843–60] All ER Rep 77, 11 ER 140, HL.

Gartner v Kidman (1962) 108 CLR 12, Aust HC.

Gerrard v Crowe [1921] 1 AC 395, [1920] All ER Rep 266, PC.

Gibbons v Lenfestey (1915) 84 LJPC 158.   b

Goldman v Hargrave [1966] 2 All ER 989, [1967] 1 AC 645, [1966] 3 WLR 513, PC.

Hurdman v North Eastern Rly Co (1878) 3 CPD 168, [1874–80] All ER Rep 735, CA.

Job Edwards Ltd v Birmingham Navigations [1924] 1 KB 341, CA.

Leakey v National Trust for Places of Historic Interest or Natural Beauty [1980] 1 All ER 17,
    [1980] QB 485, [1980] 2 WLR 65, CA.

Mason v Hill (1833) 5 B & Ad 1, [1824–34] All ER Rep 73, 110 ER 692.   c

Overseas Tankship (UK) Ltd v Morts Dock and Engineering Co Ltd, The Wagon Mound (No 1)
    [1961] 1 All ER 404, [1961] AC 388, [1961] 2 WLR 126, PC.

Polemis and Furness Withy & Co Ltd, Re [1921] 3 KB 560, [1921] All ER Rep 40, CA.

R v Pagham, Sussex, Sewers Comrs (1828) 8 B & C 355, [1824–34] All ER Rep 711, 108 ER
    1075.

Read v J Lyons & Co Ltd [1946] 2 All ER 471, [1947] AC 156, HL.   d

Rylands v Fletcher (1868) LR 3 HL 330, [1861–73] All ER Rep 1, HL; affg LR 1 Exch 265,
    Ex Ch.

Sedleigh-Denfield v O'Callagan (Trustees of St Joseph's Society for Foreign Missions) [1940] 3 All
    ER 349, [1940] AC 880, HL.

Smith v Kenrick (1849) 7 CB 515, [1843–60] All ER Rep 273, 137 ER 205.

Solloway v Hampshire CC (1981) 79 LGR 449, CA.   e

Southport Corp v Esso Petroleum Co Ltd [1953] 2 All ER 1204, [1956] AC 218, [1953] 3
    WLR 773; rvsd [1954] 2 All ER 561, [1954] 2 QB 182, [1954] 3 WLR 200, CA; rvsd in
    part [1955] 3 All ER 864, [1956] AC 218, [1956] 2 WLR 81, HL.

Wagon Mound, The (No 2), Overseas Tankship (UK) Ltd v Miller Steamship Pty Ltd [1966] 2
    All ER 709, [1967] 1 AC 617, [1966] 3 WLR 498, PC.   f

Whalley v Lancashire and Yorkshire Rly Co (1884) 13 QBD 131.

Wilson v Waddell (1876) 2 App Cas 95, HL.

Action

By a writ dated 24 January 1978 and an amended statement of claim the plaintiffs, Home
Brewery Ltd, claimed against the defendants, William Davis & Co (Loughborough) Ltd
(sued as William Davis & Co (Leicester) Ltd), damages for nuisance and an injunction   g
requiring the defendants to take all necessary steps to prevent flooding over their land.
The action was heard in Nottingham, where at the conclusion of the hearing judgment
was given on the facts. Judgment on the issue of liability was reserved to be given in
London. The facts are set out in the judgment.

Harold W Burnett QC and Susan Hunter for the plaintiffs.   h
I A B McLaren for the defendants.

                                                                            Cur adv vult

31 July. The following judgment was delivered.   j

PIERS ASHWORTH QC. This is a claim by the plaintiffs in respect of flooding of
their property which they allege was caused by operations carried out by the defendants
on their adjoining property. I heard the case at Nottingham and in order to narrow the
issues I gave judgment on the facts in Nottingham. It will be convenient if I summarise

my conclusions of fact, without going again into the reasons, and to elaborate, if
a necessary, on any particular findings.

Prior to 1884 three separate businesses existed on the site: two brickworks and one
osier-bed. They were all in separate ownership. In the first quarter of this century all the
businesses and the whole site came into the common ownership of a firm called Tuckers.
Each of the brickworks required a clay pit. Over the century these have been deepened
and extended and eventually, by about 1950, had been joined together. Before 1925 the
b osier-bed had ceased to be used for an osier business. By about this date, as the clay pits
deepened and needed large quantities of water to be pumped out, the osier-bed began to
be used as an intermediate stage in this operation. Water was pumped from the pits into
the osier-bed where solids settled out and the water ran off through a pipe into a public
drain in Beacon Road. This pipe was installed 100 years or more ago. It has a slight fall
from Beacon Road to the osier-bed and originally was used to keep the osier-bed topped
c up with water from the drain in Beacon Road. When pumping from the pits took place
into the osier-bed the pipe worked in the reverse direction, preventing the osier-bed overflowing and draining the water into the Beacon Road drain. The general fall of the land
over the site is in a south-west to north-east direction. The osier-bed was in a saucer-
shaped depression in the slope. It is impossible to conclude from the evidence whether
this was a natural depression caused by, for example, glacial action, or man-made in
d whole or in part, or, if man-made, whether made 100, 500 or 5,000 years ago. If man-
made it was made at least 100 years ago, that is, before 1884, and no material alterations
have been made to it in subsequent years, until it was filled. In particular, no alteration
was made to it when it came to be used as an adjunct to the clay pits in or about 1925.
The soil of the site is keuper marl, which is largely impervious, but with irregular strata
or lenses of pervious material, such as sand and gravel. On top of the clay, there is top-
e soil. The natural drainage follows the general contours of the site, with water percolating
through the soil and through the lenses. To a slight extent it can percolate through the
marl itself.

The effect of excavating the clay pits was to create large catchment basements for
water. This had the effect of lowering the natural water table, but it is impossible to say
f by how much.

The plaintiffs bought their site in 1962 and constructed a public house, which was
completed and opened at the end of 1963. In constructing it the plaintiffs took advantage
of the natural contours of the ground and constructed a patio and skittle alley on lower
ground in the north-east corner. They had to excavate some ground to get a level surface,
but the overall level of the patio was not below the level of adjoining ground to the
north-east, and that adjoining ground continued to fall away towards the osier-bed.
g In constructing the public house the plaintiffs did not alter or interfere with the
natural drainage, and save in one respect did not discharge any extra burden of water
onto the defendant's land. That one respect was a pipe discharging water from the rear
roof of the public house and also from a washing machine onto the defendants' land. (I
interpose my recital of facts to say that, as a matter of law, the plaintiffs were not entitled
h to do that.) This was remedied in early 1977 and had no material effect on the flooding
with which I am concerned.

The drainage from the other built-up parts of the public house and the site was taken
by drainpipes into public sewers; drainage from the patio and the car park areas continued
to be by natural seepage through the surface of the ground. At this time ground water
from the plaintiffs' land drained naturally down the adjacent land to the osier-bed and
j into the bottom clay pit. Water which drained from adjoining higher land to the south-
west into the plaintiffs' land also continued through to the osier-bed and clay pit. None
of this water ran through defined channels; the drainage was all by percolation through
or over the soil.

In 1969 the defendants bought the remainder of the site for the purpose of
development for housing. At that time the top clay pit had largely been back-filled. The

defendants completed this and also filled the adjoining land. This had no material effect on the water draining into the plaintiffs' land. The defendants' land to the south-west *a* had been generally higher than the plaintiffs' land and filling it did not increase the natural drainage through the plaintiffs' land. At the same time the defendants commenced the back-filling of the bottom clay pit. Because of the smell emanating from the pit and resulting complaints the defendants filled the pit more quickly and less economically than they would otherwise have done; but they filled it in a proper manner and in accordance with approved practice. *b*

For the first nine years of the public house's life the patio and skittle alley remained dry, but in 1972 dampness was observed in the patio and thereafter some minor flooding. The cause of this was the partial filling of the bottom pit, which the defendants had done. The effect of the filling was to restrict the flow of water from the osier-bed into the pit, which in turn restricted the flow of water from the plaintiffs' land into the osier-bed. In effect the defendants had erected a partial barrier against the flow of water from the *c* plaintiffs' land.

In 1973 the plaintiffs constructed a sump and installed a small pump, which for a time coped with this flooding. However, over succeeding years the flooding increased, and in 1977 the plaintiffs had to construct a larger sump and installed two larger pumps. For a time even these pumps had difficulty in coping, but as time has gone by the flooding has diminished and these pumps now have no difficulty in keeping the patio and skittle alley *d* dry.

The water flow into the sumps peaked about 1977 and has fallen steadily since then. The situation has now stabilised and no increase in water flow is to be anticipated in the future.

The cause of the increased flooding after 1973 was twofold: (1) completion of back-filling of the bottom pit and consolidation of that fill, with the result that the flow from *e* and through the osier-bed was much more substantially impeded and the ground water level raised, although whether it was raised to or above the pre-1884 level it is impossible to tell. In effect, the defendants' barrier against the flow of water from the plaintiffs' land had been made much more effective; (2) in this period the defendants filled the osier-bed and raised the level of the land considerably. This had the effect of squeezing out large *f* quantities of water onto the plaintiffs' land.

The cause of the decrease of the flow of water after 1977 was that the filling of the osier-bed had been completed and the fill had largely consolidated, with the result that the amount of water squeezed out diminished and then virtually stopped. It is impossible to put a precise date on this but it was probably about five years ago. Since then, and if I did not make this finally clear in Nottingham I make it clear now, the squeezing out has *g* had no material effect on the flooding of the plaintiffs' land, the sole effective cause of which is the 'barrier' erected by the defendants on their land against the flow of water from the plaintiffs' land. Again I make clear, if I did not in Nottingham, that the plaintiffs would in any event, even without the squeezing out, have had to construct their second sump and install the larger pumps to cope with the barring of the flow of water from their land to the defendants' land. The pumps as installed were just able, although *h* sometimes with difficulty, to cope with the extra water squeezed out.

On these findings of fact two major questions of law arise. Firstly, does the owner or occupier of higher land have a right to discharge water percolating through or over his land onto lower lying land? Conversely, is the owner or occupier of the lower lying land obliged to accept that water or is he entitled to prevent it from entering his land? (For convenience I shall refer to the higher and lower occupier.) If that question is answered *j* in the plaintiffs' favour, that is that the higher occupier is entitled to discharge and the lower occupier is bound to accept that water, that concludes the case in the plaintiffs' favour; but if the answer is in the negative, the second question of law that arises is whether, even if the plaintiffs had no right to compel the defendants to receive their water, nevertheless were the defendants guilty of the tort of nuisance in carrying out

such operations on their land as prevented the water flowing naturally off the plaintiffs'
a land?

The first question of law

I find it surprising that such a question falls to be decided for the first time in England
in 1986. I should have expected it to have been established in the last century, if not
earlier, when many decisions on rights and duties in respect of water are to be found.
b There are decisions and dicta in other jurisdictions, but, as one textbook writer has
expressed it, there is no worthwhile English authority. There can be no doubt that by
common law the proprietor or occupier of land on the banks of a natural watercourse is
both entitled to have and bound to accept the flow of water past or through his land. He
is not entitled to deprive those lower down the stream of its flow, nor to pen it back on
the lands of his upstream neighbour. This law was established certainly by 1833 (see
c *Mason v Hill* 5 B & Ad 1, [1824–34] All ER Rep 73) and was described by the House of
Lords in 1859 as 'conclusively settled by a series of decisions' (see *Chasemore v Richards* 7
HL Cas 349 at 374, [1843–60] All ER Rep 77 at 81). These rights and obligations do not
depend on any presumed grant or prescription. They are natural rights and obligations
incidental to the ownership or lawful occupation of land. The law is the same whether
the watercourse runs on the surface or underground. An occupier who dams a natural
d watercourse may be liable to actions at the suit of both higher occupiers, whose land may
have been flooded as a result of the damming, and lower occupiers, who may have been
deprived of the benefit of the water flowing through their land.

The law relating to water not flowing in defined channels but running freely over the
surface, or percolating through the soil, is different. In *Broadbent v Ramsbotham* (1856) 11
Exch 602, 156 ER 971 it was held that a higher occupier had the right to appropriate
e surface water which flowed over his land in no defined channel, even though this
deprived the lower landowner of the benefit of that water and even though he had
enjoyed that benefit for over 50 years. In *Chasemore v Richards* the House of Lords
affirmed that decision and held that the same principle applied to water percolating
underground. Thus, the higher occupier is entitled to abstract water flowing over or
f through his land, other than in defined channels, even though such abstraction is to the
detriment of the lower occupier. Lord Wensleydale suggested that a higher occupier's
right of abstracting such water was subject to the restriction that he must exercise that
right in a reasonable manner, but in *Mayor of Bradford v Pickles* [1895] AC 587, [1895–9]
All ER Rep 984 the House of Lords rejected this restriction and held that as a higher
occupier had the right to abstract the water his motive was irrelevant and that accordingly
no action lay at the suit of the lower occupier, even if he could prove malice on the part
g of the higher. Thus, although a lower occupier has the right to receive water flowing
through a natural watercourse, he has no corresponding right to water percolating under
or over the surface. It might, therefore, be argued that he could be under no duty to
receive such water corresponding to the duty to receive water flowing through a natural
watercourse. But this does not follow. There is no reciprocal basis for natural rights. For
h example, the natural right of a higher occupier to support for his land from lower land
does not depend upon any reciprocal obligation on his part to provide land to be so
supported. Accordingly, it does not necessarily follow that because a lower occupier has
no right to receive percolating water he is under no duty to receive it if the higher
occupier so desires. There can be no doubt that an occupier of land has no right to
discharge onto his neighbour's land water that he has artificially brought onto his land
j (*Baird v Williamson* (1863) 15 CBNS 376, 143 ER 831) or water that has come naturally
onto his land but which he has artificially, even if unintentionally, accumulated there
(*Whalley v Lancashire and Yorkshire Rly Co* (1884) 13 QBD 131) or which by artificial
erections on his land he has caused to flow onto his neighbour's land in a manner in
which it would not, but for such erections, have done (*Hurdman v North Eastern Rly Co*
(1878) 3 CPD 168, [1874–80] All ER Rep 735).

If an occupier does any of these things he is liable to an action of the suit of his neighbour. Furthermore, if he brings water onto and accumulates it on his land he may *a* well be liable to his neighbour if that water escapes, even though he has no wish to discharge it and has taken every precaution against discharging it (*Rylands v Fletcher* (1868) LR 3 HL 330, [1861–73] All ER Rep 1).

On the other hand, an occupier is under no obligation to prevent water that has come naturally onto his land and has not been artificially retained there or artificially diverted from passing naturally to his neighbour's land (*Smith v Kenrick* (1849) 7 CB 515, [1843– *b* 60] All ER Rep 273). Indeed, in that case it was held that the occupier was not liable if he had himself removed the barrier between his and his neighbour's land, thereby permitting the water to flow naturally from one land to the other. However, it is perhaps doubtful whether the principle laid down in that case is still good law in its widest application or can stand with the decision of the Court of Appeal in *Leakey v National Trust for Places of Historic Interest or Natural Beauty* [1980] 1 All ER 17 at 31, [1980] QB *c* 485 at 520 per Megaw LJ.

There is another line of cases to which I must refer before atttempting to answer the question posed in this case. These are the cases concerning flooding. It is well established that an occupier is entitled to protect his land against floodwater, be it from the sea or from overflowing rivers, by erecting an embankment on his land, and, if the erection of such an embankment causes floodwater to flow onto his neighbour's land in greater *d* quantities or with greater violence than it would otherwise have done, he is under no liability to his neighbour. If the neighbour wishes to protect his land it is for him to erect his own embankment. The law was so stated in *R v Pagham, Sussex, Sewers Comrs* (1828) 8 B & C 355, [1824–34] All ER Rep 711 by Lord Tenterden who referred to the sea as 'a common enemy' to all the landowners on that part of the coast. In *Gerrard v Crowe* [1921] 1 AC 395, [1920] All ER Rep 266 the Privy Council followed this decision and *e* held that floodwater from a river was equally the common enemy of all adjacent landowners and they were each entitled to protect their own lands from it, even though it might have serious consequences for neighbouring landowners.

None of these cases provides the answer to the question of law I have to decide, but both counsel have relied on them to a greater or lesser extent in supporting their *f* arguments. The one clear statement on the point in a case decided in this country, although not concerned with English or Scottish law, appears in the Privy Council case of *Gibbons v Lenfestey* (1915) 84 LJPC 158. Giving the judgment of the Board Lord Dunedin said (at 160):

'The law of Guernsey, differing in this respect from some other systems, does not allow of the constitution of ordinary servitudes or easements except by grant. But *g* the right of the superior proprietor to throw natural water on the lower land is not an ordinary servitude to which this rule can apply. It is a natural right inherent in property; it is a question of nomenclature whether it is or is not called a servitude. Their Lordships do not doubt that the law of Guernsey in this matter is the same as that of every other country whose jurisprudence is traceable to Roman sources. Indeed, even the countries ruled by the common law have accepted the Roman *h* rules. It is true that the Romans designated this right as servitude, but they explained the distinction by dividing servitude into three classes—natural, legal, and conventional—and it is to the first class that this belongs. The law may be stated thus: Where two contiguous fields, one of which stands upon higher ground than the other, belong to different proprietors, nature itself may be said to constitute a servitude on the inferior tenement, by which it is obliged to receive the water which *j* falls from the superior. If the water, which would otherwise fall from the higher grounds insensibly, without hurting the inferior tenement, should be collected into one body by the owner of the superior in the natural use of his property for draining or otherwise improving it, the owner of the inferior is, without the positive constitution of any servitude, bound to receive that body of water on his property.'

This was an appeal from Guernsey and so it cannot be binding in this country. Further,
a the law of Guernsey is neither the common law, nor based on the common law and,
accordingly, anything said about the common law can only be obiter. Nevertheless it is a
dictum of the highest authority and counsel for the plaintiffs rightly placed much
reliance on it.

The only reference to such a rule which anyone has been able to trace in any English
case is in *Smith v Kenrick*, to which I have already referred. Creswell J said ((1849) 7 CB
b 515 at 566, [1843–60] All ER Rep 273 at 279):

> 'The water is a sort of common enemy,—as was said by Lord Tenterden, in *Rex* v.
> *The Commissioners of Sewers for Pagham Level* ((1828) 8 B & C 355 at 360)—against
> which each man must defend himself. And this is in accordance with the civil law,
> by which it was considered that land on a lower level owed a natural servitude to
c > that on a higher in respect of receiving, without claim to compensation, the water
> naturally flowing down to it.'

I confess to some difficulty in understanding this passage. The two sentences appear to
be mutually contradictory. How can a duty to receive water flowing from a higher level
be consistent with a right to erect a barrier against it? I think that the only way these
sentences can be reconciled is to read them as meaning simply that a lower occupier has
d no right of action against a higher occupier if water runs naturally from higher land onto
his land, and that his only relief is to defend himself against it.

Despite the absence of cases in England there have been many cases in other
jurisdictions, including common law jurisdictions. They have been exhaustively
reviewed in the High Court of Australia in the judgment of Windeyer J in *Gartner v
Kidman* (1962) 108 CLR 12. I do not propose to repeat this exercise. Suffice to say
e decisions have gone both ways, even in different courts within the same country.

Counsel for the defendants submits that floodwater cases are conclusive in his favour.
Water is a common enemy and every landowner is entitled to defend himself against it.
No distinction can be drawn between floodwater and any other type of water. Further,
the dictum of Creswell J, read as I have read it, might be said to support his argument.

f I reject this argument. I do not think that these cases are conclusive in his favour.
Although in one sense water is water and always has the same properties it does not
always have the same effect. Floodwater can properly be described as a common enemy,
but water as such is not an enemy of man or beast or land. Indeed, in most circumstances,
water can be described as a common friend. Certainly the human race could not survive
long without it. Rainwater is generally beneficial and the same can be said of rainwater
g percolating naturally through the ground.

Perhaps nearer the defendants' case is the dictum of Lord Cairns LC in *Rylands v
Fletcher* (1868) LR 3 HL 330 at 338–339, [1861–73] All ER Rep 1 at 12–13 where he said:

> '. . . if, by the operation of the laws of nature, that accumulation of water had
> passed off into the close occupied by the Plaintiff, the Plaintiff could not have
> complained that the result had taken place. If he had desired to guard himself
h > against it, it would have lain upon him to have done so, by leaving, or by interposing,
> some barrier between his close and the close of the Defendants in order to have
> prevented that operation of the laws of nature.'

Although Lord Cairns there referred to the natural accumulation of water, he did not
refer to it in the context of the common enemy. But this also is inconclusive.
j However, although I reject the argument that these cases are conclusive of the
defendants' case, they are certainly not contrary to it. In *Gartner v Kidman* the majority
of the High Court of Australia (Dixon CJ and Windeyer J), having considered the
multitude of authorities from various jurisdictions, came to the conclusion that the
correct view was that the rule of civil law, that the owner of higher land has a right to
insist on his lower neighbour receiving surface water running off his land, was not part

of the common law so far as it existed in Australia. That decision is not binding on me
and the common law may well have followed different paths on opposite sides of the *a*
world. But, if I may say so, with respect, I find Windeyer J's reasoning wholly convincing
and I think the conclusion that he has come to, as to the common law of Australia, applies
also to the common law of England. In so saying I am conscious that I am rejecting the
dictum of Lord Dunedin.

I hold that the common law rule is that the lower occupier has no ground of complaint
and no cause of action against the higher occupier for permitting the natural, *b*
unconcentrated flow of water, whether on or under the surface, to pass from the higher
to the lower land, but that at the same time the lower occupier is under no obligation to
receive it. He may put up barriers, or otherwise pen it back, even though this may cause
damage to a higher occupier. However, the lower occupier's right to pen back the water
is not absolute , as I shall demonstrate below. Accordingly, counsel for the plaintiffs fails
in his primary submission.   *c*

However, this is not the end of the case. Counsel for the plaintiffs submits in the
alternative that even if the plaintiffs had no right to discharge this water onto the
defendants' land, and to compel the defendants to receive it, nevertheless, as the plaintiffs
were not acting unlawfully in so discharging it, the defendants were guilty of the tort of
nuisance in carrying out such operations on their land as prevented the water from
flowing naturally off the plaintiffs' land. This was not a case of the defendants deliberately *d*
erecting a barrier along their boundary. The clay bund they did erect had little effect
upon the underground flow of water. What the defendants did was, by their work of
reclamation of their land and particularly their filling in of the bottom clay pit, to prevent
the natural flow of water from the plaintiffs' land to the osier-bed and into the clay pit.
This caused the water to be trapped on the plaintiffs' land to a small extent in 1972 and
to a much greater extent after 1976 when the filling of the clay pit had been completed *e*
and consolidation had taken place and the osier-bed had also been filled. This is still the
position today and is likely to remain so, unless and until the defendants install land
drains when they come to develop their land. In addition, in 1976 and for a few years
thereafter, the defendants were forcing water from their land onto the plaintiffs' land by
the squeezing effect of the filling of the osier-bed. I find that this has finished and the *f*
condition has stabilised and this has caused only a minor part of the plaintiffs' damage. I
shall consider this separately.

For the present I am concerned with the major part of the plaintiffs' claim, which I am
satisfied has been caused by the defendants, by their operations on their land, preventing
the percolating water draining off the plaintiffs' land onto their land.

Counsel for the plaintiffs submits that any user of land which causes damage to *g*
another's land or to his use and enjoyment of it is a nuisance, although he concedes that
it is not necessarily actionable. I say at once that I find it difficult to understand how
something can be a nuisance in the legal sense if it is not actionable, although, of course,
it can be a nuisance in common parlance. A nuisance in law is a tort and where there is a
tort there is a remedy.

Counsel for the plaintiffs then submits that for the nuisance to be actionable there *h*
must be some fault on the part of the defendant. Alternatively, he submits that there is
strict but not absolute liability for nuisance, subject to certain defences. If by the latter
submission he means no more than that when he has established a prima facie nuisance
the burden of proof shifts to the defendants he may well be right, but the plaintiffs must
first establish a prima facie nuisance. By the form of these submissions I take counsel to
be conceding that it is not any user but any 'faulty' user of land which causes damage etc *j*
which is a nuisance in law. But whether or not he is conceding this I think this comes
nearer to the true definition. I prefer the words from *Winfield on Tort* (8th edn, 1967)
p 353 that a private nuisance is 'an unlawful interference with a person's use or enjoyment
of land or some right over or in connection with it'. But I acknowledge that this is not an
all-embracing definition, and in any event it leaves unanswered the question of what is

a unlawful in this context. Similarly, the Latin maxim sic utere tuo et alienum non laedas, while possibly a convenient shorthand expression, is not a comprehensive definition, because it suggests an absolute bar on any activity on your land which injures your neighbour. This does indeed fit in with counsel's original submission, but in my view it is clearly contrary to authority. Indeed it is difficult to see how cases such as *Mayor of Bradford v Pickles* [1895] AC 587, [1895–9] All ER Rep 984 could have been decided as they were if this were the law.

b   Counsel for the defendants makes three primary submissions: (1) that to establish a nuisance the plaintiffs must establish that the defendants' use of land was unreasonable, in other words, that the unlawful interference in the *Winfield* definition means 'interference resulting from unreasonable use'. He goes on that on the facts as I have found them, the defendants' user was reasonable; (2) that to establish a nuisance the plaintiffs must establish that their damage was reasonably foreseeable by the defendants;

c (3) that even if the defendants' user of their land was unreasonable there is still no actionable nuisance in law because there are special rules that apply to (a) water and (b) mineral workings.

I shall consider these submissions in reverse order.

Special rules for water and/or minerals

d   Counsel for the defendants received some support for this submission from the authors of textbooks, particularly Professor Fleming, who in *The Law of Torts* (5th edn, 1977) p 414 asserted that in all probability different rules apply to water and in the 6th edition (1983) p 399 stated that it was still unclear whether water still goes its own way. There are certainly suggestions to be found in older authorities that special rules might apply to water and also to mineral extraction. But although I have been taken through many

e authorities I do not think there are any which bind me to hold that I should apply any different tests or rules to actions for nuisance based on water or on mineral working. The tendency of the law as it has developed over the last century has been to assimilate all these categories into the general law of nuisance, reaching its culmination in the judgment of the Court of Appeal in *Leakey v National Trust for Places of Historic Interest or Natural Beauty* [1980] 1 All ER 17, [1980] QB 485. Accordingly, I reject counsel's

f submission and hold the law I should apply is that set out in the dissenting judgment of Scrutton LJ in *Job Edwards Ltd v Birmingham Navigations* [1924] 1 KB 341 at 360, as adopted by the House of Lords in *Sedleigh-Denfield v O'Callagan (Trustees for St Joseph's Society for Foreign Missions)* [1940] 3 All ER 349, [1940] AC 880, which was itself approved by the Privy Council in *Goldman v Hargrave* [1966] 2 All ER 989, [1967] 1 AC 645 and applied by the Court of Appeal in *Leakey v National Trust*.

g *Foreseeability*

Counsel for the defendants submits that foreseeability of damage is a necessary ingredient of the tort of nuisance. He bases this submission primarily upon the judgment of Lord Reid in *The Wagon Mound (No 2), Overseas Tankship (UK) Ltd v Miller Steamship Pty Ltd* [1966] 2 All ER 709 at 716–717, [1967] 1 AC 617 at 640. But it seems to me that

h in that passage and in the case in general Lord Reid was considering not liability but damage. The question was whether the rule in *Re Polemis and Furness Withy & Co Ltd* [1921] 3 KB 560, [1921] All ER Rep 40 which had been overruled by *Overseas Tankship (UK) Ltd v Morts Dock and Engineering Co Ltd, The Wagon Mound (No 1)* [1961] 1 All ER 404, [1961] AC 388 in the assessment of damages for negligence, still applied to the assessment of damages for nuisance. Their Lordships held that it did not. However, I

j agree that if foreseeability of damage is a prerequisite to recovery of compensation for that damage, it follows from this judgment that there must be foreseeability of some damage before liability can be established in nuisance, because damage is an essential ingredient of nuisance. In any event, the matter has been put beyond doubt by the decisions of the Court of Appeal in *Leakey v National Trust* and *Solloway v Hampshire CC* (1981) 79 LGR 449. However, I reject the submission of counsel for the defendants that

damage of the nature claimed by the plaintiffs was not reasonably foreseeable as a result
of his clients' operations. Their whole case, as advanced through their expert evidence, **a**
was that far from this flooding being unforeseeable it was inevitable. If the plaintiffs had,
for example, stowed paintings in their skittle alley and these had been damaged by the
flooding, such storage and consequent damage might well have been unforeseeable. But
the plaintiffs did no such thing. The flooding and damage in respect of which the
plaintiffs claim was eminently foreseeable.
                                                                                        b

Reasonableness
    I come to counsel's first submission. I accept his submission that unreasonable user is
an essential ingredient in the tort of nuisance, although I think the burden of proof
probably lies on the defendant to establish reasonableness, rather than on the plaintiff to
establish the contrary; but no question of the burden of proof arises in this case. Further,
the test must be objective rather than subjective. For example, it may be perfectly **c**
reasonable for a professional trumpeter to spend 12 hours a day practising his trumpet
blowing; but if viewed objectively it might be totally unreasonable to subject neighbours
to such unremitting noise.
    It follows that in my opinion, although the plaintiffs had no right to require the
defendants to accept the percolating water from their land, the defendants' right to reject
it was not absolute, but was subject to the qualification that such rejection must be **d**
reasonable and in particular in the reasonable user of their land. It follows that if a lower
occupier erects barriers maliciously and not for the purpose of the reasonable user of his
land, he is or may be guilty of the tort of nuisance. I do not think this conflicts with the
decision of the House of Lords in *Mayor of Bradford v Pickles*, because there the defendant
was extracting something that he was entitled to extract from his own land, whereas here **e**
the defendants in the use of their own land were simply turning back something coming
from the plaintiffs' land. It may be a fine distinction, but I think it is a valid one.
    Again, I gratefully adopt the words of Windeyer J in *Gartner v Kidman* (1962) 108 CLR
12 at 49:

    'Although he has no action against a higher proprietor because of a natural
    unconcentrated flow of water from his land, he is not bound to receive it. He may **f**
    put up barriers and pen it back, notwithstanding that doing so damages the upper
    proprietor's land, at all events if he uses reasonable care and skill and does no more
    than is reasonably necessary to protect his enjoyment of his own land. But he must
    not act for the purpose of injuring his neighbour. It is not possible to define what is
    reasonable or unreasonable in the abstract. Each case depends upon its own
    circumstances.'
                                                                                        g

I emphasise the last words: 'Each case depends upon its own circumstances.'
Neighbourhood, duration, time of day may all be relevant. I refer also to the considerations
set out in the judgment of Megaw LJ in *Leakey v National Trust*.
    In the present case I am satisfied that there was no question of malice in what the
defendants did. They back-filled their clay pits so that they could develop their land **h**
commercially. To some extent it was very much in the public interest that the pits
should be filled in, both from the view of safety (deep pits are dangerous, particularly in
residential neighbourhoods) and health, even if the hazard was smell rather than disease.
But I do not impute altruistic motives to them. They bought the land to develop it for
profit; they would not have bought it if they had not had a reasonable expectation of
such profit. Their primary object was commercial; but their motives and user are none **j**
the worse for that. Commercial enterprise is perfectly respectable and may well be
reasonable from an objective point of view. It all depends on the circumstances.
    Applying the objective test, I am satisfied that it was a completely reasonable user of
the land to fill in the clay pits and to fill the land generally with a view to developing it
as a residential estate. This would necessarily involve building access roads and also

leaving some areas of open space. Whether any particular piece of land is to be used for
a housing or roads or recreation is immaterial. I find that the defendants' operations on
their land were reasonably necessary for their enjoyment of their land. Further, I find
the operations were carried out in accordance with reasonable practice and certainly
without any negligence on the part of the defendants.

In the end I do not think the plaintiffs seriously contended that the defendants' user
and operations were unreasonable. Counsel for the plaintiffs' final submission was that if
b reasonable user was a defence to an action for nuisance and if it was reasonable for the
defendants to use their land in this way, by building it up, it was also reasonable for them
to put in drains and/or pumps to take away the water from the plaintiffs' land, or to
compensate the plaintiffs for putting in such drains and pumps. He based this submission
on the passage of the judgment in *Leakey v National Trust* [1980] 1 All ER 17 at 35, [1980]
QB 485 at 524 where Megaw LJ said:

c
'In the example which I have given above, I believe that few people would regard
it as anything other than a grievous blot on the law if the law recognises the existence
of no duty on the part of the owner or occupier. But take another example, at the
other end of the scale, where it might be thought that there is, potentially, an
equally serious injustice the other way. If a stream flows through A's land, A being
d a small farmer, and there is a known danger that in times of heavy rainfall, because
of the configuration of A's land and the nature of the stream's course and flow, there
may be an overflow, which will pass beyond A's land and damage the property of
A's neighbours: perhaps much wealthier neighbours. It may require expensive
works, far beyond A's means, to prevent or even diminish the risk of such flooding.
Is A to be liable for all the loss that occurs when the flood comes, if he has not done
e the impossible and carried out these works at his own expense? In my judgment,
there is, in the scope of the duty as explained in *Goldman v Hargrave* [1966] 2 All ER
989, [1967] 1 AC 645, a removal, or at least a powerful amelioration, of the injustice
which might otherwise be caused in such a case by the recognition of the duty of
care. Because of that limitation on the scope of the duty, I would say that, as a matter
of policy, the law ought to recognise such a duty of care.'
f
He later said ([1980] 1 All ER 17 at 37, [1980] QB 485 at 526–527):

'Take, by way of example, the hypothetical instance which I gave earlier: the
landowner through whose land a stream flows. In rainy weather, it is known, the
stream may flood and the flood may spread to the land of neighbours. If the risk is
one which can readily be overcome or lessened, for example by reasonable steps on
g the part of the landowner to keep the stream free from blockage by flotsam or silt
carried down, he will be in breach of duty if he does nothing or does too little. But
if the only remedy is substantial and expensive works, then it might well be that
the landowner would have discharged his duty by saying to his neighbours, who
also know of the risk and who have asked him to do something about it, "You have
h my permission to come onto my land and to do agreed works at your expense", or,
it may be, "on the basis of a fair sharing of expense". In deciding whether the
landowner had discharged his duty of care, if the question were thereafter to come
before the courts, I do not think that, except perhaps in a most unusual case, there
would be any question of discovery as to the means of the plaintiff or the defendant,
or evidence as to their respective resources. The question of reasonableness of what
j had been done or offered would fall to be decided on a broad basis, in which, on
some occasions, there might be included an element of obvious discrepancy of
financial resources. It may be that in some cases the introduction of this factor may
give rise to difficulties to litigants and to their advisers and to the courts. But I
believe that the difficulties are likely to turn out to be more theoretical than
practical.'

As I read it, Megaw LJ was there considering cases such as the landslips in *Leakey v National Trust* and the burning tree in *Goldman v Hargrave*, or the flooded stream in his *a* example, where a condition has occurred naturally on one person's land which causes him little damage, but might cause his neighbour enormous damage and which would be expensive to remedy. I do not read this part of his judgment as applying to cases such as the present, where all the landowner is doing is exercising his right to reject water coming onto his land and is doing so in a reasonable manner. To accept the submission of counsel for the plaintiffs would, in effect, be to say that a higher occupier has indeed a *b* right to force a lower occupier to accept water percolating through his land, subject only to a right of the lower occupier to buy off his obligation for a reasonable price. I can find no warrant for such a principle.

It follows that I find the defendants' operations on their land which resulted in the blocking of the natural drainage for percolating water from the plaintiffs' land were reasonable and, accordingly, the plaintiffs have no cause of action in respect of such *c* blockage.

This leaves the squeezing out. It is perhaps doubtful whether the cause of action in respect of this arises in nuisance or in trespass (see *Southport Corp v Esso Petroleum Co Ltd* [1953] 2 All ER 1204 at 1208, [1956] AC 218 at 225 per Devlin J). In my view it makes no difference to the result.

Counsel for the defendants submits that flooding resulting from such squeezing out *d* was not reasonably foreseeable by the defendants. They appreciated there was a risk that water would be squeezed onto the plaintiffs' land and they erected a clay bund on their land, a little distance from the boundary to minimise this; but obviously this could not prevent water being squeezed through the soil underground. Further, they tipped some fill on the outside of this bund, between it and the defendants' boundary. In any event, such a bund could not be totally watertight. Nevertheless, counsel for the defendants *e* submitted that if the defendants had taken expert advice they would have been advised by Mr Truswell, a chartered civil engineer who was their expert, that at most about one gallon per hour would have been squeezed onto the plaintiffs' land. This is obviously an insignificant amount.

Although I have rejected Mr Truswell's evidence on this point, counsel for the *f* defendants submits that if an occupier takes expert advice he is not at fault in acting on it, even though it proves to be wrong. There are three answers to this submission. (1) In fact the defendants took no such advice. (2) If they had done so I am far from satisfied that this is the advice they would have received. It is true that Mr Truswell gave evidence to this effect, but it is not a matter that appeared in his report and he produced no calculations to support his evidence. I do not say that he was deliberately giving false *g* evidence. I suspect that, as so often happens during the course of a trial, an expert makes quick calculations without having the time to consider the matter in detail and may come up with the wrong answer. If he had been asked to advise before the defendants commenced filling the osier-bed, I am far from satisfied that, after detailed calculations, his advice would have been the same. (3) A layman does not necessarily escape liability by employing independent advisers. A developer carrying out a large scale development *h* would generally have a team of expert advisers. But if in the course of the development something is done that causes damage to others he does not necessarily escape personal liability by saying that he relied on independent experts; although, of course, he may have a right over against them. Cases on collateral negligence of independent contractors are in point.

For all these reasons, and I also observe the point has never been pleaded, I reject this *j* defence advanced by counsel for the defendants. I find the flooding of the patio and skittle alley, as a result of squeezing out of water by the filling of the osier-beds, was reasonably foreseeable by the defendants.

The plaintiffs also put their case in two other ways, with which I must deal briefly. They allege the defendants were negligent. In so far as the filling of the osier-bed was concerned I think that there may have been some negligence, for the reasons given

a above, in that the defendants ought to have foreseen, if they did not foresee, the flooding, and ought to have taken steps to prevent it; but this matter has not been fully argued, because it adds nothing to the plaintiffs' claim in nuisance or trespass on this part of the case, and the burden of proof in negligence undoubtedly lies on the plaintiffs.

In so far as the filling of the pits and the remainder of the site is concerned, I am satisfied and have already found that the defendants in all respects complied with good

b practice and were not negligent.

The final head of liability on which counsel for the plaintiffs relied heavily in opening, but largely abandoned in reply, was *Rylands v Fletcher* (1868) LR 3 HL 330, [1861–73] All ER Rep 1. There has been interesting argument as to the precise scope of this decision. It is to be observed that a basis of the judgment of the Court of Exchequer Chamber given by Blackburn J was that a person is absolutely liable for the escape of anything that

c he brings onto his land that was not naturally there. This judgment was approved by the House of Lords. But the House also based its test on non-natural user of land. As Viscount Simon pointed out in *Read v J Lyons & Co Ltd* [1946] 2 All ER 471 at 473–474, [1947] AC 156 at 166, these are different tests. This difference has doubtless given rise to academic criticism of Blackburn J's categorisation of the grazing of cattle on land as the non-natural user. He had not so categorised it. He was considering the bringing onto land of

d something not naturally there. Nevertheless, the concept of non-natural user of land is now well enshrined in the law and was adopted by Blackburn J himself, then Lord Blackburn in *Wilson v Waddell* (1876) 2 App Cas 95. But interesting though this argument has been, I do not need to consider it in detail. This is not a case, save possibly in respect of the squeezing out, of water escaping from the defendants' land. It is primarily a case of preventing water entering their land, to which *Rylands v Fletcher* can have no

e application. In so far as the squeezing out is concerned, *Rylands v Fletcher* adds nothing to my findings in nuisance.

It follows that the plaintiffs succeed in respect of the damage resulting from the squeezing out, but fail in respect of damage resulting from the general filling of the clay pits and land. I find that it was this general filling that was the cause of the major part of

f the damage and the squeezing out caused only a minor part of it, and only for a limited period.

I have been concerned primarily with the issue of liability in this case and have heard evidence of damage only incidentally to the issue of liability, but I have been asked to indicate the principles on which the damages should be assessed and which heads are or are not recoverable. In respect of the squeezing out the only damage recoverable is in

g respect of the additional cost of pumping and maintenance of the pumps (the pumps would have been necessary in any event) and the costs, which are largely unquantifiable, associated with this. This took place over a period of five years, perhaps seven years, from about 1976 onwards. All I can really do is to give an overall figure in the region of which I think adequate compensation is to be found. In my view that figure is in the region of £1,000. I am prepared to give judgment for the plaintiffs in that figure, but if the parties

h wish the matter to be referred for the assessment of damages, then, of course, I shall bow to their request.

Judgment for the plaintiffs for damages to be assessed by district registrar. No order for costs.

Solicitors: *Browne Jacobson & Roose*, Nottingham (for the plaintiffs); *Moss Toone & Deane*,
j Loughborough (for the defendants).

K Mydeen Esq   Barrister.

R v Nanayakkara and another

a

COURT OF APPEAL, CRIMINAL DIVISION
LORD LANE CJ, McCOWAN AND SIMON BROWN JJ
2, 16 DECEMBER 1986

Criminal law – Procuring execution of valuable security by deception – Execution – Acceptance
of security – Acceptance – Stolen US social security orders handed to bank for clearing – Whether
'acceptance' having ordinary meaning of receiving or taking into possession – Whether 'acceptance'
to be given proper commercial meaning – Whether receipt of orders by bank an 'acceptance' –
Bills of Exchange Act 1882, s 17 – Theft Act 1968, s 20(2).

b

In December 1984 some 4,000 United States social security orders, worth about $US5m, c
were stolen in the United States. The orders were for the payment of money drawn on
the United States Treasury payable in America. In 1985 the appellants received 317 of
the orders in London, and one of the appellants, N, handed them to S, who indorsed the
orders and handed them to his bank in the expectation that his account would be credited
after the orders had been cleared in the United States. Following inquiries made by the
bank's head office N and the other appellant, T, were charged with others with conspiracy d
to procure the dishonest execution of valuable securities. At the trial the prosecution
alleged that the execution consisted of the 'acceptance' of the securities by S's bank,
within s 20(2)[a] of the Theft Act 1968, which defined the substantive offence. The
appellants were convicted. They appealed, contending that 'acceptance' in s 20(2) denoted
the commercial meaning of that term derived from s 17[b] of the Bills of Exchange Act
1882. The Crown contended that 'acceptance' had its ordinary colloquial meaning of e
receiving or taking into possession.

Held – The term 'acceptance' in s 20(2) of the 1968 Act was to be given its proper
commercial meaning, derived from s 17 of the 1882 Act, of a written and signed
'signification by the drawee [of the bill] of his assent to the order of the drawer'.
Accordingly, the mere handing over to and receipt of the orders by S's bank did not f
amount to an 'acceptance' within s 20(2) and the appellants had not engaged in dishonest
execution of the orders by causing them to be accepted. The appeals would therefore be
allowed and the convictions quashed (see p 653 h j and p 655 g h, post).

R v Beck [1985] 1 All ER 571 distinguished.

Notes
g
For obtaining property by deception, see 11 Halsbury's Laws (4th edn) paras 1278, 1280,
and for cases on the subject, see 15 Digest (Reissue) 1386–1387, 12131–12137.

For the Bills of Exchange Act 1882, s 17, see 5 Halsbury's Statutes (4th edn) 356.

For the Theft Act 1968, s 20, see 12 ibid 531.

Cases referred to in judgment
h
R v Beck [1985] 1 All ER 571, [1985] 1 WLR 22, CA.
Treacy v DPP [1971] 1 All ER 110, [1971] AC 537, [1971] 2 WLR 112, HL.

Appeals
Basil Chanrarahra Nanayakkara and Tang Loong Tan appealed under a certificate of the
trial judge under s 1(2) of the Criminal Appeal Act 1968 against their convictions in the
j

---

a   Section 20(2) is set out at p 652 d e, post
b   Section 17, so far as material, is set out at p 652 j, post

Crown Court at Southwark before his Honour Judge Lowe and a jury on a charge of
a conspiracy to procure the execution of valuable securities by deception contrary to s 1(1)
of the Criminal Law Act 1977. The appellant Nanayakkara was sentenced to 4 years'
imprisonment and the appellant Tan was sentenced to 4½ years' imprisonment and
recommended for deportation. The facts are set out in the judgment of the court.

b *Desmond de Silva QC* and *Kim Salariya* (both assigned by the Registrar of Criminal Appeals)
for Nanayakkara.
Christopher Sallon (assigned by the Registrar of Criminal Appeals) for Tan.
Victor Temple and *James Richardson* for the Crown.

Cur adv vult

c

16 December. The following judgment of the court was delivered.

LORD LANE CJ. On 1 November 1985 Nanayakkara and Tan were convicted at the
Crown Court at Southwark of conspiracy to procure the execution of valuable securities
d by deception. They were sentenced as follows: Nanayakkara to 4 years' imprisonment;
and Tan to 4½ years' imprisonment and recommended for deportation. They appeal
against conviction by certificate of the trial judge and apply for leave to appeal against
sentence.
The certificate of the trial judge reads as follows:

e 'The learned judge may have erred in law in: (1)(i) ruling that there was
jurisdiction in the court to try the alleged offence; (ii) rejecting the appellants'
submissions that the evidence disclosed the alleged offence was only triable outside
the jurisdiction of the court. (2)(i) ruling that the meaning of "acceptance" (as set
out in a material allegation in the indictment) was merely "taking in or taking
possession"; (ii) rejecting the appellants' submissions that the Bills of Exchange Act
f 1882 applied to and assisted in the interpretation of that material allegation of
"acceptance".'

The facts of the case are these. On or about 29 December 1984 some 4,000 United
States Treasury social security orders (described in the indictment as 'cheques') worth
about $US5m were stolen from the mail in California. By 14 January 1985 some 317
g (worth $US250,000) were in London; 82 had been indorsed by a co-defendant called Foo
and the remainder by a man called Peter Tang. The orders were for the payment of
money drawn on the United States Treasury payable in America.
Nanayakkara was staying at a hotel in London. After one abortive attempt to pass the
orders at Barclays Bank he got in touch with a man called Strassborg, who was jointly
indicted with the appellants but acquitted. Nanayakkara and Strassborg went to
h Strassborg's bank, the Indo-Suez Bank in Berkeley Square, where Strassborg indorsed the
orders again and handed them to an official of the bank. The orders were passed by the
bank to their head office, but suspicions were aroused, inquiries made, and as a result the
police were informed. No money was sought directly from the bank. Strassborg expected
his account to be credited only after clearance in the United States.
The case for the prosecution was that the appellants were all party to a joint enterprise
j to cash the orders through a London bank, knowing full well that they had been acquired
dishonestly and that they had no lawful authority to encash them. There was ample
evidence that the appellants were knowingly engaged in the fraudulent enterprise of
turning the stolen orders into money for their own benefit.
The indictment read as follows:

'STATEMENT OF OFFENCE

Conspiracy to procure the execution of valuable securities by deception, contrary *a*
to s 1(1) of the Criminal Law Act, 1977.

PARTICULARS

[The defendants] on divers days between the 1st day of December 1984 and the
20th day of January 1985 conspired together and with Peter Tang and other persons
unknown to procure, dishonestly and with a view to gain for themselves or another, *b*
the execution of valuable securities, namely the acceptance of US Treasury Social
Security Cheques, by deception, namely by falsely representing that:—(i) those
presenting the said cheques for acceptance were lawfully entitled to negotiate the
same, and (ii) each of the said cheques had been endorsed by the original payee.'

At the close of the prosecution case submissions were made by counsel on behalf of the *c*
appellants inviting the judge to rule that the prosecution had failed to prove any
agreement on the part of the appellants to procure the execution of valuable securities.
The judge ruled against that submission and the case proceeded.

That submission is now repeated before us by counsel for Nanayakkara. His argument
runs as follows. In order to succeed the prosecution had to prove that there was a
conspiracy to procure the execution of a valuable security. Section 20(2) of the Theft Act *d*
1968 defines the substantive offence as follows:

'A person who dishonestly, with a view to gain for himself or another or with
intent to cause loss to another, by any deception procures the execution of a valuable
security shall on conviction on indictment be liable to imprisonment for a term not
exceeding seven years; and this subsection shall apply in relation to the making,
acceptance, indorsement, alteration, cancellation or destruction in whole or in part *e*
of a valuable security, and in relation to the signing or sealing of any paper or other
material in order that it may be made or converted into, or used or dealt with as, a
valuable security, as if that were the execution of a valuable security.'

It was open to the prosecution to choose any of the activities as set out to found their
allegation of 'dishonest execution'. Had they for example chosen 'alteration' or *f*
'indorsement' the result might, with hindsight, have been different. They did, however,
choose to rely on 'acceptance'. Their case was based on the contention that the receipt of
these securities by the Indo-Suez Bank was an 'acceptance' within the meaning of that
word in s 20(2). In other words that 'acceptance' has its ordinary colloquial meaning of
'receiving' or 'taking into possession'. It was conceded by the prosecution that their case
depended on that interpretation being correct. *g*

Counsel for Nanayakkara submits that that interpretation is wrong, that 'acceptance'
has its technical meaning derived from the Bills of Exchange Act 1882, that there was no
acceptance when the documents were handed over to the Indo-Suez Bank and therefore
no execution. Indeed, even if they were capable of such acceptance at all, which is highly
unlikely, that could only take place in the United States and that would mean that the
substantive offence which the defendants were conspiring to commit would be *h*
committed outside the jurisdiction. It would follow that the Crown Court would have
no jurisdiction to try this matter.

The argument goes as follows. The second half of s 20(2) of the 1968 Act sets out in
chronological order all stages in the life of a bill of exchange, and is in effect the skeleton
of the Bills of Exchange Act 1882. Section 3 deals with the making; s 17 with acceptance: *j*

'(1) The acceptance of a bill is the signification by the drawee of his assent to the
order of the drawer.
(2) An acceptance . . . (a) . . . it must be written on the bill and be signed by the
drawee . . .'

Sections 31 to 35 deal with indorsements, s 64 with alterations and s 63 with cancellation.

a   Next, if one traces the history of s 20(2) of the 1968 Act, it becomes apparent, submits counsel for Nanayakkara, that 'acceptance' is being used throughout in its technical sense. The Act 21 & 22 Vict c 47 (law of false pretences (1858)) provided as follows:

> 'If any person shall by any false pretence obtain the signature of any other person to any bill of exchange, promissory note, or any valuable security, with intent to cheat or defraud, every such offender shall be guilty of a misdemeanor . . .'

b

One notes the necessity of proving a signature.

That statute was repealed in 1861 by the Criminal Statutes Repeal Act 1861. It was replaced by the Larceny Act 1861, s 90 of which read as follows:

> 'Whosoever, with intent to defraud or injure any other person, shall by any false
c   pretence fraudulently cause or induce any other person to execute, make, accept, endorse or destroy the whole or any part of any valuable security, or to write, impress, or affix his name, or the name of any other person . . . upon any paper or parchment, in order that the same may be afterwards made or converted into or used or dealt with as a valuable security, shall be guilty of a misdemeanor . . .'

In the same year came the Forgery Act 1861, s 22 of which read as follows:

d
> 'Whosoever shall forge or alter, or shall offer, utter, dispose of, or put off, knowing the same to be forged or altered, any bill of exchange, or any acceptance, indorsement, or assignment of any bill of exchange or any promissory note for the payment of money, or any indorsement or assignment of any such promissory note, with intent to defraud, shall be guilty of felony . . .'

e   It seems clear from the terms of that section that the word 'acceptance' is certainly being used in its technical sense. By parity of reasoning, it is submitted that the same consideration must apply to s 90 of the Larceny Act 1861. Both statutes are using the word in the same sense. In both statutes writing is involved or a signature. This is consonant with s 17 of the Bills of Exchange Act 1882 to which reference has already
f   been made.

The Forgery Act 1861 was repealed and replaced by the Forgery Act 1913. By s 2(2)(a) it was provided as follows:

> 'Forgery of the following documents, if committed with intent to defraud, shall be felony and punishable with penal servitude for any term not exceeding fourteen years:—(a) Any valuable security or assignment thereof or endorsement thereon,
g   or, where the valuable security is a bill of exchange, any acceptance thereof.'

It can be said, of those words at least, that acceptance is being used in its strictly technical sense.

The Larceny Act 1916 replaced the Larceny Act 1861. Section 32(2) re-enacted s 90 of the 1861 Act with no material change.

h   It seems to us that up to this point the arguments of counsel for Nanayakkara are convincing. There can be no doubt but that the term 'acceptance' had been used up to this point in its technical sense. Can it be said that the Theft Act 1968 is using the term in any different sense from that in which up to that point it had been used? In so far as we are entitled to look at the Criminal Law Revision Committee's Eighth Report, Theft and Related Offences (Cmnd 2977 (1966)) para 107, it seems that there was no intention
j   to make any such alteration. Section 20 on the face of it merely re-enacts s 32(2) of the 1916 Act and it follows in our view that there is no real basis for saying that 'acceptance' has, relating to valuable securities, any other meaning than its proper commercial meaning. It is true that many valuable securities will not be the subject of 'acceptance' in this sense at all. That is very far from saying, however, that they cannot be 'executed'.

Counsel for the Crown submits that the Theft Act 1968 is intended to be couched in simple and uncomplicated terms which can readily be understood by the ordinary man. *a* He draws our attention to part of the speech of Lord Diplock in *Treacy v DPP* [1971] 1 All ER 110 at 124, [1971] AC 537 at 565:

'The Theft Act 1968 makes a welcome departure from the former style of drafting in criminal statutes. It is expressed in simple language as used and understood by ordinary literate men and women. It avoids so far as possible those terms of art *b* which have acquired a special meaning understood only by lawyers in which many of the penal enactments which it supersedes were couched.'

We think that the word 'acceptance' was one of those terms of art which it was not possible to avoid.

Counsel for the Crown next draws our attention to the Forgery and Counterfeiting Act 1981, s 1 of which provides as follows: *c*

'A person is guilty of forgery if he makes a false instrument, with the intention that he or another shall use it to induce somebody to accept it as genuine, and by reason of so accepting it to do or not to do some act to his own or any other person's prejudice.'

We do not think that that use of the word 'accept', which, from the context, is clearly *d* its ordinary colloquial use, assists counsel for the Crown in his argument as to the meaning of s 20(2).

The main contention of the Crown is based on the decision of another division of this court in *R v Beck* [1985] 1 All ER 571, [1985] 1 WLR 22. In that case a large number of traveller's cheques were stolen and later unlawfully cashed in the south of France. 400 of *e* them were then presented to Barclays Bank International through normal banking channels in France and England. All these cheques had been forged by the appellant and he had thereby obtained property in the south of France. A Diners Club credit card was also stolen and used to obtain goods in France. Both Barclays Bank, in respect of the traveller's cheques, and Diners Club, in respect of the credit card, reimbursed the French traders for the money which they had paid out, although it was known to both *f* organisations that the cheques and the card had been stolen. This was because the French traders had complied with all the necessary conditions. The appellant was indicted and convicted on three counts of procuring the execution of a valuable security by deception, contrary to s 20(2). He appealed on the grounds, inter alia, (1) that no offence had been committed by him within the jurisdiction of the Crown Court and (2) that the trial judge was wrong in law in ruling that the final acceptance of a valuable security when it was a *g* traveller's cheque was when it was paid. Watkins LJ, giving the judgment of the court, said ([1985] 1 All ER 571 at 574–575, [1985] 1 WLR 22 at 26–27):

'We heard much argument about the definition properly to be given to the word "execution". It is a term of art, counsel for the appellant contended. It bears the meaning it would bear in relation to a legal instrument. It means the due *h* performance of all formalities necessary to give validity to a document. Seeing that the traveller's cheques were all forged, none of them could be said to have been executed. If that, he submits, be wrong, it was beyond doubt that all acts of execution were performed in France. Counsel for the Crown argued that execution in this context means no more than giving effect to. The terms of s 20(2) of the 1968 Act envisage more than one kind of execution. A shopkeeper executes, in *j* other words gives effect to, a valuable security, namely a bill arising out of the use of a Diners Club card, by demanding payment of the bill. A forged traveller's cheque is a valuable security, forged or not, and capable of being executed. In our view, having regard only to the facts of this case, execution bears one of the extended *a* meanings given to it in s 20(2). Thus it is clear that, for example, the alteration, cancellation or destruction of a valuable security can amount to an execution of it. So may an acceptance of it. To attribute to the word the very restricted meaning counsel for the appellant would have us accept and even to the somewhat more expansive definition provided by counsel for the Crown would be, in our judgment, to fail to recognise the plain indication of its meaning in the subsection itself. Thus, when a traveller's cheque is accepted as genuine by a payer who pays the monetary

b value of it to the holder, he executes it. Likewise, when Diners Club (France) accepts a bill for payment signed by the actual or ostensible holder of a club card and pays it, execution takes place . . . we see no good reason why there should not be a series of acceptances, ie executions, in respect of a traveller's cheque and provided the last of them, namely when the final act of payment on the cheque is made, occurs here, the Crown Court has jurisdiction to deal with the offence. We use the expression

c "final act of payment" because when Barclays Bank International Ltd have paid the eventual holders the traveller's cheque becomes valueless; it is no longer a valuable security as a traveller's cheque. In this respect the bill rendered to the Diners Club poses no difficulty. It was merely passed through Diners Club (France) and presented for payment here to Diners Club (UK). There seems to have been no act committed by Diners Club (France) which could be said to be an execution. If that be right,

d execution can only have occurred when the bill was accepted and paid here. If that be wrong and Diners Club (France) paid the bill to the original holder, we would apply the same reasoning to that situation as we think it sensible to apply to traveller's cheques.'

e The court in that case was not presented with the historical survey of the use of the words in s 20(2) which counsel for Nanayakkara gave to us, and the interpretation of the word 'acceptance' which he submitted before us, which we think to be correct, was not argued. However, it is in any event clear from the words we have cited that Watkins LJ was confining his decision to the facts of that particular case and that those facts, unlike those in the present case, included the payment out of money in the United Kingdom on the basis of the stolen valuable securities, which is a very different situation from that

f which obtains here, where all that happened in the United Kingdom was that the orders were handed to the bank. In *R v Beck* there was clearly an execution, and an execution within the jurisdiction and we respectfully agree with the result of that case.

We have come to the conclusion that, whatever may have been the situation on the facts in *R v Beck*, the mere handing over of the valuable securities to the Indo-Suez Bank in the present case cannot possibly have amounted to an 'acceptance'. Moreover, whatever

g interpretation is to be put on the word 'acceptance', it seems to us that by no stretch of the imagination could it be said that there was an 'execution' when the orders were handed over to the Indo-Suez Bank.

In our judgment the prosecution failed to establish what was admittedly the foundation stone of their whole case (as they presented it), namely that the appellants had executed a

h valuable security by procuring its 'acceptance' by the Indo-Suez Bank. One can understand the reasons why the prosecution presented the case in the way that they did. Nevertheless, we have no alternative but to quash the conviction.

Appeals allowed. Convictions quashed.

j The court refused leave to appeal to the House of Lords, declined to make an order under s 37 of the Criminal Appeal Act 1968, but certified, under s 33(2) of that Act, that the following point of law of general public importance was involved in the decision: whether the technical meaning of 'acceptance' as defined in s 17 of the Bills of Exchange Act 1882 is to be applied to the construction *of the word 'acceptance' in s 20(2) of the Theft Act 1968 (bearing in mind that many valuable securities not being bills of exchange are not capable of technical acceptance)?*   *a*

Solicitors: *Crown Prosecution Service.*

N P Metcalfe Esq   Barrister.

b

Maxwell v Pressdram Ltd and another

COURT OF APPEAL, CIVIL DIVISION
KERR AND PARKER LJJ   *c*
10, 11 NOVEMBER 1986

Evidence – Privilege – Press – Newspaper reporter – Source of information – Disclosure of source – Disclosure necessary in the interests of justice – Necessary – Disclosure of source relevant to issue of damages and whether defendant guilty of aggravating behaviour – Whether disclosure 'necessary' – Contempt of Court Act 1981, s 10.   *d*

The plaintiff issued a writ for libel against the defendants alleging that articles published in the defendants' satirical magazine libelled him by stating that he had financed a politician's trips abroad in order to be recommended for a peerage. The plaintiff claimed both aggravated and exemplary damages. The defendants pleaded in their defence that they intended to justify the articles and stated on affidavit that they were based on highly   *e* placed sources of information. Despite the fact that some ten months before the trial the defendants knew that their alleged sources would not give evidence and that they intended not to reveal their sources at the trial, the defendants did not withdraw their plea of justification until the trial had commenced. When asked by the plaintiff at the trial to reveal their sources the defendants refused, relying on the general protection from disclosure of sources afforded by s 10[a] of the Contempt of Court Act 1981. The *f* plaintiff submitted that disclosure could be ordered under s 10 because it was 'necessary in the interests of justice' to determine whether the defendants had published the articles recklessly or knowing them to be false and were thus liable for aggravated and exemplary damages. The judge ruled that the effect of the defendants' behaviour on the amount of damages could be dealt with adequately by a strong direction to the jury in his summing up and that therefore disclosure of the defendants' sources was not 'necessary' in the *g* interests of justice. The plaintiff appealed against the ruling.

Held – In determining whether the disclosure of sources was 'necessary' in the interests of justice, for the purposes of s 10 of the 1981 Act, the court had first to identify and define the issue for which disclosure was required and then to decide whether, having regard to the nature of the issue and the circumstances of the case, it was in fact 'necessary' *h* to order disclosure. Although disclosure of sources might be relevant and important in determining whether the defendants had acted disgracefully and whether that should be reflected in an award of aggravated or exemplary damages, that did not make disclosure 'necessary' in the interests of justice. Accordingly, the judge had not erred in his ruling and the appeal would therefore be dismissed (see p 665 *d e h* to p 666 *d g* to *j* and p 667 *b c e,* post). *j*

Dictum of Lord Diplock in *Secretary of State for Defence v Guardian Newspapers Ltd* [1984] 3 All ER at 606–607 applied.

a   Section 10 is set out at p 657 *g*, post

Notes

a For disclosure of a journalist's sources of information, see 37 Halsbury's Laws (4th edn) para 1070.

For the Contempt of Court Act 1981, s 10, see 11 Halsbury's Statutes (4th edn) 189.

Cases referred to in judgments

Associated Leisure Ltd v Associated Newspapers Ltd [1970] 2 All ER 754, [1970] 2 QB 450,
b [1970] 3 WLR 101, CA.
Secretary of State for Defence v Guardian Newspapers Ltd [1984] 3 All ER 601, [1985] AC
339, [1984] 3 WLR 986, HL.

Interlocutory appeal

By a writ issued on 24 July 1985 the plaintiff, Ian Robert Maxwell, claimed damages for
c libel against the defendants, Pressdram Ltd and Richard Ingrams, in respect of words
published about the plaintiff in articles in the issues of Private Eye dated 12 July and 26
July 1985. The defendants pleaded justification and said that they relied on the truth of
alleged highly placed and reliable sources of information for the articles. At the trial of
the action the second defendant, Mr Ingrams, refused to disclose the sources of the
information and the plaintiff applied for an order of disclosure of the sources, pursuant
d to s 10 of the Contempt of Court Act 1981, on the ground that the disclosure was
necessary in the interests of justice. On 10 November 1986 the trial judge, Simon Brown
J, ruled that he would not make a disclosure order under s 10. The plaintiff appealed to
the Court of Appeal against the ruling. The facts are set out in the judgment of Kerr LJ.

Richard L Hartley QC and Thomas Shields for Mr Maxwell.
e A J Bateson QC and Desmond Browne for the defendants.

KERR LJ. This is an appeal from a ruling given by Simon Brown J yesterday in the
course of a libel action by Mr Robert Maxwell MC against Pressdram Ltd and Mr Richard
Ingrams: in other words, against the publishers and editor of Private Eye. The judge
f gave leave to appeal; he clearly found the point to be finely balanced. We heard part of
the argument yesterday until the late afternoon; we have heard the remainder this
morning and we now give judgment at short notice because the judge and jury are
awaiting the outcome of this appeal.

The issue concerns the disclosure or non-disclosure of journalists' sources of
information; it turns on s 10 of the Contempt of Court Act 1981, which is in the
g following terms:

'No court may require a person to disclose, nor is any person guilty of contempt
of court for refusing to disclose, the source of information contained in a publication
for which he is responsible, unless it be established to the satisfaction of the court
that disclosure is necessary in the interests of justice or national security or for the
prevention of disorder or crime.'

h The issue here turns on the words 'interests of justice'. This means the administration
of justice in the course of legal proceedings: see per Lord Diplock in Secretary of State for
Defence v Guardian Newspapers Ltd [1984] 3 All ER 601 at 607, [1985] AC 339 at 350, in a
passage which I think was concurred in by all, or certainly the majority, of their
Lordships. In that context Lord Diplock said:

j 'The exceptions include no reference to "the public interest" generally and I would
add that in my view the expression "justice", the interests of which are entitled to
protection, is not used in a general sense as the antonym of "injustice" but in the
technical sense of the administration of justice in the course of legal proceedings in
a court of law . . .'

I need not read any further; Lord Diplock goes on to deal with the meaning of the word 'court'. I shall have to return to a later passage on the same page.   *a*

Mr Maxwell is of course a well-known person; in particular he is chairman of Mirror Group Newspapers Ltd, who publish the Daily Mirror. The original publication complained of was in the issue of Private Eye dated 12 July 1985. It is unnecessary to read the paragraph in full; it clearly alleges, in what one might call inimitable style, that Mr Maxwell financed trips by Mr Kinnock, the leader of the Labour Party, to East Africa and Moscow and that he also financed a Central American tour. The words in relation to *b* East Africa are to the effect that Mr Maxwell was acting as paymaster for the trip, in relation to Moscow it was said that he subsidised the trip, and in relation to the Central American tour that he 'picked up the tab'. The paragraph ended as follows: 'How many more Kinnock freebies will Maxwell have to provide before he is recommended for a peerage?'

On 15 July 1985 Mr Maxwell denied these allegations; I should read in full what he *c* wrote:

'Dear Mr Ingram
    There is not a word of truth in the allegations published in the 12th July issue of Private Eye alleging that I am "acting as paymaster for Mr Kinnock's trip to East Africa", nor that I subsidised Mr Kinnock's trip to Moscow, nor that I picked up the *d* tab for Kinnock's Central American tour. Finally, the disgraceful allegation that I provide Mr Kinnock with "freebies" (which presumably is intended to mean "bribes") for the purpose of securing for myself a peerage recommendation is as insulting as it is mendacious. I call upon you, your printers and publishers to withdraw these allegations unreservedly and to publish prominently in the next edition of Private Eye a retraction and suitable apology, the draft of which I enclose *e* herewith, and to pay £10,000 to the Mirror's Ethiopia Appeal Fund. Failing which I will issue proceedings for libel and damages against you, Pressdram Ltd and its printers without further notice.'

In the next issue of Private Eye dated 26 July, that letter was published on p 11, as well as a letter from Patricia Hewitt, Mr Kinnock's press secretary, equally denying that there *f* was any truth in these allegations. But at the same time Mr Maxwell contends that on p 6 of that issue a fresh libel was published in an article which in effect wholly neutralised the publication of the apology and made matters worse. It referred to Mr Maxwell as Mr Kinnock's 'Master's Voice' with a cartoon which illustrated that description, and it referred to the letter from Mr Maxwell by saying that he 'lamely denies' financing the East African trip. In other words, what Mr Maxwell is saying is that it made matters worse instead of better, apart from containing another alleged libel concerning Mr *g* Maxwell's reaction to the possibility that Mr Kinnock might not turn up for a party; I need not go into that further.

Mr Maxwell saw that issue on Wednesday, 24 July, when Private Eye was evidently available, although it is not generally on sale until Friday, in this case 26 July, the date of the issue. Having seen that, Mr Maxwell immediately applied to the Queen's Bench *h* Division (I think it was to McNeill J), for an interlocutory injunction to restrain the publication on Friday and to recall unsold copies. That application was refused. There was then an immediate appeal to this court, consisting of Sir John Donaldson MR, Parker and Balcombe LJJ, and the hearing began on Wednesday, 24 July. We have a truncated transcript of the proceedings on that day and the following day. The issue was whether or not the defendants were going to justify, bearing in mind that if they persuaded the *j* court that they were going to justify, then no interlocutory injunction would be granted.

On that day the journalist who had written the first article, and possibly the second one as well, was not available. But Mr Eady QC, who appeared for Private Eye, informed the court that the defendants did intend to justify. He also said that the journalist, who a   turned out to have been a Mr Christopher Sylvester (to whom I shall have to refer again) had given Mr Eady a thumbnail sketch of the nature of the evidence at Mr Eady's request, and Mr Eady said to the court:

> '. . . I have probed a little further and I do know the identity of the witnesses and the nature of the evidence that they will give in relation to the Moscow and South American trips; but simply because the journalist who wrote it is not available, I have not been in a position to obtain similar evidence in relation to Africa [meaning
b   the trip to Africa] . . .'

The matter was then adjourned and came back before the court on the following day, Thursday, 25 July. On that occasion there was before the court an affidavit by Mr Sylvester, who said that he was the political correspondent for Private Eye. He said in that affidavit:

c   > '6. The Defendants' position is that they intend to justify the statements of fact about which the Plaintiff both in his document . . . and his Counsel before the Court of Appeal on the 24th July made complaint.
> 7. The sources for the Defendants' statements are reliable and highly placed. The Defendants also have evidence by which they can identify the method whereby
d   > funds from the Plaintiff were channelled to Mr. Kinnock's private office; the amount of such funds being calculated by reference to expenditure on his overseas trips to Moscow and to Central America. It will be the Defendants' contention that at least until publication of Private Eye on 12th July 1985 the same method would have been used in relation to the East African trip.'

e   With regard to the circulation position Mr Sylvester said in para 13:

> 'The magazine's distribution pattern is a follows:—The subscription copies numbering 47,000 will already be with subscribers. Distribution of the wholesalers' copies will have been completed by 6.30 a.m. on the 25th July [ie the following day].'

f   What is said in that regard is that the total circulation of Private Eye is in excess of 200,000 copies, and that it is accordingly relevant to consider whether a substantial proportion of these copies could still have been recalled, or whether the motive was to go ahead with publication, recklessly and relentlessly, for profit.

Despite that affidavit, Mr Hartley QC, who appeared for Mr Maxwell, continued to submit that an injunction should be granted. But the matter was really closed by Sir John
g   Donaldson MR saying to him: 'In the face of that, I do not know whether Mr Hartley is pressing the matters.' Although Mr Hartley continued to press, not surprisingly an injunction was refused.

Meanwhile, the writ had been issued on 24 July, and on 26 July the statement of claim was served. I shall have to refer to a number of passages in the pleadings. In para 4 of the statement of claim Mr Maxwell pleaded:

h   > 'The said words [he is referring there to the first publication] in their natural and ordinary meaning meant and were understood to mean that the Plaintiff had acted or was acting as paymaster for trips made by Mr. Neil Kinnock, the Leader of the Labour Party, to East Africa, Central America and Moscow and was thereby guilty of bribery or attempted bribery.'

j   In para 8 there was a claim for exemplary damages in respect of the publication in the second issue, to which I have also referred; that is particularised by reference to the denial which was printed, and to the other matters which appeared in the subsequent issue. The particulars include the following:

'No apologies were published in the said issue, but instead the Defendants chose
to repeat the libel against the Plaintiff in as offensive and, having regard to the
cartoon, as eye-catching a manner as possible. In the premises the Plaintiff will
invite the Court to conclude that the Defendants published or caused to be published
the said words and cartoon with the motive or the expectation that the gain to
themselves would outweigh any loss or penalty.'

While that is an accurate paraphrase, and the basis of the claim for exemplary damages,
counsel for the defendants has pointed out that as a pleading it is insufficient, as required
by RSC Ord 18, r 8(3). That provides that a claim for exemplary damages must be
specifically pleaded, as it was, but it goes on to say, 'together with the facts on which the
party pleading relies'. Counsel for the defendants pointed out that there is no specific
allegation of knowledge of falsity, or recklessness. On this technical pleading point, he is
right in saying that; however, it does not appear to me to affect the broad issues which
arise on this appeal.

There then followed the defence and counterclaim on 15 August 1985, including the
defence of justification which had already been heralded. In para 7 it was pleaded that
the words complained of in both publications were true in substance and in fact.

A number of particulars were given, but I do not propose to read them all. But I must
read sub-paras (3) and (4), which are the most important and were subsequently dropped
in the course of the trial, as I shall explain later on. These were as follows:

'(3) Some of the financial support that the Plaintiff has provided to the Labour
Party has gone to fund visits abroad by the leader of the Labour Party, Mr Neil
Kinnock, including visits to Moscow and Central America. Such funds were made
available to Mr Kinnock's private office by being channelled through the Transport
and General Workers' Union or its officers. Until after discovery of documents and/
or by interrogatories herein, the Defendants cannot provide further particulars as to
the precise dates upon which such funds were made available or the exact amounts
thereof.

(4) In July 1985, Mr Kinnock made a visit to East Africa. At least until publication
of the words complained of in (the first issue), this visit was to be funded by or on
behalf of the plaintiff in the manner set out . . .'

Further particulars were ordered to be given, and of course these have also been
dropped. These included the following:

'In 1984 Mr Kinnock (the newly elected Labour Party Leader) paid visits to
Moscow and Central America. The plaintiff provided funds to Mr Alex Kitson, the
Deputy General Secretary of the Transport and General Workers' Union,
approximately equivalent to the cost of such visits, and those funds were then paid
over by the union to Mr Kinnock's private office in order to finance the said trips by
Mr Kinnock.'

And:

'The Defendants will ask the Court to infer from the manner in which Mr
Kinnock's Moscow and Central American trips were funded by the Plaintiff that his
visit to East Africa would have been funded in the same way. Furthermore, there
was an unspent surplus of funds provided by the Plaintiff for the Moscow trip which
Mr Kinnock's private office intended to use towards the cost of the East African
visit.'

Lest I forget it later, it should be mentioned that counsel for Mr Maxwell points out,
in my view with entire justification, that nothing more has been heard of any of these
allegations, either those in Mr Sylvester's affidavit or in the detailed particulars which I
have read. No doubt that will be taken into consideration by the jury at the outcome of
this trial, but it does not go directly to the issue which we have to decide.

The defence also included a plea of fair comment on a matter of public interest,
a namely the funding of the Labour Party leadership and the political activities of a
national newspaper proprietor. In addition, there was a counterclaim, which I think I
should mention briefly, though in the event it did not play any direct part in this appeal.
That is not to say that it may not play a further part, even on the issues which we have to
consider, at the trial. The counterclaim is as follows:

b '14. In the issue of the Mirror for 15th July 1985 the plaintiff published under
the headline "Another Whopper" the following words which are defamatory of the
Defendants:—"Private Eye, or Public Lie as it ought to be called, last week alleged
that Mirror publisher Robert Maxwell was paying for Neil Kinnock's trip to Africa
this week and that he had financed Kinnock's visit to Moscow last year. Not so".

15. By the said words in their natural and ordinary meaning the plaintiff meant
and was understood to mean that the Defendants had deliberately published a lie
c about the plaintiff paying for overseas visits by Mr Neil Kinnock.

16. It is widely known by readers of the Mirror that the First Defendant
[Pressdram Ltd] is the publisher and the Second Defendant [Mr Ingrams] is the
editor of Private Eye. Such readers would have understood the words complained
of in paragraph 14 hereof to refer to the Defendants.'

d I do not suppose there is any dispute about that. Then it is said (in para 17) that—

'By the publication of the said words the Defendants have been gravely defamed
and seriously injured in their character credit and reputation.'

There was a reply and defence to counterclaim. The plea of fair comment was met by
e a plea of express malice, which included a large number of withdrawals and apologies
which Private Eye had had to publish in the past, with a view to showing that they were
ready to publish matters recklessly which they subsequently had to withdraw. In relation
to the present case it was alleged that the words complained of had been published by the
defendants, 'knowing them to be false or recklessly not caring whether they were true or
false, the predominant motive being to injure the plaintiff's character and reputation'.
f Finally there was also a plea of justification in the defence to the counterclaim, relying
on the withdrawals and apologies mentioned above.

Meanwhile, preparations for the trial were continuing. Counsel for Mr Maxwell has
told us that throughout the defendants made matters as difficult as they could for Mr
Maxwell by pressing for discovery to what Mr Maxwell regarded as an unfair and
oppressive extent, and in other ways. Counsel for Mr Maxwell asks us to infer (and no
g doubt he will put all this before the jury) that the defendants hoped to deter Mr Maxwell
from proceeding with the action in the hope that he would drop it. For present purposes
I accept this. But Mr Maxwell was not deterred and the matter came to trial. It began on
Monday of last week and has therefore been going on for about $5\frac{1}{2}$ days. We are told that
Mr Maxwell gave evidence and that he also called Mr Kitson and a Mr Clements. Mr
h Kitson, who had been mentioned in the particulars which I have read, was, or is, the
deputy-general secretary of the Transport and General Workers Union. Mr Clements is a
highly placed assistant in Mr Kinnock's private office. All three of them denied that any
payments such as were referred to in these publications had been made by Mr Maxwell;
they had not been channelled through Mr Kitson and they had not been received in Mr
Kinnock's office. The witnesses were not cross-examined to suggest that they were not
j telling the truth.

Next (and I am inevitably only giving a brief summary of the course of the trial, which
we have gathered from what counsel have told us) the defendants called Mr Sylvester.
The issue about the duty to disclose sources first arose, as I understand it, in the course of
his evidence. He stood by the affidavit which he had sworn before the Court of Appeal.
He maintained that there was an original source, which was reliable and highly placed,

and that he continued to believe in the truth of the information supplied by that source. In relation to the major source, which I think has been called 'source A', he said that it *a* was a respected figure in the Labour Party and a Parliamentary candidate, but he refused to disclose anything further about it. He also said, as I understand, that he was told by that source that the payments alleged had been mentioned by Mr Kitson, although Mr Kitson had denied it in evidence and had not been cross-examined when he denied it.

Finally on this aspect he said that, if Mr Kitson is referred to as 'source B', whose identity was disclosed, there was, as I understand it, a further 'source C', a person in the *b* private office of Mr Kinnock, whom he also refused to name. That was in relation to the alleged libels with which we are concerned on this appeal. With regard to the second publication he said that there were two moles in the Daily Mirror, whom he again refused to name, but we are not concerned with that.

Mr Sylvester went so far as to say that he believed that Mr Maxwell, Mr Kitson and Mr Clements had all lied on their oath in the witness box, although in fact they had not been *c* cross-examined to suggest this. That, of course, is a matter for the strongest possible comment, but at the moment I am only concerned with a recital of events.

Mr Sylvester also said that originally his primary source, or sources, have informed him that they would be willing to give evidence, and that it was in reliance on this that he swore the affidavit to which I have referred, and that the defendants pleaded justification. But he said that towards the end of last year, some ten months or so ago, his *d* source, or sources, told him that their positions had changed, or that they had changed their minds, and that they would not give evidence.

The practice is of course quite clear: I read from *The Supreme Court Practice 1985* vol 1, para 28/12/18, p 285, headed 'Justification', words based on Lord Denning MR's judgment in *Associated Leisure Ltd v Associated Newspapers Ltd* [1970] 2 All ER 754 at 757, [1970] 2 QB 450 at 456: *e*

> 'Justification, like fraud, should not be pleaded unless there is "clear and sufficient evidence to support it".'

The plea of justification in the present case was not drafted by either of the counsel who are now appearing on behalf of the defendants. But it is not suggested by counsel for Mr Maxwell, particularly in the light of what he has been told by counsel for the defendants *f* with regard to such information as counsel for the defendants has about the sources, that there was never any basis for pleading justification in this case, nor indeed for the affidavit sworn by Mr Sylvester. What is said by counsel for Mr Maxwell, again with considerable justification, is that when the defendants knew months ago that their sources were not going to give evidence, the only honourable thing would have been to withdraw the plea or justification. I shall have to come back to that point later. *g*

That having been the nature of the evidence given by Mr Sylvester so far as it has been put before us (and I hope I am doing justice to it) counsel for Mr Maxwell asked Mr Sylvester to reveal his sources and he refused. The judge then ruled, though evidently with some hesitation, that he need not answer, in other words that the exception under s 10 of the 1981 Act did not require him to do so.

Yesterday, as I understand it, Mr Ingrams, the second defendant, was called. He said *h* that he had not been directly involved in the publication, nor with the affidavit, but left those matters to Mr Sylvester, being satisfied from what Mr Sylvester said that he had a basis for doing what he did. He intimated that the source was not 'at first hand' but in some way at second hand, and there followed exchanges similar to those which I have already mentioned in relation to Mr Sylvester. Mr Ingrams maintained that there was a *j* source or sources; that they were reliable and highly placed, and he also maintained that he continued to believe in the truth of what they had said. On being asked to reveal the sources, he also refused, and so the judge was called on to rule for a second time.

Meanwhile, or at about the same time, two further developments had taken place in

the course of the trial. The defendants had abandoned the main part of their plea of
a justification in para 7(3) and (4) of the defence, which I have read, dealing with the
financing of the trips, because they could not prove them. When I say they could not
prove them, it might be said that they elected not to prove them, because they declined
to disclose their sources and also declined, presumably on the same basis of ethical
journalism, to subpoena their sources.

As a result of the main part of the plea of justification having been dropped, the judge
b struck out the defence of fair comment. He was clearly right in doing so, because since
the defendants accepted that they could not prove the truth of the matters published, it
became impossible for them to seek to maintain that their comment on those matters
was fair. There is now no appeal against that ruling. With the disappearance of the
defence of fair comment went the reply of malice.

One may therefore ask: what really remains by way of defence in this action? However,
c it is said that something does remain, apart of course from the important question of
damages.

What remains has been encapsulated by the judge as follows (I paraphrase what we
were told by counsel for the defendants). The defendants continued to maintain that the
plaintiff, Mr Maxwell, seeks to achieve his ambition to be a Labour peer by patronage of
the Labour Party by various payments which are admitted, and self-publicity in Mirror
d Group Newspapers. When I say that the payments are admitted, this was on the basis
that they were perfectly normal payments in support of a political party, and nobody
could possibly suggest that there was anything wrong with them. What is still maintained
is that in making these payments to the Labour Party, and by what is called self-publicity
in the Mirror Newspapers, Mr Maxwell is seeking to achieve his ambition to be a Labour
peer. I mention that for the sake of completeness, but it does not seem to me to affect the
e issue which we have to decide, to which I shall come in a moment. That is the claim for
damages, which in this case obviously includes a claim for aggravated damages and
indeed, but for a defect in pleading which can readily be remedied, a claim for exemplary
damages.

When Mr Ingrams gave the evidence to which I have just referred, the judge had to
give a formal ruling. He did so after argument by counsel and of course in the absence
f of the jury. I think I ought to read all that he said; what we have here is a summary
agreed between junior counsel. The judge said:

g '[Counsel for Mr Maxwell] now renews his application in the course of Mr
Ingrams's evidence that, pursuant to s 10 of the Contempt of Court Act 1981, I
should require Mr Ingrams and perhaps, on his recall, Mr Sylvester to disclose the
source of the information for the first article. [Counsel] contends the position has
been a developing one in the course of the evidence and that it is even more apparent
now that it is necessary for the source to be disclosed than appeared during Mr
Sylvester's evidence. As to that, I recognise that there is a marginally stronger case
now made out but, in my judgment, the ruling I give does not turn on that and is
irrespective of the previous position and of my previous ruling. [Counsel] based his
h application on a number of grounds. The first, malice, disappears in the light of my
ruling on fair comment. As to that I would have been disposed to agree that the
evidence of the source went to the issue even though no relevant particulars have
been pleaded save for the general particular consisting in the three lines starting "In
the premises . . .".'

j Those three lines are:

'In the premises the Defendants published the said words knowing them to be
false or recklessly not caring whether they were true or false or with the dominant
motive of injuring the Plaintiff's character and reputation.'

So at that point the judge was saying that if that plea had remained alive, his conclusion might have been different, so that an order to disclose sources might in his view have been appropriate. Coming back to his ruling, he said: *a*

'His [counsel for Mr Maxwell's] other grounds can be summarised thus: that it is necessary to have the sources revealed so that the jury may better judge the strength and value of the defendants' evidence that they were relying on the source as both well placed and reliable. This assertion clearly goes to whether or not they were *b* reckless in (a) publishing in the first place, and (b) more particularly, highly relevant to the issue of exemplary damages, whether they were reckless and less than straightforward with the Court of Appeal having regard to the serious possibility of not resisting the injunction sought against them. As a final point [counsel] contends that there is a risk, however clear my direction, that the jury will regard the evidence given by the defendants on information from sources as properly going to the issue *c* of justification even though the relevant passages have now been struck out and conceded to be insupportable.'

Those were the submissions; then the judge continued as follows:

'Powerful though the arguments are in favour of an order for disclosure, I still on balance have decided to adhere to my earlier ruling, for this reason above all others. *d* As the evidence now goes solely to issues of damages and as I believe the plaintiff's legitimate interests can be met by the strong comment I propose to make in my summing up, the public interest of non-disclosure of sources which underlies the section should still be regarded as outweighing the requirement in the interests of justice for those sources to be named. I propose to comment to the jury as I have already indicated to counsel that, given the primary source must be regarded as *e* having expressly waived his anonymity and has acquitted the defendants of the strict journalist's ethic viewed at its strictest of withholding names of sources, the jury might well be disposed to regard the defendants' evidence of their reliance on that source and their continued belief in its accuracy as doubtful. This ruling covers all sources.'

f

It may well be that when it comes to directing the jury the judge will in any event invite them to consider the position in even stronger terms than this. The issue before us, however, is whether he was wrong in deciding that he could, and would, deal with the matter by a strong ruling and not by making an order for disclosure. In that connection I must read a further passage from the speech of Lord Diplock from *Secretary of State for Defence v Guardian Newspapers Ltd* [1984] 3 All ER 601 at 607, [1985] AC 339 *g* at 350, where I had stopped reading before. He said:

'The onus of proving that an order of the court which has or may have the consequence of disclosing the sources of information falls within any of the exceptions lies on the party by whom the order is sought. The words "unless it be established to the satisfaction of the court" make it explicit and so serve to emphasise *h* what otherwise might have been left to be inferred from the application of the general rule of statutory construction: the onus of establishing that he falls within an exception lies on the party who is seeking to rely on it. Again, the section uses the word "necessary" by itself, instead of using the common statutory phrase "necessary or expedient", to describe what must be established to the satisfaction of the court, which latter phrase gives to the judge a margin of discretion; expediency, *j* however great, is not enough; s 10 requires actual necessity to be established; and whether it has or not is a question of fact that the judge has to find in favour of necessity as a condition precedent to his having any jurisdiction to order disclosure of sources of information.'

Counsel for Mr Maxwell submits that this is a case, judging by the history as I have
_a_ summarised it on the basis of what we were told, in which the defendants have clearly
behaved disgracefully. He says that they cannot have the best of both worlds, or, perhaps,
of more than two worlds. On their own story, which he does not accept and which will
be a matter for the jury, they knew, at any rate since the end of 1985, that their alleged
source, or sources, would not give evidence. But they did not withdraw the plea of
justification, although they also knew that in due course they themselves would refuse
_b_ to reveal their alleged source(s) and claim the protection of s 10 of the 1981 Act. Counsel
for Mr Maxwell says that, on the contrary, they then did everything to pressurise the
plaintiff to drop the action. Finally, they only dropped the relevant parts of the plea of
justification during the trial.

There can be no doubt that the jury will have their attention drawn to all these aspects
in the clearest terms. But counsel for the defendants says by way of an excuse that the
_c_ source(s) might have changed his or her or their minds at the last moment, and might
have come to give evidence after all. All I can say to that is: 'Tell it to the jury.' There is
no doubt that this is a case in which the jury may conclude that the defendants have
behaved disgracefully.

However, as the judge points out, all that goes to the issue of damages. This is
extremely important. In order to apply the test formulated by Lord Diplock whether or
_d_ not an order to divulge sources of information is 'necessary' in fact, it is essential first to
identify and define the issue in the legal proceedings which is said to require the
disclosure of sources, and then to decide whether, having regard to the nature of the issue
and the circumstances of the case, it is in fact 'necessary' to make such a far-reaching
order. It is not enough to say that the defendants have behaved disgracefully in a general
way. So in my view the judge was quite right when he said that for the purposes of the
_e_ point which he had to decide, the only relevant issue was damages. I think counsel for
Mr Maxwell recognises that.

I should say in passing in this connection that I suggested that another relevant issue
was the maintenance of the counterclaim. I was surprised to hear this morning that the
defendants proposed to maintain the counterclaim after they had been forced to abandon
the whole of the gist of their claim for justification. Counsel for Mr Maxwell said that
_f_ under the pressure of the trial it had not occurred to him that the counterclaim could be
relevant, and he had therefore not advanced that argument below. On reflection, he
recognised that it could be important, but he had to accept that he could not submit that
the judge was wrong in his ruling on a basis which he had never argued. Whether he
seeks to revive that matter or not will be a matter for him and the judge.

In the upshot, therefore, we are left with this. Not only, as in all libel actions, is there
_g_ a claim for damages; not only, as in many such actions, is there a claim for aggravated
damages; but there is also a claim for exemplary damages. It may well be that this claim
should be regarded as a plausible claim, that is to say one which may succeed and is
perhaps prima facie justifiable.

So one comes to the ultimate issue, that is whether or not, even in the particularly
_h_ strong circumstances of this case, the fact that Mr Maxwell has claimed aggravated, and
indeed exemplary, damages renders it _necessary_, not merely relevant and desirable, to
make an order under s 10 of the 1981 Act ordering journalists to disclose the source of
their information. Counsel for Mr Maxwell submits, with considerable force as it seems
to me, that the jury will not be able to know the truth of the matters on which the claim
for exemplary damages rests without knowing whether there was any truth in Mr
_j_ Ingrams's statement on oath that there was a reliable source of high standing. He says
that they must know, if not the name of the source, at any rate a great deal more about
the nature of the source than has been divulged so far.

There is much force in that, but the judge did not accept the argument. I agree. I can
see many difficulties about the consequence that a draconian order to reveal their sources

of information should be made against journalists merely because of an apparently plausible claim for aggravated, or even exemplary, damages. One can think of other less extreme cases where the defendants may say that they had a reliable source, that they were entitled to justify, but were then let down by the source at the last moment. They would say, 'We cannot, under the ethics of our profession, reveal that source, and for the same reason we cannot subpoena the source. But we have now been let down by the source'. It would then follow that, merely because the plaintiff has also claimed aggravated, and in particular exemplary, damages, they could be forced to reveal their source.

I have not found this issue easy in the context of the present case, but the judge ruled on it in the way which I have set out. He is in charge of this trial. He clearly did not regard it as 'necessary' (a word to which he must have attached great importance) to make the order, even in the perhaps somewhat extreme circumstances of this case, but concluded that the matter could be dealt with adequately by a strong direction in his summing up to the jury, as well as by what they had seen and heard by way of cross-examination of all the witnesses. Clearly this is not the best evidence on which the jury might wish to act. But one has to consider the consequence for other cases and the importance of the public interest which is enshrined in s 10.

I have come to the conclusion that it is impossible to say that the judge was wrong. Accordingly, with some reluctance, due to the facts of this case, I would dismiss this appeal.

PARKER LJ. I agree. In *Secretary of State for Defence v Guardian Newspapers Ltd* [1984] 3 All ER 601 at 606, [1985] AC 339 at 349 Lord Diplock said:

'The nature of the protection [ie the protection afforded by s 10 of the Contempt of Court Act 1981] is the removal of compulsion to disclose in judicial proceedings the identity or nature of the source of any information contained in the publication, even though the disclosure would be relevant to the determination by the court of an issue in those particular proceedings; and the only reasonable inference is that the purpose of the protection is the same as that which underlay the discretion vested in the judge at common law to *refuse* to compel disclosure of sources of information, viz unless informers could be confident that their identity would not be revealed sources of information would dry up.'

The public interest which s 10 of the 1981 Act serves is therefore the preservation of sources of information and ensuring that they come forward.

There is recognised in the passage that I have read a competing public interest, namely that a court of law should have before it information which is relevant to the determination of any issue which falls for determination in proceedings before it. That requirement, however, is clearly not one which would be sufficient to override in general the public interest which s 10 seeks to serve, and it is for that reason that the section provides that there shall be no disclosure unless it is established to the satisfaction of the court that disclosure is *necessary* in the interests of justice (I need not trouble about the other two public interests which are identified).

It cannot therefore be sufficient merely to say that the information which it is sought to obtain within the exceptions of s 10 is information which is relevant to the determination of an issue before the court. Were that so, it would always be possible to obtain an order for disclosure, because unless the information was relevant it would not be admissible, and if it was merely admissible and that was sufficient, an order could always be made.

One must clearly go further and decide in each particular case whether a situation has been created which makes it necessary in the interests of justice that the source should be revealed. It is sometimes supposed that the reluctance of a journalist or a newspaper to reveal a source stems from the belief that, if they do, their case will be weakened. I would wish to say that that is not the case. The newspaper may be well served by revealing a

a   source; it may equally be escaping from a difficult situation by refusing to reveal a source. But it should not be supposed that refusal indicates that the disclosure would be against the newspaper's interests. It often is not; it sometimes is.

In the present case the circumstances are very strange. I adopt the criticisms which have fallen from Kerr LJ of what has gone on in the present case. It is clearly of vital importance, on the issue of exemplary damages, to know whether the source was indeed

b   a 'reliable and highly placed' source, or whether it was, for example, a cleaner in the offices of the Leader of the Opposition, or the union through whom the funds were alleged to have been channelled. Indeed, in the course of argument counsel for the defendants accepted that, on the issue of exemplary damages, it would be most important, but it does not follow that because it is important it is necessary in the interests of justice that it should be disclosed.

c   In the instant case the judge considered that he could deal with the matter with an adequate direction to the jury as to how they might view the protestations of belief in the source, in the light of what had occurred during the case. As Lord Diplock pointed out, it was a matter for the judge to decide. The judge took the view that it had not become necessary in the interests of justice to disclose the sources. It does not follow that that position need necessarily remain so until the end of the case. I do not wish to

d   encourage further applications, but it is abundantly apparent that as a trial proceeds the situation may change from time to time, and the situation might arise, as the result of some evidence being given on behalf of one side or another, that the judge concluded, albeit at a late stage and contrary to what he had felt earlier, that the interests of justice did now make it necessary that the sources should be disclosed.

However, I am not satisfied that the judge erred in concluding that he could deal with

e   the matter as he did at the time when he did it.

Accordingly, I too would dismiss this appeal.

Appeal dismissed.

Solicitors: *Nicholson Graham & Jones* (for Mr Maxwell); *Wright Webb Syrett* (for the defendants).

Wendy Shockett   Barrister.

Ogwo v Taylor

a

COURT OF APPEAL, CIVIL DIVISION
DILLON, STEPHEN BROWN AND NEILL LJJ
24 NOVEMBER, 16 DECEMBER 1986

Negligence – Duty to take care – Persons to whom duty owed – Fireman – Duty of care owed to
fireman – Nature of duty – Fireman attending premises to put out fire – Fire caused by occupier's
negligence – Fireman injured by steam created by fighting fire with water – Fireman wearing
protective clothing – Whether person starting fire owing duty of care to fireman – Whether
fireman's injuries reasonably foreseeable – Whether duty of care to fireman limited to special or
exceptional risks.

b

The defendant negligently started a fire by using a blowlamp to burn off the paint on the
fascia board under the guttering of the roof of his house thereby causing the roof timbers
to catch fire. The plaintiff, a fireman, went into the roof space to tackle the fire and
sustained serious injuries caused by steam generated by water poured onto the fire
notwithstanding that he was wearing standard protective clothing. There was no
suggestion that the contents of the roof space were unusually combustible or that there
was any special danger from some hidden cause. The plaintiff brought an action in
negligence against the defendant, contending that because the fire had been started
negligently and because he had been injured as a result, he was entitled to recover
damages from the defendant. The judge held that the defendant had been negligent but
that he could not reasonably have foreseen the injury suffered by the plaintiff and rejected
the claim. The plaintiff appealed.

c

d

e

Held – Even in the absence of special circumstances not known to the fireman, a person
who negligently started a fire was liable for any injury sustained by a fireman or another
person fighting the fire which was a foreseeable consequence of the negligent starting of
that fire. Although a fireman undertook to bear the ordinary risks of his calling he could,
when injured in the course of his duties while fighting a fire started by negligence,
recover damages from the person responsible for the fire. The injury to the plaintiff was
a predictable consequence of the defendant's negligence in starting the fire, since the
injury caused by steam was damage which was in no way different in kind from damage
caused by flames themselves, and the defendant could not rely on the efficiency of the
fireman's protective clothing to prevent the fireman being injured. Accordingly, the
defendant was liable to the plaintiff. Furthermore, the defendant was also liable on the
principle that a person who by negligence created some peril to the life or safety of others
owed a duty to a third person who, acting reasonably, came to the rescue to deal with the
emergency. The appeal would therefore be allowed (see p 671 *f* to *h*, p 672 *c d f* to p 673
c, p 674 *c* to *e g h* and p 675 *d*, post).

f

g

Haynes v G Harwood & Son [1934] All ER Rep 103 and *Hughes v Lord Advocate* [1963] 1
All ER 705 applied.

Dictum of Woolf J in *Salmon v Seafarer Restaurants Ltd (British Gas Corp, third party)*
[1983] 3 All ER at 736 approved.

h

Notes

For the duty to take care, see 34 Halsbury's Laws (4th edn) para 5, and for cases on the
subject, see 36(1) Digest (Reissue) 17–32, 34–103.

j

Cases referred to in judgments

Brandon v Osborne Garrett & Co Ltd [1924] 1 KB 548, [1924] All ER Rep 703.
Christensen v Murphy (1984) 296 Ore 610, Ore SC.
Donoghue (or M'Alister) v Stevenson [1932] AC 562, [1932] All ER Rep 1, HL.

Hartley v British Rlys Board (1981) 125 SJ 169, CA.

a   Haynes v G Harwood & Son [1935] 1 KB 146, [1934] All ER Rep 103, CA; affg, [1934] 2
     KB 240.
Hughes v Lord Advocate [1963] 1 All ER 705, [1963] AC 837, [1963] 2 WLR 779, HL.
Krauth v Geller (1960) 157 A 2d 129, NJ SC.
Merrington v Ironbridge Metal Works Ltd [1952] 2 All ER 1101, Salop Assizes.
Russell v McCabe [1962] NZLR 392, NZ CA.

b   Salmon v Seafarer Restaurants Ltd (British Gas Corp, third party) [1983] 3 All ER 729, [1983]
     1 WLR 1264.
Sibbald or Bermingham v Sher Bros 1980 SLT 122, HL.
Wagon Mound, The (No 2), Overseas Tankship (UK) Ltd v Miller Steamship Pty Ltd [1966] 2
     All ER 709, [1967] 1 AC 617, [1966] 3 WLR 498, PC.
Walters v Sloan (1977) 20 Cal 3d 199, Cal SC.

c

Appeal

The plaintiff, Michael Chiagoro Ogwo, appealed against the decision of Nolan J dated 25
November 1985 dismissing his claim for damages for personal injuries against the
defendant, R A Taylor. The facts are set out in the judgment of Dillon LJ.

d   *Benet Hytner QC* and *John Leighton Williams QC* for the plaintiff.
W R H Crowther QC and *R Moxon Browne* for the defendant.

Cur adv vult

e   16 December. The following judgments were delivered.

DILLON LJ. The plaintiff appeals against a decision of Nolan J of 25 November 1985
whereby his claim for damages against the defendant was rejected, and the defendant
was awarded his costs of the action.

     The defendant was at the material time the occupier of a house, 91 Laburnum Avenue,
f   at Hornchurch in Essex. The plaintiff was, and is, a member of the local fire brigade. 91
Laburnum Avenue is a two-storey terrace house with a roof and roof space above. On the
morning of 11 August 1982 the defendant set about burning off the paint on the fascia
board under the guttering of the roof, using a blowlamp for the purpose. Realising that
the use of a blowlamp involved a risk of fire, he had a bucket of water at hand, but
despite that precaution, such as it was, the roof timbers caught fire. The fire brigade was
g   summoned, and among the team who came was the plaintiff, then an acting leading
fireman.

     The fire was only in the roof space, or loft, which was a confined space. On the
evidence, the rafters at the rear of the house were burning more or less from the eaves to
the ridge and the fire was spreading. There was a lot of smoke. The plaintiff went up
into the roof space to tackle the fire. He was wearing normal fireman's gear and breathing
h   apparatus with a mask over his face. He took a hose with him to play water on the fire,
and the impact of the water on the fire necessarily caused steam. A colleague, Leading
Fireman Cannon, followed him into the roof space. After a bit the plaintiff came out
from the roof space because of the intense heat, but he went back in again when Leading
Fireman Cannon needed help, and together they succeeded in putting out the fire. When
the fire was out they came down, and the plaintiff found that he had suffered very serious
j   burns under his fireman's tunic. These would have been caused by steam rather than by
direct flames; the fireman's tunic cannot, and is not intended to, provide complete
protection against steam or flames. The plaintiff was taken to hospital, and Leading
Fireman Cannon also went to hospital suffering from heat exhaustion. The plaintiff's
injuries were severe and very painful. The figure for damages has been agreed, if liability
is established, at £12,902 including interest. The issue is over liability.

There is no suggestion of any fault or contributory negligence on the part of the
plaintiff; he acted bravely and efficiently in tackling the fire. There is also no suggestion *a*
that the contents of the roof space or loft were unusually combustible or that there was
any special danger from some hidden cause. It was an ordinary fire, in a confined space,
with nothing unusual about it.

The plaintiff put his case against the defendant on the ground that the defendant had
been negligent at common law in starting the fire and allowing it to get out of the
defendant's control. Alternatively, he alleged that the defendant was in breach of his *b*
statutory duty under the Occupiers' Liability Act 1957. The judge had no hesitation in
finding that the defendant had been negligent, and that finding has not been, and could
not be, challenged in this court. It is therefore unnecessary for us to consider the 1957
Act, since it is common ground that the Act does not impose any higher duty on the
defendant in the circumstances of this case than he is under at common law. We have to
consider whether a person who negligently starts a fire (and it matters not whether he is *c*
the occupier of the premises in question, a contractor or licensee or even a trespasser)
may in the absence of special circumstances not known to the fireman be liable to a
fireman who is injured in fighting that fire.

We have been referred to a number of cases where claims for damages by injured
firemen or by the dependants of firemen killed on duty have been considered by the
courts, but most of these are readily distinguishable from the present case and do not *d*
really assist.

Thus in *Merrington v Ironbridge Metal Works Ltd* [1952] 2 All ER 1101 and in *Hartley v
British Rlys Board* (1981) 125 SJ 169 it was held that an injured fireman could recover
from the occupier of premises where there was a fire, if the fireman had, in fighting that
fire, been exposed to a special danger through the negligence of the occupier of the
premises. In the former case there was an exceptional risk of explosion in the premises *e*
of which the occupier knew, or ought to have known, but of which the fireman did not
know. In the latter case the fireman was, by the negligence of an employee of the owner
of the premises, exposed to the unnecessary risk of going into an upper room in blazing
premises to see if it was occupied. In the light of the explanation by counsel for the
plaintiff of how that case was argued (viz that though the findings in the lower court that
the fire had not been caused by negligence were challenged the case was argued on the *f*
basis of special danger only), it would not be safe to treat it as authority for any wider
proposition. In the present case, though the fire was started by the negligence of the
defendant, there was no special danger from any source not known to the firemen.

In *Sibbald or Bermingham v Sher Bros* 1980 SLT 122 Lord Fraser commented that a
fireman was no doubt a 'neighbour' of the occupier of the relevant premises in the sense
of Lord Atkin's famous dictum in *Donoghue v Stevenson* [1932] AC 562 at 580, [1932] All *g*
ER Rep 1 at 11, so that the occupier owed him *some* duty of care, such as a duty to warn
firemen of an unexpected danger or trap of which the occupier knew or ought to have
known. But that was a case in which it had not been made out that the fire had been
started by the negligence of the occupier, and so the House was not considering the
consequences of negligence in starting the fire. The points actually decided, viz that the *h*
occupier did not owe a duty to the fireman to provide a safe means of escape from the
premises throughout a fire and was not liable for a sudden extension of the fire which
neither the occupier nor the firemen could have foreseen, do not assist in the present
case.

Much more germane to the present case is that it is well established that a person who
negligently starts a fire in a house is liable for any damage to an adjoining house caused *j*
by the spread of the fire. So equally he is liable for any injury to any person which is a
foreseeable consequence of the negligent starting of the fire and its consequent spread.
The foreseeability of the injury is the crux of the matter, since in the present case Nolan J
held that the defendant could not reasonably have foreseen, as neither the plaintiff
himself nor his colleague the leading fireman foresaw, the injury which the plaintiff
would suffer from an ordinary fire in an ordinary loft of an ordinary house.

That approach by Nolan J is however, in my judgment, extremely difficult to reconcile
a with the decision of Woolf J in *Salmon v Seafarer Restaurants Ltd (British Gas Corp, third
party)* [1983] 3 All ER 729, [1983] 1 WLR 1264. In that case a fire had been started in
premises through the negligence of the defendants, the occupiers. The fire brigade were
predictably called in to put the fire out. The plaintiff, a fireman, was told to use a ladder
to get to the second floor via a flat roof. As he was doing so outside the premises, there
was an explosion inside the premises because the fire had reached the gas meter, and the
b plaintiff was injured by the explosion. Woolf J held that the defendants were liable in
damages to the plaintiff. He said ([1983] 3 All ER 729 at 735, [1983] 1 WLR 1264 at
1272):

> 'The leaving of the fish or chip fryer ignited created the unnecessary hazard in the
> form of the fire which occurred. There is a direct link between the fire breaking out
c > and the explosion, and to try and divide one from the other and say that because the
> precise explosion was not foreseeable the defendants are not responsible seems to
> me to be contrary to the ordinary approach as to causation where the acts of an
> individual which are negligent give rise to a series of events all of which are linked
> one to the other.'

d He then considered whether there was any basis for limiting, because they are specially
trained to deal with the dangers inherent in any outbreak of fire, the duty which is owed
to firemen. He concluded ([1983] 3 All ER 729 at 736, [1983] 1 WLR 1264 at 1272):

> 'Where it can be foreseen that the fire which is negligently started is of the type
> which could, first of all, require firemen to attend to extinguish that fire, and where,
> because of the very nature of the fire, when they attend they will be at risk even
e > though they exercise all the skill of their calling, there seems no reason why a
> fireman should be at any disadvantage when the question of compensation for his
> injuries arises.'

Woolf J's phrase 'because of the very nature of the fire' is perhaps a bit cryptic, but in
general I respectfully agree with him. In the present case the nature of the fire was that
f it was a fire in the confined space of the loft.
Fire is inherently dangerous. If a person, as the defendant did, negligently starts a fire
and allows it to get out of his control, it is predictable that the fire brigade will be called
in, as happened here. If the fire thus started and which has got out of control is a fire in a
confined space such as this loft, with the rafters burning and the fire spreading, it is
predictable in my judgment that a fireman tackling the fire in the loft may be injured
g for all his skills and protective clothing. The person who has negligently started the fire
cannot assume that the fireman's protective clothing makes him immune from all injury
from the fire.
The general principles which illustrate the ordinary approach which the court should
apply to causation and foreseeability have been laid down in *Hughes v Lord Advocate*
[1963] 1 All ER 705, [1963] AC 837 and *The Wagon Mound (No 2), Overseas Tankship (UK)
h Ltd v Miller Steamship Pty Ltd* [1966] 2 All ER 709, [1967] AC 617. In the former case a
boy had been injured by the explosion of a paraffin lamp which workmen had left
burning near an open manhole. Lord Reid said ([1963] 1 All ER 705 at 706, [1963] AC
837 at 845):

> 'But a defender is liable, although the damage may be a good deal greater in
j > extent than was foreseeable. He can only escape liability if the damage can be
> regarded as differing in kind from what was foreseeable.'

Lord Jenkins found the distinction between injury by burning from the paraffin in
the paraffin lamp and injury by explosion too fine to warrant acceptance (see [1963] 1 All
ER 705 at 710, [1963] AC 837 at 850). It was predictable that the boy might be burned,
and injury by the explosion was of the same kind.

Lord Pearce took the same view where he said ([1963] 1 All ER 705 at 715, [1963] AC 837 at 858):

> '... by some curious chance of combustion, it exploded and no conflagration occurred, it would seem, until after the explosion. There was thus an unexpected manifestation of the apprehended physical dangers. But it would be, I think, too narrow a view to hold that those who created the risk of fire are excused from the liability for the damage by fire because it came by way of explosive combustion. The resulting damage, though severe, was not greater than or different in kind from that which might have been produced had the lamp spilled and produced a more normal conflagration ...'

In the present case injury to the plaintiff from the flames of the fire was predictable. Injury from steam was perhaps, as the judge thought, less predictable. But the steam is the natural consequence of playing water on a fire in a confined space in order to extinguish the fire. It is damage in no way different in kind from damage caused directly by the flames. It must follow therefore that the injury to the plaintiff was a predictable consequence of the defendant's negligence in starting the fire and the defendant is liable for it.

The defendant takes as an additional or alternative point that he owed no relevant duty to the plaintiff, because the plaintiff, as a trained fireman, undertook to take all the risks inherent in endeavouring to extinguish an ordinary fire. The defendant does not put this plea on the ground of 'volenti' but on the ground of absence of duty. The defendant has not pleaded volenti, since in *Merrington v Ironbridge Metal Works Ltd* [1952] 2 All ER 1101 it was held, rightly in my judgment, whether or not all the authorities cited truly support the conclusion, that a defence of volenti is not available against a fireman who is injured in the course of fighting a fire under orders. It is said rather that there was no duty of care owed to the plaintiff in the case of an ordinary fire like this, because the plaintiff undertook to bear the ordinary risks of his calling. That seems to me to mean just the same as volenti, albeit set out in a greater number of words. I cannot see that it follows, because the plaintiff undertakes for the benefit of the public to use his skills to fight fires, that he also undertakes, vis-à-vis the defendant, not to make any claim if by the defendant's carelessness he suffers injury in fighting in the course of his duties an unnecessary extra fire. Beyond that the answer is, in my judgment, provided by the decision of this court in the well-known case of *Haynes v Harwood* [1935] 1 KB 146, [1934] All ER Rep 103. There it was held that a policeman on duty, who had a general duty to protect the life and property of the inhabitants, could, when injured while endeavouring to stop some runaway horses in a crowded street, recover damages from the person by whose servant's negligence it had come about that the horses were runaways. The policeman was entitled to recover because he was endeavouring to save the people in danger from death or injury. In the present case there is no indication that any other persons were in imminent danger of death or injury while the plaintiff was engaged in extinguishing the fire. But the nature of fire is such that, if unchecked, it will spread and create increasing danger to people as well as property. Accordingly, in my judgment, the 'rescue' principle is as fully applicable as if other human beings were in immediate jeopardy when the plaintiff went into the loft to fight the fire.

It follows that I do not agree with the reasons and conclusion of the judge. For the reasons which I have given, I would allow this appeal, discharge the order of the judge and enter judgment for the plaintiff. I see no reason why people who negligently cause fires and permit them to get out of hand should not be liable in damages to firemen, as well as others, who are foreseeably injured by such fires.

STEPHEN BROWN LJ. In this instance the plaintiff suffered injury as a direct consequence of fighting a fire which had broken out as the immediate result of the defendant's negligence. By virtue of his calling he was under an obligation to attend the fire. He did nothing wrong.

a   In my judgment it was clearly foreseeable that he might suffer injury as a result of the conditions of intense heat which were inherently likely to occur in the case of a fire in a confined roof space. The chain of causation was complete and intact.

The judge found that the defendant was guilty of negligence, but held that the injury to the plaintiff was an 'unforeseen consequence'. I do not agree. On the application of the ordinary principles of liability for a negligent act, the plaintiff is entitled to recover against the defendant.

b   I would add that I agree with the submission of counsel for the plaintiff that this is not strictly a case for consideration in the context of the Occupiers' Liability Act 1957. In point of fact the plaintiff in this instance suffered injury directly from the effect of heat generated by the fire rather than as a result of any defect in the premises. It so happened that this fire was a house fire, but the plaintiff's position in law would have been the same had he been attending a fire negligently started in an open space and he had sued

c   the author of the fire.

For these reasons and for the reasons given by Dillon LJ I would allow the appeal.

NEILL LJ. The basic facts have been set out by Dillon LJ, whose judgment I have had the advantage of reading in draft. I need not repeat them.

On 7 June 1984 the writ in the present action was issued. In the statement of claim
d   which was served on 30 June 1984, the plaintiff put his claim for damages on two grounds: (1) negligence at common law; (2) a breach of the common duty of care owed by the defendant as the occupier of the premises in accordance with s 2 of the Occupiers' Liability Act 1957.

I propose to deal first with the claim based on s 2 of the 1957 Act. Before I do so, however, it will be convenient to set out certain matters which can be treated as not
e   being in dispute in this appeal. (a) The fire was started by the negligence of the defendant. (b) The contents of the attic were not unusually combustible and there was nothing unusual about the fire. Indeed attendance at fires in terraced houses is a regular part of the work of firemen in this part of Essex. (c) The plaintiff was wearing the standard protective clothing, but such clothing did not provide complete protection to the plaintiff against the steam generated by the water which he and his colleague were pouring on
f   the fire. (d) The plaintiff was not guilty of any contributory negligence.

The claim based on s 2 of the 1957 Act

I can deal with this part of the case quite shortly because it is common ground that the duty of the defendant to the plaintiff at common law as the person who started the fire
g   negligently is no lower, and may well be higher, than his duty to the plaintiff as the occupier of the premises. It is sufficient to say that there is authority for the proposition that a fireman can recover damages against an occupier of property if through the negligence of the occupier he has been exposed to and injured by some unusual or unnecessary hazard at the premises: see *Merrington v Ironbridge Metal Works Ltd* [1952] 2 All ER 1101 and *Hartley v British Rlys Board* (1981) 125 SJ 169. Thus, for example, an
h   occupier may be liable if, having an opportunity to do so, he fails to warn a fireman of the presence of some dangerous chemical or explosive material or other 'unexpected danger or trap': see *Sibbald or Bermingham v Sher Bros* 1980 SLT 122 at 125 per Lord Fraser. In the present case, however, the fire had no unusual features and the attic, although a dangerous place in which to fight a fire, contained no special hazard.

I turn therefore to examine whether the defendant owed a wider duty at common law
j   as the person whose negligence started the fire and indeed allowed it to take hold.

The claim at common law

As Dillon LJ has pointed out, it is well established as a general proposition that a person who negligently starts a fire in a house is liable for any damage to an adjoining house caused by the spread of the fire. The damage is foreseeable and in the ordinary way the existence of a duty of care to the owner and to the occupiers of the adjoining house will be easy to establish. Similarly, the tortfeasor will owe a duty of care to persons and property present in the house in which the fire is started. More difficult questions may arise, however, in relation to those who are passing in the street or come into the house after the fire has started. It would serve no useful purpose to consider all the possible cases which may arise. I confine my attention therefore to the present case, where the plaintiff entered the house for the specific purpose of fighting the fire. He did so as a professional fireman acting in the course of his duties in order to ensure that the fire was put out with the least possible risk to the persons and property of those who were in the house or in adjoining premises.

It seems clear that a person who by negligence creates some peril to the life or safety of others owes a duty to a third person who, acting reasonably, comes to the rescue to deal with the emergency. If that person is injured in effecting or trying to effect a rescue, and the peril is the proximate cause of the injury, he may be entitled to recover damages against the wrongdoer. Moreover, it seems that this duty is owed even where the peril is to the life or safety of the wrongdoer himself. The duty is an independent duty owed to the rescuer and it is unnecessary to establish a tortious breach of a duty of care owed to some other person. A similar duty will also be owed in appropriate cases where the peril is to property rather than to the person, but in the instant case I do not propose to explore this point further. The fire with which we are concerned was in a terraced house and it obviously created a dangerous situation with which the fire brigade had to deal.

I draw attention to these general propositions, however, to explain that in my view the correct approach to this case is by way of what are called the rescue cases. In this country these cases really start with the decision of Finlay J in *Haynes v Harwood* [1934] 2 KB 240, though it is right to draw attention to the earlier decision of Swift J in *Brandon v Osborne Garrett & Co Ltd* [1924] 1 KB 548, [1924] All ER Rep 703. In *Haynes v Harwood* the plaintiff, a police constable, was on duty inside a police station in a busy street. He saw the defendants' runaway horses with a van coming down the street. He rushed out and eventually stopped the horses but sustained an injury in consequence. Finlay J upheld the plaintiff's claim. His decision was affirmed by the Court of Appeal, which held that, as the defendants must or ought to have contemplated that someone might attempt to stop the horses in an endeavour to prevent injury to life and limb, and as the police were under a general duty to intervene to protect life and property, the act of, and injuries to, the plaintiff were the natural and probable consequence of the defendants' negligence) (see [1935] 1 KB 146, [1934] All ER Rep 103).

In the present case the defendant must or ought to have contemplated that the fire brigade was likely to be summoned. Fire officers such as the plaintiff were under a general duty to intervene to protect life and property by extinguishing the fire. The possibility of injury to the plaintiff by flame or heat was therefore predictable. I can see no satisfactory basis on which this court could distinguish the position of the plaintiff here from that of Pc Haynes. Nor have I been able to detect in any of the English rescue cases any support for an argument that firemen and other professional rescuers are or should be in some special category. It is true that in a number of states of the United States of America an exception has been developed to limit the rights of firemen and, in some states, of members of other rescue services including the police. The basis for this so-called 'firemen's rule' was explained by Weintraub CJ in the Supreme Court of New Jersey in the leading case of *Krauth v Geller* (1960) 157 A 2d 129 at 130 as follows:

'That the misfortune here experienced by a fireman was well within the range of foreseeability cannot be disputed. But liability is not always co-extensive with foreseeability of harm. The question is ultimately one of public policy, and the answer must be distilled from the relevant factors involved upon an inquiry into what is fair and just ... it is the fireman's business to deal with that very hazard [the fire] and hence, perhaps by analogy to the contractor engaged as an expert to remedy dangerous situations, he cannot complain of negligence in the creation of the very

a
occasion for his engagement. In terms of duty, it may be said there is none owed the fireman to exercise care so as not to require the special services for which he is trained and paid. Probably most fires are attributable to negligence, and in the final analysis the policy decision is that it would be too burdensome to charge all who carelessly cause or fail to prevent fires with the injuries suffered by the expert retained by public funds to deal with those inevitable, although negligently created, occurrences.'

b
This exception has provoked criticism and judicial comment, but it has been widely applied: see, for example, the cases cited in *Walters v Sloan* (1977) 571 P 2d 609 at 611 in the Supreme Court of California; though in at least one state, Oregon, the exception has been effectively removed by legislation: see *Christensen v Murphy* (1984) 678 P 2d 1210.

c
It is also to be observed that in *Russell v McCabe* [1962] NZLR 392 at 406, where a temporary fire fighter recovered damages in respect of injuries received fighting a tussock fire started negligently by the defendant in the course of farming operations, the New Zealand Court of Appeal specifically reserved the question whether the position might have been different if someone employed by a regular fire brigade had been injured.

There is, however, no 'firemen's rule' to be found in the cases decided in this country. Furthermore, in the argument before us no reliance was placed on any developments
d
which may have taken place in other jurisdictions. Accordingly, I too would allow the appeal and I would concur in the order proposed by Dillon LJ.

Appeal allowed. Leave to appeal to the House of Lords refused.

18 February. The Appeal Committee of the House of Lords gave leave to appeal.

e
Solicitors: *Robin Thompson & Partners,* Ilford (for the plaintiff): *Berrymans* (for the defendant).

Celia Fox   Barrister.

R v Bristol Justices, ex parte Broome

a

QUEEN'S BENCH DIVISION (CROWN OFFICE LIST)
BOOTH J
28 NOVEMBER 1986

Children and young persons – Detention – Place of safety order – Release of detained child – b
Child detained by constable in place of safety – Whether police entitled to be heard on application
for release of detained child – Children and Young Persons Act 1969, s 28(2)(5).

The police have a right to be heard on the hearing of an application under s 28(5)[a] of the
Children and Young Persons Act 1969 for the release of a child who has been detained by
a constable under s 28(2)[b], since without evidence from the police as to why the child was c
detained and whether the detention should be continued the magistrate hearing the
application will be unable properly to determine whether the child 'ought to be further
detained in his own interests' (see p 678 d to g, post).

Notes
For detention of a child by a constable, see 24 Halsbury's Laws (4th edn) para 777. d
    For the Children and Young Persons Act 1969, s 28, see 6 Halsbury's Statutes (4th edn)
270.

Application for judicial review
The Chief Constable of Avon and Somerset, Ronald Broome, applied pursuant to RSC
Ord 53 for judicial review of an order made by the justices for the petty sessional division e
of Bristol on 11 May 1986 for the release of a child detained pursuant to s 28(2) of the
Children and Young Persons Act 1969. The chief constable sought (1) an order of
certiorari to quash the order of 11 May 1986 and (2) a declaration that on the hearing of
an application under s 28(5) of the 1969 Act the police were entitled to be notified of the
application, to be present at the hearing and to give evidence. The facts are set out in the
judgment. f

David Fletcher for the chief constable.
The justices did not appear.

BOOTH J. This is an application by the Chief Constable of Avon and Somerset for
judicial review of an order made by the justices for the petty sessional division of Bristol g
on 11 May 1986 whereby they released a child detained pursuant to s 28(2) of the
Children and Young Persons Act 1969 on an application made to them under sub-s (5) of
that same section.
    The facts can be very briefly stated. The police had reason to believe that on 9 May
1986, an eight-year-old child was engaged in criminal offences. Having the necessary
information, they took action under s 28(2) of the 1969 Act and detained the child on h
the basis that the criteria of s 1(2) of that Act were satisfied inasmuch as she was in moral
danger. Having detained her, she was placed with foster parents.
    Two days later, on 11 May, an application was made on behalf of the child by her
parents with a solicitor to a magistrate under s 28(5) seeking her release. The hearing was
specially convened for the purpose. The police came to know of that application and they
wished to be heard on it. They applied to the magistrate to be allowed to attend the j
hearing and to give evidence if necessary. The single magistrate, who was advised by her
clerk, came to the conclusion that the application under s 28(5) was an application which
should be made, as it was termed, 'ex parte', that is by the child's representative alone and

---

a   Section 28(5), so far as material, is set out at p 678 b, post
b   Section 28(2) is set out at p 677 h j, post

a
in the absence of the police or indeed any other person. So the police were excluded from the hearing.

What appears to have happened was this; the magistrate had evidence from a social worker, who had information with regard to the circumstances in which the child was detained, and the magistrate on that evidence came to the conclusion that the child should be released from detention. That in fact occurred.

b
The chief constable does not seek in any way to criticise the magistrate for the conclusion to which she came on the evidence before her. No relief is sought on the facts of the case.

The issue which I have to determine, and which is the subject matter of this application for judicial review, is whether an application under s 28(5) of the 1969 Act is one that should properly be made in the absence of the police.

c
It is necessary to look in some detail at s 28. It is a section which is commonly used for the purposes of protecting children at risk. Subsection (1) contains provisions by which a place of safety order, as it is generally known, may be applied for and obtained from a justice. That is a procedure which ensures the protection of a child who is in immediate need of it. Subsection (1), so far as material, provides:

d
'If, upon an application to a justice by any person for authority to detain a child or young person and take him to a place of safety, the justice is satisfied that the applicant has reasonable cause to believe that—(a) any of the conditions set out in section 1(2)(a) to (e) of this Act is satisfied in respect of the child or young person; or (b) an appropriate court would find the condition set out in section 1(2)(b) of this Act satisfied in respect of him; or (c) the child or young person is about to leave the United Kingdom in contravention of section 25 of the Act of 1933 . . . the justice may grant the application; and the child or young person in respect of whom an authorisation is issued under this subsection may be detained in a place of safety by virtue of the authorisation for twenty-eight days . . .'

e

f
That is a commonly used subsection. The invariable procedure, in my experience, although it is not dictated in the terms of the 1969 Act, is that the application is made to a magistrate as an emergency application and ex parte, that is, without notice to any other person. Speaking personally, I have never had experience of a case where a parent or any other carer of a child has been given notice of an application for a place of safety order. It is relevant to notice in respect of that subsection that the magistrate has to be satisfied, if an order is to be made, that the applicant has reasonable cause to believe that one or other of the criteria specified in s 1(2) of the 1969 Act is satisfied and that thereby the child is in need of protection which requires him or her to be taken to a safe place.

g
Subsection (2) of s 28 is another means of protecting a child at risk. But this is a means of protecting a child without the necessity of first going to a magistrate to obtain an order. It is the provision by which the child in this case was detained by the police constable. Subsection (2) reads:

h
'Any constable may detain a child or young person as respects whom the constable has reasonable cause to believe that any of the conditions set out in section 1(2)(a) to (d) of this Act is satisfied or that an appropriate court would find the condition set out in section 1(2)(b) of this Act satisfied or that an offence is being committed under section 10(1) of the Act of 1933 (which penalises a vagrant who takes a juvenile from place to place).'

j
The criteria are similar to, although not precisely the same as, the criteria required in s 28(1). By sub-s (2) the constable is able to detain a child without first going to a magistrate. But in those circumstances specific provision is made in s 28 for the matter to come before a magistrate. In this respect the statutory provisions differ from those in respect of sub-s (1) where no provision is made for an application to be made to a magistrate for the discharge of the place of safety order. But where a constable has detained a child and no such order has been obtained, then sub-s (5) provides for an application to be made for the child to be released. It first of all qualifies sub-s (2) by

providing that after the expiration of eight days beginning with the day on which the child in question was arrested or, as in this case, detained, the period of detention must come to an end. Subsection (5) goes on to provide—

> 'and if during that period [ie the eight-day period] the person in question [ie the child] applies to a justice for his release, the justice shall direct that he be released forthwith unless the justice considers that he ought to be further detained in his own interests or, in the case of an arrested child, because of the nature of the alleged offence.'

On an application for the release of the child under s 28(5) the magistrate has to consider whether in his own interests the child should be further detained. This requires the magistrate to have regard, not to the belief of the constable as to the reasons why detention was necessary, but to the interests of the child and whether those interests require his further detention. As counsel for the applicant has so ably argued, that is a very different issue from the issue that is before the magistrate under s 28(1).

The gravamen of the argument of counsel for the applicant is that the rules and principles of natural justice entitle the police constable who detained the child to be heard on the application under sub-s (5) as to the reasons why the detention was necessary and to give evidence, if so required, to enable the magistrate to come to a conclusion, in the light of that evidence as well as evidence presented on behalf of the child, as to what is in the best interest of the child. That is a necessary step in order to ascertain the truth and to enable the magistrate to fulfil his duty under the subsection. It also enables the police to state the reason that they had for detaining the child. What counsel for the applicant suggests was likely to have happened in this case was a confusion between the duty of the magistrate under sub-s (1) of s 28 to protect a child in an emergency and the duty of the magistrate under sub-s (5) of that Act to consider whether it is in the child's best interests that he should continue to be detained. In the latter case, counsel for the applicant argues that there can be no reason at all to deny the police the right to be heard: public interest does not require that, nor do the child's interests require it. The emergency which called for immediate action has passed and the child is in a safe place. The matter can be dealt with speedily, because the police can always be summoned at short notice to such a hearing so that no delay should be involved. In those circumstances there is no reason which would justify the exclusion of the principle of audi alteram partem.

I accept the arguments of counsel for the applicant. Quite apart from the right of the police to be heard as to the reasons why they took action under sub-s (2), it appears to me to be necessary for the magistrate to consider those reasons in discharging the duty that he has under sub-s (5) to determine the interests of the child. For that reason it seems to me that on the facts of this particular case, that the police who wished to be heard on the application should have been heard. In order to enable a magistrate properly to fulfil his duty under the subsection, in my judgment it is necessary that the police should be given notice of the application for the release of the child concerned and should be given the opportunity to be heard and to give evidence.

For those reasons I will make the declaration that is now sought by the chief constable in the terms that he seeks. That is a declaration that on the hearing of an application pursuant to s 28(5) of the 1969 Act for the release of a detained child, the police are entitled to be notified of the application and to be heard and give evidence. But because all matters now relating to this child have been otherwise dealt with, it seems to me not to be necessary to make any other order in respect of the magistrate's order of 11 May.

Declaration granted.

Solicitors: *Blyth Dutton,* agents for *Crown Prosecution Service,* Bristol (for the chief constable).

Bebe Chua   Barrister.

a Rickless and others v United Artists Corp and others

COURT OF APPEAL, CIVIL DIVISION

SIR NICOLAS BROWNE-WILKINSON V-C, STEPHEN BROWN AND BINGHAM LJJ

2, 3, 6, 7, 8, 9 OCTOBER, 10 DECEMBER 1986

b

Copyright – Infringement – Right of action – Performer – Performer dead – Defendants making film after death of actor – Defendants using clips and out-takes from actor's previous films without permission – Whether breach of performers' protection legislation giving rise to civil right of action – Whether contracts between defendants and actor permitting use of clips and out-takes in other films – Whether causes of action surviving actor's death and passing to personal representatives c *– Dramatic and Musical Performers' Protection Act 1958, s 2.*

Between 1962 and 1977 the defendants, a film company and a well-known film director, made and distributed a series of five films starring a famous actor. Contracts for the actor's services for each film (except one) were made between the defendants and a 'loan-out' company which was controlled by the actor and lent out his services for a fee. The d films were highly successful and after the actor's death in 1980 the defendants made a new film using clips and discarded material (out-takes) from the previous films without securing the consent of the plaintiffs, who were the personal representatives of the actor, and without paying them for use of the material. The plaintiffs, who owned the rights to the actor's services as a performer, brought an action claiming damages for, inter alia, (i) breach of s 2[a] of the Dramatic and Musical Performers' Protection Act 1958 in not e obtaining the consent of the actor or his executors to use the clips and out-takes and (ii) wrongful interference with contractual rights belonging to the owners of the rights to the actor's services. The judge found for the plaintiffs and awarded them damages of $US1m, together with a limited account of the profits from the exhibition of the new film. The defendants appealed, contending, inter alia, (i) that breach of s 2 of the 1958 f Act did not give rise to a private cause of action, (ii) that the contracts between the loan-out company and the defendants for the making of each film permitted the defendants to use material shot for that film in other films, (iii) that neither cause of action on which the plaintiffs' claim was founded survived the actor's death and (iv) that the defendants could not be held liable for inducing a breach of purely negative covenants in a contract which had otherwise been fully performed.

g
Held – The appeal would be dismissed for the following reasons—

(1) On its true construction s 2 of the 1958 Act, as well as imposing the criminal penalty of a fine for a breach, imposed an obligation or prohibition for the benefit of a particular class of individuals, namely performers, and thus conferred a right to civil remedies at the suit of a performer whose performance was exploited by others without h his written consent. Furthermore, the right to give or withhold consent to the reproduction of a performance was not purely personal to the performer but vested in his personal representative when he died. Since the defendants had breached s 2 by their use of the actor's previous performances without first obtaining the consent of the actor's personal representatives that breach gave the personal representatives a civil cause of action (see p 685 b c j, p 686 b to d, p 687 h, p 688 e h to p 689 a e to h and p 699 e, post); j dictum of Lord Diplock in *Lonrho Ltd v Shell Petroleum Co Ltd* [1981] 2 All ER at 462–463 applied; *Ex p Island Records Ltd* [1978] 3 All ER 824 and *RCA Corp v Pollard* [1982] 3 All ER 771 considered.

(2) Under the terms of the agreements entered into between the defendants and the

---

a Section 2, so far as material, is set out at p 684 *e f*, post

loan-out company, or in one case the actor, the defendants had expressly or impliedly
undertaken that the actor's performance would be used only for the purposes of the film   *a*
to which a particular contract related and the right to enforce that negative covenant
passed to his personal representatives on his death. Moreover, the defendants were liable
for inducing a breach of a purely negative obligation under the agreements
notwithstanding that in other respects they had since been performed (see p 689 *f g*,
p 694 *c e*, p 695 *c* to *e* and p 698 *f g j* to p 699 *a d e*, post); *British Motor Trade Association v
Salvadori* [1949] 1 All ER 208 applied.   *b*

Notes

For protection of performers of dramatic works, see 9 Halsbury's Laws (4th edn) para
962, and for a case on the subject, see 13 Digest (Reissue) 158, *1332*.

   For civil actions in respect of a breach of duty imposed by statute, see 44 Halsbury's
Laws (4th edn) para 961, and for cases on the subject, see 45 Digest (Reissue) 525–526,   *c*
5481–5489.

   For the tort of interference with contractual relationships, see 45 Halsbury's Laws (4th
edn) paras 1518–1524, and for cases on the subject, see 46 Digest (Reissue) 571–587,
6326–6377.

   For the Dramatic and Musical Performers' Protection Act 1958, s 2, see 11 Halsbury's
Statutes (4th edn) 337.   *d*

Cases referred to in judgments

British Motor Trade Association v Salvadori [1949] 1 All ER 208, [1949] Ch 556.
Cutler v Wandsworth Stadium Ltd [1949] 1 All ER 544, [1949] AC 398, HL.
Dean v Wiesengrund [1955] 2 All ER 432, [1955] 2 QB 120, [1955] 2 WLR 1171, CA.
Island Records Ltd, Ex p [1978] 3 All ER 824, [1978] Ch 122, [1978] 3 WLR 23, CA.   *e*
Lonrho Ltd v Shell Petroleum Co Ltd [1981] 2 All ER 456, [1982] AC 173, [1981] 3 WLR 33,
    HL.
Musical Performers' Protection Association Ltd v British International Pictures Ltd (1930) 46
    TLR 485.
RCA Corp v Pollard [1982] 3 All ER 771, [1983] Ch 135, [1982] 3 WLR 1007, CA.
Thomson (D C) & Co Ltd v Deakin [1952] 2 All ER 361, [1952] Ch 646, CA.   *f*

Cases also cited

Chaplin v Boys [1969] 2 All ER 1085, [1971] AC 356, HL.
Darlington v Roscoe & Sons [1907] 1 KB 219, CA.
Grieg v Insole [1978] 3 All ER 449, [1978] 1 WLR 302.
Peebles v Oswaldtwistle UDC [1896] 2 QB 159.   *g*
Rose v Buckett [1901] 2 KB 449, CA.
Staffordshire Area Health Authority v South Staffordshire Waterworks Co [1978] 3 All ER 769,
    [1978] 1 WLR 1387, CA.
Swiss Bank Corp v Lloyds Bank Ltd [1981] 2 All ER 449, [1982] AC 584, HL.
Tophams Ltd v Sefton [1966] 1 All ER 1039, [1967] 1 AC 50, HL.   *h*
Wilson v William Harper Son & Co [1908] 2 Ch 370, [1908] All ER Rep 239.
Young v Bristol Aeroplane Co Ltd [1944] 2 All ER 293, [1944] KB 718, CA; *affd* [1946] 1 All
    ER 98, [1946] AC 163, HL.

Appeal

The defendants, United Artists Corp, Blake Edwards and Lakeline Productions Ltd,   *j*
appealed against the judgment and order of Hobhouse J on 10 June 1985 whereby he
held the defendants were liable to the plaintiffs, Elwood Abraham Rickless and Michael
Barry Wolf (suing as the executors of the estate of Peter Sellers deceased), Satchitananda
Ltd and Motion Picture Factoring SA, for the unauthorised use of celluloid material,
which was filmed during the lifetime of the actor Peter Sellers in a film entitled 'The

a   Trail of the Pink Panther' which was made and distributed by the defendants after the death of Peter Sellers. The judge awarded the plaintiffs $US1m in damages and a limited account of the profits from the exhibition of the film. The facts are set out in the judgment of Sir Nicolas Browne-Wilkinson V-C.

A J Bateson QC, M G Tugendhat QC and *David Parsons* for the defendants.
Colin Ross-Munro QC, Robert Englehart QC and *Anthony Peto* for the plaintiffs.

b
                                                  Cur adv vult

10 December. The following judgments were delivered.

SIR NICOLAS BROWNE-WILKINSON V-C. This is an action brought by the
c   personal representatives of the well-known film star Peter Sellers and two of his companies against the makers and distributors of a film, 'The Trail of the Pink Panther' (Trail). 'Trail' was made after the death of Peter Sellers from material filmed during his lifetime. Hobhouse J held the defendants liable for unauthorised use of this material and awarded the plaintiffs damages of $1m, together with a limited account of the profits from the exhibition of 'Trail'. The defendants, the makers and distributors of 'Trail', appeal against
d   that decision.
    The full history of the matter is set out in the exceptionally detailed judgment of the judge. I will only summarise the matters which are directly relevant to the issues argued in this court.
    During his lifetime Peter Sellers made a series of five films in which he played the main character, Inspector Clouseau, an eccentric and accident-prone French detective.
e   The first film in the series, 'The Pink Panther, was made in 1962. The character Inspector Clouseau was based on an idea of the second defendant, Blake Edwards, and was first acted by Peter Sellers. The four other films in the series were as follows: 1963, 'Shot in the Dark'; 1974, 'Return of the Pink Panther' (Return); 1976, 'The Pink Panther Strikes Again' (Strike); 1977, 'The Revenge of the Pink Panther' (Revenge). They were known as
f   the Pink Panther films.
    When a film is made far more film is shot than is eventually incorporated in the final film released for exhibition. Footages not incorporated in the final version are called 'out-takes', which comprise not only film which at the time of shooting was found unsatisfactory but also sequences which, though in themselves satisfactory, were discarded in the process of editing. 'Clips', on the other hand, are excerpts from the final film as exhibited to the public.
g
    During Peter Sellers's lifetime Blake Edwards had the idea of making a Pink Panther film using out-takes from the earlier films together with new additional material. Peter Sellers refused to agree. Peter Sellers died in July 1980. The earlier Pink Panther films had been very successful and profitable. In 1981 United Artists and Blake Edwards decided to make 'Trail'. 'Trail' purports to be a feature film starring Peter Sellers, but is
h   in fact made up to a considerable extent of out-takes or clips of Peter Sellers's performances in the earlier films. The defendants tried to get the agreement of the plaintiffs, as personal representatives of Peter Sellers, but terms could not be agreed. Having failed to get the agreement of the plaintiffs, the defendants took legal advice and then decided to make 'Trail' using the out-takes and clips from the earlier films without the specific consent either of Peter Sellers himself or of his personal representatives. 'Trail' was made by the
j   defendant, Lakeline Productions Ltd (a company controlled by Blake Edwards), as a film starring Peter Sellers. 'Trail' was financed and distributed by United Artists. The defendants have paid nothing for the use of the material containing Peter Sellers's performance in 'Trail'.
    Clips from each of the five films are incorporated in 'Trail'. The only out-takes used come from 'Strikes'. Out of the total running time of 'Trail', 97 minutes, out-takes from

'Strikes' make up 23 minutes and clips from the five films make up 14 minutes, a total of 37 minutes.

The defendants say that they were entitled to make use of the clips and out-takes because the ownership of both the physical celluloid and the copyrights in the out-takes and clips is vested in them or their associates. The plaintiffs, on the other hand, say that the terms of the individual contracts under which Peter Sellers provided his services for each of the films preclude the use of the out-takes and clips in a wholly different film, 'Trail'. It is therefore necessary to consider the contracts in some detail. But at this stage I will seek merely to explain the nature of the contractual background.

Each of the films was made by a separate company (the production company) which was the creature of Blake Edwards, a producer and director. All the films were distributed by United Artists, who also financed all the films save 'Return'. Contrary to normal practice, United Artists do not themselves produce films. As a result, in relation to the making of each film there was a separate contract for Peter Sellers's services entered into by the production company responsible for the production of that film.

On the other side of the bargain, save in one case, Peter Sellers himself did not directly contract to provide his services. No doubt for fiscal reasons, Peter Sellers entered into contracts with what are called 'loan-out companies' (controlled by Peter Sellers) under which the loan-out company was authorised to contract with producers to provide Peter Sellers's services. As a result, in the case of most of the films, the contract under which Peter Sellers provided his services as an actor was made between one of Peter Sellers's loan-out companies on the one side and one of Blake Edwards's production companies on the other.

At the expense of strict accuracy, the contractual arrangements regulating the provision of Peter Sellers's services in the making of each film were therefore as follows. In relation to each of the films there was a contract between one or more of Peter Sellers's loan-out companies and one of Blake Edwards's production companies: this contract is referred to as 'the loan-out agreement'. The loan-out agreement regulated the terms on which Peter Sellers was providing his services for that particular film. Under the finance and distribution agreements between the production company and United Artists, all the rights of the production company were assigned to United Artists. It follows that none of the defendants to this action were parties to the contracts under which Peter Sellers's services were rendered. Accordingly, even if the plaintiffs are right as to the effect of the loan-out agreements, they have no remedy for breach of contract against these defendants, since these defendants are not parties to the loan-out agreements. There is one exception to this, namely the first film, 'The Pink Panther'; in relation to that film United Artists entered into a direct contract with Peter Sellers for the provision of his services.

The plaintiffs' claim against the defendants is put in four different ways. Firstly, it is alleged that the making of 'Trail' constituted a breach of s 2 of the Dramatic and Musical Performers' Protection Act 1958 as amended, which makes it an offence knowingly to make a film directly or indirectly from, or by means of, the performance of a dramatic or musical work without the consent in writing of the performer. The plaintiffs' case is that the 1958 Act confers on a performer private rights of action enforceable in the civil courts and that those rights have been infringed in that the use of the clips and out-takes involves the indirect use of Peter Sellers's performances. The defendants contend that the 1958 Act gives the performers no civil remedy, that the contracts for the provision of Peter Sellers's services in each of the earlier films contained his consent to the use of clips and out-takes in 'Trail', that they had not 'knowingly' made 'Trail' without the necessary consents and, finally, that the 1958 Act does not apply to a film made (as was 'Trail') after the death of the performer.

On this aspect of the case the judge held substantially in favour of the plaintiffs. He held that a breach of the 1958 Act does give the performer a personal remedy by way of injunction or damages in lieu, that the 1958 Act renders unlawful the unauthorised reproduction of a performance even after the death of the performer and that the loan-

out agreements did not contain consents to the making of 'Trail' from clips or out-takes,
a save in relation to the use of the clips from 'Strikes' and 'Revenge'. Under this head,
therefore, the judge held the defendants liable in damages under the 1958 Act for the
use of all the clips and out-takes from the earlier films, save that the defendants were not
liable under the 1958 Act for the use of the clips from 'Strikes' and 'Revenge'.

The second way in which the plaintiffs put their claim is breach of contract. This claim
relates only to 'The Pink Panther' and is made against United Artists only. It is alleged
b that the use of the clips in the making of 'Trail' was a breach of an express or implied
term of 'The Pink Panther' agreement and that United Artists were parties to that
agreement. Before the judge United Artists denied that they were parties to the agreement
and argued that use of the clips was in any event not a breach of such agreement. The
judge held that United Artists were parties to the agreement and were in breach.

The third way in which the plaintiffs put their case is founded on the tort of unlawful
c interference with contract (the tort). They argue that the use of the clips and out-takes by
the defendants in the making of 'Trail' involved a breach by the production companies
of the loan-out agreements in that there was an implied contractual undertaking by the
production companies not to use the performance of Peter Sellers save for the purposes
of the individual film which was the subject matter of the particular agreement, that the
defendants knew of these contractual duties of the production companies and had the
d necessary intention to cause them to be breached. Accordingly, the plaintiffs contend
that the necessary constituents of the tort were present.

The defendants, on the other hand, argued that there were no such implied obligations
on the production companies, that, even if there were, the defendants did not have the
necessary knowledge and intention to render them liable for the tort, that the defendants
had not interfered in the performance by the production companies of their contracts,
e but merely exercised their rights as owners of the physical celluloid and copyright in the
clips and out-takes, and that they did not commit the tort by interfering with a purely
negative contractual obligation, the contract being otherwise fully performed.

The judge held that under the loan-out agreements there was an implied obligation
not to use the clips from 'The Pink Panther', 'Shot in the Dark' and 'Return' and the out-
takes from 'Strikes' other than for the purposes of the film in question. However, the
f judge held that there was no such obligation restricting the use of the clips from 'Strikes'
and 'Revenge'. The judge further held that the defendants had the necessary knowledge
and intention to be liable for the tort and that, save in the case of 'Shot in the Dark', had
interfered in the performance by the production companies of their contracts.
Accordingly, under this head the judge held that all the defendants had wrongfully
interfered with the production companies' contractual obligations by using the clips
g from 'Return' and the out-takes from 'Strikes'. He also held the defendants, other than
United Artists, liable in tort for the use of the clips from 'The Pink Panther'.

Finally, the plaintiffs claim that, if the use of the clips or out-takes was authorised by
the loan-out agreements, those agreements provided for Peter Sellers to have a share of
the receipts of the film in question and the plaintiffs are entitled to a share of the receipts
from 'Trail'. The judge held that the defendants were accountable for a share of such
h receipts in respect of the use of the clips from 'Strikes' and 'Revenge'.

In the result the judge held that the defendants were liable under one or other of the
heads in respect of the use of all the out-takes and clips from the Pink Panther films. He
assessed the damages at $1m and ordered the defendants to account for 3·15% of the
gross receipts from 'Trail' in respect of the use of the clips from 'Strikes', and 1·36% of the
j gross receipts in respect of the clips from 'Revenge'.

This summary of the issues before the judge (which is not fully comprehensive) shows
that he had to consider a very large number of issues both of construction and law. His
very full judgment runs to some 106 pages and has made our task much easier.
Fortunately, the issues raised on appeal in this court lie in a much narrower compass.
They are as follows.

1 *The 1958 Act*

(a) Does the Act give a performer a civil right of action or does it only create a criminal
offence? (b) Does the Act render unlawful the reproduction of a performance without
the consent of the performer after the death of the performer? (c) On the true construction
of the loan-out agreement for each film, did Peter Sellers consent to his performance for
that film being used in other films, such as 'Trail'?

2 *Breach of contract and interference with contract*

(a) On the true construction of each of the loan-out agreements, did the production
company expressly or impliedly undertake that Peter Sellers's performance would be
used only for the purposes of the film to which such contract related? (b) Should such
term be limited so as to prohibit the use of such performances for other purposes only
during the lifetime of Peter Sellers? (c) Can the defendants be held liable for inducing a
breach of a purely negative obligation under a loan-out agreement which in other
respects has long since been performed?

The issues under 2(a) and (b) above turn primarily on the construction of the loan-out
agreements; so does question 1(c), ie whether Peter Sellers gave his consent for the
purposes of the 1958 Act. In this judgment I deal with the effect of the 1958 Act. The
judgment of Bingham LJ deals with the construction of the individual loan-out
agreements and the contractual issues.

1(a) *Does the 1958 Act confer a civil remedy?*

Section 2 of the 1958 Act reads as follows:

> 'Subject to the provisions of this Act, if a person knowingly—(*a*) makes a
> cinematograph film, directly or indirectly, from or by means of the performance of
> a dramatic or musical work without the consent in writing of the performers, or (*b*)
> sells or lets for hire, or distributes for the purposes of trade, or by way of trade
> exposes or offers for sale or hire, a cinematograph film made in contravention of
> this Act, or (*c*) uses for the purpose of exhibition to the public a cinematograph film
> so made; he shall be guilty of an offence under this Act, and shall be liable, on
> summary conviction, to a fine . . .'

The section, on its face, only creates a criminal offence. However, in certain
circumstances such a statutory provision can confer private rights of action enforceable
under the civil law. Whether any particular statute does give rise to such private rights
of action depends on 'a consideration of the whole Act and the circumstances, including
the pre-existing law, in which it was enacted': see *Cutler v Wandsworth Stadium Ltd* [1949]
1 All ER 544 at 548, [1949] AC 398 at 407. Further guidance is contained in the speech
of Lord Diplock in *Lonrho Ltd v Shell Petroleum Co Ltd* [1981] 2 All ER 456 at 461, [1982]
AC 173 at 185. The general rule is that 'where an Act creates an obligation, and enforces
the performance in a specified manner . . . that performance cannot be enforced in any
other manner'. There are two classes of exception to this general rule. The first is: 'Where
on the true construction of the Act it is apparent that the obligation or prohibition was
imposed for the benefit or protection of a particular class of individuals'. The second
exception is where the statute creates a public right and a particular member of the
public suffers special damage.

In the instant appeal the judge held that this case fell within the first exception referred
to by Lord Diplock, since the 1958 Act was expressly made for the protection of
performers. The defendants contend that he was wrong and that there is binding
authority to the contrary.

In order to understand the arguments, it is necessary to refer to the statutory history.
The Dramatic and Musical Performers' Protection Act 1925 made it a criminal offence to
make a gramophone record without the consent of the performers. The Copyright Act
1956 amended the 1925 Act by introducing for the first time the provisions for the

protection of film actors now to be found in s 2 of the 1958 Act. Then the 1958 Act
a consolidated these provisions for the protection of performers against unauthorised
reproduction, s 1 dealing with records and s 2 with films. For the purpose of legal
analysis, the protection afforded to performers on film under s 2 of the 1958 Act is,
mutatis mutandis, the same as that provided by s 1 to performers on records. Therefore,
in considering whether Parliament intended to create a civil right of action for
performers, the two sections are equally relevant.

b   I will first consider the matter apart from authority. Does the 1958 Act, on its true
construction in the light of the pre-existing law, disclose an intention to create private
rights of action? First and foremost, it is apparent from the short titles of both the 1925
Act and the 1958 Act that they were passed for the protection of performers. This is a
very strong pointer in favour of the Act creating private rights as being within the first
exception to the general rule. But counsel for the plaintiffs accepts, to my mind correctly,
c that this factor is not decisive if there are other factors which demonstrate that Parliament
did not intend to create private rights.

In my judgment there are a number of factors which point strongly against the 1958
Act creating anything other than a criminal offence.

(1) The wording of ss 1 and 2 points in that direction. The 1958 Act does not declare
the doing of an act to be unlawful and then separately provide a criminal penalty for
d breach. The form of both sections is that the doing of an act is simply made a criminal
offence. In my judgment, although this point is far from decisive, it is easier to spell out
a civil right if Parliament has expressly stated the act is generally unlawful rather than
merely classified it as a criminal offence.

(2) It had been decided in 1930 that the 1925 Act did not confer civil rights of action
on musical performers: see *Musical Performers' Protection Association Ltd v British*
e *International Pictures Ltd* (1930) 46 TLR 485. It must be presumed that Parliament knew
this to be the law when in 1956 it introduced for film performers the same protection as
the 1925 Act gave to musical performers and when it consolidated both protections in
the 1958 Act.

(3) The Copyright Act 1956 was passed after the 1952 report of the Gregory Committee
(Report of the Copyright Committee (Cmd 8662)). That committee stated that the 1925
f Act did not create private rights for performers and advised against the introduction of
such a right. On the other hand, in 1977 the Whitford Committee reported that it was
not certain whether or not the Acts created private rights, and advised in favour of
performers having civil remedies such as an injunction and damages (Copyright and
Designs Law (Cmnd 6732)).

(4) If the sections give performers private rights, the result is that performers have a
g quasi-property right akin to copyright without any of the safeguards and provisions as to
duration, compulsory licensing and enforcement which Parliament has attached to
copyright. For example, if each performer has a civil right of action, in the case of a film
no reproduction could be made (even for educational purposes) without the consent of
all the actors in the film, since each actor would have a right of veto. Again, unless there
h can be read into the 1958 Act some limitation under which the ban on reproduction is to
last only during the life of the performer, the right of the performer to veto any
reproduction will be of indefinite duration, far outlasting the statutory protection of
copyright given to the script, the film and the musical score.

These are formidable arguments against the Act conferring private rights of action.
But the fact remains that the Act is in its terms for the protection of performers, ie it falls
j squarely within that exceptional class of case in which the statute has been held to confer
private rights. Moreover, under the International Convention for the Protection of
Performer, Producers of Phonograms and Broadcasting Organisations (Rome, 26 October
1961; TS 38 (1964); Cmnd 2425) the contracting states (of which the United Kingdom
was one) undertook to protect, inter alia, 'the rights of performers' on records. Article
7(1) of the convention provides that 'the protection provided for performers by this
Convention shall include the possibility of preventing' the broadcasting, fixation or

reproduction of the fixation of the performance without the consent of the performers. Two things seem to be clear. Firstly, under the convention the performer himself was to have 'rights'. Secondly, the perfomer's rights were to include something which, in some circumstances, would make it possible to *prevent* unauthorised reproduction, ie a quia timet injunction. Therefore, compliance with the Rome Convention required that there should be an English Act of Parliament which enabled the performer to obtain an injunction to prevent unauthorised reproduction on records. The Performers' Protection Act 1963 was passed expressly 'to enable effect to be given to' the Rome Convention. The 1963 Act merely altered the class of acts which infringe ss 1 and 2 of the 1958 Act, ie the Act continued on its face as one imposing criminal sanctions only. In my judgment Parliament must have considered that the Performers' Protection Acts gave rise to civil rights to obtain an injunction, since otherwise Parliament would not have been carrying out its declared intention of giving effect to the convention.

Therefore, in my judgment, it has been demonstrated that Parliament did have the necessary intention that the limited class of persons for whose protection the 1958 Act was passed (ie performers) were to have private rights, and, were it not for authority, I would reach the conclusion that performers do have a civil right of action under the 1958 Act. Unhappily, there are a number of cases on s 1 of the 1958 Act which present a confusing picture. Counsel for the defendants submits that we are bound by authority to hold that the 1958 Act does not give a civil right of action.

In *Ex p Island Records Ltd* [1978] 3 All ER 824, [1978] Ch 122 there were two groups of plaintiffs: (a) recording artists and (b) record companies with whom the artists had exclusive recording contracts. The plaintiffs claimed Anton Piller relief ex parte against bootleggers who made and sold unauthorised recordings of artists' public performances. The sole cause of action relied on was breach of s 1 of the 1958 Act. Walton J held the plaintiffs had no cause of action. But the Court of Appeal reversed his decision and held that the plaintiffs did have a cause of action, drawing no distinction between performers and record companies. However, the members of the court reached the result by a number of different routes.

Shaw and Waller LJJ held that the case did not fall within the first exception to the general rule. They took the view that, in order to come within the first exception under which a civil right of action is given to members of a class for whose protection the Act is passed, the words of the Act have to lay down a defined duty owed to that class: a statutory provision such as s 1 of the 1958 Act did not in their judgment satisfy this requirement since all it did was to render certain acts criminal. I will call this 'the textual argument'. Lord Denning MR expressed no view on this point. Lord Denning MR held that the plaintiffs had a cause of action on the basis of a new doctrine, viz that a man carrying on a lawful trade or calling has a right to be protected from unlawful interference with it, and on the basis of such right can obtain an injunction to restrain the commission of a criminal act which would interfere with such trade or calling. I will call this 'the injury to property argument'. Waller LJ agreed with Lord Denning MR on the injury to property argument, albeit on rather narrower grounds. Shaw LJ dissented on this point.

In *Lonrho Ltd v Shell Petroleum Co Ltd* [1981] 2 All ER 456, [1982] AC 173 Lonrho alleged that its lawful trade had been interfered with by the defendant oil company's breach of the provisions of a statutory instrument which rendered criminal the supply of oil to Southern Rhodesia. Lonrho relied on the decision in *Ex p Island Records Ltd* based on the injury to property argument. The textual argument was not directly in point since Lonrho did not claim that their case fell within the first exception to the general rule. The House of Lords held that Lonrho had no civil right of action under the statutory instrument. It did not fall within either exception to the general rule. The statutory instrument was not passed for the protection of a specified class, nor did it create a legal right to be enjoyed by every member of the public, breach of which could be enforced by a person who had suffered special damage. However, Lord Diplock, with whose speech the other members of the House concurred, commented adversely on the decision

in *Ex p Islands Records Ltd*. After pointing out that the plaintiffs in *Ex p Island Records Ltd*
a were both performers and record companies, he said ([1981] 2 All ER 456 at 462–463,
[1982] AC 173 at 187):

> 'So far as the application by performers was concerned, it could have been granted
> for entirely orthodox reasons. The Act was passed for the protection of a particular
> class of individuals, dramatic and musical performers; even the short title said so.
> Whether the record companies would have been entitled to obtain the order in a
b > civil action to which the performers whose performances had been bootlegged were
> not parties is a matter which for present purposes it is not necessary to decide. Lord
> Denning MR, however, with whom Waller LJ agreed (Shaw LJ dissenting) appears
> to enunciate a wider general rule, which does not depend on the scope and language
> of the statute by which a criminal offence is committed, that whenever a lawful
> business carried on by one individual in fact suffers damage as the consequence of a
c > contravention by another individual of any statutory prohibition the former has a
> civil right of action against the latter for such damage. My Lords, with respect, I am
> unable to accept that this is the law.'

In my judgment the decision in the *Lonrho* case establishes that the injury to property
argument on which the majority in the *Island Records* case based itself was wrong. The
d correctness of that argument was directly in point in *Lonrho* and its rejection is part of the
ratio decidendi of *Lonrho*. On the other hand, I consider the passage which I have quoted
in which Lord Diplock says that the decision in the *Island Records* case could be justified
so far as performers are concerned on the grounds that the 1958 Act was for their
protection is obiter dictum. The 1958 Act was not in issue in *Lonrho*, nor was there any
detailed argument concerning it. *Lonrho* was not claiming as a member of a special class
e for whose protection s 1 was passed. However, although only obiter dictum, the remarks
must provide powerful support for the view that I have formed.

Since the decision in the *Lonrho* case, there have been a number of cases at first instance
in which differing views have been taken as to whether any part of the decision in the
Island Records case survives as good law. It is unnecessary to review them because the
f point has been considered by this court in *RCA Corp v Pollard* [1982] 3 All ER 771, [1983]
Ch 135. In that case the only plaintiffs were recording companies. They claimed relief
against the defendant who was making and selling unauthorised recordings of
performances by artists who had exclusive recording contracts with the plaintiffs, ie the
facts were identical with those in *Island Records*, save that none of the plaintiffs were
performers. This court held that the *Lonrho* case had overruled the majority decision in
Island Records based on the injury to property argument, but the decision of Shaw and
g Waller LJJ in *Islands Records* that the 1958 Act did not give *record companies* a right of
action was still binding on them. That part of the decision, they held, was unaffected by
the decision in the *Lonrho* case, since Lord Diplock had expressly left open the question
whether the 1958 Act was passed for the protection of record companies. Oliver LJ
expressed the view that Lord Diplock in the *Lonrho* case was not saying that relief could
h properly have been given to the performers in the *Island Records* case (see [1982] 3 All ER
771 at 780, [1983] Ch 135 at 150). With respect, I am unable to read Lord Diplock's
words as saying anything other than that performers in the *Island Records* case were
entitled to injunctive relief, ie they did have a civil right of action.

The decision in *RCA Corp v Pollard* raises considerable difficulties. It asserts the binding
authority of the conclusion reached by Shaw and Waller LJJ in *Island Records* that the
j 1958 Act did not fall within the first exception to the general rule. That conclusion was
based on the textual argument. The textual argument applies as much to performers as
to record companies; the reasoning is that the 1958 Act provides no civil right because it
is drafted in a way which does not impose a defined duty either to record companies or
to performers. Yet in the *Lonrho* case the House of Lords plainly thought the performers
did have a civil right of action.

The present state of the authorities is not a happy one and the sooner the matter is clarified, either by legislation or by a definitive decision of the House of Lords, the better. How are we to decide the case in the present state of the authorities? We are bound by the ratio decidenti in *Island Records*, unless it has been overruled by the House of Lords. The ratio decidendi of a case is the reason given by the court for making the order it actually makes. In my judgment we are not technically bound by reasons given, on an independent issue, for *not* reaching the decision actually reached, although such reasons are normally of compelling weight: see *Cross on Precedent in English Law* (3rd edn, 1977) p 82. The decision in *Island Records* was that performers *did* have a civil right of action. Therefore, the reasons of Shaw and Waller LJJ on one aspect of the case (the textual argument) cannot be binding on us as the ratio of the decision. It is, of course, very persuasive and in *RCA Corp v Pollard* was treated as binding so far as the record companies were concerned, because in the *Lonrho* case the House of Lords had left open the question whether record companies had a right of action. However, so far as performers are concerned, the House of Lords expressed the unanimous view that the actual decision in *Island Records* was right so far as the performers (as opposed to record companies) were concerned, thereby impliedly disapproving the textual argument. In these circumstances it is not necessary to treat as technically binding on us the decision of Shaw and Waller LJJ on the independent issue (ie the textual argument), and I am free, so far as performers are concerned, to give effect to my own views and the obiter dictum of the House of Lords in the *Lonrho* case. Of course, so far as record companies are concerned, the decision in *RCA Corp v Pollard* is binding, but that is not the case before us.

For these reasons I agree with the judge that the plaintiffs have a civil right of action under s 2 of the 1958 Act.

1(b) *Does the 1958 Act render unlawful the making of a film without the consent of the performer after the death of the performer?*

On its face, the 1958 Act prohibits the making of a film without the consent of the performer at any time. However, the defendants contend some restriction on the literal meaning must be implied so as to limit the act rendered unlawful to the making of a film during the lifetime of the performer without his consent. If this contention is correct, the making of 'Trail' after the death of Peter Sellers, even without his consent, would not have been an infringement of s 2 of the 1958 Act, and therefore could not give rise to any civil liability under this head.

The defendants contend that, unless so limited, the effect of the 1958 Act is to impose an indefinite ban on the reproduction of a performance. They submit that the personal representatives of a deceased performer cannot give the necessary consent to any reproduction and that, even if they can, the power indefinitely to veto any such reproduction is inconsistent with the intention of Parliament. They identify this intention as being to ensure that the performer obtains further engagements to perform which he might not obtain if his performances were to be reproduced. Once the performer has died, the need for this protection comes to an end.

These arguments obviously have much greater force if the defendants are right in saying that the personal representatives of the performer cannot give the necessary consent. I can see no reason for so holding. The right to give or withhold consent is the same as any other right. It will vest in a man's personal representatives after his death. Some rights are purely personal and die with the person (for example, the right to consent to the exercise of a power of appointment). But the question in every case is whether or not the right is personal and dies with him; if it is not personal it vests in his personal representatives. So one is thrown back to the question: did Parliament intend the right to be purely personal? It has been held that prima facie a right conferred on a man by statute survives his death and that clear words are required if it is to be held that the right dies with the person given that right: see *Dean v Wiesengrund* [1955] 2 All ER 432, [1955] 2 QB 120. There are no such clear words in this case. Therefore, in my judgment the a right to give or withhold consent survives the death of the performer and vests in his personal representatives after his death.

The judge held that the personal representatives were given the power to consent by s 7 of the 1958 Act. I cannot agree with this view. Section 7 is dealing with the ostensible authority of an agent to give consent on behalf of a performer; it depends on a representation that the agent is authorised by the performer to give such consent on his behalf. If the performer has died, no such authority to consent as agent could exist: such
b authority dies with the performer. Personal representatives are not the agents of the deceased; their powers rest not on the authority given to them by the deceased, but on a quite separate authority given to them by law to stand in the place of the deceased.

If, as I think, the right to consent vests in the personal representatives after the death of the performer, I can see no compelling reason for limiting the section in the way suggested. Like the judge, I consider that the 1958 Act was not passed just to protect the
c performer's interests by prohibiting the reproduction of a performance which might damage the performer's chances of getting further employment. The 1958 Act is to protect performers generally. Although the protection of his reputation and future employment is important, so is the protection of a performer's economic interests by ensuring that he is paid for the use of his performance

This leaves only the point that an indefinite embargo on reproduction without consent
d gives to performers' rights which, unlike copyright, are both of indefinite duration and unregulated by statute. This is a genuine point. But in my judgment it is not sufficient by itself to justify implying a limitation into a statutory provision so as to alter its literal meaning. To justify such an implication the circumstances must compel one to the view that Parliament must have intended such a limitation. I am far from satisfied that Parliament did so intend.
e For these reasons I agree with the judge that the 1958 Act does confer a civil right of action on the plaintiffs and that the making of 'Trail' constituted a breach of those rights. I have had the advantage of reading the judgment of Bingham LJ and I agree with him that, save in relation to the use of clips from 'Strikes' and 'Revenge', Peter Sellers did not consent to the reproduction of his performance in 'Trail' for the purposes of the 1958
f Act. Accordingly, in my judgment, on this aspect of the case the judge's decision was entirely correct.

As to the other aspects of the case I entirely agree with the judgment of Bingham LJ. The appeal must be dismissed.

STEPHEN BROWN LJ. I have had the advantage of reading in draft the judgments prepared by Sir Nicolas Browne-Wilkinson V-C and Bingham LJ. I agree with them that
g the appeal should be dismissed for reasons which they give.

BINGHAM LJ. I have had the advantage of reading in draft the judgment of Sir Nicolas Browne-Wilkinson V-C. I fully agree with all that he has said about the Dramatic and Musical Performers' Protection Act 1958 and the plaintiffs' rights under it. There is
h nothing I wish to add on that aspect of the case.

In this judgment I shall consider the plaintiffs' claims made, independently of the 1958 Act, for breach of contract (in the case of 'The Pink Panther') and wrongful interference with contractual rights (in the case of 'Shot in the Dark', 'Return' and 'Strikes'). I can ignore 'Revenge', because no issue concerning it arises on this appeal. I can also, for the same reason, ignore the clips from 'Strikes'. On this part of the case the
j issues to be decided are these. (a) On the true construction of each of the loan-out agreements, did the production company expressly or impliedly undertake that Peter Sellers's performance would be used only for the purposes of the film to which such contract related? (b) Should such term be limited so as to prohibit the use of such performances for other purposes only during the lifetime of Peter Sellers? (c) Can the defendants be held liable for inducing a breach of a purely negative obligation under a

loan-out agreement which in other respects has long since been performed? Issues (a) and
(b) raise problems of construction which I shall consider with reference to each of the *a*
four relevant agreements in turn. I shall then consider issue (c), which raises a question
of pure legal principle.

1 *The Pink Panther*

The agreement for Peter Sellers's appearance in this film opened in this way:

> 'This will constitute the agreement to the use by us of the services by you, PETER *b*
> SELLERS (hereinafter referred to as "Artist") as an actor in the part of "Inspector
> Clouseau", (hereinafter referred to as the Artist's role) in connection with our motion
> picture photoplay tentatively entitled "THE PINK PANTHER". The term "photoplay" as
> used herein shall be deemed to include, but not be limited to, a photoplay produced,
> exhibited with and/or accompanied by sound and voice recording, reproducing and/ *c*
> or transmitting devices, radio devices, television devices, and all other improvements
> and devices which are now or may hereafter be used in connection with the
> production, exhibition and/or transmission of any present or future kind of motion
> picture productions, and Artist agrees that the Artist's services may be required
> hereunder in connection with a photoplay so produced and/or exhibited.'

The agreement then continued with a number of detailed provisions. Many of these *d*
reappear in later agreements, but for this film (unlike later films) Peter Sellers was to be
paid only a salary during the period of shooting and no percentage on the earnings of the
film. For present purposes the most important clause is cl 6, which was in these terms,
the emphasis being added by me:

> 'We shall have the right to photograph the Artist and the Artist's performances, *e*
> and thereby or otherwise to reproduce the Artist's likeness and any and all of the
> Artist's acts, poses, plays and appearances of any and all kinds hereunder, by any
> present or future methods or means, and the right to record the Artist's voice and
> all instrumental, musical and other sound effects produced by the Artist hereunder,
> and to reproduce and/or transmit the same, either separately or in conjunction with
> such acts, poses, plays and appearances as aforesaid, as we may desire. We (and our *f*
> successors and assigns) shall be entitled to and shall own solely, exclusively and
> perpetually, all rights of every kind in and to all of the foregoing, and in and to all
> other results and proceeds of the Artist's services hereunder, without restriction or
> limitation of any kind, including (but not limited to) the sole, exclusive and
> perpetual right to reproduce and record all or any of said photographs, reproductions
> and recordations, by any present or future methods or means, and to perform, *g*
> exhibit and reproduce said photographs, recordings, and reproductions or any of
> them at any time or times, either separately or in combination, in and in connection
> with said photoplay and otherwise, and in combination with photographs,
> recordations and reproductions of or made by any other person or persons. *Artist*
> *hereby transfers and assigns to us all of the results and proceeds of the Artist's services*
> *hereunder, and all rights therein, including but not being limited to, the rights specified above,* *h*
> *without reservations, condition or limitation of any kind.* We shall also have the right to
> "dub" the Artist's voice, in English (subject as hereinafter provided) and any other
> languages, and all instrumental, musical and other sound effects produced by the
> Artist, in and in connection with the advertising and exploitation of said photoplay;
> also, in and in connection with the advertising or services in so-called commercial
> tie-ups relating to said photoplay. All rights granted or agreed to be granted to us *j*
> hereunder shall vest in us immediately and shall remain vested in us, our successors
> and assigns, whether this agreement expires in normal course or whether the Artist's
> employment hereunder is terminated for any cause or reason. Notwithstanding the
> provisions contained in this Paragraph 6, we shall not have the right to involve the

Artists in commercial tie-ups or endorsements; provided, however, that we shall have the right to make commercial tie-ups involving the photoplay without obtaining Artist's consent and in such commercial tie-ups shall have the right to include production stills containing the Artist's photograph with the photograph of at least one other member of the cast and shall have the rights to include the Artist's name as appearing in the photoplay in connection with any commercial tie-ups which we make, but we shall at no time associate the Artist directly with any commodity nor hold him out as approving or endorsing any commodity or thing. *Our use of all of the results and proceeds of the Artist's services acquired by this agreement shall be related to the photoplay, but otherwise we and/or our assignees shall solely, exclusively and perpetually use said results and proceeds in accordance with the rights granted to us in this paragraph and elsewhere in this agreement . . .'*

Two further clauses were relied on in argument and should perhaps be mentioned. They were to this effect:

'(12) Artist warrants and represents to us and agrees that the Artist is or will be a member in good standing of the governing union or guild prior to the commencement of the term hereof, and will remain so for the duration of this contract. None of the provisions hereof shall be construed so as to conflict with any of the provisions of the existing agreement between us and the Screen Actors' Guild Inc, or the provisions of the agreement between the British Film Producers' Association and British Actors' Equity.

'(13) Artist agrees that we may transfer or assign this agreement or all or any of our rights hereunder to another person, firm or corporation, and this agreement shall inure to our benefit and to the benefit of our successors and assigns. Such successors and assigns shall be entitled to all of the obligations without in any way relieving us of our responsibility to Artist for the fulfillment of said obligations, and without in any way relieving us of our responsibility to provide Blake Edwards as director of the photoplay subject to the provisions hereinafter contained.'

The substance of this agreement is in my judgment made quite plain by its terms. United Artists agreed to engage Peter Sellers and he agreed to make his services available as an actor to play the part of Inspector Clouseau in a film of which the provisional title was 'The Pink Panther'. The film was not at that stage, like a finished book, a defined physical object in any final form, because the photography of the film had yet to be undertaken, and from the film shot a selection would have to be made, and no doubt the screenplay might be modified in course of production. But even at that stage there would exist a screenplay which would contain the script and describe the scenes, together with most of the key actions. It was known that Blake Edwards would be the director (and Peter Sellers was entitled to be consulted if he for any reason fell out). The main casting decisions had been taken. All concerned had (as the judge found) a reasonably clear idea of the film to which they were committing themselves, which already existed as a definable concept. It was to play the role in that film, and no other, that Peter Sellers agreed to make himself available and United Artists agreed to engage him.

I do not regard that conclusion as weakened in any way by the second sentence (beginning 'The term "photoplay" as used herein . . .') of the introductory paragraph which I have set out above. That sentence is intended to ensure that the agreement is binding whatever present or future means of production, exhibition, reproduction or transmission are employed in connection with the film. It cannot sensibly be read as altering or extending the work, namely the film, to which the contract related.

The defendants relied strongly on the language of cl 6. That clause, they rightly submitted, contained a most comprehensive grant of rights by Peter Sellers to United Artists. In their submission the effect of the clause was to give United Artists an absolute and unfettered right to use the product of Peter Sellers's services under the agreement (which would include footage not included in the final edited film, out-takes, as well as footage so included). If the closing sentence of the clause, as quoted, purported to cut down the wide rights already granted, then it should be given a restricted meaning.

That is not only, as I think, an illegitimate approach to construction, but it also fails to reflect what I regard as the plain meaning of this clause. Peter Sellers made, as I have said, a comprehensive grant of rights to United Artists, but he did so on the express undertaking of United Artists that their *use* of the results and proceeds of his services acquired by the agreement would be related to 'the photoplay', namely the film provisionally called 'The Pink Panther'. The antithesis between the passages I have emphasised is in my view clear and unambiguous. It also seems to me comprehensible and sensible. I have no hesitation in giving effect to it. It seems to me to follow that the use of clips from this film to form part of another film, such as 'Trail', not contemplated by the agreement was expressly forbidden by agreement between the parties.

A point arises on cl 12 of this agreement which arises on later agreements also but which can be conveniently considered now. The purpose of this clause is, I think, twofold: to provide that Peter Sellers should be a member of his governing union, whether the Screen Actors' Guild Inc or British Actors' Equity; and to provide that the agreement should not be construed so as to conflict with a collective agreement made by either union. I think this latter provision was probably intended to refer to the governing union (whichever it was) of which the actor was a member, but the clause does not in terms say so. Peter Sellers was a member of British Actors' Equity. The relevant collective agreement negotiated by that union gave producers the right to alter, add to and use the film performances, recordings, photographs and other work of the actor as the producer might deem fit. That provision was, however, to be read in the context of an agreement by the actor to play a named part in a named film and could not reasonably be read as conferring rights quite unrelated to performance of that agreement. The collective agreement also provided for the giving of all consents required under the Dramatic and Musical Performers' Protection Act 1925, but that Act did not apply to cinematograph films. The construction I have given to the agreement with United Artists does not conflict with any term of this collective agreement. The SAG collective agreement in force at the time was more specific. It contained this term:

'(11) Reuse of Film   (a) No part of the photography or sound track of an actor shall be used in any picture other than the one for which he was employed, without separately bargaining with the actor and reaching an agreement regarding such use, prior to the time reuse is made. The actor may not agree to such reuse at the time of original employment. The foregoing shall apply only if the actor is recognisable, and as to stunts, only if the stunt is identifiable. This provision shall not limit Producer's right to use photography or sound track in exploiting the picture, or in trailers or in advertising, as provided in the Basic Agreement . . .'

The defendants' construction of 'The Pink Panther' agreement would conflict with this term, and it would (I think) be surprising to find a requirement that this agreement should be construed so as not to conflict with a provision with which it so obviously did conflict. Since, however, Peter Sellers was not a member of SAG, I do not think much weight should be attached to this.

The judge reached the same conclusion as I have done on the construction of this contract; but he went further. He said:

'Therefore I conclude on the true construction of this agreement that the production company is not entitled to use the performance of Peter Sellers in 'The Pink Panther' in the film 'Trail'. I also as a matter of necessary implication in order to give this agreement business efficacy imply that the restriction imposed by the sentence on which the plaintiffs rely shall apply not only to any use to be made of *a* the artist's services by the actual production company but also by any assignee or transferee of the production company.'

The judge was able to put the matter thus briefly because he had, earlier in his judgment, fully described the factual context in which this agreement was made. He found that at all relevant times it was standard practice on both sides of the Atlantic, where a licence was to be given by a copyright holder to someone who was going to reuse *b* copyright material, for there to be an express stipulation about the obtaining of the relevant actors' consents. He found as a fact—

'that at the material times none of the relevant parties would have contemplated that these out-takes would be used by anyone for the making of some other film, that is to say a film other than that with regard to which the parties had specifically *c* contracted. If an officious bystander had asked any of the relevant parties about it at the time I find that the response he would have received would be: "No, of course we are only going to use the material we are shooting for this film." If pressed further by the officious bystander I consider that the relevant party would sooner or later have referred either to the relevant provision of the SAG agreement or to the Performers' Protection Act 1958 and would have acknowledged that any use of out-*d* takes for subsequent films would require the consent of any performers appearing in those out-takes.'

He also said:

'A final point that must be mentioned as being within the contemplation of the parties at the time the relevant contracts were made was that the film would be *e* financed and distributed by someone other than the actual production company and that the copyright would be assigned to a person other than the production company. This would be known not only from the ordinary structure of the industry but also from the specific involvement of United Artists because United Artists was, as I have stated, well known to be a company which did not produce the films which it financed and distributed. Therefore it would be contemplated by the *f* parties to the contracts under which Peter Sellers's services were provided that the stipulations which were made by the producer would have to enure for the benefit of the financing and distributing company and, by a parity of reasoning, the restrictions which the production company was accepting would, if they were to be fully effective, also have to apply to the financing and distributing company. It would deprive the contracts of their business effect if the provisions were to be read *g* as applying exclusively to the production company and not to any other person who was exploiting or making use of the film. Similarly, notwithstanding the intervention of the loan-out company, it would be contemplated that the contract would be for the benefit of Peter Sellers as well.'

h The second of these passages is not directly relevant to this contract, to which United Artists were themselves a party. But cl 13, which I have quoted, expressly contemplated assignment by the employing party 'without in any way relieving us of our responsibility to Artist for the fulfilment of said obligations'. It would plainly have stultified the contractual intentions of the parties had the employer been able to deprive Peter Sellers of the protection which both parties thought he was to receive by simply making out-*j* takes and clips available to a third party to use as he wished. I fully agree with the reasoning and the conclusion of the judge. In my judgment both parties plainly intended not only that United Artists' use of the results and proceeds of Mr Sellers's services should be 'related to the photoplay', but also that United Artists should ensure that the use of these results and proceeds by any party deriving title from them should be similarly limited.

Whether this negative covenant is to be treated as lapsing on the death of Peter Sellers depends again on the correct construction of the agreement in its factual context. There is no legal reason why the benefit of this negative covenant, a chose in action, should not pass to Peter Sellers's personal representatives. There are good business reasons why this benefit should pass, but it may be doubted whether the parties had these in mind in 1962. There is, however, nothing whatever in the language of the agreement to suggest that this right should lapse when Peter Sellers died. One purpose of the clause may perhaps have been to strengthen Peter Sellers's claims to future employment, a purpose which would die with him, but I think it likely that there were other purposes, such as to prevent use of sub-standard material rejected for inclusion in the film itself. Overall, this clause was intended to give Peter Sellers a right to control the use made of the product of his services for extraneous purposes, and it seems to me that this was a right which both parties would have intended to endure even though Peter Sellers personally was no longer alive to enforce it.

Like the judge, I would on the construction of this agreement answer question (a) affirmatively and question (b) negatively.

2 *Shot In The Dark*

The judge concluded that the relevant provisions of the contract for Peter Sellers's appearance in this film were indistinguishable from those in 'The Pink Panther' (although there was in this case no direct contractual relationship between Peter Sellers and United Artists).

It has not been argued that he was wrong. The same construction must accordingly be given to this agreement.

3 *Return*

The parties to this agreement were the producing companies, Peter Sellers's loan-out company and Independent Television Corp (ITC), who financed the film. The recitals to the agreement read as follows:

'(1) The Co-producers have contracted with ITC to produce a colour feature film at present entitled "The Return of the Pink Panther" (hereinafter called "the Film") starring Peter Sellers and Christopher Plummer which will be shot in the United Kingdom of Great Britain, France, Switzerland and Morocco and elsewhere and to deliver the Film within six months of the completion of principal photography in consideration of ITC providing the necessary finance.

(2) The Lender is a company incorporated under the laws of Panama and is entitled to the services of the said Peter Sellers (hereinafter called "the Artist") which it has agreed to make available to the Co-producers in connection with the Film upon and subject to the terms and conditions hereinafter set out.'

Clause 1 began in this way:

'(1) THE Co-producers hereby engage and the Lender agrees to make available the Artist's services at first call which he has agreed to render to play the part of Inspector Clouseau in the Film upon and from a date . . .'

Under the agreement the loan-out company was to receive a fixed fee plus a percentage of gross receipts earned by the distributor from exhibition of the Film. Clause 6.1 was in these terms:

'THE Co-producers shall be entitled to use the name and likeness of the Artist both [in] real life and as depicted in his part in the Film for the purpose of the promotion and publicity of the Film including illustrations in books of the Film on condition that neither the Lender nor the Artist is in any way shown as having used or endorsed any particular product. The Lender confirms the consent of the Artist under the Performers' Protection Acts for the recording and reproduction of his performance in the Film or any part thereof by any means including broadcasting and television. The entire copyright for all purposes in the Film and in any such picture photograph or record so made shall be the property of ITC.'

No doubt in recognition of Peter Sellers's crucial role in the Pink Panther films, it was agreed that he should be consulted on the major casting for 'the Film', that he should be entitled to approve a substitute for Blake Edwards as producer and director and that he should be entitled to be consulted on the screenplay for the film during its development.

I do not think there are any other provisions of this agreement which I should mention. Again, as it seems to me, the agreement was plainly one for the provision of Peter Sellers's services to play a named part in a named film. The opening words of cl 6.1 would not have been necessary had the production company acquired a right to use clips from 'the Film' for any purpose it chose, including the making of another film. It is also, to my mind, inconceivable that Peter Sellers would not have negotiated to receive a share in the takings of that other film had the parties contemplated such a use. The consent which Peter Sellers gave under the Performers' Protection Acts was to 'the recording and reproduction of his performance in the film or any part thereof by any means including broadcasting and television' and cannot be understood as extending to the incorporation of clips of his performance in this film to make another feature film. It would be absurd if his rights of consultation under this agreement could be defeated by incorporating clips of his performance in another film in respect of which he would have no rights whatever.

For all purposes relevant to this appeal there is in my judgment no material distinction between the construction of this agreement and that for 'The Pink Panther'. I would again, like the judge, answer questions (a) and (b) in the same way.

4 Strikes

The making of 'Trail' depended very much more heavily on the use of the 'Strikes' out-takes than on the use of the clips from the earlier films. The 'Strikes' agreements are therefore of central importance to this appeal. There were, for tax reasons, two loan-out agreements made by Peter Sellers's loan-out companies with Blake Edwards's production company. There was a financing agreement between the production company and United Artists and a distribution agreement between the same parties. All these agreements were made on 10 December 1975. They were clearly intended to provide a coherent contractual scheme for the production and exploitation of the film.

One of the loan-out agreements referred to exploitation of the film in (broadly) the United Kingdom, the other in the rest of the world. There is no significant difference between the two. I shall for convenience confine myself to citations from the worldwide agreement. Clause 2 of this agreement defined the basic obligation of the parties:

'Lender agrees to furnish to Producer, and Producer agrees to engage, the services of Artist to render Artist's services as an actor to portray the role of "Inspector Clouseau" in the motion picture photoplay tentatively entitled "The Pink Panther Strikes Again" (hereinafter referred to as the "Film"). The term "Film" as used herein, shall be deemed to include, but not be limited to, a motion picture production produced and/or exhibited with or accompanied by sound and voice recording, reproducing and/or transmitting devices, radio and television devices and all other improvements or devices which are now or hereafter may be used in connection with the production exhibition and/or transmission of any present or future kind of motion picture productions'

Clause 3 read:

'The term of Artist's services hereunder shall commence on or after 1 February 1976, on which date Lender agrees to cause Artist to report to Producer at such place

as Producer shall notify to Lender and shall continue thereafter for such time as
Producer may require Artist's services in connection with the production of the
Film. From and after said commencement date Artist shall render his services
exclusively to Producer as it may require, for a period of fifteen (15) consecutive
weeks (hereinafter referred to as the "production period") and thereafter, at no cost
to Producer, in connection with such post-production work (as more particularly
described in para 7 hereof) as may be required to complete Artist's part in the Film.'

Clause 4 provided that the loan-out company should receive 5% rising to 10%, of the
world gross receipts earned from parties exhibiting 'the Film'. There was a requirement
for additional services by Peter Sellers before and after the production period, and these
services were to be rendered 'without any additional compensation inasmuch as the
compensation payable to Lender pursuant to the provisions of para 4 shall be deemed to
include payment for such services'. There was, as usual, a term governing the credit to
which Peter Sellers was to be entitled in publicity and advertising 'in connection with
the Film'.

At the heart of the argument lay cl 12 of this agreement which (long though it is) I
must in large measure quote:

'(a) Lender grants to Producer all rights of every kind whatsoever, whether now
known or unknown, exclusively and perpetually, in and to Artist's services
performed pursuant to this Agreement and in and to all the results and proceeds
thereof. Without limiting the generality of the foregoing, said rights shall include
the sole and exclusive right to photograph or otherwise reproduce all or any part of
Artist's performances, acts, poses, plays and appearances of every kind and nature
made or done by Artist in connection with the Film; to record or otherwise
reproduce, by any present or future methods or means, Artist's voice and all
musicial, instrumental or other sound effects produced by artist and to reproduce,
re-record and transmit the same either separately or in conjunction with such
performances, acts, poses, plays and appearances as Producer may desire, but only in
connection with the exploitation of the Film; and perpetually to exhibit, transmit
and reproduce, and license others to exhibit, transmit and reproduce (by means of
printing, motion pictures, radio, television, televised motion pictures, whether
theatrically or non-theatrically, including all forms of commercially sponsored,
sustaining, pay-as-you-go, or other kinds of television, and in conjunction with the
advertising of any commodity, service or product, or otherwise, undertaken solely
in connection with the exploitation of the Film, as Producer may determine in its
sole discretion, or any other means now known or unknown) any of such
reproductions, recordations and transmissions in connection with the Film, or the
advertising or exploitation of the Film . . . (c) Lender agrees that all material, works,
writings, ideas, "gags" or dialogue composed, submitted, or interpolated by Artist
in connection with the preparation or production of the Film shall automatically
become the property of Producer, which shall for this purpose be deemed to be the
author thereof. Lender and Artist acknowledge and agree that the names and
characterisations of the role to be portrayed by Artist in the Film, the title of the
Film and all material performed by Artist hereunder belongs exclusively to
Producer, that neither Lender nor artist has any right, title or interest whatsoever
therein or thereto and, except as may be undertaken at the specific written request
of Producer or its assigns in connection with the exploitation of the Film, neither
has any right to make use thereof whether in the employ of another or on their own
behalf (subject however to Lender's and Artist's rights and the provisions of para 21
hereof) and Producer reserves to itself all rights therein, including, but not limited
to, merchandising rights. Lender shall, at the request of Producer, execute such
assignments certificates or other instruments as Producer may from time to time
deem necessary or desirable to evidence, establish, maintain, protect, enforce or

defend its rights or title in or to any such material. All rights granted or agreed to
be granted to Producer under this para 12 shall vest in Producer immediately and
shall remain vested in Producer its successors and assigns, whether this Agreement
expires in the normal course or is terminated or whether Artist's services hereunder
are terminated for any cause or reason.'

Reference was also made to cl 13:

'Producer shall have complete control of the production of the Film, including
but not limited to all artistic controls and the right to cut, edit, add to, subtract
from, arrange and revise the Film in any manner . . .'

Finally, I should quote cll 26 and 27:

'26. Producer shall be entitled to assign this Agreement to any person, firm or
corporation upon the express assumption by any such assignee of all of Producer's
executory obligations then remaining to be discharged, and this Agreement shall
inure to the benefit of Producer, its successors and assigns. Producer shall have the
right, at its discretion, to lend Artist's services hereunder to any person, firm or
corporation which may produce the Film, and in such event Lender shall cause
Artist to render Artist's services to such other person, firm or corporation to the best
of Artist's ability and Producer may grant to any such other person, firm or
corporation any and all rights and services to which it is entitled during the period
of such lending.

27. Producer shall not be obligated actually to utilise the services of Artist, or to
include all or any of Artist's performance in the Film, or to produce or to release or
to continue the distribution or release of the Film once released. Nothing herein
contained in this para 27 shall be deemed to relieve Producer of its obligation to pay
Lender the compensation payable to Lender pursuant to this Agreement . . .'

I do not think it is necessary to refer in detail to the distribution and financing
agreement for 'Strikes' made between the production company and United Artists. It is
plain, and was not disputed, that the production company made a most comprehensive
grant of rights to United Artists. Whatever rights it had acquired, broadly speaking, it
assigned. For present purposes the question is whether those rights included a right to
use the 'Strikes' out-takes to make another feature film.

Here again, the loan-out agreement was for the provision of Peter Sellers's services to
play a named part in a named film. The second part of cl 2 has, I think, the same meaning
and intention as the corresponding (and very similar) provision in 'The Pink Panther'
agreement. It may even be that a contrast is here intended (although imperfectly drafted)
between 'the Film' and 'Film'. The defendants' argument rested on the opening words of
cl 12(a). That, it was said, gave the production company an exhaustive right to Peter
Sellers's services 'performed pursuant to this Agreement and in and to all the results and
proceeds thereof'. Those results and proceeds included out-takes, because they represented
footage shot of Peter Sellers's performance under the agreement. Such rights vested in
the production company immediately, and at that stage it could not be known whether
any particular shots would form part of the film as exhibited or whether they would
become out-takes, because that was subject to the production company's decision. 'The
Film' should not, therefore, be held to mean 'the Film as exhibited', because rights in 'the
Film' vested before it could be known what film would be exhibited. The defendants
relied on the opening words of the second sentence of cl 12(a) ('Without limiting the
generality of the foregoing . . .') as governing everything which followed in the sub-
clause.

The judge was critical of the drafting of cl 12, and I agree with him that it is 'long-
winded and typifies some of the inelegant drafting which is to be found in these
contracts'. Nevertheless, one must construe the agreement in its factual context in order

to ascertain the parties' intentions from the words they have used. Read in isolation, the first sentence of cl 12 would in my opinion give the production company an exclusive *a* and perpetual right to use for any purpose it chose any product (including out-takes) of Peter Sellers's performance under the agreement. The words immediately following that sentence would also, on ordinary principles of construction, be read as showing that the examples which followed had the purpose of illustrating, particularising or clarifying, but not limiting the scope of, the first sentence. The provisions which follow in cl 12, however, including cl 12(b), which I have not set out, stipulate over and over again that *b* the exercise of rights apparently falling within the broad first sentence of cl 12(a), may be exercised 'in connection' or 'only in connection' with the exploitation of 'Strikes'. Either these limitations should be ignored (which is unacceptable, because the draftsman plainly attached considerable significance to them), or the opening words, for all their apparent breadth and despite the saving words which follow, should be given a meaning restricted to the film 'Strikes' identified in cl 2. If the problem fell to be resolved on the *c* wording of cl 12 alone, I would prefer this second solution. But it does not, and when account is taken of the agreement as a whole (against the background summarised by the judge to which I have already referred), the defendants' construction is in my judgment seen to be untenable.

On the defendants' construction Peter Sellers is entitled to no remuneration whatever if a film is made using the 'Strikes' out-takes. This is a very surprising conclusion, bearing *d* in mind both the very substantial share which Peter Sellers was to have in the earnings of 'Strikes' and the great care taken in drafting the agreement to provide expressly that certain services should entitle Peter Sellers to no additional compensation. The defendants accepted that certain clauses of the agreement could only be interpreted as referring to 'the Film' as exhibited, and accepted that Peter Sellers's entitlement to credits on any later film made from 'Strikes' out-takes would be unprotected. Since, under cl 27, the *e* production company was not obliged to include any or all of Peter Sellers's performance in 'Strikes' or to produce or release that film (although he would still be entitled to his flat fee), one could even reach the absurd position that 'Strikes' would not be made or released at all, so that Peter Sellers would receive no percentage, but another different film could be made from the 'Strikes' out-takes for which he would receive nothing. Had *f* this construction been put to Peter Sellers or his advisers, I think the series would have come to a premature end.

The construction of this agreement is more difficult than that of the agreements I have already considered, but on the points relevant to this appeal the upshot is the same. I agree with the reasoning and the conclusions of the judge, and I would answer questions (a) and (b) in the same way.

Having therefore concluded that under the four relevant agreements the production *g* companies did undertake that Peter Sellers's performance would be used only for the purposes of the film to which each agreement related, and that such undertakings survived the death of Peter Sellers, I can turn to question (c). Where those negative covenants were all that survived of the loan-out agreements, which had otherwise been fully performed, could the defendants be held liable (if other ingredients of the tort were *h* present) for inducing a breach of those negative covenants?

The defendants argued that they could not. I found that contention startling, and a familiar example will show why. Take the case of an employment contract containing a valid covenant against competition for 12 months after termination. The contract comes lawfully to an end. The employee has performed all the service required of him and has received all the pay to which he is entitled. The only contractual term remaining in force *j* is the employee's negative covenant not to compete. A third party, knowing of the covenant, induces the employee to work for him during the period of the covenant and in obvious breach of it. It is accepted that an action would lie (and an injunction in all probability be granted) against the employee. But if the defendants are right, no action would lie against the third party. They contend that it would not. I can find no basis in

principle for such an anomalous result, which conflicts with both the law and the practice
as I have long believed them to be.

I hope I shall not be thought discourteous if I do not discuss the authorities cited by
the defendants in support of their submission. It is, I think, enough to say that in my
judgment there is no authority which does support it. By contrast, the plaintiffs do gain
support from the decision of Roxbugh J in *British Motor Trade Association v Salvadori*
[1949] 1 All ER 208, [1949] Ch 556. The plaintiffs complained, among other things, that
the defendants had wrongfully induced or procured breaches of a negative covenant
given by buyers of new cars. They succeeded. Roxburgh J said ([1949] 1 All ER 208 at
211, [1949] Ch 556 at 565):

'... but, in my judgment, any active step taken by a defendant, having knowledge
of the covenant, by which he facilitates a breach of that covenant is enough. If this
be so, a defendant, by agreeing to buy, paying for, and taking delivery of a motor
car known by him to be offered to him in breach of covenant, takes active steps by
which he facilitates a breach of covenant, and it is not seriously contended that in
any of the cases with which I am concerned the defendant did not know of the
existence of the covenant or thought that the covenantor had obtained a release.'

This authority was referred to without disapproval by Jenkins LJ in the leading case of
D C Thomson & Co Ltd v Deakin [1952] 2 All ER 361 at 378, [1952] Ch 646 at 694, and has
never to my knowledge been doubted. I regard it as good law. If, therefore, authority to
counter the defendants' argument is needed, it exists. I should, however, add that I do
not in any event regard the factual basis of the defendants' argument as made out: the
loan-out agreements are not, apart from these negative covenants, fully performed,
because Peter Sellers's right to a share in the earnings of 'Shot in the Dark', 'Return' and
'Strikes' continues. But that does not affect the result.

For these reasons, in addition to those Sir Nicolas Browne-Wilkinson V-C has given, I
would dismiss this appeal.

*Appeal dismissed. Leave to appeal to House of Lords granted to extent that appeal be limited to
point on Dramatic and Musical Performers' Protection Act 1958.*

Solicitors: *Wright Webb Syrett* (for the defendants); *Herbert Oppenheimer Nathan & Vandyk*
(for the plaintiffs).

Vivian Horvath   Barrister.

A J Dunning & Sons (Shopfitters) Ltd v Sykes & Son (Poole) Ltd

COURT OF APPEAL, CIVIL DIVISION

SIR JOHN DONALDSON MR, DILLON AND CROOM-JOHNSON LJJ

16, 17, 30 OCTOBER 1986

Sale of land – Conveyance – Parcels – Reference to plan – Conveyance of land edged with red on plan – Land edged red mistakenly including land to which vendor had no title – Inference to be drawn from plan – Whether conveyance including land to which vendor had no title.

Land registration – Register of title – Charges and other interests appearing or protected on register – Rights and interests appearing on adjoining title – Covenant for title – Adjoining owner's land mistakingly included in conveyance of registered land – Whether 'register' referring to register of individual title of which vendor was registered proprietor – Whether 'register' extending to global register of all registered titles – Whether covenant for title only subject to charges and other interests appearing on vendor's title – Law of Property Act 1925, s 76, Sch 2 – Land Registration Rules 1925, r 77(1)(a).

The defendants were the registered proprietors of certain land. In 1969 they sold part of it but a portion (the yellow land) of the land sold was mistakenly fenced in with the land retained by the defendants and in 1978 was included in a transfer of part of the retained land (the red land) from the defendants to the plaintiffs. The transfer stated that the defendants transferred to the plaintiffs 'All that freehold property edged with red on the plan annexed hereto being another part of the property registered [in the defendants' title]'. When the plaintiffs came to register their title under the transfer they discovered that they had no title to the yellow land because the defendants in turn had had no title to it. The plaintiffs brought an action against the defendants claiming, inter alia, damages for breach of the covenants for title implied by s 76 of and Sch 2[a] to the Law of Property Act 1925. The defendants contended (i) that on its true construction the transfer did not purport to include the yellow land and (ii) that, if it did, there was not to be implied into the transfer any covenant that the defendants had power to convey the yellow land. The judge held that the transfer included the yellow land but that the implied covenant for title was subject to r 77(1)(a)[b] of the Land Registration Rules 1925 so that the implied covenant took effect 'subject to all charges and other interests appearing or protected on the register' including the rights and interests of the registered proprietor of the yellow land, with the result that any breach by the defendants of the implied covenant was immaterial. The judge accordingly dismissed the plaintiffs' claim. The plaintiffs appealed, contending that r 77(1)(a) only applied to charges and other interests appearing or protected on the register of the title with which the parties to the transfer were dealing and which the purchaser could check by inspection of the register, so that the registration of the yellow land under a different title number and proprietor did not constitute a 'charge or other interest' for the purposes of r 77(1)(a).

Held – (1) (Sir John Donaldson MR dissenting) Where parcels of land in a conveyancing document were described by reference to a plan attached thereto the natural inference was that it was intended that the parties concerned should see from the plan what land the document was purporting to pass. On the facts, the effective description of the subject matter expressed to be conveyed by the transfer was the land 'edged with red on the plan annexed'. The reference to property comprised in the defendants' title number was

---

a   Schedule 2, so far as material, is set out at p 704 *b c*, post

b   Rule 77(1) is set out at p 704 *g h*, post

subordinate, and, although believed to be accurate, the transfer was in fact inaccurate
with regard to the yellow land. Accordingly, since the red land on the plan included the
yellow land, the yellow land was part of the subject matter expressed to be conveyed by
the transfer (see p 705 *h* to p 706 *c* and p 708 *f h j*, post).

(2) On the true construction of r 77(1)(*a*) of the 1925 rules, 'the register' referred to the
register of the individual title of which the vendor was the registered proprietor and did
not extend to the global register of all registered titles, or to matters which were the
subject of entries which the purchaser could not inspect. Furthermore, the 'register' did
not include the property register of the adjoining title. Accordingly, the implied covenant
for title imposed on the defendants was, under r 77(1)(*a*), subject only to charges and
other interests appearing or protected on the register of the defendants' title to the red
land and since there were none the defendants were in breach of the covenant for title
implied by virtue of s 76 of and Sch 2 to the 1925 Act. The plaintiffs appeal would
therefore be allowed (see p 707 *c* to *h*, p 708 *e f j* and p 709 *a*, post).

Notes

For description by reference to a plan of parcels of land being conveyed, see 42 Halsbury's
Laws (4th edn) para 302, and for cases on the subject, see 40 Digest (Reissue) 404–407,
3610–3621.

For the effect of the implied covenant for title, see 26 Halsbury's Laws (4th edn) para
1155.

For the Law of Property Act 1925, s 76, Sch 2, see 27 Halsbury's Statutes (3rd edn) 455,
664.

For the Land Registration Rules 1925, SR & O 1925/1093, r 77, see 18 Halsbury's
Statutory Instruments (4th reissue) 246.

Cases cited in argument

Boreman v Griffith [1930] 1 Ch 493.
Page v Midland Rly Co [1894] 1 Ch 11, [1891–94] All ER Rep 1005, CA.
Strand Music Hall Co Ltd, Re, ex p European and American Finance Co Ltd (1865) 35 Beav
153, 55 ER 853.
Willson v Greene (Moss, third party) [1971] 1 All ER 1098, [1971] 1 WLR 635.

Appeal and cross-appeal

The plaintiffs, A J Dunning & Sons (Shopfitters) Ltd, appealed against the order of Donald
Rattee QC, sitting as a deputy judge of the High Court on 26 July 1985, dismissing their
action for damages against the defendants, Sykes & Son (Poole) Ltd, for breach of the
covenant for title relating to a piece of land at Creekmoor, Poole, Dorset, coloured yellow
on a plan annexed to a transfer dated 7 September 1978 by which, in consideration of the
sum of £80,000 paid by the plaintiffs to the defendants, the defendants purported to
convey to the plaintiffs certain land coloured red on the plan. By a respondent's notice
dated 18 September 1985 the defendants cross appealed, contending that the judge's
decision should be confirmed on the grounds, inter alia, that the transfer dated 7
September 1978 did not purport to transfer the yellow land, but that, if it did, the judge
had been wrong to reject the defendants' contention that the implied covenant for title
was not breached. The facts are set out in the judgment of Dillon LJ.

Peter Rawson for the appellants.
Nicholas Warren for the respondents.

Cur adv vult

30 October. The following judgments were delivered.

DILLON LJ (giving the first judgment at the invitation of Sir John Donaldson MR). This is an appeal by the plaintiffs in the action against a decision given on 12 July 1985 by Donald Rattee QC, sitting as a deputy judge of the High Court in the Chancery Division. There is also a respondent's notice given by the defendants, respondents to the plaintiffs' appeal, whereby they challenge the deputy judge's conclusions on a number of points which he decided in favour of the plaintiffs. The case is concerned with the implication of the traditional 'beneficial owner' covenants for title in a transfer of registered land.

The defendants were registered in April 1933 as the proprietors at HM Land Registry with absolute title under title no P 7608 of an area of land at Poole in Dorset. Over the years prior to 1978 the defendants from time to time sold off parts of that land to various purchasers. When each sale was completed, the relevant purchaser was registered as the proprietor, under a fresh title number, of the land comprised in the transfer to that purchaser, and the Land Registry removed that land from the title no P 7608. The defendants continued to be the proprietors, under that title number, merely of the remainder of the land which they had not sold off.

One of the pre-1978 sales, and the only one relevant to the issues in these proceedings, was a sale in 1969 of an area of land to a company called Elkins & Larby Ltd. That was duly completed and at the Land Registry the whole of the land comprised in the sale to Elkins & Larby was removed from the defendants' title no P 7608 and was registered in the name of Elkins & Larby under a new title number. The filed plan of title no P 7608 which provides the only description on the register of the land comprised in that title was amended accordingly. Unfortunately, when the land sold to Elkins & Larby came to be fenced off on the ground from the land still retained by the defendants, someone made a mistake and the fence was put in the wrong place. A small area of land sold to Elkins & Larby was cut off, by the fence as actually erected, from the rest of the land sold to Elkins & Larby, and was left apparently part of the defendants' retained land. That small area of land is shown coloured yellow on the plan annexed to the statement of claim, and has been referred to throughout the proceedings as 'the yellow land'; it is very small, only about 10 ft by 10 ft in area, but unfortunately it has been crucial for the plaintiffs' purposes.

In early 1978 a company called F W Cook (Mechanical Services) Ltd (Cooks) entered into negotiations with the defendants to buy part of the defendants' land, for development as industrial premises. The judge found that all concerned with those negotiations, including those acting for the defendants, proceeded on the footing that what the defendants had to sell included the yellow land, as appeared to be the case from the line of the fence on the ground.

The outcome of those negotiations was a contract for sale between the defendants and Cooks dated 10 July 1978. Whatever the intention of the parties, it is common ground that the parcels in that contract as drawn up do not include the yellow land. The solicitors who prepared the contract did not use any fresh plan to describe the land which was to be sold to Cooks. They described the land being sold as being the whole of the property registered at HM Land Registry under the title no P 7608 other than that part of the property which was comprised in a particular lease in favour of a named third party. That did not include the yellow land because the yellow land was no longer by then registered under title no P 7608.

However, Cooks assigned the benefit of that contract to an associated company, Donron (Alberice Meters) Ltd (Donron) and Donron sub-sold part of what it thought it was acquiring to the plaintiffs. Accordingly, when the time came for completion of the sale and sub-sale, it was necessary to distinguish between the land sub-sold to the plaintiffs, the land to be sold to Donron as successor to Cooks and not sub-sold and, because of covenants and exceptions and reservations not otherwise material to these

proceedings, the land retained by the defendants, being the land comprised in the lease
a in favour of a third party mentioned above.

The sale and sub-sale were accordingly completed by a transfer in the Land Registry
form dated 7 September 1978.

This transfer is headed:

b
'HM Land Registry
Transfer of Part of land comprised in
Title

County and District:	Dorset—Poole
Title Number:	P. 7608
Property:	Industrial Site at Creekmoor, Poole, Dorset.'

c The transfer has attached to it a plan which shows an area of land edged in green, another
area of land edged in red and another area of land edged in blue. The area of land edged
in red has been referred to throughout these proceedings as 'the red land'. On the plan
on the transfer part of the red land is shown hatched blue and another part is shown
coloured brown; those markings are irrelevant to these proceedings. What is fundamental,
however, is that the plan on the transfer was prepared to show what all the parties
d thought they were dealing with, as it appeared on the ground, and therefore on the plan
the red land included the yellow land, although in truth the defendants had no title to
the yellow land. The solicitors concerned did not notice the discrepancy, admittedly
small in area, between the plan of the red land on the transfer and the filed plan on the
register of title no P 7608, and everyone supposed that the whole of the red land,
including the yellow land, was comprised in that title.

e By cl 1 of the operative part of the transfer the defendants as beneficial owner
transferred to Donron—

'ALL THAT freehold property situate at Creekmoor in the County of Dorset and
shown edged with green on the plan annexed hereto... and being part of the
property registered at HM Land Registry under Title Number P. 7608.'

f By cl 2, the operative clause for present purposes, the defendants as beneficial owner
transferred to the plaintiffs—

'ALL THAT freehold property edged with red on the plan annexed hereto being
another part of the property registered at HM Land Registry under Title Number
P. 7608.'

g Clauses 3 and 4 contain exceptions and reservations and covenants for the benefit of
'the residue of the land comprised in such title and retained by the Transferor shown
edged blue on such plan'. The three areas are respectively referred to in the transfer as
'the green land', 'the red land' and 'the blue land'.

The plaintiffs bought with a view to putting up an industrial building on what they
h thought they were buying, and having obtained planning permission they proceeded to
do that. But the building in question was designed to have one corner built on the yellow
land. When they came to register their title under the transfer, they discovered that they
had no title to the yellow land because, whatever the transfer had purported to achieve,
the defendants had had no title to the yellow land. They therefore bought in the yellow
land from a successor in title of Elkins & Larby and by these proceedings they claim
j damages against the defendants for breach of the covenants for title which they say are to
be implied in the transfer because the defendants were expressed to transfer to them 'as
beneficial owner'.

With unregistered conveyancing, it is provided by s 76 of the Law of Property Act
1925 that in a conveyance there are to be implied, from the use of certain conventional
phrases such as 'beneficial owner', certain covenants for title which are set out in the

various parts of Sch 2 to that Act. These replaced with amendments certain provisions in
the Conveyancing Act 1881. In effect the conventional phrases were a form of statutory *a*
shorthand to avoid the need to set out at length in every conveyance the covenants for
title which for over a hundred years before 1881 had traditionally been set out in every
conveyance.

The covenant to be implied, under s 76 and Sch 2, in a conveyance for valuable
consideration by a person who conveys and is expressed to convey as beneficial owner is,
so far as material, a covenant— *b*

'That, notwithstanding anything by the person who so conveys or any one
through whom he derives title otherwise than by purchase for value, made, done,
executed, or omitted . . . the person who so conveys has . . . full power to convey the
subject-matter expressed to be conveyed, subject as, if so expressed, and in the
manner in which, it is expressed to be conveyed . . .' *c*

The covenant is thus not an absolute covenant of good title. But, since it was by the
defendants' own act in transferring the yellow land to Elkins & Larby that the defendants
lost their title to the yellow land, it is not in doubt that, under the system of unregistered
conveyancing, if the defendants had on 7 September 1978 purported to convey the
yellow land as beneficial owner to the plaintiffs in fee simple, the defendants would have
been in breach of the implied covenant for title above set out and liable to the plaintiffs *d*
in damages.

So far as registered land is concerned, s 38(2) of the Land Registration Act 1925
provided that rules might be made for prescribing the effect of covenants implied by
virtue of the Law of Property Act 1925 in dispositions of registered land. The relevant
rules are the Land Registration Rules 1925, SR & O 1925/1093, and, in particular, rr 76
and 77(1), which provide as follows: *e*

'**76.** For the purpose of introducing the covenants implied under Sections 76 and
77 of the Law of Property Act, 1925, a person may, in a registered disposition, be
expressed to execute, transfer, or charge as beneficial owner, as settlor, as trustee, as
mortgagee, as personal representative of a deceased person, as committee of a lunatic, *f*
or as receiver of a defective, or under an order of the court: and an instrument of
transfer or charge, and any instrument affecting registered land, or a registered
charge, may be expressed accordingly, but no reference to covenants implied under
Section 76 aforesaid shall be entered in the register.

77. Pursuant to sub-section (2) of Section 38 of the Act, it is hereby provided
that—(1) Any covenant implied by virtue of Section 76 of the Law of Property Act,
1925, in a disposition of registered land shall take effect as though the disposition *g*
was expressly made subject to—(*a*) all charges and other interests appearing or
protected on the register at the time of the execution of the disposition and affecting
the title of the covenantor; (*b*) any overriding interests of which the purchaser has
notice and subject to which it would have taken effect, had the land been
unregistered . . .' *h*

When this action came on for trial before the deputy judge, it was agreed that he
should only decide liability. If the plaintiffs succeeded in establishing liability, damages
should be referred to an inquiry.

On liability, the first question he had to decide was whether the subject matter
'expressed to be conveyed' (the wording in the covenant in Sch 2 to the Law of Property *j*
Act 1925) by cl 2 of the transfer of 7 September 1978 did or did not include the yellow
land. This is a question of construction of the parcels in the transfer. On their true
construction, do those parcels purport to convey to the plaintiffs the whole of the red
land, or do they only purport to convey to them so much of the red land as was actually
then registered under title no P 7608? The deputy judge decided this point in favour of

the plaintiffs, but his decision on it is challenged in this court by the defendants'
respondent's notice.

The next point which the judge had to consider at the trial was a claim by the
defendants that if on its true construction the transfer purported to convey the yellow
land to the plaintiffs the transfer ought to be rectified to exclude the yellow land. This
claim for rectification the judge rejected, and his rejection of it is not challenged in this
court. He held that it was the common intention of all parties that the yellow land should
be included in the transfer and be thereby transferred to the plaintiffs.

There was, however, an alternative claim for rectification before the judge. The
plaintiffs claimed that if on their true construction the parcels in cl 2 of the transfer of 7
September 1978 did not purportedly include the yellow land the transfer ought to be
rectified to include the yellow land, so as to give effect to the common intention of all
parties. The judge made no ruling on this claim for rectification since, on his construction
that the parcels did include the yellow land, rectification did not arise. In this court it is
agreed between the parties that, if we hold, contrary to the judge's view, that on their
true construction the parcels in the transfer do not purport to include the yellow land,
then, if the plaintiffs win on all other points argued on the appeal, we should remit the
case for decision at first instance on this outstanding claim of the plaintiffs for rectification
of the parcels in cl 2 of the transfer to include the yellow land.

Apart from the question of construction and the rival claims for rectification already
mentioned, the judge had also to consider a range of other points taken by the defendants,
particularly under rr 76 and 77 of the 1925 rules, as a result of all or any of which the
defendants urged that the plaintiffs could not recover damages in respect of the yellow
land under the implied covenant for title. On all but one of these other points the judge
was against the defendants; some have been argued in this court on the respondent's
notice and to these I will return. On one point, however, the judge was with the
defendants and against the plaintiffs; the result of that was that, as the plaintiffs have to
win on all points to win the action, the action failed, and was by the judge's order
dismissed with costs.

The one point of which the plaintiffs failed arises under r 77(1)(a) of the 1925 rules.
Under that rule a covenant for title implied in 'a disposition of registered land' is to take
effect as though 'the disposition' was expressly made subject to 'all charges and other
interests appearing . . . on the register at the time of the execution of the disposition'.
The judge held that the interests there referred to included the interest of the true
proprietor of the yellow land appearing on the Proprietorship Register of the title
number, not P 7608, in which the yellow land was in truth comprised at 7 September
1978. If the covenant is indeed so limited, it would follow that the fact that the
defendants have no title to the yellow land gives the plaintiffs no claim under the
covenant for title because the covenant is to be treated as subject to an express qualification
as to the true proprietor's ownership. But the plaintiffs say that the charges and other
interests referred to in r 77(1)(a) are only those which appear on the register of title no
P 7608 itself since that is the only title to which the transfer refers and the only title as to
which the defendants had power to give the plaintiffs authority to inspect the entries on
the register.

Such being the scope and history of the proceedings, I turn first to the issue of the true
construction of the parcels in the transfer of 7 September 1978. This is perhaps a question
of first impression. For my part, however, I agree entirely with the conclusion of the
deputy judge that the parcels do, as a matter of construction, include the yellow land,
and the yellow land is therefore part of the subject matter 'expressed to be conveyed' by
cl 2 of the transfer. The factors which taken together lead me to this conclusion are
briefly as follows. First, the transfer is concerned to differentiate between three parcels of
land, that to be transferred to Donron, that to be transferred to the plaintiffs and that
retained by the defendants, and it does so exclusively by reference to the plan on the
transfer and the colouring on that plan, the green land, the red land and the blue land.

The colouring on the plan is thus the dominant description of each parcel, including the red land. Second, the other part of the description of the red land, 'being another part of the property registered . . . under Title Number P. 7608' in itself describes nothing, since it does not say what further part is meant. Third, where parcels in a conveyancing document are described by reference to a plan attached to the document, the natural inference is that it was the intention that anyone concerned should see from the document alone, which means from the plan on it, what land the document was purporting to pass. But, if in the present case the defendants are right in their argument that cl 2 of the transfer imposed two cumulative conditions and only purported to pass land which (a) was within the red edging on the plan and also (b) was part of title no P 7608, that would not be so, and the reader would have to look beyond the plan on the transfer to the filed plan on the register to see what the parties were intending to deal with. That would not, to my mind, be a natural approach. I prefer the judge's conclusion that the effective description of the subject matter expressed to be conveyed by cl 2 of the transfer is the red edging on the plan on the transfer; the reference to property comprised in the title number is subordinate, believed to be accurate, but to be rejected as falsa demonstratio in so far as it is, qua the yellow land, inaccurate.

As for the defendants' arguments based on rr 76 and 77 of the 1925 rules, the function of those rules is, under s 38(2) of the Land Registration Act 1925, to prescribe the effect, in registered conveyances of the covenants implied by virtue of the Law of Property Act 1925. The first stage in this is that under r 76 a person may introduce the relevant implied covenants by being expressed, in a registered disposition, to transfer as beneficial owner. There must, therefore, for the covenants to be introduced, be a registered disposition. But in the present case there unquestionably was a registered disposition, in that the transfer was a registered disposition of at any rate so much of the red land as was still comprised in title no P 7608. The 'beneficial owner' covenants are therefore to be implied in the transfer, which means that the relevant wording in Sch 2 to the Law of Property Act 1925 is to be read into the transfer.

One argument for the defendants, discussed on the respondent's notice, is that the transfer is only a registered disposition of so much of the red land as was comprised in the title number and it was not a registered disposition of the yellow land, because the defendants had no title to the yellow land; so it is said that the beneficial owner's covenants are only implied qua the land which was effectively transferred by the transfer, and not qua the yellow land. That, however, does not follow. The registered disposition referred to in r 76 of the 1925 rules is the equivalent in registered conveyancing of the conveyance referred to in s 76 of the Law of Property Act 1925, which under s 205 has to be a conveyance of the property. But it is plain from the wording of s 76, as of Sch 2 to the Law of Property Act 1925, that the covenants implied under s 76 apply not merely to the property conveyed by the conveyance referred to, but to the whole of the subject matter expressed to be conveyed by it. The same must apply to a registered disposition. Therefore I find nothing in r 76 that helps the defendants.

I find it unnecessary to explore the question argued by the defendants whether the covenants for title are implied by virtue of s 76 of the Law of Property Act 1925 or by virtue of r 76 of the 1925 rules. It does not matter. The wording to be applied is that the covenants implied by s 76 are introduced by r 76 into the registered disposition.

The scope of the covenants thus introduced is limited by r 77(1). The primary object, at any rate, of this is to simplify the form of transfers in registered conveyancing, by making it unnecessary to refer expressly in every transfer to the matters covered by sub-paras (a) and (b) of r 77(1): charges and other interests appearing or protected on 'the register' and overriding interests of which the purchaser has notice. The crucial question is what is meant by 'the register'. It is very probable that the draftsman of the rule only had in mind the simple case where a registered proprietor transfers land of which he is registered proprietor; in that case the only relevant register would be the register of the

registered proprietor's own title. I find it hard to suppose that the draftsman ever
a envisaged that solicitors would so arrange matters that a registered proprietor would
purport to include in one transfer land of which he himself was the registered proprietor
and also land to which he had no title and of which someone else was the registered
proprietor under a different title number. These considerations, however, cannot answer
the crucial question in the present case.

The scheme of the Land Registry is that, although there is a global register of all
b registered titles, there is also a separate register for each individual title. This appears
particularly from the form of office copy entries for the individual title which are
regularly issued by the Land Registry under r 296 of the 1925 rules and which under
s 113 of the Land Registration Act 1925 are themselves admissible in evidence to the
same extent as the originals. The register for the individual title comprises a property
register, a proprietorship register and a charges register for that individual title. The way
c title is made to registered land on a sale is, under s 110 of the Land Registration Act 1925,
that the vendor furnishes the purchaser with an authority to inspect 'the register' and if
required with a copy of the subsisting entries in 'the register' and of any filed plan. In
that context 'the register' must mean the register in respect of the relevant individual
title of which the vendor is the registered proprietor, since under r 287 only the
proprietor of land (or of any charge or incumbrance thereon) can authorise anyone to
d inspect any entry in the register relating to that land. The plaintiffs, therefore, as
purchasers under their contract with Donron which preceded the transfer of 7 September
1978 had no general right to inspect anything in the global register maintained at the
Land Registry in respect of all registered land; they could inspect two things only: first,
with the defendants' authority which was given, the entries on the register of title no
P 7608, and, second, under r 288, as contracting purchasers of adjoining land, the
e Property Register and filed plan only of the title which included the yellow land and
other adjoining land.

The reference in r 77(1)(a) to charges and other interests appearing or protected on the
register could not, in my judgment, extend to matters the subject of entries which the
plaintiffs as purchasers could not have inspected. Therefore 'the register' referred to
f cannot mean the global register of all registered land. Therefore I construe the reference
to 'the register' in r 77(1)(a) as referring only to the register of the individual title, viz in
the context of the present case the title no P 7608 of which the defendants were the
registered proprietors. It was that proprietorship alone which under the scheme of the
Act empowered them to make the disposition referred to in r 77(1)(a) which I take to be
the same as the registered disposition referred to in r 76.

g I have considered whether in view of r 288 the reference to 'the register' in r 77(1)(a)
ought to be construed to include also the Property Register of the adjoining title which
in fact included the yellow land. But in my judgment, though the special power to
inspect the Property Register and filed plan is given by r 288, the emphasis of the Act
and rules between vendor and purchaser is so strongly on mere inspection of the register
of the title of which the vendor is the registered proprietor that the reference to 'the
h register' in r 77(1)(a) ought to be similarly so limited. I therefore, with all respect to the
deputy judge, disagree with him on the point on which he decided this action against
the plaintiffs.

There remains, however, one further point taken by the defendants under their
respondent's notice. They point out that the transfer to the plaintiffs in cl 2 of the transfer
of 7 September 1978 does not contain the words of limitation 'in fee simple'. They
j therefore submit that, even if the parcel in cl 2 purports to include the yellow land, the
defendants, who had no contract with the plaintiffs, have never undertaken to the
plaintiffs to pass to the plaintiffs more than whatever title they might have in the land
the subject of cl 2. The title they had happened to be the fee simple in relation to the red
land in so far as it was comprised in title no P 7608 and happened to be nothing in

relation to the yellow land, but that, the defendants submit, does not give the plaintiffs any claim to damages under the 'beneficial owner' implied covenant, because the *a* defendants never purported to transfer more than whatever they actually had.

Section 60 of the Law of Property Act 1925, which has been referred to in relation to this argument, provides that a conveyance of freehold land to any person without words of limitation or any equivalent expression shall pass to the grantee the fee simple or other the whole interest which the grantor had power to convey in such land, unless a contrary intention appears in the conveyance. Despite this, it has remained the practice in *b* unregistered conveyancing to include in the habendum of the conveyance the words of limitation 'in fee simple' where it is intended that the fee simple will pass, or where that is not intended to state that the grantor conveys only such estate title or interest (if any) as he may have in the land concerned. In the notes in *Wolstenholme and Cherry's Conveyancing Statutes* (13th edn, 1972) vol 1, p 134 it is stated:

> 'Though words of limitation are no longer essential the words "in fee simple" will *c* generally be employed in deeds to show the intention of the parties and to facilitate the construction of the implied covenants for title.'

The words of limitation 'in fee simple' are, however, never used in registered conveyancing. The form of transfer commonly used is prescribed by r 98 of the 1925 rules in mandatory terms and it contains no words of limitation. What is clear, however, *d* from s 18(1) of the Land Registration Act 1925 is that the only relevant power which the defendants had as proprietors of the land comprised in title no P 7608 was to transfer the fee simple in possession. That consequently was what they purported to do, and did, in relation to the part of the red land actually comprised in that title. But cl 2 of the transfer treated the whole of the red land alike. Therefore in my judgment they equally purported to transfer the fee simple in the yellow land. That was the manner in which it was *e* expressed to be conveyed. Consequently, the implied covenant for title bites.

For my part, therefore, I would allow this appeal, set aside the order of the deputy judge and order an inquiry as to damages.

CROOM-JOHNSON LJ. I have read the judgment of Dillon LJ and agree with it. I *f* wish to add only a few words on the question of the proper construction of the parcels clause in the transfer.

The judge rejected the defendants' submission that the words 'being another part of the property registered ... under Title Number P. 7608' should be taken to be the primary definition of the land transferred, because it was quite impossible by those words to identify any boundaries of the part of title no P 7608 intended to be transferred. He held that there was then no answer to the inevitable question: Yes, but *what* other part of *g* the property registered under title no P 7608?

In the context of the document as described in the judgment of Dillon LJ, with its references to the green land and the blue land, the plan of the red land was the primary description of that was expressed to be conveyed. It was clear and unambiguous, and was not referred to as being 'for identification only'.

Nor would it be permissible to read into the description any additional words so as to *h* make it read 'All that freehold property which is both edged with red on the plan annexed hereto and another part of the property registered ...' where the wording as it stands is straightforward.

I come to this conclusion simply on the wording of the transfer and without stepping outside it in order to ascertain the intentions of the parties. In my view the judge arrived *j* at the right answer to the interpretation of the transfer.

Accordingly I also would allow the appeal for the reasons given by Dillon LJ.

SIR JOHN DONALDSON MR. It is common ground that if, as is contended by the defendants in their cross-appeal, the judge erred in his construction of the transfer, the

matter would have to be remitted to the Chancery Division in order that the plaintiffs'
a claim to rectification should be considered. Nevertheless, it was also common ground
that the parties would be assisted if we gave judgment on the other matters which arise
if the judge's construction was correct. I agree with the judgment of Dillon LJ in all
respects, save as to the construction of the transfer and therefore confine myself to
explaining why I disagree on that one point.

Registration of land titles has only a limited utility if it is not clear to what land the
b registered title and other particulars relate. On the other hand, it is obviously impossible
to define and register boundaries for all properties overnight or even, perhaps, 'over-
century'. However, it is possible to aim in that direction and rr 272 to 285 of the Land
Registration Rules 1925 point the way. There is to be a parcels index based on the
Ordnance Survey map with provision for the boundaries to be fixed (r 276), although if
this procedure is not adopted the filed plan shall be deemed to indicate general boundaries
c only (r 278).

I mention this by way of preamble, because I think that it is not only permissible, but
is the natural and desirable course to adopt when transferring registered land, to treat the
primary unit as being the registered parcel and, if this is not being transferred as a whole,
to indicate what part or parts are being transferred.

This seems to me to be precisely what happened on this occasion. The defendants as
d the beneficial owners of the registered land constituting registered parcel Dorset–Poole
P 7608 were minded to dispose of two parts of this parcel and there is absolutely nothing
on the face of the transfer to suggest that they intended to transfer any part of any other
parcel. (In fact, although this is not a permissible aid to construction, we know that they
did not so intend. Their error lay in believing that the 'yellow land', a ten-foot square,
was part of the parcel.) In each case the land to be transferred is described in the transfer
e as 'being part' or 'being another part of the property registered at HM Land Registry
under Title Number P. 7608'. The transferor had then to identify each part of the land
comprised in the title and for that purpose used a plan and edged the parts in green and
red respectively.

On the judge's construction of the transfer, the references to the parcel number are
largely unnecessary and are certainly subordinate to the colourings on the plan.
f Furthermore, in relation to the land edged in red, the words 'being part of . . . P. 7608'
are simply not correct, since the ten-foot square 'yellow land' included in the land edged
in red is not within the parcel. On my construction the whole of the land transferred is,
as the transfer states, part of the registered parcel and full effect is given to the coloured
edging as indicating the boundary between (a) the part of the parcel transferred to
Donron (Alberice Meters) Ltd, (b) that transferred to the plaintiffs and (c) that, if any,
g retained by the defendants. The unfortunate deviation of the red line across the boundary
of parcel P 7608 and into another parcel is immaterial, since at this point the boundary is
defined by the registered particulars of parcel P 7608 as a whole and not by the red line.

In the light of my view of the construction of the transfer, I would have remitted the
matter to the Chancery division for consideration of the plaintiffs' claim to rectification.

h
Appeal allowed. Cross-appeal dismissed. Leave to appeal to House of Lords refused.

Solicitors: *Barker Son & Isherwood*, Andover (for the appellants); *Trethowans*, Salisbury (for
the respondents).

Frances Rustin   Barrister.

Smith and others v Littlewoods Organisation Ltd (Chief Constable, Fife Constabulary, third party) and conjoined appeal

HOUSE OF LORDS

LORD KEITH OF KINKEL, LORD BRANDON OF OAKBROOK, LORD GRIFFITHS, LORD MACKAY OF CLASHFERN AND LORD GOFF OF CHIEVELEY

13, 14 OCTOBER 1986, 5 FEBRUARY 1987

Negligence – Duty to take care – Act of third party – Duty of owner of building to occupier of adjoining building in respect of act of third party – Respondents purchasing cinema and closing it prior to redeveloping site – Children gaining access to empty and unattended cinema – Respondents unaware of children's incursions – Children starting fire in cinema – Fire demolishing and damaging adjoining properties – Whether respondents owing duty of care to owners of adjoining properties – Whether respondents liable for adjoining owners' loss.

The respondents purchased a cinema with a view to demolishing it and replacing it with a supermarket. They took possession on 31 May 1976, closed the cinema and employed contractors to make site investigations and do some preliminary work on foundations, but from about the end of the third week in June the cinema remained empty and unattended by the respondents or any of their employees. By the beginning of July the main building of the cinema was no longer lockfast and was being regularly entered by unauthorised persons. Debris began to accumulate outside the cinema and on two occasions attempts to start fires inside and adjacent to the cinema had been observed by a passer-by but neither the respondents nor the police were informed. On 5 July a fire was started in the cinema which seriously damaged two adjoining properties, one of which had to be demolished. The appellants, the owners of the affected properties, claimed damages against the respondents on the ground that the damage to their properties had been caused by the respondents' negligence. The judge found the claims established and awarded the appellants damages. An appeal by the respondents was allowed by the Court of Session. The appellants appealed to the House of Lords, contending that it was reasonably foreseeable that if the cinema was left unsecured children would be attracted to the building, would gain entry and would cause damage which, it was reasonably foreseeable, would include damage by fire which, it was reasonably foreseeable, would in turn spread to and damage adjoining properties.

Held – The appeal would be dismissed for the following reasons—

(1) (Per Lord Keith, Lord Brandon, Lord Griffiths and Lord Mackay) The respondents were under a general duty to exercise reasonable care to ensure that the condition of the premises they occupied was not a source of danger to neighbouring property. Whether that general duty encompassed a specific duty to prevent damage from fire resulting from vandalism in the respondents' premises depended on whether a reasonable person in the position of the respondents would foresee that if he took no action to keep the premises lockfast in the comparatively short time before the premises were demolished they would be set on fire with consequent risk to the neighbouring properties. On the facts and given particularly that the respondents had not known of the vandalism in the area or of the previous attempts to start fires, the events which occurred were not reasonably foreseeable by the respondents and they accordingly owed no such specific duty to the appellants. Furthermore (per Lord Mackay), where the injury or damage was caused by an independent human agency the requirement that the injury or damage had

to be the probable consequence of the tortfeasor's own act or omission before there could
a be liability referred not to a consequence determined according to the balance of
probabilities but to a real risk of injury or damage, in the sense of the injury or damage
being a highly likely consequence of the act or omission rather than a mere possibility.
The more unpredictable the conduct in question, the less easy it was to affirm that any
particular result from it was probable and, unless the court could be satisfied that the
result of the human action was highly probable or very likely, it might have to conclude
b that all the reasonable man could say was that it was no more than a mere possibility (see
p 712 *h*, p 713 *b* to *e j* to p 714 *b*, p 719 *e* to *j*, p 721 *f* to *j*, p 727 *f* and 728 *h*, post); *P Perl
(Exporters) Ltd v Camden London BC* [1983] 3 All ER 161 explained; *Hay (or Bourhill) v
Young* [1942] 2 All ER 396, *Smith v Leurs* (1945) 70 CLR 256, *Lamb v Camden London
Borough* [1981] 2 All ER 408 and *King v Liverpool City Council* [1986] 3 All ER 544
considered.
c   (2) (Per Lord Goff, Lord Keith concurring) There was no general duty at common law
to prevent persons from harming others by their deliberate wrongdoing, however
foreseeable such harm might be if a defendant did not take steps to prevent it.
Accordingly, liability in negligence for such harm caused by third parties could only be
made out in special circumstances, namely (a) where a special relationship existed
between the plaintiff and the defendant, (b) where a source of danger was negligently
d created by the defendant and it was reasonably foreseeable that third parties might
interfere and cause damage by sparking off the danger and (c) where the defendant had
knowledge or means of knowledge that a third party had created or was creating a risk of
danger on his property and he failed to take reasonable steps to abate it. On the facts, no
such special circumstances were present, and accordingly the respondents owed no duty
of care to the appellants (see p 712 *h*, p 728 *j* to p 729 *a c*, p 730 *b c f g*, p 731 *g h*, p 732 *h*
e to 733 *b* and p 736 *h*, post); *Stansbie v Troman* [1948] 1 All ER 599, *Haynes v G Harwood &
Son* [1934] All ER Rep 103, *Goldman v Hargrave* [1966] 2 All ER 989 and *Thomas Graham
& Co Ltd v Church of Scotland General Trustees* 1982 SLT (Sh Ct) 26 considered; *Squires v
Perth and Kinross DC* 1986 SLT 30 disapproved.

Cases referred to in opinions
f *Anns v Merton London Borough* [1977] 2 All ER 492, [1978] AC 728, [1977] 2 WLR 1024,
HL.
Arneil v Schnitzer (1944) 173 Ore 179, Ore SC.
Bolton v Stone [1951] 1 All ER 1078, [1951] AC 850, HL.
British Rlys Board v Herrington [1972] 1 All ER 749, [1972] AC 877, [1972] 2 WLR 537,
HL.
g *Carrick Furniture House Ltd v Paterson* 1978 SLT (Notes) 48.
Cattle v Stockton Waterworks Co (1875) LR 10 QB 453, [1874–80] All ER Rep 220.
Donoghue (or M'Alister) v Stevenson [1932] AC 562, [1932] All ER Rep 1, HL.
Evans v Glasgow DC 1978 SLT 17.
Fraser v Glasgow Corp 1972 SC 162.
h *Glasgow Corp v Muir* [1943] 2 All ER 44, [1943] AC 448, HL.
Goldman v Hargrave [1966] 2 All ER 989, [1967] 1 AC 645, [1966] 3 WLR 513, PC.
Graham (Thomas) & Co Ltd v Church of Scotland General Trustees 1982 SLT (Sh Ct) 26.
Hay (or Bourhill) v Young [1942] 2 All ER 396, [1943] AC 92, HL.
Haynes v G Harwood & Son [1935] 1 KB 146, [1934] All ER Rep 103, CA.
Home Office v Dorset Yacht Co Ltd [1970] 2 All ER 294, [1970] AC 1004, [1970] 2 WLR
j 1140, HL.
Hughes v Lord Advocate [1963] 1 All ER 705, [1963] AC 837, [1963] 2 WLR 779, HL.
Job Edwards Ltd v Birmingham Navigations [1924] 1 KB 341, CA.
Junior Books Ltd v Veitchi Co Ltd [1982] 3 All ER 201, [1983] 1 AC 520, [1982] 3 WLR 477,
HL.
King v Liverpool City Council [1986] 3 All ER 544, [1986] 1 WLR 890, CA.

Lamb v Camden London Borough [1981] 2 All ER 408, [1981] QB 625, [1981] 2 WLR 1038, CA.

Leigh & Sillavan Ltd v Aliakmon Shipping Co Ltd, The Aliakmon [1985] 2 All ER 44, [1985] QB 350, [1985] 2 WLR 289, CA; *affd* [1986] 2 All ER 145, [1986] AC 785, [1986] 2 WLR 902, HL.

Paterson Zochonis & Co Ltd v Merfarken Packaging Ltd (1982) [1986] 3 All ER 522, CA.

Perl (P) (Exporters) Ltd v Camden London BC [1983] 3 All ER 161, [1984] QB 342, [1983] 3 WLR 769, CA.

Prince v Chehalis Savings and Loan Association (1936) 186 Wash 372; *affd* on rehearing 186 Wash 377, Wash SC.

Scott's Trustees v Moss (1889) 17 R (Ct of Sess) 32.

Sedleigh-Denfield v O'Callagan (Trustees for St Joseph's Society for Foreign Missions) [1940] 3 All ER 349, [1940] AC 880, HL.

Smith v Leurs (1945) 70 CLR 256, Aust HC.

Squires v Perth and Kinross DC 1986 SLT 30, Inner House.

Stansbie v Troman [1948] 1 All ER 599, [1948] 2 KB 48, CA.

Torrack v Corpamerica Inc (1958) 144 A 2d 703, Del Super.

Wagon Mound, The (No 2), Overseas Tankship (UK) Ltd v Miller Steamship Co Pty Ltd [1966] 2 All ER 709, [1967] 1 AC 617, [1966] 3 WLR 498, PC.

Weld-Blundell v Stephens [1920] AC 956, [1920] All ER Rep 32, HL.

Consolidated appeals

The appellants in the first appeal, the Rev F T Smith, W G Kerr and A D Crawford, respectively the minister, session clerk and clerk of the deacon's court of St Paul's Church of Scotland, Dunfermline, and the appellant in the second appeal, Angelo Maloco, appealed against the interlocutors of the First Division of the Court of Session (the Lord President (Lord Emslie), Lord Grieve and Lord Brand) on 19 November 1985 allowing the reclaiming motion by the respondents, Littlewoods Organisation Ltd (Littlewoods), against the interlocutors of the Lord Ordinary (Cowie) on 23 March 1984 awarding the first appellants £605,000 and the second appellant £45,900 by way of damages in the appellants' actions against Littlewoods to recover damages for loss and damage resulting from a fire on 5 July 1976 which the appellants averred was caused by the negligence of Littlewoods. The two actions, which proceeded concurrently, were conjoined by order of the House of Lords dated 25 February 1986. The decision of the Lord Ordinary to grant the third party, the Chief Constable, Fife Constabulary, absolvitor was not reclaimed. The facts are set out in the opinion of Lord Mackay.

R N M MacLean QC and D S MacKay (both of the Scottish Bar) for the appellants.
A C M Johnston QC and D A Y Menzies (both of the Scottish Bar) for Littlewoods.

Their Lordships took time for deliberation.

5 February. The following opinions were delivered.

LORD KEITH OF KINKEL. My Lords, I have had the advantage of considering in draft the speeches to be delivered by my noble and learned friends Lord Mackay and Lord Goff. I agree with them, and for the reasons they give would dismiss these appeals.

LORD BRANDON OF OAKBROOK. My Lords, it is axiomatic that the question whether there has been negligence in any given case must depend on the particular circumstances of that case. That being so, I do not think that these appeals can in the end be determined by reference to other reported cases in which the particular circumstances were different, even though some degree of analogy between such other cases and the present one can legitimately be drawn. Nor do I think that it is possible, however helpful it might otherwise be, to lay down any general principle designed to apply to all cases in

which the negligence alleged against a person involves the unauthorised acts of
a   independent third parties on premises owned or occupied by that person.

The particular facts of the present case appear to me to raise two, and only two,
questions, on the answers to which the determination of the appeals depends.

The first question is: what was the general duty owed by Littlewoods, as owners and
occupiers of the disused cinema, to the appellants, as owners or occupiers of other
buildings near to the cinema? The answer to that question is, in my view, that
b   Littlewoods owed to the appellants a duty to exercise reasonable care to ensure that the
cinema was not, and did not become, a source of danger to neighbouring buildings
owned or occupied by the appellants.

The second question is whether that general duty encompassed a specific duty to
exercise reasonable care to prevent young persons obtaining unlawful access to the
cinema and, having done so, unlawfully setting it on fire. The answer to that question,
c   in accordance with general principles governing alike the law of delict in Scotland and
the law of negligence in England, must depend on whether the occurrence of such
behaviour was reasonably foreseeable by Littlewoods. It should have been reasonably
foreseeable by Littlewoods if they had known of the activities of young persons observed
by certain individuals in the locality. But they did not know of such activities because
the individuals concerned did not inform either Littlewoods or the police of them, nor
d   did the police themselves observe them. In the absence of information about such
activities, either from the individuals referred to or from the police, I am of opinion that
the occurrence of the behaviour in question was not reasonably foreseeable by Littlewoods.
I conclude, therefore, that the general duty of care owed by Littlewoods to the appellants
did not encompass the specific duty referred to above.

For these reasons I would dismiss the appeals.

e   **LORD GRIFFITHS.** My Lords, I regard these appeals as turning on the evaluation and
application of the particular facts of this case to a well-established duty and standard of
care. I agree so fully with the statement and evaluation of the facts appearing in the
speech of my noble and learned friend Lord Mackay, that I can state my own reasons for
dismissing these appeals very shortly.

f   The duty of care owed by Littlewoods was to take reasonable care that the condition of
the premises they occupied was not a source of danger to neighbouring property.

The standard of care required of them was that stated in general terms by Lord
Radcliffe in *Bolton v Stone* [1951] 1 All ER 1078 at 1087, [1951] AC 850 at 868–869 and
expanded in more particularity by Lord Wilberforce in *Goldman v Hargrave* [1966] 2 All
ER 989 at 995–996, [1967] 1 AC 645 at 662–663 when dealing with a fire on premises
g   caused by an outside agency. I refrain from citing these passages as both appear in the
speech of my noble and learned friend Lord Mackay.

Listening to the seductive way in which counsel for the appellants developed his
argument on the facts step by step, as described by Lord Mackay, I was reminded of the
fable of the prince who lost his kingdom but for the want of a nail for the shoe of his
horse. A series of foreseeable possibilities were added one to another and, hey presto,
h   there emerged at the end the probability of a fire against which Littlewoods should have
guarded. But, my Lords, that is not the common sense of this matter.

The fire in this case was caused by the criminal activity of third parties on Littlewoods'
premises. I do not say that there will never be circumstances in which the law will
require an occupier of premises to take special precautions against such a contingency
j   but they would surely have to be extreme indeed. It is common ground that only a 24-
hour guard on these premises would have been likely to prevent this fire, and even that
cannot be certain, such is the determination and ingenuity of young vandals.

There was nothing of an inherently dangerous nature stored in the premises, nor can I
regard an empty cinema stripped of its equipment as likely to be any more alluring to
vandals than any other recently vacated premises in the centre of a town. No message

was received by Littlewoods from the local police, fire brigade or any neighbour that
vandals were creating any danger on the premises. In short, so far as Littlewoods knew, *a*
there was nothing significantly different about these empty premises from the tens of
thousands of such premises up and down the country. People do not mount 24-hour
guards on empty properties and the law would impose an intolerable burden if it
required them to do so save in the most exceptional circumstances. I find no such
exceptional circumstances in this case and I would accordingly dismiss the appeals.

I doubt myself if any search will reveal a touchstone that can be applied as a universal *b*
test to decide when an occupier is to be held liable for a danger created on his property
by the act of a trespasser for whom he is not responsible. I agree that mere foreseeability
of damage is certainly not a sufficient basis to found liability. But with this warning I
doubt that more can be done than to leave it to the good sense of the judges to apply
realistic standards in conformity with generally accepted patterns of behaviour to
determine whether in the particular circumstances of a given case there has been a breach *c*
of duty sounding in negligence.

LORD MACKAY OF CLASHFERN. My Lords, the defenders and respondents in
these consolidated appeals, to whom I shall refer as 'Littlewoods', purchased the Regal
Cinema in the centre of Dunfermline from its previous owners with entry on 31 May
1976. Littlewoods' intention was to demolish the cinema within a short time and to *d*
replace it by a supermarket. On 5 July 1976, in consequence of a fire which began in the
cinema, a café and billiard saloon which lay close to the cinema on the west known as the
Café Maloco was seriously damaged and St Paul's Church which lay also to the west but
at a slightly greater distance from the cinema was so substantially damaged that it had to
be demolished. Dunfermline lies within the area of the Fife Constabulary. The issues in
both actions are the same and they have been heard together at every stage. The owners *e*
of the affected properties, to whom I shall refer as 'the appellants', claimed against
Littlewoods for the damage done to their properties alleging that the damage was caused
by negligence on the part of Littlewoods. Littlewoods, in turn, claimed that if they were
at fault the Chief Constable of the Fife Constabulary or his officers were also at fault and
he should be held liable to make a contribution to the award made against Littlewoods. *f*
The Lord Ordinary (Cowie) held that the claims had been established against Littlewoods
and pronounced awards in favour of both owners. He found that Littlewoods' case
against the Chief Constable had not been established. Littlewoods accepted the decision
relating to the Chief Constable but reclaimed against the awards which had been made
against them. The First Division of the Inner House of the Court of Session unanimously
allowed the reclaiming motions and recalled the Lord Ordinary's interlocutors (see 1986
SLT 272). The First Division also dealt with matters relating to the size of the award *g*
made in favour of the owners of St Paul's Church.

The appellants have now appealed to this House and have argued that the Lord
Ordinary's interlocutors should be restored, subject to alteration in the amount awarded
in favour of the owners of St Paul's Church. No question relating to the size of the awards
remains outstanding between the parties; they are agreed on the amounts to be awarded *h*
if the appeals succeed.

The cinema comprised a substantial brick-built auditorium with a balcony at the north
end and a flat timber and felt covered roof on a steel frame. It was reached from the High
Street by a lengthy foyer partly of similar construction and otherwise traditionally stone-
built and slated, three storeys in height. The main building of the cinema was set back a
considerable distance from the High Street. To the east of the cinema entrance in the *j*
High Street there was a passageway known as Macpherson's Close which ran down the
length towards the south on the east side of the main building. Immediately to the south
of the main building lay the car park, to which entry was gained from Canmore Street
lying to the south of the property. Macpherson's Close was regularly used by the public
as a short cut from Canmore Street to the High Street. Another close, known as the West

a Close, ran from the north side of the car park round the west side of the main building and then at the north end of the main building turned eastwards to join Macpherson's Close. This last section of the West Close passed under the section of the cinema which connected its main building with the front entrance in the High Street. On the west side of West Close was the Café Maloco and to the south-west of the cinema and beyond certain properties lying immediately to the west of the West Close lay St Paul's Church, which was a Victorian Gothic building with a small wooden turret. The main building

b of the cinema had a number of exit or fire doors with locking bars designed to be opened only from the inside which were set in the walls of the cinema.

The last showing of a film in the cinema took place on 29 May 1976. Although legal entry was given on 31 May 1976 the keys were not handed over to Littlewoods until about 14 June. During that period the previous owners employed contractors to remove fittings and equipment from the cinema which were worth taking away but which were

c of no interest to Littlewoods. Before these contractors had finished their task contractors employed by Littlewoods arrived at the premises to make certain site investigations and to do some preliminary work on foundations. Littlewoods' contractors were present and working for about three weeks; the first two were spent in the area of the cinema car park and thereafter they spent about four days working inside the premises. From about the end of the third week in June 1976 the cinema remained empty and unattended by

d any persons employed by or giving services to Littlewoods.

The evidence established that children began to overcome the security of the cinema building by breaking into it in one way or another in the period of about four days when Littlewoods' contractors were doing preliminary work inside the premises during or towards the end of the third week in June 1976. Although these contractors locked and secured the premises when they finished work each night, they discovered on their

e return in the morning clear signs that the premises had been forcibly entered. Some of the fire doors had been forced open from inside and the locking bars had been broken. The contractors then had to secure the doors which had been so affected by tying them with rope to the stage. When they finished their work they left the premises as secure as they could make them. Thereafter the security of the premises was again overcome by children and young persons and children and young persons resorted to the premises

f with increasing regularity for play, horseplay and the pleasure of making a mess and breaking whatever they could find to break. The Lord Ordinary held that it was amply established that by the first few days of July 1976 anyone with half an eye who made use of Macpherson's Close could have seen that the main building of the cinema was no longer lockfast and was being regularly entered by unauthorised persons. Paper and debris were scattered about the auditorium and in Macpherson's Close outside the

g building debris increased, consisting of bricks, glass and old films. During the time that the Littlewoods' contractors were working inside the main building one of the contractors' employees saw lengths of old cinema film lying in Macpherson's Close and noticed signs of someone having attempted to set fire to them. The type of film used in the cinema was non-inflammable and no fire had occurred. About the end of June Mr Scott, who

h was the beadle of St Paul's Church and of another church in the vicinity, saw signs of someone having tried to light a fire inside the building. His attention had been attracted because some children had run out of the building as he approached. When he went inside he found that the carpet, where oil had been spilled on it, was burning. He put it out very easily by stamping on it and told Mr Kerr, the session clerk of St Paul's, about it. Neither Mr Scott nor anyone else informed the police or Littlewoods about any of these

j matters. As the Lord Ordinary put it:

'Nevertheless, in spite of these obvious signs of the building having been violated by unauthorised persons, no one saw fit to report the matter to the police or to attempt to bring it to the attention of the defenders or their representatives.'

A notice at the front of the cinema contained the necessary particulars of Littlewoods.

On 5 July 1976 about 6.30 pm a large ceramic sink from a toilet on the top floor of the main building of the cinema landed on the roof of the billiard saloon in the Café Maloco. It was thrown from a window on the west side of the cinema by boys of 13 or 14 years of age. The police were called and detained two boys.

Between 8.00 and 9.00 pm on the same day a passer-by noticed three teenagers come out of Macpherson's Close and soon after she saw smoke coming from the close. The police and the fire brigade were called but the fire which started in the south-west corner of the balcony soon engulfed the whole building. The efforts of the fire brigade were impeded by inability to get a supply of water from the fire hoses.

The Lord Ordinary concluded, and there was no challenge to the correctness of his conclusion, that the fire which started on 5 July 1976 was deliberately started by children or teenagers and that the teenagers that the passer-by saw emerging from Macpherson's Close shortly before the smoke started to come out were probably responsible. Apart from the contractors employed by Littlewoods, to whom I have referred, the only person employed by Littlewoods who gave evidence was a member of the architectural department who was responsible for the design and supervision of the construction of buildings for the company. He visited the cinema about the middle of June and according to his evidence it was secure at that time.

The claims are based on the allegation that Littlewoods, as owners and occupiers of the Regal Cinema, had a duty to take reasonable care for the safety of premises adjoining, that they knew or ought to have known that a disused cinema would be a ready target for vandals, and that they knew or ought to have known that their cinema was, in fact, the subject of extensive vandalism and that if they did not take steps to prevent the entry of vandals they would cause damage not only to their own property, whether by fire or otherwise, but further such fire might spread and cause damage to adjoining properties. In these circumstances, it was claimed that Littlewoods had a duty to take reasonable care to keep and maintain the premises lockfast, to cause frequent and regular inspection to be made and to lock and board up any doors and windows found to be open or smashed and to employ a caretaker to watch over the premises and to prevent the entry of vandals. In the course of the hearing before your Lordships counsel for the appellants accepted that, in the light of the evidence, the only precaution that was likely to be effective in preventing the entry of vandals was to arrange for a 24-hour watch to be maintained on the premises. Littlewoods, while accepting that as owners and occupiers of the premises they had a duty to take reasonable care for the safety of premises adjoining, strenuously denied that they owed the duties on which these claims are founded.

The Lord Ordinary, after examining the authorities, concluded that whether such duties were owed by Littlewoods or not depended on the answer to the question—

'bearing in mind that [Littlewoods] had no control over the children and teenagers, was it reasonably foreseeable by [Littlewoods] that, by failing to keep the cinema lockfast and to inspect it regularly during the last half of June and the first few days of July 1976, children and young persons would not only enter it, but start a fire?'

He considered that it was appropriate that he should treat this as a jury question and try to answer it as a jury would. He said:

'In the absence of any evidence about the lighting of fires, it would have been difficult to say that it was "very likely" that children and young persons breaking into these premises would start a fire, but in the present instance there is evidence that on two occasions shortly before 5 July 1976 witnesses saw signs of someone having tried to start a fire . . . I accept that there is a very narrow dividing line in the circumstances of this case between bare foreseeability and reasonable foreseeability, but having applied my mind to that problem I have reached the conclusion that the lighting of a fire in the premises by children or teenagers was in the circumstances reasonably foreseeable.'

This conclusion he reached with some hesitation.

Before the First Division it was accepted by the appellants that, on the evidence, Littlewoods had no knowledge of the attempts to start fires to which the Lord Ordinary referred in the passage I have quoted and that, accordingly, in considering whether Littlewoods were bound reasonably to foresee that as a consequence of their inaction a fire would be started in their building and not only engulf it but cause damage to buildings nearby, these required to be left out of account unless it could be said that they had a duty to know of them. If they had not such a duty the Lord Ordinary's decision on this crucial matter was open for review by the judges of the First Division. The judges of the First Division unanimously concluded that the question was at large for their consideration and that in the circumstances it had not been shown that it was reasonably to be foreseen by Littlewoods that if they took no steps to discourage widespread use of the cinema by youngsters, including vandals, one or more of them, or some other intruder, would be likely deliberately to set fire to the building or deliberately to set such a fire in such a place as would be likely to engulf the building.

Counsel for the appellants in his very persuasive submissions to your Lordships suggested that this crucial question should be approached in stages. First he submitted that by reason of the particular features of this building it was reasonably foreseeable by Littlewoods that young persons were likely to be attracted to the building and would attempt to overcome such security as there was and would attempt to gain entry. The second submission was that it was reasonably foreseeable that if the building was insecure and remained insecure it would be entered. Further, it was reasonably foreseeable that a proportion of such young persons would be intent on causing damage within the building which might have an effect on adjoining property. The fourth step in the argument was that it was reasonably foreseeable that such damage would include damage by fire, which, being unpredictable, was likely to take hold of the fabric of the building. And the final step in the logical progression was that it was reasonably foreseeable that if the fire took hold of the building it would engulf the building and, since the building was large, the fire would readily spread to adjoining properties.

In support of these submissions and particularly the submission that it was reasonably foreseeable that such damage would include damage by fire, counsel referred to three decisions in which conduct of this kind had come to the notice of the courts: *Evans v Glasgow DC* 1978 SLT 17, in which it was alleged that one of the forms vandalism had taken in that case was that ignited material had been dropped through damaged floors of a flat above the pursuer's premises with the consequence that the contents of these premises were destroyed almost entirely; *Carrick Furniture House Ltd v Paterson* 1978 SLT (Notes) 48, in which it was alleged that persons had entered and deliberately set fire to the premises in question; and, thirdly, *Thomas Graham & Co Ltd v Church of Scotland General Trustees* 1982 SLT (Sh Ct) 26, in which vandals had entered a church and set it on fire. Counsel also referred to s 78 of the Criminal Justice (Scotland) Act 1980, in which while defining the statutory offence of vandalism as committed by 'any person who, without reasonable excuse, wilfully or recklessly destroys or damages any property belonging to another' Parliament excepted from that offence what would constitute the offence of wilful fire-raising. From that statutory provision, and these instances, counsel argued that it was right that the court should take notice that one of the forms in which persons wilfully or recklessly destroy or damage property belonging to others is by wilful fire-raising.

He further referred to *Hughes v Lord Advocate* [1963] 1 All ER 705, [1963] AC 837 as demonstrating the unpredictability of children's behaviour as a factor to be taken into account in dealing with a question such as is raised here.

Counsel submitted further, and anticipating what might be urged against him, that, although the actions that caused the fire were those of vandals over whom Littlewoods *a* had no control, his case was founded on the need that arose in consequence of the likely results of allowing vandals into the building to take precautions to keep them out. The test of whether such precautions should be taken was, in counsel's submission, whether it was reasonably foreseeable by Littlewoods that if they did not take these precautions there was a substantial risk that the neighbouring properties would be damaged. He referred particularly to *Home Office v Dorset Yacht Co Ltd* [1970] 2 All ER 294 esp at 297, *b* [1970] AC 1004 esp at 1027 per Lord Reid where, referring to the well-known passage in Lord Atkin's speech in *Donoghue v Stevenson* [1932] AC 562 at 580, [1932] All ER Rep 1 at 11, Lord Reid said:

'[It] should I think be regarded as a statement of principle. It is not to be treated as if it were a statutory definition. It will require qualification in new circumstances. But I think that the time has come when we can and should say that it ought to *c* apply unless there is some justification or valid explanation for its exclusion.'

Counsel submitted that it would not be right to regard damage caused by persons over whom the defender has no control as excluded from this statement of principle. Rather, said counsel, one should take account of actions of third parties over whom the defender has no control in considering the consequences of acts or omissions on the defender's *d* part. He referred in support of this submission to the later passages in Lord Reid's speech where he dealt with this question. As an illustration of this approach being taken in Scotland, he referred to *Squires v Perth and Kinross DC* 1986 SLT 30, in which jewellers successfully sued building contractors who were working in a flat above their shop for not adequately securing the flat against entry by thieves. A thief entered the jewellers' premises through the flat by climbing up a drain pipe at the back of the property to *e* which he obtained access by climbing over a building. A substantial quantity of jewellery was stolen.

Counsel for Littlewoods submitted that on the findings of fact in the present case the appellants had not established, applying the test of reasonable foreseeability, the existence of a risk sufficient to have obliged Littlewoods to adopt in advance of the catastrophic fire the only one of the prescribed remedies that might have avoided that occurrence, namely *f* having the premises watched all the time. He also advanced a broader proposition that the policy of the law should deny these claims, firstly, because they involved an unwarranted invasion of the basic right of a person to use his property as he pleased and, secondly, because affirming these claims implied potential obligations on those who leave property unoccupied for a comparatively short time that would be unduly heavy having regard to the purpose intended to be served. Or, putting the matter another way, *g* he submitted that the law should put the responsibility for securing the safety and security of property against vandals on the owner or occupier of the property and not on neighbouring owners or occupiers from whose property damage by vandals and thieves might be caused. In support of the submission that affirming the claims in the present case would have the result of placing unduly heavy burdens on the owners or occupiers *h* of property, he pointed out that there was no evidence that this building was in any way a special fire hazard, nor was there evidence that this part of Dunfermline was specially subject to vandalism.

In approaching these rival submissions it has to be borne in mind that the damage to the neighbouring properties, on which the claims against Littlewoods are founded, is damage by fire or otherwise resulting from vandalism in Littlewoods' premises. A duty *j* of care to prevent this damage is the only duty alleged to be incumbent on Littlewoods relevant to this case. From this it follows that, unless Littlewoods were bound reasonably to anticipate and guard against this danger, they had no duty of care, relevant to this case, requiring them to inspect their premises. Unless, therefore, Littlewoods, on taking

control of these premises without any knowledge of the subsequent history of the
a property after they assumed control, ought reasonably to have anticipated that they
would be set on fire and thus or otherwise create a substantial risk of damage to
neighbouring properties if they did not take precautions, the claims must fail. By
approaching the matter in five logical steps, counsel for the appellants made it appear
easier to reach the result for which he contended than it would be if one assumed only
Littlewoods' proved state of knowledge and asked whether, in that state of knowledge,
b they were to anticipate, as a reasonable and probable consequence of their inaction, that
a substantial risk of fire damage to their neighbours was created. As I have said, the Lord
Ordinary's answer to the basic question in the case depended, and depended critically, on
his assumption that Littlewoods were to be taken as aware of the evidence relating to the
attempt to start a fire in the lane with the abandoned film and to the smouldering carpet
which Mr Scott extinguished. It is plain from the way in which the Lord Ordinary
c expresses his opinion that, had it not been for his reliance upon that evidence against
Littlewoods, he would not have found against them. There was no evidence that
Littlewoods knew of these matters. Unless they had a duty to inspect there is no basis on
which it can be alleged that they ought to have known of them. Since the only basis on
which any relevant duty of care is said to arise is that damage to neighbouring properties
was to be anticipated unless it were exercised, in considering whether such damage
d should have been anticipated one cannot assume that any of the relevant duties should
have been performed. I conclude that the Lord Ordinary was not entitled to assume that
Littlewoods should have known of these matters. The First Division concluded, as I have
said, that the matter was at large for their consideration. In my opinion, their Lordships
of the First Division applied their minds to the correct question. In my opinion, the
question whether, in all the circumstances described in evidence, a reasonable person in
e the position of Littlewoods was bound to anticipate as probable, if he took no action to
keep these premises lockfast, that, in a comparatively short time before the premises
were demolished, they would be set on fire with consequent risk to the neighbouring
properties is a matter for the judges of fact to determine. Once it has been determined
on the correct basis, an appeal court should be slow to interfere with the determination:
f see, for example, Lord Thankerton in *Glasgow Corp v Muir* [1943] 2 All ER 44 at 47,
[1943] AC 448 at 454 and Lord Porter in *Bolton v Stone* [1951] 1 All ER 1078 at 1082,
[1951] AC 850 at 860.

The cases to which counsel for the appellants drew attention in his argument, and s 78
of the 1980 Act, illustrate that a consequence of this kind, if premises are left unoccupied,
is a possibility, but the extent to which such an occurrence is probable must depend on
the circumstances of the particular case. While no doubt in this case, as the judges in the
g courts below have found, it was probable that children and young persons might attempt
to break into the vacated cinema, this by no means establishes that it was a probable
consequence of its being vacated with no steps being taken to maintain it lockfast that it
would be set on fire with consequent risk of damage to neighbouring properties. A
telling point in favour of Littlewoods is that, although Littlewoods' particulars were
h shown on a board prominently displayed at the front of the premises, no one made any
protest to them about the state of the premises, or indicated to them any concern that,
unless they took some action, neighbouring premises were at risk. If, in the light of the
common knowledge in the neighbourhood, it had been anticipated that the cinema
might be set on fire, with consequent risk to adjoining properties, I should have thought
the persons concerned with the safety of adjoining properties, who were certainly among
j those acquainted with the situation, would have communicated their anxieties to
Littlewoods. Neither is there evidence that the police were ever informed of the situation
with regard to the cinema, and this I would take as further confirmation that, in the
circumstances, no one anticipated any adverse consequences arising from it. It is true
that Mr Scott, the beadle, spoke of anxiety for the safety of children, and also made some

reference, in that connection, to the possibility of fire, but any concern he had was not apparently sufficiently substantial to prompt him to take any action whatever in the way of seeking to have the situation remedied by the owners or the police.

This is sufficient for the disposal of this appeal but in view of the general importance of some of the matters raised in the parties' submissions it is right that I should add some observations on these.

First, counsel for the appellants urged us to say that the ordinary principle to be deduced from Lord Atkin's speech in *Donoghue v Stevenson* should apply to cases where the damage in question was caused by human agency. It is plain from the authorities that the fact that the damage, on which a claim is founded, was caused by a human agent quite independent of the person against whom a claim in negligence is made does not, of itself, preclude success of the claim, since breach of duty on the part of the person against whom the claim is made may also have played a part in causing the damage. In dealing with the submission in *Home Office v Dorset Yacht Co Ltd* [1970] 2 All ER 294 at 300, [1970] AC 1004 at 1030 that the claim must fail because there was a general principle that no person can be responsible for damage caused by the acts of another who is not his servant or acting on his behalf, Lord Reid, having quoted from *Haynes v Harwood* [1935] 1 KB 146, [1934] All ER Rep 103 and from *Scott's Trustees v Moss* (1889) 17 R (Ct of Sess) 32, said:

'These cases show that, where human action forms one of the links between the original wrongdoing of the defendant and the loss suffered by the plaintiff, that action must at least have been something very likely to happen if it is not to be regarded as novus actus interveniens breaking the chain of causation. I do not think that a mere foreseeable possibility is or should be sufficient, for then the intervening human action can more properly be regarded as a new cause than as a consequence of the original wrongdoing. But if the intervening action was likely to happen I do not think that it can matter whether that action was innocent or tortious or criminal. Unfortunately tortious or criminal action by a third party is often the "very kind of thing" which is likely to happen as a result of the wrongful or careless act of the defendant. And in the present case, on the facts which we must assume at this stage, I think that the taking of a boat by the escaping trainees and their unskilful navigation leading to damage to another vessel were the very kind of thing that these borstal officers ought to have seen to be likely.'

It has to be borne in mind that Lord Reid was demonstrating only that the submission with which he was dealing was incorrect. If a person can be responsible for damage caused by acts of another who is not his servant or acting on his behalf that sufficed to answer the question that Lord Reid had before him in the respondent's favour. It was accordingly not critical whether the test was foreseeability of that damage as likely or very likely. At the stage at which Lord Reid used the phrase 'very likely' he was giving his view on what the two cases he had cited showed. In the first of these, the phrase used is 'the very kind of thing which is likely to happen' (see [1935] 1 KB 146 at 156, [1934] All ER Rep 103 at 107 per Greer LJ) and, in the second, the consequence that was being considered was described in the passage quoted from the Lord President (Inglis) as 'the natural and almost inevitable consequence' of the defender's action which was the foundation of the claim (see 17 R (Ct of Sess) 32 at 36). When Lord Reid turns to state his own position, he does so on the basis that the intervening action was likely to happen. In *Glasgow Corp v Muir* [1943] 2 All ER 44, [1943] AC 448 the issue was whether the defender's manageress was negligent in allowing two members of a picnic party to bring a tea urn along a passage in her tea room without taking certain precautions. The damage in question, in that case, might therefore have arisen from the conduct of the two persons carrying the tea urn, who were not employees of the defenders or in any way accountable to them. The test of liability set out by Lord Macmillan in *Hay (or Bourhill) v Young* [1942] 2 All ER 396 at 403, [1943] AC 92 at 104, namely:

a

'The duty to take care is the duty to avoid doing or omitting to do anything the doing or omitting to do which may have as its reasonable and *probable* consequence injury to others and the duty is owed to those to whom injury may reasonably and *probably* be anticipated if the duty is not observed' (my emphasis),

was expressly used by Lord Thankerton and Lord Macmillan. Lord Wright said ([1943] 2 All ER 44 at 52, [1943] AC 448 at 465):

b

'As to negligence, the two men [who were carrying the urn] were not their [ie the defenders'] servants; they were not responsible for their acts; that the men should be negligent in so simple an operation was not likely to happen. It was a mere possibility, not a reasonable probability. The men, if negligent, were no doubt responsible for their own negligence, but from the standpoint of the appellants, the risk of negligence was a mere unlikely accident which no responsible person in [the

c

manageress's] position could naturally be expected to foresee.'

Lord Romer expressed it only slightly differently when he said ([1943] 2 All ER 44 at 54, [1943] AC 448 at 467–468):

d

'In my opinion, the appellants can only be fixed with liability if it can be shown that there materialised a risk that ought to have been within the appellants' reasonable contemplation.'

Lord Clauson said ([1943] 2 All ER 44 at 54, [1943] AC 448 at 468):

e

'... the crucial question in this matter appears to me to be whether [the manageress] ought as a reasonable woman to have had in contemplation that, unless some further precautions were taken, such an unfortunate occurrence as that which in fact took place might well be expected.'

There is no hint that any special qualification fell to be introduced into the test in consequence of the urn being carried by two persons not in the employment of the defenders and for whom they would have no vicarious responsibility.

f

It is true, as has been pointed out by Oliver LJ in *Lamb v Camden London Borough* [1981] 2 All ER 408 at 418, [1981] QB 625 at 642, that human conduct is particularly unpredictable and that every society will have a sprinkling of people who behave most abnormally. The result of this consideration, in my opinion, is that, where the only possible source of the type of damage or injury which is in question is agency of a human being for whom the person against whom the claim is made has no responsibility, it may not be easy to find that as a reasonable person he was bound to anticipate that type of

g

damage as a consequence of his act or omission. The more unpredictable the conduct in question, the less easy to affirm that any particular result from it is probable and in many circumstances the only way in which a judge could properly be persuaded to come to the conclusion that the result was not only possible but reasonably foreseeable as probable would be to convince him that, in the circumstances, it was highly likely. In this type of

h

case a finding that the reasonable man should have anticipated the consequence of human action as just probable may not be a very frequent option. Unless the judge can be satisfied that the result of the human action is highly probable or very likely he may have to conclude that all that the reasonable man could say was that it was a mere possibility. Unless the needle that measures the probability of a particular result flowing from the conduct of a human agent is near the top of the scale it may be hard to conclude that it

j

has risen sufficiently from the bottom to create the duty reasonably to foresee it.

In summary I conclude, in agreement with both counsel, that what the reasonable man is bound to foresee in a case involving injury or damage by independent human agency, just as in cases where such agency plays no part, is the probable consequences of his own act or omission, but that, in such a case, a clear basis will be required on which to assert that the injury or damage is more than a mere possibility. To illustrate, it is not necessary to go further than the decision of this House in *Home Office v Dorset Yacht Co Ltd,* where I consider that all the members of the majority found such a possible basis in *a* the facts that the respondents' yacht was situated very close to the island on which the borstal boys escaped from their custodians, that the only effective means of avoiding recapture was to escape by the use of some nearby vessel and that the only means of providing themselves with the means to continue their journey was likely to be theft from such nearby vessels. These considerations so limited the options open to the escaping boys that it became highly probable that the boys would use, damage or steal *b* from one or more of the vessels moored near the island.

The matter is further illustrated by *Thomas Graham & Co Ltd v Church of Scotland General Trustees* 1982 SLT (Sh Ct) 26, in which Sheriff Macvicar QC found that the area in which the defenders' church lay was subject to vandalism on a large scale, that on an inspection of the church in which representatives of the owners of the church took part shortly before the final fire evidence existed of small fires having already been lit in its interior *c* and that, on that inspection, the official reporting to the local authority concerned with public safety had reported that the building should be demolished since it constituted a serious fire hazard. Sheriff Macvicar concluded that by not taking the very obvious and inexpensive precaution of securing the side door of the church by which apparently access had been gained the defenders had failed in their duty to take reasonable care for the safety of their neighbour's property. This decision appears to me to be in accordance *d* with the decision of your Lordship's House in *Sedleigh-Denfield v O'Callagan (Trustees for St Joseph's Society for Foreign Missions)* [1940] 3 All ER 349, [1940] AC 880 establishing the occupier's liability with regard to a hazard created on his land by a trespasser, of which he has knowledge, when he fails to take reasonable steps to remove it. On Sheriff Macvicar's findings, the empty church building constituted a serious fire hazard unless it were effectively secured against further trespass. *e*

Before leaving cases relating to fires, I should mention *Evans v Glasgow DC* 1978 SLT 17 and *Carrick Furniture House Ltd v Paterson* 1978 SLT (Notes) 48, already referred to as illustrations cited by counsel for the appellants of vandalism taking the form of wilful fire-raising. In the first of these, *Evans's* case, the defenders had demolished premises which adjoined the pursuer's premises, which were also leased from the defenders, and in doing so had damaged the lock securing the pursuer's doors which had been replaced *f* with inadequate locks. The pursuer suffered loss as a result of (1) theft of goods by the persons who broke the new and inadequate locks, (2) fire caused by vandals dropping lighted material through gaps left by the defenders in floorboards above the pursuer's premises and (3) water which escaped from the defender's premises as a result of vandals interfering with the plumbing there. The case is reported at the stage of relevancy where the defenders were arguing that the pursuer's allegations, even if fully established, would *g* not justify their claim. In these circumstances, Lord Wylie said (1978 SLT 17 at 19):

'it seems to me that it would be entirely in accordance with principle to hold that in such circumstances there was a general duty on owners or occupiers of property, particularly property of the tenement type, where they chose to leave it vacant for any material length of time, to take reasonable care to see that it was proof against *h* the kind of vandalism which was calculated to affect adjoining property.'

I do not read Lord Wylie as there deciding that such a duty in the circumstances necessarily had been incumbent on the defenders. He was simply saying that principle would allow the claim and therefore it would not be right to sustain the defenders' submission. In my view that amounted only to a decision that depending on the facts as *j* they emerged a duty of the scope alleged might be incumbent on owners or occupiers of such property in some circumstances that fell within the allegations made by the pursuer. The *Carrick Furniture* case which followed is explicable on the same ground. Counsel for Littlewoods founded his argument on the decision in *Fraser v Glasgow Corp* 1972 SC 162 esp at 173 per the Lord Justice Clerk (Grant), but the circumstances in which he declined a   to hold a injury foreseeable were so different from those in the present case and so special that I find it of no assistance in this case.

I turn now to consider the cases in the Court of Appeal in England founded on by counsel for Littlewoods in support of his broad submission. The first of these, *Lamb v Camden London Borough* [1981] 2 All ER 408, [1981] QB 625, was a decision that a workman damaging a water pipe with his pick in such a way that settlement was occasioned to the foundations of the plaintiff's house was not reasonably bound to foresee

b   as a consequence of that for which he and his employers should be liable damage done to the plaintiff's house by squatters who obtained access because the house was not adequately secured against their entry when it was empty in order that repairs might be carried out. Both Lord Denning MR and Oliver LJ dealt fully with the speech of Lord Reid in *Home Office v Dorset Yacht Co Ltd* [1970] 2 All ER 294, [1970] AC 1004, to which I have already referred, and concluded that he was propounding 'highly likely' as the

c   degree of probability required before liability for the wrongful act of a third party could be established against a defendant. It will be apparent that my understanding of Lord Reid's speech, in its context, is somewhat different from theirs. While I do not consider that it is correct to base the decision in *Lamb v Camden London Borough* on a proposition as a matter of policy that no wrongdoer could ever be liable for outrageous or anti social conduct that had followed his wrongdoing and had contributed to the damage resulting

d   therefrom, I respectfully and entirely agree with the result to which the Court of Appeal came in that case, and particularly with the reason for it expressed by Oliver LJ where he said ([1981] 2 All ER 408 at 419, [1981] QB 625 at 643).

> 'I confess that I find it inconceivable that the reasonable man, wielding his pick in the road in 1973, could be said reasonably to foresee that his puncturing of a water
e   main would fill the plaintiff's house with uninvited guests in 1974.'

The next case referred to was *P Perl (Exporters) Ltd v Camden London BC* [1983] 3 All ER 161, [1984] QB 342, in which the plaintiffs were tenants of the defendants who used the basement of the demised premises in accordance with the terms of the lease for the storage of garments. The defendants were also the owners of the adjoining premises.

f   These premises had a broken lock on the front door. Unauthorised persons were often seen on those premises and burglaries had also taken place there, but the defendants had done nothing about complaints regarding lack of security. During a weekend, intruders entered the basement of the premises adjoining the plaintiffs' premises, knocked a hole through the wall separating that basement from the plaintiffs' basement, and stole some knitwear belonging to the plaintiffs from their basement. The plaintiffs brought an

g   action against the defendants claiming damages for negligence. The Court of Appeal held that the claim failed. Waller and Oliver LJJ held that, although it was a foreseeable possibility that thieves might gain access through the defendants' property to the plaintiffs' property, the defendants were not reasonably bound to foresee as the natural and probable consequence of their omission to secure their premises that persons over whom they had no control would steal the plaintiffs' goods. My noble and learned friend

h   Lord Goff, as Robert Goff LJ, gave the third judgment (see [1983] 3 All ER 161 at 171–172, [1984] QB 342 at 358–360). He quoted from Dixon J in *Smith v Leurs* (1945) 70 CLR 256 at 262, a passage which was cited with approval in *Home Office v Dorset Yacht Co Ltd*. The full passage, cited in the *Dorset Yacht Co Ltd* case [1970] 2 All ER 294 at 307, [1970] AC 1004 at 1038, is:

> 'But, apart from vicarious responsibility, one man may be responsible to another
j   for the harm done to the latter by a third person; he may be responsible on the ground that the act of the third person could not have taken place but for his own fault or breach of duty. There is more than one description of duty the breach of which may produce this consequence. For instance, it may be a duty of care in reference to things involving special danger. It may even be a duty of care with

reference to the control of actions or conduct of the third person. It is, however, exceptional to find in the law a duty to control another's actions to prevent harm to strangers. The general rule is that one man is under no duty of controlling another man to prevent his doing damage to a third. There are, however, special relations which are the source of a duty of his nature.'

(See 70 CLR 256 at 261–262.)

Robert Goff LJ continued:

'It is of course true that in the present case [the plaintiffs] do not allege that [the defendants] should have controlled the thieves who broke into their storeroom. But they do allege that [the defendants] should have exercised reasonable care to prevent them from gaining access through their own premises; and in my judgment the statement of principle by Dixon J is equally apposite in such a case. I know of no case where it has been held, in the absence of a special relationship, that the defendant was liable in negligence for having failed to prevent a third party from wrongfully causing damage to the plaintiff.'

Earlier he had made reference to *Stansbie v Troman* [1948] 1 All ER 599, [1948] 2 KB 48, in which a decorator who had contracted to carry out work in the plaintiff's home went out for a time when no one else was in the house, leaving the door unsecured. In consequence, a thief entered and removed some of the plaintiff's property from the house and the plaintiff succeeded in recovering damages against the decorator. There was in that case no special relationship between the decorator and the thief although there was a contract between the decorator and the plaintiff. I should have thought that, on the same facts, a guest of the plaintiff's who had left property in the house, if it had been stolen, might also have succeeded in recovering damages in respect of that theft from the decorator. That case proceeded on the basis that the decorator was liable because it was as 'a direct result of his negligence that the thief got in through this door which was left unlocked' (see [1948] 1 All ER 599 at 600, [1948] 2 KB 48 at 52 per Tucker LJ). I think it could be said that the purpose of the security arrangements at the door of the house was to prevent unlawful intrusion, that a reasonable man, in the decorator's position, would have secured the door, and that, on anlaysis, his reason for doing so would be to prevent the consequence which he ought reasonably to foresee of unauthorised intrusion and theft from the house whose door it was. On the other hand, if the thief, instead of confining his attention to the house whose door it was, bored a hole through the wall into the house next door, and stole items from the adjoining proprietor, assuming the first house was in a terrace or semi-detached, I consider that the decorator would not be liable in respect of the adjoining proprietor's loss, in the absence of circumstances from which this was shown to be reasonably foreseeable.

If the proprietor of the first house returned in time to find the thief boring a hole in the wall with the intention of effecting entry to the adjoining house, in the light of the decision in *Sedleigh-Denfield v O'Callagan (Trustees for St Joseph's Society for Foreign Missions)* [1940] 3 All ER 349, [1940] AC 880 I consider the first proprietor would be under a duty of care to the second proprietor to take what reasonable steps were open to him to cause the boring to cease. In some sense a thief who goes through one proprietor's property in order to reach the adjoining property of his neighbour creates a special relationship between himself and the first proprietor as a user of the first proprietor's land. In my opinion, therefore, the reason that in the circumstances of *P Perl (Exporters) Ltd v Camden London BC* [1983] 3 All ER 161, [1984] QB 342 no duty was owed by the defendants to Perl was that the defendants were not bound as reasonable occupiers to foresee that, if they took no steps to improve the security of their property, a probable consequence of that was that thieves would first unlawfully enter their property and then, by making an opening in the dividing wall or otherwise, use the defendants' property to make an entry into the property of Perl for the purpose of stealing goods belonging to Perl. Although a

duty to prevent a person from unlawfully entering my property may, in a sense, be
described as a duty to control that person, I would not consider this a very natural use of
the word 'control'. Control signifies, to my mind, a more extended relationship than
would be involved in simply keeping another off my property. If this be right, the duty
alleged by Perl to be incumbent on Camden was a duty falling under the earlier part of
Dixon J's dictum, as giving rise to responsibility on the ground that the act of the thief
could not have taken place but for the fault or breach of duty of the defendant but not to
a duty of care with reference to the control of actions or conduct of the thief. Like Oliver
LJ in the *Perl* case, I would regard the mode of entry in question in that case to the
plaintiffs' premises as a foreseeable possibility and no more, and in my view, that
reasoning amply supports the decision of the Court of Appeal in the *Perl* case.

The somewhat analogous case of *Squires v Perth and Kinross DC* 1986 SLT 30, to which
I have already referred, in the Second Division of the Court of Session, so far as it was
based on the fact that the defending contractors, having by their work seriously reduced
the security of the flat above the shop premises, failed to take adequate steps temporarily
to secure it when they were absent, was decided by an application of what, in my opinion,
was the correct test. Like Lord Dunpark, I have the greatest difficulty in seeing, in view
of the mode of entry which the thief actually used, that the alleged breach of duty was in
any way related to the particular manner in which the theft occurred.

The decision in the *Perl* case was applied in *King v Liverpool City Council* [1986] 3 All ER
544, [1986] 1 WLR 890, in which the question of damage by vandals to property again
arose. The plaintiff was the tenant of a flat in a block of flats owned by the defendants.
When the flat immediately above the plaintiff's flat became vacant, she requested the
defendants to board it up so as to secure it against intruders. The defendant took no
effective steps to secure the upper flat and on three occasions vandals broke in and
damaged water pipes in that flat allowing water to escape down into the plaintiff's flat
where it caused damage. The plaintiff claimed damages against the defendants, alleging
that they owed her a duty of care so to secure the vacant flat as to prevent vandals gaining
access to it. The trial judge found that it would not have been possible to take effective
steps in the situation disclosed in the evidence which could defeat the activities of vandals
and dismissed the plaintiff's claim. The plaintiff appealed.

The Court of Appeal (Purchas, Nicholls LJJ and Caulfield J) dismissed the appeal. After
referring to a number of authorities, Purchas LJ said ([1986] 3 All ER 544 at 552–553,
[1986] 1 WLR 890 at 901):

> 'The judge's finding is, in my judgment, determinative of this appeal.
> Summarising his judgment, he said: "Regrettably . . . I find that it is not possible for
> effective steps to be taken in a situation like this which could defeat the activities of
> vandals." Whether this finding, together with the established circumstances of the
> defendants, should operate to restrict the ambit of the duty to take any positive steps
> to secure the property, or duty arising in relation to an omission to take such steps;
> or whether it operates to break the chain of causation, may, as Robert Goff LJ
> suggested in the passage which I have just cited from [*Paterson Zochonis & Co Ltd v
> Merfarken Packaging Ltd* (1982) [1986] 3 All ER 522 at 540–542], not be essentially
> material. Personally I prefer the former approach and would limit the area of the
> duty itself in the circumstances prevailing in this case. In either event, in my
> judgment the judge was right to hold that the council owed no duty to the plaintiff
> in respect of the acts of the vandals in this case and accordingly I would dismiss this
> appeal.'

Nicholls LJ agreed but added ([1986] 3 All ER 544 at 553, [1986] 1 WLR 890 at 901–
902), in relation to an argument for the plaintiff that *King's* case was to be distinguished
from the *Perl* case:

> 'I am unable to accept that any material ground of distinction exists between the

two cases. In the *Perl* case, as in the instant case, the plaintiff sought to make the defendant occupier liable in negligence for the wrongdoing of a third party. In his *a* judgment Robert Goff LJ ([1983] 3 All ER 161 at 171–172, [1984] QB 342 at 359) set out . . . some examples of circumstances where there may be liability for a third party's wrongdoing, and concluded that those instances were very different from that case where, as in the present case, the allegation was that the defendant failed to exercise reasonable care to prevent a third party from causing damage to the plaintiff. In his preface to that passage Robert Goff LJ assumed that there might well *b* be cases where the occupier could reasonably foresee that thieves might use the unprotected property as a means of access to neighbouring property. But he, in common with the other members of the court, rejected the existence of the broad duty of care contended for by the plaintiff's counsel, and his conclusion was to the effect that in the absence of a special relationship, there was no duty to prevent thieves from so using one's property. I cannot see any distinction in principle *c* between a case where the damage arises from the third party using the defendant's property as a means of obtaining unauthorised access to the plaintiff's property and there committing theft, and one where the damage arises from a third party so conducting himself on the defendant's property as to damage the plaintiff's property by causing water to escape from the former property to the latter. Nor can I see that it is material that the defendant had a responsibility to take reasonable steps to *d* prevent the escape from its property of water in an ordinary domestic water system. I do not consider that there is a greater responsibility on the defendant because the third party caused damage by creating an escape of water than if the damage had been caused by the third party lighting a fire on the defendant's property or, if the defendant's property had been on the top floor of the building, by the third party stripping lead from the roof and thereby permitting rain to enter and eventually to *e* reach and damage the plaintiff's property.'

Caulfield J agreed with both judgments.

The conclusion of fact that no effective precautions on the lines suggested by the plaintiff could be taken by the defendants to prevent the damage suffered by the plaintiff was amply sufficient to justify the conclusion reached by the Court of Appeal in *King v* *f* *Liverpool City Council*. Leave to appeal to this House from the decision was refused to the plaintiff.

However, while it may well be true that no distinction of legal principle falls to be made between the various cases referred to by Nicholls LJ, I consider that there may be important differences in the facts which could justify different results.

Cases of theft where the thief uses a neighbour's premises to gain access to the premises *g* of the owner of the stolen goods are, in my opinion, in an important respect different from cases of fire such as that with which your Lordships are concerned in the present appeal. In the case of fire, a hazard is created on the first occupier's premises and it is that hazard which operating from the first occupier's premises creates danger to the neighbouring properties. As I have said, even though that hazard is created by the act of a trespasser on the first premises the occupier of these premises, once he knows of the *h* physical facts giving rise to the hazard, has a duty to take reasonable care to prevent the hazard causing damage to neighbouring properties. In the ordinary case of theft where the thief uses the first proprietor's property only as an access to the property of the person from whom the stolen property is taken there is no similar hazard on the first proprietor's land which causes the damage to the neighbouring property. Success of the theft depends very much on its mode and occasion being unexpected. The only danger consists in the *j* thief or thieves who, having passed from trespassing on the first proprietor's property, go on to trespass on his neighbour's. There is also a sense in which neighbouring proprietors can, independently, take action to protect themselves against theft in a way that is not possible with fire. Once the fire had taken hold on Littlewoods' building, St Paul's a proprietors could not be expected to take effective steps to prevent sparks being showered over on their property. On the other hand, in the jewellery case (*Squires v Perth and Kinross DC* 1986 SLT 30) there was no reason why the pursuers if they had anticipated the risk of theft as sufficiently serious should not have had a burglar alarm which would prove effective to warn of burglars whatever their mode of entry although this would not, of itself, prevent their entry.

b Where the question is whether or not the duty to take a particular precaution is incumbent on a defendant, the probability of the risk emerging is not the only consideration, as was pointed out by Lord Reid giving the opinion of the Board in *The Wagon Mound (No 2), Overseas Tankship (UK) Ltd v Miller Steamship Co Pty Ltd* [1966] 2 All ER 709 at 718, [1967] 1 AC 617 at 642–643 in reference to *Bolton v Stone* [1951] 1 All ER 1078, [1951] AC 850. Lord Reid said:

c 'The House of Lords held that the risk was so small that in the circumstances a reasonable man would have been justified in disregarding it and taking no steps to eliminate it. It does not follow that, no matter what the circumstances may be, it is justifiable to neglect a risk of such a small magnitude. A reasonable man would only neglect such a risk if he had some valid reason for doing so: e.g., that it would involve considerable expense to eliminate the risk. He would weigh the risk against the difficulty of eliminating it. If the activity which caused the injury to Miss Stone

d had been an unlawful activity there can be little doubt but that *Bolton v. Stone* would have been decided differently. In their lordships' judgment *Bolton v. Stone* did not alter the general principle that a person must be regarded as negligent if he does not take steps to eliminate a risk which he knows or ought to know is a real risk and not a mere possibility which would never influence the mind of a reasonable man.

e What that decision did was to recognise and give effect to the qualification that it is justifiable not to take steps to eliminate a real risk if it is small and if the circumstances are such that a reasonable man, careful of the safety of his neighbour, would think it right to neglect it.'

In my opinion this observation demonstrates that, when the word 'probable' is used in this context in the authorities, it is used as indicating a real risk as distinct from a mere

f possibility of danger. It is not used in the sense that the consequence must be more probable than not to happen, before it can be reasonably foreseeable. And again, in *Goldman v Hargrave* [1966] 2 All ER 989 at 995–996, [1967] 1 AC 645 at 662–663, Lord Wilberforce giving the opinion of the board, referring to a number of textbooks as well as an article by Dr A L Goodhart, says:

g 'All of these endorse the development, which their lordships find in the decisions, towards a measured duty of care by occupiers to remove or reduce hazards to their neighbours. So far it has been possible to consider the existence of a duty, in general terms; but the matter cannot be left there without some definition of the scope of his duty. How far does it go? What is the standard of the effort required? What is the position as regards expenditure? It is not enough to say merely that these must

h be "reasonable" since what is reasonable to one man may be very unreasonable, and indeed ruinous, to another: the law must take account of the fact that the occupier on whom the duty is cast, has, ex hypothesi, had this hazard thrust on him through no seeking or fault of his own. His interest, and his resources whether physical or material, may be of a very modest character either in relation to the magnitude of the hazard, or as compared with those of his threatened neighbour. A rule which

i required of him in such unsought circumstances in his neighbour's interest a physical effort of which he is not capable, or an excessive expenditure of money, would be unenforceable or unjust. One may say in general terms that the existence of a duty must be based on knowledge of the hazard, ability to foresee the consequences of not checking or removing it, and the ability to abate it. Moreover in many cases, as for example in SCRUTTON, L.J.'s hypothetical case of stamping out a fire [see *Job Edwards Ltd v Birmingham Navigations* [1924] 1 KB 341 at 357] or the *a* present case, where the hazard could have been removed with little effort and no expenditure, no problem arises; but other cases may not be so simple. In such situations the standard ought to be to require of the occupier what it is reasonable to expect of him in his individual circumstances. Thus, less must be expected of the infirm than of the able bodied: the owner of a small property where a hazard arises which threatens a neighbour with substantial interests should not have to do so *b* much as one with larger interests of his own at stake and greater resources to protect them: if the small owner does what he can and promptly calls on his neighbour to provide additional resources, he may be held to have done his duty: he should not be liable unless it is clearly proved that he could, and reasonably in his individual circumstances should, have done more.'

My Lords, I think it is well to remember as Lord Radcliffe pointed out in *Bolton v Stone* *c* [1951] 1 All ER 1078 at 1087, [1951] AC 850 at 868–869:

'. . . a breach of duty has taken place if [the facts] show the appellants guilty of a failure to take reasonable care to prevent the accident. One may phrase it a "reasonable care" or "ordinary care" or "proper care"—all these phrases are to be found in decisions of authority—but the fact remains that, unless there has been *d* something which a reasonable man would blame as falling beneath the standard of conduct that he would set for himself and require of his neighbour, there has been no breach of legal duty . . .'

This is the fundamental principle and in my opinion various factors will be taken into account by the reasonable man in considering cases involving fire on the one hand and *e* theft on the other, but since this is the principle the precise weight to be given to these factors in any particular case will depend on the circumstances and rigid distinctions cannot be made between one type of hazard and another. I consider that much must depend on what the evidence shows is done by ordinary people in like circumstances to those in which the claim of breach of duty arises.

In my view, if the test of the standard of the reasonable man is applied to the steps an *f* occupier of property must take to protect neighbouring properties from the hazard of fire arising on his property no further consideration of policy arises that should lessen the responsibility of the occupier in a case such as this.

The broad submission of counsel for Littlewoods does not therefore add anything to his narrow submission in the circumstances of this case since, in my opinion, no undue burdens are put on property occupiers by the application of the principle of *Donoghue v* *g* *Stevenson* [1932] AC 562, [1932] All ER Rep 1, nor is there any undue interference with the freedom of a person to use his property as he pleases.

In my opinion, these appeals should be refused and the interlocutors of the First Division affirmed. The appellants must pay Littlewoods' costs of the appeals.

LORD GOFF OF CHIEVELEY. My Lords, the Lord President (Lord Emslie) founded *h* his judgment on the proposition that the defenders, who were both owners and occupiers of the cinema, were under a general duty to take reasonable care for the safety of premises in the neighbourhood.

Now if this proposition is understood as relating to a general duty to take reasonable care *not to cause damage* to premises in the neighbourhood (as I believe that the Lord *j* President intended it to be understood) then it is unexceptionable. But it must not be overlooked that a problem arises when the pursuer is seeking to hold the defender responsible for having failed to *prevent* a third party from causing damage to the pursuer or his property by the third party's own deliberate wrongdoing. In such a case, it is not possible to invoke a general duty of care; for it is well recognised that there is no *general* duty of care to prevent third parties from causing such damage. The point is expressed

a very clearly in Hart and Honoré *Causation in the Law* (2nd edn, 1985) p 196, where the authors state:

> 'The law might acknowledge a general principle that, whenever the harmful conduct of another is reasonably foreseeable, it is our duty to take precautions against it . . . But, up to now, no legal system has gone so far as this . . .'

b The same point is made in Fleming *The Law of Torts* (6th edn, 1983) p 200, where it is said: '. . . there is certainly no *general* duty to protect others against theft or loss.' (Fleming's emphasis.)

I wish to add that no such general duty exists even between those who are neighbours in the sense of being occupiers of adjoining premises. There is no general duty on a householder that he should act as a watchdog, or that his house should act as a bastion, to

c protect his neighbour's house.

Why does the law not recognise a general duty of care to prevent others from suffering loss or damage caused by the deliberate wrongdoing of third parties? The fundamental reason is that the common law does not impose liability for what are called pure omissions. If authority is needed for this proposition, it is to be found in the speech of Lord Diplock in *Home Office v Dorset Yacht Co Ltd* [1970] 2 All ER 294 at 326, [1970] AC

d 1004 at 1060, where he said:

> 'The very parable of the good Samaritan (Luke 10:30) which was evoked by Lord Atkin in *Donoghue v Stevenson* [1932] AC 562, [1932] All ER Rep 1 illustrates, in the conduct of the priest and of the Levite who passed by on the other side, an omission which was likely to have as its reasonable and probable consequence damage to the
>
> e health of the victim of the thieves, but for which the priest and Levite would have incurred no civil liability in English law.'

Lord Diplock then proceeded to give examples which show that, carried to extremes, this proposition may be repugnant to modern thinking. It may therefore require one day to be reconsidered especially as it is said to provoke an 'invidious comparison with affirmative duties of good-neighbourliness in most countries outside the Common Law

f orbit' (see Fleming *The Law of Torts* (6th edn, 1983) p 138). But it is of interest to observe that, even if we do follow the example of those countries, in all probability we will, like them, impose strict limits on any such affirmative duty as may be recognised. In one recent French decision, the condition was imposed that the danger to the claimant must be 'grave, imminent, constant . . . nécessitant une intervention immédiate', and that such an intervention must not involve any 'risque pour le prévenu ou pour un tiers': see

g Lawson and Markesinis *Tortious Liability for Unintentional Harm in the Common Law and the Civil Law* (1982) vol 1, pp 74–75. The latter requirement is consistent with our own law, which likewise imposes limits on steps required to be taken by a person who is under an *affirmative* duty to prevent harm being caused by a source of danger which has arisen without his fault (see *Goldman v Hargrave* [1966] 2 All ER 989, [1967] 1 AC 645), a point

h to which I shall return later. But the former requirement indicates that any affirmative duty to prevent deliberate wrongdoing by third parties, if recognised in English law, is likely to be strictly limited. I mention this because I think it important that we should realise that problems like that in the present case are unlikely to be solved by a simple abandonment of the common law's present strict approach to liability for pure omissions.

Another statement of principle, which has been much quoted, is the observation of

j Lord Sumner in *Weld-Blundell v Stephens* [1920] AC 956 at 986, [1920] All ER Rep 32 at 47:

> 'In general . . . even though A. is in fault, he is not responsible for injury to C. which B., a stranger to him, deliberately chooses to do.'

This dictum may be read as expressing the general idea that the voluntary act of another, independent of the defender's fault, is regarded as a novus actus interveniens which, to use the old metaphor, 'breaks the chain of causation'. But it also expresses a general perception that we ought not to be held responsible in law for the deliberate wrongdoing of others. Of course, if a duty of care is imposed to guard against deliberate wrongdoing by others, it can hardly be said that the harmful effects of such wrongdoing are not caused by such breach of duty. We are therefore thrown back to the duty of care. But one thing is clear, and that is that liability in negligence for harm caused by the deliberate wrongdoing of others cannot be founded simply on foreseeability that the pursuer will suffer loss or damage by reason of such wrongdoing. There is no such general principle. We have therefore to identify the circumstances in which such liability may be imposed.

That there are special circumstances in which a defender may be held responsible in law for injuries suffered by the pursuer through a third party's deliberate wrongdoing is not in doubt. For example, a duty of care may arise from a relationship between the parties which gives rise to an imposition or assumption of responsibility on or by the defender, as in *Stansbie v Troman* [1948] 1 All ER 599, [1948] 2 KB 48, where such responsibility was held to arise from a contract. In that case a decorator, left alone on the premises by the householder's wife, was held liable when he went out leaving the door on the latch and a thief entered the house and stole property. Such responsibility might well be held to exist in other cases where there is no contract, as for example where a person left alone in a house has entered as a licensee of the occupier. Again, the defender may be vicariously liable for the third party's act; or he may be held liable as an occupier to a visitor on his land. Again, as appears from the dictum of Dixon J in *Smith v Leurs* (1945) 70 CLR 256 at 262, a duty may arise from a special relationship between the defender and the third party, by virtue of which the defender is responsible for controlling the third party: see, for example, *Home Office v Dorset Yacht Co Ltd*. More pertinently, in a case between adjoining occupiers of land, there may be liability in nuisance if one occupier causes or permits persons to gether on his land, and they impair his neighbour's enjoyment of his land. Indeed, even if such persons come onto his land as trespassers, the occupier may, if they constitute a nuisance, be under an affirmative duty to abate the nuisance. As I pointed out in *P Perl (Exporters) Ltd v Camden London BC* [1983] 3 All ER 161 at 172, [1984] QB 342 at 359, there may well be other cases.

These are all special cases. But there is a more general circumstance in which a defender may be held liable in negligence to the pursuer, although the immediate cause of the damage suffered by the pursuer is the deliberate wrongdoing of another. This may occur where the defender negligently causes or permits to be created a source of danger, and it is reasonably foreseeable that third parties may interfere with it and, sparking off the danger, thereby cause damage to persons in the position of the pursuer. The classic example of such a case is, perhaps, *Haynes v Harwood* [1935] 1 KB 146, [1934] All ER Rep 103, where the defendant's carter left a horse-drawn van unattended in a crowded street and the horses bolted when a boy threw a stone at them. A police officer who suffered injury in stopping the horses before they injured a woman and children was held to be entitled to recover damages from the defendant. There, of course, the defendant's servant had created a source of danger by leaving his horses unattended in a busy street. Many different things might have caused them to bolt, a sudden noise or movement, for example, or, as happened, the deliberate action of a mischievous boy. But all such events were examples of the very sort of thing which the defendant's servant ought reasonably to have foreseen and to have guarded against by taking appropriate precautions. In such a case, Lord Sumner's dictum in *Weld-Blundell v Stephens* [1920] AC 956 at 986, [1920] All ER Rep 32 at 47 can have no application to exclude liability.

Haynes v Harwood was a case concerned with the creation of a source of danger in a public place. We are concerned in the present case with an allegation that the defenders should be held liable for the consequences of deliberate wrongdoing by others who were trespassers on the defenders' property. In such a case it may be said that the defenders are entitled to use their property as their own and so should not be held liable if, for example, trespassers interfere with dangerous things on their land. But this is, I consider, too sweeping a proposition. It is well established that an occupier of land may be liable to a trespasser who has suffered injury on his land; though in *British Rlys Board v Herrington* [1972] 1 All ER 749, [1972] AC 877, in which the nature and scope of such liability was reconsidered by your Lordships' House, the standard of care so imposed on occupiers was drawn narrowly so as to take proper account of the rights of occupiers to enjoy the use of their land. It is, in my opinion, consistent with the existence of such liability that an occupier who negligently causes or permits a source of danger to be created on his land, and can reasonably foresee that third parties may trespass on his land and, interfering with the source of danger, may spark it off, thereby causing damage to the person or property of those in the vicinity, should be held liable to such a person for damage so caused to him. It is useful to take the example of a fire hazard, not only because that is the relevant hazard which is alleged to have existed in the present case, but also because of the intrinsically dangerous nature of fire hazards as regards neighbouring property. Let me give an example of circumstances in which an occupier of land might be held liable for damage so caused. Suppose that a person is deputed to buy a substantial quantity of fireworks for a village fireworks display on Guy Fawkes night. He stores them, as usual, in an unlocked garden shed abutting onto a neighbouring house. It is well known that he does this. Mischievous boys from the village enter as trespassers and, playing with the fireworks, cause a serious fire which spreads to and burns down the neighbouring house. Liability might well be imposed in such a case; for, having regard to the dangerous and tempting nature of fireworks, interference by naughty children was the very thing which, in the circumstances, the purchaser of the fireworks ought to have guarded against.

But liability should only be imposed under this principle in cases where the defender has negligently caused or permitted the creation of a source of danger on his land, and where it is foreseeable that third parties may trespass on his land and spark it off, thereby damaging the pursuer or his property. Moreover, it is not to be forgotten that, in ordinary households in this country, there are nowadays many things which might be described as possible sources of fire if interfered with by third parties, ranging from matches and firelighters to electric irons and gas cookers and even oil-fired central heating systems. These are commonplaces of modern life; and it would be quite wrong if householders were to be held liable in negligence for acting in a socially acceptable manner. No doubt the question whether liability should be imposed on defenders in a case where a source of danger on his land has been sparked off by the deliberate wrongdoing of a third party is a question to be decided on the facts of each case, and it would, I think, be wrong for your Lordships' House to anticipate the manner in which the law may develop; but I cannot help thinking that cases where liability will be so imposed are likely to be very rare.

There is another basis on which a defender may be held liable for damage to neighbouring property caused by a fire started on his (the defender's) property by the deliberate wrongdoing of a third party. This arises where he has knowledge or means of knowledge that a third party has created or is creating a risk of fire, or indeed has started a fire, on his premises, and then fails to take such steps as are reasonably open to him (in the limited sense explained by Lord Wilberforce in *Goldman v Hargrave* [1966] 2 All ER 989 at 995–996, [1967] 1 AC 645 at 663–664) to prevent any such fire from damaging neighbouring property. If, for example, an occupier of property has knowledge, or means of knowledge, that intruders are in the habit of trespassing on his property and starting fires there, thereby creating a risk that fire may spread to and damage neighbouring property, a duty to take reasonable steps to prevent such damage may be held to fall on him. He could, for example, take reasonable steps to keep the intruders out. He could also inform the police; or he could warn his neighbours and invite their assistance. If the defender is a person of substantial means, for example a large public company, he might even be expected to employ some agency to keep a watch on the

premises. What is reasonably required would, of course, depend on the particular facts
of the case. I observe that in *Goldman v Hargrave* such liability was held to sound in
nuisance; but it is difficult to believe that, in this respect, there can be any material
distinction between liability in nuisance and liability in negligence.

I turn to the authorities. Your Lordships were referred in the course of argument to
two Scottish cases concerned with fire hazards. The first was *Carrick Furniture House Ltd v
Paterson* 1978 SLT (Notes) 48. In that case, in allowing proof before answer, the Lord
Ordinary (Allanbridge) found on the facts that the building in question, which contained
considerable quantities of inflammable material, constituted a fire hazard, and that the
risk of a vandal setting fire to the premises was not too remote. The case is only briefly
reported; but it provides an indication that cases of this kind cannot normally be disposed
of on a plea to the relevancy but have to be allowed to go to proof. In the second case,
Thomas Graham & Co Ltd v Church of Scotland General Trustees 1982 SLT (Sh Ct) 26, Sheriff
Macvicar QC held that the defenders, who were occupiers of a disused church, were liable
to the pursuers whose neighbouring property suffered damage by reason of a fire started
in the church by unknown vandals. He relied, inter alia, on the facts: that the church
was situated in an area of Glasgow which was subject to vandalism on a large scale; that,
to the knowledge of the defenders, on a number of previous occasions vandals
had entered the church and caused damage there; that the vandals had also lit small fires in
the church, and that a responsible inspector had expressed the opinion that the building
was a serious fire hazard; that there was no evidence that the defenders, or anyone on
their behalf, had applied their minds to the question of fire hazard, and that there was
ample evidence to support the view that, if they had, and had taken advice on the matter,
they would have been told that the building was a serious fire risk; and that for two
months before the fire the building was not lockfast. I incline to the opinion that this
case can best be classified under the second of the two heads of liability to which I have
referred, on the basis that the defenders had the means of knowledge that a risk of fire
had been created or was being created by third parties on their land, and yet they did
nothing to prevent such risk of fire from damaging neighbouring property. The leading
Commonwealth case, in which an occupier of land was held liable for damage caused to
his neighbour's property by a fire which started on his own land without his fault (when
lightning struck a tall tree) and which he negligently failed to prevent from spreading
onto his neighbour's land, is *Goldman v Hargrave* itself. But a case more similar to the two
Scottish cases to which I have referred is perhaps the American case of *Torrack v
Corpamerica Inc* (1958) 144 A 2d 703, where it was alleged that the defendant's derelict
property was frequented by children and vagrants and had been condemned by the fire
marshal as a fire menace and that thereafter a fire was deliberately started by a third
person on the property which spread to and damaged the plaintiff's neighbouring
property; there the defendant's motion for summary judgment was denied. In so
holding, Judge Christie relied on earlier cases to the same effect, viz *Prince v Chehalis
Savings and Loan Association* (1936) 186 Wash 372, and *Arneil v Schnitzer* (1944) 173 Ore
179.

Turning to the facts of the present case, I cannot see that the defenders should be held
liable under either of these two possible heads of liability. First, I do not consider that the
empty cinema could properly be described as an unusual danger in the nature of a fire
hazard. As the Lord President pointed out (*Squires v Perth and Kinross DC* 1986 SLT 272
at 276):

'There was nothing about the building, so far as we know from the evidence, to
suggest that it could easily be set alight.'

This conclusion was, in my judgment, entirely justified on the evidence in the case; and
it is, I consider, fatal to any allegation that the defenders should be held liable on the
ground that they negligently caused or permitted the creation of an unusual source of
danger in the nature of a fire hazard.

a   Nor can I see that the defenders should be held liable for having failed to take reasonable steps to abate a fire risk created by third parties on their property without their fault. If there was any such fire risk, they had no means of knowing that it existed. If anybody (for example, the police) considered that there was such a risk they could and should have contacted the defenders (a well-known public company, whose particulars were given on a notice outside the cinema) by telephone to warn them of the situation; but they did not do so. But in any event, on the evidence, the existence of such a risk was

b   not established. As the Lord President observed (at 276–277):

> 'It is, in my opinion, significant that no witness who spoke about the increasing use of the cinema by intruding children, and the witnesses included the minister of St. Paul's Church, the session clerk and the beadle, and also Mr. Maloco, reported to the police or the defenders what they had observed. If it had crossed their minds that it was likely that the children would set fire to the building and put neighbouring properties at risk, it is inconceivable that they would not have taken immediate steps, by reporting to the police and the defenders, to bring the use of the premises by children to an end. My experience of life, which I am entitled to bring to bear as a juryman would, has not taught me that empty buildings to which vandals gain access, are likely to be set on fire by them . . .'

c

d   In the course of his argument before your Lordships, counsel for the appellants placed reliance on the decision of the Inner House of the Court of Session in *Squires v Perth and Kinross DC* 1986 SLT 30. That was a case concerned not with liability in respect of a fire hazard, but with liability in respect of a theft by a burglar who had gained access to the pursuer's jeweller's shop through a flat above, which was empty because it was being renovated by building contractors who were held to be in occupation of the flat. It was

e   held that the contractors, as occupiers, were liable in negligence to the pursuers for the loss of the jewellery stolen from the shop, on the ground that any person in occupancy and control of the flat above would have readily foreseen the likelihood of what in fact occurred. It appears that the fact that the flat above was empty was plainly apparent from, in particular, the presence of scaffolding at the front of the building; and complaints had been made on a number of occasions that the contractors did not keep

f   the flat secure, for example, because windows were left open and unglazed to accommodate scaffolding. It was a remarkable feature of the case that the burglar himself, one Sneddon, gave evidence at the trial; and it transpired from his evidence that, although his attention was drawn to the possibility of breaking into the jeweller's shop through the empty flat by seeing the scaffolding and open windows of the flat facing the High Street, he in fact approached the flat from behind, climbing over a building of about 12

g   to 15 feet high overall. He found the door into the yard behind the shop and flat unsecured, but nevertheless climbed over a wall into the yard and then climbed a drainpipe to a balcony, from which he entered the flat through a door which was open. Having entered the flat, he broke into the jeweller's shop through the floor of the flat and the ceiling of the shop. In these circumstances, assuming that the defenders were in

h   breach of duty in leaving the flat insecure, I feel, with all respect, serious doubts about the decision on the issue of causation, since it is difficult to imagine that an experienced and practised housebreaker, as Sneddon was held to be, would have been deterred from entering the flat even if the door on the balcony had been secured. I am not surprised therefore to find that Lord Dunpark shared the same doubts (at 40). Furthermore, I find it difficult to understand why the question of contributory negligence on the part of the

j   pursuers was not considered. The pursuers were just as aware of the risk as the defenders were; yet, although (as was found) an alarm system is often fitted to the roof of premises such as those of the pursuers, and is relatively inexpensive, they did not take this precaution. They seem to have assumed that, although it was their shop which was likely to attract thieves, they were entitled to rely on the contractors working above, rather than on themselves, to prevent thieves entering through the ceiling of the shop. Indeed, if it had been thought appropriate, in the circumstances, to employ a watchman to guard the jeweller's shop, the pursuers would apparently have considered that that expense should fall not on themselves but on the contractors working above. I do not think that that can be right.

In truth the case raises a more fundamental question, which is whether an occupier is under a general duty of care to occupiers of adjacent premises to keep his premises lockfast in order to prevent thieves entering his premises and thereby gaining access to the adjacent premises. Let us suppose that in *Squires v Perth and Kinross DC*, the defenders had expressly warned the pursuers, by notice, that extensive work was going to be done to the flat above, and that this would mean that for a period of time scaffolding would be erected and all the windows of the flat would be removed. Would it then be objectionable that the pursuers should have to look to their own defences against thieves, in the light of these circumstances? I do not think so. Then, should it make any difference that no such notice was given, but it was obvious what the contractors were doing? Again, I do not think so. Then, suppose that the occupiers of the flat above the shop were an ordinary family and, when they went away on holiday, in all the hustle and bustle of getting their children and animals and possessions into their car, they forgot to lock their front door. While they were away a passing thief, seeing that the flat was unoccupied because the curtains were drawn, went up and tried the front door and, finding it unlocked, gained access to the flat and thence entered the jeweller's shop below and robbed it. Should the occupiers of the flat be held liable to the jewellers in negligence? Again, I do not think so; and I add that I do not think that it would make any difference that it was well known that burglars were operating in the neighbourhood. It is not difficult to multiply these homely examples of cases where a thief may gain access to a house or flat which is not lockfast: for example, where an old lady goes out to spend the day with her married daughter and leaves a ground floor window open for her cat; or where a stone deaf asthmatic habitually sleeps with his bedroom window wide open at night; or where an elderly gentleman leaves his french windows open when he is weeding at the bottom of his garden, so that he can hear the telephone. For my part, I do not think that liability can be imposed on an occupier of property in negligence simply because it can be said that it is reasonably foreseeable, or even (having regard, for example, to some particular temptation to thieves in adjacent premises) that it is highly likely, that if he fails to keep his property lockfast a thief may gain access to his property and thence to the adjacent premises. So to hold must presuppose that the occupier of property is under a general duty to *prevent* thieves from entering his property to gain access to neighbouring property, where there is a sufficient degree of foresight that this may occur. But there is no general duty to *prevent* third parties from causing damage to others, even though there is a high degree of foresight that they may do so. The practical effect is that everybody has to take such steps as he thinks fit to protect his own property, whether house or flat or shop, against thieves. He is able to take his own precautions; and, in deciding what precautions to take, he can and should take into account the fact that, in the ordinary course of life, adjacent property is likely to be from time to time unoccupied (often obviously so, and sometimes for a considerable period of time) and is also likely from time to time not to be lockfast. He has to form his own judgment as to the precautions which he should take, having regard to all the circumstances of the case, including (if it be the case) the fact that his premises are a jeweller's shop which offers a special temptation to thieves. I must confess that I do not find this practical result objectionable. For these reasons I consider, with all respect, that *Squires v Perth and Kinross DC* was wrongly decided.

The present case is, of course, concerned with entry not by thieves but by vandals. Here the point can be made that, whereas an occupier of property can take precautions against thieves, he cannot (apart from insuring his property and its contents) take effective precautions against physical damage caused to his property by a vandal who has gained access to adjacent property and has there created a source of danger which has resulted in

a
damage to his property by, for example, fire or escaping water. Even so, the same difficulty arises. Suppose, taking the example I have given of the family going away on holiday and leaving their front door unlocked, it was not a thief but a vandal who took advantage of that fact; and that the vandal, in wrecking the flat, caused damage to the plumbing which resulted in a water leak and consequent damage to the shop below. Are the occupiers of the flat to be held liable in negligence for such damage? I do not think so, even though it may be well known that vandalism is prevalent in the neighbourhood.

b
The reason is the same, that there is no general duty to *prevent* third parties from causing damage to others, even though there is a high degree of foresight that this may occur. In the example I have given, it cannot be said that the occupiers of the flat have caused or permitted the creation of a source of danger (as in *Haynes v Harwood* [1935] 1 KB 146, [1934] All ER Rep 103 or in the example of the fireworks which I gave earlier) which they ought to have guarded against; nor of course were there any special circumstances

c
giving rise to a duty of care. The practical effect is that it is the owner of the damaged premises (or, in the vast majority of cases, his insurers) who is left with a worthless claim against the vandal, rather than the occupier of the property which the vandal entered (or his insurers), a conclusion which I find less objectionable than one which may throw an unreasonable burden on ordinary householders. For these reasons, I consider that both *Lamb v Camden London Borough* [1981] 2 All ER 408, [1981] QB 625 and *King v Liverpool*

d
City Council [1986] 3 All ER 544, [1986] 1 WLR 890 were rightly decided; but I feel bound to say, with all respect, that the principle propounded by Lord Wylie in *Evans v Glasgow DC* 1978 SLT 17 at 19, viz that there is—

> 'a general duty on owners or occupiers of property . . . to take reasonable care to see that it [is] proof against the kind of vandalism which was calculated to affect
e
> adjoining property,'

is, in my opinion, too wide.

I wish to emphasise that I do not think that the problem in these cases can be solved simply through the mechanism of foreseeability. When a duty *is* cast on a person to take precautions against the wrongdoing of third parties, the ordinary standard of foreseeability applies; and so the possibility of such wrongdoing does not have to be very great before

f
liability is imposed. I do not myself subscribe to the opinion that liability for the wrongdoing of others is limited because of the unpredictability of human conduct. So, for example, in *Haynes v Harwood* [1935] 1 KB 146, [1934] All ER Rep 103, liability was imposed although it cannot have been at all likely that a small boy would throw a stone at the horses left unattended in the public road, and in *Stansbie v Troman* [1948] 1 All ER 599, [1948] 2 KB 48 liability was imposed although it cannot have been at all likely that

g
a thief would take advantage of the fact that the defendant left the door on the latch while he was out. Per contra, there is at present no general duty at common law to prevent persons from harming others by their deliberate wrongdoing, however foreseeable such harm may be if the defender does not take steps to prevent it.

Of course, if persons trespass on the defender's property and the defender either knows

h
or has the means of knowing that they are doing so and that in doing so they constitute a danger to neighbouring property, then the defender may be under an affirmative duty to take reasonable steps to exclude them, in the limited sense explained by Lord Wilberforce in *Goldman v Hargrave* [1966] 2 All ER 989 at 995–996, [1967] 1 AC 645 at 663–664, but that is another matter. I incline to the opinion that this duty arises from the fact that the defender, as occupier, is in exclusive control of the premises on which

j
the danger has arisen.

In preparing this opinion, I have given careful consideration to the question whether *P Perl (Exporters) Ltd v Camden London BC* [1983] 3 All ER 161, [1984] QB 342, in which I myself was a member of the Court of Appeal, was correctly decided. I have come to the conclusion that it was, though on rereading it I do not think that my own judgment was very well expressed. But I remain of the opinion that to impose a general duty on occupiers to take reasonable care to prevent others from entering their property would impose an unreasonable burden on ordinary householders and an unreasonable curb on *a* the ordinary enjoyment of their property; and I am also of the opinion that to do so would be contrary to principle. It is very tempting to try to solve all problems of negligence by reference to an all-embracing criterion of foreseeability, thereby effectively reducing all decisions in this field to questions of fact. But this comfortable solution is, alas, not open to us. The law has to accommodate all the untidy complexity of life; and there are circumstances where considerations of practical justice impel us to reject a *b* general imposition of liability for foreseeable damage. An example of this phenomenon is to be found in cases of pure economic loss, where the so-called 'floodgates' argument (an argument recognised by Lord Blackburn as long ago as 1875 in *Cattle v Stockton Waterworks Co* LR 10 QB 453 at 457, [1874–80] All ER Rep 220 at 223, the force of which is accepted not only in common law countries but also in civil law countries such as the Federal Republic of Germany) compels us to recognise that to impose a general *c* liability based on a simple criterion of foreseeability would impose an intolerable burden on defendants. I observe that in *Junior Books Ltd v Veitchi Co Ltd* [1982] 3 All ER 201, [1983] 1 AC 520 some members of your Lordships' House succumbed, perhaps too easily, to the temptation to adopt a solution based simply on 'proximity.' In truth, in cases such as these, having rejected the generalised principle, we have to search for special cases in which, on narrower but still identifiable principles, liability can properly be imposed. *d* That is the task which I attempted to perform in *Leigh Sillavan Ltd v Aliakmon Shipping Co Ltd, The Aliakmon* [1985] 2 All ER 44, [1985] QB 350, by identifying a principle of transferred loss, a principle which has not, so far, achieved recognition by other members of your Lordships' House. As the present case shows, another example of this phenomenon is to be found in cases where the plaintiff has suffered damage through the deliberate wrongdoing of a third party; and it is not surprising that once again we should find the *e* courts seeking to identify specific situations in which liability can properly be imposed. Problems such as these are solved in Scotland, as in England, by means of the mechanism of the duty of care; though we have nowadays to appreciate that the broad general principle of liability for foreseeable damage is so widely applicable that the function of the duty of care is not so much to identify cases where liability is imposed as to identify those where it is not (see *Anns v Merton London Borough* [1977] 2 All ER 492 at 498–499, *f* [1978] AC 728 at 752 per Lord Wilberforce). It is perhaps not surprising that our brother lawyers in France find themselves able to dispense with any such concept, achieving practical justice by means of a simple concept of 'faute'. But since we all live in the same social and economic environment, and since the judicial function can, I believe, be epitomised as an educated reflex to facts, we find that, in civil law countries as in common law countries, not only are we beset by the same practical problems, but broadly speaking *g* we reach the same practical solutions. Our legal concepts may be different, and may cause us sometimes to diverge; but we have much to learn from each other in our common efforts to achieve practical justice founded on legal principle.

For these reasons I would dismiss these appeals.

Appeals dismissed.   *h*

Solicitors: *Denton Hall Burgin & Warrens*, agents for *Simpson & Marwick WS*, Edinburgh (for the appellants); *Herbert Smith & Co*, agents for *Brodies WS*, Edinburgh (for Littlewoods).

Mary Rose Plummer   Barrister.   *j*

John Fox (a firm) v Bannister King & Rigbeys (a firm)

COURT OF APPEAL, CIVIL DIVISION

SIR JOHN DONALDSON MR AND NICHOLLS LJ

15, 19 DECEMBER 1986

Solicitor – Undertaking – Undertaking given by one solicitor to another – Statement that defendants would retain sum in client account until plaintiffs had 'sorted everything out' – Defendants paying sum to client on his demand – Whether statement amounting to undertaking to plaintiffs – Whether payment to client breaching undertaking – Whether court would order defendants to compensate plaintiffs for their loss.

Solicitor – Undertaking – Summary jurisdiction – Material facts in issue to be resolved by court – Whether summary jurisdiction appropriate.

The plaintiffs were a firm of solicitors instructed by a client to undertake particular business. The same client also instructed the defendants, another firm of solicitors, to conduct different business, including the sale of certain property. Part of the money from that sale, some £18,000, was subsequently held by the defendants to the client's account. When the client failed to meet the plaintiffs' professional fees the plaintiffs obtained from him a form of authority authorising the defendants to give an undertaking that they would retain the £18,000 in their account for payment to the plaintiffs. The defendants wrote to the plaintiffs stating that they would retain the sum 'until you have sorted everything out'. Subsequently the plaintiffs requested the defendants to release the sum to them, but on the client's demand the defendants transferred the amount to him. Subsequently the client became bankrupt. The plaintiffs applied to the court to exercise its inherent jurisdiction over solicitors and to enforce the undertaking contained in the defendants' letter. The defendants contended, inter alia, that no undertaking had been given, that the words in their letter were ambiguous and that alternatively, if there had been such an undertaking, they had not acted in breach of it. The judge held that the words constituted an undertaking on which the plaintiffs had been entitled to rely and that the defendants had acted in breach of that undertaking. He accordingly ordered the defendants to pay the sum of £18,000 into a deposit account to the credit of the client to remain there until further order of the court. The defendants appealed, contending that the court's jurisdiction, as in proceedings for summary judgment under RSC Ord 14, was summary in nature and did not fall to be exercised in cases where there were triable issues of fact.

Held – The court's inherent jurisdiction over solicitors, although summary in nature, was not analogous to the jurisdiction which it exercised pursuant to RSC Ord 14. Accordingly, where material facts were in issue the court would still exercise its jurisdiction so long as it was satisfied that on the evidence before it the case against the solicitor had been clearly established. On the facts, the defendants had made a clear and unequivocal statement to the plaintiffs that they would retain the sum of money, and that statement constituted an undertaking given by the defendants as solicitors, and as officers of the court they were expected to abide by it. It followed that the defendants had breached that undertaking to the plaintiffs in paying the sum to the client and accordingly they were required to make good the plaintiffs' loss. However, since the client was bankrupt, it was inappropriate to order the defendants to pay the sum into an account to the client's credit or to pay the sum into a joint account or into court. The court would therefore direct an inquiry to determine the actual loss sustained by the plaintiffs, and any loss so established was to be made good by the defendants. To that extent the appeal would be allowed (see p 740 *j* to p 741 *b g*, p 742 *f* to *h* and p 743 *b* to *d j*, post).

Geoffrey Silver & Drake v Baines [1971] 1 All ER 473 considered.

Notes

For the liabilities of solicitors as officers of the Supreme Court generally, see 44 Halsbury's Laws (4th edn) para 252.

For liability on undertaking given as a solicitor, see ibid para 255, and for cases on the subject, see 44 Digest (Reissue) 410–420, 4470–4572.

Cases referred to in judgments

Grey, Re [1892] 2 QB 440, CA.

Marsh v Joseph [1897] 1 Ch 213, [1895–9] All ER Rep 977, CA.

Silver (Geoffrey) & Drake v Baines [1971] 1 All ER 473, [1971] 1 QB 396, [1971] 2 WLR 187, CA.

Solicitor, Re a [1966] 3 All ER 52, [1966] 1 WLR 1604.

United Mining and Finance Corp Ltd v Becher [1910] 2 KB 296, [1908–10] All ER Rep 876; *on appeal* [1911] 1 KB 840, CA.

Cases also cited

Gertrud, The (1927) 138 LT 239.

Solicitor, Re a, ex p Hales [1907] 2 KB 539, [1904–7] All ER Rep 1050, DC.

Appeal

The defendants, Bannister King & Rigbeys (a firm), appealed against the decision of his Honour Judge Tibber sitting as a judge of the High Court on 4 October 1985 whereby, in an action by the plaintiffs, John Fox (a firm), claiming payment of the sum of £18,000 wrongfully released by the defendants to Mr G J O Watts in breach of an undertaking given to the plaintiffs on 30 September 1982, he ordered that the defendants pay the sum of £18,000 into a deposit account to the credit of Mr Watts, such sum to remain there until disposed of by further order of the court. The facts are set out in the judgment of Nicholls LJ.

Roger Toulson QC and *Iain Hughes* for the defendants.
Anthony Cripps QC and *Susan Cooper* for the plaintiffs.

Cur adv vult

19 December. The following judgments were delivered.

NICHOLLS LJ (giving the first judgment at the invitation of Sir John Donaldson MR). This is a dispute between two firms of solicitors, both of whom at various times acted for a Mr Geoffrey Watts. The issue concerns a solicitor's undertaking said to have been given in 1982 by Mr J W Bannister, a partner in the defendant firm, to Mr John Fox, who is the senior partner of the plaintiff firm. Before the court is an appeal from a decision, given on 4 October 1985, of his Honour Judge Tibber sitting as a judge of the High Court.

From about the middle of 1981 the plaintiff firm, which I shall refer to simply as 'John Fox', acted as solicitors for Mr Watts and companies of his in various pieces of litigation, all of which eventually were compromised in July 1982. A substantial amount of complicated legal work had been involved, and John Fox's taxed fees and disbursements, including value added tax, amounted to £59,311. Mr Watts paid sums totalling £27,760 on account.

Mr Watts's previous solicitors had been the defendant firm, to which I will refer as 'Bannisters'. Mr Watts had been a client of that firm for some time. When John Fox started to act for Mr Watts they did not take over the conduct of all Mr Watts's affairs, and it was Bannisters, and not John Fox, who acted for Mr Watts in selling two properties

of his. One of these was known as King Street Coach Station, Stourbridge. The other was
a 14 Cemetery Road, Lye, Stourbridge.

Mr Fox was very anxious about his lack of security for his firm's costs. His firm had
incurred a substantial bank overdraft during the litigation. In February 1982 Mr Fox
obtained from Mr and Mrs Watts a charge over the Cemetery Road property, to secure
his liabilities to John Fox, but that charge ranked behind a first charge granted to a bank,
and it seems there was or will be no surplus remaining after discharging the liabilities to
b the bank. It seems that Mr Fox also obtained a charge over the King Street property but
that this was never registered.

In 1982 the King Street property was sold, but part of the purchase price was retained
by the purchaser pending the carrying out of demolition works on the site. In July 1982
Mr Fox obtained from Mr Watts a form of authority signed by him and addressed to
Bannisters. It read as follows:

c
'I Hereby authorise and request you to give an Undertaking to account to Messrs.
John Fox, Solicitors, of P.O. Box No. 2, Broadway, Worcestershire for the balance of
the Retention moneys in connection with the sale of the King Street Garage and also
the balance Proceeds of Sale of the Cemetery Road property.'

On 22 July 1982 John Fox sent that form of authority to Bannisters with a request for
d Bannisters' undertaking. Despite reminders from John Fox, the undertaking was not
forthcoming.

By the end of September the demolition work was finished. On 29 September Mr Fox
spoke to Mr Watts. Mr Watts, it seems, had had second thoughts about applying the
balance of the price of the King Street property in paying John Fox's costs and
disbursements and was considering using the money as a deposit for the purchase of an
e airfield. On the same day Mr Fox wrote an agitated letter to Mr Watts, reminding him
of how much was owing, and pointing out reasons why Mr Watts could not embark on
the purchase of the airfield. Mr Fox insisted that no part of the balance of the sale price
should be used for that purchase until his firm's costs had been paid, and he told Mr
Watts that he was asking Mr Bannister to account to Mr Fox for the proceeds 'in
accordance with the irrevocable authority he holds'.
f
I now come to the crucial day, 30 September. According to the undisputed affidavit
evidence, on that day Mr Bannister met Mr Fox and gave him a cheque for £11,500. Mr
Bannister retained £18,000, representing the balance of the proceeds after deducting
Bannisters' own costs. Mr Bannister retained that sum in accordance with instructions
given to him by Mr Watts. Mr Bannister told Mr Fox that he would not part with that
sum of £18,000 without referring to Mr Fox. When giving Mr Fox the cheque for
g £11,500 Mr Bannister also handed to Mr Fox a letter on Bannisters' headed paper, the
material part of which read as follows:

'... this leaves a balance in hand of £29,553.10 as I told you Geoff [Watts] wanted
me to retain the £18,000.00 and I enclose a cheque for £11,500.00 in your favour.
h I see your letter of the 29th September and no doubt you and Geoff will sort out as
to the £18,000.00 which is still in my account and which of course I shall retain
until you have sorted everything out.'

On the following day Mr Fox wrote to Mr Bannister thanking him for his efforts. He
sent Mr Bannister a copy of a further letter he had written to Mr Watts, on 1 October, in
j which he had said that unless Mr Watts authorised Mr Bannister to pay over to Mr Fox
the £18,000, he (Mr Fox) would do no further work for Mr Watts or his companies and
would commence proceedings to recover the balance due. Mr Fox commented to Mr
Bannister that so far there had been no response from Mr Watts, and added that he would
be grateful if Mr Bannister would kindly retain the £18,000 pending resolution of the
problem.

Mr Bannister's response to that letter, on 4 October, was to inform Mr Fox that he had
told Mr Watts that he would not part with the £18,000 until Mr Fox and Mr Watts had *a*
'decided what to do about this'.

Unfortunately Mr Fox was unable to sort out the position with Mr Watts. On 18
October Mr Watts wrote to Mr Bannister asking for payment of the £18,000, which he
proposed to use as a deposit for the purchase of the airfield, and three days later this was
followed by a further written demand, delivered by hand, from another firm of solicitors,
Messrs Cove & Co, acting for Mr Watts.   *b*

Meanwhile, on 19 October Mr Fox had written to Mr Bannister asking for the release
of the money to him in view of the original authority given by Mr Watts in July. On 21
October he followed this up with a letter asking Mr Bannister under no circumstances to
part with the £18,000.

By now Mr Watts's financial problems had become more pressing: an auction sale held
on 20 October of other properties belonging to Mr Watts or his companies had been *c*
unsuccessful, and a winding up petition had been presented against one of his companies.
Mr Watts was threatening to hold Bannisters liable for the loss if they held on to the
£18,000 and as a result his company was forced into liquidation. Bannisters considered
the matter and decided they had no alternative but to hand over the money to Mr Watts.
Whereupon, without reference to Mr Fox, they did so. John Fox then made efforts to
recover their unpaid costs from Mr Watts and his companies but without success. None *d*
of them has any money. Mr Watts is now bankrupt.

On 11 December 1984 John Fox issued an originating summons against Bannisters,
seeking an order for payment of the sum of £18,000 wrongfully released in breach of an
undertaking given on 30 September 1982 or, alternatively, damages for breach of the
undertaking. This was supported by an affidavit sworn by Mr Fox in December 1984,
and a short further affidavit sworn in September 1985. Bannisters adduced no evidence. *e*

The judge decided that the letter of 30 September 1982 from Mr Bannister to Mr Fox
contained an undertaking, which had subsequently been broken, and that Bannisters
should now put John Fox in the same position as if the undertaking had been honoured.
To achieve this he ordered that Bannisters should pay £18,000 into court or into a joint
deposit account to the credit of Mr Watts, that sum to remain there until further order *f*
of the court. He granted a stay pending appeal.

The basic principles applicable in the present case are not in doubt. The jurisdiction
being invoked here is the inherent jurisdiction which the Supreme Court has over
solicitors, who are its officers. It is a jurisdiction which is exercised, not for the purpose
of enforcing legal rights, but for the purpose of enforcing honourable conduct on the
part of the court's own officers: see *Re Grey* [1892] 2 QB 440 at 443 per Lord Esher MR.

One of the areas in which this principle falls to be applied is the enforcement of *g*
undertakings given by solicitors in their capacity as solicitors. As officers of the court
solicitors are expected to abide by undertakings given by them professionally, and if they
do not do so they may be called on summarily to make good their defaults: see *United
Mining and Finance Corp Ltd v Becher* [1910] 2 KB 296 at 305, [1908–10] All ER Rep 876
at 881 per Hamilton J. Where a solicitor, directly or indirectly, still has it in his power to *h*
do the act which he undertook to do, the court may order him to do that act. Where the
solicitor does not have it in his power, he may be ordered to make good the loss flowing
from his failure to perform the undertaking, as loss flowing from a breach of duty
committed by a solicitor as an officer of the court: see *Marsh v Joseph* [1897] 1 Ch 213 at
245, [1895–9] All ER Rep 977 at 981 per Lord Russell CJ.

So I turn to consider whether any undertaking was given in the present case by Mr *j*
Bannister and, if it was, whether it was given by him in his capacity as a solicitor.

In my view Mr Bannister did give an undertaking to Mr Fox. On 30 September 1982
Mr Bannister had in his possession money belonging to his client Mr Watts. He knew
that in instructing him to retain £18,000 and not pay that amount to Mr Fox, Mr Watts
was going back on the authority he had signed in July. Mr Bannister also knew that this

change of attitude was a matter of great concern to Mr Fox, who had been hoping for
a some time that this sum would be the source from which part of his outstanding bill
would be paid. When, in these circumstances, Mr Bannister wrote to Mr Fox in the terms
of his letter of 30 September, he made to Mr Fox a clear and unequivocal statement that
he would not part with the sum of £18,000. I can see no reason why Mr Fox was not
entitled to rely on that as a commitment by Mr Bannister. Mr Fox's evidence is that he
did rely on that undertaking as the security for counsel's outstanding fees which
b amounted to over £23,000. Moreover, that was a commitment given by Mr Bannister
in his capacity as a solicitor, for it was in that capacity he was holding the £18,000 in
question.

For Bannisters it was pointed out that both firms of solicitors knew that Mr Watts
wished the sum of £18,000 to be retained so that the money could be used as a deposit
for the airfield purchase. It was submitted that Mr Bannister had no authority to give
c any undertaking regarding this sum and, moreover, that Mr Fox knew this.

There are two separate points here. The first point is whether Mr Bannister had
authority from his client to give the undertaking and, if he did not, what is the
consequence of that in these proceedings. As to this, there is no evidence that Mr
Bannister was acting without authority, but in any event, whether Mr Bannister had
authority from Mr Watts is irrelevant to the question of whether he gave an undertaking
d to Mr Fox. Mr Bannister wrote the letter of 30 September. Whether his statement in that
letter amounted to an undertaking is a question of construction of that letter in the light
of the surrounding circumstances.

The second point is whether, even assuming Mr Bannister lacked authority, Mr Fox is
to be taken as having known of this and, if so, what would be the consequence of that in
these proceedings. As to this, I accept that if the circumstances were that when the
e undertaking was given Mr Fox was aware of Mr Bannister's lack of authority, this might
well have affected the attitude which the court would adopt to the undertaking in these
proceedings. But on the affidavit evidence I do not think that any such knowledge is
made out. Mr Fox knew that Mr Watts had countermanded his original instructions to
pay the money to Mr Fox, and that he had told Mr Bannister to hold on to the money.
Mr Fox knew, too, of Mr Watts's plans about the airfield deposit. But Mr Fox also knew
f that Mr Watts's plans in that regard were fraught with difficulties (and, indeed, the
money was never used as a deposit on the airfield). All in all, I am not satisfied that from
· these facts it would be right to infer that Mr Fox knew that Mr Bannister was acting
without authority in writing the letter of 30 September (if, indeed, that was the case).

Nor can I accept the further submission that the words relied on were not sufficiently
clear in their meaning to amount to a solicitor's undertaking. To my mind there is no
g material ambiguity. Mr Bannister stated that he would hold on to the money until Mr
Fox had come to some arrangement regarding it with their mutual client. This did not
mean, however, that if Mr Fox was unable to come to some such arrangement, Mr
Bannister's obligation would have continued indefinitely. Mr Bannister could have
terminated his obligation on giving reasonable notice to Mr Fox. So that, if Mr Watts
h sought payment, Mr Bannister would have been at liberty to pay over the money to him
but only after giving reasonable advance warning of this to Mr Fox, thus affording Mr
Fox an opportunity to take whatever steps he wished to protect his position. In this way
the object for which Mr Bannister's undertaking was given, to provide Mr Fox with some
immediate protection against the dissipation of the £18,000, would have been achieved
as intended at the time. (It will be recalled that at the same time as the cheque for
j £11,500 was handed over with the letter of 30 September, Mr Bannister had said to Mr
Fox that he would not part with the balance of £18,000 without referring to him.)

What, then, should now be done? The undertaking was broken. For Bannisters it was
submitted that, since the £18,000 has gone, the undertaking is incapable of performance.
It was submitted, in reliance on *Re a Solicitor* [1966] 3 All ER 52, [1966] 1 WLR 1604,
that in general the court will not make a committal order against a solicitor without first

ordering him to perform the undertaking, and that the court will not order a solicitor to
perform an undertaking which it is impossible for him to perform. *Re a Solicitor* was a   a
case where a solicitor was sought to be committed to prison for failing to comply with
certain undertakings given by him. Pennycuick J pointed out that in practice the court
makes an order on the solicitor to do the act which he had undertaken to do, and only if
the solicitor disobeys that order would a committal order be made (see [1966] 3 All ER
52 at 56, [1966] 1 WLR 1604 at 1608). But that case is no authority for the proposition
now being advanced, to the effect that if a solicitor undertakes not to part with a fund   b
and then in breach of his undertaking does so, the court is powerless to take any steps to
require the solicitor to make good his default, but must leave the party to whom the
undertaking was given to his remedy, if any, at law.

That said, however, the present case is not a straightforward one. The breach of the
undertaking occurred over four years ago, and the parties' positions have changed much
in the meantime. The £18,000 was paid to Mr Watts, and he is now bankrupt. Thus to   c
order Bannisters now to re-create a fund of £18,000, and place this in an account to the
credit of Mr Watts cannot, with all respect to the judge, be right. The one person who
can have no claim to the new fund is Mr Watts or his trusteee in bankruptcy. Again, if
the sum of £18,000 is ordered to be paid into a joint account or into court, what is the
issue between John Fox and Bannisters which will decide the entitlement to that fund?

I approach the matter in a different way. The purpose of the undertaking was as I have   d
sought to describe. What Mr Fox lost by the breach of the undertaking was the
opportunity to take whatever steps might have been open to him at the time to stop the
£18,000 being paid to Mr Watts and, ultimately, to have recourse to that money to meet
his bill. What those steps were, and whether they would have been successful, are not
matters canvassed adequately in the evidence in its present form. On the present evidence
I am not satisfied that, if the undertaking had been faithfully honoured, John Fox would   e
necessarily have obtained payment to them of the £18,000. Nor, conversely, am I
persuaded that they would necessarily have been left empty-handed.

That being so, I consider that the appropriate course is to direct an inquiry, in these
proceedings, as to what loss, if any, John Fox suffered by reason of the breach of the
undertaking. If, as contended by Bannisters, John Fox suffered no loss, Bannisters will   f
not be required to make any payment to John Fox. If, however, John Fox can prove loss
to the satisfaction of the master who will conduct the inquiry, it would only be right that
Bannisters as officers of the court should now make good to John Fox the amount of that ·
loss suffered as a result of the breach of the undertaking.

There is one final point I should add. Counsel for Bannisters submitted that to succeed
with an application such as this the applicant has to show he has a plain and obvious case,
and that where serious or difficult questions are involved, the case is not one appropriate g
to be dealt with under the court's summary jurisdiction over its officers. I am unable to
accept this submission expressed in such wide terms. If this submission were well
founded it would mean that if, for example, a dispute arose over whether a solicitor had
given an oral undertaking, or had given a written undertaking the only copy of which
had been destroyed or lost, the court would be precluded from investigating the matter.   h
That cannot be right. Since the jurisdiction is disciplinary as well as compensatory, the
court must be satisfied that there has been misconduct in that there has been a breach of
an undertaking given by the solicitor acting professionally. But, in an appropriate case,
the court can resolve issues of fact with the assistance of cross-examination of deponents.
If necessary, an order for discovery can be made. Again, if there is a dispute about the
true construction of a document, the court can resolve that issue having heard argument   j
on it.

The court, however, will always have in mind that a solicitor is not necessarily to be
regarded as having misconducted himself by failing to honour an undertaking when, for
example, the issue of whether the words amounted to an undertaking, or the further
issue of whether there has been a breach, turns on the answer to a fine or subtle point of

a construction. Likewise where there was real scope for genuine misunderstanding on what was said or meant by a solicitor on a particular occasion. In that sense this supervisory jurisdiction will only be exercised in a clear case.

b Moreover, although the court has the means to resolve disputed issues as mentioned above when exercising its summary jurisdiction over solicitors, the court will be careful to ensure that the solicitor defendant is not prejudiced by the course which is being followed in the circumstances of the particular case, and it will exercise the discretion which it has regarding this summary jurisdiction with that in mind.

None of that applies to this case. John Fox's evidence of the history, including what occurred on and after 30 September 1982, is clear and not disputed. To my mind this is a clear case.

c Accordingly I would uphold the judge's view that there was a breach of an undertaking given professionally by Mr Bannister, but allow the appeal to the extent of substituting for the judge's order for payment an order directing an inquiry in the terms I have indicated, with an order for payment of the sum found due in answer to that inquiry.

SIR JOHN DONALDSON MR. I agree with the judgment of Nicholls LJ and wish only to add a word on the nature of the 'summary' jurisdiction of the Supreme Court over solicitors as officers of that court.

d Counsel for Bannisters submitted that it was equivalent to the 'summary' jurisdiction under RSC Ord 14 and that, accordingly, if it could be shown that the solicitor had an arguable defence, the court should dismiss the application, leaving it to the applicant to bring such other 'normal' or 'non-summary' proceedings as he thought fit. He supported this argument by reference to the decision of this court in *Geoffrey Silver & Drake v Baines* *e* [1971] 1 All ER 473 at 475, [1971] 1 QB 396 at 402 in which Lord Denning MR said:

'This summary jurisdiction means, however, that the solicitor is deprived of the advantages which ordinarily avail a defendant on a trial. There are no pleadings; no discovery; and no oral evidence save by leave. The jurisdiction should, therefore, only be exercised in a clear case.'

f And Megaw LJ said ([1971] 1 All ER 473 at 478, [1971] 1 QB 396 at 405):

'If in any particular case where it is sought to invoke this extraordinary jurisdiction it appears to the court that justice requires that another procedure should be followed rather than this special procedure, then the court must exercise its discretion to refuse to allow this extraordinary procedure to be used. In my judgment in the present case, having regard to the serious and difficult issues which *g* are raised, it would be quite wrong against the will of [the respondent to the application] to allow this matter to be dealt with otherwise than by means of an ordinary action in the court with evidence given orally and with the opportunity for cross-examination.'

The jurisdiction is indeed 'extraordinary', being based on the right of the court to see *h* that a high standard of conduct is maintained by its officers acting as such (see *Cordery on Solicitors* (7th edn, 1981) p 116). It is, in a sense, a domestic jurisdiction to which solicitors are only amenable because of their special relationship with the court and it is designed to impose higher standards than the law applies generally. Thus, for example, it is no answer to a complaint that a solicitor acted in breach of an undertaking given by him that there was no consideration for it (*United Mining and Finance Corp Ltd v Becher* [1910] *j* 2 KB 296 at 303, [1908–10] All ER Rep 876 at 880).

Its 'summary' character lies not in the burden or standard of proof, although it is only exercisable where there has been a serious dereliction of duty, but in the procedure whereby it is invoked. This is normally by originating summons, although it can be by simple application in an action where the conduct complained of occurred in the course of that action, and will not automatically or usually involve pleadings, discovery or oral

evidence, although the court can, in appropriate circumstances, require a definition of
the issues (by pleadings or otherwise), discovery and oral evidence.   *a*

In *Geoffrey Silver & Drake v Baines* [1971] 1 All ER 473, [1971] 1 QB 396 what I think
that the judges were saying was that the court will only exercise this jurisdiction where
in the end it is clearly established that there has been a serious dereliction of professional
duty by a solicitor as such. Both Lord Denning MR and Widgery LJ held that Mr Baines,
the solicitor, was not acting in that capacity and so could not have been guilty of any such
breach of duty (see [1971] 1 All ER 473 at 476–477, [1971] 1 QB 396 at 403–404). On   *b*
the other hand, the plaintiff might have had a claim in contract against Mr Batts, the
employee of Mr Baines, and against Mr Baines as an individual, but not as a solicitor, if
Mr Batts had acted with his authority. Such a claim, even if successfully established,
would not however fall within the special jurisdiction invoked by the plaintiff, not
because of its 'summary' nature but because its application is limited to professional
conduct.   *c*

Appeal allowed in part. Leave to appeal to the House of Lords refused.

Solicitors: *James Chapman & Co*, Manchester (for the defendants); *Kidd Rapinet Badge &
Co* (for the plaintiffs).   *d*

Diana Procter   Barrister.

Watts and others v Yeend
e

COURT OF APPEAL, CIVIL DIVISION
KERR LJ AND SWINTON THOMAS J
24, 25 NOVEMBER 1986

*Agricultural holding – Tenancy – Agreement in contemplation of use of land for grazing during
specified period of year – Licence for seasonal grazing – Licence not fixing dates of beginning and* *f*
*end of seasonal grazing period – Whether licence for grazing 'during some specified period of the
year' – Whether licence amounting to tenancy from year to year – Whether protected tenancy –
Agricultural Holdings Act 1948, s 2(1) proviso.*

A seasonal grazing licence, ie a licence to take grass from land during the grazing season,
which is granted for successive years but without specifying the dates of the grazing *g*
season is nevertheless a licence to occupy land for grazing 'during some specified period
of the year' for the purposes of the proviso to s 2(1)*a* of the Agricultural Holdings Act
1948 and is therefore not a tenancy from year to year within s 2(1) and thus not a
protected tenancy under that Act (see p 748 *j* to p 749 *a f g*, p 750 *a* to *d*, p 753 *d* and
p 754 *c d*, post).

Dictum of Denning LJ in *Scene Estate Ltd v Amos* [1957] 2 All ER at 328 and *Mackenzie* *h*
v Laird 1959 SC 266 applied.

Notes
For tenements which are not agricultural holdings, including a letting of land for grazing
or mowing during a specified period of a year, see 1 Halsbury's Laws (4th edn) para 1005.
For the Agricultural Holdings Act 1948, s 2, see 1 Halsbury's Statutes (4th edn) 718. *j*

Cases referred to in judgments
Butterfield v Burniston (1961) 111 L Jo 696.
James v Lock (1977) 246 EG 395, CA.

---

a Section 2, so far as material, is set out at p 747 *b c*, post

Lampard v Barker (1984) 272 EG 783, CA.

a *Luton v Tinsey* (1978) 249 EG 239, CA.

Mackenzie v Laird 1959 SC 266, Ct of Sess.

Reid v Dawson [1954] 3 All ER 498, [1955] 1 QB 214, [1954] 3 WLR 810, CA.

Scene Estate Ltd v Amos [1957] 2 All ER 325, [1957] 2 QB 205, [1957] 2 WLR 1017, CA.

Appeal

b By particulars of claim in the Bristol County Court the plaintiffs, Sylvia May Ann Watts, Joan Elizabeth Bendall and Freda Doreen Davis, the personal representatives of Mrs Violet Elizabeth Ann deceased, claimed against the defendant, Brian C Yeend, possession of four fields, damages for trespass and mesne profits, on the ground that the defendant merely had the use of the fields under a grazing licence. By his defence the defendant pleaded that on the true construction of the agreement between him and Mrs Ann he c held a protected tenancy of the fields under the Agricultural Holdings Act 1948. By a judgment delivered on 18 September 1985 his Honour Judge Sir Ian Lewis held that the defendant merely had a grazing licence and made an order for possession of the fields in the plaintiffs' favour and ordered the defendant to pay mesne profits of £450 up to 1 November 1985. The defendant appealed seeking an order setting aside the judgment and a declaration that he held a protected tenancy of the fields. The facts are set out in d the judgment of Kerr LJ.

Mark West for the defendant.

Colin F Sara for the plaintiffs.

e **KERR LJ.** This is an appeal by the defendant from a judgment given by his Honour Judge Sir Ian Lewis at the Bristol County Court on 18 September 1985. The plaintiffs are the personal representatives of the estate of Violet Elizabeth Ann (to whom I shall refer as 'Mrs Ann'). The defendant, Mr Brian C Yeend, is a farmer in the same locality.

    Mrs Ann died on 18 October 1982. She had been the owner of a house and a number of fields at Rockhampton Green, Rockhampton, Berkeley, in the county of Avon. The f dispute is the familiar one: whether an agreement or arrangement between a landowner and a local farmer in relation to some fields was for a grazing licence or a tenancy protected by the Agricultural Holdings Act 1948.

    An agreed plan shows that apart from her house and a driveway, Mrs Ann owned an adjoining orchard with some derelict farm buildings and four fields, one of which was a large one adjoining the orchard and the house, and the other three all separate. The g ordnance survey number of the orchard was 116 and the numbers of the fields were 117, 126, 184 and 187. It is common ground that the defendant had some use of those fields, the issue being whether he merely had a grazing licence or a tenancy.

    The particulars of claim plead as follows in para 3:

h   'At the date of her death [Mrs Ann] had permitted the Defendant to take the grass keep from [the four fields to which I have referred] during a specified part of the year pursuant to the proviso to section 2 of the Agricultural Holdings Act 1948. The Licence so to take the grass keep was terminated upon the death of [Mrs Ann] the deceased, or, alternatively, at the end of the period of the Licence then current, and has not since been renewed.'

j Asked for particulars of that agreement, the plaintiffs said that the agreement had been made orally, and then I read from the further and better particulars:

      'The Plaintiffs have no knowledge of the oral words used by either the Deceased [Mrs Ann] or the Defendant nor when such agreement was made. The Plaintiffs rely on the fact that the Deceased considered there was an agreement for the sale of the grass keep for a specified portion of the year as evidenced by the Deceased's return to the Ministry of Agriculture in 1979 when the Deceased stated, in writing, that 5 hectares of land was let seasonally in 1979 to another person for cropping, haymaking or grazing.'   *a*

The five hectares referred to the area of the four fields, and there was an additional 0·1 hectare referred to in some of these returns which related to the orchard. The acreage of the area is about 12½.

The amended defence and counterclaim pleaded in substance as follows:

'4 By an oral agreement made between the Defendant and the deceased in or   *b* about [it was originally December 1970, and that was amended to the Spring of 1968; nothing turns on the fact that there was a second thought about the date] granted to the Defendant the exclusive occupation of approximately 12.5 acres of agricultural land, together with the use of certain buildings and a yard adjacent thereto, all situate at Rockhampton Green at an annual rent of [it was originally £100, but that has been amended to £60] payable half-yearly in advance on 1st   *c* December and 1st June in each year.'

Then particulars are given of the agricultural land, buildings and yard with reference to the ordnance survey numbers, including the orchard and the farm buildings in it. The reference to the yard is to the area surrounded by those buildings.

The defence gives lengthy particulars of what the defendant claims to have done on   *d* the land to make good his claim that he was a tenant. There was then a counterclaim for one of two alternative declarations. The first was that he had a tenancy of the land and buildings. The alternative declaration claimed was that he had a licence in respect of the land and buildings which took effect as a tenancy from year to year pursuant to the provisions of s 2 of the 1948 Act, and a declaration that this was a protected tenancy.

The defendant farmed other land in partnership with his father, who also gave   *e* evidence and played a part in the history. He also rented some other land, and had a normal, formal written tenancy agreement concerning that other land. But, as can be seen from what I have already mentioned, it is common ground that the agreement with which this appeal is concerned was informal, oral and was never referred to in any document which passed between the parties during the 14 years or so from 1968 to 1982,   *f* when it is common ground that it was in existence.

It is also common ground, I think, that the originally required annual payment was £60; it then rose to £100, and in about 1976 (although nothing turns on the date) it went up to £150. It was payable in two instalments, one on 1 July, as the defendant says, and one in December. Whatever the arrangement between Mrs Ann and the defendant was, it is also clear from some earlier documents which have survivied that it followed on from another yearly arrangement which she had, in that case certainly limited to the   *g* taking of the grass, with a firm called Sandoe Luce Panes & Johns. That was on any view of a different nature. They had the right to take and dispose of the grass each year, I think from 1966 to 1968, but on the basis that if they took it by mowing, as appears to have been the position throughout, they would then advertise and sell it and charge Mrs Ann with the expenses and a commission. Both sides have sought to draw attention to the   *h* difference between that arrangement and the one with the defendant which was certainly concerned with his actually making use of the land. But the judge clearly felt unable to draw any conclusion as to the reasons why different arrangements were made. I am in exactly the same position. It seems to me that no conclusion can be drawn as to whether, in making a change, Mrs Ann wanted to create a tenancy or merely what I have referred to as a grazing licence. It should be mentioned that she and the Yeend family were   *j* originally close friends; in particular she was friendly with the defendant's mother, and also with his father. But there was then some falling out because Mrs Ann had not been invited to the christening of a child of the family. That again is not something on which I can base any inference, let alone conclusion; and nor did the judge. That is the background.

I should say at once that the judge, having heard witnesses on both sides for a
considerable time, came to the clear conclusion that the right which the defendant had
was limited to a grazing licence which, although he does not mention the point expressly,
in his view obviously fell within the proviso to s 2(1) of the 1948 Act. He reached the
conclusion on a number of grounds, to which I shall be referring.

First I must read s 2:

'(1) Subject to the provisions of this section, where under an agreement made on
or after the first day of March, nineteen hundred and forty-eight, any land is let to a
person for use as agricultural land for an interest less than a tenancy from year to
year, or a person is granted a licence to occupy land for use as agricultural land, and
the circumstances are such that if his interest were a tenancy from year to year he
would in respect of that land be the tenant of an agricultural holding, then ... the
agreement shall take effect, with the necessary modifications, as if it were an
agreement for the letting of the land for a tenancy from year to year ...'

That states the general position that the grant of an interest less than a tenancy from year
to year, or for a licence in relation to agricultural land, will take effect as an agreement
for the letting of the land for a tenancy from year to year; and that of course has the effect
that it enjoys the protection of the Act and other statutory provisions in a number of
respects.

There then follows the important proviso, and it is on this that most of the cases have
turned:

'Provided that this subsection shall not have effect in relation to an agreement for
the letting of land, or the granting of a licence to occupy land, made (whether or not
the agreement expressly so provides) in contemplation of the use of the land only
for grazing or mowing during some specified period of the year ...'

Before I come to the evidence, I should deal with two points of law which, as counsel
for the defendant submitted, show that the judge had approached the matter on an
erroneous basis. Unlike counsel who represents the plaintiffs, counsel for the defendant
did not appear below. In connection with the submission of counsel for the defendant it
should also be noted that this is a very experienced judge sitting habitually in that part of
the country, and that the problem raised by this case is not at all an unfamiliar one in
that county court and, no doubt, many county courts in rural areas.

The first point of law is based on the fact that the judge makes no express reference to
the proviso to s 2(1). Counsel for the defendant does not go so far as to suggest that the
judge did not have the proviso in mind. It was pleaded, and of course he had it in mind.
But what counsel for the defendant submits is that the judge did not have in mind the
words 'during some specified period of the year in the proviso'.

The position in that regard is as follows. It is clear from the judgment and the
pleadings, and from what counsel for the plaintiffs has told us, that the contested issue in
the court below was, on the one hand, the plaintiffs' contention that this was a grazing
licence, that is to say a grass-keep agreement or whatever expression one chooses to use,
and on the other hand the defendant's positive contention that he had a full tenancy from
year to year. That was the issue, and everyone, the judge, the parties and their legal
advisers, assumed, and had in mind, that, if the agreement was only in the nature of
what I have called a grazing licence, then it would fall within the proviso.

Counsel for the defendant's position is this. He does not dispute, indeed he cannot
dispute, that that was how the case was conducted and contested below. But, as I follow
his submission, he says that this involves the conclusion that everyone proceeded on an
erroneous basis of law. What he submits is that, having regard to the evidence, which
undoubtedly gave the defendant some rights in relation to the land, it was not sufficient
to conclude, as the judge did, that the agreement was merely one for a grazing licence, or
as he referred to it, a seasonal grazing licence, because so to look at it ignores the words

'during some specified period of the year'. On this appeal counsel for the defendant accordingly seeks to take a point which I am quite satisfied was never taken below. But *a* of course, if he is right in law he is entitled to take it. At any rate I proceed on this basis without deciding whether it is possible for parties, by some agreement, implied or tacit, to produce the same effect as the proviso even if its precise terms are not satisfied.

But I am quite clear that the judge did not err in his approach to the proviso to s 2(1), although he makes no reference to it. He referred repeatedly to a grazing licence, or a seasonal grazing licence, and he clearly had in mind that that would be sufficient, if *b* established, to attract the protection of the proviso. For instance, he says in his judgment:

> 'The defendant contends that he had a protected agricultural tenancy. The plaintiffs contend that it was a grazing licence. So far as the onus of proof is concerned each had a liability to establish what he or she contends for.'

I shall come back to the last sentence. Then he refers to one of the agricultural returns *c* which were put in evidence in this case, to which he clearly attaches considerable importance. He quotes from that by saying:

> 'It specifically states "I include land on this holding let by you for seasonal grazing".'

Finally on this aspect, having reviewed some of the evidence and contentions, he says: *d*

> 'All this confirms the grazing agreement. There was a further friendly and informal arrangement that it was to continue on indefinitely but the land was not to be used throughout the year.'

Pausing there, counsel for the defendant sought to submit that this meant that what was not to continue throughout the year was the 'further friendly and informal arrangement', *e* not the grazing agreement. In my view that is a clear misconstruction of this passage. When he said 'all this confirms the grazing agreement', and went on to say that there was 'a further friendly and informal arrangement that it was to continue on indefinitely', he was saying that there was a grazing agreement, and there was a further informal arrangement that 'it', the grazing agreement, was to continue on indefinitely, that is to *f* say in successive years, unless somebody changed their mind. Then he went on to say 'but the land was not to be used throughout the year'. That was clearly his view of what had been agreed. At the end of the judgment he said:

> 'As to the terms of that arrangement, what was agreed here, I am quite certain was a grazing licence.'
> *g*

The issue on this aspect is therefore whether a seasonal grazing licence, not related to any specified period in the year but merely to the grazing or mowing periods, falls within the proviso so s 2(1) of the 1948 Act. In that regard I am clear that counsel for the defendant is not correct in submitting that by approaching the case on that basis which, as I have said, was the basis on which both sides and the judge approached it, there was any error of law. *h*

We have been referred to a number of cases, and I begin by mentioning them all for the sake of completeness. They were: *Reid v Dawson* [1954] 3 All ER 498, [1955] 1 QB 214; *Scene Estate Ltd v Amos* [1957] 2 All ER 325, [1957] 2 QB 205; *Butterfield v Burniston* (1961) 111 L Jo 696, a decision from the Harrogate County Court; *Luton v Tinsey* (1978) 249 EG 239, a decision of this court; *James v Lock* (1977) 246 EG 395; *Lampard v Barker* (1984) 272 EG 783; and finally, because I noticed a reference to it in *Butterfield v Burniston*, *j* the court referred both parties to an important decision of the Court of Session, *Mackenzie v Laird* 1959 SC 266.

It seems to me that on the authorities, particularly *Scene Estate Ltd v Amos* and *Mackenzie v Laird*, the judge was clearly entitled to conclude that if the parties contemplated a seasonal grazing licence which, being seasonal, would ipso facto be for less than a year, *a*   then the requirement that the licence must be for some specified period of the year was satisfied.

In *Scene Estate Ltd v Amos* [1957] 2 All ER 325 at 328, [1957] 2 QB 205 at 211 Denning LJ put the position quite generally as follows in the context of the proviso:

b   'I do not think the word "contemplation" in the proviso should be given the meaning which leading counsel for the tenant seeks to put on it. In my opinion the object of the word "contemplation" in the proviso is this: It is to protect a landlord who has not expressly inserted a provision that it is for grazing only or for mowing only or that it is for a specified part of the year: when nevertheless both parties know that that is what is contemplated. Often a landlord may let a field to a man by word of mouth saying: "You can have the field th⋅ year the same as you had it last year". Both sides mean it to be for grazing only, and mean it to be only for a few weeks of *c*   the spring, but they do not say so expressly. In such circumstances, even though nothing is expressed in the agreement, nevertheless the landlord can still take advantage of the proviso. That seems to me to be the real object of introducing the "contemplation" of the parties.'

d   Denning LJ's reference to 'a few weeks of the spring' was clearly given only as an illustration or in the context of the facts of that case, which was concerned with periods of three months in each year. Parker LJ said that he agreed and that the words 'specified period of the year' were equivalent to 'specified part of the year' (see [1957] 2 All ER 325 at 329, [1957] 2 QB 205 at 212).

In *Butterfield v Burniston* (1961) 111 LJo 696 in the Harrogate County Court a grazing tenancy granted, or understood to have been granted, by reference to the grazing season *e*   was treated as a term well understood by farmers and to be within the scope of the proviso. His Honour Judge McKee cited and followed *Mackenzie v Laird* 1959 SC 266, the Scottish case to which I have referred.

In that case there was a written agreement which provided expressly for a seasonal let for grazing purposes. The issue was whether this satisfied the requirement of the proviso, viz an agreement for the use of the land only for grazing or mowing during some *f*   specified period of the year. The three members of the Court of Session all concluded that the proviso was satisfied.

The Lord Justice Clerk (Thomson) said (1959 SC 266 at 269–270):

'The only question at issue is whether in the absence of definite terminal dates it can be said that what was in contemplation was some specified period of the year. In the present case there are no dates fixed as the beginning and end of the period *g*   but I do not see that fixed or specific dates for the beginning and end are essential. What the proviso is excepting is the use of land only for grazing or mowing and those uses are in essence seasonal. None can give in advance in any particular year, or indeed in any particular locality, a specific date when the land will be ready for the start of either operation nor can it be said in advance when either will finish. What matters to the agriculturalist is the state of the land ... What the tenant wants *h*   and what the landlord is prepared to give is the season's grass from the appropriate moment which nature directs and to the subsequent moment when nature calls a halt. Accordingly, once it is admitted that what we have to do with is grazing and grazing for part of a year only, and once one accepts, as the arbiter accepted, that what is meant by "grazing season" or "seasonal let" is unambiguous and well *j*   understood in farming circles, there is no difficulty in saying that this case falls within the proviso, as what was in contemplation was "the use of the land only for grazing or mowing during some specified period of the year".'

Lord Patrick agreed and said, referring to the findings of the arbiter (at 271):

'... some such lettings may specify particular dates as termini in the spring and autumn, but it is a common practice not to specify dates; and that farmers know well what is comprehended in a let of seasonal grazing ... The sole argument against that view is that the contemplated use must be use for some *definite* period **a** of days, weeks or months in the year. I do not find any such requirement in the language of the proviso to section 2(1). The period must be specified, not exactly defined, and, if the period of the year is one which is capable of reasonably clear ascertainment, the language of the proviso is satisfied.' (Lord Patrick's emphasis.)

Lord Mackintosh agreed, and said (at 272):   **b**

'I think that the expression "specified period" as used in the said proviso is not limited in its meaning to a period fixed by dates but includes any period which is so named or described as to be identifiable by persons versed in agricultural matters.'

He said that he agreed with the sheriff in his conclusion that a seasonal let of grazings—

'means a let of grazings for a specified period, i.e., for a period so named or **c** described as to be identifiable in agricultural circles, and that accordingly the proviso applied ...'

(See 1959 SC 266 at 272.)

I unhesitatingly follow that decision. The 1948 Act, or at any rate that part of it, applies in Scotland just as it does in England. It would obviously be undesirable for the Court of **d** Appeal to differ from the Court of Session. But the conclusion is really a matter of common sense. The courts might of course have interpreted the words 'for a specified period' very strictly. For good reason they have not done so. On every occasion when this issue arose directly, they have approached it in the same way as the parties and the judge in this case. That deals with the first point raised by counsel for the defendant.

I can take the second point much more shortly. Counsel for the defendant submitted **e** that the judge had misdirected himself about the burden of proof. He submitted, undoubtedly rightly, that in order to attract the protection of the proviso the burden of proof is on the landowner. The question is therefore whether this judgment shows that the judge misdirected himself in that regard. In my view it shows no such thing.

I have already referred to the passage in question where the judge said that the defendant contends that he had a protected agricultural tenancy and the plaintiffs **f** contended that it was a grazing licence, and added:

'So far as the onus of proof is concerned each had a liability to establish what he or she contends for.'

Given that there was a counterclaim claiming the declarations which I have read, that statement is perfectly correct. Moreover, I do not think that the judge overlooked the **g** fact that in order to recover possession, against the background of the undisputed evidence that the defendant had some rights in relation to this land, the effective onus of proof was on the plaintiffs.

Further on in his judgment the judge said:

'The important thing is that the inference is that the arrangement is to be treated **h** as a protected tenancy unless there is evidence to the contrary.'

And he went on: 'I find that here there is evidence to the contrary.'

In relation to the provision for payment, to which I have already referred, the judge said:

'I have to bear in mind that it does not appear to be in dispute that the money was **j** to be paid half-yearly. I don't overlook that this points to a tenancy.'

Finally, at the end of his judgment, I have already read the final sentence, in which he said: 'As to the terms of that arrangement, what was agreed here, I am quite certain was a grazing licence.'

a   Having regard to those passages I find it impossible to conclude that the judge misdirected himself as to the onus of proof, which he obviously realised lay on the plaintiffs, to bring themselves within the proviso.

Counsel for the defendant also faintly argued that the judge may have gone wrong when he said that the inference was that the arrangement was to be treated as a protected tenancy 'unless there is evidence ... [and] I find that here there is evidence to the contrary'. He clearly did not merely mean 'unless there is *some* evidence to the contrary'.
b   As shown by his judgment as a whole, he meant that he had to be satisfied that there was sufficient evidence to satisfy the burden of proof on the plaintiffs to displace the prima facie inference that an agreement for the use of land referable to a year, whether it be a tenancy or a licence, is a protected tenancy.

I then come to the third aspect of which counsel for the defendant relied. This concerns the bulk of the evidence and the main parts of the judgment concerned with the findings
c   of fact. Counsel for the defendant submits that the judge's decision was contrary to the weight of the evidence. The position in that regard is as follows: Mrs Ann, as I have already mentioned, was dead. A number of witnesses were called on both sides and the judge had to do his best with the evidence before him. The witnesses on the side of the plaintiffs included some relations of Mrs Ann and a Mr Freeman, who had worked for Mrs Ann and had had the use of her garden for a number of years, and also a Mr Child,
d   who farms an adjacent farm. On the side of the defendant the main witness was of course Mr Brian Yeend himself. In addition a Mr Weston, who had worked for him for a number of years, gave evidence on the defendant's behalf. Finally, Mr Christopher Yeend, Mr Yeend senior, at the ripe age of 81, also gave evidence.

The only witness who could speak about the actual arrangement was of course Mr Yeend, the defendant. In that regard I am bound to say that the judge was quite clear
e   about the impression which he formed of his evidence, after hearing him for a long time, as can be seen from the lengthy notes of evidence. He said:

'Let me say at the outset that I have come to the clear conclusion that Mr Yeend is not a witness on whom I can rely.'

f   In the last paragraph of his judgment he said:

'I have therefore come to the clear conclusion that the right granted here is that of a grazing licence. I have said that I do not accept Mr Yeend's evidence. He was confused about a whole series of matters and his recollection was at fault regarding the date of the original arrangement and the amounts and dates of variations in payment.'

g   I have already read the last sentence of the judgment. I also notice from the judge's notes of evidence that Mr Yeend said at one point:

'It was arranged that I could mow and graze cattle as I wanted—nothing said of the time of the year I could use the building.'

h   So it is quite clear that the judge did not accept from Mr Yeend that the original agreement was for a full agricultural tenancy.

I must now briefly refer to the evidence on which the judge mainly relied for his conclusion that this was a seasonal grazing licence. The first part of his judgment is concerned with certain returns which were made by Mrs Ann for agricultural purposes. We have returns for a few of the 14 years covered by the agreement and I do not propose
j   to go through them all. But for instance, in 1975 there is a reference to land let for seasonal grazing, against which the words 'Let to B.C. Yeend' appear. I should say in that connection that Mr Yeend senior who, as I have said, was a fairly close friend of Mrs Ann, helped her to complete these returns, and a number of the entries appear in his writing. In the return for 1978 a number of boxes had to be completed by ticks where applicable. Box 92 had to state the total number of cattle and calves and the figure 6 was there

inserted by Mr Yeend senior. There followed box 93, which also contained a tick against the following wording: 'Please tick this box if all the cattle entered at 92 above belong to *a* someone else, and you are only providing grazing.' Similarly in relation to the return for 1979, there was the following entry. Under the heading 'Seasonal Use of Land', box 41 contained the following wording: 'Area of land let seasonally, this year, to another person for cropping, hay-making or grazing'. The words 'five hectares' were inserted, which the judge thought, no doubt correctly, referred to the area of the four fields to the exclusion of the orchard. There was the same type of entry as before in boxes 92 and 93, with a *b* slight increase in the number of cattle and calves. It is true that at the end of that return, in what was apparently Mrs Ann's handwriting in a box headed 'Land Given Up', she put the words 'No Change', and then added 'Land is Let to B.C. Yeend', giving his address. But that is of no weight against the entries referring to grazing. Mr Yeend senior said, in relation to those entries which clearly and expressly point to seasonal grazing, that they must have been mistaken, although he agreed that he had helped Mrs Ann to complete *c* these returns.

As I have already mentioned, Mr Yeend senior farmed in partnership with his son, the defendant. He was clearly experienced and must have known, as, I think, did everybody in this case, the crucial difference between a seasonal grazing licence on the one hand and an agricultural tenancy on the other. It must also be borne in mind that Mrs Ann was only required to make these returns if she had *not* let the land in question to Mr Yeend. *d* On the other hand it was for Mr Yeend to make returns which included this land if he had had a tenancy of it as he claimed. The fact is that it was Mrs Ann who made the returns with the knowledge and assistance of Mr Yeend senior, and that the defendant, Mr Yeend junior, made no returns including this land. Those facts speak for themselves. Of course I agree with counsel for the defendant when he emphasises that Mr Yeend, the *e* defendant, never saw these returns and had no part in them, and that they could be construed as having been used by Mrs Ann to serve her own purposes. But in the circumstances that is an extremely far-fetched suggestion.

Counsel for the defendant has also submitted that one should not look at events after the original agreement in order to interpret its effect. But, rightly, he does not seek to go to the full length of that submission, which would often be impracticable in circumstances *f* such as those envisaged by this proviso. The cases show that one has to have regard to what was in fact done on the land. The court is not concerned with construing or interpreting a written agreement and therefore precluded from deciding what the parties meant by the words which they used by looking at their subsequent conduct. The proviso refers to what was in the contemplation of the parties concerning the use of the land. In that context one must have regard to what was happening on the ground, *g* particularly if the arrangement continued over a period of years.

Accordingly, I conclude that the judge was entitled to take these returns into account. For the reasons which I have explained, they clearly point in only one direction.

The remainder of the evidence was concerned with accounts of the various activities which according to the various witnesses, Mr Yeend carried on or did not carry on in relation to the land; to what extent he used the buildings; to what extent he worked the *h* land as if he were a tenant of it; or whether what he did was consistent with his only having a seasonal grazing licence. In that regard two main aspects were important. firstly, his use of the buildings, and whether or not he used them and the land for the whole of the year or only during the grazing season. Secondly, whether the work that he did on the land was compatible with his being a tenant, with full responsibilities for the land, or whether Mrs Ann retained these responsibilities on the ground that she had not *j* let it. In that connection there were references to hedging, ditching, gates and matters of that kind.

What the judge said about those parts of the evidence is as follows:

'So far as the buildings are concerned I accept Mr Bendall's [the husband of Mrs Ann's niece] evidence that he did not see the buildings used in the winter months.

a So far as the buildings are concerned I accept that the buildings were used at times but not throughout the year. I believe that the buildings were used contemporaneously with the grazing and that if the land was wet it was reasonable that they may have been.'

A little later on, dealing with hedging and ditching, his finding is favourable to Mr Yeend to the extent that Mr Yeend did the work, or had it done. But the important
b question was who paid for it. The judge said:

'I accept that Mr Yeend did the hedges and ditches and fixed the gates. But I bear in mind that Mrs Ann was asked by him to pay the bill and she agreed. The importance of this was that he asked her for money though she died before she could pay. This would not be the position if it was a tenancy. He also asked her about the draining. If Mr Yeend had a tenancy he would have drained without
c asking. Also with the draining he asked her for money although she could not in fact afford it. This was done really to improve the grazing for his own benefit and to make better use of the land subject to the grazing licence.'

That was the judge's conclusion on a very large part of the evidence through which counsel for the defendant had taken us. Some aspects supported either view. But I find it
d quite impossible to hold that the judge was not entitled to reach the conclusions about the buildings, the hedging and ditching and so forth, which I have just read. On the contrary, on the weight of the evidence, I think it supported his findings.

In all the circumstances I am left in no doubt but that this appeal must be dismissed.

e **SWINTON THOMAS J.** As I see it, the first of the two main issues which arise on this appeal is whether the defendant's occupation was by way of a tenancy or by way of a grazing licence, and whether before the judge it was proved by the plaintiffs that the occupation was by way of a grazing licence.

On that issue the trial judge found quite clearly that the occupation was by way of a grazing licence. At the end of his judgment the judge said:

f 'As to the terms of that arrangement, what was agreed here, I am quite certain was a grazing licence.'

That issue was a question of fact; in my judgment there was ample evidence on which the judge was entitled to come to the conclusion to which he in fact came. Kerr LJ has reviewed that evidence in the course of his judgment and it is not necessary for me to do
g so again. The judge was entitled to rely, as he did, on the fact that he found the defendant to be an unsatisfactory witness, on whose evidence he could not rely.

The second, and in my view crucial, question is whether the grazing licence was made in contemplation of use of the land for grazing during some specified period of the year, as set out in the proviso to s 2(1) of the 1948 Act. As has been pointed out, those words are set out in para 3 of the particulars of claim; in the defence that paragraph is formally
h denied but, more relevantly for this purpose, there is a counterclaim. In para 12 of the amended defence and counterclaim the defendant alleges:

'On a true construction of the said agreement and in the events which have happened the plaintiff at all material times held the said land, buildings and yard from the deceased as a tenant thereof and such tenancy is protected by the provisions
j of the Agricultural Holdings Act 1948.'

He then makes two alternative counterclaims:

'(a) A declaration that on the true construction of the said agreement made between the Defendant and the deceased in or about the Spring of 1968 and in the events which have happened, the Defendant holds a tenancy of the said land,

buildings and yard and that such tenancy is protected by the Agricultural Holdings
Act 1948.'   *a*

Then:

      'ALTERNATIVELY (b) A declaration that if the said agreement made between the
Defendant and the deceased in or about the Spring of 1968 was a licence to occupy
the said land, buildings and yard such licence had taken effect as a tenancy from
year to year pursuant to the provisions of section 2 of the said Act and that such   *b*
tenancy is protected thereby.'

    In those circumstances, and bearing in mind the experience of the judge, I find it quite
impossible to accept that he would not have had in the forefront of his mind in this case
the terms of the proviso to s 2(1) of the 1948 Act.
    The judge had said in his judgment, that there was a further friendly and informal   *c*
arrangement that 'it' (quite clearly that refers to the grazing agreement) was to continue
on indefinitely, but the land was not to be used throughout the year.
    Clearly in my view, the judge was there finding that the defendant's occupation was
by way of a seasonal grazing licence. 'Seasonal grazing' is a term which is well understood
in agricultural circles and, as was said in *Mackenzie v Laird* 1959 SC 266 seasonal grazing
does not have to be for the same period of time during every year, but is none the less in   *d*
contemplation of the use of the land for grazing during some specified period of the year.
In my judgment, that clearly is exactly the position in the instant case.
    Accordingly, I am quite satisfied that the plaintiffs were entitled to possession of the
land the subject matter of the claim, and that the judge came to the right conclusion, and
therefore I too would dismiss this appeal.

                                                          e

Appeal dismissed; possession within 28 days of date of Court of Appeal's judgment.

Solicitors: *Blakemores*, Tetbury (for the defendant); *Kirby Simcox*, Bristol (for the plaintiffs).

                                        Wendy Shockett   Barrister.

Ashton and others v Sobelman

CHANCERY DIVISION
JOHN CHADWICK QC SITTING AS A DEPUTY JUDGE OF THE HIGH COURT
24, 25, 26, 27, 28 FEBRUARY, 29 APRIL 1986

Landlord and tenant – Re-entry – Arrears of rent – Peaceable re-entry by landlord – Landlord changing locks but permitting underlease to continue – Whether lease forfeited by re-entry – Whether continuation of underlease consistent with re-entry – Whether tenant entitled to relief from forfeiture.

A freehold title of property consisting of a lock-up shop with a flat above was leased to the plaintiffs' predecessor in title for 80 years from 24 October 1932 at a rent of £50 pa under a lease which provided for re-entry by the landlord for non-payment of rent. By an underlease dated 29 April 1976 the premises were let to C for a period of ten years at a rent of £3,500 pa. The rent payable under the headlease was not paid when due on 29 September 1983 or on any of the following four quarter days. On 19 October 1984 the head landlords sought to forfeit the lease and purported to re-enter the premises by changing the locks with the acquiescence of the underlessee, who was assured that he could remain in possession, that his underlease would be unaffected by the re-entry and that he would merely become a direct lessee of the landlords 'under the provisions of the underlease'. In November 1984 the property was sold by the landlords to the defendant, who believed that the underlease comprised the only charge on the freehold title. The plaintiffs subsequently discovered what had happened and offered to pay the defendant the arrears of rent owing under the 1932 lease but the defendant refused to accept payment. The plaintiffs sought, inter alia, a declaration as against the defendant that there had been no forfeiture of the 1932 lease.

Held – The actions taken by the head landlords on 19 October 1984 could not be regarded as amounting to a re-entry under the provision for re-entry contained in the 1932 lease because the continuation of the 1976 underlease was wholly inconsistent with the termination by forfeiture of the 1932 lease. Accordingly, the 1932 lease had not been forfeited and the declaration sought by the plaintiffs would be granted (see p 764 h j and p 765 d j to p 766 a, post).

Baylis v Le Gros (1858) 4 CBNS 537 and *London and County (A & D) Ltd v Wilfred Sportsman Ltd* [1970] 2 All ER 600 distinguished.

Notes

For forfeiture of a lease by re-entry, see 27 Halsbury's Laws (4th edn) paras 422–428, and for cases on the subject, see 31(2) Digest (Reissue) 808–811, 6790–6818.

For relief against forfeiture for non-payment of rent, see 27 Halsbury's Laws (4th edn) paras 442–443, and for cases on the subject, see 31(2) Digest (Reissue), 816–820, 6790–6818.

Cases referred to in judgment

Baylis v Le Gros (1858) 4 CBNS 537, 140 ER 1201.
Howard v Fanshawe [1895] 2 Ch 581, [1895–9] All ER Rep 855.
London and County (A & D) Ltd v Wilfred Sportsman Ltd (Greenwoods (Hosiers and Outfitters) Ltd, third party) [1970] 2 All ER 600, [1971] Ch 764, [1970] 3 WLR 418, CA.
Lovelock v Margo [1963] 2 All ER 13, [1963] 2 QB 786, [1963] 2 WLR 794, CA.

Cases also cited

Bishop v Bedford Charity Trustees (1859) 1 E & E 714, 120 ER 1078, Ex Ch.
Canas Property Co Ltd v KL Television Services Ltd [1970] 2 All ER 795, [1970] 2 QB 433, CA.

Doe d Chawner v Boulter (1837) 6 Ad & El 675, 112 ER 260.
Doe d Baker v Coombes (1850) 9 CB 714, 137 ER 1073.   *a*
Ewart v Fryer [1901] 1 Ch 499, CA; *affd* [1902] AC 187, HL.
Jones v Carter (1846) 15 M & W 718, 153 ER 1040.
Ladup Ltd v Williams & Glyn's Bank plc [1985] 2 All ER 577, [1985] 1 WLR 851.
Relvok Properties Ltd v Dixon (1972) 25 P & CR 1, CA.
Serjeant v Nash Field & Co [1903] 2 KB 304, [1900–3] All ER Rep 525, CA.
Thatcher v C H Pearce & Sons (Contractors) Ltd [1968] 1 WLR 748.   *b*

Action

The plaintiffs, Leila Ashton, John Michael Stockbridge and Verena Evans, the children of
Norman Stockbridge deceased, in whose name a leasehold interest in the property known
as 195 Burnt Oak Broadway, Edgware, Middlesex, under a lease dated 24 October 1932
for an 80-year term commencing on 29 September 1932 at a yearly rent of £50, had been   *c*
registered in the charges register of the Land Registry, and who had been the registered
proprietor of that leasehold interest at all times between 2 July 1938 and 22 October
1985, brought an action against the defendant, Samuel Sobelman, the purchaser of the
freehold of the property, when the property was offered for sale by auction held on 20
November 1984, seeking (1) a declaration that the lease of 1932 had not been forfeited,
(2) alternatively, relief from forfeiture of the lease, and (3) a declaration that the plaintiffs   *d*
were entitled to give a good receipt for the sum of £875 being the rent under the
underlease on 25 December 1984 and for all subsequent rent payable thereunder. The
facts are set out in the judgment.

David Burton for the plaintiffs.
Caroline Hutton for the defendant.   *e*

Cur adv vult

29 April. The following judgment was delivered.

JOHN CHADWICK QC. The property known as 195 Burnt Oak Broadway, Edgware,   *f*
Middlesex, comprises a lock-up shop with a flat above. The freehold title to the property
is registered at the Land Registry under title no NGL27938. Between 17 March 1982 and
17 January 1985 the registered proprietor of the property was Twogates Properties Ltd.
On 17 January 1985 the defendant, Samuel Sobelman, was registered as proprietor in the
place of Twogates Properties Ltd.
    At all material times since the first registration of the property, entry no 3 in the   *g*
charges register has shown the property to be subject to a lease dated 24 October 1932 for
a term of 80 years from 29 September 1932 at the yearly rent of £50. The leasehold
interest under the lease of 1932 is itself registered at the Land Registry, formerly under
title no P115020, but now under title no NGL540312. At all times between 2 July 1938
and 22 October 1985 the registered proprietor of the leasehold interest was Norman   *h*
Frederick Stockbridge.
    Norman Frederick Stockbridge died on 23 September 1950. On 22 October 1985 the
plaintiffs in this action, who are the three children of Norman Frederick Stockbridge and
the persons who, in the events which have happened, are now entitled beneficially to the
real property devised by his will, were registered as the proprietors of the leasehold
interest. The questions raised in this action are whether the 1932 lease was forfeited by a   *j*
peaceable re-entry made on behalf of the then freeholders, Twogates Properties Ltd, on
19 October 1984, and, if so, whether the plaintiffs should be relieved from such a
forfeiture.
    The 1932 lease contains a proviso for re-entry in the following terms, so far as material:

'PROVIDED ALWAYS AND THESE PRESENTS ARE UPON THIS CONDITION that if the said
yearly rent hereby reserved or any part thereof shall at any time be in arrear and

a unpaid for twenty-one days after the same shall have become due and whether legally demanded or not ... then and in any case it shall be lawful for the lessor or any person or persons duly authorised by him in that behalf into or upon the hereby demised premises or any part thereof in the name of the whole to re-enter and the said premises peaceably to hold and enjoy thenceforth as if this demise had not been made ...'

b The yearly rent of £50 payable under the 1932 lease was to be paid by equal quarterly payments on the usual quarter days in each year. It is admitted by the plaintiffs that rent was not paid on 29 September 1983 or on any of the four quarter days thereafter. Accordingly, by 19 October 1984, the arrears of rent owing by the plaintiffs to Twogates Properties Ltd amounted to not less than £62·50.

At the relevant time in 1984 the directors of Twogates Properties Ltd included Mr
c Michael Moss, his brother, Mr Sydney Moss, and Mr Bryan David Lipson, a partner in the firm of solicitors Messrs Cowen Lipson & Rumney. Mr Michael Moss and Mr Sydney Moss were chartered surveyors who carried on business under the name Quennell Moss & Co. It is clear that, by February, 1984, Mr Sydney Moss and his brother were giving consideration to the remedies which might be open to Twogates Properties Ltd as landlords in relation to the non-payment of rent under the 1932 lease; and, in particular,
d to the possibility of forfeiture of the lease. In a memorandum dated 27 February 1984, Mr Lipson advised Mr Sydney Moss as to the legal position: after setting out what he conceived to be the relevant legal principles, Mr Lipson continued,

'On these basic principles if you wish to effect a forfeiture by peaceable re-entry then in my opinion you must take the following steps on the day on which you peaceably re-enter the premises:—1. Peaceably enter the premises (which will
e obviously have to be done with the consent of the occupation lessee who is in any event unlikely to refuse consent) 2. Take physical possession of the premises by changing the locks on the door 3. Accept the present sub-tenant as your tenant by giving that sub-tenant a set of keys to the new lock 4. Inform the sub-tenant in writing of the steps you have taken with a request that he should pay all future rent
f to Twogates Properties Limited.'

As appears from that memorandum it was appreciated by the landlords at the time that the property was then in the occupation of a subtenant. The subtenancy was on the terms of a lease dated 29 April 1976 made between Ada Lillian Stockbridge, the widow of Norman Frederick Stockbridge, and Gerald Clayton for a term of ten years from 25 March 1976. Following a rent review in 1983, the rent payable by Mr Clayton under the
g 1976 underlease was £3,500 per annum. Mr Clayton carried on the business of a retail furniture shop at the property. He used the flat premises above the shop for storage purposes in connection with that business. Mr Clayton also carried on the business of a retail do-it-yourself shop under the name 'Home Handyman' at 188 Burnt Oak Broadway, which was on the opposite side of the street from the property.

It is clear that by the middle of September 1984 Twogates Properties Ltd had decided
h to take steps to forfeit the 1932 lease. The property was entered for sale at an auction which was to be held by Messrs Harman Healy & Co on 20 November 1984. On 13 September 1984 Cowen Lipson & Rumney sent to Mr Barnett at Harman Healy & Co draft special conditions of sale in respect of the freehold interest, and a copy land certificate of the freehold title. Although the land certificate showed the property to be
j subject to the 1932 lease, it is clear from the draft special conditions that it was intended to be sold free from that lease, and subject only to the occupation lease; although this was, at that stage, wrongly described as a 15-year lease granted in 1971 at a current rent of £2,600 per annum.

The third quarter's rent under the 1932 lease was due on 29 September 1984. I will assume, but without deciding, that a demand for that rent was sent by Quennell Moss and Co, on behalf of Twogates Properties Ltd, to Mrs Verena Evans on behalf of the plaintiffs. Some three weeks went past and no rent was received. It was decided by

Twogates Properties Ltd and Mr Lipson that they would effect a forfeiture on 19 October 1984. In preparation, Mr Lipson dictated two letters. I set out the first of these in full. *a* The letter is addressed to Mr Clayton at 195 Burnt Oak Broadway, and reads:

'*Re: 195 Burnt Oak Broadway, Edgware*
We act for Twogates Properties Limited, the freeholders of the above property which they own subject to the following Leases:—1. A lease dated 24th October 1932 made between Robert Wilson Black (1) and The Oak Property Company *b* Limited (2) for a term of 80 years from 29th September 1932 at a rent of £50 per annum payable quarterly in arrears on the usual quarter days in each year. 2. An Underlease made in or about 1971 for a term of 15 years at a current rent of £2,600 per annum payable quarterly in advance on the four usual quarter days in each year. We understand that you are in occupation of the above premises under the provisions of the Underlease referred to in 2 above, but we do not know whether *c* that Underlease was granted to you direct by the Head Lessees or whether you subsequently acquired it by way of an assignment. Our clients acquired the freehold on 17th December 1981 and from that date until in or about June 1983, they sent rent demands to Stockbridge Holdings Limited, care of Mrs V. Evans, The Old Crispin, Windsor Forest, Berkshire and the rent was always paid. Since 28th September 1983, despite sending demands, the rent owing to our clients has not *d* been paid and as at today's date, our clients are owed rent for the period from 29th September 1983 to 29th September 1984 (five quarters) at £50 per annum amounting to £62·50. We have advised our clients that in these circumstances, they are entitled to forfeit the Lease dated 24th October 1932 on the grounds of non-payment of rent by peaceably re-entering the premises and re-taking possession. Our clients propose to exercise their legal rights today by taking the following *e* steps:—(1) Peaceably re-entering the premises. (2) Changing the locks on the front door. (3) Instructing you to pay all future rent payable by you under the Underlease referred to in 2 above to our clients or as they may direct. Our representative, Mr L. M. Bloch, a partner in this firm (who will probably be accompanied by another member of our staff, Miss A. Prizeman) will call at your premises today together with our clients' locksmith and they will hand you this letter and will supervise the *f* changing of the locks, and when that work has been completed they will hand you the following:—(1) A complete set of keys to the new lock. (2) A letter of authority relating to the payment of future rent. We would like to make it perfectly clear that our clients are not in any way challenging your right to remain in occupation of the premises under the provisions of the Underlease under which you are the present Lessee. Their sole concern is to enforce their legal rights of forfeiture against their *g* tenant and the effect of the steps which our clients propose to take will be that after the forfeiture has been effected, you will become our clients' direct Lessee. As our clients would like to know the exact terms upon which you occupy the premises, we would be grateful if you would kindly hand Mr Bloch a copy of your Underlease. If you do have a copy available, then we will be quite prepared at our clients' expense to make a photocopy of the original in your presence at a nearby photocopying *h* agency so that the original document never leaves your possession. We hope that we have made the position clear, but if there is any further information you require, Mr Bloch will be able to provide it and the writer of this letter (Mr B.D. Lipson) will also be available to answer any questions you may have on the telephone.'

Mr Bloch gave evidence before me. He told me that he had been asked by Mr Lipson *j* on 18 October 1984 to attend at the property, 195 Burnt Oak Broadway, on the following day for the purpose of making a peaceable re-entry. Mr Bloch told me that he had had no experience in effecting a peaceable re-entry, and that he had no detailed knowledge of the relevant law other than what was stated in the letter which I have set out above and which was handed to him by Mr Lipson. Mr Bloch's evidence, which was confirmed by Miss Prizeman (then an articled clerk with Cowen Lipson & Rumney) and which was not seriously at variance with that given by Mr Clayton, may be summarised as follows.

a   At 10 am on 19 October 1984, Mr Bloch and Miss Prizeman went to 195 Burnt Oak Broadway. They found Mrs Clayton there, and she directed them to the do-it-yourself shop at 188 Burnt Oak Broadway on the other side of the road. Mr Clayton was busy in his shop and Mr Bloch joined the queue and waited for customers to be served. When his turn came Mr Bloch told Mr Clayton that he was a solicitor, and that there was a matter which he wanted to discuss privately. He said that he acted for the landlords, but

b   he assured Mr Clayton that nothing that he wanted to discuss would be prejudicial to Mr Clayton personally. Mr Clayton told Mr Bloch that he was busy and asked him to return at 11 o'clock.

When Mr Bloch and Miss Prizeman returned to 188 Burnt Oak Broadway at 11 o'clock the shop was less busy. Mr Bloch again told Mr Clayton that he acted for the landlords, and on this occasion he showed him the letter of 19 October 1984, which I have set out

c   above. Mr Clayton read the letter and, as it appeared to Mr Bloch, understood what was proposed. Mr Clayton expressed his concern as to his own position, and Mr Bloch assured him that he would not be prejudiced. Mr Bloch told me that he did not think that he had applied his mind to the question whether forfeiture of the head lease would involve a forfeiture of the underlease when he told Mr Clayton that he would remain in possession under his underlease. He accepted, under cross-examination, that it would be

d   consistent both with the terms of the letter dated 19 October 1984 and with his, Mr Bloch's, probable understanding at that time, that Mr Clayton's underlease was not to be affected by what was being done.

Mr Clayton was content with these assurances. Understandably he did not wish to incur unnecessary legal costs; but he telephoned his solicitors and asked them to let Mr Bloch have a copy of the underlease. Mr Bloch recalls that Mr Clayton told his solicitors

e   in the course of that telephone call that what Mr Bloch was proposing to do would not prejudice him. I am satisfied, firstly, that Mr Bloch did not seek to influence Mr Clayton against consulting his solicitors, but, secondly, that Mr Clayton was content not to do so because of the assurances that he was being given. Mr Clayton then telephoned his wife, at 195 Burnt Oak Broadway, to tell her that Mr Bloch would be coming to change the

f   locks with a locksmith and that he was to be allowed to do this.

Mr Bloch and Miss Prizeman then went to 195 Burnt Oak Broadway, with the locksmith, and instructed him to start changing the locks. Miss Prizeman and the locksmith remained there with Mrs Clayton. Mr Bloch went to Mr Clayton's solicitors to collect a copy of the underlease. When he returned to the property he found that there had been some difficulty with the locks, but that the locksmith had finally succeeded in

g   fitting a new lock. Mr Bloch told me that he wanted to be sure that the new lock did in fact work and that he satisfied himself of this. He then gave all the keys to the new lock to Mrs Clayton, and he returned to 188 Burnt Oak Broadway where he handed to Mr Clayton the second of the two letters which had been dictated by Mr Lipson on the previous day. The second letter was also addressed to Mr Clayton and was in these terms:

h

'Re: 195 Burnt Oak Broadway, Edgware

We act for Twogates Properties Limited, the freeholders of the above property, and write to give you formal notice that our clients have today forfeited the Lease of the above premises dated 24th October 1932 and made between Robert Wilson Black (1) and The Oak Property Company Limited (2) by peaceably re-entering the premises and re-taking possession. As a result of our clients having taken physical

j   possession of the premises, you are now our clients' direct Lessee. Will you please accept this letter as our clients' formal request and authority to you to pay all future rent payable by you under the provisions of the Underlease under which you hold the premises to this firm on behalf of Twogates Properties Limited.'

After handing over that letter, Mr Bloch thought that the act of forfeiture by re-entry had been completed. He returned to the offices of Cowen Lipson & Rumney. In due

course, he made a statutory declaration, dated 29 October 1984, setting out the events of
19 October.   *a*

As I have said, Mr Clayton's evidence did not differ substantially from that of Mr
Bloch. He confirmed that Mr Bloch had assured him that he had nothing to worry about
and that his lease was safe. Mr Clayton thought that he had suggested to Mr Bloch that
he, Mr Clayton, should telephone Mrs Evans. I accept that Mr Clayton considered this
possibility; but I do not think that it was the subject of discussion between him and Mr
Bloch, nor that Mr Bloch made any attempt to persuade him against such a course. In   *b*
my judgment, the true position was that Mr Clayton took the view, on reading the first
of the two letters of 19 October 1984, that Mr Bloch was entitled to do what he was
proposing to do; that it was inconceivable that Mrs Evans could be unaware of what was
to be done; and that having been given assurances that the course proposed was not going
to affect his own underlease, he was not concerned to object.

After Mr Bloch had left, Mr Clayton found that the new lock which had been installed *c*
at 195 Burnt Oak Broadway was unsatisfactory. He told me that although the locksmith
had changed the lock, he had not changed the locking plate; with the consequence that
the tongue of the new lock would not enter into the stile of the door. He telephoned
Cowen Lipson & Rumney during the afternoon of that day to complain about this. His
complaint was met by a third letter dated 19 October 1984 from Cowen Lipson &
Rumney. The second paragraph of that letter is of some significance: *d*

> 'We confirm that our Clients have asked us to apologise for any inconvenience
> that may have been caused and we further confirm that we told you on the telephone
> this afternoon to arrange for a new lock to be fitted and we stated that as long as the
> cost was reasonable our Clients would pay the bill. We invite you to send us an
> invoice for the installation of the new lock and as long as the figure is reasonable we *e*
> have instructions to pay the cost on our Clients' behalf direct to your locksmith.'

In the event, Mr Clayton replaced the new lock with the original lock that had been
left behind. The matter progressed towards the auction. On 29 October 1984, Cowen
Lipson & Rumney sent to Mr Barnett at Harman Healy & Co amendments to the special
conditions of sale relating to the property at 195 Burnt Oak Broadway, and a copy of the *f*
statutory declaration made by Mr Bloch and the exhibits thereto. The amendment to the
special conditions was in these terms:

> '2 . . . The purchaser shall assume (as is the case) that the Lease dated the 24th
> October 1932 and made between The Oak Property Company Limited (1) and
> Robert Wilson Black (2) referred to in Entry Number 3 in the Charges Register in
> the said title was forfeited on the grounds of non-payment of rent by a peaceable re- *g*
> entry on the 19th October 1984 on which date the Vendor re-took physical
> possession of the property and authorised and instructed Gerald Clayton, the Lessee
> under the provisions of the Underlease referred to in Special Condition 3 hereof to
> pay all future rent due from him to the Vendor. On completion, the Vendors'
> Solicitors shall hand the Purchaser a Statutory Declaration approving the facts which
> amounted to a lawful re-entry on the 19th October 1984. A copy of the said *h*
> Statutory Declaration is available for inspection at the offices of the Auctioneers and
> the Vendor's Solicitors, and the Purchaser having had an opportunity to inspect it
> prior to the date hereof shall be deemed to purchase with full knowledge of the
> contents thereof and shall raise no requisition or objection in relation thereto. The
> Purchaser shall not be entitled to require the Vendor to procure the deletion of
> Entry No 3 from the Charges Register of the said title prior to completion and shall *j*
> not be entitled to refuse or delay completion by reason of the fact that the Charges
> Register of the said title still retains an entry of the said lease dated 24th October
> 1932.'

On 12 November 1984, Cowen Lipson and Rumney sent a further amendment to the
special conditions to Harman Healy & Co. That was in the following terms:

a   'The property is sold subject to and with the benefit of a Lease dated the 29th April 1976. By reason of the matters referred to in Special Condition 2 hereof the Vendor does not have in its possession the original Counterpart of the said Lease and can only provide a copy thereof. The Purchaser shall not be entitled to refuse or delay completion by reason of the fact that the Vendor does not hand over either the original Counterpart Lease or a certified copy thereof and only has in its possession a copy thereof referred to in paragraph 4 of the said Statutory Declaration

b   referred to in Special Condition 2 hereof. The Purchaser shall not be entitled to base any claim against the Vendor whether for damages for breach of Contract, compensation for loss of bargain, interest or otherwise by reason of any of the matters referred to in Special Conditions 2 and 3 hereof.'

c   Some time prior to the auction, the defendant obtained copies of the auction particulars and the special conditions in their un-amended form. It is, I think, clear that there is nothing in the particulars or the conditions (as printed, and before amendment) which would put a prospective purchaser on notice that the property was subject to the 1932 lease. The defendant attended the auction on 20 November 1984. The auction was conducted on behalf of Harman Healy & Co by Mr Barnett. Mr Barnett is a fellow of the Royal Institution of Chartered Surveyors, an experienced auctioneer and has been a

d   partner in Harman Healy & Co for some 21 years.
       Mr Barnett told me that he was well aware, and had expressed the view to Cowen Lipson & Rumney, that it had to be made abundantly clear to any purchaser that the property at 195 Burnt Oak Broadway had been the subject of a ground lease which had been forfeited. In particular, it had to be made clear that the landlords would not have the original counterpart of the 1976 underlease to produce to a purchaser.

e   There were over 90 lots to be sold on 20 November 1984; and I accept that it would not be unusual in a sale of this nature for there to be a number of last minute addenda to the particulars and conditions as published in the printed catalogue. To meet this point Harman Healy & Co produced a series of pink roneod sheets drawing attention to the additions. On one of those sheets there is found the entry: 'Lot 35—195 Burnt Oak Broadway, Edgware, Middlesex. Extra special conditions together with revised plan

f   available at the rostrum.'
       Mr Barnett told me, and I accept, that some 500 copies of these sheets were produced and were placed on every chair in the room at the auction hall.
       The property, which was lot no 35, was to be sold at the beginning of the afternoon session. I have had the advantage of hearing in the course of the trial a tape recording of Mr Barnett's introduction to the afternoon session. That recording was, I understand, taken as a matter of normal procedure. It is clear from that recording, and Mr Barnett

g   confirmed in his oral evidence before me, that he drew specific attention to the addendum and to the entry relating to lot 35. I read from a transcript of the relevant parts of that recording. At the beginning of the afternoon session Mr Barnett said this;

       'On lot 35 there is a two page extra special condition together with a revised plan.
h   I'll just mention that one in particular now. If there is anyone contemplating bidding on lot 35, which is Burnt Oak Broadway, I would like you to be aware of what is in the additional special conditions. Don't ask me in the middle of the bidding, so please, anyone for lot 35 who hasn't seen the additional three page special conditions and the plan, please make sure you see it before I get to that because it is only in two lots' time.'

j   And, immediately before offering lot 35 for sale, he said:

       'Lot 35 is 195 Broadway Burnt Oak, Edgware, Middlesex. It is a lock-up shop with a self-contained flat above. A separate lock-up shop at the side plus a rear building. It's freehold. It is let on the tenancy as set out. They have paid £3,500 a year, it is worth quite a lot more, you will see the reference to the comparable, and I would just again tell you that there are these special conditions that we are selling subject to, so don't anyone come in at the very last minute not knowing what is in these special conditions. The plan will show the additional land at the back that **a** wasn't shown on the catalogue. I advise you that you shouldn't bid unless you have read these special conditions. That is all.'

The defendant did not recall seeing the pink addenda sheets in the auction hall. But he did recall Mr Barnett's speech; and, in particular, he recalled that Mr Barnett had said that anyone interested in lot 35 should come up and take the special conditions. The **b** defendant went to the rostrum and asked for the special conditions for lot 35. He told me that he was handed one white sheet of paper; and it is clear that this was the first of the two additional special conditions. He read the document sitting in his seat in the auction hall and appreciated that there was an additional lease referred to in the special condition about which he had not previously been aware. He told me that he thought it was an old lease which had expired before Mr Clayton had taken possession, and that his **c** knowledge of it had no effect on his bidding. It is clear from his evidence that he was aware that some step had been taken to obtain peaceable re-entry within the previous months, but I accept that he had little time to consider the matter, and no time on which to take legal advice, and that he would not have appreciated the full significance of what was stated in the special condition.

The property was offered for auction on the afternoon of 20 November 1984, and was **d** knocked down in the course of the auction to the defendant at the price of £54,500. It is common ground that this price would reflect the value of the property at that time on the basis that it was subject only to the 1976 underlease. The value of the freehold subject to the 1932 lease would be very substantially less. At the conclusion of the auction, the defendant signed a memorandum evidencing his purchase. In due course, after the title had been investigated by his solicitors, the defendant took a transfer of the freehold **e** interest dated 8 December 1984 at a purchase consideration of £54,500. He charged the property to his bank to secure an advance of some £30,000 which he applied towards the purchase price. I should, perhaps, mention, that the bank has taken no part in these proceedings, although I have been informed that it is aware of them.

On 2 January 1985 Cowen Lipson & Rumney sent to Messrs Brecher & Co, the **f** solicitors acting for the defendant in the purchase, the executed transfer, the land certificate, the counterpart lease of 1932, the original statutory declaration of Mr Bloch and the exhibits thereto, and a letter of authority addressed to Mr Clayton in respect of all rent falling due on or after 24 December 1984.

On 4 January 1985 Brecher & Co sent that letter of authority to Mr Clayton and requested him to forward to them a cheque for the current quarter's rent due under the 1976 underlease, an amount of £875. On 11 January 1985 Mr Clayton replied to the **g** effect that, although he had been about to send the rent to Brecher & Co in response to their letter, he had now had a demand from Stockbridge Trust, who were astounded to be told of the events of the past two months. Mr Clayton asked Brecher & Co to 'get together with Stockbridge Trust and resolve the matter'.

At about the same time, the plaintiffs, through their solicitors Messrs Charlsley Harrison, by a letter dated 10 January 1985, tendered the arrears of rent due under the **h** 1932 lease. That tender was not accepted, and shortly thereafter, on 13 February 1985, the present proceedings were commenced by the plaintiffs.

The first question which I have to consider is, of course, whether there was a re-entry by the landlords on 19 October 1984. If there was no re-entry, then there was no forfeiture. There appears to be little authority on the nature of the acts required to effect **j** a re-entry against an intermediate tenant in a case where the premises are in the occupation of a subtenant. I was referred to a passage in *Woodfall's Law of Landlord and Tenant* (28th edn, 1978) vol 1, para 1–1899:

'Peaceable re-entry may be effected by the forfeiture landlord accepting as tenant a subtenant who is already in occupation, or by letting into occupation some third

party and maintaining him there as tenant. But, it is clear that some unequivocal
act or words are necessary to constitute a peaceable re-entry.'

The authority cited in support of the first sentence of that passage is *London and County
(A & D) Ltd v Wilfred Sportsman Ltd (Greenwoods (Hosiers and Outfitters) Ltd, third party)*
[1970] 2 All ER 600, [1971] Ch 764. But that was a case in which the defendants had
gone into possession as trespassers against the tenant. The position was explained by
Russell LJ ([1970] 2 All ER 600 at 607, [1971] Ch 764 at 785):

'Finally, the plaintiff argued that there was in fact here no re-entry. There could
be none by the third party until the reversion was vested in it on 31st August 1965.
Prior to that date the situation was that 5 Upper High Street was being occupied by
the defendant at the instance of the third party in trespass against Mr Miah as the
lessee. Mere continuation of that situation (it was argued) could not operate as a re-
entry. It would have been necessary for the third party and the defendant in some
way to withdraw from the premises and then return physically in order to achieve
a re-entry. As it was put, the trespass must be discontinued before there can be
forfeiture by re-entry. I am not able to accept that argument. I see no point in the
law requiring what was described in *Baylis v Le Gros* (1858) 4 CBNS 537, 140 ER
1201 as an "idle ceremony"—a case in which there was sufficient re-entry by
acceptance of sub-tenant already in occupation as tenant of the forfeiting landlord.
Before 31st August 1965 the third party was supporting the defendant in occupation
in trespass against Mr Miah. Thereafter the third party was reversioner, entitled to
forfeit, and by asserting the right in law to keep the defendant in occupation as
tenant of the third party could only be understood in law to be asserting the
determination of Mr Miah's lease by reason of a forfeiture.'

The right in law which the third party, Greenwoods, was asserting in that case was the
right to maintain the defendants, Sportsman, in occupation of the premises known as 5
Upper High Street, Bargoed, Glamorgan, as their tenants under a new tenancy on the
terms of a draft lease which had been negotiated and agreed between Greenwoods and
Sportsman. That was not a case in which Sportsman had ever been the subtenants, in
respect of 5 Upper High Street, of the tenant, Miah, whose lease Greenwoods were held
to have determined by re-entry. In my judgment *London and County (A & D) Ltd v Wilfred
Sportsman Ltd* is no authority for the proposition that a landlord may effect a re-entry of
premises against his tenant by an arrangement made with an existing subtenant under
which the subtenant is to remain in occupation of the premises as the tenant of the
landlord for the residue and otherwise on the terms of his existing sublease. But, although
it appears to me clear that the *Wilfred Sportsman* case does not, on its own facts, afford the
defendant any assistance in the present case, the dictum of Russell LJ to which I have
referred does suggest that *Baylis v Le Gros* (1858) 4 CBNS 537, 140 ER 1201 may be
authority for that proposition.

In *Baylis v Le Gros* the facts were these. Factory premises at Tottenham were let under
a lease dated 28 September 1850 by one Barnewell to the plaintiff's father for a term of
21 years at the yearly rent of £165 15s, payable quarterly. The lease contained a proviso
for re-entry in the event of non-payment of rent or breach of covenant. The plaintiff's
father died on 23 October 1850, having by his will bequeathed the leasehold premises to
his executors, namely his wife, one Joseph Fletcher and the plaintiff, on his attaining age
21. The widow alone proved the will; and she continued to carry on business at the
factory premises.

On 1 June 1851 the widow deposited the lease with Fletcher as security for a debt of
£2,500, and also secured the same debt by a chattel mortgage over the plant and
machinery on the premises. On 22 June 1852 the plaintiff came of age, but he did not
then come in to prove his father's will. On 1 November 1852 Fletcher died, and his will
was proved by his executors. In February 1853 the widow died intestate.

At some time after the widow's death the defendants, Messrs Le Gros & Co, went into possession of the premises. On 24 October 1853, the landlord Barnewell, having inspected *a* the premises and found them out of repair, allowed the defendants to remain in possession as his tenants under an oral agreement until Lady Day 1854 at a yearly rent of £150 and on condition that they should purchase the plant and machinery from Fletcher's executors. This they did by an assignment dated 5 November 1853.

On 9 January 1854 the defendants gave Barnewell notice of their intention to quit the premises at Lady Day 1854. Nevertheless, they remained in possession, and a tenancy for *b* a further year was agreed at the same rent. On 21 December 1854 the plaintiff took out letters of administration to his mother's estate; and on 24 February 1855 he took probate of his father's will. By a writ dated 12 February 1855 he brought an action of ejectment to recover possession of the premises from the defendants.

The question for the court was whether the lease dated 28 September 1850 had been determined by a re-entry by Barnewell. The court were unanimous in holding that there *c* had been a re-entry. Cockburn CJ said (4 CBNS 537 at 554, 140 ER 1201 at 1208):

> 'Finding the premises in a dilapidated state, the landlord comes upon them and enters into an agreement with a man he finds in possession, to become his tenant, intending thereby to act upon the forfeiture and to oust the lessee. I think that was quite sufficient to constitute an entry by the landlord so as to put an end to the lease.' *d*

Williams J was of the same view. He said (4 CBNS 537 at 555, 140 ER 1201 at 1208):

> 'As to the other point, if Barnewell had entered and desired the person he found upon the premises to go out, and then desired him to resume possession as his tenant, the case would have been clear beyond all doubt. They did not go through that idle ceremony: but the facts set out in the special case show a re-entry by the *e* landlord, and something more.'

It was urged on me on behalf of the defendant that *Baylis v Le Gros* had been decided on the basis that Le Gros & Co had been let into possession by the plaintiff. Some support for this contention can be found in an answer given by counsel for the plaintiff to a question put by the court in the course of the argument in that case (see 4 CBNS 537 at 553, 140 ER 1201 at 1208). But it appears to me that, on a true analysis of the facts, there *f* was no evidence to explain how the defendants in that case came to be occupying the premises before 24 October 1853, and, in particular, no evidence that they had ever been subtenants of, or paid rent to, the plaintiff before that date. But, whether Le Gros & Co were subtenants, licencees or trespassers in relation to the plaintiff immediately before 24 October 1853, it is clear that the arrangement which they made with Barnewell on that date was not that they should remain in possession under any existing tenancy, but *g* rather that they should be allowed to remain only on the basis that they became the tenants of Barnewell under a new tenancy, and for a different term.

It follows that, notwithstanding the dictum of Russell LJ in *London and County (A & D) Ltd v Wilfred Sportsman Ltd* [1970] 2 All ER 600 at 607, [1971] Ch 764 at 785, to which I have referred, I am unable to regard *Baylis v Le Gros* as an authority for the proposition *h* which I have set out above. In my judgment, the most that can be derived from *Baylis v Le Gros* is that a landlord may effect a re-entry against his tenant by an arrangement with an existing subtenant under which the subtenant is to remain in occupation as the tenant of the landlord on the terms of a new tenancy. So understood, I do not think that that authority assists the defendant in the present case.

In the present case, it appears to me apt to describe the changing of the lock at 195 *j* Burnt Oak Broadway as 'an idle ceremony'. This is, I think, illustrated by the fact that, when told by Mr Clayton that the new lock was unsatisfactory, Twogates Properties Ltd, through their solicitors, were content that the lock should be replaced by Mr Clayton himself. There was never any intention on the part of the landlords to exclude the subtenant from possession. There is, to my mind, no doubt that Mr Bloch and his locksmith would not have been permitted by Mr Clayton to interfere with the existing

lock if Mr Clayton had been told that that act was intended in any way to interfere with
a his rights under his existing sublease. Mr Clayton was not told this. On the contrary he
was assured, by Mr Bloch in person and by the first of the letters dated 19 October 1984,
that Twogates Properties Ltd were not in any way challenging his right to remain in
occupation of the premises at 195 Burnt Oak Broadway under the provisions of his
existing underlease. If there was a re-entry in the present case, it was not effected by the
changing of the lock.

b The real question on this part of the case, as it appears to me, is whether the landlords
effected a re-entry, constructively, by obtaining Mr Clayton's consent to their actions on
the terms of the first letter of 19 October 1984. In my judgment, even if it could be said
that Mr Clayton attorned tenant to Twogates Properties Ltd by tacitly accepting the
terms of that letter, such an attornment would not be evidence of an unequivocal
intention on the part of the landlords to re-enter under the provisions of the 1932 lease.
c It is clear that both Twogates Properties Ltd and Mr Clayton were acting on the basis that
the 1976 underlease would continue. If Mr Clayton was making an attornment at all he
was doing so as tenant under that underlease.

It is equally clear, although perhaps not appreciated at the time, that the continuation
of the 1976 underlease was wholly inconsistent with the determination, by forfeiture, of
the 1932 lease. In these circumstances, it is, in my judgment, impossible to regard the
d arrangements which Twogates Properties Ltd made on 19 October 1984 as amounting
to a re-entry under the 1932 lease.

On the view which I take of the matter, it is unnecessary to consider whether an
attornment by Mr Clayton on the terms of the 1976 underlease would be made void by
the provisions of s 151(2) of the Law of Property Act 1925. It is, I think, a question of
some difficulty whether a landlord who is asserting that notwithstanding that the head
e lease has been forfeited nevertheless the underlease survives, is 'a person claiming to be
entitled to the interest of the land of the lessor (meaning the intermediate lessor)' for the
purposes of that subsection. It seems to me that that difficulty arises because the
subsection is not framed to meet a situation which the draftsman would have recognised
as being incapable of existing at law.

It is, strictly, unnecessary also for me to go on to consider the second question raised in
f the action; namely whether, if the 1932 lease had been determined by forfeiture, this
would be a proper case for the court to grant relief from forfeiture.

Nevertheless, in case this matter should go further, it may be of assistance if I express
the view that this would have been a proper case for relief. The principles on which relief
from forfeiture for non-payment of rent is granted are well known, and they may be
found in the line of authority of which *Howard v Fanshawe* [1895] 2 Ch 581, [1895–9]
g All ER Rep 855 and *Lovelock v Margo* [1963] 2 All ER 13, [1963] 2 QB 786 are leading
examples. It was urged on me, on behalf of the defendant, that relief ought not to be
granted where to do so would prejudice the rights of third parties. The defendant, so it
was argued, had purchased the freehold at auction on the basis that it was not encumbered
by the 1932 lease. I do not think that it would be right to give weight to this
h consideration. Before the defendant made his bid at the auction on 20 November 1984,
he had in his possession the first of the additional special conditions, which he had
obtained from the auctioneers. This disclosed that the property had been subject to the
1932 lease and that, if that lease had determined, it was by reason of a peaceable re-entry
for non-payment of rent which had been effected within the past few weeks. Knowing
these facts, the defendant was on notice, before he purchased the property, that the tenant
j under the 1932 lease was likely to have an unanswerable claim for relief from forfeiture.
Whether or not the defendant was actually aware that such a claim could or would be
made, I do not know of any grounds on which (if they had need to do so) the plaintiffs
should have been unable to pursue that claim against the defendant to as full an extent as
they could have done against his predecessors, Twogates Properties.

Accordingly, I declare that the lease dated 24 October 1932 has not been forfeited by
the events which took place on 19 October 1984 and, further, that the plaintiffs are

entitled to give a good receipt to Gerald Clayton for the sum of £875, being the rent due under the underlease on 25 December 1984, and for subsequent rent payable thereunder.   *a*

Declaration accordingly.

Solicitors: *Gamlens* (for the plaintiffs); *Duke-Cohan & Co* (for the defendant).

Hazel Hartman   Barrister.   *b*

H v B (formerly H)   *c*

FAMILY DIVISION
HOLLINGS J
2 OCTOBER 1986

Divorce – Financial provision – Application – Investigation by registrar – Extent of registrar's   *d*
jurisdiction – Questionnaire as to means – Ancillary proceedings settled by consent order 'in full
and final settlement' of all claims – Wife subsequently serving questionnaire as to means on
husband – Husband refusing to answer – Whether ancillary proceedings at an end – Whether
registrar having jurisdiction to order husband to answer questionnaire – Matrimonial Causes
Rules 1977, r 77(4).

The husband and wife were divorced in 1977. In 1981 a consent order was made in   *e*
ancillary proceedings whereby the husband agreed to convey a house into their joint
names on trust for the parties in equal shares and also agreed to make periodical payments
to the wife. The order was expressed to be made 'in full and final settlement' of all
financial claims by either party. The transfer and trust were duly executed by the
husband. In 1986 the wife served a questionnaire on the husband under r 77(4)[a] of the   *f*
Matrimonial Causes Rules 1977 regarding the husband's financial affairs. The husband
refused to answer and the wife applied to the registrar for an order directing the husband
to answer the questionnaire. No application was made to set aside the consent order. The
registrar held that the ancillary proceedings were still subsisting, that the wife was
accordingly entitled to make the application for discovery and further, that under r 77(4)
the wife could make such an application at any stage. He accordingly granted the wife   *g*
leave to serve the questionnaire on the husband, who appealed.

Held – Since the material part of the 1981 consent order had already been executed and
the order was a final order in full settlement of all financial claims, the ancillary
proceedings had come to an end. An application directing compliance with a
questionnaire under r 77(4) of the 1977 rules could only be made in proceedings which   *h*
were pending, and since in the circumstances there were no pending proceedings, either
to appeal out of time or to set aside the order for non-disclosure, it followed that the
registrar had no jurisdiction to grant the wife's application. The appeal would accordingly
be allowed (see p 769 *d j* and p 770 *b h*, post).

Thwaite v Thwaite [1981] 2 All ER 789 distinguished.

Livesey (formerly Jenkins) v Jenkins [1985] 1 All ER 106 considered.   *j*

---

a   Rule 77(4), so far as material, provides: 'Any party to an application for ancillary relief may by
letter require the other party to give further information concerning any matter contained in any
affidavit filed by or on behalf of that other party or any other relevant matter ... and may, in
default of compliance by such other party, apply to the registrar for directions.'

Notes

a For consent orders embodying the spouses' agreement on financial provisions, see 13 Halsbury's Laws (4th edn) para 1158.

For the Matrimonial Causes Rules 1977, see 10 Halsbury's Statutory Instruments (5th reissue) 248.

Cases referred to in judgment

b *Livesey (formerly Jenkins) v Jenkins* [1985] 1 All ER 106, [1985] AC 424, [1985] 2 WLR 47, HL.

Thwaite v Thwaite [1981] 2 All ER 789, [1982] Fam 1, [1981] 3 WLR 96, CA.

Appeal

c The respondent husband appealed out of time with leave against the order of Mr Registrar Segal made on 22 May 1986 whereby he ordered that the respondent deliver particulars pursuant to a questionnaire given under r 77(4) of the Matrimonial Causes Rules 1977 to the petitioner wife. The appeal was heard and judgment was given in chambers. The case is reported by permission of Hollings J. The facts are set out in the judgment.

d *John Friel* for the respondent.
Peter Duckworth for the petitioner.

HOLLINGS J. This is an application by the husband who was the respondent in the divorce proceeding between him and his wife for leave to appeal out of time from an order of Mr Registrar Segal made on 22 May 1986. The appeal was lodged on 4 August
e 1986, the delay being caused by the necessity for the former husband to obtain legal aid. I understand that this is not disputed.

The order of the registrar which is sought to be appealed from, and I can say at once I propose to give leave to appeal out of time and to hear the appeal now, was to the effect that the respondent should answer a questionnaire purported to be submitted under r 77(4) of the Matrimonial Causes Rules 1977, SI 1977/344, directed to certain accounts,
f and to obtaining a schedule of property disposed of and acquired over a considerable period of time by him.

That application for the administration of a questionnaire and an order that that questionnaire should be answered was made purportedly, apparently, in proceedings for ancillary relief which had commenced very many years ago, and I relate now the relevant dates.

g The respondent had married the petitioner in November 1958 in Nicosia. They were divorced by decree nisi on 6 October 1977 and decree absolute on 18 November 1977. On 18 July 1981 the respondent applied for ancillary relief and the matter came before the court on 30 July 1981 when, both sides being represented, a consent order was made by Mr Registrar Stranger-Jones. This order was to the effect that, the respondent having bought a house which the petitioner had agreed to use as the new family home for her
h and the children instead of the formal matrimonial home, into which the petitioner had moved and lived with the five children of the family, the new house should be held by the petitioner and the respondent as trustees for themselves in equal shares. It was further ordered that the respondent should transfer to the petitioner and to himself jointly his title in the new house on the above trusts within three months. There was a further provision with regard to a mortgage which is not relevant to this appeal. The transfer
j into joint names on this trust was completed long ago.

It was provided in para 3 of the order that in consideration of that, the petitioner undertook (in the words of the order)—

'not to make any claim whatsoever hereinafter and to take no further proceedings for financial provisions, a lump sum or sums or any adjustment of property order for herself and further, the petitioner agrees to abandon and relinquish all her claims, shares and interests in property at [certain addresses and in certain companies].'

By para 4 it was ordered that the respondent should pay to the petitioner during their joint lives until she should remarry periodical payments at the rate of £30 per week, payable weekly, and certain payment to the children of the family until they reached a certain age. It was by para 5 provided that 'this order is made in full and final settlement of all claims by either party for lump sum payment and/or property adjustment', and then was provision for costs.

Matters proceeded without further court action until October 1985, when the petitioner applied ex parte to prevent the respondent from disposing of certain assets, alleging that, in particular, he was attempting to dispose of the house referred to in the consent order.

An interim order was made on 8 October 1985, pending a full hearing, restraining the respondent from such a course, and the matter came for a full hearing before his Honour Judge Quentin Edwards QC on 24 October 1985. Judge Quentin Edwards then ordered, having heard counsel for both parties and considered the affidavit evidence, that on the respondent undertaking not to take any steps to dispose of this particular house until further order, there should be no order on the petitioner's application. He ordered that the petitioner should pay the respondent's costs, such order not to be enforced without the leave of the court.

There matters rested until, on 24 March 1986, the solicitors acting for the petitioner served the questionnaire to which I have referred. The respondent refused to answer and so the application to which I have referred came before the registrar.

No appeal has been lodged by the petitioner against the making of the consent order on 30 July 1981. No application has been made on her behalf to set that consent order aside as, of course, there is jurisdiction to do if the evidence justifies it, in accordance with the decisions in *Thwaite v Thwaite* [1981] 2 All ER 789, [1982] Fam 1 and *Livesey (formerly Jenkins) v Jenkins* [1985] 1 All ER 106, [1985] AC 424. So the registrar was asked to deal with this without there being any formal application or, indeed, any application at all.

It is apparent from what I am told by counsel that the reason, or one of the reasons, indeed, the primary reason at that point in time, for seeking to administer the questionnaire was to see if the answers to the questionnaire would provide material on which the petitioner could obtain legal aid.

Counsel for the respondent has set out a number of grounds in his notice of appeal against the decision of the registrar. The first of the grounds is that the registrar had no jurisdiction to make the order and the other grounds are, in the alternative, that the registrar wrongly exercised his discretion in making the order that the evidence on which it was based was insufficient and the order was unduly onerous and too wide in its terms, and that, as regards the evidence before the court, issue estoppel applied.

I have been furnished with a note of the registrar's judgment, which has been approved by him. The first part of his judgment refers to whether or not he considers himself bound by the facts as found by Judge Quentin Edwards in the later proceedings in October 1985, and he went on to refer to counsel for the respondent's submission, he said:

'It is said that [counsel for the petitioner's] application is fatally flawed and that no application is made in accordance with the rules. This point fails as a thoroughly shabby, unmeritorious and technical point, which would result in a rehearing of this application. I am satisfied that if r 77 can apply to compel the use of Forms 11 and 13 it will be unrealistic to say that an application cannot be made unless a form of application is issued.'

That does not, it is conceded by both counsel, clearly set out what it is believed the registrar intended to say. It is believed that what the registrar intended to say is that it

was unrealistic in the circumstances to say that the application could not be heard by him
a because there was no form of application in issue. The registrar continued by saying:

> 'The proceedings are still in being. No notice of an intention to make an
> application is necessary and such a notice is not relevant. The wife was still a party
> to an application for ancillary relief. If this was a hearing for leave to appeal before a
> judge, an application for discovery could be made, and I find this supports my
> *b* decision here. The right to apply for discovery exists until the proceedings are
> disposed of. If I am wrong, r 77(6) applies and allows the wife at any stage of the
> proceedings to make this application and gives me power to grant it. The next point
> made is that this is a fishing expedition. [Counsel for the petitioner] satisfies me that
> there is a prima facie case for supposing that there are matters to investigate. So if
> no application is made to pursue this matter at the end of the day this does not deter
> *c* me. If [counsel for the petitioner's] questionnaire shows that the husband was not
> frank in 1981 this will influence the judge',

and he then went on to deal with the other grounds submitted by counsel for the
respondent.

In my judgment there was, indeed, no jurisdiction on which the registrar could make
the order that he did. Counsel for the petitioner has referred me to the decisions I have
d already mentioned, *Thwaite v Thwaite* and *Livesey v Jenkins*. But in both those cases it is to
be observed that there were, from the inception, applications by the relevant party to
appeal out of time or to set aside the order the court was concerned with. In *Thwaite v
Thwaite*, Ormrod LJ gave the judgment of the court. Counsel has referred me to a passage
where, after Ormrod LJ had referred to a passage in the judgment of the court below, he
said ([1981] 2 All ER 789 at 793, [1982] Fam 1 at 7):
e

> 'The judge might have left the matter there because under the consent order of
> 30th April 1979 the dismissal of the wife's application for ancillary relief took effect
> only from the date of the conveyance. It was open to her to restore her application
> immediately or later. But he, not unreasonably, thought that this state of affairs was
> unsatisfactory, particularly because he concluded that the die was cast, and that the
> *f* children's future now lay in Australia and that the circumstances under which the
> order had been made had wholly changed.'

And so, in that way, the judge proposed to make a new order in favour of the wife.

In *Thwaite v Thwaite* the order was an executory order, in that the wife's application for
ancillary relief was to be dismissed only upon the conveyance of the matrimonial home,
and in that case the conveyance had not taken place. As I read the judgment in that
g passage, it was because the order was executory that it was open to the wife to restore her
application immediately or later.

I referred also to part of the judgment as follows ([1981] 2 All ER 789 at 795, [1982]
Fam 1 at 9):

> 'The judge was entitled, in his discretion, to make a new order for ancillary relief
> *h* in favour of the wife, notwithstanding the refusal of the wife to consent to his doing
> so. His jurisdiction arose not from the liberty to apply, as he held, but from the fact
> that the wife's original application for ancillary relief was still before the court and
> awaiting adjudication. It had not been dismissed since the conveyance had never
> been executed, so that that part of the order of 30th April 1979, by which her
> application was dismissed, had never come into effect. We think that the judge
> *j* correctly exercised his descretion in this respect.'

There again, it seeems to me that the judgment of the Court of Appeal was based on
the fact that in that case the order was an executory one. In the present case, the material
part of the order, for one is not concerned in this case with the periodical payments part
of it, that relating to the matrimonial home, had become executed. The home had long
ago been transferred by the respondent to the petitioner.

I refer now to the 1977 rules. It is submitted by counsel for the petitioner that even though there was no application for leave to appeal out of time, even though there was *a* no application to set aside for non-disclosure, for that is what is in the contemplation of the petitioner, nevertheless the proceedings for ancillary relief are still pending so that a questionnaire can, without any further application, be applied for under r 77.

I have considered a certain number of other rules and it is, first of all, plain that under the 1977 rules, an application for a questionnaire can only be made in proceedings which are pending. There is no provision in the 1977 rules equivalent to the comparatively new *b* provision for discovery in civil actions which allows discovery before the issue of a writ. The 1977 rules are derived from the RSC Ord 24, r 1, where, in relation to discovery (and, of course, this questionnaire is a form of discovery), it is provided:

> '... there shall ... be discovery by the parties to the action of the documents which are or have been in their possession, custody or power relating to matters in *c* question in the action.'

Firstly, there is no action here (there was no application before the registrar) and, secondly, as I said earlier in this judgment, it is conceded that this questionnaire is administered not for the immediate purpose of a proposed application to the court but for the purpose of an application for legal aid, which is an added reason why, in my judgment, there was no jurisdiction to accede to this application, or at least why, in the *d* exercise of his discretion, the registrar should have refused to make the order.

Counsel for the petitioner has also referred me to a passage in *Livesey (formerly Jenkins) v Jenkins* [1985] 1 All ER 106 at 113, [1985] AC 424 at 436 where Lord Brandon referred to the terms of s 25(1) of the Matrimonial Causes Act 1973 being of crucial importance in relation to the matters raised in that appeal, which is another case of non-disclosure, and he said: *e*

> 'It follows that, in proceedings in which parties invoke the exercise of the court's powers under ss 23 and 24, they must provide the court with information about all the circumstances of the case, including, inter alia, the particular matters so specified. Unless they do so, directly or indirectly, and ensure that the information provided is correct, complete and up to date, the court is not equipped to exercise, and cannot *f* therefore lawfully and properly exercise, its discretion in the manner ordained by s 25(1).'

That, of course, must be accepted and, with respect, is plainly right and must follow. But counsel for the petitioner has not, in my judgment, got his case off the ground; that is his difficulty. There is not even an affidavit filed in an application; not even an affidavit *g* filed without an application, in fact, purporting to show that there has been any non-disclosure with regard to any of these matters under the sections referred to by Lord Brandon. If ever there was a fishing expedition, as counsel for the respondent submitted this is, this seems, in my judgment, to be one. For that additional reason, I consider that the application was misconceived, and I think, with the greatest respect to the registrar, he should have dismissed the application, or rule that he had no jurisdiction to hear it. *h*

For those reasons, having given leave to appeal out of time, I allow the appeal.

Appeal allowed.

Solicitors: *Rose & Birn* (for the respondent); *Hallewell & Co* (for the petitioner).

Bebe Chua   Barrister.

R v Howe and another
and another appeal

HOUSE OF LORDS

LORD HAILSHAM OF ST MARYLEBONE LC, LORD BRIDGE OF HARWICH, LORD BRANDON OF OAKBROOK, LORD GRIFFITHS AND LORD MACKAY OF CLASHFERN

17, 18, 19, 20 NOVEMBER 1986, 19 FEBRUARY 1987

Criminal law – Duress as a defence – Murder – Whether defence of duress available to charge of murder – Whether any distinction to be drawn between principal in first degree and principal in second degree.

Criminal law – Accomplice – Alternative offence – Accessory before fact prevailing on another to commit criminal act – Whether accused can be convicted of offence more serious than that committed by principal.

Criminal law – Duress as a defence – Test of duress – Whether test objective or subjective – Whether defendant required to have self-control of ordinary citizen in his situation.

The defence of duress is not available to a person charged with murder whether as principal in the first degree (the actual killer) or as principal in the second degree (the aider and abettor) (see p 778 *a* to *d*, p 782 *j*, p 784 *b* to *h*, p 789 *g j*, p 790 *b c* and p 798 *d* to *h*, post); *R v Dudley and Stephens* [1881–5] All ER Rep 61 and *Abbott v R* [1976] 3 All ER 140 considered; *Lynch v DPP for Northern Ireland* [1975] 1 All ER 913 overruled.

Where an accessory before the fact has by duress incited or procured another to commit a criminal act, he can properly be convicted of a more serious offence than that committed by the principal in the first degree (see p 775 *d e*, p 782 *j* to p 783 *a*, p 784 *g h*, p 790 *f* and p 799 *j*, post); *R v Richards (Isabelle)* [1973] 3 All ER 1088 overruled.

The test of whether a defendant was impelled by duress to act as he did is objective, not subjective, and accordingly a defendant is required to have the self-control reasonably to be expected of an ordinary citizen in his situation (see p 775 *e* to *g*, p 782 *j*, p 784 *g h*, p 790 *f* and p 800 *h*, post); *R v Graham* [1982] 1 All ER 801 applied.

Decision of the Court of Appeal [1986] 1 All ER 833 affirmed.

Notes

For duress as a defence to a criminal charge, see 11 Halsbury's Laws (4th edn) para 24, and for cases on the subject, see 14(1) Digest (Reissue) 57–59, 266–280.

Cases referred to in opinions

Abbott v R [1976] 3 All ER 140, [1977] AC 755, [1976] 3 WLR 462, PC.
Anderton v Ryan [1985] 2 All ER 355, [1985] AC 560, [1985] 2 WLR 968, HL.
Hyam v DPP [1974] 2 All ER 41, [1975] AC 55, [1974] 2 WLR 607, HL.
Lynch v DPP for Northern Ireland [1975] 1 All ER 913, [1975] AC 653, [1975] 2 WLR 641, HL.
Myers v DPP [1964] 2 All ER 881, [1965] AC 1001, [1964] 3 WLR 145, HL.
Note (judgment: judicial decisions as authority: House of Lords) [1966] 3 All ER 77, [1966] 1 WLR 1234.
R v Bourne (1952) 36 Cr App R 125, CCA.
R v Brady and Hindley (6 May 1966, Chester Assizes).
R v Brown and Morley [1968] SASR 467, SA SC (Full Ct).
R v Cogan [1975] 2 All ER 1059, [1976] QB 217, [1975] 3 WLR 316, CA.
R v Dudley and Stephens (1884) 14 QBD 273, [1881–5] All ER Rep 61, DC.

R v Fitzpatrick [1977] NI 20, NI CCA.
R v Graham [1982] 1 All ER 801, [1982] 1 WLR 294, CA.
R v Hindawi (24 October 1986, unreported), CCC.
R v Hudson, R v Taylor [1971] 2 All ER 244, [1971] 2 QB 202, CA.
R v Kray [1969] 3 All ER 941, [1970] 1 QB 125, 53 Cr App R 569, CA.
R v Richards (Isabelle) [1973] 3 All ER 1088, [1974] QB 776, [1973] 3 WLR 888, CA.
R v Shivpuri [1986] 2 All ER 334, [1986] 2 WLR 988, HL.
R v Tyler and Price (1838) 8 C & P 616, 173 ER 643, NP.
Sephakela v R [1954] HCTLR 60, PC.
State v Goliath 1972 (3) SA 1, AD.
Woolmington v DPP [1935] AC 462, [1935] All ER Rep 1, HL.

Conjoined appeals and appeal

R v Howe and another

Michael Anthony Howe and John Derrick Bannister appealed with leave of the Court of Appeal, Criminal Division against the decision of that court (Lord Lane CJ, Russell and Taylor JJ) ([1986] 1 All ER 833, [1986] QB 626) on 27 January 1986 dismissing their appeals against their convictions of two counts of murder in the Crown Court at Manchester before Jupp J and a jury on 28 January 1985. The facts are set out in the opinion of Lord Hailsham LC.

R v Burke and another

Cornelius James Burke and William G Clarkson appealed with leave of the Court of Appeal, Criminal Division against the decision of that court (Lord Lane CJ, Russell and Taylor JJ) ([1986] 1 All ER 833, [1986] QB 626) on 27 January 1986 dismissing their appeals against their convictions of murder in the Central Criminal Court before the Common Serjeant (his Honour Judge Tudor Price QC) and a jury on 16 October 1984. The facts are set out in the opinion of Lord Hailsham LC.

By order of the House of Lords dated 3 November 1986 the appeals of Burke, Howe and Bannister were ordered to be conjoined.

Michael Self QC, Peter L Crichton-Gold and *Roy Warne* for Howe, Bannister and Burke.
Alan Suckling QC and *Diana Ellis* for Clarkson.
Benet Hytner QC and *Timothy Langdale* for the Crown.

Their Lordships took time for consideration.

19 February. The following opinions were delivered.

LORD HAILSHAM OF ST MARYLEBONE LC. My Lords, these appeals arise from two cases, one (Howe and Bannister) originating from a trial in the Crown Court at Manchester before Jupp J and a jury and one (Burke and Clarkson) in the Central Criminal Court before the then Common Serjeant, his Honour Judge Tudor Price QC, and a jury. Howe and Bannister were tried with two other defendants (Murray and Bailey), both of whom during the trial changed their plea to one of guilty and were appropriately sentenced. The indictment in the case of Howe, Bannister, Murray and Bailey accused the four men of two murders (Elgar and Pollitt) and a conspiracy to murder (Redfern, an intended victim who escaped in time). The three counts related to three successive days, respectively 10, 11 and 12 October 1983. Burke and Clarkson were charged with the murder of a single victim (Botton) on 9 July 1983.

The four current appellants appealed against their convictions to the Court of Appeal, Criminal Division (Lord Lane CJ, Russell and Taylor JJ) ([1986] 1 All ER 833, [1986] 1

QB 626), which dismissed all four appeals in a judgment delivered on 27 January 1986.
a In giving leave to appeal to your Lordships' House the Court of Appeal certified three questions of law of general public importance as involved in the decision. The three certified questions are:

> '(1) Is duress available as a defence to a person charged with murder as a principal in the first degree (the actual killer)? (2) Can one who incites or procures by duress another to kill or to be a party to a killing be convicted of murder if that other is
> **b** acquitted by reason of duress? (3) Does the defence of duress fail if the prosecution prove that a person of reasonable firmness sharing the characteristics of the defendant would not have given way to the threats as did the defendant?'

The first of these questions involves a reconsideration of the much discussed decisions in *Lynch v DPP for Northern Ireland* [1975] 1 All ER 913, [1975] AC 653 and *Abbott v R*
c [1976] 3 All ER 140, [1977] AC 755. In answering the second question, the Court of Appeal invited us to reconsider the decision of the Court of Appeal in *R v Richards (Isabelle)* [1973] 3 All ER 1088, [1974] QB 776, by which it considered itself bound.

In the arguments presented before your Lordships many other reported authorities and citations from established writers, including the Law Commission Report on Defences of General Application (Law Com no 83 (1977)) were cited.
d Reference to other cases will be made as and where appropriate. I take the facts of these truly horrible cases almost verbatim from the judgment of Lord Lane CJ in the instant appeal ([1986] 1 All ER 833 at 835, [1986] QB 626 at 635). First, as to the case of Howe and Bannister, Murray and Bailey, the facts were as follows.

At the time of the offences Howe and Bailey were 19, Bannister was 20 and Murray was 35. Howe had one minor conviction for motoring offences. Bannister had convictions
e for theft and burglary but none for violence. He was on probation. Bailey had convictions for burglary and theft. Murray had 25 previous court appearances, including two convictions for assault occasioning actual bodily harm, and in 1974 he had been convicted of assault with intent to rob and robbery in respect of which he had been sentenced to eight years' imprisonment.

Bannister met Murray in Risley Remand Centre. Howe and Bailey met in Stockport
f when Bailey was living in a hostel and Howe happened to be living next door with his grandmother. Murray came to visit Bailey when he was on six days' home leave from a sentence of 2½ years' imprisonment. Bailey introduced Howe to Murray. Lord Lane CJ continued ([1986] 1 All ER 833 at 835–836, [1986] QB 626 at 635–636):

> '*Count 1: murder of Elgar*
> **g**   The first victim was a 17-year old youth called Elgar. He was offered a job as a driver by Murray. On the evening of 10 October [1983] all five men were driven by Murray up into the hills between Stockport and Buxton, eventually stopping at some public lavatories at a remote spot called Goytsclough. Murray at some stage told both appellants in effect that Elgar was a "grass", and that they were going to kill him. Bannister was threatened with violence if he did not give Elgar "a bit of a
> **h** battering". From thenceforwards Elgar, who was naked, sobbing and begging for mercy, was tortured, compelled to undergo appalling sexual perversions and indignities, he was kicked and punched. Bannister and Howe were doing the kicking and punching. The coup de grâce was executed by Bailey, who strangled Elgar with a headlock. It is unnecessary to go into further details of the attack on Elgar, which are positively nauseating. In brief the two appellants asserted that they
> **j** had only acted as they did through fear of Murray believing that they would be treated in the same way as Elgar had been treated if they did not comply with Murray's directions. The prosecution were content to assent to the proposition that death had been caused by Bailey strangling the victim, although the kicks and punches would have resulted in death moments later even in the absence of the

strangulation. The body was hidden by the appellants and the other two men. On
this basis the appellants were in the position of what would have earlier been
principals in the second degree and duress was left to the jury as an issue on this
count.

Count 2: murder of Pollitt

Very much the same course of conduct took place as with Elgar. On 11 October
the men picked up Pollitt, a 19-year-old labourer, and took him to the same place
where all four men kicked and punched the youth. Murray told Howe and Bannister
to kill Pollitt, which they did by strangling him with Bannister's shoe-lace. As the
appellants were in the position of principals in the first degree, the judge did not
leave duress to the jury on this count.

Count 3: conspiracy to murder Redfern

The third intended victim was a 21-year-old man. The same procedure was
followed, but Redfern suspected that something was afoot and managed with some
skill to escape on his motor cycle from what would otherwise have inevitably been
another horrible murder. The judge left the defence of duress to the jury on this
charge of conspiracy to murder. The grounds of appeal, which are the same in
respect of each of these appellants, are as follows: that the judge erred in directing
the jury: (1) in respect of count 2, that the defence of duress was not available to a
principal in the first degree to the actual killing; (2) in respect of counts 1 and 3, that
the test whether the appellants were acting under duress contains an "objective"
element, that is to say, if the prosecution prove that a reasonable man in the position
of the defendant would not have felt himself forced to comply with the threats, the
defence fails.'

So much for the facts relating to the appellants Howe and Bannister.

Lord Lane CJ then turned to the case of Burke and Clarkson. In the case of Howe and
Bannister the defence of duress was left to the jury by Jupp J on the third count of
conspiracy to murder and rejected by the jury. However, Jupp J had directed the jury in
relation to duress. In this case Burke dressed as a policeman had killed Botton with a
sawn-off shotgun at the entrance of Botton's house. Lord Lane CJ continued ([1986] 1 All
ER 833 at 836, [1986] QB 626 at 637):

'The prosecution's case was that Burke had done this at the request of Clarkson,
who was anxious to prevent Botton from giving evidence against him. Clarkson's
defence was that he had nothing to do with the shooting at all. Burke's defence was
that he had agreed to shoot Botton because of his fear that Clarkson would kill him
if he did not, but when it came to the event, the gun went off accidentally and the
killing therefore was unintentional and amounted to no more than manslaughter.'

This defence was evidently rejected by the judge, but his defence in respect of
manslaughter was left to the jury.

A further submission on behalf of Burke was not argued before us. On the third
certified question Jupp J's direction to the jury on the nature of duress, although not
identical with that of Judge Tudor Price, equally raised the question of the objective
element in the threats required raised by the third question certified by the Court of
Appeal. The only ground of appeal separately argued before your Lordships on the part
of Clarkson depends on the answer to be given to the second certified question, to which
I will return later.

On the third certified question counsel for the appellants other than Clarkson addressed
to us an impressive argument that the test applied is not objective, ie not—

'whether the threat was of such gravity that it might well have caused a reasonable
man placed in the same situation as the defendant to act as the defendant did [nor]

would a sober person of reasonable firmness sharing the defendant's characteristics have responded to the threats by taking part in the killing . . .'

Counsel's submission was to the effect that, where the defence of duress is available to an accused, the test of duress does not contain either of these objective elements but is purely subjective to the accused and depends solely on the effect which the actual threat had on the mind of the particular accused.

From the above, it will be seen that each of the appellants other than Clarkson were actual participants, whether as principal in the first or second degree, in the perpetration of the actual killing of the respective victims in respect of the counts of murder. Clarkson's defence, which was that he had nothing whatever to do with the murder of Botton, was rejected by the jury and nothing turns on this at all except that the jury's verdict means that he was the real villain of the piece, since, on any view of the facts, Burke acted at his suggestion and was very much under his influence. The success of Clarkson's appeal depends solely on the answer to the second certified question, and only arises in the event that Burke's appeal on the first or third question succeeds or succeeds to the extent that a conviction of Burke for manslaughter should be substituted in the case for the verdict of murder. Counsel for Clarkson very properly conceded that the decision of the second question was free from authority binding on this House and open to your Lordships, both on principle and authority, since *R v Richards (Isabelle)* [1973] 3 All ER 1088, [1974] QB 776, by which the Court of Appeal regarded itself as bound, is not binding on your Lordships' House. It was conceded that, on the facts as they must be assumed to be for the purposes of the second question, apart from authority the point was totally devoid of merit, and, despite the advocacy of counsel, their Lordships did not think fit to trouble counsel for the Crown on this question. The Court of Appeal does not appear to have referred directly (although it was mentioned in argument) to the horrible case of *R v Cogan* [1975] 2 All ER 1059, [1976] QB 217, which, if the answer had not been otherwise obvious, seems to me to dispose of the matter. In the event, we also did not call on the Crown to argue the third certified question since, in my opinion, and, I believe, that of my noble and learned friend, the definition of duress, whether applicable to murder or not, was correctly stated by both trial judges to contain an objective element on the lines of their respective directions and this must involve a threat of such a degree of violence that 'a person of reasonable firmness' with the characteristics and in the situation of the defendant could not have been expected to resist. No doubt there are subjective elements as well, but, unless the test is purely subjective to the defendant, which, in my view, it is not, the answer to the third certified question, like that to the second, must be Yes.

This leaves us free to discuss the first, and principal, issue in the appeal, which is the answer to be given to the first of the three certified questions. In my opinion this must be decided on principle and authority, and the answer must in the end demand a reconsideration of the two authorities of *Lynch v DPP for Northern Ireland* [1975] 1 All ER 913, [1975] AC 653 and *Abbott v R* [1976] 3 All ER 140, [1977] AC 755. Having been myself a party to *Abbott v R*, I feel I owe it to the two noble and learned friends then with me in the majority (Lord Kilbrandon and Lord Salmon) to say that we were very conscious of the fact that our decision would only be of persuasive authority in the English jurisdiction whilst the decision in *Lynch's* case, though a Northern Irish case, which distinguished for the purposes of duress between principals in the first degree on the one hand and principals in the second degree and aiders and abettors on the other, being a decision of the House of Lords would be likely to be treated as binding throughout England and Wales as well as Northern Ireland. We did, however, say ([1976] 3 All ER 140 at 143, [1977] AC 755 at 763):

'Whilst their Lordships feel bound to accept the decision of the House of Lords in *Lynch v Director of Public Prosecutions for Northern Ireland* they find themselves constrained to say that had they considered (which they do not) that that decision was an authority which required the extension of the doctrine to cover cases like the present, they would not have accepted it.'

Speaking only for myself, it was precisely because the three noble and learned Lords in the majority (Lord Morris, Lord Wilberforce and Lord Edmund-Davies) in *Lynch's* case had expressly left open the availability of duress as a defence to the actual participant in a murder that I found it possible to accept the decision in *Lynch's* case without criticism, and then only because the *Abbott* appeal was solely concerned with the question so expressly left open. One only needs to read the facts in *Abbott v R* to be aware of exactly what the Board was being asked to do if it extended *Lynch's* case and allowed the appeal.

The present case, in my opinion, affords an ideal and never to be repeated opportunity to consider, as we were invited expressly to do by the Crown, the whole question afresh, if necessary by applying the 1966 Practice Statement (*Note* [1966] 3 All ER 77, [1966] 1 WLR 1234) to the decision in *Lynch's* case.

I therefore consider the matter first from the point of view of authority. On this I can only say that at the time when *Lynch's* case was decided the balance of weight in an unbroken tradition of authority dating back to Hale and Blackstone seems to have been accepted to have been that duress was not available to a defendant accused of murder. I quote only from Hale and Blackstone. Thus, *Hale's Pleas of the Crown* (1 Hale PC 51):

'... if a man be desperately assaulted, and in peril of death, and cannot otherwise escape, unless to satisfy his assailant's fury he will kill an innocent person then present, the fear and actual force will not acquit him of the crime and punishment of murder, if he commit the fact; for he ought rather to die himself, than kill an innocent ...'

Blackstone's Commentaries on the Laws of England (4 Bl Com (1857 edn) 28) was to the same effect. He wrote that a man under duress 'ought rather to die himself than escape by the murder of an innocent'. I forbear to quote the eloquent and agonised passage in the dissenting speech of Lord Simon in *Lynch's* case [1975] 1 All ER 913 at 931, [1975] AC 653 at 695 or the more restrained exposition of Lord Kilbrandon on the law as expressed in *R v Dudley and Stephens* (1884) 14 QBD 273, [1881–5] All ER Rep 61 (see [1975] 1 All ER 913 at 944, [1975] AC 653 at 702). These quotations are unnecessary since it seems to have been accepted both by the majority in *Lynch's* case and the minority in *Abbott's* case that, to say the least, prior to *Lynch's* case there was a heavy proponderance of authority against the availability of the defence of duress in cases of murder.

I would only add that art 8 of the Nuremberg statute (Charter of the International Military Tribunal (1945) (annex to TS 27 (1946); Cmd 6903)) which was, at the time, universally accepted, save for its reference to mitigation, as an accurate statement of the common law both in England and the United States of America, states that—

'The fact that the Defendant acted pursuant to order of his Government or of a superior shall not free him from responsibility, but may be considered in mitigation of punishment if the Tribunal determines that justice so requires.'

'Superior orders' is not identical with 'duress', but, in the circumstances of the Nazi regime, the difference must often have been negligible. I should point out that, under art 6, the expression 'war crimes' expressly included that of murder, which, of course, does not include the killing of combatants engaged in combat.

What then is said on the other side? I accept, of course, that duress for almost all other crimes has been held to be a complete defence. I need not cite cases. They are carefully reviewed in *Lynch's* case and establish, I believe, that the defence is of venerable antiquity and wide extent. I pause only to say that, although duress has, in my view, never been defined with adequate precision, two views of its nature can no longer be viewed as correct in the light of reported authority. The first is that of Stephen in his *History of the Criminal Law of England* (1883) vol 2, pp 107–108, who first promulgated the opinion a that duress was not a defence at all but, as in the Nuremberg statute, only a matter of mitigation. The fact is that, where it is applicable at all, in a long line of cases duress has been treated as a matter of defence entitling an accused to a complete acquittal. But in almost every instance where duress is so treated a cautionary note has been sounded excluding murder, in terms sometimes more and sometimes less emphatic, from the number of crimes where it can be put forward.

b The second unacceptable view is that, possibly owing to a misunderstanding which has been read into some judgments, duress as a defence affects only the existence or absence of mens rea. The true view is stated in *Lynch's* case [1975] 1 All ER 913 at 945, 951, [1975] AC 653 at 703, 709–710 by Lord Kilbrandon (of the minority) and by Lord Edmund-Davies (of the majority) in their analysis.

Lord Kilbrandon said:

c '. . . the decision of the threatened man whose constancy is overborne so that he yields to the threat, is *a calculated decision to do what he knows to be wrong*, and is therefore that of a man with, perhaps to some exceptionally limited extent, a "guilty mind". But he is at the same time a man whose mind is less guilty than is his who acts as *he* does but under no such constraint.' (The first emphasis is mine.)

d In coming to the same conclusion Lord Edmund-Davies quoted from Professor Glanville Williams's well-known treatise *Criminal Law: The General Part* (2nd edn, 1961) p 751, para 242:

'True duress is not inconsistent with act and will as a matter of legal definition, the maxim being *coactus volui*. Fear of violence does not differ in kind from fear of economic ills, fear of displeasing others, or any other determinant of choice; it would be inconvenient to regard a particular type of motive as negativing of will.'

e After approving a paragraph from Lowry LCJ, Lord Edmund-Davies went on to say that two quotations from Lord Goddard CJ in the disgusting case of *R v Bourne* (1952) 36 Cr App R 125 were subject to criticism on this score.

Before I leave the question of reported authority I must refer to two other cases. The first is *R v Kray* [1969] 3 All ER 941, [1970] 1 QB 125, which was, to some extent, relied on by the majority in *Lynch's* case, on the score of an obiter dictum of Widgery LJ (see 53 Cr App R 569 at 578). I do not myself regard this passage as authoritative. It depends on a concession by the Crown, regarding a party who was not before the Court of Appeal as his case had been disposed of at first instance, in order to found a submission by the appellants. The dictum is also open to the criticism that Widgery LJ appeared to treat duress as making a person otherwise than an 'independent actor', which is contrary to the analysis which I have accepted above.

g The other reported authority is the famous and important case of *R v Dudley and Stephens* (1884) QBD 273, [1881–5] All ER Rep 61. That is generally and, in my view, correctly regarded as an authority on the availability of the supposed defence of necessity rather than duress. But I must say frankly that, if we were to allow this appeal, we should, I think, also have to say that *R v Dudley and Stephens* was bad law. There is, of course, an h obvious distinction between duress and necessity as potential defences: duress arises from the wrongful threats or violence of another human being and necessity arises from any other objective dangers threatening the accused. This, however, is, in my view, a distinction without a relevant difference, since on this view duress is only that species of the genus of necessity which is caused by wrongful threats. I cannot see that there is any j way in which a person of ordinary fortitude can be excused from the one type of pressure on his will rather than the other.

I shall revert to *R v Dudley and Stephens* when I come to consider some of the issues of principle involved in our response to the first certified question. But at this stage I feel that I should say that in *Abbott v R* I would have been prepared to accept a distinction between *Abbott v R* and *Lynch's* case on the basis of the argument which appeared to attract Lord Morris in *Lynch's* case [1975] 1 All ER 913 at 918–919, [1975] AC 653 at 671–672. I would not myself have immersed myself in the somewhat arcane terminology of accessory, principal in the second degree, and aiding and abetting. But it did seem to me then, and it seems to me now, that there is a valid distinction to be drawn in ordinary language between a man who actually participates in the irrevocable act of murder to save his own skin or that of his nearest and dearest and a man who simply participates before or after the event in the necessary preparation for it or the escape of the actual offender. It is as well to remember that in *Abbott v R* the facts were that Abbott had dug a pit, thrown the victim into it, subjected her in co-operation with others to murderous blows and stab wounds and then buried her alive. It seems to me that those academics who see no difference between that case and the comparatively modest part alleged (falsely as is now known) in *Lynch's* case to have been played by the defendant under duress have parted company with a full sense of reality. Nevertheless and in spite of this, and in the face of the somewhat intemperate criticism to which this type of distinction has sometimes been subjected since *Abbott v R*, I am somewhat relieved to know that the views of my noble and learned friends on the main issue permit me to escape from such niceties and simply to say that I do not think that the decision in *Lynch's* case can be justified on authority and that, exercising to the extent necessary the freedom given to us by the 1966 Practice Statement (*Note* [1966] 3 All ER 77, [1966] 1 WLR 1234), which counsel for the Crown urged us to apply, I consider that the right course in the instant appeal is to restore the law to the condition in which it was almost universally thought to be prior to *Lynch's* case. It may well be that that law was to a certain extent unclear and to some extent gave rise to anomaly. But these anomalies I believe to be due to a number of factors extraneous to the present appeal and to the intrinsic nature of duress. The first is the mandatory nature of the sentence in murder. The second resides in the fact that murder is a 'result' crime, only being complete if the victim dies within the traditional period of a year and a day and that, in consequence, a different crime may be charged according to whether or not the victim actually succumbs during the prescribed period. The third lies in the fact (fully discussed amongst many other authorities in *Hyam v DPP* [1974] 2 All ER 41, [1975] AC 55) that, as matters stand, the mens rea in murder not simply consists in an intention to kill, but may include an intent to commit grievous bodily harm. It has always been possible for Parliament to clear up this branch of the law (or indeed to define more closely the nature and extent of the availability of duress as a defence). But Parliament has conspiciously, and perhaps deliberately, declined to do so. In the mean time, I must say that the attempt made in *Lynch's* case to clear up this situation by judicial legislation has proved to be an excessive and perhaps improvident use of the undoubted power of the courts to create new law by creating precedents in individual cases.

This brings me back to the question of principle. I begin by affirming that, while there can never be a direct correspondence between law and morality, an attempt to divorce the two entirely is and has always proved to be doomed to failure, and, in the present case, the overriding objects of the criminal law must be to protect innocent lives and to set a standard of conduct which ordinary men and women are expected to observe if they are to avoid criminal responsibility.

No one who has read *R v Dudley and Stephens*, whether in the law reports or in the more popular and discursive volume published by Professor Simpson *Cannibalism in the Common Law* (1984), can fail to be moved by the poignant and anguished situation to which the two shipwrecked mariners with Brooks (who was not guilty) and the innocent boy of 17, who was the victim, were exposed and which led the Home Secretary of the day to commute a death sentence for murder to one of six months' imprisonment. Nevertheless, when one comes to examine the case as one of legal principle it is, I believe, the case that the conclusion reached by the judges of the Queen's Bench Division and voiced by Lord Coleridge CJ, not with manifest compassion, has met with very wide acceptance. He said (14 QBD 273 at 286–288, [1881–5] All ER Rep 61 at 67):

a   'Now it is admitted that the deliberate killing of this unoffending and unresisting boy was clearly murder, unless the killing can be justified by some well-recognised excuse admitted by the law. It is further admitted that there was in this case no such excuse, unless the killing was justified by what has been called "necessity". But the temptation to the act which existed here was not what the law has ever called necessity. Nor is this to be regretted. Though law and morality are not the same, and many things may be immoral which are not necessarily illegal, yet the absolute

b   divorce of law from morality would be of fatal consequence; and such divorce would follow if the temptation to murder in this case were to be held by law an absolute defence of it. It is not so. To preserve one's life is generally speaking a duty, but it may be the plainest and the highest duty to sacrifice it. War is full of instances in which it is a man's duty not to live, but to die. The duty, in case of shipwreck, of a captain to his crew, of the crew to the passengers, of soldiers to women and

c   children, as in the noble case of the *Birkenhead*; these duties impose on men the moral necessity, not of the preservation, but of the sacrifice of their lives for others, from which in no country, least of all, it is to be hoped, in England, will men ever shrink, as indeed, they have not shrunk . . . It is not needful to point out the awful danger of admitting the principle which has been contended for. Who is to be the judge of this sort of necessity? By what measure is the comparative value of lives to

d   be measured? Is it to be strength, or intellect, or what? It is plain that the principle leaves to him who is to profit by it to determine the necessity which will justify him in deliberately taking another's life to save his own. In this case the weakest, the youngest, the most unresisting, was chosen. Was it more necessary to kill him than one of the grown men? The answer must be "No" . . .'

e   It was pointed out in a footnote in this case (attributed to Grove J) that, if the principle were once admitted and the castaways not rescued, in the mean time it would have been lawful for the strongest of the four men to eat his way through the whole crew of the drifting boat in order to be rescued himself (see 14 QBD 273 at 288).

I must dissent profoundly from the statement of my predecessor Francis Bacon, a greater moralist perhaps in theory than in practice, where, quoted by Lord Coleridge CJ

f   in *R v Dudley and Stephens* 14 QBD 273 at 285, [1881–5] All ER Rep 61 at 66, in his commentary on the maxim necessitas induct privilegium quoad jura privata, he writes:

'. . . if divers be in danger of drowning by the casting away of some boat or barge, and one of them get to some plank, or on the boat's side to keep himself above water, and another to save his life thrust him from it, whereby he is drowned, this is neither se defendendo nor by misadventure, but justifiable.'

g   I also dissociate myself from the view of Rumpff JA in the South African case *State v Goliath* 1972 (3) SA 1 at 25 (based, however, on Roman-Dutch law) and quoted in *Abbott v R* [1976] 3 All ER 140 at 150, [1977] AC 755 at 771 as a justification for the opinion of the dissenting minority:

h   'It is generally accepted . . . that for the ordinary person in general his life is more valuable than that of another. Only they who possess the quality of heroism will intentionally offer their lives for another. Should the criminal law then state that compulsion could never be a defence to a charge of murder, it would demand that a person who killed another under duress, whatever the circumstances, would have to comply with a higher standard than that demanded of the average person. I do

j   not think that such an exception to the general rule which applies in criminal law is justified.'

In general, I must say that I do not at all accept in relation to the defence of duress that it is either good morals, good policy or good law to suggest, as did the majority in *Lynch's* case and the minority in *Abbott v R*, that the ordinary man of reasonable fortitude is not to be supposed to be capable of heroism if he is asked to take an innocent life rather than sacrifice his own. Doubtless in actual practice many will succumb to temptation, as they did in *R v Dudley and Stephens*. But many will not, and I do not believe that as a 'concession to human frailty' (see Smith and Hogan *Criminal Law* (5th edn, 1983) p 215) the former should be exempt from liability to criminal sanctions if they do. I have known in my own lifetime of too many acts of heroism by ordinary human beings of no more than ordinary fortitude to regard a law as either 'just or humane' which withdraws the protection of the criminal law from the innocent victim and casts the cloak of its protection on the coward and the poltroon in the name of a 'concession to human frailty'.

I must not, however, underestimate the force of the arguments on the other side, advanced as they have been with such force and such persuasiveness by some of the most eminent legal minds, judicial and academic, in the country.

First, amongst these is, perhaps, the argument from logic and consistency. A long line of cases, it is said, carefully researched and closely analysed, establish duress as an available defence in a wide range of crimes, some at least, like wounding with intent to commit grievous bodily harm, carrying the heaviest penalties commensurate with their gravity. To cap this, it is pointed out that, at least in theory, a defendant accused of this crime under s 18 of the Offences against the Person Act 1861, but acquitted on the grounds of duress, will still be liable to a charge of murder if the victim dies within the traditional period of one year and a day. I am not, perhaps, persuaded of this last point as much as I should. It is not simply an anomaly based on the defence of duress. It is a product of the peculiar mens rea allowed on a charge of murder which is not confined to an intent to kill. More persuasive, perhaps, is the point based on the availability of the defence of duress on a charge of attempted murder, where the actual intent to kill is an essential prerequisite. It may be that we must meet this casus omissus in your Lordships' House when we come to it. It may require reconsideration of the availability of the defence in that case too.

I would, however, prefer to meet the case of alleged inconsistency head on. Consistency and logic, though inherently desirable, are not always prime characteristics of a penal code based like the common law on custom and precedent. Law so based is not an exact science. All the same, I feel I am required to give some answer to the question posed. If duress is available as a defence to some of the most grave crimes why, it may legitimately be asked, stop at murder, whether as accessory or principal and whether in the second or the first degree? But surely I am entitled, as in the view of the Common Serjeant in the instant case of Clarkson and Burke, to believe that some degree of proportionality between the threat and the offence must, at least to some extent, be a prerequisite of the defence under existing law. Few would resist threats to the life of a loved one if the alternative were driving across the red lights or in excess of 70 mph on the motorway. But, to use the Common Serjeant's analogy, it would take rather more than the threat of a slap on the wrist or even moderate pain or injury to discharge the evidential burden even in the case of a fairly serious assault. In such a case the 'concession to human frailty' is no more than to say that in such circumstances a reasonable man of average courage is entitled to embrace as a matter of choice the alternative which a reasonable man could regard as the lesser of two evils. Other considerations necessarily arise where the choice is between the threat of death or a fortiori of serious injury and deliberately taking an innocent life. In such a case a reasonable man might reflect that one innocent human life is at least as valuable as his own or that of his loved one. In such a case a man cannot claim that he is choosing the lesser of two evils. Instead, he is embracing the cognate but morally disreputable principle that the end justifies the means.

I am not so shocked as some of the judicial opinions have been at the need, if this be the conclusion, to invoke the availability of administrative as distinct from purely judicial remedies for the hardships which might otherwise occur in the most agonising cases. Even in *R v Dudley and Stephens* in 1884 when the death penalty was mandatory and frequently inflicted, the prerogative was used to reduce a sentence of death by hanging

to one of six months in prison. In murder cases the available mechanisms are today both
a more flexible and more sophisticated. The trial judge may make no minimum
recommendation. He will always report to the Home Secretary, as he did in the present
case of Clarkson and Burke. The Parole Board will always consider a case of this kind
with a High Court judge brought into consultation. In the background is always the
prerogative and, it may not unreasonably be suggested, that is exactly what the
prerogative is for. If the law seems to bear harshly in its operation in the case of a
b mandatory sentence on any particular offender there has never been a period of time
when there were more effective means of mitigating its effect than at the present day. It
may well be thought that the loss of a clear right to a defence justifying or excusing the
deliberate taking of an innocent life in order to emphasise to all the sanctity of a human
life is not an excessive price to pay in the light of these mechanisms. Murder, as every
practitioner of the law knows, though often described as one of the utmost heinousness,
c is not in fact necessarily so, but consists in a whole bundle of offences of vastly differing
degrees of culpability, ranging from brutal, cynical and repeated offences like the so-
called Moors murders (R v Brady and Hindley (6 May 1966, unreported)) to the almost
venial, if objectively immoral, 'mercy killing' of a beloved partner.

   Far less convincing than the argument based on consistency is the belief which appears
in some of the judgments that the law must 'move with the times' in order to keep pace
d with the immense political and social changes since what are alleged to have been the
bad old days of Blackstone and Hale. I have already dealt with this argument in my
respectful criticism of the dissent in Hyam v DPP [1974] 2 All ER 41, [1975] AC 55. The
argument is based on the false assumption that violence to innocent victims is now less
prevalent than in the days of Hale or Blackstone. But I doubt whether this is so. We live
e in the age of the Holocaust of the Jews, of international terrorism on the scale of massacre,
of the explosion of aircraft in mid-air, and murder sometimes at least as obscene as
anything experienced in Blackstone's day. Indeed, one of the present appeals may provide
an example. I have already mentioned the so-called Moors murders. But within weeks of
hearing this appeal a man was convicted at the Central Criminal Court of sending his
pregnant mistress on board an international aircraft at Heathrow, with her suitcase
f packed with a bomb and with the deliberate intention of sending the 250 occupants,
crew, passengers, mistress and all to a horrible death in mid-air (R v Hindawi (24 October
1986, unreported)). I cannot forbear to say that if Abbott v R was wrongly decided, and
had the attempt succeeded, the miscreant who did this would have been free to escape
scot-free had he been in a position to discharge the evidential burden on duress and had
the prosecution, on the normal Woolmington principles (see Woolmington v DPP [1935] AC
g 462 at 482, [1935] All ER Rep 1 at 8), been unable to exclude beyond reasonable doubt
the possibility of his uncorroborated word being true. I must also point out in this
context that known terrorists are more and not less vulnerable to threats than the
ordinary man and that a plea of duress in such a case may be all the more plausible on
that account. To say this is not to cast doubt on the reliability and steadfastness of juries.
Counsel for the appellants was able to say with perfect truth that, where duress in fact
h has been put forward in cases where it was available, juries have been commendably
robust as they were in the instant cases in rejecting it where appropriate. The question is
not one of the reliability of juries. It is one of principle. Should the offence of duress be
available in principle in such a case as that of R v Hindawi, where, of course, it was not
put forward? The point which I am at the moment concerned to make is that it is not
clear to me that the observations of Blackstone and Hale, and almost every respectable
j authority, academic or judicial, prior to Lynch's case are necessarily to be regarded in this
present age as obsolescent or inhumane or unjust owing to some supposed improvement
in the respect for innocent human life since their time which unfortunately I am too
blind to be able for myself to perceive. Still less am I able to see that a law which denies
such a defence in such a case must be condemned as lacking in justice or humanity rather
than as respectable in its concern for the sanctity of innocent lives. I must add that, at

least in my view, if *Abbott v R* were wrongly decided some hundreds who suffered the death penalty at Nuremberg for murders were surely the victims of judicial murder at the hands of their conquerors owing to the operation of art 8. Social change is not always for the better and it ill becomes those of us who have participated in the cruel events of the twentieth century to condemn as out of date those who wrote in defence of innocent lives in the eighteenth century.

During the course of argument it was suggested that there was available to the House some sort of halfway house between allowing these appeals and dismissing them. The argument ran that we might treat duress in murder as analogous to provocation, or perhaps diminished responsibility, and say that, in indictments for murder, duress might reduce the crime to one of manslaughter. I find myself quite unable to accept this. The cases show that duress, if available and made out, entitles the accused to a clean acquittal, without, it has been said, the 'stigma' of a conviction. Whatever other merits it may have, at least the suggestion makes nonsense of any pretence of logic or consistency in the criminal law. It is also contrary to principle. Unlike the doctrine of provocation, which is based on emotional loss of control, the defence of duress, as I have already shown, is put forward as a 'concession to human frailty' whereby a conscious decision (it may be coolly undertaken) to sacrifice an innocent human life is made as an evil lesser than a wrong which might otherwise be suffered by the accused or his loved ones at the hands of a wrongdoer. The defence of diminished responsibility (which might well, had it then been available to Dudley and Stephens, have prevailed there) is statutory in England though customary in Scotland, the law of its origin. But in England at least it has a conceptual basis defined in the Homicide Act 1957 which is totally distinct from that of duress if duress be properly analysed and understood. Provocation (unique to murder and not extending even to 's 18' offences) is a concession to human frailty due to the extent that even a reasonable man may, under sufficient provocation temporarily lose his self-control towards the person who has provoked him enough. Duress, as I have already pointed out, is a concession to human frailty in that it allows a reasonable man to make a conscious choice between the reality of the immediate threat and what he may reasonably regard as the lesser of two evils. Diminished responsibility as defined in the Homicide Act 1957 depends on abnormality of mind impairing mental responsibility. It may overlap duress or even necessity. But it is not what we are discussing in the instant appeal.

I must add that, had I taken a different view, in the cases of Bannister and Howe and, for rather different reasons, in the case of Burke, I would have gone on to consider the questions whether in any of these appeals the appellants had discharged the evidential burden in duress, or whether, if they had, on the facts described in the judgment of Lord Lane CJ, the proviso should not have been applied in every case. The case of Clarkson is surely beyond dispute on the assumption that the second question is not answered in his favour. But, whatever may be the characteristics of duress, even on the existing law the ingredients of immediacy and absence of voluntary association (see *R v Fitzpatrick* [1977] NI 20) must be essential components of the evidential burden more or less on the lines of the draft Bill (Criminal Liability (Duress) Bill) annexed to the Law Commission report (Law Com no 83) to which I have referred above. Even apart from this and on the assumption that the matter should properly have been left to the jury, I am rather more than doubtful whether any properly instructed jury could have acquitted on the murder charges in either of the instant cases or on the facts of *Abbott v R*. It is not necessary to express a concluded opinion on this since, for the reasons I have adumbrated above, I consider that these appeals should be dismissed and the certified questions answered respectively (1) No, (2) Yes, (3) Yes. If so, the questions relating to the proviso and evidential burden do not arise. So far as I have indicated, the decision of this House in *Lynch v DPP for Northern Ireland* [1975] 1 All ER 913, [1975] AC 653 should be regarded as unsatisfactory and the law left as it was before *Lynch's* case came up for decision. The decision in *Abbott v R* [1976] 3 All ER 140, [1977] AC 755 should be followed, and, unless

it can be distinguished on the facts, that in *R v Richards (Isabelle)* [1973] 3 All ER 1088,
a [1974] QB 776 should be overruled.

LORD BRIDGE OF HARWICH. My Lords, the defence of duress, as a general
defence available at common law which is sufficient to negative the criminal liability of
a defendant against whom every ingredient of an offence has otherwise been proved, is
difficult to rationalise or explain by reference to any coherent principle of jurisprudence.
b The theory that the party acting under duress is so far deprived of volition as to lack the
necessary criminal intent has been clearly shown to be fallacious: see *Lynch v DPP for
Northern Ireland* [1975] 1 All ER 913 at 951–952, [1975] AC 653 at 709–711 per Lord
Edmund-Davies. No alternative theory seems to provide a wholly satisfactory foundation
on which the defence can rest. The law, therefore, might have developed more logically
had it adopted the view of Stephen, expressed in his *History of the Criminal Law of England*
c (1883) vol 2, pp 107–108, that duress should be a matter, not of defence, but of
mitigation. If this course had been followed, it might sensibly have led to the further
development that, in the case of murder, duress, like provocation, would have sufficed to
reduce the offence from murder to manslaughter. But that is not the law and, though it
is open to Parliament to decide that it ought to be, that course is not open to us. We have
to accept the law as we find it and, given the lack of any clear underlying principle to
d which we can refer, we must not, I think, be wholly surprised if the solution to the
problem posed by the first certified question arising in these appeals fails to remove all
the anomalies which some may discern in this field of the law.
    If we take the majority decisions of this House in *Lynch's* case and of the Privy Council
in *Abbott v R* [1976] 3 All ER 140, [1977] AC 755 as establishing the present law, duress
is a complete defence to a murderer otherwise guilty as a principal in the second degree,
e it is no defence to a murderer guilty as a principal in the first degree. Technically, of
course, the two decisions were made in two distinct jurisdictions, though three Lords of
Appeal (Lord Wilberforce, Lord Kilbrandon and Lord Edmund-Davies) were party to
both. In this situation it is an odd quirk of the system operated by two ultimate appellate
tribunals, each deciding by a majority, that their two decisions should have the combined
f effect of affirming a distinction which four out of the seven participants in the decisions
(Lord Simon and Lord Kilbrandon in *Lynch's* case, Lord Wilberforce and Lord Edmund-
Davies in *Abbott v R*) expressly rejected as untenable. The only speech which gives any
positive, even if somewhat lukewarm, support to the distinction is that of Lord Morris
in *Lynch's* case [1975] 1 All ER 913 at 918, [1975] AC 653 at 671:

g   'The issue in the present case is therefore whether there is any reason why the
    defence of duress, which in respect of a variety of offences has been recognised as a
    possible defence, may not also be a possible defence on a charge of being a principal
    in the second degree to murder. I would confine my decision to that issue. It may
    be that the law must deny such a defence to an actual killer, and that the law will
    not be irrational if it does so.'

h
    Later, referring to the 'actual killer', he said ([1975] 1 All ER 913 at 919, [1975] AC 653
at 671): 'There, I think, before allowing duress as a defence it may be that the law will
have to call a halt.' Lord Morris supported the distinction by illustrations of theoretical
cases where principals in the second degree (as in *Lynch's* case itself) might be seen as
playing a relatively minor role in a murderous enterprise. These passages are naturally
j referred to in the majority judgment in *Abbott v R*, but this hardly strengthens support
for the distinction when one remembers, firstly, that Lord Kilbrandon was one of the
majority, secondly, that the essential attitude of the majority in *Abbott v R* to the decision
in *Lynch's* case is expressed by saying that 'their Lordships, whilst loyally accepting the
decision in *Lynch's* case, are certainly not prepared to extend it' (see [1976] 3 All ER 140
at 144, [1977] AC 755 at 764).

As is pointed out in Smith and Hogan *Criminal Law* (5th edn, 1983) p 211, there is no necessary correspondence between degrees of culpability of parties to a murder and the *a* technical distinction between principals in the first and second degrees which would make the latter a rational cut-off point at which the defence of duress ceases to be available. My noble and learned friend Lord Griffiths gives cogent examples to illustrate this. I can find nothing whatever to be said for leaving the law as it presently stands. Ineluctably, as it seems to me, we must either move forward and affirm the view of the minority in *Abbott v R* that duress is available as a defence to murder generally, or depart *b* from *Lynch's* case and restore the law as it was generally accepted before *Lynch's* case, whereby duress was not a defence available to any party otherwise guilty of murder.

All other considerations apart, I should myself have found a sufficient reason for deciding in favour of the latter course in the consideration that it was never open to the House in its judicial capacity to make such a fundamental reform of the law as the introduction of duress as a defence to murder involved. The passages in *Lynch's* case *c* [1975] 1 All ER 913 at 938–939, 942–943, [1975] AC 653 at 695–696, 699–701 in the speeches to this effect of Lord Simon and of Lord Kilbrandon seem to me to carry conviction. But that conviction is now immensely strengthened by the knowledge that Parliament, even against the background of the plainly unsatisfactory present state of the law, has in ten years taken no action on the Law Commission's Report on Defences of General Application (Law Com no 83). If duress is now to be made available generally as *d* a defence to murder, it seems to me incontrovertible that the proper means to effect such a reform is by legislation such as that proposed by the Law Commission. Not only is it for Parliament to decide whether the proposed reform of the law is socially appropriate, but it is also by legislation alone, as opposed to judicial development, that the scope of the defence of duress can be defined with the degree of precision which, if it is to be *e* available in murder at all, must surely be of critical importance.

My Lords, I have had the advantage of reading in advance the speeches of my noble and learned friends Lord Griffiths and Lord Mackay. I entirely agree with them and gratefully adopt their fuller reasoning, in addition to my own short observations, as leading to the conclusion that the appeals should be dismissed and the first certified question answered in the negative. I would wish to emphasise in particular my *f* concurrence with Lord Griffiths in the weight he attaches to the opinion of Lord Lane CJ as expressed in the judgment of the Court of Appeal, Criminal Division appealed against.

For the reasons given in the speeches of my noble and learned friends the Lord Chancellor and Lord Mackay, I would answer the second and third questions in the affirmative.

g

LORD BRANDON OF OAKBROOK. My Lords, I have had the advantage of reading in draft the speech prepared by my noble and learned friend Lord Mackay. I agree with it, and for the reasons which he gives I would dismiss the appeal.

I cannot pretend, however, that I regard the outcome as satisfactory. It is not logical, *h* and I do not think it can be just, that duress should afford a complete defence to charges of all crimes less grave than murder, but not even a partial defence to a charge of that crime. I say nothing as to treason, for that is not here in issue. I am persuaded, nevertheless, to agree with my noble and learned friend by three considerations. Firstly, it seems to me that, so far as the defence of duress is concerned, no valid distinction can be drawn between the commission of murder by one who is a principal in the first degree *j* and one who is a principal in the second degree. Secondly, I am satisfied that the common law of England has developed over several centuries in such a way as to produce the illogical, and as I think unjust, situation to which I have referred. Thirdly, I am convinced that, if there is to be any alteration in the law on such an important and controversial subject, that alteration should be made by legislation and not by judicial decision.

LORD GRIFFITHS. My Lords, as a general rule, I support the view that in criminal
a appeals to this House it is desirable wherever possible to have one speech, so that the
judges and practitioners may turn to one source for authoritative guidance. Clarity,
certainty and, wherever possible, simplicity are invaluable attributes of the criminal law
which must be understood by laymen and especially by jurymen as well as lawyers. This
will usually be better achieved by the distillation of the consensus view of the House in
one speech rather than leaving judges of first instance to pick their way through five
b speeches in an attempt to apply the principle of the decision to the trial currently taking
place before them. There are, however, exceptions to every rule and as I believe that we
should now depart from the decision of this House in *Lynch v DPP for Northern Ireland*
[1975] 1 All ER 913, [1975] AC 653 I feel that I should shortly state the reasons for my
opinion.

For centuries it was accepted that English criminal law did not allow duress as a
c defence to murder. It was so stated in *Hale's Pleas of the Crown* (1 Hale PC 51), repeated by
Blackstone in his *Commentaries on the Laws of England* (4 Bl Com (1857 edn) 28), and so
taught by all the authoritative writers on criminal law. It was accepted by those
responsible for drafting the criminal codes for many parts of the British Empire and they
provided, in those codes, that duress should not be a defence to murder. In *R v Tyler and*
d *Price* (1838) 8 C & P 616, 173 ER 643 Denman CJ told the jury in emphatic language
that they should not accept a plea of duress that was put up in defence to a charge of
murder against those who were not the actual killers. Fifty years later, in *R v Dudley and*
Stephens (1884) 14 QBD 273, [1881–5] All ER Rep 61, the defence of necessity was denied
to the men who had killed the cabin boy and eaten him in order that they might survive
albeit only Stephens was the actual killer. The reasoning that underlies that decision is
the same as that which denies duress as a defence to murder. It is based on the special
e sanctity that the law attaches to human life and which denies to a man the right to take
an innocent life even at the price of his own or another's life.

There are surprisingly few reported decisions on duress but it cannot be gainsaid that
the defence has been extended, particularly since the 1939–45 war, to a number of
crimes. I think myself it would have been better had this development not taken place
f and that duress had been regarded as a factor to be taken into account in mitigation as
Stephen suggested in his *History of the Criminal Law in England* (1883) vol 2, pp 107–108.
However, as Lord Morris said in *Lynch v DPP for Northern Ireland* [1975] 1 All ER 913 at
918, [1975] AC 653 at 670, it is too late to adopt that view. And the question now is
whether that development should be carried a step further and applied to a murderer
who is the actual killer, and, if the answer to this question is No, whether there is any
g basis on which it can be right to draw a distinction between a murderer who did the
actual killing and a murderer who played a different part in the design to bring about
the death of the victim.

The first suggestion that the defence of duress might be available to a person guilty of
murder appears to have emerged in *R v Kray* [1969] 3 All ER 941, [1970] 1 QB 125 in
the judgment of the Court of Appeal delivered by Widgery LJ (see 53 Cr App R 569 at
h 576–578). It is instructive to see the circumstances in which it arose:

'We now consider the effect of these two applicants [the Kray Brothers] of the
defence put forward by Anthony Barry. The case against Anthony Barry was that he
was an accessory before the fact to the McVitie murder, and the Crown relied
primarily on his having carried a gun from the Recency Club to Evering Road,
j knowing Reginald Kray intended to use it in the murder of McVitie. Barry admitted
from the outset that he had done this, but pleaded that he had acted under duress
being in fear for the safety of himself and his family if he failed to carry out the
order of the Krays. In support of this defence Barry gave evidence of an immediate
threat made in relation to his unwillingness to carry the gun and also to prior
conduct of the Kray twins which, he said, had placed him in terror of them. The

immediate threat was said to have been a message transmitted from Reginald Kray to Hart to the effect that, if Barry would not take the gun to Evering Road, the Krays *a* would come back to the Regency Club; a message which Barry interpreted as meaning that he would get hurt as well as McVitie. The general background of terror was supported by evidence of previous threats and acts of violence committed by the Krays or their henchmen at the Regency Club and similar acts which had been reported to Barry, but which he had not seen. Barry's counsel indicated the general nature of his defence at an early stage in the trial, and counsel for the other *b* accused were naturally apprehensive lest this should let in a great deal of otherwise inadmissible evidence detrimental to the Krays. An attempt was made at the outset to get a ruling as to the admissibility of this evidence, but the judge had no information on which to rule and wisely declined. Barry's counsel attempted to cross examine along these lines when the Crown witnesses to the Cornell murder were giving evidence, but he made little progress in the face of objections. Later, *c* however, a substantial body of evidence of the vicious and violent reputation of the Kray twins was let in either during cross examination of Crown witnesses or in Barry's own evidence and that of his witnesses. [Counsel for Ronald Kray] contended before us that the whole of this evidence was inadmissible since Barry had never laid an adequate foundation for the defence of duress. He concedes that although duress is not available in murder to a person charged as a principal it is available to an *d* accessory, but he submits the accessory must show he had no alternative and in this case Barry had the alternative of taking the gun to the police instead of Evering Road. Accordingly, says [counsel for Ronald Kray], Barry never had a viable defence of duress and the judge should have discharged the jury as soon as this became apparent. [Counsel for Reginald Kray] takes a broader view and accepts that Barry *e* had a valid defence if his will was so overcome by threats and fear that he had no independent choice and ceased to be an independent actor. He accepts that it was open to Barry to support this defence by evidence of threats and violent conduct within his own knowledge, and also by recounting incidents of which he had heard and the news of which had affected his mind. [Counsel for Reginald Kray's] complaint is that the evidence admitted went beyond these limits and related to *f* events early in 1966 which were not proved to have come to Barry's notice. He further complains that on occasions a witness called to prove that Barry had been told of a particular incident went on to testify to the truth of that information, which [counsel] submits was irrelevant and inadmissible since it did not go to the state of Barry's mind. It is evident to us that both the learned judge and counsel for the Crown did their best to confine this evidence to the limits contended for by *g* [counsel for Reginald Kray], but this was not always possible. Having examined all such incidents to which our attention has been drawn, we are satisfied that they give rise to no miscarriage of justice and do not render the verdict unsafe or unsatisfactory. We are further satisfied that Barry had a viable defence on the basis left to the jury by the learned judge, namely, that by reason of threats he was so terrified that he ceased to be an independent actor, and that the evidence of violent conduct by the *h* Krays which Barry put before the Court was accordingly relevant and admissible.'

Like the Lord Chancellor, I regard this decision as of little authority. The decision proceeded on a concession by counsel that the defence of duress was available to an accessory before the fact to murder and I have myself doubts about the correctness of allowing the defence at all if, as it appears, Anthony Barry had got himself into this *j* predicament by reason of his association with known violent criminals (see *R v Fitzpatrick* [1977] NI 20). It is, however, understandable that the judge would not wish to limit the full extent of the gangleader's villainy being laid before the jury.

Widgery LJ, who had given the judgment in *R v Kray*, repeated the same qualification in *R v Hudson, R v Taylor* [1971] 2 All ER 244 at 246, [1971] 2 QB 202 at 206, when

allowing the defence in a case of perjury. He said: '. . . it is clearly established that duress
a provides a defence in all offences including perjury (except possibly treason or murder as
a principal)'; but apart from saying that the court had been referred to much authority
he gave no reason for limiting the exception to murder as a *principal*.

In *Lynch v DPP for Northern Ireland* [1975] 1 All ER 913 at 919, [1975] AC 653 at 671,
of the majority who held that duress should be available to an aider and abettor to a
murder, in that case the driver of the getaway car, Lord Morris said of the actual killer:

b
'. . . the person is told that to save his life he himself must personally there and
then take an innocent life. It is for him to pull the trigger or otherwise personally to
do the act of killing. There, I think, before allowing duress as a defence it may be
that the law will have to call a halt.'

Lord Wilberforce said ([1975] 1 All ER 913 at 930, [1975] AC 653 at 685): 'I would leave
c cases of direct killing by a principal in the first degree to be dealt with as they arise.' Lord
Edmund-Davies ([1975] 1 All ER 913 at 956, [1975] AC 653 at 715) foreshadowed his
opinion in *Abbott v R* [1976] 3 All ER 140, [1977] AC 755 by citing a passage from Smith
and Hogan *Criminal Law* (3rd edn, 1973) p 166:

'The difficulty about adopting a distinction between the principal and secondary
d parties as a rule of law is that the contribution of the secondary party to the death
may be no less significant than that of the principal.'

To illustrate this one only has to point to the case of a 'contract' killing.

Thus it seems to me, my Lords, that even after *Lynch's* case the whole weight of
authority denied the defence of duress to the actual killer. This view had the unanimous
e support of the Supreme Court of South Australia in *R v Brown and Morley* [1968] SASR
467, when the majority denied the defence of duress to an aider and abettor to murder
and Bray CJ, who dissented on this issue, nevertheless said (at 499): 'I repeat also that as at
present advised I do not think duress could constitute a defence to one who actually kills
or attempts to kill the victim.'

In *Abbott v R* the majority in the Privy Council applied the law of duress in accordance
f with English authority and denied it as a defence to a murderer who took part in the
actual killing. The minority would have extended the defence even to the actual killer,
pointing out the illogicality of allowing it to the principal in the second degree or the
aider and abettor and denying it to the principal in the first degree.

Since that time the whole question of duress has been studied by the Law Commission:
see Report on Defences of General Application (Law Com no 83 (1977)). The report sets
g out the arguments for and against the defence and deals in particular with whether it
should apply to murder. They balanced the argument based on the sanctity of human
life that denies the defence to a murderer against the argument urged by the majority in
Lynch v DPP or Northern Ireland that the law should not demand more than human frailty
can sustain. They preferred the latter argument and accordingly recommended that a
defence of duress should be available to all crimes including murder. But in the draft Bill
h they annexed to their report (Criminal Liability (Duress Bill)) they prescribed the defence
in far narrower terms than it had hitherto been defined by the judges and they introduced
conditions which clearly go beyond the bounds of judicial creativity and would require
legislation. It is worth reminding oneself of the first two clauses:

'**1.**—(1) The following provisions of this section provide a defence (referred to
j below in this Act as "the defence of duress") in place of the defence of duress at
common law (which is consequently abolished except in relation to offences
committed before the passing of this Act).

(2) Subject to section 2 and subsection (5) below, a person shall not be guilty of
an offence by virtue of any action taken by him under duress.

(3) A person shall be regarded for the purposes of this section as having taken any action under duress if he was induced to take it by any threat of harm to himself or another and at the time when he took it he believed (whether or not on reasonable grounds)—(a) that the harm threatened was death or serious personal injury (physical or mental); (b) that the threat would be carried out immediately if he did not take the action in question or, if not immediately, before he could have any real opportunity of seeking official protection; and (c) that there was no other way of avoiding or preventing the harm threatened; provided, however, that in all the circumstances of the case (including what he believed with respect to the matters mentioned in paragraphs (a) to (c) above and any of his personal circumstances which are relevant) he could not reasonably have been expected to resist the threat.

(4) The fact that any official protection which might have been available in the circumstances would or might not have been effective to prevent the harm threatened is immaterial for the purposes of subsection (3)(b) above.

(5) The defence of duress does not apply in any case where on the occasion in question the defendant was voluntarily and without reasonable cause in a situation in which he knew he would or might be called upon to commit the offence with which he is charged or any offence of the same or a similar character under threat of death or serious personal injury (whether to himself or to anyone else) if in the event he should refuse to do so.

(6) In this section "official protection" means the protection of the police, of the authorities governing any prison or other custodial institution, or of any other similar authority concerned in the maintenance of law and order.

(7) The fact that one party to any action is exempt by virtue of this section from criminal liability for that action shall not affect the question whether anyone else is guilty of an offence by virtue of being a party to that action.

2.—(1) On a trial on indictment the defendant shall not, without leave of the court, be entitled to rely on the defence of duress unless he has served on the prosecutor at least seven clear days before the hearing a notice in writing—(a) indicating his intention to rely on the defence; (b) giving particulars of the words or conduct constituting the threat which induced him to take the action in question; and (c) giving any information then in his possession to identify or assist in identifying any persons making the threat and any persons other than himself on whom the harm threatened would have been inflicted if the threat had been carried out.

(2) In any proceedings for an offence it shall be for the prosecution to prove that the defence of duress does not apply, but only if there is sufficient evidence to raise an issue with respect to whether or not it does.'

I cannot refrain from commenting that if duress is introduced as a merciful concession to human frailty it seems hard to deny it to a man who knows full well that any official protection he may seek will not be effective to save him from the threat of death under which he has acted, but such is the effect of cl 1(3)(b) and (4) when read together.

But what, I think, is significant is the fact that although the report clearly recognised that English law did not extend the defence of duress to the actual killer and recommended that the law should be changed, Parliament never acted on this advice. The report was laid before Parliament by the Lord Chancellor in July 1977 but no steps have been taken to introduce a Bill on the lines they recommended. This must at least be some indication that the community at large are not pressing for a change in the law to remedy a perceived injustice.

Against this background are there any present circumstances that should impel your Lordships to alter the law that has stood for so long and to extend the defence of duress to the actual killer? My Lords, I can think of none. It appears to me that all present indications point in the opposite direction. We face a rising tide of violence and terrorism a against which the law must stand firm recognising that its highest duty is to protect the freedom and lives of those that live under it. The sanctity of human life lies at the root of this ideal and I would do nothing to undermine it, be it ever so slight.

On this question your Lordships should, I believe, accord great weight to the opinion of Lord Lane CJ, who by virtue of his office and duties is in far closer touch with the practical application of the criminal law and better able to evaluate the consequence of a change in the law than those of us who sit in this House. This is what he had to say in his
b judgment in this case ([1986] 1 All ER 833 at 839, [1986] QB 626 at 641):

'It is true that to allow the defence to the aider and abettor but not to the killer may lead to illogicality, as was pointed out by this court in R v Graham [1982] 1 All ER 801, [1982] 1 WLR 294, where the question in issue in the instant case was not argued, but that is not to say that any illogicality should be cured by making duress
c available to the actual killer rather [than] by removing it from the aider and abettor. Assuming that a change in the law is desirable or necessary, we may perhaps be permitted to express a view. The whole matter was dealt with in extenso by Lord Salmon in his speech in Abbott v R, to which reference has already been made. He dealt there with the authorities. It is unnecessary for us in the circumstances to repeat the citations which he there makes. It would moreover be impertinent for us
d to try to restate in different terms the contents of that speech, with which we respectfully agree. Either the law should be left as it is or the defence of duress should be denied to anyone charged with murder, whether as a principal in the first degree or otherwise. It seems to us that it would be a highly dangerous relaxation in the law to allow a person who has deliberately killed, maybe a number of innocent people, to escape conviction and punishment altogether because of a fear that his
e own life or those of his family might be in danger if he did not, particularly so when the defence of duress is so easy to raise and may be so difficult for the prosecution to disprove beyond reasonable doubt, the facts of necessity being as a rule known only to the defendant himself. That is not say that duress may not be taken into account in other ways, for example by the Parole Board. Even if, contrary to our views, it were otherwise desirable to extend the defence of duress to the actual killer, this is
f surely not the moment to make any such change, when acts of terrorism are commonplace and opportunities for mass murder have never been more readily to hand.'

My Lords, in my view we should accept the advice of the Lord Chief Justice and the judges who sat with him, and decline to extend the defence to the actual killer. If the
g defence is not available to the killer, what justification can there be for extending it to others who have played their part in the murder. I can, of course, see that as a matter of common sense one participant in a murder may be considered less morally at fault than another. The youth who hero-worships the gang leader and acts as look-out man whilst the gang enter a jeweller's shop and kill the owner in order to steal is an obvious example. In the eyes of the law they are all guilty of murder, but justice will be served by requiring
h those who did the killing to serve a longer period in prison before being released on licence than the youth who acted as look-out. However, it is not difficult to give examples where more moral fault may be thought to attach to a participant in murder who was not the actual killer; I have already mentioned the example of a contract killing, when the murder would never have taken place if a contract had not been placed to take the life of the victim. Another example would be an intelligent man goading a weak-minded
j individual into a killing he would not otherwise commit.

It is therefore neither rational nor fair to make the defence dependent on whether the accused is the actual killer or took some other part in the murder. I have toyed with the idea that it might be possible to leave it to the discretion of the trial judge to decide whether the defence should be available to one who was not the killer, but I have rejected this as introducing too great a degree of uncertainty into the availability of the defence. I am not troubled by some of the extreme examples cited in favour of allowing the defence to those who are not the killer, such as a woman motorist being highjacked and forced to act as getaway driver, or a pedestrian being forced to give misleading information to the police to protect robbery and murder in a shop. The short, practical answer is that it is inconceivable that such persons would be prosecuted: they would be called as the principal witnesses for the prosecution.

As I can find no fair and certain basis on which to differentiate between participants to a murder and as I am firmly convinced that the law should not be extended to the killer, I would depart from the decision of this House in *Lynch v DPP for Northern Ireland* [1975] 1 All ER 913, [1975] AC 653 and declare the law to be that duress is not available as a defence to a charge of murder or to attempted murder. I add attempted murder because it is to be remembered that the prosecution have to prove an even more evil intent to convict of attempted murder than in actual murder. Attempted murder requires proof of an intent to kill, whereas in murder it is sufficient to prove an intent to cause really serious injury.

It cannot be right to allow the defence to one who may be more intent on taking a life than the murderer. This leaves, of course, the anomaly that duress is available for the offence of wounding with intent but not to murder if the victim dies subsequently. But this flows from the special regard that the law has for human life; it may not be logical but it is real and has to be accepted.

I do not think that your Lordships should adopt the compromise solution of declaring that duress reduces murder to manslaughter. Where the defence of duress is available it is a complete excuse. This solution would put the law back to lines on which Stephen suggested it should develop by regarding duress as a form of mitigation. English law has rejected this solution and it would be yet another anomaly to introduce it for the crime of murder alone. I would have been more tempted to go down this road if the death penalty had remained for murder. But the sentence for murder, although mandatory and expressed as imprisonment for life, is in fact an indefinite sentence, which is kept constantly under review by the Parole Board and the Home Secretary with the assistance of the Lord Chief Justice and the trial judge. I have confidence that through this machinery the respective culpability of those involved in a murder case can be fairly weighed and reflected in the time they are required to serve in custody.

I have had the advantage of reading the speeches of my noble and learned friends the Lord Chancellor and Lord Mackay and I agree with the opinions they have expressed on the second and third questions raised before your Lordships.

LORD MACKAY OF CLASHFERN. My Lords, at the request of all parties to the appeals by Burke, Howe and Bannister, they were conjoined and have been heard together. They arise out of two separate cases and the issues in each are similar. The appeal of Clarkson arises out of one of these cases and by agreement of the parties to it and the other appeals it has also been heard with the others.

The material facts in Burke's case are that on 9 July 1983 Burke shot dead one Henry Botton at point-blank range with a sawn-off shotgun. The victim was due to give evidence at the Crown Court at Inner London Sessions on 18 July 1983 in a trial in which Burke's co-defendant, William Clarkson, was accused with others of conspiracy to handle stolen goods. The victim was to have given evidence in support of the defence of duress by Clarkson which was raised by one of Clarkson's co-defendants. Burke's defence at his trial was that he had agreed to shoot the victim only because of his fear that Clarkson would kill him if he did not but, when it came to the event, the gun actually went off accidentally and the killing was therefore unintentional and amounted to no more than manslaughter. At the trial it was submitted on behalf of Burke that he was entitled to be acquitted completely of murder and manslaughter by reason of duress and that if this submission failed he was entitled to be acquitted of murder and found guilty of manslaughter by reason of accident in an unlawful act. The judge who presided at the

trial, the then Common Serjeant, his Honour Judge Tudor Price QC, directed the jury
a that Burke, as the actual killer, was not entitled to rely on the defence of duress to the
charge of murder but since he considered there was evidence in support of the defence
of duress he left it to the jury in respect of manslaughter. He further directed the jury
that they could not convict Clarkson of murder unless they convicted Burke of murder
and that if Burke was guilty of manslaughter then Clarkson could be convicted, at most,
only of manslaughter and that if the appellant was acquitted on the grounds of duress
b then Clarkson, the author of the duress, must be convicted of manslaughter.

Howe and Bannister were indicted together with two other men, Murray and Bailey,
at the Crown Court at Manchester on two counts of murder and one of conspiracy to
murder contrary to s 1 of the Criminal Law Act 1977. The particulars of the first count
referred to the murder of Mitchell Elgar on 10 October 1983, the particulars of the
second count referred to the murder of Martin Pollitt on 11 October 1983 and the
c conspiracy to murder related to a conspiracy on 12 October 1983 to murder John
Redfern.

In October 1983 Howe and Bailey were aged 19, Bannister was aged 20 and Murray
was 35. Howe had one conviction for a motoring offence. Bannister had convictions for
dishonesty offences but none for violence. Murray had 25 previous court appearances
including appearances for offences of violence and in 1974 was sentenced to a term of
d eight years' imprisonment for offences of assault with intent to rob and robbery.
Bannister met Murray whilst at Risley Remand Centre. Howe was introduced to Murray
and Bailey and all became acquainted with each other for a period of four days prior to
the first murder and were in each other's company almost all the time from the period 6
to 13 October. Murray was the dominant figure. He was dishonest, powerful, violent
and sadistic. Through acts of actual violence or threats of violence, Murray gained control
e of each of the appellants, who became fearful of him. Mitchell Elgar, referred to in count
1, was killed at a remote spot in the Goyt Valley, Derbyshire. His death was preceded by
a savage kicking and beating, and acts of torture and sexual perversion perpetrated by
Bannister, Howe and Bailey. The coup de grâce was executed by Bailey, who strangled
Mitchell Elgar with a headlock. Before the attack, Murray had told Howe and Bannister
f that Elgar was a 'grass' and was to be killed and Bannister was threatened with violence
by Murray if he did not give Mitchell Elgar 'a bit of a battering'. Martin Pollitt, referred
to in count 2, was picked up by the four men, to whom I have referred, on 11 October
1983 and they took him to the same place as that in which Mitchell Elgar was killed on
the previous day. Murray told Howe and Bannister to kill Pollitt, which they did by
strangling him with Bannister's shoelace, each holding one end. In relation to count 3,
g the same procedure had been followed. However Redfern, the intended victim, suspected
something was afoot and managed to escape from what otherwise would have inevitably
been his death. Howe and Bannister each admitted to being parties to the killings and
the conspiracy to kill in the circumstances I have described but they alleged that they
acted in fear of their own lives because of the conduct of Murray. They alleged that they
feared that Murray would treat them in the same way as Mitchell Elgar had been treated
h if they did not comply with his directions.

At the trial counsel for the prosecution were content to assent to the proposition that,
in respect of the murder of Mitchell Elgar, death had been caused by Bailey strangling
the victim although the kicks and punches would have resulted in death moments later
even in the absence of strangulation. On that basis, the prosecution were content that the
judge who presided at the trial should leave the defence of duress to the jury in respect of
j count 1 and also in respect of count 3. On count 2, the judge rejected the submissions
made on behalf of both appellants that the defence of duress should be allowed.

In directing the jury to consider the plea of duress in respect of counts 1 and 3, the
judge directed the jury that the test to be applied was whether 'the threat was of such
gravity that it might well have caused a reasonable man placed in the same situation as
the defendants to act as the defendants did' and to pose the question 'would a sober person

of reasonable firmness sharing the defendants' characteristics have responded to the threats by taking part in the killing'.   *a*

Burke was convicted of murder and Howe and Bannister were convicted on both counts of murder with which they were charged and also on the count of conspiracy to murder. All appealed to the Court of Appeal, Criminal Division ([1986] 1 All ER 833, [1986] QB 626), where the appeals were heard together and dismissed. In dismissing the appeals the court certified three points of law of general public importance were involved in the decisions to dismiss the appeals, namely: *b*

'(1) Is duress available as a defence to a person charged with murder as a principal in the first degree (the actual killer)? (2) Can one who incites or procures by duress another to kill or to be a party to a killing be convicted of murder if that other is acquitted by reason of duress? (3) Does the defence of duress fail if the prosecution prove that a person of reasonable firmness sharing the characteristics of the defendant   *c* would not have given way to the threats as did the defendant?'

The Court of Appeal granted leave to appeal against its decision to this House. Clarkson's appeal was also heard by the Court of Appeal, Criminal Division at the same time as the others, was also dismissed and leave to appeal to this House was granted. Although he is concerned in the first question already mentioned as a basis for his concern in the second, which arises only if Burke is successful on the first, Clarkson's   *d* appeal is concerned with the second question, in respect of which he contends that if Burke was acquitted by reason of duress he could not be convicted of murder as one who had incited or procured by duress Burke to kill or to be a party to a killing.

It will be convenient to deal with the matters arising in these appeals by reference to the three questions of law which have been certified and in the order in which the   *e* questions are posed by the Court of Appeal.

Question 1

The question whether duress is available as a defence in law to a person charged with murder as a principal in the first degree (the actual killer) has not been the subject of a previous decision of this House. The matter received consideration in this House in *Lynch*   *f* *v DPP for Northern Ireland* [1975] 1 All ER 913, [1975] AC 653.

Lynch had driven a motor car containing a group of the IRA in Northern Ireland on an expedition in which they shot and killed a police officer. He was tried along with two other men on a count that he murdered the police constable and was convicted and sentenced to life imprisonment. This House, by a majority of three to two, allowed Lynch's appeal and ordered a new trial pursuant to s 13 of the Criminal Appeal (Northern   *g* Ireland) Act 1968. At the new trial Lynch was allowed to plead the defence of duress but this defence was rejected by the jury and Lynch was again convicted.

It was accepted by the majority of the House in *Lynch's* case that at that time the balance of such judicial authority as existed was against the admission of the defence of duress in cases of first degree murder. The writers were generally agreed in saying that the defence was not available in murder although later writers appear to have said so   *h* following Hale. The references are *Hale's Pleas of the Crown* (1 Hale PC (1736) 51, 434); *East's Pleas of the Crown* (1 East PC (1803) 294); *Blackstone's Commentaries on the Laws of England* (4 Bl Com (1809 edn) 30); Glanville Williams *Criminal Law: The General Part* (2nd edn, 1961), p 759, para 247; *Russell on Crime* (12th edn, 1964) vol 1, pp 90–91; Smith and Hogan *Criminal Law* (3rd edn, 1973) pp 166–167. Since the fundamental passage is that from Hale, I think it is appropriate to quote it in full: *j*

'If a man be menaced with death, unless he will commit an act of treason, murder, or robbery, the fear of death doth not excuse him, if he commit the fact; for the law hath provided a sufficient remedy against such fears by applying himself to the courts and officers of justice for a writ or precept *de securitate pacis*. Again, if a man

a   be desperately assaulted, and in peril of death, and cannot otherwise escape, unless
    to satisfy his assailant's fury he will kill an innocent person then present, the fear
    and actual force will not acquit him of the crime and punishment of murder, if he
    commit the fact; for he ought rather to die himself, than kill an innocent: but if he
    cannot otherwise save his own life, the law permits him in his own defence to kill
    the assailant; for by the violence of the assault, and the offence committed upon
    him by the assailant himself, the law of nature and necessity, hath made him his
b   own *protector cum debito moderamine inculpatæ tutelæ*, as shall be farther shewed,
    when we come to the chapter of homicide *se defendendo*.'

Counsel for Burke, Bannister and Howe in his very detailed and careful submission
accepted this position as reflecting the law up to the time of *Lynch's* case. Since that time,
on this question there has been the decision of the Privy Council in *Abbott v R* [1976] 3
c   All ER 140, [1977] AC 755, a majority decision in which the minority consisted of Lord
Wilberforce and Lord Edmund-Davies, who, along with Lord Morris, had constituted
the majority in *Lynch's* case. Counsel for these appellants submitted that your Lordships
should hold that the reasoning of the majority in *Lynch's* case should be applied and
extended to cover the present cases. He recognised that this would involve a change in
the law on this matter but argued that the change was one which your Lordships should
d   properly decide to make as the consequence of the decision of the House in *Lynch's* case.
    In approaching this matter, I look for guidance to Lord Reid's approach to the question
of this House making a change in the prevailing view of the law in *Myers v DPP* [1964]
2 All ER 881 at 885–886, [1965] AC 1001 at 1021–1022, where he said:

e   'I have never taken a narrow view of the functions of this House as an appellate
    tribunal. The common law must be developed to meet changing economic
    conditions and habits of thought, and I would not be deterred by expressions of
    opinion in this House in old cases; but there are limits to what we can or should do.
    If we are to extend the law it must be by the development and application of
    fundamental principles. We cannot introduce arbitrary conditions or limitations;
    that must be left to legislation: and if we do in effect change the law, we ought in
f   my opinion only to do that in cases where our decision will produce some finality
    or certainty. If we disregard technicalities in this case and seek to apply principle
    and common sense, there are a number of other parts of the existing law of hearsay
    susceptible of similar treatment, and we shall probably have a series of appeals in
    cases where the existing technical limitations produce an unjust result. If we are to
    give a wide interpretation to our judicial functions, questions of policy cannot be
g   wholly excluded, and it seems to me to be against public policy to produce
    uncertainty. The only satisfactory solution is by legislation following on a wide
    survey of the whole field, and I think that such a survey is overdue. A policy of
    make do and mend is no longer adequate. The most powerful argument of those
    who support the strict doctrine of precedent is that if it is relaxed judges will be
h   tempted to encroach on the proper field of the legislature, and this case to my mind
    offers a strong temptation to do that which ought to be resisted.'

In the present appeal, as I have said, the reason advanced on behalf of the appellants to
allow the defence of duress to persons in the appellants' position as the actual killers is
based on the assertion that this House in *Lynch's* case allowed it to a person who was
j   charged with murder as a principal in the second degree otherwise described as an aider
and abettor and that there was no relevant distinction between that case and the case of
the actual killer. He submitted that the reasoning of the majority in *Lynch's* case when
logically applied to the circumstances of the present case led to the result that the defence
of duress should have been admitted here and that the appeal should accordingly be
allowed.

Counsel for the Crown submitted that the appeal should be refused, that the existing law did not allow the defence of duress to an actual killer or principal in the first degree and that if no proper distinction could be made between this and *Lynch's* case the House should decline to follow *Lynch's* case because in his submission the reasoning in *Lynch's* case was flawed.

The first question, accordingly, that arises in this appeal is whether any distinction can be made between this case and *Lynch's* case. It is clear from the speech of Lord Morris that he did not regard it as a necessary consequence of his view that the defence of duress should be available to a principal in the first degree. He said ([1975] 1 All ER 913 at 918, [1975] AC 653 at 671):

> 'The issue in the present case is therefore whether there is any reason why the defence of duress, which in respect of a variety of offences has been recognised as a possible defence, may not also be a possible defence on a charge of being a principal in the second degree to murder. I would confine my decision to that issue. It may be that the law must deny such a defence to an actual killer, and that the law will not be irrational if it does so. Though it is not possible for the law always to be worked out on coldly logical lines there may be manifest factual differences and contrasts between the situation of an aider and abettor to a killing and that of the actual killer.'

He goes on to distinguish the case of a person in the position of an aider and abettor who saves his own life at a time when the loss of another life is not a certainty with the position of a person who is told that to save his life he must himself personally there and then take an innocent life. Lord Morris said ([1975] 1 All ER 913 at 919, [1975] AC 653 at 671–672):

> 'There, I think, before allowing duress as a defence it may be that the law will have to call a halt. May there still be force in what long ago was said by Hale (1 Hale PC (1800) 51)? "Again, if a man be desperately assaulted, and in peril of death, and cannot otherwise escape, unless to satisfy his assailant's fury he will kill an innocent person then present, the fear and actual force will not acquit him of the crime and punishment of murder, if he commit the fact; for he ought rather to die himself, than kill an innocent." Those words have over long periods of time influenced both thought and writing but I think that their application may have been unduly extended when it is assumed that they were intended to cover all cases of accessories and aiders and abettors.'

Lord Wilberforce said ([1975] 1 All ER 913 at 930, [1975] AC 653 at 685):

> 'I would decide that the defence is in law admissible in a case of aiding and abetting murder, and so in the present case. I would leave cases of direct killing by a principal in the first degree to be dealt with as they arise.'

Lord Edmund-Davies, referring to the opinion of Bray CJ in *R v Brown and Morley* [1968] SASR 467, said ([1975] 1 All ER 913 at 955–956, [1975] AC 653 at 715):

> 'His conclusion was that ([1968] SASR 467 at 499): ". . . the trend of the later cases, general reasoning, and the express authority of the Privy Council in *Sephakela's Case* [1954] HCTLR 60 prevent the acceptance of the simple proposition that no type of duress can ever afford a defence to the type of complicity in murder. I repeat also that, as at present advised, I do not think duress could consitute a defence to one who actually kills or attempts to kill the victim." It appears to me, with respect, that the reliance placed by Bray CJ on *Sephakela's Case* is misplaced, though I concur when he says that ([1968] SASR 467 at 496): "There is nothing, in my view, in *Sephakela's Case* to prevent us from holding that there can be circumstances in which duress can be a defence to a person charged with murder as a principal in the second

degree." Such was the role of Lynch, and this House is accordingly not now called
on to deal with the reservation of Bray CJ in relation to a person who under duress
"actually kills or attempts to kill the victim". As to the actual killer, while I naturally
seek to refrain from prejudging future cases, I think it right to say that I agree with
the observation of Smith and Hogan (*Criminal Law* (3rd edn, 1973) p 166) that: "The
difficulty about adopting a distinction between the principal and secondary parties
as a rule of law is that the contribution of the secondary party to the death may be
no less significant than that of the principal."'

In my opinion, it is plain from these quotations that the majority of this House in *Lynch's*
case, and particularly Lord Morris, were reaching a decision without committing
themselves to the view that the reasoning which they had used would apply to an actual
killer. To take one example, it would have been impossible to cite Bray CJ in support of
the proposition that the defence of duress should be allowed in a charge of murder unless
this distinction had been taken.

While therefore *Lynch's* case was decided by reasoning which does not extend to the
present case, the question remains whether there is a potential distinction between this
case and *Lynch's* case by which to determine whether or not the defence of duress should
be available. I consider that *Smith and Hogan* were perfectly right in the passage cited
from that work by Lord Edmund-Davies to which I have already referred. I have not
been able to find any writer of authority that is able to give rational support for the view
that the distinction between principals in the first degree and those in the second degree
is relevant to determine whether or not duress should be available in a particular case of
murder. Whatever may have divided Lord Wilberforce and Lord Edmund-Davies on
the one hand from Lord Simon and Lord Kilbrandon on the other, it is apparent that all
agree that this is not a distinction which should receive practical effect in the law.

I believe that the discussions of this matter have shown that at one extreme, namely
that of the person who actually kills by a deliberate assault on a person who is then
present, there is a fair body of support for the view either that the defence of duress
should not be allowed or that the practical result will be, even if it is allowed, that it will
never be established, while there is also strong support for the view that at the other
extreme minor participation which the law regards as sufficient to impute criminal guilt
should be capable of being excused by the defence of duress. A similar consideration was
no doubt present to the mind of Hume, the eminent writer on the Scottish criminal law,
where in his work *Commentaries on the Law of Scotland respecting Crimes* (3rd edn, 1829)
p 53 in relation to the defence in Scotland known as coercion, after a reference to the case
of James Graham who claimed that he had been forced by Rob Roy and his gang to take
part in an armed robbery, he says:

> 'But generally, and with relation to the ordinary condition of a well-regulated
> society, where everyman is under the shield of the law, and has the means of
> resorting to that protection, this is at least somewhat a difficult plea, and can hardly
> be serviceable in the case of a trial for any atrocious crime, unless it has the support
> of these qualifications: an immediate danger of death or great bodily harm; an
> inability to resist the violence; *a backward and inferior part in the perpetration*; and a
> disclosure of the fact, as well as restitution of the spoil, on the first safe and
> convenient occasion.' (My emphasis.)

So far, I have not found any satisfactory formulation of a distinction which would be
sufficiently precise to be given practical effect in law and at the same time differentiate
between levels of culpability so as to produce a satisfactory demarcation between those
accused of murder who should be entitled to resort to the defence of duress and those
who were not.

The House is therefore, in my opinion, faced with the unenviable decision of either
departing altogether from the doctrine that duress is not available in murder or departing

from the decision of this House in *Lynch's* case. While a variety of minor attacks on the reasoning of the majority were mounted by counsel for the Crown in the present case, I do not find any of these sufficiently important to merit departing from *Lynch's* case on these grounds. I do, however, consider that, having regard to the balance of authority on the question of duress as a defence to murder prior to *Lynch's* case, for this House now to allow the defence of duress generally in response to a charge of murder would be to effect an important and substantial change in the law. In my opinion too, it would involve a departure from the decision in the famous case of *R v Dudley and Stephens* (1884) 14 QBD 273, [1881–5] All ER Rep 61. The justification for allowing a defence of duress to a charge of murder is that a defendant should be excused who killed as the only way of avoiding death himself or preventing the death of some close relation such as his own well-loved child. This essentially was the dilemma which Dudley and Stephens faced and in denying their defence the court refused to allow this consideration to be used in a defence to murder. If that refusal was right in the case of Dudley and Stephens it cannot be wrong in the present appeals. Although the result of recognising the defence advanced in that case would be that no crime was committed and in the case with which we are concerned that a murder was committed and a particular individual was not guilty of it (subject to the consideration of the second certified question) that does not distinguish the two cases from the point of view now being considered.

To change the law in the manner suggested by counsel for the appellants in the present case would, in my opinion, introduce uncertainty over a field of considerable importance.

So far I have referred to the defence of duress as if it were a precisely defined concept, but it is apparent from the decisions that it is not so and I cannot do better in this connection than refer to what Lord Simon said on this point in *Lynch's* case [1975] 1 All ER 913 at 931, [1975] AC 653 at 686:

> 'Before turning to examine these considerations, it is convenient to have a working definition of duress—even though it is actually an extremely vague and elusive juristic concept. I take it for present purposes to denote such [well-grounded] fear, produced by threats, of death or grievous bodily harm [or unjustified imprisonment] if a certain act is not done, as overbears the actor's wish not to perform the act, and is effective, at the time of the act, in constraining him to perform it. I am quite uncertain whether the words which I have put in square brackets should be included in any such definition. It is arguable that the test should be purely subjective, and that it is contrary to principle to require the fear to be a reasonable one. Moreover, I have assumed, on the basis of *R v Hudson* [1971] 2 All ER 244, [1971] 2 QB 202, that threat of future injury may suffice, although Stephen *Digest of the Criminal Law* (1877) note to art 10 is to the contrary. Then the law leaves it also quite uncertain whether the fear induced by threats must be of death or grievous bodily harm, or whether threatened loss of liberty suffices: cases of duress in the law of contract suggest that duress may extend to fear of unjustified imprisonment; but the criminal law returns no clear answer. It also leaves entirely unanswered whether, to constitute such a general criminal defence, the threat must be of harm to the person required to perform the act, or extends to the immediate family of the actor (and how immediate?), or to any person. Such questions are not academic, in these days when hostages are so frequently seized.'

To say that a defence in respect of which so many questions remain unsettled should be introduced in respect of the whole field of murder is not to promote certainty in the law. In this connection it is worth observing that, when in their Report on Defences of General Application (Law Com no 83) the Law Commission recommended that the defence of duress should be available in murder, they suggested a definition of duress which is, I believe, considerably narrower than that generally thought to be available in the present law in respect of other offences. In particular, they required that the defendant must believe that 'the threat will be carried out immediately, before he can have any real opportunity of seeking official protection' and they suggested that the fact that any official protection which might have been available in the circumstances would or might not have been effective to prevent the harm threatened should be immaterial in this context. It is of interest and importance to notice that this point figured long before in Hale's statement which I have quoted. It is to be noted that it was of this very part of Hale's statement that Lord Wilberforce said in *Lynch's* case [1975] 1 All ER 913 at 928, [1975] AC 653 at 682:

'Even if this argument was ever realistic, he would surely have recognised that reconsideration of it must be required in troubled times.'

I notice that in the Law Commission report dated 28 March 1985 (Law Com no 143), which contains a report to the Law Commission in respect of the codification of the criminal law by a team from the Society of Public Teachers of Law, doubt is expressed on the soundness of this recommendation in Law Com no 83. This particular matter does not arise in the circumstances of the present case, but the great difficulty that has been found in obtaining a consensus of informed opinion on it is just one illustration of the uncertain nature of what would be introduced into this most important area of the criminal law if the defence of duress were to be available.

Since the decision in *Lynch's* case the Law Commission have published in their report (Law Com no 83), to which I have referred, the result of an extensive survey of the law relating to duress and have made recommendations on it which have been laid before Parliament. In my opinion the problems which have been evident in relation to the law of murder and the availability of particular defences is not susceptible of what Lord Reid described as a solution by a policy of make do and mend (see *Myers v DPP* [1964] 2 All ER 881 at 886, [1965] AC 1001 at 1002). While I appreciate fully the gradual development that has taken place in the law relating to the defence of duress, I question whether the law has reached a sufficiently precise definition of that defence to make it right for us sitting in our judicial capacity to introduce it as a defence for an actual killer for the first time in the law of England. Parliament, in its legislative capacity, although recommended to do so by the report of the Law Commission, has not taken any steps to make the defence of duress available generally to a charge of murder even where it has the power to define with precision the circumstances in which such a defence would be available.

It has also been suggested for consideration whether, if the defence of duress is to be allowed in relation to murder by the actual killer, the defence should have the effect, if sustained, of reducing the crime to that of manslaughter by analogy with the defence of provocation. Provocation itself was introduced into the law by judicial decision in recognition of human frailty, although it is now the subject of a statutory provision (see the Homicide Act 1957, s 3) and it was suggested that the same approach might be taken now with regard to duress. In the judgment in *State v Goliath* 1972 (3) SA 1, in which Rumpff JA examined the question of whether compulsion could constitute the defence on a charge of murder from which Lord Wilberforce quoted as a statement of principle a substantial passage, Rumpff JA went on in a later passage to say (in translation) (at 25):

'Whether an acquittal will follow on a charge of murder because of compulsion, will depend on the particular circumstances of each case and the whole factual complex will have to be carefully investigated and judged with the greatest circumspection. In the simple case where A kills B just to save his own life, the strength of the compulsion would be a decisive factor and the compulsion would have to be so strong that although not *vis absoluta*, it would still be comparable with it, in the sense that the reasonable man in the particular circumstances would not be able to withstand it ... For the purposes of replying to the reserved questions it is unnecessary to determine in what light the defence of compulsion must be seen i.e. whether it operates because of the lawfulness of the compelled act or whether it excludes the full fault.'

And a little later he said (at 27):

> '... I am of the opinion that the second question which was stated [that is 'whether the special defence of compulsion can ever in law constitute a complete defence to a charge of murder so as to entitle an accused to an acquittal?'] must be answered by a qualified "yes" in the sense that a complete defence will depend on the circumstances of each case.'

From this I take it that Rumpff JA was of opinion that the defence might, depending on the circumstances, either lead to an acquittal or to a reduction of the charge from murder to a lower category of unlawful killing.

In my opinion we would not be justified in the present state of the law in introducing for the first time into our law the concept of duress acting to reduce the charge to one of manslaughter even if there were grounds on which it might be right to do so. On that aspect of the matter the Law Commission took the view that where the defence of duress had been made out it would be unjust to stigmatise the person accused with a conviction and there is clearly much force in that view.

The argument for the appellants essentially is that, Lynch's case having been decided as it was and there being no practical distinction available between Lynch's case and the present case, this case should be decided in the same way. The opposite point of view is that, since Lynch's case was concerned not with the actual killer but with a person who was made guilty of his act by the doctrine of accession, the correct starting point for this matter is the case of the actual killer. In my opinion this latter is the correct approach. The law has extended the liability to trial and punishment faced by the actual killer to those who are participants with him in the crime and it seems to me, therefore, that, where a question as important as this is in issue, the correct starting point is the case of the actual killer. It seems to me plain that the reason that it was for so long stated by writers of authority that the defence of duress was not available in a charge of murder was because of the supreme importance that the law afforded to the protection of human life and that it seemed repugnant that the law should recognise in any individual in any circumstances, however extreme, the right to choose that one innocent person should be killed rather than another. In my opinion that is the question which we still must face. Is it right that the law should confer this right in any circumstances, however extreme? While I recognise fully the force of the reasoning which persuaded the majority of this House in Lynch's case to reach the decision to which they came in relation to a person not the actual killer, it does not address directly this question in relation to the actual killer. I am not persuaded that there is good reason to alter the answer which Hale gave to this question. No development of the law or progress in legal thinking which has taken place since his day has, to my mind, demonstrated a reason to change this fundamental answer. In the circumstances which I have narrated of a report to Parliament from the Law Commission concerned, inter alia, with this very question, it would seem particularly inappropriate to make such a change now. For these reasons, in my opinion, the first certified question should be answered in the negative.

It follows that, in my opinion, the House should decline to follow the decision in Lynch's case. In my opinion the reasoning which persuaded this House in R v Shivpuri [1986] 2 All ER 334, [1986] 2 WLR 988 that it was appropriate to reconsider its earlier decision in Anderton v Ryan [1985] 2 All ER 355, [1985] AC 560 applies equally to the present case, although the decision in Lynch's case is of longer standing than was that of Anderton v Ryan. Up to the present time the courts have been declining to allow an actual killer to plead the defence of duress while allowing it to a person charged with murder who was not the actual killer, as is illustrated in the circumstances of these appeals. Lord Lane CJ in R v Graham [1982] 1 All ER 801 at 804, [1982] 1 WLR 294 at 297 illustrated how technical and puzzling in practice the distinction could be. In my opinion it would not be right to allow this state of affairs to continue. I recognise that this decision leaves

certain apparent anamolies in the law but I regard these as consequences of the fact that
a murder is a result related crime with a mandatory penalty. Consequently, no distinction
is made in penalty between the various levels of culpability. Differentiation in treatment
once sentence has been pronounced depends on action by the Crown advised by the
executive government, although that may be affected by a recommendation which the
court is empowered to make. Where a person has taken a minor part in a wounding with
intent and is dealt with on that basis he may receive a very short sentence. If sufficiently
b soon after that conviction the victim dies, on the same facts with the addition of the
victim's death caused by the wounding, he may be sentenced to life imprisonment. This
is simply one illustration of the fact that very different results may follow from a set of
facts together with the death of a victim from what would follow the same facts if the
victim lived.

c Question 2

I turn now to the second certified question. In the view that I take on the first question
the second question does not properly arise. However, I am of opinion that the Court of
Appeal reached the correct conclusion on it as a matter of principle.
Giving the judgment of the Court of Appeal Lord Lane CJ said ([1986] 1 All ER 833 at
d 839–840, [1986] QB 626 at 641–642):

> 'The judge based himself on a decision of this court in R v Richards (Isabelle) [1973]
> 3 All ER 1088, [1974] QB 776. The facts in that case were that Mrs Richards paid
> two men to inflict injuries on her husband which she intended should "put him in
> hospital for a month". The two men wounded the husband but not seriously. They
> *e* were acquitted of wounding with intent but convicted of unlawful wounding. Mrs
> Richards herself was convicted of wounding with intent, the jury plainly, and not
> surprisingly, believing that she had the necessary intent, though the two men had
> not. She appealed against her conviction on the ground that she could not properly
> be convicted as accessory before the fact to a crime more serious than that committed
> by the principals in the first degree. The appeal was allowed and the conviction for
> unlawful wounding was substituted. The court followed a passage from Hawkins's
> *f* Pleas of the Crown (2 Hawk PC (8th edn) p 442): "I take it to be an uncontroverted
> rule that [the offence of the accessory can never rise higher than that of the
> principal]; it seeming incongruous and absurd that he who is punished only as a
> partaker of the guilt of another, should be adjudged guilty of a higher crime than
> the other." James LJ, delivering the judgment in R v Richards [1973] 3 All ER 1088
> at 1092, [1974] QB 776 at 780, had this to say: "If there is only one offence
> *g* committed, and that is the offence of unlawful wounding, then the person who has
> requested that offence to be committed, or advised that offence be committed,
> cannot be guilty of a graver offence than that in fact which was committed." The
> decision in R v Richards has been the subject of some criticism (see for example
> Smith and Hogan Criminal Law (5th edn, 1983) p 140). Counsel before us posed the
> situation where A hands a gun to D informing him that it is loaded with blank
> *h* ammunition only and telling him to go and scare X by discharging it. The
> ammunition is in fact live (as A knows) and X is killed. D is convicted only of
> manslaughter, as he might be on those facts. It would seem absurd that A should
> thereby escape conviction for murder. We take the view that R v Richards was
> incorrectly decided, but it seems to us that it cannot properly be distinguished from
> *j* the instant case.'

I consider that the reasoning of Lord Lane CJ is entirely correct and I would affirm his
view that, where a person has been killed and that result is the result intended by another
participant, the mere fact that the actual killer may be convicted only of the reduced
charge of manslaughter for some reason special to himself does not, in my opinion, in
any way result in a compulsory reduction for the other participant.

Question 3

I turn now to the third question. On this question Lord Lane CJ said ([1986] 1 All ER   *a*
833 at 840–841, [1986] QB 626 at 642–643):

'Finally we turn to the second ground of appeal in the case of Howe and Bannister,
namely that the judge was wrong in directing the jury that there is an "objective"
element in the defence of duress. The judge directed the jury on this point as
follows: "The test is whether the threat was of such gravity that it might well have   *b*
caused a reasonable man placed in the same situation as the defendant to act as the
defendant did." And a little later on the judge put it in this way: "Would a sober
person of reasonable firmness sharing the defendant's characteristics have responded
to the threats by taking part in the killing . . .?" It seems to us that this direction was
in accordance with the judgment of this court in *R v Graham* [1982] 1 All ER 801,
[1982] 1 WLR 294. Consequently this ground of appeal likewise fails.'   *c*

In *R v Graham* [1982] 1 All ER 801 at 806, [1982] 1 WLR 294 at 300 Lord Lane CJ, giving
the judgment of the Court of Appeal, Criminal Division, said:

'As a matter of public policy, it seems to us essential to limit the defence of duress
by means of an objective criterion formulated in the terms of reasonableness.
Consistency of approach in defences to criminal liability is obviously desirable.   *d*
Provocation and duress are analogous. In provocation the words or actions of one
person break the self-control of another. In duress the words or actions of one person
break the will of another. The law requires a defendant to have the self-control
reasonably to be expected of the ordinary citizen in his situation. It should likewise
require him to have the steadfastness reasonably to be expected of the ordinary
citizen in his situation. So too with self-defence, in which the law permits the use of   *e*
no more force than is reasonable in the circumstances. And, in general, if a mistake
is to excuse what would otherwise be criminal, the mistake must be a reasonable
one. It follows that we accept counsel for the Crown's submission that the direction
in this case was too favourable to the appellant. The Crown having conceded that
the issue of duress was open to the appellant and was raised on the evidence, the
correct approach on the facts of this case would have been as follows: (1) was the   *f*
defendant, or may he have been, impelled to act as he did because, as a result of
what he reasonably believed King had said or done, he had good cause to fear that if
he did not so act King would kill him or (if this is to be added) cause him serious
physical injury? (2) if so, have the prosecution made the jury sure that a sober
person of reasonable firmness, sharing the characteristics of the defendant, would
not have responded to whatever he reasonably believed King said or did by taking   *g*
part in the killing? The fact that a defendant's will to resist has been eroded by the
voluntary consumption of drink or drugs or both is not relevant to this test.'

In my opinion, what the Lord Chief Justice said in the present case and in *R v Graham*
was entirely correct. In my opinion this question also falls to be answered Yes.

I therefore, consider that these appeals should be dismissed, the first certified question   *h*
answered in the negative and the second and third in the affirmative.

Appeals dismissed.

Solicitors: *Hogan Harris & Co* (for Howe, Bannister and Burke); *Mackesys* (for Clarkson);
Director of Public Prosecutions.

Mary Rose Plummer   Barrister.

a Davies and another v Eli Lilly & Co and others

COURT OF APPEAL, CIVIL DIVISION
SIR JOHN DONALDSON MR, RALPH GIBSON AND BINGHAM LJJ
20, 21, 22 JANUARY 1987

b *Discovery – Production of documents – Inspection – Inspection by person unconnected with proceedings – Collateral use of information obtained – Undertakings not to make improper use of disclosed documents – Plaintiffs claiming against defendants in respect of injurious effects of defendants' drug – Numerous claims of similar nature arising out of use of drug – Plaintiffs' solicitors appointing medical journalist as adviser to co-ordinate documentation of claims – Plaintiffs' solicitors appointing journalist to undertake inspection of defendants' documents c disclosed on discovery – Defendants objecting to inspection by journalist on ground that he might use documents for collateral purpose – Whether court should permit plaintiffs' solicitors' adviser to inspect defendants' documents – RSC Ord 24, r 9.*

A large number of persons, including the plaintiffs, began actions claiming damages for personal injuries arising out of the use of a drug manufactured and marketed by the *d* defendants for the treatment of arthritis. In view of the multiple claims and their overlapping nature, the plaintiffs and their solicitors co-ordinated the preparation of their cases through six 'lead' solicitors who undertook the organisation of the extensive documentation, including medical and scientific advice and evidence. In 1984 the plaintiffs also obtained the assistance of M, a medical and scientific journalist and writer, for the purposes of (i) identifying relevant expert evidence, (ii) acting as co-ordinator of *e* the expert advisers across a number of medical and scientific disciplines, (iii) analysing the mass of evidence given in similar proceedings in the United States and (iv) computerising all such material. In June 1986 a consent order was made for discovery in the plaintiffs' actions, with inspection to follow. In response to a request by the defendants for a list of those who were to conduct the inspection, the plaintiffs stated that M was to be one of their team. The defendants objected to his inclusion on the grounds that he *f* was not an employee of the plaintiffs' solicitors and that in any event he was a journalist who had published highly critical material both of the pharmaceutical industry generally and of the defendants in particular. The plaintiffs applied for an order that the defendants be required to permit M to inspect the documents, and offered undertakings by M that he would not disclose any information he obtained as a result of the inspection, while the defendants applied for an order that M be refused inspection. Under RSC Ord 24, r 9[a] a *g* party who served a list of documents on any other party was required to allow the other party to inspect the documents referred to in the list, and the question arose (i) whether the categories of persons whom the court might authorise to inspect documents on discovery extended to a person, such as M, who was neither an employee of the plaintiffs' solicitors nor a professional expert in the accepted sense, and (ii) if they did, whether the defendants were entitled to object to the particular person chosen by the plaintiffs to *h* undertake inspection. The judge upheld the objection of the defendants and ordered that M should not undertake the inspection. The plaintiffs appealed, contending that, since M occupied a pivotal role in assembling the material necessary to their claims, if he were not permitted to inspect the documents his work to date would be wasted and he would be unable to continue to assist them. The undertakings proffered to the judge were again put forward by M. The defendants contended that M was an investigative journalist who *j* was already critical of them and whose duty to inform the public might override his duty of confidentiality to themselves, that his work as a journalist was inconsistent with

---

a Rule 9, so far as material, provides: 'A party who has served a list of documents on any other party . . . must allow the other party to inspect the documents referred to in the list . . .'

his acting as agent for solicitors conducting discovery and that accordingly they should
not be required to disclose their documents to him.   *a*

Held – The court would in exceptional circumstances permit a person who was neither
a party's legal adviser nor an employee of the legal adviser nor a professional expert in
the case to undertake inspection if it could be shown that such a person's assistance was
essential in the interests of justice and the court was satisfied that there would be no
breach of the duty of confidentiality in respect of the documents so inspected. Having   *b*
regard to the facts that the circumstances of the case were exceptional, that the plaintiffs
had shown that M's assistance was essential in the interests of justice to the preparation of
their cases, that to deprive them of that assistance by refusing to permit M to make the
inspection would effectively preclude him from giving them further help and waste
much of the work already done, that the plaintiffs had shown that M was a careful
researcher and a responsible writer on medical and scientific matters rather than a fanatic *c*
engaged on a crusade against the defendants and that the defendants had been unable to
demonstrate that they were at risk, and subject to M giving express undertakings to the
court that he would not disclose the documents and would not publish material relating
to the manufacture or marketing of the drug for a specified period, the appeal would be
allowed and the plaintiffs' application granted (see p 806 *j* to p 807 *a*, p 810 *e* to 811 *b*,
p 813 *c d*, 815 *a b* and p 817 *b h*, post).   *d*

Notes
For inspection of documents produced on discovery, see 13 Halsbury's Laws (4th edn)
para 97, and for cases on the subject, see 18 Digest (Reissue) 167–168, *1343–1357*.

Cases referred to in judgments   *e*
Bevan v Webb [1901] 2 Ch 59, [1900–3] All ER Rep 206, CA.
Church of Scientology of California v Dept of Health and Social Security [1979] 3 All ER 97,
    [1979] 1 WLR 723, CA.
Dadswell v Jacobs (1887) 34 Ch D 278, CA.
Draper v Manchester Sheffield and Lincolnshire Rly Co (1861) 3 De GF & J 23, 45 ER 786,
    LJJ.   *f*
Home Office v Harman [1982] 1 All ER 532, [1983] 1 AC 280, [1982] 2 WLR 338, HL.
Lindsay v Gladstone, Brooke v Gladstone (1869) LR 9 Eq 132.
Riddick v Thames Board Mills Ltd [1977] 3 All ER 677, [1977] QB 881, [1977] 3 WLR 63,
    CA.
S v Distillers Co (Biochemicals) Ltd [1969] 3 All ER 1412, [1970] 1 WLR 114.
                                                                                                 g
Cases also cited
G v G [1985] 2 All ER 225, [1985] 1 WLR 647, HL.
Halcon International Inc v Shell Transport and Trading Co [1979] RPC 97, Ch D and CA.
Krakauer v Katz [1954] 1 All ER 244, [1954] 1 WLR 278, CA.
Schering Chemicals Ltd v Falkman Ltd [1981] 2 All ER 321, [1982] QB 1, CA.
                                                                                                 h
Interlocutory appeals
The plaintiffs, Joy Rosalie Davies and Joseph Owen Davies, appealed against the decision
of Hirst J on 23 July 1986 dismissing their applications that the first to fifth defendants,
Eli Lilly & Co, Dista Products Ltd, Lilly Industries Ltd, Lilly Research Centre Ltd and
William Ian Hamilton Sheddon (the Lilly defendants), permit Mr Charles Medawar to
attend at their premises at Basingstoke and participate in the inspection of their *j*
documents in the actions brought by the plaintiffs against them and the sixth and seventh
defendants, the Committee on Safety of Medicines and the Department of Health and
Social Security, claiming damages for personal injuries in respect of the use of the drug
Benoxaprofen, marketed under the name 'Opren'. The facts are set out in the judgment
of Sir John Donaldson MR.

David Sullivan QC and *Christopher Carling* for the plaintiffs.

a *Michael Spencer* for the Lilly defendants.

Andrew Collins QC and *Justin Fenwick* for the Attorney General on behalf of the Committee on Safety of Medicines and the Department of Health and Social Security.

SIR JOHN DONALDSON MR. Over 1,000 plaintiffs have brought individual actions claiming damages for personal injury consequent on their treatment with the drug

b benoxaprofen, marketed in the United Kingdom under the name 'Opren'. The first five Defendants are in effect the United States manufacturers of the drug and their United Kingdom subsidiaries (to whom I will refer as the 'Lilly defendants'). The sixth and seventh defendants are the Committee on the Safety of Medicines and the Department of Health and Social Security as the licensing authority under the Medicines Act 1968. The cause of action alleged is negligence, but for present purposes it is unnecessary to be

c more specific.

Manifestly there will be some issues which will be common to all these actions, some which are common to many of them and some which are peculiar to particular actions. In these circumstances it was clearly in the interests of all concerned that some of the actions should be treated as test cases and that a particular judge should be appointed to assist the parties, by making directions or otherwise, so to arrange this litigation that the

d minimum of delay and expense was involved. Hirst J has been so appointed and under his guidance certain interlocutory 'lead actions' have emerged. One such is the claim by the plaintiff Joy Davies.

The particular order which is the subject of this appeal relates to inspection of documents disclosed by the defendants. It raises an issue which is common to all the actions and our decision on this appeal will directly or indirectly affect them all. The

e matter is therefore of some importance.

With great good sense, the plaintiffs and their solicitors have co-ordinated their activities through the medium of six 'lead solicitors', the chairman or principal co-ordinator being Mr Pannone, who is a partner in the firm of Messrs Goldberg Blackburn & Howards of 123 Deansgate, Manchester, chairman of the Law Society's Contentious

f Business Committee and has unrivalled experience in the field of multiple claims for personal injuries.

At an early stage, some two years ago, it appeared to the plaintiffs' solicitors that the problem of assembling and organising the documentation in this action and co-ordinating the expert advice and evidence which were required would be uniquely difficult for two reasons. First, the subject matter is highly technical and involves medical and scientific specialities of many different kinds. Second, the extent of the documentation would

g demand that it be computerised if particular documents were ever to be available as and when required. To indicate the extent of the problem, it is perhaps only necessary to record that discovery in *S v Distillers Co (Biochemicals) Ltd* [1969] 3 All ER 1412, [1970] 1 WLR 114 (the *Thalidomide* case) involved the disclosure of some 30,000 documents, which was itself a record, but in the present litigation it is thought that the documents

h will number some 1·2m, many of which will consist of several pages.

While the essential tasks facing any solicitor preparing any action for trial are the same, problems of the scale of this order call for a special approach. In these circumstances, the plaintiffs' solicitors considered that they needed the assistance of someone who was capable of (a) acting as a go-between, co-ordinator and interpreter in their dealings with their expert medical and scientific advisers, (b) undertaking research designed to identify

j the relevant experts and to uncover supporting evidence in scientific publications, (c) analysing a mass of evidence given in similar United States proceedings and (d) computerising all this material together with the material which would in due course become available on discovery. It was not to be expected that they would find anyone with these qualifications in their own offices and indeed I am surprised that they found anyone who was not employed in the pharmaceutical industry or otherwise employed in

circumstances in which he would be quite unable to devote perhaps three or four years
of his life to this project on a more or less wholetime basis. However, they did find such _a_
a man, a Mr Medawar. He is a United Kingdom subject whose parents were scientists
and scientific writers, his father being a Nobel Prize winner. He has devoted his life to
medical and scientific journalism and, whilst not claiming to be an expert in any
particular field of medicine or science, has acquired a sufficient knowledge of a wide
range of medical and scientific specialities to be able to understand what the experts are
saying and to interpret it for the benefit of those who are, in this context, laymen. In _b_
addition, he is familiar with the art or science of computerisation.

With the approval of the legal aid authorities, the plaintiffs' solicitors engaged Mr
Medawar and he has been assisting the plaintiffs and their solicitors for the greater part
of each working week since December 1984. In the course of this work he has undertaken
research and attended many conferences with experts and by now must have an unique
knowledge of the case which the plaintiffs seek to make. What does not seem to have _c_
occurred to any of the solicitors concerned was that the Lilly defendants would object to
him seeing the documents to be disclosed by them in the actions, but that is what has
happened.

On 2 June 1986 a consent order was made for discovery, inspection to follow. On 1
July the plaintiffs asked for inspection in the following week and the Lilly defendants
inquired who would be conducting the inspection. The inquiry was perhaps unusual, _d_
but was fully justified because the documents were held at the Lilly defendants'
Basingstoke research establishment, which, like similar establishments, has in recent
years become a potential target for those concerned with animal rights and other more
or less violent protest groups. The plaintiffs' solicitors promptly supplied a list including
the name of Mr Medawar. Initially the Lilly defendants objected solely on the ground
that he was not an employee of the solicitors, but they then did some research and _e_
discovered that, in his capacity as a medical and scientific journalist, he had published
matter highly critical of the pharmaceutical industry in general and the Lilly defendants
in particular.

Let me emphasise that the plaintiffs' right to discovery of all relevant documents,
saving all just exceptions, is not in issue. The right is peculiar to the common law _f_
jurisdictions. In plain language, litigation in this country is conducted 'cards face up on
the table'. Some people from other lands regard this as incomprehensible. 'Why,' they
ask, should I be expected to provide my opponent with the means of defeating me?' The
answer, of course, is that litigation is not a war or even a game. It is designed to do real
justice between opposing parties and, if the court does not have _all_ the relevant
information, it cannot achieve this object. But, that said, there have to be safeguards. The _g_
party who is required to place all or most of his cards face up on the table is entitled to
say, 'Some of these cards are highly confidential. You may see them for the purpose of
this litigation but, unless their contents are disclosed to all the world as part of the
evidence given in open court, those contents must be used for no other purpose.' This is
only fair, because, as has been well said, discovery of documents involves a serious
invasion of privacy which can be justified only in so far as it is absolutely necessary for _h_
the achievement of justice between the parties.

Nor is it now in issue that if the plaintiffs need someone of Mr Medawar's expertise to
assist them in the conduct of this litigation, it is for them, and not for the defendants, to
choose who that person should be. What is in issue is whether the plaintiffs have such a
need at this stage when the case is being prepared for trial, and whether the choice of Mr
Medawar will, or may, deprive the defendants of essential protection disclosed by them _j_
to the plaintiffs. It is for the plaintiffs to satisfy the court of the need for a scientific co-
ordinator with access to disclose documents and it is for the defendants to satisfy the
court that the choice of Mr Medawar is not one which they should be required to accept.

I must digress for a moment to explain the position of the Attorney General on behalf
of the Committee on Safety of Medicines and of the DHSS. Before the judge his counsel

supported the Lilly defendants' opposition to inspection by Mr Medawar. Counsel for
a the Attorney General has told us that they did so for two reasons. The first was that the
issue arose so suddenly that they had difficulty in obtaining instructions and wished to
preserve whatever rights they might have. The second was that some, and probably the
majority, of the relevant documents in their possession or power emanated from the
Lilly defendants and they felt that it would be wrong for them to disclose them if the
Lilly defendants were held not to be required to do so. In the interval between the
b decision at first instance and the hearing of the appeal, counsel for the Attorney General
has been able to obtain full instructions and now adopts a wholly neutral attitude. If the
Lilly defendants are required to allow Mr Medawar to inspect their documents, the
Committee on Safety of Medicines and the DHSS would do likewise without objection.
If the Lilly defendants are not required to allow Mr Medawar to inspect their documents,
the Committee on Safety of Medicines and the DHSS would resist any order that they
c allow such inspection. This attitude is entirely intelligible and cannot be criticised. The
only positive stance of these defendants is that they wish Mr Medawar to give an express
undertaking to the court, in terms to be agreed, which reflects and records the implied
obligation of confidentiality which is inherent in his being given access to the documents
to be disclosed.

The judge held that the plaintiffs had established the need for the services of a specialist
d co-ordinator in these cases and, whilst accepting that inspection of documents by such a
co-ordinator, not being an expert witness or an employee of the plaintiffs or their
solicitors, might be an extension of the categories of permissible inspectors as presently
established, held that the categories of permissible inspectors was not closed and that, if
there was no other objection, he had jurisdiction to permit inspection by Mr Medawar.
The judge continued:
e

'That, however, still leaves the other crucial question, namely whether the
defendants have established (the burden of proof being by common consent on
them) that they have a reasonable objection to Mr Medawar personally, which ought
to prevail. There can be no doubt that it is open to the court to entertain this
objection and rule on it, having regard to the interpretation of RSC Ord 24, r 9
f applied in *Church of Scientology of California v Dept of Health and Social Security* [1979]
3 All ER 97, [1979] 1 WLR 723, following the line of *Dadswell v Jacobs* (1887) 34
Ch D 278 and *Bevan v Webb* [1901] 2 Ch 59, [1900–3] All ER Rep 206. At the
forefront of [counsel for the plaintiffs'] argument was a submission that the
defendants are in effect seeking to impose on the plaintiffs a choice of agent, which
James V-C in *Lindsay v Gladstone* (1869) LR 9 Eq 132 held impermissible. I do not
g accept this argument. The essential objection here is to Mr Medawar seeing the
defendants' documents, not to his general role as adviser, which can still continue,
though I accept that its usefulness will be seriously curtailed if he is debarred from
seeing those documents. Nor can I accept [counsel for the plaintiffs'] argument that
it is incumbent on the defendants to produce evidence that Mr Medawar would not
honour his obligation of confidentiality. The authorities seem to me clearly to
h demonstrate that a reasonable apprehension that he might not is sufficient. On the
other hand, of course, the objection must be shown to be a reasonable one, and there
is no right of veto, as [counsel for the Lilly defendants] accepts; in the final analysis
the court must exercise its discretion taking into account all relevant considerations.
In my judgment the objections of both groups of defendants are valid, reasonable
j and extremely powerful. At one stage [counsel for the plaintiffs] suggested that the
court might be led to disapprobate campaigning medical journalism as such; of
course the court will do nothing of the kind, and Mr Medawar is fully entitled to
campaign in this manner so long as he keeps himself within the limits of the general
law. But, having regard to the tone and content of his writings, I am quite satisfied
that, as [counsel for the Lilly defendants] submitted, Mr Medawar's main work, at

all events in recent years, has been a powerful and public crusade against practices
in the pharmaceutical industry of which he so strongly disapproves, and whether *a*
that disapproval is right or wrong is irrelevant. His writings speak clearly for
themselves. The practices in the pharmaceutical industry which he reprobates are
not only their attitudes and promotional activities, but also their secretiveness, and
in this latter respect he also criticises the government's attitude. I also accept [counsel
for the Lilly defendants'] argument that, in consequence, it would be very difficult,
if not impossible, for Mr Medawar, even with the best will in the world, to be sure *b*
he could honour his proffered undertaking (the genuineness of which I do not
question), and to segregate in his mind the information derived from the Lilly and
government documents from that derived elsewhere, and to seal off the former in a
separate compartment in his mind. As [counsel for the Lilly defendants] well put
the point, there is a direct conflict between his duty to keep the confidences, and the
main tenor of his life's work to castigate publicly the wrongs of the pharmaceutical *c*
industry as he sees them. Consequently I am unable to accept [counsel for the
plaintiffs'] argument that the implied undertaking would solve the problem, and I
consider that the sanction of contempt of court is really "illusory" since it would be
virtually impossible for the defendants to establish the source of any particular item
for criticism or comment in his future publications. Lilly's private documents and
information, whose confidentiality they are so anxious to preserve, are clearly and *d*
justifiably of great importance to them, and [counsel for the plaintiffs] has not
sought to argue the contrary. What are the considerations on the other side?
[Counsel for the plaintiffs] stresses the crucial role which Mr Medawar has played
hitherto: the extra expenditure on costs, falling substantially on the legal aid fund,
if he has to be replaced, coupled with the considerable delay setting back the process
of discovery; and the loss of overall efficiency in the conduct of the plaintiffs' case. *e*
He asked me to bear in mind the imbalance of power between the plaintiffs as a
group of small individuals who have combined together and the defendants on the
other side with their powerful and continuous organisation and ready access to all
relevant experts; the court, he submits, should rectify that disparity by recognising
the great importance of Mr Medawar as a key figure in the plaintiffs' humbler
organisation. I bear all these points in mind, though I think that the difficulty and *f*
delay may not be as serious as [counsel for the plaintiffs] submits; and delay must be
viewed in the conspectus of the case as a whole, which will inevitably be a very long
haul indeed before the trial stage even on the issues of liability can be reached.
Equally I think it very unlikely that any of Mr Medawar's work hitherto will be
wasted, and he will still be available to assist the plaintiffs, albeit on a circumscribed
footing. Nor am I persuaded that Mr Medawar is completely irreplaceable. Taking *g*
all these matters into account, in the exercise of my discretion I consider that the
defendants' reasonable objections to Mr Medawar are entitled to prevail, and that in
consequence it would be wrong for the court to insist that the defendants should
allow him so see their documents. It follows that I grant the defendants' application
and reject that of the plaintiffs, it being agreed that the two summonses stand or fall *h*
together. Let me stress in conclusion that I cast no reflection on Mr Medawar's basic
integrity. I simply say, in the words of Knight Bruce LJ in *Draper v Manchester
Sheffield and Lincolnshire Rly Co* (1861) 3 De G F & J 23 at 26, 45 ER 786 at 787 that
there is a personal exception to him inspecting the defendants' documents.'

j

In this court the Lilly defendants do not seriously challenge the judge's finding that
this was a suitable case for the employment by the plaintiffs of a scientific co-ordinator in
the initial stages and that in a proper case a special order might be made for inspection
by a person who is not a professional and thus subject to the discipline of his profession.
However, they do challenge the judge's implied conclusion that justice could not be done
in this case if inspection were limited to solicitors and counsel assisted by expert witnesses

in the usual way. Suffice it to say that I entirely agree with the judge that in the

_a_ exceptional circumstances of this litigation inspection by Mr Medawar or someone with his qualifications is essential if justice is to be achieved, subject always to the need to provide proper protection for the defendants from any abuse of the process of the court.

The real issue is thus whether to allow inspection by Mr Medawar would deprive the defendants of the essential protection from an abuse of the process of the court to which they are undoubtedly entitled. Before the judge, and before this court, Mr Medawar was

_b_ characterised as an 'investigative journalist'. In some circles this is regarded as an accolade to be recognised by the award of a Pullitzer prize. In others it is regarded as highly defamatory and as indicating one who, in what he alleges to be the public interest, but is, in reality, his private interest or that of his employer, will not hesitate to make unbridled use of confidential information obtained by dubious, if not illegal, means. This is not a controversy in which we need, or should, become involved. The issue is one of discretion,

_c_ balancing the legitimate needs of the Lilly defendants against the legitimate needs of the plaintiffs. As in all appeals against a discretionary decision, I am very conscious of the need for caution on the part of an appellate court. Prima facie, the discretion is that of the judge sitting at first instance and not of this court. With this in mind it was submitted to us on behalf of the plaintiffs that the judge had erred in law in holding that the issue was whether the defendants had a reasonable objection to Mr Medawar as an inspector,

_d_ as opposed to whether there was a real risk that if he was permitted to inspect the documents he would use the information for a collateral purpose. For my part I doubt whether there is any difference but, in any event, I do not think that the judge erred in his self-direction on the law. However we have had the benefit of additional evidence and, in the light of that evidence, I consider that the judge inadvertently did an injustice both to Mr Medawar personally and to the plaintiffs.

_e_   At the opening of this appeal I drew attention to the fact that the work being undertaken by Mr Medawar, although highly unusual in the scope and the expertise required, is essentially the work of a kind undertaken by all litigation solicitors and their admitted and unadmitted staffs. It would be unusual, if not unprecedented, for a party giving discovery to object to any such person inspecting his documents. In the case of the solicitors it may be said that this stems from the fact that they are subject to the very

_f_ strict ethical and disciplinary codes of their profession and are also of course officers of the court. But in the case of the unadmitted staff the basis of this trust is that the solicitor on the record accepts personal responsibility for the activities of his staff. In these circumstances I asked whether the six lead solicitors of Mr Pannone had considered taking Mr Medawar into their employment in the capacity of a 'solicitor's clerk', albeit, and I stress this, as a clerk with exceptional qualifications and with exceptionally onerous

_g_ and skilled duties. The answer was that this had been considered, but not pursued because of administrative problems. However, we were told that if necessary the lead solicitors would do so or would enter into some analogous joint contract with Mr Medawar, and in any event they were wholly content to accept the same responsibility in relation to Mr Medawar's activities as they were in relation to anyone in their employ.

_h_ This is a very impressive tribute and not something of which the judge was aware.

The judge held on the evidence before him that Mr Medawar's role as a general adviser could continue notwithstanding that he could not be allowed to see any of the disclosed documents. Counsel for the Lilly defendants supported this view, submitting that all the know-how acquired by Mr Medawar could be passed on to his successor or to solicitors and counsel. The new evidence shows that this is an unduly optimistic view to take. Mr

_j_ Medawar's future usefulness would be non-existent if lawyers and experts could only talk to him about the cases on a basis which excluded all reference to disclosed documents. Three consultant experts have paid tribute to what one described as 'the unique expertise' of Mr Medawar in this field and all thought that not only would he be irreplaceable, but that his expulsion from the team would create very substantial delay. Each was dismayed at the judge's order. Their evidence also disclosed that Mr Medawar had up to now played what I can only describe as a pivotal role in the preparation of the cases. Counsel for the

Lilly defendants sought to persuade us that, even if this was true heretofore, a point had now been reached at which all that remained was for solicitors and counsel to master the *a* cases with a view to their presentation in court. I am quite unable to accept this submission. Counsel must be instructed by solicitors and the solicitors must master and evaluate the mass of evidence which will be relevant. Part of that evidence is already to hand, and the master of that evidence is Mr Medawar. Further evidence will emerge on discovery. The same person must master, evaluate and reconcile the evidence from both sources before counsel can be adequately instructed. If Mr Medawar cannot undertake *b* this task, his successor, whether solicitor, scientist or journalist, will have to start virtually from scratch. This is, to me, a quite appalling prospect.

Counsel for the Lilly defendants says that if this is the case, which he does not admit, the fault is that of the plaintiffs and their advisers who should have foreseen this problem. I agree that they might well have foreseen it, but it was an oversight which is very understandable in the light of the unique problems which confronted the various *c* solicitors seeking to co-ordinate over 1,000 overlapping actions. But I am not sure that it matters where the fault lies. Justice must be done in these actions and that involves protecting not only the plaintiffs, but also the defendants. Whatever the delay, whatever the expense, if the defendants are faced with a significant risk that documents disclosed to Mr Medawar will be used for an extraneous purpose, they must not be so disclosed.

I therefore turn to consider the risk. I suppose that there must always be some risk *d* that solicitors, counsel or expert witnesses may suddenly decide that some higher duty than that owed to their clients, to the opposing party and to the court compels them to breach the obligation of confidentiality which they have undertaken. Happily that very rarely, if ever, happens in practice. Counsel for the Lilly defendants, however, submits that journalists have quite different standards from those of members of other professions. Their whole raison d'etre is investigation, discovery and publication, he says. They will *e* readily conclude that their duty to inform the public overrides all other duties. I am bound to say that this seems to me to be an unfounded generalisation about the profession of journalism. Without doubt there are journalists who confuse the public interest with what the public is interested in. Without doubt there are journalists who feel free to make use of documents and information which they have received from someone who to their knowledge is himself acting in breach of confidence. But I would not accept that *f* a journalist who himself receives information under seal of confidentiality is any more likely than anyone else to breach that confidence. To give but one example, the whole parliamentary lobby system of 'off the record' briefing gives this the lie. Such journalists pass on only what they are authorised to pass on.

In fact, I doubt whether Mr Medawar is to be regarded as a journalist in any ordinary sense and certainly not as an investigative journalist. He is a writer on medical and *g* scientific subjects with a specialist interest in the pharmaceutical industry. In an affidavit sworn after the hearing in the court below, he has denied the judge's finding that 'his main life's work, at all events in recent years, has been a powerful and public crusade against practices in that industry of which he so strongly disapproves'. He says:

'My main work has been to promote positively the rational and economic use of *h* medicines worldwide and in particular in the developing countries. The guiding principles of the policies which I promote are those of the World Health Organisation's "Global Strategy for Health for All by the Year 2000". This policy originates from the WHO 1978 declaration, to which Britain and other WHO member nations have expressed themselves solemnly pledged. In particular, I have been concerned to promote the WHO's policies on "Essential Drugs" for developing *j* countries; and it is through such work that I have recently participated by invitation in, for example, the WHO Conference of Experts referred to in my previous affidavit, and have undertaken assignments for the Dag Hammarskjold Foundation, the London School of Hygiene and Tropical Medicine and the Nordic School of

Public Health. More recently, I have been acting as a consultant to the WHO's
a   European Office at the first of two symposia on behavioural teratogenicity. I have
also been invited, by representatives of the *pharmaceutical industry*, to share the
platform with Sir Gerard Vaughan and Sir Douglas Black, at the Opening Session of
next year's Sixth International Meeting of Pharmaceutical Physicians. In such work,
I have been associating with experts in many different fields and carrying out work
which I believe is generally regarded as professional, both in terms of its quality and
b   in the sense that it is directed towards the ordered and responsible provision of an
important public service. In the course of this work, but as only one aspect of it, I
have on occasion criticised the actions of individual companies whose practices have
seemed to me and to many other health care professionals to have fallen far short of
the standards that the pharmaceutical industry claims to observe. Over the past
eight years, I have been involved in what might reasonably be called campaigning
c   criticism of four companies: none had any connection with the Defendant companies
and all concerned the provision of medicines in developing countries. The actions
subsequently taken by all of the companies concerned suggest that such intervention
was not inappropriate: one company withdrew the offending product; two withdrew
or radically revised all product promotion; and the fourth withdrew an indication
for use of the medicine by children. I still enjoy cordial relations with the two
d   European companies concerned. Inevitably, the conduct and outcome of such
exchanges also involved and implied criticism of the international pharmaceutical
industry's efforts to control malpractice through enforcement of its International
Code of Pharmaceutical Marketing Practice. However, I regard all such criticisms as
only part of the much wider issues. They fall far short of any crusade, and still less
do they constitute my main life's work. My book, "The Wrong Kind of Medicine?",
e   which Dr. Gennery exhibits, has a very much wider subject matter than criticism
of drug companies. As well as referring to the general nature of medicine and some
of the main characteristics of more and less useful drugs, this book discusses also the
involvement of doctors as prescribers; of government as licensing authority and in
other roles; and of patients, individually as the consumers of drugs and collectively
as the beneficiaries of a National Health Service remarkable of its kind. However, I
f   again emphasise that this book represents only part, and not even the principal part,
of my work which relates to the international scene and particularly developing
countries. Moreover I should point out that other people have criticised the present
situation, and the present government has substantially reduced the numbers of
such drugs available on the National Health Service.' (My emphasis.)

g   Mr Medawar may be an unwelcome critic of the pharmaceutical industry, but I can
find no evidence that he is a fanatic or would be in the least likely to breach the duty of
confidentiality which he has expressly acknowledged to exist if he is allowed to inspect
the defendants' documents. The judge on the more limited evidence available to him
expressly accepted the genuineness of Mr Medawar's undertaking to observe his
confidentiality of the defendants' disclosed documents. His fear was different. It was that
h   such was Mr Medawar's disapproval of pharmaceutical companies that he might
inadvertently do so. In the light of the totality of the new evidence now available, I really
cannot accept this view. All the evidence points to the fact that Mr Medawar writes with
careful regard to the need to research the facts even if his opinions may not be universally
accepted. He would thus know where his facts came from and that they were confidential.
j   Finally I must refer to an offer made by Mr Medawar set out in paras 16 to 18 of his
second affidavit, sworn, as I say, after judgment had been given in the court below. It is
in the following terms:

'16. I have no plans to write or publish about the drug Opren; nor about the role
of the Defendants in marketing or licensing it. However, if it were thought

necessary by the Court, I would be prepared to give (in addition to the usual undertaking which I fully and freely give) a specific undertaking to the Court that *a* until further order from the Court I will not seek to republish or communicate anything (save of course to the Plaintiffs and their advisers) about the drug Opren nor about the role of the Defendants in marketing or licensing it.

17. For the consideration of the Court in its decision as to whether such an express undertaking is necessary, I wish (as one who is not a party in these proceedings) to state my personal view and to submit that it would be unfair if I had *b* to give such an undertaking, for two reasons: (a) even if the litigation resulted in a lengthy trial and judgment, with extensive evidence admitted in open court, the undertaking would place me under a unique and personal inability (greater than the limitations imposed in such a situation by the usual implied obligation); and (b) in practice even in such a situation, it would be impossible for me to obtain the Court's leave for release from such an undertaking, because the cost would be *c* prohibitive for me to engage in a contested application, as it would inevitably be in view of these Defendants' attitude towards me.

18. However, I am prepared to submit to the Court's decision as to what is right and just, in the light of the Plaintiffs' and Defendants' respective interest; and if the Court thinks it right to impose a condition that I give such an undertaking, I will comply with it to the full. However, in view of what I have already said in this *d* affidavit I ask that the Court should accept that I can and will scrupulously observe the obligation as to confidentiality by which I would in any event be bound, and that I should not be compelled to submit to a condition as to a wider obligation.'

I agree that a restriction in these terms would be an unfair one to place on Mr Medawar.

I would allow the appeal and require the defendants to allow Mr Medawar to inspect *e* the disclosable documents. However, I recognise that this is an exceptional order in that Mr Medawar is not in a category of persons who would normally be allowed inspection. It is made in the exceptional circumstances of this particular litigation. It would therefore be right to take exceptional measures to reassure the defendants, although I do not think that they are necessary for their protection. Had I thought that, I would not have been in favour of allowing the appeal. *f*

The exceptional measures which I propose are twofold. First, Mr Medawar should be required to give the court an express undertaking to preserve the confidentiality of the defendants' disclosed documents in terms which reflect what would otherwise be his implied obligation. This is the undertaking for which the governmental defendants asked and it is not resisted. It has the practical advantage that if Mr Medawar, contrary to my confident expectations, were to act in breach of his duty to the court and to the *g* defendants, anyone seeking to publish his writings could be served with notice of the undertaking, and would thereafter publish at his peril. This express undertaking, like the implied obligation, should be without limit of time. Its exact terms can be agreed.

Second, Mr Medawar should be required to give the court an express undertaking not without the leave of the court or the consent of the defendants to publish or communicate anything (other than to the plaintiffs and their advisers) about the drug Benoxaprofen as *h* manufactured and marketed by the defendants under whatever name or about the role of the defendants in marketing or licensing it, subject however to a right to publish such matter in written form not less than 28 days after giving the defendants a sight of the terms of the intended publication unless restrained by further order of the court. This undertaking should expire on 31 December 1992 unless earlier varied by the court, that is to say, in six years by which time all issues of liability should have been determined *j* and the topicality of the dispute should have passed.

Counsel for the Lilly defendants submitted that this was an illusory protection for the defendants who would be unable to prove that any particular written communication breached Mr Medawar's obligations. I do not accept this. I repeat that I have no reason to believe that Mr Medawar will breach his obligations, but if he does I think that it will be

readily apparent to the defendants that he has done so. If it is not so apparent, I think that
a the defendants' cause for complaint will be technical rather than substantive.

I would allow the appeal accordingly.

RALPH GIBSON LJ. I agree that the appeal should be allowed. The consent order for
discovery and inspection was made on 2 June 1986. On 1 July the solicitors for the Lilly
b defendants received a request that the plaintiffs' solicitors be allowed to start on the work
of inspection on 4 July with a party including Mr Charles Medawar.

The Lilly defendants' solicitors asked to be told who Mr Medawar was and in what
capacity he would be attending. Some information was given. The Lilly defendants on 3
July refused to allow Mr Medawar to take part in the inspection.

On 4 July the plaintiffs applied by counsel to Hirst J for an order that Mr Medawar be
c allowed to take part in inspection. No evidence was offered. The defendants maintained
their objection before the judge on the ground that Mr Medawar was not a qualified
expert and that the defendants reasonably objected to him by reason of his past activities
as a journalist and publicist. Inevitably, as I think, Hirst J adjourned the application to be
heard by himself on affidavit evidence on 10 July, on which date he dismissed the
plaintiffs' application and, in substance, upheld the defendants' objection.

d It seems that it had not previously occurred to the plaintiffs (by which I mean of course
the solicitors and counsel concerned in the litigation as a whole) that objection might
reasonably and would probably be taken by the Lilly defendants to the participation of
Mr Medawar in the process of inspection. By June 1986 Mr Medawar had already done
much work and had established a position of great importance in the work being done
for the plaintiffs in the Opren litigation as a whole. That position has been described by
e Sir John Donaldson MR in the judgment just given.

The judge had before him affidavits from Mr Pannone and Mr Medawar which
described the nature of the work which Mr Medawar was doing and the need for his
services to the plaintiffs, and the qualifications and experience of Mr Medawar. The Lilly
defendants had issued separate summonses asking for an order that Mr Medawar be
excluded from inspection of documents. The Lilly defendants tendered affidavits in
f support of their application, including that of Dr Gennery, the group medical director
(Europe) of Lilly Research Centre Ltd. They were supplied to the plaintiffs on 9 July.
The hearing was on 10 July. The plaintiffs' advisers decided to proceed without asking
for time to answer the evidence put in for the defendants.

Dr Gennery's affidavit set out the grounds on which the Lilly defendants objected to
Mr Medawar taking part in the inspection. The documents disclosed by the Lilly
g defendants were as to a large proportion highly confidential. The documents concerned
five primary areas: (a) the discovery and development of Benoxaprofen, (b) the testing of
Benoxaprofen both in animal tests and otherwise, (c) the clinical trials of Benoxaprofen,
(d) applications for clinical trial certificates and product licences, and (e) the promotion
and sale of Benoxaprofen. It was said that documents (a) contained highly secret data: it
would be highly damaging if such trade secrets were disclosed in any form. Documents
h (b) might reveal information of a similar character. Documents (c) would reveal the
names of doctors and patients.

Next Dr Gennery referred to Mr Medawar's work as a medical journalist and to the
book *The Wrong Kind of Medicine?* (1984) and to passages from that book in which the
Lilly defendants and Opren were mentioned. Dr Gennery contended that Mr Medawar's
. role as a publicist was inconsistent with his role as agent for a firm of solicitors for
j inspecting highly confidential documents.

On the first question before him Hirst J held that the plaintiffs had made out their case
that the nature of the litigation justified in principle the employment by them of a
specialist co-ordinator such as Mr Medawar without whose services the plaintiffs would
be gravely handicapped in carrying out inspection. That holding was, in my judgment,
clearly right.

Hirst J then in a passage from his judgment which Sir John Donaldson MR has set out in his judgment directed himself as to the test to be applied; considered the factors on *a* each side of the case relevant to the exercise of his discretion, and concluded that the reasonable objections to Mr Medawar of the defendants should prevail. I agree with Sir John Donaldson MR that the judge is not shown to have gone wrong in law in his approach to the assessment of the facts.

In two respects the case before this court differs from that presented to Hirst J. First, the attitude of the two government defendants, the Committee on Safety of Medicines *b* and the licensing authority under the Medicines Act 1968, is no longer to support the objections to Mr Medawar as it was before the judge but is neutral, as Sir John Donaldson MR has described. The second matter is that further evidence was admitted from the plaintiffs. For my part I was not greatly impressed by the suggested explanation of pressure of time for the failure by the plaintiffs to reply to the defendants' evidence before proceeding with their application before the judge. The defendants' counsel had *c* made it clear on 4 July that the defendants objected to Mr Medawar on personal grounds based on his work as a publicist demonstrated by the book to which I have referred and of which a copy was produced. The plaintiffs' advisers underestimated in my view the weight of the defendants' objections as the circumstances appeared to the defendants on what they then knew. It seemed right to me that in the exercise of this court's discretion that further evidence should be admitted because of the importance of the present *d* question in the litigation as a whole and because the error, as I think it was, on the part of the plaintiffs' advisers, to which I have referred, seemed to me to be one easily made. This was unusual litigation with unusual problems facing the plaintiffs' advisers.

The further evidence consists of additional affidavits of Mr Pannone and Mr Medawar. Mr Pannone says that the plaintiffs have no interest in part of the highly confidential documentation mentioned by Dr Gennery, namely documents dealing with the discovery *e* of the drug or with technical development and production which are trade secrets. Such documents the defendants, he says, are entitled not to disclose. As to the other areas of confidentiality, the plaintiffs already hold a large number of documents of the defendants, both published and internal, including the records and the depositions of 33 witnesses from several United States cases, numbered among which is the deposition of Dr Gennery *f* himself of 280 pages and of Dr Shedden, the fifth defendant, of 320 pages. All these documents have already been examined and analysed by Mr Medawar, and the defendants have a list of all the documents held by the plaintiffs.

As I understand it, most of the documents already held by the plaintiffs are documents of the first defendants, a corporation of Indiana in the United States, and not of the United Kingdom defendants.

Next, Mr Pannone explained in greater detail the part played by Mr Medawar in the *g* litigation: it is not limited to the inspection and collation of the defendants' documents, but has included the preparation of papers and briefing on the major issues in the litigation by research in and analysis of published documents, the interpreting of technical issues and evidence at conferences of lawyers and experts, the locating and briefing of suitable experts and the provision of information on the manner and working *h* of pharmaceutical companies in marketing and promotion. Mr Pannone expressed his belief that it would not be possible to find an adequate substitute for Mr Medawar, who could not continue in the litigation if he was precluded from seeing copies of the documents of the Lilly defendants. He is supported in his estimate of the importance and value of the work of Mr Medawar to those advising the plaintiffs, and of the difficulty of replacing him, by letters from Professor Jayson of the Rheumatic Disease Centre of *j* the University of Manchester, from Dr John Ward, a consultant clinical pharmacologist, and Professor Woods, Professor of Clinical Pharmacology and Therapeutics of Sheffield.

Lastly, Mr Medawar in his further affidavit dealt with the inference drawn by the judge on the affidavit of Dr Gennery that Mr Medawar's 'main life's work, at all events in recent years, has been a powerful and public crusade against practices in that industry of

which he so strongly disapproves'. He contended that that was inaccurate. His main
a work has been to promote positively the rational and economic use of medicine
worldwide, in particular in the developing countries. It is in the course of that work that
he has criticised the actions of individual pharmaceutical companies whose practices have
appeared to fall short of the standards which the pharmaceutical industry claims to serve.
His book *The Wrong Kind of Medicine?* has a much wider subject matter than the criticisms
of those companies. Mr Medawar then dealt with the alleged difficulty in distinguishing
b between different sources of information. He was confident that as a writer who has
always worked very closely from documentary sources he could segregate information
obtained from different sources. Finally, if the court should find it necessary, despite his
intention to observe the obligation of confidentiality by which he would in any event be
bound, he was willing to give an undertaking not to publish anything about the drug, as
Sir John Donaldson MR has described. The defendants, on order of this court admitting
c the further evidence, did not ask leave to reply to it.

The judge, as I have said, found that the objections of both groups of defendants should
prevail. For my part, in the light of all the material now before the court, that assessment
is shown to be unsustainable as based on an incomplete picture of some aspects of the
facts of the case.

First, the judge was left with an inadequate description of the part played by Mr
d Medawar: he referred to him as having been 'clearly appointed for the special purpose of
dealing with the documents'. That task is an important part of the work he has done and
will do, but, as set out above, he has other functions of great value and importance to the
plaintiffs.

Next, I think that the judge was caused to underestimate the effect on the plaintffs and
the Opren litigation as a whole of the loss of Mr Medawar. The knowledge of the papers
e and the issues in the case acquired through the work done to date would be effectively
lost to the plaintiffs, and I accept that they could not usefully continue to employ him on
the basis that he could not be told of the contents of documents obtained on inspection
from the Lilly defendants. The difficulty in replacing Mr Medawar, if it could be done at
all, would constitute at least a substantial set-back in the preparation of the litigation.

f Third, the basis of the conclusion of the judge that Mr Medawar would find it difficult,
if not impossible, to honour his undertaking, was the judge's acceptance that Mr
Medawar's 'main life's work has been a powerful and public crusade against practices in
the pharmaceutical industry of which he disapproves'. Mr Medawar's additional
explanation of the nature of his work and the relationship to that work of his published
creticisms of pharmaceutical companies shows that the judge's description of his main
g life's work was not accurate. I see nothing to indicate from Mr Medawar's work put
before the court that he suffers from the uncritical zeal of the crusader which may cause
lack of respect for objective truth.

On the other side of the case, the reasonable apprehension as to Mr Medawar not
honouring the obligation of confidentiality which the judge held to be established on the
evidence was, as submitted by counsel who then appeared for the Lilly defendants, that—

h   'it would be very difficult, if not impossible, for Mr Medawar, even with the best
will in the world, to be sure he could honour his proffered undertaking (the
genuineness of which I do not qestion), and to segregate in his mind the information
derived from the Lilly and government documents from that derived elsewhere,
[and that there was] a direct conflict between his duty to keep the confidences, and
j the main tenor of his life's work to castigate publicly the wrongs of the
pharmaceutical industry as he sees them.'

The judge did not find that there was any risk of Mr Medawar deliberately breaking
his obligations and it is not clear that he was invited to reach the conclusion that there
was such risk. The judge said in terms that he did not question the genuineness of the
proffered undertaking. But in this court counsel for the Lilly defendants contended that

there would be a risk of deliberate disclosure by Mr Medawar if he should find in the papers something which he thought should be published in the public interest as he *a* judged the public interest. He contended, in short, that there was a risk of deliberate disclosure because of a conflict of duties as opposed to undeliberate disclosure resulting from a conflict between the duty to observe the confidence and the pursuit of his work as a publicist against pharmaceutical companies.

On the evidence I see no risk whatever that Mr Medawar would be guilty of deliberate disclosure in breach of his duty. He is an educated, intelligent man whose work is of *b* serious purpose. Such a person is well able to understand and to abide by an undertaking not to disclose information from a particular source. He has published works containing criticisms of pharmaceutical companies. But the evidence of the defendants does not suggest that he has been in any instance wrong or irresponsible in this use of facts or of the reports and statement of others. I reject this new submission of counsel for the Lilly defendants.   *c*

When the plaintiffs applied for their order, the Lilly defendants had to make up their minds quickly on the matter. They had not been told earlier because it had not occured to the plaintiffs that any difficulty would arise. These defendants put before the court what they had been able to learn about Mr Medawar in the time available, and it does not surprise me that they were disturbed and alarmed. It must have seemed highly unusual and distasteful to the Lilly defendants and to their advisers that the scientific co- *d* ordinator in the plaintiffs' team to carry out inspection should be a person with no technical or professional qualification who had published a book in which criticism appeared of these defendants relative to an issue in the action. There was a rational basis for anxiety that such a person might without deliberate intention fail to comply with the duty not to disclose, but it is the task of the court in a case of this nature to assess as best it can the gravity of any risk which is apprehended and the nature of the injury which *e* might result if the risk became fact. On all the evidence now before this court, the risk seems to me to be non-existent and, if I should be wrong about that, any possible injury not to be great.

It is not suggested that Mr Medawar has any interest in trading secrets as such or that there is any risk of him seeing in the papers disclosed mention of some commercially *f* useful idea of which he thereafter might make use. A risk of information of that nature being used as a springboard for development of the idea may be of particular gravity in a commercial context because the person who inspects the papers may be able credibly to claim that he got the idea elsewhere. The submissions by counsel for the Lilly defendants were directed mainly to the discovery in these papers of matters adverse to the Lilly defendants or 'scandal', as he called it, affecting them or others. With reference to such *g* matters, in my judgment, the risk of undeliberate disclosure is non-existent. If the matter is of significant importance to the Lilly defendants, I would expect Mr Medawar to be aware whence he got the information, ie from papers disclosed in these proceedings as contrasted with documents already in the possession of the plaintiffs from other sources, and I would further expect the Lilly defendants to know where such information is recorded and to be able to demonstrate that it had come from documents disclosed in *h* these proceedings, if that were the case.

The judge thought that the sanction of contempt for breach of the implied undertaking was illusory, since it would be virtually impossible for the defendants to establish the source of any particular item of criticism or comment in his future publications. I do not regard the sanction as illusory, and it is not the only sanction. Mr Medawar has been challenged as to his personal capacity to honour such an undertaking. He cannot I think *j* complain about the challenge being made. He has responded to it by asserting his ability fully to comply with the undertaking (an assertion which for my part I find credible), and his determination to do so. He has thus added the commitment of his ability as a writer and researcher to keep distinctly in his mind the sources of his information and the commitment of his personal honour.

a The defendants are entitled to be protected so far as is reasonably possible against any abuse of the process of discovery.

For the reasons I have given, it seems to me that the judge's assessment of the gravity of any risk of failure by Mr Medawar to comply with the obligations of confidentiality cannot be sustained on the evidence now before this court. Having regard to the protection which will be afforded to the defendants by the express undertakings which Mr Medawar has offered to give, the discretion of the court must in my judgment be
b exercised by directing that on the terms proposed by Sir John Donaldson MR Mr Medawar be allowed to take part in the process of inspection of the documents of the Lilly defendants.

BINGHAM LJ. Few if any common lawyers would doubt the importance of documentary discovery in achieving the fair disposal and trial of civil actions. The
c requirement that a party to civil litigation should disclose his private papers for inspection by his opponent in the litigation does none the less involve a very serious invasion of the privacy and confidentiality of his affairs. This has been recognised in a number of cases: see for example *Riddick v Thames Board Mills Ltd* [1977] 3 All ER 677 at 687–688, [1977] QB 881 at 896, *Home Office v Harman* [1982] 1 All ER 532 at 534, 540, 543, 552, [1983]
d AC 280 at 300, 308, 312, 323. A number of strict safeguards have accordingly been developed over the years to preserve a party's privacy so far as possible consistent with the administration of justice. This is done by controlling the documents which are required to be disclosed, the conditions on which inspection is to be made and copies taken, and the persons by whom inspection may be made. The present appeal turns, unusually, on the last of these points.

e RSC Ord 24, r 9 simply requires a party to allow 'the other party' to inspect the documents in his list. This rule does not call for inspection by the other party personally. The inspection is usually made by the other party's solicitor or one of the solicitor's employees. Sometimes inspection is authorised to be made by agents of other kinds, such as accountants. The first question argued before the judge here was whether Mr Charles Medawar fell within any category of agent previously recognised as appropriate to carry
f out the inspection of documents in litigation. Viewing Mr Medawar as a scientific co-ordinator employed by the plaintiffs' solicitors to handle this litigation alone, the judge held that he did not. This was a large historical inquiry and the judge's conclusion appears, with respect, to have been plainly right. But the judge then went on to consider whether, in the special circumstances of this extensive, complex and important litigation, the previously recognised categories of agent should be extended to include someone
g doing the work described as being done by Mr Medawar. He concluded that they should. No complaint is made of that conclusion, and I agree with it.

The judge then turned to consider the question which has given rise to this appeal: whether, assuming that an agent in the position of Mr Medawar was an appropriate person to inspect the defendants' documents on behalf of the plaintiffs, the defendants had good grounds for objecting to inspection by Mr Medawar personally. The ground
h on which the defendants objected to Mr Medawar personally was made clear by their affidavit evidence before the judge: he was, they contended, a publicist antagonistic to pharmaceutical companies and to the pharmaceutical industry, already on record as strongly critical of the defendants' conduct in relation to Benoxaprofen (or Opren), the very drug with which this litigation is concerned. The defendants submitted that they should not be required to show their private and confidential papers to an avowedly
j hostile critic such as Mr Medawar: the knowledge he obtained on inspection was likely either consciously or unconsciously to be reflected in his further publications; and, however stringent the conditions imposed, proof of breach would be difficult or impossible, so that the defendants would in effect be unprotected.

The burden of establishing a reasonable objection to Mr Medawar personally lay on the defendants. Their affidavit advancing the objection reached the plaintiffs' counsel on

the day of the hearing before the judge, having been delivered the evening before. That
was not because they had been in any way dilatory but because the matter was brought *a*
before the court at very short notice. The result, however, was that there was no affidavit
of the plaintiffs to answer the defendants' criticisms of Mr Medawar. It may be that the
plaintiffs should have anticipated these criticisms. It may also be that the plaintiffs should
have sought an adjournment to answer the criticisms. Neither of these things happened,
largely (I think) because the plaintiffs did not foresee how the issue would develop. But
the matter did come before the judge in a somewhat one-sided way.   *b*

In the passage of his judgment, which Sir John Donaldson MR has quoted, the judge
concluded that the defendants' objections to Mr Medawar personally were 'valid,
reasonable and extremely powerful'. Crucial to that conclusion was the judge's acceptance
that 'Mr Medawar's main life's work, at all events in recent years, has been a powerful
and public crusade against practices in the pharmaceutical industry of which he so
strongly disapproves'. In exercising his discretion, the judge was clearly impressed by the *c*
risk of irreparable harm to the defendants if Mr Medawar were allowed to inspect; in
contrast, he saw the harm to the plaintiffs if he were not as being largely administrative
and financial, and even so perhaps a little exaggerated.

On the material before him I do not for my part find the judge's conclusion of fact or
his exercise of discretion surprising or suggestive of error. It had been stated on oath that
making public that which he considered to be wrongfully kept secret appeared to be part *d*
of Mr Medawar's life's work. He had been described as a social campaigner. To oblige the
defendants to permit inspection by such a person was entirely novel. On the plaintiffs'
side, I do not think that Mr Medawar's role in the handling of this litigation had been
very clearly described.

In this court new evidence has been admitted and additional undertakings have been
offered to safeguard the defendants' right to protection against improper disclosure. *e*
These factors in my view entitle this court to consider the issue as it now stands.

The judge accepted that Mr Medawar would not deliberately break the implied
undertaking binding on anyone who undertakes inspection of another party's documents.
The defendants did not in argument before us accept that. They suggested that Mr
Medawar, as a journalist, might regard his duty to publish as a duty higher than and *f*
overriding his duty to comply with his undertaking to the court. Even if Mr Medawar
were to be regarded (wrongly, as I think) simply as a journalist, there are in my judgment
two compelling reasons for rejecting this suggestion. First, while it is well known that
journalists accept and observe certain ethical obligations, there is no reason to think that
a responsible journalist would flout a solemn undertaking given to the court, and no
ground has been demonstrated for regarding Mr Medawar as other than responsible. *g*
Second, even if Mr Medawar might otherwise be inclined to break his undertaking
(which I do not accept) I have no reason to doubt that he would, like any other rational
person, be deterred from doing so by consideration of the penalty which would be likely
to follow.

The judge was concerned at the risk of unconscious or inadvertent breach. I do not
find it easy to visualise how this would occur, since in anything he wrote Mr Medawar *h*
would be likely to stick close to the documents and I do not think he could easily overlook
their provenance. But, if there is a risk, the defendants are in my view very substantially
protected by the undertaking not to publish without notice which Sir John Donaldson
MR proposes. Counsel for the defendants rejects such an undertaking as being useless to
them. I do not agree. It will of course be useless if Mr Medawar does not publish at all, or
if any proposed publication is based on material plainly available to him without recourse *j*
to the defendants' documents disclosed in the action. In neither case will the defendants
have any ground of complaint. But if he unconsciously and inadvertently transgresses,
the proposed order will in my view enable the defendants to consider the proposed text
and if necessary seek relief if the transgression is of any significance. There remains a
theoretical possibility that Mr Medawar might, without publishing himself, feed

a illegitimate material to a sympathetic third party, but I do not think this could be inadvertent or unconscious and the third party would run the same risk as Mr Medawar.

In the light of the new evidence and undertakings, including the expression of willingness by the plaintiffs' solicitors to accept responsibility for Mr Medawar as if he were their clerk, I do not think there is a real risk (or a danger) that improper use will be made of documents inspected by Mr Medawar. I do not accordingly hold the defendants' objection to be reasonable. Their counsel accepted that their objection was in part b emotional. I am sure he was right. But to the extent that the objection was emotional, it was not (I think) reasonable, even if it was understandable.

I turn to consider the effect on the plaintiffs' conduct of this litigation if inspection by Mr Medawar is ruled out. When these claims were taking shape, I have no doubt that those acting for the plaintiffs were vividly aware of the great difficulty of preparing and co-ordinating claims by numerous plaintiffs in an unfamiliar and very complex field c spanning many specialist disciplines. The need for someone scientifically literate to guide, direct and oversee this preparation and co-ordination must have been clear. Mr Medawar must have appeared an ideal person to fill this role, his very lack of a specialist qualification being an asset as sparing him from the tunnel vision which not infrequently afflicts the most highly qualified specialists and enabling him to take a broader (though d necessarily more superficial) view of the whole field. His known opinions on this subject must of course have commended him to the plaintiffs' advisers, but I feel sure that they saw him as an informed and socially-concerned commentator rather than as the irresponsible publicist of the defendants' portrayal. I also feel sure that at the outset the plaintiffs' advisers were concentrating on their problems in preparing and presenting these cases and gave little thought to the difficulties or sensitivities of the defendants. I e doubt if at that stage anyone looked ahead very intently to the distant horizon of discovery. The initial engagement of Mr Medawar therefore strikes me as a practical, if imaginative, response to a difficult problem, and I see no reason to suspect any deliberate concealment of his engagement from the defendants (which, indeed, is not suggested).

The affidavit evidence persuades me that over the first 18 months (now two years) of his engagement Mr Medawar's services were of very great benefit to the plaintiffs, in f marshalling the plaintiffs' own material and (perhaps even more importantly) finding appropriate experts for the plaintiffs, communicating with them and interpreting their opinions. The continued engagement of Mr Medawar, if he were unable to see the defendants' documents, would (I think) be more of an embarrassment to the plaintiffs than a help, and I do not think that if he were to withdraw anyone else could take over his role at the point he had reached. No doubt it is true that he is not irreplaceable. No g one ever is. But I think it would be very hard to find anyone to fulfil his role, and even then I am sure there would be considerable disruption, expense and delay, delay alone being a serious consequence for elderly plaintiffs. The defendants' primary contention was that inspection of their documents by Mr Medawar was not necessary for the attainment of justice. In the extraordinary circumstances of this case I think that it is. I should, however, add that the picture has, for me, become very much clearer as a result h of Mr Pannone's further affidavit.

For these reasons I agree that the appeal should be allowed and the order made as proposed by Sir John Donaldson MR.

Appeal allowed on undertakings agreed between the parties. Leave to appeal to the House of Lords refused.

j Solicitors: *Owen White*, Feltham (for the plaintiffs); *Davies Arnold & Cooper* (for the Lilly defendants); *Treasury Solicitor.*

Diana Procter Barrister.

Dinch v Dinch

HOUSE OF LORDS
LORD KEITH OF KINKEL, LORD TEMPLEMAN, LORD GRIFFITHS, LORD OLIVER OF AYLMERTON AND
LORD GOFF OF CHIEVELEY
13, 14 JANUARY, 19 FEBRUARY 1987

*Divorce – Financial provision – Variation of order – Jurisdiction – No jurisdiction where final
order made – Consent order incorporating terms agreed between spouses – Wife applying for
variation of consent order – Whether jurisdiction to entertain application – Matrimonial Causes
Act 1973, ss 23(1), 24(1).*

The husband and wife were divorced in 1979. In 1980 a consent order was made on
consolidated applications by the wife for ancillary relief and by the husband for an order
for the sale of the matrimonial home. Under the terms of the order it was agreed that
the husband would make periodical payments to the wife and to the remaining minor
child of the family until he reached the age of 17 or ceased full-time education, that the
husband would also pay half the mortgage on the matrimonial home, that the
matrimonial home would be sold and the proceeds divided equally, but that the sale
would be postponed until the child reached 17 years or ceased full-time education,
whichever was the later. In 1981, when the husband failed to pay the periodical payments
and fell into arrears, the wife was granted a charging order on the husband's share of the
proceeds of the sale of the house. In 1983, when the child had reached 17 and ceased full-
time education, the husband applied for a variation of the periodical payments order
reducing the payments to a nominal sum, for the arrears to be remitted and for the
immediate sale of the matrimonial home. The wife responded by applying for a further
charging order in respect of arrears and also for a lump sum order, a transfer of property
order and an order postponing the sale of the matrimonial home. The judge granted the
husband's application, and dismissed the wife's application on the grounds that the
original consent order was an order made pursuant to s 24(1)[a] of the Matrimonial Causes
Act 1973, that therefore he had no jurisdiction to make any further order which would
in effect be a variation of the original consent order and that even if he had jurisdiction
the altered circumstances of the parties were insufficient to justify a variation of the
consent order. The wife appealed to the Court of Appeal, which allowed her appeal and
ordered the husband's interest in the matrimonial home to be transferred to the wife
subject to a charge in favour of the husband. The husband appealed to the House of
Lords.

Held – Once the court had either exercised or declined to exercise its powers under
ss 23(1)[b] and 24(1) of the 1973 Act to make a lump sum or property adjustment order in
relation to particular property, then, subject to its limited powers under s 31 to vary the
order, no further application for an order in respect of that property, whether original or
by way of variation of an existing order, could be made. Furthermore, where the order
was intended to be a final and conclusive once-for-all financial settlement, either overall
or in relation to a particular property, the order precluded any further claim to relief in
relation to that property. In the circumstances, the consent order was not capable of

---

a   Section 24(1), so far as material, provides: 'On granting a decree of divorce . . . the court may make
    . . . (a) an order that a party to the marriage shall transfer to the other party, to any child of the
    family or to such person as may be specified in the order for the benefit of such a child such
    property as may be so specified, being property to which the first-mentioned party is entitled,
    either in possession or reversion . . .'
b   Section 23(1), so far as material, provides: 'On granting a decree of divorce . . . the court may make
    . . . (c) an order that either party to the marriage shall pay to the other such lump sum or sums as
    may be so specified . . .'

being construed other than as finally and conclusively determining the rights of the
a parties in the property. Accordingly, the husband's appeal would be allowed (see p 820
e f, p 825 *a b*, p 826 *j* to p 827 *b j* and p 828 *b d f g*, post).

Minton v Minton [1979] 1 All ER 79 and de Lasala v de Lasala [1979] 2 All ER 1146
applied.

Carson v Carson [1983] 1 All ER 478 approved.

Per curiam. It is the imperative professional duty of those advising parties to a
b matrimonial dispute to consider with due care the impact which terms that they agree
on behalf of their clients will have and are intended to have on any outstanding
application for financial relief and to ensure that such appropriate provision is inserted in
any consent order as will leave no room for any future doubt or misunderstanding or
saddle the parties with the wasteful burden of wholly unnecessary costs. Furthermore,
although the primary duty lies on those concerned with the negotiation and drafting of
c the terms of the order, it is also the duty of any court called on to make a consent order
to consider for itself, before the order is drawn up and entered, the jurisdiction which it
is being called on to exercise and to make clear what claims for ancillary relief are being
finally disposed of (see p 820 *e f j* to p 821 *b* and p 828 *f g*, post).

Notes
d For consent orders embodying spouses' agreement on financial provision, see 13
Halsbury's Laws (4th edn) para 1158.

For the Matrimonial Causes Act 1973, ss 23, 24, 31, see 27 Halsbury's Statutes (4th
edn) 724, 726, 741.

Cases referred to in opinions
e Brown v Brown [1959] 2 All ER 266, [1959] P 86, [1959] 2 WLR 776, CA.
Brown v Kirrage (1980) 11 Fam Law 141, CA.
Carson v Carson [1983] 1 All ER 478, [1983] 1 WLR 285, CA.
de Lasala v de Lasala [1979] 2 All ER 1146, [1980] AC 546, [1979] 3 WLR 390, PC.
Henderson v Henderson (1843) 3 Hare 100, [1843–60] All ER Rep 378, 67 ER 313.
f Minton v Minton [1979] 1 All ER 79, [1979] AC 593, [1979] 2 WLR 31, HL.
Sandford v Sandford [1986] 1 FLR 412, CA.
South American and Mexican Co, Re, ex p Bank of England [1895] 1 Ch 37, [1891–4] All ER
Rep 680, CA.

Cases also cited
g Bedson v Bedson [1965] 3 All ER 307, [1965] 2 QB 666, CA.
Blake v O'Kelly (1874) 9 IR Eq 54.
Bothe v Amos [1975] 2 All ER 321, [1976] Fam 46, CA.
Burke v Burke [1974] 2 All ER 944, [1974] 1 WLR 1063, CA.
Chaterjee v Chaterjee [1976] 1 All ER 719, [1976] Fam 199, CA.
Empson v Empson (1979) 1 FLR 269, CA.
h H v H [1966] 3 All ER 560.
Leake (formerly Bruzzi) v Bruzzi [1974] 2 All ER 1196, [1974] 1 WLR 1528, CA.
McDowell v McDowell (1957) 107 LT 184, CA.
National Provincial Bank Ltd v Hastings Car Mart Ltd [1965] 2 All ER 472, [1965] AC 1175,
HL.
Thompson v Thompson [1985] 2 All ER 243, [1986] Fam 38, CA.
j Thwaite v Thwaite [1981] 2 All ER 789, [1982] Fam 1, CA.
Ward v Ward and Greene [1980] 1 All ER 176, [1980] 1 WLR 4, CA.

Appeal
Oral Ahmet Dinch (the husband) appealed with leave of the Appeal Committee of the
House of Lords granted on 11 June 1986 against the order of the Court of Appeal (Fox

and Purchas LJJ) dated 10 July 1985 whereby it allowed the appeal of the respondent, Dilys Enid Dinch (the wife), against the order of his Honour Judge Main QC dated 21   *a* January 1985 and ordered (i) that the order for the sale of the matrimonial property at 1 Eversley Crescent, Isleworth, Middlesex be set aside, (ii) that the order dismissing the wife's application for a property transfer order and/or an order postponing sale be set aside, (iii) that the husband and wife transfer to the wife on or before 1 October 1985 all their legal and beneficial interest in the matrimonial property such transfer to be in full satisfaction of the wife's claim for a property transfer order and a lump sum order and in   *b* full satisfaction of all moneys due or accruing in respect of periodical payments and (iv) that forthwith on such transfer (a) the matrimonial property stand charged in favour of the husband in the sum of £20,000 such sum to be paid to the husband on (1) the wife remarrying or (2) the voluntary removal of the wife from the property or (3) the death of the wife, and (b) the wife's claim for periodical payments be dismissed. The facts are set out in the opinion of Lord Oliver.   *c*

Robert L Johnson QC and *Robert Beecroft* for the husband.
Michael Irvine for the wife.

Their Lordships took time for consideration.   *d*

19 February. The following opinions were delivered.

LORD KEITH OF KINKEL. My Lords, I have had the opportunity of reading in draft the speech to be delivered by my noble and learned friend Lord Oliver. I agree with it, and for reasons he gives would allow the appeal.   *e*

LORD TEMPLEMAN. My Lords, for the reasons given in a speech which has been prepared by my noble and learned friend Lord Oliver, I would allow this appeal.

LORD GRIFFITHS. My Lords, I have had the advantage of reading in draft the speech   *f* prepared by my noble and learned friend Lord Oliver. I agree with it and would allow this appeal.

LORD OLIVER OF AYLMERTON. My Lords, this is an appeal brought by the respondent in matrimonial proceedings with the leave of your Lordships' House against an order of the Court of Appeal dated 10 July 1985 allowing the petitioner's appeal from   *g* an order made on 21 January 1985 by his Honour Judge Main QC, directing that the former matrimonial home of the parties be sold and dismissing the petitioner's application for lump sum and transfer of property orders and for an order that the sale of the property be postponed. The appeal is yet another example of the unhappy results flowing from the failure to which I ventured to draw attention in *Sandford v Sandford* [1986] 1 FLR 412 to take sufficient care in the drafting of consent orders in matrimonial   *h* proceedings to define with precision exactly what the parties were intending to do in relation to the disposal of the petitioner's claims for ancillary relief so as to avoid any future misunderstanding as to whether those claims, or any of them, were or were not to be kept alive. The hardship and injustice that such failure inevitably causes, particularly in cases where one or both parties are legally aided and the only substantial family asset consists of the matrimonial home, are so glaring in the instant case that I feel impelled   *j* once again to stress in the most emphatic terms that it is in all cases the imperative professional duty of those invested with the task of advising the parties to these unfortunate disputes to consider with due care the impact which any terms that they agree on behalf of their clients have and are intended to have on any outstanding application for ancillary relief and to ensure that such appropriate provision is inserted in

any consent order made as will leave no room for any future doubt or misunderstanding
a or saddle the parties with the wasteful burden of wholly unnecessary costs. It is, of course, also the duty of any court called on to make such a consent order to consider for itself, before the order is drawn up and entered, the jurisdiction which it is being called on to exercise and to make clear what claims for ancillary relief are being finally disposed of. I would, however, like to emphasise that the primary duty in this regard must lie on those concerned with the negotiation and drafting of the terms of the order and that any
b failure to fulfil such duty occurring hereafter cannot be excused simply by reference to some inadvertent lack of vigilance on the part of the court or its officers in passing the order in a form which the parties have approved. Having said this, I must add that the consent order which has given rise to such unfortunate consequences in the instant case is not one which was drawn by any of the counsel appearing before your Lordships or for which they can be held in any way responsible.

c My Lords, the appellant and the respondent (to whom I will hereafter refer as 'the husband' and 'the wife' respectively) were married on 19 October 1957. There were two children of the marriage, namely Errol, who was born on 8 August 1958, and Timur, who was born on 28 April 1965. The latter has completed his full-time education but lives with his mother in the matrimonial home, which, at all material times, consisted of a three-bedroom, freehold dwelling house at 1 Eversley Crescent, Isleworth, Middlesex,
d which had been purchased in the joint names of the husband and the wife. Having formed a liason with another woman, the husband left the matrimonial home on 9 April 1978, and on 25 May 1978 the wife presented in the Brentford County Court a petition for dissolution of the marriage based on the husband's adultery. That petition contained prayers for ancillary relief by way of periodical payments, secured provision orders, lump sum orders and a property adjustment order. The husband, who was at that stage
e unrepresented, filed an answer and the cause was thereafter transferred to the High Court. There were, during the summer of 1978, a number of applications to the court which it is unnecessary to mention, save that your Lordships have been told that an injunction was, at some stage, granted to prevent the husband until further order from returning to the matrimonial home save for the purpose of collecting his personal belongings. That order remained in force at the date of the consent order to which I will
f refer in a moment, so that the factual situation was that the wife was in sole possession of the matrimonial home from April 1978 onwards. It was subject to a mortgage in favour of the Alliance Building Society. Your Lordships have not been told and it does not appear from the papers by whom the mortgage instalments had been paid prior to the presentation of the petition, but it does not appear ever to have been in dispute that the
g wife, as a beneficial joint tenant, was entitled to some share in the property or the proceeds of its sale. Notwithstanding that the cause had been transferred to the High Court on the filing of the husband's answer, he applied on 17 July 1978 to the Brentford County Court for an emergency hearing of an application for an immediate sale of the property with vacant possession on the ground that he was out of possession, was paying rent for lodgings and was paying the whole of the outstanding mortgage instalments,
h the balance then outstanding being, it seems, some £6,400. His proposal at that point was that he should pay the wife £18,000 out of the proceeds of sale and should retain the balance himself after discharging the mortgage. That application was treated by the court as an originating application under s 17 of the Married Women's Property Act 1882 and a pre-trial review was fixed for 4 August 1978. Thereafter the husband consulted solicitors, who came on the record. A formal summons under the Act was filed
j and leave was given to file an amended affidavit in support. At this stage the husband, no doubt on advice, had abandoned his original proposal and was seeking simply a declaration of a joint beneficial interest, an order for sale, and an order for the division of the net proceeds between the parties in equal shares, together with certain relief in respect of jointly owned chattels which is immaterial for present purposes. Thus, at this point, the petition and the wife's claim for ancillary relief were proceeding in the High

Court and the husband's separate application under the 1882 Act was proceeding in the
Brentford County Court. On 1 February 1979, however, the husband's answer in the
matrimonial proceedings was struck out, a decree nisi was pronounced on the wife's
petition, and an order was made for her to have the custody of Timur. Her outstanding
application for ancillary relief was adjourned to chambers and subsequently transferred
back to the Brentford County Court. On 2 July 1979 there was heard by the registrar of
that court an application by the wife for interim maintenance, and an order was made
for payment of £50 a month for the wife and £40 a month for Timur from 19 June
1979, the latter to continue until Timur attained the age of 17 years or until further
order. At the same time leave was given for the decree to be made absolute. On 25 July
1980 the wife gave notice of the hearing on 20 October 1980 of her application for
ancillary relief. At that time there were considerable outstanding arrears due to the wife
under the order for interim maintenance.

I have set out this history in full because it is, I think, important that there should be
borne in mind exactly what the matters in issue between the parties then were. So far as
the husband was concerned, he was pressing for an order for the immediate sale of the
property and an equal division of the proceeds. He was also seriously in arrears with his
payments under the interim maintenance order. So far as the wife was concerned, she
was in sole possession of the property and had the custody of Timur who was then aged
15 and was living with her. Her application for a periodical payments order, a lump sum
order and a property adjustment order had not been dealt with and was to be brought
before the court on 20 October 1980.

The parties duly appeared by counsel before the registrar on 20 October 1980, and on
that occasion a consent order was made for the two applications to be considered and for
the matter to be adjourned to 26 November 1980. Your Lordships know nothing of
what negotiations then took place between the parties' respective legal advisers, but it is
clear that some did take place because, on 26 November 1980, the date of the adjourned
hearing of the now consolidated applications, the court received letters from the solicitors
on both sides consenting to an order in the terms of an agreed draft, which had, it
appears, been settled by counsel and was written out in longhand. The terms of that draft
order (and particularly, in the light of the arguments addressed to your Lordships, the
manner in which it was intituled) are important and must be set out in full. It was in
these terms:

'Nos 78D 06360
and 79D 1177A

IN THE BRENTFORD COUNTY COURT

Between

DILYS ENID DINCH   Petitioner
                              and
ORAL AHMET DINCH   Respondent
                              and
LYNN DINCH (formerly REED)   Co-Respondent

and IN THE MATTER OF THE MARRIED WOMENS PROPERTY ACT 1882

Between

ORAL AHMET DINCH   Applicant
                              and
DILYS ENID DINCH   Respondent

Upon hearing Counsel for the Petitioner and Counsel for the Respondent, the Co-
Respondent not appearing nor being represented BY CONSENT IT IS ORDERED that (i)
the Respondent do pay to the Petitioner the sum of £100 per month (calendar) from

a   the date hereof until further order (ii) the Respondent do pay to the child Timur
     Dinch the sum of £66·66 per month (calendar) until he reaches the age of 17 or
     ceases in full time education, whichever is later or until further order (iii) the
     Respondent do pay direct to the Alliance Building Society such sum monthly as
     represents one half the capital repayment element of mortgage from date hereof (iv)
     the matrimonial home (known as 1 Eversley Crescent, Isleworth, Middx) and jointly
     owned contents thereof to be sold and the net proceeds thereof to be divided equally
b   between Petitioner and Respondent, the Petitioner entitled to deduct from the
     Respondent's share (a) the sum of £1350 plus interest at 12½% p.a. from date hereof
     to date of sale (b) a sum representing one half of the capital element of any mortgage
     instalments paid by the Petitioner to the Alliance Building Society from the 1st
     November 1979 to date hereof. Such sale not to be effected until the child Timur
     reaches the age of 17 or ceases full time education, whichever is later (v) the
c   Petitioner to receive the said sum of £1350 plus interest in full and final settlement
     of all sums due and owing to the Petitioner and Timur under the Order dated 2nd
     June 1979 from the Respondent (vi) that there be no Order as to costs, save Petitioner
     to have Legal Aid Taxation and Certificate for Counsel.'

     The reference in para (v) to the order of 2 June 1979 was clearly a mistake for 2 July 1979
d   but nothing turns on this.
        For some reason which is not easy to understand, the order actually drawn up by the
     court on the basis of this document departed from it in a number of material respects, in
     particular, in omitting any reference whatever in the title to the husband's application
     under the 1882 Act. However, it has very sensibly been agreed at all stages of the
     proceedings leading to the appeal to your Lordships' House that the order is to be treated
e   as having been made in the terms of the agreed draft.
        At the date of the order there was no reason to doubt the husband's ability to meet the
     monthly periodical payments of £100 and £66·66. He had paid nothing under the
     interim maintenance order but his explanation of that, which was subsequently accepted
     by the court, was that its existence had been concealed from him by the co-respondent
     with whom he was living. He had, however, been employed for many years by Pan
f   American World Airways Inc as a traffic controller at a substantial salary and up to the
     latter part of 1981 no difficulty arose in meeting the prescribed payments. At the end of
     1981, however, largely, it seems, as a result of financial and emotional difficulties arising
     from his marriage to the co-respondent, he accepted voluntary redundancy and thus
     disabled himself from complying with the order. The wife subsequently applied for and
     obtained an order charging arrears of some £1,472 on the husband's share in the proceeds
g   of sale of the matrimonial home. Timur had ceased full-time education in August 1972,
     but the matrimonial home was not then sold pursuant to the consent order, the wife
     continuing to live there with him. On 21 June 1983, however, the husband applied to
     the court for a variation of the periodical payments order by reducing the sum payable
     to a nominal sum, for an order remitting the arrears and for an immediate sale of the
     matrimonial home. The wife responded on the following day with an application for a
h   further charging order in respect of arrears of some £476. Both applications came before
     Mr Registrar Rees and, after an adjournment for evidence, were finally heard by him on
     12 October 1983, when he made an order for an immediate sale and for the proceeds to
     be deposited in the joint names of the parties' solicitors pending the restoration of the
     matter for consideration of the division of the proceeds of sale. This was manifestly
     inconvenient, since it entailed the wife giving up her home without either knowing
j   finally the amount of her share of the proceeds, or having that share available for the
     purchase of an alternative home. She appealed to the judge and on 17 November 1983
     gave notice of her intention to proceed with an application for a secured order. On 4
     December 1984 she gave notice of the restoration of applications for a lump sum order,
     a transfer of property order and an order further postponing the sale. Her appeal in these

further applications were, by agreement, heard together by Judge Main, who, on 21 January 1985, in a reserved judgment made an order reducing the husband's periodical *a* payments to the wife to a nominal sum and remitting all unsecured arrears and an order for the immediate sale of the property, the husband's solicitors to have the conduct of the sale. The wife's appeal against that part of the registrar's order which directed the proceeds of sale to be paid into the joint names of the parties' solicitors and a further consideration of the division of the proceeds was allowed, but her applications for a further charging order, for secured provision, for a lump sum order and for a property *b* transfer order and an order postponing the sale were dismissed.

My Lords, it is, I think, plain from his judgment that Judge Main considered that he had no jurisdiction to make the transfer of property order and the order postponing the sale of the property which the wife sought, although he did not say this in terms. He clearly took the view that the original consent order was an order made pursuant to the provisions of s 24 of the Matrimonial Causes Act 1973 and that, that being so, he had no *c* jurisdiction to make any further order which would, in effect, be a variation of that order. But having reviewed the circumstances of the parties, he took the view that, even if he had jurisdiction to do so, no facts had been demonstrated which would justify him in varying the order.

With the leave of the judge, the wife appealed to the Court of Appeal against the dismissal of her applications for ancillary relief. That court allowed the appeal, holding, *d* first, that the consent order did not constitute an exercise of the court's power to make a property adjustment order under s 24 of the 1973 Act and, second, that the judge was wrong in his view that the altered circumstances were insufficient to justify a variation of the consent order. In delivering the first judgment, Purchas LJ pointed out that the husband's voluntary decision to accept redundancy, albeit brought about by circumstances not wholly within his control, had dramatically changed the financial position of the *e* parties and compelled the wife to seek support from supplementary benefit payments. In November 1984, following the death of her mother, she received a modest legacy of some £9,000 as a result of which she became disentitled to further maintenance from public funds and was compelled to have resort to her own capital resources for her support. She used part of the legacy to discharge the outstanding balance of the mortgage, *f* but because this was a voluntary disposition on her part, she remained disentitled to supplementary benefit. I would add that the existence of these modest capital resources has also disabled her from receiving legal aid to resist the husband's appeal to your Lordships' House. In the circumstances, the Court of Appeal considered that the interests of the parties ought to be adjusted to reflect the relief of the husband from liability for the wife's future maintenance and the fact that he had utilised for his own purposes the *g* capital sum which he received on his redundancy. Accordingly, the court ordered that the husband's interest in the matrimonial home be transferred to the wife, but that there be charged on the property a sum of £20,000 representing the husband's entitlement based on current values after taking into account the discharge of the mortgage and the sums already charged on his share, such charge not to be enforced until the death of the wife or until her remarriage or voluntary removal from the property, whichever should *h* first occur.

My Lords, I have to say that, in my judgment, and I venture to suppose that none of your Lordships will be disposed to disagree with this, the order of the Court of Appeal is one which, in the circumstances of this case, does substantial justice between the parties. But the question which has been primarily debated before this House and which has to be answered in limine is whether it is an order which it was within the jurisdiction of *j* the court to pronounce; and, as to that, I have to say also that I cannot, for my part, see that this appeal raises any question of principle that has not already been dealt with by this House. The issue between the parties is simply and solely one of the proper construction of the consent order.

Section 31 of the 1973 Act enables the court to vary lump sum or property adjustment

orders made pursuant to the provisions of ss 23 and 24 of the Act only in the limited
_a_ circumstances prescribed in the section, none of which is applicable in the instant case. It
is well established that, subject to the provisions of that section, once the court has either
exercised or declined to exercise its power to make such an order in relation to particular
property, no further application for an order in respect of the property at least, whether
original or by way of variation of an existing order, can be obtained. That was clearly laid
down by this House in _Minton v Minton_ [1979] 1 All ER 79, [1979] AC 593, the effect of
_b_ which is conveniently set out in the following passage in the judgment of the Privy
Council, delivered by Lord Diplock in _de Lasala v de Lasala_ [1979] 2 All ER 1146 at 1154,
[1980] AC 546 at 559:

> 'In _Minton v Minton_ the House of Lords decided that the policy of the English
> legislation, to which effect was given by the language that has been cited above, was
_c_ > to permit parties to a marriage that had irreparably broken down, to make "a clean
> break" also as respects financial matters from which there could be no going back.
> The means provided for achieving this result were for the parties to agree on a once
> and for all financial settlement between them and to obtain the court's approval to
> it and an order of the court either of a once and for all type or dismissing the parties'
> claims to any court order against one another for financial relief.'

_d_ A case very similar to the instant case and raising very much the same issues, save that
the order there concerned was not a consent order, was _Carson v Carson_ [1983] 1 All ER
478, [1983] 1 WLR 285. In that case the wife, in proceedings for ancillary relief, had
obtained an order for periodical payments and an order under s 24(1)(_b_) of the 1973 Act,
directing that the matrimonial home be transferred to trustees and held on trust for sale
_e_ for the parties in equal shares, the sale being postponed until the children of the marriage
attained full age or ceased full-time education. The husband having fallen seriously into
arrears with the periodical payments which he had been ordered to make, the wife
applied for an order transferring the whole property to her or, alternatively, for a lump
sum. It was held that no such application could be entertained, and the ratio of the
decision appears from the following passage from the judgment of Ormrod LJ ([1983] 1
_f_ All ER 478 at 481, [1983] 1 WLR 285 at 289–290):

> 'The argument before Ewbank J on the matter proceeded on the basis that, under
> s 24 of the Matrimonial Causes Act 1973, she was entitled, in the words of sub-s (1),
> "On granting a decree of divorce . . . or at any time thereafter . . ." to make
> application for one or other of the orders set out in that subsection. The difficulty
> for her was that an order had already been made by Payne J in 1975, and counsel for
_g_ > the wife argued that, although an order had been made under s 24(1)(_b_) ordering a
> settlement of the property, that did not preclude the judge later from making
> another property adjustment order, this time under para (_a_), for a transfer of
> property to the wife. The judge held that he had no such power and, in my
> judgment, he was plainly right. This is a case where an attempt was being made to
> obtain a second property adjustment order in relation to the same capital asset and
_h_ > it is not necessary in this judgment to consider what the position might have been
> if some other capital asset was involved. In my judgment the judge in the court
> below was completely right in rejecting that application by the wife. If he had
> entertained it, he would clearly have been running counter to the provisions of s 31
> of the 1973 Act, which make it clear that the court has no power to vary a property
> adjustment order in any circumstances.'

_j_ Indeed, the principle is not and never has been in dispute between the parties. What is in
dispute is whether the consent order in this case was one by which the court either
exercised or declined to exercise its jurisdiction under s 24 of the Act to make a property
adjustment order. In the Court of Appeal Purchas LJ expressed the view that it was not.
He observed:

'I do not consider that the consent order did anything other than declare the interests of the parties under the provisions of the Married Women's Property Act 1882, and order the sale of the property and the distribution of the proceeds after due postponement; but did not affect any transfer of property in the sense that the rights of the parties were in any way adjusted from the position already existing in law and equity.'

My Lords, I have found myself, albeit reluctantly, unable to accept this view of the matter. The purchase of the property in the joint names of the parties beneficially constituted a post-nuptial settlement. That may have seemed a surprising proposition to Chancery practitioners more accustomed to the familiar type of marriage settlement, but it was clearly established by the decision of the Court of Appeal in *Brown v Brown* [1959] 2 All ER 266, [1959] P 86, which has been followed and applied for over a quarter of a century since. Under the trusts of the post-nuptial settlement as they existed at the date of the presentation of the petition the parties were entitled to the property in possession as beneficial joint tenants and it was subject to an immediate trust for sale which could, theoretically at least, have been enforced by either party by an application either under s 30 of the Law of Property Act 1925 or under s 17 of the 1882 Act. As a result of the injunction the husband was excluded from physical possession of the property but remained, again theoretically, entitled to a share in the rents and profits. It was against this background and against a background of, apparently, some initial disputes as to the quantum of their respective beneficial entitlements that the consent order was made. It had a number of significant effects on the husband's interest and it is the contention of counsel for the husband that these effects made the order one made under the provisions of either para (c) or para (d) of s 24(1) of the 1973 Act. First and foremost, it imposed on the husband's right to call for an immediate sale a fetter preventing him from realising his entitlement until the occurrence of one or other of the events specified in the order. Second, and against the background of the injunction excluding him from actual possession, an order for the ultimate division of the net proceeds in equal shares without any provision for any account being taken of the value of any rents and profits in the mean time (save to the extent that they came to be reflected in the interest payments under the mortgage which were, by implication, to be made by the wife) had the effect of reducing the husband's beneficial entitlement, whilst at the same time the order sought to impose on him an obligation to continue his contributions to the reduction of the capital outstanding under the mortgage. I cannot, therefore, agree with the view that the order made no adjustment of the rights of the parties as they previously existed in law and equity, although I entirely concur with the view which Purchas LJ went on to express that the mere accounting provision for deducting the arrears of maintenance from the husband's ultimate share did not constitute the making of a lump sum provision under s 23 of the 1973 Act.

But, in any event, to determine the effect of the order by reference only to the narrow question of whether a particular part of it was made in purported exercise of the jurisdiction conferred by one Act or another is, in my judgment, to approach the case too restrictively. Your Lordships have listened to a number of interesting submissions in favour of and against the view that para (iv) of the order could have been made only under s 17 of the 1882 Act, or only under s 24 of the 1973 Act, or only under a combination of the two. Counsel has argued for the husband that, inasmuch as there is no specific jurisdiction conferred by s 17 of the 1882 Act to postpone the sale of a property and direct it to take place at a particular date, or on the happening of a particular event, that part of the order must have been made, in part at least, under the jurisdiction conferred by s 24 of the 1973 Act. Counsel for the wife, with equal ingenuity, has argued that since at the date of the consent order there was no power actually to order a sale under s 24, the order must have been made under s 17 of the 1882 Act. These submissions, however, interesting though they were, missed the essential issue, which is

simply whether, to use the words of Lord Diplock in *de Lasala v de Lasala* [1979] 2 All ER
1146 at 1154, [1980] AC 546 at 559, the parties were agreeing on 'a once-for-all financial
settlement between them and [obtaining] the court's approval to it'. If they were, then
the order is wholly inconsistent with any notion that any application by the wife for
ancillary relief in respect of a particular property specifically dealt with in the order could
thereafter remain alive. The starting point is that the questions both of the beneficial
interests of the parties and of the future disposition of the property had been put in issue
by both sides in proceedings which were, by agreement, consolidated. The question of
the shares in which the property was owned and the question of whether any, and if so
what, order should be made under the ancillary jurisdiction invoked by the petition were
both clearly before the court. Counsel on behalf of the husband has argued for the
proposition that as a matter of general principle and in every case, if an application is
made for ancillary relief and, whether consensually or otherwise, no order is made, it is
necessarily implicit that the application is dismissed. He has referred to a number of
dicta in support of this view. For instance, in *Henderson v Henderson* (1843) 3 Hare 100 at
115, [1843–60] All ER Rep 378 at 381–382 Wigram V-C observed:

> 'The plea of res judicata applies, except in special cases, not only to points upon
> which the court was actually required by the parties to form an opinion and
> pronounce a judgment, but to every point which properly belonged to the subject
> of litigation, and which the parties, exercising reasonable diligence, might have
> brought forward at the time.'

Again, in *Re South American and Mexican Co, ex p Bank of England* [1895] 1 Ch 37 at 50,
[1891–4] All ER Rep 680 at 682, Lord Herschell LC, in relation specifically to consent
orders, said:

> 'The truth is, a judgment by consent is intended to put a stop to litigation between
> the parties just as much as is a judgment which results from the decision of the
> Court after the matter has been fought out to the end. And I think it would be very
> mischievous if one were not to give a fair and reasonable interpretation to such
> judgments, and were to allow questions that were really involved in the action to be
> fought over again in a subsequent action.'

On the other hand, in *Brown v Kirrage* (1980) 11 Fam Law 141 Brandon LJ regarded
the dismissal of a wife's claim for ancillary relief as a matter of such seriousness that the
court ought to be extremely cautious about implying a dismissal where none is actually
expressed in the order. The burden of establishing that there was a final and unequivocal
dismissal of the claim was, he said, on the husband.

My Lords, for my part, I think that counsel for the husband puts the matter too high.
There cannot, in my judgment, be any irrebuttable presumption that an order which is
silent as to a claim which, on the record, appears to have been put in issue necessarily and
always has to be construed as containing a dismissal of that claim. It must, in each case,
be a question of construction of the particular order under consideration, and whilst I do
not dissent from the proposition that a proper caution should be exercised before
reaching a conclusion that will effectively preclude a wife from making a further claim
for relief, I do not, for my part, derive much help from consideration of where the
burden lies. One has, as it seems to me, simply to look at the order and any admissible
material available for its construction, and determine what the court intended, or, in the
case of the consent order, what the parties intended, to effect by the order. If the
conclusion is that what was intended was a final and conclusive once-for-all financial
settlement, either overall or in relation to a particular property, then it must follow that
that precludes any further claim to relief in relation to that property. *Carson v Carson*
[1983] 1 All ER 478, [1983] 1 WLR 285 was a case where the court's order was clearly
intended to be final and to preclude any further application for relief although it
contained no express dismissal of the claims, and a similar result was reached in relation

to a consent order in *Sandford v Sandford* [1986] 1 FLR 412. I confess to having very considerable sympathy with the view expressed by Lord Fraser in *Minton v Minton* [1979] 1 All ER 79 at 81, [1979] AC 593 at 602 that it would be preferable if the jurisdiction of the court to vary an order were invariably preserved as a matter of general law. But, as he pointed out, the relevant legislation cannot be construed so as to lead to that result. In the instant case, the consent order, on its face and in the light of the issues which were clearly before the court, is not, in my judgment, capable of being construed in any other sense than as finally and conclusively determining the rights of the parties in the property, and Judge Main was, in my judgment, right in entertaining the doubt which he expressed whether he had any jurisdiction to make the order. I confess to having reached this conclusion with the great reluctance and regret, for not only has the wife lost without any compensation the periodical payments for which she stipulated when the consent order was negotiated but her share of the proceeds of the house which she will now be compelled to vacate will be considerably reduced by the legal aid costs incurred by her before the judge and in the Court of Appeal, costs which would never have been incurred if what was clearly the parties' intention as regards the claims for ancillary relief had been, as it should have been, expressly reflected in the order. But to hold otherwise would be to fly in the face of what I apprehend to be the legislature's intention in circumscribing, as it did, the court's power to vary orders made under ss 23 and 24, and of a construction which has for many years been placed by the courts on those provisions. Regretfully, therefore, I would allow this appeal and restore the order of Judge Main. I cannot help reflecting that it seems to me a matter for regret, in all the circumstances, that the arrears of maintenance were remitted and that the order for periodical payments was reduced to a purely nominal sum, but there has been no appeal against that part of the order and it is not, of course, for this House to speculate upon what might be the fate of any future application to vary the latter order when the proceeds of sale are received by the husband. Although, if the views which I have expressed commend themselves to your Lordships, the husband will have succeeded on this appeal, I would not, in the circumstances of this unhappy case, make any order as regards the costs before your Lordships or in the courts below, save for the usual order for taxation of the husband's legal aid costs.

LORD GOFF OF CHIEVELEY. My Lords, I have had the advantage of reading in draft the speech prepared by my noble and learned friend Lord Oliver. I agree with it and would allow this appeal.

Appeal allowed. No order for costs in the House of Lords or below.

Solicitors: *Bates & Partners*, agents for *Allin & Watts*, Bournemouth (for the husband); *Vickers & Co* (for the wife).

Mary Rose Plummer   Barrister.

Baljinder Singh v Hammond

QUEEN'S BENCH DIVISION
GLIDEWELL LJ AND OTTON J
29 OCTOBER 1986

Immigration – Immigration officer – Examination of entrant – Examination away from place of entry – Whether immigration officer entitled to conduct examination of immigrant away from place of entry – Whether immigration officer entitled to conduct examination of immigrant at date after entry – Immigration Act 1971, Sch 2, para 2.

An immigration officer is entitled under para 2[a] of Sch 2 to the Immigration Act 1971 to conduct an examination of a person who has arrived in the United Kingdom away from the place of entry and on a date after the person has already entered if he has information in his possession which causes him to inquire whether the person being examined is a British citizen, and if not whether he may enter the United Kingdom without leave, and if not whether he should be given leave and on what conditions (see p 832 *j* to p 833 *a d e*, post).

Notes
For general offences in connection with the administration of the Immigration Act 1971, see 4 Halsbury's Laws (4th edn) para 1029.

For the Immigration Act 1971, Sch 2, para 2, see 41 Halsbury's Statutes (3rd edn) 61.

Case referred to in judgments
R v Clarke [1985] 2 All ER 777, [1985] AC 1037, [1985] 3 WLR 113, HL.

Case stated
Baljinder Singh appealed by way of a case stated by the justices for the North East London commission area acting in and for the petty sessional division of Redbridge in respect of their adjudication as a magistrates' court sitting at Barkingside on 15 May 1985 whereby, on an information laid by the respondent, Pc Charles Hammond, they convicted the appellant of making to an immigration officer lawfully acting in the execution of the Immigration Act 1971 a statement which he knew to be false or did not believe to be true, contrary to s 26(1)(*c*) of the Immigration Act 1971. The facts are set out in the judgment of Glidewell LJ.

Ghulam Yazdani for the appellant.
Donald Gordon for the respondent.

GLIDEWELL LJ. This is an appeal by way of case stated by the justices for the petty sessional division of Redbridge in the North East London commission area, sitting as a Magistrates' Court at Barkingside.

On 26 April 1985 the appellant, Baljinder Singh, appeared to answer an information laid by the respondent, Pc Hammond, alleging three offences. One was that on 10 October 1984, at Ilford in Essex, he had made to an immigration officer, lawfully acting in the execution of the Immigration Act 1971, a statement or representation which he knew to be false, or did not believe to be true, contrary to s 26(1)(*c*) of the Immigration Act 1971.

---

a Paragraph 2, so far as material, is set out at p 831 *h* to p 832 *a*, post

There were two other offences alleged, also under the same Act. On 15 May 1985 the justices convicted the appellant of the offence under s 26(1)(c) but acquitted him of the other two offences. The case stated does not tell us what, if any, penalty they imposed.

The facts are carefully set out and I must summarise them because the case does turn very much on its own facts. The justices found that the appellant, who is an Indian citizen, is resident in this country. On 9 October 1984 the appellant returned to this country from the United States. He presented himself at immigration control at Heathrow where he presented an Indian passport issued in London on 20 October 1983 in the name of Agit Singh born at Gamtala on 20 December 1951. The appellant was admitted for his continued residence. On 10 October 1984 the appellant was visited at his home by an immigration officer and the respondent. The respondent and the immigration officer were invited into the appellant's home. On that occasion, during the course of an interview conducted by the respondent and the immigration officer, the appellant stated that his name was Agit Singh, son of Swarn Singh, born on 2 December 1951, and admitted that he had entered this country illegally in July 1972. The appellant told the immigration officer that he had never used any name but Agit Singh, that he had not travelled to this country before July 1972, and that he had never been sent away from this country.

On 28 October 1984 the appellant was again visited at his home address by two immigration officers. During this second visit the appellant told the officers that his name was Baljinder Singh, the son of Mohan Singh, born on 2 December 1949, and he said that he had been refused entry at London Airport in 1971. The appellant said he had legally changed his name to Agit Singh.

I shall pause for one moment before continuing to relate the facts. If what the appellant said on the second occasion, added to part of what he had said on the first occasion, was correct, what the justices were finding was that the appellant was born and named Baljinder Singh, son of Mohan Singh. He was refused entry at London airport in 1971, had changed his name legally to Agit Singh (they do not say when the legal change came about), came back to this country and entered illegally in July 1972.

The case continues as follows. The appellant had been given leave to remain in the United Kingdom as a result of the amnesty of 1974 to 1975. The questions put to the appellant on 10 October 1984 by the immigration officer were directed to discovering the appellant's true identity and ascertaining whether, if he was not a British citizen, he might re-enter the United Kingdom without leave. The answer given by the appellant that he had never been refused entry to this country was untrue, as was his statement made on 10 October 1984 that he had never used any name other than Agit Singh and that he had not travelled to this country before July 1972.

The 'amnesty' referred to in part of those findings is the name given to a policy adopted by the Home Secretary originally in 1974, and then extended on 29 November 1977, under which the Home Secretary announced that he would not use his powers of removal to send away from the United Kingdom Commonwealth citizens who had entered the United Kingdom illegally between 9 March 1968 and 1 January 1973. These people had thus been in this country for a number of years when the Home Secretary made his original announcement in 1974 and his later announcement in 1977. The amnesty had to be claimed; that is to say persons who wanted the benefit of it had to go to the police or the immigration officials and admit that they had entered the country illegally, show when they had done so, and then claim the benefit of the amnesty. The effect was that if they were granted the benefit of the amnesty, as the justices found the appellant was, thereafter they would not be sent out of this country unless some circumstance arose under which they might be deported. That may happen, for example, where a person is convicted of a serious offence.

A person entitled to the benefit of the amnesty, if he remained in the United Kingdom for sufficiently long, would then become settled in the United Kingdom and be entitled not merely to continue to reside here without interruption, but also, if he left the United

Kingdom for a short visit overseas, to be given leave to re-enter upon his presenting
a himself at immigration control. That is the other matter referred to in the case as being
the purpose to which the questions asked on 10 October were directed; that is to say that
the justices were finding that the immigration officer's questions on that occasion were
directed to finding first of all whether the appellant was Agit Singh or Baljinder Singh
and whether he was a British citizen, and having ascertained that he was not and did not
claim to be, then whether he was settled here so that he was entitled to re-enter, as indeed
b he had done the day before on 9 October.
   The justices concluded that—

   'an Immigration Officer is entitled to conduct an examination under paragraph 2
   outside the port area to determine whether or not a person is or is not a British
   citizen, and that if the questions put during such an interview are relevant to that
c purpose the person being examined is under an obligation to answer truthfully. In
   our view the questions put to the Appellant during the interview of the 10th of
   October were relevant to that purpose and therefore the Appellant was obliged to
   answer them truthfully. As the Appellant made three untrue statements during the
   course of the interview we determined to convict the Appellant. The question for
   the opinion of the High Court is whether we were wrong in law to convict the
d [appellant].'

   Not all the submissions which were made in the magistrates' court were pursued
before us. The points made by counsel for the appellant, which he has made with great
clarity, come essentially to one, but it is an important point because it affects a great
many people who are in the position where, at some time in the past, they may or may
not have entered illegally, where they have been permitted to enter the United Kingdom,
e and where circumstances arise where the Home Secretary or his officials come to suspect
that they may have obtained leave to enter by deception.
   The point can be expressed in this way. On 10 October the immigration officer was
not entitled to examine the appellant. Thus, since the offence is only committed, to refer
back to the words of s 26(1)(c)1—

f 'if on any such examination or otherwise he makes or causes to be made to an
   immigration officer . . . a . . . statement or representation which he knows to be
   false or does not believe to be true,'

counsel submits that the interview on 10 October was not such an examination or
otherwise. Thus, the untruthful answers to the questions did not constitute an offence
within s 26(1)(c).
g In order to see whether that submission is correct, it is necessary to look at further
provisions of the Act. Section 26 begins as follows:

   '(1) A person shall be guilty of an offence . . . in any of the following cases—(a) if,
   without reasonable excuse, he refuses or fails to submit to examination under
   Schedule 2 to this Act . . . (c) if on any such examination or otherwise . . .'
h
So the phrase 'such examination' is an examination under Sch 2 to the Act. Turning to
Sch 2, it is para 2 that deals with examination by immigration officers. Paragraph 2(1)
provides:

   'An immigration officer may examine any persons who have arrived in the
   United Kingdom by ship or aircraft . . . for the purpose of determining—(a) whether
j any of them is or is not a British citizen; and (b) whether, if he is not, he may or may
   not enter the United Kingdom without leave; and (c) whether, if he may not, he
   should be given leave and for what period and on what conditions (if any), or should
   be refused leave.'

Paragraph 2(3) provides: 'A person, on being examined under this paragraph by an

immigration officer ... may be required in writing by him to submit to further
examination ...' This was not a further examination under para 2(3), because a further   *a*
examination takes place when, at the end of the initial examination, the immigration
officer makes it clear that a further examination is required. That was not the situation
here.

Counsel for the appellant submits that the power under para 2(1) to examine is limited
to an examination at the time and place at which the person being examined arrives in
the United Kingdom; that is to say at the port or airport of entry. That is an examination   *b*
which is conducted before he is either given or refused leave to enter. Counsel says that
that examination, subject to the power to require a further examination under para 2(3),
is the only examination which can be conducted under para 2(1).

When a person is examined under para 2(1), or indeed under para 2(3), then under
para 4 of Sch 2 he is under a duty 'to furnish to the person carrying out the examination
all such information in his possession as that person may require for the purpose of his   *c*
functions under that paragraph.' In other words, a person who is the subject of an
examination properly carried out under para 2(1) is not entitled to refuse to answer the
questions. He is under a duty to answer them. The duty is enforced by s 26(1)(*b*) under
which it is an offence not to furnish the information that he is required to furnish.

Counsel for the appellant sought support for his submission in passages from the
speech of Lord Bridge in *R v Clarke* [1985] 2 All ER 777, [1985] AC 1037. That was a case   *d*
in which a police officer who was investigating another matter, nothing to do with the
1971 Act, asked questions of the appellant whether the appellant was lawfully in the
United Kingdom. It was held by the Court of Appeal and upheld by the House of Lords
that the police officer was not, when he asked those questions and was given replies
which may or may not have been untruthful, a person lawfully acting in the execution
of the 1971 Act within s 26(1)(*c*). Although that authority deals generally with a problem   *e*
related to that with which we are concerned, it does not touch directly on the point at
issue here. I, for my part, do not find in it anything of assistance to the decision which
we have to make.

To come back to the issue, counsel for the respondent draws our attention to s 4 of the
Act, which relates to Sch 2. Section 4(2), so far as material, provides: *f*

> 'The provisions of Schedule 2 to this Act shall have effect with respect to ... (*b*) the
> examination of persons arriving in or leaving the United Kingdom by ship or
> aircraft, and the special powers exercisable in the case of those who arrive as, or with
> a view to becoming, members of the crews of ships and aircraft; and (*c*) the exercise
> by immigration officers of their powers in relation to entry into the United
> Kingdom, and the removal from the United Kingdom of persons refused leave to   *g*
> enter or entering or remaining unlawfully ... and for other purposes supplementary
> to the foregoing provisions of this Act.'

Counsel for the respondent accepts that s 4(2)(*b*) relates specifically to an examination
of persons arriving in or leaving the United Kingdom. Such an examination, he accepts,
must take place at the place and time of arrival, or it may be adjourned under the   *h*
provisions of para 2(3) of Sch 2. But he submits that an examination can be conducted
under s 4(2)(*c*) in respect of somebody who has been admitted into the United Kingdom
if it is later suspected that he may have been admitted as a result of deception.
Section 4(2)(*c*) reads as follows:

> 'The provisions of Schedule 2 to this Act shall have effect with respect to ... (*c*)   *j*
> the exercise by immigration officers of their powers in relation to ... the removal
> from the United Kingdom of persons ... entering or remaining unlawfully ...'

Counsel for the respondent submits that the immigration officer in this case, once it
came to his notice that the appellant had entered in one name, had entered illegally and
had previously entered under another name before his original entry, had reason to

believe that the appellant might be remaining unlawfully. He was thus entitled to
a conduct an examination under para 2 which was a provision falling within s 4(2)(c). He
says it is true that s 4(2)(c) does not talk about examinations as s 4(2)(b) does, but
nevertheless an examination is part of the powers of immigration officers forming an
integral part of their functions and duties in relation to investigating persons who have
entered or remained unlawfully.

Alternatively, counsel argues, even if the examination which was being conducted was
b not an examination within para 2, then going back to s 26(1)(c), untruthful answers were
given otherwise than on an examination on an occasion which was not an examination
under para 2, but still a valid exercise of the immigration officer's powers. Counsel, I take
it, is suggesting that if the immigration officer is not conducting an examination in the
strict sense, he nevertheless is entitled to ask questions and, if the person who is being
asked them does answer them and does not decline to do so, then, if the answers to those
c questions are false, they constitute the offence.

This is a matter on which, as I see it, there is no direct authority at all. As I have said, it
is of importance because if counsel for the appellant's argument is correct, the powers of
immigration officers are much more circumscribed than I imagine the Home Office has
thought they were in relation to those who it is suspected are here unlawfully. That, in
itself, is not a consideration that assists in relation to the proper interpretation of the Act.
d For my part, I take the view that counsel for the respondent's first argument is correct.
An examination, I would hold, can properly be conducted by an immigration officer
away from the place of entry and on a later date after the person the subject of the
examination has already entered, if the immigration officer has some information in his
possession which causes him to inquire whether the person being examined is a British
citizen, and, if not, whether he may enter the United Kingdom without leave, and, if not
e (which is the relevant question in this case), whether he should have been given leave
and on what conditions. The question whether he should have been given leave was
dependent, of course, on deciding whether he was here lawfully or not.

On the facts found by the justices, albeit in my conclusion the examination was lawful,
it follows that if the appellant had answered the questions truthfully in the first place,
had disclosed that he had tried to enter once and was turned away, and then entered
f illegally the second time he made his attempt, and that he used two names having
changed his name from Baljinder to Agit, he would not have committed any offence
under s 26(1)(c). He may, of course, have been frightened that if he told the truth some
attempt would be made to say that he was not here legally. But if, as the justices found,
he was entitled to the benefit of the amnesty, he need have had no such fear. Whether he
feared it or not, that did not justify the false statements which they found he made.
g On the question of law, I conclude that the justices' conclusion was correct, save for
this. They concluded that the immigration officer was entitled to conduct the
examination 'to determine whether or not a person is or is not a British citizen'. I would
add to that the following: 'and, if not, whether he is entitled to be given leave to re-enter,'
which was really the question at issue in this case. Subject to that, I agree with the
h justices' approach and their conclusion, and I would dismiss the appeal.

OTTON J. I agree.

Appeal dismissed.

Solicitors: *B C Mascarenhas* (for the appellant); *D M O'Shea* (for the respondent).

N P Metcalfe Esq   Barrister.

Thomas v University of Bradford   *a*

HOUSE OF LORDS

LORD BRIDGE OF HARWICH, LORD BRANDON OF OAKBROOK, LORD GRIFFITHS, LORD MACKAY OF
CLASHFERN AND LORD ACKNER

1, 2, 3, 4, 8 DECEMBER 1986, 26 FEBRUARY 1987

b

*University – Academic staff – Dismissal – Action for wrongful dismissal – Jurisdiction –
Jurisdiction of court – Contract of service providing that dismissal only to be in accordance with
university's charter, statutes, ordinances and regulations – Lecturer bringing action for wrongful
dismissal – Lecturer alleging that dismissal wrongful because of failure to follow procedure set out
in charter etc – Whether court having jurisdiction to hear action – Whether court entitled to
construe charter etc – Whether construction of charter etc within exclusive jurisdiction of visitor*   *c*
of university.

In 1973 the plaintiff took up an appointment as a lecturer at a university under a contract
of service which provided, inter alia, that her employment and her status as a member of
the university were to be coterminous, that she was not to be dismissed without due
fulfilment of all procedures governing removal from office and that she was to be subject   *d*
to and entitled to the benefit of the disciplinary rules and procedures in the university's
charter, statutes, ordinances and regulations relating to permanent members of the
academic staff. In 1983 the university purported to dismiss her. She brought an action
against the university seeking a declaration that her dismissal was wrongful or ultra vires
and null and void and claiming damages or alternatively arrears of salary. She alleged
that her dismissal was in breach of the terms of her contract of service because the   *e*
procedures set out in the university's charter, statutes etc had not been followed. The
university contended that the matters pleaded in the statement of claim were matters
falling within the exclusive jurisdiction of the visitor of the university and sought a stay
of the plaintiff's action pending a petition to the visitor for the determination of her
complaint. The judge refused the application for a stay of proceedings, and on appeal the   *f*
Court of Appeal upheld the refusal. The university appealed to the House of Lords.

Held – The jurisdiction of a university visitor, which was based on his position as the
sole judge of the internal or domestic laws of the university, was exclusive and was not
concurrent with the courts' jurisdiction. The scope of the visitor's jurisdiction included
the interpretation and enforcement not only of those laws themselves but also of internal
powers and discretions derived from them, such as the discretion which necessarily had   *g*
to be exercised in disciplinary matters. Accordingly, if a dispute between a university
and a member of the university over his contract of employment with the university
involved questions relating to the internal laws of the university or rights and duties
derived from those laws, the visitor had exclusive jurisdiction to resolve that dispute.
Furthermore, in exercising that jurisdiction the visitor could order the university to   *h*
reinstate a member and pay arrears of salary or to pay damages in lieu of reinstatement.
Since the plaintiff's dispute centred on the charter, statutes, ordinances and regulations
of the university and whether they were correctly applied and fairly administered, it
followed that the visitor had exclusive jurisdiction. The appeal would accordingly be
allowed (see p 836 *d e*, p 839 *e f*, p 842 *a* to *c*, p 843 *a* to *c*, p 846 *a b g* to p 847 *d*, p 848 *j*
to p 849 *d*, p 850 *c d*, p 851 *e g h*, p 852 *h j* and p 853 *b*, post).   *j*

Dictum of Burt CJ in *Murdoch University v Bloom* [1980] WAR at 198, *Re Wislang's
Application* [1984] NI 63 and *Hines v Birkbeck College* [1985] 3 All ER 156 approved.

Thomson v University of London (1864) 33 LJ Ch 625 considered.

Dictum of Lord Hailsham LC in *Casson v University of Aston in Birmingham* [1983] 1 All
ER at 91 disapproved.

Per curiam. Parliament has by the Employment Protection (Consolidation) Act 1978
a implicitly provided that industrial tribunals are to have concurrent jurisdiction with
university visitors in matters relating to unfair dismissal of university staff and if in the
course of proceedings under that Act any question arises concerning the interpretation
or application of the internal laws of the university it must be resolved by the tribunal
hearing the case. To the extent that the 1978 Act affords wider protection, the jurisdiction
of the visitor has been largely superseded (see p 836 *d e*, p 849 *e* to *g*, p 850 *d* and p 852 *j*
b to p 853 *a*, post).

Decision of Court of Appeal [1986] 1 All ER 217 reversed.

Notes

For the nature of visitatorial powers, and for a visitor's powers and jurisdiction, see 5
Halsbury's Laws (4th edn) paras 872–873, 877, 879–885, and for cases on the subject, see
c 8(1) Digest (Reissue) 452–453, 456, 2018–2030, 3078–3089.

For the Employment Protection (Consolidation) Act 1978, see 16 Halsbury's Statutes
(4th edn) 381.

Cases referred to in opinions

Appleford's Case (1672) 1 Mod Rep 82, 86 ER 750.
d *A-G v Dedham School* (1857) 23 Beav 350, 53 ER 138.
A-G v Magdalen College Oxford (1847) 10 Beav 402, 50 ER 637.
A-G v Talbot (1747) 3 Atk 662, 26 ER 1181, LC.
Berkhampstead Free School, Ex p (1813) 2 Ves & B 134, [1803–13] All ER Rep 714, 35 ER
270, LC.
Casson v University of Aston in Birmingham [1983] 1 All ER 88, Visitor.
e *Chichester (Bishop) v Harward and Webber* (1787) 1 Term Rep 650, 99 ER 1300.
Green v Rutherford (1750) 1 Ves Sen 462, [1558–1774] All ER Rep 153, 27 ER 1144, Ch
Ct.
Herring v Templeman [1973] 2 All ER 581; *affd on different grounds* [1973] 3 All ER 569,
CA.
Hines v Birkbeck College [1985] 3 All ER 156, [1986] Ch 524, [1986] 2 WLR 97.
f *Kirkby Ravensworth Hospital, Ex p* (1808) 15 Ves 305, 33 ER 770, LC.
Murdoch University v Bloom [1980] WAR 193, W Aust Full Ct.
Norrie v Senate of the University of Auckland [1984] 1 NZLR 129, NZ CA.
Patel v University of Bradford Senate [1978] 3 All ER 841, [1978] 1 WLR 1488; *affd* [1979]
2 All ER 582, [1979] 1 WLR 1066, CA.
Philips v Bury (1694) Skin 447, 1 Ld Raym 5, [1558–1774] All ER Rep 53, 90 ER 198, HL.
g *R v Bishop of Chester* (1747) 1 Wm Bl 22, 96 ER 12.
R v Bishop of Ely (1794) 5 Term Rep 475, 101 ER 267.
R v Dean and Chapter of Chester (1850) 15 QB 513, 117 ER 553.
R v Dunsheath, ex p Meredith [1950] 2 All ER 741, [1951] 1 KB 127, DC.
R v Hertford College (1878) 3 QBD 693, CA.
St John's College Cambridge v Todington (1757) 1 Burr 158, 97 ER 245.
h *Thomson v University of London* (1864) 33 LJ Ch 625.
Thorne v University of London [1966] 2 All ER 338, [1966] 2 QB 237, [1966] 2 WLR 1080,
CA.
United Australian Ltd v Barclays Bank Ltd [1940] 4 All ER 20, [1941] AC 1, HL.
Whiston v Dean and Chapter of Rochester (1849) 7 Hare 532, 68 ER 220.
Wislang's Application, Re [1984] NI 63, NI HC.
j *Wrangham, Ex p* (1795) 2 Ves 609, 30 ER 803, LC.

Appeal

The defendants, the University of Bradford, appealed with leave of the Court of Appeal
granted on 30 October 1985, against the decision of the Court of Appeal (Fox, Lloyd LJJ
and Sir George Waller) ([1986] 1 All ER 217, [1986] Ch 381) dated 30 October dismissing

an appeal against the decision of Whitford J ([1985] 2 All ER 786, [1986] Ch 381) dated 17 January 1985 whereby he refused an application by the university for a stay of *a* proceedings in an action brought by the plaintiff, Brenda Thomas. On the appeal to the House of Lords the university applied for and were granted leave to amend the relief sought from an order staying the proceedings to an order striking out Miss Thomas's claim, and the appeal was argued on that basis. The facts are set out in the opinion of Lord Griffiths.

b

Leolin Price QC and *Hubert Picarda* for the university.
Michael Beloff QC and *Brian Langstaff* for Miss Thomas.

Their Lordships took time for consideration.

25 February. The following opinions were delivered.   *c*

LORD BRIDGE OF HARWICH. My Lords, for the reasons given in the speeches of my noble and learned friends Lord Griffiths and Lord Ackner, with both of which I agree, I would allow this appeal.

d

LORD BRANDON OF OAKBROOK. My Lords, I have had the advantage of reading in draft the speeches prepared by my noble and learned friends Lord Griffiths and Lord Ackner. I agree with them, and for the reasons which they give I would allow the appeal.

e

LORD GRIFFITHS. My Lords, in March 1973 Miss Thomas accepted the offer of an appointment as lecturer in sociology at Bradford University. She took up her appointment in October 1973. After a probationary period, she became a permanent member of the academic staff. In February 1983 the university dismissed her. Miss Thomas disputes the validity of the dismissal and the issue before your Lordships is whether that dispute falls *f* within the jurisdiction of the High Court or that of the university visitor.

It is common ground that as from 1 October 1973 Miss Thomas became (i) a member of the academic staff of the university, (ii) an employee of the university under a contract of service, (iii) the holder of office in and a member of the university within the meaning of the charter and statutes. It is also common ground that the contract of service included the following terms, namely (a) that the employment of Miss Thomas and her status as a member of the university were coterminous, (b) that Miss Thomas would be subject to *g* the burden and entitled to the benefit of the disciplinary rules and procedures established and set out in the charter, statutes, ordinances and regulations such as related to permanent members of the academic staff, (c) that Miss Thomas should not be dismissed from her employment without the due fulfilment of all the procedures governing removal from office. *h*

A member of the permanent academic staff of the university, such as Miss Thomas, has security of tenure until retirement age unless removed from office by the council of the university for 'good cause': see statute 30(2) and ordinance 12.0(4)(a). 'Good cause' is defined by statute 30(4) in the following terms:

> '"Good cause" when used in reference to removal from office, membership or place means: (A) Conviction of any offence which the Court or the Council (as the *j* case may be) considers to be such as to render the person concerned unfit for the execution of the duties of his office. (B) Any physical or mental incapacity which the Court or the Council (as the case may be) considers to be such as to render the person concerned unfit for the execution of the duties of his office. (C) Conduct which the Court or the Council (as the case may be) considers to be such as to

constitute failure or inability of the person concerned to perform the duties of his
office or to comply with the conditions of tenure of his office.'

The charter, statutes, ordinances and regulations of the university provide an elaborate
code of procedures that are to be followed before the council arrives at a decision to
remove a member of the academic staff from office and thus terminate his employment
by the university. The object of the procedure is to ensure that any complaint is carefully
investigated and that the member of staff has a full and fair opportunity to answer the
complaint.

Miss Thomas alleges that the university failed to follow the correct procedure in the
investigation of the complaint against her and that accordingly the decision of the council
to dismiss her was ultra vires, null and void. She alleges that the university should have
investigated the complaint against her through the procedure provided under ordinance
13 and reg 23. The university admit that they did not so proceed but say that they
followed the correct procedure which is that prescribed by statute 30. It is unnecessary
to consider this dispute in any further detail as it is not for your Lordships to adjudicate
on it. I would observe, however, that as at present advised, I do not agree with the view
expressed by Whitford J and Sir George Waller that it presents no difficulty of
construction. I think it may be a matter of considerable difficulty to determine which
was the appropriate procedure in the present case.

Against this background Miss Thomas determined to challenge her dismissal, and
chose to do so by issuing a writ in the Chancery Division of the High Court on 18
September 1984, some 18 months after the date of her dismissal. By her statement of
claim of the same date, she claimed a declaration that the decision taken by the council
to dismiss her was ultra vires null and void, a declaration that the dimissal from her
employment was ultra vires null and void and damages or alternatively arrears of salary
from 12 February 1983 until judgment together with interest on damages and loss of
salary. The grounds of her claim were confined to allegations that in breach of the terms
of her contract of service the university had failed to follow the procedures prescribed by
ordinance 13 and reg 23 and further that irregularities in the procedure in fact adopted
amounted to breaches of natural justice. The statement of claim did not raise the issue as
to whether or not there was 'good cause' for dismissing Miss Thomas, and your Lordships
remain in ignorance of the underlying reasons for Miss Thomas's dismissal.

The university took the view that this dispute which is confined to the proper
interpretation and execution of their internal disciplinary procedures as provided in their
charter, statutes, ordinances and regulations, fell within the exclusive jurisdiction of the
university visitor and not with the courts of law. Accordingly, by notice of motion dated
12 November 1984, the university applied for an order to stay the proceedings until Miss
Thomas should have petitioned the visitor of the university and he had adjudicated on
the issues raised in her statement of claim.

It is now conceded by the university that this was not the appropriate form of relief
that they should have sought and that it may to some extent have misled Whitford J in
his approach to the case. The university's submission to Whitford J included a concession
that, after the visitor had determined the questions concerning the construction and
application of the internal rules, Miss Thomas could then bring an action for damages in
the courts and the court would not be bound by the visitor's determination. As
Hoffmann J said in *Hines v Birkbeck College* [1985] 3 All ER 156 at 165, [1986] Ch 524 at
543:

> 'In those circumstances it is not surprising that Whitford J thought that the
> plaintiff might as well start her action in the courts in the first place. No such
> concession was made before me and in my judgment it was wrong.'

The university should have taken out a summons to strike out the statement of claim on
the ground that the court had no jurisdiction in respect of the subject matter of the
claim, as was done in *Hines v Birkbeck College*. Your Lordships, at the request of the

university and without objection by Miss Thomas, allowed an amendment to the relief
sought by the university and the appeal has been argued on the basis that the relief a
sought is an order to strike out the statement of claim.

Whitford J dismissed the application of the university and said in the final paragraph
of his judgment ([1985] 2 All ER 786 at 795, [1986] Ch 381 at 394–395):

> 'I have referred to the suggestion that in the first instance the matter ought to go
> before the visitor for consideration of questions arising under paras 1 to 10 of the b
> statement of claim and then come back to the court. I cannot imagine a procedure
> more inconvenient or more likely to involve a wholly unnecessary waste of time
> and money than this. This is an allegation of a simple breach of contract. By writing
> the rules into the contract the question at issue has been brought within the
> jurisdiction of the court, and the application for a stay pending a reference to the
> visitor must, in my judgment, accordingly fail.' c

The Court of Appeal dismissed the appeal of the university (see [1986] 1 All ER 217,
[1986] Ch 381). Although the reasons they gave for their decision were different each
member of the court held that the dispute fell within the jurisdiction of the courts and
not the visitor. The underlying reason common to each judgment was that as the issue
in the case concerned a breach of a contract the courts retained jurisdiction to adjudicate
on it. There is, however, a marked difference of approach to the solution of the problem. d

Fox LJ accepted that the visitor's jurisdiction was exclusive but, as I understand his
judgment, would confine it to such matters as the court chose to concede to the visitor in
which he included the admission and amotion (the removal from office) of members,
the resolution of academic standards of a university teacher or student, and other matters
that in practical terms he considered unsuitable to the jurisdiction of the courts and in
which he included the marking of examination papers, the awarding of prizes and the e
choice of fellows. It is obvious that disputes raising such issues can be formulated as
breaches of contract or torts and Fox LJ acknowledged that this could not be the criterion
on which such claims should be judged to fall within or without the visitor's jurisdiction.
However, he considered that the present case, which alleged a contractual failure to
follow the university's internal procedures, should be adjudicated on by the court as a f
part of the general law of contract. Fox LJ's view is summed up in the following passage
from his judgment ([1986] 1 All ER 217 at 227, [1986] Ch 381 at 407):

> 'His [the visitor's] jurisdiction derives from the status of membership and where
> the issue, as in the case of breach of contract, does not derive from status, it seems to
> me that he has no jurisdiction except that which the court may concede to him.'
g

Lloyd LJ adopted the approach of the Court of Appeal in New Zealand in *Norrie v
Senate of the University of Auckland* [1984] 1 NZLR 129 and held that the jurisdiction of
the courts and the visitor were no longer mutually exclusive and that the jurisdiction of
the visitor was now subordinate to that of the courts. Applying that approach, he held
that the issue in this case did not have the 'necessary domesticity' to be left to the
jurisdiction of the visitor, and that as the claim was one for wrongful dismissal it h
remained within the jurisdiction of the courts.

Sir George Waller, although accepting the exclusivity of the jurisdiction, emphasised
what he described as the truly domestic situations in which in modern cases the visitor
had been held to have exclusive jurisdiction. He distinguished two cases in which the
dismissal of, in one case, a schoolmaster and the other, a chorister, were held to fall within
the jurisdiction of the visitor on the grounds that they were dealt with simply as a matter j
of status and no question of contract arose: see *Whiston v Dean and Chapter of Rochester*
(1849) 7 Hare 532, 69 ER 220 and *R v Dean and Chapter of Chester* (1850) 15 QB 513, 117
ER 533. He summarised his reasons in the final paragraph of his judgment ([1986] 1 All
ER 217 at 238, [1986] Ch 381 at 422):

a
'In this case there is a clear allegation of breach of contract. It is true that the breach of contract which is alleged is a failure to comply with the provisions of the statutes of the university, but in my judgment the provisions are clear, and whether there was a breach or not is a simple question of fact. It is not something peculiar to the visitor. To say that this case has to be retained in the visitatorial jurisdiction is to deprive the plaintiff of her rights at law. In my opinion, therefore, this is something which can properly be dealt with by the ordinary courts of law. It is not necessary

b
to refer the interpretation of rules to the visitor.'

I have already expressed my dissent from the view that no question of the interpretation of the statutes arises and I am not clear what would have been the view of Sir George Waller if he had considered that the present dispute depended, at least in part, on the interpretation of the university statutes and ordinances.

c
Clause 29 of the charter of the university provides for the appointment of a visitor by the Crown on the petition of the court of the university. No petition has been received and no visitor appointed under this power. However, it is common ground that in the absence of such an appointment the Crown as founder of the university is the visitor of the university and that the visitatorial powers will be exercised by the Lord Chancellor (or such other person as he may advise Her Majesty to nominate) on behalf of the Crown:

d
see *A-G v Dedham School* (1857) 23 Beav 350, 53 ER 138 and the judgment of Megarry V-C in *Patel v University of Bradford Senate* [1978] 3 All ER 841, [1978] 1 WLR 1488.

It has been conceded by Miss Thomas that the jurisdiction of the visitor is an exclusive jurisdiction, and the argument before your Lordships has been principally devoted to exploring the limits of the jurisdiction. However, as Lloyd LJ has questioned the exclusivity of the jurisdiction, it is right to consider whether the concession was properly

e
made.

My Lords in my opinion the exclusivity of the jurisdiction of the visitor is in English law beyond doubt and established by an unbroken line of authority spanning the last three centuries from *Philips v Bury* (1694) Skin 447, [1558–1774] All ER Rep 53 to *Hines v Birkbeck College* [1985] 3 All ER 156, [1986] Ch 524. This aspect of the jurisdiction has been examined and expounded with clarity and learning in articles by Dr J W Bridge

f
'Keeping Peace in the Universities: The Role of Visitor' (1970) 86 LQR 531 and Dr Peter Smith 'The Exclusive Jurisdiction of the University Visitor' (1981) 97 LQR 610, 'Visitation of the Universities: A Ghost from the Past' (1986) 136 NLJ 484, 519, 567, and with their assistance, for which I am indebted, I select judicial statements which have over the years reiterated the principle that the courts of law will not trespass upon matters that lie within the jurisdiction of the visitor.

g
To start with in *Philips v Bury* Skin 447 at 485, [1558–1774] All ER Rep 53 at 58 Holt CJ said in his dissenting judgment, subsequently upheld by the House of Lords, speaking of the jurisdiction of the visitor:

'It is not . . . material whether he hath a Court or no; all the matter is, whether he hath a jurisdiction; if he hath jurisdiction, and consuance of the matter and the

h
person, and he gives a sentence in the matter, his sentence must have some effect to make a vacancy, be it never so wrong; but there is no appeal, if the founder hath not thought fit to direct an appeal; that an appeal lieth in the Common Law Courts of the kingdom, is certainly not so.'

In the next century it is sufficient to cite two cases, one in the Chancery Court and one in the King's Bench in which the court declined jurisdiction on the ground that the

j
dispute fell within the jurisdiction of the visitor. In *A-G v Talbot* (1747) 3 Atk 662, 26 ER 1181 an unsuccessful candidate for a fellowship applied to the Chancery Court for a declaration that within the terms of the fellowship he should have been preferred to the fellow elected. Lord Hardwicke LC refused to entertain the application on the grounds that such a dispute fell within the jurisdiction of the visitor. In *St John's College Cambridge*

v Todington (1757) 1 Burr 158, 97 ER 245 the unsuccessful candidate on this occasion
appealed to the visitor and it was the college authorities that tried to prevent him doing
so by seeking a prohibition in the King's Bench. They failed because the court held that
the dispute fell within the jurisdiction of the visitor. In the course of his judgment Lord
Mansfield said (1 Burr 158 at 200, 97 ER 245 at 269):

'The visitorial power, if properly exercised, without expence or delay, is useful
and convenient to colleges. However, (be that as it may,) we must take it, as it is
now established by law: and it is now settled and established, (since the case of *Philips
v. Bury* in Dom. Proc. "that the jurisdiction of the visitor is summary and without
appeal from it".'

In *R v Dean and Chapter of Chester* (1850) 15 QB 513, 117 ER 553 a chorister who had
been removed from his office by the dean and chapter of the cathedral applied for
mandamus to restore him to his office. The application was refused, the court holding
that mandamus did not lie, as the remedy for the wrongful amotion complained of was
by application to the visitor who had sufficient and exclusive jurisdiction. Lord Campbell
CJ said (15 QB 513 at 520–521, 117 ER 553 at 556):

'Lastly, it was contended before us that, although Mr. Humphreys'might have
appealed to the visitor, he was not bound to do so, and that he may still call for the
interference of this Court: but this notion of a concurrent jurisdiction is expressly
contradicted by the language of Lord Hale in *Appleford's Case* ((1672) 1 Mod Rep 82,
86 ER 750), and by the whole current of decisions upon the subject.'

In *R v Hertford College* (1878) 3 QBD 693 one Tillyard complained that the college had
refused to examine him for a lay fellowship and wrongly elected another person to the
fellowship after examination. He obtained a mandamus in the Queen's Bench Division
directed to the principal, fellows and scholars of Hertford College, Oxford commanding
them to examine Tillyard as a candidate for a vacant fellowship in the college and to
proceed to the election of a fellow pursuant to the statutes of the college. The Court of
Appeal reversed the judgment of the Queen's Bench Division and set aside its order. The
Court of Appeal held that there was in fact no refusal to examine Tillyard but even if
there had been such a refusal the remedy was not by way of mandamus but by appeal to
the visitor. Lord Coleridge CJ said (at 706):

'For these reasons, then, upon the facts of this particular case, we think there is no
ground for issuing the mandamus. The prosecutor was not refused examination, he
did not place himself in a condition to claim more of the college than the college
had offered; if he had and if they had improperly refused him his wrong would be
one corrigible by the visitor and not by the courts of law ...'

In *Thomson v University of London* (1864) 33 LJ Ch 625 at 634, a case to which I shall
have to return later, Kindersley V-C spoke of the case falling within 'the exclusive
cognizance of the visitor'.

In the course of his review of the modern authorities in *Patel v University of Bradford
Senate* [1978] 3 All ER 841 at 847, [1978] 1 WLR 1488 at 1493–1494 Megarry V-C said:

'In *R v Dunsheath, ex parte Meredith* [1950] 2 All ER 741, [1951] 1 KB 127 a King's
Bench Divisional Court refused to grant an order of mandamus directing the
chairman of Convocation of London University to summon an extraordinary
meeting of convocation in accordance with one of the university statutes, on the
ground that the proper remedy was to apply to the visitor. The court, said Lord
Goddard CJ ([1950] 2 All ER 741 at 743, [1951] 1 KB 127 at 132), "will not interfere
in a matter within the province of the visitor." Perhaps the strongest authority is
Thorne v University of London [1966] 2 All ER 338, [1966] 2 QB 237. There, an
unsuccessful candidate for the London LLB sued the University of London for

damages for negligently misjudging his examination papers, and for an order of
mandamus requiring the university to award him the grade that his papers justified.
The Court of Appeal refused leave to appeal from a decision which had struck out
the writ and statement of claim, and dismissed the action. In the words of Diplock
LJ ([1966] 2 All ER 338 at 339, [1966] 2 QB 237 at 242)—". . . actions of this kind
relating to domestic disputes between members of London University (as is the case
with other universities) are matters which are to be dealt with by the visitor and the
court has no jurisdiction to deal with them." This case makes it plain that the
question is not merely one of refusing discretionary remedies or requiring alternative
forms of relief to be pursued first, but is truly a matter of jurisdiction. Two
interlocutory observations by Diplock LJ ([1966] 2 QB 237 at 240) emphasise that
the visitor has the sole and exclusive jurisdiction, and that at common law the court
has no jurisdiction to deal with the internal affairs or government of the university,
because these have been confided by the law to the exclusive province of the visitor.'

The Vice-Chancellor expressed his conclusion in the following words ([1978] 3 All ER
841 at 846, [1978] 1 WLR 1488 at 1493): 'On the authorities it seems to be clear that the
visitor has a sole and exclusive jurisdiction, and that the courts have no jurisdiction over
matters within the visitor's jurisdiction.' This statement of the law has since been
accepted by Kelly LJ in *Re Wislang's Application* [1984] NI 63 and by Hoffmann J in *Hines
v Birkbeck College* [1985] 3 All ER 156, [1986] Ch 524.

In *Herring v Templeman* [1973] 2 All ER 581 a student teacher who had been requested
to withdraw from a teacher-training college on academic grounds commenced an action
against the governors for a declaration that the resolution of the governing body
dismissing him was ultra vires null and void; he alleged breach of the internal regulations
of the college and a breach of natural justice. The case is of interest because the plaintiff
conceded that his matters of complaint fell within the jurisdiction of the visitor but
submitted that in so far as the allegations were of a breach of natural justice the court
retained a concurrent jurisdiction. Brightman J rejected this submission and struck out
the statement of claim. He said (at 591):

'In the action with which I am concerned, the plaintiff's case is that he did not
have a hearing before the academic board, that he did not have a fair hearing before
the governing body and that the procedure of his dismissal was defective. In my
judgment, these are essentially matters which touch the internal affairs or
government of the college and are therefore matters confined by law to the exclusive
province of the visitor.'

It should be noted that during the hearing of this case in the Court of Appeal it
emerged for the first time that the plaintiff was not a member of the college, which had
been the basis of his case at first instance. The Court of Appeal allowed the plaintiff to
amend his statement of claim and affirmed the judgment of Brightman J on other
grounds which are not material to the present appeal (see [1973] 3 All ER 569).

In New Zealand the Court of Appeal has taken a different view of the visitor's
jurisdiction as it applies to their universities. In *Norrie v Senate of the University of Auckland*
[1984] 1 NZLR 129 Woodhouse P and Cooke J, whilst acknowledging that the English
authorities showed that in England the visitor had an exclusive jurisdiction, nevertheless
held that in New Zealand it should be considered as subordinate to the courts. In that
case the courts in fact refused judicial review to a medical student who had been refused
enrolment in the faculty of medicine after failing his final examination in the previous
year. The court held that such an issue should be dealt with by the visitor. There may be
much to be said for this approach in which the scope of the visitor's jurisdiction will be
developed in New Zealand on a case by case basis although uncertainty as to the extent of
the jurisdiction will reign until a sufficient body of precedent has built up to indicate
what issues the court will consider should be left to the visitor. However, this is not the

way in which our law has developed and in my view it is not open to your Lordships to follow Lloyd LJ and adopt the New Zealand solution. I agree with Hoffmann J when he said in *Hines v Birkbeck College* [1985] 3 All ER 156 at 162, [1986] Ch 524 at 539:

> 'It is conceded that the jurisdictions of the visitor and the courts are mutually exclusive. The courts in New Zealand have felt able to take a different view (see *Norrie v Senate of the University of Auckland*) but in this country this matter is concluded by a line of decisions commencing with that of the House of Lords in *Philips v Bury* (1694) Skin 447, [1558–1774] All ER Rep 53.'

I turn now to consider the scope of the visitatorial jurisdiction. The jurisdiction stems from the power recognised by the common law in the founder of an eleemosynary corporation to provide the laws under which the object of his charity was to be governed and to be sole judge of the interpretation and application of those laws either by himself or by such person as he should appoint as a visitor. In *Philips v Bury* as reported in 1 Ld Raym 5 at 8, 91 ER 900 at 903 Holt CJ described it thus:

> '. . . the office of the visitor by the common law is to judge according to the statutes of the college, to expel and deprive upon just occasions, and to hear appeals of course. And from him, and him only, the party grieved ought to have redress; and in him the founder hath reposed so entire confidence that he will administer justice impartially, that his determinations are final, and examinable in no other court whatsoever.'

In *Ex p Kirkby Ravensworth Hospital* (1808) 15 Ves 305 at 311, 33 ER 770 at 772 Sir Samuel Romilly said in a passage in his argument which has long been accepted as authoritative:

> 'A visitor is . . . a Judge, not for the single purpose of interpreting laws, but also for the application of laws, that are perfectly clear: requiring no interpretation; and, farther, for the interpretations of questions of fact; involving no interpretation of laws.'

As the jurisdiction stems from the power to provide and administer the domestic law of the foundation, it can as a general rule be said only to apply to those who are members of the foundation because only they are subject to those domestic laws. Nevertheless, the jurisdiction has always been held to apply both to admission to and removal from office in the foundation and many of the old cases concern the election or amotion of fellows at Oxford and Cambridge colleges. I am not sure whether these cases concerning fellowships touched directly on the principal means of livelihood of those concerned although I suspect they did. There are, however, other cases in which the visitatorial jurisdiction undoubtedly governed the question of employment in the sense of earning a living which one would suppose loomed larger for those affected, than the status involved in the employment. Thus in *A-G v Magdalen College Oxford* (1847) 10 Beav 402, 50 ER 637 the appointment of a master and usher to the college school were held to fall within the jurisdiction of the visitor even though they were not corporators and in *Whiston v Dean and Chapter of Rochester* (1849) 7 Hare 532, 68 ER 220 the dismissal of the headmaster from the cathedral grammar school was also held to fall within the exclusive jurisdiction of the visitor. In *R v Dunsheath, ex p Meredith* [1950] 2 All ER 741 at 743, [1951] 1 KB 127 at 132 Lord Goddard CJ said:

> 'Any question that arises of a domestic nature is essentially one for a domestic forum, and this is supported by all the authorities which deal with visitatorial powers and duties, and, although the question has generally arisen with regard to election to fellowships, I see no difference in principle between the question whether a particular person ought to be elected to a fellowship or whether a particular person

is a fit and proper person to be appointed or retained as a teacher at a university or a
school.'

The explanation for the visitor's jurisdiction extending in cases of admission and
removal from office (amotion) to those who are not corporators lies in the basis of his
jurisdiction, namely as the judge of the internal or domestic laws of the foundation. It is
because those laws invariably provide for the conditions governing admission to and
removal from membership of the foundation and sometimes of offices on the foundation
short of membership that jurisdiction in such matters lies with the visitor.

It is a mistake to consider that the visitor's jurisdiction derives from the status of
membership, as Fox LJ said in the course of judgment in the Court of Appeal. That is,
with respect, putting the cart before the horse. The jurisdiction derives from the visitor's
position as a judge of the internal laws of the foundation, and he has jurisdiction over
questions of status because it is on those laws that status depends.

A similar issue to that which arises in this appeal was considered by Kelly LJ in *Re
Wislang's Application* [1984] NI 63. The facts are sufficiently set out in the headnote:

'In 1981 the applicant was appointed by the Senate of the Queen's University of
Belfast to a lectureship (medical) in anatomy, subject to a period of probation until
30 September 1983. His conditions of appointment provided for an annual
assessment of his "teaching, research and scholarly ability" by an ad hoc group
consisting of his head of department and senior colleagues. The ad hoc group made,
in September 1982, an adverse assessment of the applicant's progress and, in
February 1983, reported that it was unable to recommend to the Board of Curators
that he be confirmed in post. The Board of Curators invited the applicant to attend
for interview but he failed to do so. In his absence the board decided that it could
not recommend to the senate that he be confirmed in post and informed him of
their decision. In April 1983 the applicant exercised his right of appeal to a
committee appointed by the senate. The appeal committee, after considering the
oral and written submissions of the applicant, dismissed the appeal and so reported
to the Senate which in May 1983 resolved to terminate the applicant's employment
with effect from 27 May 1983, informing him that his salary up to the end of the
academic year (30 September 1983) would be paid to him in a lump sum. The
applicant appealed to the visitor and in July 1983 a board of visitors was appointed,
taking up office on 1 October 1983. In November the board informed the applicant
that it proposed to consider the appeal on the documents submitted to it. The
applicant sought an oral hearing and also legal representation but in January 1984
this was refused. The applicant then sought, and, on appeal, was granted leave to
apply for judicial review. It was contended for the university that the matters in
dispute were within the exclusive jurisdiction of the board of visitors. The applicant
contended that the board had no jurisdiction because (a) the board had not been in
existence at the time of the appeal and had subsequently delayed unduly, (b) that
the board, containing a member of the Convocation of the university and a former
secretary of the university, was improperly constituted and had acted unfairly by
refusing an oral hearing and legal representation; (c) the issues in dispute involved
questions of contract and the legality of the proceedings of several bodies of the
university, and (d) the board could not grant effective remedies.'

Kelly LJ in an impressive judgment containing a comprehensive review of the
authorities held that the matters in dispute were exclusively within the visitatorial
jurisdiction. Dealing with the argument that the issues in dispute involved questions of
contract and were thus outside the jurisdiction of the visitor, he said (at 80–81):

'That the matters in dispute were internal matters lying within the visitatorial
jurisdiction was of course strongly challenged by Dr Wislang. They were not, he
said, because they included the question of the validity of the decision to dismiss

him, the authority of the Vice-Chancellor and the Secretary of the University, the
legality and regularity of the proceedings before the Board of Curators and the *a*
Appeal Committee and the Senate. All these were matters he submitted outside the
jurisdiction of the board of visitors, because they were or many of them were in
breach of his contract of employment. But what the authorities show, as I read
them, is that matters may well be in breach of a contract of employment, yet within
visitatorial jurisdiction, if those matters are of an internal domestic character or
touch upon the interpretation or execution of private rules and regulations of the *b*
university. Of course the applicant has the right under his contract to have the
criteria relating to the assessment of his fitness as a lecturer observed and the special
procedures of the university bodies who determine this and as a result terminate his
employment, regularly and fairly followed. But this right while a right under a
contract of employment seems to me to relate to the regular and fair execution of
procedures in accordance with the internal rules and regulations at the university. *c*
If the matters in dispute under his contract of employment related to purely
common law or statutory rights and not to private or special rights of the university,
then of course visitatorial jurisdiction could not determine them and Dr Wislang's
remedies would be in the ordinary courts or the appropriate statutory tribunals.
This must follow from the nature of visitatorial jurisdiction itself as analysed and
explained by the case-law, as well as the relationship between the university and a *d*
lecturer and who by his contract of employment becomes a member of the
university and submits himself to its internal rules on matters touching his standing
and progress at the university. Undoubtedly a contract of employment may contain
terms some of which are concerned with private or special rights given as a member
of the university and other terms express or implied which give purely contractual
or statutory rights. In these circumstances the visitatorial and the common law or *e*
industrial jurisdiction co-exist. The common law or statutory rights are enforceable
in the courts of the appropriate statutory tribunals, but the visitatorial jurisdiction
is not ousted.'

In *Hines v Birkbeck College* [1985] 3 All ER 156, [1986] Ch 524 Hoffmann J in an equally
impressive judgment considered the same issue. Again I take the facts from the headnote *f*
([1986] Ch 524):

'In 1971 the Senate of the University of London, with the consent of the governing
body of Birkbeck College, appointed the plaintiff to a chair of economics at the
college and conferred upon him the title of "Professor," with the status of "appointed
teacher." His salary was paid by the college, which had the power to dismiss him.
The university senate had power to deprive him of his title and status. He was ex *g*
officio a member of the academic board of the college. His duties included
conducting such classes, and giving such lectures and other teaching as might be
necessary, and also research work. In the academic year 1980/81 he was given paid
leave by the college in order to engage upon a research project. In 1981/82 he was
given unpaid leave so that he could continue work on his project. At the beginning *h*
of the academic year 1982/83 he sought a further extension of his leave in order to
complete his project, but that was refused and certain teaching duties were assigned
to him, which, however, he refused to perform. On 16 February 1983, the master
of the college initiated procedures which led first to suspension and finally, on 7 July
1983, to dismissal for alleged serious misconduct. On 29 July 1983 the master of the
college wrote to the principal of the university reporting that the plaintiff had been *j*
dismissed, enclosing a copy of the report of the consultative group, composed of
members of the academic staff and officers of the college, which had found the
plaintiff guilty of gross misconduct, and inviting the senate of the university to take
steps to deprive him of his title and his status as an appointed teacher. A report of
the university committee, which was set up to consider the matter, recommended

a
that the plaintiff be deprived of his title. On 17 May 1985 the plaintiff, shortly
before the committee's report was to be considered by the senate of the university,
issued a writ claiming, as against the college, that its purported decision to dismiss
him forthwith if he did not resign within seven days, and its purported dismissal of
him pursuant thereto, were ultra vires, null and void, and an injunction to restrain
the university from depriving him of his title of professor and status as an appointed
teacher.'

b
The university and the college moved to strike out the plaintiff's claims on the
grounds, inter alia, that the High Court lacked jurisdiction to deal with the matters
involved.

The argument for the plaintiff was the same as that which was accepted by the Court
of Appeal in the present case and is summarised in Hoffmann J's judgment ([1985] 3 All
c
ER 156 at 163–164, [1986] Ch 524 at 541):

'Counsel for Professor Hines says with equal truth that he does not seek to enforce
the customs, procedures or statutes of the college as such. He relies on them only to
the extent that they may be taken to have been incorporated as terms of the
professor's contract of employment. If that contract was, in accordance with his
primary submission, made with the university, he says that the college by excluding
d
the professor and depriving him of his salary has committed the tort of wrongful
interference with contract. If the contract was with the college then it has been
broken. In either case he founds his claim on the general law of contract or tort,
neither of which are within the jurisdiction of the visitor.'

Dealing with the argument Hoffmann J said ([1985] 3 All ER 156 at 164–165, [1986] Ch
e
524 at 542–543):

'Counsel for Professor Hines has argued that the test of whether the dispute is
domestic should be whether it is conveniently justiciable in the courts. The marking
of examination papers, as in *Thomson* and *Thorne* or the question in *Patel* of whether
Mr Patel was sufficiently qualified to enter for a degree in mathematics were
obviously matters in which the courts declined jurisdiction with relief. But the
f
courts have no difficulty in deciding whether principles of natural justice have been
observed or rules of procedure incorporated into contracts of employment correctly
applied. If one were seeking to devise a new system from scratch, it might well be
thought fair to allow the courts full concurrent jurisdiction in all claims based on
causes of action at common law or in equity, subject to a discretionary power to stay
proceedings on the ground that some or all of the matters in issue are more suitable
g
for adjudication by the university's internal tribunals. Something along these lines
seems to have been canvassed by the New Zealand Court of Appeal in *Norrie v Senate
of the University of Auckland* [1984] 1 NZLR 129. This might avoid anomalies such as
occurred in *Casson's* case in which the petitioner's claim in the county court was
struck out because the matter was said to be one for the visitor and the visitor
h
declined jurisdiction because the claim was one for the courts. It would also avoid
problems in obtaining interlocutory relief, about which there are obvious
administrative difficulties when the visitor is the Privy Council. It is however far
too late for this court to adopt such a scheme. For one thing, it is settled law that the
jurisdictions are mutually exclusive. The authorities also make it clear that,
irrespective of whether the courts would be as well or better qualified to deal with
j
the particular case, a dispute has the necessary domesticity if it involves members of
the corporation and the interpretation or application of its internal rules, customs or
procedures. Further, as Sir Samuel Romilly said in argument in *Ex p Kirkby
Ravensworth Hospital* (1808) 15 Ves 305 at 311, 33 ER 770 at 772 (a passage quoted
in Dr Smith's article "The Exclusive Jurisdiction of the University Visitor" ((1981)
97 LQR 610 at 614)): "A visitor is ... a Judge, not for the single purpose of

interpreting laws, but also for the application of the laws, that are perfectly clear: requiring no interpretation; and, further, for the interpretations of questions of fact ..."'

In both these cases it was held that the dispute lay within the visitatorial jurisdiction and, in my view, both these cases were rightly decided.

The Court of Appeal, laying emphasis on the 'domestic' nature of the visitatorial jurisdiction, did not follow these decisions. Lloyd LJ relied particularly on a quotation from the judgment of Kindersley V-C in *Thomson v University of London* (1864) 33 LJ Ch 625. The facts of that case were far different from the present: it concerned a dispute over the award of a gold medal in the examination for the LLD degree which, not surprisingly, was held to fall within the visitatorial jurisdiction. However, it appears to be the first of the cases in which the question of contract was argued. In the course of his judgment the Vice-Chancellor said (at 634):

'... the line of demarcation between that class of questions which comes under the jurisdiction of the visitor on the one hand, and that class of cases which comes under the jurisdiction of this court, as a court of equity, on the other, is this,— whatever relates to the internal arrangements and dealings with regard to the government and management of the house, of the domus, of the institution, is properly within the jurisdiction of the Visitor, and only under the jurisdiction of the Visitor, and this Court will not interfere in those matters; but when it comes to a question of right of property, or rights as between the university and a third person *dehors* the university, or with regard, it may be, to any breach of trust committed by the corporation, that is, the university, and so on, or any contracts by the corporation, not being matters relating to the mere management and arrangement and details of their domus, then, indeed, this Court will interfere.'

Lloyd LJ said, in commenting on this passage ([1986] 1 All ER 217 at 229, [1986] Ch 381 at 410): 'I am tempted to say that the present case does not relate to the 'mere management and arrangement and details' of the University of Bradford, and leave it at that'. The Vice-Chancellor's judgment is clearly extempore and I would hesitate to place too much reliance on any particular phraseology used in the course of this discursive judgment. What is however of importance is that the Vice-Chancellor did not treat the allegation of a cause of action in contract as necessarily ousting the jurisdiction of the visitor.

This then leads me to consider what is meant by the reference in the cases to the 'domesticity' of the visitatorial jurisdiction. The word is clearly not used with the width of its everyday meaning. Nothing could be more domestic in its everyday sense than the arrangements in the kitchens or for the cleaning of the premises, but no one suggests that the domestic staff of a university fall within the visitatorial jurisdiction. I am satisfied that in referring to the domestic jurisdiction the judges are using a shortened form of reference to those matters which are governed by the internal laws of the foundation. This will include not only the interpretation and enforcement of the laws themselves but those internal powers and discretions that derive from the internal laws such as the discretion necessarily bestowed on those in authority in the exercise of their disciplinary functions over members of the foundation. It is only if 'domesticity' is understood in this sense that any principle emerges that can be of general application to determine whether or not a given matter falls within the visitatorial jurisdiction. What is not permissible is to regard 'domesticity' as an elastic term giving the courts freedom to choose which disputes it will entertain and which it will send to the visitor. This approach necessarily involves the concept of a concurrent jurisdiction and, as I have endeavoured to show, this is not the way in which our law has developed.

I would adopt the following passage from Dr Smith's latest article 'Visitation of the Universities: A Ghost from the Past' (1986) 136 NLJ at 568:

'Once it is recognised that the supervision of the statutes, ordinances, regulations
a   etc of the foundation is the basis of the visitatorial jurisdiction, then it becomes a
relatively simple matter to define the scope of the visitor's powers, for any matter
concerning the application or the interpretation of those internal laws is within his
jurisdiction, but questions concerning rights and duties derived otherwise than
from such internal laws are beyond his authority. Thus a matter or dispute is
"domestic" so as to be within the visitatorial jurisdiction if it involves questions
b   relating to the internal laws of the foundation of which he is visitor or rights and
duties derived from such internal laws. Conversely, an issue which turns on the
enforcement of or adjudication on terms entered into between an individual and
his employer, notwithstanding that they may also be in the relationship of member
and corporation, and which involves no enforcement of or adjudication concerning
the domestic laws of the foundation, is *ultra vires* the visitor's authority and is
c   cognizable in a court of law or equity (see "The Exclusive Jurisdiction of the
University Visitor" (1981) 97 LQR 610 at 644).'

In the present case, the entire dispute is centred on the statute, ordinances and
regulations of the university. Were they correctly applied and were they fairly
administered? Such a dispute in my view falls within the jurisdiction of the visitor and
d   not the courts of law, notwithstanding that its resolution will affect Miss Thomas's
contract of employment.

It has, however, been urged on your Lordships that such an approach rooted as it is in
medieval law has no place in a modern society and will by denying university teachers
access to the courts in cases affecting contracts of employment place them at a grave
disadvantage to all others who can turn to the courts to resolve such disputes, and
e   particularly in comparison to the majority of their colleagues in the teaching profession.
If such shackles ever existed as prevented a court entertaining a claim for breach of a
contract of employment, the time has come to strike them off, and to restore so important
a matter to the jurisdiction of the courts.

The appeal of such an argument is readily understood. All are jealous of their own
territory and in the ordinary course of events nothing falls more naturally within the
f   territory of the courts than disputes between master and servant. It being a well-
recognised function of the common law to resolve such disputes, they must, it is said, fall
outside the visitatorial jurisdiction. In support of this argument Miss Thomas relied on
the decision of Lord Hailsham LC, sitting as visitor, in *Casson v University of Aston in
Birmingham* [1983] 1 All ER 88. The facts were that the two petitioners had been accepted
by the university to read a course in 'human communication'. The university
g   subsequently found that they were unable to provide the course and offered an alternative
course in 'human psychology' which was accepted by the petitioners and they were
admitted to the university to read that course. They then sued the university in the
county court for damages for breach of contract in respect of the course in 'human
communication'. The registrar and the judge declined jurisdiction holding that the
dispute fell within the jurisdiction of the visitor. They then petitioned the visitor, but
h   the Lord Chancellor acting as the visitor, also declined jurisdiction. The Lord Chancellor
relied on the first of the articles by Dr Smith. He said (at 90–91):

'It is, perhaps, unfortunate that none of the parties to this dispute have referred to
the exhaustive and up-to-date article by Dr Peter M Smith "The Exclusive Jurisdiction
of the University Visitor" (1981) 97 LQR 610. If they had, I believe much trouble
j   would have been avoided.'

In giving his principal reason for declining jurisdiction, the Lord Chancellor said (at 91):

'I agree, however, with Dr Smith that a visitor can have no jurisdiction in any
matter governed by the common law, eg contract (see 97 LQR 610 at 615). I regard

each of the petitions as claims for damages for breach of a contract entered into *before* the petitioners became members of the university and for nothing else.' (My emphasis.)

As the contract relied on was one between the university and third parties who were not members of the university at the time it was entered into, I accept this case as correctly decided. However, the headnote puts the decision on a far wider basis and reads:

'*Held* – The petitions would be dismissed for the following reasons—(1) A visitor of a foundation had no jurisdiction in any matter governed by the common law, and, once a relationship with the foundation had been established which was governed by the general laws of the realm over which the visitor could have no jurisdiction, the visitor was wholly excluded from considering any question concerning that relationship. Since the relationship of contract was governed by the general laws of the realm, the visitor had no jurisdiction over contracts entered into with the foundation, and the fact that the other contracting party was also a member of the foundation did not have the effect of excluding the jurisdiction of the courts and putting the matter exclusively within the visitor's authority . . .'

If, which I doubt, the Lord Chancellor did intend to put the decision on so broad a base as excluding any relationship which, apart from visitatorial jurisdiction, would otherwise be governed by the common law, I must respectfully disagree with him. I have already pointed out that almost any dispute between a member and the university can be framed in either contract or tort, which relationships are apart from the visitatorial jurisdiction governed by the common law. To adopt this approach would entirely emasculate the visitatorial jurisdiction leaving it with virtually no content. Dr Smith in his recent article in the New Law Journal, to which I have already referred, has made it plain that he was not to be understood as suggesting in his article in the Law Quarterly Review any such sweeping approach to the visitatorial jurisdiction. It might be apposite at this point to say a word about trusts as they are referred to in the passage cited by the Lord Chancellor from Dr Smith's article as being analogous to contracts. The reason why the courts have maintained their jurisdiction over trusts, whether or not they benefit members of the foundation, is that the terms of the trust are to be derived from the construction of the trust instrument and not by any application of the laws of the foundation. Thus the construction of a trust must be a matter for the courts and not the visitor, nor is there any reason why the supervision of the trust should not remain with the courts. The cases on trusts well illustrate the principle that only those matters governed by the laws of the foundation are within visitatorial jurisdiction: see *Green v Rutherford* (1750) 1 Ves Sen 462, [1554–1774] All ER Rep 153 and *Ex p Berkhampstead Free School* (1813) 2 Ves & B 134, [1803–13] All ER Rep 714 and *A-G v Magdalen College Oxford* (1847) 10 Beav 402, 50 ER 637. Other cases are to be found discussed by Dr Smith (see 97 LQR 610 at 634–637).

Miss Thomas relied also on the view expressed by the Lord Chancellor that a university has no power to award damages. He said ([1983] 1 All ER 88 at 91):

'After considerable research, I have been unable to find any precedent in the long history of visitatorial powers in which a visitor has made such an order and in my view he has no such power.'

This view is to be contrasted with that expressed by Burt CJ in *Murdoch University v Bloom* [1980] WAR 193 at 198, in which he said on the assumption that a breach of contract fell within visitatorial jurisdiction:

'If it were then I can see no reason why an action for damages if brought upon the breach of such a contract would not equally be a matter within the exclusive jurisdiction of the Visitor . . .'

a I prefer the view expressed by Burt CJ. I can see no reason why the visitor as judge of the laws of the foundation should not have the power to right a wrong done to a member or office holder in the foundation by the misapplication of those laws. The visitor would be a poor sort of judge if he did not possess such powers. Suppose, first, a case in which on appeal the visitor concluded that there had been no 'good cause' for the dismissal of a member of the academic staff and ordered the reinstatement of the member; I cannot entertain a doubt that the visitor would have power to order payment of arrears of salary

b between the date of dismissal and reinstatement. Suppose, second, a case in which the visitor concluded there had been no 'good cause' for the dismissal but relations between the dismissed member and the other members of the academic staff had so deteriorated that it would be inimical to the general health of the university to order reinstatement. Why in these circumstances should the visitor not proceed to right the wrong done to the member by ordering that a monetary recompense should be paid by the university

c in lieu of reinstatement. No doubt in calculating the sum he would be guided by those principles that the courts have worked out in cases of wrongful dismissal in which the courts refuse to enforce a contract of service wrongfully terminated but give monetary recompense instead, which the law labels as damages. To deny a visitor such a power is to deny him one of the fundamental functions of a judge which is to right a wrong, in so far as money can.

d My Lords, I cannot accept that the continuation of the visitatorial jurisdiction with the scope and powers I have discussed will leave the academic staff of universities at a significant or at any disadvantage to their colleagues working in other fields of education. In the first place the action for wrongful dismissal has largely been superseded by the far wider protection afforded to employees by the Employment Protection (Consolidation) Act 1978. All these rights are available to all university academic staff because Parliament

e can of course invade the jurisdiction of the visitor if it chooses to do so. If in the course of such proceedings any question arises concerning the interpretation or application of the internal laws of the university, it will have to be resolved for the purpose of the case by the tribunal hearing the application. Such power must be implicit in the remedies provided by the Act, and to this extent, Parliament has given rights that enter and

f supersede the jurisdiction of the visitor. I cannot accept the suggestion that, if in the course of a tribunal hearing a question arises concerning the interpretation of university statutes etc, the case should be adjourned pending a decision by the visitor. This would be altogether too unwieldly a procedure and cannot have been the intention of Parliament.

Secondly, if what is really sought is reinstatement, it is more likely to be achieved by

g appeal to the visitor than to the courts. As a general rule the courts will not enforce a contract of service and the delay that inevitably results between the dismissal and the date on which the case comes before the court makes reinstatement all the less likely, for by the time the case is heard the plaintiff's post will have already been filled. The appeal to the visitor is, however, a speedy and informal procedure and reinstatement can be considered without the constraints imposed by the passage of time.

h It is true that the decision of the visitor is final and the parties are thus deprived of challenging a decision in that Court of Appeal and perhaps the House of Lords. But is this a disadvantage or an advantage? I rather think it is an advantage. Today the visitors of universities either are or include independent persons of the highest judicial eminence. Would not most people consider it better to accept the decision of such a person rather than face the risk of the matter dragging on through the years until the appellate process

j has finally ground to a halt. There is also the advantage of cheapness, lack of formality and flexibility in the visitatorial appeal procedure which is not bound by the intimidating and formalised procedures of the courts of law.

Finally, there is the protection afforded by the supervisory, as opposed to appellate, jurisdiction of the High Court over the visitor.

It has long been held that the writs of mandamus and prohibition will go either to

compel the visitor to act if he refused to deal with a matter within his jurisdiction or to
prohibit him from dealing with a matter that lies without his jurisdiction. On mandamus *a*
see *R v Bishop of Ely* (1794) 5 Term Rep 475, 101 ER 267 and *R v Dunsheath, ex p Meredith*
[1950] 2 All ER 741, [1951] 1 KB 127 and on prohibition see *R v Bishop of Chester* (1747)
1 Wm Bl 22 and *Bishop of Chichester v Harward and Webber* (1787) 1 Term Rep 650, 99 ER
1300. Although doubts have been expressed in the past as to the availability of certiorari,
I have myself no doubt that in the light of the modern development of administrative
law, the High Court would have power, on an application for judicial review, to quash a *b*
decision of the visitor which amounted to an abuse of his powers.

These considerations lead me to the conclusion that the visitatorial jurisdiction subject
to which all our modern universities have been founded is not an ancient anachronism
which should now be severely curtailed, if not discarded. If confined to its proper limits,
namely the laws of the foundation and matters deriving therefrom, it provides a practical
and expeditious means of resolving disputes which it is in the interests of the universities *c*
and their members to preserve.

For these reasons, my Lords, I would allow this appeal.

LORD MACKAY OF CLASHFERN. My Lords, I have had the advantage of reading
in draft the speeches prepared by my noble and learned friends Lord Griffiths and Lord
Ackner. I agree with them, and for the reasons which they give I would allow the appeal. *d*

LORD ACKNER. My Lords, the proposition that the visitor's jurisdiction may be an
unwelcome survivor from the past, like the ghosts, in Lord Atkin's famous phrase in
United Australian Ltd v Barclays Bank Ltd [1940] 4 All ER 20 at 37, [1941] AC 1 at 29,
standing 'in the path of justice, clanking their mediæval chains' was firmly, and in my
judgment correctly, rejected by Lloyd LJ in his judgment in the Court of Appeal *e*
dismissing Bradford University's appeal. He accepted that the visitor still had a valuable
function to perform in a modern university. Indeed, he said ([1986] 1 All ER 217 at 233,
[1986] Ch 381 at 415):

'Within its proper limits the jurisdiction of the visitor is wholly beneficial. So
much so that, if the visitor did not exist, it might have been necessary to invent *f*
him.'

Megarry V-C in *Patel v University of Bradford Senate* [1978] 3 All ER 841 at 851–852,
[1978] 1 WLR 1488 at 1499–1500 posed and answered the following question: why
should most university students be precluded from access to the courts in many matters
of dispute with the university authorities? He said:
g

'I think that there is much that can be said in answer. I shall take three examples.
First, there is no question of the students being denied access to a tribunal that can
resolve the dispute: the only question is whether that tribunal is to be the visitor or
the courts. For students who seek to have a university decision set aside or reversed
the advice in most cases should be "Go to the visitor, not to the courts". Second,
there is much to be said in favour of the visitor as against the courts as an appropriate *h*
tribunal for disputes of the type which fall within the visatatorial jurisdiction. In
place of the formality, publicity and expense of proceedings in court, with pleadings,
affidavits and all the apparatus of litigation (including possible appeals to the Court
of Appeal and, perhaps, the House of Lords), there is an appropriate domestic
tribunal which can determine the matter informally, privately, cheaply and speedily,
and give a decision which, apart from any impropriety or excess of jurisdiction, is *j*
final and will not be disturbed by the courts. This aspect of the matter has been the
subject of repeated high judicial approval: see *Attorney-General v Talbot* (1748) 3 Atk
662 at 674, 676, 26 ER 1181 at 1187–1188 per Lord Hardwicke LC; *St John's College,
Cambridge v Todington* (1757) 1 Burr 158 at 199-200, 97 ER 245 at 269 per Lord
Mansfield CJ; *Ex parte Wrangham* (1795) 2 Ves Jun 609 at 619, 30 ER 803 at 808 per

Lord Loughborough LC; *Thomson v University of London* (1864) 33 LJ Ch 625 at 635
a   per Kindersley V-C; *R v Dunsheath, ex parte Meredith* [1950] 2 All ER 741 at 743,
[1951] 1 KB 127 at 132 per Lord Goddard CJ. Third, the extent of visitatorial
jurisdiction in university life has greatly expanded in recent years. When Oxford
and Cambridge were the only universities in England, a relatively small portion of
the small university population was within the visitatorial jurisdiction, and then
only in relation to the colleges; and for those universities that remains true today.
b   But with the founding of the 19th century universities came the general extension
of the visitatorial jurisdiction to all the undergraduate members, instead of only the
scholars. The same applies to the 20th century universities, as appears from a
valuable article by Dr J W Bridge "Keeping Peace in the Universities: the Role of the
Visitor" (1970) 86 LQR 531) to which counsel referred me. (I am indebted to this
article as well as to the lucid restatement of the law governing visitors which is set
c   out in a book which counsel studiously refrained from citing, Picarda's Law and
Practice Relating to Charities (1977) pp 422–433.) The general picture of only a
small part of the small undergraduate population of the universities being within
the visitatorial jurisdiction has changed into a picture of the great majority of the
far larger undergraduate population of the universities being within it. The
visitatorial jurisdiction exercisable by the Lord Chancellor on behalf of the Crown
d   must now be of formidable dimensions; for in most of the modern universities the
Crown appears to be the visitor.'

It is common ground that where the visitatorial jurisdicton exists it is an exclusive
jurisdiction. The review of the authorities by my noble and learned friend Lord Griffiths
clearly establishes this principle. Accordingly, the essential issue for decision by your
e   Lordships is the scope of that jurisdiction. Miss Thomas's submission is encapsulated in
the final sentence of the judgment of Whitford J ([1985] 2 All ER 786 at 795, [1986] 1
Ch 381 at 395 where he says: 'By writing the rules into the contract the question at issue
has been brought within the jurisdiction of the court . . .'

In the Court of Appeal Fox LJ stated the matter equally shortly in these terms ([1986]
1 All ER 217 at 228, [1986] Ch 381 at 408):
f
'But, as at present advised, I think that (subject to judicial review) the visitor must
decide who is or who is not to be a member of the house. Remedies for breaches of
contract are for the courts.'

In order to consider the scope of the visitatorial jurisdiction the historic basis and
g   justification for the jurisdiction must first be considered. An eleemosynary corporation
is a corporation founded for the purpose of distributing the founder's bounty. The
purpose of the visitor's jurisdiction is the supervision of the internal rules of the
foundation so that it is governed in accordance with those private laws which the founder
has laid down to regulate the objects of his benefaction. Clearly, this supervision cannot
be restricted merely to interpreting the statutes. For the supervision to be effective it
h   must involve ensuring that the statutes, properly interpreted, are also being properly
applied and observed.

The clearest modern statement of the scope of the jurisdiction is to be found in the
Irish case of *Re Wislang's Application* [1984] NI 63 at 81 where Kelly LJ, sitting in the
Queen's Bench, said:

j   'But what the authorities show, as I read them, is that matters may well be in
breach of a contract of employment, yet within visitatorial jurisdiction, if those
matters are of an internal domestic character or touch upon the interpretation or
execution of private rules and regulations of the university. Of course, the applicant
has the right under his contract to have the criteria relating to the assessment of his
fitness as a lecturer observed and the special procedures of the university bodies who
determine this and as a result terminate his employment, regularly and fairly

followed. But this right while a right under a contract of employment seems to me
to relate to the regular and fair execution of procedures in accordance with the   a
internal rules and regulations of the university. If the matters in dispute under his
contract of employment related purely to common law or statutory rights and not
to private or special rights of the university, then of course visitatorial jurisdiction
could not determine them and Dr. Wislang's remedies would be in the ordinary
courts or the appropriate statutory tribunals. This must follow from the nature of
visitatorial jurisdiction itself as analysed and explained by the case-law, as well as the   b
relationship between the university and a lecturer and who by his contract of
employment becomes a member of the university and submits himself to its
internal rules on matters touching his standing and progress at the university.
Undoubtedly, a contract of employment may contain terms some of which are
concerned with private or special rights given as a member of the university and
other terms express or implied which give purely contractual or statutory rights. In   c
these circumstances the visitatorial and the common law or industrial jurisdictions
co-exist. The common law or statutory rights are enforceable in the courts or the
appropriate statutory tribunals, but the visitatorial jurisdiction is not ousted.'

This statement is consistent with the view expressed by Hoffmann J in *Hines v Birkbeck
College* [1985] 3 All ER 156 at 165, [1986] Ch 524 at 543 where he said: d

'In my judgment the dispute is no less domestic because the rules, customs or
procedures in issue are alleged to constitute terms of a contract or because their
construction or the questions of fact involved in their application are equally
conveniently justiciable in a court.'

The view expressed by Hoffmann J is also equally consistent with that expressed by   e
Brightman J in *Herring v Templeman* [1973] 2 All ER 581 at 591:

'In the action with which I am concerned, the plaintiff's case is that he did not
have a hearing before the academic board, that he did not have a fair hearing before
the governing body and that the procedure of his dismissal was defective. In my
judgment, these are essentially matters which touch the internal affairs or   f
government of the college and are therefore matters confined by law to the exclusive
province of the visitor. The dismissal of a student teacher for failing, in the opinion
of those charged with the task of forming an opinion, to match up to the standard
required of a teacher is the inevitable duty of an educational establishment which
holds examinations and passes out students whom it considers fit to be teachers. The
training of a student teacher and the assessment of his competence is the main and   g
indeed the only object of a teacher-training college. The construction of the
regulations of the college and the carrying into effect of those regulations in relation
to persons who subject themselves to those regulations are, in my view, matters
which the decided authorities have committed to the exclusive jurisdiction of the
visitor.'
                                                                                    h
The source of the obligation on which Miss Thomas relies for her claim is the domestic
laws of the university, its statutes and its ordinances. It is her case that the university has
failed either in the proper interpretation of its statutes or in their proper application.
Miss Thomas is not relying on a contractual obligation other than an obligation by the
university to comply with its own domestic laws. Accordingly, in my judgment, her
claim falls within the exclusive jurisdiction of the visitor, subject always to judicial   j
review.
    As regards the visitor's jurisdiction to award 'damages' I see no practical problem. The
visitor in the course of his supervisory jurisdiction must be entitled, in order to ensure
that the domestic law is properly applied, to redress any grievance that has resulted from
the misapplication of that domestic law. Such redress may involve ordering the payment

a of arrears of salary in the case in which the visitor decides that the employment has not been determined, or compensation where the complainant has accepted the wrongful repudiation of his contract of employment. It has not been submitted to your Lordships that where such an order is made, there would be any realistic risk of the university failing to comply with the order.

Accordingly, I would allow the appeal.

b **Appeal allowed. Cause remitted to Chancery Division with a direction that the action be struck out. No order for costs in the House of Lords.**

Solicitors: *Robbins Olivey & Blake Lapthorn*, agents for *Sampson Wade*, Bradford (for the university); *Kenneth Shaw & Co*, agents for *Goldsmith Williams*, Birkenhead (for Miss Thomas).

c

Mary Rose Plummer   Barrister.

d # Goldsworthy v Brickell and others

COURT OF APPEAL, CIVIL DIVISION

PARKER, NOURSE LJJ AND SIR JOHN MEGAW

16, 17, 18, 19 JUNE, 16 JULY, 30 OCTOBER 1986

e *Equity – Undue influence – Presumption of undue influence – Relationship of parties – Relationship of trust and confidence – Elderly farmer and neighbour – Neighbour involved in farmer's business and testamentary affairs – Neighbour persuading farmer to sign tenancy agreement containing option to purchase farm on farmer's death – Option at very advantageous price to neighbour – Independent legal advice as to effect of agreement not obtained – Farmer accepting rent from neighbour under agreement – Whether tenancy agreement liable to be set aside – Whether*
f *necessary to show dominating influence of party benefiting from transaction – Whether farmer affirming agreement by accepting rent.*

Costs – Bullock order – Plaintiff's right to order – Different causes of action – Whether court can make order even though plaintiff's causes of action against defendants are different.

g The plaintiff was the freehold owner of a farm comprising some 436 acres which he valued at about £1m. Between 1970 and 1976 he ran the farm with his son as his only employee. Relations between the plaintiff and his son were somewhat strained and the farm was run down and losing money. From November 1976 the defendant, a neighbouring farmer, began to give the plaintiff advice and help in running the farm. The plaintiff came to trust the defendant implicitly and to rely on him and his employees,
h so that by early 1977 the defendant was effectively managing the farm. In April 1977 the plaintiff, then aged 85 but in full possession of his faculties, granted a tenancy of the farm to the defendant at an annual rent of £500 with an option to purchase the farm at the 'prevailing value' on the death of the plaintiff. The agreement (i) provided that the plaintiff could remain in the house on the farm, (ii) prohibited the plaintiff as landlord from making any rent increases and (iii) although the intention was that the defendant
j would carry out necessary improvements, merely permitted, but did not oblige, the defendant to make improvements to the farm. A further agreement made the plaintiff and the defendant equal partners in the farm business. The plaintiff was reluctant to and did not receive independent advice in respect of the agreements and neither agreement made any reference to the plaintiff's son. In 1979 the partnership agreement was terminated by agreement, the defendant bought out the plaintiff's half interest and

thereafter worked the farm solely for his own benefit paying an annual a rent of £3,000
to the plaintiff. The market rent was about £12,500. In 1983 the plaintiff, who had   *a*
become reconciled with his son and had executed a power of attorney in his favour and a
will bequeathing the bulk of his estate to him, received advice that the tenancy agreement
was not only very unfavourable to the plaintiff, particularly if the 'prevailing value' at
which the defendant could exercise the option to purchase was on a sitting-tenant basis,
but might also be invalid. He issued a writ against the defendant seeking rescission of
the tenancy agreement on the ground of undue influence. The judge found (i) that,   *b*
arising out of the association between the two men and the defendant's advisory capacity,
the defendant had put himself in a position of influence over the plaintiff, which
although well short of domination made it his duty to take care of the plaintiff in any
transaction between them, (ii) that although there had been no actual undue influence
the confidential relationship between the two gave rise to a presumption of undue
influence, but (iii) that the subsequent conduct of the plaintiff in continuing to accept   *c*
rent amounted to affirmation of the agreement thereby giving rise to a promissory
estoppel which prevented the plaintiff from having the agreement set aside. The judge
accordingly dismissed the plaintiff's action. The plaintiff appealed. The defendant cross-
appealed against the finding of undue influence, contending that there was no evidence
to show that the plaintiff had been under his domination.
                                                                                        d

Held – (1) In order for the presumption to arise that a gift or transaction had been
procured by the undue influence of one person over another there had to be a relationship
wherein the latter had ceded such a degree of trust or confidence to the former that the
former was in a position to influence the latter into making the gift or effecting the
transaction, but it was not necessary to show that the person in whom the trust and
confidence had been placed had assumed a dominating influence over the donor or   *e*
grantor. However, the presumption remained inoperative until the party who had ceded
the trust and confidence made a gift so large or entered into a transaction so improvident
as not to be reasonably accounted for on the ground of friendship, relationship, charity
or the other ordinary motives on which ordinary men acted. Provided the gift or
transaction was manifestly and unfairly disadvantageous to the donor or grantor it would
be set aside unless it was proved to be a spontaneous act on his part in circumstances   *f*
enabling him to exercise an independent will and which justified the court in holding
that the gift or transaction was the result of a free exercise of his will. On the facts, there
was ample evidence to support the judge's finding of presumed undue influence.
Accordingly, the tenancy agreement was liable to be set aside unless the plaintiff had
subsequently affirmed it by his words or conduct and was estopped from having it set
aside (see p 865 *e* to *j*, p 868 *a*, p 869 *f* to *j*, p 870 *a e*, p 871 *j*, p 874 *a* and p 877 *c d j*, post);   *g*
dictum of Lindley LJ in *Allcard v Skinner* [1886–90] All ER Rep at 100–101 and *Tufton v
Sperni* [1952] 2 TLR 516 applied; *National Westminster Bank plc v Morgan* [1985] 1 All ER
821 considered.

(2) Since the defendant had failed to establish either a clear and unequivocal
representation by the plaintiff that he would not enforce his right to set aside the tenancy
agreement or that the defendant had acted in any way to his detriment, it could not be   *h*
said that the plaintiff had affirmed the agreement. In the circumstances, it was just and
equitable that the tenancy agreement be set aside and the plaintiff granted possession of
the farm. The appeal would accordingly be allowed and the cross-appeal dismissed (see
p 873 *b d f j*, p 874 *a* and p 877 *f* to *j*, post).

Per curiam. The authority of the court over costs is very wide, and even where there   *j*
are different causes of action there is no restriction on the making of a Bullock order (ie
an order that, where judgment is recovered against one only of two or more defendants,
the unsuccessful defendant pay to the plaintiff the costs payable by him to the successful
defendant) (see p 878 *d e*, post).

Notes
For persons in a confidential relationship, see 16 Halsbury's Laws (4th edn) para 1454.

For presumption of undue influence, see 18 ibid paras 334–343, and for cases on the subject, see 12 Digest (Reissue) 125–142, 687–820.

For Bullock orders, see 37 Halsbury's Laws (4th edn) para 219, and for cases on the subject, see 37(3) Digest (Reissue) 264–266, 4501–4510.

Cases referred to in judgments

Aiden Shipping Co Ltd v Interbulk Ltd, The Vimeira [1986] 2 All ER 409, [1986] AC 965, [1986] 2 WLR 1051, HL.

Allcard v Skinner (1887) 36 Ch D 145, [1886–90] All ER Rep 90, CA.

Antony v Weerasekera [1953] 1 WLR 1007, PC.

Billage v Southee (1852) 9 Hare 534, 68 ER 623.

Brocklehurst (decd), Re [1978] 1 All ER 767, [1978] Ch 14, [1977] 3 WLR 696, CA.

Craig (decd), Re, Meneces v Middleton [1970] 2 All ER 390, [1971] Ch 95, [1970] 2 WLR 1219.

Harrison-Broadley v Smith [1964] 1 All ER 867, [1964] 1 WLR 456, CA.

Holder v Holder [1968] 1 All ER 665, [1968] Ch 353, [1968] 2 WLR 237, CA.

Huguenin v Baseley (1807) 14 Ves 273, [1803–13] All ER Rep 1, 33 ER 526, LC.

John v James (29 November 1985, unreported), Ch D.

Lloyds Bank Ltd v Bundy [1974] 3 All ER 757, [1975] QB 326, [1974] 3 WLR 501, CA.

Mulready v J H & W Bell Ltd [1953] 2 All ER 215, [1953] 2 QB 117, [1953] 3 WLR 100, CA.

National Westminster Bank plc v Morgan [1985] 1 All ER 821, [1985] AC 686, [1985] 2 WLR 588, HL; *rvsg* [1983] 3 All ER 85, CA.

Pauling's Settlement Trusts, Re, Younghusband v Coutts & Co [1961] 3 All ER 713, [1962] 1 WLR 86; *affd in part* [1963] 3 All ER 1, [1964] Ch 303, [1963] 3 WLR 742, CA.

Poosathurai v Kannappa Chettiar (1919) LR 47 Ind App 1, PC.

Tate v Williamson (1866) LR 1 Eq 528; *affd* LR 2 Ch App 55.

Tufton v Sperni [1952] 2 TLR 516, CA.

Zamet v Hyman [1961] 3 All ER 933, [1961] 1 WLR 1442, CA.

Cases also cited

James v Heim Gallery (London) Ltd (1980) 41 P & CR 269, CA.

Johnson v Moreton [1978] 3 All ER 37, [1980] AC 37, HL.

Payman v Lanjani [1984] 3 All ER 703, [1985] Ch 457, CA.

Telfair Shipping Corp v Athos Shipping Co SA, The Athos [1981] 2 Lloyd's Rep 74; *on appeal* [1983] 1 Lloyd's Rep 127, CA.

Yerkey v Jones (1939) 63 CLR 649, Aust HC.

Appeal and cross-appeal

The plaintiff, Charles Matthew Arnold Goldsworthy, appealed from the decision of Goulding J given on 1 March 1985 whereby he (1) declared the first defendant, Robert James Brickell, to be the tenant of the property known as Chasewoods Farm, Hailey, Witney, Oxford, on the terms of a tenancy agreement dated 13 April 1977, on the grounds that although there had been undue influence on the part of the first defendant in procuring the plaintiff's agreement to the tenancy, the plaintiff had subsequently affirmed the agreement by accepting rent from the first defendant and was therefore not entitled to rescind the agreement, and (2) dismissed the plaintiff's action for professional negligence against the second defendants, Jefferson Cooper & Co (a firm), his former solicitors. By a respondent's notice dated 11 April 1985 the first defendant cross-appealed against the finding of undue influence. The facts are set out in the judgment of Nourse LJ.

Peter Scott QC, Jeremy Griggs and *Charles Falconer* for the plaintiff.
Robert Pryor QC and *Joanne Moss* for the first defendant.
W R H Crowther QC and *Jonathan Simpkiss* for the second defendants.

Cur adv vult

16 July. The following judgments were delivered.

NOURSE LJ (giving the first judgment at the invitation of Parker LJ). On 13 April 1977 the plaintiff in this action, Mr Charles Goldsworthy, then a widower aged 85, granted a tenancy of Chasewoods Farm, Witney in Oxfordshire, a property of some 436 acres of which he had bought the freehold in 1934, to the first defendant, Mr R J Brickell the younger, who comes from another family of farmers nearby. On 1 March 1985 Goulding J, in a reserved judgment given after a three-week trial in the Chancery Division, decided that the tenancy agreement had been entered into by the plaintiff under the undue influence of Mr Brickell, but he held that the plaintiff had afterwards affirmed it. He also held that the second defendants, Messrs Jefferson Cooper & Co, a firm of solicitors who had acted for the plaintiff subsequently to the granting of the tenancy, had not been negligent. The judge accordingly dismissed the action as against both defendants. Against that dismissal the plaintiff has appealed. Mr Brickell, to whom, like the judge, I shall refer simply as 'the defendant', has put in a respondent's notice asking for the judge's order to be affirmed on the ground that there was no undue influence in the first place. Argument has been heard first on the questions of undue influence and affirmation, and it is on those questions that judgment is now given.

As is often necessary in cases of this kind, the facts of this remarkable story, most of which I can take verbatim from the excellent statement by the judge, must be set out at some length.

The plaintiff was born on 17 December 1891. He served in the 1914–18 war and rose through the ranks to be a captain. For many years afterwards he traded as a retail grocer and provision merchant in North Oxford. In 1934 he purchased Chasewoods Farm. Until his wife's death in about 1970, and with her help, he ran the farm and shop. The farm is a stock farm, used for raising beef cattle and sheep, with some pigs at the farmhouse.

The plaintiff has a son, Mr Tom Goldsworthy, who was born in 1923. In 1976, when the story begins, Tom was employed by the plaintiff as an agricultural labourer at a low wage. He supplemented his income by an egg round. He lived with his wife and daughter in a cottage on the farm. Years before he had quarrelled with the plaintiff, apparently over his treatment of Tom's mother. There were periods when he and the plaintiff communicated only in writing. The plaintiff did not believe that Tom was capable of being a successful farmer, although the judge thought that he probably underestimated Tom's capacities. Nevertheless, the judge was sure that Tom was far less able than his father.

The plaintiff and Tom had for some time known the defendant and his father, Mr R J Brickell the elder, who himself appears to have been the second of that name. They were large and successful farmers in the same part of Oxfordshire. The judge found that there had been a suggestion, possibly in 1974, and possibly more than once, that the defendant might buy Chasewoods for £100,000 or thereabouts. The judge regarded it as more probable that that low figure was offered by the defendant than that the plaintiff proposed it. In 1976 the defendant was aged about 39. He had recently lost his wife and been left with two small children, and he had gone back to live with his parents.

In 1976 the plaintiff was living alone in the farmhouse at Chasewoods, as he had done since his wife's death. The judge found that he was in good health and physically strong. He was remarkably well preserved for his years and the like was true of his mental condition. His manner was authoritative and he was used to getting, and expected to get, his own way. He was not at all the sort of person who could be overborne in argument or influenced by strength of personality. However, the judge found that he had two major difficulties which must have made him receptive to suggestions capable of improving his situation. The judge was satisfied that both these matters were very serious and that together they made the plaintiff unhappy. The first was his relationship with Tom. The second was the condition of Chasewoods. The plaintiff employed no regular labour except his own and Tom's, and would not spend freely on the needs of the land *a* and of his stock. Hence, the pastures were in a poor state, the hedges overgrown, the fences broken down and the farm was making a substantial loss.

In November 1976, possibly early December, there was what the judge described as a disaster at Chasewoods, which resulted in the death of several of the plaintiff's cattle and the serious illness of others. The plaintiff asked the defendant for advice or help, which was freely given. From then on the defendant or one or more of his employees went to Chasewoods on most days and helped with the livestock or the garden. A young woman

b employee of the defendant's, Sandra Laity, did washing or cleaning in the house or shopping for the plaintiff. Sandra and the defendant quite frequently visited the plaintiff and sat with him for an hour or two in the evening. The defendant did not require payment for the services he supplied, but the plaintiff from time to time made gifts to Sandra, including one of £500 and a save-as-you-earn bond of £1,200. He also lent her a further £2,000. On the other side, the defendant made gifts to the plaintiff, including a

c portable television set.

Speaking of this relationship, the judge found that the plaintiff came to trust the defendant implicitly, and to rely on him and his employees to make his life reasonably comfortable. He went on to record that Sandra had agreed in cross-examination that, before the date of the tenancy agreement, the plaintiff had become utterly dependent on the defendant as far as farming was concerned and that, from quite early on, he became

d dependent in a sense on her too. He also recorded that the defendant accepted in cross-examination that, at this time, the plaintiff trusted him, though only trusting anyone to a degree, and relied on him as to the running of the farm. The judge then found that, from late 1976, or a very early date in 1977, the defendant was effectively managing the farm. He proceeded as follows:

e   'I feel no doubt that, by that time and certainly before the date of the tenancy agreement, the defendant had acquired an influence over the plaintiff, based on and arising out of a particular association and an advisory capacity, well short, no doubt, of domination, which nevertheless made it his duty to take care of the plaintiff in any transaction between them.'

f This finding is one of crucial importance in the case and I shall have to return to it later.

Here it is convenient to interrupt the narrative in order to say something about the evidence which was before the judge. The trial started in the last week of November 1984 and continued until the end of the Michaelmas term. The plaintiff, who was by then aged 93, was not able to come to London. His evidence was taken on commission during the course of the trial before an examiner, sitting at a hotel in Oxford. All parties

g had requested the judge to take evidence himself, but he thought that he ought not to do so. No criticism of that decision has been proffered in this court and I make none myself. However, the result was not an ideal one in that the only material available to the judge himself was a transcript of the evidence. Having studied the transcript, the judge was of the view that the plaintiff's evidence was wholly unreliable. He did not find it necessary to inquire whether its poor quality was due to the mental deterioration that comes with

h old age, or to disregard of the truth, or to a compound of both.

The judge also had serious reservations about the evidence of both Mr Tom Goldsworthy and the defendant. He regarded Tom's evidence with considerable caution, coloured as he believed it to be by his animosity towards the defendant, with whom he had waged a long war for the favour of the aged plaintiff. He referred also to the voluminous extracts from Tom's diaries and from records which he had made from

j conversations surreptitiously overheard. Although the general authenticity of those writings had not been questioned, the judge regarded them as selective records, coloured throughout by Tom's own wishes, hopes and fears. Having said that about Tom's evidence, the judge said that he found the defendant's evidence still more suspect. He said that it contained numerous inconsistencies and improbabilities which could not be explained away by faulty memory.

There were many other witnesses, to some of whose evidence I shall refer in due

course. They included three solicitors, one of whom was Mr C S H Cooper, the partner
in the second defendant firm who was alone responsible for the acts or omissions alleged   *a*
against them in the action, and two land agents. The judge, while recognising that on
the scores of recollection and impartiality they were not all equal, accepted each of them
as a witness of candour. Inevitably, from January 1977 onwards, when the professional
men first became involved in the matter, both they and the judge relied mostly on their
contemporary attendance notes and correspondence. Indeed, between 12 January and 4
April 1977 there is little other evidence to which reference need be made.   *b*

The judge described the plaintiff at the beginning of 1977 as desiring to leave behind
him not a dilapidated but a respectable farm to be sold (as he then intended) for the
benefit of the charitable institutions who were the residuary legatees under his existing
will. On the other hand, he was, like most aged people, increasingly close with money,
and he did not want to deplete his substantial deposits in building societies. Nor did he
wish ever to leave the farmhouse. The defendant had for many weeks been helping at   *c*
Chasewoods, and not charging for the labour he supplied. Hence it was the most natural
thing in the world to consider whether the defendant might not assume control of
Chasewoods, get it into an improved condition at his own expense and buy it on the
plaintiff's death. On the face of it, that would be a good solution of the plaintiff's problem
bearing in mind that he was already 85.   *d*

In the early part of January 1977 Tom, who was at that time resentful of the defendant's
influence and jealous of his position at Chasewoods, was watching and spying and
making notes of conversations between the plaintiff and the defendant. By 12 January
he had become aware that the plaintiff was proposing to come to some arrangement with
the defendant. However, it appears that from the start the arrangement was to include
Tom, who was to go into partnership with the defendant under a tenancy granted by the
plaintiff. The judge thought that this was probably the defendant's suggestion, although   *e*
he found his motive hard to ascertain. In any event, on 17 January Tom and the
defendant had a long meeting with Mr F R Williamson, the senior partner of Messrs
Morrell Peel & Gamlen, solicitors, of Oxford, who had acted for Tom in connection with
another matter in 1972 or 1973. The judge described Mr Williamson in giving evidence
as a model of impartiality and candour. I would add that at the time of his involvement   *f*
in the matter he made many full and clear attendance notes of meetings and telephone
conversations to which he was a party. He wrote many letters, some of them long and all
of them careful. From these materials it is clear that Mr Williamson's advice was sound
throughout and his conduct of the matter quite admirable. If his advice had been
followed, the story might have had a different ending.

At the meeting on 17 January 1977 Tom and the defendant told Mr Williamson that   *g*
the plaintiff proposed to let the farm to them at a nominal rent of £500 and that the
defendant planned to put capital into the farm. The plaintiff was to have the farmhouse
for his life, free of rent and rates. Tom and the defendant were to work the farm in
partnership on a fifty-fifty basis. The defendant did not want to instruct his solicitor at
that stage. Mr Williamson said that while he might be prepared to act for the tenant
partners he could not in any circumstances act for the plaintiff. It was up to the plaintiff   *h*
whether he appointed a lawyer or not but there were obviously very considerable legal
problems for him in the plan which was envisaged. Mr Williamson quoted capital
transfer tax and capital gains tax as examples. Tom and the defendant clearly wanted
something to be done quickly, but Mr Williamson said that it was a difficult business
and that in no circumstances would he proceed unless he had the backing of a valuer
who could say that the terms of the arrangement were commercially fair. It was agreed   *j*
to instruct the defendant's valuer, Mr A L Hanks, of Messrs Tayler & Fletcher of Stow-
on-the-Wold. Mr Williamson prepared a draft tenancy agreement in favour of the
defendant and Tom on a printed form supplied by Mr Hanks. It provided for a yearly
tenancy from 1 February 1977 at an annual rent of £500 and permitted the plaintiff to
continue to reside in the farmhouse without payment of rent. It also contained a clause
exonerating both landlord and tenant from any obligation to put the holding in any

better state of repair than it was at the date of the agreement, as evidenced by a schedule

a of condition which was to be annexed thereto.

As early as 20 January 1977 Tom appeared to be having second thoughts about the proposal. He told Mr Williamson that he was being put off to some extent by the pressing away in which the defendant was proceeding. On the same day Mr Williamson wrote to Mr Hanks enclosing an amended copy of the standard form of tenancy agreement. He ended his letter by observing that it was an odd situation where considerable care must

b be taken. He said that his firm did not and could not act for the plaintiff, who should in their view have separate legal advice.

On 21 January Mr Hanks inspected Chasewoods and found that it was in a very run-down condition throughout. In view of that he considered that the suggested rental of £500 for the initial period would be reasonable, because it was obvious that the tenants would have to expend a fairly large amount of money from which they would not

c receive any income for some time. Mr Hanks took the draft tenancy agreement with him in order to explain the details to the plaintiff and also to fill in the blanks at the same time. He urged the plaintiff to consult his solicitor, but the plaintiff declined and insisted on signing the draft then and there, even though the schedule of condition had not yet been prepared. On 27 January the defendant paid the plaintiff the sum of £8,729, representing half the value of the livestock. On 2 February Mr Williamson saw Tom

d alone, and then him and the defendant together. On the following day he wrote a three-page letter to the defendant, with copies to Tom and Mr Hanks, in order to summarise the position which they had reached after two meetings. Early on he repeated that he could not act for the plaintiff. He added that he thought that the defendant should instruct his own solicitor to advise him on the terms of the partnership. He also pointed out that Mr Hanks could not properly act for the plaintiff as well as for him and Tom

e and continued as follows:

> 'It follows that Mr. Goldsworthy senior should instruct someone to act for him. He has refused to do so to date. He should instruct both a solictor and a valuer. If he will not engage both then he simply must have one or the other and if it comes to a choice I think that a solicitor is the more important.'

f

Later Mr Williamson said:

> 'From my talk with Tom yesterday I gather that his father has the idea that he will hold on to some of the stock; we really must avoid uncertainties of this kind. Before we go any further we must make sure that Mr. Goldsworthy senior (with the
> *g* help of professional advice) understands that he is giving up the farm (apart from the house and the garden and paddock) and that he will in future have no say over what happens there. He must also understand that the stock, apart from the pigs, will not be his to sell or to deal with in any way. This is absolutely fundamental and I cannot stress it too strongly.'

After Mr Williamson had dealt with the partnership provisions and another matter,
h he ended as follows:

> 'It is difficult to over-emphasise the delicacy of the position which has been reached now. Mr. Goldsworthy senior has, without proper advice, signed a draft tenancy agreement intended to be effective from the 1st February. You have, without advice from us, paid him a sum representing one half of the value of the
> *j* stock. Mr. Goldsworthy senior shows every sign of wanting to continue to control the stock and he cannot do so without retaining the farm or part of it. As between you and Tom there are many points to be thrashed out so that both of you know where you are and are fully protected. I am sending copies of this letter to Tom and to Mr. Hanks. The next step is for you and Tom to see Mr. Goldsworthy senior, make sure that he properly understands that the arrangements include his giving up the farm completely (apart from the pigs) and that he will take separate advice.

Mr. Hanks must deal with the Schedule of Condition and we must discuss in more detail the partnership terms. Until these things are done your money is at risk and *a* Tom's position unprotected.'

On 3 February the defendant consulted his own solicitor, Mr R Q H Jaggar, of Messrs Jaggar & Co of Swindon, on the telephone. However, it appears that the defendant did not go back to him again until the beginning of April and neither he nor Tom went back to Mr Williamson until the middle of March. What seems to have happened was that the *b* defendant was running the farm with some, perhaps not much, help from Tom. He was in close contact with the plaintiff, but neither of them was talking much to Tom. It appears that during this period the plaintiff wrote out some instructions for a new will. The second page of these is dated 1 March 1977. From them it appears that the plaintiff, after giving various small legacies, and annuities to Tom and a woman friend of £2,000 and £1,000 respectively, wanted his residue to be divided between two charitable *c* institutions. The instructions also provided for the defendant to have the first refusal on Chasewoods at a price agreed between agents on both sides. Those instructions must have been handed by the plaintiff to the defendant, although it is not known when. They reappear in the story at the end of June 1977. The defendant said in evidence that the plaintiff had told him that he had left provisions in his will for him to buy Chasewoods. He said that the plaintiff had told him that before he went there in the autumn of 1976, *d* but I think it more likely that it was not until February or March 1977.

On 21 March 1977 Mr Williamson advised Tom to bring matters to a head with the defendant in order to prevent him from being able to claim that he had acted on the unexchanged tenancy agreement. It seems to have had the desired effect because on 24 March the defendant wrote to Tom maintaining the offer of a partnership, but offering as an alternative to pay £10,000 cash 'and you carry on working with me as we have *e* been doing the last few months'. The £10,000 was in fact offered in respect of the half interest in the stock which on 2 February the defendant had said that the plaintiff intended to give to Tom. The defendant said that he had discussed the matter with the plaintiff and that it had got to be settled by 31 March as after that date he was going to consult the plaintiff again about the whole matter. On 25 March the defendant spoke on the telephone and wrote to Mr Williamson in similar terms, complaining that Tom had *f* not been pulling his weight. He reiterated that if Tom did not decide to agree by 31 March he would withdraw his offer and return to the plaintiff to renegotiate the situation. In fact there was a burglary at Chasewoods on 30 March and the defendant extended the deadline until the evening of Monday 4 April. On the same day the defendant spoke again to Mr Williamson on the telephone and asked what he should do if the negotiations broke down. When Mr Williamson told him that he should pull out, he said that he had *g* already done a lot of work and that he was not prepared to do so.

I have now arrived at a period crucial to the question of undue influence. On the afternoon of 4 April there was a meeting at Chasewoods attended by the plaintiff, Tom, the defendant and the defendant's father. Also there was a Mr Brian Elliott, a friend of Tom, who gave evidence at the trial. The judge found that the meeting was inconclusive, that the plaintiff maintained his reluctance to have independent advice and that the *h* Brickells, if they did not actually encourage him in his refusal, at least did nothing to alter it. The judge accepted Mr Elliott as a witness of honesty, notwithstanding his intense dislike of the Brickells. The judge found that the ultimatum for Tom's decision was extended until 12 April, but he was not satisfied that any clear arrangement was made for an adjourned meeting on that day.

During the rest of that week, which was Holy Week, there was much activity on all *j* sides. Both Tom and the defendant, separately, consulted Mr Williamson; the defendant consulted Mr Jaggar; and the two solicitors were in communication with one another. All this was on the footing that the draft tenancy agreement signed by the plaintiff was to be perfected and that a partnership agreement between the defendant and Tom was to be negotiated and drawn up. The judge found it difficult to say to what extent and for

how long the proposed partners were sincere in their instructions at this time. Earlier in
a his judgment, but speaking, I think, also of this period, he had said that Tom was not in
earnest in the negotiations, that he saw very well that the defendant meant to acquire the
freehold on the plaintiff's death and that there was no secure future for him in the
arrangements. One thing which is clear is that the defendant's father did not mean the
partnership with Tom to take place if he could help it. During that week he called five
times on Mr Elliott, whom he no doubt regarded as the best channel of approach to Tom,
b pressing the defendant's offer to buy Tom out for £10,000, which he increased on the
second visit to £15,000. The defendant swore that he knew nothing of those conversations
at the time, or at least that he did not know that his father made more than one visit to
Mr Elliott. The judge did not find it easy to accept the defendant's ignorance of these
visits. He also found that the defendant's father played an active part in the matter. He
did not elaborate, but I think he may have inferred that the father advised the defendant
c not to enter into partnership with Tom and to secure an option to purchase the freehold
on the plaintiff's death.

After Easter, as the judge found, no more was in fact heard of partnership with Tom.
On Tuesday, 12 April the defendant saw the plaintiff alone. He had already made an
appointment to attend at Mr Hanks's office next morning for the preparation of a fresh
tenancy agreement in his name alone. Mr Hanks was not going to be in the office, but
d he said that his secretary, Miss Page, could type the necessary alterations on a printed
form, and so instructed her. Mr Hanks assumed that nothing more than a change of
tenants was required. Miss Page, who also gave evidence, did not remember the occasion
clearly, but thought that on 13 April the defendant gave her an agreement to copy and
that he dictated two new clauses from two scraps of paper. The tenancy agreement did
in fact contain two new clauses as follows:
e

'25. The Tenant shall be given the first option to purchase the Holding at the
prevailing value upon the demise of the Landlord.

34. The rent to remain at the figure stated hereon during the life of the Landlord
without any increase to allow the Tenant to improve the Holding.'

f It is hardly necessary to point out that these two new clauses were on their face very
beneficial to the defendant. Although cl 34 contemplated that the defendant would
improve the holding, there was no obligation on him to do so and the clause exonerating
either party from any obligation to put the holding in any better state of repair remained
unaltered. Furthermore, no schedule of condition was annexed to the agreement, as
contemplated by its terms.

g Although the judge asked himself how this revision of the document came about, he
did not, as I understand his judgment, feel able to answer that question. He evidently
did not think that it was a crucial one and in the light of his findings on the question of
undue influence that was no doubt right. Speaking for myself, I would think it quite
possible that the plaintiff drafted the clauses on 12 April for the defendant to dictate to
Miss Page the next day. But that does not mean that the proposal for their inclusion
h originated with him rather than with the defendant or his father.

On Wednesday, 13 April, after his visit to Mr Hanks's office, the defendant visited the
plaintiff at Chasewoods once more. He went in a van driven by Sandra Laity. They were
accompanied by a retired superintendent of police, Mr A T Smith, who gave evidence at
the trial. Mr Smith sat in the front with Sandra and the defendant in the back. The judge
thought that a van was used rather than a car in order to conceal the proceedings as much
j as possible from Tom's prying eyes. However, that wish did not seem to him of itself to
discredit the defendant in any way. When they got to the farm Sandra remained in the
van while Mr Smith and the defendant went into the house. The defendant asked Mr
Smith to wait in the scullery. He said that he waited there for quite a long time, at least
ten minutes, perhaps a little more, and that he was in the house altogether for about half
an hour. He could hear the sound of conversation between the plaintiff and the defendant

in the kitchen, but could not distinguish the words spoken. When he was called in to witness the signatures on the two documents, each of them prepared in duplicate parts, he was rather peeved to find that the plaintiff had already signed them. However, the plaintiff acknowledged his signature and told Mr Smith that he was satisfied with the contents. The defendant signed in Mr Smith's presence. Mr Smith attested the signatures and saw to the dating of the documents. One of them was the tenancy agreement, which had been typed in the morning by Miss Page. The other, which according to the defendant had been prepared by his deceased accountant, Mr Dawson, was a brief fifty-fifty partnership agreement between the plaintiff and the defendant. Neither document made any reference to Tom.

I have now stated all the material facts down to the execution of the tenancy agreement whose validity is in issue in these proceedings. I must now deal with subsequent events in so far as they are material to the questions of undue influence and affirmation.

Mr Hanks's firm saw to the stamping of the tenancy agreement and its counterpart and then returned them to the defendant. He said that he gave the counterpart to the plaintiff, but it was not forthcoming at the trial. In late April the defendant's father brought the tenancy agreement and one part of the partnership agreement to Mr Jaggar, who knew nothing of their origin. Mr Jaggar, quite correctly, then registered a land charge class C(iv) in respect of the option to purchase the freehold in cl 25 of the tenancy agreement. On 4 May Mr Jaggar told Mr Williamson that he suspected that Tom had been bypassed as a result of an agreement between the plaintiff and the defendant. At the end of that month Tom, who had seen a cheque book on a joint account at a bank in Swindon, told Mr Williamson that he was fairly sure that the plaintiff had gone into some form of partnership with the defendant. In early June Tom wrote to Mr Williamson to say that he had decided to take fresh advice and asking him to send on the papers to another firm of solicitors.

Mr Williamson's last action in the matter was to speak informally to Mr Cooper, who had acted for the plaintiff before 1977. The result of that conversation was that on 23 June Mr Cooper wrote to the plaintiff, out of the blue as it were, suggesting that the will which he had made for him in 1973 before the introduction of capital transfer tax ought to be reconsidered in the light of that tax. On the following day, presumably after a conversation with the plaintiff, the defendant's father called on Mr Jaggar in his office and handed him the plaintiff's handwritten instructions for a new will dated 1 March 1977 earlier referred to. They of course included the provision for the defendant to have the first refusal on Chasewoods and Mr Jaggar was very properly reluctant to accept instructions to draw a will from someone who was a close relation of a prospective beneficiary. However, Mr Brickell senior put it to Mr Jaggar as what the latter described as a sort of welfare exercise, it being explained to him that the plaintiff was having difficulty in communicating with his own solicitor because Tom was intercepting his mail. Mr Jaggar was thus persuaded to prepare a draft will and to visit the plaintiff on 30 June in order to obtain his instructions on it.

At that meeting Mr Jaggar told the plaintiff straight away that he was instructed on the other side and could not act for him. The plaintiff appeared to be disappointed. He explained that he and Tom were not on speaking terms and that he found it difficult to get into Oxford to see his solicitor. The plaintiff then produced Mr Cooper's letter of 23 June and Mr Jaggar was delighted to find that he had prepared the plaintiff's existing will. Mr Jaggar then told the plaintiff that he was prepared to go through the will with him, to take his instructions and pass the whole thing over to Mr Cooper the following day. On 1 July he did indeed telephone Mr Cooper and he wrote to him later that day enclosing a copy of the draft that he had prepared in accordance with the plaintiff's instructions and asking for Mr Cooper's comments on it. The letter continued:

'I will then pass a copy to Mr. Goldsworthy through my client Mr. R. J. Brickell of Witney; and, when the Testator has given his final approval, you will be able to engross and obtain his signature. I know the allegation will be that Mr. Goldsworthy was not of a testamentary capacity when he made this Will or was under undue influence. This is why I recommended to him that he had two Doctors to witness it. He laughed at the thought and said that he would accept the advice and would arrange for his G.P. and a lady Doctor friend of many years standing to act as witnesses.'

Mr Jaggar added that he held the original of the 1973 will, although whether this was handed to him by the defendant's father on 24 June or by the plaintiff on 30 June is not, I think, clear. Then Mr Jaggar said that he had the plaintiff's handwritten instructions dated 1 March 1977 which, he said, clearly showed that, at that date at any rate, he had all his faculties about him and knew exactly what he was doing. There was then further correspondence between the two solicitors. On 5 September Mr Jaggar sent Mr Cooper an engrossment of the will. On 7 September he wrote again, saying that it would be quite wrong for the defendant to have anything to do with the signing of it:

'Anticipating as we do that it will be challenged by Tom Goldsworthy, Mr. Brickell's involvement would inevitably lead to an allegation of undue influence, in view of the option in Mr. Brickell's favour to purchase Chasewoods Farm in the new Will.'

Between then and the spring of 1978 Mr Cooper tried several times unsuccessfully to make an appointment with the plaintiff for the execution of the will. In the mean time he received several letters from Mr Jaggar on the subject which were presumably written on the instructions of the defendant. In the end, the plaintiff sent for the will and at the beginning of April 1978 he informed Mr Cooper that it had been duly executed and witnessed by two doctors.

The partnership between the plaintiff and the defendant, which was treated in their accounts as having commenced on 1 February 1977, continued for two years. During that time the defendant managed the farm. He supplied labour from his other farms without charging wages against the partnership. The plaintiff kept the books and instructed the firm's accountants. The partnership was terminated after two years' trading, on the footing that the defendant acquired and paid cash for the plaintiff's half interest. It is the plaintiff's case that it was terminated by the defendant, but the judge thought that it was terminated by agreement. The point is not, I think, an important one. What is important is that the tenancy agreement, having been in the sole name of the defendant and not in the joint names of the partners, has since enabled the defendant to farm Chasewoods for his own benefit.

The judge found that up to the termination of the partnership the defendant had not ploughed back any substantial profit into the improvement of Chasewoods. The only significant item seems to have been the sum of £1,725 which the defendant expended in the year ended 31 January 1978 in repairing the roof of the farmhouse. I should add that up to 31 January 1982 the only further significant item was the sum of £2,455 expended during the year ended 31 January 1980 in repair and renewal of fences and gates. The judge also found that, roughly speaking, the defendant used his initial cash contribution to the partnership capital and his share of the two years' profit to buy the plaintiff out. Notwithstanding cl 34 of the tenancy agreement, the annual rent paid by the defendant was on dissolution increased to £3,000, the extra £2,500 having been sometimes, but not consistently, referred to as a consultancy fee. That figure is still considerably below the market rent, which on one estimate made just before the trial was as high as £12,696. The defendant has paid the rates on the farmhouse and, it appears, on the cottage occupied by Tom.

The next phase of the matter, as the judge put it, began almost accidentally. In or about August 1979 the defendant instructed Mr R C Cheeseman, a solicitor practising in Witney, to write to Tom complaining of his alleged interference on the farm. This letter got into the hands of the plaintiff, who thought that it was directed at him, and consulted Mr Cooper. The position was quickly clarified by Mr Cheeseman to Mr Cooper but it led, between October 1979 and May 1980, to correspondence between the two solicitors as to the terms and effect of the tenancy agreement and to two discussions of an hour or so each between Mr Cooper and the plaintiff at Chasewoods, the first in January and the second in May 1980.

The claim against the second defendant firm made it necessary for the judge to deal with the events of this period at some length, but in regard to the questions of undue influence and affirmation the salient points can be summarised as follows. Mr Cooper, who had never seen the tenancy agreement before, realised that, if, as Mr Cheeseman was contending, the expression 'at the prevailing value' in cl 25 required a valuation on a sitting tenant basis, the arrangement had been very unfavourable to the plaintiff. Taking the plaintiff's spot valuation with vacant possession at £1m, Mr Cooper told him, in a letter written after their January discussion, that he was virtually giving the defendant £½m. Secondly, and despite the evidence of notes made by Tom whilst he was eavesdropping on the January and May discussions, the judge found that the plaintiff did understand that the defendant would on his death get Chasewoods for far less than its value with vacant possession. It also appears that the plaintiff was not greatly surprised or perturbed when he was told of this. Thirdly, whatever may or may not have been Mr Cooper's duty to go behind the tenancy agreement and investigate the circumstances in which it was entered into, he never did make any such investigation and neither he nor the plaintiff knew at that time that the latter had, or might have, a right to set it aside. Fourthly, whatever may have passed between the plaintiff and Mr Cooper, the latter never did or said anything which could have led Mr Cheeseman to understand that the plaintiff knew that he had a right to set the tenancy agreement aside or, if he did, that he was not going to enforce that right. Mr Cooper's efforts were confined to advancing such arguments as he could against Mr Cheeseman's construction of the tenancy agreement.

In the summer of 1982 the plaintiff consulted a land agent, Mr G P Candy of the firm of Messrs Carter Jonas based at their Kidlington office, apparently with a view to raising the defendant's rent. It was Mr Candy's involvement in the matter which led to the plaintiff's receiving advice as to the validity of the tenancy agreement. At about the same time the plaintiff was becoming reconciled to Tom. He executed a general power of attorney in Tom's favour in September 1982. In February 1983 he executed a will bequeathing his whole estate to Tom after payment of pecuniary legacies totalling £4,000. As the judge observed, the reconciliation with Tom made litigation inevitable. On 4 January 1983 the writ in this action was issued.

The statement of claim, as well as alleging that the plaintiff was induced to sign the tenancy agreement by the defendant's undue influence, pleaded that he was induced to do so by the defendant's representation that it was in standard form and contained no unusual clauses. That contention was rejected by Goulding J. He also did not believe the plaintiff's evidence that the defendant pressed him to sign the tenancy and partnership agreements without reading them, that he asked the defendant to let him first take the advice of his land agent and was refused, and that the whole business on 13 April 1977 was over in a few minutes. It is clear from this and other passages in his judgment that the judge did not regard the case as one where express or actual undue influence, dishonest persuasion as it was called in argument, was proved.

I now come to the question of undue influence. On this question the argument of counsel for the defendant was mainly founded on four propositions. Firstly, since the plaintiff's case has throughout been one of dishonest persuasion, it can only succeed if there is proved to have been some form of dishonesty or conscious abuse of power by the defendant. Secondly, the plaintiff must prove a relationship which can properly be described as one of domination of the plaintiff by the defendant. Thirdly, the judge's findings as to the situation, physical and mental condition, character and disposition of the plaintiff in 1976–77 are wholly inconsistent with the existence of such a relationship. Fourthly, the transaction effected by the tenancy and partnership agreements was not manifestly and unfairly disadvantageous to the plaintiff. The fourth of these propositions

a stands on its own and can be treated separately. The first three run more or less together and, since they have proceeded on some notable misconceptions as to the circumstances in which courts of equity have set aside transactions on the ground of undue influence, require those circumstances to be restated.

Undue influence is of two kinds: (1) express or, as it is nowadays more usually known, actual undue influence; and (2) that which in certain circumstances is presumed from a

b confidential relationship, by which in this context is meant a relationship wherein one party has ceded such a degree of trust and confidence as to require the other, on grounds of public policy, to show that it has not been betrayed or abused. In cases where there is no confidential relationship actual undue influence must be proved. In cases where there is such a relationship it is sometimes alleged, but need not be proved and may never have occurred. Occasionally, even where there is no direct evidence of influence, it is found

c that there is both a confidential relationship and actual undue influence; cf *Re Craig (decd), Meneces v Middleton* [1970] 2 All ER 390, [1971] Ch 95.

At least since the time of Lord Eldon LC, equity has steadfastly and wisely refused to put limits on the relationships to which the presumption can apply. Nor do I believe that it has ever been distinctly held that there is any relationship from which it cannot in any circumstances be dissociated. But there are several well-defined relationships, such as

d parent and child, superior and member of a sisterhood, doctor and patient and solicitor and client, to which the presumption is, as it were, presumed to apply unless the contrary is proved. In such relationships it would seem that you only have to look at the relative status of the parties in order to presume that the requisite degree of trust and confidence is there. But there are many and various other relationships lacking a recognisable status to which the presumption has been held to apply. In all of these relationships, whether

e of the first kind or the second, the principle is the same. It is that the degree of trust and confidence is such that the party in whom it is reposed, either because he is or has become an adviser of the other or because he has been entrusted with the management of his affairs or everyday needs or for some other reason, is in a position to influence him into effecting the transaction of which complaint is later made. And with respect to certain

f arguments which have been advanced in the present case it is here necessary to state the obvious, which is that, in cases where functions of this sort constitute the substratum of the relationship, there is no need for any identity of subject matter between the advice which is given or the affairs which are managed on the one hand and the transaction of which complaint is made on the other. Nor, as will be shown, is it necessary for the party in whom the trust and confidence is reposed to dominate the other party in any sense in

g which that word is generally understood.

Because they have occasioned little or no debate on this appeal, three further general observations may be briefly made. Firstly, it is not every relationship of trust and confidence to which the presumption applies. No generalisation is possible beyond the definition already attempted. Secondly, with relationships to which it does apply the presumption is not perfected and remains inoperative until the party who has ceded the

h trust and confidence makes a gift so large, or enters into a transaction so improvident, as not to be reasonably accounted for on the ground of friendship, relationship, charity or other ordinary motives on which ordinary men act. Although influence might have been presumed beforehand, it is only then that it is presumed to have been undue. Thirdly, in a case where the presumption has come into operation the gift or transaction will be set aside, unless it proved to have been the spontaneous act of the donor or grantor

j acting in circumstances which enable him to exercise an independent will and which justify the court in holding that the gift or transaction was the result of a free exercise of his will.

The first proposition of counsel for the defendant ignores the distinction between actual and presumed undue influence. It is true that no actual influence was found. But, if the judge was correct in holding, first and expressly, that there was a confidential relationship, secondly and impliedly, that the transaction was so improvident as not to be reasonably accounted for by ordinary motives and, thirdly and expressly, that it was a not the spontaneous act of the plaintiff acting in the requisite circumstances, no further proof was required. To say that a plaintiff who fails to establish a primary case of actual influence must fail in his attempt to establish a confidential relationship to support the presumption is, with all due respect, a non sequitur.

The second proposition of counsel for the defendant is based on some observations which were made in the House of Lords in *National Westminster Bank plc v Morgan* [1985] b 1 All ER 821, [1985] AC 686.

I would readily accept the third proposition, which is that on the facts found by the judge the relationship was not one of domination of the plaintiff by the defendant. The question here is whether, as a matter of law, the presumption can apply if it was not.

In the passage from his judgment which I have already quoted Goulding J found that the defendant had acquired an influence over the plaintiff, based on and arising out of a c particular association and an advisory capacity, well short, no doubt, of domination, which nevertheless made it his duty to take care of the plaintiff in any transaction between them. He added that those phrases were suggested by the language of Evershed MR in *Tufton v Sperni* [1952] 2 TLR 516. There the plaintiff's case at trial had been that the defendant had acquired a complete control or domination over the plaintiff, so that he ceased to be a free agent and his mind became a mere vehicle or channel for the d defendant's schemes. The case so made was not one of actual undue influence, but an extreme case based on the presumption. Romer J rejected it on the facts and it was not pursued in this court. The sole question on the appeal was, therefore, as Jenkins LJ expressed it (at 528):

> '... whether the defendant, though not in a position of actual domination over e the plaintiff, was, nevertheless, placed in such a relation of confidence and trust to the plaintiff as to make it incumbent on the defendant to show that the transaction now impeached was not brought about by an abuse of that relation and of the influence arising therefrom.'

That question, after a full consideration of some leading nineteenth century cases, was f unanimously answered in the affirmative. Although the facts of the case were somewhat special, it was held that the defendant had indeed reposed the requisite degree of trust and confidence in the defendant. In the passage on which Goulding J mainly relied, Evershed MR said (at 525):

> 'In my judgment, the question is not of domination but of influence, well short, g no doubt, of domination, based on and arising out of a particular association and an advisory capacity.'

Jenkins LJ, in reference to the effect on the mind of the plaintiff of any advice given him, or proposal made to him, by the defendant, said (at 532):

> '... I think ... it must be assumed that his advice would, by reason of their special h relationship, carry more weight with, and be more likely of acceptance by, the plaintiff than the advice of a stranger, and for the purposes of the principle here in question, I think this provides a sufficient degree of potential influence.'

Morris LJ said (at 534):

> 'I have reached the conclusion that a relationship of confidence existed, and that j the defendant was in a position to exert influence over the plaintiff ...'

It cannot be doubted that in *Tufton v Sperni* all three members of this court held that domination of one party by the other was not necessary in order to make out a case based on the presumption. In expressing that opinion they were doing no more and no less than to subscribe to the test laid down in the leading nineteenth century authorities.

Thus in *Huguenin v Baseley* (1807) 14 Ves 273 at 300, [1803–13] All ER Rep 1 at 13 Lord Eldon LC said:

'Take it, that she intended to give it to him: it is by no means out of the reach of the principle. The question is, not, whether she knew what she was doing, had done, or proposed to do, but how the intention was produced: whether all that care and providence was placed round her, as against those, who advised her, which, from their situation and relation with respect to her, they were bound to exert on her behalf.'

In *Tufton v Sperni* [1952] 2 TLR 516 at 521 Evershed MR said of this passage:

'In other words, the relation must be one which makes it the duty of one party to take care of the other . . .'

That observation was cited with approval by the Privy Council in *Antony v Weerasekera* [1953] 1 WLR 1007 at 1011, where it was said to be clear from what Evershed MR had said that the duty of taking care included the duty of giving advice.

In *Billage v Southee* (1852) 9 Hare 534 at 540, 68 ER 623 at 626 Turner V-C said:

'The jurisdiction is founded on the principle of correcting abuses of confidence, and I shall have no hesitation in saying it ought to be applied, whatever may be the nature of the confidence reposed, or the relation of the parties between whom it has subsisted. I take the principle to be one of universal application, and the cases in which the jurisdiction has been exercised—those of trustees and *cestui que trust*, guardian and ward, attorney and client, surgeon and patient—to be merely instances of the application of the principle.'

In *Tate v Williamson* (1866) LR 1 Eq 528 at 536–537 Page Wood V-C (later Lord Hatherley LC) said:

'The broad principle on which the Court acts in cases of this description is that, wherever there exists such a confidence, of whatever character that confidence may be, as enables the person in whom confidence or trust is reposed, to exert influence over the person trusting him, the Court will not allow any transaction between the parties to stand, unless there has been the fullest and fairest explanation and communication of every particular resting in the breast of the one who seeks to establish a contract with the person so trusting him.'

On appeal Lord Chelmsford LC said (LR 2 Ch App 55 at 61):

'Wherever two persons stand in such a relation that, while it continues, confidence is necessarily reposed by one, and the influence which naturally grows out of that confidence is possessed by the other, and this confidence is abused, or the influence is exerted to obtain an advantage at the expense of the confiding party, the person so availing himself of his position will not be permitted to retain the advantage, although the transaction could not have been impeached if no such confidential relation had existed.'

In *Allcard v Skinner* (1887) 36 Ch D 145 at 171, [1886–90] All ER Rep 90 at 93 Cotton LJ referred to the second class of case:

'. . . where the relations between the donor and donee have at or shortly before the execution of the gift been such as to raise a presumption that the donee had influence over the donor.'

Lindley LJ said (36 Ch D 145 at 181, [1886–90] All ER Rep 90 at 98):

'The second group consists of cases in which the position of the donor to the donee has been such that it has been the duty of the donee to advise the donor, or even to manage his property for him.'

It will be observed that none of these eminent judges thought it necessary, in order to make out a case based on the presumption, to show that the relationship was one of domination of one party by the other. Everything which they said is consistent with the notion that it is enough to show that the party in whom the trust and confidence is reposed is in a position to exert influence over him who reposes it. The improbability of there being any other standard is emphasised by a consideration of some of the well-defined relationships, for example doctor and patient or solicitor and client. The reason why the presumption applies to those relationships is that doctors and solicitors are trusted and confided in by their patients and clients to give them conscientious and disinterested advice on matters which profoundly affect, in the one case, their physical and mental and, in the other, their material well-being. It is natural to presume that out of that trust and confidence grows influence. But it would run contrary to human experience to presume that every patient is dominated by his doctor or every client by his solicitor. Even in jest such cases must be rare. And while that may not be equally true of other relationships, for example, parent and child, it is not the function of a presumption to presume the generally improbable.

For these reasons I would have taken it to be clear that the second proposition of counsel for the defendant was contrary to established principle and incorrect. However, he has referred us to several passages in Lord Scarman's opinion in *National Westminster Bank plc v Morgan* [1985] 1 All ER 821 at 829–831, [1985] AC 686 at 707–709 where it is said that he and the other members of the House have now held that the presumption of undue influence can only apply to a relationship in which one party assumes a role of dominating influence over the other. The opinions in that case were delivered about a week after Goulding J gave judgment in this.

In order to see whether counsel for the defendant can make anything of this point, it is first of all necessary to observe that the relationship which was there under consideration was that between banker and customer. The House of Lords, distinguishing the decision of the majority of this court in *Lloyds Bank Ltd v Bundy* [1974] 3 All ER 757, [1975] QB 326 on the facts, held that that relationship is not one which ordinarily gives rise to the presumption of undue influence. It would seem that the decision could have been based on that ground alone, that is to say on the proposition that a banker, being a person having a pre-existing and conflicting interest in any loan transaction with a customer, cannot ordinarily be trusted and confided in so as to come under a duty to take care of the customer and give him disinterested advice. On that footing it would have been enough to say that a banker is not ordinarily in a position to exert influence over his customer and no question of domination need have arisen. However, the main ground of their Lordships' decision was that before any transaction can be set aside for undue influence, whether actual or presumed, it has to be shown that the transaction has been wrongful in that it has constituted a manifest and unfair disadvantage to the person seeking to avoid it. And it is in that part of Lord Scarman's opinion that the references to dominating influence are, incidentally as it appears, to be found.

In developing his reasoning in support of the main ground of the decision, Lord Scarman relied partly on the decision of the Privy Council in *Poosathurai v Kannappa Chettiar* (1919) LR 47 Ind App 1. That was a case under the Indian Contract Act 1872, s 16(3), which provided:

> 'Where a person who is in a position to dominate the will of another enters into a contract with him, and the transaction appears on the face of it, or on the evidence, to be unconscionable, the burden of proving that such contract was not induced by undue influence shall lie upon the person in the position to dominate the will of the other.'

What was decided in that case, and it was for this that the House of Lords relied on it, was that a person who sought to set a contract aside under s 16 had to establish not only that the other party was in a position to dominate his will, but also that the other party

had used that position to obtain an unfair advantage over him. It appears that it had not
a been suggested that there was any difference between Indian and English law on the
question of unfair advantage. However, it seems possible that Lord Scarman may have
thought that the similarities were more numerous, because he said ([1985] 1 All ER 821
at 829, [1985] AC 686 at 706):

b 'Lord Shaw, after indicating that there was no difference on the subject of undue
influence between the Indian Contract Act 1872 and English law quoted the Indian
statutory provision . . .'

What Lord Shaw in *Poosathurai v Kannappa Chettiar* LR 47 Ind App 1 at 3 said was:

'The real and only point at issue between the parties is whether the deed in
question should be cancelled on the ground of undue influence . . . It is not necessary
c to speculate whether the provisions of the Indian Contract Act differ in any
particulars from the doctrines of the English law upon this subject. For no such
differences are suggested to have any bearing on the issue between these parties.
The issue in the present suit is an issue of fact . . .'

That passage seems clearly to leave open the question whether the similarities went
beyond the one point of unfair advantage.
d In the circumstances it seems impossible to regard the judgment of the Privy Council
in *Poosathurai v Kannappa Chettiar*, in which I may add no reference was made to any of
the English cases, as any authority for the proposition that in English law the presumption
of undue influence can only apply to a relationship in which one party assumes a role of
dominating influence over the other. If, which I very much doubt, the House of Lords
intended to hold the contrary, then I would respectfully disagree with them and point
e out that the holding was not necessary to the decision in that case. I will add that it is to
my mind inconceivable that their Lordships could have intended, sub silentio, to overrule
not only *Tufton v Sperni* but many other leading cases from *Huguenin v Baseley* onwards.
It follows that Goulding J, in adopting the language of Evershed MR in *Tufton v Sperni*,
applied an entirely correct test in the present case. The next question, arising on the third
f proposition of counsel for the defendant, is whether, if that test is applied, the facts
support the judge's conclusion that there was a confidential relationship to which the
presumption of undue influence applied. In my judgment there was ample and satisfying
material to support that conclusion. In addition to the facts and matters specifically found
and recorded by the judge when speaking of the relationship, I would refer in particular
to the marked and continuing involvement of the defendant and his father in the
g plaintiff's testamentary affairs. In the end this must primarily be a question for the judge,
who, although he did not see or hear the plaintiff and thought nothing of his evidence as
transcribed, did see and hear the defendant give evidence for the best part of two days in
all. It was he who was at the best advantage to decide whether the degree of trust and
confidence reposed by the plaintiff in the defendant was such that the latter was in a
position to influence the former into entering into the tenancy agreement. In my view
h the judge was well entitled to conclude that the defendant had become a business adviser
of the plaintiff and had been entrusted with the management of his farming business
and some at least of his personal affairs and everyday needs. Finally, bearing in mind that
it was the defendant who seemed to offer to the plaintiff the resolution of the two serious
difficulties which made him unhappy, namely his poor relationship with Tom and the
poor condition of his farm, I think that the case is in this respect an overwhelming one. I
j think that the judge's decision on the facts is unimpeachable.
The fourth proposition of counsel for the defendant is based on the main ground of
the decision in *National Westminister Bank plc v Morgan* [1985] 1 All ER 821, [1985] AC
686. In a case like the present the test is in practice no different from that which is built
into the requirement that the transaction should be so improvident as not to be reasonably
accounted for by ordinary motives. The judge did not make an express finding on this

point. He appears to have taken it for granted and in that he can hardly be blamed. Although some time was spent in seeking to persuade us of the validity of the fourth proposition on the facts, I have to say at once that it seems to me to be clear beyond doubt that the transaction was both manifestly and unfairly disadvantageous to the plaintiff and so improvident as not to be reasonably accounted for by ordinary motives. I propose to state my reasons as briefly as I can.

The judge recorded that the evidence suggested that the value of Chasewoods in the plaintiff's hands might have been almost halved by the execution of the tenancy agreement. He went on to say that the low rent and the option to purchase the freehold added to the improvidence, but were of secondary importance, bearing in mind that the plaintiff was 85 and that the estate would almost certainly have to be sold on his death. It is certainly true that the option is not in itself decisive of this question, because on a sale of an agricultural freehold the sitting tenant is usually the obvious purchaser and will usually offer the best price. However, I think that the judge may somewhat have underestimated the significance of the low rent, even assuming, as I am prepared to do, that counsel for the defendant was correct in saying that notwithstanding cl 34 of the tenancy agreement the plaintiff could, under s 8 of the Agricultural Holdings Act 1948, have obtained an increased rent after three years. The real point here is that the £500 rent was regarded by Mr Hanks as reasonable only because it was obvious that the tenant (ie the defendant) would have to expend a fairly large amount of money from which he would not receive any income for some time. But in this respect the plaintiff was left entirely unprotected, both in law, because the tenancy agreement did not oblige the defendant to expend any money, and in fact, because during the three-year period his only significant expenditure was the sum of £1,725 in repairing the roof of the farmhouse. I therefore think that the low rent, although no doubt of secondary importance in terms of money, was in itself a manifest and unfair disadvantage to the plaintiff.

The suggested advantages to the plaintiff on which counsel for the defendant relied were that it secured him in the occupation of his home free of rent and rates and that it brought in a farmer who was willing and able to run the farm efficiently and profitably, so that the plaintiff did not have to rely on Tom. The tenancy and partnership agreements together eliminated the substantial loss and provided instead an immediate income of £500 per annum plus a half share in the profits of the partnership. Counsel for the defendant added that the plaintiff had no interest in the value of his estate after his death, because he knew that Chasewoods would have to be sold and that the proceeds were going to charity. In this connection he relied on the facts, as the judge found, that when Mr Cooper explained to the plaintiff the financial advantages of the tenancy agreement in January 1980 there was not any outburst of indignation on the plaintiff's part, and it appeared to suit him well enough to have his free occupation of the farmhouse secured during his life and to have the farm looked after by the defendant.

The short answer to these submissions is that all the advantages of the arrangement could have been secured to the plaintiff without any of the disadvantages, not by granting a tenancy to the defendant alone or even to the plaintiff and defendant jointly, but by granting a licence to them jointly to occupy the land during the continuation of their partnership and no longer. If the transaction had been so effected, the defendant would not have been entitled to exclusive occupation of the land as against the plaintiff. The licence would therefore have remained such and would not have taken effect as a tenancy from year to year under s 2(1) of the Agricultural Holdings Act 1948: see *Harrison-Broadley v Smith* [1964] 1 All ER 867, [1964] 1 WLR 456. Quite apart from the priceless advantage of avoiding security of tenure, it appears that in 1977 there might well have been fiscal advantages in arranging matters in this way. In this respect it must be of some significance that at his first meeting with Tom and the defendant on 17 January of that year Mr Williamson quoted capital transfer and capital gains taxes as examples of the very considerable legal problems which made it desirable for the plaintiff to consult a

lawyer. As for the suggestion that the plaintiff had no interest, either in 1977 or in 1980,
a in the value of his estate after his death, I do not think that that consideration, although
it may be material for other purposes, is of any weight in relation to the fourth
proposition. The test there must be an objective one.

On the question of undue influence it only remains to consider whether the plaintiff's
entering into the tenancy agreement is proved to have been his spontaneous act acting in
circumstances which enabled him to exercise an independent will and which justified
b the court in holding that it was the result of a free exercise of his will. That was how it
was put by Cotton LJ in *Allcard v Skinner* (1887) 36 Ch D 145 at 171, [1886–90] All ER
Rep 90 at 93, although it is nowadays more usual to adopt the shorter test propounded
by Evershed MR in *Zamet v Hyman* [1961] 3 All ER 933 at 938, [1961] 1 WLR 1442 at
1446. Such was the course taken by Goulding J and the question which he had to answer
was whether the defendant had proved that the tenancy agreement was entered into by
c the plaintiff 'only after full, free and informed thought about it'. The judge answered
that question in the negative and it has not been seriously suggested before us, given the
correctness of his decision on the other points, that he was wrong. In the circumstances,
I need do no more than express my entire agreement with the following passage in his
judgment:

d   'Did the plaintiff fully understand what he was doing? I do not doubt that he
      knew that he was granting a tenancy and entering into a partnership, and that he
      was happy to accept a low rent in return for the promise of improvements. I have
      no doubt that he knew security was given to agricultural tenants by law. I think
      that, if the point were in his mind, he could at once understand, and indeed probably
      knew already, that the value of a tenanted holding was less than the value with
e   vacant possession. But there is no evidence that that aspect of the matter ever came
      to his attention, still less that he had any idea of the magnitude of the sacrifice. Nor,
      in my view, can he have observed the incongruity, and possible danger, of a tenancy
      granted to the defendant alone, when the farming was to be carried on by himself
      and the defendant in partnership. Moreover, the obtaining of the tenancy by the
      defendant is surrounded by a number of suspicious circumstances. The defendant
f   had been advised it was essential that the plaintiff should be independently
      represented, but he did little or nothing to overcome the plaintiff's unwillingness to
      consult a solicitor. The events of 12 and 13 April come all too suddenly after the
      appearance of continued negotiations given by the defendant to Mr Williamson and
      Mr Jaggar during the previous week. It is not easy to accept the defendant's
      ignorance of his father's repeated interviews with Mr Elliott or his belated account
g   of the revision of the tenancy agreement. The defendant's father, who certainly
      played an active part in the matter and who might corroborate the defendant on
      some points, has not been called as a witness. The defendant deliberately kept Mr
      Smith out of the room at the fatal interview when the tenancy agreement was
      signed. In face of all these questionable matters I cannot hold that the defendant has
      discharged the burden cast on him by his confidential association with the plaintiff
h   of establishing that the plaintiff executed the tenancy agreement after free and
      informed thought about it. The whole history and circumstances of the case have
      an entirely different flavour from the facts in *Re Brocklehurst (decd)* [1978] 1 All ER
      767, [1978] Ch 14, with which [counsel for the defendant] pressed me in argument.'

It follows from the views above expressed that Goulding J was in my opinion correct
j in holding that the tenancy agreement was in the first instance liable to be set aside at the
suit of the plaintiff. I turn now to consider whether he was also correct in holding that
the plaintiff had afterwards affirmed it and thereby lost his right to do so.

Before explaining how this question was pleaded, argued and decided in the court
below, I think it desirable to consider in general terms both the nature of the plaintiff's
right and the defences which could have defeated it.

The characteristics of the right which are material for present purposes were these. Firstly, it was an equitable right and as such liable to be defeated by equitable defences. *a* Secondly, although it was a right to set aside a contractual transaction, it arose outside of and not under the contract. Thirdly, it was in substance no different from other equitable rights to set aside completed transactions, for example a beneficiary's right to set aside a purchase by his trustee of the trust property.

The equitable defences which would usually be regarded as being available to defeat such a right are laches, acquiescence and confirmation: see for example the judgment of *b* Lindley LJ in *Allcard v Skinner* (1887) 36 Ch D 145 at 186–189, [1886–90] All ER Rep 90 at 101–103. By any of these means the transaction could have been affirmed, in the first two cases impliedly and in the third expressly. These expressions are not uniformly used. Sometimes laches is taken to mean undue delay on the part of the plaintiff in prosecuting his claim and no more. Sometimes acquiescence is used to mean laches in that sense. And sometimes laches is used to mean acquiescence in its proper sense, which involves a *c* standing by so as to induce the other party to believe that the wrong is assented to. In this sense it has been observed that acquiescence can bear a close resemblance to promissory estoppel: see for example *Holder v Holder* [1968] 1 All ER 665 at 680–681, [1968] Ch 353 at 403 per Sachs LJ; cf also the approach of Bowen LJ in *Allcard v Skinner* (1887) 36 Ch D 145 at 192, [1886–90] All ER Rep 90 at 104. This is not an occasion for a close analysis of the differences between acquiescence and promissory estoppel. I would *d* merely observe, first, that promissory estoppel is usually concerned with rights *under* a contract whose validity is not in dispute and, second, that the conditions for its operation have almost certainly become more formalised than those on which acquiescence depends.

The defence of affirmation was pleaded as follows:

e

'21. If, which is denied, the Plaintiff was induced to enter into the Tenancy Agreement by undue influence or misrepresentation on the part of the Defendant the said Agreement has been affirmed by the Plaintiff and ought not to be rescinded by reason of the matters hereinafter set out.

PARTICULARS
a) The Plaintiff was fully aware of all the terms of the said agreement by the 22nd *f* January 1980 by which time he had consulted his own solicitors Messrs. Jefferson, Cooper & Co. b) With knowledge of the terms of the Agreement he continued to accept rent from the Defendant and stood by whilst to his knowledge the Defendant expended substantial sums in improving Chasewoods Farm. The Defendant will rely in particular on fencing he carried out during the year 1982 to the value of *g* approximately £17,629.'

That paragraph, as the judge observed, alleged that the plaintiff knew all the terms of the tenancy agreement, but it did not allege that he knew of his right to rescind it. As I have already said, it is clear on the evidence that the plaintiff did not have that knowledge, and that allegation, if it had been made, would not have been proved. However, counsel and *h* the judge then appear to have assumed that it was not open to the defendant to rely on the defence of acquiescence, on the ground, as they thought, that that required the plaintiff to have had knowledge of his right to rescind. Instead, counsel for the defendant relied only on the defence of promissory estoppel. That defence was accepted by the judge and it has again been relied on this court.

If the defence of promissory estoppel is to succeed in this case the defendant must *j* establish the following: firstly, a clear and unequivocal representation, either by words or conduct, that the plaintiff would not enforce his right to set the tenancy agreement aside; secondly, that the representation was made with the knowledge or intention that it would be acted on by the defendant in the manner in which it was acted on; thirdly, that the defendant, in reliance on the representation, acted to his detriment, or in some a   other way which would make it inequitable to allow the plaintiff to go back on his representation.

The first point to be made is that para 21 of the defence does not in my view contain a properly pleaded defence of promissory estoppel. Secondly, perhaps as a consequence of that, the evidence at the trial did not establish either a clear and unequivocal representation by or on behalf of the plaintiff that he would not enforce his right to set the tenancy agreement aside or that the defendant, in reliance on any such representation, acted

b   either to his detriment or at all. As to the first of those matters the judge said:

'If he thought about it, the defendant might reasonably have concluded that the plaintiff was choosing to treat the tenancy as valid, notwithstanding the discovery of terms dishonestly concealed (as I assume for the purposes of this argument) when he signed the document.'

c   It cannot in my view have been enough that the defendant might reasonably have arrived at that conclusion. There could only have been a clear and unequivocal representation if he could not reasonably have arrived at any other conclusion. With regard to the second matter, the judge made no finding at all, and it was indeed accepted by counsel for the defendant that no evidence was given by or on behalf of the defendant to the effect that he had, in reliance on any material representation, acted to his detriment.

d   Finally, I would add that it is very difficult to see how, on the evidence, the defendant did in fact act to his detriment or in some other material way. The payment of rent was no detriment, because that was no more than the price which he had to pay for his occupation of the land from day to day. Moreover, the sums of £1,725 and £2,455 which he expended during the years ended 31 January 1978 and 1980 respectively antedated the first date on which any material representation could have been made, and

e   it appears that no further sums were expended up to 31 January 1982, which was less than a year before the writ was issued. In general it seems very doubtful whether the arguments on this question which have now been put to us by counsel for the plaintiff were advanced before the judge.

For these reasons, I am of the opinion that Goulding J's decision on the question of

f   affirmation cannot be supported. But I would not wish to leave the question there. I am exceedingly doubtful whether the assumption made below that it was not open to the defendant to rely on the defence of acquiescence was correct. It seems to me that that plea was open to the defendant on para 21 of his defence and I do not think that the contrary has been suggested. Moreover, it was held by this court in *Holder v Holder* [1968] 1 All ER 665, [1968] Ch 353, following Wilberforce J in *Re Pauling's Settlement Trusts, Younghusband v Coutts & Co* [1961] 1 All ER 713, [1962] 1 WLR 86, that in the analogous

g   case of a right to set aside a purchase by a trustee of the trust property there is no hard and fast rule that ignorance of the right is a bar to the defence of acquiescence, but that the whole of the circumstances must be looked at to see whether it is just that the complaining beneficiary should succeed. That test was recently adopted by Nicholls J as being applicable to a case of undue influence: see *John v James* (29 November 1985,

h   unreported).

I add only this. After it had been pointed out in argument that the assumption made below might not have been correct, counsel for the defendant took time to consider whether he should seek leave to advance the defence of acquiescence in this court. No such application was made. I therefore express no view on whether, if it had been made and granted, the defence would have prevailed, beyond saying that it must have been

j   very well arguable that if all the circumstances of the present case had been looked at it would still have been just that the plaintiff should succeed.

Having decided the questions of undue influence and affirmation in favour of the plaintiff, I would (1) allow the appeal as against the first defendant and declare that the tenancy agreement ought to be set aside and (2) dismiss the appeal as against the second defendant firm.

PARKER LJ. I agree with the judgment of Nourse LJ and have little to add.

On the question whether, apart from affirmation, the tenancy agreement ought to be *a* set aside for undue influence, the judgment appealed from is in my view unassailable, unless it follows from the decision of the House of Lords in *National Westminster Bank plc v Morgan* [1985] 1 All ER 821, [1985] AC 686, which was given six days later, that the judge proceeded on a mistaken view of the law.

The submission that it does so follow involves the proposition that the House of Lords in *National Westminster Bank plc Morgan* impliedly overruled the decision of this court in *b* *Tufton v Sperni* [1952] 2 TLR 516 and many earlier cases which were referred to in argument before it without in any way criticising such cases, much less giving any reasons for departing from them.

This somewhat remarkable proposition stems from: (1) the fact that the judge held that the influence which, prior to the date of the tenancy agreement, the first defendant, Mr Brickell, had acquired over the plaintiff was described as follows: '. . . based on and *c* arising out of a particular association in an advisory capacity, well short, no doubt, of domination, which nevertheless made it his duty to take care of the plaintiff in any transaction between them'; (2) passages in Lord Scarman's speech (with which all other members of the Appellate Committee agreed) which are said to amount to a decision that nothing short of domination will suffice to shift the burden of proof to the defendant to justify the impugned transaction. It is therefore necessary to consider Lord Scarman's *d* speech in, and the circumstances of, *National Westminster Bank plc v Morgan* in some detail.

The impugned transaction was a legal charge taken by the bank on property of which the respondent and her husband were joint owners. The property was their home. The charge was signed by both husband and wife. Both were customers of the bank. In order to obtain the wife's signature the bank manager had gone to the property. He had there *e* had a conversation with her which lasted for no more than five minutes. The charge was to secure a bridging loan. On failure to repay the loan the bank took possession of the property. The wife's defence was that in obtaining her signature the bank manager had exercised undue influence.

This defence was rejected by the county court judge, who held that the charge was not *f* manifestly disadvantageous to the wife, that the manager had not exercised any actual undue influence on her and that the relationship between the wife and the bank was not such as to give rise to any presumption of undue influence.

On appeal to the Court of Appeal (Dunn and Slade LJJ) ([1983] 3 All ER 85) it was held that although, prior to the manager's visit to the house, the relationship between the wife and the bank was the normal business relationship of banker and customer, it ripened *g* into one sufficient to give rise to the presumption of undue influence in the five minutes during which the manager conversed with the wife and that it was not necessary in order to raise the presumption to establish that the transaction was manifestly disadvantageous to the wife. It being conceded that if the presumption was raised it was not rebutted, the appeal therefore succeeded.

I can now turn to an examination of Lord Scarman's speech in *National Westminster* *h* *Bank plc v Morgan*. Having first set out the facts in detail, ending with the crucial interview he said ([1985] 1 All ER 821 at 825–826, [1985] AC 686 at 701–702):

'Such was the interview in which it is said that Mr Barrow crossed the line which divides a normal business relationship from one of undue influence. I am bound to say that the facts appear to me to be a far cry from a relationship of undue influence *j* or from a transaction in which an unfair advantage was obtained by one party over the other. The trial judge clearly so thought, for he stated his reasons for rejecting the wife's case with admirable brevity. He made abundantly clear his view that the relationship between Mr Barrow and the wife never went beyond that of a banker and customer, that the wife had made up her own mind that she was ready to give the charge, and that the one piece of advice (as to the legal effect of the charge) which *a* Mr Barrow did give, though erroneous as to the terms of the charge, correctly represented his intention and that of the bank. The judge dealt with three points. First, he ruled on the submission by the bank that the transaction of loan secured on the property was not one of manifest disadvantage to the wife ... Second, he rejected the submission made on behalf of the wife that Mr Barrow put pressure on her ... Third, he rejected the submission that there was a confidential relationship between the wife and the bank such as to give rise to a presumption of undue

b influence... The Court of Appeal disagreed. The two Lords Justices who constituted the court (Dunn and Slade LJJ) (surely it should have been a court of three) put an interpretation on the facts very different from that of the judge; they also differed from him on the law. As to the facts, I am far from being persuaded that the trial judge fell into error when he concluded that the relationship between the bank and the wife never went beyond the normal business relationship of banker and

c customer.'

This was sufficient to dispose of the appeal. Lord Scarman then proceeded to consider the view of this court that it was unnecessary in order to raise the presumption of undue influence to show, in addition to the required relationship, that the transaction impugned was manifestly disadvantageous to the party asserting undue influence. Having concluded

d that this court had erred and that it was so necessary (see [1985] 1 All ER 821 at 827, [1985] AC 686 at 704), he then, by way of elaboration, quoted extensively from the judgment of Lindley LJ in *Allcard v Skinner* (1887) 36 Ch D 145, [1886–90] All ER Rep 90, which he regarded as establishing the principle justifying the court in setting aside a transaction for undue influence, and said ([1985] 1 All ER 821 at 828, [1985] AC 686 at 706):

e 'Subsequent authority supports the view of the law as expressed by Lindley LJ in *Allcard v Skinner*. The need to show that the transaction is wrongful in the sense explained by Lindley LJ before the court will set aside a transaction whether relying on evidence or the presumption of the exercise of undue influence has been asserted in two Privy Council cases.'

f The second of the Privy Council cases referred to is *Poosathurai v Kannappa Chettiar* (1919) LR 47 Ind App 1, a case under the Indian Contract Act 1872, s 16(3) of which provides:

'Where a person who is in a position to dominate the will of another enters into a contract with him, and the transaction appears on the face of it, or on the evidence,

g to be unconscionable, the burden of proving that such contract was not induced by undue influence shall lie upon the person in the position to dominate the will of the other.'

It is in the quotation of this section that the concept of 'domination' first appears in Lord Scarman's speech. It appears again in a passage from the judgment of Lord Shaw in

h the Indian case (see LR 47 Ind App 1 at 4) which was cited by Lord Scarman, not in connection with the nature of the relationship required, but to support the proposition that in addition to the relationship unfair disadvantage must be shown.

This is clear from the fact that the quotation is immediately followed by the sentence ([1985] 1 All ER 821 at 829, [1985] AC 686 at 707):

j 'The wrongfulness of the transaction must, therefore, be shown: it must be one in which an unfair advantage has been taken of another.'

Having used the word 'domination' once in a quotation from the Indian Contract Act 1872 and once in a quotation from Lord Shaw, in neither case for the purpose of defining the requirements of the relationship, Lord Scarman then continued to use it in a passage principally relied on by the defendants. That passage is in the following terms ([1985] 1

All ER 821 at 829, [1985] AC 686 at 707):

> 'The doctrine is not limited to transactions of gift. A commercial relationship can *a*
> become a relationship in which one party assumes a role of dominating influence
> over the other. In *Poosathurai's* case the Board recognised that a sale at an undervalue
> could be a transaction which a court could set aside as unconscionable if it was
> shown or could be presumed to have been procured by the exercise of undue
> influence. Similarly, a relationship of banker and customer may become one in *b*
> which the banker acquires a dominating influence.'

It is true that in this passage Lord Scarman envisages the existence of a 'dominating
influence' as being the necessary ingredient of a relationship of undue influence, but he
does not attempt to define what is meant by the word 'dominating' and I cannot regard
its use as being intended to have any significance in the light of the facts (1) that the
precise nature of the relationship required was not under discussion, (2) that Lord *c*
Scarman regarded the principle as having been established by Lindley LJ, who does not
refer to domination at all, (3) that if there had been an intention to go further it would
necessarily have involved overruling *Tufton v Sperni* [1952] 2 TLR 516, on which
Goulding J founded his judgment, (4) that Lord Scarman expressly approved the
following passage in the judgment of Sir Eric Sachs in *Lloyds Bank Ltd v Bundy* [1974] 3
All ER 757 at 772, [1975] QB 326 at 347 (see [1985] 1 All ER 821 at 830–831, [1985] AC *d*
686 at 708–709):

> 'There remains to mention that counsel for the bank, whilst conceding that the
> relevant special relationship could arise as between banker and customer, urged in
> somewhat doom-laden terms that a decision taken against the bank on the facts of
> this particular case would seriously affect banking practice. With all respect to that *e*
> submission, it seems necessary to point out that nothing in this judgment affects the
> duties of a bank in the normal case where it obtains a guarantee, and in accordance
> with standard practice explains to the person about to sign its legal effect and the
> sums involved. When, however, a bank, as in this case, goes further and advises on
> more general matters germane to the wisdom of the transaction, that indicates that
> it may—not necessarily must—be crossing the line into the area of confidentiality *f*
> so that the court may then have to examine all the facts, including, of course, the
> history leading up to the transaction, to ascertain whether or not that line has, as
> here, been crossed. It would indeed be rather odd if a bank which vis-à-vis a
> customer attained a special relationship in some ways akin to that of a "man of
> affairs"—something which can be a matter of pride and enhance his local
> reputation—should not where a conflict of interest has arisen as between itself and *g*
> the person advised be under the resulting duty now under discussion. Once, as was
> inevitably conceded, it is possible for a bank to be under that duty, it is, as in the
> present case, simply a question for "meticulous examination" of the particular facts
> to see whether that duty has arisen. On the special facts here it did arise and it has
> been broken.'

h

Having approved this passage Lord Scarman continued ([1985] 1 All ER 821 at 831,
[1985] AC 686 at 709):

> 'This is good sense and good law, though I would prefer to avoid the term
> "confidentiality" as a description of the relationship which has to be proved. In
> truth, as Sir Eric recognised, the relationships which may develop a dominating
> influence of one over another are infinitely various. There is no substitute in this *j*
> branch of the law for a "meticulous examination of the facts".'

Again he refers to the development of a dominating influence but again the expression
is not defined and in my view it is quite deliberately not defined, for Lord Scarman
concludes ([1985] 1 All ER 821 at 831, [1985] AC 686 at 709):

a '... I would wish to give a warning. There is no precisely defined law setting limits to the equitable jurisdiction of a court to relieve against undue influence. This is the world of doctrine, not of neat and tidy rules. The courts of equity have developed a body of learning enabling relief to be granted where the law has to treat the transaction as unimpeachable unless it can be held to have been procured by undue influence. It is the unimpeachability at law of a disadvantageous transaction

b which is the starting point from which the court advances to consider whether the transaction is the product merely of one's own folly or of the undue influence exercised by another. A court in the exercise of this equitable jurisdiction is a court of conscience. Definition is a poor instrument when used to determine whether a transaction is or is not unconscionable: this is a question which depends on the particular facts of the case.'

c This last passage in my view makes it clear that Lord Scarman did not, when using the expression 'dominating influence', intend to hold that the law had been previously misunderstood, much less to hold that a long line of cases were to be overruled. He used the expression as no more than a convenient means of describing a relationship in which one party is in a position to exercise influence over the other and that other naturally relies on the first party for advice or places such trust and confidence in him that the

d court considers it necessary that a transaction between them, which cannot 'be reasonably accounted for on the ground of friendship, relationship, charity, or other ordinary motives on which ordinary men act' (see *Allcard v Skinner* (1887) 36 Ch D 145 at 185, [1886–90] All ER Rep 90 at 100–101 per Lindley LJ), should be shown not to have been the result of the influence of the one and the reliance, trust or confidence of the other.

I have ventured on a perhaps over-long consideration of Lord Scarman's speech in

e *National Westminster Bank plc v Morgan* because it appears to me to be important that no one should in future be led by it to suppose that the necessary ingredient of the presumption of undue influence is the existence of a relationship in which the will of one party is under the domination of the will of another.

With regard to the question of affirmation, were we not differing from the judge, I would add nothing to the judgment of Nourse LJ, with which I wholly agree. As it is I

f add only this.

(1) On whatever precise basis it is sought to uphold a transaction which was originally obtained by undue influence it is an essential ingredient that it would be inequitable to allow the influenced party to set aside the transaction. I can see no possible inequity in allowing the plaintiff to set aside the transaction in the present case. The defendant has had more than full value for the rent he has paid and his expenditure on the farm was

g nothing but an expense of the farming business at first carried on in partnership and later alone. Indeed I would regard it as wholly inequitable to allow him to retain what is in effect a gift obtained by undue influence of something in the order of £½m.

(2) In so far as the defendant relies on estoppel he neither pleaded nor tendered evidence in support of the necessary ingredients.

h (3) The judge's finding that 'if he thought about it the defendant might reasonably have concluded that the plaintiff was choosing to treat the tenancy as valid' is wholly insufficient to support a defence of affirmation in whatever guise.

For the above reasons, as well as those given by Nourse LJ, I would therefore allow the appeal as against the defendant, Mr Brickell. The appeal as against the second defendant firm must in the circumstances be dismissed.

j **SIR JOHN MEGAW.** I agree with both the judgments.

The main contention of counsel for the defendant on the issue of undue influence was that the House of Lords in *National Westminster Bank plc v Morgan* [1985] 1 All ER 821, [1985] AC 686 had changed the law by defining undue influence by reference to the noun 'domination' or the adjective 'dominating'. To my mind, it would be odd beyond

the limit of credulity that Lord Scarman, in his speech with which the others of their
Lordships agreed, had intended to do any such thing. So to have intended would, quite *a*
simply, have been wholly inconsistent with Lord Scarman's approval of the passage in
the judgment of Lindley LJ in *Allcard v Skinner* (1887) 36 Ch D 145 at 183, [1886–90]
All ER Rep 90 at 99 the first sentence of which includes these words: '. . . no Court has
ever attempted to define undue influence . . .' It would be wholly inconsistent also with
the concluding words of Lord Scarman's speech ([1985] 1 All ER 821 at 831, [1985] AC
686 at 709): 'Definition is a poor instrument when used to determine whether a *b*
transaction is or is not unconscionable . . .'

*Appeal allowed as against first defendant. Appeal dismissed as against second defendants. Leave
to appeal to House of Lords refused.*

30 October. The parties applied for further orders including an order for costs.   *c*

PARKER LJ delivered the following judgment of the court. So far as the question of
costs is concerned, we are entirely satisfied not only that it was reasonable for the plaintiff
to join the second defendants as soon as the matter in para 21 had been raised, but that it
would have been extraordinarily ill-advised not to join the second defendants at that *d*
stage.

That being so, it is plain that we have a discretion with regard to the costs of all parties.
We only mention this: that the note to RSC Ord 62, r 2 in *The Supreme Court Practice
1985* vol 1, p 874, para 62/2/46 which suggests that a Bullock order will not be made
when there are different causes of action (which is said to be supported by *Mulready v J H
& W Bell Ltd* [1953] 2 All ER 215, [1953] 2 QB 326) is not sustained by that authority, *e*
which deals with a very special case.

The true position is that the authority of the court over costs is very wide, as is made
clear in the recent case of *Aiden Shipping Co Ltd v Interbulk Ltd, The Vimeira* [1986] 2 All
ER 409, [1986] AC 965.

The order will be as follows: 'The plaintiff recovers his costs, both here and below,
against the first defendant including all such costs as were incurred as a result of the *f*
joinder of the second defendants.'

The first defendant's suggestion that there should be any disallowance of full costs is
rejected, as is also his suggestion that he should recover any costs against the plaintiff.

With regard to the second defendants, they will recover their costs here and below
against the first defendant; that is to say there will be a Sanderson order rather than a
Bullock order. [His Lordship then proceeded to deal with matters not relevant to the *g*
report herein.]

Order accordingly.

6 November. The Appeal Committee of the House of Lords (Lord Keith of Kinkel, Lord Templeman
and Lord Griffiths) refused the first defendant leave to appeal.   *h*

Solicitors: *Burges Salmon*, Bristol (for the plaintiff); *Jaggar & Co*, Swindon (for the first
defendant); *Wansbroughs*, Bristol (for the second defendants).

Carolyn Toulmin   Barrister.

Practice Direction
(Chancery 1/86)

CHANCERY DIVISION

Chancery Division – Practice – Practice directions – Index of directions in force

1. The object of this Practice Direction is to delete those Chancery (other than Companies Court) directions which are no longer required as they are out of date or found elsewhere and to indicate those still in force which the practitioner is most likely to encounter. This is an index primarily of Chancery Practice Directions but some Central Office and Queen's Bench Practice Directions have been included which are applied in the Chancery Division.

2. The following directions are hereby cancelled:
Practice Note [1907] WN 44
Practice Note [1929] WN 105
Practice Note [1940] WN 155
Practice Note [1945] WN 210
Practice Direction [1953] 2 All ER 1159, [1953] 1 WLR 1365
Practice Direction [1953] 2 All ER 1408, [1953] 1 WLR 1452
Practice Directions [1955] 1 All ER 30, [1955] 1 WLR 36, paras 2 and 3
Practice Note [1959] 2 All ER 629, [1959] 1 WLR 743
Practice Direction [1969] 2 All ER 639, [1969] 1 WLR 974, paras 1, 3 and 4
Practice Direction [1970] 1 All ER 671, [1970] 1 WLR 520, paras 3, 5 and 6
Practice Direction [1970] 2 All ER 280, [1970] 1 WLR 977
Practice Direction [1974] 2 All ER 566, [1974] 1 WLR 708
Practice Direction [1975] 1 All ER 576, [1975] 1 WLR 321
Practice Direction [1976] 1 All ER 672, [1976] 1 WLR 201, paras 1, 3 and 4
Practice Direction [1979] 1 All ER 364, [1979] 1 WLR 204

3. The following is an index of the practice directions now in force in the Chancery Division (other than the Companies Court):

AFFIDAVITS
Acceptance of affidavits sworn before proceedings have commenced: *Practice Direction* [1969] 2 All ER 639, [1969] 1 WLR 974, para 2.

APPEALS FROM MASTERS
Notice of appeal Two copies of the notice of appeal are lodged at room 157 within 5 days after the order is made. Appeals are heard in chambers in the non-witness list: *Practice Direction* [1982] 3 All ER 124, [1982] 1 WLR 1189, para 10

Appellant opens The appellant opens but even if the appeal is against only part of the master's order the whole of the summons is treated as being before the judge who will make such order on it as he thinks fit: *Practice Direction* [1983] 1 All ER 131, [1983] 1 WLR 4, para 7

Grounds of appeal Notice of appeal need not state the grounds of appeal: *Practice Direction* [1984] 1 All ER 720, [1984] 1 WLR 447, para 3

CHANCERY CHAMBERS
Administrative structure The structure of Chancery Chambers is fully explained: *Practice Direction* [1982] 3 All ER 124, [1982] 1 WLR 1189

Termination by consent When proceedings are terminated by consent these should be reported at room 156 and the solicitor should collect his exhibits: *Practice Direction* [1963] 1 All ER 416, [1963] 1 WLR 246

CHANCERY REGISTRY
   Change of name Notice of change of name must be filed in room 157 and a copy served on every other party: *Practice Direction* [1984] 1 All ER 720, [1984] 1 WLR 447, para 4
   Description of parties: Practice Direction [1969] 2 All ER 1130, [1969] 1 WLR 1259
   Documents for use abroad Where a certified copy of a judgment is required a copy must be obtained from room 157 and authenticated by a master: *Practice Direction* [1971] 2 All ER 160, [1971] 1 WLR 604
   Judgment: foreign currency Particulars to be inserted in writ and pleadings: *Practice Direction* [1976] 1 All ER 669, [1976] 1 WLR 83

CHARGING ORDER
   A judgment creditor may apply to a master ex parte by affidavit for an order to inspect the land register relating to the title of a judgment debtor: *Practice Direction* [1983] 1 All ER 352, [1983] 1 WLR 150

CONSENT ORDERS
   The Tomlin form Where terms are inserted in the schedule: *Practice Note* [1927] WN 290 and *Practice Direction* [1960] 3 All ER 416, [1960] 1 WLR 1168, para 2[1]
   Orders made in court The normal conditions for the making of a consent order in the absence of a party are set out: *Practice Direction* [1985] 1 All ER 1040, [1985] 1 WLR 593

COSTS
   Assessment in chambers The limit of costs which may be assessed in chambers is now £2,500: *Practice Direction* [1985] 2 All ER 1024, [1985] 1 WLR 968

CROSS-EXAMINATION OF DEPONENTS
   The master may make such an order either ex parte or at a hearing and the form is set out in the schedule to the Practice Direction: *Practice Direction* [1969] 2 All ER 736, [1969] 1 WLR 983

DOCUMENTATION
   Directions about marking of affidavits, numbering and binding of documents and marking of exhibits: *Practice Note* [1983] 3 All ER 33, [1983] 1 WLR 922

ESTATE AGENTS' AND AUTIONEERS' FEES
   Fees should normally not exceed 2½% of sale price exclusive of value added tax: *Practice Direction* [1983] 1 All ER 160, [1983] 1 WLR 86

EVIDENCE
   Filing All documents in support of a master's summons are filed in room 156. All other documents are filed in room 157. Office copies can be obtained in room 157 on payment of the proper fee: *Practice Direction* [1982] 3 All ER 124, [1982] 1 WLR 1189, para 11
   Grants of representation Grants of probate and letters of administration may be accepted as evidence of death for procedural purposes but not as part of the proof of title: *Practice Direction* [1970] 1 All ER 671, [1970] 1 WLR 520, para 4

---

1 Editor's note: Notwithstanding the revocation of *Practice Direction* [1960] 3 All ER 416, [1960] 1 WLR 1168 by *Practice Direction* [1982] 3 All ER 124, [1982] 1 WLR 1189, para 22, the former direction is intended to be revived hereby

EXECUTION

a   Notice must be given to a mortgagor if the mortgagee wishes to enforce a suspended order and a summons must be issued. Notice must also be given when leave to issue execution is required because six years have elapsed since the date of the order: *Practice Direction* [1972] 1 All ER 576, [1972] 1 WLR 240

EX PARTE APPLICATIONS

b   Some applications may be made to a master merely by lodging an affidavit at room 156, eg (1) garnishee order nisi, (2) order to carry on proceedings, (3) substituted service: *Practice Directions* [1955] 1 All ER 30, [1955] 1 WLR 36, para 1

FAMILY PROVISION

c   *Appeals from masters* Notice of appeal is given in the usual way and a transcript of any oral evidence and the judgment should be obtained: *Practice Direction* [1978] 2 All ER 167, [1978] 1 WLR 585

     Indorsement of order All orders under the Inheritance (Provision for Family and Dependants) Act 1975 including 'Tomlin' orders are indorsed on the original grant of representation and sent to the Principal Registry of the Family Division for noting:

d   *Practice Direction* [1978] 3 All ER 1032, [1979] 1 WLR 1

INTERLOCUTORY PROCEDURAL APPLICATIONS

     These should be made by summons to a master and not by motion unless for good reason: *Practice Direction* [1984] 1 All ER 720, [1984] 1 WLR 447, para 2

e

JUDGMENT BY DEFAULT

     Applications To be made to room 157, in the first instance, together with an affidavit of service of the writ of summons: *Practice Direction* [1982] 3 All ER 124, [1982] 1 WLR 1189, para 17

     Claims for interest Directions as to the manner in which claims for interest should be

f   pleaded and what conditions must be fulfilled before a default judgment for interest can be obtained: *Practice Direction* [1983] 1 All ER 934, [1983] 1 WLR 377

LANDLORD AND TENANT

     Masters will give early appointments for the hearing of joint applications to authorise agreements excluding ss 24 to 28 of the Landlord and Tenant Act 1954 on two or three

g   days' notice: *Practice Direction* [1973] 1 All ER 796, [1973] 1 WLR 299

LISTING

     Full details of the lists: *Practice Direction* [1983] 1 All ER 1145, [1983] 1 WLR 436

     Revenue listing The listing of revenue appeals is dealt with in room 163: *Practice Note*

h   [1982] 3 All ER 904, [1982] 1 WLR 1474

MASTERS' POWERS

     Generally: *Practice Direction* [1975] 1 All ER 255, [1975] 1 WLR 129

     Powers under para 3(b), (l)(ii) and (m) of above direction extended to cases where

j   amount does not exceed £30,000: *Practice Direction* [1983] 1 All ER 131, [1983] 1 WLR 4, para 3

     Power to make orders authorising agreements to exclude the provisions in ss 24 to 28 of the Landlord and Tenant Act 1954: *Practice Direction* [1971] 2 All ER 215, [1971] 1 WLR 706

     Extending time for making applications under s 4 of the Inheritance (Provision for

Family and Dependants) Act 1975: *Practice Direction* [1975] 1 All ER 640, [1975] 1 WLR 405, para 2

Exercising powers under s 27 of the Leasehold Reform Act 1967 (enfranchisement where landlord cannot be found): *Practice Direction* [1976] 2 All ER 610, [1967] 1 WLR 637

MOTIONS

Hearing A full code for the hearing of motions: *Practice Direction* [1980] 2 All ER 750, [1980] 1 WLR 751 and *Practice Direction* [1985] 1 All ER 384, [1985] 1 WLR 244

Agreed adjournment (1) Signed consents to be lodged at room 180: *Practice Note* [1976] 2 All ER 198, [1976] 1 WLR 441

(2) Court file must be bespoken from room 157 before application can be made: *Practice Direction* [1982] 3 All ER 124, [1982] 1 WLR 1189, para 18

(3) This procedure extended to cases in which an undertaking to the court has been given and is to continue unchanged: *Practice Direction* [1983] 1 All ER 131, [1983] 1 WLR 4, para 4

ORDERS

Procedure for solicitors to draw up orders made on motion by agreement: *Practice Direction* [1970] 1 All ER 281, [1970] 1 WLR 249

By judges Details of procedure: *Practice Direction* [1982] 3 All ER 124, [1982] 1 WLR 1189, para 14

By masters Final orders are drawn up by the court but interlocutory orders may be drawn up by the solicitors if the master agrees: *Practice Direction* [1982] 3 All ER 124, [1982] 1 WLR 1189, para 13

Minutes of order If the drafting section does not agree with minutes settled by counsel they should be referred back to counsel through the solicitors: *Practice Direction* [1960] 3 All ER 416, [1960] 1 WLR 1168, para 1[1]

Form of order Any party dissatisfied with the form of the order must notify room 180. If the differences cannot be resolved the objecting party may apply by motion or summons for the order to be amended: *Practice Direction* [1982] 3 All ER 124, [1982] 1 WLR 1189, para 15

Copies of orders Copies may be obtained from room 157 on payment of the appropriate fee: *Practice Direction* [1982] 3 All ER 124, [1982] 1 WLR 1189, para 16

ORIGINAL DOCUMENTS

On the construction of a will or document the original probate or original document should be available in court: *Practice Note* [1949] WN 441

ORIGINATING MOTION

Procedure for the issue and hearing of originating motions: *Practice Direction* [1984] 3 All ER 512, [1984] 1 WLR 1216

Agreed directions for the rectification of the register of trade marks may be obtained by lodging the documents at room 180: *Practice Direction* [1980] 2 All ER 750, [1980] 1 WLR 751, para 9

This procedure extended to register of patents and registered designs: *Practice Direction* [1985] 1 All ER 192

PATENT ACTIONS

Summons for directions An agreed order signed by counsel for the parties will be made without any attendance before the master. If the parties are not agreed application is

---

1 Editor's note: Notwithstanding the revocation of *Practice Direction* [1960] 3 All ER 416, [1960] 1 WLR 1168 by *Practice Direction* [1982] 3 All ER 124, [1982] 1 WLR 1189, para 22, the former direction is intended to be revived hereby

made by motion to one of the assigned judges: *Practice Direction* [1974] 1 All ER 40,
[1973] 1 WLR 1425, paras 1 and 2[1]

Interlocutory applications (1) Procedure when adjournment into court likely: *Practice Direction* [1970] 1 All ER 17, [1970] 1 WLR 94

(2) Agreed orders will be made as on a summons for directions: *Practice Direction* [1974] 1 All ER 40, [1973] 1 WLR 1425, para 3[1]

POSSESSION UNDER RSC ORD 113

Details of practice: *Practice Direction* [1983] 1 All ER 131, [1983] 1 WLR 4, para 1

POST OR TELEPHONE

Details of what can be done by post and telephone: *Practice Direction* [1983] 2 All ER 541, [1983] 1 WLR 791

PROBATE

Accounts of administrator pending suit The administrator to swear an affidavit exhibiting an inventory as well as a cash account: *Practice Direction* [1973] 2 All ER 334, [1973] 1 WLR 627, paras 1 to 5

Compromise Terms of compromise to be set out in the schedule to the order and the scheduled terms can, unless the contrary is provided, be enforced forthwith by execution: *Practice Direction* [1972] 3 All ER 319, [1972] 1 WLR 1215

Copies of scripts When a party lodges an original script he should at the same time lodge a copy for court file: *Practice Direction* [1973] 2 All ER 334, [1973] 1 WLR 627, paras 6 and 7

Transmission of scripts It is the convenient practice for a probate action which is to be heard outside London to be set down in London so that the scripts can be sent to the district registry concerned: *Practice Direction* [1974] 3 All ER 752, [1974] 1 WLR 1349, paras 3 and 4

Verification of will The formalities for verification: *Practice Direction* [1974] 3 All ER 752, [1974] 1 WLR 1349, paras 1 and 2

PROCEEDINGS OUTSIDE LONDON

Liverpool, Manchester, Preston, Leeds and Newcastle upon Tyne are places authorised for trial of Chancery actions in the Northern Area within the jurisdiction of the Vice-Chancellor of the County Palatine of Lancaster: *Practice Direction* [1972] 1 All ER 103, [1972] 1 WLR 1

Birmingham, Bristol and Cardiff are also places authorised for Chancery trials: *Practice Direction* [1982] 3 All ER 124, [1982] 1 WLR 1189, para 3

Powers of circuit judge exercising Chancery jurisdiction at Birmingham, Bristol and Cardiff to be same as Vice-Chancellor of the County Palatine of Lancaster: *Practice Direction* [1985] 1 All ER 256, [1985] 1 WLR 109

Interlocutory applications in the Northern Area and in Birmingham, Bristol and Cardiff should be made to the judge exercising Chancery jurisdiction in the area of the circuit within which the registry is situated: *Practice Direction* [1984] 1 All ER 750, [1984] 1 WLR 417

The special provisions for hearing business from Liverpool and Manchester in London on a Thursday are extended to Preston: *Practice Direction* [1972] 1 WLR 53, para 2

RECEIVERS

Accounts Directions about examination of accounts: *Practice Direction* [1982] 3 All ER 124, [1982] 1 WLR 1189, para 21

---

1 Editor's note: Notwithstanding the cancellation of paras 1 and 3 of *Practice Direction* [1974] 1 All ER 40, [1973] 1 WLR 1425 by para 14(d) of *Practice Direction* [1977] 2 All ER 173, [1977] 1 WLR 421 and the revocation of para 2 of the former direction by the final paragraph of *Practice Direction* [1983] 2 All ER 541, [1983] 1 WLR 791, the former direction is intended to be revived hereby

Powers A receiver may without leave effect small repairs estimated not to cost over £1,000 in one accounting period: *Practice Direction* (1 July 1985, unreported), Ch D   *a*

REVIEW OF TAXATION

Procedure on a review of taxation: *Practice Direction* [1983] 1 All ER 131, [1983] 1 WLR 4, para 5

SERVICE BY POST   *b*

Service will be effected on the second working day after posting in the case of first class mail and on the fourth working day after posting for second class mail: *Practice Direction* [1985] 1 All ER 889, [1985] 1 WLR 489

SETTING DOWN

Leave of the court or the consent of the other parties is not required for setting down   *c* for trial out of time provided RSC Ord 3, r 6 is complied with: *Practice Direction* [1981] 1 All ER 752, [1981] 1 WLR 322

SPEEDY TRIAL

A judge hearing a motion may give directions for pleadings and discovery and specify a date for further hearing before a master: *Practice Direction* [1974] 1 All ER 1039, [1974]   *d* 1 WLR 339

SUMMARY JUDGMENT

A summons for judgment under RSC Ord 14 or Ord 86 when an injunction is sought may be issued in room 157 so as to be returnable directly before a judge: *Practice Direction* [1984] 1 All ER 720, [1984] 1 WLR 447, para 1   *e*

TITLE AND PARTIES

Contents of title: *Practice Direction* [1983] 1 All ER 131, [1983] 1 WLR 4, para 2
Numbering and arrangement of parties in title: *Note: Re Brickman's Settlement, Brickman v Goddard Trustees (Jersey) Ltd* [1982] 1 All ER 336, sub nom *Practice Note* [1981] 1 WLR   *f* 1560

TRUSTEES

Evidence on removal of trustee under disability *Practice Direction* [1948] WN 273
Lodgment in court under s 63 of the Trustee Act 1925 of less than £500 must be authorised in writing by the Chief Master or vacation master: *Practice Direction* (1975)   *g* 119 SJ 872
Investments of property in Scotland should be set out in a separate schedule so that trustees may apply for vesting order from the Scottish court: *Practice Direction* [1945] WN 80

VARIATION OF TRUSTS   *h*

Undertaking required from solicitors having the carriage of the order to submit the order to Commissioners of the Inland Revenue within 30 days of entry of order for adjudication of stamp duty: *Practice Note* [1966] 1 All ER 672, [1966] 1 WLR 345
Where any minor or unborn beneficiary will be affected by the proposed arrangement an affidavit should be filed by the guardian ad litem or trustees supporting the arrangement and exhibiting a case to counsel and his opinion to this effect: *Practice*   *j* *Direction* [1976] 3 All ER 160, [1976] 1 WLR 884

By direction of the Vice-Chancellor.

R D MUNROW
Chief Master.

8 December 1986

Kemp v Liebherr-GB Ltd

QUEEN'S BENCH DIVISION
GLIDEWELL LJ AND OTTON J
22 OCTOBER 1986

Magistrates – Summary trial – Offence triable summarily or on indictment – Time limit for trying information – Whether time limit for trying summary offences applicable to summary trial of offences triable either way – Interpretation Act 1978, Sch 1, definition of 'indictable offence' – Magistrates' Courts Act 1980, s 127(1)(2).

On the true construction of s 127(2)[a] of the Magistrates' Courts Act 1980 (but subject to any time limit that may be specified in the enactment creating the offence) a magistrates' court has jurisdiction to try an information alleging the commission of an offence which is triable either way notwithstanding that the alleged offence was committed more than six months before the information was laid, since by virtue of Sch 1[b] to the Interpretation Act 1978 an offence triable either way is an 'indictable offence' and hence s 127(2) applies to exclude it from the time limit for the trial of summary offences laid down by s 127(1) of the 1980 Act (see p 887 *h j*, p 888 *c d g h* and p 889 *g* to *j*, post).

Notes

For the time limit for prosecution of offences in magistrates' courts, see 29 Halsbury's Laws (4th edn) para 291, and for a case on the subject, see 33 Digest (Reissue) 123, 819.

For the Interpretation Act 1978, Sch 1, definition of 'indictable offence', see 48 Halsbury's Statutes (3rd edn) 1324.

For the Magistrates' Court Act 1980, s 127, see 27 Halsbury's Statutes (4th edn) 280.

Case stated

Charles William Kemp, one of Her Majesty's inspectors of factories, appealed by way of a case stated by the justices for the county of Hampshire acting in and for the petty sessional division of Portsmouth in respect of their adjudication as a magistrates' court at Portsmouth on 4 February 1986 whereby they dismissed an information laid by the appellant against the respondents, Liebherr-GB Ltd, alleging that the respondents on or about 1 August 1983 at the Marconi Space and Defence Systems, Brown Lane, Portsmouth, Hampshire contravened s 6(1)(a) of the Health and Safety at Work etc Act 1974 in that they supplied to Laden Lifting and Engineering Ltd a Liebherr LT1200 mobile crane which was not, so far as reasonably practicable, so designed and constructed as to be safe when properly used and that therefore the respondents were guilty of an offence under s 33(1)(a) of the 1974 Act and liable to a penalty as provided by s 33(3) of that Act. The justices concluded that they had no jurisdiction to hear the information as it had not been laid within the time limit laid down by s 34(3) of the 1974 Act. The facts are set out in the judgment of Glidewell LJ.

Philip N Havers for the appellant.
Seddon Cripps for the respondents.

GLIDEWELL LJ. On 4 February 1986 the justices for the county of Hampshire, sitting in the magistrates' court at Portsmouth, heard an information alleging that the respondents, on or about 1 August 1983 had contravened s 6(1)(a) of the Health and

---

a   Section 127, so far as material, is set out at p 887 *f* to *h*, post
b   Schedule 1, so far as material, is set out at p 887 *e f*, post

Safety at Work etc Act 1974 in that they supplied to Laden Lifting and Engineering Ltd
a Liebherr mobile crane which was not, so far as reasonably practicable, so designed and   *a*
constructed as to be safe when properly used, and that they were thus guilty of an offence
under s 33(1)(*a*) of the 1974 Act.

The appellant, who is one of Her Majesty's inspectors of factories, requested a summary
trial, the respondents consented to it and the justices agreed.

At the conclusion of that trial the justices decided that the information had not been
laid within the appropriate time limit and dismissed the information. The appellant now   *b*
appeals by way of case stated against that decision.

By the time the justices reached their decision they had heard the whole of the evidence
both for the appellant and respondents and had heard submissions by the appellant
himself and by counsel on behalf of the respondents.

Apart from the time point a number of other defences were raised, in the sense that
submissions were made relating to them, by the respondents, but the justices have   *c*
specifically reached no conclusion on any of those other matters.

In the case stated, which I must say is a most clear and admirable one on which I would
congratulate both the justices and their clerk, the following facts are found. In July 1983
the respondent company sold to Laden Lifting and Engineering Ltd a telescopic mobile
crane. It was delivered to Laden in August 1983. The crane had been manufactured by a
German company which, from its name, I take to be associated with the respondent   *d*
company, in Germany. It had been tested and certified to be sound in Germany in July
1982.

In February 1984 the respondents also delivered to Laden a part to be used in
conjunction with the crane, a luffing fly jib. After delivery of that jib the crane and jib
were again tested on 1 March 1984 in this country, and a certificate saying they had
passed the test was issued. Laden then put the crane and jib into use.   *e*

On 23 February 1985, when the crane was lifting a load which was not abnormal, it
collapsed. On 1 March 1985 the appellant, accompanied by an engineer, inspected the
crane. According to them (and I should say there is no finding of fact about this) they
found that the collapse was due to the faulty welding of an anchor plate.

On 26 September 1985 the information was laid. The justices held that the time limit   *f*
for the prosecution was provided by s 34(3) and (4) of the 1974 Act. As far as it is material
s 34(3) provides:

'Summary proceedings for an offence to which this subsection applies may be
commenced at any time within six months from the date on which there comes to
the knowledge of a responsible enforcing authority evidence sufficient in the
opinion of that authority to justify a prosecution for that offence . . .'   *g*

Section s 34(4) provides:

'The preceding subsection applies to any offence under any of the relevant
statutory provisions which a person commits by virtue of any provision . . . to which
he is subject as the . . . supplier of any thing . . .'   *h*

Since the respondents were charged as the supplier of the crane they came within the
wording, the justices held, of s 34(4) and thus s 34(3) applied, and the time limit for the
commencement of summary proceedings was six months from the date on which there
came to the knowledge of the appellant evidence sufficient to justify a prosecution. That,
it is accepted, happened no later than 1 March 1985, but since the information was laid
more than six months after that date the justices held that it was outside the time laid   *j*
down by s 34(3).

Counsel for the appellant submits that the justices' approach was wrong. He starts by
inviting our attention to s 33 of the 1974 Act, the section constituting the offence with
which the respondents were charged.

Section 33(1) contains offences of various kinds, described by paragraphs lettered (*a*) to

(o). We are concerned only with para (a), which says that it is an offence for a person 'to
a fail to discharge a duty to which he is subject by virtue of sections 2 to 7'.

That takes one back to s 6. Section 6(1) provides, so far as is material:

'It shall be the duty of any person who . . . supplies any article for use at work—
(a) to ensure, so far as is reasonably practicable, that the article is so designed and
constructed as to be safe and without risk to health when properly used . . .'

b
Section 33(2), again so far as material, provides:

'A person guilty of an offence under paragraph (d), (f), (h) or (n) of subsection (1)
above, or of an offence under paragraph (e) of that subsection consisting of
contravening a requirement imposed by an inspector under section 20, shall be
liable on summary conviction to a fine . . .'

c
Section 33(3), subject to provisos which do not here apply, provides:

'. . . a person guilty of an offence under any paragraph of subsection (1) above not
mentioned in the preceding subsection . . . being an offence for which no other
penalty is specified, shall be liable—(a) on summary conviction, to a fine not
exceeding [the prescribed sum]; (b) on conviction on indictment . . . (ii) if the offence
d is not one to which the preceding sub-paragraph applies, to a fine.'

Counsel for the appellant submits, and it is correct, that since the offence charged is
not one of those consisting of or defined in one of the paragraphs specified in sub-s (2) it
thus falls within sub-s (3). As it is within sub-s (3) the offence may be tried either
summarily or on indictment. In other words, in the modern terminology, the offence is
e one which is triable either way.
   Section 5 of and Sch 1 to the Interpretation Act 1978 defines 'indictable offence' as
meaning: 'an offence which, if committed by an adult, is triable on indictment, whether
it is exclusively so triable or triable either way . . .'. Therefore, an offence triable either
way is, unless the context so requires, an indictable offence.
   Counsel then takes us to the Magistrates' Courts Act 1980, s 127 of which provides, so
f far as material:

'(1) Except as otherwise expressly provided by any enactment and subject to
subsection (2) below, a magistrates' court shall not try an information or hear a
complaint unless the information was laid, or the complaint made, within 6 months
from the time when the offence was committed, or the matter of complaint arose.
   (2) Nothing in—(a) subsection (1) above; or (b) subject to subsection (4) below,
g any other enactment (however framed or worded) which, as regards any offence to
which it applies, would but for this section impose a time-limit on the power of a
magistrates' court to try an information summarily or impose a limitation on the
time for taking summary proceedings, shall apply in relation to any indictable
offence . . .'

h The proviso in relation to sub-s (4) has no effect in the circumstances of the present case.
   Counsel for the appellant submits, therefore, that the effect of sub-s (2) is that sub-s (1),
the normal six months' time limit for summary trial, does not apply and, under sub-s
(2)(b), no other enactment having the effect of imposing a time limit for summary
proceedings, which includes s 34(3), applies either. Thus, he submits, since the offence is
an indictable offence there is no time limit for either mode of trial. Put another way, his
j submission is that one must first ascertain whether the offence is triable only summarily.
If it is triable either way it is an indictable offence and thus, by reference to s 127(2), there
is no time limit.
   Counsel for the respondents takes us back to s 33(2) of the 1974 Act. That defines, by
reference to the paragraphs in sub-s (1) of that section, the offences under the Act which
are triable summarily only. Such offences do not include an offence under s 33(1)(a), that

is to say failing to discharge a duty to which the defendant is subject by virtue of, in this case, s 6. Counsel says that only offences against s 33(1)(a) would come within s 34(4), *a* since that section applies to an offence which a person commits by virtue of a provision to which he is subject as the supplier of any thing. This is an argument ad absurdum. If counsel for the appellant is correct, says counsel for the respondents, there is now no offence, at least under the 1974 Act, to which s 34(3) currently applies at all; and it cannot be conceived that Parliament intended to have two subsections, so to speak, hanging in a void unsupported by any offence to which they apply. I think counsel meant, although *b* he did not say it, that the only sensible conclusion to which the court should come is that the justices were correct, since the law must, if possible, apply common sense.

Counsel for the appellant, in reply to that, makes two points. Firstly, he reminds us that in 1974 when the Health and Safety at Work etc Act was passed by Parliament the classification of offences was different. It was a historical classification with which many of us grew up. But the law was altered, and the present classification by mode of trial, *c* that is to say either by summary trial, by indictment only or triable either way, was introduced by the Criminal Law Act 1977. What is now s 127(2) of the 1980 Act is a repeat of what was s 18(1) of the 1977 Act; that was its genesis. The 1977 Act, submits counsel for the appellant, in this respect overrode, and now the 1980 Act overrides, provisions of the 1974 Act about time limits in so far as the later Act is inconsistent with the former.   *d*

The second argument of counsel for the appellant takes us off to yet another section of the 1974 Act, namely s 15. Section 15(6)(c) empowers the Secretary of State, or various other ministers, to make health and safety regulations which—

'exclude proceedings on indictment in relation to offences consisting of a contravention of a requirement or prohibition imposed by or under any of the *e* existing statutory provisions, sections 2 to 9 or health and safety regulations.'

Therefore, submits counsel, although it has not happened yet, if the Secretary of State thought it right to make a regulation that a breach of a duty under s 6(1)(a) of the 1974 Act should be triable only summarily, then s 34(3) would immediately bite on it and the time limit for the summary trial of such an offence would be six months from the date *f* of the discovery of the evidence by the prosecuting authority, in general terms. In other words, counsel is submitting that sub-ss (3) and (4) of s 34 are not dead, they but sleep awaiting the awakening kiss of the Secretary of State.

I have the greatest sympathy with the magistrates and their clerk. Many who have listened to me for the last 25 minutes and have not been concerned in this case might think that it is really little short of absurd to go through the tortuous process of hopping *g* from one subsection of a statute to another, in the way I have done, in order to decide whether or not the prosecution was in time. Nevertheless, it is necessary. Having followed that tortuous path to its conclusion, I am persuaded that counsel for the appellant is correct and that there is no time limit for the prosecution of this offence by either mode of trial. I would, therefore, allow the appeal. But counsel for the respondents has another shot in his locker.   *h*

What counsel says is that we have had the entire hearing, he has put all his arguments in front of the bench and now they are in front of this court, so that it is in just as good a position as the bench of magistrates to decide whether they are right or not, because it has got all the material before it either by way of findings of fact by the magistrates or in the documents. He therefore invites us to reach a conclusion on the other matters he raised by way of defence and to say that he is right in relation to one or more of them, *j* and thus it would be a waste of time to send the matter back to the magistrates as they would be bound to acquit.

It may be that counsel for the respondents has persuaded counsel for the appellant and those sitting behind him that that is correct. If so, it would of course be a waste of time to send the matter back to the magistrates. But if there are still remaining issues as to the

arguments on the merits, and indeed on the technicalities, for my part I would think it
a wrong for this court to express any view about the other defences in advance of the
magistrates themselves doing so. They have carefully refrained from doing that, as I have
said, and expressed their view very carefully only in relation to the time point. I think
that we should not ourselves deal with these questions.

There is, however, one exception, whatever else happens. The case stated sets out in
proper form the contentions of the parties. At para 3(k) there is set out, as one of the
b contentions of the appellant, the following:

> 'The respondents should themselves have carried out a system of thorough testing
> upon the highly stressed units, subsequent to the tests completed by Crane Test and
> Inspection Limited in March 1984 as this was only a limited test covering only the
> luffing fly jib assembly.'

c   Counsel for the respondents made the point that that cannot give any validity in
relation to an offence alleged to have been committed in August 1983. Whether or not
they failed to carry out proper tests after March 1984 is nothing to the point, says counsel.
With that counsel for the appellant expressed his agreement. If this matter is remitted to
the magistrates, says counsel for the respondents, it should go not merely with our
opinion about the time limitation point, but also with the agreed view that the argument
d expressed in para 3(k) on behalf of the appellant is an invalid argument. With that I
agree. I would remit the case to the justices with a direction to continue the hearing,
subject to our direction as to para 3(k) of the case stated.

OTTON J. For my part, I doubt whether ss 33 and 34 of the Health and Safety at Work
etc Act 1974 are otiose. The Secretary of State may well wish to make regulations under
e s 15. If so, then s 33 and 34 would still be of relevance.

Whether or not the sections are now otiose, it is clear, in my opinion, that ss 33 and 34
were of full effect until the Criminal Law Act 1977. This Act was passed after the James
Report (Distribution of Criminal Business between the Crown Court and Magistrates'
Courts (Cmnd 6323)), and reduced the categories of offences from five to three, namely
summary, indictable and those triable either way, as defined by s 64.
f   Section 18(1) of the 1977 Act provides:

> 'Nothing in—(*a*) section 104 of the Magistrates' Courts Act 1952 (limitation of
> time for trial of information); or (*b*) subject to subsection (3) below, any other
> enactment (however framed or worded) which, as regards any offence to which it
> applies, would but for this section impose a time-limit on the power of a magistrates'
g court to try an information summarily or impose a limitation on the time for taking
> summary proceedings, shall apply in relation to any indictable offence.'

In my judgment, the language of that section clearly had the effect of overriding any
other enactment, however framed or worded, which would impose a time limit etc.
Thus, ss 33 and 34, in so far as they impose time limits, were overridden by s 18 of the
h 1977 Act.

Section 127(2) of the Magistrates' Courts Act 1980 re-enacts s 18(1) of the Criminal
Law Act 1977. The language is the same, and so is the effect. The result is that there is no
time limit on proceedings which are triable either way.

I too have sympathy with the difficulties with which the magistrates were undoubtedly
faced. In my judgment, the appeal should be allowed.

j
Appeal allowed. Case remitted to justices.

Solicitors: *Treasury Solicitor* (for the appellant); *Slaughter & May* (for the respondent).

N P Metcalfe Esq   Barrister.

Re International Tin Council
a

CHANCERY DIVISION
MILLETT J
8, 9, 11, 12, 15, 16, 17 DECEMBER 1986, 22 JANUARY 1987

Company – Compulsory winding up – Unregistered company – International organisation – *b*
International Tin Council – Council established by treaty between independent sovereign states –
Council having headquarters in London – Council becoming insolvent and owing substantial debts
– Whether court having jurisdiction to wind up council – Companies Act 1985, s 665 –
International Tin Council (Immunities and Privileges) Order 1972, para 6(1).

The International Tin Council (the ITC) was an international organisation which was *c*
established by treaty between a number of independent sovereign states, including the
United Kingdom, and which had its headquarters in London. Its main functions were to
provide for adjustment between world production and consumption of tin, to alleviate
surpluses or shortages of tin and to prevent excessive fluctuations in the price of tin and
in export earnings from tin. It maintained and operated a buffer stock of tin and engaged
in buying and selling tin by entering into sale and purchase contracts, for both immediate *d*
and forward delivery, on recognised markets. In 1985, in an attempt to support the
falling world price of tin, the ITC ran out of money and collapsed. In October 1985 it
announced that it was unable to meet its commitments and ceased to trade. The
petitioner, which claimed to be owed some £5·3m, was one of a large number of
creditors who were left unpaid by the failure of the ITC. In November 1986 the
petitioner, which had obtained an arbitration award in its favour, presented a petition *e*
for the compulsory winding up of the ITC, on the grounds that the ITC was an
unregistered company within the meaning of s 665[a] of the Companies Act 1985, that it
could accordingly be wound up by the court and that it was insolvent and was unable to
pay its debts. The ITC applied to strike out the petition on the grounds that as an
international organisation established by treaty between independent sovereign states it
was not subject to the winding-up jurisdiction of the court under the 1985 Act or, *f*
alternatively, that it was immune from such jurisdiction by virtue of of the International
Tin Council (Immunities and Privileges) Order 1972, para 6(1)[b] of which provided that
the ITC should have immunity from suit and legal process except, inter alia, in respect of
the enforcement of certain arbitration awards.

Held – (1) On its true construction s 665 of the 1985 Act did not confer on the court *g*
jurisdiction to wind up an international organisation established by treaty between
sovereign states, including an organisation of which the United Kingdom was itself a
member, since to hold otherwise would impute to Parliament an intention to confer, by
general words only, a jurisdiction which was incompatible with United Kingdom
constitutional practice and with established principles of international law, and which
would be incapable of exercise, in the case of an organisation of which the United *h*
Kingdom was a member, without putting the United Kingdom in breach of its treaty
obligations. An international organisation such as the ITC, whether incorporated or not,
was merely the means by which a collective enterprise of member states was carried on
and through which their relations with each other in a particular sphere of common
interest were regulated, and any attempt by one member state to assume responsibilities *j*
for the administration and winding up of the organisation would be inconsistent with
the arrangements made by all the member states as to the manner in which the enterprise
was to be carried on and their relations with each other in that sphere were to be

a   regulated. It followed that the court had no jurisdiction to wind up the ITC and the petition would accordingly be struck out (see p 899 *f g*, p 900 *j* to p 901 *a*, p 902 *g h*, p 903 *f* to *j*, p 906 *g* and p 907 *a*, post).

(2) In any event, para 6(1) of the 1972 order made the ITC immune from jurisdiction, because the winding up process was not a method of enforcing a judgment or arbitration award and the presentation of a winding-up petition was not simply a means of enforcing a judgment or award, and semble the presentation and hearing of a winding up petition,

b   as distinct from the proof of debt in the winding up, was part of the court's adjudicative rather than its enforcement jurisdiction (see p 906 *b* to *j*, post); dictum of Fletcher Moulton LJ in *Re a bankruptcy notice* [1907] 1 KB at 482 applied; dictum of Brightman LJ in *Re Lines Bros Ltd* [1982] 2 All ER at 194–195 applied.

Notes

c   For winding up of unregistered companies, see 7 Halsbury's Laws (4th edn) paras 1749–1754, and for cases on the subject, see 10 Digest (Reissue) 1275–1278, 8048–8076.

For the Companies Act 1985, s 665, see 8 Halsbury's Statutes (4th edn) 619.

Cases referred to in judgment

d   *A-G for Canada v A-G for Ontario* [1937] AC 326, PC.
Bankruptcy notice, Re a [1907] 1 KB 478, CA.
Blackburn v A-G [1971] 2 All ER 1380, [1971] 1 WLR 1037, CA.
British Airways Board v Laker Airways Ltd [1983] 3 All ER 375, [1984] QB 142, [1983] 3 WLR 544, CA; *rvsd in part* [1984] 3 All ER 39, [1985] AC 58, [1984] 3 WLR 413, HL.
Collco Dealings Ltd v IRC [1961] 1 All ER 762, [1962] AC 1, [1961] 2 WLR 401, HL.
Company, Re a [1915] 1 Ch 520, CA.
e   *Cook v Sprigg* [1899] AC 572, [1895–9] All ER Rep 773, PC.
Lazard Bros & Co v Midland Bank Ltd [1933] AC 289, [1932] All ER Rep 571, HL.
Lines Bros Ltd, Re [1982] 2 All ER 183, [1983] Ch 1, [1982] 2 WLR 1010, CA.
Matheson Bros Ltd, Re (1884) 27 Ch D 225.
Pan-American World Airways Inc v Dept of Trade [1976] 1 Lloyd's Rep 257, CA.
f   *Parlement Belge, The* (1879) 4 PD 129; *rvsd* (1880) 5 PD 197, [1874–80] All ER Rep 104, CA.
Reparation for Injuries suffered in the Service of the United Nations, Case of [1949] ICJR 174.
Russian and English Bank v Baring Bros & Co [1936] 1 All ER 505, [1936] AC 405, HL.
Secretary of State in Council of India v Kamachee Boye Sahaba (1859) 13 Moo PCC 22, 15 ER 9.
g   *Thomson v Henderson's Transvaal Estates Ltd* [1908] 1 Ch 765, CA.

Cases also cited

Adams v Adams (A-G intervening) [1970] 3 All ER 572, [1971] P 188.
Alcom Ltd v Republic of Columbia [1984] 2 All ER 6, [1984] AC 580, HL.
Allobrogia Steamship Corp, Re [1978] 3 All ER 423.
h   *Arabian Banking Corp v International Tin Council* (15 January 1986, unreported), QBD.
Arcot (Nabob) v East India Co (1791) 3 Bro CC 292, 29 ER 544, LC.
A-G v De Keyser's Royal Hotel Ltd [1920] AC 508, [1920] All ER Rep 80, HL.
Barton-upon-Humber and District Water Co, Re (1889) 42 Ch D 585.
Bradford Navigation Co, Re (1870) LR 10 Eq 331; *affd* LR 5 Ch App 600, LJJ.
Buttes Gas and Oil Co v Hammer (Nos 2 & 3) [1981] 3 All ER 616, [1982] AC 888, HL.
j   *Caledonian Employees' Benevolent Society, Re* 1928 SC 633.
Chapel House Colliery Co, Re (1883) 24 Ch D 259, CA.
Cia Merabello San Nicholas SA, Re [1972] 3 All ER 448, [1973] Ch 75.
Council of Civil Service Unions v Minister for the Civil Service [1984] 3 All ER 935, [1985] AC 374, HL.
Crigglestone Coal Co Ltd, Re [1906] 2 Ch 327, [1904–7] All ER Rep 894, CA.
East African Airways Corp, Re (20 June 1977, unreported), Ch D.

Eloc Electro-Optieck and Communicatie BV, Re [1981] 2 All ER 1111, [1982] Ch 43.
Garland v British Rail Engineering Ltd [1982] 2 All ER 402, [1983] 2 AC 751, HL.   *a*
General Rolling Stock Co, Re (1872) LR 7 Ch App 646, [1861–73] All ER Rep 434, LJJ.
GUR Corp v Trust Bank of Africa Ltd [1986] 3 All ER 449, [1986] 3 WLR 583, QBD and
     CA.
Hall v Truman Hanbury & Co (1885) Ch D 307, CA.
Harris, Re, Cope v Evans [1945] 1 All ER 702, [1945] Ch 316.
Hibernian Merchants Ltd, Re [1957] 3 All ER 97, [1958] Ch 76.   *b*
India (Government), Ministry of Finance (Revenue Division) v Taylor [1955] 1 All ER 292,
     [1955] AC 491, HL.
Italy (Republic) v Hambros Bank Ltd [1950] 1 All ER 430, [1950] Ch 314.
Kinder v Taylor (1825) 3 LJOS, Ch 68, LC.
Malone v Comr of Police of the Metropolis [1979] 1 All ER 256, [1980] QB 49, CA.
Oriental Bank Corp, Re (1885) 54 LJ Ch 481, CA.   *c*
Oriental Inland Steam Co, Re, ex p Scinde Rly Co (1874) LR 9 Ch App 557, LJJ.
Parker Davies & Hughes Ltd, Re [1953] 2 All ER 1158, [1953] 1 WLR 1349.
Quazi v Quazi [1979] 3 All ER 897, [1980] AC 744, HL.
R v Secretary of State for Transport, ex p Iberia Lineas Aereas de Espana (8 July 1985,
     unreported), QBD.
Roberts Petroleum Ltd v Bernard Kenny Ltd (in liq) [1983] 1 All ER 564, [1983] 2 AC 192,   *d*
     HL.
Salomon v Customs and Excise Comrs [1966] 3 All ER 871, [1967] 2 QB 116, CA.
Simpkin Marshall Ltd, Re [1958] 3 All ER 611, [1959] Ch 229.
Union Accident Insurance Co Ltd, Re [1972] 1 All ER 1105, [1972] 1 WLR 640.
Walker, Ex p (1855) 6 De GM & G 752, 43 ER 1424.   *e*
Walker v Baird [1892] AC 491, PC.
Wey and Arun Junction Canal Co, Re (1867) LR 4 Eq 197.
Zoernsch v Waldock [1964] 2 All ER 256, [1964] 1 WLR 675, CA.

Motion

On 12 November 1986 Amalgamated Metal Trading Ltd, which claimed to be owed   *f*
£5·3m by the International Tin Council (the ITC), presented a petition for the ITC to be
compulsorily wound up by the court under Pt XXI of the Companies Act 1985. By notice
of motion dated 26 November 1986 the ITC applied to the court for an order that the
petition be struck out on the grounds (i) that, as an international organisation established
by treaty between independent sovereign states, the ITC was not subject to the winding-
up jurisdiction of the court under the 1985 Act, (ii) alternatively, that by virtue of the
provisions of the International Tin Council (Immunities and Privileges) Order 1972, SI   *g*
1972/120, the ITC was immune from such jurisdiction. Kleinwort Benson plc, a loan
creditor claiming to be owed some £7m, was added as a respondent to the motion,
opposing it, and the Attorney General was joined as a further respondent, supporting the
motion. The facts are set out in the judgment.

     h

Robert Alexander QC, Richard Sykes QC, Nicholas Chambers QC, Rosalyn Higgins QC, Peter
     Irvin and *Leslie Kosmin* for the ITC.
Andrew Morritt QC, Elihu Lauterpacht QC, Sir Ian Sinclair QC, Patrick Howell and *Richard*
     Plender for the petitioner.
Stanley Burnton QC, Michael Crystal QC, Mark Barnes, David Lloyd Jones and *Richard Sheldon*
     for Kleinwort Benson.   *j*
Sir Maurice Bathurst QC, Anthony Grabiner QC, Nicolas Bratza and *David A S Richards* for
     the Attorney General.

Cur adv vult

22 January. The following judgment was delivered.

a
MILLETT J. The International Tin Council (the ITC) is an international organisation established by treaty concluded between a number of independent sovereign states, of which the United Kingdom is one, and having its headquarters and principal office in London. Thirty-two nations, including the United Kingdom, together with the European Economic Community, are members. The ITC was formed for the purpose of
b administering the treaty and carrying out the functions prescribed by the treaty. Its main functions were to provide for adjustment between world production and consumption of tin and to alleviate serious difficulties arising from surplus or shortage of tin, whether anticipated or real, and to prevent excessive fluctuations in the price of tin and in export earnings from tin. To these ends, it maintained and operated a buffer stock of tin and engaged in the buying and selling of tin by entering into sale and purchase contracts,
c both for immediate and forward delivery, on recognised markets including the London Metal Exchange. In 1985, in a vain attempt to support the world price of tin, the ITC ran out of money and collapsed. In October 1985 the ITC announced that it was unable to meet its commitments. Dealings in tin on the London Metal Exchange were suspended and the ITC ceased to trade in tin.

The failure of the ITC to meet its obligations has left a host of unsatisfied creditors
d with debts totalling several hundred million pounds arising from the ITC's commercial activities in the United Kingdom. No proposals have been made for payment. Among the many creditors is Amalgamated Metal Trading Ltd (the petitioner), which claims to be owed £5·3m. It has obtained an arbitration award in its favour for that sum and applied to the ITC for payment, but the award remains unsatisfied.

In November 1986 the petitioner presented a petition for the ITC to be compulsorily
e wound up by the court under Pt XXI of the Companies Act 1985. The petition alleges that the ITC is an unregistered company within the meaning of s 665 of that Act and is, accordingly, liable to be wound up by the court, that it is insolvent and unable to pay its debts, that unpaid creditors or claimants have already obtained or sought to obtain for themselves the benefit of assets belonging to the ITC in satisfaction of their individual
f claims, and that in the circumstances it is just and equitable that the ITC should be wound up and that an orderly realisation and distribution of such assets as may be available for its creditors should be conducted by a liquidator appointed by the court. The petition also alleges that in a winding up there will be available to the creditors the right to enforce against Her Majesty's government in the United Kingdom and the other member states their liability to contribute to the debts and liabilities of the ITC pursuant
g to s 671 of the 1985 Act and otherwise.

The ITC promptly responded by serving a notice of motion to strike out the petition on a number of grounds, which can be collected under one or other of two alternative heads: (1) that as an international organisation established by treaty between independent sovereign states the ITC is not subject to the winding-up jurisdiction of the court under the 1985 Act, or (2) alternatively that by virtue of the provisions of the International Tin
h Council (Immunities and Privileges) Order 1972, SI 1972/120, the ITC is immune from such jurisdiction. That motion is now before me.

Shortly before the hearing of the motion, I gave leave to Kleinwort Benson plc, a loan creditor which claims to be owed over £7m but has not yet obtained an arbitration award in its favour (though it appears to be in a position to do so) and which wishes to support the petition and participate in the winding up, to be added as a respondent to the
j motion and oppose it. At the hearing of the motion, I also gave leave to the Attorney General to be joined as a further respondent on certain terms as to costs. The Attorney General has appeared and argued in support of the motion.

Many international organisations have their headquarters in London, and others have assets in this country, though none has ever previously become insolvent. Whether such an organisation can be compulsorily wound up by the English court is, therefore, a

question of some importance. It calls for a consideration of some basic principles of both
public and private international law, as well as English constitutional and company law. *a*

The ITC

The ITC was originally established by the First International Tin Agreement (London,
1 March 1954; TS (1956); Cmnd 12) on 1 July 1956 and is now constituted under the
provisions of the Sixth International Tin Agreement (New York, 30 April 1982; Misc 13
(1982); Cmnd 8546) (the ITA) which came into force on 1 July 1982. The ITA is an *b*
international treaty concluded between the government of the United Kingdom, the
governments of 22 other member states, and the European Economic Community. A
further nine states are members as parties to the Fifth International Tin Agreement (New
York, 30 April 1976; TS 110 (1977); Cmnd 6424) but not to the ITA. The headquarters
of the ITC were established in London under the terms of the Headquarters agreement
between the Government of the United Kingdom of Great Britain and Northern Ireland *c*
and the ITC (London, 9 February 1972; TS 38 (1972); Cmnd 4938). The relevant
provisions of the two treaties can be summarised as follows.

The ITA

Article 1 of the ITA sets out the objectives of the ITC. Article 2 contains definitions
and provides, inter alia, that members shall be liable to the ITC up to the amount of *d*
certain financial obligations entered into by them. Article 3 provides that the ITC
established by the previous International Tin Agreements shall continue in being for the
purpose of administering the ITA, with the membership, powers and functions provided
for in the ITA; that the seat of the ITC shall be in the territory of a member; and that
subject thereto the seat of the ITC shall be in London unless the ITC by a prescribed
majority decides otherwise. Article 4 provides that the ITC shall be composed of all the *e*
members.

Article 7 provides that the ITC shall have such powers, including a power to borrow
and perform such functions as may be necessary for the administration and operation of
the ITA. Article 11 provides for the appointment of an independent executive chairman.

Article 13 provides that the executive chairman is to be responsible to the ITC for the *f*
administration and operation of the ITA in accordance with the decisions of the ITC; and
that in the performance of their duties neither the executive chairman nor members of
the staff are to seek or receive instructions from any government or power or authority
other than the ITC or a person acting on behalf of the ITC under the terms of the ITA.
They must refrain from any action which might reflect on their position as international
officials responsible only to the ITC. Each member state also undertakes to respect the
exclusively international character of the responsibilities of the executive chairman and *g*
the members of the staff and not to seek to influence them in the discharge of their
responsibilities.

Article 16 provides that the ITC shall have legal personality and, in particular, the
capacity to contract, acquire and dispose of movable and immovable property and
institute legal proceedings. It requires the ITC to be accorded all necessary exemption *h*
from taxation and currency exchange facilities to enable it to discharge its functions and
provides for the status, privileges and immunities of the ITC in the territory of the host
government to be governed by a headquarters agreement between the host government
and the ITC.

Article 41 contains undertakings by the members during the currency of the ITA to
use their best endeavours and to co-operate to promote the attainment of its objectives *j*
and to accept as binding all decisions of the ITC.

Article 48 requires any complaint that a member has committed a breach of the ITA
for which a remedy is not provided elsewhere in the ITA to be referred at the request of
the member making the complaint to the ITC for decision and provides that except
where otherwise provided in the ITA no member shall be found to have committed a
breach of the ITA unless a resolution to that effect is passed by the members.

Article 49 requires any dispute concerning the interpretation or application of the ITA
which is not settled by negotiation to be referred to the ITC for decision. Article 57
provides for amendment of the ITA. Article 58 provides for withdrawal by a member
from the ITA. Article 59 provides for the duration of the ITA, which is to be five years
from the date of its entry into force unless extended by resolution of the prescribed
majority. Article 60 provides for the procedure on termination of the ITA. It requires
the liabilities of the ITC to be met in full and assumes the continued solvency of the ITC.

The Headquarters Agreement

Article 2 of the Headquarters Agreement provides that it is to be interpreted in the
light of the primary objective of enabling the ITC at its headquarters in the United
Kingdom fully and efficiently to discharge its responsibilities and fulfil its purposes and
functions.

Article 3, which is in the same terms as art 16(1) of the ITA, provides that the ITC is to
have legal personality and, in particular, the capacity to contract and to acquire and
dispose of movable and immovable property and to institute legal proceedings. Article 4
provides that the archives of the ITC, which are widely defined, are to be inviolable.
Article 5 provides for the inviolability of the premises of the ITC and imposes a special
duty on the government of the United Kingdom to take all appropriate steps to protect
the premises of the ITC against intrusion. No official of the government of the United
Kingdom or person exercising any public authority is to enter the premises of the ITC
except with the consent of the executive chairman.

Article 8 confers on the ITC the immunities which give rise to the second question on
the present motion.

Articles 16 to 19 confer extensive privileges and immunities on the executive
chairman, staff, experts and representatives of the ITC. Article 21 provides that these
privileges and immunities are accorded for the purpose of ensuring in all circumstances
the unimpeded functioning of the ITC and the complete independence of the persons to
whom they are accorded. The immunity of the executive chairman may be waived by
the ITC; that of the staff, experts and representatives by the executive chairman, but only
if it is possible to do so without prejudicing the interests of the ITC.

Article 23 requires any formal contract entered into by the ITC with a person resident
in the United Kingdom or a body incorporated or having its principal place of business
in the United Kingdom to include an arbitration clause. Article 24 provides for the
submission of certain other disputes to an international arbitration tribunal. Article 28
provides that any dispute between the government of the United Kingdom and the ITC
concerning the interpretation or application of the Headquarters Agreement or any
question affecting the relations between the government and the ITC which is not settled
by negotiation or by some other agreed method is to be referred to a special panel of
arbitrators.

Article 29 provides that the Headquarters Agreement may be terminated by agreement
between the government of the United Kingdom and the ITC. Otherwise, it is to
terminate only in the event of the headquarters of the ITC being moved from the
territory of the United Kingdom, when it is to terminate on the expiry of the period
reasonably required for the transfer and disposal of the ITC's property in the United
Kingdom.

Those are the relevant terms of the treaties. The relevant statutory provisions of
English domestic law are to be found in the International Organisations Act 1968 and
the 1972 order.

The 1968 Act

Section 1 of the 1968 Act applies to any organisation declared by Order in Council to
be an organisation of which (a) the United Kingdom or Her Majesty's government in the
United Kingdom and (b) one or more foreign sovereign powers, or the government or
governments of one or more such powers, are members. Section 1(2) authorises Her

Majesty, by Order in Council made under the subsection, to specify an organisation to *a* which the section applies and to make provision for the organisation so specified. The provisions which may be made include conferring on the organisation the legal capacities (but not, it should be observed, the legal status) of a body corporate, according to it, to such extent as may be specified in the order, the privileges and immunities set out in Pt I of Sch 1 to the Act and according to its representatives, officers, staff and experts the privileges and immunities set out in other parts of that schedule. These include the like inviolability of official archives and premises as are accorded to the official archives and *b* premises of a diplomatic mission. Section 1(6) requires any Order in Council to be so framed as to secure that the privileges and immunities conferred by the order are not greater in extent than those required by the relevant treaty to be conferred.

The 1972 order
    The 1972 order specifies the ITC as an organisation of which Her Majesty's government *c* in the United Kingdom and the governments of foreign sovereign powers are members. Paragraph 5 provides that the ITC shall have the legal capacities of a body corporate. Paragraph 6 confers the immunities which give rise to the second question on the present motion: I shall set it out in full hereafter. Other provisions of the order accord to the ITC the like inviolability of official archives and premises as are accorded to the archives and premises of a diplomatic mission and confer appropriate privileges and immunities on *d* the executive chairman, staff, experts and representatives of the ITC.
    Thus the ITC is an international body corporate created by treaty. It has legal personality in international law. The power of sovereign states acting in sufficient numbers in conformity with international law to bring into being an organisation possessing objective international personality, and not merely personality recognised by *e* them alone, together with the capacity to bring international claims, has been recognised by the International Court of Justice: see *Case of Reparation for Injuries suffered in the Service of the United Nations* [1949] ICJR 174. As the International Court of Justice there pointed out, to say that an international organisation is an international person—

> 'is not the same thing as saying that it is a State, which it certainly is not, or that *f* its legal personality and rights and duties are the same as those of a State. Still less is it the same thing as saying that it is a "super-State", whatever that expression may mean. It does not even imply that all its rights and duties must be upon the international plane, any more than all the rights and duties of a State must be upon that plane. What it does mean is that it is a subject of international law and capable of possessing international rights and duties, and that it has capacity to maintain its rights by bringing international claims.' *g*

    The making of a treaty is an act of the executive, not of the legislature, and it is therefore a fundamental principle of our constitution that the terms of a treaty do not, by virtue of the treaty alone, have the force of law in the United Kingdom. This does not mean that they are to be disregarded. Our courts take notice of the acts of the executive, and the terms of a treaty entered into by the United Kingdom may fall to be considered *h* by them, either because Parliament has expressly or impliedly required them to be considered (as, for example, for the purposes of s 1(6) of the 1968 Act) or to enable domestic legislation to be construed wherever possible in conformity with, rather than in breach of, pre-existing international obligations undertaken by the United Kingdom. But it does mean that the terms of a treaty cannot effect any alteration in our domestic law, or deprive the subject of existing legal rights, unless and until enacted into domestic *j* law by or under the authority of Parliament. When so enacted, the court gives effect to the English legislation, not to the terms of the treaty. For authoritative statements of these well-recognised principles, reference can be made to *A-G for Canada v A-G for Ontario* [1937] AC 326 at 347–348, *Blackburn v A-G* [1971] 2 All ER 1380 at 1381–1382, [1971] 1 WLR 1037 at 1039–1041 and *Pan-American World Airways Inc v Dept of Trade* [1976] 1 Lloyd's Rep 257 at 261.

Accordingly, the status, capacities and immunities of the ITC in English domestic law
are governed by the 1968 Act and the 1972 order and not by the treaties. Its existence is
recognised by the 1972 order, which has granted it the legal capacities of a body corporate,
but it is not incorporated thereby, and it is not a statutory body. It is not incorporated in
the United Kingdom or anywhere else. It is neither an English nor a foreign corporation,
but the creation of treaty. Significantly, Parliament has not granted it the status, but only
the legal capacities, of a body corporate and has not provided, as it could easily have done,
that it should be deemed to be a company or that it should be capable of being wound
up under the Companies Acts: see, for example, s 8 of the Building Societies Act 1984
and s 55 of the Industrial and Provident Societies Act 1965.

The first question is whether such a body is amenable to the winding-up jurisdiction
of the English court.

Jurisdiction

Part XXI of the 1985 Act consists of ss 665 to 674. Section 665 provides:

> 'For the purposes of this Part, the expression "unregistered company" includes . . .
> any partnership (whether limited or not), any association and any company, with
> the following exceptions . . .'

The exceptions are not material.

Section 666 provides, inter alia:

> '(1) Subject to the provisions of this Part, any unregistered company may be
> wound up under this Act; and all the provisions of this Act about winding up apply
> to an unregistered company, with the exceptions and additions mentioned in the
> following subsections . . .
> (5) The circumstances in which an unregistered company may be wound up are
> are follows—(a) if the company is dissolved, or has ceased to carry on business, or is
> carrying on business only for the purpose of winding up its affairs; (b) if the company
> is unable to pay its debts; (c) if the court is of opinion that it is just and equitable
> that the company should be wound up . . .'

Other provisions of Pt XXI of the 1985 Act which should be mentioned are ss 671 and
674. Section 671 provides:

> '(1) In the event of an unregistered company being wound up, every person is
> deemed a contributory who is liable to pay or contribute to the payment of any debt
> or liability of the company, or to pay or contribute to the payment of any sum for
> the adjustment of the rights of members among themselves, or to pay or contribute
> to the payment of the costs and expenses of winding up the company.
> (2) Every contributory is liable to contribute to the company's assets all sums due
> from him in respect of such liability as is mentioned above . . .'

Section 674 provides:

> '(1) The provisions of this Part with respect to unregistered companies are in
> addition to and not in restriction of any provisions of Part XX with respect to
> winding up companies by the court; and the court or liquidator may exercise any
> powers or do any act in the case of unregistered companies which might be exercised
> or done by it or him in winding up companies formed and registered under this
> Act . . .'

Section 665 is quite general in its terms. It is well established that it includes companies
incorporated abroad, even though these are not referred to expressly: see, for example,
Re Matheson Bros Ltd (1884) 27 Ch D 225. An international organisation, however, is not
to be equated with a foreign corporation as a body incorporated under some legal system
other than our own. The status of a foreign corporation is a matter of private international
law, and is governed by the law of the country of incorporation. It—

'depends on territorial enactments of the country of incorporation according to which either the existence or the non-existance of the corporation is recognised by the law of other countries.' *a*

(See *Lazard Bros & Co v Midland Bank Ltd* [1933] AC 289 at 302, [1932] All ER Rep 571 at 579 per Lord Wright.)

An international organisation, by contrast, is created not by the territorial enactment of any single state, but by international treaty; it is not, or not normally, made the subject of any territorial system of law; and its recognition by the courts of a member state is a matter, not of that state's private international law, but of its constitutional law. *b*

If the ITC's corporate status is not recognised by our domestic law, however, this is of no consequence for present purposes, for s 665 is not confined to bodies corporate. It applies to—

'countless cases of partnerships, associations and companies which are merely names for groups of individuals, and which are not companies at all.' *c*

(See *Russian and English Bank v Baring Bros & Co* [1936] 1 All ER 505 at 522, [1936] AC 405 at 432 per Lord Russell.)

It is plainly capable of applying to an association, whether incorporated or not, which like the ITC has been recognised by our own domestic legislation and accorded thereby the legal capacities of a body corporate, notwithstanding that it was created by treaty and that its members are not individuals but sovereign states. Whether it does so, however, is another matter. That depends on the presumed intention of Parliament in enacting s 665, for the fact that an organisation has been recognised by our domestic legislation and granted the legal capacities of a body corporate is not by itself sufficient to make it subject to the winding-up jurisdiction. *e*

In order to ascertain the presumed intention of Parliament, it is necessary to begin by considering the effect of a winding-up order. A convenient summary of the effect of such an order may be found in McPherson *Law of Company Liquidations* (2nd edn, 1980) p 4: *d*

'Liquidation in either form effects an alteration in the status of the company. It does not destroy its corporate identity or powers, but it does place the company and those who control its affairs under certain disabilities. Generally speaking, it terminates the power of the company to carry on business except for the limited purpose of winding up its affairs; it puts an end to its capacity to dispose of assets, and it restricts the rights of creditors to take legal proceedings and to enforce their ordinary remedies against the company or its property. Liquidation also results in a transfer of power to manage the affairs of the company from the directors and members to the liquidator and the creditors . . .' *f*

The statement that a winding up, even a voluntary winding up, effects an alteration in the status of the company derives from an often quoted dictum of Buckley LJ in *Thomson v Henderson's Transvaal Estates Ltd* [1908] 1 Ch 765 at 778. In my judgment it is amply justified. *h*

The making of a winding-up order divests the company of the beneficial ownership of its assets, which cease to be applicable for its own benefit. It brings into operation a statutory scheme for dealing with the assets for the benefit of the creditors and members. The custody and control of all the property of the company and the power to manage its affairs are taken from the persons entrusted with them by the company's constitution and entrusted instead to a liquidator, whose powers are limited to carrying on the company's activities for the purpose of winding up its affairs, and who acts under the ultimate direction of the court. *j*

Any disposition of the property of the company and any alteration in the status of the company's members made after the presentation of the petition are void unless the court otherwise orders. Antecedent transactions of the company made before the presentation

of the petition are liable to be set aside. All proceedings against the company are
a automatically stayed, as is the power of the creditors to enforce their remedies against the
company. In performing his duties in a compulsory winding up, the liquidator acts as an
officer of the court. One of his duties is to take into his custody or under his control all
the property and choses in action to which the company is or appears to be entitled (see
s 537). It was submitted that in the case of an unregistered company this is made a matter
for the discretion of the liquidator by virtue of s 674. I disagree. Section 537 is
b mandatory: it imposes a statutory duty. Section 674, which applies to every kind of
unregistered company, English and foreign, corporate and unincorporated, does not give
the liquidator a discretion whether or not to perform his duties: it is there to ensure that
the liquidator has the necessary power to enable him to perform them.

The assets must be applied in satisfaction of the company's liabilities, and if there is a
surplus it must be distributed among the members according to their respective rights
c under the company's constitution. If there is a deficiency, calls may be made on the
members according to their respective obligations under the company's constitution. On
completion of the winding up, the company is dissolved. As Lord Atkin pointed out in
Russian and English Bank v Baring Bros & Co [1936] 1 All ER 505 at 517, [1936] AC 405 at
426, it is the company which is wound up, not the affairs of the company. The language
of the Act testifies to this: see, for example, ss 517, 519, 666(1), 674(1), and contrast this
d with ss 539(2)(h) and 568.

Although a winding up in the country of incorporation will normally be given extra-
territorial effect, a winding up elsewhere has only local operation. In the case of a foreign
company, therefore, the fact that other countries, in accordance with their own rules of
private international law, may not recognise our winding-up order or the title of a
liquidator appointed by our courts, necessarily imposes practical limitations on the
e consequences of the order. But in theory the effect of the order is world-wide. The
statutory trusts which it brings into operation are imposed on all the company's assets
wherever situate, within and beyond the jurisdiction. Where the company is
simultaneously being wound up in the country of its incorporation, the English court
will naturally seek to avoid unnecessary conflict and, so far as possible, to ensure that the
f English winding up is conducted as ancillary to the principal liquidation. In a proper
case, it may authorise the liquidator to refrain from seeking to recover assets situate
beyond the jurisdiction, thereby protecting him from any complaint that he had been
derelict in his duty. But the statutory trusts extend to such assets, and so does the
statutory obligation to collect and realise them and to deal with their proceeds in
accordance with the statutory scheme.

g It is obvious that the making of a winding-up order against the ITC would be
inconsistent with the continued operation of the treaties in accordance with their terms
and would compel the government of the United Kingdom either to be in breach of its
treaty obligations or to seek to withdraw from the ITA. Attempts were made to avoid
this result, or at least to minimise it, even at the expense of conceding that a winding-up
order against the ITC would have a more limited effect than usual. It was submitted, for
h example, that the court had power, and would be bound, to give effect to the inviolability
of the archives and premises of the ITC, guaranteed not only by the treaties but by the
1972 order, by giving appropriate directions to the liquidator and thereby excluding
such assets from the liquidation. I agree. If the 1972 order stood alone, it may well be
that the inviolability of the archives and premises would not survive the winding up, for
the taking of possession by the liquidator, as the agent of the ITC and the person entitled
j by virtue of the winding-up order to manage its properties and affairs, would not infringe
it. But the 1972 order does not stand alone: it falls to be construed in the light of the
treaties. And in this context I have no doubt that it means that the premises of the ITC
are not to be entered by, and its archives are not to be taken into the custody of, the
public authorities of the host state without the consent of the persons entrusted with the
management of its affairs by the terms of the ITA.

Again, it is inconceivable that the court would, or could, make a winding-up order against a solvent international organisation at the suit of one of the member states under s 666(5)(c) on the ground that the conduct of other member states made it just and equitable that their association together should be brought to an end. Such questions are not justiciable by domestic courts. They must be solved by diplomacy, not domestic litigation. But it is doubtful whether the court would entertain a petition by a contributory to wind up an ordinary foreign company, and when account is taken of the great variety of organisations, English and foreign, which are within s 665, it does not make nonsense of the statutory provisions to suppose that there are some which may be wound up on one ground but not on another.

Similarly, in my judgment, there can be no question of enforcing contributions from member states under s 671(2). Their obligations depend on the provisions of the organisation's constitution, that is to say the treaty which creates it and which constitutes the contract between the members under which the liability arises. To enforce such obligations would require the court to interpret and enforce the treaty, but it is well established that the court has no jurisdiction to do so: see *British Airways Board v Laker Airways Ltd* [1983] 3 All ER 375, [1984] 1 QB 142, CA; *rvsd in part* [1984] 3 All ER 39, [1985] AC 58, HL. This does not mean, as was somewhat flippantly suggested to me, that the court may read a treaty but may not understand it. It means that the interpretation and enforcement of a treaty between two or more states are not matters on which the decision of the courts of one party is binding on the other or others. A fortiori, it may be added, a decision of the courts of a country which is not a party to the treaty is not binding on those countries which are. The assumption of jurisdiction by the court would transgress the general and basic principle of law stated by Lord Kingsdown in *Secretary of State in Council of India v Kamachee Boye Sahaba* (1859) 13 Moo PCC 22 at 75, 15 ER 9 at 28–29:

'The transactions of independent States between each other are governed by other laws than those which Municipal Courts administer: such Courts have neither the means of deciding what is right, nor the power of enforcing any decision which they may make.'

The first part of that sentence was repeated by Lord Halsbury LC in *Cook v Sprigg* [1899] AC 572 at 578, [1895–9] All ER Rep 773 at 776, where he added that if there was a bargain between two sovereign powers, that was only a bargain which could be enforced by sovereign against sovereign in the ordinary course of diplomatic pressure. As will be seen, this objection is not met by arguing that the court would be enforcing a statutory liability arising under s 671(2) and not a treaty obligation, or (which comes to the same thing) that s 671(2) confers a jurisdiction to enforce treaty obligations. Again, however, it does not make nonsense of the statutory provisions to suppose that there may be some bodies within s 665 which are capable of being wound up under s 666 but which are outside s 671.

The facts that, if the jurisdiction exists, it can be exercised on only one of the grounds available and that some at least (and perhaps the most valuable) of the assets must be excluded from any order madeare of only peripheral significance and cannot be decisive. Of far greater importance is the fact that a winding-up order would put an end to the continued existence and operation of the ITC as provided by the treaties. All the powers of the ITC over its assets, other than its archives and premises, would cease, at least in the United Kingdom. The organisational and administrative machinery provided by the ITA would be displaced. The powers of the ITC and its executive chairman, which include the administration of the ITA, would become vested in the liquidator. The ITC could no longer carry out any of its functions, at least in the United Kingdom, the place where the ITA requires it to carry on its activities. It would be compelled, by the decision of the court of a single member state, to remove its headquarters from the United Kingdom, a matter which under the terms of the ITA is for the members by a prescribed majority to

a
decide. In my judgment, the conclusion is inescapable that the making of a winding-up order would be inconsistent with the ITA and would interfere with the continued activities of the ITC, its continued presence in the United Kingdom, its administration of the ITA, and whatever arrangements the member states may make to deal with the unforeseen situation which has arisen and to contribute to or make good the shortfall.

b
The petitioner's answer to all this was to say that it was irrelevant. Reliance was placed on the principle, to which I have already referred, that a treaty cannot of itself effect any alteration in our domestic law, or deprive the subject of his existing legal rights, unless and until it has been enacted into domestic law by legislation. The corollary of this principle is that the court will give effect to rights which are recognised by English domestic law without regard to the consequences of doing so in international law. It will not withhold relief to which the subject is entitled merely because the result of granting it would put the government of the United Kingdom in breach of its treaty obligations.

c
This was clearly established in the famous case of *The Parlement Belge* (1879) 4 PD 129. By a treaty concluded between the United Kingdom and Belgium, arrangements were made for mail packets to run between Dover and Ostend. The vessels themselves were the property of the Belgian state. One of the articles of the treaty provided that they were to be considered and treated in Dover and other British ports as vessels of war and that they should not be liable to seizure. One of the vessels was in collision with a steam tug. The
d
owners of the steam tug sought the arrest of the vessel. On the footing, later held to be incorrect, that the vessel, being engaged in a commercial activity, was not entitled by the common law to immunity from arrest, Phillimore J ordered the warrant to issue. This was plainly inconsistent with the treaty and put the government of the United Kingdom in breach of the express terms of the treaty. But the contention that this deprived the
e
court of the jurisdiction which it would otherwise possess was rejected as 'a use of the treaty-making prerogative of the Crown which I believe to be without precedent, and in principle contrary to the law of the constitution' (see 4 PD 129 at 154).

But this principle, which is not of course challenged by the ITC, has no bearing on the issue in the present case. There is no question of the ITA depriving the court of an existing jurisdiction to wind up the ITC. On the contrary, the ITC itself, the collective
f
enterprise of the members which it was formed to carry on, and the petitioner's claim to have it wound up, exist only by virtue of the ITA. Without the treaty, there would be nothing to wind up.

In fact, the petitioner's contentions presuppose that the necessary jurisdiction has been conferred by s 665. While, however, the Crown cannot, by the process of diplomacy and without the authority of Parliament, grant a foreigner immunity from action at the suit
g
of a subject who has suffered injury at his hands, it by no means follows that the general words of a statute must be construed so as to authorise the court to assume a jurisdiction to manage, regulate and wind up the affairs of a body whose very existence is the creation of that process.

It was urged on behalf of the petitioner that the words of s 665 are plain and unambiguous, that the word 'association' is apt to describe the ITC and that if a statute is
h
unambiguous effect must be given to it even if it is contrary to international law. For these propositions great reliance was placed on the decision of the House of Lords in *Collco Dealings Ltd v IRC* [1961] 1 All ER 762, [1962] AC 1. But it is one thing to give effect to plain and unambiguous language in a statute. It is quite another to insist that general words must invariably be given their fullest meaning and applied to every object which falls within their literal scope, regardless of the probable intentions of Parliament.
j
Far from supporting the petitioner's case, *Collco Dealings Ltd v IRC* undermines it. It was a case in which a taxpayer sought to escape the clear language of a tax-avoidance provision in a Finance Act by claiming that it was contrary to the terms of a double-taxation agreement, even though both parties to that agreement had stipulated that it might at any moment be brought to an end by the legislature of either country. The taxpayer's arguments were rejected. But the principle that general words in a statute may in a

proper case be given a more limited meaning than they are capable of bearing was
recognised by almost all their Lordships. Thus Viscount Simonds said ([1961] 1 All ER   *a*
762 at 765, [1962] AC 1 at 19):

'... I know of no case in which at the same time the words of a statute were
unambiguously clear and it was sought to vary them on grounds which could not
be justified by broad considerations of justice or expediency nor could be supposed
to commend themselves to that sovereign power whose citizens relied on them.'   *b*

Lord Morton said ([1961] 1 All ER 762 at 767, [1962] AC 1 at 21):

'... in the cases where wide words have been given a narrower meaning, there
has always been some reason to think that the legislature could not have intended
the wide words to have their full effect.'

Lord Reid said ([1961] 1 All ER 762 at 767, [1962] AC 1 at 22):   *c*

'I am not satisfied that it would be wrong in any circumstances to attach a limited
meaning to the words of s. 4(2) of the Finance (No. 2) Act, 1955. In some of the
authorities cited to your Lordships, words to my mind equally unambiguous have
been so limited, and, if the result of holding that these words cannot be given a
limited meaning were that Parliament must be held to have created a jurisdiction   *d*
wider than anything consistent with the broad principles of international law, I
would at least hesitate ...'

Lord Radcliffe said ([1961] 1 All ER 762 at 768, [1962] AC 1 at 23):

'It is, no doubt, true that statutory words apparently unlimited in scope may be   *e*
given a restricted field of application if there is admissible ground for importing
such a restriction; and the consideration that, if not construed in some limited sense,
they would amount to a breach of international law is well recognised as such a
ground ... The principle depends wholly on the supposition of a particular
intention in the legislature ...'

Both ss 665 and 671 are enacted in general terms. Literally construed, they are both   *f*
capable of applying to international organisations, including international organisations
of which the United Kingdom is a member. But it is obvious that s 671 at least does not
do so. Parliament cannot be taken to have intended to confer, by general words alone,
the jurisdiction to interpret the terms of an international treaty and to enforce the
obligations arising thereunder between independent sovereign states, a jurisdiction at   *g*
once unprecedented and incompatible with basic principles of English law.
The remaining question, therefore, is whether Parliament should be taken to have
intended, by the general words of s 665, to confer on the court jurisdiction to wind up
an international organisation established by treaty between sovereign states, including
an organisation of which the United Kingdom is itself a member. When the nature and
effect of a winding-up order are considered, I have no doubt that the answer here also   *h*
must be in the negative. An affirmative answer to that question would impute to
Parliament an intention to confer, by general words only, a jurisdiction incompatible
with our constitutional practice and with established principles of international law, and
which would be incapable of exercise, in the case of an organisation of which the United
Kingdom was a member, without putting the government of the United Kingdom in
breach of its treaty obligations. The exercise of the jurisdiction would constitute an   *j*
interference by the court with the ability of the executive, albeit in a limited sphere, to
conduct its relations with foreign states, a function which under our constitution is
reserved to the royal prerogative, and with the ability of other sovereign states to conduct
their relations with each other. It would alter the status of the organisation charged with

the function of administering the provisions of an international treaty and would be

a incompatible with the independence and international character of the organisation.

In *The Proper Law of International Organisations* (1962) pp 3, 8 Dr Wilfred Jenks wrote:

'If a body has the character of an international body corporate the law governing its corporate life must necessarily be international in character; it cannot be the territorial law of the headquarters of the body corporate or any other municipal

b legal system as such without destroying its international character. The law governing its corporate life will naturally cover such matters as the membership of the body, its competence, the composition and mutual relations of its various organs, their procedure, the rights and obligations of the body and its members in relation to each other, financial matters, the procedure of constitutional amendment, the rules governing the dissolution or winding up of the body, and the disposal of

c its assets in such a contingency . . . In the case of an international body corporate, as in that of a foreign corporation of municipal law, the personal law of the corporation must be considered together with the territorial law when we pass from the sphere of the law governing its corporate life to that of the law governing its operations within a particular jurisdiction. There is, however, a significant distinction between the two cases. In the case of foreign corporations the personal law yields to the

d territorial law in respect of such operations. The extent to which a foreign corporation is subject to the territorial law is determined primarily by the territorial law . . . Each State determines how far its own public policy requires it to exercise authority over the operations of foreign corporations within its jurisdiction. It may well be considered an essential element in the concept of an international body corporate that the extent to which its operations within the jurisdiction of a

e particular State are subject to the law of that State is limited by the obligations accepted by the State in recognising it as an international body corporate . . . In [such] event the personal law of the international body corporate, so far from yielding to the territorial law, will by virtue of its character as an international obligation of the State concerned, determine the extent of operation of the territorial

f law.'

In my judgment, the position can be considered broadly. An international organisation like the ITC, whether incorporated or not, is merely the means by which a collective enterprise of the member states is carried on, and through which their relations with each other in a particular sphere of common interest are regulated. Any attempt by one

g of the member states to assume responsibility for the administration and winding up of the organisation would be inconsistent with the arrangements made by them as to the manner in which the enterprise is to be carried on and their relations with each other in that sphere regulated. Sovereign states are free, if they wish, to carry on a collective enterprise through the medium of an ordinary commercial company incorporated in the territory of one of their number. But if they choose instead to carry it on through the

h medium of an international organisation, no one member state, by executive, legislative or judicial action, can assume the management of the enterprise and subject it to its own domestic law. For if one could, then all could; and the independence and international character of the organisation would be fragmented and destroyed. And if a member state has no such right, then a fortiori a non-member state has none. In my judgment, to impute to Parliament an intention, by general words only, to confer on the court a

j jurisdiction contrary to these principles and without precedent is unacceptable.

In my judgment, therefore, the court has no jurisdiction to wind up the ITC. This makes it unnecessary to consider the question of immunity, for there is no need for immunity from a jurisdiction which does not exist. But the question has been fully argued, and it is right that I should deal with it.

Immunity

Article 8(1) of the Headquarters Agreement provides that the ITC 'shall have immunity **a** from jurisdiction and execution' with certain exceptions which have been reproduced in the 1972 order. Paragraph 1 of Pt I of Sch I to the 1968 Act authorises the grant of 'immunity from suit and legal process'. Paragraph 6(1) of the 1972 order is in the following terms:

'The [ITC] shall have immunity from suit and legal process except: (*a*) to the **b** extent that the [ITC] shall have expressly waived such immunity in a particular case; (*b*) in respect of a civil action by a third party for damage arising from an accident caused by a motor vehicle belonging to or operated on behalf of the [ITC], or in respect of a motor offence involving such a vehicle; and (*c*) in respect of the enforcement of an arbitration award made under Article 23 or Article 24 of [the Headquarters Agreement].'   **c**

It has not been suggested that these exceptions are narrower, and the immunity correspondingly wider, than are required by the Headquarters Agreement, so that the 1972 order is ultra vires.

It was submitted on behalf of the petitioner that the word 'suit' in the 1972 order corresponds with, but is less extensive than, 'jurisdiction' in the Headquarters Agreement, and that the phrase 'legal process' in the one corresponds with 'execution' in the other. **d** By the process of construing the latter phrase in conformity with the treaty obligation and the former inconsistently with it, it was contended that the winding-up process is outside the immunity granted by the 1972 order. It is not 'suit', it was said, which is a word not normally used in English legal writings to describe a winding-up petition, and it is not 'execution'. If there is any ambiguity, it was submitted, it should be resolved in **e** favour of jurisdiction, on the ground that clear words are necessary in order to deprive the court of jurisdiction.

If there were an ambiguity, I would for my part resolve it in favour of immunity, on the grounds (1) that any ambiguity in an enactment passed in fulfilment of an obligation undertaken by treaty is to be resolved if possible so as to bring the enactment into conformity with the treaty obligation and (2) that the phrase 'suit and legal process' in **f** the 1972 order derives from and must mean the same as the corresponding phrase in the enabling Act, and there it must have been intended to bear a wide meaning in order to enable the as yet unknown requirements of future treaties to be met. The protection for the subject lies not in a narrow construction of the phrase 'suit and legal process' in the 1972 order but in the terms of s 1(6) of the 1968 Act.

But in my judgment there is no ambiguity. The phrase 'suit and legal process' in the **g** 1972 order corresponds with the phrase 'jurisdiction and execution' in the Headquarters Agreement, embraces all forms of adjudicative and enforcement jurisdiction, and clearly includes the winding-up process. The phrase in each case is a composite one, but the dividing line between the two component elements is not necessarily the same in each case; though in the present context I take the view that it is, 'suit' extending to all forms of the adjudicative, and 'legal process' to all forms of the enforcement, jurisdiction. But **h** if, contrary to my view, the word 'suit' is to be narrowly construed, then the ambit of the phrase 'legal process' which is apt to describe all the steps in any legal proceedings from the issue of the originating process to the levying of execution, must be correspondingly expanded.

The question, therefore, is whether a petition for the winding up of the ITC on the ground that it is insolvent and presented by a creditor with the benefit of an arbitration **j** award in its favour is a proceeding 'in respect of the enforcement of an arbitration award'. Great reliance was placed on behalf of the petitioner on the description of the winding-up process by Brightman LJ in *Re Lines Bros Ltd* [1982] 2 All ER 183 at 194–195, [1983] Ch 1 at 8:

a 'The liquidation of an insolvent company is a process of collective enforcement of debts for the benefit of the general body of creditors. Although it is not a process of execution, because it is not for the benefit of a particular creditor, it is nevertheless akin to execution because its purpose is to enforce, on a pari passu basis, the payment of the admitted or proved debts of the company. When, therefore, a company goes into liquidation a process is initiated which, for all creditors, is similar to the process, which is initiated, for one creditor, by execution.'

b It is to be observed that Brightman LJ was careful to refer to enforcing the payment of the debts, not to enforcing a judgment or award. In the ordinary case a winding-up petition is a means of recovering a debt, not of enforcing a judgment or award, which merely establishes the existence of the debt and is not a procedural requirement: see Re a company [1915] 1 Ch 520 at 528 per Phillimore LJ. It was sought to get over this difficulty c as well as the further difficulty that, by presenting a winding-up petition, the creditor does not seek to recover for himself alone but for the benefit of all the creditors, by relying on the ITC's immunity. In the present case, it was submitted, the existence of an arbitration award was a procedural requirement. Without such an award in its favour, a creditor could neither present nor support a petition, nor prove for the debt in the winding up. Accordingly, whatever might be the position in other cases, a petition to d wind up the ITC presented by a creditor with an arbitration award in its favour could enure for the benefit only of other creditors with similar awards in their favour; and this made it a process for the collective enforcement of arbitration awards.

The argument is ingenious but not persuasive. In the first place, the 1972 order refers to 'the enforcement of an arbitration award' (in the singular), not to the collective enforcement of arbitration awards (in the plural); and where the phrase is derived from e an international treaty, to which the Interpretation Act 1978 does not apply, I doubt that the singular includes the plural. In the second place, the creditor with the benefit of an arbitration award is not the only creditor who can bring himself within the exceptions in the 1972 order. There are two others: the creditor in respect of whose debt the ITC has waived its immunity; and the creditor with a claim for damages arising from an accident f caused by a motor vehicle. Either class of creditor could support the present petition and prove in the winding up. How, then, is it possible with any kind of accuracy to describe the petition, even of the present petitioner, as a process for 'the enforcement of an arbitration award'? On the contrary, the petitioner's arguments lead only to the conclusion that it is a process for the collective enforcement of all such debts as are provable in the liquidation, which if true is true of any winding-up petition and is not g what para 6(1)(c) of the 1972 order says. In any event, I doubt that, in considering the nature or character of a winding-up petition, it is right to take account of more than the nature of the petitioner's debt and the grounds on which the order is sought, and in particular I doubt that it is right to take account of the extent of any immunity or other defence the debtor may have. The question is whether a winding-up petition presented by a creditor with the benefit of an arbitration award and alleging insolvency is the h enforcement of an arbitration award. The answer cannot depend on the extent of the debtor's immunity, and whether there is only one or more than one exception to it. In my view, the fact that, unusually, the present petitioner has to prove an arbitration award, not to establish his locus standi to present the petition but to meet an anticipated defence of immunity, is irrelevant, because it does not alter the essential character of the winding-up process.

j In the context of sovereign, diplomatic and other immunity, a crucial distinction is made between the adjudicative and enforcement jurisdictions. Waiver of immunity from the one does not waive immunity from the other, even in respect of the same claim. In the case of the ITC there is no waiver of or exception to its immunity from the adjudicative jurisdiction of the court in respect of claims arising from its commercial activities. Instead, such claims are required to be referred to arbitration. Paragraph 6(1)(c) of the 1972 order is concerned exclusively with the enforcement of any award resulting **a** from such arbitration. In respect of its commercial activities, therefore, the ITC enjoys complete immunity from the court's adjudicative jurisdiction, and has only a limited exposure to its enforcement jurisdiction.

I am not satisfied that, in this context, the presentation and hearing of a winding-up petition, as distinct from the proof of debt in the winding up, are properly to be classified as falling within the enforcement jurisdiction at all. It is fallacious to suppose that, **b** because the petitioner is not seeking to establish his debt, the court is exercising its enforcement jurisdiction. Even if the petitioner has previously resorted to litigation to establish his debt, the presentation of a petition marks the commencement of an entirely new lis. The issue at the hearing is not whether the petitioning and other creditors, some of whom will not yet have established their claims, should be paid, but whether the company is insolvent and, if so, whether it should be wound up or allowed to try to trade **c** out of its difficulties. There is much to be said for the view that, in deciding whether or not the company should be wound up, the court is engaged in a new process of adjudication, separate and different from any that may previously have been involved in establishing the petitioning creditor's debt.

But it is not necessary to decide this, for in my judgment the winding-up process is plainly not a method of enforcing a judgment or arbitration award, and there is nothing **d** in the language of Brightman LJ in *Re Lines Bros Ltd*, which in any case is descriptive and not intended to be by way of classification, to suggest the contrary. Far from enabling any judgment or award to be enforced, the making of a winding-up order prevents it. The great object of insolvency law, whether individual or corporate, is to protect the debtor from harassment by the creditors, and the assets from piecemeal realisation and unequal distribution as the creditors scramble for them. Whether the petition is presented **e** by a creditor or by the debtor, its purpose is to obtain an order which will preclude the creditors from enforcing any judgments or awards which they may have obtained, and substitute the right to participate in a pari passu distribution out of an insufficient fund in full satisfaction of their claims. That is not the enforcement of their judgments or awards, but the opposite. **f**

In any case, whatever else it may be, the presentation of a winding-up petition is not simply a means of enforcing a judgment or award; as Fletcher Moulton LJ said of an application for a bankruptcy notice in *Re a bankruptcy notice* [1907] 1 KB 478 at 482: '[It] is not a method of enforcing a judgment. It is the commencement of proceedings of far wider effect.' No one asked to waive his organisation's immunity from the enforcement of an adverse judgment or arbitration award would think for a moment that it was being **g** invited to submit to being compulsorily wound up. It was submitted that to come within para 6(1)(c) of the 1972 order it is sufficient if the proceedings include the enforcement of an arbitration award; they need not be confined to that. I disagree. The submission makes nonsense of the paragraph and cannot be accepted.

Conclusion **h**

I conclude that s 665 of the 1985 Act confers no jurisdiction to make a compulsory winding-up order against the ITC, and that in any case para 6(1) of the 1972 order makes the ITC immune from such jurisdiction.

The failure of an international organisation to meet its obligations is without precedent. The possibility was obviously not foreseen when the treaties which established or continued the ITC were concluded. The responsible course now would be for the **j** member states, by diplomatic means, to negotiate suitable arrangements to meet the shortfall. Failing this, there is much to be said for the view that an unprecedented situation calls for an unprecedented solution. But under our constitution it is for Parliament to decide whether the United Kingdom, as the host state, should intervene and, contrary to the terms of the treaties and without the consent of the other member states, claim the right to subject the affairs of an insolvent international organisation to a   its own domestic jurisdiction and wind it up. All I decide is that by the general words of existing legislation Parliament has not already demonstrated any such intention. I accede to the motion and strike out the petition.

Petition struck out. Leave to appeal granted.

b   Solicitors: *Cameron Markby* (for the ITC); *Allen & Overy* (for the petitioner); *Slaughter & May* (for Kleinwort Benson); *Treasury Solicitor.*

Jacqueline Metcalfe   Barrister.

c

R v Maginnis

HOUSE OF LORDS

LORD KEITH OF KINKEL, LORD BRANDON OF OAKBROOK, LORD MACKAY OF CLASHFERN, LORD OLIVER OF AYLMERTON AND LORD GOFF OF CHIEVELEY

d   21, 22 JANUARY, 5 MARCH 1987

Drugs – Controlled drugs – Possession with intent to supply – Supply – Defendant in temporary possession of drug – Defendant holding drug for owner and intending to return it to owner in due course – Whether intention to 'supply' drug to owner – Whether necessary that transfer of physical control from one person to another be for purposes of that other – Misuse of Drugs Act 1971, s 5(3).

e

A package of cannabis resin was found in the defendant's car when he was arrested in connection with an alleged assault. The defendant claimed that the package was not his but had been left in the car on the previous evening by a friend of his whom he expected would collect it from him. He was charged with and convicted of, inter alia, possession of a controlled drug with intent to supply it to another, contrary to s 5(3)[a] of the Misuse f   of Drugs Act 1971. He appealed, contending that his intention to return the package to its owner did not amount to an intention to 'supply' drugs within s 5(3). The Court of Appeal allowed his appeal. The Crown appealed to the House of Lords.

Held (Lord Goff dissenting) – A person who was in unlawful possession of a controlled drug which had been deposited with him by another person for safekeeping had the g   necessary 'intent to supply it to another' within s 5(3) of the 1971 Act if his intention was to return the drug to that other person and for that other person's purposes. Although 'supply' connoted more than the mere transfer of physical control of a chattel or object from one person to another (since the handing over had to be for the purpose of enabling the recipient to use the chattel or object for his own purposes), it was not a necessary h   element that the supply be made out of the provider's own personal resources. It followed that the defendant had been rightly convicted. The Crown's appeal would accordingly be allowed (see p 909 h to b, p 912 h to p 913 d, post).

R v Delgado [1984] 1 All ER 449 applied.
Donnelly v HM Advocate 1985 SLT 243 approved.
Decision of the Court of Appeal [1986] 2 All ER 110 reversed.

j   **Notes**

For possession of a controlled drug with intent to supply, see 11 Halsbury's Laws (4th edn) para 1093 and 30 ibid para 746, and for cases on the subject, see 15 Digest (Reissue) 1077–1078, 9170–9173.

For the Misuse of Drugs Act 1971, s 5, see 28 Halsbury's Statutes (4th edn) 505.

a   Section 5(3) is set out at p 909 c, post

Cases referred to in opinions

Donnelly v HM Advocate 1985 SLT 243.

R v Delgado [1984] 1 All ER 449, [1984] 1 WLR 89, CA.

R v Dempsey (1985) Times, 22 November, CA.

R v Gould [1968] 1 All ER 849, [1968] 2 QB 65, [1968] 2 WLR 643, CA.

R v Harris [1968] 2 All ER 49, [1968] 1 WLR 769, CA.

R v Mills [1963] 1 All ER 202, [1963] 1 QB 522, [1963] 2 WLR 137, CCA.

Young v Bristol Aeroplane Co Ltd [1944] 2 All ER 293, [1944] KB 718, CA; *affd* [1946] 1 All ER 98, [1946] AC 163, HL.

Appeal

The Crown appealed with leave of the Court of Appeal, Criminal Division given on 10 March 1986 against the decision of that court (Parker LJ, French and Mann JJ) ([1986] 2 All ER 110, [1986] QB 618) on 16 December 1985 for reasons given on 20 December 1985 allowing the appeal of the defendant, Patrick Terrance Maginnis, against his conviction on 20 June 1985 in the Crown Court at Inner London Sessions before his Honour Judge Pullinger and a jury of possessing a controlled drug, 227g of cannabis resin, with intent to supply it to another contrary to s 5(3) of the Misuse of Drugs Act 1971. The Court of Appeal certified that a point of law of general public importance (set out at p 906 *b*, post) was involved in its decision to allow the appeal. The facts are set out in the opinion of Lord Keith.

Michael Kalisher QC and *Michael Birnbaum* for the Crown.
Keith Stones and *Douglas Taylor* for the defendant.

The Lordships took time for consideration.

5 March. The following opinions were delivered.

LORD KEITH OF KINKEL. My Lords, the respondent (the defendant) was charged on indictment with three counts alleging contraventions of the Misuse of Drugs Act 1971. The first count charged him with possessing a controlled drug with intent to supply it unlawfully to another, contrary to s 5(3) of the Act, and the second count, which was alternative to the first and related to the same package of drugs, charged him with unlawful possession of it contrary to s 5(2) of the Act. The third count charged unlawful possession of a different smaller quantity of drugs. The present appeal is not concerned with that count and it need not be further mentioned. At the trial, before his Honour Judge Pullinger and a jury in the Crown Court at Inner London Sessions, the defendant pleaded not guilty to the first count, but guilty to the second. The plea of guilty to the second count was not accepted by the prosecution, and the trial proceeded on the first count. Evidence was led by the prosecution to the effect that a package containing 227g of cannabis resin, a controlled drug, having a street value of about £500, was found under the driver's seat of the defendant's car after he had been arrested in connection with an alleged assault. The defendant stated to police officers that he did not deal in drugs and that the package had been left in the car on the previous evening by a friend. He declined to name the friend and said: 'I expected him to come round and pick it up.' At the close of the prosecution case counsel for the defendant asked the judge to direct the jury that if they accepted that his intention was merely to return the package of drugs to the person who had left it in the car that would not have been an intent to supply it to another in contravention of s 4(1)(b) of the 1971 Act, and that he should therefore be acquitted on count one. The judge ruled that the intention to return the package to the person who had left it in the car did constitute the requisite intent for conviction, and the defendant thereupon changed his plea on the first count to one of guilty. He was sentenced to 12 months' imprisonment on that count.

The defendant appealed, and on 20 December 1985 the Court of Appeal, Criminal
a Division ([1986] 2 All ER 110, [1986] QB 618) (Parker LJ, French and Mann JJ) allowed
the appeal and quashed the conviction. On the application of counsel for the Crown, it
certified that a point of law of general public importance was involved in its decision,
and later granted leave to appeal to this House. The certified question is as follows:

> 'I. Whether a person intends to supply a controlled drug if:—(a) He intends to
b transfer physical control of the drug to another; or (b) He intends to transfer physical
control of the drug to another for the benefit of the other. II. If (b) above is correct,
whether such benefit is constituted by the return of physical control of the drug to
a bailor by a bailee.'

Section 5(3) of the 1971 Act provides:

c > 'Subject to section 28 of this Act, it is an offence for a person to have a controlled
drug in his possession, whether lawfully or not, with intent to supply it to another
in contravention of section 4(1) of this Act.'

Section 4(1) provides:

> 'Subject to any regulations made under section 7 of this Act for the time being in
d force, it shall not be lawful for a person—(a) to produce a controlled drug; or (b) to
supply or offer to supply a controlled drug to another.'

No question arises as to the possible application of s 28 or s 5(4) or of any regulations
made under s 7.

The issue in the appeal is concerned with the meaning properly to be attributed to the
word 'supply' in ss 4(1) and 5(3). This is to be ascertained in the usual way by reference
e to the ordinary natural meaning of the word together with any assistance which may be
afforded by the context. Counsel for the Crown sought also to derive some assistance
from the Misuse of Drugs Regulations 1973, SI 1973/797, made under the powers to that
effect contained in the 1971 Act, which came into force at the same time as the principal
provisions of the Act. This is not, however, one of those exceptional cases where a guide
to the construction of a statute may be obtained from regulations made under it, and the
f regulations in question are not, in my opinion, admissible for the purpose sought to be
made of them. The same applies, a fortiori, to the Misuse of Drugs Regulations 1985, SI
1985/2066, to which reference was also made.

The word 'supply', in its ordinary natural meaning, conveys the idea of furnishing or
providing to another something which is wanted or required in order to meet the wants
or requirements of that other. It connotes more than the mere transfer of physical control
g of some chattel or object from one person to another. No one would ordinarily say that
to hand over something to a mere custodier was to supply him with it. The additional
concept is that of enabling the recipient to apply the thing handed over to purposes for
which he desires or has a duty to apply it. In my opinion it is not a necessary element in
the conception of supply that the provision should be made out of the personal resources
h of the person who does the supplying. Thus, if an employee draws from his employer's
store materials or equipment which he requires for purposes of his work, it involves no
straining of language to say that the storekeeper supplies him with those materials or
that equipment, notwithstanding that they do not form part of the storekeeper's own
resources and that he is merely the custodier of them. I think the same is true if it is the
owner of the business who is drawing from his own storekeeper tools or materials which
j form part of his own resources. The storekeeper can be said to be supplying him with
what he needs. If a trafficker in controlled drugs sets up a store of these in the custody of
a friend whom he thinks unlikely to attract the suspicions of the police, and later draws
on the store for the purposes of his trade, or for his own use, the custodier is in my
opinion rightly to be regarded as supplying him with drugs. On the assumed facts of the
present case (they were never tested before the jury), the defendant had been made

custodier of the drugs by his unnamed friend, who, having regard to the quantity of the
drugs, may legitimately be inferred to have been a trader. If on a later occasion the   *a*
defendant had handed the drugs back to his friend, he would have done so in order to
enable the friend to apply the drugs for the friend's own purposes. He would accordingly,
in my opinion, have supplied the drugs to his friend in contravention of s 4(1). It follows
that, in so far as he was in possession of the drugs with the intention of handing them
back to the friend when asked for by the latter, he was in possession with intent to supply
the drugs to another in contravention of s 4(1) and was thus guilty under s 5(3).   *b*

The reason why the Court of Appeal, Criminal Division gave leave to appeal in this
case was that it believed that it perceived a conflict between two earlier decisions of that
court. These two decisions were *R v Delgado* [1984] 1 All ER 449, [1984] 1 WLR 89 and
R v Dempsey (1985) The Times, 22 November. In *R v Delgado* the accused had been a
passenger in a minicab which was stopped by police because it was not displaying a tax
disc. He ran away leaving in the car a holdall containing 6.31 kg of cannabis. At his trial   *c*
on a charge of contravening s 5(3) he gave evidence that two acquaintances had told him
that they had stolen the cannabis and had nowhere to keep it. They asked him to look
after it for a couple of hours and he agreed to do so. He was on his way to deliver it back
to them when he was arrested. The judge ruled that returning the cannabis to those who
had given it to him would be an act of supplying, and the accused thereupon pleaded
guilty to the charge. On his appeal the Court of Appeal, Criminal Division, consisting of   *d*
Lord Lane CJ, Skinner and McCowan JJ, held that the ruling of the trial judge was correct
and dismissed the appeal. Skinner J, delivering the judgment of the Court of Appeal said
([1984] 1 All ER 449 at 452, [1984] 1 WLR 89 at 92):

> 'Thus we are driven back to considering the word "supply" in its context. The
> judge himself relied on the dictionary definition, which is a fairly wide one. This   *e*
> court has been referred to the *Shorter Oxford English Dictionary* which gives a large
> number of definitions to the word "supply", but they have a common feature, viz
> that in the word "supply" is inherent the furnishing or providing of something
> which is wanted. In the judgment of this court, the word "supply" in s 5(3) of the
> 1971 Act covers a similarly wide range of transactions. A feature common to all of
> those transactions is a transfer of physical control of a drug from one person to   *f*
> another. In our judgment questions of the transfer of ownership or legal possession
> of those drugs are irrelevant to the issue whether or not there was intent to supply.
> In the present case on his own evidence the appellant had possession of a substantial
> quantity of cannabis. His intention was to transfer control of it to his two friends at
> an agreed time and place. In those circumstances it seems to us that the judge was
> entirely right in his ruling, and that therefore the argument put forward by counsel   *g*
> for the appellant has no foundation.'

In *R v Dempsey* the first accused, Michael, was a registered drug addict who had
lawfully obtained from a medical practitioner ampoules of a controlled drug Physeptone.
His account was that, while in the street accompanied by the second accused, Maureen,
he gave her some of the ampoules to look after while he went into a public lavatory to   *h*
inject himself from another ampoule. This was observed by police officers who arrested
both accused. Michael was charged with supply of a controlled drug to Maureen under
s 4(3)(a) of the 1971 Act and Maureen with possession under s 5(2). The trial judge ruled
that, assuming Michael's account was true he had no defence to the charge of supply, and
he thereupon changed his plea to guilty. On his appeal to the Court of Appeal, Criminal
Division that court, consisting of Lord Lane CJ, Boreham and McCowan JJ, held that the   *j*
ruling of the trial judge was incorrect and quashed the conviction. Lord Lane CJ, giving
the judgment of the court, said:

> 'Michael Dempsey was charged under s 4(3)(a) of the Misuse of Drugs Act 1971,
> which makes it an offence for any person to supply a controlled drug to another.

a   The question in his case is whether by handing the ampoules to Maureen to hold for him temporarily, he can be said to have supplied the ampoules to her. The word "supply" is defined in the *Shorter Oxford English Dictionary* as follows: ". . . to fulfil, satisfy (a need or want) by furnishing what is wanted. To furnish, provide, afford (something needed, desired or used) . . ." Those are the two definitions which seemed to be relevant to the particular circumstances. It is an act, so it seems, which is designed to benefit the recipient. It does not seem to us that it is apt to describe

b   the deposit of an article with another person for safe keeping, as was the case here. The example was canvassed in argument of a person who hands his coat to a cloakroom attendant for safe keeping during the show in a theatre or cinema. It could scarcely be said that the person handing the coat supplies it to the cloakroom attendant. Nor do we think it makes any difference that the cloakroom attendant wishes in one sense to get his coat, thinking that he may get a tip at the end of the

c   evening. That is not the sort of wish or need which is envisaged by the definition of the offence. That sort of transfer is a transfer for the benefit of the transferor rather than the transferee. In our judgment therefore the learned recorder was in error in ruling as he did. He should have left it to the jury to decide whether or not this transfer to Maureen of the controlled drug Physeptone was so that she could use the drug for her own purposes, for example to hand on to someone else or to use on her

d   own body, in which case there would have been a supply, or may simply have been for safe keeping and for return to Michael, who was lawfully entitled to the drug, it having been prescribed for him, in which case there was not. We have been referred to a number of decisions, particularly the decisions in *R v Delgado* [1984] 1 All ER 449, [1984] 1 WLR 89, *R v Harris* [1968] 2 All ER 49, [1968] 1 WLR 769 and *R v Mills* [1963] 1 All ER 202, [1963] 1 QB 522. We do not think that those decisions

e   assist us in the interpretation of the word "supply". If there is any ambiguity in the word, it must be resolved in favour of the defendant. That is clear from the passage to which we have been referred in *Maxwell on Interpretation of Statutes* (12th edn, 1969) p 239. There is no need for us to read that. We do not think there is an ambiguity. But as I say, if there is, the principles set out in *Maxwell* applies, namely

f   that the ambiguity must be resolved in favour of the defendant.'

In the present case Mann J, giving the judgment of the court, said of these two decisions ([1986] 2 All ER 110 at 113–114, [1986] QB 618 at 623–624):

'We find it impossible to reconcile the meaning put on the word "supply" in *R v Delgado* with the meaning put on that word in *R v Dempsey*. The decision in *R v Delgado* is that the word is satisfied if there is a transfer of physical control of the

g   drug in question. However in *R v Dempsey* there was a transfer of physical control, yet the conviction was quashed. The cases cannot be composed on the basis that *R v Delgado* concerned s 5(3) of the 1971 Act, whereas *R v Dempsey* concerned s 4(3)(a). Each offence is drawn in terms of supply in contravention of s 4(1). We are faced with two decisions of this court which conflict. In that circumstance we are bound to decide which of them to follow: see *Young v Bristol Aeroplane Co Ltd* [1944] 2 All

h   ER 293 at 300, [1944] KB 718 at 729; *R v Gould* [1968] 1 All ER, [1968] 2 QB 65. In our judgment, the meaning put on the word "supply" in *R v Dempsey* is to be preferred. With respect to the members of the court in *R v Delgado* who thought otherwise, we cannot think that the word "supply" as a matter of ordinary language is apt to mean merely transfer of physical control. We agree with the view of the

j   court in *R v Dempsey*, that for there to be a supply there must be a transfer of physical control which is for the benefit of the recipient of the article. Counsel for the Crown accepted that this was the correct formulation but argued that the transferee obtains a benefit when he receives back an article which he has placed in the custody of another. The only discernible benefit is the resumption of actual possession. We do not accept that this is sufficient to constitute the return of an article an act of supply.

In ordinary language the cloakroom attendant, the left luggage officer, the warehouseman and the shoe mender do not "supply" to their customers the articles *a* which those customers have left with them. In each case the lawyer would perceive the translation of the right to possession into actual possession, but even so the user of ordinary language does not perceive a "supply". To hold that A, in possession of a controlled drug, does not supply B when he hands the substance to B for safe keeping whilst he makes a telephone call from a telephone box, and is therefore not guilty of possession with intent to supply when he decides to hand the substance to B, but *b* that when B returns the substance to A he supplies A and is thus guilty of possession with intent to supply from the moment when he accepts the substance into his custody whilst A telephones, is in our judgment unacceptable. It would be to attribute to Parliament an intention which we can only regard as bordering on the farcical. If B, when found holding the drug, were to be asked, "Do you intend to supply it to anyone?"? he would surely reply, "No, it belongs to A. I'm holding it *c* for him while he telephones in that call-box over there". We cannot give the word "supply" a meaning that would render this appellant guilty of possession with intent to supply. Accordingly, there was a wrong direction on a question of law, and for that reason we allowed the appeal against conviction on count 1.'

In my opinion, there is a clear distinction between the decision in *R v Delgado* and that *d* in *R v Dempsey*. In *R v Delgado* a custodier was found to have the necessary intent to supply because his intention was to hand back controlled drugs to the persons who had deposited them with him so as to enable those persons to apply the drugs to their own purposes, and thus put them back into circulation. In *R v Dempsey* there was a mere placing in temporary custody, and no intention of enabling the custodier to use the drugs for her own purposes. Maureen did not want the drugs for any purpose of her own. One *e* who deposits controlled drugs of which he is in unlawful possession with a temporary custodier has no legal right to require the drugs to be handed back to him. Indeed, it is the duty of the custodier not to hand them back but to destroy them or to deliver them to a police officer so that they may be destroyed. The custodier in choosing to return the drugs to the depositor does something which he is not only not obliged to do, but which he has a duty not to do. Any analogy with bailment is false in a situation where the *f* depositor has no right to ownership which the law would recognise and certainly none to immediate possession.

It is worth noting that, in a decision which was not cited in the Court of Appeal, the High Court of Justiciary in Scotland accepted a construction of s 5(3) which is in line with *R v Delgado*, of which it expressed approval. That decision is *Donnelly v HM Advocate* *g* 1985 SLT 243. The appellant had claimed that a quantity of controlled drugs, of which she had been found in possession, had been placed in her custody by a man called Colin Stewart. In the course of the opinion of the court it was said (at 244):

'. . . if the appellant intended to part with all or some of the drugs in her possession to Colin Stewart, even for his own use, she intended to supply Colin Stewart, and it matters not whether his intention was to use them himself or to supply others.' *h*

It is, I think, a misinterpretation of the grounds of judgment in *R v Delgado* to regard them as holding that a mere transfer of physical control of a drug from one person to another may constitute supply within the meaning of the subsection. If, however, this was the intention of the judgment, it is not, in my view, entirely correct. For the reasons I have earlier expressed, it is necessary that the transfer be for the purposes of the *j* transferee, and the decision in *Donnelly v HM Advocate* accords with that view. The desirability of these statutory provisions, applicable as they are both in England and in Scotland, being interpreted alike in both jurisdictions needs no emphasis.

My Lords, for these reasons I would allow the appeal. The certified question is not in all respects apt to raise the true issue in the case. I would amend it so as to read: 'Whether a person in unlawful possession of a controlled drug which has been deposited with him *a* for safe keeping has the intent to supply that drug to another if his intention is to return the drug to the person who deposited it with him,' and answer the question as so amended in the affirmative.

LORD BRANDON OF OAKBROOK. My Lords, I have had the advantage of reading in draft the speech prepared by my noble and learned friend Lord Keith. I agree with it, and for the reasons which he gives I would allow the appeal, and answer the

b certified question, amended in the manner which he proposes, in the affirmative.

LORD MACKAY OF CLASHFERN. My Lords, I have had the advantage of reading the speech prepared by my noble and learned friend Lord Keith. I agree that the certified question should be amended in the manner indicated by my noble and learned friend and that the appeal should be allowed and the amended question answered in the

c affirmative for the reasons which he has given.

LORD OLIVER OF AYLMERTON. My Lords, I have had the advantage of reading the speech prepared by my noble and learned friend Lord Keith. I agree that the certified question should be amended in the manner indicated by my noble and learned friend

d and that the appeal should be allowed and the amended question answered in the affirmative for the reasons which he has given.

LORD GOFF OF CHIEVELEY. My Lords, we are concerned in this case with the meaning of the word 'supply' as used in the expression 'with intent to supply it to another' in s 5(3) of the Misuse of Drugs Act 1971; though, since there is no reason to

e suppose that the word 'supply' in s 5(3) is intended to have any different meaning from the same word in s 4(1)(b) of the Act, which makes it unlawful 'to supply or offer to supply a controlled drug to another', we are really concerned with the meaning of the word in both subsections.

The primary rule of construction is that we should attribute to words their natural and ordinary meaning, unless the context otherwise requires. So what is the natural and

f ordinary meaning of the word 'supply'? I hesitate to attempt a definition, especially as the word under consideration is not always very precisely used; but to me the word, as used in relation to goods, connotes the idea of making goods available to another from resources other than those of the recipient. This approach is, I consider, consistent with some of the dictionary meanings in the *Shorter Oxford English Dictionary*, for example, 'The act of making up a deficiency, or of fulfilling a want or demand' and 'The act of

g supplying something needed'. It is also, I believe, consistent with the ordinary use of the word in everyday speech. So to deliver goods to a buyer or his agent under a contract of sale would obviously be to supply goods to that person, and, indeed, would perhaps provide the typical example of a supply of goods; though I can see no reason why the delivery of goods by way of gift should not also amount to a supply of goods.

But we are concerned in the present case with a deposit of goods; and I do not feel able

h to say that either the delivery of goods by a depositor to a depositee or the redelivery of goods by a depositee to a depositor can sensibly be described as an act of supplying goods to another. I certainly cannot conceive of myself using the word 'supply' in this context in ordinary speech. I ask myself: why should I not do so? I answer: I would not describe the delivery by the depositor to the depositee as a supply of goods, because the goods are not being made available to him but are rather being entrusted to him; and I would not

j describe the redelivery by the depositee to the depositor as a supply of goods, because the goods are simply being returned to him, rather than being made available to him from resources other than his own.

The context does not, as I see it, require any departure from the natural and ordinary meaning of the word. Moreover, the interpretation which I would give to the word, which I derive from my understanding of the use of the word 'supply' in ordinary speech,

is consistent with the conclusion of the Court of Appeal in the present case. I must
confess that, in a case where I am looking for the ordinary meaning of an ordinary word   *a*
like 'supply', I am much influenced by the fact that the three members of the Court of
Appeal, having searched like myself for the ordinary meaning of the word, and having
considered the earlier authorities, have reached the same conclusion as I myself have
reached. In delivering the judgment of the court, Mann J said ([1986] 2 All ER 110 at
113–114, [1986] QB 618 at 624):

> 'In ordinary language the cloakroom attendant, the left luggage officer, the   *b*
> warehouseman and the shoe mender do not "supply" to their customers the articles
> which those customers have left with them.'

I entirely agree. I cannot imagine ordinary people using the word 'supply' to describe
any of those four transactions. They would rather talk about redelivering or returning
the goods to the customer or, more colloquially, handing them back to him. It follows   *c*
that, in respectful agreement with my noble and learned friend Lord Keith, I cannot
accept the submission of the Crown that a mere transfer of possession of itself necessarily
constitutes a supply. But I find myself, with all respect, unable to agree with my noble
and learned friend that it is a sufficient qualification to characterise a transfer of possession
as a supply that it should be made in order to meet the wants or requirements of the
recipient, such expression being understood to include circumstances where the want or   *d*
requirement of the recipient is simply to get his own goods back again. Moreover, in the
case where a man deposits his own goods with a storeman, and draws on those goods
from time to time, I do not think that it would be an appropriate use of the word 'supply'
to describe the storeman as supplying the depositor when he releases part of the goods to
him. Even if the word 'supply' were to be used in such a context, I would regard it as a
loose or aberrant use of the word which should not be regarded as providing any   *e*
foundation for the proposition that the word can be appropriately used, or is normally
used, in every case where a depositee returns the goods to a depositor.

There remains, however, a problem. We are concerned in the present case with
controlled drugs; and, in cases which come before the courts, an agreement by a depositee
of controlled drugs to return them to the depositor will ordinarily be unlawful. In such
circumstances the depositor will have no enforceable right that the drugs should be   *f*
restored to him. Can it therefore be said that, in those circumstances, since the depositee
is not bound to return the drugs to the depositor, he can, if he does so, be described as
supplying them to the depositor? I do not think so. The point is for me too legalistic. Let
us forget about controlled drugs for the moment; and let us suppose that, owing to some
technical rule of law, a contract of deposit of goods is unenforceable. But the depositee is
an honourable man, and returns the goods to the man who deposited them with him.   *g*
Nobody would, I think, describe him in ordinary language as supplying the goods to the
depositor, simply because he was not legally bound to return them. The fact is that the
goods came from the depositor's own resources; and all the depositee was doing was
returning them to him. True it is that, in the case of controlled drugs with which we are
concerned, not only has the depositor no enforceable right to recover them from the   *h*
depositee, but the depositee has a duty to hand them over to the authorities. But I cannot,
for my part, see that this means that, if the depositee does not comply with his duty and
instead hands the drugs back to the depositor, he is 'supplying' them to the depositor. I
cannot imagine myself so describing his act; I would say that the depositor had, in breach
of his duty, returned the controlled drugs to the depositor. To use the word 'supply' in
such a case would not, in my opinion, accord with the natural and ordinary meaning of   *j*
that word.

I wish to add that the conclusion which I have reached as to the meaning of the word
'supply' in s 5(3) of the 1971 Act seems to me to accord with the purpose of that
subsection. The subsection creates an offence which is evidently directed at those who
are 'pushing' controlled drugs. But a person with whom controlled drugs are deposited

is not, in my opinion, necessarily involved in 'pushing' them. He may be so involved;
a but if so he can then be charged and convicted as an accessory. But to impose a meaning
on the word 'supply' in the subsection which would have the effect that every depositee
of controlled drugs would be in possession of them with intent to supply them to another
could, in my opinion, result in persons being convicted of that offence when they should
only be convicted of the offence of having been in unlawful possession of them. It is not
to be forgotten that, even for the latter offence, it is open to the court to impose, in an
b appropriate case a substantial penalty of up to five years' imprisonment. If, however,
contrary to my understanding, it were to be thought that any depositee of controlled
drugs should be held to be in possession of them with intent to supply another when his
intention was simply to return them to the depositor, then the appropriate course, in my
opinion, would be for Parliament to enlarge the definition of 'supplying' in s 37 of the
Act to include such a case.
c   In my opinion, therefore, the Court of Appeal reached the right conclusion for the
right reasons. I also find myself to be in agreement with the conclusion of the Court of
Appeal in *R v Dempsey* (1985) Times, 22 November; but I would, for my part, hold that
R v Delgado [1984] 1 All ER 449, [1984] 1 WLR 89 (and the Scottish case of *Donnelly v
HM Advocate* 1985 SLT 243, in which *R v Delgado* was, very understandably, followed)
were, with all respect, wrongly decided.
d   For the reasons I have given, I would dismiss the appeal and answer the question (as
amended) in the negative.

Appeal allowed.

Solicitors: *Crown Prosecution Service*; *Huntley Millard & Co* (for the defendant).

Mary Rose Plummer   Barrister.

Hamblett v Godfrey (Inspector of Taxes)   *a*

COURT OF APPEAL, CIVIL DIVISION
PURCHAS, NEILL AND BALCOMBE LJJ
16, 17 DECEMBER 1986

Income tax – Emoluments from office or employment – Receipt 'from' employment – Payment *b*
made in return for acting as or being an employee and for no other reason – Payment made in
return for continuing in employment with loss of rights under employment protection legislation –
Whether payment 'emolument' from employment – Income and Corporation Taxes Act 1970,
ss 181, 183(1).

In December 1983 the right of civil servants employed at the Government *c*
Communications Headquarters (GCHQ) to belong to a trade union and certain other
rights under the employment protection legislation were withdrawn by the Crown. The
employees were offered the option of accepting the withdrawal of those rights or being
transferred to another branch of the civil service. Staff who chose to remain at GCHQ, of
whom the taxpayer was one, were paid £1,000 each, expressed to be in recognition of
the loss of rights previously enjoyed. The taxpayer was assessed to income tax for the *d*
year 1983–84 on that payment on the grounds that the payment constituted an
emolument from her employment within s 183(1)[a] of the Income and Corporation Taxes
Act 1970 and was chargeable to income tax under Sch E, or alternatively, that the
payment was chargeable under s 61[b] of the Finance Act 1976 as a benefit paid to a higher-
paid employee for which no consideration had been given. The taxpayer appealed to the
Special Commissioners, contending that the payment was not paid in return for services *e*
but merely compensated her for the loss of a general freedom and was therefore a
solatium not chargeable to tax under either head. The commissioners determined that
the payment was not an emolument from the taxpayer's employment because it was not
remuneration for services but they dismissed the appeal on the ground that the payment
was chargeable under s 61 of the 1976 Act. An appeal by the taxpayer was dismissed by
the judge, who held that the definition of 'emoluments' in s 183(1) of the 1970 Act *f*
indicated a wider meaning than mere remuneration and included payments made for
the loss of rights which formed part of the employer–employee relationship and were an
incident of the particular employment. The judge accordingly held that the taxpayer
was chargeable to tax on the payment under s 181[c] of the 1970 Act. The taxpayer
appealed.

g

Held – In order to determine whether the £1,000 payment was, for the purpose of s 181
of the 1970 Act, an emolument arising 'from' the taxpayer's employment it was necessary
to consider the status of the payment and the context in which it was made. Furthermore,
'emoluments' as defined in s 183(1) of the 1970 Act were not restricted to payments
made by an employer in return for the performance of the duties of an office or
employment. On the facts, the payment to the taxpayer was made in recognition of the *h*
loss of specified rights all of which were directly connected with her employment. It
followed, therefore, that the payment constituted an emolument from her employment
and accordingly was chargeable to tax under Sch E. The appeal would therefore be
dismissed (see p 925 *b c f* to *h*, p 927 *g j* and p 928 *b c*, post).
    Dicta of Walton J in *Brumby (Inspector of Taxes) v Milner* [1975] 2 All ER 784 at 787, *j*
Hochstrasser (Inspector of Taxes) v Mayes [1959] 3 All ER 817, *Laidler v Perry (Inspector of*

---

a   Section 183(1), so far as material, is set out at p 919 *h*, post
b   Section 61, so far as material, is set out at p 919 *j*, post
c   Section 181, so far as material, is set out at p 919 *f g*, post

a Taxes) [1965] 2 All ER 121 and *Tyrer v Smart (Inspector of Taxes)* [1979] 1 All ER 321 considered.

Decision of Knox J [1986] 2 All ER 513 affirmed.

Notes

For voluntary payments to a holder of an office or employment, see 23 Halsbury's Laws (4th edn) para 644, and for cases on the subject, see 28(1) Digest (Reissue) 335–337, *1211–*
b *1218.*

For the Income and Corporation Taxes Act 1970, ss 181, 183, see 33 Halsbury's Statutes (3rd edn) 250, 260.

For the Finance Act 1976, s 61, see 46 ibid 1672.

Cases referred to in judgments

c *Brumby (Inspector of Taxes) v Milner* [1975] 2 All ER 773, [1975] 1 WLR 958; *affd* [1975] 3 All ER 1004, [1976] 1 WLR 29, CA; *affd* [1976] 3 All ER 636, [1976] 1 WLR 1096, HL.

Council of Civil Service Unions v Minister for the Civil Service [1984] 3 All ER 935, [1985] AC 374, [1984] 3 WLR 1174, HL.

Edwards v Bairstow (Inspector of Taxes) [1955] 3 All ER 48, [1956] AC 14, [1955] 3 WLR
d 410, HL.

Hochstrasser (Inspector of Taxes) v Mayes [1959] 3 All ER 817, [1960] AC 376, [1960] 2 WLR 63, HL.

IRC v Duke of Westminster [1936] AC 1, [1935] All ER Rep 259, HL.

Laidler v Perry (Inspector of Taxes) [1965] 2 All ER 121, [1966] AC 16, [1965] 2 WLR 1171, HL.

e *Tyrer v Smart (Inspector of Taxes)* [1979] 1 All ER 321, [1979] 1 WLR 113, HL.

Cases also cited

Henley v Murray (Inspector of Taxes) [1950] 1 All ER 908, CA.

Holland (Inspector of Taxes) v Geoghegan [1972] 3 All ER 333, [1972] 1 WLR 1473.

f *Hose v Warwick (Inspector of Taxes)* (1946) 27 TC 459.

Jarrold (Inspector of Taxes) v Boustead [1964] 3 All ER 76, [1964] 1 WLR 1357.

Owen v Pook (Inspector of Taxes) [1969] 2 All ER 1, [1970] AC 244, HL.

Tilley v Wales (Inspector of Taxes) [1943] 1 All ER 280, [1943] AC 386, HL.

Appeal

g June Winifred Hamblett (the taxpayer) appealed against the judgment of Knox J ([1986] 2 All ER 513, [1986] 1 WLR 839) given on 3 March 1986 whereby he allowed an appeal by the Crown from the determination of the Commissioners for the special purposes of the Income Tax Acts (set out at [1986] 2 All ER 514–520) made on 1 May 1985 holding that a sum of £1,000 paid by the Crown to the taxpayer was not a taxable emolument for the year 1983–84 in circumstances where the Crown had unilaterally withdrawn
h certain rights enjoyed by the taxpayer under the provisions of the Employment Protection Act 1975 and the Employment Protection (Consolidation) Act 1978, which rights included the right to belong to a trade union or to resort to an industrial tribunal in certain circumstances. The facts are set out in the judgment of Purchas LJ.

Robin Mathew for the taxpayer.
j *Alan Moses* for the Crown.

PURCHAS LJ. This is an appeal by June Winifred Hamblett, the taxpayer, from a judgment delivered by Knox J ([1986] 2 All ER 513, [1986] 1 WLR 839) on 3 March 1986. The judgment was delivered on an appeal from the Commissioners for the special purposes of the Income Tax Acts by way of case stated under s 56 of the Taxes

Management Act 1970. The judge declared that a sum of £1,000 paid to the taxpayer by her employer in the tax year 1983–84 was an emolument from her employment chargeable under Sch E by virtue of s 181 of the Income and Corporation Taxes Act 1970. The Special Commissioners had held that the payment was an emolument, but that it qualified for that purpose not under the 1970 Act but under s 61(1) of the Finance Act 1976. The facts can be shortly stated. I take them from the case stated.

In January 1984 the government had decided that for security reasons it was necessary to restrict the staff's right to have recourse to an industrial tribunal and their rights also in connection with union membership and activities.

The taxpayer was employed at the Government Communications Headquarters (GCHQ) at Cheltenham as a trainee typist, starting in that capacity in October 1964. By January 1984 she had risen to the grade of executive officer and was responsible for running a section of the office with a number of people under her. Her salary was £8,118.

It is not necessary to go in detail into the conditions of service, except to refer in particular to the relevant aspects so far as this appeal is concerned.

On her starting employment, it was made clear to her that she was permitted and, indeed, encouraged to join a staff association or trade union. The taxpayer initially joined a trade union, but she resigned from it in 1972 and has not been a member of any union since that date.

In January 1984, following on the policy decision to which I have just referred, each member of the staff at GCHQ Cheltenham received a communication from the director, which has been referred to by a serial number, GN 100/84, accompanied by an option form. The letter informed the staff of the reasons for the minister's decision which I have already mentioned, and it set out a number of paragraphs in a document headed 'Changes in Conditions of Service'. It is necessary only to refer to two of those paragraphs:

'11. *Special Payment to all Staff who continue to work at GCHQ*

In recognition of the withdrawal from GCHQ staff of the statutory rights, referred to above [those were the employment protection legislation provisions], a special ex-gratia payment of £1,000 (subject to tax) will be made to all full-time UK based industrial and non-industrial staff (in grades and equivalents up to and including Assistant Secretary) who remain with the Department and sign the option form to that effect . . .

12. The payment will be made by the end of March 1984 or as soon as possible thereafter to all staff whose option forms indicating that they wish to remain with GCHQ have been received by 1 March [then there are a number of special provisions].'

Paragraphs 13 to 16 explained that those who elected to leave CGHQ, and had not reached retirement age, would be transferred to another department if possible. Under para 17, those who refused to express an option or to accept an alternative posting would be dismissed, but would keep their accrued pension rights.

The option form required the staff to complete either A or B. Option A was in the following terms:

'I [and then the name of the individual concerned] have read and understood General Notice 100/84 and wish to continue to be employed at GCHQ. I agree to resign from membership of any trade union to which I belong. I also undertake not to join a trade union or to engage in its affairs or to discuss with its officials my terms of employment or conditions of service or any other matter relating to my employment at GCHQ. I understand, however, that I may join a Departmental staff association approved for the time being by Director GCHQ.'

Option B simply stated that the individual did not wish to continue to be employed at GCHQ, but wished to be considered for a transfer elsewhere in the Civil Service.

a   As a result of the exercise of the prerogative to withdraw those rights which had been made without prior consultation on the part of the ministry, the trade unions involved challenged the decision in the courts. That challenge was unsuccessful: see *Council of Civil Service Unions v Minister for the Civil Service* [1984] 3 All ER 935, [1985] AC 374.

In the mean time, the matter had attracted publicity. On 21 February 1984 the director of GCHQ sent a letter to all members seeking to clarify the position and to correct various opinions and inferences that had arisen in the ensuing public debate. The
b   relevant part of the letter reads as follows:

> 'One further point: the £1,000 offered to those of you who accept the new conditions of service is in some quarters being represented as a bribe. It is nothing of the sort and was never intended as such. It represents a genuine recognition that, because of the special nature and critical importance of their work, GCHQ staff will
> *c*   lose certain statutory rights under the Employment Protection legislation which they previously enjoyed. It was thought that these rights should not be removed without any recognition and this is why the payment of £1,000 will be made.'

The taxpayer did not hesitate long over the choice presented to her. She considered
d   that the offer of £1,000 was made so that she would sign away her right to rejoin a union and her statutory rights under the Employment Protection Acts, but that did not worry her. She had no wish to rejoin a union at that time. She knew that the payment was made ex gratia, and presumed that it was offered in order to pacify in advance those who might otherwise have objected to the changes. Although the option form did not include any undertaking by the staff to stay on indefinitely at GCHQ, she considered that
e   acceptance of the £1,000 would impose a moral obligation to remain there, at any rate for some time to come.

The taxpayer signed option A on 26 January 1984. The payment was in fact included, together with her monthly pay cheque, for the period to 31 March 1984.

Those then are the basic facts against which this appeal is brought to this court. It is convenient at this point to refer shortly to the relevant statutory provisions. They are
f   found first of all in the 1970 Act. Section 181, Sch E, reads:

> '(1) The Schedule referred to as Schedule E is as follows:—
>
> SCHEDULE E
>
> 1. Tax under this Schedule shall be charged in respect of any office or employment on emoluments therefrom which fall under one, or more than one, of the following Cases—Case I: where the person holding the office or employment is resident and
> *g*   ordinarily resident in the United Kingdom, any emoluments for the chargeable period . . .'

There are then exceptions which are not relevant.

The only other section to which I should refer is s 183(1), which, by reference to Cases 1, 2 and 3 of Sch E, defines the expression 'emoluments'. It reads as follows:
h

> '..."emoluments" shall include all salaries, fees, wages, perquisites and profits whatsoever.'

Section 61(1) of the 1976 Act provides:

> '... where in any year a person is employed in director's or higher-paid
> *j*   employment and—(a) by reason of his employment there is provided for him, or for others being members of his family or household, any benefit to which this section applies; and (b) the cost of providing the benefit is not (apart from this section) chargeable to tax as his income, there is to be treated as emoluments of the employment, and accordingly chargeable to income tax under Schedule E, an amount equal to whatever is the cash equivalent of the benefit.'

Section 61(2) defines the benefits to which the section applies as including entertainment, domestic or other services, or other benefits or facilities of whatsoever nature. It then mentions other exclusions which are not relevant.

Section 63(1) merely provides:

'The cash equivalent of any benefit chargeable to tax under section 61 above is an amount equal to the cost of the benefit, less so much (if any) of it as is made good by the employee to those providing the benefit.'

The Special Commissioners came to the conclusion that, whilst the payment was not an emolument within Sch E of the 1970 Act, it was caught by s 61 of the 1976 Act.

After being referred to a number of leading authorities, some of which I must mention later, the Special Commissioners reached, inter alia, two conclusions which counsel for the Crown submits either contained or were based on errors of law, and were correctly identified subsequently by the judge. It is convenient to refer to three short passages of the case stated which is before us. First of all, in dealing with the submissions made before them by counsel who appeared for the Crown, the case stated reads as follows ([1986] 2 All ER 513 at 519):

'Counsel for the Crown called no evidence on this point [that is a reference to the letter issued on 21 February 1984] and is content that the documents should speak for themselves. He accordingly adopts the director's explanation of the reason why the payment was made; and he accepts that the signing of the option form was of no significance in this respect. The argument of counsel for [the taxpayer] also treats the payment as being related to the unilateral withdrawal of statutory rights and not part of a bargain as to the terms on which the staff would provide their services in the future. Counsel for the Crown argues, nevertheless, that the payment has the colour of a reward for services because it was paid only to those who stayed on and was proportionately reduced for part-timers. But that is not, as we understand it, the principal ground on which he seeks to support the assessment. His main argument is that a payment, even if not paid as a reward for services, may yet be an emolument from the employment if it is paid to employees in return for acting as or being employees or "in their capacity as employees and because they were employees" and if there is no other source of the payment than the employment. In so far as that argument involves the proposition that there are two separate approaches to the question whether a payment is an emolument from the employment we feel unable to accept it.'

The case stated then continues to refer to the leading case of *Hochstrasser (Inspector of Taxes) v Mayes* [1959] 3 All ER 817, [1960] AC 376, which I shall mention later. It also goes on to refer to *Laidler v Perry (Inspector of Taxes)* [1965] 2 All ER 121, [1966] AC 16 and *Brumby (Inspector of Taxes) v Milner* [1976] 3 All ER 636, [1976] 1 WLR 1096. I now continue to read a conclusion contained in the case which is directly material to this appeal. The conclusion reads as follows ([1986] 2 All ER 513 at 519):

'The term "reward" may not be entirely apt to cover the whole range of payments which constitute emoluments, including Christmas gifts and inducement payments, but we can detect only one line of reasoning in the authorities. It seems to us that an emolument is essentially a payment made by way of remuneration in return for the performance of the duties of an office or employment and for no other purpose.'

I pause at this stage to indicate that one of the bases of the submission of counsel for the Crown is that in that statement the Special Commissioners did not go sufficiently far faithfully to rehearse the test that they purported to derive from the speech of Lord Radcliffe in *Hochstrasser's* case, and that they should have gone further to lay emphasis on the fact that it is not merely the performance of the duty but the status of being an employee which is also relevant to that consideration.

I now turn to a second part of the statement where the Special Commissioners appear
a to announce the conclusion that they have reached ([1986] 2 All ER 513 at 520):

'In *Hochstrasser v Mayes* [1959] 3 All ER 817, [1960] AC 376 the payment was
made to indemnify the employee against a loss incurred in consequence of the
employment but not as a reward for services, and it was held not to be an
emolument. Similarly in this case we find that the payment was made to recognise
b a disadvantage imposed on [the taxpayer] as a civil servant working at GCHQ, but it
was not paid in return for her services and it lacked the element of remuneration
which, in our judgment, is necessary to constitute a taxable emolument. It was, of
course, offered "subject to tax" but counsel for the Crown takes no point on that.
For the reasons explained above we hold that this payment is not assessable to tax
under s 181 of the Income and Corporation Taxes Act 1970.'

c
The judge held that the payment was an emolument within Sch E and that the Special
Commissioners had erred in point of law in particularly the third of the three extracts
which I have just cited from the statement.
The judge said, in referring to that passage ([1986] 2 All ER 513 at 523, [1986] 1 WLR
839 at 844):

d   'The last sentence contains a finding of fact regarding the purpose of the payment.
It is repeated a little later in a sentence which also contains a conclusion of law and
which reads as follows [the judge then sets out the passage which I have just recited].
The factual finding is that the £1,000 was not paid in return for [the taxpayer's]
services. The conclusion of law is that that finding prevents the payment from being
an emolument. There is a very great weight of authority on what is primarily the
e   meaning of two words, "emoluments therefrom".'

He then continued to consider the authorities, to which I shall come in a moment.
Counsel for the taxpayer, in his appeal, asserts that the judge in that passage of his
judgment is, in fact, disturbing or interfering with a finding by the Special Commissioners
of fact, and he was not therefore entitled to do that. But I shall come to develop counsel's
f submission in a little more detail in a moment.
After referring to the speeches in *Hochstrasser v Mayes*, the judge returned to his
conclusions in these terms ([1986] 2 All ER 513 at 524, [1986] 1 WLR 839 at 845):

'Bearing those principles in mind, I start with the Special Commissioners'
conclusions, which I have already read. Accepting, as I do, their findings of fact that
the £1,000 was not paid to [the taxpayer] in return for her services, I do not accept
g   their conclusion of law that this is necessarily determinant. The Special
Commissioners' view of what constitutes an "emolument" for the purposes of s 181
appears from the case stated, where they said: "It seems to us that an emolument is
essentially a payment made by way of remuneration in return for the performance
of the duties of an office or employment and for no other purpose."'

h The judge then, by way of analysis, inverted the proposition in these terms:

'That can be put negatively by way of the proposition that if a payment is not
remuneration it is not an emolument. I find that conclusion unacceptable for a
variety of reasons.'

j Counsel for the Crown frankly recognised that that expression by the judge might
have been put perhaps in a clearer way than it has been expressed. The real issue in this
appeal is not, in fact, whether the £1,000 is an emolument or not. It is accepted that it is
an emolument, but the question is whether it is an emolument arising from the
employment.
I wish now to revert to one other passage of the judgment ([1986] 2 All ER 513 at 528,
[1986] 1 WLR 839 at 850):

'Weighing the factors on either side, I conclude that this payment can properly
and should be described as being from the employment. In my judgment, *a*
Hochstrasser v Mayes, which was sheet anchor of counsel for [the taxpayer], was itself
close to the borderline: see per Lord Radcliffe ([1959] 3 All ER 817 at 823, [1960]
AC 376 at 391), where he said the case was, as Viscount Simonds said, near the line.
In fact, Viscount Simonds is not recorded in the law reports as having said exactly
that but that there was little doubt on which side of the line that case fell. However
that may be, all their Lordships, except Lord Keith, who merely agreed, presumably *b*
with the conclusion rather than all the reasoning in all the speeches, and Lord
Denning, who could see no profit from employment, found a separate source for
the payment in question, namely the housing agreement, and that dealt with Mr
Mayes's individual position as householder. In this case, there is no such independent
source other than the Crown's desire to recognise the loss of rights intimately linked
with employment.' *c*

In that passage, in my respectful view, is to be found the real ratio of the judge's decision
in this case.

In prosecuting his appeal, counsel for the taxpayer attacked the judgment on the basis
that the Special Commissioners were right, and that their conclusion should not have
been disturbed. That is a point to which I have already adverted. Counsel for the taxpayer *d*
says that the Special Commissioners correctly applied the law to the facts they were
entitled to find, particularly those facts which I have already cited, and in applying, as the
Special Commissioners did, their view of the authorities, *Hochstrasser v Mayes*, *Laidler v
Perry* and *Brumby v Milner*.

Secondly, counsel for the taxpayer submits that since the judge did not, as it was not
necessary for him to do so, consider the position under s 61 of the 1976 Act, counsel *e*
found himself in the position of having, and rightly so, to attack the reasoning and
findings of the Special Commissioners under s 61 of the 1976 Act.

The two limbs of his appeal can, however, conveniently be considered separately. That
is the basis on which I propose to approach the submissions of counsel for the taxpayer.

On the first limb, counsel for the Crown immediately conceded that, unless he can
show that the judge was correct in his view that the Special Commissioners had erred in *f*
law, then the appeal on the first limb must succeed. Indeed, it was on that basis and on
that basis alone that counsel for the Crown argued the case before the judge.

In this case the issue can be refined to a narrow point of construction, a point that has
on numerous occasions received the attention of distinguished jurists, although simply
stated, and that is the significance of the two words 'emoluments therefrom' to be found
in s 181 of the 1970 Act. *g*

The convenient starting point is *Hochstrasser (Inspector of Taxes) v Mayes* [1959] 3 All
ER 817, [1960] AC 376. That appeal related to a payment made under a housing scheme
run by Imperial Chemical Industries (ICI) for the benefit of their employees. The
payment was made to the taxpayer because the house that he had been occupying under
the scheme had to be sold because he had been posted to another factory. On the sale, the
market had dropped, and he sustained a loss of £350 which ICI under the scheme saw fit *h*
to compensate him by the payment of that sum.

Counsel for the taxpayer submits that in this appeal all that counsel for the Crown is
in fact doing is repeating the submissions made unsuccessfully by John Pennycuick QC,
and he relies on the speeches in that case, particularly of Viscount Simonds and Lord
Radcliffe.

It is necessary to look only at two passages in the speeches for the purpose of dealing *j*
with the issues on that front. Viscount Simonds, having earlier considered the issues and
an approach made by Parker LJ which it is not necessary to rehearse here, said ([1959] 3
All ER 817 at 822, [1960] AC 376 at 389–390):

'There is nothing express or implicit in the agreement which suggests that the
payment is a reward for services except the single fact of the relationship of the

parties [the agreement there is the agreement under which the housing scheme was
operated] and it is clear enough from *Inland Revenue Comrs. v. Duke of Westminster*
([1936] AC 1, [1935] All ER Rep 259) that that fact alone will not justify such a
conclusion. On the other hand, there is the significant fact that the salary earned by
the employee compares favourably with salaries paid by other employers not
operating a housing scheme, and is the same whether or not he takes advantage of
the housing scheme. This at once suggests that there is some other reason for the
payment than services rendered or to be rendered . . . My Lords, in the course of the
argument a considerable number of authorities were cited, some of them decisions
of this House. In nothing that I have said have I intended to cast any doubt on them.
I should not be justified in doing so. But I do not apologise for going back to the
very words of the statute and ignoring explanatory words like "as such", nor do I
think it useful to examine whether an agreement under which payment is made is
"collateral". The question is one of substance not form.'

Having reviewed the position of the contract under which the housing arrangement
was operated, Viscount Simonds came to this conclusion ([1959] 3 All ER 817 at 823,
[1960] AC 376 at 391):

'It was not established by the facts found by the commissioners nor was it a
legitimate inference from those facts that the sum of £350 paid to the respondent
was a reward for his services.'

Lord Radcliffe, having also referred to what he described as the 'glosses' on the
expression 'under review', said ([1959] 3 All ER 817 at 823, [1960] AC 376 at 391–392):

'But it is, perhaps, worth observing that they do not displace those words [ie the
glosses]. For my part, I think that their meaning is adequately conveyed by saying
that, while it is not sufficient to render a payment assessable that an employee would
not have received it unless he had been an employee, it is assessable if it has been
paid to him in return for acting as or being an employee. It is just because I do not
think that the £350 which are in question here were paid to the respondent for
acting as or being an employee that I regard them as not being profits from his
employment.'

On the one hand, counsel for the taxpayer relies on these speeches as indicating that it
is necessary to establish that the payment is made in relation to performance of service or
services rendered before it can come within the expressions which find themselves within
the section. Counsel for the Crown, on his part, emphasises the expression to be found in
both speeches that their Lordships distinguished the payment of £350 as being a
payment for 'another reason' and not being profit from his employment. That authority
directs one's attention to the expression 'from no other source' which is to be found
elsewhere in the authorities.

I come next to a brief reference in *Tyrer v Smart (Inspector of Taxes)* [1979] 1 All ER
321, [1979] 1 WLR 113. I wish to refer to part of the speech of Lord Diplock. It is
unnecessary to rehearse in detail the facts. They involved a scheme for employee
participation as shareholders, and the employee had rights to take up at a minimum
price shares that would be issued in the company. Lord Diplock, having referred to the
value of the right to acquire shares as found by the commissioners, said ([1979] 1 All ER
321 at 325, [1979] 1 WLR 113 at 117–118):

'That seems to me a clear finding that the offer was made as a reward for past
(since he had to have served five years to qualify for the offer) and more particularly
for future services and accordingly was made to him in return for acting as or being
an employee. In my view it is not possible to bring the commissioners' finding within
this effect within the well-known principle stated by Lord Radcliffe in *Edwards
(Inspector of Taxes) v Bairstow* [1955] 3 All ER 48 at 57, [1956] AC 14 at 36 . . .'

In this case, counsel for the Crown has not essayed that exercise either.

That indicates that Lord Diplock was following the same path as Lord Radcliffe. In *a* *Laidler v Perry (Inspector of Taxes)* [1965] 2 All ER 121, [1966] AC 16, and particularly in the speech of Lord Reid, the matter is taken a stage further. Having referred to the provisions of the relevant Act at that time, Lord Reid said ([1965] 2 All ER 121 at 124, [1966] AC 16 at 29–30):

> 'It is not disputed that this definition [ie the definition of emoluments and the *b* expression 'on emoluments therefrom'] is wide enough to include these vouchers [the vouchers were £10 vouchers issued to employees at Christmas], and it is not now disputed that by reason of the very wide range of choice in spending them, each is worth its face value of £10. Section 156, however, applies only to "emoluments *therefrom*", i.e., from the office or employment of the recipient, and it is well settled that not every sum or other profit received by an employee from his *c* employer in the course of his employment is to be regarded as arising from the employment. So the question in this case is whether these profits or emoluments of £10 did or did not arise from the taxpayer's employment. There is a wealth of authority on this matter and various glosses on or paraphrases of the words in the [Income Tax Act 1952] appear in judicial opinions, including speeches in this House. No doubt they were helpful in the circumstances of the cases in which they were *d* used, but in the end we must always return to the words in the statute and answer the question—did this profit arise from the employment? The answer will be no if it arose from something else.' (Lord Reid's emphasis.)

Whilst with that case I would like also to refer to the speech of Lord Donovan ([1965] 2 All ER 121 at 128, [1966] AC 16 at 35–36):
e

> 'My Lords, the taxpayer's argument is that these receipts of £10 each did not arise from his office or employment. The admitted facts are that the company disbursed these sums to "help to maintain a feeling of happiness among the staff and to foster a spirit of personal relationship between management and staff". In less roundabout language that simply means in order to maintain the quality of service given by the staff. Looked at in this way, the payments were an inducement to each recipient to *f* go on working well; and none the less so in the case of the taxpayer than in the case of employees less exalted in position. It looks, of course, to be a very unreal inducement in the case of the taxpayer, who was earning over £2,000 per annum; but, though much play was made of this in argument, the present appeal has clearly · been brought as a test case with the rest of the two thousand or so employees much in mind. If it is found that the general purpose of the company was to maintain the *g* quality of the service it received, no distinction can be made because of Dr. Laidler's rank and pay. Nor, indeed, is one suggested.'

Finally, I wish to refer to *Brumby (Inspector of Taxes) v Milner* [1975] 2 All ER 773, [1975] 1 WLR 958. I adopt, with gratitude and respect, the approach of Walton J in that case ([1975] 2 All ER 773 at 784, [1975] 1 WLR 958 at 964):
h

> 'The crucial question is at once seen to lie within an extremely small legal compass. Did the terminal payments so received by Mr Milner and Mr Quick arise "therefrom"—that is to say, from their office or employment with the company?'

I pause at this stage to record that the payment in question, the terminal payment, was the final distribution of a trust fund which had been set up for the benefit of the *j* employees of the company, which received its funds from the dividends and profits of the company, and distributed them year by year to the employees. But the event which gave rise to the appeal was either the amalgamation or cessation in its formal shape of the company, requiring the distribution of the funds of the trust.

Later Walton J, summarising in particular *Hochstrasser v Mayes*, said ([1975] 2 All ER
a 773 at 787, [1975] 1 WLR 958 at 968):

> 'It appears to me that the correct test as stated by Lord Radcliffe is that, for any
> sum paid to the employee to be assessable to income tax, it must be paid to him "in
> return for acting as or being an employee", and for no other reason.'

So, in my judgment, the approach that the court should take, and, indeed, that Knox J
b did in fact take, is to consider the status of the payment and the context in which it was
made. The payment was made to recognise the loss of rights. I am now going to
paraphrase, I hope accurately, from the findings of the Special Commissioners and the
employers' letter and other records.

The rights, the loss of which was being recognised, were rights under the employment
protection legislation, and the right to join a union or other trade protection association.
c Both those rights, in my judgment, are directly connected with the fact of the taxpayer's
employment. If the employment did not exist, there would be no need for the rights in
the particular context in which the taxpayer found herself. So, I start from the position
that those are rights directly connected with employment. Purely by way of contrast, to
underline that approach, if for instance the employers had for some reason or other best
known to themselves objected to some social or other activity which their employees or
d some of them enjoyed, such as joining a golf club or something of that sort (I think Lord
Diplock mentioned payments in the hunting field), but whatever it is, activities not
connected with the employment, then a payment made by an employer to recognise the
voluntary or, indeed, the compulsory withdrawal if the employer had sufficient influence
with the committee of the golf club concerned would, I can readily acknowledge, would
be a payment made to a person who was an employee but was not made in the
e circumstances which would satisfy the words of s 181, that is that the payment must
arise 'therefrom'. I only mention that analogy to emphasise the point which I seek to
make.

There is no doubt in this case that the employment protection legislation goes directly
to the employment of the taxpayer with the employer. The right to join a union, in my
f judgment, also falls directly to be considered as in connection with that employment,
because without the employment there is no purpose in joining the union except for
esoteric or personal reasons which are not relevant in this case. But I can again see a
situation in which persons involved in particularly sensitive areas of government service
might be required to abandon their right of freedom of speech. In such a case, it would
clearly have to be considered on the facts involved in the individual case to see whether
the abandonment of that fundamental right was in fact connected and arose on the
g employment or not, and it would clearly differ from case to case.

I hope that I have said sufficient in this short judgment to confirm that, in my
judgment, the judge was correct in holding that the Special Commissioners erred in law
in the passages which I have cited at the beginning of this judgment. In my judgment,
he was correct to intervene, and, having intervened, he did so correctly. This payment is
h rightly to be assessed under Sch E and the provisions of s 181 of the 1970 Act.

Having reached that conclusion, I find it unnecessary to consider the somewhat more
complicated issues which would or might have arisen under s 61 of the 1976 Act as
involving, for instance, whether a payment in cash can be a benefit in kind. I am grateful
not to have to resolve those difficult problems. In my judgment, therefore, this appeal
should be dismissed.

j
NEILL LJ. The circumstances giving rise to the present appeal against the judgment of
Knox J ([1986] 2 All ER 513, [1986] 1 WLR 839) dated 3 March 1986 have been set out
in the judgment of Purchas LJ. I can therefore deal with the facts as they appear in the
case stated quite shortly.

On 25 January 1984 the taxpayer received a copy of a general notice, GN 100/84, and an option form as well as an accompanying letter from the director of the Government *a* Communications Headquarters (GCHQ). The other members of the GCHQ staff at Cheltenham received copies of the same three documents. The general notice was headed 'GCHQ: CHANGES IN CONDITIONS OF SERVICE'.

As the general notice explained, the changes in the conditions of service included the withdrawal of the right to belong to a trade union and of the right to take advantage of the provisions of the Employment Protection (Consolidation) Act 1978 in so far as they *b* applied to persons in Crown employment (see s 138(1) of that Act).

Paragraph 11 of the general notice was in these terms:

> '*Special Payment to all Staff who continue to work at GCHQ*
> In recognition of the withdrawal from GCHQ staff of the statutory rights, referred
> to above, a special ex-gratia payment of £1,000 (subject to tax) will be made to all *c*
> full time UK-based industrial and non-industrial staff (in grades and equivalents up
> to and including Assistant Secretary) who remain with the Department and sign the
> option form to that effect . . .'

The change in the conditions of service gave rise to some controversy.

On 21 February 1986 the director of GCHQ wrote a further letter to the staff, including the taxpayer, to deal with a suggestion which had been made in some quarters that the *d* payment represented a bribe. He wrote, in para 7 of his letter:

> '. . . the £1,000 offered to those of you who accept the new conditions of service
> . . . represents a genuine recognition that, because of the special nature and critical
> importance of their work, GCHQ staff will lose certain statutory rights under the
> Employment Protection legislation which they previously enjoyed. It was thought *e*
> that these rights should not be removed without any recognition and this is why
> the payment of £1,000 will be made.'

Meanwhile, the taxpayer had completed the option form by signing Option A, thereby signifying her wish to continue to be employed at GCHQ.

In the case stated the Special Commissioners made a number of relevant findings *f* which I can summarise as follows. First, they found that the payment of £1,000 was offered as an ex gratia payment solely in recognition of the withdrawal of statutory rights which the GCHQ staff, in common with other employed persons, had previously enjoyed. Second, they found that these statutory rights had been enjoyed within the employer-employee relationship, and the payment arose out of that relationship. Third, they found that the payment was made to recognise a disadvantage imposed on the taxpayer as a *g* civil servant working at GCHQ. Fourth, they found that the payment was not made in return for the taxpayer's services and lacked the element of remuneration. Finally, because the payment was not made in return for the taxpayer's services and lacked the element of remuneration, it did not constitute a taxable emolument.

Those findings have to be read in conjunction with an earlier passage in the case stated, where the Special Commissioners said ([1986] 2 All ER 513 at 519): *h*

> 'It seems to us that an emolument is essentially a payment made by way of
> remuneration in return for the performance of the duties of an office or employment
> and for no other purpose.'

When the matter came before the judge, he held that the Special Commissioners had *j* applied too narrow a test in deciding that the payment was not a taxable emolument. Having concluded that the Special Commissioners had applied the wrong test and had therefore erred in law, the judge considered the facts again. He stated his conclusion in these terms ([1986] 2 All ER 513 at 528, [1986] 1 WLR 839 at 850):

'Weighing the factors on either side, I conclude that this payment can properly
a   and should be described as being from the employment.'

He therefore decided that the payment was an emolument and assessable accordingly.
It is against that decision of Knox J that the taxpayer appeals in the first part of the
appeal in this court. In the course of the hearing of the appeal, we have been referred to
a number of authorities in which guidance has been given as to the meaning of the
relevant words in s 181(1) of the Income and Corporation Taxes Act 1970.
b   Purchas LJ has already referred to many of the authorities. It would serve no useful
purpose for me to repeat these citations again. I shall therefore only refer to two short
passages which I have found to be of particular assistance. In *Hochstrasser (Inspector of
Taxes) v Mayes* [1959] 3 All ER 817 at 823, [1960] AC 376 at 391–392 Lord Radcliffe
said:

c   'The test to be applied is the same for all. It is contained in the statutory
        requirement that the payment, if it is to be the subject of assessment, must arise
        "from" the office or employment. In the past several explanations have been offered
        by judges of eminence as to the significance of the word "from" in this context . . .
        For my part, I think that their meaning [ie the meaning of the words] is adequately
        conveyed by saying that, while it is not sufficient to render a payment assessable
d   that an employee would not have received it unless he had been an employee, it is
        assessable if it has been paid to him in return for acting as or being an employee.'

The other passage to which I should refer is in the same case in the speech of Viscount
Simonds where, having referred to the fact that a considerable number of authorities had
been cited to their Lordships, he went on as follows ([1959] 3 All ER 817 at 822, [1960]
e   AC 376 at 390):

        'But I do not apologise for going back to the very words of the statute and ignoring
        explanatory words like "as such", nor do I think it useful to examine whether an
        agreement under which payment is made is "collateral". The question is one of
        substance not form. I accept, as I am bound to do, that the test of taxability is
        whether from the standpoint of the person who receives it the profit accrues to him
f   by virtue of his office . . .'

Though one must never lose sight of the fact that these explanations cannot provide a
substitute for the statutory words, they are valuable and authoritative. Thus these
passages, as well as those to which Purchas LJ has already referred in greater detail,
demonstrate to my mind that emoluments from employment are not restricted to
g   payments made in return for the performance of services.
With this introduction, I return to the facts of the instant case. It is plain that the
taxpayer received her payment as a recognition of the fact that she had lost certain rights
as an employee, and by reason of the further fact that she had elected to remain in her
employment at GCHQ.
Accordingly, if I may adopt the language of Lord Radcliffe in the passage I have
h   referred to, the payment to the taxpayer was made in return for her being and continuing
to be an employee at GCHQ, or to use the words of Viscount Simonds, the payment
accrued to the taxpayer by virtue of her employment. But in the end I think it is right to
base my decision on the wording of the statute.
It is clearly not enough that the payment was received from the employer. The
question is: was the payment an emolument from the employment? In other words, was
j   the employment the source of the emolument?
It was argued by counsel for the taxpayer in the course of his cogent submissions that
the rights lost by the taxpayer were mere personal rights, and that, indeed, this was a
stronger case from the taxpayer's point of view than *Hochstrasser v Mayer* since the rights

given to the employee in that case were part of a composite contract. With respect, I find it impossible to accept this argument. As the Special Commissioners held, the rights had *a* been enjoyed within the employer–employee relationship. The removal of the rights involved changes in the conditions of service. The payment was in recognition of the changes in the conditions of service.

I have been driven to the conclusion that the source of the payment was the employment. It was paid because of the employment and because of the changes in the conditions of employment and for no other reason. It was referable to the employment *b* and to nothing else. Accordingly, in my judgment, the £1,000 was a taxable emolument.

In these circumstances, I find it unnecessary, as did Purchas LJ, to go on to consider the alternative basis of assessment under s 61 of the Finance Act 1976. For these reasons and for the reasons given by Purchas LJ, I too would dismiss this appeal.

BALCOMBE LJ. In my judgment Knox J came to the right conclusion for the right *c* reasons. I cannot usefully add anything to what he has said, and to what has fallen from Purchas and Neill LJJ, and I too would dismiss this appeal.

Appeal dismissed. No order for costs. Leave to appeal to the House of Lords refused.

Solicitors: *Whitelock & Storr*, agents for *Lane & Co*, Cheltenham (for the taxpayer); *Solicitor* *d* *of Inland Revenue*.

Rengan Krishnan Esq   Barrister.

e

Practice Note

COURT OF APPEAL, CIVIL DIVISION
SIR JOHN DONALDSON MR, WOOLF AND RUSSELL LJJ
13 MARCH 1987

f

Court of Appeal – Practice – Judgment under appeal – Copy of judgment for Court of Appeal – Counsel wishing to argue from published report of judgment – Court of Appeal to be provided with photocopies of report.

SIR JOHN DONALDSON MR gave the following direction at the sitting of the *g* court. If the judgment under appeal has been reported before the hearing and counsel wish to argue from the published report rather than from the official transcript, the court should be provided with photocopies of the report for the use of the judges in order that they may be able to annotate it as the argument proceeds.

Diana Procter   Barrister.

a

Ainsbury v Millington

HOUSE OF LORDS

LORD BRIDGE OF HARWICH, LORD BRANDON OF OAKBROOK, LORD ACKNER, LORD OLIVER OF
AYLMERTON AND LORD GOFF OF CHIEVELEY

19 FEBRUARY, 12 MARCH 1987

b

Practice – Appeal – Pending appeal – No live issue – Publicly funded litigation – Event occurring which disposes of issue between parties – Duty of counsel and solicitors – Duty to ensure appeal is withdrawn or to seek directions.

It is the duty of counsel and solicitors in any pending appeal in publicly funded litigation,
c whenever an event occurs which arguably disposes of the lis, either to ensure that the
appeal is withdrawn by consent or, if there is no agreement to that course, to bring the
facts promptly to the attention of the Court of Appeal or of the House of Lords, as the
case may be, and to seek directions (see p 931 *c* to *g*, post).

Dictum of Viscount Simon LC in *Sun Life Assurance Co of Canada v Jervis* [1944] 1 All
ER at 470–471 applied.

d Appeal from decision of Court of Appeal [1986] 1 All ER 73 dismissed without hearing
argument on the merits.

Notes

For restriction on appeals where there has ceased to be a live issue, see 37 Halsbury's Laws
(4th edn) para 682, and for a case on the subject, see 36(1) Digest (Reissue) 548, 41.

e

Case referred to in opinions

Sun Life Assurance Co of Canada v Jervis [1944] 1 All ER 469, [1944] AC 111, HL.

Appeal

Susan Ainsbury appealed, with the leave of the Appeal Committee of the House of Lords
f given on 19 February 1986, against the decision of the Court of Appeal ([1986] 1 All ER
73) on 8 August 1985 dismissing an appeal by the appellant (by her next friend and
mother Daisy Emmett) against that part of the order of his Honour Judge Galpin made
in the Basingstoke County Court on 24 July 1984 whereby on a preliminary issue in
proceedings brought under the Guardianship of Minors Act 1971 and the Guardianship
Act 1973 the judge declined to exercise jurisdiction to hear the appellant's application for
g an interlocutory injunction to exclude the respondent, Derek Millington, from 24
Marlow Close, Basingstoke, Hampshire and to restrain him from returning thereto. In
the events which happened there was no live issue between the parties when the appeal
was called on for hearing and their Lordships declined to hear argument on the merits of
the decision of the Court of Appeal. The facts are set out in the opinion of Lord Bridge.

h *Joseph Jackson QC* and *Lindsey Oliver* for the appellant.
John E A Samuels QC and *Nicholas Wood* for the respondent.

Their Lordships took time for consideration.

j 12 March. The following opinions were delivered.

LORD BRIDGE OF HARWICH. My Lords, the appellant lived with the respondent
as his mistress and bore him a child on 19 December 1983. The Basingstoke and Deane
Borough Council granted them the joint tenancy of a council house at 24 Marlowe Close,
Popley. In September 1984 the respondent was sentenced to 18 months' youth custody.

While he was in custody the appellant married another man, who moved into 24
Marlowe Close with her. When the respondent was released he returned to 24 Marlowe   *a*
Close and the appellant and her husband moved out. They went to live with the
appellant's mother. The accommodation available to them there was unsatisfactory. In
July 1985 the appellant applied to the Basingstoke County Court for custody of the child
and for an injunction requiring the respondent to vacate 24 Marlowe Close. The judge
awarded interim custody of the child to the appellant, but held that he had no jurisdiction
to grant the injunction. The appellant's appeal to the Court of Appeal was dismissed on 8   *b*
August 1985 (see [1986] 1 All ER 73). On 19 February 1986 leave to appeal was granted
by your Lordships' House. On 14 March 1986 the local authority obtained an order for
possession of 24 Marlowe Close and in fact resumed possession in June. Meanwhile the
local authority granted the appellant and her husband the tenancy of a different council
house on 28 April 1986. The respondent is now once again in custody serving a sentence
of imprisonment. As one might expect, both parties have throughout the proceedings   *c*
been legally aided with nil contributions and no order for costs, save for legal aid taxation,
had been made in the courts below.

When the appeal was called on for hearing before the Appellate Committee your
Lordships required to be satisfied that the appeal could properly be entertained having
regard to the termination of the parties' tenancy of 24 Marlowe Close to which the
respondent's case had directed attention. The principle was clearly stated by Viscount   *d*
Simon LC in *Sun Life Assurance Co of Canada v Jervis* [1944] 1 All ER 469 at 470–471,
[1944] AC 111 at 113–114, where he said:

> 'I do not think that it would be a proper exercise of the authority which this
> House possesses to hear appeals if it occupies time in this case in deciding an
> academic question, the answer to which cannot affect the respondent in any way. If   *e*
> the House undertook to do so, it would not be deciding an existing *lis* between the
> parties who are before it, but would merely be expressing its view on a legal
> conundrum which the appellant hopes to get decided in its favour without in any
> way affecting the position between the parties . . . I think it is an essential quality of
> an appeal fit to be disposed of by this House that there should exist between the
> parties a matter in actual controversy which the House undertakes to decide as a   *f*
> living issue.'

The *Sun Life* case was one where the original issue between the parties related to the
terms of a policy of insurance and where leave had been granted by the Court of Appeal
on an undertaking by the appellant insurer to pay the respondent's costs as between
solicitor and client in the House of Lords in any event and not to ask for the return of
any money which the respondent had recovered in the action. In the instant case counsel   *g*
for the appellant has submitted that Viscount Simon LC's principle should be confined
in its application to cases where the point of law at issue is peculiar to the facts of the case
or arises on the construction of particular documents and should not inhibit the House
from resolving, even in the absence of any live issue between the parties, a question of
law of general importance which, as is said to be the case here, different decisions of the   *h*
Court of Appeal have left in doubt. Assuming without deciding that this is such a case, I
cannot see that it makes any difference, nor can I accept that the principle as stated by
Viscount Simon LC is to be limited as suggested. In the *Sun Life* case the outcome of the
appeal, if the House had been prepared to entertain it, would at least have been of some
concern to the appellant, since the ruling it sought would presumably have affected its
obligations to other policy holders. In the instant case neither party can have any interest   *j*
at all in the outcome of the appeal. Their joint tenancy of property which was the subject
matter of the dispute no longer exists. Thus, even if the House thought that the judge
and the Court of Appeal had been wrong to decline jurisdiction, there would be no order
which could now be made to give effect to that view. It has always been a fundamental
feature of our judicial system that the courts decide disputes between the parties before

them; they do not pronounce on abstract questions of law when there is no dispute to be

a resolved.

Different considerations may arise in relation to what are called 'friendly actions' and conceivably in relation to proceedings instituted specifically as a test case. The instant case does not fall within either of those categories. Again litigation may sometimes be properly continued for the sole purpose of resolving an issue as to costs when all other matters in dispute have been resolved. Realistically counsel did not suggest that the

b possibility in this case of either party being ordered to pay the costs of the other, which in practice is so remote as to be negligible, could be regarded as affording a sufficient lis inter partes to keep the appeal alive.

It is regrettable in the circumstances that the matter should have come before your Lordships at public expense as a full dress appeal. I do not suggest that any blame attaches to anyone. The legal aid authorities were kept fully informed of the relevant developments

c and acted on counsel's opinion in deciding that legal aid for the appeal could properly be continued. For the future, however, it should be understood that it is the duty of counsel and solicitors in any pending appeal in publicly funded litigation, whenever an event occurs which arguably disposes of the lis, either to ensure that the appeal is withdrawn by consent or, if there is no agreement to that course, to bring the facts promptly to the attention of the Court of Appeal or of this House, as the case may be, and to seek

d directions.

At the hearing before the Appellate Committee your Lordships unanimously determined not to hear argument on the merits of the decision of the Court of Appeal. For the reasons I have expressed I think that was the correct course to take and for the same reasons I would dismiss the appeal.

e **LORD BRANDON OF OAKBROOK.** My Lords, I have had the advantage of reading in draft the speech prepared by my noble and learned friend Lord Bridge. I agree with it and for the reasons which he gives I would dismiss the appeal.

LORD ACKNER. My Lords, I have had the advantage of reading in draft the speech

f prepared by my noble and learned friend Lord Bridge. I agree with him and for the reasons he gives would dismiss the appeal.

LORD OLIVER OF AYLMERTON. My Lords, I have had the advantage of reading in draft the speech prepared by my noble and learned friend Lord Bridge. I agree with him and for the reasons he gives would dismiss the appeal.

g **LORD GOFF OF CHIEVELEY.** My Lords, I have had the advantage of reading in draft the speech prepared by my noble and learned friend Lord Bridge. I agree with him and for the reasons he gives would dismiss the appeal.

Appeal dismissed.

h

Solicitors: *Church Adams Tatham & Co*, agents for *Snow & Bispham*, Basingstoke (for the appellant); *Park Nelson*, agents for *Brain & Brain*, Basingstoke (for the respondent).

Mary Rose Plummer   Barrister.

Coltman and another v Bibby Tankers Ltd
The Derbyshire

COURT OF APPEAL, CIVIL DIVISION
O'CONNOR, LLOYD AND GLIDEWELL LJJ
15, 16, 27 JANUARY 1987

Employment – Liability of master – Defective equipment – Ship – Whether 'equipment' including ship – Employer's Liability (Defective Equipment) Act 1969, s 1(1)(3).

In September 1980 a ship owned by the defendants sank off the coast of Japan with the loss of all hands. The plaintiffs, who represented the estate of a crew member and who alleged that the ship was unseaworthy because of defects in the hull attributable to the ship's builders, brought an action against the defendants claiming damages on the ground, inter alia, that the crew member's death was caused in the course of his employment in consequence of defects in equipment, namely the ship, provided by the defendants. Under s 1[a] of the Employer's Liability (Defective Equipment) Act 1969, where an employee suffered personal injury or loss of life in the course of his employment in consequence of a defect in equipment provided by his employer for the purpose of the employer's business and the defect was attributable to the fault of a third party, the injury or loss of life was deemed to be also attributable to negligence on the part of the employer. By s 1(3) of the 1969 Act 'equipment' was defined as including 'any plant and machinery, vehicle, aircraft and clothing'. The question whether the ship was 'equipment' provided by the defendants was tried as a preliminary issue. The judge held that it was and the defendants appealed.

Held (Lloyd LJ dissenting) – A ship was not 'equipment' within the ordinary meaning of that word because 'equipment' denoted something ancillary to something else and could not apply to the workplace provided by an employer, whether the workplace consisted of fixed premises on land or a movable chattel at sea or in the air. Furthermore, although s 1(3) extended the normal meaning of 'equipment', it did not expressly include ships, nor could ships come within the meaning of 'plant', because 'plant' signified the aggregate of the machinery, implements, apparatus and fixtures used in the carrying on of an industrial process, and nor could they come within the meaning of 'vehicle', which was limited to a means of conveyance on land. It followed that the ship was not 'equipment' provided by the defendants, and the appeal would accordingly be allowed (see p 934 *a* to *d*, p 935 *e*, p 938 *g* to *j* and p 939 *d* to *h*, post).

Decision of Sheen J [1986] 2 All ER 65 reversed.

Notes

For employers' liability for defective equipment, see 16 Halsbury's Laws (4th edn) para 718, and for cases on the subject, see 20 Digest (Reissue) 490–494, 511–514, 3844–3864, 3965–3991.

For the Employers' Liability (Defective Equipment) Act 1969, s 1, see 16 Halsbury's Statutes (4th edn) 180.

Cases referred to in judgments

Davie v New Merton Board Mills Ltd [1959] 1 All ER 346, [1959] AC 604, [1959] 2 WLR 331, HL.
Dilworth v Comrs of Stamps [1899] AC 99, PC.

---

[a]   Section 1, so far as material, is set out at p 933 *h* to p 934 *a*, post

Donoghue (or M'Alister) v Stevenson [1932] AC 562, [1932] All ER Rep 1, HL.

a   *IRC v Parker* [1966] 1 All ER 399, [1966] AC 141, [1966] 2 WLR 486, HL.

Robinson v Local Board of Barton-Eccles Winton and Monton (1883) 8 App Cas 798, HL.

Appeal

The defendants, Bibby Tankers Ltd, the owners of the ore/bulk/oil carrier Derbyshire, appealed from the judgment of Sheen J ([1986] 2 All ER 65, [1986] 1 WLR 751) given in

b   the Admiralty Court of the Queen's Bench Division on 14 March 1986 whereby he determined, on the trial of a preliminary issue in an action brought against the defendants by the plaintiffs, Eugenia Margaret Coltman and Alisa Elizabeth Martin, the administratrices of the estate of Leo Thomas Coltman deceased, that the vessel was 'equipment' provided by the defendants within s 1 of the Employer's Liability (Defective Equipment) Act 1969. The facts are set out in the judgment of O'Connor LJ.

c

Robin Hay for the defendants.
Belinda Bucknall for the plaintiffs.

Cur adv vult

d

27 January. The following judgments were delivered.

O'CONNOR LJ. In September 1980 the Derbyshire was lost with all hands in a typhoon off the coast of Japan. She was a large ship, 91,000 tons gross, 964 feet long, laden with 157,000 tons of iron ore on a voyage from Canada to Japan. She was built by

e   Swan Hunter in 1975. The plaintiffs are the personal representatives of a crew member. The defendants, who owned or operated the ship, were his employers. The plaintiffs allege that the ship sank because she broke in half, that she broke in half because of defects in the hull, and by para 7 of their amended statement of claim plead:

> 'Further or alternatively the Deceased's death was caused in the course of his
> *f*   employment by reason of defects in the equipment, namely the vessel, provided to
> him by the Defendants, which defects are attributable wholly or in part to the fault
> of the manufacturers, Swanhunter Shipbuilders Limited.'

Particulars of fault are given alleging negligent construction of the hull, and by para 8 they plead:

> *g*   'By reason of the provisions of the Employer's Liability (Defective Equipment)
> Act 1969 the said faults of the manufacturers are attributable to negligence on the
> part of the Defendants.'

The registrar ordered a preliminary issue of law to be tried whether this ship was 'equipment provided within the meaning of the Act'. Sheen J has held that she was (see [1986] 2 All ER 65, [1986] 1 WLR 751) and the defendants appeal.

h   The relevant provisions of s 1 of the Employer's Liability (Defective Equipment) Act 1969 are:

> '(1) Where after the commencement of this Act—(a) an employee suffers personal
> injury in the course of his employment in consequence of a defect in equipment
> provided by his employer for the purposes of the employer's business; and (b) the
> *j*   defect is attributable wholly or partly to the fault of a third party (whether identified
> or not), the injury shall be deemed to be also attributable to negligence on the part
> of the employer (whether or not he is liable in respect of the injury apart from this
> subsection), but without prejudice to the law relating to contributory negligence
> and to any remedy by way of contribution or in contract or otherwise which is
> available to the employer in respect of the injury . . .

(3) In this section ... "equipment" includes any plant and machinery, vehicle, aircraft and clothing ... "personal injury" includes loss of life ...'

Despite the lucid and persuasive submissions made by counsel for the plaintiffs I am in no doubt that this ship was not equipment within the meaning of the Act. I start by considering sub-s (1)(a) on its own. The ordinary meaning of 'equipment' must I think denote something ancillary to something else. The *Oxford English Dictionary* establishes that this is so and I quote the two main paragraphs:

'1. a. The action or process of equipping or fitting out. b. The state or condition of being equipped; the manner in which a person or thing is equipped ... 2. Anything used in equipping; furniture; outfit; warlike apparatus; necessaries for an expedition or voyage ...'

I think that it is clear that the employee's workplace is not 'equipment'. Counsel for the plaintiffs accepts that the fabric of a factory or, for example, a hotel cannot be 'equipment'. Counsel submitted, however, that a distinction should be drawn between fixed premises on land and movable chattels, and that all chattels provided by an employer for the purposes of his business should qualify as 'equipment'. In the present case the ship was a chattel and was provided by the employers for the purposes of their business of carrying goods from one part of the world to another. As I have said I do not think that the workplace provided by an employer is 'equipment' within the meaning of the subsection and I do not think it matters whether the workplace is on land or at sea or indeed in the air.

The meaning of equipment in sub-s (1)(a) must be construed in the light of sub-s (3). The effect of an interpretation section drafted in this way has been considered many times. In *Dilworth v Comr of Stamps* [1899] AC 99 at 105–106 Lord Watson, giving the advice of the Privy Council, said:

'The word "include" is very generally used in interpretation clauses in order to enlarge the meaning of words or phrases occurring in the body of the statute; and when it is so used these words or phrases must be construed as comprehending, not only such things as they signify according to their natural import, but also those things which the interpretation clause declares that they shall include. But the word "include" is susceptible of another construction, which may become imperative, if the context of the Act is sufficient to shew that it was not merely employed for the purpose of adding to the natural significance of the words or expressions defined. It may be equivalent to "mean and include," and in that case it may afford an exhaustive explanation of the meaning which, for the purposes of the Act, must invariably be attached to these words or expressions.'

In *Robinson v Local Board of Barton-Eccles Winton and Monton* (1883) 8 App Cas 798 at 801 the Earl of Selborne LC said:

'An interpretation clause of this kind is not meant to prevent the word receiving its ordinary, popular, and natural sense whenever that would be properly applicable; but to enable the word as used in the Act, when there is nothing in the context or the subject-matter to the contrary, to be applied to some things to which it would not ordinarily be applicable.'

I think it is quite clear that sub-s (3) is enacted to extend the ordinary and natural meaning of 'equipment'. I do not think that a large commercial airliner would be 'equipment', certainly so far as the crew are concerned. I am not satisfied that even a light aircraft supplied by an employer engaged in a crop spraying business would be 'equipment' so far as the pilot was concerned. However, the status of aircraft is resolved by the terms of sub-s (3).

a   In a like manner I am not satisfied that plant, machinery, vehicles and clothing would in all circumstances be 'equipment'. For example, whereas I would think that protective clothing in an industrial context such as boots or gauntlets would be equipment, I very much doubt that ordinary overalls or uniforms would qualify. The same is true of the other items, plant and machinery and vehicles; for example, I think that the engine of a large motor lorry is part of the vehicle and could not be separated as equipment, so that if the vehicle itself was not equipment nor would that particular item of machinery be

b   such.

It may be that the terms of sub-s (3) are in part declaratory but I have no doubt that the main purpose is to extend the meaning of 'equipment'.

Counsel for the plaintiffs has submitted in the alternative that the ship was a 'vehicle' for the purposes of the subsection. She relied on the seventh main definition in the *Oxford English Dictionary*: 'Any means of carriage, conveyance, or transport; a receptacle

c   in which anything is placed in order to be moved.' The quotations from literature in support of this definition are not helpful to counsel's submission and this is not surprising for, as counsel for the defendants pointed out, I think that the real meaning of 'vehicle' is to be found in the sixth definition:

d   'A means of conveyance provided with wheels or runners and used for the carriage of persons or goods; a carriage, cart, wagon, sledge, or similar contrivance.'

Counsel for the defendants submitted that if 'vehicle' was to have the apparently limitless meaning in the seventh definition, as for example: 'It was a cup . . in which Hercules passed the seas; and the same history is given of Helius, who was said to have traversed the ocean in the same vehicle', it would have been quite unnecessary to have picked out aircraft in the definition. I am satisfied that a ship is not a vehicle for the purposes of this

e   Act. I am also satisfied that a ship is not 'plant' and in my judgment the Derbyshire was not 'equipment' for the purposes of this Act.

It is said that such a decision produces anomalies; it is said that if hostesses in aircraft and dining-car crew on trains can assert that the aircraft and the train itself are equipment for the purposes of the Act so too should stewards and stewardesses on board ship be able

f   to say that the ship is equipment. This sort of anomaly can frequently be found and in my judgment the answer is that Parliament has chosen to enact this statute in the words that are used and on their true construction they do cover aircraft and trains but do not cover ships. I am mindful of the mischief that the statute was intended to correct, namely the decision in *Davie v New Merton Board Mills Ltd* [1959] 1 All ER 346, [1959] AC 604, where the plaintiff was unable to recover for personal injuries sustained as a result of a

g   defect in a drift supplied for his use by his employers because the defect was not known to the employers or reasonably discoverable by them but was due to negligent manufacture in hardening the metal of the drift. However purposive a construction is put on the Act I am not persuaded that 'equipment' is to be given a meaning which in my judgment it quite plainly does not bear.

Counsel for the defendants has submitted that on the true construction of the Act the

h   equipment must be provided to a person or for use by a person. I do not find it necessary to come to any conclusion on that submission for, as I have said, I am clear that the Derbyshire was not 'equipment'. I would allow this appeal.

LLOYD LJ. The sole question for decision in this case is whether a ship is 'equipment' for the purposes of s 1 of the Employer's Liability (Defective Equipment) Act 1969. The

j   judge has held that it was (see [1986] 2 All ER 65, [1986] 1 WLR 751). Was he right? Although he does not state the precise ground of his decision, in my view he was.

The defendants are, or were, the owners of the Derbyshire. On 9 September 1980 she was carrying a cargo of 157,000 tons of iron ore from Canada to Japan when she broke in two off the Japanese coast, with the loss of all 45 lives on board, including the third engineer, Mr Leo Coltman. This action is brought on behalf of his estate. It is the

plaintiffs' case that the death of the deceased was caused by a defect in the vessel, and that
the defect was attributable to the fault of the shipbuilders, Swan Hunter Shipbuilders
Ltd. If that is right, and if the ship is 'equipment' within the meaning of s 1(1) of the
1969 Act, then the plaintiffs have a cause of action against the defendants, even if the
defendants were not negligent. The defendants deny that the ship was equipment
provided by them for the purposes of their business.

On 13 February 1986 the court ordered, by consent, that the question of construction
be tried as a preliminary point of law. It was that preliminary point of law which was
decided by Sheen J in favour of the plaintiffs; there is now an appeal to this court.

The substantive provisions of the 1969 Act are contained in a single section, with four
subsections. It is common ground that the Act was passed as a consequence of the decision
of the House of Lords in *Davie v New Merton Board Mills Ltd* [1959] 1 All ER 346, [1959]
AC 604. Section 1 of the Act provides:

'*Extension of employer's liability for defective equipment.*—(1) Where after the
commencement of this Act—(a) an employee suffers personal injury in the course
of his employment in consequence of a defect in equipment provided by his
employer for the purposes of the employer's business; and (b) the defect is
attributable wholly or partly to the fault of a third party (whether identified or not),
the injury shall be deemed to be also attributable to negligence on the part of the
employer (whether or not he is liable in respect of the injury apart from this
subsection), but without prejudice to the law relating to contributory negligence
and to any remedy by way of contribution or in contract or otherwise which is
available to the employer in respect of the injury.

(2) In so far as any agreement purports to exclude or limit any liability of an
employer arising under subsection (1) of this section, the agreement shall be void.

(3) In this section—"business" includes the activities carried on by any public
body; "employee" means a person who is employed by another person under a
contract of service or apprenticeship and is so employed for the purposes of a
business carried on by that other person, and "employer" shall be construed
accordingly; "equipment" includes any plant and machinery, vehicle, aircraft and
clothing; "fault" means negligence, breach of statutory duty or other act or omission
which gives rise to liability in tort in England and Wales or which is wrongful and
gives rise to liability in damages in Scotland; and "personal injury" includes loss of
life, any impairment of a person's physical or mental condition and any disease.

(4) This section binds the Crown, and persons in the service of the Crown shall
accordingly be treated for the purposes of this section as employees of the Crown if
they would not be so treated apart from this subsection.'

It is often said of questions of construction that they are matters of first impression. In
the present case that could be misleading. One's first impression of the word 'equipment',
standing alone, might well be that it does not include an ocean-going vessel capable of
carrying 157,000 tons of iron ore. For one normally thinks of equipment as something
with which a factory, workshop or other premises are equipped. But the word equipment
does not stand alone. It is qualified by the words 'provided by his employer for the
purposes of the employer's business'. Clearly 'business' is not confined to the sort of
business that is carried on in a factory. Indeed, by definition, business includes the
activities carried on by any public body. So the business of being a shipowner, or of
carrying goods by sea, is plainly included within s 1(1)(a).

What then is the equipment which a shipowner provides for the purposes of his
business? The answer must surely include his ships. The word equipment is certainly
capable of including ships as a matter of language. Thus one would talk naturally of a
fleet being equipped with battleships, cruisers and destroyers, or of the equipment of an
expedition as including supply ships. In my judgment counsel for the plaintiffs was right
when she submitted that equipment in s 1(1) includes all chattels provided for the

purpose of the employer's business other than materials and work in progress. Counsel
a for the defendants drew an analogy between a ship and a factory in which people work.
But the analogy is superficial. A factory is realty, whereas a ship is a chattel. It has long
been accepted that a ship is 'goods' for the purposes of the Sale of Goods Act 1979. If so, I
see no difficulty in regarding it as equipment. If a ship does not cease to be goods merely
because it is large enough for people to live in and work on board, why should it not be
equipment?

b   Counsel for the defendants was half inclined to accept that small ships such as pleasure
craft and river steamers might be equipment, though he did not extend that concession
to dredgers and fishing boats. But, if pleasure craft and river steamers can be equipment,
I can see no reason for distinguishing between such vessels and ocean-going vessels
merely by reason of their size.

        Counsel for the defendants argued that 'provided by his employer' in s 1(1) of the 1969
c Act must mean 'provided to the employee', and a ship could not be said to be provided *to*
the crew. Rather the crew is provided *for* the ship. I cannot accept that argument. For I
can see no justification for reading in the suggested words.

        So even if s 1(1) had stood on its own, I would have held that a ship is equipment
provided by a shipowner for the purposes of his business. But the matter becomes even
clearer when one looks at the definition of equipment in s 1(3). It includes both vehicles
d and aircraft. This shows that the word equipment is used in the widest possible sense.
Counsel for the defendants submitted that aircraft must be limited to the sort of small
aircraft which are used for spraying crops, and does not include a Boeing 747. But I can
see no basis for that limitation on the ordinary meaning of the word. And if a Boeing
747 is to be included in s 1(1) as equipment provided by the airline for the purposes of
its business, I can see no ground for excluding a ship as equipment provided by the
e shipowner.

        Counsel for the defendants argued that it is of the utmost significance that the
draftsman included vehicles and aircraft in s 1(3) but did not include ships. I agree that
it is odd. But it is no more than odd. To argue that because ships are not specifically
included they are impliedly excluded is fallacious. It is to stand the maxim expressio
f unius est exclusio alterius on its head. The definitions of 'employee' and 'fault' are
exhaustive. To attempt to add a new element to those definitions would indeed infringe
the maxim. But the definition of 'equipment', like the definitions of 'business' and
'personal injury', in inclusive. Inclusive definitions necessarily imply that there are
matters covered by the word defined that are *not* included in the definition. Occasionally
the context will make it clear that the word 'include' is equivalent to 'mean and include'
(see *Dilworth v Comr of Stamps* [1899] AC 99 at 105–106). But here the context points the
g other way. It would be as difficult to argue in the present case that ships are impliedly
excluded from 'equipment' by the express inclusion of aircraft as to argue that activities
carried on by a private body are impliedly excluded from 'business' by the express
inclusion of activities carried on by a public body, or cable-cars (to take another illustration
mentioned by counsel for the plaintiffs) by the express inclusion of vehicles.

h   Counsel for the defendants argued that s 1(3) is what is sometimes called an enlarging
definition. I do not agree. In my judgment it is a clarifying definition. As Viscount
Dilhorne said in *IRC v Parker* [1966] 1 All ER 399 at 404, [1966] AC 141 at 161:

        'It is a familiar device of a draftsman to state expressly that certain matters are to
        be treated as coming within a definition to avoid argument on whether they did or
j   not.'

        I do not find it necessary to deal with the argument of counsel for the plaintiffs that a
ship is in any event included within the ordinary meaning of 'plant' and 'vehicle',
although I am inclined to think that 'vehicle' in this context means any type of
conveyance. If so, ships would be included.

Finally, if I were in doubt, I would not hesitate to construe the legislation in accordance
with the beneficent intention which Parliament had in mind. It would be difficult to   *a*
imagine a case in which the legislative purpose is clearer. Nobody has been able to
suggest any good reason, or any reason at all, why, to take counsel for the plaintiffs'
example, the steward on board a Boeing 707 should have the benefit of the statute, but
not the steward on board a ship. Of course we cannot fill in gaps left by Parliament, even
if they are clearly accidental. But to give the word 'equipment' the full meaning of which
it is capable is not to fill a gap.   *b*
   The argument of counsel for the defendants' leads to absurd distinctions and anomalies.
Thus an employee injured by a defect in a winch on board ship would have the benefit
of the Act, but not an employee injured by a defect in the main engine; for the main
engine, says counsel, is part of the structure of the ship. Similarly a dredging company
which provides buckets and spades for dredging a channel would be providing
equipment, but not if it provides a dredger. The necessity for such distinctions should be   *c*
avoided if possible. By contrast the distinction between chattels and realty is clean-cut
and workable; and it corresponds to the purpose which Parliament must presumably
have had in mind in passing the Act, namely to cast on employers the liability which
would otherwise fall on the manufacturer of a defective product under *Donoghue v
Stevenson* [1932] AC 562, [1932] All ER Rep 1. The fact that the product may be large
enough to be regarded as the employee's place of work is, to my mind, irrelevant.   *d*
   Both sides, as usually happens, relied on the plain and ordinary meaning of the word.
But the plain and ordinary meaning of a word may be elusive. When a word has a
relatively narrow meaning, then the plain and ordinary meaning is almost always the
best guide to the legislative intention. But, when a word has, potentially, a very wide
meaning, there is a danger of mistaking the plain and ordinary meaning for the meaning
most frequently used in practice. I would accept that the word 'equipment' is not often   *e*
used to include ships any more than it is often used to include aircraft. But that does not
mean that ships and aircraft do not come within the plain and ordinary meaning of the
word. In any event, the question we have to ask ourselves is what the word means in the
context of this particular Act. Having regard to the natural width of the word (it is
difficult, off hand, to think of a wider word that Parliament could have used), the
immediate context in which the word appears, and in particular the inclusion of aircraft   *f*
in the definition, and the evident legislative purpose, I would hold, in agreement with
the judge, that the question should be answered in favour of the plaintiffs. I would
therefore, for my part, dismiss the appeal.

GLIDEWELL LJ. I have had the advantage of reading in draft the judgments of
O'Connor and Lloyd JJ. They set out the relevant facts, which I therefore need not repeat.   *g*
The preliminary issue to be decided can be expressed in the following terms: is a 90,000-
ton cargo ship equipment provided by the shipowners for the purposes of their business?
I agree with O'Connor LJ that this question should be answered No. Thus I respectfully
disagree with the reasoning of both Sheen J ([1986] 2 All ER 65, [1986] 1 WLR 751) and
Lloyd LJ.   *h*
   I accept that in s 1(1) of the Employer's Liability (Defective Equipment) Act 1969 it is
the whole phrase, 'equipment provided by his employer for the purposes of his business',
which has to be construed, though the normal meaning of the single word 'equipment'
is an aid to that construction. Like Lloyd LJ I think it right to start by considering the
normal meaning of the phrase, without reference to the definition in s 1(3). Unlike Lloyd
LJ, however, I do regard this as a matter of impression. In my view, neither the normal   *j*
meaning of the word 'equipment' nor that of the whole phrase includes a 90,000-ton
vessel. In ordinary usage, I believe one would speak of 'a ship and its equipment'. The
equipment includes machinery, fixtures and fittings inside the ship, and all portable
chattels which are needed for the conduct of the shipowner's business. It may be that
there would be argument whether certain items are part of the ship itself or part of its

equipment; the main engines are a case in point. But, if the dichotomy is valid, there can
a be no doubt that the hull of the vessel (which is what is alleged to have failed in this case)
is part of the ship, not part of its equipment.

I accept that one might in some contexts properly describe a fleet of small boats as
'equipment provided', e g by the proprietors of a sailing school. But I reject the submission
that no distinction can be made, for the purposes of s 1(1) of the 1969 Act, between a
fleet of 12-foot dinghies and a very large ocean-going vessel.

b I turn, therefore, to consider the definition in s 1(3), viz: '"equipment" includes any
plant and machinery, vehicle, aircraft and clothing.' In my view this definition achieves
two purposes. In part it resolves possible doubts whether 'plant and machinery' are
'equipment' in the ordinary meaning of the word. In part, the definition extends the
normal meaning of 'equipment'. Thus some clothing provided by an employer would in
my view be 'equipment' in the ordinary sense, e g protective boots and headgear; equally,
c some would not, e g a car-park attendant's uniform jacket. In the latter respect the
definition extends the normal meaning of the word. So too, in my judgment, it does
with 'vehicle' and 'aircraft'. A dumper truck might well be 'equipment' in the normal
sense: a car used by a salesman would not in my view. So too, a crop-spraying aircraft
might be 'equipment' in the ordinary sense; a transatlantic Boeing 747 would not be. In
both instances, the definition extends the normal meaning to include any vehicle and
d any aircraft provided by the employer for the purpose of his business.

Is a very large cargo vessel 'plant', as counsel for the plaintiffs, to whom we are indebted
for her clear and attractive address, submits? In my view it is not. The word 'plant', in
this context and in its ordinary meaning, signifies the aggregate of the machinery,
implements, apparatus and fixtures used in the carrying on of an industrial process.

Counsel's alternative submission, that a large cargo vessel is a 'vehicle', is nearer the
e mark, but in my judgment still misses it. The word 'vehicle' has a variety of meanings
according to its context. One meaning of the word is 'any means of conveyance'. I have
not failed to note an advertisement of the Cunard Steamship Co (which appeared after
the hearing of this appeal had concluded) which described their cruising ships as
'luxurious vehicles'. But this meaning is in the language of hyperbole or poetry. In its
normal meaning, in the context of this statute, a vehicle is a means of conveying people
f or goods on land. That this is the meaning of the word in s 1(3) is, in my view, clear from
the inclusion in the definition of 'aircraft'. If the word 'vehicle' includes any means of
conveyance, so as to comprehend a ship, it includes also aircraft. The specific reference to
'aircraft' can only, in my view, point to the word 'vehicle' being limited to conveyance
on land.

In s 1(3) Parliament has in my judgment expressly included in the definition of
g 'equipment' means of conveyance on land and in the air, and specifically excluded means
of conveyance on the sea. Why it should have done this I do not know. That this is what
it has done I have no doubt.

For these reasons I also would allow the appeal and hold that the Derbyshire was not
'equipment provided by [the defendants] for the purposes of' their business within s 1(1)
h of the 1969 Act.

Appeal allowed. Leave to appeal to the House of Lords granted.

Solicitors: *Holman Fenwick & Willan* (for the defendants); *Evill & Coleman* (for the
plaintiffs).

Patricia Hargrove   Barrister.

Bugdaycay v Secretary of State for the Home Department
and related appeals

HOUSE OF LORDS

LORD BRIDGE OF HARWICH, LORD BRANDON OF OAKBROOK, LORD TEMPLEMAN, LORD GRIFFITHS AND LORD GOFF OF CHIEVELEY

10, 11, 13 NOVEMBER 1986, 19 FEBRUARY 1987

Immigration – Leave to enter – Refugee – Asylum – Jurisdiction of court – Applicants entering United Kingdom intending to seek asylum – Secretary of State deciding claims for asylum not made out – Secretary of State treating applicants as illegal entrants and ordering their removal – Whether court having jurisdiction to decide whether applicants refugees – Immigration Act 1971, s 4(1).

Immigration – Appeal – Deportation – Deportation pending appeal – Illegal entrant – Entrant claiming refugee status – Whether illegal entrant claiming refugee status entitled to remain in United Kingdom pending appeal – Whether removal of entrant prior to appeal contrary to United Kingdom's obligations under international convention on refugees – Immigration Act 1971, s 13(3) – Convention and Protocol relating to the Status of Refugees, art 35.

Immigration – Leave to enter – Non-patrial – Right of entry – Duty to disclose facts – Material facts – Failure to disclose intention to claim refugee status and asylum – Whether relevant that disclosure of intention to seek asylum might have caused leave to be granted – Whether failure to disclose intention to seek asylum a non-disclosure of a 'material' fact – Whether leave to enter vitiated by non-disclosure of material fact.

Immigration – Leave to enter – Refugee – Asylum – Deportation to country which would send applicant back to country where he would be persecuted – Ugandan national entering United Kingdom from Kenya – Applicant seeking asylum because of fear of persecution in Uganda – Secretary of State proposing to remove applicant to Kenya – Secretary of State not taking into account Kenyan repatriation of Ugandan nationals – Whether Secretary of State's decision should be quashed – Convention and Protocol relating to the Status of Refugees, art 33.

In separate appeals by persons who claimed asylum in the United Kingdom as refugees the issue arose whether the exercise by the Secretary of State under s 4(1)[a] of the Immigration Act 1971 of the power under that Act to refuse leave to enter or remain in the United Kingdom conflicted with the United Kingdom's obligations under art 33(1)[b] of the 1951 Geneva Convention on Refugees, which provided that 'No Contracting State shall expel or return . . . a refugee . . . to . . . territories where his life or freedom would be threatened on account of his race, religion, nationality, membership of a particular social group or political opinion'.

In the first appeal the appellants obtained leave to enter the United Kingdom by falsely stating to the immigration officer that they wished to enter only for a short period for a particular purpose. They failed to disclose that their real intention was to seek asylum as refugees who feared persecution in their own countries. Having gained entry they subsequently applied for asylum as refugees but the Secretary of State decided that the

---

a　Section 4(1), so far as material, provides: 'The power under this Act to give or refuse leave to enter the United Kingdom shall be exercised by immigration officers, and the power to give leave to remain in the United Kingdom, or to vary any leave . . . shall be exercised by the Secretary of State . . .'

b　Article 33(1) is set out at p 944 d, post

claims for asylum had not been made out and that the appellants were to be treated as
a illegal entrants. The appellants applied for judicial review of the Secretary of State's
decision but their applications were dismissed. They appealed to the Court of Appeal,
which dismissed their appeal. The appellants appealed to the House of Lords, contending
(i) that the court had jurisdiction to decide whether they were in fact refugees, because
the power to remove them from the United Kingdom depended on proof that they were
not refugees and if they were refugees their removal would be a breach of the United
b Kingdom's obligations under the Geneva convention, (ii) that the removal of the
appellants as illegal entrants before they exercised their right to appeal against the refusal
of refugee status, although in accordance with s 13(3)^c of the 1971 Act, which provided
that a person was not entitled to appeal against a refusal of leave to enter so long as he
remained in the United Kingdom, was contrary to the United Kingdom's obligation
under art 35^d of the convention to have regard to the recommendations of the United
c Nations High Commissioner for Refugees on the procedure to be adopted for determining
refugee status, and (iii) that their original misrepresentations on entry were not material
since they would not necessarily have been refused leave to enter if they had originally
applied to enter as refugees.

In the second appeal the appellant originally sought leave to enter the United Kingdom
as a visitor from Kenya, where he had lived for six years between 1974 and 1982, and
d when that was refused he claimed political asylum as a refugee from Uganda, his country
of origin, on the ground that if he was removed to Kenya it was highly likely that he
would be returned by the Kenyan authorities to Uganda, where he feared he would be
arrested and killed. His claim was rejected on the ground that he had come from a 'safe
country', ie Kenya, and the Secretary of State refused to withdraw directions for his
removal to Kenya despite evidence that in the past Kenya had broken its obligations
e under the convention by returning Ugandan refugees to Uganda. The appellant applied
for judicial review of the Secretary of State's decision but his application was refused by
the judge and on appeal that refusal was upheld by the Court of Appeal. He appealed to
the House of Lords, contending that the United Kingdom would be in breach of its
obligations under art 33(1) of the convention if it returned him to Kenya when it was
likely that Kenya would return him to Uganda.
f

Held – (1) The resolution of any issue of fact and the exercise of any discretion in relation
to an application for asylum as a refugee were matters which lay exclusively within the
discretion conferred on immigration officers and the Secretary of State by s 4(1) of the
1971 Act, subject only to the court's supervisory jurisdiction to ensure that the decision
was not flawed in any way. Accordingly, where a person who would otherwise be an
g illegal entrant claimed asylum as a refugee the question whether he was in fact a refugee
was a matter to be determined by the immigration authorities and not the courts. It
followed that the appellants in the first appeal were not entitled to judicial review of the
Secretary of State's refusal to treat them as refugees or of his decision to remove them
from the United Kingdom. Their appeals would accordingly be dismissed (see p 945 *d* to
h *f*, p 954 *b c*, p 956 *e f* and p 957 *b c*, post); *Khawaja v Secretary of State for the Home Dept*
[1983] 1 All ER 765 distinguished.

(2) Since s 13(3) of the 1971 Act expressly prohibited an appeal by a person against
refusal of leave to enter so long as he remained in the United Kingdom and since an
illegal entrant could have no better right of appeal against his removal, it followed that
an illegal entrant who claimed to be a refugee was not entitled to remain in the United
j Kingdom pending an appeal, even if that was contrary to the UN High Commissioner's
recommendations on the procedure to be adopted for determining refugee status (see
p 946 *j* to p 947 *b*, p 954 *b c*, p 956 *f g* and p 957 *b c*, post).

---

c   Section 13(3), so far as material, provides: '. . . a person shall not be entitled to appeal against a
refusal of leave to enter so long as he is in the United Kingdom . . .'

d   Article 35, so far as material, is set out at p 946 *b*, post

(3) A material misrepresentation made by an intending entrant was not made any less material because of the fact that if he had told a different story and had put forward a different reason for seeking entry he might well have been granted leave. Accordingly, the misrepresentations made by the appellants in the first appeals were relevant to the Secretary of State's decision that they were illegal entrants (see p 947 d to g, p 954 b c and p 957 b c, post).

(4) Where it was shown that if an applicant for refugee status were to be removed from the United Kingdom the country to which he would be returned might, contrary to its obligations under art 33 of the Geneva convention, send him back to another country where, on good grounds, he feared persecution, the Secretary of State was under an obligation to determine whether the danger of the applicant being returned to that other country was sufficiently substantial for his removal to involve a potential breach of art 33. In such a case, however, the court could not interfere if the Secretary of State decided, in the light of all the evidence, that the removal of the applicant to a safe country would not place him substantially at risk of return to a country where he feared persecution. On the facts, the Secretary of State had not taken into account or adequately resolved whether the appellant in the second appeal would, if returned to Kenya, be sent back to Uganda. The appellant's appeal would accordingly be allowed and the Secretary of State's decision quashed (see p 952 g to p 953 a h j, p 954 b c and p 956 j to p 957 b c, post).

Decision of the Court of Appeal sub nom *R v Secretary of State for the Home Dept, ex p Bugdaycay* [1986] 1 All ER 458 affirmed.

Notes

For illegal entrants, see 4 Halsbury's Laws (4th edn) paras 1008, 1027.

For control of immigration with respect to refugees, see ibid para 981.

For refugees and stateless persons under the Geneva Convention on Refugees, see 18 ibid paras 1717–1722.

For the Immigration Act 1971, ss 4, 13, see 41 Halsbury's Statutes (3rd edn) 22, 34.

Cases referred to in opinions

Associated Provincial Picture Houses Ltd v Wednesbury Corp [1947] 2 All ER 680, [1948] 1 KB 223, CA.

Khawaja v Secretary of State for the Home Dept [1983] 1 All ER 765, [1984] AC 74, [1983] 2 WLR 321, HL.

Consolidated appeals and appeal

Bugdaycay v Secretary of State for the Home Dept
Nelidow Santis v Secretary of State for the Home Dept
Norman v Secretary of State for the Home Dept

Huseyin Bugdaycay, Michael Nelidow Santis and Daniel Tawiah Norman each appealed, with leave of the Appeal Committee of the House of Lords granted on 14 April 1986, against the decision of the Court of Appeal (Oliver, Neill and Balcombe LJJ) ([1986] 1 All ER 458, [1986] 1 WLR 155) on 5 November 1985 dismissing their appeals against the orders of Taylor J on 28 June 1985 in relation to Mr Bugdaycay and Mr Nelidow Santis and the order of Woolf J on 24 January 1984 in relation to Mr Norman dismissing their respective applications for orders of certiorari, in the case of Mr Bugdaycay to quash a decision of an immigration officer dated 23 May 1984 that he was an illegal entrant and a decision of the Secretary of State for the Home Department in September 1984 that he had not substantiated a claim to asylum in the United Kingdom, in the case of Mr Nelidow Santis to quash a decision of the Secretary of State dated 3 July 1984 refusing him asylum in the United Kingdom and a decision of an immigration officer dated 16 July 1984 to treat him as an illegal entrant, and in the case of Mr Norman to quash a decision of an immigration officer made on 4 January 1983 to treat him as an illegal

entrant. Leave to consolidate the appeals was granted by the Appeal Committee of the
a House of Lords on 22 May 1986. The facts are set out in the opinion of Lord Bridge.

Musisi v Secretary of State for the Home Dept

Herbert Crispian Musisi appealed, with leave of the Appeal Committee of the House of
Lords granted on 19 November 1985, against the decision of the Court of Appeal
(Watkins, Purchas and Dillon LJJ) on 24 May 1985 dismissing his appeal against the
order of Mann J dated 1 November 1984 whereby his application for judicial review of a
b series of removal orders made against him by the Secretary of State for the Home
Department was refused. The facts are set out in the opinion of Lord Bridge.

The appeals were heard together by consent of the parties.

Michael Beloff QC, Alper Riza and *Andrew Nicol* for the first three appellants.
c *Andrew Collins QC* and *Christa Fielden* for Mr Musisi.
John Laws and *Philip Havers* for the Secretary of State.

Their Lordships took time for consideration.

19 February. The following opinions were delivered.

d **LORD BRIDGE OF HARWICH.** My Lords, these four appeals were heard together
by consent of all parties. All are concerned with questions as to the treatment in domestic
law of those who claim to be refugees under the Convention and Protocol relating to the
Status of Refugees (Geneva, 28 July 1951, TS 39 (1954), Cmd 9171; New York, 31 January
1967, TS 15 (1969), Cmnd 3906), which I shall refer to as 'the convention'. The
background material in the Immigration Act 1971, the rules made thereunder and the
e convention itself is common to all four appeals. The issues which arise in the first three
appeals are identical. The issues raised in the appeal of Musisi overlap to some extent
with the issues in the first three appeals. The appeal of Musisi, however, raises difficult
and entirely distinct issues which will require examination in some detail of the facts
peculiar to that case. At the outset it will be convenient to give a brief outline of the facts
so far as necessary for the proper examination of the common issues.
f   The first three appellants separately obtained leave to enter the United Kingdom under
the 1971 Act. Bugdaycay was granted leave to enter as a student, Nelidow Santis as a
holiday visitor, Norman as a business visitor. In due course each claimed to be entitled to
asylum in this country as a refugee from his country of origin. The claim in the case of
Santis was made before the expiry of his temporary leave to enter, but the other two only
made their claims after the expiry of their leave to enter and after they had been arrested
g as overstayers. The Secretary of State refused each of the claims to asylum and directions
were given in each case for the removal of the appellant as an illegal entrant pursuant to
para 9 of Sch 2 to the Act. Each applied for judicial review. The applications of Bugdaycay
and Nelidow Santis were refused by Taylor J, that of Norman by Woolf J. Their appeals
were heard together by the Court of Appeal (Oliver, Neill and Balcombe LJJ) ([1986] 1
All ER 458, [1986] 1 WLR 155) and dismissed. A fuller account of the facts which I have
h very briefly summarised will be found in the judgment of Neill LJ (see [1986] 1 All ER
458 at 460–462, [1986] 1 WLR 155 at 157–158). The appellants now appeal by leave of
your Lordships' House.
    The appellant Musisi applied for leave to enter as a visitor from Kenya. Pending a
decision on that application he was temporarily admitted to the United Kingdom
j pursuant to para 21 of Sch 2 to the 1971 Act. His application for leave to enter was
refused, but he thereupon immediately applied for asylum as a refugee from Uganda.
His temporary admission was extended indefinitely pending consideration of that
application. I shall later have to examine the history of his case in detail but at this stage
it suffices to say that a final decision was made refusing him leave to enter and directions
were given for his removal and return to Kenya in January 1984. His application for
judicial review was refused by Mann J and his appeal against that refusal was dismissed

by the Court of Appeal (Watkins, Purchas and Dillon LJJ). He, too, now appeals by leave
of your Lordships' House.   *a*

This is the first time your Lordships' House has had to consider the convention. The
questions arising from its impact on domestic law are of undoubted importance both to
those claiming refugee status and to the authorities responsible for the operation of the
system for the control of immigration established by the 1971 Act and rules made
thereunder.

The relevant definition of 'refugee' in the convention is: *b*

'any person who . . . owing to well-founded fear of being persecuted for reasons
of race, religion, nationality, membership of a particular social group or political
opinion, is outside the country of his nationality and is unable or, owing to such
fear, is unwilling to avail himself of the protection of that country . . .'

The provisions in the convention of primary importance are the following: *c*

'ARTICLE 32 . . . 1. The Contracting States shall not expel a refugee lawfully in
their territory save on grounds of national security or public order . . .
ARTICLE 33 . . . 1. No Contracting State shall expel or return ("refouler") a refugee
in any manner whatsoever to the frontiers of territories where his life or freedom
would be threatened on account of his race, religion, nationality, membership of a *d*
particular social group or political opinion.'

The relevant rules laid down by the Secretary of State pursuant to s 3(2) of the 1971
Act 'as to the practice to be followed in the administration of this Act for regulating the
entry into and stay in the United Kingdom of persons required by this Act to have leave
to enter' are found in the Statement of Changes in Immigration Rules (HC Paper (1982–
83) no 169). The rules are divided into two sections: section 1 relates to 'Control on   *e*
Entry'; section 2 relates to 'Control after Entry'. Paragraph 16 in section 1 and para 96 in
section 2, each headed 'Refugees', are in identical terms as follows:

'Where a person is a refugee full account is to be taken of the provisions of the
Convention and Protocol relating to the Status of Refugees. Nothing in these rules
is to be construed as requiring action contrary to the United Kingdom's obligations *f*
under these instruments.'

The paragraphs headed 'Asylum' in sections 1 and 2 are respectively paras 73 and 134,
which provide as follows:

'73. Special considerations arise where the only country to which a person could
be removed is one to which he is unwilling to go owing to well-founded fear of   *g*
being persecuted for reasons of race, religion, nationality, membership of a particular
social group or political opinion. Any case in which it appears to the immigration
officer as a result of a claim or information given by the person seeking entry at a
port that he might fall within the terms of this provision is to be referred to the
Home Office for decision regardless of any grounds set out in any provision of these
rules which may appear to justify refusal of leave to enter. Leave to enter will not *h*
be refused if removal would be contrary to the provisions of the Convention and
Protocol relating to the Status of Refugees.
134. A person may apply for asylum in the United Kingdom on the ground that,
if he were required to leave, he would have to go to a country to which he is
unwilling to go owing to well-founded fear of being persecuted for reasons of race,
religion, nationality, membership of a particular social group or political opinion. *j*
Any such claim is to be carefully considered in the light of all the relevant
circumstances.'

The primary submission made on behalf of the first three appellants is that the
immigration rules prohibit their removal and return to their own countries whence they

came unless and until the courts have adjudicated on and rejected their claim to be
a   refugees from those countries. The argument proceeds by stages. Each claims to be a
refugee from the country of his nationality. To return him to that country, therefore,
would contravene art 33(1) of the convention. Paragraph 73 of HC Paper (1982–83) no
169 prohibits removal contrary to the provisions of the convention. It follows, so it is
said, that the Secretary of State cannot give himself power to make a decision leading to a
person's removal contrary to the rules by finding as a fact that he is not a refugee if in
b   truth he is. The conclusion, it is submitted, is that if the Secretary of State has purported
to make such a decision the court, on an application for judicial review, is not confined
to considering whether there was evidence to support the decision of the Secretary of
State, but must examine the evidence and make its own decision. Only if the court is
satisfied on a balance of probabilities that the person claiming asylum is *not* a refugee can
the decision to remove him to his country of origin be affirmed.

c   This line of reasoning is said to be supported by analogy by the decision in *Khawaja v
Secretary of State for the Home Dept* [1983] 1 All ER 765, [1984] AC 74 that, when
directions given pursuant to para 9 of Sch 2 to the 1971 Act for the removal of an illegal
entrant are challenged on an application for judicial review, it is for the immigration
officer or the Secretary of State, as the case may be, to establish the fact of illegal entry.

        The reason why this argument cannot be sustained is that all questions of fact on
d   which the discretionary decision whether to grant or withhold leave to enter or remain
depends must necessarily be determined by the immigration officer or the Secretary of
State in the exercise of the discretion which is exclusively conferred on them by s 4(1) of
the 1971 Act. The question whether an applicant for leave to enter or remain is or is not
a refugee is only one, even if a particularly important one required by para 73 of HC
Paper (1982–83) no 169 to be returned to the House Office, of a multiplicity of questions
e   which immigration officers and officials of the Home Office acting for the Secretary of
State must daily determine in dealing with applications for leave to enter or remain in
accordance with the rules, as, for example, whether an applicant is a bona fide visitor,
student, businessman, dependant etc. Determination of such questions is only open to
challenge in the courts on well-known *Wednesbury* principles (see *Associated Provincial
Picture Houses Ltd v Wednesbury Corp* [1947] 2 All ER 680, [1948] 1 KB 223). There is no
f   ground for treating the question raised by a claim to refugee status as an exception to this
rule. For the reasons explained at length in the speeches in *Khawaja's* case the court's
fundamentally different approach to an order for removal on the ground of illegal entry
is dictated by the terms of the statute itself, since the power to direct removal under para
9 of Sch 2 is only available in the case of a person who is in fact an 'illegal entrant'.

g   All four appellants next submit that before their claims to asylum as refugees can be
finally refused and before they can be required to leave this country they are entitled, by
one route or another, to appeal to the appellate authorities under Pt II of the 1971 Act.
Section 13(1) gives a right of appeal to an applicant against refusal of leave to enter, but
s 13 prevents its exercise, subject to exceptions not presently relevant, so long as the
intending appellant is in the United Kingdom. Section 14(1) gives a right of appeal to a
h   person who has a limited leave to enter or remain against refusal to vary that leave.
Section 15 gives a right of appeal against a decision of the Secretary of State to make a
deportation order. Section 17 gives a right of appeal against directions for a person's
removal to a particular country on the ground that 'he ought to be removed (if at all) to a
different country or territory specified by him'. At one time counsel for Musisi presented
an ingenious argument that s 17 gives to a person claiming asylum who objects to
j   removal to the country named in the directions appealed against, but can specify no
other, an effective opportunity to appeal while still in the United Kingdom even though
he has been refused leave to enter. A careful reading of s 17(5), however, shows, as
counsel in due course accepted, that in the case of a person refused leave to enter an
appeal against removal directions lies only in three exceptional cases, none of which is
applicable to Musisi.

A further argument advanced in the written case for Musisi, of which counsel was not the author, but which he did not feel he could properly abandon, was that the necessary reference to the Home Office for decision, pursuant to para 73 of HC Paper (1982–83) no 169, of a claim to asylum should be taken as the grant, by implication, of temporary leave to enter, giving the person claiming asylum a right of appeal under s 14(1) against a refusal to extend that leave. This is, however, wholly inconsistent with the language of the concluding sentence of para 73, 'Leave to enter will not be refused etc'.

The main argument on this aspect of the case was advanced by counsel for the first three appellants. He drew attention to art 35(1) of the convention, whereby 'The Contracting States undertake to co-operate with the Office of the United Nations High Commissioner for Refugees . . . in the exercise of its functions'. The office of the UN High Commissioner for Refugees published in 1979 a 'Handbook on Procedures and Criteria for Determining Refugee Status'. From para 192 of that publication we learn that in 1977 the executive committee of the High Commissioner's programme recommended that the procedures to be adopted by states adhering to the convention for determination of applications for refugee status should satisfy certain basic requirements. The relevant recommendations read as follows:

'. . . (iii) There should be a clearly identified authority—wherever possible a single central authority—with responsibility for examining requests for refugee status and taking a decision in the first instance . . .

(vi) If the applicant is not recognized, he should be given a reasonable time to appeal for a formal reconsideration of the decision, either to the same or to a different authority, whether administrative or judicial, according to the prevailing system.

(vii) The applicant should be permitted to remain in the country pending a decision on his initial request by the competent authority referred to in paragraph (iii) above, unless it has been established by that authority that his request is clearly abusive. He should also be permitted to remain in the country while an appeal to a higher administrative authority or to the courts is pending.'

It is submitted that the basic requirements set out in paras (vi) and (vii) can only be satisfied if an unsuccessful applicant is accorded a right of 'appeal . . . according to the prevailing system', which in the United Kingdom must mean an appeal to the appellate authorities under Pt II of the 1971 Act, exercisable before he is required to leave the country. Removal of the appellants as illegal entrants would deprive them of any such right of appeal. On the other hand the alternative course of making deportation orders in the case of Bugdaycay and Norman and simply refusing to extend leave to remain in the case of Nelidow Santis would have opened an avenue of appeal in each case in which the decision of the Secretary of State could have been challenged. In deciding to proceed against them as illegal entrants and neglecting the alternative, the Secretary of State, it is submitted, must have failed to have regard to the UN High Commissioner's recommendations.

My Lords, there was some discussion in the courts below of the question whether the practice of the Home Office complied with recommendation (vi). I express no opinion on that question, since it is, as it seems to me, neither necessary nor desirable that this House should attempt to interpret an instrument of this character which is of no binding force in either municipal or international law.

The fact that the first three appellants are proposed to be removed summarily as illegal entrants obscures the true implication of the argument advanced by counsel on their behalf. If the effect of the UN High Commissioner's recommendations were to require the Secretary of State to treat every applicant for refugee status in such a way as to enable the application, if initially unsuccessful, to be tested by way of an appeal under Pt II of the 1971 Act while the appellant remained in the United Kingdom, this would apply not only to those who had secured entry illegally, but to every applicant for refugee status who, on arrival in this country, was refused leave to enter. The result would then be that

the Secretary of State's duty to act in conformity with the obligation of the United
Kingdom under the convention to co-operate with the office of the UN High
Commissioner and to have regard to his recommendations would override the express
terms of s 13(3) of the 1971 Act, which prohibits an appeal against refusal of leave to
enter so long as the intending appellant is in the United Kingdom. This is plainly
untenable. It is equally plain that a person who has secured entry illegally can be in no
better position in this regard than a person refused leave to enter. Counsel's argument
must therefore be rejected.

The first three appellants finally challenge the decision to remove them summarily by
direction under para 9 of Sch 2 on the ground that they are not illegal entrants. It is
common ground that each committed an offence under s 26(2)(c) by misrepresenting to
an immigration officer on arrival in this country the true nature and purpose of his visit.
It is submitted, however, that the misrepresentations were not material, since the
appellants would not necessarily have been refused leave to enter if they had originally
claimed to enter as refugees.

After setting out the argument and the citations from authority on which this
submission relies for support, Neill LJ disposed of it as follows ([1986] 1 All ER 458 at
463–464, [1986] 1 WLR 155 at 160–161):

> 'In my judgment it is impermissible to extend the concept of material facts so as
> to allow an intending entrant to seek leave to enter for a particular purpose on the
> basis of a statement of particular facts and then later, on admitting that the purpose
> had been misrepresented and the facts had been misstated, to contend he was not an
> illegal entrant because if he had told a different story and had put forward a different
> reason for his visit he might well have been given leave. The question whether facts
> are material or decisive has to be answered in the context of the leave which was in
> fact given. The 1971 Act makes this clear. Thus the appellants were seeking to enter
> the United Kingdom by making statements or making representations to the
> immigration officers which they knew to be false or did not believe to be true. The
> misstatements or misrepresentations were not on matters of detail but constituted
> versions of the appellants' intentions which were in fundamental respects at variance
> with the truth. The decisions that these appellants were illegal entrants appears to
> me to be unassailable.'

I cannot improve on this reasoning, with which I agree and which I gratefully adopt. I
would, therefore, dismiss the first three appeals.

The case of Musisi raises first a distinct issue of law. The decision to refuse him leave
to enter was not based on the denial of his claim to refugee status quoad Uganda, which
is the country of his nationality, but on a conclusion by the Secretary of State that even if
he is properly to be treated as a refugee from Uganda, within the definition of 'refugee'
under the convention, this presents no obstacle to his return to Kenya, whence he came
to this country. The primary submission made by counsel on his behalf is that if he is a
refugee, as is to be assumed, he is protected not only by art 33(1) of the convention
against return to the country where he fears persecution, but also by art 32(1) against
return to any other country because he is now 'lawfully in [the] territory' of the United
Kingdom and cannot, therefore, be expelled save on grounds of national security or
public order. The temporary admission, pursuant to para 21 of Sch 2 to the 1971 Act, of
an applicant for leave to enter pending a decision on his application has the effect, it is
submitted, of making the applicant's presence in the United Kingdom lawful for the
purpose of his entitlement to the protection of art 32(1) of the convention.

Section 11(1) of the Act provides:

> 'A person arriving in the United Kingdom by ship or aircraft shall for purposes of
> this Act be deemed not to enter the United Kingdom unless and until he disembarks,
> and on disembarkation at a port shall further be deemed not to enter the United
> Kingdom so long as he remains in such area (if any) at the port as may be approved

for this purpose by an immigration officer; and a person who has not otherwise entered the United Kingdom shall be deemed not to do so as long as he is detained, *a* or temporarily admitted or released while liable to detention, under the powers conferred by Schedule 2 to this Act.'

Counsel for Musisi was constrained to concede that, if his argument is right, it must apply equally to any person arriving in this country at a regular port of entry and presenting himself to the immigration authorities, whether he is detained or temporarily *b* admitted pending a decision on his application for leave to enter. It follows that the effect of the submission, if it is well founded, is to confer on any person who can establish that he has the status of a refugee from the country of his nationality, but who arrives in the United Kingdom from a third country, an indefeasible right to remain here, since to refuse him leave to enter and direct his return to the third country will involve the United Kingdom in the expulsion of 'a refugee lawfully in their territory' contrary in art *c* 32(1).

The United Kingdom was already a party to the convention when the 1971 Act was passed and it would, to my mind, be very surprising if it had the effect contended for. But I am satisfied that the deeming provision enacted by s 11(1) makes counsel's submission on this point quite untenable.

My Lords, I now turn to the most difficult issue, which arises from the unusual facts *d* in the case of Musisi. The question is whether there is any available ground on which the discretionary administrative decision to remove the appellant to Kenya can properly be challenged in judicial review proceedings. Not the least surprising feature of the case is that this question was raised for the first time in your Lordships' House. The different counsel who appeared for the appellant in the courts below advanced only a single argument, which has now been abandoned, but, furthermore, the very experienced *e* counsel appearing before Mann J expressly disclaimed any challenge to the decision of the Secretary of State on *Wednesbury* principles. Nevertheless, a detailed examination of the way in which the application made by the appellant for asylum was dealt with by the immigration authorities gives cause for grave concern.

The appellant Musisi arrived at Heathrow airport on a flight from Nairobi on 23 *f* January 1983. He sought leave to enter the United Kingdom for the purpose of visiting his two half-sisters, both now settled in the United Kingdom and one of whom was his sponsor. He and his sponsor were both interviewed by an immigration officer on the day of his arrival. There were discrepancies in what they told the officer, who was not satisfied and decided to make further inquiries. The appellant was granted temporary admission until 26 January. On that day he was again interviewed by another immigration officer and the decision was then taken to refuse him leave to enter as a visitor. His temporary *g* admission was extended to the following day, when he was to be removed by the airline with which he had arrived.

On the morning of 27 January, however, a claim by the appellant to political asylum as a refugee from Uganda was communicated to the Home Office on his behalf by the United Kingdom Immigration Advisory Service. This resulted in a further extension of *h* the appellant's temporary admission 'pending further consideration of your case' which remains in operation to this day.

Nothing, I think, now turns on any inaccuracies or discrepancies in the account which the appellant gave of himself when posing as an intending visitor, save that his omission to claim political asylum in the first instance has naturally engendered a degree of scepticism about the claim. But the appellant has always put forward the explanation *j* that he had been advised to try to gain entry as a visitor and then to seek asylum through the 'refugee office' in London, which seems not to be wholly implausible and which, so far as the evidence shows, has not been rejected by the Home Office as untrue.

On 27 January 1983 the appellant was interviewed in connection with his claim to asylum by an immigration officer at Heathrow. This was an interview of first importance, since it was the only occasion in these protracted proceedings when the appellant was ever questioned face-to-face by an official acting on behalf of the Secretary of State. The

a immigration officer gives an account of this interview in an affidavit sworn in the proceedings and also exhibits his contemporary notes in a document entitled 'Political Asylum Interview Questionnaire'. I shall endeavour to extract from these discursive documents a summary of the relevant factual information presented by the appellant. He was born on 30 June 1960. He was educated in Uganda until 1973. In 1973 his father fled from Uganda to Kenya, but was arrested there and returned to Uganda. He was

b never seen again and was believed to have been murdered by the Ugandan secret police. The appellant and his mother were in Kenya from 1974 to 1979, where the appellant continued his schooling. They both returned to Uganda in 1979. The mother left in 1980 to return to Kenya once more, where she has since remained. Other siblings are also in Kenya. The appellant's two half-sisters, now in England, had been harrassed by soldiers in Uganda. I interpolate that, according to the appellant's own affidavit, he was

c in 1982 living in Uganda with an aunt and two cousins. At about this time he told the immigration officer that he was himself accused of being a guerilla and beaten up. One of his cousins was arrested and taken to a barracks where he died of injuries inflicted on him. Before he died he gave the authorities particulars of his friends and relatives, including the appellant. His other cousin had since been arrested and killed. The appellant feared the same fate awaited him in Uganda if he returned. The appellant last

d left Uganda in June 1982. He claimed that he had applied or attempted to apply for political asylum in Kenya but had been unsuccessful. His temporary permit to remain in Kenya would expire on 5 March 1983.

In his contemporary note of the interview with the appellant the immigration officer writes:

e 'The passenger is an educated, intelligent, plausible individual who comes from the upper strata of Ugandan society. He would have me believe that Uganda is still a turbulent and violent country and should he return there he feels his life would be in danger. Significantly he did not claim political asylum upon his arrival in the U.K. but sought to pass himself off as a bona-fide visitor who was coming for a 3 week visit to see his sisters.'

f In the final paragraph he concludes:

'The passenger appeared in good health, was alert and confident at interview. My feelings are that he is moving away from Uganda because a better life awaits him somewhere else. Perhaps our people in Kampala can give a report on the current political, social and law and order position at present pertaining in Uganda.'

g In his affidavit sworn 18 months later the immigration officer expresses his conclusion differently in the following paragraph:

'I formed the view that the Applicant, who appeared to be in good health, was alert and confident at interview, was moving away from Uganda because a better life awaited him somewhere else and that this was not a genuine application for

h asylum.'

I find it strange that such an important interview as this should be entrusted to an immigration officer at the port of entry with no knowledge of conditions in the country of origin of a claimant for asylum. It seems even stranger that having suggested that local conditions should be investigated, presumably with the object of assessing the background

j to the claim for asylum, the interviewer should later assert that he was in a position to, and did, reject it as not being genuine. Fortunately this view has never been adopted by the Home Office as the basis for a decision on the appellant's application for leave to enter. The department has, in effect, been content to leave open and undecided the question whether the appellant is a bona fide 'refugee' as defined in the convention. But it does little to inspire confidence in the procedure that the Home Office should have based its further consideration of the case on the immigration officer's report.

The next stage in the consideration of the application for leave to enter is explained in the main affidavit sworn on behalf of the Secretary of State by Mr McDowall, a senior principal in the Immigration and Nationality Department of the Home Office. Two long paragraphs of his affidavit examine in minute detail various aspects of the appellant's account, as reported by the immigration officer, casting inferential doubts on various aspects of that account, in particular the appellant's assertion that he had applied for and been refused political asylum in Kenya. The conclusion reached at this stage is expressed in the affidavit as follows:

'In considering the above mentioned matters due regard was had to the problem of harrassment and intimidation which the Applicant and his family had experienced in Uganda but it was considered to be of significance that the Applicant had spent 6 out of 8 years during the period 1974–1982 in Kenya where his mother, a brother and 2 sisters reside and where he had been living for the 6 months immediately prior to his departure for the United Kingdom. In these circumstances it was concluded that the Applicant had come to the United Kingdom from a safe country and that were he to be refused entry then he would not be required to go to Uganda but could return to Kenya instead and his application for asylum in this country was therefore refused.'

The formal refusal of the application for asylum and directions for the appellant's removal to Kenya were communicated to the appellant on 12 March 1983. Before these directions were acted on Mr John Tilley MP intervened on the appellant's behalf writing to the Minister of State and enclosing a long statement by the appellant amplifying in considerable detail the account he had given of the persecution of his family in Uganda and of the difficulties he had encountered in seeking to establish a basis on which to remain in Kenya. The Minister of State, in his reply dated 8 July 1983, summarised the history and expressed his conclusion, confirming the decision to refuse the appellant leave to enter, in the phrases I have already quoted from the affidavit of Mr McDowall that the appellant had come from 'a safe country' and 'would not be required to go to Uganda but could return to Kenya instead'. Fresh directions for the appellant's removal on 21 July were issued but again were not acted on.

This time the appellant's case was taken up by Mr Stuart Holland MP, who wrote to the Minister of State on 9 August 1983, enclosing a letter dated 30 July from Mr Anthony Rose of the Stockwell and Clapham Law Centre who was now acting for the appellant. Mr Rose wrote:

'The Home Office's decision to remove Herbert Musisi to Kenya appears to ignore the fact that Mr. Musisi will not be allowed to enter Kenya and will almost certainly be immediately removed to Uganda where he has a well-founded fear that he will be deliberately killed. This is because the situation in Kenya has changed drastically since the troubles last year as a result of which their immigration control has been considerably tightened up. I in fact spoke on the telephone on Tuesday to the First Secretary of the Kenyan High Commission who confirmed that Mr. Musisi could only be given leave to enter Kenya if he possessed a work permit (obtainable only in similar circumstances to a work permit for the U.K.) or a student visa in which case he would have to have been accepted by an appropriate educational institution for a course of study which he has paid for. She further confirmed that if Mr. Musisi were to arrive in Kenya without permission to enter he would be removed to Uganda.'

In his reply, dated 5 October 1983, the Minister of State comments on this letter as follows:

'The enclosed letter suggests that Mr. Musisi might be in danger of being refused entry on his arrival back in Kenya and removed at once to Uganda, but given his residential and family ties with Kenya and the fact that Kenya is a signatory to the *a* 1951 UN Convention Relating to the Status of Refugees and would not knowingly remove a Ugandan citizen to Uganda if there was reason to believe he would be persecuted there, summary removal to Uganda strikes me as unlikely in the circumstances.'

The Minister of State's letter goes on to suggest that the appellant should enlist the assistance, through the London representative of the UN High Commissioner, of the *b* Nairobi office of that organisation.

Mr Rose acted on this suggestion and in further lengthy correspondence, which was submitted to the Minister of State by Mr Stuart Holland, set out what he had been told by representatives of the UN High Commissioner which he regarded as the reverse of reassuring. In his final reply, dated 13 January 1984, the Minister of State contented himself by saying that he did not 'accept Mr. Rose's pessimistic interpretation of the *c* advice given by [the UN High Commissioner's office]'. He confirmed his previous decisions. Notice was given to the appellant, dated 16 January 1984, directing his removal to Kenya by a flight leaving on 19 January 1984. Presumably notice to the Home Office of an intention to apply for judicial review prevented the implementation of these directions. Leave to apply for judicial review in these proceedings was granted on 1 February 1984.

d Following the passage to which I have earlier referred, the affidavit of Mr McDowall gives a short account of the exchanges between the members of Parliament who intervened on the appellant's behalf and the Minister of State, and concludes as follows:

> 'It is international practice that where foreign nationals embark from a country other than their own for a third country and that third country refuses them
> *e* permission to land that they are returned to and accepted by the country from which they embarked and in such circumstances, it is not open to the Kenyan Authorities to refuse this Applicant leave to enter and should he satisfy the Kenyan Authorities that he is indeed a refugee in that he has a well founded fear of persecution for the reasons referred to above then Kenya as a signatory to both the United Nations Convention on the Status of Refugees 1951 and the African
> *f* Convention on Refugees 1969 is unlikely to return him to Uganda in breach of such international obligations.'

In addition to the evidence originally filed in support of the appellant's application for judicial review, two further affidavits sworn in October 1984 were put in evidence. One is by a Ugandan lawyer, now himself a refugee from that country. He gives a long and *g* detailed account of the difficulties experienced in Kenya by Ugandans seeking to establish their status as refugees from their own country and of their frequent repatriation to whatever fate might await them in Uganda. The second deponent is a former Attorney General and President of Uganda who testifies to the practice of the Kenyan authorities in arresting and repatriating refugees from Uganda. The reply to this evidence is contained in the affidavit of Mr Handley, a senior executive officer in the Immigration *h* and Nationality Department of the Home Office. In this affidavit Mr Handley states, echoing the language used by the Minister of State in his letter of 5 October 1983, that—

> 'it is the [Secretary of State's] belief that Kenya as a signatory to the United Nations Convention relating to the Status of Refugees would not knowingly remove a Ugandan Citizen to Uganda if there was reason to believe he would be persecuted there.'

j
He refers to the evidence alleging repatriation of Ugandan refugees from Kenya and comments as follows:

> 'I can say that although it has been the case that Kenya has returned Ugandan Nationals to Uganda in the past the [Secretary of State] has no evidence that this continues to be the case and indeed earlier this year after representations had been

made to it by the United Nations High Commissioner for Refugees the Kenyan
Government confirmed its position as a signatory to the said Convention.'   a

I approach the question raised by the challenge to the Secretary of State's decision on
the basis of the law stated earlier in this opinion, viz that the resolution of any issue of
fact and the exercise of any discretion in relation to an application for asylum as a refugee
lie exclusively within the jurisdiction of the Secretary of State subject only to the court's
power of review. The limitations on the scope of that power are well known and need b
not be restated here. Within those limitations the court must, I think, be entitled to
subject an administrative decision to the more rigorous examination, to ensure that it is
in no way flawed, according to the gravity of the issue which the decision determines.
The most fundamental of all human rights is the individual's right to life and, when an
administrative decision under challenge is said to be one which may put the applicant's
life at risk, the basis of the decision must surely call for the most anxious scrutiny.   c
  This is not, of course, a case where the claim to refugee status itself is in issue. The
decision of the Secretary of State, as already pointed out, proceeds on the implicit
assumption that the appellant has or may have a well-founded fear of persecution in
Uganda. On this premise, to remove him directly to Uganda would be a clear breach of
the convention. The troublesome question is how far the provisions of the convention,
to the extent that they are incorporated in the relevant immigration rules, should be d
regarded as prohibiting the removal of a person who is a refugee from the country of his
nationality to a third country in the face of an alleged danger that the authorities in that
third country will send him home to face the persecution he fears.
  My Lords, I can well see that if a person arrives in the United Kingdom from country
A claiming to be a refugee from country B, where country A is itself a party to the
convention, there can in the ordinary case be no obligation on the immigration authorities e
here to investigate the matter. If the person is refused leave to enter the United Kingdom,
he will be returned to country A, whose responsibility it will be to investigate his claim
to refugee status and, if it is established, to respect it. This is, I take it, in accordance with
the 'international practice' of which Mr McDowall speaks in his affidavit. The practice
must rest on the assumption that all countries which adhere to the convention may be f
trusted to respect their obligations under it. On that hypothesis, it is an obviously sensible
practice and nothing I say is intended to question it. It is not, however, difficult to
imagine a case where reliance on the international practice would produce the very
consequence which the convention is designed to avoid, ie the return of refugees to the
country where they will face the persecution they fear. Suppose it is well known that
country A, although a signatory to the convention, regularly sends back to its totalitarian
and oppressive neighbour, country B, those opponents of the regime in country B who g
are apprehended in country A following their escape across the border. Against that
background, if a person arriving in the United Kingdom from country A sought asylum
as a refugee from country B, assuming he could establish his well-founded fear of
persecution there, it would, it seems to me, be as much a breach of art 33 of the
convention to return him to country A as to country B. The one course would effect h
indirectly, the other directly, the prohibited result, ie his return 'to the frontiers of
territories where his life or freedom would be threatened'.
  For the sake of illustration, I have necessarily taken cases at opposite ends of a spectrum.
In the ordinary case of a person arriving here from a third country and claiming asylum
as a refugee from the country of his nationality, there will be no ground to apprehend
that his removal to the third country whence he comes would put him at risk. But at the j
other end of the spectrum the risk may be obvious. Between these two extremes there
may be varying degrees of danger that removal to a third country of a person claiming
refugee status will result in his return to the country where he fears persecution. If there
is some evidence of such a danger, it must be for the Secretary of State to decide as a
matter of degree the question whether the danger is sufficiently substantial to involve a

potential breach of art 33 of the convention. If the Secretary of State has asked himself
a that question and answered it negatively in the light of all relevant evidence, the court
cannot interfere.

With these considerations in mind, I return to consider the evidence. Whatever doubts
I may entertain as to the sufficiency of the interview by the immigration officer on 27
January 1983 as a basis for subsequent decisions by the Secretary of State, I recognise that
the initial decision in March 1983 to return the appellant to the 'safe country' from which
b he had come could not be faulted. The point in the story at which I first find grounds to
entertain serious doubts as to the basis of the decision is in the reply by the Minister of
State on 5 October 1983 to the representations by Mr Stuart Holland MP. In Mr Rose's
letter of 30 July 1983 a senior diplomatic representative of Kenya was reported as stating
quite categorically that, if returned to Kenya without permission to enter, the appellant
would be removed to Uganda. There is no indication that the Home Office, either
c directly or indirectly, made any inquiry to verify or controvert this statement or to
ascertain whether it was qualified by reference to any possible claim for asylum in Kenya.
The statement remains uncontroverted save by implication by the statement in the
Minister of State's letter that Kenya is a signatory to the convention and 'would not
knowingly remove a Ugandan citizen to Uganda if there was reason to believe he would
be persecuted there'.

d   Even at this stage, however, it would be difficult not to accept the statement by the
Minister of State in his letter, effectively repeated in the concluding passage of Mr
McDowall's affidavit, that the appellant's removal to Uganda was 'unlikely' as a sufficient
and unchallengeable answer to the relevant question which the Secretary of State was
bound to ask himself. But it is to be noted in each case that the essential foundation for
the assessment was the expressed confidence in Kenya's observation of its obligations
e under the convention.

It is the additional evidence filed on behalf of the appellant in October 1984 directly
alleging breaches by Kenya of the convention by the return to Uganda of Ugandan
refugees and more particularly the reply to that evidence filed on behalf of the Secretary
of State which put a different complexion on the matter. The affidavit of Mr Handley is
f at worst self-contradictory, at best, ambiguous. He asserts 'the [Secretary of State's] belief'
that Kenya, as a signatory to the convention, 'would not knowingly' return Ugandan
refugees to Uganda. But the very next sentence seems to amount to an admission that
Ugandan refugees have been returned to Uganda by Kenya. If this is not the meaning, I
do not understand the relevance, in the context, of the statement that 'it has been the case
that Kenya has returned Ugandan Nationals to Uganda in the past', still less why this
g should have led to representations to the Kenyan government by the UN High
Commissioner. The inference one is entitled to draw from this obscurely drafted affidavit
is that Kenya has at some unspecified time in the past been guilty to an unspecified extent
of returning Ugandan refugees to Uganda in breach of art 33 of the convention and that
the breaches were at least sufficient to evoke a protest from the UN High Commissioner.
The reaffirmed belief of the Secretary of State that Kenya 'would not knowingly' act in
h breach of the convention may perhaps be referable to the Kenyan government's response
to the protest 'confirming its position as a signatory' to the convention.

However that may be, I cannot escape the conclusion that the Secretary of State's
decisions in relation to the appellant were taken on the basis of a confidence in Kenya's
performance of its obligations under the convention which is now shown to have been,
at least to some extent, misplaced. Since Mr Handley's affidavit does not condescend to
j particularity we do not know when Kenya's breaches of art 33 in respect of Ugandan
refugees occurred or when they came to the attention of the Home Office. The fact of
such breaches must be very relevant to any assessment of the danger that the appellant,
if returned to Kenya, would be sent home to Uganda. Since the decisions of the Secretary
of State appear to have been made without taking that fact into account, they cannot, in
my opinion, now stand.

In point of form the only relief sought by the appellant in his notice of application under RSC Ord 53, r 3(2) is an order to quash the removal orders dated 12 March 1983, *a* 13 July 1983 and 16 January 1984. Those orders directed the appellant's removal to Kenya by specified flights on dates now long past. It may be that, even if the appeal had failed, the Secretary of State would have felt obliged to reconsider the issue of the propriety of returning the appellant to Kenya in circumstances which may have changed radically after the lapse of three years. But for the reasons I have given I am of the opinion *b* that the appeal should be allowed and the orders formally quashed.

LORD BRANDON OF OAKBROOK. My Lords, I have had the advantage of reading in draft the speeches prepared by my noble and learned friends Lord Bridge and Lord Templeman. I agree with them, and for the reasons which they give I would dismiss the first three appeals and allow the fourth.
c

LORD TEMPLEMAN. My Lords, s 1(1) of the Immigration Act 1971 provides that persons having the right of abode in the United Kingdom shall be free to live in, and to come into, the United Kingdom without let or hindrance, but by s 1(2) all other persons—

'may live, work and settle in the United Kingdom by permission and subject to *d* such regulation and control of their entry into, stay in and departure from the United Kingdom as is imposed by this Act . . .'

By s 3(1) a person who is not a British citizen—

'(a) . . . shall not enter the United Kingdom unless given leave to do so in accordance with this Act; [and] (b) . . . may be given leave to enter . . . or . . . remain *e* in the United Kingdom . . . either for a limited or for an indefinite period . . .'

By s 3(2) the Secretary of State shall from time to time lay before Parliament statements of the rules laid down by him as to the practice to be followed in the administration of the Act for regulating the entry into and stay in the United Kingdom of persons required to have leave to enter. *f*

By s 4(1) the power to give or refuse leave to enter the United Kingdom shall be exercised by immigration officers and the power to give leave to remain in the United Kingdom shall be exercised by the Secretary of State. By s 4(2) the provisions of Sch 2 to the Act shall have effect with respect to the appointment and powers of immigration officers, the examination of persons arriving in or leaving the United Kingdom, the exercise by immigration officers of their powers in relation to entry into the United *g* Kingdom, the removal from the United Kingdom of persons refused leave to enter or entering or remaining unlawfully, and the detention of persons pending examination or pending removal from the United Kingdom.

By para 1 of Sch 2 immigration officers for the purposes of the Act shall be appointed by the Secretary of State and shall act in accordance with such instructions (not inconsistent with the immigration rules) as may be given to them by the Secretary of *h* State. By para 2 an immigration officer may examine any person who has arrived in the United Kingdom, and by para 8 where a person is refused leave to enter an immigration officer may give directions for his removal from the United Kingdom. By para 9 an immigration officer may direct the removal from the United Kingdom of an illegal entrant. By para 10 powers of removal are also given to the Secretary of State. By paras 16 and 21 any person liable to be examined or removed may be either detained or *j* temporarily admitted to the United Kingdom.

Sections 13 to 21 of the 1971 Act enable any person refused leave to enter or directed to be removed from the United Kingdom to appeal to an adjudicator and from the adjudicator to the Immigration Appeal Tribunal but, save in specific and limited cases not material in these proceedings, a person is not entitled to appeal so long as he is in the United Kingdom.

The restrictions and limitations imposed by the 1971 Act on entry into and stay in the
United Kingdom create a control and regulation of individuals and numbers by the
decisions of the immigration authorities, ie immigration officers and the Secretary of
State. An appeal from a decision lies only to an adjudicator and the appeal tribunal, and
then only if the appellant has left the United Kingdom. This is not surprising. The
numbers of appellants and possible appellants would not permit all appellants to be
released into the United Kingdom or detained pending the completion of the appellate
process. If it is necessary to control entry into the United Kingdom, immediate effect
must in general be given to the decisions of the immigration authorities unless in any
individual case the immigration authorities direct otherwise if such control is not to
break down.

The 1971 Act does not allow the courts of this country to participate in the decision-
making or appellate processes which control and regulate the right to enter and remain
in the United Kingdom. This also is not surprising. Applications for leave to enter and
remain do not in general raise justiciable issues. Decisions under the Act are administrative
and discretionary rather than judicial and imperative. Such decisions may involve the
immigration authorities in pursuing inquiries abroad, in consulting official and unofficial
organisations and in making value judgments. The only power of the court is to quash
or grant other effective relief in judicial review proceedings in respect of any decision
under the 1971 Act which is made in breach of the provisions of the Act or the rules
thereunder or which is the result of procedural impropriety or unfairness or is otherwise
unlawful.

The appellants are not British citizens. Three of them are illegal entrants liable to be
removed from the United Kingdom under the 1971 Act. The appellant Mr Musisi has
been refused leave to enter the United Kingdom and is also liable to be removed under
the Act. The appellants are entitled to appeal to an adjudicator or the appeal tribunal
once they have been removed from the United Kingdom but this appellate procedure is
useless to them because they all seek to remain in the United Kingdom on the grounds
that they fear persecution if they are removed from the United Kingdom. Nevertheless,
the courts remain powerless to intervene unless the appellants demonstrate that they are
entitled to the protection afforded by the process of judicial review.

The United Kingdom is a signatory to the Convention and Protocol relating to the
Status of Refugees (Geneva, 28 July 1951, TS 39 (1954), Cmd 9171; New York, 31 January
1967, TS 15 (1969), Cmnd 3906). Article 1 of the convention defines a refugee as a person
who—

'owing to well-founded fear of being persecuted for reasons of race, religion,
nationality, membership of a particular social group of political opinion, is outside
the country of his nationality and is unable or, owing to such fear, is unwilling to
avail himself of the protection of that country; or who, not having a nationality and
being outside the country of his former habitual residence, is unable or, owing to
such fear, is unwilling to return to it.'

Each of the appellants claims to be a refugee. By art 33(1) of the convention, the
United Kingdom as a signatory to the convention, has undertaken not to return—

'a refugee in any manner whatsoever to the frontiers of territories where his life
or freedom would be threatened on account of his race, religion, nationality,
membership of a particular social group or political opinion.'

By the 1971 Act a person who is not a British Citizen but claims to be a refugee must
nevertheless obtain leave from the immigration authorities to enter or remain in the
United Kingdom and is liable to be removed from the United Kingdom if the
immigration authorities do not accept his claim to be a refugee.

By para 73 of the Statement of Changes in Immigration Rules (HC Paper (1982–83)
no 169) laid before Parliament on 9 February 1983 under s 3(2) of the 1971 Act—

'Special considerations arise where the only country to which a person could be *a*
removed is one to which he is unwilling to go owing to well-founded fear of being
persecuted for reasons of race, religion, nationality, membership of a particular
social group or political opinion. Any case in which it appears to the immigration
officer as a result of a claim or information given by the person seeking entry at a
port that he might fall within the terms of this provision is to be referred to the
Home Office for decision regardless of any grounds set out in any provision of these
rules which may appear to justify refusal or leave to enter. Leave to enter will not *b*
be refused if removal would be contrary to the provisions of the Convention and
Protocol relating to the Status of Refugees.'

Paragraph 16 directs that where a person is a refugee full account is to be taken of the
provisions of the convention and protocol and nothing in the rules is to be construed as
requiring action contrary to the United Kingdom's obligations under those instruments. *c*
    It follows that any claim by a person to enter or remain in the United Kingdom on the
grounds that he is a refugee must be carefully considered and decided by the Secretary of
State. No appeal from the decision of the Secretary of State denying refugee status lies to
the courts and no effective appeal lies to the adjudicator or the appeal tribunal if the
person claiming refugee status is denied that status by the Secretary of State and is
removed pursuant to the provisions of the 1971 Act to the country where, contrary to *d*
the view formed by the Secretary of State, he is in fact in danger of persecution.
    The claims of the first three appellants to be refugees have been considered and rejected
by the Secretary of State and orders have been made for their removal from the United
Kingdom. Mr Musisi claims to be a refugee but has been refused leave to enter the
United Kingdom and his removal has been ordered. The appellants now claim judicial
review of the orders for their removal. *e*
    The first three appellants contend that the court is entitled and bound to decide
whether they are refugees protected by the convention but this contention is inconsistent
with the 1971 Act, which entrusts to the immigration authorities the right and duty to
determine whether any person who is not a British citizen shall be given leave to enter
or remain in the United Kingdom.
    In the alternative, these appellants contend that they are entitled to remain in the *f*
United Kingdom until their right to refugee status has been considered by the adjudicator
and appeal tribunal system. This contention is inconsistent with ss 13(3) and 16(2), which
in the present circumstances deny the appellants power to appeal so long as they are in
the United Kingdom.
    My noble and learned friend Lord Bridge has dealt in more detail with the contentions
adopted by the appellants. The actions of a statutory decision-making body may be *g*
controlled by the court in judicial review proceedings if there has been a defect in the
decision-making process. In the case of Mr Musisi but not in the case of any of the other
appellants, the evidence discloses that there may have been such a defect. The action of
an authority entrusted by Parliament with decision making can be investigated by the
court— *h*

'with a view to seeing whether it has taken into account matters which it ought
not to take into account, or, conversely, has refused to take into account or neglected
to take into account matters which it ought to take into account.'

(See *Associated Provincial Picture Houses Ltd v Wednesbury Corp* [1947] 2 All ER 680 at 685,
[1948] 1 KB 223 at 233–234 per Lord Greene MR.) *j*
    In my opinion where the result of a flawed decision may imperil life or liberty a special
responsibility lies on the court in the examination of the decision-making process. In the
case of Mr Musisi, a first reading of the evidence filed on behalf of the Secretary of State
and Mr Musisi gives rise to a suspicion that the dangers and doubts involved in sending
Mr Musisi back to Kenya have not been adequately considered and resolved. As a result
of the analysis of the evidence undertaken by my noble and learned friend Lord Bridge,

I am not satisfied that the Secretary of State took into account or adequately resolved the
a ambiguities and uncertainties which surround the conduct and policy of the authorities
in Kenya. With relief I gratefully concur in the reasoning of my noble and learned friend
Lord Bridge, and agree that the orders made in respect of Mr Musisi should be quashed.
The appeals of the other appellants against the refusal of the Court of Appeal and the
Divisional Court to quash the order made against them must be dismissed.

b **LORD GRIFFITHS.** My Lords, I have had the advantage of reading in draft the speech
prepared by my noble and learned friend Lord Bridge. I agree that for the reasons he
gives the first three appeals should be dismissed and the fourth appeal allowed.

LORD GOFF OF CHIEVELEY. My Lords, I have had the advantage of reading in
draft the speech prepared by my noble and learned friend Lord Bridge. I agree that for
c the reasons he gives the first three appeals should be dismissed and the fourth appeal
allowed.

Appeals of first three appellants dismissed. Appeal of Mr Musisi allowed.

Solicitors: *Winstanley-Burgess* (for the first three appellants); *Fisher Meredith & Partners*
d (for Mr Musisi); *Treasury Solicitor.*

Mary Rose Plummer   Barrister.

President of India v Lips Maritime Corp
e
The Lips

COURT OF APPEAL, CIVIL DIVISION
NEILL, NICHOLLS LJJ AND SIR ROUALEYN CUMMING-BRUCE
10, 11 JULY, 31 OCTOBER 1986

f

Damages – Special damages – Currency exchange loss – Damages arising from late payment of
money – Demurrage – Late payment of demurrage – Charterparty providing for demurrage to
be calculated in US dollars but paid in sterling – Dispute over demurrage resolved by arbitration
– Sterling exchange rate falling between period of charter and date of arbitration award –
Whether loss arising from late payment of money recoverable as special damages – Whether loss
g recoverable only if reasonably within contemplation of parties at time of contract – Whether
currency exchange loss recoverable as special damages.

In July 1980 the owners chartered their vessel to the charterer for the carriage of a cargo
of phosphate from Mississippi to India. Under the terms of the charterparty freight and
demurrage were to be calculated in US dollars but were to be paid in sterling at the mean
h exchange rate ruling on the date of the bill of lading. At that date the exchange rate was
$2·37 to the pound. A dispute arose between the parties over demurrage which was
referred to arbitration in England. In February 1983 the umpire published an award in
favour of the owners. By the date of the award the sterling exchange rate had dropped to
$1·54 to the pound. The umpire held that the charterer was liable for demurrage
amounting to $24,250 and that because the charterer was liable for the exchange loss
j suffered by the owners due to the fall in the sterling exchange rate the damages should
be awarded in sterling at the $1·54 rate of exchange (making the award £15,746). In a
further award the umpire held that the exchange loss was recoverable as special damages.
On appeal by the charterer the question arose whether the exchange loss was recoverable
as general or special damages. The judge allowed the charterer's appeal, holding that the
exchange loss caused by the late payment of demurrage could not be recovered as special

damages, and he varied the award by converting the demurrage into sterling at the $2·37   *a*
exchange rate (thus reducing the award to £10,232). The owners appealed.

Held – Damages arising from the late payment of money were only recoverable if the
loss suffered was foreseeable in the particular circumstances of the case because of special
matters known to both parties at the time of making the contract, since the court would
not impute to the parties knowledge that damages flowed naturally from a delay in
payment. Therefore, in order to recover such damages, the plaintiff had to prove not only   *b*
that he had suffered the additional special loss and that it was caused by the defendant's
default but also that the parties had knowledge of facts or circumstances from which it
was reasonable to infer that delay in payment would lead to that loss. Provided that
knowledge of the facts and circumstances from which such an inference could be drawn
were proved, it was not necessary to prove further that the facts or circumstances were
unusual or unique to the particular contract. On the proved facts, the inference from the   *c*
circumstances in which the contract was made was that loss resulting from the
devaluation of sterling was reasonably within the contemplation of, the parties and
accordingly, the exchange loss suffered by the owners because of the late payment of
demurrage was recoverable as special damages. The appeal would therefore be allowed
(see p 967 *e* to *h*, p 968 *a* to *d j* to p 969 *f*, post).
    Hadley v Baxendale [1843–60] All ER Rep 461 applied.   *d*
    Dictum of Hobhouse J in *International Minerals and Chemical Corp v Karl O Helm AG*
[1986] 1 Lloyd's Rep at 104 approved.
    London Chatham and Dover Rly Co v South Eastern Rly Co [1893] AC 429 distinguished.

Notes
For damages for late payment, see 12 Halsbury's Laws (4th edn) para 1179.   *e*

Cases referred to in judgments
Arnott v Redfern (1826) 3 Bing 353, 130 ER 549.
Aruna Mills Ltd v Dhanrajmal Gobindram [1968] 1 All ER 113, [1968] 1 QB 655, [1968] 2
    WLR 101.
Biggin & Co Ltd v Permanite Ltd [1950] 2 All ER 859, [1951] 1 KB 422; *rvsd* [1951] 2 All   *f*
    ER 191, [1951] 2 KB 314, CA.
Cook v Fowler (1874) LR 7 HL 27.
Hadley v Baxendale (1854) 9 Exch 341, [1843–60] All ER Rep 461, 156 ER 145.
International Minerals and Chemical Corp v Karl O Helm AG [1986] 1 Lloyd's Rep 81.
Knibb v National Coal Board [1986] 3 All ER 644, [1986] 3 WLR 895, CA.
London Chatham and Dover Rly Co v South Eastern Rly Co [1893] AC 429, HL.   *g*
Mehmet Dogan Bey v G G Abdeni & Co Ltd [1951] 2 All ER 162, [1951] 2 KB 405.
Monarch Steamship Co Ltd v A/B Karlshamns Oljefabriker [1949] 1 All ER 1, [1949] AC 196,
    HL.
Page v Newman (1829) 9 B & C 378, 109 ER 140.
President of India v La Pintada Cia Navegacion SA [1984] 2 All ER 773, [1985] AC 104,   *h*
    [1984] 3 WLR 10, HL.
Trans Trust SPRL v Danubian Trading Co Ltd [1952] 1 All ER 970, [1952] 2 QB 297, CA.
Victoria Laundry (Windsor) Ltd v Newman Industries Ltd [1949] 1 All ER 997, [1949] 2 KB
    528, CA.
Wadsworth v Lydall [1981] 2 All ER 401, [1981] 1 WLR 598, CA.
          j

Cases also cited
Eleftherotria (owners) v Despina R (owners), The Despina R [1979] 1 All ER 421, [1979] AC
    685, HL.
Hammond & Co v Bussey (1888) 2 QBD 79, CA.
Heron II, The, Koufos v C Czarnikow Ltd [1967] 3 All ER 686, [1969] 1 AC 350, HL.

President of India v Taygetos Shipping Co SA [1985] 1 Lloyd's Rep 155.
Ramwade Ltd v W J Emson & Co Ltd (1986) Times, 11 July, CA.

Appeal

Lips Maritime Corp, the owners of the vessel Lips, appealed with leave against the judgments of Lloyd J dated 30 July 1984 and of Staughton J dated 3 April 1985 whereby they allowed an appeal by the President of India, the charterer of the Lips under a charterparty in the Ferticon form dated 1 July 1980 against a final award by Mr Frank Rehder as umpire dated 22 February 1983 awarding the owners the sum of $24,250, converted at the rate of $1·54 to the pound to £15,746·75, by way of damages for the payment of demurrage. The facts are set out in the judgment of Neill LJ.

Steven Gee for the owners.
Roger Buckley QC and *Angus Glennie* for the charterer.

Cur adv vult

31 October. The following judgments were delivered.

NEILL LJ. This case has an unusual history and, though the sum at stake is quite small, the point at issue is of importance.

The appeal is brought pursuant to the leave of Staughton J granted on 3 April 1985, when he gave leave under s 1(7)(a) of the Arbitration Act 1979 to appeal both from his own decision of that date and from the earlier decision of Lloyd J dated 30 July 1984. At the same time Staughton J certified that the question of law to which his decision related was one of general public importance. The question of law was not formulated, however, in the order of the court and I shall have to examine the ambit of the question a little later.

On 1 July 1980 the President of India (whom I shall call 'the charterer') chartered the mv Lips, owned by Lips Maritime Corp (whom I shall call 'the owner') to carry a cargo of diammonium phosphate from Mississippi ports to India. The charterparty provided in cll 19 and 9 respectively that freight and demurrage were to be calculated in US dollars. By cl 18, however, it was provided that freight should be paid in London in British sterling. By cl 30 it was provided that demurrage should be paid in British external sterling at the mean exchange rate ruling on the date of the bill of lading. The charterparty also contained an arbitration clause providing for the reference of any dispute to two arbitrators in London, each party appointing an arbitrator, and the arbitrators in the event of disagreement appointing an umpire, the arbitrators to be commercial men.

The vessel completed loading at Donaldsonville on 8 July 1980. She discharged at Visakhapatnam and at Calcutta, discharge being completed on 11 October 1980 after some considerable delay. The parties were unable to agree, however, as to the period of time for which demurrage was payable and the dispute was referred to arbitration.

On 22 February 1983 the umpire, who had entered on the reference when the two arbitrators nominated by the parties had failed to reach agreement, published his final award. He awarded the owners the sum of £19,896·14 which included interest amounting to £4,658·28. The umpire found that the vessel was on demurrage for 28 days 1 hour 47 minutes, of which 24 days and 47 minutes had been admitted and paid for by the charterer. He therefore awarded damages at the agreed rate of $6,000 a day for a period of 4 days and 1 hour. This calculation resulted in a figure of $24,250 which the umpire converted into sterling at the rate of exchange prevailing at the date of his award ($1·54 to the pound) thus producing a starting sum, from which certain commission fell to be deducted, of £15,746·75.

Before the umpire it was argued on behalf of the owner that the award should be made in US dollars. On behalf of the charterer it was argued that if the award was in sterling the conversion rate should be the rate at the date of the bills of lading ($2·37 to the pound). The umpire rejected both these arguments in para 4 of his reasons, which states:

> 'In what Currency should the Claim be Awarded?
>
> Exchange Rate Losses
>
> 4.1 The currency of account was United States dollars (see Clause 19 in respect of freight and Clause 9 in respect of demurrage); the currency of payment was British Sterling (see Clauses 18 and 30). Accordingly, it is in my view correct that the calculations under this Award should be made in United States Dollars which must then be converted to British Sterling and the Award made in the latter currency.
>
> 4.2 On the date of the Bills of Lading the rate of exchange was about $2·37 = £1. At the present time it is about $1·54 = £1. Thus, if, as Charterers contended, conversion of the amount awarded is made at the rate as at the Bill of Lading date, Owners will suffer a considerable loss. Charterers were in breach in not making payment at the proper time, and the damages for that breach is the difference between the respective rates of exchange, and I have awarded accordingly.'

The charterer was dissatisfied with the decision of the umpire and sought leave to appeal. Paragraph 3(a) of the notice of motion dated 14 March 1983 sought an order—

> 'That the said award be varied (a) so as to provide in paragraph 4 of the Reasons attached thereto that the correct conversion rate to be adopted is $2·37 = £1 and to state that the Charterers (Applicants) are not liable, by way of damages or otherwise for all or any part of the difference between that rate of exchange and the rate of exchange prevailing at the time of the Award.'

On 15 July 1983 Hobhouse J granted leave to appeal the award in respect of para 3(a) of the motion. It is to be observed that in the notice of motion the grounds of the application and of the intended appeal were stated, so far as material, to be as follows:

> '(A) As to the exchange rate point, that the Umpire was wrong in law (i) in holding that the appropriate conversion rate was $1·54 = £1 rather than $2·37 = £1; (ii) that the Umpire in so holding disregarded the express terms of clause 30 of the Charterparty; (iii) that the Umpire was wrong in law in holding that the Applicants were liable in damages for the difference between the two exchange rates; and/or (iv) even if the Umpire was right in principle in holding that the applicants were liable in damages, the damages awarded should not have been based on the difference between the exchange rates [at] the date of the bill of lading and at the time of the award [but] should have been based on the difference between such rates at the time when demurrage ought to have been paid and at the time of the Award.'

On 26 July 1984 the appeal came before Lloyd J. On 30 July Lloyd J remitted the final award to the umpire for further consideration of para 4.2 of his reasons. In his reserved judgment delivered on 30 July Lloyd J said:

> 'I am bound to say that when I first read [para 4.2], it seemed to me inevitable that I should have to allow this appeal. For there is no better established rule of English common law than the rule that a creditor cannot, in absence of some express or implied agreement, recover damages for late payment of a debt: see *Page v Newman* (1829) 9 B & C 378, 109 ER 140, *London Chatham and Dover Rly Co v South Eastern Rly Co* [1893] AC 429 and *President of India v La Pintada Cia Navegacion SA* [1984] 2 All ER 773, [1985] AC 104. But the rule, so stated, is not without exceptions. It forbids the recovery of general damages for late payment of a debt, but not special damages: see *Trans Trust SPRL v Danubian Trading Co Ltd* [1952] 1 All ER 970 at 977, [1952] 2 QB 297 at 306, per Denning LJ, and *Wadsworth v Lydall* [1981] 2 All ER 401 at 405–406, [1981] 1 WLR 598 at 603 where Brightman LJ

a   said: "If a plaintiff pleads and can prove that he has suffered special damage as a result of the defendant's failure to perform his obligation under a contract, and such damage is not too remote on the principle of *Hadley v Baxendale* (1854) 9 Exch 341, [1843–60] All ER Rep 461, I can see no logical reason why such special damages should be irrecoverable merely because the obligation on which the defendant defaulted was an obligation to pay money and not some other type of obligation."

b   That decision was expressly approved by the House of Lords in *President of India v La Pintada Cia Navegacion SA*. The effect of that approval has been, as Lord Brandon observed, to reduce considerably the scope of *London Chatham and Dover Rly Co v South Eastern Rly Co* as previously understood. The difference between general damages and special damages in this connection is the difference between damages recoverable under the first part of the rule in *Hadley v Baxendale* (1854) 9 Exch 341,

c   [1843–60] All ER Rep 461, ie damages foreseeable as flowing naturally and probably from the breach of contract in the ordinary course of events; and damages recoverable under the second branch of that rule, ie damages foreseeable in the particular circumstances of the case because of special matters known to both parties at the time of making the contract. It is not clear from para 4.2 of the award . . . whether the umpire regarded the damages which he has awarded as coming within the first or second branch of the rule. This is not altogether surprising since he made

d   his award and composed his reasons before the decision of the House of Lords in *President of India v La Pintada Cia Navegacion SA*. If, as I suspect, the umpire regarded the case as coming within the first branch of the rule, ie general damages foreseeable as flowing naturally and probably from the late payment, then, on the authority of *President of India v La Pintada Cia Navegacion SA*, his conclusion was wrong in law. On that view, the claimants would be limited to recovering simple interest under

e   s 19(a) of the Arbitration Act 1950, by virtue of s 15 of the Administration of Justice Act 1982. But if, on the other hand, the umpire thought that the case could be brought within the second branch of the rule in *Hadley v Baxendale*, ie special damages foreseeable in the particular circumstances of the case, then his conclusion in law was correct.'

f   On 23 November 1984 the umpire, having received further written submissions, published his further award. He said:

'7. In July 1980 and at all material times the general expectation amongst businessmen was that the value of Sterling would gradually decline, and in particular that it would decline as against the United States Dollar. I am supported in this view

g   by a letter from Charterers' solicitors dated 3rd September 1984 where they refer to the 'Pearl Merchant' and other similar cases which had arisen as a result of the heavy fall in the value of Sterling.

8. I have no doubt that Charterers had this in mind when they designed clause 30 which, as Charterers' solicitors have stated, is included in every charter entered into by the Indian Government. The Government is a major charterer of vessels,

h   and, although no doubt they as Charterers on the one hand and shipowners on the other are free to negotiate on equal terms, every owner knows that if he contracts with the Indian Government, that clause will be included in the charterparty.

9. I have no doubt that in drafting that clause the Indian Government had in mind the gradual decline in the value of Sterling as against the United States Dollar, and no doubt, by fixing the rate of exchange as at the date of the Bills of Lading,

j   anticipated that there might in general be some saving of money. There would inevitably be a delay of three, four, five or perhaps more, months before payment of the balance of freight and the demurrage would have to be made. In the present case, as an example, with regard to the demurrage, the delay was some five months between the bill of lading date and the date when the demurrage should have been paid. By that time, the rate had fallen from \$2·37 to \$2·32 = £1. Charterers would

have profited by buying Sterling more cheaply, and owners would have lost by   *a*
buying Dollars, their business currency, with the Sterling more dearly.

10. The fact that Charterers insisted on clause 30 being included in their Charters
must also have concentrated the minds of the Owners with whom they contracted
on the question of Sterling exchange rates. In accepting a fixture with the Indian
Government, Owners, who operate their business in Dollars, must have had in
mind that there was a real danger that Sterling on the date when they were paid
would have been of less value than the same Sterling on the date of conversion when   *b*
the Bills of Lading were signed. It was a risk that they accepted; it was part of the
deal.

11. The vessel was Greek-owned. Charterers knew, or should have known, that
it is the almost universal practice that Greek owners, as well as owners of many
other nationalities, operate their business in Dollars and that, if a Sterling sum due
under the Charter was paid late, Owners were likely to sustain an exchange loss.   *c*

12. Accordingly, I find that loss by the devaluation of Sterling was something
which was "reasonably foreseeable" by, or "within actual or assumed contemplation"
of, the parties, and that such loss was "liable to result" or "a real danger", if payment
at the appropriate time was not made. This case in my view comes therefore within
the second rule in *Hadley v Baxendale*.'   *d*

On 29 March 1985 the case returned to the Commercial Court. It came before
Staughton J who delivered a reserved judgment on 3 April 1985. He said:

'... the case now comes before me, as I see it, to continue the hearing of the
appeal. No doubt it would have been restored before Lloyd J if he were still a judge
of this court, as he was then but now is not. I consider that, as between these parties,
I am bound by the conclusions of law which Lloyd J pronounced. I emphasise that   *e*
not because I feel any tendency to depart from those conclusions, but because I am
saved the task of considering afresh what was decided at the previous hearing. Lloyd
J gave, in effect, a direction to the umpire as judge of fact. The umpire has responded
with the facts that he found and the conclusion drawn from them. It is my task to
consider whether his conclusion accords with the judge's direction in the light of   *f*
the facts which he found. Having said that, I hope that I may observe what a
difficult task English law now imposes on a judge or arbitrator in such a case.
Damages for late payment of money, as Lord Brandon held in *President of India v La
Pintada Cia Navegacion SA* [1984] 2 All ER 773 at 787, [1985] AC 104 at 127, are not
recoverable if they are general damages within the first part of the rule in *Hadley v
Baxendale* (1854) 9 Exch 341, [1843–60] All ER Rep 461, but are recoverable if they   *g*
are special damages within the second part of the rule. If it is plain and obvious to
all and sundry that loss would be suffered in the event of late payment, it cannot be
recovered; but if the loss only results from peculiar circumstances known to the two
parties to the contract, it can be. In other contexts there is a tendency to regard
Hadley v Baxendale as laying down not two rules, not even one rule with two parts,
but simply one rule extending across a wide spectrum (see *McGregor on Damages*   *h*
(14th edn, 1980) para 195): "These considerations go to show that there can be no
rigid division between 'the first rule' and 'the second rule', and that the modern
restatement of the rule as a totality is a salutary trend." There are impressive
authorities cited in the footnote to that passage. Nevertheless, a line has to be drawn
for present purposes, as the House of Lords has held.'   *j*

The judge then set out the further facts found by the umpire as stated in paras 7 to 12
of the further award. I have already recited these paragraphs and I need not repeat them.
Staughton J continued:

'So the umpire did not, as the learned judge suspected he would, find that it was
within the first rule but within the second rule. I do not find in those paragraphs

a   any special fact communicated by the owners to the charterer which would not
have been apparent to any other businessman in the same trade. What the umpire
is saying is that if a shipowner of Greek or any another nationality contracts for
payment in sterling, he is liable to suffer loss in the event of delayed payment at a
time when the pound is falling against the dollar; and businessmen generally
expected the pound to decline in July 1980. In those circumstances, it seems to me
that the umpire should have held, in the terms of the direction of Lloyd J, that the
b   damages were foreseeable as flowing naturally and probably from the breach of
contract in the ordinary course of events; they were not damages foreseeable in the
particular circumstances of the case because of special matters known to both parties
at the time of making the contract; or to use the test of Lord Wright in *Monarch
Steamship Co Ltd v A/B Karlshamns Oljefabriker* [1949] 1 All ER 1, [1949] AC 196 at
221 (see *McGregor on Damages* (14th edn, 1980) para 16), it is not a case of special and
c   extraordinary circumstances beyond the reasonable prevision of the parties.
Accordingly, I hold that the umpire's conclusion in para 12, that this case "comes
within the second rule in *Hadley v Baxendale*", cannot stand. Counsel for the owners
submitted that remoteness is a question of fact, as was held by McNair J in *Mehmet
Dogan Bey v G G Abdeni & Co Ltd* [1951] 2 All ER 162, [1951] 2 KB 405. There is no
appeal under the Arbitration Act 1979 on questions of fact. But one cannot in my
d   judgment classify any question in the abstract as one of law or fact, without regard
to the particular issue between the parties. The issue here is whether the further
facts found by the umpire are capable, in law, of bringing the case within the second
part of the rule in *Hadley v Baxendale* as opposed to the first. In my view they are
not.'

e   The judge therefore allowed the appeal and varied the award by substituting the
sterling equivalent of $24,250 at the exchange rate of $2·37 to the pound instead of $1·54
to the pound. The owner now appeals to this court.
In support of the appeal counsel for the owners submitted that there were three issues
to be determined. These issues were conveniently set out in his skeleton argument as
follows. (a) Did cl 30 of the charterparty preclude the umpire from awarding damages to
f   the owners? (b) If cl 30 did not preclude the granting of damages did Staughton J err in
upsetting the award of the umpire either in his holding that the further award was
incapable in law of coming within the second branch of the rule in *Hadley v Baxendale* or
through the application of the conclusions of law reached by Lloyd J? (c) Should the
award have been made in US dollars?
With two of these issues I can deal quite shortly. On the first issue it was argued on
g   behalf of the charterer that cl 30 of the charterparty provided that demurrage should be
paid in sterling at a fixed rate of exchange and that the owner was entitled to recover at
that rate and at no other rate. Clause 30, it was said, contained a comprehensive code.
This argument was rejected both by the umpire and by Staughton J. The judge said:

'Clause 30 is concerned with apportionment of the risk of currency fluctuation:
h   between the date of the charter and the date of the bill of lading that risk depends
on the rise or fall of the US dollar; from the date of the bill of lading to the date
when payment is due it depends on the rise or fall of the pound sterling. But there
is in my judgment nothing in cl 30 to displace the ordinary rules of law in respect
of loss arising between the due date for payment and the date of a judgment or
award so far as concerns a claim for damages for late payment.'

j   I agree with the judge on this issue. In my view cl 30 determines what the rate of
exchange is to be if the contract is performed; it does not apply, however, where the
paying party is in breach. Accordingly, if damages for late payment are otherwise
recoverable a claim for damages is not barred by cl 30. Moreover, I find support for this
conclusion in the decision of Donaldson J in *Aruna Mills Ltd v Dhanrajmal Gobindram*
[1968] 1 All ER 113 at 199, [1968] 1 QB 655 at 667.

I turn to the third issue. On this aspect of the case it is necessary to bear in mind that leave to appeal was given by Hobhouse J only in relation to para 3(a) of the original notice of motion. It seems to me to be plain from the terms of para 3(a) and of the grounds which were advanced in the notice of motion in support of this paragraph that it was concerned with what was there described as the 'exchange rate point'. Moreover, para 3 of the affirmation filed on behalf of the charterer in support of the application for leave to appeal contained the following passage:

'There are two points on which my clients seek leave to appeal. The first is concerned with the question of the currency in which the award of demurrage should be made and the rate of exchange to be applied. In paragraph 4 of the reasons attached to his award the umpire has correctly decided that the calculations of demurrage under the award should be made in US dollars which must then be converted to British sterling for the purpose of the award. My clients do not disagree with this. However, he goes on in paragraph 4.2 and at the end of the demurrage calculation effectively to apply the rate of exchange between sterling and US dollars which prevailed at the date of the award. In my respectful submission he was wrong to do so . . .'

It was argued by counsel for the owners, however, that the words 'or otherwise' in para 3(a) were wide enough to embrace an argument to the effect that the award should have been in dollars. I am unable to accept this argument. It does not appear that at that stage there was any cross-application by the owners or other challenge concerning the decision of the arbitrator that the award should be in sterling, and it was plainly accepted by the charterer that the umpire had reached the right conclusion on this point.

In my judgment, despite the fact that the umpire made a finding in his further award that the owners operate their business in dollars it would not be right at this stage to entertain an argument that the award should have been in dollars. The question of law in respect of which leave was given concerned the rate of exchange at which the dollars should be converted. As I see it, this question does not embrace the preliminary point as to whether the award should have been in dollars rather than in sterling.

I come therefore to the second issue around which the greater part of the debate before us revolved. On this issue counsel for the owners put forward two main arguments: (1) that in the present case the exchange loss suffered by the owner was capable of falling within the second rule in *Hadley v Baxendale*, and that the umpire had found as a fact that the loss did so fall; (2) but that if the loss only fell within the first rule in *Hadley v Baxendale* the damages were still recoverable because (a) the case of *President of India v La Pinta da Cia Navigacion SA* [1984] 2 All ER 773, [1985] AC 104 was concerned with a claim for interest and not with a claim in respect of an exchange loss, (b) there was no direct authority for the proposition that an exchange loss could not be recovered unless it fell within the second rule in *Hadley v Baxendale* and (c) the speech of Lord Brandon in *President of India v La Pintada Cia Navegacion SA* should not be interpreted so as to bring a claim for an exchange loss within the rule in *London Chatham and Dover Rly Co v South Eastern Rly Co* [1893] AC 429.

In principle it is difficult to see why in an appropriate case damages should not be recoverable for a late payment of money in the same way as damages are recoverable for the late delivery of a chattel. Indeed, at one stage it looked as though, despite the hostility with which usury was regarded by both church and state from the earliest times, the common law would give a right to damages to anyone whose money had been unjustly detained by another and who had taken some steps to recover it. Thus, in *Arnott v Redfern* (1826) 3 Bing 353 at 359, 130 ER 549 at 551 Best CJ sitting in the Court of Common Pleas said:

'However a debt is contracted, if it has been wrongfully withheld by a Defendant after the Plaintiff has endeavoured to obtain payment of it, the jury may give interest in the shape of damages for the unjust detention of the money.'

But this proposition was not accepted as a correct statement of the law. Three years
a later, in *Page v Newman* (1829) 9 B & C 378, 109 ER 140, the Court of King's Bench
presided over by Lord Tenterden CJ refused to acknowledge that there was such a general
right to damages. Lord Tenterden said (9 B & C 378 at 380–381, 109 ER 140 at 141):

> 'If we were to adopt as a general rule that which some of the expressions attributed
> to the Lord Chief Justice of the Common Pleas in *Arnott v. Redfern* would seem to
b > warrant, viz. that interest is due wherever the debt has been wrongfully withheld
> after the plaintiff has endeavoured to obtain payment of it, it might frequently be
> made a question at Nisi Prius whether proper means had been used to obtain
> payment of the debt, and such as the party ought to have used. That would be
> productive of great inconvenience. I think that we ought not to depart from the
> long-established rule, that interest is not due on money secured by a written
c > instrument, unless it appears on the face of the instrument that interest was intended
> to be paid, or unless it be implied from the usage of trade, as in the case of mercantile
> instruments.'

In the following decade some relaxation of the common law rule as laid down in *Page
v Newman* was introduced by the Civil Procedure Act 1833 which allowed the court a
discretion to award interest on debts or damages in certain cases. Furthermore, by the
d Judgments Act 1838 it was provided that judgment debts should carry interest at a
certain rate. But otherwise the rule in *Page v Newman* as a rule of common law remained
unchanged for over a century.

In 1893 the matter was examined by the House of Lords in *London Chatham and Dover
Rly Co v South Eastern Rly Co* [1893] AC 429. The leading speech was delivered by Lord
Herschell LC, who said (at 440):
e

> 'I cannot profess to be altogether satisfied with the reason which Lord Tenterden
> gives, although of course for so eminent a judge one entertains the greatest respect.
> To say that it might be made a question at nisi prius whether proper means had
> been used, and that it might be productive of great inconvenience, does not seem to
> me a satisfactory reason for excluding altogether any claim to interest by way of
f > damages in cases where justice requires that it should be awarded . . . Nevertheless,
> so far as I am aware, from that time down to the present the rule which Lord
> Tenterden lays down has been followed, and no attempt has been made (or at all
> events has received the sanction of the Courts) to revert to the earlier and, as I think,
> more liberal views of those who preceded him. And one cannot shut one's eyes to
> the fact that Lord Tenterden, who presided and delivered that judgment, was the
g > author of the statute [the Civil Procedure Act 1833] . . . under which interest can
> now be allowed; and when he dealt with the allowance of interest in this statute he
> certainly introduced language which kept such claims within very narrow limits;
> speaking for myself, they seem to be too narrow for the purposes of justice.'

Lord Herschell therefore concluded that it was by then too late to reopen the question
h even in the House of Lords.

It is to be noted, however, that no reference was made to *Hadley v Baxendale*, in which
the conditions in which damages for breach of contract can be recovered were defined.
Nor was any reference made to the suggestion put forward in Bullen and Leake *Precedents
of Pleadings* (3rd edn, 1868) p 51 that interest considered as damages would as a rule not
be recoverable as being too remote. Furthermore (as Dr Mann has noted in his valuable
j article 'On Interest, Compound Interest and Damages' (1985) 105 LQR 30) the House
was not referred to their earlier decision in *Cook v Fowler* (1874) LR 7 HL 27.

The common law rule established in *Page v Newman* was considered again by the
House of Lords in *President of India v La Pintada Cia Navegacion SA* [1984] 2 All ER 773,
[1985] AC 104, where the House was invited to take advantage of the 1966 Practice
Statement (*Note* [1966] 3 All ER 79, [1966] 1 WLR 1234) and to depart from the previous

decision in *London Chatham and Dover Rly Co v South Eastern Rly Co*. The House felt
unable, however, to take this step for the reasons which were set out in the leading speech *a*
of Lord Brandon. One of these reasons was that the greater part of the injustice to
creditors which resulted from *London Chatham and Dover Rly Co v South Eastern Rly Co* had
been removed, to a large extent by legislative intervention, and to a lesser extent by
judicial qualifications of the scope of the decision itself (see [1984] 2 All ER 773 at 789,
[1985] AC 104 at 129–130).

The judicial qualifications to which Lord Brandon referred were introduced by the *b*
Court of Appeal in *Trans Trust SPRL v Danubian Trading Co Ltd* [1952] 1 All ER 970,
[1952] 2 QB 297 and in *Wadsworth v Lydall* [1981] 2 All ER 401, [1981] WLR 598. It
seems clear that the relevant passages in the judgments of Denning and Romer LJJ in the
Trans Trust case were strictly speaking no more than obiter dicta, but the passages are
important because of the references made to remoteness. Denning LJ took the view that
the only real ground on which damages could be refused for non-payment of money was *c*
that interest was generally presumed not to be within the contemplation of the parties.
He continued ([1952] 1 All ER 970 at 977, [1952] 2 QB 297 at 306):

'It is because the consequences are as a rule too remote. But when the circumstances
are such that there is a special loss foreseeable at the time of the contract as the
consequence of non-payment, then I think such loss may well be recoverable.' *d*

More importance, however, was attached by Lord Brandon to the decision of the Court
of Appeal in *Wadsworth v Lydall*. The facts of that case, as stated in the headnote, were as
follows ([1981] 1 WLR 598):

'The defendant, the owner of a dairy farm, entered into an informal partnership
agreement with the plaintiff under which the partnership was granted an *e*
agricultural tenancy and the plaintiff lived in the farmhouse and ran the farm. On
the dissolution of the partnership, an agreement was made which provided inter
alia that the plaintiff would give up possession of the farm on or before May 15,
1976 and on that event would receive £10,000 from the defendant. On May 10 the
plaintiff, expecting to receive £10,000 in five days time and having no other capital,
entered into an agreement for the purchase of a property from G., by which £10,000 *f*
of the purchase price was to be paid on completion. On May 15 the plaintiff gave
up possession of the farm but the defendant did not pay him the £10,000. On July
21, G.'s solicitors served a 28-day notice to complete. In October the defendant paid
the plaintiff £7,200. The plaintiff passed that sum on to G. and raised the balance of
the money due on completion by taking out a mortgage from G. on which he had
to pay the legal costs. In an action brought against the defendant, the plaintiff *g*
claimed as special damages £335 in respect of interest that he had had to pay G. for
late completion and £16·20 in respect of the mortgage costs. Smith J awarded the
plaintiff damages, but disallowed these two items of special damage on the ground
that they were too remote.'

The plaintiff appealed to the Court of Appeal. Before that court the defendant sought *h*
to rely on the decision in *London Chatham and Dover Rly Co v South Eastern Rly Co* as
precluding the recovery of damages for breach of contract consisting only in the late
payment of a debt. He also contended that the only remedy available to the plaintiff was
an award of interest under the Law Reform (Miscellaneous Provisions) Act 1934. These
contentions were not accepted by the Court of Appeal. Brightman LJ, who gave the
principal judgment, said ([1981] 2 All ER 401 at 405–406, [1981] 1 WLR 598 at 603): *j*

'In my view the court is not so constrained by the decision of the House of Lords.
In *London Chatham and Dover Railway Co v South Eastern Railway Co* . . . the House of
Lords was not concerned with a claim for special damages. the action was an action
for an account. The House was concerned only with a claim for interest by way of
general damages. If a plaintiff pleads and can prove that he has suffered special

a damage as a result of the defendant's failure to perform his obligation under a contract, and such damage is not too remote on the principle of *Hadley v Baxendale* (1854) 9 Exch 341, [1843–60] All ER Rep 461, I can see no logical reason why such special damage should be irrecoverable merely because the obligation on which the defendant defaulted was an obligation to pay money and not some other type of obligation'.

b This passage in the judgment of Brightman LJ was recited by Lord Brandon in his speech in *President of India v La Pintada Cia Navegacion SA* [1984] 2 All ER 773 at 787, [1985] AC 104 at 126. Lord Brandon continued as follows:

'The distinction which Brightman LJ was there drawing between general and special damages is the difference between damages recoverable under the first part of the rule in *Hadley v Baxendale* (1854) 9 Exch 341, [1843–60] All ER Rep 461 *c* (general damages) and damages recoverable under the second part of that rule (special damages). On the facts of the case before him Brightman LJ found that, by reason of special matters known to both parties at the time of contracting, the two items of special damages claimed by the plaintiff came within the second part of that rule. Accordingly, treating the *London Chatham and Dover Rly* case as applying only to damages falling within the first part of the rule in *Hadley v Baxendale* (general *d* damages), he saw no reason why the plaintiff should not recover the two disputed items of special damages under the second part of that rule. In my opinion the ratio decidendi of *Wadsworth v Lydall* [1981] 2 All ER 401, [1981] 1 WLR 598, that the *London Chatham and Dover Rly* case applied only to claims for interest by way of general damages, and did not extend to claims for special damages, in the sense in which it is clear that Brightman LJ was using those two expressions, was correct and *e* should be approved by your Lordships. On the assumption that your Lordships give such approval, the effect will be to reduce considerably the scope of the *London Chatham and Dover Rly* case by comparison with what it had in general previously been understood to be.'

f What then is the present law as to the recovery of damages at common law for a breach of contract which consists of the late payment of money? I would venture to state the position as follows.

(1) A payee cannot recover damages by way of interest merely because the money has been paid late. The basis for this principle appears to be that the court will decline to *impute* to the parties the knowledge that in the ordinary course of things the late payment of money will result in loss. I would express my respectful agreement with the way in *g* which Hobhouse J explained the surviving principle in *International Minerals and Chemical Corp v Karl O Helm AG* [1986] 1 Lloyd's Rep 81 at 104:

'In my judgment, the surviving principle of legal policy is that it is a legal presumption that in the ordinary course of things a person does not suffer any loss by reason of the late payment of money. This is an artificial presumption, but is *h* justified by the fact that the usual loss is an interest loss and that compensation for this has been provided for and limited by statute'.

(2) In order to recover damages for late payment it is therefore necessary for the payee to establish facts which bring the case within the second part of the rule in *Hadley v Baxendale*. In *Knibb v National Coal Board* [1986] 3 All ER 644 at 646, [1986] 3 WLR 895 *j* at 899 Sir John Donaldson MR stated the effect of the decision in *President of India v La Pintada Cia Navegacion SA* in these terms:

'From this [the decision] it emerges that there is no general common law power which entitles courts to award interest ([1984] 2 All ER 773 at 778, [1985] AC 104 at 115) but that if a claimant could bring himself within the second part of the rule in *Hadley v Baxendale* (1854) 9 Exch 341, [1843–60] All ER Rep 461 he could claim special damages, notwithstanding that the breach of contract alleged consisted in the nonpayment of a debt ([1984] 2 All ER 773 at 787, [1985] AC 104 at 127).'   *a*

It may be said that the line between the two parts of the rule in *Hadley v Baxendale* has become blurred so that the division has lost much of its utility. It may also be said that since the restatement of the rule in *Victoria Laundry (Windsor) Ltd v Newman Industries Ltd* [1949] 1 All ER 997, [1949] 2 KB 528 there is only one area of indemnity to be explored: see *Biggin & Co Ltd v Permanite Ltd* [1950] 2 All ER 859 at 869, [1951] 1 KB 422 *b* at 436 per Devlin J. But it is clear, as Staughton J recognised in the instant case, that the court must find the dividing line because it is only if the claim falls within the second part of the rule that the loss can be recovered.

(3) It is important to keep in mind that the question in each case is to determine what loss was reasonably within the contemplation of the parties at the time when the contract was made. As I understand the matter, the principle in *London Chatham and Dover Rly Co* *c* *v South Eastern Rly Co*, in its modern and restricted form, goes no further than to bar the recovery of claims for interest by way of general damages. Thus, in the case of a claim for damages for the late payment of money the court will not determine in favour of the plaintiff that damages flow from such delay 'naturally, that is, according to the usual course of things'. But a plaintiff will be able to recover damages in respect of a special loss if it is proved that the parties had knowledge of facts or circumstances from which it was *d* reasonable to infer that delay in payment would lead to that loss.

Moreover, I do not understand that, provided that knowledge of the facts and circumstances from which such an inference can be drawn can be proved, it is necessary further to prove that the facts or circumstances were unusual, let alone unique to the particular contract. Here again, I would express my respectful agreement with the words of Hobhouse J in *International Minerals and Chemical Corp v Karl O Helm AG* [1986] 1 *e* Lloyd's Rep 81 at 104:

'It follows that a plaintiff, where he is seeking to recover damages for the late payment of money, must prove not only that he has suffered the alleged additional special loss and that it was caused by the defendant's default, but also that the defendant had knowledge of the facts or circumstances which make such a loss a not *f* unlikely consequence of such a default. In the eyes of the law, those facts or circumstances are deemed to be special, whether in truth they are or not, and knowledge of them must be proved. Where, as in the present case, the relevant facts or circumstances are commonplace, the burden of proof will be easy to discharge and the courts may well be willing to draw inferences of knowledge; in other cases, there may be a question which would, in any event, have had to be dealt with under *g* the second rule in *Hadley v Baxendale* and then the burden of proof will be more significant.'

I return to the facts of the present case. In his further award the umpire found that—

'loss by the devaluation of Sterling was something which was "reasonably foreseeable" by, or "within actual or assumed contemplation" of, the parties, and *h* that such loss was "liable to result" or a "real danger", if payment at the appropriate time was not made.'

As I understand it, the umpire based this finding on the fact that the parties knew or should have known the following: (a) that it was the general expectation among businessmen that sterling would decline and in particular would decline against the US *j* dollar (para 7); (b) that cl 30 was designed to protect the Indian government against a devaluation of sterling between the date of the bills of lading and the due date for the payment of demurrage (paras 8 to 10); (c) that it was the almost universal practice of Greek shipowners to operate their business in dollars so that if a sterling sum were paid late the owner was likely to suffer an exchange loss on conversion.

a Staughton J came to the conclusion that none of these facts constituted a 'special fact communicated by the owners to the charterer which would not have been apparent to any other businessman in the same trade'. With the greatest respect to the judge, it seems to me that in reaching this conclusion he took too narrow a view of the limitations now imposed on the rule in *London Chatham and Dover Rly Co v South Eastern Rly Co*.

b As I have stated earlier, the question in each case is to determine what loss was reasonably within the contemplation of the parties at the time when the contract was made. In dealing with this question the court will not impute to the parties the knowledge that damages flow 'naturally' from a delay in payment. But where there is evidence of what the parties knew or ought to have known the court is in a position to determine what was in their reasonable contemplation. For this purpose, the court is entitled to take account of the terms of the contract between the parties and of the surrounding circumstances, and to draw inferences. In drawing inferences as to the

c parties' actual or imputed knowledge, the court is not obliged to ignore facts or circumstances of which other people doing similar business might have been aware.

In view of the continued existence of the rule in *London Chatham and Dover Rly Co v South Eastern Rly Co* the court cannot make the *assumption* in favour of a plaintiff that the parties contemplated that the late payment of money would result in loss, but where the

d proved facts are such as to lead to the inference that the parties would have reasonably contemplated the relevant special loss the loss can be properly recovered. Accordingly, in my view, the exchange loss which was suffered by the owners by reason of the late payment of demurrage is recoverable as damages falling within the second part of the rule in *Hadley v Baxendale*.

For my part therefore I would allow the appeal.

e Strictly speaking, the damages should be assessed on the basis of the difference between the exchange rate at the date when the demurrage should have been paid ($2·32) and the date of the award ($1·54). I would be disposed to hear argument on the question whether it is now too late for this minor adjustment between $2·37 and $2·32 to be made.

NICHOLLS LJ. I agree. The only comment I would add concerns the second issue.
f The charterer's submissions on this lead to the bizarre result that where it was obvious to the contracting parties that a currency exchange loss was not unlikely in the event of late payment, the more the defaulting party can show that this was not because of some unusual or 'special' circumstance of the particular contract but because of the well-known way in which the relevant trade or business is normally carried on, the less likely will it be that the plaintiff can recover his loss. I am pleased to be able to conclude, for the

g reasons stated by Neill LJ, that this does not represent the state of the law in this field.

SIR ROUALEYN CUMMING-BRUCE. I agree.

Appeal allowed. Leave to appeal to the House of Lords refused.

h *5 February 1987. The Appeal Committee of the House of Lords gave the charterer leave to appeal.*

Solicitors: *Richards Butler* (for the owners); *Zaiwalla & Co* (for the charterer).

Celia Fox Barrister.

Re Tepper's Will Trusts
Kramer and another v Ruda and others

CHANCERY DIVISION
SCOTT J
19, 20 NOVEMBER 1986

Will – Condition – Religion – Jewish faith – Marriage outside Jewish faith – Condition that beneficiaries remain within and not marry outside Jewish faith – Whether condition void for uncertainty – Whether extrinsic evidence admissible to establish meaning of 'Jewish faith' as practised by testator and his family.

The testator, a devout Jew, died in 1959 leaving his residuary estate on trust for M, L and P, three of his five daughters, and his grandchildren. Clause 4(d) of his will provided, inter alia, that on P's death the share of income otherwise payable to her should be paid for the education and advancement of her children in equal shares and, on their attaining 25 years of age, should be paid to them absolutely 'Provided that they shall remain within the Jewish faith and shall not marry outside the Jewish faith'. Clause 4(e) provided that on the death of M, L and P the residuary estate was to be divided amongst all his grandchildren living at the date of his death, and paid to them on their attaining 25 years of age 'Provided However that they shall not marry outside the Jewish faith'. The testator had six grandchildren, four of whom married persons who were Jewish and two of whom married persons who were not Jewish. In 1984 P died and the question arose which grandchildren were or would become entitled to share in the residuary estate. The plaintiffs, the trustees of the will, took out a summons seeking, inter alia, the determination by the court of the question whether the provisos in paras (d) and (e) of cl 4 were void for uncertainty. It was contended by the four grandchildren who had married within the Jewish faith that the provisos were valid and that the two grandchildren who had married outside the Jewish faith were precluded from claiming under the will. It was contended by those two grandchildren and also by the next of kin that the provisos were void for uncertainty.

Held – (1) Having regard to the language of the provisos in paras (d) and (e) of cl 4 of the will and the context in which they were to be construed, on their true construction they amounted to conditions of defeasance, in that interests otherwise conferred by the will, whether contingent or vested, were subject to termination by the events specified in the provisos. Accordingly, the standard of certainty required of the provisos was that governing conditions subsequent, namely that they had to be sufficiently certain for the persons affected by the condition to know with certainty and from the outset the exact event which if it happened would divest their interest (see p 981 *j* to p 882 *f h* and p 983 *g h*, post); *Clayton v Ramsden* [1943] 1 All ER 16, *Re Allen, Faith v Allen* [1953] 2 All ER 898, *Re Selby's Will Trusts, Donn v Selby* [1965] 3 All ER 386 and *Re Tuck's Settlement Trusts, Public Trustee v Tuck* [1978] 1 All ER 1047 considered.

(2) On the evidence before the court the provisos appeared to be void for uncertainty but that conclusion was not inevitable or final. The validity of the provisos depended on what the testator had meant by the use of the expression 'the Jewish faith' in his will and, while direct evidence of his intention was not admissible, extrinsic evidence of the Jewish faith as practised by the testator and his family might well be adduced which could make it possible to attribute to the expression a meaning sufficiently certain to enable the test as to certainty to be satisfied. Accordingly, the summons would be adjourned so that the parties could file further evidence as to the meaning of the expression 'the Jewish faith' as used in the will (see p 983 *c* to *h*, post).

Notes

a For uncertain conditions as to religion in wills, see 50 Halsbury's Laws (4th edn) para 328, and for cases on the subject, see 50 Digest (Reissue) 375–376, 3555–3558.

Cases referred to in judgment

Allen, Re, Faith v Allen [1953] 2 All ER 898, [1953] Ch 810, [1953] 3 WLR 637, CA.
Blathwayt v Lord Cawley [1975] 3 All ER 625, [1976] AC 397, [1975] 3 WLR 684, HL.
b Clavering v Ellison (1859) 7 HL Cas 707, 11 ER 282, HL.
Clayton v Ramsden [1943] 1 All ER 16, [1943] AC 320, HL; rvsg [1941] 3 All ER 196, [1942] Ch 1, CA.
Lowry's Will Trusts, Re, Barclays Bank Ltd v Board of Governors of the United Newcastle-upon-Tyne Hospitals [1966] 3 All ER 955, [1967] Ch 638, [1967] 2 WLR 401.
Samuel, Re, Jacobs v Ramsden [1941] 3 All ER 196, [1942] Ch 1, CA.
c Selby's Will Trusts, Re, Donn v Selby [1965] 3 All ER 386, [1966] 1 WLR 43.
Tuck's Settlement Trusts, Re, Public Trustee v Tuck [1978] 1 All ER 1047, [1978] Ch 49, [1978] 2 WLR 411, CA.

Cases also cited

d Abraham's Will Trusts, Re, Caplan v Abrahams [1967] 2 All ER 1175, [1969] 1 Ch 463.
Dunster, Re, Brown v Heywood [1909] 1 Ch 103.
Shaw v M'Mahon (1843) 4 Dr & War 431.

Originating summons

The plaintiffs, Abraham Kramer and Jonathan Michael Kramer, sought by an originating
e summons dated 20 March 1986 the determination of the court on the following questions, namely: (1) whether on the true construction of cl 4(d) of the will of Nathan Tepper (the testator) and in the events which had happened the proviso attaching to the gift of income to the children of the testator's daughter Priscilla Kester that they 'shall remain within the Jewish faith and shall not marry outside the Jewish faith' was (a) wholly valid, (b) partially valid, and if so, to what extent, or (c) wholly void, and if that
f question was answered in sense (a) or (b) whether the marriage of the defendant Jonathan Kester to Sally Kester in April 1980 disentitled him from receiving the share of the income otherwise payable to him under cl 4(d) from the death of Priscilla Kester on 30 September 1984 and if so how that share devolved; (2) whether on the true construction of cl 4(e) of the said will and in the events which had happened the proviso attaching to the gift of capital of residue in favour of the testator's grandchildren living at his death
g directed to take effect on the death of the survivor of the testator's three daughters named in the will, provided that 'they shall not marry outside the Jewish faith' was (a) valid, (b) partially valid, and if so, to what extent, or (c) void, and if that question was answered in sense (a) or (b) whether the proviso was infringed by any grandchild marrying outside the Jewish faith before the date of death of the survivor of the testator's said three daughters, and whether the marriage of the defendant Jonathan Kester and the marriage
h of Shirley Kutz to Stan Kutz disentitled them, or either of them, from receiving the shares of capital residue to which they (or either of them) would otherwise be entitled on the death of the survivor of the testator's three daughters and how such shares would devolve if that question were answered in the affirmative. The defendants to the summons were (1) Laurence Ruda, (2) Gertrude Hantman, (3) Harvey Cohen, (4) Michael Kester, (5) Jonathan Kester, (6) Shirley Kutz and (7) Lily Tepper, representing the next of
j kin interested in property to which he died intestate. The facts are set out in the judgment.

Miles Shillingford for the plaintiffs.
Sonia Proudman for the first four defendants.
Thomas Dumont for the fifth, sixth and seventh defendants.

SCOTT J. I have before me an originating summons for the construction of the will of Nathan Tepper deceased. The deceased died on 11 November 1959. He made his will on *a* 11 August 1953. Probate of that will was granted on 12 June 1961 to the executors therein named. They included one of his daughters, one of his sons-in-law and a solicitor, Abraham Kramer, who is the first plaintiff in this originating summons. The second plaintiff is Jonathan Michael Kramer, who has subsequently to the death of the testator been appointed a trustee of the will.

The issue of construction brought before the court for decision is whether a proviso, *b* or more accurately two provisos, in the will, affecting the destination of gifts made in the will, are or are not void for uncertainty. One proviso requires that the relevant beneficiaries 'shall remain within the Jewish faith and shall not marry outside the Jewish faith'. The other proviso requires that they 'shall not marry outside the Jewish faith'.

It is apparent from the terms of those provisos that the deceased was a man to whom the Jewish faith was of considerable importance. That is indeed apparent from his will *c* read as a whole. After appointing his executors he went on under paras 2 and 3 to provide for certain specific and pecuniary legacies. The specific legacies include what he describes as 'my other books of Judaica' and other Hebrew works; the pecuniary legacies include one to the Old Age Home for Jews, another to the Jewish Orphanage of Norwood, another to the Jewish Home for the Blind and three gifts, two of £50 each and the third *d* of £100, on condition that the respective legatees recite the Kaddish on the anniversary of his death. There is to my mind from the terms of those legacies a strong indication that the deceased was a devout Jew who placed importance on the observance of the rites of the Jewish faith.

The provisos which raise the issues of construction with which I must deal relate to the manner in which the deceased left his residuary estate. He was predeceased in the event by his wife, and his residuary estate was left on trusts for certain of his daughters *e* and for his grandchildren. I think I should read the relevant parts of the will in full. He directed his trustees—

'. . . (c) . . . to pay the income thereof as to 35% upon trust for my daughter MILLIE absolutely, as to 35% unto my daughter LILY absolutely, as to 20% unto my daughter *f* PRISCILLA, as to 5% to be utilised by my Trustees towards the education and advancement of my grandchildren MICHAEL and JONATHAN KESTER the children of my daughter PRISCILLA and as to the remaining 5% to be divided in the absolute discretion of my Trustees amongst such charitable institutions including the Yeshivoth and the Yesodeth Torah, as I shall have contributed to in my lifetime and as shall be from time to time determined upon by my Trustees (d) Upon any of my *g* said daughters dying then the share of my income otherwise payable to my said daughter in the event of her being one of my unmarried daughters shall be shared between my remaining daughters and in such proportion as is provided by this my will but upon the death of my daughter Priscilla the share of income otherwise payable to her shall be paid for the education and advancement of her children in equal shares and upon their attaining the age of 25 years shall be paid to them *h* absolutely Provided that they shall remain within the Jewish faith and shall not marry outside the Jewish faith (e) Upon the death of my said daughters Millie, Lily and Priscilla then the residue of my estate shall be held upon trust by my Trustees to be divided amongst all my grandchildren as shall be living at the date of my death including the children of my daughter Priscilla such share to be paid to them upon their attaining the age of 25 years Provided However that they shall not marry *j* outside the Jewish faith.'

I do not think it necessary to read any of the other contents of the will.

The terms of those residuary gifts make the identity of the various members of the family and their respective marital states important. The deceased had, as appears from a *a* family tree which is before me, five daughters. It will be recalled that three of them were named in the residuary gifts, Millie, Lily and Priscilla. A fourth was Clara, who married and had three children. Her three children are Gertrude Hantman (the second defendant), Laurence Ruda (the first defendant) and Shirley Kutz (the sixth defendant). The fifth daughter was Fanny. She died in 1984 having had one son, Harvey Cohen, the third defendant.

b Of the three daughters named in the residuary gift, Millie died in 1964, unmarried. Lily, who was born in 1916 and is still unmarried, is still alive. Priscilla died on 30 September 1984. She had the two sons mentioned in the residuary gifts, namely Michael and Jonathan Kester, who are respectively the fourth and fifth defendants.

The seventh defendant, Lily Tepper, was joined as a party to the original summons to represent the next of kin.

c It will be recalled that the provisos refer to the grandchildren of the testator marrying outside the Jewish faith. Laurence Ruda, Gertrude Hantman, Harvey Cohen and Michael Kester are all married. There is no question but that they did not marry outside the Jewish faith. The other two grandchildren, Jonathan Kester and Shirley Kutz, are also both married. Jonathan Kester married in April 1980; he had, and this may be relevant, already attained the age of 25 years. His wife was not and is not of the Jewish faith.

d Shirley Kutz, one of the daughters of the testator's daughter Clara, married a Mr Stanley Kutz. She was married to him by a rabbi in Chicago. But he was not and is not a member of the Jewish faith. Accordingly, if the provisos are valid they operate to defeat the claims of Shirley Kutz and Jonathan Kester respectively to participate in the deceased's residuary estate.

e Counsel for Shirley Kutz and Jonathan Kester has naturally argued that the provisos ought to be held void for uncertainty. He has represented also the seventh defendant, Lily Tepper, who is interested as one of the class of next of kin and whose interest also is that the provisos should be void for uncertainty. That is the only basis on which any intestacy in which next of kin could share could be held to arise.

Counsel representing the first four defendants has been concerned to submit that the provisos are valid and that Jonathan Kester and Shirley Kutz are precluded by the terms *f* of the provisos from claiming under the will.

The question whether the provisos are or are not void for uncertainty is sadly not able to be approached simply on a consideration of the language, the relatively simple language, used by the testator in his will. It is a question which has become complicated (I might say bedevilled) by authority. I must therefore refer to the relevant authorities and then come back to consider where those authorities leave the question in issue.

g I start with the decision of the House of Lords in *Clayton v Ramsden* [1943] 1 All ER 16, [1943] AC 320. In that case the testator had given a testamentary gift to an unmarried daughter, but had provided by a clause in his will that if his unmarried daughter should at any time after his death marry a person 'not of Jewish parentage and of the Jewish faith', the gift to her should fail and his will should operate as if she had died at the date of the marriage. The headnote to the report reads ([1943] AC 320): 'The testator having *h* died, the daughter married a man who was not of Jewish parentage or faith.' The question for the court therefore was whether the provision to which I have referred was valid. If it was, it defeated the daughter's claim; if it was invalid her entitlement to the gift was not affected by the provision. The House of Lords held that the provision was void. They were unanimous in concluding that the condition relating to the person whom the daughter married being 'not of Jewish parentage' was too uncertain to be *j* upheld. For present purposes, however, it is of more interest to notice what was held in regard to the other limb of the condition, namely, that the gift would fail if the person married was not of the Jewish faith.

The test to be applied to the case was dealt with by Lord Russell and Lord Romer in particular. Taking the judgments in the order in which they appear in the report, it is of interest that Lord Atkin expressed disfavour as to the power of testators, as he put it, 'to control from their grave the choice in marriage of their beneficiaries' (see [1943] 1 All ER 16 at 17, [1943] AC 320 at 325). He said that he would not be dismayed if the power *a* were to disappear, 'but at least the control by forfeitures imposed by conditions subsequent must be subject to the rule as to certainty prescribed by this House in *Clavering* v. *Ellison* (1859) 7 HL Cas 707, 11 ER 282 and, judged by the test there prescribed, this forfeiture fails'.

Lord Russell expressed the principle touched on by Lord Atkin more fully. He said ([1943] 1 All ER 16 at 18, [1943] AC 320 at 326):   *b*

'The courts have always insisted that conditions of defeasance, in order to be valid, should be so framed that the persons affected (or the court, if they seek its guidance) can from the outset know with certainty the exact event on the happening of which their interests are to be divested. The principle was enunciated many years ago by Lord Cranworth in *Clavering* v. *Ellison* ((1859) 7 HL Cas 707 at 725, 11 ER 282 at *c* 289) in the following words: "... where a vested estate is to be defeated by a condition on a contingency that is to happen afterwards, that condition must be such that the court can see from the beginning, precisely and distinctly, upon the happening of what event it was that the preceding vested estate was to determine." In all such cases that is the test which has to be applied to the particular condition which the testator has chosen to impose ... Let me now apply the principle to this *d* condition. The crucial words are "who is not of Jewish parentage and of the Jewish faith".'

Lord Russell dealt first with the words 'of Jewish parentage'. He was in no doubt that there was insufficient certainty in the condition to enable the test derived from *Clavering* v *Ellison* to be satisfied. He went on to say that it was, in view of his decision on the Jewish parentage point, unnecessary to express an opinion on the certainty of the words 'of the *e* Jewish faith'. He said, however ([1943] 1 All ER 16 at 19, [1943] AC 320 at 328–329):

'... had it been necessary, I should have felt a difficulty in holding that their meaning was clear or certain. It seems to me that (apart from the difficulty which arises from the existence of the three varieties of Judaism referred to by Lord Greene, M.R.) the testator has given no indication of the degree of attachment or *f* adherence to the faith which he requires on the part of his daughter's husband. The requirement that a person shall be of Jewish faith seems to me too vague to enable it to be said with certainty that a particular individual complies with the requirement.'

Lord Wright agreed with Lord Russell as to the uncertainty of the expression 'of Jewish parentage'. He disagreed so far as the expression 'the Jewish faith' was concerned but his *g* decision on the first point meant that he accepted in the result that the appeal succeeded.

Lord Romer, with whose judgment Lord Atkin and Lord Thankerton agreed, concurred in the view that the expression of 'of Jewish parentage' lacked the requisite certainty. Having dealt with that matter, he said: 'My Lords, this is sufficient to dispose of the appeal', but he went on to consider the other point and said ([1943] 1 All ER 16 at *h* 23, [1943] AC 320 at 334–335):

'Even if the clause could be read as though it merely provided for a forfeiture in the event of the daughter being married to a man not of the Jewish faith, I am of opinion that it would still be void for uncertainty. For how is it to be ascertained whether a man is of the Jewish faith? It will have been observed from what I have . already said that in the Court of Appeal they answered this question by saying that *j* whether a man was or was not of the Jewish faith was a mere question of fact to be determined on evidence and that the assertion by the man that he was of that faith was well nigh conclusive. I should agree entirely with the Court of Appeal as to this if only I knew what was the meaning of the words "of the Jewish faith". Until I

a
know that, I do not know to what the evidence is to be directed. There are, of course, an enormous number of people who accept every tenet of and observe every rule of practice and conduct prescribed by the Jewish religion. As to them there can be no doubt that they are of the Jewish faith. But there must obviously be others who do not accept all those tenets and are lax in the observance of some of those rules of practice and of conduct, and the extent to which the tenets are accepted and the rules are observed will vary in different individuals. Now, I do not doubt that each

b
of these last mentioned individuals, if questioned, would say, and say in all honesty, that he was of the Jewish faith. On the other hand I do not doubt that one who accepted all the tenets and observed all the rules would assert that some of the individuals I have mentioned were certainly not of the Jewish faith. It would surely depend on the extent to which the particular individual accepted the tenets and observed the rules. My Lords, I cannot avoid the conclusion that the question

c
whether a man is of the Jewish faith is a question of degree. The testator has, however, failed to give any indication what degree of faith in the daughter's husband will avoid and what degree will bring about a forfeiture of her interest in his estate. In these circumstances the condition requiring that a husband shall be of the Jewish faith would, even if standing alone, be void for uncertainty.'

d
I must return to the manner in which Lord Romer and Lord Russell in particular dealt with the question of certainty or uncertainty of the concept of a person being of the Jewish faith. For the moment it is sufficient to observe that this case is binding authority for the proposition that a clause of defeasance will only be upheld if it is so framed (and I am now reading again the passage from the judgment of Lord Russell) 'that the persons affected . . . can from the outset know with certainty the exact event on the happening

e
of which their interests are to be divested'. That, I repeat, is the test for a condition of defeasance.

The principle authoritatively stated in *Clayton v Ramsden* was considered by the Court of Appeal in *Re Allen, Faith v Allen* [1953] 2 All ER 898, [1953] Ch 810. In that case a testator had made certain testamentary gifts to certain of his relations 'who shall be a member of the Church of England and an adherent to the doctrine of that Church'. The

f
question for the court was whether that condition was or was not void for uncertainty. The Court of Appeal (Evershed MR and Birkett LJ, Romer LJ dissenting) held that the gift was not void for uncertainty. The importance of the case is that the *Clayton v Ramsden* approach was held applicable only to conditions of defeasance and not applicable to conditions precedent. Where conditions precedent were concerned it was held that the test of certainty would be satisfied if the condition was sufficiently clear to enable it to be

g
said of a particular person whether he did or did not come within the language of the condition.

The distinction between the sort of condition with which the court had been dealing in *Clayton v Ramsden* and the sort of condition with which the court was dealing in *Re Allen* [1953] 2 All ER 898 at 900, [1953] Ch 810 at 816 was expressed by Evershed MR thus:

h
'A condition subsequent operates to divest or determine a gift or estate previously or otherwise vested, so that if the condition be void the gift or estate remains. It has been long established that the courts (which are inclined against the divesting of gifts or estates already vested) will hold a condition subsequent void if its terms are such that (apart from mere difficulties of construction of the language or of the

j
ascertainment of the facts) it cannot be clearly known in advance or from the beginning what are the circumstances the happening of which will cause the divesting or determination of the gift or estate. The strictness of the special rule as to conditions subsequent was the basis of all the opinions of the noble Lords in *Clayton v. Ramsden* and was thus expressed by LORD RUSSELL OF KILLOWEN . . .'

Evershed MR then set out part of the speech of Lord Russell that I have already cited and
referred also to the dictum by Lord Cranworth in *Clavering v Ellison* (1859) 7 HL Cas 707   *a*
at 725, 11 ER 282 at 289. He went on:

> 'I feel, therefore, no doubt that if the present formula constituted a condition
> subsequent it would, for the reasons fully set out by VAISEY, J., be held to be void—
> its second part falls clearly, I think, within the reasoning and language of LORD
> RUSSELL and LORD ROMER in *Clayton v. Ramsden* to which I shall later again refer.'   *b*

Then Evershed MR dealt with the approach to conditions precedent. He said ([1953] 2
All ER 898 at 901, [1953] Ch 810 at 817):

> 'In any case, and whether the formula be a condition precedent or a qualification,
> it seems to me that no such general or academic test is called for as a condition
> subsequent requires. All that the claiming devisee has to do is at the relevant date to   *c*
> establish, if he can, that he satisfies the condition or qualification whatever be the
> appropriate test . . . The essential difference which, I think, exists, and to which I
> have alluded, was well illustrated by counsel for the third defendant in the course of
> argument. A condition subsequent divesting an estate vested in A. if A. at some
> relevant date should not be a tall man would, as it seems to me, be held void for
> uncertainty. For tallness being a matter of degree, by what standard is it, for the   *d*
> supposed purposes, to be judged? If "tallness" is achieved by being above the
> "average" height, then what average is contemplated? The average of A.'s town or
> neighbourhood, the average of Englishmen, the average of all mankind? And
> would a man in height above the average, say, of all Englishmen by however small
> a fraction of an inch, be called "tall" in any ordinary sense? But questions of this
> kind, which might be fatal to the supposed formula as a condition subsequent,   *e*
> might have no application in the case of a condition precedent or qualification, for a
> claimant who was six feet six inches tall might fairly say that he satisfied the
> testator's requirement judged by any reasonable standard.'

Then he said ([1953] 2 All ER 898 at 901, [1953] Ch 810 at 818):

> 'I am not persuaded that where a formula constitutes a condition precedent or a   *f*
> qualification it is right for the court to declare the condition or qualification void for
> uncertainty so as thereby to defeat all possible claimants to the gift, unless the terms
> of the condition or qualification are such that it is impossible to give them any
> meaning at all or such that they involve repugnancies or inconsistencies in the
> possible tests which they postulate as distinct, for example, from mere problems of
> degree.'   *g*

Having thus stated that approach Evershed MR upheld the condition. He held that
there was no reason why a particular individual should not be able, on appropriate
evidence, to satisfy the court that he was a member of the Church of England and was an
adherent to the doctrine of that church.

That decision is of course binding on me, as is the decision in *Clayton v Ramsden*. I   *h*
must, however, respectfully say that very great difficulty seems to me to remain.
Evershed MR was contemplating evidence in relation to a particular person so as to satisfy
the court that that person was an adherent to the doctrine of the Church of England. But
the doctrine of the Church of England must itself be the subject of evidence before it can
be clear to what doctrine the adherence of the person in question is being sought.
However, the decision in *Re Allen* establishes, and will continue to establish until upset   *j*
by some court of appropriate authority, a distinction between conditions of defeasance
on the one hand, to which the rule in *Clayton v Ramsden* applies, and conditions precedent
or qualifications, as it was put by Evershed MR, to which the principle expressed by him
applies, namely that it is sufficient if the condition is couched in language that permits a

particular individual to come with evidence before the court and show that he satisfies or
a does not satisfy, as the case may be, that condition.

The dichotomy between the two approaches has been underlined by subsequent cases.
In *Re Selby's Will Trusts Donn v Selby* [1965] 3 All ER 386, [1966] 1 WLR 43 Buckley J was
faced with a clause of a will in which a testator declared 'No beneficiary who shall have
married, or who before, or on attaining a vested interest shall marry out of the Jewish
faith shall take any interest or benefit'. Naturally enough it was argued before Buckley J
b that that provision was void for uncertainty. *Clayton v Ramsden* was of course relied on.
As against that, it was said that the provision in the context of the will constituted a
condition precedent, that it was possible for an individual to come before the court and
satisfy the court that he or she had not married out of the Jewish faith, and, accordingly,
on the test proposed by *Re Allen* there was no uncertainty in the condition requiring it to
be declared void.

c   Buckley J held first that the provision was in truth a condition precedent and not a
condition subsequent. That conclusion was I think particularly prompted by the language
of the provision itself whereby the testator declared that 'no beneficiary who shall have
married . . . shall take any interest or benefit'. It is cogently put that that language
precludes any suggestion that the provision could be regarded as a condition subsequent:
no interest was able to be taken unless the condition was complied with.

d   Buckley J's remarks as to certainty, as opposed to his remarks as to the character,
condition subsequent or condition precedent, of the provision, are, as it seems to me,
very relevant to some of the arguments which I have heard. He said ([1965] 3 All ER 386
at 389, [1966] 1 WLR 43 at 47), having cited lengthy passages from the judgments of
Lord Russell and Lord Romer in *Clayton v Ramsden*:

e   'Those are observations which give strong support to the submission that the
          question whether the particular person is or is not of the Jewish faith is a question
          which the court cannot answer with certainty, but it must be remembered, as I have
          already indicated, that those are observations which are made in the context of
          conditions subsequent in respect of which it is well settled that the person liable to
          suffer a forfeiture must be able to understand precisely what act or acts will be liable
f   to work forfeiture. Such cases are to be distinguished from cases of conditions
          precedent or qualifications to take a benefit. That that is so, is made clear by a
          decision of the Court of Appeal in *Re Allen*.'

      Buckley J then referred to *Re Allen* and cites from the judgment of Evershed MR. He
g then said ([1965] 3 All ER 386 at 391, [1966] 1 WLR 43 at 49):

          'Now could it be said in the present case that an inquiry whether a partner whom
          one or other of the testator's children had married during the relevant period was or
          was not of the Jewish faith would be doomed to failure? Sɪʀ Rᴀʏᴍᴏɴᴅ Eᴠᴇʀꜱʜᴇᴅ,
          M.R., clearly thought that that was not the position and I think that that is not the
h   position. I have no evidence before me of an expert nature relating to the Jewish
          faith. I can conceive that there might be a difference of substance between, for
          instance, this condition and that under consideration in *Re Allen* which related to
          membership of the Church of England, which is an organised and identifiable body,
          membership of which may be demonstrated by reference to certain formal acts such
          as baptism and confirmation and certain conduct such as regular attendance at
          Church services or even by certain professional activities such as being a priest or
j   dignitary of the Church of England . . . I cannot believe, however, that in the case
          at any rate of some people the court would not find it easy to determine whether
          they are or are not of the Jewish faith. For instance, a professing and practising
          Christian would manifestly not be of the Jewish faith. A devout and practising Jew,
          whatever kind of Jewish faith he practices, would, I should have thought, qualify as

being of the Jewish faith. Although for the purposes of a forfeiture provision, where he who is liable to forfeiture is protected by law in the sense that the law will not *a* enforce a forfeiture clause unless the person liable to forfeiture can see clearly beforehand what will work a forfeiture, membership of the Jewish faith may well be, and indeed has been held to be, too indefinite a concept to justify holding such a forfeiture provision good, nevertheless, for the purpose of a qualifying clause of this kind, notwithstanding the difficulties that may arise in borderline cases—and the border might be a fairly extensive area—it seems to me that in loyalty to the *b* decision of the Court of Appeal in *Re Allen*, I am bound to take the view that this is a sufficiently defined concept to make it clear that in many instances the court would have no difficulty in saying one way or another whether a particular person was or was not of the Jewish faith.'

The relevant phrase, it will be recalled, in *Re Selby's Will Trusts* was 'shall have married *c* or shall marry out of the Jewish faith'. It is relevant for the purposes of the present case to notice that Buckley J said ([1965] 3 All ER 386 at 387, [1966] 1 WLR 43 at 45):

'In my judgment, according to the ordinary meaning of the English language, to marry out of the Jewish faith means to marry someone who is not an adherent of that faith at the time of the marriage.'

d

I should refer, but I think happily I can do so quite briefly, to *Blathwayt v Lord Cawley* [1975] 3 All ER 625, [1976] AC 397. That was a case where a provision, that was on any footing one of defeasance, came into effect if the beneficiary should 'be or become a Roman Catholic'. It was argued that the provision lacked certainty. That argument was rejected. It was argued that the nature of such a provision might offend against public policy. That too was rejected. That latter point recalls the remarks made by Lord Atkin *e* in *Clayton v Ramsden*. Lord Atkin expressed his distaste for forfeiture clauses whereby testators sought after the grave to control the manner of marriages their descendants or the beneficiaries under their will might contract.

More relevant is the Court of Appeal decision in *Re Tuck's Settlement Trusts, Public Trustee v Tuck* [1978] 1 All ER 1047, [1978] Ch 49, a case which in many respects I find difficult to understand. One of the reasons, perhaps, why I find the case difficult to follow *f* is that the testamentary provisions were of very great complexity. The will was that of one Sir Adolph Tuck, who had been made a baronet and who wanted to try to ensure that his successors in the baronetcy should remain members of the Jewish faith and be married to members of the Jewish faith. By his will Sir Adolph Tuck introduced the concept of what he called an 'approved wife'. The will defined an 'approved wife' as 'a wife of Jewish blood by one or both of her parents who has been brought up in and has *g* never departed from and at the date of her marriage continues to worship according to the Jewish faith'; the will went on to provide, 'as to which facts in case of dispute or doubt the decision of the Chief Rabbi in London of either the Portuguese or the Anglo German Community . . . shall be conclusive'.

Clause 3(b) of the will contained a gift of income to—

h

'the baronet for the time being if and when and so long as he shall be of the Jewish faith and shall be married to an approved wife and shall either continue to live with her or, if separated . . . he shall be certified by the Chief Rabbi . . . to have in no way caused such separation by any fault of his own . . .'

By cl 3(e) the testator provided that—

j

'whenever the baronet for the time being shall be either (1) a pervert from the Jewish faith; (2) a bachelor; (3) married to a person who does not fall within the foregoing definition of an approved wife; (4) a widower under the age of 55 without male issue or (5) judicially or by agreement separate from an approved wife . . .'

Then, and in each of those cases, the baronet was to receive no more than the annual sum of £400 from the trust estate until he should be received again formally into the Jewish

a faith or until he should live again with any separated wife or being a bachelor or widower marry and live with an approved wife.

What had happened to give rise to the question that was brought before the court was that Sir Adolph Tuck's grandson had married an approved wife, had succeeded his father in 1954, in 1964 had been divorced from his approved wife and in 1968 had married a lady who was not an approved wife. The question raised by the originating summons,

b the question at least on which the case is reported, was whether the decision of one or other of the chief rabbis was conclusive in the case of doubt whether a particular wife was or was not of Jewish blood, or had or had not ever departed from the Jewish faith, or had or had not been brought up in the Jewish faith, or did or did not continue to worship according to the Jewish faith.

The case came before the court at a time when, if the trusts of the will were valid, the

c baronet had on any footing lost the original income interest to which he had succeeded on the death of his father. That loss would have been occasioned by his divorce. But was he, on his remarriage, once more entitled to resume his income interest? And were the trusts, taken as a whole, valid or void for uncertainty? The Court of Appeal treated the condition as a condition precedent. There is not a great deal of, or indeed any, discussion of the nature of the conditions. Lord Russell said ([1978] 1 All ER 1047 at 1055, [1978]

d Ch 49 at 64):

> 'Although some of the language of cl 3(e) is suggestive of conditions subsequent, in my opinion the substance of the clause is to release the baronet up to £400 from the need to fulfil the qualifying conditions or conditions precedent in the earlier part of the settlement. Accordingly, in my judgment, the question of uncertainty

e > must be decided upon the footing that we are here concerned with conditions precedent.'

On that footing Lord Russell regarded the decision in the case as concluded by Re Allen, Faith v Allen [1953] 2 All ER 898, [1953] Ch 810. He could see no sufficient uncertainty to render the condition precedent void for uncertainty. He said ([1978] 1 All ER 1047 at

f 1056, [1978] Ch 49 at 65):

> 'No doubt there are variations in rites, practices and, for aught I know, beliefs among the different groups of Jews who practise their religious faith. But I would not wish to destroy a settlement and defeat a settlor's intentions on the supposition that adherence to the Jewish faith is an unintelligible concept, any more than had the references been to Christianity, however diverse have become attitudes to the

g > latter.'

Lord Russell did not rest his opinion on the provision in the will for disputes to be resolved by one or other of the chief rabbis. He treated the condition as a condition precedent, and, applying Re Allen, held that the condition was not void for uncertainty.

Lord Denning MR did not express a view as to whether the condition should be treated

h as a condition precedent or as a condition of defeasance. He said ([1978] 1 All ER 1047 at 1054, [1978] Ch 49 at 62):

> '... if there is any conceptual uncertainty in the provisions of this settlement, it is cured by the chief rabbi clause. That was the view of Whitford J, and I agree with it. If the chief rabbi clause is inoperative, then I would so construe the settlement as

j > to hold there is no conceptual uncertainty. This is the view of Lord Russell of Killowen ... And I agree with it too.'

Eveleigh LJ, the third member of the court, agreed with Lord Russell that the condition was a condition precedent. He, too, thought the condition was valid. 'Jewish faith' meant, he held, in the context in which the phrase appeared in the will, the same as the chief rabbi's definition. And the chief rabbi could, he said, give evidence of what he, the chief rabbi, meant by the phrase and thereby render certain the meaning of the phrase in the will.

Apart from underlining the applicability of the approach adopted by the Court of Appeal in *Re Allen* to a case where there is truly a condition precedent, *Re Tuck* does not seem to me to assist a great deal for the purposes of the present case. In particular it does not, in my view, assist on the question whether or not the provisions in the present case are conditions subsequent or conditions precedent. The conditions in *Re Tuck* were as sui generis as conditions ever could be. The line of reasoning whereby Lord Russell concluded that the conditions were not conditions of defeasance does not appear from his judgment. The conditions were, as it seems to me, of a dual character. They had to be complied with before an income interest under the will could be enjoyed. To that extent they were conditions precedent. But they might also operate to bring to an end an income interest for the time being in possession. To that extent they would operate, I would have thought, as conditions of defeasance.

The importance of *Re Tuck* for the purposes of the present case is, firstly, that it shows an inclination on the part of the court to uphold, if it can, the testatator's testamentary provisions, and, secondly, that it establishes the admissibility of extrinsic evidence to elucidate the meaning in the will of such phrases as 'the Jewish faith'. On the other hand, *Re Tuck* did not, and could not, detract from the authority of *Clayton v Ramsden* [1943] 1 All ER 16, [1943] AC 320. It remains the law that a testamentary condition of defeasance must satisfy the test of certainty that requires it to be known 'with certainty the exact event on the happening of which their interests are to be divested'.

The authorities lead, in my judgment, to this position. If the right view of the two provisions of the testator's will is that they were of the nature of conditions precedent, ie qualifications to be satisfied by the beneficiaries in order to enable them to participate in the testamentary gifts, then there is no basis on which they could be said to be void for uncertainty. Buckley J's approach in *Re Selby's Will Trusts* [1965] 3 All ER 386, [1966] 1 WLR 43 would be exactly in point. It has not been suggested by counsel for the fifth, sixth and seventh defendants that if these conditions are conditions precedent they lack sufficient certainty for validity. If, on the other hand, they are properly to be regarded as conditions of defeasance, ie as conditions subsequent, then if *Clayton v Ramsden* is taken as an authoritative guide they may lack sufficient certainty to stand.

So, the first question is whether these provisions are conditions precedent or conditions subsequent. I have been referred to one authority on this point, apart from *Re Tuck*, namely *Re Lowry's Will Trusts, Barclays Bank Ltd v Board of Governors of the United Newcastle-upon-Tyne Hospitals* [1966] 3 All ER 955, [1967] Ch 638. A testator had given certain interests to members of his family. The interests were not absolute interests; there was a possibility that they might all in the end fail. The testator provided that if the interests should fail then 'subject to the trusts aforesaid I direct that [the] fund or so much thereof as shall not have been applied under the trusts aforesaid or any power incidental thereto shall be divided among the following charities in equal shares'. The will then specified a number of charities and there followed this proviso: 'Provided always that if at the time of the failure of the trusts aforesaid any of the said charities shall have ceased to exist as an independent charity [the] fund shall be divided in equal shares among such of the said charities as shall then be in existence.' Cross J held, first, that the proviso should be read 'divided in equal shares among such of the said charities as shall then be in existence as independent charities'. He was of opinion that if the proviso was to be regarded as a defeasance provision it was insufficiently certain to be valid. He regarded the phrase 'ceased to exist as an independent charity' as insufficiently precise to comply with the test of certainty expressed in *Clayton v Ramsden*. But if the proviso was to be regarded as a condition precedent, as simply part of the qualification to be fulfilled by a claiming charity, then he regarded the proviso as valid. It would be possible for any of the specified charities to come forward and show that it was an independent charity. Alternatively, it would be possible for the other charities to show of one particular charity that it was not an independent charity.

a   Cross J held that the proviso was not a defeasance provision but was a condition precedent or a qualification. He regarded the testator's requirement that the charities which were to receive his bounty should be independent charities as a qualification which they had to satisfy at the time the gift to them came into effect, that is to say at the time the prior trusts failed. He said ([1966] 3 All ER 955 at 960, [1967] Ch 638 at 650):

b   'I think that the interest which the charities took on the death of the testator were future contingent interests. If the testator had inserted between the words "Sunshine Homes for Blind Babies" and the words "Provided always", the words "being respectively in existence as independent charities", it could not have been suggested that the charities took vested interests. Those words, however, are implicit in the gift, and can it really make any difference that they are not expressed? I must, of course, remember that the court in any case of doubt construes a condition as a

c   condition subsequent rather than a condition precedent. Further, it is to be observed that the contention that the gift and the condition if read together amounted to a qualification was rejected by the House of Lords in *Clavering* v. *Ellison* ((1859) 7 HL Cas 707, 11 ER 282); but the will there was totally different in character. There the testator clearly gave vested equitable estates tail in remainder by one clause and clearly imposed a condition subsequent divesting them by another clause. To turn

d   the interests given into future gifts on a contingency, one would have had to rewrite the whole of the disposition. Here, however, the testator was not saying to the charities, "See, I am making gifts in your favour, but be careful that you do not lose your independence because if you do, you will lose your gift". He was saying "If it so happens that Selby Dalgliesh has no issue to take the capital of his mother's share, then I want that share, on the failure of the prior trusts, to go to such of these

e   charities which I have named as are there in existence as independent charities".'

   The answer to the question as to the status and character of the provisos in the present case must depend on their language and the context in which they find themselves. I would start with the proviso in para (d). That paragraph, it will be recalled, contains a substitutionary gift to the two sons of Priscilla, Michael and Jonathan, of the share of

f   income payable to Priscilla. On her death that share is to go to Michael and Jonathan. I should, perhaps, read the paragraph again:

   '... the share of income otherwise payable to her shall be paid for the education and advancement of her children in equal shares and upon their attaining the age of 25 years shall be paid to them absolutely Provided that they shall remain within the Jewish faith and shall not marry outside the Jewish faith.'

g   Counsel for the first four defendants has presented the proviso as a condition precedent. She has submitted that it is to be read as a qualification which Michael and Jonathan must fulfil if they are to take the gift of income. I find it impossible to read it in that sense; to my mind such a reading is an unnatural one if the clause is read as a whole. On the death of Priscilla income goes to Michael and Jonathan. Both counsel for the defendants agreed

h   that the reference to the two sons attaining the age of 25 years did not represent a contingency. It was suggested by counsel for the first four defendants that it indicated the time by which the qualification represented by the provision had to be fulfilled. It was suggested by counsel for the other defendants that it indicated the time after which the condition of defeasance could no longer operate. Be that as it may, once income becomes payable under para (d) to the two sons it will continue to be payable to them

j   unless and until the proviso bites. If, following the death of Priscilla, one of them was no longer to remain within the Jewish faith or one of them was to marry outside the Jewish faith, then and in that event his income interest under the sub-paragraph would, in my view, fail. That is the substance of the intended effect of the proviso. That being its substance it is in my view a provision of defeasance.

   I do not myself think it matters whether the interests of Michael and Jonathan under the aragraph are contingent or vested. In my view, they are vested; but, whether they

are contingent or vested, if the interests are subject to determination by the events
specified by the proviso, then, in my judgment, the proviso must be regarded as a   *a*
condition of defeasance, not as a condition precedent or as a qualification. Counsel for
the first four defendants accepted that, on Priscilla's death, the events specified in the
proviso not having happened, income would at once be payable to Michael and Jonathan.
If, in relation to one of them, the events then happened, income would no longer be
payable to him. I do not see how a proviso which operates in that way can be regarded as
other than a condition of defeasance. Counsel argued that it represented a condition   *b*
precedent to the right of each son to receive income as the income from time to time
accrued. Each time income came into the hands of the trustees for distribution, the
condition would have to be satisfied. I am unable to accept this, to my mind, highly
artificial construction. The paragraph contains one gift of income, not several. If the
proviso operates so as to bring to an end the right to receive income, it is, in my view, a
condition of defeasance and cannot be described as a failed condition precedent to the   *c*
right to receive future income.

If it is right, as I think it is, that the proviso in para (d) is a condition of defeasance, a
condition subsequent, it would be strange if the proviso in similar, although not identical,
form in para (e) were not of the same character. In my view, it is of the same character. I
reach this conclusion both for the reason that prima facie a consistent construction should   *d*
be given to the two provisos and also having regard to the language of the proviso in para
(e). Under para (e) the testator has directed that on the death of the survivor of the three
named daughters, Millie, Lily and Priscilla, the residue of his estate shall be held in trust
to be divided among all his grandchildren as shall be living at the date of his death. I do
not read that language as introducing the contingency that the grandchildren shall
survive until the death of the survivor of the three daughters. On a natural reading of
the paragraph, as it seems to me, the grandchildren achieve vested interests at once. Here   *e*
again both counsel for the defendants agree that the words 'such share to be paid to them
upon their attaining the age of 25 years' do not introduce any contingency. But, if it is
right to regard the grandchildren as attaining vested interests at once, then the proviso
'Provided however they shall not marry outside the Jewish faith' cannot be other than a
condition of defeasance.   *f*

If, contrary to the view I have expressed, it were right to regard the interests of the
grandchildren under para (e) as contingent on surviving the survivor of Millie, Lilly and
Priscilla, even so the proviso would, in my judgment, represent a provision of defeasance.
It would bring to an end the contingent interest of the grandchild in question.

In my view, the reference to the grandchildren attaining the age of 25 years in para (e)
was intended to limit the period during which the proviso could operate. Once the date   *g*
of distribution had arrived, whether it be the death of the survivor of Millie, Lily and
Priscilla or whether it be the attainment by the particular grandchild of the age of 25
years (whichever should be the later) the proviso would, in my view, no longer bite. I
think that the testator intended that after the death of the last survivor of his three named
daughters each grandchild who attained the age of 25 years, provided that the grandchild
had not married outside the Jewish faith, should receive his or her share. What marriage   *h*
the grandchild might thereafter contract would not matter.

Be that as it may, I am of the opinion that the proviso in para (e), like the proviso in
para (d), is one of defeasance defeating the interests given to the grandchildren and,
accordingly, that the principles of certainty expressed in *Clayton v Ramsden* [1943] 1 All
ER 16, [1943] AC 320 ought to be applied.

The next question is where that leaves this case. Counsel for the fifth, sixth and seventh   *j*
defendants has submitted, understandably, that if I were to come to the conclusion that
the provisos are conditions of defeasance, I ought to declare them void for uncertainty.
That was the result in *Clayton v Ramsden*. It may be that that would have been the result
in *Re Selby's Will Trusts* [1965] 3 All ER 386, [1966] 1 WLR 43 if Buckley J had regarded
the condition as a condition of defeasance instead of regarding it, as he did, as a condition
precedent.

a I am reluctant, however, to find these provisos void for uncertainty. I do not accept that the conclusion of uncertainty is an inevitable one. There does not seem to have been any evidence before the court in *Clayton v Ramsden* relevant to the meaning of the expression 'of the Jewish faith' (see *Re Samuel, Jacobs v Ramsden* [1941] 3 All ER 196, [1942] Ch 1). It may be that there was no relevant or admissible evidence which could be adduced. It may be that in that event, for the reasons advanced by Lord Russell and Lord Romer, it was not possible to give any certainty to the expression.

b But lack of certainty as to the meaning of 'the Jewish faith' does seem to me to be bound to be the case where every testator and every will are concerned. I have already remarked that the contents of Nathan Tepper's will, read as a whole, show him to have been a devout Jew and, I think, a practising Jew. He practised his religion according to some tenets and in some community of Jewry; I do not know which and I do not know in what manner: there is no evidence of that. But a will falls to be construed, it is c sometimes said, from the testator's armchair. The question is what the testator, sitting in his armchair, meant by 'the Jewish faith'. Direct evidence of his intention is not admissible; but I would have regarded as admissible extrinsic evidence of the Jewish faith as practised by the testator and his family. It would, in my view, be well arguable that when the testator in his will referred to 'the Jewish faith' he meant the Jewish faith in accordance with which he practised his religion. I would have regarded it as possible and, d indeed, likely that objective evidence might be available as to what was the Jewish faith in accordance with which he practised his religion. If evidence of that character were adduced it might well, in my view, be possible to attribute to the expression 'the Jewish faith' a meaning sufficiently certain to enable the *Clayton v Ramsden* test to be satisfied. This approach to construction is, in my view, supported by that of the Court of Appeal in *Re Tuck's Settlement Trusts* [1978] 1 All ER 1047, [1978] Ch 49 and, in particular, by e that of Eveleigh LJ.

A question of construction of a will depends on the language of the particular will construed with the aid of admissible evidence of relevant surrounding circumstances. A decision by another court, even a court as august as the House of Lords, is not binding on the question whether in Nathan Tepper's will a sufficiently certain meaning can be f attributed to the expression 'the Jewish faith' so as to enable the conditions of defeasance to be upheld.

Counsel for the plaintiffs and counsel for the first four defendants, in the event that I should decide against her on the condition precedent or condition of defeasance point, and I have done so, have asked for an opportunity to adduce extrinsic evidence of surrounding circumstances in order to elucidate the meaning of the expression 'the Jewish faith' as used by the testator in his will. I think I should give them an opportunity g to do so.

If there is no more evidence than that which is before me now, it seems to me inevitable that the provisos must be declared void for uncertainty. The case would, in the event, be on all fours with *Clayton v Ramsden*. But, as I have said, that state of affairs does not seem to me to be inevitable.

h I would therefore deal with the questions raised by the originating summons before me by declaring, if it be appropriate and useful, that the provisos represent conditions of defeasance and by adjourning the originating summons with liberty to the parties to file further evidence as to the meaning in this will of the expression 'the Jewish faith'.

Declaration accordingly. Summons adjourned.

j
Solicitors: *A Kramer & Co* (for all parties).

Jacqueline Metcalfe   Barrister.

Polkey v A E Dauton Services Ltd a

COURT OF APPEAL, CIVIL DIVISION

NEILL, NICHOLLS LJJ AND SIR GEORGE WALLER

17, 18 JULY, 22 OCTOBER 1986

Unfair dismissal – Determination whether dismissal fair or unfair – Reasons justifying dismissal b
– Determination of whether employer acted reasonably – Redundancy – Employer failing to
consult employee prior to dismissal – Industrial tribunal concluding that failure to consult not
making any difference to decision to dismiss employee – Whether any distinction between reason
for dismissal and manner in which dismissal effected – Whether industrial tribunal bound to
consider whether failure to consult made any difference to result – Whether dismissal unfair –
Employment Protection (Consolidation) Act 1978, s 57(3). c

The appellant was employed as a van driver by the employers. In 1982 in order to stem
their financial losses the employers decided to make redundant three van drivers,
including the appellant. Accordingly, with no prior consultation, the appellant was told
that he was being made redundant and handed a letter of redundancy. The appellant
complained to an industrial tribunal that he had been unfairly dismissed. The tribunal d
held that, notwithstanding that there had been no consultation with the appellant prior
to his dismissal, the question whether the appellant had been unfairly dismissed depended
on whether the result (ie his dismissal) would have been the same if there had been
consultation, and they concluded that it would. They accordingly dismissed the claim,
and on appeal their decision was affirmed by the Employment Appeal Tribunal. The
appellant appealed to the Court of Appeal, contending that the effect of the failure to e
consult and whether it would have made any difference to the result were only relevant
in considering the question of remedies for unfair dismissal, and that since the fact of the
failure to consult was by itself sufficient for the employers to be held to have 'acted
unreasonably in treating [the redundancy] as a sufficient reason for dismissing the
employee' the tribunal should have decided under s 57(3)[a] of the Employment Protection
(Consolidation) Act 1978 that the dismissal was unfair. f

Held – In questions relating to unfair dismissal there was a crucial distinction between
the reason for a dismissal and the manner in which it was effected, and in determining
whether an employer had acted reasonably or unreasonably in treating redundancy as a
sufficient reason for dismissing an employee for the purposes of s 57(3) of the 1978 Act
an industrial tribunal were entitled to investigate and evaluate the practical effect of a g
failure to consult or warn the employee. It followed that the industrial tribunal had been
right to regard themselves as bound to inquire whether the employers' failure to consult
the appellant prior to his dismissal would have made any difference to the result. The
appeal would accordingly be dismissed (see p 989 d f to h and p 990 c d g to p 991 g, post).
    British Labour Pump Co Ltd v Byrne [1979] ICR 347 and *W & J Wass Ltd v Binns* [1982]
ICR 486 applied. h

Notes

For fair and unfair dismissal, see 16 Halsbury's Laws (4th edn) paras 626–630, and for
cases on the subject, see 20 Digest (Reissue) 403–407, 3357–3374.
    For the Employment Protection (Consolidation) Act 1978, s 57, see 16 Halsbury's
Statutes (4th edn) 439. j

Cases referred to in judgments

Bailey v BP Oil (Kent Refinery) Ltd [1980] ICR 642, CA.

---

a   Section 57(3) is set out at p 987 g h, post

British Home Stores Ltd v Burchell [1980] ICR 303, EAT.

a *British Labour Pump Co Ltd v Byrne* [1979] ICR 347, EAT.

Devis (W) & Sons Ltd v Atkins [1977] 3 All ER 40, [1977] AC 931, [1977] 3 WLR 214, HL.

Sillifant v Powell Duffryn Timber Ltd [1983] IRLR 91, EAT.

Wass (W & J) Ltd v Binns [1982] ICR 486, CA.

West Midlands Co-op Society Ltd v Tipton [1986] 1 All ER 513, [1986] AC 536, [1986] 2 WLR 306, HL.

b *Williams v Compair Maxam Ltd* [1982] ICR 156, EAT.

Cases also cited

Barley v Amey Roadstone Corp (No 2) [1978] ICR 190, EAT.

British United Shoe Machinery Co Ltd v Clarke [1978] ICR 70, EAT.

Gibson v British Transport Docks Board [1982] IRLR 228, EAT.

c *Henderson v Granville Tours Ltd* [1982] IRLR 494, EAT.

Kearney & Trecker Marvin Ltd v Varndell [1983] IRLR 335, CA.

Murray MacKinnon v Forno [1983] IRLR 7, EAT.

Pirelli General Cable Works Ltd v Murray [1979] IRLR 190, EAT.

Pritchett v J McIntyre Ltd [1986] IRLR 97, EAT.

Siggs & Chapman (Contractors) v Knight [1984] IRLR 83, EAT.

d *Weddel (W) & Co Ltd v Tepper* [1980] ICR 286, CA.

Appeal

Dennis Polkey appealed with the leave of the Employment Appeal Tribunal against the decision of that tribunal (Popplewell J, Mr T S Batho and Mrs M L Boyle) given on 2 October 1984 whereby it dismissed his appeal against the decision of an industrial

e tribunal (chairman Miss N Healey) sitting at Nottingham on 9 February 1983 dismissing his claim that he had been unfairly dismissed by the respondents, A E Dauton Services Ltd (formerly Edmund Walker (Holdings) Ltd) (the employers). The facts are set out in the judgment of Neill LJ.

f *Robin Allen* and *Martha Cover* for Mr Polkey.

Frederic Reynold QC and *John Wardell* for the employers.

Cur adv vult

22 October. The following judgments were delivered.

g

NEILL LJ. This is an appeal by Mr Dennis Polkey against the decision of the Employment Appeal Tribunal given on 2 October 1984 whereby it dismissed Mr Polkey's appeal against the order of the industrial tribunal dated 23 February 1983 rejecting his application for a finding that he had been unfairly dismissed by his former employers, A E Dauton Services Ltd (formerly Edmund Walker (Holdings) Ltd). The

h appeal to this court is brought pursuant to the leave of the Employment Appeal Tribunal.

The employers are members of a large group of companies dealing with components for the motor industry. Mr Polkey, who is now aged 57, was employed by the employers as a van driver. He entered their employment on 19 June 1978 and was responsible for delivering components to a number of regular customers engaged in the stripping and reconditioning of engines whose works lay on the route from Nottingham to Derby and

j Mansfield.

In the summer of 1982 the employers had to consider a reduction in overheads in order to stem the financial losses which had been incurred during the previous months. Matters came to a head when the figures for July 1982 became available. At that time the employers employed four van drivers, three men, including Mr Polkey, and a woman, Mrs Brenner. It was decided that the company could not afford to lose storekeepers or stockkeepers and that the reductions in staff including some reorganisation of duties would have to be made among the van drivers.   *a*

The decision to declare redundancies was made on 16 or 17 August 1982. On 18 August a discussion took place between Mr French, the divisional general manager, and Mr Marlow, the branch manager, in the course of which it appears to have been agreed that the four van drivers would be replaced by two van salesmen and a representative.

On 20 August Mr Marlow told Mr French that he had come to the conclusion that none of the three male van drivers was capable of working as a van salesman, that only   *b* Mrs Brenner was suitable for transfer to the new duties, and that accordingly three van drivers, including Mr Polkey, would have to be made redundant.

The first that Mr Polkey himself knew of the matter was when he was called to Mr Marlow's office at 2 pm on 27 August 1982 and was told that he had been made redundant. He was handed a redundancy letter setting out the payments which were due to him. He was then driven home.   *c*

Not surprisingly, the industrial tribunal commented unfavourably on the fact that there had been no consultation whatever with the employees who were to be made redundant and on the fact that Mr Polkey had been given no warning. They said:

> 'The respondents like all employers are under an obligation to consult both in accordance with the Code of Practice and now under the guidance of the recent case   *d* of *Williams v Compair Maxam Ltd* [1982] ICR 156. They are also required to give employees as much notice as possible of forthcoming redundancies. In this case we accept that the decision was not made until 16 or 17 August but the existence of a redundancy situation had been known for a long time. Mr Marlow called Mr Polkey into his office at 2 pm on 27 August, told him quite out of the blue that he was redundant and handed to him his redundancy letter. He then called in Mr Ward,   *e* one of his fellow drivers, got him to take Mr Polkey home and on his return made him redundant also. There could be no more heartless disregard of the provisions of the Code of Practice than that ... We feel that the respondents have behaved extremely badly. There is nothing that excuses their failure to consult ...'

The reference to the code of practice was a reference to the Industrial Relations Code   *f* of Practice issued by the Advisory Conciliation and Arbitration Service pursuant to s 6(1) of the Employment Protection Act 1975. The purpose of the Code of Practice is to give practical guidance for promoting good industrial relations.

Having expressed their disapproval of what had happened, however, the industrial tribunal continued as follows:

> 'The Tribunal unfortunately cannot stop there. It has to consider whether had   *g* there been consultation the result would have been any different. Mr Polkey has told us that one of his duties was to take telephone calls from customers before he commenced his round and that frequently he made telephone calls to customers to see if there was anything they would be likely to be needing before he set out, and that having completed a delivery he would then ask if there was anything needed on the next round. To that extent he kept the supply of spare parts flowing easily,   *h* and conveniently. He has also produced a document which confirms that he had previously been employed in a telephone sales capacity. The fact, however, is that his own customers had disappeared. Selling in this undertaking requires familiarity with very complicated catalogues. Mr Ward has told us that he on occasions looked up items for Mr Polkey in the catalogue. Mr Polkey told us that on occasions   *j* customers already knew the numbers and supplied them. He and Mr Ward have said that Mrs Brenner did not have knowledge of the garages upon whom calls were made and was not familiar with the catalogue. Mr Marlow's evidence was that she had the personality necessary for a sales position and that she had already brought back former customers ... At the end of the day we have no alternative but to find

a
that in this case had they acted in accordance with the Code of Practice, as interpreted in the recent case, the result would not have been any different, and we have therefore unhappily to reject this application.'

Mr Polkey appealed against the rejection of his application to the Employment Appeal Tribunal.

b
At the hearing of the appeal, however, it was accepted on Mr Polkey's behalf that the Employment Appeal Tribunal had no alternative but to dismiss his appeal because it was bound by previous authorities. Nevertheless, leave to appeal to this court was sought and obtained from the Employment Appeal Tribunal.

The main argument addressed to this court by counsel for Mr Polkey was that once the industrial tribunal had determined that in the course of the dismissal the employers had failed to observe material provisions of the code of practice relating to consultation

c
they should have found that Mr Polkey had been unfairly dismissed. The question whether the failure to consult had made any difference was only relevant when the tribunal came to consider what remedies might be available, but on the proper construction of s 57(3) of the Employment Protection (Consolidation) Act 1978 the issue of unfair dismissal should have been determined in Mr Polkey's favour. It was also argued by way of an alternative that even if the tribunal might have been free to inquire

d
whether the failure to consult had made any difference they misdirected themselves in holding that they were under an obligation to make this inquiry and that this misdirection provided a further ground of appeal.

Counsel for Mr Polkey did not pursue, however, a further submission adumbrated in the amended notice of appeal, but not argued before the Employment Appeal Tribunal, to the effect that the finding of the industrial tribunal that the failure to consult made no

e
difference was perverse. I need say no more therefore about this third argument.

By s 54 of the 1978 Act every employee in qualifying employment has 'the right not to be unfairly dismissed by his employer'. Accordingly, where a question is raised whether the dismissal of an employee was fair or unfair, it is first necessary for the employer to show what was the reason or the principal reason for the dismissal and that it was a reason falling within s 57(2) of the 1978 Act or 'some other substantial reason of

f
a kind such as to justify the dismissal of an employee holding the position which that employee held.'

In the instant case, the employers satisfied this burden by showing that Mr Polkey was redundant, which is a reason specified in s 57(2)(c). It therefore became necessary for the industrial tribunal to apply the statutory test which is set out in s 57(3) of the 1978 Act in these terms:

g
'Where the employer has fulfilled the requirements of subsection (1), then, subject to sections 58 to 62, the determination of the question whether the dismissal was fair or unfair, having regard to the reason shown by the employer, shall depend on whether in the circumstances (including the size and administrative resources of the employer's undertaking) the employer acted reasonably or unreasonably in

h
treating it as a sufficient reason for dismissing the employee; and that question shall be determined in accordance with equity and the substantial merits of the case.'

The case for Mr Polkey was that by failing to consult him and by acting in flagrant disregard of the code of practice the employers had acted unreasonably in treating redundancy as a sufficient reason and that, in accordance with equity and the substantial merits of the case, the question whether the dismissal was fair or unfair should be

j
determined against the employers.

At this stage, submitted counsel for Mr Polkey, it was unnecessary and impermissible to speculate what action the employers might have taken if they had done what ex hypothesi they had not done and had consulted Mr Polkey before they declared him redundant.

In developing this argument, counsel drew our attention to the remedies for unfair dismissal set out in the 1978 Act and stressed that the primary remedy for unfair *a* dismissal was reinstatement or re-engagement. Moreover, he argued, even though reinstatement or re-engagement were not practicable (see s 69(5)(*b*) and (6)(*b*)) and even though no compensation for lost wages was payable under s 72 because dismissal was inevitable, the employee might still have a right to recover some sum in respect of loss sustained by him in consequence of the dismissal including any expenses reasonably incurred: see s 74(1) and (2)(*a*). *b*

The scheme of the 1978 Act suggested that a finding of unfair dismissal should be made where the procedure involved in the dismissal was manifestly unfair and that any inquiry as to what might have happened in any event should be postponed to the stage when remedies were being investigated.

Counsel for Mr Polkey further argued that this approach was in accordance with the principle established in *W Devis & Sons Ltd v Atkins* [1977] 3 All ER 40, [1977] AC 931 *c* that employers could not justify an unfair dismissal by relying on subsequently discovered facts. Moreover, an inquiry by the industrial tribunal as to what effect consultation might have had on the minds of the employers appeared to run counter to the well-established rule in *British Homes Stores Ltd v Burchell* [1980] ICR 303 that the industrial tribunal should not substitute their own judgment for that of the employers themselves.

In addition, counsel for Mr Polkey drew our attention to the recent decision in *West* *d* *Midlands Co-op Society Ltd v Tipton* [1986] 1 All ER 513, [1986] AC 536, where it was held that an industrial tribunal were entitled to make a finding of unfair dismissal where the employers in a case which did not involve any undisputed serious misconduct had refused to entertain the employee's contractual right of appeal. The basis of the decision was that evidence in such an appeal would have been admissible for the purpose of considering whether the employer's real reason for dismissal could reasonably be treated *e* as sufficient. Counsel submitted that in the present case the fact that Mr Polkey had been denied the opportunity of putting forward some alternative to redundancy entitled and indeed required the industrial tribunal to make a finding that the dismissal was unfair.

In support of his submissions, counsel for Mr Polkey placed reliance on the judgment of the Employment Appeal Tribunal, delivered by Browne-Wilkinson J, in *Sillifant v* *f* *Powell Duffryn Timber Ltd* [1983] IRLR 91.

In *Sillifant's* case the Employment Appeal Tribunal expressed the opinion that what was there described as the *British Labour Pump* principle (see *British Labour Pump Co Ltd v Byrne* [1979] ICR 347) was logically inconsistent with the provisions of s 57(3) of the 1978 Act, but it held that the validity of the principle was part of the ratio decidendi of the decision of the Court of Appeal in *W & J Wass Ltd v Binns* [1982] ICR 486 and that it was bound by authority to hold that the *British Labour Pump* principle was good law. *g*

If this analysis by the Employment Appeal Tribunal is right, then of course this court too is bound by the decision in *W & J Wass Ltd v Binns* [1982] ICR 486. Nevertheless, I propose to start by considering the matter on the basis that this court is not so bound. At the same time, it is necessary to remember that the present case is one of redundancy.

It will be convenient to set out again the relevant provisions of s 57(3) of the 1978 Act: *h*

> 'Where the employer has fulfilled the requirements of subsection (1), then . . . the determination of the question whether the dismissal was fair or unfair, having regard to the reason shown by the employer, shall depend on whether in the circumstances (including the size and administrative resources of the employer's undertaking) the employer acted reasonably or unreasonably in treating it as a sufficient reason for dismissing the employee; and that question shall be determined *j* in accordance with equity and the substantial merits of the case.'

It is apparent therefore that in determining the issue whether the dismissal was fair or unfair the industrial tribunal have to decide whether in the circumstances the employer *a* acted reasonably or unreasonably in treating the proved reason (or principal reason) for dismissal as a sufficient reason for dismissing the employee.

It is further apparent from the decision of the House of Lords in *W Devis & Sons Ltd v Atkins* [1977] 3 All ER 40, [1977] AC 931 that an employer is not entitled to justify a dismissal by reliance on facts which were not known to him at the time of the dismissal.

b On the other hand, in a misconduct case, an employer can justify dismissal if he acted fairly on the facts and in the circumstances known to him or of which he ought to have been aware at the time of dismissal even though the employee was in fact innocent of the misconduct attributed to him.

c The question can then be asked: if an employer cannot justify dismissal and if an employee cannot complain of a dismissal on the basis of facts not known to the employer at the time of dismissal, how can it be right for an industrial tribunal to embark on the speculative exercise of examining facts which were not known to the employer at the time of dismissal in order to decide whether a procedural defect made any difference?

At first sight, this question appears to require the answer that such an exercise would be contrary to the decision in *W Devis & Sons Ltd v Atkins* because it would allow an employer to rely on facts not known to him at the time of dismissal, or, where an internal appeal procedure has been put in operation, not known to him at the time when the final decision to uphold the dismissal was taken.

d On further analysis, however, it seems to me that an answer on these lines overlooks the crucial distinction between the reason for a dismissal and the manner in which the dismissal is effected.

Section 57(1) of the 1978 Act provides:

e 'In determining for the purposes of this Part [Pt V] whether the dismissal of an employee was fair or unfair, it shall be for the employer to show—(*a*) what was the reason (or, if there was more than one, the principal reason) for the dismissal, and (*b*) that it was a reason falling within subsection (2) or some other substantial reason of a kind such as to justify the dismissal of an employee holding the position which that employee held.'

f I have already set out a little earlier the terms of s 57(3) of the 1978 Act.

It will be seen therefore that a complaint of unfair dismissal will succeed where the employer fails to establish that the reason for dismissal was one of those specified in s 57(2) or where the tribunal reaches the conclusion that even though the employer has fulfilled the requirements of s 57(1) he acted unreasonably in treating the reason shown by him as a sufficient reason for dismissing the employee. But, on the other hand, a *g* complaint of unfair dismissal will not succeed *merely* because of the manner in which the dismissal was carried out.

A failure to observe a proper procedure may make a dismissal unfair, but this is not because such failure by itself makes the dismissal unfair but because the failure, for example, to give an employee an opportunity to explain may lead the tribunal to the conclusion that the employer, in the circumstances, acted unreasonably in treating the *h* reason for dismissal as a sufficient reason. The tribunal will look at the practical effect of the failure to observe the proper procedure in order to decide whether or not the dismissal was unfair.

Where an employee is dismissed for alleged misconduct and he then complains that he was unfairly dismissed, it is to be anticipated that the industrial tribunal will usually need to consider (a) the nature and gravity of the alleged misconduct, (b) the information *j* on which the employer based his decision, (c) whether there was any other information which the employer could or should have obtained or any other step which he should have taken before he dismissed the employee.

Similarly, in a case of alleged redundancy, it is to be anticipated that the industrial tribunal will usually need to consider (a) the information on which the employer based his decision to dismiss the employee as redundant and the method of selection which he used and (b) whether there was any other information which the employer could or *a* should have obtained or any other step which he should have taken before he dismissed the employee.

In some cases of misconduct, however, the misconduct may be so grave and the information available to the employer so clear that the tribunal will be likely to conclude that no further inquiries by the employer were necessary. Indeed, counsel for Mr Polkey was prepared to concede that there are cases where serious misconduct will justify instant *b* dismissal and the failure to comply with a disciplinary procedure agreement will be irrelevant: see *Bailey v BP Oil (Kent Refinery) Ltd* [1980] ICR 642 at 648, where Lawton LJ gave the example of an employee who was seen by the works manager and others to stab another man in the back with a knife.

But in many cases of misconduct the tribunal will need to consider whether the employer, either in accordance with some disciplinary procedure or otherwise, should *c* have taken steps to obtain further information either from the employee or from elsewhere because such information might throw light on the sufficiency of the employer's reason for dismissal.

But the failure to obtain this information does not ipso facto render the dismissal unfair, and it seems to me to be both logical and desirable to require the industrial tribunal to try to evaluate the effect in practice of the failure. Thus, as counsel for Mr *d* Polkey acknowledged, there may be cases where the evidence of misconduct is not so clear as to justify instant dismissal and which could be capable of explanation, but where on examination, the employee has no explanation to put forward. In such a case, the failure to seek an explanation from the employee, which fairness would in principle require, will not make any difference.

In a case where dismissal is on the ground of redundancy, the matter may have to be *e* looked at rather differently because the system adopted for the selection of the individual for redundancy may be at the very centre of the inquiry when the tribunal comes to determine whether the employer has acted reasonably or unreasonably in treating redundancy as a sufficient reason for dismissing the employee concerned.

The decision of the Employment Appeal Tribunal in *Williams v Compair Maxam Ltd* *f* [1982] ICR 156 demonstrates the importance of the use of a fair system. Furthermore, it is to be noted that s 59 of the 1978 Act contains special provisions rendering a dismissal on the ground of redundancy unfair in certain specified circumstances, including cases where the selection for dismissal was in contravention of a customary arrangement or agreed procedure relating to redundancy and there were no special reasons justifying a departure from that arrangement or procedure. *g*

But where s 59 does not apply, it seems to me to be proper and indeed necessary for the tribunal to investigate the effect of the failure to consult the employee or to warn him or to hold discussions or as the case may be.

In some cases, the facts may show beyond peradventure that no discussions or other steps could have made any difference whatever because the state of the company was so grave. In other cases, the matter will be more evenly balanced. But, for my part, I can see *h* no objection in principle to the tribunal seeking to evaluate the effect in practice of any failure by the employer to observe the provisions of a code of practice or of the guidelines prescribed in cases such as *Williams v Compair Maxam Ltd*.

But even if this analysis of the law is wrong, I agree that the Employment Appeal Tribunal was bound, as this court is bound, by the decision of the Court of Appeal in *W & J Wass Ltd v Binns* [1982] ICR 486. In that case the Court of Appeal held that there *j* was nothing in the speech of Viscount Dilhorne in *W Devis & Sons Ltd v Atkins* [1977] 3 All ER 40, [1977] AC 931 to throw doubt on the decision of the Employment Appeal Tribunal in *British Labour Pump Co Ltd v Byrne* [1979] ICR 347.

It follows, therefore, that in my judgment, the industrial tribunal did not misdirect themselves in law when they undertook an inquiry on the lines indorsed by the decision *a* of the Employment Appeal Tribunal in *British Labour Pump Co Ltd v Byrne* and by this court in *W & J Wass Ltd v Binns*. Indeed, in the light of the authorities, it was right to regard itself as bound to undertake this inquiry.

Prima facie, as the reason for dismissal was redundancy, the reason was a valid reason. The failure to consult did not automatically render the dismissal unfair: it was for the tribunal to determine whether that failure showed that the employers had acted reasonably or unreasonably in treating redundancy as a sufficient reason for the dismissal

b of Mr Polkey. For that purpose, they had to look at all the circumstances including the consequences of the failure.

Accordingly, for the reasons which I have endeavoured to explain, I would dismiss this appeal.

c **NICHOLLS LJ.** I agree.

SIR GEORGE WALLER. I agree with the judgment of Neill LJ. I will briefly express my view. In my opinion, a distinction has to be drawn between the reasons for dismissal and the manner of dismissal. In this case, the reason for dismissal was redundancy: it was urgently necessary to reduce costs and the employers decided to dispense with van drivers

d and employ van salesmen instead. There were four van drivers, one of whom was a woman. The employers decided to make the three men redundant and to continue to employ the woman as a van salesman because they thought that she had potential as a salesman.

The employers then dismissed Mr Polkey (and the other two male drivers) in a manner fully described by the industrial tribunal. The manner was not only about as tactless as anything could be, but was also not in accord with the provisions of the code of practice.

e The industrial tribunal, having inquired into what would have happened if the code of practice had been complied with, came to the conclusion that it would have made no difference. In other words, the employer acted reasonably in treating redundancy as a sufficient reason for dismissing Mr Polkey. I agree with Neill LJ that the industrial tribunal did not misdirect themselves in law in carrying out that inquiry. They were

f saying that prima facie the reasons of the employer were good. But they allowed the employee to call evidence which might have thrown doubt on that conclusion. Having regard to the manner of dismissal, and in particular the failure to follow the code of practice, it was only right to allow the employee to call this evidence. The evidence did not throw doubt on the conclusion. I would dismiss this appeal.

g *Appeal dismissed. Leave to appeal to the House of Lords granted.*

Solicitors: *Seifert Sedley Williams*, agents for *Gregsons*, Nottingham (for Mr Polkey); *Gorna & Co*, Manchester (for the employers).

Celia Fox   Barrister.

R v Corby Juvenile Court, ex parte M

QUEEN'S BENCH DIVISION
WAITE J
10, 17 OCTOBER 1986

Child – Care – Local authority – Access – Application by parent for access order – Right of access to children in care – Child taken into care before enactment of legislation introducing right of access to children in care – Whether parental right of access applying to children taken into care before introduction of right – Interpretation Act 1978, s 17 – Child Care Act 1980, ss 3, 12A(1), 12C.

In 1977 the applicant's two children were taken into voluntary care by a local authority. In 1978 the local authority resolved under s 2(1) of the Children Act 1948 to assume parental rights and duties over the children thereby putting them into compulsory care. The children were placed with foster parents with a view to eventual adoption and in 1985 as a preliminary to adoption the local authority served notice of its intention to terminate parental access under Pt IA (ss 12A–12G) of the Child Care Act 1980. Section 2 of the 1948 Act was consolidated in s 3ᵈ of the 1980 Act, which, as amended, introduced the rights of a parent to object to the termination of access and to apply for access to children in compulsory care. Section 12A(1)(a) to (h)ᵇ of the 1980 Act, which set out the categories of children in compulsory care which were affected, made no specific reference to children who, as a result of a resolution passed under s 2 of the 1948 Act, were in compulsory care prior to the coming into force of the 1980 Act. The applicant's application for an access order under s 12C(1)ᶜ of the 1980 Act was refused by the juvenile court on the ground that it had no jurisdiction. The applicant applied for an order of mandamus requiring the juvenile court to hear and determine her application. The question arose whether the category of children in care as the result of a resolution passed under s 2 of the 1948 Act was deemed by s 17ᵈ of the Interpretation Act 1978 to be included in s 12A of the 1980 Act notwithstanding the absence of an express provision to that effect.

Held – Since the intention of Parliament in enacting the 1980 Act and amendments thereto was that parents of all children in compulsory care should have a right to be heard in objection to the termination of parental access, the failure of s 12A of the 1980 Act to enumerate exhaustively every category of children in care was not sufficient to show to a 'contrary intention' to refer to a re-enacted provision, for the purposes of s 17 of the 1978 Act. Accordingly, a resolution passed under s 2 of the 1948 Act was deemed to take effect under s 17(2)(b) of the 1978 Act as if it had been passed under s 3 of the 1980 Act. It followed that the juvenile court had had jurisdiction to entertain the applicant's application for an access order. In any event, the applicant fell within the scope of Pt IA of the 1980 Act because, construing s 12A(1)(h) in the light of that Act's manifest purpose, the reference to a resolution passed under s 3 was by necessary

---

a   Section 3, so far as material, provides:
      '(2) If the local authority know the whereabouts of the person whose parental rights and duties have vested in them by virtue of a resolution passed [by them], they shall forthwith after it is passed serve notice in writing of its passing on him.
      (3) Every notice served by a local authority under subsection (2) above shall inform the person on whom the notice is served of his right to object to the resolution and the effect of any objection made by him . . .'

b   Section 12A(1), so far as material, is set out at p 995 g, post

c   Section 12C(1) provides: 'A parent, guardian or custodian on whom a notice under section 12B above is served may apply for an order under this section (in this Part of this Act referred to as an "access order").'

d   Section 17, so far as material, is set out at p 994 j to p 995 a, post

a inference deemed to include a reference to any antecedent resolution passed under the provisions of the subsequently repealed s 2 of the 1948 Act. The application would accordingly be allowed and an order of mandamus would issue (see p 997 *d e g j* to p 998 *e*, post).

Notes

b For the care of a child by a local authority, see 24 Halsbury's Laws (4th edn) para 787, for the assumption of parental rights by a local authority, see ibid paras 790–793, and for cases on the subject, see 28(2) Digest (Reissue) 940–943, 2432–2442.

For the Child Care Act 1980, ss 3, 12A, 12C, see 6 Halsbury's Statutes (4th edn) 535, 545, 547.

For the Interpretation Act 1978, s 17, see 48 Halsbury's Statutes (3rd edn) 1306.

c **Case referred to in judgment**
A v Liverpool City Council [1981] 2 All ER 385, [1982] AC 363, [1981] 2 WLR 948, HL.

Application for judicial review

The mother of two children in the care of Northamptonshire County Council applied,
d with leave of McNeill J given on 11 April 1986, for (i) an order of mandamus directed to the juvenile court sitting at Corby in the petty sessional division of Corby in the county of Northampton requiring them to exercise the jurisdiction conferred on them by s 12A of the Child Care Act 1980 and in particular requiring them to hear and determine an application for an access order made by the mother under s 12C(1) of that Act and (ii) further or alternatively, an order of certiorari to quash the order of the juvenile court made on 9 December 1985 dismissing the mother's application for an access order made
e under s 12C(1) of the 1980 Act on the ground of want of jurisdiction. The facts are set out in the judgment.

William Coker for the mother.
Jeremy Posnansky for the local authority.
f *Charles Wide* for the guardian ad litem.

Cur adv vult

17 October. The following judgment was delivered.

g **WAITE J.** This application for judicial review provides yet another illustration of the sad paradox that the law of child care, though designed to cater principally for the problems that press on the least advantaged and most defenceless families in our society, has nevertheless been allowed to become one of the most complex areas within the legal system. A mass of separate enactments, all with their confusing amendments and cross-references to each other, has given growth to a legislative thicket through which even
h the most practised members of the legal and social work professions have to struggle to find their way.

As for the people whose lives are most closely affected by it, there seems to be a particular harshness in requiring them, in addition to all their other difficulties, to undergo the ordeal of taking part as bewildered amateurs in a game whose rules are understood only by those who play it professionally.

j The applicant in this instance is a mother whose two children, now aged 12 and 10, were received when they were very young into the voluntary care of a local authority. That was converted into compulsory care when, shortly afterwards, the mother lost her right to recover the children as the result of the passing by the authority of a resolution assuming her parental rights.

Years later she learnt that the authority was proposing to terminate her access to the children altogether, as a preliminary to the children's adoption by foster parents. When she sought to take advantage of recent changes in the law designed to enable natural parents to obtain a court hearing before being deprived of access, she was faced with a technical objection. It was pointed out that the relevant amending legislation had omitted, perhaps by an oversight or perhaps deliberately, to make any reference at all to children whose parents' rights had been assumed (as hers had been) by resolution passed before a date in 1981. The regrettable consequence is that before the human aspects of this family problem have been able to be investigated at all, the court has had to wrestle, on a preliminary point of jurisdiction, with a complex statutory analysis of the kind that it would be natural to experience in a Revenue appeal, but which seems cruelly out of place in a forum where the future of two young lives has to be decided.

That will explain why, before giving any further description of the factual background to the case, it is necessary for me first to describe the governing statutory provisions. They are as follows.

1. *The Children Act 1948*   Section 1 created a category of voluntary care which could be terminated at any time by the parent on giving the due period of notice. Sections 2 and 3 empowered the local authority, in effect, to convert that into compulsory care by passing a resolution assuming the parental rights of the child's parents; one of the results of which was to remove the right of the parent to give notice terminating the care.

2. *The care order legislation*   Compulsory care more commonly arises as the result of a care order in court proceedings. According to the Department of Health and Social Security Review of Child Care Law (September 1985) there are no less than 20 separate sections in various statutory provisions under which such an order may be made. The governing statutes include: the Children and Young Persons Act 1969; the Domestic Proceedings and Magistrates' Courts Act 1978, repealing and in part re-enacting the Matrimonial Proceedings (Magistrates' Courts) Act 1960; the Guardianship Act 1973; and the Children Act 1975.

3. *The Child Care Act 1980*   This was a consolidating statute which repealed and re-enacted, in ss 2, 3, and 4 respectively, the provisions for voluntary care and its conversion into compulsory care by use of a parental rights resolution which had formerly been contained in ss 1, 2, and 3 of the 1948 Act. It came into force on 1 April 1981. The 1980 Act included transitional provisions which, so far as relevant, are expressed in these terms in s 89:

'(1) This Act shall have effect subject to the transitional provisions and savings set out in Schedule 4 to this Act . . .

(4) The inclusion in this Act of any express saving or amendment shall not be taken as prejudicing the operation of section 16 or 17 of the Interpretation Act 1978 . . .'

Schedule 4 mentioned in s 89(1) introduces para 1 under the rubric: 'Children in care under Children Act 1948'. It reads as follows:

'Any reference in this Act to a child in the care of a local authority under section 2 of this Act shall be construed as including a reference to a child received into the care of the authority under section 1 of the Children Act 1948.'

That is the only transitional provision dealing with children who are in care otherwise than under a care order. There is no specific saving provision either in the main body of the Act or in Sch 4 to cover the case of children who, prior to the coming into force of the 1980 Act on 1 April 1981, were in care that had become compulsory as a result of the passing of a parental rights resolution under the repealed s 2 of the 1948 Act.

4. *The Interpretation Act 1978*   Section 17 (one of the sections expressly imported by the transitional provisions of the 1980 Act) provides, by sub-s (2), as follows:

'Where an Act repeals and re-enacts, with or without modification, a previous enactment then, unless the contrary intention appears,—(a) any reference in any

a other enactment to the enactment so repealed shall be construed as a reference to
the provision re-enacted; (*b*) in so far as any subordinate legislation made or other
thing done under the enactment so repealed, or having effect as if so made or done,
could have been made or done under the provision re-enacted, it shall have effect as
if made or done under that provision.'

b 5. *The Health and Social Services and Social Security Adjudications Act 1983*   This statute
amended the 1980 Act by giving parents a limited right of objection in cases where a
local authority is proposing to terminate access to a child in compulsory care. A new Pt
IA was inserted into the 1980 Act requiring notice of termination to be given to the
parent, who was thereupon allowed a right of application to the juvenile court in
proceedings in which the child's welfare is the paramount consideration, in which there
is a power in suitable cases to order that the child be represented by an independent
c guardian ad litem, and to which a code of practice propounded under the statute is
expressed to apply.

The right thus given to parents of an opportunity of a court hearing before they can
be deprived of access to a child in care is an important one, designed to give parents a
measure of relief from the more extreme consequences of the House of Lords decision in
A v Liverpool City Council [1981] 2 All ER 385, [1982] AC 363 that the wardship
d jurisdiction of the High Court could not be used to challenge the reasonableness or
fairness of a decision taken by a local authority in the exercise of its powers under the
statutory code of the 1948 Act. It thus has constitutional as well as personal significance,
establishing as it does the right not to be deprived of access to a child in care without a
hearing as one of the ordinary liberties enjoyed by every subject.

The new remedy was not, however, defined empirically as one which applied to all
e children in compulsory care. The new s 12A introduced by the 1983 Act set out, by
explicit definition, to specify the categories of children to which it would and would not
apply. In sub-s (2) there was a specific exclusion of all children in care as a result of an
order of the High Court.

As to inclusion, there was a specific inventory in sub-s (1) of the categories of children
in compulsory care to which it applied. The first seven items listed in paras (*a*) to (*g*) are
f all instances of statutory care orders made under the enactments which I have already
mentioned in 2 above.

The only provision dealing with children in care otherwise than under an order of the
court is para (*h*), which when read in conjunction with the opening words of the main
subsection reads as follows:

g '(1) Subject to subsection (2) below, this Part of this Act applies to any child in
the care of a local authority in consequence . . . (*h*) of a resolution under section 3
above.'

That completes the account of the governing legislation. It is common ground between
counsel that so far as that specific enactment is concerned, it contains a gap or lacuna.
h Section 12A(1)(*h*) speaks only of children in local authority care 'in consequence of a
resolution under section 3' of the 1980 Act. There is no specific reference, either in the
original consolidating and transitional provisions of the 1980 Act or in the terms of
application stated for the amendments introduced by the 1983 Act, to children who at
the commencement of the 1980 Act on 1 April 1981 had already been received into care
before that date, and whose care had by then already become compulsory as the result of
a resolution passed under s 2 of the 1948 Act to extinguish the parents' rights.
j It is also common ground that the reference to children being in care 'in consequence'
of a parental rights resolution is inappositely drafted, for it elides the two entirely separate
concepts of care on the one hand and the passing of the resolution on the other, and
overlooks the fact that the care, albeit at first voluntary, must in point of time precede
the passing of the resolution, and cannot therefore be properly described as a consequence
of it. Each side is content, however, to treat that as a mere misuse of language, and no

one has invited me to draw any wider inferences from it as shedding light one way or
the other on the general legislative intention.

The sole issue in this case is whether children in the category, covered by a pre-April
1981 parental rights resolution, should be deemed, notwithstanding the absence of
express words in the two statutes, nevertheless to be included by implication.

The factual circumstances in which that issue arises can be very shortly stated, because
they are not in dispute. The two children were born respectively on 5 October 1974 and
7 July 1976. While still very young they were received, for reasons which it is not
relevant or necessary to state, into the voluntary care of the Northamptonshire County
Council on 5 May 1977. That was converted into compulsory care in the following year,
when the county council passed a resolution on 19 April 1978 under s 2 of the 1948 Act
assuming parental rights and duties in respect of both children. They remained in such
care for seven years, living with long-term foster parents who had been selected by the
county council with an eye to possible eventual adoption.

By 1985 the county council had decided that the time was ripe to pave the way for
adoption by terminating parental access. The children's mother, who is the only parent
with relevant claims to access, was served on 7 August 1985, with notices of the county
council's intention to terminate access to both children. Those notices were purportedly
served under Pt IA of the 1980 Act as amended by the 1983 Act, the county council being
at that time unaware of the statutory lacuna to which I have just referred.

The mother, purporting for her part to invoke the same statutory procedure, responded
in due course with a complaint to the juvenile court seeking an access order. Her advisers
were also unaware of any gap in the explicit legislation which might render such a
complaint unmaintainable.

The justices' clerk, however, was aware of the lacuna. Public attention has recently
been drawn to it by the commentary to s 12A given in *Clarke Hall and Morrison on Children*
(10th edn, 1986) para **A** 214. It has, no doubt, been pointed out elsewhere as well.

The issue of jurisdiction was therefore taken by the justices and dealt with at an
adjourned hearing on 9 December 1985, when the juvenile court dismissed the mother's
complaint on the grounds that they had no jurisdiction to hear it.

The mother now challenges that decision, seeking by way of judicial review an order
of mandamus requiring the juvenile court to exercise jurisdiction under s 12A and deal
with the mother's claim on its merits.

The children's guardian ad litem, while reserving his position entirely on the question
whether access should be allowed or terminated if the merits of the case are allowed to be
investigated, supports the mother's application on the ground that it would be in the
children's best interests for an investigation of such merits to take place.

For its part the county council, though entirely willing in the first instance to operate
the machinery of Pt IA of the 1980 Act as amended, has, quite reasonably and properly in
my judgment, taken the view that it ought to adopt the objection to jurisdiction raised
by the magistrates and instruct counsel in this court to ensure that the issue of law, which
is bound to affect other cases as well as this one, is fully argued.

I am grateful to both sides for their clear and succinct arguments. Counsel for the
county council rests his case on the well-established principles of statutory construction:
firstly, the words of the enactment itself, which must, if they are plain and unambiguous,
be applied as they stand, however strongly it may be suspected that the result does not
represent Parliament's real intention; and, secondly, that Parliament is strongly presumed
not to make mistakes (see 44 Halsbury's Laws (4th edn) paras 856, 862). He invites me to
see both the 1980 Act as originally enacted and the amendments to it introduced by the
1983 Act as instances of meticulously detailed specific legislation, undertaken with such
thoroughness as to provide an exhaustive definition of the Parliamentary intention which
allows no play for the implication of any unstated purpose. Both Acts list the categories
of children to which they are intended to apply, and neither includes within that list the

a category represented by children who are the subject of a parental rights resolution passed before April 1981.

The 1978 Act is of no relevance, counsel submits, for two reasons. Firstly, the phrase 'other thing done' in s 17(2)(b) of the Act falls to be construed ejusdem generis with the antecedent words 'subordinate legislation made', so as to restrict the 'thing done' to the genus of a legislative act of government in the nature of a statutory instrument, decree or byelaw. A merely administrative act of local government, such as the passing of a
b resolution to assume the private rights of an individual, would lie well outside that ambit. There is therefore no scope, he says, for treating the county council's resolution of 23 March 1978 as a 'thing done' under the repealed s 2 of the 1948 Act, and capable as such of being saved by s 17(2)(b) of the 1978 Act through being deemed to have been done under the re-enacted counterpart of s 2, ie s 3 of the 1980 Act.

He alternatively argues that if that be wrong, and s 17 does, prima facie, apply to deem
c the original resolution to have been passed under the 1980 Act and thus bring it directly within the scope of s 12A(1)(h), such deeming operates only 'unless the contrary intention appears'. The contrary intention does very much appear here, he submits, and in support of that he points to all the specific indications of parliamentary intention already mentioned; indications so specific, he argues, as to leave the court with no alternative but to apply in all its rigour the principle summarised in the maxim expressio unius exclusio
d est alterius.

Counsel for the mother, with the support of counsel for the guardian ad litem, argues that it would be illogical and wrong to attribute to Parliament so capricious an intention as to draw an arbitrary distinction between children whose compulsory retention in care happened to have resulted from a parental rights resolution passed before 1 April 1981,
e and those whose compulsory retention happened to have resulted from a similar resolution passed after that date, and then proceed to include the latter within, but to exclude the former from, the scope of the parental right to be heard in objection to a termination of access.

He acknowledges the gaps in the 1980 and 1983 Acts, so far as the legislation is explicit; but he prays in aid s 17 of the 1978 Act for the purpose already referred to, and relies
f generally on the principle (stated in 44 Halsbury's Laws (4th edn), para 860) that statutes must be so construed as to make them operative and avoid defeating the manifest intentions of the legislature. He further points out that the exclusion of children who are the subject of a pre-April 1981 resolution from the operation of the 1980 Act would result in their being deprived altogether of the protection from abduction or unlawful concealment afforded by ss 13 and 14 of that Act. If, to avoid that consequence, they are
g to be included within the scope of the 1980 Act, then it is a short and easy step from there, says counsel for the mother, to include them also by implication within the scope of the amendments introduced by Pt IA.

Making a choice, as I must, between these conflicting submissions, the arguments on the mother's side should in my judgment be allowed to prevail. Parliament cannot have intended, either when it enacted the 1980 Act, or when it introduced the 1983
h amendments, to have allowed a whole section of the child population to vanish from legislative view as though they had gone off at the heels of the Pied Piper.

It may well be that the draftsman did indeed stumble, and that despite his methodical attempt to identify for express reference every category of child in compulsory care who was intended to be covered, first by the 1980 consolidation and then by the 1983 amendment to introduce parental rights of objection to access termination, he overlooked
j provision for those who were the subject of a pre-April 1981 resolution. The deliberate reference in the transitional provisions of the 1980 Act to s 17 of the 1978 Act, whose terms I construe in the sense contended for by counsel for the mother seems to me, however, to show Parliament contemplating expressly that such an oversight might occur, and making appropriate provision for it.

The legislative intention is plain. Parliament intended the parents of all children in compulsory care, with the exception of those specifically excluded, to benefit from the *a* important and valuable rights introduced by Pt IA of the 1980 Act. The fact that a draftsman has made an unsuccessful attempt to enumerate exhaustively all the prior enactments thought to be affected by new or amending legislation cannot be enough, in my judgment, particularly in an area like this where the prior enactments are legion and widely scattered, to amount to a 'contrary intention' for the purposes of s 17(2) of the 1978 Act.   *b*

I hold, accordingly, that the county council's resolution of 19 April 1978 was a 'thing done' under the repealed s 2 of the 1948 Act within the meaning of that term as it is used in s 17(2)(*b*) of the 1978 Act, that such resolution could equally have been passed under s 3 of the 1980 Act in which s 2 was re-enacted, that there has been no contrary intention shown to displace the operation of s 17(2) and that accordingly, for the purposes of statutory interpretation, the resolution passed under the 1948 Act takes effect under *c* s 17(2)(*b*) as if it had passed under s 3 of the 1980 Act.

If follows that the juvenile court had jurisdiction to entertain the mother's complaint as relating to children in respect of whom a resolution is deemed to have been passed, for the purposes of s 12A(1)(*h*) of the 1980 Act, under s 3 of that Act.

I would add, though such a holding will necessarily be obiter, that even without the assistance of the 1978 Act, I would still have held that the applicant is within the scope of *d* Pt IA of the 1980 Act on the ground that when s 12A(1)(*h*) is construed in the light of the legislation's manifest purpose, the reference to a resolution passed under s 3 must be deemed, by necessary inference, to include a reference to any antecedent resolution passed under the provisions of the subsequently repealed s 2 of the 1948 Act.

The application will be allowed, and I give leave for the order of mandamus to issue as prayed.   *e*

Application allowed.

Solicitors: *Hopkin & Sons*, Mansfield (for the mother); *J E Fursey*, Northampton (for the local authority); *Sharman Jackson & Archer*, Corby (for the guardian ad litem).

Bebe Chua   Barrister.

Chebaro v Chebaro

COURT OF APPEAL, CIVIL DIVISION
PURCHAS, NEILL AND BALCOMBE LJJ
12 DECEMBER 1986, 5 FEBRUARY 1987

Divorce – Financial provision – Order – Order following decree – Jurisdiction – Foreign decree – Legislation giving court power to order financial relief in England and Wales after overseas divorce etc – Whether legislation having retrospective effect – Whether court having power to grant financial relief in cases where overseas divorce etc pronounced before legislation in force – Matrimonial and Family Proceedings Act 1984, s 12(1).

On its true construction s 12(1)[a] of the Matrimonial and Family Proceedings Act 1984 (which provides, inter alia, that where a marriage 'has been' dissolved by a valid foreign divorce either party to the marriage may apply to the court for financial relief) has retrospective effect. It follows that a former spouse whose marriage was dissolved by a foreign divorce before the 1984 Act came into force is entitled to apply under s 12(1) for financial provision (see p 1001 *d e*, p 1003 *f g* and p 1004 *g*, post).

Decision of Sheldon J [1986] 2 All ER 897 affirmed.

Notes

For financial relief in England and Wales after overseas divorce etc, see Supplement to 13 Halsbury's Laws (4th edn) 1180A.

For the retrospective effect of statutes, see 44 ibid paras 921–926, and for cases on the subject, see 45 Digest (Reissue) 430–439, 4246–4352.

For the Matrimonial and Family Proceedings Act 1984, s 12, see 27 Halsbury's Statutes (4th edn) 855.

Cases referred to in judgments

Bonning v Dodsley [1982] 1 All ER 612, [1982] 1 WLR 279, CA.
Carson v Carson and Stoyek [1964] 1 All ER 681, [1964] 1 WLR 511.
Chaterjee v Chaterjee [1976] 1 All ER 719, [1976] Fam 199, [1976] 2 WLR 397, CA.
Chaudhary v Chaudhary [1984] 3 All ER 1017, [1985] Fam 19, [1985] 2 WLR 350, CA.
Lewis v Lewis [1985] 2 All ER 449, [1985] AC 828, [1985] 2 WLR 962, HL; *affg* [1984] 2 All ER 497, [1984] Fam 79, [1984] 3 WLR 45, CA.
Madden v Madden [1974] 1 All ER 673, [1974] 1 WLR 247.
Powys v Powys [1971] 3 All ER 116, [1971] P 340, [1971] 3 WLR 154.
Quazi v Quazi [1979] 3 All ER 897, [1980] AC 744, [1979] 3 WLR 833, HL; *rvsg* [1979] 3 All ER 424, [1980] AC 744, [1979] 3 WLR 402, CA.
Williams v Williams [1971] 2 All ER 764, [1971] P 271, [1971] 3 WLR 92.
Yew Bon Tew v Kenderaan Bas Mara [1982] 3 All ER 833, [1983] AC 553, [1982] 3 WLR 1026, PC.

Appeal

Musbah Chebaro (the husband) appealed with leave against the decision of Sheldon J ([1986] 2 All ER 897, [1986] Fam 71) given on 26 March 1986 whereby he granted the respondent, Mona Chebaro (the wife), leave, pursuant to s 13 of the Matrimonial and Family Proceedings Act 1984, to apply for financial relief under Pt III of that Act, namely an order for periodical payments for herself, a lump sum and a property transfer order of property in Greater Manchester, and ordered that the action be transferred to the Manchester District Registry. The facts are set out in the judgment of Balcombe LJ.

---

a   Section 12(1) is set out at p 1000 *h j*, post

Donald Hart QC and *Martin Allweis* for the husband.
Robert L Johnson QC and *Deborah Lambert* for the wife.   *a*

Cur adv vult

5 February. The following judgments were delivered.

BALCOMBE LJ (giving the first judgment at the invitation of Purchas LJ). Until Pt III   *b*
of the Matrimonial and Family Proceedings Act 1984 was brought into force, our courts
had no power to grant ancillary financial relief after divorce unless the decree had been
granted in this country, notwithstanding that both the property and the parties were
within the jurisdiction. This resulted in a number of cases where the recognition of an
overseas divorce obtained by a husband was the issue before the court. The reason why
the issue arose in this way was because, if the overseas divorce was recognised as valid   *c*
here, there was no longer any marriage subsisting, so that the wife was unable to petition
for a decree of divorce, and was consequently unable to claim financial relief,
notwithstanding that there was property in this country (often the matrimonial home)
and that her ex-husband was living and working here: see e g *Quazi v Quazi* [1979] 3 All
ER 897, [1980] AC 744 and *Chaudhary v Chaudhary* [1984] 3 All ER 1017, [1985] Fam
19. The unsatisfactory nature of the law had long been recognised: see *Quazi v Quazi*   *d*
[1979] 3 All ER 424 at 427, [1980] AC 744 at 785, CA; [1979] 3 All ER 897 at 904, 912,
[1980] AC 744 at 810, 819, HL; and in 1982 the Law Commission recommended in
their report, Financial Relief after Foreign Divorce (Law Com no 117), that the High
Court should have power to entertain applications for financial provision and property
adjustment orders, notwithstanding the existence of a prior foreign divorce. This
recommendation was given statutory effect by Pt III of the 1984 Act, which came into   *e*
force on 16 September 1985 by virtue of the Matrimonial and Family Proceedings Act
1984 (Commencement No 2) Ord 1985, SI 1985/1316. The question raised by this appeal
is whether the court can entertain an application under Pt III when the overseas divorce
was obtained before 16 September 1985.

The husband and wife are Lebanese. They were married in Beirut on 26 May 1966.
They have four children born respectively in 1967, 1968, 1970 and 1971. In 1976 they   *f*
came, with their family, to this country and established their matrimonial home at Sale
in Cheshire. They separated in December 1984 and on 16 April 1985 the marriage was
formally dissolved by a decree of divorce obtained by the husband in the Lebanon, the
validity of which, prima facie, would be recognised in England. On 26 February 1986
the wife applied for leave to make an application under Pt III of the 1984 Act, and the
husband at once raised the question of jurisdiction, on the basis that Pt III does not apply   *g*
where the overseas divorce was granted, as here, before 16 September 1985. This issue
came before Sheldon J who, by a reserved judgment delivered on 26 March 1986, decided
in favour of the wife and gave her leave to pursue her application (see [1986] 2 All ER
897, [1986] Fam 71). The husband has appealed to this court.

Part III of the 1984 Act comprises ss 12 to 27 (inclusive). Section 12(1) is in the   *h*
following terms:

'Where—(*a*) a marriage has been dissolved or annulled, or the parties to a marriage
have been legally separated, by means of judicial or other proceedings in an overseas
country, and (*b*) the divorce, annulment or legal separation is entitled to be
recognised as valid in England and Wales, either party to the marriage may apply to
the court in the manner prescribed by rules of court for an order for financial relief   *j*
under this Part of this Act.'

There is a long-established principle of statutory construction that a statute shall not
be interpreted retrospectively so as to impair an existing right or obligation. A statute is
retrospective if, inter alia, it attaches a new disability in regard to events already past. For

a recent statement of this principle, see *Yew Bon Tew v Kenderaan Bas Mara* [1982] 3 All
a   ER 833 at 836, [1983] 1 AC 553 at 558. The principle is of general application, and there
are no special rules applicable to the construction of matrimonial statutes: see *Lewis v
Lewis* [1984] 2 All ER 497 at 501, [1984] Fam 79 at 89. It has been said (as in *Yew Bon
Tew*) that the principle applies unless the result is unavoidable on the language used. I
prefer the approach adopted by Brandon J in *Powys v Powys* [1971] 3 All ER 116 at 124,
[1971] P 340 at 350:

b
'The true principles to apply are, in my view, these: that the first and most
important consideration in construing an Act is the ordinary and natural meaning
of the words used; that, if such meaning is plain, effect should be given to it; and
that it is only if such meaning is not plain, but obscure or equivocal, that resort
should be had to presumptions or other means of explaining it.'

c   The reasoning of Brandon J in *Powys v Powys* was expressly approved by this court in
Chaterjee v Chaterjee [1976] 1 All ER 719, [1976] Fam 199, a decision which, unless
distinguishable, is binding on us.

However, whichever approach is here adopted, the result will be the same, since in my
judgment the meaning of the words used is plain and unequivocal. The use of the past
tense, 'where a marriage *has been* dissolved', in contradistinction to the present tense in
d   the immediately following paragraph, 'and the divorce ... *is* entitled to be recognised',
makes it clear that the section is intended to apply to a decree of divorce whenever
pronounced and whether before or after 16 September 1985. On this point I am in
complete agreement with the views of Sheldon J (see [1986] 2 All ER 897 at 904, [1986]
Fam 71 at 80). Further support for this construction is afforded by the provisions of paras
(a) and (b) of s 15(1) of the 1984 Act. These lay down the jurisdictional requirements
e   which have to be satisfied for the court to entertain an application for financial relief
under Pt III. They are if—

'(a) either of the parties to the marriage was domiciled in England or Wales ... on
the date on which the divorce, annulment or legal separation obtained in the
overseas country took effect in that country; or (b) either of the parties to the
f   marriage was habitually resident in England and Wales ... throughout the period
of one year ending with the date on which the divorce, annulment or legal separation
obtained in the overseas country took effect in that country.'

This is language which it is hard to reconcile with a construction that limits the
operation of s 12 only to those overseas divorces granted after the date when Pt III came
into force.
g
This interpretation has the added advantage of being consistent with the interpretation
placed by the courts on similar, though less obvious, words in earlier statutes dealing
with the like subject matter. In s 5(1) of the Matrimonial Causes Act 1963 the words,
imported by reference, were: 'On pronouncing a decree nisi ... or at any time thereafter.'
It was held in *Powys v Powys* that these words, on their ordinary and natural meaning,
h   were amply wide enough to cover not only cases in which a decree was pronounced after
the date of coming into force of the 1963 Act, but also cases in which a decree had been
pronounced before that date. In s 4(1) of the Matrimonial Proceedings and Property Act
1970 the words were: 'On granting a decree of divorce ... or at any time thereafter' and
these words were also held to be retrospective in their operation so as to apply to decrees
granted before the Act came into force: see *Williams v Williams* [1971] 2 All ER 764,
j   [1971] P 271 and *Powys v Powys*. Similar words in ss 23(1) and 24(1) of the Matrimonial
Causes Act 1973 were held by this court to have the like retrospective effect in relation to
the date of granting the decree of divorce: see *Chaterjee v Chaterjee* and *Bonning v Dodsley*
[1982] 1 All ER 612, [1982] 1 WLR 279. I accept the submission of counsel for the
husband that it would be possible to distinguish these decisions from the present case,
but to do so would be to introduce into this field more of those fine distinctions which

tend to bring the law into disrepute. It is noteworthy that the decision of this court in *Lewis v Lewis* [1984] 2 All ER 497, [1984] Fam 79, which did purport to introduce such a distinction, was affirmed by the House of Lords on other grounds, and this particular issue of retrospective operation, whether the words 'on granting a decree of divorce . . . or at any time thereafter' in para 1(1) of Sch 2 to the Matrimonial Homes and Property Act 1981 applied to decrees granted before that provision came into force, was expressly left open by their Lordships' House (see [1985] 2 All ER 449 at 452, [1985] AC 828 at 834).

In view of the plain meaning of the words used it is unnecessary to deal with the other grounds on which Sheldon J held that Pt III of the 1984 Act had retrospective operation, viz the 'mischief' with which these provisions were intended to deal (see [1986] 2 All ER 897 at 903–904, [1986] Fam 71 at 79–90), and the existence of the 'filter procedure', ie the necessity to obtain the leave of the court under s 13 before making an application for financial relief after an overseas divorce, which affords to the husband a safeguard against any hardship which he might otherwise suffer as a result of a retrospective construction of the provisions in question. Had it been necessary to consider these matters as an aid to construction, for my part I would have reached the same conclusion as did the judge.

In conclusion I would echo the plea of Lord Simon P in *Williams v Williams* [1971] 2 All ER 764 at 772, [1971] P 274 at 281:

'. . . I hope that it will not be thought presumptuous if I suggest that it is desirable that wherever possible a statute should indicate in express and unmistakable terms whether (and, if so, how far) or not it is intended to be retrospective. The expenditure of much time and money would be thereby avoided.'

The 1984 Act received the royal assent on 12 July 1984, over 13 years after the date of the judgment in *Williams v Williams*, and although, like the judge, I have felt able to say that the meaning of the words used is plain, the addition of some express statement that Pt III applied whether the overseas divorce, annulment or legal separation was granted before or after the commencement of the Part would have avoided the necessity for this present litigation.

I would dismiss this appeal.

PURCHAS LJ. This appeal raises a short but important point on the construction of s 12 of the Matrimonial and Family Proceedings Act 1984. The material provisions of the Act and the relevant history have already been set out in the judgment of Balcombe LJ and I only repeat some salient parts for convenience sake in this judgment. The parties are both natives of Lebanon but qualify residentially for relief in this country. Their marriage, which took place in 1966, was finally dissolved by 'a proxy divorce' obtained by the husband in Lebanon on 23 April 1985. The provisions of Pt III of the 1984 Act came into effect some five months later. Section 12(1) is in Pt III and the relevant provisions are as follows:

'Where—(a) a marriage *has been dissolved* or annulled, or the parties to a marriage *have been legally separated*, by means of judicial or other proceedings in an overseas country, and (b) the divorce, annulment or legal separation *is entitled to be recognised* as valid in England and Wales . . .'

The proxy divorce is entitled to be recognised as valid in England and Wales under s 12(1)(b). The only issue is whether the wife is entitled to relief in respect of a divorce pronounced before the coming into effect of the Act.

The judge considered at some length the recommendations of the Law Commission in their report, Financial Relief after Foreign Divorce (Law Com no 117 (1982)). It is not clear if, and if so to what extent, he was influenced in his construction of s 12(1)(a) by his consideration of the reaction of Parliament to the Law Commission's report. Counsel for the wife, in supporting the judgment on general grounds, did not seek to justify the reference to the Law Commission's report. I agree with the submissions made by counsel

for the husband in support of his appeal that the judge should not have had resort to the
a report of the Law Commission in the way that it appears that he might have done.

Counsel for the husband referred to *Yew Bon Tew v Kenderaan Bas Mara* [1982] 3 All
ER 833, [1983] AC 553 for the proposition that where a right has accrued it is not to be
taken away by conferring on a statute a retrospective operation unless such a construction
is unavoidable. Thus he submitted that, having obtained his divorce under the law of his
country of origin, the husband was entitled to plan his affairs in the light of the Lebanese
b matrimonial laws and the laws of England and Wales as existing at the date of his divorce.

I have no doubt that in appropriate cases there is a strong presumption against holding
that a statute has retrospective effect, where this would prejudice the accrued rights of
private individuals. However, since I have come to a clear view of the primary meaning
of s 12(1) of the 1984 Act it is not necessary for me to consider the construction of the
section by reference to the construction of s 4(a) of the Matrimonial Proceedings and
c Property Act 1970 to be found in *Williams v Williams* [1971] 2 All ER 764, [1971] P 271
and *Powys v Powys* [1971] 3 All ER 116, [1971] P 340. Although these decisions at first
instance were approved by the Court of Appeal in *Chaterjee v Chaterjee* [1976] 1 All ER
719, [1976] Fam 199, had it been necessary in the instant case to have followed the case
of *Chaterjee* I would have found this to be a difficult course to adopt in view of the long-
established presumption and the line of authorities dealing with s 7(4) of the Matrimonial
d Proceedings and Property Act 1970: see *Bonning v Dodsley* [1982] 1 All ER 612, [1982] 1
WLR 279 and *Madden v Madden* [1974] 1 All ER 673, [1974] 1 WLR 247. In *Carson v
Carson and Stoyek* [1964] 1 All ER 681 at 687, [1964] 1 WLR 511 at 518, which related to
the Matrimonial Causes Act 1963, s 3, Scarman J relied on the presumption in these
terms:

e 'It is a section which has effected an alteration in the substantive law. It seems to
me to be plain, therefore, that, unless Parliament expressly or by clear implication
makes such a section retrospective, it will not be retrospective so as to interfere with
rights that have accrued prior to the passing of the Act.'

In my judgment, the use of the past tense 'has been dissolved' and 'have been legally
f separated' in s 12(1)(a) contrasted with the use of the present tense 'is entitled to be
recognised' in s 12(1)(b) clearly indicates that Parliament intended that the operation of
the section should be retrospective. If this accords with the approach advocated by
Brandon J in *Powys v Powys* then I am fortified in my view.

For these reasons I agree that this appeal should be dismissed.

g **NEILL LJ.** Part III of the Matrimonial and Family Proceedings Act 1984 came into
force on 16 September 1985. Five months earlier, on 16 April 1985, the husband and
wife's marriage had been dissolved in Lebanon. The question which arises for
determination is whether the new right to apply for financial relief, which is given by
the 1984 Act to the parties to a foreign divorce which is recognised in this country, can
be exercised by the wife.

h There is a general rule of common law that all statutes, other than those which are
merely declaratory, or which relate only to matters of procedure or of evidence, are to be
interpreted in such a way that retrospective effect is not given to them unless by express
words or necessary implication it appears that this was the intention of Parliament: see
44 Halsbury's Laws (4th edn) para 922.

The decided cases, however, suggest that the way in which this general rule is to be
j applied can be approached from different standpoints. Thus in *Yew Bon Tew v Kenderaan
Bas Mara* [1982] 3 All ER 833 at 836, [1983] 1 AC 553 at 588 Lord Brightman said:

'... there is at common law a prima facie rule of construction that a statute should
not be interpreted retrospectively so as to impair an existing right or obligation
unless that result is unavoidable on the language used.'

On the other hand in *Powys v Powys* [1971] 3 All ER 116 at 124, [1971] P 340 at 350 Brandon J used these words in explaining what he considered to be the true principles to be applied:

> '... that the first and most important consideration in construing an Act is the ordinary and natural meaning of the words used; that, if such meaning is plain, effect should be given to it; and that it is only if such meaning is not plain, but obscure or equivocal, that resort should be had to presumptions or other means of explaining it.'

It is to be observed that the reasoning of Brandon J in *Powys v Powys* was expressly approved by the Court of Appeal in *Chaterjee v Chaterjee* [1976] 1 All ER 719, [1976] Fam 199, but for my part I do not think that it is necessary or desirable to try to determine in this case the precise stage at which the presumption against retrospection is to be introduced into the process of interpretation.

In my judgment the intention of the legislature can be determined with sufficient certainty by looking at the words of s 12(1) of the 1984 Act by themselves. The subsection provides as follows:

> 'Where—(a) a marriage has been dissolved or annulled, or the parties to a marriage have been legally separated, by means of judicial or other proceedings in an overseas country, and (b) the divorce, annulment or legal separation is entitled to be recognised as valid in England and Wales, either party to the marriage may apply to the court in the manner prescribed by rules of court for an order for financial relief under this Part of this Act.'

It is plain from the concluding words of the subsection that a person can apply to the court for financial relief if the conditions set out in paras (a) and (b) are satisfied. It is also to be observed that this right can be exercised by either party to the marriage.

How then should the two conditions be interpreted?

First, it seems clear that the time by reference to which the question whether the conditions are satisfied has to be decided is the date of the application. It is by reference to that date, therefore, that one seeks an answer to the two specific questions: (a) has the marriage to which the applicant was a party been dissolved (or as the case may be) by means of proceedings in a foreign country? and (b) is the divorce (or other order) made in those proceedings 'entitled to be recognised as valid in England and Wales'?

In the present case we are concerned with the first of these two specific questions.

I can see no reason to give any other than the plain meaning to the words 'has been dissolved'. The marriage of the wife has been dissolved by means of proceedings in an overseas country and the validity of the divorce is, as I understand the matter, recognised in this country. For my part I see no answer to the argument that the statutory conditions which enable the wife to apply for financial relief have been satisfied.

These are new statutory rights which are given to persons who can show that certain specified conditions have been satisfied.

I would dismiss the appeal.

Appeal dismissed.

Solicitors: *Rowleys & Blewitts*, Manchester (for the husband); *Duncan Straker & Co*, Altrincham (for the wife).

Azza M Abdallah   Barrister.

a # West Glamorgan County Council v Rafferty and others
R v Secretary of State for Wales and another, ex parte Gilhaney

b
COURT OF APPEAL, CIVIL DIVISION
SLADE, RALPH GIBSON LJJ AND SIR JOHN MEGAW
1, 2, 22 MAY 1986

c *Local authority – Caravan sites – Provision of caravan sites – Duty of local authority – Judicial review of authority's decision – Authority in breach of duty to provide caravan sites – Authority deciding to evict gipsies from site required for redevelopment – Whether authority giving sufficient weight to its own breach of duty and consequences thereof – Whether decision to evict void for unreasonableness – Caravan Sites Act 1968, s 6.*

d *Local authority – Caravan sites – Provision of caravan sites – Duty of local authority – Duty to provide adequate accommodation for gipsies 'resorting to' its area – Caravan Sites Act 1968, s 6(1).*

For some ten years a county council was in breach of its duty under s 6[a] of the Caravan Sites Act 1968 to exercise its statutory powers in order to provide adequate accommodation 'for gipsies residing in or resorting to [its] area'. The council had made unsuccessful *e* attempts over that period to provide such accommodation. In July 1985 a council-owned site forming part of an industrial redevelopment area was occupied by gipsies whose presence caused a nuisance on the site and damage to neighbouring occupiers and inhibited the letting of vacant factories on the site. On 16 September 1985 the council resolved to institute proceedings to evict the gipsies from the site because it intended to call for tenders for the redevelopment of the site, was concerned about the nuisance and *f* damage being caused to neighbouring occupiers and considered that it would be a bad example if the council was to be seen to be tolerating trespassers on its land for a long period. The council did not offer alternative accommodation to the gipsies or consider whether the gipsies might remain on a different part of the land until temporary alternative accommodation was found for them. Pursuant to its decision to evict, the council applied on 29 September for a possession order under RSC Ord 113 against the *g* gipsies. On 2 October the council was granted an ex parte possession order but on 19 December the order was set aside and a trial of the council's claim was ordered, on the ground that the gipsies had an arguable defence, namely that their trespassing was caused by a lack of lawful accommodation resulting from the council's breach of its statutory duty to provide such accommodation. In March 1986 a gipsy on the site applied for and was granted judicial review of the council's decision of 16 September 1985 to institute *h* possession proceedings. The judge granted an order of certiorari to quash the decision and made a declaration that the council was not entitled to seek possession of the site until it had made reasonable alternative provision for gipsies occupying the site. The council appealed against the order of certiorari, the declaration and the setting aside of the possession order.

j **Held** – The court was not precluded from holding that a public authority's decision was void for unreasonableness merely because there were factors on both sides of the question. If the weight of factors against a decision ought to be recognised by a reasonable council, properly aware of its duties and powers, as being overwhelming then that decision could not be upheld if challenged. Although the court would exercise restraint before

a   Section 6, so far as material, is set out at p 1009 *j*, post interfering with a decision of an elected authority made according to its lawful procedure, the court would require a council, as a reasonable authority, to recognise any breach of *a* legal duty for what it was and to give due weight to that breach and the consequences thereof in arriving at a decision affected by the breach. On the facts, the council, in deciding to evict the gipsies, had acted unreasonably in treating the interference with the redevelopment of the site as outweighing the effect the eviction would have both on the gipsies and on those to whose area they would move if evicted, when those effects were caused by the council's own breach of its duty to provide accommodation. It followed *b* that the council's appeal in both the judicial review and the possession proceedings would be dismissed and the quashing of the council's decision of 16 September 1985 upheld, although the declaration in the judicial review proceedings would be set aside because the council ought to be left free to deal with the situation as it thought best, having regard to its statutory duty and powers (see p 1009 *d e*, p 1021 *g* to p 1022 *c h j*, p 1023 *a c* to *f* and p 1024 *e*, post).

c

Associated Provincial Picture Houses Ltd v Wednesbury Corp [1947] 2 All ER 680 and *Puhlhofer v Hillingdon London BC* [1986] 1 All ER 467 applied.

Per Ralph Gibson LJ and Sir John Megaw. In considering whether a county council has failed to fulfil its obligation under s 6 of the 1968 Act the adequacy of any accommodation provided by the council is to be tested by reference to (i) the number of gipsies known to the council to be habitually residing in or resorting to its area over a *d* preceding period of reasonable length and (ii) the time required for the council to provide accommodation for them. Parliament cannot have intended to impose on a council the duty to provide accommodation for any number of persons of a nomadic habit of life who for any reason might choose at any time to resort to the council's area, in the sense of choosing to go there for however short a time and for whatever purpose. Accordingly, a county council faced with a sudden and unforeseen influx of gipsies into its area is not *e* by reason only of their presence and the absence of adequate accommodation for them necessarily in breach of its duty under s 6 (see p 1017 *d* to *h*, p 1023 *f j* to p 1024 *a*, post).

Quaere (per Sir John Megaw). Whether 'gipsies . . . resorting to' a county council's area, within s 6(1) of the 1968 Act, refers to gipsies who have come to and are in the council's area or to non-resident gipsies who go habitually and frequently to the council's area (see *f* p 1023 *g h*, post).

Notes

For the powers of local authorities with respect to the provision of caravan sites, see 29 Halsbury's Laws (4th edn) para 118.

For the Caravan Sites Act 1968, s 6, see 24 Halsbury's Statutes (3rd edn) 230.

g

Cases referred to in judgments

Associated Provincial Picture Houses Ltd v Wednesbury Corp [1947] 2 All ER 680, [1948] 1 KB 223, CA.

Bristol DC v Clark [1975] 3 All ER 976, [1975] 1 WLR 1443, CA.

Cannock Chase DC v Kelly [1978] 1 All ER 152, [1978] 1 WLR 1, CA.

Kensington and Chelsea London BC v Wells (1973) 72 LGR 289, CA. *h*

Nottingham CC v Secretary of State for the Environment [1986] 1 All ER 199, [1986] AC 240, [1986] 2 WLR 1, HL.

O'Reilly v Mackman [1982] 3 All ER 1124, [1983] 2 AC 237, [1982] 3 WLR 1096, HL.

Padfield v Minister of Agriculture Fisheries and Food [1968] 1 All ER 694, [1968] AC 997, [1968] 2 WLR 924, HL.

Puhlhofer v Hillingdon London BC [1986] 1 All ER 467, [1986] AC 484, [1986] 2 WLR 259, *j* HL.

R v Secretary of State for the Environment, ex p Hillingdon London BC [1986] 1 All ER 810, [1986] 1 WLR 192; *affd* [1986] 2 All ER 273, [1986] 1 WLR 807, CA.

R v Secretary of State for the Environment, ex p Lee (14 January 1985, unreported), QBD.

Southwark London BC v Williams [1971] 2 All ER 175, [1971] Ch 734, [1971] 2 WLR 467,
a   CA.
W (an infant), Re [1971] 2 All ER 49, [1971] AC 682, [1971] 2 WLR 1011, HL.
Wandsworth London BC v Winder [1984] 3 All ER 976, [1985] AC 461, [1984] 3 WLR
    1254, HL.
Wyatt v Hillingdon London BC (1978) 76 LGR 727, CA.

b

Appeals
West Glamorgan CC v Rafferty and others
By an originating summons dated 19 September 1985 the West Glamorgan County
Council applied, pursuant to RSC Ord 113, for an order for possession of land and
premises comprising the Briton Ferry Industrial Estate at Neath, Swansea against the
c   defendants, Edmund Rafferty, James Rafferty, Mr Fury and Mr Gaskin, being gipsies
who were in occupation of the site, on the ground that the defendants were in occupation
without licence or consent. On 2 October 1985 Tudor Price J made an order for possession
in favour of the county council. By a further order dated 19 December 1985 Peter Pain J
set aside the possession order and directed that the county council's claim for possession
of the site should proceed by way of trial in the High Court. The county council appealed
d   from that order seeking that the order for possession be restored. The facts are set out in
the judgment of Ralph Gibson LJ.

R v Secretary of State for Wales and another, ex p Gilhaney
On 13 March 1986 James Gilhaney, one of the gipsies occupying land and premises
comprising the Briton Ferry Industrial Estate at Neath, Swansea (the Briton Ferry site),
e   applied with the leave of Mann J given on 18 March 1986 for judicial review of (1) the
decision of the West Glamorgan County Council on 16 September 1985 to take
proceedings for possession of the Briton Ferry site, (2) the failure of the county council
since 1974 to provide adequate accommodation for gipsies residing in or resorting to its
area pursuant to s 6 of the Caravan Sites Act 1968 and (3) the decision of the Secretary of
f   State on 29 November 1985 not to give directions to the county council to provide
accommodation for such gipsies pursuant to s 6. Mr Gilhaney sought relief by way of (i)
an order of certiorari to quash the county council's decision of 16 September 1985, (ii) an
injunction restraining the county council from seeking possession of the Briton Ferry
site until such time as it provided adequate accommodation for gipsies residing in or
resorting to its area, (iii) an order of mandamus requiring the county council to comply
g   with its statutory duty under s 6 of the 1968 Act and with any direction given by the
Secretary of State to comply with s 6, (iv) an order of mandamus directing the Secretary
of State to give directions to the county council requiring it, pursuant to s 6 of the 1968
Act, to provide sites to accommodate such numbers of gipsy caravans as the Secretary of
State might specify and (v) a declaration that the Secretary of State was bound by law to
give such directions to the county council. On 28 April 1968 Kennedy J quashed the
h   council's decision of 16 September 1985 to institute proceedings for possession of the
Briton Ferry site and declared that the county council was not entitled to seek possession
of the site until such time as it made reasonable alternative provision for the gipsies'
accommodation. The county council appealed from that decision. The facts are set out
in the judgment of Ralph Gibson LJ.

j   *Michael Barnes QC* and *Philip Price* for the county council.
    David Marshall Evans QC and *D S Geey* for the defendants in the first appeal and for the
        applicant in the second appeal.

Cur adv vult

22 May. The following judgments were delivered.

RALPH GIBSON LJ (delivering the first judgment at the invitation of Slade LJ). West Glamorgan County Council resolved on 16 September 1985 to commence proceedings in order to evict from the Briton Ferry site at Neath a number of travelling folk or gipsies who were camped there. The gipsies were trespassers. They had gone on to the site without permission and they knew that they had no right to be there. On 2 October 1985 Tudor Price J made an order in summary proceedings under RSC Ord 113 for the county council to recover possession of the Briton Ferry site. The defendants were Mr Edmund Rafferty, Mr James Rafferty, Mr Fury, Mr Gaskin and 'persons unknown', who included a number of families (the husbands, wives and children) living in about 25 caravans. (That was the figure at 30 December 1985: see the affidavit of Mr Burgess, a solicitor in the county clerk's department who had responsibility for the council's functions under the Caravan Sites Act 1968.) A writ of possession was issued on 1 November 1985 but it was not executed. The county council held their hand at the request of a solicitor acting for the gipsies. On 19 December 1985 Peter Pain J set aside the order for possession, and directed that the claim of the county council for possession of the site proceed by way of trial in the High Court, on the ground that the breach by the county council of its statutory duty to provide adequate accommodation for gipsies in the area of the county deprived the council of any right to summary judgment. From that order of Peter Pain J the county council appeals to this court and asks that the order for possession be restored. That is the first appeal.

The gipsies at the Briton Ferry site were assisted by the National Gipsy Council and its president Mr Hughie Smith. Solicitors had been instructed with reference to the plight of gipsies in West Glamorgan before the decision was made to seek possession of this site. It was thought, and rightly in my view for reasons to be mentioned later in this judgment, that there would be no effective defence to the claim for possession of the site if the proceedings in which possession was claimed had been validly instituted in the first place by the county council. Accordingly, on 13 March 1986 application was made by Mr Gilhaney, one of the gipsies camped at Briton Ferry, for judicial review in respect of the decision of 16 September 1985 by the county council to take proceedings for possession of the site, and for an order quashing it. The application asked for other relief as well, to which reference will be made later. The main ground of the application was that on which Peter Pain J had relied in setting aside the order for possession, namely the failure since 1974 by the county council to carry out its statutory duty under s 6 of the Caravan Sites Act 1968 for the provision of adequate accommodation in their area for gipsies. It was contended that having regard to that breach of duty the decision in September 1985 to evict the gipsy families from this site was in all the circumstances a decision that no reasonable authority could make. An early hearing was obtained and on 28 April 1986 Kennedy J upheld that contention and quashed the decision by the county council to start the proceedings for eviction. From that decision also the county council appeals to this court. That is the second appeal.

It has been common ground that if in the second appeal the order of Kennedy J is upheld by this court then the proceedings for possession are aborted and no separate issues arise in the first appeal save as to costs. It is also common ground that if the order of Kennedy J is set aside then the first appeal must be allowed and the original order for possession restored.

The decision to evict the gipsies from Briton Ferry was made by the chairman of the county council committee and by the chairman of the policy and resources committee on a recommendation put to them by Mr Rush, the county clerk, at the request of Mr Burgess. This decision on that recommendation was made under the county council's Standing Order 35, a procedure known as 'chairman's action' whereby the council delegated powers of decision to the chairman, acting in consultation as required by the order, if the matter required immediate attention and did not justify the holding of a

special meeting of the committee. The document submitted to the chairman of the
a policy and resources committee which contained the recommendation for recovery of
possession of the council's land at Briton Ferry explained the subject thus:

> 'Briton Ferry Industrial Estate: tenders are due to be received shortly for the next
> stage of reclamation works. Part of the land affected by these works is at present
> unlawfully occupied by gipsy caravans.'

b Delegation by the council of the power to make decisions to one member, as contrasted
with delegation to a committee or sub-committee or to an officer, was considered by
Woolf J in *R v Secretary of State for the Environment, ex p Hillingdon London BC* [1986] 1 All
ER 810, [1986] 1 WLR 192 and held to be invalid as not within the power to delegate
given by s 101 of the Local Government Act 1972. His decision was upheld by this court
on 17 April 1986 (see [1986] 2 All ER 273, [1986] 1 WLR 807). The county council,
c having regard to the decision of Woolf J, resolved, first by committee and later by vote
of the whole council, to ratify the chairman's decision of 16 September 1985. Having
regard to that ratification it has not been argued before this court that the original
decision was invalid because made under an unlawful delegation of power. The position
therefore is that the decision of 16 September 1985 which was quashed by the order of
Kennedy J was a decision taken by an elected body under lawful procedure and must
d receive the careful respect which such a decision always receives in a court of law. The
decision was moreover one in which factors of social policy, some for and some against
eviction of the gipsies, had to be considered. It follows that the facts of this case must be
both exceptional and extreme for Kennedy J to have been driven to find that the decision
by the county council was void in law in the sense that it was such that no reasonable
council could make. In my judgment, on this main point in the case, Kennedy J was
e right and I would, subject to deletion of the declaration from the order which he made,
dismiss both the appeals by the county council. Explanation of the reasons for proposing
that course requires examination of the difficulties encountered by the county council
over many years and of their efforts to deal with the provision of permanent sites for
gipsies in their area.

f Before setting out that history, the approach of this court, as I understand it should be,
must in courtesy to the county council be explained. If my view of the law is right, it is
necessary to describe the conduct and attitude of the county council as long continued
breach of duty and an apparent inattention both to that breach of duty and to the powers
of the council by which it might be remedied. The good faith of the council in this affair
has never, of course, been questioned. No one could fail to have some sympathy with the
council and its officers in their efforts to deal with the tasks placed on the council by the
g law enacted by Parliament. Nothing that I say in this judgment is intended to criticise
the council, or its members at any date, for lack of any concern for any of the people of
its area. What has gone wrong in my view is attributable to a misapprehension of the
nature and extent of the duty placed on the council by s 6 of the 1968 Act.

h *The statutory duties*

By s 24 of the Caravan Sites and Control of Development Act 1960 local authorities
were given power to provide sites for caravans within their area, both to acquire land for
that purpose and to provide services and facilities for those occupying the sites. The
power to acquire sites includes the power to acquire them compulsorily.

Part II of the Caravan Sites Act 1968 contained provisions dealing with gipsy
j encampments. Section 6(1) provided that it shall be the duty of certain local authorities
including the council of a county—

> 'to exercise their powers under section 24 of the [1960 Act] . . . so far as may be
> necessary to provide adequate accommodation for gipsies residing in or resorting to
> their area.'

By s 16 of the 1968 Act 'gipsies' means—

> 'persons of nomadic habit of life, whatever their race or origin, but does not *a*
> include members of an organised group of travelling showmen, or of persons
> engaged in travelling circuses, travelling together as such.'

By s 7 of that Act the duty imposed by s 6 on the council of a county extends only to
determining what sites are to be provided and acquiring or appropriating the necessary
land; and it is the duty of the council of the district in which any such site is located to *b*
exercise all other powers under s 24 of the 1960 Act in relation to the site. By s 8 of the
1968 Act, before adopting a proposal to acquire or appropriate land for this purpose, the
council of a county must consult the council of the county district in which the land is
situated and such other authorities and persons as they consider appropriate. If objection
is made by a district council to any such proposal, and the objection is not disposed of in
consultation, the district council may give notice of the objection to the Secretary of *c*
State. The Secretary of State may then give directions to the county council to abandon
the proposal, or to proceed with it, or to make an application for planning permission in
respect of it. Any such application for planning permission is deemed to be referred to
the Secretary of State.

Finally, s 9 of the 1968 Act gives powers to the Secretary of State. In its present form,
s 9 provides that: *d*

> 'The Secretary of State may, if at any time it appears to him to be necessary so to
> do, give directions to any local authority to which subsection (1) of section 6 of this
> Act applies requiring them to provide, pursuant to that section, such sites or
> additional sites, for the accommodation of such numbers of caravans, as may be
> specified in the directions; and any such directions shall be enforceable on the *e*
> application of the Secretary of State, by mandamus.'

Policy statements have been made from time to time by the Department of the
Environment and the Welsh Office which have indicated the social purposes which it
was thought by government should be served, by use of the powers given to county and
district councils with reference to the provisions and management of sites for gipsies. *f*
Unless there is some statutory basis for attaching binding effect to such statements (and
the court has been referred to none) they remain as advice and no more. But in my view
the provisions of the 1968 Act to which I have referred indicate plainly enough the evils
at which the legislation was directed. First, adequate accommodation is to be provided
for gipsies in the area of the local authority in the interest of the gipsies themselves,
giving them sites to which they can lawfully go and which will be supplied with facilities *g*
and supervised so that the sites will be maintained in decent order. Given some security
of accommodation their children are more likely to get effective instruction in school.
Any gipsies not complying with the regulations of the site may be ejected. Such sites will
be better both for the travelling people who use them and for those who live near the
sites. The second purpose of the legislation is plain from ss 10 and 12 of the 1968 Act. *h*
When the Secretary of State is satisfied that the duty imposed by s 6 has been carried out,
or that it is not necessary or expedient to make provision for accommodation for gipsies
in a particular area, the Secretary of State may on the application of the local authority
designate the area of that authority as an area to which s 10 of the 1968 Act applies. The
effect of designation is that it becomes a criminal offence for any person being a gipsy to
station a caravan for the purpose of residing for any period within that area on any land *j*
situated within the boundaries of a highway, or any other unoccupied land, or any
occupied land without the consent of the occupier. Further, by s 11, in any designated
area a magistrates' court may on the complaint of the local authority by order authorise
that authority to take such steps as may be specified in the order for the removal from
land in that area of caravans stationed in contravention of s 10. The rest of the community

is thus to an extent protected from visitation by gipsies trespassing on land, and camping
a on unregulated sites so as to cause nuisance, and sometimes damage, to those areas in
which they trespass and the people living there.

The history
Kennedy J set out a summary of the events described in the affidavits before the court
and I gratefully take the substance of what follows from his account.
b   (i) Part II of the 1968 Act, relating to gipsy encampments, was brought into force in
1970. The number of gipsies 'residing in or resorting to' the area of West Glamorgan
County Council has been neither fixed nor precisely ascertainable. Figures have been
kept since at least 1975. The average number of caravans within the whole area of the
county over the period since 1975 has been 85. By far the greater part of caravans and
families have been in the area of Swansea City Council, partly by reason of the presence
c there of the dock used by the Cork ferry. A number of the travellers resorting to Swansea
have been coming from and returning to Ireland. The average number of gipsies for
whom accommodation has been required over the last 11 or 12 years, as we have been
told, has not been more than 350. The population of West Glamorgan is about 370,000.
(ii) In 1970 the then Glamorgan County Council held the view that only in the area
of Swansea was it necessary to provide sites for the accommodation of gipsies. A site at
d Clyne near Swansea was proposed but in 1971, after a public inquiry, it was rejected by
the Secretary of State.
(iii) In 1974 the newly constituted West Glamorgan County Council adopted a report
which set out criteria for the selection and regulation of gipsy caravan sites. Between
June 1974 and April 1975 officers of the county council and of the district councils
within the county, by which any sites would be managed, tried to provide a list of
e possible sites. The officers appear to have recommended the provision of one site in each
district, but in the result not one site was approved.
(iv) In 1975 gipsies occupied a site in the Morriston area of Swansea City Council,
which is one of the four district councils within the county of West Glamorgan. The city
council was proposing to evict them. Mr Hughie Smith, who tried to intervene on their
behalf, was told by the then leader of the county council that a site at Jersey Marine
f outside Swansea was under consideration and should be available by 1976. Nothing came
of that proposal.
(v) In August 1975 gipsies were camped without permission at North Dock, Swansea.
It was intended that they be evicted. On 6 August 1975 the Welsh Office wrote to the
clerk and chief officer of the county council a letter which included the following:

g   'We since understand that, in contravention of Government Policy, your Council
now propose to evict the families from this site. [The site referred to was the site at
North Dock.] As was pointed out in the Department of the Environment's letter, to
simply secure the removal of unaccommodated families is not seen as a solution to
the problem. The Department would, therefore, urge your Council to reconsider
evicting the gypsy families and again ask them to consider making temporary
h arrangements either on the existing land or on some other more suitable site, with
the provision of basic facilities. If, however, your Council feel that there is an
overriding need for the families to be moved on, it would be desirable if you would
first locate, in conjunction with the City Council, alternative areas of land on which
facilities could be provided and where the families would be free from harassment
or eviction.'
j
As stated above, government policy is not, in my view, by reason only of it being
government policy, binding in law on the county council but performance by the county
council of its statutory duty would in fact have served that policy. The letter is of
importance also because it drew attention to the lawful powers of the county council to
make temporary arrangements.

(vi) In 1976 Swansea City Council was prepared to recommend five small sites for caravans in its area, which together would accommodate a total of 30 caravans, towards a need within the county of accommodation for a considerably larger number as will appear, but the proposal depended on the other district councils also providing sites. They failed to do so. It was, of course, for the county council to act on the willingness of Swansea City Council and despite the unwillingness of the other districts, because it was the county council which had both the duty and the necessary powers.

(vii) The then view of the Welsh Office was expressed in November 1976 in a letter to the chairman of West Glamorgan County Council which pointed out that—

'failure to provide sites together with repeated eviction simply perpetuates the problems and intensifies the sense of despair and frustration arising from this situation.'

On 25 March 1977 the Department of the Environment and the Welsh Office issued a joint circular (circular 1977/28 (DOE), 1977/51 (WO)) which urged local authorities not to spend so much money on evicting gipsies from illegal sites and to concentrate instead on providing as many cheap makeshift sites as possible to deal with an acute and growing problem (see para 3.6 of the written representations by the West Glamorgan County Council dated 5 January 1978 with reference to the proposed caravan site at Garth Farm, Glais, Swansea). It is right to point out that the Secretary of State, of course, also had the powers under s 9 of the 1968 Act which have been set out above and it would have been possible for central government to have employed direction in place of exhortation.

(viii) Mr Hughie Smith in May 1977, by letter to the Secretary of State, urged that use be made of the powers under s 9 to require West Glamorgan County Council to provide sites. In July 1977 the county council selected a site at Garth Farm, Glais, which would have provided space for 20 caravans. Swansea City Council objected to that site and in 1978 there was a public inquiry in relation to it. In 1979 the Secretary of State accepted the recommendation of his inspector, and granted planning permission in relation to Garth Farm, but his decision was set aside by the High Court in July 1981 on the ground, as we have been told, that there had been a failure to consider alternative sites.

(ix) In 1978 the gipsies camped at North Dock, Swansea, had been evicted and had returned to the Morriston site, where their presence was tolerated by Swansea City Council over a period of seven years until April 1985. This toleration was effected by the grant of temporary planning permission granted and renewed at six monthly intervals. It has been agreed in this court that the procedure authorising the use of a site on a temporary basis has at all times been open to the county council.

(x) After the decision of the High Court in July 1981 with reference to Garth Farm at Glais, the county council resolved to co-operate with Swansea City Council to find an alternative site in place of that at Glais. A working group of officers from the county and the city councils were instructed to produce a report on possible sites. The report was produced in March 1984 and recommended six sites which together would have accommodated 66 caravans. All were within the area of the city council. There were local objections and during the summer of 1984 there were meetings between residents and representatives of the two councils.

(xi) In January 1985 Swansea City Council decided not to renew the temporary planning permission in respect of the Morriston site, which by then had been in use for some seven years. Further, for reasons which are not directly relevant to the issues in this case and which therefore have not been examined, any immediate prospect of the provision of sites by agreement disappeared when, on 18 March 1985, Swansea City Council resolved as follows:

'RESOLVED (1) that the City Council withdraw from the agreement with the West Glamorgan County Council for the provision of designated gipsy sites within the City; (2) that discussions be held with the Local Members of Parliament with a view to promoting legislation to amend the provisions of the Caravan Sites Act 1968; (3) that the Association of District Councils be requested to support the proposals for revised legislation; (4) that the Officers be authorised to take appropriate action to ensure the removal of gipsies from all sites within the City.'

(xii) It is clear that the councillors were being required to deal with issues which raised fierce opposition and strong feelings. The county council commented on that decision of the city council in a letter written in August 1985 to the solicitors acting for the gipsies in these cases, part of which read as follows:

'Six sites, carefully selected around the Swansea area, failed to proceed earlier this year because of the withdrawal of City Council support. You will understand that their involvement is essential in terms of running the sites. With the widespread and strong public opposition based on the previous experience which the Authority had experienced at Glais where there had been physical obstruction, and with public order and safety in mind, they feared that further obstructions would occur on the other sites proposed.'

(xiii) In April 1985 Swansea City Council began to evict gipsies from the Morriston site. In June 1985 the Welsh Office wrote to the county council with reference to the 'deferring' of 'the proposals to establish 6 gypsy sites in the Swansea area'. The letter (dated 10 June 1985) continued:

'. . . having regard to the lapse of planning permission in respect of the temporary site at Morriston the Council have not provided any accommodation for gypsies residing in or resorting to their area. Since they are, no doubt, mindful of their statutory obligation to provide such accommodation I should be pleased to know, if the 6 sites are not being proceeded with, what action the Council are now taking, or propose to take, to discharge this obligation.'

The reply of the county council, in a letter of 18 June 1985 from the county clerk, refers to two factors which made it 'impossible' to proceed with the six small sites. The first factor was the withdrawal of Swansea City Council 'which, in the normal course of events, would be responsible for site management' and the second factor (which was thought also to be the reason for the withdrawal of Swansea City Council) was that—

'the Minister of State has found himself unable to give assurances on the questions of grant, designation and the procedure for determination of objections. It was felt by both Authorities that these were aspects of the proposals which are his direct responsibility and the Authorities wished to know his attitude to these before proceeding further with the procedures for the establishment of these sites . . . it is also fair to observe that members of the Authority have never in their experience encountered such a high degree of animosity and hostility on any matter which they have ever dealt with and I think they genuinely believe that the threats of direct action to prevent the sites being implemented will be carried out. After ten years of hard effort to make some provision, first with the co-operation of the Districts, then by the County alone in the absence of such agreement, and now, once again with the co-operation of the City Council, I do not know what more the County Council can reasonably do.'

I shall refer to this letter again. It is, in my view, of importance as indicating a likely source of misapprehension as to the nature of the duty imposed on the council and of its powers to implement that duty.

(xiv) It appears from the evidence, and it has not been disputed in this court, that from the date of that letter until after the commencement of proceedings to evict gipsies from the Briton Ferry site, the county council acted in accordance with the assessment of its position set out in that letter of the chief clerk. The council did nothing towards the

carrying out of its statutory duty by taking steps towards the provision either of
permanent or of temporary sites.   *a*

(xv) In July 1985 gipsies evicted from the Morriston site moved to Briton Ferry
industrial estate at Neath. On 16 September 1985 the decision was taken by the county
council to take proceedings to evict the gipsies from the Briton Ferry site.

The Briton Ferry site

The land at Briton Ferry was formerly a steel works. Extending to 170 acres, the site is *b*
on the east side of the entrance to the Neath river. The appearance of the site from
photographs shown to the court is what might be expected in the site of dismantled
steelworks in which the process of redevelopment is in its early stages. A sum of £4·5m
of public money has been spent on the site so far and there were immediate plans for
work of landscaping to be done on part of the site. No part of it was ever proposed as
permanent or temporary accommodation for gipsies. The purpose of the county council *c*
has been to procure redevelopment of the area for industrial purposes so as to assist in the
creation of employment while removing the blight of redundant plant. The Welsh
Development Agency owns adjoining land. The effect of the unregulated presence of the
gipsies at Briton Ferry has been to cause severe nuisance to some neighbours and some
damage to neighbouring occupiers and to cause difficulty to the Welsh Development
Agency in persuading firms to acquire new or vacant factory premises in the area.   *d*

The legal proceedings

In the summary proceedings under RSC Ord 113 there was no appearance by the
defendants when Tudor Price J made the order for possession on 2 October 1985. An
application was made on 22 November 1985 to Peter Pain J to suspend the operation of
the possession order pending the outcome of an application for legal aid to enable the *e*
defendants to take proceedings by way of mandamus to enforce the obligation of the
county council under s 6 of the 1968 Act. In that shape, as Peter Pain J said in his
judgment, the application could not succeed. There is no power in the court to suspend
an order for possession to which a plaintiff can prove his right under Ord 113. The
defendants were given leave to amend their application to ask that the order for possession *f*
be set aside. On the adjourned hearing on 13 December 1985 it was contended for the
county council that the only relief available to the defendants was to apply to the court
for an order to enforce the admitted breach of duty on the part of the council and that,
meanwhile, the order for possession should be made. Peter Pain J found that to be an
unattractive argument. He acknowledged the force of the submission that, if the order
for possession were set aside, gipsies might be free to squat on the property of the county *g*
council for a period of time, but it seemed wrong to him that the council should obtain
the assistance of the court to evict from the site gipsies who had no accommodation
available to them in the area by reason of the breach of duty of the county council which
had no present intention of carrying that duty into effect. He found the conduct of the
county council to have been 'harsh and oppressive'. No submission was made to him as
to the validity of the decision of the county council to evict the gipsies. He regarded the *h*
issues at that stage under RSC Ord 113 as being whether the defendants had any arguable
defence and whether the right of the county council to possession was sufficiently clear
for the order to have been made in summary proceedings. He concluded that there was
an arguable case that the county council was not entitled to relief while the circumstances
which caused the council to ask for that relief had been caused by the breach of duty on
the part of the council and that breach of duty continued. He therefore set aside the order *j*
and gave direction for the trial of the council's claim.

In this court counsel for the defendants has not sought to uphold the order on that
ground. The fact that the county council was and is in breach of statutory duty to provide
accommodation for the defendants, or for some of them, or that their breach had caused,
or may have caused, the presence of the defendants, or some of them, on the county

a council's land at Briton Ferry, does not by itself afford to the defendants any defence, nor does it deprive the council of its right to possession: see *Southwark London BC v Williams* [1971] 2 All ER 175, [1971] Ch 734, *Kensington and Chelsea London BC v Wells* (1973) 72 LGR 289 and *Wyatt v Hillingdon London BC* (1978) 76 LGR 727. Those cases were not cited to Peter Pain J. If, however, the decision to institute proceedings for the eviction of the gipsies was void on the ground of unreasonableness, then the defendants can in law require that the proceedings be struck out. In *Bristol DC v Clark* [1975] 3 All ER 976,
b [1975] 1 WLR 1443 a tenant of a council house was in arrears of rent. The council claimed possession. The tenant disputed the claim to possession on the ground that the council did not require possession for the purposes of exercising its powers under the Housing Act 1957. This court rejected the tenant's defence on the facts but accepted that if unreasonableness or abuse of power in the sense described in *Associated Provincial Picture Houses Ltd v Wednesbury Corp* [1947] 2 All ER 680, [1948] 1 KB 223 were
c established with reference to the decision to claim possession, the tenant could raise that as a defence against the council's claim. Lord Denning MR said ([1975] 3 All ER 976 at 980, [1975] 1 WLR 1443 at 1448):

> 'The powers of the corporation are contained in ss 91 and 111 of the Housing Act
> 1957. They have the general management, regulation and control of houses
> *d* provided by them. This means that they can pick and choose their tenants at will;
> they can grant tenancies and determine them by notice to quit; and they can take
> proceedings for possession. They are not trammelled in any way by the Rent Acts
> ... Nevertheless in exercising their statutory powers I agree with counsel for the
> tenants: they must exercise them in good faith, taking into account relevant
> considerations and not irrelevant considerations. That applies not only to judicial
> *e* decisions but also to administrative decisions: see *Padfield v Minister of Agriculture
> Fisheries and Food* ([1968] 1 All ER 694, [1968] AC 997). It applies, I think, to a
> decision whether to evict a tenant or not.'

This court again, in *Cannock Chase DC v Kelly* [1978] 1 All ER 152, [1978] 1 WLR 1, rejected on the facts a similar defence raised by a council tenant but accepted that on the
f principle stated in *Associated Provincial Picture Houses Ltd v Wednesbury Corp* a tenant could challenge by way of defence the validity of the council's decision to claim possession of its property. Megaw J said ([1978] 1 All ER 152 at 156–157, [1978] 1 WLR 1 at 6–7):

> '... even though there has been no bad faith, a public authority's exercise of its
> statutory powers may properly be challenged before the court if it can be shown,
> the burden being on the challenger, that the authority has, as a material factor in
> *g* reaching its decision, taken into account a factor which as a matter of law should not
> have been taken into account or has failed to take into account a factor which should
> have been taken into account. To that extent a local authority, as landlord, is under
> a stricter obligation than a private landlord, in a case where the tenancy is not subject
> to the Rent Acts. But, if such a challenge be made, it is for the tenant to particularise
> *h* the relevant consideration or considerations alleged to have been taken into account
> or omitted, as the case may be, and to prove that erroneous taking into account or
> that erroneous omission, which constitutes the so-called "abuse of the powers". In
> the present case, no such consideration was specified. It is said that it ought to be
> inferred. Such an inference may be justified, even though the precise consideration
> erroneously taken into account or omitted, cannot be identified or proved. How
> *j* that may arise is shown, again, in Lord Greene MR's judgment in the *Wednesbury
> Corpn* case [1947] 2 All ER 680 at 683, [1948] 1 KB 223 at 230: "... it is true to say
> ... that, if a decision on a competent matter is so unreasonable that no reasonable
> authority could ever have come to it, then the courts can interfere. That, I think, is
> right, but that would require overwhelming proof, and in this case the facts do not
> come anywhere near such a thing."'

Lawton J accepted that—

'the abuse or excessive use of statutory powers by a local authority acting as a
housing authority can provide a defence for a council tenant against a claim for
possession.'

(See [1978] 1 All ER 152 at 159, [1978] 1 WLR 1 at 10.) Sir David Cairns agreed with
Megaw and Lawton LJJ.

The dicta in these cases, to the effect that invalidity of the decision to serve the notice
to quit can be raised as a defence against the claim for possession without prior application
to the High Court to quash the council's decision, are unaffected by the principles stated
by the House of Lords in *O'Reilly v Mackman* [1982] 3 All ER 1124, [1983] 2 AC 237.
That was made clear by the further decision of the House of Lords in *Wandsworth London
BC v Winder* [1984] 3 All ER 976, [1985] 1 AC 461.

In the present case the decision of the county council to start proceedings to evict the
gipsies was taken with reference to land vested in the council as freehold owners. It was
not suggested for the gipsies that in making that decision the council was acting pursuant
to any particular statutory power as was the case in *Cannock Chase DC v Kelly*, namely
powers under the Housing Act 1957; nor was it suggested for the council that the
principles stated in that case were not applicable to the decision by the county council in
the circumstances of this case if unreasonableness in the *Wednesbury* sense could be made
out on the facts.

It follows, in my judgment, that that which was common ground between the parties
on this appeal was rightly not disputed by either side: if the decision on 16 September
1985 to evict the gipsies was void for unreasonableness, the council's claim for possession
must fail. On that basis, Peter Pain J was right (although the true point had not been
clearly raised before him) to set aside the order for possession and to direct trial of the
council's claim. The point has been duly raised in amended pleadings. Further, if the
decision to evict was not void, the defendant gipsies have no defence and the original
order for possession would have to be restored.

As to the proceedings for judicial review, application was made by Mr Gilhaney on 13
March 1986: nearly six months after the decision of September 1985 by the county
council to evict gipsies from Briton Ferry. The respondents were the Secretary of State
for Wales and the county council. The relief sought was (i) the quashing of the decision
of 16 September 1985, (ii) an injunction restraining the county council from seeking
possession of the Briton Ferry site until the county council made available adequate
accommodation for gipsies residing in or resorting to the area, (iii) an order for
mandamus requiring the county council to comply with their statutory duty under s 6
of the 1968 Act, (iv) an order of mandamus directing the Secretary of State for Wales to
give directions to the county council requiring that council to provide such sites for the
accommodation of such number of gipsy caravans as the Secretary of State might specify
and (v) a declaration that the Secretary of State is bound by law to give directions to the
county council for the provision of sites pursuant to s 6 of the 1968 Act.

On 11 April 1986 for the first time there was use of power in place of exhortation, and
of the offering of advice. On that date the Secretary of State for Wales, in exercise of his
power under s 9 of the 1968 Act, directed the county council to provide within its area
accommodation for 60 caravans, which was roughly the number of caravans parked at
Briton Ferry site in March 1985. By the date of the giving of directions by the Secretary
of State the number of caravans at Briton Ferry had risen to 103, which is an aspect of the
situation to which I shall return.

The application came before Kennedy J in the week of 21 April 1986. Much was
agreed between the parties. The county council has contested the issues with complete
candour and has wasted no time whatever on peripheral matters. Kennedy J, following
Mann J in *R v Secretary of State for the Environment, ex p Lee* (14 January 1985, unreported),

a held that, irrespective of efforts which it may have been making at any time, the county council was in breach of duty under s 6 of the 1968 Act because it was demonstrated that adequate accommodation had not been provided for gipsies in the area of the county council and that the question for the court then was whether, in the exercise of its discretion, relief should be granted in respect of that breach. Mann J had said:

b 'In my judgment, the correct approach is to ask simply whether, at the moment the question is to be answered, there is adequate accommodation for gipsies residing in or resorting to the area. If the answer is No, then whether the breach of duty should be visited by relief is a matter of discretion. So simple an approach seems to me appropriate, having regard to the language of the statute and to the consideration that the court is not dealing with a mere technicality but with the ability of people to have secure accommodation for their homes (as presumably Parliament intended) and with the removal of the often grossly injurious environmental impact on the public and local residents of unauthorised gipsy encampments.'

c

Kennedy J adopted those words. On the hearing of these appeals it has not been argued that this approach was wrong.

I agree with the approach described by Mann J, and the words used by him, provided that the meaning of the phrase 'adequate accommodation for gipsies residing in or *d* resorting to their area' and the date by reference to which the adequacy of available accommodation is to be tested are first made clear. In my judgment Parliament clearly, and at least, intended to impose on a county council an obligation to exercise its powers under the 1960 Act so as to provide accommodation for the number of gipsies known to be habitually residing in or resorting to its area in the ordinary course of the year, on the basis that at any time, in considering whether that obligation has been broken, the *e* adequacy of accommodation provided would be tested by reference to the number of gipsies known to the council to be so residing or resorting over a preceding period of time of reasonable length. That period of time would be assessed by reference to the time necessary for a county council to exercise its powers to provide accommodation. Whether any more rigorous or peremptory duty was imposed on a county council by s 6 of the *f* 1968 Act need not be decided for the purposes of this case. It has not been argued before this court that on any view of the meaning of s 6, West Glamorgan County Council could be regarded as not in breach of the duty imposed by it at the relevant time. Since the extent of the duty has not been argued I shall not attempt to define what I think it is but I cannot attribute to Parliament an intention that by s 6 of the 1968 Act a duty was imposed on any county council to provide accommodation for any number of 'persons of nomadic habit of life' who for any reason might choose at any time to resort to the *g* area of the council, simply in the sense of choosing to go there for a time however short and for whatever purpose. A county council faced with a sudden and unforeseen influx of gipsies into their area would not, as it seems to me, by reason only of the presence of those gipsies and the absence of adequate accommodation for them, necessarily be in breach of duty under s 6 of the 1968 Act.

h Before Kennedy J the direction given by the Secretary of State on 11 April 1986 was attacked by counsel on behalf of the county council as being invalid in that it did not specify the sites to be provided. The direction was justified by the Secretary of State on the ground that the choice of sites was better left to the county council, which knew its area, owned some land and was in close contact with the district councils. Kennedy J held that the direction as made was within the powers of the Secretary of State and therefore *j* valid. There has been no appeal from that finding.

Counsel for the defendants before Kennedy J submitted that the direction given by the Secretary of State should be re-enforced by an order of mandamus requiring the county council to comply with its statutory duty under s 6 of the 1968 Act and with any directions given by the Secretary of State, or, alternatively, a declaration should be made

that the county council was in breach of its statutory duty. The county council informed
the court that if the direction of 11 April 1986 was found to be valid, as it was, the county   *a*
council would comply with it. Kennedy J accordingly declined in the exercise of the
court's discretion to make either the order of mandamus or the declaration sought.
Kennedy J added:

> '. . . I recognise that the direction given by the Secretary of State only requires
> provision of 60 caravan sites, which everyone agrees to be less than are needed to   *b*
> provide adequate accommodation for gipsies residing in or resorting to the county
> as a whole. But the right course, as it seems to me at this stage, is for the county
> council to be given a reasonable opportunity to comply with the direction given on
> 11 April.'

There has been no appeal against that part of Kennedy J's judgment.

As to the order of mandamus which was sought requiring the Secretary of State to   *c*
issue a further direction covering the whole of the obligation imposed on the county
council by s 6, Kennedy J declined to make any such order. He held that the Secretary of
State was not obliged by s 9 to give directions simply because a local authority had failed
to comply with its obligations under s 6. It was for the Secretary of State to decide
whether in a particular case it was necessary or desirable to give a direction. If the gipsies
then at Briton Ferry were allowed to remain there for the time being, and if the county   *d*
council complied with the directions already given under s 9, it might well be that the
Secretary of State would not consider it necessary to give any further directions. Kennedy
J saw no reason to override that decision on his part. Kennedy J drew attention to the
letter from the Welsh Office to the county council dated 11 April 1986 which
accompanied the direction and which stated:
                                                                                        e
> 'The directions require the provision of sites for 60 caravans for gipsies. The
> Secretary of State has chosen this figure having regard to information provided by
> officers of the county council and the national gipsy council as a sensible means of
> promoting the fulfilment of their statutory obligations to the county council. He
> will monitor any continuing requirement for accommodation for gipsies and will
> consider as he thinks fit further exercise of his powers under s 9 of the 1968 Act.   *f*
> The Secretary of State would be grateful if the council would inform him as soon as
> possible of their proposals for meeting the requirements of the directions.'

Kennedy J said that that seemed to him to be an entirely proper attitude for the Secretary
of State to adopt at that stage and there would be no order affecting him. From these
parts of Kennedy J's judgment there has also been no appeal and the Secretary of State has
not taken part in the hearing of the appeals before this court.   *g*

The decision to evict

After setting out the history of this matter, which has been repeated above in this
judgment, Kennedy J directed himself by reference to the principle stated by Lord
Greene MR in *Associated Provincial Picture Houses Ltd v Wednesbury Corp* [1947] 2 All ER   *h*
680, [1948] 1 KB 223. He then summarised the submission made by counsel for the
county council on the facts and continued:

> 'Having regard to the history of which I have referred, I am satisfied that the
> decision of 16 September 1985 to evict the gipsies from the Briton Ferry site without
> offering them any place in West Glamorgan to which they could go, was a decision
> which was unreasonable in the *Wednesbury* sense and which must, therefore, be   *j*
> quashed. That, of course, does not mean that the land at Briton Ferry is likely to be
> sterilised for a long time. As soon as an alternative site can be offered the situation
> will change.'

Later in his judgment Kennedy J added:

a
'Accordingly, there will be an order to quash the decision of the county council to take possession of the land at Briton Ferry. There will be a declaration that the West Glamorgan County Council are not entitled in law to seek possession of the land at Briton Ferry Industrial Estate, Neath, until such time as they make some reasonable alternative provision for the accommodation of gipsies ... it seems to me wrong to relate the obligations of the county council to the number of gipsies who happen to be at Britton Ferry at any particular time. There will be no injunction restraining

b
the county council from taking further proceedings for possession because, when some alternative accommodation does become available, further proceedings may be necessary. That may well be before the county council has discharged all of its obligations under s 6.'

Counsel for the county council has reminded this court of the respect which the law requires to be paid to the decisions of elected bodies made within their lawful procedures
c
on matters entrusted to them. He referred us, as he referred the court below, to the well-known words of Lord Greene MR in *Associated Provincial Picture Houses Ltd v Wednesbury Corp* [1948] 1 KB 223 at 230; cf [1947] 2 All ER 680 at 683:

'It is clear that the local authority are entrusted by Parliament with the decision on a matter which the knowledge and experience of that authority can best be
d
trusted to deal with. The subject-matter with which the condition deals is one relevant for its consideration. They have considered it and come to a decision upon it. It is true to say that, if a decision on a competent matter is so unreasonable that no reasonable authority could ever have come to it, then the courts can interfere. That, I think, is quite right; but to prove a case of that kind would require something overwhelming, and, in this case, the facts do not come anywhere near anything of
e
that kind.'

A more recent statement of the principle, which does not affect the substance of it but which re-emphasises the nature of what must be proved before the court can justify the striking down of such a decision, is to be found in *Puhlhofer v Hillingdon London BC* [1986] 1 All ER 467, [1986] AC 484. That case was concerned with the obligations of a local
f
authority under the Housing (Homeless Persons) Act 1977. Lord Brightman, in an opinion with which Lord Keith, Lord Roskill, Lord Brandon and Lord Mackay agreed, said ([1986] 1 All ER 467 at 474, [1986] AC 484 at 518):

'Although the action or inaction of a local authority is clearly susceptible to judicial review where they have misconstrued the Act, or abused their powers or otherwise acted perversely, I think that great restraint should be exercised in giving
g
leave to proceed by judicial review. The plight of the homeless is a desperate one, and the plight of the applicants in the present case commands the deepest sympathy. But it is not, in my opinion, appropriate that the remedy of judicial review, which is a discretionary remedy, should be made use of to monitor the actions of local authorities under the Act save in the exceptional case. The ground on which the
h
courts will review the exercise of an administrative discretion is abuse of power, e g bad faith, a mistake in construing the limits of the power, a procedural irregularity or unreasonableness in the *Wednesbury* sense (see *Associated Provincial Picture Houses Ltd v Wednesbury Corp* [1947] 2 All ER 680, [1948] 1 KB 223), ie unreasonableness verging on an absurdity: see the speech of Lord Scarman in *Nottinghamshire CC v Secretary of State for the Environment* [1986] 1 All ER 199 at 202, [1986] 2 WLR 1 at
j
5. Where the existence or non-existence of a fact is left to the judgment and discretion of a public body and that fact involves a broad spectrum ranging from the obvious to the debatable to the just conceivable, it is the duty of the court to leave the decision of that fact to the public body to whom Parliament has entrusted the decision-making power save in a case where it is obvious that the public body, consciously or unconsciously, are acting perversely.'

The decision made on 16 September 1985 to evict the gipsies on the recommendation of the county clerk was, as I have said above, a decision based on the choice of priorities *a* on a matter of social policy within the control of an elected council. There were factors on both sides of the question: some against and some for the policy of eviction. From the submissions of counsel for the county council and counsel for the defendants, which were as admirably complete as they were concise, those factors can be summarised as follows.

Those against eviction included the following. (i) The county council had failed over *b* 15 years to carry out its statutory duty so to use its powers under s 24 of the 1960 Act, as to provide adequate accommodation for gipsies resorting to or residing in the area. (ii) There was accordingly no site within West Glamorgan to which the gipsies, if evicted, could lawfully go. (iii) It is probable that as to a large number of those to be evicted their presence as trespassers on the land of the county council was caused by the breach of duty of the county council. (iv) Eviction would cause substantial hardship to a substantial *c* number of the families evicted, which hardship would be reduced only by the families resorting to the sites provided in other areas (and there was no evidence to suggest that there would be room for them), or by trespassing elsewhere within West Glamorgan. (v) Eviction would thus cause hardship not only to the gipsies evicted but also to those on whom the burden of receiving the displaced families would be transferred. (vi) Both forms of hardship (ie to the gipsies and to those affected by the presence of gipsies on *d* unapproved and unregulated sites) were within the mischief at which the enactment of the statutory duty was directed.

The factors telling in favour of eviction were as follows. (i) As stated on the documents submitted to the chairman of the policy and resources committee for approval of the recommendation to evict, tenders were due to be received shortly for the next stage of the reclamation works and 'part of the land affected by these works is at present *e* unlawfully occupied by gipsy caravans'. Reclamation of the area was part of the process of redevelopment which was aimed at the creation of employment. (ii) The presence of some of the gipsies on the site was causing nuisance and probably some damage to neighbouring occupiers. The Welsh Development Agency owns land adjoining the Briton Ferry site on which there were two vacant factories and another factory let to a *f* timber engineering firm. The agency had received a complaint from that firm in October 1985 of the offensive attitude and behaviour of some gipsies camped on the county council's land over the period 7 to 12 October 1985 which included the fouling of doorways and damage to the property. The vacant factory units were found to have been vandalised in December 1985. The agency has had to incur the expense of security patrols. The agency's senior property surveyor, Mr Piper, has stated his belief that the *g* unlawful gipsy encampment was seriously inhibiting the letting of the vacant factories and it was preventing progress on the agency-funded reclamation scheme which was required to make the land suitable for industrial development and to upgrade the appearance of the site so as to improve its attraction to companies. This evidence relates in detail some matters arising after the decision to evict in September 1985 but it describes the results of the presence of some gipsies in an unregulated and unlawful *h* encampment which must have been known to the county council before 19 September 1985. (iii) The gipsies at Briton Ferry site were there as trespassers and knew that they had no right to be there. (iv) It was a bad example to the whole community that trespassers should be seen to be tolerated or immune from eviction for any prolonged period of time.

It is necessary to emphasise that Kennedy J did not rule that the decision to evict was *j* unreasonable because the county council was in breach of statutory duty. He held that, having regard to all the circumstances, it was unreasonable to resolve to evict the gipsies from the site without making any arrangements whatever for provision of alternative accommodation for any of them.

It seems to me, in considering the factors for and against eviction, which have been set out above, that there is no effective reply in diminution of the weight of those listed against eviction but that, with reference to those listed in favour of eviction, there is much to be said which greatly reduces their weight. First, it is not shown that it was necessary, for the purposes relied on by the county council, to evict at once all the families from all the 170 acres of this site, the nature of which is clear from the account already given. The evidence indicates that it was practicable to contain the caravans within a selected part of the whole site by evicting only from defined parts of it and by permitting all or some of the caravans then on the site, which did not exceed 25 in number, to remain on or move to the selected part. The county council made a proposal in February 1986 to Mr Hughie Smith that the gipsies camped at the site should move to a less obtrusive part of the 170-acre estate (see the affidavit of Mr Burgess), and Mr Smith was invited to seek the co-operation of the gipsies to that end. The court has not been told of the details of the suggestion or offer. Neither the offer nor the refusal of it can affect the reasonableness of the decision to evict of 16 September 1985. The fact that the offer could be made, however, demonstrates in my judgment that it was at all times practicable for the county council to have sought possession of the site, or part of it only, while offering to permit caravans to remain for a period of time on that 'less obtrusive' part of the whole site. There is no evidence that this practicable alternative was considered.

Next, while the presence of gipsies on this partly reclaimed site was causing some damage and nuisance, eviction of the gipsies from the whole of the area of West Glamorgan was not, in my judgment, a lawful aim for this county council; nor was it in fact possible of achievement. Immediate eviction from the whole of this site of all the families camped on it, therefore, would not terminate that evil of damage and nuisance caused by some of the gipsies unlawfully camped, but would merely shift it to others within the area or to the land of the county council in another place.

Finally, as to the gipsies being trespassers, it is probable in my judgment that as to many of them their presence on this site as trespassers was caused directly by the long-continued breach of duty of the county council; and the 'badness of the example', if trespassers were seen to be immune, is not, I think, any worse than that provided to the community if the county council is seen, while in clear breach of its statutory duty to provide accommodation for the gipsies in the area, to be evicting the gipsies from a site of this nature without provision of any alternative accommodation. It lay within the powers of the county council to change the status of the gipsies from that of 'trespassers' into that of temporarily tolerated trespassers or into regulated licensees on some defined and temporary site.

For these reasons it is clear to me that the question to be answered by reference to the factors discussed above could only reasonably be answered against eviction, if eviction was to be carried out with no provision for alternative accommodation, but that by itself is not enough to justify the decision of Kennedy J. Reasonable men and women can 'perfectly reasonably come to the opposite conclusions on the same set of facts without forfeiting their title to be regarded as reasonable' (per Lord Hailsham LC in Re W (an infant) [1971] 2 All ER 49 at 56, [1971] AC 682 at 700).

The question is whether, within the principles of law stated above, the decision of the county council must be described as perverse or as revealing 'unreasonableness verging on an absurdity'. I have found the decision difficult but, in the end, I am driven to the same conclusion as that reached by Kennedy J for the following reasons. The court is not, as I understand the law, precluded from finding a decision to be void for unreasonableness merely because there are admissible factors on both sides of the question. If the weight of the factors against eviction must be recognised by a reasonable council, properly aware of its duties and its powers, to be overwhelming, then a decision the other way cannot be upheld if challenged. The decision on eviction was a decision which required the weighing of the factors according to the personal judgment of the councillors but the

law does not permit complete freedom of choice or assessment because legal duty must
be given proper weight.   a

The continuing breach of duty by the county council to 'gipsies residing or resorting
to' the area of West Glamorgan does not in law preclude the right of the county council
to recover possession of any land occupied by the trespassing gipsies, but that does not
remove that continuing breach of duty from the balance or reduce its weight as a factor.
The reasonable council in the view of the law is required to recognise its own breach of
legal duty for what it is and to recognise the consequences of that breach of legal duty for   b
what they are. The reasonable council, accordingly, was not in my judgment free to treat
the interference with the intended reclamation and redevelopment of this site, for such
period of time as would have resulted from the holding up of complete eviction from
the entire site while temporary accommodation was provided elsewhere, as outweighing
the effects of eviction on the gipsies then present and on those to whom the impact of
trespassing by gipsies would necessarily be transferred. The decision is only explicable to   c
me as one made by a council which was either not thinking of its powers and duties
under law or was by some error mistaken as to the nature and extent of those powers and
duties.

I have been able to reach that conclusion with greater confidence because it is, in my
view, supported and justified by the contents of the letter of 18 June 1985 sent by the
county clerk to the Welsh Office, to which I have referred above (para (xii) of the history).   d
The clerk referred to the failure to provide any sites after 'ten years of hard effort to make
some provision' and concluded that he did not know what more the county council could
reasonably do. That attitude was reflected in the conduct of the county council, from
June 1985 until the commencement of proceedings to evict the gipsies by the originating
summons issued on 19 September 1985, in doing nothing whatever and in having no
plans to do anything towards the provision of accommodation for gipsies even on   e
temporary sites. It was perhaps reflected also in the argument addressed to Kennedy J by
counsel for the county council to the effect that the county council could not be in breach
of its duty under the 1960 Act unless and until the Secretary of State should make a valid
direction under s 9 of the 1968 Act; and, further, that the county council was not in
breach of its duty under s 6 of the 1968 Act provided that it was making all reasonable   f
efforts to select and provide sites. Kennedy J rejected both submissions. They have not
been renewed in this court. It seems to me that the unreasonableness of the decision to
evict without any attempt or intention to provide or to direct the gipsies to alternative
accommodation is explained by, and probably sprang from, the mistaken view held by
the county clerk that there was nothing more to his knowledge that the county council
could reasonably do in discharge of their statutory duty. That view was, in my judgment,
wrong. It remained the duty of the county council to make provision for the   g
accommodation of gipsies by use of their powers under the 1960 Act. It has not been
disputed in this court that they could have used their powers to provide temporary
accommodation. The decision simply to evict by itself suggests the failure to consider
the consequences of eviction, both on the gipsies themselves and on others as discussed
above, and a failure to consider the county council's own powers to alleviate those   h
consequences. If those who made the decision accepted the view that there was nothing
that the county council could then reasonably do in discharge of its statutory duty under
the 1968 Act, then the holding of that mistaken opinion provides an explanation why
this decision, which in my view was void for unreasonableness, came to be made.

I would therefore, for the reasons given, uphold the decision of Kennedy J to quash
the decision of the county council to take proceedings for eviction of the gipsies at the   j
Briton Ferry site. I take a different view, however, of the declaration which Kennedy J
also made that:

> 'The County Council is not entitled in law to seek possession of the land . . . until
> such time as the County Council makes some reasonable alternative provision for
> the accommodation of gipsies.'

I would set aside that declaration, which I think should not have been made. It is not
a possible for the court to decide in advance that any decision to claim possession of the
land at Briton Ferry, or any part of it, must be perverse unless the county council has first
made 'reasonable' alternative provision for the accommodation of gipsies. The
circumstances at the site have changed since 19 September 1985 and will continue to
change. There were in September 1985 at the site many fewer caravans than there are
now. There were 25 caravans in December 1985. By 3 March 1986 there were 63. In
b April 1986 there were 103, as the court was informed by counsel for the county council.
This large increase in the number of caravans on this site shows the factual validity of the
submission made to Peter Pain J that, if he set aside the original order for possession, the
consequence would be that gipsies would be free to squat on the county council's property
and to remain there. The 103 caravans present in April 1986 is greater than the average
number of caravans in West Glamorgan over the past 10 years, namely 85. Kennedy J
c was aware of this aspect of the problem, as is clear from the passage from his judgment
which I have cited and he therefore amended the form of the declaration. In my
judgment, no declaration should be made in any terms. The county council is free, and
must be left free, to deal with the situation as it thinks best having regard to its duty and
powers, which will have been clarified by the judgment of Kennedy J and by the decision
of this court. It would be wrong for this court, as I think, to try to indicate what sort of
d plan or provision for recovery of possession of this site would be 'reasonable'. We have
neither the right nor the knowledge to formulate any such suggestion and the county
council does not need guidance from us. There is no reason to suppose that the county
council will again make a decision with reference to this matter which could be described
as perverse. If any such challenge is made hereafter to any further decision of the county
council the matter will have to be considered and decided in the usual way. For my part,
e therefore, I would allow the appeal of the county council to the extent of deleting the
declaration from the court's order in the judicial review proceedings but otherwise I
would dismiss that appeal. I would also dismiss the appeal in the RSC Ord 113
proceedings.

f **SIR JOHN MEGAW.** I agree with the order proposed, and, subject to the reservations
set out below, I agree with the reasons given by Ralph Gibson LJ.

My first reservation relates to the meaning of 'residing in or resorting to their area' in
s 6 of the Caravan Sites Act 1968. Because of the way in which this case has developed,
and because of its very special facts, this issue was not argued before us. It would be
wrong, therefore, to express any final view on the matter. But it is, in my opinion,
g desirable that nothing which has been said by this court should be interpreted as resolving
what appears to me to be a serious difficulty of construction in s 6. If 'resorting to' were
to mean, simply, 'coming to' or 'having come to', then the single word 'in' would have
expressed the intended meaning. The words 'residing in or resorting to' would be
superfluous, since 'gipsies in their area' would cover, and cover no more than would be
covered by, 'gipsies residing in or resorting to their area'. I should hesitate long before
h attributing such useless verbosity to the draftsman. But if 'resorting to' has an esoteric
meaning, what is it? Could it be the fifth meaning appearing in the *Shorter Oxford
Dictionary*: to go habitually or frequently to a place? But, if so, would that not put an
almost intolerable burden on the county council, in attempting to ascertain who or how
many qualify as non-resident 'resorters'?

My second reservation relates to the acceptance by Kennedy J of Mann J's proposition
j in *R v Secretary of State for the Environment, ex p Lee* (14 January 1985, unreported), which,
if I have not misunderstood it, means that a county council becomes in breach of its
statutory duty at the moment when the number of gipsies 'residing in or resorting to'
(whatever those words mean) the council's area exceeds the number for whom suitable
accommodation has been provided. To my mind, Parliament cannot have intended to
provide that a council would immediately, necessarily and automatically be in breach of

its statutory duty if, for example, an unforeseen, perhaps unforeseeable, influx of gipsies
'resorting to' the council's area should have the result that the accommodation which the   *a*
council had provided, adequate up to that moment, should become inadequate. I should
not find it an attractive answer to that absurdity, if it were to be suggested that, although
the council would be in breach of its statutory duty, that did not really matter because it
would be unlikely that a court of law would, in its discretion, grant judicial review.

The absence of argument on behalf of the county council in this appeal against Mann
J's view expressed in the passage quoted by Ralph Gibson LJ may well have been because,   *b*
on the special facts of this case, it would not avail the county council to show that that
view was wrong in law. If the concession went further than that, I should, respectfully,
feel serious doubt whether the concession was rightly made. Apart from any other
considerations, the duty under s 6 is to *provide* accommodation for those who qualify as
'residing in or resorting to'. It is not a duty to *have provided* accommodation in anticipation
of 'residing in' being achieved or 'resorting to' taking place by any persons or by any   *c*
number of persons.

SLADE LJ. The judgment of Sir John Megaw vividly illustrates certain problems of
interpretation to which s 6 of the Caravan Sites Act 1968 may give rise. While not
intending in any sense to indicate dissent from his illuminating analysis, I would, for my
part, prefer to venture not even a provisional answer to those problems, since they have   *d*
not been fully ventilated in argument before us. On appeal before this court, it has, I
think, been common ground that, whatever the meaning of the section, the West
Glamorgan County Council had been in long-continued breach of its duty thereunder by
the time when it resolved, on 16 September 1985, to issue proceedings against the gipsies.
This, I think, is the basis on which Ralph Gibson LJ has reached his conclusion. For the
reasons given by him, with which I respectfully agree, I would delete the declaration   *e*
from the order of the court in the judicial review proceedings, but, subject to that
deletion, would dismiss the county council's appeals both in those proceedings and in
RSC Ord 113 proceedings.

Appeal in possession proceedings dismissed. Appeal in judicial review proceedings allowed to   *f*
extent of deleting declaration in those proceedings but otherwise appeal dismissed.

Solicitors: *Sherwood & Co*, agents for *M E J Rush*, Swansea (for the county council); *Parkers*,
St Helens (for the defendants in the first appeal and the applicant in the second appeal).

Wendy Shockett   Barrister.

a

R v Secretary of State for the Home Department, ex parte Ullah and other applications

b
QUEEN'S BENCH DIVISION (CROWN OFFICE LIST)
TAYLOR J
15, 16 JANUARY 1987

c
Immigration – British citizen – Right of abode – Right to live in United Kingdom 'without let or hindrance' – Right to live in United Kingdom with spouse – British citizen marrying Bangladeshi wife in Bangladesh – Wife having no right of entry into United Kingdom – Wife arriving in United Kingdom from Bangladesh without entry certificate – Wife refused entry and having to return to Bangladesh to obtain entry certificate – Whether right to live in United Kingdom 'without let or hindrance' including right to bring forthwith into United Kingdom wife who required entry certificate – Whether delay in granting entry certificate to wife infringing husband's right of abode – Whether requirement that wife return to Bangladesh to obtain entry certificate unreasonable –

d
Immigration Act 1971, s 1(1).

The applicants were British citizens married to Bangladeshi wives who arrived in the United Kingdom without entry clearance certificates and were refused entry. The immigration officers' decisions to refuse entry, which were indorsed by the Secretary of State, meant that the wives would be sent back to Bangladesh to obtain entry certificates.

e
The applicants sought judicial review of the Secretary of State's decisions, contending that the applicants' right under s 1(1)[a] of the Immigration Act 1971 to live in the United Kingdom 'without let or hindrance' included the right to live in the United Kingdom with their spouses and that any delay in granting their wives entry clearance infringed that right.

f

Held – On the true construction of s 1(1) of the 1971 Act the term 'without let or hindrance' did not confer the right on those having a right of abode in the United Kingdom to bring forthwith to the United Kingdom a wife or relative who herself required leave to enter. Furthermore, the decision of the Secretary of State to send the wives back to Bangladesh to obtain entry certificates rather than arrange for them to be

g
interviewed in the United Kingdom was not irrational, notwithstanding the length of the delay that would be involved, since the Secretary of State had been entitled to take the view, as he had done, that it would be unfair to give priority to those who entered without an entry certificate over those who abided by the rules and took their turn in Bangladesh to obtain a certificate. It followed that the applications would be refused (see p 1029 *j*, p 1030 *g h* and p 1031 *e* to *h*, post).

h
R v Secretary of State for the Home Dept, ex p Phansopkar [1975] 3 All ER 497 distinguished.

Notes
For persons having the right of abode in the United Kingdom, see 4 Halsbury's Laws (4th
j
edn) paras 974–975.
    For the control of immigration of wives, see ibid para 976, and for cases on the subject, see 2 Digest (Reissue) 200–202, 1157–1159.
    For the Immigration Act 1971, s 1, see 41 Halsbury's Statutes (3rd edn) 16.

---

a   Section 1(1) is set out at p 1028 *a b*, post

Cases referred to in judgment

Brahmbhatt v Chief Immigration Officer, Heathrow Airport, Terminal [1984] Imm AR 202, *a*
   CA.
Nottingham CC v Secretary of State for the Environment [1986] 1 All ER 199, [1986] AC 240,
   [1986] 2 WLR 1, HL.
R v Secretary of State for the Home Dept, ex p Akhtar [1975] 3 All ER 1087, [1975] 1 WLR
   1717, DC.
R v Secretary of State for the Home Dept, ex p Phansopkar [1975] 3 All ER 497, [1976] QB *b*
   606, [1975] 3 WLR 322, DC and CA.

Case also cited

R v Secretary of State for the Home Dept, ex p Swati [1986] 1 All ER 717, [1986] 1 WLR 477,
   CA.

Applications for judicial review   *c*
                     R v Secretary of State for the Home Dept, ex p Ullah
Rofath Ullah applied, with the leave of Russell J given on 24 April 1986, for judicial
review of the refusal of the Secretary of State for the Home Department to reverse an
immigration officer's notice of refusal of leave to enter the United Kingdom, dated 5
October 1985. The relief sought was a declaration that the waiting time in the queue in
Bangladesh amounted to a delay in the exercise of a right that the applicant's wife had to *d*
come to the United Kingdom as a dependant pursuant to s 1(4) of the Immigration Act
1971. The facts are set out in the judgment.

                     R v Secretary of State for the Home Dept, ex p Ali
Soifur Rahman Ali applied, with the leave of Nolan J given on 18 August 1986, for
judicial review of the refusal by the Secretary of State for the Home Department to *e*
reverse an immigration officer's notice of refusal of leave to enter the United Kingdom,
dated 4 May 1986. The relief sought was a declaration that the applicant's right to live in
the United Kingdom without let or hindrance conferred by s 1(1) of the Immigration
Act 1971 included the right to live in the United Kingdom with his spouse and that any
delay in the exercise of that right was unlawful. The facts are set out in the judgment. *f*

                     R v Secretary of State for the Home Dept, ex p Uddin
Foriz Uddin applied, with the leave of Nolan J given on 18 August 1986, for judicial
review of the refusal by the Secretary of State for the Home Department to reverse an
immigration officer's notice of refusal of leave to enter the United Kingdom, dated 23
November 1985. The relief sought was a declaration that the applicant's right to live in
the United Kingdom without let or hindrance conferred by s 1(1) of the Immigration *g*
Act 1971 included the right to marry and live in the United Kingdom with his spouse
and that any delay in the exercise of that right was unlawful. The facts are set out in the
judgment.

Alper Riza for the applicants.   *h*
David Pannick for the Secretary of State.

TAYLOR J.   These are three applications for judicial review. They have been heard
together as they all raise the same points. In each the applicant is a British citizen married
to a Bangladeshi wife. In each the wife was refused entry into the United Kingdom since
she lacked an entry clearance certificate. The decision challenged in each case is the *j*
refusal of the Secretary of State to reverse the immigration officer's refusal.
   The facts of the three cases can be stated quite shortly. The first applicant, Rofath
Ullah, is 25 years old and was born in Bangladesh. He came to the United Kingdom in
1976 to join his father . He settled here and was registered as a British citizen in 1984. In
May 1985 he went back to Bangladesh, where he married Nurjahan Begum on 31 August

1985. She was a Bangladeshi citizen. He returned to the United Kingdom with his wife
a on 5 October 1985. They had made no application for an entry certificate in Dhaka
before coming to the United Kingdom because they knew that there would be a very
considerable delay. On arrival the wife was refused leave to enter on the grounds that she
had no entry certificate. The assistance of a member of Parliament was enlisted to seek a
reversal of that decision, but by a letter of 6 December 1985 the Secretary of State for the
Home Department maintained the refusal.
b   It is accepted in each of these three cases that the process of being interviewed with a
view to obtaining an entry certificate in Dhaka at the present time involved something
of the order of 13 months' delay.
      The second applicant is Soifur Rahman Ali. He is 27 years old. He is a British citizen
born in the United Kingdom in Coventry of Bangladeshi parents. He has lived here most
of his life, but on 13 March 1986 he married Dilara Begum in Bangladesh. On 29 March
c 1986 he and his wife visited the British High Commission in Dhaka and applied for an
entry certificate for the wife to join her husband in England. There are letters from the
High Commission indicating that no firm date could be given for an interview. The
applicant claims that he had to return to the United Kingdom for business reasons and
he was unwilling to endure any lengthy delay before his wife could join him. Accordingly
d he brought her back with him on 5 April 1986. She was given temporary admission
whilst her case was considered, but on 4 May she was refused entry again on the ground
that she had no entry clearance certificate. Once again the applicant sought help from a
member of Parliament. He also suggested by letter to the authorities that any interview
that was necessary in respect of his wife's application for entry clearance might take place
in the United Kingdom rather than in Dhaka, but again the Secretary of State turned
e down the application by letter of 18 June 1986.
      The third applicant is Foriz Uddin. He is 20 years old and was born in Bangladesh. He
became a registered British citizen on 1 June 1985. He married Ashma Begum, a
Bangladeshi citizen, in the United Kingdom on 18 December 1985. She falls to be
considered as a fiancée rather than as a wife in this case because she arrived on 23
November seeking leave to enter so as to marry the applicant. She was refused at that
f stage as she had no entry clearance, but she was granted temporary admission. She took
advantage of that to marry the applicant and thereafter in this case, as in the other two,
the assistance of a member of Parliament was sought to try to overturn the decision of
the immigration officer. But by a letter of 14 May 1986 the Secretary of State refused to
change the decision. Special reliance was placed in that case on the fact that the applicant's
wife was expecting a child imminently at the time that the approach was made to the
g Secretary of State, but unfortunately that child was stillborn in July 1986.
      It is unnecessary to recite the precise terms of the Secretary of State's decision in each
case, but the rationale of each can perhaps best be summarised by referring to the letter
which was written in the case of Soifur Rahman Ali on 18 June 1986. This paragraph
appears in the Secretary of State's letter:

h   'I attach great importance to the entry clearance requirement as an essential factor
      in maintaining an effective immigration control which is both firm and fair. It
      provides not only the opportunity for entry clearance officers to check the
      entitlement of applicants before they travel but also ensures that all are dealt with
      in a fair and orderly way. Waiving the requirement would encourage others to
      travel without entry clearance leading to long delays at ports while the necessary
j   enquiries were undertaken. For these reasons I am prepared to set aside the entry
      clearance requirement only in exceptional compassionate circumstances.'

It is right to say that counsel for the applicants does not suggest in these cases that there
are any exceptional compassionate circumstances.
      It is next convenient to look at the statutory provisions and at the rules which are

relevant. First, reference must be made to s 1 of the Immigration Act 1971, which, so far as is relevant, reads as follows:

'(1) All those who are in this Act expressed to have the right of abode in the United Kingdom shall be free to live in, and to come and go into and from, the United Kingdom without let or hindrance except such as may be required under and in accordance with this Act to enable their right to be established or as may be otherwise lawfully imposed on any person.

(2) Those not having that right may live, work and settle in the United Kingdom by permission and subject to such regulation and control of their entry into, stay in and departure from the United Kingdom as is imposed by this Act . . .

(4) The rules laid down by the Secretary of State as to the practice to be followed in the administration of this Act for regulating the entry into and stay in the United Kingdom of persons not having the right of abode shall include provision for admitting (in such cases and subject to such restrictions as may be provided by the rules, and subject or not to conditions as to length of stay or otherwise) persons coming . . . as dependants of persons lawfully in or entering the United Kingdom . . .'

Section 2(1)(a) of the 1971 Act reads as follows, in the form in which it now stands, having been substituted by s 39 of the British Nationality Act 1981:

'A person is under this Act to have the right of abode in the United Kingdom if— (a) he is a British citizen . . .'

Section 3, so far as is relevant, reads as follows:

'(1) Except as otherwise provided by or under this Act, where a person is not a British citizen—(a) he shall not enter the United Kingdom unless given leave to do so in accordance with this Act . . .

(2) The Secretary of State shall from time to time (and as soon as may be) lay before Parliament statements of the rules, or of any changes in the rules, laid down by him as to the practice to be followed in the administration of this Act for regulating the entry into and stay in the United Kingdom of persons required by this Act to have leave to enter . . .'

The relevant rules are those laid down in the Statement of Changes in Immigration Rules (HC Paper (1982–83) no 169), as amended by the Statement of Changes in Immigration Rules (HC Paper (1984–85) no 503). Paragraph 4 of HC Paper (1982–83) no 169 deals, inter alia, with the requirements for entry. The last sentence of para 4 reads as follows:

'A person who is neither a British citizen nor a Commonwealth citizen having the right of abode requires leave to enter.'

HC Paper (1984–85) no 503, by para 3, substitutes new paragraphs in relation to the obtaining of entry clearance. It is unnecessary for me to read the provisions in full. Paragraph 8 of HC Paper (1984–85) no 503 substitutes new paras 41 to 44 in HC Paper (1982–83) no 169 in respect of fiancés and deals with requirements before they can be admitted for settlement. Those requirements are that they must hold a current entry clearance granted for the purpose of entry and the entry clearance will be refused unless the officer is satisfied of various matters which I can shortly summarise as saying that the marriage is not a marriage of convenience. Similarly para 10 of HC Paper (1984–85) no 503 substitutes new paragraphs in HC Paper (1982–83) no 169 in respect of spouses which are in similar terms to those in relation to fiancés.

Counsel for the applicants accepts that the wives of these applicants do not have a right of entry to the United Kingdom. They do not have a right of abode themselves, nor does

the fact that they are married in each case to a British citizen give them any such right.
a Under the Immigration Act 1971 as originally enacted they would as Commonwealth
citizens married to British citizens have had a right of abode themselves pursuant to
s 2(2) as it then was. However, s 39(2) of the British Nationality Act 1981 amended the
1971 Act to remove that right. Now wives and fiancés of British citizens who are
themselves Commonwealth citizens require leave to enter the United Kingdom under
s 3(1)(a) of the 1971 Act. They are subject to immigration control and to the rules made
b in pursuance of ss 1(2) and (4) and 3(2) of the 1971 Act.

Counsel for the applicants seeks to meet this problem by basing his case on the rights
of the applicant husbands. His principal argument stems from s 1(1) of the 1971 Act.
Each of the applicants having a right of abode has a right under that section to live in,
come from and go to the United Kingdom without let or hindrance, subject to the
c exceptions stated. The argument is that if his wife is delayed for months in joining him
that constitutes an indirect let or hindrance to the applicant's right. Counsel for the
applicants contends that the right to live in the United Kingdom is not confined to a
right of physical presence. It includes by implication, he says, the right to live in the
United Kingdom normally with one's wife. He goes further and says not only with one's
wife, but with one's children and relatives too. Therefore, the delay occasioned by
d processing entry clearance infringes the husband's right. He recognises that the phrase
'without let or hindrance' in s 1(1) is qualified by the words 'except as may be otherwise
lawfully imposed on any person', but he maintains that once the wife is eligible to come
any extensive delay in allowing her to do so is not lawfully imposed.

Counsel for the applicants relies on *R v Secretary of State for the Home Dept, ex p
Phansopkar* [1975] 3 All ER 497, [1976] QB 606. There the Court of Appeal ruled that it
e was unlawful for a wife's certificate of patriality to be delayed without good cause and
that a desire by the authorities to be fair to all and avoid queue jumping was not a valid
reason for such delay. However, *Phansopkar*'s case was decided when s 2(2) of the 1971
Act still operated to give the patrial's wife a right to come to the United Kingdom. Each
member of the Court of Appeal emphasised the difference between one who has a right
to come and one who requires leave. Thus, Lord Denning MR said ([1975] 3 All ER 497
f at 508, [1976] QB 606 at 622):

'It is only those who have a simple straightforward case for patriality who should
get priority . . . because they are entitled as of right and not by leave.'

Similarly, Lawton LJ said ([1975] 3 All ER 497 at 508, [1976] QB 606 at 623):

'Such rules as have been made under s 3(2) would not apply to patrials, including
g wives coming within s 2(2), as they have a right to enter; they do not require leave
to enter.'

The case decided that a wife having a right of abode could not lawfully be delayed in her
exercise of it. Here it is common ground that the wives required leave.

The distinction was underlined in the subsequent case of *R v Secretary of State for the
h Home Dept, ex p Akhtar* [1975] 3 All ER 1087, [1975] 1 WLR 1717. There the wife was an
alien and had therefore no right of abode under s 2(2) even as originally enacted. The
court made it clear that the decision in *Phansopkar*'s case did not apply to a person who
did not have the right of abode.

In my judgment, the argument based on s 1(1) of the 1971 Act in this case is
misconceived. However desirable it no doubt is in human terms that husband and wife
j should live together and should not have to endure long separation, s 1 cannot by
implication give the husband a right to have his wife join him forthwith. The Act is
concerned to distinguish between different categories of persons for the purposes of
immigration. It differentiates between those who have a right of abode and those who
require leave. The phrase 'without let or hindrance' in s 1 cannot in my view carry with
it the right to bring forthwith a wife or relatives who themselves require leave. If it did

there would be no need in s 1(4) to make provision by rules for dependants to come. *a*
Moreover, s 2(2), as originally enacted, which gave the Commonwealth wives of British
citizens right of abode, would have been otiose. The amendment which replaced it has
in any event made it clear that such wives require leave and the meaning of s 1(1) cannot
have altered simply because s 2 has been amended.

Counsel for the Secretary of State referred me to a decision of the Court of Appeal on
similar facts which supports the view that the argument of counsel for the applicant is
misconceived. It is *Brahmbhatt v Chief Immigration Officer, Heathrow Airport, Terminal* *b*
[1984] Imm AR 202. In that case Slade LJ said (at 209):

'Though [counsel for the appellant applicant] made some reference to the past
history of our immigration laws going back beyond 1971, I confess that it never
became completely clear to me upon what grounds he asserted that immediately
before the passing of the [British Nationality Act 1981] a wife in the position of the *c*
appellant would have had a right to enter this country *at common law*, apart from the
statutory rights given her by section 2(2) of the 1971 Act. If I understood him
correctly, he submitted (inter alia) that a woman in this position would have
possessed such a right at common law as a by-product of the statutory right of her
husband under section 1(1) of the 1971 Act to come into the United Kingdom
"without let or hindrance". I would, for my part, find great difficulty in accepting *d*
any such submission. However, I think it unnecessary to consider further what
rights (if any) to enter this country the wife of a person who is now to be termed a
British citizen would have enjoyed at common law immediately before the passing
of the 1981 Act. For, in my opinion, it is quite clear that such common law right, if
indeed it existed, must have been removed by the 1981 Act: In this context, I need
do no more than refer to section 3(1)(a) of the 1971 Act, as amended in 1981 . . . *e*
which makes it clear that a person who is not a British citizen has no right to enter
the United Kingdom "except as otherwise provided by or under this Act", unless he
is given leave to do so. In other words, whatever may have been the position before
the passing of the 1981 Act, the rights of entry of any such person now stem from
statute and statute alone. A person such as the appellant can gain a right of entry
only by qualifying under the Act and the Rules. This, I think, is the combined effect *f*
of sections 1(1), 1(2) and 1(4) and 3(1) and 3(2) of the 1971 Act as amended in 1981.'
(Slade LJ's emphasis.)

It is true that the argument in that case was put on the basis that the wife herself acquired
a right to come as a by-product of the husband's right to live here without let or
hindrance, whereas counsel for the applicants before us simply relies on the husband's *g*
right. However, the reasoning is analogous and in my view equally fallacious. Even if
there were any merit in the broad submission that 'without let or hindrance' implies a
right to have one's wife and family, the exception here in relation to the wife requiring
entry clearance is lawfully imposed. It depends on s 3(1) and (2) and the rules made
thereunder.

Counsel for the applicants concedes that if his main submission on s 1(1) fails, as I hold *h*
it does, he is in difficulty in pursuing his remaining contentions. They are that the delay
is unreasonably long and that there is no reason why wives should not be interviewed in
the United Kingdom rather than be sent back to Dhaka.

I accept the submission of counsel for the Secretary of State that the Secretary of State's
decision is only open to challenge if it could be said to be illegal, irrational or involve a
procedural impropriety. Apart from his point on s 1(1) of the 1971 Act, counsel for the *j*
applicants does not suggest that this decision was illegal. Nor does he suggest that it
involved any procedural impropriety in the sense of denying the applicant a hearing or
failing to consult or any of the other manifestations of the phrase 'procedural impropriety'.

What he contends here is that the decision was irrational. The irrationality he relies on
is based on the factual background to the delay which has been mentioned. The delay, it

is common ground, is due to the large number of applicants and the small number of
a entry clearance officers. There is no suggestion here of bad faith on the part of the
authorities. There is no suggestion that the delay is being deliberately created in order to
slow down or bar immigration and there is no suggestion that the Secretary of State has
prescribed, as it were, a period of delay in order to postpone the arrival of those eligible
to join their spouses.

What is accepted to be the position is that, having regard to the numbers, the period
b of delay in fact works out currently at about 13 months. Counsel for the applicants says
that this could be overcome by appointing more entry clearance officers. Of course, that
would involve further expense. Counsel for the Secretary of State relies on the fact that
the expenditure is one which would have to be considered by the Secretary of State and
that he would be responsible to Parliament for considering what added expenditure
would be justified.

c In those circumstances counsel for the Secretary of State says that the court should be,
and habitually has been, slow to interfere with the exercise of discretion by a Secretary of
State. He relies further on the dicta in *Nottinghamshire CC v Secretary of State for the
Environment* [1986] 1 All ER 199, [1986] AC 240. That was a rate-capping case and it is
perhaps sufficient if I read, from the headnote, the second holding in that case, which is
as follows ([1986] AC 240 at 241):
d

> '. . . in the absence of some exceptional circumstances such as bad faith or
> improper motive on the part of the Secretary of State it was inappropriate for the
> courts to intervene on the ground of "unreasonableness" in a matter of public
> financial administration that had been one for the political judgment of the Secretary
> of State and the House of Commons.'

e So far as the second argument of counsel for the applicants is concerned, namely that
interviews could take place in the United Kingdom rather than that the applicant's wives
be sent back to Dhaka, a further consideration arises. The Secretary of State takes the
view that it would be unfair to allow priority to those who enter in defiance of the
requirement of entry certificates being obtained over those who abide by the rules and
f take their turn back in Bangladesh. In other words, it is the argument of fairness which
failed in *Phansopkar's* case because there it was sought to rely on it where there was a right
to come. Here, however, there is no such right. There is an eligibility subject to
procedural rules which it is for the Secretary of State to make and place before Parliament
and, unless it could be shown that the system was one which was irrational in the sense
that it was one which no reasonable Secretary of State could properly arrive at, such
g challenge as counsel for the applicants makes to it must fail.

In my judgment, both on the question of additional expense in providing further
entry clearance officers and in relation to the argument on interviews taking place in the
United Kingdom where someone has sought to jump the queue, the approach which has
been adopted by the Secretary of State is a reasonable one. One could not possibly say that
it was one which was irrational or which no reasonable Secretary of State could have
h reached.

In those circumstances, the challenge on that basis must fail and, accordingly, these
applications must be refused.

Applications refused.

Solicitors: *Norton & Coker* (for the applicant Ullah); *Suriya & Co* (for the applicants Ali
and Uddin); *Treasury Solicitor.*

Raina Levy   Barrister.

R v Garwood

COURT OF APPEAL, CRIMINAL DIVISION
LORD LANE CJ, CAULFIELD AND McCOWAN JJ
3, 10 FEBRUARY 1987

Criminal law – Demanding money with menaces – Menaces – Direction to jury – Whether direction on meaning of 'menaces' necessary – Circumstances when direction appropriate – Theft Act 1968, s 21(1).

Where the defendant is charged with blackmail by making an 'unwarranted demand with menaces', contrary to s 21(1)[a] of the Theft Act 1968, it is normally not necessary for the trial judge to direct the jury on the meaning of 'menaces' because it is an ordinary word the meaning of which ought to be clear to any jury. However, where appropriate, the trial judge ought to direct the jury that menaces are proved either if the threats might have affected a person of ordinary stability but did not affect the person actually addressed or if the threats in fact affected the mind of the victim although they would not have affected a person of ordinary stability providing that the defendant was aware of the likely effect of his actions on the victim (see p 1034 *b* to *e*, post).

Dictum of Cairns LJ in *R v Lawrence* (1971) 57 Cr App R at 72 applied.

Notes
For the offence of blackmail, see 11 Halsbury's Laws (4th edn) para 1277, and for cases on the subject, see 15 Digest (Reissue) 1339–1346, 11609–11675.

For the Theft Act 1968, s 21, see 12 Halsbury's Statutes (4th edn) 531.

Cases referred to in judgment
R v Clear [1968] 1 All ER 74, [1968] 1 QB 670, [1968] 2 WLR 122, CA.
R v Lawrence, R v Pomroy (1971) 57 Cr App R 64, CA.

Appeals against conviction and sentence
Patrick Augustus Garwood appealed with leave of the single judge against his conviction of and sentence for blackmail, contrary to s 21(1) of the Theft Act 1968, in the Crown Court at Acton before Mr Recorder Thayne Forbes QC and a jury on 12 September 1986. The facts are set out in the judgment.

Nigel Shepherd (assigned by the Registrar of Criminal Appeals) for the appellant.
David Farrington for the Crown.

Cur adv vult

10 February. The following judgment of the court was delivered.

LORD LANE CJ. On 12 September 1986 in the Crown Court at Acton the appellant was convicted of blackmail and was sentenced to 2½ years' imprisonment. In addition a suspended sentence of four months' imprisonment, imposed at Willesden Magistrates' Court on 22 May 1986 for theft, was activated in full and ordered to run consecutively, making a total of 34 months' imprisonment.

He now appeals against conviction and sentence by leave of the single judge.

The charge arose out of events on 3 June 1986. On that date a conversation took place

---

a Section 21(1), so far as material, provides: 'A person is guilty of blackmail if, with a view to gain for himself or another or with intent to cause loss to another, he makes any unwarranted demand with menaces . . .'

a between the appellant and the victim, an Indian youth called Sayed, aged 18, as a result of which Sayed went home and fetched £10 which he gave to the appellant. So much was not in dispute.

Sayed gave evidence that as he was passing through the flats where he lived on the way to the library, carrying a bag full of books, the appellant (whom he knew by sight) called out to him from behind. The appellant then indicated to Sayed that he should follow him into a secluded area in the vicinity of the flats. Having arrived there the appellant *b* accused Sayed of having 'done over' his house. He asked Sayed if he or his family had a television or jewellery; he asked where they were kept; he stated that he wanted something 'to make it quits' for what he alleged Sayed had done.

He then became aggressive, seizing Sayed by the shirt and pushing him up against a girder. He eventually demanded £10 and some jewellery saying that if the victim had been white he would have beaten him up by then. At that Sayed went home and got *c* £10, which he gave to the appellant. He told the appellant that he could not get any jewellery. The appellant then said to him: 'Don't tell the police or your parents or I'll get you.' He demanded that Sayed should give him a further £20 three days later; if he did this, he would be protected. On 7 June the appellant met Sayed at a bus stop and reminded him that the £20 had not been forthcoming.

When the appellant was interviewed by the police, he denied any threats or aggression *d* towards Sayed. He denied asking Sayed anything about the television or jewellery. He said that the two of them had had a conversation about sport and that he had asked Sayed if he could lend him £5. Sayed agreed and brought back £10. So he asked if he could borrow the £10, to which Sayed had agreed. He admitted that he had seen Sayed on 7 June. He was then simply apologising for not having paid back the money.

The appellant gave evidence along the lines of his statement to the police, except that *e* he said he only ever asked the victim for £10; the mention of £5 was a mistake.

After the jury had retired to consider their verdict for a short time, they sent the following note to the recorder:

f 'We think Sayed is probably rather timid—i.e. not normally stable (whatever that is). Therefore [the appellant] would appear more menacing than perhaps he was. If this seemed menacing to Sayed, does this amount to "menaces", despite the fact that others may not have found it menacing?'

That was a reference to the definition which the recorder had given to them of the word 'menaces'. What he had said was:

g 'The definition which I give you of the word "menaces", which is satisfactory for this case, is as follows: that threats or conduct of such a nature and extent that the mind of an ordinary person of normal stability and courage might be influenced or made apprehensive so as to accede unwillingly to a demand on him is menaces, that is a demand with menaces.'

In answer to the jury's question the judge gave the following further direction: 'May I *h* first of all remind you of the definition of menaces which I gave you for the purposes of your deliberation as follows . . .' He then repeated the definition of the word 'menaces' which he had given in the body of the summing up.

He then continued:

j 'Now, you must give that definition a very liberal and commonsense interpretation because it is a fact very often that people who are influenced by menaces, who are practised on, as lawyers say, are very often people who are not of average firmness and courage. They are the sort of people on whom blackmailers prey: vulnerable people. So, give those words a liberal and commonsense interpretation and if at the end of the day when you have come to a conclusion as to what you are satisfied so that you are sure of as having happened, if you get to that stage, so that you have decided what the facts are, you must acquit the defendant if your decision about the facts leads you to the conclusion that nothing that was said or done to Mr Sayed was *a* capable of influencing or making apprehensive the mind of an ordinary, normal person.'

In the judgment of this court those words might have led the jury to believe that the prosecution had proved the existence of menaces even though a person of normal stability would not have been influenced by the words or actions of the accused and the accused *b* was not aware that the victim was thus unduly susceptible to threats. To that extent we think there was a misdirection.

In our judgment it is only rarely that a judge will need to enter on a definition of the word 'menaces'. It is an ordinary word of which the meaning will be clear to any jury. As Cairns LJ said in *R v Lawrence, R v Pomroy* (1971) 57 Cr App R 64 at 72:

'In exceptional cases where because of special knowledge in special circumstances *c* what would be a menace to an ordinary person is not a menace to the person to whom it is addressed, or where the converse may be true, it is no doubt necessary to spell out the meaning of the word.'

It seems to us that there are two possible occasions on which a further direction on the meaning of the word menaces may be required. The first is where the threats might *d* have affected the mind of an ordinary person of normal stability but did not affect the person actually addressed. In such circumstances that would amount to a sufficient menace: see *R v Clear* [1968] 1 All ER 74, [1968] 1 QB 670.

The second situation is where the threats in fact affected the mind of the victim, although they would not have affected the mind of a person of normal stability. In that case, in our judgment, the existence of menaces is proved providing that the accused *e* man was aware of the likely effect of his actions on the victim.

If the recorder had told the jury that Sayed's undue timidity did not prevent them from finding 'menaces' proved, providing that the appellant realised the effect his actions were having on Sayed, all would have been well. The issue before the jury was clear-cut. If they felt sure that Sayed's version of events was true, there were plainly menaces. If *f* they thought that the appellant's version might be true, there were equally plainly no menaces. There was no need for him to have embarked on any definition of the word. It only served to confuse, as the jury's question showed.

However, if he had given a proper and full answer to the jury's question in the terms which we suggested earlier, the jury could have been in no doubt at all that, if Sayed's version was correct (which they must have felt that it was), the appellant must have *g* realised from the moment that the conversation started the effect which his actions and words were having on Sayed.

This is accordingly eminently a case for the application of the proviso to s 2(1) of the Criminal Appeal Act 1968. The appeal against conviction is accordingly dismissed.

[The court (Lord Lane CJ and McCowan J) then heard submissions on the appeal against sentence and substituted a sentence of 18 months' imprisonment for that of 2½ *h* years.]

Appeal dismissed. Sentence varied.

Solicitors: *Crown Prosecution Service*, Acton (for the Crown).

N P Metcalfe Esq   Barrister.   *j*

a R v Commissioner for the Special Purposes of the Income Tax Acts, ex parte R W Forsyth Ltd

QUEEN'S BENCH DIVISION (CROWN OFFICE LIST)

b MACPHERSON J

21, 22 OCTOBER 1986

Judicial review – Availability of remedy – Special Commissioner – Special Commissioner in London postponing tax assessment raised in Scotland – Postponement application heard in London at request of taxpayer's advisers – Taxpayer applying to English court for judicial review of
c *commissioner's decision – Whether English court having jurisdiction to review commissioner's decision – Whether application for judicial review should be stayed.*

The taxpayer company, which was incorporated and registered in Scotland, where it traded as a retailer, appealed against two assessments to corporation tax for the accounting period ended 30 September 1982 and applied for postponement of the tax assessed. All
d the proceedings relating to the two assessments were taken in Scotland except that, at the request of the company's advisers and to suit their convenience, a postponement hearing was heard by a Special Commissioner sitting in London. The commissioner postponed a small part of the tax assessed, so that the remainder was due and payable. The taxpayer company gave notice of application under RSC Ord 53 in London for judicial review of the postponement decision, and on 8 November 1985 leave to apply for judicial review
e was given and proceedings were stayed pending determination of the application. On 10 October 1986 the Court of Session pronounced a decree in favour of the Revenue in an action by the Lord Advocate for recovery of the tax not postponed and, in spite of argument that that court should heed the judicial review proceedings, the Court of Session concluded that the English court had no jurisdiction in the matter. The Crown applied to strike out the judicial review proceedings or to stay them on the grounds (i)
f that the English court had no jurisdiction over a commissioner dealing with a purely Scottish matter and (ii) that, even if there was jurisdiction, it would be right to stay the judicial review proceedings because the appropriate forum was the Scottish court, where there were concurrent proceedings in progress.

Held – (1) Tax and its assessment was a United Kingdom matter and a Special
g Commissioner's jurisdiction extended throughout the United Kingdom. Accordingly, although the only connection with England in the taxpayer company's case was the postponement application before the Special Commissioner, the court was not prepared to say that it had no jurisdiction to countenance an application for judicial review of the commissioner's decision. The court would accordingly not strike out the judicial review proceedings (see p 1036 *f*, p 1038 *a g* to *j* and p 1039 *d* to *f*, post).
h   (2) However, as a matter of common sense and convenience and in the interests of comity, the proper tribunal for any review of the Special Commissioner's decision was the Scottish court. In any event the stay ordered when leave to apply for judicial review was given did not affect the liability of the taxpayer company to pay the unpostponed tax, and a continuation of the judicial review proceedings would be unlikely to help the
j taxpayer company. The court would accordingly stay the judicial review proceedings (see p 1036 *f*, p 1037 *j*, p 1038 *e f*, p 1039 *f* and p 1040 *b d e g* to *j*, post); *The Abidin Daver* [1984] 1 All ER 470 applied.

Notes

For judicial review generally, see 37 Halsbury's Laws (4th edn) paras 567–583.

Cases referred to in judgment

Abidin Daver, The [1984] 1 All ER 470, [1984] AC 398, [1984] 2 WLR 196, HL.

MacShannon v Rockware Glass Ltd [1978] 1 All ER 625, [1978] AC 795, [1978] 2 WLR 362, HL.

R v Industrial Disputes Tribunal, ex p Kigass Ltd [1953] 1 All ER 593, [1953] 1 WLR 411, DC.

Rutherford v Lord Advocate (1931) 16 TC 145, Ct of Sess.

Application

The Crown applied to strike out or to stay proceedings in which Farquharson J had given leave on 8 November 1985 to R W Forsyth Ltd (the taxpayer company) to apply under RSC Ord 53 for judicial review of a decision on 19 June 1985 of a Commissioner for the special purposes of the Income Tax Acts, sitting in London, postponing part only of the tax assessed on the taxpayer company for its accounting period ended 30 September 1982. The grounds on which the application was made were (1) that the court had no jurisdiction over a commissioner hearing or dealing with a purely Scottish matter, so that the Ord 53 proceedings should be struck out, and (2) that even if there were jurisdiction in the High Court as well as in the Court of Session it would be right to stay the proceedings in the interests of comity so that conflicting decisions could be avoided and because the natural and appropriate forum was the Scottish court, where there were concurrent proceedings in progress in relation to the assessments. The facts are set out in the judgment.

Alan Moses for the Crown.
Harvey McGregor QC, Michael Ashe and *Penelope Reed* for the taxpayer company.
The Special Commissioner did not appear.

MACPHERSON J. Since I do not believe in suspense I say now that in this case the application for a stay succeeds, but I do not strike out the proceedings.

R W Forsyth Ltd (the taxpayer company) is a company incorporated and registered in Scotland. Its head offices are in Glasgow. Its trade is that of a retailer and is carried on in Scotland.

On 19 May 1983 the inspector of taxes in Edinburgh raised an assessment to corporation tax on the taxpayer company for the accounting period ended 30 September 1982 in the sum of £20,000. The taxpayer company appealed against the assessment and applied for the payment of the tax to be postponed. On 21 June 1984 the General Commissioners in Edinburgh North determined that there should be no postponement, so that tax in the sum of £10,400 became due and payable under the terms of s 55 of the Taxes Management Act 1970.

Then on 24 July 1984 the inspector of taxes raised a further assessment for the same accounting period in the sum of £2·73m. The assessment arose from the taxpayer company's involvement in a reverse annuity scheme entered into during the accounting period.

The taxpayer company appealed against the second assessment under s 31 of the 1970 Act. That appeal will be heard on 1 December 1986 by a Special Commissioner sitting in Edinburgh. The matter will be heard by a Special Commissioner because the taxpayer elected for such disposal under the provisions of s 31(4) of the Act. Otherwise without doubt the matter would have been before the General Commissioners sitting in Scotland under the provisions of s 44 of and para 7 of Sch 3 to the Act.

At the same time as the appeal was entered the taxpayer company applied under s 55 of the 1970 Act for postponement of the payment of tax, and made a further application under s 55(4) to postpone payment of the tax due under the first assessment, presumably on the ground that there had been a change of circumstances.

The date fixed for the hearing of the postponement application was 22 April 1985, and the place was to be Glasgow. So far the flavour and indeed the whole substance of the

case was thus Scottish. The application was in fact heard here in London on 18 April
a 1985, after the Revenue had been asked on 16 April 1985 to agree to this change of
arrangements. The change was at the behest of the taxpayer company's lawyers and was
purely to suit their convenience. Both postponement applications were heard in London,
and on 19 June 1985 the commissioner issued a written decision by which he postponed
payment of only £125,000 of the tax due under the second assessment. No doubt now
the Revenue wish that they had not been so considerate as to agree to the change of
b venue.

On 25 June and 20 September 1985 respectively, the Lord Advocate issued two
summonses in the Exchequer Court of the Court of Session seeking payment of the two
sums due under the assessments. In between those dates, namely on 13 September, the
taxpayer company gave notice of application in London under RSC Ord 53 for judicial
review of the postponement decision of 19 June. It is said in that notice that the Special
c Commissioner approached his task on a wrong basis, and the taxpayer company wishes
to argue that his decision is of no effect and that the matter should be remitted in order
to determine the amount if any in which it appears that there may be reasonable grounds
for believing that the taxpayer company is overcharged to tax, and to ask for the
postponement application to be reheard. The application itself would be a renewal of the
original application.
d In a nutshell the argument is that the commissioner went further than he should have
and effectively ruled that the annuity scheme was fatally flawed, when all that he should
have done was to consider whether there were reasonable grounds for believing that the
taxpayer company had been overcharged. And it will be argued that the payment of tax
should be postponed until the matter is fully argued on appeal.

I confess that I find the argument unattractive and doubtful, and so indeed did
e Farquharson J when he gave leave in the Ord 53 proceedings. But at this stage that is not
something which should influence me, and I must ignore my own inclinations in that
respect.

A further twist to this somewhat convoluted case is that on 23 October the Special
Commissioner signed a case stated for the opinion of the Court of Session at the taxpayer's
f behest by way of appeal from the postponement decision, but on 11 November notice of
intention not to proceed with that appeal was given in Scotland. No appeal has ever been
lodged in England.

On 18 September 1985 Lord Cameron was asked to sist or stay the proceedings in
respect of the first tax due (£10,400) pending the outcome of the present Ord 53
proceedings. No leave had then been granted in those Ord 53 proceedings, but Lord
g Cameron refused the motion to sist.

Both actions for recovery of the tax assessed came before Lord Wylie on 30 September
and 1 October 1986. By that time it must be noted that there had of course been
movement in this court. On 4 October 1985 Mann J required the application for leave to
move for judicial review to be made in open court. And on 8 November 1985
Farquharson J gave leave to move and further ordered (in these words)—

h   'that the Notice of Motion to be issued in this matter by the applicant shall by
     virtue of Order 53 Rule 3(10)(a) of the Rules of the Supreme Court operate as a stay
     of the proceedings to which this application relates until determination of the said
     application or until the court otherwise orders.'

The postponement order is not negated by the stay and it thus remains in my judgment
j in the form that it was made. In my judgment the stay does not and cannot affect the
liability of the taxpayer company to pay the unpostponed tax. I believe that Farquharson J
had no power to stay the payment of the tax, although he says in his judgment that this
was what he would do. The order actually made was correct and did not in my judgment
operate to stay the payment of tax. Even if this conclusion of mine is wrong, the Court
of Session has (in my judgment rightly) acted accordingly in granting its decree and has
refused to be put off by the existence of any stay in London or by the existence of the
Ord 53 proceedings.

On 10 October 1986 Lord Wylie pronounced decree in favour of the Crown in both actions. He did this in the face of argument that he should heed the Ord 53 proceedings. He decided the case in this respect on the basis that the sole jurisdiction in respect of these postponement applications should have been subject and only subject to the supervision of the Scottish court. His opinion is twice exhibited in the evidence before me in the instant proceedings. His decision is founded on the conclusion that the English court had no jurisdiction in the matter. I do not go so far as to find that that is so, but the conclusion which I do reach has, as will be seen, the same result in practice.

Yesterday, on 21 October 1986, counsel for the Crown applied to strike out the Ord 53 proceedings or to stay them on two grounds: (1) that this court has no jurisdiction whatsoever over a commissioner hearing or dealing with a purely Scottish case, so that the Ord 53 proceedings should be struck out as an abuse of process; (2) that even if there is jurisdiction in the High Court as well as in the Court of Session it would be right to stay the Ord 53 proceedings in the interests of comity so that conflicting decisions shall be avoided and because the natural and appropriate forum is the Scottish court, where there are concurrent proceedings in progress in relation to these assessments and this tax.

The application is made later than it could or perhaps should have been made. But in my judgment it is none the less right to consider it now, since if it is successful the decks are cleared of this additional active part of the litigation between these parties and the further cost of these Ord 53 proceedings is stemmed.

At one stage in this case I wondered whether or not it was right for me to tamper with this case at all, since leave was given to move on 8 November 1985 by Farquharson J. In the end I conclude that since that application was made ex parte, I should not be over-inhibited by the fact that leave was given. Furthermore, as I have said earlier, it is apparent to me that while the stay imposed by Farquharson J operated as a stay of the proceedings to which the application related it did not and does not operate to prevent the recovery in Scotland of the tax involved. The stay was imposed when counsel for the taxpayer company asked for a 'stay on the payment of the tax for the time being'. It may have been supposed that such a stay was implicit in Ord 53, r 3(10). As I have said it is established in my judgment that this is not so and that in any event the Ord 53 proceedings will in all likelihood do nothing to help the taxpayer company. By the time they are heard, and indeed by the time any appeal against Lord Wylie's decision is heard, the whole matter will be resolved by the main decision in connection with the assessment, namely the appeal of 1 December 1986.

If that appeal goes in favour of the taxpayer company there will be no need for postponement. If it goes against the taxpayer company any renewed application for postponement (which is all that could be available after success in the Ord 53 proceedings) would be hopeless. There is thus a certain unreality about the Ord 53 case in any event, now that it has plainly been overtaken by events.

I proceed to consider the two arms of the argument. I say at once that I am not wholly convinced that this court has no jurisdiction at all to countenance an Ord 53 application for review of a decision made in a Scottish case when the matter at issue is heard in England.

It is argued that since the Special Commissioner stands in the shoes of the General Commissioners, by reason of the taxpayer's election, so he should be taken to be in effect purely a Scottish tribunal in any Scottish case. But the position, in my judgment, is that a Special Commissioner stands in his own shoes. His office or jurisdiction starts from Turnstile House and extends throughout the United Kingdom. Tax and its assessment is a United Kingdom business, in the sense that there is no exclusive Scottish tax system.

This court must guard its position so far as review of the activities of Special Commissioners carried on in England is concerned. In the instant case the only connection with England was the postponement application, but it seems to me in the light of the arguments and the cases cited to me that I should beware of ruling that this court is wholly without jurisdiction lest that might lead to later problems.

The cases cited were *Rutherford v Lord Advocate* (1931) 16 TC 145 and *R v Industrial*
a *Disputes Tribunal, ex p Kigass Ltd* [1953] 1 All ER 593, [1953] 1 WLR 411.
   In *Rutherford v Lord Advocate* Lord Fleming was dealing with a case in which General
Commissioners in England had issued warrants, and he ruled that the English courts
alone had the jurisdiction to determine the questions as to the validity of those warrants,
but he expressly stated that he did not hold or imply that the 'Suspension is incompetent'
(at 157). He held that in the circumstances of that case it was competent for the
b complainant to invoke the preventive jurisdiction of the Court of Session but that the
real questions between the parties could and should only be determined in the English
court. In the result I am not much assisted by that decision in the present case.
   In the *Kigass Ltd* case Lord Goddard CJ and his court ruled that both the Scottish and
English courts had jurisdiction, since the dispute arose in Scotland, but the registered
office of the taxpayer company involved was in England and the tribunal sat in England,
c so that there was a strong English dimension to the case.
   There were no Scottish proceedings at all in the *Kigass Ltd* case, so that while Lord
Goddard CJ stated that it would be much better where the whole subject matter of the
dispute had arisen in Scotland that the proceedings should be taken in Scotland, yet he
found that from the point of view of comity there was no objection on the facts of that
case to the English court going into the matter. Again I do not find much direct assistance
d from that case.
   On the somewhat unreal assumption that no proceedings had started at all in Scotland
I am unable to hold that this court would have been powerless to investigate by way of
review the activities of a United Kingdom Special Commissioner sitting in London, even
in the circumstances of the present case. This court may not in my judgment be so
absolutely powerless.
e In the result I am not persuaded that these proceedings should be struck out because
of lack of jurisdiction and as an abuse of our process. That question lives to fight another
day. In Scotland Lord Wylie has answered it and his opinion may well prevail here when
and if the matter is again ventilated. For the moment I am not prepared to rule that there
can be no jurisdiction in a case of this kind.
f I am on the other hand wholly convinced that these proceedings should be stayed. As
to this aspect of the case counsel for the Crown relies on the decision of the House of
Lords in *The Abidin Daver* [1984] 1 All ER 470, [1984] AC 398. He stresses Lord Diplock's
reference to the change over the years from judicial chauvinism to judicial comity and to
the acknowledgment in cases such as *The Abidin Daver* of the Scottish legal doctrine of
forum non conveniens (see [1984] 1 All ER 470 at 476, [1984] AC 398 at 411). And in
g essence he says that in the present case the whole feel and ambit of this tax case is Scottish,
and that since the taxpayer has available to him both appeal and judicial review
procedures in Scotland it is both inconvenient, wrong and potentially confusing to allow
this English part of the case to proceed.
   In parenthesis, it seems to me fanciful to say that the Special Commissioner might
refuse to submit to the jurisdiction of the Scottish court in judicial review proceedings
h started there. That would be a most unlikely course for him to take in my judgment.
   Counsel for the taxpayer company referred to a signal distinction between this case
and *The Abidin Daver*, namely that the lis in Scotland is in form and substance quite
different from the proceedings brought here. He urges me to say that he is entitled to
have the advantage of such legitimate personal or juridical advantage as he may obtain
from Ord 53 proceedings, and that I should not be satisfied that Scotland is in judicial
j review or appeal terms a place where justice can be done at less expense or inconvenience
for his clients (see *MacShannon v Rockware Glass Ltd* [1978] 1 All ER 625, [1978] AC 795).
   The goal of delaying or holding off realisation of assets is, says counsel for the taxpayer
company, a legitimate exercise which the taxpayer is entitled to shoot at, and that goal is
available on the English Ord 53 pitch. Thus his clients should not be excluded or held
up in these proceedings.

In this context I pay much heed to the currently unappealed judgment of Lord Wylie, and to the recorded refusal of Lord Cameron to sist the first proceedings for recovery of a tax. Lord Wylie firmly rules that in his judgment the proper tribunal for any review of the commissioner's activities is the Scottish court.

I agree that on the facts of this case this is so. But even if I had doubted the matter I would have been likely to fall in with Lord Wylie's opinion as a matter of comity. Since I have no doubt, I am glad to echo his conclusion, though for different reasons, and say that this whole matter should as a matter of both convenience and common sense be left b to Scotland.

It is true that there is no immediate conflict of similar proceedings, but there must in my judgment be a risk of conflict when it is seen that the Scottish court has given judgment, yet the taxpayer wishes to repeat his demand for postponement of payment of tax to the commissioner. Furthermore the existence and operation of the Ord 53 c proceedings was referred to in the pleadings and figured largely in argument before Lord Wylie.

Perhaps more cogently it is argued that the juridical advantage sought in England by the taxpayer has little merit, and that any difficulty in Scotland as to judicial review and the position as to unfulfilled avenues of appeal may well be exactly echoed here when and if the Ord 53 proceedings come to full hearing.

As a matter of common sense and convenience it is in my judgment perfectly clear d that all activity in this case should be in Scotland. This is particularly so when I remind myself that the whole feel of the case is Scottish, and that the matter would never have crossed the border unless counsel and solicitors' convenience and their request had tempted it to London for this limited application. That application could and would otherwise have been heard in Glasgow, and counsel for the taxpayer company rightly made the important unqualified concession that if it had been heard there he could not e have expected the English court to hear him on an application for judicial review.

Farquharson J himself wondered why he was involved and asked whether the Court of Session did not have jurisdiction. He did not pursue the matter when counsel for the taxpayer company made a short reference to the facts of the *Rutherford* case, but the case was not cited and of course no argument was advanced since the matter was heard ex f parte. Farquharson J would have realised that that point could in any event be taken when the matter was fully argued. In my judgment its argument now has the result of curtailing the present proceedings.

I should mention in this context that it is right to say that Farquharson J had some information before him about the existence of the Scottish proceedings, but, as Lord Wylie said, that was not much more than a fleeting reference or glance. The matter was not then a prominent feature. It is now the commanding feature of this part of the case. g

Without wishing to be too lighthearted in a case which has serious implications generally for the taxpayer, I find myself unable to help the taxpayer in spite of the fact that a Macpherson is considering a case in which leave was granted by a Farquharson and that we have both been assisted in argument by a McGregor.

This case should in my judgment be confined to home-based Scottish judges, whose h decisions as they stand firmly indicate that they believe Scotland should supervise the whole of this affair. I agree with them, and accordingly stay these Ord 53 proceedings.

I am encouraged finally in this decision by what I have already said about the practical position which means that it is almost impossible that a continuation of the Ord 53 proceedings would bring any comfort to the taxpayer, save perhaps as to the question of the costs of this present application. That question will now be debated if necessary. j

Proceedings stayed. Leave to appeal refused.

Solicitors: *Solicitor of Inland Revenue*; *Waltons & Morse*, agents for *T P D Taylor*, Knutsford (for the taxpayer company).

Edwina Epstein   Barrister.

a

Barnet v Crozier and another

COURT OF APPEAL, CIVIL DIVISION
NOURSE AND RALPH GIBSON LJJ
9, 11 DECEMBER 1986

b   *Libel and slander – Statement in open court – Settlement of plaintiff's action against one of two defendants – Plaintiff continuing action against other defendant – Factors to be considered by court in deciding whether to allow statement to be made – Whether making of statement should be postponed until after conclusion of trial of outstanding claim – RSC Ord 82, r 5.*

c The plaintiff, who was a senior fellow and one of the founders of the Institute of Policy Studies (the IPS) in the United States of America, wrote a book which was reviewed in the second defendant's journal. The review prompted the first defendant to write a letter to the journal in which he referred to the plaintiff as 'a mainstay' of the IPS and to the IPS as 'a front for Cuban intelligence, itself controlled by the Soviet KGB' (being a reference to the Soviet intelligence service). The plaintiff brought an action against the defendants alleging that the letter was defamatory of him. Both defendants pleaded justification.

d Subsequently, however, the second defendant decided to settle the action and the plaintiff applied under RSC Ord 82, r 5ᵃ for leave to make a joint statement in open court (which would also be published in the second defendant's journal) by which the second defendant accepted that neither the plaintiff nor the IPS was a front for the Cuban intelligence service and that neither of them was controlled by the Soviet intelligence service. The first defendant contended that the statement ought not be made until after the conclusion

e of the trial of the plaintiff's action against him, on the ground that the making of the statement and consequent reporting of it were likely to prejudice the trial of that action and were defamatory of him. The judge approved the terms of the statement and directed that it be made in court at an early date. The first defendant appealed.

f **Held** – Where parties made a bona fide settlement of a defamation action and asked leave to make a statement in open court leave ought to be granted unless, taking into account the interests of all the parties affected and the risk of prejudice to the fair trial of any outstanding issue, there was sufficient reason apparent on the material before the judge for leave to be refused. For the risk of prejudice to the trial of outstanding issues to be taken into account it had to be real and not shadowy or fanciful, although the weight to be given to it would depend on the seriousness of the risk and the gravity of the

g prejudice threatened. On the facts, the making of the statement would not have the slightest effect on a jury trial taking place some months later and, even if the statement was defamatory of the first defendant, the risk of any injury to him from the content of the statement was negligible. The statement should therefore be permitted to be made and the appeal would accordingly be dismissed (see p 1042 *g*, p 1047 *a* to *c f* to *h*, p 1048 *b* to *f h* and p 1049 *b c*, post).

h **Notes**

For a statement in open court on the settlement of a libel action, see 28 Halsbury's Laws (4th edn) para 200.

---

a   Rule 5 provides:

j   '(1) Where a party accepts money paid into Court in satisfaction of a cause of action for libel or slander, the plaintiff or defendant, as the case may be, may apply to a Judge in Chambers by summons for leave to make in open Court a statement in terms approved by the Judge.

     (2) Where a party to an action for libel or slander which is settled before trial desires to make a statement in open Court, an application must be made to the Court for an order that the action be set down for trial, and before the date fixed for the trial the statement must be submitted for the approval of the Judge before whom it is to be made.'

Cases referred to in judgments

Church of Scientology of California v North News Ltd (1973) 117 SJ 566, CA.   *a*
J v R (1984) Times, 23 February.
Sievier v Wootton (1920) Times, 13 February.
Tracy v Kemsley Newspapers Ltd (1954) Times, 9 April.
Wolseley v Associated Newspapers Ltd [1934] 1 KB 448, CA.

Cases also cited   *b*

A-G v News Group Newspapers Ltd [1986] 2 All ER 833, [1987] QB 1, CA.
Eyre v Nationwide News Pty Ltd (1968) 13 FLR 180, ACT SC.
Liebrich v Cassell & Co Ltd [1956] 1 All ER 577, [1956] 1 WLR 249.
Lucas-Box v News Group Newspapers Ltd, Lucas-Box v Associated Newspapers Group plc,
[1986] 1 All ER 177, [1986] 1 WLR 147, CA.

c

Interlocutory appeal

The first defendant, Brian Crozier, appealed with leave of the Court of Appeal against the
order of Tucker J made in chambers on 27 November 1986 granting the plaintiff,
Richard Jackson Barnet, and the second defendant, The Spectator (1828) Ltd, leave to
make a statement in open court in terms approved by the judge pursuant to a proposed
or agreed settlement as between the plaintiff and the second defendant of a libel action   *d*
brought by the plaintiff against the defendants in respect of an alleged libel published in
the second defendant's journal, the Spectator, in a letter from the first defendant. The
first defendant sought to postpone the making of the statement until after the conclusion
of the trial of the plaintiff's claim against him on the ground that the making of the
statement and the reporting of it were calculated to prejudice the trial of that action and
were defamatory of him. The facts are set out in the judgment of Ralph Gibson LJ.   *e*

Roger Buckley QC and *Richard Walker* for the first defendant.
Patrick Milmo QC and *David Parsons* for the plaintiff.
Mark Warby for the second defendant.

RALPH GIBSON LJ (delivering the first judgment at the invitation of Nourse LJ).   *f*
This appeal is brought by the first of two defendants in a pending libel action in an
attempt to postpone the making of a statement in open court pursuant to a proposed or
agreed settlement of that action as between the plaintiff and the second defendant. The
appeal is from the order of Tucker J given after a hearing in chambers.

For my part, I will say at once that I have reached the conclusion that this appeal of the
first defendant must be dismissed. The argument of the first defendant has been directed   *g*
in part to the prejudice which he claims he may suffer as a result of the making of a
statement in court. I propose to say no more of the facts of the case than is necessary to
make the issues and the decision intelligible. I shall not deal with every aspect of the
alleged libel or of the justification of it because such detail is, in my view, not necessary.

The plaintiff is a senior fellow of the Institute for Policy Studies (the IPS) in Washington   *h*
DC in the United States of America. The IPS is a private institution. The plaintiff helped
to found it in 1963 and was co-director of it until 1978. He has written a number of
books. One was published in this country in April 1984 called *Allies: America and Japan
since the War*. A review of that book was published in the Spectator on 7 April 1984. The
review prompted Mr Crozier, the first defendant, to write to the Spectator. His letter
referred to the plaintiff as a mainstay of the IPS and to the IPS as a 'front for Cuban   *j*
intelligence, itself controlled by the Soviet KGB'. The plaintiff in his statement of claim,
which was served with the writ in August 1984, asserts that the words complained of
meant and were understood to mean that the plaintiff was—

'the mainstay of, and knowingly helped to run, an institution which pretended *a*   to be bona fide but was in fact a front for covert operations by Cuban intelligence at the instigation of the Soviet KGB.'

The first defendant is a journalist of distinction and a writer on international affairs. In his defence of 13 November 1984 he denied that his letter was defamatory in any way and, in particular, he denied that his letter bore the meanings alleged in the plaintiff's statement of claim. Moreover, he has asserted that the words used by him in his letter

b   are true in substance and in fact. There are some 11 pages of particulars of the matters relied on in support of that plea of justification and a further 39 pages of further and better particulars. The particulars on which the first defendant relies include many references to what were, or are said to have been, aspects of the political history of Cuba since about 1959, the setting up of the Cuban intelligence service, the relationship thereto of the Soviet Union, the setting up of the Transnational Institute (the TNI) by the IPS in

c   1974, the role and working of the TNI, the political, or apparent political, attachment of many people who have taken part in the activities of the IPS, the economic and social policies advocated by the IPS and the attitude of the IPS towards the defence and armaments policies of the United States and NATO. By reference to such matters, of which much detail is given, the first defendant will invite the jury to infer that his references to the plaintiff were true in substance and in fact. The issues are serious because

d   the first defendant says in terms that, while the IPS holds itself out as an independent centre devoted to research on public policy issues, in fact it is not such a centre but is an organisation which advocates policies which are Marxist, pro-Soviet, pro-Cuban and socialist.

The first defendant is not alleged and does not claim to have played any part in these events. His position and role are those of the historian who has attended, or who claims

e   to have attended, to what has been going on in and about the IPS and who asserts that the inference which he has drawn from what he has observed, and which the jury should draw from what he says he will put before them, is that the statements made by him in his letter to the Spectator in April 1984 are true. It appears from the affidavit of the first defendant's solicitor, Mr Pepper, that the second defendant, the publisher of the Spectator, pleaded a similar defence, relying on substantially similar particulars of justification.

f   The second defendant, however, has come to terms with the plaintiff and wishes to settle the action. The terms of the settlement would be that the second defendant makes a substantial contribution towards the plaintiff's costs and joins in making a statement in open court to the effect that the second defendant accepts that neither the plaintiff nor the IPS is a front for Cuban intelligence and that neither is controlled by the KGB. An agreed term of the settlement is that the terms of the statement in open court would also

g   be published in the Spectator.

The plaintiff applied under RSC Ord 82, r 5 for an order that the action be set down for trial, and the proposed statement was submitted to Tucker J for his approval with a view to the statement being made before him in court. On 27 November Tucker J approved the terms of the statement and directed that it be made in court at an early date. The first defendant had opposed the giving of approval and the making of the

h   order. He contended that no such statement should be made until after the conclusion of the trial of the plaintiff's claim against him on the ground that the making of the statement and the reporting of it are calculated to prejudice the trial of the plaintiff's claim against the first defendant and were defamatory of him. The first defendant now appeals to this court and asks this court to set aside the judge's order.

j   Before coming to the reasons given by Tucker J for his decision it is necessary to say something about the practice of the courts, which has been established over many years, when an action for libel or slander has been settled, to permit the plaintiff to say on oath in court that the statements made of him are untrue, or to permit counsel for the parties to make statements in court which have been agreed between the parties and approved by the judge (see *Gatley on Libel and Slander* (8th edn, 1981) paras 1179, 1192).

Parties to an action do not need the consent of the court to make an effective settlement of their dispute; nor do they need the consent of the court to announce to the world that *a* they have settled it on stated terms. The importance of the making of a statement in open court is, first, that it is likely to come to the attention of the press, who will give to it such attention as its public interest is seen by them to merit and, second, since the statement is part of a judicial proceeding, it is made on an occasion of absolute privilege. Thus, the parties to the statement are protected and, moreover, the statement can be reported without the publisher of the report incurring the risk of being sued in respect *b* of it. *Tracy v Kemsley Newspapers Ltd* (1954) Times, 9 April, which some of us can vividly recall, is an example of publishers, after an apology by them for statements made in a story published by them, being held liable in an action brought by the author of the statements in respect of the defamatory effect of the apology. The case is referred to in *Gatley on Libel and Slander* (8th edn, 1981) para 1174.

It seems to me that the protection obtained from the fact that the approved statement *c* is made in open court is not to be seen as an unintended and undeserved consequence of the procedure, but as a useful attribute of it which is obtained, of course, only if the court permits it to be used. The daunting burden of the risk in costs in such litigation must weigh intolerably on most litigants. The procedure offers a means by which settlement can be reached and, when appropriate, announced in appropriate terms between two parties without risk of further litigation arising out of that announcement. It is, in my *d* view, a grievous burden to be sued in a defamation action even if you win it in the end.

The judge's reasons for making the ruling which he did are in a note approved by him. He noted that the practice of making a statement in open court and the principles which should guide the court with reference thereto are not laid down in any rule of court, although there is reference to the procedure in Ord 82, r 5. It is within the discretion of the judge to allow a statement to be made and, if so, in what form. In exercising that *e* discretion, the judge should, said Tucker J, take into account the interests of all the parties affected and the risks of prejudice to the fair trial of any outstanding issue. To that point there has been no criticism of the judge's approach. The judge continued:

'I do not regard either party as having a burden of proof. The judge must weigh up the interests of both sides and all the circumstances of the case. On the one hand, *f* it is desirable that settlement should be encouraged and facilitated. It is to the advantage of society generally and of the court and the parties that costly and lengthy litigation should be avoided. It is equally desirable that once a settlement is reached it should be implemented. This is particularly so on settlement of a libel action. A plaintiff should have the opportunity of making a statement in open court by way of reparation of the damage caused to his reputation. On the other hand, *g* where only one defendant to an action reaches a settlement, it is clearly important that a fair trial of the remaining issues in the action should not be prejudiced. In considering this matter, I take into account that this is a jury action. But the trial is not imminent and may not be for several months, probably not for many months. It is also relevant to take into account the nature of the case, which I do not consider to be unduly sensational or likely to attract considerable national or international *h* publicity. The court should consider also the notoriety or otherwise of the parties concerned and the extent to which the publication of the statement may impinge on the minds of potential jurors. It is not sufficient that there be a shadowy or fanciful risk of prejudice for it to be decided that a statement should not be made in open court. There must be a real risk. Balancing the interests of all the parties, this is not an unduly sensational case and none of the parties are famous or notorious. It *j* does not seem to me that a statement in open court made in November 1986 will have the slightest effect on a trial taking place in March to May or June [1987]. Potential jurors will be unaffected. Any publicity resulting from such a statement will have passed out of their minds long before the trial. As between the plaintiff a   and the second defendant, a settlement has been achieved. I am told that if it is not implemented there is a risk that it will break down. Costly and lengthy litigation may ensue as a result. In my view it is right that the statement should be allowed to be made forthwith.'

This matter came before this court as an application for leave to appeal and leave was granted. Affidavit evidence before us has dealt with the probable date of the hearing. It
b   is said that the case will take six weeks when it is tried. The judge's reference to a trial in March to May or June 1987 is not shown to be wrong. The approved statement in open court and the proposed publication in the Spectator which will follow are before the court. It is said that the acceptance by the second defendant that the IPS is not a front for Cuban intelligence directly contradicts the letter written by the first defendant and what, in his plea of justification, he will be seeking to prove. Publication of this apology and
c   statement constitutes, it is said, a declaration by a co-defendant who has pleaded a defence of justification with substantially the same particulars that the words complained of are false and such publication may prejudice the fair trial of the action. It is said to be a damaging form of prejudgment of the issue. Further, it is asserted that, while neither the plaintiff nor the first defendant is famous in the sense that neither is a prominent public figure, the action is nevertheless of considerable public interest. An affidavit from
d   Mr Sykes, the solicitor for the second defendant, shows that negotiations for settlement have been taking place with varying degrees of urgency since August 1985. There is, he says, a concluded settlement between the plaintiff and the second defendant, but it is conditional on the reading of the statement in open court and on it being read immediately and not postponed. The fear is expressed that, if the appeal of the first defendant should be allowed, the second defendant will be forced to continue to defend
e   an action of which it has achieved a concluded agreement for settlement and to incur the expense of taking part in a trial lasting six weeks. It is stated that, if the appeal is allowed, it is the intention of the second defendant 'To rely on the settlement in mitigation of damages' and to 'put before the jury the concluded agreement, including the agreed statement in open court'.

Counsel for the first defendant submitted that the judge had been wrong in several
f   respects. There is, he said, no urgency for any statement to be made. The publication was in April 1984, the writ issued and served in August 1984. It cannot seriously affect the plaintiff if the making of the statement is held up until May or June 1987. The publication of the apology and statement will, he said, directly affect the issue to be tried and will create a risk of prejudice. The judge, first, misdirected himself when he said that 'he did not regard either party as having a burden of proof'. Save in exceptional
g   circumstances, which counsel for the first defendant said were not present, it must be wrong to permit the making of such a statement before trial which touches the main issue to be tried, and it must be for those who seek to make the statement to show good cause why it should be permitted. Second, the statement approved is, according to counsel for the first defendant, defamatory of the first defendant. It may be taken to mean that he was not honest when he wrote as he did of the plaintiff, or at least that he
h   was careless and incompetent as a journalist or historian. The court should not, at least without compelling reason and none is advanced, lend its aid to enable a defamatory statement to be published under the protection of absolute privilege. This point was argued before the judge and no mention of it appears in his reasons. He thus misdirected himself. In the absence of any justification for thus protecting a defamatory publication
j   leave to make the approved statement should be set aside and the plaintiff and first defendant left to make whatever settlement they choose to make and to make whatever publication of that settlement they can lawfully make at this time, or wait until after the trial to make a statement protected by the privilege of legal proceedings.

I will deal first with the nature and practice and procedure by which a statement in open court is approved and made. There is no reported authority on the issues raised in this appeal. The practice has certainly existed since before 1920 (see *Sievier v Wootton* (1920) Times, 13 February, cited in *Gatley* para 1179). In 1933 there were changes in the rules and in *Wolseley v Associated Newspapers Ltd* [1934] 1 KB 448 at 453 Greer LJ said:

'The rule of law, before this new rule was passed [ie RSC 1883 Ord 22, r 4, added in 1933], was that there could not be a plea of payment into Court in a libel action with a denial of liability, for the obvious reason that what a plaintiff who had been, or who said that he had been, libelled or slandered wanted, just as much as money compensation, was the opportunity of stating in open Court, and proving if necessary, that he was not the villain he was alleged to be by the defendant, and it was felt, when these new Rules were made, that it was right, if the privilege was granted to the defendant of paying money into Court with a denial of liability and the money was sufficient to satisfy the plaintiff's claim, so that the plaintiff went on at his peril, that the plaintiff should have that which he would have had before— namely, an opportunity to make a statement in open Court with the approval of the judge in Chambers, so as to clear his character from the alleged slander, and that was the reason for the provision in sub-r. 4.'

That passage which I have read I have in fact taken from the judgment of Balcombe J on 20 February 1984 in a case in chambers in Liverpool which I have found of great assistance (see *J v R* (1984) Times, 23 February).

There is another passage referred to by the judge and that is from Lawton LJ in *Church of Scientology of California v North News Ltd* (1973) 117 SJ 566. This is another case, unlike this one, in which the plaintiff had taken money out of court, but the observations of Lawton LJ appear to me to be of assistance. He said:

'In my judgment a judge who is asked to exercise his discretion under Ord 82, r 5 should take into consideration the realities of litigation in defamation actions. One of these realities is that the defendants often wish to get rid of the litigation at the cheapest price they can, even though they may think they have a good defence. Another reality is that writs for defamation are frequently issued in anger. When a plaintiff gets the defence and realises that he has got to fight for his reputation, his anger is very often diminished and he is in a frame of mind in which he is prepared to settle; and it is in those circumstances that defendants frequently make payments into court. Plaintiffs may not do themselves any good by going on with their claims, and defendants often want to avoid the trouble and expense of litigation, particularly as plaintiffs in defamation cases frequently have not the wherewithal to pay any order for costs which may be made against them. The motives for paying money into court and taking it out are often self-interest on both sides. In my judgment it is wrong for plaintiffs to assume that, if they do take money out of court, they are entitled as of right to be whitewashed by defendants. The judge dealing with applications under Ord 82, r 5 should look at all the circumstances of the case, and, in particular, should look at the relationship between the gravity of the allegations in the alleged libel and the amount of money which is paid into court.'

As I have said, the court was not there dealing with a case in which the interests of the defendant who had not taken money out of court or who had not settled the case against him required to be considered. Nevertheless, looking at those authorities, it seems to me that an opportunity to make a statement in open court was thus seen more than 50 years ago as something which was an incident, or part of the available procedure, in a defamation action which the plaintiff was at least entitled to expect to be available to him, provided that the terms of the statement were approved by the judge and there was nothing in the case which made it unfair to another party to the statement to be made.

The present rule, Ord 82, r 5, which derives from the previous Ord 22, r 2 introduced in 1933, provides for the making of a statement in open court with the leave of the judge, both when there has been acceptance of money paid in and when the action is settled before trial without a payment into court.

a   The judge was right, in my view, to regard the settlement of proceedings as a public good which the court should encourage and facilitate if, having regard to the interests of all the parties, it is right and just so to do. Although a party has no right to make a statement in open court, on which he can insist if the circumstances are such that the judge cannot in his discretion approve that course, it seems to me that parties who have made a bona fide settlement of a defamation action and ask leave to make a statement in open court may expect to be allowed to do so unless some sufficient reason appears on

b   the material before the judge why leave should be refused to them. By saying that he did not regard either party as having a burden of proof, while acknowledging that it is desirable for settlement to be facilitated, I think the judge meant, as he said, that he must have regard to the interests of all parties; but, if there is no sufficient reason to refuse it, a plaintiff who has reached a settlement with a defendant should be allowed to make an approved statement. I think the judge was right in his approach.

c   As to prejudging the fair trial of the pending action by the making and reporting of the proposed statement, I consider that the judge was right in his conclusion and in the reasons he gave. The court was pressed by counsel for the plaintiff and counsel for the second defendant to accept that the test for proof of prejudice to the trial of the issue between the plaintiff and the first defendant is that laid down in s 2 of the Contempt of Court Act 1981. By s 1 of that Act:

d

> 'In this Act "the strict liability rule" means the rule of law whereby conduct may be treated as a contempt of court as tending to interfere with the course of justice in particular legal proceedings regardless of intent to do so.'

By s 2(2):

e

> 'The strict liability rule applies only to a publication which creates a substantial risk that the course of justice in the proceedings in question will be seriously impeded or prejudiced.'

It was argued for the plaintiff and the second defendant that it would be irrational to have any stricter or other test so that the court should only decline to approve the making

f   of a statement in open court if there was shown to be a substantial risk of serious prejudice. I do not accept that submission. Tucker J said that there must be a real risk, not shadowy or fanciful, and I take him to mean that the risk of prejudice must be real for it to be taken into account at all in the balancing exercise which he set himself to carry out. The weight to be given to it would depend on the seriousness of the risk and the gravity of the prejudice threatened. He did not mean that, if there was any real risk of prejudice, the making of a statement must, for that reason alone, be refused. Again, I

g   think his approach was right.

On the facts of the case, his view was that the making of this statement would not have the slightest effect on a jury trial of those issues taking place in March to June 1987. It seems to me that his assessment is right. If there should happen to be any jurors who notice and remember any report of the statement, what are they likely to conclude? In

h   my judgment, the very great probability is that they would think that the second defendant, after consideration of the material available and pleaded by them in their defence, had concluded or formed the opinion that the words cannot be shown to be true and must, therefore, be acknowledged to be untrue. Such jurors would not, therefore, conclude that the second defendant's opinion must dictate their opinion or that the first defendant must be wrong. They would listen to the evidence and, as they would be

j   directed to do, make up their own minds on what they hear in court. The opinion formed by the second defendant does not suggest the possession by it of any information tending to discredit the first defendant or any primary evidence he has to lay before the jury.

As to the defamatory nature of the terms of the approved statement, this court is considering the reasons given by Tucker J in an extempore judgment in chambers. I do not accept, and counsel for the first defendant did not suggest, that the absence of

references to the issue of defamation means that the judge did not consider it. Nourse LJ
suggested, in the course of argument, that the explanation, in all probability, is that   *a*
Tucker J considered it but thought nothing of it.

For my part, I was at first troubled by this part of the case. There seemed to me to be
force in the contentions of counsel for the first defendant that the court could not
properly lend its aid by affording the protection of absolute privilege to the making and
further reporting of the statement of which there is any risk that it could be held to be
defamatory. The plaintiff and the first defendant should be left, said counsel for the first   *b*
defendant, to do whatever they choose to do without that protection bestowed on them
by the court. In the end, however, I am driven to the conclusion that any risk of
defamation of the first defendant is not such as to require or justify refusal of leave to
make the statement.

In the first place, I am not persuaded that the statement is defamatory of the first
defendant. The nature of the case is such that justification of what the first defendant   *c*
wrote does not depend on his account of events which he has seen or in which he has
participated; so that to say of him that what he wrote is untrue means that his account is
false to his knowledge, or that he is not competent in his job as a journalist or modern
historian. It seems to me that writers on international affairs can and do differ in the
inferences which they draw from the actions and words of others, and it is not, I think,
supposed by ordinary people that, if some of them do differ amongst themselves, for that   *d*
reason one must be lying or incompetent.

Next, if there is any real risk of the publication being injurious to the first defendant
because defamatory of him, I regard the extent of any injury likely to be caused to him
as negligible. The first defendant will be deprived of the right to damages for the
publication but he will have a full opportunity to vindicate himself in the verdict of the
jury in the trial itself. I would add that, in saying that, I have not been unmindful of the   *e*
fact which was urged on us that, if leave to make the statement in open court were
refused, the plaintiff also would not be deprived of the opportunity of vindicating his
reputation because he too will obtain the verdict of the jury, whichever way it goes.

Finally, for the reasons already given, the opportunity to make a statement in open
court is an incident of the court's procedure, which parties who settle such an action can   *f*
be expected to be allowed to use unless there is some sufficient reason to cause the court
to refuse to approve that course. In that context, I regard any risk of injury to the first
defendant from any defamatory content of the statement as negligible. There is no
reason to doubt the bona fide nature of the settlement. The statement itself has been
drafted with care to avoid any unnecessary reference to or imputation against the first
defendant. The plaintiff and the second defendant have agreed further minor changes in
the course of argument which have marginally improved it. (It is not necessary to detail   *g*
them.) The court should be vigilant to see that the benefit of the procedure of making a
statement in open court is not used to the unfair disadvantage of a third party. There
will, no doubt, be cases in which, on balancing the interest of all the parties, where one
or more defendants continue in the action after a settlement by the plaintiff with one or
more of them, the court will conclude that the facts are such that the making of a   *h*
statement must be postponed until after the trial of the remaining issues. The judge held
that this was not such a case and, for my part, I agree with him.

I must mention one or two other matters. The argument before us ranged over many
aspects of the law of defamation including the questions whether, if the making of the
statement were not approved, it would be open to the second defendant to put in
evidence the terms of the conditional settlement which would have been thus aborted   *j*
and whether the first defendant's position would, on any view of the probable course of
the trial, be significantly improved. Aspects of these questions included the assessment
of damages against the two defendants in respect of one publication and the matter of
contribution between the defendants. There was also raised the issue whether that which
the second defendant admits in the proposed statement is exactly the same allegation or

a meaning as put forward by the first defendant in his plea of justification. I intend no discourtesy to counsel, whose arguments on these matters were compelling and relevant, if I had taken a different view on other aspects of the case, in not dealing with them, but I have not found it necessary to resolve them.

I would mention only one further matter. The judge mentioned the fact that, as he had been told, there was a risk that the settlement might break down. The point urged on the court was that the plaintiff required as a condition of the settlement a statement *b* in open court. I was, for my part, unable to attach any great weight to this risk, such as it is, as adding anything to the general principle that the settlement of litigation is to be facilitated by recourse to the procedure of a statement in open court if it can be done without unfair impact on the interests of other parties.

For these reasons I would dismiss this appeal.

c **NOURSE LJ.** I agree and do not wish to add anything.

Appeal dismissed.

d Solicitors: *Peter Carter-Ruck & Partners* (for the first defendant); *Bindman & Partners* (for the plaintiff); *Richard C M Sykes* (for the second defendant).

Mary Rose Plummer   Barrister.

e
R v Cook

COURT OF APPEAL, CRIMINAL DIVISION
WATKINS LJ, DRAKE AND OGNALL JJ
13 NOVEMBER, 9 DECEMBER 1986

f *Criminal evidence – Identity – Photofit picture – Admissibility – Whether photofit picture admissible in evidence – Whether admission of photofit picture contrary to hearsay rule.*

A photofit picture of a defendant is admissible at his trial as part of a witness's evidence and does not constitute a breach of either the hearsay rule or the rule against the admission of earlier consistent statements (see p 1054 *j*, post).

g *R v Tolson* (1864) 4 F & F 103 applied.
R v Percy Smith [1976] Crim LR 511 considered.

Notes

For proof of identity, see 11 Halsbury's Laws (4th edn) para 363, and for cases on the subject, see 14(2) Digest (Reissue) 486–490, 4008–4038.

h For hearsay evidence, see 11 Halsbury's Laws (4th edn) 437–439, and for cases on the subject, see 14(2) Digest (Reissue) 596–598, 4841–4842.

Cases referred to in judgment

Jones v Metcalfe [1967] 3 All ER 205, [1967] 1 WLR 1286, DC.
Myers v DPP [1964] 2 All ER 881, [1965] AC 1001, [1964] 3 WLR 145, HL.
j *R v O'Brien, Nicholson and Nicholson* [1982] Crim LR 746.
R v Okorodu [1982] Crim LR 747, Crown Ct.
R v Percy Smith [1976] Crim LR 511, CA.
R v Tolson (1864) 4 F & F 103, 176 ER 488, Assizes.
R v Turnbull [1976] 3 All ER 549, [1977] QB 224, [1976] 3 WLR 445, CA.
Sparks v R [1964] 1 All ER 727, [1964] AC 964, [1964] 2 WLR 566, PC.

Case also cited

R v Christie [1914] AC 545, [1914–15] All ER Rep 63, HL.   *a*

Appeals against conviction and sentence

Christopher Cook appealed with leave of Roch J against his conviction on 27 March 1986 in the Crown Court at Acton before his Honour Judge Palmer and a jury on one count of robbery and one count of indecent assault for which he was sentenced to concurrent terms of three years' youth custody. He also appealed against the sentences. The facts are   *b* set out in the judgment of the court.

R D Roebuck for the appellant.
Sally O'Neill for the Crown.

Cur adv vult   *c*

9 December. The following judgment of the court was delivered.

WATKINS LJ. On 27 March 1986, before his Honour Judge Palmer, the appellant was at the Crown Court at Acton convicted on the first of three indictments of robbery and indecent assault. For these offences he was sentenced to concurrent terms of youth   *d* custody. On a second indictment for burglary, to which he had pleaded guilty, he was sentenced to one year's youth custody concurrent with the first indictment. On a third indictment for a number of offences of taking a vehicle without consent, driving whilst disqualified and common assault he was sentenced to concurrent terms of one year's youth custody to run consecutively to the second indictment. For breach of a probation   *e* order he was sentenced to one year's youth custody concurrent. He was also disqualified from holding a driving licence for three years. He appeals, inter alia, against his convictions for robbery and indecent assault.

The evidence which resulted in the convictions can be summarised in this way. Miss Diane Tanswell lives in Edgware. On 17 October 1984, at about 6 pm, when making   *f* her way home from work, she was walking along Broadfields Avenue when a man suddenly grabbed her from behind. She fell to the ground. He demanded money and jewellery. He tried without success to pull a ring from her finger. He grabbed her right wrist and touched her vaginal area over her clothing and made repeated further demands for money. Her handbag had when she fell spilt its contents on the pavement. Her assailant pulled down his trousers, exposed his penis and threatened her with more violence. He then took money from her purse and ran away.   *g*

The following day she reported the matter to the police. She described her assailant as a tall, thin, coloured man, about 20 years of age with a puckered or pock-marked face. He was, she said, wearing a grey tracksuit with a black stain on the trousers and a black woollen peaked cap. She maintained that she had a clear view of him from the light of a nearby street lamp when she was assaulted. From her description of him on 19 October a photofit picture was pieced together and photographed by a police officer.   *h*

On 26 November 1984 the appellant was arrested for another offence. His home was searched and a pair of tracksuit trousers with a black stain on them were found. When the appellant was questioned about the robbery of Miss Tanswell he denied being involved in it.

On 4 February 1985 he was again arrested in connection with other matters. During   *j* the course of an ensuing interview a detective sergeant referred to the robbery of Miss Tanswell. The file on the case was not to hand, but a report sheet and the photofit were. The photofit was shown to the appellant and he agreed that it looked like him and that it might point to his having been involved in the robbery. He went on to make full and detailed admissions of both the robbery and the indecent assault. The interview was

contemporaneously recorded. At its conclusion the appellant was charged with robbing
a and indecently assaulting Miss Tanswell.

The evidence of confession given by the police officers to the jury was challenged by
the appellant, who claimed that admissions had been extracted from him by bullying
and violence. They were, he said, untrue. He had agreed to suggestions put to him
merely in order to obtain bail. In any event the admissions he actually made were not,
he claimed, in the form recorded at the time of the interview.

b   Sometime between 26 November 1984 and 4 February 1985 an unsuccessful attempt
was made to hold an identification parade. On 30 July 1985 the police decided to hold an
alternative process of identification. They took Miss Tanswell to the Brent Cross shopping
centre and asked her to stand at the top of an escalator. The appellant, with five or six
men of similar appearance, was brought up the escalator. They were bunched together
apparently so that Miss Tanswell was unable to see any of them clearly. She became
c agitated at being unable to make any kind of identification. However, as she was walking
away, accompanied by a friend, from the shopping centre she saw the appellant on his
own in the street and began to cry. A police inspector asked her what was troubling her,
whereupon she pointed the appellant out as the man who had attacked her. It was
suggested to her in cross-examination that the only reason why she was distressed on that
occasion was because she badly wanted someone to be charged for assaulting her.
d   During the course of the trial it was submitted in the absence of the jury by counsel
for the defence that the photofit was inadmissible in evidence. To put it before the jury
would be, it was said, to introduce a previous consistent statement. Further, a basic
principle of the hearsay rule would be offended against. Reference was made to *R v Percy
Smith* [1976] Crim LR 511 (we have seen the full transcript), *R v O'Brien, Nicholson and
Nicholson* [1982] Crim LR 746 and *R v Okorodu* [1982] Crim LR 747.
e   The judge ruled as follows:

'I rule that this photofit picture is admissible evidence to go before the jury. It is
admissible on the basis that it is part of the circumstances of the identification of the
defendant and the proper identification of the defendant, and, if that in itself is not
a good enough reason, I rely on the fact that it was shown to the defendant in
f   interview and, although that might have been excluded if the witness herself was
not going to be called, here she is going to be called and I see no reason why the
photofit picture should not be permitted in evidence and shown to the jury even if
it does differ from a written statement describing the defendant, describing his
features, clothing and so on. This is a likeness of the defendant in the same way that
a photograph is a likeness of the defendant and so, therefore, in my judgment, it is
g   admissible.'

Counsel for the appellant (who did not appear in the court below) has made to us
broadly speaking similar submissions to those made to the judge before counsel for the
prosecution opened the case to the jury. In addition to the cases already mentioned, he
has referred to us to the well-known case on identification, namely *R v Turnbull* [1976] 3
h All ER 549, [1977] QB 224, as well as to passages in *Phipson on Evidence* (13th edn, 1982)
pp 336–340, paras 16-09–16-10, *Cross on Evidence* (6th edn, 1985) p 472 and *Archbold's
Pleading, Evidence and Practice in Criminal Cases* (42nd edn, 1985) pp 953–954, 2201, paras
11-3 and 27-11. He has also reminded us that in *Sparks v R* [1964] 1 All ER 727 at 735,
[1964] AC 964 at 981 Lord Morris stated: 'There is no rule which permits the giving of
hearsay evidence merely because it relates to identity.'
j   It is submitted that the judge was wrong to allow counsel for the Crown to refer in
opening to the photofit and wrong to allow it to be introduced into evidence whilst Miss
Tanswell was giving evidence-in-chief. This, he argues, constituted a material irregularity
which should cause us to quash the convictions. A photofit is, he asserts, a self-serving
previously consistent statement. Unlike what is said at an identification parade it does

not constitute an exception to the rule against hearsay. Exceptions to the rule can only be made by statute. A photofit is not, he argues, a photograph or even similar to a   *a* photograph. It is no more than an attempted description of someone.

In *R v Percy Smith* [1976] Crim LR 511, a case of attempted murder, a sketch of the defendant had been made by a police officer in accordance with a description of him provided by a young girl who had seen him at a relevant time near the scene of the crime. An unsuccessful objection was made by counsel for the defence to the admissibility of that sketch. On appeal Lawton LJ, giving the judgment of the court, observed: *b*

> 'Then came the trial. At the trial the prosecution sought to put in the sketch which had been made by the police officer under the direction of Karen. [Counsel for the defendant] objected to it. The objection was that it was not Karen Barton's document and therefore it was not admissible in evidence. Before us the argument put forward on behalf of the appellant by [counsel] was that the document could   *c* only have come into existence as a result of the conversation between Karen and the police officer making the sketch, and that what Karen had said to the police officer and what he had said to her was not admissible evidence because it was hearsay. That was right. But the prosecution at the trial never sought to put in evidence what was said by Karen to the police officer and vice versa. It was submitted that what was said was a necessary link between Karen and the sketch. In our judgment it was   *d* not. Karen, using her memory, had directed the sketching hand of the police officer. The result of exercising her memory in that way was to produce a sketch which was admissible in evidence. It was her sketch made through the hand of the police officer. We can see no reason for saying that that sketch was not admissible in evidence.'

Counsel for the appellant says, rightly in our view, that the argument as to admissibility   *e* addressed to the court in *R v Percy Smith* was altogether different from the challenge which is here made to the admissibility of the photofit. As appears from the foregoing extract from the judgment the objection to the admissibility of the sketch was based on the contention that it was not Karen's document and further that the document could only have come into existence as a result of the conversation between Karen and a police   *f* officer. No submission was made to the effect that the sketch was a self-serving previously made consistent statement. That, so it is said, may account for the court feeling able to say that there was no reason why the sketch was not admissible in evidence. It might have ruled differently if arguments similar to those presented to us had been made to the court in *R v Percy Smith*.

The single judge in giving leave stated: *g*

> 'The appeal against conviction raised the issue whether admitting a photofit picture as part of the complainant's evidence-in-chief is a breach of the general rule against the admission of earlier consistent statements. This point which does not appear to have been argued in *R v Percy Smith* seems to be one of some importance.'

We think it undoubtedly is of importance and we agree that the issue arising for our   *h* decision was not argued in *R v Percy Smith*.

The opinion as to admissibility of a sketch expressed in that case has been criticised by a number of well-known academics. It was followed in *R v Okorodu* [1982] Crim LR 747 but not in *R v O'Brien, Nicholson and Nicholson* [1982] Crim LR 746. The objection to it is as clearly stated as anywhere else in the commentary on those two cases, which quotes from Murphy *A Practical Approach to Evidence* (1980) p 130 (see [1982] Crim LR at 748).   *j* The relevant passage is as follows:

> 'There is some authority on the point. In *Percy Smith* a sketch of a man made by a police officer at the direction of a witness was ruled admissible to show likeness. The hearsay rule was not broken, said the Court of Appeal, because there was no need to

a rely on any conversation between the witness and the officer in order to link the witness to the sketch. This seems, with respect, to miss the point, and indeed to demonstrate that what is being relied on *is* the witness's out of court identification. The point is well put by Murphy: "If the eyewitness had made a written statement of the man's description to the police, such statement would have amounted to a previous consistent statement, and would not have been admissible. It is true that, *b* if contemporaneous, she might have used it to refresh her memory while giving evidence, and this would surely apply equally to the sketch; but it is hard to see why the sketch should itself be admissible, whether made by the eyewitness or by the officer at her direction. One can hardly fail to sympathise with the plight of any court which is obliged to apply such inconvenient and surely unnecessary rules of law, but piecemeal judicial reform of such a fundamental topic often involves, as here, a process of reasoning which is not at all happy." On the law, then, *O'Brien* is *c* closer to the truth than *Okorodu*. What part common sense plays in the result is for the reader to judge.'

We have no doubt that the common sense of the matter leans heavily in the direction of indorsing the opinion expressed in *R v Percy Smith*. It is right to add that in our experience photofits have been admitted to evidence without objection in a number of *d* cases, in recent times anyway. That does not, of course, mean that they really are strictly speaking admissible. So we must confront the issue and endeavour to resolve it.

We begin by stating what on authority is in our judgment beyond dispute, namely that Miss Tanswell when in the witness box could have been permitted to see the photofit which she had observed being composed for the purpose of refreshing her memory. In *Jones v Metcalfe* [1967] 3 All ER 205, [1967] 1 WLR 1286 an independent witness to a *e* collision between two cars caused by the action of a lorry going in the opposite direction gave the registration number of the lorry to a police officer. When in the witness box in the magistrates' court he could not remember it and could not be permitted to be assisted by anyone or anything to remember it.

Diplock LJ, agreeing with Lord Parker CJ in the result, said ([1967] 3 All ER 205 at 208, [1967] 1 WLR 1286 at 1290–1291):
f
'I reluctantly agree. Like LORD PARKER, C.J., I have every sympathy with the magistrates because the inference of fact that the appellant was the driver of the lorry at the time of the accident is irresistible as a matter of common sense; but this is a branch of the law which has little to do with common sense. The inference that the appellant was the driver of the lorry was really an inference of what the *g* independent witness had said to the police when he gave them the number of the lorry, and since what he had said to the police would have been inadmissible as hearsay, to infer what he said to the police is inadmissible also. What makes it even more absurd is, as LORD PARKER, C.J., pointed out, that if when the independent witness gave the number of the lorry to the policeman, the policeman had written it down in his presence, the policeman's note could have been shown to the *h* independent witness and he could have used it, not to tell the magistrates what he told the policeman, but to refresh his memory. This case does illustrate the need to reform the law of evidence, in order to overcome these difficulties, on the lines which are set out in the recent report of the Law Reform Committee (13th Report (Hearsay Evidence in Civil Proceedings) (Cmnd 2964)); but the law of evidence being still as it is, I reluctantly agree that the conviction must be set aside.'
j
Using a photofit for the purpose of refreshing memory may be regarded as a step in the right direction but it cannot of itself have the effect of rendering the photofit admissible so as to enable the jury to see it. If either the hearsay rule or the rule against the admission of a previous consistent statement is applicable to this situation, the evidence of photofit being, as must be acknowledged, no exception to these rules there

would be no reason in our view why the submission made on the appellant's behalf should not succeed. But we question whether either of those rules apply to evidence of a photofit.

The rule against hearsay is described in *Cross on Evidence* (6th edn, 1985) p 453 as one of the oldest, most complex and most confusing of the exclusionary rules of evidence. The author quotes Lord Reid as having said in *Myers v DPP* [1964] 2 All ER 881 at 884, [1965] AC 1001 at 1019–1020: 'It is difficult to make any general statement about the law of hearsay evidence which is entirely accurate . . .'

We agree with all that. What, however, is clear is that what was said by a prospective witness to a police officer in the absence of a defendant is hearsay and cannot, therefore, be admissible as evidence. But admissibility of a photofit is not dependent on a recital by a witness when giving evidence of what that person said to the police officer composing it. So that aspect of hearsay need no further be considered.

The rule is said to apply not only to assertions made orally, but to those made in writing or by conduct. Never so far as we know has it been held to apply to this comparatively modern form of evidence, namely the sketch made by the police officer to accord with the witness's recollection of a suspect's physical characteristics and mode of dress and the even more modern photofit compiled from an identical source. Both are manifestations of the seeing eye, translations of vision onto paper through the medium of a police officer's skill of drawing or composing which a witness does not possess. The police officer is merely doing what the witness could do if possessing the requisite skill. When drawing or composing he is akin to a camera without, of course, being able to match in clarity the photograph of a person or scene which a camera automatically produces.

There is no doubt that a photograph taken, for example, of a suspect during the commission of an offence is admissible. In a bigamy case, namely *R v Tolson* (1864) 4 F & F 103 at 104, 176 ER 488, Willes J said:

'The photograph was admissible because it is only a visible representation of the image or impression made upon the minds of the witnesses by the sight of the person or the object it represents; and, therefore is, in reality, only another species of the evidence which persons give of identity, when they speak merely from memory.'

That ruling has never since been doubted and is applied with regularity to photographs, including those taken nowadays automatically in banks during a robbery. Such photographs are invaluable aids to identification of criminals. It has never been suggested of them that they are subject to the rule against hearsay.

We regard the production of the sketch or photofit by a police officer making a graphic representation of a witness's memory as another form of the camera at work, albeit imperfectly and not produced contemporaneously with the material incident but soon or fairly soon afterwards. As we perceive it the photofit is not a statement in writing made in the absence of a defendant or anything resembling it in the sense that this very old rule against hearsay has ever been expressed to embrace. It is we think sui generis, that is to say the only one of its kind. It is a thing apart, the admissibility to evidence of which would not be in breach of the hearsay rule.

Seeing that we do not regard the photofit as a statement at all it cannot come within the description of an earlier consistent statement which, save in exceptional circumstances, cannot ever be admissible in evidence. The true position is in our view that the photograph, the sketch and the photofit are in a class of evidence of their own to which neither the rule against hearsay nor the rule against the admission of an earlier consistent statement applies.

For these reasons we think the judge was correct in this case in his decision to admit to evidence the photofit. Accordingly, the appeal against conviction is dismissed.

a   [The court heard further submissions from counsel on the appeal against the sentence
but, being satisfied that the sentences were appropriate, dismissed the appeal.]

*Appeals dismissed. The court refused to certify, under s 33(2) of the Criminal Appeal Act 1968,
that a point of law of general public importance was involved in the decision.*

    Solicitors: *S B Gilinsky & Co*, Edgware (for the appellant); *Crown Prosecution Service*, Acton
b   (for the prosecution).

                                                              Raina Levy   Barrister.

Post Office v Aquarius Properties Ltd

c   COURT OF APPEAL, CIVIL DIVISION
SLADE, RALPH GIBSON LJJ AND SIR ROGER ORMROD
26, 27 NOVEMBER, 18 DECEMBER 1986

*Landlord and tenant – Repair – Construction of covenant – Covenant to keep premises in repair
– Covenant by tenant to keep demised premises in good and substantial repair – Demised premises*
d   *having defect in original construction caused by bad workmanship – Defect resulting in flooding
of basement – No damage caused to premises by defect – Whether building in disrepair – Whether
tenant liable under covenant to eradicate defect.*

    In 1969 the landlords let a newly constructed office building to tenants for a term
expiring in 1991. The lease contained a covenant by the tenants 'to keep in good and
e   substantial repair . . . the demised premises and every part thereof'. There was a defect
in the structure of the basement of the building by reason of porous concrete and
defective construction joints used in the construction of the building which caused water
to enter the basement whenever the water table rose, as it did between 1979 and 1984
when the basement was permanently ankle deep in water. In 1984 the water table
receded and the basement became dry. No damage had been caused to any part of the
f   building by the defect, which had not been aggravated but was in the same condition as
when the building was built. In an action brought by the tenants against the landlords,
the questions arose (i) whether the building was out of repair so as to give rise to an
obligation on the tenants under the repairing covenant to put it into repair, and (ii)
whether, assuming the building was in a state of disrepair by reason of the defect, the
remedial work required to cure the defect and make the basement waterproof was work
g   of repair or involved structural alterations and improvements. The trial judge held that
the remedial work would involve structural alterations and improvements and therefore
did not fall within the tenants' obligations under the repairing covenant and he made a
declaration to that effect. The landlords appealed.

h   **Held** – A covenant by a tenant to keep the demised premises in good and substantial
repair did not impose an obligation on the tenant to remedy a defect in the structure of
the premises, whether resulting from faulty design or workmanship, which had been
present from the time of the construction of the building and which had caused no
damage to the demised premises. Since no damage to the building had been proved and
the wetting of the basement floor coupled with the inconvenience caused thereby did
j   not constitute disrepair, it followed that the tenants were under no liability to the
landlords under the repairing covenant to carry out any work to the premises in order to
remedy the defect. The appeal would therefore be dismissed (see p 1063 d e h j, p 1064 c,
p 1065 b to j and p 1066 g, post).
    Quick v Taff-Ely BC [1985] 3 All ER 321 applied.
    Proudfoot v Hart [1886–90] All ER Rep 782 distinguished.

Notes

For covenants to repair, see 27 Halsbury's Laws (4th edn) paras 284–299, and for cases on　*a*
the subject, see 31(2) Digest (Reissue) 606–621, 4929–5069.

Cases referred to in judgments

Anstruther-Gough-Calthorpe v McOscar [1924] 1 KB 716, [1923] All ER Rep 198, CA.
Brew Bros Ltd v Snax (Ross) Ltd [1970] 1 All ER 587, [1970] 1 QB 612, [1969] 3 WLR 657,
　CA.　　　　*b*
Elmcroft Developments Ltd v Tankersley-Sawyer (1984) 270 EG 140, CA.
Halliard Property Co v Nicholas Clark Investments Ltd (1983) 269 EG 1257.
Pembery v Lamdin [1940] 2 All ER 434, CA.
Proudfoot v Hart (1890) 25 QBD 42, [1886–90] All ER Rep 782, CA.
Quick v Taff-Ely BC [1985] 3 All ER 321, [1986] QB 809, [1985] 3 WLR 981, CA.
Ravenseft Properties Ltd v Davstone (Holdings) Ltd [1979] 1 All ER 929, [1980] QB 12,　*c*
　[1979] 2 WLR 897.
Wright v Lawson (1903) 19 TLR 203; *affd* 19 TLR 510, CA.

Cases also cited

Lister v Lane [1893] 2 QB 212, [1891–4] All ER Rep 388, CA.
Lurcott v Wakely & Wheeler [1911] 1 KB 905, [1911–13] All ER Rep 41, CA.　　*d*
Smedley v Chumley & Hawke Ltd (1981) 44 P & CR 50, CA.
Sotheby v Grundy [1947] 2 All ER 761, CA.

Appeal

The defendants, Aquarius Properties Ltd (the landlords), appealed against the judgment
of Hoffmann J given ([1985] 2 EGLR 105) on 26 July 1986 whereby he granted the　*e*
plaintiffs, the Post Office (the tenants), a declaration that, on the true construction of an
underlease dated 25 June 1969 and made between the tenants and the landlords, the
tenants were not liable to the landlords by virtue of their repairing covenant in the
underlease to carry out work for preventing the ingress of water into the basement of the
demised premises at Abbey House, 74–76 St John Street, London EC1 and dismissed the　*f*
landlords' counterclaim for damages for breach of that covenant. The facts are set out in
the judgment of Ralph Gibson LJ.

Malcolm Spence QC and *Anthony Dinkin* for the landlords.
Paul Morgan for the tenants.

Cur adv vult　*g*

18 December. The following judgments were delivered.

RALPH GIBSON LJ (delivering the first judgment at the invitation of Slade LJ). This
is an appeal by landlords from the decision of Hoffman J ([1985] 2 EGLR 105) given on　*h*
26 July 1985 by which he made a declaration at the suit of the Post Office, who are the
tenants and the plaintiffs in the action, that on the true construction of an underlease
dated 25 June 1969 the tenants are not liable to carry out certain work to the basement
floor and walls at Abbey House, 74–76 St John Street, London EC1. The appeal raises
questions of principle on the proper construction in law of repairing covenants in
common form. The facts which have given rise to these questions, however, appear to　*j*
be highly unusual. In short, there is shown to be a defect in the structure of the basement
of an office building which was present from the time of the construction of the building.
During a period of time when the water table rose at the place where the building stands,
the defect permitted ground water to enter the basement so that water stood ankle deep
on the floor for some years. The defect has not grown worse but is in the same condition

a   as when the building was built. Apart from permitting water to enter, which disappeared
when the water table dropped, leaving the basement dry for the last two years, no damage
to any part of the building is shown to have been caused by the defect.

The first question, accordingly, is whether it has been proved that the building was
out of repair so as to give rise to an obligation under the covenant to put it into repair.
The second question, which appears to have been treated as the main, if not the only,
question at the trial, is whether, assuming the building to be in a state of disrepair by
b   reason of the existence of the defect, any of the schemes of treatment put forward for
curing the defect were capable of being regarded as work of repair as opposed to being
structural alterations and improvements.

On this appeal the findings of fact of the judge have not been questioned. I set out his
primary findings in his words ([1985] 2 EGLR 105 at 105–106):

c   'Abbey House is an office building in the City of London constructed in the mid-
    1960s. Since 1969 it has been let to the [tenants] on a full repairing lease by [the
    landlords]. For most of the time between 1979 and 1984 the basement was ankle
    deep in water. This appears to have been the result of a rise in the level of the local
    water table combined with defects in the construction and possibly the design of
    the building. In 1984 the water table subsided again and since then the basement
d   has been dry. The tenants' lease expires in 1991, but the building has a life
    expectancy of many years and it is therefore agreed by landlords and tenants that
    remedial work is necessary to make the basement waterproof in case the water table
    should rise again . . . The building consists of front and rear sections. The basement
    runs under both. It has 12-in thick reinforced concrete walls. Under the front
    section of the building the basement floor is a reinforced concrete raft 3 ft thick
e   which, together with the walls, supports the ground and six upper storeys. At the
    rear there are only two upper storeys and the basement slab is of lighter construction.
    For the most part it is 8 in thick . . . The floor has been constructed integrally with
    the walls by forming a 5-in upstand around the edge of the floor and then using that
    as the base for the walls. This upstand is called the "kicker". Concrete has to be cast
    in sections with each new section of wet concrete being poured alongside or above a
f   section which has already dried. There is also a tendency for concrete to shrink as it
    dries, partly from chemical reaction and partly on account of evaporation. The
    result is to produce a construction joint between sections of concrete which, unless
    suitably bridged, may admit water. In the design of Abbey House, basement pvc
    water bars were specified for insertion at the construction joints beneath the concrete
    floor and on the outside of the walls up to a height of 6 ft from a datum line
g   corresponding to the surface of the basement concrete floor. These water bars are,
    in effect, strips of pvc which are keyed into the concrete and overlay and construction
    joints by some inches on each side . . . The contract documents record that in
    November 1964 trial holes had shown the water table to lie 1¾ ft below the datum
    line to which I have referred, that is about a foot below the 8-in section of the rear
    basement floor. In May 1965 the engineer engaged for the construction of the
h   building reported the water table 3 in higher. In 1979 it appears to have risen to at
    least 6 in above the basement floor and the flooding took place. There is no evidence
    that ground water entered at any higher level . . . I have had the benefit of the views
    of two eminent structural engineers on the causes of the flooding and the remedies
    which should be adopted. Both agreed that there had been a failure of the kicker
j   joint between the floor and the walls. This was caused by poor workmanship which
    had produced weak areas of concrete or what Mr Reith, the [tenants'] expert,
    described as honeycombing of the concrete. This means that the concrete consists in
    places almost entirely of aggregate and is deficient in sand and cement. It is therefore
    relatively porous. Unless care is taken, this phenomenon tends to occur at the
    bottom of the section being cast and in this case affected the concrete immediately

above the kicker. There was also evidence that some construction joints had not been formed with care and that the water bars had therefore been inadequate to prevent the ingress of water.'

The judge then considered whether, in addition to the porous concrete above the kicker joint and the inadequate water bars, other causes of the entry of ground water had been proved. He considered shrinkage of concrete as a possible cause of the detachment of water bars, which may have allowed water to enter between them and the concrete, and possible cracks in the 8-inch slab, but no such defects were positively shown to have existed.

Next the judge considered the remedial measures proposed by the two experts. He approached the matter in that way because he had defined the issues in the case as whether the remedial work necessary to make the basement waterproof was 'repair' within the meaning of the tenants' covenants. Mr Reith, the tenants' expert, recommended the more elaborate and expensive asphalt scheme, costing, at £175,000, rather more than twice the less elaborate rendering scheme, at £86,000, recommended by Mr Deverill, the landlords' expert. Reliance by the tenants on evidence showing more expensive work to be necessary and by the landlords on evidence showing that much less expensive work would suffice resulted no doubt from the concern of the parties over whether this work could properly be regarded in law as work of repair.

The scheme proposed by Mr Reith at £175,000 was, as described by the judge, as follows (at 106):

'Mr Reith recommends the tanking of the basement with a layer of asphalt covering the floor and the walls up to a height of 5 ft. Since asphalt does not bond very well with concrete it would have to be held in place by an additional concrete slab of 12-in thickness laid over the floor and an inner concrete skin 6 in thick within the walls. In order to add additional weight to the floor, he also recommends the extension of the inner concrete walls to the ground-floor slab so as to enable its weight to be transmitted to the basement floor and the construction of heavy internal partitions for the same purpose.'

Mr Deverill proposed two alternative schemes. The judge described them as follows (at 106):

'One is an asphalt tanking scheme similar to that of Mr Reith. The differences are that Mr Deverill considers that it would be excessive to allow for the possibility of a 5-ft head of water. In his opinion 3 ft would be enough . . . he agrees that it would be advisable to cover the asphalt on the floor with an additional 12-in concrete slab. Mr Deverill's second and preferred scheme involves the use of waterproof rendering in place of asphalt. This would be strongly bonded to the floor and walls and would not, therefore, need an inner concrete skin or covering. On the floor, however, Mr Deverill still thinks it advisable to add another 9 in of concrete slab firmly bonded to the existing slab and reinforced on the upper side. The waterproof rendering would then be applied to the upper surface of the new slab. Mr Deverill proposed the rendering scheme as a cheaper and more elegant solution than the traditional asphalt scheme. He agreed that the application of rendering was technically more demanding than asphalt and that unless the workmanship was good there was a higher risk of failure. Mr Reith said that his experience taught that the rendering scheme was too risky and that asphalt was worth the additional expense.'

The judge observed that the choice between the schemes involved an evaluation of the additional risk in the cheaper scheme and the likely damage and inconvenience if the risk eventuated against the additional cost. The question before him was whether the work required to waterproof the basement amounted to repair within the meaning of the tenant's covenants. The answer to that question might have depended on the scheme

which he thought appropriate but in this case in his view the answer to that question was
a the same whichever of the three schemes is adopted. In the result the judge expressed no
view between the schemes proposed.

Finally, the judge found certain facts which he later considered as relevant to the
question whether in all the circumstances any of the schemes of remedial work were
shown to be work of repair. The landlords held the property under a long lease for 125
years from 29 September 1966 granted in consideration of the rents and covenants and
b the erection of the building. The tenants had an underlease dated 25 June 1969 for a
term from 25 March 1969 until 19 September 1991, or about 22½ years. The rent was
£11,250 until a rent review at 24 March 1983. Thereafter the rent was to be the market
rent at the rent review date on the assumption that the tenants had complied with their
covenants. Since the parties had been unable to agree on whether that meant that the
tenants must be assumed to have waterproofed the basement, the determination of the
c new rent awaited the outcome of these proceedings. On the assumption that the
basement was waterproof, the annual rent would be in the region of £50,000 to £60,000.
The capital value of the building was about £687,000, but the cost of rebuilding it today
would be a good deal more.

It was said at the beginning of this judgment that this appeal raised questions of
principle on the proper construction in law of repairing covenants in common form.
d The judge referred to the repairing covenant in this case in cl 2(3) of the tenants'
underlease as in fairly standard form. He set out only what he called the critical words:
'... keep in good and substantial repair ... the demised premises and every part thereof
...' In the course of argument Slade LJ pointed to the fact that the covenant includes also
the following: '... during the said term ... well and substantially to repair ... amend
... renew and keep in good and substantial repair and condition ...' No reliance has
e been placed in this case on any contention that the words 'amend' or 'renew' or 'condition'
add anything to the words referred to by the judge as the critical words.

Finally, the judge approached the question for decision thus ([1985] 2 EGLR 107):

f 'I have found most assistance in the judgment of Sachs LJ in *Brew Brothers Ltd v
Snax (Ross) Ltd* ([1970] 1 All ER 587, [1970] 1 QB 612). This says, in effect, that the
whole law on the subject may be summed up in the proposition that "repair" is an
ordinary English word. It also contains a timely warning against attempting to
impose the crudities of judicial exegesis upon the subtle and often intuitive
discriminations of ordinary speech. All words take meaning from context and it is,
of course, necessary to have regard to the language of the particular covenant and
the lease as a whole, the commercial relationship between the parties, the state of
g the premises at the time of the demise and any other surrounding circumstances
which may colour the way in which the word is used. In the end, however, the
question is whether the ordinary speaker of English would consider that the word
"repair" as used in the covenant was appropriate to describe the work which has to
be done. The cases do no more than illustrate specific contexts in which judges, as
ordinary speakers of English, have thought that it was or was not appropriate to do
h so.'

After considering the submissions of counsel and noting that it was agreed by counsel
that the question was one of degree, and, to a large extent, one of impression on which
different people could reasonably give different answers, the judge continued (at 107):

j 'I think one is entitled to take into account, first, as part of the context, the
commercial relationship between the parties at the time of the demise. This was
that the landlords had a headlease of 125 years and the tenants had been given an
underlease of about 22 years. Second, in considering whether the work was
improvement rather than repair, one must have regard to its substantiality. In this
case both experts advise that whatever scheme of waterproofing is adopted, there
should be a very substantial structural addition to the basement ... Third, I think I

am entitled to take into account the probable cost of the work . . . This [at the lower end of the range] is twice the likely annual market rent for the whole building with a waterproof basement and over 15% of its total capital value . . . Taking these matters into consideration and deploying my ordinary understanding of language, I do not think it would be appropriate to describe any of the three schemes of treatment as work of repair. In my judgment, they involve structural alterations and improvements to the basement. Consequently, they do not fall within the tenants' b obligations under the lease and I shall so declare.'

By their notice of appeal the landlords asked, inter alia, that the declaration made by the judge be set aside and that this court should declare that on a true construction of the underlease the tenants are liable to carry out one of the schemes of works considered in evidence. The main contentions in the notice of appeal were that, in reaching his conclusion, the judge had failed to apply the correct legal tests. In particular, it was said c that (i) he failed properly to apply the test whether the work would involve giving back to the landlords a wholly different thing from that which was demised and (ii) he failed to hold that works can constitute repair notwithstanding that they may also constitute a substantial addition or alteration or improvement if those works are the only reasonable way in which the defect can be remedied.

On opening the appeal in this court counsel for the landlords, who did not appear d below, contended primarily that the work required to be done would be work of repair to cure the failure of the kicker joint between the floor and the walls caused by poor workmanship and would not give the landlords a wholly different thing from that which they demised; and that as such it would be work to a portion, a subsidiary portion of the demised property, and not to the whole or substantially the whole. Reliance was placed e on the test stated by Forbes J in *Ravenseft Properties Ltd v Davstone (Holdings) Ltd* [1979] 1 All ER 929 at 937, [1980] QB 12 at 21. There, in holding that the cost of certain work to a building was recoverable under the tenant's covenant to repair, Forbes J said:

> 'The true test is, as the cases show, that it is always a question of degree whether that which the tenant is being asked to do can properly be described as repair, or f whether on the contrary it would involve giving back to the landlord a wholly different thing from that which he demised.'

In that case under the terms of an underlease the tenants covenanted to be liable for the repairs of the demised building. The building had been constructed in concrete with an external cladding of stone. No expansion joints had been included when the building was being constructed because it had not been realised that the different coefficients in g expansion of stone and concrete made it necessary to include such joints. The stones had not been tied in properly to the building, so, instead of cracking as a result of pressure as the building expanded, they bowed away from the concrete frame and there was danger of stones falling. The landlords required the tenants to carry out the necessary work, but the tenants denied that they were liable under the covenant to repair the damage caused by the inherent defect in the building of the exclusion of expansion joints. The landlords h carried out the necessary work of taking down the cladding stones, retying the stones and inserting expansion joints. Forbes J gave judgment for the landlords. He rejected the contention that, if the cause of the want of reparation was an inherent defect, the tenant was thereby given a complete defence (see [1979] 1 All ER 929 at 937, [1980] QB 12 at 21). It is to be noted that the inherent defect, ie the absence of an expansion joint, had j caused damage and deterioration to the building and the making good of the inherent defect was a necessary part of the making good of the damage and deterioration suffered by the building. This authority had, of course, been relied on by counsel who appeared for the landlords before the judge.

On 29 July 1985, some three days after the decision of Hoffmann J in this case, the decision of Forbes J in *Ravenseft Properties Ltd v Davstone (Holdings) Ltd* was considered by a this court (Lawton, Dillon and Neill LJJ) in *Quick v Taff-Ely BC* [1985] 3 All ER 321, [1986] QB 809. In that case the plaintiff was the tenant of a house owned by the defendant council. As a result of severe condensation throughout the house, decorations, woodwork, furnishings, bedding and clothes rotted, and living conditions were appalling. The condensation was caused by lack of insulation of window lintels, single-glazed metal frame windows and inadequate heating. The plaintiff brought proceedings in the county court, alleging that the council was in breach of its covenant, implied in the tenancy

b agreement by s 32(1) of the Housing Act 1961 'to keep in repair the structure and exterior' of the house and seeking an order for specific performance of the covenant. The judge held that the council was in breach of the repairing covenant in respect of, inter alia, the condensation and made an order requiring the council to insulate the lintels and to replace the metal frame windows. This court allowed the appeal of the council. Liability under the covenant did not arise because of lack of amenity or inefficiency, but

c only when there existed a physical condition which called for repair to the structure or exterior of the dwelling house; and, as there was no evidence to indicate any physical damage to, or want of repair in, the windows or lintels themselves or any other part of the structure and exterior, the council could not be required to carry out work to alleviate the condensation. The decision of Forbes J in *Ravenseft Properties Ltd v Davstone (Holdings) Ltd* was approved. Dillon LJ described the reasoning in the careful judgment of the judge

d as follows ([1985] 3 All ER 321 at 324–325, [1986] QB 809 at 817):

'... (1) recent authorities such as *Ravenseft Properties Ltd v Davstone (Holdings) Ltd* [1979] 1 All ER 929, [1980] QB 12 and *Elmcroft Developments Ltd v Tankersley-Sawyer* (1984) 270 EG 140 show that works of repair under a repairing covenant, whether by a landlord or a tenant, may require the remedying of an inherent defect in a

e building, (2) the authorities also show that it is a question of degree whether works which remedy an inherent defect in a building may not be so extensive as to amount to an improvement or renewal of the whole which is beyond the concept of repair, (3) in the present case the replacement of windows and the provision of insulation for the lintels does not amount to such an improvement or renewal of the whole, (4) therefore, the replacement of the windows and provision of the insulation to

f alleviate an inherent defect is a repair which the local authority is bound to carry out under the repairing covenant.'

Dillon LJ continued:

'But ... this reasoning begs the important question. It assumes that any work to eradicate an inherent defect in a building must be a work of repair, which the

g relevant party is bound to carry out if, as a matter of degree, it does not amount to a renewal or improvement of the building.'

Later in his judgment Dillon LJ said ([1985] 3 All ER 321 at 325, [1986] QB 809 at 818):

'In my judgment, the key factor in the present case is that disrepair is related to the physical condition of whatever has to be repaired, and not to questions of lack of

h amenity or inefficiency. I find helpful the observations of Atkin LJ in *Anstruther-Gough-Calthorpe v McOscar* [1924] 1 KB 716 at 734, [1923] All ER Rep 198 at 206 that repair "connotes the idea of making good damage so as to leave the subject so far as possible as though it had not been damaged". Where decorative repair is in question one must look for damage to the decorations but where, as here, the

j obligation is merely to keep the structure and exterior of the house in repair, the covenant will only come into operation where there has been damage to the structure and exterior which requires to be made good. If there is such damage caused by an unsuspected inherent defect, then it may be necessary to cure the defect, and thus to some extent improve without wholly renewing the property as the only practicable way of making good the damage to the subject matter of the repairing covenant. That, as I read the case, was the basis of the decision in *Ravenseft*.'

Lawton LJ said ([1985] 3 All ER 321 at 328, [1986] QB 809 at 822):   **a**

'It follows that, on the evidence in this case, the trial judge should first have identified the parts of the exterior and structure of the house which were out of repair and then have gone on to decide whether, in order to remedy the defects, it was reasonably necessary to replace the concrete lintels over the windows, which caused "cold bridging", and the single-glazed metal windows, both of which were among the causes, probably the major causes, of excessive condensation in the   **b** house.'

Later Lawton LJ said ([1985] 3 All ER 321 at 329, [1986] QB 809 at 823):

'... there must be disrepair before any question arises whether it would be reasonable to remedy a design fault when doing the repair. In this case, as the trial judge found, there was no evidence that the single-glazed metal windows were in   **c** any different state at the date of the trial from what they had been in when the tenant first became a tenant. The same could have been said of the lintels.'

When asked early in the course of argument by Slade LJ whether the first question in this case was not more accurately to be stated as whether the premises were shown to have been out of repair, counsel for the landlords accepted that that was the correct   **d** approach. Counsel for the tenants told the court that the point, which is not expressly discussed in the judgment of Hoffmann J, had been argued for the tenants before the judge, namely that there was no proof of disrepair or of damage or deterioration resulting from any inherent defect, and that reliance had been placed on the dictum of Atkin LJ in *Anstruther-Gough-Calthorpe v McOscar* cited by Dillon LJ in *Quick v Taff-Ely BC*.

Addressing the question whether disrepair had been proved, counsel for the landlords   **e** relied on the findings by the judge as to the failure of the kicker joint due to porosity of the concrete and as to the construction joints not having been formed with care. At one stage counsel for the landlords suggested that the porosity of the concrete due to honeycombing had not necessarily existed since the date of the underlease in 1969 or from any earlier date, but had 'come on over the years'. On consideration of the words used by the judge in his findings of fact, which indicate that the defects had existed since   **f** the building was constructed, and in the absence of any finding of deterioration or worsening of the condition caused by the presence of the water when the water table rose, or from the passing of the water through the porous concrete, counsel for the landlords was unable to pursue the contention. It is clear to me that the defects which were found by the judge to have caused the flooding were present in the condition in which they now are from the time that the building was constructed.   **g**

Counsel for the landlords submitted that it was not relevant to inquire whether the original defects in the concrete or construction joints had grown worse or had caused any other damage or deterioration to the demised premises. In summary form his submission was as follows. (i) At the date of the lease the premises were defective in that by reason of the porosity of the concrete and the defective construction joints ground water could enter the basement and did enter when the water table rose. (ii) The defects existed by   **h** reason of bad workmanship and not from a decision as a matter of design not to incorporate some amenity or advantage: the defects, accordingly, constituted disrepair. (iii) To hold that such a state of a building did not constitute disrepair (and such a holding would be applicable to the terms of a similar covenant whether by landlord or tenant) would be a departure from, or an undesirable limitation of, the important principle established in *Proudfoot v Hart* (1890) 25 QBD 42 at 50, [1886–90] All ER Rep 782 at 784   **j** per Lord Esher MR and never since doubted, namely:

'... under a contract to keep the premises in tenantable repair and leave them in tenantable repair, the obligation of the tenant, if the premises are not in tenantable repair when the tenancy begins, is to put them into, keep them in, and deliver them up in tenantable repair.'

(iv) The reference in *Quick's* case to deterioration or damage, such as the statement by
a Lawton LJ that 'that which requires repair is in a condition worse than it was at some
earlier time', or that of Dillon LJ that a covenant to repair the structure or exterior 'will
only come into operation where there has been damage to the structure and exterior
which requires to be made good' are not to be taken as applicable to a case of this nature,
and their Lordships in *Quick's* case did not have such a case as this in mind. In particular,
they were not dealing with a case like this where the defective part of the premises is
b such that it has and may again interfere with the ordinary use and occupation of the
premises contemplated by the demise and, having been caused by defective work, was
'worse' than it was required to be if that part of the premises was to be regarded as in
good repair.

For my part I am unable to accept the submission made by counsel for the appellant
landlords. The facts of this case seem to me to be, as I have said, highly unusual. I found
c it at first to be a startling proposition that, when an almost new office building lets
ground water into the basement so that the water is ankle deep for some years, that state
of affairs is consistent with there being no condition of disrepair under a repairing
covenant in standard form whether given by landlord or tenant. Nevertheless, as was
pointed out in the course of argument, the landlord of such a building gives no implied
warranty of fitness merely by reason of letting it; and neither a landlord nor a tenant,
d who enters into a covenant to repair in ordinary form, thereby undertakes to do work to
improve the demised premises in any way. I see no escape from the conclusion that, if
on the evidence the premises demised are and at all times have been in the same physical
condition (so far as concerns the matters in issue) as they were when constructed, no want
of repair has been proved for which the tenants could be liable under the covenant.

When the water entered by reason of the original defects, damage might have been
e done to the premises, whether to plaster on walls, or to the flooring, or to electrical or
other installations. But no such damage was proved. If such damage is done, the
authorities show that the resulting state is a condition of disrepair: see *Ravenseft Properties
Ltd v Davstone (Holdings) Ltd* [1979] 1 All ER 929, [1980] QB 12 and *Elmcroft Developments
Ltd v Tankersley-Sawyer* (1984) 270 EG 140. As to the submission that the court in *Quick
f v Taff-Ely BC* was not considering a defect which had been caused by defective work, I
accept that such were the facts in that case: the house was built in accordance with the
regulations in force and standards accepted at the time (see [1985] 3 All ER 321 at 324,
[1986] QB 809 at 816). In my judgment, however, the reasoning of the court in *Quick's*
case is equally applicable whether the original defect resulted from error in design, or in
workmanship, or from deliberate parsimony or any other cause. If on the letting of
g premises it were desired by the parties to impose on landlord or tenant an obligation to
put the premises into a particular state or condition so as to be at all times fit for some
stated purpose, even if it means making the premises better than they were when
constructed, there would be no difficulty in finding words apt for that purpose.

Neither counsel for the landlords nor counsel for the tenants could refer the court to
any reported case in which a defect, whether of design or workmanship, and present
h unaltered since construction of the premises, and which had caused or permitted entry
of water into the premises, had nevertheless caused no damage to the premises demised.
It seems to me that the unusual facts of this case are covered by the plain meaning of the
word 'repair' and by the decision of the court in *Quick's* case. It is not possible to hold that
the wetting of the basement floor, or the presence of the water on the floor, coupled with
the inconvenience caused thereby to the tenant, constitutes damage to the premises
j demised. There is, accordingly, no disrepair proved in this case and therefore no liability
under the tenant's covenant to repair has arisen.

So to hold is not, in my judgment, to depart from, or to cast doubt on, the principles
established by the decision of the Court of Appeal in *Proudfoot v Hart*. On examination
of the judgment of Lord Esher MR in that case, it is apparent that he was only directing
his observations to premises of which the condition has deteriorated from a former better
condition. Counsel for the landlords accepted that that was so. It might be said that there

is no difference in principle between, on the one hand, imposing a liability on a tenant to put premises into a better condition than they were at the date of the demise by reference   *a*
to an earlier state before deterioration had occurred, and, on the other hand, imposing on a tenant, as counsel for the landlords asks the court to do, liability to put premises into a better condition than ever they were in by reference to a state in which they ought to have been if they are to be in some state of fitness or suitability. That, however, in my judgment is not the point. This court in this case is not laying down rules to govern the relationships and mutual responsibilities of landlords and tenants of office buildings.   *b*
Our task is to construe a repairing covenant in a particular underlease. The decision may be of some general importance, despite the unusual set of facts, because the covenant so far as concerns the words on which reliance is placed is in common form. But landlords and tenants of such premises are free to modify the repairing covenants as they think appropriate and can agree. There is no basis to be found in the decision in *Proudfoot v Hart* for holding that the tenant can be held liable under an ordinary repairing covenant   *c*
to carry out work merely to improve premises so as to remove a defect present since construction of the building.

That conclusion, if right, is sufficient to dispose of this appeal. The questions considered by the judge whether, as a matter of degree, any of the schemes of work qualified as 'repair', as contrasted with works of improvement or alteration, do not arise. These issues were, however, argued before us and I think it is appropriate to make some comments   *d*
on them. The main criticism advanced by counsel for the landlords was that the judge had failed to have due regard to, or to apply correctly the test enunciated by, Forbes J in *Ravenseft Properties Ltd v Davstone (Holdings) Ltd*, namely that it was a question of degree whether work carried out on a building was repair or work that so changed the character of the building as to involve giving back to the landlord 'a wholly different thing' from that which he demised. It was said that if the judge had given sufficient force to the fact   *e*
that the necessary work in this case was directed to a subordinate part only of the building he must have reached a different conclusion. For my part I do not accept that the judge is shown to have misapprehended or misapplied in this way the appropriate test. The relationship of the part on which work is required to the whole of the subject matter of the demise is also in my judgment, and as Slade LJ suggested in argument, a question of   *f*
proportion and degree. At one end of the scale there has never been any doubt that a party liable under a covenant to repair may have to renew in effect a whole part such as a floor, or a door, or a window. An example of a substantial part is the stone cladding of the building in *Ravenseft Properties Ltd v Davstone (Holdings) Ltd*. I do not accept, however, that it is only open to the court to hold that work involves giving back a wholly different thing if it is possible to say that the whole subject matter of the demise, or a whole building within the subject matter of the demise, will by the work be made different.   *g*

Counsel for the tenants in a comprehensive review of the authorities, which lost nothing by its brevity of reference to them, drew attention to cases in which, applying the substance of the test propounded by Forbes J, courts have held that liability for work could not be imposed on a party bound by the covenant although the work was required only to a part of the relevant premises: e g the bay window in *Wright v Lawson* (1903) 19   *h*
TLR 203; *affd* 19 TLR 510; the basement walls in *Pembery v Lamdin* [1940] 2 All ER 434; and the roofing of the back addition in *Halliard Property Co v Nicholas Clark Investments Ltd* (1983) 269 EG 1257.

The notice of appeal in this case included as a ground of appeal complaint that the judge had wrongly taken into account, in considering as a question of degree whether the proposed works were works of repair or of alteration and improvement, the respective   *j*
lengths of the landlords' and tenants' leasehold interests and the cost of the scheme of work proposed. On the hearing of this appeal counsel for the landlords did not argue that ground. He conceded that those matters were relevant but argued that they could be of little weight. In my judgment counsel for the landlords was right to concede the relevance of those matters and I accept also that in a case of this nature, assuming disrepair

a to have been proved, the weight that could properly be given to those factors would not be large.

As to whether on the evidence before the judge he was right to reach the conclusion which he did on the assumption that the premises were in a state of disrepair, I have seen in draft the judgment of Slade LJ and I too prefer to express no view on that matter. For these reasons I would dismiss this appeal.

b **SLADE LJ.** In agreement with the judgment of Ralph Gibson LJ, I think that there is quite a short answer to the landlords' claims under present circumstances.

The only provision of the tenants' covenants contained in the tenants' underlease on which reliance has been placed by the landlords in argument is that which obliges the tenants to 'keep in good and substantial repair . . . the demised premises and every part thereof'. The tenants cannot yet be under any obligation to do any work pursuant to this c covenant unless the demised premises are at present out of repair. However, a state of disrepair, in my judgment, connotes a deterioration from some previous physical condition. I would have reached this conclusion even in the absence of authority, but its correctness is shown by the decision of this court (later in time than that of Hoffmann J in the present case) in *Quick v Taff-Ely BC* [1985] 3 All ER 321, [1986] QB 809. As Lawton d LJ there observed ([1985] 3 All ER 321 at 328, [1986] QB 809 at 821):

'As a matter of the ordinary usage of English that which requires repair is in a condition worse than it was at some earlier time.'

Dillon LJ, adopting a similar train of thought, said ([1985] 3 All ER 321 at 325, [1986] QB 809 at 818):

e 'Where decorative repair is in question one must look for damage to the decorations but where, as here, the obligation is merely to keep the structure and exterior of the house in repair, the covenant will only come into operation where there has been damage to the structure and exterior which requires to be made good.'

f In the present case there was evidence at the trial that, in the original construction of the building, poor workmanship (or perhaps, in the case of the construction joints, poor design) had produced weak areas in the concrete or the kicker joint and also in some construction joints, so as to allow the ingress of flood water. However, despite the prolonged flooding in past years, there was, as Ralph Gibson LJ has pointed out, no finding (and we have been referred to no evidence) that any part of this defective building had suffered deterioration since its original construction. Thus, there was no finding at g the trial that any of the building was out of repair.

In these circumstances, there would in my opinion have been no grounds on which the judge could properly have held that the words of the repairing covenant quoted above imposed any present obligation on the tenants to do work to the premises. Counsel for the landlords suggested that any such decision would conflict with the principle h established by *Proudfoot v Hart* (1890) 25 QBD 42, [1886–90] All ER Rep 782 that a tenant's covenant to keep premises in good repair obliges the tenant, if the premises are not in good repair when the tenancy begins, to put them into that state. However, as he accepted in the course of argument, the relevant statements of the law in that case were only directed to the case where the condition of premises has deteriorated from an earlier better condition. They were not directed, and in my judgment have no application, to a j case such as the present where the structural defect complained of by the landlords has existed from the time when the premises were originally built. Though counsel for the landlords sought to draw a distinction in this context between structural defects due to errors in design and those due to faulty workmanship, I can see no grounds on principle or authority for drawing any such distinction.

For these reasons, albeit different from those of the judge, I think that he was right to conclude that the tenants are under no present liability to the landlords by virtue of the repairing covenants and to dismiss the landlords' counterclaim. I do not reach this *a* conclusion with regret on the very unusual facts of this case. It seems to me that, if, as in the present case, landlords let to tenants newly built premises of which parts are defectively constructed, clear words are needed to impose a contractual obligation on the tenants to remedy the defects in the original construction, at least at a time before these have caused any damage. This is not an obligation which tenants under a commercial lease might reasonably be expected readily to undertake.   *b*

It is, however, possible that, before the underlease expires in 1991, the original defects in construction could result in actual damage to the demised premises. For example, if there was another rise in the water table, there might be further flooding and this might cause damage to the plaster work or electrical fittings of the building. I would like to leave entirely open any questions as to the liability of the tenants in that event.

Forbes J in *Ravenseft Properties Ltd v Davstone (Holdings) Ltd* [1979] 1 All ER 929 at 936– *c* 937, [1980] QB 12 at 21 specifically rejected a contention that, if it can be shown that any want of reparation has been caused by an inherent defect in a building, then that want of reparation is necessarily not within the ambit of a covenant to repair. He considered that, whether or not the lack of repair has been caused by an inherent defect—

> 'it is always a question of degree whether that which the tenant is being asked to *d*
> do can properly be described as repair, or whether on the contrary it would involve
> giving back to the landlord a wholly different thing from that which he demised'.

The *Ravenseft Properties* decision was referred to by this court in *Elmcroft Developments Ltd v Tankersley-Sawyer* (1984) 270 EG 140 without criticism and in *Quick v Taff-Ely BC* with approval.

In the future contingency now under discussion, the extent of the liability of the *e* tenants would, in my opinion, depend on precisely what works they were being asked to do by way of so-called repair and in what circumstances. In that contingency those works would not by any means necessarily be the same as those envisaged by any of the schemes of work now proposed. On the further evidence then available, the questions of degree involved might be different from those considered by Hoffmann J on the evidence before him. For these reasons I would prefer to express no opinion on any of these particular *f* schemes beyond saying that *under present circumstances* none of them can properly be described as repair and the tenants are *at present* under no obligation to carry out any of them.

I agree that this appeal should be dismissed.

SIR ROGER ORMROD. I agree with both judgments.   *g*

Appeal dismissed.

Solicitors: *Grangewoods* (for the landlords); *B A Holland* (for the tenants).

Mary Rose Plummer   Barrister.   *h*

a

Practice Note

COURT OF APPEAL, CIVIL DIVISION
SIR JOHN DONALDSON MR, GLIDEWELL LJ AND SIR FREDERICK LAWTON
23 MARCH 1987

b *Court of Appeal – Practice – Long vacation – Sittings of Civil Division during long vacation – RSC Ord 64, r 2(1).*

SIR JOHN DONALDSON MR gave the following direction at the sitting of the court. Having determined that sittings are necessary for the purpose of hearing appeals and applications during vacation, in the exercise of the powers conferred on me by RSC Ord 64, r 2(1), and with the concurrence of the Lord Chancellor, I direct that the Civil c Division of the Court of Appeal shall sit during August and September 1987 and in the months of August and September in future years until further notice. Details of the number of courts sitting in August and September will be published each year, normally before Easter.

The sittings in the Civil Division of the Court of Appeal in August and September d 1987 and the number and constitution of the courts expected to sit will be as follows:

3 to 7 August	one 3-judge court and one 2-judge court
10 to 14 August	one 2-judge court
14 to 30 September	one 3-judge court and three 2-judge courts

Frances Rustin   Barrister.

Re Poulton's Will Trusts
Smail and another v Litchfield and another

CHANCERY DIVISION

WARNER J

13, 14, 18 NOVEMBER 1986

Will – Gift – Specific donees – Relatives – Testatrix's daughter empowered by will to divide estate among her own 'relatives' at her discretion – Daughter appointing cousin's three daughters to take – Whether appointment limited to next of kin – Whether appointment to cousin's three daughters valid.

By a handwritten will dated 16 September 1935 the testatrix bequeathed to P, her only daughter, the whole of her estate for life and on P's death 'whatever remains to be divided amongst her own relatives according to her own discretion'. The testatrix died in 1936 leaving an estate which included two freehold houses. By a will dated 15 November 1938 P bequeathed the rents and income arising from the two houses to her cousin L and directed that on L's death the houses were to be sold and the proceeds of sale divided equally between those of L's children who had attained the age of 21. P died in 1948 and L died in 1982 leaving three children over 21, who were not statutory next of kin of P. In an action brought by two of the trustees of the testatrix's will, it was not disputed that the testatrix's will gave P a life interest in the entirety of the testatrix's estate and a special power of appointment in favour of her own relatives over what remained of the estate at her death. However, the question arose whether relatives of P other than her next of kin could take under an exercise of that special power or whether the gift to L's children failed and the property fell to be distributed among P's next of kin.

Held – The rule that a disposition to the 'relations' of the testator would be restricted to the testator's next of kin was an artifical rule designed to prevent the failure of a bequest for uncertainty and the rule did not apply if the effect of the disposition was not uncertain. It followed that the disposition by P to L's three children was valid (see p 1072 *b c*, p 1073 *f g* and p 1074 *b*, post).

Re Gansloser's Will Trusts, Chartered Bank of India Australia and China v Chillingworth [1951] 2 All ER 936 considered.

Re Deakin, Starkey v Eyres [1894] 3 Ch 565 not followed.

Notes

For construction of wills in accordance with the testator's intention, see 50 Halsbury's Laws (4th edn) paras 370–372, 414, and for cases on the subject, see 50 Digest (Reissue) 487–488, 491–492, 4654–4686, 4733–4744.

Cases referred to in judgment

Bridgen, Re, Chaytor v Edwin [1937] 4 All ER 342, [1938] Ch 205.

Deakin, Re, Starkey v Eyres [1894] 3 Ch 565.

Finch v Hollingsworth (1855) 21 Beav 112, 52 ER 801.

Gansloser's Will Trusts, Re, Chartered Bank of India Australia and China v Chillingworth [1951] 2 All ER 936, [1952] Ch 30, CA.

Harding v Glyn (1739) 1 Atk 469, 26 ER 299.

Lawlor v Henderson (1876) IR 10 Eq 150.

Pope v Whitcombe (1810) 3 Mer 689, 36 ER 264.

Wilson v Duguid (1883) 24 Ch D 244.

Cases also cited

a   *Grant v Lynam* (1828) 4 Russ 292, [1824–34] All ER Rep 522, 38 ER 815.
Hughes, Re, Hughes v Footner [1921] 2 Ch 208, [1921] All ER Rep 310.

Originating summons

The plaintiffs, Ena Smail and Ronald Litchfield, two of the trustees of the will of Sarah Poulton deceased, sought by an originating summons dated 1 April 1985 the
b   determination of the court on the question whether on the true construction of the testatrix's will the bequest in the will of Mabel Eleanor Poulton (Miss Poulton) of the net proceeds of sale of 33 and 35 Frederick Street, Luton to the children of her cousin Eleanor Mary Litchfield (Mrs Litchfield), was a valid exercise of the power of appointment conferred on Miss Poulton by the testatrix's will empowering her to divide the testatrix's estate among her own relatives according to her own discretion, and if the gift was not a
c   valid exercise of the power of appointment, how the net proceeds of sale of the properties should devolve. The defendants to the summons were Haydon William Litchfield, representing the children of Mrs Litchfield, and Ralph Frank Buckingham, representing the next of kin of Miss Poulton. The facts are set out in the judgment.

d   *Martin Roth* for the plaintiffs.
Geraint Thomas for the children of Mrs Litchfield.
Teresa Peacocke for the next of kin of Miss Poulton.

Cur adv vult

e   18 November. The following judgment was delivered.

WARNER J. This is an originating summons raising questions as to the effect of the wills of the late Sarah Poulton (whom I will call 'Mrs Poulton') and of her daughter, the late Mabel Eleanor Poulton (whom I will call 'Miss Poulton').

Mrs Poulton made her will on 16 September 1935. It is a handwritten will made on a
f   piece of note paper. At the top are her address and the date. The text of the will is as follows.

> 'I, Sarah Poulton, of the above address, do hereby Give and Bequeath to my daughter Mabel Eleanor Poulton, the whole of my possessions for her life, and at her decease, whatever remains to be divided amongst her own relatives according to her own discretion. As my executors, I appoint Horace Ward Clements of 100
g   Wenlock Street, Luton, Beds, and my own daughter Mabel Eleanor Poulton.'

Mrs Poulton died on 14 January 1936 and her will was proved on 23 March 1936 by the executors therein named. Her estate included two freehold houses, 33 and 35 Frederick Street, Luton.

By her will, which was dated 15 November 1938, Miss Poulton provided, so far as
h   material, as follows:

> 'I DEVISE my two dwellinghouses and premises Numbers 33 and 35 Frederick Street Luton aforesaid to my Trustees Upon trust that my Trustees shall let the same to such person or persons at such rents and on such conditions as they shall think fit and shall pay the net rents and income arising from the said premises to my Cousin
j   the said Eleanor Mary Litchfield during her life to whom I bequeath the same for her own use and enjoyment and from and after the death of the said Eleanor Mary Litchfield I direct my Trustees to sell the said premises Numbers 33 and 35 Frederick Street Luton aforesaid and to pay and divide the net proceeds arising from such sale unto and equally between all the children of the said Eleanor Mary Litchfield who

have attained or shall attain the age of twenty one years and if there shall be only
one such child the whole to go to that one child to whom in the events aforesaid I   *a*
give and bequeath the same absolutely.'

Miss Poulton died on 19 October 1948 and her will was proved on 29 September 1949.
Eleanor Mary Litchfield (whom I will call 'Mrs Litchfield') died on 24 January 1982.
She had three children, all of whom have attained the age of 21, and are parties to these
proceedings. Until her death Mrs Litchfield occupied 33 Frederick Street and received   *b*
the rents of no 35. After her death the trustees sold no 33. Number 35 is occupied by an
elderly gentleman as tenant and the trustees have refrained for the time being from
selling it. The property now remaining subject to the trusts of the will of Mrs Poulton
consists of no 35, the net proceeds of sale of no 33 and a small holding of $3\frac{1}{2}\%$ war stock
which is bound to be absorbed by the costs of these proceedings.

There is before me a family tree which shows that Miss Poulton was born in about   *c*
1887, that she was Mrs Poulton's only child and that she never married. The family tree
also shows that Mrs Poulton had four sisters, two of whom had children. Mrs Litchfield
was one of the daughters of one of them. Arthur Poulton, the husband of Mrs Poulton
and father of Miss Poulton, had three brothers and a sister, all of whom have descendants.
The statutory next of kin of Miss Poulton number over 20. They included Mrs Litchfield,
but do not include her children.   *d*

It is undisputed that the effect of Mrs Poulton's will was to confer on Miss Poulton a
life interest in the entirety of Mrs Poulton's estate (probably coupled with a right to resort
to capital) and a special power of appointment in favour of her own relatives over what
remained of the estate at her death. The question that has been argued before me is
whether relatives of Miss Poulton other than her next of kin could take under an exercise
of that special power. If not, the gift in Miss Poulton's will in favour of Mrs Litchfield's   *e*
children fails and the property now held by the trustees of Mrs Poulton's will must be
distributed among Miss Poulton's next of kin.

The relevant law is conveniently set out in *Hawkins and Ryder on the Construction of
Wills* (3rd edn, 1965) pp 174–178. I will read the more pertinent passages of that:

'The word "relations" in its ordinary meaning extends to all persons related to the   *f*
propositus, however remotely. But if the word were construed in this sense in a gift
to the relations of a specified person, the gift would fail for uncertainty. To avoid
this result the courts in construing wills made before 1926 adopted the rule that a
gift to the "relations" of A, or the testator, should be construed to mean the persons
who would be entitled as next of kin under the Statutes of Distribution. The rule
was first applied to bequests of personalty and was subsequently extended to devises   *g*
. . . The rule applied whenever the testator had used an expression equivalent to
"relations" . . . The terms "relatives" and "blood relations" are equivalent to
"relations" . . . Since the rule was adopted in order to save gifts which would
otherwise have failed for uncertainty, it does not apply where the restriction of the
meaning of relations to a defined class is unnecessary, *i.e.* where the disposition is
valid even though "relations" is construed in the ordinary sense . . . A simple power   *h*
of appointment (*i.e.*, one not coupled with any trust in favour of the class of object
of the power) is valid even though the class of objects is incapable of being
exhaustively enumerated, provided that the qualification for membership of the
class is one which makes it possible to decide whether any given person is or is not
within the class. Where, on the other hand, a power is coupled with a trust in favour
of the whole class of objects of the power, (*i.e.*, where there is a duty to exercise a   *j*
power, or an implied gift in favour of all the objects in default of appointment) the
power is invalid unless the class of objects is ascertainable in the sense that all its
members can be enumerated. [That that is no longer quite accurate does not matter
for present purposes.] The class of the blood relations of a given person is not
ascertainable in this sense, though it may be possible to state with certainty that

a particular persons are within the class. Thus where a testator has given a power to appoint to such of A's "relations" as the donee shall select, the whole disposition must fail if it is construed as a power in the nature of a trust in favour of A's blood relations. The courts might have solved the difficulty by simply treating "relations" as equivalent to statutory next-of-kin. In fact, however, they have treated such dispositions as creating a power to appoint amongst blood relations, with a trust in default of appointment in favour of statutory next-of-kin. The rule was thus stated

b by Chitty J. in *Wilson v. Duguid* ((1883) 24 Ch D 244 at 251): "It is now established that where there is a power to appoint among relations so as to give the donee of the power the right of selection—the donee of the power can appoint any relations, but in modelling the trusts to be applied in default or arising from the power being coupled with the duty, the court has found itself under the necessity of confining the class of relations to a particular set of relations, and has adopted the rule that

c relations who take in default of the exercise of the power in that case are those who are next-of-kin according to the statute" ... Before 1874 the rule allowing an appointment to be made in favour of any blood relations only applied where the power was an exclusive power or power of selection, i.e., where the donee was entitled to appoint the whole fund to one or some only of the objects and to exclude the others. Where the power was a non-exclusive power or power of distribution

d (i.e., where the donee was not entitled to appoint in such a way that some of the objects were excluded) an appointment could only be made in favour of statutory next-of-kin of the propositus. Where the testator had done no more than create a power which was simple on the face of it, i.e., not in the nature of a trust, a similar distinction was made: if the power was exclusive an appointment could be made in favour of any blood relations, but if it was non-exclusive the donee could only

e appoint to statutory next-of-kin. It was necessary to draw this distinction between exclusive and non-exclusive powers, since a non-exclusive power (whether simple or in the nature of a trust) to appoint to an unascertainable class would have been void, and therefore in order to save the validity of a non-exclusive power to appoint to "relations" it was necessary to construe the term so as to confine its meaning to the ascertainable class for statutory next-of-kin. But since the passing of the Powers

f of Appointment Act 1874, which provided that no appointment under any power should be invalid on the ground that any object was excluded, the distinction between exclusive and non-exclusive powers has been obsolete: all powers are now in effect exclusive. It was, nevertheless, held by Stirling J. in *Re Deakin* ([1894] 3 Ch 565) that the former rule of construction had not been altered by the Act, i.e., that

g where the power to appoint to relations is not in terms exclusive, where it is on the face of it a power of distribution as opposed to one of selection, the word "relations" must still be construed as limited to statutory next-of-kin.'

There is then this comment by Professor Ryder:

h 'It is doubtful whether this case would be followed in a higher court; the reasoning on which the earlier decisions were based is no longer valid, and there can be no justification for determining the meaning of the testator's words by applying a technical and artificial rule based on a distinction which is now only a matter of history. It is submitted that at the present day the true principle is that a power to appoint amongst the "relations" of a person should be construed as a power to

j appoint among blood relations whether it is framed as a power of selection or one of distribution, though if it is a power in the nature of a trust the persons to take in default of appointment will be the statutory next-of-kin of the propositus.'

Without reading more from *Hawkins and Ryder* I will add that the provisions of the Powers of Appointment Act 1874, together with those of the Illusory Appointments Act 1830, are now replaced by s 158(1) of the Law of Property Act 1925, and that, where a

gift to relations or relatives is contained in a will taking effect after 1925, the persons to
take as next of kin are those who would have taken under the Administration of Estates   *a*
Act 1925.

It is submitted by counsel for the next of kin of Miss Poulton that I should follow *Re
Deakin, Starkey v Eyres* [1894] 3 Ch 565 and accordingly hold that the gift to the children
of Mrs Litchfield fails.

Counsel for those children contends first that I should construe the will of Mrs Poulton
as conferring on Miss Poulton an exclusive power, or power of selection, and not a non-   *b*
exclusive power or mere power of distribution, so that *Re Deakin* is not in point. If the
matter were free from authority I should have no hesitation in giving effect to that
contention. It seems to me highly improbable that, when Mrs Poulton used the words
'whatever remains to be divided amongst her own relatives according to her own
discretion', she meant Miss Poulton to ensure that every 'relative' of hers received
something out of the estate. I would have thought that an absurd intention to attribute   *c*
to Mrs Poulton, particularly in view of the large number of relatives that she must have
known that her daughter had.

Counsel for Miss Poulton's next of kin has however drawn my attention to a number
of cases where, in the past, judges have held testamentary provisions in very similar form
to create only powers of distribution: *Pope v Whitcombe* (1810) 3 Mer 689, 36 ER 264,
Finch v Hollingsworth (1855) 21 Beav 112, 52 ER 801, *Lawlor v Henderson* (1876) IR 10 Eq   *d*
150 and *Re Deakin* itself. I am inclined to think that a full analysis of those cases would
show that none of them is an entirely satisfactory authority on the point, but my
attention has also been drawn to cases where, absurdly though it may seem to me,
twentieth century testators have unambiguously directed their property to be divided
equally among all their relations, or among someone else's relations: see *Re Bridgen,
Clayton v Edwin* [1937] 4 All ER 342, [1938] Ch 205 and *Re Gansloser's Will Trusts,*   *e*
Chartered Bank of India Australia and China v Chillingworth [1951] 2 All ER 936, [1952] Ch
30. In the circumstances, without expressing any concluded view on the matter, I will
assume in counsel's favour that the will of Mrs Poulton, on its true construction and apart
from s 158(1) of the Law of Property Act 1925, conferred on Miss Poulton a mere power
of distribution.

Counsel for Mrs Litchfield's the children contended in the alternative that, in so far as   *f*
Stirling J in *Re Deakin* held that, despite the Powers of Appointment Act 1874, where a
power to appoint among relations was on the face of it a power of distribution and not of
selection, it should still be construed as limited to statutory next of kin, his decision was
wrong and I should not follow it. What Stirling J said about that was this ([1894] Ch 565
at 577–578):
   g
'That [ie the 1874 Act] relieves the donee of a power from the necessity of either
making an appointment to every object of the power, or of leaving something
unappointed. It does not purport to alter any rule of construction which has been
laid down as to the meaning of powers, nor to affect the class of objects to take under
them. The Act does not seem to me to be directed to such a question as I have to
consider; there is nothing to shew that the Legislature had such a question as this in   *h*
contemplation. It is said, however, that if we go back to the beginning of the series
of cases of which *Lawlor v. Henderson* ((1876) IR 10 Eq 150) is one of the latest, and
try to ascertain the reasoning on which they were based, we shall arrive at the
conclusion that if the law had been then the same as it now is the word "relations"
would always be construed as it is when a power is exclusive. I am not so persuaded.
It is difficult to find the origin of the rule. *Harding v. Glyn* ((1739) 1 Atk 469, 26 ER   *j*
299) is the first case, and no reasons are given for the decision. It seems to me that I
ought not to speculate as to what might have been done if the law had been different
from what it was when those early cases were decided. I hold that the class to take is
the same as it would have been before the passing of the Act in question, viz., the
statutory next of kin of the testatrix at her death.'

a I have the advantage, which Stirling J did not have, of the guidance afforded by the judgments in the Court of Appeal in *Re Gansloser's Will Trusts*. Those judgments show that what Stirling J called 'the origin of the rule' is not, as he thought, a matter for speculation. As to that, Evershed MR said ([1951] 2 All ER 936 at 940, [1952] Ch 30 at 37):

b '... it becomes clear that the court has adopted what is called a "rule" for the purpose of saving from invalidity, through vagueness, a gift expressed in favour of a class which would be so wide, according to its proper meaning, as to be incapable of any sensible or possible ascertainment ... There has been some discussion whether this rule (and I have so far tried to avoid using language which would prejudge the matter) is regarded as a rule of convenience or a rule of construction—
it being assumed that there is some antithesis between the two. Of course, in a sense
c it is a rule of construction, *i.e.*, it is a rule which the courts apply in construing wills which use the word "relations" in such a context as the present. It is equally a rule of convenience in the sense that it is a rule which the courts apply under compulsion of the argument *ab inconvenienti*, because on any other view the will would be rendered nugatory.'

d Jenkins LJ said ([1951] 2 All ER 936 at 946, [1952] Ch 30 at 46–47):

'The rule, whether it be called a rule of construction or a rule of convenience, under which the word "relations" is held to be limited to the next of kin of the propositus according to the statutes, is an artificial rule which the court in its benevolence has adopted to prevent a testator's disposition failing from uncertainty. That was considered sufficient justification for imputing a wholly conventional and
e artificial intention to the testator by limiting his meaning of the word "relations", or the meaning he might attach to the word "relations," to the next of kin according to the statutes. The alternative of uncertainty was the justification for the procedure.'

Morris LJ expressed his agreement with the judgments of Evershed MR and Jenkins
f LJ.
So the reasoning that led Stirling J to reject the argument based on the 1874 Act started from an erroneous premise. It seems to me that, as Professor Ryder suggests in his criticism of *Re Deakin*, it would be wrong to apply an artificial rule, which may have the effect of defeating a testator's intention, in a case where the circumstances justifying the rule do not exist. Indeed that is, in a way, what the Court of Appeal decided in *Re Gansloser's Will Trusts*. The actual question there, so far as material to the present point,
g was whether the Statutes of Distribution should be resorted to, not only to ascertain the identity of the next of kin to take, but also to determine the manner in which they should take. As to that, Evershed MR said ([1951] 2 All ER 936 at 944, [1952] Ch 30 at 43):

h 'There is here, according to the language of the testator himself, no reference to the Statutes of Distribution. The statutes are introduced because a court, to save the will, is compelled so to construe the word "relations." But to read into this word not only a reference to the statutes for the purposes of discovering the objects, but also a direction that the division is to be in such shares and in the manner in which the persons concerned would take under the statutes seems to me to be asking a great deal and to be going beyond what the rule, strictly so-called authorises ...'

j But Jenkins LJ put it in this way in a passage that follows immediately the passage that I have already read ([1951] 2 All ER 936 at 946, [1959] Ch 30 at 47):

'But, that procedure having been gone through and the problem of uncertainty thus resolved, I cannot see what justification there can be for going on to impute to the testator a further entirely artificial intention that the fund, or subject-matter of

the gift, should be divided amongst the next of kin according to the statutes in the
shares and manner provided for by the statutes. That is a matter with which
uncertainty has nothing to do, and in a case of this kind, where there is a gift to
"relations," and the reference to the Statutes of Distribution is imported simply and
solely by force of the benevolent rule of the court, I think there is no sufficient
justification for applying it beyond the point necessary to avoid uncertainty.'

Similarly, to my mind, there being in the present case no need to apply the rule to
avoid uncertainty, it would be wrong to apply it. I am conscious, of course, of Professor
Ryder's reference to 'a higher court', but a High Court judge is free, indeed bound, not
to follow another if convinced that he was wrong. I therefore hold that the gift in this
case to Mrs Litchfield's children is valid.

Order accordingly.

Solicitors: *Neves*, Harpenden (for all parties).

Vivian Horvath   Barrister.

Porzelack KG v Porzelack (UK) Ltd

CHANCERY DIVISION
SIR NICOLAS BROWNE-WILKINSON V-C
20 JANUARY 1987

*Costs – Security for costs – Plaintiff ordinarily resident out of jurisdiction – Plaintiff resident in
EEC – West German plaintiff seeking injunction against defendant resident in UK – Defendant
seeking order for security of costs against plaintiff – Discretion to order security for costs –
Factors to be taken into account in exercising discretion – Civil Jurisdiction and Judgments Act
1982, Sch 1 – RSC Ord 23, r 1(1).*

The plaintiff was a West German organisation carrying on business in the manufacture
and supply of car care products. B, its sole promoter and director, set up and controlled a
limited company, PIL, in the United Kingdom trading in car care products sold under a
particular brand name. In 1986, when PIL was wound up, the defendant company was
set up by former distributors of its products and a former executive of PIL to sell car care
products of the same kind under the same brand name. The plaintiff sought an injunction
against the defendant restraining it from passing off its car care products as being
products of the plaintiff. The defendant applied under RSC Ord 23, r 1(1)(a)[a] for security
for costs to be given against the plaintiff on the ground that the plaintiff was ordinarily
resident out of the jurisdiction.

Held – In exercising its discretion to order security for costs under RSC Ord 23, r 1(1)(a)
where the plaintiff was ordinarily resident out of the jurisdiction, the court would take
into account, as an important but not a decisive factor, the substantial and improved
rights of enforcement available to a defendant under the Civil Jurisdiction and Judgments
Act 1982, which gave effect to the Convention on Jurisdiction and the Enforcement of
Judgments in Civil and Commercial Matters set out in Sch 1 to that Act. Whether the
court would make such an order depended on what was just having regard to all the
circumstances of the case. On the facts, the court would take into account (a) that if no
security was given the defendant could enforce an order for costs under the law of West

---

Germany in accordance with the convention, (b) that, if security was ordered on the scale
a asked for, the plaintiff's action would in fact be stifled and (c) that the defendant had no
possible right itself to use the goodwill attached to the brand name and there was likely
to be confusion in the public mind between the plaintiff's product and that of the
defendant. In the circumstances, it would not be right to grant security for costs. The
application would therefore be dismissed (see p 1077 *b c* and p 1079 *f* to 1080 *g* post).

b **Notes**

For the court's power to order security for costs where the plaintiff is ordinarily resident
out of the jurisdiction, see 37 Halsbury's Laws (4th edn) para 299.

For the Civil Jurisdiction and Judgments Act 1982, Sch 1, see 22 Halsbury's Statutes
(4th edn) 374.

c **Cases referred to in judgment**

Cie Française de Television v Thorn Consumer Electronics Ltd [1981] FSR 306.
DSQ Property Co Ltd v Lotus Cars Ltd [1987] 1 WLR 127.
Kohn v Rinson & Stafford (Brod) Ltd [1947] 2 All ER 839, [1948] 1 KB 327.
Landi den Hartog BV v Stopps [1976] CMLR 393.
Meijer v John H Taylor Ltd [1981] FSR 279.
d *Raeburn v Andrews* (1874) LR 9 QB 118.

Cases also cited

Aeronave SPA v Westland Charters Ltd [1971] 3 All ER 531, [1971] 1 WLR 1445, CA.
Oertli (T) AG v E J Bowman (London) Ltd (No 3) [1957] RPC 388, CA; *affd* [1959] RPC 1,
HL.
e

Motion

The plaintiff, Porzelack KG, an organisation resident in West Germany, sought an
injunction restraining the defendant, Porzelack (UK) Ltd, from passing off the car care
products it was selling as being the products of the plaintiff. By a notice of motion dated
f 19 November 1986 the defendant applied under RSC Ord 23, r 1(1)(*a*) for security for
costs to be given by the plaintiff on the ground that the plaintiff was ordinarily resident
out of the jurisdiction. The facts are set out in the judgment.

Michael Silverleaf for the defendant.
A Kynric Lewis QC for the plaintiff.

g **SIR NICOLAS BROWNE-WILKINSON V-C.** I have before me a motion by the
defendant, Porzelack (UK) Ltd, asking for security for costs to be given by the plaintiff, a
German organisation called Porzelack KG. The background to this application is shortly
as follows. The moving spirit behind the plaintiff German organisation is a Mr Bendel,
himself a West German now resident in West Germany, as is the plaintiff organisation.
h Mr Bendel, through a number of companies, has over a long period of years carried on
business in the manufacture and supply of car polishes, car paints and other car care
products.

The plaintiff organisation is, as I have said, resident in West Germany. There is no
expert evidence as to its legal status and I am far from clear as to what it is. In the
statement of claim it is alleged that Mr Bendel is the sole promoter and director of the
j plaintiff organisation and that he has unlimited liability for its debts; but on the
information before me it is quite impossible to form any clear view as to what is its
position under the law of West Germany.

Mr Bendel at one stage had an Irish company also carrying the name 'Porzelack', which
traded until 1979. In this country Mr Bendel has had no less than three limited
companies. The first, which started trading in 1964, was called Porzelack Ltd. It went
into receivership in 1970 and ceased trading, and was struck off the register in 1983.

Almost simultaneously with it going into receivership, Mr Bendel formed a new
company in this country called Continental Chemicals Ltd, which started trading on   **a**
1 June 1970, went into receivership in November 1983 and a winding-up order was
made in December 1983. Not a whit abashed, Mr Bendel then started trading under the
guise of a new limited company, Porzelack International Ltd (which I will call 'PIL').
That started trading in June 1983, ceased trading in January 1985 and was wound up on
3 February 1986. Each of those companies was apparently controlled by Mr Bendel, not
by the plaintiff organisation. They traded in this country in car care products under the   **b**
name attached to the products, 'Porzelack'.

The defendant company, despite its name, has no connection with Mr Bendel or the
plaintiff company. Following the final demise of PIL, the defendant company was set up
in 1986 apparently by former distributors of PIL's products, with the help of a former
executive of PIL. The defendant company is selling car care products of the same kind
under the same name, 'Porzelack', in this country. It neither sought nor obtained any   **c**
consent, either from the plaintiff organisation or from Mr Bendel so to do. There have
been negotiations with the Official Receiver as liquidator of PIL for the defendant
company to acquire from the liquidator the goodwill in the name 'Porzelack', but, so far,
those negotiations have not reached any conclusion.

Simultaneously with the defendant company trading and selling goods in the market
under the name 'Porzelack', it appears that the plaintiff organisation has also re-entered   **d**
the United Kingdom market by importing products of the same kind and selling them
under the name 'Porzelack' in the United Kingdom. The resulting confusion in the
public mind must, I would have thought, be substantial. The name 'Porzelack' has never
been registered as a trade mark.

In the action the plaintiff organisation claims an injunction against the defendant
company to restrain it from passing off the car care products it is selling as being the   **e**
products of the plaintiff organisation. The plaintiff has applied for an interim injunction.
That application has yet to be heard, having been stood over to be heard as a motion by
order. The defendant has, at this very early stage, applied for security for costs and there
is in evidence before me a costed statement of costs already incurred and an estimate of
the costs to be incurred by the defendant down to the completion of pleadings and the   **f**
completion of the motion. That bill produces a figure of rather over £19,000, a figure
which I confess I find staggering for interlocutory proceedings in a comparatively small
matter. I am very far from satisfied that a bill of that size could ever be justified on a
taxation in a matter of this kind.

The evidence discloses that another quite separate organisation has a judgment for a
comparatively small sum (less than £20,000) against the plaintiff organisation which it
is seeking to enforce in West Germany. It has not received payment in full. Provisions   **g**
for payment by instalments have not been adhered to. The latest information is that
payments of some £1,500 have been made on two occasions, those payments barely
keeping pace with the rate of interest chargeable.

I have little doubt that the plaintiff organisation would be unable to provide security
for costs if I were to order it on this application. I also have little doubt that there may be   **h**
great difficulty in recovering the costs against the plaintiff, not by reason of its residence
in West Germany, but by reason of its lack of funds to meet the order.

The application is made under RSC Ord 23, r 1(1)(a), which provides:

'Where . . . it appears to the Court—(a) that the plaintiff is ordinarily resident out
of the jurisdiction . . . then if, having regard to all the circumstances of the case, the
Court thinks it just to do so, it may order the plaintiff to give such security for the   **j**
defendant's costs of the action or other proceeding as it thinks just.'

The purpose of ordering security for costs against a plaintiff ordinarily resident outside
the jurisdiction is to ensure that a successful defendant will have a fund available within
the jurisdiction of this court against which it can enforce the judgment for costs. It is

not, in the ordinary case, in any sense designed to provide a defendant with security for
a costs against a plaintiff who lacks funds. The risk of defending a case brought by a
penurious plaintiff is as applicable to plaintiffs coming from outside the jurisdiction as it
is to plaintiffs resident within the jurisdiction. There is only one exception to that, so far
as I know, namely in the case of limited companies, where there is provision under the
Companies Act 1985, s 726 for security for costs. Where the plaintiff resident outside the
jurisdiction is a foreign limited company, different factors may apply (see *DSQ Property*
b *Co Ltd v Lotus Cars Ltd* [1987] 1 WLR 127).

Under Ord 23, r 1(1)(a) it seems to me that I have an entirely general discretion either
to award or refuse security, having regard to all the circumstances of the case. However,
it is clear on the authorities that, if other matters are equal, it is normally just to exercise
that discretion by ordering security against a non-resident plaintiff. The question is what,
in all the circumstances of the case, is the just answer.

c   The matters urged before me have spread over a fairly wide field. First there have been
attempts to go into the likelihood of the plaintiff winning the case or the defendant
winning the case, presumably following the note in *The Supreme Court Practice 1985*
vol 1, para 23/1–3/2, which says: '. . . A major matter for consideration is the likelihood
of the plaintiff succeeding . . .' This is the second occasion recently on which I have had a
major hearing on security for costs and in which the parties have sought to investigate in
d considerable detail the likelihood or otherwise of success in the action. I do not think that
is a right course to adopt on an application for security for costs. The decision is necessarily
made at an interlocutory stage on inadequate material and without any hearing of the
evidence. A detailed examination of the possibilities of success or failure merely blows
the case up into a large interlocutory hearing involving great expenditure of both money
and time.

e   Undoubtedly, if it can clearly be demonstrated that the plaintiff is likely to succeed, in
the sense that there is a very high probability of success, then that is a matter that can
properly be weighed in the balance. Similarly, if it can be shown that there is a very high
probability that the defendant will succeed, that is a matter that can be weighed. But for
myself I deplore the attempt to go into the merits of the case unless it can be clearly
demonstrated one way or another that there is a high degree of probability of success or
f failure.

In the present case the plaintiff company, amongst other things, alleges that it granted
a licence to the English companies to use the name 'Porzelack' and that, as a result, the
goodwill in that name belongs to it as the licensor or to Mr Bendel, who claims to be its
alter ego, as licensor. Therefore, it is said that the existing plaintiffs can now sue in the
United Kingdom for unlawful use of the name 'Porzelack' by the defendant. Whether or
g not that case will succeed at the trial, I really cannot say: it will depend very much on the
facts as proved, but it is plainly an arguable case.

So far as the defendant is concerned, I think counsel for the defendant really accepts
that, at the present stage, it has not demonstrated any right to the use of the goodwill
attached to the name 'Porzelack'. Its defence depends in this action on showing that the
h plaintiff company itself has no right to restrain it from using the name. The case is,
therefore, one which is arguable and will have to go to trial. As a result, costs will have to
be incurred. Beyond that, I find it unnecessary to go into the merits of the case one way
or the other.

The second point urged arises under the Civil Jurisdiction and Judgments Act 1982,
which contains provisions giving effect, in the domestic law of the United Kingdom, to
j the Convention on Jurisdiction and the Enforcement of Judgments in Civil and
Commercial Matters (Brussels, 27 September 1968; EC 46 (1978); Cmnd 7395), which is
set out in Sch 1 to the Act. By way of background, I should say a word as to what the law
is apart from that Act. The purpose of requiring security from an overseas resident
plaintiff is, as I have said, to provide a fund subject to the jurisdiction against which an
order for costs can be readily enforced. If the plaintiff outside the jurisdiction is resident

in the United Kingdom, for example, in Scotland or Northern Ireland, it is established
that no security for costs ought to be awarded, since the judgment of the court in England   *a*
is readily enforceable in the Scottish and the Irish courts under the Judgments Extension
Act 1868 (see *Raeburn v Andrews* (1874) LR 9 QB 118).

   An attempt was made to extend the *Raeburn v Andrews* principle to resist an application
for security for costs against a plaintiff resident in a country to which the Foreign
Judgments (Reciprocal Enforcement) Act 1933 applied. That Act contains provisions
under which in certain countries the judgments of this court are enforceable in the   *b*
overseas jurisdiction. That attempt to extend the *Raeburn v Andrews* principle was
rejected by Denning J in *Kohn v Rinson & Stafford (Brod) Ltd* [1947] 2 All ER 839, [1948]
1 KB 327. He did not think that the provisions for enforcement under the 1933 Act were
sufficiently close to those provided by the 1868 Act to render the 1933 Act an exception
to the rule.

   After the United Kingdom joined the Common Market, a further point was put   *c*
forward in resisting security for costs by urging that the award of security against a
plaintiff resident in the EEC would contravene the EEC Treaty on the ground that it
would discriminate against a national of a country within the EEC. That argument was
rejected in two cases, *Meijer v John H Taylor Ltd* [1981] FSR 279 and *Cie Française de
Television v Thorn Consumer Electronics Ltd* [1981] FSR 306. On the other hand, it was
treated as being a relevant factor in *Landi den Hartog BV v Stopps* [1976] CMLR 393.   *d*

   That is the background against which the 1982 Act was enacted. The Act did not
immediately come into force; but it is common ground that it came into force at the
latest on 1 January 1987. Section 2 of the 1982 Act simply provides that the 1968
convention, amongst others, 'shall have the force of law in the United Kingdom, and
judicial notice shall be taken of them'. Schedule 1 then sets out the 1968 convention.
Title II of the convention deals with jurisdiction and lays down a code applicable to all   *e*
member states of the EEC as to the circumstances in which the member states shall or
shall not have jurisdiction over litigation involving two or more members of the EEC.

   Then Title III deals with 'Recognition and Enforcement'. Article 26 provides, in part,
as follows: 'A judgment given in a Contracting State shall be recognised in the other
Contracting States without any special procedure being required . . .' Articles 27 to 30 set   *f*
out various grounds on which a judgment of one member state shall not be recognised
in another member state. Article 27, for example, provides that judgment shall not be
recognised if it is contrary to public policy in the state in which recognition is sought, or
where it is given in default of appearance and there is no service, or the judgment is
irreconcilable with a judgment given in a dispute in the state in which enforcement is
sought. Article 28 provides that the judgment shall not be recognised if it conflicts with   *g*
the provisions as to jurisdiction, or some of them, in Title II. Article 29 provides as
follows: 'Under no circumstances may a foreign judgment be reviewed as to its substance.'

   Then art 31 and those following deal with enforcement. Article 31 provides as follows:

> 'A judgment given in a Contracting State and enforceable in that State shall be
> enforced in another Contracting State when, on the application of any interested   *h*
> party, the order for its enforcement has been issued there . . .'

Article 33 provides that the procedure for the application is to be governed by the law of
the state in which enforcement is sought. Article 34 provides as follows:

> 'The court applied to shall give its decision without delay; the party against whom
> enforcement is sought shall not at this stage of the proceedings be entitled to make   *j*
> any submissions on the application. The application may be refused only for one of
> the reasons specified in Articles 27 and 28. Under no circumstances may the foreign
> judgment be reviewed as to its substance.'

Article 35 provides for enforcement without delay. Then art 36 provides as follows: 'If

enforcement is authorised, the party against whom enforcement is sought may appeal
against the decision . . .' Then there are provisions for the appeal.

Article 45 provides as follows:

'No security, bond or deposit, however described, shall be required of a party who
in one Contracting State applies for enforcement of a judgment given in another
Contracting State on the ground that he is a foreign national or that he is not
domiciled or resident in the State in which enforcement is sought.'

It is common ground that that article is dealing only with the requirement of security
for costs on the enforcement of a judgment in a foreign state; it has no direct bearing on
the present case.

Those, in outline, are the provisions of the convention which now forms part of the
law of England. To my mind, they are not the same as the provisions of the 1868 Act.
Under the 1868 Act, mere registration of the decision of the English court renders it as
enforceable in the courts of, for example, Scotland as if the order had been made in
Scotland. From the passages that I have read, that is plainly not the position under the
1968 convention. There has to be an application to the foreign court for recognition
before the order becomes enforceable and there are grounds on which it can be challenged
in the other member state's court.

On the other hand, I do not think that the provisions of the 1968 convention can be
treated as being exactly on the same footing as the Foreign Judgments (Reciprocal
Enforcement) Act 1933 cases. First, the convention lays down a common system for the
whole group of EEC countries as to their respective jurisdictions within the EEC.
Questions of jurisdiction are regulated by the convention itself. Second, although the
convention provides for challenge to the order when it is sought to be enforced, those are
very limited rights of challenge, circumscribed in the way that I have sought to illustrate.
Third, the whole purpose of the convention, as I understand it, was to produce a common
system of enforcement within the European Community. It was designed to produce
'free movement of judgments within the EEC'.

As the Act has so recently come into force, there is of course no experience as to how it
works in practice. But, at the present stage, I think that in exercising my discretion it is
right to take into account the fact that the defendant has substantial and improved rights
of enforcement under the convention and that as an alternative to enforcing any order
for costs in this country there is a realistic alternative which makes it comparatively
simple to enforce such an order in an EEC country. This country has now been a member
of the EEC for a long time and I think it is right to take into account the flow of trade
between the United Kingdom and the other members of the Community giving rise to
litigation between residents of member states, which the convention is designed to
regulate and to provide for enforcement without special provisions. I, therefore, think it
is right to attach considerable importance to the rights of enforcement under the 1968
convention.

However, I do not think that the convention is a decisive factor in the way that *Raeburn
v Andrews* (1874) LR 9 QB 118 treats the 1868 Act. There is a real difference between
going to a foreign system of law using a different language and a different system and
going to Scotland which, though the system is different in detail, is still part of the United
Kingdom. Moreover, as I pointed out, the judgment is not automatically enforceable in
the other EEC country as though the judgment had been made in that country. There
are limited powers of challenge.

In exercising my discretion in this case, I therefore take into account as an important
matter the possibility that, if no security is given, the defendants can enforce an order for
costs under the law of West Germany in accordance with the convention. I do not treat
it as decisive. It is a factor to be weighed.

The next matter that I take into account is that, on the evidence before me, there is little doubt that if I order security on anything like the scale asked for, the plaintiff's action will in fact be stifled. It simply does not have the means to put up the money. It is *a* always a matter to be taken into account that any plaintiff should not be driven from the judgment seat unless the justice of the case makes it imperative. I am always reluctant to allow applications for security for costs to be used as a measure to stifle proceedings.

Next I take into account the defendant's conduct in this case. As I see it, the defendant company has no possible right itself to use the goodwill attached to the 'Porzelack' name. What the defendant company and its promoters have done is to step into the void left by *b* the winding up of PIL and the vesting of its assets in the Official Receiver and have sought to annex the goodwill for themselves. They may well be entitled to do that; I do not know. But undoubtedly what is going on at the moment must produce confusion in the mind of the public. Both the plaintiff and the defendant are selling very similar, though different, goods under the same name and, as I understand from the evidence, in certain respects similar get-up. The defendant says that its product is different from the *c* plaintiff's and indeed better. But, to my mind, that will merely increase the confusion in the public mind, because one has two different products both being sold under the same name. I think that the public is likely to be substantially misled by what is going on in this case.

In the case of a registered trade mark, counsel for the defendant accepts that a defendant who is trading deceptively can be deprived of his costs, even if successful in the action. *d* However, counsel submits that such an order cannot be made in a passing-off action and that the court in this action will be bound to order the defendant, if successful, to get its costs. I can see no ground which justifies that distinction being drawn between a registered trade mark and an unregistered trade mark or passing-off. The essence of the matter is that the defendant's conduct, leading as it does to confusion in the mind of the public, is such as to disentitle it to an order for costs in its favour. I am far from saying *e* that that will be the outcome in this case; but it is certainly a possibility. Accordingly, I am far from satisfied that, even if it wins in this case, the defendant will necessarily get an order for costs against the plaintiff.

Weighing all these factors and all the circumstances of the case, subject to one point I do not think that it is right to grant security for costs. The one matter that I am concerned about is the status of the plaintiff company, as to which I remain in a state of unknowing. *f* Mr Bendel, the moving spirit behind it, has offered to be joined as a plaintiff. Provided I have an undertaking that Mr Bendel is joined as a plaintiff and, therefore, any order for costs is enforceable against him directly, I will dismiss this application for security for costs.

Order accordingly.   *g*

Solicitors: *Hopkins & Wood* (for the defendant); *Stocken & Lambert* (for the plaintiff).

Celia Fox   Barrister.

a

Re Tom's Settlement
Rose and others v Evans

CHANCERY DIVISION

SIR NICOLAS BROWNE-WILKINSON V-C

b 4, 5 DECEMBER 1986

Settlement – Class gift – Distribution date – Defined closing date – Deed of appointment providing for fund to be held for beneficiaries reaching 18 before 'vesting day' and those living at vesting day – Deed further providing for fund income to be distributed on 'closing date' – Closing date defined as earlier of vesting day or 25 years from date of appointment – Whether class closing rule
c *applying – Whether class closing when eldest beneficiary reaching 18.*

The plaintiffs were trustees of a settlement dated 19 August 1955. By a deed of appointment dated 25 March 1977 they provided for the creation of, inter alia, a 'specified beneficiaries' fund' of some £12m, the specified beneficiaries being defined as the future grandchildren and existing and future great-grandchildren of the settlor. The deed of
d appointment provided that the trustees were to hold the fund on trust absolutely for such of the specified beneficiaries who attained the age of 18 before the 'vesting day' or who were living at the vesting day and further provided that at the 'closing date' each specified beneficiary then living was to receive a share in the distribution of income, so that on the closing day each beneficiary would acquire an interest in possession in the whole or part of the fund. The deed of appointment defined the 'closing date' as the
e vesting day (as defined by the settlement) or 25 years from the date of execution of the deed, whichever was earlier. At the date of the appointment there were nine great-grandchildren then living. The trustees brought an action to determine whether the class of specified beneficiaries closed when the oldest of the great-grandchildren living at the date of the appointment attained the age of 18. At the time of the proceedings there were 20 great-grandchildren, with the possibility of more to come. The defendant, the eldest
f great-grandchild, having attained 18 years of age had become entitled to call for payment of his share under the terms of the appointment. The issue arose whether the rule that the class of persons entitled to a share of a fund closed when one member of the class became absolutely entitled in advance of the others applied so as to close the class of specified beneficiaries automatically at the time when the defendant became entitled to call for his share, since unless the class of specified beneficiaries was closed the defendant
g could not receive his share because its amount could not be quantified until the maximum number of possible beneficiaries had become certain.

Held – Where a trust instrument showed two conflicting intentions, namely an intention to give a share under a settlement to all the members of a certain class whenever born and an intention to permit each member of the class to enjoy his share when he became
h entitled to do so, the class closing rule provided a presumption resolving the conflict in favour of early enjoyment by the member of the class who became so entitled. However, if the trust instrument showed that the draftsman had specifically considered the date at which the class was to close there could not be said to be a conflict of intention and the rule could not apply. Since the deed of appointment expressly defined the category of
j future born beneficiaries not simply by reference to a named propositor and their ages, but also by reference to a period the beginning and end of which was clearly defined, namely beneficiaries born after the date of the deed of appointment and before the closing date, the deed had excluded the class closing rule, because the unequivocal intention of the deed was for the class to remain open until the defined date. Furthermore, the express reference in the deed to future great-grandchildren 'living at the closing date'

clearly showed an intention that the class would remain open until the defined date. Accordingly, the class had not closed when the defendant attained the age of 18 but *a* remained open (see p 1084 *b c* and p 1085 *a* to p 1086 *c f g*, post).

Re Edmondson's Will Trusts, Baron Sandford of Banbury v Edmondson [1972] 1 All ER 444, dicta of Bridge LJ and Sir John Pennycuick in Re Chapman's Settlement Trusts, Jones v Chapman [1978] 1 All ER at 1127, 1129 and of Megarry V-C in Re Clifford's Settlement Trusts, Heaton v Westwater [1980] 1 All ER at 1016 applied.

Andrews v Partington [1775–1802] All ER Rep 209 distinguished.   *b*

Notes
For the class closing rule, see 50 Halsbury's Laws (4th edn) paras 492–495.

Cases referred to in judgment
Andrews v Partington (1791) 3 Bro CC 401, [1775–1802] All ER Rep 209, 29 ER 610, LC.   *c*
Chapman's Settlement Trusts, Re, Jones v Chapman [1978] 1 All ER 1122, [1977] 1 WLR 1163, CA.
Clifford's Settlement Trusts, Re, Heaton v Westwater [1980] 1 All ER 1013, [1981] Ch 63, [1980] 2 WLR 749.
Coventry v Coventry (1865) 2 Drew & Sm 470, 62 ER 699.
Edmondson's Will Trusts, Re, Baron Sandford of Banbury v Edmondson [1972] 1 All ER 444,   *d*
[1972] 1 WLR 183, CA.
Faux, Re (1915) 84 LJ Ch 873.
Hagger v Payne (1857) 23 Beav 474, 53 ER 186.
Paul's Settlement Trusts, Re, Paul v Nelson [1920] 1 Ch 99.
Wernher's Settlement Trusts, Re, Lloyds Bank UK Ltd v Mountbatten (Earl) [1961] 1 All ER   *e*
184, [1961] 1 WLR 136.

Summons
By a summons dated 8 August 1986, the plaintiffs, Christopher Alan Rose, Stephen Michael Farrell, Maureen Smith, Gerald Leslie Brown, John Gregory Tom and Elizabeth Wendy Ruth Evans, the trustees of a settlement made by Leonard Gregory Tom, sought *f* the determination of the court on the question whether the special beneficiaries' fund referred to in a deed of appointment made on 25 March 1977 by the trustees was to be held on trust for such of the specified beneficiaries therein defined who before the vesting day therein defined attained the age of 18 or who were living at the vesting date or for such of the beneficiaries as were born on or before 22 November 1986, being the date when the defendant, Richard Gregory Evans (Richard), the eldest beneficiary, attained *g* the age of 18, and before the vesting date attained the age of 18 or who were living at the vesting date. The facts are set out in the judgment.

Donald Rattee QC and Kenneth Farrow for the trustees.
J Maurice Price QC and Michael Hart for Richard.

                                                                  h
SIR NICOLAS BROWNE-WILKINSON V-C. This case raises the question whether the class closing rule, commonly referred to as the rule in Andrews v Partington (1791) 3 Bro CC 401, [1775–1802] All ER Rep 209, applies to the trusts of a fund known as the specified beneficiaries fund (having a current value of some £12m) appointed by a deed of appointment date 25 March 1977.

The appointment was made by the trustees of a settlement dated 19 August 1955, *j* under a power contained in that settlement. The settlor was Leonard Gregory Tom (who is referred to throughout as 'the settlor'). No question arises as to the validity of the appointment made by the trustees, and it is only necessary to refer to the main settlement for two purposes. First, the 'vesting day' is defined as being the day before that on which will expire the period of 60 years from the date of the execution thereof, coupled with the perpetuity limitation linked to the 21 years after the death of the survivor of the

a settlor and his issue then living, whichever shall first occur. Second, under cl 7 every
trustee of the settlement, other than the settlor and his wife, are entitled whilst they
continue to be trustees to receive a yearly sum of £50.

The appointment, dated 25 March 1977, was made by the trustees under the power in
the settlement. Broadly it divided the trust fund into three parts: the children's fund
which comprises some 40% of the whole, the grandchildren's fund comprising some
b 35% and the fund with which I am concerned, the specified beneficiaries fund which
comprises the remaining 25%. The children's fund was appointed in favour of the six
surviving children of the settlor, either absolutely or in some cases in settlement. The
grandchildren's fund was appointed on certain trusts for the benefit of the existing
grandchildren of the settlor, who are ten in number. Nothing directly turns on the trusts
of those two funds.

c   Under the appointment, the annual payment of £50 to each of the trustees was
specifically charged exclusively on the specified beneficiaries' fund. The beneficial trusts
of that fund are declared by cl 7(1) and (2) as follows:

'(1) THE Trustees shall hold the Specified Beneficiaries' Fund and the income
thereof (subject to the yearly sums of fifty pounds (£50) payable under Clause 7 of
d the Settlement) upon the following trusts (that is to say):—(a) upon trust absolutely
for such of the Specified Beneficiaries as shall before the Vesting Day attain the age
of eighteen years or (not having attained that age) shall be living at the Vesting Day
if more than one in equal shares per capita And subject thereto (b) upon trust for
the Existing Grandchildren absolutely in equal shares per capita.

(2) AS from the Closing Date the provisions of Section 31 of the Trustee Act 1925
e ... shall apply in relation to the income of the Specified Beneficiaries' Fund as if all
the Specified Beneficiaries for the time being in existence had already attained the
age of eighteen years TO THE INTENT that each minor Specified Beneficiary who shall
be living at the Closing Date shall upon that Date acquire an interest in possession
in the whole or some part of the Specified Beneficiaries' Fund.'

f   The trusts of the specified beneficiaries' fund include the statutory power of
maintenance in s 31 of the 1925 Act, the trustees being given an unfettered discretion.
The statutory power of advancement, but unlimited as to amount, was also applicable.

The crux of those trusts, of course, is the definition of the specified beneficiaries. The
definitions are contained in cl 1 of the appointment, from which I must read the
following definition:

g   '... (b) "the Closing Date" means the twenty-fifth anniversary of the date of
execution of this Deed or the Vesting Day whichever shall be the earlier ... (e) "the
Future Grandchildren" means the grandchildren of the Settlor born after the date
hereof and before the Closing Date (f) "the Existing Great-Grandchildren" means
the Great-Grandchildren now living of the Settlor (being the persons whose names
are set forth in Part III of the Schedule hereto) (g) "the Future Great-Grandchildren"
h means the great-grandchildren of the Settlor born after the date hereof and before
the Closing Date (h) "the Specified Beneficiaries" means:—(i) the Future
Grandchildren (ii) the Existing Great-Grandchildren and (iii) the Future Great-
Grandchildren ...'

At the date of the appointment there were nine great-grandchildren living, the oldest
j being the defendant in these proceedings, Richard Gregory Evans, whom I shall call
'Richard'. He was born on 22 November 1968 and has therefore just attained the age of
18. No further grandchildren have been born since the date of the appointment but,
since six of the children (including three sons) are still alive, there is a possibility (albeit
very remote) that there might still be a future grandchild. It is clear that the specified
beneficiaries' fund was primarily for the benefit of great-grandchildren, the children's
fund and the grandchildren's fund having dealt with the earlier generations. However,
future grandchildren also come into the class of specified beneficiaries.

The question I have to decide is whether the class of specified beneficiaries closed under the class closing rules when Richard attained the age of 18 years. If the class did so close, *a* all specified beneficiaries now living (which consist of 20 great grandchildren) will be included, but all great-grandchildren hereafter born will be excluded. The ages of the grandchildren are such that the birth of further great grandchildren is far from improbable.

The class closing rules operate on class gifts so as to close the class automatically and artificially at the time when the first member of the class would be entitled to call for *b* payment of his share were it not for the possibility of the birth of future members of the class. Unless the class closing rules operate a beneficiary so entitled could not receive his share, since its amount cannot be quantified until the maximum number of possible beneficiaries has become certain.

In general the rules operate only when, apart from the uncertainty as to the number of beneficiaries in the class, there is a member of the class entitled to call for payment of *c* his share. Thus, in the case of an immediate gift to the children of A who attain the age of 21, the class will close when the first child of A attains 21. In the case of gifts to A for life remainder to his children who attain 21, the class does not close during A's life time, since his children are not then entitled to receive their share: the class only closes when A dies or the first of his children attains the age of 21, whichever is the later, that being the first time at which any member of the class of children is entitled to call for payment. *d*

So, in this case, Richard having attained 18 years of age is entitled to call for his share of the specified beneficiaries' fund, and if the class closing rules apply they will close the class of possible specified beneficiaries at that date. However, it is clear that the class closing rules can be excluded by the trust instrument. The main question I have to decide is whether the class closing rules have or have not been excluded in this case.

Before dealing with that main point, I must mention a subsidiary point taken by *e* counsel on behalf of the trustees, who have presented the argument on behalf of persons not yet born and who would come within the definition of specified beneficiaries. Counsel submitted that the £50 per annum for each trustee charged on the specified beneficiaries' fund prevented the class closing rules from applying at all since the time for the application of the rules had not yet arrived: the trustees' right to their £50 was a *f* charge on the whole income and, therefore, no distribution could in any event be made. He relied on the decisions in *Re Faux* (1915) 84 LJ Ch 873 and in *Re Paul's Settlement Trusts, Paul v Nelson* [1920] 1 Ch 99. On the other side, counsel for Richard submitted that those cases had no application: the trustees' right is comparable to the right of an annuitant against a fund, and it was well established that in the case of an annuity charged on a fund the class closing rules were not affected by the existence of that *g* annuity. The class closes when a member of the class becomes entitled to payment, subject to any right of the annuitant. He relied on the statement in *Jarman on Wills* (8th edn, 1951) p 1666 and *Hagger v Payne* (1857) 23 Beav 474, 53 ER 186.

I find it difficult to accept the argument that the trustees' minimal income right charged on a fund of £12m is sufficient to alter the beneficial interests in the whole fund. But, in the light of the cases to which counsel for the trustees has referred, I think there *h* is here a difficult point. On the one hand *Hagger v Payne* and *Coventry v Coventry* (1865) 2 Drew & Sm 470, 62 ER 699 suggest that an annuity or a life interest existing under a separate trust does not prevent the class closing rules being applied immediately in relation to the fund into which the annuity fund later sinks. On the other hand *Re Faux* and *Re Paul's Settlement Trusts* suggest the opposite. In the light of the view that I have formed on the other aspect of the case, I do not think it is necessary for me to express any *j* concluded view on that point.

The main question is whether the terms of the appointment are such as to exclude the class closing rules. The applicable principles have been considered many times in recent years, particularly in *Re Wernher's Settlement Trusts, Lloyds Bank UK Ltd v Mountbatten (Earl)* [1961] 1 All ER 184, [1961] 1 WLR 136. The principles are I think now well established and I will seek merely to summarise them as they apply to this case.

a (1) The reason lying behind the class closing rules is, as I have stated, to enable distribution to take place as soon as there is one member of the class entitled to receive his share.

(2) The rules operate even in a case where, applying ordinary rules of construction, the normal construction of the trust instrument would be to leave the class open, eg a gift to the children of A at 21, whether now living or hereafter to be born, would as a matter of ordinary construction leave the class open even if a child of A had attained 21.

b But the class closing rules operate to close the class when the first child of A attains 21, even though A is still alive.

(3) The modern rationalisation of the rule is that in such a case the trust instrument shows two conflicting intentions. One to include *all* the children of A, whenever born; the other an intention to permit each child of A to enjoy his share as soon as he becomes entitled so to do. It is said that the class closing rules provide a presumption resolving

c this conflict of intention in favour of early enjoyment by the member of the class who becomes entitled, that is to say in favour of the class closing rule: see *Re Chapman's Settlement Trusts, Jones v Chapman* [1978] 1 All ER 1122 esp at 1127, 1129, [1977] 1 WLR 1163 esp at 1169, 1170 per Bridge LJ and Sir John Pennycuick.

(4) Such presumption in favour of the class closing can only be rebutted by express provisions of the trust instrument which are inescapably incompatible with the intention

d being to close the class artificially. Megarry V-C in *Re Clifford's Settlement Trusts, Heaton v Westwater* [1980] 1 All ER 1013 at 1016, [1981] Ch 63 at 67 said:

'. . . it is not enough to find provisions which merely point to the exclusion of the rule if they nevertheless are capable of operating in conformity with it. There must

e be an inescapable incompatibility with the operation of the rule.'

(5) If the words of the trust document contain a particular reference to the future expressly unlimited in point of time (eg 'whenever born') the class closing rules are excluded as being incompatible with such provision: see *Re Edmondson's Will Trusts, Baron Sandford of Banbury v Edmondson* [1972] 1 All ER 444, [1972] 1 WLR 183.

f Turning to apply those principles to this appointment, in my judgment the first thing to notice is that the reported cases hitherto have all been dealing with what might be called traditional forms of limitation, eg to a single class of children or grandchildren of a named propositor. The definition of such a class is dependent on the form of the gift itself. There is no specific reference to the date on which the class is to close. The present case in my judgment is different. The form is that there is an express definition of 'the

g closing date'. The very words of the definition show that the draftsman and the makers of the deed have specifically directed their minds to the question of when the class is to close. The category of future born beneficiaries, namely future grandchildren and future great-grandchildren, are expressly defined not simply by reference to their relationship to a named propositor and to their ages, but also by reference to a period, the beginning and end of which is expressly defined: they have got to be born after the date of the

h appointment and before the closing date. This factor alone would in my judgment probably be sufficient to exclude the rule in *Andrews v Partington* (1791) 3 Bro CC 401, [1775–1802] All ER Rep 209. If the document shows that the mind of the draftsman has been specifically directed to the date on which the class is to close, there is in my judgment no room for saying that there are two possible conflicting intentions which have to be reconciled by the class closing rules. The document itself shows unequivocally

j that the intention is for the class to remain open until the defined date. There is only one possible intention. The case is analogous to a gift to a class 'whenever born'. In *Re Edmondson's Will Trusts* the draftsman had specifically directed himself to the date when the class was to close and put in the word 'whenever', showing that the class was to remain open indefinitely. In the present case, though it is not to remain open indefinitely, the draftsman has directed his mind to the date when it is to close; he has specifically said it is to remain open until the closing date. To apply the class closing rules in such a case would be wholly incompatible with the express intention of the draftsman and the makers of the deed.

Whether or not I am right on that, in my judgment cl 7(2) puts the matter beyond all doubt. To quote again the final words of cl 7(2):

'. . . TO THE INTENT that each minor Specified Beneficiary who shall be living at the Closing Date shall upon that Date acquire an interest in possession in the whole or some part of the Specified Beneficiaries' Fund.'

There may well yet be further great-grandchildren born hereafter who will be living on the closing date. If the class closed under the class closing rules on Richard attaining the age of 18, such after born great grandchildren would not take any share in the specified beneficiaries fund. Yet the words I have quoted show that the intention was that each minor specified beneficiary living on the closing date should acquire an interest. Therefore, there is, in my judgment, an inescapable incompatibility between the words of the appointment and any application of the class closing rule. Therefore, on the principles that I have sought to summarise, the rules are excluded in the present case.

Counsel for Richard submitted that I should not attach such importance to the definition of the closing date or to the provisions of cl 7(2). He submitted, I suspect rightly, that the purpose behind the making of the appointment was to obtain the fiscal benefits for capital transfer tax purposes attaching to maintenance and accumulation settlements. Those benefits can only be obtained if there are excluded from the possible class of beneficiaries persons born more than 25 years after the date of the appointment, and care is taken to ensure that all persons taking beneficial interests should within that period take an interest in possession. He says, again rightly, that there is nothing in the fiscal background to the case which prevents beneficiaries from taking interest earlier than that date. All that may well be true. But the fiscal background does not in my judgment permit me to depart from the plain meaning of the words used by the draftsman which I have sought to elucidate. Moreover, the fiscal background might, for all I know, lead one to think that there was an intention to take advantage of the benefits for capital transfer tax purposes of maintenance and accumulation settlement for as long as possible and to include as wide a class as possible. Quite apart from fiscal purposes there may will have been, and indeed are likely to have been, other non-fiscal purposes in the mind of the person making the appointment.

In those circumstances, it cannot in my judgment be right to limit the words purely so as to give effect to those factors necessary to achieve the fiscal advantages.

For those reasons I would declare that the class did not close on Richard attaining the age of 18 on 22 November 1986, but remains open.

Order accordingly.

Solicitors: *Freshfields* (for the trustees); *Fishers,* Ashby-de-la-Zouch (for Richard).

Vivian Horvath   Barrister.

a
Practice Direction

FAMILY DIVISION

*Practice – Transfer of proceedings between High Court and county courts – Family business and
family proceedings – Proceedings which may and may not be transferred – Adoption Act 1968,*
b *s 6 – Guardianship of Minors Act 1971, s 15(3) – Matrimonial Causes Act 1973, ss 1(2)(e), 5,
19, 45(1) – Domicile and Matrimonial Proceedings Act 1973, s 5(6) – Children Act 1975, ss 14,
24 – Matrimonial and Family Proceedings Act 1984, Pt III (ss 12–27), ss 37, 38, 39.*

1. These directions are given under s 37 of the Matrimonial and Family Proceedings Act
1984 by the President of the Family Division, with the concurrence of the Lord
c Chancellor, and apply to all family proceedings which are transferable between the High
Court and county courts under ss 38 and 39 of that Act. They supersede the directions
given on 28 April 1986 ([1986] 2 All ER 703, [1986] 1 WLR 1139). They do not apply to
proceedings under the following provisions (which may be heard and determined in the
High Court alone):

    (*a*) s 45(1) of the Matrimonial Causes Act 1973 (declaration of legitimacy or validity
d of a marriage);

    (*b*) the Guardianship of Minors Acts 1971 and 1973 in the circumstances provided by
s 15(3) of the Guardianship of Minors Act 1971;

    (*c*) s 14 of the Children Act 1975 where the child is not in Great Britain (freeing for
adoption);

    (*d*) s 24 of the Children Act 1975 or s 6 of the Adoption Act 1968 (Convention
e adoptions);

    (*e*) Pt III of the Matrimonial and Family Proceedings Act 1984;

to an application for an adoption order where the child is not in Great Britain, or to an
application that a minor be made, or cease to be, a ward of court.

2. (1) Family proceedings to which these directions apply (including interlocutory
f proceedings) shall be dealt with in the High Court where it appears to the court seised of
the case that by reason of the complexity, difficulty or gravity of the issues they ought to
be tried in the High Court.

    (2) Without prejudice to the generality of sub-para (1), the following proceedings shall
be dealt with in the High Court unless the nature of the issues of fact or law raised in the
case makes them more suitable for trial in a county court than in the High Court:

g   (*a*) petitions under s 1(2)(e) of the Matrimonial Causes Act 1973 which are opposed
pursuant to s 5 of that Act;

    (*b*) petitions in respect of jactitation of marriage;

    (*c*) petitions for presumption of death and dissolution of marriage under s 19 of the
Matrimonial Causes Act 1973;

    (*d*) proceedings involving a contested issue of domicile;

h   (*e*) application under s 5(6) of the Domicile and Matrimonial Proceedings Act 1973;

    (*f*) applications to restrain a resident from taking or continuing with foreign
proceedings;

    (*g*) proceedings for recognition of a foreign decree;

    (*h*) suits in which the Queen's Proctor intervenes or shows cause and elects trial in the
High Court;

j   (*i*) proceedings in relation to a ward of court (i) in which the Official Solicitor is or
becomes the guardian ad litem of the ward or of a party to the proceedings, (ii) in which
a local authority is or becomes a party, (iii) in which an application for blood tests is made
or (iv) where any of the matters specified in (*j*) below are in issue;

    (*j*) proceedings concerning children in divorce and under the Guardianship Acts
where (i) an application is opposed on the grounds of want of jurisdiction, (ii) there is a

substantial foreign element or (iii) there is an opposed application for leave to take a child permanently out of the jurisdiction or where there is an application for temporary removal of a child from the jurisdiction and it is opposed on the ground that the child may not be duly returned;

(*k*) applications for adoption or for freeing for adoption (i) which are opposed on the grounds of want of jurisdiction, (ii) which would result in the acquisition by a child of British citizenship;

(*l*) interlocutory applications involving (i) Anton Piller orders, (ii) Mareva injunctions, (iii) directions as to dealing with assets outside the jurisdiction.

3. In proceedings where periodical payments, a lump sum or property are in issue the court shall have regard in particular to the following factors when considering in accordance with para 2(1) above whether the complexity, difficulty or gravity of the issues are such that they ought to be tried in the High Court:

(*a*) the capital values of the assets involved and the extent to which they are available for, or susceptible to, distribution or adjustment;

(*b*) any substantial allegations of fraud or deception or non-disclosure;

(*c*) any substantial contested allegations of conduct.

An appeal in such proceedings from a registrar in a county court shall be transferred to the High Court where it appears to the registrar, whether on application by a party or otherwise, that the appeal raises a difficult or important question whether of law or otherwise.

4. Subject to the foregoing, family proceedings may be dealt with in a county court.

5. Proceedings in the High Court which under the foregoing criteria fall to be dealt with in a county court or a divorce county court, as the case may be, and proceedings in a county court which likewise fall to be dealt with in the High Court shall be transferred accordingly, in accordance with rules of court, unless to do so would cause undue delay or hardship to any party or other person involved.

23 February 1987

J L ARNOLD P

a
Miles v Wakefield Metropolitan District Council

HOUSE OF LORDS

LORD BRIDGE OF HARWICH, LORD BRANDON OF OAKBROOK, LORD BRIGHTMAN, LORD TEMPLEMAN
AND LORD OLIVER OF AYLMERTON

b
3, 4, 5 JUNE, 9, 10 DECEMBER 1986, 12 MARCH 1987

*Registrar – Superintendent registrar of births, deaths and marriages – Remuneration – Registrar
paid by local authority – Powers of dismissal for failure to perform duties exercisable by Registrar
General – Whether registrar employed by local authority – Whether office-holder or employee –
Whether local authority bound to pay full salary despite registrar's failure to perform duties –*
c *Registration Service Act 1953, s 6(3)(4).*

*Employment – Remuneration – Industrial action – Refusal to perform full duties – Employee
refusing to perform part of his services as form of industrial action – Whether employer entitled
to withhold remuneration for period in which services not fully performed – Whether employer*
d *entitled to decline to accept partial performance of employee's duties without dismissing employee.*

The plaintiff was a superintendent registrar of births, deaths and marriages in the
defendant council's area. By s 6(3)[a] of the Registration Service Act 1953 the council was
responsible for paying the plaintiff's salary. Section 6(4) provided that superintendent
registrars held office during the pleasure of the Registrar General. The plaintiff worked
e 37 hours per week including 3 hours on Saturday mornings. From August 1981 until
October 1982, as part of industrial action and in breach of his duties, the plaintiff refused
to conduct marriage ceremonies on Saturday mornings, although he carried out his other
duties on that morning. The council informed him that he would not be paid for work
on Saturday unless he was prepared to undertake the full range of his duties, and when
he refused the council withheld part of his salary. An action by the plaintiff to recover
f the amount withheld was dismissed by the judge, but an appeal by the plaintiff was
allowed by the Court of Appeal on the grounds that the plaintiff was a statutory office-
holder who had no contractual relationship with the council, which was under an
unqualified obligation to pay the plaintiff's salary for as long as he held office, that the
council was not entitled to take disciplinary action against the plaintiff by way of
withholding salary and that the only remedy for the plaintiff's failure to perform his
g duties lay in the Registrar General's power of dismissal. The council appealed.

Held – (1) The salary which the plaintiff received from the council constituted
remuneration for work done and not simply an honorarium for the tenure of an office.
Although there was no contract between the plaintiff and the council, and notwithstanding
h that the power of dismissal was vested in the Registrar General, the nature of the
plaintiff's remuneration and the terms of his tenure of office were so closely analogous to
a contract of employment that his claim to salary payable under the 1953 Act was to be
considered in the same way as a claim to salary or wages under a contract of employment
(see p 1091 d, p 1092 b to d, p 1095 fg, p 1102 f to j and 1103 j to 1104 a, post).
        (2) A plaintiff in an action for remuneration under a contract of employment had to
j aver and prove that he was ready and willing to render the services required of him by
the contract and he could not do that if he refused to perform the full duties required of
him. It followed that if an employee offered partial performance of the contract, eg by
refusing to perform part of his duties as a form of industrial action, the employer was

---

a   Section 6, so far as material, is set out at p 1094 c, post entitled, without terminating the contract of employment, to decline to accept the partial performance offered by the employee, in which case the employee would not be able to sue for payment for his unwanted services. Since the plaintiff had refused to carry out part of his duties, his action to recover remuneration for the period when he withheld part of his services had been rightly dismissed by the judge. The council's appeal would therefore be allowed (see p 1091 g h, p 1092 b to f, p 1093 b, p 1098 h to 1099 e, p 1101 g to j, p 1104 c to e, p 1105 j to 1106 a, p 1108 j and p 1109 h to 1110 a, post); *Cuckson v Stones* [1843–60] All ER Rep 390, *Henthorn and Taylor v Central Electricity Generating Board* [1980] IRLR 361, *Cresswell v Board of Inland Revenue* [1984] 2 All ER 713 and *Sim v Rotherham Metropolitan BC* [1986] 3 All ER 387 considered.

Quaere. Whether an employee engaged in certain kinds of industrial action, such as a 'go slow' or 'work to rule', may be entitled to claim remuneration on a quantum meruit basis for work actually done (see p 1091 j to p 1192 c f to p 1093 a, p 1099 c and p 1110 a b, post).

Decision of the Court of Appeal [1985] 1 All ER 905 reversed.

Notes

For an employee's right to remuneration, see 16 Halsbury's Laws (4th edn) paras 532–535, and for cases on the subject, see 20 Digest (Reissue) 290–295, *2645–2668*.

For the appointment and remuneration of superintendent registrars, see 39 Halsbury's Laws (4th edn) para 1072.

For the Registration Service Act 1953, s 6, see 27 Halsbury's Statutes (3rd edn) 1057.

Cases referred to in opinions

Boston Deep Sea Fishing and Ice Co v Ansell (1888) 39 Ch D 339, [1886–90] All ER Rep 65, CA.

Cresswell v Board of Inland Revenue [1984] 2 All ER 713.

Cuckson v Stones (1858) 1 E & E 248, [1843–60] All ER Rep 390, 120 ER 902.

Denmark Productions Ltd v Boscobel Productions Ltd [1968] 3 All ER 513, [1969] 1 QB 699, [1968] 3 WLR 841, CA.

Gilbert-Ash (Northern) Ltd v Modern Engineering (Bristol) Ltd [1973] 3 All ER 195, [1974] AC 689, [1973] 3 WLR 421, HL.

Graham (Alexander) & Co v United Turkey Red Co Ltd 1922 SC 533.

Hanak v Green [1958] 2 All ER 141, [1958] 2 QB 9, [1958] 2 WLR 755, CA.

Hanley v Pease & Partners Ltd [1915] 1 KB 698, [1914–15] All ER Rep 984, DC.

Healey v SA Française Rubastic [1917] 1 KB 946.

Henthorn and Taylor v Central Electricity Generating Board [1980] IRLR 361, CA.

Johnston v Robertson (1861) 23 Dunl (Ct of Sess) 646.

Laurie v British Steel Corp (23 February 1978, unreported), Ct of Sess.

McClenaghan v Bank of New Zealand [1978] 2 NZLR 528, NZ SC.

Marrison v Bell [1939] 1 All ER 745, [1939] 2 KB 187, CA.

Mondel v Steel (1841) 8 M & W 858, [1835–42] All ER Rep 511, 151 ER 1288.

Morgan & Son Ltd v S Martin Johnson & Co Ltd [1948] 2 All ER 196, [1949] 1 KB 107.

National Coal Board v Galley [1958] 1 All ER 91, [1958] 1 WLR 16, CA.

Photo Production Ltd v Securicor Transport Ltd [1980] 1 All ER 556, [1980] AC 827, [1980] 2 WLR 283, HL.

Ramsden v David Sharratt & Sons Ltd (1930) 35 Com Cas 314, HL.

Secretary of State for Employment v Associated Society of Locomotive Engineers and Firemen (No 2) [1972] 2 All 949, [1972] 2 QB 455, [1972] 2 WLR 1370, CA.

Sim v Rotherham Metropolitan BC [1986] 3 All ER 387, [1986] 3 WLR 851.

Suisse Atlantique Société d'Armement Maritime SA v NV Rotterdamsche Kolen Centrale [1966] 2 All ER 61, [1967] 1 AC 361, [1966] 2 WLR 944, HL.

Turnbull v M'Lean & Co (1874) 1 R 730, Ct of Sess.

Welbourn v Australian Postal Commission [1984] VR 257, Vict SC.

Williams v North's Navigation Collieries (1889) *Ltd* [1906] AC 136, [1904–7] All ER Rep 907, HL.

Appeal

a Wakefield Metropolitan District Council appealed, with leave of the Appeal Committee of the House of Lords given on 1 April 1985, against the decision of the Court of Appeal (Fox and Parker LJJ, Sir Edward Eveleigh dissenting) ([1985] 1 All ER 905, [1985] 1 WLR 822) on 8 February 1985 allowing the appeal of Henry Gladstone Miles against the order and judgment of Nicholls J given on 9 November 1983 dismissing his claim for £774·06 plus interest as money had and received by the council to Mr Miles's use or as a debt
b owed by the council to Mr Miles. The facts are set out in the opinion of Lord Templeman.

Alexander Irvine QC and *M R Taylor* for the council.
Stephen Sedley QC and *Antony White* for the plaintiff.

c Their Lordships took time for consideration.

12 March. The following opinions were delivered.

LORD BRIDGE OF HARWICH. My Lords, I have had the advantage of reading in draft the speeches of my noble and learned friends Lord Templeman and Lord Oliver. I
d agree, for the reasons they give, that the salary payable to the respondent (the plaintiff) by the appellants (the council) was not an honorarium for the mere tenure of an office but had the character of remuneration for work done. The salary was paid for a working week of 37 hours. The more difficult question at the heart of this appeal is whether the council were entitled, in the circumstances, to deduct and withhold a proportion of the weekly salary corresponding to the three hours of work required to be done on Saturday
e mornings during the weeks when the plaintiff was refusing to perform his duty of celebrating marriages on Saturdays. This depends, in turn, on whether in the like circumstances, if there had been a straightforward contract of employment, the employer would have the right to make such a deduction independently of any set-off of damages for breach of contract. By their letter of 8 October 1981 the council made clear that the
f partial and imperfect performance of his Saturday duties which the plaintiff was willing to undertake was not acceptable. If he was not prepared to celebrate marriages on Saturdays, which was part of the duty required by his terms of service, he was not to attend at his office and would not be paid if he did. I regard this attitude manifested by the council as a central feature in the dispute, which serves to narrow and define the question of law falling for decision. If an employee refuses to perform the full duties
g which can be required of him under his contract of service, the employer is entitled to refuse to accept any partial performance. The position then resulting, during any relevant period while these conditions obtain, is exactly as if the employee were refusing to work at all. It follows that the central question of law can be stated thus: if an employee entitled to a weekly salary for a working week of a defined number of hours refuses to work for the whole or part of a week, is the employer entitled, without terminating the
h contract of employment and without relying on any right to damages for breach of contract, to withhold the whole or a proportion of part of the week's salary?

My Lords, the penetrating analysis of the authorities undertaken by my noble and learned friend Lord Oliver and the reasoning he bases on that analysis seem to me to lead convincingly to an affirmative answer to this question. I do not believe that any wider question relating to the effect on contractual rights and obligations of industrial action
j designed to put pressure on employers falls for consideration. Industrial action can take many different forms and there are a variety of options open to an employer confronted by such action. In particular I should, for my part, have preferred to express no opinion on questions arising in the case of an employee who deliberately 'goes slow' or otherwise does his work in a less than satisfactory way, when the employer nevertheless acquiesces in his continuing to work the full number of hours required under his contract. There may be no single, simple principle which can be applied in such cases irrespective of

differences in circumstances. But I find it difficult to understand the basis on which, in such a case, the employee in place of remuneration at the contractual rate would become *a* entitled to a quantum meruit. This would presuppose that the original contract of employment had in some way been superseded by a new agreement by which the employee undertook to work as requested by the employer for remuneration in a reasonable sum. This seems to me to be contrary to the realities of the situation.

I would allow the appeal.

b

LORD BRANDON OF OAKBROOK. My Lords, I have had the advantage of reading in draft the speeches prepared by my noble and learned friends Lord Templeman and Lord Oliver. I agree that for the reasons which they give the appeal should be allowed. Like my noble and learned friend Lord Oliver, however, I should prefer to reserve my opinion on the question whether an employee engaged in certain kinds of industrial action may be entitled to claim remuneration on a quantum meruit basis for *c* work actually done.

LORD BRIGHTMAN. My Lords, for the reasons so convincingly expressed by my noble and learned friends Lord Templeman and Lord Oliver in their speeches, which I have had the privilege of reading in draft, I agree that the plaintiff's action was rightly dismissed by the trial judge. It was rightly dismissed because in an action by an employee *d* to recover his pay it must be proved or admitted that the employee worked or was willing to work in accordance with his contract of employment, or that such service as was given by the employee, if falling short of his contractual obligations, was accepted by the employer as a sufficient performance of his contract. I leave out of account a failure to work or work efficiently as a result of illness or other unavoidable impediment, *e* to which special considerations apply.

If an employee offers partial performance, as he does in some types of industrial conflict falling short of a strike, the employer has a choice. He may decline to accept the partial performance that is offered, in which case the employee is entitled to no remuneration for his unwanted services, even if they are performed. That is the instant case. Or the employer may accept the partial performance. If he accepts the partial *f* performance as if it were performance which satisfied the terms of the contract, the employer must pay the full wage for the period of the partial performance because he will have precluded or estopped himself from asserting that the performance was not that which the contract required. But what is the position if the employee offers partial performance and the employer, usually of necessity, accepts such partial performance, the deficient work being understood by the employer and intended by the employee to *g* fall short of the contractual requirements and being accepted by the employer as such? There are, as it seems to me, two possible answers. One possible answer is that the employer must pay the full wage but may recover by action or counterclaim or set-off damages for breach of contract. The other possible answer is that the employee is only entitled to so much remuneration as represents the value of the work he has done, i e quantum meruit. My noble and learned friend Lord Templeman prefers the latter *h* solution, and so do I. My reason is this. One has to start with the assumption that the employee sues for his pay; the employer is only bound to pay the employee that which the employee can recover by action. The employee cannot recover his contractual wages because he cannot prove that he has performed or ever intended to perform his contractual obligations. If wages and work are interdependent, it is difficult to suppose that an employee who has voluntarily declined to perform his contractual work can *j* claim his contractual wages. The employee offers partial performance with the object of inflicting the maximum damage on the employer at the minimum inconvenience to himself. If, in breach of his contract, an employee works with the object of harming his employer, he can hardly claim that he is working under his contract and is therefore entitled to his contractual wages. But nevertheless in the case supposed the employee has

provided *some* services, albeit less than the contract required, and the employer has
a received those (non-contractual) services; therefore the employer must clearly pay
something, not the contractual wages because the contractual work has deliberately not
been performed. What can he recover? Surely the value of the services which he gave
and which the employer received, ie quantum meruit.

My Lords, some of my conclusions travel outside the ambit of this case. The fact that
they are obiter does not deter me from expressing them. I express my thoughts in the
b hope that they may, perhaps, be of some assistance to those who seek a correct approach
to the rights of the parties in the common case of industrial action which falls short of a
withdrawal of labour.

My Lords, I would allow this appeal.

LORD TEMPLEMAN. My Lords, the respondent plaintiff is the superintendent
c registrar of births, deaths and marriages for the district of Wakefield. The plaintiff was
appointed by the appellant defendants, Wakefield Metropolitan District Council. The
plaintiff is paid a salary by the council, and he works a 37-hour week. One of the most
important functions of the plaintiff as superintendent registrar is to conduct civil
wedding ceremonies, and the most popular time for such weddings is Saturday morning,
when the register office provided by the council is open for three hours between nine
d o'clock and midday. On instructions from his trade union, NALGO, the plaintiff by way
of industrial action, refused to conduct weddings on Saturday morning. The object of
the union was, by inconveniencing the public, to obtain publicity and support for the
campaign conducted by the union in the interests of its members for a higher scale of
salary to be paid to superintendent registrars. The plaintiff remained willing to work a
37-hour week and to work on Saturday but he refused to conduct weddings on Saturday.
e By a letter dated 8 October 1981 the council—

> 'made it clear to the Registration Officers that whilst ever they are not prepared
> to undertake the full range of their duties on Saturdays they are not required to
> attend for work and accordingly will not be paid. If the Registrars attend at their
> offices on Saturdays that is entirely a matter for them.'

f Thus the council treated the plaintiff as being under a duty to work 3 out of his 37 hours
on Saturday morning for the purpose of conducting weddings if required. The plaintiff
refused to conduct weddings on Saturday and the council treated him as working for
only 34 hours. In refusing to conduct weddings on Saturday, the plaintiff, as he now
frankly concedes, acted in breach of his duties as superintendent registrar. The council
g deducted 3/37ths of the salary of the plaintiff while he remained unwilling to conduct
weddings on Saturday, between August 1981 and October 1982, when the salary dispute
was settled. The plaintiff now seeks payment of the sums deducted, amounting to £774.
Nicholls J decided against the plaintiff. The Court of Appeal by a majority (Parker and
Fox LJJ) held that the plaintiff was entitled to be paid his full salary unless and until he
was dismissed. Sir Edward Eveleigh dissenting, agreed with Nicholls J that the plaintiff
h was not entitled to be paid for the time he refused to work in accordance with his duties.
The council now appeal with the leave of the House.

The rights and obligations of the plaintiff derive from the Registration Service Act
1953. The question is whether, on the true construction of the 1953 Act and the terms
of the appointment of the plaintiff, he was entitled to be paid for a Saturday morning
when in pursuit of industrial action he was not willing to work normally.
j By s 45 of the Marriage Act 1949:

> '(1) Where a marriage is intended to be solemnized on the authority of a
> certificate of a superintendent registrar, the persons to be married may state in the
> notice of marriage that they wish to be married in the office of the superintendent
> registrar ... to whom notice of marriage is given, and where any such notice has

been given ... the marriage may be solemnized in the said office, with open doors, in the presence of the superintendent registrar ... and in the presence of two witnesses ...' *a*

Section 1 of the 1953 Act created the office of Registrar General for the purposes of the 1949 Act and the Births and Deaths Registration Act 1953, which regulate the reporting and registration of births and deaths and the conduct and registration of civil marriages. Section 5 of the 1953 Act, as amended by the Local Government Act 1972, created the office of superintendent registrar of births, deaths and marriages for every registration district consisting of or comprised in a non-metropolitan county or metropolitan district. The 1953 Act, as amended, and so far as material for present purposes, also provided by s 6(1): *b*

'Every superintendent registrar ... shall be appointed by the council of the non-metropolitan county or metropolitan district in which his district ... is situated ...' *c*

Pursuant to this provision, the council appointed the plaintiff to be the superintendent registrar for the district of Wakefield. Section 6 further provides:

'... (3) Every superintendent registrar ... shall be a salaried officer paid by the council ...
(4) Every superintendent registrar ... shall hold office during the pleasure of the Registrar General.' *d*

Thus the plaintiff is paid by the council but can only be dismissed by the Registrar General. Section 13 provides:

'(1) There shall be in force for each non-metropolitan county and metropolitan district a scheme or schemes (in this Act referred to as "the local scheme") ... *e*
(2) Provision shall be made by the local scheme for ... (*e*) fixing ... the salary and other remuneration, if any, to be attached to each office ... (*f*) fixing ... the conditions on which an office is to be held, so, however, that nothing in the scheme shall affect the power of the Registrar General to remove from office an officer in any case in which the Registrar General is satisfied that the officer has been guilty of serious default in the performance of the duties imposed on him by the Registration Acts or any regulations made thereunder ...' *f*

The plaintiff was a competent and conscientious officer and the Registrar General did not exercise his power of removal when the plaintiff, under instructions from his union and no doubt in agreement with the view that superintendent registrars were underpaid, took industrial action by declining to conduct weddings on Saturday. *g*

Section 13(2)(*g*) required the local scheme to make provision for—

'applying with any necessary modifications, adaptation and exceptions the provisions of the Local Government Act, 1929, relating to the transfer, superannuation and compensation of officers.'

These officers were in the main employed by local authorities under contracts of employment. *h*

Section 13(2)(*h*) required the local scheme to make provision for—

'conferring on the proper officer [appointed by the council for the purposes of the Act] powers with respect to—(i) the fixing of the hours of attendance of officers; (ii) the distribution of business between officers ...'

Section 13(3)(*b*) authorised the local scheme to— *j*

'confer on the proper officer ... such general powers of supervising the administration within the ... county or ... district of the provisions of the Registration Acts as may be specified in the scheme.'

Section 14 directed that the local scheme be prepared by each council and approved by the Minister of Health, now the Secretary of State for Social Services.

The Wakefield registration scheme, duly made by the council and approved by the Minister, assimilated a superintendent registrar with an appropriate local government officer in relation to salary scales, overtime pay, sick leave, travel expenses, superannuation and other matters. Under the Wakefield scheme the plaintiff became entitled to a fixed salary and became bound to work a 37-hour week. Thus the position of the plaintiff was in many respects similar to the position of an employee. He was appointed by the council and paid a salary by the council out of public money, for a fixed number of hours of work, and he worked on council premises for the benefit of the public. The main differences between the position of the plaintiff and the position of an employee of the council were that the plaintiff could only be dismissed by the Registrar General and that the plaintiff performed tasks which were imposed by the central government in the interests of the nation generally.

Counsel for the plaintiff submitted, and the majority of the Court of Appeal accepted, that significance was to be attached to the fact that the plaintiff was not a servant under a contract of employment but the holder of an office. In the olden days satirised by Dickens and Thackeray a gentleman appointed to an office, for example, in the Chancery Registry or in the Department of Circumlocution and Sealing Wax, carried out his ill-defined duties at his leisure and pleasure. Trollope explained that a special Act of Parliament was necessary in order to control the functions and the stipend of the holder of the office of Warden of Hiram's Hospital. It is unusual for the holder of an office to take industrial action and the consequences will depend on the rights and obligations conferred and imposed on the office-holder by the terms of his appointment. But if an ambassador and the embassy porter were both on strike then I would expect both to be liable to lose or both to be entitled to claim their apportioned remuneration attributable to the period of the strike. A judge and an usher on strike should arguably be treated in the same manner. The ambassador might be required to decode a declaration of war on Sunday, and a judge might devote his Christmas holidays to the elucidation of legal problems arising from industrial action, so that it would be necessary to divide their annual salaries by 365 to define a daily rate applicable to the period of strike, whereas the weekly, daily or hourly wages of the porter and the usher provide a different basis for apportionment, but in principle it is difficult to see why there should be any difference in treatment. To decide this appeal it suffices that there is no logical distinction between a superintendent registrar who is paid a weekly salary for a 37-hour week and a municipal dustman who is paid a weekly wage for a 37-hour week if both are on strike, both are supported by their unions and both claim from the council payment in full of their salary and wages for the duration of the strike. Middle class morality must not be allowed to place Mr Dolittle in an inferior position in this respect.

Counsel for the plaintiff contended that the power to dismiss a superintendent registrar conferred on the Registrar General was a penalty and the only penalty which could be inflicted on a superintendent registrar if he committed a breach of his duties. In my opinion this power was only intended to deal with transgressions which in the opinion of the Registrar General rendered a superintendent registrar unfit to continue in office. It does not follow that all other breaches of duty can be committed with impunity.

The 1953 Act and the local scheme do not expressly authorise a deduction from the salary of a superintendent registrar if he declines to carry out his duties. It does not follow that the legislature intended to confer on a superintendent registrar the right to be paid if he declines to work. The 1953 Act does not state the obvious, namely that a superintendent registrar may be removed from office if he is guilty of serious default in the performance of his duties. The Act states that which would otherwise not be obvious, namely that the power of removal shall be exercisable by the Registrar General and not by the council. It does not follow that the legislature intended to impose on the council the obligation to pay a superintendent registrar for doing nothing. If the plaintiff worked more than 37 hours in a week he was entitled to overtime pay in accordance with the provisions regarding overtime contained or incorporated in the local scheme. The council *a* say that if the plaintiff in breach of duty worked less than 37 hours he is only entitled to be paid for his hours of work.

Counsel for the plaintiff said that by the 1953 Act the council were bound to pay the salary of the plaintiff; the council were not concerned to see whether the plaintiff gave value for money and were not entitled to benefit from the plaintiff's breach of duty by retaining any part of his salary. These submissions ignore the fact that the council are a *b* public authority paying out public money for the purpose of securing a public service from a public official. The result of the local scheme and the appointment of the plaintiff was that the council promised to pay the plaintiff his weekly salary determined from time to time under the scheme and the plaintiff promised to devote 37 hours each week to the due performance of his duties.

Next, counsel submitted that the plaintiff was entitled to be paid for 37 hours if he *c* carried out his duties as a superintendent registrar (other than his marriage service duties) for three hours on Saturday and carried out all his duties as a superintendent registrar for 34 hours between Monday and Friday. Alternatively, the plaintiff was entitled to be paid for 37 hours if he carried out his duties for 37 hours between Monday and Friday. But the plaintiff refused to conduct marriage services on Saturday because he knew that it was his duty to conduct marriage services on Saturday and that his refusal would cause *d* serious inconvenience to the public he was paid to serve. The plaintiff could not perform his Saturday duty of conducting marriage ceremonies by carrying out other tasks of a superintendent registrar on that day. Nor could the plaintiff perform his Saturday duty of conducting marriage ceremonies on that day by conducting marriage ceremonies on other days and by working for 37 hours between Monday and Friday. Between Monday and Friday the plaintiff was only entitled to work 34 hours. On Saturday the plaintiff was *e* entitled to work for three hours but only if he was willing to conduct marriage ceremonies.

Parker LJ was impressed by the fact that under the 1953 Act an additional registrar is paid by fees and certain superintendent registrars may elect to be paid by fees. Parker LJ appears to have assumed that the council were bound to acquiesce in industrial action by *f* a registrar paid by fees and were therefore bound to acquiesce in industrial action by a registrar paid by salary. But if a registrar paid by fees declines to work on Saturday he receives no remuneration for that day. The plaintiff declined to work efficiently on Saturday but claims his full remuneration attributable to that day. A registrar cannot be compelled to work; but the present dispute concerns the question whether a registrar on strike is entitled to be paid without working. By their letter dated 8 October 1981 the *g* council made it clear that a registrar would not be paid for work on Saturday unless he was prepared to undertake the full range of his duties. Sir Edward Eveleigh rightly summed up the position of the plaintiff as follows ([1985] 1 All ER 905 at 917, [1985] 1 WLR 822 at 838–839):

> '... the local scheme indicates that a superintendent registrar's salary is like most other salaries payable for work which he is required to do according to the terms of *h* his appointment ... the local scheme is to the effect that the salary is payable in respect of services rendered and I see nothing in this case to show that the [council] are required to pay when services were not rendered.'

If the plaintiff is in no better position for present purposes than a worker under a contract of employment, he is no worse position. Counsel submitted that, unless and *j* until an employer puts an end to a contract of employment by dismissing the worker, the employer must pay the worker his full contractual wages even though the worker is on strike. The plaintiff was not dismissed and was therefore entitled to his full salary.

My Lords, industrial action involves a worker, in conjunction with all or some of his fellow workers, declining to work or declining to work efficiently, in each case with the

object of harming the employer so that the employer will feel obliged to increase wages
a or improve conditions of work or meet the other requirements put forward by the
workers' representatives. The form of industrial action which consists of declining to
work is a strike. The form of industrial action which consists of declining to work
efficiently has many manifestations, including the 'go slow' and the refusal by the
plaintiff to carry out some of his functions on Saturday. In essence, the plaintiff was
employed by the public and his industrial action took the form of declining to work
b efficiently on Saturday with the object of inconveniencing the public and advancing the
claim of his union for higher salaries. Industrial action is an effective method of
enhancing the bargaining power of the workers' representatives. The courts are not
competent to determine and are not concerned to determine whether a strike or other
form of industrial action is justified or malicious, wise or foolish, provoked or exploited,
beneficial or damaging; history has proved that any such determination is speculative
c and liable to be unsound. Any form of industrial action by a worker is a breach of
contract which entitled the employer at common law to dismiss the worker because no
employer is contractually bound to retain a worker who is intentionally causing harm to
the employer's business.

The Employment Protection (Consolidation) Act 1978 provides that a worker who is
lawfully dismissed shall nevertheless be entitled to prove to an industrial tribunal that he
d has been unfairly dismissed and is entitled to reinstatement or compensation. An
individual worker is unfairly dismissed if the only reason for his dismissal is that he has
taken part in industrial action unless all workers who take part are also dismissed. In
practice, the Act protects a worker against losing his job as a direct consequence of his
industrial action unless the employer goes out of business or is able to enagage a wholly
new and different work force. The legislation does not protect the worker against losing
e his wages during a period of industrial action. If the worker were protected against losing
both his job and his wages, nearly every threat of industrial action would result in the
capitulation of the employer. As a result of the 1978 Act, there is little point in an
employer dismissing a worker who is engaged in industrial action which is expected to
end in a negotiated settlement. If counsel for the plaintiff is right, however, the worker
f engaged in industrial action is entitled to his wages unless and until the employer serves
a formal notice of dismissal, which in the vast majority of cases will never affect the
worker. Counsel concedes that a worker is not entitled to his wages if the employer
serves formal notice of dismissal. Counsel, in effect, denies the right of the employer to
say, expressly or by implication, to the worker engaged in industial action: 'I have no
present intention of dismissing you but I will only pay you wages if you work.' A worker
g who is on strike (as opposed to a worker who is locked out) does not usually line up for
his pay packet on pay day during a strike. The worker thus recognises and accepts that,
whether or not he is dismissed for industrial action, he is not entitled to be paid if he
declines to work. The worker hopes that the damage inflicted on or feared by the
employer by industrial action will drive the employer to the bargaining table before the
loss of wages suffered by the worker drives him back to work. In the present case the
h council refrained from calling on the Registrar General to dismiss the plaintiff but by
their letter dated 10 October 1981 announced that they would only pay for normal work.
According to counsel for the plaintiff the law of contract is so formalistic and inflexible
that an employer may not keep a worker in his employ and refuse to pay him while he
is engaged in industrial action. The employer must either dismiss the worker or pay him
in full. Counsel submitted that where a worker under a contract of employment commits
j a breach of contract by declining to work the remedies of the employer are rescission and
damages. The employer may treat the conduct of the worker as repudiation of the
contract and may accept the repudiation; in plain language, the employer may dismiss
the worker. The employer will then cease to be liable to pay wages and may sue the
worker for any additional damages caused by the breach of contract. Alternatively, the
employer may treat the contract as still subsisting; in that case the employer will be

bound to pay the worker his full wages but may then sue the worker for unliquidated damages caused by the breach of contract. The same choice between dismissal and *a* payment confronts an employer where the worker takes industrial action in the form of declining to work efficiently. The plaintiff has not been dismissed; the council must pay his full salary, and the council can then sue the plaintiff for damages. But then, according to counsel, the council have suffered no damages and will not be able to recover any damages from the plaintiff; the only effect of the refusal of the plaintiff to conduct wedding ceremonies on Saturday was that members of the public who wished to be *b* married on that day at the Wakefield District Registry were disappointed. If counsel is right, the difficulty about damages applies to most forms of industrial action, so that in effect an employer must either dismiss a worker or pay his full wages albeit that the worker is either idle or is working in a manner calculated to harm the employer. A strike may involve the employer in a loss of profits but it is impossible to show that any particular proportion of the loss is attributable to the industrial action of any individual *c* worker. If a chauffeur goes on strike for one day, his employer may suffer only the inconvenience or enjoyment of driving his own car for once. My Lords, an employer always suffers damage from the industrial action of an individual worker. The employer suffers the loss of the services of the worker. The value of those services to the employer cannot be less than the salary payable for those services, otherwise most employers would *d* become insolvent.

In the present case, if the council were obliged to pay for the services of the plaintiff on Saturday morning, the council would suffer the loss of the money thus paid for services to the public which the plaintiff declined to perform. A man who pays something for nothing truly incurs a loss. The value of the lost services cannot be less than the value attributable to the lost hours of work. Indeed, the plaintiff embarked on industrial action *e* because his union believed that the value of his services exceeded his current salary.

Counsel for the plaintiff's next contention is that unless a worker is dismissed he is nevertheless entitled to his full wages on the due date in each week, although the employer can recover damages in proceedings which will eventually result in a judgment. But, if the damages suffered by the employer are the wages for the lost hours, it would be purposeless to require the employer to pay the wages and then to recover a like *f* amount by way of damages. If 10,000 workers earn £100 a week and go on strike for a week, no logical system of law will compel the employer to pay out £1m at the end of the week, and then to issue 10,000 writs against 10,000 defendants to recover £100 from each.

For the past two years teachers have been engaged in sporadic strike action, usually on one day in a week. If counsel for the plaintiff is right, educational authorities must pay *g* for strike days unless after each day's strike they issue dismissal notices. To show that the educational authorities have no intention of ruining the educational system by insisting on dismissal, the dismissal notice must presumably be accompanied by a reinstatement notice. This would finally submerge the teaching profession in paper.

The consequences of counsel's submissions demonstrate that his analysis of a contract of employment is deficient. It cannot be right that an employer should be compelled to *h* pay something for nothing whether he dismisses or retains a worker. In a contract of employment wages and work go together. The employer pays for work and the worker works for his wages. If the employer declines to pay, the worker need not work. If the worker declines to work, the employer need not pay. In an action by a worker to recover his pay he must allege and be ready to prove that he worked or was willing to work. Different considerations apply to a failure to work due to sickness or other circumstances *j* which may be governed by express or implied terms or by custom. In the present case the plaintiff disentitled himself for his salary for Saturday morning because he declined to work on Saturday morning in accordance with his duty.

Where industrial action takes the form of working inefficiently, the employer may decline to accept any work and the worker will not then be entitled to wages.

a   I agree with my noble and learned friend Lord Bridge that industrial action can take many forms and that the legal consequences of industrial action will depend on the rights and obligations of the worker, the effect of the industrial action on the employer and the response of the employer. For my part however I take the provisional view that on principle a worker who, in conjunction with his fellow workers, declines to work efficiently with the object of harming his employer is no more entitled to his wages under the contract than if he declined to work at all. The worker whose industrial action

b   takes the form of 'going slow' inflicts intended damage which may be incalculable and non-apportionable but the employer, in order to avoid greater damage, is obliged to accept the reduced work the worker is willing to perform. In those circumstances, the worker cannot claim that he is entitled to his wages under the contract because he is deliberately working in a manner designed to harm the employer. But the worker will be entitled to be paid on a quantum meruit basis for the amount and value of the reduced

c   work performed and accepted. In the present case, the council by their letter dated 18 October 1981 refused to accept any work from the plaintiff unless he worked normally and discharged all his duties. The plaintiff offered to work inefficiently on Saturday but could not compel the council to accept that offer, and on their refusal to accept that offer he ceased to be entitled to be paid for Saturday. My present view is that a worker who embarks on any form of industrial action designed to harm his employer gives up his

d   right to wages under his contract of employment, in the hope that the industrial action will be successful in procuring higher wages in the future, and possibly in the hope that negotiations which end the industrial dispute will provide for some payment for the period of the industrial action.

  Industrial action is largely a twentieth century development introduced with success by the Bermondsey matchworkers at about the turn of the century. Industrial action is

e   unique in that in order to be effective the action must involve a repudiatory breach of contract designed to harm the employer. Most of the 50-odd authorities cited in the course of this appeal were ancient and irrelevant. There are, however, some authorities which concern or have some relevance to claims and defences arising out of industrial action.

f   The authorities disclose that a breach of some contracts affords the injured party the remedy of abatement, and that in many other circumstances a right to damages may be set off against a duty to pay.

  The remedy of abatement applies to a contract for goods where the vendor agrees to supply 15 bottles of wine for £30 and only supplies 12 bottles. In that case the purchaser is entitled to pay £24 for the bottles received. That principle is apt to apply equally to a

g   contract of employment where the worker agrees to work for 15 hours for £30 and only works for 12 hours, so that the employer is entitled to pay £24 for the hours worked.

  In *Mondel v Steel* (1841) 8 M & W 858 at 871–872, [1835–42] All ER Rep 511 at 516 Parke B said:

> '... in all these cases of goods sold and delivered with a warranty, and work and

h   > labour, as well as the case of goods agreed to be supplied according to a contract ... it is competent for the defendant, in all of those, not to set-off, by a proceeding in the nature of a cross action, the amount of damages which he has sustained by breach of the contract, but simply to defend himself by shewing how much less the subject-matter of the action was worth, by reason of the breach of contract; and to the extent that he obtains, or is capable of obtaining, an abatement of price on that

j   > account, he must be considered as having received satisfaction for the breach of contract ...'

  In *Hanley v Pease & Partners Ltd* [1915] 1 KB 698 [1914–15] All ER Rep 984, where a worker absented himself without leave for one day, the employer suspended him from work the following day, and, as the worker was ready and willing to work on the following day, he was held entitled to be paid for the following day. It does not appear

that the worker was paid for the day's absence when he was not ready and willing to
work or that he claimed for that day's pay.

In *National Coal Board v Galley* [1958] 1 All ER 91, [1958] 1 WLR 16 workers in an
industrial dispute refused to work on Saturday. The board suffered a loss of profit due to
the impossibility of working the Saturday shift. The board were not entitled, as against
each worker, to recover a proportion of the loss of profit. Pearce LJ delivering the
judgment of the court said ([1958] 1 All ER 91 at 103, [1958] 1 WLR 16 at 29): 'We do
not think it can be said that any damage has been proved against him beyond the cost of
a substitute, say £3 18s.2d.' The cost of a substitute will not be less than the value placed
by the contract on the services of the worker.

In *Hanak v Green* [1958] 2 All ER 141 at 143, [1958] 2 QB 9 at 16 Morris LJ, in a
judgment approved by Lord Diplock in *Gilbert-Ash (Northern) Ltd v Modern Engineering
(Bristol) Ltd* [1973] 3 All ER 195 at 215, [1974] AC 689 at 717, referred to the right of
equitable set-off by a defendant who possessed a liquidated or unliquidated claim arising
out of the same contract, citing, as an example, *Morgan & Son Ltd v S Martin Johnson & Co
Ltd* [1948] 2 All ER 196, [1949] 1 KB 107. In that case the plaintiffs claimed a sum
payable for storing the defendants' vehicles, and the defendants were held to be entitled
to plead an equitable set-off in respect of damages for one of the vehicles which had been
stolen as a result of the negligence of the plaintiffs.

In *Gilbert-Ash (Northern) Ltd v Modern Engineering (Bristol) Ltd* [1973] 3 All ER 195 at
215, [1974] AC 689 at 717 Lord Diplock said that the remedy of abatement—

'is a remedy which the common law provides for breaches of warranty in contracts
for sale of goods and for work and labour. It is restricted to contracts of these types
... It is independent of the doctrine of "equitable set-off" developed by the Court of
Chancery to afford such relief in appropriate cases to parties to other types of
contracts...'

In *McClenaghan v Bank of New Zealand* [1978] 2 NZLR 528 Chilwell J held that bank
employers were in breach of the New Zealand Wages Protection Act 1964, which
provided by s 4(1) that 'the entire amount of wages payable to any worker shall be paid
to the worker in money when they become payable'. The bank employees went on strike
for two days. The bank employers deducted two subsequent days' pay and were held to
be in breach of the 1964 Act. Chilwell J said that the employer banks had a claim for
damages for breach and if the Act had not stood in the way they would have had a set-off
for those damages but that the banks had not sought damages nor an amendment to the
pleadings to let it in, nor had they established any damage (at 536). The judge remarked
that to work 12 days out of 14 was substantial performance if the contract were regarded
as entire. But delivery of 12 bottles out of 14, though in some respects substantial
performance, does not oblige the purchaser to pay for the two missing bottles.

In a decision of Lord Cowie in the Outer House of the Court of Session, *Laurie v British
Steel Corp* (23 February 1978, unreported), workers took industrial action by declining to
work normally. They were suspended, their wages were not paid during the period of
suspension and Lord Cowie held that they were not entitled to recover the amounts
deducted. It was argued that the only remedies of British Steel were to rescind the
contract, with or without a claim for damages, or simply to claim damages which they
had not proved. Lord Cowie held that a contract of employment gave rise to mutual
obligations, and that if one party failed to fulfil his obligations he could not call on the
other party to fulfil his.

In *Henthorn and Taylor v Central Electricity Generating Board* [1980] IRLR 361 workmen
employed by the CEGB took part in an unofficial 'work to rule'. The CEGB were of the
opinion that the workmen were not performing their contracts of employment and
refused to pay the men for the days on which they were working to rule. Lawton LJ,
with whose judgment Bridge and Shaw LJJ agreed, held that, in order to recover, the
workmen must allege and prove that they were ready and willing to perform their part
under the contract of employment.

In *Welbourn v Australian Postal Commission* [1984] VR 257 postal workers refused to
a perform certain work which had been banned by their union. The postal authorities did
not order the workers to cease performance of the balance of their work and did not
dismiss them, but indicated that the workers would not be permitted to leave the post
office and that leaving the post office or not attending in future would be regarded as a
serious dereliction of duty. Fullagar J held that in those circumstances the post office
were not entitled to withhold pay for the period during which each worker refused to
b carry out banned work. Of course, where an employer insists that a worker engaged in
industrial action shall nevertheless attend, and the worker does attend, it is impossible
for the employer to maintain that the worker is not entitled to be paid for his attendance.
In the present case, however, the council made it clear that if the plaintiff was not
prepared to conduct wedding ceremonies on Saturday, he was neither required nor
entitled to attend at the register office.
c   In *Sim v Rotherham Metropolitan BC* [1986] 3 All ER 387, [1986] 3 WLR 851, where a
teacher in breach of contract refused to work during his 'free hours', Scott J held that the
principle of equitable set-off applied to contracts of employment and that the local
authority employers were entitled to make deduction from the teacher's salary by way of
equitable set-off of amounts calculated to represent the financial loss suffered by those
authorities. In that case the amounts of the deductions were accepted by the teacher as
d reasonable. In the present case, since the deductions made by the council is less than the
value placed on the services of the plaintiff by his union in their industrial dispute for
higher salaries, the deduction can hardly be unreasonable.
    Two of the authorities (*Laurie v British Steel Corp* and *Henthorn and Taylor v Central
Electricity Generating Board*) held that a contract of employment does not entitle a worker
to wages but entitles him to claim wages for work which he carries out or is willing to
e carry out pursuant to the contract. Some authorities (*National Coal Board v Galley* and *Sim
v Rotherham Metropolitan BC*, and other cases) proceed on the footing that a contract of
employment entitles a worker to wages and that a refusal to work only founds a claim
for damages by the employer. Whether a refusal to work prevents a claim by the worker
or affords a defence to the employer, workers taking industrial action have not recovered
their wages save in two cases. The first case, *McClenaghan v Bank of New Zealand* [1978] 2
f NZLR 528, was decided on the construction of a New Zealand statute with which your
Lordships are not concerned, and the obiter remarks of the judge concerning the position
at common law do not commend themselves to me. In the second case, *Welbourn v
Australian Postal Commission* [1984] VR 257, the employers were obliged to pay wages
because they insisted that the workers attend for work and the workers complied. In my
opinion, wages are remuneration which must be earned; in a claim for wages under a
g contract of employment, the worker must assert that he worked or was willing to work.
The principle is elegantly expressed in the speech prepared by my noble and learned
friend Lord Oliver and is supported by the additional authorities to which he refers.
When a worker in breach of contract declines to work in accordance with the contract,
but claims payment for his wages, it is unnecessary to consider the law relating to
h damages and unnecessary for the employer to rely on the defences of abatement or
equitable set-off. The employer may or may not sustain and be able to prove and recover
damages by reason of the breach of contract for each worker. But, so far as wages are
concerned, the worker can only claim them if he is willing to work. The plaintiff is in no
better position than a worker under a contract of employment in declining to work in
accordance with the duties of his office.
j   I would allow the appeal and dismiss the action.

LORD OLIVER OF AYLMERTON. My Lords, the factual background from which
this appeal arises has already been set out in the speech delivered by my noble and learned
friend Lord Templeman, which I have had the advantage of reading in draft. The appeal
raises, essentially, three questions. First, on the true construction of the relevant legislation
and of the local scheme made thereunder, is the salary of a superintendent registrar of

births, deaths and marriages an honorarium attached to mere tenure of the office, regardless of whether the office-holder chooses to perform all or any of the duties attached *a* to it (as the majority in the Court of Appeal held), or is it in the nature of remuneration for work done (as was the view of Sir Edward Eveleigh in his dissenting judgment in the Court of Appeal and of Nicholls J in the court of first instance)? Second, if the true nature of the plaintiff's salary is remuneration for work done and thus to be equiparated to the salary or wages of an employee under a contract of employment, would the appellant council, in the circumstances of this case, have been entitled to withhold all or part of the *b* salary in respect of a period in which the plaintiff declined to carry out the duties of his office if he had in fact been employed by the council to carry out those duties? Third, it having been conceded in the council's written case that the evidence before Nicholls J could not support a contention that the plaintiff was in fact employed by the council under a contract of employment, is it permissible, as Sir Edward Eveleigh and Nicholls J concluded, to apply to the statutory relationship between them arising from the holding *c* by the plaintiff of his office as superintendent registrar the analogy of a contractual employment and, if so, what is the consequence of so doing?

As to the first of these questions, there appear to me to be a number of indications pointing to the conclusion that the salary was intended to be the reward for the work done in carrying out the duties of the office and not simply an honorarium for its mere tenure. Prior to the Local Government Act 1929, a registration officer's remuneration *d* was derived from the fees which were payable to him for carrying out his functions. If he failed to perform a particular function on a particular occasion he was not paid for it. By s 22(1) of the 1929 Act it was provided that on any vacancy occurring after the appointed day in the office of a registration officer the office should become a salaried office and, by sub-s (2) of the same section, existing registration officers were given the option of becoming salaried officers. The 'salary or remuneration to be attached to any *e* salaried office' was to be determined by the responsible council (s 22(4)(a)). After the Registration Service Act 1953 all registration officers became salaried. It is difficult to see any reason why the legislature should have intended to substitute for a system of remuneration which originally depended entirely on the volume of work done an honorarium entirely unrelated to the work done and payable for the mere holding of the *f* office regardless of whether or not the holder carried out the duties of the office. There is no provision of the 1929 Act or of the 1953 Act which compulsively leads to this conclusion as a matter of construction. On the contrary, the more natural construction of the 'salary and other remuneration' which is to be fixed by the local authority under s 13(2)(e) of the 1953 Act is that these words connote a financial reward for services rendered. Again, s 13(2)(f) imposes on the local authority the duty to fix the conditions *g* on which the office of a superintendent registrar is held, a duty which, while it may not establish a contractual nexus between the authority and the appointee, certainly assimilates his position to that of an employee, an assimilation which is strengthened by the power of supervision conferred on the proper officer of the local authority by s 13(2)(h). Moreover, as was pointed out by Sir Edward Eveleigh in his dissenting judgment in the Court of Appeal, the salary fixed by the local authority under para 5 of *h* the local scheme is directly related to the number of hours required for the proper performance of the duties of the office. For my part, therefore, I am persuaded that the true nature of the salary for which statutory provision is made by s 13 of the 1953 Act is that it is a remuneration for work done and not simply an honorarium for the tenure of office.

My Lords, it does not of course follow from this that a failure on the part of the office- *j* holder to perform the duties of his office necessarily entitles the local authority to withhold payment of the whole or part of his remuneration, but if that is to be justified at all the determination of the nature of the salary is a first and essential step. If the authority would have no right at common law to withhold any part of the salary were it payable pursuant to a contract of employment, there is certainly nothing in the 1953 Act which would give the local authority any higher right than that possessed by an employer.

a Counsel for the plaintiff has drawn attention to a number of authorities in support of the proposition that an employer under a contract of employment has no such right. He submits that, in a case where an employee is in breach of the terms of his employment, the employer has only two options. He may, if the failure to carry out contractual duties is sufficiently serious, treat it as a repudiatory breach of contract and accept the repudiation, thus bringing the contract to an end and excusing himself from further

b performance of his own obligation to pay the contractual wage or salary. Alternatively, he may affirm the contract and sue for damages for the breach which has occurred. That claim is one which, if he is sued by the employee for wages, he can exert by means of a counterclaim or set-off, so that effectively he can, in practice, make a deduction from the employee's wages. If he does, however, he must be prepared to justify the deduction by reference to the damage which he has suffered. That the options in case of breach of

c contract are thus restricted is, counsel submits, clearly established by decisions of this House in, for instance, *Suisse Atlantique Société d'Armement Maritime SA v NV Rotterdamsche Kolen Centrale* [1966] 2 All ER 61, [1967] 1 AC 361 and *Photo Production Ltd v Securicor Transport Ltd* [1980] 1 All ER 556, [1980] AC 827. The same principle equally applies, counsel submits, to contracts of employment. Thus in *Sim v Rotherham Metropolitan BC* [1986] 3 All ER 387, [1986] 3 WLR 851, where a teacher had declined to perform part of

d his duties but the employing authority had affirmed the contract and continued to accept his services, a deduction from the employee's wages was justified only by reference to a set-off of the employer's claim for damages for breach of contract. In the instant case what is said is that, even if the entitlement of the plaintiff to salary under the statute is analogous to the contractual right of an employee, the council cannot justify the withholding of salary by reference to either option. The council cannot accept the refusal

e of the plaintiff to carry out his statutory duties as a repudiation disentitling him to claim the salary because, ex hypothesi, there is no contract with the council which can be repudiated. Further and in any event, the plaintiff continued to perform the other duties of his office and certainly no claim has been made by the council that he is not entitled to any salary at all. Equally, the alternative option is closed to the council because they

f are unable either to show any damage which they have suffered (such damage as there was as a result of the inconvenience caused having been damage to the general public and not to the council) or to demonstrate any juristic basis for a counterclaim for damages by the council arising otherwise than from a breach of contract.

My Lords, I see much force in these arguments and were it not for the principles to which I am about to refer I would, for my part, feel bound to reach the same conclusion

g as that reached by the majority of the Court of Appeal. But the critical point in this case and the point which, in my judgment, answers counsel for the plaintiff's contentions is that the action which was tried by Nicholls J and which gave rise to this appeal was an action in which the plaintiff claimed certain sums as due to him by way of salary and in which, therefore, he assumed the burden of pleading and proving each essential allegation necessary to establish his entitlement. Although, speaking for myself, I question whether

h the mere fact that the plaintiff was appointed to his office under the provisions of the 1953 Act necessarily precludes the existence of a parallel contract between him and the council for the carrying out of his statutory duties, it has been accepted for the purposes of the present appeal that no contractual nexus exists between him and the council. Nevertheless, the nature of his remuneration and the terms of his tenure of office are so closely analogous to those of a contract of employment that any claim by him to salary

j payable pursuant to the statutory provisions and the local scheme made thereunder ought, in my judgment, to be approached in the same way as a claim to salary or wages under such a contract. The relationship between the council and the plaintiff has all the incidents which one would expect from a contract of employment save that the power of dismissal is vested in the Registrar General and not in the appointing authority which has the responsibility for paying the plaintiff, providing him with premises and regulating his hours and conditions of work. If, as a matter of law, he were employed by the council I do not, for my part, see any difficulty in finding a juristic basis for the *a* retention of salary which the council have made. The simple fact would be that the council had suffered damage to the extent that they were liable to pay for what was, in effect, a period of voluntary absence from work and I see no particular difficulty in quantifying that damage, since the employee could hardly contend successfully that that of which his employer had been deprived by his absence (ie his services) was worth less than the sum which he was claiming to be paid for them. And, in my judgment, on the *b* facts of the case, the proper inference to be drawn is that the plaintiff was refusing to work on Saturdays and was thus, in effect, voluntarily absent on that day. It is true that he attended the office on Saturday but it was, at the outset, made clear to him by the council, whose proper officer had under the statute the task of supervising the administration of the Registration Acts and fixing the hours of attendance, that if he was not prepared to carry out his proper function of conducting weddings his attendance at *c* the office on Saturdays was not required and would not be recognised as a performance of his duties. Thus, applying the contractual analogy, the plaintiff's position was no different from that of an employee voluntarily absenting himself from work. The question to be asked, therefore, is not so much: has the employer a *right* to withhold from an employee who voluntarily absents himself from work wages for the period in which he is absent? but: is the employee entitled to sue for and recover from his employer *d* wages in respect of a period during which he has made it perfectly clear that he is not ready and willing to perform his own contractual obligations? To put it another way, is it sufficient for the employee simply to plead a contract for his employment over a given period or must he, in order to substantiate his claim, aver and prove something more than the mere formation of the contract? Counsel has submitted that to deny to the plaintiff his claim for salary in respect of the period not worked would be to contradict a *e* long line of authority establishing the employee's right to wages for periods of involuntary absence due to sickness. Speaking for myself, I have found this a useful analogy, for there is, I think, to be found in those cases the answer to the question posed above. The line of cases referred to was reviewed by Scott LJ in *Marrison v Bell* [1939] 1 All ER 745, [1939] 2 KB 187, and they all stem from and follow the decision in *Cuckson v Stones* (1858) 1 *f* E & E 248, [1843–60] All ER Rep 390, where the distinction is clearly drawn between voluntary and involuntary non-performance by a servant of the duties of his employment. The plaintiff in that case had pleaded a contract of employment at a wage of £2 10s od per week and that—

> 'although all things have happened and been performed in order to entitle the plaintiff to the performance of the said promise of the defendant, yet the defendant *g* ... refused to pay the said plaintiff the said sum of 2l.10s. a week for divers, to wit thirteen, weeks.'

(See 1 E & E 248 at 249–250, [1843–60] All ER Rep 390 at 391.)

To that the defendant pleaded in his fourth plea—

> 'to so much of the first count as relates to the claim therein for wages: that the *h* plaintiff was not, during any part of the time for and in respect of which such wages are by that count claimed, ready and willing or able to render, and did not in fact during any part of such time render, the agreed or any service.'

(See 1 E & E 248 at 250, [1843–60] All ER Rep 390 at 391.)

The plaintiff demurred to the fourth plea and issue was joined. Cockburn CJ at the *j* trial directed a verdict for the plaintiff with leave to move to enter a verdict for the defendant, or for a nonsuit. The defendant then obtained a rule to show cause why the verdict should not be set aside and the verdict entered for the defendant—

> 'on the ground that, upon the evidence, the plaintiff is not entitled to a verdict

a   upon the fourth plea; and that the plaintiff is not entitled to recover the weekly wages for the time during which he has not performed the service.'

(See 1 E & E 248 at 251, 120 ER 902 at 903–904.)

The demurrer was directed to come on for argument with the rule. The judgment of the court as to the demurrer to the fourth plea was delivered by Lord Campbell CJ. It is instructive and, so far as material was as follows (1 E & E 248 at 255–256, [1843–60] All

b   ER Rep 390 at 392):

'We are of opinion that this plea is good. It is pleaded only to the claim for wages; and it avers "that the plaintiff was not, during any part of the time for and in respect of which such wages are by that count claimed, ready and willing or able to render, and did not in fact during any part of such time render, the agreed or any service." We think the gist of the plea is that the plaintiff, during the time in question, was

c   not ready and willing to render, and did not render, any service, in the sense that he voluntarily and wilfully refused or omitted to serve. If so, we think he could not claim the wages to be paid to him in consideration of his service. It was objected that his breach of the contract would only be the subject of a cross-action. But the alleged breach of the contract on his part seems to go to the whole consideration for the wages: we must treat the demurrer as if the action were brought for the wages

d   only: and, to avoid circuity of action, it may well be considered that this action should be barred, so as to prevent an unjust advantage in this action, and to put an end to further litigation, rather than that the plaintiff should be allowed to recover wages when he had refused to serve, and that another action should afterwards be brought against him to recover back the amount. On the rule as to entering the verdict on the fourth plea. Whether, when issue is joined on such a plea, the want

e   of ability to do the act proves, in point of law, a want of readiness and willingness, depends upon whether the want of ability is necessarily a breach of the contract to perform a condition precedent, or the consideration for the promise sued upon. In an action for not accepting goods purchased, issue being joined on a plea that the plaintiff was not ready and willing to deliver them, the defendant would be entitled

f   to a verdict, on proof that the plaintiff never was in possession of the goods he undertook to deliver. But, looking to the nature of the contract sued upon in this action, we think that want of ability to serve for a week would not, of necessity, be an answer to a claim for a week's wages, if in truth the plaintiff was ready and willing to serve had he been able to do so, and was only prevented from serving during the week by the visitation of God, the contract to serve never having been

g   determined.'

Thus the distinction between voluntary and involuntary inability is clearly brought out. It has been the council's contention before this House and was, as I read his judgment, also the contention before Nicholls J that the council's obligation to pay salary and the plaintiff's willingness at least to perform his contractual duties were interdependent. That certainly derives support from the case cited. But the matter does

h   not end there. I entirely accept that in the case of the ordinary contract of employment there is no entitlement in the employer to withhold wages for bad work (save in the case of special stipulation to that effect), or, without treating a breach of contract by the employee as a repudiation, to accept such services as the employee is prepared to render under his contract and deduct from his remuneration self-assessed damages for such work as he fails to perform or fails to perform properly. Whether in such a case the

j   employer is entitled to any set-off in respect of damage which he may have suffered is a matter which must depend on the facts of each individual case. But where the employee declines to work at all for a particular period (and I have already said that, in my judgment, this case has to be approached on the basis that the plaintiff was simply withholding his services on Saturdays) then, subject to the question of whether the wages or salary payable are apportionable on a periodic basis, I see no ground on which the employee who declines to perform that condition on which payment depends can *a* successfully sue for the remuneration which is dependent on its performance. An employee, for instance, who is rightly dismissed from his employment can recover salary which has become due and payable at the date of his dismissal but cannot recover sums becoming due and payable at some later date and on the condition that he has performed his contractual duties down to that date (see *Boston Deep Sea Fishing and Ice Co v Ansell* (1888) 39 Ch D 339 at 364, [1886–90] All ER Rep 65 at 73 per Bowen LJ).   *b*

My noble and learned friend Lord Templeman has referred in the course of his speech to the Scottish case of *Laurie v British Steel Corp* (23 February 1978, unreported). This is a good example of the practical interdependence of the employee's willingness to perform on the one hand and the employer's obligation to pay wages on the other. That too was a case where employees had absented themselves from work but had nevertheless taken on themselves the burden of averring and proving their entitlement to wages for the *c* period of absence. The interdependence of the obligations on both sides is aptly summarised in the following extract from the opinion of Lord Cowie in the Outer House of the Court of Session:

> 'Counsel [for the pursuers] pointed out that no rescission of the pursuers' contracts of employment had taken place, and so the defenders were not entitled to refuse to *d* fulfil their obligations. For the defenders it was argued that they were not seeking a remedy against the pursuers for breach of contract. Their position was that, these being contracts of employment, they gave rise to mutual obligations and if one party failed to fulfil his obligations he could not call on the other party to fulfil his. That was all that had happened here. The defenders maintained that the pursuers had failed to fulfil their obligation to work during a specific period; this was a *e* breach of their contracts of employment and so they could not call on the defenders to fulfil their obligations to pay their salaries during the relevant period.'

After referring to *Turnbull v M'Lean & Co* (1874) 1 R 730 and *Alexander Graham & Co v United Turkey Red Co Ltd* 1922 SC 533, Lord Cowie continued:

> 'The feature of all these cases referred to in *Graham* was, of course, that the *f* contracts had, in each case, terminated, whereas in the present case the contracts of employment continued and the defenders simply refused to fulfil their obligation to pay the pursuers' salaries during a specific period of the currency of the contracts. In spite of this apparent specialty, however, I do not see why the general principle should not still apply. That general principle embodies the fundamental rule that if one party does not fulfil his part of the mutual contract he cannot turn round and *g* demand performance by the other of his part of the contract . . . It seems to me that, assuming that the pursuers were in material breach of their contracts in June 1976, there were certain remedies open to the defenders, and they could have exercised them if they so desired. It does not follow, however, that because the defenders did not exercise their remedies the pursuers had the right to demand performance of the defenders' part of the contract when they had not carried out their own part. In *h* principle it does not seem to me to matter that the defenders have not taken the formal step of rescinding the contract. If the pursuers have not carried out their obligations, they cannot sue for performance by the defenders of their obligations. No reference is made in any of the cases to the necessity of rescinding the contract before putting forward the defence that the other party cannot sue for performance because he has not fulfilled his own obligations. In my opinion it is not necessary to *j* do so, and in these circumstances, if the defenders can establish a material breach of contract by pursuers in June 1976, the latter would have no right of action to enforce payment by the defenders of their salaries or indeed to obtain the declarator sought.'

The 'general principle' referred to was stated thus in *Turnbull v M'Lean & Co* 1 R 730 at 738:

'With us . . . all the conditions of a mutual contract are dependent on their
counterparts, as a general rule, when they are of the substance of or material to the
subject matter of the contract itself.'

The same approach appears from the opinion of Lord Salvesen in *Alexander Graham &
Co v United Turkey Red Co Ltd* 1922 SC 533 at 546. There was, it appears, nothing
particularly novel in this so far as the law of Scotland is concerned. The same principle
appears as long ago as 1861 in *Johnston v Robertson* 23 Dunl (Ct of Sess) 646. The Lord
Justice Clerk (Inglis) observed (at 656):

'. . . in a mutual contract, where one party seeks performance of the stipulations
in his favour, he must show that he has given or tendered performance of his part
of the contract. Every action on a mutual contract implies that the pursuer either
has performed, or is willing to perform, his part of the contract; and it is, therefore,
always open to the defender to say that under the contract a right arises also to him
to demand performance of the contract before the pursuer can insist in his action.'

The same principle has been applied in England. In *Henthorn and Taylor v Central
Electricity Generating Board* [1980] IRLR 361 the plaintiffs were two employees at a power
station. They engaged in the practice known as 'working to rule'. The facts are not
entirely clear but the point which arose for decision was essentially one of pleading. In
the case of the plaintiff Henthorn, his claim indicated that he had presented himself for
work but that the employer had declined to accept his services. In the case of the plaintiff
Taylor, the pleading was less clear and indicated that he had in fact been admitted for the
purpose of working and that his services had been accepted. To both claims the employer
pleaded simply that the plaintiffs were taking unofficial industrial action in breach of
their contracts of employment and on that ground resisted the plaintiffs' claim for wages
for the days on which the industrial action had taken place. The claims having been
referred to arbitration under s 92 of the County Courts Act 1959, the arbitrator treated
the employer's pleading as a confession and avoidance and made an award in favour of
the plaintiffs on the basis that the burden was on the employer to show that the plaintiffs
had not been willing to work on the days for which the wages were claimed. The matter
came before the Court of Appeal on an appeal from the refusal of the judge to set aside
the award. The appeal was allowed and the award set aside. Lawton LJ, in delivering the
leading judgment, said that the arbitrator—

'seems to have assumed that because the defendants were admitting that the
plaintiffs were employed by them and were alleging that they had not done their
job as they should have done it, they were assuming a burden of proof. In other
words, he was approaching the problem on the basis that the particulars of defence
constituted a confession and an avoidance. I am satisfied that the defendants'
pleading was not such a plea. When a plaintiff claims that he is entitled to be paid
money under a contract which he alleges the defendant has broken he must prove
that he was ready and willing to perform the contract. That, in my judgment, is a
rule of the common law as is shown by the precedents of pleadings in *Bullen & Leake,
Precedents of Pleadings* (3rd edn, 1868) . . . Mr. Henthorn, in his particulars of claim,
was following what was in the third edition of *Bullen & Leake, Precedents of Pleadings*,
because he was saying that he was ready and willing to work and presented himself
for work. There have, of course, been many changes in the law since the publication
of the third edition of *Bullen & Leake, Precedents of Pleadings*, but the burden of proof
in contract cases of this kind has not been shifted by any of the statutory changes in
procedure which have been made in the last 100 years . . . It follows, so it seems to
me, that all the defendants were doing was to put in issue, by their particulars of
defence, the question whether the plaintiffs were ready and willing to perform their
contracts of employment, and on the authorities to which I have referred, the
burden of proof rested on the plaintiffs. It follows that when Judge Davies took the
view, as he did, that it was for the defendants to establish their allegation that the

plaintiffs were not ready and willing to perform their contracts, he misdirected
himself on the very fundamentals of the case.'   *a*

(See [1980] IRLR 361 at 362–363.)

Another case in which wages were claimed for what was, effectively, a period of
absence from work was *Cresswell v Board of Inland Revenue* [1984] 2 All ER 713. In that
case employees of the Board of Inland Revenue refused their employer's lawful
instructions to operate a computerised system. Their contracts of employment contained   *b*
powers of suspension, but the board made it clear that it was not relying on this. Equally
it did not accept the employees' refusal as a repudiation. It simply indicated that the
employees would not be permitted to work so long as they refused its lawful instructions
and that it would not pay for the manual services which the employees were willing to
tender but which the board, acting within its rights under the contract, was not prepared
to accept as a performance of the employees' obligation. Walton J dismissed the plaintiffs'   *c*
claim and it is worth quoting from his judgment, where the principle is thus pithily
expressed (at 723–724):

> 'On this part of the case, which, if the plaintiffs were correct, would mean that
> the board would have to go on paying them all during the time they were refusing
> to carry out the perfectly lawful requirements of their employer, counsel for the   *d*
> board rested his case on the very simple ground that, so far as an employer and an
> employee are concerned, the promises of pay and work are mutually dependent. No
> work (or, at any rate, readiness to perform whatever work it is the employee ought
> to be willing to perform if physically able to do so) no pay. This is such an obvious
> principle, founded on the simplest consideration of what the plaintiff would have to
> prove in any action for recovery of pay in respect of any period where he was   *e*
> deliberately absent from work of his own accord, that direct authority is slight,
> slight but sufficient. See e g *Denmark Productions Ltd v Boscobel Productions Ltd* [1968]
> 3 All ER 513 at 527–528, [1969] 1 QB 699 at 731–732 per Winn LJ, *Secretary of State
> for Employment v ASLEF (No 2)* [1972] 2 All ER 949 at 966–967, [1972] 2 QB 455 at
> 491–492 per Lord Denning MR, and in particular the unreported Scottish case of
> *Laurie v British Steel Corp* (23 February 1978), a decision of Lord Cowie.'   *f*

Thus it is the submission of counsel for the council that there is no necessity to engage
in a tortuous process of seeing whether the council can establish by way of set-off some
valid counterclaim for damages quantified so as to equal or exceed the amount of the
plaintiff's claim. The plaintiff, he submits, fails at an earlier stage because he simply is
not able to aver and prove that he was ready and willing to perform the services which   *g*
formed the consideration for the payment claimed and on the performance of which it
depended. His claim simply fails for want of proof of an essential allegation. The essential
question is whether what counsel has termed the theory of interdependent obligation is
consistent with the authorities relied on by counsel for the plaintiff in support of his
proposition that, short of accepting the employee's breach as a repudiation determining
the contract altogether, there is no way in which an employer can resist a claim for the   *h*
full contractual remuneration other than the establishment of a counterclaim for
damages.

My Lords, I confess that I have not found the question an easy one to answer but in the
end I am persuaded by the submissions of counsel for the council. A plaintiff in an action
for remuneration under a contract of employment must, in my judgment, assume the
initial burden of averring and proving his readiness and willingness to render the services   *j*
required by the contract (subject, no doubt, to any implied term exonerating him from
inability to perform due, for instance, to illness). I do not, for my part, find this
inconsistent with the cases to which counsel for the plaintiff has drawn attention and
which preclude the employer from accepting the services tendered whilst at the same
time seeking to penalise the employee for some other breach of his contractual

obligations. For instance, *Hanley v Pease & Partners Ltd* [1915] 1 KB 698, [1914–15] All
a ER Rep 984 was a case in which the employer unsuccessfully sought to withhold from
his employee, as a punishment for absence on a previous day on which he had not
worked, wages for a day on which the employee had worked. It is interesting to note
that there does not appear to have been any dispute that that employee was not entitled
to be paid for the day on which he was absent. *Healey v SA Française Rubastic* [1917] 1 KB
946, a decision approved by this House in *Ramsden v David Sharratt & Sons Ltd* (1930) 35
b Com Cas 314, was a case not of absence but of misconduct. The claim there was for salary
in respect of a period properly worked by the employee prior to his dismissal, which he
was held entitled to recover. *Williams v North's Navigation Collieries* (1889) *Ltd* [1906] AC
136, [1904–7] All ER Rep 907 was another case concerned with a claim to deduct from
wages due for a period properly worked a sum due in respect of a previous period of
absence. The decision, in any event, turned on the provisions of the Truck Act 1831. *Sim*
c *v Rotherham Metropolitan BC* [1986] 3 All ER 387, [1986] 3 WLR 851 contains a lucid
analysis by Scott J but was not concerned with the point argued by counsel for the
council. It was not itself an action for wages but was an action for a declaration that the
employer had no right to make any deduction from the employee's wages for the non-
performance of certain of the employee's duties, the services of the employee having
been continued and accepted by the employer. The deduction was there justified by the
d employer's cross-claim for damages for breach of contract, there being no dispute about
quantum. Two cases particularly relied on by counsel for the plaintiff were *McClenaghan
v Bank of New Zealand* [1978] 2 NZLR 528 and *Welbourn v Australian Postal Commission*
[1984] VR 257. The former was concerned with the withholding by the employer of
wages in respect of a period during which the employee had worked in accordance with
his contract which was sought to be justified on the ground of a breach of contract in a
e previous period. There was no cross-claim by the employer for damages and, in any
event, the decision turned on the provisions of the New Zealand Wages Protection Act
1964. In *Welbourn* the employee had presented himself for duty but indicated his
unwillingness to perform certain functions. The employer nevertheless accepted the
services tendered, but at the same time sought to withhold the payment of wages. The
f employer in that case, having not only accepted the benefit of the services offered but
insisted on the employee staying at the place of work to perform them, was hardly in a
position to refute that the employee was ready and willing to perform contractual services
which the employer was prepared to accept. But in any event the decision ultimately
turned on the specific provisions of the Australian Postal Services Act 1975. I do not for
my part find that any of these cases touches the point which, as I read his judgment,
g ultimately formed the basis for Nicholls J's decision and which, in my judgment,
concludes this appeal in the council's favour. It may well be that different considerations
apply where an employer claims to withhold remuneration under a subsisting contract
on the ground of past misconduct or where the employer has, by accepting and directing
the employee's services, precluded himself from denying that the employee was ready
and willing to perform (albeit possibly incompletely) the services which his contract
h obliged him to render. But for the reasons which I have endeavoured to expound I do
not consider that the instant case is in pari materia and I prefer to reserve any comment
about such a case until it arises.
      As I have already indicated, the position of the plaintiff is very closely analogous to that
of an employee employed by the council under a contract of service and embraces
substantially all the incidents normally associated with such an employment save that
j the power of dismissal lies elsewhere than in the paymaster. In the context of a claim
against the paymaster for remuneration for his services, where the question is: has the
plaintiff earned the salary which he claims?, the analogy appears to me to be exact and in
my judgment the burden which the plaintiff has to assume in order to succeed in a claim
for his statutory remuneration is no different from that required of an employee. I
would, for my part therefore, answer the third question postulated above in the

affirmative. Applying the contractual analogy, the plaintiff cannot, for the reasons which I have given, successfully claim that he was at the material time ready and willing to perform the work which he was properly required to do on Saturdays and his action for the remuneration attributable to that work must fail. I would also prefer to reserve my opinion with regard to the question whether there may not be circumstances in which an employee engaged in industrial action might be entitled to claim remuneration on a quantum meruit basis for work actually done.

Appeal allowed.

Solicitors: *Sharpe Pritchard & Co*, agents for *Lawrence A Tawn*, Wakefield (for the council); *Penelope Grant* (for the plaintiff).

Mary Rose Plummer   Barrister.

Hua Chiao Commercial Bank Ltd v Chiaphua Industries Ltd

PRIVY COUNCIL
LORD BRIDGE OF HARWICH, LORD BRANDON OF OAKBROOK, LORD OLIVER OF AYLMERTON, LORD GOFF OF CHIEVELEY AND SIR IVOR RICHARDSON
27, 28 OCTOBER, 25 NOVEMBER 1986

Landlord and tenant – Covenant – Covenant running with land – Lease – Deposit paid by tenant to landlord returnable at end of term if tenant's covenants observed – Whether assignee of reversion liable to return deposit – Whether covenant to repay touching and concerning land.

In 1979 the tenant was granted a lease of factory premises in Hong Kong for a term of five years. The lease provided that the 'landlord' and the 'tenant' therein included their respective assigns. The lease required the tenant to pay to the landlord on or before the signing of the lease a liquidated sum as a deposit which was to be 'returned' to the tenant at the expiration of the term if it observed the covenants, but otherwise was to be forfeited absolutely to the landlord as liquidated damages without prejudice to the landlord's right of action against the tenant for breach of covenant. In 1982 the landlord mortgaged its interest in the reversion to a bank by way of assignment with provision for reassignment on repayment of capital and interest. No reference was made to the tenant's deposit in the assignment. The landlord later defaulted on the mortgage, the bank entered into possession of the property and subsequently the landlord went into liquidation. On the expiry of the lease the tenant, which had not committed any breach of covenant, issued an originating summons in the High Court of Hong Kong seeking a declaration that the bank was liable to return the deposit. The master dismissed the tenant's claim and the judge affirmed that decision, on the ground that the landlord's obligation to return the deposit did not run with the reversion. On further appeal by the tenant, the Court of Appeal of Hong Kong allowed the appeal and granted the declaration sought, on the ground that the obligation to return the deposit touched and concerned the land and, accordingly, was an obligation the burden of which passed to, and was binding on, the bank. The bank appealed to the Privy Council.

Held – The obligations of the tenant to pay a deposit on the execution of the lease and of the landlord to return the deposit on the expiration of the term were obligations which were personal to the original parties to the lease, because although the tenant's obligation

was intended to secure its performance of the tenant's covenants, which did touch and
a concern the land demised, the landlord's obligation to return the deposit if those
covenants were observed was by its nature simply an obligation to repay, on the stipulated
condition, money which the landlord had received in the capacity of payee rather than
in the capacity of landlord. Accordingly, the landlord's obligation to return the deposit
was personal to it and did not pass to the bank as assignee of the reversion. It followed
that the appeal would be allowed (see p 1115 h to p 1116 a h to p 1117 d, post).

b   Re Dollar Land Corp Ltd and Solomon [1963] 2 OR 269 applied.
      Mansel v Norton (1883) 22 Ch D 769, Lord Howard de Walden v Barber (1903) 19 TLR
183 and Moss' Empires Ltd v Olympia (Liverpool) Ltd [1939] 3 All ER 460 distinguished.

Notes

c For the passing of benefit and burden of covenants in a lease, see 27 Halsbury's Laws (4th
edn) paras 388–404, and for cases on the subject, see 31(1) Digest (Reissue) 371–378,
2967–3014.

Cases referred to in judgment

d Congleton Corp v Pattison (1808) 10 East 130, 103 ER 725.
Dollar Land Corp Ltd and Solomon, Re [1963] 2 OR 269, Ont HC.
Horsey Estate Ltd v Steiger [1899] 2 QB 79, [1895–9] All ER Rep 515, CA.
Howard de Walden (Lord) v Barber (1903) 19 TLR 183.
Hunter's Lease, Re, Giles v Hutchings [1942] 1 All ER 27, [1942] Ch 124.
Mansel v Norton (1883) 22 Ch D 769, CA.
e Moss' Empires Ltd v Olympia (Liverpool) Ltd [1939] 3 All ER 460, [1939] AC 544, HL.
Thomas v Hayward (1869) LR 4 Exch 311, [1861–73] All ER Rep 290.

Appeal

The defendant, Hua Chiao Commercial Bank Ltd, appealed with leave of the Court of
f Appeal of Hong Kong against the decision of that court (Huggins, McMullin V-PP and
Cons JA) on 18 April 1985 allowing the appeal of the plaintiff, Chiaphua Industries Ltd
(formerly known as Chiap Hua Clocks and Watches Ltd) (the tenant), against the
judgment of Mayo J in the High Court of Hong Kong dated 14 January 1985 whereby
he dismissed the tenant's appeal from the order of Master Boa dated 19 September 1984
dismissing the tenant's application by originating summons dated 20 June 1984 for a
g declaration that the bank as mortgagee in possession was liable to return to the tenant the
sum of $277,896·80, being rental deposit for factory premises in Hong Kong paid by the
tenant under a lease made between the tenant and the bank's predecessor-in-title. The
facts are set out in the judgment of the Board.

Michael Barnes QC and John Furber for the bank.
h Jonathan Sumption QC for the tenant.

25 November. The following judgment of the Board was delivered.

LORD OLIVER OF AYLMERTON. By a lease dated 29 March 1979 Fook Kin
Enterprises Co Ltd (Fook Kin) as landlord granted to the present respondent, Chiaphua
j Industries Ltd (formerly known as Chiap Hua Clocks and Watches Ltd) (the tenant), as
tenant a lease of certain premises in Hong Kong for a term of five years from 1 February
1979. It was provided in the lease that the expression 'the landlord' 'where the context so
admits shall include its executors administrators and assigns' and that the expression 'the
tenant' 'where the context so admits shall include its executors administrators and
assigns'. The crucial provision of the lease for present purposes is cl 4(h). It provides:

'The Tenant shall pay to the Landlord a sum of DOLLARS TWO HUNDRED SEVENTY SEVEN THOUSAND EIGHT HUNDRED NINETY SIX AND CENTS EIGHTY ($277,896·80) as a security deposit on or before the signing of this Lease. The deposit shall bear no interest and if there shall be no breach of any of the terms and conditions on the part of the Tenant herein contained, the deposit shall be returned to the Tenant at the expiration of the term of this Lease or sooner determination of the same but shall if otherwise be absolutely forfeited to the landlord as liquidated damages without prejudice to the Landlord's right of action against the Tenant for any of its breaches thereof.'

On 5 February 1982 Fook Kin mortgaged its interest in the reversion to Hua Chiao Commercial Bank Ltd by way of assignment with provision for reassignment on repayment of capital and interest. Nothing was expressed in relation to the security deposit. Following default by Fook Kin under the mortgage, on 15 January 1983 the bank took possession of the mortgaged property and took receipt of the rents and profits. Fook Kin subsequently went into liquidation and the bank remained in possession of the property.

The security deposit payable under cl 4(h), which was equivalent to two months' rent under the lease, had been paid by the tenant to Fook Kin at the commencement of the lease. On 31 January 1984 the lease expired. The tenant was not then in breach of any of the terms and conditions of the lease nor was it suggested that it had been in such breach at any time before or after the assignment of the reversion to the bank.

The tenant issued an originating summons in the High Court of Hong Kong seeking a declaration that the bank was liable to return the deposit to the tenant. On 19 September 1984 Master Boa dismissed the claim and an appeal against that decision was dismissed by Mayo J on 14 January 1985. However, on further appeal the Court of Appeal, in a judgment delivered on 18 April 1985, allowed the appeal and granted the declaration sought. It held that the obligation to return the security was one which touched and concerned the land and, accordingly, was an obligation the burden of which passed to and was binding on the bank. The bank now appeals.

There is a considerable measure of common ground between the parties. It is not in dispute that the bank constitutes, by assignment, 'the landlord' for the purposes of the lease. Equally it is not in dispute that the test of whether the original landlord's covenant to return the amount of the deposit is enforceable against a successor in title is the same as it would be if the lease had been a lease of land in England, that is to say whether the covenant is one 'entered into by a lessor with reference to the subject matter of the lease' or, to use the common law terminology, whether it is a covenant which 'touches and concerns the land'. Nor is there any disagreement about the formulation of the test for determining whether any given covenant touches or concerns the land. Their Lordships have been referred to and are content to adopt the following passage from Cheshire and Burn *Modern Law of Real Property* (13th edn, 1982) pp 430–431:

'If the covenant has direct reference to the land, if it lays down something which is to be done or is not to be done upon the land, or, and perhaps this is the clearest way of describing the test, *if it affects the landlord in his normal capacity as landlord or the tenant in his normal capacity as tenant*, it may be said to touch and concern the land. Lord Russell CJ said [in *Horsey Estate Ltd v Steiger* [1899] 2 QB 79 at 89, [1895–9] All ER Rep 515 at 519]: "The true principle is that no covenant or condition which affects merely the person, and which does not affect the nature, quality, or value of the thing demised or the mode of using or enjoying the thing demised, runs with the land"; and Bayley J at an earlier date asserted the same principle [in *Congleton Corp v Pattison* (1808) 10 East 130 at 138, 103 ER 725 at 728]: "In order to bind the assignee the covenant must either affect the land itself during the term, such as those which regard the mode of occupation, or it must be such as per se, and not merely from collateral circumstances, affects the value of the land at the end of

a
the term." If a simple test is desired for ascertaining into which category a covenant falls, it is suggested that the proper inquiry should be whether the covenant affects either the landlord *qua* landlord or the tenant *qua* tenant. A covenant may very well have reference to the land, but, unless it is reasonably incidental to the relation of landlord and tenant, it cannot be said to touch and concern the land so as to be capable of running therewith or with the reversion.' (*Cheshire and Burn's* emphasis.)

b
The two points on which the parties divide are (a) whether as a matter purely of the construction of the clause it can be said to contemplate a payment by or to anyone other than the two original parties to the lease and (b) whether, assuming that the covenant is apt in its terms to impose an obligation between persons other than the two original parties, the obligation is one which, whatever the parties may have intended, touches and concerns the land so as to impose, through privity of estate, a financial obligation on
c
a successor in title to 'return' that which he has never had.

As regards the question of construction, the arguments are finely balanced. On any analysis the clause is, to say the least, infelicitously drawn. It seems tolerably clear that the parties can never have addressed themselves here specifically to the event of an assignment either of the reversion or of the lease even though cl 5 of the lease clearly shows that they entertained the possibility of the term being assigned. On the one hand,
d
it can be said that the initial references to the tenant and the landlord can refer only to the original parties and that there is no necessary context for reading the subsequent references in the clause as having any wider connotation, particularly having regard to the use of the word 'return' which hardly seems appropriate to a payment by a person who has never received money to a person who has never paid it. On the other hand, where, as here, the reversion changes hands, there seems little sense, if the covenant is a
e
purely personal one, in postponing repayment until the end of the lease. Moreover, as counsel for the tenant has forcefully pointed out, the reference to the 'return' being without prejudice to the landlord's right of action appears to contemplate that the 'landlord' obliged to return the payment will be the same person as the 'landlord' having then the right of action for damages for breach of covenant. If it were otherwise, then
f
the original tenant, if in breach of covenant, would be liable to an action for damages at the suit of the new landlord without any countervailing obligation on the new landlord to give credit for the deposit forfeited to the original landlord.

It is, indeed, doubtful whether it is possible to apply any totally rational construction to the clause without a wholesale implication of terms which the parties have not thought fit themselves to express. That in itself is not an easy exercise although it is not one from
g
which their Lordships would or could shrink if it were necessary to make the attempt. But it is not, in the final analysis, necessary for their Lordships to express any concluded view on the proper construction of the clause, because there remains in any event the critical question of whether, even assuming that, as a matter of construction of the clause, there can be deduced the intention by the original parties that the benefit and burden of the landlord's obligation for payment should pass without express assignment or novation
h
to and against successors in title, that is a result which, having regard to the nature and purpose of the obligation, is capable of achievement. And as regards this question, their Lordships have found themselves unable to agree with the decision reached by the Court of Appeal of Hong Kong.

In the High Court Mayo J, in holding that the landlord's obligation to 'return' the deposit was not one which ran with the reversion, relied on the decision of Uthwatt J in
j
Re Hunter's Lease, Giles v Hutchings [1942] 1 All ER 27, [1942] Ch 124 and on a decision of Grant J in the Ontario High Court, *Re Dollar Land Corp Ltd and Solomon* [1963] 2 OR 269, where the relevant facts were substantially indistinguishable from those in the instant case. In the former, the original lessor had covenanted to pay to the lessee a sum of £500 on the determination of the lease, but subject to a proviso that if he was unwilling to pay the covenanted sum the lessee would be entitled to remain in occupation and to call for a

new lease for five years subject to the same conditions as to determination and as to payment of £500. The question raised by the originating summons was whether, the *a* reversion having changed hands, the obligation to pay £500 on the determination of the lease was one which bound a transferee of the reversion. Although it was conceded that a bare covenant by the lessor to pay a sum of money on the determination of the term clearly did not touch and concern the land, it was argued that the obligation in that case was one which was part of an arrangement governing the continued occupation of the premises by the lessee and therefore passed to the transferee of the reversion. Uthwatt J *b* rejected that argument, quoting from the judgment of Channell B in *Thomas v Hayward* (1869) LR 4 Exch 311 at 312, cf [1861–73] All ER Rep 290 at 291:

> 'A covenant runs with the land only when it touches, that is, when its operation directly, and not merely collaterally, affects the thing demised.'

In the Canadian authority relied on by Mayo J, *Re Dollar Land Corp Ltd and Solomon*, *c* the clause in question provided, so far as material, that the lease was executed by the lessor on condition that the lessee would forthwith deposit with the lessor a sum of $165 'in order to assure the performance by the Lessee of all terms, conditions and provisions herein contained' (at 270). It further provided:

> '... under no condition shall the Lessee be entitled to ask for or demand the *d* return or a rebate of any part or all of the said sum of $165·00 until the expiration of the period provided for in this Lease ... and then only if the Lessee has fulfilled all the terms, conditions and provisions herein contained ...'

Grant J, after an extensive review of the English authorities, concluded thus (at 274):

> 'It would appear from the cases above quoted that such an arrangement as is set *e* forth in the guarantee clause of the lease ... is a personal obligation only between the immediate landlord and his lessee. It is not such an arrangement as deals with "the subject-matter of the lease". As Dollar Land received no part of the $165 paid by the tenant Solomon, I do not find any obligation on its part to now repay the same to Solomon.'

The Court of Appeal of Hong Kong declined to follow the Canadian authority, *f* observing that although the cases cited to Grant J did support the general proposition that a covenant by a party to a lease to pay a sum of money at the end of the term was personal to the original parties, he did not have (and nor did Mayo J in the High Court) the benefit of the citation of the two English cases which put a gloss on that general proposition. The first was *Mansel v Norton* (1883) 22 Ch D 769, a decision of the Court of *g* Appeal, where the question which fell to be decided was whether the responsibility for the performance of a covenant in the lease of a farm for the purchase by the lessor of the lessee's tenant right at valuation on the expiration of the term fell on the landlord's estate or on the devisee under his will who had entered into possession. It was held that the landlord's covenant was one which passed with the reversion and that the burden therefore fell on the devisee in possession. The second case relied on by the Court of *h* Appeal in the instant case was a decision of Wright J in *Lord Howard de Walden v Barber* (1903) 19 TLR 183, which was concerned with a tenant's covenant not to do or suffer anything which should be, or tend, to the annoyance, nuisance or damage of the person or persons for the time being entitled in reversion. The lease contained a specific provision that if the premises should at any time during the term be used as a brothel or disorderly house the tenant should pay to the landlord a sum of £800 by way of *j* liquidated damages. The question in issue was whether an assignee of the term who had permitted the premises to be used as a brothel was liable to pay the sum of £800. The judgment is reported shortly and only in oratio obliqua. The report states (at 184):

> 'It was a strong thing to hold that a covenant to pay damages could run with the land. It seemed to him that the only way to regard it was that the covenant was

inserted for the express purpose of binding the assignee. It was not a separate provision, but an annex to the general covenant. If it was treated as a buttress to the general covenant there was no objection to treating it as running with the land . . .'

There is, of course, no doubt that the mere fact that a covenant, whether on the part of the landlord or of a tenant, involves an obligation to pay a liquidated sum of money does not of itself demonstrate that the covenant is not one which touches and concerns the land but, with respect to the Court of Appeal, their Lordships do not find either of these two cases of great assistance in the solution of the question raised by this appeal. The covenant in *Mansel v Norton* 22 Ch D 769 was, as both Jessel MR and Lindley LJ observed, a covenant to purchase the tenant right of cultivation. In his judgment Jessel MR said (at 771–772):

'Before the present state of agricultural depression a new tenant could always be found who came in and paid the outgoing tenant, and the landlord was not called upon to pay. The landlord, however, was the person liable to the outgoing tenant, and in the view of the law he paid the outgoing tenant and received the amount back from the incoming tenant.'

The liability, he observed, was 'a liability in respect of the cultivation of the land' (at 772). As such it was plainly a covenant which directly affected the value and quality of the land. Similarly, in *Lord Howard de Walden v Barber* 19 TLR 183 the liability to pay damages for breach of the covenant not to cause damage to the reversion was clearly and on any analysis a covenant which touched and concerned the land. The covenant to pay a liquidated sum for a breach of a particular nature was no more than the quantification of the damage and was, quoad that particular type of breach, not so much a buttress for the covenant but part and parcel of the covenant itself.

The tenant argues, however, that inasmuch as the tenant's obligation to pay over the deposit on the execution of the lease was an obligation to secure the performance of covenants which touched and concerned the land, it was an obligation inextricably associated with covenants whose benefit and burden would pass with the reversion in the lease respectively. The landlord's obligation to repay if those covenants are observed is, it is argued, inseparable from that associated obligation and must therefore possess the same characteristics as the covenants whose performance is secured by the associated obligation. To put it another way the obligation to pay a deposit is an obligation of the tenant assumed by him qua tenant and it follows that the correlative obligation of the landlord is an obligation assumed by him qua landlord. This argument is reflected in the judgment of McMullin V-P, in the Court of Appeal, who observed:

'The plain fact is that the provisions of clause 4(h) are so clearly intended to encourage compliance with the very many covenants enjoining the lessee to make proper use of the land and not to cause a diminution in its value that it would be wholly unrealistic to regard it as being otherwise than inextricably bound up with those undertakings generally.'

That the original tenant's obligation to make the deposit is 'bound up' with his obligation to perform the tenant's covenants in the lease is undeniable, but the former is, of course, a once-for-all contractual obligation between the original parties as regards which no question of transfer with the term or with the reversion can arise. The sum deposited is to be paid on or before the execution of the lease. What this appeal is concerned with, however, is only the landlord's obligation to repay once the lease has expired without breach of covenant, there being neither any obligation on the original landlord to pay over the amount of the deposit to an assignee of the reversion nor any obligation on the original tenant to assign to an assignee of the term his contractual right to receive back the amount of the deposit when and if the condition for its repayment is fulfilled. It is bound up with the tenant's covenant only, as it were, at one remove, as being an obligation correlative to a contractual obligation which is itself connected with

the performance of covenants touching and concerning the land. The expression
'inextricably bound' appears to derive from the speech of Lord Atkin in *Moss' Empires Ltd* a
v Olympia (Liverpool) Ltd [1939] 3 All ER 460, [1939] AC 544, a case strongly relied on by
the tenant. The question in that case arose out of a lease which contained a series of
repairing and decorating covenants on the part of the tenant numbered (iv) to (viii)
inclusive. The covenant numbered (vii) obliged the tenant in each year of the term to
expend at least £500 on the performance of the covenants to repair and decorate for
which receipts were to be produced to the lessor, any shortfall in any year in the amount b
expended to be paid to the lessor and any excess in expenditure over the amount of £500
in any year to be treated pro tanto as a satisfaction of the liability for future years. An
assignee of the lease having failed to expend the full sum of £500 in certain years, the
question arose whether the obligation was one which bound the assignee as one touching
and concerning the land or whether it was merely a collateral covenant binding only as
between the original parties. Lord Atkin observed ([1939] 3 All ER 460 at 463, [1939] c
AC 544 at 551):

> '... this is not a bare obligation to pay money which does not touch the thing
> demised. On the contrary, the performance of the repairing covenants and the
> obligations under subcl. (vii) are so inextricably bound together that it would be
> impossible to sever subcl. (vii) and treat it as a collateral promise to pay money. The d
> relevant clauses read as a whole provide a scheme whereby, if things work smoothly,
> the obligation of the tenant over the term is limited to £500 per annum, less than
> one-sixth of the total rent, while the lessor is provided with sums which, if he
> chooses, he may apply towards meeting the obligation which he has assumed of
> performing structural repairs. In my opinion, the clause in question closely touches
> the thing demised, and runs with the land.' e

Similarly, Lord Porter said ([1939] 3 All ER 460 at 469, [1939] AC 544 at 560):

> 'This is not a bare or mere covenant to pay £500, or even to pay the difference
> between the sum spent and proved and £500. It is part of a number of covenants
> whereby the mutual obligations of landlord and tenant in repairing and redecorating
> the premises are fulfilled, and is inextricably bound up with them.' f

On the facts of that case the decision is scarcely a surprising one, for the obligation was to
expend not less than the stipulated sum on the preservation of the estate in the proper
performance of the repairing covenants in the lease, an obligation clearly affecting the
value of the lessor's estate and so directly touching and concerning the thing demised.
That was, however, a very different case from the present and their Lordships are not g
persuaded that it is, or was ever intended to be, authority for the proposition that every
covenant which is related, however obliquely, to some other obligation which touches
and concerns the land necessarily takes on from that very relationship, the same character
as regards transmissibility to or against successors in title. To say that the obligation to
'return' the amount of the deposit is 'inextricably bound up with' covenants which touch
and concern the land in the sense in which the expression was used by McMullin V-P in h
the instant case, i e that, in order to determine whether or not the obligation to pay could
have arisen against anyone, it would be necessary to survey the other covenants, does not,
in their Lordships' view, answer the critical question of whether it itself touches and
concerns the land. It certainly does not per se affect the nature, quality or value of the
land either during or at the end of the term. It does not per se affect the mode of using
or enjoying that which is demised. And to ask whether it affects the landlord qua j
landlord or the tenant qua tenant is an exercise which begs the question. It does so only
if it runs with the reversion or with the land respectively. There is not, on any conceivable
construction of the clause, anything which either divests the original tenant of his
contractual right to receive back after assignment the deposit which he has paid or which
entitles an assignee from him to claim the benefit of the sum to the exclusion of his

assignor; and, plainly, the money cannot be repaid more than once. Equally, there is not
on any conceivable construction anything in the clause which entitles the assignee of the
reversion to take over from his assignor the benefit of the sum deposited or which obliges
the assignee, in enforcing the covenants against the tenant for the time being, to give for
money which he himself has never received and to which he has no claim. Whilst it is
true that the deposit is paid to the original payee because it is security for the performance
of contractual obligations assumed throughout the term by the payer and because the
payee is the party with whom the contract is entered into, it is, in their Lordships' view,
more realistic to regard the obligation as one entered into with the landlord qua payee
rather than qua landlord. By demanding and receiving this security, he assumes the
obligation of any mortgagee to repay on the stipulated condition and that obligation
remains, as between himself and the original payer, throughout the period of the lease,
even though neither party may, when the condition is fulfilled, have any further interest
in the land demised. The nature of the obligation is simply that of an obligation to repay
money which has been received and it is neither necessary nor logical, simply because
the conditions of repayment relate to the performance of covenants in a lease, that the
transfer of the reversion should create in the transferee an additional and coextensive
obligation to pay money which he has never received and in which he never had any
interest or that the assignment of the term should vest in the assignee the right to receive
a sum which he has never paid.

Their Lordships consider that *Re Dollar Land Corp Ltd and Solomon* [1963] 2 OR 269
was rightly decided. In all material respects it is indistinguishable from the instant case.
They will accordingly humbly advise Her Majesty that the appeal should be allowed and
that the order of Mayo J in the High Court dismissing the tenant's action with costs
should be restored. The tenant must pay the bank's costs before their Lordships' Board
and in the Court of Appeal.

Appeal allowed.

Solicitors: *Clifford-Turner* (for the bank); *Turner Kenneth Brown* (for the tenant).

Mary Rose Plummer   Barrister.

Lloyd and others v McMahon

COURT OF APPEAL, CIVIL DIVISION
LAWTON, DILLON AND WOOLF LJJ
9, 10, 14, 15, 16, 17, 18, 21, 22, 31 JULY 1986

HOUSE OF LORDS
LORD KEITH OF KINKEL, LORD BRIDGE OF HARWICH, LORD BRANDON OF OAKBROOK, LORD
TEMPLEMAN AND LORD GRIFFITHS
26, 27, 28, 29 JANUARY, 2, 3 FEBRUARY, 12 MARCH 1987

Local government – Audit – Surcharge – Auditor's inquiry – Procedure – Whether auditor required to invite oral representations before issuing certificate of surcharge – Whether auditor acting unfairly in inviting written representations only – Whether unfairness by auditor curable on appeal – Whether court can investigate merits and itself give certificate of surcharge – Local Government Finance Act 1982, s 20(1)(3)(b).

The appellants formed the majority group of a city council. In the hope of persuading the government to provide a larger grant to the city than had been announced, the appellants refused, in February 1985, to arrange a meeting of the council to set a rate for the year 1985–86. On 10 April and 21 May the district auditor warned the council that failure to set a rate would be a clear breach of duty. The council failed to set a rate until 14 June. On 26 June the district auditor notified the appellants that he proposed to consider whether he should certify under s 20(1)[a] of the Local Government Finance Act 1982 that the sum of £106,103 was due from the appellants on the ground that the loss of that sum by the council had been caused by their wilful default in preventing the council from setting a rate until 14 June. Documents enclosed with the notice identified (i) specific losses resulting from the delay in setting a rate, and (ii) the appellants as councillors who by their voting or absences might have been guilty of wilful misconduct causing the loss. The notice further stated that they could make written representations to the district auditor before he reached a decision. On July 19 the appellants made a collective and detailed response in writing. None of the appellants requested an oral hearing. On September 6 the district auditor issued a certificate under s 20(1) that the sum of £106,103 was due from the appellants. The appellants appealed to the Divisional Court against the making of the certificate but that court dismissed their appeal and that decision was affirmed by the Court of Appeal. The appellants appealed to the House of Lords, contending that the district auditor's decision to issue the certificate was vitiated by his failure to offer the appellants an oral hearing. At the hearing of the appeal the issue also arose whether if the district auditor had acted unfairly the court could decide for itself whether a certificate should be issued.

Held – A district auditor who proposed to issue a certificate under s 20(1) of the 1982 Act to the effect that members of a local authority had been guilty of wilful misconduct which had caused the authority to incur a loss was required to act fairly and to give the affected members an opportunity to make representations before issuing the certificate, but he was not obliged in every case to offer the affected members the opportunity of making oral representations. Since the district auditor had given the appellants adequate notice of the case they had to meet and had given them adequate opportunity to make representations, which opportunity they had taken up, he had not acted unfairly before issuing the certificate. The appeal would therefore be dismissed (see p 1156 c to h, p 1157 f, p 1161 d e, p 1164 d to f, p 1165 e f, p 1166 g h, p 1170 c to g and p 1172 c, post).

Per curiam. Where a district auditor's decision to issue a certificate under s 20(1) is vitiated by unfairness the court can investigate the merits and decide for itself whether a

---

a Section 20, so far as material, is set out at p 1162 d to h, post

a certificate of wilful misconduct should be issued, under the power conferred on the court by s 20(3) to 'give any certificate which the auditor could have given' (see p 1157 *a* to *e*, p 1166 *c d f h*, p 1171 *f g j* to p 1172 *b d*, post).

Notes

For district auditors' duties, see 28 Halsbury's Laws (4th edn) paras 1306, and for cases on the subject, see 33 Digest (Reissue) 36–42, *108–129*.

b   For the Local Government Finance Act 1982, s 20, see 25 Halsbury's Statutes (4th edn) 677.

Cases referred to in judgments and opinions

Asher v Lacey [1973] 3 All ER 1008, [1973] 1 WLR 1412, DC.
Asher v Secretary of State for the Environment [1974] 2 All ER 156, [1974] Ch 208, [1974] 2 WLR 466, CA.
c Bushell v Secretary of State for the Environment [1980] 2 All ER 608, [1981] AC 75, [1980] 3 WLR 22, HL.
Calvin v Carr [1979] 2 All ER 440, [1980] AC 574, [1979] 2 WLR 755, PC.
Council of Civil Service Unions v Minister for the Civil Service [1984] 3 All ER 935, [1985] AC 374, [1984] 3 WLR 1174, HL.
d Denton v Auckland City [1969] NZLR 256, NZ SC.
George v Secretary of State for the Environment (1979) 38 P & CR 609, CA.
Graham v Teesdale (1981) 81 LGR 117.
Hornal v Neuberger Products Ltd [1956] 3 All ER 970, [1957] 1 QB 247, [1956] 3 WLR 1034, CA.
Jeffs v New Zealand Dairy Production and Marketing Board [1966] 2 All ER 863, [1967] 1 *e* AC 551, [1967] 2 WLR 136, PC.
King v University of Saskatchewan [1969] SCR 678, Can SC.
Leary v National Union of Vehicle Builders [1970] 2 All ER 713, [1971] Ch 34, [1970] 3 WLR 434.
Malloch v Aberdeen Corp [1971] 2 All ER 1278, [1971] 1 WLR 1578, HL.
O'Reilly v Mackman [1982] 3 All ER 1124, [1983] 2 AC 237, [1982] 3 WLR 1096, HL.
f R v Hackney London BC, ex p Fleming [1986] RVR 182.
R v Hull Prison Board of Visitors, ex p St Germain (No 2) [1979] 3 All ER 545, [1979] 1 WLR 1401, DC.
R v Local Government Board, ex p Arlidge [1914] 1 KB 160, CA; rvsd [1915] AC 120, [1914–15] All ER Rep 1, HL.
R v Roberts [1908] 1 KB 407, CA.
g R v Roberts, ex p Scurr [1924] 2 KB 695, CA; rvsd sub nom Roberts v Hopwood [1925] AC 578, [1925] All ER Rep 24, HL.
Reid v Rowley [1977] 2 NZLR 472, NZ CA.
Rothnie v Dearne UDC (1951) 50 LGR 123, DC.
Smith v Skinner [1986] RVR 45.
Smith & Fawcett Ltd, Re [1942] 1 All ER 542, [1942] Ch 304, CA.
h Twist v Randwick Municipal Council (1976) 12 ALR 379 Aust HC.
White v Kuzych [1951] 2 All ER 435, [1951] AC 585, PC.
Wiseman v Borneman [1969] 3 All ER 275, [1971] AC 297, [1969] 3 WLR 706, HL.

Cases also cited

Associated Provincial Picture Houses Ltd v Wednesbury Corp [1947] 2 All ER 680, [1948] 1 *j* KB 223, CA.
Bromley London BC v Greater London Council [1982] 1 All ER 129, [1983] 1 AC 768, CA and HL.
Builders Licensing Board (NSW) v Sperway Constructions (Sydney) Pty Ltd (1976) 51 ALJR 260, Aust HC.
Cinnamond v British Airports Authority [1980] 2 All ER 368, [1980] 1 WLR 582, CA.
Coltman v Wembley BC (District Auditor) (1962) 60 LGR 247.

District Auditor's Decision, Re [1947] 2 All ER 47, sub nom *Dickson v Hurle-Hobbs (District Auditor)* [1947] KB 879, DC; *affd* sub nom *Re Dickson* [1948] 1 All ER 713, [1948] 2 KB 95, CA.

Glynn v Keele University [1971] 2 All ER 89, [1971] 1 WLR 487.

Indian Zoedone Co, Re (1884) 26 Ch D 70, CA.

Jones v National Coal Board [1957] 2 All ER 155, [1957] 2 QB 55, CA.

Lamb v Camden London BC [1981] 2 All ER 408, [1981] QB 625, CA.

London and Clydesdale Estates Ltd v Aberdeen DC [1979] 3 All ER 876, [1980] 1 WLR 182, HL.

Love v Porirua City Council [1984] 2 NZLR 308, NZ CA.

Maxwell v Dept of Trade and Industry [1974] 2 All ER 122, [1974] QB 523, CA.

Maynard v Osmond [1977] 1 All ER 64, [1977] QB 240, CA.

Pentecost v London District Auditor [1951] 2 All ER 330, [1951] 2 KB 759.

Pergamon Press Ltd, Re [1970] 3 All ER 535, [1971] 1 Ch 388, CA.

Pickwell v Camden London BC [1983] 1 All ER 602, [1983] QB 962, DC.

Powell v Streatham Manor Nursing Home [1935] AC 243, [1935] All ER Rep 58, HL.

Puhlhofer v Hillingdon London BC [1986] 1 All ER 467, [1986] AC 484, HL.

QT Discount Food Stores Ltd v Warley General Comrs [1982] STC 40.

R v Ghosh [1982] 2 All ER 689, [1982] QB 1053, CA.

R v Brent London BC, ex p Gunning (1985) Times, 30 April.

R v Liverpool City Council, ex p Ferguson, R v Liverpool City Council, ex p Grantham (1985) Times, 20 November, DC.

R v Secretary of State for the Environment, ex p Brent London BC [1983] 3 All ER 321, [1982] QB 593, DC.

R v Secretary of State for Transport, ex p Gwent City Council [1987] 1 All ER 161, CA.

Raymond v Honey [1982] 1 All ER 756, [1983] 1 AC 1, HL.

Ridge v Baldwin [1963] 2 All ER 66, [1964] AC 40, HL.

Taylor v Munrow [1960] 1 All ER 455, [1960] 1 WLR 151, DC.

Appeal

David John Lloyd and 46 others, all being members of Liverpool City Council, appealed against the decision of the Divisional Court of the Queen's Bench Division (Glidewell LJ, Caulfield and Russell JJ) (sub nom *Gladden v McMahon* [1986] RVR 45) on 5 March 1986 dismissing appeals by the appellants against a certificate issued on 6 September 1985 and served on them by the respondent, Thomas Irving McMahon, the district auditor for the Chester district, pursuant to s 20(1) of the Local Government Finance Act 1982, certifying that a surcharge of £106,103 was due from them jointly and severally, being the amount of a loss caused by their wilful default in deferring the making of the rate for the council for the year 1985–86 until 14 June 1985. The facts are set out in the judgment of Lawton LJ.

Louis Blom-Cooper QC, Beverley Lang and *Heather Williams* for the appellants.
Anthony Hidden QC and *Mark Lowe* for the district auditor.
Charles Cross for the council.

Cur adv vult

31 July. The following judgments were delivered.

LAWTON LJ. This is an appeal by 47 councillors of Liverpool City Council, all being members of the majority party on that council, against the judgment of the Divisional Court (Glidewell LJ, Caulfield and Russell JJ) ([1986] RVR 45) whereby it was adjudged that a certificate dated 6 September 1985 issued by the respondent district auditor pursuant to s 20(1) of the Local Government Finance Act 1982 should take effect in law.

The issues

a   The appeal raises three issues. First, did the district auditor act fairly in issuing the certificate? Second, if he did not, did the appellants' appeal to the Divisional Court cure any unfairness? Third, if any unfairness was cured, did the facts prove that the appellants, and each of them, had been guilty of wilful misconduct.

b   *The background to the appeal*

Ever since 1979 central government has wanted to curb local government expenditure. Parliament has passed three Acts which has enabled it to take action towards this end ie the Local Government Planning and Land Act 1980, the Local Government Finance Act 1982 and the Rates Act 1984. The way in which these Acts work is set out in the judgment of Glidewell LJ and need not be repeated in this judgment.

c   Central government's policy of curbing local government expenditure has been opposed by many councillors all over the country, and in particular it has been opposed by the majority of the councillors on the Liverpool City Council. The main grounds of opposition have been that central government was encroaching on the independence of local authorities and that it was preventing them from meeting what they considered to be the needs of their areas. The appellants were, of course, entitled to take such steps as

d   they wished in order to persuade central government to change its policy. What they were not entitled to do was to allow their political efforts in this respect to interfere with or impede the performance of their statutory duties, which included a duty to make a rate without unreasonable delay. The district auditor alleges that for the financial year beginning 1 April 1985 they unlawfully delayed making a rate, with the result that they had, by their wilful misconduct in that respect, caused the city council to incur a loss of

e   £106,103.

In the years before 1984 the city council had normally made a rate at the end of March or the beginning of April so that rate demands could go out in April. Delays in making rates are likely to cause loss to local authorities. There may be cash flow problems and a need to borrow money on the short-term money market.

f   In the spring of 1984 the majority on the city council were of the opinion that central government, under the spending curbs imposed by the three Acts to which I have referred, had deprived Liverpool of large sums and that the rates ought not to be increased to cover the shortfall. On 26 March 1984 the performance review and financial control sub-committee (which was the sub-committee primarily concerned with rate making), under the chairmanship of the appellant, Mr Byrne, proposed that for the

g   rating year starting on 1 April 1984 there should only be a rate increase of 9% notwithstanding that such an increase would not provide for the estimated total expenditure which would be incurred during the coming rating year. A lawful rate would have to provide for such expenditure and it was the duty of the appellants to see that such a rate was made: see s 2 of the General Rate Act 1967, as amended. The chief executive, the city solicitor and the city treasurer of the council advised the sub-

h   committee that this proposal, if implemented, would produce an unlawful rate. That advice was minuted and ignored by the sub-committee, who sent the resolution forward to the city council. The city council considered it at a meeting held on 29 March 1984. It was again advised to the same effect as the sub-committee had been. Once again the advice was minuted and ignored. The resolution was passed. It was not put into effect because on 13 April 1984 negotiations started between the city council and the Secretary

j   of State for the Environment with the object of getting more central funds made available to cover the shortfall in rates. The city council did get more money from central government and was able to make a lawful rate on 11 July 1984. The minutes and reports circulated to all members of the city council between March and 11 July 1984 show that they were told in clear terms that if they delayed making a lawful rate or made an unlawful one they would not be performing their statutory duty and would be likely to cause a loss to the city council which might lead to their being surcharged for wilful misconduct. The inference to be drawn from what happened in the summer of 1984 *a* (and it is a strong one) is that the majority on the council were using the rate-making process to threaten central government with financial chaos in Liverpool if the shortfall on rates was not made good from central funds. The delay in making a rate in 1984 almost certainly caused some loss to the city council, but the then district auditor took no action against anyone under s 20(1) of the 1982 Act.

The history of the making of a rate for the financial year beginning 1 April 1984 is of *b* importance in this case for three reasons. First, the appellants' case has been that the city council's success in 1984 in persuading the Secretary of State to make more money available from central government funds led them to think that they could repeat that success for the financial year beginning 1 April 1985. The needs which the Secretary of State in 1984 had recognised as needing alleviation still had to be met in 1985. Second, the district auditor's omission to take any action over the delay in making a rate in 1984 *c* led them to think, at least until 16 April 1985, that the making of a rate could be delayed, and after 16 April that it could be delayed until 20 June. 16 April is an important date because on that day Woolf J delivered a judgment in *R v Hackney London BC, ex p Fleming* [1986] RVR 182. It got considerable publicity. It seems to me likely that many members of the city council would, about this date, have learnt something of what had been decided. The fact that judgment was going to be given on 16 April 1985 was reported to *d* the performance review and financial control sub-committee by the city solicitor on that very day. Woolf J adjudged that for a local authority not to make a rate by the beginning of the rating year had obvious disadvantages of a financial nature which increased as time went by. The members of the city council had been told this by the city solicitor in 1984. The law, however, said Woolf J, did not specify by what date a rate had to be made. He *e* went on as follows (at 184):

'No generally applicable period can be laid down as to by when the rate must in any event be made so that an authority can be said to be in breach of its duty by that date. The facts of each case must be examined. However, in the absence of a reasonable explanation, not to make a rate by the beginning of a financial year or within a reasonable time thereafter—I have in mind weeks rather than months— *f* would *prima facie* be unreasonable and, therefore, in breach of duty.'

The making of the 1985–86 rate

In November 1984 the district auditor perceived that the city council was likely to have difficulty in making a lawful rate for 1985–86 because the performance review and financial control sub-committee had forecast that by 31 March 1985 expenditure would *g* exceed the budget provision and a substantial deficiency would arise. He issued a report to the city council pursuant to s 15(3) of the 1982 Act. It contained the following warning:

'It is opportune for me to remind the Council that they have a duty to levy a rate sufficient to provide for their estimated total expenditure to be incurred during the *h* period covered by the rate together with such amount as is sufficient to cover expenditure previously incurred. The Council does not now have the benefit of being able to levy supplementary rates to restore any shortfall in the original rate levy and it is therefore important that budget predictions are accurate and achievable, if a deficit which will affect the level of the subsequent year's rate is to be avoided ... A number of opportunities to secure better value for money which may assist *j* the Council in the longer term have been identified in audit work during the current year. These have been discussed with your officers and will shortly be discussed with members. However, some four months only of the current financial year remain in which the Council can act to contain expenditure within the original budget. Unless a determined effort is made now to achieve the budget intentions a for the current year it is clear that the rate making process in the coming year will commence with the Council in a seriously disadvantaged position. They are asked to review as a matter of urgency their achievements against budget expectations and to take corrective action.'

b Despite that warning not much seems to have been done before 16 April 1985. During the early months of 1985 financial reviews were carried out from time to time and the education and social services committees did prepare budgets. At council meetings when budget matters were discussed the majority on the council seem to have had their thinking dominated by what they considered to have been the mandates on which they had been elected. On occasions resolutions were proposed by members of the minority on the city council that progress should be made with the rate-making procedure. These resolutions were always defeated. During the early part of 1985 the city council had been c associated with a group of local authorities who were trying to put political pressure on central government to change its policy about local government expenditure and to make more money available from central funds for local needs. On 7 March 1985, acting in concert with other local authorities, the city council passed a resolution which was nothing more than a political manifesto expressed in intemperate language. Resolutions in the same kind of terms had been passed in 1984 and earlier in 1985. The first, fourth d and fifth paragraphs of this resolution were as follows:

'(i) this Council re-endorses the policies upon which the people of Liverpool elected the Labour Party to power, viz:—(a) to defend existing City Council jobs and services; (b) to create additional jobs and improve services; (c) to build houses for rent; (d) to end the threat of privatisation of City Council services; and (e) to e refuse to impose increases in Rates, Rents and Charges to compensate for Government cuts in Grants.

(iv) this Council requires a budget of £265·4 million but, with a target of only £222·1 million—representing another £90 million stolen from the City in grant penalty—this Council considers it will be impossible to make a rate. The Council therefore calls upon the Secretary of State to—(a) remove the meaningless and f arbitrary targets; (b) remove the deliberately punitive penalties; (c) establish a realistic level of Rate Support Grant—the minimum being that which was offered in 1979; and (d) establish a level of Housing Environmental and Partnership allocations commensurate with the needs of Liverpool; and

(v) in particular, this Council demands the return of resources stolen by the Tory Government since 1979, viz:—(a) £170 million in Rate Support Grants; (b) £24 g million from Further Education; (c) £69 million in Housing Subsidy; and (d) £96 million in the Housing Investment Programme.'

Those who voted for this resolution have only themselves to blame if it was construed as a threat to hold up rate-making in order to put pressure on central government.

h On 16 April 1985 there was a meeting of the performance review and financial control sub-committee. It had before it a joint report of the chief executive, city solicitor and city treasurer which set out what were the statutory duties of the city council in relation to rate-making and what were likely to be the consequences of making a substantially insufficient rate or failing to make one. The sub-committee also had before it a budget report of the city treasurer and summaries of the committees' income and expenditure and the detailed summaries of the expenditure and income of the education and social j services committees. Nothing effective was done at this meeting to carry the rate-making procedure forward. Members of the minority party on the sub-committee moved a number of resolutions directed to the need to make progress with rate-making. All were defeated, as was a resolution that all members of the city council should be sent a report by the city solicitor as to the significance for the city council of Woolf J's judgment in *R v Hackney London BC, ex p Fleming* which was expected to be delivered that day. No

effective action towards rate-making was taken between 16 April 1985 and 21 May 1985
when the district auditor who, on 1 May 1985 had succeeded his predecessor as district   *a*
auditor, wrote to all the members of the city council drawing their attention to the
serious consequences to them which would follow 'from the continued delay in making
a rate sufficient for the Council's requirements for the current financial year ending 31
March 1986'. He suggested that a rate had to be made before the end of May 1985. This
letter had effect. Committees did produce budgets before the end of May 1985. No
committee met to consider what rate would be necessary to provide for the city council's   *b*
requirements. There were, however, informal discussions between the city treasurer and
the chairman of the performance review and financial control sub-committee as to what
the rate should be. At a special meeting of the city council held on 14 June 1985 it was
resolved that the rate should be increased by 9%. This increase did not begin to be
sufficient for the city council's requirements. The estimated expenditure for 1985–86
was £265m. A deficit of £5·938m had to be brought forward, making a total estimated   *c*
expenditure of £270·938m. With an increase of 9% the total rate was estimated to bring
in £125·031m which, after adjustments, left a shortfall of £117m. This was clearly an
unlawful rate. No explanation has ever been given as to why an increase of 9% was agreed
on.

The intervention of the district auditor   *d*
    The rate-making activities of the city council were much publicised. The Audit
Commission, pursuant to s 22 of the 1982 Act, directed the district auditor to hold an
extraordinary audit of the city council's accounts for the financial year commencing on 1
April 1985 in so far as they related to the failure to make a rate or the delay in the making
of a rate for that financial year. As a result of what he found out when carrying out the
audit it seemed to him that a loss to the city council might have been caused by the   *e*
wilful misconduct of those members of the majority on the city council who, between
January and June 1985, had voted for a number of resolutions before the city council
which had held up rate-making during 1985. Not all members of the majority party had
so voted. He decided to exercise his powers under s 20(1) of the 1982 Act in order to
recoup this loss from those who had caused it. He sent each member of the city council
whom he suspected of causing a loss a notice dated 26 June 1985, the relevant parts of   *f*
which are as follows:

        'NOTICE is given that at the extraordinary audit of the accounts of the Liverpool
    City Council for the year commencing 1 April 1985 I have to consider in pursuance
    of my duty under Section 20(1) of the Local Government Finance Act 1982 whether
    I should certify the sum of £106,103, or any other sum, consequent upon the failure   *g*
    to make a rate or the delay in the making of the same for that financial year as due
    from you on the ground that a loss of such sum has been incurred or deficiency
    caused by your wilful misconduct. NOTICE is also given that you may make
    representations in writing to me before I reach a decision. Any such representations
    must reach me by no later than 19 July 1985. I enclose a note of the matters to
    which I have had regard in deciding to issue this NOTICE.'   *h*

The accompanying note set out what he was alleging, namely that by delaying the
making of a rate without lawful justification each of the recipients of the notice had acted
in breach of statutory duty and that the breaches had caused two readily assessable losses
which he identified in an appendix. He also identified the documents, mostly minutes
and reports, which he thought revealed the breaches of statutory duty.   *j*
    The appellants decided that they would put before the district auditor a joint answer
to the allegations made against them. This they did. There were advantages for them in
putting forward a joint answer. It could be carefully drafted and there would be no
danger of individuals contradicting one another. The answer was contained in a typed
document on foolscap paper consisting of 29 pages, together with a number of appendices.

One of them set out the text of a letter dated 29 June 1984 which the Secretary of State
a had written to the leader of the city council. The last paragraph of that letter was as
follows:

> 'Against that background, and bearing in mind the constraints set out in the two
> preceding paragraphs of this letter, I can give you an assurance that I will do my
> very best to ensure that allocations to Liverpool next year under the Housing
b > Investment Programme and the Urban Programme, taken together, will enable the
> council to make positive progress in dealing with the City's severe needs, having
> regard to the scale of your capital commitments and the resources (including
> possible proceeds of sales of Council dwellings and freeholds) available to you.'

No request was made to the district auditor for him to hear any of the appellants or for
them to be legally represented.
c   On 6 September 1985 the district auditor made a report to the city council pursuant to
his duties under s 15(3) of the 1982 Act. He stated that he had considered the
representation which he had received and had concluded that he had a duty under s 20
to certify that a sum of £106,103 was due from 49 members of the city council jointly
and severally, being the amount of a loss incurred or deficiency caused by their wilful
misconduct. Of the 49 members so certified, two have since died, leaving 47 councillors
d before this court. The district auditor's way of exercising his powers under s 20 was said
by the appellants to be unfair. Whether it was so necessitates this court considering what
are the powers, duties and practices of district auditors.

The powers, duties and practices of district auditors
     The office of district auditor was created by the Poor Law Amendment Act 1844 (s 32).
e Before then justices, either in petty or quarter sessions, had dealt with problems relating
to the collection and administration of the poor rate. The district auditor was given
powers to deal with illegality and misconduct in relation to the collection and
administration of the poor rate and to 'charge' persons in default. The Poor Law Audit
Act 1848 specified what procedure the district auditor was to follow when exercising his
charging jurisdiction. He was required, when he found possible cause to 'surcharge' any
f person, to give him notice in writing of a right to attend to 'show cause against' the
making of a surcharge. After the hearing the district auditor was to determine the matter
according to the 'Law and Justice of the Case': see s 8. By the Public Health Act 1848 the
district auditor's jurisdiction was extended to the supervision of rates collected under that
Act; but in it there was no provision similar to s 8. Between 1848 and 1929, when by the
Local Government Act of that year great changes were made in the scheme for poor
g relief, the district auditor exercised in parallel two jurisdictions over rate making. In
respect of one, the poor rate, he had been under a statutory obligation to offer oral
hearings to those whom he was minded to surcharge; in respect of other rates he was not
under any such obligation. The Poor Law Audit Act 1848 had been largely repealed by
the Poor Law Act 1927; but s 8 of the 1848 Act had been replaced by s 153 of the 1927
h Act. In practice district auditors seem to have offered all suspects an oral hearing,
whatever the nature of the rate: see A Carson Roberts *District Audit* (1919) vol 1 (Audit
Law and Audit Work) p 112:

> 'The principle laid down in Sec 8 of the Poor Law Audit Act, 1848, is one which
> should be observed most punctiliously in every case where the Auditor has to make
> any decision which involves the purse or character of any person who is not present
j > at the audit. This principle should be followed in all cases and not only in poor law
> audits (Memo. of 1909, par. 75).'

The Local Government Act 1933 amended the Local Government Act 1929 and
contained detailed provisions relating to the powers and duties of district auditors. The
nineteenth century concept that an audit was a public proceeding which any local

government elector could attend still continued: see s 226(1). Such an elector could object to the accounts before the district auditor. It is clear from the enabling section, *a* s 226(1), that he was entitled to be present or to be represented. Section 228, which dealt with surcharging any person 'by whose negligence or misconduct' the loss had been incurred or a deficiency had been caused contained no procedural directions as to how the district auditor was to discharge his duty; but it seems to have been accepted that he had to act judicially. In order to do so in practice district auditors offered oral hearings: see C R H Hurle-Hobbs *The Law Relating to District Audit* (1949) p 100, where there is a *b* footnote in these terms:

> 'In practice, district auditors invariably afford persons likely to be affected by their decisions an opportunity of being heard at audit.'

From the context and certain forms which he suggested could be used, it is clear that by 'heard' he meant heard orally.   *c*

The Local Government Act 1933 was repealed by the Local Government Act 1972 which effectively came into force on 1 April 1974. It made some changes in relation to the law governing the powers and duties of district auditors. Those relating to objectors were substantial; but they continued to have a right to attend before the district auditor: see s 159. The power to surcharge was limited to a loss incurred or deficiency caused by 'wilful' misconduct. Save for this charge and the abandonment of the concept that audits *d* were public proceedings, the 1972 Act followed the provisions of the 1933 Act. In Reginald Jones *Local Government Audit Law* (1981) pp 277–278 it is stated:

> 'It would seem in principle that in order to give a person the fullest rights to answer a case against him it is necessary to hold an oral hearing so that witnesses may be seen and questioned . . . However, some statutory tribunals have power to *e* dispense with oral hearings and in other instances where matters have required judicial consideration it has been held that it is not contrary to justice to determine them on written communications only . . . District audit practice has generally been to hold oral hearings . . . But if all parties are agreeable to a matter being decided on the basis of written representations possibly after initial attendance by an objector . . . it seems, on the basis of the precedents cited above, that this may be admissible, *f* provided that all parties are given a fair opportunity to comment on statements adverse to them.'

Between January 1974 and 1980 14 certificates were issued by district auditors for wilful misconduct surcharges. In all but one of these cases an oral hearing was offered and in 11 of them the offer was accepted. All these cases, however, involved only one person. The case in which no oral hearing was offered related to a man who had been *g* convicted and sent to prison for what was alleged to be his wilful misconduct. The history of the office and practices of district auditors establishes that certainly from about 1909 at least until 1982 it was the normal, perhaps invariable, practice for district auditors to offer oral hearings. The reported cases relating to surcharging, starting with *R v Roberts, ex p Scurr* [1924] 2 KB 695 and ending with *Asher v Lacey* [1973] 3 All ER 1008, *h* [1973] 1 WLR 1412, all reveal that before issuing his certificate the district auditor gave the suspect an oral hearing.

The Local Government Finance Act 1982 repealed the provisions of the 1972 Act which dealt with the powers of district auditors. By s 11 an Audit Commission was established which was to be responsible for auditing the accounts of a large number of public bodies, including those of local authorities. The respondent is an officer of the *j* Audit Commission and is generally referred to as a district auditor. The Audit Commission is not an organ of the central government, nor are its officers servants of the government. By s 14 a code of practice was to be prepared and presented to Parliament for approval. This was done (see the Code of Local Government Audit Practice for England and Wales, which came into effect on 7 November 1983). As in the 1933 and

1972 Acts, the 1982 Act envisaged that an objector to any accounts could appear before
a the district auditor (see s 17) and the code of practice envisaged too that any person
adversely affected by an objection should be offered an oral hearing: see paras 17 and 18.
As in the 1933 and 1972 Acts, the 1982 Act made no statutory provision for anyone
suspected of wilful misconduct to be offered an oral hearing.

Fairness

b   When exercising his powers under s 20 of the 1982 Act the district auditor had a
constitutional duty to act fairly towards each of the appellants. There has been no dispute
about that in this case. What did he have to do in order to act fairly? Counsel for the
appellants submitted that when he sent out the notices dated 26 June 1985 he should
have afforded each recipient an opportunity of an oral hearing and that his failure to do
so was such a grave affront to fairness (I avoid using the words 'natural justice') that his
c certificate ought not to be enforced. Alternatively, counsel for the appellants submitted
that even if it was permissible for the district auditor to start by inviting written
representations, when he received them and appreciated that the appellants were giving
explanations on matters which he thought pointed towards wilful misconduct, and
above all when he learned that they were denying that they had done anything which
could be reasonably adjudged to be wilful misconduct, he should then have given them,
d and each of them, an opportunity of an oral hearing or, at the very least, an opportunity
of having their cases presented by a lawyer. They were entitled, he submitted, to have a
fair opportunity to comment on statements in the district auditor's reasons, given on 6
September 1985, which were adverse to them.
     Counsel for the appellants' first submission of fairness was not put to the Divisional
Court. Counsel then appearing had made his submission in the alternative way in which
e counsel for the appellants has made his in this court. It seems that he did not know of
the history of the office of district auditor which the research of counsel for the appellants
has revealed. It was on this history that counsel for the appellants based his first
submission. His argument was that Parliament in 1933, 1972 and 1982 should be
deemed to have known how district auditors in practice exercised their powers by always
offering oral hearings. We should infer that Parliament intended that the practice should
f continue as an essential feature of district auditors' jurisdiction under s 20 of the 1982
Act. This reasoning can be turned on itself. Between 1848 and 1929, probably for
historical reasons going back to the days when justices sat in sessions, Parliament provided
in relation to the poor rate that suspects should be given an opportunity of an oral
hearing. It made no such provision in relation to other rates. I would infer from this
legislative history that in the subsequent Acts Parliament left it to the discretion of
g district auditors what procedure to adopt when exercising their powers to surcharge. In
exercising their powers they had to do so fairly, honestly and to the best of their ability:
see *Bushell v Secretary of State for the Environment* [1980] 2 All ER 608 at 612, [1981] AC 75
at 94–95 per Lord Diplock.
     In my judgment, on the facts of this case, the district auditor should not be criticised
h for the way he started his inquiry. It was likely to be complex. If he offered oral hearings
at the outset and before he knew what kind of answers each of the appellants was going
to make, his inquiry might taken an inordinate time. Time did matter. If the appellants,
or some of them, had been guilty of wilful misconduct, the sooner they were disqualified
from holding public office the better; but if they had not been so guilty, the threat of
disqualification should be removed without delay. Further, by inviting written
j representations the district auditor might have been able to discover quickly whether
any of the appellants had a satisfactory answer or none at all. A councillor, for example,
who claimed that making a rate was contrary to some political theory he believed in
would have had no answer; it would have been a waste of his and the district auditor's
time to give him an opportunity of explaining his answer in person. I infer from the
facts of this case that the appellants themselves were content with the procedure adopted

by the district auditor. As I have already commented, it had some advantages for them. Amongst the appellants there were two magistrates and a solicitor who would, I feel sure, have protested had they thought that there was anything unfair in not being offered oral hearings at the outset. I do not accept the first part of the submission of counsel for the appellants.

In order to deal with his alternative submission it is necessary to consider some of the reasons which the district auditor gave for his decision. In their joint answer the appellants made three basic averments: first, that they had acted in good faith and in the interests of the citizens and ratepayers of Liverpool; second, that until 6 June 1985 they had believed that central government would make funds available to the council which would enable it to make a lawful rate; and third, that this belief justified them in delaying making a rate until 20 June 1985 at the latest. The district auditor's findings on these averments were, first, that they had not acted in good faith: they had followed 'a course of conduct aimed at conducting a political battle without regard to statutory and other obligations and duties'; and second, that the reasons advanced to support the delay in commencing the budget-making process were not the real reasons for the delay. The district auditor was in effect saying that he did not believe their explanations. They were contrived excuses which hid the reality. He queried their creditibility and honesty and found them wanting.

Counsel for the district auditor submitted that this followed inevitably from the facts which were set out in the city council's own minutes and documents. What the appellants were saying was wholly inconsistent with what was in these minutes and documents. An example is provided by their assertion that they had acted 'in good faith and after taking advice from their officers'. They had not acted on the advice of their officers in March 1984, and again in April 1985 and on 14 June 1985. Their assertion that they believed until 6 June 1985 that central government would provide further money was so contrary to the facts that no rational person could have believed anything of the kind. The evidence relied on by the district auditor for rejecting the appellants' assertion that they believed that more money would be forthcoming was strong; but it is a matter of human experience that political zealots, as some of the appellants seem to have been, can so delude themselves about reality that lying is unnecessary for them. The courts are chary, however, about disbelieving people and attributing bad faith to them without an oral hearing: see *Re Smith & Fawcett Ltd* [1942] 1 All ER 542 at 545, [1942] Ch 304 at 308 per Lord Greene MR and *Jeffs v New Zealand Dairy Production and Marketing Board* [1966] 3 All ER 863 at 870, [1967] 1 AC 551 at 568 per Viscount Dilhorne. Had the appellants been given an opportunity of commenting on the adverse opinion of their conduct which the district auditor had formed they, or some of them, might have been able to persuade him of their good faith and credibility. Maybe on the facts of this case they would have had difficulty in so doing; but, in my judgment, they should have been given a chance of doing so. It was unfair not to have given them that chance.

The consequences of the appeal to the Divisional Court

Two questions now have to be answered. First, was the appellants' appeal to the Divisional Court capable of curing the unfairness which I have identified in the district auditor's conduct of the s 20 inquiry? Second, if it was, on the facts of this case did it?

The first of these questions raises a point of law which has been considered both in this country and in the Commonwealth and has engendered much academic comment (see Wade *Administrative Law* (5th edn, 1982) pp 487–489 and de Smith *Judicial Review of Administrative Action* (4th edn, 1980) pp 240–246). There are two broad lines of authority bearing on the question whether unfairness at first instance can be cured by an appeal. I do not propose to review them because, in my opinion, the starting point in any inquiry of this kind is to construe the statutory provisions which confer the originating and appellate jurisdictions, with the object of finding out whether Parliament intended to provide a legal framework in which aggrieved persons could be assured of justice. As I

have come to a firm conclusion about the effect of the statutory framework in this case
there would be no point in my examining the statutory or contractual frameworks
which have been considered in other cases.

The 1982 Act is silent about the procedure to be followed by a district auditor when
considering whether to surcharge anyone suspected of wilful misconduct. District
auditors are required to have professional qualifications as accountants but not as lawyers.
When exercising their powers under s 20(1) they may get both the law and the procedure
wrong and take wrong-headed views of the facts. A mistake under any of these heads
would be likely to give rise to a grievance. Parliament would have appreciated this.
Hence the provision for appeals which is contained in s 20(3) of the 1982 Act. An appeal
is available to any person 'who is aggrieved' by a decision of an auditor and on the hearing
of the appeal 'the court may confirm, vary or quash the decision and give any certificate
which the auditor could have given'. This must mean that the court rehears the case.
There are no limitations on what the aggrieved person can complain about. In this case
the appellants wanted to complain, inter alia, about not having been afforded any
opportunity for an oral hearing. There was nothing in s 20(3) to stop them doing so; and
they did. In my judgment the statutory framework of s 20 reveals an intention on the
part of Parliament that all complaints, whatever their nature, against the decision of a
district auditor, should be brought before the court so that at the end of the appellate
process justice can be done. It would not have been right, as was submitted by counsel
for the district auditor before the Divisional Court, for the appellants, because of the
alleged unfairness, to have applied for judicial review, instead of appealing. Glidewell LJ
was of the opinion that in principle they should have done so, but considered that he was
bound by the decision of this court in *Asher v Secretary of State for the Environment* [1974]
2 All ER 156, [1974] Ch 208 (see [1986] RVR 45 at 55). He was so bound and so are we.
It is, however, my opinion that that case was rightly decided. In this court counsel for
the district auditor reserved the point. In my judgment the Divisional Court was capable
of curing such unfairness as there was in the way the district auditor exercised his powers.

Did the appeal cure the unfairness?

As the amount of the certified loss exceeded the amount over which county courts
have jurisdiction the appeal was to the High Court: see s 20(9) of the 1982 Act. It was
heard by a Divisional Court. The procedure to be followed on an appeal under s 20(3) is
set out in RSC Ord 98. Rule 4(2) of that order is in these terms:

'Except in so far as the Court directs that the evidence on any such application or
appeal shall be given orally, it shall be given by affidavit.'

All the appellants filed affidavits: the leader of the city council, Mr Hamilton, filed four;
the chairman of the performance review and financial control sub-committee, Mr Byrne,
filed three. Mr Hamilton and Mr Byrne put forward detailed explanations on comments
and findings which were adverse to or critical of the appellants as a body or of themselves
in particular. Some of the appellants who were chairmen of committees made detailed
comments about matters of which they had personal knowledge. All deposed that they
agreed with what Mr Hamilton had sworn in his first affidavit. Before the Divisional
Court all the appellants were represented by the same counsel. Counsel did not ask the
court to direct that any evidence should be given orally. When the court itself asked
counsel to consider whether there should be a direction for an oral hearing or for any
deponent to be cross-examined, counsel said that such a direction would not be
appropriate. I am satisfied that the Divisional Court gave the appellants every opportunity
of leading any evidence they wished and, through experienced counsel, of making all
relevant submissions. The proceedings before that court were truly a rehearing and not,
as counsel for the appellants suggested, a critical examination of a reasoned decision. In
my judgment the appellants, and each of them, had a fair and adequate opportunity of
dealing with any findings and comments which were critical of or adverse to them in

the district auditor's written reasons dated 6 September 1985. Such unfairness as there
was in the way he performed his duties was cured by the appeal.   a

Were the appellants, and each of them, guilty of wilful misconduct?

It is trite law that when a number of persons are charged with having combined
together to commit an offence the jury or magistrates must consider the case of each
defendant separately. The same principle applies in this case. The application of it,
however, is not difficult because those of the appellants, who were not leaders, by their   b
votes at council and committee meetings, supported the leaders and encouraged them to
go on pursuing the course of conduct which is under scrutiny in this case. Further, when
the time came for answering accusations of wilful misconduct they expressly stated that
they adopted what the leader of the council, Mr Hamilton, had said in his and their
defence. On the facts of this case I can see no valid reason for distinguishing between any
of the appellants.   c

For the purpose of considering whether the appellants were proved to have been guilty
of wilful misconduct I shall not review the evidence in detail. The Divisional Court did
so. Reference can be made to the judgments there (see [1986] RVR 45).

I start by considering what constitutes 'wilful misconduct' and by what standard of
proof it should be established. Wilful misconduct is a more serious charge than
'negligence or misconduct', which was the criterion under the Local Government Act   d
1933. In *Graham v Teesdale* (1981) 81 LGR 117 at 123 Webster J adjudged that for the
purposes of s 161(4) of the 1972 Act (s 20 of the 1982 Act is in the same kind of context)
wilful misconduct meant 'deliberately doing something which is wrong knowing it to
be wrong or with reckless indifference as to whether it is wrong or not'. I agree. As to
the burden of proof, although a s 20 inquiry is not a criminal proceeding, nevertheless,
following what Denning LJ said in *Hornal v Neuberger Products Ltd* [1956] 3 All ER 970,   e
[1957] 1 QB 247 it should take a lot of evidence to tip the balance in favour of a positive
finding because the accusation is serious and the consequences of such a finding are grave.

The appellants were elected to the city council on a manifesto which pledged them to
maintain and improve jobs and services and to refuse to impose increases in rates. The
evidence establishes that they tried to do what they had pledged themselves to do; but   f
what they wanted to do cost money, which could only be got from the ratepayers or
central government. There was, however, an insuperable difficulty in their way.
Parliament had given central government powers to curb local government expenditure.
This it could do by reducing grants from central funds. In 1984 the majority party on
the city council had made clear to the Secretary of State that if he did not authorise the
payment of more money from central funds they would make an unlawful rate which   g
would have caused financial chaos in Liverpool and might have had repercussions
elsewhere. The Secretary of State did make more money available and wrote the letter
dated 29 June 1984 to which I have already referred. When, at the end of 1984, the time
was approaching for the city council to start thinking about rate-making for the financial
year beginning 1 April 1985 the majority on the city council decided to repeat the tactics
which had been successful in 1984. The letter dated 29 June 1984 gave some hope of   h
another success. An essential move in these tactics was to delay making a rate. Nothing
effective was done about making a rate before 16 April 1985. In my judgment the reason
for this inactivity, about which all members of the city council had been warned by the
district auditor, was the wish of the majority party to exert political pressure on the
Secretary of State. By 16 April 1985, however, no rational member of the majority party
(and I assume all the appellants are rational) could have believed that there was any hope   j
of persuading central government to make further grants out of central funds to
Liverpool. In January 1985 Parliament had approved the Rate Support Grant Report
(England) (HC Paper (1984–85) no 142) and the associated proposals intended to deter
excessive spending. In February 1985 the Secretary of State in strong terms had written
to the leader of the city council telling him that no more money was going to be made

available. More letters in similar terms were written in March 1985. On 14 March 1985,
a in a written answer to a parliamentary question, the Secretary of State said (75 HC Official
Report (6th series) written answers col 217):

> 'I wish to make two things clear. First, there is no question of the Government
> reconsidering the rate limits or the precept limits or the rate support grant settlement
> for 1985/86, all of which Parliament has approved. There will be no "negotiations".
> *b*   Second, while I am prepared to meet the local authority associations to discuss issues
> of general concern, or to meet individual authorities where they have genuine local
> issues to raise with me, I see no purpose in a further meeting with the ad hoc and
> unrepresentative group led by Councillor Blunkett . . . No rating authority can now
> have any excuse for delay in carrying out its duty to make a lawful rate. But if any
> authorities are still considering delay they should be clear about the consequences
> *c*   . . . Finally, I should remind all councillors that if a failure to make a rate leads to
> loss or deficiency and the auditor considers that this results from wilful misconduct,
> then those responsible may be surcharged.'

There was a local issue in Liverpool about grants under the Inner Urban Areas Act 1978
but the maximum amount which could have been obtained was so small that it would
not have made much difference to the rate which would have to be levied in order to
d comply with s 2 of the General Rate Act 1967 as amended. After that parliamentary
answer, in my judgment, it is inconceivable that any of the appellants could genuinely
have believed that central government would willingly make more money available.
What they did believe, so I infer, was that the Secretary of State would in the end have to
make more money available in order to avoid the financial chaos in Liverpool which
would result if a rate was not made or there was a long delay in making a rate. What
e happened on and after 16 April 1985 supports this inference. Despite Woolf J's judgment
in *R v Hackney London BC, ex p Fleming* [1986] RVR 182, the advice of the city's principal
officers and the efforts of the minority party, inactivity in the rate-making process
continued until the district auditor, by his letter dated 21 May 1985, made clear to all the
members of the city council that if they did not make a rate soon they were likely to be
surcharged. Then and only then did the majority of the city council bestir themselves to
f prepare budgets. When a rate was made it was an unlawful one, which all the appellants
must have appreciated it was. The district auditor did not charge the appellants with
making an unlawful rate but the fact that they did reveals their thinking during the six
weeks before 14 June 1985. Pursuit of their political objectives was not a valid excuse for
not performing their statutory duty under the General Rate Act 1967. In my judgment
there was ample evidence on which the Divisional Court could find wilful misconduct.
g   As a result of the delay in making a rate until 14 June 1985 the city council did not
receive at the beginning of that financial year either the rate rebate element of the
housing benefit subsidy or any contribution from the Treasury in lieu of rates on Crown
property. These were the two items of loss identified by the district auditor. The
Department of Health and Social Security warned the city council early in 1985, as they
h had done in 1984, that the rate rebates element of the housing benefit subsidy would not
be paid until a rate had been made. The Treasury valuer had done the same in respect of
contributions in lieu of rates on Crown property. As a result of the delay in making a
rate these sums were not paid when otherwise they would have been. In my judgment
the delay caused the resulting losses. It is immaterial that central government were under
no legal obligation to make these payments.
j   I would dismiss the appeal.

DILLON LJ. This court has, in my judgment, to consider three questions on this appeal
viz (1) Was the procedure of the district auditor, before he issued the certificate of
surcharge of 6 September 1985, fair to the appellants? (2) If not, was the unfairness cured
by the hearing on appeal in the Divisional Court? (3) If the answer to either of those

questions is in the affirmative, was the decision of the Divisional Court correct on the merits of the appellants' appeal against the district auditor's certificate?

I have qualified the third question in this way because if the procedure of the district auditor was unfair and the unfairness was *not* cured by the hearing in the Divisional Court, the appellants are entitled to succeed in this appeal and have the certificate of surcharge set aside without further inquiry into the merits.

I do not need to set out the facts in this judgment since they are comprehensively set out in the judgment of Glidewell LJ in the Divisional Court ([1986] RVR 45), and have been summarised by Lawton LJ, so far as necessary for the purposes of this appeal.

I turn to the first question.

It is not suggested that the district auditor was biased or prejudiced against the appellants, or that he intended to treat them unfairly. What is said is that the procedure which he adopted, and required them to follow, was, even if inadvertently, fundamentally unfair to them, and unjust in the result, because he should, either at the outset, or after considering their collective representations of 19 July 1985 and before making his findings, have given the appellants the opportunity of an oral hearing, or alternatively, at the lowest, he should, after considering their collective representations and before making his findings, have given them the opportunity to comment on the principal findings which he was minded to make. By one or other of these routes the district auditor should, it is said, have given the appellants a fair opportunity of correcting what he was minded to find against them, and of disabusing his mind of any misconceptions which he might have formed.

Additionally or alternatively, it is submitted that the procedure adopted by the district auditor lacked fairness, because in his statement of reasons which accompanied the notices of his certificate of 6 September 1985 he introduced new matters with which the appellants had had no opportunity of dealing.

It is not in doubt that in deciding, in the course of carrying out an audit, whether or not a loss has been incurred by the wilful misconduct of any person, a district auditor is acting in a quasi-judicial capacity. He must, therefore, act fairly by that person or, as it used to be put, he must observe the requirements of natural justice. This has been established law for a very long time. It is equally well established, however, that a person who has to decide a question in a quasi-judicial capacity can, in general, lay down his own procedure. Whether or not, therefore, the district auditor ought ultimately to have offered the appellants an oral hearing on any ground, I can see no objection whatsoever to the course he adopted, in the first place, of inviting written representations from the appellants.

The district auditor put to the appellants the case they had to meet fairly and in sufficient detail, by reference to the minutes and reports listed in Appendix 2 to his note which accompanied each of the notices to the appellants of 26 June 1985. He asked for their written representations. The result was that they produced for him a very carefully drawn and thorough document which served to clarify the issues considerably. I cannot think that fairness required the district auditor to launch out on an oral hearing involving no less than 49 councillors, against a very complicated background, without any previous request for written representations or attempt to define the issues.

It remains to consider whether, after he had received and considered the appellants' representations and before he made his findings, he should have offered the appellants an oral hearing, or at the least an opportunity of commenting on the findings he was minded to make. Our attention has been drawn to the observations of Hamilton LJ in *R v Local Government Board, ex p Arlidge* [1914] 1 KB 160 at 191 that—

'the question whether the deciding officer "hears" the appellant audibly addressing him or "hears" him only through the medium of his written statements, is in a matter of this kind one of pure procedure.'

Conversely there are, I apprehend, cases where a fair chance of exculpation cannot be
given without the offer of an oral hearing: see the observations of Geoffrey Lane LJ in *R
v Hull Prison Board of Visitors, ex p St Germain (No 2)* [1979] 3 All ER 545 at 551, [1979] 1
WLR 1401 at 1407.

Historically every person threatened with surcharge by a district auditor for negligence
or misconduct has almost invariably been given, or offered, an oral hearing. This practice
has no doubt arisen in part from the fact that the audits, in the course of which questions
of surcharge arose, were, under the earlier statutes, required to be held in public: see eg
s 247 of the Public Health Act 1875. Also s 8 of the Poor Law Audit Act 1848 expressly
required the district auditor, at poor law audits, to give notice to any person whom he
saw cause to surcharge and to allow that person an oral hearing. But the practice has also,
in my judgment, arisen from the recognition that the district auditor, in deciding on
questions of negligence, misconduct and surcharge, is discharging a quasi-judicial
function: see the successive books on audit practice published by HMSO ie A Carson
Roberts (*District Audit* (1919) vol 1 (Audit Law and Audit Work)), C R H Hurle-Hobbs
(*Law Relating to District Audit* (1949) and Reginald Jones *Local Government Audit Law*
(1981). Importance has been attached for over 75 years to the observations of Farwell LJ
in *R v Roberts* [1908] 1 KB 407 at 440 that—

> 'I fail to see how the auditor can discharge the duties put upon him by [s 247(7)]
> of the Public Health Act 1875] unless he hears and determines the questions of
> illegality, negligence and misconduct mentioned in the sub-section in the only way
> consonant with the elementary principles of justice, viz., after hearing the evidence
> and the arguments of the parties.'

Counsel for the district auditor submits that this deep-rooted practice has been swept
away, sub silentio, by the changes in the law, and to some extent in procedure, embodied
in the Local Government Act 1972, as compared with the Local Government Act 1933
and earlier Acts. For my part, I have difficulty in accepting this, since the function of the
district auditor in these matters remains a quasi-judicial function since the 1972 Act as it
was before, and in one important respect the burden on him is now increased, in that it
is now for the district auditor to decide whether the misconduct of any person referred
to in s 20(1)(b) of the Local Government Finance Act 1982 was wilful. The information
supplied to us indicates that it has continued to be the practice of district auditors since
1972 to offer an oral hearing to any person threatened with a surcharge for wilful
misconduct. The present case of the Liverpool councillors, and the parallel case of the
Lambeth councillors (see *Smith v Skinner* [1986] RVR 45 heard together with the present
case in the Divisional Court), are virtually the first cases where that practice has not been
followed.

Counsel for the district auditor submits, alternatively, that the practice of offering oral
hearings to persons threatened with surcharge has rested on an unchallenged assumption
since audits ceased being held in public and that the decision whether or not to offer an
oral hearing is in truth a matter of pure procedure within the discretion of the district
auditor. He claims that there is no valid basis for challenging the way in which the
district auditor exercised his discretion in the present case, and he points out that none of
the appellants ever asked for an oral hearing.

As to this, there are in my judgment, three factors to be taken together. One is the
practice of district auditors referred to above, though again there is no evidence from the
appellants that any of them felt deprived of a legitimate expectation when he or she was
not offered an oral hearing. The second is the seriousness of the surcharge to the
individual appellants: it carries the penalty of disqualification from office for five years
for people, many of whom have been active in local government in Liverpool for a long
time, and it also carries a liability to pay an amount of £106,103 for which they are
jointly and severally liable if the surcharge stands, which, though small compared with

the annual needs of the City of Liverpool, could spell bankruptcy and financial ruin for many of the appellants. The third factor, which to my mind points strongly in favour of the view that the district auditor ought to have offered an oral hearing before he gave his certificate, is that what the district auditor did in his statement of the reasons for his decision to issue the certificate, was to reject as untrue the explanation of their conduct and motives which the appellants had put forward in their collective representations. He found in clear terms in his reasons that 'The reasons adduced by members to support the delay in commencing the budget-making process are not the real reasons for the delay'. A court of law could not, in my judgment, in the circumstances of this case, have reached that stark conclusion of fact on mere documentary evidence without according the appellants at least the opportunity of an oral hearing: see *Re Smith & Fawcett Ltd* [1942] 1 All ER 542 at 545, [1942] Ch 304 at 308 per Lord Greene MR.

A district auditor is, of course, not bound to follow all the procedures of a court of law; but the gravity of the finding which he proposes to make on documents alone is a factor which calls for an oral hearing to be offered.

Because of these three factors, I am for my part inclined to the view that the district auditor ought, after he had considered the appellants' collective representations, to have offered them an oral hearing before he made his findings and issued his certificate. I find it unnecessary, however, to reach a final conclusion.

On the separate submission, to which I referred above, that the district auditor acted unfairly in that in his statement of reasons which accompanied the notices of his certificate of 6 September 1985 he introduced new matters with which the appellants had had no opportunity of dealing, I agree with Glidewell LJ that there were no new matters (see [1986] RVR 45 at 58). The point most strongly pressed as a new matter is that it is said that he found against the appellants that the rate for the year 1985–86, which by the appellants' votes the council set on 14 June 1985, was an illegal rate. I do not, however, read the statement of reasons as containing any such finding. The district auditor there records, first, that the rate made at the council meeting of 14 June 1985 was inadequate to meet the council's approved estimated expenditure for the year concerned and, second, that, before the resolution to make that rate was passed at the meeting of 14 June the city solicitor advised the council that if passed the resolution would be contrary to law. These are facts which appear from the minutes of the meeting of 14 June 1985, and those were among the minutes which the district auditor had listed in Appendix 2 to his note which accompanied the notices to the appellants of 26 June 1985. The district auditor had used these facts as a test of the credibility of the appellants in the explanation of their motives put forward in their collective representations, and in particular he has contrasted the making of the rate despite the city solicitor's advice that it would be contrary to law with the assertion in para 2 of the collective representations that in all these matters the appellants have throughout acted in good faith and after taking advice from their officers. But the district auditor has not found that the rate made on 14 June 1985 *was* illegal; it was not necessary for him to do so. I have already referred to the factor, as pointing in favour of an oral hearing, that the district auditor was in his findings rejecting the appellants' explanations as untruthful; I cannot see that the appellants make out the additional claim that the district auditor relied on new matter which they had not had a chance of dealing with.

Before I pass to the second of the three questions listed at the outset of this judgment, I should refer to a point taken by Caulfield J in his judgment in the Divisional Court. Caulfield J has said that the question which had troubled him most in the case was whether natural justice required the district auditor to do more than to invite, as he did, the appellants to put forward written representations (see [1986] RVR 45 at 83). He concluded that no more was requred of the district auditor because there was no matter of fact or comment or argument which could have been added to the written representations and which might have affected the auditor's determination. With every respect, I am unable to agree with this conclusion. There were matters, in my judgment,

which, if given a further opportunity, the appellants would have wanted to urge on the
a district auditor, such as their prospects, whatever they may have been in September
1985, of balancing the books despite the apparent shortcomings of the rate fixed on 14
June, and the facts as to the progress made at the beginning of April 1985 in determining
the estimated income and expenditure for the year 1985–86 of the various committees
and in particular of the education committee and the social services committee. It may
be that no further facts which were available to be put forward, and no amount of
b argument, would in the event have caused the district auditor to change his mind; but
that is not relevant if there was unfairness by their not being given a chance of putting
forward further representations, oral or written, and if that unfairness has not been cured
by the appellate hearing in the Divisional Court.
      I turn, therefore, to consider the effect, on the assumption that there was such
unfairness, of the appellate hearing in the Divisional Court.
c   The appeal is provided for by statute in s 20(3) of the 1982 Act, and the Divisional
Court is given very wide power to confirm, vary or quash the decision of the district
auditor and to give any certificate which he could have given. I agree entirely with the
Divisional Court that the appeal hearing before the Divisional Court required an
examination de novo of the questions which the district auditor had to consider and the
appeal fell to be decided on the evidence and arguments placed before the Divisional
d Court, whether or not they had been placed before the district auditor. In that sense the
Divisional Court was exercising an original as well as an appellate jurisdiction. Moreover,
any challenge to the fairness of the district auditor's decision on grounds of natural justice
was within the scope of the appeal; this is clear from the decision of this court in *Asher v
Secretary of State for the Environment* [1974] 2 All ER 156, [1974] Ch 208, which is binding
on us, and expecially from the observations of Lawton LJ ([1974] 2 All ER 156 at 170,
e [1974] Ch 208 at 228) with which I respectfully agree.
      It follows, incidentally, though it is not relevant to the disposal of this appeal, that with
all deference to Glidewell LJ I do not agree that a challenge to the fairness of a district
auditor's procedure ought to be made by an application for judicial review rather than
by an appeal to the Divisional Court. The procedure for an appeal is laid down by statute
f as the procedure for challenging a certificate of a district auditor, and questions of the
validity of a district auditor's decision on procedural grounds should also be taken on
such an appeal and not by other procedure. The 'decision' of the district auditor referred
to in s 20(3) of the 1982 Act must mean his 'conclusion', which is susceptible of an appeal
under the section, even if reached in breach of natural justice and therefore for certain
purposes void: see the observations of Lord Wilberforce in *Calvin v Carr* [1979] 2 All ER
g 440 at 446, [1980] AC 574 at 590 and of Viscount Simon in *White v Kuzych* [1951] 2 All
ER 435 at 441, [1951] AC 585 at 600.
      The question whether a decision vitiated by a breach of the rules of natural justice, i e
by unfairness, e g by failure to allow a person an opportunity to be heard, can be cured or
made good by a subsequent hearing has been considered in a number of cases recently.
It is plain that no clear and absolute rule can be laid down: see per Lord Wilberforce in
h *Calvin v Carr* [1979] 2 All ER 440 at 447, [1980] AC 574 at 592 and per Barwick CJ in
Twist v Randwick Municipal Council (1976) 12 ALR 379 at 384. If the scope of any
permissible appeal is limited, so that it does not involve an examination of the
circumstances of the case de novo on evidence not limited to that which was before the
original tribunal, it may well be that the appellate hearing will not cure the defects of the
original decision.
j   Where, however, as here, the appeal does require an examination of the circumstances
of the case de novo on whatever evidence may be put before the appellate court, then the
major question for consideration is, I apprehend, whether, in the context of this particular
case, the procedure as a whole gave the appellants an opportunity for a fair hearing.
      As to that, the appellants' objections to the procedure of the district auditor are that
they did not have an opportunity of an oral hearing and did not have an opportunity of

dealing with the district auditor's proposed findings. But on the appeal they were able to put in, and did put in, as much evidence as they wished to deal with those findings and to answer every point taken against them by the district auditor, and they were given, though they did not take advantage of it, the opportunity of giving oral evidence. Their complaint on the ground of overall fairness therefore comes down to this, that to appeal after an order has been made is much less advantageous than an opportunity to advance reasons against the making of the order before it has been made. That, as a fundamental ground of complaint on the score of fairness, was rejected by the High Court of Australia in *Twist v Randwick Municipal Council*; it could really only stand as a fundamental ground of complaint if, contrary to *Calvin v Carr*, the observations of Megarry J in *Leary v National Union of Vehicle Builders* [1970] 2 All ER 713 at 720, [1971] Ch 34 at 49 were to be treated as validly laying down a rule of general application that a failure of natural justice in the trial body cannot be cured by a sufficiency of natural justice in an appellate body.

In *Twist v Randwick Municipal Council* (1976) 12 ALR 379 at 387 Mason J attached importance to the factor that in certain Privy Council and Canadian cases the party affected had elected to treat the decision of an administrative body as a valid, though erroneous, decision, by appealing from it in preference to asserting his right to a proper performance by the authority of its duty at first instance. That factor is not relevant in the present case, since in my view, as explained above, the appellants were bound to appeal against the decision of the district auditor if they wanted to challenge that decision. But the absence of that factor does not preclude the application to the present case of the reasoning of the members of the court in *Twist's* case, which was said in *Calvin v Carr* to be close to the views of their Lordships in the latter case.

The general principle is formulated in *Calvin v Carr* [1979] 2 All ER 440 at 449, [1980] AC 574 at 594 as being that what is required is examination of the hearing process, original and appeal as a whole, and a decision whether after it has been gone through the complainant has had a fair deal of the kind that he bargained for. *Twist's* case is of particular relevance to the present case in that the procedure was laid down by statute, rather than by contract or by the rules of a domestic body or trade union, and in that the appeal prescribed by that procedure was to a court of law rather than to a domestic tribunal. The reasoning in *Twist's* case, is however, as it seems to me, in line with the reasoning of the Supreme Court of Canada in *King v University of Saskatchewan* [1969] SCR 678 to which we were also referred, where it was held that a hearing before the ultimate appeal tribunal, in which the appellant was accorded a full measure of natural justice, cured any absence of natural justice in the inferior tribunals.

Applying the law as I take it to have been laid down in *Calvin v Carr* and in *Twist's* case, I have no doubt that in the present case, if there was any failure of fairness on the part of the district auditor, either in not offering the appellants an oral hearing or not offering them an opportunity to comment on his proposed findings before he rejected the appellants' representations as untrue, that failure was fully cured by the hearing in the Divisional Court under the statutory appeal process.

There remains the third question in this appeal, namely whether the decision of the Divisional Court was correct on the merits.

As to this, it has been common ground between the parties that the law as it was at the relevant time as to the duty of a local authority to make a rate has been correctly stated by Woolf J in his judgment in *R v Hackney London BC, ex p Fleming* [1986] RVR 182 delivered on 16 April 1985. In the absence of a reasonable explanation, it was a breach of duty for the Liverpool council not to have made a rate by the beginning of the financial year or within a reasonable time thereafter. It was accepted by leading counsel for the appellants in this court, as in the Divisional Court, that it was not a justifiable excuse for the council's delay in making the rate until 14 June 1985 to say merely that the council was endeavouring to exort money from central government by the threat that the council would not perform its legal duty to make a lawful rate.

a It is said for the appellants that there was a reasonable excuse for not making the rate earlier than 14 June 1985 because until very shortly before that date the council was negotiating, or endeavouring to negotiate, with central government to obtain more government money for Liverpool, as had been achieved in the corresponding months of 1984. It is said further for the appellants, and this is really the gravamen of their appeal on the merits, that the appellants were not guilty of 'wilful misconduct', as that term was interpreted by Webster J in *Graham v Teesdale* (1981) 81 LGR 117 in the light of the

b earlier authorities, because (a) the appellants genuinely thought that further government money would be forthcoming for the city and (b) the appellants, though realising that there was a duty to make that rate not later than 20 June, never appreciated that there was any *obligation* on the council to make the rate earlier than 20 June.

Finally, and as a separate point, it is said for the appellants that the loss to the City of Liverpool relied on by the district auditor in making the surcharge was not caused by

c any act or omission of the appellants, but was caused by the voluntary decision of the government not to pay estimated rate rebates or estimated sums in lieu of rates in respect of Crown property until the council had made its rate for the year. This last point I regard as unarguable. The loss was plainly foreseeable as the government had repeatedly declared its intentions, and the prospective loss had also been mentioned in reports from the council's own officers. The loss was caused by the appellants' acts and omissions just

d as much as those acts and omissions caused other rate payers, e g commercial ratepayers in the city, not to make payments in advance of the rate being set and the rate demands being sent out.

On the facts, the government had again and again and again made its position as clear as anyone possibly could that there would be no extra money available for Liverpool for the year 1985–86 and that the government would not go back on, or reopen, the Rate

e Support Grant Report which had been approved by Parliament in January or February 1985. The appellants say that it was to be expected that the government would say that, and that the government had said much the same in the spring of 1984 and yet had made further money available for Liverpool. But the council's principal officers had clearly pointed out, in their joint memorandum of 16 April 1985 to the key performance review and financial control sub-committee, that the circumstances of 1985 were not

f necessarily comparable to those surrounding the deferment of the rate in 1984.

For my part, I have no doubt that, from 1 April 1985 to 14 June 1985, no reasonable person could have expected that any further government money, of any significant amount beyond what had already been specifically agreed, would be made available to Liverpool for the year 1985–86. If the appellants, despite all appearances and the utterances of the government, believed to the contrary and deferred making the rate in

g that belief, they acted recklessly in so doing. They knew that there would be an element of loss to the city if the making of the rate was delayed and they had no reasonable prospect of achieving any countervailing benefit from the government.

There is the further point that the only financial matter even tenuously under discussion in April and May 1985 with the Merseyside Task Force or the Department of

h the Environment in London was in the context trivial: how much the council would be allowed in respect of two outstanding items (management support and monitoring and enhanced maintenance of environmental sites) in the urban programme for the previous year 1984–85. The total amount of government money in issue was about £1·75m and the expenditure had already been incurred by the council in 1984. If the government was prepared to provide the money, a larger sum (because penalties would be avoided) of

j around £5m would fall to be deducted from the city's opening deficit in its accounts for the year 1985–86, but there would be no other effect on the budget-making process for that year. The council had not yet got around, apparently, to putting forward specific urban programme projects for the year 1985–86.

It is said in the appellants' collective representations to the district auditor that the arrival of the letter of 8 May from the Merseyside Task Force confirming that no further

government money would be forthcoming in respect of these two outstanding items of
the urban programme for 1984–85 'had a profoundly disruptive effect upon the approach
to budget-making' for the year 1985–86. Without doubting Cllr Hamilton's integrity, I
cannot see how that can have been so, since the opening deficit for the year 1985–86 in
the figures put before the council on 14 June 1985 when the rate was made was precisely
the same as the figure for the opening deficit given in a memorandum of the city
treasurer of 16 April 1985 prepared, obviously, on the footing that the amounts of
government money available for the urban programme of 1984–85, even in respect of
these two outstanding or final items, was already known. It would seem to be more
correct to say that the receipt of the letter of 8 May, and of a further final warning from
the district auditor dated 21 May 1985, accelerated the budget-making process which
had been in abeyance since 16 April; we find that committees, such as the library and
leisure activities committee, the general services committee, the housing and building
committee and the planning and land committee, which had done nothing before, were
all approving their budgets for 1985–86 in the last days of May.

I conclude therefore that the possibility or hope of obtaining further money from the
government does not on the facts provide any reasonable explanation or excuse for the
failure to set a rate until 14 June and, furthermore, the appellants were acting recklessly
in so far as they delayed setting the rate in the belief or hope that further government
money would be forthcoming.

It remains to consider the appellants' case that they were not guilty of wilful default
because they never appreciated that there was any *obligation* on the council to make the
rate earlier than 20 June.

The appellants were selected for surcharge because of the pattern of their voting at
meetings of the council on 30 January, 27 February, 7 March and 14 June 1985 when a
number of highly political resolutions were passed and an opposition amendment, on 7
March, which called for estimates to be prepared and considered and for a meeting to be
held to fix a rate, was defeated. The case argued by counsel for the district auditor was
that, from at least 30 January, the appellants had been conducting a political battle
without regard for statutory and other obligations and duties; this had been the finding
of the district auditor in para 55 of his statement of reasons of 6 September 1985.

Members of the council were told very many times by the district auditor and his
predecessor throughout 1984 and in the first five months of 1985 that the council had a
duty to make an adequate rate. There is no reason to doubt that all the members
understood this. They were also told, in a report of 19 March 1984, of which a reminder
was sent later, that they could be personally at risk if a rate was not made because no vote
was taken or there was unreasonable delay in making a rate. They were also told in June
1984 that a rate had to be set by 20 June at the latest because of the statutory right of
ratepayers to discharge their rate liability by ten instalments in the financial year. In fact
in 1984 the rate was not made until July and in the circumstances of that year no action
was taken on the score of delay in not having fixed the rate earlier.

Against that background, various of the appellants, such as Cllr Hamilton, Cllr G A
Lloyd and Cllr Mrs Adams, have deposed to the effect that they believed that so long as a
rate was made by 20 June they were not acting unlawfully or improperly. That may well
have been a tenable view up to 16 April 1985 when Woolf J gave judgment in *R v
Hackney London BC, ex p Fleming* [1986] RVR 182. However, on 16 April the three
principal officers placed a joint memorandum before the performance review and
financial sub-committee which made it clear to any councillor who read it: (1) that there
was this important and highly relevant case involving the Hackney borough council
being decided that day; (ii) that while 20 June remained the final date for fixing a rate
there had to be a good reason for deferring the making of the rate at all; (iii) that the
circumstances of 1985 were not necessarily comparable to those surrounding the
deferment of the making of the rate in 1984; and (iv) that deferment would involve loss
to the council, not least in that the government had made it plain that rate rebates would
not be paid to any council so long as that council had not set a rate for 1985–86.

What actually happened, despite that memorandum, was that on 16 April 1985

a progress towards making the rate for the year 1985–86 ceased. There had been progress in that on 26 March 1985 the policy and finance committee had resolved that the city treasurer be requested to prepare summaries of all committees' income and expenditure, and that the income and expenditure of the education and social services committees be submitted to special meetings of those committees for consideration prior to the meeting (a special meeting) of the performance review and finance control sub-committee on 16

b April; that had all been done, the special meetings of the education and social services committees which approved their budgets being held on 12 and 10 April respectively. But on 16 April the performance review and financial control sub-committee rejected opposition proposals deploring the delay in fixing the rate, demanding the calling within ten days of a meeting of the city council to determine the budget and fix a rate, and requiring the circulation to all members of the city council of, inter alia, the joint

c memorandum of the three principal officers which I have mentioned and, instead, the sub-committee carried a motion which, after a long political preamble, referred the further budget-making process to meetings of the committees (other than the education and social services committees) and a further meeting of the sub-committee itself, which in the event were never convened. These proceedings of the performance review and financial control sub-committee were approved by the policy and finance committee,

d despite further opposition amendments, on 7 May 1985.

In these circumstances, and as the appellants had every opportunity of putting in as much evidence as they wished before the Divisional Court in relation to the matters set out in the district auditor's statement of reasons, including the opportunity of giving oral evidence, I would for my part conclude that those of the appellants (whichever they may have been) who decided the policy of the majority party on the city council in the first

e six months of 1985 knew perfectly well from 16 April onwards that they were acting illegally and in breach of their statutory duty in delaying setting an adequate rate; alternatively, if they were not deliberately acting illegally, they were acting with blatant recklessness in disregarding the principal officers' advice.

As for the others (and I do not know which they were), they have chosen to follow

f their leaders. All the appellants joined in the collective representations to the district auditor. All have been represented together before the Divisional Court and in this court. In his judgment Glidewell LJ records that in the hearing in the Divisional Court neither counsel for the Lambeth councillors nor counsel for the Liverpool councillors was able to point to any feature which distinguished any of their clients from the remainder; they both treated their task as being to present a single case on behalf of all their clients (see

g [1986] RVR 45 at 47).

The observations of Devlin J in *Rothnie v Dearne UDC* (1951) 50 LGR 123 at 125–126 are, in my judgment, apposite where he said:

h '. . . it may seem, on the face of it, to be very drastic that 17 out of 27 members of an urban district council should be disqualified from election for five years because they either voted for or failed to vote against an illegal resolution. I confess that I find it a little surprising that we are asked to determine the matter on the basis that the position of these 17 members is exactly the same. I should have thought that different considerations might well have applied in different cases . . . But the case has been presented to us with one affidavit on behalf of all 17 members which their state of mind is stated to be exactly the same, and upon that basis the order which

j my Lord has proposed is, in my judgment, inevitably the right one.'

As they have all, whether leaders or not, chosen to stand together, without any being distinguished from the remainder, the conclusion must be that all acted recklessly in delaying the making of the rate until 14 June 1985. The finding which I have referred to in para 55 of the district auditor's statement of reasons is, on the full evidence before the

Divisional Court, justified in relation to all the appellants, and all were guilty of wilful misconduct, with the consequences which follow from that.   *a*

I agree that this appeal should be dismissed.

WOOLF LJ. I am fortunate in that as the facts leading up to this appeal have been fully set out in the judgment of Glidewell LJ in the Divisional Court ([1986] RVR 45) and in the judgment of Lawton LJ in this court it is possible for me to turn directly to the principal issues raised on this appeal. They are: (a) whether the district auditor can   *b* lawfully issue a certificate under s 20(1) of the Local Government Finance Act 1982 without holding an oral hearing at which the persons to whom the certificate relates have an opportunity for presenting evidence and making representations (the oral hearing issue); (b) whether, if there is no statutory requirement to hold an oral hearing, the principles of fairness in the circumstances of this case require the auditor either to hold an oral hearing or to give the appellants an opportunity to make additional representations,   *c* having regard to the conclusions to which the auditor was minded to come (the fairness issue); (c) whether the auditor and the Divisional Court correctly came to the conclusion that the appellants had been guilty of 'wilful misconduct' (the wilful misconduct issue); (d) whether the auditor and the Divisional Court were correct in concluding that the alleged loss of £106,103 had been incurred or caused by the wilful misconduct of the appellants (the loss issue).   *d*

In his admirable opening argument in this appeal on behalf of the 47 councillors he now represents, counsel contended with justification that in coming to a decision on the issues raised in this appeal it is necessary to have in mind the background of severe urban deprivation which undisputedly exists in the City of Liverpool. For this reason he referred to the Report of the Archbishop of Canterbury's Commission on Urban Priority Areas, *Faith in the City* (1985), and in particular the passages in the report stressing the   *e* urgent need to stop the decay and begin the regeneration of inner city areas such as exist in Liverpool. He submitted that when viewed against this background his clients had behaved perfectly properly and were justified in stating on the first page of their representations to the auditor of 19 July 1985:

> 'In all these matters, Members of the Council have, throughout, acted in good   *f* faith and after taking advice from their Officers. They have never at any time sought to avoid their duty to make a rate, or introduce unnecessary delay in its discharge. They have at all times had at the forefront of their minds the interests of the citizens and ratepayers of Liverpool in seeking to maximise the resources available to finance services, and to make improvements in living conditions of Liverpool people. In doing so, they claim that they were entitled to exercise that   *g* degree of discretion which, as elected representatives, the law allows them—and which the Courts have frequently protected from undue interference by outside bodies.'

With this submission in mind I now turn to deal with the principal issues I have identified.   *h*

The oral hearing issue

This issue can be dealt with as part of the next issue but I can deal with it separately since, as I understood the submissions of counsel for the appellants as developed in argument, he was submitting for the first time in this court that the auditor was required as a matter of statutory construction of s 20 of the 1982 Act to hold an oral hearing. No   *j* such argument was advanced in the Divisional Court. Indeed, it was conceded that there was no such statutory requirement. However, counsel for the appellants was entitled to advance the argument on the appeal and I recognise that the argument has considerable force. It can be summarised in this way: the origin of the present jurisdiction of the auditor can be traced to s 8 of the Poor Law Audit Act 1848; that section gave the person *a* who it was proposed to surcharge the right to be notified and attend and make oral submissions before the auditor and although the express right no longer appears in the current legislation it is unthinkable that Parliament intended to take away this right particularly as an objector is still given the right to attend before the auditor by s 17(3) of the 1982 Act. Counsel for the appellants in support of his argument referred us to the successive editions of the authoritative textbooks on the law relating to district audits by Mr Carson Roberts (*District Audit* (1919) vol 1 (Audit Law and Audit Work)), Mr Hurle-

b Hobbs (*Law Relating to District Audit* (1949)) and the more recent and current editions by Mr Reginald Jones (*Local Government Audit Law* (1981 and 1985)). These works are published by HMSO and are undoubtedly highly authoritative, and while they have become less dogmatic over the question of the need for an oral hearing in the more recent editions, the earlier editions certainly express the view that an oral hearing is necessary and the later editions regard such a hearing as highly desirable. Furthermore,

c they contain precedents which presuppose such a hearing. Counsel for the appellants also strongly relies on the fact that as a matter of practice, of which Parliament should be taken to be aware (subject to a sole exception in 1978 when the person surcharged was already convicted and in prison in relation to matters giving rise to the surcharge), so far as is known an oral hearing has always been offered before persons are surcharged and in fact has normally taken place.

d The terms of s 8 of the 1848 Act are as follows:

'. . . if an Auditor shall see Cause to surcharge any Person now liable by law to be surcharged by him, and to whom no Notice is now required by Law to be given, with any Sum of Money in reference to any Payment considered by him to have been illegally or improperly made, he shall, if a Person be not present at such Audit,

e cause Notice in Writing of his Intention to make such Surcharge to be given, by Post or otherwise to the Person against whom he shall propose to make this Surcharge . . . and shall adjourn the Audit, so far as it shall relate to such particular Matter, for a sufficient Time to allow of such Person appearing before him, and showing Cause against such Surcharge, and at such Time the said Auditor shall hear the Party, if present, and determine according to the Law and Justice of the Case.'

f It is to be noted that the obligations on an auditor now are greater than they were at the time of the original legislation because of the requirement in s 20 of the 1982 Act that not only must misconduct be established, it must also be established that the misconduct was 'wilful' which clearly adds to the gravity of the finding.

Support for the argument of counsel for the appellants is to be found in Hurle-Hobbs

g *Law Relating to District Audit* (1949) p 100, where it states:

'The absence from the present statutory provisions relating to District Audit of any requirement respecting the giving of notice to show cause against any action contemplated by the auditor can scarcely indicate an intention on the part of Parliament to withdraw from persons likely to be affected by his decisions the right to receive notice and be heard: the more likely explanation is that the obligation of

h any tribunal or person exercising judicial functions to afford an opportunity for appearance and to listen fairly to both sides has become so fundamental a principle of English law as to render unnecessary any statutory provision in relation thereto . . .'

The probable reason for the change of emphasis in the textbooks on this subject is that

j in *Graham v Teesdale* (1981) 81 LGR 117 Webster J, when dealing with the question of fairness in an appeal arising out of the grant of a certificate by a district auditor under s 161(4) of the Local Government Act 1972 (the predecessor of s 20 of the 1982 Act), accepted that there was no statutory requirement to have an oral hearing. However, in that case the appellant appeared in person and the full argument advanced by counsel for the appellants before this court would not have been before Webster J. I therefore do not pay the attention which I otherwise would to the view expressed by Webster J. In addition, in *Asher v Secretary of State for the Environment* [1974] 2 All ER 156 at 163, [1974] Ch 208 at 219, Lord Denning MR assumed that there was to be an oral hearing and that the person to be surcharged should have an opportunity of answering questions and of calling witnesses if desired, but this comment was obiter.

In considering whether the submission of counsel for the appellants is correct, it is possible to distinguish the position under the 1848 Act from that under the current legislation because in the nineteenth century the auditor was conducting his activities in public and the process of surcharging therefore took place in the same way, and this is no longer the situation. It is also possible to contrast the provisions of s 17(3) of the 1982 Act which expressly provides that 'any local government elector for any area to which those accounts relate, or any representative of his, may attend before the auditor and make objections', with the absence of any express provision as to attendance where the auditor is exercising his power under s 20 without there being an objection. However, I do not regard these points as being of significance. Indeed, the reference to an objector having to attend in s 17(3) is surprising and probably explicable because of the historical background to this legislation, which is detailed in the judgment of Lawton LJ. The fact that the elector is required to attend to make an objection does not mean that today the auditor is required to inquire into the objections in public or to hear oral representations or evidence relating to the objection.

An objection can be made with the intention that the auditor should take action under ss 19 or 20 of the 1982 Act. However, the auditor can exercise his powers whether or not there is an objection and it appears to me clear that whether or not there is an objection the procedure under ss 19 and 20 must be the same. If an oral hearing is required where there is an objection, an oral objection must equally be required where there is objection. Likewise, if an oral hearing is necessary before the auditor exercises his power under s 19(1) to apply to the court for a declaration that an item of account is contrary to law, there must be a requirement for an oral hearing before the auditor exercises his powers to certify under s 20 which can have more immediate financial consequences to and can affect the status of the person to whom the certificate relates.

The solution has to be found in accordance with the general principles applied by the courts where they are considering supplementing the provisions of legislation so as to give effect to what must have been deemed to be the intention of Parliament in passing the legislation in the terms used. Undoubtedly, having regard to the function which the auditor has to perform under s 20, Parliament must be taken to have intended that he should perform his duties fairly, but must it have intended he should do so by an oral hearing? The judicial activity of supplementing the express provisions of the legislation as to fairness has now been the subject of many judicial comments of the highest authority. An example, in a case which was cited on this appeal, is to be found in Lord Reid's speech in *Wiseman v Borneman* [1969] 3 All ER 275 at 277, [1971] AC 297 at 308:

> 'Natural justice requires that the procedure before any tribunal which is acting judicially shall be fair in all the circumstances, and I would be sorry to see this fundamental general principle degenerate into a series of hard and fast rules. For a long time the courts have, without objection of Parliament, supplemented procedure laid down in legislation where they have found that to be necessary for this purpose. But before this unusual kind of power is exercised it must be clear that the statutory procedure is insufficient to achieve justice and that to require additional steps would not frustrate the apparent purpose of the legislation.'

Applying this approach, it would only be right to establish a 'hard and fast' requirement for an oral hearing in addition to the general requirement of fairness if this was necessary having regard to the auditor's functions under s 20. In my view it is not so necessary. Counsel for the appellants was not able to point to any precedent for inferring a statutory requirement for an oral hearing in the performance of a quasi-judicial function of this

sort and there clearly can be cases where justice can be done and the auditor can certify
a under s 20 without the need for an oral hearing and Parliament cannot be presumed to
have required an oral hearing in all cases, if it may not be necessary in some cases. In this
situation implying into the legislation a general requirement to act fairly, which alters
depending on the circumstances, provides all the protection that is needed and so,
notwithstanding the legislative history, it is this general requirement of fairness that I
would import into s 20 and not the rigid requirement for an oral hearing for which
b counsel for the appellants contends. In expressing my reasons on this issue I have not
made reference to the Code of Local Government Audit Practice for England and Wales,
since I did not find that it provided any assistance on this issue.

The fairness issue
As there is no statutory requirement placed on the auditor to hold an oral hearing
c before he exercises his power to certify under s 20, he has a discretion whether to hold an
oral hearing. This does not mean that the court's powers of intervention are limited to
those which normally apply to the exercise of administrative discretions. The discretion
of the auditor is limited by the requirement that he must ensure that the proceedings are
fair, and if in the view of the court the procedure adopted by the auditor is unfair, the
procedure is unlawful and the court can intervene even though the auditor cannot be
d regarded as having acted unreasonably in adopting the procedure which he did.
In deciding whether in any particular case there was unfairness it is necessary to
consider the particular function which was being performed by the auditor in making
the decision, the nature and consequence of the decision and the matters in issue.
Therefore, before examining precisely what happened in this case, it is helpful to examine
the statutory framework under which the auditor was operating and in particular the
e effect of the right of appeal which is given by s 20, which counsel for the district auditor
in his helpful submissions argued could cure any failure of fairness on the part of the
auditor in this particular case.
The first point that has to be made with regard to s 20 in the circumstances of this case
is a point to which I have already alluded. This is, that although it gives the auditor other
f powers, the power which he was exercising in this case was to certify that loss or
deficiency had occurred due to wilful misconduct. Such a certificate in itself could cast a
serious reflection on the character of the person to whom it relates, can have grave
financial consequences and where, as here, the persons concerned are members of a local
authority and the amount involved is in excess of £2,000 the certificate has the further
consequence of disqualification for the substantial period of five years. It is next to be
noted that both under s 19 and under s 20, before the auditor exercises any of the powers
g given to him by those sections, the same initial requirements is laid down by the statute,
namely that 'it appears to the auditor'. I only draw attention to this because under s 19
the auditor has no direct powers other than to apply to the court for a declaration,
whereas under s 20, where he decides to certify in the absence of an appeal, the certificate
becomes the final decision.
h Whether the auditor is acting under ss 19 or 20, his role is at least in part inquisitorial.
While he would always be under an obligation to look fairly into the objection and deal
fairly with any person who can be affected by his decision, both under s 19 and under
s 20 his role is not identical to that of a judge in court.
The power of appeal which is given by s 20 to the court is a wide one. It is accepted
that the court grants a hearing de novo, a full rehearing, and sub-s (3) provides:

j
'. . . (*a*) in a case of a decision to certify that any sum or amount is due from any
person, the court may confirm, vary or quash the decision and given any certificate
which the auditor could have given; (*b*) in the case of a decision not to certify that
any sum or amount is due from any person, the court may confirm the decision or
quash it and give any certificate which the auditor could have given; and any

certificate given under this subsection shall be treated . . . as if it had been given by
the auditor . . .'   *a*

There has been some uncertainty as to the effect of an appeal provision of this sort in
relation to the adoption of an unfair procedure which, in the absence of a right of appeal,
would undoubtedly result in the quashing of a decision.

In *Leary v National Union of Vehicle Builders* [1970] 2 All ER 713, [1971] Ch 34 Megarry J
dealt with the position with characteristic clarity. He was of the view that, in general, a   *b*
right of appeal could not cure a breach of the rules of natural justice. He said ([1970] 2
All ER 713 at 719–720, [1971] Ch 34 at 48–49):

> 'What is required is a venire de novo and not the process of appeal, whereby the
> person aggrieved may be treated as bearing the burden of displacing an adverse
> decision which, for the lack of natural justice, ought never to have been reached . . .
> That is not all. If one accepts the contention that a defect of natural justice in the   *c*
> trial body can be cured by the presence of natural justice in the appellate body, this
> has the result of depriving the member of his right of appeal from the expelling
> body. If the rules and law combine to give the member a right to a fair trial and the
> right of appeal, why should he be told that he ought to be satisfied with an unjust
> trial and a fair appeal? Even if the appeal is treated as a hearing de novo, the member
> is being stripped of his right to appeal to another body from the effective decision to   *d*
> expel him. I cannot think that natural justice is satisfied by a process whereby an
> unfair trial, although not resulting in a valid expulsion, will nevertheless have the
> effect of depriving the member of his right of appeal when a valid decision to expel
> him is subsequently made. Such a deprivation would be a powerful result to be
> achieved by what in law is a mere nullity; and it is no mere triviality that might be
> justified on that ground that natural justice does not mean perfect justice. As a   *e*
> general rule, at all events, I hold that a failure of natural justice in the trial body
> cannot be cured by a sufficiency of natural justice in the appellate body.'

As a matter of general principle, bearing in mind the importance of the requirement
of fairness to any adjudicating process, I have considerable sympathy with the approach
adopted by Megarry J where there is no right to a rehearing. However, counsel for the   *f*
district auditor relied strongly on the decision of the High Court of Australia in *Twist v
Randwick Municipal Council* (1976) 12 ALR 379. That case concerned the power of a
council to order the demolition of a building where there was a right of appeal against
the order to a district court. Twist failed to exercise his right of appeal but instead sought
a declaration that the order directing the demolition of his building was null and void,
on the basis that before the order was made he should have been given an opportunity to   *g*
be heard. The appellant's appeal against the refusal of a declaration was dismissed by the
High Court. Barwick CJ was of the view that, because of the right of appeal there was no
enforceable right to a hearing before the order was made. However, Mason and Jacobs JJ
took the view that the right of appeal did not in itself mean that there was no right to a
hearing before the order was made, it merely alters the consequences of a failure to
accord such a hearing. Mason J said (at 387):   *h*

> 'Further, the earlier cases should not be regarded as deciding that the presence of
> an appeal to another administrative body is an absolute answer to a departure from
> natural justice or the standard of fairness. The existence of such an appeal does not
> demonstrate in itself that an inferior tribunal is at liberty to deny a hearing. But if
> the right of appeal is exercised and the appellate authority acts fairly and does not   *j*
> depart from natural justice the appeal may then be said to have "cured" a defect of
> natural justice or fairness which occurred at first instance.'

The judge then referred to a series of cases, concluding with a reference to *Denton v
Auckland City Council* [1969] NZLR 256 and *Leary v National Union of Vehicle Builders,*

where a different approach had been taken. Mason J then went on to say that he preferred
the earlier line of cases rather than the *Denton* and *Leary* cases (at 387–388):

> '... first, because the party affected has elected to treat the administrative decision
> as a valid, though erroneous decision, by appealing from it, in preference to asserting
> his right to a proper performance by the authority of its duty at first instance; and
> secondly, because in some cases the court will be compelled to take account of the
> public interest in the efficiency of the administrative process and the necessity for
> reasonable prompt despatch of public business and balance that interest against the
> countervailing interest of the individual in securing a fair hearing—in appropriate
> cases that balance will be achieved if the individual secures a fair hearing on his
> appeal.'

Jacobs J put it somewhat differently, saying (at 390):

> 'However the second question remains. Is an order made without giving any
> opportunity to be heard invalid, that is to say, void and a nullity? Whether or not
> an order made without an opportunity to be heard will be wholly invalid depends
> on the legislative provision read in the light of the nature of the subject matter and
> the provisions for review. Though the nature of the subject matter would tend to
> support an intention of total invalidity, I regard the wide provision for appeal in
> sub-s (5) [of s 317B of the NSW Local Government Act 1919] as indicating a contrary
> legislative intention. The appeal is to a judicial body in the fullest sense of that term.
> The determination must be made upon the evidence before the District Court. I do
> not think that it would at all accord with the legislative intention that an owner
> should be able to ignore rights of appeal of the kind given by sub-s (5) and instead
> rely on an absolute invalidity in the order which a council had made. A different
> view might be open if the appeal were to anything less than a court of the wide
> jurisdiction and consequent legal standing possessed by the District Court; but in
> my opinion it was not the legislative intention that an order under the section,
> subject to appeal to the District Court, should, without any resort to the right of
> appeal, be able to be treated for all purposes as void and of no effect upon the ground
> that the principle of the natural justice had not been observed.'

One of the cases which Mason J preferred to the decision of Megarry J in *Leary v
National Union of Vehicle Builders* was the decision of the Supreme Court of Canada in *King
v University of Saskatchewan* [1969] SCR 678. In that case Spence J (at 689), giving the
judgment of the court, took the view that any failure of natural justice before inferior
bodies of the university was unimportant—

> 'when the senate, the appeal body under the provisions of the *University Act*, and
> also the body in control of the granting of degrees, has exercised its function with
> no failure to accord natural justice.'

In his judgment Megarry J had distinguished *King v Universities of Saskatchewan* and
preferred *Denton v Auckland City Council*, in which the High Court in New Zealand held
that as the decision of a town planning committee lacked natural justice, the appeal board
could not supply the deficiency of natural justice because the committee's decision was a
nullity. However, although Megarry J found some support in this decision, he was
correctly careful in my view not to base his decision on the use of the terms 'void' and
'voidable' which was the approach adopted in the New Zealand case.

The final authority to which it is necessary for me to refer on this point is the decision
of the Privy Council in *Calvin v Carr* [1979] 2 All ER 440, [1980] AC 574. That was a case
involving the Australian Jockey Club. There had been a preliminary hearing before the
stewards in which it was alleged that there was a breach of the rules of natural justice and
there was then an appeal to the committee of the Jockey Club which was a hearing de
novo when witnesses were present and available for cross-examination. The opinion was

delivered by Lord Wilberforce who indicated that Megarry J had stated the position too broadly when he had said that a failure of natural justice of a trial body could not be *a* cured by a sufficiency of natural justice in an appellate body (see [1979] 2 All ER 440 at 448, [1980] AC 574 at 592–593). Lord Wilberforce also indicated that the passage in the judgment of Mason J in *Twist v Randwick Municipal Council* to which I have already made reference, was 'close to their Lordships' view'.

The approach of the Privy Council, having analysed the various earlier decisions in different jurisdictions, was as Lord Wilberforce stated ([1979] 2 All ER 440 at 447–448, *b* [1980] AC 574 at 592), that—

> '... no clear and absolute rule can be laid down on the question whether defects in natural justice appearing at an original hearing, whether administrative or quasi-judicial, can be "cured" through an appeal proceedings. The situations in which this issue arises are too diverse, and the rules by which they are governed so various, that *c* this must be so. There are however a number of typical situations as to which some general principles can be stated.'

Lord Wilberforce then dealt with three different categories:

> 'First, there are cases where the rules provide for rehearing by the original body, or some fuller or enlarged form of it. This situation may be found in relation to *d* social clubs. It is not difficult in such cases to reach the conclusion that the first hearing is superseded by the second, or, putting it in contractual terms, the parties are taken to have agreed to accept the decision of the hearing body whether original or adjourned ... At the other extreme there are cases, where, after examination the whole hearing structure, in the context of the particular activity to which it relates (trade union membership, planning, employment etc) the conclusion is reached *e* that a complainant has a right to do nothing less than a fair hearing both at the original and at the appeal stage.'

The third category was the intermediate category as to which Lord Wilberforce said ([1979] 2 All ER 440 at 448–449, [1980] AC 574 at 593):

> 'In them it is for the court, in the light of the agreements made, and in addition *f* having regard to the course of proceedings, to decide whether, at the end of the day, there has been a fair result, reached by fair methods, such as the parties should fairly be taken to have accepted when they joined the association. Naturally there may be instances where the defect is so flagrant, the consequences so severe, that the most perfect of appeals and rehearings will not be sufficient to produce a just result. Many rules (including those now in question) anticipate that such a situation may arise by *g* giving power to remit for a new hearing. There may also be cases when the appeal process is itself less than perfect; it may be vitiated by the same defect as the original proceedings, or short of that there may be doubts whether the appeal body embarked on its task without predisposition or whether it had the means to make a fair and full inquiry ... In such cases it would no doubt be right to quash the original *h* decision.'

The appeal procedure under s 20 of the 1982 Act obviously falls within Lord Wilberforce's intermediate category.

Finally, Lord Wilberforce quoted with approval a judgment of Cooke J in *Reid v Rowley* [1977] 2 NZLR 472 and, having done so, went on to say that their Lordships did not— *j*

> 'understand the Court of Appeal [of New Zealand] to be subscribing to a view that cases of "insulation" or "curing", after a full hearing by an appellate body, may not exist; on the contrary Cooke J expresses the opinion that the court, in the exercise of its discretion, when reviewing the domestic or statutory decision, should

a   take into account all the proceedings which led to it, the conduct of the complaining
     party and the gravity of any breach of natural justice which may have occurred.
     This, though perhaps with some difference in emphasis, is their Lordships' approach.'

(See [1979] 2 All ER 440 at 451, [1980] AC 574 at 596.)
     Counsel for the appellants criticises the reasoning advanced by Mason J for his
conclusion in the *Twist* case, and I consider that there is justification for that criticism
and I certainly would not apply that reasoning to the present case. Counsel for the
b   appellants also sought to distinguish the *Twist* case and *Calvin v Carr*, and while he does
not quarrel with those decisions on the facts which were before the court he submits that
there is a distinction to be drawn between domestic tribunals where contract has a part
to play and bodies who are exercising judicial functions under a statute, particularly
where the decision can affect the personal interests of the complainant. In this approach
c   counsel for the appellants receives some support from Sir William Wade in his
authoritative textbook on *Administrative Law* (5th edn, 1982) p 488. However, I do not
regard it as right to treat what Lord Wilberforce stated as being confined to non-statutory
tribunals and in my view the approach of Jacobs J in *Twist* and Lord Wilberforce in *Calvin
v Carr* provides considerable guidance as to the approach to be adopted in this case.
     In my view in cases such as this the question the court should ask is whether, taking
d   into account the complainant's rights of appeal and if those rights have been exercised
what happened on the appeal, the complainant, viewing the combined proceedings as a
whole, has had a fair hearing? I regard this approach as appropriate because if Parliament
makes provision for an initial hearing followed by appeal then what Parliament should
be presumed to intend is that the persons affected by those proceedings should be treated
fairly in the proceedings as a whole. Where there are shortcomings in the initial
e   proceedings but the appellant has in fact been dealt with fairly when the proceedings as
a whole are considered, to regard the proceedings as invalid would be to condemn
something as being unfair because of a flaw in a part when, if the whole was considered,
the flaw would be sufficiently insignificant to enable the whole procedure to be regarded
as unblemished. Expressing the matter slightly differently, if the whole procedure is
properly regarded as being fair, then to strike that procedure down because of a flaw in
f   part will be to apply an unduly technical approach. My view of the test receives some
support in de Smith *Judicial Review of Administrative Action* (4th edn, 1980) p 242 ff and is
in accord with Lord Wilberforce's opinion in *Calvin v Carr*. Furthermore, it does not
have the flaw to which Megarry J referred because it presupposes Parliament gave the
complainant no more than a right to a fair hearing in the proceedings as a whole.
     Counsel for the district auditor also submitted that in this case even if there was a
g   breach of natural justice, the court should not intervene because the result would
inevitably have been the same even if there had not been the defect in procedure. I
recognise that there can be cases where such a submission will have to be considered by
the court. However, I regard the authorities on which counsel for the district auditor
relies, including *George v Secretary of State for the Environment* (1979) 38 P & CR 609 and
Malloch v Aberdeen Corp [1971] 2 All ER 1278 at 1294, [1971] 1 WLR 1578 at 1595, as
h   having application in very limited circumstances, and certainly I would not regard them
as applying here.
     What, then, is the result of applying this test to the circumstances of this case? Counsel
for the appellants submits that the auditor's decision, in particular, was unfair because he
rejected the truthfulness of the explanation which the appellants put forward without
their knowing that he was minded to do this and without his having the opportunity to
j   assess their credibility in the manner which would have been possible at an oral hearing.
In addition, in his reasons for his decision the auditor relied on five matters of which the
appellants did not have notice. The appellants, it is contended, were thus prevented from
dealing with these matters. Finally, counsel for the appellants says the period which the
appellants had in which to make their representations was unduly short and that when

the district auditor wrote to the appellants on 21 May 1984 he could have given more information than he did. I regard the last two complaints as being manifestly without *a* substance and I do not propose to take up any more time dealing with them. The other points are, however, of greater substance.

In the circumstances of this particular case, having regard to the history as to oral hearings before the district auditor in the past, it is surprising that both in this case and in the *Lambeth* case (*Smith v Skinner* [1986] RVR 45) the councillors were not given the offer of an oral hearing. They could have but did not allege they had a legitimate *b* expectation of such a hearing. I appreciate that where 49 councillors are involved an oral hearing might give rise to administrative problems and create delay, and the situation which existed in Liverpool could have been regarded by the auditors as one which required prompt action. However, in my view it would have been preferable to have invited representations whether there should be an oral hearing. This does not mean, however, that the procedure was unfair as a whole because this was not done. In this *c* country we attach considerable importance to the benefits of oral hearings in the administration of justice. It has been suggested that we attach excessive importance to orality. I would refer here to the dissenting judgment of Hamilton LJ in *R v Local Government Board, ex p Arlidge* [1914] 1 KB 160 at 192–193, which was subsequently indorsed in the House of Lords ([1915] AC 120, [1914–15] All ER Rep 1):

d

> 'It is said that a written argument is an illusory thing, that there is no eloquence or at least no persuasion but in speech. Parliament should know something about that, and it has left the matter to the Board. I find the contention bewildering. Are reasoning and writing mutually exclusive processes? The appellant desires to enjoy what Mr. Upjohn felicitiously calls "the bound and rebound of ideas and arguments between the Bench and Bar." This invests with authority a practice (or should I say *e* a foible) of judges, which I had believed to be pardonable and hoped to be not without its uses, but I am unable to see that it is the very pith of the administration of natural justice. It is said again that the appellant is entitled to a reply . . . I think this is only procedure again.'

In this case, in the note accompanying his notice to each individual appellant dated 26 *f* June 1985, the auditor sets out the charge, specifies the duty which is placed on the council under s 2(1) of the General Rate Act 1967 and indicates that the rate was not made for the year commencing 1 April 1985 by the council until 14 June 1985, and then adds:

> '4 ... The facts leading up to this decision by the Council are to be found principally in the minutes of the proceedings of meetings of the Council, of its *g* Policy and Finance Committee and of its Performance Review and Financial Control Sub-Committee and also in reports of officers referred to in these minutes ...
> 5. The facts show that there was no lawful justification for the delay in making of the rate. The Council thus disregarded the advice and warnings given by me my predecessors and its officers. On the evidence the Council would appear to be in breach of its statutory duty. *h*
> 6. To the extent that a breach of statutory duty results from a deliberate failure by any member to discharge his or her own duty then such a member is guilty of wilful misconduct ...'

Finally, the note identifies the loss which is alleged to arise as the result of the breach of duty. It is important that the note either in its appendices or by means of the documents *j* which accompanied the note identifies the evidence on which the auditor relied.

At the outset of this judgment I indicated the general nature of the appellants' case advanced in their representations. If the representations which they were making were correct then they were inconsistent with the view which the district auditor was provisionally expressing as being his interpretation of the facts set out in the documents

to which he referred. In these circumstances it should have been apparent that the
a representations could be rejected as being inconsistent with the contents of those
documents. This is what happened and although the appellants may not have anticipated
the district auditor's precise reasoning it should also have been anticipated that he could
reject their representations and in doing so could impugn their motives and credibility.
With regard to the alleged unfairness due to the failure to offer an oral hearing, my
conclusion is that the proceedings remained fair notwithstanding the absence of an offer
b of an oral hearing at the earlier stage. It is quite clear, as the appellants themselves said,
that they wished to make a collective response. Such a response can satisfactorily be made
in writing. The appellants made no request for an oral hearing which they could have
done although the district auditor had indicated that he intended to deal with the matter
in writing. In the Divisional Court the appellants had their opportunity for an oral
hearing and they were offered and declined the opportunity to give evidence. While,
c therefore, it may have been preferable to offer an oral hearing, justice did not require
such an offer at the earlier stage, and it is doubtful whether even if an offer had been
made it would have been accepted.

I turn to the new matters on which counsel for the appellants relies. In his reasons the
district auditor did not in fact find that the rate which was made was unlawful. He used
the inadequacy of the rate as being an example of the contravention by the appellants of
d their officials' advice, which was a matter referred to in the note.

The second matter on which counsel for the appellants relies is the events of 1984 and
their significance for 1985 and 1986. As the auditor referred to various documents
relating to the previous year, he had done sufficient, in my view, to make it clear that he
was relying on the events in the previous year in coming to his conclusion as to what
occurred in the year directly under consideration.
e The next matter relied on by counsel for the appellants, namely the lack of progress in
the budget-making process, I also regard as being adequately dealt with in the allegations
of delay which appear in the note. The same is true on the remaining matters on which
counsel for the appellants relies, namely the failure to act on the advice from the officers
and the negotiations with the Department of the Environment. I accept that there was
further material which could have been put forward and was subsequently put forward
f before the Divisional Court by the appellants, but I do not consider that it can be said
that the fact that there was not sufficient opportunity to put it forward earlier meant the
proceedings as a whole were rendered unfair or the auditor was required to give an
opportunity for further representations.

Accordingly, I have come to the conclusion that when the proceedings, including the
hearing before the Divisional Court, are considered as a whole the allegation of unfairness
g is not made out.

The wilful misconduct issue

It is convenient first to consider the question whether there was misconduct on the
part of the appellants and then consider whether the alleged misconduct was wilful.
h The argument on behalf of the appellants that there was no misconduct stems from
the fact that the rating legislation contains no express statutory provision setting out the
date by which the rate has to be made. In my judgment given on 16 April 1985, in *R v
Hackney London BC, ex p Fleming* [1986] RVR 182, I indicated what I considered to be the
position.

Subject to two qualifications made by Glidewell LJ to which I should refer, both in the
j court below and before this court it has been accepted that what I said in the *Hackney* case
generally reflected the legal position. The first reservation was that I may have been
unduly generous in talking of weeks and it would have been preferable to talk of a few
days rather than weeks. I would not dissent from this qualification. The second
qualification arises because the General Rate Act 1967, s 50 and Sch 10 as amended gives
to all ratepayers the right to pay rates by instalments and provides that a person wishing

to pay by instalments may do so by not less than ten instalments payable at intervals of at least one month. This provision did not arise for consideration in the *Hackney* case, and I *a* agree with Glidewell LJ that in order that ratepayers are able to complete their payments by the end of the following March they must start by the end of the preceding June, and as at least ten days' notice must be given of the rate the last day on which a rate can be made is 20 June if the ratepayers are to have this opportunity of paying by instalments. However, whether the stricter approach indicated by Glidewell LJ or the approach I indicated in the *Hackney* case is adopted, it is quite clear in this case that the council would *b* be in breach of duty unless there was a valid reason for deferring making the rate until 14 June 1985.

In their joint representations to the auditor, the appellants put forward as the explanation for the delay in making the rates that they wished to seek—

> 'to take maximum advantage of every avenue of negotiation open to them to *c* maximise the resources available to the Council. Negotiations in 1984/85 had a marked measure of success. There was every reason to suppose in the light of that success that Liverpool could present its case in a manner which would again command respect and response. To attempt to add to Liverpool's resources—or to shield Liverpool from the worst consequences of the Target—and Penalty system is in fact evidence on the part of those making the attempt that they have acted with *d* the highest degree of public responsibility . . . In the present case, the motivation of the Councillors has been throughout to ensure that the resources available to combat the deprivation in Liverpool and to sustain the services it offers to Liverpool people are as large as possible.'

This reasoning is amplified by Mr Hamilton and Mr Byrne in their affidavits. I do not propose to set out all the relevant paragraphs. However, I should refer to what Mr *e* Hamilton describes in his first affidavit as being 'Our reasons for not making a rate until the 14th June'. This, he said, could be stated very simply and shortly:

> 'Our financial problems were so severe that it appeared that we could not meet our budget costs without an unacceptable rise in the rates or an unacceptable cut in jobs and services. We believed that there was a reasonable prospect of obtaining *f* increased financial resources that would alter the calculations and hence the level of rate we would need to set. We believed this for a whole number of reasons which I will endeavour to set out below. Furthermore, we believed that there was no legal obligation to set a rate before 20th June 1985.'

This statement was accepted by the other deponents. Mr Byrne, who was chairman of *g* the performance review and financial control sub-committee, which was the primary committee dealing with the finances of the city, concludes his first affidavit by saying:

> 'The decision to delay making the rate whilst attempting to seek substantial financial resources for the City of Liverpool at the risk of incurring possible increased interest charges by the withholding of apparently discretionary payments was, in my opinion, a purely political decision which the Council was entitled to make and *h* which it believed (wrongly as it turned out) would be more likely to produce a financial advantage, and an enormously greater financial advantage at that, to the City.'

Although this may not be explicit in the passages to which I have made reference, it is implicit, and it was undoubtedly the case, that the reason that it was the policy of the *j* majority party to delay making a rate was to use the absence of a rate as a lever or weapon in the negotiations to obtain additional resources from central government. Even if the policy was adopted because it was thought that it was in the best interests of the people of Liverpool it does not alter the fact that to delay making a rate as part of this tactic is unlawful. As must have been appreciated by those who were responsible for choosing

this tactic, it involves a threat that unless central government provides additional
a resources a rate would not be made and Liverpool's resources would be reduced so that
eventually a state of financial chaos would result, as in fact very nearly happened as is
illustrated by the purported dismissal of all teachers in Liverpool. What this amounts to
is threatening not to perform a duty so as to take advantage of the undesirable
consequences which will flow from the failure to perform that duty. This constitutes the
clearest possible example of misconduct.

b   In addition, having regard to the history of the negotiations with the Secretary of State,
and in particular the relatively small sum which it was hoped could be obtained as a
result of the negotiations, when compared to the extent of the deficiency with which
Liverpool was faced, the desire to negotiate could not be a reasonable explanation for the
delay in making the rate. It would be wholly unreasonable to delay making a rate until
14 June merely to ascertain what additional provision, if any, by way of housing and
c urban benefit could be obtained.

The next question is whether this misconduct should be regarded as wilful? It would
only be wilful if the appellants were doing something which they knew to be wrong or
about which they were recklessly indifferent whether it was wrong or not: see *Graham v
Teesdale* (1981) 81 LGR 117.

Even without my judgment in the *Hackney* case it should have been obvious to any
d councillor familiar with the rate-making process that it was not lawful to use the
deferring of making a rate as a weapon or lever in the way that I have described. I regard
it as significant that there is no evidence that the appellants sought advice whether it was
permissible to use tactics of this sort. In addition, I consider that if there was any doubt
in the matter the position was made abundantly clear by the reports of the district auditor
and the council's officers in 1984 and 1985. I do not propose to lengthen this judgment
e by citations from those reports. It is sufficient if I draw attention to the fact that in March
1984 the chief executive, city solicitor and city treasurer, in their joint report, dealt
clearly and explicitly with the practical consequences not only of failing to make a rate
but of delaying making a rate, and in the same officers' report of 16 April 1985 delay in
making a rate was dealt with in terms which made it clear that, while there might have
been good reasons the previous year for delay, that did not apply to the current year. As
f the district auditor pointed out in his reasons, the rate which was in fact made by the
council indicated that the appellants were prepared to act in disregard of the advice
which they received. I agree with the Divisional Court that if the appellants collectively
were not acting knowing what they were doing was wrong they were most certainly
acting recklessly whether what they were doing was wrong.

g   So far I have dealt with the position on a collective basis. I was, at one stage, concerned,
after having read all the affidavits of the appellants, whether it was right to condemn all
the appellants merely because they were prepared to cast their votes for the critical
resolutions because they were the policies of the party of which they were members.
However, although they filed individual affidavits, which in many cases indicate that
they are otherwise not in the habit of indulging in unlawful conduct, I have come to the
h conclusion that it is not possible to distinguish between the appellants. They made
collective representations as a matter of policy to the district auditor. They advanced a
collective argument before the Divisional Court, and in this court no ground for
distinguishing between them has been advanced. Therefore, although regrettably steps
were taken by the majority party to avoid the wider dissemination of the report of the
officers on 16 April 1985 at the meeting of the performance review and financial control
j sub-committee of that date, and the report which would have been a further warning
was not seen by all the appellants, it is not possible, in the circumstances of this appeal, to
make a distinction between any of the appellants.

The loss issue
The argument of the appellants is that because it was a decision of central government

to refuse to make the payments amounting to £106,103 this loss was not incurred or
caused by the appellants' wilful misconduct. However, warnings had been given that the
payments would not be made until such time as the rate was made, and undoubtedly the
cause of the payments being withheld was the failure to make the rate. Although,
therefore, decisions were no doubt made by the Department of Health and Social Security
and Treasury valuer not to pay the rate rebate element of housing benefit subsidy or to
make the contributions in lieu of rates on Crown property, this was still the direct
consequence of the council's action and therefore the resultant loss falls within s 20 of the
1982 Act.

There is one further matter with which I should deal which I consider of some
importance. Before the Divisional Court Mr Scrivener, on behalf of the district auditor,
submitted that it was not open to the appellants to challenge the validity of the auditor's
decision on the grounds of procedural impropriety on an appeal under s 20(3) because he
argued that an appeal presupposes that there has been a valid decision. He submitted that
the correct procedure would be to apply for judicial review, and at the same time to enter
an appeal which would only be heard if the decision were to be held invalid.

Glidewell LJ considered, in principle, that this submission was correct. However, he
regarded himself as being bound by the decision in *Asher v Secretary of State for
Environment* [1974] 2 All ER 156, [1974] Ch 208, a decision of this court, that the validity
of the auditor's decision could be challenged on an appeal, but he went on to say that
Asher's case was only authority for the fact that an auditor's decision—

> 'may be challenged by way of appeal under s 20(3), not that it cannot be challenged
> in any other way. That challenge, of course, arose after the appeal had been heard
> and decided. The decision, therefore, does not prevent the procedure suggested by
> counsel for the auditors [Mr Scrivener] from being adopted, and it is my clear view
> that if the same situation arises again, this is the course which should be followed.'

(See [1986] RVR 45 at 55.)

Before this court counsel for the district auditor did not repeat Mr Scrivener's argument
but reserved the point having regard to the *Asher* decision in case there should be a
further appeal.

In case the position is not clarified by a further appeal I feel it right that I should make
it clear that I do not regard Mr Scrivener's argument as being right in principle. Nor do I
consider that it would be desirable that in the normal way decisions as to the procedural
propriety of an auditor's decision should be challenged by judicial review and not by way
of statutory appeal. Mr Scrivener, in support of his suggestion that the only appropriate
method of raising this matter was by way of judicial review, relied on *O'Reilly v Mackman*
[1982] 3 All ER 1124, [1983] 2 AC 237. However, in that case there was no statutory
right of appeal. The normal approach in relation to judicial review is that if there is an
appropriate statutory procedure that procedure should be followed rather than judicial
review. This is of importance in relation to appeals from district auditors. First of all, the
ordinary time limit in respect of the statutory appeal is, under RSC Ord 98, r 3(2), only
28 days, rather than the general requirement in Ord 53 that an application should be
made promptly, and in any event within three months. Of more significance is the fact
that the powers expressly given to the court under s 20 of the 1982 Act, as has already
been pointed out, are wide. In addition to the power, which is equivalent to that on an
application under Ord 53, to quash the decision, there is power to vary the decision and
to give any certificate which the auditor could have given. This could be of very
considerable significance in a case where a certificate has wrongly been refused by an
auditor because he had, for example, refused to hear an objector fairly. If application has
to be made first for judicial review by the objector, if the objector was successful the
matter would have to be remitted to the auditor, whereas if the objector could appeal
this would be unnecessary and the court could give the certificate which the auditor

should have given if he had acted fairly. It can also be of significance in the case of an
a allegation of unfairness where there is no objection, as the facts of this case indicate.

I appreciate that the additional inconvenience of bringing two sets of proceedings is
not a substantial argument against the course which was recommended in the Divisional
Court. However, if there is no requirement to have two sets of proceedings I cannot see
that there is any advantage in recommending a course which must involve limited
additional expense. There are many statutory appeals by applicants in respect of decisions
b by ministers and others where questions of fairness are regularly considered by the courts
without any necessity for judicial review, and if the court considers that it is desirable for
an allegation of procedural impropriety to be taken first this can always be done. My
principal concern, however, is that I can foresee considerable delay and disruption being
caused to the very important role of the auditor under s 20 if persons aggrieved by a
decision as to procedure can seek to apply for judicial review independently of the right
c to appeal. In the normal case it would certainly be most undesirable if the High Court
should be asked to intervene by way of judicial review before the auditor had come to
his decision on the merits.

For these reasons, as well as the reasons given in the judgments of Lawton and
Dillon LJJ, I agree that these appeals must be dismissed.

d *Appeals dismissed. Expenses incurred by district auditor as a result of the appeal, not of the
original hearing, to be paid by the council. Leave to appeal to the House of Lords granted.*

Appeal
The appellants appealed.

e *Louis Blom-Cooper QC, Beverley Lang* and *Heather Williams* for the appellants.
Anthony Hidden QC and *Mark Lowe* for the district auditor.
Charles Cross for the council.

Their Lordships took time for consideration.

f 12 March. The following opinions were delivered.

LORD KEITH OF KINKEL. My Lords, the appellants are a group of Liverpool city
councillors. The respondent is the district auditor for the city. In respect of the financial
year beginning 1 April 1985 the appellants brought it about that a rate for the city was
g not set until 14 June 1985. The council were advised by their officers that the rate then
proposed to be set was an illegal one, in respect that it fell far short, taken along with
other sources of income, of meeting the city's expenditure for the year as then estimated.
But that is not the point. The point is that the delay in setting the rate led to delay in
receiving various items of income, including government contributions in respect of
payments in lieu of rates on Crown properties and in respect of rate rebates.
h There had been trouble over the making of a rate also in respect of the financial year
1984–85, when in the event a rate was made on 10 July 1984. On 19 March 1984 the
district auditor's predecessor had sent to the council a report expressing concern at
indications that the council might deliberately make a rate for the year which would not
be sufficient to meet its outgoings for that year. The report drew attention to possible
consequences to individual councillors, both financial and by way of disqualification, if
an adequate rate were not made. In the penultimate paragraph it was stated: 'Members
j would in my view also be at risk if a rate was not made because no vote was taken or
there was unreasonable delay in making a rate.'

On 10 April 1985 the district auditor's predecessor had sent to the council a report
expressing concern at the council's failure to make a valid rate for the year commencing

1 April 1985, drawing attention to his report dated 19 March 1984 and reiterating the
duties of councillors and the possible consequences to the city and to individual   *a*
councillors if these duties were not carried out. The report concluded by urging the
council in its own best interests, as well as those of individual members, employees and
the local community, that a rate should be made at a very early date. On 7 May 1985 the
policy and finance committee of the council rejected a motion that the chairman of the
committee submit proposals to the next meeting of the council to enable it to fix a rate,
and this was approved at a meeting of the council on 21 May.   *b*

On 21 May 1985 the district auditor had made a further report to the council, copies
of which he sent to all councillors. In it he referred to earlier reports and gave notice that
unless the council made a lawful rate at the earliest opportunity and in any event before
the end of May he would forthwith commence action under s 20 of the Local Government
Finance Act 1982 to recover any losses occasioned by the failure to make a rate from the
members responsible for incurring them.   *c*

On 6 June 1985 the Audit Commission directed that an extraordinary audit be carried
out. On 26 June the district auditor sent to each of the appellants a notice stating that he
had to consider in pursuance of his duty under the 1982 Act whether he should certify
the sum of £106,103, or any other sum, consequent on the failure to make a rate or the
delay in making a rate for the financial year 1985–86, as due from the appellants on the
ground that a loss of such sum had been incurred or deficiency caused by the appellants' *d*
wilful misconduct. The appellants were further notified that they might make
representations in writing to the district auditor before he reached a decision, and that
any such representations should reach him by 19 July 1985. There was enclosed with the
notice a note of the matters to which the district auditor had had regard in deciding to
issue it. This note set out the council's duty under s 2(1) of the General Rate Act 1967 to
make a rate, and the district auditor's responsibility under s 20(1) of the 1982 Act, which *e*
provides:

> 'Where it appears to the auditor carrying out the audit of any accounts under this
> Part of this Act . . . (b) that a loss has been incurred or deficiency caused by the wilful
> misconduct of any person, he shall certify that . . . the amount of the loss or the
> deficiency is due from that person and . . . both he and the body in question . . . may *f*
> recover that . . . amount for the benefit of that body; and if the auditor certifies
> under this section that any . . . amount is due from two or more persons, they shall
> be jointly and severally liable for that . . . amount.'

There were appended to the note copies of earlier reports by the district auditor and his
predecessors, including those of 19 March 1984, 10 April 1985 and 21 May 1985, and
also a list of minutes of meetings of the council and certain of its committees between   *g*
March 1984 and June 1985 and of reports by the council's officers between the same
dates. The facts gathered from these documents were stated to show that there was no
lawful justification for the delay in the making of the rate for the year 1985–86. The
note went on to identify certain specific losses resulting from the delay. These were the
loss of interest on sums which would, but for the delay, have been paid at an earlier date *h*
than was actually the case by the Department of Health and Social Security in respect of
the rate rebates element of housing benefit subsidy and by the Treasury valuer in respect
of contributions in lieu of rates on Crown property. The total of such loss was stated to
be £106,103. The appellants were identified as persons who by their voting or absence
might have failed to discharge their duty as members of the council and might therefore
be guilty of wilful misconduct resulting in the losses in question.   *j*

The appellants chose to make a collective response to the district auditor's notice. This
was prepared with the assistance of the chief executive of the council, who was legally
qualified and had great experience in local government, and was sent to the district
auditor on 19 July 1985. The appellants relied on various matters which they claimed
rebutted the district auditor's provisional view that they had been guilty of wilful

misconduct. Their principal contention was that, considering that the relevant legislation

a laid down no date by which a rate must be set, it was sufficient if they did so within a reasonable time after the start of the financial year, and that the delay until 14 June 1985 had been reasonable because they had hoped or expected to be able to persuade ministers to make larger grants available to Liverpool than ministers had previously expressed themselves as willing to do. In this respect they founded on the circumstance that in relation to the year 1984–85 their efforts in this direction had met with some success,

b and that the then district auditor in his report of 7 June 1984 had stressed the importance of 20 June as the latest date for making a rate, in order to permit of ratepayers exercising their statutory right to pay rates by ten monthly instalments. It was contended that the appellants had been influenced throughout by a sincere desire to maximise the resources available to the people of Liverpool and thus to do their best to alleviate the unsatisfactory conditions prevailing there. There were sent along with the representations various

c documents to which it was desired that the district auditor should have regard as supporting the appellants' contentions. It is to be observed at this point that the representations did not face up to the circumstance that, whether or not additional funds might be secured from government sources, delay in making a rate must inevitably have an adverse effect on the city's finances through delay in the receipt of items of income which depended on a rate having been set. Nor did the representations draw attention to

d any records, whether of meetings of the council and its committees or meetings of the ruling political group represented by the appellants, describing the reasons for the delay in making a rate.

On 6 September 1985 the district auditor issued a certificate under s 20(1) of the 1982 Act to the effect that a loss of £106,103 had been incurred by the wilful misconduct of the appellants. The certificate was accompanied by a lengthy statement of reasons for its

e issue setting out the history of the matter and dealing in considerable detail with the appellants' representations before setting out the district auditor's conclusions. These were that the delay in making a rate was deliberate, that the intention of the delay was to use the non-making of the rate as a lever in an attempt to prise additional money from central government, that there was no justifiable reason for supposing that delay would influence central government to increase rate support grant, and that the council knew

f that to delay unreasonably was a wrongful act or was recklessly indifferent whether or not it was a wrongful act. Finally, it was concluded that a loss of £106,103 was a direct consequence of the delay in making a rate and the appellants were identified as those responsible for the delay.

The appellants appealed to the High Court under s 20(3) of the 1982 Act. The appeal was heard by a Divisional Court consisting of Glidewell LJ, Caulfield and Russell JJ,

g together with a similar appeal by a number of Lambeth councillors. Counsel then acting for the appellants appear to have concentrated on the merits of the appeal rather than on allegations of procedural irregularity on the part of the district auditor. Affidavits were lodged by all the appellants and also a considerable amount of documentary evidence which had not been before the district auditor. Though invited to do so by the court,

h none of the appellants gave any oral evidence. Counsel for the appellants submitted that it would be inappropriate for the court to investigate the proceedings of the political caucus represented by the appellants. The Divisional Court dismissed the appeal (see [1986] RVR 45), and their decision was affirmed by the Court of Appeal (Lawton, Dillon and Woolf LJJ) (see p 1120, ante), who gave leave to appeal to your Lordships' House.

The argument by counsel for the appellants did not invite your Lordships to enter

j deeply into the merits of the question whether or not they had been guilty of wilful misconduct, nor was attention drawn to any details of the affidavits and other material placed before the Divisional Court. The substance of the argument was that the district auditor's decision had been vitiated by his failure to offer the appellants an oral hearing before reaching it, and should therefore have been quashed. The argument was supported by an examination of earlier legislation in regard to local government audits, starting with the Poor Law Amendment Act 1844, where oral hearings were the order of the day, and by reference to the Code of Local Government Audit Practice for England and Wales, *a* made under s 14 of the 1982 Act and approved by resolution of both Houses of Parliament. The code, by paras 16 to 20, contemplates that an oral hearing will be held where the auditor is dealing with a notice of objection given under s 17(3) of the 1982 Act, which itself refers to the objector attending before the auditor. The code does not deal with the procedure to be followed where the auditor takes action under s 20(1). Counsel produced a list of all instances since 1972 where a district auditor had occasion *b* to consider an issue of wilful misconduct, indicating that in all but one of them an oral hearing had been offered. This had the effect, so it was maintained, of creating a legitimate expectation on the part of the appellants that they would be offered an oral hearing before the district auditor arrived at his decision.

My Lords, if the district auditor had reached a decision adverse to the appellants without giving them any opportunity at all of making representations to him, there can *c* be no doubt that his procedure would have been contrary to the rules of natural justice and that, subject to the question whether the defect was capable of being cured on appeal to the Divisional Court, the decision would fall to be quashed. In the event, written representations alone were asked for. These were duly furnished, in very considerable detail, and an oral hearing was not requested, though that could very easily have been done, and there is no reason to suppose that the request would not have been granted. *d* None of the appellants stated, in his or her affidavit before the Divisional Court, that they had an expectation that an oral hearing, though not asked for, would be offered. The true question is whether the district auditor acted fairly in all the circumstances. It is easy to envisage cases where an oral hearing would clearly be essential in the interests of fairness, for example where an objector states that he has personal knowledge of some facts indicative of wilful misconduct on the part of a councillor. In that situation justice would *e* demand that the councillor be given an opportunity to depone to his own version of the facts. In the present case the district auditor had arrived at his provisional view on the basis of the contents of documents, minutes of meetings and reports submitted to the council from the auditor's department and their own officers. All these documents were appended to or referred to in the notice of 26 June sent by the district auditor to the *f* councillors. Their response referred to other documents, which were duly considered by the district auditor, as is shown by his statement of reasons dated 6 September 1985. No facts contradictory of or supplementary to the contents of the documents were or are relied on by either side. If the appellants had attended an oral hearing they would no doubt have reiterated the sincerity of their motives from the point of view of advancing the interests of the inhabitants of Liverpool. It seems unlikely, having regard to the *g* position adopted by their counsel on this matter before the Divisional Court, that they would have been willing to reveal or answer questions about the proceedings of their political caucus. The sincerity of the appellants' motives is not something capable of justifying or excusing failure to carry out a statutory duty, or of making reasonable what is otherwise an unreasonable delay in carrying out such a duty. In all the circumstances I am of opinion that the district auditor did not act unfairly, and that the procedure which *h* he followed did not involve any prejudice to the appellants.

It is to be added that counsel for the appellants founded on certain matters which it was maintained were relied on by the district auditor in his statement of reasons dated 6 September 1985 without having been included in the notice of 26 June 1985 so as to give the appellants the opportunity of dealing with those matters. In my opinion there is no merit in this point. One of the matters, the alleged unlawfulness of the rate made on 14 *j* June 1985, was not founded on by the district auditor as a ground for issuing his certificate. The statement of reasons does not assert that the rate was unlawful. It does no more than mention that, as was the fact, the city solicitor had advised the council that the proposed rate would be unlawful. The substance of the other matters was broadly covered in the statement which accompanied the notice of 26 June 1985.

On the view which I take, that the district auditor's decision was not vitiated by
a procedural unfairness, the question whether such unfairness, had it existed, was capable
of being cured by the appeal to the High Court does not arise directly for decision. It is,
however, my opinion that the particular appeal mechanism provided for by s 20(3) of
the 1982 Act, considered in its context, is apt to enable the court, notwithstanding that it
finds some procedural defect in the conduct of an audit which has resulted in a certificate
based on wilful misconduct, to inquire into the merits of the case and arrive at its own
b decision thereon. Section 20(3)(*b*) empowers the court to 'confirm the decision or quash
it and give any certificate which the auditor could have given'. The relevant rules of
court enable a rehearing of the broadest possible scope to take place. Evidence may be
given on oath, which is not possible before the auditor, and there is no limit to the
further material which may be introduced so as to enable the whole merits to be fully
examined. There is no question of the court being confined to a review of the evidence
c which was available to the auditor. In the circumstances, it would be quite unreasonable
and not in accordance with the intendment of the enactment to hold that the court,
where an issue is raised as to the fairness of the procedure adopted by the auditor, is
confined to a judicial review species of jurisdiction so as to have power only to quash or
affirm the auditor's certificate without entering on its own examination of the merits of
the case. No doubt there may be cases where the procedural defect is so gross, and the
d prejudice suffered by the appellant so extreme, that it would be appropriate to quash the
auditor's decision on that ground. But in my opinion the court has a discretion, where it
considers that justice can properly be done by its own investigation of the merits, to
follow that course. I may add that I agree entirely with all that is said on this aspect of the
appeal in the speech of my noble and learned friend Lord Bridge.
　　The final argument for the appellants was that the loss of £106,103 was not shown to
e have been caused by the wilful misconduct of the appellants. This argument was fully
considered and rejected by the Divisional Court and the Court of Appeal. I agree entirely
with their reasons for rejecting that argument, to which I find it unnecessary to add.
　　My Lords, for these reasons I would dismiss the appeal. The appellants must pay the
district auditor's costs, subject to any protection available to those of them who hold legal
f aid certificates. This is a suitable case for directing, under s 20(3) of the 1982 Act, that
any unrecovered costs shall not be paid by the city of Liverpool.

LORD BRIDGE OF HARWICH. My Lords, on 6 June 1985 the Audit Commission
exercised its power under s 22(1)(*b*) of the Local Government Finance Act 1982 to order
an extraordinary audit of the accounts of the Liverpool City Council for the financial
g year which commenced on 1 April 1985 in so far as they related to the failure to make a
rate or the delay in making a rate for that financial year. By notice dated 26 June 1985
the respondent district auditor informed each of the present appellants, who were
members of the majority party on the Liverpool City Council, of the extraordinary audit
and that he intended to consider in pursuance of his duty under s 20(1) of the 1982 Act
whether he should certify the sum of £106,103 or any other sum, consequent on the
h failure to make a rate or the delay in making a rate for the financial year commencing on
1 April 1985, as due from him or her on the ground that a loss of such sum had been
incurred or a deficiency caused by his or her wilful misconduct. The notice was
accompanied by a note referring to the relevant statutory provisions, summarising the
history, enclosing a number of reports made to the council by the district auditor and his
predecessor, and identifying all relevant minutes of the council and its committees and
j reports made to the council by the council's own officers. The note indicated that this
was the material to which the district auditor had had regard and continued as follows:

　　　'5. The facts show that there was no lawful justification for the delay in the
　　making of the rate. The Council has thus disregarded the advice and warnings given
　　by me, my predecessor and its officers. On the evidence the Council would appear

to be in breach of its statutory duty. 6. To the extent that a breach of statutory duty results from a deliberate failure by any member to discharge his or her own duty then such a member is guilty of wilful misconduct. My predecessor referred to the members' duty in his reports of 19 March 1984 and 10 April 1985.'

The note then proceeds to indicate how the district auditor had assessed such losses or deficiencies as he could then identify as caused by the delay in making a rate and concludes:

'11. I have reviewed the resolutions of the Council to determine how individual members discharged their duty. It at present seems to me that members listed below by their voting, abstention from voting or absence may have failed to discharge their duty as members and may therefore be guilty of wilful misconduct occasioning the loss or deficiency identified in paragraph 9 above. But I will defer making any decision until I have had the opportunity to consider any representations in writing you may wish to make.'

The formal notice indicated that representations in writing should be made not later than 19 July 1985.

On 19 July the leader of the city council, Cllr Hamilton, wrote to the district auditor in the following terms:

'The Liverpool Labour Group have held several meetings to discuss their response to your letter of 26 June 1985 regarding the audit of Liverpool City Council's accounts 1985–86. It is the unanimous view of those concerned that our response to you should be a collective one and accordingly the Labour Group's response is attached and signed by those councillors who are in receipt of your letter of 26 June. I would, however, wish to point out, that in the case of Councillor James Hackett, he has been away on holiday for the last three weeks and has not had the opportunity to sign the document. It would therefore be appreciated if you would allow Councillor Hackett to reply to you upon his return.'

On his return from holiday a few days later Cllr Hackett adopted the response of his fellow councillors.

The response enclosed with Cllr Hamilton's letter was a carefully drafted and closely reasoned document of 30 pages accompanied by 349 pages of appendices. A paragraph headed 'Conclusion' contained the following:

'In preparing this response, and in assembling the accompanying material, the councillors have sought to comply with the relatively short time allowed in the district auditor's notice. They would wish, however, to reserve the right to add to or develop their response, as appropriate, in the light of events.'

Concurrently with the extraordinary audit of the accounts of Liverpool City Council a similar extraordinary audit had been ordered of the accounts of the Lambeth London Borough Council. In the course of that audit a notice similar to the notice date 26 June 1985 in the Liverpool case had been sent to the Lambeth councillors and they too had made a collective response. On 7 August 1985 Cllr Hamilton wrote again to the district auditor saying:

'The Liverpool councillors would wish, as part of their response to the notices issued to them and in exercise of the right reserved therein, to associate themselves with the legal submissions made by the Lambeth councillors in so far as they have not been explicitly covered in their own response.'

No individual Liverpool councillor submitted any separate written representations on his own behalf or asked for the opportunity to make representations orally.

On 6 September 1985 the district auditor issued his certificate pursuant to s 20(1)(b) of
a the 1982 Act that £106,103 was due from each of the appellant councillors on the ground
that it appeared to him that a loss or deficiency in that amount had been caused by their
wilful misconduct, accompanied by a statement in writing of the reasons for his decision
to issue the certificate. The appellant councillors all appealed against the decision under
s 20(3)(a). A decision to issue a similar certificate in respect of a number of Lambeth
councillors was also under appeal. The appeals were heard together by the Divisional
b Court (Glidewell LJ, Caulfield and Russell JJ) ([1986] RVR 45) over ten sitting days from
3 to 14 February 1986. As in the written representations to the district auditor, so on the
hearing of the appeals the stance adopted by the appellants was a united and collective
one. They were all represented by the same counsel. Although the affidavit material was
voluminous and different appellants deposed in their affidavits to different detailed
aspects of the facts, all expressed their agreement with the main affidavit made by Cllr
c Hamilton, the leader of the council, and neither by affidavit nor through counsel did any
individual appellant invite the court to distinguish his responsibility for what the
majority group on the city council did or failed to do from that of any other member of
the group.

The main issue canvassed in the Divisional Court was the issue on the merits, whether
the appellants had been guilty of wilful misconduct and, if so, whether it had caused any
d loss. The court took the view urged by counsel for the district auditor and supported by
counsel for the Lambeth councillors that, in relation to that issue, the scope of the hearing
on appeal was unlimited and that they could consider whatever evidence and arguments
were put before them, whether or not they had been before the respective auditors. At
an early stage in the hearing, the court raised the question whether any party wished to
give oral evidence. None did. Counsel then appearing for the appellants went further
e and submitted that it would be inappropriate for the court to hear oral evidence. When
invited by the court to disclose when and in what circumstances the rate at a figure
representing a 9% increase over the 1984 rate (which the Liverpool City Council had
eventually adopted and which would have left a deficit of £117m on estimated
expenditure) had been decided on by the appellants, he submitted that the court was not
f entitled to investigate the activities of a political caucus. As Glidewell LJ put it ([1986]
RVR 45 at 52):

'It is clear to me, therefore, that the highly experienced counsel who appeared for
the councillors were satisfied that justice could be done by our hearing their clients'
appeals on affidavit and documentary evidence.'

g The judgments in the Divisional Court examined the issue on the merits at length and
concluded that wilful misconduct causing the loss certified by the district auditor was
fully established.

Submissions that the district auditors' certificates against both Liverpool and Lambeth
councillors were vitiated by procedural unfairness, in that the appellants had not had a
proper opportunity to answer some of the points relied on in the reasons for the respective
h decisions to certify, were made by counsel for both the Liverpool and the Lambeth
councillors after their submissions on the merits. The court took the view that these
should have been taken as preliminary points and, if well-founded, would lead to the
quashing of the auditors' decisions. But they concluded that there had been no procedural
unfairness and that the appellants had had a sufficient opportunity to meet the case put
against them. The Divisional Court gave judgment dismissing the appellants' appeals on
j 5 March 1985.

The Liverpool councillors appealed. The Lambeth councillors did not. In the Court of
Appeal there was both a change of counsel and a change of emphasis. Counsel now
presented the case for the appellants, as he has done before your Lordships. The hearing
occupied the court for nine days from 9 to 22 July 1986. The merits were once more
fully canvassed and the Court of Appeal (Lawton, Dillon and Woolf LJJ) unanimously

affirmed the view of the Divisional Court that the appellants had been guilty of wilful
misconduct causing the certified loss. But my impression is that the procedural complaint a
by which the decision of the district auditor was sought to be impugned loomed much
larger in the Court of Appeal than it had in the Divisional Court. Counsel for the
appellants introduced elaborate new arguments based on the history of the legislation
relating to the auditing of local government accounts from the Poor Law Amendment
Act 1844 to the Local Government Finance Act 1982 and on the practice followed by
district auditors over a long period to support a submission, repeated before your b
Lordships, that a district auditor, before certifying that a loss or deficiency has been
caused by the wilful misconduct of any person under s 20(1)(b) of the 1982 Act, is obliged,
as a matter of law, to offer that person an oral hearing and that, if he does not do so, any
certificate issued is a nullity. The Court of Appeal unanimously rejected this submission.
They expressed marginally different views, however, on the complaint that there had
been a lack of fairness in the proceedings. Put shortly, Lawton LJ thought that, in so far c
as the district auditor's reasons for his decision impugned the good faith and credibility
of the appellants' response to his notice of 26 June 1985, he ought, before taking the
decision, to have given them the opportunity of addressing him orally on that issue.
Dillon LJ inclined to the same view, though he found it unnecessary to reach a final
conclusion. Both based their decision on the ground that the full hearing on the merits
before the Divisional Court could, as a matter of law, and did, as a matter of fact, remove d
any ground of complaint arising out of the procedure followed by the district auditor in
reaching his decision. Woolf LJ approached the matter more broadly. He went no
further than to say that it would be preferable to have invited representations whether
there should be an oral hearing. But he concluded that when the proceedings, including
the hearing before the Divisional Court, were considered as a whole, the allegation of
unfairness was not made out. The Court of Appeal gave judgment dismissing the appeals e
on 31 July 1986 but granted leave to appeal to your Lordships' House.

My Lords, it is appropriate to emphasise at the outset that the conclusion reached by
the district auditor, the Divisional Court and the Court of Appeal that the appellants
were guilty of wilful misconduct causing the certified loss is no longer the subject of any
substantial challenge. I use the qualifying epithet 'substantial' for two reasons. First, f
counsel for the appellants renewed shortly before your Lordships a submission made
below to the effect that, if there was wilful misconduct, it did not cause the relevant loss
which the district auditor certified. The point is shortly dealt with in the judgments of
Glidewell LJ in the Divisional Court and Lawton and Woolf LJJ in the Court of Appeal.
They demonstrate clearly that, if there was misconduct, the certified loss was caused by
it. I need say no more than that I agree with and adopt their reasons. Second, the g
document headed 'The Issues on the Appeal' which counsel for the appellants helpfully
handed in at the opening of his submissions contains a paragraph which reads:

'Did the district auditor and the courts below, in concluding that the [appellants]
were guilty of wilful misconduct in delaying the making of the rate for the financial
year 1985–86, apply the right test in judging the decisions and actions of the h
[appellants]?'

Whatever faint argument, in the course of counsel's oral submissions, may have been
addressed to this issue, it signally failed to identify any misdirection in law by the courts
below in their consideration of the issue of wilful misconduct. It seems to me abundantly
clear that they applied the right test and the question whether they came to the right
conclusion is one not of law but of fact. Your Lordships were never invited by counsel j
for the appellants to examine the voluminous material in the affidavits and exhibits on
which any challenge to the finding of wilful misconduct must depend and the fact of
wilful misconduct, therefore, must be accepted as established.

The only challenge which must now be considered is procedural. There are, I think, three facets to the challenge. First, it is said that, as a matter of law, there is an absolute

a obligation on a district auditor, before issuing a certificate under s 20(1) of the 1982 Act, to ask any person on whom the certificate will impose a liability whether he wishes to make oral representations. Second, in the circumstances of this case, it is said that there were matters of complaint against the appellants relied on by the district auditor in his reasons for decision dated 6 September 1985 of which the appellants were not informed by, and could not have anticipated from, the terms of the notice given to them dated 26

b June 1985. Third, it is said that, apart from any general obligation to offer the appellants an oral hearing, the district auditor was under a particular obligation to do so before he could properly reject as unacceptable any explanation of their conduct put forward by the appellants relating to their intention, motivation or good faith. If any one of these three propositions is established, then it is submitted that there was such a want of natural justice in the proceedings leading to the decision of the district auditor as to

c invalidate the certificate, with the result that, on appeal, the Divisional Court, irrespective of its view on the merits, was obliged to quash it.

My Lords, the so-called rules of natural justice are not engraved on tablets of stone. To use the phrase which better expresses the underlying concept, what the requirements of fairness demand when any body, domestic, administrative or judicial, has to make a decision which will affect the rights of individuals depends on the character of the

d decision-making body, the kind of decision it has to make and the statutory or other framework in which it operates. In particular, it is well established that when a statute has conferred on any body the power to make decisions affecting individuals, the courts will not only require the procedure prescribed by the statute to be followed, but will readily imply so much and no more to be introduced by way of additional procedural safeguards as will ensure the attainment of fairness. It follows that the starting point for

e the examination of all the appellants' submissions on this aspect of the case is the 1982 Act. It will be convenient here to set out all the provisions which, in my opinion, throw light on the issues to be decided. They are as follows:

'**17.**—(1) At each audit by an auditor under this Part of this Act any persons interested may inspect the accounts to be audited and all books, deeds, contracts,

f bills, vouchers and receipts relating to them and make copies of all or any part of the accounts and those other documents.

(2) At the request of a local government elector for any area to which those accounts relate, the auditor shall give the elector, or any representative of his, an opportunity to question the auditor about the accounts.

(3) Subject to subsection (4) below, any local government elector for any area to

g which those accounts relate, or any representative of his, may attend before the auditor and make objections—(*a*) as to any matter in respect of which the auditor could take action under section 19 or 20 below . . .

(4) No objection may be made under subsection (3) above by or on behalf of a local government elector unless the auditor has previously received written notice of the proposed objection and of the grounds on which it is to be made . . .

h **19.**—(1) Where it appears to the auditor carrying out the audit of any accounts under this Part of this Act that any item of account is contrary to law he may apply to the court for a declaration that the item is contrary to law except where it is sanctioned by the Secretary of State.

(2) On an application under this section the court may make or refuse to make the declaration asked for, and where the court makes that declaration, then, subject

j to subsection (3) below, it may also—(*a*) order that any person responsible for incurring or authorising any expenditure declared unlawful shall repay it in whole or in part to the body in question and, where two or more persons are found to be responsible, that they shall be jointly and severally liable to repay it as aforesaid; (*b*) if any such expenditure exceeds £2,000 and the person responsible for incurring or authorising it is, or was at the time of his conduct in question, a member of a local authority, order him to be disqualified for being a member of a local authority for a specified period; and (c) order rectification of the accounts.

(3) The court shall not make an order under subsection (2)(a) or (b) above if the court is satisfied that the person responsible for incurring or authorising any such expenditure acted reasonably or in the belief that the expenditure was authorised by law, and in any other case shall have regard to all the circumstances, including that person's means and ability to repay that expenditure or any part of it.

(4) Any person who has made an objection under section 17(3)(a) above and is aggrieved by a decision of an auditor not to apply for a declaration under this section may—(a) not later than six weeks after he has been notified of the decision, require the auditor to state in writing the reasons for his decision; and (b) appeal against the decision to the court, and on any such appeal the court shall have the like powers in relation to the item of account to which the objection relates as if the auditor had applied for the declaration . . .

(6) The court having jurisdiction for the purposes of this section shall be the High Court except that, if the amount of the item of account alleged to be contrary to law does not exceed the amount over which county courts have jurisdiction in actions founded on contract, the county court shall have concurrent jurisdiction with the High Court . . .

20.—(1) Where it appears to the auditor carrying out the audit of any accounts under this Part of this Act—(a) that any person has failed to bring into account any sum which should have been so included and that the failure has not been sanctioned by the Secretary of State; or (b) that a loss has been incurred or deficiency caused by the wilful misconduct of any person, he shall certify that the sum or, as the case may be, the amount of the loss or the deficiency is due from that person and, subject to subsections (3) and (5) below, both he and the body in question (or, in the case of a parish meeting, the chairman of the meeting) may recover that sum or amount for the benefit of that body; and if the auditor certifies under this section that any sum or amount is due from two or more persons, they shall be jointly and severally liable for that sum or amount.

(2) Any person who—(a) has made an objection under section 17(3)(a) above and is aggrieved by a decision of an auditor not to certify under this section that a sum or amount is due from another person; or (b) is aggrieved by a decision of an auditor to certify under this section that a sum or amount is due from him, may not later than six weeks after he has been notified of the decision require the auditor to state in writing the reasons for his decision.

(3) Any such person who is aggrieved by such a decision may appeal against the decision to the court and—(a) in the case of a decision to certify that any sum or amount is due from any person, the court may confirm, vary or quash the decision and give any certificate which the auditor could have given; (b) in the case of a decision not to certify that any sum or amount is due from any person, the court may confirm the decision or quash it and give any certificate which the auditor could have given; and any certificate given under this subsection shall be treated for the purposes of subsection (1) above and the following provisions of this section as if it had been given by the auditor under subsection (1) above.

(4) If a certificate under this section relates to a loss or deficiency caused by the wilful misconduct of a person who is, or was at the time of such misconduct, a member of a local authority and the amount certified to be due from him exceeds £2,000, that person shall be disqualified for being a member of a local authority for the period of five years beginning on the ordinary date on which the period allowed for bring an appeal against a decision to give the certificate expires or, if such an appeal is brought, the date on which the appeal is finally disposed of or abandoned or fails for non-prosecution.

a
(5) A sum or other amount certified under this section to be due from any person shall be payable within fourteen days after the date of the issue of the certificate or, if an appeal is brought, within fourteen days after the appeal is finally disposed of or abandoned or fails for non-prosecution.

(6) In any proceedings for the recovery of any sum or amount due from any person under this section a certificate signed by an auditor appointed by the Commission stating that that sum or amount is due from a person specified in the

b
certificate to a body so specified shall be conclusive evidence of that fact; and any certificate purporting to be so signed shall be taken to have been so signed unless the contrary is proved...

(9) The court having jurisdiction for the purposes of this section shall be the High Court except that, if the sum or amount alleged to be due does not exceed the amount over which county courts have jurisdiction in actions founded on contract,

c
the county court shall have concurrent jurisdiction with the High Court...'

All these provisions except s 17(1) and (2) apply to an extraordinary audit under s 22 as they apply to an ordinary audit.

I draw attention at the outset to two striking features of this statutory machinery. The first is that both the exercise of the power to declare items of account unlawful under

d
s 19 and the ultimate power to control the issue of certificates under s 20 are entrusted to the regular courts, the county court if the amount in issue is within the county court's contractual jurisdiction, the High Court if it is not. Under s 19 the auditor can take no effective step without invoking the jurisdiction of the court. Under s 20 the auditor's certificate will be effective unless appealed against. The second striking feature is this.

e
The auditor may act of his own motion either in applying to the court for a declaration under s 19 or in issuing a certificate under s 20. But where, for any reason, he fails or declines to act under either section, after he has been invited to do so by a local government elector exercising his right of objection under s 17(3)(a), that elector has an unfettered right to invoke the jurisdiction of the court himself. In a case under s 19 the court will in every case be exercising its jurisdiction at first instance, but the auditor may be either seeking or opposing the declaration. In a case under s 20, the auditor may, if he

f
has been invited to act under s 17(3)(a), be described as the tribunal of first instance, but whichever way he decides, an unfettered right of appeal to the courts lies at the instance either of the aggrieved elector or of the party from whom the relevant loss has been certified to be due. In either case if the court falls into error the error can be corrected by the Court of Appeal or, if necessary, by your Lordships' House.

g
So far as procedure is concerned, s 14 of the 1982 Act provides for the issue of a code of audit practice to be approved by each House of Parliament. The code currently in force contains detailed provisions relating to objections under s 17, but none relating to the procedure to be followed when an auditor contemplates the issue of a certificate under s 20 of his own motion. The gravity of the consequences of a certificate for the person from whom the amount of a loss is certified to be due, particularly if he is a

h
member of a local authority and the amount exceeds £2,000, are obvious enough. No one doubts that the auditor must give to such a person adequate notice of the case against him and an adequate opportunity to present to the auditor his defence to that case. I followed with interest counsel for the appellants' carefully researched review of the history of local government audit legislation, but I did not find that it threw any light on what, in particular, is required to provide such an opportunity in the circumstances of

j
any particular case under the statute presently in force. Still less do I attach any significance to the fact that since 1972, when provisions substantially to the like effect as those which we find in the 1982 Act first reached the statute book, auditors have, as a matter of practice, always invited oral representations from members of local authorities before certifying the amount of any loss or deficiency as due from them. When a single individual is thought to have failed to bring a sum into account or by his wilful

misconduct to have caused a loss or deficiency, it is no doubt a very appropriate practice
to invite his explanation orally. But I fail to understand how that practice can constrain *a*
the courts to construe the statute as requiring an auditor proposing to act under s 20 to
invite oral representations as a matter of law in every case. In this case the auditor seems
to have intelligently anticipated that the appellants who constituted the majority group
would want to present a united front in their response to his notice of 26 June 1985 as
they had done in their conduct of the city council's affairs during the previous year. Cllr
Hamilton's letter of 19 July 1985 amply confirmed his expectation. If any councillor had *b*
wanted to put forward his own independent and individual grounds in rebuttal of the
charge of wilful misconduct against himself, I have no doubt he would have done so. If
any had asked to be heard orally and the auditor had refused, there would have been clear
ground for a complaint of unfairness. I suppose it is conceivable that the appellants
collectively might have wished to appoint a spokesman to present their case orally rather
than in writing, though the case they did present, embracing as it did such a large volume *c*
of documentary material, clearly lent itself more aptly to written than oral presentation.
It has never been suggested that it was unfair that the auditor did not invite the appellants
to address arguments to him through solicitor or counsel. The proposition that it was,
per se, in breach of the rules of natural justice not to invite oral representations in this
case is quite untenable.

The second facet of the complaint of unfairness alleges that the notice of 26 June 1985 *d*
did not sufficiently particularise the case which the appellants had to meet and that new
matters were relied on by the auditor in the reasons for his decision given on 6 September
1985. This is exhaustively examined in the judgments of the courts below and it would
serve no good purpose to re-examine it in detail. The notice dated 26 June was sent with
copies of all previous reports sent to the council by the district auditor and his predecessor
and identified by reference all the relevant council and committee minutes and reports *e*
made to the council by their own officers. I am fully satisfied that this gave adequate
notice of the grounds on which the auditor was provisionally minded to proceed against
the appellants under s 20 and, indeed, the character of the response shows that they were
in no doubt as to the nature of the case they had to meet. The point that troubled Lawton
LJ and, to a lesser extent, Dillon LJ was that the auditor in giving the reasons for his *f*
decision rejected the protestations of good faith in the appellants' response to his notice
of 26 June and did not accept that their motivation in acting as they did was as they
claimed. The relevant passage from the judgment of Lawton LJ reads as follows (p 1128,
ante):

> 'What the appellants were saying was wholly inconsistent with what was in these
> minutes and documents. An example is provided by their assertion that they had *g*
> acted "in good faith and after taking advice from their officers". They had not acted
> on the advice of their officers in March 1984, and again in April 1985 and on 14
> June 1985. Their assertion that they believed until 6 June 1985 that central
> government would provide further money was so contrary to the facts that no
> rational person could have believed anything of the kind. The evidence relied on by
> the district auditor for rejecting the appellants' assertion that they believed that *h*
> more money would be forthcoming was strong; but it is a matter of human
> experience that political zealots, as some of the appellants seem to have been, can so
> delude themselves about reality that lying is unnecessary for them. The courts are
> chary, however, about disbelieving people and attributing bad faith to them without
> an oral hearing: see *Re Smith & Fawcett Ltd* [1942] 1 All ER 542 at 545, [1942] Ch *i*
> 304 at 308 per Lord Greene MR and *Jeffs v New Zealand Dairy Production and
> Marketing Board* [1966] 3 All ER 863 at 870, [1967] 1 AC 551 at 568 per Viscount
> Dilhorne. Had the appellants been given an opportunity of commenting on the
> adverse opinion of their conduct which the district auditor had formed they, or
> some of them, might have been able to persuade him of their good faith and

a   credibility. Maybe on the facts of this case they would have had difficulty in so doing; but, in my judgment, they should have been given a chance of doing so. It was unfair not to have given them that chance.'

With respect, I cannot agree that the authorities referred to had any relevance to the circumstances of the instant case. There was here no room for dispute as to what the council, for whose action or inaction the appellants were responsible, had done or failed to do. There was no room for dispute as to the factual information and legal advice which
b   had at all material times been available to the appellants. It was never claimed on behalf of the appellants that they acted under any misapprehension. In so far as there was an issue whether the course on which the appellants quite deliberately embarked was one in which they acted 'in good faith' or as to the motives which underlay their action or inaction, it was in essence a matter for argument rather than for evidence. When a group
c   of 49 people act collectively they may, of course, have different subjective reasons for acting. But, if they assert that their collective action was prompted by a single collective state of mind, this is inevitably to some extent a fiction. A group can have no single subjective mind. On the other hand, the objective state of mind of the group can only be inferred from what the group concurred in doing or omitting to do in given circumstances. In this case it would not have advanced the appellants' case at all if each
d   appellant had appeared in person before the auditor and asserted his sincere belief in what had been said in the collective written response. On the other hand, if each had given his own explanation and volunteered to submit to questioning as to his own individual state of mind in relation to the council's proceedings, this would have been a departure from the collective stance which the appellants had deliberately adopted and to which they have throughout resolutely adhered. For these reasons I think the auditor
e   was fully entitled to draw inferences from the undisputed facts which involved a rejection of the appellants' protestations of good faith and purity of motive and that his doing so without further reference to the appellants after he received their response dated 19 July 1985 involved no unfairness to them.

These conclusions would be sufficient to dispose of the appeals. But I return to the question of more general importance whether, if there had been any unfairness in the
f   procedure followed by the auditor, this would necessarily have led, as the Divisional Court thought, to the quashing of the certificate or whether, as the Court of Appeal concluded, the full hearing of the appeal to the court on the merits was in law able to make good any deficiency in the auditor's procedure. It was in order to set this question in its proper context that I thought it necessary, earlier in this opinion, to set out the relevant statutory provisions in extenso. The question how far in domestic and
g   administrative two-tier adjudicatory systems a procedural failure at the level of the first tier can be remedied at the level of the second tier was considered by the Privy Council in *Calvin v Carr* [1979] 2 All ER 440, [1980] AC 574 in which all the relevant previous authorites on the subject are reviewed. I do not find it necessary in this case to examine the general principles there discussed, nor would I think it appropriate in this case to seek to lay down any principles of general application. This is because the question arising in
h   the instant case must be answered by considering the particular statutory provisions here applicable which establish an adjudicatory system in many respects quite unlike any that has come under examination in any of the decided cases to which we were referred. We are concerned with a point of statutory construction and nothing else.

As I have pointed out, the court acts at first instance under s 19 in deciding whether or not to make a declaration and so acts either on the application of the auditor or at the
j   instance of an objector against the auditor's opposition. Under s 20, although the auditor acts at first instance in deciding whether or not to certify, either of his own motion or at the instance of an objector, the jurisdiction of the court may be invoked by a person aggrieved by either an affirmative or a negative decision. Once issued a certificate is valid until it is quashed or varied. This clearly follows from the provisions of s 20(6) making

the certificate conclusive evidence in proceedings for recovery of the certified sum or amount of the loss. Apart from the provisions for appeal in s 20(3) a certificate could, no *a* doubt, be the subject of an application to the High Court for judicial review. But I cannot see any reason why it should be necessary to seek leave to invoke the supervisory jurisdiction of the court when any party aggrieved by the certificate is entitled as of right to invoke the much more ample appellate jurisdiction which the statute confers. It is the very amplitude of the jurisdiction which, to my mind, is all-important. Whether the auditor has decided to certify or not to certify, the court is empowered to confirm or *b* quash the decision, to vary the decision if a certificate has been issued by the auditor, and in any case to give any certificate which the auditor could have given. The language describing the court's powers could not possibly be any wider. Procedurally there is nothing either in the statute or in the relevant rules of court to limit in any way the evidence which may be put before the court on either side. In the light of these considerations I can find no reason whatever to construe the statute in such a way as to *c* limit the discretion of the court as to the action it will take to provide an appropriate remedy where the matter of complaint, or one of them, is of unfairness in the procedure followed by the auditor. I can well see that, if the auditor has certified of his own motion without giving any proper notice to the person against whom the certificate operates, the court would probably decide to quash it without entering on the merits. But if, on the other hand, a local government elector had objected under s 17(3)(*a*) seeking a certificate *d* against a councillor whom he accused of wilful misconduct causing loss and the auditor had improperly dismissed his objection out of hand, it might well be that the most expeditious and appropriate remedy would be for the court, on appeal by the objector, to determine the issue itself. If the court decided to proceed in that way, it would be effectively determining at first instance the issue whether the councillor had been guilty of wilful misconduct causing loss or deficiency. The councillor might, in such *e* circumstances, have heard nothing of the matter until the proceedings before the court, but, if the objector could prove the case against him, the councillor would have no ground of complaint on that score.

In every case it must be for the court, as a matter of discretion, to decide how in all the circumstances its jurisdiction under s 20(3) can best be exercised to meet the justice of *f* the case. But I am clearly of opinion that when the court has, as here, in fact conducted a full hearing on the merits and reached a conclusion that the issue of a certificate was justified, it would be an erroneous exercise of discretion nevertheless to quash the certificate on the ground that, before the matter reached the court, there had been some defect in the procedure followed.

I would dismiss the appeals and make orders for costs as proposed by my noble and *g* learned friend Lord Templeman.

LORD BRANDON OF OAKBROOK. My Lords, I have had the advantage of reading in draft the speeches prepared by my noble and learned friends Lord Keith, Lord Bridge and Lord Templeman. I agree with all of them, and for the reasons which they give I would dismiss the appeal. *h*

LORD TEMPLEMAN. My Lords, this appeal is the culmination of a conflict between a local authority and Parliament. In 1985 the will of the local authority, Liverpool City Council, was exercised by the appellants, an united majority of elected councillors. The will of Parliament was exercised by ministers supported by an united majoirty of elected members of the House of Commons. Liverpool's revenues mainly consisted of grants *j* from national taxes controlled by the ministers and the products of local rates controlled by the appellants. The appellants asked that Liverpool's grants from national taxes be made at a level which the ministers declined to accept. The ministers asked that Liverpool's expenditure be maintained and Liverpool's budget balanced at levels which

the appellants declined to accept. The ministers could lawfully make grants from national
a taxes at the level decided by the ministers with the approval of Parliament. The appellants
could not lawfully maintain Liverpool's expenditure at a level which exceeded Liverpool's
income derived from grants, rates and other sources of revenue. A local authority is
created by Parliament; must perform the duties imposed by Parliament; and can only
exercise powers conferred by Parliament in the manner and for the purposes intended
by Parliament. If a majority of councillors who control the local authority procure the
b local authority to reject or neglect its statutory duty, each councillor is guilty of
misconduct, even though the councillor may have been democratically elected to oppose
the performance of that duty. If a councillor is advised or is otherwise conscious that
action contemplated by him will amount to misconduct, he is guilty of wilful misconduct
and is liable to statutory penalties if he persists. In the present case the appellants appeal
against a finding of wilful misconduct.
c   By s 2(1) of the General Rate Act 1967:

> 'Every rating authority shall . . . make such rates as will be sufficient to provide
> for such part of the total estimated expenditure to be incurred by the authority
> during the period in respect of which the rate is made as is not to be met by other
d   means . . .'

By s 1 of the Local Government Finance Act 1982 a rating authority shall not have
power '(b) to make a rate for any period other than a financial year', and by s 7(1) of the
same Act '"financial year" means a period of twelve months beginning with 1st April'.
Liverpool was a rating authority and was therefore under a duty to make a rate for each
e year beginning with 1 April sufficient to meet its expenditure for that year. Collection
of rates and payment of other revenues begin as soon as the rate is made and notified.
The rates should be made by or soon after 1 April in order to facilitate collection and
payment. Any delay in making the rate involves a loss to the authority of interest or
borrowing charges by imposing a delay on collection and payment.
The 1982 Act established the Audit Commission charged with appointing auditors to
f audit the accounts of local authorities. Each auditor must be a professionally qualified
accountant. By s 20(1) where it appears to the auditor carrying out an audit that '(b) that
a loss has been incurred or deficiency caused by the wilful misconduct of any person' the
auditor is to certify the amount involved and the Act provides for the recovery of that
amount from the person guilty of wilful misconduct. If a local authority does not make
an adequate rate or delays in making a rate, then the resultant loss of revenue or of
g interest or borrowing charges may be investigated by the auditor. If a councillor does not
support the making of an adequate rate or shares responsibility for delay in making a
rate, he shares responsibility for the loss thereby inflicted on the local authority and the
auditor may find the councillor guilty of misconduct. If the councillor knows that he is
failing in his duty to ensure that the local authority receives as much revenue from rates
as is necessary and as soon as possible, the auditor may find that the councillor is guilty of
h wilful misconduct.
In March 1984 the Liverpool City Council was under a duty to consider making a rate
for the financial year beginning 1 April 1984. In a report dated 19 March 1984, sent to
all councillors, the district auditor explained the duty of the local authority and the duty
of the appellants, indicated the liability of the appellants for breach of duty and warned
that—
j
> 'I should find it difficult to see how the deliberate making of an inadequate rate
> could be anything other than wilful misconduct . . . Members would in my view
> also be at risk if a rate was not made because no vote was taken or there was
> unreasonable delay in making a rate.'

In the event, negotiations between central government and the local authority for an increase in government grant continued long after 1 April and no action was taken to challenge the conduct of the appellants, notwithstanding that no rate was fixed until July 1984. A copy of the report dated 19 March 1984 was subsequently sent to all councillors elected after that date in order that they too should be aware of their responsibilities and liabilities.

In December 1984 the council indorsed—

'the policies upon which the people of Liverpool elected the Labour Party to power, viz. (inter alia) to refuse to impose increases in rates, rents and charges to compensate for government cuts in grants',

and called for the reinstatement of cuts in grants said to amount to some £216m.

On 27 February 1985 the council rejected the proposal that a meeting of the council be arranged in order to set a rate for 1985–86. On 7 March 1985 the council resolved that—

'this council requires a budget of £265·4 million but, with a target of only £222·1 million—representing another £90 million stolen from the City in grant penalty—this Council considers it will be impossible to make a rate.'

On 14 March 1985, in a parliamentary answer which was drawn to the attention of the council, the Secretary of State for the Environment made it clear that no more government money would be provided, that 'No rating authority can now have any excuse for delay in carrying out its duty to make a lawful rate', and that government grants for 1985–86 would not be paid until a rate had been fixed. The minister reminded—

'all councillors that if a failure to make a rate leads to loss or deficiency and the auditor considers that this results from wilful misconduct, then those responsible may be surcharged.'

(See 75 HC Official Report (6th series) written answers col 217.)

On 10 April 1985 the district auditor, in a report to the council, expressed his concern at 'the council's failure to make a valid rate for the financial year which commenced on 1 April 1985'. He advised that 'failure to make a lawful rate would be a clear breach of duty and that deliberate failure to do so would be wilful misconduct'. He concluded by urging—

'the council in its own best interests, as well as those of individual members, employees and the local community, that a rate should be made at a very early date. That rate needs to be matched with plans to operate within available resources.'

In May the council again declined to consider making a budget or a rate. On 21 May 1985 the auditor made a further report to the council and sent a copy of his report to each councillor. After referring to the reports dated 19 March 1984 and 10 April 1985, the auditor continued:

'By its continued failure to make a rate the Council and individual members have placed themselves seriously at risk ... I must now give the Council notice that unless it makes a lawful rate at the earliest opportunity and in any event before the end of May I shall forthwith commence action under section 20 to recover any losses occasioned by the failure to make a rate from the members responsible for incurring them ... Yet again and for the last time I urge the Council most strongly to comply with its statutory duty to make a lawful rate and to do so with the utmost speed.'

On 6 June 1985 the Audit Commission directed an extraordinary audit to be carried out. On 14 June 1985 the council considered a resolution that, inter alia—

'a rate increase of 9% be approved and the difference of £29 million be made up

by the return of grant monies stolen from the people of Liverpool by the Tory
a government since 1979.'

It appears from the revised budget summary, however, that the difference between
budgeted revenue and budgeted expenditure on the basis of the increased rate proposed
would amount to £117m. The rate proposed to be fixed was therefore inadequate and
the city solicitor advised the council before they passed the resolution that the resolution
b would be contrary to law. The resolution fixing a rate based on a 9% increase was,
however, passed with the support of the appellants.

The respondent auditor was appointed auditor for the purpose of the extraordinary
audit and on 26 June 1985 gave notice to each of the appellants that he was considering
certifying that the appellants had been guilty of wilful misconduct. The auditor asserted
that the documentary evidence which he particularised and which consisted of the
c relevant minutes of the meetings of the council and its committees and the relevant
reports of its officers including the reports of the district auditor—

> '. . . show that there was no lawful justification for the delay in the making of the
> rate. The Council, has thus disregarded the advice and warnings given by me, my
> predecessors and its officers.'

d The auditor invited representations in writing by 19 July 1985 and intimated that he
would defer making a decision until he had considered the appellants' representations.

On 19 July 1985 the appellants submitted detailed and careful representations which
had been drafted with the assistance of the chief executive of Liverpool. The facts to
which the auditor had drawn attention could not be and were not disputed. The
appellants denied wilful misconduct on three grounds. First, they said that at all times
e they had acted in what they sincerely believed to be the best interests of the ratepayers
and citizens of Liverpool. My Lords, political leaders from Robespierre, the sea-green
incorruptible, to Gandhi, the prophet of non-violence, have acted in the sincere belief
that it was necessary to break the nation's laws in the interests of the nation's citizens.
Only Gandhi, who broke the salt laws, acknowledged in a celebrated exchange of
f courtesies with the British magistrate the correctness of his conviction and the appropriate
imposition of a sentence of imprisonment which, however, hastened the repeal of the
salt tax and the dawn of independence for India. The sincerity of the appellants provides
no defence to a charge that they deliberately delayed after they had been warned that it
was wrong of them to do so. Second, the appellants contended that they were entitled to
delay in the hope and expectation that the government would thereby be compelled or
g persuaded to provide more money for Liverpool. But the government in March 1985
had made it quite clear that the appellants would be responsible if they did not make a
rate based on current government grants. The appellants' belief that the government did
not mean that which the government stated does not justify a delay which was bound to
cause loss to Liverpool whatever the government might do. Third, the appellants
contended that they had delayed in 1984 without dire consequences to themselves, and
h were entitled to believe that they would escape from the consequences of delay in 1985.
But both the government and the officers of Liverpool, at an early stage, made plain to
the council that 1985 circumstances were different from 1984 circumstances, and that
delay in 1985 would not be tolerated or excused. An offender cannot successfully plead
by way of defence that he was not prosecuted for a similar offence on a previous occasion.

The appellants did not ask the auditor for an oral hearing but it is now said that the
j auditor should have invited the appellants to make oral representations before he
ultimately made up his mind. My Lords, a councillor might have persuaded the auditor,
if he was not already persuaded, that the councillor was sincere in his belief that he could
not sacrifice the policy for which he had been elected and sincere in the belief that a rigid
adherence to the policy would enure for the benefit of the citizens of Liverpool even if it
entailed a breach of the councillor's duty promptly to make an adequate rate to provide

for the year's expenditure. But the councillor's beliefs could not alter the councillor's
duty or excuse a deliberate breach of that duty. In the voluminous evidence and in the　*a*
addresses of counsel I have been unable to discern any grounds for the assertion that the
oral representations of a councillor could have supplied a defence which was lacking
from the written representations of the appellants or could have validated or reinforced
possible defences foreshadowed in those written representations. The facts disclosed by
the documents were incontrovertible and damning. The auditor had no choice but to
find the appellants guilty of wilful misconduct. He certified on 6 September 1985 that　*b*
the loss for which the appellants were liable amounted to £106,103.

Counsel for the appellants urged that the auditor should have invited the appellants to
make oral representations before he reached the decision based on the written material.
If any councillor had requested an oral hearing, I think that it would have been desirable
for the auditor to have granted that request, first, so that the councillor could reiterate
the sincerity of his motives and, second, so that the councillor might satisfy himself as to　*c*
the judicial and impartial quality of the auditor. But sincerity is no excuse. An oral
hearing could not detract from the force of the documentary evidence or supplement the
written defence of the appellants in any material respects. I do not consider that the
auditor was bound to follow a procedure which the appellants, acting under competent
advice, did not suggest. The judicial and impartial qualities of the auditor are not in
question.　*d*

Counsel for the appellants urged that although the appellants did not request an oral
hearing, they were deprived of a 'legitimate expectation' of being invited to an oral
hearing. Counsel for the appellants does not allege that the appellants in fact expected to
be invited to an oral hearing and does not speculate whether they would have accepted
an invitation. He submits that a legitimate expectation of being invited to an oral hearing
is an objective fundamental right which, if not afforded, results in a breach of law or　*e*
breach of natural justice which invalidates any decision based on written material. This
extravagant language does not tempt me to elevate a catch-phrase into a principle. The
true principle is that the auditor, like any other decision-maker, must act fairly. It was
not unfair for the auditor to reach a decision on the basis of the written material served
on and submitted by the appellants. In *Council of Civil Service Unions v Minister for the Civil*　*f*
Service [1984] 3 All ER 935, [1985] AC 374 it was unfair for the government to decide to
deprive a civil servant of his right to belong to a trade union without first consulting the
civil servant or his union; this House would have quashed the decision but for the
overriding interests of national security which justified the government's decision. Lord
Roskill pointed out that 'legitimate expectation' is a manifestation of the duty to act fairly
(see [1984] 3 All ER 935 at 954, [1985] AC 374 at 415). A decision may be unfair if the　*g*
decision-maker deprives himself of the views of persons who will be affected by the
decision. In the present case the appellants were afforded ample opportunity to express
their views, and the auditor was enabled to reach a decision in the light of every defence
which it was possible for the appellants to urge.

The certificate of the auditor that a loss of £106,103 had been incurred by the wilful
misconduct of the appellants was given pursuant to s 20(1) of the Local Government　*h*
Finance Act 1982, which provides:

> 'Where it appears to the auditor . . . (b) that a loss has been incurred or deficiency
> caused by the wilful misconduct of any person, he shall certify that . . . the amount
> of the loss or the deficiency is due from that person and . . . may recover that . . .
> amount for the benefit of [the relevant authority]; and if the auditor certifies . . .
> that any . . . amount is due from two or more persons, they shall be jointly and　*j*
> severally liable for that . . . amount.'

By s 20(3) any person who is aggrieved by a decision of an auditor to certify that an
amount is due from him may appeal against the decision to the court and 'the court may
confirm, vary or quash the decision and give any certificate which the auditor could have

given', and any certificate given by the court 'shall be treated . . . as if it had been given
a by the auditor . . .'

On 6 October 1985 the appellants appealed under s 20(3) to the High Court. By RSC
Ord 98 the appeal was brought by notice of motion supported by an affidavit setting out
the facts on which the appellants intended to rely at the hearing. Order 98, r 4(2) provides
that evidence at the hearing shall be given by affidavit, except in so far as the court directs
that the evidence shall be given orally. The appellants filed numerous affidavits and there
b were exhibited all the relevant documents which were considered by the auditor or to
which the councillors wished to refer. The appeal was heard by a Divisional Court
(Glidewell LJ, Caulfield and Russell JJ). The appellants asked that the certificate given by
the auditor be set aside and discharged. The appellants were invited to give oral evidence
but declined the invitation. After a hearing lasting ten days the appellants' appeals were
dismissed (see [1986] RVR 45). The appellants appealed to the Court of Appeal (Lawton,
c Dillon and Woolf LJJ). The appeal was dismissed and, with leave of the Court of Appeal,
this present appeal has been brought to this House. Any oral evidence which could have
been given by the appellants to the auditor could have been given on affidavit or orally
to the Divisional Court. In these circumstances, counsel for the appellants did not urge
the merits of the appellants' case. Having submitted that the procedure of the auditor
was defective because he did not invite the appellants to give oral evidence, he next
d submitted that in those circumstances the Divisional Court had no power to affirm the
decision of the auditor.

My Lords, in reaching a decision an auditor may make mistakes of fact, law or
procedure. The auditor does not take evidence on oath and the information available to
him may be incomplete. On an appeal from his decision, the court is entitled to consider
any evidence from any appellant or from any auditor or other expert. Such evidence is
e given on oath, either in the form of an affidavit or in the form of oral testimony.
Evidence may be produced before the court which was never available to the auditor.
The judges will draw their own conclusion from the evidence before the court, will apply
the law as judicially construed, and will adhere to court procedure. If the Divisional
Court errs in law a further appeal lies. In my opinion, the court hearing an appeal under
s 20 of the 1982 Act is not powerless to confirm or vary the decision of an auditor merely
f because the decision of the auditor was defective, whether the defect relates to a matter
of evidence, law or procedure. It is for the court to consider a certificate under s 20(3) in
substitution for the certificate of the auditor.

Counsel for the appellants relied on the dictum of Megarry J in *Leary v National Union
of Vehicle Builders* [1970] 2 All ER 713 at 720, [1971] Ch 34 at 49 that 'a failure of natural
justice in the trial body cannot be cured by a sufficiency of natural justice in an appellate
g body'. This dictum was enunciated in connection with an appeal from one domestic
tribunal to an appellate domestic tribunal. In *Calvin v Carr* [1979] 2 All ER 440 at 448,
[1980] AC 574 at 593 Lord Wilberforce, delivering the advice of the Board, demurred to
this dictum as being 'too broadly stated' and recognised and asserted—

h   'that no clear and absolute rule can be laid down on the question whether defects
         in natural justice appearing at an original hearing, whether administrative or quasi-
         judicial, can be "cured" through appeal proceedings.'

(See [1979] 2 All ER 440 at 447, [1970] 2 All ER 713 at 592.)

My Lords, when by statute an appeal lies from a tribunal to a court of law, the statute
j must be construed to determine whether the court is free to determine the appeal on the
basis of the evidence before the court or is bound by the evidence or information laid
before the tribunal. In the present case I have no doubt that it was for the court of law to
consider whether 'wilful misconduct' was proved and for that purpose to consider the
evidence laid before the court. The task of the court was to 'give any certificate which the
auditor could have given' (s 20(3) of the 1982 Act). The court was not concerned with

any defects in the procedure adopted by the auditor because those defects (if any) did not hamper the prosecution or conduct of the appeal. Different considerations apply if a *a* statute only allows an appeal to a court of law on a question of law, or entitles or obliges the court of law to rely on the facts found by the tribunal. And the defects in the inquiry conducted by the tribunal may be so prejudicial to the aggrieved person that the court in its discretion may decide to quash the decision and not to proceed with an appeal on the merits in the absence of the views of the tribunal after a proper inquiry. In the present case the Divisional Court was entitled to consider the appeal on its merits and on the basis *b* of the evidence presented to the court.

The auditor on the basis of the information available to him came to the conclusion that the appellants were guilty of wilful misconduct. The Divisional Court on the basis of that information supplemented by the additional evidence put forward by the appellants affirmed the decision of the auditor. I would dismiss this appeal. As regards costs there are technically 47 appeals before this House. Some appellants are legally aided, *c* some are not. I would order each appellant to pay one forty-seventh of the auditor's costs of the appeal to this House, subject to the usual protection afforded by the legal aid certificates. If and so far as the auditor does not recover a due proportion from a legally-aided appellant and subject to any application of the Law Society, the auditor should be entitled to recover from the legal aid fund pursuant to s 13 of the Legal Aid Act 1973.

d

LORD GRIFFITHS. My Lords, I have had the advantage of reading in draft the speeches prepared by my noble and learned friends Lord Keith, Lord Bridge and Lord Templeman. For the reasons they give I too would dismiss the appeal.

Appeal dismissed.

e

Solicitors: *Christian Fisher & Co* (for the appellants); *Clifford-Turner* (for the district auditor); *William Murray,* Liverpool (for the council).

Mary Rose Plummer   Barrister.

Hill v Chief Constable of West Yorkshire

COURT OF APPEAL, CIVIL DIVISION
FOX, GLIDEWELL LJJ AND SIR ROUALEYN CUMMING-BRUCE
1, 2, 3 DECEMBER 1986, 19 FEBRUARY 1987

Police – Negligence – Duty to take care – Negligence in investigation of crime – Persons to whom duty owed – Victim of crime – Plaintiff's daughter murdered by notorious criminal – Police failing to apprehend criminal prior to murder of plaintiff's daughter – Whether police owing duty of care to plaintiff's daughter – Whether special relationship existing between police and criminal – Whether plaintiff having cause of action for negligence against police – Police Act 1964, s 48(1).

Between 1969 and 1980 13 murders and 8 attempted murders were committed by S, who became notorious for his attacks on unaccompanied young women. The plaintiff, the mother and administratrix of his last victim, brought an action under s 48(1)[a] of the Police Act 1964 claiming damages for negligence against the chief constable in whose area most of S's attacks had occurred. The plaintiff contended that the circumstances of the earlier murders and attacks were so similar that it was reasonable to infer that they were committed by the same person, that it was foreseeable that unless apprehended that person would commit further offences, that it was the duty of the police in the conduct of their investigations to exercise all reasonable skill and care in apprehending him and that they had been in breach of their duty in failing to detect him prior to the murder of her daughter. The chief constable applied to strike out the plaintiff's claim under RSC Ord 18, r 19 as disclosing no cause of action. The question arose whether the police owed a duty of care to a member of the public in respect of an attack made on him by another member of the public. The judge held that the police owed no such duty in the circumstances and accordingly struck out the action. The plaintiff appealed to the Court of Appeal.

Held – In the absence of any special relationship between the police and a criminal arising out of the fact that the criminal either was in police custody or had escaped from it, the general duty owed by the police to the public to suppress crime did not give rise to a duty owed to individual members of the public in respect of damage caused to them by a criminal whom the police failed to apprehend in circumstances when it was possible to do so. On the facts no special relationship had existed between the police and S since S had neither been in police custody nor escaped from it. Accordingly, the plaintiff's statement of claim disclosed no cause of action and had been properly struck out. The appeal would therefore be dismissed (see p 1179 b, p 1180 d e j, p 1181 a b d e, p 1182 c to f j, p 1183 c to f and p 1184 b, post).

Dicta of Lord Wilberforce in *Anns v Merton London Borough* [1977] 2 All ER at 498, of Lord Wilberforce and of Lord Edmund Davies in *McLoughlin v O'Brian* [1982] 2 All ER at 303, 308 and of Lord Keith in *Governors of the Peabody Donation Fund v Sir Lindsay Parkinson & Co Ltd* [1984] 3 All ER at 534 applied.

Home Office v Dorset Yacht Co Ltd [1970] 2 All ER 294 distinguished.

Smith v Leurs (1945) 70 CLR 256 and *R v Metropolitan Police Comr, ex p Blackburn* [1968] 1 All ER 763 considered.

---

a Section 48(1) provides: 'The chief officer of police for any police area shall be liable in respect of torts committed by constables under his direction and control in the performance or purported performance of their functions in like manner as a master is liable in respect of torts committed by his servants in the course of their employment, and accordingly shall in respect of any such tort be treated for all purposes as a joint tortfeasor.'

Notes

For the nature of negligence and the duty to take care generally, see 34 Halsbury's Laws *a*
(4th edn) paras 1–5, and for cases on the subject, see s 36(1) Digest (Reissue) 5–55, 31–
177.

For the Police Act 1964, s 48, see 25 Halsbury's Statutes (3rd edn) 363.

Cases referred to in judgments

Anns v Merton London Borough [1977] 2 All ER 492, [1978] AC 728, [1977] 2 WLR 1024, *b*
HL.

Davis Contractors Ltd v Fareham UDC [1956] 2 All ER 145, [1956] AC 696, [1956] 3 WLR
37, HL.

Donoghue (or M'Alister) v Stevenson [1932] AC 562, [1932] All ER Rep 1, HL.

Hedley Byrne & Co Ltd v Heller & Partners Ltd [1963] 2 All ER 575, [1964] AC 465, [1963]
3 WLR 101, HL. *c*

Home Office v Dorset Yacht Co Ltd [1970] 2 All ER 294, [1970] AC 1004, [1970] 2 WLR
1140, HL.

McLoughlin v O'Brian [1982] 2 All ER 298, [1983] 1 AC 410, [1982] 2 WLR 982, HL.

Marshall v Osmond [1983] 2 All ER 225, [1983] QB 1034, [1983] 3 WLR 13, CA.

Peabody Donation Fund (Governors) v Sir Lindsay Parkinson & Co Ltd [1984] 3 All ER 529,
[1985] AC 210, [1984] 3 WLR 953, HL. *d*

R v Metropolitan Police Comr, ex p Blackburn [1968] 1 All ER 763, [1968] 2 QB 118, [1968]
2 WLR 893, CA.

Rondel v Worsley [1967] 3 All ER 993, [1969] 1 AC 191, [1967] 3 WLR 1666, HL.

Smith v Leurs (1945) 70 CLR 256, Aust HC.

Weld-Blundell v Stephens [1920] AC 956, [1920] All ER Rep 32, HL.

Williams & Humbert Ltd v W & H Trade Marks (Jersey) Ltd [1986] 1 All ER 129, [1986] *e*
AC 368, [1986] 2 WLR 24, HL.

Cases also cited

Glasbrook Bros Ltd v Glamorgan CC [1925] AC 270, [1924] All ER Rep 579, HL.

Haynes v G Harwood & Son [1935] 1 KB 146, [1934] All ER Rep 103, CA. *f*

King v Liverpool City Council [1986] 3 All ER 544, [1986] 1 WLR 890, HL.

Knightley v Johns [1982] 1 All ER 851, [1982] 1 WLR 349, CA.

Newby v General Lighterage Co [1955] 1 Lloyd's Rep 273, CA.

Paterson Zochonis & Co Ltd v Merfarken Packaging Ltd (1982) [1986] 3 All ER 522, CA.

Philco Radio and Television Corp of GB Ltd v J Spurling Ltd [1949] 2 All ER 882, [1949] 2 KB
33, CA.

R v Chief Constable of the Devon and Cornwall Constabulary, ex p Central Electricity Generating *g*
Board [1981] 3 All ER 826, [1982] QB 458, CA.

R v Metropolitan Police Comr, ex p Blackburn (No 3) [1973] 1 All ER 324, [1973] QB 241,
CA.

Rigby v Chief Constable of Northamptonshire [1985] 2 All ER 985, [1985] 1 WLR 1242.

Squires v Perth and Kinross DC 1986 SLT 30, Inner House. *h*

Stansbie v Troman [1948] 1 All ER 599, [1948] 2 KB 48, CA.

Ward v Cannock Chase DC [1985] 3 All ER 537, [1986] Ch 546.

Interlocutory appeal

The plaintiff, Doreen Hill, suing as administratrix of the estate of Jacqueline Hill deceased,
appealed with leave granted by the judge against the order of Sir Neil Lawson, sitting as *j*
a judge of the High Court on 19 December 1985, directing that the writ and statement
of claim issued in the action brought by the plaintiff against the defendant, the Chief
Constable of West Yorkshire, claiming damages for negligence in respect of the death of
Jacqueline Hill at Leeds on 17 November 1980 be struck out and the action be dismissed.
The facts are set out in the judgment of Fox LJ.

Richard Clegg QC and *John M Collins* for Mrs Hill.
a   *Alan Rawley QC* and *Richard Rains* for the chief constable.

Cur adv vult

19 February. The following judgments were delivered.

b   **FOX LJ.** This is an appeal from an order of Sir Neil Lawson, sitting as a judge of the High Court, that the writ and statement of claim be struck out as disclosing no cause of action.

The plaintiff is the mother and sole personal representative of Jacqueline Hill (to whom I will refer as 'Miss Hill') who died aged 20 on or about 17 November 1980. It is the plaintiff's case that about 9.30 pm on 17 November 1980 Miss Hill was attacked in a *c*   street in Leeds by one Peter Sutcliffe and thereby suffered injuries from which she died on or about the same day. On 22 May 1981 Sutcliffe was found guilty at the Central Criminal Court of the murder of Miss Hill on or about 17 November 1980. The plaintiff's pleaded case is broadly as follows. Between 1969 and 17 November 1980, and in particular between 1 July 1975 and 17 November 1980, Sutcliffe committed a series of offences against young or fairly young women and mostly in the metropolitan police *d*   area of West Yorkshire (of which area the defendant is the chief officer of police). Those offences consisted of 8 cases of attempted murder and 13 cases (including that of Miss Hill, who was the last to be killed) of murder. Sutcliffe has been commonly referred to as the Yorkshire Ripper. Although his victims were women he was not, we were told, a rapist. He killed or attempted to kill.

The mode of assault and the circumstances of the offences, it is pleaded, resembled one *e*   another to such an extent that it was reasonable to infer that the offences were committed by the same man; and that accordingly it was at all material times foreseeable that if he were not apprehended the man would commit further similar offences.

Accordingly, it is contended, it was the duty of the chief constable and of the officers under his direction to exercise all reasonable skill and care to apprehend the perpetrator of the crimes, but in breach of that duty the police failed to use sufficient skill or care to *f*   detect the perpetrator prior to the murder of Miss Hill. The statement of claim sets out, at length, particulars of alleged failures by the police to use information which they obtained and to conduct investigations which would have been appropriate.

Inter alia, it is alleged that the police failed to collate relevant information and to investigate records relating to Sutcliffe; failed to make sufficient use of photo-fit pictures; attached undue importance to hoax letters and telephone calls; failed to re-evaluate *g*   suspects who had been eliminated; and failed to take account of the fact that Sutcliffe had been provided with an alibi for offences only by his wife.

In the premises, the plaintiff claims on behalf of the estate of Miss Hill (a) damages for loss of expectation of life and pain and suffering caused to Miss Hill prior to death, (b) funeral expenses and (c) damages in respect of Miss Hill's loss of earnings during the lost *h*   years. The main element in this claim is item (c), the lost years' claim. Such claims on behalf of the estate of a deceased person were abolished by Parliament in 1982. That was done by s 4 of the Administration of Justice Act 1982. The plaintiff is only able to assert the claim in this case because Miss Hill died before s 4 of the 1982 Act came into force.

The defendant is sued under the provisions of s 48(1) of the Police Act 1964 under which the chief officer of police for the police area is liable for torts committed by *j*   constables under his direction and control. The statement of claim contains no allegation that the alleged breach of duty by the police caused the death of Miss Hill but that could be cured by amendment. The plaintiff was not a dependant of Miss Hill and we were informed by counsel that although she is the sole residuary beneficiary of the estate, she does not seek to recover damages for her own benefit but wishes to use them to establish a charitable trust to commemorate her daughter.

The defendant applied to strike out the statement of claim as disclosing no cause of
action. The judge, in acceding to that application, held that Miss Hill was not in such a   *a*
relationship with the defendant or his officers as to give rise to any duty of care in relation
to the apprehension of Sutcliffe.

The case comes before the court, not by way of preliminary issue but under RSC Ord
18, r 19 on an application to strike out as disclosing no cause of action. For the purposes
of such an application it must be assumed, in the plaintiff's favour, that all the facts
pleaded in the statement of claim are true. The issue, which was argued before us, is   *b*
whether under the law of England any cause of action lies against the police for the
consequences of a direct physical attack on one citizen (Miss Hill) by another (Sutcliffe)
in circumstances where the attacker was not a police officer and was not in police custody
or, having been arrested, was allowed to escape from police custody but where reasonable
care on the part of the police would have resulted in the attacker's previous arrest. If the
answer is No, then the plaintiff must fail and there will be no need for the lengthy trial   *c*
which the examination of the pleaded facts would otherwise entail. Since the question is
purely one of law and will probably have to be determined sooner or later whatever
course the action takes, it seems appropriate to decide it at this juncture. It is, of course, a
novel point (in the sense that it has not previously been decided) and cannot be said to be
unarguable in the sense that there is a short answer to it. But if at the end of the
argument, be it short or long, the court is satisfied that no cause of action lies, I apprehend   *d*
that the court is entitled to decide the matter accordingly (see *Williams & Humbert Ltd v
W & H Trade Marks (Jersey) Ltd* [1986] 1 All ER 129 at 139, [1986] AC 368 at 435–436).
No objection to the procedure is in fact raised and the matter has been argued at length
before us.

In dealing with the case I will assume that, if the police owed Miss Hill a duty of care
in the conduct of their investigations into the Yorkshire Ripper murders, the facts   *e*
pleaded in the statement of claim would, if proved, constitute a breach of that duty. The
question is whether the duty of care existed.

I begin with some familiar quotations. Lord Atkin's 'general conception of relations
giving rise to a duty of care' was:

> 'You must take reasonable care to avoid acts or omissions which you can reasonably   *f*
> foresee would be likely to injure your neighbour. Who, then, in law is my
> neighbour? The answer seems to be—persons who are so closely and directly
> affected by my act that I ought reasonably to have them in contemplation as being
> so affected when I am directing my mind to the acts or omissions which are called
> in question.'

(See *Donoghue v Stevenson* [1932] AC 562 at 580, [1932] All ER Rep 1 at 11.)   *g*

Lord Reid in *Home Office v Dorset Yacht Co Ltd* [1970] 2 All ER 294 at 297, [1970] AC
1004 at 1027 observed that Lord Atkin's formulation was not to be treated as a statutory
definition; it would require qualification in new circumstances. Lord Reid said:

> 'But I think that the time has come when we can and should say that it ought to
> apply unless there is some justification or valid explanation for its exclusion. For   *h*
> example, causing economic loss is a different matter . . .'

Lord Wilberforce in *Anns v Merton London Borough* [1977] 2 All ER 492 at 498, [1978]
AC 728 at 751–52 said:

> 'Through the trilogy of cases in this House, *Donoghue v Stevenson* [1932] AC 562,
> [1932] All ER Rep 1, *Hedley Byrne & Co Ltd v Heller & Partners Ltd* [1963] 2 All ER   *j*
> 575, [1964] AC 465 and *Home Office v Dorset Yacht Co Ltd* [1970] 2 All ER 294, [1970]
> AC 1004, the position has now been reached that in order to establish that a duty of
> care arises in a particular situation, it is not necessary to bring the facts of that
> situation within those of previous situations in which a duty of care has been held

to exist. Rather the question has to be approached in two stages. First one has to ask
whether, as between the alleged wrongdoer and the person who has suffered damage
there is a sufficient relationship of proximity or neighbourhood such that, in the
reasonable contemplation of the former, carelessness on his part may be likely to
cause damage to the latter, in which case a prima facie duty of care arises. Secondly,
if the first question is answered affirmatively, it is necessary to consider whether
there are any considerations which ought to negative, or to reduce or limit the scope
of the duty or the class of person to whom it is owed or the damages to which a
breach of it may give rise (see the *Dorset Yacht* case [1970] 2 All ER 294 at 297–298,
[1970] AC 1004 at 1027, per Lord Reid).'

Applying this statement, the plaintiff contends first that there was a sufficient
relationship of neighbourhood or proximity that it must have been within the reasonable
contemplation of the police that failure to exercise due care in their investigations could
put at risk the life of an unaccompanied young woman and, second, it is said that there
is no consideration which ought to negative or limit the scope of that duty.

In *Governors of the Peabody Donation Fund v Sir Lindsay Parkinson & Co Ltd* [1984] 3 All
ER 529 at 534, [1985] AC 210 at 240–241 Lord Keith, with whom the other members of
the House agreed, after referring to the above observation of Lord Wilberforce put the
question thus:

'There has been a tendency in some recent cases to treat these passages as being
themselves of a definitive character. This is a temptation which should be resisted.
The true question in each case is whether the particular defendant owed to the
particular plaintiff a duty of care having the scope which is contended for, and
whether he was in breach of that duty with consequent loss to the plaintiff. A
relationship of proximity in Lord Atkin's sense must exist before any duty of care
can arise, but the scope of the duty must depend on all the circumstances of the case.
In *Home Office v Dorset Yacht Co Ltd* [1970] 2 All ER 294 at 307–308, [1970] AC 1004
at 1038–1039 Lord Morris, after observing that at the conclusion of his speech in
Donoghue v Stevenson [1932] AC 562 at 599, [1932] All ER Rep 1 at 20 Lord Atkin
said that it was advantageous if the law "is in accordance with sound common sense"
and expressing the view that a special relation existed between the prison officers
and the yacht company which gave rise to a duty on the former to control their
charges so as to prevent them doing damage, continued: "Apart from this I would
conclude that in the situation stipulated in the present case it would not only be fair
and reasonable that a duty of care should exist but that it would be contrary to the
fitness of things were it not so. I doubt whether it is necessary to say, in cases where
the court is asked whether in a particular situation a duty existed, that the court is
called on to make a decision as to policy. Policy need not be invoked where reasons
and good sense will at once point the way. If the test whether in some particular
situation a duty of care arises may in some cases have to be whether it is fair and
reasonable that it should so arise the court must not shrink from being the arbiter.
As Lord Radcliffe said in his speech in *Davis Contractors Ltd v Fareham UDC* [1956] 2
All ER 145 at 160, [1956] AC 696 at 728, the court is 'the spokesman of the fair and
reasonable man'." So in determining whether or not a duty of care of particular
scope was incumbent on a defendant it is material to take into consideration whether
it is just and reasonable that it should be so.'

It is, therefore, proper in the present case to inquire whether it is just and reasonable
that such a duty of care as the plaintiff contends for should be established. In considering
that, it is necessary to bear in mind throughout that Miss Hill was not killed by the West
Yorkshire police. She was killed by the deliberate, and murderous, act of Sutcliffe.

Now it is clear that the police have no general exemption from the ordinary law of the
land. Thus if a police car is driven negligently on the highway, the police may incur

liablity to a person who is injured in consequence. In *Marshall v Osmond* [1983] 2 All ER
225, [1983] QB 1034 the plaintiff was a willing occupant of a car which had been driven *a*
away without the consent of its owner and which was being pursued by the police. The
car eventually came to a halt and the occupants got out. The plaintiff was hit by the
police car as the latter was drawing to a halt. Dealing with a plea of volenti non fit injuria,
Sir John Donaldson MR said ([1983] 2 All ER 225 at 227, [1983] QB 1034 at 1038):

> 'For my part I am bound to say that I do not believe that the defence of volenti *b*
> non fit injuria is really applicable in the case of the police pursuing a suspected
> criminal. I think that the duty owed by a police driver to the suspect is, as counsel
> on behalf of the plaintiff has contended, the same duty as that owed to anyone else,
> namely to exercise such care and skill as is reasonable in all the circumstances.

Further, the police are liable for assault, unlawful arrest, wrongful imprisonment and
malicious prosecution. *c*
All the above are, however, cases where the injury suffered by the complainant is the
direct consequence of the acts of the police. Thus the complainant is directly injured by
the negligent driving or assault of a police officer or his liberty is directly interfered with
by police action or he is subjected to an improper prosecution by the positive act of the
police. The present case is quite different. The death of Miss Hill was the direct result of
the criminal act of a third party. *d*
No case has been cited to us, in any of the United Kingdom or Commonwealth or USA
jurisdictions where the police have been made liable for the acts of a criminal on the
ground that they should previously have apprehended him. The case must be determined
on principle and, if necessary, policy.
The police have a duty to enforce the law. Thus in *R v Metropolitan Police Comr, ex p*
Blackburn [1968] 1 All ER 763 at 771, [1968] 2 QB 118 at 138 Salmon LJ said: 'In my *e*
judgment the police owe to the public a clear legal duty to enforce the law.' And Edmund
Davies LJ said ([1968] 1 All ER 763 at 777, [1968] 2 QB 118 at 148): '... the law
enforcement officers of this country certainly owe a legal duty to the public to perform
those functions which are the raison d'etre of their existence.'
Although the duty to the public exists, it is not as wide as it looks. Lord Denning MR *f*
in the *Blackburn* case [1968] 1 All ER 763 at 769, [1968] 2 QB 118 at 136 said:

> 'I hold it to be the duty of the Commissioner of Police, as it is of every chief
> constable, to enforce the law of the land. He must take steps so to post his men that
> crimes may be detected; and that honest citizens may go about their affairs in peace.
> He must decide whether or no suspected persons are to be prosecuted; and, if need
> be, bring the prosecution or see that it is brought; but in all these things he is not *g*
> the servant of anyone, save of the law itself. No Minister of the Crown can tell him
> that he must, or must not, keep observation on this place or that; or that he must,
> or must not, prosecute this man or that one. Nor can any police authority tell him
> so. The responsibility for law enforcement lies on him. He is answerable to the law
> and to the law alone ... Although the chief officers of police are answerable to the
> law, there are many fields in which they have a discretion with which the law will *h*
> not interfere. For instance, it is for ... the chief constable ... to decide in any
> particular case whether enquiries should be pursued, or whether an arrest should be
> made, or a prosecution brought. It must be for him to decide on the disposition of
> his force and the concentration of his resources on any particular crime or area. No
> court can or should give him direction on such a matter. He can also make policy *j*
> decisions and give effect to them, as, for instance, was often done when prosecutions
> were not brought for attempted suicide ...'

The policy decision not to prosecute young teenage boys who have had sexual intercourse
with girls under 16 is another example of the latter kind of decision referred to by Lord
Denning MR.

The passage from Lord Denning MR's judgment is dealing largely with powers and
a discretions, but it shows that the duty of the police to suppress crime is no ordinary duty.
In particular, the fact that the chief constable may decide as a matter of policy not to
prosecute for certain crimes does not lie easily with the notion that the police in the
conduct of their investigations owe a duty to individual members of the public to prevent
harm to them by criminals. Quite apart from that, it seems to me that the existence of a
general duty in the police to suppress crime does not necessarily carry with it a liability
b to individuals for damage caused to them by criminals whom the police have failed to
apprehend in circumstances when it was possible to do so. The police have a very wide
range of activities to perform and limited resources with which to perform them. The
performance of a duty in relation to one group of persons may involve its neglect in
relation to another group.

The risk of injury to a citizen if a violent criminal is not apprehended is of course
c something which can be said to be foreseeable. But foreseeability is not necessarily the
test of whether a duty of care exists (see *McLoughlin v O'Brian* [1982] 2 All ER 298 at 303,
308, [1983] 1 AC 410 at 420, 426 per Lord Wilberforce and Lord Edmund-Davies). The
matter has to be considered more widely in the light of relevant principles and of policy.

The general principle was stated by Lord Sumner in *Weld-Blundell v Stephens* [1920] AC
d 956 at 986, [1920] All ER Rep 32 at 47 as follows:

'In general (apart from special contracts and relations and the maxim Respondeat
superior), even though A. is in fault, he is not responsible for injury to C. which B.,
a stranger to him, deliberately chooses to do.'

In *Smith v Leurs* (1945) 70 CLR 256 at 261–262 Dixon J said:

e   '... apart from vicarious responsibility, one man may be responsible to another
for the harm done to the latter by a third person; he may be responsible on the
ground that the act of the third person could not have taken place but for his own
fault or breach of duty. There is more than one description of duty the breach of
which may produce this consequence. For instance, it may be a duty of care in
reference to things involving special danger. It may even be a duty of care with
f   reference to the control of actions or conduct of the third person. It is, however,
exceptional to find in the law a duty to control another's actions to prevent harm to
strangers. The general rule is that one man is under no duty of controlling another
man to prevent his doing damage to a third. There are, however, special relations
which are the source of a duty of this nature. It appears now to be recognized that it
is incumbent upon a parent who maintains control over a young child to take
g   reasonable care so to exercise that control as to avoid conduct on his part exposing
the person or property of others to unreasonable danger. Parental control, where it
exists, must be exercised with due care to prevent the child inflicting intentional
damage on others or causing damage by conduct involving unreasonable risk of
injury to others.'

h   In *Home Office v Dorset Yacht Co Ltd* [1970] 2 All ER 294, [1970] AC 1004 some borstal
boys who were working on an island in Poole Harbour under the control of borstal
officers escaped during the night and went aboard a yacht which they found nearby.
They set the yacht in motion and collided with the plaintiff's yacht which was moored
in the vicinity. They then boarded the latter yacht; much damage was done to it both by
the collision and by the boys when they boarded it. The House of Lords, on a preliminary
j issue, held that the borstal officers owed the plaintiff a duty to take such care as was
reasonable in all the circumstances with a view to preventing the boys under their control
from causing damage of which there was a manifest risk if they neglected that duty and
that public policy did not require that there should be immunity from action in such a
case.

The *Dorset Yacht* case is said by the plaintiff to bear a close similarity on its facts to the present. I do not think it does. In the first place, the boys had been charged and sentenced and committed to the borstal institution. They were in the custody of the borstal officers *a* when they escaped. That was the basis of the special relationship which existed in that case. In the present case, Sutcliffe was never in the custody of the police at all in relation to his assaults. Certainly he had been interviewed by the police on a number of occasions. But many people must have been interviewed in the course of the long series of investigations between 1969 and 1980. Secondly, the duty of care which the House of Lords held to exist in the *Dorset Yacht* case was very limited. It was not a duty to any *b* person who might suffer damage or injury at the hands of the boys while they were at large. Thus Lord Morris said ([1970] 2 All ER 294 at 307, [1970] AC 1004 at 1039):

> 'There was a special relation in that the officers were entitled to exercise control over boys who to the knowledge of the officers might wish to take their departure and who might well do some damage to property near at hand. The events that are *c* said to have happened could reasonably have been foreseen . . . A duty arose . . . It was not a duty to prevent the boys from escaping or from doing damage but it was a duty to take such care as in all the circumstances was reasonable in the hope of preventing the occurrence of events likely to cause damage to the [plaintiff].'

In the present case the duty which is being contended for (ie the duty of care in the conduct of investigations into crime) is a duty of great width. It is a duty, in effect, to all *d* unaccompanied young women in the West Yorkshire police area. Indeed, if the duty exists at all, it is difficult to see why it should be restricted to the West Yorkshire police area. Sutcliffe might attack women in adjoining areas in Yorkshire and, for that matter, anywhere else in Britain. And there is no reason why the duty should be restricted to young women; if it exists it should extend to anybody who goes to the help of a woman who was attacked. Is it just and reasonable to impose such a duty on the police in relation *e* to the consequences of the acts of a criminal? Lord Diplock in the *Dorset Yacht* case [1970] 2 All ER 294 at 333–334, [1970] AC 1004 at 1070 said:

> 'It is common knowledge, of which judicial notice may be taken, that borstal training often fails to achieve its purpose of reformation, and that trainees when they have ceased to be detained in custody revert to crime and commit tortious *f* damage to the person and property of others. But so do criminals who have never been apprehended and criminals who have been released from custody on completion of their sentences or earlier pursuant to a statutory power to do so. The risk of sustaining damage from the tortious acts of criminals is shared by the public at large. It has never been recognised at common law as giving rise to any cause of action against anyone but the criminal himself. It would seem arbitrary and *g* therefore unjust to single out for the special privilege of being able to recover compensation from the authorities responsible for the prevention of crime a person whose property was damaged by the tortious act of a criminal, merely because the damage to him happened to be caused by a criminal who had escaped from custody before completion of his sentence instead of by one who had been lawfully released or who had been put on probation or given a suspended sentence or who had never *h* been previously apprehended at all.'

Lord Diplock went on to say that to give rise to a duty of care by a custodian to members of the public to take reasonable care to prevent an escape, there must be some relationship between the custodian and the persons to whom the duty was owed which exposes that person to a particular risk of damage which is different in incidence from *j* the general risk of damage from the criminal acts of others which he shares with all members of the public. That risk in the *Dorset Yacht* case he regarded as extending only to persons who had property situate near the place of detention (the island) which the detainee was likely to steal or appropriate or damage in the course of eluding immediate pursuit. This is because the detainee is likely to steal property in the immediate vicinity in order to make good his escape (for example breaking in and stealing money to get

a transport).

   In my opinion (and looking at the matter, for the moment, apart from the state compensation scheme) it would not be a satisfactory state of the law that persons who suffer injury to their person or are killed by the direct acts of a criminal, should have an effective cause of action if they can show carelessness by the police but not otherwise. I say 'effective' because a cause of action will lie against the criminal himself, but that is

b normally worthless. The problem is sharply illustrated by the position of Sutcliffe's victims. It is not fitting, and it would indeed be distasteful, that the compensation to (or to the estate of) the various victims of Sutcliffe should depend on whether their deaths occurred, or their injuries were sustained, early or late in the sequence of his crimes. In the case of the earlier, and certainly the first, of the attacks the likelihood of the police having information which might have prevented them is remote. All the victims met

c their deaths or were injured by a man who was an enemy of society and there is no valid reason why the general approach to compensation should vary according to the amount of information available to the police as to the identity of the criminal at a particular time. Nor, I think, would it be reasonable that if, for example, on the day when Miss Hill was murdered, another woman who had no dependants was murdered by a killer of whom the police have no previous knowledge, the approach to compensation should be

d totally different in the two cases. Both suffered the same consequence from the acts of criminals. As to the question of 'special relationship', there is in my view no special relationship here. Sutcliffe was not under the control of the police. The fact that the police have a general duty to the public at large to suppress crime does not mean that the police have a special relationship with the possible perpetrator of a crime which they are investigating. Sutcliffe was of course a great danger. It was in the interests of the public

e at large that he should be caught. And the police had a general duty to the public to try and catch him. But the fact that they attempted to perform that duty does not create a special relationship between them and Sutcliffe. So long as Sutcliffe was at large he might of course commit further crimes. But escaped borstal boys might until recapture commit offences up and down the country; but the only cause of action held to exist was the very limited one in relation to property in the vicinity which I have mentioned. The Home

f Office was not held to be answerable for any offences which the boys might commit before recapture.

   I now come to the Criminal Injuries Compensation Scheme established by the Government. Historically, English law has left the consequences of the tortious acts of criminals to be borne by the members of the public who suffered them. What we are concerned with in this case is whether it is just and reasonable (or, if it be preferred,

g whether as a matter of policy) that a cause of action should lie against the police in the alleged circumstances of the present case which I have assumed (solely for the purposes of this application) would constitute a breach of duty if one exists. If the state made no provision at all for criminal injuries that might be a reason for imposing a legal duty of care on the police in the conduct of their investigations, though, for the reasons which I

h have indicated, I think that would produce unfair results between the victims of crime. In fact however the state has provided a scheme of compensation for criminal injuries since 1964 or thereabouts when the Criminal Injuries Compensation Board was established. Claims for ex gratia payments of compensation can be made to the Board by a victim of a crime of violence. A claim is entertained where an applicant, or, in the case of an application by a dependant of a deceased person, the deceased, suffered personal

j injury attributable to, inter alia, a criminal offence or the arrest or attempted arrest of a suspected offender or to the prevention of crime. Compensation is, in general, assessed on the basis of common law damages. The scheme has not, up to the present, been statutory but is now intended to be given statutory effect with amendments (see the Criminal Justice Bill 1986, cll 73 to 82).

   Apart from damage to clothing and some personal effects arising from the injury, the

scheme is not concerned with damage to property. That will normally be covered by
insurance. The scheme does not provide for claims by a parent of an unmarried victim   *a*
over 18 (though the Bill, it seems, may do so). That however is not I think of consequence
for present purposes. What is important in my view is this. The scheme (and the Bill)
make quite wide provision for compensation for such persons as are likely to suffer
financial loss as a result of a crime of violence. It is not desirable that inequalities should
be produced by providing additional remedies for negligence. Either such remedies will
merely duplicate the scheme, or they will give rise to inequalities which may be offensive   *b*
to the families of other victims of crimes of violence in cases where no negligence by the
police was involved. I quite appreciate that Mrs Hill is not seeking financial benefit for
herself and that nothing can compensate here for the tragic loss of her daughter. But I
think that the problems of compensation for injury from crimes of violence are best
dealt with in the framework of the scheme as it may be enacted which has been developed
for more than 20 years with a view to dealing with the particular difficulties of the   *c*
subject matter and to the establishment of an acceptable system of compensation.

I summarise the position thus. (1) It is not sufficient, in order to establish a duty of
care, to show that the defendant could reasonably foresee damage in consequence of his
alleged carelessness. The matter has to be considered much more widely and in particular
by reference to the test whether the imposition of such a duty is just and reasonable at
all. (2) The cause of action contended for would impose a duty of care of undue width   *d*
and does not fall within the principle of the *Dorset Yacht* case. (3) There is already in
existence a compensation scheme, financed by the government, for the provision of
compensation for criminal injuries and which the Bill now before Parliament seeks to
put into statutory form. (4) The cause of action could lead to unfair and unacceptable
differences in the remedies available in consequence of criminal injuries. (5) In the
circumstances, I do not think that the courts would be justified in extending the law by   *e*
providing a remedy for criminal injury which has never previously been given.

I think therefore that the judge was right to strike out the proceedings. I would
dismiss the appeal.

GLIDEWELL LJ. I have had the advantage of reading in draft the judgment delivered   *f*
by Fox LJ. I agree with both his reasoning and his conclusion that this appeal should be
dismissed. I add some further observations because of the importance of the issue raised
in these proceedings.

That issue can be expressed as follows: do police officers who are conducting an
investigation into crimes of violence committed by a person who has not yet been
arrested owe a duty of care to members of the public, the breach of which duty is likely
to result in the offender remaining at liberty and killing or attacking further victims?   *g*

Paragraph 6 of the statement of claim asserts (for present purposes we must assume
correctly) that:

'... the circumstances of the said offences resembled one another to such an
extent that it was reasonable to infer that the said offences were committed by one
and the same man and in the premises it was at all material times foreseeable that if   *h*
he were not apprehended the said man would commit further similar offences.'

As Fox LJ says, in order to establish the existence of such a duty of care, it does not suffice
merely to show that if the criminal remains at large it is reasonably foreseeable that he
will attack other victims. 'That foreseeability does not of itself, and automatically, lead to
a duty of care is, I think clear' (see per Lord Wilberforce in *McLoughlin v O'Brian* [1982] 2   *j*
All ER 298 at 303, [1983] 1 AC 410 at 420).

It is commonplace that where a particular activity carries with it the risk of direct
injury or damage to other persons, the actor may owe a duty of care to many people over
a wide area. The driver of a car travelling from London to Leeds owes a duty to drive
with reasonable skill and care to the many thousands of people, to him unknown, who

are in his vicinity throughout his journey on or near the roads or in vehicles on the roads.
a A chemical manufacturer must ensure that dangerous substances do not escape from his plant, and owes a duty in this respect to many millions of people to whom the wind may convey the pollutant.

The present case, however, is one where the lack of reasonable care by the defendant is alleged to have caused the death of Miss Hill indirectly through the agency of the killer Sutcliffe. The plaintiff's claim is founded on the decision in *Home Office v Dorset Yacht Co*
b *Ltd* [1970] 2 All ER 294, [1970] AC 1004. As Fox LJ says, their Lordships in that case held that the duty of care arose out of the special relationship between the borstal trainees and the prison officers, and that it was owed to a limited class of people, namely those in the vicinity of the island from which the youths escaped: see the passage quoted by Fox LJ from the speech of Lord Morris ([1970] 2 All ER 294 at 307, [1970] AC 1004 at 1039; see also [1970] 2 All ER 294 at 321–322, 327, 334, [1970] AC 1004 at 1054–1055, 1062,
c 1070 per Lord Pearson and Lord Diplock).

In the present case, the matters alleged in the statement of claim do not, in my judgment, establish such a special relationship between Sutcliffe and the chief constable as that found in the *Dorset Yacht* case. In this respect there is, in my view, a vital difference between a person in custody being allowed to escape by the negligence of those who have
d him in their charge and a person not in custody remaining at large as a result of negligence in the investigation of crime. Moreover, I agree with Fox LJ that a duty allegedly owed, as this must be, to all young or fairly young women in Yorkshire and Lancashire, if not the whole of Great Britain, is not within the ambit of the decision in the *Dorset Yacht* case. In my view, the law does not recognise a duty of care owed to so wide a class of persons to avoid injury at the hand of a third person.

There is another reason why, in my judgment, the statement of claim in this case
e discloses no cause of action. Whether one asks, in the words of Lord Wilberforce in *Anns v Merton London Borough* [1977] 2 All ER 492 at 498, [1978] AC 728 at 752, whether there are considerations which ought to negative the duty or, in those of Lord Keith in *Governors of the Peabody Donation Fund v Sir Lindsay Parkinson & Co Ltd* [1984] 3 All ER 529 at 534, [1985] AC 210 at 241, whether it is fair and reasonable that a duty of care should arise, a court confronted by a novel set of facts has in the end to give the answer
f which it thinks justice and public policy require. Counsel for the chief constable submits that public policy clearly dictates that, in the circumstances of the present case, no duty should arise. Like Sir Neil Lawson, I agree with him.

If the police were liable to be sued for negligence in the investigation of crime which has allowed the criminal to commit further crimes, it must be expected that actions in
g this field would not be uncommon. Investigative police work is a matter of judgment, often no doubt dictated by experience or instinct. The threat that a decision, which in the end proved to be wrong, might result in an action for damages would be likely to have an inhibiting effect on the exercise of that judgment. The trial of such actions would very often involve the retrial of matters which had already been tried at the Crown Court. While no doubt many such actions would fail, preparing for and taking part in
h the trial of such an action would inevitably involve considerable work and time for a police force, and thus either reduce the manpower available to detect crime or increase expenditure on police services. In short, the reasons for holding that the police are immune from an action of this kind are similar to those for holding that a barrister may not be sued for negligence in his conduct of proceedings in court: see *Rondel v Worsley* [1967] 3 All ER 993, [1969] 1 AC 191.
j Fox LJ has already referred to the Criminal Injuries Compensation Scheme as providing a remedy for victims of criminal violence. The existence of that remedy would, if I had any doubt whether there is a duty of care, have been a relevant matter to take into account.

There is one other consideration which supports the judge's decision. In *R v Metropolitan Police Comr, ex p Blackburn* [1968] 1 All ER 763 at 769–771, [1968] 2 QB 118

at 136–139 both Lord Denning MR and Salmon LJ made clear their view that, while the
police owe a duty to members of the public to enforce the law, the way in which the   *a*
courts should, if necessary, enforce that duty was by an order of mandamus. It is true
that no question of an action in tort arose in that case, but the decision is a pointer to the
conclusion that the judicial remedy for a failure by the police to carry out their duty lies
(in modern phraseology) in the field of public rather than private law.

   For these reasons I would uphold the decision of the judge to strike out the writ and
statement of claim and dismiss the action. I would dismiss this appeal.   *b*

SIR ROUALEYN CUMMING-BRUCE. I agree with the judgments of Fox and
Glidewell LJJ.

Appeal dismissed. Leave to appeal to the House of Lords granted.
                                                                                          c
Solicitors: *Appleby Hope & Matthews*, Middlesbrough (for Mrs Hill); *S Walker*, Wakefield
(for the chief constable).

                                                           Diana Procter   Barrister.

                                                                                          d

Practice Note

QUEEN'S BENCH DIVISION (CROWN OFFICE LIST)
MANN J
3 APRIL 1987   *e*

*Practice – Crown Office list – Estimated length of hearing – Notice of estimate – Duty of counsel's
clerks.*

MANN J made the following statement at the sitting of the court. I make the following
observations with the approval of Watkins LJ. The practice direction handed down by   *f*
Lord Lane CJ on 3 February 1987 (*Practice Note* [1987] 1 All ER 368, [1987] 1 WLR 232)
prescribed the arrangements which as from 2 March 1987 apply to the listing of cases
included in the Crown Office list. Part B of that list contains cases ready to be heard. Part
D is the expedited list. The pressure on both of those parts is great. Particularly is it so
when the case is to be heard by the single judge. In regard to both parts it is the
responsibility of counsel's clerks to inform in writing the head clerk of counsel's time   *g*
estimate for a case and of any variation in an estimation previously given. Dealing with
the list is critically dependant on the reasonable accuracy of estimates. Plainly precision
is impossible but there have been a number of cases recently where the estimate can be
described only as an ill-judged underestimate. In the interests of the dispatch of business
and of those who have business in this court, close attention must be paid to the reality
of an estimate. I emphasise, should there be a belief to the contrary, that underestimation   *h*
now secures no advantage in the listing of a case.

                                                           N P Metcalfe Esq   Barrister.

Thomas v Wignall and others

COURT OF APPEAL, CIVIL DIVISION

SIR JOHN DONALDSON MR, LLOYD AND NICHOLLS LJJ

24, 25, 26 NOVEMBER, 10 DECEMBER 1986

Damages – Personal injury – Loss of future earnings – Multiplier – Effect of taxation on award – Higher rate of tax payable on income of large award – Whether multiplier can be increased to allow for higher tax payable on income of large award.

In 1976 the plaintiff, then 16 years old, underwent a routine minor operation in hospital in the course of which she suffered severe permanent brain damage as the result of negligence in the administration of the anaesthetic. The defendants, the anaesthetist and the local health authority responsible for the hospital, admitted liability for negligence and the issue before the judge was limited to quantum. In determining the amount payable for the cost of future care and loss of earnings the judge considered that although the appropriate multiplier would ordinarily be 14 it ought to be increased to 15 to make some allowance for the high incidence of taxation on the award of damages. The total award was £679,264, which, properly invested, would produce an annual income in excess of £30,000. The defendants appealed against, inter alia, the amounts awarded in respect of future care and loss of past and future earnings contending, inter alia, that the judge had been wrong to increase the multiplier to take account of the effect of high taxation on the award.

Held (Lloyd LJ dissenting) – There was no reason in principle why the court should not consider the effect of high rates of taxation on an award of damages in personal injury cases. Although prudent investment planning could mitigate or offset some of the rigours of higher rates of taxation, it was unrealistic to approach the assessment of damages with complete disregard for the incidence of such higher rates on a large income. The judge had thus been entitled to adopt some method of allowing for high tax rates and his adjustment of the multiplier from 14 to 15 was a reasonable method of achieving that result. Furthermore (Lloyd LJ concurring), the defendants had not established that the judge's assessment of the multiplicand was wrong. It followed therefore that the appeal would be dismissed (see p 1188 *j* to p 1189 *a c d h*, p 1190 *e f*, p 1191 *b c*, p 1192 *a*, p 1193 *c d*, p 1195 *g h* and p 1196 *f* to *j*, post).

Dictum of Lord Fraser in *Cookson v Knowles* [1978] 2 All ER at 616 and *Lim Poh Choo v Camden and Islington Area Health Authority* [1979] 2 All ER 910 considered.

Notes

For the measure of damages in personal injury cases, see 12 Halsbury's Laws (4th edn) paras 1145–1158, and for cases on the subject, see 17 Digest (Reissue) 113–118, 169–199.

Cases referred to in judgments

Auty v National Coal Board [1985] 1 All ER 930, [1985] 1 WLR 784, CA.

Carrick v Camden London BC (25 July 1979, unreported), QBD.

Chapman v Lidstone (3 December 1982) referred to in Kemp and Kemp *The Quantum of Damages* vol 2, para 1–210.

Cookson v Knowles [1978] 2 All ER 604, [1979] AC 556, [1978] 2 WLR 978, HL; *affg* [1977] 2 All ER 820, [1977] QB 913, [1977] 3 WLR 279, CA.

Harris v Harris [1973] 1 Lloyd's Rep 445, CA.

Hartin v Scott (4 December 1978, unreported), QBD.

Housecroft v Burnett [1986] 1 All ER 332, CA.

Hughes v McKeown [1985] 3 All ER 284, [1985] 1 WLR 963.

Lim Poh Choo v Camden and Islington Area Health Authority [1979] 1 All ER 332, [1979] QB
196, [1978] 3 WLR 895, QBD and CA; *affd* [1979] 2 All ER 910, [1980] AC 174, [1979] **a**
3 WLR 44, HL.
Moriarty v McCarthy [1978] 2 All ER 213, [1978] 1 WLR 155.
Moser v Enfield and Haringey Area Health Authority (1982) 133 NLJ 105, referred to in
Kemp and Kemp *The Quantum of Damages* vol 2, para 1–721.
Seton v Elliott (6 April 1979) referred to in Kemp and Kemp *The Quantum of Damages* vol
2, para 1–716.	**b**
Taylor v O'Connor [1970] 1 All ER 365, [1971] AC 115, [1970] 2 WLR 472, HL.

Cases also cited
Birkett v Hayes [1982] 2 All ER 710, [1982] 1 WLR 816, CA.
Croke (a minor) v Wiseman [1981] 3 All ER 852, [1982] 1 WLR 71, CA.
Mitchell v Mulholland (No 2) [1971] 2 All ER 1205, [1972] 1 QB 65, CA.	**c**
Robertson v Lestrange [1985] 1 All ER 950.

Appeal
The defendants, Mr J R Wignall and the South Glamorgan Area Health Authority,
appealed from the order of Hutchison J sitting in the Queen's Bench Division in Cardiff
on 20 December 1985 awarding the plaintiff, Linda Thomas (suing by her next friend **d**
Frank Lack Maffey), damages of £679,264 for personal injuries caused by the negligence
of the first defendant in respect of which the second defendants were vicariously liable.
Liability was admitted by the defendants and the only issue at the trial was quantum.
The facts are set out in the judgment of Nicholls LJ.

Piers Ashworth QC and *Michael Baker* for the defendants.	**e**
Malcolm Pill QC and *Vernon Pugh QC* for the plaintiff.

Cur adv vult

10 December. The following judgments were delivered.	**f**

NICHOLLS LJ (delivering the first judgment at the invitation of Sir John Donaldson
MR). This is a tragic case. On 6 March 1976 Linda Thomas was married, at the early age
of 16½ years. She had left school some time previously, and was working locally as a sales
assistant in a chemist's shop. She had become engaged on her 16th birthday. Two weeks
after her marriage she underwent a routine operation for the removal of her tonsils in
the University Hospital of Wales in Cardiff. That was on 25 March. The anaesthetic went **g**
wrong. Linda suffered severe permanent brain damage. Mercifully, she is not aware of
what has happened to her or of what she has lost. The defendants, who are the anaesthetist
and the local area health authority, admitted liability for negligence, and so the issue
before Hutchison J at the trial of the action was limited to the amount of the damages.
By his decision, given on 20 December 1985, the judge awarded the plaintiff the sum of **h**
£679,264. We were told that this is the largest award ever made in a personal injuries
case. The defendants have now appealed against that decision.
	The plaintiff was born on 10 October 1958. Thus at the time of the trial she was 27
years old. She is now very seriously disabled, physically and intellectually. For practical
purposes she is confined to a wheelchair, and she will need constant care and attention
for the rest of her life. She is incontinent, particularly at night. She also has serious **j**
behavioural problems, exhibiting very disturbed and even aggressive behaviour. One of
the doctors described her as a profoundly damaged and difficult lady. Save for very short
periods she cannot be left alone, and she needs help in virtually every aspect of daily
living. The doctors were agreed that for the foreseeable future she will need a high
degree of individual attention. She requires a house of her own in which she can live,

with suitable nursing and other care. She is not now expected to live beyond the age of
a 55 years, so her expectation of life at the time of the trial had been reduced to about 28
years.

The principal items in the very large sum awarded by the judge are as follows. First,
general damages were agreed between the parties at the sum of £60,000, plus £6,396
interest thereon. Second, £10,000 in respect of recoverable loss of earnings up to the
time of the trial. Third, £52,662 as the cost of the plaintiff's care up to the time of the
b trial, and a further £14,906 as the cost of care until 14 February 1986, when it was
expected that the plaintiff's house would be ready for occupation. Fourth, £5,000 in
respect of the cost of parental visits to the plaintiff when she was in hospital in Cardiff,
and for extra care and work by her parents on her visits home, and a further £2,896 for
the cost of parental visits to Northampton and London, and damage done to the parents'
house on her visits home. Fifth, £39,000 for loss of future earnings. Sixth, £25,000 in
c respect of the difference between the cost of the house when converted to suit the
plaintiff's particular requirements and its then market value, and an allowance for
increased running costs, and a further £2,000 for the extra cost of furnishing a house
suitable for the plaintiff. Finally, the judge awarded the sum of £435,000 in respect of
the cost of the plaintiff's future care.

Of these items the defendants have sought to challenge only some elements in the
d amounts awarded in respect of future care and loss of past and future earnings.

Cost of future care: the multiplier

I turn first to the cost of future care. The judge arrived at the sum of £435,000 by
applying a multiplier of 15 to the estimated annual cost of future care. He took the sum
of £34,000 as representing the present annual expenditure on care, and the sum of
e £24,000 as being the annual cost of care exclusive of extra night care. He applied one
half of the multiplier (7½) to the larger sum and one half to the smaller sum. He did this
to give effect to his finding that there was no greater chance that the plaintiff's
incontinence, which necessitates night nursing, would be substantially cured than that it
would continue unabated.

f The judge arrived at the multiplier of 15 in respect of the cost of future care as follows.
This was the multiplier he had used in respect of loss of future earnings. Since the
plaintiff was not expected to live to be older than 55, and at the time of the trial she was
aged 27, he equated her position to that of a 37-year-old person due to retire at the age of
65. He considered that the appropriate multiplier for such a person would ordinarily be
14. To make some allowance for the high incidence of taxation on the damages award he
g increased the multiplier to 15.

The defendants submitted that the appropriate multiplier in this case, where the
period in question was just under 28 years, was 13 and not 14. Moreover, and this was a
point much stressed by the appellants, to increase the multiplier by one as an allowance
for the high incidence of taxation was wrong in law and not supported by evidence.

Our attention was drawn to certain authorities. The first of these was the decision of
h the House of Lords in *Cookson v Knowles* [1978] 2 All ER 604, [1979] AC 556, a case under
the Fatal Accident Acts 1846 to 1959. In that case both Lord Diplock and Lord Fraser
observed that conventionally the multipliers generally adopted are those appropriate to
interest rates of 4% to 5% and that, in a rough and ready way, this takes care of inflation,
in that in times of high inflation much higher interest rates will readily be obtainable as
one of the consequences of inflation (see [1978] 2 All ER 604 at 611, 615, [1979] AC 556
j at 571, 577).

The second authority relied on by the defendants was *Lim Poh Choo v Camden and
Islington Area Health Authority* [1979] 2 All ER 910, [1980] AC 174. In that case Lord
Scarman said of those passages in the speeches of Lord Diplock and Lord Fraser in *Cookson
v Knowles* that he did not read them as modifying the law in any way, which is 'now
settled that only in exceptional cases, where justice can be shown to require it, will the

risk of future inflation be brought into account in the assessment of damages for future loss' (see [1979] 2 All ER 910 at 923, [1980] AC 174 at 193).

The present case is not one where any allowance was made, or is being claimed, for the prospect of future inflation. But counsel for the defendants prayed in aid those decisions in this way. The sum awarded in *Lim Poh Choo v Camden and Islington Area Health Authority* was £250,000. The trial in that case took place in December 1977. In 'real' terms, £250,000 in December 1977 corresponds to a sum of about £500,000 at the date of the trial in the present case (November 1985). Thus the award in *Lim Poh Choo v Camden and Islington Area Health Authority* was a very substantial one. The burden of higher rates of tax was much heavier in December 1977 than it is now, but despite this, and even though the award there was a very substantial one, in *Lim Poh Choo v Camden and Islington Area Health Authority* the House of Lords did not suggest that it would be appropriate to adjust the multiplier or make some other allowance for the incidence of higher rates of tax.

Furthermore, it was pointed out that there was before the judge no evidence of the likely burden of taxation in this case. In *Cookson v Knowles* [1978] 2 All ER 604 at 615, [1979] AC 556 at 577 Lord Fraser observed that what the dependant loses by inflation will be roughly equivalent to what she gains by the high rate of interest, 'provided she is not liable for a high rate of income tax'. He added ([1978] 2 All ER 604 at 616, [1979] AC 556 at 577):

> 'In exceptional cases, where the annuity is large enough to attract income tax at a high rate, it may be necessary for the court to have expert evidence of the spendable income that would accrue from awards at different levels and to compare the total annuity with the amount of the lost dependency having regard to the net income (after tax) of the deceased person. Whether in such cases it might be appropriate to increase the multiplier, or to allow for further inflation in some other way would be a matter for evidence in each case.'

So here, it was submitted, the observation made by Lord Fraser regarding expert evidence of the spendable income accruing from awards at different levels is equally applicable where the comparison is with the amount of the cost of future care and lost earnings.

The plaintiff's answer was that the appropriate multiplier in this case falls between about 13 and 15, and that she does not contend that tax reasons make this a case for a multiplier outside the normal, conventional bracket. This is not an exceptional case. Within the reasonable range of appropriate multipliers the judge was entitled to take higher incidence of tax into account as one of the factors.

I shall consider the matter first without reference to authority. Higher rates of income tax are a fact of life. In general, the larger an individual's income, the greater is the percentage of it which goes in tax. Further, all the signs are that a taxation system having this broad effect will continue to exist in this country for the foreseeable future, although the figures and the percentages will vary from time to time. Thus, other things being equal, taxation bears and will continue to bear more heavily on the income of a large award of damages than on the income of a small one. In percentage terms, the net yield after tax of a substantial fund is likely to be lower than the net yield after tax of a small fund the income whereof is subject to little or no tax.

Hence, and still speaking in general terms, there is, in this respect, a material distinction from the outset between a very large award and a comparatively modest one. In principle one would expect that distinction to be taken into account by the court when determining the amount of the award. Take two examples, at opposite ends of the spectrum. In one the court is concerned with assessing the amount of an award to make good an income loss of £3,500 pa, or to provide for annual expenditure at that rate. In the other, the facts are the same save that the income loss or the expenditure is £35,000 pa. If 14 were the appropriate multiplier in the first case, in my view it would be wrong, and import an

inflexible rigidity neither justifiable nor necessary, if the court were not able to make
a some adjustment to the multiplier in the second case to reflect the increased incidence of
tax.

The point can be illustrated by some simple figures, using the income tax rates put
before us by counsel for the defendants, which were the rates current at the time when
the judge made his award in this case. The overall percentage of a single person's income
of £3,500 pa which disappears in tax is about 10%. With an annual income of £35,000
b the percentage rises to 36%. £3,500 is, of course, a very small figure, but at £10,000 pa
the percentage (which is 23%) is still 13% below the percentage applicable to a yearly
income of £35,000. Again, let it be supposed that funds which have been quantified to
produce, at a notional 5% interest rate, £10,000 and £35,000 pa respectively, are invested
and yield, say, 10% pa gross, so that the actual income of the two funds would be £20,000
and £70,000: income tax would absorb about 27½% overall of the smaller fund's income,
c but 47% of the larger fund's income.

Of course prudent investment planning can mitigate or offset some of the rigours of
higher rates of tax. For example, advantage can be taken of capital gains, including
capital gains not chargeable to capital gains tax, and better investment opportunities may
be available with a larger fund than a small one. But, and here I have in mind the facts of
the instant case relating to future care and future earnings, where the fund will have an
d annual income of over £30,000, it is unrealistic to approach the matter on the footing
that the incidence of higher rates of tax on such a large income should be wholly ignored.
For my part I can see no reason in principle why the court should be constrained to deal
with a case such as this in such an artificial way.

Nor do I see why a judge needs evidence to inform him of facts so well known as those
I have mentioned. Mustill J considered this point in *Seton v Elliott* (6 April 1979) referred
e to in Kemp and Kemp *The Quantum of Damages* vol 2 para 1–716, where he said:

'If it is right to accept that in principle some allowance ought to be made for the
incidence of tax on the fund, yet the strictly arithmetical method is rejected, how is
the allowance to be assessed? One possibility would be to receive evidence from
bankers and accountants as to the way in which a prudent investor might lay out
f the sums in question, with a view to minimising the incidence of tax and providing
a hedge against inflation, whilst at the time exhausting the fund at the end of the
anticipated working life. Sample calculations would then provide the court with a
general idea of the level at which tax would be likely to impinge on the fund. I
doubt whether such a method would be appropriate, except in cases where the term
is sufficiently short to justify the assumption that the pattern of investment will
g remain substantially unchanged throughout. No such assumption can be made
here, nor is there any sufficient evidence to found a calculation, although the
defendant has submitted one or two examples of how savings in tax would be made.
In these circumstances I consider that the right course is to proceed in the same way
as when allowing at other stages of the calculation for contingencies which can be
foreseen but not accurately quantified; namely, by an adjustment of the multiplier.'

h
With that I respectfully agree. In doing so I recognise that the amount of any
adjustment made to the multiplier to reflect the incidence of higher rates of tax will,
inevitably, be somewhat arbitrary, such are the uncertainties involved. But there are
many items brought into the calculation of the amount of an award which could be
similarly criticised. I do not see why making some comparatively small adjustment is,
j for this reason, to be rejected altogether.

I turn to the authorities. In *Taylor v O'Connor* [1970] 1 All ER 365, [1971] AC 115, a
Fatal Accidents Act case, all their Lordships, as I read their speeches, considered that in a
case where the figures are high the incidence of tax should be borne in mind. Moreover,
in that case there seems to have been no evidence before the court of the precise burden
of income tax and surtax on the widow, but none of their Lordships considered that for

that reason no allowance at all could be justified. It seems to me that one of the
conclusions to be distilled from all the speeches is that, where high figures are involved   *a*
and the trial judge makes a modest adjustment, he is not to be faulted solely because of
the absence of expert evidence on the likely impact of taxation. Lord Morris dealt with
this point as follows ([1970] 1 All ER 365 at 372, [1971] AC 115 at 134):

> 'In fixing a multiplier judges do the best they can to make fair allowance for all
> the uncertainties and possibilities to which I have earlier referred. It may well be
> that, in cases where high figures are involved, courts could derive assistance from   *b*
> skilled evidence concerning ways in which a sum of money could be used and
> managed to the best advantage. Such evidence should, however, only afford a check
> or a guide. It could not resolve those matters which in the nature of things must be
> uncertain or decide those issues to which the art of judgment must be directed.'

In *Cookson v Knowles* the observation of Lord Fraser cited above was made in the context   *c*
of a question different from, albeit closely related to, the one now under consideration.
The question Lord Fraser was considering was whether an award should be increased to
make allowance for inflation after the date of the trial. His conclusion was that, for the
reason I have already stated, what a plaintiff loses by inflation will be roughly equivalent
to what he gains by the high rates of interest prevailing in times of inflation. To that
general rule he made an exception where the dependant's assumed annuity would be   *d*
large enough to attract income tax at a high rate.

The question arising in the present appeal is not whether some allowance should be
made to compensate the plaintiff for the risk that, because of high tax rates, the high
rates of interest obtainable in times of inflation will not provide her with an adequate
degree of protection against the effects of future inflation. The question in the instant
case is whether, irrespective of any future inflation, some allowance should be made for   *e*
the incidence which high rates of tax will have on the income of this large award from
the outset. Nevertheless, although the questions are different, it seems to me that Lord
Fraser's approach to the question before him is consistent with the incidence of high rates
of tax being a factor properly to be taken into account when answering the question
arising in the present case. Furthermore, I cannot read Lord Fraser's statement that in
exceptional cases 'it may be necessary for the court to have expert evidence' as indicating   *f*
that in every case such evidence is an essential prerequisite to making any allowance for
tax reasons.

In *Lim Poh Choo v Camden and Islington Area Health Authority* [1979] 1 All ER 332, [1979]
QB 196 Bristow J made an allowance for future inflation in the multiplier for Dr Lim's
loss of future earnings and in the multiplier for the cost of her future care. On appeal
this court upheld him. On further appeal the House of Lords disapproved of that course   *g*
(see [1979] 2 All ER 910, [1980] AC 174). In the leading speech Lord Scarman said
([1979] 2 All ER 910 at 923, [1980] AC 174 at 193):

> 'The correct approach should be, therefore, in the first place to assess damages
> without regard to the risk of future inflation. If it can be demonstrated that, on the
> particular facts of a case, such an assessment would not result in a fair compensation   *h*
> (bearing in mind the investment opportunity that a lump sum award offers), some
> increase is permissible. But the victims of tort who receive a lump sum award are
> entitled to no better protection against inflation than others who have to rely on
> capital for their future support.'

That, therefore, was another case in which the issue concerned making an allowance   *j*
to compensate for the possible future erosion of the 'real' value of the fund by inflation.
What the House of Lords rejected was making any such anti-inflation allowance in that
case.

What the House of Lords did not reject, or have to consider, was whether in assessing
damages in the first place without regard to the risk of future inflation, any adjustment

should have been made to reflect the heavier incidence of tax on the large fund involved
a in that case. That such an adjustment should have been made does not seem to have been
argued in that case. In those circumstances it seems to me that this decision is an insecure
base for the structure which counsel for the defendants seeks to erect on it.

In the present case, in my view, the judge's initial choice of 14 as a multiplier was
within the reasonable range of possible awards. Further, the figures involved in this
award are high, and the adjustment of one to the multiplier then made by the judge, 'in
b an effort', as he stated, 'to make some allowance for the high incidence of taxation on the
income from this award', was not unreasonable in amount. For a female with an
expectation of life of just under 28 years, a multiplier of 14 represents a rate of interest of
about $5\frac{1}{4}\%$. A multiplier of 15 represents a rate of interest of about $4\frac{1}{2}\%$. Put differently,
the adjustment represents an overall increase in the notional income of the fund of about
15%. This is quite a generous adjustment, but not an excessive one. In my view the judge
c was entitled to make that adjustment in this case.

The defendants also submitted that some reduction in the multiplier ought to have
been made because of the risk, which the judge accepted was a real risk, that during the
latter part of her life the plaintiff would have to go into an institution. He did not think
it could be assumed that if and when institutional care were needed again there would
be any saving. On this the defendants pointed out that over the period of about nine
d years from the accident to the trial the plaintiff was in hospitals or institutions operated
by the national health service for some seven years, and that only for a period of about 18
months was she in a private hospital. It was submitted that the chances are that, if the
plaintiff has to have long-term institutional care again at some time in the future, she
will go into a national health service institution.

In my view this submission lacks the necessary supporting evidence. There was no
e evidence that any long-term institutional care which may be needed by the plaintiff in
future will not be available in the private sector, to use a currently fashionable expression.

Cost of future care: the multiplicand

I turn to the other factor in this equation: the annual cost of future care. The judge
f accepted the care scheme propounded by the defendants, namely that a husband and
wife would be resident housekeepers in the plaintiff's house and share the task of caring
for the plaintiff, with additional help being provided as necessary. The judge costed this
scheme at £33,958 pa.

The defendants criticised this calculation on two counts. First, it was submitted that
the appropriate weekly figure for the housekeepers was £150 and not £175, and that in
arriving at the higher figure the judge had misunderstood part of the evidence of Mrs
g Stephens (a witness called by the defendants who is the director of an agency which has
experience in providing help for home care) when she said that the cost for a resident
couple could be more than £150 per week. Having read the transcript of the evidence,
in my view the judge was fully justified in reaching the conclusion he did on this point.

Second, two of the items in the judge's costings were '(c) Night cover: 10 hours per
h night, for 7 nights per week, and for 52 weeks, at £2·80 per hour ... £10,192' and
'(e) Holiday care: £300 per week for 4 weeks plus £300 for contingencies ... £1,500'. It
was submitted that there was duplication in these two items to the extent that the cost of
night cover is included for every night in the year even though the four weeks' holiday
care allowance would include the cost of night cover in the holiday periods, when the
plaintiff would be away from her house.

j I cannot accept this. There was evidence that the cost of specialist holidays varied from
£100 to £260 per week, plus the cost of attendants. Furthermore if, as the defendants
contended, holiday care includes night cover, the consequences would be that exclusive
of night cover normally costing £28 per night, which equals £196 per week, holiday
care would cost some £104 per week. This is a far lower sum than the regular weekly
cost of care exclusive of night cover, the regular cost being £175 per week for the

housekeepers and £100 for nursing relief. It seems improbable that this can be right. The defendants have not satisfied me that the cost of holiday care allowed by the judge *a* included the cost of night cover.

Loss of earnings

I come now to loss of future earnings. On this the judge awarded the sum of £39,000, being £2,600 a year times 15. The defendants challenged the multiplier of 15. *b*

The judge found that at the time of the accident the plaintiff and her husband were saving for a house and were intending to have a family, but that nevertheless, and although not career-minded, the plaintiff would have continued to work so far as her domestic and family commitments permitted. He approached the assessment of damages on the basis that there was at any rate a real prospect that the plaintiff would have continued 'part-time and/or full-time work' throughout her married life. *c*

The judge reached the figure of 15 as the multiplier by the route I have already explained. In doing so he followed the approach of Leonard J in *Hughes v KcKeown* [1985] 3 All ER 284, [1985] 1 WLR 963, who, in turn, adopted the approach of O'Connor J in *Carrick v Camden London BC* (25 July 1979, unreported), who, in his turn, in that case adopted the approach of Kilner Brown J in *Hartin v Scott* (4 December 1978, unreported). That approach was to disregard the intervention of marriage when assessing a plaintiff's *d* economic loss, on the footing that in a period of child-bearing the plaintiff would still be working, but in a different capacity, and would be supported by her husband, and that to disregard the intervention of marriage when calculating the loss of earnings was preferable to arriving at the same result by the different route adopted in *Moriarty v McCarthy* [1978] 2 All ER 213, [1978] 1 WLR 155, namely by making a deduction from the loss of earnings compensation but adding an equivalent sum to general damages. *e*

The defendants submitted that the judge's approach was based on the erroneous assumption that the plaintiff would have either (a) worked full-time for the rest of her working life or (b) been supported by her husband at the same rate. As to (a), it was submitted that on the judge's findings uninterrupted full-time work was unlikely and that, even if the plaintiff had returned to full-time work after the youngest child started school, this would have been well into the future. Further, her earnings would partly *f* have gone supporting the children. As to (b), it was submitted that this approach was contrary to the decision of this court in *Harris v Harris* [1973] 1 Lloyd's Rep 445, where, compensation for loss of prospect of marriage having been included in the general award for loss of amenity, this court reduced an award for loss of earnings on the ground that allowance had to be made for career interruption in the event of marriage. Moreover, it was submitted, the plaintiff's husband would not have been able to support the plaintiff *g* to the full extent of her lost wages. When a wife stops work for the children, her income and the income of the household falls.

Similar arguments were addressed to the judge's award of pre-trial loss of earnings, which was calculated on the footing that for the whole of the period of over nine years the plaintiff would have worked full-time.

The authorities mentioned above were all considered by this court in *Housecroft v* *h* *Burnett* [1986] 1 All ER 332. There O'Connor LJ said (at 345):

'*Harris v Harris*, which is binding on us, has been considered a number of times at first instance, most recently in *Hughes v McKeown* [1985] 3 All ER 284, [1985] 1 WLR 963. Leonard J, relying on two unreported decisions (by coincidence one of *j* mine, the other of Kilner Brown J) held that, as it was the plaintiff's economic loss that was being assessed, then, so long as no account was taken of loss of marriage prospects in the award for loss of amenity, there was no need to reduce the multiplier from that which would be appropriate had the plaintiff been a man. In *Moriarty v McCarthy* [1978] 2 All ER 213, [1978] 1 WLR 155 I reduced the multiplier from the male equivalent of 15 to 11 in assessing the loss of earnings, but added the missing a four years to the award for loss of amenity. I do not think that the approach adopted by Leonard J is in conflict with *Harris v Harris* and it is a convenient way of assessing the plaintiff's economic loss in this very limited class of case. I must not be taken as approving the multiplier used in *Hughes*. However, the judge must be careful not to duplicate the damage . . .'

b Thus the question which arises is whether there has been duplication of damages in this case. On this there is the complication that general damages were not determined by the judge but were agreed between the parties.

However, let me assume, in favour of the defendants, that the sum of £60,000 was intended to cover loss of amenity, including loss of prospect of marriage. Even so, the multiplicand used by the judge was arrived at by reducing the agreed figure of the plaintiff's net annual wage loss of (about) £3,070 to £2,600 to allow for the 'possible' cost

c of earning the sums in question. That reduction, which is a substantial one, was not the subject of evidence. In my view, even if the judge fell into error in not reducing the multiplier to take account of the career interruption likely to be caused by marriage, the substantial cost of earnings deduction he made, the justification for which is not easy to discern in this case, produced an end result which was not unfair. The one broadly balances out the other. An award of £39,000 for future loss of earnings, and an award of

d £10,000 for loss of earnings from March 1976 to December 1985, taken in the round, are not excessive in this case.

For these reasons I do not think that any of the defendants' criticisms of the amount of the judge's award succeed, and for my part I would therefore dismiss this appeal.

LLOYD LJ. We were told that this is, or at any rate was, the largest award of damages

e for personal injuries ever made in this country. The size of the award, the complexity of the calculation and the social and financial consequences likely to result from similar awards in the future, all underline what has been said on many occasions, that it is time for a radical reform of this branch of the law. But that is a task for the legislature, not the courts: see *Lim Poh Choo v Camden and Islington Area Health Authority* [1979] 2 All ER 910 at 914, [1980] AC 174 at 182 per Lord Scarman.

f On the law as it stands, Hutchison J, in a judgment to which I would pay my respectful tribute, reached a total sum which, though very large, is not obviously too large; and he reached it by a process of reasoning which, save in one respect, cannot be criticised. The one criticism which I would make is of his selection of a multiplier of 15 rather than 14, in order to allow, as he said, for the high incidence of taxation.

Ordinarily a difference of one in the multiplier would not justify this court in

g intervening; it lies well within the discretion of the judge. But in this case it seems to me that, in so far as the judge was increasing the multiplier to take account of taxation, he erred in principle. I would therefore for my part feel it the duty of this court to say so, even though the difference in the outcome is not great.

Both sides accept that we ought to adopt the conventional approach in assessing damages for loss of future earnings, namely that we should take a multiplier and a

h multiplicand, the multiplier being based on a discount of 4 or 5% pa. We are not therefore concerned with the question agitated in Kemp and Kemp *The Quantum of Damages* vol 1, ch 7. It is forcefully argued in that chapter that, with the advent of index-linked securities, a discount of 2% is more appropriate. A 2% discount would, of course, result in a much higher multiplier. However, in the light of the very recent decision of this court in *Auty v National Coal Board* [1985] 1 All ER 930, [1985] 1 WLR 784, where

j the argument favoured in *Kemp and Kemp* was advanced and rejected, it is not surprising that counsel for the plaintiff was content to accept, at any rate before us, the traditional approach.

In applying the traditional approach, the judge said:

'I approach this case as I would that of a 37-year-old person due to retire at the age of 65. I consider that the appropriate multiplier for such a person would ordinarily be 14. In an effort to make some allowance for the high incidence of taxation on the income from this award, I increase the multiplier to 15.'

     a

Counsel for the defendants advanced two arguments. His first argument was that the judge was wrong to regard 14 as the multiplier which would ordinarily have been appropriate. He should have taken 13. Counsel relied in particular on the multiplier of 12 taken by the House of Lords in *Lim Poh Choo v Camden and Islington Area Health Authority* [1979] 2 All ER 910, [1980] AC 174, where the life expectancy was 37 years. Here the life expectancy is only 28 years. He also relied on *Housecroft v Burnett* [1986] 1 All ER 332, where this court approved a multiplier of 13 on a life expectancy of 27 years, and *Moser v Enfield and Harringey Area Health Authority* (1982) 133 NLJ 105, where Michael Davies J took a multiplier of 11 on a life expectancy of 20 years.

     b

I think I would myself have taken 13 years as the multiplier in the present case. But I am certainly not prepared to disturb the judge's finding that the appropriate multiplier would ordinarily have been 14. In *Chapman v Lidstone* (3 December 1982) referred to in Kemp and Kemp *The Quantum of Damages* vol 2, para 1–210 Forbes J took a multiplier of 14 on an expectancy of 23 years. It was argued that this was too high. But this court refused to interfere. The choice of 14 lay clearly within the realm of the judge's discretion. I would take the same view in this case. So I would reject the first argument of counsel for the defendants, which, to be fair, he did not strongly press.

     c

     d

His second argument is more formidable. The judge increased the multiplier from 14, which he would otherwise have regarded as appropriate, to 15, because of the high incidence of taxation. Was this legitimate? In *Cookson v Knowles* [1978] 2 All ER 604, [1979] AC 556 one of the main questions for decision was whether the award for future loss of earnings should be increased to cover the risk of continuing inflation. The House of Lords held not. But the House also dealt incidentally with the question of tax. A discount of 4 or 5% takes account of tax at ordinary rates. Should the award be increased where the recipient pays tax at a high rate? Lord Fraser said ([1978] 2 All ER 604 at 616, [1979] AC 556 at 577):

     e

'In exceptional cases, where the annuity is large enough to attract income tax at a high rate, it may be necessary for the court to have expert evidence of the spendable income that would acrue from awards at different levels and to compare the total annuity with the amount of the lost dependency having regard to the net income (after tax) of the deceased person. Whether in such cases it might be appropriate to increase the multiplier, or to allow for future inflation in some other way would be a matter for evidence in each case.'

     f

In *Lim Poh Choo v Camden and Islington Area Health Authority* [1979] 1 All ER 332, [1979] QB 196 the judge awarded a total of £254,765 after allowing for future inflation. The Court of Appeal upheld the award, holding that the case fell within the class of exceptional cases to which Lord Fraser had referred. Lord Denning MR said ([1979] 1 All ER 332 at 342, [1979] QB 196 at 218):

     g

'So far as inflation is concerned, we have it established by the House of Lords that it is not to be taken into account in the oridinary run of cases, but there are exceptional cases (where the sum awarded attracts high tax) where allowance may be made for future inflation . . .'

     h

Lawton LJ said ([1979] 1 All ER 332 at 348, [1979] QB 196 at 224):

'As to inflation I have read the speech of Lord Fraser . . . in the same sense as Lord Denning MR has done and as meaning that in exceptional cases where there is a high tax factor, inflation can be taken into account when calculating the heads of damage for which the assumed annuity method is appropriate.'

     j

Browne LJ said ([1979] 1 All ER 332 at 356, [1979] QB 196 at 234):

'The present case seems to me to be one of the exceptional cases referred to by *a*   Lord Fraser; the high incidence of tax on the assumed annuity in this case is shown on Mr Eccleshall's exhibit. In my view, the judge (who seems to have had premonition of what the House of Lords was going to say in *Cookson v Knowles*) made no mistake in principle on this point and I am not satisfied that he made any excessive allowance.'

b   But the House of Lords held that the Court of Appeal had been wrong. The high incidence of tax to which all three members of the court had referred did not justify an increase in the conventional multiplier.

c   Counsel for the defendants put hypothetical figures before us designed to show that the notional tax on the income from the present award is no higher, indeed considerably lower, than it would have been when *Lim Poh Choo v Camden and Islington Area Health Authority* was decided in 1979. It is unnecessary to go into the figures in detail, since counsel for the plaintiff did not seek to contend that the present case was in any way exceptional from the taxation point of view. He conceded that the tax would fall to be paid at ordinary rates, and is therefore covered by the ordinary discount of 4 or 5%. This concession should put an end to what counsel for the defendants described as a prevalent myth that the very high awards of today are attracting very high rates of tax. They are not. Here was the highest ever award made by the courts. Yet it is conceded that the tax payable does not bring the case within the exceptional category envisaged by Lord Fraser in *Cookson v Knowles*.

d   I would only add that I do not find the decision of Mustill J in *Seton v Elliott* (6 April 1979) referred to in Kemp and Kemp *The Quantum of Damages* vol 2, para 1–716 of any real assistance on this point, since it was decided on the basis of *Lim Poh Choo v Camden and Islington Area Health Authority* in the Court of Appeal before it went to the House of Lords.

e   How then does counsel for the plaintiff seek to justify the judge's multiplier of 15? He says, very simply, that the range of multiplier in the present case was 13 to 15, and that the judge was entitled to take tax into account in choosing a figure at the top of the range.

   I regret that I cannot accept that argument. It does not do justice to the language which the judge himself used, and which must presumably reflect his reasoning. He did not take a figure 'at the top of the range'. He has said that he would ordinarily have taken 14 as the appropriate multiplier. He has then increased that figure *above* what he would otherwise have regarded as appropriate, because of the high incidence of taxation. With great respect to the judge, this seems to be precisely the same error as was made by this court in *Lim Poh Choo v Camden and Islington Area Health Authority*. In that case it was possible for the House of Lords to justify the multiplier chosen on grounds other than high taxation. But no other grounds have been suggested in this case. I would therefore, for my part, allow the appeal to the extent of reducing the multiplier from 15 to 14. In all other respects I would dismiss the appeal for the reasons given by Nicholls LJ.

f

g

SIR JOHN DONALDSON MR. I would have been content to have said that I agreed that the appeal be dismissed for the reasons given by Nicholls LJ. I add to that in *h* deference to the views expressed by Lloyd LJ on the question of whether the judge was entitled to increase the multiplier from 14 to 15 'in an effort to make some allowance for the high incidence of taxation on the income from this award'.

   I do not understand Lord Scarman, when giving the leading judgment in *Lim Poh Choo v Camden and Islington Area Health Authority* [1979] 2 All ER 910 at 923, [1980] AC 174 at 193, to have been intending to depart from the decision of the House of Lords in *Cookson* *j* *v Knowles* [1978] 2 All ER 604, [1979] AC 556, to which he was a party, when he said:

   'The law appears to me to be now settled that only in exceptional cases, where justice can be shown to require it, will the risk of future inflation be brought into account in the assessment of damages for future loss.'

I therefore feel justified in going back to *Cookson v Knowles*.

Both Lord Diplock and Lord Fraser founded their decisions on the fact that, where the
real value of a sum paid to a plaintiff pursuant to an award of damages was thereafter *a*
eroded by inflation, wise investment policies enabled the loss to be made good in the
form of increased income derived from the sum, or what remained of it, because inflation
produced increased rates of interest. Lord Salmon made the same point. However, he
also adverted to the possibility that the lost wages would also have been affected by
inflation, but that the effects might become out of phase with those on the value of
money and interest rates. This is a separate point. So far as I can see, only Lord Fraser *b*
seems to have considered the subsidiary point that, whilst in an inflationary period
increased interest rates leading to higher income might indeed compensate for the loss
in real value of the plaintiff's compensation fund, that *increased* income might attract a
high rate of tax thus distorting the built-in anti-inflationary mechanism to the
disadvantage of the plaintiff. He was not referring to the effect of tax otherwise than in
the context of inflation. This, I think, is clear if one eliminates the break in his speech *c*
indicated by the new paragraph so that it reads ([1978] 2 All ER 604 at 616, [1979] AC
556 at 577–578):

> 'The fact is that, as was demonstrated from tables shown to us, inflation and the
> high rates of interest to which it gives rise is automatically taken into account by the
> use of multipliers based on rates of interest related to a stable currency. It would *d*
> therefore be wrong for the court to increase the award of damages by attempting to
> make a further specific allowance for future inflation. In exceptional cases, where
> the annuity is large enough to attract income tax at a high rate, it may be necessary
> for the court to have expert evidence of the spendable income that would accrue
> from awards at different levels and to compare the total annuity with the amount of
> the lost dependency having regard to the net income (after tax) of the deceased *e*
> person. Whether in such cases it might be appropriate to increase the multiplier, *or
> to allow for future inflation in some other way* would be a matter for evidence in each
> case.' (My emphasis.)

In the instant case, loyally following *Cookson v Knowles*, the judge has taken no account
of inflation whatsoever. What he has done is to take account of a quite different problem *f*
which arises irrespective of inflation, although it could be aggravated by it. This is that,
in a case in which the claim in respect of lost wages of very moderate amount is swollen
by very large claims for added expenditure, the income element in the compensation
will inevitably attract significant amounts of tax, whether or not there is inflation. To
ignore this factor would be an injustice and I can see no error of principle in dealing with
it in the way in which the judge did, namely by increasing the multiplier by one. This
gave the plaintiff a mini fund of about £29,000 to meet the tax payable over some 28 *g*
years.

I am not persuaded that this approach is wrong because tax rates have fallen since *Lim
Poh Choo v Camden and Islington Area Health Authority* was decided. There Bristow J, giving
judgment before the decision in *Cookson v Knowles*, made allowance for inflation as such,
the Court of Appeal sought to justify it on the grounds of Lord Fraser's exception and the *h*
House of Lords admitted further evidence and started all over again. By then I think that
everyone was thoroughly bemused. However that may be, I can detect no discussion of
the effect of tax, apart from inflation. Perhaps it should have been considered, but in the
instant case where, as Nicholls LJ points out, the fund will have an annual income of over
£30,000, it would have been a denial of justice not to have taken it into account.

Appeal dismissed.   *j*

Solicitors: *Hempsons* (for the defendants); *Hermer & Flacke*, Cardiff (for the plaintiff).

Frances Rustin   Barrister.

a
Peatfield v General Medical Council

PRIVY COUNCIL
LORD KEITH OF KINKEL, LORD BRANDON OF OAKBROOK AND LORD MACKAY OF CLASHFERN
7 NOVEMBER, 2 DECEMBER 1985

b *Medical practitioner – Professional misconduct – Charge of professional misconduct – Duplicity – Single charge of improperly supplying drugs to 'individual patients' over four-year period – Whether charge bad for duplicity – Whether charge alleging single course of professional misconduct.*

The appellant, a registered medical practitioner, was charged by the Professional Conduct
c Committee of the General Medical Council with a single charge of supplying certain
drugs to what were described as 'individual patients' over a four-year period without first
adequately examining each patient or seeking adequate information as to the patient's
medical history, without consulting the patients' doctors about the proposed treatment
or notifying the doctors after treatment had commenced and without making adequate
inquiries on each occasion about the effect of treatment on the patient's health. The
d patients were not particularised in the charge. At the hearing before the committee
evidence was given regarding nine patients, two of whom were identified merely as 'Mr
X' and 'Mrs Y'. The committee, having found the facts alleged against the appellant to be
proved to their satisfaction, held that he was guilty of serious professional misconduct
and directed that his name be struck off the register. The committee did not give reasons
for their decision and did not indicate in detail what facts they had found to be established.
e The appellant appealed to the Privy Council, contending, inter alia, (i) that the charge
was bad for duplicity because it indicated a number of charges of serious professional
misconduct in respect of each of the individual patients referred to, thereby contravening
the principle of criminal law that a charge should allege only one offence, (ii) that
evidence about the unidentified patients would be inadmissible in a criminal trial and
the committee had failed to comply with the proviso to r 56(1)[a] in the appendix to the
f General Medical Council Preliminary Proceedings Committee and Professional Conduct
Committee (Procedure) Rules Order of Council 1980, which required the committee to
consult the legal assessor before receiving such evidence, and (iii) that the committee had
failed to give reasons for their decision as required by r 30(1)[b] of the 1980 rules.

Held – The appeal would be dismissed for the following reasons—
g   (1) Although it was inappropriate for a charge laid by the General Medical Council
against a medical practitioner to refer to 'individual patients', the charge could be read,
and had in fact been treated by the committee and all parties, including the appellant
himself, as alleging a course of conduct by the appellant in the conduct of his practice
over the stated period and that it was that course of conduct which amounted to serious
professional misconduct. It followed that in the circumstances the charge was not bad
h for duplicity (see p 1201 *b* to *d*, post); *R v General Medical Council, ex p Gee* [1987] 1 All
ER 1204 distinguished.
     (2) Although the evidence regarding Mr X and Mrs Y would not have been admissible
in criminal proceedings and the committee had not followed the procedure laid down in
the proviso to r 56(1) of the 1980 rules, that evidence did not materially add to the case
against the appellant and, on the facts, no injustice had resulted from the committee's
j failure to follow the procedure (see p 1201 *j* to p 1202 *a*, post).

---

a   Rule 56(1) is set out at p 1201 *e f*, post
b   Rule 30(1), so far as material, provides: 'On the conclusion of proceedings . . . the Committee shall
    consider and determine as respects each charge which remains outstanding which, if any, of the
    facts alleged in the charge have been proved to their satisfaction.'

(3) Although the committee had not spelt out the reasons for their decision they had given sufficient details to discharge their duty under r 30(1) of the 1980 rules, since the details provided had enabled the appellant's counsel to make his submissions adequately to the committee in the light of the committee's findings. Taking a comprehensive view of the evidence as a whole, the committee had held a fair and proper inquiry and made a proper finding (see p 1202 *j* to p 1203 *b f g*, post); *Fox v General Medical Council* [1960] 3 All ER 225 applied.

Notes

For serious professional misconduct, see 30 Halsbury's Laws (4th edn) para 125, and for cases on the subject, see 33 Digest (Reissue) 294–297, 2360–2368.

For appeals against being struck off the register, see 30 Halsbury's Laws (4th edn) para 131.

For the General Medical Council Preliminary Proceedings Committee and Professional Conduct Committee (Procedure) Rules Order of Council 1980, App, r 56, see 13 Halsbury's Statutory Instruments (4th reissue) 195.

Cases referred to in judgment

Bebbington v General Optical Council (22 May 1985, unreported), PC.
Fox v General Medical Council [1960] 3 All ER 225, [1960] 1 WLR 1017, PC.
R v General Medical Council, ex p Gee [1987] 1 All ER 1204, [1986] 1 WLR 226, QBD.
Rai v General Medical Council (14 May 1984, unreported), PC.
Rodgers v General Medical Council (19 November 1984, unreported), PC.

Cases also cited

R v Greenfield [1973] 3 All ER 1050, [1973] 1 WLR 1151, CA.
R v Immigration Appeal Tribunal, ex p Khan (Mahmud) [1983] 2 All ER 420, [1983] QB 790, CA.
Tarnesby v General Medical Council (20 July 1970, unreported), PC.

Appeal

Dr Barry John Durrant Peatfield appealed from a determination of the Professional Conduct Committee of the General Medical Council of 12 July 1985 that by reason of serious professional misconduct his name should be removed from the Register of Medical Practitioners. The facts are set out in the judgment of the Board.

Michael Beloff QC and *Thomas Shields* for the appellant.
Ann Curnow QC and *M J Dennis* for the respondent.

2 December. The following judgment of the Board was delivered.

LORD MACKAY OF CLASHFERN. On 12 July 1985 the appellant, who was a registered practitioner, was judged by the Professional Conduct Committee of the General Medical Council, the respondent to the appeal, to have been guilty of serious professional misconduct. The committee directed that his name should be erased from the register. The appellant has exercised his statutory right to appeal from the decision of the committee to Her Majesty in Council.

Originally the appellant faced two charges but the second was not established and need not be further considered. The first charge was in these terms:

'That, being registered under the Medical Act, (1) between about June 1980 and about November 1984 or later, at your practice premises in Purley and in South Croydon, you abused your professional position as a medical practitioner by supplying to individual patients in return for fees, quantities of drugs including phentermine or amphetamine with dexamphetamine, thyroid extract and other drugs, repeatedly, over extensive periods: (a) without first adequately examining each patient, or seeking adequate information as to his or her medical history;

(b) without first consulting the patients' general practitioners about the proposed treatment, or in all cases notifying those general practitioners after treatment had first commenced of the details of any drugs supplied and the dosages prescribed; (c) without making adequate inquiries on each occasion about the effect of the treatment on the patient's health.'

The hearing took place on 11 and 12 July 1985. At the hearing both the appellant and the respondent were represented by leading counsel. Prior to the hearing the statements of the witnesses to be adduced by the respondent were sent to the solicitors for the appellant. These statements referred to patients some of whom had not been mentioned in earlier correspondence between the parties.

After the case was opened by counsel for the respondent, evidence was led from four patients of the appellant, one of whom spoke also about two other members of her family, from a senior inspector at the Home Office Drugs Branch and from seven medical practitioners. The appellant then gave evidence. He was the only witness on his own behalf. In the course of the evidence of the medical practitioners, reference was made to three other patients of the appellant, two of whom were identified only by letters as Mr X and Mrs Y.

At the conclusion of the evidence counsel in turn addressed the committee and after being addressed by their legal assessor the committee was required in terms of r 30 of the applicable procedural rules, which are appended to the General Medical Council Preliminary Proceedings Committee and Professional Conduct Committee (Procedure) Rules Order of Council 1980, SI 1980/858, to consider and determine as respects each charge which remained outstanding which, if any, of the facts alleged in the charge had been proved to their satisfaction. At this stage the chairman, on behalf of the committee, announced their decision in these terms:

'Dr. Peatfield, the committee have determined that the following facts alleged against you in the charge have been proved to their satisfaction: that between about June 1980 and November 1984 or later, at your practice premises in Purley and in South Croydon you abused your professional position as a medical practitioner by supplying to individual patients in return for fees, quantities of drugs including phentermine or amphetamine with dexamphetamine, thyroid extract and other drugs, repeatedly, over extensive periods: (a) without first adequately examining each patient, or seeking adequate information as to his or her medical history; (b) without first consulting the patients' general practitioners about the proposed treatment, or in all cases notifying those general practitioners after treatment had first commenced of the details of any drugs supplied and the dosages prescribed; (c) without making adequate inquiries on each occasion about the effect of the treatment on the patient's health.'

At this stage they also recorded a finding of not guilty on the other charge which the appellant had faced in respect that the facts alleged in that charge had not been proved. Counsel for the respondent then addressed the committee and was followed by counsel for the appellant. At that stage counsel for the appellant pointed out that there were obvious difficulties in his making submissions when the findings of the committee were bound to be very general in their terms and could cover a very wide spectrum of seriousness. At that stage the main point which he drew to the committee's attention was that the question of adequacy which was in issue so far as heads (a) and (c) of the charge were concerned were questions of degree and judgment and that it was accordingly not the sort of gross abuse of the appellant's position as a medical practitioner which could amount to serious professional misconduct. So far as head (b) was concerned, he accepted that the appellant admitted that head as being factually correct in any event but he questioned the basis on which it could be said that head (b) could give rise to serious professional misconduct. Counsel for the appellant also handed to the committee for their consideration a bundle of documents relating to reports obtained from consultants to whom the appellant had sent patients and with whom he had come into professional contact. One of those may be taken as typical of the tone of this correspondence. A consultant wrote:

'Those patients who he has referred to me as a consultant over the years have come with a comprehensive referral letter, indicating that a proper assessment of the patient's whole condition had been made, appropriate investigations carried out where necessary and suitable drug therapy prescribed.'

After considering their decision, the chairman, on behalf of the committee, announced it in the following terms:

'Dr Peatfield, the committee take a serious view of the evidence which they have heard in this case concerning that part of your practice in which you have accepted patients for a period of treatment for obesity. The committee are appalled that you prescribed potent drugs to some patients in such circumstances without first adequately examining them, seeking adequate information as to his or her medical history, and without notifying your treatment to other doctors who, over the same periods, were concurrently undertaking responsibility for comprehensive management of the patients' medical care. They deplore the evidence that you supplied repeat prescriptions without making adequate inquiries on each occasion about the effect of the treatment on the patients' health. The committee have accordingly judged you to have been guilty of serious professional misconduct in relation to the facts which have been proved against you in the charge and have directed the registrar to erase your name from the register.'

On the hearing of this appeal before the Board, counsel for the appellant, who was not the counsel who represented the appellant before the Professional Conduct Committee, elaborated on the matters which had been raised in the very clearly drawn case presented for the appellant in this appeal. He did so under five heads.

Counsel first drew attention to the form of the charge. He pointed out that although there was reference therein to 'individual' patients, these patients were not particularised in the charge. He went on to submit that the charge should be read as indicating a number of instances of serious professional misconduct in respect of each of the individual patients referred to. He pointed out that it was a well-established principle of English criminal law, which should also apply in proceedings such as those from which this appeal arose, that a charge should allege only one offence and that to allege two distinct offences within one charge rendered the charge bad for duplicity. In support of this submission, counsel referred to a recent decision of Mann J in *R v General Medical Council, ex p Gee* [1987] 1 All ER 1204, [1986] 1 WLR 226[1].

That case was concerned with two applications for judicial review at the instance of a doctor who faced a charge under four heads, the first three of which were in terms as to their substance almost identical to the charges in the present case, although the drugs in question were not absolutely identical to those referred to here. In that case it had been submitted to the judge that the charge related to the way in which the doctor's practice was carried on and the particular way of which complaint was made was that of irresponsible prescribing and it mattered not whether there were eight patients or one. The judge did not agree that the charge was so drawn; he pointed to the reference to 'individual patients' and noted that the charge had been particularised by reference to eight patients, material about four of whom had been submitted to the Preliminary Proceedings Committee but material about the balance had not. The judge, in these circumstances and having regard to the correspondence in that case, concluded that the charge in question there alleged separate offences of serious professional misconduct, each being in regard to a different patient and that accordingly the charge in the form before him was bad for duplicity and that the Professional Conduct Committee should

---

1   Subsequent to the decision reported herein Mann J's decision was reversed by the Court of Appeal on, inter alia, the issue of duplicity: see [1987] 1 All ER 1204 at 1218, [1986] 1 WLR 1247

not be allowed to proceed to its consideration until that vice was cured. He also considered
a that it was appropriate that further particulars should be given of the charge in that case
before it went to inquiry before the Professional Conduct Committee. In the present
case, this matter has been raised for the first time after the inquiry before the Professional
Conduct Committee has been concluded.

In terms of r 24(2) of the applicable rules, the practitioner may, if he so desires after
the reading of the charge or charges, object to the notice of inquiry, or to any part of it,
b in point of law. No such objection was taken in the present case.

Their Lordships take the view that, in the present case, the charge can be fairly read as
alleging a course of conduct by the appellant in the conduct of his practice over the
period stated in which patients were treated with the drugs specified in the three
circumstances referred to under heads (a), (b) and (c) and that it was this course of conduct
which amounted to serious professional misconduct. They agree, and counsel for the
c respondent accepted this, that the use of the word 'individual' was inappropriate but it is
apparent from the record of the hearing that both parties before the committee treated
the charge as a complaint with regard to a course of conduct and the appellant in his own
evidence dealt with the matter very much from the point of view of what his ordinary
practice and manner of operation were. Indeed the appellant and his counsel laid stress
on the number of patients dealt with in respect of whom there was no complaint.
d In this circumstance, their Lordships consider that this point taken by itself is not a
good reason for allowing this appeal. Their Lordships will later consider its relationship
to one of the other matters raised at the hearing.

The next issue raised was based on r 56(1) of the applicable rules, which is in these
terms:

e   'The Committee may receive oral, documentary or other evidence of any fact or
matter which appears to them relevant to the inquiry into the case before them;
Provided that, where any fact or matter is tendered as evidence which would not be
admissible as such if the proceedings were criminal proceedings in England, the
Committee shall not receive it unless, after consultation with the Legal Assessor,
they are satisfied that their duty of making due inquiry into the case before them
f   makes its reception desirable.'

Here it was said that evidence which would not be admissible as such if the proceedings
were criminal proceedings in England was tendered. The evidence referred to was the
evidence given relating to the patients identified no further than as Mr X and Mrs Y. It
was accepted by counsel for the respondent that at least some of the evidence tendered
relating to Mr X and Mrs Y would not have been admissible if the proceedings were
g criminal proceedings in England. It follows that the procedure laid down in the proviso
should have been adopted at least in respect of such evidence.

The rules make no provision for the consequences of a failure to follow the provisions
of this rule. The rule imposes an obligation on the committee whether or not objection
is taken on behalf of the doctor. In the present case the appellant, as has been noted, was
h represented before the committee by leading counsel, who took no objection to the
leading of the evidence in question although he did point out very plainly to the
committee that such evidence put him in considerable difficulty and the chairman stated
that he was quite clear about the appellant's position in this matter.

When this point is taken at the present stage, it is possible to consider the evidence
which is in question in relation to the other evidence in the case and their Lordships
j consider that the evidence which is the subject of this objection did not materially add to
the case against the appellant and that the appellant, in his evidence, dealt with the
matter from the point of view of his ordinary practice in a way which if the committee
had accepted it would have dealt adequately with this particular evidence even although
he was not able to identify the particular patients who were the subject of it. It is fairly
plain that counsel for the appellant before the committee took the view that it was not
wise to take an objection of this kind in the circumstances and that it was better in the
interests of the appellant to deal fully with the whole case tendered against him, pointing

out as he did so the special difficulty that prevented him from dealing in detail with this
evidence. Their Lordships see the wisdom of the course adopted by counsel and are of *a*
opinion that no injustice has in the circumstances resulted from the committee's omission
to follow the procedure laid down in the proviso.

The third point taken on the appeal was that the committee wrongly received evidence
of the alleged effects of the drugs prescribed for his patients by the appellant when there
was no allegation facing him of any adverse effect from his supply of these drugs actually
having been experienced by any patient.   *b*

It is clear that the issue on this aspect of the case was not whether patients had suffered
adverse consequences from the supply to them by the appellant of the drugs in question,
but whether the potential for damage was such that he should have anticipated it and
taken the steps suggested in the charge to guard against such adverse consequences
arising. It is true that in the course of the evidence the question of effects experienced by
patients was canvassed but on this aspect, in his closing submission on the facts, counsel *c*
for the appellant before the committee said:

> 'The important point is that there are assertions made without any supporting
> expert evidence which makes it impossible for us to answer the points. I hope you
> will feel, at the end of the day, that it would be quite wrong to conclude that there
> is any evidence here at all that there were deleterious effects being sustained by the *d*
> patients of any significance, which were caused by a failure to monitor the treatment
> that was being provided by Dr Peatfield and his colleagues. One would have
> expected, had there been such a lack of monitoring, to have had some indication
> from doctors of patients for whom there were such problems which were
> identifiable, but we have not heard them; particularly when you consider the
> concern that was obviously being expressed by general practitioners in Croydon *e*
> who, you can bet your bottom dollar, have been watching this situation of patients
> of Dr. Peatfield with eagle eye!'

The question of whether or not there were deleterious effects shown in the case of any
patient was thought to be relevant as indicating whether or not there had been a lack of
monitoring and in this passage we find counsel for the appellant founding strongly on *f*
the absence of any identifiable consequence as indicating that the case of inadequate
monitoring was not established.

There is nothing in the findings made by the committee to suggest that they went
beyond the matters referred to in the charge and their Lordships consider that evidence
relating to actual effects admitted in a way which made it possible for the appellant's
counsel to make submissions on the lines just indicated was not improperly admitted. *g*

The next matter raised on the appeal was that the Professional Conduct Committee
had given no reason for their decision and had not indicated in detail what facts they had
found established. Observations of this Board in *Rai v General Medical Council* (14 May
1984, unreported), *Rodgers v General Medical Council* (19 November 1984, unreported)
and *Bebbington v General Optical Council* (22 May 1985, unreported), were referred to.
Counsel submitted that having regard to the form of the charge in the present case to *h*
which he referred in his first submission, it was particularly necessary for the committee
to make findings that dealt separately with the facts found relating to each patient who
had been dealt with in the evidence. While there are cases in which it would be extremely
helpful if the committee gave reasons for their decision, their Lordships have no difficulty
in appreciating how in the present case the committee could have reached their decision
and they take that decision to amount to a finding that the facts alleged in the charge *j*
were substantially proved against the appellant. While their Lordships appreciate that
after the announcement of findings in fact, the appellant's counsel stated that he had
some difficulty in making submissions, they see no reason to doubt that he was able
adequately to represent to the committee the appellant's position in the light of their
findings. In a case such as the present it would have been open to the committee if they

so chose to make more detailed findings in fact, but in the circumstances of the present
a case, their Lordships consider that the committee's findings were made in sufficient
detail to discharge the obligation imposed on them by r 30(1) of the rules.

Their Lordships consider that counsel for the appellant, in making his submissions at
this stage, said everything that could have been urged on behalf of the appellant and they
cannot see that he was in any way prejudiced in making his submissions by the form
that the findings took. It was open to him to urge, as he did, that the findings in the
b circumstances should not yield the inference that there had been serious professional
misconduct on the appellant's part.

Their Lordships would only add that the decision which the committee intimated on
the question whether the appellant had been guilty of serious professional misconduct
makes it clear that the committee did not attribute any significance to their finding that
the appellant had prescribed without first consulting the patients' general practitioners
c about the proposed treatment, while on the other hand they did attribute significance to
the absence of adequate examination, to the absence of adequate information about the
patients' medical history, to the absence of notification of the appellant's treatment of the
patients to other doctors who, over the same period, were concurrently undertaking
responsibility for comprehensive management of the patients' medical care, and to the
absence of adequate inquiries about the effect of the treatment on the patients' health
d before the supply of repeat prescriptions. It is clear further that the absence occurred
according to the committee's findings in the case of more than one patient and in their
Lordships' opinion it is clear that the committee had sufficient evidence before them on
the points that they regarded as critical to enable them properly to reach the verdict
which they announced that the appellant had been guilty of serious professional
misconduct.
e

Their Lordships are mindful, in the light of the authorities to which they have been
referred, of the critical importance to a person in the appellant's position of the decision
of the committee but they are satisfied that the points made by the appellant taken singly
or together do not justify their Lordships interfering with the decision to which the
committee has come. Taking a comprehensive view of the evidence as a whole and
f endeavouring to form their own conclusion on it in accordance with the duty imposed
under the present statute and its predecessors as it has been interpreted for example in
Fox v General Medical Council [1960] 3 All ER 225 at 227, [1960] 1 WLR 1017 at 1021,
the Board have reached the conclusion that a fair and proper inquiry was held and a
proper finding made on it.

The final point made by the appellant was that the sentence imposed was unduly
g severe and the appellant invited their Lordships to substitute either a suspension or a
direction that the appellant's registration should be conditional on his observance of
conditions to be prescribed.

The question of the appropriate penalty to be imposed in respect of serious professional
misconduct is a matter peculiarly within the discretion of the committee and interference
would be justified only if it was plain that the sentence imposed was inappropriate. On a
h consideration of the whole circumstances here including in particular those relied on by
the appellant's counsel at the hearing, their Lordships are of opinion that no ground has
been put forward which would justify their interference.

For these reasons their Lordships will humbly advise Her Majesty that the appeal
should be dismissed. The appellant must pay the costs of the General Medical Council
before the Board.

j

Appeal dismissed.

Solicitors: *Royds Barfield* (for the appellant); *Waterhouse & Co* (for the respondent).

Mary Rose Plummer   Barrister.

R v General Medical Council, ex parte Gee   *a*

R v General Medical Council Professional Conduct Committee, ex parte Gee

QUEEN'S BENCH DIVISION (CROWN OFFICE LIST)

MANN J   *b*

7, 8, 9, 10 OCTOBER, 1 NOVEMBER 1985

COURT OF APPEAL, CIVIL DIVISION

DILLON, LLOYD AND NICHOLLS LJJ

30 APRIL, 1, 19 MAY 1986   *c*

*Medical practitioner – Professional misconduct – Charge of professional misconduct – Duplicity
– Single charge of improperly supplying drugs to 'individual patients' on different occasions –
Whether charge bad for duplicity – Whether charge alleging single course of professional
misconduct.*

Medical practitioner – Professional misconduct – Disciplinary proceedings – Procedure –   *d*
*Whether charge of professional misconduct required to be considered by General Medical Council's
preliminary proceedings committee before being referred to professional conduct committee –
Whether charge can be amended by professional conduct committee by adding further particulars
without being referred back to preliminary proceedings committee – General Medical Council
Preliminary Proceedings Committee and Professional Conduct Committee (Procedure) Rules*   *e*
Order of Council 1980, App, rr 10(2), 11.

*Medical practitioner – Professional misconduct – Charge of professional misconduct – Particulars
of charge – Whether accused practitioner entitled to know particulars of improper conduct
charged.*

f

Complaints of serious professional misconduct were made to the General Medical Council
against the applicant, a general medical practitioner, concerning his treatment of patients
for obesity. The council referred complaints relating to four of the applicant's patients to
the preliminary proceedings committee of the council, which determined that a charge
of serious professional misconduct should be formulated against the applicant and that
the case should be referred to the professional conduct committee of the council for   *g*
inquiry pursuant to r 11[a] in the appendix to the General Medical Council Preliminary
Proceedings Committee and Professional Conduct Committee (Procedure) Rules Order
of Council 1980. Notice of the charge was given to the applicant alleging that over a
period of 13 months he had abused his professional position by repeatedly supplying to
'individual patients' certain drugs in circumstances which amounted to serious
professional misconduct. In response to requests for particulars of the individual patients   *h*
referred to in the charge the council identified eight patients by name, including four
patients whose cases had not been before the preliminary proceedings committee, and
stated which allegation related to which patient. The applicant claimed that the charge
was bad for duplicity since it contained a number of separate allegations relating to eight
different patients, thereby contravening the principle of criminal law that a charge
should allege only one offence, and he requested that the charge be amended and that   *j*
further particulars be given of the allegation of improper prescribing of drugs. The
council refused to direct amendment of the charge or to supply the particulars requested.

---

a   Rule 11, so far as material, is set out at p 1210 *e*, post

The applicant sought judicial review of the council's refusal to amend the charge and the proceedings pending before the professional conduct committee. The judge held (i) that the charge as formulated was bad for duplicity, (ii) that the proceedings before the professional conduct committee were ultra vires on the ground that the cases concerning four of the patients had not been referred to the preliminary proceedings committee for inquiry pursuant to rr 10(2)[b] and 11 of the 1980 rules and (iii) that the council should have given the applicant the further particulars of the charge requested. The council appealed.

Held – (1) Although as a matter of elementary fairness the rule of criminal law that a charge should not be duplicitous applied (Dillon LJ dissenting) by analogy to a charge laid before the professional conduct committee of the General Medical Council, the charge as formulated was not bad for duplicity (Lloyd LJ dissenting) because it was to be read as a single charge of serious professional misconduct arising out of a course of conduct adopted by the applicant in the course of his professional work, notwithstanding that it embraced allegations in respect of eight different patients on different occasions. Moreover, it would not be confusing or unfair to the applicant if the committee were to have regard to those allegations when considering and determining whether the applicant had been guilty of serious professional misconduct or for those allegations to be included in a single charge, nor would the applicant be prejudiced if the case was proceeded against him on that charge. Accordingly, the appeal on the issue of duplicity would be allowed (see p 1221 e f, p 1223 f, p 1225 f to j, p 1226 g and p 1229 d to g, post).

(2) Furthermore (Lloyd LJ dissenting), since the case was the same case regarding a course of conduct as it was when referred by the preliminary proceedings committee to the professional conduct committee, it was permissible for additions to be made to the charged facts by way of further particulars of the four further patients without further reference to the preliminary proceedings committee and (per Nicholls LJ) for the charge to be amended under r 22[c] of the 1980 rules, since the further particulars did not widen or alter the substance of the course of conduct alleged. Accordingly, the proceedings before the professional conduct committee were not ultra vires and the appeal on that issue would be allowed (see p 1227 d e and p 1229 g h, post).

(3) The applicant was entitled to the particulars of improper prescribing of drugs which he had requested, since he was entitled to know in advance the standard against which he was to be judged. The judge had been right therefore to order the council to supply those further particulars and the appeal on that issue would be dismissed (see p 1217 b to e, p 1223 c d, p 1227 f and p 1229 h j, post).

Per Dillon and Nicholls LJJ. In expressing the decision of the professional conduct committee of the General Medical Council under r 30(3)[d] of the 1980 rules that a medical practitioner is guilty of the charge laid, the chairman of the committee is under a duty to announce in clear terms which facts alleged in the charge, including the particulars of the charge subsequently given, have been proved to their satisfaction and which have not (see p 1227 b c and p 1228 f g, post).

Notes

For procedure on inquiry into professional misconduct by the General Medical Council, see 30 Halsbury's Laws (4th edn) paras 164–177.

For the General Medical Council Preliminary Proceedings Committee and Professional Conduct Committee (Procedure) Rules Order of Council 1980, App, rr 10, 11, 22, 30, see 13 Halsbury's Statutory Instruments (4th reissue) 186, 188, 190.

---

b Rule 10(2), so far as material, is set out at p 1210 d, post
c Rule 22, so far as material, is set out at p 1210 g, post
d Rule 30(3) is set out at p 1220 a, post

Cases referred to in judgments

Bhattacharya v General Medical Council [1967] 2 AC 259, [1967] 3 WLR 498, PC.   **a**
Crompton v General Medical Council (No 2) [1985] 1 WLR 885, PC.
Datta v General Medical Council (27 January 1986, unreported), PC.
General Medical Council v Spackman [1943] 2 All ER 337, [1943] AC 627, HL.
Johnson v Miller (1937) 59 CLR 467, Aust HC.
Peatfield v General Medical Council [1987] 1 All ER 1197, [1986] 1 WLR 243, PC.
R v Greenfield [1973] 3 All ER 1050, [1973] 1 WLR 1151, CA.   **b**
R v Jones (John) [1974] ICR 310, CA.
R v Pharmacy Board of Victoria, ex p Broberg [1983] 1 VR 211, Vict SC.
R v Thompson [1914] 2 KB 99, CCA.
R v West [1948] 1 All ER 718, [1948] KB 709, CCA.
Tarnesby v General Medical Council (20 July 1970, unreported), PC.

   c

Cases also cited

Abrol v General Dental Council (10 April 1984, unreported), PC.
Allinson v General Medical Council [1894] 1 QB 750, [1891–4] All ER Rep 768, CA.
Felix v General Dental Council [1960] 2 All ER 391, [1960] AC 704, PC.
Fox v General Medical Council [1960] 3 All ER 225, [1960] 1 WLR 1017, PC.
Gardiner v General Medical Council (1961) 105 SJ 525, PC.   **d**
Hadmore Productions Ltd v Hamilton [1982] 1 All ER 1042, [1983] 1 AC 191, HL.
Haggart v General Medical Council (8 December 1975, unreported), PC.
Leeson v General Medical Council (1889) 43 Ch D 366, [1886–90] All ER Rep 78, CA.
Libman v General Medical Council [1972] 1 All ER 798, [1972] AC 217, PC.
McCoan v General Medical Council [1964] 3 All ER 143, [1964] 1 WLR 1107, PC.
McEniff v General Dental Council [1980] 1 All ER 461, [1980] 1 WLR 328, PC.   **e**
National Enterprises Ltd v Racal Communications Ltd [1974] 3 All ER 1010, [1975] Ch 397, CA.
Ong Bak Hin v General Medical Council [1956] 2 All ER 257, [1956] 1 WLR 515, PC.
R v Brent London BC, ex p Gunning (26 April 1985, unreported), QBD.
R v Huntingdon DC, ex p Cowan [1984] 1 All ER 58, [1984] 1 WLR 501.   **f**
R v Secretary of State for the Home Dept, ex p Tarrant [1984] 1 All ER 799, [1985] QB 251, DC.
R v General Medical Council [1930] 1 KB 562, CA.
R v Morry [1945] 2 All ER 632, CCA.
Rai v General Medical Council (14 May 1984, unreported), PC.
Rodgers v General Medical Council (19 November 1984, unreported), PC.
Sivarajah v General Medical Council [1964] 1 All ER 504, [1964] 1 WLR 112, PC.   **g**

Applications for judicial review

Dr Sidney Gee applied, with the leave of Webster J given on 14 December 1984, for (i) an order of certiorari to quash the order made and direction given by the president of the General Medical Council (the GMC) in a letter dated 19 November 1984 refusing to order **h** the amendment of a charge of serious professional misconduct against the applicant pursuant to r 22(1) of the General Medical Council Preliminary Proceedings Committee and Professional Conduct Committee (Procedure) Rules Order of Council 1980, SI 1980/ 858, (ii) an order of prohibition directed to the GMC and the professional conduct committee thereof prohibiting them from further proceeding with an inquiry into the charge made against the applicant unless the charge be amended so as to charge the **j** applicant separately with each allegation of professional misconduct made, and (iii) an order of mandamus directed to the president of the GMC requiring him to order that the charge be amended so as to charge the applicant separately with each allegation of professional misconduct made. The applicant also applied, with the leave of Woolf J given on 2 July 1985, for (i) an order of prohibition directed to the GMC and the

professional conduct committee thereof prohibiting them from further proceeding with
a an inquiry into the charge made against the applicant to be held by the committee
pursuant to a notice of inquiry dated 13 June 1984, unless, inter alia, the charge and/or
the particulars were amended and the particulars requested by the applicant were given
by the solicitor appointed by the GMC, (ii) an injunction to restrain the professional
conduct committee from proceeding further with the inquiry until the charge and/or
the particulars were amended and particulars given, (iii) an order of mandamus directed
b to the president of the GMC requiring him to order that the charge and/or the particulars
thereof be amended and the particulars given, (iv) an order of certiorari to quash the
refusal of the solicitor to the GMC to amend the charge and give particulars thereof, and
(v) a declaration that the inquiry to be held by the professional conduct committee into
the charge set out in the notice of inquiry and in the particulars given thereof was ultra
vires the professional conduct committee. The applications were heard together. The
c facts are set out in the judgment of Mann J.

Michael Beloff QC and *Charles Flint* for the applicant.
Raymond Sears QC and *Timothy Straker* for the GMC.

Cur adv vult

d

1 November. The following judgment was delivered.

MANN J. There are before the court two applications for judicial review. Leave to move
the first application was given by Webster J on 14 December 1984. Leave to move the
e second application was given by Woolf J on 2 July 1985. In each case the applicant is Dr
Sidney Gee and the respondent is the General Medical Council, to which I shall refer as
'the GMC'. The first application relates to a direction given by the president of the GMC
on 19 November 1984, whereby he refused to order the amendment of a charge of
serious professional misconduct against the applicant. The second application seeks to
prohibit the GMC's professional conduct committee from inquiring into certain matters
f until certain conditions are met.
    The applicant is a registered medical practitioner. He practices at surgeries in London
and Rochester. He has an especial interest in the treatment of obesity. In the course of
treating his patients for obesity he prescribed for them or supplied to them
dexamphetamine sulphate and thyroid extract. The applicant's conduct does not seem to
have been the subject of comment or complaint until 26 June 1983, when the British
g Broadcasting Corp (the BBC) broadcast a comment on him with particular reference to
his treatment of Mrs Elizabeth Ann Day, who had for many years been overweight. The
applicant responded to the comment with a writ for libel, which he issued on 26 August
1983. The hearing of the action commenced on 23 October 1984, but it was settled
during the plaintiff's case on 23 April 1985. The settlement was in the plaintiff's favour
in that the BBC agreed to pay to him £75,000 and his costs.
h   After the date of the broadcast, but not necessarily because of it, complaints were made
to the GMC. On 12 April 1984 the GMC's registrar wrote to the applicant as follows:

    'The Chairman of the Preliminary Proceedings Committee of the Council, who is
    the member appointed under Rule 4(3) of the Preliminary Proceedings Committee
    and Professional Conduct Committee (Procedure) Rules 1980 to undertake the
j initial consideration of cases, has asked me to notify you in accordance with Rule
    6(3) of the Procedure Rules that the Council has received from Dr A.C.S. Mitchell,
    Dr B.K. Attlee and Mr A.L. White complaints, and from the Solicitor to the Council
    information, which appear to raise a question whether, as a registered medical
    practitioner, you have committed serious professional misconduct within the
    meaning of section 36(1) of the Medical Act 1983. A copy of the relevant provisions

is enclosed, together with copies of the Procedure Rules and of a pamphlet, "Professional Conduct and Discipline: Fitness to Practise". In the complaints and *a* information it is alleged that over a period including May, 1982 to August, 1983, at your practice premises in Harley Street and in Rochester, you abused your professional position as a medical practitioner by supplying to individual patients, in return for fees, quantities of drugs including dexamphetamine sulphate and thyroid extract, repeatedly, over extensive periods, (a) without first adequately examining the patients, or seeking adequate information as to their medical history; *b* (b) without first consulting the patients' general practitioners about the proposed treatment, or notifying to those general practitioners after treatment had first commenced the details of any drugs supplied and the dosages prescribed; (c) without making adequate inquiries on each occasion about the effect of this treatment on the patients' health; (d) without offering appropriate advice when a patient reported to you the harmful effects upon her of the drugs which you had supplied. The *c* complaints are supported by statutory declarations by Dr A. C. S. Mitchell, Mrs E. A. Day, Dr B. K. Attlee and Mr A. L. White, copies of which are enclosed. Also enclosed is a copy of a statement by Mrs L. Twyman. As matters stand, the Chairman intends to direct me, as Registrar, in accordance with the provisions of Rule 10 of the Procedure Rules, to refer the complaints and information to the Preliminary Proceedings Committee of the Council; in this event it will be the duty of that *d* Committee to consider the complaints and information and any explanation furnished by you, and to determine whether the case shall be referred to the Professional Conduct Committee for inquiry into a charge against you. The next meeting of the Preliminary Proceedings Committee will be held on 17th May, 1984. It is in your interest that the Committee should have time to give careful consideration to any explanation you may wish to offer. I am accordingly inviting *e* you to submit to the Council not later than 8th May, 1984, any explanation of the foregoing matters which you have to offer for consideration at that meeting...'

This letter cannot be appreciated without reference to statute and an Order of Council. The GMC is a body corporate whose existence is now given by s 1(1) of the Medical Act 1983. It has by the Act four committees (see s 1(3)). Amongst the four are the preliminary *f* proceedings committee and the professional conduct committee. The professional conduct committee has the power when it judges a registered person to have been guilty of serious professional misconduct to direct that his name should be erased from the Medical Register (see s 36(1) of the 1983 Act). An exercise of that power means that the practitioner's medical career is ended subject to an exercise of the discretion to restore to the register under s 41 of the Act. There is, however, an appeal to Her Majesty in Council *g* against a decision directing erasure (see s 40(1)(a) and (4) of the 1983 Act).

Sections 42 and 43 of the 1983 Act provide, so far as is material, as follows:

'**42.**—(1) The Preliminary Proceedings Committee shall have the functions assigned to them by this section.

(2) It shall be the duty of the Committee to decide whether any case referred to *h* them for consideration in which a practitioner is alleged to be liable to have his name erased under section 36 above or his registration suspended or made subject to conditions under section 36 or 37 above ought to be referred for inquiry by the Professional Conduct Committee...

(3) If the Committee decide that a case ought to be referred for inquiry by the Professional Conduct Committee... (a) they shall give a direction designating the *j* Committee which is to inquire into the case...

43. Schedule 4 to this Act (which contains supplementary provisions about proceedings before the Professional Conduct Committee... and the Preliminary Proceedings Committee) shall have effect.'

Schedule 1 to the 1983 Act is given effect by s 1 of that Act. The schedule contains
a provisions about the four committees of the GMC. Amongst those provisions are these
paragraphs:

'The Preliminary Proceedings Committee

20. The Preliminary Proceedings Committee shall be constituted as provided by
the General Council by rules under this paragraph.

b   *The Professional Conduct Committee*

21. The Professional Conduct Committee shall be constituted as provided by the
General Council by rules under this paragraph.'

Schedule 4 to the 1983 Act is given effect by s 43 of the Act, as will have appeared. The
schedule contains provisions about proceedings before the preliminary proceedings
c committee and the professional conduct committee. They are as follows:

'1.—(1) Subject to the provisions of this paragraph, the General Council shall
make rules for the Professional Conduct Committee . . . with respect to the times
and places of the meetings of the Committee and the mode of summoning the
members, the reference of cases to the Committee (whether by the Preliminary
Proceedings Committee or otherwise) and the procedure to be followed and rules of
d   evidence to be observed in proceedings before the Committee.
(2) Rules made under this paragraph for the Professional Conduct Committee
shall include provision—(*a*) securing that notice that the proceedings are to be
brought shall be given, at such time and in such manner as may be specified in the
rules, to the person to whose registration the proceedings relate; (*b*) securing that
e any party to the proceedings shall, if he so requires, be entitled to be heard by the
Committee; (*c*) enabling any party to the proceedings to be represented by counsel
or a solicitor, or (if the rules so provide and the party so elects) by a person of such
other description as may be specified in the rules; (*d*) requiring proceedings before
the Committee to be held in public except in so far as may be provided by the rules;
(*e*) requiring that where, in a case in which it is alleged that a person has been guilty
f of serious professional misconduct, the Committee judge that the allegation has not
been proved they shall record a finding that the person is not guilty of such
misconduct in respect of the matters to which the allegation relates . . .
(4) Before making rules under this paragraph the General Council shall consult
with such bodies of persons representing medical practitioners, or medical
practitioners of any description, as appear to the Council requisite to be consulted.
g   (5) Rules under this paragraph shall not come into force until approved by order
of the Privy Council, and the Privy Council may approve such rules either as
submitted to them or subject to such modifications as appear to them to be requisite;
but where the Privy Council propose to approve any rules subject to modifications
they shall notify to the General Council the modifications they propose to make and
consider any observations of the General Council on them.'

h
Rules have not been made under the schedules to the 1983 Act. Rules were made
under the Medical Act 1978 and that Act was repealed and re-enacted by the 1983 Act.
Accordingly, the General Medical Council Preliminary Proceedings Committee and
Professional Conduct Committee (Procedure) Rules Order of Council 1980, SI 1980/858
remains in force by virtue of s 17(2)(*b*) of the Interpretation Act 1978. I shall refer to the
j rules contained in the appendix to that order as 'the rules'.
The relevant provisions of the rules are as follows:

'4.—(1) No case shall be considered by the Preliminary Proceedings Committee
unless it has first been considered by the member of the Council appointed under
this rule and referred by him to that Committee . . .

6.—(1) Where a complaint in writing or information in writing is received by the Registrar and it appears to him that a question arises whether conduct of a practitioner constitutes serious professional misconduct the Registrar shall submit the matter to the President.

(2) Unless the complaint or information has been received from a person acting in a public capacity the matter shall not proceed further unless and until there has been furnished to the satisfaction of the President one or more statutory declarations in support thereof; and every such statutory declaration shall state the address and description of the declarant and the grounds for his belief in the truth of any fact declared which is not within his personal knowledge.

(3) Unless it appears to the President that the matter need not proceed further he shall direct the Registrar to write to the practitioner—(a) notifying him of the receipt of a complaint or information and stating the matters which appear to raise a question whether the practitioner has committed serious professional misconduct; (b) forwarding a copy of any statutory declaration furnished under paragraph (2) of this rule; (c) informing the practitioner of the date of the next meeting of the Preliminary Proceedings Committee to which the case may be referred; and (d) inviting the practitioner to submit any explanation which he may have to offer . . .

10 . . . (2) Subject to the foregoing rules the President may direct the Registrar to refer any case of conduct to the Preliminary Proceedings Committee together with any statutory declaration [or] explanation . . . furnished under rule 6 . . .

11.—(1) Where a case has been referred to the Preliminary Proceedings Committee as aforesaid, that Committee shall consider the case and, subject to these rules, determine:—(a) that the case be referred to the Professional Conduct Committee for inquiry, or (b) that the case shall be referred to the Health Committee for inquiry, or (c) that the case shall not be referred to either Committee.

(2) When referring a case to the Professional Conduct Committee the Preliminary Proceedings Committee shall indicate . . . the matters which in their opinion appear to raise a question whether the practitioner has committed serious professional misconduct, to be so referred . . .

17.—(1) As soon as may be after a case has been referred to the Professional Conduct Committee for inquiry, the Solicitor shall send to the practitioner a "Notice of Inquiry" which shall—(a) specify, in the form of a charge or charges, the matters into which the inquiry is to be held, and (b) state the day, time and place at which the inquiry is proposed to be held . . .

22.—(1) Where before a hearing by the Professional Conduct Committee it appears to the President that a charge should be amended, the President shall give such directions for the amendment of the charge as he may think necessary to meet the circumstances of the case, unless, having regard to the merits of the case, the required amendments cannot be made without injustice . . .'

The reference in the rules to 'the Solicitor' means 'any Solicitor, or any firm of Solicitors, appointed by the [GMC] or any member of such a firm': see r 2. Messrs Waterhouse & Co is the firm which has been appointed by the GMC and its predecessors for the last 85 years.

I observe that the letter of 12 April was written in conformity with r 6(3) and return to the correspondence. The applicant made representations in consequence of the letter of 12 April, but on 22 May 1984 the GMC's deputy registrar wrote, so far as is material, as follows:

'I am writing to inform you that the Preliminary Proceedings Committee of the Council have now considered the complaints and information to which reference was made in the Council's letter of 12th April, 1984. The Committee also had before them letters of 4th May and 16th May, 1984 from Messrs. Beachcrofts, solicitors, on your behalf, and five reports which were sent to the Council by Messrs. Beachcrofts *a* with a further letter of 16th May 1984. The Committee determined that a charge should be formulated against you on the basis of the complaints and information, and that an inquiry into the charge should be held by the Professional Conduct Committee.'

On 13 June a charge was formulated in accordance with r 17 and, so far as is material, it was in these terms:

b 'On behalf of the General Medical Council notice is hereby given to you that in consequence of a complaint made against you to the Council an inquiry is to be held into the following charge against you:—"That, being registered under the Medical Act, 'Between about June, 1982 and about July, 1983, at your practice premises in Harley Street and in Rochester, you abused your professional position as a medical practitioner by supplying to individual patients, in return for fees, quantities of

c drugs including dexamphetamine sulphate and thyroid extract, repeatedly, over extensive periods, (a) without first adequately examining the patients, or seeking adequate information as to their medical history; (b) without first consulting the patients' general practitioners about the proposed treatment, or notifying to those general practitioners after treatment had first commenced the details of any drugs supplied and the dosages prescribed; (c) without making adequate inquiries on each

d occasion about the effect of this treatment on the patients' health; (d) without offering appropriate advice when a patient reported to you the harmful effects upon her of the drugs which you had supplied.' And that in relation to the facts alleged you have been guilty of serious professional misconduct." Notice is further given to you that on Wednesday the 18th day of July 1984, a meeting of the Professional Conduct Committee will be held at 44 Hallam Street, London, W1N 6AE, at

e 11.30 am to consider the above-mentioned charge against you, and to determine whether or not they should direct the Registrar to erase your name from the Register or to suspend your registration therein, or to impose conditions on your registration pursuant to section 36 of the Medical Act 1983.'

The applicant considered that he had an inadequate time to answer the charge against

f him. He applied for an adjournment but on 21 June he was told that his application had been refused by the president of the GMC. On 4 July Glidewell J granted leave to move for a judicial review of the decision to refuse an adjournment. The application came before McNeill J, who on 13 July quashed the refusal of an adjournment. The charge of 13 June awaits for its further advance on the determination of the applications now before the court.

g I again return to the correspondence. On 28 June the applicant's solicitors wrote a letter of length and complexity, in which particulars of the charge were sought and matters of discovery and evidence raised. I need not recite it.

The response to the long and complex letter was dated 29 June and was, so far as is material, as follows:

h 'Thank you for your letter dated 28th June. In response we shall deal with the matters raised in the same order, although it is our view that we have already complied with the rules to which you have referred, having served a charge which is clearly expressed and statements which really need no further interpretation.

Particulars

j 1. The patients referred to are, as you already know: Mrs. E. A. Day, Mrs. J. Foster, Mrs. Spain, the late Mrs. White, Mrs. Twyman, Mrs. Holland, Mrs. Downs, Master Chaplain.

2. It is intended to allege that it was an abuse of your client's professional position as a medical practitioner to supply in the circumstances of the case the drugs in question *and* that he did so in the circumstances listed in (a) to (d) of the charge.

We refer you to the relevant entries in the extracts in the British National Formulary of which copies are enclosed. (i) Where the drugs are capable of being identified, the details are clearly set out in the witnesses' statements. Where they are not, it is due in part to your client's reluctance to tell either the patients or their medical advisors. Presumably your client has his own record and will be the best person to know what precisely was being prescribed. (ii) This is set out above and dealt with in the statements of the medical witnesses, the medical literature enclosed and the well known general medical practice.

3. It is, in our view, unnecessary to rehearse again each such allegation, as these are quite clearly set out in the statements.

4. (a) Each patient has adequately described the occasions when an examination took place or when no examination took place. (b) When prescribing the drugs alleged, it seems to us obvious that *a full examination* of the patient should have been conducted, both at the commencement of the supply of drugs and thereafter and particularly (i) when the patients, as alleged, complained of side effects and (ii) having regard to the nature of the drugs supplied. In many cases no examination took place at all. On those occasions no "adequate examination" could have taken place. In relation to those occasions when some examination took place, the allegation is that such examination was inadequate based upon the evidence of the witnesses which is already in your possession.

5. (a) Where [the applicant] did seek information it is contained in the statements. (b) First and foremost, at initial interview the name and address of the patients' regular general medical practitioner and a full medical history to include all relevant diseases, surgical operations, heart disease and family medical history, e.g. Mrs White's previous medical history and Mrs Day's. The best method of ascertaining would have been for your client himself to communicate with the patients' general practitioner.

6. In the booklet issued by the Council in September 1981 and August 1983, the Council's views are clearly expressed. Similarly the Council's Annual Report sent to all registered medical practitioners in about mid 1982 again provided adequate advice to the profession. We enclose a copy of each section. In the B.M.A. Handbook issued in 1981 (page 16) the same recommendation was made. Copy enclosed. These we suggest reflect the proper medical practice.' (Emphasis as in letter.)

At once it must be observed that the 'individual patients' referred to in the charge are now particularised and that in the process of particularisation new patients are introduced into the proceedings. They are Mrs Spain, Mrs Holland, Mrs Downs and Master Chaplain. [His Lordship considered the correspondence between the applicant's solicitors and the GMC's solicitors relating to whether the charge as formulated was bad for duplicity on the ground that it contained a number of separate allegations relating to eight different patients, read the application made on 1 November 1984 on the applicant's behalf under r 22(1) of the 1980 rules for the charge to be amended and the decision of the president of the GMC by letter dated 19 November 1984 refusing that application, and continued:]

That decision was the decision in respect of which Webster J gave leave to move on 14 December 1984.

On 29 May 1985 the applicant's solicitors wrote to Waterhouse & Co a letter referring to many matters, but which in particular requested the particulars contained in an enclosed schedule. That schedule is:

'1. State whether it is or is not alleged that it is serious professional misconduct for a doctor to supply *in the course of treatment for obesity* the drugs referred to in the Notice of Inquiry:—(a) at all, or (b) otherwise than under certain conditions. 2. If it is permissible for a doctor to supply such drugs in the course of treatment for obesity state what conditions must be fulfilled if such prescription is not to constitute serious professional misconduct. 3. Is it alleged that [the applicant] was guilty of

a
serious professional misconduct in using particular drug therapy on any particular occasions for any particular patients? If so:—(i) Give the name of each individual patient concerned; (ii) In relation to each particular patient, give the date or dates when the impugned drug therapy was given; (iii) state the particular drugs and doses given to each particular named patient at each date identified under (ii); (iv) (insofar as not covered by answers to 1 and 2 stated above) the ground or grounds upon which it is alleged it was serious professional misconduct to prescribe the

b
particular drugs on the particular dates. 4. If the drug therapy as part of the *treatment for obesity* is impugned under 1, then list any medical articles relied upon, explain the precise medical basis on which the therapy is impugned, and specify any research work and results upon which reliance is to be placed. 5. Specify the precise rule or rules or advice which it is alleged gave rise to an obligation on the part of [the applicant] to consult a patient's General Practitioner. In your letter of 29th June you

c
referred generally to the booklets issued by the GMC and the BMA Handbook but you have not specified which paragraph or paragraphs of those documents you rely upon, or which Edition (giving the date of publication). 6. In relation to sub-paragraph (d) of the Notice state which drug or drugs are referred to and what dose or doses and give proper particulars of the alleged harmful effects of such drug or drugs, specifying each alleged harmful effect of each dose. 7. The purported Charge

d
alleges that [the applicant] prescribed the drugs "... without first adequately examining the patients ..." The following points arise:—(i) In relation to each individual patient what examination should have been carried out (which was allegedly not carried out) and the reason(s) for such examination, setting out the particular medical grounds and the particular facts relied upon; (ii) In relation to the alleged insufficient examination of each patient, whether it is alleged that such

e
examination was negligent or alternatively whether it is alleged that the conduct was worse than negligent and if so precisely what is alleged and on what grounds. 8. The purported Charge in Part (a) alleges that [the applicant] prescribed the drugs, "... without seeking adequate information ..." State:—(i) in relation to each patient what should [the applicant] have done, which he failed to do, and when? (ii) what information was not obtained as a result? (iii) whether it is alleged that such failure

f
was negligent or alternatively worse and if worse than negligent precisely what is alleged and on what grounds. 9. In regard to Part (c) of the Charge in relation to each individual patient what should [the applicant] have done and when, in what way were his inquiries "inadequate", whether it is alleged that [the applicant] was acting negligently or worse and if it is alleged that the conduct was worse than negligent precisely what is alleged? 10. In regard to Part (d):—(i) which patients

g
reported harmful effects? (ii) in relation to each such patient, when such report was made, in what words, what were the "harmful effects", and what advice should have been given and why? (iii) whether it is alleged that the failure to give advice was negligent or worse, if worse precisely what is alleged and on what grounds.' (Emphasis as in letter.)

h
The particulars were refused on 18 June in a letter which also refused to countenance the suggestion that the cases of Mrs Spain, Mrs Holland, Mrs Downs and Master Chaplain could not be considered by the professional conduct committee as they had not been before the preliminary proceedings committee. On reading that letter and other documents, Woolf J gave leave to move the second application.

j
Four questions are before the court. They are: (i) are the matters complained of justiciable? (ii) is there here an ultra vires decision? (iii) is there here a charge bad for duplicity? and (iv) should particulars of the charge be given as asked? I take the four questions in turn.

I have no doubt that the matters complained of are susceptible to judicial review. The applications are applications in the field of public law in that they relate to the exercise of statutory powers against an individual. Counsel for the GMC did not contend to the

contrary. He accepted that the cases with which I am concerned are justiciable. My lack
of doubt and counsel's acceptance accord with the decision of McNeill J on 13 July 1983   *a*
and with the decision of the Supreme Court of Victoria in *R v Pharmacy Board of Victoria,*
ex p Broberg [1983] 1 VR 211. I see no cause for reticence in approaching a threatened act
in excess of a statutory jurisdiction or of a threatened abuse of the principles of fairness
in the exercise of that jurisdiction.

I turn to the question of vires. It is said by counsel for the applicant and correctly so,
that the GMC, its committees, its president and its solicitor derive their disciplinary   *b*
powers wholly from statute. Therefore, he argues, those powers are exercisable only in
accordance with the scheme embodied in the statute and the rules. The particular point
is that the professional conduct committee has no jurisdiction to consider a 'case' which
has not been referred to it by the preliminary proceedings committee. The submission
bites in the present application because the preliminary proceedings committee never
considered the cases of Mrs Spain, Mrs Holland, Mrs Downs and Master Chaplain (to   *c*
whom I shall refer as the group B patients). The submission of counsel for the applicant
is based on the natural meaning of the words employed in the rules and on the purpose
of the mechanism established by the statute and rules. He referred in particular to
rr 10(2) and 11(2). Under r 10(2) the president may direct the registrar to refer 'any case
of conduct' to the preliminary proceedings committee. Under r 11(1) the committee is
obliged to consider the case and amongst the options which they may exercise is that of   *d*
referring the 'case' to the professional conduct committee. In referring that case, the
preliminary proceedings committee must, according to r 11(2), indicate 'the matters
which in their opinion appear to raise a question whether the practitioner has committed
serious professional misconduct'. The preliminary proceedings committee did not and
could not indicate any matter in relation to the group B patients. As they could not have
done so, it is difficult to see how the solicitor could have sent (as he did not) the   *e*
practitioner under r 17(1) a 'notice of inquiry' specifying amongst the matters into which
the professional conduct committee inquiry is to be held matters concerning the group
B patients.

Counsel for the GMC argued that it was unnecessary for the group B patients to have
been before the preliminary proceedings committee. He submitted that the inquiry is to
be an inquiry into 'conduct' which can arise from behaviour in regard to an individual   *f*
patient or from the way in which a practice is carried on. This charge related he said, to
the way in which a practice is carried on. The particular way of which complaint was
made was that of irresponsible prescribing and it mattered not whether there were eight
patients or one. I do not agree that the charge is so drawn. The charge is in terms drawn
by reference to 'individual patients'. It was particularised on 29 June 1983, by reference
to eight patients. Material about four patients was before the preliminary proceedings   *g*
committee. Material about the group B patients was not. Each patient occasions a
different 'case' in regard to which there are 'matters' into which an inquiry can be made.

The language of the rules, together with their purpose, that is to say the creation of a
protective filter, have together the result that the professional conduct committee cannot
as a matter of jurisdiction consider a 'case' which has not been considered by the   *h*
preliminary proceedings committee. The practitioner is as much entitled to have the
process observed as is an accused to have the process of committal observed. The
professional conduct committee must not entertain any case or matter in regard to the
group B patients unless and until the case or matter has been referred to it by the
preliminary proceedings committee.

I add that the preliminary proceedings committee cannot consider a case unless it has   *j*
first come in as a complaint or as an information under r 6 and then been passed to the
preliminary proceedings committee under r 10(2). It would be odd if the preliminary
proceedings committee could refer a 'case' which had not been referred to them. Counsel
for the GMC said that the preliminary proceedings committee could do so in that r 6 was
only 'directory'. I cannot accept that submission. Rules 6, 10 and 11 supply a coherent

and (from the point of view of the practitioner) important filter process which must be
a observed.

I turn to the third question, which has a relationship with the second. The applicant
submits that the charge is duplicitous in that it alleges the commission of the same
offence, serious professional misconduct, on a number of occasions. It follows from what
I have said in regard to the second question that I accept that it does so allege. It alleges
separate offences of misconduct, each being in regard to a different patient.

b   It is a rule of the criminal law that a charge must not be duplicitous. The rule is a
common law rule and, although it relates to form, it has a substantive consequence (see
R v Thompson [1914] 2 KB 99, *R v West* [1948] 1 All ER 718, [1948] 1 KB 709 and *R v
Jones (John)* [1974] ICR 310). A person should know of what it is that he has been found
guilty (if guilty he should be found). He cannot know if he has been found guilty on a
duplicitous charge whether he has been found guilty of one offence or of many. He
c should have the opportunity of submitting that there is no case to answer in relation to a
particular occasion. That he cannot do if he is confronted with a duplicitous charge. A
person cannot make a sensible plea in mitigation unless he knows of the number of his
offences. The rule concerning duplicity seems to me to be a rule of elementary fairness
which should apply to a charge before the professional conduct committee. As it seems
to me, the only answer of counsel for the GMC to the argument is that the charge is a
d single one of general irresponsible prescribing. I have said that I do not agree.
Accordingly, in my judgment, the charge in its present form is bad for duplicity and the
professional conduct committee must not proceed to its consideration until that vice is
cured.

I find support for my view that the rule concerning duplicity should apply to charges
before the professional conduct committee in the opinion of the Privy Council in
e *Tarnesby v General Medical Council* (20 July 1970, unreported), where their Lordships
observed:

'The main complaint against the form of the charges was that the vital allegation
of wrongful intention, contained in the words "with a view to attracting patients
and promoting your own financial benefit", was put in an introductory paragraph
f or passage and the allegations of acts done were put in separate later paragraphs. The
alleged acts done would have been innocuous without the alleged intention. The
alleged intention might have been clearer and more definite in relation to some of
the alleged acts than to others. It would have been more orthodox according to long-
established practice in the courts, and more informative for the disciplinary
committee, and conducive to clarity in the presentation of the case, if the alleged
g intention had been associated directly with each set of alleged acts done, so as to
make it clear from the outset that both the acts done and the intention with which
they were done constituted the facts of the case and must both be proved in relation
to each matter. This complaint (which is additional to the general disadvantages of
a long and complicated charge) has some substance in it and merits consideration in
relation to the formulation of charges in future cases. Their Lordships, however, are
h satisfied that the form of the charges did no appreciable harm in this case.'

In my judgment the professional conduct committee (and the solicitor) should observe
the long-established practice of the courts in regard to duplicitous charges. The
professional conduct committee would, I think, find it helpful when deliberating either
on guilt or on sentence to have their attention guided by a charge which isolated the
j different occasions on which the offence of misconduct is said to have occurred or to have
been found. Certainly an advocate who appeared before the professional conduct
committee to mitigate would find it helpful. If a charge is duplicitous the advocate is at
a loss.

I turn to the fourth question, that is to say whether the particulars of the charge should
be given. Counsel for the applicant submitted that the giving of particulars was but an

aspect of fairness. He referred me to two authorities and to a rule. The first authority was
the decision of the Supreme Court of Victoria, in *R v Pharmacy Board of Victoria, ex p*　*a*
Broberg, to which I have already adverted. Faced with an allegation that the Pharmacy
Board of Victoria should not proceed further with its inquiry in the absence of furnishing
to the applicant sufficient particulars of the charge against him, O'Bryan J said ([1983]
1 VR 211 at 213–214):

> 'The argument in relation to ground b. can be conveniently considered first.　*b*
> [Counsel for the applicant] argued firstly, that the applicant should know with
> reasonable clarity the case he has to meet and secondly, that the particulars which
> have been given to date do not provide the applicant with reasonable information
> of the case he has to meet. In support of the first proposition [counsel for the
> applicant] referred the court to *Johnson v. Miller* ((1937) 59 CLR 467), a case in which
> a complaint had been dismissed in the Magistrates' Court because the informant　*c*
> had failed to furnish particulars giving reasonable information as to the nature of
> the charge. The matter eventually reached the High Court. There Dixon, J., as he
> then was, observed (at 489): "a defendant is entitled to be apprised not only of the
> legal nature of the offence with which he is charged but also of the particular act,
> matter or thing alleged as the foundation of the charge". Evatt, J., (at 497) said: "It
> is of the very essence of the administration of justice that a defendant should, at the　*d*
> very outset of the trial, know what is the specific offence which is being alleged
> against him." The principle expressed in those passages obviously has an application
> to an inquiry by a professional disciplinary tribunal into the conduct of one of its
> members.'

I gratefully adopt what the judge said.

The second authority is the decision of the Privy Council in *Crompton v General Medical*　*e*
Council (No 2) [1985] 1 WLR 885 at 895–896, where their Lordships expressed the
opinion:

> 'It is clearly desirable that the mental condition which triggers section 37 of the
> Medical Act 1983 should be notified to the practitioner with as much particularity
> as is reasonable and practical, so that he knows what case he has to meet.'　*f*

Counsel for the GMC submitted, and I agree, that there is no sensible distinction between
medical condition and serious professional misconduct.

The rule to which I was referred is r 17(1), which requires the solicitor to 'specify, in
the form of a charge or charges, matters into which the inquiry is to be held'. The word
'specify' indicates, said counsel for the GMC, that there must be particularity.

Counsel for the GMC accepted that the professional conduct committee must act　*g*
fairly. He initially was disposed to argue that in the circumstances of the case the
principles of fairness did not require the applicant to be supplied with any of the
particulars which had been requested in the schedule of 29 May 1985. After an
examination of a perplexing correspondence, to which I need not now refer, he resiled
from the proposition. The following schedule was supplied after the midday adjournment　*h*
on 10 October:

> 'As far as [the applicant] is concerned: 1. It is alleged to be capable of amounting
> to serious professional misconduct if he supplies such drugs when the conditions in
> charges (a)–(d) obtain. 2. In relation to 2 reference is made to the preceding answer.
> 3. The answer to 3 is No. 4. 4 is not applicable. 5. There are no precise rules. The
> blue book has never attempted to be comprehensive rules affecting the profession.　*j*
> The need to consult general practitioners is a matter which speaks for itself. 6. This
> relates to those patients who came within D. The drugs are dexamphetamine
> sulphate and/or thyroid extract. 7, 8, 9. We do not consider it appropriate to answer
> these. 10. (i) This appears from the Statements served upon you. (ii) Other than

a repeating (i) above, we do not consider it appropriate to answer this request. (iii) We
do not consider it appropriate to answer this request.'

Counsel for the GMC asked me to record that the supply of these particulars was made
in order to be fair in the case of the applicant. He said that it was a supply applicable only
in the circumstances of that case. I record the request.

b In relation to the inappropriateness of answering the requests in paras 7, 8, 9, 10(ii)
and (iii), counsel for the GMC said that they were particulars which would be appropriate
in a civil action for professional negligence, but which were inappropriate in disciplinary
proceedings for serious professional misconduct. I cannot appreciate the force of his
submission which was unsupported by any reason. The professional conduct committee
has, to use the words of Lord Wright, the power to 'close a man's professional career': see
General Medical Council v Spackman [1943] 2 All ER 337 at 342, [1943] AC 627 at 639. If
c the provision of particulars would be appropriate in civil litigation for professional
negligence, then it must be appropriate in proceedings with so grave a consequence as
Lord Wright has stated. The only reason given for refusing to answer the particulars is
an inadequate one. The particulars must be given.

Counsel for the applicant, whilst welcoming the particulars which had been given,
made some observations on them. In regard to answer 5 he said that that was inconsistent
d with para 6 in the solicitor's letter of 29 June 1985 in that the letter refers to particular
rules. I agree that there is an apparent inconsistency between the letter and the particulars.
It is an inconsistency which should and could be resolved. In regard to the particular in
para 6, counsel for the applicant asks why should not the harmful effects of the drugs be
particularised. He also asks why should not the dose and the drug be particularised. I
agree. There is no reason why the particulars should not be supplied and it is fair that
e they should be supplied.

In regard to his response to para 10(i) counsel for the applicant says that a statement is
not as good as a particular in that the former does not give a focus. I agree, but the
matters sought do clearly appear in the statements.

Counsel for the GMC gave to me an interesting résumé of the history and powers of
the GMC, of the professional conduct committee and of their predecessors. He also
f referred to the attitude which the Privy Council has adopted in regard to the decisions of
those bodies. I hope that counsel for the GMC will not think me discourteous if I do not
recite that resumé and reference. I am not concerned with an attempt to review the
judgments of medical men on medical or ethical matters; I am concerned with
jurisdiction and procedural fairness. Where the court is confronted with the threat either
of an ultra vires act or of procedural unfairness in the area of public law it will intervene.
g I recognise the reticence with which the court considers the judgments of professional
men on the conduct of colleagues (see *Bhattacharya v General Medical Council* [1967] 2 AC
259 at 265). However, reticence is not appropriate when the court is confronted with
allegations of illegality and procedural impropriety.

h *Applications granted. Undertaking that the GMC would not proceed further on the charge as
presently formulated and particularised. Liberty to apply.*

Appeal
The GMC appealed.

j
Vivian Robinson QC and *Timothy Straker* for the GMC.
Michael Beloff QC and *Charles Flint* for the applicant.

Cur adv vult

19 May. The following judgments were delivered.

a

LLOYD LJ (giving the first judgment at the invitation of Dillon LJ). The facts which give rise to this appeal, and the statutory background, are so fully and accurately set out in the judgment of Mann J (see pp 1207–1213, ante) that it would be a waste of time to repeat them. The case concerns proceedings taken by the General Medical Council (the GMC) for alleged professional misconduct on the part of the applicant, Dr Gee. There were four questions for the judge's determination: first, whether the matters complained *b* of by the applicant are justiciable at all; in other words, whether they are properly the subject of an application for judicial review; second, whether the charge laid against the applicant is bad for duplicity; third, whether the proceedings currently before the professional conduct committee are ultra vires on the grounds that they have not been properly referred for inquiry by the preliminary proceedings committee; and fourth, whether the GMC should give further particulars of the charge as laid. The judge has *c* answered all four questions in favour of the applicant. There is now an appeal to this court.

Counsel for the GMC does not seek to argue the first point. He concedes that the applicant's complaints are properly the subject of an application for judicial review.

On the second question, I shall start by referring to the charge as drawn in the notice of inquiry dated 13 June 1984:

d

'That, being registered under the Medical Act, "Between about June, 1982 and about July, 1983, at your practice premises in Harley Street and in Rochester, you abused your professional position as a medical practitioner by supplying to individual patients, in return for fees, quantities of drugs including dexamphetamine sulphate and thyroid extract, repeatedly, over extensive periods, (a) without first adequately *e* examining the patients, or seeking adequate information as to their medical history; (b) without first consulting the patients' general practitioners about the proposed treatment, or notifying to those general practitioners after treatment had first commenced the details of any drugs supplied and the dosages prescribed; (c) without making adequate inquiries on each occasion about the effect of this treatment on the patients' health; (d) without offering appropriate advice when a patient reported *f* to you the harmful effects upon her of the drugs which you had supplied." And that in relation to the facts alleged you have been guilty of serious professional misconduct.'

In deciding whether a count is duplicitous at common law, it is, of course, permissible to consider not only the count itself, but also any particulars that may have been given: see *R v Greenfield* [1973] 3 All ER 1050, [1973] 1 WLR 1151.

g

In the present case the applicant asked for particulars, inter alia, of the individual patients referred to in the charge. Certain particulars were furnished on 29 June 1984. I need only mention one paragraph which identifies eight patients by name. The applicant then asked for further particulars, stating which of the allegations set out in paras (a) to (d) of the charge related to which of the patients. The answer came back on 18 September *h* 1984. Again, I need only refer to one paragraph as follows:

'As to the charge, we note your comments and whilst the statements submitted to you make it quite clear what is alleged, for the purpose of simplification we set out here-under the patients' names as relating to the paragraphs (a) to (d) in the charge.

j

(a) [eight names].
(b) [eight names].
(c) [seven names].
(d) [five names].'

Counsel for the applicant submitted that the charge as laid, including the particulars, is bad for duplicity, in that it charges more than one offence. The answer of counsel for

the GMC is it charges one offence only, namely serious professional misconduct. At one
a stage it looked as if counsel for the GMC was going so far as to submit that in a case of
serious professional misconduct there *could* be only one charge. But that was plainly
unsustainable in the light of the General Medical Council Preliminary Proceedings
Committee and Professional Conduct Committee (Procedure) Rules Order of Council
1980, SI 1980/858, and in particular rr 17(1)(*a*), 27, 28 and 30 which clearly contemplate
that the notice of inquiry may contain more than one charge of serious professional
b misconduct, as does the form of notice of inquiry set out in Sch 2.

To be fair to counsel for the GMC, he conceded that, if there were distinct allegations
of misconduct, such as, for example, misprescription of drugs and indecent assault, then
those matters should be drawn as separate charges. But, if the alleged misconduct consists
of a course of conduct, such as a succession of indecent assaults, then those indecent
assaults could all be charged in a single charge as part of a single course of conduct. He
c accepted that indecent assaults committed on different occasions against different patients
would have to be charged in separate counts in a criminal indictment. But he said that
the procedure before the professional conduct committee of the GMC is different. There
is no direct analogy with criminal procedure; and in all the many cases that have come
before the Privy Council on appeal from the GMC there has never been any suggestion,
to counsel's knowledge, that a charge could be bad for duplicity, until the very recent
d decision in *Peatfield v General Medical Council* [1987] 1 All ER 1197, [1986] 1 WLR 243.

The consequence of the submission of counsel for the GMC, a consequence which he
readily accepted, is that a doctor might be placed in the position of having to plead both
guilty and not guilty to the same charge; guilty in respect of the facts relating to one
patient, not guilty in respect of the facts relating to another. The same difficulty would
face the committee when coming to make their findings. It may be that it was this
e difficulty which prompted an observation at the conclusion of another even more recent
decision of the Privy Council in *Datta v General Medical Council* (27 January 1986,
unreported). The facts of that case do not matter for present purposes. But at the
conclusion of the judgment delivered by Lord Griffiths there appears this paragraph:

f   'Before parting with this case, their Lordships would like to observe that their
        understanding of the committee's conclusions was not assisted by the somewhat
        delphic form in which their findings of fact concluded, namely "they have recorded
        a finding that you are not guilty of serious professional misconduct in respect of
        those other facts alleged which have not been proved". We were told by counsel
        that this was the consequence of a procedural format which has been evolved and is
g   applied in all cases of professional misconduct. Their Lordships suggest that the
        procedure requires re-examination. If all the sentence means is that the committee
        are not going to find the accused guilty of something that has not been proved, it is
        a statement of the obvious which should not require saying. If as we suspect it is
        intended to serve some other purpose, that purpose is far from clear to their
        Lordships.'

h
It was not possible, of course, for the GMC to 're-examine the procedure' before the
present proceedings were initiated. But there is no reason why the procedure should not
be re-examined now. I would respectfully echo Lord Griffiths' observation.

There is another aspect of the procedure which is open to criticism. Rule 30(1) provides
that at the conclusion of the hearing the committee shall consider and determine as
j respects each charge which, if any, of the facts alleged in the charge have been proved.
Rule 30(2) and (3) provides as follows:

        '(2) If under paragraph (1) of this rule the Committee determine, as respects any
        charge, either that none of the facts alleged in the charge has been proved to their
        satisfaction, or that such facts as have been so proved would be insufficient to
        support a finding of serious professional misconduct, the Committee shall record a

finding that the practitioner is not guilty of such misconduct in respect of the matters to which that charge relates.

    (3) The Chairman shall announce the determination or the finding of the Committee.'

At the conclusion of the hearing in *Peatfield v General Medical Council* the chairman announced the determination as follows:

'The Committee have determined that the following facts alleged against you in the charge have been proved to their satisfaction.'

The chairman then read out verbatim the terms of the charge, a charge which, incidentally, is very similar to the charge in the present case. If that procedure were adopted in the present case, the applicant would have no means of knowing in respect of which of the eight individual patients the facts had been found proved, and which not. Counsel for the GMC told us that the committee is encouraged to spell out the facts in some detail, and he referred us to a number of cases in which this appeared to have been done. But the applicant wishes to have reassurance in advance. The best way of achieving this would be to ensure that separate incidents of misconduct are charged separately, and not as part of an omnibus charge of professional misconduct.

Counsel for the GMC submits that it is important that the GMC should be able to look at a doctor's conduct in the round. It may be that a series of incidents might be sufficient to support a finding of serious professional misconduct, if considered together, but insufficient if considered separately. I see the force of that. But there is nothing in the Medical Act 1983, or the rules, which entitles the GMC to roll up separate offences in a single charge by describing the offence as a course of conduct. Indeed, r 30(2), to which I have already referred, clearly contemplates that it is the duty of the committee to consider whether the facts proved are sufficient to support a finding of serious professional misconduct in respect of *each* charge in the notice of inquiry.

I now return to *Peatfield v General Medical Council* [1987] 1 All ER 1197, [1986] 1 WLR 243. In that case Dr Peatfield faced a charge which was divided into two halves. The first half is very similar, if not identical, to the charge in the present case. The second half referred to the doctor's conduct in relation to a particular patient, alleging that he had made statements in relation to that patient which were untrue or misleading. At the conclusion of the charge, which was, I emphasise, drafted as a single charge, appear the words: 'and that in relation to the facts alleged you have been guilty of serious professional misconduct.' The facts relating to the second half of the charge were not established. It is not without significance that Lord Mackay, who delivered the judgment of the Privy Council, referred in his narrative to Dr Peatfield as having originally faced *two* charges, the second of which had not been established. After referring to the decision of Mann J in the present case, Lord Mackay observed that the duplicity point had been taken much later than in the present case. In *Peatfield v General Medical Council* the point was only raised for the first time after the inquiry before the professional conduct committee had been concluded. There then comes the following passage ([1987] 1 All ER 1197 at 1201, [1986] 1 WLR 243 at 248):

'Their Lordships take the view that, in the present case, the charge can be fairly read as alleging a course of conduct by the appellant in the conduct of his practice over the period stated in which patients were treated with the drugs specified in the three circumstances referred to under heads (a), (b) and (c) and that it was this course of conduct which amounted to serious professional misconduct. They agree, and counsel for the [GMC] accepted this, that the use of the word "individual" was inappropriate but it is apparent from the record of the hearing that both parties before the committee treated the charge as a complaint with regard to a course of conduct and the appellant in his own evidence dealt with the matter very much from the point of view of what his ordinary practice and manner of operation were.

Indeed the appellant and his counsel laid stress on the number of patients dealt with
a in respect of whom there was no complaint. In this circumstance, their Lordships
consider that this point taken by itself is not a good reason for allowing this appeal.'

Counsel for the GMC relied strongly on that passage in support of his submission. But it
is to be noticed that that passage contains no criticism of Mann J's decision in the present
case, nor is there any suggestion elsewhere in the judgment that Mann J's decision might
b be wrong. On the contrary, the Privy Council appear to have gone out of their way to
distinguish *Peatfield's* case from the present case on the ground that in *Peatfield's* case both
parties had at the hearing been content to treat the charge as properly relating to a course
of conduct. No objection was taken at that stage. The manner in which the Privy Council
expressed its conclusion suggests to me that they were, so to speak, applying the proviso.
That the proviso to s 2(1) of the Criminal Appeal Act 1968 may be applied in criminal
c cases where a count is bad for duplicity on the ground that no miscarriage of justice has
actually occurred appears clearly from *R v Thompson* [1914] 2 KB 99.
So I do not think counsel for the GMC can get much assistance from *Peatfield's* case.
But, equally, I do not think that counsel for the applicant can get much assistance either.
The fact that Mann J's decision was not overruled or even criticised does not help him.
For the Privy Council may have anticipated that his decision would be the subject of an
d appeal to this court.
I accept the submission of counsel for the GMC that domestic tribunals should not be
hedged around with unnecessary legal technicalities. I accept his submission that the
procedure on inquiries into professional misconduct by the GMC is not exactly analogous
to the procedure on indictment, and that the rule against duplicity cannot be exactly
applied. But the reasons underlying the rule are the same for both cases. Those reasons
e are that to charge what are essentially two separate offences in the same count is both
confusing and unfair. The rule against duplicity, despite its name, is not a legal
technicality. It is a rule of common law grounded in elementary justice. Experience has
shown that it is a rule which is not always easy to apply. It may be that it will be even
more difficult to apply in cases before the professional conduct committee, as in cases
before other committees with a disciplinary jurisdiction, such as the professional conduct
f committee of the Bar Council. But that is no reason why the attempt should not be
made. So I would reject the submission of counsel for the GMC that the rule against
duplicity does not apply at all in proceedings before the professional conduct committee
of the GMC. In my judgment, it does.
Then does the rule apply here? One of the difficulties in applying the rule is that, like
many other rules, it involves drawing a line. It depends on a question of fact and degree.
g So when the subject matter of the inquiry is a doctor's course of conduct, it will be
necessary to decide whether the inquiry in truth demands an investigation into separate
instances. In the present case, where the eight patients are all particularised, and where
some of the allegations relate to some of the patients and not others, I am left in no doubt
that the misconduct alleged in relation to each of the patients should have been the
h subject of a separate charge. There would have been no difficulty in adopting that course.
It would not have added one minute to the length of the inquiry. If necessary, the
inquiry could have been limited to fewer patients; it could have been made clear that the
charges were in the nature of specimen or sample charges. To charge what are essentially
distinct offences in the same charge, even though they form part of what may be regarded
as a course of conduct, can only, in my judgment, lead to confusion and unfairness. For
j the reasons which I have mentioned, and for the reasons mentioned by Mann J, with
which I fully agree, I regard that as being the position here. I would answer the second
question in the same way as he did.
The third question is closely related to the second, and I can deal with it quite shortly.
The rules provide for a preliminary investigation by the preliminary proceedings
committee, corresponding roughly, but only roughly, to proceedings before examining

magistrates. If the preliminary proceedings committee is satisfied that there is a question
to be investigated, they can refer the matter for inquiry to the professional conduct
committee. At the time of the reference in this case, the allegations related to four
patients only. If I am right in my answer to the second question, those allegations should
have been made the subject of four separate charges in the notice of inquiry. Subsequently,
the GMC obtained evidence from four more patients. It follows from what I have said
that those allegations should also have been made the subject of separate charges. The
question is whether that could be done without a further preliminary investigation by
the preliminary proceedings committee.

Counsel for the GMC submits that it could. He refers to the language of r 11(1), which
provides:

> 'Where a case has been referred to the Preliminary Proceedings Committee ...
> that Committee shall consider the case and ... determine:—(a) that the case be
> referred to the Professional Conduct Committee for inquiry ...'

Rule 17 is couched in similar language. Although 'case relating to conviction' and 'case
relating to conduct' is defined in r 2, the word 'case' itself is not defined. Counsel for the
GMC argues that it means the case as a whole. He accepted that, where the fresh
complaint relates to a completely different subject matter, as in his example of a doctor
charged with misprescription, who is then alleged to be guilty of indecent assault, the
fresh complaint must first be investigated by the preliminary proceedings committee.
But he submitted that, where the fresh complaint is sufficiently similar to an existing
charge, then a fresh charge can be added at any stage without going back to the
preliminary proceedings committee.

I cannot accept the argument of counsel for the GMC. Mann J was, in my judgment,
correct in saying that the purpose of proceedings before the preliminary proceedings
committee, as in proceedings before examining magistrates, is to act as a filter. It is an
essential safeguard to ensure that a doctor is not harrassed by groundless complaints.
That safeguard is equally important whether one is considering the original allegation or
a fresh allegation which might or might not give rise to a new charge.

Counsel for the GMC submitted that in a case such as the present, where there were
already four charges properly referred to the professional conduct committee, an
investigation by the preliminary proceedings committee of four more allegations which
are so similar to the existing allegations would be a pure formality. I sincerely hope that
that would not be so. But, even if it were so, that is no reason why the rules should not
be obeyed.

Counsel for the GMC further argued that it would be an intolerable burden if every
piece of fresh evidence had to be considered by the preliminary proceedings committee
before being put before the professional conduct committee. But that misses the point.
Relevant fresh evidence would always be admissible in support of an existing charge. It
is only where it gives rise to what should be a *new* charge that it should be considered
first by the preliminary proceedings committee.

There was some discussion of r 22(1) which empowers the president to give such
directions as he may think necessary for the amendment of a charge. But, as I read the
rule, it does not authorise the addition of a new charge. Thus, in the present case, the
power could have been exercised so as to split the original charge into four separate
charges covering the original four complainants. But it cannot be used to add four
further charges.

The third and last point relates to particulars. Counsel for the GMC did not suggest
that any question of principle was involved here. In those circumstances, I would be
content to say that there is no ground on which we could interfere with the judge's
discretion. But, out of deference to the argument of counsel for the GMC, I will assume
that we are approaching the matter afresh. I will take only one of the outstanding

requests by way of illustration. On 29 May 1985 the applicant asked for particulars of
a para (a) of the charge in the following terms:

> 'The purported Charge alleges that [the applicant] prescribed the drugs ...
> "without first adequately examining the patients..." The following points arise:—
> (i) In relation to each individual patient what examination should have been carried
> out (which was allegedly not carried out) and the reason(s) for such examination
> setting out the particular medical grounds and the particular facts relied upon; (ii)
> b In relation to the alleged insufficient examination of each patient, whether it is
> alleged that such examination was negligent or alternatively whether it is alleged
> that the conduct was worse than negligent and if so precisely what is alleged and on
> what grounds.'

The answer came back that it was not appropriate to answer the request.
c   It was, I think, accepted by counsel for the GMC that the applicant would have been
entitled to these particulars in a medical negligence action. But it was said that he is not
entitled to the particulars in proceedings before the professional conduct committee
because it is for the committee to set the standards, and because the committee is vested
with a very wide discretion vested in the committee.
        I do not accept that suggestion for one moment. The consequences of a finding that
d the applicant is guilty of serious professional misconduct are of the utmost importance
to the applicant. The applicant is entitled to know in advance what is the standard against
which he is to be judged. Like the judge, I can see no reason at all why the particulars
should not be given. The same applies to the other particulars, which have been requested
and not supplied. I would answer the third question in the same way as the judge, and
dismiss the appeal.
e

NICHOLLS LJ.

Duplicity
        This appeal raises the question of what factual allegations may properly be included in
a single charge of serious professional misconduct against a registered medical practitioner.
f I approach this question on the premise, accepted by Mann J and which I also accept,
that, as a rule of elementary fairness, the rule of the criminal law that a charge should not
be duplicitous should apply by analogy to a charge before the professional conduct
committee of the General Medical Council (the GMC).
        Whether a charge as formulated breaches the rule necessitates consideration of the
relevant offence or offences and the terms of the particular charge. In the present case,
g and leaving aside as irrelevant for present purposes conviction of a criminal offence, there
is only one relevant offence, under s 36(1) of the Medical Act 1983: 'serious professional
misconduct'. The nature of this offence is apparent from its name. Its essential factual
ingredients are not further defined or identified in the statute. In my view, this makes it
particularly important, when considering the factual allegations that can properly be
included in a single charge, to keep in mind what is meant by a single charge in the
h context of these disciplinary proceedings and, also, the consequence of including several
factual allegations in a single charge or, conversely, of requiring them to be separated
into separate charges. Rule 17(1) of the 1980 rules provides that the solicitor shall send to
the practitioner a notice of inquiry which is to specify 'in the form of a charge or charges'
the matters into which the inquiry is to be held. Rule 17(3) provides that the notice of
inquiry shall be in the form set out in Sch 2 to the rules, with such variations as
j circumstances may require. The material part of the prescribed form reads:

> 'Dear Sir/Madam,
>   On behalf of the General Medical Council notice is hereby given to you that in
> consequence of [a complaint made against you to the Council] or [information

received by the Council] an inquiry is to be held into the following charge [charges]
against you:—

a

(If the charge relates to conviction) That you were on the . . . . day of
. . . . at (specify court recording the conviction) convicted of (set out
particulars of the conviction in sufficient detail to identify the case).

OR

(If the charge relates to conduct) That, being registered under the Medical Acts, *b*
you (set out briefly the facts alleged): and that in relation to the facts alleged you
have been guilty of serious professional misconduct.

(Where there is more than one charge, the charges are to be numbered
consecutively, charges relating to conviction being set out before charges relating
to conduct.)

c

Notice is further given to you that on [day of the week] the . . . . day of
. . . . 19. ., a meeting of the Professional Conduct Committee will be held
at . . . ., at . . . . a.m./p.m. to consider the above-mentioned charge [charges]
against you, and to determine whether or not they should direct the Registrar to
erase your name from the Register or to suspend your registration therein, or to
impose conditions on your registration pursuant to section 7 of the Medical Act *d*
1978.

You are hereby invited to appear before the Committee at the place and
time specified above, for the purpose of answering the above-mentioned charge
[charges] . . .'

Thus, as might be expected, although there is only one offence relating to conduct, the *e*
prescribed form of notice of inquiry envisages (as, indeed, do other provisions in the
1980 rules) that a single notice may include more than one charge relating to conduct.

Further, in much the same way as a charge in an indictment contains a statement of
the offence and particulars of the offence, so the prescribed form provides that, if the
charge relates to conduct, the charge shall contain a statement of the offence ('you have
been guilty of serious professional misconduct') and brief particulars of the facts alleged, *f*
the only difference from an indictment being that the statement of the offence follows
rather than precedes the statement of the alleged facts.

As I understand these provisions, a charge relating to conduct remains a single charge
even if the facts alleged are numerous, and even if, for convenience, they appear in
separate, numbered paragraphs. A charge to the effect that 'being registered under the
Medical Acts you failed to visit X on Christmas Day 1985 when requested and when the *g*
patient's condition so required, and that in relation to the facts alleged you have been
guilty of serious professional misconduct' is a single charge, and it would remain so even
if the words 'and also on New Year's Day 1986' were added after the words 'Christmas
Day 1985'. It would also remain a single charge if the alleged failure to visit was in
respect of (1) patient X on one or more dates, (2) patient Y on one or more dates, and (3) *h*
patient Z on yet other dates. Whether a single charge can properly be so framed is what
is in issue on this appeal.

For there to be more than one charge, on the other hand, there must be separate
allegations of the offence and of the facts alleged. Thus, an example of notice of more
than one charge relating to conduct would be to the following effect: '1. That being
registered under the Medical Acts you failed to visit X on Christmas Day 1985 when *j*
requested and when the patient's condition so required, and that in relation to the facts
alleged you have been guilty of serious professional misconduct. 2. That being registered
under the Medical Acts you failed to visit Y on Boxing Day 1985 when requested and
when the patient's condition so required, and that in relation to the facts alleged you
have been guilty of serious professional misconduct.'

I have set out the above at some length and at the risk of being thought to labour the
a obvious, because a clear appreciation of what is meant by a single charge or a separate
charge in the context of the present disciplinary proceedings is, to my mind, helpful
when considering what properly can be made the subject of a single charge, for this
reason. In deciding whether serious professional misconduct has been established, the
professional conduct committee must, where there is more than one charge, consider the
facts proved in relation to each charge separately. If the facts alleged and proved in
b relation to one charge are not sufficiently serious to warrant a finding of serious
professional misconduct, the practitioner is entitled to a finding of not guilty of such
misconduct in respect of the matters to which that charge relates, regardless of what
other charges there may be or of what facts are proved in respect of any other charge: see
r 30(2). There can be no question of aggregating the facts proved in relation to one charge
with the facts proved in relation to another charge and making a finding of serious
c professional misconduct under either or both charges if, considered separately, the facts
proved in relation to each charge would not justify such a finding.

With that introduction I turn to the issue raised by the present appeal. Whether a
number of wholly unrelated incidents involving the same type or different types of
misconduct can properly be made the subject of a single charge in all circumstances does
not arise for determination in this case, because on this appeal the submission for the
d GMC was that, properly construed, the charge laid is one alleging a course of conduct. If
for my part, I am unable to see any reason in principle why a charge cannot so be laid. If
the misconduct alleged is a practice said to have been followed by the practitioner in the
conduct of his professional work, which is what I understand is meant by the phrase 'a
course of conduct', I do not see why the charge should not be so formulated, as a single
charge, even though a properly particularised statement of the practice may involve
e identifying several different patients and several different occasions.

Counsel for the applicant, at any rate at one stage during his submissions, was not
disposed to quarrel with this, but he submitted that a single charge of a course of conduct
was not permissible if the allegations therein in relation to each individual patient would
be capable of amounting to serious professional misconduct in each instance. I feel unable
to accept this as a rigid limitation on what may properly be made the subject of a single
f 'course of conduct' charge. If the particular incidents alleged can fairly and reasonably be
regarded as showing that, in the conduct of his practice, the practitioner has adopted a
course of conduct in relation, for example, to the treatment of obesity, I am unable to see
any reason in principle why the GMC's ability to formulate a charge in respect of that
course of conduct should depend on the seriousness or triviality of the incidents regarded
as separate incidents.
g Moreover, I suspect there may well be cases where it will be unclear whether each
alleged instance, taken alone, does or does not amount to serious professional misconduct.
Take the present appeal. The case of counsel for the applicant is that the complaint in
respect of each patient should be made the subject of a separate charge. If this were done,
it would mean that, when considering under r 30(2) whether the facts proved amounted
to serious professional misconduct, the facts proved in relation to each patient would
h have to be viewed in isolation. I can see no good reason why the professional conduct
committee should be put into such an artificial position. If (and I stress if, because no
inquiry has yet taken place and the applicant may be wholly innocent of all the matters
of which he is charged) all the charged facts were proved against the applicant, I do not
consider it would be unfair for the committee to be able to have regard to all those facts
j when considering and determining whether the applicant has been guilty of serious
professional misconduct or, hence, for all those charged facts to be included in a single
charge.

I confess that on this point I am acutely conscious that others have much greater
experience in the field of criminal law and practice. But, for my part, I derive comfort
from the decision of the Privy Council in *Peatfield v General Medical Council* [1987] 1 All

ER 1197, [1986] 1 WLR 243. In every material respect the charge there was on all fours
with the charge in the instant case. After consideration of the decision of Mann J in the   *a*
present case, and after having the benefit of hearing submissions for the practitioner
from the same leading counsel (Mr Beloff) as appeared for the applicant before Mann J
and before this court, their Lordships' view was stated in this way by Lord Mackay
([1987] 1 All ER 1197 at 1201, [1986] 1 WLR 243 at 248):

> 'Their Lordships take the view that, in the present case, the charge can be fairly   *b*
> read as alleging a course of conduct by the appellant in the conduct of his practice
> over the period stated in which patients were treated with the drugs specified in the
> three circumstances referred to under heads (a), (b) and (c) and that it was this course
> of conduct which amounted to serious professional misconduct.'

In that case there was the further fact that both parties before the professional conduct
committee had treated the charge as a complaint with regard to a course of conduct, and   *c*
it was in that circumstance their Lordships did not consider that the duplicity point
taken by itself was a good reason for allowing the appeal. But, and this is the importance
of *Peatfield*'s case for the present purpose, nowhere in the judgment of Lord Mackay is
there any suggestion that, read and treated as a single charge of a course of conduct, the
charge was not a proper form of charge either generally or in that particular case, even
though (as I have said) in that case the nature of the charged facts was in all material   *d*
respects the same as in the present case.

So I turn to consider whether, properly construed, the charge in the present case is one
alleging a 'course of conduct' rather than one alleging a number of unrelated incidents in
regard to eight patients. It has to be said that the charge is not happily drafted. As in
Peatfield's case, the use of the word 'individual' is inappropriate to a course of conduct
allegation. Particulars were supplied in this case, initially of four patients, and   *e*
subsequently of a further four, but I do not think service of these particulars really assists
one way or the other. If the conduct complained of is disputed, as in the present case, the
practitioner must be entitled to particulars of the patients on whose treatment the charge
is founded, whether or not the charge is of a course of conduct. Again, it can be said that,
if the allegation is of a course of conduct, it has taken the GMC a long time to make its   *f*
case clear in one important respect, for it was not until further particulars were produced
during the hearing before Mann J that it became clear that the complaint regarding the
supply of drugs mentioned in the charge was confined to a complaint of the supply of
those drugs 'when the conditions in charges [sic] (a)–(d) obtain'.

In the end, however, as in *Peatfield*'s case, so in the present case, this charge can fairly
be read as alleging a course of conduct adopted by the practitioner in the course of his   *g*
practice. The substance of what is being said is that, over a period of about 13 months at
his practice premises, the applicant supplied dexamphetamine sulphate and thyroid
extract to patients repeatedly, and over extensive periods, (a) without first adequately
examining them or seeking adequate information as to their medical histories, (b)
without first consulting their general practitioners or notifying them after the start of
treatment of the drugs or dosages, (c) without making adequate inquiries about the effect   *h*
of the treatment on the patients' health, and (d) without offering appropriate advice
when patients reported the harmful effects of the drugs. Heads (a) and (b) apply in the
case of all eight patients, head (c) in the case of seven of the eight, and head (d) in the case
of five of the eight. Furthermore, the GMC has made it plain that the complaint is one
of a course of conduct (and, as I understand it, is prepared to amend the charge by
deleting the word 'individual' if its presence gives rise to any embarrassment). In those   *j*
circumstances, I do not think that the court would be justified in making an order whose
effect would be to require the present charge to be abandoned, and in place eight separate
charges formulated, with the consequence spelled out above.

Nor, I add, if the charged facts may properly be made the subject of a single charge, as
in my view they may, can I see any justification for the court making an order whose

only effect would be to require the present formulation of the charge, as now
a particularised, to be abandoned and a new, and no doubt improved, formulation of a
single charge to be produced, the substance of which, however, would remain the same
as the present formulation. I am unable to see what useful purpose would be served by
that course in this case, either in the interests of the applicant or otherwise. Admittedly,
the piecemeal manner in which particulars have been forthcoming (and there are still
more to come) has made the task of identifying the factual issues more difficult, but both
b parties have the benefit of experienced legal advisers and I see no reason to doubt that the
inquiry can be conducted properly and fairly.

In passing I mention, because this was canvassed before us, that one matter on which
the committee will need to exercise particular care is the manner in which the chairman
announces the determination or finding of the committee under r 30(3). If, in the event,
some but not all the facts alleged in the charge should be proved to the satisfaction of the
c committee, I consider that fairness to the applicant will require that the announcement
in this case should be in terms that make plain which facts have been proved and which
have not.

Vires
I turn to the question of vires. Where the charge is one of a course of conduct I can see
d nothing in the 1980 rules which expressly or by implication precludes the charge being
amended, by additions being made to the charged facts, where the additional facts do not
widen or alter the substance of the allegation. Indeed, r 22 expressly empowers the
president to give directions for the amendment of a charge unless that cannot be done
without injustice.

In the present case, the additional facts do not widen or alter the substance of the
e course of conduct alleged. Adding to the charged facts particulars of the four 'group B'
patients, as they have been called, left the substance of the allegation unaltered.

For these reasons, for my part, I would allow the appeal so far as it relates to the
duplicity and vires points.

f *Further particulars*
With regard to the third issue (further particulars), I agree entirely with Mann J's views
set out in his judgment regarding the particulars sought under paras 5 to 10 of the
schedule accompanying the letter of the applicant's solicitors of 29 May 1985.

DILLON LJ. The main question on this appeal, on which Lloyd and Nicholls LJJ have
g differed, is whether the disciplinary proceedings against the applicant, Dr Gee, can
proceed before the professional conduct committee on the charge as at present formulated,
or whether that charge is bad for duplicity. As hereafter appears, I find this an artificial
question with little relation to reality.

The main reason, as I understand the law, why a duplicitous charge is not allowed in a
criminal case is that the jury can, in general, only give a simple verdict of guilty or not
h guilty on each charge in the indictment. They cannot state their findings of fact or bring
in a verdict of partly guilty. Consequently, if a charge is duplicitous and in truth
embraces several charges, the judge, when he comes to pass sentence, has no means of
knowing on which of those charges the jury have really convicted. All that, however, has
no application to a disciplinary hearing before the professional conduct committee.
There is no jury on such a hearing and the members of the committee who make the
j finding of fact, and are bound by the rules to state those findings, are the same persons as
will pass sentence if they have found serious professional misconduct proved.

Serious professional misconduct is (apart from conviction of a criminal offence which
is not in question in the present case and which I therefore ignore for the purposes of this
judgment) the only offence for which the General Medical Council (the GMC) can
discipline, or punish, a registered medical practitioner. This is under s 36 of the Medical

Act 1983. Under the relevant rules, the General Medical Council Preliminary Proceedings Committee and the Professional Conduct Committee (Procedure) Rules Order of Council 1980, SI 1980/858, as soon as may be after a case has been referred to the professional conduct committee for inquiry, the solicitor appointed by the GMC is to send to the practitioner a 'notice of inquiry' which is to be in the form set out in Sch 2 to the rules with such variations as circumstances may require and is to specify in the form of a charge or charges the matters into which the inquiry is to be held (see r 17). Plainly, there can be more than one charge, although there need not be and, on the prescribed form, there is at the end of the charge or charges to be an averment that, in relation to the facts alleged, the practitioner has been guilty of serious professional misconduct.

Under r 30, the committee is, on the conclusion of the first stage of the hearing of the case, to consider and determine as respects each charge which remains outstanding which, if any, of the facts alleged in the charge have been proved to their satisfaction. If the committee determine as respects any charge either that none of the facts alleged in the charge has been proved to their satisfaction or that such facts as have been proved would not support a finding of serious professional misconduct, the committee is to record a finding that the practitioner is not guilty of such misconduct in respect of the matters to which that charge relates. Then, under r 30(3), the chairman is to announce the determination or the finding of the committee.

Rule 31 then provides that, if under r 30 the committee have determined as respects any charge that the facts or some of the facts alleged in the charge have been proved to their satisfaction, and the committee have not on those facts recorded (under r 30) a finding of not guilty, there is to be opportunity for argument as to the extent to which such facts are indicative of serious professional misconduct, and for pleas and evidence in mitigation. The committee is then under r 33 to determine whether in relation to the facts proved they find the practitioner to have been guilty of serious professional misconduct.

It appears from the observations of Lord Griffiths in giving the judgment of the Privy Council in the recent case of *Datta v General Medical Council* (27 January 1986, unreported) that the professional conduct committee have felt some difficulty about how the chairman's announcement under r 30(3) ought to be expressed (see p 1219, ante). I have no doubt at all in the context of these rules that the chairman's duty must cover announcing the determination of the committee, as respects each outstanding charge, as to which, if any, of the facts alleged in the charge have been proved to their satisfaction. The facts alleged in the charge include, of course, the facts alleged in particulars of the charge subsequently given, in particular, in the applicant's case the names of the patients allegedly concerned in each of the sub-heads (a) to (d) of the charge. The chairman must say, concisely, no doubt, but clearly, which of the facts alleged in each charge, with reference to the names in the particulars, have been found proved.

Even if, therefore, the charge is technically duplicitous, the practitioner will be told which parts of the charge, or which charges within the charge, have been found proved.

The charge against the applicant as at present formulated is in a comprehensive form, embracing allegations in respect of eight patients in a single charge. It is very similar to the charge which was held proved against Dr Peatfield in the recent case, heard on appeal by the Privy Council, of *Peatfield v General Medical Council* [1987] 1 All ER 1197, [1986] 1 WLR 243. There are indications from other recent disciplinary cases that this type of comprehensive charge is currently much favoured by the GMC or its advisers.

In giving the judgment of the Privy Council in *Peatfield's* case Lord Mackay expressed the view of their Lordships that the charge could be fairly read as alleging a course of conduct by the doctor in the conduct of his practice over the period stated. It was this course of conduct, in which patients were treated with the drugs specified in the circumstances referred to under the sub-heads in the charge, which was held to amount to serious professional misconduct. In considering the doctor's appeal against the decision

of the professional conduct committee, the Privy Council found nothing in the form of
a the charge to warrant allowing the appeal, because, at the hearing before the committee,
both parties had treated the charge as a complaint with regard to a course of conduct and
the doctor in his own evidence had dealt with the matter very much from the point of
view of what his ordinary practice and manner of operation were.

Of course, it does not follow that the approach of the High Court or of this court in
considering before a hearing whether a case can proceed without reformulation of the
b charge, and the approach of the Privy Council in considering an appeal after a hearing,
should be the same. The value of *Peatfield's* case lies in their Lordships' understanding of
the nature of the charge. But this highlights, to my mind, the unreality of the question
we have to consider. The choice is between a single charge, as put forward by the GMC,
of a course of conduct in the respects set out in the sub-heads (a) to (d) in the charge,
which is intended to be proved by reference to the circumstances of eight individual
c patients and, on the other hand, eight separate charges, one in respect of each of the eight
named patients, as specimens from which a course of conduct in the respects set out in
the sub-heads (a) to (d) in the present charge is to be inferred. I cannot see that the
difference between these alternatives will have any meaning to a tribunal such as the
professional conduct committee which is composed of doctors and not of lawyers, and
d whichever alternative is adopted will, so far as I can see, make no difference at all to the
course and scope of the hearing by the committee of the applicant's case.

I can well see that, from the point of view of the GMC, a course of conduct on the part
of a doctor in prescribing drugs with potentially harmful side effects to patients without
examining the patients adequately or without warning of the side effects, or without
advising the patients' general practitioners of what had been prescribed, could more
easily be regarded as indicative of serious professional misconduct than a single instance.
e I see no reason why the GMC should not be entitled to lay a charge of a course of conduct.

It is undesirable that the proceedings of domestic tribunals should be hedged around
with unnecessary legal technicalities. The procedure for the hearing of a case by the
professional conduct committee under the rules which I have mentioned is very different
from the procedure at a criminal trial. For my part, I cannot see that the form of the
f charge against the applicant in the notice of inquiry, read with the particulars which
have been given and are to be given under the order of Mann J, is either confusing or
unfair. I see no prejudice to the applicant if the case against him proceeds on that charge.
A fortiori, if it be a relevant consideration, the president was not, in my judgment, acting
unreasonably in declining to amend the charge.

It follows that, in my judgment, the judge was not justified in his ruling that the
g charge as formulated was bad for duplicity. On this point, therefore, I would allow this
appeal.

If the charge stands as formulated, it is not necessary for there to be any further
reference to the preliminary proceedings committee. The case is the same case of a course
of conduct as when it was referred by the preliminary proceedings committee to the
professional conduct committee. The addition of the names of four further patients by
h way of additional particulars makes no difference. On this point also I would allow this
appeal.

But, on the question of the further particulars ordered by the judge, I see no basis for
interfering with the judge's decision and that order should stand. It is not enough to say,
as counsel for the GMC appeared at one time to suggest, that the standards of professional
conduct required of a registered medical practitioner depend on the collective wisdom
j and experience of the eminent members from time to time of the professional conduct
committee, and so cannot be anticipated or divulged.

*Appeal on issue of particulars dismissed. Appeal on the issues of duplicity and vires allowed. On
the undertaking of the GMC the GMC are released from their undertaking below. Applications*

for judicial review dismissed. GMC to have three-quarters of their costs in Court of Appeal and below. Leave to appeal to the House of Lords refused.

a

24 July. The Appeal Committee of the House of Lords gave leave to appeal.

Solicitors: *Waterhouse & Co* (for the GMC); *Beachcrofts* (for the applicant).

Mary Rose Plummer   Barrister. *b*

C and another v S and others

QUEEN'S BENCH DIVISION
HEILBRON J
17, 18, 20, 21, 23 FEBRUARY 1987

c

COURT OF APPEAL, CIVIL DIVISION
SIR JOHN DONALDSON MR, STEPHEN BROWN AND RUSSELL LJJ
23, 24, 25 FEBRUARY 1987

Abortion – Legal abortion – Power of father to prevent mother having abortion – Unmarried *d* *mother 18 to 21 weeks pregnant – Mother wishing to have abortion – Mother obtaining necessary medical certificates for legal abortion – Father applying for injunction to stop abortion – Father contending that fetus old enough to be 'capable of being born alive' – Whether abortion in such circumstances constituting an offence – Whether injunction preventing abortion should be granted – Infant Life (Preservation) Act 1929, s 1(1) – Abortion Act 1967, s 1.*

Abortion – Legal abortion – Power of father to prevent mother having abortion – Locus standi – *e* *Unmarried mother wishing to terminate pregnancy – Father applying for injunction restraining termination – Father applying as next friend of child en ventre sa mère – Whether father having locus standi to apply as next friend of child – Whether child en ventre sa mère having any right to be party to such proceedings.*

Court of Appeal – Judgment – Effect – Act done in reliance on judgment of Court of Appeal – *f* *Judgment given in circumstances of real emergency – Whether parties entitled to act in reliance on judgment without waiting to see if there will be appeal to House of Lords.*

The first defendant, a single woman who was between 18 and 21 weeks pregnant, wished to terminate the pregnancy. Two medical practitioners certified, in accordance with s 1(1)(a)[a] of the Abortion Act 1967, that the continuance of her pregnancy would involve *g* risk of injury to her physical or mental health greater than if the pregnancy were terminated. The father sought, on his own behalf and as next friend of the child en ventre sa mère, an injunction restraining the first defendant from undergoing the termination and restraining the second defendants, the area health authority, from performing the termination. By s 1(1)[b] of the Infant Life (Preservation) Act 1929 it was an offence for any person, with intent to destroy the life of a child capable of being born *h* alive, to cause it to die before it had an existence independent of its mother. The father contended that a fetus of between 18 and 21 weeks was 'capable of being born alive' because, if delivered, it would demonstrate real and discernible signs of life, namely a primitive circulation and movements of its limbs, and that consequently termination of such a pregnancy would constitute an offence under s 1(1) of the 1929 Act. He conceded that as father of the child he had no locus standi to make the application but contended *j* that he had a sufficient personal interest to do so because the proposed termination would be a crime concerning the life of his child. He further contended that the unborn child

---

a   Section 1(1), so far as material, is set out at p 1233 *h j*, post
b   Section 1(1), is set out at p 1242 *d e*, post

was a proper party to the proceedings since it was the subject of the threatened crime.
a The judge refused to grant an injunction, holding that the fetus had no right to be a
party and that the father had failed to establish that an offence under the 1929 Act would
be committed if the termination was carried out. The father appealed to the Court of
Appeal.

Held – Although a fetus of a gestational age of between 18 and 21 weeks could be said to
b demonstrate real and discernible signs of life, the medical evidence was that such a fetus
would be incapable of breathing either naturally or with the aid of a ventilator. It
followed therefore that such a fetus could not properly be described as being 'capable of
being born alive' within s 1(1) of the 1929 Act and accordingly the termination of a
pregnancy of that length would not constitute an offence under that Act. The appeal
would therefore be dismissed (see p 1242 *f* to *h* and p 1243 *j*, post).
c   Per Sir John Donaldson MR. The Court of Appeal is the final court of appeal in
circumstances of real urgency and litigants are entitled to act on its judgments in such
circumstances without waiting to see whether there will be an appeal to the House of
Lords (see p 1243 *c d*, post).
      Per Heilbron J. A fetus has no right of action until it is subsequently born alive and
therefore while it is unborn it cannot be a party to an action (see p 1234 *h j* and p 1235
d *c d*, post); dictum of Baker P in *Paton v Trustees of BPAS* [1978] 2 All ER at 990 followed.

Notes
For the medical termination of pregnancy, see 30 Halsbury's Laws (4th edn) para 44.
      For offences under the law relating to abortion, see 11 ibid paras 1176, 1191–1194.
      For the Infant Life (Preservation) Act 1929, s 1, see 12 Halsbury's Statutes (4th edn)
e 222.
      For the Abortion Act 1967, ss 1, 5, see ibid 414, 418.

Cases referred to in judgments
Dehler v Ottawa Civic Hospital (1979) 25 OR (2d) 748, Ont HC; *affd* (1980) 29 OR (2d)
f   677n, Ont CA.
Gouriet v Union of Post Office Workers [1977] 3 All ER 70, [1978] AC 435, [1977] 3 WLR
      300, HL.
Medhurst v Medhurst (1984) 46 OR (2d) 263, Ont HC.
Mullick v Mullick (1925) LR 52 Ind App 245.
Paton v Trustees of BPAS [1978] 2 All ER 987, [1979] QB 276, [1978] 3 WLR 687.
g *R v Enoch* (1833) 5 C & P 539, 172 ER 1089, NP.
R v Handley (1874) 13 Cox CC 79, NP.
R v Poulton (1832) 5 C & P 329, 172 ER 997, NP.
R v Wright (1841) 9 C & P 754, 173 ER 1039, NP.
Roe v Wade (1973) 410 US 113, US SC.
Thellusson v Woodford (1799) 4 Ves 227, 31 ER 117, LC; *affd* (1805) 11 Ves 112, [1803–
h   13] All ER Rep 30, 32 ER 1030, HL.

Cases also cited
Caller v Caller [1966] 2 All ER 754, [1968] P 39, DC.
Carruthers v Langley [1984] 5 WWR 538, BC SC.
Cayne v Global Natural Resources plc [1984] 1 All ER 225, CA.
j *Elliott v Joicey* [1935] AC 209, [1935] All ER Rep 578, HL.
George and Richard, The (1871) LR 3 A & E 466.
Gillick v West Norfolk and Wisbech Area Health Authority [1985] 3 All ER 402, [1986] AC
      112, CA and HL.
Island Records Ltd, Ex p [1978] 3 All ER 824, [1978] Ch 122, CA.
Jones v Smith (1973) 278 So 2d 339, Fla 4th DCA; *cert denied* (1974) 415 US 958.

Montreal Tramways Co v Leveille [1933] SCR 456, Can SC.
NWL Ltd v Woods [1979] 3 All ER 614, [1979] 1 WLR 1294, HL.
Pinchin NO v Santam Insurance Co Ltd 1963 (2) SA 254, WLD.
R v Brain (1834) 6 C & P 349, 172 ER 1272, NP.
R v Shephard [1919] 2 KB 125, [1918–19] All ER Rep 374, CA.
R v West (1848) 2 Car & Kir 784, 175 ER 329, NP.
Redland Bricks Ltd v Morris [1969] 2 All ER 576, [1970] AC 652, HL.
Royal College of Nursing of the UK v Dept of Health and Social Security [1981] 1 All ER 545, [1981] AC 800, QBD, CA and HL.
Scattergood v Edge (1699) 12 Mod Rep 278, 88 ER 1320.
Villar v Gilbey [1907] AC 139, [1904–7] All ER Rep 779, HL.

Application

The first plaintiff, Mr C, applied on his own behalf and on behalf of the second plaintiff, named as 'a child en ventre sa mère' as his father and next friend, for orders (i) restraining the first defendant, Miss S, from causing or permitting an abortion to be carried out on her or otherwise in any way physically harming or causing the death of the child en ventre sa mère and (ii) restraining the second defendants, the area health authority, by itself its servants or agents from causing or permitting, counselling or procuring Miss S to undergo an abortion or to suffer an act whereby the second plaintiff might be physically harmed. On an ex parte application for an injunction, Turner J refused the application. On appeal, the Court of Appeal directed that the matter be heard expeditiously inter partes. The application was heard in chambers but judgment was given by Heilbron J in open court. The facts are set out in the judgment.

Gerard Wright QC and *Tonya Pinsent* for Mr C.
Peter Sheridan QC and *Caroline Harry Thomas* for Miss S.
Allan Levy as amicus curiae.
The health authority were not represented.

HEILBRON J. The first defendant, Miss S, a single woman, 21 years of age and a university student, is approximately 18 weeks pregnant and wishes to have an abortion. She obtained a certificate signed by two doctors, as required by the terms of the Abortion Act 1967. The operation should have taken place on Monday, 23 February, that is to say today, at a hospital for which the health authority are responsible.

The first plaintiff, Mr C, a single man and a postgraduate student, is the father of the second plaintiff, who is named as 'a child en ventre sa mère' and sues by his father and next friend.

Mr C applies on his own behalf, and on behalf of the second plaintiff, for orders restraining Miss S from having an abortion and the area health authority, the second defendants, from causing or permitting, by itself or its servants or agents, the abortion to be performed. The second defendants have adopted a neutral position and have taken no part in the proceedings.

This matter first came before Turner J on an ex parte application by the plaintiffs for an injunction, which was refused, and on appeal the Court of Appeal directed that the matter be heard speedily. The hearing before this court began last Tuesday, as a matter or urgency, but, due to its anticipated length, the doctors agreed with some reluctance to a short postponement of the proposed termination, if it was to take place, until Thursday, 26 February at the latest.

There were a number of affidavits put before the court, one from Mr C, two from Miss S, one from her solicitor and several from three consultants, namely two from Mr Norris, two from Professor Newton and one from Professor Rivers. None has been personally involved in the factual events or with the parties.

The facts briefly are that Miss S and Mr C met in or about October 1985. Sexual

intercourse occurred for the first time and unexpectedly on 17 October 1986 when no
a precautions were taken and, as was discovered much later, conception had occurred.

Miss S visited her college doctor on 20 October to seek his advice and help to try and
avoid the possibility of a pregnancy, and he prescribed a pill for her to take for this
purpose. Subsequently bleeding occurred for two weeks, followed a month later by the
onset of a normal period. Not long after, she began to suffer from depression and her
doctor prescribed anti-depressants and referred her to a psychiatrist.

b Intercourse had continued intermittently and casually for a few weeks and precautions
were taken. The brief affair came to an end at the end of November. By that date, Miss S
was feeling very ill indeed with persistent depression, vomiting and nausea, and she
developed a chest infection, but she had no idea she was pregnant. She went to stay with
her parents in December but continued to feel very ill and her local doctor sent her for
chest X-rays. She was X-rayed twice, on one occasion unshielded.

c She went to see the college doctor again, after she missed a period in January, in order
to have a check-up. The doctor arranged for her to have a scan on 27 January, when her
pregnancy was revealed for the first time. She has now been informed by the doctor that
the unshielded X-ray could cause complications with her pregnancy, in that there might
be some damage to the fetus.

She saw the consultant the day following the discovery of her pregnancy and he
d discussed with her in detail all the circumstances of the pregnancy, the possible medical
complications concerned with its continuation, and explained that it would be appropriate
for her to have a termination if she wished and that she should return in a week.

During that week she told Mr C of her condition and they discussed the situation. She
denies telling him, as he asserts, that she was not contemplating an abortion; she told
him that she was considering the options.

e When she next saw the college doctor on 6 February she told him that she wanted a
termination, and on 9 February he signed the certificate of opinion, having seen her and
examined her on a number of occasions. This is the certificate required by the terms of
the Abortion Regulations 1968, SI 1968/390, before an abortion can be performed. She
saw a consultant at the hospital two days later, who also examined her, as he was required
f to do, and he signed the certificate. The ground was number 2 on the form, namely that
the continuance of the pregnancy would involve risk of injury to her physical or mental
health greater than if the pregnancy was terminated.

Miss S further stated in her affidavit that she believed her mental state was now
precarious and that these proceedings have caused her more anxiety and distress, and no
one has doubted that, except Mr C, for he asserted in his affidavit that she was healthy
and would suffer no risk to her health, either mental or physical. That was directly
g contrary to the views of two doctors. It is not suggested that Mr C is possessed of any
medical qualifications or that he has any medical knowledge as to Miss S's condition,
which, on the evidence before me, indicates that her health has been adversely affected
by a difficult and complicated pregnancy with all the attendant anxieties which she
mentions.

h The Abortion Act 1967 provides by s 1(1):

'... a person shall not be guilty of an offence under the law relating to abortion
when a pregnancy is terminated by a registered medical practitioner if two registered
medical practitioners are of the opinion, formed in good faith—(*a*) that the
continuance of the pregnancy would involve risk ... of injury to the physical or
mental health of the pregnant woman ... greater than if the pregnancy were
j terminated ...'

Section 5 provides:

'(1) Nothing in this Act shall affect the provisions of the Infant Life (Preservation)
Act 1929 (protecting the life of the viable foetus).

(2) For the purposes of the law relating to abortion, anything done with intent to procure the miscarriage of a woman is unlawfully done unless authorised by section 1 of this Act.'

By the Infant Life (Preservation) Act 1929, s 1(1) the offence of child destruction, for which the maximum penalty is imprisonment for life, occurs where—

'any person who, with intent to destroy the life of a child capable of being born alive, by any wilful act causes a child to die before it has an existence independent of its mother . . .'

By sub-s (2):

'For the purposes of this Act, evidence that a woman had at any material time been pregnant for a period of twenty-eight weeks or more shall be prima facie proof that she was at that time pregnant of a child capable of being born alive.'

The 1968 regulations, made under s 2 of the 1967 Act, set out the conditions relating to the certificate of opinion to be provided by two medical practitioners prior to commencement of the treatment for the termination of the pregnancy. There is, in those regulations, a restriction on disclosure of information other than to certain limited and specified persons. Neither the husband nor a father is within that group. Furthermore, there is no provision requiring or referring to consultation with or obtaining the consent of a husband, if any, or father. Neither is given any power of veto.

Miss S contends that the termination which she wishes to be performed is a lawful one, that neither the first nor the second plaintiff has the locus standi to maintain this suit, and she seeks dismissal of the applications.

Counsel's case on behalf of Mr C is that he has the locus standi to bring these proceedings, based on his personal interest, which he does not put as high as a legal right, and because the proposed termination encompasses, he submits, a threatened crime concerning the life of his child.

If it were to be decided that there was no such threat, he concedes that he has no standing qua father, for he does not contend that as a father he has any special rights. He concedes too that a husband has no special rights qua husband, and he accepts the correctness of the decision in *Paton v Trustees of BPAS* [1978] 2 All ER 987, [1979] QB 276 in that regard.

As to the position of the second plaintiff and his claim that the unborn child has the locus standi to make this application, counsel produced a wealth of authorities from far and wide, some of which he cited. His research and that of his junior was extensive, but it would serve no useful purpose, nor do I propose, to refer to most of them, for they did appear to be somewhat remote from the issue whether or not the unborn child could be a party to this motion. Counsel indeed referred me to *Mullick v Mullick* (1925) LR 52 Ind App 245, a Privy Council case relating to the right of an Indian idol to participate in legal proceedings. The facts of that case were so exceptional and so far removed from anything I have to decide as to be of little assistance.

The authorities, it seems to me, show that a child, after it has been born, and only then in certain circumstances based on his or her having a legal right, may be a party to an action brought with regard to such matters as the right to take, on a will or intestacy, or for damages for injuries suffered before birth. In other words, the claim crystallises on the birth, at which date, but not before, the child attains the status of a legal persona, and thereupon can then exercise that legal right.

This also appears to be the law in a number of Commonwealth countries. In *Medhurst v Medhurst* (1984) 46 OR (2d) 263 Reid J held in the Ontario High Court that an unborn child was not a person and that any rights accorded to the fetus are held contingent on a legal personality being acquired by the fetus on its subsequent birth alive. Nor could its father, the husband in that case, act as the fetus's next friend.

A similar decision was taken in *Dehler v Ottawa Civic Hospital* (1979) 25 OR (2d) 748,
a quoted with approval by Reid J, and affirmed by the Ontario Court of Appeal (see (1980)
29 OR (2d) 677n).

In *Paton v BPAS Trustees* [1978] 2 All ER 987 at 990, [1979] QB 276 at 279 Baker P, in
a case where a husband sought, and was refused, an injunction to prevent his wife
obtaining an abortion, said:

b   '... there can be no doubt, in my view, that in England and Wales, the foetus has
no right of action, no right at all, until birth. The succession cases have been
mentioned. There is no difference. From conception the child may have succession
rights by what has been called a "fictional construction" but the child must be
subsequently born alive.'

I agree entirely.
c   In his reply, counsel's final position was summarised in this way: (1) he no longer
relied on the numerous succession cases but he wished to retain some reliance on the
position of the unborn child in *Thellusson v Woodford* (1799) 4 Ves 227, 31 ER 117; (2) he
did not claim that a child had either a right to be born or a right to life in view of the
terms of the 1967 Act; but (3) he maintained that the unborn child had a right to be a
party because it was the subject of a threatened crime, that is to say that of child
d destruction. If there was no such threat, then this claim too failed.

In my judgment, there is no basis for the claim that the fetus can be a party, whether
or not there is any foundation for the contention with regard to the alleged threatened
crime, and I would dismiss the second plaintiff from this suit and the first plaintiff in his
capacity as next friend.

The question of the plaintiff's locus standi both as husband and father was also
e considered in *Paton's* case by Baker P, who decided that, since an unborn child had no
rights of its own and since a father had no rights at common law over his illegitimate
child, the plaintiff's right to apply for an injunction had to be made on the basis that he
had the status of a husband and had rights of consultation and consent under the 1967
Act. But the judge pointed out that that Act gives the husband no such rights and, in his
view, therefore, the husband had no legal right, enforceable at law or in equity (a
f necessary basis for issuing the injunction) to stop his wife having the abortion or to stop
the doctors from carrying it out.

Counsel for Mr C does not seek to argue the contrary; but he submits that the instant
case is distinguishable, because no suggestion was made in *Paton's* case, as here, that there
is a potential criminal abortion and that, if it is carried out, the doctor would be
contravening the provisions of s 1 of the 1929 Act and would be guilty, because he would
g be aborting a fetus of 18 weeks. Indeed, he further submitted that any doctor who since
1967 had aborted, or who proposed to abort, a fetus of that duration must be found
guilty of the offence.

Counsel did not resile from the implications of that assertion, relying for it on the
terms of the 1929 Act and the statements of Mr Norris in his affidavits, particularly in
h that which stated that 'an unborn child of eighteen weeks gestation were it to be delivered
by hysterotomy *would be* live born' (my emphasis).

The affidavits are important. They indicate very clearly the wide difference in thinking
and interpretation between medical men, all of high reputation and great experience, in
regard to the language used in the 1929 Act. I will now read the affidavits, so as to
incorporate their explanation of certain phrases and terms into this judgment. I begin,
j because it was the first, with that of Mr Norris, emeritus consultant gynaecologist at St
Peter's Hospital, Chertsey. He stated in para 2 of his first affidavit that 'an unborn child
of eighteen weeks gestation were it to be delivered by hysterotomy would be live born'.
He then went on to refer to a definition of this expression or condition by the World
Health Assembly under art 23 of the Constitution of the World Health Organisation in
1976 (subsequent to both the Acts in this matter) as being—

'the complete expulsion or extraction from its Mother of a product of conception irrespective of the duration of pregnancy, which after such separation breathes or [and I emphasise the 'or' in his affidavit] shows any other evidence of life such as beating of the heart, pulsation of the umbilical cord or definite movement of voluntary muscle whether or not the umbilical cord has been cut or the placenta is attached'.

To that affidavit Professor John Richard Newton replied. He did so, in his first affirmation, on 16 February. He said:

'I am the Layson Tait Professor of Obstetrics and Gynaecology and Head of Department at the Birmingham University Medical School Queen Elizabeth Hospital Edgbaston Birmingham. I have been a Gynaecologist for twenty years and held my present position since 1979.'

He had been shown a copy of Mr Norris's affidavit and asked to comment on it and in regard to para 2 he said:

'I believe it confusing in the circumstances to use the words "live born" for a foetus of 18 weeks gestation. As Mr. Norris says the term has been defined by Article 23 of the World Health Assembly in 1976. There is now produced . . . a copy of a report known as "Report on Foetal Viability and Clinical Practice" which was prepared in August 1985 by a representative committee on behalf of the Royal College of Obstetricians and Gynaecologists, the British Paediatric Association, Royal College of General Practitioners, Royal College of Midwives, British Medical Association and the Department of Health and Social Security . . . I refer in particular to the twelfth page of that report in which reference is made to the recommendation of the World Health Organisation concerning perinatal statistics. The committee to which I have referred above was charged with the task of considering foetal viability and comparison is made between the World Health Organisation definition and the concept of foetal viability. As will be seen from the report the purpose behind the World Health Organisation definition was to standardise the perinatal statistics for member countries of births. The purpose behind the definition was specifically not to define independent foetal viability and the committee go on to consider that concept and I believe that to be the important concept in these circumstances. Foetal viability means that the foetus is capable of independent human existence separate from the mother.'

He then refers to the contents of this report of the various prestigious colleges and associations of doctors and says:

'It will be seen that in the survey of 29 neo-natal intensive care units in the United Kingdom during 1982 no foetus of less than 23 weeks survived after delivery. It is my conclusion therefore that a foetus of anything below 23 weeks cannot survive independent of its mother and has therefore no viability.'

A few days later Mr Norris swore a second affidavit, in order to amplify the first. He then suggested that the period of gestation was 2, or possibly 3, weeks more than the 18 weeks which had been mentioned. He went on to explain the expression 'live born' which had been used in his first affidavit:

'4 . . . In case there is any ambiguity I wish to assert that in so stating I mean that in my opinion any foetus of eighteen weeks or longer gestation is capable of being born alive and that by "alive" I mean showing real and discernible signs of life within the meaning of the World Health Organisation definition set out in my original Affidavit and of the Births and Deaths Registration Act 1926 current when the Infant life (Preservation) Act 1929 was passed and also of the Births and Deaths Registration Act 1953 now current. Under the provisions of both these statutes such a child shall be registered as a live birth.'

5. A child of eighteen or even twenty-one weeks gestational age although capable
a of being born alive and capable of surviving for some time outside the womb is not
generally regarded by the medical profession as being viable because present
paediatric skills are insufficient to assist it to remain alive for more than a limited
time.'

On the same day, 19 February, Professor Newton, having read the second affidavit of Mr
b Norris, stated in a further affidavit:

'1 . . . Although he uses the expression "live born" in [his first] affidavit he does
not mention, nor did I understand that he was specifically referring to the words
actually appearing in an Act of Parliament namely the words "born alive" in Section
1 Infant Life (Preservation) Act 1929. This has now been drawn to my attention and
I give my comments.
c 2. The expression "born alive" used in the Infant Life (Preservation) Act 1929
raises difficulties before the expiration of 28 weeks of gestation.
3. Although it is difficult to generalise, for reasons which I will refer to in
paragraph 4 after 8 weeks of gestation some fetuses will exhibit some primitive fetal
movement, have a primitive heart tube which contracts and the circulation has
started to develop but these fetuses will be quite incapable of life separate from the
d mother.
4. Each individual fetus in each individual mother develops differently and at
different rates . . .'

He then refers to the difficulty of the medical assessment of the gestational period in any
particular case, which must be approximate and which may be complicated, as indeed in
e this case, by irregular menstruation. However, there are some firm generalisations on
development which could be made:

'In a fetus of 18–21 weeks gestation the cardiac muscle is contracting and a
primitive circulation is developing, but in my opinion lung development does not
occur until after 24 weeks gestation; before this time the major air passages have
been formed and there is gradual development of the bronchioles but these
f terminate in a blind sac incapable of gas exchange prior to 24 weeks.'

He says that a fetus of 18 to 21 weeks gestation could be delivered by hysterotomy but
that would not be routinely used on such a fetus, and he describes the type of operation:

'Once placental separation occurs whether the delivery has been by hysterotomy
or vaginally it will not be able to respirate . . . What constitutes "born alive" is
g controversial among the medical profession and often turns not only on medical
knowledge but on the moral views of the person giving his opinion. I would
mention that the development of each particular fetus in each particular mother is
an individual process, the progress of which [at] any stage before 28 weeks can best
be ascertained by an examination of the particular mother in question or at the very
h least detailed knowledge of that individual person.'

With that I must entirely agree, and counsel for Mr C conceded that that must be so. It is
an important aspect of this case, to which I will later refer. Professor Newton continued:

'Whether or not a fetus up to 24 weeks of gestation is delivered by hysterotomy
or vaginal delivery it will not be capable of surviving once the placental separation
j occurs. Up to 24 weeks in my opinion the lungs are incapable of sustaining life
because they are not adequately developed. The development of other organs within
the fetus is at an equally primitive stage incapable of sustaining life. I do not consider
the indicia referred to in paragraph 3 hereof to equate with being "alive". I equate
"alive" with being able to sustain a separate independent existence and in my
opinion this a fetus is clearly not capable of being able to do until after 24 weeks of
gestation.'

Finally, I draw attention to the affidavit of Professor Rivers FRCP, a reader in paediatrics at St Mary's Hospital Medical School since 1978 and having a special interest in new-born intensive care. He stated:

> '2. Although a foetus of 18/21 weeks gestation displays some signs of life in the womb in my opinion such foetuses are unable to perform the function of lung respiration without which they cannot live separate from their mothers once the umbilical cord is clamped and/or the placenta is removed. Obviously therefore a foetus of such gestation cannot even be mechanically ventilated since the lungs are not sufficiently developed for lung inflation and gas exchange to occur.
>
> 3. Whether such a foetus is "born" before the umbilical cord is clamped and or the placenta is removed or whether it is to be considered "alive" after this has happened are matters which cause difficulty and controversy to such an extent that, for example, the medical profession prefer to use the words "viable" foetus rather than the very difficult expression "born alive".'

Counsel for Mr C submitted that 'being born alive' is a much more restrictive concept than viability, for that embraces not only being born alive but surviving, for however short a time, thereafter, that the 1929 Act is unconcerned with viability, but that there is no ambiguity in the words used and they cannot be extended to cover the other concept. Therefore, if a doctor aborts an 18-week fetus, counsel argued, he is inevitably doing so on one capable of being born alive, regardless of the fact, which he accepted, that not all fetuses are either identical or in the same condition in different mothers, even though of the same period of gestation. If Mr Norris's view is correct, he continued, 'all fetuses' must necessarily include the one in this case.

Abortion itself is a very controversial subject. It has been; it still is. Many people feel genuinely and sincerely for and against its operation. It involves sociological, moral and profound religious aspects which arouse anxieties. Parliament itself has been much exercised over this subject for many years. None of these matters concern or affect my considerations or my ultimate decision. The court endeavours, to the best of its ability, to interpret the law and, as Baker P said in *Paton v Trustees of BPAS* [1978] 2 All ER 987 at 989, [1979] 1 QB 276 at 278: 'My task is to apply the law free of emotion or predilection'.

Since the enactment of the 1929 Act there have undoubtedly been rapid, extensive and truly remarkable developments in medical science, not least in the field of obstetrics. Some matters have become much clearer, some have remained obscure and difficult to determine; so it is perhaps understandable that the questions when life begins, when a fetus is capable of being born alive and when a child is actually alive are all problems of complexity for even the greatest medical minds. The determination of when life ends is now also a matter of concern and dispute.

Having said that, this case, I remind myself, concerns to some extent the meaning of the phrase 'capable of being born alive'. Unless Mr Norris' unequivocal assertion that *all* fetuses of 18 weeks' gestation *are* capable of being born alive is taken at face value as credible, then in reality and in the hospital where the decisions are taken it is the doctor (one of a team and probably one not yet designated) who has to make his decision on that problem in respect of Miss S's unborn child. We do not know on what basis he will make his prognosis, for that is what is entailed, or indeed, if by now he has been nominated, whether he has made the decision and on what criteria.

That the phrase *is* ambiguous would seem to follow from the differing points of view as disclosed in the affidavits and the exhibits.

In the nineteenth century, on charges of murder of a very young infant who died or was killed before or not long after separation from its mother at birth, I found some, perhaps a little, assistance, for the judge, after hearing medical evidence, sometimes in agreement but often in conflict, would direct the jury on the meaning of 'born alive', not, be it noted, 'born alive and surviving', which was a necessary pre-condition for a conviction. Such directions, based on interpretation of that very phrase, prior to the 1929 Act, interpretations which one can presume would be known to the draftsmen of the Act

and which might have been of some assistance, were, except for one case that has been
a produced (though there may of course be more), based on interpretations culled from
the doctors and bear a certain similarity to those in the affidavits of Professor Newton
and Professor Rivers, rather than in that of Mr Norris.

In *R v Handley* (1874) 13 Cox CC 79 Brett J, a very distinguished judge, directed the
jury that a child was considered to have been 'born alive' when it existed as a live child,
that is to say breathing and living by reason of its breathing through its own lungs alone,
b without deriving any of its living or power of living by or through any connection with
its mother.

In *R v Poulton* (1832) 5 C & P 329, 172 ER 997 even the fact of the child having
breathed was said not to be conclusive proof of it having been in 'a living state' after
birth. In that case three doctors had given evidence and the judge told the jury (5 C & P
329 at 330, 172 ER 997 at 998):

c
'... if there is all this uncertainty among these medical men, perhaps you would
think it too much for you to say that you are satisfied that the child was born alive.'

In *R v Enoch* (1833) 5 C & P 539, 172 ER 1089, and similarly in *R v Wright* (1841) 9 C
& P 754, 173 ER 1039, the judge directed the jury that to be alive there must be, in
addition to breathing, a circulation independent of the mother. The limited indicia of
d life which Mr Norris said was sufficient would not at any rate have accorded with those
directions.

Counsel's case that Mr C was entitled to an injunction because a crime was threatened
depended, it appears, partly, as counsel for Miss S submitted, on the extraordinary and
dogmatic assertion with regard to the ability to be born alive of *every* 18 week fetus,
without any personal knowledge or examination of any of these countless unborn
e children, partly on his interpretation of 'being born alive' and partly on the view
adumbrated by counsel for Mr C that, if any doctor was intending to perform an abortion
on an 18-week fetus, it would be perverse of him or her to assert other than that the fetus
was capable of being born alive. Counsel, though not Mr Norris, submitted that no other
interpretation of 'live born' than that of Mr Norris is within the words of the Act.

I disagree. Counsel for Mrs S pointed out that Mr Norris did not disagree with Professor
f Newton that an 18-week fetus cannot breathe and cannot even be mechanically ventilated.
I would have thought that to say, as he has, that a child is live born or alive, even though
it cannot breathe, would surprise not only doctors but many ordinary people.

The word 'viable' is, I believe from what I have heard in this case, sometimes used
interchangeably and in a number of cases where others might use the words 'born alive'.
g In the United States of America, in the Supreme Court, in *Roe v Wade* (1973) 410 US 113
at 163 it was said:

'With respect to the State's important and legitimate interest in potential life, the
"compelling" point is at *viability*. This is so because the fetus then presumably has
the capability of meaningful life outside the mother's womb. State regulation
protective of fetal life after viability thus has both logical and biological justifications.'
h (My emphasis.)

As far as the phrase in the 1929 Act is concerned, counsel for Mr C submits, it either
contains an ambiguity or the phrase is a technical one. In my view, one or both of those
submissions is or are correct. That expression, in my judgment, does not have a clear and
plain meaning. It *is* ambiguous. It is a phrase which is capable of different interpretations,
j and probably for the reason that it is also a medical concept and, as with the example of
earlier days, the expertise of doctors may well be required and gratefully received to assist
the court.

Even distinguished medical men have found considerable difficulties but have
discovered that it is more helpful to equate that phrase with viability, possibly with the
example from the parliamentary draftsman in mind.

I cannot accept counsel for the plaintiff's submission that this is not, at any rate in this court, even partly a matter of expert opinion as to the meaning of 'alive', for I have to point out that the first expert, namely Mr Norris, who produced an affidavit on that very topic was introduced by him. Professor Newton replied later.

Counsel on behalf of the Official Solicitor, acting as amicus curiae, submitted that the alleged threatened criminality raised a difficult question of interpretation and pointed out that s 5(1) of the 1967 Act itself incorporates the word 'viable' in the phrase which refers to 'protecting the life of the viable foetus', a section to which I have already referred. By that date, he argued, Parliament would no doubt be aware of the controversies over the law on abortion and it is possible that the use of that word is some indication that Parliament thought it necessary to use that particular qualifying word. I think that that is possible too, though I would not attach too much weight to the parenthesis containing that word as an aid to construction.

Perhaps it is more significant that, though the reference to a fetus of 28 weeks or more being deemed 'capable of being born alive' is referable to the burden of proof, it is probably dealing with a fetus of an age that would be known or expected to be viable in 1929.

Mr Norris, of course, does not limit his statement to a question of presumption. He goes much further and in effect makes his 18 weeks an irrebuttable presumption, thus, at a stroke, as it were, reducing the 28 weeks to 18.

Council for the Official Solicitor submitted that the court should reject Mr Norris's interpretation of 'born alive' as the minimum indicia, without breathing, possibly without circulation and minus a number of indications referred to by Professor Newton.

In considering this submission, I find Mr Norris's statements as to the inevitability of every 18-week fetus being born alive unacceptable. It is not necessary for me, nor would I want, to try to decide on affidavit evidence in a somewhat limited sphere the answer, which baffles men and women with great scientific expertise, to a very profound question. I would, however, say that I am not greatly attracted to the very limited definition relied on by Mr Norris and I do not accept it as a realistic one.

I now, finally, come to consider the alleged criminality and to decide, as I am asked to do, whether or not I should grant the injunction which is sought. I note, first of all, that this is a matter of the utmost urgency and importance.

Counsel for Mr C no longer claims qua father, but it is not unimportant to point out, as Baker P did in *Paton v Trustees of BPAS* [1978] 2 All ER 987 at 990, [1979] QB 276 at 279–280, that, apart from a right to apply for custody of or access to an illegitimate child, the father has no other rights whatsoever, and the equality of parental rights provision in s 1(1) of the Guardianship of Minors Act 1971 and s 1(7) of the Guardianship Act 1973 expressly does not apply to an illegitimate child; parental rights are exclusively vested in the mother.

An injunction of the nature sought is rare. Indeed, a case of this sort is rare. The *Paton's* case was, I understand, the first to be heard in this country. Such an injunction should not issue, in any event, on evidence which is conflicting, or uncertain, as here, and, in my opinion, for such an injunction to issue there must, most importantly, be strong evidence against the proposed defendant and virtual certainty that what is being complained of constitutes a defined criminal offence. Every case depends on its own facts and circumstances and none more so than this, for the graver the offence the more vital it is that, before an injunction issues to interfere with the operative procedures being prepared because of the risk to the health of Miss S, it is shown that an offence is virtually certain to be committed if no injunction issues. Moreover, the statute whose terms have to be interpreted in order to found this alleged offence is a penal one and the offence which it is said will be committed is one which attracts a penalty, as I have indicated, of life imprisonment. Such statute must be strictly construed.

I ask myself, first of all, how can an unknown, unascertained doctor, one who will be personally responsible for making the necessary clinical judgments, particularly pre-operatively, be said at this stage to be about to commit a criminal offence because another a doctor, namely Mr Norris, gives it as his opinion, unsupported by any other evidence or examination, that the hospital doctor will be, must be, committing this offence because, it is said, if he intends to do this operation, he must know that the fetus could be born alive, 'alive' meaning what Mr Norris says it means, and that if he nevertheless continues the termination he is not only perverse but guilty of the offence of child destruction.

On the other hand, there is before me compelling evidence that Mr Norris's opinion is not accepted by a wide body of eminent medical opinion and by many reputable doctors.

b I am not satisfied that a potential crime has been proved. If a doctor were to be charged, which is difficult to envisage, any such offence would have to be proved to the standard of certainty, the burden of proof, a heavy one, would be on the prosecution to produce evidence to establish all the elements of their case, including proof of the accused's requisite men rea (because such an offence would not be provable on an objective basis) and Mr Norris's evidence as to the notional 'perverse doctor' would not avail in any

c attempt to prove an offence under the 1929 Act.

In my view, there is no sufficient basis for saying that there is a threatened crime and, if a case were brought, the judge would in my judgment be bound to stop the case, as I would. I have no hesitation in coming to the conclusion that counsel for Mr C has not made out his case for an injunction.

In view of my conclusion, which disposes of the matter, I have not thought it necessary

d to add to this already long judgment by considering another hurdle that counsel might have encountered by reason of the decisions with regard to a private individual seeking to prevent the commission of an offence by way of an injunction, following the *Gouriet* line of cases (see *Gouriet v Union of Post Office Workers* [1977] 3 All ER 70, [1978] AC 435).

The applications are dismissed.

e *Application dismissed.*

Bebe Chua   Barrister.

Appeal
f Mr C appealed to the Court of Appeal.

Gerard Wright QC and *Tonya Pinsent* for Mr C.
Peter Sheridan QC and *Caroline Harry Thomas* for Miss S.
Allan Levy as amicus curiae.
The health authority were not represented.

g **SIR JOHN DONALDSON MR** delivered the following judgment of the court. In this appeal the court has been concerned with an application for an injunction to restrain the termination of a pregnancy. The applicants are the putative father, Mr C, and, if this is permissible in English law, 'a child en ventre sa mère' suing by its father. The respondents are Miss S, the mother, and the health authority under whose aegis any

h termination is likely to take place.

An ex parte application for such an injunction was refused both by Turner J and, on appeal, by this court. The application was renewed last week on an inter partes basis before Heilbron J, who refused it in a judgment given yesterday morning. In view of the possible danger to the health of the mother if this application remained unresolved for longer than was absolutely necessary, we offered to hear the appeal within an hour of the

j judge having completed giving judgment and, with the consent of the parties, have begun to do so.

The urgency precludes our giving full reasons for our conclusion that any injunction should be refused but the public interest also requires that, so far as possible, we indicate the basis of this conclusion. Expanded reasons dealing more fully with the arguments of counsel appearing for Mr C on this first issue will be delivered at a later date.

There is more than one way of measuring the duration of a pregnancy, but it is common ground that, however measured, this pregnancy has continued for between 18 and 21 weeks. Shortly after the time when conception must have taken place, Miss S was prescribed and took medicine designed to prevent pregnancy developing. Later she was prescribed and took anti-depressant drugs. Later still, in ignorance that she was pregnant, she was twice subjected to X-ray examination for a chest infection. On one such occasion there was no shielding to prevent damage to the fetus, whose presence was unknown. The pregnancy was revealed by a later body scan.

All these treatments could damage a fetus and Miss S wishes to terminate the pregnancy. It is common ground that all the steps required by the Abortion Act 1967 as a precondition to such a termination have been taken and, in particular, that in accordance with s 1(1)(a) of the Act it has been certified by two doctors that in their opinion the continuance of the pregnancy would involve risk of injury to the physical or mental health of Miss S greater than if the pregnancy were terminated.

What is said by counsel for Mr C is that termination of a pregnancy at this stage will necessarily involve the commission of a criminal offence under s 1(1) of the Infant Life (Preservation) Act 1929, the provisions of which are unaffected by the 1967 Act.

That subsection is in the following terms:

> 'Subject as hereinafter in this subsection provided, any person who, with intent to destroy the life of a child capable of being born alive, by any wilful act causes a child to die before it has an existence independent of its mother, shall be guilty of felony, to wit, of child destruction, and shall be liable on conviction thereof on indictment to penal servitude for life: Provided that no person shall be found guilty of an offence under this section unless it is proved that the act which caused the death of the child was not done in good faith for the purpose only of preserving the life of the mother.'

The key words for present purposes are 'destroy the life of a child capable of being born alive'.

We have received affidavit evidence from three doctors, none of whom has examined Miss S. Their evidence is thus necessarily directed at the stage in the development of a fetus which can normally be expected to have been reached by the 18th to 21st week. On this, as one would expect, they are in substantial agreement. At that stage the cardiac muscle is contracting and a primitive circulation is developing. Thus the fetus could be said to demonstrate real and discernible signs of life. On the other hand, the fetus, even if then delivered by hysterotomy, would be incapable ever of breathing either naturally or with the aid of a ventilator. It is not a case of the fetus requiring a stimulus or assistance. It cannot and will never be able to breathe. Where the doctors disagree is as to whether a fetus, at this stage of development, can properly be described as 'a child capable of being borne alive' within the meaning of the 1929 Act. That essentially depends on the interpretation of the statute and is a matter for the courts.

We have no evidence of the state of the fetus being carried by Miss S but, if it has reached the normal stage of development and so is incapable ever of breathing, it is not in our judgment 'a child capable of being born alive' within the meaning of the 1929 Act and accordingly the termination of this pregnancy would not constitute an offence under that Act.

I say no more at this stage because that disposes of the first issue, and counsel for Mr C, with the agreement of counsel for Miss S, wishes us to continue and deal with the other issues.

Sheridan QC for Miss S. My Lord, we have in the time that your Lordships were out of court made inquiries of the second defendants (the hospital), whose stance is that they will not carry out this operation on Thursday or at all if there is any question of appeal to the House of Lords. If we have to wait out time because the House of Lords cannot sit for some time, we will be run out of time. Accordingly, our suggestion is that your

a Lordships may favour a two-stage approach to these questions: that if there is to be an appeal to the House of Lords on the first, the terminative, matter, that should proceed now if leave is given, and we do our best to see if somebody can hear us over there. That is the only way that we can keep our date for next Thursday or within a period of time which is still, according to this judgment, uncontroversial. Otherwise we simply will not have our operation and the effect of the plaintiffs' application will be as if they had

b obtained an injunction here.

SIR JOHN DONALDSON MR. Mr Sheridan, I am bound to say that all three of us are astonished at the attitude of the regional health authority. It is a fact that some 1,000 appeals are heard by this court every year, of which about 50 go to the House of Lords, either because the House of Lords does not consider them appropriate or because there

c may be other reasons, but it is a tiny proportion which go to the House of Lords. So in practical terms in the everyday life of this country this court is the final court of appeal and it must always be the final court of appeal in circumstances of real urgency. In those circumstances, no one could be blamed in any way, a fortiori could they as a practical matter be prosecuted, for acting on a judgment of this court. If that be wrong, which it is not, the life of the country in many respects would grind to a halt. The purpose of any

d supreme court, including the House of Lords, is to review historically and on a broad front; it is not to decide matters of great urgency which have to be decided once and for all. That said, since we cannot compel the authority to appreciate what the position is in the system of jurisprudence in this country, what we propose to do is to say that the appeal on the other issues will continue, but that will not in any way prevent you from going to see the Appeal Committee or whoever you wish to see in the House of Lords

e with a view to seeing whether you can make an application to the committee or to the full House or whatever may be appropriate; and, if it emerges at any stage of the argument that your presence or the presence of your junior or of the solicitors is required to attend before the House, we will immediately adjourn to enable you to do that.

f The court heard further argument on the question of leave to appeal.

SIR JOHN DONALDSON MR. Let me say what I would otherwise have said. Technically, and now in substance in the light of what counsel for Mr C has said, the questions whether a putative father has any right to be heard on an application of this nature and whether a fetus is a legal person in law capable of suing do not arise, and of

g course we do not rule on them. But I have also to say that, if we had been in favour of Mr C on all other points, we should have had to have given very considerable thought to the words of Baker P in *Paton v Trustees of BPAS* [1978] 2 All ER 987 at 992, [1979] QB 276 at 282 where he said:

'... not only would it be a bold and brave judge ... who would seek to interfere with the discretion of doctors acting under the [Abortion Act 1967], but I think he

h would really be a foolish judge who would try to do any such thing, unless possibly, there is clear bad faith and an obvious attempt to perpetrate a criminal offence. Even then, of course, the question is whether that is a matter which should be left to the Director of Public Prosecutions and the Attorney-General.'

So, with that addendum on behalf of the court, we dismiss the appeal.

j

Appeal dismissed. Leave to appeal to the House of Lords refused.

24 February. The Appeal Committee of the House of Lords (Lord Bridge of Harwich, Lord Griffiths and Lord Oliver of Aylmerton) refused leave to appeal.

25 February. In the Court of Appeal.

SIR JOHN DONALDSON MR. When delivering judgment yesterday, we said that considerations of urgency precluded the giving of full reasons, but that fuller reasons would be given later. The expanded reasons would have been concerned with technical arguments on the construction and interrelation of the Births and Deaths Registration Acts 1836 to 1926, the Births and Deaths Registration Act 1953 and the Infant Life (Preservation) Act 1929. In view of the fact that the matter has since been considered by the House of Lords on the basis of the reasons already given, we now consider that it would be inappropriate to add to that judgment.

STEPHEN BROWN LJ. I agree.

RUSSELL LJ. I agree.

Solicitors: *Gamlens*, agents for *Clifford Poole & Co*, Salford (for Mr C); *Edwin Coe & Calder Woods*, agents for *Rigbey Loose & Mills*, Birmingham (for Miss S); *Official Solicitor*.

Diana Procter   Barrister.

R v Oxford City Justices, ex parte Berry

QUEEN'S BENCH DIVISION

MAY LJ AND RUSSELL J

28 NOVEMBER, 5 DECEMBER 1986

Criminal law – Committal – Preliminary hearing before justices – Confession – Representation that confession not voluntary – Justices failing to determine whether accused's confession voluntary – Whether failure a ground for granting judicial review of committal proceedings – Whether sufficient reason to quash committal proceedings – Police and Criminal Evidence Act 1984, s 76(2).

If in the course of committal proceedings it is represented that a confession made by an accused person which the prosecution proposes to give in evidence was or may have been obtained from him by oppression or in circumstances likely to render any confession made by him unreliable, but contrary to s 76(2)[a] of the Police and Criminal Evidence Act 1984 the examining justices allow the confession to be given in evidence without requiring the prosecution to prove beyond reasonable doubt that it was voluntary, that omission may be a ground for granting judicial review of the committal proceedings, but, save in exceptional circumstances, the court will not quash the committal proceedings on that ground alone (see p 1248 *d g*, post).

R v Carden (1878) 5 QBD 1 and *R v Marsham* [1892] 1 QB 371 considered.

Notes

For the admissibility in evidence of confessions in committal proceedings, see 11 Halsbury's Laws (4th edn) paras 136, 140, 153, 156, 410–415, and for cases on the subject generally, see 14(1) Digest (Reissue) 233–235, 1677–1700, 14(2) ibid 562–565, 582–586, 4578–4601, 4662–4708.

For the Police and Criminal Evidence Act 1984, s 76, see 17 Halsbury's Statutes (4th edn) 213.

Cases referred to in judgment

a   *Anisminic Ltd v Foreign Compensation Commission* [1969] 1 All ER 208, [1969] 2 AC 147,
        [1969] 2 WLR 163, HL.
     R v Carden (1879) 5 QBD 1, DC.
     R v Highbury Corner Magistrates' Court, ex p Boyce (1984) 79 Cr App R 132, DC.
     R v Ipswich Justices, ex p Edwards (1979) 143 JP 699, DC.
     R v Marsham [1892] 1 QB 371, CA.
b   *R v Norfolk Quarter Sessions, ex p Brunson* [1953] 1 All ER 346, [1953] 1 QB 503, [1953] 2
        WLR 294, DC.

Cases also cited

     R v Cripps, ex p Muldoon [1984] 2 All ER 705, [1984] QB 686, CA.
     R v Horsham Justices, ex p Bukhari (1981) 74 Cr App R 291, DC.
c

Application for judicial review
John Andrew Berry applied, with the leave of Taylor J given on 15 July 1986, for an
order of certiorari to bring up and quash his committal for trial on five charges of alleged
burglary by the Oxford City justices on 11 February 1986. The facts are set out in the
judgment of May LJ.
d
James F Gibbons for the applicant.
Richard Jenkins for the Crown.

                                                                            Cur adv vult

e
5 December. The following judgments were delivered.

MAY LJ. In this matter counsel moved with leave on behalf of one John Andrew Berry
for judicial review in the nature of certiorari to bring up and quash his committal for
f   trial on five charges of alleged burglary by the Oxford City Magistrates' Court on 11
February 1986.
     The grounds on which this application was made were based on the provisions of
s 76(2) of the Police and Criminal Evidence Act 1984:

        'If, in any proceedings where the prosecution proposes to give in evidence a
        confession made by an accused person, it is represented to the court that the
g   confession was or may have been obtained—(*a*) by oppression of the person who
        made it; or (*b*) in consequence of anything said or done which was likely, in the
        circumstances existing at the time, to render unreliable any confession which might
        be made by him in consequence thereof, the court shall not allow the confession to
        be given in evidence against him except in so far as the prosecution proves to the
        court beyond reasonable doubt that the confession (notwithstanding that it may be
h   true) was not obtained as aforesaid.'

     The only evidence against the applicant on four of the burglary charges were
confessions said to have been made by him to the police when they were investigating
the offences. The evidence against him on the fifth charge was circumstantial and, it was
contended before us, weak in the extreme. I shall have to return to this later in this
j   judgment.
     At the committal proceedings, at which the applicant appeared in person, he indicated
to the magistrates and to their clerk that he wished to challenge the admissibility of his
alleged confessions on the grounds that they had not been voluntary under the provisions
of s 76(2) of the 1984 Act. In an affidavit sworn by the clerk to the magistrates and filed
in these proceedings, the clerk said:

'I considered Section 76(2) of the Police and Criminal Evidence Act 1984 in light
of Section 6(1) of the Magistrates' Courts Act 1980 in that examining Justices were   *a*
concerned in finding a prima facie case only. Further, in the light of observations
made in earlier decided cases concerning the proper forum for the consideration of
such matters I advised the Magistrates that the issue of a confession improperly
obtained was a matter for a Judge in the Crown Court to decide, if prima facie
evidence existed to commit the defendant for trial. The Magistrates followed this
advice and the committal continued.'   *b*

The applicant accepted that prior to the coming into force of the 1984 Act, if examining
justices followed the procedure for committal proceedings prescribed by the Magistrates'
Courts Act 1980 and the Magistrates' Courts Rules 1981, SI 1981/552, this court would
not interfere with a committal for trial on the ground that during the committal
proceedings inadmissible evidence had been received: see *R v Norfolk Quarter Sessions, ex*   *c*
p Brunson [1953] 1 All ER 346, [1953] 1 QB 503, *R v Ipswich Justices, ex p Edwards* (1979)
143 JP 699 and *R v Highbury Magistrates' Court, ex p Boyce* (1984) 79 Cr App R 132.

Counsel for the applicant contended, however, that, since the passing of the 1984 Act,
where, as here, examining justices have not merely received inadmissible evidence but
have refused to enter on the inquiry prescribed by s 76(2) of the 1984 Act before receiving
evidence of a confession, when it has been represented that it was or may not have been   *d*
voluntary, the situation is different. By so refusing, he submitted, the justices thereby
declined to enter on an inquiry on which they were bound to enter; they did not merely
receive inadmissible evidence, but they declined jurisdiction and thus the resulting
committal can be challenged by certiorari.

In support of this argument counsel for the applicant referred us first to *R v Carden*
(1879) 5 QBD 1. In that case the question was whether on an information for maliciously   *e*
publishing a defamatory libel the examining magistrate should have received evidence
as to the truth of the libel before deciding whether or not to commit the defendants for
trial. The facts of that case were wholly different from those of the instant application
and so also were the relevant statutory provisions. But it had been argued that the
magistrate had declined jurisdiction and in the course of his judgment Cockburn CJ said
(at 5–6):   *f*

'It is said that in this case the magistrate has declined jurisdiction. That involves
the question whether he had jurisdiction to hear this evidence. I am clearly of
opinion that he had not. The duty and province of the magistrate before whom a
person is brought, with a view to his being committed for trial or held to bail, is to
determine, on hearing the evidence for the prosecution and that for the defence, if   *g*
there be any, whether the case is one in which the accused ought to be put upon his
trial. It is no part of his province to try the case. That being so, in my opinion, unless
there is some further statutory duty imposed on the magistrate, the evidence before
him must be confined to the question whether the case is such as ought to be sent
for trial, and if he exceeds the limits of that inquiry, he transcends the bounds of his
jurisdiction.'   *h*

Counsel for the applicant argued that today there is a further statutory duty imposed on
the examining justices, namely that of making the inquiry into the question whether
any confession relied on by the prosecution had been made voluntarily by virtue of
s 76(2) of the 1984 Act.

We were also referred to *R v Marsham* [1892] 1 QB 371. There, on the hearing of a   *j*
summons against the owner of property in a new street to enforce payment of his
apportioned share of the expenses of paving it, the defendant sought to give evidence to
show that the amount alleged to have been expended had not actually been expended, or
that it included expenses other than paving expenses. The magistrate refused to receive
such evidence. An application for an order nisi for a mandamus directed to the magistrate
requiring him to hear and determine the summons, that is to do so according to law, was

refused by a Divisional Court but was subsequently granted and thereafter made absolute
a in the Court of Appeal. In the course of his judgment Lord Halsbury LC said (at 375–
376):

> 'No doubt a magistrate may improperly reject evidence, and the Court may be
> unable to set him right, and the question is, whether this case comes within that
> category. I think that it does not; the act of the magistrate was not a mere rejection
> of evidence, but amounted to a declining to enter upon an inquiry on which he was
b > bound to enter; he has not merely rejected evidence, but has declined jurisdiction,
> and, therefore, the right of the applicants to call upon him to exercise his jurisdiction
> is enforceable by mandamus... The magistrate was asked to enter upon an inquiry
> whether the subject-matter was paving or not, and it was suggested that the board
> had expended money on works which were wholly outside paving works. The
c > magistrate took the view that he could not enter into the inquiry, and declined to
> do so, and the question for us is whether he was right. If so, no mandamus will lie;
> but if he was wrong, it is manifest that he absolutely refused to enter upon the
> inquiry and declined jurisdiction.'

Lord Esher MR said (at 378):

d > '... there is now an application for a mandamus upon the ground that the
> magistrate declined to exercise the jurisdiction given him by law. Now, the form in
> which he is said to have declined jurisdiction is, that he refused to hear certain
> evidence which was tendered before him, and it is suggested on behalf of the board
> that such refusal, at the most, only amounted to a wrongful refusal to receive
> evidence, and not to a declining of jurisdiction. The distinction between the two is
e > sometimes rather nice; but it is plain that a judge may wrongly refuse to hear
> evidence upon either of two grounds: one, that even if received the evidence would
> not prove the subject-matter which the judge was bound to inquire into; the other,
> that whether the evidence would prove the subject-matter or not, the subject-matter
> itself was one into which he had no jurisdiction to inquire. In the former case the
> judge would be wrongly refusing to receive evidence, but would not be refusing
f > jurisdiction, as he would in the latter. Here the magistrate does not say that the
> evidence tendered would not prove the fact that the claim of the board included
> matters outside the statute; he has refused to hear the evidence, even though it
> would prove that fact; he has, therefore, declined jurisdiction.'

Although the circumstances of that case were again different from the present one,
g nevertheless it was argued that the applicable principle of law was the same. Where a
magistrate is asked to enter on an inquiry on which he is bound by statute to enter, then
judicial review will lie to quash a decision reached by him without undertaking that
obligatory inquiry.

In answer to these submissions counsel for the Crown argued that the failure of the
justices, on advice, to consider whether the alleged confessions by the applicant had or
h had not been improperly obtained did not affect their jurisdiction to decide whether a
prima facie case had been made out against him and thus whether he should be
committed for trial, even having regard to the provisions of s 76(2) of the 1984 Act. All
that the justices may have done was to admit evidence which might prove to be
inadmissible and there was ample authority, indeed it was accepted, that this court would
not interfere with a committal by justices on this ground alone.

j Counsel for the Crown, secondly, submitted that in any event certiorari was a
discretionary remedy and that in circumstances such as obtained in the instant case, this
court ought not to exercise its discretion in favour of the applicant: there would be ample
opportunity at the trial to investigate the voluntariness or otherwise of the alleged
confessions.

Finally, counsel for the Crown submitted that the evidence relied on to raise a prima
facie case against the applicant on the fifth charge of burglary did not include any alleged

confession by him. Consequently his committal on this charge could not validly be
challenged. By virtue of proviso (i) to s 2(2) of the Administration of Justice (Miscellaneous
Provisions) Act 1933 the indictment against the applicant could then include further
counts founded on the facts or evidence disclosed in the depositions, for instance counts
charging the four burglaries in respect of which the evidence led against the applicant in
the committal proceedings had included the disputed confessions. On this ground also,
the argument continued, it would be wrong to quash the committal of the applicant of
any charges against him.

I very much doubt whether the draftsman of s 76(2) of the 1984 Act ever had in mind
the possible impact that its provisions could have on committal proceedings before
justices. I do not think that it can ever have been intended to produce such a radical
change in such proceedings. As is well known the question of the voluntariness or
otherwise of alleged confessions by an accused has hitherto seldom, if ever, been
investigated in committal proceedings before justices, save perhaps to have some matters
of fact established in the cross-examination of prosecution witnesses to found a subsequent
challenge to a confession at the ultimate trial on indictment.

Nevertheless, on the authorities to which I have referred and remembering Lord Reid's
classic dictum on the meaning of 'jurisdiction' in *Anisminic Ltd v Foreign Compensation
Commission* [1969] 1 All ER 208 at 214, [1969] 2 AC 147 at 171, I think that as a matter
of law judicial review could go to quash a committal in circumstances such as in the
instant case, where the justices have refused to undertake the inquiry contemplated by
s 76(2). Nevertheless I am quite satisfied that, save in the exceptional case, this court
should not quash any committal on this ground alone. Judicial review is a discretionary
remedy, and, if it were allowed to go in the circumstances of the instant case, 'I tremble
to think what would be the result to the criminal practice of this country' (to use the
words of Lord Goddard CJ in *R v Norfolk Quarter Sessions, ex p Brunson* [1953] 1 QB 503 at
505). As Geoffrey Lane LJ said in similar vein in *R v Ipswich Justices, ex p Edwards* (1979)
143 JP 699 at 706:

'No hardship results. If the evidence is found to be inadmissible at the trial, then
the prosecution will have to do without it, to put it bluntly.'

In any event, in the instant case, I think that, despite counsel for the applicant's valiant
argument to the contrary, there was sufficient evidence before the justices to support
their committal of him on the fifth burglary charge. On the third argument raised by
counsel for the Crown therefore, it would I think be clearly wrong to accede to this
application and for my part I would refuse it.

RUSSELL J. I agree.

Application refused.

Solicitors: *Darby & Son*, Oxford (for the applicant); *Crown Prosecution Service*.

Carolyn Toulmin   Barrister.

End of Volume 1